Rev. Steven VanderMolen
12/93

# Dictionary OF Paul AND HIS Letters

Editors:

Gerald F. Hawthorne

Ralph P. Martin

Associate Editor:

Daniel G. Reid

InterVarsity Press

DOWNERS GROVE, ILLINOIS 60515

LEICESTER, ENGLAND

*InterVarsity Press*
*P.O. Box 1400, Downers Grove, IL 60515, USA*
*38 De Montfort Street, Leicester LE1 7GP, England*

*InterVarsity Press®, U.S.A., is the book-publishing division of InterVarsity Christian Fellowship®, a student movement active on campus at hundreds of universities, colleges and schools of nursing in the United States of America, and a member movement of the International Fellowship of Evangelical Students. For information about local and regional activities, write Public Relations Dept., InterVarsity Christian Fellowship, 6400 Schroeder Rd., P.O. Box 7895, Madison, WI 53707-7895.*

*Inter-Varsity Press, England, is the book-publishing division of the Universities and Colleges Christian Fellowship (formerly the Inter-Varsity Fellowship), a student movement linking Christian Unions in universities and colleges throughout the United Kingdom and the Republic of Ireland, and a member movement of the International Fellowship of Evangelical Students. For information about local and national activities write to UCCF, 38 De Montfort Street, Leicester LE1 7GP.*

*All Scripture quotations, unless otherwise indicated, are the authors' own translations. Those identified NIV are taken from the American edition of the HOLY BIBLE, NEW INTERNATIONAL VERSION®. NIV®. © 1973, 1978, 1984 by International Bible Society, used by permission of Zondervan Publishing House and published in Great Britain by Hodder and Stoughton Ltd. All rights reserved. Those identified RSV are from the Revised Standard Version of the Bible, copyright 1946, 1952, 1971 by the Division of Christian Education of the National Council of the Churches of Christ in the U.S.A., and used by permission. Those identified NRSV are from the New Revised Standard Version of the Bible, copyright 1989 by the Division of Christian Education of the National Council of the Churches of Christ in the U.S.A., and used by permission.*

*USA ISBN 0-8308-1778-6*
*UK ISBN 0-85110-651-X*

*Printed in the United States of America.* ∞

---

**Library of Congress Cataloging-in-Publication Data**

*Dictionary of Paul and his Letters/editors, Gerald F. Hawthorne,*
   *Ralph P. Martin; associate editor, Daniel G. Reid.*
      *p.    cm.*
   *Includes bibliographical references and indexes.*
   *ISBN 0-8308-1778-6 (alk. paper)*
    *1. Bible. N.T. Epistles of Paul—Criticism, interpretation, etc.*
  *2. Bible. N.T. Epistles of Paul—Dictionaries.  3. Paul, the*
  *Apostle, Saint—Dictionaries.  I. Hawthorne, Gerald F., 1925-*
  *II. Martin, Ralph P.  III. Reid, Daniel G., 1949-*
  *BS2650.2.D53  1993*
  *227'.03—dc20*                      *93-36044*
                                                     *CIP*

---

**British Library Cataloguing in Publication Data**

*A catalogue record for this book is available from the British Library.*

---

| 19 | 18 | 17 | 15 | 14 | 13 | 12 | 11 | 10 | 9 | 8 | 7 | 6 | 5 | 4 | 3 | 2 | 1 |
|----|----|----|----|----|----|----|----|----|----|----|----|----|----|----|----|----|----|
| 07 | 06 | 05 | 04 | 03 | 02 | 01 | 00 | 99 | 98 | 97 | 96 | 95 | 94 | 93 | | | |

# InterVarsity Press

*Executive Director*
Kenneth DeRuiter

## Editorial Staff

*Editorial Director*
Andrew T. Le Peau

*Managing Editor*
James Hoover

*Reference Book Editor*
Daniel G. Reid

*Editorial Assistants*
Kathleen Carlson
Gloria Duncan
Cynthia M. Reid
Rhonda Skinner

*Proofreaders*
Helen Kelly
Michele Pelton
Robin Sheffield

## Production Staff

*Production Manager*
Nancy Fox

*Production Coordinator*
Don Frye

*Design*
Kathy Lay Burrows

*Design Assistant*
Carla Sonheim

*Typesetters*
Marjorie Sire, Gail Munroe

*Programming Consultant*
Richard E. Ecker

# Contents

# Preface

"It has long been a matter of controversy among New Testament scholars how best we should interpret the theology of Paul." If this remark of W. D. Davies was true when he first made it in 1948, the last several decades have seen no resolving of the matter and very few points of consensus.

Yet areas of agreement are to be found, and they are significant. They range from Paul's Jewish-rabbinic background and the setting of his missionary life and work in a Greco-Roman environment to, and above all, the decisive turning point in his thought and vocation when he became a Christian apostle. To be sure, each of these fields of inquiry has provoked animated discussion, even if there is general agreement among students of Paul that it is within these three sectors of investigation that the ultimate meaning of Paul's life and ministry and its legacy to the subsequent history of the church is to be located.

The present time is surely opportune to harvest the gains of such inquiries, proposals and investigations. We are sufficiently distant from E. P. Sanders's epoch-making volume *Paul and Palestinian Judaism* (1977), rightly praised, if then pertinently criticized, by J. D. G. Dunn (in his essay "The New Perspective on Paul," 1983) as breaking the mold of current Pauline research and posing a new set of agenda questions, to attempt a reevaluation and assessment. The team of essayists who have contributed to the *Dictionary of Paul and His Letters* mainly stand in the shadow of this major new appraisal of Paul's attitude to the Law, the covenant and the people of Israel, and reflect their reaction, whether positive or cautious, to the "new look" on Paul's gospel of righteousness by faith and the elements of continuity with the ancestral faith.

This perhaps is the chief reason why the ensuing volume should prove serviceable to a new generation of seminary and college students wishing to interact with the "new look" on Paul and his place in Christian and world history. Parish ministers too will value an up-to-date survey of Paul's leading ideas as well as find helpful background data in seeking to place the apostle in his time frame. Key articles, however, show the relevance of the Pauline message to the Christian pulpit today, and would-be preachers will not be slow to glean useful insights based on the best modern scholarship, both critical and conservative. The editors venture to believe that their fellows in the professional guild of teachers and researchers will find here a working tool and a conspectus of bibliographical aids and summarized discussions to assist them in their classroom courses and to provoke further discussion.

Yet a wider audience should equally benefit from a handbook like *DPL*. Editorial policy has striven to keep in view the needs of a vast company of lay people who are interested in these letters of the New Testament. We have tried to make each contribution readable to and understandable by the educated person-in-the-pew who, we believe, will welcome this comprehensive study of Paul's life and labors, his teaching and influence—and the enduring witness he still stands for, centered on the new life in Christ and the church. If this volume serves to introduce Paul to any who are curious about his role in early Christian history and takes Paul out of the study and the sanctuary into the marketplace and the hectic world where moral values are threatened and ethical decisions made, it will have achieved part of its purpose.

It remains to pay tribute to all who have made possible a venture like this. When two of the editors sat down at a noon meal during the Society of Biblical Literature meetings in 1987 to talk over the possibilities of a dictionary like the present one, we had little idea of the complexity and scope of the task. Subsequent editorial meetings, at SBL conferences and at Wheaton College, were soon to impress us with the vast nature of our undertaking. Yet such occasions were memorable as we wrestled with editorial (and theological) decisions in the interest of making a serviceable volume.

Whether we succeeded, the readers will tell. One thing is clear. We would never have come close to our aim without the willing collaboration of the IVP staff and the army of cooperative contributors whose work we were privileged to edit.

Two names need to be mentioned in this regard. The piece by F. F. Bruce ("Paul in Acts and Letters") was composed within weeks of his lamented death and may represent one of his final contributions to a well-nigh prodigious literary output, chiefly in the field of Pauline studies. The assignment of the major article on "God" was accepted by Donald Guthrie. Alas, he too was to be taken from us before this could even be sketched; yet it was thought fitting if his last written contribution, to crown his life's work, could be assembled from what he had previously written in his *New Testament Theology*. With family and collegial consent, this has been attempted by one of the editors who has striven to retain as much of Dr. Guthrie's wording as seemed feasible, with a modicum of updating and reworking.

The entire project is issued in the expectation that it will be of service to readers across the world and will represent a not too unworthy contribution to Pauline scholarship, composed by a wide circle of writers who with the editors have sought to discharge their tasks, in the ancient phrase, *amore Pauli*.

*Gerald F. Hawthorne*
*Ralph P. Martin*
*Daniel G. Reid*

# How to Use This Dictionary

**Abbreviations**
Comprehensive tables of abbreviations for general matters as well as for scholarly, biblical and ancient literature may be found on pages xiii-xxiii.

**Authorship of Articles**
The authors of articles are indicated by their first initials and last name at the end of each article. A full list of contributors may be found on pages xxvii-xxix, in alphabetical order of their last name. The contribution of each author is listed.

**Bibliographies**
A bibliography has been appended to each article. The bibliographies include works cited in the articles and other significant related works. Bibliographical entries are listed in alphabetical order by the author's last name.

Full bibliographical information has been supplied whenever possible. In cases where a volume has been published in English on both sides of the Atlantic, only the North American publisher has been listed. Abbreviations used in the bibliographies appear in the tables of abbreviations.

Bibliographies for each Pauline letter include a special listing of commentaries on the respective letter.

**Cross-references**
The *Dictionary* has been extensively cross-referenced in order to aid readers in making the most of material appearing throughout the volume. Four types of cross-referencing will be found:

1. One-line entries appearing in alphabetical order throughout the *Dictionary* direct readers to articles where a topic is discussed:

    **Abba.** *See* Adoption, Sonship; God; Son of God.

2. An asterisk after a single word in the body of an article indicates that an article by that title appears in the *Dictionary*. For example, "Christ*" directs the reader to an article entitled **Christ.**

3. A cross-reference appearing within parentheses in the body of an article also directs the reader to an article by that title. For example, (*see* Dying and Rising)

directs the reader to an article entitled **Dying and Rising with Christ.** Such cross-references are used either to prevent the confusion an asterisk might introduce (i.e., Son of God* could refer to either an article on "God" or "Son of God") or to direct the reader's attention to an article of related interest.

4. Cross-references have been appended to the end of articles, immediately preceding the bibliography, to direct readers to articles significantly related to the subject:

*See also* JUSTIFICATION; RIGHTEOUSNESS, RIGHTEOUSNESS OF GOD.

## Indexes

Since most of the *Dictionary* articles cover broad topics in some depth, the *subject index* is intended to assist readers in finding relevant information on narrower topics that might, for instance, appear in a standard Bible dictionary. For example, while there is no article entitled "Hellenists," the subject index might direct the reader to pages where the Hellenists are discussed in the articles on "Antioch," "Gentiles," "Hellenism," "Jerusalem" and "Mission."

A *Pauline Letters index* is provided to assist readers in gaining access to information related to various Pauline texts.

An *index of articles* in the dictionary allows readers to review quickly the breadth of topics covered and select the ones most apt to serve their interests or needs.

For those who wish to identify the articles written by specific contributors, they are listed with the names of the contributors in the list of contributors.

## Transliteration

Hebrew and Greek words have been transliterated according to a system set out in the table of transliterations (xxv). Greek verbs appear in their lexical form (rather than infinitive) in order to assist those with little or no knowledge of the language in using other reference works.

# Abbreviations

## General Abbreviations

| | | | |
|---|---|---|---|
| κτλ | etc. (Greek) | n.d. | no date |
| 2d ed. | second edition | n.s. | new series |
| 3d ed. | third edition | NT | New Testament |
| A | Codex Alexandrinus | o.s. | old series |
| B | Codex Vaticanus | OT | Old Testament |
| bis | twice | p. or pp. | page or pages |
| C | Codex Ephraemi Syri | *pace* | with due respect to, but differing from |
| c. | circa, about (with dates); column | par. | parallel passage in another/other Gospel(s) |
| cent. | century | | |
| cf. | *confer,* compare | passim | elsewhere |
| chap(s). | chapter(s) | pl. | plural |
| D | Codex Bezae | Q | Quelle ("sayings" source for Synoptic Gospels) |
| DSS | Dead Sea Scrolls | | |
| e.g. | *exempli gratia,* for example | repr. | reprint |
| ed. | edition; editor(s), edited by | rev. | revised |
| esp. | especially | s.v. | *sub verbo* ("under the relevant word") |
| ET | English translation | sy | Syriac |
| EVV | English versions of the Bible | Tg. | Targum |
| Gk | Greek | v. or vv. | verse or verses |
| Heb | Hebrew | v.l. | *vario lectio* ("variant reading") |
| i.e. | *id est,* that is | vol. | volume |
| km. | kilometer | x | times (2 x = two times, etc.) |
| LXX | Septuagint | § or §§ | section or paragraph number(s) (usually indicating Loeb Classical Library numbering system for Josephus) |
| mg. | margin | | |
| MS or MSS | manuscript or manuscripts | | |
| MT | Masoretic Text (of the Old Testament) | א | Codex Sinaiticus |

## Translations of the Bible

| | | | |
|---|---|---|---|
| ASV | American Standard Version (1901) | NEB | New English Bible |
| AV | Authorized Version (= KJV) | NIV | New International Version |
| GNB | Good News Bible | NRSV | New Revised Standard Version |
| JB | Jerusalem Bible | REB | Revised English Bible |
| KJV | King James Version (= AV) | RSV | Revised Standard Version |
| NASB | New American Standard Bible | RV | Revised Version (1881-85) |

## Books of the Bible

| *Old Testament* | Job | Mic | 1-2 Cor |
|---|---|---|---|
| Gen | Ps | Nahum | Gal |
| Ex | Prov | Hab | Eph |
| Lev | Eccles | Zeph | Phil |
| Num | Song | Hag | Col |
| Deut | Is | Zech | 1-2 Thess |
| Josh | Jer | Mal | 1-2 Tim |
| Judg | Lam | | Tit |
| Ruth | Ezek | *New Testament* | Philem |
| 1-2 Sam | Dan | Mt | Heb |
| 1-2 Kings | Hos | Mk | Jas |
| 1-2 Chron | Joel | Lk | 1-2 Pet |
| Ezra | Amos | Jn | 1-2-3 Jn |
| Neh | Obad | Acts | Jude |
| Esther | Jon | Rom | Rev |

## The Apocrypha and Septuagint

| 1-2-3-4 Kgdms | 1-2-3-4 Kingdoms | 1-2-3-4 Macc | 1-2-3-4 Maccabees |
|---|---|---|---|
| Add Esth | Additions to Esther | Pr Azar | Prayer of Azariah |
| Bar | Baruch | Pr Man | Prayer of Manasseh |
| Bel | Bel and the Dragon | Sir | Sirach (or Ecclesiasticus) |
| 1-2 Esdr | 1-2 Esdras | Sus | Susanna |
| 4 Ezra | 4 Ezra | Tob | Tobit |
| Jdt | Judith | Wis | Wisdom of Solomon |
| Ep Jer | Epistle of Jeremiah | | |

## The Old Testament Pseudepigrapha

| Adam and Eve | Life of Adam and Eve | Pss. Sol. | Psalms of Solomon |
|---|---|---|---|
| Ahiq. | Ahiqar | Pseud.-Phoc. | Pseudo-Phocylides |
| Apoc. Abr. | Apocalypse of Abraham | Sib. Or. | Sibylline Oracles |
| 2-3 Apoc. Bar. | Syriac, Greek Apocalypse of Baruch | T. 12 Patr. | Testament of the Twelve Patriarchs |
| Asc. Isa. | Ascension of Isaiah | T. Reub. | Testament of Reuben |
| Apoc. Mos. | Apocalypse of Moses | T. Sim. | Testament of Simeon |
| As. Mos. | Assumption of Moses (or Testament of Moses) | T. Levi | Testament of Levi |
| | | T. Judah | Testament of Judah |
| Apoc. Elijah | Apocalypse of Elijah | T. Iss. | Testament of Issachar |
| Apoc. Zeph. | Apocalypse of Zephaniah | T. Zeb. | Testament of Zebulon |
| Bib. Ant. | Biblical Antiquities of Pseudo-Philo | T. Dan. | Testament of Dan |
| 1-2-3 Enoch | Ethiopic, Slavonic, Hebrew Enoch | T. Naph. | Testament of Naphthali |
| Ep. Arist. | Epistle of Aristeas | T. Gad. | Testament of Gad |
| Ep. Diognetus | Epistle to Diognetus | T. Asher | Testament of Asher |
| Jos. and As. | Joseph and Asenath | T. Jos. | Testament of Joseph |
| Jub. | Jubilees | T. Benj | Testament of Benjamin |
| Liv. Proph. | The Lives of the Prophets (followed by prophet abbreviated) | T. Abr. | Testament of Abraham |
| | | T. Job | Testament of Job |
| Mart. Isa. | Martyrdom of Isaiah | T. Mos. | Testament of Moses (or Assumption of Moses) |
| Odes Sol. | Odes of Solomon | | |

## Early Christian Literature

**Aristides**
| | |
|---|---|
| Apol. | Apologia |

**Augustine**
| | |
|---|---|
| Civ. D. | De Civitate Dei |
| Conf. | Confessiones |
| De cons. | De consensu evangelistarum |
| Hom. | Homilia |
| Quaest. Evan. | Quaestiones Evangeliorum |
| Barn. | Barnabas |

**Chrysostom**
| | |
|---|---|
| Hom. Mt. | Homilies on Matthew |
| Regno | De Regno |

**Clement of Alexandria**
| | |
|---|---|
| Paed. | Paedagogus |
| Protr. | Protreptikos |
| Strom. | Stromateis |

**Clement of Rome**
| | |
|---|---|
| 1-2 Clem. | 1-2 Clement |

**Cyprian**
| | |
|---|---|
| Ep. | Epistulae |

**Cyril of Jerusalem**
| | |
|---|---|
| Cat. | Catechesis |
| Did. | Didache |
| Diogn. | Epistle to Diognetus |

**Epiphanius**
| | |
|---|---|
| Haer. | Haereses |
| Weights | Treatise on Weights and Measures |

**Eusebius**
| | |
|---|---|
| Eccl. Theol. | De Ecclesiastica Theologia |
| Hist. Eccl. | Historia Ecclesiastica |
| Dem. Ev. | Demonstratio Evangelica |
| In Ps. | Commentary on the Psalms |
| Praep. Ev. | Praeparatio Evangelica |

**Gospels:**
| | |
|---|---|
| Gos. Bar. | Gospel of Bartholomew |
| Gos. Eb. | Gospel of the Ebionites |
| Gos. Eg. | Gospel of the Egyptians |
| Gos. Heb. | Gospel of the Hebrews |
| Gos. Naass. | Gospel of the Naassenes |
| Gos. Pet. | Gospel of Peter |
| Gos. Thom. | Gospel of Thomas |

**Hippolytus**
| | |
|---|---|
| Apos. Trad. | Apostolic Tradition |

**Ignatius**
| | |
|---|---|
| Eph. | Letter to the Ephesians |
| Magn. | Letter to the Magnesians |
| Phld. | Letter to the Philadelphians |
| Pol. | Letter to Polycarp |
| Rom. | Letter to the Romans |
| Smyrn. | Letter to the Smyrneans |
| Trall. | Letter to the Trallians |

**Irenaeus**
| | |
|---|---|
| Haer. | Adversus haereses |

**Jerome**
| | |
|---|---|
| Ep. | Epistulae |
| Vir. | De Viris Illustribus |

**Justin Martyr**
| | |
|---|---|
| Apol. I, II | Apology I, II |
| Dial. Tryph. | Dialogus cum Tryphone Judaeo |
| Mart. Pol. | Martyrdom of Polycarp |

**Origen**
| | |
|---|---|
| Comm. Joh. | In Johannem Commentarius |
| Comm. Mt. | In Matthaeum Commentarius |
| Contra Celsum | Contra Celsum |

**Polycarp**
| | |
|---|---|
| Phil. | Letter to the Philippians |

**Pseudo-Clementines**
| | |
|---|---|
| Hom. | Homilies |
| Recogn. | Recognitions |

**Tertullian**
| | |
|---|---|
| Nat. | Ad Nationes |
| De An. | De Anima |
| De Car. | De Carne Christi |
| De Praesc. | De Praescriptione Haereticorum |
| De Bapt. | De Baptismo |
| Marc. | Adversus Marcionem |
| Pud. | De Pudicitia |

**Theophilus**
| | |
|---|---|
| Autol. | Ad Autolycum |

## Classical and Hellenistic Writers and Sources

**Aeschylus**
| | |
|---|---|
| Sept. c. Theb. | Septem contra Thebas |
| Suppl. | Supplices |

**Ammonius**
| | |
|---|---|
| Adfin. Vocab. Diff. | De adfinium Vocabulorum Differentia |

**Antipater**
| | |
|---|---|
| Anth. Pal. | Anthologia Palatina |

**Appian**
| | |
|---|---|
| Mith. W. | Mithridatic Wars |
| Civ. W. | The Civil Wars |

| | | | |
|---|---|---|---|
| Apuleius | | *Inscr. Cos* | *The Inscriptions of Cos*, ed. W. R. |
| *Met.* | *Metamorphoses* | | Paton and E. L. Hicks (1891) |
| Aratus | | Isocrates | |
| *Phaen.* | *Phaenomena* | *Dem.* | *Demonicus* |
| Aristophanes | | *Panath.* | *Panathenaicus* |
| *Thes.* | *Thesmophorizousai* | *Paneg.* | *Panegyricus* |
| Aristotle | | Josephus | |
| *Cael.* | *De Caelo* | *Ant.* | *Antiquities of the Jews* |
| *Eth. Nic.* | *Ethica Nicomachea* | *J.W.* | *Jewish Wars* |
| *Pol.* | *Politica* | *Life* | *Life of Flavius Josephus* |
| *Prob.* | *Problemata* | *Ag. Ap.* | *Against Apion* |
| Aulus Gellius | | Justinian | |
| *Noc. Att.* | *Noctes Atticae* | *Digest* | *Digest of Roman Law* |
| Cicero | | Juvenal | |
| *De Div.* | *De Divinatione* | *Sat.* | *Satirae* |
| *De Leg.* | *De Legibus* | Livy | |
| *De Offic.* | *De Officiis* | *Epit.* | *Epitomae* |
| *De Orat.* | *De Oratore* | *Hist.* | *History of Rome* |
| *Phil.* | *Orationes Philippicae* | Lucian of Samosata | |
| *Rab. Perd.* | *Rabirio Perduellionis* | *Herm.* | *Hermotimus* |
| *Tusc.* | *Tusculanae Disputationes* | *Philops.* | *Philopseudes* |
| *Corp. Herm.* | *Corpus Hermeticum* | Nicolaus of Damascus | |
| Demosthenes | | *Vit. Caes.* | *Vita Caesaris* |
| *Lacrit.* | *Against Lacritus* | *Orphic Fragments* | *Orph. Frag.* |
| Dio Cassius | | Pausanias | |
| *Epit.* | *Roman History* | *Descr.* | *Description of Greece* |
| *Hist.* | *Roman History* | Philo | |
| Dio Chrysostom | | *Abr.* | *De Abrahamo* |
| *De Homero* | *De Homero et Socrate* | *Aet. Mund.* | *De Aeternitate Mundi* |
| *Disc.* | *Discourses* | *Agric.* | *De Agricultura* |
| *Or* | *Orationes* | *Cher.* | *De Cherubim* |
| Diodorus | | *Conf. Ling.* | *De Confusione Linguarum* |
| *Bib. Hist.* | *Bibliotheca Historica* | *Congr.* | *De Congressu Eruditionis Gratia* |
| Diogenes Laertius | | *Decal.* | *De Decalogo* |
| *Vit.* | *Vitae* | *Det. Pot. Ins.* | *Quod Deterius Potiori Insidiari* |
| Dionysius of Halicarnassus | | | *Soleat* |
| *Ant. Rom.* | *Antiquitates Romanae* | *Deus Imm.* | *Quod Deus Sit Immutabilis* |
| Epictetus | | *Ebr.* | *De Ebrietate* |
| *Disc.* | *Discourses* | *Flacc.* | *In Flaccum* |
| *Diss.* | *Dissertationes* | *Fug.* | *De Fuga et Inventione* |
| Euripides | | *Gig.* | *De Gigantibus* |
| *Hipp.* | *Hippolytus* | *Jos.* | *De Josepho* |
| Eustathius | | *Leg. All.* | *Legum Allegoriae* |
| *on Homer Od.* | *Commentary on Homer's Odyssey* | *Leg. Gai.* | *Legatio ad Gaium* |
| Firmicus Maternus | | *Migr. Abr.* | *De Migratione Abrahami* |
| *De Errore Prof.* | | *Mut. Nom.* | *De Mutatione Nominum* |
| *Rel.* | *De Errore Profanarum Religionum* | *Omn. Prob. Lib.* | *Quod omnis Probus Liber sit* |
| Galen | | *Op. Mund.* | *De Opificio Mundi* |
| *De Placitis* | *De Placitis Hippocratis et Platonis* | *Poster. C.* | *De Posteritate Caini* |
| Hesiod | | *Praem. Poen.* | *De Praemiis et Poenis* |
| *Op.* | *Opera et Dies* | *Quaest. in Ex.* | *Quaestiones in Exodum* |
| Iamblichus | | *Quaest. in Gen.* | *Quaestiones in Genesin* |
| *De myst.* | *De Mysteriis* | *Rer. Div. Her.* | *Quis Rerum Divinarum Heres sit* |

| | | | |
|---|---|---|---|
| *Sacr.* | *De Sacrificiis Abelis et Caini* | Polybius | |
| *Som.* | *De Somnis* | *Hist.* | *Histories* |
| *Spec. Leg.* | *De Specialibus Legibus* | Proclus | |
| *Virt.* | *De Virtutibus* | *In Tim.* | *In Platonis Timaeum* |
| *Vit. Cont.* | *De Vita Contemplativa* | | *Commentarius* |
| *Vit. Mos.* | *De Vita Mosis* | Quintilian | |
| Philostratus | | *Inst. orat.* | *Institutio oratoria* |
| *Vit. Ap.* | *Vita Apollonii* | Seneca | |
| Pindar | | *De Clem.* | *De Clementia* |
| *Isth.* | *Isthmia* | *Ep. Mor.* | *Epistulae Morales* |
| Plato | | Sophocles | |
| *Alc.* | *Alcibiades* | *Elec.* | *Electra* |
| *Apol.* | *Apologia* | Stobaeus | |
| *Crat.* | *Cratylus* | *Ecl.* | *Ecloge* |
| *Leg.* | *Leges* | Strabo | |
| *Rep.* | *Respublica* | *Geog.* | *Geography* |
| *Soph.* | *Sophista* | Suetonius | |
| *Symp.* | *Symposion* | *Claudius* | *The Twelve Caesars* |
| *Tim.* | *Timaeus* | *Domitian* | *The Twelve Caesars* |
| Pliny (the elder) | | *Julius* | *The Twelve Caesars* |
| *Nat. Hist.* | *Naturalis Historia* | *Nero* | *The Twelve Caesars* |
| Pliny (the younger) | | *Tiberius* | *The Twelve Caesars* |
| *Ep.* | *Epistolae* | *Vespasian* | *The Twelve Caesars* |
| Plutarch | | Tacitus | |
| *Alex.* | *De Alexandro* | *Ann.* | *Annales ab excessu divi Augusti* |
| *Anton.* | *De Antonio* | *Hist.* | *Historiae* |
| *Caesar* | *De Caesar* | Thucydides | |
| *Conv.* | *Quaestiones Conviviales* | *Hist.* | *History of the Peloponnesian* |
| *Def. Orac.* | *De Defectu Oraculorum* | | *War* |
| *Fac. Lun.* | *De Facie in Orbe Lunae* | Valerius Maximus | |
| *Gen. Socr.* | *De Genio Socratis* | *Fact. ac Dict.* | *Factorum ac Dictorum* |
| *Lib. Educ.* | *De Liberis Educandis* | | *Memorabilium Libri* |
| *Mor.* | *Moralia* | Xenophon | |
| *Non Posse Suav.* | *Non Posse Suaviter Vivi* | *Hist. Gr.* | *Historia Graeca* |
| | *Secundum Epicuram* | *Mem.* | *Memorabilia Socratis* |
| *Pomp.* | *De Pompeio* | | |
| *Rom.* | *Quaestiones Romanae* | | |
| *Ser. Num. Pun.* | *De iis qui sero a numine* | | |
| | *puniuntur* | | |

## Dead Sea Scrolls and Related Texts

| | | | |
|---|---|---|---|
| CD | Cairo (Genizah text of the) *Damascus (Document/Rule)* | 1QH | *Hôdāyôt* or *Thanksgiving Hymns* from Qumran Cave 1 |
| P | Pesher (commentary) | 1QIsa$^{a,b}$ | First or second copy of Isaiah from Qumran Cave 1 |
| 1Q, 3Q, 4Q etc. | Numbered caves of Qumran yielding written material (e.g., 1Q = Qumran Cave 1); followed by abbreviation or number of document | 1QM | *Milḥāmāh* or *War Scroll* from Qumran Cave 1 |
| | | 1QpHab | *Pesher on Habakkuk* from Qumran Cave 1 |
| 1QapGen | *Genesis Apocryphon* from Qumran Cave 1 | 1QS | *Serek hayyaḥad* or *Rule of the Community, Manual of Discipline* from Qumran Cave 1 |

| | | | |
|---|---|---|---|
| 1QSa | Appendix A, *Messianic Rule*, to 1QS from Qumran Cave 1 | 4QMess ar | Aramaic "Messianic" text from Qumran Cave 4 |
| 1QSb | Appendix B, *Rule of Benediction*, to 1QS from Qumran Cave 1 | 4QMMT | *Miqsat Ma'aseh Torah* (unpublished) from Qumran Cave 4 |
| 3Q15 | *Copper Scroll* from Qumran Cave 3 | 4QPhyl | Phylacteries from Qumran Cave 4 |
| 4Q Ps DanAᵃ | Pseudo-Danielic Writings from Qumran Cave 4 | 4QPrNab | *Prayer of Nabonidus* from Qumran Cave 4 |
| 4Q139 | Ordinances or commentaries on biblical laws from Qumran Cave 4 | 4QPssJosh | *Psalms of Joshua* from Qumran Cave 4 |
| 4Q169 | Pesher on Nahum from Qumran Cave 4 | 4QShirShabb | *Songs of Sabbath Sacrifice* or *Angelic Liturgy* from Qumran Cave 4 |
| 4Q171 | Pesher on Psalms from Qumran Cave 4 | 4QTestim | *Testimonia* text from Qumran Cave 4 |
| 4Q176 | *Tanhumim*, or *Consolations*, from Qumran Cave 4 | 4QtgJob | *Targum of Job* from Qumran Cave 4 |
| 4Q186 | (see 4QMess ar) | 4QtgLev | *Targum of Leviticus* from Qumran Cave 4 |
| 4Q246 | (see 4QPs DanAᵃ) | 4QZodiac | Magical text from Qumran Cave 4 |
| 4Q400-407 | (see 4QShirShab) | 5Q15 | *New Jerusalem* from Qumran Cave 5 |
| 4Q504 | *Words of the Luminaries* from Qumran Cave 4 | 11QMelch | *Melchizedek* from Qumran Cave 11 |
| 4Q513-14 | Ordinances or commentaries on biblical laws from Qumran Cave 4 | 11QpaleoLev | Copy of Leviticus in paleo-Hebrew script from Qumran Cave 11 |
| 4QCryptic | Magical text from Qumran Cave 4 | 11QPsᵃ | *Psalms Scroll* from Qumran Cave 11 |
| 4QEn Giantsᵃ⁻ᵉ | *1 Enoch* fragments from Book of Giants from Qumran Cave 4 | 11QTemple | *Temple Scroll* from Qumran Cave 11 |
| 4QEnᵃ⁻ᵍ | *1 Enoch* fragments from Qumran Cave 4 | 11QtgJob | *Targum of Job* from Qumran Cave 11 |
| 4QEnastrᵃ⁻ᵍ | *1 Enoch* fragments from Astronomical Book from Qumran Cave 4 | | |
| 4QFlor | *Florilegium* or *Eschatological Midrashim* from Qumran Cave 4 | | |

## Targumic Material

| | | | |
|---|---|---|---|
| *Tg. Onq.* | *Targum Onqelos* | *Tg. Neof.* | *Targum Neofiti I* |
| *Tg. Neb.* | *Targum of the Prophets* | *Tg. Ps.-J.* | *Targum Pseudo-Jonathan* |
| *Tg. Ket.* | *Targum of the Writings* | *Tg. Yer. I* | *Targum Yerušalmi I* |
| *Frg. Tg.* | *Fragmentary Targum* | *Tg. Yer. II* | *Targum Yerušalmi II* |
| *Sam. Tg.* | *Samaritan Targum* | *Yem. Tg.* | *Yemenite Targum* |
| *Tg. Isa* | *Targum of Isaiah* | *Tg. Esth I, II* | *First or Second Targum of Esther* |

**Order and Tractates in the Mishna, Tosepta and Talmud** Same-named tractates in the Mishna, Tosepta, Babylonian Talmud and Jerusalem Talmud are distinguished by *m.*, *t.*, *b.* and *y.* respectively.

| | | | |
|---|---|---|---|
| 'Abot | *'Abot* | *Nazir* | *Nazir* |
| 'Arak. | *'Arakin* | Ned. | *Nedarim* |
| 'Abod. Zar. | *'Aboda Zara* | Neg. | *Nega'im* |
| B. Bat. | *Baba Batra* | Nez. | *Neziqin* |
| Bek. | *Bekorot* | Nid. | *Niddah* |
| Ber. | *Berakot* | Ohol. | *Oholot* |
| Beṣa | *Beṣa (= Yom Ṭob)* | 'Or. | *'Orla* |
| Bik. | *Bikkurim* | *Para* | *Para* |
| B. Meṣ. | *Baba Meṣi'a* | *Pe'a* | *Pe'a* |
| B. Qam. | *Baba Qamma* | Pesaḥ. | *Pesaḥim* |
| Dem. | *Demai* | *Qinnim* | *Qinnim* |
| 'Erub. | *'Erubin* | Qidd. | *Qiddušin* |
| 'Ed. | *'Eduyyot* | Qod. | *Qodašin* |
| Giṭ. | *Giṭṭin* | Roš Haš. | *Roš Haššana* |
| Ḥag. | *Ḥagiga* | Sanh. | *Sanhedrin* |
| Ḥal. | *Ḥalla* | Šabb. | *Šabbat* |
| Hor. | *Horayot* | Šeb. | *Šebi'it* |
| Ḥul. | *Ḥullin* | Šebu. | *Šebu'ot* |
| Kelim | *Kelim* | Šeqal. | *Šeqalim* |
| Ker. | *Keritot* | Soṭa | *Soṭa* |
| Ketub. | *Ketubot* | Sukk. | *Sukka* |
| Kil. | *Kil'ayim* | Ta'an. | *Ta'anit* |
| Ma'aś. | *Ma'aśerot* | *Tamid* | *Tamid* |
| Mak. | *Makkot* | Tem. | *Temura* |
| Makš. | *Makširin (= Mašqin)* | Ter. | *Terumot* |
| Meg. | *Megilla* | Ṭohar. | *Ṭoharot* |
| Me'il. | *Me'ila* | Ṭ. Yom | *Ṭebul Yom* |
| Menaḥ. | *Menaḥot* | 'Uq. | *'Uqṣin* |
| Mid. | *Middot* | Yad. | *Yadayim* |
| Miqw. | *Miqwa'ot* | Yebam. | *Yebamot* |
| Mo'ed | *Mo'ed* | Yoma | *Yoma (= Kippurim)* |
| Mo'ed Qaṭ. | *Mo'ed Qaṭan* | Zabim | *Zabim* |
| Ma'aś. Š. | *Ma'aśer Šeni* | Zebaḥ. | *Zebaḥim* |
| Našim | *Našim* | Zer. | *Zera'im* |

## Other Rabbinic Works

| | | | |
|---|---|---|---|
| 'Abot R. Nat. | *'Abot de Rabbi Nathan* | Pesiq. R. | *Pesiqta Rabbati* |
| 'Ag. Ber. | *'Aggadat Berešit* | Pesiq. Rab Kah. | *Pesiqta de Rab Kahana* |
| Bab. | *Babylonian* | | |
| Bar. | *Baraita* | Pirqe R. El. | *Pirqe Rabbi Eliezer* |
| Der. Er. Rab. | *Derek Ereṣ Rabba* | Rab. | *Rabbah* (following abbreviation for biblical book: Gen. Rab. = *Genesis Rabbah*) |
| Der. Er. Zuṭ. | *Derek Ereṣ Zuṭ* | | |
| Gem. | *Gemara* | Ṣem. | *Ṣemaḥot* |
| Kalla | *Kalla* | Sipra | *Sipra* |
| Mek. | *Mekilta* | Sipre | *Sipre* |
| Midr. | *Midraš* (cited with abbreviation for biblical book; but Midr. Qoh. = *Midraš Qohelet*) | Sop. | *Soperim* |
| | | S. 'Olam Rab. | *Seder 'Olam Rabbah* |
| | | Talm. | *Talmud* |
| Pal. | *Palestinian* | Yal. | *Yalquṭ* |

## Periodicals, Reference Works and Serials

| | | | | |
|---|---|---|---|---|
| *AB* | Anchor Bible | | *Bib* | *Biblica* |
| *ABQ* | *American Baptist Quarterly* | | BibO | Biblica et orientalia |
| *ABR* | *Australian Biblical Review* | | *BibRes* | *Biblical Research* |
| ACNT | The Augsburg Commentary on the New Testament | | *BibS(F)* | Biblische Studien (Freiburg, 1895-) |
| *AGJU* | Arbeiten zur Geschichte des antiken Judentums und des Urchristentums | | *BibS(N)* | Biblische Studien (Neukirchen, 1951-) |
| | | | *BJRL* | *Bulletin of the John Rylands University Library of Manchester* |
| *AGSU* | Arbeiten zur Geschichte des Spätjudentums und Urchristentums | | BJS | Brown Judaic Studies |
| *AJBI* | *Annual of the Japanese Biblical Institute* | | BMI | The Bible and Its Modern Interpreters |
| *AJT* | *American Journal of Theology* | | *BRev* | *Bible Review* |
| *ALGHJ* | Arbeiten zur Literatur und Geschichte des hellenistischen Judentums | | BS | Bollingen Series |
| | | | *BSac* | *Bibliotheca Sacra* |
| *ALUOS* | *Annual of Leeds University Oriental Society* | | *BT* | *The Bible Translator* |
| *AnBib* | Analecta Biblica | | *BTB* | *Biblical Theology Bulletin* |
| *ANF* | *Ante-Nicene Fathers*, ed. A. Roberts and J. Donaldson, (10 vols.; 1951 [c. 1890]) | | BU | Biblische Untersuchungen |
| | | | *BZ* | *Biblische Zeitschrift* |
| *ANRW* | Aufstieg und Niedergang der römischen Welt | | BZNW | *Beihefte zur Zeitschrift für die Neutestamentliche Wissenschaft* |
| *ASNU* | Acta seminarii neotestamentici upsaliensis | | *CAH* | *Cambridge Ancient History* |
| | | | *CBQ* | *Catholic Biblical Quarterly* |
| *ATANT* | Abhandlungen zur Theologie des Alten und Neuen Testaments | | CCWJCW | Cambridge Commentaries on Writings of the Jewish and Christian World 200 B.C. to A.D. 200 |
| *ATLABibS* | American Theological Library Association Bibliography Series | | *CD* | *Church Dogmatics*, Karl Barth |
| *AusBR* | *Australian Biblical Review* | | CG | Nag Hammadi Gnostic Codices |
| *ATR* | *Anglican Theological Review* | | CGTC | Cambridge Greek Testament Commentary |
| *AUS* | American University Studies | | | |
| *BA* | *Biblical Archaeologist* | | *CIG* | *Corpus Inscriptionum Graecarum* I-IV (1828-1877) |
| *BAGD* | W. Bauer, W. F. Arndt, F. W. Gingrich and F. W. Danker, *Greek-English Lexicon of the New Testament and Other Early Christian Literature* | | *CII* | *Corpus Inscriptionum Iudaicarum* I-II, J. B. Frey (1936-1952) |
| | | | *CIL* | *Corpus Inscriptionum Latinarum* I-XI (1862-1943, 2d ed. 1893-) |
| BBB | Bonner biblische Beiträge | | CNT | Commentaire du Nouveau Testament |
| *BBR* | *Bulletin for Biblical Research* | | ConB | Coniectanea biblica |
| BCJ | Brown Classics in Judaica | | CRINT | *Compendia Rerum Iudaicarum ad Novum Testamentum*, ed. S. Safrai et al. (Philadelphia: Fortress, 1974—) |
| BDB | F. Brown, S. R. Driver and C. A. Briggs, *Hebrew and English Lexicon of the Old Testament* | | | |
| | | | *CT* | *Christianity Today* |
| BDF | F. Blass, A. Debrunner and R. W. Funk, *A Greek Grammar of the New Testament and Other Early Christian Literature* (Chicago: University of Chicago, 1961) | | *CTM* | *Concordia Theological Monthly* |
| | | | *CTR* | *Criswell Theological Review* |
| | | | *CurTM* | *Currents in Theology and Mission* |
| | | | *CV* | *Communio Viatorum* |
| | | | DJD | Discoveries in the Judaean Desert |
| BETL | Bibliotheca ephemeridum theologicarum lovaniensium | | *DJG* | *Dictionary of Jesus and the Gospels* |
| | | | *DRev* | *Downside Review* |
| BG | Berlin Gnostic Codex | | DSB | Daily Study Bible |
| BGU | Ägyptische Urkunden aus den Museen zu Berlin: Griech. Urkunden I-VIII (1895-1933) | | *DTT* | *Dansk teologisk tidsskrift* |
| | | | EB | Études bibliques |
| | | | EBC | The Expositor's Bible Commentary |
| BHT | Beiträge zur historischen Theologie | | *EBT* | *Encyclopedia of Biblical Theology* |

| | | | |
|---|---|---|---|
| EDNT | Exegetical Dictionary of the New Testament, ed. H. Balz and G. Schneider | JCBRF | Journal of the Christian Brethren Research Fellowship |
| EGT | The Expositor's Greek Testament | JCSR | Journal of Comparative Sociology and Religion |
| EKK | Evangelisch-katholischer Kommentar zum Neuen Testament | JES | Journal of Ecumenical Studies |
| ELS | Enchiridion Locorum Sanctorum. Documenta S. Evangelii Loca Respicientia | JETS | Journal of the Evangelical Theological Society |
| EncJud | Encyclopaedia Judaica | JJS | Journal of Jewish Studies |
| EvQ | Evangelical Quarterly | JR | Journal of Religion |
| EvT | Evangelische Theologie | JRE | Journal of Religious Ethics |
| ExpT | Expository Times | JRH | Journal of Religious History |
| FB | Facet Books | JRS | Journal of Roman Studies |
| FF | Foundations and Facets | JSJ | Journal for the Study of Judaism in the Persian, Hellenistic and Roman Period |
| FIRA | Fontes Iuris Romani Antejustiniani | | |
| FJ | The Foundation of Judaism | JSNT | Journal for the Study of the New Testament |
| FN | Filologia Neotestamentaria | JSNTSup | Journal for the Study of the New Testament Supplement Series |
| FRLANT | Forschungen zur Religion und Literatur des Alten und Neuen Testaments | | |
| | | JSOT | Journal for the Study of the Old Testament |
| GBL | Das Große Bibellexikon | JSOTSup | Journal for the Study of the Old Testament Supplement Series |
| GNS | Good News Studies | | |
| GNTE | Guides to New Testament Exegesis | JSPSup | Journal for the Study of the Pseudepigrapha and Related Literature Supplement Series |
| GTJ | Grace Theological Journal | | |
| HBD | Harper's Bible Dictionary | | |
| HBT | Horizons in Biblical Theology | JTS | Journal of Theological Studies |
| HDB | A Dictionary of the Bible (ed. J. Hastings) | JTSA | Journal of Theology for South Africa |
| HDR | Harvard Dissertations in Religion | KNT | Kommentar zum Neuen Testament |
| Herm | Hermeneia | KP | Der Kleine Pauly, ed. K. Ziegler |
| HeyJ | Heythrop Journal | LAE | Light from the Ancient East, A. Deissmann |
| HNT | Handbuch zum Neuen Testament | Louw-Nida | Greek-English Lexicon, ed. J. P. Louw and E. A. Nida |
| HNTC | Harper's New Testament Commentaries | | |
| | | LQHR | London Quarterly and Holborn Review |
| HSS | Harvard Semitic Studies | LSJ | Liddell-Scott-Jones, Greek-English Lexicon |
| HTKNT | Herders theologischer Kommentar zum Neuen Testament | | |
| | | LTJ | Lutheran Theological Journal |
| HTS | Harvard Theological Studies | LW | Luther's Works, ed. J. Pelikan and H. T. Lehmann |
| HZ | Historische Zeitschrift | | |
| IBS | Irish Biblical Studies | MBTh | Münsterische Beiträge zur Theologie |
| ICC | International Critical Commentary | MeyerK | Meyer Kommentar |
| IDB | Interpreter's Dictionary of the Bible | MM | J. H. Moulton and G. Milligan, The Vocabulary of the Greek Testament, Illustrated from the Papyri and Other Non-Literary Sources (1930) |
| IDBSup | Interpreter's Dictionary of the Bible, Supplementary Volume | | |
| IEJ | Israel Exploration Journal | | |
| ILS | Inscriptiones Latinae Selectae (Berlin, 1892) | | |
| | | MNTC | Moffatt New Testament Commentary |
| Int | Interpretation | MPAT | A Manual of Palestinian Aramaic Texts |
| IntC | Interpretation Commentaries | MSB | Monographic Series of Benedictina |
| ISBE | International Standard Bible Encyclopedia (rev. ed.) | NA26 | Nestle-Aland, Novum Testamentum Graece 26th ed. |
| | | | |
| IVPNTC | InterVarsity Press New Testament Commentary | NAC | The New American Commentary |
| | | NCB | New Century Bible |
| | | NClB | New Clarendon Bible |
| JAC | Jahrbuch für Antike und Christentum | NedTTs | Nederlands theologisch tijdschrift |
| JAOS | Journal of the American Oriental Society | NewDocs | New Documents Illustrating Early Christianity, ed. G. H. R. Horsley |
| JBL | Journal of Biblical Literature | | |

| | | | |
|---|---|---|---|
| NICNT | The New International Commentary on the New Testament | SCJ | Studies in Christianity and Judaism |
| NIDNTT | New International Dictionary of New Testament Theology | Schürer | E. Schürer, The History of the Jewish People in the Age of Jesus Christ (175 B.C.– A.D. 135), rev. and ed. G. Vermes et al. (3 vols.; Edinburgh: 1973-87) |
| NovT | Novum Testamentum | | |
| NovTSup | Supplement to Novum Testamentum | SE | Studia Evangelica |
| NRT | La nouvelle revue théologique | SEÅ | Svensk Exegetisk Årsbok |
| NTAbh | Neutestamentliche Abhandlungen | SEG | Supplementum Epigraphicum Graecum (Leiden, 1923-) |
| NTD | Das Neue Testament Deutsch | | |
| NTG | New Testament Guides | SESJ | Suomen Ekseegeettisen Seuran Julkaisuja |
| NTOA | Novum Testamentum et Orbis Antiquus | | |
| | | SSEJC | Studies in Scripture in Early Judaism and Christianity |
| NTR | New Theology Review | | |
| NTS | New Testament Studies | SIG³ | Sylloge Inscriptionum Graecarum (3d ed.; Leipzig, 1915-24) |
| OBO | Orbis Biblicus et Orientalis | | |
| OBT | Overtures to Biblical Theology | SJ | Studia Judaica |
| OCD | Oxford Classical Dictionary | SJLA | Studies in Judaism in Late Antiquity |
| OTP | The Old Testament Pseudepigrapha, ed. J. H. Charlesworth | SNTSMS | Society for New Testament Studies Monograph Series |
| PC | Proclamation Commentaries | SO | Symbolae osloenses |
| PEQ | Palestine Exploration Quarterly | SP | Studia Patristica |
| PG | Patrologia graeca, ed. J. P. Migne | SPP | Studien zur Palaeographie und Papyruskunde |
| PRS | Perspectives in Religious Studies | | |
| PTMS | Pittsburgh Theological Monograph Series | SR | Studies in Religion |
| | | SSRH | Sociological Studies in Roman History |
| PTR | Princeton Theological Review | SJT | Scottish Journal of Theology |
| QD | Quaestiones Disputatae | SJTOP | SJT Occasional Papers |
| RAC | Reallexikon für Antike und Christentum | SOTBT | Studies in Old Testament Biblical Theology |
| RB | Revue biblique | | |
| RE | Real-Encyklopädie der klassischen Altertumswissenschaft, Pauly-Wissowa | ST | Studia theologica |
| | | StBT | Studia Biblica et Theologica |
| RelS | Religious Studies | Str-B H. | Strack and P. Billerbeck, Kommentar zum Neuen Testament |
| RelSRev | Religious Studies Review | | |
| RevExp | Review and Expositor | StudLit | Studia Liturgica |
| RevQ | Revue de Qumrân | SUNT | Studien zur Umwelt des Neuen Testaments |
| RHPR | Revue d'histoire et de philosophie religieuses | | |
| RQ | Restoration Quarterly | SWJT | Southwestern Journal of Theology |
| RSB | Religious Studies Bulletin | TB | Theologische Bücherei |
| RST | Regensburger Studien zur Theologie | TD | Theology Digest |
| RTR | Reformed Theological Review | TDNT | Theological Dictionary of the New Testament, ed. G. Kittel and G. Friedrich |
| SA | Studia Antiqua | | |
| SAJ | Studies in Ancient Judaism | TDGR | Translated Documents of Greece and Rome, ed. R. K. Sherk |
| SANT | Studien zum Alten und Neuen Testament | | |
| | | THKNT | Theologische Handkommentar zum Neuen Testament |
| SBEC | Studies in the Bible and Early Christianity | | |
| | | TI | Theological Inquiries |
| SBLASP | Society of Biblical Literature Abstracts and Seminar Papers | TJ | Trinity Journal |
| | | TLZ | Theologische Literaturzeitung |
| SBLDS | SBL Dissertation Series | TNTC | Tyndale New Testament Commentary |
| SBLMS | SBL Monograph Series | TPINTC | Trinity Press International New Testament Commentaries |
| SBLSBS | SBL Sources for Biblical Study | | |
| SBT | Studies in Biblical Theology | TQ | Theologische Quartalschrift |
| ScrHier | Scripta hierosolymitana | TRE | Theologische Realenzykopädie |

| | | | |
|---|---|---|---|
| *TS* | *Theological Studies* | WBC | Word Biblical Commentary |
| *TSFBul* | *Theological Students Fellowship Bulletin* | *WTJ* | *Westminster Theological Journal* |
| *TToday* | *Theology Today* | WUNT | Wissenschaftliche Untersuchungen zum Neuen Testament |
| *TWOT* | *Theological Wordbook of the Old Testament* | *WW* | *Word and World* |
| *TynB* | *Tyndale Bulletin* | *ZSTh* | *Zeitschrift für Systematische Theologie* |
| *TZ* | *Theologische Zeitschrift* | *ZTK* | *Zeitschrift für Theologie und Kirche* |
| UBSGNT | United Bible Societies Greek New Testament | ZBNT | Züricher Bibelkommentare: Neues Testament |
| *USQR* | *Union Seminary Quarterly Review* | *ZNW* | *Zeitschrift für die neutestamentliche Wissenschaft* |
| *VC* | *Vigiliae Christianae* | | |
| *VoxEv* | *Vox Evangelica* | *ZRG* | *Zeitschrift für Religions- und Geistesgeschichte* |
| *VT* | *Vetus Testamentum* | | |
| VTSup | Vetus Testamentum, Supplements | | |
| WA | Weimar Ausgabe | ZS: NT | Zacchaeus Studies: New Testament |

# Transliteration

**Hebrew**
*Consonants*

| Hebrew | Translit. |
|---|---|
| א | = ' |
| בּ | = b |
| ב | = ḇ |
| ג | = g |
| ג | = ḡ |
| ד | = d |
| ד | = ḏ |
| ה | = h |
| ו | = w |
| ז | = z |
| ח | = ḥ |
| ט | = ṭ |
| י | = y |
| כ | = k |
| כ | = ḵ |
| ל | = l |
| מ | = m |
| נ | = n |
| ס | = s |
| ע | = ' |
| פ | = p |
| פ | = p̄ |
| צ | = ṣ |
| ק | = q |
| ר | = r |
| שׂ | = ś |
| שׁ | = š |
| תּ | = t |
| ת | = ṯ |

*Long Vowels*

| | |
|---|---|
| (ה)ָ | = â |
| יֵ | = ê |
| יִ | = î |
| וֹ | = ô |
| וּ | = û |
| ָ | = ā |
| ֵ | = ē |
| ֹ | = ō |

*Short Vowels*

| | |
|---|---|
| ַ | = a |
| ֶ | = e |
| ִ | = i |
| ָ | = o |
| ֻ | = u |
| ֲ | = ᵃ |
| ֱ | = ᵉ |
| ֳ | = ᵒ |

**Greek**

| | | | |
|---|---|---|---|
| A = A | Θ = Th | ο = o | Ψ = Ps |
| α = a | θ = th | Π = P | ψ = ps |
| B = B | I = I | π = p | Ω = Ō |
| β = b | ι = i | P = R | ω = ō |
| Γ = G | K = K | ρ = r | ῾Ρ, ῥ = rh |
| γ = g | κ = k | Σ = S | ῾ = h |
| Δ = D | Λ = L | σ/ς = s | γξ = nx |
| δ = d | λ = l | T = T | γγ = ng |
| E = E | M = M | τ = t | αυ = au |
| ε = e | μ = m | Y = Y | ευ = eu |
| Z = Z | N = N | υ = y | ου = ou |
| ζ = z | Ξ = X | Φ = Ph | υι = ui |
| H = Ē | ξ = x | φ = ph | |
| η = ē | O = O | X = Ch | |
| | | χ = ch | |

# List of Contributors

Alexander, Loveday C. A., Ph.D. Lecturer in New Testament, Department of Biblical Studies, University of Sheffield, Sheffield, England: **Chronology**.

Arnold, Clinton E., Ph.D. Associate Professor of New Testament, Talbot School of Theology, Biola University, La Mirada, California, USA: **Ephesians, Letter to the; Ephesus; Magic; Power**.

Aune, David E., Ph.D. Professor of New Testament and Christian Origins, Director of Graduate Programs in Theology, Loyola University, Chicago, Illinois, USA: **Apocalypticism; Emperors, Roman; Religions, Greco-Roman**.

Banks, Robert J., Ph.D. Homer L. Goddard Professor of the Ministry of the Laity, Fuller Theological Seminary, Pasadena, California, USA: **Church Order and Government**.

Barclay, John M. G., Ph.D. Lecturer in Biblical Studies, University of Glasgow, Glasgow, Scotland: **Jesus and Paul**.

Barnett, Paul W., Ph.D. Bishop of North Sydney, Diocese of Sydney, Sydney, New South Wales, Australia: **Apostle; Opponents of Paul; Revolutionary Movements; Tentmaking**.

Barton, Stephen C., Ph.D. Lecturer in New Testment, Department of Theology, University of Durham, Durham, England: **Social-Scientific Approaches to Paul**.

Bauckham, Richard J., Ph.D. Professor of New Testament Studies, St. Mary's College, University of St. Andrews, St. Andrews, Scotland: **Apocryphal Pauline Literature**.

Beasley-Murray, George R., Ph.D. Senior Professor of New Testament Interpretation, Southern Baptist Theological Seminary, Louisville, Kentucky, USA: **Baptism; Dying and Rising with Christ**.

Beasley-Murray, Paul, Ph.D. Senior Minister, Victoria Road South Baptist Church, Chelmsford, Essex, England: **Pastor, Paul as**.

Belleville, Linda L., Ph.D. Associate Professor of Biblical Literature, North Park Theological Seminary, Chicago, Illinois, USA: **Authority; Enemy, Enmity, Hatred; Moses**.

Black, David Alan, D. Theol. La Mirada, California, USA: **Weakness**.

Blue, Bradley Byron, Ph.D. Academic Dean, Washington College Academy, Washington College, Tennessee, USA: **Apollos; Food Offered to Idols and Jewish Food Laws; Law Suit; Love Feast**.

Borchert, Gerald L., Ph.D. LL.B. T. Rupert and Louise Coleman Professor of New Testament Interpretation, The Southern Baptist Theological Seminary, Louisville, Kentucky, USA: **Light and Darkness; Wrath, Destruction**.

Bowers, W. Paul, Ph.D. Deputy Administrator, Accrediting Council for Theological Education in Africa, Nairobi, Kenya: **Mission**.

Brauch, Manfred T., Ph.D. President, Eastern Baptist Theological Seminary, Wynnewood, Pennsylvania, USA: **Righteousness, Righteousness of God**.

Bruce, F. F., D.D. Late Rylands Professor of Biblical Criticism and Exegesis, University of Manchester, Manchester, England: **Paul in Acts and Letters**.

Burge, Gary M., Ph.D. Associate Professor of New Testament, Wheaton College, Wheaton, Illinois, USA: **Barnabas; Intercession; First Fruits, Down Payment**.

Calvert, Nancy L., Ph.D. Assistant Professor of New Testament Studies, Wheaton College, Wheaton, Illinois, USA: **Abraham**.

Camery-Hoggat, Jerry A., Ph.D. Associate Professor of Religion, Southern California College, Costa Mesa, California, USA: **Visions, Ecstatic Experience**.

Campbell, William S., Ph.D. Head of Religious and Theological Studies, Westhill College, University of Birmingham, Birmingham, England: **Covenant and New Covenant; Israel; Judaizers; Olive Tree**.

Chamblin, J. Knox, Th.D. Professor of New Testament, Reformed Theological Seminary, Jackson, Mississippi, USA: **Freedom/Liberty; Psychology**.

Clines, David J. A., M.A. Professor of Biblical Studies, University of Sheffield, Sheffield, England: **Image, Image of God**.

Comfort, Philip W., Ph.D. Visiting Professor of New Testament, Wheaton College, Wheaton, Illinois, USA: **Futility; Idolatry; Temple**.

Davids, Peter H., Ph.D. Research and Theological Teacher, Langley Vineyard Christian Fellowship, Langley, British Columbia, Canada: **James and Paul**.

De Lacey, Douglas R., Ph.D. Faculties of Divinity and Oriental Studies, University of Cambridge, Cambridge, England: **Gentiles; Holy Days**.

Dockery, David S., Ph.D. Dean, School of Theology, The Southern Baptist Theological Seminary, Louisville, Kentucky, USA: **Fruit of the Spirit; New Nature and Old Nature**.

Dunn, James D. G., D.D. Lightfoot Professor of Divinity, University of Durham, Durham, England: **Romans, Letter to the**.

Ellis, E. Earle, Ph.D. Research Professor of Theology, Southwestern Baptist Theological Seminary, Ft. Worth, Texas, USA: **Coworkers, Paul and His; Pastoral Letters**.

Elwell, Walter, Ph.D. Professor of Bible and Theology, Wheaton College Graduate School, Wheaton, Illinois, USA: **Election and Predestination**.

Erickson, Richard J., Ph.D. Associate Professor of New Testament, Fuller Theological Seminary, Seattle, Washington, USA: **Flesh**.

Evans, Craig A., Ph.D. Professor of Biblical Studies, Trinity Western University, Langley, British Columbia, Canada: **Prophet, Paul as**.

Everts, Janet Meyer, Ph.D. Assistant Professor of Religion, Hope College, Holland, Michigan, USA: **Conversion and Call of Paul;**

Financial Support; Hope.

Fee, Gordon D., Ph.D. Professor of New Testament, Regent College, Vancouver, British Columbia, Canada: **Gifts of the Spirit**.

Fowl, Stephen E., Ph.D. Assistant Professor of Theology, Loyola College in Maryland, Baltimore, Maryland, USA: **Imitation of Paul/of Christ**.

Fuller, Ruth M., Ph.D. Adjunct Professor, Azusa Pacific University, Azusa, California, USA: **Rewards**.

Fung, Ronald Y. K., Ph.D. Resident Scholar and Adjunct Lecturer, China Graduate School of Theology, Hong Kong: **Body of Christ; Curse, Accursed, Anathema**.

Gaffin, Richard B. Jr., Th.D. Professor of Biblical and Systematic Theology, Westminster Theological Seminary, Philadelphia, Pennsylvania, USA: **Glory, Glorification**.

Gempf, Conrad, Ph.D. Senior Lecturer, LBC Centre for Undergraduate and Postgraduate Theological Studies, Northwood, Middlesex, England: **Athens, Paul at**.

Green, Joel B., Ph.D. Associate Professor of New Testament, American Baptist Seminary of the West and Graduate Theolgical Union, Berkeley, California, USA: **Crucifixion; Death of Christ**.

Greidanus, Sidney, Th.D. Professor of Preaching and Worship, Calvin Theological Seminary, Grand Rapids, Michigan, USA: **Preaching from Paul Today**.

Gundry-Volf, Judith M., Th.D. Associate Professor of New Testament, Fuller Theological Seminary, Pasadena, California, USA: **Apostasy, Falling Away, Perseverance; Conscience; Expiation, Propitiation, Mercy Seat; Foreknowledge, Divine; Universalism**.

Guthrie, Donald, Ph.D. Late Lecturer in New Testament Studies and Vice-Principal, London Bible College, Northwood, England: **God**.

Hafemann, Scott J., Dr. Theol. Associate Professor of New Testament, Gordon-Conwell Theological Seminary, South Hamilton, Massachusetts, USA: **Corinthians, Letters to the; Paul and His Interpreters; Suffering**.

Hansen, G. Walter, Th.D. Lecturer in New Testament, Trinity Theological College, Singapore, Republic of Singapore: **Galatians, Letter to the; Rhetorical Criticism**.

Hawthorne, Gerald F., Ph.D. Professor of Greek and New Testament Exegesis, Wheaton College, Wheaton, Illinois, USA: **Marriage and Divorce, Adultery and Incest; Philippians, Letter to the**.

Holmes, Michael W., Ph.D. Professor of Biblical Studies and Early Christianity, Bethel College, St. Paul, Minnesota, USA: **Textual Criticism**.

Hunter, W. Bingham, Ph.D. Senior Vice President of Education and Academic Dean, Professor of New Testament, Trinity Evangelical Divinity School, Deerfield, Illinois, USA: **Prayer**.

Hurtado, Larry W., Ph.D. Professor of Religion, University of Manitoba, Winnipeg, Manitoba, Canada: **Lord; Pre-existence; Son of God**.

Keener, Craig S., Ph.D. Professor of New Testament, Hood Theologcial Seminary, Salisbury, North Carolina, USA: **Man and Woman**.

Kim, Seyoon, Ph.D. Professor of New Testament, Chongshin Theological Seminary, Seoul, Korea: **Jesus, Sayings of**.

Klein, William W., Ph.D. Professor of New Testament, Denver Seminary, Denver, Colorado, USA: **Perfect, Mature**.

Kreitzer, Larry J., Ph.D. Tutor of New Testament, Regent's Park College, University of Oxford, Oxford, England: **Adam and Christ; Body; Eschatology; Intermediate State; Kingdom of God/Christ; Resurrection; Travel in the Roman World**.

Kroeger, C. C., Ph.D. Adjunct Associate Professor of Classical and Ministry Studies, Gordon-Conwell Theological Seminary, South Hamilton, Massachusetts, USA: **Head**.

Kruse, Colin G., Ph.D. Senior Lecturer in New Testament, Ridley College, University of Melbourne, Melbourne, Victoria, Australia: **Afflictions, Trials, Hardships; Call, Calling; Ministry; Servant, Service; Virtues and Vices**.

Levison, John R., Ph.D. Associate Professor of Biblical Studies, North Park College, Chicago, Illinois, USA: **Creation and New Creation**.

Lim, David S., Ph.D. Associate Dean and Pew Lecturer on TwoThirds World Theology, Oxford Centre for Mission Studies, Oxford, England: **Fullness**.

Luter, A. Boyd, Jr., Th.D. Associate Professor of Bible Exposition, Talbot School of Theology, Biola University, La Mirada, California, USA: **Gospel; Grace; Jealousy, Zeal; Name; Savior**.

McGrath, Alister E., Ph.D. Lecturer in Historical and Systematic Theology, Wycliffe Hall, University of Oxford, Oxford, England: **Cross, Theology of the; Justification**.

McKnight, Scot, Ph.D. Associate Professor of New Testament, Trinity Evangelical Divinity School, Deerfield, Illinois, USA: **Collection for the Saints**.

McRay, John R., Ph.D. Professor of New Testament and Archaeology, Wheaton College Graduate School, Wheaton, Illinois, USA: **Antioch on the Orontes**.

McVay, John K. Ph.D. (Cand.) Assistant Professor, Pacific Union College, Angwin, California, USA: **Head, Christ as**.

Maile, John F., B.D. Senior Minister, West Wickham and Shirley Baptist Church, London, England: **Exaltation and Enthronement; Heaven, Heavenlies, Paradise**.

Marshall, I. Howard, Ph.D. Professor of New Testament Exegesis, University of Aberdeen, Aberdeen, Scotland: **Lord's Supper**.

Martin, Ralph P., Ph.D. Professor, Department of Biblical Studies, University of Sheffield, Sheffield, England: **Center of Paul's Theology; Creed; Early Catholicism; God; Hymns, Hymn Fragments, Songs, Spiritual Songs; Worship**.

Meye, Robert P., Th.D., Professor Emeritus of New Testament Interpretation and Dean Emeritus, School of Theology, Fuller Theological Seminary, Pasadena, California, USA: **Spirituality**.

Michaels, J. Ramsay, Th.D. Professor of Religious Studies, Southwest Missouri State University, Springfield, Missouri, USA: **Paul in Early Church Tradition; Peter**.

Mohrlang, Roger, D.Phil. Professor of Religion, Whitworth College, Spokane, Washington, USA: **Love**.

Morrice, William G., Ph.D. Part-Time Lecturer, University of Durham, Durham, England: **Joy**.

Morris, Leon, Ph.D. Principal Emeritus, Ridley College, Melbourne, Victoria, Australia: **Faith; Forgiveness; Man of Lawlessness and Restraining Power; Mercy; Redemption; Sacrifice, Offering; Salvation; Sin, Guilt; Truth**.

Mott, Stephen Charles, Ph.D. Professor of Christian Social Ethics, Gordon-Conwell Theological Seminary, South Hamilton, Massachusetts, USA: **Civil Authority; Ethics.**

Mounce, Robert H., Ph.D. Professor, President Emeritus, Whitworth College, Spokane, Washington, USA: **Preaching, Kerygma.**

Noll, Stephen F., Ph.D. Professor of Biblical Studies, Trinity Episcopal School for Ministry, Ambridge, Pennsylvania, USA: **Qumran and Paul.**

O'Brien, Peter T., Ph.D. Vice-Principal and Head of the New Testament Department, Moore Theological College, Newtown, New South Wales, Australia: **Benediction, Blessing, Doxology, Thanksgiving; Caesar's Household, Imperial Household; Church; Colossians, Letter to the; Fellowship, Communion, Sharing; Firstborn; Letters, Letter Forms; Mystery; Mysticism.**

Onesti, Karen L., Ph.D. (Cand.). Adjunct Professor of Greek Language and Exegesis, Eastern Baptist Theological Seminary, Philadelphia, Pennsylvania, USA: **Righteousness, Righteousness of God.**

Osborne, Grant R., Ph.D. Professor of New Testament, Trinity Evangelical Divinity School, Deerfield, Illinois, USA: **Hermeneutics/Interpreting Paul.**

Paige, Terence P., Ph.D. (Cand.). Lecturer, Belfast Bible College, Belfast, Northern Ireland: **Demons, Exorcism; Holy Spirit; Philosophy.**

Painter, John, Ph.D., FAHA. Associate Professor and Reader in Religious Studies, La Trobe University, Melbourne, Victoria, Australia: **World, Cosmology.**

Patzia, Arthur G., Ph.D. Associate Professor of New Testament, Director, Fuller in Northern California, Fuller Theological Seminary, Menlo Park, California, USA: **Canon; Philemon, Letter to.**

Porter, Stanley E., Ph.D. Associate Professor of Religious Studies, Trinity Western University, Langley, British Columbia, Canada: **Fear, Reverence; Holiness, Sanctification; Peace, Reconciliation.**

Reasoner, Mark, Ph.D. Assistant Professor of Biblical Studies, Bethel College, St. Paul, Minnesota, USA: **Citizenship, Roman and Heavenly; Political Systems; Purity and Impurity; Rome and Roman Christianity.**

Reid, Daniel G., Ph.D. Reference and Academic Books Editor, InterVarsity Press, Downers Grove, Illinois, USA:

**Angels, Archangels; Elements/ Elemental Spirits of the World; Principalities and Powers; Prison, Prisoner; Satan, Devil; Triumph.**

Robeck, Cecil M. Jr., Ph.D. Associate Professor of Church History and Ecumenics, Fuller Theological Seminary, Pasadena, California, USA: **Knowledge, Gift of Knowledge; Prophecy, Prophesying; Tongues.**

Rupprecht, Arthur A., Ph.D. Professor of Classical Languages, Wheaton College, Wheaton, Illinois, USA: **Legal System, Roman; Slave, Slavery.**

Schmidt, Thomas E., Ph.D. Associate Professor of New Testament, Westmont College, Santa Barbara, California, USA: **Discipline; Riches and Poverty.**

Schnabel, E. J., Ph.D. Dozent, Bibelschule Wiedenest, Freie Theologische Akademie, Bergneustadt, Giessen, Germany: **Wisdom.**

Schreiner, Thomas R., Ph.D. Associate Professor of New Testament, Bethel Theological Seminary, St. Paul, Minnesota, USA: **Circumcision; Law of Christ; Works of the Law.**

Scott, James M., Th.D. Assistant Professor of Biblical Studies, Trinity Western University, Langley, British Columbia, Canada: **Adoption, Sonship; Restoration of Israel.**

Scott, J. Julius, Jr., Ph.D. Professor of Biblical and Historical Studies, Wheaton College Graduate School, Wheaton, Illinois, USA: **Immortality; Life and Death.**

Seifrid, Mark A., Ph.D. Assistant Professor of New Testament Interpretation, The Southern Baptist Theological Seminary, Louisville, Kentucky, USA: **In Christ.**

Silva, Moisés, Ph.D. Professor of New Testament, Westminster Theological Seminary, Philadelphia, Pennsylvania, USA: **Old Testament in Paul.**

Simpson, John W. Jr., Ph.D. Theology and Biblical Studies Editor, Wm. B. Eerdmans Publishing Co., Grand Rapids, Michigan, USA: **Thessalonians, Letters to the.**

Stegner, William R., Ph.D. Professor of New Testament, Garrett-Evangelical Theological Seminary, Evanston, Illinois, USA: **Diaspora; Jew, Paul the.**

Stein, Robert H., Ph.D. Professor of New Testament, Bethel Theological Seminary, St. Paul, Minnesota, USA: **Jerusalem.**

Thielman, Frank, Ph.D. Associate

Professor of Divinity, Beeson Divinity School, Samford University, Birmingham, Alabama, USA: **Law.**

Thompson, Michael B., Ph.D. Lecturer in New Testament Studies, St. John's College, Nottingham, England: **Stumbling Block; Strong and Weak; Teaching/Paraenesis; Tradition.**

Tidball, Derek J., Ph.D. Head of Department of Mission, Baptist Union of Great Britain, Didcot, Oxfordshire, England: **Social Setting of Mission Churches.**

Towner, Philip H., Ph.D. Research Fellow, Department of New Testament, University of Aberdeen, Aberdeen, Scotland: **Households and Household Codes.**

Travis, Stephen H., Ph.D. Vice-Principal and Lecturer in New Testament, St. John's College, Nottingham, England: **Judgment.**

Trebilco, Paul, Ph.D. Professor of New Testament Studies, Knox Theological Hall, Dunedin, New Zealand: **Itineraries, Travel Plans, Journeys, Apostolic Parousia.**

Trites, Allison A. Ph.D. The John Payzant Distinguished Professor of Biblical Studies, Acadia Divinity College, Acadia University, Wolfville, Nova Scotia, Canada: **Witness.**

Twelftree, Graham H., Ph.D. Minister, Hope Valley Uniting Church, Adelaide, South Australia, Australia: **Healing, Illness; Signs, Wonders, Miracles.**

Watson, Duane F., Ph.D. Associate Professor of New Testament Studies and Chair of Department of Religion and Philosphy, Malone College, Canton, Ohio, USA: **Diatribe.**

Winter, Bruce W., Ph.D. Warden, Tyndale House, Cambridge, England: **Rhetoric.**

Witherington, Ben III, Ph.D. Professor of Biblical and Wesleyan Studies, Ashland Theological Seminary, Ashland, Ohio, USA: **Christ; Christology.**

Wright, David F., M.A. Senior Lecturer in Ecclesiastical History, New College, The University of Edinburgh, Edinburgh, Scotland: **Homosexuality; Sexuality, Sexual Ethics.**

Wu, Julie L., Ph.D. Resident Faculty of New Testament Studies, Logos Evangelical Seminary, Pasadena, California, USA: **Liturgical Elements.**

Yamauchi, Edwin M., Ph.D. Professor of History, Miami University, Oxford, Ohio, USA: **Gnosis, Gnosticism; Hellenism.**

**ABBA.** *See* ADOPTION, SONSHIP; GOD; LITURGICAL ELEMENTS; PRAYER.

## ABRAHAM

Paul uses Abraham as a key figure in the development of his argument in his letters to the Galatians* and Romans.* He uses Abraham in a less significant way in 2 Corinthians.* Abraham figured prominently in Jewish literature contemporary with Paul, and these traditions provide a background against which Paul's use of Abraham in his letters may be better understood.

1. Abraham in the OT and Jewish Literature
2. Abraham in Galatians
3. Abraham in Romans
4. Abraham in 2 Corinthians

**1. Abraham in the OT and Jewish Literature.**
The role played by the patriarchs became increasingly important to the Jewish people after they returned from exile in Babylon. Abraham was one of these important figures whose stature is reflected in extrabiblical Jewish literature and in the NT.

*1.1. Abraham in the OT.* Later accounts of Abraham are based on the Genesis stories of the patriarch. The depiction of the life of Abraham is found in the first book of the Hebrew Bible, from his inclusion in the genealogy of his father, Terah (Gen 11:27), to his death and burial (Gen 25:7-10). The major events in Abraham's life are his leaving his father and birthplace (Gen 12:1), his sojourns in Egypt and Gerar (Gen 12:10-20; 20:1-18), his battle with the kings (Gen 14:1-16), his meeting with Melchizedek (Gen 14:17-20), God's* covenant with him (Gen 15:7-21; 17:2, 4), his union with Hagar and the birth of Ishmael (Gen 16:1-15), God's commandment of circumcision for Abraham and his descendants (Gen 17:9-14), the promise of the birth of Isaac (Gen 17:15-21), the birth of Isaac (Gen 21:1-7), the proposed offering of Isaac (Gen 22:1-19) and the death and burial of Sarah (Gen 23:1-20).

Four primary themes are found in the Genesis account: the promises from God that Abraham would have many descendants (Gen 12:2; 13:16; 15:5; 17:2, 4; 22:17) and the gift of a land (Gen 12:7; 13:14-15; 15:7), the obedience of Abraham (12:1-4; 17:1; 22:16-18) and the subsequent blessing of all nations through Abraham (Gen 12:3; 22:18).

Within the OT Abraham functions in three primary ways. First, he is the *father of the Jewish people* (Gen 25:19; 26:15, 24; 28:13; 32:9; 48:15-16; Ex 3:6; Deut 1:8; 6:10; 9:5; 30:20; Josh 24:3; 1 Chron 1:27-28, 34; 16:13; Ps 105:6; Is 41:8; Jer 33:26; Mic 7:20). Second, he is the *original source of blessing for the Jewish people* (Gen 26:24; 28:4; 35:12; 50:24; Ex 2:24; 6:3-8; 32:13; 33:1; Num 32:11; Deut 1:8; 6:10; 9:5, 27; 29:13; 30:20; 34:4; 2 Kings 13:23; 1 Chron 16:15-16; 2 Chron 20:7; Ps 105:7-11, 42; Is 51:2; Mic 7:20). Third, his name is used to identify the God of the Jewish people as "the *God of Abraham*" (Gen 28:13; 31:42, 53; 32:9; Ex 3:6, 15-16; 4:5; 1 Kings 18:36; 1 Chron 29:18; 2 Chron 30:6; Ps 47:9).

Abraham functions in three additional noteworthy ways. His obedience to God and his laws (Gen 26:4-5; see also Neh 9:7-8) was the basis for the blessing of his descendants. God's compassion toward the Jewish people is sometimes invoked on the basis of his covenant with Abraham (Deut 9:27; 2 Kings 13:23; Mic 7:18-20). Finally, God brings Abraham out of the midst of idolatry* (Josh 24:2-3).

*1.2. Abraham in Early Jewish Literature.* The authors of Jewish literature from 200 B.C. to A.D. 200 used many of the same themes found in the OT accounts in accordance with their particular situations. Josephus and Philo portray Abraham as one who assimilates pagan, particularly Hellenistic, culture (e.g., Josephus *Ant.* 1.8.2 §§166-68; Philo *Abr.* 88). In other texts Abraham is one who isolates himself from Gentile influence (*Jub.* 22:16; Pseudo-Philo *Bib. Ant.* 6:4). The authors of these texts have both apologetic and didactic motives. The Jews are instructed to live in their respective situations in the same way that Abraham is portrayed as living in a particular context.

Four major themes are found in these texts. First,

the stress on Abraham as a tenacious monotheist, often portrayed as the first of his kind, is prevalent in texts from both Palestine and the Diaspora from 200 B.C. to A.D. 200 (*Jub.* 11:16-17; 12:1-5, 16- 21; 20:6-9; Pseudo-Philo *Bib. Ant.* 6:4; Josephus *Ant.* 1.7.1 §§154-57; Philo *Abr.* 68-71, 88; *Apoc. Ab.* 1-8). Second, God establishes a covenant* with Abraham through which his descendants are blessed (*Jub.* 15:9-10; Pseudo-Philo *Bib. Ant.* 7:4; 1QapGen 21:8-14) and are shown compassion (Pseudo-Philo *Bib. Ant.* 30:7; *Pss. Sol.* 9:8-11; *T. Levi* 15:4; *As. Mos.* 3:8-9). However, sometimes one must obey the stipulations of the covenant in order to remain within it (*Jub.* 15:26-27). Eventually other nations would be blessed as well (Sir 44:21). Third, Abraham's character is extolled. He is righteous (*T. Abr.* 1:1A), hospitable (*T. Abr.* 1:1-3A; Philo *Abr.* 107-110; Josephus *Ant.* 1.11.2 §196) and virtuous (Josephus *Ant.* 1.7.1 §154; Philo *Abr.* 68). He is faithful (Sir 44:20; 1 Macc 2:52; *Jub.* 17:17-18), he loves God (*Jub.* 17:18) and is even called the friend of God (CD 3:2-4). Josephus maintains that Abraham and his seed are rewarded because of the patriarch's virtue and piety (*Ant.* 1.13.4 §234). Fourth, Abraham lived according to the Mosaic Law (*Jub.* 15:1-2; 16:20; Sir 44:20) or the natural/philosophical law (Philo *Abr.* 3-6). Abraham is alive (4 Macc 7:19; 16:25; *T. Levi* 18:14; *T. Jud.* 25:1; *T. Benj.* 10:6) and praises those who die for keeping the Law (4 Macc 13:13-18). Abraham established the covenant by being circumcised (Sir 44:20). Additionally, Abraham is noted for his powers of intercession (*T. Abr.* 18:10-11A) and his ascension to the heavens where he receives revelation (Pseudo-Philo *Bib. Ant.* 18:5; *T. Abr.* 10—14; *Apoc. Abr.* 15:4- 30).

## 2. Abraham in Galatians.

### 2.1. The Situation in Galatia.
From the letter itself it is evident that Gentile Christians were part of the community at Galatia (Gal 4:8) and that some persons came among them who contradicted Paul's gospel and confused these recent converts (Gal 1:7-9; 5:8-10). These persons persuaded Gentile converts to obey stipulations of Mosaic Law* (Gal 3:1-2; 4:8-10), especially circumcision* (Gal 5:2-3; 6:12-13). In view of the evidence in the letter, it seems most likely that Paul's opponents* were Jewish Christians (Gal 4:30; Paul refers to them as preaching "another gospel" in Gal 1:6-9; *see* Judaizers).

Many scholars have noted that Abraham must have played a central role in the arguments of Paul's opponents. For example, J. C. Beker maintains Paul's opponents were those who thought that the Gentiles'* turning to Christ was not enough. In order to be sure that God's blessing was upon them and that they were true children of Abraham, they had to participate fully in the Torah (Beker, 42-44).

### 2.2. The Text of Galatians.
#### 2.2.1. Galatians 3:1—3:14.
Paul's angry tone is evident from the beginning of his letter to the Galatians, omitting as it does the thanksgiving section usually found in his letters. He calls them "foolish" (Gal 3:1, 3) for having been "bewitched" (Gal 3:1) into obeying the requirements of the Law (Gal 3:2, 3, 5). His scathing questions in Galatians 3:1-5 serve to pinpoint his themes in his discussion which follows.

In his barbed questions, Paul sets up an antithesis between "works of the Law"* (*ergōn nomou*) and "hearing with faith" (*akoēs pisteōs*). Did God work miracles among them by their doing "works of the Law" or by their "hearing with faith?" (Gal 3:5). Paul's major concern here is to alert his readers to the contrast between "hearing with faith" and "works of the Law" and for them to consider the gross error into which they have fallen.

Paul's argument from Scripture, which is his answer to his own previous rhetorical questions (Betz, 130), revolves around Abraham: "just as Abraham believed God, and it was reckoned to him as righteousness" (Gal 3:6). B. Byrne points out that the use of *kathōs* ("just as") implies that what follows corresponds to what has just been described (Byrne, 148). Abraham becomes the one who believed in God and, by God's action, was reckoned righteous. This corresponds to the Spirit supplied by God because of the faith of the Galatian believers. The receipt of the Spirit by the Galatian believers is parallel to Abraham's receipt of righteousness* (Barclay, 80; *see* Holy Spirit).

In using Abraham to discuss the contrast of faith versus works, Paul is using Abraham in a new way. Previously Judaism had viewed Abraham's faith and his works together. For example, in *Jubilees* Abraham is not only the first to separate from his family and worship* the one Creator God* (*Jub.* 11:16-17; 12:16-21), but he also observes stipulations of the Mosaic Law such as the Feast of Tabernacles (*Jub.* 16:20; cf. 22:1-2). In Philo's works Abraham is portrayed as following the natural law (Philo *Abr.* 275-76). To Philo, the law of nature and the Law of Moses are identical. Only law which was revealed by God, the creator of nature, can really be in accordance with natural law. By following the natural law Abraham becomes an example of obedience to the Law for his descendants (Philo *Abr.* 6).

Philo is the only one who actually tells us that Genesis 15:6 was interpreted to mean that Abraham believed in the one Creator God in contrast to other gods or philosophies. Genesis 15:6 states "and Abraham believed God, and it was reckoned to him as righteousness." Philo describes Abraham by saying "he is spoken of as the first person to believe in God, since he first grasped a firm and unswerving conception of the truth that there is one Cause above all and that it provides for the world and all that there is therein" (Philo *Virt.* 216). Abraham is the first one to be spoken of in both the LXX and the Hebrew Bible as believing in God. Most often those who spoke of the faith of Abraham spoke of it as faith in the one God (Josephus *Ant.* 1.7.1 §§155-56; *Apoc. Abr.* 7:10; Pseudo-Philo *Bib. Ant.* 6:4; 23:5) in contrast to idolatry. The law, whether Mosaic or natural (see above), was a necessary corollary to his belief in God. Because Abraham was believed to have embodied these characteristics, he functioned as an ideal representative of the Jewish people.

In Galatians 3:7 Paul commands the Galatian believers to recognize from his proof in Galatians 3:6 (cf. Gen 15:6; Betz, 141) that "it is the people of faith who are the sons of Abraham." Anyone among them who was at all familiar with the traditions of Abraham as the first monotheist and anti-idolater would realize that the Jewish people had interpreted Abraham as the man of faith* all along. This statement of Paul's would ring true. To them the descendants of Abraham—the Jews—would be the people of faith in God.

Paul again uses Scripture to back up his claim that the children of Abraham are those who have faith in God. In Galatians 3:8-9 he states, "And the Scriptures, seeing that God would justify the Gentiles by faith, declared the gospel beforehand to Abraham saying that 'All the Gentiles will be blessed in you.' " Paul personifies the Scripture, saying that it saw in advance that God would justify the Gentiles by faith and declared the gospel beforehand to Abraham that all the Gentiles would be blessed in him (Gal 3:8; Gen 12:3). Paul understands the promise to Abraham that he would be a blessing to the nations (Gentiles) as the anticipatory preaching of the gospel* to Abraham. Because the message of the gospel was that justification* comes by faith, and thus Gentiles were included in justification, the announcement that God would bless the Gentiles through Abraham anticipated the gospel.

In the meantime Paul picks up the other thread of his argument, the "works of the Law" (Gal 3:10). Using Deuteronomy 27:26, Habakkuk 2:4 and Leviticus 18:5 Paul argues that obedience to Law does not bring righteousness. He uses Deuteronomy 21:23 to show that the era of faith has now arrived through Christ's becoming a curse* and providing redemption from the curse of the Law (Gal 3:13; Byrne, 156). It is probable that Paul is dealing here with the very passages that his opponents used in their message in support of the Law (Longenecker, 116-21, 124).

In Galatians 3:14 Paul includes two purpose clauses. Christ became a curse and provided redemption* from the curse of the Law in order that in Christ Jesus the blessing of Abraham might come upon the Gentiles (cf. Gal 3:8). The second purpose clause is parallel to the first: "In order that we might receive the promise of the Spirit through faith" (3:14b). The Spirit becomes the blessing of Abraham which has come upon the Gentiles (Betz, 143). This blessing is by faith (Gal 3:1-5) in Christ (Gal 3:14). Formerly the promise to Abraham referred to land and descendants. But now the promise refers to the Spirit which is a foretaste of the inheritance of the world to come (Byrne, 156-57). And if the Gentiles in Galatia have the Spirit, which is the blessing promised to Abraham in Christ, they have the sign that they are members of the descendants of Abraham.

What is noteworthy in the letter thus far is that Paul alludes to two aspects of Judaism that are also related to the major traditions about Abraham found in Jewish texts mentioned above: faith and Law. Paul has argued forcefully against the Law. The Gentiles have received the blessing of Abraham, the Spirit, solely according to their faith. If the opponents are using Abraham in their arguments to convince the Gentiles that they must be obedient to the Mosaic Law, especially with regard to circumcision, it would seem that they are aware of the tradition of Abraham's obedience to the Law and are making use of that tradition (see also Hansen, 172).

*2.2.2. Galatians 3:15-18.* Paul begins this section by referring to an everyday example, namely a person's testament or will, which is neither annulled nor added to once it has been ratified. Paul uses this example to discuss Abraham by showing that the promises, originally made to Abraham and his seed (Gal 3:16), were made not to many but to one, which actually refers to Christ (Gen 12:7; 22:17-18). Paul plays upon the word *seed*, which, in both Hebrew and Greek (Heb *zera'*; Gk *sperma*), is a collective singular (Ellis, 73). The one descendant, Christ, represents not only the fulfillment of the promises to Abraham (Gal 3:8, 14) but also represents the head of the spiritual race and, subsequently, the solidarity of believers. Gentiles, who were formerly considered to be outside of the descendants of Abraham, are now included within the realm of his descendants by virtue of their faith in Christ.

Paul next argues from a chronological standpoint. The Law actually came 430 years after the covenant that God ratified with Abraham (Gal 3:17); in fact the Law was "added" (Gal 3:19). God's promise to Abraham is foundational and unchanging (Gal 3:16, 18). Those who are children of Abraham "in Christ" benefit from the promise and inheritance he received before the coming of the Law.

If the opponents of Paul in Galatia are using the popular tradition that Abraham obeyed the Law (see above), the opponents must also have argued that Abraham was obedient to the Law before it was given by Moses. If this was the example of Abraham which the opponents were giving to the believers in Galatia, Paul must argue forcefully that the Mosaic Law actually came after the promise had been made to Abraham. If the Mosaic Law arrived centuries after the promise to Abraham, then Abraham could not have been obedient to that Law. This new chronology (overturning the rabbinic exegetical "principle" that in the Torah there is no before or after) establishes the priority of Paul's gospel of justification by faith over the opponents' insistence of obedience to the Law.

*2.2.3. Galatians 3:19-22.* In this section Paul addresses the reasons why Law was necessary (Gal 3:19). It was added because of transgressions until the offspring (Christ) should come to whom the promises had been made (Gal 3:19; cf. Gal 3:16). According to Paul, God gave Abraham this inheritance directly through promise: "For if the inheritance is based on Law, it does not come from the promise; but God granted it to Abraham through the promise" (Gal 3:18). Paul states that the Law, however, was "ordained through angels by means of a mediator" (Gal 3:19). The giving of the Law by angels* was a common Jewish tradition (LXX Deut 33:2; LXX Ps 67:18 *Jub.* 2:2; *1 Enoch* 60:1; also NT, Acts 7:38, 53; Heb 2:2). Paul deviates from the tradition in that he argues that the giving of the Law by angels is taken as a point against the Law. In his contrast between the direct communication of the promises to Abraham and the indirect mediation of the Law, Paul is drawing attention to the inferiority of the Law. Not only is God's promise to Abraham prior to the Law (Gal 3:16-17), but it is superior because it was communicated directly to Abraham without a mediator.

In Galatians 3:20 Paul makes a statement that has long puzzled interpreters of Galatians: "but the mediator is not one, but God is one." The plurality associated with the "mediator" has been understood in several ways (Longenecker, 141-42). Interpreters have searched for Paul's exact referent in his allusion to the plurality of angels who served as mediators involved in giving the Law (cf. Wright for the view that Moses is the mediator). But this is to miss Paul's overall point. The most important item to glean from Paul's state-

ment is that somehow the Law coming through angels via the agency of a mediator implies more than one intermediary in contrast to God, who gave the promise to Abraham and who is one. In reference to Jewish monotheism of the day, this kind of statement, which contrasts the oneness of God* who gave the promise to Abraham with the plurality of intermediaries through whom the Law was given, clearly demonstrates again the superiority of the promise to Abraham over the Law.

It was noted above that popular traditions of Abraham found in Jewish literature included the notion that Abraham was the first monotheist and that he obeyed the Law before it was given. If these traditions were also held by Paul's opponents, their appeal to the example of Abraham probably had something to do with his monotheism and obedience to Law. In Galatians 3:20, using the opponents' own contentions and the popular traditions which linked Abraham to monotheism and Law, Paul demonstrates that the Law is actually second-rate when compared to God's promises to Abraham. Consequently, if the promises are superior to the Law, and if it is through the promises to Abraham that the inheritance comes to those united in Christ (the "one" seed, Gal 3:16), the Law becomes superfluous. Not only does being a descendant of Abraham no longer mean that one has to follow Jewish Law, but obedience to the Law which is based upon a plurality is now a contradiction of the oneness of God.

*2.2.4. Galatians 3:23-29.* In this section Paul uses the example of the *paidagōgos* (NRSV "disciplinarian") to explain the function of the Law. The use of a *paidagōgos* was a prevalent custom in Paul's day. It entailed placing one's child or children under the care or oversight of a trusted slave until the child reached late adolescence. Just what Paul had in mind when he related the *paidagōgos* to the Law has been much debated. Rather than viewing the *paidagōgos* in terms of severity as had previously been the case (Betz, 177-78), more recently scholars have concentrated upon positive aspects of the *paidagōgos*. For example, the guardianship of the *paidagōgos* protected the charge from outside immoral influences (Young, Gordon). In Galatians 3:24 Paul associates the Law with *paidagōgos* which functioned "until Christ came, in order that we might be justified by faith" (Gal 3:24). Once faith came, the *paidagōgos* was no longer necessary (Gal 3:25).

Jewish literature testifies that one of the primary functions of the Law was that it served to separate and protect Israel from her Gentile neighbors (*Jub.* 20:6-10; 21:21-24; 22:16-19; Josephus *Ant.* 1.10.5 §192). Another aspect of the Law, particularly circumcision, was to identify the Jewish people (*Quaest. in Gen.* 3.49; cf. *Jub.* 15:26). In the context of Paul's letter to the Galatians he speaks primarily of those aspects of Law that were especially known to identify the Jewish people (circumcision, food* laws, and the observation of the Sabbath and festival days; *see* Holy Days). One way that the Law functioned as a *paidagōgos* was to guard the Jewish people from outside influences of idolatry and immorality. Paul says that now that faith has come, the Law is no longer necessary. The Law as a protective device in a community like the one at Galatia, where both Gentile and Jewish Christians exist side by side, is obsolete because they all have faith and belong to the same community "in Christ"* (Gal 3:26). Separation by means of Law is now unnecessary. Additionally, the identifying symbol of circumcision is no longer necessary. All the believers in Galatia were now one in Christ Jesus (Gal 3:28). Because the believers in Galatia are one by virtue of their faith in Christ, they are Abraham's descendants and heirs of the promise made to him (Gal 3:29; cf. Gal 3:8).

*2.2.5. Galatians 4:1-11.* In Galatians 4:1-2 Paul uses the imagery of an heir who, as a child, is under "guardians and trustees" until the date set by his father. Paul is probably referring to practices in Roman law in which guardians were appointed over a minor by the father either in a will or in a court of law (Belleville, 63). The father could also stipulate the age at which the child would no longer be under such guardians. Paul asserts the temporary nature of the Law, and it is apparent that the heir is not in control of his own affairs. In this sense the heir is no better than a slave.*

It is the minors, probably Jews (cf. Gal 3:23, 25; 4:1-2; Longenecker, 165), who were enslaved to the "elements of the world"* (*stoicheia tou kosmou*). However, now that the "fullness of time has come" (Gal 4:4; cf. Gal 4:2) both Gentiles and Jews are heirs, the Spirit being proof that they are no longer slaves (Gal 4:6-7).

In Galatians 4:8 Paul addresses the Gentiles alone. In the previous age they neither knew God nor were they recognized by God. They were enslaved by things which by nature "were not gods." The phrase "were not gods" is a familiar one in Septuagintal literature where it refers to idols (2 Chron 13:9-10; Is 37:18-19; Jer 2:11-28). Paul accuses them of returning to their former idolatry (Gal 4:9).

In the context of the situation in Galatia, these Gentile believers are being persuaded to obey different aspects of Jewish Law (Gal 5:2-3; 6:12-13; 4:10; see also above). Paul compares their obedience to the Law with their former idolatry (Gal 4:8-9) and to their ens-

lavement under the "elements of the world" (*stoicheia tou kosmou*). Both obedience to the Law and idolatry are forms of enslavement under these "elements of the world." Obedience to the Law has become tantamount to idolatry.

It was noted above that in Jewish traditions about Abraham he was portrayed as believing in the one Creator God in contrast to other gods or philosophies.* Most often Jews who spoke of the faith of Abraham thought of it as faith in the one God in contrast to idolatry (*Jub.* 11:16-17; 12:2-8, 16-24; Pseudo-Philo *Bib. Ant.* 6:4; 23:5; Philo *Abr.* 68-71; *Apoc. Abr.* 1—8). For Paul both Jewish and Gentile believers are now true children of Abraham (Gal 3:29; 4:6-7). As such they are no longer to be enslaved to the elements of the world, which formerly functioned as Gentile paganism and Jewish Law. In equating the observance of Law with idolatry, Paul makes the Law the ultimate taboo for a true child of Abraham. Like Abraham the anti-idolater, these children of Abraham are to avoid idolatry. In Galatians 4:1-10, however, now that these children of Abraham have a new identity "in Christ," the idolatry to be avoided is obedience to the Law.

*2.2.6. Galatians 4:12-20.* In Galatians 4:12-20 Paul speaks of the Galatians' response to his first preaching of the gospel and his desire to see them again. In Galatians 4:14 Paul states that when he visited them they welcomed him "as an angel of God, as Christ Jesus." This is the only place in his letters where Paul compares himself to an angel. His commendation of the Galatians for welcoming him as a superhuman being (Longenecker, 192) is cryptic; it may go back to the allusion in Galatians 1:8 or even the story in Acts 14:8-18.

Another major tradition about Abraham is that he was known for his hospitality (*T. Abr.* 1:2A; 1:10B; Josephus *Ant.* 1.11.2 §196; Philo *Abr.* 107), a quality particularly exhibited in Genesis 18:1-8 where Abraham welcomes the three angelic visitors. It may be that in Galatians 4:14 Paul's intention is to imply that the believers in Galatia are true descendants of Abraham by the way that they too show hospitality to others as if they are angels.

*2.2.7. Galatians 4:21—5:1.* Paul's final discourse on Abrahamic descendants is found in his allegory of Sarah and Hagar (Gal 4:21—5:1). Paul's apparently arbitrary exegesis in this allegory may indicate that this was not his choice of text (Gen 16:15; 21:2-12), but that it was being used by his opponents to their own advantage (Lincoln, 12; Barclay, 91). Paul constructs the allegory around the literal sons of Abraham, Isaac and Ishmael. Hagar is interpreted to represent the covenant of slavery, the Law (Gal 4:24-25). Sarah is interpreted to represent the covenant of freedom (Gal 4:24, 26). Anyone (even those at Jerusalem,* Gal 4:25) who is in bondage to the Law (Gal 4:24) is actually enslaved and will not inherit with the true children. The children of promise, who are born of Isaac (Gal 4:28), are members of the heavenly Jerusalem (Gal 4:26) and are more numerous than those in bondage (Gal 4:27).

Paul concludes the allegory in Galatians 4:28—5:1. He identifies the Galatians as being like Isaac, the children of promise (Gal 4:28). At the present time the persecution they are experiencing is like that which Isaac experienced at the hand of Ishmael (Gen 21:9; Gal 4:29; see also Betz, 249-50). Paul uses Genesis 21:10 as instruction for the present: the Galatians who are being persecuted for not being obedient to the Law are to "cast out" those who are persecuting them (Gal 4:30; Lincoln, 22-29). They are children of the free woman; Christ has set them free from the Law. They are commanded not to submit again to the Law, the "yoke of slavery" (Gal 5:1; see also Gal 4:3, 9).

### 3. Abraham in Romans.

Most of the discussion of Abraham is found in Romans 4 where Paul uses the patriarch to show how Gentiles as well as Jews can now be righteous before God by virtue of their faith in Jesus Christ. In Romans 9—11 Paul again refers to Abraham in order to show how God's promises to his chosen people have not failed (Rom 9:6).

*3.1. The Situation in Rome.* Paul's purpose in writing Romans* has been a matter of debate (Donfried; *see* Rome). It is likely that the house churches (Rom 16:5, 10-11, 14-15) to which Paul writes were influenced to some degree by the Jewish community (Dunn, xlvi, xlvii; Calvert, "Traditions") and struggled over the relationship Gentile Christians now had with God (Rom 4:2, 11-12) especially in light of practices related to Jewish Law (Rom 14:2, 5, 6, 21; Wedderburn, 33-34).

*3.2. The Text in Light of Abrahamic Traditions.*

*3.2.1. Romans 1:1—3:26.* After his section of thanksgiving and travel plans (Rom 1:8-15; *see* Itinerary), Paul announces his thesis statement, proclaiming that the gospel is the "power* of God for salvation to everyone who has faith," both Jew and Greek (Rom 1:16), and that through faith in this gospel the righteousness* of God is revealed (Rom 1:17; Ziesler, 186-87). In Romans 1:1—3:20 Paul shows that both idolatrous and immoral Gentiles (Rom 1:18-32; cf. *Jub.* 22:11-23; *1 Enoch* 91:7-10; although Jews may be idolaters implicitly, see Hays, 93-94), and Jews who boast in their relationship to God and the Law (Rom 2:1- 29, esp. Rom 2:17), are condemned before God (Rom 3:9-20).

In Romans 3:21-26 Paul shows how God has continued to be righteous, but now apart from Law (Rom 3:21 cf. Rom 1:17). Participation in the realm of the righteousness of God (Ziesler, 186-87) is now to be found through faith in Jesus Christ for both Jew and Gentile (Rom 3:22): there is no distinction.

*3.2.2. Romans 3:27—4:25.* Romans 3:27—4:25 functions both as a clarification of what Paul has already discussed and as an introduction to the example of faith provided by Abraham. Paul uses the principle of Jewish monotheism against a common contention of Jewish particularism. Because God is one, he is the God of both Jews and Gentiles (Rom 3:29). And because God is one, he justifies both Jews and Gentiles on the basis of the same criterion—faith (Rom 3:30). Jews and Gentiles then have equal access to salvation. "This is, in effect, an argument against the law as being in any way necessary for salvation" (Sanders 1977, 489). Through his example of Abraham, Paul will show how his interpretation actually upholds the Law (Rom 3:31).

Paul first identifies Abraham in a strictly Jewish sense as "our forefather according to the flesh" (Rom 4:1) and asks what it was that Abraham "found" (the verb is *heuriskō*). Several traditions of Abraham depicted him finding the one God (see above; especially Philo *Abr.* 68-71 and Josephus *Ant.* 1.7.1 154-57, where he discerns God's existence from the creation). It is generally held that Paul in Romans 1:18-32 is indebted to the Hellenistic Jewish thought that lies behind Wisdom 12—15, if not to that text itself (Dunn, 56-57; Calvert, "Traditions"). Wisdom 13:6-9 speaks of people seeking to find (*heuriskō*) God. Additional texts which refer to people "finding" (*heuriskō*) God through intellectual discovery are also present in the LXX (Is 55:6; 65:1), the works of Philo (*Spec. Leg.* 1.36; *Leg. All.* 3.47) and the NT (Acts 17:26-27; Rom 10:20). In Romans 4:17 Paul also refers to Abraham as believing in God the Creator (see below). This belief in the one God as the Creator was foundational to Jewish monotheism. Only if the God of the Jews was the Creator was he the one, true God (cf. *Sib. Or.* Fr. 1.7). In the context of Paul's discussion of idolatry in Romans 1, in his use of "one God" in proving that both Jew and Gentile are justified by faith (Rom 3:29-30) and in his introduction of the example of Abraham, it may be that he expects his readers to assume he will speak of Abraham who "found" the one, true Creator God.

A second natural response of someone who was familiar with the traditions of Abraham would be that not only was he the first monotheist, but that he obeyed the Law (see 1.2 above) even before it was given. Paul foresees this interpretation in his statement in Romans 4:2: "For if Abraham was justified by works, he has something to boast about, but not before God." Paul already used the term for boasting* to describe the boasting by the Jews in reference to their perceived privileged status (Rom 2:17, 23; 3:27). Abraham, who was understood to have been obedient to the Law before it was given and who represented the ideal Jew, could indeed boast—but not before God (Rom 4:2). If Abraham could not boast in his works, who among the Jewish Christians could then be so bold as to boast in their obedience to the Law?

Paul proves why it is that Abraham cannot boast in his works before God by citing Genesis 15:6, "Abraham believed God and it was reckoned to him as righteousness." Abraham becomes a paradigmatic type of how it is that God makes human beings righteous (Sanders 1983, 33). In clarifying what he means by "reckoned" Paul uses the analogy of one who works and to whom wages are paid, not as a gift but as what is due (Rom 4:4), in contrast to one who believes in him who justifies the ungodly (Rom 4:5). All of this is given in order that Paul may answer his first question about what Abraham found. Through his faith Abraham found grace* (Rom 4:4; cf. Gen 18:3; 30:27; 32:5; 33:8, 10, 15; 34:11; 39:4; 47:25, 29; 50:4).

In Romans 4:9-12 Paul shows how Abraham is the father of both the Jews (circumcised) and the Gentiles (uncircumcised). The figure of Abraham was connected with circumcision* in the Jewish world because Abraham was the first to participate in the covenant of circumcision (Gen 17:9-14; Sir 44:20). Referring to the "blessed" whose sins are forgiven (Rom 4:7-8; cf. Ps 32:1-2), Paul asks whether this blessedness is "pronounced on the circumcised alone, or also upon the uncircumcised?" (Rom 4:9). In order to answer the question Paul begins by paraphrasing Genesis 15:6: It was Abraham's faith that resulted in God's forgiveness* because Abraham as a result of his faith was reckoned righteous. Through further rhetorical questions in Romans 4:10-12 Paul proves that Abraham was reckoned righteous while he was uncircumcised (Rom 4:10; cf. Gen 15:6, Gen 17). For Paul circumcision was a seal of the righteousness Abraham had by faith while he was yet uncircumcised (Rom 4:11). Thus Abraham is the father of all those who believe who are not circumcised and who are reckoned righteous (Gentiles; Rom 4:11), and of those who are not only circumcised but who also follow the example of the faith of Abraham while he was still uncircumcised (Jews; Rom 4:12). Whereas circumcision once marked one as a descendant of Abraham (Gen 17:9-14), Paul has shown that by virtue of their common faith in

Christ, both Gentiles and Jews have Abraham as their father.

Paul's concern in Romans 4:13-17 is the promise to Abraham and his seed. He states that the promise did not come through the Law but through the "righteousness of faith" (Rom 4:13). What Abraham was to inherit here, as in other Jewish literature, was not just the land of promise but the *world* (Rom 4:14; Sir 44:21; *Jub.* 17:3; 22:14; 32:19; Philo *Som.* 1.175; Dunn, 213). The necessity of the Law for the Jewish people was a major part of their identity. Paul is refuting the idea that in order to be an heir of the promise of Abraham, one has to be Jewish in terms of obedience to the Mosaic Law. Paul further states that if "those of the Law" (*hoi ek nomou*) are the heirs, then "faith is empty and the promise is nullified" (Rom 4:14). According to Dunn the phrase should be taken to mean those who saw their continuing existence as Jews arising out of the Law, which determined all that was characteristic and distinctive in all that they were and did as God's people (Dunn, 213-14). If those who identify themselves as the people of God by their obedience to the Law are heirs, then faith is empty because it is not the basis for the inheritance. Additionally, the Law brings wrath* and reveals transgression (Rom 4:15).

Most Jews would have seen the function of the Law in a positive light as that which both identified them and separated them from other nations. Instead Paul here points out negative functions of the Law. Paul's gives a further reason why the promise must be according to faith: the promise must be according to grace so that it may be guaranteed to all the descendants of Abraham. It is not only for those Christians who identify themselves as the people of God by virtue of their obedience to the Law (Rom 4:16) but also for those Christians who share the faith of Abraham who is the "father of many nations" (Rom 4:17; 12:3; 22:18). Abraham is not merely the father of the chosen nation Israel.

Abraham's faith is described by two familiar phrases from Jewish literature (Rom 4:17). Abraham's faith was in God's creative ability to call into being that which existed from that which did not exist (*2 Apoc. Bar.* 21:4; 48:8; Philo *Rer. Div. Her.* 36; *Spec. Leg.* 4.187; 2 Macc 7:28). And Abraham had faith in the God "who gives life to the dead" (Rom 4:17). This description of God was also popular in Judaism as is attested by its use to describe the conversion of Gentiles (*Jos. and As.* 27:10). However in Romans 4:18-22 Paul explains Abraham's faith in the God who gave life to the dead by referring to the Genesis narrative. Abraham's faith in God's promise that he would become the father of many nations (Rom 4:18; Gen 15:5) did not weaken even when he considered his own body which was already "as good as dead" (impotent; Rom 4:19) or when he considered that Sarah's womb was "dead." Paul is describing Abraham's faith in God (Rom 4:21) and his promise of offspring (Rom 4:20) in spite of the physical incapability on the part of the marriage partners, himself and Sarah. Therefore it was written that Abraham's faith was "reckoned to him as righteousness" (Rom 4:21; cf. Gen 15:6 and above), not for the sake of Abraham alone, but for the sake of Paul and his readers as well (Rom 4:23-24). Faith will be reckoned as righteousness to those who believe in him who raised Jesus Christ from the dead, who was handed over to death for their trespasses and raised for their justification (Rom 4:25).

The monotheistic faith of Abraham which was so central in Jewish tradition has been transformed by Paul. The faith of believers who follow after the faith of Abraham is now in the one creator God who raised Jesus Christ from the dead so that they too could be made righteous.

*3.2.3. Romans 9—11.* In Romans 9—11 Paul proceeds generally to show how it is that God's word to Israel has not failed (Rom 9:6). The foundational patriarch Paul uses in his discussion is Abraham (Rom 9:3-9; 11:1). Paul's first point in his argument is that God's word has not failed because "not all of Abraham's children are his true descendants" (Rom 9:7). For proof he cites Genesis 21:12: "through Isaac descendants will be named for you." Paul further clarifies in Romans 9:8 that the children of the flesh (all ethnic Jews) are not the children of God, but the children of promise are reckoned as the descendants of Abraham (*see* Israel).

By using Genesis 21:12 Paul is making the point that the Jewish Christians at Rome already know that ethnic descent from Abraham is not the same as being his true descendant. It was through Isaac that Abraham's true descendants were named (cf. Rom 9:10, 13). Neither Ishmael nor the sons of Keturah (Gen 25:1-4) were counted as the true descendants of Abraham. According to Paul's proof, this is because Isaac was the descendant of the promise of God. To further support his argument Paul includes the promise from the angel to Abraham, "About this time I will return and Sarah will have a son" (Rom 9:9; Gen 18:10). Neither Hagar nor Keturah were the women through whom the promise was actualized. Only Sarah, whose childbearing years were long over (Rom 4:19), was the woman through whom God fulfilled his promise of a descendant to Abraham.

Paul's final use of Abraham in Romans occurs in Romans 11:1 where he calls himself "an Israelite, a descendant of Abraham." In view of Paul's previous discussion about the definition of a true descendant of Abraham (Rom 4:13-18; 9:7-8), it is reasonable to assume that here Paul is not simply referring to his ethnic Jewish heritage. Paul continues to argue that God's word has not failed (Rom 9:6) by showing that the stumbling of Israel has brought salvation to the Gentiles (Rom 11:11-13), who have been grafted into the people of God because of their faith (Rom 11:20). In Paul's argument "hardening" has come upon a part of Israel, and in their present unbelief (Rom 11:29) ethnic Jews have been broken off (Rom 11:20). The Jews, however, can be grafted back into the olive* tree (Rom 11:24). This leads Paul to state that with respect to the gospel, ethnic Jews are enemies,* but with respect to their election they are beloved "for the sake of their fathers" (Rom 11:28). In this case Paul gives evidence of knowing the tradition of Abraham's ethnic descendants receiving special consideration (*Bib. Ant.* 30:7; 35:3). God's original word has not failed (Rom 9:6). Ethnic Jews will also be among the true descendants of Abraham once again, not by virtue of their identity found in obedience to the Law but by reason of their faith. This faith will be after the example of Abraham's faith (Rom 4:17-25), a faith which has been deepened from its starting point in Jewish monotheism to incorporate faith in Jesus Christ (*see* God).

**4. Abraham in 2 Corinthians.**
In 2 Corinthians 11:22 Paul, in response to the boasts of his opponents in Corinth, calls himself a descendant of Abraham. Most scholars agree that by designating himself a "descendant of Abraham" Paul has more in mind than ethnic derivation. For example, R. P. Martin suggests that Paul is using the term for himself "as a badge of honor to mark out his Christian self-identity over against his rivals" (Martin, 375).

*See also* Circumcision; Faith; Galatians, Letter to the; Gentiles; Israel; Judaizers; Justification; Law; Moses; Old Testament in Paul; Righteousness, Righteousness of God; Romans, Letter to the; Works of the Law.

BIBLIOGRAPHY. J. Barclay, *Obeying the Truth: A Study of Paul's Ethics in Galatians* (Edinburgh: T. & T. Clark, 1988); J. C. Beker, *Paul the Apostle: The Triumph of God in Life and Thought* (Philadelphia: Fortress, 1980); L. L. Belleville, " 'Under Law': Structural Analysis and the Pauline concept of Law in Galatians 3:21—4:11," *JSNT* 26 (1986) 53-78; H. D. Betz, *Galatians: A Commentary on Paul's Letter to the Churches in Galatia* (Philadelphia: Fortress, 1979); B. Byrne, *Son of God—'Seed of Abraham': A Study of the Idea of the Sonship of God of All*

*Christians in Paul against the Jewish Background* (Rome: Biblical Institute, 1979); N. L. Calvert, "Abraham and Idolatry: Paul's Comparison of Obedience to the Law to Idolatry in Galatians 4:1-10," in *Paul and the Scriptures of Israel,* ed. C. A. Evans and J. A. Sanders (JSNTSup83; Sheffield: JSOT, 1992); idem, "Traditions of Abraham in Middle Jewish Literature: Implications for the Interpretation of Paul's Epistles to the Galatians and to the Romans" (Ph.D. diss., University of Sheffield, 1993); K. P. Donfried, ed., *The Romans Debate* (rev. ed.; Peabody, MA: Hendrickson, 1991); J. D. G. Dunn, *Romans* (WBC 38; Dallas: Word, 1988); E. E. Ellis, *Paul's Use of the Old Testament* (Edinburgh: Oliver & Boyd, 1957); T. D. Gordon, "A Note on *ΠΑΙΔΑΓΩΓΟΣ* in Galatians 3:24-25," *NTS* 35 (1989) 150-54; G. W. Hansen, *Abraham in Galatians: Epistolary and Rhetorical Contexts* (Sheffield: JSOT, 1989); R. B. Hays, *Echoes of Scripture in the Letters of Paul* (New Haven: Yale University, 1989); A. T. Lincoln, "Abraham Goes to Rome: Paul's Treatment of Abraham in Romans 4," in *Worship, Theology and Ministry in the Early Church,* ed. M. J. Wilkins and T. Paige (JSNTSup 87; Sheffield: JSOT, 1992); idem, *Paradise Now and Not Yet: Studies in the Role of the Heavenly Dimension in Paul's Thought with Special Reference to His Eschatology* (SNTSMS 43; Cambridge: University Press, 1982; repr., Grand Rapids: Baker, 1991); R. N. Longenecker, *Galatians* (WBC 41; Dallas: Word, 1990); R. P. Martin, *2 Corinthians* (WBC 40; Waco, TX: Word, 1986); E. P. Sanders, *Paul, the Law, and the Jewish People* (Philadelphia: Fortress, 1983); idem, *Paul and Palestinian Judaism* (Philadelphia: Fortress, 1977); J. M. Scott, *Adoption as Sons of God* (WUNT 2.48; Tübingen: J. C. B. Mohr, 1992); A. J. M. Wedderburn, *The Reasons for Romans* (Minneapolis: Fortress, 1991); N. T. Wright, "The Seed and the Mediator: Galatians 3.15-20," in *The Climax of the Covenant* (Minneapolis: Fortress, 1991) 157-74; N. H. Young, "*Paidagōgos*: The Social Setting of a Pauline Metaphor," *NovT* 29.2 (1987) 150-76; J. A. Ziesler, *The Meaning of Righteousness in Paul* (SNTSMS 20; Cambridge: University Press, 1972).

N. L. Calvert

**ACCURSED.** *See* CURSE, ACCURSED, ANATHEMA.

**ACTS.** *See* CHRONOLOGY OF PAUL; ITINERARIES, TRAVEL PLANS, JOURNEYS, APOSTOLIC PAROUSIA; PAUL IN ACTS AND LETTERS.

# ADAM AND CHRIST

Although references to the OT figure of Adam in the Pauline corpus are by no means extensive, its use is highly significant in that Adam serves as a vehicle to communicate tremendous theological truths about marriage,* sin,* death (*see* Life and Death), human nature and eschatological hope.* Most importantly, "Adam" stands as a theological counterpart within Paul's christological teaching, with Adam and Christ* as the two halves of an analogy explicitly formulated in both Romans 5 and 1 Corinthians 15.

This analogy presents Adam and Christ as corporate heads of two contrasting orders of existence and may be taken as one of the most revealing ways in which the apostle's theological thought is expressed: Adam embodies fallen humanity and Christ embodies redeemed humanity. Thus, within these two chapters we see the intersection of several key theological concerns, namely anthropology, christology, soteriology and ecclesiology. It is because of the fact that so many central Pauline themes come together in connection with the Adam-Christ analogy that it could be said to lie close to the heart of Paul's thought (*see* Center). It is precisely because of its central significance that the Adam-Christ analogy has remained an important focus of NT interpretation over the years.

1. Adam: The Generic Sense of the Term
2. Adam: The Historical Figure
3. Adam: The Typological Figure
4. Adam and the Image of God
5. Adam and the Body of Christ

**1. Adam: The Generic Sense of the Term.**
The name *Adam* occurs within the Pauline corpus only seven times (Rom 5:14 [twice]; 1 Cor 15:22, 45 [twice]; 1 Tim 2:13, 14), although some would see a few of the more generalized discussions about "man" (*anthrōpos*) as also having an Adamic background in Paul's thought. This is due to the fact that the Hebrew term *'ādām* can refer to not only "Adam" the individual but to the generic "humankind" as well. It is entirely proper to view Paul's use of Adam as closely connected to a number of other anthropological images and expressions he uses to communicate the Christian experience, the new life found in Jesus Christ. Included among these are: old man/new man (Rom 6:6; Col 3:9-10; Eph 2:15; 4:22-24; *see* New Nature and Old Nature); outer man/inner man (2 Cor 4:16; Rom 7:22; Eph 3:15); physical man/spiritual man (2 Cor 2:14-16; *see* Psychology). Related to this larger anthropological sense of Adam are those passages where Paul uses the pronoun "I" in such a way as to suggest that he has in mind Adamic humankind, or humankind outside of the new experience which for believers is found in Christ (*see* In Christ). A good example of this is found in Romans 7:7-25 where the apostle appears to use the "I" in a corporate sense

which demonstrates some overlap with the generic sense of the more explicit Adam motif.

It is virtually certain that the narrative of Genesis 2—3 underlies the use of *Adam* within the Pauline letters and provides the background for it. The same fascination for the figure of Adam can also be seen in a number of first-century Jewish and Christian documents, including 4 Ezra, 2 Baruch and the Apocalypse of Moses, as Levison has duly noted. Speculation about Adam is also well documented within the Qumran materials and in the writings of Paul's contemporary, Philo of Alexandria. In light of the fact that Adam figures regularly in Gnostic* materials, such as the Nag Hammadi texts, some scholars have attempted to see a link between the Adamic motif and Gnostic ideas of "a second man." Generally, this has not been well received, the evidence probably representing precisely the reverse flow of influence (it is more likely that the biblical theme is taken up by the later Gnostic writers).

All of these relevant background documents help us understand the interest that the tradition of Adam, the first created human being, generated among ancient writers and how they came to rely on it and express it in their writing. When this is recognized the Pauline discussion of the theme is seen to be wholly consistent with other documents of its day, although the specifically christological use to which it is connected distinguishes Paul's treatment. Paul seems to be the first to describe Jesus Christ as "the Last (or Second) Adam" (1 Cor 15:45, 47), a description which points unambiguously to the eschatological character of the apostle's thought.

**2. Adam: The Historical Figure.**
Clearly the figure Adam was understood by many first-century people to be the first historical person; this explains why Jude 14 (quoting *1 Enoch* 1:9) describes Enoch as "the seventh generation from Adam" (NSRV). Luke offers similar assessment when he includes Adam within the genealogy of Jesus (Lk 3:38). The historicity of Adam as the first created person appears to have been taken for granted by the apostle Paul, although such historicity is not the primary focal point of the two key Pauline texts which discuss the Adam/Christ motif.

*2.1. Adam (and Eve) As Ethical Example(s).* The historicity of Adam (and Eve) does, however, seem to underlie teaching within the Pauline letters concerning the man-woman relationship and, by extension, the relationship that exists between Christ and his church. Similarly, the figures of Adam and Eve are used sparingly within the Pauline letters to make a point about authority* within the divine order of creation. In both of these ways the role(s) of Adam (and Eve) as ethical example is preeminent, although the historicity of the first man (and woman) seems to be assumed as part of the ethical argument. The use of Adam (and Eve) as ethical model(s) anticipates the more typological use of Adam within the Adam/Christ analogy in Romans 5 and 1 Corinthians 15.

*2.1.1. Adam (and Eve): Marriage and Sexual Roles.* Paul alludes to the story of Adam and Eve in 1 Corinthians 6:16 via his quotation of Genesis 2:24. Although the names of the first couple are not used here, it is clear that they stand as key ethical models for how proper sexual relationships (*see* Sexuality) between man and woman should function in the life of the church. Paul here emphasizes the importance and sanctity of the sexual union of a man and a woman as a means to exhort the Corinthian believers to a more worthy lifestyle and impress upon them the fact that they belong to the body of Christ (*see* Body of Christ). The story of Adam and Eve also underlies the advice offered on the union of the marriage* relationship in Ephesians 5:22-33. Here, once again, Ephesians builds on the OT imagery of Adam and Eve and an understanding of their union with that "mystery"* which exists between Christ and the church (especially seen in Eph 5:32).

*2.1.2. Adam (and Eve): Sin and the Order of Creation.* 1 Timothy 2:13-14 also clearly demonstrates reliance upon the Adam and Eve story of Genesis 2—3. In a section given over to ethical teaching (1 Tim 2:9-15; *see* Ethics), the argument turns to the story of Adam and Eve in Genesis for scriptural support of an understanding of the authority structure, the order of creation, which exists between men and women (*see* Man and Woman). The emphasis is on the priority of Adam's creation (1 Tim 2:13) and the priority of Eve's deception (1 Tim 2:14) in the Garden of Eden. Adam and Eve are called into service as normative examples of how men and women should interrelate and what can happen if the proper authority structure is adhered to by subsequent peoples. In short, the point is that 1 Timothy presents Adam and Eve in a specific way, as a means of regulating conduct within the life of the church, particularly in its worship* practices. They are put forward as ethical examples from the past both to follow (as in the case of Eve's proper submission to Adam based upon her creational dependence upon him), and as models of behavior to guard against (as in the case of Eve's deception and its aftermath). Again, the historicity of the Genesis account seems to be taken for granted within this ethical explication of the story.

## 3. Adam: The Typological Figure.

When we turn to consider the relevant passages in Romans 5 and 1 Corinthians 15, we find a much more complicated and extended use of *Adam* by Paul. Here the focus shifts from Adam as a mere historical figure to Adam as a typological or figurative character set over against Jesus Christ (in Rom 5:14 the actual term *typos*, "type," is used of Adam). Commenting on the significance of Adam in the apostle's thought, C. K. Barrett remarks that "Paul sees history gathering at nodal points, and crystallizing upon outstanding figures—men who are notable in themselves as individual persons, but even more notable as representative figures" (Barrett, 5). Thus we see that in both Romans 5 and 1 Corinthians 15 Paul juxtaposes Adam and Christ and uses several key features of OT background to communicate christological truths about Jesus Christ who encompasses humanity in himself. We could even summarize Paul's understanding of Christian redemption as the transition from being "in Adam" to being "in Christ" as the saving movement from one sphere of life, one realm of existence, to another. Given the fact that Paul's theology arises out of an eschatological mindset (*see* Eschatology), with its emphasis on the new creation having supplanted the old (*see* Creation), it is entirely proper to see the Adam/Christ motif as expressing his teaching concerning what Scroggs has described as "eschatological humanity."

*3.1. Adam and Eschatological Humanity.* 1 Corinthians 15 is a self-contained discussion of the resurrection* of the dead, the primary purpose of which is not so much to assert the truth of the resurrection of Jesus (since this is assumed), as to explain its significance for the life of the faithful. Thus the chapter deals with the reality of the resurrection of Christ and its implications in the lives of the Christian believers. Within this discussion the Adam/Christ analogy is explicitly used at two points, in 1 Corinthians 15:20-22 and in 1 Corinthians 15:44-49. Christ's resurrection is the event which inaugurates and constitutes his being the "first fruits"* of those who have died (1 Cor 15:20, 23); it is in connection with this idea that the Adam/Christ analogy is initially introduced. It has been suggested (by Thrall) that the christological debate which develops in Corinth arises out of Paul's previous introduction of the Adamic motif (and the Corinthian church's misunderstanding of it). Such an idea is far from certain and assumes a vacillation in Paul's thought which is much more deliberate than this suggests.

*3.1.1. Christ As Last Adam: The First Fruits.* The first use of the Adam/Christ analogy is introduced by a statement (1 Cor 15:20), built upon the declaration of Christ's resurrection stated in 1 Corinthians 15:3-5. In the second half of 1 Corinthians 15:20 the meaning of Christ's resurrection is amplified—Christ is also the "first fruits of those who are asleep." In this way a new point is injected into the discussion of Christ's resurrection, namely, the unity of the risen Lord with those who believe in him. The resurrection bodies (*see* Body) of the redeemed (it is important to note that the focus of the discussion is on this "somatic" point) are to correspond to and flow from Christ's in the same way that the harvest corresponds to and flows from the first fruits.

It is to amplify further and explain the relationship between Christ and his believers that the Adam/Christ analogy is used by Paul; the Adam/Christ typology becomes an argument for the certainty of the resurrection of the believing community and (in Lambrecht's words) sets us a "temporal, as well as a casual," relationship between the Lord* and those who believe in him. In 1 Corinthians 15:21-22 Paul sets forth a double parallelism showing this relationship:

21a  For since by a man came death,
21b  so also by a man came the resurrection of the dead,

22a  For as in Adam all die,
22b  so also in Christ shall all be made alive.

The two verses should be taken together, as the second serves to clarify the meaning of the first. The essentially eschatological outlook of the analogy is demonstrated by the use of the future passive verb in 22b.

Some debate arises as to the universal salvation implied in verse 22. How much weight should be given to the two uses of "all" in 22b? Is Paul teaching the ultimate salvation of all humankind in Christ in the same way that he asserts the universal death of all humankind in Adam? Most commentators agree that such an idea is incompatible with the rest of Paul's teaching; throughout this letter Paul has spoken of those who perish (1 Cor 1:18; 3:17; 5:13; 6:9; 9:27). In light of this it seems that we are left to limit both (or at least the second) "all" clauses of verse 22 and have them act as modifiers of "in Adam" and "in Christ." Thus we can take the meaning of the verse to be "all who are in Adam die, while all who are in Christ shall be made alive."

*3.1.2. Christ As Last Adam: The Life-Giving Spirit.* 1 Corinthians 15:45-49 is a quotation of the midrashic commentary on Genesis 2:7. The section is founded on Paul's statement in 44b: "If there is a physical body, there is also a spiritual body" (NRSV). This statement in 1 Corinthians 15:44 is a summary of the preceding paragraph, beginning in 1 Corinthians 15:35, which contains a discussion about the nature of the resurrection body. Paul speaks here of both a *sōma psychikon* ("physical body") and a *sōma pneumatikon* ("spiritual body"), effectively outflanking his Corinthian opponents (as Dunn 1973, notes). The exact identification of these opponents has remained a matter of considerable scholarly debate over the years. B. Pearson, however, has identified their use of *pneumatikos-psychikos* terminology as forming one of the points of friction with Paul. It is in attempting to explain the relationship that exists between these two *sōmata* ("bodies," both *psychikon* and *pneumatikon)* that Paul turns once again to the Adam/Christ analogy in 1 Corinthians 15:45-49.

Paul quotes Genesis 2:7 from the LXX, adding the words "first" and "Adam" to the OT text in order to set up the typological contrast with Christ which follows in 1 Corinthians 15:45b: "the last Adam became a life-giving spirit" (NRSV). In setting up the contrast in the way he has, Paul is addressing the question of the "bodies" of physical and spiritual existence as can readily be seen in the use of the neuter definite articles in 1 Corinthians 15:46 (the antecedent being *sōma*, "body") instead of masculine ones (which would refer to *anthrōpos*, "man"). The point is that Adam, in having a "physical body" (NRSV), also became a "living being" (NRSV); Christ, in becoming a "spiritual body" (NRSV), also became a "life-giving spirit" (NRSV). Paul is not merely making an anthropological claim about Christ as "Last Adam" here; his meaning goes beyond that. He is also making a christological statement about the risen Lord who has manifested himself as the regenerating Spirit within the church. The passage in Genesis lent itself toward that purpose, although (as Wright notes) the connection of this christological point with the primary discussion about the "spiritual body" is not immediately obvious.

In a sense, therefore, Paul's use of the Adam/Christ analogy is not entirely consistent. In calling Christ the "life-giving spirit" Paul is making a statement about the work of Christ within the church which has no parallel on the Adamic side of the analogy. The motivating factor in Paul's use of the analogy was his desire to show that a relationship exists between Adam and the rest of humankind. But the wonder of what God had done for humankind through Christ was so great that the Adam/Christ analogy broke down. It was employed by the apostle insofar as it was useful in demonstrating the solidarity of the two Adams with

their respective followers, but when it could no longer communicate or contain the message of Christ's life-transforming power in the life of the believer, it was laid aside.

It is significant that both structured references to the Adam/Christ analogy in 1 Corinthians 15 (verses 21 and 45) are followed by passages that speak of Jesus Christ in very exalted terms and are sometimes taken to express a Pauline understanding of preexistence.* Thus, in 1 Corinthians 15:25-28 there is the christological use of Psalm 8:6 and Psalm 110:1, while in 1 Corinthians 15:47-49 there is repeated reference to the "heavenly man." The question then becomes: Is there any relationship between Paul's calling Jesus Christ the "last Adam" and the exaltation/heavenly man language (*see* Exaltation) ascribed to him in 1 Corinthians 15:25-28 and 47-49? If there is such a relationship, a link might be discovered between Paul's Adamic theology and his belief in the preexistence of Christ, or even a vestigial "Son of man" figure. Many (like Dunn) feel that this is purely speculative and that it presses the evidence too far; we must proceed with caution. In any event, we should not allow the fascinating question of an overlap between preexistence ideas and exaltation/heavenly man language to distract us from the essentially eschatological character of the Christ/Adam analogy as it is found in this letter.

*3.2. Adam and the Origin of Sin.* Largely because of the narrative of Genesis 3, the figure of Adam has been one of the focal points for discussions about human sinfulness in both Judaism and Christianity (*see* Sin). Romans 5:12-21 contains the fullest treatment of this theme within the Pauline letters. These verses have exerted an enormous influence upon Christian theology over the centuries as various interpreters have sought to plumb the depths of the apostle's teaching about the origin of sin. Clearly Paul associates the entry of sin and death into the world with the transgression of Adam. Although in Romans 5 he is (presumably) thinking historically of the fall, it is readily apparent that he had far more in mind than a historical assessment of Adam and his rebellious act. In effect, Paul's use of Adam in Romans 5:12-21 is protological (pointing back to the beginning) in its emphasis; Adam serves as a means to describe the entry of sin and death into the world and (by extension) the condition of humankind following that first transgression. There is a shift from a focus on Adam and Christ as corporate *persons* in 1 Corinthians to their respective *acts* in Romans 5.

This is not to say that the whole perspective of Romans 5 is simply a retrospective (backward-looking) one, for there is at the same time a real sense in which all that has happened in Adam is transcended by what happens in Jesus Christ, the Last Adam. As Paul says in Romans 5:14, Adam is "a type of the one who was to come" (NRSV). Adam's act of disobedience is contrasted with Christ's act of obedience, which carries with it a promise of future life within the new creation. Indeed, in Romans 5:15-21, within a highly structured section of his argument, Paul goes to great lengths to make it clear that Jesus Christ has met the negative effects of Adam's transgression in every way: transgression is met by obedience, condemnation by justification,* death by life.* The argument *a minori ad maius* ("from the lesser to the greater") is employed throughout, and the tremendous truth concerning the surpassing of sin and its effects by God's grace* in Christ is emphasized. However, the protological dimension of the Adam/Christ analogy does come to the fore here in a way that it does not in 1 Corinthians 15.

The fact that Romans 5:12 is an unfinished sentence in Greek has led to a variety of attempts to interpret the direction in which Paul's argument was heading. As Danker has noted, part of the dilemma is the difficulty in deciding what the antecedent for the dative relative pronoun *hō* is (sin, death, Adam or neither, but with the preposition *epi* [eph'], an idiom meaning "for which reason," "because"). In addition, the Augustinian rendering of Romans 5:12 as "in whom (Adam) all sinned" (Latin *in quo omnes peccaverunt*) has ever since, for better or worse, governed the church's theological interpretation of the Adam declaration (Cranfield lists six major possibilities for interpreting Rom 5:12d alone and notes that support for each can be found within church history). Bonner laments that Augustine did not "concentrate more upon the rich and profound conception of the antithesis between the two Adams, rather than on the macabre theory of the participation of unbegotten humanity in the first Adam's primal sin" (Bonner, 247).

It is important to note that while Paul does turn to Adam as the means whereby sin enters the world, he does not tell us the means whereby that sin is transmitted from one generation to another. The mechanics are left unexplained, beyond the simple declaration that "all humankind sinned" (a more correct rendering of Rom 5:12). Adam's responsibility for the origin of sin's introduction into the world is affirmed by Paul alongside an affirmation of the individual's responsibility for the presence of sin in his or her life. For Paul both elements (personal guilt and responsibility as well as universal guilt and sin in Adam) are active. This paradox becomes clear by the way in which Paul's thought flows quite freely from the in-

tensely personal statement in Romans 5:12 ("because all men sinned" [NRSV], to the more deterministic statement of Romans 5:19 ("by the one man's disobedience the many were made sinners" [NRSV]. Paul's teaching is echoed in 2 Baruch 54:15, 19: "For although Adam sinned first and has brought death upon all who were not in his own time, yet each of them who has been born from him has prepared for himself the coming torment. . . . Adam is, therefore, not the cause, except only for himself, but each of us has become our own Adam" (Charlesworth edition).

## 4. Adam and the Image of God.

Adamic theology has also had an important role to play in several other key passages within the Pauline letters, notably those, such as the hymnic materials (*see* Hymns) in Philippians 2:6-11 and Colossians 1:15-20 and the declaration in 2 Corinthians 4:4, which speak of Jesus Christ in terms of his being "the image of God" (*see* Image). Here the OT background of Adam as one who is created "in the image of God" (*morphē* is used in Phil 2:6 and *eikōn* in Col 1:15 and 2 Cor 4:4). The description of the "glory of God (or man)" also figures in the discussion at this point (*see* Glory). This confluence of imagery and description has recently led some scholars to see the preponderance of "image of God" language found throughout the Pauline letters as another expression of Adamic theology. Dunn (1980), for instance, argues strongly for such an Adamic understanding of the Philippian hymn; Hooker sees an Adamic motif underlying Romans 1:18-32 where the apostle describes humankind's predicament in terms of Adam's fall (Wedderburn offers some clarifications to Hooker's suggestion). In addition, there is some justification for seeing the fall of Adam as underlying the declaration made by Paul in Romans 3:23.

*4.1. Image of God: Nature and Existence in Romans 5.* Closely related to this matter is the consideration of how being made "in the image of God" stands as a description of human nature and existence. This is a matter which has long occupied the attention of Christian commentators, many of whom, like Calvin (as R. Prins notes), have concentrated on Paul's letters in addressing the issue. It is interesting to note that the whole of Romans 5, particularly the Adam/Christ analogy in verses 12-21, becomes critical in this regard.

The interpretations of Romans 5 offered by Barth and Bultmann are helpful comparisons on this point, standing as interpretations concentrating on the christological and anthropological halves of the analogy respectively. Thus Barth focuses on the christological element within the analogy and sees the passage as essentially one expressing humankind's *nature*. Bultmann, on the other hand, focuses on the anthropological element within the analogy and sees the passage as essentially expressing humankind's *existence*. In short, the crucial question concerns how we understand humankind (Adam) to be made "in the image of God." Is it in Adam or Christ that we truly see "the image of God"? Do we begin with Christ and move to interpret humankind as the image of Christ (Barth's position)? Or do we begin with humankind and move to interpret Christ as the true expression of what the image of God means (Bultmann's position)?

These two interpretative approaches are dependent, in part, on the way in which the two halves of Romans 5 (verse 1-11 and 12-21) are seen to fit together. Thus, Barth effectively places Romans 5:12-21 (with its description of Adamic humankind) within the boundaries of Romans 5:1-11 (which states the real condition of humankind in Christ). Bultmann, on the other hand, grounds Romans 5:12-21 in the lifestyle motivated by Christ's example of faith and stresses that Romans 5:1-11 concerns the paradoxical existence of believers in hope. In other words, Romans 5:12-21 is taken to express this life of the believer more fully, and it is only at that point that the christological component, as it were, is introduced into the scheme.

*4.2. Image of God: Stages of Salvation History.* Another way to express this essential difference of interpreting the meaning of humankind (be it Adamic humankind or the new humankind in Christ) as being made "in the image of God" is via an illustration of successive stages which are negotiated in salvation history. The eschatological framework which underlies the whole of Paul's thought sees the old age, in the light of the Christ event, as having given way to a new age (as texts such as 2 Corinthians 5:17 demonstrate).

Ziesler sets this out in terms of a possible three-stage scheme in which "original state—fall—restored state" serves as a description of this development. Such a three-stage scheme would tend toward the kind of interpretation offered by Bultmann. However, Ziesler argues that Paul's view of man is so overwhelmingly directed toward the eschatological vision of the Last Adam that such a three-stage scheme becomes irrelevant to any discussion of Paul. He notes that nowhere does Paul talk of Adam in terms of his being "in the image of God" and on that basis suggests that a two-stage scheme is closer to Paul's central teaching. This would trace the steps in salvation history as a simpler movement (fall—restored state) and would tend toward the kind of interpretation offered by Barth.

Is such a radical break between Adam and Christ as the image of God justified? Ziesler's ideas need to be modified somewhat by a more rigorous consideration of 1 Corinthians 11:3-9 where Paul employs the creation story of Genesis as a basis for proper ethical behavior among men and women with respect to covering one's head during worship. The crucial verse is 1 Corinthians 11:7: "For a man ought not to have his head veiled, since he is the image and reflection of God; but woman is the reflection of man" (NRSV). The point here is that Paul shows some flexibility in his usage of "image of God" and is willing to apply the concept broadly if it suits his purposes, even if it is true that the passage does, as Ziesler notes, occur in a nonsoteriological context. Nevertheless, we should not overlook the Adamic undertone of this verse—Paul means to say that man, that is, every human being, bears in some way the image and glory (or "reflection" as in the NRSV) of God just as the first Adam did.

This is not to deny that, according to Paul, there is a strong sense in which humankind's glory as the image of God finds its fulfillment in Christ. In Philippians 3:20-21 we find this clearly expressed in terms of the believer's transformation from a "body of humility" into "the body of his (Christ's) glory," and in Romans 8:29 the believer is described as one who is "conformed to the image of his (God's) Son."

*4.3. Image of God: Christophany.* Is it possible to determine the origin of Paul's understanding of Jesus Christ in terms of the Last Adam and its connection with an "Image of God" motif? There appears to be a close relationship between image-Christophany and descriptions of the risen Lord Jesus Christ which build upon the OT tradition of theophany and are properly described as christophany. This means that those passages where Paul describes or alludes to his own conversion experience and his vision of Christ, can be taken as supplementing an Adamic christology. This brings passages such as 1 Corinthians 9:1; 15:8-10; 2 Corinthians 3:4—4:6; Galatians 1:13-17 and Philippians 3:4-11 into the discussion and sees within them an underlying Adamic theme. Kim argues that this brings together two different bases of christological thought in Paul, a wisdom* christology and an image christology, both of which converge in the person of Jesus Christ, the Second Adam within Paul's thought.

## 5. Adam and the Body of Christ.

In that Paul viewed humankind as embodied in both Adam and Christ, unredeemed and redeemed respectively, he demonstrated (or contributes to) a conceptual overlap between an Adamic theology and the idea of the body of Christ (*see* Body of Christ). In other words, this body of Christ is made up of believers who are all joined together so as to form a united humanity, that of the last Adam. Although explicit reference to Adam is not made within the key texts under discussion here, it is clear that fallen Adamic humankind is spiritually reconstituted (Eph 1:10) in Christ in such a way that Adamic language and body of Christ imagery merge. We see this particular emphasis at various points in the Pauline letters, including Colossians 3:12-17 and Ephesians 2:13-18.

In the modern era W. D. Davies has spearheaded investigation into this matter by pointing out the Jewish rabbinic background to such an understanding of Adam and its relevance to a study of Paul's teaching about a corporate Christ. Central to this issue is the recognition that discussion about Adam in these terms is not primarily about humankind per se, so much as about the nation of Israel* viewed from an eschatological perspective, as N. T. Wright argues. The contribution brought by a sense of the corporate, whether it be seen in terms of an Adamic humankind or in terms of the body of Christ, to an analysis of the Pauline letters should not be underestimated. Such a reinterpretation of the OT promises to the nation of Israel in terms of the new creation in Christ seems implied in Galatians 6:15-16, and is certainly made unambiguous within some of the writings of later Christian leaders, such as Justin Martyr who declared that the Christian church is "the true spiritual Israel" (Justin *Dial. Tryph.* 11.5). However, who constitutes "Israel" is a difficult matter to decide throughout Paul's letters and a one-for-one exchange between the nation and the church cannot be easily sustained, especially in light of difficult verses such as Romans 11:26.

*See also* BODY OF CHRIST; CHRISTOLOGY; CREATION AND NEW CREATION; IMAGE, IMAGE OF GOD; NEW NATURE AND OLD NATURE.

BIBLIOGRAPHY. C. K. Barrett, *From First Adam to Last* (London: A. & C. Black, 1962); K. Barth, *Christ and Adam: Man and Humanity in Romans 5* (SJTOP 5; Edinburgh: Oliver & Boyd, 1956); G. Bonner, "Augustine on Romans 5,12," in *Studia Evangelica* V, ed. F. L. Cross (Berlin: Akademie Verlag, 1968) 242-47; R. Bultmann, "Adam and Christ According to Romans 5," in *Current Issues in New Testament Interpretation: Essays in Honor of O. A. Piper*, ed. W. Klassen and G. F. Snyder (London: SCM, 1962) 143-65; C. E. B. Cranfield, *The Epistle to the Romans* (2 vols.; Edinburgh: T & T Clark, 1975); F. W. Danker, "Romans 5:12: Sin Under Law," *NTS* 14 (1967-68) 424-39; W. D. Davies, *Paul and Rabbinic Judaism* (4th ed.; Philadelphia: Fortress, 1980); J. D. G. Dunn, "1 Corinthians 15.45—Last Adam, Lifegiving Spirit," in *Christ and Spirit in the New Testament:*
*Studies in Honour of C. F. D. Moule,* ed. B. Lindars and S. Smalley (Cambridge: University Press, 1973) 127-41; idem, *Christology in the Making* (Philadelphia: Westminster, 1980) xviii-xix, 98-128; M. D. Hooker, *From Adam to Christ: Essays on Paul* (Cambridge: University Press, 1990); S. Kim, *The Origin of Paul's Gospel* (Grand Rapids: Eerdmans, 1982); L. J. Kreitzer, "Christ as Second Adam in Paul," *CV* 32 (1989) 55-101; J. Lambrecht, "Paul's Christological Use of Scripture in 1 Corinthians 15.20-28," *NTS* 28 (1982) 502-27; J. R. Levison, *Portraits of Adam in Early Judaism* (JSPSup 1; Sheffield: Academic Press, 1988); B. Pearson, *The Pneumatikos-Psychikos Terminology in 1 Corinthians* (Missoula, MT: Scholars, 1973); R. Prins, "The Image of God in Adam and the Restoration of Man in Jesus Christ," *SJT* 25 (1972) 32-44; R. Scroggs, *The Last Adam* (Oxford: Basil Blackwell, 1966); M. Thrall, "Christ Crucified or Second Adam? A Christological Debate Between Paul and the Corinthians," in *Christ and Spirit in the New Testament: Studies in Honour of C. F. D. Moule,* ed. B. Lindars and S. Smalley (Cambridge: University Press, 1973) 143-56; A. J. M. Wedderburn, "Adam in Paul's Letter to the Romans," in *Studia Biblica* 1978: III. *Papers on Paul and Other New Testament Authors,* ed. E. A. Livingstone (JSNTSup 3: Sheffield: Academic Press, 1980) 413-30; N. T. Wright, "Adam, Israel and the Messiah," in *The Climax of the Covenant* (Minneapolis: Fortress, 1991) 18-40; J. A. Ziesler, "Anthropology of Hope," *ExpT* 90 (1978-79) 104-9.

L. J. Kreitzer

## ADOPTION, SONSHIP

In the Pauline letters the Greek word *huiothesia* is used either of the Israelites (Rom 9:4) or of believers (Gal 4:5; Rom 8:15, 23; Eph 1:5) as sons of God. There is, however, some disagreement as to how to translate the term, whether as "adoption" or, more generally, as "sonship." This problem must be resolved before the specific background of the term can be discussed.

1. The Meaning of *Huiothesia* in Paul
2. The Background of Divine "Adoption as Sons" in Paul
3. The Sonship of Believers in Paul

### 1. The Meaning of *Huiothesia* in Paul.

The fact that Paul uses *huiothesia* in the sense of "adoption" has sometimes been denied in favor of the translation "sonship" (e.g., B. Byrne), but the overwhelming lexical evidence hardly supports this contention (see Scott 1992). In Paul, as in contemporary extra-biblical sources, *huiothesia* always denotes either the process or the state of being adopted as son(s). This is substantiated not only by the univocal and widespread usage of the term in literary and non-literary sources, but also by ancient Greek lexicographers dating to the time of the NT (e.g., Ammonius, *Adfin. Vocab. Diff.* s.v. *apokēryktos*). Paul's use of *huiothesia* obviously appropriates this normal usage of the term, because the construction in Galatians 4:5 is closely paralleled in Hellenistic literature (cf. Nicolaus of Damascus *Vit. Caes.* 130.55). Hence any attempt to translate the term more generally as "sonship" sets the study of the background off on the wrong foot from the start.

## 2. The Background of Divine "Adoption as Sons" in Paul.

Among those authors who agree that *huiothesia* denotes "adoption," there is diversity of opinion as to the background of the term. This is due in part to the fact that Paul seems to be the first to use the term in a theological context (let alone of divine adoption) and yet he never explains what he means by the term. The apostle evidently assumes that his readers would know what was meant by *the* adoption as sons of God.

*2.1. Adoption as a Theological Abstraction.* Some scholars treat Paul's concept of adoption simply as an abstraction which is linked with another Pauline concept. In this way the question of background is obviated altogether. For example, H. Hübner takes adoption as a synonym of "freedom" (*eleutheria*) in the sense of freedom* from the Law.* R. Bultmann and others following him treat adoption as a forensic-eschatological term parallel to "righteousness"* (*dikaiosynē*). S. Kim considers Paul's concept of *huiothesia* a secondary deduction of the Damascus Road christophany, in which Paul perceived the risen Lord as the image of God (*see* Image, Image of God) or the Son of God (*see* Son of God). Other kinds of abstractions of the concept can be found in the works of N. R. Petersen and D. von Allmen.

*2.2. Adoption Against a Greco-Roman Background.* When, as is more commonly done, Paul's concept of divine adoption is considered against a Greco-Roman background, it is usually compared either to a particular case of divine adoption in Greco-Roman mythology or to the actual practice of adoption in Greco-Roman jurisprudence.

*2.2.1. Divine Adoption in Greco-Roman Mythology.* Divine adoption plays very little role in Greco-Roman sources. Outside of Paul *huiothesia* is not used of such adoptions in the period under consideration. The few unequivocal examples of divine adoption which can be adduced from Greco-Roman sources using other terms of adoption do not provide a background for Paul's concept (cf. the adoption of Heracles by Hera

[Diodorus Siculus 4.39.2], that of Alexander the Great by Amon-Zeus [Plutarch *Alex.* 50.6], that of Solon by Fortune [Plutarch *Mor.* 318C] and that of the Lybian goddess "Athena" by Ammon-Zeus [Herodotus 4.180]). The mystery religions have sometimes been suggested as a possible background (cf. H. D. Betz), but there is no evidence for divine adoption in the mysteries (*see* Religions).

*2.2.2. Adoption as a Legal Metaphor.* Many scholars have suggested that Paul's concept of adoption is a legal metaphor which Paul constructed ad hoc from his Greco-Roman background. Among them, a few have considered it a metaphor drawn from Hellenistic law, because there adoption is an institution connected especially with inheritance, and Galatians 4:5 speaks of the adoption which makes believers heirs (cf. Wenger). More often, however, proponents of this kind of approach (e.g., Lyall, Bruce) have seen Paul's concept of adoption in light of the elaborate Roman ceremony of *adoptio,* in which the minor to be adopted was emancipated from the authority of his natural father and placed under the new authority of his adoptive father, often for the purpose of social and/or political maneuvering (cf. Kurylowicz). Galatians 4:5 does indeed put redemption* and adoption in parallel, but the notion that the witness* of the Spirit (*see* Holy Spirit) in Romans 8:16 reflects the witnesses in the Roman ceremony hardly deserves serious consideration. Circumstantial evidence such as Paul's Roman citizenship* and the prevalence of Roman adoptions in Paul's day also fails to establish the case for a legal metaphor.

*2.3. Adoption Against an Old Testament/Jewish Background.* The term *huiothesia* occurs in the NT only in Paul and never in the Septuagint or other Jewish sources. Despite frequent claims to the contrary, however, the concept of adoption—even divine adoption—was certainly known to the OT and Judaism, regardless of whether it was ever actually practiced (see Scott 1992, Malul). Therefore, it is not impossible that the roots of Paul's concept could be found here.

*2.3.1. Galatians 4:5.* The context of the earliest occurrence of the term, in Galatians 4:5, does in fact give a decisive clue to understanding *huiothesia* against an OT/Jewish background. For when Galatians 4:1-2 is properly understood not as an illustration from Greco-Roman law but as an allusion to the OT (see Scott 1992), it is clear that Galatians 4:5 is set within a context framed by Exodus typology (Gal 4:1-7): just as Israel,* as heir to the Abrahamic promise (*see* Abraham), was redeemed as son of God from slavery in Egypt at the time appointed by the Father (Gal 4:1-2; cf. Hos 11:1; Gen 15:13), so also believers were redeemed to adoption as sons of God from slavery under the "elements of the world" (*see* Elements/Elemental Spirits) at the fullness of time and thereby became heirs to the Abrahamic promise (Gal 4:3-7).

The fact that "the" *huiothesia* is to be seen here against a particular OT/Jewish background is further substantiated both by Romans 9:4, where the articular term occurs in a list of Israel's historical privileges (cf. Ex 4:22; Hos 11:1), and more specifically, by the broader context of Galatians 3—4 itself, which makes it clear that believers are sons and heirs as they participate by baptism (Gal 3:27) in the Son of God who was sent to redeem them (Gal 4:4-5; cf. Gal 3:13-14). For, strictly speaking, Christ* is the seed of Abraham (Gal 3:16) and the messianic Son of God promised in 2 Samuel 7:12 and 14, respectively. Seen in context, therefore, "the adoption" in Galatians 4:5 must refer to the Jewish eschatological expectation based on 2 Samuel 7:14.

It can be shown that 2 Samuel 7:14 ("I will be to him [the Davidide] a Father, and he will be to me a son") contains an adoption formula (cf. Ex 2:10; Esther 2:7; Gen 48:5), which subsequent Judaism applied not only to the Davidic Messiah but, under influence of New Covenant theology (cf. Hos 2:1, cited in Rom 9:26; *see* Covenant and New Covenant), also to the eschatological people of God. In accordance with the Deuteronomic framework of Sin-Exile-Restoration (see esp. O. H. Steck), this 2 Samuel 7:14 tradition expects that at the advent of the Messiah, God* would redeem his people from Exile in a Second Exodus; he would restore them to a covenantal relationship; and he would adopt them, with the Messiah, as his sons (cf. *Jub* 1:24; *T. Judah* 24:3; 4QFlor 1:11). In fact 2 Corinthians 6:18 actually cites the adoption formula of 2 Samuel 7:14 (+Is 43:6), and that in the context of the same Exodus typology, the same New Covenant theology and in the same generalized form as in the Jewish tradition. As in the 2 Samuel 7:14 tradition, furthermore, Galatians 4:4-6 connects divine adoption with the reception of the Spirit (of the New Covenant) in the heart. Hence, while the context of *huiothesia* in Galatians 4:5 gives no reason to suspect a Greco-Roman background for the term, the whole line of argumentation in Galatians 3—4, together with Pauline parallels, leads unambiguously to an OT/Jewish background for the term (cf. Rom 9:4) and particularly to the 2 Samuel 7:14 tradition (cf. 2 Cor 6:18). In other words, believers who are thus baptized (*see* Baptism) into the messianic Son of God and take up his very cry of "Abba!" to the Father (Gal 4:6; Rom 8:15; cf. Mk 14:36) participate with him in the Davidic promise of divine adoption and in the Abrahamic promise of universal sovereign-

ty (cf. Gal 4:1).

*2.3.2. Romans 8:15, 23.* This interpretation of *huiothesia* in Galatians 4:5 applies equally to the use of the term in the closely parallel passage of Romans 8. For here, too, participation by adoption in the messianic Son of God who is sent (Rom 8:3; cf. Gal 4:4) is so integrally connected with the reception of the indwelling Spirit that the Spirit can now be called the "Spirit of adoption" (Rom 8:15), the Spirit by which also the righteous requirement of the Law* is fulfilled (Rom 8:4). Like Galatians 4:5, furthermore, the context of *huiothesia* in Romans 8 contains elements of Exodus typology, and divine adoptive sonship implies heirship with Christ in the Abrahamic promise (Rom 8:17). Unlike Galatians 4:5, however, Romans 8 develops the point that participation in the messianic Son of God by adoption extends not only to the present (Romans 8:15) but, by means of the Spirit, to the future as well (Romans 8:23). For just as Jesus once received the Spirit at his baptism and was pronounced the Son of God (cf. Mk 1:11 pars.), so also believers presently receive the Spirit of adoption at their baptism, the Spirit by which, again, believers share in the Son's cry of "Abba!" to the Father (Rom 8:15). Likewise, just as Jesus as the seed of David was set as messianic Son of God in power* by the Holy Spirit at the proleptic resurrection* of the dead (Rom 1:3-4; cf. 2 Sam 7:12, 14), so also believers, who have the Spirit as the means of resurrection (Rom 8:11), eagerly await their revelation (Rom 8:19), their predestined (*see* Election and Predestination) resurrection/adoption into the glorified image of the resurrected Son (Rom 8:23, 29; cf. Eph 1:5), when the Son will be the firstborn* among many brothers and sisters (Rom 8:29; cf. Ps 89:27). At that time the sons of God will share in the Abrahamic promise of universal sovereignty as fellow-heirs with Christ the Messiah (Rom 8:17; cf. Rom 4:13; 8:32; Gal 4:1). Hence the present and future aspects of *huiothesia* in Romans 8 reflect successive stages of participation in the Son by the Spirit and, as such, constitute ways that believers share with the Son in the Davidic promise.

*2.3.3. Conclusion: The Place of Adoption in Pauline Theology.* In sum, there is a coherent and specific OT/Jewish background of "adoption as sons" (*huiothesia*) in the Pauline letters: the word occurs four times in the sense of adoption expected by the 2 Samuel 7:14 tradition (cf. 2 Cor 6:18), and that in either a present (Gal 4:5; Rom 8:15) or future aspect (Rom 8:23; Eph 1:5), depending on the christological and salvation-historical moment stressed in each context. Once the word occurs in the sense of the Exodus type which underlies this *huiothesia* of messianic salvation in the other four occurrences (Rom 9:4; cf. Gal 4:1-2). The whole concept must be seen in light of Paul's restoration theology (cf. Sanders, who, although failing to discuss the full Deuteronomic framework, does unwittingly present a major Jewish alternative to business-as-usual "covenantal nomism" [cf. J. M. Scott, "Gal 3:10"]; *see* Restoration of Israel).

### 3. The Sonship of Believers in Paul.

The foregoing interpretation of *huiothesia* against the background of the 2 Samuel 7:14 tradition provides the logical and necessary starting point for interpreting Paul's more general references to the sonship of believers; for adoption as sons of God provides the means of entry into divine sonship. Hence the Pauline passages which attribute *huiothesia* to believers also call them "son(s)" (*huioi*; cf. Gal 3:26; 4:6, 7; Rom 8:14, 19; 9:26) or, without specifying gender, "children" (*tekna;* cf. Rom 8:16, 17, 21) of God. 2 Corinthians 6:18, under the influence of Isaiah 43:6, explicitly broadens the concept of adoption to "daughters." Hence both males and females are included in Paul's concept of divine "sonship." In Philippians 2:14-15, Paul instructs his readers to "do everything without grumbling and dispute, in order that you may be faultless and pure, blameless children of God in the midst of a crooked and perverse generation." The reference here to the "children" (*tekna*) of God being "blameless" (*amōma*) alludes to Deuteronomy 32:5, where because they had sinned, the Israelites are characterized as "blameful" (*mōmēta*) and as "not his children" (*tekna*) in the context of the Song of Moses which predicts the Sin-Exile-Restoration. In this way Paul contrasts the situation which led up to the punishment of the Israelites as sons of God with the way in which believers as sons of God should now behave (cf. 2 Cor 6:14—7:1; Rom 8:4, 12-14).

*See also* BAPTISM; HOLY SPIRIT; SON OF GOD.

BIBLIOGRAPHY. D. von Allmen, *La famille de Dieu: La symbolique familiale dans le paulinisme* (OBO 41; Fribourg: Éditions Universitaires; Göttingen: Vandenhoeck & Ruprecht, 1981); H. D. Betz, *Galatians: A Commentary on Paul's Letter to the Churches in Galatia* (Herm; Philadelphia: Fortress, 1979); F. F. Bruce, *The Epistle to the Galatians: A Commentary on the Greek Text* (NIGTC; Grand Rapids: Eerdmans, 1982); R. Bultmann, *Theology of the New Testament* (2 vols.; New York: Scribner's, 1951, 1955); B. Byrne, *'Sons of God'—'Seed of Abraham': A Study of the Idea of the Sonship of God of all Christians against the Jewish Background* (AnBib 83; Rome: Biblical Institute, 1979); M. Hengel, *The Son of God: The Origin of Christology and the History of Jewish-Hellenistic Religion* (Philadelphia: Fortress, 1976); H. Hübner, *Law in Paul's Thought* (Edinburgh: T. & T. Clark, 1984); S. Kim, *The Origin of Paul's Gospel* (Grand Rapids: Eerdmans, 1981); M. Kurlowicz, *Die Adoptio im klassischen römischen Recht* (SA 6; Warsaw: University of Warsaw, 1981); F. Lyall, *Slaves, Citizens, Sons: Legal Metaphors in the Epistles* (Grand Rapids: Zondervan, 1984); M. Malul, "Foundlings and their Adoption in the Bible and in Mesopotamian Documents: A Study of Several Legal Metaphors in Ezek 16:1-7," *JSOT* 46 (1990) 97-126; N. R. Petersen, *Rediscovering Paul: Philemon and the Sociology of Paul's Narrative World* (Philadelphia: Fortress, 1985); E. P. Sanders, *Jesus and Judaism* (Philadelphia: Fortress, 1985); J. M. Scott, *Adoption as Sons of God: An Exegetical Investigation into the Background of ΥΙΟΘΕΣΙΑ in the Corpus Paulinum* (WUNT 2.48; Tübingen: J. C. B. Mohr, 1992); idem, " 'For as many as are of works of the law are under a curse' (Gal 3:10)," in *Paul and the Scriptures of Israel*, ed. C. A. Evans and J. A. Sanders (JSNTSup; Sheffield: JSOT, forthcoming); O. H. Steck, *Israel und das gewaltsame Geschick der Propheten. Untersuchungen zur Überlieferung des deuteronomischen Geschichtsbildes im Alten Testament, Spätjudentum und Urchristentum* (WMANT 23; Neukirchen-Vluyn: Neukirchener, 1967); L. Wenger, "Adoption," *RAC* 1.100.
J. M. Scott

**ADULTERY.** *See* MARRIAGE AND DIVORCE, ADULTERY AND INCEST; SEXUALITY, SEXUAL ETHICS.

## AFFLICTIONS, TRIALS, HARDSHIPS

Paul refers frequently to his trials and afflictions, sometimes cataloging them in his letters. He appears to have found persecution at the hands of the Jews the most difficult of his afflictions to bear. Paul's letters nevertheless reflect a positive attitude toward afflictions.

1. Catalogs of Afflictions
2. Persecution at the Hands of Jews
3. Paul's Attitude Toward Trials and Afflictions

### 1. Catalogs of Afflictions.

The trials and afflictions which Paul experienced were many and varied, and this is reflected in the catalogs found in his letters (Rom 8:35; 1 Cor 4:9-13; 2 Cor 4:8-9; 6:4-5; 11:23-29; 12:10).

*1.1. The Most Comprehensive Catalog.* In 2 Corinthians 11:23-29 Paul's trials and afflictions are listed in great detail. The passage falls into four parts, each reflecting a different aspect of these afflictions:

(1) Verses 23b-25: imprisonments, beatings and being near death, including five occasions when he received the thirty-nine lashes (i.e., the maximum allowed minus one) at the hands of the Jews, three times

when he was beaten with rods by Gentiles, one stoning and three shipwrecks.

(2) Verse 26: frequent journeys, with their accompanying dangers of rivers, bandits and Jews as well as Gentiles; dangers in the city, in the wilderness and at sea; and dangers from false Christians.

(3) Verse 27: toil and hardship, including sleepless nights (whether as privations or vigils), hunger, thirst, cold and nakedness.

(4) Verses 28-29: anxiety for all the churches.

*1.2. Parallels in Ancient Literature.* The attitude reflected in the writings of the Hellenistic moralists (e.g., Epictetus *Diss.* 3.12.10; 4.8.31; Seneca *Ep. Mor.* 13.1-3; Dio Chrysostom *Diss.* 3.3) and in some Jewish writings of the period (e.g., Wis 3:5-6; Sir 2:1-5; Jdt 8:25-26; Pss. Sol. 16:14-15; T. Jos. 2:7; 4 Macc 17:11-16) is that hardship functions as a test of character.

Lists of afflictions were used by the Hellenistic moralists to depict serenity in the midst of suffering and to provide a model of endurance for their readers. They believed that sufferings played a part in the divine plan. In these respects they parallel Paul's attitude to hardships and his use of lists of afflictions. However, Paul differed radically from those who minimized the impact of afflictions and saw in their triumph over them a demonstration of their own power.* Paul frankly admitted the distress caused by his afflictions (2 Cor 1:8-9), and gloried in the fact that it was God's power, not his own, which enabled him to endure (2 Cor 12:9-10). These similarities and differences suggest that, if Paul was familiar with the lists of the Hellenistic moralists, he adopted and adapted the genre to suit his own purposes. Such adaptation was influenced by OT traditions about the sufferings of the righteous, by Jewish apocalyptic* ideas of endtime woes, and most importantly by Paul's own theology of the cross.*

## 2. Persecution at the Hands of Jews.

Of the afflictions which Paul experienced, none receives more attention in his letters than persecution on account of the gospel.* He was persecuted by Jews, Gentiles and false Christians (2 Cor 11:26), but it was persecution at the hand of the Jews to which he referred most frequently (cf., e.g., Rom 15:31; 2 Cor 11:24, 26; Gal 5:11; 1 Thess 2:14-16), suggesting he found this hardest to bear. Paul's letters provide several hints concerning the reasons for this persecution.

*2.1. He Preached the Faith He Once Sought to Destroy.* According to Acts 9:1-2, Paul formerly persecuted the church with the backing of the high priest. Following his conversion he switched sides and preached the faith he once sought to destroy (Gal 1:23; *see* Jealousy,

Zeal). It is no wonder that the Jewish leaders felt a great antipathy toward him, leading to his persecution.

*2.2. He Regarded Cherished Elements of Judaism as Rubbish.* Following his conversion Paul underwent a reversal of values. He now regarded the most cherished elements of Judaism as "rubbish" compared with the excellency of knowing Christ (Phil 3:4-8). If he was known to have adopted such an attitude towards Judaism, and to be promoting a similar attitude among others, it is little wonder he drew down Jewish persecution upon his head.

*2.3. He Encouraged Jews to Neglect the Law of Moses.* Paul strongly rebuked Jewish believers for not being prepared to free themselves from the Law's* demands for ritual purity* when these kept them from sharing table fellowship with Gentiles (Gal 2:11-21). Thus it would not be surprising if he fell foul of zealous Jews who persecuted those of their nation who encouraged violations of the Law.

*2.4. He Did Not Preach Circumcision.* The reasons why Paul suffered Jewish persecution mentioned so far can only be inferred from hints found in his letters. For this fourth reason we have the evidence of an explicit statement: "Why am I still being persecuted if I am still preaching circumcision? In that case the offense of the cross has been removed" (Gal 5:11 NRSV; *see* Circumcision).

*2.5. He Relaxed Ethical Demands.* While Paul would have pleaded guilty to the charges lying behind the reasons for persecution suggested above, he strongly denied the charge that he relaxed ethical demands. It was, as far as he was concerned, a piece of blasphemous slander (Rom 3:7-8). Nevertheless, because this was what his Jewish opponents believed of him, it probably contributed to the reasons why he suffered persecution at their hands.

## 3. Paul's Attitude Toward Trials and Afflictions.

The apostle did not offer a comprehensive solution to the problem of suffering. However his letters do reveal something of the ways in which he came to understand its meaning.

*3.1. The Destiny and Privilege of Believers.* When seeking to encourage his converts, Paul reminded them that they had been granted the privilege "not only of believing in Christ, but of suffering for him as well" (Phil 1:29 NRSV). This was something for which they had been destined (1 Thess 3:3-4; cf. 2 Tim 3:12).

*3.2. Sharing Christ's Sufferings.* Paul believed that his sufferings* filled up what was lacking in Christ's afflictions for the sake of the church (Col 1:24). This should not be taken to mean that there was something lacking in Christ's atoning sacrifice.* Rather Paul shared the sufferings of the Servant-Messiah (*see* Christ) inasmuch as he too suffered for the sake of the elect in bringing the gospel to them (cf. 2 Tim 2:10).

*3.3. The Discipline of Afflictions.* One of the fruits of justification* is that believers are enabled to rejoice in afflictions (Rom 5:3). Believers do not find affliction less hurtful than others, but they know that under God's good hand it produces endurance, character and hope* in God* (Rom 5:3-4). It was through despair of life itself that Paul learned not to rely on himself but on God (2 Cor 1:8-9).

*3.4. Suffering and Comfort.* During the struggle with his "thorn in the flesh" Paul was comforted when the Lord told him that the power of Christ is made perfect in human weakness* (2 Cor 12:8-9). Paul came to understand that one of the reasons why he suffered was that, as he experienced the comfort of God in the midst of his sufferings, so he might be able to comfort others (2 Cor 1:3-7).

*See also* APOSTLE; CROSS, THEOLOGY OF THE; HEALING, ILLNESS; OPPONENTS OF PAUL; POWER; SUFFERING; WEAKNESS.

BIBLIOGRAPHY. J. T. Fitzgerald, *Cracks in an Earthen Vessel: An Examination of the Catalogue of Hardships in the Corinthian Correspondence* (SBLDS 99; Atlanta, GA: Scholars, 1988); A. Fridrichsen, "Zum Stil des paulinischen Peristasenkatalogs. 2 Cor. 11, 23ff.," *SO* 7 (1928) 25-29; idem, "Peristasenkatalog und res gestae: Nachtrag zu 2 Cor. 11, 23ff.," *SO* 8 (1929) 78-82; S. R. Garrett, "The God of this World and the Affliction of Paul: 2 Cor 4:1-12," in *Greeks, Romans, and Christians: Essays in Honor of Abraham J. Malherbe,* ed. D. L. Balch, et al. (Minneapolis: Fortress, 1990) 99-117; E. Kamlah, "Wie beurteilt Paulus sein Leiden?" *ZNW* 54 (1963) 217-32; C. G. Kruse, "The Price Paid for a Ministry Among Gentiles: Paul's Persecution at the Hands of the Jews," in *Worship, Theology and Ministry in the Early Church: Essays in Honor of Ralph P. Martin,* ed. M. J. Wilkins and T. Paige (Sheffield: JSOT, 1992) 260-72; W. Schrage, "Leid, Kreuz und Eschaton: Die Peristasenkataloge als Merkmale paulinischer theologia crucis und Eschatologie," *EvT* 34 (1974) 141-75.

C. G. Kruse

**AGE TO COME.** *See* APOCALYPTICISM; ESCHATOLOGY; WORLD, COSMOLOGY.

**ALLEGORY.** *See* OLD TESTAMENT IN PAUL.

**ALLUSIONS TO OLD TESTAMENT.** *See* OLD TESTAMENT IN PAUL.

**AMEN.** *See* LITURGICAL ELEMENTS; PRAYER.

**ANATHEMA.** *See* CURSE, ACCURSED, ANATHEMA.

## ANGELS, ARCHANGELS

The English word *angel* is derived from and is frequently used to translate the Greek word *angelos,* "messenger." In the Greek translation of the OT (LXX) *angelos* translates the Hebrew word *mal'ak,* or "messenger." Both *angelos* and *mal'ak* could be used to refer to either a human or a spiritual emissary. Each of the fourteen usages of *angelos* (usually plural) in Paul's letters seems to refer to, or assume a comparison with, a supernatural being or beings, either good or evil. *Archangelos,* or "archangel" (appearing only once in Paul, 1 Thess 4:16), refers to an angel of highest rank, such as the archangel Michael.

1. Angels in the OT and Judaism
2. Angels in Paul
3. Angels and Christology

### 1. Angels in the OT and Judaism.

Although angels are frequently called *mal'akîm* ("sent ones") in the OT, they may also be referred to as *qᵉdôšîm* ("holy ones"), *bᵉnê 'ēlîm* ("sons of gods"), *bᵉnê (hā) ᵉlōhîm* ("sons of God"), *sᵉbā'ôt* ("hosts"), *mᵉšārᵉtîm* ("ministers") or in certain instances they may be given the title *śar* ("commander," Josh 5:14). Angels in the OT appear as messengers or representatives of the heavenly world, frequently sent by Yahweh himself. They are part of the created order and serve God's purposes, assisting and carrying out important transactions between God and humans, but primarily between God and Israel. They mediate revelation (2 Kings 1:3), come to the assistance of individuals (Gen 16:9), are associated with manifestations of Yahweh (Gen 18; 32:1), serve as part of the heavenly council (Ps 89:6-9) and make up the heavenly army (Deut 33:2; Zech 1:11). An angel is sent to accompany and direct Israel through the wilderness journey (cf. Ex 23:23 and Ex 33:2), and an angel brings judgment against Jerusalem (2 Sam 24:16). In visionary and apocalyptic settings angels take on more distinct roles as manlike figures who guide the seer within visions and serve as interpreters (Ezek 40:3; Zech 1:7-17). In Daniel angels take on a variety of roles, the most notable being that of the great archangel Michael, the protector of Israel (Dan 10:13; 12:1).

The title "angel of the Lord" seems to refer to an angel of rank or stature who carries out special missions for Yahweh. Such an angel appears to Moses in the flaming bush (Ex 3:2), leads Israel out of Egypt and into the land of promise (cf. Josh 5:13-15 and

Judg 2:1-5) and appears to Gideon (Judg 6:11) at an hour of crisis.

Jewish texts outside of the OT testify to an expanded understanding of the nature and role of angels in some sectors of Second Temple Judaism. Much of this was simply an extension and development of what was to be found in the OT. Angels protect individuals (*1 Enoch* 100:5), execute judgment (*1 Enoch* 56:1-8), act as heavenly scribes (*Jub* 1:27-29), populate the heavenly court (*1 Enoch* 14:18-24), take part in the heavenly liturgy (*1 Enoch* 61:9-13; 4Q400-407), come to the aid of Israel in warfare (3 Macc 6:18-21), are differentiated by rank and name (*1 Enoch* 61:10; *2 Enoch* 20; *T. Levi* 3), and guide heavenly visions and interpret mysteries (*1 Enoch* 17—36). One notable new development is the notion of two opposing forces of angelic powers: a force of good angels led by God or an archangel, and a force of evil angels led by an evil angelic power known as Satan, Mastema or Belial.

### 2. Angels in Paul.

*2.1. Angels as Witnesses.* In several instances angels are referred to as observers or witnesses of Christ* or believers. In 1 Corinthians 4:9 Paul contrasts the plight of true apostles with that of the Corinthians who, according to their notion of realized eschatology,* had "already become kings" (1 Cor 4:8). In contrast, the true apostles* in their afflictions* and foolishness had become a spectacle to the world, to angels and to humans (1 Cor 4:9). In this case the nature of the angels, whether good or evil, is not immediately clear. Quite possibly Paul is ironically placing the angels alongside the eschatologically complete Corinthians,* who observe the apostles as a curiosity. But the fact that the angels are listed with the "world" (*kosmos*) and "humans" (*anthrōpoi*) could suggest that Paul had in mind inimical spirits.

1 Timothy 3:16 has been identified as a piece of preformed tradition, perhaps a hymn,* setting forth a series of contrasts between Jesus' earthly life and his exalted status. The six lines of the hymn form three pairs of contrast between the mundane and spiritual spheres (following an a b b a a b pattern). The third line, "he [Christ] was seen by angels" corresponds with the second and sixth lines: "he was vindicated by (or "in") the Spirit"; "he was taken up in glory.*" The positive note struck in these three lines would suggest that Christ's appearance before angels refers to his exaltation in the presence of angels of glory who acclaimed honor and praise to the exalted Lord, perhaps in triumphal procession. The notion of angels accompanying God and the exalted Christ reappears in 1 Timothy 5:21, where Timothy is warned "in the

presence of God and of Christ Jesus and of the elect angels" to keep the instruction of church discipline.*

In 1 Corinthians 11:10 Paul instructs that "a woman should have authority on her head, because of the angels." The context (1 Cor 11:2-26) raises several complex exegetical problems (see commentaries) and calls for broader treatment (*see* Authority; Head; Man and Woman); here the focus is limited to the nature and role of the angels. Clearly the issue for Paul is right order in worship* where women, as well as men, pray* and prophesy* (1 Cor 11:4-5). The suggestion that the angels, like the "sons of God" in Genesis 6:2, might be sexually tempted by the uncovered heads of women (a woman's hair being a sexual attraction) or that the women would be subject to the assault of evil, demonic angels lacks compelling exegetical support and assumes that the "authority"* on the woman's head is a head covering (see Fee, 490-530). Paul's interest in liturgical order suggests that the angels are concerned with the maintenance of that order. Evidence from Qumran attests to Jewish belief in the presence of angels "in the congregation," for which reason a person with physical defect was to be excluded from the sectarian assembly (1QSa 2:4-10; see Cadbury; Fitzmyer). A similar understanding may have been introduced at Corinth, with "authority" on the woman's head satisfying the angelic requirements for right order. Later, in 1 Corinthians 13:1, Paul refers to speaking "in the tongues of mortals and of angels." This may allude to prophetic speech, or speaking in tongues,* and suggests again a relationship between Spirit-inspired worship and that of the angels.

*2.2. Angels as Evil.* It is clear that early Christians, like Jews, thought that some angels were evil. Jesus in Matthew 25:41 speaks vividly of "the eternal fire prepared for the devil and his angels," and while Paul does not employ such striking language, in Romans 8:38 it seems that he does count angels as among the hostile forces of the universe that might threaten to separate believers from the love* of God* in Christ. Paul may have had in mind the angels of the lower spheres of heaven who some may have regarded as blocking access to God, or he may have been referring to the angels of the nations (Deut 32:8; Dan 10:13; Sir 17:17; *Jub.* 15:31-32) who, as national deities, might be perceived as thwarting the Gentiles'* access to the redemptive love of God in Christ. Ordinarily, however, when Paul speaks of angelic beings inimical to Christ and his people, he employs the variety of names associated with the "principalities and powers"* (note *archai* in Rom 8:38).

In 2 Corinthians 11:14 Paul warns that even Satan*

can disguise himself as an angel of light. Paul takes the Jewish tradition of Satan disguising himself (cf. *Life of Adam and Eve* 9; *T. Job* 6:4) and applies it to his opponents at Corinth who had disguised themselves as apostles. In fact, Paul maintains, they are ministers of Satan (2 Cor 11:15). Another metaphorical use of *angelos* occurs in 2 Corinthians 12:7 where Paul speaks of his "thorn in the flesh"—perhaps a physical disability or illness*—as an *angelos Satana*, an "angel" or "minister" of Satan.

*2.3. Angels as Inferior or Obstructions to the Divine Will.* As highly as Paul could regard angels in some contexts—even likening his warm reception by the Galatians to their receiving "an angel of God" (Gal 4:14)—he could also employ angels as foils for the surpassing glory of the gospel* of Christ. Even if Paul "or an angel from heaven should preach a different gospel" (Gal 1:8) from the one they originally had received, it was to be regarded as anathema. Or again, the fact that, as in some Jewish traditions, the Law* had been ordained through angels (Gal 3:19; cf. Acts 7:53; Heb 2:2) and by a mediator sets it in contrast with the work of God in Christ. This notion of the role of angels in giving the Law at Sinai seems to stem from the LXX translation of Deuteronomy 33:2 and is found in later rabbinic interpretation of Psalm 68:18.

The eschatological authority of believers is underscored in 1 Corinthians 6:3 where Paul puts to the Corinthians a rhetorical question: "Do you not know that we are to judge angels—to say nothing of ordinary matters?" (NRSV). The context is one of grievances between believers being taken into a court of law (*see* Lawsuit). Paul argues from the greater, eschatological role and authority of believers, to the mundane, temporal realm of behavior in social relationships. While it is not certain whether the angels to be judged are good or evil, the more likely interpretation is that Paul was referring to the judgment of evil powers (cf. 2 Peter 2:4; Jude 6). In this case Paul would be reminding the Corinthians that believers, having been exalted with Christ who rules over all powers, will play a role in the final judgment* of those powers.

Colossians 2:18 warns against those who would persuade the Colossians of the necessity of self-abasement and the "worship of angels" (*thrēskeia tōn angelōn*). This allusion to "worship of angels" is problematic in two respects: (1) whether the genitive "of angels" is to be read as an objective (worship directed toward angels) or subjective genitive (worship led by angels); and (2) in either case, what the religious setting of the practice might have been. The exegetical solution to this problem involves wider issues related to the false teaching at Colossae (*see* Colossians). If the

angels are equivalent to the "elements of the world"* (*stoicheia tou kosmou*, Col 2:8, 20), they appear to be powers that intrude between believers and the rightful object of worship, God in Christ. Paul would then be warning against a spiritual teaching or practice that dwells on angels to such an extent that they are virtually worshiped—or a teaching that in fact advocates their worship.

If Paul is speaking of worship promoted by angels (subjective genitive), the picture would be one of religious practices of abstinence and spiritual discipline aimed at achieving visionary* experiences in which one shares in the heavenly worship of angels (see Francis). This teaching might be akin to the understanding of worship alluded to in the Qumran* texts in which humans take part in the angelic liturgy (4Q400-407), or to the esoteric Merkabah visionary tradition attested in later Jewish texts in which spiritual adepts penetrate the heavens to the very throne of God and take part in the celestial liturgy (cf. *3 Enoch*).

*2.4. Angels at the Parousia.* When Paul speaks of the parousia of Christ he employs the traditional imagery of the Lord being revealed from heaven "in blazing fire with his powerful angels" (2 Thess 1:7) and of the Lord Jesus coming "with all his holy ones" (1 Thess 3:13). The notion of angels accompanying the divine warrior may be observed in Zechariah 14:5, where on the Day of the Lord, Yahweh will come "and all the holy ones with him"—clearly a reference to the heavenly army (cf. Deut 33:2; *1 Enoch* 1:9; Jude 14). In a similar manner, in 1 Thessalonians 4:16 Paul speaks of the "call" of the archangel, along with the "trumpet call of God." It has also been suggested that "the restrainer" mentioned in 2 Thessalonians 2:6, 7 refers to an angelic figure, possibly Michael (cf. Dan 10:13, 20; see Goulder, 99), who restrains evil for the sake of the preaching of the gospel (Marshall, 199-200).

## 3. Angels and Christology.
Research into the origin of NT christology* has appealed to Jewish angelology as an existing conceptual category of divine agency that would have assisted early Christians in coming to terms theologically with the exalted Christ (see Hurtado). Within Judaism certain principal angels were understood to be in a position of power, honor and authority that was surpassed only by God. Such angels were human-like in form and were known by the names Gabriel (Dan 8:15-26; 10:2-9; *1 Enoch* 9:1; 10:9; 40:9-10), Michael (Dan 10:13-21; 12:1; *1 Enoch* 9:1; 40:9-10; 1QM 17:6-8; 13:10), Raphael (*1 Enoch* 10:4; 40:9-10; Tob 12:15), Melchizedek (11QMelch; cf. Ps 82:1-2) and Yahoel

(*Apoc. Abr.* 10:3-4; 11:1-4). These principal angels are probably to be understood in continuity with the angel of the Lord, who appears in the Pentateuchal narratives (cf. Gen 16:7-14; 22:11-18; Ex 14:19-20). The tradition may have received significant impetus from texts such as Ezekiel 1:26-28; 8:2-4, where the "glory of the Lord" appears in human-like form, and Daniel 7:9-14; 10:2-9, where a heavenly "one like a son of man" and chief angels appear. In some Jewish texts of approximately the first century, these principal angels act as chief servants or agents of God, and seem to have contributed to a bifurcation in the Jewish conception of the image of God. The angel Yahoel may have been conceived as a personification of the divine name (Fossum) or an indwelling of that name (Yahweh and El = Yahoel; cf. Ex 23:20-21) in an angelic being (Hurtado). Thus, while other factors must also be considered, a fruitful line of investigation has been uncovered for understanding how early Christians could maintain a continuity with Jewish monotheism and yet speak of and worship Jesus as the pre-existent* Son* of God (*see* God).

*See also* ELEMENTS/ELEMENTAL SPIRITS OF THE WORLD; GOD; PRINCIPALITIES AND POWERS; QUMRAN AND PAUL; SATAN, DEVIL.

BIBLIOGRAPHY. H. Bietenhard and P. J. Budd, "Angel, Messenger, Gabriel, Michael," *NIDNTT* 1.101-5; H. Bietenhard, *Die himmlische Welt im Urchristentum und Spätjudentum* (WUNT 2; Tübingen: Vandenhoeck & Ruprecht, 1951); M. Brauch, *Hard Sayings of Paul* (Downers Grove, IL: InterVarsity, 1989) 147-53; I. Broer, "ἄγγελος," *EDNT* 1.13-16; H. J. Cadbury, "A Qumran Parallel to Paul," *HTR* 51 (1958) 1-2; G. B. Caird, *Principalities and Powers: A Study in Pauline Theology* (Oxford: Clarendon, 1956); W. Carr, *Angels and Principalities: The Background, Meaning and Development of the Pauline Phrase* hai archai kai hai exousiai (SNTSMS 42; Cambridge: University Press, 1981); M. J. Davidson, "Angels" *DJG* 8-11; idem, *Angels at Qumran: A Comparative Study of 1 Enoch 1—36, 72-108 and Sectarian Writings from Qumran* (JSPSup 11; Sheffield: Sheffield Academic, 1992); M. Dibelius, *Die Geisterwelt im Glauben des Paulus* (Göttingen: Vandenhoeck & Ruprecht, 1909); G. D. Fee, *The First Epistle to the Corinthians* (NICNT; Grand Rapids: Eerdmans, 1987); J. A. Fitzmyer, "A Feature of Qumran Angelology and the New Testament," *NTS* 4 (1957-58) 48-58; J. E. Fossum, *The Name of God and the Angel of the Lord: The Origins of the Idea of Intermediaries in Gnosticism* (WUNT 1.36; Tübingen: J. C. B. Mohr, 1985); F. O. Francis, "Humility and Angelic Worship in Col 2:18," in *Conflict at Colossae*, ed. F. O. Francis and W. A. Meeks (SBLSBS 4; 2d ed.; Missoula, MT: Scholars, 1975) 163-95; T. H.

Gaster, "Angel," *IDB* 1.128-34; M. D. Goulder, "Silas in Thessalonica," *JSNT* 48 (1992) 87-106; W. Grundmann, G. von Rad and G. Kittel, "ἄγγελος κτλ," *TDNT* I.74-87; L. W. Hurtado, *One God, One Lord: Early Christian Devotion and Ancient Jewish Monotheism* (Philadelphia: Fortress, 1988); H. B. Kuhn, "The Angelology of the Non-Canonical Jewish Apocalypses," *JBL* 67 (1948) 217-32; I. H. Marshall, *1 and 2 Thessalonians* (NCB; Grand Rapids: Eerdmans, 1983); J. Michl, "Angel," *EBT* 1.20-28; E. T. Mullen, *The Assembly of the Gods: The Divine Council in Canaanite and Early Hebrew Literature* (HSM 24; Chico, CA: Scholars, 1980); C. A. Newsom and D. F. Watson, "Angels," *ABD* I.248-55; C. Rowland, *The Open Heaven: A Study of Apocalyptic in Judaism and Early Christianity* (New York: Crossroad, 1982); D. S. Russell, *The Method and Message of Jewish Apocalyptic* (Philadelphia: Westminster, 1964).

D. G. Reid

## ANTHROPOLOGY. *See* PSYCHOLOGY.

## ANTIOCH ON THE ORONTES

Antioch of Syria, one of the principal cities of the Roman Empire, was the focal point of Christianity as it spread beyond the borders of Palestine to the Diaspora.*

When Paul first arrived in Antioch the city was bustling with activity and excitement, experiencing a time of rebuilding. The year Paul probably arrived, A.D. 43, was the year the city established its Olympic Games. Its population in the first century A.D. was estimated at about 300,000 (Strabo *Geog.* 16.2.5), which included a large number of Jews (estimates range from 22,000 to 65,000), according to Josephus (J.W. 7.3.3 §43). A huge, wealthy and cosmopolitan city where barriers of religion, race and nationality were easily crossed—and where toleration may have been a matter of civic pride—it was a perfect base of operations for the spread of Christianity. Nicolaus from Antioch, one who had been a proselyte to Judaism and one of the early converts to Christianity, was selected as one of the seven leaders of the Hellenist (*see* Hellenism) Christians in Jerusalem* (Acts 6:5).

Hellenistic Jewish Christians, fleeing from the persecution that arose in Jerusalem in connection with the martyrdom of Stephen, brought Christianity to Antioch. Soon other refugees who had fled to Cyprus and Cyrene came to Antioch and preached to "Greeks" with considerable success (Acts 11:19-21). These "Greeks" were probably "God-fearers," Gentiles attracted to Jewish monotheism (Acts 10:22; 13:16, 26, 43; 16:14; 17:4, 17; 18:7). Jews of Antioch were numerous and wealthy at this time, endowing splendidly decorated synagogues, and "constantly attracting to their religious ceremonies multitudes of Greeks" (Josephus *J.W.* 7.3.3 §45).

When the Jerusalem church heard of the growing number of believers in Antioch, they sent Barnabas* who, over a period of time, successfully ministered to the young church (Acts 11:22-24) and eventually invited Paul to join him (Acts 11:25-26). Acts tells us that Paul, the Jew of Tarsus (*see* Jew, Paul the), and Barnabas, the Levite from Cyprus, ministered together in Antioch for an entire year (Acts 11:26). But for many years thereafter they made this city of heterogeneous cultures the focal point and home base of their missionary activity among Gentiles* (Acts 13:3; 15:22-36; 18:22-23). Besides Jerusalem, no other city of the Roman Empire played as large a part in the life of the early church as did Antioch. It was at Antioch that the term *Christian* (*Christianos*, "Follower of Christ") was first used for the disciples of Jesus (Acts 11:26). And it was the Christian believers at Antioch who, during the severe famine (A.D. 45-47) that occurred during the reign of Claudius (Suetonius *Claudius* 18.2), sent relief to believers living in Judea (Acts 11:27-30).

At some point during Paul's stay in the city, Peter* came to Antioch. In the course of his visit Peter, who had been eating with Gentiles, began to withdraw from table fellowship with them (*see* Food). From Paul's account of the matter (Gal 2:11-14), Peter's withdrawal coincided with the arrival of a contingent from the Jerusalem church ("certain men" who "came from James") and arose out of fear of "those of the circumcision*" (*tous ek peritomēs*, Gal 2:12; *see* Judaizer). It is conjectured that the pressure for Peter to withdraw from fellowship may have arisen out of the Jerusalem church's practical concern for the gospel's outreach to Jews in a climate of rising Jewish nationalism. Nevertheless, Paul saw Peter's withdrawal, and the consequent withdrawal of other Jewish believers—including Barnabas—as hypocritical and destructive of the mission to the Gentiles and of Christian unity (Gal 2:13-14). Thus Antioch became the setting for a significant controversy over a matter of practice that struck at the heart of Paul's gospel.*

According to Eusebius, the first bishop of Antioch was Peter, who was succeeded by Evodius, and then by Ignatius of Antioch, who was martyred very early in the second century, during the reign of Trajan (A.D. 98-117; Eusebius *Hist. Eccl.* 3.36.2; 3.22).

Our knowledge of Antioch is derived from limited archeological excavation but also from a considerable body of ancient literature (Strabo, Evagrius, Procopius, Libanius, the Emperor Julian, John Chrysostom, and especially the *Chronographia* of John Malalas from the sixth century A.D.). The city covered an area of approximately one by two miles between the Orontes River on the east and Mount Silpius on the west. It was laid out on a Hippodamian grid plan (streets crossing at right angles and buildings placed in the rectangles), typical of Hellenistic cities, with rectangular city blocks of 367 feet by 190 feet. It was surrounded by a wall built by Seleucus I (311-281 B.C.), enlarged probably by Antiochus Epiphanes (175-164 B.C.) and rebuilt by Tiberius (A.D. 14-37).

Beginning in 67 B.C., many important buildings, including a palace and a circus, were constructed by Marcius Rex and Pompey. This building program was continued in 47 B.C. by Julius Caesar, who constructed an aqueduct to provide water for residences built on the side of Mount Silpius. Some remains of these private residences and also of small bathhouses whose construction was facilitated by the building of the aqueduct have been found. At the foot of the mountain Caesar constructed a theater in the monumental center of town and an amphitheater near the southern gate. Somewhere, undoubtedly near the center of town, he built the *Kaisareion*, perhaps the oldest basilica in the East, for use by the cult of Rome. It bore his name and housed a statue of himself. In Antioch he also rebuilt the Pantheon, which was in a state of deterioration, and built (or reconstructed) a theater on the slope of Mount Silpius.

A colonnaded street, which ran the full length of the city, north to south, and cut Antioch in half, was built by Herod the Great (Josephus, *J.W.* 1.21.11 §425; *Ant.* 16.5.3 §148). Augustus Caesar visited Antioch twice and conducted an extensive building program in the city. This he funded by the treasure he found in Egypt after the defeat of Cleopatra and Antony at Actium in 31 B.C. Several temples and other projects attributed to Tiberius were probably only completed by him, actually having been initiated by Augustus.

Some of Tiberius's building activities may have been occasioned by a fire in Antioch during his reign in A.D. 23/24. He built bathhouses in the eastern part of the city, and perhaps also on the island in the Orontes. He is also credited with the expansion of the theater, the construction of monumental gates at each main intersection of the city's streets, and the completion and improvement of the Epiphania, the city's southern section built by Antiochus Epiphanes and named after himself.

Antioch was hit by earthquakes often, two of which occurred in the time of Paul. The first happened on April 9, A.D. 37, during the reign of Caligula, to which Caligula responded quickly and generously, utilizing the considerable surplus left in the treasury at Rome by Tiberius. Substantial building and renovation were conducted as he rebuilt the devastated city. The second earthquake at Antioch, which occurred during the reign of Claudius (A.D. 41-54), also damaged Ephesus, Smyrna and other cities of Asia Minor.

The "Silver Chalice of Antioch" was purportedly discovered there in 1910. It consists of a plain silver inner cup and a heavily gilded outer silver holder. It has been speculated that the reason for making such a beautiful container for such an ordinary cup was that the latter was the cup used by Christ at the Last Supper. However, authorities generally date the cup from the second to the sixth century.

*See also* BARNABAS; MISSION; PETER.

BIBLIOGRAPHY. R. E. Brown and J. P. Meier, *Antioch and Rome: New Testament Cradles of Catholic Christianity* (New York: Paulist, 1983); F. Cimok, *Antioch on the Orontes* (Istanbul: Us Tan Tma Merkezi, 1980); Committee for the Excavation of Antioch and its Vicinity, *Antioch-on-the-Orontes*, eds. G. W. Elderkin et al. (5 vols.; Princeton: University Press, 1934-70); G. Downey, *A History of Antioch in Syria from Seleucus to the Arab Conquest* (Princeton: University Press, 1961); idem, *Ancient Antioch* (Princeton: University Press, 1963); J. D. G. Dunn, "The Incident at Antioch (Gal. 2.11-18)," *JSNT* 18 (1983) 3-57 [= idem, *Jesus, Paul and the Law* (Louisville: Westminster/John Knox, 1990) 129-82]; C. H. Kraeling, "The Jewish Community at Antioch," *JBL* 51 (1932) 130-60; J. H. W. G. Liebeschuetz, *Antioch: City and Imperial Administration in the Later Roman Empire* (Oxford: Clarendon, 1972); R. N. Longenecker, *Galatians* (WBC 41; Dallas: Word, 1990) 65-71; W. Meeks and R. Wilken, *Jews and Christians in Antioch in the First Four Centuries of the Common Era* (SBLSBS 13; Missoula, MT: Scholars, 1978); D. S. Wallace-Hadrill, *Christian Antioch: A Study of Early Christian Thought in the East* (Cambridge: University Press, 1982).

J. McRay

# APOCALYPTICISM

The term "apocalypticism" is a transliterated form of the Greek term *apokalypsis*, which means "disclosure," "revelation." The author of the Apocalypse, or Revelation of John, was the first Jewish or Christian author to use the term *apokalypsis* in describing the content of his book, which is essentially a narrative of a series of revelatory visions which disclose the events surrounding the imminent end of the present age: "[This is] the revelation [*apokalypsis*] of John, which God gave to him, to show to his servants what must soon take place" (Rev 1:1). Following Revelation 1:1, the term *apocalypse* has been used since the early nineteenth century, when it was popularized by the German NT scholar F. Luecke (1791-1854) as a generic term to describe documents with a content and structure similar to the Revelation of John.

1. Defining Apocalypticism
2. The Origins of Apocalypticism
3. Characteristics of Apocalypticism
4. Paul and Jewish Apocalyptic

### 1. Defining Apocalypticism.

The term *apocalypticism* is a modern designation widely used to refer to a worldview which characterized segments of early Judaism from c. 200 B.C. to A.D. 200, and which centered on the expectation of God's imminent intervention into human history in a decisive manner to save his people and punish their enemies by destroying the existing fallen cosmic order and by restoring or recreating the cosmos to its original pristine perfection. Knowledge of cosmic secrets (one of the contributions of the wisdom tradition to apocalypticism) and the imminent eschatological plans of God was revealed to apocalyptists through dreams and visions, and the apocalypses they wrote were primarily narratives of the visions they had received and which were explained to them by an interpreting angel. All extant Jewish apocalypses are believed to be pseudonymous, that is, written under the names of prominent ancient Israelite or Jewish figures such as Adam, Enoch, Moses, Daniel, Ezra and Baruch. Only the earliest Christian apocalypses, the Revelation of John and the Shepherd of Hermas, were written under the names of the actual authors. The most likely reason for the phenomenon of apocalyptic pseudonymity is that it was a strategy to provide credentials and thereby assure the acceptance of these revelatory writings at a point in Israelite history when the reputation of prophets had sunk to an extremely low point. *Apocalypticism* is therefore a term used to describe the particular type of eschatological expectation characteristic of early Jewish and early Christian apocalypses. The Jewish religious compositions which are generally regarded as apocalypses include Daniel 7—12 (the only OT apocalypse), the five documents which comprise *1 Enoch* (1—36, the Book of Watchers; 37—71, the Similitudes of Enoch; 72—82, the Book of Heavenly Luminaries; 83—90, the Animal Apocalypse; 92—104, the Epistle of Enoch), *2 Enoch*, 4 Ezra, *2 Baruch*, *3 Baruch* and the *Apocalypse of Abraham*. Early Christian apocalypses include the Revelation of John (the only NT apocalypse) and the Shepherd of Hermas.

There are four aspects of apocalypticism which need to be distinguished:

(1) *Apocalyptic eschatology*, a type of eschatology that

is found in apocalypses or is similar to the eschatology of apocalypses, characterized by the tendency to view reality from the perspective of divine sovereignty (e.g., the eschatologies of the Qumran Community, Jesus and Paul)

(2) *Apocalypticism* or *millennialism*, a form of collective behavior based on those beliefs (e.g., the movement led by John the Baptist, and the revolts of Theudas reported in Acts 5:36 and Josephus *Ant.* 20.5.1 §§97-98, and the unnamed Egyptian reported in Acts 21:38; Josephus *Ant.* 20.8.6 §§169-72; *J.W.* 2.13.5 §§261-63)

(3) *Apocalypse*, a type of literature in which those beliefs occur in their most basic and complete form, and which centers on the revelation of cosmic lore and the end of the age

(4) *Apocalyptic imagery*, the various constituent themes and motifs of apocalyptic eschatology used in various ways in early Jewish and early Christian literature

The focus in this article will be on Jewish apocalyptic eschatology and the ways in which Paul adapted some of the basic themes and structures of apocalyptic eschatology into his own theological thought.

## 2. The Origins of Apocalypticism.

A number of proposals have been made regarding the origins of apocalypticism, and these proposals have often reflected the positive or negative attitude which scholars have had toward the phenomenon of apocalypticism. Following the lead of F. Luecke in the mid-nineteenth century, many scholars have viewed apocalypticism favorably as a development of OT prophecy that perhaps resulted from the disillusionment of the post-exilic period which included subjection to foreign nations and tension within the Jewish community. Other scholars who discerned a sharp break between OT prophecy and later apocalypticism proposed that many of the basic features of apocalypticism originated in ancient Iran and had penetrated Jewish thought during the Hellenistic period (c. 400-200 B.C.), or more generally from the syncretistic tendencies during the Hellenistic period when there was a blending of religious ideas from both west and east.

*2.1. The Setting of Apocalypticism.* The fact that most apocalypses are pseudonymous has made it difficult to reconstruct the social situations within which they were written and to which they responded. There is nevertheless wide agreement that Jewish apocalypses were written or revised during times of social or political crisis, though such crises may run the spectrum from real to perceived. Focusing his attention on the period 400-200 B.C., Ploeger discerned a split in the

post-exilic Jewish community into two sharp divisions, the theocratic party (the ruling priestly aristocrats), which interpreted prophetic eschatology in terms of the Jewish state, and the eschatological party (forerunners of the apocalyptists), which awaited the fulfillment of the eschatological predictions of the prophets. More recently, P. D. Hanson has argued that apocalypticism is a natural development of Israelite prophecy which originated in the intramural struggle between visionary prophets and hierocratic (Zadokite) priests which took place from the sixth through the fourth centuries B.C.

*2.2. Eschatology and Apocalypticism.* A distinction has generally been made between eschatology* and apocalypticism. Eschatology is a term which began to be used in the nineteenth century as a label for that aspect of systematic theology which dealt with topics relating to the future of the individual (death, resurrection, judgment, eternal life, heaven and hell), and topics relating to corporate or national eschatology, that is, the future of the Christian church or the Jewish people (e.g., the coming of the Messiah, the great tribulation, resurrection, judgment, the Second Coming of Christ, the temporary messianic kingdom, the recreation of the universe). A distinction has often been made between prophetic eschatology and apocalyptic eschatology, which serves the useful function of emphasizing the continuities as well as the changes in Israelite-Jewish eschatological expectation. Following this model, prophetic eschatology was an optimistic perspective which anticipated that God would eventually restore the originally idyllic pristine conditions by acting through historical processes. The Israelite prophet proclaimed God's plans for Israel to both king and people in terms of actual historical and political events and processes. Prophecy sees the future as arising out of the present, while apocalyptic eschatology regards the future as breaking into the present; the former is essentially optimistic, while the latter is pessimistic (Rowley, 35).

*2.3. Prophecy and Apocalypticism.* The problem of the relationship between prophecy and apocalypticism is one aspect of the problem of the degree of continuity or discontinuity thought to exist between Jewish apocalypticism and earlier Israelite religious and political traditions. It is important to recognize that prophecy and apocalypticism exhibit both elements of continuity and discontinuity. The sharp contrasts often thought to exist between prophecy and apocalypticism are somewhat mitigated by the recognition that prophecy itself underwent many changes and that there are numerous striking similarities between late prophecy and early apocalyptic (Hanson). Late prophetic books which exhibit tendencies that were later to emerge more fully developed in Jewish apocalyptic literature include the visions of Zechariah 1—6 (with the presence of an angelic interpreter), Isaiah 24—27, 56—66, Joel and Zechariah 9—14.

**2.4. Wisdom and Apocalypticism.** Many scholars have argued that there was a fundamental break between prophecy and apocalypticism. G. von Rad, for example, rejected the view that the primary roots of apocalypticism were to be found in Israelite prophecy. Von Rad described apocalypticism as consisting in a clear-cut dualism, radical transcendence, esotericism and gnosticism, and proposed that apocalypticism arose out of the Wisdom literature of the OT. Themes common to wisdom* and apocalyptic literature, and which suggest the connection between the two types of literature include the following: (1) both sages and apocalyptists are referred to as "the wise" and preserved their teaching in written form, often emphasizing their special "knowledge" and its antiquity; (2) both exhibit individualistic and universalistic tendencies; (3) both are concerned with the mysteries of nature from a celestial perspective; and (4) both reflect a deterministic view of history.

The proposal that Israelite wisdom, not Israelite prophecy, was the mother of Jewish apocalypticism has found little scholarly support in the form in which it was proposed by von Rad. Yet there are undeniably links between wisdom and apocalyptic (Wis 7:27; Sir 24:33), both of which are *scribal* phenomena. The wisdom tradition in Israel was certainly one of the many influences upon the development of Jewish apocalypticism. Nevertheless it is important to distinguish between two types of wisdom: *proverbial wisdom* and *mantic wisdom*. The latter type is related to the role of the "wise" in interpreting dreams as reflected in the biblical traditions concerning Joseph and Daniel, both of whom were able to explain the meaning of ambiguous revelatory dreams through divine wisdom (Gen 40:8; 41:25, 39; Dan 2:19-23, 30, 45; 5:11-12). The figure of the *angelus interpres* ("interpreting angel") occurs frequently in Jewish apocalypses where he plays the analogous role of a supernatural revealer who is able to reveal the deeper significance of the dreams and visions experienced by the apocalyptist (Dan 7—12; Zech 1—6; 4 Ezra).

**2.5. Pharisaism and Apocalypticism.** The monumental three-volume work on Judaism by G. F. Moore was based on the assumption that "normative" Judaism of the first few centuries of the Christian era, "the age of the Tannaim," did not include Jewish apocalypticism. Similarly, A. Schweitzer sharply distinguished the teaching of the apocalyptists (and therefore Jesus)

from the teaching of the rabbis. However, the Pharisaic emphases on the resurrection, the age to come and the Messiah, make it difficult to distinguish sharply the religious and political concerns of apocalyptists from the Pharisees, even though Pharisees appear to have become disenchanted with many aspects of apocalypticism in the aftermath of the disastrous first revolt against Rome (A.D. 66-73). W. D. Davies has argued that there are several links between apocalypticism and Pharisaism: (1) Both share a similar piety and attitude toward the Torah. (2) Both share similar views on such eschatological topics as the travail of the Messianic era, the gathering of exiles, the days of the Messiah, the New Jerusalem, the judgment and gehenna. (3) Both have populist and scholastic tendencies.

## 3. Characteristics of Apocalypticism.

**3.1. Major Aspects of Apocalypticism.** There are a number of features of apocalyptic eschatology upon which there is some scholarly agreement:

(1) The temporal dualism of the two ages

(2) The radical discontinuity between this age and the next coupled with pessimism regarding the existing order and otherworldly hope directed toward the future order

(3) The division of history into segments (four, seven, twelve) reflecting a predetermined plan of history

(4) The expectation of the imminent arrival of the reign of God as an act of God spelling the doom of existing earthly conditions

(5) A cosmic perspective in which the primary location of an individual is no longer within a collective entity such as Israel or the people of God, and the impending crisis is not local but cosmic in scope

(6) The cataclysmic intervention of God will result in salvation for the righteous, conceived as the regaining of Edenic conditions

(7) The introduction of angels* and demons* to explain historical and eschatological events

(8) The introduction of a new mediator with royal functions

These characteristics are not exhaustive, but they serve the useful purpose of focusing on some of the distinctive features of the apocalyptic worldview.

**3.2. The Apocalyptic Scenarios.** Since narratives that describe the events attending the close of the present era and the inauguration of the future era are essentially a type of folklore, there are many divergent descriptions of expected future events with little consistency between them. In producing a synthesis of the great variety of apocalyptic scenarios found in apocalyptic literature, therefore, the emphasis must be on the more typical features found in such descriptions. Apocalypticism or apocalyptic eschatology centers on the belief that the present world order, which is both evil and oppressive, is under the temporary control of Satan and his human accomplices. This present evil world order will shortly be destroyed by God and replaced with a new and perfect order corresponding to Eden. During the present evil age, the people of God are an oppressed minority who fervently await the intervention of God or his specially chosen agent, the Messiah. The transition between the old and the new ages, the end of the old age and the beginning of the new, will be introduced by a final series of battles fought by the people of God against the human allies of Satan.* The outcome is never in question, however, for the enemies of God are predestined to be defeated and destroyed. The inauguration of the new age will begin with the arrival of God or his accredited agent to judge the wicked and reward the righteous, and will be concluded by the re-creation or transformation of the universe.

**3.3. Limited Dualism.** One of the basic features of apocalypticism is the conviction that the cosmos is divided under two opposing supernatural forces, God and Satan, who represent the moral qualities of good and evil (cosmological dualism). However, the Jewish conviction that God is absolutely sovereign implies that he is the originator of evil and that the resultant dualism of good and evil is neither eternal nor absolute (unlike the dualism of ancient Iranian religion), but limited. This essentially limited cosmological dualism was understood in various different but related types of dualistic thought in early Jewish apocalypticism: (1) *Temporal or eschatological dualism* makes a sharp distinction between the present age and the age to come. (2) *Ethical dualism* is based on a moral distinction between good and evil and sees humanity divided into two groups, the righteous and the wicked, in a way which corresponds to good and evil supernatural powers. (3) *Psychological or microcosmic dualism* is the internalization of the two-age schema which sees the forces of good and evil struggling for supremacy within each individual.

**3.3.1. Temporal or Eschatological Dualism.** The belief in two successive ages, or worlds, developed only gradually in Judaism. The earliest occurrence of the rabbinic phrase "the world to come" is found in *1 Enoch* 71:15 (c. 200 B.C.). The doctrine of two ages is fully developed by c. A.D. 90, for according to 4 Ezra 7:50, "The Most High has not made one Age but two" (see 4 Ezra 8:1). The day of judgment is considered the dividing point between the two ages (4 Ezra 7:113): the "day of judgment will be the end of this age and be-

ginning of the immortal age to come."

**3.3.2. Ethical Dualism.** Daniel 12:10 distinguishes between the "wicked" and the "wise"; *Jubilees* distinguishes between Israelites who are "the righteous nation" (*Jub.* 24:29), "a righteous generation" (*Jub.* 25:3) and the Gentiles who are sinners (*Jub.* 23:24; 24:28); the Qumran War Scroll similarly distinguishes between the people of God and the Kittim (1QM 1:6; 18:2-3); and the *Testament of Asher* contrasts "good and single-faced people" (*T. Asher* 4:1) with "people of two faces" (*T. Asher* 3:1).

**3.3.3. Psychological or Microcosmic Dualism.** In this type of dualism the antithetical supernatural cosmic powers, conceived of in the moral categories of good and evil, have an analogous correspondence to the struggle between good and evil experienced by individuals. In some strands of Jewish apocalyptic thought, notably the Qumran Community and the circles which produced the Testaments of the Twelve Patriarchs, it was believed that God created two spirits, the spirit of truth and the spirit of error (i.e., the evil spirit called Belial, 1QS 1:18-24; *T. Judah* 20:1-5; see Jn 14:17; 15:26; 16:13; 1 Jn 4:6), and humans may live in accordance with one or the other; the Prince of Lights controls the lives of the children of righteousness, while the Angel of Darkness has dominion over the children of falsehood (1QS 3:17—4:1; 4:2-11; 1QM 13:9-12). However, even the sins of the children of righteousness are ultimately caused by the spirit of error, for both spirits strive for supremacy within the heart of the individual (1QS 4:23-26; *T. Asher* 1:3-5; see Seitz). The dominion of the spirit of error is temporally limited, however, for God will ultimately destroy it (1QS 4:18-19). The doctrine that the spirit of truth and the spirit of error strive for supremacy in the heart of each person is similar to the rabbinic doctrine of the good and evil impulses.

**3.4. Messianic Expectation.** Messianism was not an invariable feature of all the various eschatological schemes which made up Jewish apocalypticism. During the Second Temple period there were at least two main types of Jewish messianism, restorative and utopian. Restorative messianism anticipated the restoration of the Davidic monarchy and centered on an expectation of the improvement and perfection of the present world through natural development (*Pss. Sol.* 17), and modeled on an idealized historical period; the memory of the past is projected into the future. Utopian messianism anticipated a future era which would surpass everything previously known. Jewish messianism tended to focus, not on the restoration of a dynasty, but on a single messianic king sent by God to restore the fortunes of Israel (*see* Restoration of

Israel). However, as a theocratic symbol, the Messiah is dispensable, since a Messiah is not invariably part of all Jewish eschatological expectation. No such figure, for example, plays a role in the eschatological scenarios of Joel, Isaiah 24—27, Daniel, Sirach, *Jubilees*, the *Assumption of Moses*, Tobit, 1 and 2 Maccabees, Wisdom, *1 Enoch* 1—36 [the Book of Watchers], 90—104 [the Epistle of Enoch], *2 Enoch*.

**3.5. The Temporary Messianic Kingdom.** There is little consistency in Jewish apocalyptic regarding the arrival of the kingdom* of God. It was conceptualized by some as the arrival of an eternal kingdom, but by others as a temporary messianic kingdom which would be succeeded by an eternal kingdom (see 1 Cor 15:24). The conception of a temporary messianic kingdom which would function as a transition between the present evil age and the age to come, between monarchy and theocracy, solved the problem of how the transition from the Messiah to the eternal reign of God (where such a conception is present) might be conceived. In Jewish apocalyptic thought generally, the kingdom of God is more centrally important than the figure of a Messiah. A messianic interregnum, therefore, functions as an anticipation of the perfect and eternal theocratic state which will exist when primordial conditions are reinstated forever. This interim kingdom was expected to be transitional since it is depicted as combining some of the characteristics of this age with those of the age to come. In Christian apocalypticism this anticipation of a temporary messianic kingdom is clearly reflected in Revelation 20:4-6, and according to some scholars is also reflected in 1 Corinthians 15:20-28 (see below). The expectation of a future temporary messianic kingdom is found in only three early Jewish apocalypses, the Apocalypse of Weeks, or 1 Enoch 91:1-10; 93:12-17 (written between 175 and 167 B.C.), 4 Ezra 7:26-44; 12:31-34 (written c. A.D. 90), and 2 Baruch 29:3—30:1; 40:1-4; 72:2—74:3 (written c. A.D. 110). Though some have claimed that the conception of a temporary messianic kingdom is found in *2 Enoch* 32:2-33:1 and *Jubilees* 1:27-29; 23:26-31, the evidence is not compelling.

*3.5.1. Apocalypse of Weeks.* In *1 Enoch* 93:3-10 and 91:11-17, an earlier apocalypse inserted into the Epistle of Enoch (*1 Enoch* 91—104), history is divided into ten weeks (i.e., ten ages), with a nonmessianic temporary kingdom appearing in the eighth week and an eternal kingdom arriving in the tenth week (*1 Enoch* 91:11-17).

*3.5.2. 4 Ezra.* According to 4 Ezra 7:26-30, the Messiah will appear in the last days and live with the righteous for four hundred years. The Messiah, together with all other people on earth, will then die

and the world will return to seven days of primeval silence. After this the resurrection will occur (4 Ezra 7:32), and the Most High will take his place on the seat of judgment and will execute judgment on all nations (4 Ezra 7:36-43). In 4 Ezra 12:31-34, on the other hand, the Davidic Messiah will sit on the seat of judgment and, after reproving the ungodly and the wicked, will destroy them (4 Ezra 12:32). This judgment exercised by the Messiah is preliminary to the final judgment which will be exercised by God after the arrival of the end (4 Ezra 12:34). Nowhere in 4 Ezra, however, does the Messiah play a role in the eternal theocratic kingdom which is inaugurated with the resurrection.

*3.5.3. 2 Baruch.* After twelve periods of tribulation (*2 Baruch* 27:1-5), the messianic kingdom is depicted as a period of phenomenal abundance inaugurated by the appearance of the Messiah (*2 Baruch* 29:3) and concluded by his return to glory (*2 Baruch* 30:1). The elect who lived during the messianic kingdom will then be joined by the resurrected righteous, but the souls of the wicked will fear judgment (*2 Baruch* 30:1-5). The author assumes rather than clearly states the fact that those who lived during the messianic kingdom will experience a transformation into a resurrection mode of existence like the resurrected righteous. In *2 Baruch* 39—40 the predicted fall of the fourth kingdom (Rome) will be followed by the revelation of the Messiah (*2 Baruch* 39:7), who will destroy the armies of the final wicked ruler, who will be brought bound to Zion where he will be judged and executed by the Messiah (*2 Baruch* 40:1-2). The kingdom of the Messiah will last "forever," that is, until the world of corruption has ended, which means that this kingdom is temporary but of unspecified duration. Finally, in *2 Baruch* 72:2—74:3, the warrior Messiah will summon all nations together, sparing some and executing others (*2 Baruch* 72:2-6). Following this period of judgment will be an era in which Edenic conditions will be restored to the earth (*2 Baruch* 73:1-7). As in 4 Ezra, the Messiah plays no role in the eternal kingdom which is inaugurated after he is taken up into heaven.

*3.6. The Eschatological Antagonist.* In Jewish apocalyptic literature there are two traditions of a wicked eschatological figure who functions as an agent of Satan, or Beliar, in leading astray, opposing and persecuting the people of God; both traditions represent historicizations of the ancient combat myth. One tradition focuses on a godless tyrannical ruler who will arise in the last generation to become the primary adversary of God or the Messiah. This Satanic agent was expected to lead the forces of evil in the final battle between the forces of evil and the people of God (1QM 18.1; 1QS 4.18-18; *T. Dan.* 5:10-11; *T. Mos.* 8).

The historicization of the combat myth is already found in the OT where the chaos monsters Rahab and Leviathan are sometimes used to symbolize foreign oppressors like Egypt (Ps 74:14; 87:4; Is 30:7; Ezek 29:3; 32:2-4). Several OT traditions provided the basis for the later apocalyptic conception of the eschatological antagonist, including the figure of Gog, the ruler of Magog in the Gog and Magog oracle in Ezekiel 38—39 (see Rev 20:8; 3 Enoch 45:5), the references to a vague "enemy from the north" found in several OT prophecies (Ezek 38:6, 15; 39:2; Jer 1:13-15; 3:18; 4:6; 6:1, 22), and the depicting of Antiochus IV, the "little horn" in Daniel 7—8, as the oppressor of the people of God. The career of the Greco-Syrian king Antiochus IV Epiphanes (175-164 B.C.), whose actions against the Jewish people are described in 1 Maccabees 1:20-61, and 2 Maccabees 5:11-6:11, is presented as a mythologized apocalyptic figure in Daniel 11:36-39, claiming to be God or to be equal with God (Dan 11:36-37; Sib. Or. 5:33-34; Asc. Isa. 4:6; 2 Enoch [Rec. J] 29:4).

Later the characteristics of the eschatological adversary were augmented and embellished by traditions about the Roman emperors* Caligula and Nero, both of whom had divine pretensions which their Roman contemporaries considered tacky and which outraged the Jews. The other tradition concerns the false prophet who performs signs and wonders to legitimate his false teaching (cf. Deut 13:2-6). Occasionally Satan and the eschatological antagonist are identified as the same person, as in Sibylline Oracles 3:63-74 and Ascension of Isaiah 7:1-7, where Nero (= the eschatological antagonist) is regarded as Beliar (= Satan) incarnate.

*3.7. The Re-creation or Transformation of the Cosmos.* In Isaiah 65:17 and 66:22 the creation of a new heaven and a new earth is predicted. The theme of the re-creation or renewal of creation was taken up into apocalyptic literature as the final eschatological act. Essentially the expectation of a new creation or a renewed creation is a particular application of the two-age schema in which the first creation is identified with the present evil age (or world) and the new or renewed creation is identified with the age (or world) to come. While there are many references to the new creation in Jewish apocalyptic literature, it is not always clear whether the present order of creation is reduced to chaos before the act of re-creation (1 Enoch 72:1; 91:16; Sib. Or. 5.212; Jub. 1:29; 4:26; Bib. Ant. 3:10; Apoc. Elijah 5:38; 2 Pet 3:13; Rev 21:1, 5; see 2 Cor 5:17; Gal 6:15), or whether the renewal or transformation of the existing world is in view (1 Enoch 45:4-5; 2 Apoc. Bar. 32:6; 44:12; 49:3; 57:2; Bib. Ant. 32:17;

4 Ezra 7:30-31, 75; see Rom 8:21). In many of these passages the pattern for the new or transformed creation is based on the Edenic conditions thought to have existed on the earth before the fall of Adam and Eve.

**4. Paul and Jewish Apocalyptic.**

*4.1. Sources and Problems.* Critical scholarship regards the seven generally acknowledged Pauline letters as providing a firm basis for analyzing Pauline theology. These letters include Romans, 1 and 2 Corinthians, Galatians, Philippians, 1 Thessalonians and Philemon. Letters whose authenticity remains in some doubt (2 Thessalonians; Colossians) or whose Pauline authorship is generally rejected (Ephesians; 1 and 2 Timothy; Titus) are used only to supplement data found in the basic corpus of seven letters. The Book of Acts is another important source for our knowledge of Paul's life, but this work too must be used only as a supplement to the core of genuine letters.

One of the major problems in the study of Paul's life and thought is that of determining the extent to which it is appropriate to label Pauline thought as "apocalyptic." There is widespread agreement that Paul was influenced by apocalyptic eschatology, but the extent to which he modified apocalypticism in light of his faith in Christ remains a central problem. Baumgarten holds that Paul demythologizes apocalyptic traditions by consistently applying them to the present life of the community.

Another problem centers on the issue of the origin of Paul's apocalyptic thought. Baumgarten (43-53) has suggested that apocalyptic traditions came to Paul through the Hellenists at Antioch.*

*4.2. The Center or Structure of Pauline Thought.* The complexity of Paul's theological thought is exacerbated by the fact that the primary evidence for his views is found in occasional letters written in a variety of specific contexts for the purpose of addressing particular problems and issues; they are historically contingent pastoral communications. Further, the basic seven-letter corpus can hardly be regarded as a representative sample of Pauline thought. Despite the difficulties, many attempts have been made to understand the coherence of Paul's thought and on that basis to identify the core or center* of his thought. Some scholars have doubted whether Paul himself thought in terms of such a "core," or whether the evidence from seven occasional letters is adequate for such a task. Some of the more important suggestions for identifying the central message of Paul's thought include: (1) the gospel,* (2) christology,* (3) the death* and resurrection* of Jesus, (4) the theme "in

Christ"* (participatory categories), (5) ecclesiology (*see* Church), (6) justification* by faith (the traditional Lutheran view) and (7) anthropology (F. C. Baur; R. Bultmann). It is evident, however, that many of these topics are closely related to others, so that the choice of a core for Pauline thought becomes a matter of nuance. It is clear, for example, that Paul's polemical doctrine of justification by faith is an aspect of his christology, and that the topics of anthropology and ecclesiology are two ways of looking at individual Christians who at the same time hold membership in the people of God.

Other scholars have proposed that it is more important to identify the structure of Paul's thought. Two of the most important proposals include: (1) salvation history, that is, God, who is the central actor in history, has had an ultimate salvific goal for humanity from the beginning, which originally centered on Israel and ultimately on all who believe in Christ, a structure particularly evident in Romans 9—11; and (2) apocalyptic eschatology. However, salvation history and apocalyptic eschatology must not be considered antithetical, since the latter is simply a more specific and particular version of the former. Further, it is a matter of continuing debate whether these suggestions constitute the horizon or kernel of Paul's thought.

*4.3. Paul as a Visionary and Mystic.* The authors of apocalypses, though they usually concealed their true identities behind pseudonyms, received divine revelations through visions* and for that reason they structured the apocalypses they wrote as narratives of the visions they had actually received or pretended to receive. There was a close relationship between Jewish merkabah mysticism (based on Ezek 1; *see* Jew, Paul the; Mysticism) and apocalypticism (Gruenwald), though out-of-body visions were more common in the former and bodily ascensions to heaven more common in the latter. While there is no evidence that Paul himself wrote an apocalypse, he claims to have been the recipient of revelatory visions or ecstatic experiences (Gal 1:11-17; 1 Cor 9:1; 15:8; *see* Acts 9:1-9; 16:9; 18:9-10; 22:6-11, 17-21; 26:12-18; 27:23-24). In Galatians 1:12 he speaks of his Damascus Road experience as an *apokalypsis* ("revelation") from Jesus Christ (*see* Conversion), and in 2 Corinthians 12:1 he speaks of "visions and revelations [*apokalypseis*] of the Lord," which are presumably descriptions of his own experience. It is likely that Paul is the man of whom he speaks, who experienced a journey to the third heaven where he heard unspeakable things (2 Cor 12:1-10).

*4.4. Apocalyptic Scenarios.* There are four relatively extensive apocalyptic scenarios in the Pauline letters,

three of which center on the Parousia of Jesus (1 Thess 4:13-18; 2 Thess 1:5-12; 1 Cor 15:51-57), and the so-called "Pauline apocalypse," which centers on the coming of the eschatological antagonist (2 Thess 2:1-12). There are also a number of shorter scenarios which appear to be formulaic in character and therefore of pre-Pauline or extra-Pauline origin (1 Thess 1:9-10; 3:13; 5:23).

*4.5. Limited Dualism.* The Pauline view of the sovereignty of God (Rom 9—11) makes it apparent that he shares the basic dualistic convictions of Jewish apocalypticism during the late Second Temple period.

*4.5.1. Temporal or Eschatological Dualism.* In continuity with the temporal dualistic thought of Jewish apocalypticism, Paul also contrasted the present evil age with the coming age of salvation* (Gal 1:4; Rom 8:18; 1 Cor 1:26; see Eph 5:16) and believed that he was living at the end of the ages (1 Cor 10:11). Yet Paul considerably modified the sharp distinction usually made in apocalyptic thought between these two ages. Paul understood the death and resurrection of Jesus in the past as cosmic eschatological events that separated "this age" (Rom 12:2; 1 Cor 1:20; 2:6), or "this present evil age" (Gal 1:4), from "the age to come." This present age is dominated by rulers, demonic powers who are doomed to pass away (1 Cor 2:6-7; *see* Principalities and Powers).

Paul's belief in the resurrection* of Jesus the Messiah convinced him that eschatological events had begun to take place within history, and that the resurrection of Jesus was part of the traditional Jewish expectation of the resurrection of the righteous (1 Cor 15:20-23). For Paul the present is a temporary period between the death and resurrection of Christ and his return in glory in which those who believe in the gospel share in the salvific benefits of the age to come (Gal 1:4; 2 Cor 5:17). This temporary period is characterized by the eschatological gift of the Spirit of God who is experienced as present within the Christian community in general as well as within particular believers who are members of the Christian community (Rom 8:9-11; 1 Cor 6:19; 12:4-11; 1 Thess 4:8; *see* Holy Spirit). While Paul did not explicitly use the phrase "the age to come" in 2 Corinthians 5:17 and Galatians 6:15, he uses the phrase "new creation,*" a phrase with apocalyptic associations (Is 65:17; 66:22; Rev 21:1). Though the final consummation still lay in the future, for Christians the new age was present because the Messiah had come.

The basic salvation-history framework of Paul's thought incorporates within it the apocalyptic notion of the two successive ages. This is evident in Romans 5:12-21 where Paul schematizes history in terms of the two realms of Adam* and Christ, which are both made part of present experience. Paul therefore made an "already"/"not yet" distinction, indicated by his use of the indicative and imperative in passages such as Galatians 5:25: "If we live [indicative] in the Spirit, let us also walk [imperative] in the Spirit." While the flesh* has been crucified with Christ (Gal 2:20; 3:24; 6:14; Rom 6:2, 6-7, 22; 8:13), the desires of the flesh still pose temptations for Christians (Gal 5:16-18; Rom 6:12-14; 8:5-8). The daily obedience of the Christian provides the continual and necessary authentication of their original act of believing in Christ until the future redemption* of creation and the freedom* of the children of God becomes a reality (Rom 8:19-20).

*4.5.2. Spatial Dualism.* Ancient Israelite cosmology conceived of a cosmos in three levels: heaven, earth and Sheol. This same conception of the universe was transmitted to early Judaism, though the emphasis on the transcendence of God which characterized late Second Temple Judaism presupposed a sharper distinction between the heavenly world and the earthly world. This spatial dualism (heaven as the dwelling place of God and his angels; earth as the dwelling place of humanity) coincided with temporal or eschatological dualism in the sense that the kingdom of God, or the age to come, was a heavenly reality which would eventually displace the earthly reality of the present evil age. For Paul, "the things that are seen are transient, but the things that are not seen are eternal" (2 Cor 4:18; see Phil 3:20; 2 Cor 5:1-5). There are therefore three cosmic realms: heaven, earth and the region below the earth (Phil 2:10), though the normal focus is on the two primary cosmic realms: heaven and earth (1 Cor 8:5; 15:47-50; see Col 1:16, 20; Eph 1:10; 3:15). Heaven* is where God and his angels dwell (Rom 1:18; 10:6; Gal 1:8; see Eph 6:9), and is the place where Christ is now seated at the right hand of God, a tradition based on the pre-Pauline Christian interpretation of Psalm 110:1 (Rom 8:34; Col 3:1). Heaven is the place from which Jesus will return in the near future as both savior and judge (1 Thess 1:10; 4:16; Phil 3:20; see 2 Thess 1:7; *see* World, Cosmology).

*4.5.3. Ethical Dualism.* For Paul the two antithetical cosmic powers were God* and Satan* who respectively represent the moral qualities of good and evil. God is the ultimate source of love* (Rom 5:5; 8:39; 2 Cor 13:14). It is God who has expressed love toward humanity by sending his Son to die an atoning death for them (Rom 5:8). The influence of the Spirit of God, that is, God's active presence in the world, is reflected in such ethical virtues as love, patience, kindness and self-control (Gal 5:22-23). There is an essential similarity between the lists in 1QS 4:2-6, 9-11, in which the

virtues* encouraged by the spirit of truth are contrasted with the vices promoted by the spirit of error, and the lists in Galatians 5:16-24, where vices are the products of the flesh, while virtues are the products of the Spirit. Satan is frequently mentioned as the supernatural opponent of God and Christians and as the source of evil in the world (Rom 16:20; 1 Cor 7:5; 2 Cor 2:11; 11:14; 12:7; 1 Thess 2:18).

*4.5.4. Psychological or Microcosmic Dualism.* Assuming that the structure of Paul's theology is in part the product of his adaptation of Jewish apocalypticism as the framework for understanding the significance of the death and resurrection of Jesus the Messiah, that same apocalyptic framework had a profound effect on the way in which he understood the effects of salvation on individual Christians. The basic structure of Jewish apocalypticism consisted of a temporal or eschatological dualism consisting of two ages, the present era (a period of oppression by the wicked), which will be succeeded by a blissful future era. While Jewish apocalypticism had a largely future orientation, Paul's recognition of the fact that Jesus was the Messiah who was a figure of the past as well as the present and future, led him to introduce some significant modifications. The most significant modification is the softening of the distinction between this age and the age to come with his emphasis on the hidden presence of the age to come within the present age.

Paul exhibits a tendency to conceptualize human nature and existence as a microcosmic version of a Christianized form of apocalyptic eschatology. In other words, the apocalyptic structure of history was considered paradigmatic for understanding human nature. In effect the Christian person is situated at the center of history in the sense that in him or her the opposing powers which dominate the cosmos are engaged in a struggle. Just as Paul's Christian form of apocalyptic thought is characterized by a historical or eschatological dualism consisting in the juxtaposition of the old and new ages, so his view of human nature reflected a similarly homologous dualistic structure. This is evident in 2 Corinthians 5:17 (NRSV): "So if anyone is in Christ, there is a new creation: everything old has passed away; see, everything has become new!" Here Paul uses the basic apocalyptic expectation of the renewal of creation (i.e., the inauguration of the age to come) following the destruction of the present evil age as a paradigm for the transformation experienced by the individual Christian who has moved from unbelief to belief. Thus the apocalyptic expectation of an impending cosmic change from the present evil age to the future age of salvation has become paradigmatic for the transformation of the individual believer (*see* Creation and New Creation).

Since this apocalyptic transformation affects only those "in Christ," the external world and its inhabitants remain under the sway of the old age. The new age is thus concealed in the old age. The phrase "new creation" refers to the renewal or re-creation of heaven and earth following the destruction of the old cosmos (Is 65:17; 66:22; *1 Enoch* 91:16; 72:1; *2 Apoc. Bar.* 32:6; 44:12; 49:3; 57:2; *Bib. Ant.* 3:10; 2 Pet 3:11-13; Rev 21:1). Bultmann's existentialist understanding of Pauline anthropological terms (i.e., the human person as a free agent responsible for his or her own decisions), and E. Käsemann's apocalyptic or cosmological understanding of Paul's anthropology (i.e., the human person is a victim of supernatural cosmic forces) are not mutually exclusive categories. Paul also conceives of the struggle within each Christian as the conflict between the Spirit and the flesh, as in Galatians 5:16: "Walk in the Spirit and you will not fulfill the desires of the flesh."

**4.6. Jesus the Messiah.** One of the major obstacles impeding Jewish belief in Jesus as the Messiah of Jewish expectation was the fact of the crucifixion* (1 Cor 1:18-25; Gal 5:11; see Heb 12:2). One of the unsolved problems in the investigation of early Christianity is the reason why early Christians recognized the messianic status of Jesus despite the fact that he fulfilled none of the central functions which the Jewish people expected of the figure of the Davidic Messiah, including his role as an eschatological high priest, a paradigmatic benevolent and all-powerful king, a judge and destroyer of the wicked, a deliverer of the people of God (*Pss. Sol.* 17; 4 Ezra 12; *2 Apoc. Bar.* 40). In the seven undisputed letters of Paul the term *Christos*, meaning "Anointed One," "Christ," or "Messiah," occurs 266 times, usually as a proper name for Jesus (e.g., "Jesus Christ"), often with some residual titular quality (evident in the name "Christ Jesus)," and occasionally as a name for a specific Messiah, Jesus (Rom 9:5), but never as a general term for an eschatological deliverer within Judaism. In the seven core Pauline letters *Christos* is never used as a predicate (e.g., "Jesus is the Christ"), *Christos* is never given a definite article following the name "Jesus" (e.g., "Jesus the Christ"), and *Christos* is never accompanied by a noun in the genitive (e.g., "the Christ of God"). It is safe to conclude that the messianic status of Jesus was not a matter of dispute or concern to Paul. Paul assumes but does not argue that Jesus is the Messiah (*see* Christ).

**4.7. The Parousia and Judgment.** The later OT prophets frequently referred to the Day of the Lord as the occasion when God would judge the world (Amos 5:18-20; Zeph 1:14-16; Joel 2:2). In Jewish apocalyptic literature the inauguration of the eschaton occurs with the coming of God or of an accredited agent of God, the Messiah, to bring both salvation and judgment.* While Paul can speak of "the Day of the Lord" (1 Thess 5:2), and God's role as eschatological judge (Rom 3:6), the center of his eschatological hope has shifted from God to Christ, so that he can speak both of the impending Day of the Lord (1 Thess 5:2), and claim that on that day God will judge the secrets of men by Christ Jesus (Rom 2:16; see 2 Tim 4:1). The Parousia is referred to by Paul both as "the revelation [*apokalypsis*] of our Lord Jesus Christ" (1 Cor 1:6) and (on the analogy of the OT expression "the Day of the Lord") as "the Day of Jesus Christ" (1 Cor 1:8; Phil 1:6; 3:12-21; Rom 14:7-12, 17-18; 2 Cor 5:10; 1 Thess 4:13-18; 1 Cor 15:20-28, 50-58; *see* Eschatology).

**4.8. The Resurrection.** For Paul the resurrection* of Jesus was not an isolated miraculous event but rather the first stage of the general resurrection of the righteous dead (1 Cor 15:20-23). As an eschatological event, Paul expects that the resurrection of the righteous will occur when Christ returns (Phil 3:20; 1 Thess 4:13-18; 1 Cor 15:51-53). Those who are raised from the dead will be transformed into a new mode of existence (1 Cor 15:51-53; Phil 3:20-21). A similar expectation occurs in Jewish apocalyptic literature (Dan 12:3; *1 Enoch* 39:4-5; 62:15; *2 Enoch* 65:10; *2 Apoc. Bar.* 49:3). But the resurrection of Jesus, which guarantees the resurrection of believers, is not simply a past event with future consequences. Nor is the death of Jesus simply a historical fact. For Christians, baptism represents a real identification with Christ in both his death and resurrection, signaling death to the old life and resurrection to the new (Rom 6:1-14; 8:10-11; see Col 3:1-3; Eph 2:1-10).

**4.9. The Eschatological Antagonist.** The Christian doctrine of the incarnation of Christ made it all but inevitable that a Satanic counterpart to Christ would be incorporated into early Christian apocalyptic expectation. In the Synoptic apocalypse the appearance of false Messiahs and false prophets at the end of the age is predicted (Mk 13:21-22; Mt 24:23-24). This figure is called the Antichrist in Johannine literature (1 Jn 2:18, 22; 4:3; 2 Jn 7). In Revelation the two major Antichrist traditions, the godless, tyrannical ruler and the false, seductive prophet, are kept separate. The evil ruler is called the Beast from the Sea (Rev 13:1-10; 16:13; 19:20), while the false prophet is called the Beast from the Land, or the False Prophet (Rev 13:11-18; 16:13; 19:20). There is a single extended discussion of the coming of the eschatological antagonist in the Pauline letters (2 Thess 2:1-12), though strangely there are no allusions to this figure elsewhere in the

Pauline letters. In 2 Thessalonians 2:1-12 Paul combines into a single figure the two major eschatological antagonist traditions, that of the godless, tyrannical ruler and that of the false, seductive prophet. This person is called both the "man of lawlessness" and the "son of perdition" (2 Thess 2:3; see Dan 11:36-37; *Sib. Or.* 5:33-34; *Asc. Isa.* 4:6; *2 Enoch* [Rec. J] 29:4), who will install himself in the temple of God, proclaim himself to be God (2 Thess 2:4) and perform miracles to legitimate his claims (2 Thess 2:9; see Mk 13:22; Mt 24:24; Rev 13:13-14; *see* Signs, Wonders). This eschatological antagonist has not yet appeared because someone or something is restraining him or it (2 Thess 2:7), though there is no agreement regarding whether this restraining force is Satan, the Roman Empire, the Roman Emperor or perhaps some supernatural force. This eschatological antagonist will be slain by the Lord Jesus when he returns in judgment (2 Thess 2:8; *see* Man of Lawlessness).

**4.10. The Problem of a Temporary Messianic Kingdom.** The relevance of 1 Corinthians 15:20-28 to the early Jewish and early Christian view of a temporary intermediate messianic kingdom is disputed, though the general view is that there is no clean and convincing evidence that Paul, like the author of Revelation (Rev 20:1-6), expected a messianic interregnum (*see* Kingdom of God/Christ).

A. Schweitzer summarized Paul's apocalyptic beliefs in this way: (1) the sudden and unexpected return of Jesus (1 Thess 5:1-4); (2) the resurrection of deceased believers and the transformation of living believers, all of whom meet the returning Jesus in mid-air (1 Thess 4:16-17); (3) the messianic judgment presided over either by Christ (2 Cor 5:10) or God (Rom 14:10); (4) the inauguration of the messianic kingdom (not described by Paul, but hinted at in 1 Cor 15:25; Gal 4:26); (5) the transformation of all nature from mortality to immortality* during the messianic kingdom (Rom 8:19-22), and the struggle with angelic powers (Rom 16:20) until death itself is conquered (1 Cor 15:23-28); (6) the conclusion of the messianic kingdom (Paul does not mention its duration); (7) the general resurrection at the conclusion of the messianic kingdom (1 Cor 6:3); (8) the judgment upon all humanity and defeated angels. According to Schweitzer, Paul introduced two resurrections although Jewish eschatology before him knew only a single resurrection, either at the beginning or the end of the messianic kingdom. This modification was motivated by Paul's belief in the death and resurrection of Jesus the Messiah. The first resurrection enables believers who have died as well as living Christians to participate in the messianic kingdom, all enjoying a resur-

rection mode of existence.

Schweitzer's reconstruction of Pauline eschatology is subject to several criticisms. (1) There is no evidence in 1 Thessalonians 4:13-18 or 1 Corinthians 15:20-28 that Paul expected an intermediate messianic kingdom (Wilcke). (2) There is no evidence to indicate that Paul expected a general resurrection of both the righteous and the wicked dead.

There are a number of reasons for thinking that it is more probable that 1 Corinthians 15:20-28 indicates that the Parousia will shortly be followed by the resurrection and judgment, which together will usher in the final consummation of history (Davies 1970, 295-97): (1) For Paul the kingdom of God is an unending kingdom (1 Thess 2:12; Gal 5:21; 1 Cor 6:9-10; 15:50; see 2 Thess 1:4-5; Col 4:11). (2) The only text which mentions the "kingdom of Christ" (Col 1:12-13) understands it as a present fact. (3) Paul connects the Parousia with the judgment of the world (1 Cor 1:7-8; 2 Cor 1:14; Phil 1:6, 10; 2:16). It is probable that Paul has essentially historicized the apocalyptic conception of a temporary messianic kingdom in terms of a temporary period between the crucifixion and resurrection of Jesus and his Parousia.

*See also* CREATION AND NEW CREATION; ESCHATOLOGY; KINGDOM OF GOD/CHRIST; MAN OF LAWLESSNESS AND RESTRAINING POWER; QUMRAN AND PAUL; RESTORATION OF ISRAEL; RESURRECTION; TRIUMPH; WORLD, COSMOLOGY.

BIBLIOGRAPHY. J. Baumgarten, *Paulus und die Apokalyptik* (Neukirchen-Vluyn, 1975); J. Becker, "Erwägungen zur apokalyptischen Tradition in der paulinischen Theologie," *EvT* 30 (1970) 593-609; J. C. Beker, *Paul's Apocalyptic Gospel: The Coming Triumph of God* (Philadelphia: Fortress, 1982); idem, *Paul the Apostle* (Philadelphia: Fortress, 1980); H. D. Betz, "On the Problem of the Religio-Historical Understanding of Apocalypticism," *Journal for Theology and the Church* 6 (1969) 134-56; V. P. Branick, "Apocalyptic Paul?" *CBQ* 47 (1985) 664-75; J. J. Collins, ed., *Apocalypse: The Morphology of a Genre* (Semeia 14; Missoula: Scholars, 1979); W. D. Davies, "Apocalyptic and Pharisaism," in *Christian Origins and Judaism* (Philadelphia: Westminster, 1962) 19-30; idem, *Paul and Rabbinic Judaism* (3d ed.; London: SPCK, 1970); I. Gruenwald, *Apocalyptic and Merkavah Mysticism* (Leiden: E. J. Brill, 1980); P. D. Hanson, *The Dawn of Apocalyptic* (Philadelphia: Fortress, 1975); E. Käsemann, "On the Subject of Primitive Christian Apocalyptic," in *New Testament Questions of Today* (Philadelphia: Fortress, 1969) 108-37; K. Koch, *The Rediscovery of Apocalyptic* (SBT, 2d ser. 22; Naperville, IL: Allenson, 1970); L. J. Kreitzer, *Jesus and God in Paul's Eschatology* (JSNTSup 19; Sheffield: JSOT, 1987); H. P. Mueller, "Mantische Weisheit und Apokalyptik," in *Congress Volume* (VTSup 22; Leiden: E. J. Brill, 1972) 268-93; O. Ploeger, *Theocracy and Eschatology* (Richmond: John Knox, 1959); G. von Rad, *Old Testament Theology* (2 vols.; New York: Harper & Row, 1962-65); C. C. Rowland, *The Open Heaven: A Study of Apocalyptic in Judaism and Early Christianity* (New York: Crossroad, 1982); D. S. Russell, *The Method and Message of Jewish Apocalyptic* (Philadelphia: Fortress, 1964); A. Schweitzer, *The Mysticism of Paul the Apostle* (New York: Holt, 1931); M. Smith, "On the History of *Apokalypto* and *Apokalypsis*," in *Apocalypticism in the Mediterranean World and the Near East*, ed. D. Hellholm (Tübingen: J. C. B. Mohr, 1983) 9-20; H.-A. Wilcke, *Das Problem eines messianischen Zwischenreichs bei Paulus* (ATANT 51; Zurich: Zwingli, 1967).

D. E. Aune

## APOCRYPHAL PAULINE LITERATURE

As with other major figures of the NT, a variety of later works were written in Paul's name or about Paul. They are usually placed in the rather loose category of "New Testament Apocrypha."

1. Letters
2. Acts
3. Apocalypses
4. Prayer

### 1. Letters.

The letter* was not a popular genre for writers of Christian apocryphal literature, and so, despite Paul's fame as a letter writer, few apocryphal Pauline letters were written. An apparent reference by Clement of Alexandria (*Protr.* 9.87.4) to a letter of Paul to the Macedonians should probably be understood as a reference to Philippians. The Muratorian Canon (late second century) refers to spurious Pauline letters used by the Marcionites and addressed to the Laodiceans and to the Alexandrians (*see* Canon). The latter has not survived. In the reference to the letter to the Laodiceans there may be some confusion, since Marcion himself thought that Ephesians was Paul's letter to the Laodiceans. If the reference is to an apocryphal letter which was Marcionite in content, then it cannot be to the *Laodiceans* which has survived in Latin. This is little more than a patchwork of Pauline phrases, mainly from Philippians* and Galatians,* and must have been composed simply to fill the gap in the Pauline correspondence indicated by Colossians 4:16. It dates from the fourth century or earlier, and in the medieval West was widely regarded as an authentic Pauline letter, though not as canonical.

The apocryphal correspondence between Paul and the Corinthians (known as *3 Corinthians*), which in-cludes a letter from the Corinthian church to Paul as well as Paul's reply, probably (though some disagree) originated as part of the *Acts of Paul* (see below), but also circulated separately. On the basis of the Corinthians' problem about the resurrection* in 1 Corinthians, it represents them as troubled by the Gnostic teaching of Simon Magus and Cleobius and gives, as it were, a Pauline response to second-century Gnosticism.*

The apocryphal correspondence between Paul and Seneca consists of fourteen letters exchanged between Paul and his contemporary, the Roman philosopher and statesman Seneca. It shows Seneca as very impressed by Paul's teaching, and presumably it served an apologetic purpose. It dates from the fourth century.

### 2. Acts.

For students of Paul and the Pauline tradition, by far the most interesting of the apocryphal Pauline works is the second-century *Acts of Paul*. Unfortunately, the complete text has not survived. Because three major parts of the work were extracted and circulated as separate works after the *Acts of Paul* itself had largely fallen out of favor (the *Acts of Paul and Thecla, 3 Corinthians* and the *Martyrdom of Paul*), these parts are still extant, but most of the rest of the work survives only in fragmentary form.

The work must have been written in the second half of the second century. According to Tertullian, who was concerned to disallow appeal to the story of Thecla for evidence that Paul permitted women to teach and baptize, the author was a presbyter in Asia, who as a result of the work was removed from office (*De Bapt.* 17.5). If this account is reliable, it cannot mean that the presbyter was deposed for attempting to pass off his work as Paul's, for the *Acts of Paul* makes no claim to be written by Paul. It was presumably rather because he attributed to Paul teaching (such as that mentioned by Tertullian or the strong advocacy of sexual abstinence) which was deemed unacceptable. It seems very likely that the author incorporated in his work traditions and legends that already circulated orally in the Pauline churches of Asia Minor. MacDonald has argued that the stories about Thecla, the story of Paul and the lion at Ephesus,* and the story of Paul's martyrdom are folkloric in content and resemble oral narrative in style.

The story of Thecla tells of a young woman of a prominent family in Iconium, who is won over by Paul's message, especially its emphasis on the need to abstain from sexual* relations, and breaks off her engagement. Condemned to be burned at the stake, she is miraculously preserved and accompanies Paul to (Pisidian) Antioch, where she repulses the advances of a city official, is thrown to the wild beasts in the arena and again is miraculously preserved. After this experience Paul permits her to become a teacher, she returns to Iconium, then moves to (Isaurian) Seleucia and spends the rest of her life as a successful evangelist and teacher. Another episode of miraculous deliverance is Paul's experience when thrown to the lions at Ephesus: the lion he encounters is the same he had once baptized, on its request, in Jericho! The *Acts* included several miracles of healing and resurrection by the apostle. The concluding section recounts his final journey by sea from Corinth to Rome, preaching in Rome, arrest by Nero and martyrdom. (For the correspondence with the Corinthians, see section 1 above.)

Various attempts have been made to identify good historical tradition about Paul behind these narratives. Thecla was most probably a real person, a convert of Paul at Iconium and well remembered as a prominent Christian leader in that area, but it is impossible to tell whether anything else in the stories about her is more than legend. (Conceivably, Ignatius *Rom.* 5.2. is a reference to the story of Thecla in the arena.) Rordorf has drawn attention to the traditions which the *Acts of Paul* share (he thinks independently) with the Pastorals,* especially 2 Timothy. Persons who appear in both are Onesiphorus, Demas, Hermogenes, Titus and Luke (both with Paul in Rome in the *Acts of Paul*, as in 2 Tim 4:10-11). He finds in the *Acts of Paul* confirmation of the theory that the personal information about Paul in the Pastorals relates to travels which took place after the end of Acts, and concludes that the account in the *Acts of Paul* of Paul's final journey to Rome (understood as a journey subsequent to that recounted in Acts) and his martyrdom rests on historical tradition.

The physical description of Paul (*Acts of Paul and Thecla 3*) is well known: "a man of small stature, with a bald head and crooked legs, in a good state of body, with eyebrows meeting and nose somewhat hooked, full of friendliness." The modern impression that this is an unflattering description is mistaken. According to ancient ideas about physiognomy, the hooked nose, bowed legs and meeting eyebrows were regarded favorably, and shortness was not necessarily a disadvantage. The reference to baldness is the most surprising feature, and might preserve a historical memory. Early catacomb paintings depict Paul with little hair.

Much recent study of the *Acts of Paul* has seen the work as valuable evidence for popular Christianity in Asia Minor in the second century and has focused especially on the role of celibate women, who are prominent generally in the second-century apocryphal Acts and are thus represented in the *Acts of Paul* especially by Thecla. S. L. Davies argued that the apocryphal Acts were written by Christian women for groups of women vowed to celibacy (widows, virgins who had renounced marriage,* like Thecla, and women who had left their husbands). MacDonald, whose work deals more specifically with the *Acts of Paul*, accepts that the presbyter mentioned by Tertullian wrote it, but argues that the oral legends he used were stories told by Christian women, for whom they served as justification for their life and ministry as celibates independent of male authority. Others agree with this view of the celibacy espoused by Thecla as an assertion of female independence of patriarchal marriage and patriarchal social structures. MacDonald further argues that these oral legends were also known to the author of the Pastorals (which he dates in the second century), who refers to them in 1 Timothy 4:7 and 2 Timothy 4:17, and wrote to counteract them. The Pastorals' restrictions on the order of widows and women teachers were intended to control and to suppress the activities of celibate women. The Pauline tradition in second-century Asia Minor thus divided between the apocalyptic social radicalism of the women who told the stories of Thecla and the social conformism and patriarchalism of the Pastorals. This feminist approach has opened up valuable new perspectives on the apocryphal Acts, but probably needs to be tested by further study of the theme of celibacy as an ideal for both men and women in the apocryphal Acts in general and in the second-century church.

Paul appears also in a number of later Acts (*Acts of Andrew and Paul, Acts of Peter and Paul, Syriac History of Paul*, etc.). An otherwise unknown *Preaching of Paul* is described in Pseudo-Cyprian, *De Rebaptismo* 17 (3rd century?).

### 3. Apocalypses.

Two apocalypses of Paul have been preserved, both inspired by Paul's reference to his ascent to heaven* (2 Cor 12:2; *see* Visions). One is a Gnostic work, probably of the second century, preserved among the Nag Hammadi texts (CG V, 2). It describes Paul's ascent through the heavens, where he sees the judgment of souls in the fourth and fifth heavens, encounters an old man on a throne in the seventh heaven, who threatens to prevent his further ascent, and passes beyond the twelve apostles in the eighth heaven (the Ogdoad) to meet his fellow spirits in the tenth heaven. The work obviously has a Jewish apocalyptic* base, but whereas in a Jewish apocalypse the seventh heaven, containing the throne of God, would be the highest heaven, this work engages in a typically Gnostic polemic against the Jewish God, represented as the demiurge, whose authority Paul escapes. It is also characteristic that Paul, the favorite apostle of many second-century Gnostics, surpasses the twelve apostles. Whether this work is the Gnostic *Ascension of Paul* to which Epiphanius refers (*Haer.* 38.2.5) seems doubtful, for the latter refers to only three heavens.

Very different is the *Apocalypse of Paul* which became the most popular of the extracanonical Christian apocalypses. Originally written in Greek, only a later redaction survives in Greek, but there are early versions in Latin, Syriac, Coptic, Armenian and Arabic. A whole series of Latin redactions, abbreviating, adapting and adding to the text, were made in the early Middle Ages, and one of these was a source for Dante's *Divine Comedy*. The continuing immense popularity of the work in the medieval period is shown by its translation into most of the European vernacular languages of the Middle Ages. There are various redactions also in other languages, such as Armenian. The *Apocalypse of Paul* is thus really the name for the whole collection of literature deriving from a Christian apocalyptic work of the patristic period. In addition, there are other influential later apocalypses, such as the Greek and Ethiopic *Apocalypses of the Virgin*, which were heavily indebted to the *Apocalypse of Paul* for their content. It would be hard to overestimate the influence which the *Apocalypse of Paul* has had on the picture of the afterlife, especially hell, in Christian imagination and art.

The earliest extant form of the work, represented by the long Latin version, has an introduction purporting to record the discovery of the work in a house in Tarsus in 388. This would seem to date it at the end of the fourth century. But there are reasons for supposing that the introduction was added to an earlier form of the *Apocalypse*. In any case, the work is certainly heavily indebted to older sources and apocalyptic traditions, some of Jewish origin, and is closely related to the early second-century *Apocalypse of Peter*, probably by way of a common source. The *Apocalypse of Peter* was the most popular account of the fate of the righteous and the wicked after death until the *Apocalypse of Paul* supplanted it.

The *Apocalypse* relates how Paul was taken up to heaven and shown the judgment and separation of souls after death, paradise and the heavenly Jerusalem, and hell, whose wide variety of types of punishment for various classes of sinners are described in detail. In response to the prayers of Paul and the arch-

angel Michael, God grants the damned in hell a day's respite from their sufferings on Sunday of each week. Like other apocalypses of this type, the work is concerned both with the justice of hell, which is depicted in order to dissuade its readers from sin, and also with compassion for those condemned to an eternity of torment.

**4. Prayer.**

A short *Prayer of the Apostle Paul* (CG I,1) is written on the front flyleaf of Codex I of the Nag Hammadi Library. It is a Gnostic, most likely Valentinian, production. There are some Pauline echoes in a strongly Gnostic framework of thought.

*See also* PAUL IN ACTS AND LETTERS; PAUL IN EARLY CHURCH TRADITION.

BIBLIOGRAPHY. F. Bovon et al., *Les Actes Apocryphes des Apôtres* (Geneva: Labor et Fides, 1981); E. Dassmann, *Der Stachel im Fleisch: Paulus in der frühchristlichen Literatur bis Irenäus* (Münster: Aschendorff, 1979); S. L. Davies, *The Revolt of the Widows: The Social World of the Apocryphal Acts* (New York: Winston/Seabury, 1980); E. Hennecke, W. Schneemelcher, *Neutestamentliche Apokryphen* (2 vols.; Tübingen: J. C. B. Mohr, 1989) 2.41-50, 193-243, 644-75; E. Hennecke, W. Schneemeicher, R. McL. Wilson, *New Testament Apocrypha* (2 vols.; London: Lutterworth, 1965) 2.91-93, 128-41, 322-90, 755-98; M. Himmelfarb, *Tours of Hell: An Apocalyptic Form in Jewish and Christian Literature* (Philadelphia: University of Philadelphia, 1983); C. Kappler, "L'Apocalypse latine de Paul," in *Apocalypses et Voyages dans l'Au-delà*, ed. C. Kappler (Paris: Éditions du Cerf, 1987) 237-66; D. R. MacDonald, *The Legend and the Apostle: The Battle for Paul in Story and Canon* (Philadelphia: Westminster, 1983); A. J. Malherbe, "A Physical Description of Paul," *HTR* 79 (1986) 170-75; W. Rordorf, "Nochmals Paulusakten und Pastoralbriefe," in *Tradition and Interpretation in the New Testament: Essays in Honor of E. Earle Ellis*, ed. G. F. Hawthorne with O. Betz (Tübingen: J. C. B. Mohr; Grand Rapids: Eerdmans, 1987) 319-27; idem, "Tradition and Composition in the *Acts of Thecla*: The State of the Question," *Semeia* 38 (1986) 43-52 (this issue of *Semeia* also contains other relevant articles).

R. J. Bauckham

# APOLLOS

Apollos was a trained rhetor, capable of demonstrating from the OT that the Messiah was Jesus. Nonetheless, we read very little about his contribution to the expansion of early Christianity. Quite the opposite; 1 and 2 Corinthians suggest that his training and ministry contributed to problems which necessitated

Paul's correspondence.
1. Apollos at Ephesus
2. Apollos and the Divisions at Corinth
3. Summary

### 1. Apollos at Ephesus.
Although the NT provides little personal information about Apollos, the details that are provided are helpful. According to Acts 18:24-28, Apollos was a Jew from Alexandria. Luke introduces him in connection with Ephesus* and Paul's recent departure from that city. At Ephesus, Priscilla and Aquila heard Apollos speaking in the synagogue. Realizing that Apollos was already familiar with John's baptism, the couple informed him of "the way of God more accurately." The text indicates that they "received him into their house," that is, into the church* meeting in their house (cf. 1 Cor 16:19, written from Ephesus). Subsequently, Apollos ministered in Corinth.*

### 2. Apollos and the Divisions at Corinth.
Apollos's ministry at Corinth precipitated a number of problems which Paul attempts to resolve in 1 and 2 Corinthians. Recent reports (1 Cor 1:11; cf. 5:1; 11:18) and a letter (1 Cor 7:1) alerted Paul to the fact that the church was divided into four groups, defined by their allegiances to Paul, Apollos, Cephas or Christ (1 Cor 1:12). Paul attempted to defuse this hazardous situation by removing any possible claims of allegiance to himself. Apart from Crispus and Gaius, and the household of Stephanus, none can claim allegiance based on their baptism* at the hands of Paul.

*2.1. Apollos and the Sophistic Tradition.* Apparently, the most significant schism at Corinth was between those who identified themselves as Paul's and those who affirmed allegiance to Apollos. This is readily seen in 1 Corinthians 3:3-9; 4:6 (see Wallis, Hooker). A careful reading of the Acts 18 text and the Corinthian correspondence provides ample evidence for the nature of the polarity.

Luke provides three pieces of information which are instructive: (1) Apollos is an *anēr logios* ("an eloquent man"). (2) With respect to his exposition of the OT, he is *dynatos* ("powerful"). (3) As far as his ability to cite the OT to the synagogue community, he is a man who is *epideiknys*, "one who shows" that the Messiah is Jesus.

B. Winter (citing the earlier work of Orth) has demonstrated that the term *anēr logios* connoted rhetorical training and the ability to speak eloquently, or a sophist (*see* Rhetoric). C. K. Barrett also supports this definition of the term, arguing that it should be translated "an eloquent man" rather than, as others suggest,

"learned"; though it is a fault of the ancient world that it often confused the two (Barrett, 22). Apollos was an eloquent man (so AV, NEB, RSV, NRSV) and this term suggests that he is deliberately introduced as a sophist, a virtuoso rhetor. Like *logos*, *dynatos* and *epideiknymi* also connote rhetorical ability (Winter, 15-19 and 160-61) and certainly rhetorical training. All three terms are indicative of the sophistic *modus operandi.*

The identification of Apollos as "a native of Alexandria" (Acts 18:24) is significant since the sophistic movement thrived in Alexandria during this period (Winter cites, e.g., *P. Oxy* 2190, Philonic *corpus* and *The Alexandrian Oration* [*OR. 32*] by Dio of Prusa—Vespasian's emmisary to Alexandria).

*2.2. Paul at Corinth: Conflict with the Sophists.* Apollos's eloquence and sophistic presence in Corinth were undoubtedly contrasted with Paul's unimpressive delivery. In 2 Corinthians 10:10 Paul quotes some at Corinth who condemn Paul for his contemptible speech or unwillingness to speak eloquently. Turning to Paul's word's in 1 Corinthians 1—4, we observe that the real contention between Paul and Apollos was evidently the matter of the ability or willingness of Paul to use eloquence in proclaiming the gospel.* Paul claims that his coming to Corinth was not characterized by *sophia logou* ("wisdom of speech," 1 Cor 1:17). A number of commentators have taken *en sophia logou* as a reference to a formal characteristic of skillful speech (which Paul may be taking up as a Corinthian slogan). Paul reiterates that he did not come in such a way as to distinguish himself in eloquence or wisdom (1 Cor 2:1; cf. 1:17). What is primarily at stake is Paul's speaking. Paul is adamant in restating in 1 Corinthians 2:4 that his speech and proclamation were not with eloquence and rhetorical skill.

In these passages *logos* is seen in a negative light and is associated with rhetorical eloquence. For Paul, a dedication to wise speech may detract from the theology of the cross* and its redemptive power, so that it becomes of no effect. Similarly, *sophia* is condemned as "of the world*" (1 Cor 1:29; cf. 3:19), merely "human" (vs. divine, 1 Cor 2:5; cf. 2:13 and the variant readings for 1 Cor 2:4 where the same thrust was made), and "of this age" and the "rulers of this age" (1 Cor 2:6; *see* Principalities and Powers). In contrast to these negative comments, Paul juxtaposes his own understanding of *logos/sophia*. According to Paul, *logos* and *gnōsis* ("knowledge"*) are given by God (1 Cor 1:5). Later, he would affirm that *logos sophias* ("words of wisdom*") and *logos gnōseōs* ("words of knowledge") are to be attributed to the Spirit (1 Cor 12:8; cf. 2:13). In this respect, we have two opposing definitions: that of Paul and that of certain Corinthians (see Pogoloff).

*2.3. The Sophists at Corinth: Additional Evidence.* In addition to the extant non-Christian literature from this period, three additional factors suggest that Corinth was frequented by the sophists who influenced the Christian communities. Paul (unlike the sophists—perhaps Apollos?) came bearing no promise of material benefaction; rather he worked with his hands (*see* Tentmaker). While Paul defends in principle the apostolic right of financial* support (1 Cor 9:7-14), he refuses to accept support from the Corinthians. According to Paul, by accepting this support he would impede the gospel (2 Cor 11:7-15; 12:13-18). As Paul states, he would not "retail" (*kapēleuō*) God's word (2 Cor 2:17). This term (from *kapēlos*, "retailer"), was frequently used to derogate sophists who charged fees for their spiritual or intellectual wares.

Second, Paul showed no concern for luxury and bodily appearance—he was self-disciplined (1 Cor 9:24-27). In contrast, the Corinthians' attitude toward Paul (2 Cor 10:10) was that in addition to his inability (or unwillingness) to speak eloquently, he had a weak physical presence (*see* Weakness). The sophists (in Alexandria) report of themselves the opposite. According to Philo, the sophists declared themselves to be

> men of mark and wealth, holding leading positions, praised on all hands, recipients of honors, portly, healthy, robust, reveling in luxurious and riotous living, knowing nothing of labor, conversant with pleasures which carry the sweets of life to the all-welcoming soul by every channel of sense. (Philo *Det. Pot. Ins.* 34B)

Third, Paul refused to align himself with any particular group or patron—he baptized no one (with exceptions!). While Paul is dependent upon the benefaction of wealthy home owners (even at Corinth, Acts 18:1-11; cf. 1 Cor 16:19), since the house church was the primary place for Christian gathering, he refuses to be "attached" to a householder. The sophistic *modus operandi*, on the other hand, suggests a predilection for attachment to the great houses at Corinth (Blue).

### 3. Summary.

Whether Apollos knew of the Corinthians' proclivity to attach themselves to eloquent teachers is difficult to determine. Moreover, it is impossible to establish the degree to which Apollos adopted the sophist *modus operandi*. Nevertheless, his presence at Corinth (before he met Paul) certainly did not help the already sensitive relationship between Paul and certain Corinthian believers. Perhaps N. Hyldahl is correct when he observes that it is no accident that we do not hear of

Apollos in any of Paul's other letters. After the exchange of letters between Paul and the Corinthians, and Paul's deliberate distancing of himself from the sophists, Apollos's influence in the Pauline churches evidently waned.

*See also* CORINTHIANS, LETTERS TO THE; PHILOSOPHY; RHETORIC; WEAKNESS; WISDOM.

BIBLIOGRAPHY. C. K. Barrett, *Essays on Paul* (Philadelphia: Westminster, 1982) 1-27; B. B. Blue, *In Public and in Private: The Role of the House Church in Early Christianity* (unpublished Ph.D. dissertation, Aberdeen University, 1989); F. F. Bruce, *Peter, Stephen, James & John: Studies in Early Non-Pauline Christianity* (Grand Rapids: Eerdmans, 1980) 65-85; E. S. Fiorenza, "Rhetorical Situation and Historical Reconstruction in 1 Corinthians," *NTS* 33 (1987) 386-403; M. D. Hooker, " 'Beyond the Things Which Are Written': An Examination of 1 Cor 4.6," *NTS* 10 (1963-64) 127-32; N. Hyldahl, "Den korintiske situation—en skitse," *DTT* 40 (1977) 18-30; E. A. Judge, "The Early Christians as a Scholastic Community," *JRH* 1 (1960) 4-15; 125-137; idem, *The Social Pattern of Christian Groups in the First Century: Some Prolegomena to the Study of the New Testament Ideas of Social Obligation* (London: Tyndale, 1960); B. Kerferd, *The Sophistic Movement* (Cambridge: University Press, 1981); A. D. Litfin, *St. Paul's Theology of Proclamation: An Investigation of 1 Corinthians 1—4 in Light of Greco-Roman Rhetoric* (unpublished D. Phil. dissertation, Oxford University, 1983); E. Orth, *Logios* (Leipzig: Obert Noske Universitatsverlag, 1926); S. M. Pogoloff, *Logos and Sophia: The Rhetorical Situation of 1 Corinthians* (SBLDS 134; Atlanta: Scholars, 1992); W. C. van Unnik, "First Century A.D. Literary Culture and Early Christian Literature," *NedTTs* 25 (1971) 28-43; P. Wallis, "Ein neuer Auslegungsversuch des Stelle 1 Kor 4, 6," *TLZ* 75 (1950) 506-8; A. J. M. Wedderburn, "ἐν τῇ σοφίᾳ τοῦ θεοῦ—1 Kor 1:21," *ZNW* 64 (1973) 132-134; L. L. Welborn, "On the Discord in Corinth: 1 Corinthians 1—4 and Ancient Politics," *JBL* 106 (1987) 85-111; B. W. Winter, *Philo and Paul among the Sophists: A Hellenistic Jewish and a Christian Response* (unpublished Ph.D. dissertation, Macquarie University, 1988).

B. B. Blue

# APOSTASY, FALLING AWAY, PERSEVERANCE

Is the perseverance of Christians in faith* and in the grace* of salvation* certain, or might they fall away, be cut off from the benefits of Christ* and come short of final salvation? Paul's response to these questions is disputed.

1. Terminology
2. Continuity in Salvation and the Eschatological

Tension
3. The Significance of Ethical Failure and Unbelief for Continuity in Salvation
4. The Pastoral Letters

## 1. Terminology.

In theological debate the terms "perseverance (of the saints)," "falling away" and "apostasy" are used in discussing the question of whether it is certain a Christian will remain in faith and salvation. Where Paul's teaching touches this issue we find the similar expressions "steadfast endurance" (in hope, good work; *hypomonē [tēs elpidos, ergou agathou]*, e.g., Col 1:11; 1 Thess 1:3; 2 Thess 1:4; Rom 2:7; 8:25), "remain in faith" (*epimenō tē pistei*, Col 1:23), "remain in [God's] kindness" (*epimenō tē chrēstotēti*, Rom 11:22) and, on the other hand, "fall [from grace]" (*[ek]piptō [tēs charitos]*, Rom 11:11; 1 Cor 10:12; Gal 5:4). The "apostasy" (*apostasia*) in 2 Thessalonians 2:3 refers to a future, widespread rebellion against God's rule through intensified ungodliness apparently prompted by the revelation of "the lawless one"; that is, the "apostasy" is one of the extraordinary phenomena which will precede the Parousia. It is not clear whether Paul has in mind a Jewish rebellion against God, as in traditional apocalyptic understanding (e.g., *Jub.* 23:14-23), or that of Christians as well (*see* Man of Lawlessness). In any case, Paul does not use the term to refer specifically to Christian apostasy, or complete abandonment of faith in Christ, during the church age (Marshall 1975, 108).

## 2. Continuity in Salvation and the Eschatological Tension.

### 2.1. Continuity in Salvation.
Paul can describe the individual's salvation* as already begun but not yet complete. Is it then certain to be completed? The question becomes acute in the face of obstacles posed by evil forces now at work against God's purposes, by persecution and temptation which threaten to break continuity in salvation, and by the prospect of the last judgment.*

The question of the certainty of believers' final salvation depends in part on whether salvation is wholly God's work or whether human beings also contribute to it. For Paul, salvation is by divine grace* alone, and thus is God's work alone. Christians have no contribution to make to salvation such that their failure to do so would jeopardize the final outcome. The command "Work out your salvation with 'fear* and trembling' " (Phil 2:12) refers to the active role of believers in sanctification based on the fact that ("for," *gar*) "*God* is the one who is working in you both the willing

and the working" (Phil 2:13). This utter dependence on God inspires humility and obedience ("fear and trembling"; *see* Holiness, Sanctification).

Further, God has purposed to bring believers' salvation to completion. God "predestined [them] to be conformed to the image* of his Son" (Rom 8:29), "chose [them] from the beginning for salvation, . . . called [them] . . . so that [they] may obtain the glory of our Lord Jesus Christ" (2 Thess 2:13-14), and "destined [them] not for wrath but for obtaining salvation" (1 Thess 5:9). Paul portrays the divine initiatives in Christians' salvation as a "golden chain" in which each link implies the preceding and bears a promise of the one to follow, the final link being glorification* (Rom 8:29-30). Paul is certain that God's intention will be realized: "the one who began a good work [of salvation] in you will finish [it] until the day of Christ Jesus" (Phil 1:6).

Since Paul traces true Christian faith to the eternal election* of God, not to arbitrary human history or human will, he can express certainty that this faith will reach its final goal (differently, Marshall 1975, 100-103). He sees another guarantee of believers' final salvation in the gift of the Spirit (*see* Holy Spirit). This Spirit is the "Holy Spirit of promise" (Eph 1:13), the "Spirit of the one who raised Jesus from the dead" (Rom 8:11), the "Spirit of life" (Rom 8:2). Paul can describe this divine power* of new, eschatological life* and hope* indwelling Christians (cf. Rom 5:5; Tit 3:5) with the metaphors of the "first fruits"* (Rom 8:23), "deposit [of our inheritance]" (Eph 1:14; 2 Cor 1:22; 5:5) and "sealing" (Eph 1:13; 4:30; 2 Cor 1:22). Because of the integral connection between the first fruits and the whole, the gift of the first fruits of salvation can function as a promise that the fullness of salvation will follow. As the deposit obligates the giver to full payment, the Spirit guarantees that God will fully redeem Christians, who are God's possession. Paul plays on the ancient function of the seal when he says that Christians are "sealed with the Holy Spirit [for the day of redemption]," which signifies that they belong to God and come under God's protective care with a view to their final salvation.

These assurances of final salvation are sometimes said to pertain to the church as a whole and not to the individual; in this case the assurances would not rule out the possibility of loss of salvation by some. On the other hand, it is the individual who benefits from God's saving work—by being called to faith, justified,* indwelt by the Spirit, and eventually glorified—and who is thus apparently the one meant to draw assurance from these divine actions. Paul's bold formulation in Romans 8:29-30 suggests that God's saving work will continue unto completion in *all* those in whom it has begun.

*2.2. Continuity and the Eschatological Tension.* Even when discussing the real and grave threats to continuity in salvation posed by present afflictions* or trials and the last judgment, Paul expresses certainty of Christians' final salvation. His confidence even reaches a mighty crescendo in his acclamations of God's* faithfulness: "God is faithful!" and "will strengthen you and keep you from the evil (one)" (2 Thess 3:3); God "will not allow you to be tested beyond what you are able [to endure] but will provide . . . the way out that you may be able to endure" (1 Cor 10:13), and "will confirm you until the end blameless at the day of our Lord Jesus Christ" (1 Cor 1:8-9). Paul prays that God may "sanctify you entirely; and may your spirit and soul and body be preserved complete, without blame at the coming of our Lord Jesus Christ" (1 Thess 5:23-24).

Further, Paul compellingly portrays the completion of believers' salvation as certain, despite great hindrances, by arguing from the omnipotent love* of God: "God demonstrated his love toward us in that while we were yet sinners Christ died for us" (Rom 5:8). With the obstacle of our own estrangement from God overcome, what can prevent God from finishing our salvation? "Since, therefore, we are now justified by his blood, much more shall we be saved through him from the [eschatological] wrath.* For if while we were enemies* we were reconciled to God through the death of his Son, much more, since we are [now] reconciled, shall we be saved by his life" (Rom 5:9-10). God's love, seen in the fact that God "did not spare his own Son but gave him up for us all" is the proof that God "will graciously give (*charisetai*) us all things with him" (Rom 8:32). God's powerful love guarantees that nothing can stand in the way of God's free gift of salvation through Christ in its fullness. Thus "who shall separate us from the love of Christ," which is the power of our salvation? Nothing can! Neither earthly nor superhuman powers (which Paul names in comprehensive lists; *see* Principalities and Powers), "nor any other created thing." "Rather, through the one who loved us we more than conquer in all these things" (Rom 8:35-39).

This victory of remaining in the love of God, and thus in salvation, a victory attributed to the loving God, extends also to the judgment day when all will meet their final destiny (*see* Eschatology). On that day the elect will not be convicted as guilty and condemned. For the Christ who loved them and died for them is the same one who was raised and now sits at the right hand of God and makes intercession* for them before the Judge who has already justified them on the basis of Christ's work (Rom 8:33-34). The love of a vindicated and exalted intercessor is surely a supreme guarantee of a positive outcome of judgment for the justified. Paul sums it up: "if God [is] for us, who [is] against us?" (Rom 8:31). That is to say, no challenge to believers' final salvation can be successfully mounted because the omnipotent, loving God has taken their part. The same love of God which guarantees final salvation "has been poured out in our hearts through the Holy Spirit," so that believers now subject to affliction are enabled to have "hope* that does not disappoint" in the eschatological test (Rom 5:5).

Present tribulation and trials do not make Christian hope less sure according to Paul. He even turns them into a positive component in God's plan of realizing salvation. Through God's direction "all things"—Paul means adversities in particular—"work together for good," the supreme good of eschatological salvation (Rom 8:28). Further, Christian suffering* manifests unity with Christ, who suffered and was glorified, and whom Christians will thus also follow in glory* (Rom 8:17). Paradoxically, therefore, believers can "boast"* in afflictions too (Rom 5:3; 2 Cor 12:1-10) because of their positive eschatological significance for the afflicted.

### 3. The Significance of Ethical Failure and Unbelief for Continuity in Salvation.

God will continue to intervene for the purpose of completing believers' salvation, according to Paul. Nevertheless, it is claimed, believers themselves can block the fulfillment of God's purpose by their misdeeds or unbelief; perseverance is in some degree up to Christians themselves. What, we must then ask, is the relationship between believers' faith and conduct, and God's saving action toward them?

*3.1. Ethical Failure and Falling Away.* Numerous passages in Paul have suggested to interpreters the possibility of loss of salvation for ethical failure (the problem of "postbaptismal sin" or "postconversion sin"). In 1 Corinthians 8 and Romans 14 Paul says the "weak" are "destroyed" if they eat certain foods, which their conscience* prohibits as foods that are "unclean" or "sacrificed to idols" (*see* Strong and Weak). "Destruction" could be eschatological here (see Marshall 1975, 113; *see* Wrath, Destruction). On the other hand, a weaker meaning is suggested both by the nature of the sin (not idolatry [contrast Sanders 1983, 110-11], but violation of conscience) and by the contrastive concern for mutual edification in both contexts (Rom 14:19; 15:2; 1 Cor 8:1; cf. 10:23). The "destruction" could therefore be existential, and consist in a setback in the Christian walk, as supported by the parallel descriptions of the consequences suffered by the weak Christian (sorrow, Rom 14:15; self-condemnation, 14:23; defilement and wounding of the conscience, 1 Cor 8:7, 12) and parallel uses of Paul's terminology in the LXX (e.g., Sir 30:23; 20:21-22).

In 1 Corinthians 11:27-34 Paul criticizes the Corinthians' practice of the Lord's Supper* as a "com[ing] together which results in judgment," and declares that those who partake inappropriately "will be guilty of the body and the blood of the Lord" and "eat and drink judgment to themselves" (1 Cor 11:27). The judgment has already struck: some Corinthians are ill and have died (1 Cor 11:30). This judgment may prefigure their eschatological judgment. Nevertheless, the phrase "will be (*estai*) guilty" probably has the future tense simply for the sake of emphasis, to stress guilt already incurred (see Gundry-Volf, 101). And, instead of aligning present and future judgments, Paul seems to juxtapose them explicitly: "when we are judged by the Lord, we are chastised so that we might not be condemned with the world" (1 Cor 11:32). Since it is unlikely that Paul presupposes that repentance forestalls future condemnation—some of the guilty have already died—he must take present judgment and future salvation as two sides of the same coin. Chastisement itself can imply exemption from final condemnation because, as in the OT-Jewish tradition of divine *paideia* ("chastisement," "education"), God's parental chastisement of God's children marks them out as being true children (Deut 8:5; Wis 11:10; also Heb 12:8), who are headed for salvation on the basis of God's faithfulness to the covenants* and promises (see Gundry-Volf, 107-11).

According to 1 Corinthians 5:5 a member of the Corinthian church who is engaged in flagrant sexual misconduct should be "deliver[ed] . . . to Satan,* with the result of the destruction of the flesh, that the spirit might be saved at the day of the Lord." Cast out of the church (cf. 1 Cor 5:2), the man might repent under Satan's* destructive influence and thus finally be saved (see Collins, Harris; *see* Discipline). Though his future salvation is not a foregone conclusion, loss of salvation is not a possibility here. For Paul goes on to indicate that a fornicator in the church is a "so-called brother" (1 Cor 5:11)—that is, one who has not yet converted—and Paul reminds the readers that believers cannot have Christian fellowship* with fornicators (1 Cor 5:9) but must "judge" the falsely professing one and "take the fornicator out" of the community (1 Cor 5:12-13; cf. 5:7-8).

The warning in 1 Corinthians 10:12, "So if you think you are standing, watch out that you do not

fall!," seems to suggest the possibility of forfeiting salvation (Sanders 1977, 455), but it may actually have in view false profession of faith in Christ. Some Corinthians mistakenly think that, protected by the Christian sacraments, they can safely participate in idolatrous practices (1 Cor 10:14-22). The wilderness generation, however, illustrates that the mere outward benefit of baptism* and eucharistic food does not protect against divine judgment for idolatry* (1 Cor 10:1-11). Therefore, "If you think you are standing" (i.e., are saved) you must make sure that you really are (i.e., have fellowship* with Christ and not with demons, 1 Cor 10:16-21), if you are not to "fall" (i.e., fail to pass the test of judgment). And God will enable those who take the warning seriously to pass the test (1 Cor 10:13).

In 1 Corinthians 6:9-10 and Galatians 5:19-21 Paul writes that evildoers will not inherit the kingdom of God (*see* Kingdom of God/Christ). Most interpreters think Paul is warning his readers against their own exclusion. On the other hand, in 1 Corinthians 6:1-11 Paul repeatedly contrasts the Corinthians ("the saints") with the people named in the vice list ("the world, the unrighteous"): "and such were some of you, but you were washed, . . . sanctified, . . . justified," and "the saints will judge the world [and] . . . angels." Paul probably wants to reinforce such distinctions in order to motivate the Corinthians to reform their behavior so it will conform to their final destiny (though 1 Cor 6:9-10 may have a secondary, warning character for falsely professing Christians; cf. 2 Cor 12:21; 13:2). In the Galatians' case no warning is called for: they are the ones who oppose the works of the flesh,* and Paul, preacher of the Law*-free gospel, must assure them that he does too, and that one need not embrace the Law to be against the works of the flesh (cf. Gal 5:16-24). Paul is thus apparently speaking in self-defense when he tells the Galatians that those whose lives are characterized by the vices will not inherit the kingdom.

Some texts seem to reveal Paul's apprehension that his own conduct will in some way disqualify him from final salvation. Yet Paul can express confidence of his final salvation (Phil 1:21, 23). It is God's approval of his apostolic service that he does not take for granted. "Lest . . . I might become disqualified [*adokimos*]" at 1 Corinthians 9:27 probably refers to Paul the apostle* instead of Paul the Christian (cf. 1 Cor 3:13-15). For when Paul uses the language of testing (*dok-*) of himself, it always has to do with divine approval of his apostolic service. Paul seeks to avoid divine disapproval as an apostle* by subduing his body through the giving up of his rights (to food and drink, pay, a wife).

He does this so as not to "put up an obstacle in the way of the gospel* of Christ" (1 Cor 9:12) but to "become the gospel's partner" in the work of salvation (1 Cor 9:23). This translation of 1 Corinthians 9:23 is preferable to the common rendering, "become a sharer of the gospel['s blessings]," which violates usage of *euangelion.*

Paul sounds uncertain about his final destiny in Philippians 3:11-12, where he writes "if somehow I may attain the resurrection* from the dead" and "I pursue if also I might obtain." It has been suggested that any uncertainty Paul expresses here pertains to the manner and not the fact of arriving at his final destiny: by martyrdom? Alternatively, Paul's further assertion, "I have been apprehended by Christ," takes the uncertainty out of his obtaining and makes it simply future, as well as suggests its dependence on divine action. Similarly, Paul's hope of attaining to the resurrection can be seen as an expectation expressing dependence on God's action and not as raising doubt about its fulfillment, as Paul's other uses of the expression *ei pōs*, here translated "if somehow," show (Rom 1:10; 11:14).

In summary, traditionally some Pauline texts have been seen to show the possibility of forfeiting salvation through unethical behavior (see Sanders 1977, 517-18; Sanders 1983, 109-11). But a rereading of these texts suggests that for Paul unethical behavior may call into question the genuineness of one's profession of faith, it may provoke divine chastisement, or it may cause regression in Christian sanctification, but it does not result in actual loss of salvation (see Gundry-Volf, 83-157, 231-60; cf. Gundry, 7-38).

**3.2. Unbelief and Falling Away.** Other Pauline passages suggest that salvation could remain incomplete because of unbelief in the gospel (Marshall 1975, 108-11, 118-19).

Israel's* "no" to the gospel, despite its election, challenges the significance Paul has attributed to election for the perseverance of believers. But in Romans 9—11, where Paul deals with the matter of unbelieving Israel, he defends the faithfulness of God and explains Israel's present unbelief in terms of God's design for salvation. It includes a "hardening" of part of Israel and a time when finally "all Israel will be saved," when Israel turns from unbelief and the Redeemer removes Israel's ungodliness (Rom 11:23, 26-27; *see* Restoration of Israel).

Just as the certain completion of God's saving work for the elect does not rule out the temporary exclusion of Israel in unbelief, so also it does not rule out the "cutting off" and not "sparing" of Gentile Christians who do not continue in faith (Rom 11:17- 24). Partic-

ipation in the benefits of salvation is dependent on faith* in Christ; faith is the only way one can "remain in the kindness," or saving mercy,* of God in Christ. Paul does not concern himself here with the final fate of Gentiles who might be cut off, but he has shown with the example of Israel that regrafting is possible (*see* Olive Tree).

A clearer statement of the consequences of abandoning faith in the gospel is found in Galatians 5:2-4. If the Galatians embrace the false gospel of justification by works* of the Law, Paul warns, "Christ will not benefit you at all. . . . You are severed from Christ, . . . you have fallen away from grace." In other words, the Galatians would cut themselves off from the hope of salvation. On the other hand, Paul cannot imagine this actually taking place: "have you experienced such great things in vain, if [at all one] really [can experience such great gifts] in vain?" (Gal 3:4). Unless this cryptic verse is a threat that it was all in vain, Paul here thinks of their losing salvation as an impossible possibility. And in the final analysis he is "confident in the Lord" (Gal 5:10) that the Galatians will not make the decisive break with the gospel (and lose salvation). This expression of confidence does not make the danger less real or the warning less urgent, but it finds the way out in the faithfulness of the Lord, through whose intervention Paul anticipates his admonitions achieving their desired result.

If Paul's converts do not stand at the day of Christ, he will have "labored or run in vain" (1 Thess 3:5; Gal 2:2; 4:11; Phil 2:16; *see* Futility). If some fail the final test, they will either have fallen from a state of grace, or prove that they were not true converts in the first place. Paul's letters show that he could have thought in terms of the latter possibility. He recognizes that his communities include both the genuine and the false (see, e.g., 1 Cor 5:5-13). Paul cannot be sure of the genuineness of the success of his apostolic efforts in the same way that he is confident of the effects of the gospel, the power of God for salvation (cf. Rom 1:16; 15:18; 1 Thess 1:5; 2:13; 2 Cor 4:7; 1 Cor 3:6; 2:4-5; 15:10). Only those who share in the eschatological life imparted through the gospel will withstand the judgment.

The Corinthians may "receive the grace of God in vain" (2 Cor 6:1) and "fail the test" of faith (2 Cor 13:5). For if they continue to contest Paul's apostleship, they imply that their own conversion and salvation through Paul's preaching was a sham. Paul clearly expects his suggestion that they are not saved to evoke their protest, a confirmation of their own faith, and (indirectly) a confirmation of himself. Similarly, Paul suggests that the Corinthians may have "believed in vain" (1 Cor 15:1) in order to shock them with the unsavory implication of the false teaching some had accepted, that "there is no resurrection of the dead" (1 Cor 15:12). Since a message that excludes the physical resurrection of the dead (based on the presumption that resurrection had already occurred in a different sense) cannot truly save anyone who believes in it, such "faith is vain" (1 Cor 15:17-18). Though these verses are often taken to imply the possibility of salvation being lost, their contexts suggest otherwise.

The perseverance which Paul affirms, therefore, can only be "in faith." Only the one who believes in Christ can know assurance of final salvation (Col 1:22-23). Perseverance is not automatic. Estrangement from the gospel through unbelief can break the continuity in salvation and bring its completion into question—or call the genuineness of a person's conversion itself into question. Nevertheless Paul can view the threat of unbelief from the ultimate perspective of his confidence in God, the gracious and faithful giver and finisher of salvation. This perspective enables Paul to hold onto perseverance in this non-automatic sense, always dependent on divine intervention.

### 4. The Pastoral Letters.

The Pastorals* use the term "endure" (*hypomenō*, 1 Tim 2:12) to express the idea of perseverance in faith. Contrasting expressions are "desert," "wander away from," "deny the faith" (*aphistēmi, apoplanaō apo tēs pisteōs, arneomai tēn pistin*, 1 Tim 4:1; 6:10; 5:8).

As regards the problem of abandoning the faith, the Pastorals anticipate such behavior "in later times" (1 Tim 4:1; cf. 2 Tim 4:3-4). But they already know of false teachers who have "missed the mark with regard to the truth/faith" and who "upset the faith" of some in the church (2 Tim 2:18; 1 Tim 6:21). Some "will depart from the faith" (1 Tim 4:1) and "will turn away from hearing the truth" (2 Tim 4:4). Departure from the faith comes from accepting "teachings of demons*" (1 Tim 4:1, referring to the demonic origin of the false teachings) characterized by asceticism, disputes about the Law and speculation (1 Tim 4:3; 1:4, 6-7; Tit 1:10; 3:9), and a denial of the future resurrection (2 Tim 2:18). The love of money and other vices can also accompany such turning away from the faith (1 Tim 6:10; 2 Tim 3:2-5). Exclusion from salvation is implied.

By contrast, Timothy and Titus should resist false teaching and hold fast the true gospel (e.g., 1 Tim 1:3; Tit 1:9, 11), even as Paul has done under pressure of persecution so that he can express confidence in his final salvation (2 Tim 1:12; 4:7-8, 18). Perseverance in the Pastorals, therefore, as elsewhere in Paul, is only

by continuance in the true gospel, "in the faith" (as defined in the Pastorals). It is also the case that the Pastorals make the same connection between the present benefits of salvation and its consummation (2 Tim 2:10-11; cf. 2:19) as seen previously in Paul, while they emphasize the significance of human endurance for believers' remaining in salvation (e.g., 2 Tim 2:10, 12). Further, the Pastorals even echo Paul's acclamation of God's faithfulness (in the "faithful saying," 2 Tim 2:11-13) for Christians in danger of "denying Christ" and becoming "faithless" (a temporary state?), while they warn in the same breath against such denial.

The Pastorals indicate that departure from the faith is thus clearly a possible ground for exclusion from salvation. Nevertheless the Pastorals can explain abandonment of faith through the notion of false profession, and not explicitly as falling from a state of grace. Those teachers who "hold the form of religion but deny its power" are not to be accepted as true Christians but are "disqualified [*adokimoi*] with regard to the faith" (2 Tim 3:5, 8). Likewise, failure to respond to admonition betrays one's true perverted and sinful self (Tit 3:10-11). Such opponents of true teaching still need "repentance so that they may come to know the truth" (2 Tim 2:25), that is, they need to convert.

Paul's delivering Hymenaeus and Alexander to Satan "that they may be taught not to blaspheme" (1 Tim 1:20) suggests treating them as non-Christians in the hope of their conversion (cf. 1 Cor 5:5; 1 Tim 1:13). "They made shipwreck with regard to the faith" (1 Tim 1:19) probably refers not to their personal faith but to faith as such in the gospel, to which they have caused damage. Only genuine Christians belong in the church. As a matter of fact, however, the church includes both those whom "the Lord knows . . . are his" and the others, as in a "big house" which has both "vessels of gold and silver . . . for honor[able use]" and "[vessels] of wood and earthenware . . . for dishonor[able use]" (2 Tim 2:19-20; cf. Rom 9:19-26). One demonstrates that one falls into the former category by "depart[ing] from iniquity" and "cleans[ing] oneself from these" other vessels (2 Tim 2:19, 21). The mixed nature of the community presently (not necessarily all will attain final salvation, for some will go astray) need not cast doubt on the final salvation of genuine believers. With respect to that, according to 2 Timothy 2:19, there is a "firm foundation of God [which] stands." On it are inscribed the words "God knows those who are his." This affirmation grounds the eschatological triumph* of true believers in divine faithfulness.

Nevertheless the possibility that the Pastorals also

have in view the apostasy of genuine Christians through abandonment of faith cannot be excluded (cf. Marshall 1975, 128-31). This possibility, however, is also present to a small degree in the undisputed Pauline letters. In light of the preceding comments, therefore, the Pastorals, while they reflect their own specific historical situation, still seem compatible with Paul's thought on perseverance and falling away.

*See also* AFFLICTIONS, TRIALS, HARDSHIPS; CALL, CALLING; DISCIPLINE; ELECTION AND PREDESTINATION; ESCHATOLOGY; FAITH; GRACE; HOLINESS, SANCTIFICATION; JUDGMENT; SALVATION; SIN, GUILT; UNIVERSALISM.

BIBLIOGRAPHY. A. Y. Collins, "The Function of Excommunication in Paul," *HTR* 73 (1980) 251-63; M. Goguel, "Les fondements de l'assurance du salut chez l'apôtre Paul," *RHPR* 17 (1938) 105-44; R. H. Gundry, "Grace, Works, and Staying Saved in Paul," *Bib* 66 (1985) 1-38; J. M. Gundry Volf, *Paul and Perseverance: Staying in and Falling Away* (WUNT 2/37; Tübingen: J. C. B. Mohr, 1990; Louisville: John Knox/Westminster, 1991); G. Harris, "The Beginnings of Church Discipline: 1 Corinthians 5," *NTS* 37 (1991) 1-21; O. Hofius, "Die Unabänderlichkeit des göttlichen Heilsratschlusses: Erwägungen zur Herkunft eines neutestamentlichen Theologumenon," *ZNW* 64 (1973) 135-45; idem, "Hoffnung und Gewissheit: Römer 8, 19-39," *Mitarbeiterhilfe* 31 (1976) 3-10; I. H. Marshall, *Kept by the Power of God: A Study of Perseverance and Falling Away* (Minneapolis: Bethany, 1975); idem, "The Problem of Apostasy in New Testament Theology," in *Jesus the Saviour: Studies in New Testament Theology* (Downers Grove, IL: InterVarsity, 1990); E. P. Sanders, *Paul and Palestinian Judaism: A Comparison of Patterns of Religion* (Philadelphia: Fortress, 1977); idem, *Paul, the Law, and the Jewish People* (Philadelphia: Fortress, 1983).

J. M. Gundry-Volf

# APOSTLE

The office of apostle, by which Paul pointedly referred to himself, is of singular importance in the appreciation of his life and ministry. There has been considerable debate over the social origins of the word *apostle* and more significantly over the criteria for apostleship and the nature of the authority* which Paul claimed over the Gentile* churches, which others questioned or rejected. The authority of Paul for modern churches and Christians is connected with these issues.

1. Greek Origin of the Word *Apostle*
2. The Quest for the Origin of the Concept of Apostle
3. The Evidence from Paul's Letters
4. Jesus the Apostle and His Apostles
5. Apostles in Paul's Letters
6. Paul's Apostleship Disputed
7. Conclusion

## 1. Greek Origin of the Word *Apostle*

The word *apostolos* ("apostle") was used only infrequently in the Greek language prior to NT times (see Rengstorf, 407-8). In classical Greek its use is more or less confined to seafaring contexts. Herodotus uses it twice for "messenger," while the LXX has it only once with the same meaning. With the word occurring thirty-five times in the Pauline corpus and eighty times in the NT, it is evident that *apostolos* must have been very important within the early Christian movement. How then can we account for the rise of this word within the NT and by Paul in particular?

## 2. The Quest for the Origin of the Concept of Apostle.

Modern study of *apostle* began with J. B. Lightfoot's essay, "The Name and Office of Apostle" (published as an excursus to his commentary on Galatians in 1890; for a useful survey of the flood of literature which has appeared since see Agnew).

Despite wide-ranging opinions of the origin, character and significance of *apostolos* within the NT, there is broad agreement that *apostolos* is used in two main senses—solemn, in the sense of bearing divine authority (e.g., "apostle of Christ Jesus," 1 Cor 1:1), and nontechnical (e.g., "messengers from the churches," 2 Cor 8:23). As we shall see, Paul uses *apostolos* with these two meanings.

There have been three main views of the origin of the concept of an apostle.

*2.1. The* Šālîaḥ *of Rabbinic Judaism.* First noticed by Lightfoot but developed by Rengstorf, this theory draws attention to parallels to the NT apostle in the *šālîaḥ*, "sent one," found in late rabbinic literature. The *šālîaḥ* was a surrogate commissioned and sent either by a private individual—for example, to negotiate a marriage (*m. Qidd.* 2:1; *t. Qidd.* 4:2; *t. Yebam.* 4:4)—or as an agent representing the religious authorities in Jerusalem to Jews of the Diaspora (*y. Ḥag.* 76d). Legally speaking, "The-one-whom-a-person-sends (*šālîaḥ*) is like the sender" (*m. Ber.* 5:5). The *šālîaḥ*'s relationship with the sender is primary, the content of the commission secondary.

Since the literature containing *šālîaḥ* postdates the NT, it has been difficult to establish what relationship may have existed between the *šālîaḥ* of late Judaism and the NT *apostolos*. Those who link *apostolos* with *šālîaḥ* point to the probability that *šālîaḥ* predates the literature in which it occurs and also to the frequency of the verbal root *šlh* in the OT (about 700 times, appearing in LXX as *apostellein* or *ex-apostellein*. It is noted that *apostolos* occurs only once in the LXX, translating the participle *šālûah* in 1 Kings 14:6). Overarching unity of concept is seen in the predominantly secular character of the references of both the OT texts and the rabbinic texts. It seems likely that Paul's nontechnical use of *apostolos* referred to below is to be traced to the *šāliah* concept.

A prime example of a text illustrating the conceptual linkage of NT *apostolos* with *šāliah* is John 13:16, "Amen, amen I say to you . . . a messenger (*apostolos*) [is not] greater than the one who sends (*tou pempsantos*) him" (see also Mk 6:30; Lk 11:49), and recalls the aphorism, "The-one-whom-a-person sends is like the sender."

*2.2. The Apostolos of Gnosticism.* W. Schmithals, the chief proponent of the Gnostic (*see* Gnosis, Gnosticism) background for *apostolos*, has forcefully declared that ". . . the late Jewish legal institution of the *shaliah* has not even the least to do with the primitive Christian apostolate" (Schmithals, 105). Schmithals points to the religious use of *apostolos* in the NT in contrast with the uniformly juridical character of *šāliah* in the rabbinical literature. Likewise, the predominantly nonreligious use of *šlh* in the OT is seen to be an improbable source for the NT apostle, who as a missionary and eschatological figure is religious in character.

Schmithals proposes that Antioch,* not Jerusalem,* is the source of the apostle concept and that the NT apostle derives from the redeemer myth of the gnostic systems. Schmithals points to two types of redeemers, heavenly and earthly, arguing that the apostles' call and ecstatic experience (receipt of *gnōsis*) and their worldwide mission identifies them as earthly redeemers. He argues that the NT apostle arose with Paul in the gnostic milieu of Syria.

Schmithals's thesis has received little support. Almost nothing is known about the religious milieu of Syria of the time. He must reconstruct his earthly redeemer figure from Paul's writings. The word *apostolos*, while used of a heavenly redeemer in Gnostic texts, which in any case postdate the NT, is not used of an earthly redeemer.

*2.3. The Apostoloi of the NT.* J. Munck and A. Ehrhardt reject the *šāliah* concept for reasons that resemble those of Schmithals mentioned above. This viewpoint argues for the Christian origin of the apostle on the basis that the new faith stimulated the rise of an appropriate leadership figure. According to Munck, "The Christian Apostles are part of something entirely new and dynamic in that the whole Christian religion

is something to be spread abroad. . . . Compared with this, the Jewish use of the apostolic idea . . . is as far removed from the Christian usage as a diplomatic envoy is from a missionary to the heathen" (Munck 1949, 100).

Generally speaking, however, this school of thought offers no specific scenario for the emergence of the apostle in the primitive church.

*2.4. The Character of Paul's Apostleship.* One of the major questions relating to Paul's apostleship is its character and authority. The traditional view that Christ's* call (*see* Conversion and Call of Paul) on the road to Damascus conferred on Paul the Lord's authority over the Gentile churches, which carries over into the canonical status of his letters for churches today, has been challenged by broader definitions of apostleship. In effect these redefinitions make Paul's apostolic authority in the churches relative and conditional. R. Schnackenburg, for example, argues that Paul found no uniform definition of apostle when he became a Christian and provided no systematic criteria for apostleship, regarding apostles only as "preachers and missionaries of Christ" (Schnackenburg, 302). J. A. Kirk states that "for Paul apostleship is proved, not by any exclusive claim, but by the fruits of those who exercise it" (Kirk, 261) and "the same apostolic ministry, in differing historical circumstances, exists to this day" (Kirk, 264).

## 3. The Evidence from Paul's Letters.

Since Paul's letters are the earliest writings of the NT, and since he uses *apostolos* more than any other NT author, all historical investigations of the origin, meaning and significance of the word properly begin with his letters.

However, lest it be thought that the concept of apostle originated with Paul, it should be noted that he writes of "those who were apostles *before me*" (Gk: *tous pro emou apostolous*). These apostles were located in Jerusalem (Gal 1:17). The creedal tradition (*see* Creed) which he repeats to the Corinthians, and which he "received" many years before, mentioned that the risen Lord* appeared [in Palestine] "to all the apostles" before he appeared to Paul (1 Cor 15:7, 8), suggesting that there were "apostles" at or close to the time of Jesus' resurrection.*

This creedal tradition (1 Cor 15:5-9) is helpful in a second respect, namely, that it distinguishes between the Twelve and "all the apostles":

| [Christ] appeared | to Cephas, | then to the twelve . . . |
|---|---|---|
| Then he appeared | to James, | then to all the apostles. |
| Last of all he appeared | also to me . . . | the least of the apostles. |

There is a symmetry here regarding the appearances of the risen Lord in Palestine. *Cephas* (*see* Peter) is placed with *the Twelve*, and *James* with *all the apostles*. Since Cephas is elsewhere referred to as an apostle (Gal 1:18-19; 2:8; cf. 1 Pet 1:1; 2 Pet 1:1), we take it that the Twelve were called apostles but that there were more apostles than twelve, and that among them were James and Paul himself, as he claimed (1 Cor 15:9).

The most logical explanation of this differentiation between *the Twelve* and *the apostles* is that the Twelve had been a term applied to the twelve disciples of Jesus from the time of the Galilean mission and that apostles were these and others, who at the first Easter were among those who were commissioned by the risen Lord.

We are able to say, then, that the apostle—so common in Paul's letters—predates those letters and goes back to the first Easter in Palestine, and indeed earlier. The same is true of the notion of the Twelve.

### 4. Jesus the Apostle and His Apostles.

The origin of the NT phenomenon of the apostle must be sought within the ministry of Jesus. This is a far more likely proposition than that the concept arose abruptly at the first Easter.

In this regard we note sayings which reveal Jesus' consciousness that he was "sent." He said: "whoever receives me receives . . . him who *sent* (*aposteilanta*) me" (Mk 9:37 pars.; cf. Mk 2:6 pars.; Mt 15:24; Lk 4:43; Jn 5:36; 9:7; 20:21). For the author of Hebrews Jesus himself is "the *apostle* . . . of our confession" (Heb 3:1).

Those he chose and called to be with him were in time "sent" to the towns of Galilee "to proclaim" the same message that he proclaimed, namely, the immediacy of the kingdom of God, the sign of which was the casting out of unclean spirits (Mk 3:14; 6:7, 12, 13; cf. Mk 1:14-15, 39). Jesus is conscious that he bears the authority (*exousia*) of God* as God's representative to fulfill his eschatological will on earth (Mk 2:10; cf. Jn 5:37). In the same way Jesus gave his "authority" (*exousia*) over the demons to the Twelve as his surrogates (Mk 3:15; 6:7). The tradition that "Jesus appointed twelve . . . that he might *send* them to preach" and "the *apostles* returned to Jesus" (Mk 3:14; 6:30) need not be regarded as anachronistic.

The best explanation of the origin of the notion of apostleship is that the *šālîaḥ* concept was current at the time of Jesus and that he took it, applied it first to himself as "the one *sent* by God" and then, by extension, to those who were *sent* by him first to Galilee and then to the Gentiles.

As to "the Twelve" we should regard them as a bridge between the beginnings of the ministry of the

historic Jesus and the establishment of early Christianity, as Gerhardsson has argued. This is confirmed in Mark, who shows little redactional interest in the place of the Twelve in the post-Easter church, and yet rather naively refers to the Twelve on a number of occasions (Mk 3:14; 4:10; 6:7; 9:35; 10:32; 11:11; 14:10, 17, 20, 43).

### 5. Apostles in Paul's Letters.

Broadly speaking, Paul uses the term *apostle* in two ways: in the nontechnical and in the solemn sense.

*5.1. Apostle: Nontechnical.* There are two references in Paul's writings to *apostle* in the nontechnical sense. In the first of these, Paul was writing from Macedonia to prepare the Corinthians for the coming of two men, about whom he writes a brief commendation (2 Cor 8:16-24). The purpose of their visit was to hasten the Corinthians' completion of the collection for the saints in Jerusalem. Paul wrote, "[With Titus] we are sending (*synepempsamen*) the brother who is famous among all the churches for his preaching of the gospel" and one whom Paul calls "our brother whom we have often tested and found earnest in many matters." Paul declared that these *two "brothers"* are "messengers [*apostoloi*] of the [Macedonian] churches" to the church in Corinth (2 Cor 8:23), sent for a practical and financial mission. This use of *apostolos* appears to resemble the *šālîaḥ* of later rabbinic writings who might be sent on a mission from Jerusalem to synagogues of the Diaspora.

In the second instance Paul wrote from prison (possibly in Rome) to the church in Philippi explaining that due to illness Epaphroditus was returning to them. Epaphroditus was the Philippian church's "messenger [*apostolos*] and minister to [Paul's] need" (Phil 2:25). This apostle's role was practical and not directly religious. Once again the similarity between the *šālîaḥ* concept and the role of Epaphroditus, the apostle of the church of Philippi, seems too close to be coincidental.

These two references support the notion that "messengers (*apostoloi*) of the churches" were well established in the Pauline churches by the middle fifties of the first century. The most probable explanation for the origin of these apostles is that Paul borrowed the idea from Jewish practice and applied it to his churches.

*5.2. Apostle: Solemn.* By this we mean "apostles of Christ" (as, e.g., 1 Thess 2:6). These apostles are not sent by ordinary people on a mundane mission. The sender is Christ, the Messiah of God. The overwhelming number of Paul's references to *apostle* belong to this category, which, however, may be further divided into other apostles and Paul himself.

*5.2.1. Other Apostles.* There are "apostles before" Paul (Gal 1:17) located in Jerusalem. It is clear from Paul's reflection on his apostolic call en route to Damascus, which we may date in the mid thirties, that there were apostles from earliest times in the primitive church, indeed from the time of the first Easter ("Christ . . . appeared . . . to all the apostles," 1 Cor 15:8).

Were there apostles *after* Paul? Is there a historical point after which, according to Paul, there were no apostles?

1 Corinthians 15:5-11 bears on these important questions. Paul's words "[Christ] appeared to Cephas, *then* to the twelve . . . *then* to more than five hundred brothers . . . *then* . . . to James . . . *then* to all the apostles. *Last of all* . . . he appeared also to me" seems to demarcate a span of resurrection appearances beginning with Cephas and ending with Paul. Paul does not say, "*Then* he appeared to me" but "*Last of all* he appeared to me," suggesting a finality of appearances. Paul is able to go on to say "I am the least of the apostles . . . by the grace of God I am [an apostle]" because the apostles are a group limited in number. He can say that he is the "least of the apostles" since he is, in reality, the "last" apostle to whom the Lord "appeared." The first and most basic test of apostolicity is that the claimant has "seen the Lord" (1 Cor 9:1).

The nature of Christ's appearance to Paul was atypical. He did not see the risen Lord in the context of the first Easter in Palestine as the other apostles before him did, but as the glorified heavenly Lord a year or two later. The unusual and much debated phrase, "As one untimely born" (*tō ektrōmati*, 1 Cor 15:8), whatever it means, reflects Paul's defense of his genuine apostleship despite the isolated and late appearance of the Lord to him. From Paul's standpoint the unusual nature of Christ's resurrection appearance to him serves to mark him out as the end point of such appearances and therefore the end point of apostolic appointment.

The apostles must have been numerous since the creed refers to "*all* the apostles" (1 Cor 15:7) and Paul can refer to "the *rest* of the apostles" (1 Cor 9:5). We do not know the exact number except that there were more than twelve who were the core group. The Twelve may have functioned as the symbolic foundation for the new community of the resurrected Christ. The apostles, on the other hand, took their character from their name: they were *sent* by Christ to go to others. At the missionary meeting in Jerusalem there were two "apostolates" (*apostolai*), which involved two "sendings": one to the circumcised (*see* Circumcision), the other to the Gentiles* (Gal 2:7-9).

We know the names of some, but not all the apostles. James is linked with "all the apostles" (1 Cor 15:7; cf. Gal 1:19), suggesting that, while James* was not counted among the Twelve, he was the most honored among the apostles. It is probable that James's relationship as "the brother of the Lord" gave him his special place (cf. Gal 1:19). The "brothers of the Lord," who are unnamed but among whom James would be included, are probably also to be thought of as apostles (see context of 1 Cor 9:5). Clearly John is to be thought of as an apostle (Gal 2:7-9). The link between Barnabas* and Paul also suggests that Barnabas is to be regarded as an apostle (1 Cor 9:6; cf. Acts 14:4). The only others named as apostles in the writings of Paul are his relatives "Andronicus and Junia(s) . . . persons of note among the apostles" (Rom 16:7). If to the Twelve we add James, Barnabas, Andronicus, Junia(s) and Paul (last and least), we know the names of seventeen apostles; but the number was greater.

Paul has a high view of apostles. As founders of churches apostles are pre-eminent persons in early Christianity. Paul declares, "God has appointed apostles *first* in the church" (1 Cor 12:28; cf. Eph 2:20; 4:11). Moreover, theirs was a prophetic, revelatory ministry, illuminating the meaning of Christ and the gospel.* Paul claims that he and the other apostles enjoyed the revelation of God through the Spirit (*see* Holy Spirit) to understand the mysteries* of the gospel (Eph 3:1-9; cf. 1 Cor 2:6-16). Apostles made known this revelation of God both verbally and in their writings (Rom 16:25-26; 1 Cor 2:13; Eph 3:3-4).

*5.2.2. Paul the Apostle.* Paul refers to himself many times as an "apostle." He frequently introduces himself to his readers as "apostle of Jesus Christ" or by similar ascription (1 Cor 1:1; 2 Cor 1:1; Eph 1:1; Col 1:1; 1 Tim 1:1; 2 Tim 1:1; Tit 1:1). It is "through Jesus Christ" that Paul has "received apostleship (*apostolē*, Rom 1:5; cf. Gal 1:1) because Jesus has "called" Paul to be an apostle and "separated" him for the gospel of God (Rom 1:1; 1 Cor 1:1) to bring about the obedience of faith* among the Gentiles (Rom 1:5; 11:13). All of this is due to the risen Christ appearing to Paul "last of all," as the persecutor was travelling to Damascus.

According to S. Kim, Paul alludes frequently to his Damascus Road encounter with Christ. In addition to more readily recognized passages such as 1 Corinthians 9:1; 15:8-10; Galatians 1:13-17; Philippians 3:4-11, there are others (e.g., Rom 10:2-4; 1 Cor 9:16-17; 2 Cor 3:4—4:6; 5:16; Eph 3:1-13; Col 1:23-29). Kim argues that to a remarkable degree the Damascus christophany has colored and shaped Paul's vocabulary and thought.

## 6. Paul's Apostleship Disputed.

There is no hint in his letters to the Thessalonians that Paul's apostleship was in dispute in the Greek churches at the time of writing (c. A.D. 50-52). Paul feels free to bracket Silvanus and Timothy with himself on equal terms and to include them with him as "apostles of Christ" (1 Thess 2:6; cf. 1 Thess 1:1). But from that time, doubtless due to mounting criticism, Paul became explicit about his status as an apostle (Gal 1:1; 1 Cor 1:1; 2 Cor 1:1; Rom 1:1), and was careful to distance himself as an apostle from various co-workers* (1 Cor 1:1; 2 Cor 1:1; Col 1:1; cf. Phil 1:1).

By about A.D. 55 Paul acknowledged that his apostleship was in dispute: "If to others I am not an apostle . . ." (1 Cor 9:1). These "others" are probably the Judaizers whose views he may have been echoing in Galatians, when he wrote that he was not an "apostle" only "from and through men" (Gal 1:1). In other words (they said), Paul was nothing more than a šālîaḥ on an errand from the Jerusalem church, a surrogate of others.

Their further criticisms may be detected from Paul's comments in 1 Corinthians 15:8-9 where he affirms his apostleship, even though he was not present when the risen Lord appeared to the apostles before him. Christ's appearance to Paul (they said) was later in time, of a different kind and to him alone. A true resurrection appearance did not occur in his case. He should not be counted among the apostles.

Paul, however, insisted that he was an apostle, notwithstanding his "untimely birth," and that he had seen the Lord in a manner different from others. If he was the "least of the apostles," it was only because he had been a persecutor. But for that he made amends by working "harder than them all." If they preached Christ crucified and risen, so too did he (1 Cor 15:3-5, 11).

*6.1. 1 Corinthians: Paul's Apostleship Questioned.* Similar defensive tones may be heard earlier in the letter reflecting local questioning of his apostleship: "Am I not an apostle? Have I not seen Jesus our Lord?" (1 Cor 9:1).

Here the question does not relate to the historical basis of Paul's claim to be an apostle but to his ministry lifestyle which some found unacceptable in the Greco-Roman environment of Corinth, namely that he did not accept remuneration (*see* Financial Support; Tentmaking). From his "defense to those who would examine me" (1 Cor 9:3) which follows (1 Cor 9:4-18), it appears that according to some Corinthians his refusal to accept patronage was his tacit recognition that he was not in any true sense an apostle. A genuine apostle would accept full payment.

Nonetheless, this was a factional, unrepresentative complaint. Paul felt able to say "At least I am [an apostle] to you [Corinthians]" (1 Cor 9:3).

*6.2. 2 Corinthians: Paul's Apostleship Opposed.* Within no more than one or two years, however, questioning of Paul's apostleship by some of the Corinthians had hardened into widespread opposition. This dramatic development is attributable to the recent arrival of a number of self-professed "ministers" or "apostles" (2 Cor 11:13, 23), who had launched a counter mission against Paul and his version of Christianity (2 Cor 2:17—3:1; 11:4, 12; *see* Opponents). The vocabulary of their ministry emerges from 2 Corinthians and includes such terms as "the word of God," "gospel," "Jesus," "Spirit" and "righteousness" (2 Cor 2:17; 4:1; 11:4, 15).

This was now a far-reaching assault on Paul's apostleship by newly arrived persons who sought to oust Paul from his place at Corinth. They were superior, Paul inferior (2 Cor 11:5, 23), whom Paul mocks as "superlative apostles" (2 Cor 11:5; 12:11). If he has come to them, they have come further (2 Cor 10:12-14—Jerusalem compared to Antioch?). If he is an apostle, where are his "signs,* wonders and mighty works " (2 Cor 12:12)? If he claimed to have "seen" the "Lord" (1 Cor 9:1; 15:8), they boast of an abundance of "visions and revelations of the Lord" (2 Cor 12:1, 7; *see* Visions), the evidence of which is their ecstatic speech (2 Cor 5:12-13; cf. 2 Cor 12:2-4; *see* Tongues). Their credentials as "Hebrews . . . Israelites . . . the seed of Abraham" are impeccable, making them superior in every way.

For his part Paul is denigrated as inadequate, powerless, worldly and a "fool" to be "tolerated" (2 Cor 2:17; 3:5; 10:1-6). Paul is a "crafty" (2 Cor 4:23; 12:16), sorry figure as he limps from defeat to defeat (2 Cor 2:14-16; 4:1, 7-8, 16; 6:3-10; 11:23—12:10). What is the proof that "Christ is speaking through" this man (2 Cor 13:3; 10:7; cf. 1 Cor 2:13; 14:36)?

How did Paul answer this devastating attack on his apostleship? Significantly he did not reiterate the Lord's appearances to him (cf. 1 Cor 9:1; 15:8; Gal 1:15-16). His opponents' "visions and revelations of the Lord" (2 Cor 12:1) had stolen that ground from him, at least in the eyes of the Corinthians.

Paul defends his apostleship in 2 Corinthians along the following lines. First, the Damascus Road call by the risen Lord is implicit throughout 2 Corinthians. He was an apostle "by the will of God" (2 Cor 1:1) who used the "authority (*exousia*) the Lord gave [him] for building up" the Gentile churches (2 Cor 10:8; 13:10; cf. 11:17; 12:19). He exercised "this ministry (of the new covenant, 3:6) by the mercy of God" (i.e., as a result of the Damascus call 2 Cor 4:1; cf. 1 Cor 15:9; Gal 1:15; 1 Tim 1:16). He spoke "from and before God" (*ek theou katenanti theou*, 2 Cor 2:17; cf. 2 Cor 12:10) and his "competence" to be a "minister of a new covenant" (*see* Covenant and New Covenant) is from God (*hikanotēs . . . ek tou theou*, 2 Cor 3:5-6).

If the Damascus Call was the basis of Paul's apostleship, its legitimacy is demonstrated by the quality of his ministry (*see* Ministry), especially when seen in contrast to the new ministers in Corinth. He "refuse[s] to tamper with God's word" (2 Cor 4:2), unlike those who "peddle God's word" (2 Cor 2:17). Whereas they promote a view of the "righteousness of God" (based on circumcision or other works of the Law? 2 Cor 11:15; *see* Righteousness, Righteousness of God), Paul is true to the message entrusted to him by God, that God's righteousness is to be found in Christ who became sin for us (2 Cor 5:19-21; cf. 2 Cor 3:9). Despite their claims for themselves and their assault on him, they are "false apostles . . . [servants of] Satan" (2 Cor 11:13-15). Through Paul's ministry, however, there is a church at Corinth, a living "letter from Christ" as proof of Paul's genuineness (2 Cor 3:2-3; 10:7) as an apostle who effectively "persuades" people to become Christians (2 Cor 5:11-13). Christ indeed speaks powerfully through Paul (2 Cor 13:4) and through Paul brings resistant people captive to obey the gospel (2 Cor 10:4-6).

Second, Paul accepted the observation about his weakness,* indeed he expanded upon it, even boasting of his sufferings in three important passages (2 Cor 4:7-8; 6:3-10; 11:23—12:10; cf. 1 Cor 4:9-13; 15:30, 32). Paul proclaimed the one who had become sin,* and that he himself had experienced in his own life, in some measure, the sufferings* of the Jesus whom he preached. Implicit in these catalogs of tribulation (*see* Afflictions) is the claim that the sufferings of Christ are reproduced in an apostle who is true to him (2 Cor 1:5). Unsaid but perhaps implied is that the powerful triumphalism (*see* Triumph) of the "superlative apostles" arises from their cross-less gospel (*see* Cross, Theology of the) and serves only to disqualify them (2 Cor 2:13; 5:16; 11:4). The "falsity" of these apostles lies in their "other" Jesus, their "different" gospel.

### 7. Conclusion.

The use of the word *apostolos* is almost completely confined to the NT writings. Since Paul makes more use of the word than other NT writers and his writings are chronologically the earliest, it is clear that study of this word must begin with Paul's letters.

It is evident from Paul's writings, however, that

there were "apostles before [Paul]," going back at least to the resurrection appearances of Jesus in Jerusalem and elsewhere in Palestine. The appearance of the *apostle* vocabulary in the Gospel of Mark makes it likely that the notion of the apostle must be taken back into the Gospel story.

Jesus, followed by Paul and other early church leaders, appear to have been influenced in their use of the word *apostle* by the Jewish notion of the *šālîaḥ* who in late Judaism represented persons and institutions to others. While it is clear that nontechnical use of "apostle" by Paul resembles the secular *šālîaḥ* of later Jewish writings, the technical, or "solemn," use of this word takes on a special character from the unique circumstances associated with the rise of early Christianity.

Galatians,* Romans* and the two Corinthian* letters reflect the rise of opposition to the recognition of Paul as an apostle of Christ. While some of this opposition arose at a local level over personal criticism of Paul, by far the greatest rejection of his apostleship arose from the Judaizers,* who at best sought to classify him as a humble *šālîaḥ* of the Jerusalem church.

Paul himself sought to establish the limited extent of the numbers of apostles. His careful words that Christ "appeared to me last of all" (1 Cor 15:8) serve to show that while there were apostles *before* him, there were no apostles *after* him. According to Paul he is both "the least" and "the last" of the apostles.

Questioning or outright rejection of Paul's authority as an "apostle of Christ" is by no means confined to Paul's own day. Some modern scholars have attempted to broaden the definition of "apostle" in such a way (e.g., as "missionary" or "church planter") that Paul's distinctive authority is dissipated. Paul strenuously resisted attempts to downgrade him in this way. If Paul's apostleship meant and means no more than that, then he had and continues to have little real authority in the churches.

There should be no doubt that Paul based his claim to be an apostle on having seen the risen Lord and having been commissioned by him to go to the Gentiles (1 Cor 9:1; 15:8; Gal 1:11-17). To be sure, he pointed to his effectiveness in establishing churches, his own sufferings as a continuation in history of the sufferings of Christ and to his own integrity, but these served only to legitimize a ministry which had its basis in Christ's confronting him on the road to Damascus.

*See also* AFFLICTIONS TRIALS, HARDSHIPS; AUTHORITY; COWORKERS, PAUL AND HIS; MINISTRY; OPPONENTS OF PAUL; PASTORAL THEOLOGY; SIGNS, WONDERS, MIRACLES.

BIBLIOGRAPHY. F. H. Agnew, "On the Origin of the Term *Apostolos*," *CBQ* 38 (1976) 49-53; idem, "The Origin of the NT Apostle-Concept: a Review of Research," *JBL* 105 (1986) 75-96; C. K. Barrett, *The Signs of an Apostle* (Philadelphia: Fortress, 1972); A. Ehrhardt, *The Apostolic Succession in the First Two Centuries of the Church* (London: Lutterworth, 1953); idem, *The Apostolic Ministry* (SJT Occasional Papers 7; Edinburgh: Oliver & Boyd, 1958); B. Gerhardsson, *The Origins of the Gospel Traditions* (London: SCM, 1977); S. Kim, *The Origins of Paul's Gospel* (Grand Rapids: Eerdmans, 1981); E. Käsemann, "Die Legitimität des Apostels," *ZNW* 41 (1942) 33-71; J. A. Kirk, "Apostleship since Rengstorf: Towards a Synthesis," *NTS* 21 (1975) 249-64; J. B. Lightfoot, "The Name and Office of Apostle" in *The Epistle of St. Paul to the Galatians* (10th ed., 1890; London: Macmillan, 1986) 92-101; J. Munck, "Paul, the Apostles and the Twelve," *ST* 3 (1949) [= *Paul and the Salvation of Mankind* (Atlanta: John Knox, 1959) 36-68]; K. H. Rengstorf, "ἀπόστολος," *TDNT* I.407-47; W. Schmithals, *The Office of Apostle in the Early Church* (Nashville: Abingdon, 1969); R. Schnackenburg, "Apostles Before and During Paul's Time," in *Apostolic History and the Gospel*, ed. W. W. Gasque and R. P. Martin (Grand Rapids: Eerdmans, 1970).

P. W. Barnett

**APOSTOLIC FATHERS.** *See* PAUL IN EARLY CHURCH TRADITION.

**APOSTOLIC PAROUSIA.** *See* ITINERARIES, TRAVEL PLANS, JOURNEYS, APOSTOLIC PAROUSIA.

**AQEDAH.** *See* DEATH OF CHRIST; SACRIFICE, OFFERING.

**ARCHANGELS.** *See* ANGELS, ARCHANGELS.

**AREOPAGUS.** *See* ATHENS, PAUL AT.

**ARMOR OF GOD.** *See* TRIUMPH.

**ARTEMIS.** *See* EPHESUS; RELIGIONS, GRECO-ROMAN.

**ASCETICISM.** *See* MARRIAGE AND DIVORCE, ADULTERY AND INCEST; PAUL IN EARLY CHURCH TRADITION; SEXUALITY, SEXUAL ETHICS.

**ASTROLOGY.** *See* ELEMENTS/ELEMENTAL SPIRITS OF THE WORLD; RELIGIONS, GRECO-ROMAN.

## ATHENS, PAUL AT

Chapter 17 of the Acts of the Apostles* preserves a speech of Paul in a city traditionally associated with pagan learning. This speech, uniquely constructed to address the historical situation, is also in harmony with Paul's letters, though this has been challenged and is a matter of continuing debate.

1. Paul in First-Century Athens
2. The Athens Speech
3. The Athens Speech and the Letters
4. Conclusions

### 1. Paul in First-Century Athens.

*1.1. The City of Athens: Its Reputation and Piety.* It strikes the modern person as ironic that Christians and Jews were regarded by most of the ancient world as "atheists" because of their refusal to recognize the gods. It is with a similar irony that Paul, having walked about the city and having been disturbed by the profusion of idols (Acts 17:16; *see* Idolatry), calls the Athenians "religious" (Acts 17:22).

The city of Athens, one of the great city-states in fifth-century B.C. Greece, is located in the southeast of the country. By the apostolic era it was no longer a world superpower nor the hub of intellectual activity as it once was, but it did have a legacy from the glories of the past in its civic pride and its reputation for matters of philosophy and piety. Full of idols, as Acts 17 records, Athens was described by ancient authors as a model of "speaking well of the gods"; so religious were the people of Athens, that in that city altars were even set up "to unknown gods" (Pausanias 1.1.4; 5.14.8; Philostratus *Vit. Ap.* 6.3).

Critics of the historicity of the speeches in Acts have frequently pointed out that none of the strands of extrabiblical evidence specifically mentions the singular "an unknown god," which is necessary for the speech's introduction (Acts 17:23). The phrase "altars to unknown gods," which is mentioned in the literature, is ambiguous, however. With only scant archeological evidence yet recovered, it is too early to conclude from silence that the singular could not have been used (contra Lüdemann, 194).

More significant is the way that the practice of this anonymous worship was linked to themes central to Paul's speech: besides being an indication of religiousness, it also is clearly presented by Diogenes Laertius as a "safety precaution." The thinking was that if the gods were not properly venerated they would strike the city. Hence, lest they inadvertently invoke the wrath of some god in their ignorance of him or her, the city set up these altars to unknown gods (Diogenes 1.110-13). Both the admission of ignorance and the desire to avoid divine catastrophe are used to great effect by Paul in his speech.

*1.2. The Mars Hill (Areopagus) Council.* It is unclear whether or not Acts is presenting Paul as formally "on trial" in Athens. The phrase "they took him to the Areopagus" (Acts 17:19) could refer either to the Council called by that name or just to the location, a hill after which the Council was named. Since there are good arguments on both sides of this controversy, it is probably best to leave the question open.

Whether it was a formal trial or not the reader should not miss the fact that the speech is a response to a very specific and serious accusation: "He seems to be advocating strange and foreign gods" (Acts 17:18), not very different from the famous charge mounted against Socrates, leading to the death of that great teacher. Luke's comment in Acts 17:21 is ironic: the Athenians are more interested in satisfying their curiosity than they are in preserving "orthodoxy." In Paul's case the charges arise from the Athenians' apparent misunderstanding of Paul's preaching; they appear to have thought he was referring to two gods (note the plural in Acts 17:18b). The terms *Jesus* and *Anastasis* ("Resurrection") could be mistaken for the names of a god and his consort.

## 2. The Athens Speech.

The speech in Acts 17 has been criticized for not being sufficiently Christian (e.g., Dibelius, 57-63). But this negative assessment of the speech is, as shall be seen, superficial. The argument is in reality a devastating attack on both the Athenians and their religion.

*2.1. Idol Worship and the True God.* Before correcting the Athenians' mistaken impression of the Christian message and satisfying their curiosity, Paul cleverly uses the altar to the Unknown God to defend himself against the charge of preaching strange and foreign gods. In effect Paul says in Acts 17:23: "What I proclaim to you is only that which you yourselves, while openly admitting your ignorance, claim to reverence." Paul is not here saying that what he worships is what they worship* without knowing it. The emphasis in the Greek construction is on the "ignorance" not the "worship." They are right only insofar as they recognize that there is something worthy of worship of which they are ignorant. In this way Paul's defense quickly turns to an attack. The speech goes on to attack various facets of the practice of idol worship: It is wrong to try to locate the Creator of all in a building fashioned by humans (Acts 17:24). It is wrong to try to give gifts to the giver of life (Acts 17:25). It is wrong to try to identify the God who created all nations with any particular city (Acts 17:26; identifying gods with cities was a regular feature of pagan religion). And finally, it is wrong to think that the one who gives life to people can be something that itself has no life, but is shaped by human hands (Acts 17:29).

Thus, far from approving idol worship, the speech asserts that their idol worship (except for their implicit acknowledgment of ignorance) is fatally flawed both in theory and in execution. It is worth noting that parts of these criticisms of idolatry,* while thoroughly Jewish (see Gärtner, passim), were not completely alien to the Stoics or the Epicureans (who are specifically mentioned in Acts 17:18). In addition, these criticisms, in their sharpest form, could be seen as having some bite against Jewish cultic practices as well (see Stephen's speech, Acts 7).

*2.2. Natural Revelation and the True God.* Dibelius, among others, thought that the speech at Athens teaches a "kinship" between God* and people that is "foreign" to Paul's thinking and to the rest of the NT (Dibelius, 74). But this reading of the speech is untenable. The language used in Acts 17:27 clearly indicates irony and tragedy. People are intended to "seek" God, it is true. The result of this "seeking" we would expect to be "finding." But the verb for "finding" is weakened in three ways. The first is the grammatical construction: the use of the optative mood in Greek introduces a tone of uncertainty, coupled with a phrase (*ei ara ge*) which is best translated "if perhaps." The "finding" is by no means certain. Second, the force of the verb is weakened by being paired with the colorful verb "groping" (*psēlaphaō*), a word used in such sources as Homer's *Odyssey* (9.416) and the Greek version of Deuteronomy (28:29) to mean a "blind feeling around." Third, the verb phrase is followed by the clause "although he is not far." The concessive nature of this clause only makes sense if the "groping" is unsuccessful.

It seems safe to conclude that while the speaker believes that knowledge of God is theoretically possible from nature, yet in practical terms there is little or no hope that this hypothetical possibility will be or has been translated into an acceptable relationship with God. It is hard to imagine a stronger contrast between the God who is in control of all (Acts 17:24-26) and the ironic pathetic state of the human predicament as here described (Acts 17:27): blindly and unsuccessfully groping for someone who stands so close and who desires to be found.

*2.3. Pagan Thinking and the True God.* Does the citation, with apparent approval, of pagan literature in Acts 17:28 provide evidence of a positive evaluation of paganism? Very likely it does not. There is reason to doubt that the first part of verse 28 is a quotation from any specific pagan work, for there is no consensus as to the alleged source for its wording, although several have been proposed. Probably, then, verse 28a is not a quotation at all, but a statement using common vocabulary and a commonly used form, the triad. While the phrase is one that Greeks and Christians could both affirm, it is much more likely that the triad is meant to be a reminder of the three main prongs in the Jewish attack on idols (they lack life, they cannot move, and they have no real existence) than that the statement is simply taken from a pagan source (Gärtner, 197, 222).

The phrase in the middle of Acts 17:28, while plural in form, is a common method of introducing a single and specific poetic quotation; without question the phrase "for we are his offspring" is a quotation from pagan literature (Aratus *Phainomena* 5). But the citation is not so much intended to indicate a close relationship between people and God (so, e.g., Haenchen, 525), as it is to show a close resemblance between people and God: since human beings are living, God must also be living; he must be greater, not less, than his creations. This is made clear by the "therefore" which links verse 28 with verse 29.

Thus, as with the words of the inscription, so the quotation from pagan literature is used to demonstrate the errors of the belief system from which it is borrowed. Even the Greeks are aware that there is something or someone worthy of worship of whom they are ignorant; even the Greeks realize that something living can only be truly represented by something living. This utilization of pagan philosophy* and literature to show its own inconsistencies may be something borrowed from Jewish apology, for the quotation from Aratus seems to have been used in a similar way by the Jewish propagandist Aristobulos (fragment 4 in Eusebius *Praep. Ev.* 8.12).

*2.4. Christianity and the True God.* The specifically Christian thrust of the speech is confined to the final two verses. In this final section the speaker answers two questions that would be on the minds of the hearers of the speech.

The question that Acts 17:30 is designed to answer is not about the guilt or innocence of the pagans, as Dibelius assumes (Dibelius, 55). The text deals only with the delay of punishment and says nothing about the Athenians' innocence before God. The historical context clarifies the reasoning: the worship of unknown gods was a type of "insurance" for the Athenians, a way of warding off divine catastrophe from some attention-demanding god with whom they were unacquainted. Paul has just argued that their efforts are mistaken and ineffectual. The obvious rejoinder from the audience would be: "If our worship is unacceptable to the unknown god, why is there no catastrophe?" The answer then focuses not on whether the Athenians are worthy of punishment, but why no pun-

ishment has followed their alleged errors. The answer is that although divine retribution has not yet come, its delay is not because of their innocent ignorance or precautionary worship, but because God has been merciful. "But now . . . ," the speaker indicates, things will be different. God, who cannot be served with human hands, does not want their offerings, he wants their repentance.

Only after explaining the deficiencies of their attempts at worship does the speech return to the main subject of the gospel message which had been misunderstood earlier (see Acts 17:18). In Acts 17:31 Paul tells the Athenians that, in complete contrast to the lifeless things with which they have chosen to represent the divine, God has appointed a living human being, Jesus Christ.* Jesus' humanity is here emphasized not only to avoid the confusion hinted at in Acts 17:18—he is not to be added to the pantheon—but also as a contrast to lifeless idols.

Any misunderstanding of "Jesus and the Resurrection" as a new god and his consort are dispelled not only by the reference to Jesus as a human being but also by an attempt to make clear what is meant by the resurrection.* This attempt at clarification, it would seem, was only too successful. The Athenians, to whom the idea of physical resurrection would have been repugnant, began to sneer, and the reported speech comes to an abrupt end.

**3. The Athens Speech and the Letters.**

*3.1. Athens and 1 Thessalonians: Convincing and Converting Gentiles.* In such an obviously abridged report of a speech by Paul as that found in Acts 17, one should not expect the whole of his gospel message to be reproduced in the detail that we have it in his letters. There is a notable parallel in 1 Thessalonians 1:9-10, however, where Paul writes of the Thessalonians'* response to his message. Their first step was toward monotheism: they "turned to God from idols to serve a living and true God" (1 Thess 1:9), reminiscent of the mainly monotheistic rather than specifically Christian thrust in the Athens speech.

Even more remarkable is the parallel between Acts 17:31 and 1 Thessalonians 1:10. Both speak about the future, but certain, divine judgment* or wrath,* which is linked to Jesus as judge or as the criterion for judgment. And in both cases the resurrection of Jesus by God is brought into view. The differences in content between the two passages are slight and consistent with the fact that the one is directed toward pagans and the other toward those who have become Christians.

*3.2. Athens and 1 Corinthians: A Change in Missionary*

*Strategy?* It has been argued that the small number of converts in Athens caused Paul to change the character of his preaching, and that this is reflected in such passages as 1 Corinthians 2:1-2 (see the references in Gärtner, 51-53, who does not agree; Stonehouse). But the situations in Athens and Corinth were radically different and called for different emphases. The Corinthians needed to be told that the Christian teachers, whom they exalted overly much, considered themselves as "fools" for Christ (1 Cor 4:10). The Athenians, who already considered Paul a fool—the term they used, *spermologos* (Acts 17:18), means something like "one who has collected scraps of learning"—needed to be taught about their own ignorance (a theme that also resonates with 1 Cor 3:18-19). Similarly, although Christ is the main subject of the gospel message in both contexts, for the Corinthians it is Christ and his humiliation and crucifixion,* whereas for non-Christians it is Christ and his vindication through the resurrection.

Once these differences are noted, the important similarities between the speech and the letter become clear, especially in terms of the style of argument. In 1 Corinthians more clearly than the other letters, Paul employs the tactic of citing slogans of his opponents with apparent approval, only to add such severe qualifications and restrictions as to reverse the meaning. An example is the Corinthian slogan "All things are lawful for me" (1 Cor 6:12) which is followed by such amendments as to negate its force. This is precisely the tactic used in the Athens speech in regard to Paul's initial apparent praise for their religiousness and worship of the Unknown God. In the end, nothing about their religion is commendable except their implicit acknowledgment that they were ignorant about something.

*3.3. Athens and Romans: Natural Theology.* The other clear tie-in with Paul's letters is his teaching on the matter of the human response to natural revelation. In the Athens speech natural observations should tell the Athenians that their worship is misguided. The God who created the earth cannot need material gifts; the God who gave life must himself be living, and so on. Indeed, there are clues in their own philosophy and poets that should have turned them to the one true God, yet they have clung to pagan practices and idolatry. What the Athenians need, according to the speech, is not education but repentance. In Romans 1 the point of Paul's discussion is identical: no one is without blame. Romans 1:22-23 might just as well have been written with the Athenians in mind: "Although they claimed to be wise, they became fools and exchanged the glory of the immortal God for images."

Both Romans and Acts 17 display the conviction that enough can be known about God from his universe to make human beings reject idolatry. Neither Romans nor Acts 17, however, holds much in the way of hope that people will come to know God by natural revelation alone.

### 4. Conclusions.

Acts 17:22-31 must be seen in the context of the historical situation of Paul's visit to Athens. It begins as a defense against the accusation brought by the Athenians, but quickly turns to an attack on idol worship. Finally, the speech answers questions that an Athenian audience could be expected to have had, questions not only arising from the speech itself, but from Paul's initial discussions in the marketplace (Acts 17:17).

If the difference in audience is taken into account, the speech shows pronounced affinities with Paul's letters. In terms of content, the presentation of the Christian message to pagan Gentiles is consistent with what we would expect from passages like 1 Thessalonians 1:10, and the ideas about natural revelation are consistent with the teaching at the beginning of Romans. In terms of the style of the argument, it is the similarities between the Areopagus speech and 1 Corinthians that stand out. In terms of his thinking, the way that thinking is expressed and the boldness in meeting opponents on their own geographical and intellectual territory, it is none other than the apostle Paul's voice we hear in the Athens speech.

*See also* IDOLATRY; PAUL IN ACTS AND LETTERS; PHILOSOPHY.

BIBLIOGRAPHY. F. F. Bruce, *The Acts of the Apostles* (Grand Rapids: Eerdmans, 1990); H. Conzelmann, "The Address of Paul on the Areopagus," in *Studies in Luke-Acts*, ed. L. E. Keck and J. L. Martyn (London: SPCK, 1968) 217-30; M. Dibelius, "Paul on the Areopagus," in *Studies in the Acts of the Apostles*, ed. H. Greeven (New York: Scribners, 1956) 26-77; B. Gärtner, *The Areopagus Speech and Natural Revelation* (Uppsala: Gleerup, 1955); E. Haenchen, *The Acts of the Apostles: A Commentary* (Philadelphia: Westminster, 1971); C. J. Hemer, "The Speeches of Acts: II. The Areopagus Address," *TynB* 40 (1989) 239-59; G. Lüdemann, *Early Christianity According to the Traditions in Acts* (Minneapolis: Fortress, 1988); N. B. Stonehouse, *Paul Before the Areopagus and Other New Testament Studies* (London: Tyndale, 1957). C. Gempf

# AUTHORITY

The term *exousia* (and the related words *exousiazō, exesti*) is used of "ability," "freedom"* and "right" in the

Pauline writings. When applied to Paul himself, *exousia* refers to a "right" that stems from his commission as apostle* to the Gentiles.* When used of the apostolate, the term carries the sense of faithful transmission and hence guarantor rather than innovator of church tradition. Within the church it has the twofold sense of individual "freedom" and corporate "warrant" that derives from the presence of Christ's* power* with those gathered in his name.*

    1. Of Paul
    2. Of Other Apostles
    3. Of Opponents
    4. In the Church

## 1. Of Paul.

*1.1. Source.* Paul defines the source of his authority as "given by the Lord*" (2 Cor 10:8; cf. Rom 1:1). This authority stems specifically from his status as "Christ's apostle" (1 Thess 2:6), which gives him the right to exert his personal influence when necessary (1 Thess 2:7). Authority and apostleship are closely linked in Paul's letters. Indeed, his ability to exercise authority stems from his commission as an apostle (*see* Conversion and Call). Requests are made "through the name of the Lord Jesus Christ" (e.g., 1 Cor 1:10), discipline is exercised "in the Lord Jesus Christ" (e.g., 2 Thess 3:12), household* instructions are given "in the name of the Lord" (1 Thess 4:2; 2 Thess 3:6) and teaching* is rendered "by the word of the Lord" (1 Thess 4:15; cf. 1 Cor 7:10).

*1.2. Challenges.* There are very few of Paul's letters where his authority is not highlighted. It may be observed in the opening section of his letters where he commonly identifies himself as "Paul, an apostle of Christ Jesus" (Rom, 1—2 Cor, Gal, Eph, Col, 1—2 Tim, Tit). But Paul's apostolic authority is particularly at issue in his letters to the Galatians* and the Corinthians.* In Galatians we read of Jewish-Christian itinerant missionaries who preach a message of circumcision* (Gal 2:3-4; 5:2-12; 6:12-13) and obedience to the Mosaic Law* (Gal 2:15-16; 3:2; 5:4), and who seek to erode Paul's authority among the Gentile churches by claiming that his apostleship is secondary (Gal 1:1; 1:13—2:10) and his gospel fashioned to be palatable to the Gentiles (Gal 1:11-12; 2:1-10). It is common among interpreters to link these opponents with those from the Pharisaic wing of the Jerusalem church ("Judaizers*"; Acts 15:5) whom James claimed had "gone out" without the church's authority (Acts 15:24) and taught the Gentiles that unless they were circumcised according to the custom taught by Moses they could not be saved (Acts 15:1). In 1 and 2 Corinthians Paul responds to those who challenge his authority by

questioning his apostleship on the grounds that he refused financial* support from his churches (1 Cor 9:3-18; 2 Cor 12:13), that he did not carry letters of recommendation (2 Cor 3:1-3), that he was not successful in reaching his own people (2 Cor 3:14—4:4) and that he was an unimpressive speaker (2 Cor 10:10-11). There also seem to have been insinuations that the Jerusalem Collection (*see* Collection) was merely a smoke screen for Paul's personal gain (2 Cor 8:18-21; 12:16-18).

*1.3. Validity.* When his authority is challenged, Paul points to the validating marks that he shares with other apostles. Witness to Christ's resurrection* is a primary credential (1 Cor 9:1; cf. 1 Cor 15:7; Gal 1:15-16). While Paul refers to financial* support as a "right" of the apostle (1 Cor 9:3-12; 2 Thess 3:9), it is one he himself waived so as not to hinder receptivity to the gospel (1 Cor 9:12; *see* Tentmaking) and to undercut rival apostles who preached for financial gain (1 Cor 9:15-18; 2 Cor 2:17; 11:7-12). Paul also referred to the "signs of the apostles" that were evident in the church planting process (2 Cor 12:12). It is difficult to know whether "signs, wonders and miracles" in 2 Corinthians 12:12 defines the content of these apostolic signs or what accompanied them, or even whether they were terms used by his opponents.* The problem is the repetition of "signs" (*sēmeia*) in the dative plural, which commonly defines instrument or accompaniment ("with signs, wonders and miracles"). Reference, however, to the "working" (*kateirgasthē*) of signs (by God: an instance of the divine passive voice of the verb), along with the frequency of this type of anacoluthon in Paul (Blass-Debrunner-Funk §467), tips the balance in favor of the former. That his preaching was not merely one of word but of "power and the Spirit" is a recurring Pauline thought (Rom 15:19; 1 Cor 2:4; Gal 3:5; 1 Thess 1:5; *see* Holy Spirit; Power).

While his opponents seek to legitimize their authority through such formalities as commendatory letters and financial support, Paul turns rather to the birth and continuing existence of a church (1 Cor 9:2; 2 Cor 3:1-2), faithful witness* to the gospel (e.g., 1 Cor 4:1-2; 2 Cor 1:18; 4:5) and endurance of missionary hardships (1 Cor 4:9-13; 2 Cor 4:7-12; 6:4-10; 11:23—12:10; *see* Afflictions, Hardships, Trials) as the chief evidences of his own apostolic authority. Lack of faithful witness in particular marks one as a "false" apostle (2 Cor 11:13-15) and "accursed" (Gal 1:8; *see* Curse).

There is some question as to the intent of Paul's second visit to Jerusalem* (Gal 2:1-10). The language of Galatians 2:2 appears to indicate that his purpose was the validation of his gospel: "I placed before those of repute the gospel that I preach among the

Gentiles lest I am running or have run in vain." This would seem to imply that Paul viewed his authority as dependent on the approval of "the Twelve." Yet elsewhere in Galatians Paul strenuously denies that his apostleship or his gospel were dependent in any way on human recognition or validation (Gal 1:1, 11-12, 15-17). Much hinges on one's interpretation of "to run in vain." That Paul did not look on the Twelve as having an authority superior to his own is clear from his indifference to their status ("their reputation means nothing to me," Gal 2:6). He, therefore, cannot have in mind the need for apostolic correction or validation. This is confirmed by *eis kenon* (*see* Futility), which elsewhere in Paul functions as an adverb of result meaning "without effect" (2 Cor 6:1; Phil 2:16; 1 Thess 3:5). Paul's meeting with "those of repute" in the Jerusalem church suggests rather that he was concerned to know whether the Judaizers' "other gospel" (Gal 1:8) has the support of the Jerusalem apostolate. Paul's mission to the Gentiles and, in the long term, Christianity itself would be compromised and so "without effect" if there were a failure of the Jewish and Gentile wings of the church to agree on the nature of the gospel.*

*1.4. Limitations.* The scope of apostolic authority was not an unlimited one. Paul sets out definite boundaries for the exercise of his own authority. These boundaries, which were agreed on by Paul and the "pillars" of the Jerusalem Church, amounted to an ethnic division of labor. Paul was to preach to the Gentiles, and James, Peter and John were to go to the Jews (Gal 2:9)—a division that accords with Paul's own commissioning as "apostle to the Gentiles" (Rom 1:5; 15:15-16; Gal 1:16; 1 Tim 2:7; *see* Mission). Even so, these boundaries were not absolute since Paul's own evangelistic strategy involved an initial outreach in the synagogue (Acts 13:5, 14; 14:1; 17:2, 10; 18:4; 19:8).

Paul also refers to "the limit of the field that God allotted" (2 Cor 10:13). This "limit" was violated in Corinth by interlopers who "overreached" themselves and tried to displace Paul from his rightful mission field (2 Cor 10:12-15). What this "allotted field" amounted to is clearly spelled out in Romans 15:18-20, where Paul speaks of preaching the gospel in uncharted areas so as not to build on another apostle's foundation. Corinth became Paul's "field" not because they were Gentiles per se but because he was the "first to reach" them (*ephthasamen*, 2 Cor 10:14).

In 2 Corinthians 10:15-16 the concept of territorial fields is introduced. Paul appears to have included within his "field" those churches, like Laodicea and Colossae, that his converts—and not he personally—established (*see* Colossians). It was Paul's practice to focus his evangelistic efforts on the large urban centers with a view to enlarging his sphere of authority (*kata ton kanona*, 2 Cor 10:15) to surrounding areas (*ta hyperekeina*, 2 Cor 10:16) through the evangelistic efforts of his converts (e.g., Acts 19:1-7; cf. Col 1:3-8; *see* Coworkers). The limiting of Paul's authority to Gentiles that he or his converts were the first to reach may indeed explain why Paul's letters are directed almost exclusively to the Gentile constituency of churches with an explicit Jew-Gentile mix (1-2 Cor, Gal, Eph, Phil, 1-2 Thess). Furthermore, if it is true that no apostle was directly responsible for the founding of the church at Rome,* this may also account for Paul's freedom to address the Roman church in an authoritative fashion (*see* Romans).

*1.5. Exercise.* Although Paul views his authority as a warrant that he possessed by virtue of his apostolic commission (Philem 8) and expected his churches to accept without debate (1 Cor 14:37; cf. 1 Cor 7:17), it was nonetheless a right that he usually waived in favor of reasoned argumentation. His relationship to his churches is articulated, with rare exception, in terms of request rather than command. *Parakaleō*, an appeal by one who has the authority to command but the tact not to (Rom 12:1; 16:17; 1 Cor 1:10; 4:13, 16; 16:15; 2 Cor 2:8; 6:1; 10:1; 12:18; Eph 4:1; Phil 4:2; 1 Thess 4:1, 10; 5:14; 1 Tim 2:1; Philem 9, 10), and *erōtaō*, a request made between equals (Phil 4:3; 1 Thess 4:1; 5:12; 2 Thess 2:1), is Paul's usual approach to instructing his churches. This approach arose out of his concept of authority as that which aims "to build up rather than tear down" (2 Cor 10:8). Pastoral ministry is conceived in nurturing versus authoritarian terms (2 Cor 1:24, "not that we lord it over your faith but work with you"). The primary images employed are ones that evoke the intimacy of familial relationships—"gentle as a nursing mother" (1 Thess 2:7; cf. Gal 4:19) and "as a father who exhorts and encourages his children" (1 Thess 2:11-12; cf. 1 Cor 4:15; 2 Cor 12:14; *see* Pastor).

Even so, Paul did on occasion use his authority as a kind of "stick" to warn his "children" what would happen if his requests were not heeded. Paul warns the arrogant at Corinth that he would, if need be, use a "rod" (1 Cor 4:21) and "deal harshly with them" on his return "in accordance with the authority given" to him "by the Lord" (2 Cor 13:10; cf. 2 Cor 10:8; *see* Discipline).

With churches that had moved beyond the request stage, Paul did not hesitate to exercise his authority. Paul commands the Thessalonian* church "in the name of the Lord Jesus Christ" to disassociate themselves from those in their community that refused to work (2 Thess 3:6-15). He similarly orders the Corinthian church, "as one who has already passed judgment," to "hand over to Satan*" a member who was sexually involved with his stepmother (1 Cor 5:3-5; see Marriage, Divorce, Adultery, Incest; Sexuality). In the so-called painful letter, intermediate to canonical 1 and 2 Corinthians (see Corinthians), Paul commands the church to discipline the individual who had publicly challenged his authority (2 Cor 2:5-11; 7:9-13). Yet the conjoining of command and request in 2 Thessalonians 3:12 shows Paul's reluctance to use a hard-line approach ("we command and ask in the Lord Jesus Christ that such people work quietly and earn their own living").

## 2. Of Other Apostles.

### 2.1. Authority and Tradition.
Apostolic authority was not innovative authority. It resided in a common core of traditions* (see Creed) about the life and teaching of Jesus, carefully preserved and transmitted by the early church. The apostolic task was that of faithful transmission (paredōka) of these traditions (tas paradoseis) to new congregations, rather than origination (1 Cor 11:2; 2 Thess 2:15). The transmission process was both oral and written (2 Thess 2:15).

Paul's letters give us glimpses of the content of these traditions, which included details of the death, resurrection* and appearances of Christ (1 Cor 15:3-8), Jesus' institution of the new covenant* (1 Cor 11:23-26; see Lord's Supper), the teachings of Jesus concerning the end time (2 Thess 2:1-15; see Eschatology) and instruction about ethical conduct (Rom 6:15-18; Phil 4:8-9; see Ethics) and communal responsibilities (2 Thess 3:6-15; cf. 1 Cor 11:2-34).

Paul frequently reminds his converts that he had faithfully transmitted the tradition (1 Cor 15:3; cf. 1 Cor 11:2, 23) and is concerned that his converts find those who, in turn, could faithfully pass it on (2 Tim 2:2). Some churches are praised for "holding to the traditions" just as Paul passed them on to them (1 Cor 11:2; cf. Rom 6:17); others were commanded to do so (Phil 4:9; 2 Thess 2:15; 3:6). The role of transmitter versus innovator explains Paul's care to distinguish between when he is drawing on tradition (1 Cor 7:10; 9:14; 11:23-26; 1 Thess 4:15) and when he is not (e.g., "judge for yourselves," 1 Cor 10:15; cf. 1 Cor 7:12, 25, 40; 2 Cor 8:10). Because of the pains taken by the apostles in transmitting the teaching of Jesus, Paul can say that he passed on to his churches what he "received from the Lord" (1 Cor 11:23; see Jesus, Sayings of).

It is puzzling then to understand what Paul means in Romans 2:16 and 16:25 (cf. 2 Tim 2:8) by "my gospel." Given his role as transmitter, in what sense could he speak of the gospel as uniquely his? It is not the content that is original, for he defines his gospel as "Jesus Christ, raised from the dead, descended from David" (2 Tim 2:8). Moreover, the ease with which he can shift between "my gospel," "the gospel" (e.g., Rom 1:1, 9, 16) and "our gospel" (e.g., 2 Cor 4:3) suggests something other than a peculiarly Pauline form of the gospel. Perhaps the key is to be found in Galatians 1:12, where Paul distinguishes between first receiving the gospel by human transmission and, as in his case, by special revelation (see Conversion and Call).

### 2.2. Authority and Gentile Instruction.
As Paul was not an innovator of the kerygma (see Preaching, Kerygma), neither was he an originator of what he preached to the Gentiles. While it is common to think of Paul as departing from the Jerusalem apostolate in preaching to and instructing those for whom he was given a special commission, Paul's own statements indicate otherwise. 1 Thessalonians 1:9-10 represents a summary of Paul's preaching at Thessalonica. The wording (alēthinō, "true"; anamenein, "await"; tōn ouranōn, "the heaven[s]") and phraseology ("to serve God," "to wait for his Son"), uncharacteristic of Paul, suggest that Paul was using the vocabulary of Jewish-Christian missionary preaching rather than introducing something that was distinctively his own. This is also suggested by the language of "turning to God from idols to serve the living and true God" (1 Thess 1:9), which is a typical description of what Gentile conversion to Christianity meant (cf. Paul's Areopagus speech in Acts 17:16-31; see Athens).

A similar conclusion can be drawn from Paul's ethical instruction in 1 Thessalonians 4:1-12, which focuses on what Jews perceived to be the three primary Gentile abuses: sexual immorality (see Sexuality), lack of love* and idleness. The fact that Paul in 1 Thessalonians 4:1 uses technical phraseology for the transmission of tradition to describe this instruction (parelabete), indicates once again that he was not an innovator but merely a transmitter of what was commonly considered to be appropriate and necessary instruction for Gentile converts. Comparison with the conditions put forward at the Jerusalem Council to ease the tension of Jew-Gentile fellowship suggests this as well (Acts 15:19-21).

### 2.3. Authority and Collegiality.
Apostolic authority is grounded ultimately in the call to preach the gospel; and while divisions of labor and allotted "fields" existed, the task of evangelism (see Mission) is viewed by Paul as a cooperative effort and likened to that of farming, where, as "colaborers" (1 Cor 3:9), one "plants" and another "waters" as the Lord assigns (1 Cor 3:5-6).

The evangelistic task, however, was not seen by all as a cooperative one. Paul likens his founding of the church* at Corinth to that of a master craftsman who, having laid the foundation of the building, finds those who have been contracted to build the superstructure departing from the master plan and even tinkering with the foundation (1 Cor 3:10-12). For such, Paul warns, a day of judgment* awaits, when the quality of one's work will be brought to light (1 Cor 3:13-15; see Rewards). It is unclear whether Paul has in mind the Judaizing efforts of the Pharisaic wing of the Jerusalem church (1 Cor 7:18) or perhaps Peter* himself (1 Cor 3:21; cf. 1 Cor 9:5). If Peter is in view, then Corinth is a violation of the division of labor agreed upon by Paul and "the pillars" (Gal 2:9), as well as an encroachment on a "field" that the Lord had assigned to Paul (1 Cor 3:10).

It is not that Paul begrudged sharing the apostolic task. He clearly welcomed other apostles as colaborers. The distinction lies in his understanding of authority. For while Paul could conceive of colaboring, he could not admit the idea of coauthority. Authority, for Paul, resided in the father-child relationship that was established through the church planting process. It was because Paul reached Corinth first with the gospel that he could address them as "beloved children" (1 Cor 4:14). It was this "begetting through the gospel" that gave Paul the right to ask his converts to "imitate" him (1 Cor 4:16; see Imitation) and explains the care Paul took, in turn, to respect James's* allotted field in Jerusalem (Acts 21:20-26).

The Corinthian situation demonstrates that apostolic authority did not exempt one from judgment. "We must all appear before the judgment seat of Christ," Paul states, "that each may receive in accordance with the good and bad done through the body" (2 Cor 5:10; cf. 1 Cor 3:13-15). Here apostolic status makes no difference, for God does not judge on the basis of position in the church (Gal 2:6). This is clear from Paul's confrontation of Peter at Antioch* "because he was in the wrong" when he withdrew from table fellowship with the Gentiles (Gal 2:11-14).

### 3. Of Opponents.

Given Paul's view of the apostolic task as one of "colaboring," it is of some consequence to find him referring to "false apostles" (2 Cor 11:13-15; see Apostle; Opponents). Wrong motivation per se did not render someone an opponent in Paul's eyes. As long as "Christ is preached" he could "rejoice" (Phil 1:18; cf. 1 Cor 15:11). Even if some preached Christ "out of envy and rivalry" or "with the intent to stir up trouble" for Paul, this mattered little to him (Phil 1:15-18).

Their "falseness" stemmed rather from an erroneous concept of apostleship and hence a wrong exercise of authority. It was specifically those who claimed the credit for missionary work that was not their own (2 Cor 10:15-16), who preached a different gospel (2 Cor 11:4; Gal 1:8) and who encroached on another's field (2 Cor 10:12-14) that Paul labels as "false." Their aim was not that of "colaborer" but of "supplanter," justifying their actions through the claim of better credentials. They brought and solicited letters of recommendation (2 Cor 3:1-3), claimed a superior heritage to Paul's (2 Cor 11:21-22) and boasted of greater spirituality* ("visions* and revelations," 2 Cor 12:1; "signs, wonders and miracles,"* 2 Cor 12:12). Their intent was not to preach the gospel but "to lead astray from a sincere and pure devotion to Christ" (2 Cor 11:3; cf. Gal 1:8). Financial gain (2 Cor 2:17; 11:20) and the desire for dominance ("enslave," "slap you in the face," 2 Cor 11:20) was their motivation. As such they masqueraded as servants* of righteousness* when in fact they were servants of Satan* (2 Cor 11:14-15), not servants of Christ (2 Cor 11:13).

Some have thought that Paul was being unduly harsh in his judgments of these rival apostles. Yet where the gospel and commitment to Christ was at stake, as at Galatia and Corinth, Paul's remarks are in line with judgments made against false prophets in the OT, whose intent was to lead Israel astray from her commitment to Yahweh and the covenant (e.g., Deut 18:20; cf. Jer 28:15-18). The label "opponent" was not given to those who challenged Paul personally but to those who undermined his role as a preacher (see Preaching) and teacher (see Teaching) of the gospel in a particular community. If in the final analysis Christ and his church are served, then personal rivalries are of little account.

### 4. In the Church.

Authority is not the sole prerogative of the apostle. Paul recognizes both individual and corporate forms of authority in the church. He calls on the Thessalonians to acknowledge "those who stand before them (proistamenous) in the Lord" (1 Thess 5:12). This is an authority that resides in their work rather than in their personal status or position. As such, they are to be held "in high esteem" (1 Thess 5:13). A sphere of authority exists as well for women within the Christian community. In distinction from Greco-Roman and Jewish society, Paul emphasizes mutuality in the marriage* relationship, where both husband and wife relinquish "rights" to one another (1 Cor 7:3-4). As a symbol of their authority, women are called upon to cover their heads when praying and prophesying

(1 Cor 11:10). Considerable scholarly effort has been expended on understanding what Paul means in 1 Corinthians 11:10 by "the woman ought to have *exousia* on her head." There is much to commend M. Hooker's interpretation that the woman's head covering was a sign of her God-given "warrant" to exercise the functions of praying (*see* Prayer) and prophesying (*see* Prophecy) specified in 1 Corinthians 11:5. Alternatively, her head covering might represent her role as "helpmate" within the creation order (1 Cor 11:9), while praying and prophesying express her function in the redemptive order (*see* Head; Man and Woman).

The church as well possesses authority by virtue of its being the "body" of which Christ is the "head" (Eph 1:22; 4:15-16; 5:23; Col 1:18; 2:19; *see* Body of Christ). The responsible exercise of corporate authority was something that Paul had great difficulty inculcating in his churches. It is the corporate responsibility of the church to "test" (1 Thess 5:19-21) and "weigh prophecies" (1 Cor 14:29), to warn the idle, encourage the timid and support the weak (1 Thess 5:14), to punish wrongdoing (2 Cor 2:6), to excommunicate in the case of persistent sin* (1 Cor 5:2, 10-13; 2 Thess 3:6, 14-15) and to reinstate the repentant (2 Cor 2:7-8). This authority derives from "the power of the Lord Jesus" that is present with believers "gathered in his name" (1 Cor 5:4; cf. Mt 18:20) and from the possession of the "mind of Christ" (1 Cor 2:16). The enforcing and waiving of penalties for sin was something that the Gentile churches had difficulty administering. On more than one occasion Paul had to rebuke a church for not exercising its authority (1 Cor 5:2; 6:1; 2 Thess 3:6; *see* Discipline).

Part of the difficulty for the Gentile churches was in understanding the relationship between corporate authority and individual freedom. While Paul is adamant in his insistence that "for freedom Christ has set us free" (Gal 5:1; 1 Cor 10:25, 29; cf. *exestin*, 1 Cor 6:12; 10:23), he nonetheless warns against its indiscriminate use (e.g., Rom 6:1-23). He is especially concerned that Christian freedom not be taken as a warrant to flout current social conventions (1 Cor 11:6, 13), to blur the distinctions between right and wrong for a "weaker" brother or sister (1 Cor 8:11; *see* Strong and Weak), to exercise the charismata (*see* Gifts of the Spir-

it) without due consideration for good order in worship* (1 Cor 14:33, 40), and the interests of the unbeliever (1 Cor 14:23-25), or to jeopardize Christian witness in the surrounding community (1 Cor 5:1).

*See also* APOSTLE; CHURCH ORDER AND GOVERNMENT; CIVIL AUTHORITY; CONVERSION AND CALL OF PAUL; DISCIPLINE; FREEDOM; OPPONENTS OF PAUL; PASTOR, PAUL AS; POWER; TRADITION.

BIBLIOGRAPHY. R. J. Banks, "Freedom and Authority in Education. II: Paul's View of Authority," *Journal of Christian Education* 56 (1976) 17-24; C. K. Barrett, "Paul's Opponents in 2 Corinthians," in *Essays On Paul* (Philadelphia: Westminster, 1982) 60-86; E. Best, "Paul's Apostolic Authority—?," *JSNT* 27 (1986) 3-25; H. von Campenhausen, *Ecclesiastical Authority and Spiritual Power in the Church of the First Three Centuries* (Stanford: Stanford University, 1969); J. D. G. Dunn, "The Relationship Between Paul and Jerusalem According to Galatians 1 and 2," *NTS* 28 (1982) 461-78 [= idem, *Jesus, Paul and the Law* (Louisville: Westminster/John Knox, 1990) 108-26]; E. E. Ellis, "Paul and His Opponents: Trends in Research," in *Christianity, Judaism and Other Greco-Roman Cults: Studies for Morton Smith*, part 1, ed. J. Neusner (Leiden: E. J. Brill, 1975); D. M. Hay, "Paul's Indifference to Authority," *JBL* 88 (1969) 36-44; B. Holmberg, *Paul and Power: The Structure of Authority in the Primitive Church as Reflected in the Pauline Epistles* (Philadelphia: Fortress, 1983); M. D. Hooker, "Authority on Her Head: An Examination of 1 Cor. XI.10," *NTS* 10 (1963-64) 410-16; R. P. Martin, "Authority in the Light of the Apostolate, Tradition and the Canon," *EvQ* 40 (1968) 66-82; K. J. Neumann, "Paul's Use of Authority and Persuasion in the Corinthian Letters," *Consensus* 5 (1979) 15-23; J. H. Schütz, *Paul and the Anatomy of Apostolic Authority* (Cambridge: University Press, 1975); R. Schnackenburg, "Apostles Before and During Paul's Time," in *Apostolic History and the Gospel*, ed. W. W. Gasque and R. P. Martin (Grand Rapids: Eerdmans, 1970) 287-303.

L. L. Belleville

## AUTOBIOGRAPHY, PAULINE. *See* CONVERSION AND CALL OF PAUL; CROSS, THEOLOGY OF THE; GALATIANS, LETTER TO THE; JEW, PAUL THE; OPPONENTS OF PAUL; RHETORICAL CRITICISM.

# B

## BAPTISM

From references to baptism in Paul's letters it is apparent that he assumes that all believers in Christ* have been baptized. A single example will suffice to show this. Paul's exposition of baptism in Romans 6 commences by citing an objection to his teaching of justification* by faith* apart from the works* of the Law*: "On that basis," says the objector, "why not sin more to give more room for God's* justifying grace*?" Paul answers by appealing to the meaning of baptism: "How can people like us who died to sin* go on living in it?" He continues, "All of us who were baptized to Christ Jesus were baptized to his death," and he concludes, "so you also must consider yourselves dead to sin and alive to God in Christ Jesus." Self-evidently, "people like us who died to sin," "all of us who were baptized to Christ Jesus," and "you also must consider yourselves dead to sin," include Paul and *all* his readers, otherwise his argument against the allegedly antinomian effect of the doctrine of justification by faith falls to the ground. Similar examples of the assumption that all Christians are baptized are to be seen in Galatians 3:26-28, Colossians 2:12, 1 Corinthians 12:13 and the exposition of baptismal ethics* in Colossians 2:20—3:15.

Since Paul himself had received baptism, and had reason to believe that all other Christians were baptized, it is clear that the rite existed prior to his conversion.* (The conversion of Paul is commonly dated four years after the death of Jesus.) Since baptism existed prior to Paul's conversion, it is reasonable to view it as coexistent with the inception of the church. That conclusion concurs with the NT evidence as to the baptizing ministry of John the Baptist (Mk 1:4-8), of Jesus (see Jn 3:25-26, 4:1-3), and of the apostles from the day of Pentecost on (Acts 2:37-41), and the missionary commission of the risen Lord, recorded in Matthew 28:19.

1. The Language and Actions of Baptism
2. Baptism and Christ
3. Baptism and the Spirit
4. Baptism and the Church
5. Baptism and Christian Ethics
6. Baptism and the Kingdom of God

### 1. The Language and Actions of Baptism.

*1.1. Baptism "in the Name of Jesus."* In Paul's letters, as in the book of Acts, baptism is typically represented as baptism "in the name" of Jesus. This is reflected in a significant manner in Paul's handling of the divisions in the Corinthian* church. He cites its members as saying, "I belong to Paul," "I belong to Apollos," "I belong to Cephas (= Peter*)," "I belong to Christ" (1 Cor 1:12). Paul, with some indignation, asks, "Has Christ been apportioned to any single group among you? Was Paul crucified for you? Or were you baptized in the name of Paul?" This final question echoes the language of baptism in the name of Jesus; its use in the context suggests that its normal usage is to make a person a follower of Jesus, even to belong to him, and somehow to be involved in his crucifixion* and enjoy a special relation to him.

There has been much discussion as to whether the phrase "in the name of" reflects a Greek or Hebrew (and Aramaic) idiom, for it is found in all three languages. W. Heitmüller showed that while the expression *eis to onoma* ("in the name") did not appear in Greek classical literature, it was very common in everyday documents with the meaning of "to the account of," alike in banking and commercial sales. He cited with approval A. Deissmann's definition of "in the name of [someone]" as denoting "the setting up of the relation of belonging." Heitmüller added, "Our word 'for,' generally speaking, would rightly reproduce the meaning" (Heitmüller, 105). In using this expression, the name of the person to whom the possession is "made over" naturally follows. According to Heitmüller, then, baptism in the name of Jesus signifies the setting up of the relation of belonging to Jesus.

This explanation, however, is denied by some in favor of a Hebrew origin of the phrase. In Jewish literature, including the OT, an equivalent of the Greek expression is frequently met, namely *lᵉšēm* (*lᵉ* = "to," *šēm* = "name"). The term has a very elastic sense. Basically it means "with respect to," but the context determines it precise connotation. P. Billerbeck gave three illustrations of its use in his discussion of baptism in Matthew 28:19. (1) When pagans were bought by Jews as slaves they were baptized "in the name of slavery," that is, with a view to becoming slaves; when they were set free they were baptized "in the name of freedom," that is, for freedom. (2) An offering is slaughtered in the name of five things: in the name of the offering (i.e., with respect to its intention, whether it be a burnt or sin or peace offering, etc); in the name of God (for his sake and glory); in the name of the altar fires (that they be properly kindled); in the name of the sweet savor (for the delight it gives to God); and in the name of the good pleasure of God (in obedience to his will). (3) An Israelite can circumcise a Samaritan, but not a Samaritan an Israelite, because the Samaritans circumcise "in the name of Mount Gerizim," that is, with the obligation of worshiping the God of the Samaritans who is worshiped there (Str-B, 1054-55). In light of such evidence Billerbeck affirmed: "Baptism grounds a relation between the triune God and the baptized, which the latter has to affirm and express through his confession to the God in whose name he is baptized."

It is evident, therefore, that the Greek and Hebrew usages of "in the name" are remarkably similar in meaning, especially when applied to baptism, and they would be similarly interpreted in Greek-speaking and Hebrew-speaking circles, despite the greater elasticity of meaning in the Hebrew language.

Sometimes one finds in Paul a shorter expression, baptism *eis Christon*, which can be rendered either as "into Christ" or "to Christ," and is possibly a conscious abbreviation of the full phrase "in the name of Christ" (see Rom 6:3-4; Gal 3:27). Significantly, both the Greek preposition *eis* and the Hebrew prefix *l*e can have the meaning "with respect to," and also a final sense or dative of interest, "for" (BAGD, 229; BDB, 514-15). In such cases the context will help to determine its intention.

An important element of interpretation arises in connection with this formula. We have noted Deissmann's affirmation that "in the name" "sets up a relation of belonging." So also Billerbeck affirmed that baptism in the name of the triune God* "grounds a relation between God and the baptized." Who is viewed as the prime mover in establishing this relationship? In the application to baptism both God and humans are involved. The baptizer invokes the name of Jesus over the baptized, and the baptized calls on the name of the Lord* as he or she is baptized (for the former cf. Jas 2:7; for the latter cf. Acts 22:16). It

is likely that Paul has both aspects in mind in Romans 10:9. It is universally acknowledged that "Jesus is Lord" is the primitive confession of faith in Christ that was made at baptism; from it all later creeds of the church were developed (*see* Creed; Worship). But the salvation granted on confession of faith is in virtue of God's once-for-all action in Christ's death* and resurrection,* and his action in the lives of those who believe. The priority of God's action applies in the reconciliation of the world in Christ and in the reconciliation of each believer who accepts it (2 Cor 5:18-21). In baptism, therefore, the Lord appropriates the baptized for his own and the baptized owns Jesus as Lord and submits to his lordship.

*1.2. Symbolism and Reality.* It is important to observe that Paul never refers to baptism as a purely external rite, whether as a "mere symbol" for confessing faith in Christ, or as a rite that effects what it symbolizes. Admittedly for Paul, as for the whole early church, the symbolic nature of baptism is plain. Most obviously it symbolizes cleansing from sin* (cf. Acts 22:16). And this meaning seems clear in a pericope that is best understood as reflecting early Christian baptismal practice and its significance for the congregation (Eph 5:25-27: see commentaries, esp. Lincoln *ad loc.*). The actions of stripping off clothes for baptism and putting on clothes after baptism affords a symbol of "putting off" the old life without Christ and "putting on" the new life in Christ, and even putting on Christ himself (Gal 3:27; Col 3:9, 12). The sinking of the baptized beneath water and rising out of it vividly symbolizes sharing in Christ's burial and resurrection (Rom 6:3-4; the baptismal actions lie in the background of Eph 5:14, often regarded by interpreters as a baptismal chant addressed to the newly initiated believers: see commentaries). None of these spiritual realities, however, can be said to happen by the mere performance of appropriate symbolic actions; they depend on God's once-for-all acts in Christ, according to the gospel, and on God's action in believers as they respond to God's call in the gospel. For that reason Paul's use of baptismal language (in 1 Cor 10:1-12) speaks to a situation where the readers imagined that sacramental action carried its effective and operative power irrespective of moral choices. Paul insists, on the contrary, that the OT "sacraments" led to judgment on an idolatrous and immoral generation.

With these considerations in mind we turn to examine Paul's statements in his letters relating to the significance of baptism.

## 2. Baptism and Christ.

Baptism "in the name of Jesus" is distinguished from

all other religious ablutions by virtue of its relation to Christ. Believers are united with Christ in his redemptive actions of death and resurrection, and so pass from the life of the old age to the life of the new (*see* Dying and Rising).

*2.1. Putting on Christ.* The relationship between baptism and union with Christ is indicated not only through its administration "in the name of Jesus" but also in Paul's foundational baptismal utterance, Galatians 3:26-27: "You are all children of God in Christ Jesus through faith, for all you who were baptized to Christ clothed yourself with Christ" (*see* Adoption, Sonship). The statement is shaped by the discussion in the context as to who the children of Abraham* are, for the promise of God that he should inherit the world to come was made to him and his descendants (Rom 4:16). To Jews the answer was plain: they are Abraham's descendants, and any who would be included with them must receive the sign of the covenant* (circumcision*) and live in obedience to the Law of Moses. Paul, on the contrary, maintained that the "offspring" of Abraham, for whom the promise was intended, is *Christ* and *all in union with him*. Hence the pertinence of Galatians 3:26: "In Christ Jesus you are all God's children through faith." They are children not merely of Abraham, but of God. For they are "in Christ,"* the unique Son* of God. This has come about "through faith" (Gal 3:26), "for all you who were baptized to Christ clothed yourself with Christ" (Gal 3:27).

We have already noticed the symbolism used in this passage. The imagery of stripping off clothes and putting on fresh ones to indicate a transformation of character is frequent in the OT (cf., e.g., Is 52:1; 61:10; Zech 1:1-5). The symbolism was peculiarly apt for Christian baptism in apostolic times, since it normally took place by immersion, and apparently often in nakedness. (That was insisted on in Jewish proselyte baptism; when women were baptized the Rabbis turned their backs on them while the women entered the water to their neck, and the latter were questioned and gave answers; they had to have their hair loose, to ensure that no part of their bodies was untouched by water. This feature reappears in Hippolytus, *The Apostolic Tradition*, c. A.D. 215. Cyril of Jerusalem later remarked on the fitness of being baptized in nakedness, as Jesus died on the cross in such a state.)

More important than the symbolism is the reality expressed through it: the baptized "took off" their old life and "put on" Christ, thereby becoming one with him, and so qualified to participate in life in the kingdom* of God (*see* New Nature and Old Nature). The two statements in Galatians 3:26 and 27 are comple-

mentary: verse 26 declares that believers are God's children "through faith," and verse 27 associates entry into God's family upon union with Christ, and Christ sharing his sonship with the baptized. It is an example of Paul's linking faith and baptism in such a way that the theological understanding of faith that turns to the Lord for salvation, and of baptism wherein faith is declared, is one and the same.

*2.2. Union with Christ in Death and Resurrection.* Because baptism signifies union with Christ, Paul saw it as extending to *union with Christ in his redemptive actions*, for the Christ who saves is forever the once crucified and now risen redeemer. Such is the message in Paul's exposition of baptism in Romans 6:1-11 (for a survey of interpretation, see Wedderburn).

First, it should be observed that in this passage Paul was not primarily giving a theological explanation of the nature of baptism, but expounding its meaning for life. He is concerned to rebut the charge that the doctrine of justification by faith logically encourages sin. Accordingly he urged that "people like us who died to sin" could not still live in sin, for "death to sin" is the meaning of our baptism. When we were "baptized to Christ Jesus" we were "baptized to his death" (Rom 6:3, echoing Gal 3:27). That is the consequence of becoming one with the Lord who died and rose for the conquest of sin and death. Moreover, "we were buried with him by baptism to death." Note that Paul did not write, "we were buried *like* him," but "buried *with* him." That is, we were laid with him in his grave in Jerusalem! So, too, the death he died on the cross was our death also. This entails a different way of looking at Christ's death for the world from what may be expected.

When we read in Romans 5 that Christ died for us while we were still sinners, we think of Christ as our *substitute*. Here, however, Paul speaks of Christ as our *representative*. If he died on the cross as our representative, and that death was accepted, then it was accepted as *our* death, so that when he died, we died (*see* Death of Christ). He was an effective representative! Taking that a step further, united with him in his death for sin, we rise in him to live the resurrection life. Through the faith expressed in baptism, what was done outside of us (*extra nos*) becomes effective faith within us. In Christ we are the reconciled children of God.

But a further element is involved in this exposition of baptism. The last two sentences echo Paul's statement of the gospel in 2 Corinthians 5:14-15: "We are convinced that one died for all, therefore all died. And he died for all that those who live might live . . . for him who died and was raised for them." "Those who live" are those who, having learned that Christ died as their representative, thankfully trust him, confess their faith in baptism, share his resurrection life and in gratitude have begun life in Christ to his glory.*

This aspect of baptism—the end of life without God and the beginning of life with God—is explicitly stated in Colossians 2:11-12. Like the Galatians passage, this rebuts an attempt to persuade Christians to submit to circumcision,* but adopts a different approach by emphasizing the needlessness of the rite of Israel, for in Christ they have suffered a more drastic circumcision: "In him (Christ) you were circumcised with a spiritual circumcision, by putting off the body* of flesh* in the circumcision of Christ." Apparently, Paul depicts Christ's death as a circumcision; cutting off the foreskin of the male sex organ is replaced by the tearing of Christ's whole fleshly body, hence his death. In him that happened to us; it happened in baptism understood as our turning-to-God-in-faith. "When you were buried with him in baptism, you were also raised with him." This is not so much an advance on Paul's teaching in Romans 6 as a clarification of what he wrote there. The person who hears the gospel, heeds it, believes it and confesses it in baptism, ends the old life apart from God and begins life in the risen Christ. Colossians 2:12 makes the point: "buried with him in baptism . . . you were *raised with him through faith in the power of God who raised him from the dead.*" Any effectiveness in baptism is due to the power of God operative "through faith." Clearly Paul is talking about conversion-baptism, a baptism that embodies both the gospel and the convert's response to it. Some find Paul's use of "sealing" (in 2 Cor 1:21) to include the latter element, as God certifies his acceptance of the human response.

Yet a third feature is inherent in baptism as Paul expounds it in Romans 6. The baptism which sets forth believers' identification with Christ in his death and resurrection, and the end of life apart from God for life in Christ, calls for renunciation of life unfit for the new age. Roman 6:4, when stripped of its parenthetical clause in the middle, reads, "We were buried with him by baptism for death . . . *that we might walk in newness of life.*" Paul thereby gives the reason the Christian can never willfully "sin that grace may abound;" in Christ's death believers died to sin, in Christ's resurrection they rose, henceforth to live for God who redeemed them in Christ (so 2 Cor 5:15).

### 3. Baptism and the Spirit.

A major consequence of the rise of modern Pentecostalism and the charismatic movement is to provoke the question of the relation of the rite of baptism to baptism in the Spirit (*see* Holy Spirit). Most members of those groups view the baptism of the Spirit as radically distinct from baptism in water, and it is the former on which emphasis is laid. The viewpoint is characteristic of the two groups, though for different reasons (see Dunn for discussion in detail); the question is whether Paul made such a distinction.

W. H. Griffith Thomas voiced a doubt commonly heard today: "How can that which is physical effect that which is spiritual?" (Griffith Thomas, 379). From that standpoint some interpreters hold that passages such as Romans 6:1-11; Galatians 3:26-27; Colossians 2:11-12; Ephesians 5:26; and Titus 3:5-7, which all conjoin baptism with "spiritual effects," refer to Spirit baptism, not water baptism, thereby eliminating most of Paul's references to baptism. But such questioning of the relationship between the physical and the spiritual logically draws into question the Pauline emphasis on the incarnation (e.g., Rom 8:3) and the physical death of Christ which results in "the redemption of the body" (Rom 8:23). The corollary of this argument for baptism as solely the work of the Spirit without baptism in water is to make Pauline Christians too ethereal and unrelated to early Christian practices (cf., e.g., Acts 18:8; 1 Pet 3:21).

Galatians 3:26-27 associates baptism with union with Christ. Now Paul makes it clear that people can be "in Christ" only through the Holy Spirit. That is plainly stated in Romans 8:9-11, and is assumed in 2 Corinthians 3:17-19. Clearly Paul associates baptism and unity with Christ and all that follows from it on the basis that for him baptism in water and baptism in the Spirit are ideally one, just as conversion and baptism are part of one process. Accordingly, the sole reference in Paul's letters to baptism in the Spirit (1 Cor 12:13) must surely relate to baptism in the sense that Paul elsewhere uses it: "In one Spirit we were all baptized to one body," and in that body all racial and social barriers are done away. Precisely that is stated in Galatians 3:26-28 in relation to baptism.

The latter half of 1 Corinthians 12:13 is generally rendered, "We were all made to drink of one Spirit" (see Cuming for a reference to baptism in this text). In all likelihood that has in mind the *outpouring* of the Spirit in the last times (Is 32:15; Joel 2:28-29) and could be paraphrased, "we all received *the floodtide of the Spirit*" (i.e., we were saturated with the Spirit). That this experience belongs to the beginning of the Christian life hints at an important consideration: conversion is not only the result of human decision, but is enabled by the Spirit. He is not only the fruit of conversion-baptism; he is the real baptizer, the agent who makes baptism what it was meant to be: entry upon life in Christ.

A similar line of understanding is in Titus 3:5, which the NRSV renders "He saved us, not because of any works of righteousness that we had done, but according to his mercy, through the water of rebirth and renewal by the Holy Spirit." The last clause may be rendered, "He saved us . . . through *the washing characterized by the new beginning and renewal which the Holy Spirit effects.*" The text continues, "This Spirit he poured out on us richly," which is an echo of Joel 2:28.

### 4. Baptism and the Church.

From the beginning baptism in the NT communities was understood as a corporate as well as an individual rite. We have already seen that for Paul this understanding of baptism was axiomatic, and at Corinth it is appealed to as a protest against individualism taken to extreme. To be baptized to Christ was to be baptized to the body of Christ (1 Cor 12:13; *see* Body of Christ). In Galatians 3:26-27 Paul's thought immediately passes from that of "putting on" Christ in baptism to that of the body in which all distinctions among human beings lose their power. The same connection is apparent in the appeal for behavior worthy of baptism in Colossians 3:5-15, in which the baptismal imagery found in Galatians 3:27 is extensively applied: "You stripped off the old nature and put on the new, which is being renewed . . . according to the image* of its creator [i.e., Christ as the perfect image of God], where there is no longer Greek or Jew, circumcised or uncircumcised, barbarian, Scythian, slave* and free, but Christ is all and in all."

The question not infrequently has been raised, "To which church does baptism give entry: to the local or universal church, to the visible or the invisible church?" The question is essentially modern. It would have been inconceivable to Paul. The church* is the visible manifestation of the people of God, whose life is "hidden with Christ in God" (Col 3:3). Baptism is a visible act with a spiritual meaning; it is therefore well adapted to be the means of entry into a visible community of God's people *and* the body which transcends any one place or time. How to give satisfactory expression to the outward and inward elements, alike of baptism and of the church, is a perpetual pastoral problem; that dilemma, however, challenges believers to reform themselves according to the Word of God rather than to accept laxity of doctrine and practice.

### 5. Baptism and Christian Ethics.

It is surely significant that the longest exposition of baptism in Paul's letters is given for an ethical purpose

(*see* Ethics). Romans 6:1-14 is filled with appeals for life consonant with participation in the redemption of Christ that lies at the heart of baptism:

> How can we who died to sin go on living in it? . . . We were buried with him by baptism to death . . . that we might walk in newness of life. . . . Our old self was crucified with him that we might no longer be enslaved to sin. . . . You also must consider yourselves dead to sin and alive to God in Christ Jesus.

This appeal is most extensively developed in Colossians 2:20—3:13. Therein the fact that the believer died and rose in Christ is not only a motive for Christlike living, but a basis to work out the baptismal pattern of dying to sin and rising to righteousness*:

> Put to death what is earthly in you. . . . Put off all such things . . . seeing that you stripped off the old nature with its practices and put on the new nature. . . . Put on therefore compassion. . . . Above all put on love.

This led G. Bornkamm to affirm that in Paul's writings, "baptism is the appropriation of the new life, and the new life is the appropriation of baptism" (Bornkamm 1958, 50). To give substance to this principle the primitive church construed a system of ethics which is reflected in the practical sections of many of the NT letters, not least in Paul's writings. To this tradition Paul refers at times, notably Romans 6:17: "Thanks be to God that although you once were slaves of sin, you became obedient from the heart to *the pattern of teaching to which you were entrusted*" (*see* Creeds). From this it is clear that the believers addressed were instructed in the elements of Christian living that follow from baptism (see further 1 Thess 4:1-7; 2 Thess 3:6, 11-13).

### 6. Baptism and the Kingdom of God.

The baptism of John the Baptist was essentially an eschatological* rite, anticipating the coming of the Messiah, the Day of the Lord and the kingdom* of God. The baptism of Jesus at his hands saw the inauguration of that kingdom: the heavens were opened, the Spirit descended on Jesus, the voice of God came to him, affirming him as the messianic Servant of the Lord (with Mk 1:11; cf. Ps 2:7; Is 42:1), and his service for the kingdom reached its climax in his death and resurrection. Paul understood Christian baptism as participation in that inauguration of the kingdom of God through Jesus. The baptized shares in the death and resurrection of the Lord that initiated the new age, hence the believer lives in it now. The same truth is expressed by Paul in terms of new creation; when Jesus rose from death the new creation* came into existence in him, hence Paul could say, "If anyone is in Christ there is a new creation: everything old has passed away; see, everything has become new!" (2 Cor 5:17). Christian existence is nothing less than life in the new creation.

Because this is so, the Christian life is a pilgrimage to the consummated kingdom, into which the believer enters by ultimate resurrection. So Paul states in Romans 6:5: "If we have been united with the form of his death, we shall be united with the form of his resurrection"—logically now, and finally in the day of his coming in this kingdom. That is expounded more fully in 1 Corinthians 15, the heart of which is in 1 Corinthians 15:20-28. Interestingly, this means that baptism, like the Lord's Supper,* sets the believer between the two poles of redemption—the death and resurrection of Jesus and the future coming of Jesus; standing in between them the Christian looks back to salvation accomplished, forward to salvation to be consummated, and to the risen Lord in the present for grace to persist to the goal and live worthily of such infinite love.

*See also* ADAM AND CHRIST; BODY OF CHRIST; CIRCUMCISION; DEATH OF CHRIST; DYING AND RISING WITH CHRIST; ESCHATOLOGY; ETHICS; HOLY SPIRIT; IN CHRIST; LIFE AND DEATH; LORD'S SUPPER; NEW NATURE AND OLD NATURE; RELIGIONS, GRECO-ROMAN; RESURRECTION; WORSHIP.

BIBLIOGRAPHY. D. M. Baillie, *The Theology of the Sacraments and Other Papers* (New York: Scribners, 1957); K. Barth, *Church Dogmatics IV, The Doctrine of Reconciliation, Part 4 (Fragment)* (Edinburgh: T & T Clark, 1969); M. Barth, *Die Taufe ein Sakrament?* (Zollikon-Zürich: Evangelischer Verlag, 1951); G. R. Beasley-Murray, *Baptism in the New Testament* (London: Macmillan, 1962); W. Bieder, "βαπτίζω κτλ," EDNT 1.192-96; G. Bornkamm, *Das Ende Des Gesetzes, Paulusstudien, Gesammelte Aufsätzen I* (München: Kaiser, 1958); idem, *Early Christian Experience* (London: SCM, 1969); idem, "Taufe und neues Leben bei Paulus (Röm. 6)," in *Das Ende des Gesetzes: Paulusstudien. Gesammelte Aufsätze 1* (BET 16; 2d ed.; Munich: C. Kaiser, 1958) 34-50; R. Burnish, *The Meaning of Baptism* (London: SPCK, 1985); R. P. Carlson, "The Role of Baptism in Paul's Thought," *Int* 47 (1993) 255-66; P. Carrington, *The Primitive Christian Catechism: A Study in the Epistles,* (Cambridge: University Press, 1940); N. Clark, *An Approach to the Theology of the Sacraments* (London: SCM, 1956); J. H. Crehan, *Early Christian Baptism and the Creeds* (London: Burns, Oates & Washburn, 1950); O. Cullmann, *Baptism in the New Testament* (Chicago: Regnery, 1950); G. J. Cuming, "*Epotisthēmen:* 1 Corinthians 12.13," *NTS* 27 (1981) 283-85; G. Delling, *Die Zueignung des Heils in der Taufe: eine Untersuchung zum neutestamentlichen Taufen auf den Namen* (Berlin: Evangelische Verlagsanstalt, 1961); J. D. G. Dunn, *Baptism in the Holy Spirit* (London: SCM, 1970); W. F. Flemington, *The New Testament Doctrine of Baptism* (London: SPCK, 1948); P. T. Forsyth, *The Church and the Sacraments* (London: Independent, 1953); A. Gilmore, ed., *Christian Baptism: A Fresh Attempt to Understand the Rite in Terms of Scripture, History and Theology* (London: Lutterworth, 1959); W. Heitmüller, *Im Namen Jesu, Eine Sprach-und religionsgeschichtliche Untersuchung zum Neuen Testament, speziell zur altchristliche Taufe* (FRLANT 1.2; Göttingen: Vandenhoeck & Ruprecht, 1903); F. J. F. Jackson and K. Lake, *The Beginnings of Christianity, Part 1, The Acts of the Apostles* (5 vols.; London: Macmillan, 1922-42); R. Jungkuntz, *The Gospel of Baptism* (St. Louis: Concordia, 1968); G. Lampe, *The Seal of the Spirit: A Study in the Doctrine of Baptism and Confirmation in the New Testament and the Fathers* (London & New York: Longmans Green, 1951); F. J. Leenhardt, *Le baptême chrétien, son origine, sa signification* (Neuchâtel-Paris, 1946); A. T. Lincoln, *Ephesians* (WBC 42; Dallas: Word, 1990); P. C. Marcel, *The Biblical Doctrine of Infant Baptism* (London: James Clarke, 1953); H. G. Marsh, *The Origin and the Significance of the New Testament Baptism* (Manchester, 1941); D. Moody, *Baptism: Foundation for Christian Unity* (Philadelphia: Westminster, 1967); W. Mundle, *Der Glaubensbegriff des Paulus, eine Untersuchung zur Dogmengeschichte des ältesten Christentums* (Leipzig: Heinsius, 1932); J. Murray, *Christian Baptism* (Philadelphia: Commission on Christian Education [The Orthodox Presbyterian Church], 1952); C. H. Ratschow, *Die eine christliche Taufe* (Gütersloh: Mohn, 1972); E. Schlink, *The Doctrine of Baptism* (St. Louis: Concordia, 1972); R. Schnackenburg, *Baptism in the Thought of St. Paul: A Study in Pauline Theology* (Oxford: Blackwell, 1964); J. Schneider, *Die Taufe im Neues Testament* (Stuttgart: Kohlhammer, 1952); G. Wagner, *Pauline Baptism and the Pagan Mysteries: The Problem of the Pauline Doctrine of Baptism in Romans 6:1-11 in the Light of its Religious-Historical Parallels* (Edinburgh: Oliver & Boyd, 1967); J. Warns, *Baptism: A Study in the Original Christian Baptism* (London: Paternoster, 1957); A. J. M. Wedderburn, *Baptism and Resurrection: Studies in Pauline Theology against Its Graeco-Roman Background* (WUNT 1/44; Tübingen: J. C. B. Mohr, 1987); idem, "The Soteriology of the Mysteries and Pauline Baptismal Theology," *NovT* 29 (1987) 53-72; R. E. O. White, *The Biblical Doctrine of Initiation* (London: Hodder & Stoughton, 1960); World Council of Churches, *One Lord, One Baptism* (London: SCM, 1960); idem, *Baptism, Eucharist, Ministry* (Geneva: WCC, 1982); J. Ysebaert, *Greek Baptismal Terminology:*

*Its Origins and Early Development* (Nijmegen: Dekker & Van de Vegt, 1962).

G. R. Beasley-Murray

## BARNABAS

Barnabas is a Greek name interpreted by Luke as *huios paraklēseōs* in Acts 4:36 and variously translated as "son of consolation" (KJV), "son of exhortation" or "son of encouragement" (RSV, JB, NIV). Barnabas was the affectionate nickname of a Levite named Joses, or Joseph (Acts 4:36), who became one of Paul's closest colleagues. This use of "son" to indicate a person's character was a common Semitic idiom. However, reconstructing its Hebrew or Aramaic original has proven difficult. "Son of Nebo" (Gk *Barnebon*) has been suggested by some, but most see the name coming from "son" (*bar*) "of prophecy" (*n°bû 'â;* cf. Heb *nāḇî',* "prophet"). The Greek *paraklēsis*, which Luke uses in his translation, effectively describes the exhorting, proclaiming functions of the prophet. And this is the sort of man Barnabas was. In Acts 13:1 "prophet and teacher" describes him and a list of other Christian leaders. In Lystra (Acts 14:12) Barnabas is even called "Zeus" by pagan worshippers. In Acts 14:14 he is listed along with Paul as an apostle.*

1. Background
2. Ministry with Paul
3. Writings

### 1. Background.

Barnabas had originally come from Cyprus (Acts 4:36) and settled in Jerusalem.* His strong Jewish roots as a Levite (Acts 4:36) and his Hellenistic background in the Jewish diaspora* gave him a background similar to Paul's, whose close friend he would become. Along with people like Stephen, Barnabas represents the large number of Hellenistic Jews who had migrated back to Jerusalem. Luke reminds us that during both Jesus' crucifixion and Pentecost many Hellenistic Jews were in the city. Barnabas was one of these. An early tradition stemming from Eusebius (who cites Clement of Alexandria, *Hist. Eccl.* 1.11.12; 2.1.1) says that Barnabas was one of the Seventy sent out by Jesus (Lk 10). But this is impossible to confirm.

Barnabas owned land in Jerusalem. His first appearance in the NT shows him among the earliest converts, selling his parcel of land and giving the proceeds to the apostles (Acts 4:36). He quickly became a highly admired and respected leader within this circle. When, after the death of Stephen, many of the Hellenists fled north (Acts 8:1), Barnabas stayed in Jerusalem with the apostles.

We also know that Barnabas had family connec-

tions in Jerusalem. His cousin (Gk *anepsios*, Col 4:10, as cousin, not his "sister's son" or nephew, so KJV) was John Mark whose mother, Mary, lived in Jerusalem and hosted the church in her home (Acts 12:12). This explains Barnabas's sympathy for John Mark when the young man turned back during Paul's first missionary tour (Acts 13:13; cf. 15:36-41).

### 2. Ministry with Paul.

Paul and Barnabas became close associates in the work of ministry. Their shared background in the diaspora and their conservative training as respectively Pharisee and Levite may have made them ready candidates for joint ministry.

*2.1. Early Association.* When Paul returned to Jerusalem after his conversion and lengthy stay in Arabia, the apostles were understandably cautious about him. But as Ananias had brought Paul into the Christian fellowship at Damascus, so Barnabas trusted the integrity of Paul's conversion (*see* Conversion and Call) and became his advocate among the Jerusalem leaders (Acts 9:27). With the help of Barnabas Paul was invited into the center of the church's life.

After fifteen days (Gal 1:18) Paul set sail from Caesarea to return to Tarsus while Barnabas remained in Jerusalem. But the church was growing rapidly, especially among the Greeks and Hellenistic Jews, and soon a Christian church was thriving in the city of Syrian Antioch.* The apostles dispatched Barnabas to travel to Antioch and to pastor the fellowship there (Acts 11:22). Under his guidance the church grew even more, with Barnabas respected "as a good man, full of the Holy Spirit and faith" (Acts 11:24). Since Tarsus was nearby and since Paul had become well known in the regions of Syria and Cilicia (Gal 1:21-24), Barnabas found Paul and invited him to join the work in Antioch. Together Paul and Barnabas co-pastored the church there for one year (Acts 11:26).

Barnabas also traveled with Paul on the so-called famine visit to Jerusalem (Acts 11:27-30). Antioch was the third-largest city in the Roman Empire (next to Rome and Alexandria) and its church, no doubt the wealthiest yet, determined to share its riches with the poorer Christians of Judea. The visit was uneventful, unless of course we allow that Galatians 2:1-10 describes one episode during the visit. This seems appropriate (hence: the South Galatian theory) since both trips are in response to a revelation (Gal 2:2; Acts 11:27-28) and fit well chronologically (*see* Chronology). Further, Galatians 2:1-10 seems an inadequate parallel to Acts 15. This means that Barnabas witnessed firsthand the dissension concerning circumcision* and, at least at this point, stood with Paul (Gal

2:9). The same cannot be said for another episode which took place after Paul and Barnabas had returned home to Antioch. Peter came to Antioch and mixed freely with the Gentile* Christians; but he withdrew from having fellowship with them when a conservative delegation from Jerusalem appeared (Gal 2:11-13). Worse yet, Barnabas was, in the words of Paul, "carried away by their insincerity" (Gal 2:13). Barnabas was a man with a mind of his own, and it probably surprised Paul to see his colleague stand against him on this still-debated issue of Gentile circumcision.

**2.2. Missionary Travels.** Following the famine visit, Acts 13 tells us that the leadership at Antioch had grown (now to include Simeon, Lucius and Manaen, Acts 13:1). Barnabas and Paul (Paul's precedence is not suggested in the text) were commissioned to travel west as missionaries.

*2.2.1. The First Tour.* The decision to sail to Cyprus may have been influenced by Barnabas since it was his home and he would have known the island well. John Mark's presence in Acts 12:25 and 13:5 implies that he had been in and around Antioch all along and had teamed up with Barnabas and Saul. But when Barnabas and Paul, after their arrival in Pamphylia, decided to leave Perga and climb the mountains toward Antioch of Pisidia, John Mark turned back. Barnabas's later defense of John Mark would prove to be the decision that would separate Barnabas from Paul on subsequent journeys. During this first tour Paul turned out to be the spokesperson for the company, often engaging synagogues in vigorous discussion. Even so, Barnabas was given recognition (and even a divine title in Lystra, Acts 14:12), but he never became the target of violence or stoning.

*2.2.2. The Jerusalem Council.* Following the first trip west, Barnabas accompanied Paul to Jerusalem* in order to settle the now divisive issue of the Law* and circumcision.* Barnabas is given equal respect with Paul (Acts 15:12) and perhaps his word, as that of a convert and leader *prior to* Paul, carried important weight. Barnabas was a disciple of the Jerusalem church who was now reporting to his mentors.

*2.2.3. The Second Tour.* The second tour witnessed the rupture of Barnabas's relation with Paul. Barnabas wanted to give John Mark another chance, but Paul refused (Acts 15:36-41). Luke uses discretion when he writes, "And there was a sharp disagreement (*paroxysmos*), so that they separated from each other" (Acts 15:39). Once again Barnabas had stood his ground and while Paul assembled a new entourage, Barnabas and John Mark returned to Cyprus where Luke lets their story fall silent.

It seems clear that Paul, Barnabas and John Mark shared a longer working relationship than Acts implies. Paul's reference to Barnabas in 1 Corinthians 9:6 shows not only that the Corinthians knew Barnabas but that Paul continued to respect him. Calvin and Luther were convinced that 2 Corinthians 8:18-19 also referred to Barnabas: "With him (Titus) we are also sending the brother who is famous among all the churches for his preaching of the gospel." Likewise, the mention of John Mark in Philemon 24 and 2 Timothy 4:11 shows that Paul and this younger disciple were later reconciled.

**3. Writings.**
Tertullian seems to have been the first to suggest that Barnabas wrote the anonymous Epistle to the Hebrews. This claim has merit inasmuch as the letter shows remarkable interest in the details of the Temple, an interest that would befit a Levite such as Barnabas. But his authorship of Hebrews cannot be proven.

*3.1. The Epistle of Barnabas.* There also exists a letter called *The Epistle of Barnabas* (collected among the writings of the Apostolic Fathers) which Origen (*Contra Celsum* 1.63) and Clement of Alexandria (*Strom.* 2.6, 7) both accepted as canonical since they were persuaded that Barnabas wrote it. Codex Sinaiticus even contains a complete copy of the letter, placing it after Revelation. But scholars today assign the letter to the second century (usually c. 132-35) and have found it difficult to associate it with Barnabas since the text nowhere even mentions his name.

*See also* ANTIOCH ON THE ORONTES; COWORKERS, PAUL AND HIS; MISSION; PAUL IN ACTS AND LETTERS.

BIBLIOGRAPHY. R. J. Bauckham, "Barnabas in Galatians," *JSNT* 2 (1979) 61-70; P. Benoit, "La deuxième visite de S. Paul à Jerusalem," *Bib* 40 (1959) 778-92; S. P. Brock, "BARNABAS: HYIOS PARAKLESEOS," *JTS* 25 (1974) 93-98; F. F. Bruce, *Men and Movements in the Primitive Church: Studies in Early Non-Pauline Christianity* (Exeter: Paternoster, 1979) 49-85; idem, *The Acts of the Apostles* (3d ed. rev. and enlarged; Grand Rapids: Eerdmans, 1989); H. Evans, "Barnabas the Bridge-Builder," *ExpT* 89 (1977/78) 248-50; B. Gärtner, "Paulus und Barnabas in Lystra. Zu Apg 14,8-15," *SEÅ* 27 (1962) 83-93; E. Haenchen, *Acts of the Apostles* (Philadelphia: Westminster, 1971); R. A. Kraft, *Barnabas and the Didache*, vol. 3, *The Apostolic Fathers*, ed. R. M. Grant (New York: Nelson, 1965).

G. M. Burge

**BASIC PRINCIPLES.** *See* ELEMENTS/ELEMENTAL SPIRITS OF THE WORLD.

**BAUR, F. C.** *See* PAUL AND HIS INTERPRETERS.

## BENEDICTION, BLESSING, DOXOLOGY, THANKSGIVING

The four terms *benediction, blessing, doxology* and *thanksgiving* and are used in the Pauline letters to describe a range of joyful responses to God's* gracious saving activity in creation* and redemption.* God's action in Christ* is that of grace*; our response should be one of gratitude. Blessing, thanksgiving, benediction and doxology describe that human response.

1. Benediction
2. Blessing
3. Doxology
4. Thanksgiving

### 1. Benediction.

Although the term *benediction* has been used in a variety of ways, in recent Pauline study it has come to refer to the apostle's* (opening and closing) greetings in which he indicates his deep prayerful concern (*see* Prayer) for his readers. Paul's benedictions are both affirmations regarding the grace and peace* of God in which they already participate and (wish-) prayers that they may appreciate and experience these blessings more fully. There is a difference of opinion as to the origin of these stylized expressions—the LXX, early Christian worship* or the sermon.

*1.1. Opening Benedictions.* Paul's opening salutations or benedictions (Rom 1:7; 1 Cor 1:3; 2 Cor 1:2; etc.) remain basically unchanged throughout his letters. They consist of three parts: (1) mention is made of the "grace" and "peace" which the apostle desires, (2) his readers ("you") to know and appreciate more fully, and finally (3) the source of these blessings is spelled out (usually "the God and Father of our Lord Jesus Christ"). With deep prayerful concern, the apostle desires that his readers may apprehend more fully the grace of God in which they already stand (cf. Rom 5:2) and the relationship of peace which God has established with them. At the same time Paul may be urging his readers "to renewed Christian living under grace appropriate to the immediate circumstances" (Wiles).

*1.2. Closing Benedictions.* Paul's concluding benedictions have a general uniformity of phraseology, structure and position (Rom 16:20, 24; Gal 6:18; Eph 6:24; etc.), although they can vary, from the shortest form ("The grace of the Lord Jesus be with you," 1 Cor 16:24) to the long "trinitarian" form of 2 Corinthians 13:14. These benedictions bring the letter to a definitive conclusion and correspond formally to the final wish of the secular letter ("Farewell!"; *see* Letters, Letter Forms). The concluding benediction, which often picks up the introductory greeting with its reference to the grace of God, also gives expression to Paul's strong desire and strikes a note of confidence.

### 2. Blessing.

Although the language of blessing (the *eulog-* word group) occurs sixty-eight times in the NT, the concept receives less prominence here than in the OT where it had considerable significance. The *eulog-* word group is used by the Synoptics (esp. Luke), Paul and Hebrews in relation to God's saving work in Christ. According to Galatians 3:8-9, 14, the blessing promised to Abraham* has been fulfilled in Paul's gospel with believing Gentiles* being justified (*see* Justification) by faith* and receiving the gift of the Spirit (*see* Holy Spirit), while in Ephesians 1:3 "every spiritual *blessing*" is a comprehensive expression to designate the whole of God's saving work in Christ (Eph 1:4-14; cf. Rom 15:29; *see* Salvation). Most instances of the word group in Paul, however, refer to the human response of praising God for his manifold blessings, especially his work of salvation, and these are the focus of attention in this article. All eight NT examples of *eulogētos* ("blessed," which renders the Hebrew *bārûk*), five of which appear in Paul, are used in this way. They are instances of "declarative praise" (C. Westermann), where the writer expresses his simple and joyous response (*see* Joy) to a definite act of God that has been experienced. Paul's eulogies do not express a wish; they describe a fact ("Blessed *is* God"), as he proclaims that God is the source of blessing.

*2.1. Introductory Blessings.* Using a typically OT and Jewish prayer* form denoting praise (cf. the doxological conclusions to the books of the Psalter: Ps 41:13; 72:19-20; etc.), Paul introduces two of his letters (2 Cor 1:3-4; Eph 1:3-14; cf. 1 Pet 1:3-5) with an introductory blessing or eulogy (*eulogētos*, "blessed"). While his introductory thanksgivings focus on God's work in the lives of others, his eulogies praise God for blessings in which he himself participates. The formula with a Jewish background was apparently more apt when he himself came within the circle of blessing.

In 2 Corinthians 1:3-4, an intensely personal paragraph, Paul praises the God of Israel* who is now known to him as "the Father of our Lord Jesus Christ." He is the merciful Father from whom all compassion comes, and this has been demonstrated in a marvelous way by his mighty intervention at a time of extreme need in the apostle's life (cf. 2 Cor 1:8-11).

Ephesians 1:3-14 is a eulogy, or blessing, of considerable length in which Paul praises God for his wide-ranging blessings "in Christ." Using highly exalted language in a long sentence he explains what this means by reference to election, adoption, God's will, his grace, redemption, etc. Here is a profound example of "declarative praise."

*2.2. Short Eulogies.* On three occasions in Paul's letters, but nowhere else in the NT, short interjections of praise appear (Rom 1:25; 9:5; 2 Cor 11:31). The nearest parallel is the well-known rabbinic interjection after the name of God (e.g., "the Holy One, blessed be he . . ."). Each has the same basic form, "Blessed is . . . for ever"—God is praised as Creator (Rom 1:25) and as the Father of the Lord Jesus (2 Cor 11:31), and Messiah is praised as the one who is [God] over all (Rom 9:5).

*2.3. Other References to Blessing.* The language of "blessing" occurs in 1 Corinthians 10:16 with reference to the cup at the Lord's Supper* over which the prayer of thanksgiving is offered to God, while in 1 Corinthians 14:16 "bless" refers to praising God in tongues* within the assembly at worship.

## 3. Doxology.

Doxologies are short, spontaneous ascriptions of praise to God which frequently appear as concluding formulae to prayers, hymnic expressions (*see* Hymns) and sections of Paul's letters. Their basic structure is threefold. First, the person to whom praise is ascribed is mentioned ("to our God and Father," Phil 4:20). Then follows the word of praise, usually *doxa* ("glory," or an equivalent), and finally, the doxology concludes with a temporal description, normally an eternity formula ("for ever and ever"). In most cases the doxology is followed by "amen."

The first element in these NT ascriptions of praise is the most variable: the one to whom glory* is given may be expressed by a relative pronoun ("whom," Gal 1:5; "him," Rom 11:36), a Greek participial expression ("God who is able to strengthen you," Rom 16:25) or a simple noun ("the King of the ages," 1 Tim 1:17). The ascription in Philippians 4:20 is particularly appropriate: Paul ascribes glory "to our God and Father." At Philippians 4:19 he used the intensely personal expression "*my* God" to assure the Philippians that his God would act on his behalf to fulfill all their needs. Now he changes to the plural "our" as he unites himself with his converts in this ascription of praise.

The second element of the doxology is the ascription of "glory" (honor, greatness or power*) which properly belongs to God and is, therefore, rightly ascribed to him. In the OT *doxa* was primarily the brightness or radiance of God's presence. To give God glory is not to add something to him; rather, it is an active acknowledgment or extolling of what he is or has already done (Ps 29:2; 96:8). Although many doxologies contain no verb, the indicative "is" or "belongs" is presupposed: the doxology is an affirmation rather than a wish. So

in Galatians 1:5 glory *belongs* to God for it was in accordance with his will that the "Lord Jesus Christ . . . gave himself for our sins to set us free from the present evil age."

The third feature of Paul's doxologies is the temporal expression "for ever and ever" (literally, "to the ages of the ages"). This eternity formula, which is unique to the NT (cf. Gal 1:5; 1 Tim 1:17; 2 Tim 4:18), is a more emphatic variation of the common LXX expression which means "for all eternity" in an unlimited sense (cf. Ps 84:5). Paul's ascription of glory to God is not restricted to "this age" but belongs to "the age to come" as well. The spontaneous endorsement of the doxology in Philippians 4:20 is uttered in the "amen" which follows, a response uttered on solemn occasions in the OT to confirm a curse* or adjuration, to accept a blessing or to associate oneself with a doxology. Each of the doxologies which conclude the first four books of the OT psalter (Ps 41:13; 72:19; 89:52; 106:48) ends with an "amen," while prayers and doxologies in the NT are strengthened and endorsed by it (Rom 1:25; Gal 1:5). The "amen" makes it clear that Paul's ascription of praise is not simply a matter of the lips, but is the spontaneous response of his whole being. Elsewhere he strikingly connects believers' response of "amen" to the faithfulness of God who has said yes to all his promises in Christ (2 Cor 1:20).

## 4. Thanksgiving.

Paul mentions the subject of thanksgiving in his letters more often, line for line, than any other Hellenistic author, pagan or Christian. The *eucharisteō* word group turns up forty-six times in the Pauline corpus and appears in many important contexts of every letter except Galatians and Titus. The apostle's thanksgiving terms consistently express the notion of gratitude which finds outward, and often public, expression in thanksgiving. By mentioning what God has graciously done in his Son (*see* Son of God), other Christians are encouraged to thank him also. As thanksgivings abound, so God is glorified (2 Cor 4:15; cf. 2 Cor 1:11).

Pauline thanksgiving approximates what we understand by "praise," for it is broader than the expression of gratitude for personal benefits received. The apostle regularly gave thanks for God's graces effected in the lives of others. Thanksgiving is a response to God's saving activity in creation* and redemption.* It is always the second word, never the first.

*4.1. Introductory Paragraphs.* The most significant Pauline references to thanksgiving occur in the opening paragraphs where the apostle, sometimes in conjunction with his associates, gives thanks to God for the progress in faith,* love* and hope* of his readers within the Gentile mission* (Rom 1:8; 1 Cor 1:4; 2 Cor 1:11; Eph 1:16; Phil 1:3; Col 1:3, 12; 1 Thess 1:2; cf. 1 Thess 2:13; 3:9; 2 Thess 1:3; cf. 2 Thess 2:13; Philem 4). These paragraphs, which open with a statement of thanksgiving to God, have an epistolary function (*see* Letters, Letter Forms), that is, they introduce and present the main themes of their letters, usually setting the tone and atmosphere and previewing the content. Many have a didactic function so that either by fresh teaching* or recall to instruction previously given the apostle sets forth theological matters he considers important (see esp. Col 1:9-14). An exhortatory purpose is also present in several of these passages (e.g., Phil 1:9-11). The thanksgivings and petitions which are included give evidence of the apostle's deep pastoral and apostolic concern for the readers (*see* Pastor).

At the same time Paul reports his actual thanksgivings and actual petitions for the readers. The thanksgivings are directed to God (1 Cor 1:4; 1 Thess 1:2; note "my God" at Rom 1:8; Phil 1:3) who is known to Paul as the "Father of Jesus Christ" (cf. Col 1:3), and they are offered "always" (1 Cor 1:4; Phil 1:4) or "unceasingly" (1 Thess 1:2; 2:13), expressions which refer not to continual prayer* but to the apostle's remembrance of them in his regular times of prayer.

Paul gives thanks for the readers, some of whom were well known to him (the Philippians,* Corinthians* and Thessalonians*), others who had been converted through the ministry of an associate (the Colossians*), while others were outside the sphere of his previous ministry (the Romans*).

The grounds for Paul's thanksgivings were manifold. Frequently the early Christian triad of faith, love and hope (1 Thess 1:2, 3; 2 Thess 1:3; etc.) was the *immediate* cause, with the prior activity of God being the *final* cause: the Thessalonians' election (1 Thess 1:4; cf. 2 Thess 2:13-14), God's good work in the Philippians (Phil 1:6), his amazing, gracious activity in Christ in the lives of the Corinthians (1 Cor 1:4-9), and his fitting the Colossians for a share in an eternal inheritance (Col 1:12-14). Particularly striking is the connection between Paul's giving of thanks and the gospel. The outworking of faith, love and hope shows that the gospel has come to the readers dynamically (1 Thess 1:3-5), that they had been called through the gospel (2 Thess 2:14), had the testimony to Christ confirmed in their midst (1 Cor 1:6), had shown their active participation in the gospel (Phil 1:5) or received a hope that was integral to that gospel (Col 1:5). Clearly God had been mightily at work in his gospel.

*4.2. Colloquial Uses.* Three examples of the verb *eucharisteō* ("give thanks") express gratitude at a conversational level: Romans 16:4, where Paul is grateful to Priscilla and Aquila for risking their lives on his account (cf. 1 Cor 1:14; 14:18).

*4.3. Thanksgivings Said over Food.* On six occasions in Paul's letters thanksgiving over food is mentioned, including the reference to Jesus' prayer of thanks over the bread at the Last Supper (1 Cor 11:24; *see* Lord's Supper). At Romans 14:6 both the Christian who eats meat and the one who abstains do so to the Lord,* for both give thanks to God over their meals (*see* Food). In 1 Corinthians 10:30 (cf. 1 Tim 4:3, 4) the note of gratitude is struck by Christians who offer their prayer of thanksgiving, recognizing that "the earth is the Lord's and everything in it" (1 Cor 10:26, from Ps 24:1).

*4.4. Exhortations to Thanksgiving.* Exhortations to thanksgiving appear often in the Pauline letters, particularly in Colossians. Whether private or public, such thanksgiving is to be offered joyfully "in all circumstances" (1 Thess 5:18), for along with prayer and rejoicing this is God's will. Thanksgiving should be the accompaniment of every activity (Col 3:17). A "thankful attitude" (Col 3:15) is inculcated, and it will show itself outwardly and corporately as the readers "sing psalms, hymns and spiritual songs with gratitude" (Col 3:16; *see* Hymns). In Ephesians 5:20 the continuity of thanksgiving ("at all times"), its corporate nature (Eph 5:19) and the fact that it is the proper outcome of those who are filled with the Spirit (Eph 5:18) are stressed, while in Colossians 2:7 firmness and strength of faith, coupled with thanksgiving, describe the Christian life.

Thanksgiving is regularly and intimately joined together with petitionary prayer (Col 4:2; Phil 4:6). Paul's own petitions for his readers were often tied in with his thanks to God for them (cf. Phil 1:3-6, 9-11). Christian thanksgiving stands in contrast with coarse vulgarity and flippancy of speech (Eph 5:4). Lips given to thanking God should not be used for language that dishonors his name.

*4.5. Thanksgivings in Didactic Contexts.* The giving of thanks to God should have been the response of all men and women on the basis of their knowledge of him as Creator (Rom 1:21). But they failed to recognize his lordship and glorify him: they were "ungrateful" (cf. 2 Tim 3:2). By contrast, as thanksgivings increase among believers so God is glorified (2 Cor 4:15; cf. 2 Cor 1:11). These may be offered for a variety of reasons, not least for the generosity shown by fellow Christians (2 Cor 9:11, 12).

*4.6. Short Expressions of Thanksgiving.* "Thanks be to God" is a short expression which occasionally appears in Paul's letters, sometimes as a spontaneous outburst for some great blessing which the apostle or his readers have received from God. Twice they function as introductory thanksgivings (1 Tim 1:12; 2 Tim 1:3), while the remaining instances occur at pivotal points in the letters denoting a change of direction in the apostle's argument (e.g., in a concluding section: Rom 7:25; 1 Cor 15:57; 2 Cor 9:15; and to begin a new theme: 2 Cor 2:14; 8:16). These short expressions of gratitude are like eulogies—examples of "declarative praise."

The grounds for the offering of thanks are wide-ranging: from the personal expression of gratitude offered to Christ for showing mercy* to Paul (1 Tim 1:12), to the triumph* over sin* and death which Christ has effected on behalf of his people (1 Cor 15:54-55, 57; cf. Rom 7:25; see Life and Death) and to the ultimate gift of God's Son (2 Cor 8:16; cf. 2 Cor 8:9).

See also HYMNS, HYMN FRAGMENTS, SONGS, SPIRITUAL SONGS; LITURGICAL ELEMENTS; PRAYER; WORSHIP.

BIBLIOGRAPHY. L. G. Champion, Benedictions and Doxologies in the Epistles of Paul (Oxford: published privately, 1934); R. Deichgräber, Gotteshymnus und Christushymnus in der frühen Christenheit (SUNT 5; Göttingen: Vandenhoeck & Ruprecht, 1967); T. Y. Mullins, "Benediction as a NT Form," AUSS 15 (1977) 59-64; P. T. O'Brien, Introductory Thanksgivings in the Letters of Paul (NovTSup 49; Leiden: E. J. Brill, 1977); idem, "Thanksgiving within the Structure of Pauline Theology," in Pauline Studies: Essays Presented to Professor F. F. Bruce, ed. D. A. Hagner and M. J. Harris (Grand Rapids: Eerdmans, 1980) 50-66; W. Schenk, Der Segen im Neuen Testament (Berlin: Evangelische Verlagsanstalt, 1967); C. Westermann, Blessing in the Bible and the Life of the Church (Philadelphia: Fortress, 1978); G. P. Wiles, Paul's Intercessory Prayers (SNTSMS 24; Cambridge: University Press, 1974).

P. T. O'Brien

**BENEFACTOR.** See FINANCIAL SUPPORT; SOCIAL-SCIENTIFIC APPROACHES TO PAUL.

**BINDING OF ISAAC.** See DEATH OF CHRIST; SACRIFICE, OFFERING.

**BLESSING.** See ABRAHAM; BENEDICTION, BLESSING, DOXOLOGY, THANKSGIVING.

**BOASTING.** See ABRAHAM; CORINTHIANS, LETTERS TO THE; LAW; OPPONENTS OF PAUL; ROMANS, LETTER TO THE; WISDOM; WORKS OF THE LAW.

# BODY

The term sōma ("body") occurs in the Pauline letters a total of ninety-one times, with a rich diversity of meanings. The bulk of the references to sōma in the Pauline letters are expressions of the body/member(s) analogy, particularly as an image of a Christian congregation (notably in Rom 12:4-5; 1 Cor 10:16-17; 12:12-27). In an important modification to the analogy, this body of Christ (see Body of Christ) is described in cosmic terms and united under the headship* of the Lord* Jesus himself (Eph 1:23; 2:16; 4:4, 12-16; 5:23; Col 1:18, 24; 2:19; 3:15). These important theological ideas are largely expressive of the corporate dimension of the somatic metaphor; there is, however, a more personal dimension to the use of sōma in the Pauline letters which is foundational to these ecclesiastical extrapolations which are based upon it. Insofar as these personal references to sōma reflect Paul's teaching concerning the ultimate hope of the individual believer (albeit always within the context of the corporate community), they overlap with his eschatological beliefs of the resurrection.* Paul's use of sōma in this sense is thus an important feature of his eschatology,* essential to his teaching concerning the resurrection and integral to his understanding of salvation* and redemption* in Christ.* The granting of this resurrection body is so timed as to coincide with the parousia of Jesus Christ. As Paul puts it in Romans 8:23, Christians eagerly "wait for adoption, the redemption of our bodies" (NRSV; see Adoption).

1. Sōma: Focal Point of Pauline Anthropology
2. The Mortal Body
3. The Spiritual Body
4. Resurrection of the Dead or Immortality of the Soul?

## 1. Sōma: Focal Point of Pauline Anthropology.

A proper understanding of Paul's teaching about the body (sōma) is inescapably bound up with the larger issue of his anthropology. What is it that constitutes the human being? How do the various components associated with the human being (body, soul, spirit, flesh) fit together? In the Pauline view is humanity essentially dichotomous or (as 1 Thess 5:23 is sometimes taken to indicate) trichotomous in nature? These questions are exceedingly complex and we need not attempt to solve them here (see Psychology). They have been the subject of considerable discussion over the years with several important studies on the subject readily available (W. D. Stacey and R. H. Gundry are two notable examples). Most scholars now agree that Paul's basic anthropological stance derives from Judaism rather than from the Hellenistic world which tended to see the sōma as evil and something from which to be redeemed; in the Platonic world the sōma was, to cite a well-known Orphic phrase, "a prison-house for the soul (psychē)."

Yet even here the issue of background is not as

simple as it might first appear, for R. Jewett argues that much of Paul's anthropological teaching arises directly out of his contact with his Hellenistic (Gnostic?) opponents. In effect, Jewett asserts, Paul borrows many of the terms and concepts of his adversaries in the course of his letters to his churches—the "wall of separation" between Greek and Jewish anthropology rapidly breaks down as a result. This is not an unreasonable thesis, although the extent to which Jewett pursues it is perhaps unwarranted. In any event, the overlap between *sōma* and *psychē* in Paul's teaching will not sustain the rigid dualism inherent within much Greek thought of the time. As E. Best remarks, "Man cannot be divided into an 'I' and a 'non-I', a soul and a body; he is a unity and can be regarded as 'body' or as 'soul' " (Best, 217).

### 2. The Mortal Body.

At several points Paul uses the term *sōma* as a shorthand expression for the physical body, the material stuff of human existence which is subject to decay and death (*see* Life and Death) and hence, by definition, mortal. The actual phrase "mortal body" (*thnēton sōma*) appears only twice in Paul (Rom 6:12 and 8:11, where it is plural). It is also implied twice in a highly stylized passage contrasting the mortal with the immortal (1 Cor 15:53, 54; cf. 2 Cor 5:4). In both instances it is still the body of human beings which is in view. Only rarely does Paul apply the term *sōma* to other physical bodies. In 1 Corinthians 15:37-40 it is used to describe a variety of physical bodies within the created order (grains of wheat, animals, sun, moon, stars, etc.), and in Colossians 2:17 it is contrasted with shadows (*skia*) and bears the sense of "substance" or "reality." In 1 Corinthians 15:47-49 the creation imagery of Genesis 2:7 is brought into play as a means of highlighting the mortality of humankind. Here Paul emphasizes that human beings are created "from dust" (*ek gēs choïkos*), contrasting this mortal existence in Adam with the heavenly one in Christ.

It is sometimes difficult to make sharp distinctions between *sōma* and *sarx* ("flesh"*) as terms of human mortality, although the latter is almost always used negatively by Paul to describe the physical side of human beings as they are driven by purely human concerns and interests. Just to demonstrate how fluid the use of terms *sarx* and *sōma* can be at times, it is worth noting that in 2 Corinthians 4:11 Paul describes the faithful as manifesting the life of Jesus in "our mortal flesh" (*en tē thnētē sarki hēmōn*), and in Colossians 1:22 Christ's act of redemption is described as the reconciliation (*see* Peace, Reconciliation) brought about in "his body of flesh" (*en tō sōmati tēs sarkos autou*). Most

notable of all is the ease with which the apostle moves from his discussion of *sōma* in 1 Corinthians 15:35-38 to insert a (somewhat distracting) reference to *sarx* in 1 Corinthians 15:39, and then goes back to the use of *sōma* in 1 Corinthians 15:42-44. In the main, however, the *sarx* acts independently of God and his Spirit,* motivated by a spirit of independence and rebellion, captivated by sin* and ultimately under the eschatological judgment* of God. In other words, here the ethical contrast operative in Paul is not so much between *sōma* and *pneuma*, but between *sarx* and *pneuma*; the latter pair are presented as mutually exclusive realms in which human beings conduct themselves.

One final question about the mortal body is worth posing. Was the human body originally created by God to be immortal (*see* Immortality)? Has it become tainted with mortality as a result of sin and disobedience? Much of the answer to this depends on how one interprets the Adam/Christ analogy (*see* Adam and Christ) of Romans 5 and the original state of humankind implied within it. These matters have perplexed NT scholars for centuries and are impossible even to begin to solve here. M. J. Harris offers a sensible summary answer when he states that Adam: "was created neither immortal (see Gn. 3:22-24) nor mortal (see Gn. 2:17) but with the potentiality to become either depending on his obedience or disobedience to God. While not created *with* immortality, he was certainly created *for* immortality" (Harris 1986, 47).

*2.1. Sōma as an Expression of Paul's Person.* Occasionally phrases containing the word *sōma* are used within the Pauline letters as a personal pronoun, the equivalent of "I," or "me" or "myself." Thus in 1 Corinthians 9:27 Paul describes his self-discipline in athletic terms, "I pummel my body [*sōma*]"; and in 1 Corinthians 13:3 he can talk about "delivering my body [*sōma*] to be burned" when it is quite clear that he means "himself." Similarly, in Philippians 1:20 he states his intention that "Christ will be honored in my body [*sōma*]," again with the sense of "in me" (see Gal 2:19-20 for an equivalent statement).

*2.2. Sōma as an Expression of the Whole Person.* Several passages use expressions containing the word *sōma* in such a way that it is clear Paul means "person," or "a human being in all his or her wholeness," the "self." A classic example is Romans 8:23 where Paul describes the Christian church as awaiting the future "redemption of our bodies." Paul's belief is that the whole person will ultimately be redeemed, not just their physical body (cf. Rom 8:10-11). Likewise, in Romans 12:1 Paul exhorts his readers to "present your bodies as a living sacrifice," meaning that they are to present the whole of their being to this end (cf. 1 Cor

6:12-20). Thus in many of the instances where Paul uses *sōma* it is possible to translate it simply with the word "person," perhaps the nearest equivalent in the English language, as in the expression "everybody" (meaning "everyone").

Two writers of significant influence in the modern theological world, R. Bultmann and J. A. T. Robinson, both follow this as a basic approach within their interpretations of *sōma* as it is used in Paul. It is not without significance that both of these interpreters (as well as others who follow the same line) have gone on to interpret the resurrection theologically by means of existential categories (albeit with different focal points; Bultmann focusing on the individual person and Robinson on the person within social structures). The result is that a physical (or "bodily") resurrection is thought to be neither needed nor desired; they present a dematerialized understanding of the resurrection.

However, not all would agree with the implications of such an approach and would want to defend strongly a more physical understanding of *sōma*, and by extension a belief in the bodily resurrection which flows from it. R. H. Gundry, for example, argues strongly that although *sōma* can *represent* the whole person, it does not necessarily *mean* the whole person (see M. J. Harris, 120, for discussion). Gundry asserts that the Pauline doctrine of *sōma* always means a physical body, pointing out that the term is always so used in the LXX (J. A. Ziesler disagrees on this key point and adduces at least seven instances where *sōma* has a more-than-physical sense; that is, it is occasionally used to indicate a "person"). The precise nuance of *sōma* in key Pauline passages is often notoriously difficult to determine. As J. D. G. Dunn remarks, "Every time σῶμα appears in Paul modern readers need to be reminded that it does not denote the physical body as such, rather a fuller reality which includes the physical but is not reducible to it" (Dunn 1988, 319).

*2.3. The "Body of Sin" and the "Body of Death."* Two additional phrases appear in Paul's letters and help us understand what he means by "the mortal body." In Romans 6:6 Paul uses an unusual phrase found nowhere else in the Pauline corpus, "the body of sin" (*to sōma tēs hamartias*; or "sinful body" RSV). This functions as the equivalent of "the flesh" and means the physical locality through which sin operates in the person. A related phrase occurs in Romans 7:24 where Paul asks the rhetorical question "Who will deliver me from this body of death [*ek tou sōmatos tou thanatou toutou*]?" Here too the emphasis seems to be on the physicality of Paul's existence, particularly as it is expressed in its mortality. The "body of death" is one that is doomed to die; the larger context of Ro-

mans 7 emphasizes the place that sinful disobedience has in causing this death (*see* Life and Death). R. Jewett posits that Paul has here taken over a phrase from his gnostic* opponents* that is not typical of Pauline theology; he also calls attention to 2 Corinthians 5:8 as a parallel, suggesting that here too Paul is citing the ideas of his opponents in the midst of his discussion.

**3. The Spiritual Body.**

In 1 Corinthians 15:35 Paul demonstrates how closely connected his doctrine of the resurrection is to the question of its bodily form. The verse has him paraphrasing the Corinthians' concerns in the form of two separate but essentially equivalent questions: "How are the dead raised? With what kind of body do they come?" (See Usami for a discussion of how these two rhetorical questions interlock). The actual phrase "spiritual body" (*sōma pneumatikon*) occurs only in 1 Corinthians 15:44, although it is implied by the use of the neuter *to pneumatikon* immediately following in 1 Corinthians 15:46. Precisely what Paul means by "the spiritual body" has been the subject of intense theological and philosophical debate. The comment by G. E. Ladd is a sound starting point for any serious exegetical discussion: "The 'spiritual body' of 1 Cor 15:44 is not a body made of spirit any more than the 'natural' (literally, *psychical*) body is a body made of *psyche*. However, it is a *literal, real body*, even though it has been adapted to the new order of existence which shall be inaugurated at the resurrection" (Ladd, 139).

*3.1. The Resurrection and Disembodied Existence.* In 1 Corinthians 15:35-41 Paul challenges a belief concerning the resurrection apparently held by the Corinthians. The precise nature of the so-called Corinthian heresy has been one of the most explored issues in twentieth-century NT scholarship and remains one of the most debated topics in Pauline studies. Were the adversaries Paul confronted a gnostic or proto-gnostic group within the congregation, who were importing Greek ideas into their Christian faith? Scholarly discussion about the Corinthian opponents of Paul is extensive, but most agree that eschatological matters, including the resurrection, figured prominently within their thinking (see D. Georgi, B. Pearson, J. H. Wilson, R. Mcl. Wilson and C. K. Barrett for treatments of the Corinthian opponents). Most scholars have approached the question from the standpoint of Paul correcting an over-realized eschatology on the part of the Corinthians. Others, notably B. A. Pearson and R. A. Horsley, have argued that the Corinthians had apparently so identified the resurrection with spiritual existence that they had detached it from any physical context; the resurrection hope thereby becomes a disembodied existence, an asomatic immortality. The question is thus switched from a consideration of an over-realized eschatology as the basis for the Corinthian position; instead it understands the Corinthians to deny the bodily resurrection altogether. On balance it seems the former interpretation has more to substantiate it than the latter, although it must be admitted that the latter position allows a much more natural reading of 1 Corinthians 15:12.

The substance of Paul's correction is to assert forcefully the somatic character of the resurrection and to place this within a future context (see 3.2 below). He asserts the somatic nature of the resurrection by an appeal to analogies drawn from nature: grains of wheat (1 Cor 15:37-38); types of animals (1 Cor 15:39); celestial bodies (1 Cor 15:40-41). The substance of the argument is that in each instance God is able to produce a new order of life (resurrection) but does so in such a way that a correlation to somatic existence is maintained. The phrase translated as "bare kernel" in the RSV (*gymnon kokkon*) is particularly interesting and has an important parallel in Jewish rabbinic literature (*b. Sanh* 90b). The image of somatic nakedness also figures in 2 Corinthians 5:3 where Paul uses it to describe existence between the time of death and the granting of a resurrection body at the parousia of Christ (*see* Intermediate State).

Most scholars accept that the heart of Paul's resurrection belief requires the materiality of the resurrection body (*sōma pneumatikon*), although it is extremely difficult to know precisely what Paul envisioned this body to be like or what bodily properties he held it to have. However, some (such as Gooch) suggest that this resurrection body is ontologically the same as the disembodied person, and that the logic of Paul's eschatological teaching leads inevitably to a breakdown of the distinction between the two. Effectively the argument here (as we noted in 2.2 above) follows the suggestion of J. A. T. Robinson that the *sōma* is best understood as constituting "the human person in his or her totality"; a disembodied *sōma* is not therefore a contradiction in terms. Most scholars (including Reichenbach) would consider this argument terminological sophistry which is contrary to Paul's teaching in the main, and fails to recognize the material meaning of *sōma* in such passages as 1 Corinthians 15:35.

It may well be that the inability to distinguish properly between a "resurrection of the body" (which Paul clearly affirms) and a "resurrection of the flesh" (which Paul nowhere mentions) is what prompts many such theological discussions. The former gives sufficient weight to the idea of discontinuity within the somatic image while the latter sacrifices too much to the idea of continuity between this mortal body and the resurrection body. In any event, the debate is another illustration of how difficult it is to discuss the material nature of the resurrection body with any degree of precision.

*3.2. The Nature of the Resurrection Body.* The NT never attempts to describe the nature of Christ's resurrection body, what it looked like or what sort of physical properties it possessed; neither does it offer much detail about what the resurrection body of the believer will be like. This is not unusual in and of itself, in spite of the fact that the only contemporaneous Jewish text which attempts to address this problem in any depth is *2 Baruch* 50:2—51:10. At best the NT evidence on such matters is circumstantial, largely drawn from Luke and Acts. It has been suggested on this basis that the risen Lord Jesus was not bound by the laws of physics as we know them, that he was able to materialize (and dematerialize) at will, that it was possible for the disciples to examine his body, that he ate fish and bread only for their sake, etc. The witness of the Pauline letters adds little, if anything, to such discussions. Indeed, J. D. G. Dunn suggests that Luke and Paul may have been at variance on this point: "What Luke affirms (Jesus' resurrection body was flesh and bones) Paul denies (the resurrection body is *not* composed of flesh and blood)!" (Dunn 1985, 74). Paul does discuss the resurrection body at some length in 1 Corinthians 15, but it is within the context of a theological debate about the nature of the resurrection body *of the believers*. Yet the two matters are not unrelated. As Harris states, "there is an interesting correspondence between the depiction of Christ's resurrection body in the gospels and Paul's description of the believer's spiritual body" (Harris 1983, 57).

In 1 Corinthians 15:42-49 Paul makes a crucial distinction between the "natural body" (*sōma psychikon*) and the "spiritual body" (*sōma pneumatikon*; cf. Phil 3:21). At the heart of the passage is the contrast built upon his Adam/Christ analogy in 1 Corinthians 15:44b-45, which sets forth the proper temporal relationship between the two. In effect Paul is countering a false anthropology being held by the Corinthians with one that understands the resurrection body as both future and somatic (Dunn, 1973, offers a stimulating discussion on this). On the stormy and uncharted seas of describing the resurrection body Paul is attempting to steer a middle course between the Scylla of a crass materialism (equating resurrection with the reanimation of corpses) and the Charybdis of spiritualistic immortality (denying materiality altogether). To avoid the first danger he asserts that it is a *spiritual* body which will be resurrected; to avoid the second he asserts that it is a spiritual *body* which will be resurrected. R. J. Sider correctly observes that the use of the *psychikos anthrōpos/pneumatikos anthrōpos* contrast in 1 Corinthians 2:14-15 lends support to a material understanding of the *sōma pneumatikon*.

How the maintenance of identity and the preservation of individuality are retained within the resurrection body of the believer are matters which are left largely unanswered by Paul, although his use of the seed analogy in 1 Corinthians 15:35-54 allows for both continuity and discontinuity between the present mortal body and the resurrected body of the believer (both Sider and Harris 1983, 125-33, discuss this at some length).

But how far dare we pursue the matter of somatic continuity? Will sexuality be an integral part of resurrection existence, or will it be an asexual existence like that of the angels? Will persons be able physically to recognize each other? How old will people be within their resurrection bodies—children, teenagers or mature adults? Will the color of hair or eyes remain the same? We may scoff at the naive simplicity of such questions, but they are inevitable given the nature of the *sōma* image itself. The issue of molecular continuity in the resurrection body is an even more perplexing problem, one which raises a host of new questions in our increasingly technological age. Such matters can, however, serve as a nexus between science and faith if they are allowed to do so. The fact that human beings are able to maintain a continuity even though their physical bodies undergo a constant change of cells challenges us to rethink the meaning of continuity itself (M. E. Dahl, 94, offers an interesting discussion of how physical molecular discontinuity in the present mortal life helps us understand the nature of the bodily resurrection to come). Most conservative scholars would argue that an enduring rationality, a consistency of personality and a persistence of memory are the minimum requirements for the idea of continuity to make sense.

However, Paul addresses none of these matters directly; his aims are much more modest (and all the more frustrating as a result; we would have liked him to offer more insight into these issues which puzzle us!). In short, Paul's line is to assert that the resurrection body, though continuous with the physical body, is not identical with it since it is a spiritual body; his whole argument in 1 Corinthians 15:35-44 pursues this. In the end we are forced to admit that Paul struggled with the limitations of language in the same way that we do today when it comes to describing the nature of the resurrection body. Paul himself acknowl-edged this, for he asserts in 1 Corinthians 2:9 (paraphrasing Is 64:4) that "what no eye has ever seen, what no ear has ever heard, what never entered the mind of man, God has prepared all that for those who love him" (Moffatt trans.).

## 4. Resurrection of the Dead or Immortality of the Soul?

One of the classic ways in which discussion about the resurrection has been pursued is by contrasting it with the immortality* of the soul. O. Cullmann, for instance, argued that the two formulations of future hope are mutually exclusive, representing a difference of perspective between Judaism and Hellenism about the afterlife. This either/or distinction has often been accepted as self-evident and is sometimes used polemically to distinguish the Christian hope over against that of the pagan religions of the NT period (as in Acts 17:18, 32). Indeed, in the course of his argument Cullmann contrasts attitudes to the death of Jesus with those to the death of Socrates.

However, it is now recognized that the distinction between resurrection of the body and immortality of the soul is somewhat artificial and does not take into account the teaching of some relevant first-century texts which blur the differences between the two (as Harris argues). Some of the Jewish pseudepigraphic documents, as well as the Dead Sea scrolls from Qumran,* demonstrate how difficult it is to maintain a rigid contrast on this particular point (Barrett, 1979, offers a helpful discussion of Cullmann's book).

As a case in point, the Book of Wisdom (which Paul may well have read) straddles these allegedly incompatible Jewish and Hellenistic conceptualizations of afterlife with little apparent difficulty. This is an especially important text for comparison (NA[26] lists forty-one allusions to the book within the Pauline corpus); it also offers some interesting parallels to Paul's use of the terms *athanasia* and *aphtharsia* within his teaching about the resurrection body. For instance, in Wisdom 2:23 the aim of man's creation is stated: "God created man for incorruption (*aphtharsia*)." At the same time, in language much more characteristic of the dualism associated with Hellenistic thought, we read in Wisdom 9:15 that "the corruptible body weighs down the soul" (*phtharton gar sōma barynei psychēn*). At several points within the book the idea of immortality is also communicated by means of the term *athanasia* (Wis 3:4; 4:1; 8:13, 17; 15:3) In short, the Wisdom of Solomon itself should make us wary of phrasing this question of afterlife in terms of a rigid choice between Hellenistic and Jewish conceptions of afterlife.

*See also* BODY OF CHRIST; FLESH; HOLY SPIRIT; IMMORTAL-

ITY; INTERMEDIATE STATE; LIFE AND DEATH; PSYCHOLOGY; RESURRECTION.

BIBLIOGRAPHY. C. K. Barrett, "Immortality and Resurrection," in *Resurrection and Immortality: Aspects of Twentieth-Century Christian Belief*, ed. C. S. Duthie (London: Samuel Bagster & Sons, 1979) 68-88; E. Best, *One Body in Christ* (London: SPCK, 1955) 215-25; R. Bultmann, *Theology of the New Testament* (2 vols.; New York: Charles Scribners's Sons, 1951, 1955) 1.192-203; H. C. C. Cavallin, *Life After Death: Paul's Argument for the Resurrection of the Dead in 1 Cor 15* (ConBNT 7,1; Lund: Gleerup, 1974); O. Cullmann, *Immortality of the Soul or Resurrection of the Dead?* (London: Epworth, 1958); M. E. Dahl, *The Resurrection of the Body* (London: SCM, 1962); J. D. G. Dunn, "I Corinthians 15:45—Last Adam, Life-Giving Spirit," in *Christ and Spirit in the New Testament: Studies in Honour of C. F. D. Moule*, ed. B. Lindars and S. Smalley, (Cambridge: University Press, 1973) 127-41; idem, *The Evidence for Jesus* (Philadelphia: Westminster, 1985); idem, *Romans 1-8* (WBC 38A; Waco: Word, 1988); E. E. Ellis, "II Cor 5:1-10 in Pauline Eschatology," *NTS* 6 (1959-60) 211-24; D. Georgi, *The Opponents of Paul in Second Corinthians* (Philadelphia: Fortress, 1986); P. W. Gooch, "On Disembodied Resurrected Persons: A Study in the Logic of Christian Eschatology," *RelS* 17 (1981) 199-213; R. H. Gundry, *Sōma in Biblical Theology* (Cambridge: University Press, 1976); M. J. Harris, *Raised Immortal: The Relation between Resurrection and Immortality in New Testament Teaching* (Grand Rapids: Eerdmans, 1983); idem, "The New Testament view of life after death," *Themelios* 11 (1986) 47-52; R. A. Horsley, "How can some of you say there is no resurrection of the dead? Spiritual Elitism in Corinth," *NovT* 20 (1978) 203-31; J. Jeremias, "Flesh and Blood Cannot Inherit the Kingdom of God," *NTS* 2 (1955-56) 151-59; R. Jewett, *Paul's Anthropological Terms: A Study of Their Use in Conflict Settings* (Leiden: E. J. Brill, 1971) 201-304; G. E. Ladd, *Crucial Questions about the Kingdom of God* (Grand Rapids: Eerdmans, 1952); R. P. Martin, *The Spirit and the Congregation* (Grand Rapids: Eerdmans, 1984); C. F. D. Moule, "St Paul and Dualism: The Pauline Conception of the Resurrection," *NTS* 13 (1966-67) 106-23; B. A. Pearson, *The 'Pneumatikos-Psychikos' Terminology in 1 Corinthians* (Missoula, MT: Scholars, 1973); B. R. Reichenbach, "On Disembodied Resurrected Persons: A Reply," *RelS* 18 (1982) 225-29; J. A. T. Robinson, *The Body: A Study in Pauline Theology* (SBT 5; London: SCM, 1952); E. Schweizer, "σῶμα κτλ," *TDNT* VII.1024-94; R. J. Sider, "The Pauline Conception of the Resurrection Body in I Corinthians XV.35-54," *NTS* 21 (1974-75) 428-39; W. D. Stacey, *The Pauline View of Man* (London: Macmillan, 1956); K. Usami, " 'How are the dead raised?' (1 Cor 15, 35-58)," *Bib* 57 (1976) 468-93; S. Wibbing, "Body, Member, Limb," *NIDNTT* 1.232-38; J. H. Wilson, "The Corinthians Who Say There Is No Resurrection from the Dead," *ZNW* 59 (1968) 90-107; R. Mcl. Wilson, "How Gnostic Were the Corinthians?," *NTS* 19 (1972-73) 65-74; J. A. Ziesler, "*Sōma* in the Septuagint," *NovT* 25 (1983) 133-45.

L. J. Kreitzer

# BODY OF CHRIST

The Pauline writings use the exact phrase "the body of Christ" only four times (*to sōma tou Christou:* Rom 7:4; 1 Cor 10:16; Eph 4:12; *sōma Christou:* 1 Cor 12:27). Equivalent expressions include "the body of the Lord" (1 Cor 11:27), "his body of flesh" (Col 1:22), "his glorious body" (Phil 3:21), "his body" (Eph 1:23; 5:30; Col 1:24) and "my body" (1 Cor 11:24). Closely related to the above are the terms "the body*" (1 Cor 11:29; Eph 5:23; Col 1:18; 2:19) and "one body" (Rom 12:5; 1 Cor 10:17; 12:13; Eph 2:16; 4:4; Col 3:15). These twenty-one phrases may be classified into the three uses set out in the following outline; significantly, however, they all relate to either the physical body (crucified or resurrected) of Christ* or the metaphorical body of Christ, the church.*

1. The Physical Body of Christ
2. The Body of Christ in Eucharistic Contexts
3. The Body of Christ As a Designation of the Church

### 1. The Physical Body of Christ.

In Romans 7:4 "the body of Christ," which is the instrument through which believers were rendered dead to and hence free from the Law,* refers to Christ's physical body in which he suffered death on the cross.* Similarly, "his body of flesh*" in Colossians 1:22 is a Hebraism (with Qumran parallels) denoting Christ's physical body, which in death became the means by which God reconciled sinners to himself: the addition "of flesh" insists, against the Colossian* heresy, on the true humanity of the incarnate Jesus. In Philippians 3:21 "his glorious body" stands in antithetical parallelism to "our lowly body" and refers to the resurrection* body with which and in which the Lord Jesus is expected to return from heaven* (cf. Phil 3:20).

### 2. The Body of Christ in Eucharistic Contexts.

Several times in 1 Corinthians the body concept appears in close conjunction with the eucharist, or Lord's Supper*; the texts reveal a close relationship between the physical body of Christ which was crucified and the church as the body of the risen Christ.

Thus, partaking of the cup and the bread in the

eucharist means participation in the blood and the body of Christ (1 Cor 10:16), that is, in the benefits of his death and in fellowship* with him (see Dying and Rising). The strict parallelism between "the body of Christ" and "the blood of Christ" shows that the former refers to the body of Jesus surrendered in death (cf. 1 Cor 11:24) just as the latter refers to his blood shed as atoning blood (cf. 1 Cor 11:25; see Jeremias). Just as there is only one loaf at the eucharist, so those who participate jointly in the single loaf constitute a single body (1 Cor 10:17). The context, with its exhortation to shun the worship* of idols (1 Cor 10:14; see Idolatry), suggests that Paul's point in making use of the body analogy in 1 Corinthians 10:16-17 is not so much the unity of the body made up of Christians as their solidarity as one body in union with Christ which forbids a similar union with demons* (cf. 1 Cor 10:21). This, in turn, implies that the "one body" of 1 Corinthians 10:17 refers to the body of Christ, the church.

A similar shift of meaning from the crucified body of Christ to the church as the body of Christ occurs in 1 Corinthians 11:23-32. The bread at the institution of the Lord's Supper signifies or represents Christ's actual body about to be offered up on the cross (1 Cor 11:24). It follows that to eat the bread in an unworthy manner is to be guilty of "the body . . . of the Lord" (1 Cor 11:27); that this phrase refers to the crucified body of Jesus is rendered certain by its linkage (cf. 1 Cor 10:16) with "the blood [of the Lord]." But in 1 Corinthians 11:29 the expression "not discerning the body" is probably a reference, not to failure to discern in the bread of the eucharist the body of the Lord surrendered on the cross (cf. 1 Cor 11:24, 27), but the failure to recognize in the group of believers gathered at the Lord's Supper the metaphorical body of Christ (cf. 1 Cor 10:17), a failure which resulted in the shameful abuses described in 1 Corinthians 11:17-22 (Bornkamm, 190-95).

### 3. The Body of Christ As a Designation of the Church.

This particular use of the body concept, of which two instances have already been referred to (1 Cor 10:17; 11:29), is unique to Paul in the NT writings. The issues of the origin and nature of the concept will be addressed before examining its usage in the remaining Pauline texts.

*3.1. The Origin of the Concept.* There have been many suggestions regarding the possible sources of Paul's "body of Christ" idea. (1) The previously fashionable attempt to trace it to the gnostic concept of the primal person, whose body was conceived of as cosmic (H. Schlier, E. Käsemann, R. Bultmann), is gener-

ally discarded today because of the lateness (third century A.D.) of the evidence. (2) That the temple of Asclepius in Corinth, with its votive offerings in the form of clay representations of dismembered parts of the body that have been healed, provided the catalyst for the formation of the Pauline image (A. E. Hill) is surely far-fetched. (3) That Paul's phrase "body of Christ" was constructed on the analogy of the phrase "body of Adam*" allegedly implicit in rabbinic usage (see Davies), or at least was probably influenced by the Jewish "body of Adam" idea (R. Jewett) appears doubtful, since no actual examples of the phrase "body of Adam" in rabbinical literature are forthcoming, and it is admitted that "the Jewish body of Adam idea does not provide us with an exact parallel to Paul's sōma Christou [body of Christ] concept" (Jewett, 245). (4) The view (A. E. J. Rawlinson, H. Conzelmann) that Paul derived his expression "body of Christ" from the eucharistic tradition—the sacramentally acquired share in the body of Christ in the eucharist makes the participants the body of Christ—faces the simple objection that "*eating* the body is not *being* the body" (Moule, 87). (5) The suggestion that Paul, from the concept of Israel as the bride of God (Jer 2:2) and through new-covenant theology, developed the concept of "the body of Christ" as its parallel for the new Israel, the church (Bass, 530-31), is not very likely, since the more logical line of development is from Israel as the bride of Yahweh to the church as the *bride* of Christ. (6) The statement that Genesis 2:24— "a man leaves his father and his mother and clings to his wife, and they become one flesh" (quoted in Eph 5:31)—"appears to provide the biblical rationale and the conceptual foundation for the Apostle's understanding, throughout his letters, of the church as the body of Christ" (Ellis, 42) calls to mind C. Chavasse's attempt to locate the origin of the Pauline phrase in the nuptial union of bridegroom and bride in the "one flesh." But F. F. Bruce thinks that "both the eucharistic . . . and the nuptial . . . applications of Paul's thought on this subject are derived from his conception of the church as the body of Christ rather than *vice versa*" (Bruce 1984, 69 n.141).

Rather than being attributable to a single source, the body of Christ concept is more likely the result of the interplay of several influences.

(1) The comparison of the state (*polis*) or world-state (*cosmopolis*) to a body consisting of interdependent members is a Stoic commonplace, and, as Moule (84-85) points out, close parallels to the Pauline use of the analogy are provided, for instance, by Seneca, who addresses Nero as "the soul of the republic [which] is your body" (Seneca *De Clem.* 1.5.1). He also speaks of

Nero as the head, on whom the good health of the body, the empire, depends (Seneca *De Clem.* 2.2.1), and says "We are limbs of a great body" (Seneca *Ep. Mor.* 95.52). Philo, with a change of context, says that the High Priest's purpose in offering sacrifice for the nation is "that every age[-group] and all the parts of the nation may be welded into one and the same family as though it were a single body" (Philo *Spec. Leg.* 3.131).

(2) Paul was familiar with the Hebrew concept of "corporate personality," with its oscillation between the individual and the corporate and its notion of the inclusion of the many in the one: a figure standing at the head (e.g., Adam,* Abraham,* Noah, Moses*) can be regarded as incorporating in his own person those represented by him. It is this idea of solidarity between the one and the many, of the union between believers and Christ, that Paul emphasizes in his presentation of the church as the body of Christ. The analogy between all men and women by natural birth being "in Adam" and all believers by new birth being "in Christ"* (Rom 5:12-21; 1 Cor 15:22, 45) is an important datum of Pauline theology.

(3) The idea of solidarity between Christ and his people finds expression in the teaching of Jesus (Mk 9:37 and par.; cf. Mt 18:5; 25:40), and is clearly implied in the risen Lord's identification of himself with his persecuted people (Acts 9:4). While it is probably impossible to be certain about the precise origin(s) of the Pauline expression, it may be that it was Paul's own coinage, based on the common image of the body in popular philosophy and the Hebrew concept of corporate personality, with the words of the risen Jesus to Paul on the Damascus road providing the germ of the conception in his mind or the catalyst for the formation of the unique Pauline expression (see Kim, 252-56).

**3.2. The Nature of the Concept.** The body of Christ concept is plainly not used allegorically: in 1 Corinthians 12, for instance, different parts of the body do not represent different individuals or sections of the Corinthian church. It has been said that the phrase "the body of Christ" (meaning the church) "is used realistically, ontologically, and *therefore* metaphorically or symbolically or analogically" (Richardson, 256-57 n.1), but it is more usual to describe its use as either realistic/ontological or analogical/metaphorical. The realistic understanding of the expression, espoused by such scholars as A. Schweitzer, who thought of the elect as coming into corporeal union with the risen Christ, and J. A. T. Robinson, for whom the church is identified as literally the resurrected body of Christ, violates the clear indication of a comparison given in

Romans 12:4-5 and 1 Corinthians 12:12 ("just as . . . so") and, besides, ignores Paul's careful distinction between Christ's resurrection in the past and believers' (yet awaited) resurrection in the future. We may, therefore, with most recent Protestant interpreters, understand the body concept metaphorically, not literally and biologically or mystically.

**3.3. The Concept in Paul's Usage.** Two stages may be distinguished in Paul's use of the body concept in reference to the church: it is used largely as a simile in 1 Corinthians* and Romans* (the church is like a body), and as a metaphor in Colossians* and Ephesians* (the church is the body of which Christ is the head). "The advance from the language of simile in 1 Corinthians and Romans to the real interpersonal involvement expressed in the language of Colossians and Ephesians may have been stimulated by Paul's consideration of the issues involved in the Colossian heresy" (Bruce 1977, 421).

*3.3.1. Earlier Letters: 1 Corinthians and Romans.* In 1 Corinthians 6:15 the bodies of believers are said to be "members of Christ"; the word "members" (*melē*) means "bodily parts" and thus implies that believers are members of the "body" of Christ. However, Paul immediately goes on to speak of his own body as "members [plural] of Christ," which he will not turn into "members [plural] of a prostitute." This shows that here his concern is with the individual believer's relationship with the Lord, and there is no reference to believers as a corporate body.

Later in the letter Paul says to the local congregation at Corinth: "You are the body of Christ" (1 Cor 12:27; the Greek phrase has no article before either "body" or "Christ," but it means the same as if both nouns had the article—this is an instance of the grammatical rule known as "Apollonius's canon"). This metaphor comes as the summary and climax of the preceding fifteen verses (1 Cor 12:12-26), in which the character of the body concept as simile is plainly indicated by the opening statement: "For just as [*kathaper*] the body is one and has many members, . . . so [*houtos*] also is Christ" (1 Cor 12:12; cf. NEB, "For Christ is *like* a single body . . ." [italics added]). Since Paul does not say "so also is the church" or even ". . . the body of Christ" but simply ". . . (the) Christ," some have derived from this a view of Christ as the whole (*totus Christus*) of which the various members are parts; but in view of 1 Corinthians 12:27-28 it seems better to regard Paul here as using the figure of metonymy ("Christ" for "the body of Christ") or as having omitted the intermediate logical step: Christ himself may be described as a body with many members since the church is the body of Christ.

Into this one body believers—here the "we all" (*hēmeis pantes*) seems to refer to a wider group than the "you" (*hymeis*) of verse 27 and could include all Christians—are baptized in the one Spirit (1 Cor 12:13; the baptizer being, presumably, Christ: cf. Mt 3:11; Lk 3:16; *see* Holy Spirit). Within this one body there is, by God's design (1 Cor 12:18), a multiplicity of members and functions (1 Cor 12:14-16) which is necessary not only for the body as a whole (1 Cor 12:17, 19-20) but for the members themselves (1 Cor 12:21), all of whom are involved in a solidarity of experience or unity of destiny (1 Cor 12:26). Hence, resentment born of a sense of inferiority (1 Cor 12:15-16) and arrogance arising from a sense of superiority (1 Cor 12:21) are alike out of place. Indeed, the so-called weaker members of the human body are actually indispensable (1 Cor 12:22), and there is at work in the human body, again by God's design (1 Cor 12:24), a certain principle of compensation or complementarity which, Paul implies, provides a pattern for Christian conduct (1 Cor 12:23-25).

The same correlatives as are used in 1 Corinthians 12:12 appear also in Romans 12:4-5: "For as [*kathaper*] in one body we have many members, . . . so [*houtōs*] we, though many, are one body in Christ" (RSV). As in 1 Corinthians 12:27, the body simile is applied to the local Christian congregation, with a change in terminology from "the body of Christ" to "one body . . . in Christ"; the latter expression brings out the thought that the organic unity of Christians as a body is grounded in their common incorporation in Christ, but since these two verses in Romans 12 may reasonably be regarded as a summary of the fuller treatment of 1 Corinthians 12:12-26, "one body . . . in Christ" refers to the same reality as "the body of Christ."

In both 1 Corinthians 12 and Romans 12, the theme of the body imagery is that of "one body, many members," of "diversity within unity" of the church as the body of Christ. So far, the body imagery emphasizes primarily the mutual relationships and obligations of believers one to another and secondarily their union with Christ, but leaves undefined the exact relation of the church as the body of Christ to Christ himself: the "head" of the body is in 1 Corinthians 12:21 apparently some self-important member of the local church.

*3.3.2. Later Letters: Colossians and Ephesians.* Despite appearances, the final words of Colossians 2:17 in the Greek (*to de sōma tou Christou*) is not a reference to "the body of Christ," but means "the *substance* [in contrast to the shadow] belongs to Christ." In Colossians 3:15 the believers in Colossae are described as having been called "in one body": they are thus members of

a single organism. If, possibly by implication, this organism is identified with the body of Christ, then the same emphasis on the unity of the body of Christ is found here as in the two earlier letters. In Colossians 1:24 the body of Christ is definitely identified as the church, clearly in an "ecumenical" sense, for whose sake the apostle suffers. Colossians 1:18 calls Christ "the head of the body, the church."

The majority view believes (1) that Colossians 1:15-20 is a pre-Pauline hymn which has been inserted into the letter's train of thought, (2) that in it the "body" whose "head"* is Christ is originally the universe or cosmos, and (3) that the words "the church" in Colossians 1:18 are a gloss added by either Paul or the final redactor of the letter so as to reinterpret the original cosmological reference along ecclesiological lines (e.g., Schweizer, 1074-77). This view has, however, been challenged (see, e.g., O'Brien 1982, 48-49) and the verse (Col 1:18) may be understood simply as it stands, with the result that the church as the body of Christ is now definitely related to Christ as its head. Although a few scholars (most notably Ridderbos, 379-83) have argued that "head" and "body" in this and other Pauline texts do not make up a composite metaphor but are to be kept distinct as two independent images, the more natural reading of the present text seems clearly to teach an organic relationship in which Christ as the head exercises control and direction over his body, the church.

In Colossians 2:19 the metaphor brings out the new element of growth: Christ as the head of the body is here the source of the body's growth (*ex hou*, "from whom [Christ]," rather than *ex hēs*, "from which [head]," is probably an instance of construction according to sense). The idea which follows of the whole body being knit together and growing together is appropriate in view of the fact that headship involves direction and control. (W. A. Grudem has adduced several texts from Philo and Plutarch as well as Plato which explicitly say that the head is the ruling or governing part of the body; but *see* Head, Headship).

Thus in Colossians the use of the body metaphor differs from that in the earlier letters in that the explicit application to the believers' mutual relationship is dropped—although the notion of their harmonious union and functioning is implied in the description of Colossians 2:19—and in its place are introduced the headship of Christ and the growth of the church as a living organism.

Whereas in the three letters already dealt with the term "body" is used in other ways as well, in Ephesians* it is employed exclusively in connection with the church. Here the metaphor is even more fully developed than in Colossians, or at least its implications are more explicitly drawn out. In Ephesians 1:22-23 the church is designated the body of Christ, and Christ its "supreme head" (NEB). The text introduces the entirely new element of Christ's filling his body just as he fills the universe. (We take the noun *plērōma,* "fullness,"* passively and the participle *plēroumenou* as middle, "filling," rather than passive, "being filled"; cf. Eph 4:10.) In Ephesians 2:16 the "one body" within which both the reconciliation* of Jew (*see* Israel) and Gentile* to God and the reconciliation of Jews and Gentiles to one another take place is a reference to the church (same as the "one new person" of Eph 2:15) rather than the crucified* body of Christ. In favor of this conclusion are the use of "one body" and not "his body," and the order of the words "[the] both in one body" (*tous amphoterous en heni sōmati*). The reference here to the unity of the body, not in terms of individuals, but in terms of the two great divisions of humankind (cf. Eph 3:6, which uses a cognate adjective, *syssōmos,* "concorporate, sharing in the same body"), again presents a new aspect to the use of the body metaphor, but the "one body" is not specifically called the body "of Christ." Similarly, in Ephesians 4:4 the "one body" vitalized by the "one Spirit" (who in Eph 2:18 creates the unity of the "one body" of Jewish and Gentile believers), is separate from the "one Lord" of Ephesians 4:5 and is simply a description of the Christian community as a unity. This unity of the body supplies the motivation for keeping the unity of the Spirit (Eph 4:3).

In Ephesians 4:12-16, where the church is again (cf. Eph 1:22-23) designated the body of Christ (Eph 1:22), the unity of the church is again (as already in Eph 4:4, and in Rom 12 and 1 Cor 12) described in terms of individual members, and their mutual dependence is seen to be necessary for the growth of the body, which is said to be both from Christ (Eph 4:16: *ex hou,* "from whom," as in Col 2:19) and to Christ (Eph 4:15: *eis auton,* "unto him"). The meaning appears to be that the growth of the body, which aims at conformity to Christ (*eis auton,* cf. Eph 4:13), takes place as (1) the body is rightly related to the head (*ex hou*), holding fast to him (cf. Col 2:19) and receiving nourishment from him (cf. Eph 1:23); and as (2) its members are rightly related to one another, each making its own contribution, according to the measure of its gift and function, to the upbuilding of the whole in love.* (An alternative view, which regards the participles, rendered in the RSV as "joined and knit together," in Eph 4:16 as indicating not the mutual relationship among believers but the relationship between believers on the one

hand and Christ on the other, is less probable. Nor is it likely that the "joints" of Eph 4:16 refer to the ministers of Eph 4:11, the thought being that they are the ligaments which bind the church to Christ, as argued for by A. T. Lincoln, ad loc.)

In Ephesians 4:25 the fact that believers are "members one of another" (cf. Rom 12:5), meaning "fellow-members in the one body which is the body of Christ," provides the motivation for honest dealings one with another. In Ephesians 5:23 the actual wording of the Greek describes Christ as "head of the church" and "the Savior of the body" (NEB) and not exactly as "the head of his body, the church" or even "the head of the church, his body" (RSV, NIV), so that it might be argued that here, at least, "head" and "body" do not make up one composite imagery. However, the fact that in Ephesians 5:30 believers are said to be "members of his body" suggests that in Ephesians 5:23 as well, the description of Christ as "the head of the church" involves the correlative figure of the church as his body (cf. Eph 1:22-23; 4:15-16), even though there is no corresponding correlative in the husband-wife relationship (*see* Man and Woman).

Thus, the body metaphor in Ephesians both combines the earlier expressions of the concept in the other three letters and advances beyond them in presenting the church as filled by Christ and as embracing Jew and Gentile in its unity. Another especially noteworthy feature of the use of the body metaphor in Ephesians is its fusion with other metaphors of the church. The building of the temple* grows (Eph 2:21) while, conversely, the body is built up (Eph 4:16, cf. 4:12). In Ephesians 5:22-33, with the concept of bodily union providing the link (Gen 2:24; Eph 5:31), the figure of the church as the bride of Christ is supplemented by that of the body. The twin aspects of Christ's lordship over the church and his union with her, which are connected with the body concept, are made to serve the interests of illustrating and emphasizing (1) the church's obligation to Christ (the wife [cf. the church as the body] is to be subject to the husband [cf. Christ as the head]) and (2) Christ's love for the church (the husband is to love the wife as his own body, as Christ [the head] loved the church [his body]).

*3.3.3. Summary and Conclusion.* By way of summary and conclusion the following statements may be derived from Paul's use of the concept of the body of Christ as a designation of the church:

(1) The figure of the body of Christ is applied by Paul to a local congregation (1 Cor 12:27), to Christians who were not necessarily members of the same congregation (Rom 12:4-5; cf. 16:3-15), as well as to a

wider group possibly inclusive of all believers in Christ (1 Cor 12:12-13). That Christ, the head of the body, is the exalted, heavenly Lord is beyond doubt (Eph 1:20-21), but to argue that in Colossians and Ephesians "the 'body' image is used to denote *a heavenly entity,*" since his body the church is also where he is, in heaven (O'Brien 1987, 112, 110; but *see* Church), is to forget the nature of the body of Christ concept as *metaphor*. When believers are said to be raised and seated in the heavenlies with Christ (Col 3:1; Eph 2:6), this is not done in conjunction with the body image.

(2) The church as the body of Christ is a living organic unity composed of a multiplicity of members (i.e., individual believers, not individual congregations), each necessary to the other and to the growth of the whole (1 Cor 10:16-17; 12:12-27; Rom 12:4-5; Col 1:24; 3:15; Eph 4:16). The unity, from another angle, is a unity between diverse races of the world (Eph 2:16-18).

(3) This "horizontal" dimension of unity is based on the "vertical" unity between the church as the body of Christ and Christ as the head of the church. The church, in terms of its members, enters into union with Christ by baptism* in the one Spirit (1 Cor 12:13; cf. Eph 2:18) and maintains it by participation in the eucharist (1 Cor 10:16-17), so that the source of the church's unity is both Christ and the Spirit (cf. Eph 4:4, 5).

(4) Christ as the head is not only united with the church, his body, as the source of its life, but also stands over it as its absolute ruler (Col 1:18; Eph 1:22-23; 4:15; 5:23) and fills it with all the resources of his power* and grace* (Eph 1:23).

(5) The church grows as its members are properly related to Christ the head and to one another as members of the same body (Col 2:19; Eph 4:16).

(6) The mingling of metaphors may indicate that no one metaphor is sufficient by itself to convey the total message concerning the nature and function of the church. Nevertheless, there can be little reasonable doubt that the picture of the body of Christ, more than any other, represents Paul's maturest reflections on the subject: for, as it has been maintained elsewhere, it is with this particular conception of the church that Paul's charisma (*see* Gifts) concept is in perfect correspondence, and it is in terms of this particular conception that the Pauline doctrine of the ministry is largely to be understood (see Fung, esp. 15-20).

(7) The image of the church as the body of Christ looks inward (to the mutual relationship of believers as members of the body) and upward (to the relationship between the body and its head) but not outward (to the relationship between the church and the world). The view that Paul regarded the church as an extension of the incarnation in the world is surely excluded by the very fact that the body metaphor maintains a clear distinction between Christ as head and the church as body; such a view also ignores the fundamental difference between Christ as sinless and the church as not yet perfect.*

(8) The body of Christ is usually the locus of the Christian ministry. The gift of evangelism, indeed, is orientated toward outsiders, and the work of "showing mercy*" (Rom 12:8) is a service which reaches beyond the confines of the Christian fellowship. But there can be no denying that Paul's emphasis in speaking of the ministry rests on how the ministry should serve the church and not on how it should serve the world, and that the stated purpose of the church's being equipped by the ministry is not that it may serve the world but that it may upbuild itself (Eph 4:12, 16). By and large it may be said that for Paul "ministry is of the body, for the body, and by the body" (Ellis, 14).

*See also* ADAM AND CHRIST; BODY; CHURCH; FULLNESS; GIFTS OF THE SPIRIT; HEAD, HEADSHIP; IN CHRIST; LORD'S SUPPER.

BIBLIOGRAPHY. C. B. Bass, "Body," *ISBE* 1.528-31; E. Best, *One Body in Christ* (London: SPCK, 1955); G. Bornkamm, *Paul* (New York: Harper & Row, 1971); F. F. Bruce, *Paul: Apostle of the Heart Set Free* (Grand Rapids: Eerdmans, 1977); idem, *The Epistles to the Colossians, to Philemon and to the Ephesians* (NICNT; Grand Rapids: Eerdmans, 1984); R. Bultmann, *New Testament Theology* (2 vols.; New York: Charles Scribner's, 1951, 1955) 2.151-52; C. Chavasse, *The Bride of Christ* (London: Faber, 1940); H. Conzelmann, *1 Corinthians* (Herm; Philadelphia: Fortress, 1975); W. D. Davies, *Paul and Rabbinic Judaism* (4th ed.; Philadelphia: Fortress, 1980) 56-57; J. D. G. Dunn, " 'The Body of Christ' in Paul," in *Worship, Theology and Ministry in the Early Church*, ed. M. J. Wilkins and T. Paige (JSNTSup 87; Sheffield: JSOT, 1992) 146-62; E. E. Ellis, *Pauline Theology: Ministry and Society* (Grand Rapids: Eerdmans, 1989); R. Y. K. Fung, "Ministry, Community and Spiritual Gifts," *EvQ* 56 (1984) 3-20; W. A. Grudem, "The Meaning of *Kephalē* ("Head"): A Response to Recent Studies," *TJ* 11 NS (1990) 3-72; R. H. Gundry, *SŌMA in Biblical Theology* (SNTSMS 29; Cambridge: University Press, 1976); A. E. Hill, "The Temple of Asclepius: An Alternative Source for Paul's Body Theology," *JBL* 99 (1980) 437-39; J. Jeremias, *The Eucharistic Words of Jesus* (New York: Charles Scribner's, 1966); R. Jewett, *Paul's Anthropological Terms* (AGJU 10; Leiden: E. J. Brill, 1971); E. Käsemann, *Leib und Leib Christi: Eine Untersuchung zur paulinischen Begrifflichkeit* (BHT; Tübingen: J. C. B. Mohr, 1933); idem, "The Theological Problem

Presented by the Motif of the Body of Christ," in *Perspectives on Paul* (Philadelphia: Fortress, 1971) 102-21; S. Kim, *The Origin of Paul's Gospel* (Grand Rapids: Eerdmans, 1981); A. T. Lincoln, *Ephesians* (WBC 42: Dallas: Word, 1990); C. F. D. Moule, *The Origin of Christology* (Cambridge: University Press, 1978) 47-96; P. T. O'Brien, *Colossians, Philemon* (WBC 44; Waco: Word, 1982); idem, "The Church as a Heavenly and Eschatological Entity," in *The Church in the Bible and the World*, ed. D. A. Carson (Grand Rapids: Baker, 1987) 88-119; A. Perriman, " 'His body, which is the church. . . .' Coming to Terms with Metaphor," *EvQ* 62 (1990) 123-42; A. E. J. Rawlinson, "Corpus Christi," in *Mysterium Christi*, ed. G. K. A. Bell and A. Deissmann (London: Longmans, 1930) 225-46; A. Richardson, *An Introduction to the Theology of the New Testament* (New York: Harper, 1958); H. Ridderbos, *Paul: An Outline of His Theology* (Grand Rapids: Eerdmans, 1975) 362-95; J. A. T. Robinson, *The Body: A Study in Pauline Theology* (SBT 5; London: SCM, 1952); H. Schlier, *Christus und die Kirche im Epheserbrief* (Tübingen: J. C. B. Mohr, 1930); A. Schweitzer, *The Mysticism of Paul the Apostle* (London: Black, 1931); E. Schweizer, "σῶμα κτλ," *TDNT* VII.1024-94; A. J. M. Wedderburn, "The Body of Christ and Related Concepts in 1 Corinthians," *SJT* 24 (1971) 74-96.                    R. Y. K. Fung

**BONDAGE.** *See* ELEMENTS/ELEMENTAL SPIRITS OF THE WORLD; LAW; LIFE AND DEATH; PRINCIPALITIES AND POWERS; SATAN, DEVIL; SIN, GUILT; TRIUMPH.

**BREAD.** *See* LORD'S SUPPER.

# C

**CAESAREA.** *See* PHILIPPIANS, LETTER TO THE.

## CAESAR'S HOUSEHOLD, IMPERIAL HOUSEHOLD

The expression "Caesar's household" (*kaisaros oikia*) appears in a concluding greeting of Paul's letter to the Philippians* (Phil 4:22). The full phrase is *"the saints of Caesar's household"* and the apostle* mentions that these believers along with other Christians in the place of his captivity send their greetings to the congregation at Philippi. The expression suggests that the gospel* had made significant progress in the city where Paul was in prison*—which may have been Caesarea (Hawthorne) but Rome* seems more likely.

1. The Meaning of Caesar's Household
2. The Gospel and Caesar's Household
3. Caesar's Household and the Greetings of Romans 16

### 1. The Meaning of Caesar's Household.

The household* of a Roman aristocrat (Gk *oikia/oikos*, Lat *familia*) included, in addition to his family, his staff of servants, especially those who were slaves, but also those who had been freed and who had obligations as his clients. Often their duties were specialized, and included all types of domestic service, professional duties (such as medicine and education) and business, literary and secretarial assistance. In the case of the Caesars (*see* Emperors), their "household" was the equivalent of a modern civil service which provided the experts in most fields of state. Accordingly, the designation "Caesar's household" (called *domus Caesaris* by Tacitus *Hist.* 2.92) included not simply the members of the imperial family or relations, but also the great number of slaves and freedmen from whose ranks the imperial service was staffed. These households were scattered throughout the provinces of the Empire, although the largest concentration was in Rome, which seems to have been large enough to include a significant number of converts to the Christian faith.

Although a good case has been made for a Caesar-ean provenance of Philippians (Hawthorne), as Reicke has put it, Rome may provide "the background for those images used by Paul in Philippians which refer to the political realm (1:27; 3:20)." He adds that the readers would have understood "the reference to Rome and Nero's clients in the greeting from 'those *of Caesar's household*' (Phil 4:22)" (Reicke, 285). These imperial slaves or freedmen may have been known to the Philippians through their employment as couriers between Rome and the East or on business (see Gillman, 34-35, for speculation about Lydia).

On a Roman provenance, Philippians 1:13, "through-out the whole *praitōrion*," denotes neither the emperor's palace situated on the Palatine hill, the barracks attached to the imperial palace nor the large permanent camp of the praetorian soldiers, but a body of men, namely, "those forming the praetorian guard." The term could thus describe either the emperor's bodyguard or the praetorian cohorts stationed in the metropolis. On a Caesarean provenance, it refers to "those in all parts of the residence of the provincial governor of Caesarea" (Hawthorne, 35).

### 2. The Gospel and Caesar's Household.

According to Acts 28:14-15 Paul was met by Roman Christians on his arrival in the imperial city. It is not known exactly how or when the gospel first reached Rome. It may have spread among Jewish believers there soon after Pentecost, or else was first taken to the capital by traders, businessmen or soldiers. Paul's arrival gave fresh impetus to the spread of the gospel (Phil 1:14). Although he was a "bound prisoner," he was able to preach and teach "with all boldness and without hindrance" (Acts 28:31). Soon after his arrival Paul was in touch with "the local leaders of the Jews" (Acts 28:17)—probably the rulers of the synagogues in Rome—and many came to him for the express purpose of hearing his views regarding "the hope of Israel" (Acts 28:20-22).

Caesar's household, because of its servile origins and the eastern responsibilities of the Caesars, contained numbers of Asiatics, many of whom were Jews and who were either slaves* or employed in the imperial court. When the gospel reached Rome and was proclaimed in the many synagogues there, these members of Caesar's household could not fail to hear about Jesus' death* and resurrection.* Further, Paul's daily contact with the soldiers who guarded him led to the introduction of the gospel to "the whole guard." It became evident that his imprisonment, which was "in Christ," was a demonstration of Christ's saving activity and thus contributed to the spread of the gospel not only among the troops but to others as well ("the gospel . . . has become known throughout the whole imperial guard and to everyone else," Phil 1:13). It is not surprising, then, to find Caesar's household well represented in the Christian group in Rome.

**3. Caesar's Household and the Greetings of Romans 16.**
If the letter to the Philippians was sent *from* Rome and the greetings of Romans 16 sent *to* Rome three or four years earlier, then it might be asked whether any of "the saints of Caesar's household" were included among the recipients mentioned in the earlier letter. J. B. Lightfoot and, more recently, F. F. Bruce have claimed that "the family of Aristobulus" and "the family of Narcissus" (Rom 16:10, 11) could well have belonged to the imperial household. The latter has been thought to have comprised the slaves of Tiberius Claudius Narcissus, a wealthy freedman of the Emperor Tiberius who was a powerful figure under Claudius but was executed after Nero's accession in A.D. 54. His household would have become imperial property but distinguished from others in the imperial household by the term *Narcissiani*. Less certain is the position of the family of Aristobulus. Lightfoot and others suggested that he was a grandson of Herod the Great who lived in Rome as a private citizen and, like his elder brother Herod Agrippa I (cf. Acts 12:1), was a friend of the Emperor Claudius. According to Philo, at an earlier date Herod Agrippa I himself was described in exactly these words, a member of "Caesar's household" (Philo *Flacc.* 35).

*See also* EMPERORS, ROMAN; PHILIPPIANS, LETTER TO THE.
BIBLIOGRAPHY. F. F. Bruce, *Philippians* (Peabody, MA: Hendricksen, 1983); F. M. Gillman, *Women Who Knew Paul* (Collegeville, MN: Liturgical, 1992); G. F. Hawthorne, *Philippians* (WBC 43; Waco: Word, 1983); J. B. Lightfoot, *Saint Paul's Epistle to the Philippians* (London: Macmillan, 1890) 171-78; B. Reicke, "Caesarea, Rome and the Captivity Epistles," in *Apostolic History and the Gospel: Biblical and Historical Essays Presented to F. F. Bruce*, ed. W. W. Gasque & R. P. Martin (Grand Rapids: Eerdmans, 1970) 277-86; P. R. C. Weaver, *Familia Caesaris: A Social Study of the Emperor's Freedmen*

*and Slaves* (Cambridge: University Press, 1972).

P. T. O'Brien

## CALENDAR. *See* HOLY DAYS.

## CALL, CALLING
The Pauline letters mention calling in three different connections: the calling of all believers, Paul's calling as an apostle,* and the calling of Israel.*
1. The Calling of All Believers
2. Paul's Calling as an Apostle
3. Israel's Calling as the People of God

### 1. The Calling of All Believers.
When Paul speaks about calling it is, more often than not, the calling of believers to faith* and salvation* that he has in mind. God* himself is the subject of that call (Gal 1:6; 5:8), even though Paul or some other person might be the human agent through whom God calls.

*1.1. Called According to God's Purpose.* God calls people according to his own will and purpose (Rom 8:28; cf. 2 Tim 1:9). This calling rests, not upon any works done by the recipients of the call, but upon the purpose and grace* of God alone (cf. 2 Tim 1:9). It is those he has predestined for salvation whom he calls (Rom 8:30), Gentiles as well as Jews (Rom 9:24-26; 1 Cor 1:24), and mostly the lowly not the exalted (1 Cor 1:26).

*1.2. Called Through the Gospel.* The call of God comes normally through the preaching* of the gospel (1 Thess 1:4-5; 2 Thess 2:14), and the preachers are ambassadors through whom God calls people to be reconciled to him (2 Cor 5:20; *see* Peace, Reconciliation). This gracious calling was made possible only by the death* of Christ, so Paul speaks not just of God calling people through the preaching of the gospel, but also through the grace of Christ* (Gal 1:6).

*1.3. Called to Future Glory.* God calls people to share in his own kingdom* and glory* (1 Thess 2:12), to share the glory of Christ (2 Thess 2:14), to obtain eternal life* (1 Tim 6:12) and to share in a glorious inheritance (Eph 1:18).

*1.4. Called to Present Privileges and Responsibilities.* Those whom God calls to future glory he also calls to enjoy peace with himself (Col 3:15) and in human relationships now (1 Cor 7:15). They are also called to freedom* (Gal 5:13)—from both legalism (trying to establish their acceptability before God by observance of the Law*) and from nomism (regarding the Mosaic Law as a regulatory norm for those already accepted by grace through faith). They are called to be "saints," people set apart for God (Rom 1:7; 1 Cor 1:2), and to holy living (1 Thess 4:7). They are to walk worthily of their high calling by practicing humility, patience, love* and unity (Eph 4:1), and by fulfilling with God's power* every good resolve and work of faith (2 Thess 1:11).

*1.5. Called to Stay with God in Particular Life Situations.* Paul gives a rule of thumb to be followed by the Corinthians: "Let each of you lead the life that the Lord has assigned, to which God called you. This is my rule in all the churches" (1 Cor 7:17 NRSV). People should normally remain in the circumstances in which they found themselves when they first responded to the gospel (whether circumcised* or uncircumcised, whether slave or free, and, Paul implies in the context, whether married* or single). Paul does not regard such circumstances as callings in the sense of Christian vocations, as some have argued. Rather he is saying that the call to faith does not necessitate a change in life circumstances for those who respond to it. Rather, in those circumstances they ought normally to "remain with God" (1 Cor 7:24).

### 2. Paul's Calling as an Apostle.

Just as believers in general are called to salvation according to God's purpose, so Paul's calling to be an apostle was also according to the purpose of God (1 Cor 1:1; see Dietzfelbinger). This calling meant that Paul's whole life was to be dedicated to the proclamation of the gospel (Rom 1:1), something for which he continued to feel quite unworthy, because he had once persecuted the church of God (1 Cor 15:9; *see* Conversion and Call of Paul).

Galatians 1:15-16, more than any other text, reveals what was involved in being called to be an apostle* as far as Paul was concerned: "But when God, who had set me apart before I was born and called me through his grace, was pleased to reveal his Son to me, so that I might proclaim him among the Gentiles, I did not confer with any human being" (Gal 1:15-16 NRSV). This text reveals several important aspects of Paul's apostolic calling: (1) He had been chosen by God for this task even before he was born (as had been some of the prophets of the OT, cf. Is 49:1, 5; Jer 1:5; *see* Prophet, Paul As). (2) His own realization of this calling came to him by a revelation from God at a time determined by God himself. (3) It had nothing to do with anything deserving on Paul's part; it came through God's grace. (4) It involved a revelation by God of his Son Jesus Christ to Paul so that he might preach Christ to others. (5) The preaching ministry to which he was called had a specific scope: to the Gentiles.* (6) It came directly from God, without human mediation.

### 3. Israel's Calling as the People of God.

One of the problems Paul wrestled with was his own people's resistance to the gospel. How could the Jews, who had been called by God to be his special possession among the nations, reject the good news God sent to them? Writing about this, Paul reveals several aspects of his understanding of Israel's calling (*see* Israel; Restoration of Israel).

*3.1. It Is Irrevocable.* Even when confronted by Israel's rejection of the gospel, Paul insists that God had not rejected his people, for, he asserts, the gifts and calling of God are irrevocable (Rom 11:28-29). It must be understood that God's calling now involves Gentiles as well as Jews (Rom 9:24-26).

*3.2. It Is a Matter of Grace and Election.* To deal with the problem of God's faithfulness to his word in the light of Israel's rejection of the gospel, Paul explains that not every member of the nation of Israel was in fact a member of the elect people (Rom 9:6-7; *see* Election). A person's status as a true Israelite depended not upon the works of that person, but rather upon the mercy* of God; that is, upon God's election and calling (Rom 9:10-16).

*3.3. God's Calling and the Remnant.* Even though many Jews had shown, by their rejection of the gospel, that they were not true Israelites, Paul insists that there is a remnant of true Israelites, of whom he is one (Rom 11:1-5). This was the remnant according to the election of grace (Rom 11:5-6).

*See also* Apostasy, Falling Away, Perseverance; Conversion and Call of Paul; Election and Predestination; Israel; Prophet, Paul As.

BIBLIOGRAPHY. C. Dietzfelbinger, *Der Berufung des Paulus als Ursprung seiner Theologie* (WMANT 58; Neukirchen-Vluyn; Neukirchener, 1985); C. G. Kruse, *New Testament Models for Ministry: Jesus and Paul* (Nashville: Thomas Nelson, 1985); I. H. Marshall, "Election and Calling to Salvation in 1 and 2 Thessalonians," in *The Thessalonian Correspondence*, ed. R. F. Collins (Leuven: University Press, 1990) 259-76; K. L. Schmidt, "καλέω κτλ," *TDNT* III.487-536.
C. G. Kruse

## CANON

Any discussion about the canonicity of Paul's letters takes place between two certainties: One is that the apostle Paul wrote letters to a number of individuals and churches; the other is that by A.D. 397 the church had canonized (i.e., accepted as authoritative and normative) fourteen letters attributed to Paul along with the other books which eventually made up the canon of the NT.

What happened between the first and the fourth centuries, however, is open to considerable speculation and debate. Sources for reconstructing this process of recognition of Paul's letters are either non-existent or subject to a variety of interpretations. There is very little scholarly consensus as to what could and did in fact happen. Hypotheses abound, and in many cases we are left with a bewildering number of probabilities.

Schmithals expressed this pessimism rather well when he wrote that "the question as to the form of the *earliest collection of Paul's epistles* has occupied the exegetes and historians so often and with so much ingenuity that one takes up this question with only slight hope of new convincing results" (Schmithals, 253-54). This study also is complicated by the fact that the concept and process of canonicity is closely related to other issues. R. P. Martin has noted that the questions of how and when Paul's letters found general acceptance cannot be understood, much less answered, apart from the larger framework of Paul's claim to authority, the apostolate and the use of tradition (Martin, 279).

1. Paul and His Letters
2. Between Paul and Clement (c. 60-100)
3. Between Clement and Justin (c. 96-165)
4. Marcion (Mid Second Century)
5. *P*[46]
6. The Muratorian Fragment
7. Some Later Church Fathers (c. 150-254)
8. Summary
9. Canonicity

**1. Paul and His Letters.**
From an uncritical reading of Paul's letters in the NT one can make the following conclusions: thirteen letters (excluding Hebrews) are attributed to Paul; most were occasional or particular, that is, they were written to specific local congregations for a definite purpose (e.g., believers in Rome, Corinth, Philippi, Thessalonica, Colossae, Ephesus, Galatia, etc.); others were written to individuals (Philemon, Timothy and Titus); Paul's letters were read in the church, probably in the context of worship* (1 Thess 5:27; Col 4:16); some were intended to be circulated to other churches (Col 4:16; Gal 1:1); and not all the letters that Paul wrote have been preserved (1 Cor 5:9; 2 Cor 2:4; Col 4:16). At the time of writing Paul had no idea that his letters would be collected or become authoritative and canonical for the universal church (on the history and development of the word *canon*, cf. Metzger 1987, Appendix I, 289-93).

A critical analysis of Paul's letters, however, questions this simplistic picture. The history of interpretation of the NT in general, and Paul in particular, has

suggested some alternate ways of understanding Paul and his letters. For one thing, there is the question of authenticity. Were all the letters attributed to Paul actually written by him? A number of scholars have postulated that certain letters are post-Pauline and probably were written by a "pupil" or "school" of Paul sometime after his death (cf. Patzia and current critical introductions to the NT such as W. G. Kümmel). The letters whose Pauline authorship is disputed are Colossians,* Ephesians,* 2 Thessalonians* and the Pastorals.* If these are indeed Deutero-Pauline, this changes the way one reconstructs the chronology* of the composition and collection of Paul's letters.

Another issue raised by scholars is the editorial and redactional work that has been applied to Paul's letters. Are the Corinthian* letters a combination of several fragments of letters that Paul wrote to Corinth? Is the phrase in 1 Corinthians 1:2, "together with all those everywhere who call on the name of our Lord Jesus Christ" (NIV), an interpolation intended to change the letter from an "occasional" to a "universal" letter, thus making it applicable to a wider body of believers (cf. Dahl, 270)? Was Romans* similarly altered in some manuscripts by omitting the words "in Rome" (Rom 1:7, 15), and did it originally circulate as a shorter letter (chaps. 1—15) with chapter sixteen added later from another piece of Paul's correspondence (cf. Gamble 1977)? Was Ephesians* written as a "circular letter" for the churches in Asia Minor before it found a permanent home in Ephesus? Both the general nature of the letter and the textual problems related to its destination (omitting *en Ephesō*, Eph 1:1, in some chief textual authorities) suggest such a possibility.

**2. Between Paul and Clement (c. 60-100).**
Clement, an early bishop of the church in Rome, appears to have been acquainted with several letters of Paul. R. M. Grant suggests that Clement knew 1 Corinthians, Romans, Galatians, Philippians, Ephesians and "perhaps has a definite allusion to Hebrews" (Grant 81-83). R. P. Martin, on the other hand, believes that "at best" Clement knew only four of Paul's letters (Martin, 277). At any rate, we need to remember that Clement may have been aware of more letters than he utilized in his correspondence.

The significance of Clement, however, lies not so much in the number of letters that he referred to as in the fact that his "letter of the Church of Rome to the Church of Corinth" (*1 Clement*) reflects an acquaintance not only with Paul's letter to the Romans (as we would expect) but 1 Corinthians as well. This means that Clement somehow had access to 1 Corinthians, either from a visit he may have made to Corinth or that this Corinthian letter—and some others—had found their way to Rome. One wonders if this acquaintance with Romans and 1 Corinthians presupposes the existence of a limited collection of Paul's letters.

What happened to Paul's letters in the period between Paul and Clement is shrouded in mystery. There does not appear to be any evidence of a significant knowledge of Paul's letters during this time. The book of Acts (dated in the range of 60 and 85) makes no mention of them even though it focuses on the life of the apostle* Paul. If Paul's letters were treasured during this time (cf. 2 Pet 3:2, 15-16), it is indeed puzzling that there is no further evidence of their use, circulation and collection (cf. Mitton). However, given the fact that Paul's letters ultimately were circulated, collected and canonized, it is obvious that some kind of process was at work during this early stage.

*2.1. The Gradual-Collection Theory.* It can be legitimately assumed that Paul's letters, because they were occasional, particular and pastoral, would have been valued and preserved by the churches to which they were written. Exceptions could include the "sorrowful letter" to Corinth (2 Cor 2:4), a possible letter to the Laodiceans which is now lost (Col 4:6) and others which may have been written but about which we do not have any knowledge or record.

At some stage, Paul's occasional letters must have been recognized to have a broader or more universal significance. This may have come about because they were soon recognized for their apostolic and pastoral value (Harnack) or through some kind of cumulative effect (Gamble 1985, 36). It appears more likely that each letter of Paul, which would have been read and reread in the church, gradually found its way to other congregations because of its practical significance. They could have been carried and circulated by significant church leaders in the same way that Paul had his letters delivered by such messengers as Timothy and others (cf. 1 Thess 5:27).

The circulation of letters and their limited collection may have begun in such regional areas as Asia Minor (Colossae, Ephesus, Hierapolis, Laodicea), Macedonia (Thessalonica, Philippi) and Achaia (Corinth). Then at some point these regional collections became part of the Pauline corpus (cf. L. Mowry; also Zuntz, 278-79). Unfortunately there is no evidence that such collections existed.

It is difficult to imagine this early circulation and collection of Paul's letters without the guidance of some significant individual(s). The editorial and redactional activity in the Corinthian correspondence,

and possibly Philippians and Romans, confirms that someone was working on the letters. Although some scholars have suggested that Paul recognized the timeless value of his own letters and may have initiated this process himself, most recommend individuals such as Luke, Timothy and Onesimus. On the other hand, B. Metzger notes that early in the 1800s, J. Eichhorn "was the first to attribute to Marcion the stimulus to collect the New Testament writings" (Metzger 1987, 18; W. Bauer also saw Marcion as "the first systematic collector of the Pauline heritage"). It appears more likely, however, that Marcion took over an existing list and then edited it to fit his theological agenda.

The process of collecting and editing Paul's letters may have been performed by a "school" of Paul. This envisions a process where, after Paul's death, a group of his disciples or coworkers met together to study his theology in order to pass on the theological traditions that they had inherited from their master. It is suggested that those letters some scholars have designated as Deutero-Pauline were attempts of the school, or certain individuals within the Pauline circle, and under the name of Paul, to interpret, reinterpret and apply Paul's theology to later generations by appealing to Paul's apostolic authority* (Patzia; Schenke).

From this perspective, the utilization of Paul's name and authority would have been especially significant as the church confronted various forms of false teaching and needed to establish "sound doctrine and practice." Certain individuals within the school, like Luke, Tychicus, Onesimus, etc., may actually have been responsible for the writing of some letters. Ephesians often is attributed to Luke (Martin) or Onesimus (Goodspeed, Knox). Suggestions for the authorship and/or final editing of the Pastoral Letters ranges from a Paulinist like Luke (Martin) to Polycarp (von Campenhausen). Most scholars are content to simply designate the author as "the Pastor"—but maintaining that it was someone who stood firmly within the Pauline heritage (cf. Collins); for arguments supporting the Pauline authorship of the Pastorals see Guthrie, 607-49, 1011-28.

Those who follow the Deutero-Pauline line of reasoning usually identify Ephesus as the place for this editorial activity (Goodspeed, Knox, Mitton, P.N. Harrison). Harnack, Zahn and Schmithals suggest Corinth. Thus Schmithals, for example, argues for the publication of a seven-letter Pauline corpus in Corinth as early as the "eighties" (Schmithals, 88, 262). Zuntz (14), Grant (121-124) and Bruce (130) see Alexandria as a likely site. Bruce, following the reasoning of Zuntz, affirms that the corpus shows signs of dependence upon "the traditions of Alexandrian scholarship" (Bruce, 129-30).

All of the above is, of course, quite hypothetical. We are not always sure how much Paul was appreciated and how widely his theology was used in the early church. And, although the reference to "all Paul's letters" in 2 Peter 3:16 (NIV) and reminiscences of Paul in the early Fathers testify to a growing appreciation of Paul—as would the phenomenon of the Deutero-Paulines—the fact remains that there is no evidence for a collection of Paul's letters before the end of the first century (even if 2 Peter is dated to around the turn of the century, the "all" would mean "all" those that were known at the time).

*2.2. E. J. Goodspeed's Theory.* Part of Goodspeed's reconstruction of the Pauline corpus involves what is commonly referred to as the "theory of lapsed interest" (Guthrie, 647). Rather than a sustained and growing appreciation of Paul, Goodspeed maintained that because Paul's letters were occasional, they had little value for anyone else, and were simply stored in church chests (Goodspeed, 21) and gradually fell into obscurity.

Briefly stated, Goodspeed's theory suggests that there was little apparent interest in Paul between the time of his death and the latter part of the first century. Only after the publication of The Acts* of the Apostles (c. 85) was interest in Paul revived. Anyone reading this history of the early church would be fascinated with Paul and undoubtedly ask questions about the apostle's literary activity. Goodspeed, followed by Knox and Mitton, identified Onesimus (Paul's friend in Philemon and perhaps the same person who was later bishop of Ephesus) as the one who eventually collected and published Paul's letters as a corpus. Ephesians was written as a cover letter for that corpus (see Goodspeed, Knox, Mitton).

This theory is challenged by scholars who have concluded that Paul's letters continued to exert a considerable influence upon the life and theology of the early church after the apostle's death. Guthrie, for example, thinks that someone like Timothy could have been responsible for collecting and publishing Paul's letters (cf. 2 Tim 4:13: "When you come, bring the cloak that I left with Carpus at Troas, and my scrolls, especially the parchments"). And the reference to "all his [Paul's] letters" (2 Pet 3:16) should be taken as proof that at least some of Paul's letters were known to Peter before 68 (Guthrie, 832).

Whether or not one regards Goodspeed's theory as "a romantic embellishment" (Bruce) or "imaginative reconstruction" (Martin, 278) one cannot help but concur with Zuntz who commends Goodspeed for "the liveliness of his imagination and the persuasiveness of his presentation" (Zuntz, 276).

*2.3. Summary.* From the preceding discussion, the following points emerge:

*2.3.1.* There is sufficient evidence to conclude that by the end of the first century some of Paul's letters were being circulated and collected in various churches.

*2.3.2.* The circulation/collection of Paul's letters indicates that they were valued for their universal and not just local significance.

*2.3.3.* We do not know how and when the editor(s) obtained copies of Paul's letters. The collector/editor may have picked them up during travels or had them sent to a location through the normal process of exchange and circulation.

*2.3.4.* For those who accept the Deutero-Pauline hypothesis, the collection and further publication of these letters was a deliberate attempt by an individual or individuals within the Pauline school to appeal to Paul's apostolic authority and commend his theology to later generations.

**3. Between Clement and Justin (c. 96-165).**
An examination of the events and literature of this period sheds some further light on our subject. References and allusions to most of Paul's letters can be found in Ignatius, bishop of Antioch (early second century), and Polycarp, bishop of Smyrna (d. c. 156). Exceptions in Ignatius include 2 Thessalonians, Philemon and the Pastorals, while Polycarp has no allusions to 1 Thessalonians, Colossians, Titus and Philemon.

The writings of Barnabas (late first to early second century), Papias (early second century) and Justin (mid second century) bear no trace of Paul's letters (cf. Grant, 62-107 for more detailed information). Such omissions are puzzling, and caution needs to be taken when arguing from silence. Papias may have omitted quotations from Paul because he treasured oral tradition ("a living and continuing voice") much more highly than written sources, and Justin, an apologist, was not necessarily writing to Christians.

The possession of most of Paul's epistles by many of the church fathers, from Clement to Justin, signifies a further development in the collection of a Pauline corpus. Polycarp, in addition to his own collection, is aware of a similar collection in the Philippian church ("when absent he [Paul] wrote you letters that will enable you, if you study them carefully, to grow in the faith delivered to you," Polycarp *Phil.* 3.2).

From the above observations it becomes clear that Paul's letters were becoming more widely known and used among the churches. However, there is less certainty regarding the status of a singular collection (or corpus).

A number of scholars feel confident that the collection—and the circulation *as a collection*—began early in the second century (Bruce, 130; Zahn, according to Metzger 1987, 23; Beare, 520-32). G. Zuntz, although he doubts that Clement would have had access to a Pauline corpus in Rome, believes that "it may conceivably have been circulating in, say, Asia Minor or Egypt for some time; but hardly for long. Thus, A.D. +/– 100 is a probable date for the collection and publication of the Corpus Paulinum; that is forty or fifty years after the Epistles were written" (14).

### 4. Marcion (Mid Second Century).

This early church leader in Rome was expelled from the church c. A.D. 144 because of his rejection of the OT and what he regarded to be its inferior view of God and the Law. Nevertheless, he remains a crucial figure in our understanding of the collection and canonicity of Paul's letters because of the ten-letter corpus found in his *Apostolikon* (in Marcion's order: Galatians, 1 Corinthians, 2 Corinthians, Romans, 1 Thessalonians, 2 Thessalonians, Ephesians [which he called the "epistle to the Laodiceans"], Colossians, Philippians and Philemon).

Assessment of the significance of Marcion's list varies considerably among scholars because there is no way of knowing with certainty what his intentions were. It is doubtful that he intended to produce a "closed canon" of Scripture as this term came to be understood by the church at a later date. Harnack and von Campenhausen see him as the first compiler of a list; others believe that he is indebted to an earlier collection or collections. The most we can say is that Marcion's list represents a deliberate selection of Paul's letters, which he viewed as supporting his rejection of the OT. This, in turn, may have driven the church to expand the collection at a later time by including other recognized letters of Paul.

### 5. $P^{46}$.

This early manuscript, known as the Chester Beatty Codex (c. A.D. 200), is recognized as the earliest extant copy of the Pauline letters. Although only 86 of its original 104 leaves have survived, it remains a significant witness to the status of the Pauline corpus at the beginning of the third century. It contains Romans (beginning at Rom 5:17), Hebrews, 1 and 2 Corinthians, Ephesians, Galatians, Philippians, Colossians and 1 Thessalonians. Metzger suggests that "the seven leaves lost from the end probably contained 2 Thessalonians but would have been insufficient for the Pastoral Epistles" (Metzger 1981, 64). The inclusion of Hebrews and its frequent agreement with texts belonging to the Alexandrian group of witnesses suggests that it is a product of the Eastern church, probably from Alexandria (Bruce, 130-31; Zuntz, 14).

Without doubt, $P^{46}$ is the most significant tangible piece in the puzzle to reconstruct the Pauline corpus. It may well represent (though it should not necessarily be identified as) the earliest collection of Paul's letters and from which all subsequent collections were made. Nevertheless, there is no way of knowing whether it was representative of the entire Eastern church.

Both Bruce (130) and Metzger (1987, 259) confidently affirm that from the beginning of the second century Paul's letters only circulated as a collection. This means that with the possible exception of Clement of Rome, all subsequent collectors, including Marcion, worked from an early *Corpus Paulinum* (for detailed discussion on a primitive archetype of the Pauline corpus and $P^{46}$ see the detailed discussion in Zuntz, esp. 14-23). H. Gamble dismisses the idea of a single archetypal corpus as untenable (cf. Gamble 1975, 415; 1989, 208). Aland voices his skepticism even more strongly:

> the opinion that a uniform 'ur-Corpus' of seven Pauline Epistles had been collected by the close of the first century, from which all later witnesses have descended, is nothing but a 'phantasy of wishful thinking'. . . . by about A.D. 90 several 'Ur-Corpora' of Pauline Epistles began to be made available at various places, and that these collections, of differing extent, could have included some or all of the following: 1 and 2 Corinthians, Hebrews, Romans, Galatians, Ephesians, Philippians. Eventually other traditional Pauline Epistles were added to the several collections and a more or less stabilized collection finally emerged. (quoted from Metzger 1987, 260-61; cf. also Gamble 1975, 415; 1989, 208)

### 6. The Muratorian Fragment.

This Fragment, a Latin translation from the seventh or eighth century, was published in 1740 and is named after its Italian discoverer L. A. Muratori (see text and translation in Metzger 1987, 305-7). Its significance for the reconstruction of the collection and canonicity of Paul's letters mainly depends upon its dating. Historically, the Fragment was considered to be the product of the western church (Rome?) near the end of the second century. Included among the NT letters (twenty-two of the present twenty-seven canonical books) are Paul's letters to the Corinthians, Ephesians, Philippians, Colossians, Galatians, Thessalonians, Romans, Philemon, Titus and "two to Timothy." As such, the Fragment could be a significant testimony to an early collection of Paul's letters. Gamble, however, refers to it as "a puzzling list of letters which perhaps never will be made wholly intelligible" (Gamble 1975, 407).

The enthusiasm for the value of the Fragment has been challenged in recent scholarship. A. C. Sundberg's detailed analysis led him to propose a fourth-century date and an Eastern setting (see similar positions in von Campenhausen and McDonald). Among Sundberg's objections to an early date for the Fragment are its attitude toward the *Shepherd of Hermas* and the fact that there are no similar lists until the time of Eusebius in the fourth century.

Not everyone, however, has been persuaded by Sundberg's critique. Both Bruce (158 n.2) and Metzger (1987, 191) are confident that E. Ferguson has adequately refuted Sundberg's arguments against an early date. Thus, in some circles at least, the Fragment is regarded as an authoritative list of NT books in the Roman church by the end of the second century.

## 7. Some Later Church Fathers (c. 150-254).

Significant individuals during this period include Tatian (c. 110-180), Irenaeus (d. c. 202), Clement of Alexandria (c. 160-215), Tertullian (c. 160-220) and Origen (c. 185-254). The general consensus among scholars is that these Fathers recognized and accepted either thirteen or fourteen (if Hebrews is included) letters of Paul. Tatian appears to reject 1 and 2 Timothy, and neither Irenaeus nor Clement mentions Philemon. Origen often uses the phrase "Paul said" or "Paul says." Thus one can fairly safely conclude that by the middle of the third century there was a broadly uniform consensus with respect to the contents of the Pauline corpus. But final confirmation of this has to await evidence from the following century.

## 8. Summary.

The following points seem well established.

*8.1.* After the first century Paul's letters circulated as a collection and not (with possible minor exceptions) as individual letters. Although *P*[46] represents the earliest extant evidence of such a collection, it may be only one of several independent collections. The other collections may have included as many as seven, ten, thirteen or fourteen letters of Paul respectively. Some later collections also included "Third Corinthians" and "The Epistle to the Laodiceans."

*8.2.* References/allusions to Paul's letters by church fathers from the second century onward indicate an increasing appeal to Paul's authority and theology in the church so that by the middle of the third century the content of the *Corpus Paulinum* was pretty well

decided although not yet canonized. Methodologically, we must not assume that the fathers felt obliged to mention all the letters they knew or that they intended to construct a "canon" of authoritative Scripture.

*8.3.* The significance of the Muratorian Fragment needs to be tempered in the light of criticisms made by Sundberg and others. If it is authentically from the second century, one cannot help being puzzled by the lack of similar lists until the fourth century (McDonald, 139).

## 9. Canonicity.

Enough has been said above to indicate that the collection of Paul's letters was a significant factor in their ultimate canonicity. Although addressed to specific congregations, they increasingly were valued for their universal applicability and apostolic authority within the first and second century. One can safely conclude that a Pauline corpus of thirteen letters existed by the beginning of the third century. These, along with the Gospels and the other letters which now make up the NT, were declared "canonical" by the Council of Carthage in A.D. 397.

There are a number of confluent factors which led to the canonicity of the entire NT generally and Paul's letters specifically. Externally, there was the problem of false teaching. What Paul faced during his own lifetime, and is reflected in the Pauline corpus, including the disputed letters, became more acute in the post-apostolic age with the development of Gnosticism and other heresies. This continually forced the church to appeal to an authoritative and widely accepted body of literature to define its theology (note the emphasis in the Pastorals on keeping "the faith" and "sound teaching," guarding "the truth" and the "good deposit," etc.). Schmithals has proposed that the earliest collection and editing of Paul's letters was motivated by an attempt to provide a universal body of Paul's letters to serve as an authoritative weapon against Gnosticism (cf. the critique of Schmithals by Gamble 1975).

Marcion played a significant role in the development of the Pauline canon when he published his list of ten Pauline letters in the mid second century. The question whether or not he created this "hyper-Paulinist" list or utilized an earlier collection is secondary to the insight that it provides on the status of Paul and his letters. It may have stimulated the church to clarify and enlarge its position on the content of the Pauline corpus because succeeding lists contain additional letters. However, too little is known about the effects of Marcion's canon to suggest that it forced the church to formulate a canon of its own in opposition to his.

Montanism (c. 140-180), on the other hand, with its claim to new revelations, prophecies and inspiration, undoubtedly made it necessary for the church to establish additional norms of authority.

The internal criteria that determined the canon include such concepts as apostolicity, orthodoxy and catholicity. Since Paul was regarded as a legitimate and inspired apostle by the church, his letters were considered part of the "apostolic deposit of faith" and thus authoritative for the church. This reverence for Paul contributes to the argument for a Deutero-Pauline school which would have appealed to his apostolic authority in addressing the theological needs of later generations (Ephesians, Pastorals).

Nevertheless, there were factors other than the concepts of inspiration and apostolicity at work in the second and third century. Certain apocryphal Gospels, Letters, Acts, etc., claimed to be apostolic (e.g., Peter, Thomas, Philip) but were rejected. Even Paul's "Epistle to the Laodiceans" was judged to be spurious and hence not included among the canonical letters of Paul. The antiquity of a document (i.e., that it was written during the apostolic age), its orthodoxy and its usage in the church also helped to shape the canon. The Muratorian Fragment, for example, rejects the "Shepherd of Hermas" because it was written too recently and cannot be included "among the prophets whose number is settled or among the apostles to the end time" (section 6).

In spite of a general consensus regarding the canonical status of Paul's letters by the end of the second century, there are a few interesting scenarios that continued into and beyond the fourth century. We noted above that the Pastorals were not included in such early collections as those of Marcion or $P^{46}$. Philemon also is missing from $P^{46}$, although it, along with 2 Thessalonians, may have been part of the missing seven leaves at the end.

The book of Hebrews had a curious and checkered career. In Alexandria (the eastern church), it was held in high regard, was used in the church and considered to be Pauline. Hence its inclusion in $P^{46}$ as one of Paul's letters. Rome (the western church), on the other hand, doubted Hebrew's apostolic (Pauline) authorship and did not include it among the Pauline letters. This may account for its absence from the Muratorian Fragment, a creation of the western church. According to Bruce, it was not until the fourth century, and only due to the persuasive influence of Athanasius, that Rome consented to include Hebrews in the Pauline corpus (Bruce, 220).

The order or sequencing of Paul's letters varies in most lists. Many group the letters written to churches followed by those written to individuals. Occasionally letters to the same community (Corinth, Thessalonica) appear as a single reference. Other arrangements utilize the principle of decreasing length.

Finally, we should note that there are a number of divergences within the canon of the NT even after the Third Council of Carthage (A.D. 397). Letters like "Third Corinthians" and "The Epistle to the Laodiceans" continued to be used in some churches. Codex Sinaiticus (fourth century) includes *Barnabas* and *The Shepherd of Hermas* in its list; Alexandrinus (fifth century) has *1 Clement* and *2 Clement* 1:1—12:5; and Claromontanus (sixth century) mentions *Barnabas, The Shepherd,* the *Acts of Paul* and the *Apocalypse of Peter.* Thus we do well to heed Metzger who wisely notes, "It would be a mistake to represent the question of the canon as finally settled in all Christian communities by the beginning of the fifth century" (Metzger 1987, 239).

*See also* APOCRYPHAL PAULINE LITERATURE; AUTHORITY; PASTORAL LETTERS; PAUL AND HIS INTERPRETERS; PAUL IN ACTS AND LETTERS; PAUL IN EARLY CHURCH TRADITION; TEXTUAL CRITICISM.

BIBLIOGRAPHY. A. E. Barnett, *Paul Becomes a Literary Influence* (Chicago: University of Chicago, 1941); F. Beare, "Canon of the New Testament," *IDB* 1.520-32; F. F. Bruce, *The Canon of Scripture* (Downers Grove: InterVarsity, 1988); H. von Campenhausen, *The Formation of the Christian Bible* (Philadelphia: Fortress, 1972); R. F. Collins, *Letters That Paul Did Not Write* (Wilmington: Michael Glazier, 1988); N. A. Dahl, "The Particularity of the Pauline Epistles as a Problem in the Ancient Church," in *Neotestamentica et Patristica: Eine Freundesgabe Herrn Prof. Dr. Oscar Cullmann zu seinem 60. Geburtstag* (NovTSup 6; Leiden: Brill, 1962) 261-71; E. Ferguson, "Canon Muratori: Date and Provenance," *Studia Patristica* 18 (New York: Pergamon, 1982) 677-83; H. Y. Gamble, *The New Testament Canon* (Philadelphia: Fortress, 1985); idem, "The Redaction of the Pauline Letters and the Formation of the Pauline Corpus," *JBL* 94 (1975) 403-18; idem, "The Canon of the New Testament," in *The New Testament and Its Modern Interpreters,* ed. E. J. Epp and G. W. MacRae (Atlanta: Scholars, 1989) 201-43; idem, *The Textual History of the Letter to the Romans* (Grand Rapids: Eerdmans, 1977); E. J. Goodspeed, *The Formation of the New Testament* (Chicago: University of Chicago, 1926); R. M. Grant, *The Formation of the New Testament* (London: Hutchinson University Library, 1965); D. Guthrie, *New Testament Introduction* (rev. ed.; Downers Grove, IL: InterVarsity, 1990); J. Knox, *Philemon Among the Letters of Paul* (Nashville: Abingdon, 1959); R. P. Martin, *New Testament Foundations 2* (Grand Rapids: Eerdmans, 1986);

L. M. McDonald, *The Formation of the Christian Biblical Canon* (Nashville: Abingdon, 1988); D. G. Meade, *Pseudonymity and Canon* (Tübingen: J. C. B. Mohr, 1986); B. M. Metzger, *Manuscripts of the Greek Bible* (Oxford: University Press, 1981); idem, *The Canon of the New Testament: Its Origin, Development, and Significance* (Oxford: University Press, 1987); C. L. Mitton, *The Formation of the Pauline Corpus of Letters* (London: Epworth, 1955); L. Mowry, "The Early Circulation of Paul's Letters," *JBL* 63 (1944) 73-86; A. G. Patzia, "The Deutero-Pauline Hypothesis: An Attempt at Clarification," *EvQ* 52 (1980) 27-42; E. R. Richards, *The Secretary in the Letters of Paul* (WUNT 2/42; Tübingen: J. C. B. Mohr, 1991); H.-M. Schenke, "Das Weiterwirken des Paulus und die Pflege seines Erbs durch die Paulusschule," *NTS* 21 (1975) 505-18; W. Schmithals, *Paul and the Gnostics* (Nashville: Abingdon, 1972); A. C. Sundberg, "Canon Muratori: A Fourth Century List," *HTR* 66 (1973) 1-41; D. Trobisch, *Die Entstehung der Paulusbriefsammlung* (Göttingen: Vandenhoeck & Ruprecht, 1989); G. Zuntz, *The Text of the Epistles: A Disquisition upon the Corpus Paulinum* (Oxford: University Press, 1963). A. G. Patzia

**CAPTIVE.** *See* PRISON, PRISONER; TRIUMPH.

**CATHOLICISM.** *See* EARLY CATHOLICISM.

**CELIBACY.** *See* MARRIAGE AND DIVORCE, ADULTERY AND INCEST; SEXUALITY, SEXUAL ETHICS.

# CENTER OF PAUL'S THEOLOGY

The endeavor to ascertain whether there is a central organizing principle in Paul's theology has been pursued actively in recent studies. All students agree that Paul's thinking is not so much systematic as "occasional." But there the agreement stops. When we ask about a "Pauline center," or the underlying principle of coherence in Paul's theology, we are faced by a bewildering variety of answers. Usually the suggestions made range from being too narrow to being too wide. Proposals that say no more than "Jesus Christ is the center of Paul's life and thought" or "he saw life under the lordship of Christ" (see Gibbs; Dunn, 369-72) are of course true, but they hardly touch upon the complexity of this man's mind. Nor do they account for the flexibility of Paul's sensitive response to situations he met. The same criticism has to be leveled at proposals that concentrate on single christological titles (e.g., "Son of God," so Cerfaux, 4) or more vaguely on a generalized summary of Christ's saving work (e.g., "christological soteriology," so Fitzmyer, 16).

    1. Some Recent Proposals

    2. The Need for Criteria
    3. Patterns of Pauline Theology
    4. The Theme of Reconciliation
    5. Conclusion

**1. Some Recent Proposals.**

The classic Lutheran position (stated by Käsemann, 168-69; but cf. Conzelmann, 159-60, in critique of Bultmann) is to affirm the centrality of justification* by faith.* But this assertion has been challenged in recent times by a variety of interpreters (listed in Plevnik, 461-62).

    At the other extreme we encounter suggestions that have been too far-reaching. For example, Sanders draws attention to "two readily identifiable and primary convictions which governed Paul's Christian life: (1) that Jesus Christ is Lord, that in him God provided for the salvation of all who believe . . .; (2) that he, Paul, was called to be the apostle to the Gentiles" (441-42). Again both statements stand out as clearly demonstrable, but they do not bring us directly to the heart of Paul's message.

    C. J. A. Hickling accepts these two propositions as essentially accurate but goes on to add a rider: "God has already brought about in Christ a decisive and final *transformation of time*" (199-214). Hickling's position brings us nearer to the Pauline center, since it recognizes the new age and the new life that came into the world through Christ; and Hickling rightly praises the novelty of divine grace.* Nonetheless, his dualistic framework remains somewhat of an abstraction, requiring to be filled out with personal content and application. J. C. Beker adopts a similar apocalyptic* framework and regards "apocalyptic [as] the indispensable means for [Paul's] interpretation of the Christ-event" (Beker 1980; this entire work is an explication of his seminal essay of 1978). He matches this schema, however, with an interface of Paul's use of "symbolic" terms in applying the conviction he had about the cosmic triumph* of God to particular contingencies in the situations of his readers. This "interaction between coherent center and contingent interpretation" is offered as the key to Paul's hermeneutic, and indeed his theology. The outstanding question remains, however: how can a series of events on a cosmic scale be made normative for, and binding on, various human situations? (Beker's response to this critique is treated in his second edition preface. See too Beker 1990.)

    The most comprehensive discussion of a *centrum Paulinum*, by Plevnik, reverts in its conclusion to a broad spectrum of components which, it is said, go to make up the range of Paul's convictional base, namely:

Any center of Pauline theology must therefore include all those components of the apostle's gospel: his understanding of Christ and of God, his understanding of God's salvific action through Christ, involving the Easter event and its implications, the present Lordship, the future coming of Christ, and the appropriation of salvation. (Plevnik, 477-78)

Not surprisingly, the conclusion is then drawn that "the center is thus not any single aspect of Christ . . . but the whole Christ." The net is so widely cast that almost everything in Paul's preaching* is included or regarded as equally significant.

### 2. The Need for Criteria.

Clearly, before entering the field with any further suggestions as to a Pauline center, the question must be asked about the criteria by which any proposal may be justified. There is here the obvious danger of a hermeneutical circle since the criteria are drawn from the same body of data that hypothetically contains the organizing principle; so, it may well be objected that we are selecting criteria which we know in advance will serve the interests of our proposed term. There seems to be no way to escape this dilemma unless we are prepared to abandon the quest and treat Paul's theology as fragmentary responses delivered ad hoc. Yet, provided we continue to test the criteria by the data as they are uncovered and provided we are willing to revise the initial theoretical proposal in the light of the reconstructed criteria, the enterprise is worthwhile and may be honestly and conscientiously pursued. The better way of putting the process then is to speak of a "hermeneutical spiral" by which we rise from one level to a more adequately framed hypothesis as new data are fed into the inquiry and it moves upward and forward.

In general terms the set of criteria needed to determine a Pauline core may include the following: (1) Paul's attested awareness of a central affirmation or cluster of affirmations that embody his chief message: the "center" is thus the primal reality from which he draws his entire theology; (2) the role of tradition which implies that Paul can and did take over preformed creedal statements (*see* Creeds), hymnic/poetic fragments (*see* Hymns) and baptismal reminders that he thereby made his own possession (e.g., Phil 2:6-11; Rom 3:24-26; 1 Cor 8:6; *see* Liturgical Elements). To this truism should be added a factor that is often overlooked (e.g., by Plevnik, 465), that Paul often redacted the tradition where it was deemed to be inadequate or misleading (e.g., on Col 1:15-20); (3) the extent of Paul's correspondence, which is determined by the interpreter's choice of letters claimed to

be indisputably authentic. Obviously, if, for instance, Colossians* is held to be Deutero-Pauline, the best that may be claimed is that it represents an extension (and perhaps a modification) of Paul's thought adapted to a new situation arising after his death; and (4) the bid to locate what is unique in Paul so that "anything that is derived from something else in Pauline theology is not the center" (Plevnik, 466, interpreting A. Schweitzer's and Sanders's contributions).

### 3. Patterns of Pauline Theology.

The basic patterns of Paul's theological teaching, derivable mostly from his generally undisputed letters, are as follows:

*3.1. God's Grace.* The primacy of God's grace* which takes the initiative and promotes human recovery (Rom 8:29-30; Phil 1:6; 1 Cor 15:10; 2 Cor 5:18-21; cf. 2 Thess 2:13; Eph 2:1-10).

*3.2. The Cosmos.* Such an operation, while entering human history in the person of Jesus of Nazareth and at a given point of time (Gal 4:4; cf. Eph 1:10), has repercussions that affect the cosmic scene and involve even the mysterious spiritual intelligences often referred to in Paul's worldview (*see* Angels; Elements; Principalities and Powers). These cosmic forces are regarded as both created by God and alienated from him (Col 1:15-20; cf. Eph 3:9-10; Rom 8:38-39; 1 Cor 8:5-6).

*3.3. The Cross.* The cross remains crucial to Paul's salvation teaching both as an event in time and as related to creation's recovery and humanity's need as sinners. But with equal insistence Paul regards the cross as the instrument of self-denial by which the "flesh"* is overcome and a new life, cruciform in shape and diaconal in character, is made possible (Gal 2:20; 6:14; *see* Cross, Theology of the).

*3.4. Ethical Imperative.* Thus the gap between historical "is"-ness and ethical "ought"-ness has to be bridged (see the texts in Dahl), and a rationale provided for the apostolic claim that the death and resurrection* of the man Jesus impinge upon human activity both as a power to break the stranglehold of evil and as an effectual summons to new life (Rom 6:1-23; Gal 1:4; 5:13-26; 1 Cor 15:20-28, 34; 2 Cor 5:18-21; 1 Thess 5:9-10; *see* Ethics; Dying and Rising).

*3.5. Missionary Mandate.* Nor can we overlook the way Paul's theology was bound up with his professed vocation. He was both a Christian and a missionary (*see* Mission), charged with a mandate to proclaim and live out the saving truth he claimed to have found in Jesus Christ (Rom 1:1-5; Gal 1:15-16; 1 Cor 9:16-18; Rom 10:14-17). Word and life for Paul went hand in hand; and missionary theology meant just as obviously both the kerygma and the way of life Paul exemplified and enacted in his pastoral dealings with awkward people (at Corinth) and ugly situations (at Philippi).

### 4. The Theme of Reconciliation.

It is the overall theme of reconciliation (*see* Peace, Reconciliation), we propose, that meets most of—if not all—these tests (see Martin). This is not to say that the word-group *katallass-* is prominent in Paul's writings; manifestly it is not. Nor is it claimed that "reconciliation" is used with the same nuance in those places where it does occur; obviously it does not. But the contention stands, namely, that reconciliation provides a suitable umbrella under which the main features of Paul's kerygma and its practical outworking may be set (see Lemcio 1988, 3-17; 1990, 3-11, for a bold assertion of what these features or "categories" were, summed up as "God [who] sent or raised Jesus. A response towards God brings benefits"). Moreover, justice is done to some of the main motifs in Pauline missionary theology.

The term *reconciliation* has a pre-history in the tradition Paul gladly took over, as in 2 Corinthians 5:18-21 and Colossians 1:15-20. However, he was not content to leave the term open to misunderstanding; and there is form-critical, linguistic and tradition-historical evidence to show how he has changed the word's meaning by subtle editorial adaptations to the surrounding context. In particular, he has disinfected the term of its gnosticizing taint by anchoring reconciliation in the historical events of Jesus' passion and tying in the effect of reconciliation to moral transformation in human lives.

The counterarguments in Paul are always on the level of personal relationships, of which the forgiveness of sins is the great reality shared alike by apostle and people. To that experience he appeals under a variety of images—new creation,* justification,* redemption,* sonship (*see* Adoption, Sonship), the gift of the Spirit (*see* Holy Spirit) and the promise of resurrection.*

Against those enthusiastic followers who believed that their baptism brought the completion of salvation* here and now, and against the intruding teachers who discounted morality as irrelevant once the spirit had been saved, Paul entered the plea of the "eschatological proviso," the "not-yet" of reconciliation which, unlike justification, is still going on and needs to be renewed continually. Hence the call to Christians at Corinth, "Be reconciled to God" (2 Cor 5:20), lest they receive God's grace to no purpose (2 Cor 6:1) and fail to see his proffered forgiveness

(2 Cor 2:5-11; 6:11-13). Reconciliation is thus admirably suited to express and safeguard the existential element in Paul's moral theology. God has achieved a final reconciliation of the world but men and women need to learn to live with moral sensitivity and vigilance until the end comes.

The blend of God's deed and Paul's role as a reconciling agent at Corinth and in the note to Philemon illustrates how the transition from historical factuality to ethical obligation may be made. The middle term is Paul's "ministry of reconciliation" (2 Cor 5:18)—the one clear job description Paul has left on record. What God did expressed his great love,* with Christ's cross at the center (Rom 5:1-11). As Paul gratefully rejoiced in that love as a fact of experience, conveyed by the Spirit, he saw his mission as modeling what God had done in recalling the Corinthians to their true allegiance and in urging Philemon* to consider the social implications of the new life on which he had embarked. The skeleton of an adequate ethical theory is here seen in embryo—even if it took Christians eighteen centuries to work out the force and relevance of this admonition.

Equally, the same may be said about the teaching in Ephesians 2:11-22. Here reconciliation takes on a horizontal direction. The inveterate hostility between Jews and non-Jews (*see* Gentiles) is overcome in the cross of Jesus who has reconciled both groups in one body (*see* Body of Christ). The "one new person" in place of two suggests the vision of a "third race," a new species of humankind, who in becoming part of the divine family form a microcosm of that new society which is a token in God's design to place all of conscious life under the headship* of the cosmic Christ (Eph 1:10).

### 5. Conclusion

These far-ranging and distinctive ideas—covering cosmic, personal, societal and ethnic areas of our human story—are nevertheless part of a pattern, whose picture fills the tapestry. The various strands are closely textured and intricately woven together. Yet they are not aimlessly put into a frame. There is an emerging design and a coherent picture. And the most adequate and meaningful title for the result is, we submit, "reconciliation."

*See also* CHRISTOLOGY; CROSS, THEOLOGY OF THE; JUSTIFICATION; PAUL AND HIS INTERPRETERS; PEACE, RECONCILIATION; RIGHTEOUSNESS, RIGHTEOUSNESS OF GOD.

BIBLIOGRAPHY. J. C. Beker, "Contingency and Coherence in the Letters of Paul," *USQR* 33 (1978) 141-50; idem, *Paul the Apostle* (Philadelphia: Fortress, 1980); idem, *The Triumph of God: the Essence of Paul's Thought*

(Philadelphia: Fortress, 1990); L. Cerfaux, *Christ in the Theology of St. Paul* (New York: Herder & Herder, 1959); H. Conzelmann, *An Outline of the Theology of the New Testament* (London: SCM, 1969); N. A. Dahl, "Form-Critical Observations on Early Christian Preaching," in *Jesus in the Memory of the Church* (Minneapolis: Augsburg, 1976) 30-36; T. Deidun, "Some Recent Attempts at Explaining Paul's Theology," *Way* 26 (1986) 230-42; J. D. G. Dunn, *Unity and Diversity of the New Testament* (Philadelphia: Westminster, 1977); J. A. Fitzmyer, *Pauline Theology: A Brief Sketch* (Englewood Cliffs, NJ: Prentice-Hall, 1967); J. G. Gibbs, *Creation and Redemption* (Leiden: E. J. Brill, 1971); C. J. A. Hickling, "Centre and Periphery in Paul's Thought," in *Studia Biblica III. Papers on Paul and Other NT Authors*, ed. E. A. Livingstone (Sheffield: Academic Press, 1978) 199-214; E. Käsemann, *New Testament Questions of Today* (London: SCM, 1979); E. E. Lemcio, "The Unifying Kerygma of the New Testament," *JSNT* 36 (1988) 3-17; 38 (1990) 3-11; R. P. Martin, *Reconciliation: A Study of Paul's Theology* (rev. ed.; Grand Rapids: Zondervan, 1990); J. Plevnik, "The Center of Paul's Theology," *CBQ* 51 (1989) 460-78; J. Reumann, *Variety and Unity in New Testament Thought* (Oxford: University Press, 1991); E. P. Sanders, *Paul and Palestinian Judaism* (Philadelphia: Fortress, 1977).

R. P. Martin

**CEPHAS.** *See* PETER.

**CHAINS.** *See* PRISON, PRISONER.

**CHARISMATA.** *See* GIFTS OF THE SPIRIT.

**CHILDREN OF ABRAHAM.** *See* ABRAHAM.

**CHILDREN OF GOD.** *See* ADOPTION, SONSHIP.

# CHRIST

Paul's extraordinarily frequent use of the term *Christos* calls for explanation. Paul often used the term as a virtual second name for Jesus, or as a way of distinguishing this particular Jesus from others. Various texts also show that Paul was well aware of the larger significance of the term *Christos/Māšîah*. It is also notable that there are certain ways Paul refrained from using the term *Christos;* for instance, we never find the phrase "Jesus the Christ." Careful study of the Jewish and Greek background does not explain the frequency and manner in which Paul used the term *Christos*. His usage is best explained by the fact that Paul received a tradition associating the term *Christ* with the core of the early Christian message: the death and resurrection* of Jesus (cf. 1 Cor 15:3-4). This received tradition,* coupled with the singular experience Paul had of Christ on the Damascus Road (*see* Conversion and Call), go far in explaining the distinctive ideas the apostle associated with Jesus being the Christ. There is, however, no clear explanation or rationale for the particular permutations and combinations that we find in Paul's letters where he juxtaposes Christ with various other names and titles. *Christos* most often seems to appear where Christ's death, resurrection and return are under discussion. The *en Christō* formula in many ways best encapsulates Paul's view of the condition and position of Christians—they are "in Christ." The use of the term *Christos* in the disputed Pauline letters differs little from what we find in those letters generally regarded as authentic, except that there is more emphasis on what may be called cosmic christology.

1. Jewish Background
2. Greek Usage
3. Origin of the Christian *Christos* Usage
4. Pauline Usage
5. The *En Christō* Formula
6. *Christos* in the Contested Pauline Letters

## 1. Jewish Background.

The Greek verbal adjective *christos* (which came to be used as a noun) and its Hebrew analog *māšîah* are terms which were used in early Judaism and Christianity to refer to an anointed person set apart for a special task and, in particular, to a royal and/or messianic figure. In the political realm the term was used of Davidic kings (Ps 18:50; 89:20; 132:10-17). In this regard 2 Samuel 7:8-16 is especially crucial as it expresses the hope that God* would provide the ideal Davidic ruler. It should be noted, however, that none of the later OT prophetic books use the term *māšîah* for the future royal one like unto David (cf., e.g., Zech 9:9-10; 12:7—13:1). Indeed, in Isaiah 45:1 the term refers to Cyrus, and in Habakkuk 3:13 it appears to refer to a presently reigning king. Furthermore, in early Jewish literature the term is found infrequently (cf. *Pss. Sol.* 18:5; 4QPBless 3; CD 12:23-24; 14:19; 19:10-11; *1 Enoch* 48:10; 52:4) and does not seem to have been "an essential designation for any future redeemer" (De Jonge 1966, 147).

There were various forms of messianic expectation in early Judaism, but it does not appear that the terms translated into English as "Messiah" were used with any frequency, and they probably were not technical terms for a future redeemer figure. The messianic hope of early Judaism could incorporate the idea of one or more messianic figures, as in the royal and priestly anointed figures at Qumran (e.g., 1QS 9:10-11; CD 12:22-23), or none at all when it was believed that Yahweh himself would finally rescue his people (e.g., 1QM 11—12).

### 2. Greek Usage.

It is surprising that the term *Christos* is used so frequently by Paul (270 out of a total of 531 uses in the NT) and that it seems to be used as a name for Jesus rather than as a title or descriptive term. This is especially remarkable since in the main Paul was writing to Gentiles* who may or may not have been familiar with the Jewish background for this term. In secular Greek usage the term *christos* simply means an ointment or cosmetic, but apparently it never referred to the one anointed (cf. Euripides *Hipp.* 516; Moule, 32). A fragment from a manuscript written by Diodorus Siculus (1b;38-39, 4) shortly before the time of Jesus uses the term *neochristos* to refer to a building "newly plastered." Thus the prolific Pauline use of the term *Christos,* almost as a name for Jesus, requires an explanation. This is especially so since there was a perfectly good Greek word available for speaking of an anointed person, *ēleimmenos* (from the verb *aleiphō,* "anoint"). And in fact Aquila used this term to render the Hebrew *māšîaḥ* in his Greek translation of the OT.

The suggestion that the term *Christos* as a surname for Jesus arose in Gentile Christianity, where its original royal or messianic Jewish connotations were no longer understood, fails to explain why Paul, a Jew, is the chief employer of this term among NT writers (Hengel). Paul's understanding of the meaning of the term is clear from 2 Corinthians 1:21 where we find the play on words "God establishes us in Christ (*eis Christon)* and has anointed us (*chrisas*)." Yet, strikingly, Paul rarely speaks of *the Christ,* but rather *Iēsous Christos* (Jesus Christ) or sometimes *Christos Iēsous* (Christ Jesus) or even *ho Kyrios Iēsous Christos* (the Lord Jesus Christ). This usage strongly suggests that before Paul wrote his letters the term *Christos* was used widely in early Christianity as part of the name of Jesus. Were this not the case, we would expect Paul somewhere to explain to his audience(s) what the term meant. We must consider briefly the evidence that points to a pre-Pauline use of the term *Christos* for Jesus.

### 3. The Origin of the Christian *Christos* Usage.

In one of Paul's earliest letters, 1 Thessalonians, probably written in the 50s if not earlier, a variety of uses of *Christos* appear. For example, Paul speaks of the "Lord Jesus Christ" (1 Thess 1:1; cf. 1 Thess 5:23, 28), "Christ" (1 Thess 2:6), "in Christ Jesus" (1 Thess 2:14) and, what was to become one of Paul's favorite

phrases, "in Christ" (1 Thess 4:16). This suggests that in the early 50s, and even earlier, the term *Christos* had already become a virtual name for Jesus and would be recognized as such by Paul's audience in Macedonia. A similar variety of usage and assumptions can be observed in 1 Corinthians. There, for instance, we find not only the phrase "Christ Jesus" (1 Cor 1:1-4) but also "Christ" (1 Cor 1:6) as well as "our Lord Jesus Christ" and "Jesus Christ our Lord" (1 Cor 1:2, 7-10). There is no obvious significance to this variation; all these terms and phrases refer to the same person in his relationship to his people. Detailed studies about Paul's use of the term *Christ* have made clear that Paul uses the term in a variety of ways and combinations with other names and titles, and only rarely is it possible to explain these permutations. It would appear that there is no theological rationale for Paul sometimes using the phrase "Christ Jesus" rather than "Jesus Christ," or sometimes preferring the phrase "the Lord Jesus Christ" as opposed to "Christ."

It can be shown that Paul uses the term *Christos* and its variants especially in contexts where he is drawing upon pre-Pauline tradition or is reflecting on the eschatological significance of Christ's death, resurrection and parousia (*see* Eschatology). These epochal events are the primary reason Paul is willing to call Jesus *Christos* (cf. Hengel, 146-48). A summary of Paul's theology of Christ can be found in 2 Corinthians 5:14-21. Christ is the one who died—once for all—and was raised so that those whom he has redeemed might live for him. These events bear witness to the self-sacrificial love that Christ expressed for his people and which they in turn are to emulate. Christ then is the great reconciler of humans to God (2 Cor 5:19; *see* Reconciliation) and of humans to each other (Gal 3:28). It is the climactic salvific events at the close of Jesus' life that especially cause Paul to call Jesus the *Christ.* The significance of these events for defining the Christ is also made clear by Paul's virtual silence regarding Jesus' miracles. Furthermore, though Paul does draw on the tradition of Jesus' sayings in 1 Corinthians 7 and elsewhere, he does not cite such sayings as of the essence of his gospel* or kerygma (*see* Preaching, Kerygma), nor as the heart of the early Christian confession of faith about Christ.

It is important to note that when Paul rehearses the *paradosis,* the sacred "tradition" of early Christians which he and others handed on, he indicates that it included the confession that "*Christos* died for our sins" (1 Cor 15:3). This extraordinary formula, having no known precedent in early Judaism, is regarded as the heart of Christian faith by Paul, who had learned of it from those who were "in Christ" before him. This means that in the period between A.D. 30 and the point at which Paul received this tradition (surely prior to his missionary journeys) the term *Christos* was not only being used by Christians as a term having exclusive reference to Jesus, but already it was being closely linked to Jesus' death as the means of eschatological salvation.

It is possible, as Dahl concluded (1974), that this development can be traced back to the fact that Jesus was crucified as a messianic pretender. There is room for doubt about this, however, since the title on the cross may well have read *Basileus, Melek* and *Rex* rather than *Christos, Māšîaḥ* and *Christus*. It is perhaps more probable that the early and even pre-Pauline use of the word *Christos*, virtually as a name for Jesus, is explained by the fact that Jesus during his ministry in some way identified himself as God's final agent (*Māšîaḥ*) and also spoke of his death in terms something like we find in Mark 10:45 (cf. Witherington, 251-56). Perhaps also the early Hellenistic-Jewish Christians knew that the average Greek speaker might easily take the word *Christos*, like the more familiar term *Chrestos* (cf. Suetonius *Claudius* 25, where evidently *Christus* is read as *Chrestus*) to be a name, distinguishing this Jesus from others by that name. Furthermore, it is possible that the double name *Jesus Christ* in part became common because early Christians wished to suggest the royal dignity of their savior and thus gave him a double name like other notable figures of the era, such as Caesar Augustus.

## 4. Pauline Usage.

Paul, wherever he may have first heard of Jesus being called *Christos* as a virtual second name, did not lose sight of the fact that *Christos* was originally likely to have been a title. This is shown by several pieces of evidence. First, Paul never juxtaposes *Kyrios* with *Christos* alone, for this would amount to awkwardly combining two titles (Grundmann, 542-43). The one possible exception to this rule is found in Colossians 3:24 where we find *tō kyriō Christō douleuete* ("you serve/are slaves to the Lord Christ"), but there *kyriō* may well carry its secular meaning of "master," not divine Lord (cf. Col 3:22-23). Second, Paul never adds a genitive to the term *Christos* (as may be observed in early Judaism, e.g., "the Anointed of the Lord"). In fact, he does not use the term in any sort of possessive expression, such as "God's Christ" (but cf. 1 Cor 3:23). Neither is *Christos* ever used as a simple predicate in the Pauline letters. Nor is the expression "Jesus the Christ" ever found (Dahl, 37). In fact, Paul never feels it necessary to state the formula "Jesus *is* the Christ," nor does he argue for the idea. On the other hand, he among

others utilized what is commonly regarded as the earliest of Christian confessions "Jesus is Lord" (Rom 10:9; *see* Creeds). This evidence strongly suggests that the messiahship of Jesus was not under debate in the Pauline communities, and that Paul himself took it as a presupposition for all other confessions. In his letters he did not, for example, try to demonstrate by prooftexts the messiahship of Jesus. J. D. G. Dunn puts it this way:

> [Paul] makes no attempt to prove that Jesus really is "the Christ" despite his suffering and death. "Christ" is no longer a title whose fitness in its application to Jesus has to be demonstrated. The belief in Jesus as the Christ has become so firmly established in his mind and message that he simply takes it for granted, and "Christ" functions simply as a way of speaking of Jesus, as a proper name for Jesus (so even in 1 Cor. 15.3). (Dunn, 43)

One of the most important ways Paul uses the term *Christos* is in a daring phrase meant to characterize his preaching: *Christos estaurōmenos* ("Christ crucified," 1 Cor 1:23). The phrase must have had some shock value for Jewish listeners since there is no conclusive evidence that early Jews expected a crucified Messiah. Crucifixion* was a punishment reserved for the worst criminals and revolutionaries. Jews, on the basis of a certain reading of Deuteronomy 21:23 (cf. Gal 3:13), seem to have understood crucifixion to be a sign that the crucified person was cursed by God. There is no conclusive evidence that Isaiah 53 was ever applied to the Messiah before Jesus' day (the significance of the evidence from *Tg. Isa* 53 is debatable).

Careful scrutiny of Paul's usage of the term *Christ* suggests that in the main Paul's meaning was not derived from early Jewish ideas about God's anointed, but rather from traditions about the conclusion of Jesus' life and its sequel, coupled with Paul's own Damascus Road experience. These events forced Paul to rethink what it meant for someone to be the Davidic Messiah (Kim). The fact that Paul and other early Christians used the term *Christos* to refer to someone who had died on the cross and had risen from the dead, indicates the extent to which the meaning of the term was transformed. *Christos* brought redemption to his people by dying, rising and being exalted (*see* Exaltation) to authority* and power* at the right hand of God over all the principalities (*see* Principalities and Powers). He did not bring redemption by throwing off the yoke of Roman rule during his earthly ministry. In short, Paul has something rather different in mind from what is found in such texts as *Psalms of Solomon* 17—18 where Messiah is seen as a conquering hero throwing off the yoke of a foreign rule.

Yet it would not be quite true to say as Grundmann does that "the understanding of the Messiah loses its national, political, and religious significance and the significance of the Messiah in human history is attested and expounded. This is the distinctive theological achievement of Paul" (Grundmann, 555). In Romans 15:8 Paul very clearly recounts the fact that Christ became a servant to the circumcision,* and he holds out the hope of the salvation* of many Jews at the eschaton (Rom 11:25-26). Christ is only now a savior to the Gentiles through his ministers and apostles* like Paul (cf. Rom 15:16-18), but in Paul's mind this does not nullify the significance of Christ's prior mission and service to Jews. Indeed, Paul wishes to insist to his largely Gentile audience that salvation is from and for the Jew first and also the Gentile (Rom 1:16; *see* Israel).

Paul was well aware of early Jewish ideas about Messiah being a Jew born under the Law* (cf. Gal 4:4) and of Davidic ancestry (cf. Rom 1:3), and he is happy to affirm these things of Jesus. There are also various places where Paul referred to the fully human character of this *Christos* (Rom 5:17-19; Phil 2:7; Rom 8:3). He was also aware that early Jews by and large did not think of Messiah as some sort of superhuman figure, but rather as an exemplary human being especially anointed with God's Spirit (Grundmann, 526; but cf. the parables of *1 Enoch* which suggest a more-than-human figure, and possibly the Son of man of Dan 7). Yet here too Paul appears to have gone far beyond the majority of his Jewish contemporaries in his understanding of the Davidic Messiah, for the most natural way to read the grammatically difficult phrase in Romans 9:5 is as follows: "comes the Christ who is over all God blessed forever" (Metzger). This suggests that Paul saw the Christ as not only assuming divine functions in heaven but in some sense properly being called God.* This comports with Philippians 2:11, where Jesus *Christos* is called by the divine name used in the LXX, *kyrios* ("Lord"*), as well as with Colossians 1:19 ("for in him all the fullness* [*plērōma*] was pleased to dwell"). It should be noted that in Romans 9:5 Paul very clearly speaks of "the Christ," which once more indicates his understanding of the larger significance of the term.

Paul's use of *Christos* in the salutations of his letters* also points to an exalted view of Jesus. Thus, for instance, in Philippians 1:2 grace and peace are said to come not only from God the Father but also from the Lord Jesus Christ. As Moule puts it, "The position here occupied by Jesus in relation to God, as well as in many other opening formulae of the New Testament letters, is nothing short of astounding—especially when one considers that they are written by mono-

theistic Jews with reference to a figure of recently past history" (Moule, 150). In these instances Jesus Christ is seen as one who dispenses what only God can truly give—shalom (*see* Peace, Reconciliation).

Romans 1:16 provides a possible clue indicating why Paul so persistently used the term *Christos* and occasionally gave hints that it was originally a title, rather than using a term such as *Sōtēr* ("Savior"*) to refer to Jesus. Though Paul was the apostle to the Gentiles, he wished to continue to affirm to his audience, and perhaps on occasion even stress, that salvation is from the Jews and for the Jews before it is for others. One way of doing this was to continue to juxtapose the two terms *Iēsous Christos*. Paul, as a Jew, wished it never to be forgotten that Jesus, who is savior of the world, is such only as the Jewish Messiah—the *Christos*. Thus it may be that Paul's use of the term *Christos* as a virtual name for Jesus, as well as the manner in which he refrained from using the term, was not just a matter of habit. On the other hand, it was an attempt by Paul to remind an increasingly Gentile church of the Jewish origin and character of the Savior and his salvation.

The term *Christos*, if studied in the context of its varied uses in the Pauline corpus, reveals how the apostle drew on, amplified, transformed and transcended some early Jewish ideas about the Messiah. For Paul the content of the term *Christos* was mainly derived from the Christ event and his experience of that event. This led to three elements in his preaching about Christ that were without known precedent in early Judaism: (1) Messiah is called God; (2) Messiah is said to have been crucified, and his death is seen as redemptive; (3) Messiah is expected to come to earth again. Non-Christian Jews did not speak of a crucified Messiah much less of a Second Coming of Messiah. Nor do we have any evidence that early Jews were willing to call the Messiah "God," or one in whom the fullness of deity dwells.

### 5. The *En Christō* Formula.

It was probably due to careful reflection on some of the three elements listed above that Paul came to use the phrase *en Christō* ("in Christ") as he did (*see* In Christ). *En Christō* was unquestionably one of Paul's favorite phrases, appearing 164 times in the chief Pauline letters and another half dozen in the form *en Christō Iēsou* ("in Christ Jesus") in the Pastorals. This total is especially remarkable in view of the fact that other NT writers hardly ever used the phrase (but cf., e.g., 1 Pet 3:16; 5:10, 14). Paul never used the term *Christianos* ("Christian"), rather *en Christō* seems to be his substitute for this adjective (cf. 1 Cor 3:1). At other points the phrase *en Christō* seems to have a more pregnant sense indicating the environment or atmosphere in which Christians live, that is, they are "in Christ." A. Deissmann in his pioneering study *Die Neutestamentliche Formel "in Christo Jesu"* (1892) argued that this formula had both a local and mystical meaning in which Christ, as a sort of universal Spirit, was the very atmosphere in which believers lived.

A good example of this usage is found in 2 Corinthians 5:17: "If anyone is in Christ, that person (or "there") is a new creation" (cf. Phil 3:8-9; *see* Creation and New Creation). In fact whole congregations could be said to be "in Christ" in the same way they were said to be "in God" (cf. Gal 1:22 and Phil 1:1 with 1 Thess 1:1). There are a variety of other passages which seem to have a locative sense (1 Thess 4:16; Gal 2:17; 1 Cor 1:2; 15:18). A. Schweitzer in *The Mysticism of Paul the Apostle* (1931), rejecting much of Deissmann's reasoning, argued that the solidarity that Paul envisioned Christians having with Christ and with each other is a corporate one of a quasi-physical nature which occurs through the material rite of water baptism* and not through some subjective experience brought about through faith.* This surely goes beyond the evidence and contradicts such texts as Galatians 2:16 and Romans 5:2. Schweitzer's view seems to have been more indebted to his own understanding of early Jewish eschatology than to Paul.

Paul does speak of Christ being in the believer (Gal 2:20; Rom 8:10), but this is not nearly so characteristic of the apostle as the phrase *en Christō*. It does not seem possible either to argue that Paul is simply using the language of transfer from one dominion to another or to eliminate completely the locative sense of *en Christō* in various instances. Nor can these texts simply be explained as another way of saying one belongs to Christ or that things are accomplished for the believer through Christ. Rather, for Paul both logically and theologically the concept of being *en Christō* is central. One cannot do something for or with Christ unless one is first *en Christō*. One cannot approach the Father through the Son (*see* Son of God) unless one is *en Christō*. If one is *en Christō* then one is in his body—the *ekklēsia* (*see* Church). The effects of being in Christ are varied: human spiritual transformation by means of death to sin,* possession of the Spirit (*see* Holy Spirit), being made a new creation or creature, having one's inner person and mind renewed, being given both hope* and assurance of a bodily resurrection* like unto Christ's, and being united spiritually with a great host of other believers in a living entity Paul likens to a body.*

The christological implications of this use of *en Christō* have been ably summed up by C. F. D. Moule:

"if it is really true that Paul thought of himself and other Christians as 'included' or 'located' in Christ; . . . it indicates a more than individualistic conception of the person of Christ . . . a plurality of persons can find themselves 'in Christ', as limbs are in the body." (Moule, 62, 65)

This means that Paul conceives of the exalted Christ as a divine being in whom Christians everywhere can dwell. Put another way, Paul's views on both incorporation into Christ and its result, being in Christ, suggest a view of Christ as a divine being "in" whom all believers can dwell and at the same time a divine being who can be "in" all believers, through the presence of the Spirit.

### 6. *Christos* in the Contested Pauline Letters.

In Colossians* and Ephesians* we find a further development of Paul's christology focusing on what is called "the mystery* of Christ." This mystery is that God in Christ has provided salvation and reconciliation for all peoples, Jews and Gentiles, and even for the whole cosmos (*see* World, Cosmology). The cosmic scope of Christ's role becomes particularly evident in these two letters. It is thus not surprising that these letters place more emphasis on the ongoing role of the exalted Christ than do most of Paul's earlier letters, though reference to Christ's death and resurrection is not absent. In these two letters Christ is seen not only as a personal savior for individuals but also as a cosmic ruler. In Christ is found the storehouse of God's wisdom* and knowledge* (Col 2:2-10), although the mystery is not esoteric since it has to do with Christ's public work on the cross and in both letters the mystery is carefully related to the community of faith. According to Ephesians 1:22 Christ rules over the cosmos for the church, and in Ephesians 5:32 the mystery has to do with the relationship of Christ to his church. Furthermore, the relationship between Christ's headship over both the cosmos and the church becomes evident in the Christ hymn of Colossians 1:15-20, where the two are mentioned in the same breath.

Among the "faithful sayings" that characterize the Pastoral Epistles (*see* Pastoral Letters), only two add anything new to the concept of Christ revealed in Paul's earlier letters. In 1 Timothy 6:13 Christ's witness is made before Pilate, thus tracing moments of christological significance back to an event prior to Christ's death. Earlier, in 1 Timothy 1:15 we read that Christ "came into the world" for the specific purpose of saving sinners. This theme presses the moments of christological significance even further back into the story of Christ, at least to the inception of Jesus' human life, and possibly alludes to Christ's preexistence (*see* Christology). The latter idea is expressed elsewhere in Paul, most clearly in the Christ hymns* of Philippians 2:6-11 and Colossians 1:15-20. In 1 Timothy 2:5 the stress is on the humanity of Jesus as the mediator between God and humanity. Finally, it should be noted that the Pastorals reflect a certain predilection for the phrase "Christ Jesus" or occasionally "Christ Jesus" combined with "our Lord."

The study of Paul's use of the term *Christos* provides a window on the character of Paul's christological thought, but it must be supplemented with detailed study of other important christological ideas such as Lord,* last Adam* and Son of God.*

*See also* ADAM AND CHRIST; CHRISTOLOGY; IN CHRIST; LORD; SAVIOR; SON OF GOD.

BIBLIOGRAPHY. O. Cullmann, *The Christology of the New Testament* (rev. ed.; Philadelphia: Westminster, 1963); N. A. Dahl, "The Messiahship of Jesus in Paul," in *The Crucified Messiah and Other Essays* (Minneapolis: Augsburg, 1974) 37-47; M. De Jonge, *Christology in Context* (Philadelphia: Westminster, 1988); idem, "The Earliest Christian use of χριστός. Some Suggestions," *NTS* 32 (1986) 321-43; idem, "The Use of the Word 'Anointed' in the Time of Jesus," *NovT* 8 (1966) 132-48; J. D. G. Dunn, *Unity and Diversity in the New Testament: An Inquiry into the Character of Earliest Christianity* (Philadelphia: Westminster, 1977); W. Grundmann, "χριστός," *TDNT* IX.540-62; M. Hengel, " 'Christos' in Paul," in *Between Jesus and Paul* (Philadelphia: Fortress, 1983) 65-77; J. Jeremias, "Artikelloses Christos," *ZNW* 57 (1966) 211-15; idem, "Nochmals: Artikelloses Christos in 1K 15.3," *ZNW* 60 (1969) 215-17; S. E. Johnson, "Christ," *IDB* 2.567-68; S. Kim, *The Origin of Paul's Gospel* (Grand Rapids: Eerdmans, 1982); W. Kramer, *Christos Kyrios Gottessohn* (AThANT 44; Zurich: Zwingli, 1963); S. V. McCasland, "Christ Jesus," *JBL* 65 (1946) 377-83; I. H. Marshall, *The Origins of New Testament Christology* (Downers Grove, IL: InterVarsity, 1990 [1976]); B. M. Metzger, "The Punctuation of Romans 9.5," in *Christ and Spirit in the New Testament: Studies in Honour of C. F. D. Moule*, ed. B. Lindars and S. S. Smalley (Cambridge: University Press, 1973) 95-112; C. F. D. Moule, *The Origin of Christology* (Cambridge: University Press, 1977); F. Neugebauer, "Das Paulinische 'in Christo,' " *NTS* 4 (1957-58) 124-38; J. Neusner, W. S. Green, E. Frerichs, *Judaisms and Their Messiahs at the Turn of the Christian Era* (Cambridge: University Press, 1987); K. H. Rengstorf, "χριστός," *NIDNTT* 2.334-43; C. C. Torrey, "χριστός," in *Quantulacumque* (Kirsopp Lake Festschrift) ed. R. P. Casey et al. (London: Christopher, 1937) 317-24; B. Witherington, *The Christology of Jesus* (Minneapolis: Fortress, 1990). B. Witherington III

**CHRIST HYMN.** *See* CHRISTOLOGY; HYMNS, HYMN FRAGMENTS, SONGS, SPIRITUAL SONGS; PHILIPPIANS, LETTER TO THE; WORSHIP.

**CHRISTOLOGICAL MONOTHEISM.** *See* CHRISTOLOGY; GOD; SON OF GOD.

# CHRISTOLOGY

Pauline christology has frequently been discussed under the headings of the prominent titles Paul employed—Christ,* Lord,* Son of God,* Savior*—and prominent analogies such as Adam* and Wisdom.* Important as this christological nomenclature may be, however, it does not engage the full picture of Pauline christology. In an attempt to enlarge on the perspective gained through an account of the individual facets of Paul's christology, this article will focus on the origins of Paul's christology, its narrative framework, its dual focus on the divinity and humanity of Christ, the significance of Paul's christology for the early church and its distinctive contribution in comparison and contrast with other canonical christologies.

1. The Origins of Paul's Christology
2. The Narrative Framework of Paul's Christology
3. The Divinity and Humanity of Jesus Christ in Paul's Christology
4. The Impact and Influence of Paul's Christology
5. The Distinctiveness and Commonality of Paul's Christology

### 1. The Origins of Paul's Christology.

There are various possible starting points for discussing the sources or origins of Paul's christology.

*1.1. Judaism.* One approach is to attempt to extrapolate from the NT documents and extracanonical sources Paul the Pharisee's (*see* Jew, Paul the) beliefs about the coming Messiah. How much of a debt did Paul's christology owe to his pre-Christian messianic beliefs? This enterprise, however, involves a tremendous amount of conjecture not only about messianic faith in pre-A.D. 70 Pharisaism, but also about Paul's unique appropriation of his heritage (for the complexity of the evidence representing the "Judaisms" of Paul's day, see Neusner et al.). Unfortunately, apart from a few references here and there, Paul says little about his pre-Christian beliefs about Messiah. The most one can assume, judging from a text such as Romans 9:5, is that he must have believed in a coming human and Davidic Messiah. While Paul's debt to Jewish messianism, and particularly Pharisaic messianism, was surely greater than this, the evidence for discovering the degree or character of this debt is not available (but see Hengel 1991).

**1.2. Hellenism.** Another method of ferreting out the origins of Paul's christological thinking has been the *religionsgeschichtliche* ("history-of-religions") approach. Perhaps the paramount and most influential example of this approach is W. Bousset's classic work *Kyrios Christos* (1913). There the christology of Paul and the early church is compared with ideas from the Greco-Roman world, particularly those found in its various forms of pagan religious thought. For example, it was assumed that Paul appropriated the title *kyrios* ("Lord"*) from pagan usage and so reflected the Hellenizing influence on early Christian thought. An underlying premise of this approach, however, assumes a radical distinction between Hellenism* and Palestinian Judaism, an assumption that has been severely discredited by the work of M. Hengel and others (Hengel 1974; *see* Hellenism). Research has shown, for example, that documents such as Sirach and the Maccabean corpus attest to the influence of Hellenism on Palestinian Jewish thinking about God and other religious matters well before the Christian era.

But apart from these more general considerations, there is evidence that the title *kyrios* arose from an early chapter in the emergence of the church and was not a product of the later Hellenization of Christianity. The Aramaic cry *Marana tha*, "Our Lord, come" (1 Cor 16:22; *see* Liturgical Elements), which surely goes back to Aramaic-speaking Palestinian or bilingual Antiochean Jewish Christians, shows that prior to the writing of Paul's extant letters, Jesus was being invoked and beckoned as a divine Lord who would return to his people. Had early Christians believed Jesus was simply a deceased Palestinian Jewish teacher, this sort of address would never have arisen (cf. Moule, Longenecker). And its preservation in Aramaic, transliterated into Greek, attests to its revered place in early Christian devotion to Christ (*see* Worship).

**1.3. Paul's Conversion/Call and Early Christian Tradition.** For reasons such as we have just given, modern research into the origins of Paul's christology has found a more promising approach in examining early christological confessions (*see* Creed) embedded in Paul's letters and in exploring Paul's own statements about his call/conversion (*see* Conversion and Call). From this evidence conclusions may be drawn about how that experience and his encounter with early Christian confessions may have shaped his christology.

Galatians 1:11-23 provides the clearest and probably the earliest statement from Paul about his own conversion and its immediate consequences. Here Paul is adamant in stating that he did not receive his

gospel* through human beings, nor was it human in origin nor the result of some human instruction he received. To the contrary, Paul claims to have received his gospel by revelation directly from God.* It must be stressed that in this passage Paul is primarily defending the source and substance of his gospel, *not* his conversion to Christ, and this goes a long way toward explaining the differences that have been noted between this narrative and the Acts accounts, particularly those of Acts 9 and 22. Let us assume, for the sake of argument, that Acts does provide us with some reliable data on the matter of Paul's call/conversion. Both in Paul's letters, and certainly in the third Acts account of his conversion/call (Acts 26), it is clear that Paul did not see his commission, mission and essential message as deriving from a human source. We read of no Christian instruction delivered to Saul prior to his Damascus Road experience and, as Acts 26 makes clear, Ananias was not the ultimate source of Paul's commission and mission.* All three elements are traced to his encounter with the exalted Lord. This point is equally clear in Acts 9:15 and, to a lesser but significant degree, in Acts 22:14.

**1.3.1. "The Gospel of Christ."** The real issue for Paul in Galatians* is not to establish that he is an authentic Christian, or that he received a missionary commission or even to identify the source of the Pauline Gospel; the issue is the content of his gospel. In Galatians 1:7 Paul identifies his gospel with "the gospel of Christ," a gospel which his opponents in Galatia were seeking to pervert. This phrase "the gospel of Christ" could be understood as "the gospel that comes from Christ" or "the gospel of which Christ is the content." The difference is significant, and a clue to Paul's meaning is found within the immediate context when Paul says that "God . . . was pleased to reveal his Son to me" (Gal 1:15-16). Paul appeals to a revelation, the content of which was the "Son of God." This is likely the meaning of "gospel of Christ" in Galatians 1:7 as well. If this is so, then it is germane to this argument that in the accounts of Acts 9 and 22 Ananias does not teach Saul *about* Jesus Christ. Rather, in Acts 9 he tells him to arise, receive his sight and be baptized, while in Acts 22 Ananias expounds the meaning of Paul's commission. In any event, in light of the word of the Lord that comes to Ananias in Acts 9:15-16, we are probably to understand Ananias as speaking a prophetic word to Paul, not offering mere human instruction or counsel.

Furthermore, whatever Paul may have meant by "the gospel of Christ," he was well aware that subsequent to his conversion he had received traditions about Jesus and his teachings from other Christians, probably including Peter when Paul first visited Jerusalem (Gal 1:18; *see* Tradition; Jesus, Sayings of). And we can scarcely believe that when Paul went up to Jerusalem* again "after fourteen years," Peter,* James* and John only listened quietly as Paul laid before them the gospel he had been proclaiming among the Gentiles* (Gal 2:1-10). It is reasonably certain that while Paul can say "those leaders contributed nothing to me," their words with Paul amounted to more than simply an endorsement of his commission. Paul's point in Galatians 2 is that his "gospel of Christ," the distinctive and essential insights he received directly from Christ either during or as a result of reflecting on the Damascus Road experience, was left undisturbed. What were the elements that he may have learned from this firsthand encounter on the Damascus Road?

*1.3.2. The Risen and Exalted Christ.* First, the apostle* learned that Jesus was still alive—though in a form transcending mere flesh and blood. Since Paul was a Pharisee and believed in resurrection,* he probably came to the immediate conclusion that the Christian claims about Jesus having risen must have been true. We know from his statement in 1 Corinthians 9:1, "Have I not seen the risen Lord?" (cf. 1 Cor 15:8), that Paul did draw such a conclusion, whether at his conversion/call or later. In Paul's mind certain things necessarily would have followed from this conclusion. If Jesus after his death* had been exalted in heaven,* then this surely meant Jesus' claims, or at least the claims made about Jesus, had been vindicated. Thus Paul in Romans 1:4 says that Jesus was vindicated as or designated to be the Son of God in power* by his resurrection from the dead (*see* Life and Death). Inasmuch as Jesus did not reject the claim to be Messiah Paul could have concluded that if Jesus was alive in heaven, then he must be God's anointed one. Why else would God vindicate someone who had died a death by crucifixion,* a death that, in light of early Jewish understanding of Deuteronomy 21:22, meant the crucified was accursed (*see* Curse, Accursed) by God? As Galatians 3:13 makes clear, Paul came to believe that Christ had become a curse for believers in order to redeem them from the curse of the Law* (cf. 1 Cor 12:3). In short, Paul's experience of a risen and exalted Jesus occasioned a complete reversal of his estimate of Jesus and his crucifixion.

Paul had once regarded Jesus from a purely human point of view (2 Cor 5:16)—a failure, perhaps a fool and certainly not the Jewish Messiah—but after the Damascus Road experience he did so no longer. He now viewed Jesus as the Son of God. This does not mean Paul had no use for apostolic traditions about Jesus or for the actual sayings of Jesus.

*1.3.3. The Corporate Christ.* The second thing Paul is likely to have deduced from his Damascus Road encounter was that Jesus closely identified himself with the Christians Paul had been persecuting. As Acts attests, the risen Lord asked Saul, "Why are you persecuting *me*? . . . I am Jesus whom you are persecuting" (Acts 9:4-5; cf. Acts 22:7-8; 26:14-15). This would have suggested to him that the Christians must be God's people. If God's special Son was so closely identifying himself with those whom Saul was persecuting, Saul needed to reevaluate his understanding of the people of God. Far from doing God's will in persecuting Christians, he found himself to be opposing God's Christ and thus opposing God. It is possible that Paul's later theology of the body of Christ (*see* Body of Christ) owed something to his Damascus Road experience, where he learned that the afflictions* of Christians were also the afflictions of Christ (cf. Robinson, 58; Kim, 252-56).

*1.3.4. The Savior Christ.* Third, Saul may have learned that he had been saved or converted on the road to Damascus quite *apart* from his own actions and deserts. Indeed, Christ had laid claim on him in spite of Paul's actions. This could only lead to the conclusion that salvation* in its forgiving* and transforming power was a gift of grace* (see Dunn 1977, 190).

This experience of grace in turn meant that Paul had to assume a new attitude toward the Law. Whereas previously the Law had been the center point of his religious life before God, Christ and the experience of Christ was now the integrating factor in his life. All of life had to be seen through the eyes of Christ, not through the lens of the Law. For Paul, Christ was the terminus of the Law, insofar as the Law might be understood as a means of salvation. Salvation by works,* or even salvation by responding to the initial work and grace of God by obedience to the Mosaic Law (covenantal nomism; *see* Law), was no longer—if it ever had been—possible. Life before God could no longer be a matter of "do this and you shall live." Rather, it became a matter of a righteousness* received by grace through faith* which enabled one to obey the law of Christ (a different matter from Moses' Law; *see* Law of Christ) out of gratitude.

Nevertheless, none of this meant that Paul saw no value in the Mosaic Law. Indeed he saw it as holy, just and good, and some of its instruction was seen as a valuable moral guide for Christian living, particularly the narrative portions which could be in a typological manner (cf. 1 Cor 10). The Law's problem was that while it could often inform a person about what was evil and what was good, it could not enable one to shun the evil or do the good. It could not provide the life and power that was available from Christ through the Spirit (*see* Holy Spirit), which made possible a lifestyle pleasing to God. In addition the Law, though splendid, had but a partial and fading splendor which was eclipsed by Christ—the fuller and final revelation of God's good and perfect will and character (cf. 2 Cor 3:4-18).

It is not surprising that Paul concentrated on preaching Christ crucified and risen, for in his mind these were the decisive events which had changed the human situation before God. One who formerly had stood under the Law and its condemnation could now in Christ stand under grace and its justification.* If salvation was by grace through faith in the Lord Jesus who was crucified and risen, nothing stood in the way of anyone, Gentiles included, being saved apart from the Mosaic Law. For Paul the removal of the Mosaic Law as a means of right-standing with God, as a way of being saved *or* working out one's salvation, had broken down the barrier between Jew and Gentile (cf. Eph. 2:14-15). If faith in the risen Lord was the way of salvation, then it could be offered to all without prior religious commitment to the Jewish requirements of circumcision,* food* laws and keeping the whole of Torah.

Paul, according to Galatians 1:16, saw the purpose of his conversion to be his call as a missionary to the Gentiles. This call complemented his experience of God's grace. If one's standing before God was all of grace, there was no reason why grace could not be offered to all without the preconditions of the Mosaic Law. Thus it is quite possible that Paul deduced the heart of his gospel from his conversion experience. When Paul spoke of the revelation (*apokalypsis*) of Christ (Gal 1:12, 16), or of Christ as the glory* (*doxa*) of God (2 Cor 4:6), he may have been reflecting the experience recorded in Acts of a blinding light that accompanied the revelation of the risen Lord. In Paul's mind the revelation of Jesus in glory on the Damascus Road probably signaled the arrival of the eschatological age (*see* Eschatology) in which old things were passing and would pass away and new things were coming into existence (Kim 71-74; cf. also Burton, 42-43). The arrival of the new age initiated for Paul a new christocentric view of the Law and ethics* in general. This was but a part of his larger enterprise of revisioning the story of Israel* in light of the story of Christ.

## 2. The Narrative Framework of Paul's Christology.
The universe of Paul's thought revolved around the Son of God, Jesus Christ. Paul's christology illumined his thought in its entirety, sometimes shedding its light on aspects of his thought that one might have expected would have gone relatively untouched by christology. For instance, who would have expected Paul, in midrashic fashion, to tell his Corinthian listeners that the rock that gave forth water to the Israelites during their period of wilderness wanderings *was* Christ (1 Cor 10:4)? Here he draws on sapiential ideas about the role of personified Wisdom* in Israel (cf. Wis 11:2-4, "They journeyed through the uninhabited wilderness. . . . When they were thirsty, they called upon [Wisdom], and water was given them out of flinty rock"). Paul's view of Christ was so broad that he could conceive of him as being involved in God's dealings with his people long before he was born and began his earthly ministry. This is apparently because he saw Christ as Wisdom come in the flesh* (cf. 1 Cor 1:24), and therefore whatever had been said of Wisdom in early Jewish thought, including its existence in heaven before creation* (cf. Prov 8; Sir 24; Wis 7), was now predicated of Christ (cf. Witherington 1993, chaps. 7—8).

*2.1. Christology and Theology.* Two opposite dangers must be avoided in the study of Pauline christology. First is the danger of underestimating the significance and weight of Pauline christology for Paul's thought world. Paul's christology should be seen as a subspecies of his theology. For Paul "Jesus is Lord" is not merely a functional description of Jesus' work since his resurrection. Many, though not all, of the names, titles, roles and functions of God were predicated of Christ precisely because Paul believed that he was dealing with God in Christ, and God as Christ (though in neither respect did Paul define this with the precision of the later church councils). Christ was one way God had manifested himself to the world. Christ could be an object of confession and worship for Paul and other early Jewish Christians precisely because Christ was seen as divine. Paul was not advocating a violation of Jewish monotheism (*see* God) by advocating the worship* of Christ, because he believed that Christ was divine. L. W. Hurtado has demonstrated that early Jewish monotheism could include the idea of divine agency, which on occasion involved seeing a human figure of the distant past, such as an Enoch or a patriarch, as a divine agent of God (cf. Hurtado, 17-92). In such a context seeing the Messiah as a divine agent of God, or as Wisdom in person, was not such a radical departure from Jewish orthodoxy as has sometimes been thought.

Paul's letters do not present a developed doctrine of the Trinity or a lengthy explanation of the interrelationships in the Godhead, but in predicating divinity of Father, Son and Spirit, Paul provided the raw data for later Christian trinitarianism. Christology was a form of theology for Paul, though by no means the only form. When Paul spoke of Christ handing over the kingdom to the Father "so that God may be all in all" (1 Cor 15:28) he was not dissolving christology into theology (cf. Beker, 200, 344).

Likewise, Paul was not christomonistic, a perspective which regards christology as the exclusive or near-exclusive form of theology. While Paul reenvisioned the world and even God from a christocentric point of view, he maintained a significant place in his theology for the Father and the Spirit. For Paul it was the Father alone who had sent the Son, the Son alone who had died on the cross* and the Spirit alone by whom believers were baptized into the one body of Christ. Paul not only distinguished these three by their functions, but also by their nature—inasmuch as they might be compared to Christ's human nature (i.e., the Father and the Spirit do not have a human nature). Casting Paul's theology as a christomonism fails to appreciate the apostle's differentiation between the distinctive roles, functions and characteristics of Father, Son and Spirit.

Too often discussions of Paul's christology, while recognizing it to be a subspecies of his theology, have approached the subject piecemeal, analyzing christological titles in isolation from one another. The frequent outcome is a display of ideas torn from the fabric of Paul's thought with little accounting for the coherent core of Paul's christology as it was expressed in the contingencies of the situations he addressed. J. C. Beker rightly points to both the coherency of Paul's thought through time *and* its contingency as it addresses particular situations and concerns. The study of christological titles can be helpful, but it can also be reductionistic, treating elements of Paul's thought as permutations in the history of theological ideas. This approach overlooks the fact that Paul's theological thought is woven together with his ethical and practical thinking as well as with his social concerns. Isolating christology at the cost of neglecting the rest of his thought world often results in an imbalanced picture. The whole of Paul's christology is much greater than the sum of its parts.

*2.2. The Fourfold Narrative.* A more adequate approach to Paul's christology recognizes its narrative shape (cf. Hays). That is to say, Paul's christology implies a story in which four aspects may be identified: the story of Christ, the story of Israel, the story of the world and the story of God.

*2.2.1. The Story of Christ.* The narrative structure follows the course of one who was in the very form of God (Phil 2:6) but set aside his divine prerogatives and status in order to take the status of a slave and die a slave's death; for this reason God exalted him. Paul may have derived this much of the story from reflecting on already existing christological hymns* that were part of early Christian worship (cf. Phil 2:6-11; Col 1:15-20; Heb 1:2-4; and also Jn 1:1-14). These hymns ascribed to Christ traits that early Judaism had ascribed to personified Wisdom (cf. Witherington 1993, chap. 7). Paul, however, continues the story in relating Christ's ongoing role in heaven and his future return to earth as divine judge* and triumphant* Lord. Thus Paul's story of Christ transcends the more familiar pattern of *Endzeit = Urzeit* (endtime = primal time). Christ's exalted state does not simply recapitulate his pre-existent state. A few examples will illustrate some of these points.

First, the christological hymn in Philippians 2:6-11 indicates that the career of Christ determines how he should be confessed. Jesus was given a throne name of "Lord" precisely because God highly exalted him as a result of his finished work on earth, which included death on a cross. The *dio kai* of Philippians 2:9 is crucial, and should be translated "and therefore" or "and that is why." Ever since his death, and precisely because of his earthly life and death as a servant,* Jesus has been highly exalted (*see* Exaltation) to a place of divine honor and power, and so he is now functioning as Lord. This is why in the present age he may be properly confessed using the divine throne name "Lord."*

Second, the title *Christ** became, among early Christians, another name for Jesus. But Jesus was a human being, just as various early Jews seem to have expected Messiah to be. *Christ*, on the rare occasions when it functions as a title in Paul, refers primarily to the role of Jesus during his earthly career, climaxing in the cross. For this reason Paul can resolve to know nothing among the Corinthians but "Christ crucified" (cf. 1 Cor 1:23). It can also on occasion be used to refer to Christ's roles after his death and resurrection, and even in his pre-existence* (cf. 1 Cor 10:4). Thus it is critical to understand the christological titles within the narrative framework of Paul's story of Christ.

*2.2.2. The Story of Israel.* A larger story, the story of Israel,* also informed Paul's christology. Jesus was born of woman and born under the Law (Gal 4:4). For Paul this meant a *sending* of God's Son to be the human Jesus. Moreover, this Son was sent to redeem those under the Law, Israel, a fact that clearly presupposes the lostness of Israel (*see* Restoration). More importantly, this story of Israel influenced how Paul viewed both the name and the roles of the Christ. He is God's royal and even pre-existent Son, sent to redeem God's people. For it was to Israel that the promise of a Messiah had been made and from Israel the Messiah was to come (Rom 9:4-5). For Paul the sonship of Jesus was another way of speaking of Jesus as a Jewish royal or messianic figure who came to set his people free. For this reason Paul can speak of the gospel as for the Jew first (Rom 1:16).

*2.2.3. The Story of the World.* The story of Christ and of Israel are a part of yet a larger story, the story of the world.* For Paul the world is fallen (cf. Rom 1) and living on borrowed time; the present form of this world is passing away (1 Cor 7:31; cf. Gal 1:4). On the one hand this fact relativizes relationships and other social realities that may have seemed of paramount importance in the past. On the other hand, the fact of the world's gradual demise makes decisions about the critical issues in life all the more crucial. The world is bent on self-destruction yet longs for liberation, and this is true not just of the human world but of the whole material creation (Rom 8:20-22). In addition, Paul can speak of malevolent supernatural powers (*see* Principalities and Powers), including Satan* and demons,* who are part of the present age (cf. 1 Cor 10:20-21; 2 Cor 2:11; 4:4).

It is against this dark backdrop and in the very midst of this world that the drama of Israel and her Messiah and the Christian community is played out (cf. Wright, chap. 2).

*2.2.4. The Story of God.* Transcending the story of the world is the story of the Son as part of the ongoing life of God. This is a story of the interrelationship of Father, Son and Spirit, and it too informs Paul's christology. The story of God is intertwined with the story of the world. The christological hymn of Colossians 1:15-20 (cf. 2 Cor 4:4) indicates that the Son played a role in the creation of all things, including humankind. Thus the role of Christ as redeemer (*see* Redemption) is part of the divine initiative to reconcile (*see* Peace, Reconciliation) all things to God. And the Incarnation is part of the story of God. Moreover, the subduing and reconciling of the powers and principalities* is also part of the larger story of God, though this cosmic mission is also intertwined with the story of Christ as redeemer of humankind (1 Cor 15:24). The place of this cosmic christology in Paul's thought is well founded, for whatever one may conclude about the authorship or contingent circumstances being addressed in Colossians,* the elements of this christology were already evident in Paul's christology as it was expressed in 1 Corinthians 15:24-26. Moreover, this is an eschatological story, for in relating God's final action toward his creation, the story is eschatological in

both framework and substance (*see* Eschatology).

## 3. The Divinity and Humanity of Jesus Christ in Paul's Christology.

*3.1. Christ's Divinity.* We have already seen that Paul, in appropriating the language of the christological hymns, subscribed to the christological notion that Christ existed prior to taking on human flesh. Paul spoke of Jesus both as the wisdom of God, his agent in creation (1 Cor 1:24, 30; 8:6; Col 1:15-17; see Bruce, 195), and as the one who accompanied Israel as the "rock" in the wilderness (1 Cor 10:4). In view of the role Christ plays in 1 Corinthians 10:4, Paul is *not* founding the story of Christ on the archetypal story of Israel, but rather on the story of divine Wisdom, which helped Israel in the wilderness.

*3.1.1. "Christ . . . the Wisdom of God."* Furthermore, it seems likely that the sapiential ideas we find in 1 Corinthians 1:24, 30 and 8:6 blossomed into Paul's concept of the cosmic Christ—not only Lord over land and universe but also involved in its creation. The full flower of this christological wisdom thinking came to expression in the hymn in Colossians 1:15-20 where Christ is said to be the "image* of the invisible God," the "firstborn"* of creation, and the means and goal of creation. Here the qualities that Judaism could attribute to Wisdom are transferred to Christ, as illustrated by a text such as Wisdom of Solomon 7:25-26:

> For she is the breath of the power of God, and a
> pure emanation of the glory of the Almighty;
> therefore nothing defiled gains entrance into her.
> For she is a reflection of eternal light, a spotless
> mirror of the working of God, and an image of his
> goodness. (NRSV)

While Paul adopted and adapted this understanding of Wisdom to his own ends, the implications of its use are important—the apostle ascribed divine attributes to Jesus Christ.

Did Paul think of Jesus as being divine? Two difficult texts call for investigation: Romans 9:5 and Philippians 2:6-7.

*3.1.2. "Messiah . . . God Blessed" (Rom 9:5).* This verse comes at the outset of Paul's discussion of the advantages of the nation Israel; but it poses an exegetical problem in the form of punctuation. F. C. Burkitt once said, with some exaggeration, that the punctuation of Romans 9:5 has probably been more discussed than that of any other sentence in literature. Since there is little or no punctuation in the earliest Greek manuscripts, it must be supplied by the reader or exegete. In the case of Romans 9:5 this has resulted in the text being read in various ways (see Metzger). The argument turns on whether Romans 9:5b should be read with the NRSV's "Messiah, who is over all, God blessed forever," or with the NRSV margin's "Messiah, who is God over all, blessed forever" or with the NEB "Messiah. May God supreme over all be blessed for ever." In the latter case 5b becomes a separate sentence from 5a, or at least a separate clause. The JB, NIV and NKJV support the reading "who is over all, God blessed for ever," as qualifying Christ. It appears that both the context and the grammar favor the reading of the NRSV or the NRSV margin.

Romans 9:5a has the phrase *ho Christos to kata sarka*. As Metzger points out, in the instance of Romans 1:3-4 and elsewhere it is normal to expect a contrast when we come to the phrase *kata sarka* ("according to the flesh"). So in Romans 1:3-4 the contrast is *kata sarka* ("according to the flesh") and *kata pneuma* ("according to spirit"). *Kata sarka* in Romans 9:5a is unnatural in its present form if the speaker does not go on to say what Christ is according to something else besides the flesh.

Secondly, the phrase "who is" (*ho ōn*) is normally taken as introducing a relative clause, and 2 Corinthians 11:31 ("who is blessed forever," *ho ōn eulogētos eis tous aiōnas*) provides a good parallel to Romans 9:5. As N. Turner puts it:

> The text of the N.E.B. simply closes the sentence at 'Messiah' and begins anew with an exclamation 'May God, supreme above all, be blessed for ever!' So it avoids assigning the quality of godhead to Jesus Christ, but it introduces asyndeton and there is no grammatical reason why a participle agreeing with 'Messiah' should first be divorced from it and then be given the force of a wish, receiving a different person as its subject. It would in fact be unnatural to divorce it from its antecedent. (Turner, 15)

It is better to follow the NRSV margin and read, "sprang the Messiah, who is God over all, blessed forever."

Metzger also notes that Pauline doxologies (*see* Benediction, Blessing, Doxology) elsewhere are always attached to some previous antecedent; they are not asyndetic (i.e., lacking a conjunction). Furthermore, it is almost a universal pattern for doxologies in the Hebrew and LXX to be "blessed be God," not "God blessed," as we have here if one translation is followed. So the likelihood is that "God blessed" does not express a wish that God be blessed forever, but that the Messiah, who is God, is by nature blessed forever (but cf. Dunn 1988, 528-29, 535-36). The early versions also favor the reading represented in the NRSV or the reading listed in the NRSV margin. If it is asked why Paul nowhere else so explicitly calls

Christ "God," Metzger's response is a good one.

> The reason why there are so few statements in Paul's epistles bearing on the essential nature of Christ . . . is doubtless connected with a feature often noticed by others, namely that the apostle, for purposes of instruction bearing on Christian nurture, usually prefers to speak of the functional rather than the ontological relationships of Christ. (Metzger, 111-12)

We conclude that in Romans 9:5 Paul calls Christ God, thus demonstrating the extent to which Paul's experience of the risen Lord had caused him to qualify or transform his Jewish monotheism (cf. Wright, 237). This means that Paul had a high christology even before he used the Christ hymn in Philippians 2 (assuming Philippians* is later than Romans,* and that Paul did not already know the Christ hymn before he wrote Romans).

*3.1.3. "Who Being in the Form of God . . ." (Phil 2:6-7).* A portion of the christological hymn of Philippians 2 must now be explored more fully. The argument turns on several key terms and phrases: (1) *morphē* ("form"), found in the NT only here and in Philippians 2:7 (except in Mk 16:12 which is part of a later addition to Mark); (2) *to einai isa theō* ("to be equal with God"); and (3) *harpagmos* ("a snatching, grasping"; "a desire to acquire").

It is entirely likely that *morphē* ("form") carries the same general meaning in verse 7 as it does in verse 6. In addition, the *alla* ("but") at the beginning of verse 7 suggests a contrast is being drawn between the before and after of Jesus becoming human. *Morphē* has been translated as "form," "appearance," "condition," "status," "image" or "mode of being." If one translates *morphē* as "status," "condition" or "appearance," it would seem to indicate Jesus' outward form, status, appearance or function, not what he was in his being. It is unlikely that Paul in Philippians 2:7 is saying that Jesus in his earthly ministry merely "looked like" or "appeared to be" or "functioned" as a servant.* Rather, he became this—he was a servant. The parallel between the two states is not exact since the text says that he was *in* the form of God, but then also *took on* the form of a servant. Elsewhere Paul clearly states that Jesus became "poor" and generously gave himself to his people (cf. 2 Cor 8:9). For Paul this was part and parcel of the meaning of Christ's taking on the condition and status of humanity.

Second, we note that Paul does not say Jesus *was* the form of God, but that he was *in* the form of God. Thus the translation "likeness" in itself seems lexically improbable (unless one imports a Last Adam idea into this text, cf. Rom 5:18-19; 1 Cor 15:45-47). Paul is not calling Jesus the "image" or "likeness" of God. Rather, as G. F. Hawthorne has pointed out,

> from earliest Greek texts μορφή was at least used to express the way in which a thing, being what it is in itself, appears to our sense. "Μορφή always signifies a form which truly and fully expresses the being which underlies it" (MM417). Thus, when this word is applied to God, his μορφή must refer to his deepest being, to what he is in himself, to that "which cannot be reached by our understanding or sight, precisely because God is ἀόρατος: in fact the word has meaning here only as referring to the reality of God's being" (Cerfaux, *Christ*, 305). Μορφὴ θεοῦ, then, may be correctly understood as "the essential nature and character of God." (Hawthorne, 83-84)

We thus translate Philippians 2:6a and 7b, "being in the form (i.e., "character," "nature") of God . . . he went on to take on the character, nature of a servant."

Third, *to einai isa theō* (Phil 2:6c) has a definite article with it: "*the* being equal with God." This probably indicates that this second phrase is closely connected to the first, pointing to what Christ already is. But Paul is going to move on to state what that meant for Jesus in view of his later actions.

Fourth, the word *harpagmos* has been taken to mean either groping for something one doesn't have, perhaps snatching at something, or it has been taken to mean clutching on to something one already has. More likely than either of these two views is that of R. W. Hoover who demonstrates that it means "taking advantage of something that is already rightfully yours." The Christ hymn portrays Jesus in his self-giving. He did not consider being equal with God a matter of taking full advantage of his rights (or glory), but rather (*alla*) of giving them up and taking on the form of a servant.

We conclude that Philippians 2:6-7 indicates Paul saw Jesus as having preexistence* and equality with God (against Dunn 1980), but that in his preexistence he did not take advantage of all the prerogatives of deity.

Fifth, one more matter needs to be dealt with at this juncture—what does it mean to say Christ *heauton ekenōsen*, usually translated, "he emptied himself"? Philippians 2:7 begins with the word *alla* ("but"), probably suggesting a contrast followed by a verb and its object. This may be interpreted to mean either he "stripped himself" or "emptied himself." One may ask, emptied himself of what? Although Hawthorne argues that one cannot determine from this statement alone what Christ emptied himself of (Paul does not say), the context may give some clues. So-called kenotic christol-

ogy, based chiefly on this text, suggests that Jesus emptied himself of certain divine attributes—omniscience, omnipotence and omnipresence—when he became a human being. The text must surely be referring to what Christ did at the point of taking on a human nature, not at his death (cf. Martin 1976, 97). The kenotic view might be thought to derive some support from a text like Mark 13:32, "no one knows . . . not even the Son." Mark 13:32, however, can just as easily be taken to suggest that Jesus limited himself, and to say that Christ limited himself is not the same as saying he emptied himself of various divine attributes. It is also important to remember that Mark 13:32 does not attempt to answer the christological question addressed in Philippians 2.

Thus, it seems likely that Paul in Philippians 2 means one of two things: (1) Jesus emptied himself of the prerogatives and glory* of being divine, or of the right to claim such prerogatives (which Phil 2:6 seems to suggest if we are right about *harpagmos*). These prerogatives would entail glory and lordship, which belonged to Christ by virtue of his being equal with God. (2) Hawthorne suggests it simply means Jesus totally gave himself, poured himself out, rather than telling us what he gave up. The former seems more likely.

*3.1.4. "In Christ."* A third category of texts speak of Christ as a sort of omnipresent being in whom believers are included. The evidence cannot be rehearsed here (*see* Christ; Moule 1977, 62-65), but the essence is that when Paul speaks of believers being "in Christ" he often suggests that Christ has attributes that only a divine being could properly be said to have.

*3.1.5. Christ and the Spirit.* Finally, our understanding of Paul's view of the divinity of Christ is enhanced by comparing what Paul says about Christ in comparison to what he says about God's Holy Spirit. It has been noted often how closely Paul identifies Christ and the Spirit (*see* Holy Spirit) in his letters—indeed, at points they seem to be identical. Paul can speak of the Spirit coming to believers only because Christ is risen and ascended. For instance, in discussing Jesus' resurrection Paul speaks of Jesus, the last Adam, as a "life-giving spirit" (1 Cor 15:45). He is the one who sends the Spirit and without his resurrection and exaltation the Spirit would not have come. Romans 1:3-4 indicates that it was through the power of the Spirit that Jesus was enabled to be Son of God in power. The Spirit empowered him, and he sends that power to believers. It is Christ who makes the eschatological age possible, and that age focuses on him.

Frequently in Pauline thought the functions of Jesus and the Spirit are identified, so much so that being in Christ is simply another way of speaking about being in the Spirit (*pace* Smalley). Consider the following:

(1) Believers are righteous in Christ (Phil 3:8, 9) but also in the Spirit (Rom 14:17).

(2) Believers have life* in Christ (Col 3:4) but also in the Holy Spirit (Rom 8:11).

(3) Believers have hope in Christ for life to come (1 Cor 15:19) and in the power of the Spirit to give them eternal life (Gal 6:8).

(4) Believers rejoice and have joy* in the Holy Spirit (Rom 14:17) but also in the Lord (Phil 4:4).

(5) Believers have truth* in Christ (Rom 9:1), and truth is also spoken in the Spirit (1 Cor 12:3-6).

(6) Believers have fellowship* in Christ (1 Cor 1:9) but also fellowship of Spirit (2 Cor 13:13).

(7) Believers are consecrated and sanctified (*see* Holiness, Sanctification) in Christ (1 Cor 1:2) but also in the Spirit (Rom 15:16).

(8) Believers are sealed both in Christ (Eph 1:13) and in the Spirit (Eph 4:30).

This identification between Christ and Spirit is taken even further when Paul ascribes to Christ various features characterizing the Spirit in the OT. Thus, for instance, Psalm 104:29 states that it is the Spirit that gives life (cf. Ezek 31), but in 1 Corinthians 15:45 it is Christ who gives life. This means that at his resurrection and exaltation Jesus assumed the functions previously ascribed to the Spirit. This characteristic of Paul has led some to ask whether he held to a binitarian rather than trinitarian view of God. Is the Lord the Spirit for Paul?

This is in fact what Paul seems to be saying in 2 Corinthians 3:17: "The Lord is the Spirit, for where the Spirit of the Lord is, there is freedom." On the one hand, it is sometimes pointed out that Paul in 2 Corinthians 3:14 identifies Christ with God. This is not quite correct, for Paul in fact says that *in* Christ the veil is lifted, not *by* Christ. Throughout this text Paul has in mind the OT context of Exodus 34:34-35. In 2 Corinthians 3:16 it does appear that on the surface Paul is referring to Christ, who is being identified with Yahweh in his role in Exodus. C. K. Barrett notes a subtle distinction: while "the Lord" in 2 Corinthians 3:11 is Christ, the one to whom people turn, the function of removing the veil from over a person's heart is for Paul preeminently the work of the Spirit, as Christ's agent. Christ in 2 Corinthians 3:11 is identified with his agent but only in his activity, and so it is not proper to speak of Paul having a Spirit christology. Rejecting a binitarianism on the part of Paul, Barrett concludes:

> It is certainly true that for Paul Christ the Lord, and the Spirit, were two very closely related terms, each of which was unthinkable apart from the oth-

er, since the objective status of being in Christ carried with it the subjective accompaniment of receiving the Spirit, who was manifested in particular gifts . . . ; he was however capable of distinguishing them, as for example in the phrase 'Spirit of Christ' (Rom. viii.9). It is in the realm of action . . . rather than of person . . . that the terms Lord and Spirit are identified. (Barrett 1973, 123)

What Paul is saying, according to Barrett, is that the Spirit is Lord in such situations, illuminating believers and giving them freedom. Another way of looking at this, however, is to assume that Paul is commenting on Exodus 34 in a manner we may paraphrase as follows: "now the 'Lord' in this text is the 'Spirit,' and where the Spirit of the Lord is . . ."

In any case, Paul speaks of "the Spirit of the Lord," which seems to imply a distinction between "Spirit" and "Lord." More clearly in Romans 8:9 the two seem to be distinguished in the phrase "the Spirit of Christ." Thus for Paul the "Spirit of Christ" = "Spirit of God" (cf. Rom 8:8) = "Spirit of the Lord." We must conclude then that the Spirit is Christ's agent, and he functions for Christ, one might almost say, as Christ, here on earth during the church age. This identity in function and effect surely implies the deity of Christ, for from the perspective of the OT it is only God who can send or be a life-giving Spirit.

Nevertheless, so far as their being is concerned, Christ and the Spirit are not to be equated and may even be distinguished in some of their activities. It was Christ, not the Spirit, who died and was raised. It is Christ, not the Spirit, who will return and judge (1 Cor 4:5). It was Christ, not the Spirit, who came in the flesh. In one sense the Spirit is the bridge between believers and Christ on this earth. But it is also interesting how Paul attributes tasks to Christ that in the OT were attributed to the Spirit. In Psalm 33:6 the world is said to have been created by the Spirit, but in Colossians 1:16 we read "by him [Christ] all things are created." In the OT it often appears that the Spirit is simply God on the move in creation and history. What was said of the Spirit is now predicated of the exalted Christ who is on the move and active in his church and in history.

To summarize: in the church age Christ and Spirit are not one but two in identity, but they are one in function because the Spirit is Christ's agent on earth (recalling the Rabbinic adage, "a person's agent [*šaliah*] is as their self"). This also implies that receiving Christ and receiving the Spirit are simultaneous events. Paul knows no doctrine of a second baptism, for by the Spirit one enters Christ's body, and that is the only occasion which Paul speaks of as being baptized by the Spirit (cf. 1 Cor 12:13; *see* Baptism).

*3.2. The Humanity of the Christ.*

*3.2.1. Christ as Son.* As a preface to examining what Paul meant when he called Jesus Son of David, Last Adam* or a human being, it is helpful to summarize what Paul meant by the term *Son of God* (*see* Son of God).

M. Hengel has provided the valuable insight that for Paul " 'Son of God', with its more complicated language, was kept for exceptional usage, at the climax of certain theological statements" (Hengel 1976, 14). By this title Paul signified the unique relationship between the exalted Christ and God. Its further significance for Paul is summed up by I. H. Marshall:

> it is the Son who is the theme of the gospel (Rom. 1:3, 9), and it is by means of this title that Paul emphasizes the supreme value of the death of the One who stood closest to God as the means of reconciling men with God (Rom. 5:10; 8:32; Gal. 2:20; Col. 1.13 f.). . . . For Paul Jesus was God's Son during his earthly life, and . . . it was as God's Son that he died. Consequently, he did not cease to be divine in his earthly existence, and his self-emptying cannot mean that he gave up his divine nature to assume human nature. (Marshall, 644-45)

Romans 1:3-4 is an important christological statement which speaks of the Son in two aspects, his earthly descent and his resurrection glory. Here we focus on Romans 1:3: in the sphere of the flesh (*kata sarka*), Jesus is said to have been "born of the seed of David" (a phrase we find again at the end of the Pauline corpus in 2 Tim 2:8). This phrase in itself indicates not only Jesus' Jewishness and humanity, but also focuses on the pedigree warranting his title Messiah/Christ. This surely implies some stress on his royalty. The only other place where Paul highlights this fact is Romans 15:12 ("the shoot of Jesse shall come forth"), where he quotes from Isaiah 11:10 (LXX). Romans 1:3-4 indicates two stages of Jesus' career epitomized in what seems to be a primitive christological formula which Paul adopted and endorsed. Jesus' Davidic descent is well attested in various strands of NT material (Mt 1:1; Acts 2:30; Rev 5:5). Paul introduces this christological formulation by appealing to God's promises through the prophets in Holy Scripture (Rom 1:2). Jesus Christ is the promised and prophesied Messiah.

For most Jews it appears that *messiah* was a term referring to a human being, not divine even if he was given certain divine gifts or authority* (though cf. the picture of the "Elect One" in *1 Enoch* 55—69; see Neusner et al.). It is thus appropriate, in a context where messiahship is mentioned, to stress Jesus' humanity born of David's seed. Indeed, it is telling that

Paul uses the term *Christ* of Jesus more than he does any other, suggesting that salvation comes to believers only through one who was human like them, who lived and *died* for them. The term *Christ,* coupled with a stress on his crucifixion, characterized Paul's preaching* to a significant degree (cf. 1 Cor 1:23). In order to speak of salvation,* Paul had to stress Jesus' humanity in various ways (cf. Dunn 1977, 43). The story of Jesus (i.e., his death) brought about a redefinition of Paul's understanding of the Davidic Messiah, a process which appears to have taken place prior to the writing of Paul's extant letters (*see* Christ).

If Paul had no difficulty identifying Jesus as Christ, and Jesus as a human who had died, how did he view Jesus' humanity in general? What little he had to say about this can be summed up in a few short phrases. There is enough to suggest that Paul understood Jesus to have been fully human, but not enough to spell out in any detail how he defined that humanity. This may be because the facts of Jesus and his ministry were assumed knowledge on the part of Paul and his readership. It may also reflect Paul's chosen emphasis in his letters on Jesus' death and resurrection, and issues of life in the Spirit and in the church. Paul was not a Gospel writer or historian; he was a pastoral theologian called upon to deal with matters of theological weight and direct bearing on the issues which arose in the churches (*see* Jesus, Sayings of; Jesus and Paul).

The christological events of first importance for Paul seem to have been Christ's taking on true human nature and humbling himself to the status of a servant, his death on the cross and his resurrection. The significant events of Jesus' earthly career between his Incarnation and death is scarcely mentioned (cf. 2 Cor 8:9, though this may also refer to the circumstances into which Jesus was born).

*3.2.2. Born of a Woman.* Paul could affirm that Jesus was born of woman (Gal 4:4). His appearance in this world was as a normal human being, who came forth from his mother's womb into this world. As F. F. Bruce pointed out (195), Paul's word choice (*genomenon*), is applicable to anyone born of a woman. The text implies nothing peculiar about Jesus' manner of birth. Nor does Paul mention the virginal conception, though we cannot be sure that he did not know of it.

Paul also states in Galatians 4:4 that Jesus was born under the Law. His mother was a Jew and so was he. And when Paul says Jesus was born under the Law "to redeem those who were under the Law" (Gal 4:5), he seems to imply that Jesus' earthly ministry was essentially directed toward Israel.* Paul's apostleship to the Gentiles* may go some distance in explaining why he said so little about Jesus' earthly ministry, which was directed to the lost sheep that made up Israel. When Israel did not respond, a new door was opened to take the gospel to the Gentiles (cf. Rom 9—11). If Christ's death and resurrection was the decisive event for the mission to the Gentiles, it is not surprising that Paul focuses on those events in the story of Jesus that affected and involved the Gentiles.

*3.2.3. Born in Human Likeness.* In Philippians 2:7 we are told that Christ was born in human likeness (cf. Phil 2:8). In other words, Jesus took on human flesh, becoming a man who was subject to human frailty, even death. Romans 8:3 also comments on this point in similar and carefully worded terms. Jesus condemned sin in the flesh, taking on human flesh to do so. Thus any sort of docetism is ruled out. Jesus was real flesh and blood. But Romans 8:3 is probably worded as it is to indicate that Jesus did not participate in the sinfulness of flesh (*see* Sin). Barrett stresses:

> One possible suggestion is that Paul distinguished between flesh as it was created by God, and 'flesh of sin', that is, flesh which had fallen under the dominion of sin. Christ (on this view) had perfect, unfallen flesh, which nevertheless was indistinguishable in appearance from 'flesh of sin'; he came in flesh, so that the incarnation was perfectly real, but only in the likeness of 'flesh of sin', so that he remained sinless. (Barrett 1957, 156),

It seems plausible that the very reason the word *likeness* (*homoiōma*) is used in Romans 8:3 is intentionally to avoid saying he came in sinful flesh (cf. Cranfield 1979, 381). This is compatible with Paul's emphasis in Romans and elsewhere that Jesus was a new Adam, starting a new creation and race. As such he did not participate in the fallen nature of the old Adam.

Paul may have spoken of Christ as being in the "likeness of sinful flesh" not to deny Jesus' sinlessness (2 Cor 5:21), nor to deny his sinless human nature, but to affirm that he took on human flesh and was like all humans in this respect. Perhaps part of the reason Paul worded Romans 8:3 as he did was because he thought of Jesus as the Paschal lamb (*see* Sacrifice, Offering, Passover Lamb), metaphorically speaking (cf. 1 Cor 5:7). An atoning sacrifice must be unblemished and spotless. Like Adam, Jesus was born with an unfallen nature that had the capacity to sin; unlike Adam, Jesus remained sinless and so in due course became an unblemished sacrifice.

Paul's letters yield little else about the earthly Jesus except for what is implied in his recital of the Last Supper tradition (1 Cor. 11:23-26; *see* Lord's Supper). There he indicates Jesus was a person who broke bread, who poured wine, who gave thanks and thus was human, thanking the heavenly Father for such earthly gifts. Paul does not say Jesus ate at the Last Supper, but it is certainly implied. Apart from the references to Jesus' death and burial, indicating he truly died and was resurrected, there is little else that needs mentioning (cf. 1 Cor 15:4).

*3.2.4. Last Adam.* We turn now to Paul's theme of Christ as the last Adam. It has often been noted that Paul does not call Jesus the Son of man (none of the authors of the NT letters do). This may be due to the Jewish background and meaning of the title. To Gentile ears it may have been too easily assumed to mean simply that Jesus was a real human being, or as a title it may have been considered too obscure or too simple for the Gentile mission and the expanding church (cf. Moule 1977). On the other hand, Paul uses the Adam typology of Jesus and in 1 Corinthians 15:45 calls Jesus the last Adam. Perhaps in Paul's case reflection on Jesus as truly human led to a comparison between Jesus and the first and archetypal human being. In preparation for examining Paul's typology involving Adam and the man Christ, we must first examine certain references to Jesus as *the human being*.

For instance, in Romans 5:15, in the midst of developing the Adam-Christ typology (*see* Adam and Christ), Paul writes that just as death came by "the one," Adam, so God's grace and the gift that accompanied it (righteousness, Rom 5:17) came by "the one," Jesus. Again, in 1 Corinthians 15:21 death comes through a human being (*anthrōpos*), Adam, and the resurrection of the dead comes through a human being (*anthrōpos*), Jesus. In the later and disputed Paulines, 1 Timothy 2:5 shows a further development along these lines when it speaks of Christ as mediator between God and humans, and he is said to be the human being Christ Jesus. What is Paul's point in saying that grace comes to us, as does resurrection and reconciliation, by a human being? Sin was a human problem that could only be resolved for humanity by a human being. Some may think the efficacy of salvation for humankind was due to Jesus being divine, but Paul wishes to emphasize the opposite. If Jesus had not been human, humanity would not have received grace, resurrection or, as Colossians* and Ephesians* stress, reconciliation (*see* Peace, Reconciliation). The extraordinary thing is that the human Jesus died and rose again. God—apart from the mystery of the Incarnation—is not subject to death.

1 Timothy 2:5 goes beyond this in stressing Christ's mediatorial role. Jesus, this text seems to imply, had to be fully God and fully human in order to properly represent God to humans and humans to God. He had to stand on both sides of the fence in order to experience and fully know both the God who grieves

over sin and the sinner who causes God grief. In short, for salvation to reach humans, and to redeem humans, it had to be mediated through one who shared in humanity.

The "last" or "eschatological" Adam motif in 1 Corinthians 15:21-23, 44-49 calls for comment in some detail. This passage is quite unlike the other Adam references we find in Paul. Here we have the responsibility for sin and its consequences placed squarely on Adam's shoulders, while Eve is not mentioned. To J. Jeremias we owe the insight that Paul may have avoided using the term "Son of man" because he addressed a Gentile audience (Jeremias, 141-42). But he goes on to stress how Paul appears to know of the "Son of man" tradition because in 1 Corinthians 15:27 Paul makes a messianic application of Psalm 8:6 to Jesus, "for he has made all things subject under his feet." This psalm is well known for the line that shortly precedes the part Paul is quoting—"or the son of man that you care for him" (Ps 8:4).

There are both similarities and differences between Adam the type and Christ the antitype. Both were truly human, both are representative heads of a race and both had a dramatic effect on their physical/spiritual progeny. However, in some ways the differences outweigh the similarities. The powerful effect of Adam's action on all humanity was death (1 Cor 15:21), but the powerful effect of Christ's action was life (in the specific form of the resurrection of the dead). Now the question may be raised, "Is the parallelism in 1 Corinthians 15:22 a perfect one?" In Adam *all* die. Does the *all* in 1 Corinthians 15:22b mean that *all* humans will one day be made alive in Christ? 1 Thessalonians 4:16 makes it quite clear that elsewhere when Paul spoke of human resurrection he meant the resurrection of the dead in Christ. This may also be true of 1 Corinthians 15:22. In fact, 1 Corinthians 15:23 lends strength to this interpretation when it speaks of the resurrection of those "who belong to him." Thus the parallelism of 1 Corinthians 15:22a and 22b is not perfect. Jeremias provides us with the following chart of the pertinent elements in 1 Corinthians 15:44-49 (Jeremias, 142).

| 15:45 | the first Adam | the last Adam |
| | a living being | a life-giving spirit |
| 15:47 | the first human being | the second human being |
| 15:47-48 | from the dust of the earth | from heaven |

In order to understand Paul's Adam-Christ typology, several things must be borne in mind. First is the idea of collective personality or at least representative headship. In some sense all persons were in Adam—

he was humankind and sinned for humanity. The human race died in him. This may suggest the idea of collective personality, that is, in some sense the whole race was present (seminally?) in Adam. Perhaps a better way to view this matter, however, would be to say that as the head and progenitor of the race Adam sinned for all, and thus all human beings felt the effects of this act. By analogy, it is like when a king in an absolute monarchy declares war on a nation. All the king's subjects are then at war with that nation, quite apart from their own individual choices or predilections. The idea in Paul is perhaps of a corporate head who acts for all (cf. Rom 5:12 *eph' hō* with Col 1:14 *en hō*).

Secondly, salvation only comes "in Christ." A person must be in Christ to receive the benefits of Christ's work. On the other hand, believers have died and risen in Christ (Rom 6:3-4). The idea of representative headship, when applied to the last Adam, means that Christ as head of a new race performed deeds that subsequently shaped that race. He died in the believer's place as his or her corporate head, just as Adam sinned in humanity's place and for humankind.

It will be seen from the chart above that Jesus is called the last Adam, which does not mean the last human being. Rather, it is an eschatological claim. Christ, as the first fruits* of the dead, is the beginning of a new creation (*see* Creation and New Creation). But in another sense he is the end and goal of the human race. He is bringing in the last age, the new creation, the end of God's plan.

Further, Jesus is the "second" human being, in the corporate sense. He is the start of a second human race, but with a significant difference. Adam, from one perspective, was strictly an earth creature—he came from the earth, he returned to the earth, and his body and life was natural and physical. Insofar as humanity descends from him, humankind is earthly, physical, contingent and has a natural life in the body. Christ, on the other hand, was from heaven and of heaven. He was not of earth. In what sense? He was also a life-giving Spirit.

Several points may be drawn from this: (1) Christ is not merely living, like Adam; he is life-giving, whereas Adam gave us death. (2) When Paul calls Christ a life-giving spirit he does not mean to imply Jesus had or has no body, but that he lived in a form of life characterized by the Spirit. (3) 1 Corinthians 15:45 ("The first man Adam became a living being") is a quote from Genesis 2:7, except that Paul has added the word "first" and the word "Adam." When Genesis speaks of Adam as a "living being" (Heb *nepeš ḥayāh*), it does not mean Adam gained a soul, but that God animated his body and he became a living body, a living being (*see* Psychology). It is unlikely that the Greek *psychē* in 1 Corinthians 15:45 means soul. Rather, here as in elsewhere in the NT (as with the Heb *nepeš*), it means "being"—Adam was a living being. (4) When Paul uses the term "spiritual body" (*sōma pneumatikon*) he does not mean a body consisting of nonmaterial substance, but a body empowered by the Spirit. Notice that Jesus did not become a life-giving Spirit until after he rose from the dead, and the life he gave was everlasting life, unlike the life Adam gave. Moreover, it was given to believers by the Spirit—in part now, in full later.

It could be that Paul derived the raw material for these ideas from Jewish speculation about Adam and the coming Messiah. The Jewish philosopher Philo understood the created humanity of Genesis 1 as an ideal being, a Platonic type, whereas he interpreted the Adam of Genesis 2 in the same way as Paul. In 1 Corinthians 15, however, it is not the first founder of the human race who is the ideal or true model, but the last one. Moreover, never in rabbinic literature is the redeemer described as a last Adam. It would seem that Paul, reflecting on the Christian gospel and the ministry, death and resurrection of Jesus—all in the light of his own revelation of the ascended Lord—modified any previous ideas he may have held.

In closing we turn to Romans 5:12-18. In Romans 5:12 we are told that not only sin, but death, entered the world through Adam. Death came through or because of sin. Paul apparently accepted Genesis 1—3 as a straightforward account of historical events, but here he is concerned with its theological significance. He wishes to add that whatever believers may have inherited from Adam, and whatever effect his sin may have had on humanity, there is a real sense in which human beings dig their own graves. God has not unjustly punished any with death. Nonetheless, it is also true in the primary sense that none of the human race would be dying if Adam had not sinned in the first place. So Paul can add in Romans 5:15, "many died by the trespasses of the one man." Through Adam's transgression death reigned (Rom 5:17), but Paul wishes to make perfectly clear that God's antidote is not merely an equal and opposite reaction. The gift is not like the trespass (Rom 5:17); salvation is not just paradise regained, as if the negativity of sin was counteracted by an equally positive force. If one trespass could effect so much and affect so many, how much more effective was the overflowing grace and gift of righteousness for believers (Rom 5:15). The death penalty followed just one sin, but God's grace came after many sins and, quite apart from what humans

deserved, it brought about their right standing with God.

Romans 5:17 implies quite clearly that the life believers have in Christ is not merely more powerful than the death Adam bequeathed to the human race, it is of a wholly different order. As 1 Corinthians 15 makes clear, it comes from the Spirit and heaven, and as such it transcends natural life and triumphs over natural death. Romans 5:10 goes on to point out that Christ's obedience even unto death (his righteous conduct and sinlessness) made possible the undoing of all that was brought about by the first Adam's disobedience (cf. Cranfield 1975, 290; Barrett 1957, 117).

### 4. The Impact and Influence of Paul's Christology.

*4.1. Paul's Christology in His Thought World.* We have earlier spoken of how christology, as an aspect of Paul's thought, was the greatest shaping force on the rest of Paul's thought world. This can be shown in a number of ways.

*4.1.1. Eschatology.* Paul's eschatological outlook was surely transformed once he became a follower of Jesus. There is no evidence that early Jews were expecting *two* comings of Messiah; yet that is precisely what Paul believed, and it dictated how he viewed the future and the life of believers. The future course of history had for Paul taken on an eschatological character. There was a sense in which the age to come had *already* arrived, the redemptive effect of God's reign had already broken into space and time in the coming of Christ, but redemption had *not yet* been completed. The form of this world was passing away (1 Cor 7:31), but it was not yet gone. Powers and principalities could no longer separate the believer from the love* of God in Christ (Rom 8:38) because Christ's death had disarmed the supernatural forces of evil (Col 2:15). Likewise, the inner life of the believer was caught up in the tension between the already and not yet. The believer was already a new creature in Christ (2 Cor 5:17), but had not yet experienced physical resurrection, the full redemption of the body (Rom 8:21-22).

There is likewise no evidence of an early Jewish expectation of an isolated resurrection, much less an isolated resurrection of Messiah prior to the resurrection of believers. Yet on the basis of the story of Jesus' earthly career, that is precisely what Paul proclaimed. This enabled Paul to explain the connection between Christ's resurrection and believers' resurrection (1 Cor 15).

*4.1.2. Soteriology.* Paul's christology changed the shape of his soteriology. Unless new finds from the Qumran* scrolls change matters, there is no conclusive evidence that early Jews were expecting a *crucified* Messiah. It was the story of the death and resurrection of Jesus that caused Paul to rethink how salvation would be accomplished. This message was a scandal to Jews and folly to Gentiles precisely because it ran in the face of expectations (1 Cor 1:23). Even in the case of the Suffering Servant of Yahweh referred to in Isaiah 53, there is no firm evidence that anyone in early Judaism prior to the ministry of Jesus had applied that text to the coming Messiah (though cf. *Tg. Isa.* 53). Furthermore, in light of Deuteronomy 21:23 ("anyone who is hung on a tree is under God's curse" NIV), even if the text *had* been thought to refer to a suffering Messiah, it is highly unlikely that it was understood to speak of a *crucified* Messiah.

Salvation also was an already/not yet matter. Already large numbers of Gentiles were being saved, but God had not yet completed his plan of salvation for the Jews (Rom 9—11). Already the believer had right standing and peace with God (Rom 5:1), but that same believer was not yet fully sanctified or glorified, as is clear from the ongoing tension between flesh and spirit in the believer's life (Gal 5:16-26).

*4.1.3. People of God.* Paul's thinking about the people of God was changed, especially regarding the basis of one's inclusion in that group. If God's people consisted of Jews and Gentiles united in Christ (Gal 3:28), and if that group could be called the "Israel of God" (Gal 6:16; *see* Israel), then neither heredity nor obedience to Torah could any longer be the basis for securing or maintaining a place in true Israel (cf. Rom 3:23—4:8). In Christ the Law, at least as a means of obtaining or keeping right standing with God, was at an end (Rom 10:4). Paul clearly stated that it was no longer necessary to follow the dietary laws since no food was unclean (Rom 14:14). Thereby for Paul the very basis of fellowship with and marks of identity among God's people were changed.

If the three great pillars of early Judaism—Torah, Temple and territory—are evaluated in light of Paul's theology, we discover how radically Paul had reconceptualized the people of God. We have already spoken of Paul's view of the Law, but what does he say about Temple and sacrifice? On the one hand, it is Jew and Gentile united in Christ that make up the temple* of God's Spirit (1 Cor 6:19; on the individual believer as temple cf. 1 Cor 3:16-17). On the other hand, Christ is the once-for-all sacrificial lamb who made all other literal sacrifices no longer necessary (cf. 1 Cor 5:7). Finally, it is not clear that Paul reaffirmed the territorial doctrine, though it is possible that he made room for such an idea once the full number of Gentiles are saved and then all physical

Israel is saved (cf. Rom 11:23-25). It is striking however that in his list of what God promised Israel according to the flesh, land is not mentioned (Rom 9:4-5, unless it is included under "the promises"; cf. Davies). Colossians 1:12 ("inheritance"), on the other hand, may reflect Paul's appropriation of the territorial idea, but there it is apparently transferred to a nonmaterial realm—heaven.

*4.1.4. God.* Earlier in this article it was pointed out how Paul's vision of God changed as a result of affirming Jesus as the divine and human Christ. Not only were the functions of God as Lord now assumed and exercised by Christ (cf. 1 Cor 15:24-27), but it was Christ who would return to judge the world and even believers (cf. 2 Cor 5:10; 1 Thess 5:4-10). In addition, Paul understood Christ and the Spirit as sharing many of the same functions, their earthly work and effect being seen as virtually interchangeable. Though Paul did not elaborate a trinitarian theology, the raw elements of such a theology were already evident in his letters, especially in his doxologies and benedictions* (cf. e.g., 2 Cor 13:14). Paul only invoked blessing in God's name, but now God had three names by which he could be called (see Wright, 120-36).

*4.2. The Wider Impact of Paul's Christology.* Paul's christology also seems to have had an impact on early Christianity outside his own writings. Hebrews especially seems to know and draw on Pauline modes of thought about Christ and other matters. It appears that the author of Hebrews had a special indebtedness to elements of Paul's thought as it is known to us in Galatians, and perhaps also 1 Corinthians and Romans (cf. e.g., 1 Cor 15:24-28, 45-49 with Heb 2:6-13; Witherington 1991).

It is worth pondering the possible impact of Paul's christology on the Fourth Evangelist. Not only does the Gospel of John begin with a christological hymn displaying motifs similar to Paul's, but the Gospel also presents a "Pauline" notion of believers being incorporated into Christ (though under a different image, that of the vine and branches of Jn 15). There we also find an exalted view of Christ's sacrificial death, associated with the slaughter of the Passover lamb (cf. e.g., Jn 1:29; Jn 19:28-31). The pneumatology of the Fourth Gospel is also related to the death and resurrection of Christ (cf. Jn 14:18-21) in a way that finds its only full NT parallel in Paul.

Possible Pauline influence, particularly christological, may be present elsewhere in the NT. For instance, in 1 Peter the presence of the "in Christ"* formula, and the use of the phrases "Lord Jesus Christ" or "revelation of Jesus Christ" (1 Peter 1:3, 13; 5:10, 14) may indicate Pauline influence (*see* Christ). The speech of Paul in Acts 20:18-32 is noteworthy for its Pauline themes, a fact that may be accounted for by the author epitomizing Paul's gospel as it was known from his letters or, if Luke was a firsthand witness to the speech, by recording what he spoke on the occasion (see Hemer). In any event, the author of 2 Peter (3:15-16) testifies to the impact of Paul's letters among the "Petrine" churches of the first century, though he confesses that Paul is difficult to comprehend.

### 5. The Distinctiveness and Commonality of Paul's Christology.

In discussing the distinctiveness of Paul's christology we need to be reminded that we are not exploring its uniqueness among NT christologies. To pursue its uniqueness would entail discussing what it is that completely sets Paul's christology apart from other NT christologies. Rather, we wish to discuss what *characterizes* Paul's christology. It can hardly be claimed that there is anything in Paul's christology that is unique, totally without analogy elsewhere in the NT. The preexistence, divinity and humanity of Christ can all be found outside of Paul. The emphasis on Christ crucified is found in the Gospels, as well as in Acts, Hebrews, 1 Peter and elsewhere in the NT. The stress on Jesus' Jewishness, or on his resurrection, also finds analogies. Finally, the idea of Christ as the embodiment of God's Wisdom can be found in Matthew and possibly in the Gospel source Q, though with differing emphases (cf. Witherington 1993).

We have pointed to the absence of any reference to Jesus as Son of man in Paul's christology. In this sense Paul is distinct from the Gospels. But it can also be argued that the most distinct aspect of Paul's christology is his Last Adam typology. This christological theme was not simply an attempt to transpose the Son of man christology into a new key for Gentiles. For one thing, the sources are different; Paul's Last Adam christology draws on Genesis, while the Son of man material in the Gospels draws on Daniel 7 (and less possibly on Ezekiel and the Parables of *1 Enoch*). Moreover, the Son of man christology has nothing to do with the founder of a new race of human beings; it is more specifically focused on a representative of and for Israel who comes before the presence of the Almighty and is given dominion. In short, the Last Adam christology is more universal than the Son of man in scope. By comparing and contrasting Christ with the progenitor of the whole human race Paul forged a concept in which both Jews and Gentiles had a stake simply because they were human.

Paul's use of the "in Christ" formula (*see* Christ; In Christ) to speak of the spiritual union between Christ and Christians is also remarkable. The Pauline idea transcends the use found in 1 Peter or the parallel ideas found in the Fourth Gospel, both in depth and breadth of implication. This formula more than any other explains how Paul viewed the condition of believers—they were "in Christ." This goes well beyond the claim that Christians by God's grace have been conformed to the pattern of Christ's death and resurrection (Rom 6:3-11). Their burial with Christ was a one-time event that occurred in the past at their conversion, whereas their union and communion with Christ is an ongoing reality. Indeed, it was such a profound reality in the apostle's mind that it was incompatible with other forms of union that were spiritually antithetical to it (cf. 1 Cor 6:15-17). The person united to Christ through Christ's body (made up of believers) was one spirit with Christ. This union "in Christ" was also the very basis of Paul's imperatives to imitate the sacred story or character of Christ (cf. e.g., Phil 2:5; 1 Cor 11:1). "In Christ" is a concept developed by Paul in a way and degree without parallel in the NT canon.

Paul's christology has continued to have an impact on the church through the ages, a fact that plays a part in our evaluating it. For Protestants who draw their charter of foundation directly or indirectly from Martin Luther, John Calvin or John Wesley, Paul's christology continues to be central, sometimes even eclipsing the variety of other canonical NT christologies. But that fact is also testimony to the compelling force of Paul's christological vision. It is a christology which cannot be neatly summarized under the headings of the titles Paul employs. The whole of Paul's christology is much greater than the sum of its parts. It is grounded in the sacred story of the Christ, which in turn is grounded in the story of Israel and, by way of the Last Adam christology, rooted in the story of the whole human race.

It is this sacred story of a Jesus who was born of woman, who took on human nature, who died on the cross and who arose from the dead—for the salvation of all human beings—which Paul held in common with the other NT theologians. This shared story, more than any influence of one NT writer upon another, best explains the similarities between the christologies of Paul and the Fourth Gospel or Hebrews or Peter. They all shared this story and, from the evidence of christological hymns and hymn fragments in these works, it appears that they all sang this story in one form or another as they worshipped Christ. Christ crucified and risen, both human and divine, was the core of the gospel these early missionaries proclaimed and taught throughout the first-century Mediterranean world.

*See also* ADAM AND CHRIST; BODY OF CHRIST; CHRIST; ESCHATOLOGY; FIRSTBORN; GOD; HOLY SPIRIT; IMAGE; IN CHRIST; JESUS AND PAUL; LORD; PRE-EXISTENCE; SAVIOR; SON OF GOD; WISDOM.

BIBLIOGRAPHY. C. K. Barrett, *A Commentary on the Epistle to the Romans* (New York: Harper & Row, 1957); idem, *A Commentary on the First Epistle to the Corinthians* (New York: Harper & Row, 1968); idem, *A Commentary on the Second Epistle to the Corinthians* (New York: Harper & Row, 1973); J. C. Beker, *Paul the Apostle: The Triumph of God in Life and Thought* (Philadelphia: Fortress, 1980); W. Bousset, *Kyrios Christos* (Nashville: Abingdon, 1970); R. E. Brown, *The Virginal Conception and Bodily Resurrection of Jesus* (New York: Paulist, 1973); F. F. Bruce, *The Epistle to the Galatians* (NIGNT; Grand Rapids: Eerdmans, 1982); E. DeW. Burton, *A Critical and Exegetical Commentary on the Epistle to the Galatians* (ICC; Edinburgh: T. & T. Clark, 1920); M. Casey, "Chronology and the Development of Pauline Christology," in *Paul and Paulinism: Essays in Honour of C. K. Barrett*, ed. M. D. Hooker and S. G. Wilson (London: SPCK, 1982) 124-34; L. Cerfaux, *Christ in the Theology of St. Paul* (New York: Herder & Herder, 1959); C. E. B. Cranfield, *A Critical and Exegetical Commentary on the Epistle to the Romans* (ICC; 2 vols.; Edinburgh: T. & T. Clark, 1975, 1979); O. Cullmann, *Christ and Time* (rev. ed.; Philadelphia: Westminster, 1975); idem, *The Christology of the New Testament* (Philadelphia: Westminster, 1959); W. D. Davies, *The Gospel and the Land: Early Christianity and Jewish Territorial Doctrine* (Berkeley: University of California, 1974); J. D. G. Dunn, *Christology in the Making* (Philadelphia: Westminster, 1980); idem, *Romans* (WBC 38; Dallas: Word, 1988); idem, *Unity and Diversity in the New Testament* (Philadelphia: Westminster, 1977); P. Fredriksen, *From Jesus to Christ: The Origins of the New Testament Images of Jesus* (New Haven: Yale University, 1988); G. F. Hawthorne, *Philippians* (WBC 43; Waco: Word, 1983); R. B. Hays, *Echoes of Scripture in the Letters of Paul* (New Haven: Yale University, 1989); C. J. Hemer, *The Book of Acts in the Setting of Hellenistic History* (Winona Lake, IN: Eisebrauns, 1989); M. Hengel, *Judaism and Hellenism* (2 vols.; Philadelphia: Fortress, 1974); idem, *The Pre-Christian Paul* (Philadelphia: Trinity Press International, 1991); idem, *The Son of God* (Philadelphia: Fortress, 1976); R. W. Hoover, "The Harpagmos Enigma: A Philological Solution," *HTR* 64 (1971) 95-119; L. W. Hurtado, *One God, One Lord* (Philadelphia: Fortress, 1988); J. Jeremias, "ἀδάμ," *TDNT* I.141-43; M. de Jonge, *Christology in Context: The Earliest Christian Responses to Jesus* (Philadelphia: Westminster, 1988); S. Kim. *The Origin of Paul's Gospel* (Grand Rapids: Eerdmans, 1982); J. B. Lightfoot, *St. Paul's Epistle to the Philippians* (London: Macmillan, 1894); R. N. Longenecker, *The Christology of Early Jewish Christianity* (London: SCM, 1970); J. G. Machen, *The Virgin Birth of Christ* (New York: Harper & Row, 1930); I. H. Marshall, "Son of God," *NIDNTT* 3.644-45; R. P. Martin, *Carmen Christi: Philippians 2:5-11 in Recent Interpretation and in the Setting of Early Christian Worship* (rev. ed.; Grand Rapids: Eerdmans, 1983); idem, *Philippians* (NCB; Grand Rapids: Eerdmans, 1976); B. M. Metzger, "Punctuation of Rom. 9.5," in *Christ and the Spirit in the New Testament*, ed. B. Lindars and S. S. Smalley (Cambridge: University Press, 1973) 95-112; C. F. D. Moule, *The Origin of Christology* (Cambridge: University Press, 1977); idem, "Further Reflexions on Philippians 2.5-11," in *Apostolic History and the Gospel*, ed. W. W. Gasque and R. P. Martin (Grand Rapids: Eerdmans, 1970) 264-76; idem, "The Manhood of Jesus in the NT," in *Christ, Faith, and History*, ed. S. W. Sykes and J. P. Clayton (Cambridge: University Press, 1972) 95-110; J. Neusner et al., ed. *Judaisms and their Messiahs* (Cambridge: University Press, 1987); J. A. T. Robinson, *The Body: A Study in Pauline Theology* (Philadelphia: Westminster, 1977); S. S. Smalley, "The Christ-Christian Relationship in Paul and John," in *Pauline Studies*, ed. D. A. Hagner and M. J. Harris (Grand Rapids: Eerdmans, 1980) 95-105; N. Turner, *Grammatical Insights into the New Testament* (Edinburgh: T. & T. Clark, 1966); B. Witherington III, *The Christology of Jesus* (Minneapolis: Fortress, 1990); idem, "The Influence of Galatians on Hebrews," *NTS* 37 (1991) 146-52; idem, *Jesus, Paul and the End of the World* (Downers Grove, IL: InterVarsity, 1992); idem, *Jesus the Sage and the Pilgrimage of Wisdom* (Minneapolis: Fortress, 1993); N. T. Wright, *The Climax of the Covenant* (Minneapolis: Fortress, 1992).

B. Witherington III

## CHRONOLOGY OF PAUL

Pauline chronology is concerned to establish the sequence and (where possible) the dates of events in Paul's life. It is an area which has attracted much complex theorizing: this article will attempt simply to set out the parameters of the problem as clearly as possible.

1. Sources and Types of Evidence
2. The Outer Framework
3. Chronological Data in the Letters
4. Chronological Data in Acts
5. Integration of the Letters and Acts

### 1. Sources and Types of Evidence.

There are two main sources for the chronology of Paul, Acts and the letters, and two kinds of chronological indicators, internal and external.

***1.1. Internal and External Chronology.*** Acts provides a narrative account of Paul's ministry which recounts events in a particular sequence and gives some indication (though not as much as we would like) of the lapse of time between one event and another (internal chronology). Acts also from time to time links events in Paul's life with people or events known to historians from sources outside the NT, like the proconsul Gallio at Acts 18:12. These provide the possibility of anchoring the narrative at certain points in relation to the known history of the Roman world (external chronology). Less obviously, the letters also contain some reference to external history (external chronology) and some indications of sequence (internal chronology). In the latter case it is important to clarify the types of data most useful for purposes of chronology. It is tempting to try to sequence the letters on the basis of theological development, but in practice it has proved difficult to avoid subjectivity in this area (Jewett, 75-78). For this reason it seems safer to build up a chronological sequence from concrete indicators such as travel details, and then to use this framework to date the development of Paul's theology, rather than the other way round.

***1.2. Primary and Secondary Evidence.*** The letters were written by Paul himself and thus rank as "primary evidence" in historical terms; Acts by the same token ranks as "secondary evidence" in that it was written about Paul by somebody else. (This is a distinction of principle common to historical practice, not an expression of theological prejudice.) For this reason a number of scholars have argued in recent years that a methodologically sound chronology must proceed by working outward from the evidence of the letters (see especially Knox, Jewett, Lüdemann). In what follows we shall try to distinguish the chronological data that can be deduced from the letters (internal and external) and from the data provided by Acts before attempting a synthesis.

## 2. The Outer Framework.

We have no independent evidence for the date of Paul's birth, and only tradition for the date of his death. For the NT his life begins with his conversion* and ends with his imprisonment in Rome* (*see* Paul in Acts and Letters).

***2.1. The Beginning.*** Neither Acts nor the letters tell us much about Paul's life before his conversion (*see* Paul the Jew), though both agree that his life-changing encounter with the risen Christ was separate from, and later than, the resurrection appearances to the other apostles* (1 Cor 15:3-9; Acts 9:3-5). Both also concur that prior to this Paul was a persecutor of the church (1 Cor 15:9; Gal 1:13; Acts 7:58; 8:1; 9:1-2). Acts states that at the time of the death of Stephen, Paul (Saul) was "a young man" (Acts 7:58), and Galatians 1:14 also implies that the "persecutor" was at least a young adult. This gives us at least a *terminus ante quem non*: Paul's public career cannot begin before Jesus' death and the events of Pentecost the same year. In what follows we shall assume a date for the crucifixion of A.D. 33 (see Hoehner). This date is also accepted by Jewett as a baseline for Pauline chronology; Lüdemann and Hemer, for different reasons, prefer an earlier date (27 or 30). How long a time elapsed between the events of Acts 2 and Paul's conversion in Acts 9 is not clear, since neither of our major sources gives us any precise chronological information, but we shall work here with the assumption that Paul began his Christian life as a young adult within a year or two of Pentecost A.D. 33.

***2.2. The End.*** The "captivity" letters, traditionally linked with the end of Paul's life, provide little chronological information (see 3.2.5 below). Acts does not narrate Paul's death, but does give a detailed account of Paul's voyage to Rome which can be dated with some precision. The transfer of office from Felix to Festus should probably be dated to A.D. 59 or 60 (see 4.2.7 below). Seasonal data suggest that the year 59 provides the best fit with the journey details of Acts 27, and this suggests that Paul could have arrived in Rome in February 60 (Jewett, 50-52). The two years' captivity of Acts 28:30 would take us to 62, but Luke simply does not tell us what happened after that. A longstanding church tradition associates the martyrdom of Peter and Paul with the persecution of Nero at the time of the great fire of A.D. 64. Clement of Rome (*1 Clem.* 5), writing at about A.D. 95, says that Paul "bore witness before rulers" after preaching "in the East and in the West," which seems to imply that Paul was able to implement his plan to travel to Spain (Rom 15:28) before his death. The trip to Spain may however be simply an inference from the text of Romans. All we can say is that the evidence we have is consistent with a death in Rome in the early sixties.

***2.3. Conclusion.*** Paul's missionary journeys (*see* Itineraries) and letters must thus be fitted into a time span of thirty-odd years or less, between the outer limits of A.D. 33 and 64.

## 3. Chronological Data in the Letters.

The letters provide us with two clear tripartite sequences plus a mass of miscellaneous unsequenced detail.

***3.1. Direct Chronological Indicators.***

*3.1.1. External Chronology.* In 2 Corinthians 11:32 Paul mentions that the "ethnarch of King Aretas" was guarding Damascus at the time of his dramatic escape in a basket (2 Cor 11:33). The Nabatean king Aretas IV died between 38 and 40 (probably 39), and Nabatean control of Damascus is unlikely before 37, when the accession of Caligula signaled a new Roman policy toward client kings. This escape must therefore have taken place between 37 and 39/40 (Jewett, 30-33; but Hemer, 264, warns against placing too much reliance on this datum).

*3.1.2. The Galatians Sequence.* Galatians 1:11—2:14 seems (on the most obvious reading) to yield the following sequence of events:

| | |
|---|---|
| Gal 1:16 | Conversion |
| Gal 1:16-17 | Three-year interval (Arabia, Damascus) |
| Gal 1:18-20 | First Jerusalem visit of 15 days |
| Gal 1:21—2:1 | Interval of 14 yrs (Syria, Cilicia: preaching to Gentiles) |
| Gal 2:1-10 | Second Jerusalem visit for private conference on Gentile mission |
| Gal 2:11-14 | Incident at Antioch (Lüdemann, 75-77, places the Antioch incident just before the conference, but this makes little difference to the chronology overall.) |

The writing of Galatians* must have occurred after all the events described, most likely (given the passionate nature of Paul's concern here) quite soon after: and this implies that the founding of the "Galatian" churches (wherever they are) took place before the Jerusalem* conference. Certainly the account of the conference implies strongly that Paul's Gentile* mission* was well established by then: in other words, substantial missionary activity had taken place during the "fourteen years" (Lüdemann, 70-71). Note that Paul does not say that he stayed in Syria and Cilicia for fourteen years, only that he went there (Gal 1:21) and that "fourteen years later" (Gal 2:1) he was back in Jerusalem. What is not clear is how precisely we should take these figures: are the three and fourteen years reckoned inclusively or exclusively? And should the two time spans be read consecutively (3 yrs + 14 yrs = 17 yrs) or concurrently (3 yrs + 11 yrs = 14 yrs in total)? At first sight the consecutive reading seems more natural, but the concurrent cannot be ruled out (Jewett, 52-54; Hemer, 262 n.37).

*3.1.3. The Hardship Catalogs.* In 2 Corinthians 6:4-10; 11:21-33; and 12:1-10 Paul lists a prodigious series of toils and travels, many of which are not recorded in Acts, including three shipwrecks and several beatings and imprisonments (*see* Afflictions, Trials, Hardships). No sequence can be reconstructed from these

details, but they presuppose several years' travels. Moreover, whatever the identity of the "man in Christ," 2 Corinthians 12:2 indicates that Paul had been a Christian for at least fourteen years. This suggests that at least 2 Corinthians 10—13 must have been written at an advanced stage of Paul's ministry; but there are no good grounds for identifying this "fourteen years" with the "fourteen years" of Galatians 2:1, as Knox proposed (Jewett, 54-55).

*3.1.4. Synthesis.* We can deduce from Galatians 1:17 that Paul was in Damascus twice, once at or near his conversion, and once on his return from Arabia. It is reasonable to conjecture that the basket episode of 2 Corinthians 11:32 took place on one of these visits, since there is no indication that Paul was operating in this area in his later years. Given that the ethnarch of Aretas must probably be dated between 37 and 39/40 (see 3.1.1 above), it would make sense to date this incident to the time of Paul's departure for Jerusalem, three years after the conversion in 34 or 35. If the fourteen-year span is reckoned consecutively, this would date the conference to 51/52; a concurrent reckoning would bring the conference back to 48/49. Galatians must be written after the conference; 2 Corinthians presupposes several years of ministry.

| Summary: consecutive reckoning: | |
|---|---|
| 34/35 (A) Conversion, Arabia, Damascus | 3 yrs |
| 37/38 (B) Jerusalem visit 1; to Syria and Cilicia Fourteen-year span including mission in Galatia | 14 yrs |
| 51/52 (C) Jerusalem visit 2, conference, Antioch incident | |
| TOTAL: | 17 yrs |

| Summary: concurrent reckoning: | |
|---|---|
| 34/35 (A) Conversion, Arabia, Damascus | 3 yrs |
| 37/38 (B) Jerusalem visit 1; to Syria and Cilicia Eleven-year span including mission in Galatia | 11 yrs |
| 48/49 (C) Jerusalem visit 2, conference, Antioch incident | |
| TOTAL: | 14 yrs |

*3.2. The Travel Sequence.* The travels and travel plans of the apostle and his associates contain valuable chronological clues, some of which can be sequenced (see Itineraries, Travel Plans).

*3.2.1. First Macedonian Journey.* 1 Thessalonians seems to have been written from Achaia (1 Thess 1:9) or Athens,* where Paul waited alone for Timothy to return with reassurance from Thessalonica* (1 Thess 3:1-8). Paul wishes to return to Thessalonica himself, but has been unable to do so (1 Thess 2:17). The fact that there are no greetings from other "brothers and sisters" at the end of 1 Thessalonians suggests (though it does not prove) that this letter was written at an early stage in the first Achaian mission, not long after Paul had left Thessalonica. Philippians 4:15-16 makes it clear that Philippi* was evangelized before Thessalonica. The support Paul received in Corinth (2 Cor 11:8-9) may also belong to this first visit, although it could belong to a later visit to Corinth. This yields a sequence of visits as follows: Philippi—Thessalonica—Athens, with believers recorded in Philippi, Thessalonica and Achaia (which could include both Athens and Corinth).

*3.2.2. Final Macedonian Journey.* The visit to Macedonia which Paul projects in 1 Corinthians 16:5-9, and from which he apparently writes 2 Corinthians 7:5-16, clearly reflects a later journey, when both the Corinthian and the Macedonian churches are well established and Paul is busy organizing the collection.* In 1 Corinthians 16:2-4 Paul is uncertain whether or not he will accompany the collection, but by the time he writes Romans 15:25 (apparently from Corinth) he has made firm plans to go to Jerusalem. The visit to Illyricum (Rom 15:19) may have been made during this last Macedonian tour. At this stage Paul feels that his mission in Europe is fully accomplished (Rom 15:19, 23); despite some apprehensiveness about Jerusalem (Rom 15:30-32), he intends to continue his mission in the west, passing on to Spain via Rome, which he has never visited (Rom 15:22-24, 28-29).

*3.2.3. Ephesian Ministry.* Between these two tours lies an extended period in Ephesus,* from where Paul writes 1 Corinthians (16:8-9) and where he suffered a life-threatening "affliction" (2 Cor 1:8-11, cf. 1 Cor 15:32). The instructions about the collection in Galatia (1 Cor 16:1) seem to have been made at about this time, perhaps en route for Ephesus, or perhaps by messenger from there: the extant letter to the Galatians contains no such instructions. When he left Ephesus, Paul travelled by way of Troas (2 Cor 2: 12-13), where he preached and (by implication) left a small body of believers.

*3.2.4. Galatians.* The letter to the Galatians is difficult to place (*see* Galatians). It is the only letter to mention the conference, and could reasonably be placed soon after it. The collection appears (as Lüdemann plausibly argues, 77-80) as the only condition imposed on Paul by the "pillars" (Gal 2:10), but Paul does not seem yet to be involved with detailed planning for its assembly and delivery. Despite this, Lüdemann dates Galatians at the same time as 2 Corinthians, after 1 Corinthians and three years after the conference (Lüdemann, 83-87). Jewett's date shortly after the conference (Jewett, 103) seems on the face

of it more likely. Galatians 4:12-15 contains the incidental information that Paul's initial evangelization of the area was "because of a bodily ailment," which suggests that he was on a journey to (or returning from) another destination at the time. This implies that there was at least one missionary journey (originally intended to go beyond Galatia) before the conference.

*3.2.5. Paul's Imprisonments.* The "captivity" letters, traditionally linked with Paul's final years in prison in Rome, contain few chronological indicators. Ephesians* and Colossians* are too general to be of much help. 2 Timothy is clearly located in Rome (2 Tim 1:17) and depicts the apostle facing imminent martyrdom (see Pastoral Letters). Philippians and Philemon,* however, may be associated with earlier imprisonments (cf. 2 Cor 11:23): the number and frequency of Paul's visitors suggests Ephesus as a more probable location. However, Hemer (272-76) makes the point that the imperial postal service (cf. Phil 4:22) could have made communications with Rome fast and efficient. Whatever the verdict on this, it is clear that these letters do not provide secure foundations for chronology.

*3.2.6. Synthesis.* The evidence of Paul's travels makes it clear that Paul undertook at least two major journeys to Macedonia and Achaia. On the initial, founding visit he came round from the north, visiting Philippi first, then Thessalonica, before heading south for Athens and Corinth. On his last journey (which does not rule out the possibility of intervening visits) he came from Ephesus, where he had been working for some time, via Troas and Macedonia to Corinth. On this trip he was supervising the final assembly of the collection, incorporating contributions from the churches in Macedonia and Achaia, which he eventually decided to accompany to Jerusalem. Our last glimpse of Paul is in Romans 15, where he announces his intention to turn west after Jerusalem, visiting Rome (which he has never seen) en route for Spain; but no letter tells us what happened in Jerusalem. The prison letters date traditionally from after this period, though some may come from earlier episodes. The travel sequence thus provided runs as follows:

(D) First journey to Macedonia and Achaia
    [1 Thess]

(E) Ephesus ministry, time unspecified, perhaps including 2 imprisonments: [?Phil, ?Philem]—Galatians—organization of collection by letter [1 Cor; 2 Cor 1—9; 2 Cor 10—13; message or visit to Galatia]

(F) Final journey, Ephesus to Corinth via Troas and Macedonia, en route for Jerusalem with collection

There are few indicators of time in this material, and no external chronological data.

**3.3. Conclusions.** Using the letters alone, we are able to construct a surprisingly full picture of Paul's ministry, but the evidence falls short of providing a full chronology. Attempts to achieve greater precision on this basis tend to rely on theological or stylistic development, on which it is difficult to reach general agreement, or to lay greater weight on details than they can properly bear.

The above analysis seeks to set out the minimum chronological information which is clearly stated or implied in the letters. What is not yet clear is how the two sequences relate to each other: are they successive or interlocking? If Galatians 2:10 refers to the institution of the collection, then the last Macedonian journey at least must date from after the conference of Galatians 2:1-10: but how long after it is not clear. We know that the churches in Galatia were founded before the conference, and (purely on the internal evidence of the letters) it seems likely that those in Macedonia and Achaia were too, both because the early letter 1 Thessalonians contains no mention of either conference or collection, and because Paul is unlikely to have delayed many years over fulfilling his obligation (Rom 15:31). This would give an interlocking sequence A B D C E F:

34/35 (A) Conversion, Arabia, Damascus (3 yrs)
37/38 (B) Jerusalem visit 1; to Syria and Cilicia
        Fourteen-year span including mission in
        Galatia and
        (D) First Macedonian journey
51/52 (C) Jerusalem visit 2, conference, Antioch incident
        (E) Ephesus ministry and organization of collection
        (F) Final Macedonian journey, en route for Jerusalem with collection

However, this is a matter of probability only: a successive order is also possible, yielding the sequence A B C D E F:

34/35 (A) Conversion, Arabia, Damascus (3 yrs)
37/38 (B) Jerusalem visit 1; to Syria and Cilicia
        Fourteen-year span including mission in
        Galatia
51/52 (C) Jerusalem visit 2, conference, Antioch incident
        (D) First Macedonian journey
        (E) Ephesus ministry and organization of collection
        (F) Final Macedonian journey, en route for Jerusalem with collection

A reading of the fourteen years (3 + 11 = 14) gives a conference date of 48/49 in both cases, but does not affect the sequence.

## 4. Chronological Data in Acts.

### 4.1. Internal Chronology.

*4.1.1. The Sequence of Events.* Acts, being narrative in form, has to arrange events in a clear sequence, which may be tabulated as follows:

(1) Conversion at Damascus (Acts 9:1-19), escape in a basket (Acts 9:25)

(2) Jerusalem visit 1 (Acts 9:26), to Tarsus via Caesarea (Acts 9:30)

(3) Jerusalem visit 2: from Antioch with famine relief (Acts 11:19-30, 12:25)

(4) First missionary journey: Antioch-Cyprus-Pamphylia-Pisidia-Iconium-Lystra-Derbe-Antioch (Acts 13:1—14:28)

(5) Jerusalem visit 3, conference (Acts 15:1-35)

(6) Second missionary journey: Syria & Cilicia, Phrygia-Galatia-Philippi-Thessalonica-Berea-Athens-Corinth (Acts 15:36—18:17)

(7) Miscellaneous travels: Corinth-Ephesus-Caesarea-"up" to greet the church (= Jerusalem visit 4?)-Antioch-Galatia-Phrygia-Ephesus (18:18—19:20)

(8) Return to Jerusalem:Ephesus-Macedonia-Greece-Macedonia-Troas-Miletus-Caesarea-Jerusalem (Acts 19:21—21:16)

(9) Final Jerusalem visit: arrest in Temple, trial before Sanhedrin under high priest Ananias, removal to Caesarea, two-year imprisonment under Felix (Acts 21:17—24:27)

(10) Journey to Rome: trial before Festus and Agrippa, voyage to Rome, two-year imprisonment (25:1—28:31)

*4.1.2. The Passing of Time.* Luke is notoriously vague about time: precise travel details alternate with vague indications like "after many days." His episodic style inclines him to focus often on the events of a single day, or to give a detailed timetable for a voyage of a few weeks, while explicit indications of the chronological relationship between one episode and another are rare. The most precise indications of longer time lapses are:

A year in Antioch (Acts 11:26)
"A long time" in Iconium (Acts 14:3)
"No little time" in Antioch (Acts 14:28)
Eighteen months in Corinth (Acts 18:11)
Three months + two years + "a while" in Ephesus (Acts 19:8, 10, 22)
Three months in Greece (Acts 20:3)
Two years in Caesarea (Acts 24:27)
Two years in Rome (Acts 28:30)

Even on a generous estimate, this accounts for no more than eleven out of the thirty possible years of

Paul's ministry. Implicit indicators such as travelling speed and seasonal conditions can also be used, but caution is needed here: thus, for example, Jewett estimates that the second missionary journey (6) should be allowed no less than "three or four years" (Jewett, 57-62), but Hemer (267-69) points out that it is dangerous to assume that we know what was "normal" for Paul: Hemer's own estimate for the same journey is eighteen months (*see* Travel).

*4.2. External Chronology.* Acts mentions a number of names and events which provide possible anchor points in Roman history.

*4.2.1. The Famine.* Acts 11:27-30 speaks of a widespread famine "in the days of Claudius" (A.D. 41-54). External evidence suggests a number of possible dates for this famine: Bruce (276-77) concludes "not later than A.D. 48, and possibly 2 or 3 years earlier." Note that Acts actually describes two events here: the prophecy of Agabus, and a future famine which he correctly predicts. This Jerusalem visit is thus difficult to date precisely and need not have happened before the death of Herod Agrippa which is recounted in Acts 12: "Luke completes one phase of his narrative before going back in time to deal with another phase" (Bruce, 277).

*4.2.2. Herod Agrippa.* The death of Herod Agrippa I (Acts 12:20-23) took place in early March, A.D. 44 (Josephus *Ant.* 19.8.2 §§ 343-52). This event is related rather loosely as a coda to the Peter story of Acts 12:1-19: compare Luke 3:18-20, where the story of John's imprisonment (related by Mark in a quite different context) is attached by Luke to the baptism story. Similarly here: Acts 12:25 appears to have Saul and Barnabas return shortly after Herod's death, but this arrangement may be topical rather than chronological.

*4.2.3. Sergius Paulus.* A Sergius Paulus (Acts 13:7) is known from inscriptional evidence to have had a connection with Cyprus (Ogg, 60-65; Bruce, 297), but the data are not sufficient to allow a precise dating.

*4.2.4. Claudius and the Jews.* There is dispute over the date of the expulsion of Jews from Rome mentioned in Acts 18:2. Dio Cassius (60.6.6) dates Jewish disturbances to A.D. 41, but states that a ban on assembly was imposed because expulsion was impossible. Suetonius (*Claudius 25.4*) records an expulsion of Jewish agitators (possibly confused with Christians), but gives no date: a later church historian dates it in Claudius's ninth year, A.D. 49. Lüdemann (157-75) argues for the earlier date and has Paul meet Aquila and Priscilla in Corinth in 41; the Gallio incident (which he accepts as genuine tradition) must therefore be dated during a later visit in 51. Most scholars prefer

the later date, having Aquila and Priscilla arrive shortly before Paul in 49/50 (Smallwood, 210-16; Jewett, 36-38; Bruce, 390-91).

*4.2.5. Gallio.* The proconsulship of Gallio (Acts 18:12) is widely regarded as a "pivotal date" (Jewett) for Pauline chronology. Inscriptional evidence means that Gallio's period of office can be dated with some precision to A.D. 51/52: Roman governors took office in early summer. (See Bruce, 394-95; Jewett, 38-40. Ogg, 104-11, gives the relevant inscriptions in full.)

*4.2.6. Ananias the High Priest.* Ananias (Acts 23:2; 24:1) was appointed in 47. He was sent to Rome in chains in 52 (Josephus *Ant.* 20.6.2 §131), but since Claudius decided the dispute in the Jews' favor (Josephus *Ant.* 20.6.3 §136), we can assume that Ananias was restored to his office. No other high priest is mentioned until the appointment of Ishmael (Josephus *Ant.* 20.8.8 §179), which Josephus links with the transfer of power from Felix to Festus, i.e., around 59/60 [see 4.2.7 below]).

*4.2.7. Felix and Festus.* Paul's final hearing in Caesarea is linked fairly precisely by Luke with Festus's arrival as procurator (Acts 25:1, 6, 13, 23). Unfortunately, although both Felix and Festus are known from Josephus and other ancient sources, the date of transfer of office cannot be determined precisely. Jewett (40-44) gives a clear account of the data, which can be summarized as follows: Josephus (*Ant.* 20.8.9 §182) states that when Felix was accused of misdemeanors against the Jews at the end of his term in office, he was protected by Nero because of his brother Pallas. Since Pallas fell from favor in 55, many have assumed that the transfer took place in 54/55. But there is no reason to suppose that Pallas' influence ceased immediately after his demotion (Jewett, 42-43), and the activities which Josephus assigns to Felix's procuratorship (including the Egyptian agitator of Acts 21:38 and Josephus *J.W.* 2.13.5 §261) seem to require that he was in office several years under Nero (Josephus *J.W.* 2.13.1-7 §§250-70), that is, after October 54. For this reason many historians prefer a later date: Smallwood (269 n.40) suggests 58/59, Jewett 59 or 60.

*4.3. Conclusions.* Taken by itself, the evidence of Acts allows us to reconstruct the following tentative chronology:

34/35 (1) Conversion at Damascus (9:1-19), escape in a basket (9:25)

(2) Jerusalem visit 1 "after many days," to Tarsus

41-48 (3) Jerusalem visit 2 (famine relief)

(4) First missionary journey

(5) Jerusalem visit 3, conference

47-51 (6) Second missionary journey: arrival of Aquila and Priscilla in Corinth could be either 41/42 or 49/50. Paul's stay in Corinth at least eighteen months. Hearing before Gallio must be 51-52

(7) Miscellaneous travels: two-and-a-half to three years in Ephesus

56-57 (8) Return to Jerusalem: three months in Greece

57-59 (9) Final Jerusalem visit, two-year imprisonment in Caesarea

59-62 (10) Trial before Festus, voyage to Rome, two-year imprisonment

## 5. Integration of the Letters and Acts.

*5.1. Sequential Integration.* Purely in terms of chronological sequence, there is little difficulty in integrating the two sequences derived from the letters with the fuller and more circumstantial narrative provided by Acts. The two sets of data are remarkably coherent: Acts has the same two tripartite sequences, integrated successively A B C D E F. Thus Luke begins with the conversion in Damascus (A = 1), a basket escape from Damascus, and a visit to Jerusalem (B = 2), followed by a withdrawal to Tarsus (Cilicia) and activities in Antioch* (Syria). Acts 9:23 gives a vague "after many days" in place of Paul's "three years," but unless we are to doubt Paul's solemn asseveration (Gal 1:20), the two visits must be regarded as equivalent (Bruce, 241). The planning of this chapter suggests that Luke has grouped all his information about Damascus together in topical fashion.

Some time later (no interval specified, but the arrangement of topics suggests that some years have elapsed) we have a conference on the Gentile mission (C = 5), preceded by missionary activities in the area of Syria, Cilicia and "South Galatia." Whether or not this is the area addressed in Galatians, there is space in this period for the founding of the churches addressed there. The conference is followed by a missionary journey which takes in Philippi, Thessalonica, Athens and Corinth (D = 6), then by an obscure period of travel circling around Ephesus (E = 7), and finally by a carefully planned journey (Acts 19:21) from Ephesus via Macedonia and Achaia to Jerusalem, with a distant intention of visiting Rome (F = 8). The final outcome, with the arrest in Jerusalem and journey to Rome as a captive, fills in the hiatus left at the end of the travel sequence in the letters.

There are however two major problems with this synthesis, one connected with the date of Gallio, and the other with the second Jerusalem visit recorded in Acts 11.

*5.2. The Date of Gallio.* Acts 18:12 dates Paul's dispute in Corinth securely to the year A.D. 51/52. This event comes after an eighteen-month stay in Corinth (Acts 18:11), so Paul must have been in Corinth at least since January 50. The visit comes at the end of the long missionary journey from Antioch through to Macedonia, which at Paul's normal rate of progression should take three to four years; even on a minimum calculation this would take eighteen months, which means that Paul must have left Jerusalem in 48. But the date of the conference, according to our calculations based on the letters, is fourteen years after the Aretas incident. This cannot be earlier than 37, which means that the earliest possible conference date is 51.

Pushing the crucifixion (and thus Paul's conversion) back to an earlier date will not help: it is the Aretas incident which causes the problem here. Lüdemann, who dates the conference to 47, simply discounts the Aretas date (similarly Hemer). Theoretically we could argue that 2 Corinthians 11:32-33 refers to a different occasion altogether, an unrecorded third Damascus visit: but this seems to be straining credibility. An alternative is to attack the fixity of the fourteen-year time span of Galatians 2:1. Inclusive reckoning can shorten this to thirteen years, and concurrent reading of the three-year and fourteen-year spans means that the conference can be placed as early as 47.

A number of scholars believe, however, that the simplest solution is to reverse the order of the second missionary journey and the conference, giving the sequence A B D C E F. On this view Paul left Corinth soon after Gallio's arrival (July/August 51) to arrive in Jerusalem for the conference in October 51. On the evidence of the letters, as we saw above, this sequence is perfectly feasible (and indeed marginally preferable), and the reversal in Acts is easily explained if we argue that Luke had good Pauline tradition for both the journey and the conference but had no information as to their correct sequence (the letters, as we have seen, provide no such information). In fact it is possible to see a relic of the correct position in Acts 18:22-23, which has all the necessary stages: Jerusalem, Antioch, Galatia and Phrygia, Ephesus (Bruce, 399-400, accepts that Acts 18:22 contains a reference to Jerusalem, although he does not agree that this is the conference visit). Jewett (78-85) lists the scholars who have followed this solution: Jewett himself prefers it, and on this basis is able to integrate virtually every detail from the Acts narrative and the letters into a precise chronology.

*5.3. The Famine Relief Visit.* The other difficulty of integration concerns Acts' second Jerusalem visit (3). If we identify the conference of Galatians 2 with the one described in Acts 15 (C = 5), we are left with two problems: the accounts of the conferences differ in significant details, and the Acts 11 visit contradicts Paul's express statement in Galatians that the conference visit was only his second visit to Jerusalem. Acts 15 is his third. Of these the first can be explained in a variety of ways (the different accounts may represent different perspectives on the same event), but the second seems intractable: Paul's statement in Galatians is no passing remark, but a solemn asseveration. If Acts 11 is correct, then Paul is being (to put it mildly) economical with the truth.

One simple and longstanding solution to this problem is to argue that the conference described in Galatians 2 took place on the Acts 11 visit (C = 3). Jewett (69-75) lists and describes the various hypotheses which have followed this route. It disposes neatly of both the objections to the C = 5 identification. Acts 15 can be read as describing a later, more formal conference which is not reflected in the letters (Bruce, 29-32), and there is no contradiction with Galatians 1. It does however raise some problems of its own. The stated motivation for the two visits is not the same: we would have to argue that Paul's "by revelation" (Gal 2:2) alludes obliquely to the prophetic basis for the visit described in Acts, and that Paul's stress on a private meeting does not preclude the possibility that the public reason for the visit was quite different (Hemer, 248).

But our immediate concern here is that this identification appears to raise acute problems for chronology. The fourteen-year span of Galatians 2:1 now has to be fitted in between Acts 9 and Acts 11. This is clearly impossible if the conference took place before the death of Herod (Acts 12:23) in 44. The situation is eased if we agree that (as argued at 4.2.1 above) the visit of Acts 11:30 is not closely tied to the events of Acts 12, but is simply reckoned to have happened "in the days of Claudius" (Acts 11:28), that is, somewhere in the period 41-54. Famines are known up to at least 48 (see 4.2.1 above), and a concurrent reckoning of the fourteen years could bring the conference down to this date. But the later we put the conference, the greater the difficulties, given that now both missionary journeys (4 and 6), as well as Paul's eighteen months in Corinth, must be fitted in before Paul meets Gallio in 51/52. Again, some scholars believe that it is simpler to conclude that the Acts 11 visit is out of sequence, most probably because the information Luke received did not enable him to align it correctly with the journey traditions. It may reflect a separate line of tradition from the church at Antioch, which did not originally include Paul, or possibly it may allude to the collection, which Luke does not mention elsewhere.

**5.4. Conclusions.** The two tripartite sequences deduced from the letters can be integrated with Acts in one of two ways. An interlocking sequence (on the assumption that Luke has reversed the conference and the first Macedonian journey) gives the order A B D C E F, with (3) as a floating tradition reflecting either (C) or (F):

| | | |
|---|---|---|
| 34 | (A = 1) | Conversion, Arabia, Damascus (3 years) |
| 37 | (B = 2) | Jerusalem visit 1; to Syria and Cilicia Fourteen-year span including mission in Galatia and |
| | (4) | First missionary journey |
| 49-50 | (D = 6) | Second missionary journey = First Macedonian journey |
| 50-51 | | Eighteen months in Corinth, Gallio July 51, conference October 51 |
| 51 | (C = 5) | Jerusalem visit 2, conference, Antioch incident |
| | (E = 7) | Ephesian ministry (2 1/2—3 yrs) and organization of collection |
| 56-57 | (F = 8) | Final Macedonian journey to Jerusalem with collection |
| 57-59 | (9) | Final Jerusalem visit, two-year imprisonent in Caesarea |
| 59-62 | (10) | Trial before Festus, voyage to Rome, two-year imprisonment |

This schedule enables us to make sense of all the chronological data in the letters and Acts, except for two points at which Luke did not have sufficient information to allow him to sequence his material clearly. He appears to have followed the same procedure as the Gospel writers, who sometimes arrange material topically rather than in chronological sequence. Exactly the same problem occurs in the ancient historians (Josephus, Suetonius), whose vagueness or lack of information about sequence means that first-century chronology can rarely attain a high degree of precision.

If, on the other hand, we follow the order of events as given in Acts, the two sequences must be arranged successively in the order A B C D E F, thus:

| | | |
|---|---|---|
| 34 | (A = 1) | Conversion, Arabia, Damascus (3 yrs) |
| 37 | (B = 2) | Jerusalem visit 1; to Syria and Cilicia Eleven-year span including mission in Galatia |
| 48 | (C = 3) | Jerusalem visit 2, conference, Antioch incident |
| 48 | (4) | First missionary journey |
| 49 | (5) | Acts 15 conference |

| 49-50 | (D = 6) | Second missionary journey = First Macedonian journey |
| 50-51 | | Eighteen months in Corinth followed by meeting with Gallio |
| | (E = 7) | Ephesian ministry (2 1/2—3 yrs) and organization of collection |
| 56-57 | (F = 8) | Final Macedonian journey to Jerusalem with collection |
| 57-59 | (9) | Final Jerusalem visit, two-year imprisonment in Caesarea |
| 59-62 | (10) | Trial before Festus. voyage to Rome, two-year imprisonment |

This results in a very tight timetable between the conference and the meeting with Gallio. An earlier date for the crucifixion (and thus the conversion) would help, but only if we ignore the Aretas datum. If we keep the same sequence but eliminate the famine relief visit (3), this gives an easier schedule, though the time for the second missionary journey is still tight:

| 34 | (A = 1) | Conversion, Arabia, Damascus (3 yrs) |
| 37 | (B = 2) | Jerusalem visit 1; to Syria and Cilicia Eleven-year span including mission in Galatia and |
| | (4) | First missionary journey |
| 48 | (C = 5) | Jerusalem visit 2, conference, Antioch incident |
| 48-50 | (D = 6) | Second missionary journey = First Macedonian journey |
| 50-51 | | Eighteen months in Corinth followed by meeting with Gallio |
| | (E = 7) | Ephesus ministry (2 yrs) and organization of collection |
| 56-57 | (F = 8) | Final Macedonian journey to Jerusalem with collection |
| 57-59 | (9) | Final Jerusalem visit, two-year imprisonment in Caesarea |
| 59-62 | (10) | Trial before Festus, voyage to Rome, two-year imprisonment |

Given the imprecision of most of our chronological data and the limitations of the evidence, it would be unrealistic to look for a more definitive chronology. Within these limitations, the chronology of Paul is as well founded as any historian would expect for a comparable figure of his time and place.

*See also* CORINTHIANS, LETTERS TO THE; EPHESUS; GALATIANS, LETTER TO THE; ITINERARIES, TRAVEL PLANS, JOURNEYS, APOSTOLIC PAROUSIA; JERUSALEM; PASTORAL LETTERS; PAUL IN ACTS AND LETTERS; PHILIPPIANS, LETTER TO THE; ROME AND ROMAN CHRISTIANITY; THESSALONIANS, LETTERS TO THE; TRAVEL IN THE ROMAN WORLD.

BIBLIOGRAPHY. F. F. Bruce, *The Acts of the Apostles: Greek Text with Introduction and Commentary* (3d ed.; Grand Rapids: Eerdmans, 1990); K. P. Donfried, "Chronology: New Testament," *ABD* I.1011-22; J. J. Gunther, *Paul: Messenger and Exile: A Study in the Chronology of His Life and Letters* (Valley Forge, PA: Judson, 1972); C. J. Hemer, *The Book of Acts in the Setting of Hellenistic History* (Winona Lake, IN: Eisenbrauns, 1990); H. W. Hoehner, "Chronology," *DJG* 118-22; R. Jewett, *A Chronology of Paul's Life* (Philadelphia: Fortress, 1979); J. Knox, *Chapters in a Life of Paul* (Nashville: Abingdon, 1950); G. Lüdemann, *Paul, Apostle to the Gentiles: Studies in Chronology* (Philadelphia: Fortress, 1984); G. Ogg, *The Chronology of the Life of Paul* (London: Epworth 1968); E. M. Smallwood, *The Jews under Roman Rule* (Leiden: E. J. Brill, 1976).

L. C. A. Alexander

## CHURCH

More than one hundred different terms, metaphors and images are used in the NT to describe God's* people with whom he has entered into a saving relationship in Christ.* In addition to these descriptions several activities are said to characterize Christian believers. Integral to Paul's teaching about the people of God is his use of the important word *ekklēsia*, a term meaning "congregation," "church," "gathering" or "assembly."

1. *Ekklēsia* Outside the Bible
2. *Ekklēsia* in Paul
3. The Origin of the Church
4. Some Images of the Church
5. The Purpose of the Church's Gathering
6. Authority in the Church

### 1. *Ekklēsia* Outside the Bible.

*1.1. Ekklēsia in the Greek City-State.* The term *ekklēsia* ("assembly"), derived from *ek-kaleō* ("call out," a verb used for the summons to an army to assemble), is attested from the time of Euripides and Herodotus onward (fifth century B.C.) and denoted the popular assembly of the full citizens of the *polis,* or Greek city state. During this period it met at regular intervals, though in cases of emergency the term could describe an extraordinary gathering. Every citizen had the right to speak and to propose matters for discussion. Centuries before the translation of the OT and the time of the NT, the term *ekklēsia* was clearly characterized as a political phenomenon; it was the assembly of full citizens, functionally rooted in the Greek democracy, an assembly in which fundamentally political and judicial decisions were taken (cf. Acts 19:39; where at 19:32 and 41 even an unconstitutional assembly is called an *ekklēsia*). It was regarded as existing only when it actually assembled (as such it was distinct from the *dēmos*, "people," "crowd," "populace").

**1.2. Ekklēsia *in the LXX, Josephus and Philo*.** In the LXX *ekklēsia* frequently was a translation of the Hebrew *qāhāl*, a term that could describe assemblies of a less specifically religious or nonreligious kind, such as the gathering of an army in preparation for war (1 Sam 17:47; 2 Chron 28:14) or the "coming together" of an unruly and potentially dangerous crowd (Ps 26[LXX 25]:5). (*Ekklēsia* never renders *ʿēḏāh*, "congregation," which represented the people as a national unit.) Of particular significance are those instances of *ekklēsia* (rendering *qāhāl*) which denote the congregation of Israel when it assembled to hear the Word of God on Mt. Sinai, or later on Mt. Zion where all Israel was required to assemble three times a year. Sometimes the whole nation appears to be involved, as when Moses addresses the people prior to their entry into the promised land. Deuteronomy 4:10 describes "the day when you stood before the Lord your God, in Horeb, when he said to me, 'Assemble the people before me to hear my words' " (the LXX uses the term *ekklēsia* and its cognate verb *ekklēsiazō*; note also Deut 9:10; 18:16; 31:30; Judg 20:2; etc.). At other times it is only the chief representatives that seem to be present, as with the congregation of tribal leaders, or patriarchal chiefs, at Solomon's dedication of the Temple of Jerusalem (1 Kings 8:14, 22, 55, etc.).

Josephus also used the word frequently (some forty-eight times, of which eighteen are LXX quotations), always of a gathering. These vary in character, for example, religious, political and spontaneous assemblies are mentioned (Josephus *Ant.* 4.45 §309; *Life* §268; *J.W.* 1.4 §654; 1.8 §666). Philo employs the term some thirty times, all but five of which are in quotations from the LXX. These five appear in a classical Greek sense.

So in the Greek and Jewish worlds prior to and contemporaneous with the NT *ekklēsia* meant an assembly or gathering of people. It did not designate an "organization" or "society." Although it had no intrinsically religious meaning and could refer to meetings that were secular in character, of special significance are those occurrences of *ekklēsia* in the LXX which refer to the congregation of Israel when it assembled to hear the Word of God.

## 2. *Ekklēsia* in Paul.

The word *ekklēsia* appears 114 times in the NT, with sixty-two instances in Paul (three instances are in Matthew, twenty-three in Acts, twenty in Revelation and in the non-Pauline letters six occurrences). Since Paul's uses all predate the other instances in the NT it is important to determine the meaning he attaches to it in various contexts.

**2.1. *A Local Assembly or Congregation of Christians*.** Chronologically, the first use occurs at 1 Thessalonians 1:1 (cf. 2 Thess 1:1) in the greeting to the Christians at Thessalonica: "Paul, Silas and Timothy. To the church (*ekklēsia*) of the Thessalonians in God the Father and the Lord* Jesus Christ." The term is employed in the same way as in Greek and Jewish circles, that is, like other assemblies (*ekklēsiai*) in the city, it is described as "a gathering of the Thessalonians." But it is distinguished from the regular political councils by the addition of the words "in God the Father," and from the regular synagogue meetings by the use of the term *ekklēsia* and the additional phrase "in the Lord Jesus Christ" (Banks). From the closing remarks of the letter it is clear that Paul has in mind an actual gathering of the Thessalonian* Christians. So he requests that his letter "be read to all the brothers and sisters" and that they "greet them all with a holy kiss" (1 Thess 5:26-27).

Other instances of *ekklēsia* (singular) and *ekklēsiai* (plural) in Paul's letters also denote a *local assembly or gathering of Christians* in a particular place: it is thus not a metaphor, but a term descriptive of an identifiable object. In the two Thessalonian letters reference is made to "the churches of God" (2 Thess 1:4) and "the churches of God in Judea" (2:14). Other letters such as Galatians* (Gal 1:2), the two letters to the Corinthians* (1 Cor 7:17; 11:16; 14:33, 34; 2 Cor 8:19, 23, 24; 11:8, 28; 12:13) and Romans* (Rom 16:4, 16) also employ the plural when more than one church is in view (the only exceptions are the distributive expression "every church," 1 Cor 4:17, and the phrase "the church of God," 1 Cor 10:32, in a generic or possibly localized sense). So reference is made to "the *churches* in Galatia" (Gal 1:2; 1 Cor 16:1), "the *churches* of Asia" (1 Cor 16:19), "the *churches* in Macedonia" (2 Cor 8:1) and "the *churches* of Judea" (Gal 1:22). This suggests that the term was applied only to an actual gathering of people, or to a group that gathers when viewed as a regularly constituted meeting (Banks). Although we often speak of a group of congregations collectively as "the church" (i.e., of a denomination), it is doubtful whether Paul (or the rest of the NT) uses *ekklēsia* in this collective way. Also, the notion of a unified provincial or national church appears to have been foreign to Paul's thinking. An *ekklēsia* was a meeting or an assembly. This primary sense of "gathering" comes out clearly in 1 Corinthians 11—14 where expressions are used, such as "when you assemble in church" (1 Cor 11:18) and "to speak in church" (1 Cor 14:35; cf. 14:4, 5, 12, 19, 28).

In one or two NT instances *ekklēsia* is found as an extension of the literal, descriptive use of "an assembly" to designate the persons who compose that gathering, whether they are assembled or not. This is a natural extension or linguistic development of group words (note our use of the word "team"), and may explain references such as Acts 8:3; 9:31; 20:17. However, two significant observations need to be made: first, the primary use of the word *ekklēsia* as gathering predominates overwhelmingly in the NT—and indeed through the Apostolic Fathers to the Apologists. Secondly, no theological constructs are made on the basis of these very few *extended* uses.

It is of particular significance that at the beginning of the two Corinthian letters (1 Cor 1:1; 2 Cor 1:1; cf. 1 Cor 10:32; 11:22; Rom 16:16) the church is described as belonging to the one who brought it into existence, that is, God, or the one through whom this has taken place, namely, Christ. Such an *ekklēsia* was not simply a human association or a religious club, but a divinely created entity. As in the case of ancient Israel, the gatherings referred to by our term were in order to hear the word of God and to worship.* Paul's reference in Galatians (Gal 1:13; cf. 1 Cor 15:9; Phil 3:6) to his original persecution of "the church of God" does not necessarily contradict this suggestion, since the expression may point to the church at Jerusalem* before it was distributed into a smaller number of assemblies in various parts of Judea, or that it was as the believers met together that the arrests were made—their gathering provided evidence of their Christian associations (cf. Banks).

*2.2. A House Church.* In a second group of references *ekklēsia* is again used as a descriptive term of an identifiable object—as distinct from a metaphor—this time of a gathering that met in a particular home, a *house-church* (*see* Sociology). On occasion, a whole congregation in one city might be small enough to meet in the home of one of its members, and it must be remembered that it was not until about the middle of the third century that early Christianity owned property for purposes of worship. In other places house churches appear to have been smaller circles of fellowship within the larger group. In addition to Nympha's house in Laodicea (Col 4:15), we know that in Colossae Philemon's* house was used as a meeting place (Philem 2). At Philippi Lydia's home seems to have been used in this way (Acts 16:15, 40), while at Corinth Gaius is described as "host . . . to the whole church" (Rom 16:23; the qualification "whole" would be unnecessary if the Christians at Corinth only met as a single group, and implies smaller groups also existed in the city; cf. 1 Cor 14:23; note also 1 Cor 16:19; Rom 16:5).

*2.3. A Heavenly Gathering.* Of particular significance for our study of the church are those instances in Paul's later letters where *ekklēsia* has a *wider reference than either a local congregation or a house-church*, and describes a heavenly and eschatological entity. We begin with Colossians 1:18 where it is stated that Christ is "the head of the body, that is the church." At Colossians 1:24 a similar expression is employed in the context of Paul's sufferings ("on behalf of his body, which is the church"). Most commentators interpret these references in Colossians (and the similar instances in Eph 1:22; 3:10, 21; 5:23-24, 27, 29, 32) of "the church universal, to which all believers belong" (Bauer) and which is scattered throughout the world. But there are two serious criticisms that may be leveled against this view: (1) The term *ekklēsia* can no longer have its usual meaning of "gathering" or "assembly," since it is difficult to envisage how the worldwide church could assemble, and so the word must be translated in some other way to denote an organization or society. (2) The context of Colossians 1:15-20 which is moving on a heavenly plane suggests it is not an earthly phenomenon that is being spoken of in Colossians 1:18, but a supernatural and heavenly* one.

This is not to suggest that believers have no relationships with one another if they do not gather together in church. As members of the body of Christ or of God's people, they are not only related to Christ himself but also to one another even when separated by time and distance. But the point being made here is that *ekklēsia* is not the term used in the NT of those wider, universal links. Earlier in the Letter to the Colossians* it had been mentioned that the readers have been fitted for a share in the inheritance of the saints in the kingdom* of light,* and have been transferred from a tyranny of darkness to a kingdom in which God's beloved Son* holds sway (Col 1:12-14). On the one hand, the Colossians are obviously members of an earthly realm (note the exhortations of Col 3:4—4:6 which show they have important earthly responsibilities), and the apostle looks forward to their being presented as "holy, irreproachable, and blameless" before God on the last day (Col 1:22). On the other hand, they are described as presently existing in a heavenly realm. Since they have been raised with Christ, they are to seek the things that are above, where Christ is, seated at God's right hand (Col 3:1; *see* Dying and Rising with Christ). Because they live with Christ in this heavenly dimension (note that Christ who is their life is already in heaven, Col 3:1, 3), they are assured that when he appears they will also appear with him in glory* (Col 3:4).

Later references in Ephesians are thought to point

in this same direction of a heavenly gathering: it is expressly mentioned that God "made us alive with Christ . . . raised us up with him and seated us in the heavenly realms in Christ Jesus" (Eph 2:5-6). The same readers of this circular letter have been "blessed . . . in the heavenly realms with every spiritual blessing in Christ" (Eph 1:3). Again reference is made to Christ's headship* over the "church" (*ekklēsia*) which is his body (Eph 1:22-23). If the term *ekklēsia* is to be understood here as "church" or a gathering taking place in heaven, then this would mean that Christians participate in it as they go about their ordinary daily tasks. They are already gathered around Christ, and this is another way of saying that they now enjoy fellowship* with him. Further references in Ephesians (Eph 3:10, 21; 5:23, 25, 27, 29, 32), though usually taken by interpreters to refer to "the church universal," could also be understood as designating that heavenly gathering around Christ.

An important passage outside the Pauline letters where *ekklēsia* refers to a "gathering" that is both *heavenly* and *eschatological* is Hebrews 12:23 where the unusual expression "the assembly (*ekklēsia*) of the firstborn" appears. Although the heavenly city is still the goal of the Christian's pilgrimage (Heb 13:14), Christians in their conversion have already come to that heavenly assembly.

*2.4. The Relationship of Paul's Uses of* **Ekklēsia.** The NT does not discuss the relationship between the local church and the heavenly gathering. The link is nowhere specifically spelled out. Certainly the local congregation was neither a *part* of the church of God nor *a* church of God. This is made plain in several places, including 1 Corinthians 1:2 where the apostle writes "to *the church* of God which is at Corinth." But we may suggest that local congregations, as well as house groups that met in the homes of Nympha and Lydia, for example, were concrete, visible expressions of that new relationship which believers have with the Lord Jesus. Local gatherings, whether in a congregation or a house church, were earthly manifestations of that heavenly gathering around the risen Christ.

If this heavenly meeting with Christ is a figurative or metaphorical way of speaking about believers' ongoing fellowship with him, then it was appropriate that this new relationship with the ascended Lord should find concrete expression in their regular coming together, that is, "in church." Apparently, the responsibility of meeting together in this way was not immediately obvious to some of the early Christians since they still needed to be exhorted not to forsake "the assembling of . . . [themselves] together" (Heb 10:25).

Men and women were called into membership of this one church of Christ, the heavenly assembly, through the preaching of the gospel. They were brought into fellowship with God's Son (cf. 1 Cor 1:9), and to speak of their membership of this heavenly gathering assembled around Christ is another way of referring to this new relationship with him. They and other Christians were to assemble in local congregations here on earth, for this was an important way in which their fellowship with Christ was expressed. Further, as they came together with others who were in fellowship with him, so they not only met with each other—they also met with Christ himself who indwelt them corporately and individually.

### 3. The Origin of the Church.

*3.1. "The Church of God."* It has been claimed that whenever *ekklēsia* appears by itself it is to be understood as an abbreviation of the original term *hē ekklēsia tou theou* ("the church of God": 1 Cor 1:2; 10:32; 11:22; 15:9; 2 Cor 1:1; Gal 1:13; plural in 1 Cor 11:16, 22; 1 Thess 2:14; 2 Thess 1:4). Accordingly, the genitive *of God* is not merely an addition which defines more precisely the preceding word *church*, but was part of an original fixed formulation. "The church of God" was the self-designation of the early Jerusalem church (1 Cor 15:9; cf. Gal 1:13; Phil 3:6), which understood itself to be the eschatological community of salvation.* The full expression "the church of God" came to be applied to other congregations as well (1 Thess 2:14), including those in the Gentile* mission* ("the church of God which is at Corinth," 1 Cor 1:2; cf. 2 Thess 1:4). The genitive *of God* indicates that he is the source or origin of the church's life and existence. He summons men and women to himself through the preaching of Christ crucified and forms them into his *ekklēsia*.

*3.2. Christ and the Church.* On occasion, Paul mentions Christ in connection with the term *ekklēsia*: for example, "the churches of Christ greet you" (Rom 16:16). 1 Thessalonians 2:14 ("you became imitators of the churches of God in Christ which are in Judea") shows that Christ has not replaced God as the source of the church's life. God's act of founding the *ekklēsia* is mediated through Jesus Christ and his gospel. This was true of the *ekklēsia* in Thessalonica, no less than the churches in Judea. So, the churches of the NT are the congregations *of God in Christ*, the churches *in* Jesus Christ (1 Thess 2:14; Gal 1:22), or the churches *of* Jesus Christ (Rom 16:16).

### 4. Some Images of the Church.

In addition to his use of the important term *ekklēsia*

("church, congregation"), Paul employs many significant images and metaphors of God's people in Christ. These images are not always synonymous or coterminous with *ekklēsia*. For example, the body metaphor can refer to Christians generally in their relationships in Christ, without suggesting that they are members of the same *ekklēsia*. But often in his letters the apostle applies these images to the same entity as the *ekklēsia*—for example, the congregation at Corinth. These metaphors have different or nuanced connotations, and therefore it is important to ask what point is being conveyed or taught through the image. More than a hundred are used in the NT generally. We shall confine our remarks to a limited number which throw special light on Paul's understanding of the church. (For a discussion of the wider issues relating to any one image, see the separate entry.)

*4.1. The Temple.* The figure of *the temple*\* is used metaphorically in the NT to denote God's people. The apostle, in particular, develops this picture of the church as the community of the redeemed which, through the sanctifying activity of the Holy Spirit,\* is constituted as the dwelling place of God: this idea appears in 1 Corinthians 3:16-17; 2 Corinthians 6:16-18 and Ephesians 2:20-22 (cf. 1 Cor 6:19).

*4.1.1. 1 Corinthians 3:16-17.* In a context where he seeks to combat party strife in the church at Corinth (1:10-17; 3:5-9), Paul uses *naos theou* ("the temple of God") specifically of the local congregation. By means of the temple imagery he makes plain, first, that the congregation at Corinth is the temple of God because his Spirit dwells among God's assembled people (1 Cor 10:16). Second, the church is itself the dwelling place of God. His tabernacling on earth is not apart from his people; instead, it is an indwelling *within them* (1 Cor 10:16-17). Third, Paul stresses the unity and holiness of God's temple. All the Corinthians together constitute God's dwelling place, and as such it is holy. To defile it by internal schism, divisions or party spirit is to destroy it, and any attempt to do this will incur divine judgment.\*

*4.1.2. 2 Corinthians 6:16-18.* In one of the clearest statements in his letters about the idea of believers as God's temple, Paul, referring primarily to the members of the congregation at Corinth, states: "we are the temple of the living God." He quotes OT texts which speak of God's presence with his people (Lev 26:12; Ezek 37:27; etc.); however, it may be implied that for the apostle God's dwelling in his people goes beyond OT notions of his "presence with or among" them; now it is an actual "dwelling in" them. Although it is not explicitly stated that this temple is *holy*, it is clearly implied from the admonition where the Corin-

thians are exhorted to separate from all that is unclean (2 Cor 6:17, quoting Is 52:11).

*4.1.3. Ephesians 2:20-22.* The third major temple reference in Paul's letters occurs in a passage where the apostle reminds his Gentile converts that through Christ's death they have been made heirs of God's promises. Here the church is set forth as the *heavenly* temple—teaching that is akin to the heavenly dimension we have already observed in relation to *ekklēsia*. According to OT prophecy the temple at Jerusalem was to be the place where all nations at the end time would come to worship and pray\* (Is 66:18-20; cf. Is 2:1-5; Mic 4:1-5). The temple imagery here is to be understood in fulfillment of these promises. Through Christ Gentiles have been brought near to God and along with Jews have become the new temple, the place where God's presence dwells. Christ's preeminent place in the temple is stressed: he is the "cornerstone," either the stone at the foot of the building, set in the corner to determine the line of the walls and so of the building as a whole, or the final stone set over the gate which holds the building together. "A holy temple in the Lord" and "a dwelling place of God in the Spirit" (Eph 2:21, 22) are parallel descriptions. The temple is God's heavenly abode, the place of his dwelling. Yet that temple is his people in whom he lives by his Spirit. Believers on earth, recipients of this circular letter, are linked with the heavenly realm in and through the Spirit of the risen Lord. Finally, the metaphor of the body is combined with that of the building to draw attention to the element of growth (Eph 2:21a, 22). Viewed as the temple the church is a dwelling inhabited by God; but from the point of its being a building it is still under construction.

*4.2. The Body.* The metaphor of the body of Christ (*see* Body of Christ), employed by Paul to describe the church, is a highly significant one, and is applied to a number of entities and with a range of connotations. It is used by the apostle in his earlier letters of a local congregation (at Corinth), of *Christians* (at Rome) *in their relationships* with one another—Christians who were not necessarily members of the same congregation (Rom 12:4-5)—and of a wider group, possibly including *all Christians* (1 Cor 12:13), that is, all who have been united to the Lord Jesus Christ. In Colossians\* and Ephesians,\* the body image denotes *a heavenly*\* *entity,* that is, all Christians united to him. He is their life and is seated in heaven at God's right hand while believers themselves have not only been raised with Christ, but also have been made to sit with him in the heavenly places. We shall treat only those references which throw light on Paul's use of *ekklēsia*.

*4.2.1. The Earlier Letters.* At 1 Corinthians 12:12-27,

where the apostle is concerned to impress on the Corinthian Christians that they have mutual duties and common interests which they must not neglect, he asserts, "You are the body of Christ and severally members of it" (1 Cor 12:27). Within the body which is one, there is true diversity—a multiplicity of functions which are necessary to its being a real body (1 Cor 12:17-20). Each member with his or her gifts is necessary to the other members for the good of the body as a whole (1 Cor 12:17-21). The Spirit's activity is specifically mentioned: it is through baptism in or by the Spirit (*en heni pneumati*, 1 Cor 12:13) that members are added to the body of Christ. The Spirit then refreshes them just as he graciously gives them gifts* for the common good (cf. 1 Cor 12:7, 11). The explicit reference to "you" (*hymeis*) at the conclusion of the paragraph (1 Cor 12:27) makes it plain that this metaphor of "the body of Christ" is predicated of the local congregation (*ekklēsia*) at Corinth. This church is neither a *part* of the body of Christ nor "*a* body of Christ." Such a description is similar to that in the opening words of the letter where the congregation is called "the church (*ekklēsia*) of God which is at Corinth" (1 Cor 1:2)—it is neither a *part* of the church of God nor *a* church of God in Corinth. Yet the statement in 1 Corinthians 12:13 about "we" being baptized into one body suggests that the image of the body of Christ can be used of Christians generally (or at least a wider group than the believers at Corinth). There are thus two entities being referred to by the one expression—the local congregation at Corinth, which is specifically in mind at 1 Corinthians 12:27, and a wider group including Paul and possibly others (the "we" of 1 Cor 12:13). The phrase "the body of Christ" can be used comprehensively of all who are united in him, and also of a particular manifestation of that body, in this case the local congregation. This notion fits exactly with our interpretation of *ekklēsia* (and the temple motif) where the term can describe a local manifestation (in either a specific congregation or a house church) and a heavenly entity.

At Romans 12:4-5 the body metaphor has reference to believers generally in their relationships with one another (perhaps scattered throughout the capital in Rome*), rather than describing them as a single congregation.

*4.2.2. The Later Letters.* In Colossians and Ephesians there is an advance in Paul's thought, involving the setting forth of the relationship which the church, as the body of Christ, bears to Christ as head* of the body (note the household code* of Eph 5:22-33 which is an occasion for instruction about the relationship between Christ and the church). The church as the body of Christ occupies a highly significant role in the purposes of God. This is brought out particularly in Ephesians 1:23 where it is asserted that Christ's rule over all things is for, or on behalf of, the church, and at Ephesians 3:10 where it is stated that through the *ekklēsia* the wisdom* of God is made known even to the cosmic powers (Eph 3:10; *see* Principalities and Powers). Christ's headship over the church is presented in terms of an organic relationship in which he exercises control over his people as the head of a body exercises control over its various parts. The living relationship between the members is kept in view, while the dependence of the members on Christ for life and power, as well as his supremacy, is reiterated. The element of the body's growth is made plain in Colossians 2:19 and even more so in Ephesians. Its upbuilding is mentioned in the context of unity in diversity; such a growth derives from Christ and leads to Christ as members are rightly related to him as the head, and to one another (Eph 4:1-16). The church as the body of Christ is described as Christ's fullness (Eph 1:23). In one sense it is complete, for it is already a body just as there is already a Lord (Eph 4:4-6). On the other hand, it grows and will be completed on the final day. The body thus partakes of the tension regularly seen in the NT between the "already" and the "not yet," between what it is and what it will be. The body is a present reality and yet it is an eschatological, that is, future, entity.

*4.3. The Household.* Throughout the NT God's people are regularly spoken of as a family, and a cluster of terms, drawn from family life, is used in discussions of the church and early Christian communities (*see* Household). God is "Father" (Rom 8:15; Gal 4:9), and those who are redeemed by Jesus Christ are God's children (Gal 4:1-7), with Jesus Christ being the firstborn* of the family (Rom 8:29). Paul speaks in warm terms when he addresses fellow Christians as "brothers" (note, for example, Phil 4:1; *adelphoi*, lit. "brothers," includes both "brothers and sisters"). The theme of family relationships is particularly prominent in 1 Timothy, where the church (*ekklēsia*) is described as "the household (*oikos*) of God, and the pillar and bulwark of the truth" (1 Tim 3:15; cf. Heb 3:1-6). The purpose of this letter as a whole is to indicate "how one ought to behave in God's household." The order of the church is analogous to that of a human household. Members are to treat one another as they would the members of their own family (1 Tim 5:1-2). They are to care for one another in need (1 Tim 5:5, 16), while overseers are to be skillful at managing the household of God, as demonstrated by their skill with, and care for, their own immediate families (1 Tim 3:1-7).

## 5. The Purpose of the Church's Gathering.

We have seen that coming together is an essential element of the *ekklēsia*. In many languages today the equivalent word for *church* is still used in relation to the act of gathering together: so expressions such as "it is time for church," "before [or after] church" or "in church" are used. The sense is always that of Christians congregating for a given reason. What, then, is the purpose of believers gathering together?

**5.1. Edification.** Although it is almost universally claimed that Christians meet together in church "to worship God," Paul's revolutionary teaching is that they are meant to worship him in every sphere of life (Rom 12:1). Worship terminology is transformed by the apostle and applied to the work of Christ (Rom 3:24-25; cf. Eph 5:2), the preaching* of the gospel* (Rom 1:9; 15:16; Phil 2:17), and the new lifestyle of believers (Rom 6:13, 16; 12:1; Phil 2:17; 1 Thess 1:9-10). It cannot be worship alone, therefore, that brings believers to church (cf. 1 Cor 14:25). Instead of the language of worship, Paul regularly uses the terminology of upbuilding, or *edification*, to indicate the purpose and function of Christian gatherings (1 Cor 14:3-5, 12, 17, 26; 1 Thess 5:11; Eph 4:11-16). "Edification" (*oikodomē*), which refers to the growth and progress of believers, is not to be interpreted individualistically. There is a corporate as well as a personal dimension in the apostle's teaching on edification. According to Ephesians 4:7 the Messiah builds his church (cf. the OT promises of God preparing a people for himself: Jer 24:6; 31:4; 33:7) through the people he gives as apostles,* prophets,* evangelists and pastor*-teachers. The focus of attention here is on the ministries of the word (cf. Eph 2:20-22) which are to "equip the saints for works of service for building up the body of Christ" (Eph 4:12). The ultimate goal of this ministry, and therefore the purpose of the gathering, is to prepare believers for full maturity when they meet their Lord (Eph 4:13). Edification occurs through prophecy* (1 Cor 14:3) and other verbal ministries of exhortation, comfort and admonition by congregational members (Eph 4:26; cf. 1 Thess 4:18; 5:11, 14; Eph 4:15). Of primary importance in the process of building up God's people is the regular and systematic exposition of Scripture, together with the teaching of "sound doctrine" by those equipped and appointed for the task (cf. 1 Tim 4:6, 11, 13; 5:17; 2 Tim 2:1-2, 14-15; 4:1-5; Tit 1:9). "When Christians gather together to minister to one another the truth of God in love, *the church is manifested, maintained and advanced in God's way*" (Peterson, 214; emphasis added). The well-being and strengthening of the congregation is a fundamental aim of the members gathering together.

In 1 Corinthians 11:17-34, although the terminology of "edification" is not used in Paul's discussion of the Lord's Supper* at Corinth, the issue of upbuilding is clearly prominent. The apostle appears to be speaking about different aspects of the same meetings throughout the chapter (*ekklēsia* occurs in 1 Cor 11:18, 22). The Christian congregation is not an ordinary association or club in which members have the same interests; rather, it is a gathering that arises out of a sharing together in the benefits of Christ's saving work. When the members met together, divisions of a social kind occurred. As long as individuals were pre-occupied with consuming their own private meals, they were not holding a meal in honor of the Lord Jesus. By disregarding one another they were negating the very point of Christ's sacrifice for them. He had made it possible for them to share in the life of the age to come, but by their self-centered behavior they had failed to understand their partnership in the body of Christ. Rather than building up or edifying their fellow believers they were showing "contempt for the church of God" (1 Cor 11:22). Thus, by not caring for their fellow believers, they were not worshiping God or serving him acceptably.

**5.2. Meeting with Christ.** When NT believers met with one another and shared a whole range of ministries of the word in the congregation, so that the body of Christ was *edified*, they met with Christ himself. As the members sang psalms, hymns* and spiritual songs with gratitude in their hearts, and thus fulfilled the apostolic injunction to let the word of Christ dwell among them richly (Col 3:16; cf. Eph 5:19-20), so Christ himself was present in their midst. "Any gospel-based ministry of encouragement or admonition will be a means by which Christ engages with his people" (Peterson, 198). This would take place when the Scriptures were formally expounded and taught, or when believers informally exhorted one another in the congregation to live out their obedience to the gospel. The model of the NT assembly was the congregation (*ekklēsia*) of Israel* gathered at Mt. Sinai to hear the word of the Lord. Now, however, under the new covenant there is a significant difference. The Lord himself meets with his people *wherever* they gather in his name and under his authority.

The assembling of believers "in church" was an appropriate and natural outworking of their relationship with Christ; meeting together in the congregation was obviously an important way in which this relationship with their Lord was expressed.

At the same time, their coming together was a foretaste and anticipation of the life of heaven. Reference has already been made to believers' membership in the heavenly gathering assembled around Christ. The end will bring the assembling of God's children to meet him (2 Thess 2:1), the moment when Christ is glorified in his saints (1 Thess 4:17; cf. 2 Thess 1:12), and when they obtain the glory of our Lord Jesus Christ (2 Thess 2:14). God's ultimate intention for them is the joy* of fellowship, the restoration and enrichment of the relationships so rudely shattered in Eden. In this sense, fellowship with God and his Son, the Lord Jesus Christ, was not a means to an end, but the end itself. Every authentic Christian gathering is not simply an expression of the heavenly church as it presently gathers round Christ in heaven; it is also an anticipation of that blessed consummation.

The OT hope for the nations (*see* Gentiles) was that they too might be united with Israel and with one another in serving God (Is 56:6-7; Rev 7). This hope should be anticipated in the gathering of God's people on earth in the here and now, and fulfilled on the final day. Accordingly, the *ekklēsia* as it gathers was to keep looking "upward" or "forward," rather than simply "inward" at itself, or even "outward" at the world and its needs.

*5.3. Worshiping God?* If the worship terminology of the OT has been transformed by the NT writers, especially Paul, so that Christians are urged to worship the Living God in every sphere of life (Rom 12:1), is it appropriate to speak of their gathering together in church for "the worship* of God"? Also, how are we to understand the prayers, praises and thanksgivings which believers offer when they meet together in Christ's name? Should not these responses be viewed as significant elements in the corporate worship of God? If the emphasis is placed upon believers gathering together *for the purpose of edification*, how did Paul view the relationship between the "horizontal" and the "vertical" dimension of worship?

Central to Christian gatherings was the concern to proclaim and apply the truths of the gospel so as to stimulate and maintain saving faith.* Prayers and praises were clearly part of "the worship of God" as faith responses to the gospel. Yet even these were to be expressed in church in a way that would build up the congregation. Prayers and thanksgivings were not to be purely private, God-directed activities when others were present. Whether inspired or not, they were to be intelligible, for otherwise they would fall short of the fundamental goal of building up other members of the assembly (1 Cor 14:16-17).

It seems "best to speak of congregational worship as *a particular expression of the total life-response that is the worship of the New Covenant*" (Peterson, 220; emphasis added). As the word of Christ was ministered and re-

ceived in the congregation, so the body of Christ was built up. Christ himself was encountered in and through the "edification" (*oikodomē*). And, it was in building up the congregation that God was worshiped and glorified. A wedge should not be driven, therefore, between Paul's understanding of the "vertical" and "horizontal" dimensions of what took place in worship. Edification and worship, for example, were different sides of the same coin. Participating in the upbuilding of the church was an important expression of the believing community's devotion and service to God. It was, as Peterson puts it, an element of believers "engaging with God" (220). Therefore, one part of the meeting could not have been viewed as "worship time" (e.g., prayer and praise), and another part as "edification time," since the apostle's teaching encourages us to view the same activities from both points of view.

**6. Authority in the Church.**

*6.1. Christ's Authority and the Apostolic Word.* From Paul's letters it is plain that the churches in his care stood under the authority* of the Lord Jesus Christ. The church is Christ's body. He is its head,* not only in the sense of being the source of its life and power, but also as the one who exercises authority over it. The church of God (in a particular place) has been brought into existence through the proclamation of the apostolic gospel (cf. 1 Cor 1:4-9); its members have come into a living relationship with God's Son through his word. Christ continues to rule their lives by that same word. It is through the gospel that believers stand firm and by which they will be saved (1 Cor 15:1-2).

In the first instance that authority was exercised by Christ's apostles*—initially through their preaching and later through their apostolic writings. They were his witnesses,* emissaries and representatives (2 Cor 5:20), whose tasks were to found, build up and regulate the churches (2 Cor 10:8; 13:10; Gal 2:7-9). They appointed "men of good standing," or deacons (Acts 6:3, 6) and elders (Acts 14:23; cf. Tit 1:5-9), while their teaching was presented as Christ's truth, which was Spirit-given in its content and form of expression (1 Cor 2:9-13; cf. 1 Thess 2:13), and was a norm of faith (2 Thess 2:15; cf. Gal 1:8) and behavior (2 Thess 3:4, 6, 14). The church at Corinth, for example, was to realize that what the apostle wrote to them was a command of the Lord (1 Cor 14:37), while the Thessalonians were bound under oath to read and obey Paul's letters since they came with the authority of Christ himself (1 Thess 5:27; 2 Thess 2:15; 3:14).

*6.2. The Authority of the Congregation.* The authority

of an apostle, however, was not without limit. It came from the risen Lord Jesus Christ, and was to be exercised within the sphere of the apostolic commission, while an apostle was to preach and teach what was consistent with the gospel (1 Cor 15:1-11; Gal 1:6-17).

Congregations, too, had a derived authority. Their elders and leaders were to rule over the church, teaching the members, and urging them to follow the apostolic gospel and traditions* (1 Thess 5:12-13; 1 Tim 3:5; 5:17; cf. 1 Cor 16:15-16). At 1 Corinthians 5, in the context of a serious pastoral problem involving immorality, Paul expects the congregation to make an important decision in relation to the offending Christian. The apostle gives his advice in no uncertain terms: "you are to hand this man over to Satan for the destruction of the flesh" (1 Cor 5:5; *see* Discipline). But the congregation itself is to make the decision. The Corinthians are to assemble, conscious that the guidance and power of the Lord Jesus will be with them as they pronounce a disciplining judgment in his name on their disobedient member (1 Cor 5:4-5; *see* Church Order and Government).

Concerning the problem of discipline at the Lord's Supper in Corinth (1 Cor 10:14-22; 11:23-32), the apostle Paul lays down a number of principles which he expects the Corinthians to follow. But the actual details, the form of service,* the way in which their errors were to be corrected, lay with the congregation itself. The apostle's instructions were addressed to the whole congregation, not to any particular leader or presiding elder within it (*see* Pastor).

*See also* BODY OF CHRIST; CHURCH ORDER AND GOVERNMENT; FELLOWSHIP, COMMUNION, SHARING; GENTILES; HEAD, CHRIST AS; HOUSEHOLDS AND HOUSEHOLD CODES; ISRAEL; PASTOR, PAUL AS; SOCIAL SETTING OF MISSION CHURCHES; TEMPLE; WORSHIP.

BIBLIOGRAPHY. R. Banks, *Paul's Idea of Community: The Early House Churches in Their Historical Setting* (Grand Rapids: Eerdmans, 1980); K. Berger, "Volksversammlung und Gemeinde Gottes. Zu den Anfängen der christlichen Verwendung von 'ekklesia,' " *ZTK* 63 (1976) 167-207; L. Cerfaux, *The Church in the Theology of St. Paul* (New York: Herder, 1959); L. Coenen, "Church," *NIDNTT* 1.291-307; G. Delling, "Merkmale der Kirche nach dem NT," *NTS* 13 (1966-67) 297-316; R. Y. K. Fung, "Some Pauline Pictures of the Church," *EvQ* 53 (1981) 89-107; W. Klaiber, *Rechtfertigung und Gemeinde* (FRLANT 127; Göttingen: Vandenhoeck & Ruprecht, 1982); H. Küng, *The Church* (London: Burns & Oates, 1968); A. T. Lincoln, *Paradise Now and Not Yet* (SNTSMS 43; Cambridge: University Press, 1981); I. H. Marshall, "How far did the early Christians *worship* God?" *Churchman* 99 (1985) 216-29; idem, "New Wine

in Old Wine Skins: V. The Biblical Use of the Word 'Ekklēsia,' " *ExpT* 84 (1972-73) 359-64; H. Merklein, "Die Ekklesia Gottes. Der Kirchenbegriff bei Paulus und in Jerusalem," in *Studien zu Jesus und Paulus* (Tübingen: J. C. B. Mohr, 1987) 296-318; P. T. O'Brien, "The Church as a Heavenly and Eschatological Entity," in *The Church in the Bible and the World*, ed. D. A. Carson (Grand Rapids: Baker, 1987) 88-119, 307-11; D. G. Peterson, *Engaging with God: A Biblical Theology of Worship* (Grand Rapids: Eerdmans, 1993); J. Roloff, "ἐκκλησία," *EDNT* 1.410-15; K. L. Schmidt, "ἐκκλησία," *TDNT* III.501-36; W. Schrage, " 'Ekklesia' und 'Synagoge' Zum Ursprung des urchristlichen Kirchenbegriffs," *ZTK* 60 (1963) 178-202; B. W. Winter, "The Problem with 'Church' for the Early Church," in *In the Fullness of Time: Biblical Studies in Honour of Archbishop Donald Robinson*, ed. D. Peterson and J. Pryor (Homebush West, NSW: Lancer, 1992) 203-17.

P. T. O'Brien

## CHURCH ORDER AND GOVERNMENT

During the last half-century Paul's teaching and practice regarding how the Christian communities were ordered and led has undergone frequent investigation. (1) Exegetical work on Paul has rediscovered the charismatic dimension in Paul's approach to church order, developed a more contextual understanding of his approach and emphasized the indigenous leadership of his communities. (2) Socio-historical and sociological investigation of Paul has explored connections between Paul's churches and other first-century institutions, authority* and power,* charisma and its routinization. In addition feminist perspectives on Paul have discussed the role of women in ministry in the light of a cultural analysis of his writings.

What follows is an exegetical survey of Paul's approach to church order and government with a clear sociological interest. It begins by considering distinctive aspects and terminology involved in Paul's approach. This is followed by an examination of the chief metaphors he uses and models he identifies. Attention is then given to key dynamics and roles in the church. Finally the influence of Paul and his colleagues within these congregations will be assessed.

1. Perspective and Terminology
2. Metaphors and Models
3. Dynamics and Functions
4. Remuneration and Commissioning
5. Apostles and Colleagues
6. Conclusion

**1. Perspective and Terminology.**

*1.1. Differences between Modern and Ancient Mentali-*

*ties.* For modern people questions of order and government are often of primary interest. Organization and leadership are central concerns in any democratic and bureaucratic-rational society. This is also the case in church life, which is more democratized and bureaucratic than in previous times. In our social and religious arrangements we prize order: it is not only a preoccupation but a virtue, not only a means but an end. We are also fascinated by the issue of leadership, with chains of command, lines of authority and so forth. As a result we are in constant danger of reading the priority we accord these matters into Paul's ideas about the church.* He was certainly concerned that the church conduct itself in an orderly manner and that members were properly cared for and guided. But except where these were inadequate or threatened in some way, he says very little about them. For him they appear to be secondary rather than primary issues. Where more fundamental aspects of church life are given priority, church order and government should largely look after themselves.

*1.2. Order as a Secondary Concern.* If we begin by looking simply at the basic words Paul uses in speaking about these issues, what first strikes us is the infrequency of terms related to organization and to authority. The word *order* (*taxis*), appears infrequently in Paul (1 Cor 14:40; Col 2:5), and only once is it clearly associated with the church, coming at the close of his instructions to the Corinthians about what should happen in their meetings (1 Cor 14:13-40). This usage of *order* sums up a series of appeals relating to different aspects of the Corinthians' gatherings; appeals designed to prevent confusion from reigning (1 Cor 14:13-19, 22-23, 27-30, 34-35). Interestingly Paul does not use the word in connection with abuses surrounding the Lord's Supper (1 Cor 11:17-34). The opposite of order is "unruliness" (*akatastasia*), which is associated with disharmony (1 Cor 14:33; cf. 2 Cor 12:20). Paul never suggests that it is the role of certain people in the assembly to regulate its gatherings. Unlike the Greeks, he does not use the word *taxis* of an office that is responsible for ensuring that order is maintained (Epictetus 1.29, 39; Josephus *Ant.* 7.1.5 §36). This is everyone's responsibility as they share what the Spirit grants them (1 Cor 12:7-11) and discern what the Spirit is contributing through others (1 Cor 14:28, 30, 32). The church's "liturgy" is a communal construction. Order stems from a highly participatory and charismatic process and is not determined in advance by a few. Though neither purely spontaneous nor fully egalitarian, it is dynamic and mutually created. It is not constitutive of the church but functional and instrumental.

*1.3. Authority as a Background Issue.* The idea of authority* is a key sociological category in any discussion of government. It has to do with the way power is interpreted and communicated. The word *authority* (*exousia*) appears several times in Paul's writings in a specific sense of a reward for service performed (1 Cor 9:4-6, 12, 18; 2 Thess 3:9), a right he does not take up (2 Cor 11:7-10). Only in two places does Paul use the word more broadly of his own position—never of those in leadership in local churches—and only then when his apostolic link with a church is under challenge (2 Cor 10:8; 13:10). In view of the widespread use of this term in Greek for those in positions of influence over others, Paul's reticence in using the term can only be intentional. At Corinth he certainly wishes to reestablish his unique relationship with the church as its founder (2 Cor 10—13), but he wants to disassociate himself from the authoritarian way the "false apostles" conduct themselves. He does not seek to influence the members by improper means (2 Cor 10:3), boast to them of his preeminence (2 Cor 10:12-15), dazzle the church with rhetoric (2 Cor 11:5-6), or manipulate and control his converts (2 Cor 11:16-19; cf. 2 Cor 1:24). The "authority" God has given him is for "building up" not "tearing down," and he does not wish to use it in a harsh way when he arrives. Indeed he gives the church an opportunity to correct their attitude beforehand so that there will be no conflict when he arrives. This type of authority is basically charismatic, and therefore different from that found in traditional societies or in modern organizations: it is the authority of an unusual founder figure, though one who does not normally assert his position.

**2. Metaphors and Models.**

Though terms relating to organization and authority are not central to Paul's discussion of church organization or government, he does deploy certain metaphors and identify certain role models to convey what he has in mind. These word pictures and these "living epistles" begin to provide an overall frame of reference or paradigm for Paul's view. They form important components of the symbolic world from which his thinking proceeds.

*2.1. Family as the Root Metaphor.* Fundamental to interpreting his and his colleagues' relationship to the churches they founded are metaphors and analogies drawn from family life. This is not surprising, for it is the primary language for the relationship between God and his people. Just as God* is viewed as "Father" and believers as "children," so Paul describes himself as a "father" to his "offspring" in the faith (1 Cor 4:14-15; 2 Cor 12:14; 1 Thess 2:11). This should not be viewed as a patriarchal, even purely paternal, affair but as a parental one (*see* Pastor). Paul also speaks of himself as a "mother" who suffers labor pains (Gal 4:19) and as a nurse who cares for her charges (1 Thess 2:7 cf. 1 Cor 3:2). Instructions to Timothy in the Pastorals (1 Tim 5:2) retain this Pauline emphasis. Though this cluster of metaphors emphasizes the affectionate bond between Paul and his converts, we should not psychologize this as we tend to do in speaking of families today, nor fail to remember the greater influence fathers then had upon their children. This does not entail a childlike dependency of the churches upon Paul. He urged them to "grow up" in Christ and become adults in the faith (e.g., 1 Cor 14:20; Eph 4:14). This involved granting them a considerable degree of autonomy.

Other metaphors in Paul drawn from the world of work, such as builder (1 Cor 3:6-9) and farmer (1 Cor 3:10-15), reveal little by the way of detail about the nature of the relationship between the apostle and his churches. They do, however, stress his fundamental role in starting and designing the church. The metaphor of the body (1 Cor 12:12-27; Eph 4: 1-16), especially the reference to the unifying and structuring role of the "ligaments" (*haphai*), does tell us something about the central role of key people in the church whose primary responsibility is to help maintain unity and engender growth.

*2.2. Primary Models to Follow.* Alongside these metaphors Paul points to specific persons who embody his understanding of authority. Chief among these is Christ.* Christ is certainly presented as a model to believers of how they should care for one another (Rom 15:7; Gal 6:1) as well as engage in mutual instruction and work for harmony in the congregation (Col 3:15-16). Significantly these words are addressed to all members of the church, not just to a core group. Paul also presents himself as a model, precisely because he models himself upon Christ (Acts 20:34-35; 1 Cor 4:16; 11:1; Phil 3:17; 4:9). Believers are also encouraged to imitate those among their number who, like Epaphroditus, "almost died for the work of Christ" (Phil 2:28; *see* Imitation). Even other churches as a whole should be imitated (2 Cor 8:1-7; 1 Thess 1:7-10). Others, like Stephanas and his household who "devote themselves to the service of the saints" (1 Cor 16:15), are not so much held up to be imitated as to be recognized, or to be regarded as the one under whom the people are to "order" their own corporate life. Since the word *household*\* generally refers to slaves, this group in the church at Corinth crosses status lines (*see* Social Setting). Indeed Paul goes on to say that "everyone who joins in the work, and labors

at it" should be so regarded (1 Cor 16:16).

So then, the list of exemplars is open-ended. The criteria for who can become a role model are functional, not formal. It does not depend on a person's being appointed to a position in the church. Paul's emphasis upon models rather than positions itself indicates that it is the person, not the office, that is central for him and that government of the church has more to do with a way of life than a designated post.

Paul does not treat authority, then, as something official or sacral. He views it primarily in relational and functional terms. It does not result in the formation of a leadership elite, formally marked off from others in the church. Only Christ has this distinction and he is the ultimate criterion of who should be regarded as a fundamental role model for others. Aspiring to this is apparently open to a wide range of people, including those with lower social status, and can be embodied in a group as well as individuals.

### 3. Dynamics and Functions.

The social analysis of institutions is interested in examining their dynamics and functions. In considering Paul, we should stress that it is again important to pay careful attention to his language, especially that used to describe the church's gatherings and those who play a significant part in directing its affairs.

*3.1. Range and Diversity of Contributions.* For Paul what happens at church gatherings originates in the Spirit and flows through the whole membership for the benefit of all. Everyone is caught up in this divine operation (1 Cor 12:7). The process itself is described through the use of active verbs to stress its dynamic character: contributions to the meetings are "energized," "manifested" and "distributed" by the Spirit (1 Cor 12:7, 11). He uses a variety of nouns to capture the diversity of what takes place. It is an exercise of "gifts"\* or "presents," a variety of "services" or "ministries," a range of "activities" or "operations" (1 Cor 12:4-6). The concrete speech events and activities that result from this are listed, with differences, three times in Paul's letters (Rom 12:4-8; 1 Cor 12:8-11; Eph 4:11-13). These lists highlight the versatility and diversity of the Spirit's working. Since, for Paul, everyone in church is under an obligation to discern the validity of contributions to the meeting, "liturgy" is fundamentally the people's work (*see* Worship). It is not in the hands of one person, a leadership team or a worship committee, even if certain people play a more prominent role in shaping what takes place, for example, those with greater prophetic or spiritual discernment (1 Cor 12:10; 14:30).

**3.2. Freedom and Form in the Meetings.** Paul does enunciate some guiding principles that should shape members' sensitivity to the Spirit when they come together. Just as in his moral teaching he pursues a principled contextual approach, rather than one based solely on absolutes, so here he exhibits what may be described as a principled charismatic perspective. What takes place should be intelligible, even to outsiders (1 Cor 14:9, 16, 21), constructive or edifying to all the members (1 Cor 14:26; Eph 4:12), under the control of those taking part (1 Cor 14:32), aware of what should have greatest priority (1 Cor 14:6) and be motivated by love* (1 Cor 13:1-3; Eph 4:15). This set of guidelines gives texture to what Paul says about the need for "order" in the meetings. He does not have in mind some spiritual or charismatic free-for-all. If these guidelines are adhered to there is no need for a planned order of service. There is certainly room for the reading of Scripture or apostolic letters,* hymns* and psalms, set doxologies, blessings (see Benediction) and responses, and for creedal confessions or formulas (see Creeds). We do not find here any opposition between the charismatic and liturgical or between spirit and institution, but rather a transcending of these religious and sociological distinctions.

**3.3. The Unofficial Nature of Sacramental Rites.** The central corporate action in Paul's churches was the Lord's Supper.* This was probably a weekly affair and was undoubtedly a full, not just token, meal. The social dynamics of this corporate action match those just described in connection with other aspects of the church's gatherings. Even where abuses are present that divide the congregation and nullify Christ's presence in the meal, Paul calls upon the whole church to take responsible action (1 Cor 11:22, 27) and upon each person to have a proper discernment of other's needs (1 Cor 12:28, 34). Nowhere in Paul's letters, disputed or undisputed, is anyone identified as the presider or celebrant of this meal. Most probably this was undertaken by the host or hostess of the meeting in whose home the meal was being held. Baptism also took place through other than leading figures in a group (1 Cor 1:14-17).

**3.4. Absence of Priests and Clergy.** Reference to certain people in the community playing a greater role than others leads us into a consideration of key people within Paul's churches. Koine Greek abounds in terms for people in official positions in organizations. The word priest (*hiereus*) only appears metaphorically in Paul of a wide range of devotional, compassionate, financial and evangelistic activities (cf. Rom 15:16, 27; Phil 2:17, 25, 30; 2 Cor 9:12), activities in which not only apostles but other Christians engage. This radi-

cally desacralizes the role of those who have a significant part to play in the church and sociologically places early Christianity, like post-Temple Judaism, in a distinctive position vis-à-vis other religions. So far as the language for secular offices is concerned, only one of these terms, *office* (*archē*), appears in Paul's writings but is used exclusively of the governing role played by Christ in the church (Col 1:18). Instead the language of servanthood dominates.

We should note, however, that this language of servanthood did not always conjure up ideas of lowly people undertaking inferior tasks such as waiting on tables. Servants of important social and political figures had considerable status and carried on high-level managerial and bureaucratic work. It is who is one's "master" that is determinative of a servant's status, and many servants had a higher social standing than free men or women who belonged to socially inferior families. Since Christ is the Lord of Christians, this gives a dignity and respect to their servant work that should be respected (see Servant).

**3.5. Emphasis upon Function rather than Position.** Alongside the verb *serve* (*diakoneō*), or its nominal form *servant* (*diakonos*), verbs rather than nouns tend to be used more frequently of those making a fundamental contribution to the church. This means that it is the functions people perform rather than the positions they occupy which is crucial. So, for example, Paul refers to those who "labor," "aid," "admonish" and "teach" (1 Thess 5:12; Gal 6:6). Or, it is the way people have proven themselves (*hoi dokimoi*) through conflict in the church which marks them out from others (1 Cor 11:19). Where nouns are used, as of those who are "helpers" or "administrators" (1 Cor 12:28), they are sometimes given a lower ranking than those who have more dramatic healing* or miracle-working skills. Apart from the Pastoral letters (e.g., 1 Tim 5:1-2; Tit 1:5-9), the term *elders* (*presbyteroi*), referring to older, respected Christians who probably had a corporate responsibility for a cluster of churches in a city, does not occur in Paul's writings (but cf. Acts 14:23). The words *episkopoi* and *diakonoi* appear just once in these writings, in the plural and not presumably as titles (Phil 1:1), and as ancillary to the "saints" in general. In the Pastorals,* where more is said about them, they probably respectively refer to persons hosting a house church and their female assistants or wives (1 Tim 3:1-7, 8-13).

**3.6. Pastoral Care and Family Experience.** As the qualifications listed in the Pastorals indicate, such people as *episkopoi* and *diakonoi* should only be encouraged to function as overseers and helpers in the community if they have first proven themselves in their households and are well regarded in their wider community. This suggests that it was the household, not synagogues or voluntary associations, that provided the basic model for leadership in the church. Also that it was the dealings with people, not—except for some aptitude to teach—the manifestation of charismatic gifts (1 Tim 3:1-11; cf. Tit 1:5-8), that was most determinative. This is the background for such hosts of the churches as Titius Justus (Acts 18:7), Aquila and Priscilla (Rom 16:3), Gaius (Rom 16:23), Nympha (Col 3:15), Philemon and Apphia (Philem 1-2). The social status of such people would provide the basis for their having pre-eminence in the group if, like Stephanas and his household, they "devoted themselves to the service of the saints" (1 Cor 16:15-16). This is not to say that traditional authority here replaces charismatic authority, for these people need more than their status to qualify for this responsibility. What we find is a more dialectical approach to authority, one that gives place to but goes beyond purely charismatic or traditional elements.

Notable is the way Paul names women among this pastoral group, indicating that they often played a significant role in congregational life. Women are also involved in the first group, as among the apostles* (Rom 16:6-7 NRSV) and as prophets* (1 Cor 11:5). For him these are the two most fundamental contributions one can make in church (cf. Eph 2:20; 3:5). Women may also have operated as evangelists (Phil 4:3), while among his associates was a wife-and-husband team involved in at least occasional high-level instruction (Acts 18:26). Here Paul rises above the gender as well as status distinctions of his own time.

## 4. Remuneration and Commissioning.
What kind of reimbursement and acknowledgment did such people receive? We live in a day when people's value is generally indicated by the amount of money they receive and by the official character of the position they hold. This stress upon financial reward and formal position was not without parallel in the first century, but even among other religious groupings these did not have the same significance they possess today. In a consumer-oriented and accreditation-conscious society such factors feature more strongly (*see* Financial Support).

*4.1. Financial Support, not a Salary.* The majority of key people in local congregations appear to have worked independently for a living, as Paul himself frequently did. So, for example, Aquila and Priscilla had their own tentmaking business (Acts 18:3), Lydia was a seller of fabrics (Acts 16:14) and Gaius worked as the city treasurer (Rom 16:23). When Paul refers to the setting aside of money for charitable purposes, it is to help the impoverished saints overseas, not to provide support for the ministry of a local person in the church (1 Cor 16:1-4). According to the evidence of the Corinthian correspondence, Paul does not even avail himself of such recompense when he is with a particular congregation, even though it would be proper for him as an itinerant apostle to do so (1 Cor 9:4-15). Yet he does encourage those who consistently benefit spiritually from others' teaching ministry to share materially with them (Gal 6:6; cf. the analogy in Rom 15:27). This may well be the meaning of the injunction in the Pastorals to give a "double honor" (i.e., "ample remuneration") to elders who do their work well, especially those who focus on teaching (1 Tim 5:17). So, while full-time employment by the local church of pastors, teachers, overseers, and so on, was not a feature of congregational life, some support for those who gave time and effort to serving others was appropriate. These people were not full-time professionals in the church but part-time servants of it who occasionally received, but did not necessarily depend on, reimbursement for their efforts.

*4.2. Ecclesial Recognition but not Ordination.* Ordination, as we know it, does not appear in the Pauline letters. There is reference to laying on of hands, but this was a multi-purpose procedure, used for such diverse procedures as receiving the Spirit (Acts 8:17), healing from illness (Acts 9:17), restoring a person to the church (1 Tim 5:22, though many see here a reference to ordination of elders) and commissioning for itinerant service (Acts 13:2; cf. 2 Tim 1:6). While, according to Acts, Paul and Barnabas* are said to "appoint elders" in every church (Acts 14:23), this could have involved ratifying the community's choice, as was earlier the case with the laying on of hands upon the Seven (Acts 6:3-4, see probably also Acts 16:2). The word *appoint* can certainly be used in this way. When in his undisputed writings Paul identifies certain people in the church in Corinth as having a fundamental contribution to its life, he merely asks the congregation to "order themselves" (*hypotassesthe*) under such people, and instructs them to extend this attitude "to everyone who joins in the work, and labors at it" (1 Cor 16:16). This suggests a non-formal, community-based recognition, one based on the quality of the ministry people are already engaged in rather than on any external qualifications. Moreover it is always a group that is referred to when the local church is in view, indicating that pastoral work in the congregation was always a corporate rather than solo affair (cf. Acts 20:17).

## 5. Apostles and Colleagues.

What role did the apostle* and his associates play in ordering and governing the affairs of the churches they founded? From what has been noted already they obviously played a vital role, but in what areas and of what kind? If the relationship between the churches and Paul was an interdependent affair, not independent or dependent, let alone codependent, where and how were the lines drawn and how, sociologically, would we describe this relationship today (*see* Co-workers)?

*5.1. The Extent and Limits of Apostolic Authority.* Paul played a visible role in the birth and ongoing life of the churches he founded. With other churches he cannot and does not assume a pre-eminent position (cf. Rom 1:11-13). But he also distinguished between the churches themselves and his work which brought them into existence. This is not the same distinction as that between sodalities and modalities that has become widely used in missionary circles. In sociological terms, a congregation was a "community," an organic phenomenon focusing primarily on the quality of its common life and the overflow of that into the lives of others. Paul's work, and that of other apostles, was an "association," with its primary focus outside itself on evangelism and church planting.

*5.2. The Language of Persuasion not Command.* So then, the main day-to-day ordering and governing of affairs of Paul's churches lay in the hands of the congregations themselves. In churches, as at Philippi, where things were going relatively well, Paul could address problems without reminding them of his foundational role in their life or of his apostolic authority. In other churches, as at Corinth, where things were not going so well and his role was under challenge, Paul had to remind his converts of his seminal role in their life (1 Cor 4:15) and, from a distance at least, play a more directive part in their affairs. But nowhere does he exhibit an authoritarian stance. Generally in his writings he is more concerned that his converts should "imitate" rather than "obey" him (cf. also 1 Thess 3:6; 1 Cor 11:1; Gal 4:12; Phil 3:17), and his instruction is consistently expressed through the language of an "appeal" (1 Cor 4:16) based on love (Philem 8) rather than, except occasionally, of "command" (cf. 1 Cor 14:37). His rare calls for obedience have more to do with responding appropriately to his loving urgings (2 Cor 2:9), remaining faithful to the gospel* (Philem 21; cf. Phil 2:12) or yielding to the promptings of the Spirit (1 Thess 4:8).

*5.3. Christ not Apostles the Fundamental Authority.* All this is in accord with certain characteristic features of Paul's method of operation. Having left with them the gospel (1 Cor 15:3), certain basic instruction (1 Thess 4:1) and his own example (Acts 20:34-35)—as well as the OT Scriptures (1 Cor 14:34), certain sayings of Christ (1 Cor 7:10) and several rules operating in all his churches (1 Cor 11:16)—he is confident that his communities now have the resources to mature in their common life. He is there if they need advice on certain matters (e.g., 1 Cor 7:1; 1 Thess 4:13) and will occasionally visit them to see how they are doing (Acts 15:36). In a situation requiring discipline,* he can still "lay down the line," not however as an external, hierarchical authority so much as a significant fellow member whose spirit is present in their deliberations even when he is absent (1 Cor 5:3-5; Col 2:5). Even those with little status have the wisdom to deal with some disputes in the community (1 Cor 6:4-5), though on other occasions the whole church should do so (1 Cor 5:1-5). His aim is to build up the community's ability to look after such matters, "working with" them rather than "lording it over" them (2 Cor 1:24). If he is forced to confront them, the "rod" that he brings is the rod of the "word" (2 Cor 10:3-6), and his preference is to come "with love in a gentle spirit" (1 Cor 4:21). His basic authority stems from the gospel he has been commissioned to preach, not by right from his apostolic commission itself. Only so long as his words reflect that gospel (Gal 1:9), or are in accord with the Spirit (1 Cor 7:40), should his churches give him a hearing. His authority is instrumental not inherent and, though powerful because of God's call, subject to his converts' Christian discernment.

*5.4. The Derivative Power of Paul's Colleagues.* Associates such as Timothy and Titus have only functional or derived authority, based upon the reputation of the work they have undertaken or upon transmitting Paul's message to his churches. They do not have any automatic right of entry. Often he has to argue their case, pointing out their involvement with him and knowledge of his affairs as well as their fidelity to the apostolic task, sometimes at risk to their own lives (Phil 2:19-23; Col 4:7-8; 1 Cor 8:17, 23; 16:10-11). When visiting churches these colleagues have a role to play but as itinerants (cf. 2 Cor 7:15), not in some resident capacity.

The Pastoral Letters are revealing here. Although there are hints that they reflect a later, more structured state of affairs, Paul's associates still have no settled, formal role in the congregations but an ambassadorial, exemplary one (1 Tim 2:12-15; 6:11-12; 2 Tim 1:8; 2:22-24; 3:10; Tit 2:7). They are to relate to people in the churches in a familial way, reflecting their limited age and experience, rather than from a position of command (1 Tim 5:1-2). They provide instruction on how the churches are to order certain aspects of their worship and govern themselves, but they do not provide regulations to control these (1 Tim 3:6; 2 Tim 2:2-7; Tit 2:1-9). The key roles in the congregations are to be taken up by proven individuals and couples within their own ranks (1 Tim 3:1-13; Tit 1:5-9), which Paul's associates could only help identify through knowledge provided by the churches themselves.

Clearly, for all his close ties with his churches, Paul gave them considerable freedom to develop their own life and to do so in ways that were not identical to one another. Diversity within unity is the rule here as well. To view the Pastorals as changing and routinizing this situation is to ignore the temporary nature of his associates' role in these churches. Some degree of formalizing appears to have taken place, as for example in what is said about women, but this may have been partly induced by certain local problems. For all that, the Pastorals still breathe much the same air as the other Pauline letters.

### 6. Conclusion.

Did Paul's understanding of church order and government undergo development during his lifetime? Occasional attempts have been made to plot this but, given the summary nature of much that he wrote, and the indirect evidence we have of the contexts he was addressing, it is difficult to draw definite conclusions. No doubt his understanding did grow as he dealt with the different problems he encountered. But the main lines of his approach are clearly discernible in his earliest writings. So while we should always be open to detecting changes of emphasis or even content in his treatment of these issues, we are unlikely to find a great deal or be able to plot a simple learning trajectory. It is easier to identify certain differences between what is said in the undisputed writings and in the Pastorals, though even there more caution is needed than is often exercised.

*See also* APOSTLE; AUTHORITY; BODY OF CHRIST; CHURCH; COWORKERS, PAUL AND HIS; DISCIPLINE; FELLOWSHIP, COMMUNION, SHARING; FINANCIAL SUPPORT; GIFTS OF THE SPIRIT; HOLY SPIRIT; HOUSEHOLDS AND HOUSEHOLD CODES; IMITATION OF PAUL/OF CHRIST; MAN AND WOMAN; MINISTRY; PASTOR, PAUL AS; POWER; SERVANT, SERVICE; WORSHIP.

BIBLIOGRAPHY. R. Banks, *Paul's Idea of Community: The Early Churches in Their Historical Setting* (Grand Rapids: Eerdmans, 1980); E. Best, *Paul and His Converts* (Edinburgh: T. & T. Clark, 1988); M. M. Bourke, "Reflections on Church Order in the New Testament," *CBQ* 30 (1969) 161-79; V. Branick, *The House Church in the Writings of Paul* (Wilmington: Michael Glazier, 1989); U. Brockhaus, *Charisma und Amt* (Wuppertal: Brockhaus, 1975); J. N. Collins, *DIAKONIA: Re-interpreting the Ancient Sources* (New York: Oxford, 1990); H. Doohan, *Leadership in Paul* (Wilmington: Michael Glazier, 1984); K. Giles, *Patterns of Ministry Among the First Christians* (Melbourne: Collins Dove, 1989); J. Hainz, *Ekklesia: Strukturen paulinischer Gemeinde-Theologie und Gemeinde-Ordnung* (Regensburg: Pustet, 1972); A. E. Harvey, "Elders," *JTS* 25 (1974) 315-32; B. Holmberg, *Paul and Power: Authority in the Primitive Church as Reflected in the Pauline Epistles* (Philadelphia: Fortress, 1980); E. Käsemann, "The Cry for Liberty in the Worship of the Church," in *Perspectives on Paul* (Philadelphia: Fortress, 1971) 122-37; M. Y. MacDonald, *The Pauline Churches: A Socio-historical Study of Institutionalisation in the Pauline and Deutero-Pauline Writings* (SNTSMS 60; Cambridge: University Press, 1988); W. A. Meeks, *The First Urban Christians: The Social World of the Apostle Paul* (New Haven: Yale University, 1983); W. Munro, *Authority in Peter and Paul* (New York; Cambridge University, 1983); P. Perkins, *Ministering in the Pauline Churches* (New York: Paulist, 1982); J. H. Schütz, *Paul and the Anatomy of Apostolic Authority* (New York: New York University, 1975); E. Schüssler-Fiorenza, *In Memory of Her* (Philadelphia: Westminster, 1983); E. Schweizer, *Church Order in the New Testament* (London: SCM, 1964); H. von Campenhausen, *Ecclesiastical Authority and Spiritual Power in the Church of the First Three Centuries* (London: A. & C. Black, 1969); A. Warkentin, *Ordination: A Biblical Historical View* (Grand Rapids: Eerdmans, 1982).

R. Banks

## CIRCULATION OF PAUL'S LETTERS. *See* CANON.

## CIRCUMCISION

Paul's insistence that circumcision not be imposed on Gentile* converts led to one of the most serious and fundamental controversies in the early church. The controversy over Paul's stance on circumcision is reflected in Acts 15, the letters to the Galatians* and to the Romans,* Philippians 3 and perhaps Colossians 2.

1. The View of Paul's Opponents on Circumcision
2. Paul's Response to His Opponents
3. The Circumcision of Timothy and Titus

### 1. The View of Paul's Opponents on Circumcision.

Those who opposed Paul on the circumcision question have traditionally and probably rightly been called Judaizers.* Judaizers were Jews who confessed Jesus as Messiah,* believing also that the Mosaic Law* and particularly the rite of circumcision should be required of Gentiles. The views of the Judaizers are explicitly cited in Acts 15:1, 5 and can be inferred from Galatians, Philippians 3 and Romans 2:25-29; 4:1-12.

**1.1. The Scriptures.** The Judaizers found support in the OT for their understanding of circumcision, for Genesis 17:9-14 says that circumcision was the covenant sign for the people of God, and that refusal to take on the covenant sign would result in being cut off from the people of God. Moreover, Genesis 17:13 specifies that this covenant is an "everlasting" one. Therefore, the Judaizers probably concluded from Genesis 17 (see also Ex 4:24-26; Lev 12:3; Josh 5:2-9) that circumcision was an indispensable sign of the covenant, and thus they taught that "unless you are circumcised according to the custom of Moses,* you cannot be saved" (Acts 15:1).

**1.2. Other Jewish Literature.** Evidence from extrabiblical literature also shows that the majority of Jews considered circumcision as necessary for conversion (cf. Esther 8:17 LXX; Jdt 14:10; Josephus *Ant.* 13.9.1 §§257-258; 13.11.3 §§318-319; 20.2.4 §§38-41; *J.W.* 2.17.10 §454; Philo *Mig. Ab.* 89-93). J. Nolland *contra* N. J. McEleney argues persuasively that in the intertestamental period circumcision was typically required for one to become a proselyte to Judaism. Moreover, during the reign of Antiochus Epiphanes Jews had practiced circumcision at the risk of losing their lives (1 Macc 1:60-61; cf. 2 Macc 6—7). Thus any diminution of the rite would naturally inflame both the cultural and religious passions of Jews.

## 2. Paul's Response to His Opponents.

This brief examination of the OT and the intertestamental period demonstrates that circumcision was considered to be crucial for membership in the people of God. The question that arises is, How could Paul defend the idea that Gentiles could be part of the people of God without being circumcised? Paul marshalled at least four arguments for his position.

**2.1. Argument from the Spirit.** The presence of the Spirit* in the lives of the Galatian believers, apart from their being circumcised, proved that circumcision was unnecessary for membership in the people of God (Gal 3:1-5). No one could be a part of the new community who has not received the Spirit (Rom 8:9), and since God had seen fit to give the Galatians the Spirit apart from circumcision, it followed that circumcision was not essential for membership among the people of God (cf. Acts 15:8-9).

**2.2. Argument from the Scriptures.** In order to convince Jewish believers of the tenability of his theology, Paul had to defend his view from the OT. Paul pinned his case on Abraham,* arguing from Genesis 15:6 that Abraham was justified by faith, not by his performance of the Law (Gal 3:6-9; Rom 4:1-8). Indeed, circumcision could not have been decisive for Abraham's entrance into the people of God because Abraham was already righteous in God's sight *before he was circumcised* (Rom 4:9-12). In this latter passage, Paul claims that circumcision was a "seal" (*sphragis*) of Abraham's righteousness* by faith gained before he was circumcised, indicating that righteousness does not depend on circumcision. Circumcision as a seal ratifies and confirms one's faith. Abraham was circumcised so that he could be the father of Jewish believers in the covenant God, and his righteousness by faith prior to circumcision made him the father of Gentile believers in Christ (Rom 4:11-12).

**2.3. Argument from Salvation History.** Paul's view of circumcision raises the question of the place of the Law in salvation history. Granted that Abraham was righteous before he was circumcised, objectors might still point out that the OT commands circumcision. In Galatians 3:15—4:7 Paul provides his perspective on salvation history (cf. also 2 Cor 3:4-18).

The Mosaic covenant, as a means by which the people of God were identified, was never intended to be in force forever. It was a temporary covenant designed for an interim period until the promise that was made to Abraham reached its fulfillment. Now that the Christ has come the promise made to Abraham has been fulfilled, and thus the covenant with Moses is no longer in force. Paul considered circumcision to be part of the covenant with Moses, and so he concluded that since the Mosaic covenant was no longer operative, circumcision was unnecessary. Moreover, the arrival of the new covenant (Jer 31:31-34; Ezek 36:26-27), which is really a fulfillment of the covenant made with Abraham, involved the outpouring of the Holy Spirit who enables believers to fulfill what circumcision in the OT pointed to—inclusion in the people of God. For now the true circumcision, the circumcision of the heart, has become a reality (Rom 2:28-29; Phil 3:3).

In Paul's thinking circumcision and the Law are intertwined in yet another way. Those who think they can be righteous before God by receiving circumcision (Gal 5:2-6; Phil 3:2-11)—that is, by doing the works of the Law*—are deceived. No one can be justified by the works of the Law (Gal 3:1-5, 10-14), for no one can perform perfectly the works required by the Law.

**2.4. Argument from the Cross.** P. Borgen has also pointed out that for Paul the cross* had replaced circumcision as the way of entrance into the people of God. In Galatians Paul wages a consistent polemic against circumcision and the Law because they diminish the cross (Gal 1:4; 2:21; 3:1, 13; 5:11; 6:12, 14). And the context of Colossians 2:11-14 suggests that Jesus' death is portrayed as his circumcision in Colossians 2:11, indicating that the new circumcision for believers is accomplished in the cross.

### 3. The Circumcision of Timothy and Titus.

The explanation offered above explains why Paul refused to circumcise the Gentile Titus (Gal 2:3-5). The requirement of circumcision for salvation* was a compromise of the gospel* of grace* and a denial of the arrival of the age of fulfillment. Paul's decision to circumcise Timothy (Acts 16:3) consequently seems inconsistent, and many scholars claim that the incident is not historically credible. The traditional resolution of this problem postulates that Paul did agree to circumcise Timothy since Timothy's mother was Jewish. This would, according to Jewish Law, make Timothy a Jew. According to this interpretation, Paul circumcised Timothy for cultural reasons so that he could bring his Jewish brother with him into synagogues when he preached the gospel.

S. J. D. Cohen, however, has raised three objections to this common resolution. (1) The most natural reading of Acts 16:3 is that Timothy was circumcised because he was a Gentile, not because he was a Jew, for Luke does not inform the reader that Timothy's mother was Jewish in this verse but simply says that "they all knew that his father was Greek." (2) Most interpreters from the second to the eighteenth century believed that Timothy was a Gentile. (3) There is no firm pre-mishnaic evidence that in Jewish circles a son born to a Jewish mother and a Gentile father was considered a Jew.

C. Bryan has shown that Cohen's conclusion is not as convincing as it appears on first examination. Acts 16:1 introduces Timothy by saying that "he was the son of a Jewish woman who was a believer." Since Luke particularly notes that Timothy was the son of a Jewish woman and a Greek father, he has hinted to the reader before he describes Timothy's circumcision in verse 3 that the latter's national status is ambiguous. Moreover, it is difficult to see how the circumcision of Timothy as a Gentile fits the Lukan story line. In Acts 15 Paul has just won a victory over those who would require circumcision of Gentile converts, and in Acts 16:4 he delivers the results of this decree to the churches. It contradicts the Lukan context if in Acts 16:3 he portrays Paul as circumcising the Gentile Timothy contrary to the decree.

Nevertheless, Cohen is right in asserting that there is no evidence contemporary with the NT that sons of a Jewish mother and a Gentile father were legally considered Jewish. Such a fact is not damaging to the theory that Paul circumcised Timothy because the latter was considered to be Jewish. The Rabbinic Law on the status of children born to a Jewish mother and a Gentile father was probably established by early in the second century of the Common Era, and thus it is likely that in the previous century there was ongoing discussion and uncertainty about the status of such cases. Paul agreed to circumcise Timothy because there was some doubt regarding his nationality. He wanted to show that he did not forbid circumcision if there was any connection with the Jewish people. Thus by circumcising Timothy Luke shows that Paul did not forbid Jews from practicing the Law (Acts 21:21-26; cf. 1 Cor 9:19-23). Paul had no animosity toward circumcision as a cultural practice; neither circumcision nor uncircumcision were anything significant in themselves (Gal 5:6; 6:15; 1 Cor 7:19). But when circumcision was required for salvation, then Paul resisted it adamantly.

*See also* ABRAHAM; LAW; WORKS OF THE LAW.

BIBLIOGRAPHY. J. M. G. Barclay, *Obeying the Truth: A Study of Paul's Ethic in Galatians* (Edinburgh: T. & T. Clark, 1988) 45-60; P. Borgen, "Observations on the Theme 'Paul and Philo': Paul's Preaching of Circumcision in Galatia (Gal 5:11) and Debates on Circumcision in Philo," in *The Pauline Literature and Theology*, ed. S. Pederson (Göttingen: Vandenhoeck & Ruprecht, 1980) 85-102; idem, "Paul Preaches Circumcision and Pleases Men," in *Paul and Paulinism: Essays in Honour of C. K. Barrett*, ed. M. D. Hooker and S. G. Wilson (London: SPCK, 1982) 85-102; C. Bryan, "A Further Look at Acts 16:1-3," *JBL* 107 (1988) 292-94; S. J. D. Cohen, "Was Timothy Jewish (Acts 16:1-3)? Patristic Exegesis, Rabbinic Law, and Matrilineal Descent," *JBL* 105 (1986) 251-68; G. F. Dowden, "Circumcision of Christ," *CQR* 162 (1961) 400-407; M. E. Glasswell, "New Wine in Old Wine Skins: VIII, Circumcision," *ExpT* 85 (1974) 328-32; N. J. McEleney, "Conversion, Circumcision and the Law," *NTS* 20 (1974) 319-41; R. Meyer, "Περιτέμνω κτλ," *TDNT* VI.72-84; J. Nolland, "Uncircumcised Proselytes?" *JSJ* 12 (1981) 173-94; W. O. Walker, "The Timothy-Titus Problem Reconsidered," *ExpT* 92 (1981) 231-35.

T. R. Schreiner

## CITATIONS OF OLD TESTAMENT. *See* OLD TESTAMENT IN PAUL.

## CITIZENSHIP, ROMAN AND HEAVENLY

Roman citizenship was a matter of considerable advantage for travel* in the Mediterranean world of the first century. Paul's Roman citizenship greatly enhanced his ministry. His acquaintance with the issues of citizenship allowed him to use it as a fitting metaphor for participation in the kingdom* of God.

1. Roman Citizenship
2. Heavenly Citizenship

## 1. Roman Citizenship.

The biblical case for Paul's legal standing as a Roman citizen rests primarily on three texts in Acts. Paul's mention of the Roman citizenship he and Silas enjoyed provides the context for their release from jail in Philippi (Acts 16:37-39). Then at the end of his speech before the people in Jerusalem, Paul's citizenship is once again helpful in allowing for his protection by the Roman garrison from the angry crowd (Acts 22:25-29). At his hearing in Caesarea before Festus over two years later, after Festus offered to conduct a full trial back in Jerusalem, Paul used his right as a Roman citizen to reject the offer and to appeal for trial before Caesar (Acts 25:7-12). Agrippa II mentions this appeal to Festus after Paul testifies before them (Acts 26:32).

*1.1. Paul's Roman Citizenship.* Arguments advanced against Paul's Roman citizenship, most recently by Stegemann, have been soundly answered by Hengel. Roman historians also accept Paul's citizenship as most probable. According to traditions preserved in Jerome (Philemon commentary; *Vir.* 5) and Photius (*Quaest. Amphil.* 116), Paul's parents were carried off as prisoners of war from the Judean town of Gischala to Tarsus. Presumably enslaved to a Roman, they were freed and granted citizenship. The rights of a Roman citizen included *provocatio* (the right to appeal after trial), *muneris publici vacatio* (exemption from imperial duties such as military service), and the right of an accused citizen to choose either a local or a Roman trial. A right that was usually (but not always) honored in the provinces was that Roman citizens were exempt from flogging. The best explanation for Paul's silence about his Roman citizenship in Philippi until after his scourging (Acts 16:22-23) is that he wanted to follow Jesus in suffering* (Phil 3:10-11; Col 1:24; 2 Cor 4:7-10; 6:4-10). It is likely that there were other occasions also in which Paul kept silent and so surrendered this Roman right (2 Cor 11:25). When Paul did claim Roman citizenship (Acts 16:37; 22:25-28), it is most likely that he produced as evidence a birth certificate or certificate of citizenship, which Roman citizens carried with them.

*1.2. Paul's Appeal to Caesar.* Against Lyall and Sherwin-White, the evidence favors Garnsey's reconstruction of Paul's appeal not as a *provocatio* appeal, but as

a rejection of one court in favor of another (*reiectio*). This was a right Paul had as a Roman citizen, subject to Festus's approval. Garnsey notes that Acts 25 is the only example ever cited for evidence of *provocatio* before trial. Elsewhere such an appeal always occurs after trial. A close reading of Acts 25:9-12 shows that what is at issue is the location for Paul's trial. Paul did not want to be tried in Jerusalem as Festus suggested, for it was there that he was first imprisoned because of Jewish antipathy (Acts 22:22-29) and because it was clear that Festus wanted to please the Jews (Acts 25:9). It is also clear that Paul's rejection of trial in Jerusalem for trial in Rome was not automatically accepted. Festus only agreed after conferring with his advisors (Acts 25:12), for he had the authority to override Paul's plea. What occurred in Caesarea was not a complete trial, therefore, but a preliminary hearing. Paul's appeal to Caesar was not simply because he wanted to go to Rome, but also because he did not want to stand trial in Jerusalem.

*1.3. Implications of Paul's Roman Citizenship.* As a Roman, Paul writes of his mission plans with a map of the Roman Empire in mind (Rom 15:19, 24) and gives no indication that he plans to evangelize in places outside the Empire's boundaries. His Roman citizenship shows in his recognition that citizens were accountable for two kinds of taxes, *tributum* (direct taxes) and *vectigalia* (sales taxes on slave transactions and customs fees), as Romans 13:7 shows, making use of comparable Greek terms for these taxes. The fact that his section on obedience to the government ends with tax payment shows his own recognition that taxes were a duty (*munus*) one carried as a citizen, and an unpopular one at that time (cf. Tacitus *Ann.* 13.50-51). Other language in Romans that perhaps indicates Paul's Roman citizenship includes his allusion to Roman military policy when he describes his apostolic commission in Romans 1:5 and his acknowledgement of the Roman preoccupation with legal matters (Rom 7:1). But in most of Paul's letters he does not give evidence of his Roman citizenship, for to him another citizenship was more important.

## 2. Heavenly Citizenship.

While explicit language related to heavenly citizenship is rare in Paul, the metaphor of heavenly* citizenship is clearly an influential force in his theology. In both ethical injunctions and eschatological descriptions, it is clear that Paul uses this citizenship to describe the believer's participation in the kingdom of God.

*2.1. Ethical Injunctions.* Paul's idea of heavenly citizenship is communicated with full cognizance of his church members' participation in their local societies as citizens (1 Cor 5:9-10; Rom 13:1-7). In this sense it is possible that Paul has in mind the legal status of dual citizenship (see Phil 1:27). The fact that Christians are citizens of both earth and heaven leads to Paul's ambassadorial language in 2 Corinthians 5:18-21 and Ephesians 6:19-20. As citizens of heaven, Christians have the responsibility to think consistently with their citizenship (Col 3:1-4) and live holy* lives (Rom 13:12-14). Paul's own idea of his heavenly citizenship allowed him to live in a way that freed him to be all things to all people (1 Cor 9:19-23). Paul's doctrine of heavenly citizenship and its implications for living are close to 1 Peter 2:11, although Paul does not use the metaphor of sojourning as strongly as Peter. Philippians 3:20 (in the light of Phil 1:27) provides the best example of heavenly citizenship terminology in Paul. This citizenship here provides the ground for Paul's commands to avoid thinking in an earthly way (Phil 2:3-4; 3:19), and instead to follow his example (Phil 3:17) as befits one who rejoices in God's goodness, praying and thinking in a God-centered way (Phil 4:1-9). The description of Christians' heavenly citizenship in Philippians 3:20 also is linked to the expectation of the *parousia* and the physical transformation to occur at that time (Phil 3:20-21).

*2.2. Eschatological Descriptions.* The sense that Christians are headed for a citizenship in the next life is a powerful force in Paul's theology. Thus we see in 1 Thessalonians 4:13—5:24 how an understanding of the rights and destiny of the heavenly citizen leads to a certain pattern of behavior. In Romans 8:12-30, the prospect of participation as a citizen in the new creation* is inextricably linked both to one's status as a child of God and the concomitant behavior that such future citizenship and adoption* necessarily implies for the present. Paul's eschatological understanding of heavenly citizenship includes the conviction that the Christian is not ultimately subject to death, and ought therefore to live for values that will outlast life on earth (1 Cor 15:53-58).

*See also* CIVIL AUTHORITY; LEGAL SYSTEM, ROMAN; POLITICAL SYSTEMS.

BIBLIOGRAPHY. J. D. G. Dunn, *Romans 9-16* (WBC 38B; Waco: Word, 1988); P. Garnsey, "The *Lex Iulia* and Appeal under the Empire," *JRS* 56 (1966) 167-89; M. Hengel, *The Pre-Christian Paul* (Philadelphia: Trinity Press International, 1991); F. Lyall, *Slaves, Citizens, Sons: Legal Metaphors in the Epistles* (Grand Rapids: Zondervan, 1984); A. N. Sherwin-White, *The Roman Citizenship* (2d ed.; Oxford: Clarendon, 1973); idem, *Roman Society and Roman Law in the New Testament: The Sarum Lectures 1960-1961* (Oxford: University Press,

1963; repr. ed., Grand Rapids: Baker, 1978); W. Stegemann, "War der Apostel Paulus ein römischer Bürger?" *ZNW* 78 (1987) 200-29; H. Strathmann, "πόλις κτλ," *TDNT* VI.529-35.

M. Reasoner

# CIVIL AUTHORITY

Civil authority is the centralized control in society whose power to formulate and to enforce the basic formal rules of the society is granted to it by the groups which possess social power. Paul's teaching regarding civil authority is not direct or comprehensive but comes in the context of correcting misunderstandings of the freedom* of the gospel. He experienced persecution from civil authorities but also appealed to them for protection.

1. Civil Authorities
2. Romans 13:1-7

## 1. Civil Authorities.

The civil authority ranged from the emperor* to governors (proconsuls, procurators and kings) (representing the emperor) to civil magistrates carrying out local rule (*see* Political Systems). The local rule in Judea included the high priest and the Sanhedrin.* According to the presentation in Acts,* the role of government in the persecution of Paul came from local authorities (Acts 16:22-24; 24:1-8; cf. 1 Thess 2:2). (The severe punishments in 2 Cor 11:25 may be cases of civil authorities disregarding the limits of their authority.) The incident related in Acts 14:5 has the character of mob action. More commonly, Paul is shown to have found civil authority as a source of deliverance (Acts 23:10). He appeals to his rights as a Roman citizen (Acts 16:37; 21:39; 22:25; *see* Citizenship). As such he was entitled to trial in Rome for statutory charges (*see* Legal System). He accordingly appealed to the emperor (Acts 25:10-12, 25). The picture of Roman citizenship in Acts is quite compatible with our knowledge of the mid-century period, which it fits better than it does the situation at the end of the century. In addition it should be noted that serving in municipal office apparently was acceptable conduct for a believer (Rom 16:23).

## 2. Romans 13:1-7.

The occasion for Paul's mention of civil authority in Romans 13:1-7 most likely was a recurring problem faced by him in his missionary preaching*: the temptation of some to use their Christian freedom in a way deemed to violate responsible social relationships with respect to marriage,* labor and slavery (*see* Slave, Slavery), or to see themselves as freed from moral codes. As earlier in Romans he had to deal with undue freedom from the Mosaic Law* (Rom 6:15), Paul in Romans 13 deals with undue freedom from civil law.

1 Corinthians 6 provides an example of the element of freedom in Paul's message and its potentiality to create the problem faced in Romans 13. Paul admonishes his readers not to sue one another in the civil courts (see Lawsuit). He reminds them of their eschatological role of ruling the world, and describes the civil authorities as "unjust" (1 Cor 6:1) and "unbelievers" (1 Cor 6:6). In 1 Peter 2:16, a passage parallel to Romans 13:1-7, Peter makes the issue of freedom explicit: "[Subordinate yourselves] as free persons and not using your freedom as a covering for vice, but as slaves of God" (1 Pet 2:16). Although this problem could easily have occurred in the church at Rome,* the occasion as one of responsibility within Christian freedom fits well the interpretation of Romans as a letter dealing with general problems of Christians among Paul's churches. His emphasis upon paying the tribute (phoros, Rom 13:6) would support the churchwide reference since this tax on subject peoples was not collected in the capital.

Other hypotheses regarding the occasion of Romans 13:1-7 suggest special situations in Rome. Tacitus mentions tax protests under Nero in A.D. 58 (Tacitus Ann. 13.50-51). Earlier (c. A.D. 49-50), Claudius had expelled the Jews from Rome for "disturbances at the instigation of Chrestus" (Suetonius Claudius 25.4). The suggestion is made that Chrestus (an alternative spelling for Christus) had been a messianic pretender. With increased turmoil in Palestine, Paul in A.D. 56 warned the Christians, who had close contacts with the Jewish community, against involvement in a repetition of such insurrection or against associated tax protests. The motivation behind such actions of disobedience, it is proposed, would have been a just protest; not vice or antinomianism. The general hypothesis is weakened, however, not only by its speculative character but also by the fact that on the one hand Tacitus cites the tax petitions as an example of Nero's popular spirit of clemency and gives no evidence of insubordination or antigovernment resistance. On the other hand, there is little evidence of later disturbances among Jews in Rome related to the Palestinian turmoil, even during the Jewish Revolts.

The close parallels between Romans 13 and 1 Peter 2:13-17 indicate the likelihood that both authors used common tradition, probably derived from Hellenistic Judaism.

Romans 13:1-7 comes within a framework determined by Romans 12:1-2. Subordination to civil government, particularly in the symbolic act of paying taxes, is an aspect of the call to spiritual worship* in the everyday life of the world. The injunction is to be subordinate (hypotassō, Rom 13:1; cf. Tit 3:1), putting one's own interest below what is required for relationships with the civil authorities. The subordination is a discriminating one supported by conscience* (syneidēsis, Rom 13:5). The civil authorities at all levels are agents of God.* Their service to God is at the same time for the people, restraining evil and promoting their good (Rom 13:4). Paul does not identify his conception of the good (to agathon), but the Hellenistic-Jewish and OT conception of the ruler is pastoral and paternal in character. In a later Pauline text, 1 Timothy 2:2, the civil authorities are said to be instruments of a peaceful order which the author may consider to be instrumental for the missionary task (1 Tim 2:4; see Mission).

The negative perspective on authorities is most clearly implied in Paul's conception of the "principalities and powers,"* angelic beings who have responsibility for God's creation,* including its government (Dan 10:13, 20-21; 12:1), but who, from the Jewish apocalyptic* viewpoint, are fallen. In Romans 8:35, 38-39 Paul links these powers with the persecution of believers. In speaking of angelic powers Paul employs the terminology commonly used for human political powers, but the context is determinative of meaning. It should not be assumed that because Paul employs these terms in Romans 13 or 1 Corinthians 2:8, he is there referring to angelic, cosmic powers and not to human political powers.

See also CITIZENSHIP, ROMAN AND HEAVENLY; EMPERORS, ROMAN; ETHICS; FREEDOM; LAWSUIT; LEGAL SYSTEM, ROMAN; POLITICAL SYSTEMS; PRINCIPALITIES AND POWERS.

BIBLIOGRAPHY. M. Borg, "A New Context for Romans xiii," NTS 19 (1973) 205-18; C. J. Cadoux, The Early Church and the World: A History of the Christian Attitude to Pagan Society and the State Down to the Time of Constantinus (Edinburgh: T. & T. Clark, 1925); C. E. B. Cranfield, A Commentary on Romans 12-13 (SJT Occasional Papers 12; Edinburgh: Oliver & Boyd, 1965); J. Friedrich et al., "Zur historischen Situation und Intention von Röm 13, 1-7," ZTK 73 (1976) 131-66; D. Georgi, Theocracy in Paul's Praxis and Theology (Minneapolis: Fortress, 1991); E. Käsemann, "Principles of the Interpretation of Romans 13," in New Testament Questions of Today (Philadelphia: Fortress, 1969) 196-216; S. C. Mott, Biblical Ethics and Social Change (New York: Oxford University, 1982); B. Reese, "The Apostle Paul's Exercise of His Rights as a Roman Citizen as Recorded in the Book of Acts," EvQ 47 (1975) 138-45; E. G. Selwyn, The First Epistle of St. Peter (2d ed.;

Grand Rapids: Baker, [1947] 1981 reprint); A. N. Sherwin-White, *Roman Society and Roman Law in the New Testament* (Oxford: University Press, 1963) 48-119; W. Wink, *Naming the Powers: The Language of Power in the New Testament* (Philadelphia: Fortress, 1984).

S. C. Mott

**CLEAN.** *See* PURITY AND IMPURITY.

## COLLECTION FOR THE SAINTS

The specific campaign which Paul led to collect funds to relieve the poverty of the Jerusalem* church is commonly called "the collection for the saints." While on the surface the general notion of the collection is quite simple, the question of Paul's purpose leads to some complex issues. Paul calls the collection a "fellowship"* (*koinōnia*, Rom 15:26; see Hainz), "service"* (*diakonia*, Rom 15:25, 31; 2 Cor 8:20; 9:1, 12, 13), "gift" (*charis*, 1 Cor 16:3; 2 Cor 8:6, 7, 19), "generous gift" (*eulogia*, 2 Cor 9:5), "collection" (*logeia*, 1 Cor 16:1), "liberal gift" (*adrotēs*, 2 Cor 8:20) and "service that you perform" (*hē diakonia tēs leitourgias*, 2 Cor 9:12). 2 Corinthians 8:4 uses three terms at once: "they urgently pleaded with us for the *privilege* (*charis*) of *sharing* in this *service* to the saints" (on the terms, see Dahl, 37-38).

1. The Data for the Collection
2. The Historical Context for the Collection
3. The Purpose of the Collection
4. The Results of the Collection

### 1. The Data for the Collection.

Paul's second visit to Jerusalem, recorded in Galatians 2:1-10 (and probably Acts 11:27-30; 12:25), resulted in a sort of peace accord that sought to demonstrate the unity of the gospel* alongside a diversity of audience. Paul, it was decided, would work among the Gentiles* while Peter* carried on his ministry among the Jews. The Jerusalem "pillars" asked Paul only that he would continue to remember the "poor" (Gal 2:10). Paul assured them that he was most willing to do so. This exhortation reflects the Jerusalem leaders' perception of the need for the Diaspora* communities to help with the economic problems in Jerusalem, and, indeed, the occasion of Paul's second visit to Jerusalem (which may correspond with the occasion of his receiving this exhortation) was to help in the relief of the "saints" (cf. Acts 11:27-30). Little did the Jerusalem leaders know that their suggestion would become Paul's *obsession* for nearly two decades. Some scholars have also detected an allusion to the collection in Galatians 6:6-10 (Hurtado).

Evidently, as soon as Paul left Jerusalem and began his second missionary journey throughout the northern Mediterranean, he started a campaign for funds to relieve the poverty of the Jerusalem community ("saints" is Paul's reference to Jewish Christians). (A traditional view of Pauline chronology is assumed here; for another view, see Luedemann.) The next trace we find of his concern comes in 1 Corinthians 16:1-4, where we learn that Paul had been encouraging others among his churches to set aside funds weekly in an orderly fashion so when he arrived there would be a full allotment for the saints. There we also learn that official representatives from each church would accompany the funds to Jerusalem.

Paul's second letter to the Corinthians contains two chapters that are largely devoted to the collection for the saints (2 Cor 8—9). Included in these directions are such things as the need for generosity (2 Cor 8:12; 9:5-11), the goal of equality (2 Cor 8:13-15) and the need for careful administration of the funds (2 Cor 8:18-21). Finally, Paul mentions the collection in his letter to the Romans. At Romans 15:27 he speaks to the ultimate socio-theological purpose of the campaign: "If Gentiles have shared in the Jews' spiritual blessings, they owe it to the Jews to share with them their material blessings" (NIV). But Paul may have worried over its reception, for he says, "Pray that I may be rescued from the unbelievers in Judea and that my service in Jerusalem [*hē diakonia mou hē eis Ierousalēm*] may be acceptable to the saints there" (Rom 15:31). Paul apparently saw the collection as his sacrificial offering to the Jerusalem community (see Hill, 177-78).

The evidence in Acts complements these data. There we learn that Paul was most eager to arrive in Jerusalem before Pentecost (Acts 20:16), although he was unsure of what would happen (Acts 20:22). This latter comment by Luke may well reflect Paul's concern about the response of the Jerusalem church, for Paul thought the credibility of his mission and the unity of the church were at stake. Later, before Felix, Paul says that he had come to Jerusalem "to bring my people gifts for the poor and to present offerings" (Acts 24:17; perhaps Felix thought that Paul still had the money and hoped for a bribe from Paul; cf. Acts 24:26).

From both the book of Acts and Paul's letters we can discern the magnitude of Paul's campaign, for it appears that Paul was able to derive both funds and sponsors from all his churches. Thus he had the following funds and/or people representing his missionary efforts: from the Galatian region (1 Cor 16:1) we hear of Derbe (Acts 20:4) and Lystra (Acts 20:4); from Macedonia (2 Cor 8:1-5; 9:2, 4) we hear of Berea (Acts

20:4), Thessalonica (20:4) and Philippi (cf. Acts 16:16 and 20:6; an inference about the "we" sections of Acts; see Nickle, 68); from Achaia we hear of Corinth (Rom 15:26; 1 Cor 16:1-4); from Mysia and Lydia we hear of Ephesus (Acts 20:4) and perhaps Troas (Acts 20:5-6); it is possible that funds came from Tyre (Acts 21:3-4), Ptolemais (Acts 21:7), and from both Cyprus and Caesarea (Acts 21:16). It is even possible that funds were collected from Rome (cf. Rom 12:13; 15:26 with 2 Cor 8:4; 9:13; and Rom 1:13 with 2 Cor 9:6-10). It is hard to imagine any campaign more embracing of the northern Mediterranean and any project that occupied Paul's attention more than this collection for the saints.

Perhaps the most puzzling aspect of the evidence from Acts is its almost total silence regarding the collection campaign (cf. Acts 24:17). Luke's silence, no doubt, is to be explained by recourse to Luke's designs; he obviously did not think descriptions of it were necessary for his purposes. M. Hengel wryly notes that "Luke does not always say everything that he knows, and when he does, he can mention facts which are important—to us—only in passing" (Hengel, 119). Some have suggested that Luke did not bring it up because it ended in failure or because the collection led to charges that Paul was taking money from the Temple* tax itself. The absence of any reference to it in Acts 15 shows that the collection was largely stimulated by Paul and not by the Jerusalem authorities. They did not seek the Gentile funds; the collection was Paul's attempt to show the unity of the church. It is indeed probable that many Jerusalem leaders did not even see the generous funds as something that demonstrated the unity of the church.

The complexity of the evidence is apparent. Involved in Paul's collection were the credibility of his apostolic mission* and the legitimacy of the Gentile mission (Gal 2:1-10), the recognition of the priority of Israel* in God's redemptive plan (Rom 15:27), the goodwill of Christian communities (2 Cor 8—9), as well as the need for individual Christians to trust in God to supply their needs if they were to give generously (2 Cor 9). It is likely that the collection itself gained different theological arguments as Paul's ministry developed and as his relationship to Jerusalem shifted back and forth.

## 2. The Historical Context for the Collection.

*2.1. Conditions in the Jerusalem Church.* The historical occasion for the collection of Paul was *the poverty of the Jerusalem church.* Scholars have traced several possible causes of this poverty (Martin, 256): (1) the relief of more and more widows (Acts 6:1-7); (2) the pilgrim-ages to Jerusalem of both the elderly and Galileans, who burdened the communities; (3) the potential problems arising from Jerusalem's early experimentation with communal life (Acts 4:32—5:11); (4) the economic hardships caused by famine (Acts 11:27-30); and (5) the personal stresses due to economic persecutions (cf. Jas 1:9; 2:6-7; 5:1-6). Whatever the underlying reasons, one thing remains sure: the churches in Jerusalem were poor and in need of relief (see Jeremias, 87-144; Goppelt, 25-60). Paul assumed the task of demonstrating his commitment to the founding community in Jerusalem by campaigning for relief funds (*see* Riches and Poverty).

*2.2. Administration of the Collection.* The precise mode of administering funds to the mother church seems to have been similar to the procedures of the Jewish Temple tax and its attendant gifts that were annually offered at the feasts of Passover, Pentecost and Tabernacles (see Nickle, 74-99). We now know that Diaspora Jews regularly helped support the Jerusalem Temple by sending in the annual two-drachma tax. Along with this, Jews seemed regularly to have added some supplementary gifts (*aparchai*; see Sanders, 49-51, 283-308). The Temple tax, so it seems, was carefully monitored and protected by Roman authorities (Josephus *Ant.* 14.10.2-8 §§190-216) and we can only surmise that the funds Paul was collecting were related somehow to this Temple tax payment. Thus, it is possible that Paul encouraged the Christian communities throughout the Mediterranean to set aside gifts for the Christian community in Jerusalem along with their Temple tax. He, along with sponsors from each church, would accompany the funds and hand them over to the Temple and to the Jerusalem community so as to ensure that each was given to the proper authority.

Paul's evident concern for the administration of the collection may have had two fronts: (1) his concern that the Jerusalem authorities should know for whom the funds were intended and (2) his concern that the Roman authorities might question the legitimacy of such gifts. (We assume that Roman authorities would have been nervous about too much money leaving individual districts.) In a classic essay K. Holl went so far as to argue that the Jerusalem Church exercised its prerogative and right to tax the Diaspora Gentile churches, although his view is seen today as an exaggeration of the situation.

## 3. The Purpose of the Collection.

Scholars have debated vigorously the precise purpose of Paul's campaign to collect funds for the saints in Jerusalem. Of the various proposals, four can be mentioned.

**3.1. Help for the Poor.** The traditional viewpoint has been that Paul wanted to help the poor Christians in Jerusalem (cf. Gal 6:10) as a demonstration of the love* of God* that the Gentiles had found in Christ (2 Cor 8:8-9, 19; 9:12-15). In general, the collection was charity in that it might create "equality." As Paul wrote to the Corinthians, the collection was so that "at the present time your plenty will supply what they need, so that in turn their plenty will supply what you need. Then there will be equality" (2 Cor 8:13-14).

Paul teaches elsewhere that love of Christ and others ought to motivate believers to show compassion (Gal 5:6, 14; 6:10; 1 Cor 13; 2 Cor 5:14; Rom 12:13). Thus Paul's motivation is love for the churches of Christ, and in this he follows in a long line of deeds of mercy so typical of ancient Judaism (Ex 23:10-11; Deut 14:28-29; 24:19-22; *m. Pe'a* 1:2, 4; see *Str-B* 4.1.536-610; Nickle, 93-95), the teaching of Jesus (Lk 6:20-21; Mt 6:2-4; 11:2-6) and the early church (Acts 2:43-47; 4:32-37; 6:1-7). Paul's campaign could well have been motivated by little more than his Jewish piety and his desire to see the economic stress in Jerusalem alleviated (Nickle, 100-111). Yet other motives are also feasible.

**3.2. Unity of the Church.** Scholars have recognized that Paul's collection was motivated by more than providing aid for the poor (though that would have been motivation enough). Hand in hand with providing aid, Paul was motivated to demonstrate to Jerusalem that, just as there was one Lord* and one gospel,* so there was one church.* That church was comprised of both Gentiles in the Diaspora and Jews in Judea. Paul wanted to show that his gospel was in harmony with the Jerusalem churches, and so a gift from his churches would demonstrate their thanksgiving to God for the covenant* he had made with Israel. This perspective on the collection is explicitly stated in Romans 15:27: "For if the Gentiles have shared in the Jews' spiritual blessings, they owe it to the Jews to share with them their material blessings."

This motivation, no doubt, greatly influenced Paul. Many interpreters have detected some nervousness on the part of Paul, and it was his concern for Jerusalem's acceptance of the collection as a demonstration of their acceptance of his "Law-free" gospel that caused the anxiety (Rom 15:31; see Dunn 1988, 2.879-80). The tension between Paul and Jerusalem, whether or not it was only between Paul and factions in Jerusalem, is well known and well documented and need not be enlarged upon here (cf. Gal; Acts 15; 21:28-29; see Nickle, 112-15; Dunn 1991; *see* Opponents).

On Paul's part, there was a battle going on over the proper definition of the gospel of Jesus Christ (Galatians). Contrary to Peter's actions at Antioch (Gal 2:11-14) and the message of the Judaizers (cf. Gal 3:1-5), there was but one gospel that was to be accepted by faith* (not by works* of the Law) and this gospel of Christ did not need supplementation from the Law of Moses. Further, there was a continual emphasis upon the internal unity of the church, which is achieved in the Spirit who creates the body* of Christ (1 Cor 12:4-31; Eph 2:11-22). This unity owed its origins, of course, to the Jewish nation (Rom 9:1-5; 10:1-4; 11:1-6, 17-24) and to the Jerusalem community (Rom 15:27; Acts). For these three reasons—the singularity of the gospel, the organic unity of the church, and the temporal priority of the Jewish people in God's redemptive plan—the church should act as a unity. This gave Paul a theological foundation for his collection.

Accordingly, Paul urged his churches to give voluntarily (1 Cor 16:1; 2 Cor 8:3, 8, 11-12; 9:1-5) and generously (2 Cor 8:2-4; 9:6-15) as a demonstration to the Jerusalem churches that the Gentile Christians of the Diaspora wanted to be involved in the relief efforts and, in so doing, to show to the mother church (Acts 24:17) their thanksgiving for their spiritual heritage (Rom 15:27; Dahl). Thus the presented collection would be "proof of your love" (2 Cor 8:24).

In fact, several have observed that the collection was the culminating act of Paul's apostolic ministry in the East (Bartsch). Paul describes the collection as the "fruit" and "seal" of his ministry as he now prepares for a wider ministry to Spain (Rom 15:23-24, 28). We may infer from this that the collection and its successful presentation in Jerusalem were together to be the crowning jewel of the first phase of his apostolic ministry (the only phase he actually completed).

It ought to be observed that Paul's perception(s) of his collection may not have been identical to those of the Jerusalem churches. The Jerusalem believers may well have seen the gifts and funds as obligations on the part of the Gentile churches and as the Gentiles' expression of their dependence upon the founding churches. They may have argued that, since they had salvation-historical priority, they also had rights to support from the newer areas (cf. Rom 15:27; see Holmberg).

**3.3. Substitute for Jewish Entry Rites.** Although this view is not been held by many, K. Berger argues that the collection itself was seen as almsgiving on the part of the Diaspora Gentile church and, as such, was seen as a substitute action for their sacrifices and circumcision.* Money gifts for Israel were seen as the act whereby the Gentile demonstrated his or her allegiance to the covenant of Abraham* and to the people of Israel (Sir 29:12; 40:24; Tob 4:10-11; 12:9; 14:11; Acts 10:2, 35). According to Berger's hypothesis, the collected funds and gifts were a symbol of the Gentile commitment to Israel and its Law, a visible sign of their recognition of the priority of the Jewish nation in salvation-history. Such would have been Paul's argument if he had so regarded the collection.

*3.4. Eschatological Provocation.* The unbelief of Israel was problematic to Paul, and he looked and longed for the day when Israel would turn to its Messiah, Jesus Christ.* Paul did not doubt that that day would come (Rom 11:25-26). Paul believed, furthermore, that the salvation* of the Gentiles would turn out for the conversion of Israel (Rom 11:11-24; cf. 11:9-11 in general; *see* Restoration of Israel). Some have contended that the collection fits into this scheme (Munck; Nickle, 129-142; Bruce, 22-25): the presentation by Paul and his retinue of Gentile sponsors of the funds to the Jerusalem churches would provoke the nation of Israel to believe in the Messiah, for they would see in that act the fulfillment of the promise that the Gentiles would bring gifts to Zion (Is 2:2-4; 60:6-7, 11; Mic 4:13; see McKnight, 47-48). Thus the collection was for Paul an eschatological provocation of Israel; by it he hoped to convert Israel to faith in the Messiah. It is possible that this is the meaning of 2 Corinthians 9:10: borrowing language from Isaiah 55:10, Paul contends that the gifts of the Corinthians will actually turn out to enlarge their harvest (the conversion of Israel?). This view might also lie behind 2 Corinthians 9:11-12, where the increase of thanksgivings could refer to the conversion of Israelites (*see* Eschatology).

We are probably on firmest ground if we recognize that Paul might have had more than one purpose in conducting the collection for the saints. It may well be that what began as largely an adventure in charity became, as a result of growing tensions, an act of theological unity and eschatological provocation. We can hardly be certain about these matters.

### 4. The Results of the Collection.
Neither Luke nor Paul tell of the results of the offering of the collection. Paul never mentions it in any of his extant later correspondence. However, Luke records the trip and the period during which the collection was handed over to the leaders. His first few lines may reveal that the collection was received with profound gratitude. Acts 21:17-26 speaks of the church receiving them "warmly" (Acts 21:17). Paul and his retinue greeted the Christian leaders, especially James,* in Jerusalem (Acts 21:18) and Paul then declared what God was doing in the Gentile world (Acts

21:19). Luke states that "when they heard this, they praised God" (Acts 21:20). Then they asked Paul to demonstrate his commitment to the Law and to the Jewish people by undertaking a vow of purification, which he did—perhaps gladly (Acts 21:21-26). We can probably infer from this that the collection was received with gratitude, with perhaps some residual suspicions regarding the Gentile Christians' commitment to the Law* (a suspicion which may have lingered for some time thereafter).

Some scholars, however, have argued that the collection did not accomplish its purposes. The saints remained poor, the act of charity notwithstanding; the tension between Jewish Christians and Gentile Christians continued; and the conversion of Israel never took place. The presence of those Gentiles who aided in the collection led to the very occasion for Paul's arrest (Acts 21:29). While we must contend that Israel did not convert, we must also say that it is not entirely clear that Paul saw the conversion of Israel as a major motivation for his collection. Furthermore, there is no evidence that Paul thought all traces of poverty would be eliminated. Paul was realistic enough, we might suppose, to realize that his collection of funds, as large as it may have been, would not alter permanently the economic conditions of Christians. Finally, Paul's gospel may have continued to remain a sore spot for the Jerusalem Christians; but we have no traces in the concluding chapters of Acts that the Jerusalem Christians refused to stand behind him. Relations between Jewish and Gentile churches probably remained in tension, but we must also accept the implications of what such a gift might have communicated. There can be no doubt that the majority of Judean Christians would have been greatly impressed by the generosity of the Diaspora Christians and, therefore, would have drawn the conclusion that the church has one gospel, one Lord and one Spirit—even if that same church was characterized by a considerable amount of diversity.

*See also* CORINTHIANS, LETTERS TO THE; FELLOWSHIP, COMMUNION, SHARING; FINANCIAL SUPPORT; GENTILES; ISRAEL; JERUSALEM; LOVE; MISSION.

BIBLIOGRAPHY. H.-W. Bartsch, ". . . wenn ich ihnen diese Frucht versiegelt habe. Röm 15:28," *ZNW* 63 (1972) 95-107; K. Berger, "Almosen für Israel," *NTS* (1976-77) 180-204; F. F. Bruce, "Paul and Jerusalem," *TynB* 19 (1968) 3-25; N. A. Dahl, "Paul and Possessions," in *Studies in Paul* (Minneapolis: Augsburg, 1977) 22-39; W. D. Davies, *The Gospel and the Land* (Berkeley: University of California, 1974) 195-208; J. D. G. Dunn, *Romans* (WBC 38; Dallas: Word, 1988); idem, *The Partings of the Ways* (Philadelphia: Trinity

Press International, 1991); D. Georgi, *Remembering the Poor: The History of Paul's Collection for Jerusalem* (Nashville: Abingdon, 1992); L. Goppelt, *Apostolic and Post-Apostolic Times* (London: A. & C. Black, 1970); J. Hainz, *Koinonia: 'Kirche' als Gemeinschaft bei Paulus* (BU 16; Regensburg: F. Pustet, 1982) 123-61; M. Hengel, *Acts and the History of Earliest Christianity* (Philadelphia: Fortress, 1979) 118-19; C. C. Hill, *Hellenists and Hebrews* (Minneapolis: Fortress, 1992) 173-78; K. Holl, "Der Kirchenbegriff des Paulus in seinem Verhältnis zu dem der Urgemeinde," in *Gesammelte Aufsätze zur Kirchengeschichte* (Tübingen: J. C. B. Mohr, 1928) 2.44-67; B. Holmberg, *Paul and Power* (Lund: CWK Gleerup, 1978) 35-44; L. W. Hurtado, "The Jerusalem Collection and the Book of Galatians," *JSNT* 5 (1979) 46-62; J. Jeremias, *Jerusalem in the Time of Jesus* (Philadelphia: Fortress, 1969); G. Luedemann, *Paul, Apostle to the Gentiles: Studies in Chronology* (Philadelphia: Fortress, 1984) 77-100; S. McKnight, *A Light Among the Gentiles: Jewish Missionary Activity in the Second Temple Period* (Minneapolis: Fortress, 1991); R. P. Martin, *2 Corinthians* (WBC 40; Waco: Word, 1986) 256-58; J. Munck, *Paul and the Salvation of Mankind* (Atlanta: John Knox, 1959); K. F. Nickle, *The Collection: A Study in Paul's Strategy* (SBT 48; Naperville: Allenson, 1966); E. P. Sanders, *Jewish Law from Jesus to the Mishnah* (Philadelphia: Trinity Press International, 1990); F. Watson, *Paul, Judaism and the Gentiles* (SNTSMS 56; Cambridge: University Press, 1986) 174-76; J. R. Willis, "Collection," in *Dictionary of the Apostolic Church*, ed. J. Hastings (New York: Charles Scribner's Sons, 1916) 1.223-25.                                    S. McKnight

**COLLECTION OF PAUL'S LETTERS.** *See* Canon.

**COLOSSAE.** *See* Colossians, Letter to the.

**COLOSSIAN HERESY.** *See* Colossians, Letter to the; Opponents of Paul.

## COLOSSIANS, LETTER TO THE

Colossians, one of Paul's shortest letters, was written to the infant church at Colossae in the Lycus valley of the province of Asia. This Christian community had not been founded by Paul but came into existence during his Ephesian ministry (c. A.D. 52-55; *see* Ephesus) through the efforts of Epaphras, one of his colleagues. Although not a theological treatise, Colossians has much to say about the importance of the gospel, the person and work of the Lord* Jesus Christ,* especially as Lord in creation* and author of reconciliation (Col 1:15-20; *see* Peace, Reconciliation),

the people of God, eschatology,* freedom* from legalism and the Christian life.

1. Colossae and Its Citizens
2. The Church at Colossae
3. The Occasion of the Letter
4. The Threat to Faith and the "Colossian Heresy"
5. Paul's Handling of the Colossian Philosophy
6. Some Critical Questions

### 1. Colossae and Its Citizens.

*1.1. The City.* The ancient city of Colossae was situated 100 miles east of Ephesus in Phrygia on the southern bank of the river Lycus (in modern Turkey), and its fertile valley produced large crops of figs and olives. Colossae lay on the main road from Ephesus and Sardis to the Euphrates. In the fifth and fourth centuries B.C. it was described as populous, large and wealthy, its commercial significance being due to its wool industry. Later the city declined in importance so that in Roman times it had become a "small town" (Strabo *Geog.* 12.8.13, though the text is debatable) and had been surpassed by Laodicea and Hierapolis which were also in the Lycus valley. By the time Paul wrote to the Christians living at Colossae the commercial and social importance of the town was already on the wane, though coins and inscriptions attest to the civic life of the town in the second and third centuries A.D.

*1.2. Its People.* Laodicea, Hierapolis and Colossae belonged to the proconsular province of Asia. Colossae's population consisted mainly of indigenous Phrygian and Greek settlers, but in the early part of the second century B.C. two thousand Jewish families from Babylon and Mesopotamia were settled in Lydia and Phrygia by Antiochus III (Josephus *Ant.* 12.3.4 §§147-53). According to grave inscriptions in the area Jews had become part of the Asian culture by the first century B.C. So the Colossae of Paul's day seems to have been a cosmopolitan place in which differing cultural and religious elements mingled.

### 2. The Church at Colossae.

The believers at Colossae, who are addressed as faithful brothers and sisters in Christ (Col 1:2), were not converted through the ministry* of Paul himself. This Christian community had come into existence during a period of vigorous missionary and evangelistic activity (*see* Mission) associated with Paul's Ephesian ministry (c. A.D. 52-55) recorded in Acts 19. But the apostle himself during his missionary work in Asia Minor had not reached Colossae in the upper valley of the Lycus (cf. Col 2:1). His daily evangelistic "dialogues" held in the hall of Tyrannus in Ephesus were so effective that

Luke can claim "all the residents of Asia heard the word of the Lord, both Jews and Greeks" (Acts 19:10). While the work was directed by Paul, he was assisted by several coworkers* through whom a number of churches were planted in the province of Asia. Among these were the congregations of Colossae, Laodicea and Hierapolis, which, we infer, were the fruit of Epaphras's evangelistic efforts (Col 1:7; 4:12, 13). Epaphras, a native of Colossae (Col 4:12), who may have become a Christian during a visit to Ephesus, was "a faithful minister of Christ" and as Paul's representative (Col 1:7) he had taught the Colossians the truth of the gospel.*

The many allusions to the non-Christian past of the readers suggest that most of them were Gentile* converts. They had once been utterly out of harmony with God, enmeshed in idolatry* and slavery to sin,* being hostile to God* in mind and godless in their actions (Col 1:21; cf 1:12, 27). They had been spiritually dead because of their sins and "the uncircumcision of . . . [their] flesh"—a statement which indicates they were both heathen and godless (Col 2:13).

But God had effected a mighty change in their lives: he had reconciled them to himself in an earth-shattering event, namely, Christ's physical death* on the cross* (Col 1:22). He had delivered them from a tyranny of darkness and transferred them into a kingdom* in which his beloved Son* ruled (Col 1:13). They now possessed redemption* and the forgiveness* of sins (Col 1:14; 2:13; 3:13).

Because the congregation had received Christ Jesus the Lord as their tradition* (parelabete, Col 2:6) when they accepted the gospel at the hands of Epaphras, they are admonished to conduct their lives as those who have been united to Christ in his death and resurrection.* Since Christ Jesus was a more-than-adequate safeguard against empty human traditions, they are urged to see to it that their way of life and thought conform continually to Christ's teaching (Col 2:6-8).

The picture is therefore drawn of a Christian congregation obedient to the apostolic gospel and for which the apostle* can give heartfelt thanks to God (Col 1:4-6). He knows of their love* "in the Spirit" (Col 1:8) and was delighted to learn of their orderly Christian lives and the stability of their faith* in Christ (Col 2:5).

### 3. The Occasion of the Letter.

Epaphras had paid Paul a visit in Rome (see 6.2 below) and informed him of the progress of the gospel in the Lycus valley. While much of the report was encouraging (cf. Col 1:8; 2:5), one disquieting feature was the attractive, but false, teaching that had recently been introduced into the congregation and which, if it went unchecked, would subvert the gospel and bring the Colossians into spiritual bondage. Paul's letter then is written as a response to this urgent need. Perhaps Epaphras found it difficult to cope with the specious arguments and the feigned humility of those spreading this teaching, and so needed the greater wisdom of the apostle.

### 4. The Threat to Faith and the "Colossian Heresy."

*4.1. Was There a "Colossian Heresy"?* Nowhere in the letter does the apostle give a formal exposition of the "heresy"; its chief features can be detected only by piecing together and interpreting his positive counterarguments. Several recent scholars have questioned whether these counterarguments point to the existence of a "Colossian heresy" at all. They prefer to speak in terms of tendencies rather than a clear-cut system with definite points and suggest that the young converts were under external pressure to conform to the beliefs and practices of their Jewish and pagan neighbors (Hooker). This view rightly stresses Paul's positive statements about the life and stability of the congregation (Col 1:3-8; 2:5) and warns against the danger of arguing in a circle when reconstructing the situation behind Paul's writings. However, in the light of Colossians 2:8-23 with its references to "fullness,"* specific ascetic injunctions (Col 2:21), regulations about food and holy days (see Holy Days), unusual phrases which seem to be catchwords of Paul's opponents and the strong emphasis on what Christ has *already achieved* by his death and resurrection, it seems appropriate to speak of a "heresy" which had just begun to make some inroads into the congregation.

*4.2. Some Distinguishing Marks of the "Heresy."* The teaching was set forth as "philosophy"* (Col 2:8), based on "tradition" (paradosis denotes its antiquity, dignity and revelational character), which was supposed to impart true knowledge* (Col 2:18, 23). Paul seems to be quoting catchwords of the opponents in his attack on their teaching: "all the fullness" (Col 2:9); "delighting in humility and the worship* of angels,*" "things which he has seen upon entering" (perhaps "entering into visions"; Col 2:18); "Don't handle, don't taste, don't even touch!" (Col 2:21); and "voluntary worship," "humility" and "severe treatment of the body" (Col 2:23). Further, the keeping of these taboos in the "philosophy" was related to obedient submission to "the elemental spirits of the world" (Col 2:20; see Elements/Elemental Spirits).

*4.3. Interpreting These Distinguishing Marks.* No complete agreement has been achieved among scholars as to the nature of the teaching. Basically the heresy seems to have been Jewish, because of the references to food regulations, the Sabbath* and other prescriptions of the Jewish calendar. Circumcision* is mentioned (Col 2:11) but did not appear as one of the legal requirements. (Wright argues for an exclusively Jewish background to the heresy.)

But what kind of Judaism? Apparently it was not the more straightforward kind against which the Galatian* churches had to be warned, but was one in which asceticism and mysticism* were featured and where angels and principalities played a prominent role in creation and the giving of the Law.* They were regarded as controlling the communication between God and man, and so needed to be placated by keeping strict legal observances.

A number of important suggestions has been made as to the nature of the Colossian "philosophy," ranging from a pagan mystery cult (Dibelius) and a syncretism of gnosticized Judaism and pagan elements (Bornkamm)—the "worship of angels" (Col 2:18) was regarded as a pagan element in the false teaching, but should be understood as "the angelic worship [of God]"—to Essene Judaism of a gnostic* kind (Lightfoot) and Judaizing syncretism (Lyonnet).

Many recent scholars, however, consider that the false teaching, which advanced beyond Epaphras's elementary gospel, is to be read against the background of ascetic and mystical forms of Jewish piety (as evidenced, for example, at Qumran*). It was for a spiritual elite who were being urged to press on in wisdom and knowledge so as to attain true "fullness." "Self-abasement" (Col 2:18, 23) was a term used by opponents to denote ascetic practices that were effective for receiving visions of heavenly mysteries* and participating in mystical experiences. The "mature" were thus able to gain entrance into heaven and join in the "angelic worship of God" as part of their present experience (Col 2:18).

### 5. Paul's Handling of the Colossian Philosophy.

Although there is a build-up in Paul's presentation in the first chapter, it is not until Colossians 2:4 ("I am saying this in order that no one may deceive you with persuasive language") that the apostle *expressly* points to the dangers facing the congregation. He is aware of the methods of the false teachers and issues a strong warning to the Colossians to be on their guard lest they be carried off as spoil (Col 2:8, *sylagōgeō*, "kidnap, carry off as booty," is a rare and vivid word, showing just how seriously Paul regarded the evil designs of those seeking to influence the congregation); these spiritual charlatans were trying to ensnare them by their "philosophy and empty deceit" (Col 2:8). Al-

though they set forth their teaching as "tradition," Paul rejects any suggestion of divine origin. It was a human fabrication ("according to *human* tradition") that stood over against the tradition of Christ—the tradition which stems from the teaching of Christ, which also finds its embodiment in him (Col 2:6).

In a magnificent passage of praise exalting Christ as the Lord in creation and reconciliation (Col 1:15-20), Paul asserts that Christ is the one through whom all things were created, including the principalities and powers (*see* Principalities and Powers) which figured so prominently in the Colossian heresy. All things have been made *in* him as the sphere, *through* him as the agent and *for* him as the ultimate goal of all creation (Col 1:16).

Those who have been incorporated into Christ have come to fullness of life in the one who is master over every principality and power (Col 2:10). They need not seek perfection anywhere else but in him. It is in him, the one in whose death, burial and resurrection they have been united (Col 2:11-12), that the totality of wisdom* and knowledge is concentrated and made available to all his people—not just an elite group.

Christ Jesus is the sole mediator between God and humankind. The Colossians are not to be misled by the false teachers into thinking it was necessary to obey the angelic powers who were said to control the communication between God and humankind. That way was now controlled by Christ who by his death is revealed as conqueror of the principalities and powers (Col 2:13-15; *see* Triumph).

The apostle's criticisms of the advocates of the Colossian philosophy, with their false notions and aberrant behavior, are devastating (Col 2:16-23). Because of their legalism, the false teachers failed to recognize God's good gifts and his purpose in giving them, namely, that all of them should be enjoyed and consumed through their proper use (Col 2:22). The things covered by the taboos were perishable objects of the material world, destined to pass away when used. The taboos themselves, which belonged to a transitory order (Col 2:17), were merely human inventions that laid no claim to absoluteness but stood over against the revelation of the will of God (cf. Col 2:22). To place oneself under rules and regulations like those of Colossians 2:21 is to go back into slavery again—under the personal forces overthrown by Christ (Col 2:20). By his death he had freed the Colossians from bondage to the principalities and powers. They must not turn their backs on that life-changing event. Although the prohibitions (cf. Col 2:21) carried a reputation for wisdom in the spheres of voluntary worship, humility and severe treatment of the body, these practices were in fact spiritually and morally bankrupt. Such energetic endeavors could not hold the flesh in check. Instead, these self-made regulations actually pandered to the flesh* (Col 2:23).

In his reply to the false teaching Paul expounds the doctrine of the cosmic Christ more fully than in his earlier letters (see Christology). Hints had previously appeared in Romans 8:19-22 and 1 Corinthians 1:24; 2:6-10; 8:6 but a more detailed exposition is given in Colossians 1:15-20 and 2:13-15. Against the false teachers who boasted in their exalted spiritual experiences, their fresh revelations and their participation in the divine fullness, the apostle's criticisms are trenchant: they are arrogant and in danger of being separated from Christ (Col 2:18-19).

In his handling of the Colossian false teaching Paul places his emphasis on realized eschatology* (see especially Col 2:12; 3:1-4). Within the "already-not yet" tension the stress is upon the former, called forth by the circumstances of the letter. The Colossians have a hope laid up for them in heaven (Col 1:5; cf. 3:1-4), they have been fitted for a share in the inheritance of the saints in light (Col 1:12), having already been delivered from a tyranny of darkness and transferred into the kingdom of God's beloved Son (Col 1:13). Not only did they die with Christ; they were also raised with him (Col 2:12; 3:1; cf. 3:3). Although the "not yet" of salvation does feature in the letter (esp. Col 3:4), the "already" needed to be asserted again and again over against those who were interested in "fullness" and the heavenly* realm, but who had false notions about them, believing they could be reached by legalistic observances, a special knowledge, visionary experiences and the like (see Visions). Christ has done all that was necessary for the Colossians' salvation. They had died with Christ, been raised with him and given new life with him (see Dying and Rising with Christ). Let them now zealously seek the things above (Col 3:1-2), that new order centered on the exalted Christ (see Exaltation), and let them as a consequence show true heavenly-mindedness (cf. Col 3:5, 8, 12 and 3:18—4:1).

### 6. Some Critical Questions.

**6.1. Authorship.** The letter makes clear that the apostle Paul is the writer, not only in the opening greeting (Col 1:1), but also in the body of the letter (Col 1:23) and at its conclusion (Col 4:18). The character of Paul, as we know it from other letters, shines throughout this letter. There was no dispute over the authenticity of Colossians in the early period of the church, and the letter was included in Marcion's canonical list as

well as in the Muratorian canon (see Canon). However, the Pauline authorship has been challenged on a number of occasions in the last one hundred and fifty years. The grounds presented concern the language and style of the letter, and the supposed differences between Colossians and the theology of the main Pauline epistles.

**6.1.1. Language and Style.** Many of the formal features of Colossians show similarities with the other Pauline letters, including its structure (the introduction, Col 1:1-2; conclusion, Col 4:18; and thanksgiving prayer,* Col 1:3-8), connecting words and phrases (Col 2:1, 6, 16; 3:1, 5) as well as the list of messages and greetings (cf. Col 4:8, 10, 12, 15).

Many expressions are Pauline in style: for example, the superfluous use of "and" after "therefore" (Col 1:9; cf. 1 Thess 2:13; 3:5), phrases like "his saints" (Col 1:26; cf. 1 Thess 3:13) "in regard to" (Col 2:16; cf. 2 Cor 3:10; 9:3), as well as verbs such as charizomai, with the meaning "to forgive" (Col 2:13; 3:13; cf. 2 Cor 2:7, 10). The similarities extend to the theological terminology such as "in Christ"* (Col 1:2, 4, 28), "in the Lord" (Col 3:18, 20, etc.), expressions about being united with Christ in baptism* (Col 2:11, 12), about being freed from the power of the regulations (Col 2:14, 20, 21), the contrast between the old and the new person (Col 3:5-17), and the relation between the indicative and the imperative in exhortations (Col 3:5-17).

Yet there are linguistic differences between Colossians and the other Pauline letters: thirty-four words appear in Colossians but nowhere else in the NT, twenty-eight words do not occur in the other Pauline letters, and ten words Colossians has in common only with Ephesians. But in assessing these statistics it ought to be borne in mind that many of these words appear in the hymnic* paragraph of Colossians 1:15-20 or in interaction with the false teaching, either as catchwords of the Colossian philosophy or as part of the author's polemic. Further, hapax legomena and unusual expressions turn up in considerable numbers in the other Pauline letters; the absence of a word or concept may be due to the different subject matter being discussed.

Characteristic features of style, as distinct from vocabulary, include liturgical material with long clauses introduced by relative pronouns, inserted causal and participial phrases, combined and synonymous expressions ("strengthened with all power," Col 1:11; "praying and asking," Col 1:9), a series of dependent genitives ("the word of truth, of the gospel," Col 1:5) and loosely joined infinitival constructions ("to walk worthily of the Lord," Col 1:10).

These stylistic peculiarities have been understood as evidence of an author who, for all his dependence on Paul, argues differently from the apostle (so Bujard). But such a judgment appears to be unduly negative and presupposes an almost infallible understanding of what Paul could or could not have written. Further, it does not explain the close similarities between Colossians and the generally accepted Pauline letters. Rather, the stylistic peculiarities would seem to have their basis in the letter's content which is clearly connected with the particular situation which necessitated the letter.

*6.1.2. Teaching.* For scholars such as E. Lohse the supposed theological differences between Colossians and the generally accepted Pauline letters are decisive against the apostolic authorship of Colossians, even if the grounds of language and style are not. Some have argued that the post-Pauline author's christology belonged to a later period of church history when classical Gnostic influences had begun to assert themselves. But it is unnecessary to resort to full-blown Gnostic influences of the second century as a possible background. If a Jewish background of an ascetic mystical kind is likely, then there is no need to look beyond the apostolic age, and certainly Pauline authorship is not ruled out on this account.

The objections to Paul's authorship on the grounds of theology are:

*6.1.2.1. Christology.* It has been claimed that Colossians develops its christology* on the basis of Colossians 1:15-20 and goes beyond Paul's statements in 1 Corinthians 8:6 and Romans 8:31-39 in its teaching that in Christ the entire fullness of deity dwells "bodily" (Col 2:9) and that he is the "head* of every principality and power" (Col 2:10). But this latter statement spells out the implications of Colossians 1:15-20, which is central to the letter, while Colossians 2:9 applies the words of the hymn to the Colossian situation, making clear how the entire fullness of deity dwells in Christ, that is, in bodily form by his becoming incarnate. The cosmic dimension of Christ's rule is a fuller and more systematic exposition of the theme of Christ's universal lordship that is found in Paul's earlier letters (1 Cor 8:6; cf. Col 1:24; 2:6-10), and it is spelled out in relation to and as a correction of the false teaching at Colossae. There is no need to look for an author other than Paul as the source of such ideas.

*6.1.2.2. Ecclesiology.* The notion of Christ as the "head of the body, the church" is said to reflect a post-Pauline development. In 1 Corinthians 12:12-27 and Romans 12:4-5 Paul uses the body (*see* Body of Christ) terminology and its constituent parts to refer to the

mutual relations and obligations of Christians. In these references the "head" of the body has no special position or honor; it is counted as an ordinary member (cf. 1 Cor 12:21). In Colossians (and Ephesians) there is an advance in the line of thought, from the language of simile (as in 1 Cor and Rom) to that of a real and interpersonal involvement. This advance has probably been stimulated by Paul's reflection on the issues involved in the Colossian heresy, and is entirely appropriate. Further, the term *church** (Col 1:18), while usually taken to refer to the people of God all over the world, the universal or worldwide church where Christ here and now exercises his cosmic lordship, is best understood of a heavenly assembly gathered around the risen and exalted Christ (cf. Col 3:1-4; Eph 2:6). This heavenly gathering with Christ at its center is manifested here and now on earth. The same word *church* can be used of a local congregation at Colossae or even of a small house community (Col 4:15-16). The congregation in heaven finds its manifestation and becomes visible as the domain of Christ's rule where saints and faithful brothers and sisters in Christ gather (Col 1:2).

*6.1.2.3. Eschatology.* Future eschatology has receded in Colossians, it is argued, with Colossians 3:4 the only explicit reference to this future event. Instead, spatial concepts are said to dominate, while none of the typically Pauline ideas—Parousia, resurrection of the dead and judgment* of the world—is encountered in the letter. Further, unlike the genuine Pauline letters Colossians states that believers have already been raised with Christ (Col 2:12-13; 3:1), and this serves as the basis of the ethical imperative (*see* Ethics).

There is indeed an emphasis on realized eschatology in Colossians, but this has been called forth by the particular circumstances. Also, there is future eschatology not only at Colossians 3:4, 6, 24, but at Colossians 1:22, 28 (cf. Col 4:11) as well. Spatial concepts are used in the service of eschatology, while the antithesis between eschatological and transcendent perspectives is found together in the undisputed Paulines and at Colossians 3:1-4. There is an eschatological motivation in Colossians; it may not be dominant but is present nevertheless (Col 3:5 is based on Col 3:1-4 with its eschatological emphasis). At the same time there are other grounds for exhortation than eschatology in the generally accepted Pauline letters.

*6.1.2.4. Tradition.* The alleged differences in the above-mentioned areas are thought to derive from a "Pauline school tradition" probably based in Ephesus. The post-Pauline author took over the hymn now found in Colossians 1:15-20 and other traditional materials in order to combat heresy in the subapostolic age (Käsemann). Epaphras's name is especially emphasized in the list of greetings in Colossians. This document, which is a kind of pastoral letter, was to provide an apostolic authorization for Epaphras, whose teaching represents the mind of Paul. According to M. Kiley the author of Colossians used Paul's two prison letters (Philippians* and Philemon*) as models for writing a letter of recommendation for Epaphras. The letter, which bears the marks of the "early catholicism"* of the subapostolic age, was intended to show that "Paul's teaching is not strictly limited to the exigencies of time and place" (Kiley, 107). The "author of Colossians affirms to the communities the message of the Apostle in a powerful new formulation" (Lohse, 183).

But in Colossians 1:23—2:5 the gospel gives validity to Paul's ministry; the paragraph does not legitimate the gospel through the apostolic office of Paul and then assert (Col 1:7; 4:7-13) the legitimation of Epaphras because of his relationship to the apostle. Both serve the gospel as coworkers and ministers of that word. No attempt is made in these passages to give an apostolic authorization to Epaphras (or anyone else) because he stands in an apostolic succession and his teaching represents the mind of Paul.

The so-called differences between Colossians and the generally accepted Pauline letters do not constitute sufficient grounds for rejecting the apostolic authorship of this letter. Differences of emphasis there are, but these are best interpreted as being called forth by the circumstances at Colossae.

*6.2. Place and Date of Origin.* The traditional view that Paul wrote Colossians during his imprisonment in Rome* is more likely than that he penned the letter in Ephesus or Caesarea. No other imprisonment recorded in Acts seems a real alternative (there are difficulties regarding the Caesarean imprisonment of Acts 24:27; but *see* Philippians). The greetings from colleagues in Colossians 4 suggest they had direct access to him, and this is consistent with the Roman imprisonment of Acts 28:30, while the reference to Onesimus (which brings into account the Letter to Philemon) could be understood in the context of the imperial capital even though some have argued that the distance between Colossae and Rome is an obstacle to its Roman origin. It is precarious to place any weight on the progression in Pauline thought as a criterion for dating Colossians.

If the Roman hypothesis is accepted, then the most likely date is fairly early in Paul's (first) Roman imprisonment, that is, about A.D. 60-61. Those advocating an Ephesian alternative place the letter around A.D. 54-57, or even earlier, A.D. 52-55.

*6.3. The Hymn in Praise of Christ.* Colossians 1:15-20 is a magnificent passage of praise exalting Christ as the Lord in creation (Col 1:15-17) and author of reconciliation (Col 1:18-20). As to the structure of the hymn* no scholarly consensus has been reached about the number and content of the stanzas. It is better to speak of certain parallels (cf. Col 1:15 and 18), with relative clauses being followed by causal clauses (Col 1:16, 19), the frequent use of "all," and the formal chiasmus in verses 16c and 20 (note also Col 1:17, 18).

Although the backgrounds in pre-Christian Gnosticism and rabbinic Judaism have been suggested as the source of the hymn's ideas, a general Wisdom* milieu in the OT and Hellenistic Judaism (E. Schweizer) is probably correct. But how the predicates and activities ascribed to Wisdom came to be applied to Jesus of Nazareth, recently crucified and risen from the dead, cannot be explained by the background itself.

This hymnic paragraph is not a christological digression or excursus but is clearly central to the context in which it stands. Paul's lengthy prayer* (Col 1:9-14) leads up to the hymn, and themes from it are taken up and applied throughout the rest of the letter (cf. Col 1:19 with 2:9; Col 1:20 with 1:21-23 and 2:15). Although the passage praises Christ, surprisingly the names "Jesus," "Christ" and "Lord" do not appear with it. The stanza simply begins, "He is . . ." However, it is clear that the words of praise can apply to no one else.

The Pauline authorship of the "hymn" has been challenged on linguistic and structural grounds. The arguments for and against Paul's authorship are not decisive either way, so we should accept the passage as authentic. Thus, there has been considerable debate whether the apostle here incorporated an existing "hymn" into his letter. This is possible, but if so he has woven the rest of the letter around it, and the focus on the supremacy of Christ is intended to strengthen the readers and correct the erroneous views of the false teachers. Whether pre-Pauline or not, the passage perfectly suited the apostle's purposes in writing to the Colossians.

*See also* CHRISTOLOGY; EPHESIANS, LETTER TO THE; FULLNESS; GNOSIS, GNOSTICISM; MYSTICISM; PRINCIPALITIES AND POWERS; TRIUMPH; WISDOM.

BIBLIOGRAPHY. **Commentaries:** T. K. Abbott, *The Epistles to the Ephesians and to the Colossians* (ICC; Edinburgh: T. & T. Clark, 1897); F. F. Bruce, *The Epistles to the Colossians, to Philemon, and to the Ephesians* (NICNT; Grand Rapids: Eerdmans, 1984); G. B. Caird, *Paul's Letters from Prison* (Oxford: University Press, 1976); M. Dibelius, *An die Kolosser, Epheser, an Philemon* (3d ed.; HNT 12; Tübingen: J. C. B. Mohr, 1953); J. L. Houlden, *Paul's Letters from Prison* (Philadelphia: Westminster, 1970); J. B. Lightfoot, *Saint Paul's Epistles to the Colossians and to Philemon* (London: Macmillan, 1890); E. Lohmeyer, *Die Briefe an die Philipper, an die Kolosser und an Philemon* (13th ed.; MeyerK; Göttingen: Vandenhoeck & Ruprecht, 1964); E. Lohse, *Colossians and Philemon* (Herm; Philadelphia: Fortress, 1971); R. P. Martin, *Colossians and Philemon* (NCB; Grand Rapids: Eerdmans, 1981); idem, *Ephesians, Colossians, and Philemon* (Int; Louisville: John Knox, 1991); C. F. D. Moule, *The Epistles of Paul the Apostle to the Colossians and to Philemon* (CGTC; Cambridge: University Press, 1957); P. T. O'Brien, *Colossians, Philemon* (WBC 44; Waco: Word, 1982); A. G. Patzia, *Colossians, Philemon, Ephesians* (San Francisco: Harper & Row, 1984); E. Schweizer, *The Letter to the Colossians: A Commentary* (Minneapolis: Augsburg, 1982); N. T. Wright, *The Epistles of Paul to the Colossians and to Philemon* (TNTC; Grand Rapids: Eerdmans, 1986). **Studies**: G. Bornkamm, "The Heresy of Colossians," in *Conflict at Colossae*, ed., F. O. Francis and W. A. Meeks (2d ed.; SBLSBS 4; Missoula, MT: Scholars, 1975) 123-45; W. Bujard, *Stilanalytische Untersuchungen zum Kolosserbrief* (SUNT 11; Göttingen: Vandenhoeck & Ruprecht, 1973); G. E. Cannon, *The Use of Traditional Materials in Colossians* (Macon, GA: Mercer, 1983); M. Dibelius, "The Isis Initiation in Apuleius and Related Initiatory Rites," in *Conflict at Colossae*, ed. F. O. Francis and W. A. Meeks (SBLSBS 4; 2d ed.; Missoula, MT: Scholars, 1975) 61-121; F. O. Francis and W. Meeks, ed., *Conflict at Colossae* (SBLSBS 4; Missoula: Scholars, 1975); M. D. Hooker, "Were There False Teachers in Colossae?" in *Christ and Spirit in the New Testament: Studies in honour of Charles Francis Digby Moule*, ed. B. Lindars and S. S. Smalley (Cambridge: University Press, 1973) 315-31; E. Käsemann, "A Primitive Christian Baptismal Liturgy," in *Essays on New Testament Themes* (SBT; Naperville: Allenson, 1964) 149-68; M. Kiley, *Colossians as Pseudepigraphy* (Sheffield: JSOT, 1986); A. T. Lincoln, *Paradise Now and Not Yet* (SNTSMS 41; Cambridge: University Press, 1981); S. Lyonnet, "Paul's Adversaries in Colossae," in *Conflict at Colossae*, ed. F. O. Francis and W. A. Meeks (2d ed.; SBLSBS 4; Missoula, MT: Scholars, 1975) 147-61; J. T. Sanders, *The New Testament Christological Hymns* (SNTSMS 15; Cambridge: University Press, 1971); R. C. Tannehill, *Dying and Rising with Christ* (BZNW 32; Berlin: Töpelmann, 1967); N. T. Wright, "Poetry and Theology in Col. 1:15-20," *NTS* 36 (1990) 444-68.

P. T. O'Brien

**COMMUNION.** *See* COLLECTION FOR THE SAINTS; FELLOWSHIP, COMMUNION, SHARING.

**COMMUNITY.** *See* CHURCH; CHURCH ORDER AND GOVERNMENT; FELLOWSHIP, COMMUNION, SHARING; HOUSEHOLDS AND HOUSEHOLD CODES; SOCIAL SETTING OF MISSION CHURCHES; SOCIAL-SCIENTIFIC APPROACHES TO PAUL.

**CONFESSIONS.** *See* CREED; LITURGICAL ELEMENTS.

## CONSCIENCE

Paul uses the term and idea of "conscience" frequently in his instructions to the Corinthians* on eating meat sacrificed to idols (*see* Food). *Conscience* is mentioned in the context of Paul's apostolic ministry. It appears once in connection with Christians' obedience to the state (*see* Civil Authority) and with Gentiles' doing the Law* by nature. The Pastoral Letters contrast the "good conscience" of Christian ministers with the "defiled" or "seared" conscience of false teachers. Interpreters of Paul express both difference of opinion and some ambiguity regarding the meaning of "conscience" in Paul. This is due not least to the considerable interpretive difficulties faced in many of his uses of the term.

1. Usage and Definition
2. Conscience in Romans and 1 and 2 Corinthians
3. Conscience in the Pastoral Epistles

### 1. Usage and Definition.

In Romans and 1 and 2 Corinthians Paul uses the substantive *syneidēsis*, "conscience," fourteen times and the reflexive verb phrase *emautō synoida ti*, "I know something against myself," only once (1 Cor 4:4). *Syneidēsis* appears six times in the Pastorals, usually with an attributive adjective (*agathē*, "good," or *kathara*, "pure"). Paul may have taken over the term *conscience* as a Christian ethical term from the Corinthians (seeing that he uses it first and most frequently in his letters to them, so Pierce, 64-65).

The meaning of *syneidēsis* varies widely in Greco-Roman antiquity, where it is common since the first century B.C. (cf. the Hebrew *lēb*, "heart," in the OT; see Eckstein, 35-135). R. Bultmann understands the term in Paul as "knowledge shared with oneself . . . of good and evil and of the corresponding conduct" (Bultmann, 1.216-17). But H.-J. Eckstein (311-14) argues that *syneidēsis* in 1 Corinthians and Romans refers uniformly to the inner tribunal which determines whether behavior (in the broad sense, including thinking, willing, speaking and acting) agrees with the moral norms and requirements affirmed by the mind and which testifies of this verdict to the subject. C. A. Pierce's (78) interpretation of conscience as "pain" has been challenged on exegetical grounds.

## 2. Conscience in Romans and 1 and 2 Corinthians.

*2.1. Conscience as Universally Human.* Paul ascribes conscience to Christians and unbelievers alike. Pagans have a conscience, as evidenced by the fact that "their conflicting thoughts accuse or defend," depending on whether or not their behavior corresponds to "the work of the law written in their hearts" (Rom 2:15). Here Paul understands conscience as an inner tribunal which tests and so helps guide behavior by internalized moral norms.

*2.2. Conscience and Moral Norms.* The moral norms according to which the conscience tests behavior are a given for the conscience (*see* Ethics). The conscience does not establish these norms nor provide knowledge* of them. Knowledge of moral norms is prior to the activity of the conscience and not to be equated with the conscience itself (see Eckstein, 312). Norms which are already internalized thus come to the conscience as criteria for its use in evaluating behavior.

The moral norms which the conscience uses are the internalized norms of the subject which may or may not correspond to the will of God. These norms may differ from person to person, with the result that the judgments by different consciences on the same type of behavior will differ (1 Cor 8:7-12; 10:25-29).

*2.3. Function of Conscience.* The conscience can register the agreement between behavior and norms (Rom 9:1; 2 Cor 4:2; 5:11; also 1 Cor 10:25, 27). As an independent judge over a person's behavior it can also be called as witness to such agreement: "my conscience bears me witness . . ." (Rom 9:1; also 2 Cor 1:12; but not Rom 2:15, where conscience as a *phenomenon* bears witness). The conscience may, on the other hand, deliver a verdict of disagreement between behavior and norms (1 Cor 10:29b). In Paul the conscience pronounces its verdict on past behavior and also on future behavior (cf. Rom 2:15; 13:5; 1 Cor 8:10; 10:25-29). Conscience thus makes possible "objective" evaluation by oneself of one's behavior. Yet conscience is still an anthropological designation and does not refer to an "authority beyond man" (*contra* Bultmann, 1.219).

*2.4. Conscience and Divine Judgment.* Paul distinguishes the verdict of this human tribunal from God's own judgment.* The conscience operates only on the basis of internalized norms, but those norms may not match the standard of divine judgment. Indeed, they can err (e.g., because of lack of knowledge, or because of social pressure or custom [*synētheia,* cf. the secondary variant *syneidēsei*], 1 Cor 8:7), as Paul's call for the "renewal of your mind" (Rom 12:2) reminds us. The

judgments of the conscience tell whether behavior is truly right in God's eyes only insofar as they are based on norms corresponding to God's will. In the final analysis, for Paul conscience is a neutral faculty and is ultimately only as right as are the norms it uses (which are right if they correspond to God's will). Judgment according to the norms of the conscience is not finally determinative. Only the Lord's judgment is: "I am conscious (*synoida*) of nothing against myself, but I am not thereby acquitted. Rather the one who judges me is the Lord" (1 Cor 4:4). Thus in Romans 9:1 Paul seeks to back up the testimony of his conscience with his references to Christ and the Spirit: "I am speaking the truth in Christ . . . ; my conscience bears me witness in the Holy Spirit." (But Paul by no means implies here that the conscience operates only under the rule of the Spirit, nor does 2 Corinthians 4:2 support the understanding of the conscience as a "divine voice," *vox Dei; see* Holy Spirit.)

*2.5. Relative Value of Conscience.* Paul thus relativizes the conscience in the light of divine judgment. Yet he ascribes to it independent (though relative) value. Paul believes that human beings ought to heed their conscience not only when the internalized norms by which it judges correspond to God's will (cf. Rom 13:5, "be subject . . . on account of conscience"; Maurer [915-16] discusses possible interpretations), but also when those norms neither correspond to nor contradict God's will. For Paul the "integrity" of a person— as the harmonious relationship between one's beliefs and practice—is a value in itself, and the conscience helps achieve such integrity and avoid dissonance.

*2.6. "Weak" Conscience.* Paul therefore wants to protect the conscience so it can continue to fulfill its function. The conscience of the "weak" (1 Cor 8:10-11; *see* Strong and Weak), who lack "knowledge" (1 Cor 8:7) and whose conscience thus operates according to faulty norms and can therefore also be described as "weak" (1 Cor 8:7, 12), may be "defiled" (1 Cor 8:7) and "wounded" (1 Cor 8:12) by the strong.* The example of the strong leads the weak to eat meat sacrificed to idols despite the fact that such behavior is not permitted according to *their* own norms. "Wounding (*typtontes*) the conscience" apparently suggests damage to the function of the conscience (it fails to preserve one's integrity, though its judgments themselves do not err) through encouragement to use alien norms for its evaluations. The expression "the conscience is defiled (*molynetai*)" more easily refers to the state of consciousness of those who reckon themselves to have become morally contaminated by eating meat offered to idols (similarly, Jewett, 425; *see* Food). H.-J. Eckstein (241) takes *syneidēsis* here to stand for the whole person (*pars pro toto*) and so sees not merely subjective but objective defilement and wounding of the person. The weak conscience should not be artificially "built up" (Paul says ironically, 1 Cor 8:10; cf. 8:1: "knowledge puffs up") through the adoption of alien norms so as to make judgments which result in people's behaving according to norms contrary to their real convictions. The same concern probably stands behind the injunction to the dinner guest, "don't eat!" on account of the conscience of the one who supplied the information that the meat served was sacrificed to idols (1 Cor 10:28-29; the informer is probably a weak Christian in danger of violating his or her convictions through an artificially built-up conscience).

When these things happen to the conscience there are negative consequences: the weak "stumbles" (1 Cor 8:13; cf. 8:9) and "is destroyed" (1 Cor 8:11). Sin is committed (the sin of acting contrary to one's convictions, Rom 14:23; but not the sin of idolatry, see Gundry Volf, 93) and regression in the Christian life occurs (including "grief" and self-condemnation instead of "peace* and joy*" and upbuilding, Rom 14:15-23). (The parallels with Rom 14 are close, though conscience is not mentioned there; see Bultmann, 1.220.) A properly functioning conscience, on the other hand, helps protect one from these objective and subjective setbacks.

*2.7. Qualifications.* Paul wants Christians to heed their conscience when it comes to matters where there is freedom* for Christians to behave differently as in the case of sacrificial food, even when the conscience uses faulty norms. Paul's intention is to preserve the "integrity" of the person and avoid inner dissonance. He explicitly denies, however, that one person's conscience may judge another person's behavior in the case of matters where Christians disagree (*adiaphora*): "why should my freedom be judged by another's conscience?" (1 Cor 10:29b; personal "integrity" is not endangered by violation of *another's* conscience). (Nevertheless, Paul is willing that the trustworthiness of his apostolic conduct [but not the truth of the gospel*] be measured by the consciences of his converts, 2 Cor 4:2; 5:11.)

The conscience may give a positive verdict on a particular behavior *as such*, but that verdict does not suffice as a justification for engaging in that behavior (possibly against explicit Corinthian claims to the contrary). The "strong" ignore this truth when they eat meat offered to idols in the presence of the weak. Paul would probably say that the conscience's verdict on a particular behavior *in a concrete situation* must be heard, and that verdict must be based on all the applicable norms before one can engage in that behavior and claim

conscience as a witness to its rightness. The green light may turn red when one gets to the intersection, and then one must put on the brakes. Love* and the glory* of God are the norms which determine whether the strong may exercise freedom in a given situation (1 Cor 8:1, 11-13; 10:31-33; cf. Rom 14:15-21).

### 3. Conscience in the Pastoral Letters.

*3.1. "Good Conscience."* In the Pastorals* the Christian teacher and deacon should be characterized by a "good" (*agathē*, 1 Tim 1:5, 19), or "clean" (*kathara*, 1 Tim 3:9; 2 Tim 1:3), conscience. This use of *syneidēsis* with qualifying adjectives suggests not conscience as a tribunal but as a state of consciousness: consciousness of having behaved in agreement with given norms. Christian ministers must "keep a good conscience" and "keep the mystery of faith with a clean conscience" (1 Tim 1:19; 3:90), and Paul can be said to assert "I serve [God] with a clean conscience" (2 Tim 1:3; cf. Acts 23:1; 24:16). The good/clean conscience ranks alongside keeping faith* and practicing love as prime aims for Christian servants* (1 Tim 1:5, 19; 3:9).

*3.2. "Defiled Conscience."* "Rejecting" (*apōsamenoi*) a good conscience and having a "defiled" (*memiantai*) and "seared" (*kekaustēriasmenon*) conscience characterize the false teachers in the Pastoral letters (1 Tim 1:19; 4:2; Tit 1:15). General immorality is apparently not in view, however, for they are not criticized as libertines (though as avaricious and contentious, 1 Tim 6:5; Tit 1:11) but as perpetrators of ascetic teaching (1 Tim 4:3). Their "purity" does not earn them a clean conscience, rather they are said to have "defiled" and "seared" consciences. These labels hardly describe their subjective consciousness—they were no doubt full of satisfaction not guilt (though Roloff, 221-22, suggests that "seared" alludes to the shame which they in fact cannot escape). Do the descriptions instead denote the state of consciousness which they *should* have because in reality they are "defiled," "detestable, disobedient, unfit for any good deed" (Tit 1:15-16)? We can ask further whether they paradoxically defile themselves by their asceticism (by rejecting what God "created good" and "to be received with thanksgiving," 1 Tim 4:3-4), or whether through their disguised moral faults they "deny [God] by their deeds" (Tit 1:16). Alternatively, should we take the defiled or seared conscience not as consciousness but as an inner judge between right and wrong which has become impaired, or as the brand-mark indicating Satan's* ownership of the false teachers (Kelly, 94)?

Appealing to Hebrews 10:22 and 1 Peter 3:21, some take *syneidēsis* in the Pastorals as synonymous with "heart," and the "good/clean conscience" as the result of forgiveness* of sins* and the end-time renewal of the heart (so Roloff, 68-70). Along the same line, the "seared" and "defiled conscience" could be identified with the unrenewed heart, and rejection of a good conscience with unbelief in the gospel, whether apostasy* (so Wolter, 217) or false profession might be in view. In any case, in the Pastorals the ideas of "keeping" and not "rejecting" a good conscience, and of "serving God" with a good conscience, relate conscience more to the imperative than to the indicative. Therefore even if we understand conscience here in the terms of "renewal . . . by the new creation in faith" (Maurer, 918), the interest of the Pastoral letters lies in the aspect of human responsibility, in particular, that of Christian ministers.

It is sometimes argued that the "good conscience" of the Pastorals is a support for a bourgeois Christian morality. But this interpretation would be possible only if the text were speaking of human responsibility to live in a Christian way. This view further assumes that the moral code of the Pastorals fits the popular ethos of their day. But W. D. Davies urges caution: "In the Pastorals also the Christian life is a battle and conscience is tied to faith" (676).

*See also* APOSTASY, FALLING AWAY, PERSEVERANCE; ETHICS; FOOD OFFERED TO IDOLS AND JEWISH FOOD LAWS; LAW; LAW OF CHRIST; PSYCHOLOGY; STRONG AND WEAK.

BIBLIOGRAPHY. R. Bultmann, *Theology of the New Testament* (2 vols; New York: Scribners, 1951, 1955) 1.211-20; W. D. Davies, "Conscience," *IDB* 1.671-76; H.-J. Eckstein, *Der Begriff Syneidēsis bei Paulus: Eine neutestamentlich-exegetische Untersuchung zum Gewissenbegriff* (WUNT 2/10; Tübingen: J. C. B. Mohr, 1983); P. W. Gooch, " 'Conscience' in 1 Corinthians 8 and 10," *NTS* 33 (1987) 244-54; J. M. Gundry Volf, *Paul and Perseverance: Staying in and Falling Away* (WUNT 2/37; Tübingen: J. C. B. Mohr, 1990; Louisville: John Knox/ Westminster, 1991) 85-97; R. Jewett, *Paul's Anthropological Terms: A Study of Their Use in Conflict Settings* (AGJU 10; Leiden: E. J. Brill, 1971) 402-46; J. N. D. Kelly, *A Commentary on the Pastoral Epistles* (Grand Rapids: Baker, 1981); C. Maurer, "σύνοιδα, συνείδησις," *TDNT* VII.899-919; C. A. Pierce, *Conscience in the New Testament* (SBT 15; London: SCM, 1958); J. Roloff, *Der erste Brief an Timotheus* (EKK 15; Zürich: Benziger; Neukirchen-Vluyn: Neukirchener, 1988); C. Spicq, "La conscience dans le Nouveau Testament" *RB* 47 (1938) 50-80; J. Stelzenberger, *Syneidēsis im Neuen Testament* (Paderborn: Schöningh, 1961); W. L. Willis, *Idol Meat in Corinth: The Pauline Argument in 1 Corinthians 8 and 10* (SBLDS 68; Chico, CA: Scholars, 1985); M. Wolter, "Gewissen" II, *TRE* 13.213-18.

J. M. Gundry-Volf

**CONTENTMENT.** *See* MYSTICISM; PHILOSOPHY; RICHES AND POVERTY.

## CONVERSION AND CALL OF PAUL

One of the best known narratives in the NT is the story of Paul's conversion and call to be the apostle* to the Gentiles.* Scholars have often disagreed about whether this experience of Paul is best understood as a conversion or a call to a specific mission* as apostle to the Gentiles. References to Paul's conversion/call experience are found in Galatians 1, Philippians 3, Acts 9, Acts 22 and Acts 26.

1. History of the Interpretation of Paul's Conversion/Call
2. Accounts of Paul's Conversion/Call
3. Some Critical Questions

### 1. History of the Interpretation of Paul's Conversion/Call.

Several decades ago many biblical scholars would have agreed that Paul's remarkable experience on the road to Damascus was a paradigmatic instance of Christian conversion. Today many biblical scholars would describe the same experience as Paul's unique call to be apostle to the Gentiles. This shift in understanding has set the agenda for many recent studies of Paul's conversion/call.

The traditional way of understanding Paul's Damascus Road experience as a conversion has a long history in Western thought, going back to Augustine and his understanding of his own conversion. William James's psychological study of conversion was heavily dependent on this traditional view. James defined conversion as the process by which a person who struggles with a sense of guilt and inferiority becomes a person with a conscious sense of being right and unified as a consequence of achieving a firmer hold of religious realities. From this traditional perspective Paul's Damascus Road experience is seen as a prime example of conversion. A Pharisaic Jew* who is very conscious of his failure to keep the Law* experiences a profound inner change when it is revealed to him that he can be justified* by faith* in Jesus Christ. The Jewish persecutor becomes the Christian convert who preaches the message of justification by faith in Christ Jesus. Until quite recently, this understanding of Paul's conversion dominated biblical scholarship (see Nock, Stewart).

But in the past few decades this view of Paul's conversion has come under profound suspicion. The biblical scholar who is largely responsible for raising questions about the traditional way of understanding Paul's conversion is K. Stendahl in his book *Paul*

*Among Jews and Gentiles* (1976). Stendahl claims that the Western understanding of Paul owes more to the introspective readings of Augustine and Luther than it does to the NT documents. Paul's experience on the Damascus Road was not the inner experience of conversion which Western theology has taken for granted, nor was it a conversion from the works righteousness of Judaism. In fact, Paul's experience on the road to Damascus was not really a conversion at all, according to traditional definitions of conversion. Paul did not change religions nor did he suffer from an inner experience of guilt or despair. Stendahl suggests that Paul's experience is better understood as a call to be the apostle to the Gentiles. Because of this call he begins to ask questions about what happens to the Law now that the Messiah (*see* Christ) has come and what the Messiah's coming means for relationships between Jews and Gentiles. Paul arrives at a new view of the Law as he answers these questions, not as he struggles with the meaning of the Law in his own life. Paul's Damascus Road experience is part of his unique apostolic call and is not meant to be an example of a Christian conversion.

Stendahl's understanding of Paul's Damascus Road experience as a call and his challenge to traditional understandings of Paul's conversion have created a whole new set of questions for biblical scholars who study Paul's conversion/call: How are we to define conversion and how are modern definitions applied to Paul? Did Paul remain a Jew or did he change religions? Is his experience best understood as a call or a conversion? Is Paul's experience meant to be an example for Christians? How did Paul's conversion/call experience influence his theology? But even more importantly, Stendahl's challenge forced biblical scholars to return to the NT texts about Paul's conversion/call to answer these questions.

## 2. Accounts of Paul's Conversion/Call.

Accounts of Paul's conversion/call are found in two different places in the NT—Paul's letters and the book of Acts. Galatians 1:11-17 and Philippians 3:4-17 are two passages in which Paul writes about his conversion/call experience. In addition, 1 Timothy 1:12-17 and Romans 7 are sometimes considered autobiographical descriptions of this experience. Acts contains three different accounts of Paul's Damascus Road experience: Acts 9:1-20, 22:1-21 and 26:2-23. One of the issues involved in studying Paul's conversion/call is how to use the NT evidence. Historical research values the letters, which are Paul's own accounts of his experience, over Acts, which is a later interpretation of Paul from a particular perspective. So

methodologically it seems best to start with the accounts in Paul's letters and then examine the Acts material. It is also important to ask how the accounts in the letters and Acts are related to each other (*see* Paul in Acts and Letters).

**2.1. Galatians 1:11-17.** The autobiographical references in Galatians 1:11-17 are part of Paul's defense of his gospel.* Many scholars see Paul's opponents* as Judaizers,* those who believed that Gentile Christians should keep the Law and be circumcised.* In Galatians Paul argues against these Judaizers and claims that, in Christ, Gentiles should not keep the Law or be circumcised. Paul makes his own experience a part of his argument in order to emphasize the revelatory nature of the Law-free gospel he preaches among the Gentiles.

The divine origin of the gospel Paul preaches (Gal 1:11-12) is also seen in the divine source of Paul's call (Gal 1:15-17). Paul's discussion of the revelation he received (Gal 1:15) is couched in the language of OT prophetic calls (cf. Jer 1:5; *see* Prophet, Paul as). Such language emphasizes Paul's role as one called to proclaim the word of God and points to the divine origin of the word that is proclaimed. The object of this divine revelation is Jesus Christ; this is the word of God that Paul is called to proclaim among the Gentiles (Gal 1:16). Although Paul relates almost nothing of the events surrounding this revelation he does report that subsequent to this experience he was not influenced by any human agency (Gal 1:16-17). Paul uses the experience of his conversion/call to show that his gospel to the Gentiles is rooted in divine revelation and divine calling (*see* Call, Calling).

It is in this context that Paul's mention of his earlier life in Judaism (Gal 1:14-15) needs to be understood. There is no human explanation for his experience; nothing prepared him for the revelation he received. The Jew who was so zealous for the traditions* of his ancestors that he persecuted those who believed in Christ is now the champion of a Law-free gospel for the Gentiles. The contrast between Paul's former life as a Jew and his new life as apostle to the Gentiles is seen as evidence for the divine origin of the gospel Paul preaches as apostle to the Gentiles.

**2.2. Philippians 3:3-17.** The occasion which calls forth Paul's autobiographical statements in Philippians 3:3-17 is not as clear as that of Galatians 1:1-17. But it is probable that Paul is again arguing against Judaizing tendencies in the church. This is suggested by the reference to those who mutilate the flesh* (Phil 3:2) and Paul's claim to be the true circumcision (Phil 3:3). Although Judaizing tendencies do not appear to be a major problem at Philippi, Paul uses his own life as an example of what it means to be the true circumcision. Paul sees his experience as a paradigmatic expression of the great contrast between life under the Law and the transforming grace* of the new life in Christ.

Paul is willing to compare himself with those who think they have reason for confidence in the flesh, for he has even better reasons for such confidence (Phil 3:4-6). Three of Paul's reasons for having confidence in the flesh are based on hereditary factors: he was born a Jew,* circumcised according to the Law and raised as a culturally pure, Hebrew-speaking Jew. Paul's personal convictions while a Jew also gave him reason to boast*: his attitude toward the Law was that of the strict sect of the Pharisees, he was a zealous persecutor of the church and was blameless in his observance of the Law. Paul's background establishes him as one who is fully competent to judge any issue involving the Law.

But coming to know Christ Jesus brought about a reversal in Paul's life. His judgment on all these former advantages, everything that he considered gain, is that he now considers it loss (Phil 3:7-8). The result of the conversion/call experience in which Paul came to know Christ is a complete transformation. Being found in Christ means that Paul is no longer found in the Law (Phil 3:9). Now Paul's whole life is shaped by his sharing in Christ's death* and resurrection* (Phil 3:10-11). This process of being transformed in Christ is a continuing process in Paul's life as he responds to the call of God in Christ Jesus (Phil 3:12-14).

Because Paul's experience of conversion/call has resulted in a total transformation of his life, Paul sees his relation to his readers as that of a type to be imitated (Phil 3:15-17). This idea of himself as an example of the life in Christ is the underlying purpose of Paul's account of his experience in Philippians 3:3-17.

**2.3. Other Pauline Accounts?** Two other passages in the Pauline letters are often considered autobiographical accounts of Paul's conversion: 1 Timothy 1:12-16 and Romans 7:7-25.

1 Timothy 1:12-16 is clearly an account of Paul's conversion. But many scholars do not think Paul wrote 1 Timothy, and so its value as an autobiographical statement is questioned. In this passage, the contrast between Paul's former life and his life in Christ (*see* In Christ) is again strongly emphasized. But two aspects of this contrast are different from the passages in Philippians and Galatians 1. The first is that there is no mention of Judaism. The second difference is that Paul identifies himself as the foremost of sinners, a judgment Paul does not make in either of the other

passages. However, just as it is in Philippians 3, the transformation in Paul's life is held up as an example to believers. Whether or not it is Pauline, this passage certainly represents the Pauline tradition and is useful as evidence of the way Paul's conversion/call experience was understood in the Gentile churches* Paul founded.

The autobiographical character of Romans 7:7-25 is not just disputed, it is the center of a major controversy in Pauline studies. The central issue is how the "I" of Romans 7:7-25 is to be understood. (For a historical summary of the various ways this "I" has been interpreted see Cranfield, 342-47.) Is Paul speaking of his personal experience, either as a Jew or a Christian? Is he speaking in a general way about Jewish, Christian or general human experience? Or is he using the "I" as a way of talking about the Law in a more general sense?

The traditional view of Paul's conversion/call usually understands this passage as Paul's autobiographical account of his pre-Christian experience as a Jew. Romans 7:7-25 is seen as evidence of Paul's feelings of guilt and inferiority as a Jew because he is unable to keep the Law perfectly. But this reading of Romans 7:7-25 is directly contradictory to Paul's statements in Galatians 1 and Philippians 3 about his life as a Jew. So most historical scholars now reject this possibility. Instead they usually understand this passage as Paul examining the Law from a Christian perspective in a general sense; the "I" represents his deep personal involvement in the issue of the Law. A. F. Segal offers a different and compelling interpretation of Romans 7:7-25. He suggests that Paul is describing Jewish-Christian experience with the Law after conversion. Paul uses "I" because he speaks as a Jewish-Christian for Jewish-Christians. The struggle with the Law is a struggle no Christian can win as long as observance of the Law is a serious option in the Christian community. A Law-free gospel is the only solution. Thus Romans 7:7-25 is a description of the personal struggle experienced by any Jewish-Christian who tries to keep the Law as a Christian.

Given the multiplicity of readings of Romans 7:7-25 and the lack of direct biographical information in the text, it seems best not to consider this passage as an account which refers to Paul's conversion/call.

**2.4. The Acts Accounts.** Paul's letters give us little information about the actual conversion/call event. Instead the Pauline accounts reflect the radical change in Paul's values and commitments when he received a revelation of Christ. But the three accounts in Acts focus on the events surrounding the conversion/call. The fact that the conversion/call account occurs three times suggests that this event has major significance for Luke's narrative. The first account, in Acts 9:1-20, is told as part of the historical narrative; the other accounts, in Acts 22:1-21 and 26:2-23, are contained in Paul's speeches before the Jews and King Agrippa. There has been a tendency in NT scholarship to isolate these conversion/call narratives from the rest of Acts and then to compare them with Paul's accounts. However, it is important to see these passages in their context in Acts. Luke uses them to show the progress of the church from a Jewish to a Gentile community and to justify the Pauline mission* to the Gentiles. Because of Luke's definite apologetic stance, some scholars question the historical reliability of the Acts accounts. It is true that Luke does not have first-hand knowledge of the conversion/call event. But he does have the advantage of a historical perspective and may be able to see the importance of Paul's conversion/call in ways that Paul himself could not.

The events of Acts 9:1-19 mark a major turning point in the narrative of Acts. Here Luke takes a piece of historical storytelling and describes an event of crucial importance for the Christian mission. The story of Paul's dramatic conversion/call is placed just before the story of Cornelius and introduces the beginning of the mission to the Gentiles. At the beginning of Acts 9 Paul is presented as the persecutor of the church, who completely opposes the disciples of the Lord. But as he pursues the disciples to Damascus, his journey is interrupted. Jesus appears to Paul in a vision. The blinding light, the double vocative ("Saul, Saul"), Saul's falling to the ground and the questions he asks clearly mark this extraordinary event as a theophany, similar to the theophanies of prophetic calls. Paul emerges from this experience a different person, but he has not yet received his call. That call comes through a disciple at Damascus, one of the people Paul had been persecuting. The fact that the call comes in a separate vision gives it greater emphasis, but it is still part of the same event. The new description of Saul given through Ananias, indicates that Saul is a "chosen vessel" and has been picked for a particular role. The very name he has persecuted he will now bear before the Gentiles, kings and the people of Israel and will suffer* for its sake. This call is far more than a call which belongs to any believer; it is an apostolic commissioning. Although the Acts 9:1-19 account certainly presents Paul as a person who has experienced a dramatic reversal in his life, it emphasizes his call to be apostle to the Gentiles more than the change in his life.

Acts 22:1-21 and Acts 26:2-23 tell the same basic story but have a different emphasis and seem to be serving a different purpose in the Acts narrative. Both speeches draw attention to Paul's relationship to Judaism and may reflect controversy between Jews and Christians about the validity of the Gentile mission. This emphasis on Paul's relationship to Judaism is especially evident in Acts 22:1-21, where Paul is presented as a pious and loyal Jew. In fact, most of the differences between Acts 9 and Acts 22 can be accounted for by the emphasis on Paul as a devout Jew. This is particularly clear in Paul's report of his commissioning. Here Ananias is also presented as a devout Jew and the call is couched in language acceptable to Jewish sensibilities. The call to go to the Gentiles is not given by Ananias but by Jesus himself in another vision* during a time when Paul is praying in the Temple.* Here there is no doubt that it is the mission to the Gentiles that is the problem for Jewish/Christian relations. When Paul claims that the call to go to the Gentiles came in the Temple, his Jewish listeners create an uproar.

Acts 26:2-23 has an only slightly different emphasis. Here Paul emphasizes his obedience to his call. It is in this passage that the expression "It hurts you to kick against the goads" appears. Even though many interpreters have seen this as a reference to Paul's inner struggle before his conversion, it more probably refers to his future task and the cost of obeying the call he is about to receive. This phrase indicates that the call of Christ will constrain Paul and conform his whole life to the goal of making Christ known among the Gentiles.

Luke has one tradition about Paul's conversion/call which he uses in different ways to further his purposes in the Acts narrative. Paul is the driving force behind Christianity's Gentile mission and Luke uses Paul's conversion/call experience to justify that mission and the Gentile Christianity it produced.

*2.5. Paul's Conversion/Call in the NT.* Comparing the Acts account of Paul's conversion/call with Paul's own accounts is not as straightforward a task as it might appear. Paul is making comments about his life as he writes letters to various churches. Luke is telling a story with an overarching narrative purpose. Even though historical research values the letters over Acts, the Acts material is essential to understanding the events surrounding Paul's conversion/call experience. What are the major similarities and differences between the material in Acts and Paul's own accounts?

It is important to note that all five accounts of Paul's conversion/call occur in contexts where the relationship between Judaism and Christianity is an issue. In Acts the validity of the Gentile mission is at stake; in Galatians 1, and probably Philippians 3 as well, the validity of Paul's Law-free gospel is the issue. In these contexts the revelatory nature of Paul's conversion/call is stressed.

Paul's former life as a zealous Jew and persecutor of the church and his transformation into a follower of Christ is an important part of all five passages. This theme of the contrast between Paul's former and present life is especially prominent in the autobiographical passages in Galatians 1 and Philippians 3. This strong sense of contrast is one of the arguments for seeing 1 Timothy 1 and Romans 7 also as autobiographical.

All three Acts passages and Galatians 1 describe a call to proclaim Christ to the Gentiles as part of the revelatory experience. But it is noteworthy that Philippians 3 does not even hint at a special apostolic call. Instead, Paul speaks of a general "heavenly call of God in Christ Jesus." Why is a perspective that is so prominent in the other accounts entirely absent from the Philippians 3 account? Perhaps since Paul's Gentile mission and his gospel* to the Gentiles is not being immediately threatened, he does not need to stress the divine origin of his gospel. Another possible explanation is that since Paul is stressing his role as an example to be imitated, he doesn't mention a part of his experience that is so obviously unique to him. If 1 Timothy 1 is taken as genuinely Pauline, another possibility emerges. As the Gentile mission became established and Paul needed to justify his gospel less frequently, Paul himself saw the transformation of his life as the most important part of his experience and understood being an example of the transforming grace of Christ as an integral part of his apostolic role.

The differences between Luke's and Paul's accounts of the conversion/call are rooted in their different purposes. Luke wants to show the progress of the church from the Jewish to the Gentile community; Paul is concerned with his relationship as apostle to the Gentile communities he has founded. But Paul and Luke ultimately understood Paul's conversion/call in similar ways. Both are concerned with the relationship between Jew and Gentile and see Paul's call as apostle to the Gentiles as an important factor in that relationship. Both see Paul's conversion/call as a revelatory and transforming event in Paul's life and the life of the church. And both Paul and Luke see Paul's experience as a model of the transforming grace of God for the church. These similarities make it possible to speak of the NT understanding of Paul's conversion/call experience.

### 3. Some Critical Questions.

The questions which biblical scholarship addresses to

the NT text often challenge traditional assumptions about the text. This is especially true of the questions scholars ask about Paul's conversion/call experience. Not only has Stendahl challenged traditional Western understandings of Paul's experience, but other scholars have challenged Stendahl's interpretation. These challenges have resulted in several critical questions which need to be addressed in any study of Paul's conversion/call experience. The answers to these several questions are all related to the major issue. Is Paul's experience better understood as a conversion or a call?

*3.1. Defining Conversion.* If the term *conversion* is to be useful in understanding Paul, it needs to be defined. As Stendahl pointed out, Western definitions of conversion have been strongly influenced by Augustine's and Luther's views of Paul's conversion. These views of conversion dominated early psychological research, which tended to focus on dramatic conversion and understood conversion as a solution to unbearable sin* and guilt. Social scientists as well as biblical scholars have questioned this definition of conversion and have tried to offer models that are more useful to those who seek to understand conversion from either a theological or social-scientific perspective.

Most recent studies of conversion have taken a sociological approach and defined conversion as a person transferring from one community to another (*see* Social-Scientific Approaches). Such studies also point out that the main characteristic of converts is a predisposition to reinterpret their past from the perspective of their new communities. Conversion represents a conscious choice to socialize to a new group and accept the reality structure of that group (see Berger and Luckmann, 144-50). The analogies between this sociological definition of conversion and Paul's experience are striking. Paul came from a Pharisaic community and entered a community that included Gentiles. This new community helped him understand his revelatory experience and reinterpret his past. This reinterpretation of his past as a Pharisee is evident in Paul's autobiographical accounts in Galatians 1 and Philippians 3; Paul's statements about his past are greatly influenced by his present commitments.

Helpful as these modern sociological definitions are, we need to be careful in applying them to Paul's experience. We simply do not have enough historical data on Paul for an adequate psychological or sociological analysis. We need to be careful not to reduce Paul's unique experience to a formula or let modern studies define his experience. But we can use modern categories to illuminate certain aspects of his experience for us.

### 3.2. Did Paul Change Religions?

Did Paul remain a Jew even after he changed communities? According to a sociological definition of conversion, this would be entirely possible and would answer one of Stendahl's objections to calling Paul's experience a conversion. Stendahl asserts that Paul did not really change religions. He had a new calling, but still served the same God; as a Jew, he was to bring God's message to the Gentiles. His experience led not to a new religion, but to a new understanding of the Law in relation to the Gentiles. When Paul was transformed by his experience, Christianity was not yet defined as a different religion from Judaism, so it might be best to say that Paul changed communities within Judaism.

But this reading of Paul fails to take into account the radical nature of Paul's reinterpretation of Judaism. His claim that Gentiles did not have to be circumcised to enter the Christian community was more than a minor reinterpretation of the Law. In addition, he claimed that he received this new understanding of the Law in a revelatory event that changed his life. These claims got him into trouble even within the Christian community. Comparing Paul to the Pharisaic Christians of Acts 15 and Galatians 2, who wanted Gentile Christians to be circumcised, shows how radical his reinterpretation of Judaism was. Paul left the Pharisaic community and was completely rejected by that community. Paul's claim in Philippians 3:7-8 that he regards his Jewish reasons for confidence as "rubbish" indicates a complete break with his Jewish past. Although the Acts accounts of Paul's experience present him as a devout Jew, they also indicate that Paul's life and values were radically changed by his Damascus Road experience and that he was uncompromising in his insistence that Gentiles need not be circumcised. If Paul's entering the Christian community involved such a radical reorientation of his life and his religious values, it seems misleading to assert that Paul remained a Jew with a new calling. Paul may indeed have thought of himself as a Jew throughout his entire life. But he also insisted on a reinterpretation of Torah so radical that it eventually created a new pattern of religion.

### 3.3. Conversion or Call?

In many ways the question of whether Paul's Damascus Road experience was a call or a conversion is an artificial one. The question itself seems to impose modern categories on ancient descriptions of a complex religious event. But asking the question also allows us to realize that Paul's experience is far too rich to fit neatly into any of our categories. It is both call and conversion. So when we ask if Paul's experience is a call or a conversion, we are not only asking which term best describes Paul's experience, we are also asking whether any single term can do justice to that event.

Paul's call to be the apostle to the Gentiles is central to the accounts in Acts and Galatians 1. But it seems much more important in the Acts accounts, which are seeking to justify the mission to the Gentiles, than it does in Paul's accounts. Paul mentions it in defense of his gospel in Galatians 1, but there is no mention at all of an apostolic call in Philippians 3. This would suggest that Paul himself did not understand his revelatory experience primarily as a call, even though his call to be apostle to the Gentiles was certainly part of that experience. Those who see Paul's experience primarily as a call are probably being more influenced by Luke and his purposes than by Paul's own interpretation of his experience.

The central theme of the autobiographical passages in Galatians 1 and Philippians 3 is the contrast between Paul's former life in Judaism and his present life in Christ. In Philippians 3 Paul claims that this contrast is due to the transforming character of his experience of knowing Christ. This same contrast is also found in all three Acts accounts. Does this evidence of a profound change in Paul's life mean that the Damascus Road experience is best understood as a conversion? The answer to this question depends on how conversion is defined.

The traditional Western understanding of conversion, when imposed on the NT texts, leads to a distorted understanding of Paul's experience. This view of conversion sees Paul as a Jew who struggles with guilt over his failure to keep the Law. Paul says that he was "as to righteousness* under the Law, blameless" (Phil 3:6). It also sees Paul's conversion as an experience of being justified by faith rather than an experience of knowing Christ and being called to proclaim him to the Gentiles. Although this is not a serious distortion of the NT texts, it is still an example of trying to fit Paul into traditional Protestant categories rather than trying to understand the complexities of Paul's experience.

Sociological definitions of conversion seem to be more consistent with the NT descriptions of Paul's experience. If conversion results in a change of communities and a reinterpretation of one's past life, Paul's experience certainly qualifies as a conversion. Even though sociological definitions of conversion do not distort Paul's experience, they do not really do justice to it either. Paul's experience had a powerful revelatory dimension to it and Paul claims that both his experience and the gospel he received were of divine origin. The event which caused him to change communities was a call to be apostle to the Gentiles and the event which caused him to re-evaluate his life was a direct revelation of Christ. Social-scientific definitions of conversion cannot describe these revelatory elements in Paul's conversion experience.

No single term seems to be able to describe the complexities of Paul's Damascus Road experience. Because strong contrasts are part of every account of Paul's experience, it certainly qualifies as some sort of conversion experience. But it is also important to include the revelatory dimensions of Paul's experience and recognize it as an experience of call. In other words, Paul's call to be apostle to the Gentiles is part of a profound and transforming conversion experience. Call and conversion are both aspects of a divine revelation of Christ to Paul. The changes in Paul's life and his mission to the Gentiles are the results of this profound experience of knowing Christ.

*3.4. Paul's Experience as a Model for Christians.* To what extent is Paul's Damascus Road experience meant to be a model for Christians? In Philippians 3:17 Paul urges his readers to "join in imitating me, and observe those who live according to the example you have in us" (*see* Imitation). What aspects of his experience is Paul urging his readers to imitate? In answering this question it is important to maintain a distinction between the call and conversion aspects of Paul's experience.

It is interesting that the only passage referring to Paul's Damascus Road experience in which Paul urges his readers to follow his example is the passage in which no mention of his apostolic call is made. There is no indication that Paul ever suggested that anyone imitate him in his role as apostle to the Gentiles. In fact, there is every indication in Galatians 1—2 that Paul saw his call as unique and that he zealously defended his unique mission and perspective. The Acts accounts also present him as *the* apostle to the Gentiles and give him credit for the early church's Gentile mission. This is why scholars like Stendahl, who see Paul's experience primarily as a call, are suspicious of attempts to make Paul's experience normative for the church.

So what does Paul mean when he urges his readers to "join in imitating me"? In Philippians 3 Paul is reflecting on his personal experience of knowing Christ. Paul discusses knowing Christ in such a way that it can only be something gained in the process of being transformed. All Christians must be part of the community of those being transformed by Christ if they are truly to know Christ. In Philippians 3:14 Paul says that this transformation continues as he follows the "call of God in Christ Jesus." Here Paul is not talking about his apostolic call but about the call to be

transformed—one that is addressed to all believers. Being transformed involves "forgetting what lies behind" and "straining forward to what lies ahead." So the dynamic of this transformation is very similar to the dynamic of conversion, in which one completely rethinks the past in the light of present commitments. Paul shares with the Philippian community the "call of God in Christ Jesus" and the experience of being transformed by that call. All Christians must be part of the community of those being transformed by Christ if they are to truly know Christ. When Paul urges the Philippians to imitate him, he is urging them to join him in responding to that call and allowing Christ to transform their lives. Knowing Christ has led to a total transformation of Paul's life and values. It is this experience of being transformed by Christ that Paul urges his readers to imitate.

*3.5. Paul's Experience and His Theology.* Most scholars either ignore the issue of Paul's experience and dismiss it as irrelevant or see it as the key to understanding Paul's theology. But those who think Paul's conversion/call affects his theology are not in agreement on exactly what influence the experience might have had. A great deal of this lack of agreement stems from the different ways Paul's experience is understood. Those who see it as a call think it has a very different influence on his theology from those who see it as a conversion.

The traditional view of Paul's conversion, which sees it as an experience of being justified by faith, also views the center of Paul's theology as the doctrine of justification* by faith (*see* Center). Paul arrives at his view of the Law because of his struggle with the Law as a Jew and his subsequent experience of being freed by Christ from this struggle. He rejects the "works-righteousness" of Judaism in favor of the Christian way of justification by faith. Although most biblical scholars no longer define Paul's conversion in the traditional way, this view of the relationship between Paul's experience and his theology is still presented in modified forms (see Theissen, 177-265).

Those who see Paul's experience as a call have a very different view of the relationship of this experience to Paul's theology. For these scholars, the center of Paul's theology lies in his call as apostle to the Gentiles (so, partly, Sanders). This call created questions about the Law for Paul: If Gentiles are now included in the people of God, do they have to keep the Law? What happens to the Law now that the Messiah has come? What does this mean for Jew-Gentile relations and the place of Gentiles in the church? Paul arrived at his view of the Law from answering these questions, not from his experience of the Law before or after his call (see Stendahl, Munck, Dunn).

In recent years scholars who understand Paul's experience as a conversion have linked it to his theology in ways that are quite different from the traditional "justification by faith" model. These scholars think that all of Paul's theology, not just his doctrine of justification by faith, is derived from his Damascus Road experience.

S. Kim takes seriously Paul's claim to have received his gospel "through a revelation of Jesus Christ" (Gal 1:12) and argues that Paul's conversion experience on the Damascus road was the source for both his apostolic call and his theological understanding of the gospel. Paul's christology comes from his recognition that the glory of God was revealed in the face of Christ (2 Cor 4:6). This revelation leads to Paul's proclamation of salvation* as a present reality which will be consummated at the eschaton, when the glory* of Christ will be fully visible (see Newman). This Christ is the embodiment of God's plan of salvation that includes both Jews and Gentiles; Christ is the end of the Law.* This is why Paul surrendered his righteousness based on the Law to receive God's righteousness, which is based on faith in Christ. This experience of the reconciling grace of God allowed Paul to develop his distinctive doctrine of the atoning death of Christ as God reconciling (*see* Peace, Reconciliation) the world to himself through Christ. Seeing this glorified Christ as the image of God who has restored the divine image* and glory lost by Adam* led directly to Paul's conception of believers being conformed to the image of Christ and becoming a new creation.* In other words, Paul really did receive his gospel as part of his conversion experience and all of his theology is derived directly from that experience.

A. F. Segal makes a very strong case for the close connection between Paul's conversion experience, understood from a sociological perspective as a change of communities, and his theology. Paul's understanding of the Law comes from both his conversion experience and his subsequent experience in the Gentile church. Paul's legal principle in Romans 7:4, that those who have died with Christ are dead to the Law, is a metaphor for his own conversion. His experience of radical change led to a radical new evaluation of the Law. Much of his theology of the Law-free gospel was formed in battles with Jewish Christians about the role of the Law in Gentile-Christian communities. Paul's understanding of transformation, which is the result of his conversion experience, plays a crucial role in his understanding of Christian community. All Christians must be part of an evolving, transformed, redeemed community and all who are members of that community are equally members of Christ. In fact all of Paul's theology can ultimately be traced to his experience of conversion: "Having begun with his own personal experience, Paul thereafter expands his theory not simply to involve his own salvation, and the salvation of the Gentiles, but also the entire history of humanity, from Adam to the eschaton" (Segal, 183). Since Paul's life, as well as much as his writings, embodied the solution to the issues facing the earliest church, Christianity received the influence of his personality and was seen as a community of converts. Paul's conversion not only influenced his theology, it defined Christianity.

*See also* APOSTLE; CALL, CALLING; JEW, PAUL THE; JUSTIFICATION; LAW; MYSTICISM; PAUL IN ACTS AND LETTERS; PROPHET, PAUL AS; VISIONS, ECSTATIC EXPERIENCE.

BIBLIOGRAPHY. P. Berger and T. Luckmann, *The Social Construction of Reality: A Treatise on the Sociology of Knowledge* (Garden City, NY: Doubleday, 1966); H. D. Betz, *Galatians: A Commentary on Paul's Letter to the Churches in Galatia* (Herm; Philadelphia: Fortress, 1979); M. Bouttier, *Christianity According to Paul* (Naperville, IL: Alec R. Allenson, 1966); C. E. D. Cranfield, *Romans: I-VIII* (ICC; Edinburgh: T. & T. Clark, 1975); J. D. G. Dunn, " 'A Light to the Gentiles': The Significance of the Damascus Road Christophany for Paul," in *Jesus, Paul and the Law: Studies in Mark and Galatians* (Louisville: Westminster/John Knox, 1990); B. R. Gaventa, *From Darkness to Light: Aspects of Paul's Conversion in the New Testament* (Philadelphia: Fortress, 1986); E. Haenchen, *The Acts of the Apostles: A Commentary* (Oxford: Basil Blackwell, 1971); W. James, *The Varieties of Religious Experience* (New York: Collier MacMillan, 1961); S. Kim, *The Origin of Paul's Gospel* (Grand Rapids: Eerdmans, 1982); G. Lohfink, *The Conversion of St. Paul: Narrative and History in Acts* (Chicago: Franciscan Herald, 1976); R. P. Martin, *The Epistle of Paul to the Philippians* (TNTC; Grand Rapids: Eerdmans, 1959); J. Munck, *Paul and the Salvation of Mankind* (Atlanta: John Knox, 1977); C. Newman, *Paul's Glory-Christology: Tradition and Rhetoric* (NovTSup 69; Leiden: E. J. Brill, 1992); A. D. Nock, *Conversion: The Old and New in Religion from Alexander the Great to Augustine of Hippo* (Oxford: Oxford University, 1933); E. P. Sanders, *Paul and Palestinian Judaism* (Philadelphia: Fortress, 1977); A. F. Segal, *Paul the Convert: The Apostolate and Apostasy of Saul the Pharisee* (New Haven: Yale University, 1990); K. Stendahl, *Paul Among Jews and Gentiles* (Philadelphia: Fortress, 1976); J. S. Stewart, *A Man in Christ: The Vital Elements of St. Paul's Religion* (New York: Harper & Brothers, 1935); G. Theissen, *Psychological Aspects of Pauline Theology* (Philadelphia: Fortress, 1987).

J. M. Everts

**CONVERTS.** *See* COWORKERS, PAUL AND HIS; SOCIAL SETTING OF MISSION CHURCHES.

**CORINTH.** *See* CORINTHIANS, LETTERS TO THE.

## CORINTHIANS, LETTERS TO THE

1 and 2 Corinthians represent at least two of the four or more letters that Paul wrote to his church in Corinth together with the churches in the region of Achaia which surrounded this important Roman city (1 Cor 1:2; 2 Cor 1:1; cf. Rom 16:1). As its founder (cf. 1 Cor 4:14-15; 2 Cor 10:13-14), Paul knew well the church's history, character and problems. 1 Corinthians provides the most detailed example within the Pauline corpus of the way in which Paul applied his theological convictions, especially his christology* and eschatology,* to the practical issues facing the church. In contrast, due to the circumstances which later developed in Corinth with the arrival of Paul's opponents,* 2 Corinthians contains Paul's most sustained apologetic for his apostolic authority* of any of the Pauline letters. In addition, both letters deal with the collection for the saints in Jerusalem, which was so important to Paul (cf. 1 Cor 16:1-9; 2 Cor 8—9; *see* Collection).

1. The Contents of 1 Corinthians
2. The Contents of 2 Corinthians
3. The City and Its Citizens
4. The Church and Its Apostle
5. Some Critical Questions
6. Theological Themes of 1 and 2 Corinthians

### 1. The Contents of 1 Corinthians.

*1.1. The Salutation.* Paul's salutation in 1 Corinthians 1:1-3 is typical of ancient letters in that it first identifies the sender and then the recipients, after which a greeting is extended. Paul's salutation in 1 Corinthians is distinct, however, in that he expands both the identification of the sender (Paul and Sosthenes) and the recipients (to the church in Corinth, "together with all those who are calling upon the name of our Lord Jesus Christ in every place," 1 Cor 1:2). On the one hand, joint authorship of an ancient letter is rare. We are not sure who Sosthenes was (cf. the same name in Acts 18:17 for the ruler of the synagogue in Corinth), or what contribution he made in writing the letter, for as 1 Corinthians unfolds it becomes clear that Paul alone is speaking. Moreover, Paul's position as "an apostle of Christ Jesus" is clearly distinguished from that of Sosthenes, who is identified merely as "our brother" (1 Cor 1:1). On the other hand, this is the most extensive elaboration of the recipients found among Paul's letters. In it Paul indicates that he views

the church in Corinth to be the center of a cluster of house churches in the surrounding area.

But what is most striking in the salutation are the two supporting clauses which give the general reason both for Paul's writing (i.e., because he has been called by the will of God to be an apostle of Christ Jesus), and for his writing to the Corinthians (i.e., because they too have been called to be "saints" as those "set apart" or "sanctified in Christ Jesus"). In both cases the focus on Christ* in the salutation points forward to the christological foundation of Paul's arguments in 1 Corinthians. The prayer*/wish in 1 Corinthians 1:3, "grace (*charis*) . . . to you," is a Christianized form and expansion of the typical greeting used in ancient letters: "greetings (*chairein*) to you."

*1.2. The Opening Thanksgiving.* Again according to his normal custom, Paul follows his salutation with a thanksgiving for his church in 1 Corinthians 1:4-9 (*see* Benediction). More than merely a spontaneous expression of personal praise, the thanksgiving introduces the central theme of the letter as a whole (*see* Letters). Despite the Corinthians' current problems, Paul begins by expressing his gratitude to God* for the sufficiency of their spiritual gifts* (i.e., the concrete expression of the "grace"* of God given to them), since Paul is thereby assured that God has irrevocably called the Corinthians and will therefore sustain them faithfully until judgment* day. Hence, the problem in Corinth is not their spiritual gifts *per se*, but their attitude toward and use of them (cf. 1 Cor 12—14). As will become clear, the Corinthians are boasting in the very calling and gifts (= grace) for which God alone is to be thanked (cf. 1 Cor 1:26-31; 4:7).

*1.3. Responses to Reports About Corinth.* 1 Corinthians 1:10 begins the body of Paul's letter and introduces the first major section, which runs from 1 Corinthians 1:10 to 6:20. This section contains Paul's responses to the issues which he has heard about from "Chloe's people" (1 Cor 1:11, i.e., a certain group, most likely from Ephesus, in contact with the Corinthian situation) and from other oral reports (1 Cor 5:1; cf. 16:15-18). In this first major section Paul also attempts to clear up the Corinthians' misunderstanding of his earlier correspondence (1 Cor 5:9, 11).

In the first unit within this section (1 Cor 1:10—6:20), Paul deals with the causes of and the solution to the dissension and rivalry that has developed between some of the Corinthians based on their loyalty to various Christian leaders, including Paul himself (to posit actual divisions or "parties" within the church is too strong a reading of 1 Cor 1:10-12). The many attempts to ascertain the origin and distinctive theological perspective of those who claimed to belong to Paul, Apollos,* Cephas (*see* Peter) and, more generally, to Christ (1 Cor 1:12) have not been successful. The attempt to read this text as evidence for a pervasive conflict within the early church between Peter, representing the Jewish Christians, and Paul, representing the Gentiles,* as first championed by F. C. Baur, has also failed (*see* Paul and His Interpreters).

What can be said with confidence is that the root of the problem was the Corinthian addiction to the power, prestige and pride represented in the Hellenistic rhetorical* tradition, with its emphasis on the glory of human wisdom and attainment and its corresponding flagrant and flamboyant lifestyle. It is this Hellenistic "wisdom of the word" (1 Cor 1:17, 20, 26; 2:1; 3:19) that Paul combats by calling attention to the contrary "wisdom"* and "power"* of God as manifested first in the cross* of Christ (1 Cor 1:18-25), then in the calling of the Corinthians themselves (1 Cor 1:26-31), and finally in the intentional nature of Paul's own ministry* and apostolic way of life (1 Cor 2:1-5; 4:1-13).

Yet since "the word of the cross is foolishness* to those who are perishing" (1 Cor 1:18; cf. 2:14), only those whose hearts have been transformed by the work of the Spirit will be able to accept the true wisdom and power of God as revealed in the gospel* (1 Cor 1:20-24; 2:6-16). Paul therefore warns the Corinthians that their boasting in themselves and in their various spiritual leaders is a dangerous sign that the Spirit is not prevailing in their lives, since they are acting like those who are still "natural" or "unspiritual" (1 Cor 2:14—3:4). Should such an attitude and its behavior continue, they too will thus find themselves under the judgment of God, who will destroy the wisdom of this world* and all those who work to destroy the church* as the temple* of the Spirit, built on the foundation of the cross of Christ (1 Cor 1:19-20; 3:10-23). The Corinthians must consequently repent of their boasting, recognize that everything they have is a gift, and follow in the pattern of their own apostle, whose life of weakness* and suffering manifests both the power of the kingdom* of God and the reality of the cross (1 Cor 1:31; 2:3-5; 4:6-13, 14-21).

The same arrogance and spiritual competition based on one's spiritual gifts and leaders, which some Corinthians had wed to a boasting in the achievements of Hellenistic wisdom (1 Cor 1:10—4:21), had also manifested itself in flagrant immorality within the church and in lawsuits* between fellow believers (cf. 1 Cor 5:2, 6; 6:9). In 1 Corinthians 5:1—6:20 Paul now addresses these problems and their underlying causes.

In the first case Paul responds by exercising his own authority. With the cooperation and consent of the Corinthian church, he disciplines* the man who is living with his father's wife with excommunication for the sake of his ultimate restoration (1 Cor 5:3-5). Paul then proceeds to make it clear that one's new position in and worship* of Christ demand a corresponding purity and separation, not from the world, but within the world (1 Cor 5:6-13), since "the unrighteous will not inherit the kingdom of God" (1 Cor 6:9). The Corinthians' present status of having been justified* and sanctified (*see* Holiness) in Christ must work itself out in a corresponding life of growing obedience to the demands of God, for they are the temple of God's own Spirit (1 Cor 6:11, 12-20). Though all things are "lawful" for the believer, the Spirit does not free one from the call to holiness in this age; it frees one for it (1 Cor 6:12).

In the midst of this discussion, Paul addresses the fact that the Corinthians are taking their disputes to the secular courts for arbitration. Here too the Corinthians' spirituality* ought to equip them to express God's wisdom, rather than allowing them to capitulate to the world, especially when they are being equipped as God's people to share in God's ultimate judgment of the world (1 Cor 6:1-6). And in the event that no settlement can be reached, those who are spiritual ought to be willing and able to suffer wrong unjustly for the sake of Christ (1 Cor 6:7-8). As 1 Corinthians 8:1—11:1 and 1 Corinthians 13 will make clear, this is the true way of Christ-like love* and the true expression of one's spiritual power, maturity and giftedness.

*1.4. Responses to the Letter from Corinth.* Beginning with 1 Corinthians 7:1, Paul turns his attention to the issues concerning which the Corinthians have recently written to Paul for clarification of his views and their implications. Paul's treatment of these matters constitutes the second major section of the letter, which extends to 1 Corinthians 16:12 (cf. the repeated use of the "concerning" formula in 1 Cor 7:1; 8:1; 12:1; 16:1; 16:12).

In 1 Corinthians 7:1-40 Paul discusses marriage* and celibacy. Here he is mindful of the tensions and anxieties caused by living in an evil age between the first and second comings of Christ (1 Cor 7:25-35), and of the God-given physical and emotional needs and desires of his people (1 Cor 7:1-5, 36-38). The basis of Paul's instruction is once again the determinative role that the calling and gifting of God play in one's life (cf. 1 Cor 7:15, 17-24 with 1:26-31). And here again, though Paul himself prefers being single as the way of life most suited to serving God (cf. 1 Cor 7:8, 32-34, 38), the goal is to live, whether married, widowed or single, in the kind of devotion to the Lord that corresponds to God's work in one's life and reflects God's character (cf. 1 Cor 7:19-20, 35).

In 1 Corinthians 8:1—11:1 Paul confronts the problems that have arisen due to the fact that the more knowledgeable within the church are eating food* which has been sacrificed in a pagan temple. These individuals have come to understand that idols* do not actually exist (1 Cor 8:4-6). But their behavior has become a stumbling block for those who do not yet share this understanding, defiling their weaker consciences and destroying their faith (1 Cor 8:7, 9, 11-12). Paul considers such disregard for the disposition of others, based on one's own rights and knowledge, to be a sin not only against them but against Christ himself. Those who truly know God and are known by him will employ their freedom* and knowledge* for the sake of building up others in their faith, even when this entails denying one's own legitimate rights as a believer (1 Cor 8:1-3; 13). This is the "love that builds up," rather than knowledge alone, which merely "makes one arrogant" (1 Cor 8:1).

To support his point Paul illustrates this principle of love by pointing to his own decision to support himself financially while in Corinth (1 Cor 9:1-27; see Tentmaking). Although the Corinthians accepted Paul as an apostle (1 Cor 9:1-2), others criticized him for not exercising his legitimate apostolic right to financial support (1 Cor 9:3-14; see Financial Support) even when this meant much undue hardship and suffering* on Paul's part (cf. 1 Cor 4:11-13). Paul's answer is that he has given up his rights as an apostle for the sake of the progress of the gospel and for the reward God has promised for such acts of love (1 Cor 9:15-18). Paul thus makes himself "a slave to all, that [he] might win the more" (1 Cor 9:19) even though he is free to do as it is appropriate in Christ. This is the training in love that all must engage in, who, like Paul, are called to persevere in self-control in order to pursue the prize of the gospel (1 Cor 9:23-27).

In chapter ten Paul goes on to warn the Corinthians of what will happen if they too fail to persevere in love, and misuse their knowledge and experience as an excuse for continual immorality and evil (cf. 1 Cor 10:11-12). Like Israel in the wilderness, they will be destroyed (1 Cor 10:1-10). Indeed, God has provided a way of escape from overwhelming temptation, so that there is no excuse for not enduring in the love that is produced by genuine faith (1 Cor 10:13). As an example of this Paul gives theological parameters and practical advice for dealing with the temptation to partake of food offered to idols. This temptation was common among the Corinthians in general, for whom it was a common social practice to eat in the precincts

of a pagan temple (see Idolatry). But Paul warns of the inherent spiritual dangers, arguing that even if an idol is "nothing," those who partook of food offered to idols were partaking of the table of demons* (1 Cor 10:14-30). Finally, Paul returns once again to his own apostolic lifestyle of not seeking his own advantage but living to please others for Christ's sake (1 Cor 10:31-32). Here too this is an example for the Corinthians themselves, calling them once more to be "imitators" of him, as he is of Christ (1 Cor 11:1; cf. 4:16; see Imitation).

In 1 Corinthians 11:2-34 and 1 Corinthians 12—14 Paul turns his attention to three matters concerning Christlike behavior in worship*: (1) the relationship between men and women in worship as expressed in the cultural practice of women wearing veils (1 Cor 11:2-16 [see Man and Woman]; unlike his response to the following two problems, Paul here praises the Corinthians and merely writes to give them a theological grounding for their practice), (2) the setting up of class distinctions during the celebration of the Lord's Supper* as an abuse of its very meaning (1 Cor 11:17-34), and (3) the proper use of prophecy* and tongues* in worship (1 Cor 14:1-40) against the backdrop of the significance of spiritual gifts* in general (1 Cor 12:1-31).

In view of Paul's arguments thus far in 1 Corinthians it is not surprising that in each of these cases Paul's approach is to make it clear that true spirituality and giftedness are not compatible with arrogant boasting and competition based on one's place in the body of Christ (see Body of Christ) or in society, or with parading one's gifts before others (cf. 1 Cor 11:18-22; 12:14-26; 14:6-12). Genuine spirituality manifests itself in mutual interdependence and complementarity, both among men and women in view of their distinct roles, and among those within the church due to the variety of their spiritual gifts. The same principles are to be manifest in dealing with their cultural diversity and economic distinctions (cf. 1 Cor 11:11, 33-34; 12:4-31; 14:26-40). And in each case this practical spirituality is grounded in theology, whether that be the creative work of God (1 Cor 11:2-16), the redemptive work of Christ (1 Cor 11:17-34), or the gifting of the Spirit (1 Cor 12—14).

Finally, as "the more excellent way" outlined in 1 Corinthians 13 makes evident, the criterion for establishing the appropriate application of this theology is that of "love,"* the character of which is outlined in 1 Corinthians 13:4-7 (cf. its application in 1 Cor 12:4-11; 14:6-19). Hence, apart from faith in Christ working itself out in love for the body of Christ, participation in the Lord's Supper and apparent possession of spiritual gifts do not ensure one's right standing before God. In fact, they bring one under the judgment of God (cf. 1 Cor 11:16, 27-32; 14:37-38), since only love, as the outward expression of faith* and hope,* remains forever (1 Cor 13:1-3, 8-13). Paul can thus admonish the Corinthians, who pride themselves on their spiritual gifts and experiences, that "since you are eager for spiritual things and experiences, strive that you may abound in building up the church" (1 Cor 14:12).

Having begun by grounding his opening section in the cross of Christ (cf. 1 Cor 1:18-25), Paul now concludes his application of theological truths to practical problems by dealing in 1 Corinthians 15:1-58 with the surety and nature of the future resurrection* in view of the resurrection of Christ. Paul first calls attention in 1 Corinthians 15:1-5 to the death and resurrection of Christ as the center point of the gospel, which Paul had received as the common tradition* of the church and then passed on to the Corinthians as the basis of their salvation. This is the earliest account we have of the contours of the early Christian message and its historical evidence. Paul then supplements this evidence with the recital of Christ's further resurrection appearances. He concludes with his own experience of the resurrected Christ and its consequences for his life as the "least of the apostles" (1 Cor 15:9-11).

In turning his attention to the Corinthians, Paul draws out a threefold significance from the fact of Christ's resurrection. First, no one can conclude that there is no resurrection from the dead (1 Cor 15:12-19, 29-34). Second, Christ's resurrection is the "first fruits"* of what will happen to all "in Christ"* at his second coming when God's "final enemy," death (see Life and Death), is destroyed and all authorities are put back under subjection to the reign of God. Hence, contrary to the Corinthians' belief that they were *already* experiencing the fullness of the resurrection age to come in their own current life of the Spirit (i.e., their "over-realized eschatology"), the final resurrection is by no means merely an experience of spiritual power and gifting in the present (1 Cor 15:20-28). Rather, it is a qualitatively different bodily existence which can only be gained through the granting of a new, resurrected and spiritual body (1 Cor 15:35-56). Third, believers now live "between" the two resurrections, Christ's and their own. They live in the midst of an age which is still evil, but which can be endured and overcome by the sure confidence that Christ's resurrection experience and victory over death as the "last Adam*" will be shared by them because they are "in Christ" (1 Cor 15:42-54). The practical implication of this hope is that the believer is encouraged to "be steadfast, immovable, always abounding in the work

of the Lord, knowing that in the Lord your labor is not in vain" (1 Cor 15:58).

As the last of the matters raised by the Corinthians' letter, Paul ends his responses by outlining his instructions concerning the management of the collection being taken for the poor believers in Jerusalem,* noting his future travel plans, providing a recommendation for Timothy (*see* Coworkers), and then giving a brief explanation of Apollos's* reason for not visiting Corinth (1 Cor 16:1-12).

*1.5. Concluding Remarks.* The letter ends with a final series of admonitions and greetings from Paul and those with Paul in Asia (1 Cor 16:13-24). As a fitting capstone to the letter as a whole, these admonitions center on the need for perseverance in one's faith as it works itself out in love (1 Cor 16:13-14) and the corresponding pronouncement of God's judgment on those who "have no love for the Lord," with Paul himself longing for the return of Christ (1 Cor 16:22).

**2. The Contents of 2 Corinthians.**

*2.1. The Salutation.* The salutation in 2 Corinthians 1:1-2 follows the same pattern as 1 Corinthians 1:1-3, though in comparison both the identification of the sender and of the recipients are now abbreviated. Paul's apostolic identity by means of the will of God is again expressed, with Timothy now noted as the letter's cosender. But as in the case of Sosthenes, here too Timothy is identified merely as a "brother," once again clearly highlighting Paul's apostolic office. Though there has been considerable discussion concerning whether the first person plurals in 2 Corinthians 1—7 refer to a wider circle of apostles or coworkers* (cf., e.g., 2 Cor 1:19; 8:16-23), the internal evidence of the letter suggests that Paul alone remains the subject *and* object of the discussion throughout 2 Corinthians, apart from those texts where it is explicitly indicated otherwise (e.g., 2 Cor 3:18; the focus on the Corinthians in 2 Cor 6:14—7:1; 8—9). The recipients of the letter remain the house churches in Corinth and those believers scattered in small groups around this center. The greeting is also the same as in 1 Corinthians.

*2.2. The Opening Thanksgiving.* But unlike the situation he faced in 1 Corinthians, Paul now finds himself in a new polemical situation in which his own legitimacy as an apostle had been severely called into question at Corinth and still is being doubted by a significant minority within the church (see 4.2 below). This polemical situation and the corresponding apologetic tone which characterizes much of 2 Corinthians are evident from the beginning of the letter. In contrast to Paul's opening thanksgiving in 1 Corinthians 1:4-9, Paul begins 2 Corinthians not by thanking God for God's work of grace among the Corinthians, but by praising God for his work of comfort and deliverance from adversity in his own life (2 Cor 1:3-11). In doing so, Paul uses a formula in 2 Corinthians 1:3 which is typical of Jewish worship ("blessed be God . . .") and which calls attention to blessings in which he himself has participated (see Liturgical Elements). These thanksgivings function in Paul's letters to introduce the main themes of his writing, to express his perspective on them, and to introduce an implicit appeal to his readers in response.

Second Corinthians 1:1-11 thus establishes the apologetic tone and central theme of what is to follow: rather than calling his apostleship into question, Paul's suffering* validates his call.* God has called Paul to suffer in order that through the merciful "comfort" of God's sustaining power and ultimate deliverance, which Paul experiences in his affliction,* he will be able to make God's power and comfort known to others (2 Cor 1:6-7, 10). Paul can thus interpret his own suffering (= "death") in terms of the death of Christ, and his deliverance from this suffering as a type of the resurrection (2 Cor 1:9). As such, these too become a means by which the church is encouraged in its faithfulness in the midst of adversity (2 Cor 1:7). Paul's suffering, being the vehicle through which the comfort God provides is made manifest, is therefore the very mark of his genuine apostolic calling. Paul consequently concludes this section by calling the Corinthians to join him in thanking God for his suffering and deliverance, the very thing his opponents claimed disqualified him as an apostle (2 Cor 1:11).

### 2.3. Paul's Defense of the Change in His Travel Plans.
In the first major section of Paul's letter, 2 Corinthians 1:12—2:13, Paul explains the theological rationale for the recent unexpected change in his travel plans (2 Cor 1:15-16; see Itineraries, Travel Plans). Paul's purpose is to demonstrate that his behavior has been an expression of the sincerity of motives which only God can discern (2 Cor 1:12). Conversely, Paul's actions have not been the result of "fleshly wisdom" (2 Cor 1:12) and the vacillations of one who makes his plans "according to the flesh.*" This may reflect an allegation, apparently made by his opponents, that Paul was guilty of an elaborate scheme to defraud the Corinthians in connection with the collection for Jerusalem and his own practice of preaching for free (2 Cor 1:17; cf. 2:17; 7:2; 8:20-21; 11:7-11; 12:13-18).

Paul's point in 2 Corinthians 1:15—2:4 is that his earlier decision not to visit Corinth on his way to Jerusalem from Macedonia (cf. 1 Cor 16:5-9), but to come directly to Corinth first (2 Cor 1:15), as well as his later decision not to return to Corinth a second time (2 Cor 1:23), were all the actions of one who is "sealed by the Spirit" and is therefore acting in a Christ-like manner. As the full realization of the promises of God (2 Cor 1:19-20), Christ makes it clear that God's purpose in acting toward his people is to establish mercy* before judgment. In the same way, Paul's changes in travel plans were all motivated by his desire to extend mercy to the Corinthians in order to effect their restoration, rather than to come in judgment (2 Cor 1:23-24). Paul changed his travel plans in order to give the Corinthians the chance for repentance (2 Cor 7:8-13), deciding not to come back to Corinth after his "painful visit," but writing the "sorrowful letter" instead (2 Cor 2:1-5). Far from being an expression of fleshly behavior, Paul's changes in plans were thus an extension of God's action in Christ.

In 2 Corinthians 2:5-11 Paul turns his attention back to those Corinthians who have already repented of their disloyalty to Paul in response to his previous "sorrowful letter" (cf. 2 Cor 2:5, 8-9; 7:7-16). Paul admonishes them to follow in his footsteps. Just as Paul acted to extend mercy to the Corinthians, they too should extend mercy to the repentant offender who caused Paul so much pain. They must welcome this one back, lest he be "overwhelmed by excessive sorrow" (2 Cor 2:7). Moreover, just as Paul's actions toward the Corinthians demonstrate his genuine apostolic standing, their willingness to extend mercy to this person takes on the character of a test of their faith* (2 Cor 2:9). Those who have experienced God's mercy have no choice but to extend mercy to those who have sinned against them, but have now repented. Paul therefore ends this section by reminding the Corinthians of the ultimate purpose of his admonitions: to prevent Satan* from using this situation against the church (2 Cor 2:11).

Finally Paul provides the transition to the next major section of his letter by calling attention to his most recent change in plans. When Titus failed to arrive as prearranged, Paul could not use opportunities for ministry in Troas but went to meet with Titus in Macedonia (cf. 2 Cor 7:5-7) because of his overwhelming concern for Titus and his earnest desire to hear the news Titus was to bring from Corinth (2 Cor 2:12-13). In view of 2 Corinthians 11:28 this anxiety over his "brother" and the Corinthians was yet another expression of Paul's greatest suffering as an apostle. This apparently insignificant transition thus calls us back to the central theme of the letter.

### 2.4. Paul's Direct Defense of His Apostolic Authority.
Rather than calling the legitimacy of his apostleship

into question, Paul's suffering as related in 2 Corinthians 2:12-13 leads him once again to praise God in 2 Corinthians 2:14, just as it did in 2 Corinthians 1:3-11. Moreover, here too Paul employs a typical Jewish thanksgiving formula in 2 Corinthians 2:14 ("thanks be to God") in order to signal the introduction of the central theme of the next section, which now runs from 2 Corinthians 2:14 to 7:16: "Thanks be to God who always leads us in a triumphal procession (*thriambeuō*) *unto death* in Christ, and in so doing manifests the fragrance of the knowledge of him through us in every place" (see Hafemann for a defense of this translation).

Just as in 1 Corinthians 4:9 Paul could picture himself as sentenced to death by God as a spectacle in the Roman arena, and in 2 Corinthians 1:9 as having been given the "sentence of death," Paul now portrays his suffering as an apostle in terms of the Roman triumphal procession in which those taken captive by the victor (like Paul by Christ!) are led like slaves to their death (2 Cor 2:14; *see* Triumph). Paul thus views his suffering as the divinely orchestrated means by which the knowledge of God is revealed in the world. With this as its introduction, this section sets forth Paul's most detailed defense of his apostolic ministry. Here his defense is aimed at those who called Paul's apostleship into question on account of his suffering (cf. 2 Cor 4:7-15; 6:3-10; 11:23-33), his weak personal appearance (cf. 2 Cor 10:10; 1 Cor 2:1-5) and his commitment to preach the gospel at his own expense. His opponents took these things to be signs of his inferiority as an apostle, of the worthlessness of his message and as part of his scheme to defraud the Corinthians (2 Cor 2:17; 11:7-15; 12:13-19).

At the heart of Paul's self-defense is the twofold argument in 2 Corinthians 2:14—3:6 for his sufficiency and boldness as an apostle.* On the one hand, Paul argues that he *is* sufficient for the apostolic calling (2 Cor 2:16) precisely because his apostolic life of suffering, as the means of revealing the knowledge of God, brings about the same dual effect in the world that Paul attributed to the word of the cross in 1 Corinthians 1:18-25 (2 Cor 2:15-16). Moreover, unlike his opponents, Paul has willingly taken up this suffering by preaching the gospel free of charge as evidence of his sincerity and divine call (2 Cor 2:17). On the other hand, Paul can point to the Corinthians themselves as additional concrete evidence for his sufficiency, since their own conversion and life in the Spirit, brought about through Paul, testify to the genuine nature of Paul's ministry among them (2 Cor 3:2-3). Paul's ministry of suffering and the Spirit thus combine to support his assertion that his sufficiency is from God and

that God has made him a minister of the "new covenant" of the Spirit in fulfillment of Ezekiel 36 and Jeremiah 31 (2 Cor 3:4-6; *see* Covenant).

In 2 Corinthians 3:7-18, one of the most complex passages in the Pauline corpus, Paul proceeds to compare his role as an apostle of the "new covenant" established by Christ to that of Moses'* role as mediator of the "old covenant" established at Sinai. Such a comparison is necessitated by the fact that in 2 Corinthians 2:16 and 3:5 Paul's sufficiency as an apostle is based on his call according to the pattern of the call of Moses as portrayed in Exodus 4:10 (LXX, *ouk hikanos eimi*). If Paul has been called *like* Moses, how then is his ministry *different* from that of Moses?

Paul answers this question by contrasting the events of Exodus 32—34 and their significance for understanding the nature and purpose of the old covenant to the new covenant in Christ. Paul's main point is that from the very beginning the Law functioned to "kill" Israel* by condemning it for its sinfulness. This was not because the Law itself was somehow deficient, but because the vast majority of Israel was left in a hardened condition so that it was unable to keep the covenant (cf. Ex 32:1-10; 33:3, 5; 34:9). As a result, Israel could not endure the glory of God without being destroyed (cf. Ex 33:3, 5). Moses had to veil himself, therefore, not because the glory* was fading, but so that the effects of God's glory against a stiff-necked people might be brought to an end (*katargeō*; 2 Cor 3:7, 11-12, in view of Ex 34:29-35). This would make it possible for God's presence to continue in Israel's midst in spite of Israel's hardened nature. The veil of Moses thus becomes a metonomy for the hardness of Israel's hearts under the old covenant (2 Cor 3:14-15).

The "letter" (*gramma*) of 2 Corinthians 3:6 is therefore the Law* apart from the power of the Spirit, which by itself can only declare God's will and pronounce judgment for not doing it, but cannot empower one to keep it. Only God's Spirit, which is now being poured out in the new covenant as a result of the work of Christ, can "make one alive" (2 Cor 3:6) and bring about this righteousness* (2 Cor 3:8-9). Hence, believers may now encounter in the Spirit the same glory of God that Moses encountered "with unveiled faces" (2 Cor 3:16-17). As a result, rather than being judged and destroyed by the presence of God, they are transformed by it into the very image* of God himself (2 Cor 3:18). Whereas Moses had to veil himself (2 Cor 3:12-13), as an apostle of the new covenant Paul can be bold in his declaration of the gospel because he is confident that he has been called to a ministry of the Spirit (2 Cor 3:8). Inasmuch as Paul's ministry thus mediates the glory of God to those whose hearts have been changed and thus need not fear their destruction, his ministry "outshines" that of the old covenant (2 Cor 3:10-11).

In 2 Corinthians 4:1-6 Paul draws the necessary conclusion from his preceding argument. On the one hand Paul's apostleship is legitimate in that it functions, both through his preaching and his way of life, to make known the "light of the gospel of the glory of Christ, who is the image of God" (2 Cor 4:4). This was the purpose of Paul's own call, pictured in 2 Corinthians 4:6 in terms of a new creation in which God "shone in our hearts to give the light of the knowledge of the glory of God in the face of Christ" (see Conversion and Call). On the other hand, this can only mean that those who reject Paul and his message do so because their own minds have been hardened by Satan, the "god of this age" (2 Cor 4:3-4).

In 2 Corinthians 4:7—6:13 Paul returns once again to the theme of his suffering, this time by both introducing and concluding this unit of thought with the second and third of his "catalogues of suffering" (2 Cor 4:7-15 and 6:3-13 respectively; cf. 1 Cor 4:11-13; see Afflictions). Having argued for the legitimacy and function of his suffering thus far, Paul now addresses the question of the actual necessity for his suffering, which he says in 2 Corinthians 4:7 is to demonstrate that the power and glory that is revealed in him is clearly God's and not his own. The way in which this is accomplished is through Paul's repeated experience of suffering (i.e., "carrying around in our body the death of Jesus," 2 Cor 4:10; "being handed over to death for Jesus' sake," 2 Cor 4:11; and having "death at work in us," 2 Cor 4:12) in order that God's power to sustain him might be seen (i.e., "that the life of Jesus might also be manifested in our [mortal] body," 2 Cor 4:10, 11) and experienced by others (2 Cor 4:12). Paul thus follows in the footsteps of the suffering righteous of the OT (cf. the quote from Ps 115:1 LXX in 2 Cor 4:13) and of the suffering Righteous One, Jesus, both in enduring suffering for the sake of others (cf. 2 Cor 4:15) and in his confidence in God's righteous vindication and reward* in the future (2 Cor 4:14, 16-18).

Paul's confidence in his future vindication, when he will be "at home with the Lord" (2 Cor 5:8), is based on the guarantee of his present possession of the Holy Spirit (2 Cor 5:5). This confidence causes him not only to long with courage for its reality (2 Cor 5:2-4), but also to endeavor to be pleasing to God, knowing that all must appear before the judgment seat of Christ to be recompensed for their deeds (2 Cor 5:9-10). This healthy fear of God also motivates Paul in his ministry and in his defense of his apostleship (2 Cor

5:11), not for his own sake, but in order that the Corinthians might have just cause to be proud of Paul (2 Cor 5:12-15) and to affirm the truth of his gospel of reconciliation (2 Cor 5:14, 16-21; see Peace, Reconciliation).

The consequence of Paul's ministry is then made clear. Those who have been reconciled to God in Christ are a "new creation" (2 Cor 5:17), which in the context entails not only a new relationship with God but also a new, righteous way of life in which one takes on the very character of God in Christ by living one's life for the sake of others (2 Cor 3:18; 4:5, 14-15; 5:21). Rather than rejecting Christ because of his suffering, as Paul himself formerly did when he regarded Christ from the nonspiritual point of view (i.e., "according to the flesh"), those who have been created anew see both Christ and others in the light of God's purpose of reconciliation (2 Cor 5:16, 19, 21).

Paul concludes this section and at the same time introduces the next by calling those within the Corinthian church who are still rejecting Paul and his message to be reconciled to God and not to presume upon God's grace and mercy. By doing so they will demonstrate that their prior acceptance of God's grace has not been in vain (2 Cor 5:20; 6:1). For as an ambassador for Christ (2 Cor 5:20), Paul, like the servant* in Isaiah 49:8, is called to bring the people back to their God (2 Cor 6:2). The catalog of suffering in 2 Corinthians 6:3-13 functions to support this appeal further by demonstrating again that, rather than calling his legitimacy into question, his opponents should observe that Paul's endurance in the midst of adversity commends him as an apostle. The section therefore ends with yet another appeal to those Corinthians still under the influence of Paul's opponents to be reconciled to Paul (2 Cor 6:11-13).

In view of the fact that the Corinthian church now stands divided over the legitimacy of Paul's apostleship and his understanding of Jesus and the Spirit (cf. 2 Cor 11:4), 2 Corinthians 6:14—7:2 addresses the question of the relationship between believers and unbelievers, the latter of which are now implicitly identified as those who will not repent and be reconciled to Paul as an apostle of the gospel of God. Paul's admonition is straightforward. Based on his understanding of the church as the temple of God (2 Cor 6:16) and the biblical injunction for God's people to separate themselves from idolatry in order to be God's "sons and daughters" (2 Cor 6:17), Paul calls the faithful Corinthians to separate themselves from those among them who continue to reject Paul and his gospel (2 Cor 6:14-15; 7:1).

In 2 Corinthians 7:2-16 Paul resumes his account of

the recent events in Corinth, focusing on the good news he received when he finally did meet Titus. Although Paul initially regretted having sent them such a severe reprimand, Paul is relieved by the fact that his letter of rebuke (2 Cor 7:5-8) brought about among the majority of Corinthian believers the kind of godly sorrow which leads to repentance rather than the "worldly grief" which merely brings death (2 Cor 7:9-13). Paul's defense of his apostleship in 2 Corinthians 2:14—7:16 consequently ends with a great expression of joy,* comfort and confidence in the Corinthians as a whole, since their positive response to Paul's previous warnings and to Titus's mission was a sure sign of the genuine nature of their faith and of the bond between Paul and his church (2 Cor 7:2-5, 11-16).

*2.5. The Collection.* In 2 Corinthians 8:1—9:15 the subject matter changes completely. Paul now takes up the theological foundation and practical administration of the collection* for the believers in Jerusalem* which he had initiated in Corinth, but which due to the problems in the church had not been completed as anticipated (2 Cor 8:6-7, 10-11; 9:2; cf. 1 Cor 16:1-4). The necessity for the collection is based not only on the needs of the church in Jerusalem and the ability of the Corinthians to give (2 Cor 8:14-15) but also on the implications of Christ's own self-giving for those under his lordship (2 Cor 8:8-9). Giving to the needs of others therefore becomes a test of the genuineness of one's faith (2 Cor 8:8, 24; 9:13), with Titus providing an example of just such a genuine faith and the love it produces (2 Cor 8:16-17). Two unnamed, but well-known and respected, brothers will be sent by Paul with Titus to ensure the completion and credibility of the collection to the glory of God (2 Cor 8:18-23; 9:1-5).

In 2 Corinthians 9:6-15 Paul then concludes his discussion of the collection by returning to its theological foundation. The collection is necessary because it expresses the church's trust in God to meet their needs to such a degree that they are willing and able to give cheerfully to others (2 Cor 9:6-9). God is faithful and he will respond to such acts of faith by working to supply the needs of those who give and then by rewarding those who use their resources for the benefit of others (2 Cor 9:8, 10-12). In going forward with the collection the Corinthians will therefore glorify God by affirming with their actions the gospel of Christ (2 Cor 9:13) and causing others to join them in glorifying God (2 Cor 9:12). The collection will also create a unity of prayer* and appreciation between the Corinthians and the church in Jerusalem (2 Cor 9:14), which leads Paul in response to close this section by praising God for his own "inexpressible gift" (2 Cor 9:15).

*2.6. Paul's Final Defense and Attack on His Opponents.* In the last major section of 2 Corinthians, 10:1—13:10, the tone, style and subject matter again change dramatically from the pastoral admonitions of 2 Corinthians 7:2-15 and chapters 8—9. Here is an aggressive apologetic and counter-attack against those within the church who still oppose Paul (2 Cor 13:5-10) and against his opponents from outside Corinth who stand in the shadows behind them (2 Cor 10:10; 11:4, 12-15, 21-23). The issues are still Paul's personal weakness and suffering (2 Cor 10:1, 10; 11:23-33), his voluntary self-support (2 Cor 11:7-15; 12:13-17) and his apparent lack of charismatic power (2 Cor 12:12; 13:3). Paul's upcoming visit consequently dominates this section in the hope that it will be a constructive time of healing, rather than a time of judgment for the church (cf. 2 Cor 10:2; 12:14, 20-21; 13:1-4).

2 Corinthians 10:1-6 is Paul's final appeal to the church for reconciliation in order that he might not have to "show boldness" in punishing disobedience when he arrives—although he is ready to do so (2 Cor 10:2, 6). In 2 Corinthians 10:7-11 Paul supports this appeal by reaffirming his legitimacy both as a Christian and as an apostle on the basis of the appropriate nature of his recent conduct, including his forceful boasting in his authority over the Corinthians. The appropriateness of Paul's conduct becomes evident once the right criterion for apostolic legitimacy is applied, namely, the concrete evidence of God's own work through him as seen in Paul's apostolic activity of founding the church in Corinth (2 Cor 10:12-18). When Paul lays claim to his authority he is thus not commending himself (2 Cor 10:12) but boasting "of the Lord," of what God himself has accomplished through Paul as evidence of the fact that he is the one whom the Lord "commends" (2 Cor 10:17-18).

Since God has already commended Paul through his apostolic work, the need to boast in one's own behavior or accomplishments is "foolish" (cf. 2 Cor 11:1, 16-21; 12:11). Yet in 2 Corinthians 11:1—12:10 Paul feels forced to do just that in order to counter the claims of his opponents and to win back those who have fallen under their sway. At the heart of the issue is the opponents' claim that they, not Paul, represent and are equal to the "eminent apostles" in Jerusalem. In this section Paul endeavors to show that he is the one who is a genuine apostle, on a par with the leaders of the mother church (2 Cor 11:5; 12:11), while his opponents, claiming some connection with the Jerusalem leaders, are in fact "false apostles" and "deceitful workers" who disguise themselves as "servants of righteousness" (2 Cor 11:12-15). Thus in 2 Corinthians 11:5 and 12:11 Paul compares himself positively with the "eminent apostles," while in 2 Corinthians 11:12-15 he draws the sharpest possible distinction between himself and his opponents.

In this section Paul therefore "boasts" first in his decision to preach the gospel free of charge in Corinth (2 Cor 11:7-12), and then in his other sufferings (2 Cor 11:23-33), as the true marks of his legitimacy as an apostle, only to boast finally in his own spiritual experiences. In this last case, however, Paul is exceedingly hesitant, knowing that this is the epitome of foolishness and the very thing concerning which God has given him a "thorn in the flesh" to keep him from doing (2 Cor 12:6-10). Furthermore, Paul asserts that the real reason his opponents have criticized him for his preaching free of charge, for his suffering and for his refusal to boast in his spiritual experiences is that his lifestyle and practice call their own legitimacy as apostles into question, based as it is on a demand for payment and their own tales of spiritual experiences (2 Cor 11:12). Paul's point is that neither human distinctives nor religious pedigree make one a servant of Christ (cf. 2 Cor 11:21-23), but weakness, since God has declared that his "power is made perfect in weakness" (2 Cor 12:9).

In 2 Corinthians 12:11—13:10 Paul brings the section to a close by reminding the Corinthians for the last time of his sincerity and apostolic legitimacy, as evidenced in his ministry of the Spirit and his suffering as a result of refusing to burden the Corinthians (2 Cor 12:11-18). Those who are still rejecting Paul must therefore repent in anticipation of his final visit (2 Cor 12:19—13:10). Not to do so will bring them under the judgment of God, since Paul has identified his own person and message with the glory of God in Christ and the true gospel (2 Cor 11:4; 12:21; 13:1-4). The ultimate test of the genuine nature of their faith is thus whether or not they will be reconciled with Paul (2 Cor 13:5-9). Hence, Paul's elaborate self-defense has not been for his own sake, but for the good of the Corinthians (2 Cor 12:19), since Paul is writing "these things while being absent in order that when [he is] present [he] might not have to use his authority severely, which the Lord gave [him] for building up and not tearing down" (2 Cor 13:10).

*2.7. Final Greetings.* In 2 Corinthians 13:11-13 (14) Paul ends his letter by calling his church to mend its ways, heal its rivalries, and live in unity and peace with one another. This closing appeal is based on the promise that in doing so "the God of love and peace" will be with them.

### 3. The City and Its Citizens.
More than perhaps any other of the Pauline letters, the sociological characteristics of Corinth, together with the religious and philosophical milieu of the region, influence one's interpretation of 1 and 2 Corinthians. Corinth was located at the foot of the 1,886-foot-high Acrocorinth, on the southern side of the 4.5-mile isthmus that connected the Peloponnese with the rest of Greece and separated the Saronic and Corinthian gulfs. Its location was strategic both militarily and commercially. Corinth controlled the overland movement between Italy and Asia, as well as the traffic between the two ports of Lechaeum, 1.5 miles to the north, and Cenchreae, 5.1 miles to the east. A portage between these two ports, which ran through Corinth, made it possible to avoid sailing the treacherous waters around the Peloponnesus. This portage was facilitated by a paved road across the isthmus, which was built in the sixth century B.C. Corinth was thus known as a wealthy city due to its tariffs and commerce, and as a crossroads for the ideas and traffic of the world (cf. Strabo *Geog.* 8.6.20-23). In terms of manufacturing it was especially known for its highly treasured bronze ware, one use of which was as "resonance enhancers" in the theater (cf. 1 Cor 13:1; Murphy-O'Connor, 50, 76).

The history of ancient Corinth is the history of two cities. As a political entity Corinth's history reaches back to the eighth century B.C., and until the mid-second century B.C. it flourished as a Greek city-state. But its status as the leader of the Achaean League led to Corinth's destruction by Rome in 146 B.C. Corinth then lay in ruins until 44 B.C., when it was re-founded by Julius Caesar as a Roman colony, after which it quickly rose to prominence once again (cf. Appian *Rom. Hist.* 8.136). By the first century Corinth had become the foremost commercial center in southern Greece. Beginning in 27 B.C. it was the seat of the region's proconsul and the capital of the senatorial province of Achaia until A.D. 15, when it became an imperial province. It also became famous for its control of the Isthmian games, a biennial athletic competition second only to the Olympian games in importance. This background is reflected in 1 Corinthians 9:24-27 in Paul's use of the athletic metaphor and his emphasis on the imperishable crown reserved for believers. This, for the Corinthians, would be recognized as a contrast with the crowns given in the Isthmian games, which were made out of withered celery plants (cf. Murphy-O'Connor, 17).

As a wealthy hub for commerce and seafarers, Greek Corinth was evidently renowned for its vice, especially its sexual corruption, and for its many religious temples and rites. Aristophanes (c. 450-385 B.C.) even coined the term *korinthiazesthai* ("to act like a

Corinthian," i.e., "to commit fornication") in view of the city's reputation. Plato used the term "Corinthian girl" as an euphemism for a prostitute (Murphy-O'Connor, 56). And although its historical accuracy is disputed, Strabo's account of 1,000 prostitutes in the temple of Aphrodite does reflect the city's image, in which the many temples played their own role in the immoral tenor of its life (cf. Strabo *Geog.* 8.6.20, first written in 7 B.C. and revised slightly in A.D. 18).

After Corinth was reestablished in 44 B.C. as a Roman city, it received a rapid influx of people. It soon became the third city of the empire after Rome and Alexandria. In addition to the veterans and the many from the lower classes who moved to Corinth, the city was settled largely by "freedmen" from Rome, whose status as manumitted servants was just above that of a slave. The repopulation of Corinth provided Rome a way to ease her overcrowding and the freedmen a chance to take advantage of the socioeconomic opportunity offered by this new city. Moreover, Corinth also boasted a significant community of Jews, who exercised the right to govern their own internal affairs (cf. Acts 18:8, 17). It is listed by Philo as one of the cities of the Jewish Diaspora (cf. Philo *Leg. Gai.* 281-282), and a lintel inscribed with the words "synagogue of the Hebrews" has been found, though its date cannot be determined with certainty (cf. Murphy-O'Connor, 79). By Paul's day Corinth had thus become a pluralistic melting pot of cultures, philosophies, lifestyles and religions, and had the feel of an economic "boom-town."

Paul's categories of people within the church, listed in 1 Corinthians 12:13 as Jew, Greek, slave* and free, thus reflect the make-up of the city, as do the various Jewish, Roman and Greek names mentioned in the letters (cf. the Jews Aquila, Priscilla, Crispus; the Romans Fortunatus, Quartus, Justus, etc.; the Greeks Stephanus, Achaicus, Erastus). We know from 1 Corinthians 7:20-24 that some of the believers in Corinth were slaves. Furthermore, since no landed aristocracy now existed in Roman Corinth, an "aristocracy of money" soon developed, accompanied by a fiercely independent spirit (so Fee, 2). This class distinction based on wealth is reflected in the tensions and factions that existed during the celebration of the Lord's Supper (1 Cor 11:17-34), since most of the church was apparently from the lower or middle socioeconomic class, with only a few wealthy families represented (cf. 1 Cor 1:26-27; *see* Sociology).

Roman law, culture and religion* were dominant in Corinth, and Latin was the city's official language, but the Greek traditions and philosophies of the area and the mystery cults from Egypt and Asia were also strongly represented (cf. 1 Cor 1:20-22). Diogenes, the founder of the Cynics, was associated with Corinth and Craneum, a residential area near it. Indeed, it is judged that Corinth was the "most thoroughly Hellenistic city in the NT" (Fee, 4 n.12). The Corinthian theater at the time of Paul held 14,000 people (Murphy-O'Connor, 36) and is reflected in the image behind 1 Corinthians 4:9 and 9:24-25. Moreover, although the accounts which we have of the widespread sexual immorality in Corinth are of Greek Corinth and should not be taken to apply to the Corinth of Paul's day, it is certainly the case that such a problem also came to be prevalent in the new, Roman city due to its character as a crossroads and seaport. 1 Corinthians 5:1-2 and 6:9-20 reflect just such an atmosphere. Finally, in Paul's day Corinth was filled with pagan religious sites (cf. 1 Cor 8:4-6; 10:14, 20-30). Pausanias (d. c. A.D. 180), who gives us our earliest guide book to Corinth in his *Description of Greece*, Book 2, describes at least twenty-six sacred places for the Greco-Roman pantheon and mystery cults. But it must be kept in mind that much of Corinth was destroyed in an earthquake in A.D. 77, after which there was an extensive rebuilding of the city. For the time of Paul, archaeology has thus far attested a temple of Fortune and temples or shrines to Neptune, Apollo, Aphrodite (on the Acrocorinth), Venus, Octavia, Asclepius, Demeter, Core and Poseidon (cf. Murphy-O'Connor and Wiseman).

**4. The Church and Its Apostle.**
The church in Corinth was largely, though not exclusively, Gentile, as reflected in their former background in pagan idolatry (1 Cor 6:10-11; 8:7; 12:2) and in the issue of partaking in temple feasts (1 Cor 8:1—11:1). It was also normal for Greeks and Romans to go to secular law courts with their disputes, whereas Jews were forbidden to do so, which helps explain this practice in Corinth (cf. 1 Cor 6:1-6). The acceptance of prostitution discussed in 1 Corinthians 6:12-20 and the attitudes toward marriage reflected in 1 Corinthians 7 are also more in keeping with a Gentile background.

The church* in Corinth met in various houses, since there was no possibility for a public meeting place, such as a synagogue, for a newly constituted religious movement which still lacked government recognition (cf. Rom 16:23). Based on the excavation of the four houses in Corinth from the Roman period (one from Paul's time) and the listing of the fourteen male members of the church in 1 and 2 Corinthians, Murphy-O'Connor estimates the base figure of the Corinthian church to be fifty members (Murphy-

O'Connor, 158). But such a gathering of the "whole church" was unusual, since the church usually met in smaller groups in various members' homes (cf. 1 Cor 16:19; Rom 16:5; Col 4:15; Philem 2).

*4.1. The Problems Behind 1 Corinthians.* G. D. Fee's commentary on 1 Corinthians represents the most thoroughgoing presentation of the "apologetic" view of the problems behind 1 Corinthians. In this view the historical situation behind 1 Corinthians is fundamentally one of conflict between Paul and the church as a whole, in which the Corinthians' rejection of Paul's authority as the founder of the church is perceived to be at the heart of their troubles. For Fee, therefore, the most serious division in the church is between the majority of the community and Paul himself (Fee, 8). Paul's language throughout the letter is taken to be combative, and his references to his apostleship are read to be apologetic (cf. esp. 1 Cor 4:1-21; 9:1-27; 15:8-11).

But Paul's purpose in writing 1 Corinthians is best seen not to be primarily apologetic but didactic. Nowhere in the letter does Paul argue for his own authority as an apostle *per se*, since he continues to bank on the fact that the Corinthians recognize him as their founder (1 Cor 4:15) and as a legitimate apostle, even though others *outside* the church might not (1 Cor 9:1-2). Rather, Paul writes to "remind" the Corinthians of "his ways in Christ" (1 Cor 4:17) and to call their attention to the fact that as their "father" (1 Cor 4:15) it is his "way," the way of the cross, that is to be imitated (1 Cor 4:16; 11:1). The appropriateness of Paul's suffering is therefore nowhere defended in 1 Corinthians. Instead it functions as the foundational premise for Paul's arguments (cf. esp. 1 Cor 1:10—4:21; 8:1—11:1; 13; 14:18-19), which in turn are based on his parental authority over the Corinthians in Christ (1 Cor 4:14-21). The very fact that Paul can enlist his practice of preaching free of charge to support his hortatory purpose in 1 Corinthians 8—10 indicates that Paul's apostolic lifestyle and authority were still being held in high esteem. If not, Paul's larger argument in 1 Corinthians 8—10, climaxing in his call to imitate him in 1 Corinthians 11:1, would have collapsed. Throughout 1 Corinthians the focus of Paul's arguments is thus on the Corinthians and their behavior, and the mode of Paul's address is not apologetic, but directive. Paul's ability to pronounce authoritative judgments on the Corinthians' behavior throughout the letter is based on his assumption that his apostolic authority is still in place in Corinth. The problems that 1 Corinthians addresses are essentially within the church, and not tensions between the church and its apostle.

*4.2. The Problems Behind 2 Corinthians.* By the time Paul wrote 2 Corinthians everything had changed. For a while, between the writing of 1 and 2 Corinthians, the church as a whole was in open rebellion against Paul and his gospel due to the influence of Paul's opponents who had recently arrived (cf. 2 Cor 11:4). Since then a significant segment of the church had repented and returned to Paul's side. But Paul's apostolic authority is no longer common ground between Paul and his entire church. There is still a sizeable opposition to Paul among the Corinthians, with Paul's opponents lurking behind them. As a result, the church now stands divided over Paul and his legitimacy as an apostle. This current condition is reflected in the absence of the call to imitate* Paul in 2 Corinthians, in the consistent focus on Paul's own authority as an apostle throughout most of 2 Corinthians, and most clearly in the different ways in which Paul's suffering functions in the two letters. In 1 Corinthians 4:8-13 and 9:1-27 Paul's suffering can be used to support his argument on behalf of the Corinthians, whereas throughout 2 Corinthians Paul must argue for the legitimacy of his suffering itself (cf. 2 Cor 2:17; 11:7-15; 12:13-18). Hence, whereas the problems in 1 Corinthians were within the church, the central problem to be solved in 2 Corinthians is the authority and legitimacy of Paul as an apostle.

*4.3. The Source of the Problems in Corinth and Paul's Response.* The source of the problems in Corinth, whether in 1 or 2 Corinthians, can be traced back to the Hellenistic culture which so influenced the Corinthians. The key issue was what it meant to be "spiritual" (cf. Paul's use of *pneumatikos* fourteen times in 1 Corinthians alone, over against only four times in the other undisputed Pauline letters). Even as believers, the Corinthians held on to that part of the Hellenistic body/soul or material/immaterial dualism which disdained the physical world for the "higher" knowledge and wisdom of spiritual existence. Although it is anachronistic to speak of gnostics or gnosticism in Corinth, one may thus speak of an "incipient gnosticism" in the theology of the Corinthians (so Martin, following Bruce; *see* Gnosis, Gnosticism). Under its influence the Corinthians were prone to intellectual pride, placing a high value on their "knowledge" and spiritual experiences (cf. 1 Cor 1:5; 8:1, 7, 10, 11; 12:8; 13:2; etc.). The result was an attitude of boasting and competition within the church, which was further fed by their cultural arrogance and admiration of the public power, style and polish of the Sophistic rhetorical tradition. Such a disdain for this world could also lead them to consider participation in its law courts and immorality as of no consequence on the one hand (cf. 1 Cor 5:1—6:20), and to the practice of an undue asceticism on the other (cf. 1 Cor 7:1-5).

But equally important, this dualism also provided the conceptual support which made the Corinthians so susceptible to an "over-realized eschatology*" that spiritualized the future resurrection* as already having taken place in their own experience (cf. 1 Cor 4:8; 15). One's present life was therefore viewed as already participating in the fullness of the heavenly reality of the world to come. Such an over-realized eschatology further inflated the Corinthians' estimation of their spiritual knowledge, gifts and religious experiences, especially that of tongues, which they saw as indicating that they too shared the spiritual existence of the angels* (cf. 1 Cor 13:1; 14:37). This in turn led to more boasting and disunity in the church, as well as to the eventual rejection of Paul's legitimacy as an apostle and of his gospel.

Paul's response in 1 Corinthians was decidedly based on the twofold foundation of the OT* and christology* (cf. his OT response to the problem of boasting in wisdom in 1 Cor 1:18—3:23, with direct quotes of the OT in 1 Cor 1:19; 1:31; 2:9; 2:16; 3:19-20). Both make it clear that the power and wisdom of God have now been revealed in Christ and his cross. At the same time Paul's message of the cross (1 Cor 1:17-19) and his own apostolic experience of suffering (1 Cor 4:8-13) demonstrate that the kingdom of God, though here in power, is not yet present in all of its fullness. Hence if suffering and weakness are the essential characteristics of the apostolic ministry upon which the Corinthians' lives are based, then as children of their spiritual father the lives of the Corinthians also ought to be characterized by the power of the cross and not by boasting in their own spiritual attainments or leaders. Paul's most basic advice, therefore, was to "imitate me" (1 Cor 4:16; 11:1).

By the time of 2 Corinthians, however, Paul's opponents had arrived from outside Corinth and had capitalized on the Corinthians' over-realized eschatology, preaching a view of Christ and of the Spirit that the Corinthians were open to receiving (2 Cor 11:4). Instead of calling the Corinthians to endure faithfully in the midst of adversity in hope of their future resurrection and vindication, Paul's opponents promised the Corinthians a life in the Spirit that was characterized by deliverance from suffering and by a steady diet of miraculous experience. They supported their claims to be apostles with letters of recommendation from other churches (cf. 2 Cor 3:1), by their ethnic distinctives as Jews (2 Cor 3:4-18; 11:21-22), and by boasting in their spiritual attainments and supernatural signs,

together with their rhetorical abilities (2 Cor 10:10, 12; 11:12, 18; 12:12). Paul's apologetic in 2 Corinthians 3 leads one to posit that they also tied their ministry in some way to the ministry of Moses* and the Law,* although unlike Galatians the issues of ritual purity* and circumcision* are not mentioned in 2 Corinthians. Moreover, Paul's opponents sealed their claims by demanding money from the Corinthians as a sign of the value and legitimacy of their message (2 Cor 2:17). But in order to make these claims and demand this payment they had to attack Paul himself and his apostolic legitimacy, which called both their gospel and their lifestyle into question.

In response, Paul now had to defend his own legitimacy as an apostle in order to establish the veracity of his gospel. Once again he does so by returning to the OT and to christology to demonstrate the necessity and purpose of his suffering in relationship to his ministry of the Spirit under the new covenant.

### 5. Some Critical Questions.

*5.1. Authorship.* Both 1 and 2 Corinthians are attributed to Paul in their salutations and show every historical and literary evidence of Pauline authorship. Indeed, the Pauline authorship of 1 Corinthians has never been disputed and the letter is already attested in the 90s by Clement of Rome (cf. *1 Clem.* 37:5; 47:1-3; 49:5) and in the first decade of the second century by Ignatius (cf. Ignatius *Eph.* 16:1; 18:1; *Rom.* 5:1, etc.). Although 2 Corinthians is not clearly documented until Marcion's canon (A.D. 140), it is undisputed from that point on as part of the Pauline corpus. Even the most critical modern scholarship has consistently accepted these letters as genuine, apart from 1 Corinthians 1:2b and 14:34b-35, which some scholars have argued are non-Pauline interpolations. But the evidence for removing these texts has not convinced the majority of scholars, since no manuscript tradition has ever omitted these verses and both texts can be seen to fit within Paul's flow of thought. Other scholars have argued that the distinct vocabulary and subject matter of 2 Corinthians 6:14—7:1 indicate that Paul adopted this passage from a previous Pauline writing, or from a non-Pauline Jewish source (often associated with the Essene movement or Qumran* documents) or from a Jewish-Christian tradition. But even if this hypothesis stands against the views of those who maintain that its distinct character is due to the OT texts which Paul quotes in this section, the passage has been fully integrated by Paul into his own train of thought in 2 Corinthians.

*5.2. Unity and Occasion of 1 and 2 Corinthians.* Paul's founding of the church at Corinth, recorded in Acts

18, took place in the years A.D. 49-51 as part of Paul's second missionary journey. When Paul left Corinth after eighteen months, the new church was flourishing. Sometime later Paul wrote a letter to the Corinthians from Ephesus,* a document which is no longer extant, in order to deal with some specific ethical issues now being faced by the new believers. But the Corinthians had difficulty understanding Paul's admonitions and, in fact, misapplied them to their context (cf. 1 Cor 5:9-13). The church then sent a letter to Paul by the hands of the messengers listed in 1 Corinthians 16:15-17 in order to receive further clarification. In response to this letter Paul wrote canonical 1 Corinthians. Paul's aim was to clarify his positions and to respond to the other reports he had heard about the serious problems which had arisen in Corinth (1 Cor 1:11; 5:1; cf. 16:15-18; see 4.2 above). The somewhat disjointed and topical nature of 1 Corinthians is due to the fact that Paul is responding in turn to the variety of issues and questions brought to him by the church's letter and to the reports he has heard.

At the time he wrote 1 Corinthians, Paul intended to return to Corinth after staying in Ephesus until Pentecost and then visiting Macedonia (cf. 1 Cor 16:5-8). In the meantime he sent Timothy to visit the Corinthians on his behalf (1 Cor 16:10-11; Acts 19:22). Timothy found the tension between Paul and the Christians at Corinth to have escalated, due most probably to the arrival of opponents of Paul from outside Corinth. In response, Paul set out for Corinth immediately for what became a "painful visit," during which Paul's authority and gospel were severely called into question by the church. Paul himself was opposed and offended by one of its leaders (cf. 2 Cor 2:1, 5-8; 7:8-13; 11:4).

Paul left Corinth under attack, determined not to make another such "painful visit" to the Corinthians (2 Cor 2:1-2). Instead he sent Titus to them with a "tearful letter" of rebuke and a warning as an attempt to win them back (cf. 2 Cor 2:3-9; 7:8-12). The fact that Titus was also to organize the collection (cf. 2 Cor 8:6) indicates, however, that Paul still held out hope for the Corinthians and did not consider them beyond repentance. This "tearful letter" is now lost, though some scholars have attempted to identify it with canonical 1 Corinthians or the four chapters of 2 Corinthians 10—13. But 1 Corinthians is neither severe nor painful enough to qualify, nor does its subject matter fit the nature of the description in 2 Corinthians 2:1-4, since in 1 Corinthians there is no consistent treatment of the theme of the Corinthians' rejection of Paul, the influence of Paul's opponents within Co-

rinth, or the offender of 2 Corinthians 2:5-11.

As Paul waited for Titus to return with his report concerning the impact of this letter, his mind could not rest due to his anxiety over the Corinthian situation (2 Cor 2:12-23). So Paul left Troas to find Titus, and when he did, Titus gave Paul the good news that his "tearful letter" had indeed won back the majority of the Corinthians (2 Cor 7:6-13). Moreover, because the church had responded so positively, Paul could now plan to visit them once again (cf. 2 Cor 2:3; 9:5; 12:20—13:1).

In anticipation of this third visit, Paul wrote canonical 2 Corinthians, or at least chapters 1—9 of the document as we now have it. The fact that the majority of the church had repented and returned to Paul, while a significant segment still resisted his authority and gospel, explains the mixed nature of this section. In it Paul both comforts and encourages the majority of the church, while at the same time defending his apostleship in order to strengthen those who have repented and to win back the recalcitrant minority. Moreover, behind the Corinthians lurk Paul's opponents, whom Paul does not address directly, but who are the most direct source of the problem. Paul's goal in writing, therefore, is to prepare for his next visit to the Corinthians in which he will have to judge those who persist in their rejection of him and his gospel. Paul did in fact return to Corinth (cf. Acts 20:2), where less than a year later he wrote his letter to the Romans.*

In view of this scenario the question of the literary unity of 2 Corinthians has been answered in various ways because of the seemingly abrupt transitions and change of subject matter within the letter. The key issues are the apparent breaks in thought between 2 Corinthians 2:13 and 2:14, 7:4 and 5, 6:13 and 14, and 7:1 and 2; the seemingly separate treatments of the collection in chapters 8 and 9; and the distinct unit of 2 Corinthians 10:1—13:14. If each of these transitions marks out a separate document, 2 Corinthians becomes a composite of the following six major fragments, which were then later unified into a single letter: 2 Corinthians 1:1—2:13 and 7:5-16; 2:14—6:13; 6:14—7:1; 8; 9; 10—13.

A minority of scholars still maintain, however, the literary unity of the entire letter. Those who hold this position attempt to explain the integrity of the transitions within the letter at each point. In addition, they view the changes in subject matter throughout 2 Corinthians as the result of the mixed nature of the Corinthian community. Chapters 10—13 are Paul's last direct defense and attack against his opponents, after primarily addressing the reconciled majority of the church in chapters 1—9, and perhaps after some lapse in time or the arrival of new, menacing information. This is the approach taken in the overview of 2 Corinthians above.

At the other extreme a few scholars have sought to isolate each of these sections as originally part of a separate writing and to assign them to the history of Paul's interaction with the Corinthians outlined above. In this scenario, as we noted, some view 2 Corinthians 10—13 to be part of the "tearful letter;" 2 Corinthians 2:14—6:13 to be part of a lost letter of defense; 2 Corinthians 1:1—2:13 and 7:5-16 to be Paul's letter of reconciliation after Titus' report; 2 Corinthians 6:14—7:1 to be part of yet another lost Pauline or non-Pauline writing, part of the "tearful letter," or even part of the "previous letter" of 1 Corinthians 5:9. The growing consensus is that chapters 1—9 are in fact a unified composition written after Paul's encounter with Titus (cf. 2 Cor 7:5-13). Chapters 10—13 are then taken as a subsequent work which was written after a fresh outbreak of trouble in Corinth and appended to the previous section at some time early on in the history of these traditions, since there is no textual-critical evidence that chapters 10—13 ever circulated independently of chapters 1—9 (see, e.g., the commentaries by Martin and Furnish).

*5.3. Place and Date.* First Corinthians was written from Ephesus between the time Paul left Corinth in A.D. 51-52 and three years later, in the autumn of A.D. 52 to the spring of 55, depending on the following factors: the dating of the edict of Claudius and the term of office of Gallio (cf. Acts 18:2, 12); the time of Paul's departure from Corinth (Acts 18:18); and the subsequent length of his later stay in Ephesus (*see* Chronology). 2 Corinthians (taken as a whole, or at least chapters 1—9) was completed in the next year or so after 1 Corinthians, and was written from Macedonia.

*5.4. Paul's Opponents.* The key passages for identifying Paul's opposition in Corinth have traditionally been 1 Corinthians 1:12; 3:22; 9:2-5; 2 Corinthians 3:1-18; 11:4 and 11:22-23. From these texts it is clear that Paul's opponents were Jews who were familiar with the Hellenistic world and espoused Sophist values and rhetorical techniques on the one hand, and relied on their own spiritual heritage as Jews on the other (see 4.3 above). But beyond this bare sketch, the more exact identity and theology of the opponents must remain a matter of scholarly reconstruction, since 1 and 2 Corinthians themselves are our only available evidence, though material from Philippians* (when dated in Paul's Ephesian period) has been introduced by some scholars (see commentaries).

Since the seventeenth century scholars have offered three basic theories concerning the identity of Paul's opponents in 2 Corinthians. These hypotheses have been constructed predominantly by reading Paul's arguments as a direct contrast to the positions of his opponents (the so-called mirror technique). The proposals are basically as follows: (1) gnostics; (2) legalistic Judaizers* on a par with those Paul fought elsewhere; or (3) a mixture of legalistic and gnostic and/or enthusiastic or pneumatic elements of various persuasions (*see* Opponents; Paul and His Interpreters). These basic positions have repeatedly been refined and combined in various ways, so that Machalet could list no less than eleven different positions on 2 Corinthians between 1908-1940. Since then these three basic positions have again been forcefully argued by R. Bultmann and W. Schmithals (the gnostic hypothesis), C. K. Barrett (the Judaizer hypothesis), and Dieter Georgi (Hellenistic Jewish pneumatics and missionaries of Palestinian origin with a "divine man" [*theios anēr*] theology centered on Moses).

The only major study of Paul's opponents in general to appear after these studies, J. J. Gunther's *St. Paul's Opponents and their Background* (1973), offered neither a new methodology nor a clear way out of this scholarly impasse. Gunther's thesis is that the backdrop for Paul's opponents is to be found in the Qumran and Jewish apocryphal writings, so that Paul's opponents were from a mystic, apocalyptic,* ascetic, non-conformist, syncretistic Judaism, more like Essenism than any other group (Gunther, 315). But in his attempt to forge a consensus among the thirteen different views he catalogued, Gunther cast his net so wide that his description becomes nondescript.

Hence, Sumney's recent proposal of a methodology based upon a "minimalist approach" for identifying Paul's opponents is to be welcomed. Sumney's proposal includes: (1) an emphasis on the priority of exegesis in a "text-focused method"; (2) an insistence upon a sound evaluation of proper sources; (3) a "stringently" limited application of the "mirror technique" (i.e., the practice of reading Paul's statements as a direct reflection of his opponents' contrary views); and (4) a rejection of the attempt to approach the text with a previously determined, externally based, reconstruction. But in view of the history of research it is significant that when Sumney applies his method to 2 Corinthians, he offers no new insights into the identity of Paul's opponents. Sumney ends up agreeing basically with the previous proposal of Käsemann that the opponents behind 2 Corinthians 10—13 were pneumatics, rather than Judaizers, gnostics or Georgi's "divine men," and that the short time span between the letter fragments of 2 Corinthians 1—9 and 10—13 leads one to "reasonably conclude" that the opponents in both cases are part of the same group (Sumney, 183).

Today, the gnostic hypothesis has died due to a lack of evidence for gnosticism in the pre-Christian or NT era. And Georgi's proposal has met with serious criticism concerning his reconstruction both of early Jewish missionaries and of their understanding of Moses as a "divine man." The way out of the remaining impasse will be to realize that the Judaizers' concern with the Law* was motivated not only by their desire to uphold their tradition, but also by a desire to gain access to a deeper experience of the Spirit (see Holy Spirit). The artificial divorce between the Law and the Spirit, which leads scholars to posit two distinct types of opponents, must therefore be overcome. The question raised by Paul's opponents, based on their Jewish heritage, was essentially the same one being raised by the Corinthians, based on their Hellenistic worldview: how does one participate fully in the power of the Spirit? The opponents' answer was based on a theology of "over-realized glory," in which participation in their gospel, with its tie to the old covenant, was said to guarantee freedom from sin* and suffering in this world. At the center of the debate was the relationship between the old and new covenants as this came to expression in the question of the authority and role of Moses and the Law in regard to Paul's role as an apostle of Christ and mediator of the Spirit (cf. 2 Cor 2:16; 3:4-18).

## 6. Theological Themes of 1 and 2 Corinthians.

It is striking that most of the commands throughout 1 Corinthians center on some aspect of church unity (cf. 1 Cor 1:10; 3:1-3; 4:14, 16; 5:4, 5, 7, 8; 6:1, 4, 6-7, 18, 20; 8:9, 13; 10:14; 11:33-34; 12:14, etc.). Clearly Paul's primary concern is with the true nature and life of the church, making ecclesiology the most important theme of 1 Corinthians. As the "church of God" (1 Cor 1:1), the Corinthians are "the temple of God," due to their reception of the Holy Spirit (1 Cor 3:16-17; 14:24-25); and the "body of Christ,"* due to their submission to the lordship of Christ (1 Cor 6:17; 10:17; 11:29; 12:12-16, 27). But in focusing his attention on the Corinthians as the people of God, the eschatological framework of Paul's theology also stands out in this letter. Throughout 1 Corinthians Paul strives to make it clear that although the kingdom of God has already dawned, as evidenced by the resurrection power of Christ and the pouring out of the Spirit in the lives of the Corinthians (cf. 1 Cor 4:20), it is nevertheless not yet here in all of its fullness, a "proviso" seen clearly in Paul's own suffering and the qualita-

tively different nature of the future bodily resurrection and the end of age. At the same time, Paul must also make it clear to the Corinthians that although the kingdom of God is not yet present in all its fullness, one's ethical life (see Ethics) as a follower of Christ is still to be controlled by the dawning reality of the age to come in which the power of the Spirit enables one to keep God's commandments (cf. 1 Cor 5:7-8; 6:1-6; 7:29-31; 10:11; etc.). Paul's insistence throughout 1 Corinthians on the inextricable link between faith and obedience is therefore framed theologically by the cross (cf. 1 Cor 1:10—4:21) and the resurrection of Christ (1 Cor 15). In the end, therefore, 1 Corinthians demonstrates that both ecclesiology and eschatology are rooted in one's understanding of Christ "according to the Scriptures" (cf. 1 Cor 15:3-5).

In 2 Corinthians the central theological theme becomes the relationship between suffering and glory as this is determined and illustrated in Paul's apostolic experience. Here too Paul's arguments are grounded throughout in his eschatology and christology, both of which are developed within an OT framework and consistently applied to his own life as an apostle. Paul's point is as simple as it is profound. Rather than calling his legitimacy as an apostle into question, Paul's suffering is the very vehicle which God has ordained to validate his apostleship and to make known the knowledge of his own power and glory, now revealed in the gospel of Christ. Paul's ministry of suffering and of the Spirit does not represent an unresolved tension which calls into question his sufficiency as a true apostle. Indeed *both* the cross *and* the resurrection power of God are being revealed through Paul's life of divinely ordained suffering. And although there is no *call* for all Christians to suffer in either 1 or 2 Corinthians, nor any sign of a martyrdom theology, Paul affirms that whenever God's people are brought into the same kinds of sufferings to which he was called as an apostle, they too will become vehicles for the manifestation of the power of God in the midst of their adversity (cf. 2 Cor 1:7). In support of this main point and his corresponding apologetic for his apostolic authority, Paul outlines the nature of the new covenant in relationship to the covenant at Sinai (2 Cor 3:6-18), the nature of the new creation in the midst of the old (2 Cor 4:6—5:21) and the christological foundation for living for the sake of others because one now lives for the sake of Christ (2 Cor 5:15; 8:1—9:14).

*See also* APOSTLE; AUTHORITY; BODY OF CHRIST; COLLECTION FOR THE SAINTS; CROSS, THEOLOGY OF THE; ESCHATOLOGY; GIFTS OF THE SPIRIT; GLORY, GLORIFICATION; HOLY SPIRIT; LAW; LORD'S SUPPER; MOSES; OPPONENTS OF

PAUL; POWER; RESURRECTION; RHETORIC; SUFFERING; WISDOM.

BIBLIOGRAPHY. *Commentaries:* C. K. Barrett, *The First Epistle to the Corinthians* (HNTC; New York: Harper & Row, 1968); idem, *The Second Epistle to the Corinthians* (HNTC; New York: Harper & Row, 1973); F. F. Bruce, *1 and 2 Corinthians* (NCB; Grand Rapids: Eerdmans, 1971); R. Bultmann, *The Second Letter to the Corinthians* (Minneapolis: Augsburg, 1985); H. Conzelmann, *1 Corinthians* (Herm; Philadelphia: Fortress, 1975); E. Fascher, *Der erste Brief des Paulus an die Korinther, Erster Teil* (THKNT 7/1; 2d ed.; Berlin: Evangelische Verlagsanstalt, 1980); G. D. Fee, *The First Epistle to the Corinthians* (NICNT; Grand Rapids: Eerdmans, 1987); V. P. Furnish, *II Corinthians* (AB 32; Garden City, NY: Doubleday, 1984); P. E. Hughes, *Paul's Second Epistle to the Corinthians* (NICNT; Grand Rapids: Eerdmans, 1962); F. Lang, *Die Briefe an die Korinther* (NTD 7; Göttingen: Vandenhoeck & Ruprecht, 1986); R. P. Martin, *2 Corinthians* (WBC 40; Waco: Word, 1986); A. Plummer, *Second Epistle of St. Paul to the Corinthians* (ICC; Edinburgh: T. & T. Clark, 1925); A. Schlatter, *Paulus, Der Bote Jesus. Eine Deutung seiner Briefe an die Korinther* (4th ed.; Stuttgart: Calwer, 1969); C. H. Talbert, *Reading Corinthians: A Literary and Theological Commentary on 1 and 2 Corinthians* (New York: Crossroad, 1987); H. Windisch, *Der zweite Korintherbrief* (MeyerK 6; 9th ed.; Göttingen: Vandenhoeck & Ruprecht, 1970); C. Wolff, *Der erste Brief des Paulus an die Korinther, Zweiter Teil* (THKNT 7/II; Berlin: Evangelische Verlagsanstalt, 1982). *Studies:* L. Belleville, *Reflections of Glory: Paul's Polemical Use of the Moses-Doxa Tradition in 2 Corinthians 3:12-18* (Sheffield: Sheffield Academic, 1991); D. A. Carson, *Showing the Spirit: A Theological Exposition of 1 Corinthians 12—14* (Grand Rapids: Baker, 1987); J.-F. Collange, *Enigmes de la deuxième épître de Paul aux Corinthiens* (SNTSMS 18; Cambridge: University Press, 1972); N. A. Dahl, "Paul and the Church at Corinth according to 1 Corinthians 1:10-4:21," in *Christian History and Interpretation: Studies Presented to John Knox,* ed. W. R. Farmer et al. (Cambridge: University Press, 1976) 313-35; D. Georgi, *The Opponents of Paul in Second Corinthians* (Philadelphia: Fortress, 1986); J. J. Gunther, *St. Paul's Opponents and their Background: A Study of Apocalyptic and Jewish Sectarian Teachings* (NovTSup 30; Leiden: E. J. Brill, 1973); S. J. Hafemann, *Suffering and Ministry in the Spirit: Paul's Defense of His Ministry in II Corinthians 2:14-3:3* (Grand Rapids: Eerdmans, 1990); idem, " 'Self-Commendation' and Apostolic Legitimacy in 2 Corinthians: A Pauline Dialectic?" *NTS* 36 (1990) 66-88; E. Käsemann, "Die Legitimität des Apostels. Eine Untersuchung zu II Korinther 10-13," *ZNW* 41 (1942) 33-71; C. Machalet, "Paulus und seine Gegner. Eine Untersuchung zu den Korintherbriefen," in *Theokratia. Jahrbuch des Institutum Judaicum Delitzschianum, II. Festgabe für Karl Heinrich Rengstorf zum 70. Geburtstag,* ed. W. Dietrich et al. (Leiden: E. J. Brill, 1973) 183-203; P. Marshall, *Enmity in Corinth: Social Conventions in Paul's Relations with the Corinthians* (WUNT 2/23; Tübingen: J. C. B. Mohr, 1987); W. A. Meeks, *The First Urban Christians: The Social World of the Apostle Paul* (New Haven: Yale University, 1983); J. Murphy-O'Connor, *St. Paul's Corinth: Texts and Archaeology* (GNS 6; Wilmington, DE: Michael Glazier, 1983); idem, *The Theology of the Second Letter to the Corinthians* (NTT; Cambridge: University Press, 1991); C. Newman, *Paul's Glory-Christology: Tradition and Rhetoric* (NovTSup 69; Leiden: E. J. Brill, 1992); C. K. Stockhausen, *Moses' Veil and the Glory of the New Covenant: The Exegetical Substructure of II Cor. 3:1—4:6* (Rome: Pontificio Instituto Biblico, 1989); J. L. Sumney, *Identifying Paul's Opponents: The Question of Method in 2 Corinthians* (JSNTSup 40, Sheffield; Sheffield Academic, 1990); G. Theissen, *The Social Setting of Pauline Christianity: Essays on Corinth* (Philadelphia: Fortress, 1982); J. Wiseman, "Corinth and Rome I: 228 B.C.—A.D. 267," *ANRW* II.7.1.438-548; F. Young and D. F. Ford, *Meaning and Truth in 2 Corinthians* (Grand Rapids: Eerdmans, 1987).

S. J. Hafemann

**COSMIC POWERS.** *See* ELEMENTS/ELEMENTAL SPIRITS OF THE WORLD; PRINCIPALITIES AND POWERS.

**COSMOLOGY.** *See* WORLD, COSMOLOGY.

**COSMOS.** *See* WORLD, COSMOLOGY.

## COVENANT AND NEW COVENANT

In the letters generally accepted as Pauline there are eight occurrences of covenant (*diathēkē*): Romans 9:4; 11:27; 1 Corinthians 11:25; 2 Corinthians 3:6, 14; Galatians 3:15, 17; 4:24 (cf. also Eph 2:12). Of special note among these are Galatians 4:24 (two covenants), 2 Corinthians 3:6 (the only use in Paul of new covenant, *kainē diathēkē*, apart from the eucharistic passage in 1 Cor 11:25) and 2 Corinthians 3:14 where we find the only reference to old covenant, *palaia diathēkē*.

The above references may indicate that covenant was not a dominant theme in Paul's theology, but there is little agreement on this issue. It may be argued that what is generally presumed need not always be explicitly stated. This would certainly apply to covenant theology in the case of someone like Paul, who had been brought up in a Pharisaic tradition (*see* Jew, Paul the). Again there may have been good reasons why Paul did not use the term more frequently, such as the possibility that his opponents used it and interpreted it differently.

In view of this and being conscious of how basic to NT interpretation are the themes "old and new covenant," we will proceed cautiously by looking at the instances of the term *covenant* in each of Paul's letters, as far as possible allowing the text to stand by itself without reading too much into it from other parts of the NT.

1. Galatians
2. 1 and 2 Corinthians
3. Romans
4. Conclusion

**1. Galatians.**

Covenant theology is essentially a way of describing God's relationship with his people. Such a relationship does not exist in a vacuum, but in time and place. Thus a question arises concerning the understanding of divine revelation and activity in history and, more specifically, in relation to the history of Israel. Paul's letter to the Galatians,* though the story of Abraham* is very much part of the discussion, does not give great significance to the history of Israel as such, at least not in the way that Romans does.

In Galatians 3:15-17 Paul, by means of a human example of covenant ratification, seeks to argue for the priority and inviolability of the Abrahamic covenant. Inasmuch as human wills cannot be added to or modified except by the testator, God's covenant with Abraham into which Christians are incorporated in Christ, Abraham's "seed," is neither nullified nor added to by the later Sinai covenant which is subsidiary to it.

Galatians 4:21-32 is a midrashic passage in which Paul may be taking up both the arguments and the scriptural citations of his opponents. Hence some of the content may not be characteristically Pauline, though he doubtless shared elements of belief with other Jewish Christians and Jews. Although Paul speaks here of two covenants (*dyo diathēkai*), he explicitly describes his use of these two covenants as "allegory." Moreover the impression one receives is not of one covenant being superseded by another, but rather of two parallel covenant options that possibly allegorically refer to two concurrent missions to Gentiles*: (1) a Law-observant one led by Paul's opponents (*see* Judaizers), and in opposition to (2) that of his own Gentile mission.* The likelihood is that Paul intends the Sarah covenant to signify not Christianity (over against the Hagar covenant, i.e., Judaism) but rather the Law-free Gentile mission. The entire discussion

may be seen as two processes of begetting "children of God" (*see* Adoption, Sonship). In and through the Pauline mission the Galatians received the Spirit "by the hearing of faith*"; no counter mission advocating circumcision* or Law observance for Gentiles could add to, or improve on, the standing of those in Christ by faith. They are exhorted to stand in the freedom* of Christ (Gal 5:1). A Law-observant mission for Gentiles is now treated as an anachronism.

This understanding of the passage releases us from any interpretation that sees Paul as referring to two sequential covenants, the first with Judaism succeeded by the second with Christianity. The problem with the passage, of course, is its midrashic content and Paul's use of allegory. Nevertheless, the important point Paul wishes to stress is that in the begetting of children, the type or quality of the children is dependent on the lineage of their parents. This is in keeping with the general meaning of covenant, which necessarily has at its heart some kind of continuity, even if it may not be an earthly continuity, but only the theological continuity of those begotten by the word of God.

**2. 1 and 2 Corinthians.**

1 Corinthians 11:25 gives the rendering of Jesus' word at the Last Supper as "this cup is the new covenant (*kainē diathēkē*) in my blood." Luke also includes the adjective "new," but there is a strong scholarly tradition which regards the Markan form of the words of institution as being the oldest (Jeremias). What is important for our study is whether something substantially different is intended by the addition of the word "new." Maybe it is rather a drawing out of something already implicit in the death* of Christ (*see* Lord's Supper).

In 2 Corinthians 3:6, in a section of the letter which has spawned numerous divergent interpretations, we find the only other reference to "new covenant" in Paul. In 2 Corinthians 3:14 we meet the sole reference in Paul to "old covenant" (*palaia diathēkē*). The unique occurrence in Paul of the adjectives *old* and *new* in relation to covenant within the Corinthian correspondence probably points to some factor at Corinth which gave particular significance to these designations. For instance, D. Georgi considers that Paul's opponents* introduced the term *new covenant*. Christian theology has tended, in the past, to see in 2 Corinthians 3 a contrast between the new dispensation and the old. However warranted such a contrast may be, it is not at all clear that such a contrast was the immediate focus of Paul's thought when the letter was sent to the Corinthians. Commentators agree that Paul three times uses an *a fortiori* ("how much more") argument to contrast the amount of glory* which attaches to two different ministries. Exodus 34 is clearly under discussion here and it may also be true that midrashic interpretations of the passage lie behind Paul's comments. The introduction of Moses* into the discussion has led some interpreters to find here a simple and explicit contrast between the old and new dispensations—hence the strange RSV translation of *diakonia* as "dispensation" rather than "ministry"!

The context, however, indicates that Paul is grieved that the Corinthians are impressed by letters of commendation from rival missionaries. Paul does not wish to commend himself nor does he need, like some, such letters of commendation. Paul's "letter" is the Corinthians themselves and the author of this letter is Christ; the apostle's letter is written with the Spirit of the living God, not with ink on papyrus (*see* Holy Spirit).

Paul has in mind Ezekiel 11:19 (36:26) rather than Jeremiah 38:31 (LXX). S. J. Hafemann insists that the *heart* motif is drawn from the Ezekiel passage, which includes the motif of the Spirit, missing entirely from the Jeremiah text. He also notes that when we take as our starting point the actual passages Paul has in mind, we do not need to posit stark contrasts between ink and spirit, or stone and heart, or even to develop these into a full-blown antithesis between the dispensation of Law* and the new dispensation of gospel.* For Ezekiel the hope of the future work of God in the heart was not seen to alter the validity of the Law. The actual comparison intended here is that Paul understood his ministry to his converts to be the eschatological counterpart to the giving of the Law. Paul sees himself in the ministry* of the gospel to be the Spirit-giver just as Moses was the Law-giver.

The relationship between the activity of God in Moses the Law-giver and in his new activity in Paul the Spirit-giver is best expressed in the *qal wahomer*, "how much more," type of argument. The movement is from something glorious to something even more glorious. In any case, when Paul says in 2 Corinthians 3:13 that Moses put a veil over his face so that the Israelites might not see *to telos tou katargoumenou* ("the end of the transitory [splendor?]"), he cannot possibly have been referring to the covenant as transitory since *diathēkē* is a feminine noun, and the transitory (splendor) is indicated by a neuter participle.

The immediate issue in 2 Corinthians 3—4 is two concepts of Christian ministry. Paul is not addressing the Israelites at Sinai but the Corinthian Christians and his opponents. It is the latter whose thoughts have been dulled and over whose hearts lies a veil. We conclude therefore that despite a unique instance of

"old covenant" in this passage, we are not warranted in reading into it the stark contrast of two antithetical ways of salvation, typical of some later Christian theology.

### 3. Romans.

Covenantal relationship may be implied in Paul's addressing the Romans* as *agapētoi theou* ("beloved [of God]") and *klētoi hagioi* ("called [to be] saints"). There are only two explicit references to covenant in the letter, Romans 9:4 and 11:27. In Romans 9:4-5 Paul lists the covenant as one of the privileges belonging to Israel,* along with sonship (*see* Adoption), glory,* the giving of the Law,* worship,* the promises and the patriarchs. Whether or not we follow the singular reading of "covenant" in *P⁴⁶* or the plural "covenants" as supported by the majority of manuscripts, it appears that here Paul has primarily in view the Abrahamic covenant. The focus is on the call and election of Abraham who in Romans 4 was depicted as a paradigm of the believer.

In Romans 11:27 Paul amalgamates two citations from Isaiah 59:12 and Isaiah 27:9 to produce a promise of future redemption for Israel despite her present refusal of the gospel: "this will be my covenant with them, when I take away their sins." The argument concerning the olive tree,* and the theme of Romans 11 generally, is that despite the present enmity as regards the gospel, the election of Israel still stands. "God has not cast off Israel" (Rom 11:1, 7). The covenant is secure and Israel's election is not in doubt, for "the gifts and the call of God are irrevocable" (Rom 11:29).

Though we cannot insist that Paul's theology was covenantal in the sense that he explicitly used covenantal terminology, it may be that there existed at Rome a misunderstanding of the covenant with Israel arising from the success of Paul's Gentile mission (see Campbell). In face of this, Paul focused his thinking in Romans upon the theme of the covenant. Whereas in Galatians Christ is "the seed," in Romans the people of faith are "the seed," and there is continuity "from faith to faith," with the covenant being opened up to include Gentiles also.

### 4. Conclusion.

R. D. Kaylor argues that the role of covenant functions at two levels in Paul's theology—at the levels of *idea* and of *conviction*. Though Paul may not always have had this distinction in mind, Kaylor holds, nevertheless, that the covenant as a conviction functions as a persistent presence and a dominant reality in Paul's life, work and thought.

Had Romans been written prior to Galatians, we might have argued that covenantal or *heilsgeschichtlich* (salvation historical) thinking is a relic of Paul's Jewish past, eventually to be cast aside. But the issue is very complicated. It centers upon the problem of what "descent from Abraham" means. In the case of Sarah—where discontinuity (and covenant failure) seemed inevitable, God miraculously intervened to provide an heir (cf. Is 54:1). This could be seen to indicate God's maintenance of earthly continuity (cf. Rom 4:19); but in fact it may also be interpreted as the opposite—as the divine activity of the new creation. We should note, however, that in Sarah's case, it is divine creativity *in relation to a people of promise*. Only later in history did this creativity extend beyond Israel to Gentiles, and even then it will be through Jesus Christ—"of the seed of David."

The covenant concept indicates continuity in the divine purpose in history. It primarily depends on the faithfulness of God (e.g., Romans 3:21-26). But how can one give an adequate explanation of an earthly continuity in faith—Abraham—Isaac— Jesus? In Romans 9:21 Paul argues that it is not those of physical descent alone who are Abraham's children, it is those of physical descent who also share the faith of their father Abraham. Only in Romans 9:22-24 does Paul mention the inclusion of Gentiles. The Gentiles are included not in and of themselves but in and with the faithful in Israel (cf. Eph 2:11-22).

Käsemann rightly insists that right relationship and righteousness* can only be ours in so far as God gives them to us anew every day (i.e., in faith). But does this mean that God's revelation only comes to people in a punctiliar manner, as "a bolt from the blue"? Or does revelation tend to occur in the context of a believing family or of a wider community of faith? The problem with the latter view is that history is not simply the record of divine achievement, but also of human sinfulness. It was Jeremiah's despair at the latter that led him to posit a "new covenant."

Christians have tended to regard Jeremiah's new covenant as the clear basis for the fully developed Christian concept of a new dispensation. This is then frequently read back into Paul's writings via Hebrews. It is however, by no means clear that "new covenant" was a term widely used in earliest Christianity. It is certainly reasonably correct to hold that "old covenant" was a rare concept up to the time of the death of Paul.

For various reasons, it seems, Paul did not frequently use explicit covenant terminology. Yet it does occur at important points in some of his writings. The frequency of "calling,"* "election"* and related terms in 1 Corinthians, for example, may indicate it was significant in Paul's thought. But whatever we conclude from the above, it is clear that when Paul used the terms old or new covenant, he did not include many of the associated ideas of a later more developed Christianity. As W. D. Davies has reminded us, Jeremiah did not look forward to a new Law but to "my law," and that the adjective *ḥādāš* in Jeremiah 31:31, translated *kainē* by Paul, can be applied to the new moon which is simply the old moon in a new light.

*See also* ABRAHAM; CIRCUMCISION; CORINTHIANS, LETTERS TO THE; GALATIANS, LETTER TO THE; GENTILES; ISRAEL; JUDAIZERS; LAW; LORD'S SUPPER; MOSES; OLD TESTAMENT IN PAUL; OLIVE TREE; RESTORATION OF ISRAEL; ROMANS, LETTER TO THE; WORKS OF THE LAW.

BIBLIOGRAPHY. J. B. Agus, "The Covenant Concept—Particularistic, Pluralistic, or Futuristic," *JES* 18 (1981) 217-30; C. K. Barrett, "The Allegory of Abraham, Sarah and Hagar in the Argument of Galatians," in *Essays on Paul* (London: SPCK, 1982) 154-69; W. S. Campbell, *Paul's Gospel in an Intercultural Context: Jew and Gentile in the Letter to the Romans* (Frankfurt: Peter Lang, 1991); E. J. Christiansen, "Baptism: Covenant Ritual or Conversion Rite? A Study of Ecclesiological Identity and Baptismal Boundaries in Pauline Christianity and Palestinian Judaism" (unpublished doctoral dissertation, University of Durham, November 1992); J. Cott, "The Biblical Problem of Election," *JES* 21 (1984) 199-228; W. D. Davies, "Paul and the People of Israel," *NTS* 24 (1978) 4-39; J. D. G. Dunn, "The Theology of Galatians," in *Pauline Theology*, Vol. 1, ed. J. M. Bassler (Minneapolis: Fortress, 1991) 160-79; L. Gaston, *Paul and the Torah* (Vancouver: University of British Columbia, 1987); D. Georgi, *The Opponents of Paul in Second Corinthians* (Philadelphia: Fortress, 1986); E. Grässer, *Der Alte Bund im Neuen* (Tübingen: J. C. B. Mohr, 1985); S. J. Hafemann, *Suffering and the Spirit* (WUNT 2.19; Tübingen: J. C. B. Mohr, 1986); G. W. Hansen, *Abraham in Galatians: Epistolary and Rhetorical Contexts* (JSNTSup 29; Sheffield: JSOT, 1989); R. B. Hays, *Echoes of Scripture in the Letters of Paul* (New Haven: Yale University, 1989); M. D. Hooker, "Paul and Covenantal Nomism," in *Paul and Paulinism: Essays in Honour of C. K. Barrett*, ed. M. D. Hooker and S. G. Wilson (London: SPCK 47-56; J. J. Hughes, "Hebrews 9:15ff and Galatians 3:15ff: A Study in Covenant Practice and Procedure," *NovT* (1979) 27-96; J. Jeremias, *The Eucharistic Words of Jesus* (Philadelphia: Fortress, 1977); R. D. Kaylor, *Paul's Covenant Community: Jew and Gentile in Romans* (Atlanta: John Knox, 1988); H. J. Kraus, ed., *Der Ungekuendigte Bund* (Stuttgart: Kreuz, 1962); S. Lehne *The New Covenant in Hebrews* (JSNTSup 44; Sheffield: JSOT, 1990); U. Luz, "Der alte und der neue

Bund bei Paulus im Hebräerbrief," *EvTh* 27 (1967) 318-36; R. P. Martin, *2 Corinthians* (WBC 40; Dallas: Word, 1986); J. L. Martyn, "A Law Observant Mission to Gentiles: The Background of Galatians," *SJT* 38 (1985) 307-24; idem, "Events in Galatia: Modified Covenantal Nomism Versus God's Invasion of the Cosmos in the Singular Gospel," in *Pauline Theology*, Vol I, ed. J. M. Bassler (Minneapolis: Fortress 1991) 160-79; idem, "The Covenants of Hagar and Sarah," in *Faith and History: Essays in Honor of Paul W. Meyer*, ed. J. T. Carroll et al. (Atlanta: Scholars, 1991) 160-92; E. P. Sanders, *Paul* (Oxford: University Press, 1991); N. T. Wright, *The Climax of the Covenant: Christ and the Law in Pauline Theology* (Edinburgh: T. & T. Clark, 1991).                                    W. S. Campbell

**COVENANTAL NOMISM.** *See* LAW; PAUL AND HIS INTERPRETERS; WORKS OF THE LAW.

## COWORKERS, PAUL AND HIS

In Acts and the Pauline letters some one hundred individuals, under a score of titles and activities, are associated with the apostle at one time or another during his ministry. They are participants in his preaching and teaching and in his writing, and they define the apostle's work as a "collaborative ministry" (Harrington).

 1. The Identity and Designations of the Coworkers
 2. The Classification of Their Activities

**1. The Identity and Designations of the Coworkers.**
The total number of Paul's coworkers has been placed at ninety-five (Redlich) or eighty-one (Pölzl), depending on how broadly one defines the term. When the names mentioned only in Acts and those with unspecified and general relationships to Paul are eliminated, thirty-six coworkers under nine designations can be identified with considerable probability (see chart).

*1.1. Long-Term Coworkers.* A number of these individuals have a long-term relationship with the apostle. Barnabas,* Mark and Titus are associated with him from the time of his Antiochian ministry (c. A.D. 46; Acts 13:1-3, 5; Gal 2:1, 13). The latter two remain in relationship to his mission* from time to time until the close of his life in c. A.D. 67 (*see* Pastoral Letters), as do a number who joined him during his mission to Greece: Timothy, Luke, Priscilla (= Prisca) and Aquila, and perhaps Erastus (c. A.D. 50-52; Acts 16:1-3, 10 ["we"]; 18:2; 19:22; Rom 16:3, 21, 23; 2 Tim 1:2; 4:10-11, 19-20; Tit 1:4). Similar are certain associates who initially come into view during Paul's first Aegean ministry: Apollos,* Trophimus and Tychicus (c. A.D. 53-58; Acts 19:1; 20:4; 1 Cor 16:12; Eph 6:21; Col 4:7;

2 Tim 4:12, 20; Tit 3:13). On the probable Caesarean provenance of three letters from prison—Ephesians, Colossians and Philemon (c. A.D. 58-60)—the name Demas may be added, although he abandoned the mission near the end of Paul's life (Col 4:14; 2 Tim 4:10; Philem 24). These ten or so long-time coworkers are complemented by many others who are a part of Paul's mission for shorter periods of time.

Of these long-term associates, five appear as Paul's subordinates, serving him or being subject to his instructions. They are Erastus, Mark, Timothy, Titus and Tychicus (Acts 19:22; Phil 2:19; Col 4:7-8; 2 Tim 4:10-12; Tit 1:5; 3:12; cf. 2 Cor 12:18). Others have a cooperative relationship with Paul but work in relative independence (Apollos, Priscilla and Aquila) or join him only on specific missions (Barnabas, Silas = Silvanus, Mark; cf. Acts 13:1-3; 15:40-41; 1 Thess 1:1).

*1.2. Four Frequent Designations.* The designations most often given to Paul's fellow workers are in descending order of frequency as follows: coworker (*synergos*), brother (*adelphos*), minister (*diakonos*) and apostle* (*apostolos*).

*1.2.1. Coworker* (*Synergos*). Some of Paul's associates are termed coworkers "of Paul" "in Christ" and for the Christian community (Rom 16:3, 9, 21; 2 Cor 8:23; Phil 2:25). They are also coworkers "with God" (1 Cor 3:9; 1 Thess 3:2 [D]; see Harnack, 7; but cf. Furnish, 369: "for God") in God's work even though they are God's "servants"* (*diakonoi*), each of whom "will receive his own reward according to his own toil" (1 Cor 3:8). Coworkers, workers (*ergatai*) and "those who toil" (*hoi kopiōntes*) usually are virtually equivalent idioms for a specific group or class and are not used of believers generally. The terms are applied to itinerant or local personnel and are connected with the right to pay or support, as Christ ordained (1 Cor 9:14; 1 Tim 5:18b; cf. Lk 10:7b), including "those who toil in word and teaching" (1 Tim 5:17; 2 Tim 2:6). They are entitled to respect and obedience by the congregation (1 Cor 16:16, 18) and are, at least at times, an appointed group (1 Thess 5:12; cf. Harnack, 1-10). On the other hand, if they become idlers, they should not receive support, for "if anyone does not want to work, neither let him eat," that is, at the community's expense (2 Thess 3:10; cf. Ellis 1993, 7, 10-11, 20-21). However, their ministry was a function of their spiritual gifts, and their support and leadership role was apparently unofficial and had no contractual character.

*1.2.2. Brother (Adelphos).* The term "brothers," like "slaves"* (*douloi*), can refer either to Christians generally or to Christian workers. "Brothers" often has the latter connotation when it is used with the article (cf.

| | adelphos "brother" | apostolos "apostle" | diakonos "minister" | (syn)doulos "fellow slave" | koinōnos "partner" | ho kopiōn "toiler" | (sy)stratiōtēs "(fellow) soldier" | synaichmalōtos "fellow prisoner" | synergos "coworker" |
|---|---|---|---|---|---|---|---|---|---|
| Achaicus[1] | — | — | (1 Cor 16:15-18) | — | — | (1 Cor 16:15-18) | — | — | (1 Cor 16:15-18) |
| Andronicus[3] | — | Rom 16:7 | — | — | — | — | — | Rom 16:7 | — |
| Apollos | 1 Cor 16:12 | 1 Cor 4:9 | 1 Cor 3:5 | — | — | — | — | — | 1 Cor 3:9 |
| Apphia[1] | (Philem 2) | — | — | — | — | — | — | — | — |
| Aquila & Prisca | — | — | — | — | — | — | — | — | Rom 16:3-5 |
| Archippus | — | — | (Col 4:17) | — | — | — | Philem 2 | — | — |
| Aristarchus | — | — | — | — | — | — | — | Col 4:10 | Philem 24 (Col 4:10-11) |
| Barnabas | — | Acts 14:4, 14 (1 Cor 9:5-6) | — | — | — | — | (1 Cor 9:7) | — | (Col 4:10-11) |
| Clement[1] | — | — | — | — | — | — | — | — | Phil 4:2-3 |
| Demas | — | — | — | — | — | — | — | — | Philem 24 (Col 4:11, 14) |
| Epaphras | — | — | Col 1:7 | — | Col 1:7; 4:12 | — | — | Philem 23 | — |
| Epaphroditus[1] | Phil 2:25 | Phil 2:25 | — | — | — | — | Phil 2:25 | — | Phil 2:25 |
| Erastus | — | — | (Acts 19:22) | — | — | — | — | — | — |
| Euodia & Syntyche[1] | — | — | — | — | — | — | — | — | (Phil 4:2-3) |
| Fortunatus[1] | — | — | (1 Cor 16:15-18) | — | — | (1 Cor 16:15-18) | — | — | (1 Cor 16:15-18) |
| Junia[3] | — | Rom 16:7 | — | — | — | — | — | Rom 16:7 | — |
| Justus[1] | — | — | — | — | — | — | — | — | Col 4:10-11 |
| Luke | — | — | — | — | — | — | — | — | Philem 24 (Col 4:11, 14) |
| Mark | — | — | (2 Tim 4:11) | — | — | — | — | — | Philem 24 (Col 4:11) |
| Mary[3] | — | — | — | — | — | Rom 16:6 | — | — | — |
| Onesimus | Col 4:9 | — | — | — | — | — | — | — | — |
| Persis[3] | — | — | — | — | — | Rom 16:12 | — | — | — |
| Philemon[1] | (Philem 7) | — | — | — | Philem 17 | — | — | — | Philem 1 |
| Phoebe[1] | (Rom 16:1) | — | (Rom 16:1) | — | — | — | — | — | — |
| Quartus[2] | Rom 16:23 | — | — | — | — | — | — | — | — |
| Sosthenes[1] | 1 Cor 1:1 | — | — | — | — | — | — | — | — |
| Silas | Acts 15:22 (1 Thess 3:2) | 1 Thess 2:7 | — | — | — | — | — | — | (1 Thess 3:2) |
| Stephanas[1] | — | — | (1 Cor 16:15-18) | — | — | (1 Cor 16:15-18) | — | — | (1 Cor 16:15-18) |
| Timothy | 2 Cor 1:1 Col 1:1 1 Thess 3:2 Philem 1 | (1 Thess 2:7) | (Acts 19:22) 2 Cor 3:6; 6:4 1 Thess 3:2 | Phil 1:1 2 Tim 2:24 | — | 2 Tim 2:6 | 2 Tim 2:3 | — | Rom 16:21 (1 Cor 16:10) (1 Thess 3:2) |
| Titus | 2 Cor 2:13 (2 Cor 8:16-23) | — | — | — | 2 Cor 8:23 | — | — | — | 2 Cor 8:23 |
| Tryphaena & Tryphosa[3] | — | — | — | — | — | Rom 16:12 | — | — | — |
| Tychicus | Eph 6:21 Col 4:7 | — | Eph 6:21 Col 4:7 | Col 4:7 | — | — | — | — | — |
| Urbanus[3] | — | — | — | — | — | — | — | — | Rom 16:9 |
| Paul | — | Rom 1:1 passim | 1 Cor 3:5 passim | Rom 1:1 passim | Philem 17 | (1 Cor 15:10 passim) | (1 Cor 9:7) | — | 1 Cor 3:9 |
| Christ | Rom 8:29 Heb 2:11-12 | Heb 3:1 | Gal 2:17 cf. Lk 22:27 Rom 15:8 | Phil 2:7 | cf. 2 Cor 1:5-7 | — | — | — | — |
| Christians generally | Rom 8:29 1 Cor 3:1 | — | ?Heb 6:10 | 1 Cor 7:22 Eph 6:6 | — | — | — | — | — |

[1]Mentioned in only one passage (one letter).
[2]Mentioned only once, with Paul in a greeting.
[3]Mentioned only once, a recipient of Paul's greeting.

Ellis 1993, 13-17). This becomes apparent when "the brothers" are distinguished from "the church" (1 Cor 16:19-20) or from believers generally (Eph 6:23-24; Phil 4:21-22; Col 4:15). It also probably has this sense in Paul's letter from Antioch* (cf. Longenecker, lxxxviii) to the Galatians: "Paul . . . and all the brothers with me" (Gal 1:1-2); cosenders elsewhere are always fellow workers (1 Cor 1:1; 2 Cor 1:1; Phil 1:1; Col 1:1; 1 Thess 1:1; cf. Acts 13:1-3). "The brothers" may refer to workers in local congregations (Phil 1:14; cf. Col 1:2 with 4:15-16; cf. Acts 11:1, 29; 12:17) or to those whose ministry takes on a traveling missionary character (2 Cor 2:13; 8:18, 22-23; cf. Acts 10:23; 11:12).

*1.2.3. Minister (Diakonos).* The term *diakonos* occurs in close connection with the above designations (1 Cor 3:5, 9; 2 Cor 6:1, 4) but has a somewhat more specialized meaning. It is probably best rendered "minister" since it refers to workers with special activities in preaching* and teaching,* both among Paul and his coworkers (1 Cor 3:5; 2 Cor 3:6; 6:4; Eph 3:7-8; Col 1:7, 23; 1 Tim 4:6) and among his opponents* (2 Cor 11:15, 23; cf. Ellis 1993, 102-3; Georgi, 27-32). Like "the brothers," the *diakonoi* serve in local congregations (Rom 16:1; Phil 1:1; 1 Tim 3:8) as well as on missionary circuits and, as teachers, they are mentioned as deserving of pay (Gal 6:6; Longenecker, 278-79).

*1.2.4. Apostles (Apostoloi) of Jesus Christ.* As ministers are a special kind of worker, so apostles (*apostoloi*) of Jesus Christ are a special kind of minister. In part they fulfill the same type of work and can be called ministers (cf. 1 Cor 4:9 with 3:5; Eph 3:5, 7). However, in other respects they are a more exclusive category. They are those who have "seen Jesus our Lord" (1 Cor 9:1; cf. 15:5-8), that is, those whom the risen Jesus commissioned, since his appearances seem always to have been coupled with a commission. In this category of apostles were a large number, including "500 brothers" (1 Cor 15:6), an understanding of "apostles of Christ" that is common to the NT, also to Luke-Acts (cf. Ellis 1987, 132-35). Although the term *apostles* can be used in the NT more narrowly to refer to the Twelve (e.g., Acts 4:35-37; 5; cf. Acts 6:2 with 6:6; 9:27), the limitation of apostles to the Twelve plus Paul is a creation of the later church.

Apostles of Jesus Christ among Paul's coworkers include Apollos, Barnabas and Silas. Apollos is probably included with Paul and Peter in Paul's phrase "us apostles" (1 Cor 4:9; cf. 3:22—4:1) and placed on a par with them. Accordingly, when Apollos is described by Acts (18:24-25; cf. 19:1-7) as "instructed in the way of the Lord" (cf. Lk 3:4; 20:21) and "knowing only the baptism of John [the Baptist]," it is likely that he is identified as an apostle of the earthly Jesus, who continued his apostleship separate from, and without knowledge of, Pentecost and of the Jerusalem events (Acts 1—6). He may well have won the converts in Acts 19:1-7. If his fervor "in spirit" refers to the Holy Spirit, it could be the same Holy Spirit power that was active in the preresurrection apostolic missions (cf. Lk 10). This understanding may explain why in Luke's account Apollos, like the Twelve, remains without a "Christian" baptism,* and it quite likely underlies his later listing as one of the Seventy (ps-Hippolytus, *On the Seventy Apostles* 50; *ANF* V.256). His identification as an Alexandrian Jew refers to his birthplace and to his special political and civil rights (cf. Philo *Flacc.* 53; *Leg. Gai.* 371; Kasher, 261), and probably has no more to do with his Christian background than Tarsus had to do with Paul's (Acts 18:24; 22:3; *see* Jew, Paul the). Teaching and preaching in the Aegean area, Apollos remained in occasional association with Paul from the early fifties to the mid-sixties (Tit 3:13).

Barnabas, a native of Cyprus, was a member of the Jerusalem* church in its earliest days (Acts 4:36). He introduced the newly converted Paul to the Twelve, invited his participation in the Hellenist mission at Syrian Antioch,* and with Paul was numbered among the resident "prophets and teachers" there (Acts 9:27; 11:25-26; 13:1). Barnabas and Paul are equated with "the rest of the apostles" at 1 Corinthians 9:5-6; and they are called "apostles" at Acts 14:4, 14, texts that probably refer to those commissioned by Christ and not to "apostles of the churches" (2 Cor 8:23 = commissioned missionaries), a usage that is foreign to Luke-Acts. After working with Paul during the famine visit and on the Cyprus-Galatian mission, together with his cousin Mark (c. A.D. 46-49; Acts 13—14; Gal 2:1, 9), and at the council of Jerusalem (c. A.D. 50; Acts 15:2, 12, 22; cf. Gal 2:13), Barnabas returned with Mark to the evangelization of Cyprus (Acts 15:39). In the fifties he appears to have ministered around the Aegean and in Asia Minor, at times in Pauline congregations, since he is known to Paul's churches at Corinth (c. A.D. 53; 1 Cor 9:6) and at Colossae (c. A.D. 60; Col 4:10). Like Apollos, he is counted by later tradition as one of the Seventy apostles (see above; cf. Clement of Alexandria *Strom.* 2.20; Eusebius *Hist. Eccl.* 1.12.1; 2.1.4).

Silas, a prophet in the Jerusalem church who coauthored and distributed the decree of the Council (Acts 15:22-23: *grapsantes dia cheiros autōn*), joined Paul in his mission to Greece (c. A.D. 50-53; Acts 15:40—18:22). According to 1 Thessalonians 1:1 and 2 Thessalonians 1:1 he was a cosender and plausibly the coauthor of these letters (see 2.2.1 below). Like Mark

(Col 4:10; Philem 24; 1 Pet 5:13; cf. Ellis *Making*), Silas was later a coworker in the Petrine mission where he also had a writing role as the secretary in composing 1 Peter (1 Peter 5:12). Both he and Paul are termed Roman citizens (Acts 16:37-38), and in 1 Thessalonians 2:6 (Gk 2:7) they are jointly referred to as "apostles of Christ" (*Christou apostoloi*), an idiom that identifies both as men who were personally commissioned by Christ. With this understanding Silas, like Apollos (see above), is counted as one of the Seventy apostles in church tradition which, in a clear misconception, also makes him a different person from Silvanus. That he, Apollos and Barnabas are called prophets or teachers or ministers does not rule out their apostolic status since Paul can also identify himself with these other ministries (1 Cor 14:37; 4:17; 1 Tim 2:7; Col 1:23; cf. Ellis 1993, 132n, 138-42).

*1.2.4.1. False Apostles.* The larger circle of "apostles of Christ" included not a few unnamed opponents of Paul who, like Judas, were commissioned by Jesus but turned out to be "ministers of Satan*" (2 Cor 11:15), who preached "another gospel*" (2 Cor 11:4; cf. Gal 1:6; I Tim 4:1) and were thus "false apostles" (2 Cor 11:13). Or did they only make a false claim to have been commissioned by Jesus? Favoring the former view are Paul's earlier (caustic) recognition of their apostolic status (2 Cor 11:5; cf. Ellis 1993, 105-6) and lettered credentials (2 Cor 3:1), and the analogy with Satan. In the Judaism of the period Satan was understood to have been originally an angel* of God, an angel of light (cf. Lk 10:18; Jude 8-9; *1 Enoch* 6; Job 1:6; Zech 3:1) who, after his fall, was, with his angels, the invisible power behind earthly rulers (1 Cor 2:8; cf. Dan 10:13; Ezek 28:12-15; 1QM 1:1; perhaps, Rom 13:1 [*exousiai*]; Is 14:12) and false teachers (CD 12:2-3), and who could disguise himself in his former righteousness (2 Cor 11:14-15; cf. Mt 12:24).

*1.2.4.2. Apostles of the Churches.* "Apostles of the churches," that is, commissioned missionaries, are also present among Paul's associates. They embrace the unnamed brothers traveling with Titus, including one whose service "in the gospel" was of high renown (2 Cor 8:16-24, 23); Epaphroditus, the "apostle" (*apostolos*) of the Philippian church to Paul (Phil 2:25), and Andronicus and Junia, probably a married couple who were kinfolk of Paul and "outstanding among the apostles" (*episēmoi en tois apostolois*, Rom 16:7). Because of this phrase they have sometimes been identified as "apostles of Christ," but that meaning is precluded by the descriptions: (1) This otherwise unknown couple could hardly be described, in comparison with Peter, James or even Paul himself, as "outstanding among the apostles of Christ." (2) Also, if they were "apostles

of Christ," the phrase "who were in Christ before me" would be a meaningless redundancy (cf. 1 Cor 15:8). They are, in fact, identified as commissioned missionaries.

### 1.3. Other Categories of Coworkers.

*1.3.1. Paul's Relatives.* Near the beginning of his ministry Paul fled from enemies in Jerusalem to Tarsus in Cilicia, the city of his birth, and ministered in that area for about ten years (c. A.D. 36-46; Gal 1:21; Acts 9:30; 11:25; 15:23; 21:39; 22:3). That he had relatives there who sheltered him on his arrival is a reasonable surmise. He was later aided by his sister's son after his arrest in Jerusalem during his collection* visit (c. A.D. 58; Acts 23:16).

In Romans 16:7, 11, 21 Paul mentions six kinfolk (*syngeneis* = "relatives" not "fellow Jews"), five of whom played a more explicit role in his ministry.* The couple mentioned above, Andronicus and Junia, were very early converts, having been won to Christ before the apostle. Accordingly, they were very likely Jerusalem relatives who were missionaries from that church to Rome. Like Paul, they had suffered imprisonment for the sake of the gospel, although not necessarily at the same time and place (Rom 16:7). Jason (Rom 16:21) is probably none other than the Jason of Thessalonica who was Paul's host and apparently the patron of a house church there (Acts 17:5-9). Equally probable, Sosipater is the fuller name of Sopater, who represented the church of Berea on the collection visit to Jerusalem (Acts 20:4).

That Lucius of Romans 16:21 is to be identified with Luke, the beloved physician and author of Luke-Acts, poses the problem of Paul using one form of his name here and another at Colossians 4:14, Philemon 24 and 2 Timothy 4:11. Nevertheless, it remains quite possible since Luke could be an abbreviated form of Lucius and since Acts places Luke with Paul about this time (Acts 20:5-6, "we").

In mentioning these kinfolk coworkers Paul reveals something of the strategy of his mission. He utilized contacts with his relatives in charting the evangelization of Thessalonica and Berea and, upon their conversion, accepted them as fellow workers in the mission and their homes as house churches for his congregations. If Luke was also a relative, it would not only put to rest the traditional but mistaken view that Luke was a Gentile (cf. Ellis 1987, 52-53) but also explain Paul's mission route to Troas. He travelled there with the intention of adding a confidant to his team who was familiar with the area and was already ministering in Troas (Acts 16:10, "we"). In time he also utilized Luke's gifts to provide a gospel of the words and works of Jesus for reading in his mission congregations (cf. Lk 1:1-4).

*1.3.2. Women Coworkers.* A remarkable number of women are mentioned as Paul's associates, both in Acts and in his letters (see chart; cf. Fiorenza, Gerberding, Trebilco). Some are called ministers (*diakonoi*) or coworkers (*synergoi*) or missionaries (*apostoloi*), several of whom were engaged in ministries of teaching and preaching (Rom 16:1, 3, 7; Phil 4:2-3; cf. Acts 18:26). Those who "toiled" and "labored" were involved in unspecified church work (Rom 16:6, 12), and others were members of wealthy families who supported Paul as benefactors and who dedicated their homes for use as house churches (Rom 16:15; Col 4:15; Philem 1-2; cf. Rom 16:13, 15-16; Acts 16:14-15, 40: see Gillman).

*1.3.3. The Circumcision Party.* Ritually strict "Hebraists," or "the circumcision* party," and ritually lax "Hellenists" were in tension within the church virtually from its beginning (Acts 6:1; 11:2-3; 15:1-2, 5). The Hebraists soon divided into two factions, the "Judaizers,"* who insisted that Gentile converts be circumcized and keep the Mosaic regulations (Gal 2:4-5, 12-14; Acts 15:1, 5), and the "orthodox" Hebraists like James who, while carefully observant of Jewish traditions themselves, accepted Hellenist and Gentile believers who were not (Gal 2:9-10; Acts 15:19-21; 21:17; cf. Ellis 1993, 116-28).

Paul firmly opposed the Judaizers (2 Cor 11:22; Tit 1:10), but he sought to work in friendly and appreciative cooperation with the "orthodox" Hebraists, taking collections to their (Jacobean) mission based on Jerusalem (Gal 2:10, *mnēmoneuōmen*; Rom 15:25-27; 1 Cor 16:3; 2 Cor 8—9; Acts 11:29-30; 24:17). When Hebraist ministers like Silas, a prophet of the Jerusalem church, could accommodate to a Gentile mission, Paul incorporated them into his ministry team (Acts 15:40), and at Caesarea he had among his coworkers two adherents of the circumcision party, Mark and Justus (Col 4:10-11). In this way the apostle sought to maintain the unity of the church within a diversity of praxis (cf. Rom 14; Gal 6:15).

## 2. The Classification of Their Activities.

Coworkers are almost always present with Paul, and they participated in his mission in a variety of ways. In his traveling they occasionally conducted him (Acts 9:30; 21:16; 27:1, "we"; Acts 28:15) and, more importantly, joined in the task (Gal 2:1; Acts 11:30; 15:2; 19:29). Some accompanied him on the collection visit to Jerusalem as representatives of the various churches (2 Cor 8:19; Acts 20:4-6; cf. 1 Cor 16:3-4).

Affluent believers in various cities, including a number of women (see 1.3.2 above), became hosts to Paul, and some opened their homes for the services of a local congregation (Rom 16:3-5; 1 Cor 16:19; Philem 2; Acts 17:5-7; 18:2-3, 7; cf. Ellis 1989, 139-45).

Most important were those gifted coworkers who were Paul's associates in preaching and teaching and those who were secretaries, recipients of and contributors to his letters.

*2.1. Associates in Preaching and Teaching.* In a manner not entirely clear to us the apostle trained coworkers who were gifted in preaching and teaching (cf. Rom 12:6-8; 1 Cor 12:28; Gal 6:6; Eph 4:11) not only to learn the basic Christian proclamation and the christological interpretation of Scripture but also to enable them to transmit his and the general apostolic message to new converts. That Paul adhered to an agreed apostolic catechesis is evident in Romans 6:17 and 16:17, and when he founded a church, he instructed believers also in his own distinctive Christian doctrines. He admonished his churches to continue in the traditions that he delivered to them and praised them for doing so (1 Cor 11:1; Col 2:7-8; 2 Thess 2:15; 3:6). To mediate his teachings Paul utilized, probably from the beginning, a number of coworkers, including gifted local converts as well as those who accompanied him and who were sent out on certain occasions to establish or to give instruction to his churches.

*2.1.1. Local Coworkers.* Stephanus and other local coworkers at Corinth had a ministry (*diakonia*) that probably went beyond practical services to include a ministry of the Word (1 Cor 16:15-16; cf. 2 Cor 5:18-19). They and "the brothers" addressed in 2 Thessalonians 2:13 [B] were termed the "first fruits"* (*aparchē*), a concept that referred (also) to the consecrated firstborn sons, who were set apart for service to God (cf. Ex 22:29 LXX: *aparchē*; Ellis 1993, 8, 19-20), although in Israel the tribe of Levi served as substitutes for the firstborn of other tribes (Num 3:11-13). Such local workers, preachers and teachers, most of them trained by Paul himself, are mentioned in a number of his letters (Gal 6:6; Phil 4:2-3; cf. 1:1; 1 Thess 5:12-13; 2 Thess 3:6-11). They were at work also in the church at Colossae, which apparently was founded by Paul's "fellow slave," Epaphras (Col 1:7-8; 2:1; 3:16; 4:12, 16).

*2.1.2. Coworkers Accompanying Paul.* Several coworkers, in particular Timothy, Titus and Tychicus, accompanied Paul and were on occasion sent to teach his churches in his absence. Timothy had been well instructed by the apostle and therefore could be dispatched to Thessalonica to "strengthen and exhort you regarding your faith" (1 Thess 3:2, 6) and later to Corinth to "remind you of my ways in Christ just as I teach [them] everywhere in every church" (1 Cor 4:17). Sometime later Titus and others were delegated to Corinth on a more difficult mission in the confidence that Titus "walks in the same Spirit, in the same steps" as Paul himself (2 Cor 12:18; cf. 8:16, 24). Finally, Titus went to Dalmatia (Tit 3:12; 2 Tim 4:10).

Tychicus was sent as a letter-bearer to the Ephesians (Eph 6:21-22) and others, and to the Colossians (Col 4:7), not only to add a personal dimension to the correspondence but probably also to explain Paul's teachings as the occasion might require. With similar authority he (or Artemas) was appointed to replace Titus in supervising churches on Crete (Tit 3:12) and to serve as Paul's messenger or perhaps surrogate at Ephesus (2 Tim 4:12).

As his mission expanded, Paul depended on coworkers not only to further his evangelistic and teaching ministries but also to assist in his writing.

### 2.2. Associates in Writing.

*2.2.1. Cosenders of Letters.* Cosenders—Sosthenes, Timothy, the brothers, Silas—are mentioned in eight of Paul's thirteen letters, Timothy in six of them. In what ways they contributed is not disclosed, but the mention of them in the greetings is hardly ornamental (cf. Conzelmann, 234-35).

*2.2.2. Secretaries.* A secretary is also in evidence in virtually all of the letters, although he is named only at Romans 16:22: Tertius (*see* Letters). In all likelihood the secretary was selected from among the believers, perhaps from the household of an affluent convert, and was thus a coworker. His role in ancient letter-writing could vary from taking dictation to being a coauthor. For the Pauline letters it would have varied in accordance with his spiritual gifts, the apostle's confidence in him and Paul's own situation, whether captive or free, traveling or resident in a city. The secretary appears to have had a considerable influence in the composition of the Pastoral Letters* and of a number of other letters (cf. Richards, 128-98; Ellis, *Making*).

*2.2.3. Coauthors.* Probably the secretary in 1 and 2 Thessalonians is a coauthor and is to be identified with Silas/Silvanus, who also coauthored the Jerusalem decree (Acts 15:22-23; see 1.2.4 above; cf. Selwyn, 9-17). But the view that the secretary who wrote Colossians, whether Timothy or another, was also the coauthor (so Ollrog, 241-42) is more doubtful.

*2.2.4. Recipients of Letters.* Particular individuals were of necessity the recipients of Paul's letters, even those that were addressed and intended for the church as a whole. For churches founded by the Pauline mission, these individuals were doubtless persons whom the apostle trusted to read the letter to the congregation. In the case of Colossians and 2 Thessalonians the coworkers, that is, "the brothers" themselves, appear to have been the primary addressees of the letters (Col 1:2; 4:16; 2 Thess 2:1-2; 3:1-15; Ellis 1993, 17-22).

*2.2.5. Authors of Traditions in Paul's Letters.* Although it is difficult to document, a number of the preformed pieces—confessions, hymns, expositions—that were used by Paul in his letters were also probably the creations of one or more of these fellow prophets and teachers (Ellis, *Making*; *see* Creed; Hymns; Liturgical Elements).

Given the numerous and varied contributions of Paul's fellow ministers to his mission, it is clear that they were an essential factor in its accomplishments and that even Paul's letters were not an individual enterprise. These missioners indeed deserve the considered attention of students of Paul. For it does not detract from his greatness to bring into greater prominence those with whom he served, those he was glad to praise and pleased to call his coworkers.

*See also* APOLLOS; APOSTLE; BARNABAS; CHURCH ORDER AND GOVERNMENT; FINANCIAL SUPPORT; MAN AND WOMAN; MINISTRY; MISSION; OPPONENTS OF PAUL; PASTORAL LETTERS; SOCIAL SETTING OF MISSION CHURCHES.

BIBLIOGRAPHY. F. F. Bruce, *The Pauline Circle* (Exeter: Paternoster, 1985); H. Conzelmann, "Paulus und die Weisheit," *NTS* 12 (1965-66) 231-44; E. E. Ellis, *The Making of the New Testament Documents* (forthcoming); idem, *Pauline Theology: Ministry and Society* (Grand Rapids: Eerdmans, 1989); idem, *Prophecy and Hermeneutic in Early Christianity* (4th ed.; Grand Rapids: Baker, 1993); idem, *The Gospel of Luke* (NCB; 5th rev. ed.; Grand Rapids: Eerdmans, 1987); E. S. Fiorenza, "Missionaries, Apostles, Coworkers," *WW* 6 (1986) 420-33; V. P. Furnish, " 'Fellow Workers in God's Service' [1 Cor 3:9]," *JBL* 80 (1961) 364-70; D. Georgi, *The Opponents of Paul in Second Corinthians* (Philadelphia: Fortress, 1986); K. A. Gerberding, "Women Who Toil in Ministry, Even as Paul," *CurTM* 18 (1991) 285-91; F. M. Gillman, *Women Who Knew Paul* (ZS: NT; Collegeville, MN: Liturgical, 1992); A. Harnack, "KOPOS," *ZNW* 27 (1928) 1-10; D. J. Harrington, "Paul and Collaborative Ministry," *NTR* 3 (1990) 62-71; A. Kasher, *The Jews in Hellenistic and Roman Egypt* (Tübingen: J. C. B. Mohr, 1985); J. Knox, *Philemon Among the Letters of Paul* (2d ed.; Nashville: Abingdon, 1959); E. Lohse, "Die Mitarbeiter des Paulus im Kolosserbrief," in *Verborum Veritas*, ed. O. Böcher and K. Haacker (Wüppertal: Brockhaus, 1970); R. N. Longenecker, *Galatians* (WBC 41; Dallas: Word, 1990); W. H. Ollrog, *Paulus und seine Mitarbeiter* (Neukirchen: Neukirchener, 1979); F. X. Pölzl, *Die Mitarbeiter des Weltapostels Paulus* (Regensburg: Manz, 1911); E. B. Redlich, *S. Paul and His Companions* (London: Macmillan, 1913); E. R. Richards, *The Secretary in the Letters of Paul* (Tübingen: J. C. B.

Mohr, 1991); E. G. Selwyn, *The First Epistle of St. Peter* (London: Macmillan, 1946); P. Trebilco, "Women as Co-workers and Leaders in Paul's Letters," *JCBRF* 122 (1990) 27-36 (cited in *NTA* 35 [1991] 180).

E. E. Ellis

## CREATION AND NEW CREATION

"New creation," *kainē ktisis*, is an expression Paul uses in 2 Corinthians 5:17 and Galatians 6:15. It is closely related to the expression "new human[ity]," *kainos anthrōpos*, in Ephesians 2:15, 4:23-24 and Colossians 3:9-10. This expression is not unique to Paul. It, and ideas associated with it, occur in several literary texts and traditions of Second Temple Judaism.

1. Need for a New Creation
2. Scope of the New Creation
3. Characteristics of the New Creation

### 1. Need for a New Creation.

Many early Jewish interpreters believed that God* had created a good world through the mediation of Wisdom (Prov 8:22-31; Sir 24; Wis 7:22—8:1). Paul identified this Wisdom* with Jesus Christ (1 Cor 1:17-25; Col 1:15-20). Paul also recognized that sin* damages this good creation by subjecting humankind to death (Rom 5:12-14; 1 Cor 15:21-22; see *4 Ezra* 7:116-131; *2 Apoc. Bar.* 54:13-19; *see* Life and Death) and the natural world to decay (Rom 8:19-22; see *4 Ezra* 7:11-14; *2 Apoc. Bar.* 56:6-10; *see* Futility). Disillusionment with the present state of affairs led many early Jewish interpreters to expect a new creation in a new age to come when the entire creation would be liberated from futility and transformed into its original goodness (e.g., *4 Ezra* 7:75; *2 Apoc. Bar.* 73—74). For Paul this age would accompany the Parousia, or future appearance, of Jesus (Rom 8:18; Eph 1:9-10; Col 3:1-4; *see* Eschatology).

### 2. Scope of the New Creation.

In 2 Corinthians 5:17 Paul suggests that this future reality is already present. There are three options for explaining precisely how the new creation is to be understood: (1) through individual converts; (2) through the community of faith; or (3) through the cosmos as a whole. Each option reflects a different opinion about which particular early Jewish texts and traditions were foremost in Paul's mind when he referred to the new creation.

*2.1. Convert.* In *Genesis Rabbah* 39.4, a Gentile convert to Judaism is regarded as a new creation: "Whoever brings a heathen near to God and converts him [or her] is as though he had created him [or her]." Similarly, in the Jewish tale of Joseph and Asenath, a

heavenly man says to Asenath, upon her conversion to Judaism, "you will be renewed and formed anew" (*Jos. and As.* 15:4). It is possible that Paul, like his Jewish counterparts, believed the convert to Christ to be a new creation.

*2.2. Community of Faith.* In Isaiah 65:17-19 the author parallels a cosmic re-creation with the re-creation of Jerusalem and its inhabitants: "For I am about to create new heavens and a new earth . . . for I am about to create Jerusalem as a joy, and its people as a delight." In Isaiah 66:22-23 the author develops this thought further when he predicts that within this new creation Israel will experience the influx of Gentiles* to worship* God.

Both of these elements—the re-creation of a new community of believers and the influx of Gentiles— underlie two of the Pauline passages which contain references to the new creation or new humanity. In both passages the new creation or new humanity is a *communal* reality. In Galatians 6:15-16, Paul even parallels the new creation with a specific community, "the Israel* of God." In Ephesians 2:14-16 the new humanity is composed of communities rather than individuals: "in his flesh he has made both groups into one . . . that he might create in himself one new humanity in place of the two."

Concomitantly, in both passages *Gentiles** are the community included alongside Jews. In Galatians 6:15 the new creation is a community where "neither circumcision* nor uncircumcision is anything." In Ephesians 2:11-22 (and Col 3:11) the new humanity is composed of Jews as well as Gentiles "who once were far off" (see Is 57:19). The church, therefore, is a new Israel where Jews and Gentiles are united in peace.*

*2.3. Cosmos.* Many apocalyptic* Jewish interpreters developed in detail the anticipation of the new heavens and new earth introduced by Isaiah 56—66. The emphases of their developments varied, including: the restoration* of Israel (*Jub.* 4:26; *1 Enoch* 45:4-5); the transformation of the righteous in a final resurrection* (*2 Apoc. Bar.* 51:1-16); the liberation of the natural world (*1 Enoch* 51:4-5); and the return of the creation to its original state of goodness (*2 Apoc. Bar.* 73—74). The persistent conviction of the apocalyptic perspective is that the new age to come will be decidedly different from—and qualitatively better than—the present evil age.

Paul reflects this apocalyptic context when, in 2 Corinthians 5:17-18, he depicts a radical disjuncture between "old things" (*ta archaia*) and "new things" (*kaina*). Such words suggest much more than individual transformation. Indeed, Paul argues that God reconciled "all things" (*ta panta*) through Christ, including presumably the entire natural world. If 2 Corinthians 5:16-17 provides a glimpse of the beginning of the new creation, other passages presage the completion of the new creation. According to Romans 8:18-25 "the creation itself will be set free from its bondage to decay" (Rom 8:21), while, according to Ephesians 1:10, "all things . . . things in heaven* and things on earth" will be gathered up in Christ (see 1 Cor 15:24-28).

It is not possible to choose definitively between these options. Nor is it necessary, for all three mutually illuminate each other. The convert, as part of a community of faith, enters the cosmic drama of re-creation that God inaugurated at the resurrection of Jesus Christ and will bring to completion at the Parousia (*see* Eschatology).

### 3. Characteristics of the New Creation.

A study of the Pauline contexts of the expressions "new creation" and "new human[ity]" reveals the two quintessential values that characterize the community of faith. By embodying these values, this community anticipates the final cosmic restoration of creation's goodness.

*3.1. Reconciliation.* The key concept that accompanies Paul's references to the new creation or new humanity is reconciliation (*see* Peace, Reconciliation). The dominant theme of 2 Corinthians 5:17-21 is that believers, who themselves have been reconciled to God, must continue by the apostolic ministry* of proclamation and witness* to bear testimony to the reconciliation of the world to God, which God inaugurated through Jesus. The thrust of Galatians 6:15, Ephesians 2:11-22 and Colossians 3:10-11 is that the new creation and new humanity come about only when peoples once divided are seen to be reconciled in Christ.

*3.2. Rejection of Worldly Standards.* Reconciliation can occur only when believers cease living and judging others according to worldly standards. The presence of a new creation means that new standards of unity and peace replace old standards of judgment and divisiveness. The *racial* division of Jew and Gentile, in particular, is based upon an obsolete criterion: "For neither circumcision nor uncircumcision is anything; but a new creation is everything!" (Gal 6:15; cf. Eph 2:11-22). Similarly, *individual* rivalry has no place in the new creation. Paul's reference to "new creation" in 2 Corinthians 5:17 is polemical; with it he confronts the faulty standards of his opponents at Corinth, who judge him according to worldly standards such as rhetorical* ability and physical strength (e.g., 2 Cor 10:1-11). In the new creation, contends Paul, no one is judged "from a human point of view,"

for even Christ is no longer judged by human standards (2 Cor 5:16). These new standards apply, not only to ethnic groups or to church leaders, but also to every believer who participates in the new humanity. He or she must put away conduct that characterizes the "old humanity," such as greed, slander and abuse (Col 3:5-9; Eph 4:25-30), and put on the new humanity, "which is being renewed in knowledge according to the image of its creator," that is, which is being restored to its original goodness (Col 3:10; see Gen 1:26). This new humanity is characterized by compassion, patience, truthfulness (Col 3:12-17; Eph 4:23-24; 32) and, once again, by reconciliation of peoples once hostile to one another (Col 3:11).

*See also* ADAM AND CHRIST; CENTER OF PAUL'S THEOLOGY; CHURCH; ESCHATOLOGY; NEW NATURE AND OLD NATURE; PEACE, RECONCILIATION; RESTORATION OF ISRAEL; RESURRECTION; RIGHTEOUSNESS, RIGHTEOUSNESS OF GOD; WORLD, COSMOLOGY.

BIBLIOGRAPHY. G. Baumbach, "Die Schöpfung in der Theologie des Paulus," *Kairos* 21 (1979) 196-205; N. A. Dahl, "Christ, Creation, and the Church," in *The Background of the New Testament and Its Eschatology*, ed. W. D. Davies and D. Daube (Cambridge: University Press, 1956) 422-43; W. D. Davies, *Paul and Rabbinic Judaism* (4th ed.; Philadelphia: Fortress, 1980) 36-57, 119-31; J. D. M. Derrett, "New Creation: Qumran, Paul, the Church, and Jesus," *RevQ* 13 (1988) 597-608; V. P. Furnish, *II Corinthians* (AB 32A; Garden City, NY: Doubleday, 1984) 309-16, 329-33; G. W. H. Lampe, "The New Testament Doctrine of *Ktisis*," *SJT* 17 (1964) 449-62; M. Parsons, "The New Creation," *ExpT* 99 (1987) 3-4; L. M. Russell, "Partnership in New Creation," *ABQ* 3 (1984) 161-71; P. Stuhlmacher, "Erwägungen zum ontologischen Charakter der *kainē ktisis* bei Paulus," *EvT* 27 (1967) 1-35; L. H. Taylor, *The New Creation: A Study of the Pauline Doctrines of Creation, Innocence, Sin, and Redemption* (New York: Pageant, 1958).

J. R. Levison

**CREATOR.** *See* CHRISTOLOGY; GOD; PRE-EXISTENCE.

## CREED

It is not easy to distinguish between "creeds"—the term used of rudimentary confessions of faith expressing Christian conviction—and other types of liturgical material as they appear in the Pauline letters. Clearly a full-scale creed, in the later sense of essential articles of the Christian faith enjoying ecclesiastical sanction, is not discernible in the NT letters. But there are fragments enshrining cardinal beliefs present in the hymns,* baptismal responses and eucharistic forms which Pauline research has brought to light.

1. Marks and Usage of Creeds
2. Central Affirmation of the Creeds
3. Types of Confession

## 1. Marks and Usage of Creeds.

Some of the telltale marks indicating the presence of creedal formulae are seen in 1 Corinthians 15:3-5: (1) The four-times-repeated "that" (*hoti*) suggests Paul is consciously citing material forming a set of propositions (e.g., that "Christ died for our sins in accordance with the Scriptures"). (2) The vocabulary in these verses is full of rare terms and expressions Paul never uses in other places. (3) The introducing verbs that say that Paul "received" (*parelabon*) what follows as part of the instruction he had known in his early days as a new believer, and now in turn "handed on" (*paredōka*) to the Corinthians, are semitechnical terms for the transmission of "holy words" of the faith, both Jewish and Christian (*see* Tradition). (4) In its content this same passage looks to Isaiah 53 as a passion—and resurrection*—*testimonium*, and it is argued (by R. H. Fuller) that Paul only uses such scriptural proof of the Suffering Servant when he is consciously indebted to his predecessors.

Creedal formulations and hymnic material are not easy to separate on stylistic grounds (*see* Liturgical Elements). Bultmann has usefully made the distinction that the early confessions of faith tended to be expressed in simple, succinct sentences like "Jesus is the Christ*" or "Jesus is Lord,*" whereas the hymns represented a longer statement of the person and achievement of Christ (as in Phil 2:6-11; Col 1:15-20) capable of being analyzed in stanzas and sections. But ultimately the distinction is not important since creedal materials and hymnic compositions overlap. We confine our attention here, however, to the former type.

Recent investigation of Paul's use of rhetorical forms and structures in his letters (*see* Rhetoric) has suggested reasons for his introducing quoted materials, notably creedal fragments. Paul as letter writer put his epistolary compositions together in an artistic way, cleverly designed to make maximum appeal to his readers whom he needed to win over to his theological point of view. One way he chose to do this was to cite creedal material, sometimes with added redactional touches to emphasize or to correct a previously cherished statement, as a common basis he believes will maintain the friendly relationship (Gr. *philophronēsis*) with his readers. Evidence of this is seen in Romans 1:3-4; 3:24-26; 2 Corinthians 5:18-21 and the hymnic Philippians 2:6-11. It is not surprising that he should employ this device since he is often building his polemical case on what he regarded as "received" Christian convictions which he and his congregations shared. One sure way to recall the errant members to his gospel was to draw out the implications of a "creed" they had accepted but momentarily had deserted because of alien teachings (e.g., 2 Cor 11:12-15; Col 2:8).

## 2. Central Affirmation of the Creeds.

The Pauline churches were made up of believing men and women whose new life in Christ was oriented to the risen Lord. Paul assumed that whatever the source of the proclamation that brought the saving message, it centered on the resurrection of Christ (1 Cor 15:11). This basic conviction gave the communities a sense of identity in the social world around them (1 Cor 10:32) and a missionary impulse to proclaim and embody the gospel* in that social setting (Gal 1:8-9; 1 Cor 9:19-23; 15:1-2; 1 Thess 2:13). Moreover, possessing a body of Christian truth explains how, from the start, the church was a worshipping community with a devotion that centered on Christ as living Lord (Mt 18:20; 1 Cor 5:4; 16:22).

Gradually this limpid confession of the risen Christ (seen in the later epigraphic motto of the fish, represented in Greek by the code word *ICHTHYS*, i.e., Jesus Christ, Son of God, Savior, the Greek words' initials forming the word for fish, which in turn derives from such passages as Mk 1:17; 6:38-44 and par.; Jn 21:9-14) underwent developments according to the situations in which Christians were encouraged or required to confess their faith. Simple piety, however, still persisted, and in an unsophisticated form believers retained for several centuries an undeveloped faith in Christ's person without much theological refinement.

## 3. Types of Confession.

The life settings of the Pauline creedal forms are as follows:

*3.1. Mission Preaching.* With a body of doctrinal and practical beliefs known variously as "the word of life" (Phil 2:16), "the standard of teaching" (Rom 6:17), "the faith" (Col 2:6-7), "the truth" (Col 1:5; 2 Thess 2:13), "the gospel" (Rom 2:16; 16:25; Phil 1:7, 27), Paul's churches confronted the pagan world around them, sought to win over new converts and then to indoctrinate fledgling members. At the core of such mission proclamation was the claim that God has exalted Jesus as sovereign Lord (Rom 10:9-10; *see* Exaltation) and that faith* is seen primarily as obedience to his authority* (Rom 1:5; 14:9).

*3.2. Cultic Worship.* As new adherents were led to confess Christ as Lord (Rom 10:9-10) and to accept a new life in him (Col 2:6), it was natural that the honor paid in worship that put the risen Lord at the center would follow. The baptismal confession "Jesus is Lord" (1 Cor 12:3; Rom 10:9-10; cf. Eph 5:26) and the Lord's Supper* service which is interpreted by Paul as a "proclaiming" of Christ's death in an eschatological context (1 Cor 11:26) are the clearest ways in which Christ crucified and living, with his parousia anticipated (1 Cor 16:22), was set at the heart of worship* practices in Paul's congregations.

*3.3. Opposition.* As the Pauline churches met resistance and their beliefs were challenged, first by Jewish debaters and then from within, so the creeds became more nuanced to the situation. The primary creed confessing the messiahship of Jesus gave way to longer expositions hailing his cosmic authority over demonic powers (Phil 2:6-11; Col 1:15-20; 1 Tim 3:16; *see* Principalities and Powers) which were placed in opposition to rival christologies and cosmologies (*see* World, Cosmology). Part of Paul's response was to build on the Jewish monotheistic credo (Deut 6:4-5; Is 45:22) with its belief in one God* (1 Cor 8:6) and to christianize it with a confession of the lordship of Christ, both pre-existent* (Phil 2:6; 1 Cor 10:4; 2 Cor 8:9) and exalted (Phil 2:9-11; Rom 1:3-4).

*See also* HYMNS, HYMN FRAGMENTS, SONGS, SPIRITUAL SONGS; LITURGICAL ELEMENTS; WORSHIP.

BIBLIOGRAPHY. H. Bettenson, *Documents of the Christian Church* (London: Oxford University Press, 1943); R. Bultmann, "Bekenntnis- und Liedfragmente im ersten Petrusbrief," *Coniectanea Neotestamentica* 11 (1949) 1-14; H. Conzelmann, *1 Corinthians* (Hermeneia; Philadelphia: Fortress, 1975); O. Cullmann, *The Earliest Christian Confessions* (London: Lutterworth, 1949); R. H. Fuller, *The Mission and Achievement of Jesus* (London: SCM, 1954); G. A. Kennedy, *New Testament Interpretation through Rhetorical Criticism* (Chapel Hill: University of North Carolina, 1984); R. P. Martin, *Worship in the Early Church* (Grand Rapids: Eerdmans, 1974); V. H. Neufeld, *The Earliest Christian Confessions* (Leiden: E. J. Brill, 1963).

R. P. Martin

# CROSS, THEOLOGY OF THE

"We preach Christ crucified" (1 Cor 1:23). The centrality of the cross to Paul's proclamation of the gospel is captured in this enormously suggestive phrase from the Corinthian correspondence. Since the early sixteenth century, the phrase "theology of the cross" has come to be used to refer to a theology which centers on the crucifixion.* The origins of the phrase can be traced back to the Heidelberg Disputation (1518), in which Martin Luther contrasted a "theology of glory"

(which marginalized the cross of Christ) and a "theology of the cross," which focused on God as he revealed himself in and through the crucified Christ.* For Luther the cross was not merely the basis of human salvation; it was the basis of God's self-revelation in which "true theology and the knowledge of God" alone could be found.

This emphasis on the centrality of the cross has remained a continuing feature of Christian theology, although this fact is perhaps more fully reflected in hymns rather than works of theology. In recent years the theology of the cross has found powerful expression chiefly in the writings of J. Moltmann and E. Jüngel, although with significant contributions from D. J. Hall and others. But what about the Pauline theology of the cross? What role did the cross play in Paul's conception of Christian theology and the Christian life?

1. Defining a Theology of the Cross
2. E. Käsemann on Paul and the Theology of the Cross
3. The Cross and the Attributes of God
4. The Cross and the Resurrection: "Now" and "Not Yet"
5. The Cross and Human Redemption
6. The Cross and the Christian Life

## 1. Defining a Theology of the Cross.

What is a "theology of the cross"? In one sense, just about every Christian theology could lay some claim to this title in that it makes at least some reference to the crucifixion of Jesus Christ. Even the defective Corinthian theology attacked by Paul appears to have incorporated the cross in its reflections (*see* Corinthians). However, in its stricter sense a "theology of the cross" can be defined in the following terms (Luz):

*1.1. Ground of Salvation.* A theology of the cross treats the cross as the *exclusive ground of salvation*. All other events within the history of salvation (such as the resurrection* of Christ or his coming again in glory*) are seen as being set in their proper context by the cross. Thus, in the case of the Corinthian theology so powerfully criticized by Paul, the resurrection appears to be detached from the cross and treated as relativizing the crucifixion. The theology of the cross negates this relativizing development.

*1.2. Starting point of Christian Theology.* A theology of the cross declares that the cross is the *starting point of authentically Christian theology*. The cross is not an isolated individual aspect of theology, but is itself the foundation of that theology. Far from being an isolated chapter in a textbook of theology, the cross both dominates and permeates all true Christian theology, with its thread being woven throughout the entirety of its fabric.

***1.3. Center of Christian Thought.*** A theology of the cross treats the cross as the *center of all Christian thought* in that from its center radiate Christian statements on ethics, anthropology, the Christian life and so on. The doctrines of revelation and salvation,* so easily detached from one another, converge on the cross.

In this strong sense of the phrase, Paul and Mark (and perhaps 1 Peter) emerge as the leading representatives within the NT corpus of a theology of the cross.

## 2. E. Käsemann on Paul and the Theology of the Cross.
Recent studies of the centrality of the cross within Paul's thought have been dominated by the influence of E. Käsemann, especially his essay "The Saving Significance of the Death of Jesus in Paul." Käsemann argues forcefully for the need to reappropriate the great Reformation insights concerning Paul's theology; more accurately, those of Luther (*see* Paul and His Interpreters). Standing firmly within the Lutheran tradition of Pauline interpretation, Käsemann declares that any other approach to Paul's theology can at best embrace only some of its many aspects; it is Luther's approach which takes in Paul's theology in its totality (*see* Center). So what are the basic features of Paul's theology of the cross, according to Käsemann?

In his analysis of the Pauline texts, Käsemann draws a precise distinction between texts which Paul inherits, and which reflect the liturgical and doxological tradition (*see* Liturgical Elements) of a pre-Pauline tradition,* and those texts which may be argued to owe their origin directly to Paul himself. It is these latter, it is argued, which are more authentically Pauline. To begin with, we may consider those which are argued to derive from an earlier tradition.

Käsemann argues that passages which refer to Christ's death* on the cross as possessing salvific importance largely derive from this earlier tradition. However, he discerns a process of reinterpretation in operation, by which Paul introduces radical new elements into this traditional material. In part, this reinterpretation consists in redirecting attention from the "not-yetness" of the resurrection to the "here and now" of the crucifixion—a key element of his controversy with the Corinthian enthusiasts. Also, Jewish-Christian elements (in Rom 3:24-26) are taken over but redacted to yield a richer meaning (*see* Käsemann 1980, 91-101). But this reinterpretation is chiefly to be seen in Paul's stress on the justification* *of the ungodly.* The cross brings home the full seriousness of sin,* declares the powerlessness of fallen humanity to achieve salvation and exposes human delusions of self-righteousness.

Paul's letters include a number of instances of pre-Pauline tradition which Paul has interpreted or redacted. Two such instances are of special importance. Romans 3:24-26 illustrates the general observation that the pre-Pauline tradition lacks the radical emphasis upon the cross which appears to be so typical of Paul himself. More significantly, Paul appears to add an emphasis upon the cross to Philippians 2:6-11, which is generally regarded as a pre-Pauline tradition. The phrase "even death upon a cross" disrupts the scansion of the text, suggesting that it has been added by Paul. The significant modification of this text, which now includes an explicit and important reference to the cross, illustrates Paul's concern to focus his theology on the crucified Christ.

What, then, of those passages which are to be regarded as directly arising from Paul, his personal creations, rather than an inheritance from the pre-Pauline tradition? It is in these that the message of the scandal* of the cross, with all its theological implications, is found in its fullness and distinctiveness. Perhaps the most significant such passage is 1 Corinthians 1:18-31. It is here that one finds Paul's distinctive emphasis upon the fact that God wills to justify the ungodly through the scandalous crucifixion of Jesus as a criminal publicly cursed by God. In particular, Käsemann draws attention to two distinctive features of this theology: its *polemical* character and its *predisposition toward rejection by the world.**

Paul's theology of the cross is *polemical*, not in that it is directed against false understandings of the nature of God* current outside the church, but in that it counters misunderstandings of the gospel within the church* itself—such as the legalistic piety of Judaizing Christian circles (*see* Judaizers) or the false views concerning the resurrection current at Corinth. Paul's theology of the cross "was always a critical attack on the dominating traditional interpretation of the Christian message, and it was not by chance that it characterized Protestant beginnings" (Käsemann, 35). And that theology is orientated toward *rejection* by the world. Käsemann stresses that Paul's personal ministry may be seen as an autobiographical presentation of the impact of the cross in that it evokes affliction, suffering, rejection and persecution (*see* Afflictions, Trials, Hardships). Wherever the church takes the cross of Christ seriously, it can expect to encounter hostility.

Toward the end of his essay Käsemann introduces an important discussion on the relation between the theology of the cross and preaching,* apparently directed against those who stress the historicity and objectivity of the crucifixion. Faith cannot be allowed to become dependent on mere historical remembrances of a past event (and surely one can detect echoes here of M. Kähler's critique of purely historical approaches to christology*). The death of Christ is significant, not simply as an historical event, but through the preaching of the word (Rom 10:14) and the subsequent evoking of faith.*

Käsemann's approach to Paul's theology of the cross is brilliant and original, and he remains an enormously significant conversation partner in relation to any discussion of Paul's theology of the cross. Some obvious points of criticism of the essay may be noted, centering on his distinction between the pre-Pauline and Pauline components of the corpus.

First, why should one assume that pre-Pauline material is somehow less important than Paul's own sections? The very fact that Paul draws upon an earlier tradition may well indicate that he intended it to be taken with great seriousness, and that those sections were intended to be invested with particular interpretative weight. An obvious example is 1 Corinthians 11:23-25, where Paul clearly wishes his citation from an earlier tradition to possess enough authority* to clinch his argument (see also 1 Cor 15:1-4).

Second, how can anyone be quite so sure as Käsemann that Paul has radically modified earlier material? This question is methodologically related to the question of how a clear distinction may be drawn between traditional and redactional material, which is not necessarily as simple as Käsemann would have us believe. As far as can be seen, Paul does not always modify earlier material; there must always be a degree of doubt concerning the nature, extent and significance of Paul's reworking of the earlier tradition.

Nevertheless, Käsemann's essay, supplemented by a distinguished series of subsequent writings, may be said to have stimulated new interest in the Pauline theology of the cross, especially within German language scholarship, and increasingly within North American writings (e.g., Beker, Cousar). The remainder of this essay attempts a general survey of this theology, in the light of this work.

### 3. The Cross and the Attributes of God.

The impact of Paul's theology of the cross on the attributes of God is best seen from the analysis of 1 Corinthians 1:18—2:5. This passage appears to be addressed to a community which has lost sight of the centrality of the cross on account of a preoccupation with a quasi-gnostic (see Gnosis, Gnosticism) notion of resurrection* or heavenly existence in the present world. Significantly, Paul appears to make the demand that all talk of the divine attributes should be ground-

ed in the crucified Christ rather than human preconceptions of what counts as "wisdom."* There are strong parallels between the theology of the cross and the doctrine of justification*: just as the world tried to discern God through its own wisdom (1 Cor 1:21), so it sought to attain justification through works of the Law (Rom 3:21-26; see Works of the Law). This is not so much a suggestion that human wisdom is slightly deficient; it is an assertion that there is such a serious flaw in natural human notions of wisdom that humanity totally inverts the relation of "wisdom" and "folly." Christ becomes for us the "wisdom of God" (1 Cor 1:30)—an idea which is perhaps best understood in terms of Christ becoming the paradigm of divine wisdom. The crucified Christ is the interpretative framework for making sense of God.

The passage may be regarded as a powerful demonstration of the freedom of God. God is not bound by the limitations of human categories. Human concepts of wisdom are shown up as spurious, things that humans have invented rather than things that have been revealed. There are parallels here with the related argument developed in Romans 1:19-25, where Paul argues that sinful humans have a natural propensity to confuse the creation with the Creator, substituting created entities for their having been made by God. Paul's argument clearly centers on the fact that humanity has been allowed to define the framework of reference for understanding God, rather than allowing God to establish that framework himself. 1 Corinthians 1:30 implies that human ideas of wisdom,* righteousness,* sanctification (see Holiness, Sanctification) and redemption* are not merely relativized, but are shown to be spurious by the crucifixion of Jesus Christ. It is not simply that God"s ways are not our ways; it is that our ways of thinking preclude us from discerning those ways in the first place.

This point can be understood by considering Paul's discussion of the notion of the "righteousness of God" in relation to the justification of the ungodly (e.g., Rom 3:21-26). Alongside the hints at the covenant faithfulness of God is the notion that God is somehow *defined* in relation to the justification event. God is one who—despite all the offence given to human notions of justice—justifies the ungodly. Believers are asked to trust in the one "who justifies the ungodly" (Rom 4:5)—that is, God. Just as God justifies the ungodly (thus simultaneously offending and contradicting human ideas of justice and righteousness), so God chooses those who are weak and foolish in the eyes of the world (thus simultaneously offending and contradicting human ideas of wisdom).

The cross—more accurately, the crucified Christ—

thus acts as both the foundation of authentically Christian ways of thinking about God, and as a judge of those ways of thinking about God which humans absorb uncritically from the world around them and unconsciously incorporate into theological reflections. If Käsemann is right, and Paul's theology of the cross is indeed polemical in nature, directed toward inadequate theologies *within* the church itself, then theology must submit itself to this criterion.

### 4. The Cross and the Resurrection: "Now" and "Not Yet."

How do the cross and resurrection relate to one another? Käsemann delivered a powerful protest against those who saw the cross and resurrection as "two links in a chain"—the chain in question being the ordered sequence of events which leads from the pre-existence to the final return of Christ, taking in such landmarks as his birth (or incarnation) and ascension en route. As noted above, the theology of the cross insists upon the cross being given priority over all other events in the history of salvation. Käsemann thus declares that the cross and resurrection are to be related as "riddle and interpretation."

This contrasts with the pre-Pauline tradition (e.g., at 1 Cor 15:3-4), in which cross and resurrection are treated as events in sequence. While it could be argued that the cross is the necessary presupposition of the resurrection (in that without Christ's death, he could not have been raised again), this insight is not necessarily theologically significant. It is not that the cross is a chapter in the history of the resurrection in which the resurrection excels the cross in importance. Rather, the resurrection gives meaning to the cross, with the cross being the real center of gravity. One might almost say that the resurrection is a chapter in a book on the theology of the cross. Before Paul, the cross of Jesus formed the question which was answered by the message of the resurrection. The apostle decisively reversed this way of looking at things. In his controversy with the enthusiasts it was precisely the interpretation of the resurrection which turned out to be a problem, a problem which can only be answered in the light of the cross. The situation at Corinth illustrates this point well.

The most reasonable interpretation of the Corinthian situation could be summarized along the following lines. A section of the church had developed ideas which sound similar to those associated with Hymenaeus and Philetus (1 Tim 2:17-18)—that the resurrection has already taken place. This idea of a "realized resurrection" accounts for many of the distinctive themes associated with the situation addressed by

1 Corinthians (*see* Corinthians). The "not yet" emphasis may be directed against those who believed that they had already attained fulfillment, who were already endowed with spiritual and heavenly voices, and who were already speaking with the tongues* of angels.* Paul's emphasis on the cross appears intended to stress that the cross cannot be bypassed on the way to resurrection. Before sharing in the resurrection life and all its fullness, believers must first pass through the shadow of the cross, which continues to fall across the entire range of Christian existence (*see* Eschatology).

A similar point emerges from Paul's discussion of baptism, especially as it is found in Romans (Rom 6:1-11). A consistent eschatological reserve is maintained here, as in the earlier Corinthian correspondence. Through baptism, believers are participants in the death of Christ on the cross—and believers *shall be* participants in his resurrection. Believers have been united with him in his death; they shall be united with him in his resurrection (Rom 6:5). Believers have died with Christ; they shall live with him in his resurrection (Rom 6:8-9; *see* Dying and Rising with Christ). Baptism* thus does not lead directly to a sharing in the resurrection: sharing in Christ's death is the "here and now" to which sharing in his resurrection is the "not yet." Paul's emphasis on the present sharing of believers in the death of Christ firmly anchors the life of faith to this world and presents heaven as a future reality, present in promise, yet not in fact: *non in re sed in spe* (Luther).

### 5. The Cross and Human Redemption.

In turning to deal with the Pauline theology of the cross as it relates to human redemption, one discovers Paul presenting and endorsing ideas which appear to go back to the pre-Pauline tradition. The idea that Christ "died for (*hyper*) our sins" is deeply embedded within the Pauline corpus (e.g., Rom 5:6, 8; 14:15; Gal 1:4; 2:20). Most significantly, the phrase is cited from the pre-Pauline tradition (1 Cor 15:3) in such a way as to leave no doubt of its considerable authority both for Paul and for his readership. The historic event of the crucifixion is thus overlaid with a significant interpretative element, in which history becomes salvation history. But how is this salvation event to be explored further?

Paul's exposition of the manner in which Christ's death* on the cross is salvific is complex, often intermingling a variety of deeply suggestive and rich images in a very short space. In 2 Corinthians 5:14—6:2 a remarkable set of images is interwoven, to build up a composite picture of the manner in which the cross may be said to redeem us. In Romans 3:24-26, three significant images (to be discussed below) are integrated to give a comprehensive overview of the redemption event. Yet it is difficult to reduce Paul's statements here, or elsewhere, to the neat theories so beloved of certain theologians. For example, Paul's thought at Romans 6:1-11 is clearly participatory; the believer shares in Christ's death now, and will finally share in his resurrection. But in 2 Corinthians 5:21 vicarious language is used: there is an interchange of sin and righteousness between the believer and Christ (Hooker).

Debate has centered on a number of key images used within the Pauline corpus to describe the "benefits of Christ" (Melanchthon). Three may be noted as being of special importance.

1. The Greek word *hilastērion* is traditionally translated "expiation" or "propitiation," although the term "mercy seat" (cf. Lev 16) is increasingly finding favor among exegetes (*see* Expiation, Propitiation, Mercy Seat). This technical term occurs only once in the Pauline corpus, making its interpretation as significant as it is difficult, given its pivotal function in Romans 3:24-26. The translation "propitiation" would convey associations of "an action directed towards satisfaction of the divine wrath" (Morris). The strong link between sin and the wrath* of God (e.g., Rom 1:18; 3:5) makes this a strong possibility. To translate the term as "expiation" would imply that the death of Christ "makes amends for sin," suggesting that Christ's death is aimed at the rectification of sin rather than the appeasement of God. "The wrath of God in the case of Jesus' death is not so much retributive as preventative" (Dunn). In the end, this debate must be left open. Christ's death is clearly understood to get to the root cause of sin—however that is understood.

2. The act of God justifying the ungodly. (We have deliberately avoided the noun "justification" to remain faithful to the fact that Paul almost invariably uses the verb. *See* Justification; Righteousness.) This idea expresses a number of central Pauline ideas: God's powerful, cosmic and universal action in effecting a change in the situation between sinful humanity and God by which God is able to acquit believers, setting them in a right and faithful relation to himself. The death of Christ can be seen as a simultaneous vindication of the character of God and a genuine forgiveness of human sins (Rom 3:26).

3. The idea of "redemption"* (Rom 3:24) has strong links with the world of a slave market or prison. The dominant theme is that of liberation from being "under the power of sin" (Rom 3:9). Sin is here understood as a power or force, which exercises authority and dominion over sinful humanity. The death of Christ snaps this baleful force, enabling humans to achieve the glorious liberty of the children of God (*see* Adoption, Sonship).

It must be stressed, however, that Paul is not concerned to build up a systematic theology of redemption such as that which is found in many a scholastic theologian. It is the reality rather than any specific theory of the power* of God to deliver from sin through the death of Christ that dominates Paul's horizons. The images used toward this end are illustrative, and one would do well to avoid the selectivity and prioritization that inevitably accompany systematization of the event of redemption. The theology of the cross has much to tell us here, by reminding us that it is the cross, the crucified Christ, that lies at the heart of the Christian gospel,* not a theory.

### 6. The Cross and the Christian Life.

How does the cross affect the Christian life? It is perhaps here that the full implications of a theology of the cross become clear. For theology becomes spirituality, not spirituality in the vague humanist sense of a means of heightening human religiosity, but in the proper sense of fashioning people who are on the road to becoming spiritual. The cross shapes the Christian life, a fact which Paul develops in a powerful series of autobiographical passages in which he relates the way in which he has been shaped by the cross and conformed to the pattern of the crucified Christ. In a significant series of passages Paul indicates the manner in which the cross may be expected to affect the life of believers. We may pick up the themes in the passages that follow.

*6.1. 2 Corinthians 4:7-15.* In this list of afflictions,* which bears a significant relationship to the "hardship literature" of the classical period, Paul indicates the manner in which the cross of Christ impresses itself upon his existence. To be a believer is to bear the marks of hardship, conflict and rejection. The key idea is expressed in the enormously evocative sentence "always carrying in the body the death of Jesus" (2 Cor 4:10). For Paul, Christ and his cross are the cause and the paradigm of the suffering of the believer. There is a strong sense of the believer sharing in the life—and hence in the sufferings—of Christ, an idea perhaps expressed most fully at Romans 8:17 (cf. Col 1:24).

*6.2. Galatians 6:14.* "Far be it for me to glory except in the cross of Christ Jesus, by which the world has been crucified to me, and I to the world." This significant passage is concerned with the criticism of those who, for worldly reasons, wish to compel Christians to adopt lifestyles which are alien to the gospel. The world is seen as a power impinging upon the life of believers where it has no authority to do so. The passage implies an organic relation between three crucifixions: those of Christ, Paul and the world. On account of the cross Paul has died to the world, and the world has died to him. "Those who belong to Christ Jesus have crucified the flesh" (Gal 5:24). The power that the world once exercised over him has been broken. Paul now participates in a new creation* brought into being by the crucifixion, in which the authority and dominion of the world* has been destroyed—no, more than that: the world has been crucified.

*6.3. Philippians 3:8-12.* This powerful passage builds on the idea of sharing in the resurrection* and sufferings* of Christ on account of the believers' relationship to him. Paul expresses the passionate longing "that I may know him [Christ] and the power of his resurrection, and may share his sufferings, becoming like him in his death" (Phil 3:10). Because Christ has made them his own (Phil 3:12), believers may expect to share in all that he is and has—including both the fellowship of his sufferings, becoming like him in his death, and finally (note the "not yet" element), sharing in the resurrection. It is passages like this which caused Luther to write that "the *Christianus* must be *crucianus.*" To know Christ is to know his sufferings. Note the idea of "becoming like Christ in his death"; the Greek has perhaps the sense of "being conformed to Christ in his death," so that the Christian life can be thought of as a process of being refashioned and reforged after the image of the suffering Christ.

So how is Paul's theology of the cross to be described? We may say that, for Paul, the cross stands, immovable, as the fundamental reference point of faith. It is from here that faith began, and to here that faith will continually return, to be nourished by the crucified Christ. Through sharing in Christ, the believer shares in his sufferings and death, and will one day—*but not yet!*—share in his glorious resurrection. And that hope will and must keep us going through faith. Believers may catch glimpses of the heavenly realms, they may even hear the distant voices of angels—but they remain here, committed to Christ crucified, in the midst of a suffering world. The heavenly realms remain in the future, even if their distant music can now be heard. The cross stands as the image of the Christian life in the world, just as it stands for the hope beyond this world, which believers share with Paul.

*See also* CHRISTOLOGY; CRUCIFIXION; CURSE, ACCURSED, ANATHEMA; DEATH OF JESUS; DYING AND RISING WITH CHRIST; JUDGMENT; JUSTIFICATION; RESURRECTION; RIGHT-EOUSNESS, RIGHTEOUSNESS OF GOD; WEAKNESS; WISDOM.

BIBLIOGRAPHY. R. Barbour, "Wisdom and the Cross in 1 Corinthians 1 and 2," in *Theologia Crucis, Signus Crucis: Festschrift für Erich Dinkler,* ed. C. Andresen and G. Klein (Tübingen: J. C. B. Mohr, 1979) 57-71; C. K. Barrett, *The First Epistle to the Corinthians* (London: Black, 1965); J. C. Beker, *Paul the Apostle: The Triumph of God in Life and Thought* (Philadelphia: Fortress, 1980); C. B. Cousar, *A Theology of the Cross* (Minneapolis: Fortress, 1990); G. Delling, *Der Kreuzetod Jesu in der urchristlichen Verkündigung* (Göttingen: Vandenhoeck & Ruprecht, 1972); J. D. G. Dunn, "Paul's Understanding of the Death of Jesus," in *Reconciliation and Hope,* ed. R. Banks (Grand Rapids: Eerdmans, 1974) 137-41; R. Goetz, "The Suffering God: The Rise of a New Orthodoxy," *Christian Century* 103 (1986) 385-89; D. J. Hall, *God and Human Suffering* (Minneapolis: Augsburg, 1986); A. J. Hultgren, *Paul's Gospel and Mission* (Philadephia: Fortress Press, 1985); M. J. Hooker, "Interchange in Christ," *JTS* 22 (1971) 349-61; E. Jüngel, *God as the Mystery of the World* (Edinburgh: T. & T. Clark, 1983); E. Käsemann, "The Saving Significance of the Death of Jesus in Paul," in *Perspectives on Paul* (Philadelphia: Fortress, 1971) 32-59; idem, *Commentary on Romans* (Grand Rapids: Eerdmans, 1980); H. W. Kuhn, "Jesus als Gekreuzigter in der frühchristlichen Verkündigung," *ZTK* 72 (1975) 1-46; U. Luz, "*Theologia Crucis* als Mitte der Theologie im Neuen Testament," *EvT* 34 (1974) 116-41; A. E. McGrath, *Luther's Theology of the Cross* (Oxford: Blackwell, 1985); R. P. Martin, *Reconciliation: A Study of Paul's Theology* (2d ed.; Grand Rapids: Zondervan, 1989); J. Moltmann, *The Crucified God* (San Francisco: Harper & Row, 1974); L. Morris, *The Apostolic Preaching of the Cross* (Grand Rapids: Eerdmans, 1955); K. A. Plank, *Paul and the Irony of Affliction* (Atlanta: Scholars, 1987); E. P. Sanders, *Paul and Palestinian Judaism* (Philadelphia: Fortress, 1977); P. Stuhlmacher, "Eighteen Theses on Paul's Theology of the Cross," in *Reconciliation, Law, and Righteousness* (Philadelphia: Fortress, 1986) 155-68; D. Way, *The Lordship of Christ: Ernst Käsemann's Interpretation of Paul's Theology* (Oxford: Clarendon, 1991); H. Weder, *Das Kreuz Jesu bei Paulus* (Göttingen: Vandenhoeck & Ruprecht, 1981). A. E. McGrath

# CRUCIFIXION

A particularly cruel form of execution popular in the first-century Roman Empire. Numerous sources—both Christian and non-Christian—attest to the crucifixion of Jesus of Nazareth under Pontius Pilate (e.g., Mk 15:1-39 par.; Josephus *Ant.* 18.3.3 §§63-64; Tacitus *Ann.* 15.44). Outside the Gospels and Acts Paul is responsible for all but one use of both the verb "to crucify" (*stauroō*: 1 Cor 1:13, 23; 2:2, 8; 2 Cor 13:4; Gal 3:1; 5:24; 6:14; cf. also "to crucify with" [*sustauroō*]: Rom 6:6; Gal 2:19) and the noun "cross" (*stauros*: 1 Cor 1:17, 18; Gal 5:11; 6:12, 14; [Eph 2:16]; Phil 2:8; 3:18; Col 1:20; 2:14). For him, the historical event of Jesus' execution on the cross had enormous theological importance, even if it proved to be a major obstacle in the early Christian mission (see especially the programmatic statements in 1 Cor 1:18-25; Gal 3:1-14).

The practice of crucifixion as a form of execution (or impalement after death) dates back at least to the Persians, and was also utilized by other barbarian peoples (as they were known to Greek and Roman historiographers), including the Assyrians and, later, the Carthaginians. No regular practice of crucifixion is attested among the Jews, though some evidence suggests it was employed as a mode of execution before the time of Herod the Great (Josephus *J.W.* 1.4.6 §§97-98; *Ant.* 13.14.2 §§379-83; 11QTemple 64:6-13).

Descriptions of the act of crucifixion are rare in the extant literature of antiquity, primarily due to literary-aesthetic concerns. Greek and Roman authors who wrote about crucifixion underscored its brutality, but did not dwell long on the procedure itself. M. Hengel regards the passion narratives of the canonical Gospels as the most detailed description of their kind, but even they are noticeably brief in their accounts of the execution itself. The Evangelists simply report, "They crucified him" (Mt 27:35 par.), so we must go elsewhere to discover, for example, the tradition that Jesus was *nailed* to the cross (cf. Lk 24:39[?]; Jn 20:25; Acts 2:23; Col 2:14; *Gos. Pet.* 6.21; Justin *Dial. Tryph.* 97).

The available literary evidence suggests three general observations. First, the act of crucifixion was heinously cruel. The procedure itself damaged no vital organs, and it is unlikely that any wounds inflicted in the practice would have resulted in excessive bleeding. The likely cause of the consequently slow death, then, would have been shock or a painful process of asphyxiation as the muscles used in breathing were exhausted.

As a result, Roman citizens were generally spared this form of execution. Crucifixion was largely reserved for those of lower status and, above all, for dangerous criminals and insurrectionists. In Judea crucifixion was generally effective as a deterrent against open resistance to Roman occupation until the Jewish War.

Second, crucifixion was a public affair. Naked and fastened to a stake, cross or tree on a well-traveled route or crossroads, the executed was subjected to savage ridicule by passersby. Moreover, under Roman practice the person crucified was denied burial, the corpse left on the cross as carrion for the birds or to rot. In this way, the general populace was reminded of the fate of those who resisted the authority of the state.

Third, it is clear that no standard form of crucifixion was uniformly practiced. The victim might be bound or nailed to the cross, with or without a crossbeam, in one of a variety of positions. It is not even clear whether crucifixion always took place before or after the death of the subject. The Romans appear to have practiced a more constant form of crucifixion: It included a flogging beforehand; victims often carried the crossbeam to the place of crucifixion, where they were nailed or bound to the cross with arms extended, raised up, and perhaps seated on a *sedicula*, or small wooden peg (Hengel, 22-32). On the other hand, as Josephus reports, even among the Romans the method of crucifixion was subject to the whims of military leaders (Josephus *J.W.* 5.11.1 §§449-51).

To date, direct archeological evidence related to the practice of crucifixion is limited to one ossuary discovered in 1968 in northern Jerusalem. It contained the bones of an adult male who had died by crucifixion in the first half of the first century A.D. Initial study of the skeletal remains indicated that a nail had been driven through each of his forearms, and his heel bones had been pierced by a single iron nail. The latter nail was found still embedded in the heel bones of both feet. Wood fragments found at both ends of the nail indicated that the nail first passed through a small wooden plaque, then through the victim's feet, and then into a vertical, olivewood beam. Apparently as a *coup de grâce*, his shins had deliberately been broken.

A recent reevaluation of the skeletal remains of the ossuary, together with related photographs, casts and radiographs by Zias and Sekeles suggests a number of amendments to those earlier conclusions, however. Most importantly, they determined that the still-intact iron nail had passed from the right side to the left of the right heel bone (calcaneum) only. A different picture of the crucified man emerges, for on this reconstruction the feet were not anchored, one on top of the other, with one nail, but the victim apparently straddled the upright beam. Moreover, finding no clear evidence of traumatic injury to the bones of the forearm or hands, they propose the victim was tied to the crossbeam, not nailed. Finally, they questioned whether the bones of the lower limbs had been broken prior to death.

Although this discovery adds archeological evidence to literary descriptions of crucifixion, it is nevertheless clear that the paucity of direct anthropological evidence of this nature restricts the certainty one might attach to its interpretation.

The negative perceptions associated with crucifixion in the first-century world are suggested by two Pauline texts, 1 Corinthians 1:18-25 and Galatians 3:13. This stigma is grounded not only in the barbaric nature of crucifixion, but also, in a Jewish context, in the linkage of Deuteronomy 21:22-23 with crucifixion already by this period. In its OT context, the Deuteronomic passage—"anyone who is hung on a tree is under the curse of God" (LXX)—refers to the public display of the corpse of an executed criminal. But both Philo and the Qumran community provide evidence that, in first-century Judaism, this text was being used with reference to the practice of crucifixion (Philo *Spec. Leg.* 3.152; *Poster. C.* 61; *Som.* 2.213; 4QpNah 3-4.1.7-8; 11QTemple 64:6-13). Given these data, it would seem that a positive assessment of crucifixion within first-century Jewish circles would have been out of the question.

The theological gravity accorded the cross of Christ,* together with its overwhelmingly positive significance in early Christian circles, stands in stark contrast to this expectation, however. Interestingly, Deuteronomy 21:23 had an apparent role in early Christian reflection on the meaning of the cross, as indicated by the allusions in Acts 5:30; 13:29 and Galatians 3:13-14. The oxymoron thus produced—that the "cursed one" is, in fact, the "Anointed One" (i.e., "Christ")—is emphasized by Paul in his kerygmatic expression "Christ crucified" (*christos estaurōmenos*) in 1 Corinthians 1:23; 2:2 (cf. Gal 3:1; 2:19).

*See also* CROSS, THEOLOGY OF THE; DEATH OF CHRIST.

BIBLIOGRAPHY. E. E. Ellis, " 'Christ Crucified,' " in *Reconciliation and Hope: New Testament Essays on Atonement and Eschatology Presented to L.L. Morris on His 60th Birthday*, ed. R. Banks (Grand Rapids: Eerdmans, 1974) 69-75; J. A. Fitzmyer, "Crucifixion in Ancient Palestine, Qumran Literature, and the New Testament," in *To Advance the Gospel: New Testament Essays* (New York: Crossroad, 1981) 125-46; M. Hengel, *Crucifixion in the Ancient World and the Folly of the Message of the Cross* (Philadelphia: Fortress, 1977); M. Wilcox, " 'Upon the Tree'—Deut 21:22-23 in the New Testament," *JBL* 96 (1977) 85-99; J. Zias and E. Sekeles, "The Crucified Man from Giv'at ha-Mivtar: A Reappraisal," *IEJ* 35 (1985) 22-27.

J. B. Green

## CUP. *See* LORD'S SUPPER.

## CURSE, ACCURSED, ANATHEMA

Paul uses five different Greek terms, four of which are cognates, for a total of twelve times to express three closely related but clearly distinguishable ideas.

1. Curse As a Human Malediction
2. The Curse of the Law
3. Accursed/Anathema

### 1. Curse As a Human Malediction.

In its only NT occurrence (Rom 3:14, quoting Ps 10:7 [LXX Ps 9:28; cf. 13:3]), the noun "curse" (Gk *ara*) denotes "the content of what is expressed in a curse" (Louw-Nida, 33.473). The verb "curse" (Gk *kataraomai*), whose single Pauline usage appears in antithesis to "bless" (Rom 12:14), goes beyond asking God* to withhold his blessing and indicates rather a calling down of injury or harm on the person(s) being cursed (cf. Deut 28:15-68).

### 2. The Curse of the Law.

This unique expression (Gal 3:13) refers to the "curse" (Gal 3:10, Gk *katara* as in Gal 3:13; cf. Louw-Nida, 33.473) pronounced by the Mosaic Law* upon all who fail to observe it completely (Gal 3:10); that "all who rely on works of the law" are under this curse (Gal 3:10 RSV) implies that no one does observe the Law completely. The Greek expression in Galatians 3:10 (*hosoi ex ergōn nomou*) cannot reasonably be rendered "as many as are nomists (i.e., identify with the old covenant)" (Caneday, 194), if for no other reason than that the Greek phrase *ex ergōn nomou* in its previous five occurrences (2:16 [3 x]; 3:2, 5) consistently means "by works of the Law." It more naturally has the sense "all who rely on obedience to the law" (NEB) and this, in view of Paul's polemical purposes in Galatians, must include both Jews (the Judaizers*) and Gentiles* (those of the Galatian converts who might yield to the Judaizers' persuasion). It follows that the curse of the Law is envisaged in Galatians 3:10 as resting, not exclusively on Jews, but on Gentiles as well, so that when Christ is said to have redeemed "us" from the curse of the Law "by becoming for our sake an accursed thing [Gk *katara*; cf. Louw-Nida 33.474]" (Gal 3:13 NEB), the first person plural pronouns are most naturally understood as referring to both Jews and Gentiles. (For other considerations supporting this conclusion see, e.g., Fung, 148-49, cf. 167 n.1, 181; but cf. Wright, 143.)

In arriving at the conclusion stated in Galatians 3:13, Paul has apparently employed the Jewish exegetical principle of "equal category" (Heb *gᵉzērâ šāwâ*): by (1) bringing together the two Deuteronomic passages (Deut 21:23, cited in Gal 3:13, and Deut 27:26, cited in Gal 3:10), which in the LXX share a common verbal stem between them (Gk *katara*-; as cited by Paul, both quotations begin with the adjective "cursed" [Gk *epikataratos*]), and by (2) interpreting the former in

*199*

terms of the latter, Paul understands the death of Christ (*see* Atonement) on the cross (*see* Crucifixion) as a vicarious bearing of the curse which rightfully falls on all who fail to continue in perfect obedience to the Law. Ultimately, however, Paul's application of Deuteronomy 21:23 to the death of Christ is probably determined by his Christian hermeneutical principle of viewing the OT in the light of the Christ event.

Paul's unambiguous statement that "Christ redeemed us from the curse of the Law" by becoming the vicarious bearer of the curse would seem to militate against the suggestion that "the curse of the Law," rather than being an actuality (cf. Gal 3:10), is merely a threat—the negative potentiality associated with Torah-observances, that is, "a 'curse' in case of non-fulfilment" (Stanley, 506, 505). The "curse of the Law" is understood by J. D. G. Dunn, in accordance with his "new perspective on Paul" (cf. Dunn, 183-214) as "the curse of a wrong understanding of the law" (Dunn, 229, cf. esp. 225-32, 237; *see* Law). This novel interpretation is a logical corollary of Dunn's original exposition of "works of the Law" as denoting "those observances of the law . . . which ought to characterize the good Jew and set him apart from the Gentile" (Dunn, 231). The validity of this interpretation stands or falls with judgments regarding the soundness of Dunn's understanding of "works of the Law" (*see* Law; Romans; Works of the Law).

### 3. Accursed/Anathema.

Five times the Greek term *anathema* ("anathema"; cf. Louw-Nida 33.474) is used to refer to various persons as "(something) accursed" (cf. the sense of the second *katara* ["curse"] in Gal 3:13, above). To be "accursed/anathema" means to be delivered up to the judicial wrath* of God. Paul's references to his desire that he himself be "accursed" and separated "from Christ" for Israel's sake (Rom 9:3) and to an angel (Gal 1:8-9) as being the possible object of the anathema shows that the church discipline* of excommunication is not in view.

The widely held view that in 1 Corinthians 16:22 the reference is to a ban excluding the unworthy from participating in the Lord's Supper* has rightly been rejected by Fee in favor of its being Paul's final warning to his Corinthian opponents* who might be tempted to disobey the injunctions he has just written them (see Fee, 834-35, 837-39).

The enigma of the blasphemous cry "Jesus is/be cursed!" (1 Cor 12:3) has given rise to a plethora of reconstructed life settings, including the suggestions that the reference is (1) to the readers' (or Paul's own) pre-Christian past; (2) to a confrontation with Jewish persecutors or Roman magistrates; (3) to the radical dualism of Gnostics* at Corinth which exalted the heavenly Christ at the expense of the earthly Jesus; (4) to Christian ecstatics resisting an ecstatic experience coming upon them; (5) to Christian ecstatics yielding to an upsurge of emotion, and giving vent to an expression Paul deemed to be blasphemous. Probably the best solution is (6) to understand the cry not as an actual utterance in a Corinthian church meeting, but as a reference to what those who do not have the Holy Spirit* (i.e., non-Christians, whether Jew or Gentile) say about Jesus, in contradistinction to the Christian confession of Jesus as Lord (see Carson, 24-31; cf. the discussion in Fee, 578-81).

*See also* DEATH OF CHRIST; LAW; RESTORATION OF ISRAEL; WORKS OF THE LAW; WRATH, DESTRUCTION.

BIBLIOGRAPHY. J. M. Bassler, "1 Cor 12:3—Curse and Confession in Context," *JBL* 101 (1982) 415-18; J. P. Braswell, " 'The Blessing of Abraham' versus 'the Curse of the Law': Another Look at Gal 3:10-13," *WTJ* 53 (1991) 73-91; F. F. Bruce, "The Curse of the Law," in *Paul and Paulinism: Essays in Honour of C. K. Barrett*, ed. M. D. Hooker and S. G. Wilson (London: SPCK, 1982) 27-36; A. Caneday, " 'Redeemed From the Curse of the Law': The Use of Deut 21:22-23 in Gal 3:13," *TJ* 10 NS (1989) 185-209; D. A. Carson, *Showing the Spirit: A Theological Exposition of 1 Corinthians 12—14* (Grand Rapids: Baker, 1987) 24-31; T. L. Donaldson, "The 'Curse of the Law' and the Inclusion of the Gentiles: Galatians 3.13-14," *NTS* 32 (1986) 94-112; J. D. G. Dunn, *Jesus, Paul and the Law: Studies in Mark and Galatians* (Louisville, Kentucky: Westminster/John Knox, 1990); G. D. Fee, *The First Epistle to the Corinthians* (NICNT; Grand Rapids: Eerdmans, 1987); R. Y. K. Fung, *The Epistle to the Galatians* (NICNT; Grand Rapids: Eerdmans, 1988); R. G. Hamerton-Kelly, "Sacred Violence and the Curse of the Law (Galatians 3:13): The Death of Christ as a Sacrificial Travesty," *NTS* 36 (1990) 98-118; H.-W. Kuhn, "ἀνάθεμα," *EDNT* 1.80-81; R. P. Martin, *The Spirit and the Congregation: Studies in 1 Corinthians 12—15* (Grand Rapids: Eerdmans, 1984); C. D. Stanley, " 'Under a Curse': a Fresh Reading of Galatians 3.10-14," *NTS* 36 (1990) 481-511; W. C. van Unnik, "Jesus: Anathema or Kyrios (I Cor. 12:3)," in *Christ and Spirit in the New Testament: Studies in Honour of C. F. D. Moule*, ed. B. Lindars and S. S. Smalley (Cambridge: University Press, 1973) 113-26; N. T. Wright, "Curse and Covenant: Galatians 3.10-14," in *The Climax of the Covenant: Christ and the Law in Pauline Theology* (Minneapolis: Fortress, 1992) 137-56.

R. Y. K. Fung

**CYNICS.** *See* PHILOSOPHY.

# D

**DAMASCUS ROAD EXPERIENCE.** *See* CON-
VERSION AND CALL OF PAUL.

**DARKNESS.** *See* LIGHT AND DARKNESS.

**DAY OF THE LORD.** *See* ESCHATOLOGY.

**DAYS.** *See* HOLY DAYS.

**DEAD SEA SCROLLS.** *See* QUMRAN AND PAUL.

**DEATH.** *See* DEATH OF CHRIST; LIFE AND DEATH; RES-
URRECTION; TRIUMPH.

## DEATH OF CHRIST

The death of Christ,* often mentioned in tandem with
his resurrection,* occupies the central position in
Paul's representation of the gospel.* Paul is aware of,
employs and develops its redemptive significance
through creedal* formulae and hymnic* traditions;
he probably has some familiarity with and reminds his
readers of the story of Jesus' suffering* and death;
and he develops the importance of Christ's passion in
contexts related to all aspects of his apostolic message—especially his soteriology and christology,*
eschatology* and ethics.* This article is concerned
not exclusively but especially with Paul's attribution of
atoning significance to the suffering and death of
Christ.

1. The Centrality of Christ's Death
2. The Significance of the Cross: A Plurality of
   Images
3. The Death of Christ and the Purpose of God
4. The Death of Christ and the Human Condition
5. The Crucified Messiah and the Christian Life

### 1. The Centrality of Christ's Death.

For Paul the cross of Christ was critical for Christian
reflection and life, especially as the means by which
God has provided for salvation and as the instrument
and measure of new life in Christ.

It is of great consequence that the letters of Paul,

themselves the earliest extant literary productions of
Christianity, already document the central importance
of the cross* of Christ. This is true for our understanding of very early Christianity, for it evidences how
quickly the followers of Jesus were compelled to grapple with the theological problem of his crucifixion. It
is also true for our understanding of Paul, for it reveals the degree to which Paul himself struggled with
and valued the cross of Christ, and the degree to
which his own thought was at home in Christian reflection understood more broadly in the dawning
years of the Jesus movement.

Leaving aside for the moment the variety of traditional materials concerned with Jesus' death which
Paul incorporated into his correspondence, one can
point to the example of 1 Corinthians. Some twenty-
five years after Jesus' crucifixion* Paul writes of the
pivotal scandal and folly of the cross (1 Cor 1:18, 23),
suggesting the harsh realities encountered in early
missionary activity. Historically, Jesus' execution on a
cross encouraged an understanding of his death as
that of a common criminal, humiliated among his
people—indeed, even cursed by God (cf. Deut 21:22-
23). How could this Jesus also be the "Anointed One"
(i.e., Messiah)? Despite this problem, Paul asserts that,
while among the Corinthians, he had "resolved to
know nothing . . . other than Jesus Christ and him
crucified" (1 Cor 2:2). It is not too much to say that the
early church had to come to terms with the cross of
Christ precisely because it was this crucified-and-dead
Jesus who was being proclaimed as Messiah (Green,
157-74). As a theologian of the cross, Paul played a key
role in the exploration of the meaning of the crucified
Christ (*see* Christ; Cross, Theology of the).

It is evident that Paul borrowed from pre-existing
Christian tradition* regarding Jesus' passion, and that
such traditional materials are incorporated into his
correspondence (cf., e.g., the language of the tradi-
tioning process in 1 Cor 11:23-25; 15:3-5; cf. Kertelge,
116-24). It is equally transparent that he exercised his
own creativity in shaping the tradition. This is not
surprising, since one of the primary motivations for

his spirited opposition to the Christian movement prior to his encounter with the risen Lord* must have been the contradiction offered by the Christian kerygma as it featured the divine exaltation of the "cursed* one." Paul's embracing "the gospel of Christ" (Gal 1:6-17) entailed a theological conversion* which enabled him to move beyond his initial negative interpretation of the cross; it also suggests one of the influences behind his subsequent reflection on the cross. It is noteworthy that Paul was able to come to terms with the seeming contradiction of a crucified Christ not by denying its perplexing character, but by showing how God vindicated his Christ and filled his apparently ignominious demise with unexpected, positive significance.

On the other hand, Paul's own apostolic experience underscored the degree to which suffering and powerlessness was integral to the Christian life, this in spite of Jesus' resurrection. In the Pauline perspective, apostolic weakness* found its significance in light of the suffering of Christ. Thus, having reminded the Corinthians that among them he had sought only to present Christ and him crucified, Paul goes on to call to their attention his own manner of life while with them: "I came to you in weakness, fear, and much trembling" (1 Cor 2:2-3; cf. Col 1:24). Consequently, we see that a further inspiration for Paul's ongoing translation of the meaning of the cross was his own and the church's life in Christ—life that was no stranger to weakness, opposition and suffering. The importance of the cross for Paul is thus grounded in his encounter with the risen Lord and in the demands of his apostolic ministry.*

*1.1. The Cross and Kerygma.* How is the centrality of the cross manifest for Paul? It is implied by the phrases he uses to denote the kerygma. Thus in 1 Corinthians 1:18 "the message of the cross" is virtually a synonym for "gospel"*; in 2 Corinthians 5:19 "the message of reconciliation*" is employed similarly, in a context wherein the salvific event is presented in the parallelism: "And he died for all, so that those who live might live no longer for themselves, but for him who on their behalf died and was raised" (cf. Phil 2:16: "word of life"; Acts 13:26: "word of salvation"; Kertelge, 124-27).

*1.2. Formulaic Expressions.* A close reading of the Pauline letters also reveals two stereotypical expressions for the atoning significance of the cross (Hengel, 34-39). The first presents the "giving up" of Jesus for the salvation of humankind—either as a divine act (e.g., Rom 4:25: "who was given up on account of our trespasses"; Rom 8:32: "who did not spare his own son, but gave him up on behalf of us all") or as a self-

giving (e.g., Gal 1:4: "who gave himself up for our sins"; Gal 2:20: "gave himself up for me"). The second expression, the "dying formula," is found repeatedly—for example, in the celebrated tradition represented in 1 Corinthians 15:3: "Christ died for our sins" (cf. further: Rom 5:6, 8; 14:9; 1 Cor 8:11; 2 Cor 5:14, 15; Gal 2:21; 1 Thess 5:10). Paul's phrase "Christ died for us," according to Hengel, "is the most frequent and most important confessional statement in the Pauline epistles and at the same time in the primitive Christian tradition in the Greek language which underlies them" (Hengel, 37).

This traditional basis is important for showing the degree to which Paul aligns himself with the common faith of the early church. That is, his letters draw on the common vocabulary of the Christian communities; his innovations in theological expression build on the foundation of the shared faith. More particularly, in the face of such antagonism as Paul faced at Corinth and Galatia, his repetition of traditional materials related to the cross serves to indicate how Paul legitimized his authority* in the face of opposition (*see* Opponents).

*1.3. The Story of Jesus.* This is not to suggest that Paul was indebted only to the *formulaic* tradition he shared with early Christianity. There are also hints that he was aware of the *story* of Jesus' suffering and death, which would also have been handed down to him. Such a reference may lie behind Galatians 3:1, where Paul's language ("Before your eyes Jesus Christ was publicly portrayed as crucified") suggests the graphic quality of his proclamation, opening the possibility that his missionary preaching made use of a passion story. Similarly, his introduction to the tradition of the Last Supper, "in the night when he was delivered up" (1 Cor 11:23-25), presumes a shared knowledge of a narrative context for the eucharistic tradition. Also suggestive are the themes with which Paul describes his own suffering in 2 Corinthians; for example, in 2 Corinthians 6:3-10 he lists the sufferings, grace* and paradoxical aspects of his service in a way that echoes the story of the passion of Christ. Not unlike what one finds in the Gospel of Mark, then, Paul has his own understanding of the "way of the cross," the way of suffering through which one identifies with the manner of Christ's suffering. Finally, while Pauline only in the broad sense, 1 Timothy 6:13 alludes to Jesus' trial before Pontius Pilate in a way that presupposes at least rudimentary knowledge of the passion story. In these and other texts, we recognize that Paul's theology has about it a *narrative* quality—that is, that he understands Christian experience within the larger mural of God's activity ranging from the formation of God's people to the Parousia, and within this greater narrative and as its centerpiece is the narrative of Jesus' crucifixion. Even though Paul shows little interest in the historical details of Jesus' passion *qua* historical data, it appears that he was aware of them and was concerned with their significance for Christian faith and life (*see* Jesus and Paul; Jesus, Sayings of).

*1.4. The Pattern of Christ.* This again points to the degree to which Paul is ready to posit the cross of Christ as the basis of Christian faith and life. Indeed, Paul's reference to the Last Supper tradition is set contextually within his discussion of the community meal in order to attack the problem of divisions at Corinth (1 Cor 11:17-34; cf. 1 Cor 1:10-17); here a reminder of Jesus' sacrificial self-giving is the basis for Paul's call for a life modeled on the way of Jesus' passion, diaconal in orientation, cruciform in shape (*see* Lord's Supper).

At Corinth,* as at Colossae,* Paul reflects on the meaning of the crucified Christ in large part so as to counter competing ideas. In the case of his correspondence with the Corinthians, the word of the cross opposes wrong-headed thinking about the nature of present existence, as though this were the time for triumphalism* following the consummation of the new age. Against the "wisdom* of the world" and the status-seeking orientation of his Greco-Roman audience at Corinth, Paul posits the scandalous* cross of Christ as the "power* of God" "to us who are being saved." Social, philosophical, even soteriological norms are uprooted as Paul brings to the foreground "what is weak in the world,*" "what is low and despised in the world"—that is, "Christ crucified" and the community oriented around the crucified Christ (1 Cor 1:18-31).

For the Colossians Paul grounds his presentation of the cosmic Christ—who reconciled the whole cosmos, including the astral powers, to God—in the flesh-and-blood life and death of Christ: "through him God was pleased to reconcile to himself all things . . . by making peace* through the blood of his cross" (Col 1:20; cf. 1:14; 2:13-14; 3:13). Thus Paul both counters a lifestyle oriented around appeasing astral powers as though they were the means of human access to God and, against a quasi-gnostic* spiritualizing of the way of discipleship, affirms in an impassioned way the importance of ethical* behavior in this material world (*see* Elements/Elemental Spirits).

Elsewhere Paul presents Jesus' death as the culmination of his life. In Philippians 2:6-11 Paul has apparently added to an early hymn to Christ the words, "even death on a cross." Here, Jesus' life as God's

obedient Son is at center stage, and this obedience is seen most profoundly in his willingness to embrace rejection, human suffering and a heinous death by crucifixion. In this way, Paul contends that Christ's death "is the fullest expression of [his] life and establishes [for us] the pattern of a life of love and obedience" (Tambasco, 72). In these and many other ways, Paul shows how Christian thought and life build on the foundational event of the cross of Christ.

**2. The Significance of the Cross: A Plurality of Images.**
Just as Jesus' death lies at the foundation of Pauline theology, so Paul seems never to tire of adding new images to his interpretive vocabulary by way of explicating its significance.

It is true that Paul is much more concerned with laying out the significance of the death of Christ than with its historical circumstances, and he communicates this significance above all in terms of its benefits for humankind. In subsequent theological reflection, these benefits have been developed under the nomenclature of "atonement," and this presents the modern interpreter with two problems.

First, the word itself, *atonement*, is open to diverse definition. On the one hand, today many trace the meaning of the term back to its roots in Middle English—"at-one-ment"—and so understand the term above all as a synonym for *reconciliation* (e.g., Fitzmyer). As a consequence, a cleavage is drawn between atonement on the one hand, and notions of expiation,* propitiation and other ideas related to doctrines of substitution or satisfaction on the other; more to the point, the atoning significance of Jesus' death is thus divorced from any consideration on Paul's part regarding the means by which this at-one-ment or reconciliation is achieved (*see* Peace, Reconciliation).

On the other hand, after centuries of debate it is now difficult to read Paul without the overlay of one or more of the so-called classical theories of the atonement (see Driver, 37-67)—especially the "dramatic theory," which portrays the saving work of Christ as a cosmic drama of conflict and victory (*see* Triumph); the "satisfaction theory," which presents the cross of Christ as the means by which the barrier between God and humanity is removed, so that through Christ's death "satisfaction" is rendered to God; or the "moral influence theory," which concentrates on the cross as a demonstration to humanity of God's boundless love that is to be emulated. The ascendancy of the "satisfaction theory," with its often-held corollary, penal or forensic satisfaction (i.e., since human beings have been found guilty before

God the judge, they must be punished, but Christ is made to suffer the penalty) as the way to understand Paul's theology of the cross has proven especially problematic in contemporary theological discussion. For some, Paul seems to portray God as a sadist who inflicts punishment, and Jesus as the masochist who willingly endures it. Any attempt to sunder the interests and activity of God and Christ—as though the cross is the manifestation of God's wrath but of Christ's mercy—would be problematic on Pauline grounds (see below). And, in fact, it seems highly unlikely that those who formulated the substitutionary interpretation of the death of Christ would recognize this contemporary characterization of their view. This is true even if this classical theory of the atonement has subsequently proven itself susceptible to this problematic reading in some hymnody and popular interpretation (see the helpful discussion in Houts; Beker, 208-11.)

The bulk of this article is given over to an examination of Paul's theology of atonement. First, however, it is important that we come to terms with the more fundamental reality that Paul has no *one* way of explicating the meaning of the cross. Although the crucified Christ lies at the center of his theology, this central truth is capable of multiple interpretations. In fact, Paul seems capable of tailoring his representation of the significance of the death of Jesus to the needs of his audience in particular, contextualized circumstances (see Driver; Boff, 78-84; Cousar, 82-87). This fact has serious ramifications for the ongoing crosscultural mission of the church, for it suggests that interpreters, in drawing out the significance of Jesus' crucifixion, must continuously seek out metaphors that speak specifically to culture and/or circumstance. In their openness to shaping context-specific ways to communicate the meaning of the death of Christ, contemporary interpreters who would be faithful to Paul will be guided by apostolic testimony to the cross, grounded in the Scriptures and cognizant of the way Paul draws on them in his own hermeneutical enterprise, fully sensitive to the contemporary images and metaphors that carry redemptive meaning, and vitally concerned with the interplay between these three.

Of the several dozen metaphors Paul employs to lay bare the benefits of the death of Christ, only a handful can be mentioned here. These are conveniently brought together in two Pauline texts—2 Corinthians 5:14—6:2 and Galatians 3:10-14.

An examination of the presentation of the effects of Jesus' death in 2 Corinthians 5:14—6:2 underscores the degree to which the manifold categories by which Paul drew out the significance of the cross overlap with one another. Even though reconciliation stands at the center of this passage (2 Cor 5:18, 19, 20), other categories are in the foreground: vicarious substitution ("for us," 2 Cor 5:14, 15), representation (2 Cor 5:14, 21) or interchange (Hooker's term [1974, 1978]), sacrifice* (2 Cor 5:21; cf. Dunn, 42-43), justification (implicitly, 2 Cor 5:19, 21), forgiveness* (2 Cor 5:19) and new creation* (2 Cor 5:16-17). Moreover, the cross and resurrection of Christ appear in tandem as salvific events (2 Cor 5:15).

*Reconciliation* as a term is not found very often in the Pauline corpus. Apart from this passage it appears in Romans 5:10-11 with reference to the reconciliation of humanity to God; Colossians 1:20 with reference to the reconciliation of the cosmos to God; and in Ephesians 2:16 with reference to the reconciliation of both Jew and Gentile to God and one another. Whether Ephesians is judged to be Pauline or not, its message at this juncture is clearly Pauline, for this notion of "restored relationship" in Paul consistently embraces the dynamic presence of divine love* active to restore the divine-human relationship and extending both a call for and an enablement of persons to exhibit toward one another this same social restoration. Moreover, especially in 2 Corinthians and Colossians, the work of reconciliation is extended to the entire creation (*see* Center).

In 2 Corinthians 5 Paul's choice of terminology and logic of argumentation is tailored to its context, for here Paul not only needs to counter the triumphalistic boasting of his opponents at Corinth but also to overcome the disharmony between himself and his "children" at Corinth. Rooting the message of reconciliation fundamentally in the sacrificial death of Jesus and asserting that reconciliation entails living no longer for oneself but for Christ (and thus for others), he addresses his first aim. His impassioned appeal to the Corinthians to be reconciled to God (2 Cor 5:20; 6:1-2), followed by an affirmation of his own openheartedness to the Corinthians (2 Cor 6:11-13; 7:2) will, he hopes, accomplish the second goal of restoring his relationship with the Corinthians.

Similarly, Galatians 3:10-14 consists of a convergence of images or theological categories by which Paul expounds the salvific character of the cross of Christ. The larger unit, Galatians 3:1-14, contends that the experience of the Galatians of receiving the Spirit by faith signified the fulfillment of God's promise to bless the Gentiles through Abraham,* and that this fulfillment was made possible through the death of Christ. The benefits of the death of Christ are presented in Galatians 3:10-14 through a combination of images: Christ as the *representative* of Israel* in whose death the *covenant\** reaches its climax (Wright, 137-56; cf. the notion of interchange [Hooker]); *justification\** (Gal 3:11); *redemption\** (Gal 3:13), evoking exodus and exilic themes (cf. the corollary of *adoption\** in Gal 3:26-29); *substitution* ("for us," Gal 3:13); *sacrifice\** (implicitly, Gal 3:13; cf. Wright, 153); the *promise of the Spirit\** (Gal 3:14); and the *triumph\* over the powers* (*see* Principalities and Powers).

This last motif emerges in a similar way in Ephesians 2:14-15, where the Law\* appears as a barrier separating Jew and Gentile; there the death of Christ abolishes this "dividing wall." In Galatians, however, the Law is characterized more as a force, like the elemental spirits of this world, holding the Jewish people captive (Gal 4:1, 3). In a context-specific way, then, Paul insists that the death of Christ has triumphed not by denying the Law but by demonstrating its validity and executing the blessing of the covenant.

Taken together, the message of the cross in 2 Corinthians and Galatians (but also elsewhere in the Pauline corpus), raises two issues requiring more explicit elucidation. On the one hand, attention must be drawn to the *apocalyptic\** significance of the cross: set within apocalyptic horizons, the cross has cosmic repercussions. This is the importance of the use of such language as "new creation" in 2 Corinthians 5:17 and Galatians 6:15, for these texts must be understood not as in some modern translations as individual-focused (e.g., NIV, NAS), but as signifying the role of Jesus' death in the termination of the old epoch and the presentation of the new. The death of Christ marks the end of the rule of the apocalyptic powers (cf. Beker, 189-92; Col 2:15; *see* Triumph) and deliverance "from the present evil age" (Gal 1:4; *see* Eschatology). This intrusion of the new world into contemporary life has for Paul far-reaching consequences for those who would follow the crucified Christ and embody in their lives together the new creation revealed in the cross. Old ways of relating to one another (e.g., boasting in a continuous game of one-upmanship in the service of status-seeking) and of drawing lines between Jew and Gentile, slave and free, male and female, are shown to be just that—old, out of date, and judged as such (cf., e.g., Gal 3:26-29; Philem).

On the other hand, we see in Paul's understanding of the cross his ongoing reflection on Israel, and particularly his inclusion of believing Gentiles in the "Israel of God" (Gal 6:10). For Paul, believers, because of their inclusion in the salvific work of Christ, share in the benefits of the new creation and thus in their identity as the people of God. As Paul acknowledges, "I have been crucified with Christ. It is no longer I who live, but Christ who lives in me" (Gal 2:19b-20a; *see* Dying and Rising). Even if the question of the eschatological role of Israel in Pauline thought is not thus settled, it is nonetheless apparent that the death of Christ marks the new aeon in which Gentiles may be embraced, in Christ, as children of Abraham (*see* Israel; Restoration of Israel).

Many other interpretive categories or images might be mentioned from within the Pauline letters, for he makes use of a rich variety of metaphors by way of comprehending the cross and encouraging both understanding and response among his varied audiences. This multiplicity raises a caution against moving too quickly to positing for Paul a single (or any one as *the* central) theory of the atonement. For him the depths of the significance of the death of Christ can scarcely be plumbed.

### 3. The Death of Christ and the Purpose of God.

For Paul the question of the meaning of the cross is first a question about God—*theology*—and only then a question about anthropology and soteriology. His theology of the cross is rooted in his understanding of the divine purpose, and of God as the primary actor in the drama of salvation\* (*see* God). Although he affirms that Christ "gave himself for our sins in order to set us free from the present evil age," he goes on to affirm that Christ did so "according to the will of our God and Father" (Gal 1:4). That is, Christ's self-giving signifies his identification and solidarity with God's salvific aim. By this affirmation, any attribution to Paul of a view of the atonement that segregates the activity of God from that of God's Son is disallowed. Nevertheless, at center stage stands God's initiative (e.g.): "God was in Christ reconciling the world to himself" (2 Cor 5:19); "God . . . sent his own Son" (Rom 8:3). Paul's atonement theology is thus rooted in his understanding of God, and especially of God's righteousness,\* wrath\* and love.\*

*3.1. The Righteousness of God.* The precedence Paul gives to the question about God in his atonement theology is perhaps underscored best in the central but tightly packed passage, Romans 3:21-26. Two questions related to the character of God are raised in the verses preceding this passage (see Cousar, 37-41): (1) What are we to make of God's faithfulness vis-à-vis his covenant promises to the Jewish people? If, as Paul has earlier argued, both Jew and Gentile stand side by side before God as implicated in sin, what are we to make of God's covenantal history with Israel? "Will their faithlessness nullify the faithfulness of God?" (Rom 3:3). (2) If salvation is available outside the Law, should we not engage in evil so that God's goodness may abound all the more (Rom 3:8)? Or, to raise the question in a way more oriented around the character of God, If God's goodness is available to sinners, how can God judge the world? The first is a question about the reliability of God, the second about the moral integrity of God.

These questions place the righteousness of God in the dock, for in the OT "the righteousness of God" is a central affirmation, affirming God's faithful orientation toward the covenant and setting the pattern for the character of Israel's comportment and behavior before God. Paul is not unaware of this. First, he grounds his treatment of these two questions in the prior disclosure of the righteousness of God ("attested by the Law and the Prophets," Rom 3:21). Then he develops his present perspective on God's faithfulness, with clear echoes of occasions of covenant making and covenant keeping in Israel's past (cf. *redemption*, Rom 3:24; *sacrifice of atonement*, Rom 3:25 NRSV). Moreover, he does so via a traditional Jewish-Christian formula, demonstrating even more the rootedness of this representation of God's character in the history of God's interaction with the community of God's people.

In this context, Christ's salvific death, as it were, "proves" the reliability and integrity of God. To put it differently, the righteousness of God is manifest in his intervention to bring salvation to a humanity mired in sin.* And it is manifest precisely in the revelation of God in the cross as one who keeps his promises; who does not wink at sin but, through the faithful obedience and sacrificial death of Jesus Christ, redeems all who believe, whether Jew or Gentile; and, thus, who does not introduce a way of salvation that nullifies the Law but that actually upholds it (cf. Rom 3:31). Consequently, Paul affirms that the righteousness of God is revealed in Christ not merely as a description of God in his role as judge, but also and more so as the activity of God oriented around covenant making and covenant keeping; in the death of Christ the righteousness of God is exhibited in God's delivering people from sin (*see* Righteousness, Righteousness of God).

*3.2. The Wrath of God.* In some ways God's wrath stands as a corollary to God's righteousness: "since God's fidelity to covenant demands human response and responsibility, wrath is what one experiences when one rejects God's offer of justice" (Tambasco, 33; cf. Travis). It is imperative to recognize, however, that for Paul divine wrath is not a divine property, or essential attribute, but the active presence of God's judgment* toward "all ungodliness and wickedness" (Rom 1:18). The wrath of God is not vindictive indignation or the anger of divine retribution, but the divine response to human unfaithfulness. For Paul

God's wrath is future, eschatological (Rom 2:5, 8; 1 Thess 1:10; 5:9; Col 3:6). It is also already present, for God is now handing people over to experience the consequences of the sin they choose (Rom 1:18, 24, 26, 28; cf. Wis 11:15-16; 12:23).

In any attempt to come to terms with Paul's theology of atonement, then, it is vital to keep in mind Paul's understanding of divine wrath. Paul does not portray an angry God requiring mollification. For him divine wrath is a means of underscoring how seriously God takes sin, but it is not an affective quality or "feeling" on God's part. The righteousness of God is effective in the present to save, but as men and women resist it they experience God's righteousness as condemnation (*see* Wrath, Destruction).

*3.3. The Love of God.* According to Romans 5:6-8, the death of Christ is the ultimate expression of the boundless love of God: "But God demonstrates his love for us in that while we were still sinners Christ died for us" (Rom 5:8). This affirmation follows on the heels of the claim that the human experience of divine love guarantees that suffering will lead to a hope that will not disappoint (Rom 5:3-5). Three declarations are critical here. First, the love of God for humanity cannot be measured, for there are no anthropomorphic analogues on which to base such a measurement; even though someone might dare to die on behalf of a righteous person (Rom 5:7), Christ died for "the ungodly" (Rom 5:6), for "sinners" (Rom 5:8), for "enemies"* of God (Rom 5:10).

Second, Paul's audience can be certain that their suffering has significance because the suffering of Christ has proven to be so meaningful. Through his death "we have been *justified*," "*saved* from the wrath of God," "*reconciled* to God" (Rom 5:9-11). In the midst of our impotence, Christ took on the measure of our powerlessness and died in our place; as a result of his death, we share in his life, *and* we find that our own suffering has significance.

Third, in an unusual turn of phrase (Rom 5:8), we are told that *God* demonstrates his love by means of what *Christ* did. We might have anticipated that God's love would be manifest best in God's own deed. This way of putting things certifies that "Christ's death does not merely express his own sentiment, . . . but God's; or to put it another way, God's stance toward the world is quintessentially demonstrated in the action of Christ" (Cousar, 45). Once more, then, we find in Paul the unrelenting affirmation of the oneness of purpose and activity of God and God's Son in the cross (*see* Love).

### 4. The Death of Christ and the Human Condition.
To affirm that Paul's understanding of the death of

Christ is profoundly theocentric is not to downplay his interest in the need for atonement from the human side of the equation. Quite the contrary, it is to introduce the sharp contrast Paul sees between God and humanity—that is, between the faithfulness of God and human unfaithfulness (see, e.g., the word play in Rom 1:17-18: God's righteousness [*dikaiosynē*] versus human unrighteousness [*adikia*]). Paul's portrait of humanity "before Christ" is that of persons, collectively and individually, ensnared in sin, enslaved to powers from which they are impotent to escape. As with atonement, so with sin Paul is able to draw from a full linguistic arsenal to fill out his description of humankind apart from God.

Of special interest in this brief review of Paul's anthropology is Romans 1:18-32. Here *sin* (in the broad sense; the language Paul uses in 1:18 is *ungodliness* and *unrighteousness*) is identified not with individual acts of wickedness but with a general disposition to refuse to honor God as God and to render him thanks, to substitute things created for the Creator—that is, to turn away from authentic human existence by turning away from God.

Four aspects of Paul's reflections in this passage are of particular significance here. First, Paul is not giving the autobiography of individual persons; he is not bent on outlining how each person in his or her own experience comes to be implicated in sin. Instead, his is a universalistic presentation, a diagnosis of the condition of the human family taken as a whole (cf. Rom 3:9). Second, the acts of wickedness that Paul goes on to enumerate by way of illustration are not themselves *the* problem. Lust, gossip, envy, deceit, homosexual* activity, rebelliousness toward parents and the rest— these are expressions of *sin*. Third, within the fabric of Paul's argument, these activities are themselves expressions of the wrath of God. They evidence the moral integrity of a God who takes *sin* seriously. It is this, God's moral character, that Paul is defending here, and he does so by showing the progression from (1) the human refusal to honor God with its consequent denial of the human vocation to live in relation to God; to (2) God's giving humanity over to its own desires—giving humanity, as it were, the life apart from him it sought; and from this to (3) human acts of wickedness—which, then, do not arouse the wrath of God but are themselves already the consequences of its active presence. Finally, it is remarkable that, for Paul, *sin* marks a rupture in the divine-human relationship, but also manifests itself in human relations and in relations between humanity and the material creation. *Sin*, in this broad sense, then, can never be understood as something private or individualistic, for it always manifests itself in relation to others and to the cosmos (see Rom 1:26-32). What is more, Paul recognizes that *ungodliness* and *unrighteousness* have as their object their own self-legitimation: humanity embraces a lie (Rom 1:25) and receives a corrupt mind (Rom 1:28), with the consequence that it defines its unjust ways as just.

As a result, it is no wonder that Paul's preaching of and identification with the cross would excite opposition and misunderstanding. A humanity that has turned against itself as it turned against God will not easily sanction so revolutionary a re-ordering of the world as would be required by this accentuation of the crucified Christ. This would call for an apparently topsy-turvy way of understanding what it means to be human, for an inversion of the social system. Power* rooted in powerlessness? This emphasizes the profound role the word of the cross would have in Paul's conception and experience of the Christian life (see 5 below), but also the severity of the predicament to which God's saving activity would have to address itself (*see* Cross, Theology of the).

### 5. The Crucified Messiah and the Christian Life.

We come finally to explore more directly the question, How is the death of Christ efficacious? It is clear that for Paul the cross is the means by which God has provided salvation and that it is the instrument and measure of the new life in Christ. How is the cross operative in this way? Paul provides no single answer to this question, though we can ascertain in the Pauline letters certain parameters for this discussion.

*5.1. The Atoning Death of Christ.* For Paul, Jesus' death is not interpreted by metaphors drawn from the law court, but from within the history of God's covenant with Israel. Thus Paul does not think of Christ's having been punished by execution on the cross so as to satisfy the justice of God (Travis; Tambasco). The cross of Christ can be understood as substitutionary, but within the matrix of the OT conception of sacrifice.*

Although the rationale for the sacrificial system is not worked out fully in the OT, Dunn believes that the notion of "identification" or "representation" is basic to our understanding of it. That is, the sin-offering in some way came to represent the sinners in their sin. Thus, by laying hands on the beast's head in the ritual of sacrifice, sinners identified themselves with the beast, indicating that the beast now represented the sinner *in his or her sin* (i.e., *qua* sinner). As a consequence, the sinner's sin was identified with the beast, and its life became forfeit—"just as Christ, taking the initiative from the other side, identified himself with [human beings] in their fallenness (Rom. 8:3), and was made sin (2 Cor. 5:21)" (Dunn, 44).

This logic introduces Christ's dual role in his death—his substitution *for humanity* before God and in the face of God's justice, but also his substitution *for God* in the face of human sin.

This use of the language of representation to assist our understanding of substitution is not designed to deny the sense of Christ's having achieved something objective in his death. Indeed, according to Paul, Christ gave himself up for us *so that* we might live in him (cf. 1 Thess 5:9-10; Rom 8:3-4; 14:9; 2 Cor 5:15, 21; Travis). As significant as the theme of participation in Christ's death (and resurrection) is for Paul (cf., e.g., Phil 3:10), the possibility of such participation is grounded in his first dying "for us."

From where does Paul obtain this mode of interpretation? Attempts have been made in recent decades to find a Greco-Roman background for Paul's thought on the atoning death of Christ—either quite apart from the OT and Second-Temple Judaism (Seeley) or mediated through Hellenistic Judaism (Williams). It is not clear, however, why one must draw such strict boundaries between OT influence and Greco-Roman philosophy, particularly given the degree to which Hellenism and Judaism had coalesced by the beginning of the first century A.D.

It is more probable that the redemptive interpretations of death in Hellenistic Judaism and in Paul are drawn from the common quarry of Israel's Scriptures and sacrificial practices. The sacrificial system of the OT provides a ready source for speculation concerning the relation of innocent death and forgiveness of sins, particularly since during the Second Temple period sacrifices in general were interpreted along redemptive lines. Of course, this is not to suggest that Paul would have been unaware of such martyrological interpretations of death as one finds in texts such as 2 Maccabees 7:37-38 and 4 Maccabees 6:28-29. But these texts themselves develop OT sacrificial and Servant* themes, particularly making use of Isaianic material concerning the Suffering Servant of the Lord (Is 52:13—53:12)—just as did the early church and Paul. Moreover, the degree to which Paul might have been directly indebted to Hellenistic Judaism via the martyr tales of the Maccabean literature is modulated by the strong influence of retributive ideas in those texts. Paul, on the other hand, places a more profound stress on God's initiative in providing the sacrifice, and his evident concern is to establish the universality of Christ's atoning benefits which are not limited to Israelite cultic and memorial rites needing repetition and reenactment (Hengel, 51). In addition to the sac-

rificial system of the OT, with its concern for maintaining the relationship between God and his covenant people, the Isaianic Suffering Servant and Jewish martyrology, scholars have also found reflections of the Jewish notion of the binding of Isaac in the background of Paul's thought (cf. Tambasco, Dunn, Hengel, Brown, et al.).

As Hengel has argued, it is not enough to peruse the OT and later Jewish texts for precursors to Paul's salvific interpretation of Jesus' death. An influence of significant proportions lies much closer to hand—namely, the interpretation of the cross of Christ mediated through the repetition of the Last Supper in the early Christian communities. Paul himself knows and repeats the eucharistic words of Jesus (1 Cor 11:23-25), words that interpret Jesus' self-giving as redemptive.

*5.2. The Death of Christ and Following Christ.* According to Paul, the death and resurrection of Christ mark the beginning of a new epoch that reaches forward to the time of Christ's parousia (cf. Hanson). This fundamentally changes the way one understands life in the present. First, awareness that Christ's death and resurrection has instituted a new epoch allows one to envision new life in contrast to old ways of living, and to embrace the power of God requisite for new life. Moreover, considering the present in light of the past motivates believers to act in gratitude for deliverance from slavery to sin. Finally, recognition of this new time encourages believers' further recognition that life in the present is determined by the cross. This means that one effect of the cross is the possibility of restored humanity, restored in its relationships to God, to itself and to all creation. It also means that the definition of existence put forward by sinful humanity has been radically altered, so that those who follow Christ must look to Christ for the expression of restored humanity. "The church whose theology is shaped by the message of the cross must itself take on a cruciform life if its theology is to carry credibility" (Cousar, 186).

What this means practically is related above all to believers taking on themselves the form of obedience to God represented in Christ's life, expressed ultimately in his death. This thought lies behind Paul's use of the hymn to Christ in Philippians 2:6-11. It also lies behind his defense of his own apostolic ministry, his sense that in his weakness* and suffering* he is engaged in the imitation of Christ and participating in the suffering of the Messiah (cf. Pobee, Hanson, Bloomquist).

*5.3. The Death of Christ and the Life of God's People.* The cross of Christ has as its effect the restoration of humanity in another sense, too. The cross is understood by Paul as a boundary-shattering event (cf. Driver, esp. chap. 13). Thus, Paul can assert in 1 Corinthians that those who follow the example of Christ in his selfless death will not nurture their status-based divisions within the Christian community but will gain a fuller understanding and appreciation of the body of Christ (1 Cor 11:17—12:31; *see* Body of Christ). This, after all, is a manifestation of the new covenant in Christ's blood (1 Cor 11:25). But Paul can also assert that faithful identification with Christ in his salvific work opposes even more fundamental ethnic, social and sexual boundaries, "for in Christ Jesus you are all children of God through faith" (Gal 3:26; cf. 3:27-29; Eph 2:11-22). In this way too, then, the cross not only enables new life, it also points beyond itself to disclose the norms of that life, and thus it inaugurates the new era wherein the salvific will of God will be realized.

Clearly, the death of Christ occupies center stage in Paul's theology. He draws on an abundance of images by which he explicates its meaning, both by way of excavating the rich resources available to him in Israel's Scriptures and in the common faith of the early church, and by way of relating the message of the cross more directly to his audiences in their diverse backgrounds and with their diverse circumstances. The cross of Christ lies at the intersection of the major avenues of his theology and of his understanding of faithful living before Christ returns. For Paul, believers here and now manifest their obedience to Christ by proclaiming his death until he comes.

*See also* CENTER OF PAUL'S THEOLOGY; CHRISTOLOGY; CROSS, THEOLOGY OF THE; CRUCIFIXION; CURSE, ACCURSED, ANATHEMA; DYING AND RISING WITH CHRIST; ESCHATOLOGY; EXPIATION, PROPITIATION, MERCY SEAT; FORGIVENESS; JUSTIFICATION; LORD'S SUPPER; PEACE, RECONCILIATION; REDEMPTION; SACRIFICE, OFFERING, RESURRECTION; SALVATION; SUFFERING; TRIUMPH.

BIBLIOGRAPHY. J. C. Beker, *Paul the Apostle: The Triumph of God in Life and Thought* (Philadelphia: Fortress, 1980); L. G. Bloomquist, *The Function of Suffering in Philippians* (JSNTSup 78; Sheffield: Academic, 1993); L. Boff, *Passion of Christ, Passion of the World: The Facts, Their Interpretation, and Their Meaning Yesterday and Today* (Maryknoll, NY: Orbis, 1987); C. A. Brown, "The Peace-Offerings (שלמים) and Pauline Soteriology," in *The New Testament and Christian-Jewish Dialogue: Studies in Honor of David Flusser, Immanuel* 24-25 (1990) 59-76; C. B. Cousar, *A Theology of the Cross: The Death of Jesus in the Pauline Letters* (OBT; Minneapolis: Fortress, 1990); J. Driver, *Understanding the Atonement for the Mission of the Church* (Scottdale, PA: Herald, 1986); J. D. G. Dunn, "Paul's Understanding of the Death of Jesus as Sacrifice," in *Sacrifice and Redemption:*

*Durham Essays in Theology*, ed. S. W. Sykes (Cambridge: University Press, 1991) 35-56; J. A. Fitzmyer, "Reconciliation in Pauline Theology," in *To Advance the Gospel: New Testament Studies* (New York: Crossroad, 1981) 162-85; J. B. Green, *The Death of Jesus: Tradition and Interpretation in the Passion Narrative* (WUNT 2.33; Tübingen: J. C. B. Mohr, 1988); A. T. Hanson, *The Paradox of the Cross in the Thought of St. Paul* (JSNTSup 17; Sheffield: JSOT, 1987); M. Hengel, *The Atonement: The Origins of the Doctrine in the New Testament* (Philadelphia: Fortress, 1981); M. D. Hooker, "Interchange and Atonement," *BJRL* 60 (1978) 462-81; idem, "Interchange in Christ," *JTS* 22 (1974) 349-61; M. Houts, "Classical Atonement Imagery: Feminist and Evangelical Challenges," *Catalyst* 19 (1993) 1, 5-6; K. Kertelge, "Das Verständnis des Todes Jesu bei Paulus," in *Der Tod Jesu: Deutungen im Neuen Testament*, ed. K. Kertelge (QD 74; 2d ed.; Freiburg: Herder, 1976) 114-36; E. Lohse, *Märtyrer und Gottesknecht: Untersuchungen zur urchristlichen Verkündigung vom Sühntod Jesu Christi* (2d ed.; FRLANT 64; Göttingen: Vandenhoeck & Ruprecht, 1963); J. S. Pobee, *Persecution and Martyrdom in the Theology of Paul* (JSNTSup 6; Sheffield: JSOT, 1985); D. Seeley, *The Noble Death: Graeco-Roman Martyrology and Paul's Concept of Salvation* (JSNTSup 28; Sheffield: JSOT, 1990); S. H. Travis, "Christ as Bearer of Divine Judgment in Paul's Thought about the Atonement," in *Jesus of Nazareth: Lord and Christ. Essays on the Historical Jesus and New Testament Christology*, ed. J. B. Green and M. Turner (Grand Rapids; Eerdmans, forthcoming); A. J. Tambasco, *A Theology of Atonement and Paul's Vision of Christianity* (ZS: NT; Collegeville, MN: Liturgical, 1991); H. Weder, *Das Kreuz Jesu bei Paulus: Ein Versuch, über den Geschichtsbezug des christlichen Glaubens nachzudenken* (FRLANT 125; Göttingen: Vandenhoeck & Ruprecht, 1981); S. K. Williams, *Jesus' Death as Saving Event: The Background and Origin of a Concept* (HDR 2; Missoula, MT: Scholars, 1975); N. T. Wright, *The Climax of the Covenant: Christ and the Law in Pauline Theology* (Minneapolis: Fortress, 1991).

J. B. Green

**DECONSTRUCTION.** *See* HERMENEUTICS/INTERPRETING PAUL.

**DEITIES.** *See* IDOLATRY; RELIGIONS, GRECO-ROMAN.

## DEMONS AND EXORCISM

In Hellenistic Greek *daimones* (masculine) and *daimonia* (neuter) signified semidivine beings with powers of various sorts who could be either good or evil, similar to our popular use of the word *spirit*. The LXX used *demons* (*daimonia*) to designate heathen gods, as an epithet of contempt. Judaism in the Hellenistic era took up the term and used it to designate evil supernatural beings who caused physical harm in all sorts of ways. They also tempted people to idolatry,* witchcraft (*see* Magic), war and other things which would keep them far from God.* Philo and Josephus, however, were able to follow the older Greek usage (*daimōn* = god/angel/spirit). Later Hellenistic Jewish literature viewed the demons generally as fallen angels (*see* Principalities and Powers); they could be called "angels" or "spirits" (*pneumata*), and were associated more frequently with the work of Satan.*

Early Christianity inherited from Judaism this usage of *daimonion*, and hence in the NT it was the neuter term which was used almost exclusively (only Mt 8:31 uses the masculine). Paul shared the Jewish-Christian view of demons, though the actual term *daimonia* appears infrequently (5x, all but one in 1 Cor).

1. Demons
2. Exorcism

**1. Demons.**

In 1 Corinthians 10:14-22 Paul drew a lesson and warning from Israel's apostasy* in the wilderness (1 Cor 10:1-13; cf. Ex 32:6) with an application to current problems in the Corinthian* church*: namely, that certain Corinthian Christians had been joining pagan feasts held in the temples of their gods (*see* Religions). They seem to have believed that they could share in such festivities with impunity (1) because they possessed the powerful Christian "knowledge"* that there is only one God and idols are really "nothing" (1 Cor 8:4-7; 10:19) and (2) because their baptism* and "sharing in Christ" (*see* Fellowship) at the Eucharist (*see* Lord's Supper) had given them a heavenly status of immunity that was irrevocable regardless of conduct (implied in Paul's counterargument of 1 Cor 10:1-6 and at 1 Cor 10:21-22; cf. 1 Cor 6:12-20; 10:23).

Paul responded that though an idol image lacks any of the potency claimed for it by pagans (1 Cor 10:19), and though the object of their sacrifice* was not really a god (1 Cor 10:20; cf. 1 Cor 8:5-6), yet neither was the act of sacrifice or participation in it a matter of indifference. Behind the attraction of the pagan cultus with its ceremonies, food* (meat was a rarity for most working people) and social life, lay the activity of evil supernatural powers, the *daimonia*, or demons (1 Cor 10:20-21; cf. 1 Cor 12:2). And in the same way that the "cultic" acts of the Lord's Supper established a new reality, a new covenant* relationship with the universal Lord,* so participation in cult-related eating and drinking ("cup of demons" and "table of demons," 1 Cor 10:21) violated the *koinōnia*, or communion (*see*

Fellowship) with Christ* and established a new reality in communion with inferior evil powers. Through Paul's correctives the Corinthians were shown the danger of their excesses: that their intemperate actions displayed a dangerous presumption on God's grace parallel to Israel's* sin* in the wilderness, and that they were inviting similar consequences upon themselves.

The theme that pagan sacrifice was dedicated to demons is probably hinted at in Galatians 4:8-10, where it is said the Galatians formerly served "those things which are by nature not gods." However, it is not certain that the word *elements* (*stoicheia*, Gal 4:9; *see* Elements/Elemental Spirits) refers to celestial beings. It could just as well be a derogatory figure of speech, and may have designated the Judaizing religion of the intruders. Scholars are divided as to whether or not Paul signified demonic powers in speaking of the "rulers of this age" (1 Cor 2:6; *see* Principalities and Powers) who are perishing, who do not have God's wisdom and who were instrumental in bringing about the crucifixion of the Lord of glory (1 Cor 2:8)—though the last characteristic may suggest human government.

Both the use of *spirits* (*pneumata*) for *demons* and the theme of demons drawing humanity away from God through deception as seen in 1 Timothy 4:1 were well known in Judaism and early Christianity. In 1 Timothy the demonic activity is seen to be not only in paganism, but to have moved into the church as well, snaring some with doctrinal deception.

**2. Exorcism.**

In Acts 16:16-18 Paul and Silas in Philippi were hounded by a slave girl possessed by a spirit which enabled her to prophesy (*see* Prophecy). She was said to have a "Python-spirit" (Acts 16:16, *pneuma pythōna*), probably her owners' way of claiming that her prophecy was as good as that at Delphi (*pythō-* being a Greek designation for Delphi or the god Apollo). She proclaimed, in a fashion reminiscent of some of the demon-possessed who encountered Jesus, that the apostles* were "servants* of the Most High God." It is not clear whether her owners hoped to be paid by the apostles for this free advertising, or whether Luke intended this as a demonic attempt to label and hence gain power over the missionaries. In any case, Paul recognized the source as demonic and expelled the spirit "in the name of Jesus" (Acts 16:19). It is significant that at such an early date exorcism formulas incorporated the name of Jesus, implying that Jesus was already thought of as divine by the early Christians (cf. 1 Cor 1:2, and the invocation of the names of deities in pagan exorcism formulas; e.g., *PGM* I.27-29, 212, 220-21, 265; II.285-87).

Nowhere in his letters did Paul explicitly mention exorcism; nevertheless, it is plain that he believed evil powers to be at work on the cosmic level (Rom 8:38-39; Eph 6:10-18; *see* Principalities and Powers), in human society (1 Cor 2:6-8) and in individuals (note his characterization of sin* as an alien power within, Rom 6:17-18; 7:14-20; Eph 2:1-2; cf. 2 Cor 4:4). It is equally clear that he believed Christ had triumphed (*see* Triumph), and that God would make complete his victory over these forces (Rom 16:20; 1 Cor 15:20-28; Phil 2:9-11; Col 2:15). The Holy Spirit (*see* Holy Spirit) brings the benefits of Christ's victory to believers, overcoming the tyranny of evil forces (Rom 8:3-4, 5-9; Eph 6:10-18). It is possible that Paul might have included exorcism among the apostolic "signs" (2 Cor 12:12) or the deeds done by the Spirit's power which he referred to generally (1 Cor 2:4; 12:9-10; Gal 3:5; 1 Thess 1:5).

*See also* ELEMENTS/ELEMENTAL SPIRITS OF THE WORLD; FLESH; HEALING, ILLNESS; HOLY SPIRIT; MAGIC; PRINCIPALITIES AND POWERS; SATAN, DEVIL; TRIUMPH.

BIBLIOGRAPHY. D. Aune, "Demon," *ISBE* 1.919-23; H. D. Betz, ed., *The Greek Magical Papyri in Translation, Including the Demotic Spells* (Chicago: University of Chicago, 1986); F. Brenk, "In the Light of the Moon: Demonology in the Early Imperial Period," *ANRW* 2.16.3 (1986) 2068-145; C. Colpe et al., "Geister (*Dämonen*)" *RAC* 9.546-797, esp. 688-700; H. Conzelmann, *1 Corinthians* (Herm; Philadelphia: Fortress, 1975); M. Dibelius, *Die Geisterwelt im Glauben des Paulus* (Göttingen: Vandenhoeck & Ruprecht, 1909); G. Fee, *The First Epistle to the Corinthians* (NICNT; Grand Rapids: Eerdmans, 1987); W. Foerster, "δαίμων κτλ," *TDNT* II.1-20. T. Paige

**DESTRUCTION.** *See* ESCHATOLOGY; WRATH, DESTRUCTION.

**DEUTERONOMIC PERSPECTIVE.** *See* RESTORATION OF ISRAEL.

**DEVELOPMENT IN PAUL'S THEOLOGY.**
*See* CENTER OF PAUL'S THEOLOGY; CONVERSION AND CALL OF PAUL; ESCHATOLOGY; HERMENEUTICS/INTERPRETING PAUL; JESUS AND PAUL.

**DEVIL.** *See* SATAN, DEVIL.

**DIASPORA**

The term *diaspora* refers to the voluntary scattering or dispersion of the Jewish people throughout the an-

cient world. This voluntary departure from the Holy Land began very early. Technically, diaspora is not exile. The Babylonians carried the leadership of the nation and many of its people into exile after conquering Jerusalem. Thus while the Babylonian Exile was a forced deportation, exile became a voluntary residence outside of Palestine when the Persians allowed the exiles to return home and many chose instead to remain in Babylonia. But after the Romans destroyed the Second Temple in A.D. 70 and the last vestiges of independence were removed in A.D. 132-135, the Jews once again regarded themselves as exiles.

Here the focus is on the voluntary dispersion in the Roman Empire as it existed during the first century A.D. The Roman Diaspora is far more important than the Babylonian Diaspora for understanding Paul and the Judaism* of his time.

1. The Extent and Circumstances of the Diaspora
2. Judaism in the Diaspora and in Palestine
3. Conclusions

**1. The Extent and Circumstances of the Diaspora.**
During the Hellenistic period a great number of Jews were dispersed as Jewish mercenaries, military settlers, slaves and free wage-earners who worked in agriculture or as skilled crafts people. The largest concentrations of Jews outside Palestine were found in the two countries immediately adjacent—Egypt and Syria. Philo reports 1,000,000 Jews residing in Egypt during the first century A.D. (*Flacc.* 6.8), with Alexandria as their center where they constituted one-eighth of the population and occupied two out of five wards of the city. The large number of Jews in adjoining Cyrenaica should be considered an extension of Egyptian Jewry.

Like Egypt, Syria's population was comprised of a high percentage of Jews, particularly in the great cities such as Antioch and Damascus. And like Syria, a high percentage of the population of Asia Minor was Jewish. Colonies of Jews were also located in the Greek isles of the Eastern Mediterranean and in the cities of Greece and Macedonia. In the West, Jews settled in Carthage in North Africa and in Rome (where they numbered between 40,000 and 60,000 in the first century), as well as in the other cities of Italy (see Philo *Leg. Gai.* 36; Josephus *Ant.* 14.7.2 §§110-118).

Throughout the Roman Empire the Jews enjoyed the privilege of *religio licita*, officially recognized religion. Thus the Diaspora Jews practiced their religion openly and had their synagogues* or, as the Diaspora Jews characteristically referred to them, "prayer houses" (*proseuchai*). Far from the Temple cult of Jerusalem,* the synagogue served as a meeting place for daily and Sabbath prayer, for instruction in Torah and for various community gatherings. Like other ethnic groups in the empire, Jews in some major population centers, such as Alexandria, were organized into an officially recognized *politeuma*, a central autonomous organization run by its own board of directors and constituting the numerous synagogues of the city. As we know from records of events in Alexandria in A.D. 38-41, the *politeuma* could serve as a means for Diaspora Jews to defend their rights against Gentile hostility (Philo *Leg. Gai.* 132).

While the extent of the Diaspora as well as the social and economic causes for it have often been discussed (see Stern), the significant question today concerns the degree of difference between the Judaism of the Diaspora and that of the Holy Land (*see* Hellenism).

## 2. Judaism in the Diaspora and in Palestine.

*2.1. The Old Perspective: Inward-Looking Versus Syncretistic.* The older view posits an inward-looking, Aramaic-speaking, Torah-centered Judaism in Palestine and an open, Greek-speaking, Hellenistic Judaism in the Diaspora—syncretistic in nature and lax in observance of the Law.*

Greek was the primary language of Diaspora Judaism. Since the second century B.C. the Torah had been available in Greek translation and Diaspora authors wrote mainly in Greek. Moreover, Greek education, with its stress on rhetoric and persuasion and with its gymnasia, fostered an appreciation for Greek culture and an accommodation to it.

The Aramaic-speaking Jews of the Holy Land, on the other hand, resisted the inroads of Hellenism by clinging to the Torah. This older view has been challenged by contemporary scholarship as it has interpreted the literary evidence and recent archeological finds.

*2.2. The New Perspective: Points of Convergence.* The newer view does not deny a difference between the two Judaisms. Nevertheless, recent scholarship has emphasized points of convergence rather than divergence. Palestinian Judaism was neither self-contained nor monolithic; it was marked by variety and shared points of contact with the Judaism of the Diaspora.

*2.2.1. Points of Contact.* Diaspora Jews not only paid the Temple tax, but they also made pilgrimages to Jerusalem for the festivals (cf. Acts 2:9-11; *see* Collection). Some, like Paul, came to Jerusalem to study (*see* Jew, Paul the). Palestinian Judaism also tried to influence Diaspora Judaism by translating books into Greek. Indeed, the work of translating and editing the Septuagint continued into the second century A.D.

*2.2.2. Variety in Palestinian Judaism.* The use of Greek in Palestine perhaps best illustrates the variety in first-century Palestinian Judaism. Recent archeological finds point to Greek-speaking communities both in Jerusalem and in Galilee. Greek inscriptions on tombs and ossuaries, as well as Greek names, bear their silent but impressive testimony.

*2.2.3. The Intent of Jewish-Greek Literature.* A further point of convergence is the apologetic intent of the Greek literature both Judaisms produced. While the writers of the Diaspora employed the forms of Greek literature, they wrote primarily for Jews and for apologetic purposes. The Jewish historian Jason of Cyrene is a good example. Trained in Greek rhetoric and historiography, he wrote his five-volume history of the Maccabean revolt (which formed the basis for 2 Maccabees; see 2 Macc 2:19-25), to gain support for the Maccabean revolt among a readership in the Diaspora and in the Greek-speaking world. At the same time he exalted the piety of the Maccabean age with its strict observance of the Sabbath and the food laws. Jason had probably spent time in Palestine (Hengel 1974, 1.95-99). Quite different in outlook, Philo of Alexandria was philosophical and sought to combine Judaism and philosophy by means of allegory. He too sought to commend Judaism to both Jews and non-Jews. The extensive historical writings of Josephus best represent first-century Jewish-Greek literature from Palestine. Among other purposes, he wrote to commend Jewish history to a Hellenistic audience and to set the Jewish wars in the best possible light.

## 3. Conclusions.

The older view of two very different Judaisms was a misperception. The evidence for variety within Palestinian Judaism corresponds to the variety attested in the Diaspora. Jason and Philo represent the differences of perspective within Diaspora Judaism, with Jason illustrating the close connection between one strand of Diaspora Judaism and a pietistic variety of Palestinian Judaism. Apparently, Diaspora Judaism could be both lax and strict in its observance of the Torah, as could Palestinian Judaism. Philo, for example, observed the Law and condemned those who did not keep it. Rather than contrast the two Judaisms in terms of geography only, with R. N. Longenecker we should consider the contrast of the two Judaisms in terms of attitude and outlook: "The horizontal cleavage of geography must be noted. But more important is the vertical break between Hebraic and Hellenistic inclinations in both Palestine and the Diaspora" (Longenecker, 28). On the other hand, geography and environment cannot be ignored altogether: the

Roman Diaspora was, on the whole, tilted more toward the Hellenistic mindset and assimilation of Greek culture than was the Judaism of the homeland. *See also* HELLENISM; MISSION; RESTORATION OF ISRAEL.

BIBLIOGRAPHY. S. J. D. Cohen, *From the Maccabees to the Mishnah* (Philadelphia: Westminster, 1987); M. Hengel, *Jews, Greeks and Barbarians* (Philadelphia: Fortress, 1980); idem, *Judaism and Hellenism* (Philadelphia: Fortress, 1974); A. Kasher, *The Jews in Hellenistic and Roman Egypt* (New York: Ktav, 1975); R. N. Longenecker, *Paul, Apostle of Liberty* (Grand Rapids: Baker, 1964); J. A. Overman, "Who Were the First Urban Christians? Urbanization in Galilee in the First Century," *SBLASP* (1988); M. Stern, "The Jewish Diaspora," in *The Jewish People in the First Century: Historical Geography, Political History, Social, Cultural and Religious Life*, ed. S. Safrai and M. Stern (CRINT; 2 vols.; Philadelphia: Fortress, 1974) 1.117-83; J. A. Sanders, "Dispersion," *IDB* 1.854-56; M. Stern, "Diaspora," *EncJud* 6.8-19. W. R. Stegner

# DIATRIBE

Diatribe was a method or mode of teaching and exhortation used in the ancient schools of philosophy.* It was a facet of the Socratic method in which the teacher, using dialogue and question and answer, led the student from error to truth through censure (of incorrect thoughts and behavior) and protreptic (persuasion to a certain philosophy). Diatribe describes this teaching* activity, and also writings that offer actual school diatribes or use the typical features of the diatribe.

1. Origin and Usage
2. Characteristics
3. Paul's Use of the Diatribe
4. Value for Interpreting Paul's Letters

### 1. Origin and Usage.

The diatribe originated in both the philosophical circles and the rhetorical schools of the Sophists. It was used by itinerant philosophers who brought philosophy to the masses. Diatribe was once thought to have originated with a Cynic philosopher, Bion of Borysthenes (c. 325-255 B.C.), but this is now questioned. In any case, diatribe was given its main features by Bion's student, Teles. The diatribe came to prominence with the Stoics and, owing to its suspected origin with the Cynics, became known as the Cynic-Stoic diatribe.

Diatribe has been understood as a literary genre or style typical of the preaching of the Cynic and Stoic philosophers, but recent study has shown this to be false. Diatribe was not a part of any school curriculum, nor was it incorporated into rhetorical theory or handbooks. However, though not a literary genre, this oral teaching method could be accommodated to a literary mode. From the third century B.C. onward its typical form was a lecture or written thesis on moral and philosophical commonplaces such as divine providence, self-control and self-sufficiency.

### 2. Characteristics.

The diatribe has no typical structure or approach. Utilization of the many features of the diatribe depends upon the personality and skill of the speaker or author, and the particularities of the situation being addressed. Diatribe is characterized by rhetorical features of a dialogical nature including the introduction of imaginary opponents or interlocutors, and hypothetical objections and false conclusions. Introducing an imaginary interlocutor can take the form of a series of questions and answers between the author and interlocutor, with either one leading. Hypothetical objections and false conclusions are also commonly placed on the lips of the interlocutor, allowing the author to introduce and clarify typical objections or possible misunderstandings of the argument at hand, and to move to a new phase in the argumentation as a whole. These objections and false conclusions are rejected by the author, often beginning with a phrase like "by no means!" (*mē genoito*).

Diatribe also relies heavily upon features common to Greco-Roman rhetoric* in general. These include amplification, personification, maxims, *chreiai* (brief sayings or actions attributed to people), comparisons, historical examples, virtue* and vice lists, parallelism, antithesis, irony, sarcasm and paradox. It shares many characteristics with the philosophical dialogue and rhetorical thesis.

### 3. Paul's Use of the Diatribe.

Paul's use of the diatribe was fully recognized early in this century, particularly by R. Bultmann. In his dissertation he noted that diatribe was used by the popular philosophers and is also found in Paul's letters. He concluded that in his missionary enterprise Paul was functioning like a Cynic street preacher. However, in light of the teaching function of the diatribe it is more accurate to say that Paul taught his churches in a manner reminiscent of a philosophical-school teacher—through censure and protreptic. Diatribe's confrontive nature would not be conducive to a suitable evangelistic preaching style.

No book of the NT can be described as a diatribe. Rather, some books exhibit diatribal features, and these books are best described as "modes" of diatribe. Paul used diatribe creatively, adapting its features to the needs of the gospel, his congregations, his rhetorical style and the letter genre. Some diatribal elements are found in portions of Paul's letters (1 Cor 6:12-20; 15:29-41; and Gal 3:1-9, 19-22), but are most heavily utilized in the letter to the Romans.*

Diatribe in Romans has been extensively studied by S. K. Stowers, upon whose work most current discussion and this one are based. Romans 1—11 most heavily exhibits diatribal features, including rhetorical questions, personification, comparisons and virtue and vice lists. Two main subforms of diatribe predominate. The first subform is an address to an imaginary interlocutor (e.g., Rom 2:1-5, 17-24; 9:19-21; 11:17-24; 14:4, 10). Paul introduces a Jewish interlocutor who boasts over Gentiles* (Rom 2:17-29) and subsequently dialogues with him (Rom 3:1-9; 3:27—4:2). He also introduces a Gentile interlocutor who boasts over Jews (Rom 11:17-24). The second subform is objections and false conclusions from Paul's arguments drawn by the interlocutor. These often set forth possible misinterpretations of a point, correct them, and lead to other points in the argument. These are often rejected with the phrase "by no means!" (*mē genoito*) and given accompanying reasons for their rejection (Rom 3:1-9, 31; 6:1-3, 15-16; 7:7, 13; 9:14, 19-20; 11:1, 11, 19-20).

**4. Value for Interpreting Paul's Letters.**
The full evaluation of the role of diatribe in Paul's letters has aided in their interpretation, particularly in regard to Romans. Since diatribe was a tool of instruction in philosophical schools, it was not used for polemic, but instruction and exhortation. Thus the use of diatribe in Romans does not indicate that Paul is engaging in polemic against Judaism (e.g., Rom 2:17-29) or specific groups within the Roman congregations, but teaching the Romans his gospel prior to his imminent visit (Rom 1:8-15; 15:22-29). Interlocutors are not specific groups, but rhetorical voices that raise possible objections to or misunderstandings of Paul's gospel.*

Also, it has been argued that since Paul is using diatribe in Romans, he is not addressing any concrete situation in the Roman congregations (see Rome). Objections of interlocutors are merely teaching tools. However, teaching through diatribe does not preclude addressing a concrete situation. Knowing several members of the Roman congregations, Paul may be addressing situations in the church through the teachings selected and the approach taken for their presentation. This is certainly true of Galatians* and 1 Corinthians,* where diatribal elements address the situations of respective congregations.

*See also* PHILOSOPHY; RHETORIC; RHETORICAL CRITICISM;

ROMANS, LETTER TO THE; TEACHING/PARAENESIS; VIRTUES AND VICES.

BIBLIOGRAPHY. R. Bultmann, *Der Stil der paulinischen Predigt und die kynisch-stoische Diatribe* (FRLANT 13; Göttingen: Vandenhoeck & Ruprecht, 1910); K. P. Donfried, "False Presuppositions in the Study of Romans," *CBQ* 36 (1974) 332-55; G. L. Kustas, *Diatribe in Ancient Rhetorical Theory* (with responses), ed. W. Wuellner (Colloquy 22; Berkeley: The Center for Hermeneutical Studies, 1976); T. Schmeller, *Paulus und die 'Diatribe'* (NTAbh 19; Münster: Aschendorff, 1987); S. K. Stowers, *The Diatribe and Paul's Letter to the Romans* (SBLDS 57; Chico, CA: Scholars, 1981); idem, "The Diatribe," in *Greco-Roman Literature and the New Testament*, ed. D. E. Aune (SBLSBS 21; Atlanta: Scholars, 1988) 71-83; B. P. Wallach, "A History of the Diatribe from the Origin up to the First Century B.C. and a Study of the Influence of the Genre upon Lucretius III, 830-1094" (unpublished Ph.D. dissertation, University of Illinois at Urbana, 1974).

D. F. Watson

# DISCIPLINE

Community discipline was an emerging concept and practice among Christian groups of Paul's day. Paul probably borrowed some notions from Jewish groups such as the Pharisees, whose disciplinary procedures he knew well from his early days (*see* Jew, Paul the). From Paul's letters we learn that occasionally believers engaged in aberrant behavior and were reproved for it or made to suffer temporary isolation from other believers. In the most severe cases, permanent exclusion may have been necessary. Such measures had in view primarily the redemption of the individual and secondarily the holiness of the community.

1. Paul's Background and Experience
2. Evidence of Paul's Disciplinary Practice

**1. Paul's Background and Experience.**
*1.1. Discipline in Qumran and Pharisaic Judaism.* The Qumran sectaries developed an elaborate system of penalties intended to safeguard the purity and order of their community. Offenders were subject to immediate public reproof which was to be administered not harshly but "with truth and humbleness and affection" (1QS 5:24-26). The procedure for reproof required witnesses (1QS 6:1; CD 9:2), the number of which varied according to the offense and could be cumulative (CD 9:16-20). If reproof was ineffective or the offense serious, a range of penalties was possible, from short-term reduction in food allowance (1QS 6:25) and exclusion from ritual meals (1QS 7:20), to permanent expulsion from the community (1QS 8:20—9:2). It is not clear precisely who had jurisdic-

tion in disciplinary matters. Some texts speak of the whole community making decisions, but other texts imply a more centralized authority (a group of leaders or a single figure), and it may be that the "community" acted through its leader(s).

Rabbinic traditions suggest that the Pharisees of Paul's time commonly imposed a "ban," a state of social isolation imposed for deviation from ritual purity laws or for heretical views (*m. 'Ed.* 5:6; *m. Mid.* 2:2; *m. Mo'ed Qaṭ.* 3:1). The right to put someone under the ban was originally limited to the Sanhedrin, but some time before the destruction of the Temple it was extended to groups of scribes acting together. The ban was a temporary measure, lasting at least thirty days (*b. Mo'ed Qaṭ.* 16a), designed to recall the offender to full participation in the community. While under a ban, the offender had to exhibit signs of mourning, and everyone but his immediate family was to keep a "leper's distance" of four cubits from him (*b. B. Meṣ.* 59b). He could, however, participate in Jewish public life, including Temple worship,* and he could receive instruction. Upon his repentance he was fully restored to the community at the end of the ban period. Rabbinic sources are not clear with respect to complete expulsion from Pharisaic communities in the NT era, but it is reasonable to assume that unrepentant banned persons (cf. *t. Dem.* 2:9), and heretics like Christians would incur more severe judgment.

*1.2. Discipline of Paul by the Jews.* The "forty lashes less one" which Paul reports receiving five times at the hands of the Jews (2 Cor 11:24) was a punishment administered by synagogues (*see* Afflictions). In Paul's case it was probably administered for heretical teaching, although the Mishnah specifies only violations of ritual purity (*m. Mak.* 3:1-9). The only explicit point of contact between these regulations and Paul's career is the specification of defilement of the Temple as grounds for scourging (*m. Mak.* 3:2; cf. Acts 21:28, which of course postdates Paul's reference in 2 Cor). The number of lashes was reduced from the stipulation of "no more than forty lashes" in Deuteronomy 25:2-3, presumably in order to safeguard against excessive punishment. Detailed instructions concerning administration of the scourging are offered in Mishnah *Makkot* 3:10-14. Significantly, the scourging was understood to accomplish atonement for the presumably repentant offender (*m. Mak.* 3:15; cf. *m. Sanh.* 6:2). The same tractate of the Mishnah includes a detailed discussion of the place of two or more witnesses in accordance with Deuteronomy 19:15; 17:6.

*1.3. Non-Pauline Christian Practices.* Insufficient data concerning a pre-Pauline system of community discipline necessitate caution in concluding that Pauline

practices were the apostle's own invention or were adapted from Judaism. Luke 17:5 may represent the seed of an originally interpersonal "reproof, apology, forgiveness" formula which is expanded into community action in Matthew 18:15-17 and joined to the ascription of apostolic authority (Mt 18:19-20; 16:18-19; cf. Jn 20:23). The record of Acts suggests that the apostles presided in discipline cases from the earliest times (Acts 5:1-11; 8:20-24). Other pertinent texts from the canonical apostolic literature include the charge to bring back sinners from error (Jas 5:19-20; 1 Jn 5:16-17; Jude 22-23) and the command to keep any "root of bitterness" from springing up within the community (Heb 12:15). 2 John 10-11 calls the community to refuse hospitality to heretics, and 3 John 10 refers to the rebellious Diotrephes who expels believers from the church.

Many of these texts may postdate Pauline material, but it is significant that they display the full range of approaches, from the "early" interpersonal encounter to the "late" notion of centralized authority.* The texts exemplify most and exclude none of the measures employed by Paul. It is, therefore, not unreasonable to suppose that Paul himself made only minimal additions to a disciplinary program which was already in place when he joined the movement.

**2. Evidence of Paul's Disciplinary Practice.**
The ambiguity of what little evidence we have as well as indications of a non-Pharisaic flexibility preclude the use of words like "program" or "system" for Paul's notions of community discipline. It is possible, however, to gain some insights concerning disciplinary practice in the Pauline churches by examining key texts for evidence of procedural elements, culpable behaviors and intended effects. The key texts, in canonical order, are Romans 16:17; 1 Corinthians 5:1-13; 16:22; 2 Corinthians 13:1-2; Galatians 6:1-5; 2 Thessalonians 3:6-15; 1 Timothy 1:18-20; 5:19-22 and Titus 3:10-11.

*2.1. Procedural Elements.* It appears from Galatians 6:1-5 that the first step in correction of an erring believer was personal, private and gentle (Eph 4:29-32; Col 3:12-13; 1 Thess 5:14-15; cf. 2 Cor 2:5-11). The stress in these passages on humility and readiness to forgive (*see* Forgiveness) on the part of the person who admonishes recalls the teaching of Jesus in passages like Matthew 7:1-5; 18:21-35. The notions of self-searching censure and eagerness to effect heartfelt reconciliation (*see* Peace, Reconciliation) are practically nonexistent in Qumran and rabbinic sources, but they are pervasive in Paul's letters. It is important, then, that the similarities in procedure between Paul and his Jewish contemporaries not obscure the distinction in spirit. Paul's disciplinary practices were intended as *remedial* rather than *punitive* measures, being infused from start to finish with the single-minded desire for the good of the offending individual.

The nature of some offenses or the intransigence of some offenders required that the wider community of believers and its leaders become involved. The command to "take note of" (*sēmeiousthe,* 2 Thess 3:14) those who are disobedient may be understood as a command to "keep written records concerning" such persons (cf. *skopeō,* "keep an eye on" dissenters, Rom 16:17). This formal element, employed at Qumran, may have been appropriate in the case of more serious offenses, especially if the accumulation of witnesses would have a bearing on further action. *Rebuke* or *refutation* (*elengchō*) is a common term in the Pastoral Epistles which may include both doctrinal and moral lapses to be corrected by the community leaders (1 Tim 5:20; 2 Tim 4:2; Tit 1:9, 13; 2:15; cf. *paideuō,* 2 Tim 2:25-26). Either "taking note" or "rebuking" by the community leaders may have constituted "witnesses" as required in the case of elders in 1 Timothy 5:19 and in the case of divisive persons in Titus 3:10-11 ("after a first and second admonition"). Paul equates warnings with witnesses when he writes of his impending third visit to the Corinthians (2 Cor 13:1-2). There is some ambiguity here—for example, were warnings sometimes retroactively (*ex post facto*) construed as witnesses? This could have provided a flexibility designed to avoid the legal elaborations of the Pharisees and Qumran sectaries. It also would have allowed Paul and his delegates to "troubleshoot" freely with the immature and often contentious local communities.

A survey of the key passages does not strongly support the view that disciplinary action became increasingly centralized and formalized during and after Paul's career. Rather, it appears that a pattern existed during Paul's ministry (and/or after, depending on one's view of the date of the Pastorals; *see* Pastoral Letters) wherein jurisdiction arose in the community hierarchy according to the severity of the offense. Thus we observe that commonly occurring misbehavior is handled by all believers individually (Gal 6:1-5 and par.), warnings are administered generally by the community (Rom 16:17; 2 Thess 3:6-15), the factious and elders are disciplined by apostolic delegates (1 Tim 5:19-22; 2 Tim 2:25-26; Tit 3:10-11) and the most serious cases are taken up by the apostle* himself (2 Cor 13:1-2; 1 Tim 1:19-20; probably 1 Cor 5:3-4; see below on 1 Cor 16:22). Admittedly, the evidence is too sparse to insist on a rigid structure. It is equally possible that, as in the case of Qumran, the group acted through its local community leaders when problems were brought to their attention, and higher authorities, in this case Paul or his delegates, acted when they deemed it appropriate. As in the case of the witness/warning sequence, the church flexibly adapted contemporary Jewish practice to fit the dynamic spirit of the movement and the occasional aberrations of its local leadership.

When an individual did not respond to warning(s) or committed a serious offense, it was necessary to effect social isolation. The expressions used in the Pauline corpus to convey this idea do not specify what is meant. Romans 16:17 tells believers, "keep away" (*ekklinō*) from wrongdoers; 1 Corinthians 5:11 and 2 Thessalonians 3:14 enjoin, "do not associate" (*mē synanamignysthai*) with offenders; 2 Thessalonians 3:6 commands, "set apart" (*stellesthai*) the disobedient. 1 Corinthians 5:11 is more specific in instructing believers not to eat with those under discipline. Some have suggested that the restriction applies only to ritual meals (as in serious cases among the Qumran sectaries), which in the primitive church were the most powerful sign of inclusion (*see* Fellowship). But this does not fit Paul's wording when he makes the phrase intensive: "do not even eat with such a one." The parallel is not to be found in Qumran but in the Pharisaic ban, under which the offender was cut off socially from all but his immediate family. As in the case of the ban, the individual was "shamed" (1 Thess 3:14) and, when proven repentant (it is not clear how), welcomed back "as a believer" (2 Thess 3:15; cf. 2 Cor 2:5-11; Gal 6:1).

In several instances it appears that Paul goes beyond measures intended to recall erring individuals and seems to advocate their final expulsion from the community. The key text in this regard is 1 Corinthians 5:1-5. Paul here responds to a case of incest by invoking the name* and the power* of Jesus (1 Cor 5:4) and by twice invoking his own authority* from a distance (1 Cor 5:3-4). All of this is a solemn preface to the dramatic command to "hand this man over to Satan,*" an expression employed similarly in 1 Timothy 1:20. It is clear that the early church understood the realm of Satan to be everywhere outside the fellowship of believers (2 Cor 4:4; Gal 1:4; Eph 2:2) and that Paul's expression here denotes expulsion from the community. That the sentence is reformatory in some sense is confirmed by the fact that Paul ends the pronouncement in 1 Corinthians 5:5 with the express intent that the offender's "spirit may be saved in the day of the Lord" (*see* Eschatology); similarly, 1 Timothy 1:20 ends, "that they may learn not to blaspheme." But beyond this point there is no consensus among scholars.

Disagreement centers on the phrase in 1 Corinthians 5:5, "for the destruction of the flesh." It is unusual for Paul to use the word "flesh"* (*sarx*) for bodily existence rather than sinful nature (although he does so in 1 Cor 15:39), and an interpretation which views the phrase as a synonym for a kind of penance may appear to be more in line with 1 Timothy 1:20 and the remedial tenor of other Pauline passages. For several reasons, however, a penitential discipline is untenable: it makes Satan an agent for positive ethical change, it overlooks the unmistakable parallel in 1 Corinthians 11:29-30 to illness (*see* Healing, Illness) and death (*see* Life and Death) as judgments* for disobedience, and it misses the allusion to the exceptional circumstances of Job 2:6, where Satan is allowed to visit physical affliction on an individual as God permits. Admittedly, Job is a victim and not an offender, but the point is that Satan has power by divine consent to inflict suffering.* Paul demonstrates his understanding of this in 2 Corinthians 12:7, where his "thorn in the flesh" is a "messenger of Satan"; an evil work which ultimately serves God's purpose (cf. Deut 28:15-68).

In the case of 1 Corinthians 5:5, however, are we to understand that the handing over to Satan will result in death? If so, how could it have been remedial? One possibility is that Paul intends that the person's total exclusion from the community will effect repentance before the end. The person's sinful nature would be destroyed. Another possibility is that the suffering and death of the offender are understood to have an atoning effect, a notion affirmed by the Pharisees with the stipulation that the offender must pronounce a desire for his death to atone for his sins (*m. Sanh.* 6:2). But there is no other evidence that Paul held such a view. A third possibility is that the punishment would stop short of death if the person repented. This may be what Paul has in mind when in 2 Corinthians 2:5-11 and 7:12 he refers to his previous letter in which he had mentioned an "offender." But interpreters are divided over whether this offender who was disciplined is the same person mentioned in 1 Corinthians 5:5.

In 1 Corinthians 16:22 Paul writes in his own hand "if anyone does not love* the Lord,* let him be anathema" (*see* Curse, Accursed, Anathema) This should be understood as a pronouncement of judgment against those who reject the gospel or as an exhortation to self-examination, although some have mistakenly taken it as a pronouncement of expulsion for heretics or intransigent wrongdoers. Titus 3:10-11

contains another apparent absolute expulsion: after the second warning Titus is to "avoid" (*paraitou*) a factious person who is "self-condemned." While this seems to go further than other discipline passages, it may, like 1 Corinthians 16:22, be directed toward those outside the community. Titus 3:9 refers to controversies about genealogies and the Law, making it appear that the person in view was not one of "those who have trusted in God" (Tit 3:8).

*2.2. Types of Behavior Which Merit Discipline.* Doctrinal deviations which created division in the community were a problem early in Paul's ministry (1 Cor 1:10-11; 11:18-19), and the disciplinary measures in Romans 16:17 and 2 Corinthians 13:1-2 appear to respond to division caused by heterodoxy (cf. Gal 5:2-12). The Pastoral letters are dominated by this concern, and 1 Timothy 1:20 is a clear case in point. Heresy and its consequent factions were an obvious danger to the integrity of local communities and the Christian movement as a whole. It is not clear, however, to what extent aberrant views that did not cause splits could be tolerated.

In the two most lengthy passages, 2 Thessalonians 3:6-15 and 1 Corinthians 5:1-13 (1 Tim 5:19-22 is ambiguous), moral deviations are clearly in view. The charge that some were "idle" in Thessalonica is taken by many interpreters to denote inactivity based on the expectation of an imminent parousia, but Paul makes no explicit connection between this problem and his eschatological concerns (*see* Thessalonians). It is more likely that Paul's instruction reflects a social situation typical of a large port city, where many laborers were inactive for periods of time and dependent on patrons. Within the community of believers, some appear to have begun to presume upon the Christian goodness of patrons, and the system was in danger of degenerating into freeloading, resentment and division (perhaps echoed in 1 Cor 11:18-19).

In 1 Corinthians 5 Paul is obviously concerned about sexual immorality (*porneia/pornos*, 1 Cor 5:1, 9, 11; *see* Sexuality, Sexual Ethics), but he also condemns any "so-called" brother or sister (cf. the lack of negative qualification in 2 Thess 3:15) who is "greedy, or is an idolater, reviler, drunkard or robber" (1 Cor 5:11 NRSV). Many scholars take this list as a random enumeration of pagan vices after the fashion of contemporary moralists. But the fact that the list is expanded in 1 Corinthians 6:9-10 with special attention to sexual and property values suggests that it is consciously directed at the sins of Corinth. The list is representative and not comprehensive; that is, these are not the only offenses subject to discipline (cf. Gal 5:19-21). Although the list does not quantify (*how* greedy, *how much* reviling), it gives the impression of a moral accountability that is more strict than the church has practiced throughout most of its subsequent eras. The reason for this ethical rigorism is implied in Paul's allusion to Deuteronomy 17:7 in 1 Corinthians 5:13, "Drive out the wicked person from among you." The opposite of *wicked* for Paul is not *pure* in the sense of cultic purity but *holy* in the sense of the Spirit-controlled life of each member of the unified community (*see* Holiness). Deviation from holiness would retard the growth of the entire organism (or "leaven the lump," 1 Cor 5:5-8). For this reason, Paul views the types of behavior he lists as particularly dangerous in the life of the church.

*2.3. Intended Effects.* For the individual offender Paul's practice is clearly intended to produce repentance in an atmosphere of support and forgiveness. For the community, to hold its members accountable through disciplinary measures would maintain the moral integrity of the group. Although Paul does not develop the notion of an apologetic purpose for discipline, his practice in ethical decisions is in line with passages like Matthew 5:16 and 1 Peter 2:12. All of these principles were present at least to some extent in the contemporary Jewish practices which were apparently adapted by the primitive church, albeit in a less systematized form. What makes the Pauline concept of discipline unique and potentially potent, however, is the infusion of Christ-like love* into disciplinary practice.

Philippians 2:1-5, although it does not address discipline directly, expresses concisely the principle behind the scattered Pauline references to the subject. It is the incentive of love, the sharing of the Spirit (*see* Holy Spirit), the humble attitude—that is, the mind of Christ—which makes it possible to hold another person accountable. Thus the secret power of effective discipline is in its reflexive element. That is, the one who holds another accountable is first accountable to be a loving person. When this is true of a community of believers, isolation of an offender will be a compelling remedial force. Ultimately, then, it is not the power of persuasion or coercion that effects recall, but the power of love emanating from a transformed community.

*See also* Apostasy, Falling Away, Perseverance; Opponents of Paul.

Bibliography. H. Conzelmann, *1 Corinthians* (Philadelphia: Fortress, 1975) 95-102; G. D. Fee, *The First Epistle to the Corinthians* (NICNT; Grand Rapids: Eerdmans, 1987) 194-228; G. Forkman, *The Limits of the Religious Community* (Lund: Gleerup, 1972); G. W. H. Lampe, "Church Discipline and the Interpretation of the Epistles to the Corinthians," in *Christian History and Interpretation: Studies Presented to John Knox,* ed. W. R. Farmer, C. F. D. Moule and R. R. Niebuhr (Cambridge: University Press, 1967) 337-61; C. J. Roetzel, *Judgment in the Community* (Leiden: E. J. Brill, 1972); R. Russell, "The Idle in 2 Thess 3:6-12: An Eschatological or Social Problem?" *NTS* 34 (1988) 105-19; A. C. Thiselton, "The Meaning of SARX in 1 Corinthians 5.5: A Fresh Approach in the Light of Logical and Semantic Factors," *SJT* 26 (1973) 204-28; C. A. Wanamaker, *The Epistles to the Thessalonians* (NIGTC; Grand Rapids: Eerdmans, 1990) 279-90; P. Zaas, "Cast Out the Evil Man from Your Midst," *JBL* 103 (1984) 259-61; idem, "Catalogues and Context: 1 Corinthians 5 and 6," *NTS* 34 (1988) 622-29.

T. E. Schmidt

**DIVINE FOREKNOWLEDGE.** *See* Foreknowledge, Divine.

**DIVINE MAN.** *See* Corinthians, Letters to the; Opponents of Paul.

**DIVINE SONSHIP.** *See* Adoption, Sonship; Son of God.

**DIVORCE.** *See* Marriage and Divorce, Adultery and Incest.

**DOMINICAL SAYINGS.** *See* Jesus, Sayings of.

**DOMINIONS.** *See* Principalities and Powers.

**DOWN PAYMENT.** *See* First Fruits, Down Payment.

**DOXOLOGY.** *See* Benediction, Blessing, Doxology, Thanksgiving; Liturgical Elements; Worship.

## DYING AND RISING WITH CHRIST

The theme denoted by this title finds frequent mention in Paul's letters. Both the context and the content of these references show that it held an important place in Paul's thinking, his personal life and his apostolic ministry.

1. Origin and Development of the Metaphor
2. The Eschatological Dimension
3. Baptism as Enactment
4. Rising to New Life in Christ
5. Dying, Rising and Apostolic Ministry

**1. Origin and Development of the Metaphor.**
The best known passage in which this concept appears

is Paul's exposition of baptism* in Roman 6:3-4:

> Do you not know that all we who were baptized to Christ Jesus were baptized to his death? We were buried therefore with him through baptism to death, in order that as Christ was raised from death through the glory of the Father so we also might walk in newness of life.

The first sentence of this quotation suggests that this interpretation of baptism did not originate with Paul. He apparently assumes that the Christians at Rome* were acquainted with it. If this conclusion is correct, Paul will have received this teaching as an accepted element of Christian teaching (*see* Creed), but he grasped its profound significance more than others (as witnessed by its frequency in his writings). Some scholars have suggested that it was taken over from Greek mystery religions, in which initiation was conceived in terms of death and resurrection. From considerations of the late date of the records of these rites and differences of interpretation, particularly as to whether initiates in such cults clearly identified with a deity in death and resurrection or were offered immortality through such ritual experience, the suggestion is highly unlikely (Wagner; Wedderburn; Dunn 1988, 308-10; *see* Religions, Greco-Roman).

By contrast, others have put forward the idea that it was Paul's experience that caused him to seize on this element of Christian teaching—notably the dramatic nature of his conversion* and the acute sufferings* that he endured in his ministry. Paul's allusion in 2 Corinthians 1:8-10 to a "deadly peril" which he had recently endured led him to write:

> We were so unbearably crushed that we despaired of life itself. Indeed, we felt that we had received the sentence of death, so that we should rely not on ourselves but on God who raises the dead. (2 Cor 1:8-9)

On that text W. E. Wilson commented, "In this terrible experience the presence of Christ had been so strongly with him [Paul] that he felt himself to be going through the very Passion itself, and then, as despair was turned into joy through release, his experience of return to life seemed like being raised with Christ" (Wilson, 564). The same passage was believed by C. E. Faw to have played a decisive part in Paul's thinking; with other interpreters of Paul, Faw saw in it an indication of Paul at last accepting physical death as part of his future (in contrast to the assumption that he would survive to Christ's second coming); from that time on "Paul began to use the metaphor of death and resurrection to explain the various aspects of present religious experiences" (Faw, 296). Without minimizing the fearful nature of the experience Paul referred to

in 2 Corinthians 1:8-11, one finds it difficult to believe that it had such a drastic effect on his thinking in light of his description of his sufferings* in the service* of the gospel in 2 Corinthians 11:16—12:10, to say nothing of the doubtfulness of this interpretation of dying and rising with Christ.

Even where it is accepted that the concept of death and resurrection with Christ has deeper roots, there is a persistent tendency among English speaking interpreters to view Romans 6:1-11 as primarily concerned with Christian experience (as distinct from Christian conduct). For example, W. Sanday and A. C. Headlam explained Romans 6 as meaning, "In baptism the believer suffers a death and resurrection like Christ's" (Sanday and Headlam, 154). W. F. Flemington described baptism as "a re-enactment for the believer of what once happened to our Lord" (Flemington, 59). And J. D. G. Dunn views the passage as dealing with death to sin,* of which baptism was but one of three metaphors, the others a simile drawn from horticulture ("planted together in the likeness of his death," Rom 6:5) and the concept of the old and new creation*; he considers that baptism is in view only in Romans 6:4—"through baptism" (Dunn 1970, 139-42).

In reality the fundamental feature that lies behind the exposition of baptism in Romans 6:1-11 is the gospel of the once-for-all death and resurrection of Christ, and what that death and resurrection means for humanity. The very terms of Romans 6:3-4 echo the primitive summary of the gospel in 1 Corinthians 15:3-4, and assume the references to the redeeming power of the death and resurrection of Christ set forth in the earlier chapters of Romans (see esp. Rom 3:25-26; 4:25, 5:6—8:21).

### 2. The Eschatological Dimension.

More clearly than any other passage, however, the theology that lies behind Romans 6:1-11 is succinctly stated in 2 Corinthians 5:14-21 (see commentaries). The theme is God's reconciliation of the world to himself through Christ's redeeming acts (*see* Peace, Reconciliation). The objective facts stated therein are that Christ in his death and resurrection acted as the representative of the human race, so that when he died and rose from death all humanity was implicated in those acts. In Christ's death all died, in his resurrection all rose, and through those deeds the new creation came into being. The old age, characterized by sin and death, ended; the new age of righteousness and life began. Admittedly there is an overlap of the two ages (1 Cor 10:11), for the end is not yet, but the realities of the new creation are present in Christ and all united with him (2 Cor 5:17).

This is, of course, eschatological* language, but it is in direct line with the teaching of Jesus that in his ministry of word and deed, climaxed by his death and resurrection, the kingdom* of God was established in this world, in anticipation of its consummation at his Parousia. Accordingly in 2 Corinthians 5:14 the statement, "We have reached the conclusion that one died on behalf of all, therefore all died," must be interpreted as relating to all humanity (see Dunn 1974, 130), *not* solely to the church (but cf. Martin, 129-33). In 2 Corinthians 5:15 "those who live" are those who have learned that they were included in Christ's death and resurrection, and so have come to share in the resurrection life of the risen Lord. In 2 Corinthians 5:17, since they are "in Christ," they participate in the new creation; for them the old order has passed away, the new world has arrived (*see* Creation and New Creation).

### 3. Baptism as Enactment.

This interpretation of the new situation brought about by Christ's redemptive acts clarifies for us Paul's train of thought in Romans 6. His intention is an essentially practical one, namely that of demonstrating that justification* by faith* (expounded in Rom 3—5) does not lead to increase of sin (Rom 6:1); on the contrary, Christ's death and resurrection for humanity have in view death to sin and life* from and for God in his new world. Since baptism* in the name of Jesus means union with Christ (Gal 3:26-27), to be baptized to him means to share his death (Rom 6:3). Hence the baptized are buried *with him* (Rom 6:3)—they are laid with him in *his* grave. Sharing, then, with him his resurrection, they are called to "newness of life," that is, life in accord with the new age in God's kingdom. Paul in Romans 6:4 refrains from stating that baptism indicates sharing in the resurrection of Christ, not only because he is arguing against a proleptic eschatology (so Käsemann, 166-67), but he also is intent on emphasizing the ethical meaning of baptism; but in Romans 6:11 he clearly implies the believer's resurrection with Christ ("Reckon yourselves dead to sin *and alive to God in Christ Jesus*"), and he explicitly affirms it in Colossians 2:12: "buried with him in baptism, in which you were also raised with him through faith in the working of God who raised him from the dead."

This last sentence needs to be pondered. Baptism signifies resurrection "through faith in the God who raised Christ from the dead." If Paul is saying that participation in the resurrection of Christ in baptism is through faith, then he most surely implies that participation in Christ's death in baptism also takes place

through faith. From that time on, life without God has ended, and a new one in Christ has begun. Here justification through Christ and life in Christ by the Spirit* join hands, for the baptism so interpreted is of one who turns to the Lord in response to the gospel of Christ crucified and risen for the life of the world. Interestingly, the clearest indication in Paul's writings of present participation in the kingdom of God occurs in the introduction to a passage often thought to be a baptismal confession (Col 1:15-20): "He (the Father) has rescued us from the power of darkness and transferred us into the kingdom of his beloved Son" (Col 1:13). "Rescued us . . . transferred us into the kingdom" is another way of expressing the meaning of the believer's dying and rising with Christ.

### 4. Rising to New Life in Christ.

Because baptism signifies participation in Christ's death and resurrection, and through faith an existential participation in them, it calls for the believer's resolute death to sin and life in accord with the fellowship of the risen Lord (Rom 6:4). But it is not alone a call for such living, but with it comes an assurance of the grace of the risen Lord* and the power* of the Holy Spirit so to live ("as Christ was raised from the dead through the glory of the Father, so we also should walk" relates to the Holy Spirit as the agent of Christ's resurrection and therefore of the believer's). The link between demand and grace* runs right through Romans 6:1-14; it is spelled out in terms of the Spirit in Romans 8:1-4, and expounded in detail in the lengthy exhortation of Colossians 2:20—3:17. The two aspects of living in light of Christ's death and resurrection and life by the aid of the Holy Spirit are strikingly exhibited in Galatians 5:24-25: "Those who belong to Christ Jesus have crucified the flesh with its passions and desires. If we live by the Spirit, let us also walk by the Spirit."

That conjunction of life in union with the living Lord and life by the aid of the Spirit leads Paul to say, "For me living is Christ, and dying is gain" (Phil 1:21). "Living is Christ" means not only *for the sake of* Christ, but *by the grace* of Christ. It is otherwise expressed in the profound utterance of Galatians 2:19-20:

> I through the Law died to the Law, so that I might live to God. I have been crucified with Christ, and it is no longer I who live, but Christ lives in me; and the life that I now live in the flesh I live by faith—faith in the Son of God, who loved me and handed himself over to death for me.

For Paul, the former Pharisee who sought to live in total obedience to the Law and experienced it as a tyranny that held him in thrall, it was an inexpressible relief to know that in Christ's death and resurrection he was released for life in the new age. That element of the theology of redemption* became for him an existential reality: his life under the domination of Law* had ended, and life henceforth was fellowship* with the risen Christ; or, otherwise expressed, the risen Christ was the continuing source of his life, as he daily lived by faith in the Lord who loved him and died for him.

Paul concludes the letter to the Galatians in which this statement appears by summarizing his teaching that through Christ's redeeming work believers are emancipated for life in the kingdom of God. He writes:

> May it never happen that I should boast in anything except the cross of our Lord Jesus Christ, through which the world has been crucified to me and I to the world. For circumcision is nothing, and uncircumcision is nothing, but new creation is everything. (Gal 6:14-15)

In what sense does Paul mean that "the world*" has been crucified to him and he to the world? R. C. Tannehill points out that for the apostle the term "world" often has reference to the present evil world in which sin, death and the Law are ruling powers (*see* Principalities and Powers).

> The world has a structure which determines the life of each individual, and so human life as a whole, and man can only escape from this through an event which breaks into the all-encompassing world of sin and opens the possibility of a new existence in a new world. It is to such an eschatological event that Paul is referring when he speaks of the crucifixion of the world. (Tannehill, 64)

Once again, therefore, Paul here refers to the cataclysmic effect of the death and resurrection of Christ, in which he was implicated before he could know it, and through which life was transformed from the day that he came to know Christ; then it was that in fellowship with the once crucified and now ever-living Lord, he experienced life in the new creation. And that is all that now matters.

### 5. Dying, Rising and Apostolic Ministry.

Since Paul had died with Christ to the world and now partook of the reality of the new creation, he dedicated all his God-given powers to take this news to every creature. This ministry* he sought to carry out after the pattern of Christ's service of bringing the kingdom of God into the world, namely through death and resurrection. This is revealed with particular clarity in his description of his apostolic ministry* in 2 Corinthians 4:8-12. Remarkably, each item of suffering

mentioned is balanced by an indication of victory over it, and it is characterized as:

> always carrying about in our body the putting to death of Jesus, in order that the life of Jesus may be revealed in our body. For we are always being handed over to death for the sake of Jesus in order that the life of Jesus may be revealed in our mortal body. (2 Cor 4:10-11)

In his missionary service Paul was constantly being "handed over to death" (a frequent expression in the NT for the death of Jesus), but he also experienced the deliverance of God in a manner analogous to Jesus in his resurrection (*see* Afflictions). References that compare the apostle's sufferings and deliverances in ministry to the death and resurrection of Jesus are to be found in 2 Corinthians 13:4, Colossians 1:24 and 2 Timothy 2:8-13, but above all in Philippians 3:7-11, where Paul describes what he gave up when he became a Christian and the infinitely greater gain he found in Christ. The passage reaches its apex in Philippians 3:10-11:

> (I want) to know Christ,
> and the power of his resurrection,
> and the participation in his sufferings,
> becoming conformed to his death,
> if somehow I may attain to the resurrection
> of the dead.

"Knowing Christ" is here equated with participating in the power of his resurrection and in his sufferings. On this Tannehill comments: "Through participation in Christ's death and resurrection Christ himself is known, for it is in this way that Christ gives himself to the believer and exercises his Lordship over him" (Tannehill, 122). Such knowledge is experienced especially in the service of Christ, and it reaches its goal in the resurrection to the consummated kingdom of God. That, of course, is the ultimate end of the redemption of God in Christ, as Paul never tires of asserting (cf. Rom 14:9; 1 Cor 15:20-28; Phil 2:6-11; Eph 1:7-10; etc.)

*See also* AFFLICTIONS, TRIALS, HARDSHIPS; BAPTISM; CROSS, THEOLOGY OF THE; DEATH OF CHRIST; ESCHATOLOGY; LIFE AND DEATH; RESURRECTION.

BIBLIOGRAPHY. P. Bonnard, "Mourir et vivre avec Jésus-Christ selon saint Paul," *RHPR* 36 (1956) 101-12; M. Carrez "Souffrance et gloire dans les épîtres pauliniennes," *RHPR* 31 (1951) 343-53; J. D. G. Dunn, *Baptism in the Holy Spirit* (London: SCM, 1970) 139-42; idem, "Paul's Understanding of the Death of Jesus," in *Reconciliation and Hope*, ed. R. J. Banks (Grand Rapids: Eerdmans, 1974) 125-41; idem, *Romans* (WBC 38; Waco: Word, 1988) 308-10; C. E. Faw, "Death and Resurrection in Paul's Letters," *JBR* 27 (1959) 291-98.

W. F. Flemington, *The New Testament Doctrine of Baptism* (London: SPCK 1948) 59; H. Frankemölle, *Das Taufverständnis des Paulus: Taufe, Tod und Auferstehung nach Röm 6* (Stuttgart: KBW, 1970); T. F. Glasson, "Dying and Rising with Christ," *LQHR* 186 (1961) 186-91; E. Käsemann, *Commentary on Romans* (Grand Rapids: Eerdmans, 1980); R. P. Martin, *2 Corinthians* (WBC 40; Waco: Word, 1986); C. M. Proudfoot, "Imitation or Realistic Participation? A Study of Paul's Concept of 'Suffering with Christ,' " *Int* 17 (1963) 140-60; W. Sanday and A. C. Headlam, *The Epistle to the Romans* (ICC; 5th ed.; Edinburgh: T. & T. Clark, 1902); E. Schweizer, "Dying and Rising with Christ," *NTS* 14 (1967-68) 1-14; D. M. Stanley, *Christ's Resurrection in Pauline Soteriology* (AnBib 13; Rome: Pontifical Institute, 1961); R. C. Tannehill, *Dying and Rising with Christ* (Berlin: Töpelmann, 1967); G. Wagner, *Pauline Baptism and the Pagan Mysteries* (Edinburgh: Oliver and Boyd, 1967); A. J. M. Wedderburn, *Baptism and Resurrection: Studies in Pauline Theology against its Graeco-Roman Background* (WUNT 1/44; Tübingen: J. C. B. Mohr, 1987); W. E. Wilson "The Development of Paul's Doctrine of Dying and Rising Again with Christ," *ExpT* 42 (1930-31) 562-65.

G. R. Beasley-Murray

# E

## EARLY CATHOLICISM
1. Definition
2. Features
3. Circumstances
4. Evaluation

### 1. Definition.

The term *early catholicism* (German *Frühkatholizismus*) requires some clarification. Its use goes back to F. C. Baur in the nineteenth century; others claim it was first used by W. Heitmüller or E. Troeltsch (see Neufeld). E. Käsemann was probably the first to use the term extensively in recent debate (in 1949; cf. Käsemann 1969, 236 n.1). But it has taken on a special nuance in contemporary discussion, chiefly because of its employment in 1950 by Ph. Vielhauer in a programmatic essay which concluded that Luke-Acts "no longer stands within earliest Christianity, but in the nascent early catholic church" (Vielhauer, 49). I. H. Marshall, after summarizing the contributions of E. Käsemann, H. Conzelmann, E. Lohse and K. Wegenast to the discussion, concludes: "The expression 'early Catholicism' refers to a situation in which primitive apocalyptic expectation has been weakened, and the Church as an institution with an organized ministry and sacraments has begun to replace the Word as the means of salvation" (Marshall, 222-23).

### 2. Features.

In the above definition the data drawn from Acts are combined with those from the Pastoral Epistles, Ephesians, Jude and 2 Peter to form a composite picture of Christian theology and church life in the period between Paul and the emergence of the "catholic" church in the mid-second century. What features mark the growth of this institution of the church (a picture allegedly taken from the later, i.e., deutero-apostolic, NT books and supplemented from the Apostolic Fathers)?

*2.1. Church Order.* The organization of the church* and ministry* has become developed and structured, with charismatic, Spirit-controlled spontaneity and flexibility (reflected in 1 Cor 12—14) giving way to a regular hierarchical and monepiscopal (i.e., sole bishopric) institution of the ministry, seen in *Ignatius* and *1 Clement* 44 by way of the Pastoral* Letters (*see* Church Order and Government).

*2.2. Faith.* The understanding of the faith* has been transformed from an outgoing response to the gospel call to the possession of articles of religion which form a once-for-all "deposit" (hinted at in 1 Tim 6:20; 2 Tim 1:14) to be preserved intact and handed on. The term *pistis* ("faith") loses its eschatological and existential character and signifies one "virtue" among other qualities of the moral life (as in 2 Tim 3:10; cf. 2 Pet 1:5-7: Jude 3, 20).

*2.3. Canonical Authority.* The boundaries of the canon* are set inevitably by the later church's collecting apostolic writings, especially Paul's letters (2 Pet 3:15-16), and thereby erecting a "formal principle" of canonical authority (*sola scriptura*) as a bulwark against gnosticism* (which claimed a secret tradition handed down from the apostles) and Montanism (a movement which relied on a direct illumination of and continuous revelation from the Spirit).

*2.4. Gospel.* The character of the gospel,* it is alleged, is changed by these new features. Christian doctrine is objectified and so thereby a church of *beati possidentes* ("happy possessors"), who rejoice in their "orthodoxy," replaced the earlier Christian charismatic groups, in which the sense of living in the fresh dawn of the fulfillment in the new age is strong (e.g., 1 Cor 10:11: 2 Cor 5:17). The gospel is construed as a "new law" (*lex nova*) to be obeyed. There is a growing distinction between clergy and laity (as in *1 Clement*), and tendencies to sacramentalism appear (evidenced by Ignatius). The unity of the church becomes itself an article of belief, a conviction that some find present in the Pauline letter to the Ephesians* (Eph 4:5).

### 3. Circumstances.

What brought about this transmutation of earlier NT Christianity? E. Käsemann answers this in one phrase:

the deferment of the parousia (Käsemann 1969, 236-37). He writes, "Early catholicism means that transition from earliest Christianity to the so-called ancient Church, which is completed with the disappearance of the imminent expectation" of Christ's coming. The promise of an imminent second coming of Christ and of a cataclysmic end to the age failed to materialize, with two consequences (*see* Eschatology). First, the prospect of "church history," which pledges the church to an indefinite period of time on the earth, meant a loss of the existential dimension of the gospel; and a "formal principle" (*sola scriptura*) was accepted in place of a "material principle" (justification* by faith) in the debate over canonicity. In other words, the issue turned on which books were treated as authoritative, but not by the presence or absence of teaching on God's justification of the ungodly. Rather, the period of "saving history" in the "middle of time" is seen to be closed, and with it the boundaries of canonical authority. Hence the original title of Conzelmann's study, *Die Mitte der Zeit* (ET *The Theology of St. Luke*). Luke, as the "theologian of salvation history" and "the first Christian historian," is held responsible for this slide from the primitive Christian apocalyptic understanding of the church's role, associated with Paul.

Second, Käsemann's criterion "by grace alone, by faith alone," enshrined in the teaching of the "justification of sinners," attributed less significance to the catholic elements in the NT and thereby reduced them to a lower level of importance so that the Pauline evangelical substance, seen in Romans* and Galatians,* might shine in clearer light. In that sense early catholicism marks a departure from the apostolic faith, viewed as the essential Pauline gospel of justification and righteousness* by faith.

### 4. Evaluation.

A number of critical remarks may be offered on this enterprise of finding "early catholic" elements in the NT, and in those of Paul's writings regarded as deutero-Pauline in particular.

We may first inquire whether this analysis of the texts in the Pauline corpus is factually correct. Is it true that the Pastorals and Ephesians (and 2 Peter) contain no reference to the apostolic gospel? We may freely grant that the formulation of the *kerygma* (*see* Preaching, Kerygma) has changed in these parts of the NT. This shift in formal expression, vocabulary and mode of statement is indeed related to new situations in the later Pauline or even post-Pauline period. But this does not entail a change in substance, as can be seen from the studies which have shown the essential one-

ness of the apostolic and post-Pauline *kerygma*, which is centered in Jesus Christ crucified and risen as the ground of salvation. The inroad of false teaching, reflected in such documents as the Pastorals and Ephesians, led the Pauline writers to express Paul's teaching in a new way; but it is Paul's mind they are seeking to express, not some inferior substitute passed off as Paul's, with an intention to deceive the readers (*see* Canon).

J. W. Drane argued that the "distinction between the 'early catholic' church and the 'apostolic' church is not so marked as is often supposed" (Drane, 165-78). Käsemann (1969 and especially 1964) has insisted, on the basis of verses like 2 Peter 1:4, that there is "a relapse of Christianity into Hellenistic dualism," in which the world is evil *per se* and communion with God confers a divine nature on believers. Yet it is likely that the distinctions made by the writer here are moral and eschatological, not metaphysically dualistic; and the author of 2 Peter, a devoted follower of Paul, may be using the opponents' own terms (see Martin 1994).

It may be remarked in general that setting up a criterion and judging all else by a failure to approximate to it brings about an ever-present danger of subjectivism. Hence H. Diem has charged that Käsemann has transformed the gospel from an event to a doctrine. Diem argued that because it is an event of history it must go through transformations relative to new situations and contingencies (Diem, 229-34), a feature elaborated in J. C. Beker's works. A final allegation is that pressed home by J. H. Elliott and I. H. Marshall. They charge that Käsemann fails to see the totality of the gospel, which includes those parts of Scripture for which he has little use. For Elliott "evangelical" can be too narrowly defined and he opts for a larger content which will embrace the so-called "catholic" elements in such matters as church order and discipline. In Marshall's critique the so-called "catholic" elements detected by Käsemann form "essential constituent element(s) of the Gospel" (Marshall, 230-31).

Similarly, Hans Küng pleads for the necessity of both evangelical concentration and catholic comprehensiveness, while conceding that we must give prior place to the "original testimonies" (the Gospels and Paul) over the derived witnesses (e.g., Eph; 2 Peter). Käsemann, he says, is "more biblical than the Bible, more New Testament-minded than the New Testament, more evangelical than the Gospel, more Pauline than Paul" (Küng, 268).

*See also* AUTHORITY; CANON; CHURCH ORDER AND GOVERNMENT; COLOSSIANS, LETTER TO THE; EPHESIANS, LETTER

TO THE; GOSPEL; PASTORAL LETTERS; PAUL IN EARLY CHURCH TRADITION; PREACHING, KERYGMA; THESSALONIANS, LETTERS TO THE.

BIBLIOGRAPHY. J. C. Beker, *Paul the Apostle* (Philadelphia: Fortress, 1984); idem, *The Triumph of God* (Minneapolis: Fortress, 1990); idem, *Heirs of Paul* (Minneapolis: Fortress, 1991); H. Conzelmann, *The Theology of St. Luke* (New York: Harper & Row,1960); H. Diem, *Dogmatics* (Edinburgh: Oliver & Boyd, 1959) 229-34; J. W. Drane, "Tradition, Law and Ethics in Pauline Theology," *NovT* 16 (1974) 165-78; J. H. Elliott, "A Catholic Gospel: Reflection on 'Early Catholicism' in the New Testament," *CBQ* 31 (1969) 213-23; E. Käsemann, "Paul and Early Catholicism," in *New Testament Questions of Today* (Philadelphia: Fortress, 1969) 236-51; idem, "An Apologia for Primitive Christian Eschatology" in *Essays on New Testament Themes* (Philadelphia: Fortress, 1964) 169-95; H. Küng, *The Living Church* (New York: Sheed & Ward, 1963) 268-70; idem, *Structures of the Church* (Notre Dame, IN: University of Notre Dame, 1964) 135-54; I. H. Marshall, " 'Early Catholicism' in the New Testament" in *New Dimensions in New Testament Study*, ed. R. N. Longenecker and M. C. Tenney (Grand Rapids: Zondervan, 1974); R. P. Martin, *The Theology of Jude, 1-2 Peter* (NTT; Cambridge: University Press, 1994); L. Morris, "Luke and Early Catholicism," *WJT* 35 (1973) 121-36; K. H. Neufeld, " 'Frühkatholizismus'—Idee und Begriff," *ZKT* 94 (1972) 1-28; J. Reumann, *Variety and Unity in New Testament Thought* (New York: Oxford University Press, 1991); Ph. Vielhauer, "On the 'Paulinism' of Acts," in *Studies in Luke-Acts: Festschrift in honor of Paul Schubert*, ed. L. E. Keck and J. L. Martyn (New York: Abingdon, 1966) 33-50. R. P. Martin

**EARLY CHURCH TRADITION.** *See* PAUL IN EARLY CHURCH TRADITION.

**EBIONITES.** *See* PAUL IN EARLY CHURCH TRADITION.

**ECSTATIC EXPERIENCE.** *See* VISIONS, ECSTATIC EXPERIENCE.

**EDUCATION OF PAUL.** *See* JEW, PAUL THE; PHILOSOPHY; RHETORIC.

**ELDERS.** *See* CHURCH ORDER AND GOVERNMENT.

## ELECTION AND PREDESTINATION

The closely related ideas of election and predestination are crucial elements in the theological structure of Paul's thinking. If he nowhere develops them as themes, nor even frequently uses the words, that was because they were part of the very fabric of his thinking. When they do occur they are buried deeply within highly complex theological arguments, as indisputable theological givens, connected with other such fundamental ideas (e.g., call,* purpose, will, counsel). In Paul these terms are used primarily as redemptive ideas, but there is evidence that they extended beyond that.

1. The Electing God and His Purposes
2. The Election of God
3. The Predestination of God
4. A Summary Statement of Election and Predestination
5. Final Considerations Concerning Election and Predestination

### 1. The Electing God and His Purposes.

In order to understand Paul's doctrine of election and predestination one must begin with the doctrine of God,* because it is God who elects, who calls, who purposes and who predestinates. God, and for Paul that term must be understood as embracing Father, Son and Spirit, is the center of his thinking, not as an abstract idea reached after long theorizing, but the Supreme Reality in the universe. Everything that Paul says relates to his idea and experience of God. Yet Paul's theology was not practiced in a vacuum but came to expression in his pastoral dealings with his congregations. They in turn lived in a world influenced by skepticism and uncertainty about life's meaning and the ability of the gods to control evil and answer questions about human destiny (*see* Worship; Religions).

In theory, then, in order to understand election and predestination one would need to understand everything that Paul said about God, because it is God who elected and predestinated. For present purposes, however, only two aspects of the being of God will be considered—those qualities of God that relate directly to him as the one who elects, and those that relate to him as the one who plans or purposes.

*1.1. The Qualities of God Related to Election.* The qualities of God that one finds related to election are his love* (Eph 1:4-5; 1 Thess 1:4), mercy* (Rom 9:16), grace* (Rom 11:5), and wisdom* and knowledge* (Rom 11:33). For Paul it is the God of love and mercy, acting graciously and wisely, who is the electing God. This would be enough to silence anyone who might imagine that God was arbitrary and chose without any rationale at all, but Paul takes it one step further.

*1.2. The Plan of the Electing God.* God's election is part of an overall plan or purpose. This means there is nothing at all arbitrary about election. God has a purpose that was worked out in accordance with his love, mercy and grace, that was wise beyond imagination, and that is to be accomplished by means of election and predestination. Election and predestination are not ends in themselves but means to an end, practical ways of accomplishing God's will. So the merciful and loving God worked out a gracious plan from within the depths of himself, based on his eternal wisdom, that he effects in time by means of election and predestination.

*1.3. The Plan of God and Redemption.* Paul nowhere develops the full extent of what he means by the purpose or plan of God, but no doubt it covered the whole of God's dealings with the created order. Paul does, however, develop its redemptive aspect. God works everything according to the counsel of his own will, and his will or purpose is redemptive. Consequently, according to that purpose, he calls (Rom 8:28), he works everything together for good for those whom he has called (Rom 8:28), he predestinates those who are in Christ* (Eph 1:11; *see* "In Christ"), he elects (Rom 9:11) and he makes known his manifold wisdom through the church (Eph 3:11). This purpose of God is inscrutable, for "who has known the mind of the Lord?" (1 Cor 2:16; Rom 11:33-35, quoting Is 40:13 LXX), and, though God's ways and doings are past finding out and embody an ultimate mystery,* one is not left wholly in the dark. The Spirit (*see* Holy Spirit) has searched out the deep things of God (1 Cor 2:10-11), just as God has searched out the hearts of all human beings (Rom 8:27) and God has revealed these things to believers by the Spirit (1 Cor 2:10, 12). Christ also knows the mind of God and believers have the mind of Christ (1 Cor 2:16). So, although the mind, will and purpose of God are eternal, divine mysteries, it was God's purpose to make this known in all its manifold wisdom, to the extent that it can be known, through the church, which is the body of Christ (Eph 3:11; *see* Body of Christ).

## 2. The Election of God.

*2.1. The Vocabulary of Election.* Three cognate terms are used by Paul when he speaks of election: the verb *eklegomai*, the noun *eklogē* and the adjective *eklektos*. Paul uses the verb *eklegomai* four times (1 Cor 1:27 [2], 28; Eph 1:4). It is found frequently in classical Greek with the basic meaning in the active voice of "to pick" or "single out" (Xenophon *Hist. Gr.* 1.6.19; Plato *Rep.* 535a; *Leg.* 811a).

In the middle or passive voice it means "to pick out for oneself" or "choose" and is found less frequently in this voice in classical Greek (Plato *Alc.* 1.121e), but almost exclusively so in the LXX. It is only found in the middle or passive in the NT.

Paul uses the noun *eklogē* five times (Rom 9:11; 11:5, 7, 28; 1 Thess 1:4; elsewhere in NT, only in Acts 9:15; 2 Pet 1:10). The basic meaning of *eklogē* is "choice" or "selection," and in secular Greek this word has many shades of meaning, including "balancing an account" (*Pap. Ryl.* II.157.6) and "quotation from a book" (Antig. *Mir.* 15).

The adjective *eklektos* is used by Paul six times (Rom 8:33; 16:33; Col 3:12; 1 Tim 5:21; 2 Tim 2:10; Tit 1:1). It means basically "picked out" or "selected" (Plato *Leg.* 938.5; Thucydides *Hist.* 6.100), but can also mean "choice," "excellent" or "pure" (LXX Ex 30:23; Asclepius *Ap. Aet.* 9.12).

Paul uses these various words in three different ways which must now be considered: the election of angels,* the election of persons and the election of Israel.*

*2.2. The Election of Angels.* In 1 Timothy 5:4 we read of the elect angels. Nothing more is said of this, so the exact meaning is difficult to determine. It could reflect the idea that some angels defected from God, while some (i.e., the elect) did not. Or it could mean that some angels are "choice," that is, superior to the other angels in some indefinable way.

*2.3. The Election of Persons.* Paul speaks of the election of persons, whether of groups of individuals, no doubt synonymous with the church* (Rom 8:33; Eph 1:4; Col 3:12; 1 Thess 1:4; 2 Tim 2:10; Tit 1:1), or of a single individual (Rufus, Rom 16:13). There are two passages where Paul elaborates this idea: Romans 8:28-39 and Ephesians 1:3-5.

*2.3.1. Romans 8:28-39.* Here Paul is addressing the question of God's faithfulness. Seventeen hostile and destructive things are listed and none of them (nor all of them together) can separate the elect (Rom 8:33; "the called" Rom 8:28) from the love of Christ (Rom 8:35; "the love of God in Christ" Rom 8:39). The reason for this is that no one can bring any charge against those whom God has chosen, because it is God who has justified them (Rom 8:34), and if God has justified them and is for them, who can be against them (Rom 8:31)? The complex theological reasoning that lies behind this is compressed into an almost oversimplified list in Romans 8:29-30. Those who were foreknown were predestined to be made like Christ. In order to ensure that this would take place, they were called, justified (*see* Justification) and glorified (*see* Glory, Glorification). Although their glorification is future, because it is "in Christ" and Christ is already glorified, Paul could speak of their having been glorified as a certainty. Because of this no one can charge God's elect with guilt. They are already glorified in Christ, even if that glorification, considered historically, lies in the future as the hope of salvation.* For those in Christ it is an accomplished fact.

*2.3.2. Ephesians 1:3-5.* Here the idea of election is qualified in four ways. It is described as being (1) "in Christ,"* (2) supratemporal ("before the foundation of the world"), (3) redemptive and moral ("to make us holy and blameless before him") and (4) an act of love. The idea of predestination enters in Ephesians 1:5 and appears to be synonymous with the election mentioned in the preceding verse. The goal of predestination is adoption* into God's family.

In the eyes of the world* the thought that God would choose such inconsequential people, as were the early believers, made the idea preposterous. But, according to Paul, God has indeed elected the foolish things of the world, the weak things of the world, the lowly things of the world, the despised things, the things that are not, to confound the wisdom, strength and facticity of those things that are (1 Cor 1:27-28). God's purpose in doing this is that he would be acknowledged as God and that any boasting would be a boast in him (1 Cor 1:29-31). Here election is seen as a purposeful act of God directed to the moral end of keeping his readers' pride in check. The Corinthians are summoned to examine their calling: not many wise, powerful or well-born were among them, primarily because the means God chose to effect his calling and election, namely, the preaching of the cross,* was despised and rejected by the world (1 Cor 1:18-21). To those who believe (1 Cor 1:21), who are the called (1 Cor 1:24), who in humility acknowledge Christ as Lord,* Christ becomes wisdom,* righteousness,* sanctification and redemption* (1 Cor 1:30)—the very power* and wisdom of God (1 Cor 1:24). It is possible that these verses refer more generally to the preaching of the gospel,* which seems weak (*see* Weakness) and foolish to the world, than to the individuals who believed, in which case there would be another category of Pauline usage for election. That category would be "The election (choice) of the preached message by God to offer salvation to the world."

Putting all this together, election for Paul means that God, as an act of his love, has eternally chosen a group of individuals in Christ to be holy and without blame. This has brought about their adoption* into God's family according to a predetermined plan that included their calling, justification and glorification. Because it is God who has effectuated this plan, with justification the apparent key to understanding it, no one is able to bring any ultimately damaging charge against believers, and nothing or no one is able to drive a wedge between them and the God of love who

set the plan in motion and will surely bring it to completion.

*2.4. The Election of Israel.* Paul speaks specifically of the election of Israel* in Romans 9:11; 11:5, 7, 28. In Romans 9—11 Paul is struggling with the question of Israel's place in God's plan. He knew very well the teaching of the OT regarding God's choosing of Israel and that this covered their entire existence. God chose Israel to make them his treasured possession (Deut 7:6; 14:2). He chose who should be priests among them (Deut 18:5; 21:5), who should be king (1 Sam 17:7-13; 2 Sam 21:6; 1 Kings 8:16) and the city where they should dwell (1 Kings 14:21; 2 Chron 6:6). They were, in fact, his chosen ones (Ps 105:6, 43). So there is nothing new in Paul's speaking of the election of Israel.

What is new is Paul's probing the purpose of God in the election of Israel and locating the essence of God's purpose in his mercy (Rom 9:16), and as independent of Israel's works (Rom 9:11). From this, Paul can move to the larger idea that the Gentiles* were included from the beginning and that Israel was only Israel when it fulfilled God's ultimate purpose (already hinted in Is 56:1-8). So God's promise to Israel was to all who qualified as Israel, which included the Gentiles. Nevertheless, in Paul's day there was still an Israel—a remnant chosen by grace (Rom 11:5)—that experienced the favor of God. But the whole complex history of Israel is a mystery that would only be unraveled in the future when "all Israel will be saved" (Rom 11:26). The gifts and calling of God are irrevocable and Israel is beloved by God because of "the fathers" (i.e., the patriarchs, Rom 11:28-29).

The essence of Paul's difficulty is that he wants to say Israel's election ensured that it would forever stand, and yet it was now being set aside. He solves this by finding a deeper meaning to election in the purpose of God, by finding Israel within Israel, by pointing to himself as a saved Israelite, and by postulating Israel's future redemption. (For an interesting discussion of Israel's unbelief, see Volf, 161-95. For a revisioning of Paul's theology under the thesis that by his christology and pneumatology Paul has redefined the Jewish doctrine of election, see Wright.)

### 3. The Predestination of God.

*3.1. The Vocabulary of Predestination.* Paul uses the verb *proorizō* five times (Rom 8:29, 30; 1 Cor 2:7; Eph 1:5, 11) with the basic meaning of "determine beforehand" or "predetermine." It is not found in the LXX, and in secular Greek it is rare (if existent) before the Common Era. *Proginōskō* also has strong predestinarian overtones and is used by Paul in Romans 8:29 and

11:2. It has been suggested by some that *proorizō* and *proginōskō* are virtually synonymous terms (see Volf, 9; *see* Foreknowledge).

*3.2. The Hidden Wisdom of God Predestined.* In 1 Corinthians 2:7 Paul speaks of a secret, hidden wisdom* that has been predestined for the believers' glory. This wisdom is the entire plan of salvation that was unknown to the demonic* forces of this world, who, if they had known about it, would have attempted to thwart it (1 Cor 2:8; *see* Principalities and Powers). It was God's eternal purpose (eternal, because God is eternal) to effect salvation through the death* of Christ. It was divinely wise because the death of Christ satisfied God's love and justice at the same time, broke the power of evil, transferred believers into God's kingdom* and ultimately saves them. It was God's determination that this be so.

*3.3. Persons Predestined to be Like Christ.* In a related way Paul speaks of God's predestining persons to be conformed to the image of Christ (Rom 8:29) and adopted into the family of God (Eph 1:5). This was done in accord with the counsel of his will (Eph 1:11), and "in" (Eph 1:11) or "through" (Eph 1:5) Christ. In Ephesians 1:4 Paul parallels this divine ordination with election and defines it as being "before the foundation of the world." In Romans 8:29 the act of predestination appears to follow upon that of foreknowing, with calling consequent upon predestining. In Ephesians 1:11 foreknowledge is not mentioned, but calling follows predestination and is in accord with the counsel of God's will (the "good pleasure of his will," Eph 1:5).

### 4. A Summary Statement of Election and Predestination.

In summary, Paul teaches that in all of God's dealings with the created order he works according to a predetermined plan, as eternal as himself (but not apart from himself or Christ—the elect one par excellence), in such a way that his own inner being and divine good will are satisfied. That plan has a definite goal: to sum up all things in Christ (Eph 1:10). This encompasses objects, means and ends. The objects include angels, human beings and Israel; the means include the person and work of Christ, and the proclamation of the gospel; the ends are wholly redemptive whether for Israel or for believers (and presumably for the angels, whatever that may mean). The ultimate end is the praise of God's glorious grace (Eph 1:5, 11). With respect to human beings, it is important to emphasize that Paul speaks of the election and salvation of sinners (Rom 5:6, 8), that is, he joins means and end. The good news of the gospel is that humans do not

need to work their way into God's favor (indeed, they cannot). Rather, God's grace is given freely (Rom 3:24). This excludes human boasting and results in the eternal praise of God's goodness.

### 5. Final Considerations Concerning Election and Predestination.

Paul was aware that the doctrines of election and predestination had some problematic elements in them and, although he never dealt with them in any systematic fashion, in the course of his letters he did touch upon the two most prominent difficulties: fairness on God's part and human responsibility, or freedom.*

*5.1. The Problem of God's Fairness.* For Paul it is axiomatic that God is fair and would never do anything that shows partiality (Rom 2:11; Eph 6:9; Col 3:25). Consequently, election does not mean that some people cannot come to God for salvation, nor that those who are elected are singled out on the basis of any virtue they possess. In fact, the underlying reason Paul develops the doctrine of salvation along these lines is precisely to exclude any boasting or the imagination that election was based on works (*see* Works of the Law) or virtue. Indeed, God would not have been unfair had he not elected anyone, because all equally deserve God's judgment* due to their sin.* So, if there is apparent unfairness in this doctrine, it is only apparent and not real. In addition, Paul taught that the grace of God that brings salvation has appeared to all people (Tit 2:11), and he certainly would have agreed with Peter, "God is not willing that anyone perish, but that all come to repentance." (2 Pet 3:9). If people are not saved, the blame cannot be laid upon God.

*5.2. The Problem of Human Responsibility.* If a cynical detractor were to ask Paul, "Why does God still blame us? For who resists his will?," Paul can answer in the same sharp way, "Who are you to talk back to God? Shall what is formed say to him who formed it, 'Why did you make me like this?'" (Rom 9:19-21). For those who so misunderstand God as to imagine that God works arbitrarily and on no moral basis whatsoever, let such an answer suffice. But Paul knew very well that election and predestination included human responsibility.

His using Pharaoh as an example is a case in point (Rom 9:16-17). Paul knew that the OT spoke not only of God's hardening Pharaoh's heart (Ex 4:21; 7:3, 4, 13; 9:12, 15-17, 34-35; 10:1, 20, 27; 11:9, 10) but also of Pharaoh hardening his own heart (Ex 8:15, 32; 9:34; 1 Sam 6:6), thus making him responsible for the sins he committed. That God could work his will in and through the acts of humans in such a way that his will was done and yet the human will was not violated, coerced or ignored is fundamental to biblical thinking. (See, e.g., Prov 16:1, 4, 9, 33. This idea is also found in Rabbinic thought, e.g., *Pirqe 'Abot* 3:19, "All is foreseen, and free will is given, and the world is judged by goodness," dating from somewhat after Paul's day.)

Paul stresses the sovereign freedom of God in order to silence proud human rebellion against God, not to make God appear unreasonable and dictatorial. Conceivably, Paul would argue that it is not necessary that we know exactly how God works his will in and through the responsible acts of our will, and Paul nowhere discusses this. It is enough to know that it is the loving and gracious God and Father of the Lord Jesus Christ who calls mortals, sinners that they are, to himself, and that anyone who believes can be assured of salvation. Salvation does not depend on any merit humans might possess but on the electing grace of God that chose believers in Christ before the foundation of the world.

*See also* APOSTASY, FALLING AWAY, PERSEVERANCE; CALL, CALLING; FOREKNOWLEDGE, DIVINE; FUTILITY; GOD; ISRAEL.

BIBLIOGRAPHY. D. A. Carson, *Divine Sovereignty and Human Responsibility* (Atlanta: John Knox, 1980); L. Coenen, "Elect, Choose," *NIDNTT* 1.533-43; C. E. B. Cranfield, *Commentary on Romans* (2 vols.; ICC; Edinburgh: T. & T. Clark, 1975, 1979); F. Davidson, *Pauline Predestination* (London: Tyndale, 1946); J. D. G. Dunn, *Romans* (2 vols.; WBC 38; Dallas: Word, 1988); J. Eckert, "ἐκλέγομαι," *EDNT* 1.416-17; idem, "ἐκλεκτός," *EDNT* 1.417-19; K. Grayston, "The Doctrine of Election in Rom 8:28-30," *SE* 2 (1964) 574-83; A. T. Lincoln, *Ephesians* (WBC 42; Dallas: Word, 1990); H. H. Rowley, *The Biblical Doctrine of Election* (1950); K. L. Schmidt, "προορίζω," *TDNT* V.456; G. Schrenk and G. Quell, "ἐκλέγομαι," *TDNT* IV.144-92; N. Turner, *Christian Words* (Nashville: Nelson, 1981) 127-34; J. M. Gundry Volf, *Paul and Perseverance* (Louisville: Westminster/ John Knox, 1991); N. T. Wright, *The Climax of the Covenant* (Minneapolis: Fortress, 1992).

W. A. Elwell

# ELEMENTS/ELEMENTAL SPIRITS OF THE WORLD

The meaning or meanings Paul attached to *ta stoicheia* (*tou kosmou*) in the four instances in which he used it (Gal 4:3, 9; Col 2:8, 20; cf. Heb 5:12; 2 Pet 3:10, 12) has been a matter of exegetical debate. Interpreters have usually understood Paul's usage to fall into one of the following semantic fields: (1) basic principles of religious teaching such as the Law*; (2) essential, rudimentary substances of the universe such as earth, water,

air and fire; or (3) personal spiritual beings of the cosmos such as demons,* angels* or star deities. Studies of the usage of *stoicheia* in Greek writings outside the NT have provided evidence for these and other specific usages of the word, though the clear extrabiblical evidence for usage (3) cannot be found in texts dated prior to the second century A.D. In the final analysis, however, exegetical decisions regarding the meaning of *stoicheia* in Pauline texts must take into account particular usage and context. But interpreters of Paul, even though agreeing on this principle, have not arrived at a consensus.

1. Terminology and Contexts
2. The Elements as Basic Principles
3. The Elements as Essential Components of the Universe
4. The Elements as Spiritual Powers

## 1. Terminology and Contexts.

In three of the four Pauline usages *stoicheia* (always in the plural in Paul) is qualified by the genitive *tou kosmou*, "of the world," and the fourth usage (Gal 4:9), where *stoicheia* is not so qualified, seems by its proximity to Galatians 4:3 to be nothing more than an abbreviated reference to *ta stoicheia tou kosmou*. Thus interpreters of Paul must focus on *ta stoicheia tou kosmou* as a linguistic unit.

This characteristic Pauline usage may be usefully contrasted with the three other usages of *stoicheia* in the NT. In Hebrews 5:12 the author speaks of *ta stoicheia tēs archēs tōn logiōn tou theou*, "the basic principles about the elementary aspects of God's message," clearly referring to the basic, rudimentary teachings of the faith. In 2 Peter 3:10, 12, in the context of speaking of the Day of the Lord, it is said that the created order, with its "elements" (*stoicheia*), will be consumed with fire. Here the reference is clearly the natural substances of which the world is made.

Certain other features of Pauline usage should be noted. In Colossians 2:8-10 Paul refers to a false teaching which is according to *ta stoicheia tou kosmou* rather than according to Christ,* who is the head of every principality and power. The proximity of *ta stoicheia tou kosmou* to "principalities and powers"* has led some interpreters to correlate the two categories. Later Paul speaks of the Colossians as having died with Christ "from [*apo*] the *stoicheia tou kosmou*" (Col 2:20), who are implied to be associated with encumbering and ineffective religious rules and regulations. The allusion to spiritual disciplines associated with the "worship of angels" in Colossians 2:18 has led some interpreters to see again a parallel between *ta stoicheia tou kosmou* and angelic powers.

In Galatians *ta stoicheia tou kosmou* is used first to refer to an aspect of religious experience prior to Christ (Gal 4:3) in which people were subjected to slavery and a status as minors, a situation parallel to the Jewish experience under the Law which Paul has just described (cf. Gal 3:23-25). A few verses later Paul refers to the Galatian Gentiles' religious past when they did not know God,* likening it to an enslavement to the "weak and beggarly" *stoicheia* (Gal 4:9). This field of power to which they were formerly subject is set in parallel relationships with what Paul calls "those who by nature are not gods" (Gal 4:8). A parallel may thus be observed between Colossians 2:8, 20 and Galatians 4:8-10. In each case the *stoicheia* are closely associated with religious rules and regulations and in both letters the context is polemical.

The Greek noun *stoicheion* is related to *stoichos*, a term we know to have been employed in military contexts in reference to a "row" or "series." In that context *stoicheion* referred to that which is found in a row or series. But the word came to be applied in many contexts and could refer to the letters making up a word, whether silent or vocal; the basic components of language (letters, syllables, words) and music (notes); the basic rudiments of a subject (what contemporary English speakers would refer to as the ABC's); the basic components, or "elements," of the physical world as understood by ancient philosophers (earth, air, water, fire; cf. Plato *Theaet* 201e; Diogenes Laertius 7.136, 137; 2 Macc 12:13; Wis 7:17); the stars of the heavens, which are composed of the chief and purest element, fire; the stars as visible gods who, by some accounts, influenced events and the fate of men and women (*Ps-Calisthenes* 1.12.1); and celestial demons or spirits inimical to humankind (*T. Sol.* 8:2). (For discussion of these various meanings and references see Delling.)

## 2. The Elements as Basic Principles.

Could Paul be referring to a basic set of philosophical or religious principles which pressed their claim upon individuals prior to and apart from Christ, and which still threaten to supplant Christ? This approach has had its proponents, including E. D. Burton, C. F. D. Moule and A. J. Bandstra. Moule, while finding a reference to demonic powers "natural" in the context of Colossians 2:8, is led by "the absence of data outside the N.T. for any such sense of στοιχεῖα until later times" to define it as "simply 'elementary teaching'— teaching by Judaistic or pagan ritualists, a 'materialistic' teaching bound up with 'this world' alone, and contrary to the freedom of the Spirit" (Moule, 92). R. N. Longenecker, commenting on *stoicheia* in Gala-

tians 4:3, 9, finds " 'basic principles' of religion" to be the most satisfactory interpretation in the context of Galatians,* which in the case of Judaism is "the Mosaic Law in its condemnatory and supervisory functions" and for the Galatians was the pagan "veneration of nature and cultic rituals" (Longenecker, 166). Furthermore, he would distinguish this usage from that found in Colossians 2:8, 20. Bandstra has understood the *stoicheia* as "law" and "flesh" (unregenerate human nature), "two fundamental cosmical forces" which held men and women, whether Jew or Gentile, in their thrall and from which deliverance is available in Christ alone (Bandstra, 70). The *kosmos* in this case is "that whole sphere of human activity which stands over against Christ and His salvation" (Bandstra, 57).

But many interpreters have been struck with the fact that when Paul speaks of *ta stoicheia tou kosmou* in both Galatians and Colossians, they appear in a linguistic context in which they are associated with references to personal spiritual forces (angels, principalities and powers, gods who are not gods) and, in Colossians 2:8, set in contrast with Christ. Moreover, the selection of "law" and "flesh" as referents raises questions, for in Paul's vocabulary "sin" and "death" also appear as archetypal powers which determine the plight of humans outside of Christ. And when Paul speaks of believers "dying to/from" something, he can speak not only of the Law (Gal 2:19; cf. Rom 7:2, 4, 6) and flesh (implied in Col 2:11-14), but of dying to sin (as a power, Rom 6:2, 6-7) and to the world (Gal 6:14). Should the lack of evidence that Paul's contemporaries used *stoicheia* to refer to demonic powers discredit the possibility that Paul used *stoicheia* in such a manner? This issue needs to be re-assessed (see 4 below).

## 3. The Elements as Essential Components of the Universe.

E. Schweizer is the most notable proponent of the view that Paul, like some of his contemporaries, used *stoicheia tou kosmou* to refer to the elements earth, water, air and fire. Schweizer argues that Pythagorean ideas informed the situation at both Colossae and Galatia (*see* Philosophy). He demonstrates from a number of texts how "from Heraclitus in the sixth century B.C. up to the sixth century A.D., 'the mighty strife among the members' of the world (Aristotle *Metaphysics* 11.4 [1000ab]) dominates the Greek understanding of the cosmos" (Schweizer 1988, 456). In other words, the four elements, which were originally in equilibrium, were considered to be in "strife," and their imbalance threatened to bring either deluge or conflagration upon the cosmos. Even the Hellenistic

Jewish philosopher Philo interpreted the Jewish new year festival as a thank offering to God the peace-keeper (Philo *Spec. Leg.* 2.190-92) and could view the high priest (Philo *Vit. Mos.* 2.121, 125, 133) as playing a role in guaranteeing cosmic harmony.

With this background as well as the evidence from Colossians and Galatians, Schweizer suggests a religious milieu in which individuals regarded themselves as living in a world of futility,* bound to this world by the elements which prevented their ascent to heaven.* At Colossae* a syncretistic notion prevailed that one could escape the cosmos by means of ascetic practices that would free the soul from earthly entanglements. Moreover, by worshiping angels (as their pagan neighbors worshiped heroes and demons) they were propitiating the powers who ruled the elements and who could thus assure humans their escape through the lower spheres beneath the moon to reach heaven above. It is against this background that the author of Colossians maintains that Christ is the one through whom believers may "die out from under the elements of the world" and so find deliverance.

Schweizer admits more difficulty in bringing this interpretation to bear upon Galatians, but suggests that the adherence to "days and months and seasons and years" (Gal 4:10; *see* Holy Days) may be related to a Pythagorean notion that insight into the cosmic order (in this case the divisions of time) would purify the soul. The "ones that are by nature not gods" (Gal 4:8) might then refer to savior heroes of the Galatians' pagan past who were ineffective in providing deliverance. The "elements of the world" were not worshiped but feared; they were not deities or spirits, but earth, water, air and fire. The means of deliverance was asceticism, insight and worship of angels or "gods."

Schweizer's proposal explains Colossians better than it does Galatians, where his solution does not engage Paul's evident concern about the Law and his apparent implication that the Jews too were enslaved to the *stoicheia tou kosmou* (Gal 4:3). Moreover, in order to maintain Schweizer's view, one must be persuaded that the false teaching Paul opposed at Colossae—and at Galatia—bore further characteristics of Hellenistic philosophy (Pythagoreanism) in syncretistic relationship with Jewish ideas. Such a scenario has been suggested, but other factors need to be considered in determining the nature of the religious notions Paul was opposing.

### 4. The Elements as Spiritual Powers.

A number of interpreters, perhaps even a majority, have concluded that *ta stoicheia tou kosmou* refers to spiritual powers of some sort. The options, broadly defined, range from star deities, to demons, to angels of the nations or local tribal and national deities.

### 4.1. Star Deities and Demonic Powers.

The notion that stars and constellations in some sense control the cosmos and human destiny has an ancient lineage, traceable at least as far back as the celestial divination of Old Babylon in the second millennium B.C. (see Rochberg-Halton). In time the stars were associated with spiritual powers and then identified as spiritual powers themselves (*see* Worship). Plato could speak mythically of the deity of the stars, even calling them "visible gods" (Plato *Tim.* 40a, 40c, 40d, 41a; cf. the mythic language of Judg 5:20). Diogenes Laertius (third century A.D.) testifies to the Pythagorean notion that the sun, moon and stars are gods because they possess the element of warmth, an essential characteristic of life (Diogenes Laertius 8.28), and he can call the twelve signs of the zodiac *ta dōdeka stoicheia*, "the twelve *stoicheia*" (Diogenes Laertius 6.102; cf. PGM 39.18-21).

From Second Temple Judaism there comes ample evidence of speculation about the universe and how the heavenly bodies were related to angels. The Book of the Heavenly Luminaries in *1 Enoch* 72—82, a work dating from perhaps the first century B.C., testifies to Jewish astrological ideas and the association of an angel, Uriel, with the stars. This is set within a context in which particular attention is paid to times and seasons (for further texts relating angelic powers with natural elements, including the stars, cf. *1 Enoch* 43:1-2; 60:11-12; 80:6; *Jub.* 2:2). Stephen, in Acts 7:42-43, points to Israel's worship of the "heavenly hosts" (*stratia tou ouranou*) as evidence of Israel's disobedience in rejecting God's Law, and appeals to Amos 5:25-27 where idolatry and star worship resulted in Israel's exile. It is of some significance that Josephus could say that the woven veil separating the "holy place" from the outer vestibule of the Herodian Temple was "a kind of image of the universe." Its four colors symbolized fire, earth, air and sea, and embroidered upon it was "a panorama of the heavens," excepting "the signs of the zodiac." The latter, however, were represented by the twelve loaves upon the table while the seven lamps represented the seven planets (Josephus *J.W.* 5.5.4-5 §§212-18). Thus even at the heart of the Jerusalem Temple cultus there were symbols which suggest a necessity of penetrating the heavens in order to reach the throne of God in the Holy of Holies.

The earliest extant extrabiblical Jewish evidence for the word *stoicheia* being associated with both spirits and stars is later than the first century (second and third centuries A.D.), but it is well attested and may very well represent beliefs contemporaneous with Paul (cf. Lohse, 99 n.41). The *Testament of Solomon*, a Jewish-Christian work usually dated to the third century A.D., but possibly containing material dating to the first century, testifies to a belief in star spirits called *stoicheia*. Seven bound spirits appear before Solomon and reveal their identity: "We are the *stoicheia*, rulers of this world of darkness [*kosmokratores tou skotous*, cf. Eph 6:12] . . . our stars in heaven look small, but we are named like gods" (*T. Sol.* 8:2-4).

Thus it is not difficult to imagine a belief system, particularly at Colossae, in which Jewish and Hellenistic ideas would have been intermingled and celestial powers associated with angels, who were revered as controlling the fate of humans. These cosmic powers, which Paul may have called *stoicheia tou kosmou*, needed placating if humans were ever to escape their bondage to fate. Thus when Paul refers to a "forced piety" (Col 2:23 NEB, *ethelothrēskia*) characterized by calendrical observances, ascetic practices aimed at visionary experience and the "worship of angels," he may have had in mind a form of religion that venerated the *stoicheia* either as star deities or as astral bodies in close association with angelic cosmic powers. Paul's proclamation of Christ's triumph* over the principalities and powers (Col 2:15) and his assertion that "all the fullness*" resides in Christ (Col 1:19; 2:9)—rather than in the cosmic forces—may thus be seen as a frontal attack on such theosophical religious notions which may have been an incipient form of gnosticism* (cf. Martin, 90-96). It is interesting to observe that a text from Alexander Polyhistor, of the first century A.D. (see trans. in Schweizer 1988, 458), attests to several Pythagorean practices that bear similarity to the calendrical observances, abstention from certain foods, and worship of angels alluded to in Colossians 2:16-23.

*4.2. Local, Tribal Deities.* Finally, we may consider the suggestion that *stoicheia tou kosmou* was Paul's particular way of referring to "local presiding deities" or "national 'gods' " who rule over territories and races. N. T. Wright has argued for this meaning in Colossians, understanding Paul to be engaged in a polemic against Judaism rather than some sort of Jewish-Hellenistic syncretism, and he sees the same meaning operative in Galatians (see Wright, 101-2, 115-16). Following and developing this line of interpretation we could understand *ta stoicheia tou kosmou* as a broad, inclusive term that embraced the whole host of spiritual beings known individually as principalities, powers, dominions and rulers, the equivalent to the angels or gods of the nations (*see* Principalities and Powers). In Galatians 4:8 Paul speaks of the Galatians as for-

merly enslaved to "those beings which by nature are no gods." This analysis of the Galatian Gentiles' former situation resonates with the Jewish notion that the gods of the nations are not really what they appear to be; they are but spiritual powers appointed as national guardians by Yahweh, ultimately subservient to him alone, but falsely regarded as "gods" by the nations. Paul employs this notion elsewhere in 1 Corinthians 8:5 and 10:22 (cf. Deut 32:8-9, 17, 21; Ps 82:1, 6-7). Israel, on the other hand, was God's own possession (Deut 32:9), though he could employ angelic intermediaries in his dealings with his people.

Paul, faced with Judaizers at Galatia, would then be likening Jewish religion governed by the Law to paganism; both were characterized by bondage to religious forces that were but local, national, tribal deities. When the Judaizers* insisted on Gentile Christians submitting to the "works of the Law"—namely, circumcision, food laws and Sabbath observance—they were in effect regarding the triumph of Christ as the victory of one national deity over all others (see Dunn, 135). Thus, when Paul refers in Galatians 3:19 to the Law being "ordained through angels," he may be suggesting that the implication of the Judaizers' message (which may have emphasized the glory of the giving of the Law at Sinai with the accompaniment of angels) is that, rather than understanding Israel to be ultimately God's own possession, the means through which he would bring all nations to himself, they in effect placed Israel back under the intermediate superintendence of an angelic power and reduced God's purposes in history to the inclusion of Gentiles as proselytes in an ethnically restrictive religion. This was in effect to deny the new status of Gentiles in Christ, who now know and are known by the one true God* (Gal 4:9; cf. 1 Cor 8:3). God's oneness and universal sovereignty is now reflected in the universal extension of his blessing of salvation* through his Son,* the seed of Abraham,* to form one people who are neither Jew nor Gentile (Gal 3:28). To insist on "works of the Law"* as entry requirements is to return to the previous epoch in salvation history in which nations and ethnic groups were under the superintendence of the "weak and beggarly" *stoicheia tou kosmou*, with Israel's own situation characterized as being under the Law as a restrictive pedagogue (*paidagōgos*, Gal 3:23-25) who kept them from mingling with the nations and falling into idolatry.

This final line of interpretation may emerge as an attractive option for those who are convinced that the "new perspective" (*see* Paul and His Interpreters) has grasped the root of the matter: that Paul's critique of the Law and its "works" focuses on the misguided definition of the people of God as those who adhere to the boundary-defining works of circumcision,* food* laws and Sabbath keeping (*see* Holy Days). As in each of the possible meanings of *ta stoicheia tou kosmou* that we have reviewed, larger interpretive issues come into play and will guide interpreters in deciding what meaning or meanings Paul employed when he used the term.

*See also* ANGELS, ARCHANGELS; COLOSSIANS, LETTER TO THE; GALATIANS, LETTER TO THE; LAW; PRINCIPALITIES AND POWERS.

BIBLIOGRAPHY. C. E. Arnold, *Powers of Darkness: Principalities and Powers in Paul's Letters* (Downers Grove, IL: InterVarsity, 1992); A. J. Bandstra, *The Law and the Elements of the World* (Kampen: Kok, 1964); G. B. Caird, *Paul's Letters from Prison* (Oxford: University Press, 1976); idem, *Principalities and Powers* (Oxford: Clarendon, 1956); G. Delling, "στοιχεῖον," *TDNT* VII.670-83; J. D. G. Dunn, "The Theology of Galatians: The Issue of Covenantal Nomism," in *Pauline Theology*. Volume I: *Thessalonians, Philippians, Galatians, Philemon*, ed. J. M. Bassler (Minneapolis: Fortress, 1991) 125-46; E. Lohse, *Colossians and Philemon* (Herm: Philadelphia: Fortress, 1971) 96-99; R. N. Longenecker, *Galatians* (WBC 41; Dallas: Word, 1990); R. P. Martin, *Ephesians, Colossians, and Philemon* (Int; Louisville: Westminster/John Knox, 1991); C. F. D. Moule, *The Epistles to the Colossians and to Philemon* (CGTC; Cambridge: University Press, 1957); P. T. O'Brien, *Colossians, Philemon* (WBC 44; Waco: Word, 1982) 129-32; B. Reicke, "The Law and this World according to Paul: Some Thoughts concerning Gal 4:1-11," *JBL* 70 (1951) 259-76; E. Schweizer, *The Letter to the Colossians* (Minneapolis: Augsburg, 1982); idem, "Slaves of the Elements and Worshipers of Angels: Gal 4:3, 9 and Col 2:8, 18, 20," *JBL* 107 (1988) 455-68; F. Rochberg-Halton, "Astrology in the Ancient Near East," *ABD* I.504-7; N. T. Wright, *Colossians and Philemon* (TNTC; Grand Rapids: Eerdmans, 1986).                    D. G. Reid

## ELEUSINIAN MYSTERIES. *See* RELIGIONS, GRECO-ROMAN.

## EMPEROR CULT. *See* EMPERORS, ROMAN; LORD; RELIGIONS, GRECO-ROMAN; SAVIOR.

## EMPEROR WORSHIP. *See* EMPERORS, ROMAN; LORD; RELIGIONS, GRECO-ROMAN; SAVIOR.

## EMPERORS, ROMAN

Following the cessation of the monarchy with expulsion of the seventh and last Roman king, the Etruscan Tarquinius Superbus in 510/09 B.C., the Roman Re-public came into being and flourished until it collapsed during the economic, political and military chaos of the late Republic (133-31 B.C.). Julius Caesar emerged as a military dictator, introducing the autocratic rule which was adopted by his imperial successors. His intentions were thwarted by his assassination by a conspiracy of Republican forces in 44 B.C. At the battle of Actium in 31 B.C., Octavian defeated Antony and took control of the political and military affairs of Rome.

The Roman Imperial Period can be subdivided into the period of the Principate (27 B.C. to A.D. 180), based on a civilian conception of the role of the emperor, followed (after a period of chaos) by the reorganization of the empire under Diocletian (A.D. 284-305) and the period of the Dominate (A.D. 284-476), based on a military model. The last Roman emperor was Romulus Augustulus, who was removed from power in A.D. 476, when the center of power was transferred to the Emperor of the East in Constantinople.

1. Imperial Titles
2. The Foundation of the Principate
3. Early Imperial Dynasties
4. The Functions of the Emperor
5. Emperor Worship
6. Christians and Roman Government

### 1. Imperial Titles.

The English word *emperor* is derived from the Latin word *imperator*, meaning "one in charge, one who gives orders," and was a generic title for Roman military commanders which eventually became a title of honor retaining strong military associations (the related term *imperium* refers to the right to give orders, or the official power of higher magistrates or the emperor). Julius Caesar used this designation for himself, as did his adopted son and successor Augustus, though he favored the term *princeps* (meaning "first citizen"). Augustus took the term *imperator* as a *praenomen* (Imperator Caesar), and so did his successors. In 27 B.C. the right of *imperium maius* ("greater imperium") was granted to Augustus for life. Augustus, whose actual name was C. Julius Caesar Octavianus, took over the *cognomen* ("surname") "Caesar" because he was the adopted son of C. Julius Caesar. Later emperors used the name *Caesar* as part of their imperial titles (e.g., Lk 3:1 refers to "Tiberius Caesar"), and the term was widely used as a way of referring to the reigning emperor (Mk 12:14 and par.; Jn 19:12-16; Acts 17:7; 25:8; Phil 4:22). *Augustus* (meaning "venerable") was an honorary title conferred on Octavian by the Senate (he is referred to as "Caesar Augustus" in Lk 2:1) and later was given to his imperial successors. The Greek translation of Augustus was *Sebastos* ("revered, worthy of honor"), and is used of the emperor in Acts 25:21, 25. The Latin term *rex* ("king") was never used of the Roman emperor in the West, though the Greek equivalent, *basileus,* was sometimes used in the eastern part of the empire (1 Pet 2:13, 17; Jn 19:15), though rarely until the second century.

### 2. The Foundation of the Principate.

Augustus created the imperial system in which he retained the latent powers of an autocrat while giving the appearance of a constitutional monarch. In 27 B.C. Augustus resigned his extraordinary powers and began the process of the theoretical restoration of the Republic, all the while retaining firm control of the state. The Senate, which at this time consisted of about 600 former magistrates, was functionally subordinate to Augustus and to his successors. His achievements are catalogued in the autobiographical inscription *Res Gestae Divi Augusti* ("Achievements of the Divine Augustus"; see Brunt and Moore). The basis of the power of the *princeps* was the assumption of tribunician power (*tribunicia potestas*) by Augustus in 23 B.C., which gave him the right to convene the Senate, the right of veto, the right to initiate legislation and inviolability (*sacrosanctitas*). This title, *sacrosanctitas,* had Republican associations and emphasized the non-military nature of his role. He also assumed other important titles such as *pater patriae,* "father of the country") and *pontifex maximus* ("High Priest"), with control over the state religion. This system became inoperative under the reclusive Tiberius (A.D. 14-37), while the incompetent Gaius (A.D. 37-41) became the first truly autocratic emperor installed with the backing of the Praetorian Guard (cf. Phil 1:13).

### 3. Early Imperial Dynasties.

The first century A.D. was dominated by two imperial dynasties, the Julio-Claudian emperors (27 B.C.-A.D. 68) and the Flavian emperors (A.D. 69-96). Two of the first three Julio-Claudian emperors, Augustus (27 B.C.-A.D. 14) and Tiberius (A.D. 14-37) were the adopted sons of their predecessors. Gaius (A.D. 37-41), affectionately nicknamed "Caligula," meaning "little boots," by soldiers when he was a toddler, Claudius (A.D. 41-54) and Nero (A.D. 54-68) were all acclaimed *imperator* by the Praetorian Guard, an action which the Senate was forced to ratify. The Flavian dynasty was founded by the popular general Vespasian (A.D. 69-79), who arranged to be succeeded by his two sons, Titus (A.D. 79-81) and Domitian (A.D.81-96). Between these two dynasties was a year of political and military upheaval during which three different emperors claimed impe-

rial power in a single year (A.D. 69): Galba, Otho and Vitellius. The six Antonines followed, each adopted by his predecessor, with the exception of the last Antonine, Commodus, the natural son of Marcus Aurelius: Nerva (A.D. 96-98), Trajan (A.D. 98-117), Hadrian (A.D. 117-38), Antoninus Pius (A.D.138-61), Marcus Aurelius (A.D.161-80) and Commodus (A.D. 180-92).

### 4. The Functions of the Emperor.

In Rome, the *princeps* was expected to make public appearances at games, theaters and festivals, and (unlike Julius Caesar who used such occasions to read and sign documents) to give the appearance of enjoying such spectacles. During the early empire the primary task of the emperor was to dispense justice through reading and responding to letters and petitions, hearing cases presented orally (Roman citizens like Paul had the right to present their case before the emperor, cf. Acts 25:9-12) and receiving embassies from various cities of the empire (an embassy of Alexandrian Jews to Caligula in A.D. 39/40 is the subject of Philo's *Legatio ad Gaium).* The responses of the emperor were regarded as setting legal precedent.

In discharging this legal task, the emperor was surrounded by friends (*amici*) and advisors (*concilium*) who advised him as he made decisions. There were four types of *constitutiones principium,* or "imperial enactments": (1) *edicta* ("edicts"), announcements of the emperor made to the general public articulating orders or policies; (2) *decreta* ("decrees"), judicial decisions pronounced by the emperor in court; (3) *mandata* ("mandates"), directives from the emperor to officials in the imperial service (an excellent example of which is the correspondence between Pliny and Trajan); and (4) *rescripta* ("rescripts"), imperial correspondence consisting of written replies of the emperor either in a separate letter (*epistulae principium*) or in marginal notes on the original petition (*subscriptiones*).

### 5. Emperor Worship.

The imperial cult had religious as well as political dimensions (*see* Worship). Hellenistic ruler cults, beginning with Alexander the Great, honored living benefactors, primarily dynastic rulers of Hellenistic kingdoms, with *isotheoi timai,* "honors equal to the gods," in other words, temples, sacrifices, priests, festivals and games. Roman emperors were somewhat more reluctant to accept divine honors (particularly Augustus, Tiberius and Claudius) than Hellenistic rulers. In the eastern empire the living emperor occupied an ambiguous position between gods and mortals. Sacrifices were usually made "on behalf of" the emperor, rather than "to" him, and there is almost no evidence that people prayed to the emperor. Imperial cults were particularly popular in the Roman province of Asia, where a temple to Augusta and Roma was dedicated in 29 B.C.

While the imperial cult in the Greek East focused on the living ruler, in the Roman West the emphasis was on the worship of deified deceased emperors. The posthumous deification of Julius Caesar in 42 B.C., in a law accepted in the Senate (Plutarch *Caesar* 67.4), was a maneuver of his adopted son and successor Octavian to legitimate his rule with the title *divi filius* ("son of the god [Julius]"). Thus began the long tradition of the postmortem deification, or *apotheosis*, of deceased emperors, ritualized in the rite of *consecratio*. In violation of traditional Roman protocol, two emperors were thought to have applied the term *deus* ("god") to themselves, Caligula (Philo *Leg. Gai.* 353), and Domitian (Suetonius *Domitian* 13.2); neither was posthumously deified by the Senate.

### 6. Christians and Roman Government.

Early Christians had conflicting views of the empire and its rulers (*see* Civil Authority). Paul had a positive attitude to the Roman government and its functions (Rom 13:1-7). Paul's conception of the Eschatological Antagonist in 2 Thessalonians 2:4 (*see* Man of Lawlessness) may have been influenced by the abortive attempt of Gaius to have a statue of himself installed in the Jerusalem Temple (Josephus *Ant.* 18.8.2 §§261-62; *J.W.* 2.3.10 §§185-87; Tacitus *Hist.* 5.9; Philo *Leg. Gai.* 188, 208-28). Similarly, in 1 Peter 2:13-17 Christians are encouraged to be subject to the emperor and to honor him (here the term *basileus*, or "king," is used). On the other hand, an extremely negative and diabolical picture of the empire and the emperors is found in Revelation 13 and 17.

*See also* CAESAR'S HOUSEHOLD, IMPERIAL HOUSEHOLD; CITIZENSHIP, ROMAN AND HEAVENLY; CIVIL AUTHORITY; LEGAL SYSTEM, ROMAN; POLITICAL SYSTEMS; ROME AND ROMAN CHRISTIANITY.

BIBLIOGRAPHY. A. A. Barrett, *Caligula: The Corruption of Power* (Manchester: B. T. Batsford, 1989); P. A. Brunt and J. M. Moore, *Res Gestae Divi Augusti: The Achievements of the Divine Augustus* (Oxford: University Press, 1967); D. Fishwick, *The Imperial Cult in the Latin West* (Leiden: E. J. Brill, 1987); M. T. Griffin, *Nero: The End of a Dynasty* (New Haven and London: Yale University, 1984); K. Hopkins, "Divine Emperors or the Symbolic Unity of the Roman Empire," in *Conquerors and Slaves* (SSRH 1; Cambridge: University Press, 1978) 197-242; B. W. Jones, *The Emperor Domitian* (New York: Routledge, 1992); F. Millar, *The Emperor in the Roman World* (31 BC–AD 337) (Ithaca: Cornell University, 1977);

A. Momigliano, *Claudius: The Emperor and His Achievement* (rev. ed.; Westport, CT: Greenwood, 1981); S. R. F. Price, *Rituals and Power: The Roman Imperial Cult in Asia Minor* (Cambridge: University Press, 1984); K. Scott, *The Imperial Cult under the Flavians* (Stuttgart: Kohlhammer, 1936); L. R. Taylor, *The Divinity of the Roman Emperor* (Middletown, CT: American Philological Association, 1931); S. Weinstock, *Divus Julius* (Oxford: Clarendon, 1971).

D. E. Aune

## ENEMY, ENMITY, HATRED

The terminology of "enemy" (*echthros*), "enmity" (*echthra*), "hate" (*miseō*) and its various related images must be seen within the context of the dualism of Pauline thought. Humanity is divided by Paul into "those who are being saved" and "those who are perishing" (1 Cor 1:18; 2 Cor 2:15); those of the kingdom* of light* and those of the domain of darkness (Col 1:12-13; cf. Gal 1:4); those who belong to Christ and those who belong to this world* (Eph 2:1-10; 1 Cor 2:6-7). The backdrop for this division is the supernatural conflict between the rule of Christ and "the spiritual forces of evil in the heavenly realms" (Eph 6:12; *see* Principalities and Powers). It is to the latter categories that the term *enemy* properly applies.

1. The World and the "Unspiritual Person"
2. The Work of Christ
3. The Church
4. Personal Enemies

### 1. The World and the "Unspiritual Person."

Paul's warnings against compromise with the world are stringent (e.g., 1 Cor 6:9-10; 10:1-22). This is not because the world itself is evil but because the world is inhabited by the "unspiritual person" who stands in opposition to God* and his Law.* "The thoughts of the unspiritual person [*sarx*] are hostile [*echthra*] toward God" (Rom 8:7; cf. *theostygēs*, "hater of God," Rom 1:30; *see* Flesh). They are "alienated from God and are enemies [*echthrous*] because of their evil deeds" (Col 1:21). Their "fruits" include "hatred, strife and jealousy" (Gal 5:20), and their life is characterized by "being hated [*stygētoi*] and hating [*misountes*] one another" (Tit 3:3). In this they "follow the ruler of the domain of the air, the spirit who is now at work in those who are disobedient" (Eph 2:2; cf. 2 Cor 4:4; *exousia* can refer to a sphere of authority, i.e., "kingdom," "domain" or to supernatural, demonic "powers").

### 2. The Work of Christ.

*2.1. Past.* One aspect of Christ's redemptive work

was that of reconciling enemies. It was "while we were enemies [*echthroi*]" that "we were reconciled to God through the death of his Son" (Rom 5:10). Paul nowhere designates God as an "enemy" of humanity. It is humanity who is hostile toward God. Nonetheless, God's response to the sinful acts of humanity is "wrath"* (*orgē*) and the unspiritual person becomes an "object of wrath" (Eph 2:3). So the work of Christ was one of "making peace" between God, whose wrath is directed against sin (Col 3:6), and hostile humanity (Col 1:20-21). The initiator of this peace was God, not humanity. It was God, motivated by "his great love for us" (Eph 2:4), who through Christ "reconciled all things to himself" (Col 1:20; Rom 5:11; 2 Cor 5:18-19; *see* Peace, Reconciliation).

Christ's work of reconciliation also included putting an end to the age-old hostility between Jew and Gentile* (Eph 2:14-16). This was accomplished by nullifying the Mosaic Law, which historically set Jews apart from their pagan neighbors ("the dividing wall of hostility [*echthra*]," Eph 2:14), thus "making peace" (Eph 2:15) between Jew and Gentile.

Powers hostile to both God and humanity were dealt with as well. Paul views the ordinances of the Law (and perhaps all moral decrees) as a power "against us" (*kath' hēmōn/hypenantion hēmin*) because we have failed to discharge its obligations (Col 2:13-14). The Law's power resides in its ability to condemn and kill those who transgress its stipulations (2 Cor 3:7-11). Moreover, all powers and authorities (whether cosmic, angelic or demonic) were made a spectacle of as captive enemy by means of the cross (Col 2:15; *see* Triumph).

*2.2. Present and Future.* Christ's ongoing work is pictured as one of "subjecting enemies." "It is necessary," Paul states, "that Christ reign until all his enemies [*tous echthrous*] have been put under his feet" (1 Cor 15:25; cf. Eph 1:10). The enemies of Christ are broadly defined by Paul as "every rule, authority and power" (1 Cor 15:24). The only power specified is death, which is called "the final enemy" (*eschatos echthros*, 1 Cor 15:26), but a study of similar phraseology elsewhere indicates that he is thinking primarily of spiritual powers (cf. Eph 1:21; 3:10; 6:12; Col 1:16). The term that Paul uses to describe this subjecting process is one that means "to render powerless" (*katargeitai*, 1 Cor 15:26). In the case of Satan,* though, the language is stronger; for Paul promises the Roman Christians that "the God of peace will soon crush Satan under your feet" (Rom 16:20).

**3. The Church.**

*3.1. Enemies Without.* A number of references to enmity in Paul's writings have to do with enemies outside and inside the church.* Enemies without are those who oppose the gospel* (1 Thess 2:2). The Jews (or their leaders), in particular, are singled out by Paul as "enemies" of the church (1 Thess 2:14-15), whose rejection of the gospel incurs God's enmity (Rom 11:28)—though not without hope of Israel's salvation (Rom 11:25-28).

The destiny of the unrepentant enemy of the church is "eternal destruction" and "exclusion from the presence of the Lord" (2 Thess 1:8-9; cf. Phil 1:28). The persistent efforts of especially the Jewish synagogal leadership to prevent the preaching of the gospel to the Gentiles result in "God's wrath coming on them" (1 Thess 2:16).

For the church in the midst of persecution, Paul does not offer any immediate hope of deliverance. What is promised is "relief" (2 Thess 1:7) and vindication on Christ's return (2 Thess 1:10, "when he comes to be glorified with his saints"), as well as retribution to their enemies (2 Thess 1:6).

The preeminent external enemy is Satan, who "masquerades as an angel of light" (2 Cor 11:14), often working within the unsuspecting church through servants that Paul labels as "false apostles" and "deceitful workers" (2 Cor 11:13). The church must, therefore, arm itself against "the schemes of the devil" and his "heavenly troops" (Eph 6:10-18). It must also prepare itself for Satan's final trump card, the "man of lawlessness,"* who will be empowered to perform "signs and wonders"* (2 Thess 2:1-12).

*3.2. Enemies Within.* The enemy can also be found within the ranks of the church. Paul hopes that he will not be labeled an "enemy" (*echthros*) by telling the Galatians the truth (Gal 4:16). He commands the Thessalonian church not to associate with those who do not work to support themselves. Yet they are not to be regarded as "an enemy" but are still to be looked upon as a "brother"/"sister" (2 Thess 3:6-15).

The identity of the "many who live as enemies (*echthrous*) of the cross of Christ" in Philippians 3:18 has been intensely debated. The range of suggestions include proselytizing Jews, Jewish-Christian gnostics,* perfectionist Judaizers* (see 4.1 below), and Christian libertines. The contrast Paul makes between his example and how the "many" live, points to Christians. Beyond this, much depends on the relationship of Philippians 3:17-21 to what precedes.

**4. Personal Enemies.**

*4.1. Paul's Enemies.* Paul faced serious personal challenges throughout his ministry. The Jews stirred up trouble for him in virtually every city where he preached (Acts 13—17). Their antagonism extended at times to pursuing him from city to city (e.g., Acts 14:19; 17:13). Paul faced Gentile hostility as well (e.g., 2 Cor 11:26), but in his letters stern words of condemnation are reserved for the Jews, who "heap up their sins to the limit" (1 Thess 2:16; see Opponents).

Conservative Jewish Christians from the Jerusalem* church (= "Judaizers") tried to undercut Paul's work by raising doubts about both his gospel and his apostleship (see Apostle). Paul views them as not only personal enemies but enemies of the church because they preach circumcision* and Law-obedience for the Gentiles, in opposition to the gospel of justification* by faith alone. Some have deemed Paul's response as unduly harsh: He wishes that they would "emasculate themselves" (Gal 5:12) and he warns the church to "watch out for those dogs" (Phil 3:2). Their destiny is "eternal condemnation" (Gal 1:9).

Equally harsh are Paul's comments regarding opponents who encroached on his missionary field in Corinth and claimed credit for missionary work that was not their own (2 Cor 10:15-16). Although he does not refer to them as "enemies" per se, Paul does call them "false apostles" and "deceitful workers," who "masquerade as servants of righteousness" when in fact they are "servants of Satan" (2 Cor 11:13-15). The severity of Paul's remarks is initially surprising since he says elsewhere that even if some preach Christ "out of envy and rivalry" or "with the intent to stir up trouble," this matters little to him; for as long as Christ is preached, it is an occasion for rejoicing (Phil 1:15-18). The status of "opponent" or "enemy," however, stems not from personal rivalry but from an attempt to undermine the work of the gospel in a particular community. These so-called apostles are "false" in Paul's opinion because their intent is not to preach the gospel but "to lead astray from a sincere and pure devotion to Christ" (11:3; cf. Gal 1:8). Financial gain (2 Cor 2:17; 11:20) and the desire for dominance ("enslave," "slap you in the face," 2 Cor 11:20) is their motivation.

*4.2. God's Enemies.* It is important when approaching references to God's wrath and hatred in the NT not to read these in light of corresponding human emotions. God, unlike sinful humanity, is not given to vindictiveness, fitful rages or the urge to retaliate. Divine anger in the NT is a controlled response of a holy being to the sinful actions of humanity; divine hatred is intense aversion toward any sort of wickedness. "Because of such things," Paul says, "God's wrath comes upon those who are disobedient" (Eph 5:6). The essential incompatibility of holiness and sinfulness is evident from the fact that not even God's chosen people can escape from becoming "objects of God's

wrath" when they sin (Rom 9:22).

References to God's wrath far outnumber references to his hatred in the NT. Indeed, there is only one reference to divine hatred in the Pauline letters—albeit a widely debated one. In Romans 9:13 Paul cites from Malachi 1:2-3: "Jacob I loved, but Esau I hated [*emisēsa*]." One of the major difficulties in interpreting this text is that "hate" here is not a divine response to human sin. For it was before the twins were born, or had done anything good or bad, that God "hated Esau" but "loved Jacob." How then is one to understand this divine polarity?

It is clear from the context that what is in view is not Jacob and Esau per se but the nations they represent. Paul is concerned in the broader context with "those of my own race, the people of Israel" (Rom 9:4-5). This is confirmed by Genesis 25:23, cited by Paul in Romans 9:12, which speaks of "two nations" being in the womb and by Malachi 1:2-6, where Israel* (= Jacob) and Edom (= Esau) are specifically addressed. Moreover, what is in question in Romans 9:1-29 is not the destinies of two nations but their functions in salvation history. " 'The older will serve the younger,' just as it is written, 'Jacob I loved but Esau I hated.' " "Hate" and "love"* are therefore not to be equated with "condemnation" and "salvation."* Furthermore, God's love/hate relationship with Israel and Edom is not based on their differing characters or their respective deeds but on God's sovereign will: "not by works but by him who calls" (Rom 9:12).

How then are God's "love" and "hate" to be construed within these contextual restraints? Did God determine before the birth of either nation to love the one and hate the other? Some think that the word "hate" is an instance of the Semitic use of a direct opposite to express a lesser degree of comparison: "God loved Jacob more than Esau." But this does not take into account the overarching theme in Romans 9 of God's sovereign choosing and rejecting. Others have taken "hate" at face value to refer to God's intense animosity toward and ultimate condemnation of Esau/Edom. This, however, overlooks the intimate link in Romans 9:12-13 between "the older serving the younger" and God's hatred of Esau ("as it is written, Esau I hated"). The solution surely lies in seeing that Paul's overall argument in Romans 9:1-29 has to do with corporate "election"* and "rejection" based on promise as opposed to natural descent. Here the very act of choosing the one (= "love") by default results in rejecting the other (= "hate"). That "hate" can be used of the rejection implicit in the action of choosing one party over another is well illustrated by Matthew 4:24, where to choose between two masters is to "love" the one and "hate" the other, and by Luke 14:26, where to choose to follow Christ is effectively "to hate father and mother."

**4.3. The Believer's Enemies.** Christians are not encouraged by Paul to hate their enemies but are rather commanded to do good to them (Rom 12:21). This includes satisfying their thirst and hunger (Rom 12:20) and in "blessing" them (1 Cor 4:12; Rom 12:14). Believers are forbidden to respond in kind to their enemies (1 Thess 5:15; Rom 12:17). Vengeance is the sole prerogative of God (Rom 12:19). The regularity of this teaching in Paul indicates that it was a standard part of early Christian catechism.

Some think that there is a fundamental contradiction between Paul's "love" ethic and the *lex talionis* ("an eye for an eye") principle found in the OT. Yet Paul himself cites Leviticus 19:18 ("Do not seek revenge, . . . but love your neighbor as yourself") and Proverbs 25:21-22 ("If your enemies are hungry, give them food to eat; if they are thirsty, give them water to drink") in support of his love dictum (e.g., Rom 12:20; 13:10; Gal 5:14). The point of the OT eye-for-an-eye principle was not retribution but to guarantee legal fairness. Nor is this principle absent from the NT. But it is the prerogative of the secular courts, as ordained by God, and not the church, to ensure due process (Rom 13:1-7; cf. 1 Cor 5:12-13; *see* Civil Authority).

For Paul, love of one's enemy is grounded in the mercy* of God. Believers are to love their enemies because at one time "we all were enemies [of God]." Yet out of his great love, God sent his Son to die for those who were still his enemies (Rom 5:10). Are believers, as God's children, to do any less?

*See also* Opponents of Paul; Peace, Reconciliation; Principalities and Powers; Satan, Devil; Triumph; Wrath, Destruction.

BIBLIOGRAPHY. J. B. Bedenbaugh, "Paul's Use of 'Wrath Of God,'" *Lutheran Quarterly* 6 (1954) 154-57; G. B. Caird, *Principalities and Powers* (Oxford: Clarendon, 1956); A. Carr, "The Meaning of 'Hatred' in the NT," *The Expositor*, 6th Series, 12 (1905) 153-60; J. Piper, *'Love Your Enemies'* (SNTSMS 38; Cambridge: University Press, 1979); J. Scharbert, "Enemy," in *Encyclopedia of Biblical Theology*, ed. J. B. Bauer (New York: Crossroad, 1981) 1.220-24; J. B. Scott, "The Place of Enmity in Scriptural Teaching," in *The Law and the Prophets*, ed. J. H. Skilton (Nutley, NJ: Presbyterian & Reformed, 1974) 128-40; F. L. R. Stachowiak, "Hatred," in *Encyclopedia of Biblical Theology*, ed. J. B. Bauer (New York: Crossroad, 1981) 1:351-55; K. Stendahl, "Hate, Non-Retaliation and Love," *HTR* 55 (1962) 343-55.

L. L. Belleville

**ENMITY.** *See* Enemy, Enmity, Hatred.

**ENTHRONEMENT.** *See* Exaltation and Enthronement; Lord; Triumph.

## EPHESIANS, LETTER TO THE

The Letter to the Ephesians is unique among the letters attributed to Paul. Its language of worship* and prayer,* the depth and scope of its theology, and the many practical admonitions have led many Christians (including John Calvin) to cherish it as their favorite NT book. The letter's emphasis on the nature of the church and the present dynamic relationship of the exalted Christ* to the church makes it an important and practical book for the church today.

1. Style and Composition
2. Authorship
3. Relationship to Colossians
4. The History-of-Religions Question
5. Destination
6. Life Setting and Purpose
7. Themes in the Letter

### 1. Style and Composition.

The author's method of composition is characterized by an elevated style that reveals his affection for the subject he is discussing. He also identifies with the beliefs of the early church through his use of traditional material: hymns,* creeds,* liturgical material (*see* Liturgical Elements) and household codes.* Yet the writer is not content merely to reaffirm what the church is already confessing; he is a fresh thinker and advances his readers' understanding of Christ, the church* and eschatology.*

The first half of Ephesians is well known for its lofty and exalted style. Here the author makes use of the language of worship, prayer and doxology (*see* Benediction, Blessing, Doxology). The letter begins with an elegantly composed eulogy (*berakah*) praising God* for the election* and redemption* of his people (Eph 1:3-14). Consisting of one long sentence, the section abounds with participles, prepositional phrases and relative clauses and is punctuated with the refrain-like phrase "to the praise of his glory." In true poetic form, the passage also uses a variety of synonyms to repeat the key thoughts, such as the knowledge,* power* and will of God. Because of these poetic traits, some scholars have regarded this section as an early-Christian hymn (see Lincoln, 10-19, for discussion). The majority of scholars, however, prefer to describe it as the author's own "unified ad hoc composition, a hymnic passage in artistic, rhythmical prose" (Schlier as cited in Schnackenburg, 46). The style is distinctively Jewish and has much in common with the hymns found among the Qumran* scrolls. The switch from the first person plural ("we") to the second person plural ("you") in Ephesians 1:13 has occasioned much discussion, with some contending for an intentional contrast between Jewish Christians ("we") and Gentile* Christians ("you") (Martin, Bruce, Robinson, Barth). Since the discussion of the relationship between Jews and Gentiles does not surface as a major theme until Ephesians 2:11, it is better to take "we" as a reference to all believers and "you" as referring to the readers in particular (Schnackenburg, Lincoln, Percy).

The letter also contains two prayers (Eph 1:15-23; 3:14-21). The first actually consists of an introductory thanksgiving, an intercessory prayer report and a digression extolling the power of God which raised Jesus from the dead. The poetic language used in this praise of God's resurrection* power (Eph 1:20-23) has led some interpreters to regard it as a hymnic quotation, but it more likely reflects the author's own poetic style with possible dependence on early creedal formulations (Lincoln, Schnackenburg). The second prayer properly begins in Ephesians 3:1 but is interrupted by an excursus on Paul's apostleship* to the Gentiles (Eph 3:2-13), a topic extremely relevant to the predominantly Gentile readership. The prayer report consists of one long sentence but is structured around two requests (introduced by hina) and a summarizing request. The prayer reiterates and develops some of the themes of the first prayer (e.g., power, spirit). The exalted language of the prayer leads immediately into a doxology (Eph 3:20-21) praising God for his power effective in the lives of believers.

The first half of the letter is far from a dispassionate theological treatise. It exudes emotion in the praise and worship of the almighty God who loves and responds to his people. The author writes with intense feeling and wants to elicit the same response—praise, worship and prayer—in the lives of his readers.

The letter's most explicit citation of an early Christian hymn appears in Ephesians 5:14 where it is introduced by a technical formula normally used for the introduction to an OT citation (*dio legei;* cf. Eph 4:8 where it is used to introduce an OT quotation). The original setting of this hymn is thought by most scholars to be the occasion of baptism* (e.g., Lincoln, Martin), but this is rather speculative. Another possible hymnic fragment appears in Ephesians 2:14-18, although this identification is disputed by P. Stuhlmacher who regards it as a Christian midrash on Isaiah 57:19. The formal characteristics of the passage—the unique words, the use of participles, the intensely christological content, the parallelism of the lines, the

"we" style that interrupts the "you" style—lead most scholars to conclude that it is indeed hymnic (so Lincoln, Martin, Barth). Therefore, the author's admonition to "speak to one another in psalms and hymns and spiritual songs" (Eph 5:19) appears to be modeled by his own use of hymnic material in this letter. At the beginning of his call to unity in the second half of the letter, the author roots his appeal partly in a confession of the early church: "there is one body and one Spirit . . . one Lord, one faith, one baptism, one God and father of all" (Eph 4:4-6). It appears that he wants to remind these believers of their common confession as the beginning step to increasing the unity of the churches.

In his composition of the letter, the author also makes use of a literary form commonly identified by scholars as a "household code"* (Eph 5:21—6:9). This form was his vehicle for addressing the relationships within the household: husband-wife, parent-child and master-slave. This passage and Colossians 3:18—4:1 appear to be the first adaptations of this form from Hellenistic Judaism to describe the relationships in a *Christian* household. The use of the form here varies considerably from Colossians,* particularly in the expanded discussion of the husband-wife relationship modeled on the relationship between Christ and the church.

Although the OT quotations in Ephesians are not numerous (there are only four explicit quotations), there are many allusions evidenced by the author's dependence on OT phraseology, terminology and concepts (*see* Old Testament Citations). In one quotation of the OT (Eph 4:8), the author uses Psalm 68:18 as an introduction to his discussion of the risen Christ endowing the church with gifted people. The actual citation appears to follow a rabbinic tradition preserved in a later targum that the victorious king "gave" gifts to people rather than "received" them (so the LXX and MT; see Bruce, 340-43). It also shows the writer's knowledge of rabbinic methods of exegesis as he then (in Eph 4:9-10) explains the meaning of the text in terms of a midrash pesher technique. A section of moral exhortation such as Ephesians 5:15-18 reveals the author's indebtedness to the OT wisdom* tradition. References to such items as temple,* redemption,* God's choosing, hope,* mercy,* promise, wisdom, the Father, sons of men, helmet of salvation and many more show how deeply steeped the author was in the OT and how the language of the OT influenced his own composition.

The application of rhetorical criticism to NT documents is still in its infancy stage (*see* Rhetoric; Rhetorical Criticism), so very little has yet been written on

Ephesians from this perspective. A noteworthy beginning is A. T. Lincoln's commentary on Ephesians, which attempts to observe the rhetorical purpose of the flow of thought throughout the letter. He concludes that the writer combines the epideictic and the deliberative rhetorical genres (Lincoln, xli-xlii).

With its variety of literary forms, traditions and sources, Ephesians is far from the straightforward prose of a typical letter of antiquity (*see* Letters). What, then, is the best way to describe Ephesians? Is it even accurate to call it a "letter"?

E. Käsemann (*RGG)* described it as a "theological tract" merely dressed up like a letter. H. Schlier called it a "wisdom discourse" focusing on the role of Christ as personified wisdom (Schlier, 21; so also Bruce, 246, but who also sees it as an actual letter). J. Gnilka refers to it as a "liturgical homily" clothed in the form of a letter (Gnilka, 33). Similarly, and most recently, A. T. Lincoln characterizes it as "the written equivalent of a sermon or homily" (Lincoln, xxxix). Nevertheless, he still regards it as an actual letter adapted from the Pauline letter form.

Because Ephesians retains many conventions of the Pauline letter form, it is probably best explained as an actual letter. The language, literary and rhetorical forms, and the traditions employed primarily grant us insight into the concerns of the author in communicating to his readers. The precise nature of the content and composition need to be explained by the background and purpose of the author as well as his perceived understanding of the needs of the readers.

## 2. Authorship.

Scholarly opinion regarding the Pauline authorship of Ephesians is divided, with perhaps a majority of scholars today holding that the letter was not written by Paul. This situation is rather ironic in that a good number of scholars have esteemed Ephesians as "the crown" of Paul's thought (e.g., C. H. Dodd, J. A. Robinson). On the other hand, W. G. Kümmel can assert, "The theology of Eph makes the Pauline composition of the letter completely impossible" (Kümmel, 360).

The Pauline authorship of Ephesians was not challenged until the late eighteenth century and early nineteenth century. It was the outspoken denial of authenticity by F. C. Baur and his followers, however, which had the greatest influence on the subsequent course of scholarship. Prior to that time Ephesians was universally recognized as Pauline. As early as Ignatius (early second century) the letter was quoted as being from the hand of the apostle.

Until recently, British and American evangelical scholars unanimously affirmed Pauline authorship.

Now, some evangelicals are convinced that the evidence of the letter is inconsistent with Pauline authorship. A. T. Lincoln, for instance, concludes, "Everything points instead to a later follower of Paul who used Colossians as the basis for his own reinterpretation of the Pauline gospel" (Lincoln, lxvii). Similarly, R. P. Martin contends that the author was "a well-known disciple and companion of Paul who published this letter under the apostle's aegis either during the apostle's final imprisonment or (more probably) after his death" (Martin, 4). In an earlier writing, Martin identified this person as Luke. The arguments against Pauline authorship have been fourfold:

(1) Language and Style. The number of words in Ephesians which are not found in the other Pauline letters is proportionally insignificant. This fact is actually a point in favor of Pauline authorship. The criticism lies more in the observation that many of these unique terms are used in the apostolic fathers, thus giving the letter more of a post-apostolic atmosphere. Since most scholars, however, acknowledge that early church fathers such as Clement knew and used Ephesians, the possibility that the vocabulary of Ephesians influenced these writers needs to be considered more seriously.

The style of writing exhibited in Ephesians has been the greater stumbling block to authenticity. It is often characterized as "pleonastic," that is, a fullness of style seen in the repeated use of prepositional phrases, abundant participles, numerous relative clauses, genitive upon genitive and lengthy sentences. Schnackenburg says that "there is scarcely anything comparable in Paul" (Schnackenburg, 26). What is not often observed, however, is that this unique style predominates in the first half of the letter. It is here where the author intentionally employs a lofty style of eulogy, praise, prayer and doxology. He also appears to be relying on the use of traditional material. This half of the letter does not consist of the straightforward prose, argument or admonition that usually characterizes the Pauline letters. Nevertheless, passages such as Romans 8:38-39 and 11:33-36 demonstrate that Paul was capable of writing in an elevated style similar to what we find in the Qumran hymns. One should not underestimate Paul's resourcefulness in expressing himself.

(2) Theology. Many scholars have contended that there are significant theological divergences in Ephesians compared to the eight recognized letters. Discussion has normally focused on the cosmic christology,* the realized eschatology and the apparently advanced ecclesiology of the letter. Those denying Pauline authorship contend that there is not merely a develop-

ment in Paul's thought, but an entirely changed perspective revealing a later stage of theological reflection (see Schnackenburg, 26-28; Lincoln, lxii-lxv).

There is no doubt about the development in Ephesians of the cosmic aspect of christology and the heightened emphasis on a realized eschatology. But this emphasis may have been prompted by the writer's concern to build up the readers in light of their ongoing struggle with the principalities and powers (Arnold, 124-29, 145-58, 171; see Principalities and Powers). The teaching of the letter on both of these topics does not represent a break with the apostle's teaching, but the logical extension of his thought. A. T. Lincoln himself has done much to demonstrate that Ephesians is not totally devoid of a futurist eschatology as it was once often charged (see Lincoln, lxxxix-xc; pace A. Lindemann, H. Conzelmann et al.).

Many aspects of the ecclesiology are thought to be discontinuous with Paul and to reflect a later temporal setting: the use of "church" (ekklēsia) in a non-local sense, Christ now seen as "head"* of the church, mention of the apostles* and prophets* as "holy" and as the foundation of the church, etc. Some think that the author of the letter is looking back to the founding years of the church, emphasizing Paul as the guarantor of apostolic tradition, and building on his eschatology (see Schnackenburg, 28).

Each of these objections, however, can be met with a plausible explanation grounded in the lifetime of the apostle. (1) If the letter circulated among a network of churches, as is likely, it would be natural for the writer to use "church" in a more universal sense. (2) Christ as "head" of the church is a clear development over Paul's earlier presentation of the metaphor of the body of Christ, but is not impossible that Paul's thinking developed in this direction. The needs of the Colossian church initially prompted this development, and Paul may have reflected on it further for the benefit of the readers of Ephesians. (3) The description of the apostles and prophets as "holy" (hagios, Eph 3:5; see Holiness, Sanctification) does not necessarily point to a time when they were receiving increasing veneration. "Saints" (hagioi) was the typical Pauline designation for believers. It was used of anyone or anything set apart for a sacred purpose (see Abbott, 82). (4) Although the apostles and the prophets do indeed form the foundation of the church through their foundational witness to the life, death and resurrection of Jesus Christ, they are not presented as dead, gone and off the scene. The resurrected Christ continues to give them to the church (Eph 4:11-12). They are foundational in a dynamic continuing fashion.

In general, more consideration needs to be given to uncovering the plausible life setting of the letter in Asia Minor in the early 60s before recourse is made to the more extreme assumption of a different temporal and life setting toward the end of the first century. Furthermore, it is not irrational to assume that Paul himself could bring further development to his own ideas, especially as his circumstances and the circumstances of his readers would prompt him. Carson, Moo and Morris have recently observed, "What appears to some as impossible for one mind is for others quite a possibility for such a wide-ranging and inventive mind as Paul's" (Carson, Moo and Morris, 307).

(3) The Use of Colossians. Scholars on both sides of the issue have recognized the close similarity in vocabulary, phraseology and thought between Ephesians and Colossians. Many scholars are now contending that there is a formal relationship between the two letters in terms of a one-way literary borrowing. The precise nature of the borrowing and the alleged alteration of the thought of Colossians is considered by some to point decisively away from Pauline authorship. The nature of this relationship will be explored in more detail below.

Since each of these objections to the authenticity of Ephesians can be met with a reasonable explanation, the scales are tipped in favor of the letter being precisely what it claims to be—a letter of Paul—when two other factors are taken into consideration.

(1) Tradition. W. G. Kümmel observes (and must concede) that "Eph is extraordinarily well attested in the early church" (Kümmel, 357). It appears to have been used as a Pauline letter by many of the Apostolic Fathers, including Clement of Rome, Ignatius, Hermas and Polycarp. It was listed as a Pauline letter in the earliest canons, viz. Marcion's (c. A.D. 140) and the Muratorian Canon (c. A.D. 180; see Canon). Many of the Gnostic* writers quoted it as Paul's own words. A new line of evidence that has not entered the debate thus far is that Ephesians is quoted as Pauline in some of the Nag Hammadi documents (as early as the second century). For instance, Ephesians 6:12 is quoted in the *Hypostasis of the Archons* as from "the great apostle" (II.86.20-25). The same verse is cited in the *Exegesis on the Soul* (II.6.131) as the words of Paul.

(2) Autobiographical Information. In addition to the address of the letter which claims Paul as the author (Eph 1:1), Ephesians contains a substantial amount of material presented as a first-person address on the part of the apostle to the readers. The most significant is the reflection on his stewardship of the mystery* (Eph 3:2-6) and the nature of his apostolic ministry* (Eph 3:7-13). The first-person material also

extends to the prayers, for example, "I Paul the servant of Christ Jesus [pray] for you Gentiles" (Eph 3:1; see also Eph 1:16; 3:14), his call to unity ("I, the prisoner of the Lord" [Eph 4:1]). Paul also asks specifically that the readers would pray for him (Eph 6:19-20) and then concludes the letter with comments on the role of Tychicus when he comes to them with words that in places exactly parallel the text of Colossians (Eph 6:21-22).

Those who argue in favor of pseudonymity have variously explained the autobiographical material. Most recently, D. Meade has claimed that the literary device of pseudonymity was not only acceptable to early Christians but widely used. He contends that the author of Ephesians, an admirer of Paul, wrote in Paul's name as an attempt to secure the heritage of Paul in the Asia Minor churches after the death of the great apostle. According to Meade, by writing in Paul's name the author was able "to actualize the apostolic doctrine and lifestyle" (Meade, 139-61). Pseudonymity, he argues, "is primarily an assertion of authoritative tradition, not of literary origins" (161). A. T. Lincoln accepts Meade's thesis and attempts to provide additional exegetical support for it. According to Lincoln, "Instead of simply saying that he is passing on Pauline traditions, he [the author of Ephesians] makes it more personal, direct, and forceful by adopting the device of Paul himself appealing to the churches" (Lincoln, lxxxvii).

This thesis makes too strong a dichotomy between authoritative tradition and literary origins without corroborating it with convincing support. Meade's approach has also been criticized for presenting a facile and homogenous picture of ancient Jewish literature that blurs the distinctions of literary genre among the varied documents. With regard to Ephesians, however, the thesis is difficult to sustain in a passage like Ephesians 6:19-20 where Paul asks his readers to pray that he would be emboldened to proclaim the gospel in his prison situation. It is not enough to say that the writer is soliciting the readers' prayers for the progress of the apostolic gospel that is summed up by the image of Paul. The autobiographical information is much more naturally explained by the assumption of authenticity.

### 3. Relationship to Colossians.

Most scholars who see Ephesians as pseudonymous contend that it depends heavily on Colossians as its primary literary source (e.g., Lincoln, Schnackenburg, Lindemann, Mitton et al.). Some argue that the dependence is based on the author's memory of Colossians (so Schnackenburg, 32), but others contend that the author must have possessed a copy of Colossians which he redacted according to his own interests (so Lincoln, lv; Mitton, 230).

The most extensive point of contact is the commendation of Tychicus (Col 4:7-8; Eph 6:21-22) where there is verbatim correspondence between twenty-nine consecutive words (although *kai syndoulos* is omitted in Ephesians). Beyond this there are only three additional places where seven words are exactly paralleled and two places where there are five words. This appears to be very slim evidence for the postulation of literary dependence. It seems especially odd that the longest passage reproduced in Ephesians is not from the theological argumentation or paraenesis of Colossians, but about the sending of Tychicus. This passage is even more difficult under the assumption that the Ephesian author is reproducing the text of Colossians from memory.

Proponents of literary dependence put more stock in the similar overall structure and sequence of the letters with much of the same thematic material (e.g., Lincoln, xlvii) and the apparent dependence on certain key terms and concepts expressed in Colossians. Nevertheless, it is argued, the author of Ephesians had his own distinct interests: quite apart from being slavishly dependent, he rearranged and gave fresh expression to his source material to suit his own theological purposes.

One example of this reworking is the digression in Ephesians 3:1-13 on Paul's apostolic ministry, which is said to depend on Colossians 1:23-29. The Ephesian passage sequences many of the same themes as the Colossian text and uses a number of the same (or similar) terms and expressions. Lincoln therefore concludes that the passage "derives from the author's distinctive reworking of the Colossians passage" (Lincoln, 170). In response, it must be said that the conclusion of literary dependence is not demanded by this passage (although it could fit the hypothesis). If the author were using Colossians as source material it is surprising that he did not reproduce more of his source in his writing; he was going far beyond the work of a redactor in his complete refashioning of the material and creative elaboration on it. This passage more likely reflects the same author giving a fresh exposition of a similar theme (with different emphases) a short time later for a different audience.

Many scholars, however, find the theology of Colossians at variance with that of Ephesians. Thus, some suggest that even assuming the authenticity of Colossians (which itself is disputed), it is highly doubtful that Paul could have written Ephesians. This conclusion is based on the way the author of Ephesians alters the theology of Colossians on certain points.

For example, in Colossians 1:27 and 2:2 the content of the "mystery" appears to be Christ, whereas in Ephesians it is the fact that the Gentiles have been made fellow members, with the Jews, of the body of Christ (Eph 3:6; *see* Body of Christ). But one must ask if this is truly a discrepancy or whether it could possibly be a matter of emphasis in the use of a term which expresses a multi-faceted concept.

In a monograph on the Pauline concept of "mystery," M. Bockmuehl has argued that this use of the term reflects an emphasis on one aspect of the more comprehensive use of "mystery." In other words, it is more a matter of continuity and emphasis rather than discontinuity and a variant theology (Bockmuehl, 202; cf. C. Caragounis, 143: "they are not different *mysteria,* but wider or narrower aspects of one and the same *mysterion*—God's *mysterion* in Christ"). On the relationship of the two letters as a whole, F. F. Bruce comments that the change of perspective from Christ (Colossians) to the church (Ephesians) may go far to account for the different nuances of terms held in common by the two letters (Bruce, 231).

Some significant problems with the postulation of literary dependence still remain: (1) The influential study by H. J. Holtzmann in 1872 concluded that the evidence of some of the parallels pointed more in the direction of the dependence of Colossians on Ephesians. Others, especially Mitton and now Lincoln, have argued that all the parallels point to a one-way dependence of Ephesians on Colossians. A. van Roon, however, has once again brought this hypothesis into question. In his comparison of the two letters he found no indication of literary priority on the part of either letter, but what evidence there was pointed toward the priority of Ephesians (van Roon, 426). Although van Roon's postulation of a third document upon which both were dependent is highly questionable, he does demonstrate the difficulty of proving any literary dependence on the available evidence. (2) If the author of Ephesians did use Colossians as his literary source, it is difficult to explain why he neglected the hymn and omits any use of the polemic against the "heretics" in Colossians 2. (3) The theory does not give sufficient credit to Paul's ability and versatility as a writer and theologian. It is not unreasonable to think of Paul re-expressing, developing and modifying his own thoughts for a different readership facing a different set of circumstances. It seems that one must first prove that Paul was incapable of this versatility.

The traditional view, recently given fresh expression by Carson, Moo and Morris, still seems to have the most evidence in its favor: "The best explanation to many seems to be that the same man wrote Colos-

sians and Ephesians a little later, with many of the same thoughts running through his head and with a more general application of the ideas he had so recently expressed" (308). The precise nature, however, of the relationship between Ephesians and Colossians continues to stand in need of careful research from a literary, linguistic and theological perspective.

**4. The History-of-Religions Question.**
In the mid-nineteenth century, F. C. Baur argued that Ephesians must belong to the second century because of its dependence on Gnostic* thought. Since then the affirmation of Gnostic influence on Ephesians has been widely promulgated by such writers as R. Bultmann, H. Schlier, E. Käsemann, P. Pokorný, H. Conzelmann and A. Lindemann. They have found Gnosticism evident in such terminology and concepts as the head-body imagery, mystery, *plērōma* ("fullness"*), *aiōn* ("age"), *archōn* ("ruler"), the once-now schema, and the so-called spatial eschatology. More conservative scholars, on the other hand, argued rather for the influence of Gnosticism on the readers of the letter than on the author himself.

In recent years a dramatic shift away from the history-of-religions school's assumption of a pre-Christian Gnostic redeemer myth has taken place in NT scholarship in general, and in the study of Ephesians in particular. In light of new evidence about the origins of Gnosticism, it is now accurate to conclude that the reputed existence of any relatively coherent Gnostic system which would have been capable of influencing either the author of Ephesians or the communities to which the letter was addressed rests on a very weak foundation (Arnold, 12). Scholars are now using phrases such as "proto-Gnosticism" and "incipient Gnosticism" to describe the phenomena in the first-century A.D.

The most productive approach is to examine the local religious traditions which were known to be active and influential at the time the letter was written. For western Asia Minor this would include the phenomena commonly referred to as magic,* the Anatolian religions (such as the cults of Artemis and Cybele), astrological practices and astral religion, and the various other local cults (see Arnold, 5-40; *see* Religions). A deeper understanding of these traditions provides a firmer basis for interpreting the readers and assessing how Paul may have contextualized his theology to address their needs.

**5. Destination.**
In 1855 Charles Ellicott wrote, "That the Epistle was addressed to the Christians of the important city of

Ephesus seems scarcely open to serious doubt" (Ellicott, 1). Precisely the opposite sentiment is shared by the majority of scholars today.

The letter is traditionally understood to have been written to believers in Ephesus because the city is mentioned in the superscript "To the Ephesians," and the prescript "to the saints who are in Ephesus" (Eph 1:1). The words "in Ephesus," however, are not present in certain manuscripts generally regarded as the most reliable, viz. Sinaiticus (ℵ), Vaticanus (B) and a second-century papyrus (*P*⁴⁶)—all published after Ellicott wrote his commentary (*see* Textual Criticism). Further doubt is cast on the authenticity of the words "in Ephesus" because of the impersonal tone of the letter and the general nature of the contents. "Ephesians" does not look like an occasional letter written to one church which Paul had come to know well through his three years of ministry in Ephesus. Thus most interpreters see Ephesians as some form of a circular letter.

Various attempts have been made to explain the sense of Ephesians 1:1 without the addition of a geographical location. Some take the text as it stands in ℵ and B as original and translate it, "to the saints and to those who are faithful in Christ Jesus" (e.g., Schnackenburg, 41). But this leaves us with a very awkward participial expression (*tois ousin*) which always has a place name following it in prescripts of other Pauline letters (see Rom 1:7; 1 Cor 1:2; 2 Cor 1:1; Phil 1:1; Col 1:2).

Others resort to some form of conjectural emendation. For example, E. Best supposes that the original text may have been *tois hagiois kai pistois en Christō Iesou* ("to the saints and faithful ones in Christ Jesus"). He argues that the address given on the outside of the papyrus roll originally read "to the saints" and was later modified to "to the saints who are in Ephesus (*tois ousin en Ephesō*)." According to Best this occurred when the Pauline collection of letters was made (late first century) and the collectors realized that this letter did not conform to the rest because it had no geographical location. The phrase was then later carried into the body of the letter (Best, 3251). Against this view, one can say that it does not seem likely that such a process could have happened over the time required without at least a trace in some remaining manuscript evidence.

It is likely that there was some indication of place in the prescript of Ephesians 1:1. The participle *ousin* expects the subsequent naming of a place. Bruce, persuaded that "in Ephesus" was not original and that the letter has the appearance of a circular letter, conjectures that a space was left after *ousin* for Tychicus to insert the appropriate geographical name for each of the places to which he delivered a copy of the letter (Bruce, 240; so also Martin, 3-5). Bruce admits that such a practice is difficult to attest for the first century, but nevertheless still finds this argument the most convincing. It is problematic to this view that Ephesus was preserved as the only geographical place name when the letter was presumably written to many other cities along the west coast of Asia Minor (although Tertullian reports that Marcion thought the letter was written to Laodicea—probably Marcion's own conjecture based on Col 4:16).

A. van Roon, followed by A. T. Lincoln, suggested that there were originally two place names—Hierapolis and Laodicea. These writers claim that this has the advantage of explaining the awkward *kai* (commonly translated "also") which connects "saints" with "faithful" (van Roon, 80-85; Lincoln, 3-4). Apart from the difficulty of no textual evidence to support these locations, this view cannot explain why a scribe—often concerned with smoothing the text—would have let the *kai* stand in the text (cf. Best, 3250).

We are left with no satisfactory explanation of the original text of Ephesians 1:1 if we assume the reliability of *P*⁴⁶, ℵ and B on this reading. This is one point where it may be best to part company with these manuscripts and affirm the accuracy of the widely attested alternative tradition, that is, "in Ephesus" was the original reading. This view is finding an increasing number of supporters (e.g., Conzelmann, Gnilka, Lindemann).

The following arguments support this conclusion: (1) There is still strong manuscript support for the inclusion. The entire Western and Byzantine traditions stand behind it as well as important Alexandrian witnesses, including Alexandrinus. (2) An Ephesian destination was the unanimous tradition of the early church (for references, see Ellicott, 1) and is the only reading known in *all* the extant versions. (3) There is a reasonable explanation to account for the omission of "in Ephesus." At a very early date, churches in a different location (perhaps Egypt) universalized the address in the prescript by omitting the prescript in copies that were made for their own catechetical (or liturgical) purposes (Gnilka, 7). The contents of Ephesians, as also the book of Romans,* were especially well suited to a broad readership. For the same reason, several witnesses omit "in Rome" (Rom 1:7) in the prescript to the book of Romans. On this passage Metzger notes that the words were eliminated "as a deliberate excision, made in order to show that the letter is of general, not local, application" (Metzger, *Textual Commentary,* 505). (4) When Paul says in Ephesians 1:15 that he had "heard" of their faith and love, it does not necessarily mean that he does not know them. It could just as easily refer to the progress they had made in the five or so years he had been absent from them. There is probably also a reference here to the many converts that had joined the church since he had been with them. (5) One cannot place too much emphasis on the fact that no greetings are attached since Paul sends no extended greetings to other churches he knew well (see 1 and 2 Corinthians,* Galatians* and Philippians).

Was the letter therefore written exclusively to the one church at Ephesus? Although many interpreters assume that there was one big church present in Ephesus when the letter was written, it is far more likely that there was a network of house churches scattered throughout the city and perhaps also in the nearby villages (e.g., Metropolis, Hypaipa, Diashieron, Neikaia, etc.). Many of these could have been started after Paul left Ephesus. One must not forget that population estimates for first-century Ephesus begin at one-quarter million. Furthermore, Paul may have envisioned and even encouraged the reading of the letter to a broader circle of churches throughout the west coast of Asia Minor (e.g., Pergamum, Laodicea, Colossae and Hierapolis).

The letter was probably a circular letter in the sense that it was intended primarily to circulate among the house churches of Ephesus, its environs and perhaps even more broadly in western Asia Minor (e.g., to the Lycus valley).

### 6. Life Setting and Purpose.

Of all the Pauline letters, Ephesians is the least situational. This does not mean that the letter fails to address real needs and problems faced by its readers; Ephesians simply does not have the same sense of urgency and response to crisis as do the apostle's other letters. Consequently, a vast array of opinions have been expressed regarding why the letter was written.

Of course, one's view on the authenticity of the letter has a significant impact on how this question is answered. Among those denying the Pauline authorship, a few have seen it as something other than a letter—such as a theological tract, a wisdom discourse or a liturgical homily—as was noted above. N. Dahl has stressed a baptismal setting for the document. He thinks the pseudonymous letter was addressed to some recently founded congregations to remind the young Gentile Christians of the implications of their faith and baptism and to exhort them to live up to their calling (Dahl, 38). R. P. Martin has described Ephesians as "an exalted prose-poem on the theme

'Christ-in-his-church' " (Martin, 5-6). He explains that the document was written in response to the needs of the predominantly Gentile readership to admonish them to appreciate the Jewish background of their faith and thus also their fellow Jewish Christians. He also sees a type of "gnosticizing" teaching that has led the readers into a libertine lifestyle and a fear of astrological fate.

R. Schnackenburg, however, describes Ephesians as a genuine letter. More specifically, he sees it as "a theologically based, pastorally-oriented" pseudonymous letter written to a circle of churches in Asia Minor around A.D. 90 addressing two pragmatic concerns: the internal unity of the congregations and the need for a distinctively Christian lifestyle in a pagan environment (Schnackenburg, 22-35). A. T. Lincoln stresses the temporal setting of the letter in the period after the death of the apostle Paul (Lincoln, lxxxv-lxxxvii). He concurs with D. Meade that many of the problems seen in Ephesians stem from the loss of Paul as a unifying source of authority.* He sees the readers as consequently lacking a sense of cohesion and communal identity once the coordinating activity of the great apostle was gone.

Moving in an entirely different direction, E. J. Goodspeed, later supported by J. Knox and C. L. Mitton, argued that Ephesians was a general letter written toward the end of the first century as an introduction to the collected letters of Paul (see Canon). Mitton concedes that Ephesians may not properly have served as an "introduction" to the letters, but that it sprang from a relationship to the corpus and was used to present the message of the recently assembled Pauline letters comprehensively to a new generation (Mitton, 29). He believes that the writer was well aware of the context of the readers and thus wrote against the current Gnostic threat and the danger of the largely Gentile readership disowning their Jewish heritage (Mitton, 30-31).

There has also been a diversity of opinions offered by those affirming Pauline authorship. C. Ellicott said the letter was not prompted by any special circumstances, but was written to set forth the origin and development of the church for believers in Ephesus.* He contended that Paul wrote the letter in a general way because he intended it for circulation among all the churches coterminous to or dependent on that city (Ellicott, xv-xvi). H. A. W. Meyer described the letter simply as a written discourse by Paul to the predominantly Gentile church in Ephesus to advance their understanding of the glory of their redemption and encourage them to proper conduct in keeping with their faith. He also thought that Paul had in the back of his mind as he wrote the dangers of the possible approach of Gnosticism (Meyer, 307-8).

J. A. Robinson envisioned Paul taking advantage of his own tranquil circumstances (under house arrest in Rome, but with time to think) to write a positive exposition of the heart of his theology—"the doctrine of the unity of mankind in Christ and of the purpose of God for the world through the church" (Robinson, 10-11). Robinson thought the letter was written as an encyclical which would go first to Ephesus and then to the many churches in Asia Minor. E. F. Scott termed the letter "a private meditation," but composed as a letter for the church at Laodicea. Although a positive exposition, the letter addressed a problem of Jew-Gentile disunity in the church and the splintering effect of the heresies that were beginning to surface (Scott, 123-24). These heresies were also promoting a moral laxity and libertinism.

More recently, M. Barth has suggested that Ephesians was written by Paul to Christians in Ephesus, but only those of Gentile origin, "people whom he did not know personally and who had been converted and baptized after his final departure from that city" (Barth, 1.3-4). F. F. Bruce regarded it as a circular letter (with a blank space in Eph 1:1) written as a meditation on the divine "wisdom in a mystery" (so also Schlier, 21-22). Through this Paul also encouraged the Gentile Christians to appreciate the dignity of their calling (Bruce, 245-46).

Among all the viewpoints expressed, a few points of commonality emerge: Gentile believers are strongly in view; there is no specific crisis or problem the letter addresses; the letter gives a positive presentation of the Pauline gospel; and there is a need for the readers to receive teaching and admonishment on unity and a distinctively Christian lifestyle.

Based on the foregoing discussion and conclusions, the life setting and purpose of the letter could be described in the following way: In the period of time since Paul's ministry in Ephesus, the churches of the area had engaged in extensive evangelism among the Gentiles. These new believers lacked a personal acquaintance with Paul but respected his role as apostle. Being converts from a Hellenistic religious environment—mystery religions, magic, astrology—these people needed a positive grounding in the Pauline gospel from the apostle himself. Their fear of evil spirits and cosmic powers was also a great concern, especially the question of where Christ stands in relation to these forces. Because of their pagan past, they also needed help and admonishment in cultivating a lifestyle consistent with their salvation in Christ, a lifestyle free from drunkenness, sexual immorality, stealing and bitterness. Although there were many Jewish Christians (and former God-fearers) in the churches of the region, the flood of new Gentile converts created some significant tensions. Their lack of appreciation for the Jewish heritage of their faith prompted some serious Jew-Gentile tensions in the churches.

Ephesians is therefore a genuine letter, without a specific crisis, but addressed in a pastoral way to a multiplicity of needs shared by the readership. It was written by the apostle Paul to a network of churches in Ephesus, but also intended for a broader readership among the churches of that region.

It has traditionally been regarded as written during Paul's first Roman imprisonment (see also Robinson, Barth, Bruce et al.), but a strong case has also been made for his prior imprisonment in Caesarea (Meyer). It is least likely to have been written during a possible Ephesian imprisonment. A date of A.D. 60-62 is probable.

### 7. Themes in the Letter.

The main themes of Ephesians could be summarized in the following way (not ordered according to importance):

*7.1. The Greatness of God.* The letter begins with an exclamation of praise to God.* He is eulogized as the Father of the Lord Jesus Christ and is magnified for all that he has done for his people in and through Christ (Eph 1:3). Most notably, he has chosen for himself a people and has provided them with redemption from bondage and forgiveness of sin. With a rich variety of terminology, Paul stresses that God is fulfilling a grand plan—his "will"—that encompasses the entire sweep of human history. One of the most awe-inspiring characteristics about God is his great love* which prompts him to act on behalf of his people (Eph 1:4; 2:4). His divine power is also brought into bold relief by his act of raising Jesus from the dead (Eph 1:19-20).

*7.2. The Exalted Christ.* Ephesians is often described as presenting a "cosmic christology." This stems from Paul's stress on the exaltation* of Christ over all his enemies, especially the principalities and powers (Eph 1:21-22) and Christ's role in bringing all of history to completion (Eph 1:10). Nevertheless, the letter speaks of the suffering* of Christ; it was through his blood that redemption* was secured (Eph 1:7) and by the cross that reconciliation* was achieved (Eph 2:16). This letter builds on Paul's previous thought about the relationship of Christ to his church by depicting him as the "head"* of his body (Eph 1:23; 4:15-16) and a bridegroom that nourishes and cares for his bride (Eph 5:29).

*7.3. Salvation in its Present Dimension.* Ephesians is also often characterized as having a strongly "realized" eschatology.* Although the future aspect of eschatology is not totally absent (see Eph 1:10, 14; 4:30; 5:6, 27), there is a significant stress on salvation as present. This is clearly expressed in Ephesians 2:5, 8 by the perfect tense of *sōzō* with the emphasis of the perfect on the present state of affairs: "you have been saved and are saved." It is also accented by the declaration that believers have been raised and exalted with Christ (Eph 2:6). This represents a distinctive Pauline development on ideas already present in Romans 6:1-13 (cf. Col 3:1).

Although justification* terminology does not appear in Ephesians (perhaps because there is no Judaizing controversy in the background; *see* Judaizers), the Pauline emphasis on faith alone apart from works for salvation is clearly expressed (Eph 2:8-9). Christ's work of reconciliation is stressed (Eph 2:16) with the implication that believers now have access to God, their Father (Eph 2:18; 3:12).

*7.4. The Status of Believers.* Through use of the expression "in Christ"*—which occurs thirty-four times in Ephesians—Paul describes the corporate solidarity of believers with their resurrected and exalted Lord. The *syn-* ("with") compounds also help express this notion, especially in Ephesians 2:5: he made us alive *with* Christ, he raised us *with* him, and he seated us *with* him. As people who are united with Christ, believers have redemption, forgiveness* of sins,* a heavenly* existence, access to the Father, knowledge of the truth* and the gift of the Holy Spirit (Eph 1:13-14; *see* Holy Spirit). They possess a new existence created by God and characterized by righteousness* (Eph 4:24).

*7.5. The Unity of Jew and Gentile.* One of the central messages of the letter is that Christ has effected a reconciliation of Jew (*see* Israel) and Gentile* by incorporating them into one body through his work on the cross (Eph 2:16; 3:6). Christ has removed all of the obstacles that separated the two groups and resulted in their hostility to one another (Eph 2:12-18). What matters now is the unity of the body of Christ, the church, composed of Jews and Gentiles who have equal access to the Father.

*7.6. The Struggle with the Powers.* Believers within the young Christian communities in and around Ephesus lived in a culture where magical practices flourished (*see* Magic). These practices were reinforced by the renowned Artemis cult. Artemis was worshiped as a goddess of the underworld with cosmic supremacy; she bore the six magical *Ephesia Grammata* on her cultic image. The people of the region had an extraordinary fear of the hostile spiritual "powers." Through

magical practices and cultic rituals, people sought relief and deliverance from the dreaded realm of the powers. This fear was not immediately allayed, however, when people became Christians. Demonstrating his sincere pastoral concern, Paul addressed their fear of this realm. More than any other Pauline letter, Ephesians stresses the hostile role of the principalities and powers (*see* Principalities and Powers) against the church (see Arnold, 167-68).

In contrast to the power of the hostile supernatural realm, Paul emphasizes the superiority of the power* of God and the supremacy of Christ (Eph 1:19-23; 4:8-10; *see* Triumph). He demonstrates that believers have access to this power by virtue of their union with Christ, thereby enabling them to resist the vicious attacks of the hostile powers (Eph 6:10-20). He regards all these spiritual powers as evil and under the leadership of a being he calls "the devil" (*see* Satan).

*7.7. The Ethical Obligation of Believers.* The latter half of the letter is replete with specific ethical guidance for these believers (*see* Ethics). Paul wants them to rid their lives of vices that characterized their pre-Christian conduct and appropriate the virtues of Christ. He admonishes them to desist from such practices as lying, stealing, sexual immorality, dirty talk, excessive anger, bitterness, greed and many more (*see* Virtues and Vices). He instructs them on appropriate relationships within the Christian household.*

He affirms that behavioral change is not only possible, it is part of their divine calling and God's purpose for them (Eph 1:4; 2:10; 4:1). They have access to God's power which will enable them to resist temptation (Eph 6:10-18). They are enabled by the risen Christ himself who has endowed the church with gifted people who depend on him for leadership and provision (Eph 4:11-16). Finally, they have an example in Christ himself who modeled self-sacrificial love and service (Eph 5:2; *see* Servant, Service).

*7.8. Apostle to the Gentiles.* In a lengthy digression Paul speaks about his apostolic ministry* (Eph 3:1-13). He stresses that he has been given the special responsibility of administering God's grace* (his saving favor) to the Gentiles (Eph 3:2, 7, 8). God revealed to Paul, as he did to all the apostles, his formerly secret plan to extend his favor to the Gentiles through the work of Jesus, the Messiah. On this basis, Paul claims special insight into "the mystery," the saving plan of God disclosed in Christ. He does not want his readers to be discouraged by his recent imprisonment or see it as the result of some crime; he wants them to know that it was for his service to Christ and his ministry to them as Gentiles (cf. Acts 21:17-36; Rom 15:14-32).

*7.9. The Church.* Ephesians has a strong ecclesiological focus. Paul's teaching in this letter conceptualizes the many churches as a collective whole. In fact, the term *ekklēsia* is never used of one local church,* but in a universal sense (Eph 1:22; 3:10, 21; 5:23-25, 27, 29, 32). This may be due in part to the fact that a network of churches was addressed (if Ephesians was a circular letter), but more likely Paul is reflecting on the church as a universal, unified organism.

Some have argued that the ecclesiology of Ephesians reflects early catholicism (e.g., Käsemann 1971; *see* Early Catholicism), but this is to misconstrue the teaching of the letter. The church is still viewed as an organism (thus, the head/body imagery and the teaching on the Spirit) and not as an institution. There is no interchurch organization and no established priesthood to mediate the means of grace (see Bruce, 238-39). All members are involved in the work of the ministry (Eph 4:12, 16).

In this letter Paul depicts the church as a building, the "household of God" (Eph 2:19-22), a growing body in connection to its head which gives leadership and provision (Eph 1:23; 4:16; 5:23), and a bride in relationship to her loving and caring bridegroom (Eph 5:25-32). Each of these images shows continuity with but also advancement on Paul's prior teaching on the church.

*See also* BODY OF CHRIST; CANON; CHRISTOLOGY; CHURCH; COLOSSIANS, LETTER TO THE; EARLY CATHOLICISM; EPHESUS; EXALTATION AND ENTHRONEMENT; HEAVEN, HEAVENLIES, PARADISE; MAGIC; MYSTERY; POWER; PRINCIPALITIES AND POWERS; WORSHIP.

BIBLIOGRAPHY. **Commentaries:** T. K. Abbott, *A Critical and Exegetical Commentary on the Epistles to the Ephesians and to the Colossians* (ICC; Edinburgh: T. & T. Clark, 1897); M. Barth, *Ephesians* (AB 34; 2 vols.; New York: Doubleday, 1974); E. Best, *A Critical and Exegetical Commentary on the Epistle to the Ephesians* (ICC; Edinburgh: T. & T. Clark, in preparation); F. F. Bruce, *The Epistles to the Colossians, to Philemon, and to the Ephesians* (NICNT; Grand Rapids: Eerdmans, 1984); G. B. Caird, *Paul's Letters from Prison* (NCIB; Oxford: University Press, 1976); H. Conzelmann, "Der Brief an die Epheser," in *Die Briefe an die Galater, Epheser, Philipper, Kolosser, Thessalonicher und Philemon*, ed. J. Becker et al. (Göttingen: Vandenhoeck & Ruprecht, 1976) 86-124; C. H. Dodd, "Ephesians," *The Abingdon Bible Commentary*, ed. F. C. Eiselen et al. (New York: Abingdon, 1928) 1224-25; C. J. Ellicott, *A Critical and Grammatical Commentary on St. Paul's Epistle to the Ephesians* (2d ed.; London: Parker & Son, 1859); J. Gnilka, *Der Epheserbrief* (HTKNT X/2; Freiburg: Herder, 1971); H. W. Hoehner, *Ephesians* (Grand Rapids: Baker, in preparation); A. T. Lincoln, *Ephesians* (WBC 42; Dallas: Word, 1990); A. Lindemann, *Der Epheserbrief* (Zürich: Theologischer Verlag, 1985); R. P. Martin, *Ephesians, Colossians, and Philemon* (IntC; Louisville: John Knox, 1992); H. A. W. Meyer, *Critical and Exegetical Hand-Book to the Epistle to the Ephesians* (4th ed.; New York: Funk & Wagnalls, 1884); C. L. Mitton, *Ephesians* (NCB; Grand Rapids: Eerdmans, 1973); C. Newman, *Ephesians* (NAC; Nashville: Broadman, in preparation); P. Pokorný, *Der Epheserbrief und die Gnosis* (Berlin: Evangelische Verlagsanstalt, 1965); J. A. Robinson, *St. Paul's Epistle to the Ephesians* (2d ed.; London: Macmillan, 1907); H. Schlier, *Der Brief an die Epheser* (Dusseldorf: Patmos, 1957); R. Schnackenburg, *The Epistle to the Ephesians* (Edinburgh: T. & T. Clark, 1991); E. F. Scott, *The Epistles of Paul to the Colossians, to Philemon and to the Ephesians* (MNTC; London: Hodder & Stoughton, 1930); **Studies:** C. E. Arnold, *Ephesians: Power and Magic* (SNTSMS 63; Cambridge: University Press, 1989); F. C. Baur, *Paulus der Apostel Jesu Christi* (Stuttgart: Becker & Müller, 1845); E. Best, "Recipients and Title of the Letter to the Ephesians: Why and When the Designation 'Ephesians'?" *ANRW* II.25.4 (1987) 3247-79; M. N. A. Bockmuehl, *Revelation and Mystery in Ancient Judaism and Pauline Christianity* (WUNT 2/36; Tübingen: J. C. B. Mohr, 1990); R. Bultmann, *Theology of the New Testament* (2 vols.; New York: Scribners, 1951, 1955) 2.151-53; C. C. Caragounis, *The Ephesian Mysterion* (CB 8; Lund: Gleerup, 1977); D. A. Carson, D. Moo and L. Morris, *An Introduction to the New Testament* (Grand Rapids: Zondervan, 1992); N. A. Dahl, "Gentiles, Christians, and Israelites in the Epistle to the Ephesians," *HTR* 79 (1986) 31-39; E. J. Goodspeed, *The Meaning of Ephesians* (Chicago: University of Chicago, 1933); H. J. Holtzmann, *Kritik der Epheser- und Kolosserbriefe auf Grund einer Analyse ihres Verwandtschaftsverhältnisses* (Leipzig: Engelmann, 1872); E. Käsemann, "Epheserbrief," *RGG* 2.517-20; idem, "The Theological Problem Presented by the Motif of the Body of Christ," in *Perspectives on Paul* (Philadelphia: Fortress, 1971) 102-21; J. Knox, *Philemon Among the Letters of Paul* (Nashville: Abingdon, 1959); W. G. Kümmel, *Introduction to the New Testament* (rev. ed.; Nashville: Abingdon, 1975); D. G. Meade, *Pseudonymity and Canon* (WUNT 39; Tübingen: J. C. B. Mohr, 1986; Grand Rapids: Eerdmans, 1987); H. Merkel, "Der Epheserbrief in der neueren exegetischen Diskussion," *ANRW* II.25.4 (1987) 3156-3246; C. L. Mitton, *The Epistle to the Ephesians* (Oxford: Clarendon, 1951); E. Percy, *Die Probleme der Kolosser- und Epheserbriefe* (Lund: Gleerup, 1946, repr. 1964); A. Van Roon, *The Authenticity of Ephesians* (NovTSup 39; Leiden: E. J. Brill, 1974); P. Stuhlmacher, " 'He is our Peace' (Eph 2:14). On the Exegesis and Significance of Ephesians

2:14-18," in *Reconciliation, Law, & Righteousness: Essays in Biblical Theology* (Philadelphia: Fortress, 1986) 182-200.                                              C. E. Arnold

# EPHESUS

The city of Ephesus was situated on the west coast of Asia Minor (modern-day Turkey) at the mouth of the Cayster River. This thriving harbor city ranked with Rome, Alexandria and Syrian Antioch as one of the greatest cities of the Roman Empire. The apostle Paul spent nearly three years of his ministry in this center of Asian life. As many as six of his letters (see 6.) have been reputed to have a connection with Ephesus.

1. Pre-Roman Times
2. The Roman City
3. Artemis Ephesia and Other Deities
4. Judaism in Ephesus
5. The Lukan Account of Paul's Ephesian Ministry
6. The Ephesian Ministry As Seen from Paul's Letters

## 1. Pre-Roman Times.

According to mythology the city of Ephesus was founded by the Amazons, a race of female warriors. Although little is known about the early history of Ephesus, it was probably inhabited by a combination of Carians, Leleges and indigenous peoples. The Greek city was founded by Ionian colonists led by Androclus, son of the Athenian king Codrus c. 1100 B.C. Half a millennium later (c. 550 B.C.) Croesus, king of the province of Lydia, captured Ephesus. Croesus endeared himself to the people by contributing to the construction of the great temple of Artemis. Ephesus and all of Anatolia soon came under Persian rule which lasted until the combined Greek armies defeated the Persians c. 480 B.C. Ephesus joined the Greek alliance (called the Delian League), but the city revolted in 412 B.C. and sided with Sparta in the Peloponnesian War.

In 334 B.C. Alexander the Great took control of the city, as well as the rest of Asia Minor, on his eastward imperialistic march. Alexander's successor, Lysimachus, replanned Ephesus (c. 294 B.C.) and relocated the population from near the Artemis temple to a site next to the harbor. Here the city remained throughout the Roman and Byzantine periods. Ephesus then came under the control of the successive reigns of the Seleucids, the Ptolemies and finally the kingdom of Pergamum (c. 190 B.C.).

In 133 B.C. Attalus III, king of Pergamum, bequeathed the city to Rome. The city remained under Roman rule except for a brief interlude in which Mithridates VI, king of Pontus, took control of most of Asia Minor in a revolt against Rome. The people welcomed Mithridates as a deliverer because of harsh Roman exactions. He was eventually defeated by the Roman general Pompey in the "Third Mithridatic War" (c. 69 B.C.).

## 2. The Roman City.

Beginning in the reign of Caesar Augustus and lasting for 200 years, Ephesus experienced a more stable political history which enabled the city to prosper and thrive. Population estimates for the city during this time begin at around 250,000 people.

*2.1. The Leading City of Asia.* Ephesus may accurately be called the leading city of the richest region of the Roman Empire (Elliger, 101). Politically, the city functioned as the Roman provincial capital of Asia Minor (from 133 B.C.; *see* Political Systems). Economically, Strabo (14.1.24) called Ephesus "the greatest commercial center in Asia this side of the Taurus river." Similarly, Aelius Aristides (*Orat.* 23.24) spoke of Ephesus as the most prosperous commercial center of the time, controlling the financial affairs of western Asia Minor. A recent study of Roman milestone markers demonstrates that mileages to other cities in Asia Minor were measured from Ephesus (French, 698-729). Referred to in the inscriptions as "the metropolis of Asia," Ephesus served as the administrative and commercial hub of Asia Minor.

*2.2. Institutions and Buildings.* Since 1895, archeologists from the Austrian Archeological Institute in Vienna have worked at excavating various parts of the city. The work still continues. Many of the reconstructed edifices which one sees today were erected in the second century and later. Listed below are a few of the important buildings that were present during Paul's ministry.

*2.2.1. Theater.* One of the most impressive structures in Ephesus was the theater which had a seating capacity of 24,000 people. Situated on the side of a hill, the theater looked upon the beautiful colonnaded street that led directly to the harbor. The theater was the scene of the tumultuous mob assembly provoked by the guild of silver shrine makers for the Artemis cult (Acts 19:30-41).

*2.2.2. Prytaneion.* Directly across from the State Agora was the prytaneion, or town hall (built in the first century B.C. or first century A.D., so Akurgal, 167). Much of the city's political business was conducted in this center. The building was also used for various ceremonies, banquets and receptions for official guests of the city. Discoveries stemming from the excavation of the building in 1955 have demonstrated that the prytaneion served a strong religious function during

Paul's time. Although the goddess Hestia Boulaia was the principal deity worshiped in the prytaneion, there is inscriptional evidence pointing to the worship of Artemis, Demeter, Kore and other deities in this important building (Oster, 1688-91).

*2.2.3. Commercial Market (Agora).* The commercial market was located in the center of the city near the theater. It measured 110 meters square and was surrounded on all four sides with stoas. Most of the everyday buying and selling of produce and goods took place here. Another market, called the State Agora, was situated at the southeast part of the city across from the prytaneion. Many municipal activities, including the meetings of the law courts, took place in the basilica of this agora.

*2.2.4. Baths and Gymnasiums.* During the Roman period the city had a number of baths and gymnasiums. The largest complex was located near the harbor. The structure contained two *palaestrae* (athletic training areas), a bath and a gymnasium, complete with lecture halls and meeting rooms. Another gymnasium was located next to the theater and still another, "the East Gymnasium," at the southeastern corner of the city.

*2.2.5. Stadium.* The stadium was situated in the north part of the city. It measured 229 meters long and 30 meters wide. Various kinds of ceremonies, including athletic contests, chariot races and gladiatorial fights, took place there. Inscriptional evidence suggests that the stadium was erected during Nero's reign (A.D. 54-68).

*2.2.6. Medical School.* Literary sources point to the existence of a medical academy in Ephesus which trained doctors. Two of the most important doctors in antiquity, Rufus and Soranus, came from Ephesus. Both worked during Trajan's reign (Elliger, 85-86).

*2.3. Festivals and Athletic Contests.* Two important festivals were held each year in the city, honoring the patroness deity, Artemis Ephesia. The first, called the "Artemisia," was held in the early spring. In addition to sacrifices to the goddess, there were many musical, theatrical and athletic events. A second festival took place at the end of spring in celebration of the nativity of Artemis (Oster, 1709-10). One of the highlights of this festival was a religious procession through the city.

Another festival of regional importance was the quadrennial "Ephesia." This festival was especially noted for its athletic games. Ephesus also hosted the "Common Games of Asia" (*koinon Asias)* which had all the usual athletic events.

### 3. Artemis Ephesia and Other Deities.

"The most prominent and significant cult in Ephesus during the first three centuries of the Roman Empire was incontestably Artemis Ephesia (= Diana Ephesia)" (Oster, 1699). The people of Ephesus regarded the city's relationship to her in terms of a divinely directed covenant relationship.

Her temple, called the Artemision, was originally constructed in the sixth century B.C. This Ionic temple (c. 550 B.C.) was the largest building in the Greek world and was made entirely of marble. It was destroyed c. 350 B.C. The temple was rebuilt with the same dimensions during the first half of the third century B.C. According to Pliny (*Nat. Hist.* 36.96), the temple measured 220 x 425 feet (55.10 m. x 115 m.) and contained 127 columns, with some rising to a height of 60 feet (17.65 m.). The grandeur and beauty of the temple led Antipater (*Anth. Pal.* 9.58) to classify it as one of the seven wonders of the ancient world. The Greek historian Pausanias (*Descr.* 4.31.8) declared that the size of the temple surpassed all known buildings. The ancient site of the Artemision and its meager remains were discovered by J. T. Wood in 1869. In recent years Austrian archeologists have undertaken extensive excavations which have provided much information about the archaic temple and its predecessor.

Inscriptions give evidence that mystery rites were celebrated in the Artemis cult. The celebration of her birth marked one of the major occasions for the performance of the mysteries. We know little about the meaning attached to the mystery rites performed by her devotees. The cult of the Ephesian Artemis also had a close connection with the practice of magic* in the city and region (Arnold, 22-24). The Atticist lexicographer Pausanias (as cited by Eustathius *on Homer Od.* 19.247) reports that the six magical "Ephesian Letters" (*Ephesia Grammata)* were inscribed on the cultic image of the Ephesian Artemis. This is part of the reason why Ephesus gained a reputation as being something of a center for magical practices in antiquity.

In spite of the city's special relationship with Artemis, numerous other gods and goddesses were also worshiped there. Egyptian colonists and traders introduced the worship of Sarapis and Isis to Ephesus. Beautiful temples were erected for these deities. Material evidence also points to the veneration of the following deities in Ephesus: Agathe Tyche, Aphrodite, Apollo, Asclepius, Athena, the Cabiri, Concord, Cybele (the Mother Goddess), Demeter, Dionysus, Enedra, Hecate, Hephaestus, Heracles, Hestia Boulaia, Kore, Nemesis, Pan, Pion (a mountain god), Pluto, Poseidon, Theos Hypsistos, Tyche Soteira, Zeus and several river deities (*see* Religions).

### 4. Judaism in Ephesus.

Luke records that Paul spent three months preaching

in a Jewish synagogue in Ephesus (Acts 19:8). Although archeologists have not yet discovered the synagogue, there is substantial literary evidence and some material evidence of the Jewish presence. According to Josephus there had been a Jewish community in Ephesus since Seleucid times, and this community possessed citizenship (Josephus *Ant.* 13.3.2 §125). These Jews were exempted from military service and were permitted to send money to the Jerusalem Temple. Most importantly, they were granted the freedom to practice their religion according to their traditions (Josephus *Ant.* 14.10.11-12 §§223-27; 14.10.25 §§262-64). A few Jewish inscriptions have been found, including one which mentions the officials of the local synagogue.

**5. The Lukan Account of Paul's Ephesian Ministry.**
Luke gives us only a very abbreviated record of Paul's work in Ephesus. He narrates a few episodes that serve to further his own theological agenda, but that also provide us with a fascinating picture of the beginning of the church in this city.

*5.1. The Beginnings.* Paul first visited Ephesus only briefly on his way to Jerusalem from Corinth (Acts 18:18-22). He had attempted to preach in Ephesus earlier, but discerned clearly that the Holy Spirit (*see* Holy Spirit) was directing otherwise (Acts 16:6). Paul's preaching was well received by the Jews in the synagogue, and he promised to return. In order to continue the work he had started, he left Priscilla and Aquila, a Jewish-Christian couple.

*5.2. Apollos and the Disciples of John.* In Paul's absence an Alexandrian Jew familiar with the Jesus tradition came and began speaking in the synagogue (Acts 18:24-28). This man, Apollos,* said to have been fervent in spirit, had not received Christian baptism,* only a baptism associated with John the Baptist's teaching. Priscilla and Aquila took him into their home and provided him with a full account of early Christian tradition. Apollos apparently received their instruction favorably and continued his powerful preaching in Corinth.

Shortly after Paul arrived he encountered twelve men also inadequately instructed in Christian teaching (Acts 19:1-7) and who had not received the Holy Spirit. Priscilla and Aquila apparently had no contact with these men. The men claimed only to be familiar with the teaching of John the Baptist and had received his baptism. Paul baptized them, presumably after instructing them more fully about Jesus. After Paul laid his hands on them, they received the Holy Spirit, prophesied and spoke in tongues.*

*5.3. In the Synagogue and the School of Tyrannus.* As Paul promised, he returned to the synagogue and

taught for three months. The originally warm reception he received turned to hostility toward his preaching, and he was forced to leave the synagogue (Acts 19:8-9).

By this time, a few of the Jews (and probably Gentile God-fearers) had received Christ. Paul took these new believers with him and spoke daily in a lecture hall in the city (*scholē Tyrannou,* Acts 19:9). The western text adds the historical note that Paul taught between 11:00 a.m. and 4:00 p.m. With regard to the hall itself, no archeological or inscriptional evidence has yet been discovered to illustrate this point of the narrative (though one pillar *in situ* has the name Tyrannus, a common name). Many of the people in Ephesus and its environs now had the opportunity to hear the gospel. In fact, Luke says, "all the inhabitants of Asia heard the word of the Lord, both Jews and Greeks" (Acts 19:10). Paul made use of this hall for two years.

*5.4. Miracles, Jewish Exorcists and Magic.* Luke mentions that God accomplished many supernatural works through Paul, although he does not provide us with any specific accounts. People were healed (*see* Healing) of various illnesses, and demons* were exorcised (Acts 19:11-12).

At the same time, Luke records that there was a group of itinerant Jewish exorcists performing their exorcistic rites in the city (Acts 19:13). Probably because they saw Paul's success, they had added the name of Jesus to their exorcistic formulas. We know nothing of their relationship to the local synagogue, viz., whether they were attached to the synagogue or came from outside and acted independently. Luke tells us of one incident involving the sons of a Jewish chief priest (*archiereus*), Sceva, who unsuccessfully applied their method to a demonized man and experienced tragic results. They were physically assaulted and hurt by the man with whom they were working (Acts 19:14-16).

Word of this incident spread quickly through the city. Believers who had failed to renounce their occult practices when they were converted now confessed (Acts 19:17-20). They brought their magical books together and burned them. Luke was clearly impressed by the amount and monetary value of their books, estimating the value as equivalent to 50,000 days' wages.

*5.5. Hostility from the Artemis Adherents.* The rest of Luke's account is taken up with one major incident of hostility against Paul and, indeed, nascent Christianity. An outspoken leader of a local trade union named Demetrius fomented a dramatic mob scene at the theater to protest Paul's preaching (Acts 19:23-41). As a maker of cultic paraphernalia for the local Artemis cult, he foresaw a significant loss of income to his business. He rallied his fellow union workers and soon people from all over the city gathered at the theater to affirm their support of their patroness deity, chanting, "Great is Artemis of the Ephesians." The frenzy in the theater lasted for two hours and was finally quelled by the intervention of the city clerk (*grammateus*, also attested in local inscriptions). Luke reports that Paul left Ephesus shortly after this incident.

*5.6. Churches Begin.* One could wish that Luke had disclosed more about the founding of local churches in Asia Minor, but this was beyond the scope of his work. Presumably during this time in which "all Asia heard the word of the Lord" (Acts 19:10), churches were established not only in Ephesus but also by Paul's colleagues in Colossae (Col 1:7) and throughout Asia Minor (e.g., the churches mentioned in Rev 2—3). Given the size of Ephesus and the early tendency toward house churches, it is likely that more than one church was planted in Ephesus. Perhaps a network of house churches came into existence throughout the city and in the local villages (e.g., Hypaipa, Diashieron, Neikaia and Koloe).

**6. The Ephesian Ministry As Seen from Paul's Letters.** We are able to gain some insight into Paul's Ephesian ministry through scattered references in his correspondence.

*6.1. Ephesian Imprisonment?* While there is no explicit mention of Paul being imprisoned in Ephesus either by Luke or in the Pauline epistles, the majority of recent scholars postulate that Paul was imprisoned one or more times while he was in Ephesus. Shortly after leaving Ephesus, Paul tells the Corinthians that he had been in prison* frequently (2 Cor 11:23; cf. 1 Clem 5:6). Many have also thought imprisonment was one of the things entailed in his fighting with "wild beasts" at Ephesus (1 Cor 15:32) and part of the hardship he experienced in Asia (2 Cor 1:8). It is therefore quite possible that Paul was imprisoned during his Ephesian ministry.

*6.2. Correspondence with Corinth.* Paul wrote his first letter to the Corinthians* from Ephesus. He also appears to have written two other letters to the Corinthians, both of which are now lost (cf. 1 Cor 5:9; 2 Cor 2:4), and taken one trip to Corinth from Ephesus. We also know that a delegation from Corinth visited the apostle with a report about the Corinthian church and a list of questions during Paul's Ephesian ministry (1 Cor 16:17). Paul's explicit reference to "fighting with wild beasts" at Ephesus (1 Cor 15:32) should not be taken literally since his Roman citizenship would

have prevented such an occurrence. Rather, this is a metaphorical way of referring to the difficulty with his opponents and possible physical injury they may have inflicted on him.

*6.3. Philemon and Philippians.* If Paul was imprisoned in Ephesus, it is possible that he wrote his letters to Philemon* and to the Philippians* from there. Neither of these letters states where they were written, only that they were written during an imprisonment. Many scholars now accept this view, but there is still no consensus (*see* Philippians).

*6.4. The Epistle to the Ephesians.* The majority of scholars discount the tradition that Ephesians was intended for exclusive use by the church(es) of Ephesus. On text-critical grounds, they claim that the appearance of "in Ephesus" in Ephesians 1:1 is a spurious reading. Most are therefore content to describe the document as some kind of circular letter for churches in the Roman province of Asia.

Nevertheless, even if "in Ephesus" is not original in Ephesians 1:1—although there are good arguments in favor of its authenticity—it is still likely that Ephesus was one of the destinations for the letter, if not the primary recipient, because of its standing as the leading city of the region and because of its strategic importance for the Christianity of the province. In a general way then, Ephesians may very well give us a picture of the situation of the churches in Ephesus in the mid first century. Based on Ephesians, it appears that the churches were dealing with a problem of Jew-Gentile disunity (Eph 2:11-22) and were still struggling with the issue of divine power* and evil spirits. The letter also gives evidence of a strong, if not predominantly, Gentile presence in the churches who needed doctrinal instruction as well as ethical exhortation.

*6.5. Timothy in Ephesus.* Traditionally, 1 Timothy has been taken to be an authentic Pauline letter written to Timothy whom Paul had left as his representative in Ephesus. This view still has much in its favor, although many scholars (e.g., Schnackenburg) are inclined to deny the authenticity of the letter based on linguistic and theological grounds. At a minimum, the letter does appear to have a genuine connection with Asia Minor (and probably Ephesus) and gives us a glimpse of the incursions of false teaching during the latter third of the first century A.D.

*See also* EPHESIANS, LETTER TO THE.

BIBLIOGRAPHY. E. Akurgal, *Ancient Civilizations and Ruins of Turkey* (6th ed.; Istanbul: Haset Kitabevi, 1985); C. E. Arnold, *Ephesians: Power and Magic* (SNTSMS 63; Cambridge: University Press, 1989); E. C. Blake and A. G. Edmonds, *Biblical Sites in Turkey* (Istanbul: Redhouse, 1977); W. Elliger, *Ephesos: Geschichte einer antiken Weltstadt* (Stuttgart: Kohlhammer, 1985); D. H. French, "The Roman Road System of Asia Minor," *ANRW* II.7.2 (1983) 698-29; D. Knibbe and W. Alzinger, "Ephesos vom Beginn der römischen Herrschaft in Kleinasien bis zum Ende der Principatszeit," *ANRW* II.7.2 (Berlin: Walter de Gruyter, 1983) 748-830; R. Oster, "Ephesus as a Religious Center Under the Principate, I. Paganism Before Constantine," *ANRW* II.18.2 (Berlin: Walter de Gruyter, 1990) 1661-1728; R. Schnackenburg, "Ephesus: Entwicklung einer Gemeinde von Paulus zu Johannes," *BZ* 35 (1991) 41-64; P. Trebilco, *Jewish Communities in Asia Minor* (SNTSMS 69; Cambridge: University Press, 1991); E. Yamauchi, *New Testament Cities in Western Asia Minor* (Grand Rapids: Baker, 1980).

C. E. Arnold

**EPICUREANS.** *See* PHILOSOPHY.

**EPISTLES.** *See* LETTERS, LETTER FORMS.

**ESCHATOLOGICAL ANTAGONIST.** *See* APOCALYPTICISM; ESCHATOLOGY; MAN OF LAWLESSNESS AND RESTRAINING POWER.

## ESCHATOLOGY

Eschatology has traditionally been understood as that branch of theology which is concerned with "final" things. Topics such as the future of the world, the parousia of Jesus Christ, the coming kingdom* of God, the last judgment* of humankind, the resurrection* from the dead, heaven* and hell, the transformation of the cosmos, etc., are all generally considered under its heading. The term *eschatology* is often used interchangeably with *apocalyptic,** although in recent years the latter has been more correctly defined in terms of a distinctive literary genre which may or may not be concerned with temporal "last things" (as J. J. Collins and C. C. Rowland demonstrate). The relationship between chronological history and eschatology has been a major source of scholarly discussion in recent years. G. B. Caird has offered an important linguistic assessment of eschatological language which focuses on the *metaphorical* sense as primary to its meaning. The result of such an approach is similar to genre investigations, namely that a straightforward equation between temporal "last things" and eschatological literature, particularly apocalyptic texts, is qualified, if not challenged altogether.

Strictly speaking a distinction should be maintained between the two terms *apocalyptic* and *eschatology*, despite the fact that much earlier scholarly endeavor uses *apocalyptic* without knowledge of the genre clarification, inadvertently providing the basis for some modern confusion when these older materials are consulted (see Sturm for an overview; cf. Marshall, Barker). L. Keck has tried to address this problem when he suggests that we take *apocalyptic* as an adjective "which characterizes *a type of theology*, not merely a type of eschatology" (Keck, 233). According to Keck, Paul's apocalyptic theology is to be distinguished from his wisdom theology since it arises from a different theological base. This is true, although it is possible to see both types of theology overlapping within the Pauline letters, often within key passages (such as 1 Cor 2—3; Phil 2:5-11; Col 1:13-20).

Paul's place within the area of eschatological theology is central, not least because his writings are among the earliest Christian documents preserved, thus reflecting foundational perspectives on eschatological matters. Most of the standard introductions on Paul have a section dealing with eschatology (H. Ridderbos, D. E. H. Whiteley, G. Bornkamm, F. F. Bruce). In addition, many of the classic interpretative studies of Paul in previous generations were dependent upon critical analyses of his eschatological thought (e.g., A. Schweitzer, G. Vos, E. Käsemann, J. Munck, H. J. Schoeps, W. D. Davies). In the past decade or so several important studies of Pauline eschatology have been produced, most notably that of J. C. Beker (1980). These have served to revitalize interest in the topic and have highlighted how central eschatology is to Pauline studies as a whole.

Paul's eschatology provides the background for many other important topics which constitute the substance of Pauline theology; christology,* pneumatology, ecclesiology, soteriology and anthropology are all built upon the eschatological foundation of Paul's thought. This foundation is all pervading in Pauline studies for it is possible to see eschatological concerns or presuppositions surfacing in virtually every letter within the Pauline corpus (Gal and Philem have been suggested as possible exceptions since they do not contain explicit references to the future Day of the Lord). Eschatological material occurs in a wide variety of contexts within the Pauline letters: creedal,* polemical, pastoral,* ethical,* paraenetic* and personal pericopae all contain such teaching. The importance of Pauline eschatology is evident no matter what one's opinion about the question of the authenticity of some of the letters, namely 2 Thessalonians,* Colossians* and Ephesians* or the Pastorals.* Even if some of these letters within the Pauline corpus are taken to be the work of Paul's followers in a subsequent generation, it is clear that Paul's own eschatological viewpoint helps condition the teaching contained within them (more about this below).

## 1. The Context of Pauline Eschatology: Jewish Apocalyptic Literature.

Recognition of the importance of the eschatological milieu of the NT materials is one of the most important results of twentieth-century investigations by biblical scholars. It needs to be recognized that the production of apocalypses was by no means restricted to Jewish or Christian writers; there are examples from many parts of the ancient Near East. However, it is the apocalypses of the first-century Jewish-Christian world (such as *1 Enoch*, 4 Ezra and *2 Baruch*) that are the most important parallels to Paul since it is these materials which are closest to him in terms of date and geographical setting; they therefore afford us the best opportunity of appreciating the eschatological content of Paul's thinking.

In the memorable words of E. Käsemann, "apocalyptic was the mother of all Christian theology" (Käsemann, "Beginnings," 102). Indeed, apocalyptic* has been viewed as one of the keys for unlocking the meaning of the NT as a whole. It is for this reason that Beker has described the apocalyptic worldview as the "coherent center" of Paul's thought and "rejects those construals of Paul's thought that suppress, delimit, or compromise its apocalyptic texture" (Beker 1980, 135). Beker is here following the lead of Käsemann in defining apocalyptic eschatology in terms of a belief in the future, imminent consummation of the world, an event which is triggered by (and at times even equated with) the future parousia of Jesus Christ. At the same time Beker takes the argument a step further than Käsemann did, asserting that Paul's apocalyptic framework is not only the starting point for Paul's thought but constitutes "the indispensable framework for his interpretation of the Christ-event" (Beker 1980, 19). This stands in contrast to Käsemann, who argues that Paul later departs from such an apocalyptically conditioned perspective. In short Beker serves as the advocate for many who would see the long standing debate about the center and periphery of Paul's thought as resolved in favor of the centrality of the apocalyptic-

eschatological element of his teaching. The focus of theological discussion is thereby shifted away from earlier arguments about justification* by faith* (e.g., Käsemann) and Christ mysticism* (e.g., Schweitzer) as being the focal point(s) of Paul's theology. As an alternative Beker asserts that "the triumph of God [is] the center of Paul's thought" (Beker 1980, 355), a suggestion which arises directly out of an apocalyptic framework of Paul's thought. Beker summarizes this approach as one which recognizes Paul's thought as an interaction between "contingency" and "coherency" (*see* Center).

Some scholars have criticized the extent of Beker's approach, however, pointing out that in certain instances he imposed the apocalyptic scheme upon Paul's letters without due consideration to its appropriateness. J. L. Martyn, for example, has argued that Beker's interpretation of Galatians is misdirected and fails to take into account the role that the cross* has in the letter (the letter is not easily fitted into an apocalyptic framework since eschatological material is notably absent within it). Nevertheless, according to Martyn, Galatians forms, as it were, an "apocalypse of the cross," which initiates a cosmic battle between the flesh* and the spirit (as in Gal 5:16-25). (See Beker's response in his preface to 2d ed., *Paul the Apostle*.) A modification of the basic thesis is in order (as Beker [1991] himself now acknowledges).

Such attempts at interpreting Paul's theology from the standpoint of its eschatological foundation could legitimately be seen as a reaction to the overly realized approach of some interpreters such as Dodd or Bultmann, who build upon the (presumed) loss of an eschatological perspective as the Christian faith spread into the Hellenistic* world. However, this is not to suggest that Paul's viewpoint is completely apocalyptic in substance, merely that it lies within an eschatological framework. Clearly there is, at the same time, a dimension of realized eschatology in Paul's thought which tempers his obviously futuristic teaching (as V. P. Branick argues). Any attempt to contrast what is "present" with what is "eschatological" in Paul's thought misrepresents his position—the two are dynamically interconnected. Recognition of Paul's two-dimensional eschatology (present/future; immanent/transcendent) is particularly important when it comes to determining how the message of Pauline eschatology is applicable to us today. The two dimensions of Paul's thought are sometimes usefully described as the "vertical" and "horizontal" (or the "spatial" and "temporal") planes of his eschatology. The perceived relationship between the spatial and temporal dimensions of Paul's eschatological thought has proven to be one of the great divides among interpreters of Paul; those who emphasize the vertical dimension tend to see the conflict implied by a two-age dualism in cosmological terms (earthly versus heavenly), while those who emphasize the horizontal dimension tend to see the conflict arising out of straightforward chronological considerations (present versus future). A full examination of Paul's letters reveals that he uses the language of both time and space within his eschatological teaching (*see* Lincoln). The latter should not be neglected nor the former overemphasized; both help constitute Paul's eschatological thought. Even such a passage as Colossians 3:1-6, dominated by "spatial" language, has a wider eschatological vision behind it which hints at its "horizontal" counterpart (*see* Levison for a discussion).

Over the years considerable discussion has been given over to determining the background sources for Paul's eschatological viewpoint: does it ultimately derive from his Jewish heritage or from the wider Hellenistic world of which he was a part? Most scholars now accept that Paul's Jewish heritage and background, including its twofold division of temporal history into two aeons, the "now" and the "not-yet," is determinative for his eschatological worldview. M. C. de Boer [1989] further subdivides Jewish apocalyptic eschatology by suggesting two tracks: a cosmological-apocalyptic eschatology and a forensic-apocalyptic eschatology. De Boer argues that these correspond respectively to Käsemann's cosmological understanding of apocalyptic and Bultmann's anthropological understanding of it. Be that as it may, for Paul Jewish apocalyptic is a worldview which has had to undergo significant adaptation in light of the crucial event of Jesus' resurrection from the dead. It is the resurrection of Jesus Christ, above all, which conditions and determines Paul's eschatological teaching for it is in the resurrection that the inauguration of the eschaton has truly taken place, the new order begun. While the resurrection is central to it, Pauline eschatology is by no means monolithic in its conceptualization, nor is it uniform in its expression. A great deal of variety characterizes the letters on this score. As W. Baird puts it: "Paul does not have a clear and simple apocalyptic picture of the end. His language is drawn from external sources and is not used consistently" (Baird, 325). Before we turn to consider some of the specifics of Paul's eschatological teaching there is one additional matter of significance which must first be addressed.

## 2. The Contingency of the Pauline Letters.

One of the most important contributions in recent Pauline studies has been the increased understanding of the contingent nature of the letters which form the Pauline corpus. Even if, as we suggested above, Beker argues that apocalyptic be recognized as the "coherent center" of Paul's thought, he rightly notes that it must be translated into "the contingent particularities of the human situation" (Beker 1980, ix). More than ever before scholarship has come to appreciate how the circumstances surrounding the production of a letter help to contribute to our understanding of its contents. In short, the greater our knowledge of precisely how and why the apostle Paul (or, perhaps one of his followers, in the case of the so-called Deutero-Pauline letters) came to write a given letter, the better our chances of understanding not only its original message, but of interpreting the meaning for us today.

An informed study of the relationship that Paul (or his successors) might have had with the intended congregation better enables us to expound the text as a whole. Unfortunately, the contingent nature of many of the letters is such that we are often left with many key questions unanswered. We simply do not know enough about what actually occasioned the apostle to write to the congregations (or they to him), and are often forced to hypothesize so as to fill in the gaps of our knowledge; we do not even have the complete Pauline corpus to work with (as 1 Cor 5:9 demonstrates). Hypothetical reconstructions of the correspondence between Paul and the various congregations are needed to overcome this problem (as J. C. Hurd's seminal "backward extrapolation" theory about the Corinthian correspondence illustrates). These problems affect virtually all of the letters in the Pauline corpus and involve many theological themes, but become particularly acute in the area of eschatological teaching within several of the undisputed letters. Is Paul responding to questions arising from the congregations concerned? Have they misunderstood (or misrepresented) him? How much of what he writes in reply is dependent upon a common eschatological understanding which he shares with them (or perhaps, even was responsible for imparting to them)? How much of what he writes is designed as conscious corrective? Two examples are worth citing at this point.

*2.1. 1 Thessalonians 4:13—5:11: The Premature Death of Christian Believers?* The Thessalonian* letters both appear to have been written in response to serious questions raised by the congregation about the death of believers prior to the expected parousia of the Lord (1 Cor 11:30 and 15:18 may hint at the same issue being debated in Corinth). Paul's answer in 1 Thessalonians 4:13—5:11 attempts to deal with this concern and basically asserts that the dead suffer no disadvantage and will be joined with Christ at his coming. The difficulty here is that it is not entirely clear what eschatological beliefs were held by the church at Thessalonica, nor why they were thrown into such theological turmoil by the death of some of the members of the congregation. Did they simply misunderstand what Paul (presumably) had taught them about the future when he helped found the congregation? Or could it be that Paul himself had altered his views about the resurrection in the interim and that he is correcting his earlier teaching within the letter? Part of the problem lies, no doubt, in the imprecise nature of eschatological material itself (Klijn notes that the question of the status of the deceased was a problem common to apocalyptic literature). However, because we do not know the earlier exchange between Paul and the Thessalonians, it is not possible to be sure about the accuracy of any interpretation; it is like trying to listen to one end of a telephone conversation and deduce the matter being discussed.

*2.2. 1 Corinthians 7: The Institution of Marriage and Human Sexuality in the Face of the Parousia.* In this chapter Paul responds to some questions raised by the Corinthians about sex and marriage* in the lives of Christian believers. It appears that the Corinthians had adopted an ascetic attitude toward sexuality* in light of their belief that full salvation* in Christ had already arrived (in 1 Cor 7:1b Paul cites one of their slogans to this effect). Paul writes to correct this attitude, emphasizing in 1 Corinthians 7:2-6 the mutual obligations and responsibilities of sexual relationships between husbands and wives. This section presents little difficulty as far as eschatological matters are concerned. However, in 1 Corinthians 7:7-40 Paul continues with advice that seems much more conditioned by his views of the imminent parousia of Christ; this is particularly true in 1 Corinthians 7:25-35. There he advises those who are single (for whatever reason) to remain so in light of the "present distress" (1 Cor 7:26) and the "shortening of the time" (1 Cor 7:29). The chapter is an exegetical minefield, but most scholars agree that to some degree Paul's eschatological perspective is coloring his ethical advice to those contemplating marriage. Whatever interpretation is eventually adopted, one must give due consideration to the eschatological backdrop of Paul's thought (see Moiser for an overview).

**3. The Content of Pauline Eschatology: Some Central Tenets.**

Clearly an eschatological viewpoint underlies the whole of Pauline theology. The extent to which the perspective is determinative and the variety of form and expression which it employs makes it difficult to assess the matter simply. However, the main points may be summarized under the following eight headings.

*3.1. The Messiahship of Jesus of Nazareth.* For Paul, Jesus of Nazareth is without doubt the Messiah, the Christ promised of old. So much is this so that the title "Christ"* (*christos*) functions almost as if it is the surname of Jesus himself. Several other messianic titles and designations are accorded to Jesus within the Pauline corpus, including Son (of God)* (sixteen times in Rom 1:4, 9; 5:10; 8:3, 29, 32; 1 Cor 1:9; 15:28; 2 Cor 1:19; Gal 1:16; 2:20; 4:4, 6; Eph 4:13; Col 1:13; 1 Thess 1:10), Son of David (two times in Rom 1:3; 2 Tim 2:8) and Lord* (around 275 times, including such important christological passages as 1 Cor 8:6; Phil 2:11). Yet it cannot be forgotten that the appearance of the Messiah was regarded within many writings of first-century Judaism above all as an eschatological event, an indisputable sign that the age to come had arrived. In a sense then, it is true to say that the linchpin of Paul's eschatology is the proclamation of Jesus of Nazareth as the Messiah. At the same time it also needs to be said that the key event which guarantees, or authenticates, that messiahship is the raising of Jesus from the dead, for it is that act of resurrection which demonstrates how the eschatological age has impinged upon the present.

*3.2. The Presence of the Eschatological Age.* One of the standard features of Jewish apocalyptic literature is the division of time into two aeons (4 Ezra 7:50, "The Most High made not one age but two," is a classic statement of this). Perhaps the most demonstrable way that Paul shows his acceptance of this sort of an eschatological dualism of two aeons is in his use of the phrase "this age" (Rom 12:2; 1 Cor 1:20; 2:6-8; 3:18; 2 Cor 4:4). The corresponding phrase "the age to come," although implied at several points in the Pauline corpus, is never used in the undisputed letters (it does appear in Eph 1:21). The present age is occasionally described as evil (*ponēros*, Gal 1:4; Eph 5:16; 6:13), and the inhabitants of the world are a "wicked and perverse generation" (Phil 2:15). And yet it becomes clear that Paul believes that the eschatological hope of the future has in some way impinged upon the present. As the apostle declares in 2 Corinthians 5:17, "the old has passed away, behold the new has come." In 1 Corinthians 10:11 he asserts that "the end of the ages has come" (with a deliberate use of the perfect verb *katēntēken*), and in 1 Corinthians 7:31 he states that "the form of this world is passing away." He describes this eschatological age as a "new creation*" (*kainē ktisis*, 2 Cor 5:17; Gal 6:15). More than this, Paul associates the arrival of the eschatological age with the revelation of Jesus Christ as God's Messiah. Thus he declares in Galatians 4:4 that "when the time had fully come, God sent forth his own Son." All of this is to suggest that Paul's teaching about the presence of the eschatological age must be set against the backdrop of a temporal dualism.

Several related images are used to express this idea of two aeons, including the Adam/Christ analogy of Romans 5 and 1 Corinthians 15 (*see* Adam and Christ), and an extended anthropological image involving a contrast between the old self/new self (Rom 6:6; Col 3:9-10; Eph 2:15; 4:22-24); outer self/inner self (Rom 7:22; 2 Cor 4:16; Eph 3:15); physical person/spiritual person (2 Cor 2:14-16; *see* New Nature and Old Nature). A spatial image involving the use of "heaven"* (*ouranos*) and its related terms also offers an important means whereby eschatological truth is communicated in the Pauline letters (as Lincoln demonstrates).

The assurance of the present reality of the new age gave rise to an overly realized understanding of Christian existence within some congregations. So certain were they about the reality of eschatological existence *now* that there seemed little need for any resurrection in the *future*—the resurrection life was presently being lived (most scholars accept that 1 Cor 4:8; 15:12 and 2 Tim 2:18 can all be exegetically linked as expressive of this overrealized perspective, but see Wedderburn for a dissenting opinion). In the case of Corinth this overrealized enthusiasm seems to have manifested itself in an unhealthy preoccupation with spiritual gifts,* demonstrating how closely allied eschatology and pneumatology were in Paul's time (as Thistleton argues; *see* Holy Spirit). Surely R. P. Martin is correct at this point in suggesting that 1 Corinthians 15 must not be separated from 1 Corinthians 12—14, particularly within an exegetical framework. It is not difficult to demonstrate that the same dynamic interplay between eschatology and pneumatology persists throughout church history and holds true even today, with appeal to the Pauline letters being made by all sides over the years. Paul counters the enthusiasm of the Corinthians in two major ways: first, by the use of sarcastic rebuke (as in 1 Cor 4:8); second, by forcefully reemphasizing the futuristic dimensions of their common faith (as in 1 Cor 15). Similar overly realized understandings of Christian existence are reflected (and challenged!) in 1 Timothy 2:16-18, 2 Thessalonians 2:2 and (possibly) 1 Thessalonians 4:13. There exists in Paul a dialectic between the present and the future, particularly as it is connected to the concept of salvation.

However, despite the assurance of a present dimension of eschatological hope, it should not be overlooked that for Paul the final revelation of the eschatological age still lies in the future. The ultimate transformation of the world order, the final redemption of the believer (the granting of the resurrection body) and the final judgment are all events which are yet to be awaited. The present is conditioned by both the past (death and resurrection of Jesus Christ) and the future (the awaited parousia at the end of time).

*3.2.1. The Kingdom of God/Christ.* Although the idea of the kingdom of God/Christ is a standard feature of the Jewish eschatological perspective which Paul shares and is something which clearly underlies much of his ethical teaching, the phrase itself is not a prominent one within the Pauline letters (*see* Kingdom of God/Christ). Apparently Paul does clearly assume the life and ministry of Jesus Christ to have been in some way the inauguration of the kingdom of God on earth, despite the fact that this is never explicitly stated anywhere within his letters.

Paul tends to talk of the kingdom of God/Christ as if it is something awaited in the future, although occasionally he hints at the present reality of the kingdom in the life of the Christian (as in Rom 14:17 and 1 Cor 4:20). One of his most common statements about the kingdom is that it is something which the believer inherits (as in 1 Cor 6:9-10; 15:50; Gal 5:21) as a result of faithfulness; again, clearly it is a future inheritance which is in view. More central within Paul's teaching on the kingdom of God/Christ is the place that the resurrection of Jesus Christ has in bringing the kingdom to bear within human history.

*3.3. The Resurrection of Jesus Christ from the Dead.* For Paul the resurrection* of Jesus is primarily an eschatological event affirming the fact that the new age has arrived. At the same time it is understandably seen as the vindication of Jesus' death on the cross and is closely associated with Christ's accession to power at the right hand of God (Rom 8:34; *see* Exaltation), providing the basis for his intercession on behalf of the saints. Despite the fact that the resurrection is for Paul an eschatological act of God, it is never simply a "spiritual" event loosed from the moorings of history or distanced from some sort of physicality. For Paul the resurrection of Jesus clearly involves the risen Lord in some sort of somatic existence, although admittedly it is an existence of a different order.

*3.3.1. Romans 1:3-4: Son of God and Resurrection.* Most scholars agree that within these two verses we have the apostle alluding to a traditional creedal affirmation (*see* Creed) about Jesus Christ. Several features of the passage hint at an earlier setting of the declaration, perhaps arising from the Palestinian church. Notable among these are the unusual phrase "according to the Spirit of holiness" and the juxtaposition of Jesus' earthly credentials ("descended from David according to the flesh") with his heavenly status ("designated Son of God in power"). In short, we have here a dual affirmation of Jesus' sonship: he is both Son of David and Son of God.* What is significant in terms of Paul's eschatology is the fact that Jesus' credentials as Son of God are closely linked to his resurrection from the dead. It is no wonder that this passage is sometimes described as reflecting one of the earliest stages of theological reflection among the first Christians, where the resurrection is the act which accords Jesus his status as God's Son. When this consideration is held alongside the fact that the participial form *horisthentos* in verse 4 (translated as "designated" in the RSV, "declared" in the NRSV) is very difficult to interpret precisely, it is easy to understand how those who advocated adoptionism found the text a key one for their position.

*3.3.2. 1 Corinthians 15: An Excursus on Resurrection.* In 1 Corinthians 15 we have a semi-independent excursus on the resurrection and its implications for the believer. This is the most detailed discussion of the resurrection within the Pauline corpus. The focus of discussion within the chapter is *not* whether or not Jesus Christ has been raised from the dead (as is often assumed in popular apologetics), but what the implications of Christ's resurrection are for the believer. Thus 1 Corinthians 15:12 provides an important clue for the discussion as a whole: "Now if Christ is preached as raised from the dead, how can some of you say that there is no resurrection of the dead?" Important insight is here gained about the nature of the controversy at Corinth and the identity of the so-called Corinthian* heresy. Paul is here confronting an overrealized eschatology within the Corinthian congregation, one which suggests that the Corinthians (or at least some of them) believed there was no need for their future resurrection since they had been baptized and were living the resurrection life already. Paul's initial defense of a futuristic eschatology involves his reminding the Corinthians of his earlier teaching on the matter, one built on traditional creedal declarations about the resurrection of Jesus Christ (1 Cor 15:3-7) and his appearance to witnesses. In other words the Corinthians share Paul's acceptance of the resurrection of Jesus Christ as foundational to their Christian faith but differ as to their understanding of its significance for Christian hope.

*3.3.2.1. The First Fruits (1 Cor 15:20, 23).* Paul uses an illustration drawn from agriculture to demonstrate the connection between the resurrection of Jesus

Christ and the resurrection of the believer. In 1 Corinthians 15:20 and 15:23 he describes the risen Lord Jesus Christ as the first fruits* (*aparchē*), implying that the believer will share in the resurrection life in the same way that the full harvest is related to the initial crop. The important qualifier interjected by means of this agricultural image is that the resurrection existence of the believer is still future and yet to be awaited. The whole image is dependent upon an understanding of a dynamic unity existing between Christ and the believers; whatever happens to the risen Lord Jesus Christ is automatically transferred to the Christian community, albeit within an eschatological context. As M. J. Harris (114) puts it, the first fruits image demonstrates that Christ is "both the pledge and the paradigm of the somatic resurrection of believers."

Paul also applies the *aparchē* image to his eschatological teaching about the gift of the Holy Spirit* in Romans 8:23, as well as to Jewish/Gentile relationships within the plan of God in Romans 11:16 (the image may also be present in 2 Thess 2:13 depending on the textual variants adopted). A related image, describing the risen Christ as the "firstborn* of the dead" (*prōtotokos ek tōn nekrōn*), is contained in the pre-Pauline hymn of Colossians 1:15-20.

*3.3.2.2. The Adam/Christ Analogy (1 Cor 15:20-21, 44b-45).* Paul's use of the Adam/Christ* analogy is one of the most important features of his eschatological teaching in the chapter. Beginning in 1 Corinthians 15:20 the apostle sets up a deliberate contrast between Adam and Jesus Christ as representative figures of humanity. The analogy is further extended in 15:44b-45 where Paul once again appears to correct an overrealized understanding of resurrection existence among the Corinthians. In 1 Corinthians 15:46 he reverses the order in which the physical body and the resurrection body are to appear (the Corinthians may be exhibiting dependence upon the kind of teaching about Adamic mankind found in Philo of Alexandria at this point). The result of this is that Christ is portrayed as embodying what R. Scroggs has described as "eschatological humanity."

*3.3.2.3. Death: The Last Enemy (1 Cor 15:26).* Within the Pauline letters death is portrayed in both physical and spiritual terms. Thus, it is both the cessation of mortal life (Phil 1:21; *see* Life and Death) and the state of spiritual separation from God (Rom 7:9-14; Eph 2:1-3; Col 1:21). The destructive power of death is never downplayed in Paul (note the use of *katalyō* in 2 Cor 5:1), although it is occasionally presented as the doorway of departure to another existence (2 Cor 5:8; Phil 1:23; 2 Tim 4:6). In the midst of his extended discussion on the implications of Jesus Christ's resurrection,

Paul uses an unusual phrase in describing physical death, referring to it as "the last enemy to be destroyed." M. C. de Boer argues that this defeat of death is central to 1 Corinthians 15:20-28, the heart of Paul's eschatological teaching in the chapter. This is a highly evocative image, emphasizing the importance of the cross* for Paul's thought as it hints at a confrontation between Jesus Christ and Death, as if the latter is a personified figure who must be engaged in combat on this cross of Calvary (*see* Triumph). The figure of Death as an enemy is clearly drawn from Paul's eschatological worldview (similar instances of precisely this sort of personification of death can be found in other Jewish and Christian apocalypses such as 4 Ezra 8:53 and Rev 6:8; 20:13-14; see de Boer, 90-91, for further details).

At the same time the image sets up something of a tension within Paul's teaching on physical death, a tension which can perhaps best be highlighted by considering *when* it is that Paul views this enemy* to be destroyed. Has it already been accomplished by Christ's death on the cross (as the use of the aorist *katargēsantos* in 2 Tim 1:10 suggests)? Or is it something which is still to occur in the indefinite future, at the awaited parousia of Christ? Clearly the immediate context of 1 Corinthians 15:20-28 would suggest the latter, although how this is then to be applied to believers and what its implications are for their present ethical conduct are matters which are far from certain. To put it another way, if death and sin are interconnected (as Paul forcefully asserts in Rom 5:12), how is it that the Christian is exhorted to live a life in the present which is freed from the power and effect of sin,* and yet be expected to await the deliverance from death as something in the future? Sin (which is personified in Rom 5:14, 17, 21; 7:8-11, 13-25) is already conquered—yes; but not the physical death that is so intimately associated with it—that must await the future consummation. At the very least we must admit a theological tension being expressed here, although we need not go so far as some do to suggest that Paul is involved in a damaging self-contradiction at this point.

*3.4. The Awaited Day of the Lord and Final Judgment.*
The Day of the Lord (*yôm YHWH*) is a standard feature in OT prophetic literature, one which Paul takes over and expands within his letters. As far as can be adduced it was originally conceived as a day of future joy, when God would intervene on behalf of his people and save them from calamity, righting injustice and defeating Israel's enemies. However, many of the prophets, such as Amos, Ezekiel, Isaiah, Zechariah, Zephaniah, Malachi and Joel, in an effort to call the

people back to true obedience, shifted the focus within their message, proclaiming the Day of the Lord to be not only a time of deliverance but a time of judgment for the nation of Israel as well (see Everson). The idea of an eschatological Day of the Lord can also be found in Jewish pseudepigraphal documents (such as *1 Enoch*, 4 Ezra and *2 Baruch*) and in select Qumran* documents (such as 1QM and 1QS). In the Gospels it is most closely associated with Jesus' statements about the coming Son of man, but can be identified within all gospel strata. Paul takes over the Jewish concept of the Day of the Lord, including the twin themes of eschatological salvation and future judgment, within his teaching on the theme. However, he creatively integrates this OT hope with his own developing christology, effectively transforming the "Day of the Lord (Yahweh)" into the "Day of the Lord *Jesus Christ.*" This creativity stands as one of the most important contributions within Pauline eschatology (see 4 below).

*3.4.1. The Day of the Lord and the Parousia of Jesus Christ.* A variety of expressions are used within the Pauline letters for the eschatological Day of the Lord, particularly as it is used with reference to Jesus Christ. The simple phrase "Day of the Lord" occurs in 1 Thessalonians 5:2 and 2 Thessalonians 2:2; the phrase "Day of the Lord Jesus Christ" in 1 Corinthians 5:5; "Day of the Lord Jesus" in 1 Corinthians 1:8 and 2 Corinthians 1:14; "Day of Christ Jesus" in Philippians 1:6; "Day of Christ" in Philippians 1:10 and 2:16; "the Day" in 1 Thessalonians 5:4 and 1 Corinthians 3:13; "that Day" in 2 Timothy 1:12, 18; 4:8. In addition Paul is the major NT source for the use of the term *parousia* of the future coming of Jesus Christ (1 Cor 15:23; 1 Thess 2:19; 3:13; 4:15; 5:23; 2 Thess 2:1, 8-9). The noun *apokalypsis* ("revelation") is used in a similar way in 1 Corinthians 1:7 and 2 Thessalonians 1:7. In the Pastorals a significant change in vocabulary appears; the term *epiphaneia* is used with reference to the appearance of the Lord Jesus Christ in 1 Timothy 6:1; 2 Timothy 1:10; 4:1, 8; Titus 2:13, while the verb *epiphainō* ("appear") appears in Titus 2:11 and 3:4 (the noun *epiphaneia* ("appearance") also appears in 2 Thess 2:8). In all three Pastoral letters the immediate context of these verses suggests a future manifestation of the glory* of the Lord Jesus Christ, although the present dimension is also clearly in evidence (especially in 2 Tim 2:10). Several related verb forms are also used within the Pauline corpus to denote this future eschatological event: forms of *erchomai* ("come") appear in 1 Corinthians 4:5; 11:26 and 2 Thessalonians 2:10; *apokalyptō* ("reveal") in 2 Thessalonians 1:7; and *phaneroō* ("make manifest") in Colossians 3:4. The phrase "the Day of redemption" appears in Ephesians 4:30; while *to telos* ("the end") occurs in 1 Corinthians 1:8; 15:24; 2 Corinthians 1:13; and *ta telē* in 1 Corinthians 10:11. The future parousia of Jesus Christ is often popularly described as "the Second Coming" or "the Second Advent," although it is worth noting that neither phrase is found within the Pauline letters (nor anywhere in the NT, for that matter); the first attested distinction between a "First Advent" and a "Second Advent" is found in the writings of Justin Martyr (c. A.D. 110), although a close approximation is found in Hebrews 9:28.

At several points in the Pauline letters it appears that traditional declarations of the coming of the Messiah from heaven are cited. Generally these statements are filled with apocalyptic language and imagery, much of it drawn from OT prophetic literature (as in 1 Thess 1:9-10; 4:13—5:11). One of the most interesting is the Greek transliteration of the Aramaic phrase *Maranatha* found in 1 Corinthians 16:22. The linguistic evidence deriving from a bilingual setting makes this potentially the earliest recorded acknowledgement of the lordship of Jesus Christ. Some dispute remains about how *Maranatha* should be divided and separated and whether it should be understood as an invocation for the Lord to come (*marana tha*, "Come, our Lord!") or as a straightforward declaration that he has already come (*maran atha*, "The Lord has come!"). In any event, the context of the passage is presumably the Lord's Supper* (as in the interesting parallel in *Did.* 10:6), and it seems reasonable to take the Aramaic phrase to contain at least an element of future fulfillment within it. In short, the ejaculation *Maranatha* is a prayer, uttered within a liturgical context, that may call for the future parousia of the Lord. The parallel in Revelation 22:20 would support such an interpretation.

*3.4.2. The Delay of the Parousia.* One prominent school of thought within NT scholarship has held that the nonarrival of the parousia of Jesus Christ created a crisis early within the life of the Christian church. This "delay of the parousia" is sometimes portrayed as triggering the need for a de-eschatologization of the Christian hope, a movement away from Jewish apocalyptic ideas which see the fulfillment of God's promises as taking place in the not-too-distant return of Christ to earth; such a belief is replaced by a more Hellenistic understanding of Christ's "presence" as taking place within the life of the believer. Under the impact of the delayed parousia (so the argument goes), eschatology is necessarily dehistoricized, and the meaning of the future hope was spiritualized and transposed into a more mystical union between Christ and the church. The Pauline materials figure prominently within such theories about the crisis presented by the delay of the parousia, although there is an increasing swell of voices objecting to the assumption that the parousia presented such a theological crisis among the early Christians that is so often supposed (see Aune, Bauckham). Many scholars have concluded that the later Pauline letters (such as 2 Cor 10—13 and Phil) reflect precisely this sort of shift in perspective, a suggestion which raises the question of development within Paul's eschatological thought.

*3.4.3. The Question of Development in Pauline Eschatology.* Two basic ways of approaching this question have been employed by Pauline scholars. The first is to note the differences (even inconsistencies) between sections of Paul's letters with regard to eschatological matters and suggest that the apostle has changed his mind, or developed in his understanding of the issues, or that his follower(s) responsible for the Deutero-Pauline letters have done so (see Achtemeier and Beker 1991). Generally such an approach involves both a detailed study of Pauline chronology* and careful attention to the polemical contexts in which the letters are written. Indeed, J. W. Drane argues that the diversity of eschatological expression is directly related to the diversity of opponents against whom Paul is writing, although he rejects some of the more radical results of advocates of such an approach. In any event, the dating and circumstances surrounding the production of a letter are crucial in determining whether development of thought is detectable. In the main, the letters of the Pauline corpus are divided by scholars adopting this explanation of development into three groups, representing an increasingly Hellenistic and individualistic understanding of eschatology which occurs over time: (1) Paul's early letters (1 Thess, 2 Thess); (2) Paul's major letters (Rom, 1 Cor, 2 Cor, Gal); (3) Paul's later letters (Phil, Col, Eph, Philem) (diversity of opinion about the categorization of some letters is common).

The second approach is simply to allow the differences to stand and to explain them as inevitable given the nature of the subject matter; to accept them as the apostle trying to explain the inexplicable and, not surprisingly, creating some real theological tensions within his writing. In the words of C. F. D. Moule, such tensions are "best explained as the result, simply, of the unmanageable dimensions of the Christian verities" (Moule, 4).

In summary, the question of development in Paul's eschatology inevitably involves one in scholarly investigation on at least three separate but interconnected fronts: controversy about the integrity of the Corinthian letters (two, three or four letters?), the chronological order of the letters (notably Phil) and debates about Pauline authorship of some of the disputed letters (namely, 2 Thess, Col and Eph). However, even within the undisputed letters the controversy about development of Paul's eschatological thought arises.

The eschatological teaching contained in 1 Corinthians 15 and 2 Corinthians 5:1-10 has long been one of the major areas of discussion (Gillman offers a survey of interpretation). Many feel that in 1 Corinthians 15 we have Paul giving his clearest expression of the future hope for the believer, associating the granting of the resurrection body with the parousia of Christ (which is expected very soon, during Paul's own lifetime). However, in 2 Corinthians 5:1-10 it appears that Paul provides an alternative perspective, one in which the Christian believer is somehow united with Christ at the point of death, and the granting of the resurrection body postponed indefinitely, presumably until the parousia (*see* Intermediate State). Many scholars have attempted to explain this shift in perspective between the two letters. Dodd, for example, explains the shift to have come about because of Paul's own brush with death, something which, Dodd suggests, took place between the writing of the letters we know as 1 Corinthians and 2 Corinthians (this trauma is perhaps hinted at in 2 Cor 1:8-11). Many scholars (including F. F. Bruce and E. E. Ellis) would dispute this suggestion, arguing that it is highly improbable that Paul would have changed his mind on so central an issue within the span of a few short weeks or months (the supposed time lag between the writing of the two Corinthian letters). For them the essential teaching contained in 1 Corinthians 15 and 2 Corinthians 5:1-10 is perfectly compatible. Some scholars have attempted to explain the difference between the teaching contained within the two letters by arguing that 1 Corinthians 15 is concerned primarily with a collective eschatology and 2 Corinthians 5:1-10 is concerned primarily with an individualistic eschatology. The fact that so much attention (and variety of interpretation) is given to the problem raised by the eschatology of the Corinthian letters is some indication of its importance within Pauline studies.

Others have sought to identify a development in Paul's eschatological thought even within his earlier letters, namely 1 and 2 Thessalonians. C. L. Mearns, for example, suggests that Paul's earliest eschatological teaching was radically realized and that the death of Christian believers within the Thessalonian congregation forced a radical shift in his understanding of such matters. This sort of approach assumes that the death of believers would have come as something

unexpected and theologically worrying to Paul, resulting in him "re-conceptualizing the Parousia in the form of a 'Second Coming.' " (Mearns, 139). While the death of some of the members of the congregation is certainly an issue within the church at Thessalonica (as in 1 Thess 4:13-18), there is little to suggest that this was a result of Paul's own teaching to them. Indeed, it is difficult to imagine that in the approximately twenty years of missionary activity prior to his writing 1 Thessalonians, Paul had not yet been faced with the death of Christians nor worked out the matter theologically.

*3.4.4. The Judgment Seat of God/Christ.* Paul takes over the standard Jewish expectation that all men and women will be held accountable before God* for their lives (see Travis). There is within Paul's letters a close association between the parousia of the Lord Jesus Christ and the execution of final judgment.* A classic example of this is found in 1 Thessalonians 3:13, where declaration of the parousia is placed within a judgment context "before God" (*emprosthen tou theou*). In 1 Corinthians 3:12-15 Paul offers an extended passage about the final judgment, using an image of building materials being tested by the purifying fires of "the Day" (1 Cor 3:13). Similar imagery of giving account before God is used in Romans 2:1-11; 14:10-12 and (with reference to Paul himself) in Philippians 2:16. In Romans 2:16 God is said to judge the secrets of humankind by Christ Jesus (*dia Christou Iēsou*).

In connection with the final judgment at the consummation of this age, Paul speaks explicitly of the judgment seat (*bēma*) twice within his letters (Rom 14:10; 2 Cor 5:10), building upon the image found in Isaiah 45. The curious thing about this motif is that the judgment seat is described as belonging to God in the first reference and as belonging to Christ in the second. There is some precedent for this fluctuation between God and messianic agent within Jewish pseudepigraphal texts (such as *1 Enoch* 37—71; *T. Abr.* 13:1-2); the same is carried on in Christian writings after Paul, probably under the apostle's influence (e.g., Polycarp *Phil* 6.2). By extension, the right of judgment is extended to the Christian church* acting as Christ's agents. Thus Paul himself feels able to pass judgment on unethical behavior (1 Cor 5:3-5) and exhorts the church to do the same (1 Cor 5:11-13; *see* Discipline). He even hints that the saints will execute eschatological judgment over the world* and the angels* (1 Cor 6:2-3).

*3.4.5. The Judgment of Satan and His Angels.* Satan* is mentioned frequently in the Pauline letters, always as a power hostile to God and malevolent to the saints (Rom 16:20; 1 Cor 5:5; 7:5; 2 Cor 2:11; 11:14; 12:7;

1 Thess 2:18). The terms *Tempter* (*ho peirazōn*) and *Devil* (*diabolos*) are also used (in 1 Thess 3:5 and Eph 6:11 respectively). This is perfectly in keeping with the eschatological dualism of other Jewish apocalyptic texts which characteristically describe the present age as one in which Satan's power and authority are in evidence. Indeed, Satan is called "the god of this age" in 2 Corinthians 4:4, and "the prince of the power of the air" in Ephesians 2:2. Also in keeping with these apocalyptic texts is a developed angelology, with Satan being supported by a host of figures; in the main Paul conforms to this Jewish usage (see Carr). We find angels (sometimes friendly, but generally hostile) mentioned in passing throughout the Pauline letters (Rom 8:38; 1 Cor 4:9; 6:3; 11:10; 13:1; 2 Cor 11:14; 12:7; Gal 1:8; 3:19; 4:14; Col 2:18; 1 Thess 4:16). Related to this are the references to the "rulers of this age" (1 Cor 2:6-9); the "principalities and powers"* (Rom 8:38; 1 Cor 15:24; Eph 6:12; Col 2:15); "world rulers of this present darkness and spiritual hosts of wickedness in high places" (Eph 6:13); and "the elemental spirits of the universe" (Gal 4:3; Col 2:8, 20). Yet the ultimate judgment and defeat of Satan, together with his angelic minions, is portrayed as a certainty in several key passages, notably Romans 16:20. Thus Paul balances the present and future dimensions of this judgment of Satan, with the cross of Christ being the fulcrum of the scales of justice.

There is considerable fluidity of referents within the language of angelic powers in the Pauline corpus. At times (such as Rom 8:38-39; Col 2:15 and Eph 2:2; 3:10; 6:12) the referent is apparently a spiritual force, while at other times (such as Rom 13:1-7 and 1 Cor 2:6-8) it is clearly a political power that is in view (see Carr, Wink; *see* Principalities and Powers). The relationship between the two basic categories (spiritual and political forces) inevitably involves one in discussions about Pauline chronology* and the authorship of Colossians* and Ephesians.*

*3.4.6. The Judgment of the Man of Lawlessness (2 Thess 2).* There has been considerable debate about the identification of the "man of lawlessness (or sin)" mentioned in 2 Thessalonians 2:1-12. The fact that it is found in a letter which is disputed by some as genuinely Pauline has also contributed to the debate. The passage presents significant exegetical dilemmas in its own right, not least the difficulty in determining who the "man of lawlessness"* (2 Thess 2:3) is supposed to represent. Is he a symbol of Satan, or one of his agents? Is he a figure in the tradition of the wicked Antiochus Epiphanes from the days of Daniel, associated with the "abomination of desolation" and the Roman emperor Caligula (Mk 13:14)? Should we iden-

tify this figure with the political leadership of Rome, a representative of civil authority or perhaps even with the emperor* himself as the one who brings political upheaval (*apostasia*)? It seems clear that the underlying imagery for this ungodly figure is found in Ezekiel's passage about the King of Tyre (Ezek 28:1-19), but recognition of this does not necessarily aid in determining who is intended. Association with the antichrist figure in Revelation is understandable given the overall tone of the passage (see Mounce).

Similarly, who or what is "the restraining influence" (2 Thess 2:6-7; *see* Man of Lawlessness and Restraining Power)? Is it Paul himself (as Cullmann and Munck suggest)? Or is it the need for the gospel message to be proclaimed throughout the world (as Aus argues)? Again, one of the reasons why it is difficult to determine precisely what the author has in mind arises from an exegetical oddity, an unusual phrasing in the Greek text which provides both a neuter expression (*to katechon*, 2 Thess 2:6) and a masculine one (*ho katechōn*, 2 Thess 2:7) in successive verses.

In any event, the main thrust of the passage is to place the rise of the "man of lawlessness" within a temporal framework (as in 2 Thess 2:3), while at the same time assert his ultimate defeat by the Lord Jesus at the future parousia.

*3.4.7. The Wrath to Come.* The coming wrath* (*orgē*) is mentioned over twenty times within the Pauline letters, the noun appearing both with the definite article and without it. Several other terms and phrases, mostly drawn from the verb *krinō* ("judge") and its cognates, are also used to express the just execution of judgment by God or his designated agent at the end of the age (see Kreitzer, 99-100, for details). The fact that Paul tends not to associate God directly with the execution of this wrath has prompted some scholars (notably Dodd) to suggest that he depersonalizes wrath. There is some validity to the suggestion, although the phrase "the wrath of God" (*hē orgē tou theou*) does appear three times (Rom 1:18; Eph 5:6; Col 3:6).

*3.5. The Gentile Mission and the Fate of the Jewish Nation.* According to his own testimony Paul's calling as an apostle is intimately related to his encounter with the risen Lord Jesus (Gal 1:11-17). While the focus of Paul's "Damascus Road" experience is often placed upon it being his conversion experience, it is important to note that it might be more properly described as his calling to participate in the fulfillment of God's promises to bring all nations to him in the fullness of time (as in Is 49; see Conversion and Call). This means that Paul sees the whole of his subsequent ministry* among the nations (*see* Gentiles) as taking place within the context of an eschatological act, the resurrection of Jesus from the dead. Paul's commissioning as the "apostle to the Gentiles" (Gal 2:8) is alluded to throughout Paul's letters (see Kim, 1-31, for details). Clearly Paul sees his own apostolic ministry as part of God's eschatological activity, and an essential component of that activity is the salvation of a people called to be his own (as Wright notes). But how does this affect his understanding of the fate of the Jewish nation (*see* Israel)? Several key texts deal with precisely this question.

*3.5.1. Romans 9—11.* C. H. Dodd long ago recognized the special nature of Romans 9—11, suggesting that it was an independent source, possibly a sermon which was inserted by Paul into the letter. Certainly the fact that it is possible to read from Romans 8:38 to 12:1 without a discernible break in thought lends weight to this suggestion. However, many Pauline interpreters feel that Romans 9—11 is an integral part of the overall argument of the letter and do not feel the interpolation approach is warranted. The problem of the fate of the Jewish nation lies at the heart of this section of the letter, but this is anticipated earlier in the letter (as in Rom 3:1-8 and the Abraham image in Rom 4:1-25). Insofar as the section is concerned with the future fate of the Jewish nation, in light of their rejection of Jesus Christ as Messiah, it deals with eschatological matters.

What does Paul feel will ultimately happen to the Jewish nation (his own people)? In Romans 11:26 ("all Israel will be saved") he appears to come close to what might be described as a national universalism. How literally should we take the "all Israel*" (*pas Israēl*) in Romans 11:26 to be? It is difficult to reconcile such teaching with the theme of justification by faith so strongly emphasized elsewhere in his writing. One way to understand Romans 9—11 is that it reflects an unresolved tension within Paul's own thought, one which cannot quite seem to abandon faith in God's promises to historical Israel, yet one which is challenged by the redefinition of Israel into spiritual terms demanded by the Christ event. Traditionally Israel was seen as the instrument of God's salvation of the Gentile nations (as in Is 40—66); Paul's dilemma is how to maintain belief in this strand of prophetic proclamation in light of Israel's rejection of Jesus Christ. A volcanic eruption has taken place within Paul's thought and the place of Israel within the revised eschatological scheme is like lava that has not yet cooled; it is not yet hardened or fixed, remaining somewhat resilient.

*3.5.2. 1 Thessalonians 2:13-16.* Since the days of F. C. Baur scholars have often claimed that this pericope

breaks the flow of Paul's argument in the letter and have suggested that it is an interpolation, perhaps inserted by a later editor after the fall of Jerusalem in A.D. 70. At the heart of such an interpretation is the assumption that the pericope is incompatible with Paul's eschatological teaching elsewhere concerning the fate of the Jewish nation. Competent cases have been made for both possibilities (the section is genuinely Pauline; alternatively, it is a non-Pauline interpolation). To a large degree the argument hinges on whether a historical setting can be determined to fit the judgment on the Jewish nation implied (such as the Jewish Passover riot of A.D. 49).

*3.6. The Eschatological Gift of the Spirit.* Jewish eschatology traditionally associated the dawn of the age to come with the bestowal of the Spirit of God (see Holy Spirit). Paul carries through this idea, knitting together his doctrine of the risen Lord Jesus Christ as experienced by the indwelling presence of the Spirit of God in the life of the believer. In 1 Corinthians 15:45 the risen Christ, the last Adam, is even described as the "life-giving Spirit" (*pneuma zōopoioun*). Several images are used to express the role that the Spirit has in the life of the believer. Similar declarations about the impartation of life by the Spirit are recorded in Romans 8:2, 10 and 2 Corinthians 3:6.

*3.6.1. The Spirit as First Fruits.* Paul explicitly describes the Spirit as the first fruits* (*aparchē*) in Romans 8:23, paralleling what is said about the risen Christ himself in 1 Corinthians 15:20. This agricultural image is used extensively in the OT (as in Lev 23:10-14).

*3.6.2. The Spirit as Guarantee.* At several places within the Pauline letters the gift of the Holy Spirit is described as the guarantee (*arrabōn*) of God (2 Cor 1:22; 5:5; Eph 1:14). This unusual term is a Semitic loan word and was well established in Greek as a financial term. It denoted the promise to pay a full balance based upon the handing over of an initial down payment.* The financial metaphor lent itself readily to Paul's doctrine of the indwelling Spirit and is clearly eschatologically conditioned. The essential point is that the believer is assured of his or her ultimate redemption* based upon the present possession of the Holy Spirit.

*3.6.3. The Spirit and Inheritance.* The language of inheritance also figures within Paul's pneumatology (1 Cor 6:9-10; 15:50; Gal 5:21), where it is closely connected to his understanding of covenental blessing and the fulfillment of the promise of God to his people in Abraham.* The idea of the Christian's possession of the Spirit as the basis for the adoption* (*huiothesia*) as the children of God is declared at several places within the Pauline letters (Rom 8:15; 9:4; Gal 4:5; Eph 1:5). The use of the Greek transliteration of the Aramaic term *Abba* is linked to this (Rom 8:15; Gal 4:6). By virtue of the fact that the Christian (by definition) has the Spirit, the status of adoption exists as a present reality. Yet it is not difficult to detect a future dimension to this adoption within the passages, a feature which is consistent with the rest of Paul's eschatological teaching.

*3.6.4. The Spirit and Christian Ethical Life.* Paul's eschatological perspective informs his ethical teaching, often helping to frame the way in which he describes the Christian as one who is to live his or her life with an eye to the future (*see* Ethics). In effect this means that Paul's ethical dualism is eschatological in nature, not anthropological (as many advocating a clash with Gnosticism have suggested in the past). For Paul soteriology and eschatology are intertwined, finding the basis of expression through his christology.* For example, in Galatians 1:4 the sacrificial death of Christ is described as the means of believers' deliverance "from the present evil age." Similarly, in Romans 8:4 he defines Christian existence in terms of a "life in the flesh" which has been surrendered for a "life in the Spirit." The Spirit is also spoken of as the power of resurrection existence made operative in the Christian's ethical life (as in Rom 8:11; 1 Cor 2:4-5).

*3.7. The Transformation of the Cosmos.* One of the standard features of apocalyptic eschatology is the transformation of the created order under the effects of the emerging age to come. This cosmic redemption is also reflected at several key points within the Pauline letters, demonstrating a close connection between the ideas of creation* and redemption* (see Gibbs). Cosmic redemption is also intimately connected to anthropological redemption within the Pauline letters. The destiny of both the created order and the human race are determined by Christ's resurrection from the dead, and both find their fulfillment in his lordship. Thus Paul concludes his short excursus on creation in Romans 8:19-22 with the proclamation that this redemption includes the adoption of his children via the activity of the Spirit (Rom 8:23).

*3.7.1. Romans 8:19-23.* In the midst of an extended discussion of the effects of Jesus Christ's redeeming action for the Christian we have a short section which describes its cosmic dimensions. Paul here employs the language of Jewish apocalyptic, anthropomorphizing the created order (*hē ktisis*), and mixing in the image of birth pangs (*synōdinei*). As D. C. Allison demonstrates, "birth pangs" is something of a technical term within apocalyptic texts, often associated with the tribulations surrounding the advent of the Messiah.

Interestingly, Paul also includes the image within the passage on the parousia in 1 Thessalonians 5:3, a section built very much on the traditional OT expectations of the Day of the Lord. It is a common image within apocalyptic sections of the OT (Is 26:16-19; 66:7-14), of the Synoptics (Mk 13:8; Mt 24:8), and it occurs within other apocalypses (4 Ezra 5:1-13, 50-55; 6:21-24; 9:3). Yet the paragraph from Romans is not intended as a detailed teaching about creation as such, but is made to serve as a supporting illustration of Paul's main concern, the "adoption, the redemption of our body" (Rom 8:23 NRSV; see 7.2 below).

*3.7.2. Philippians 3:21.* In Philippians 3:20-21 we have another example of Paul's concern with the transformation of the believer's physical body into a glorious body by the power* of the resurrection. Yet at the conclusion of this couplet Paul includes a phrase which breaks out of the boundaries of the anthropological imagery and interjects a cosmic note. The resurrection is said to be the power "which enables him even to subject all things to himself." This is similar to the declaration made in 1 Corinthians 15:27 and is built upon Psalm 8:7. Once again the transformation of humankind and the subjection of the cosmos are interconnected ideas.

*3.7.3. Colossians 1:15-20.* The idea of Christ's role as creator is prominent within the pre-Pauline hymn* of Colossians 1:15-20. This creator motif is also balanced within the hymn by the proclamation of Christ as the agent of redemption (*di' autou apokatallaxai*, Col 1:20). The cosmic dimension of the redemptive action of Christ on the cross is brought out by the inclusion of *ta panta* ("all things") and *eite ta epi tēs gēs eite ta en tois ouranois* ("whether things on earth or in the heavenlies") in verse 20.

*3.7.4. Ephesians 1:10.* In Ephesians 1:9-10 the mystery* of God's plan of salvation is described as preplanned in Christ and revealed in the fullness of time. The author of Ephesians then includes an unusual verb (*anakephalaiōsasthai*) to denote the ultimate goal of this plan as it is fulfilled in Christ. This verb carries with it a strongly eschatological note, as well as a cosmological one (it is *ta panta*, "all things," which is said to be "summed up" in Christ).

*3.8* **To Telos and To Teleios.** The *telos* word group is used quite extensively within the Pauline letters, often with an eschatological meaning which is perhaps best interpreted in straightforward temporal terms. J. M. Court contends that this is part of the technical language of apocalyptic which Paul adopts. Almost certainly a temporal sense of *to telos*, "finally," is intended in 1 Corinthians 15:24 where the noun is used to describe the conclusion of a sequence of eschatological events, including the Son's handing over of the kingdom to the Father (although some interpreters take *to telos* here as a noun). A related occurrence, again bearing a temporal sense, is 1 Corinthians 10:11 where Paul describes his Corinthian audience as those "upon whom the ends of the ages (*ta telē tōn aiōnōn*) have come." The noun (*to telos*) is also used in Romans 6:21-22 to denote the contrasting end results of sin* (death) and grace* (eternal life; *see* Life and Death). *To telos* is used by Paul to communicate the time of ultimate judgment, as in Philippians 3:9 where the enemies of the cross of Christ are declared in Philippians 3:19 to have their end (*to telos*) in destruction (*see* Wrath, Destruction). Similarly, in 2 Corinthians 11:15 the servants of Satan are also said to be heading for an appropriate end (*hōn to telos estai kata ta erga autōn*); and in 1 Thessalonians 2:16 the Judaizers are condemned as under judgment of the wrath of God which will come upon them "in the end" (*eis telos*). The term can also be used to denote the time of ultimate redemption, as in 1 Corinthians 1:8, where the Lord Jesus Christ is said to sustain the believing Christians "until the end" (*heōs telous*).

*To telos* can also carry the sense of "goal" or "destination," although it is difficult to separate this completely from the temporal sense just discussed. The most celebrated instance of this meaning is Romans 10:4 where the noun is used to describe the effect of Christ's coming upon the Jewish Law: "For Christ is the end (*telos*) of the Law, that every one who has faith may be justified." It may be that Paul is here reflecting the saying of Jesus recorded in Matthew 5:17, associating the end (*to telos*) with the idea of fulfillment of the Law* (*plērōsai*). A similar use of *to telos* is found in 1 Timothy 1:5.

The neuter form (*to teleion*) of the adjective *teleios* is used as an abstract noun in 1 Corinthians 13:10, denoting "that which is perfect or completed" and thus sets up a contrast with the future eschatological age and the present imperfect world. The adjective *teleios* can also take the sense of "mature" or "adult" and is so used in 1 Corinthians 2:6; 14:20; Philippians 3:15 (*see* Perfect, Mature). In Ephesians 4:13 and Colossians 1:28 the same term is applied anthropologically to the church and the believer respectively.

### 4. Pauline Eschatology and Christology.

The interface between Paul's eschatology and his christology* is extensive, particularly as it concerns the role that Jesus Christ has as the executor of God's final judgment. Although Paul does not choose to use the title Son of man (the most prevalent language in the Synoptic Gospels) to express this, he does never-theless use equivalent ideas and images. Within the Pauline letters OT theophanic traditions about the Day of the Lord become invested with new meaning and are applied to the risen Lord Jesus Christ. This re-emphasis generally builds upon a referential shift of "Lord"* from God to Jesus Christ, or on the reapplication of "Day of the Lord" passages to the messianic agent (see Kreitzer, 112-128, for a discussion of eleven key texts where this occurs).

The central feature of Paul's eschatology, the resurrection* of Jesus Christ from the dead, is indisputably a theological declaration, as can be evidenced by the ways in which God is said to be active in Christ's resurrection. At several points within the Pauline letters God the Father is explicitly said to be responsible for Jesus' resurrection (Rom 4:24; 10:9; 1 Cor 6:14; 15:15; 2 Cor 4:14; Gal 1:1; Eph 1:20; Col 2:12; 1 Thess 1:9-10); once it is the God through his Spirit who accomplishes this (Rom 8:11); once it is the "Spirit of holiness" (Rom 1:4); and once it is the "glory of the Father" which raises Jesus (Rom 6:4). Other passages simply use an impersonal verb to denote the resurrection, generally taken to be a divine passive (Rom 4:25; 7:4; 1 Cor 15:4, 12, 20; 2 Cor 5:15; 2 Tim 2:8).

Yet Paul maintains a strong note of subordination of Jesus Christ to God the Father even in the midst of the most exalted christological passages. The two most important examples are 1 Corinthians 15:28c and Philippians 2:11c, lines which round off passages containing eschatological material.

One of the most intriguing features of Paul's eschatology (which anticipates the rise of the doctrine of the Trinity in the church) is the relationship between the risen Lord Jesus and the Holy Spirit. The Holy Spirit is described as "Christ's Spirit" (Rom 8:9; Phil 1:19) and the "Spirit of (God's) Son" (Gal 4:6). At the same time, in other passages the Holy Spirit is clearly "God's Spirit" (1 Cor 3:16; Phil 3:3; 1 Thess 4:8). The overlap between God and Christ (with reference to "the Spirit") is highlighted in 2 Corinthians 3:17, a *crux interpretum* which it is possible to take in either direction.

### 5. Pauline Eschatology and Ethics.

It is sometimes suggested that an overemphasis on eschatological matters undermines the need for a strong ethical code for living in the present (*see* Ethics). Contrary to many popular assumptions about the detachment alleged to be inherent within eschatological teaching, Paul's letters demonstrate a close connection between eschatology and ethical exhortation. This is evident within the earliest of his letters, those written to the church at Thessalonica where

Paul confronts a misguided understanding about work which is based upon an erroneous view of the imminent return of Christ (see Kaye). Similarly, the ethical exhortations contained in Romans 12—13 are wholly conditioned by an eschatological perspective; the passage begins with an appeal that the believer not be "conformed to this world but be transformed by the renewal of your mind" (Rom 12:2), and concludes with an extended paragraph warning of the approaching day of Christ (Rom 13:11-14). The same observation can be made about 2 Corinthians 5:1-10 where the eschatological teaching about the implications of a Christian's death are interwoven with the exhortation to gain Christ's approval (1 Cor 5:9).

Indeed, it is possible to see the whole of Paul's ethical teaching as providing instruction about how the Christian is to live in the interval between the death and resurrection of Jesus Christ and his future parousia. In the evocative phrase of Sampey, Paul's moral teaching involves teaching the Christian about walking "between the times."

## 6. Pauline Eschatology and Jewish Mysticism.

We have already mentioned the "horizontal" (or "spatial") dimension of eschatology (see 1 above). This feature of Paul's eschatological thought has received special treatment in recent years, particularly as it relates to the mystical traditions of Judaism. The so-called merkabah mysticism, influential within certain Jewish circles during the NT period, was built upon the opening vision of Ezekiel in which the prophet sees the throne chariot (*merkāḇâ*) of God in heaven (Ezek 1:26-27). This mystical tradition is widespread within Judaism and has produced a separate subsection of literature which offers a comparative reference point for NT studies. The critical point with reference to Paul's letters comes in the supposed relationship between the apostle's apocalyptic eschatology and his mysticism* (which manifested itself in ecstatic experiences). Some scholars have argued that the distinction between the two (apocalypticism and mysticism) is exceedingly fine, if not altogether artificial. A. F. Segal, for example, has recently argued that Jewish apocalypticism *was* mysticism in the way it was experienced and that it is entirely proper to speak of Paul as an apocalyptic mystagogue. Crucial to Segal's argument is the contention that in terms of religious experience there is no distinction between apocalypticism and mysticism, despite the fact that the two are clearly distinct literary genres. Several key passages from the undisputed letters are appealed to in support of such an interpretation of Paul.

**6.1. 2 Corinthians 12:1-10.** Most scholars rightly feel that this curious passage is reflective of Paul's own experience, although not necessarily his conversion/ call on the Damascus Road (Acts 9:1-19; 22:1-21; 26:12-23). It is noted that he combines apocalyptic language with a denial of the validity of boasting (1 Cor 12:5-6) and a brief description of the tribulations he must suffer in fulfilling his role as the missionary* to the Gentiles (1 Cor 12:7-10). He does begin this section by describing his experience as a revelation (*apokalypsis*) from the Lord (1 Cor 12:1).

**6.2. 1 Corinthians 9:1.** Paul bases a defense of his apostleship (*see* Apostle) on the fact that he has seen (*heōraka*) the Lord. The verb is usually taken to mean physical sight, but it is possible to interpret it as ecstatic insight given by means of revelation (similar descriptions of "seeing" the risen Lord occur in 2 Cor 4:4-6).

**6.3 Galatians 1:11-17.** Here too Paul employs the language of apocalyptic literature choosing to describe his commissioning as an apostle coming to him via a revelation (*apokalypsis*, Gal 1:12) of Jesus Christ (*see* Visions). Yet this revelation is not so much a revelation *to* Paul, but a revelation *in* him (*en emoi*, Gal 1:16) suggesting almost an incarnational understanding of the encounter with the risen Christ (cf. Gal 2:20; 6:4). Such highly personalized language could be taken as expressing the mystical and ecstatic experience of the visionary mind (as Segal suggests). However, it is doubtful if that is the way Paul perceived his encounter with Jesus Christ; he associates his sight of the risen Lord alongside the postresurrection appearances found in early Christian tradition* (1 Cor 15:5-7), firmly basing them in objective history and not subjective imagination. His use of the aorist passive verb *ōphthē* supports this (1 Cor 15:5, 6, 7, 8; cf. 1 Tim 3:16).

**6.4 Apocalypticism, Mysticism and Christology.** That apocalypticism* and mysticism share the common ground of religious experience seems evident; there is much insight that can be gained into one aspect of Paul's eschatological thought as a result of a comparison of the two. However, too much can be made in straightforwardly equating them, not least the seeming evacuation of Paul's eschatology of any future significance. It is not only the way that the encounter of the risen Lord Jesus is communicated to Paul that is important to him; this is merely the form of the experience. Of at least equal importance is the *content* of that experience; *who* is revealed (not only *how*) is of crucial concern for Paul. As a result perhaps the most helpful contribution that the Jewish mystical tradition has to offer to a study of Paul's eschatology is the fact that it helps provide a context in which Pauline christology can develop. There is much to suggest that the most enduring feature arising from the overlap between apocalypticism and mysticism is the importance of the theme of revealed "glory"* (Heb *kābôd*) inherent within them (see Newman for a recent study of this and a critique of Segal's thesis). When applied to christological considerations this allows the shift from a theocentric to an anthropocentric fulfillment to take place. In other words, the common ground of apocalyptic and mysticism within Judaism allows Paul (and others) to see the risen Lord Jesus Christ as the agent of the fulfillment of God's eschatological purposes. The future revelation of Jesus Christ is, in Paul's words, closely connected with the manifestation of the glory of God (1 Cor 3:18; 4:4, 6).

**7. Social Dynamics in Paul's Eschatological Teaching.**
Considerable understanding into Paul's letters has been gained in recent years by applying the insights gained through sociological approaches to the documents (*see* Social-Scientific Approaches). This has also held true with respect to his eschatological teaching, especially when it is used to assess what W. Meeks has described as the "millenarian beliefs" of the congregations to which Paul responds. D. W. Kuck has carried the investigation a step further, examining the place that the judgment theme has within Paul's Corinthian correspondence and making some important observations about how such a futuristic eschatology functioned socially within the congregation.

Much work is yet to be done on this issue, particularly as it will help explain how eschatological ideas influenced (and perhaps even determined) the beliefs and practices of the congregations. Recognition of the social dimension of eschatological beliefs (*see* Sociology; Social-Scientific Approaches) also enables us to discover the enduring relevance of Paul's teaching and begin to apply it to our own contemporary problems (as Glasswell points out). This is nowhere more acute for the contemporary situation than in the areas of human sexuality* (matters involving sexual identity and role) and creation (matters involving ecology and the created order). In both instances eschatological perspectives can dictate both the interpretations accepted for these passages and the practices adopted by the Christian church in expressing them.

*7.1. Galatians 3:27-28.* In recent years this has become one of the most debated passages within the whole of the Pauline corpus, largely because of the implications it has for social conventions. The pericope opens with a declaration about the believing community as having been "baptized into Christ" and having "clothed yourselves with Christ," two images which are powerful symbols of a resurrection theology in Paul. In Galatians 3:28 Paul goes on to assert that unity in Christ transcends various human barriers: ethnic (Jew/Greek), economic (slave/free) and sexual (male/female).

Many would argue that the focus of the passage is on the means of entry into the community of faith, and that there is no difference between male and female on that point. But what does the passage imply about Paul's eschatological understanding of male-female relationships? Is Paul giving a programmatic statement about how human relationships should be conducted in the present, a manifesto for social activism? Or is he caught up in the enthusiasm of the moment and providing us with a visionary's glimpse of what the future ultimately will be like when Christ comes at the parousia to bring everything to its accomplishment? If so, what impact might this have upon the way that women are often assigned lower places of value and service in modern societies? Does not Paul challenge us with, in the enticing phrase of Scroggs, "the eschatological woman," whose place in society must be reassessed if we are to remain true to Paul's eschatological vision?

The "visionary" interpretation has been pursued by many, particularly as it does not necessarily demand that equality of role between men and women in the present order is what Paul intends. On the other hand, it is difficult to restrict the force of Galatians 3:27-28 to the future and not recognize its relevance for the present (*see* Man and Woman). The social implications (e.g., the role and ordination of women) are wide-ranging. No doubt Galatians 3:27-28 will continue to be a major focal point for contemporary theology (see MacDonald).

*7.2. Romans 8:19-23.* In these few short verses we have the most extensive discussion within the Pauline corpus about the future of the created order. As we mentioned above (see 3.7), the primary focus of the passage is to illustrate God's ultimate redemption of his children (Rom 8:23). Nevertheless, there clearly is an indication of God's concern for the created order (*see* Creation and New Creation), despite the fact that it has been tainted and suffers under the effects of Adam's disobedience (Gen 3 underlies the whole passage). God's concern that creation itself is worthy of being transformed and set free should inform our own attitudes toward it. Thus it is possible to integrate fully a protectionist stance toward creation and the environment within Paul's eschatological perspective. Indeed, it could be argued that to do so is to demonstrate our continuing revelation as the children of God (Rom 8:19).

In conclusion, it is clear that Paul's thought is thoroughly conditioned by an eschatological perspective in which Jesus Christ's death and resurrection are seen in some way to inaugurate the long-awaited age to come. Virtually every letter within the Pauline corpus reflects, to a greater or lesser degree, this eschatological viewpoint. Many of the key areas of Pauline teaching, such as ethics, christology and ecclesiology, share as common ground this eschatological perspective. All of this helps to make Pauline eschatology one of the main arenas of modern scholarly debate.

*See also* ADAM AND CHRIST; APOCALYPTICISM; CHRISTOLOGY; CREATION AND NEW CREATION; DYING AND RISING WITH CHRIST; ETHICS; EXALTATION AND ENTHRONEMENT; FIRSTFRUITS, DOWN PAYMENT; GENTILES; GLORY, GLORIFICATION; HEAVEN, HEAVENLIES, PARADISE; HOLY SPIRIT; HOPE; IMMORTALITY; INTERMEDIATE STATE; ISRAEL; JUDGMENT; JUSTIFICATION; KINGDOM OF GOD/CHRIST; LIFE AND DEATH; MAN OF LAWLESSNESS AND RESTRAINING POWER; MYSTERY; MYSTICISM; PEACE, RECONCILIATION; RESTORATION OF ISRAEL; RESURRECTION; REWARDS; SALVATION; TRIUMPH; UNIVERSALISM; WRATH, DESTRUCTION.

BIBLIOGRAPHY. P. J. Achtemeier, "An Apocalyptic Shift in Early Christian Tradition: Reflections on Some Canonical Evidence," *CBQ* 45 (1983) 231-48; D. C. Allison, *The End of the Ages Has Come* (Philadelphia: Fortress, 1987); D. E. Aune, "(Early Christian) Eschatology," *ABD* II.594-609; idem, "The Significance of the Delay of the Parousia for Early Christianity," in *Current Issues in Biblical and Patristic Interpretation*, ed. G. F. Hawthorne (Grand Rapids: Eerdmans, 1975) 87-109; R. D. Aus, "God's Plan and God's Power: Isaiah 66 and the Restraining Factors of 2 Thess. 2.6-7," *JBL* 96 (1977) 537-53; W. Baird, "Pauline Eschatology in Hermeneutical Perspective," *NTS* 17 (1970-71) 314-27; M. Barker, "Slippery Words: Apocalyptic," *ExpT* 89 (1977-78) 324-29; R. J. Bauckham, "The Delay of the Parousia," *TynB* 31 (1980) 3-36; J. C. Beker, *Heirs of Paul: Paul's Legacy in the New Testament and in the Church Today* (Minneapolis: Fortress, 1991); idem, *Paul the Apostle: The Triumph of God in Life and Thought* (Philadelphia: Fortress, 1980, 2d ed. 1984); idem, *Paul's Apocalyptic Gospel: The Coming Triumph of God* (Philadelphia: Fortress, 1982); idem, "Recasting Pauline Theology: The Coherence-Contingency Scheme as Interpretative Model," in *Pauline Theology.* Volume I: *Thessalonians, Philippians, Galatians, Philemon*, ed. J. M. Bassler (Minneapolis: Fortress, 1991) 15-24; idem, *The Triumph of God: The Essence of Paul's Thought* (Minneapolis: Fortress, 1990); M. C. de Boer, *The Defeat of Death* (JSNTS 22; Sheffield: Academic, 1988); idem, "Paul and Jewish Apocalyptic Eschatology," in *Apocalyptic and the New Testament: Essays in Honor of J. Louis Martyn*, ed. J. Marcus and M. L. Soards (JSNTS 24;

Sheffield: Academic, 1989) 169-90; G. Bornkamm, *Paul* (New York: Harper & Row, 1969); V. P. Branick, "Apocalyptic Paul?," *CBQ* 47 (1985) 664-75; F. F. Bruce, *Paul: Apostle of the Heart Set Free* (Grand Rapids: Eerdmans, 1977) 300-13; G. B. Caird, *The Language and Imagery of the Bible* (Philadelphia: Westminster, 1980) 201-71; W. Carr, *Angels and Principalities* (SNTSMS 42; Cambridge: University Press, 1981); J. J. Collins, ed., *Apocalypse: The Morphology of a Genre. Semeia* 14 (Missoula, MT: Scholars, 1979); J. M. Court, "Paul and the Apocalyptic Pattern," in *Paul and Paulinism: Essays in Honour of C. K. Barrett*, ed. M. D. Hooker and S. G. Wilson (London: SPCK, 1982) 57-66; O. Cullmann, "Le caractère eschatologique du devoir missionnaire et de la conscience apostolique de saint Paul. Étude sur le κατέχον (-ων) de 2 Thess. 2:6-7," *RHPR* 16 (1936) 210-45; W. D. Davies, *Paul and Rabbinic Judaism* (4th ed.; Philadelphia: Fortress, 1980); J. W. Drane, "Theological Diversity in the Letters of St. Paul, *TynB* 27 (1976) 3-26; E. E. Ellis, "II Corinthians V.1-10 in Pauline Eschatology," *NTS* 6 (1959-60) 211-24; A. J. Everson, "Day of the Lord," *IDBSup* 209-10; J. G. Gibbs, *Creation and Redemption: A Study in Paul's Theology* (NovTSup 26; Leiden: E. J. Brill, 1971); J. Gillmann, "A Thematic Comparison: 1 Cor 15:50-57 and 2 Cor 5:1-5," *JBL* 107 (1988) 439-54; M. E. Glasswell, "Some Issues of Church and Society in the Light of Paul's Eschatology," in *Paul and Paulinism: Essays in Honour of C. K. Barrett*, ed. M. D. Hooker and S. G. Wilson (London: SPCK, 1982) 310-19; M. J. Harris, *Raised Immortal: The Relation Between Resurrection and Immortality in New Testament Teaching* (Grand Rapids: Eerdmans, 1983); J. C. Hurd, *The Origin of 1 Corinthians* (2d ed.; Macon, GA: Mercer, 1983); E. Käsemann, "The Beginnings of Christian Theology," in *New Testament Questions of Today* (Philadelphia: Fortress, 1969) 82-107; idem, "On the Subject of Primitive Christian Apocalyptic," in *New Testament Questions of Today* (Philadelphia: Fortress, 1969) 108-37; B. N. Kaye, "Eschatology and Ethics in 1 and 2 Thessalonians," *NovT* 17 (1975) 47-57; L. Keck, "Paul and Apocalyptic Theology," *Int* 38 (1984) 229-41; S. Kim, *The Origin of Paul's Gospel* (Grand Rapids: Eerdmans, 1982); B. Klappert, "King, Kingdom," *NIDNTT* 2.372-90; A. J. F. Klijn, "1 Thessalonians 4.13-18 and Its Background in Apocalyptic Literature," in *Paul and Paulinism: Essays in Honour of C. K. Barrett*, ed. M. D. Hooker and S. G. Wilson (London: SPCK, 1982) 67-73; L. J. Kreitzer, *Jesus and God in Paul's Eschatology* (JSNTS 19; Sheffield: JSOT, 1987); D. W. Kuck, *Judgment and Community Conflict: Paul's Use of Apocalyptic Judgment Language in 1 Corinthians 3:5—4:5* (NovTSup 66; Leiden: E. J. Brill, 1992); J. R. Levison, "2 Apoc. Bar. 48:42-52:7 and the

Apocalyptic Dimension of Colossians 3:1-6," *JBL* 108 (1989) 93-108; A. T. Lincoln, *Paradise Now and Not Yet* (SNTSMS 43; Cambridge: University Press, 1981); D. R. MacDonald, *There is No Male and Female* (HDR 20; Philadelphia: Fortress, 1987); I. H. Marshall, "Slippery Words: Eschatology," *ExpT* 89 (1977-78) 264-69; idem, "Is Apocalyptic the Mother of Christian Theology?" in *Tradition and Interpretation in the New Testament*, ed. G. F. Hawthorne with O. Betz (Tübingen: J. C. B. Mohr; Grand Rapids: Eerdmans, 1987) 33-42; R. P. Martin, *The Spirit and the Congregation* (Grand Rapids: Eerdmans, 1984); J. L. Martyn, "Apocalyptic Antinomies in the Letter to the Galatians," *NTS* 31 (1985) 410-24; C. L. Mearns, "Early Eschatological Development in Paul: The Evidence of I and II Thessalonians," *NTS* 27 (1981) 137-57; W. A. Meeks, "Social Functions of Apocalyptic Language in Pauline Christianity," in *Apocalypticism in the Mediterranean World and the Near East*, ed. D. Hellholm (Tübingen: J. C. B. Mohr, 1983) 687-705; J. Moiser, "A Reassessment of Paul's View of Marriage With Reference to 1 Cor. 7," *JSNT* 18 (1983) 103-22; C. F. D. Moule, "The Influence of Circumstances on the Use of Eschatological Terms," *JTS* 15 (1964) 1-15; R. H. Mounce, "Pauline Eschatology and the Apocalypse," *EvQ* 46 (1974) 164-66; J. Munck, *Paul and the Salvation of Mankind* (Atlanta: John Knox, 1977); C. C. Newman, *Paul's Glory-Christology: Tradition and Rhetoric* (NovTSup 69; Leiden: E. J. Brill, 1992); idem, "Transforming Images of Paul: A Review Essay of Alan Segal, *Paul the Convert*," *EvQ* 64 (1992) 61-74; H. Ridderbos, *Paul: An Outline of His Theology* (Grand Rapids: Eerdmans, 1975); C. C. Rowland, *The Open Heaven: A Study of Apocalyptic in Judaism and Early Christianity* (New York: Crossroad, 1982); J. P. Sampey, *Walking Between the Times* (Philadelphia: Fortress, 1991); R. Schippers, "Goal, Last, End, Near, Complete," *NIDNTT* 2.52-66; H. J. Schoeps, *Paul: The Theology of the Apostle in the Light of Jewish Religious History* (Philadelphia: Westminster, 1961); A. Schweitzer, *The Mysticism of Paul the Apostle* (London: Adam & Charles Black, 1931); R. Scroggs, *The Last Adam* (Oxford: Basil Blackwell, 1966); idem, "Paul and the Eschatological Woman," *JAAR* 40 (1972) 283-303; A. F. Segal, *Paul the Convert* (New Haven: Yale University, 1990); R. E. Sturm, "Defining the Word 'Apocalyptic': A Problem in Biblical Criticism," in *Apocalyptic and the New Testament: Essays in Honor of J. Louis Martyn*, ed. J. Marcus and M. L. Soards (JSNTS 19; Sheffield: Academic, 1989) 17-48; A. C. Thistleton, "Realised Eschatology at Corinth," *NTS* 24 (1978) 510-24; S. H. Travis, *Christ and the Judgment of God* (Grand Rapids: Zondervan, 1987): 31-124; G. Vos, *The Pauline Eschatology* (Princeton: University Press, 1930); A. J. M. Wedder-

burn, "The Problem of the Denial of Resurrection in 1 Corinthians XV," *NovT* 23 (1981) 229-41; D. E. H. Whiteley, *The Theology of St. Paul* (Philadelphia: Fortress, 1966); W. Wink, *Naming the Powers* (Philadelphia: Fortress, 1984); idem, *Unmasking the Powers* (Philadelphia: Fortress, 1986); B. Witherington, *Jesus, Paul and the End of the World* (Downers Grove, IL: InterVarsity, 1992); N. T. Wright, "Putting Paul Together Again," in *Pauline Theology*. Volume I: *Thessalonians, Philippians, Galatians, Philemon*, ed. J. M. Bassler (Minneapolis: Fortress, 1991) 183-211.

L. J. Kreitzer

**ETERNAL LIFE.** *See* ESCHATOLOGY; IMMORTALITY; LIFE AND DEATH; RESURRECTION.

# ETHICS

Paul demonstrated the personal character integral to the new life created by faith* in Jesus Christ as well as the obligations for personal, family, church and social relationships. The radical implications of this new creation* soon to be fully manifest at the Parousia were related to the realities of the continuing present age. The ethical struggle had become universal. The contexts for such teachings were particular situations in his churches, but the "ways in Christ Jesus" apply to all the churches (1 Cor 4:17) and general topics are introduced. Not all admonitions have the same weight, nor does Paul attempt to be comprehensive.

1. The Basis of Ethics in Grace
2. An Ethic of Love
3. The Actor and Thinker
4. The Eschatological Challenge
5. The Tension between the New and the Old
6. Universalizing the Moral Conflict

## 1. The Basis of Ethics in Grace.

*1.1. A New Reality.* God's* saving act in Christ's death* and resurrection* is the ground of ethical appeal for Paul. "The old yeast" of vice must be cleaned out "in order that you may be a fresh batch just as you are, without fermentation, because Christ our Paschal Lamb was sacrificed" (1 Cor 5:7). Ethical behavior is to correspond to what God has enabled them to be through Christ's sacrifice.* This ethical appeal has been called the "indicative and imperative" (Bultmann; cf. Gal 5:1, 25), that is, "become in your character and conduct what God's action in Christ has made you to be."

The imperative is not a secondary application of the gospel designed for the spiritually immature. Betz suggests that in Paul's early letters, as in 1 Thessalonians, ethics was a means of preserving the present state of holiness up to the day of judgment* (cf. 1 Thess 5:23). Certainly by the time of Paul's writing Romans the connection of the imperative to the indicative clearly had become implicit. God's claims upon our obedience is "a constitutive part of God's gift" (Furnish). In Romans 6 union with Christ (Rom 6:2-11) compels behavior which is consistent with it (Rom 6:12-23). Even in the section of instruction the indicative breaks through (Rom 6:13). In Philippians, where Paul is confronting rancor by an appeal to Christ's humility and exaltation* (Phil 2:6-11), he does not urge a self-conscious imitation* of Christ, representing a moral ideal. He invokes participation in the ethos of the drama of salvation* which is at the basis of their being as believers (Phil 2:5 may be so understood, but this is the occasion of recent debate; see Imitation; Hymns).

God's power* and sovereignty accordingly dominate ethics. Righteousness* does not make its appearance as the consequence of a life lived for God, except marginally, as in Galatians 5:5. It is the presupposition, as a gift in salvation.

God's grace* empowers the new being created in salvation. "Grace reigns through righteousness for eternal life" (Rom 5:21). God works through the will and actions of believers for God's own purpose (Phil 2:12-13). God's gift creates the integral response of a whole person, whose conduct (Gal 6:4) and fruit* (Gal 5:22) are described in the singular.

*1.2. Grace Corresponding to Grace.* God's grace is a power within the believers reproducing its own character. The letter to the Ephesians admonishes them to be imitators of God and "gracious to each other just as God in Christ was gracious" to them (Eph 4:32). Their conduct is to be loving because its foundation is the love* expressed in Christ's sacrifice (Eph 4:32—5:2). Paul expresses the relationship organically: since the indicative is union with Christ in baptism, they are bidden to live the life of the risen Christ himself (Rom 6:5-12).

The immeasurable inequality between the recipients of Christ's gift and Christ, who sacrificially gave himself for them, should make the believers gracious to those who are poor. In motivating the church of Corinth to give to the poor Christians in Jerusalem, Paul reminds them that Christ in grace became poor for them although he was rich (2 Cor 8:9). A genuine love will be demonstrated in care for the poor (2 Cor 8:8). 2 Corinthians 8—9 is filled with such correspondence between God's grace and the believers' generosity in contributing to the poor (see Riches and Poverty). God is the actor. Giving to the poor is prompted by God's grace (2 Cor 8:6-7), which enables believers

to give even beyond their ability (2 Cor 8:1-4). God's abundant grace provides ample means for every good action; the poor will thank God for the surpassing grace in the givers (2 Cor 9:8, 13-14). The distribution to the poor is a harvest of the seed provided by God; God's grace flowing through them is manifested in the form of justice (2 Cor 9:9-10).

The arrangement which Paul seeks among the Christians in response to God's grace is one of equality (*isotēs*, 2 Cor 8:13-14). In Hellenistic Judaism the ideal government would distribute for "the necessary needs" of life so that there would be no "excess for luxury" nor lack (Philo *Jos.* 243; cf. 2 Cor 8:15). That the recipients are the poor and that this standard of justice is applied reveals elements of a social ethic. These two chapters, however, have frequently been neglected in treatments of Paul's ethics. One factor is the interpretation that Paul's concern is missionary diplomacy, validating his mission* by an offering from the Gentiles to the Judean church (see Collection). The logic within these chapters, however, is the social requirements of grace. This applies also to the view that "the poor" (Rom 15:26; Gal 2:10) was a title of the Jerusalem Christians, denoting their piety, not their economic need. Evidence is lacking, however, for such a technical use of the term by Christians at the date of Paul's writing.

*1.3. Social Ethic as well as Community Ethic.* A further reason for the neglect of 2 Corinthians 8—9 is the view that not only here, but also in general, Paul's social concern is limited to the church; thus his ethic of sharing is a community ethic, not a social ethic. The collection was directed to the poor of the *saints* (2 Cor 8:4; Rom 15:26). The givers indeed will be praised for "their liberality of sharing to them *and to all*" (2 Cor 9:13; cf. Gal 6:10). Does this broader designation denote needy people in general, or only the needy among all Christians (not merely those in Judea)?

Indication of a more universal reference is found in other texts which apply to non-believers. In Galatians 6:10 (in a passage which may also relate to the collection for Jerusalem [cf. Gal 6:6; Rom 15:27; but in contrast 1 Cor 9:10-11]), Paul concludes his discussion of giving with the an admonition, "Do good to all people (*pros pantas*), but especially to the household* of faith." "Doing good" (*ergazesthai to agathon*) is terminology for kindly concrete acts of helping others. The first part of the phrase is the general principle, followed by the specific application to the church. Some have argued, however, that *malista de* ("but especially") should be translated with the rare rendering, "that is." The few examples of this usage that have been discovered are ambiguous, however, and differ significantly in form and context (also cf. 2 Cor 1:12).

Loving service to needy non-believers is also evident in Romans 12:13-14. Paul enjoins hospitality in its literal sense of love for or care of strangers (*philoxenia*), here meaning non-believers since it contrasts the immediately preceding injunction of sharing with fellow Christians ("saints") and the following stipulation of love to one's enemies.* (The last connection is reinforced by the repetition of the verb *diōkō: pursue* (*diōkontes*) hospitality and bless *persecutors* (*diōkontas*). Eusebius describes Polycarp as showing hospitality to his persecutors (Eusebius *Hist. Eccl.* 4.15.14). Since Paul does enjoin loving care to non-believers, the more ambiguous references of doing concrete acts of good "for each other and for all" (1 Thess 3:12; 5:15 [v. 15a would strengthen universality]; cf. 2 Cor 9:13) can be understood as pointing beyond and outside the church (cf. Phil 4:5; 2 Tim 2:24; Tit 3:2, 8).

## 2. An Ethic of Love.

Love is the specific pattern of life by which grace forms the new reality of the believer. The supernatural infusion of love through the Holy Spirit* produces the character upon which eschatological hope about the final judgment* of God is built (Rom 5:3-5). Love is the first fruit* of the Holy Spirit (Gal 5:22).

The most significant question in current scholarship pertinent to Pauline ethics is the place of the Law.* In Galatians 3—5 Paul presents the Law as a slave in sharp contrast to faith as a free woman. The Law also was a slave attendant when we were schoolchildren, having custody over us until we came to maturity with faith. Now we are set free. Love gives full expression to the Law (Gal 5:14) as we bear each other's burdens and thus fulfill the law of Christ (Gal 6:2; cf. "law of faith" in Rom 3:27; *see* Law of Christ). Some would suggest that the Law is no longer pertinent as a moral authority.* The believer has been freed to consider all kinds of ethical traditions, sifting them by the law of faith* and love.*

Others have argued effectively, however, that what is at stake in Paul's negative treatment of the Law is not the question of the source of moral authority, but that of the grounds of membership in God's community. The parallelism in Galatians 3:24-25 indicates that not being under the slave attendant (the Law) is equivalent to being justified* by faith (cf. Rom 6:14). Those who feel compelled to be circumcised* in order to enter community membership are attempting to be justified by the Law (Gal 5:4; cf. 2:16, 21; 3:11), which is what being "under the Law" means. The question of the remaining moral authority of the Law is left open.

When love is actualized, the other demands of God are fulfilled. Freedom* in Christ is not an opportunity for selfishness, but compels us to be slaves to one other in love (Gal 5:13-14; 1 Cor 9:19). The fulfillment of the Law then is not its termination but the full expression of its principles, purpose and motivation. Good and evil are determinate realities established and revealed by God, rather than, in terms of content, subjectively grounded in the relationship to God by faith. Loving one's neighbor as oneself (Lev 19:18) fulfills the second half of the Decalogue and "any other commandment" (Rom 13:8-10).

Love thus is not a replacement of the Law, but a new motivation, understanding and power for meeting and surpassing its moral demands. The combination is crucial. Obedient deeds of great justice and self-sacrifice which lack the motivation and attitude of love are empty (1 Cor 13:3; cf. Ps 112:9 LXX). The Law was good but weak in the face of the power of sin* (Rom 7:11-17; 2 Cor 3). The Spirit of God sets us free from condemnation, which comes from the weakness of the Law as the result of sin. God's purpose at the same time is that the just requirement of the Law might be fulfilled by those empowered and guided by the Spirit (Rom 8:2-4, 9). The just requirement of the Law, which is in tune with love, remains as a standard of righteous living (cf. also 2 Tim 3:16). It provides a pattern, warning, instruction and exhortation, including matters as specific as sexual* immorality and remuneration of leaders (1 Cor 9:10; 10:6-11; *see* Financial Support). The law of Christ is the criterion of love which fulfills the Law as it makes that obedience possible. For example, the obligation in the Law of responsibility to the poor is carried out through the grace of God flowing through the believer (2 Cor 9:9-10).

## 3. The Actor and Thinker.

For Paul the human being is created as a member of the material world and as a member of society. Paul uses *body* (*sōma*) to refer to the person in relationship with his or her environment. As body, one is part of the world and communicates with the world. *Flesh* (*sarx*), when used neutrally, describes human beings in relationship and solidarity with others (e.g., Philem 16). Negatively, flesh represents the sphere of worldliness in which the individuals share and from which they draw their values and goals (e.g., Rom 7:5). It does not refer to an inferior, material part of the individual. The promise that God "will give life also to your mortal bodies" (*thnēta sōmata*, Rom 8:11; cf. 1 Cor 15:42-44, 53-54) reflects the value placed by Paul upon the body. He thus reinforces the continuity of existence before and after redemption, as well as the individual's relationship to the surrounding world.

In salvation people are called into a new community, which is a new realm of social existence which God is calling forth, a believing and obedient human community founded in God's love and grace (see Church). Community needs are given priority even when they conflict with personal rights and privileges (1 Cor 10:23-24). Love toward those whose conscience remains uninformed restricts freedom in dietary and ceremonial matters that are ethically adiaphora (i.e., "matters of relative indifference"; Rom 14; 1 Cor 8, 10). In such matters Paul gives individuals considerable leeway, and in the pursuit of the good of others seeking one's own good is not excluded (Phil 2:4 [note kai, "also," though the word is textually uncertain]).

For Paul the renewed mind has a critical role in discerning good (Rom 12:2; Phil 1:9-10; 1 Thess 5:21) in conjunction with the instruction of Scripture and common moral traditions. Christ and Paul (who himself emulates Christ) provide patterns for this way of life (1 Cor 11:1; cf. Rom 15:5; see Imitation).

Considerable attention has been given recently to the Pauline use of precepts from Hellenistic moral philosophy, such as the lists of virtues* and vices. In Titus 2:12 the state to which people are brought in conversion is described by the Greek cardinal virtues. Vices define outer boundaries of behavior which are beyond dispute. Some would suggest that the Pauline ethic is distinct only in its christological motivation and empowerment.

Paul's attitude toward non-Christians provides support for that usage even if much of it was through the mediation of Hellenistic Judaism. As illustrated in Romans 1, Paul indeed is highly critical of Gentile morality. His relating morality to nature (physis, Rom 1:26; 2:14; ta kathēkonta, "what is fitting," the Stoic term for what nature teaches, Rom 1:28), however, illustrates his agreement with Hellenistic Judaism that there is an affinity between the morality in God's revealed Law and that disclosed in the created order, which God's people share with the Gentiles. Even in Romans 1 the moral problem for Paul is rooted not in the error of judgment but in a refusal of obedience.

Correspondingly, Paul recognizes knowledge of genuine values by secular people. His followers are to take into consideration "that which is morally good in the judgment of all people" (Rom 12:17; cf. 2 Cor 8:21). They are to conduct themselves becomingly (euschēmonōs) with outsiders (1 Thess 4:12; Rom 13:13). The term implies a common standard of what is decent, and traditional elements of morality are cited in both passages. Paul also conducted himself in a way which would commend him to every human conscience* (2 Cor 4:2; cf. Tit 2:5, 8-10).

### 4. The Eschatological Challenge.

Christ is King. God has exalted him. Not every knee, however, has yet bowed to him (Phil 2:9-11). The present time for Paul is situated between the initial triumph* of Christ over the powers hostile to God and Christ's securing from them full and final obedience and submission. At the Parousia every power in opposition to the will of God will be destroyed (1 Cor 15:24-26). Even the last of these, death, is already in process of being destroyed (katargeitai, present indicative, 1 Cor 15:26; though some commentators would maintain that the present tense refers to what takes place at the eschaton, v. 24). At present, life is a battlefield of the divine and the demonic.*

There is a divine purpose in history: "that God may be everything in everything" (1 Cor 15:28), the total sovereignty of God over all things (cf. Col 1:20; Eph 1:10). In the end the whole created world with its people, supernatural powers, natural forces and institutions will be conformed to the will of God. The purpose of the life in faith is the glorification of God (Rom 15:5-6).

In this ultimate purpose we have solidarity with the rest of the material world. The fallen creation retains within it a redemptive purpose. It will be set free from corruption at the time when believers' mortal bodies are redeemed from their temporality and weakness* (Rom 8:18-23). The material world thus gains significance. A privatized sphere of salvation is not partitioned off from the rest of creation. In Ephesians and Colossians the church as the body of Christ contributes to the cosmic reconciliation (see Peace, Reconciliation) of all things to God (Eph 1:22-23). Within it the hostility between Jew and Gentile is overcome (Eph 2:11-22). The church exposes the works of darkness through the word of God and deeds of goodness, justice and truth* (Eph 2:10; 5:8-11; 6:10-17; cf. Col 1:6, 10).

Paul's ethics are strongly influenced by the tension implicit in the belief that the coming new age is present already (Rom 13:11-12), yet only partially. The expectation creates moral seriousness (Rom 13:13-14). The eschatological teaching of 1 Thessalonians 4:13—5:11 is placed in the middle of the ethical sections of the letter so that 1 Thessalonians 5:12 smoothly resumes the thought of 1 Thessalonians 4:12. The eschatological reserve means that while voicing a powerful expression of Christian freedom (1 Cor 3:21-22), Paul also warns that the eschatological time is not yet: Judge not before the final judgment (1 Cor 4:5).

## 5. The Tension between the New and the Old.

A tension occurs in Paul's teaching. On the one hand he opens up radically new social relationships. In the new Christian existence there is neither male nor female, bond nor free. On the other hand Paul upholds responsibilities for the social institutions which continue. The household* codes enjoin subordination. The overall evaluation of Paul's teaching must keep both elements together.

*5.1. The New Reality.* The coming of the Spirit in conversion has conspicuous ethical and social consequences in the love, joy, kindness and self-control that it imparts (Gal 5:22-23). Colossians* presents the abolishing of false distinctions among human beings as a renewal of the situation at the creation (*see* Creation and New Creation). This new nature "is being renewed in knowledge according to the image* of its Creator" (Col 3:10). Redemption in Christ restores human relationships to creation as God intended it (*see* Adam and Christ).

When a person joins Christ in conversion, "there is a new creation" (2 Cor 5:17; Gal 6:15). One then no longer views other people according to worldly standards but as those for whom Christ has died (2 Cor 5:15-16). The old external distinctions of superior status related to nationality or slavery* cease to exist (Col 3:9-11; cf. Eph 2:14-16). By thus "putting on Christ," "there is neither Jew nor Greek; there is neither slave nor free; there is neither male nor female" (Gal 3:27-28). For Paul this equality is based on the direct access every individual has to God (Rom 10:11-12) and the need of all for redemption* (Rom 3:22-24). Each believer is distinctly marked, possessing gifts which differ in function. The gifts are equal in dignity, however, because they derive from the common Spirit (1 Cor 12:4-13).

Some have argued that the canceling of status distinctions relates only to the religious situation of grounds for justification before God. This concern provides the context of Galatians 3:28, for example. Colossians, however, draws direct consequences for human relationships from the abolishing of status distinctions (Col 3:11). "Therefore . . . put on a merciful heart, kindness, humility, patience, bearing with one another and forgiving each other; . . . and in addition to all of these put on love, which is the bond of completeness" (Col 3:12-16).

Paul does radically challenge religious privilege. Through faith in Christ all have access to God, are heirs of Abraham* and are therefore one (Gal 3:26-29). In Ephesians the terminology of the foreigner is used to describe the negative status which is overcome in the new unity in Christ of Jew and Gentile* (Eph 2:11-22). The challenge of religious status is socially significant, however. Religion had been the central status distinction in the social system so that when this distinction falls, other distinctions follow.

*5.2. Responsible Conduct While the Old Remains.* Paul also enjoins conduct which is much less challenging of the present. He recognizes the continuation of institutional relationships which are less than ideal but which serve to keep a check on sin. Daube argues that Paul's qualification, "I say this as a concession, not as a command" (1 Cor 7:6), is technical language known from concessions to sinfulness in the Jewish background. Thus a more accommodating ethic controls behavior in areas not yet transformed by the higher command. Some suggest that the primary motivation is to protect the reputation and thus the mission of the church (cf. 1 Cor 9:19-23; 1 Tim 2:1-7; 6:1).

In what has been called a "Christian patriarchism," the ongoing unequal relationships of life are not directly challenged. The "Christian" qualification, however, denotes that these instructions (*see* Households, Household Codes) are framed by the lordship of Christ (e.g., Col 3:17). This stipulation poses opportunity for the application of love, which modifies the tradition significantly. Superiors themselves are required to reciprocate with a care for those who for the time being are in a subordinate position. These subordinate persons have already been told to obey their superiors lovingly. Husbands now are admonished, not to rule their wives, but to love them with a selfless love (Eph 5:25; cf. 5:21). The rights of the husbands are not mentioned; instead the husbands have special obligations (*see* Man and Woman).

Elements of Paul's own message of freedom were exploited by his opponents.* In 1 Corinthians spiritual enthusiasts claimed to possess already full eschatological privileges. Even now they reigned as kings (1 Cor 4:8). Claiming mystical powers in a spiritual resurrection from the dead (1 Cor 15:12), they were convinced of their freedom and power in the Spirit. Their spiritual achievement could allow either antinomianism (1 Cor 5:1) or asceticism. Urging celibacy, they counseled the married to refrain from sexual intercourse (1 Cor 7:3) or to separate (1 Cor 7:10), especially from a non-Christian spouse (1 Cor 7:12), and the unmarried to remain so (1 Cor 7:8). In view of the end time, Paul does not fully disagree with the avoidance of marriage,* yet he counsels responsibility to the mutual obligations of marriage and the claims of sexual* ethics.

To slaves, who are prompted by these opponents to achieve a higher spiritual status through manumission, Paul's response is that neither slavery* nor manumission gives superior spiritual status. Slavery is not a disadvantage in relationship before God (1 Cor 7:21-24). The governing principle instead is to live according to the will of God in one's various relationships (Bartchy).

In the household code of Ephesians 5:21—6:9, the mutuality demanded of the masters is grounded in both master and slave having the same Master in heaven (Eph 6:9). The masters are to carry out "the same things" for the slaves that the slaves had been told to do (Eph 6:9): obedience (Eph 6:5) and service (Eph 6:7). (In the household code of Colossians 3:18—4:1 they are to "grant the slaves what is required by justice and equality [isotēs]," Col 4:1.) Slavery similarly is ultimately undercut in Philemon,* where Paul requests that Onesimus be received back, not only as a brother in Christ, but as a brother in social relationships (sarx, "flesh") and as a partner (Philem 16-17).

In 2 Thessalonians social responsibility means supporting oneself by working (2 Thess 3:10). Some interpret the teaching as common morality used to address a typical situation of human frailty. The passage is opened up more fully, however, by seeing eschatological enthusiasm as the motivation leading some Thessalonians to eschew labor; scholars differ, however, as to whether the excitement is over the imminence of Christ's coming or a realized eschatology* (see Thessalonians). The result in either case is abandoning labor as no longer necessary or required. There may be a link with a radical interpretation of Jesus' teaching about anxiety about material necessities (such as may have been associated with the so-called Q source of Synoptic criticism). In this teaching they found the restoration of the Edenic situation of dependence upon God's sustenance apart from labor.

The Pauline response is to describe this group as acting "in a manner which shirks responsibility" (ataktōs, 2 Thess 3:6, 11). Paul's injunction of labor shows that eschatological newness must be qualified by the concession of ongoing organizational principles required by necessities of the created world. The reply to the enthusiasts' rejection of civil authority* had also been a call to order (hypotassō, Rom 13:1, 5; cf. 1 Pet 2:13).

This concession, however, is not a retreat to a bourgeois ethic, which Dibelius saw developed not only here but particularly in the Pastoral letters. Instead a higher level of fulfillment of the new order is achieved by the concession. Concerns for mission (2 Thess 3:7-9; cf. 1 Thess 2:9; 4:11-12) and mutual love prevail. Love provides the context in which the Thessalonian believers are to work with their own hands (1 Thess 4:9, 11; 2 Thess 3:12).

In the Pauline church mutual love in labor is to be expressed not only in providing for one's own needs, but also in working in order to share with those with basic needs (Eph 4:28). Acts 20:34-35 ties these elements together. The standard for possessions is to be sufficiency (1 Tim 6:8). Riches* are not owed to the rich and are futile (1 Tim 6:7). They also are a danger to faith itself (1 Tim 6:9-10). Paul desired that his followers have a devotion to Christ freed from anxiety, which came from being tied more than necessary to the fallen social order, which is passing away (1 Cor 7:32-35). Economic relationships with the social order cannot be avoided, but they should not be overused. Purchases will have to be made but without retaining more than is needed (1 Cor 7:30-31).

### 6. Universalizing the Moral Conflict.

Evil exists in the order of society (kosmos, "world"*) and exerts an influence upon the individual (Eph 2:1; cf. Rom 12:2, with aiōn). This evil order is comprehensive in society, including necessary economic relationships (1 Cor 7:31), social stratification (1 Cor 1:27-28), status distinctions based on religion (Gal 6:14-15) and its own wisdom* (1 Cor 1:20).

The universal dimensions of evil are even clearer in view of the fallen angelic powers which, particularly in the later Pauline letters, are perceived to control the social order (see Principalities and Powers). Individual sins are patterned not only by the social order but also by "the ruler of the domain of the air" (Eph 2:2; see Satan, Devil). "Our battle is not with flesh and blood, but with the rulers, the authorities, the rulers of this [world's] order of darkness" (Eph 6:12). The background for these supernatural "principalities and powers" (cf. 1 Enoch 61:10; 2 Enoch 20:1) is to be found in the universal care of angels* over the creation (Deut 32:8; 2 Enoch 19:2-5; Jub. 4:15) who are now fallen. Understanding the powers as angels in Pauline thought (cf. Rom 8:38-39; cf. 1 Pet 3:22) is more satisfactory than the position that Paul has demythologized them as dominating principles of existence.

The Pauline understanding of structural evil gives a societal, cosmic and universal dimension to evil. Oppressive forces are not confined to particular communities. They belong to the structure of human community as a whole. The struggle against evil, grounded in Christ's conquest of these powers (Col 2:15; cf. 1:13-16), then deals with factors in the very fiber of social existence. Despite this conquest, for Paul the victory will not be completed by Christ until the end of history (1 Cor 15:24). In Ephesians the church is pivotal in the struggle against the powers of evil (Eph 3:10; 5:11).

The fallen aspect of the social order, and the control of the fallen angelic lieutenants, is not total, however. Earthly authorities are appointed by God and serve God, and this perception still guides normative behavior (Rom 13:1, 4).

Despite the influence of Hellenistic moral philosophy, Paul's view of the cosmos and history give a different cast to his ethical perspective. On one hand for Paul evil deeply penetrates the created order; on the other hand he anticipates final victory based on the present redemptive work of Christ.

At the very basis of Christian faith lies a disruptive claim which throws into disarray the sentiments upon which institutions of social and political life are founded. Not only is the righteousness* of God announced as separate from a standing based on performance of the Law; the resurrection of the crucified Jesus vindicates and exalts as Lord one who was cursed* according to the Law (Rom 1:4; Gal 3:13). The ruler of the world joins company with those in rebellion against that very ruler (Rom 5:6-8; see Georgi).

*See also* CIVIL AUTHORITY; CONSCIENCE; FREEDOM; HOMOSEXUALITY; HOUSEHOLDS, HOUSEHOLD CODES; IMITATION OF PAUL/OF CHRIST; LAW; LAW OF CHRIST; LOVE; MAN AND WOMAN; MARRIAGE AND DIVORCE; RICHES AND POVERTY; RIGHTEOUSNESS, RIGHTEOUSNESS OF GOD; SEXUALITY, SEXUAL ETHICS; STRONG AND WEAK; VIRTUES AND VICES.

BIBLIOGRAPHY. J. M. G. Barclay, *Obeying the Truth: Paul's Ethics in Galatians* (Minneapolis: Fortress, 1988); S. Bartchy, *Mallon Chrēsai: First Century Slavery and the Interpretation of 1 Corinthians 7:21* (SBLDS 11; Missoula: Scholars, 1973); M. Barth, "Jews and Gentiles," *JES* 5 (1968) 241-67; H. D. Betz, "The Foundations of Christian Ethics According to Romans 12:1-2," in *Witness and Existence*, ed. P. Devenish and G. Goodwin (Chicago: University of Chicago, 1989) 55-72; R. Bultmann, "The Problem of Ethics in the Writings of Paul," in *The Old and New Man* (Richmond: Knox, 1967 [1924]) 7-32; D. Daube, "Concessions to Sinfulness in Jewish Law," *JJS* 10 (1959) 1-13; V. P. Furnish, *Theology and Ethics in Paul* (Nashville: Abingdon, 1968); D. Georgi, *Theocracy in Paul's Praxis and Theology* (Minneapolis: Fortress, 1991); L. Keck, "Justification of the Ungodly and Ethics," in *Rechtfertigung*, ed. J. Friedrich et al. (Tübingen: J. C. B. Mohr, 1976) 199-209; J. Kilner, "A Pauline Approach to Ethical Decision-Making," *Int* 43 (1989) 366-79; E. Lohse, *Theological Ethics of the New Testament* (Minneapolis: Fortress, 1991); R. N. Longenecker, *New Testament Social Ethics for Today* (Grand Rapids: Eerdmans, 1984); S. Rostagno, "The Bible: Is an Interclass Reading Legitimate?" in *The Bible and Liberation*, ed. N. Gottwald (2d ed.; Maryknoll: Orbis, 1983) 61-73; J. P. Sampley, *Walking Between the Times* (Minneapolis: Fortress, 1991);

W. Schrage, *The Ethics of the New Testament* (Philadelphia: Fortress, 1988); B. M. Styler, "The Basis of Obligation in Paul's Christology and Ethics," in *Christ and Spirit in the New Testament*, ed. B. Lindars and S. Smalley (Cambridge: University Press, 1973) 175-87; P. Towner, *The Goal of Our Instruction: The Structure of Theology and Ethics in the Pastoral Epistles* (JSNTSup 34; Sheffield: JSOT, 1989).

S. C. Mott

**EUCHARIST.** *See* LORD'S SUPPER.

**EVANGELISM.** *See* APOSTLE; MINISTRY; MISSION; PREACHING, KERYGMA.

**EVE.** *See* ADAM AND CHRIST; MAN AND WOMAN.

## EXALTATION AND ENTHRONEMENT

The exaltation of Jesus Christ and his enthronement at the right hand of God is a significant theme in Pauline christology. They are not merely a part of that christology but form the essential core which gives significance to everything else. It is the exaltation which reveals the true identity of Jesus, gives ultimate significance to his life and death, and provides the basis for the Christian hope. Paul's own experience of the exalted Christ, his understanding of the elements comprising that exaltation, and his identification of Jesus as Lord have profound implications not only for a full understanding of the person and work of Jesus but also for the present experience and ultimate destiny of the believer.

1. Paul and the Exalted Christ
2. Aspects of Exaltation
3. Exaltation and the Lordship of Christ
4. Implications

### 1. Paul and the Exalted Christ.

*1.1. Paul's Experience.* At the heart of Paul's christology,* as represented by his letters, is the exalted Christ. The great majority of references to Christ in Paul concern the exalted one. This is due to the fact that Paul's experience of Jesus Christ, and that of those to whom he wrote, was almost certainly only of the risen and exalted Christ. While it cannot be demonstrated beyond a shadow of doubt that Paul never saw or heard Jesus during his ministry (that Paul was brought up and educated in Jerusalem has been argued by W. C. van Unnik), it still seems most probable that this was the case, and that Paul's first encounter with Jesus Christ was the overwhelming and transforming experience on the Damascus Road recorded three times in Acts (Acts 9, 22 and 26) and referred to by Paul himself in 1 Corinthians 9:1, 15:8 (*see* Conversion and Call).

This encounter with the exalted Lord* formed the dynamic center of his understanding, the starting point of his christology (cf. Kim). Whereas for the original disciples the wonder was that the Jesus whose earthly life they had shared and whose death* they had witnessed had been exalted to lordship, for Paul the amazing thing was that the one to whom had been given the name which is above every name, the pre-existent* Son* and now the Lord of glory,* should humble himself by taking human flesh and submitting to death (1 Cor 2:8; Phil 2:6-11). For Paul and those to whom he wrote, the Jesus in whom they trusted, whom they worshipped* and above all whom they experienced, was the exalted Lord.

*1.2. Earthly Jesus and Exalted Christ.* However, this should not be taken to mean that Paul had little or no interest in, or knowledge about, the historical Jesus (*see* Jesus and Paul). The lack of reference to the historical Jesus has often been exaggerated. Paul shows himself aware of the birth of Jesus and his descent from both Abraham* and David (Rom 1:3; Gal 3:16; 4:4); he knows of the betrayal of Jesus on the night on which he also instituted a fellowship meal (1 Cor 11:23-25); the crucifixion* is frequently mentioned, a death in which the Jewish leaders were implicated (1 Thess 2:15); he speaks of the burial of Jesus and of the eyewitnesses to his resurrection* (1 Cor 15:4-8). In addition, and contrary to the claims of R. Bultmann, for example, that the teaching of the historical Jesus is virtually absent from Paul's writings, there are numerous points of contact with the teaching of Jesus as depicted in the Gospels, if few verbatim quotations (*see* Jesus, Sayings of). This rules out the interpretation of 2 Corinthians 5:16 championed by W. Bousset and Bultmann, and followed by numerous continental scholars, which understands this verse as meaning that for Paul the historical Jesus was an irrelevance compared with the crucial significance of the exalted Christ of faith. Rather, Paul is contrasting his pre-conversion understanding of Jesus with the totally new outlook which has become his as a Christian.

Furthermore, Paul had no doubt as to the personal identity of the earthly Jesus and the heavenly Christ, an identity integral to the gospel he proclaimed. While clearly recognizing different modes of existence (1 Cor 15:44-50), it is clear that for Paul the Jesus who was born, lived a human life and died on a cross, is the one who now sits at the right hand of God and who will return in glory, and this identity forms the basis of Paul's understanding of the future transformation of the believer.

*1.3. Paul and the Christology of the Early Church.* While Paul speaks with a distinctive voice, and it is possible to define a Pauline christology, his understanding of Christ, including the exalted Christ, is at one with, or is a development of, other NT teaching. This is seen in his use of key OT texts like Psalm 110:1 (1 Cor 15:25) and is shown most markedly in his use of traditional "hymns"* or creedal statements, particularly when speaking of the exaltation of Christ (see, e.g., Rom 1:3-4; 1 Cor 15:3-8; Phil 2:6-11; Col 1:15-20; 1 Tim 3:16; *see* Creeds). Indeed these passages, where he "passes on" what he had "received," form the core of his teaching about the exalted Christ (*see* Tradition). Although occasionally Paul adapts this traditional material by inserting a word or phrase to make clear his meaning, he does not radically alter their meaning and so shows himself in harmony with the earlier material he uses. Whenever Paul refers to the confession of Jesus as Lord, he is clearly drawing on an early and widespread tradition which was at the heart of early Christian proclamation and confession.

## 2. Aspects of Exaltation.

There are four aspects of Paul's understanding of exaltation. They are not all present on each occasion when exaltation is the subject; sometimes they are combined and sometimes one idea will include one or more of the others. But for ease of presentation they can be separated out as follows:

*2.1. Resurrection.* The resurrection* marks the transition from the state of humiliation to that of exaltation. For Paul this was a real space-time event in which the one who had been crucified, was dead and buried, and was raised to newness of life "through the glory of the Father" (Rom 6:4). This involved not just a restoration to life, but to a new, better kind of life, imperishable, powerful and glorious, no longer subject to weakness, sickness, aging or death, a new-creation life over which no other power in the universe had any influence (Rom 6:4-19; 14:9; 1 Cor 15:20-23, 42-44; Col 2:13; 2 Tim 1:10). The resurrection confirmed his divine sonship (Rom 1:3-4), announced God's acceptance of his saving death (Rom 3:21-25; 4:25), attested his exaltation to lordship (Rom 10:9), proclaimed his entry into the power* and glory of his royal reign (Eph 1:19-21) and made possible his return from heaven (1 Thess 1:9-10). Many of these passages, and the ideas associated with resurrection in them, show that, while separable in thought, the four elements (resurrection, ascension, session, Parousia) found in Paul's understanding of exaltation together form a unity; they are four parts of one exaltation. Thus when Paul speaks of the resurrection of Jesus he includes, or implies, all that is meant by exaltation.

*2.2. Ascension.* This is equally clear when we turn to the ascension. References to the ascension of Jesus per se are relatively rare in Paul, and there is no description of the event as found in Luke 24 and Acts 1. This need not imply, as has been argued by Lohfink, for example, that Paul and the traditions with which he was familiar knew nothing of a resurrection—forty days—ascension scheme. That Paul argues in 1 Corinthians 15 that Jesus had appeared to him in just the same way as he had appeared to the other apostles need not imply that Paul had no knowledge of an ascension. On the contrary, 1 Corinthians 15:8 shows that Paul knew that the appearances of the risen Lord came to an end, and that in some way the appearance to him was unique.

There is no contradiction between Luke and Paul so long as one recognizes that Luke's ascension accounts are not descriptions of the exaltation or glorification of Jesus; rather they describe the departure of the already exalted Lord, whose exaltation coincided with his resurrection, as in Paul (Acts 2:32-36). Equally, while Paul does refer to the descent-ascent of Christ in the quotation of the traditional formula in 1 Timothy 3:16 and in Ephesians 4:8-10, in both these places it is not so much to a visible departure to heaven that he refers, as to the exaltation of the one who humbled himself in the incarnation.

*2.3. Session/Enthronement.* Although there may be no mention of a visible departure of the risen Lord, Paul does speak of the exalted Christ being in heaven. Exaltation involves being at "the right hand of God." (Paul, like many first-century thinkers, recognized that such language is metaphorical; even now it is difficult to find ways of expressing Christ's supreme authority over all things without using spatial metaphors.) Paul uses this expression only three times (Rom 8:34; Eph 1:20; Col 3:1, drawing on the testimonium of Ps 110:1; cf. Phil 2:9-11). The latter two references emphasize the sovereign authority and power which belong to Christ as Lord over every power in the universe, exercising a reign that will last until every enemy has been subdued (1 Cor 15:24-25; *see* Principalities and Powers; Triumph). That lordship is also in mind in the context of Romans 8:34, but the thought is added that the exalted Lord makes effective intercession on behalf of God's people. Not only did he die and rise for us, he returned to the Father's side for us also.

*2.4. Parousia.* The numerous references in Paul's writings to the return of Christ in triumphant glory presuppose his exaltation, especially references to his coming "from heaven" (e.g., Phil 3:20; Col 3:1-4; 1 Thess 4:16). The Parousia will reveal the now hidden glory of the exalted Lord (1 Cor 1:7), his lordship will be universally acclaimed (Phil 2:9-11), and his enemies will all be finally vanquished (1 Cor 15:24-26; *see* Eschatology).

## 3. Exaltation and the Lordship of Christ.

*3.1. Lord.* Kyrios, Lord,* is Paul's title par excellence for Jesus. This is "the name* which is above every name" given to Jesus in his exaltation (Phil 2:9-11), so called because it is God's name. It is the word frequently employed in the LXX to render the name of God, and the Philippians passage is based on Isaiah 45:23, transferring to Jesus words originally referring to Yahweh (*see* God; Old Testament). For Paul *kyrios* was the only term which could adequately express what he had come to understand as the person and work of Christ. It was not, however, a Pauline innovation, nor was it a product of Paul's Hellenistic background, although its widespread use in the Greek-speaking world made it especially appropriate. Paul inherited this title from the early Palestinian church, as is shown by its presence in the creedal formulas Paul quotes, and especially the use of the expression *maranatha* in 1 Corinthians 16:22, where *mar-* represents the Aramaic equivalent of the Greek *kyrios* (*see* Liturgical Elements).

For Paul *kyrios* is a title of majesty reflecting the regal lordship of the risen Christ over the living and the dead. God made Jesus Lord at the resurrection (Rom 1:4; 6:4; 14:9; Phil 2:10), as a consequence of which he now shares with the Father dominion over all creation and the right to universal adoration. The cosmic role of Christ's lordship, involving his triumph* over the principalities and powers, is expounded most fully in the later letters (Eph 1:21-22; Col 2:15), but it is already present in the earlier writings (1 Cor 15:24-25). The cosmic lordship, to be revealed at the Parousia, is seen and experienced now in Christ's lordship over the church* (Eph 5:23; Col 1:18), and over the individual Christian (note Paul's numerous references to being "servants"* or "slaves"* of Christ, esp. 1 Cor 7:22). This exalted language expresses Paul's belief in the deity of Christ, denoting an equality between Father and Son reflecting their functional unity; yet the distinction between Father and Son is never blurred, and Paul retains the idea of the subordination of the exalted Lord (1 Cor 15:27-28).

Similarly, Paul speaks of the closest possible relation between exalted Lord and Holy Spirit,* while maintaining a distinction between them. Romans 1:4 speaks of the role of the Spirit in the exaltation of Jesus, an exaltation in which "the last Adam*" became "a life-giving spirit" (1 Cor 15:45). The Holy Spirit, the

Spirit of sonship who inspires prayer* in Romans 8:15, is identified with the "Spirit of his Son" in Galatians 4:6 (cf. Phil 1:19), and in Romans 8:9-11 "Spirit of God" and "Spirit of Christ" are interchangeable to the extent that the expression "Christ in you" is equivalent to "Spirit in you." Nevertheless, as Romans 8:11 shows, there is a distinction between the risen Christ and "the Spirit of him who raised Jesus from the dead." Paul's thinking was clearly trinitarian, even in the much discussed 2 Corinthians 3:17-18, whose concise language appears to identify the Lord and the Spirit. In reality Paul is expounding Exodus 34:34, and he should probably be understood as saying that the Lord of whom this passage speaks is the Spirit. Clearly Paul experienced the presence of the Holy Spirit in his life, and was equally aware of the presence of the risen and exalted Lord (Gal 2:20). Thus the exalted Lord is present with and available to the believer through the indwelling Spirit.

*3.2. Son.* The terms "Son" and "Son of God"* are used less frequently by Paul, and only on occasions with reference to the exalted Christ. Like *kyrios*, it was passed on to Paul from the early church, and it had widespread currency in the Hellenistic world and in the OT and Judaism, although its messianic connotations in the latter are disputed. Galatians 4:4 implies the pre-existence of the Son; Romans 1:3-4 can be understood in terms of messianic enthronement only, but the reference to "his Son" in Romans 1:3, and the emphasis on "power" and the inclusion of "Lord" in Romans 1:4, point to the exaltation at the resurrection of the pre-existent Son to the status of lordship, thus providing a close parallel to Philippians 2:6-11. 1 Thessalonians 1:10 refers to the Son as the exalted and coming one now in heaven, and 1 Corinthians 15:28 shows that he who, in the preceding verses, reigns until all enemies are put under his feet, is the Son.

*3.3. King.* Although Paul does not use the word *king* of Jesus, and only rarely refers to the kingdom, the idea of Christ's kingly rule is present. It is into his kingdom that the believer has been brought (Col 1:13), and as exalted ruler Christ provides for the ministry* of his church (Eph 4:11-12), prays for his people (Rom 8:34; *see* Intercession), and overcomes all opposition (1 Cor 15:25; *see* Kingdom of God/Christ).

## 4. Implications.

Along with his pre-existence, the exaltation of Jesus as understood by Paul has profound implications for the person of Christ. His exalted status could be no higher, as the name he has received could be no higher. As exalted Lord he is given the name which in the LXX translates Yahweh, the name of God himself. He is, therefore, the very "image of the invisible God" (Col 1:15); not that he merely is like God, or reveals God, but in the sense that he shares the nature of God. The OT "Day of the Lord," therefore, quite naturally becomes for Paul "the Day of Christ Jesus" (Phil 1:6; cf. 2 Thess 1:9). Thus he shares with the Father in providing all the blessings of salvation* (1 Cor 1:3; 2 Cor 1:2; Gal 1:3). It is in such exalted language that Paul lays the foundation of trinitarian understanding.

Finally, the exaltation of Jesus has profound implications for both the present and the future of the believer. Here and now "in Christ"* the Christian is raised with Christ and "seated with him in the heavenly* realms" (Eph 2:6); even now the Christian is "being transformed into his likeness with ever-increasing glory" (2 Cor 3:18); and the day is coming when his people shall "bear the likeness of the man from heaven" (1 Cor 15:49-57; *see* Image).

*See also* ADAM AND CHRIST; CHRIST; CHRISTOLOGY; DYING AND RISING WITH CHRIST; GOD; HEAVEN, HEAVENLIES, PARADISE; LORD; PRE-EXISTENCE; PRINCIPALITIES AND POWERS; SON OF GOD; TRIUMPH; WORLD, COSMOLOGY.

BIBLIOGRAPHY. P. Beasley-Murray, "Colossians 1:15-20: An Early Christian Hymn Celebrating the Lordship of Christ," in *Pauline Studies*, ed. D. A. Hagner and M. J. Harris (Grand Rapids: Eerdmans, 1980) 169-83; H. Bietenhard, "Lord, Master," *NIDNTT* 2.508-20; F. F. Bruce, *Paul and Jesus* (Grand Rapids: Baker, 1974) 77-87; L. Cerfaux, *Christ in the Theology of St. Paul* (Edinburgh: Nelson, 1959); O. Cullmann, *The Christology of the New Testament* (Philadelphia: Westminster, 1959); J. D. G. Dunn, *Christology in the Making* (Philadelphia: Westminster, 1980); idem, "1 Corinthians 15:45—Last Adam, Life-Giving Spirit," in *Christ and Spirit in the New Testament*, ed. B. Lindars and S. S. Smalley (Cambridge: University Press, 1973) 127-42; M. Hengel, *The Son of God* (Philadelphia: Fortress, 1976); S. Kim, *The Origin of Paul's Gospel* (Grand Rapids: Eerdmans, 1982); W. Kramer, *Christ, Lord, Son of God* (SBT 50; London: SCM 1966); W. G. Kümmel, *The Theology of the New Testament* (Nashville: Abingdon, 1974) 151-71; G. E. Ladd, *A Theology of the New Testament* (Grand Rapids: Eerdmans, 1975); R. P. Martin, *Carmen Christi* (SNTSMS 4; Cambridge: University Press, 1967); C. F. D. Moule, *The Origins of Christology* (Cambridge: University Press, 1977); E. Schweizer, *Lordship and Discipleship* (London: SCM, 1960); idem, *Jesus Christ: The Man from Nazareth and the Exalted Lord* (London: SCM, 1987); V. Taylor, *The Person of Christ in New Testament Teaching* (London: Macmillan, 1958); J. Ziesler, *Pauline Christianity* (rev. ed.; Oxford: University Press, 1990).

J. F. Maile

**EXAMPLE OF CHRIST.** *See* Ethics; Hymns, Hymn Fragments, Songs, Spiritual Songs; Imitation of Paul/of Christ; Jesus and Paul.

**EXEGESIS.** *See* Hermeneutics/Interpreting Paul; Jew, Paul the; Old Testament in Paul.

**EXILE.** *See* Restoration of Israel.

**EXORCISM.** *See* Demons and Exorcism.

# EXPIATION, PROPITIATION, MERCY SEAT

These are three translations, each having different connotations, of one Greek word, *hilastērion*. Paul uses it in Romans 3:25 with reference to the crucified Christ* "whom God put forth [as] *hilastērion.*" Which of the three translations best reflects the interpretation of Christ's death* here? "Expiation" implies the obliteration of sin through Christ's atoning death. "Propitiation" implies that Christ's death appeased divine wrath* called forth by sin.* "Mercy seat" recalls the place in the holy of holies where God's saving mercy* was supremely manifested in atonement for sins accomplished through the OT cult. Christ would therefore be the eschatological antitype of this mercy seat. The question whether Christ's death is seen to avert the wrath of God is the crucial theological point at issue and has been the focus of a long debate. Scholars also disagree over the equally important questions of whether *hilastērion* implies the sacrificial character of Christ's death and whether this term interprets it in the light of the OT cultic ritual of atonement.

1. Occurrence and Form
2. *Hilastērion* and Cognates in Classical and Hellenistic Greek Literature
3. *Hilastērion* in Paul

## 1. Occurrence and Form.

Romans 3:25 has the only occurrence of *hilastērion* (and of the *hilask-* word group) in Paul (in the NT see also Heb 9:5; cf. *hilasmos*, 1 Jn 2:2; 4:10, and *hilaskesthai*, Heb 2:17, also of Christ's work). Grammatically *hilastērion* can be explained either as a neuter substantive ("means of propitiation/expiation," or "mercy seat"), a substantival masculine adjective ("propitiator," "reconciler," "obtainer of mercy"), or a masculine or neuter adjective ("making propitiation/expiation," "able to make propitiation/expiation"). If it is a masculine adjective, it modifies *hon* and the meaning is that Christ is the propitiatory/expiatory agent or object. Often *atonement* is used interchangeably with expiation or propitiation in such translations.

## 2. *Hilastērion* and Cognates in Classical and Hellenistic Greek Literature.

Inquiry into the meaning of *hilastērion* and cognates in the NT has engendered much discussion on their use in classical and Hellenistic Greek literature. In the LXX *hilastērion* usually renders *kappōreṭ*. It can be taken as a technical term for the "mercy seat," which was located above the ark of the covenant in the holy of holies (see Ex 25:17-22) and was sprinkled with sacrificial blood on the Day of Atonement (see Lev 16). But T. W. Manson (1-4) notes that *hilastērion* can designate other places (besides the mercy seat) where the action denoted by *hilaskesthai* takes place (either propitiation or expiation). Others, however, say the term in the LXX originally did not refer to a place but, more generally, to an agency which performs this action (they argue especially from Ex 25:16 [17]); the technical use for "mercy seat" is later (e.g., Büchsel, 319-20). Philo uses *hilastērion* as a technical term (e.g., Philo *Cher.* 25); Josephus does not (the adjective occurs in *Ant.* 16.7.1 182). *Hilastērion* at 4 Maccabees 17:22 is nontechnical and may be an adjective or noun; it connotes the propitiatory character of the Jewish martyrs' death. Outside biblical and Jewish Greek *hilastērion* (the neuter noun) means "oblation" (Büchsel, 320), usually in the form of a stele (Dio Chrysostom *Or.* 11.121; *Inscr. Cos* 81.347; MM ἱλαστήριον).

In secular Greek the verbs *hilaskesthai* and *exhilaskesthai* with a personal object generally mean "appease," "render propitious to oneself." A pagan deity could be propitiated through various human actions (Büchsel, 311). It is often claimed that Israelite religion did not exhibit a crude form of propitiation of Yahweh which amounted to celestial bribery or appeasement of capricious, vindictive wrath (although this may not always be a valid characterization of pagan religion either, cf. Kleinknecht, 385).

Going further, C. H. Dodd in an important article even argued that in Hellenistic Judaism as represented by the LXX, the *hilask-* word group does not denote propitiation (with three exceptions). He claimed that a shift in the predominant meaning had taken place and that the LXX translators used *hilaskesthai*, etc. in the sense of "expiate" (when the subject is a human) or "be gracious," "forgive" (when the subject is God). He based his conclusions on (1) comparisons of the *hilask-* class with other Septuagintal translations of the Hebrew *kipper* (whose Piel forms are usually rendered by *[ex]hilaskesthai*), and (2) comparisons of other Hebrew words which are rendered by the *hilask-* class. In support of the secondary meaning "expiate" for *exhi-*

*laskesthai* with an impersonal object in secular Greek literature, Dodd appealed to Plato's *Laws* 862c and the Men Tyrannus inscription (Dittenberger, *Syll.*, 3d ed., 1042). In line with this shift, then, Romans 3:25 describes Jesus' death not as averting the wrath of God but as delivering from the guilt of sin (Dodd, 94).

Dodd's virtual elimination of propitiation from the LXX has not proved generally persuasive. Critics have rejected his method of defining the *hilask-* class there as well as his evaluation of the evidence (cf. the discussions by Nicole, Morris, 136-56, and Hill, 23-36). For the meaning "propitiate" they refer to Zechariah 7:2; 8:22; Malachi 1:9 (the three exceptions which Dodd discounts as "contemptuous" or "standard pagan" use); Psalm 105(106):30; Sirach 45:23; Genesis 32:20, and possibly also Numbers 16:46-47; 25:13; Deuteronomy 21:8; 1 Samuel 6:3; 2 Kings 24:4; Psalm 77(78):38; Daniel 9:19 (Th.) (see Hill, 29-30; Morris, 138-40; Nicole, 134-35). Morris (154) notes the common use of *exhilaskesthai* "in a personal sense" as seen in the constructions with *peri* with the genitive of person, "to make propitiation concerning a person" (e.g., Ex 30:15-16; Lev 1:4) and with *hyper* with the genitive of person (once, Ezek 45:17). This focus on the relation between persons Morris takes to favor the meaning "propitiate." Dodd's critics also point to the wrath of God as a prominent theme in the OT and one which appears in the context of *hilaskesthai* terminology, so that the idea of turning away divine wrath seems to be implied (esp. Morris, 129-36).

Morris (155), however, seems to force the evidence in favor of his view that "the removal of wrath seems to be definitely in view when this word group is used" in the LXX. Often it is difficult to determine exactly what the intention of the action denoted by this terminology is: to avert wrath or to remove the cause of enmity or defilement? The verb *exhilaskesthai* can have an impersonal object (e.g., "sin," "altar"), which suggests the meaning "forgive," "atone," "expiate" or "cleanse." Rarely is God the object, and sometimes God is the subject of the verb (in the active voice, e.g., Sir 5:6; 2 Chron 6:30), both of which can go against the meaning "propitiate." In the LXX, then, the complex *hilask-* word group shows itself able to accommodate new meanings (cf. Hill, 36). The main question therefore is whether the original connotations of removal of wrath still adhere to these new usages. The LXX's retention of the terminology for propitiation could suggest that they do. But the change in usage (God as subject; use of an impersonal object) giving rise to other translations suggests that they do not. The context will probably be determinative in each case in deciding whether *hilask-* implies propitiation or expiation.

### 3. *Hilastērion* in Paul.

In the light of the previous discussion on the usage of the *hilask-* terminology, we must now ask whether *hilastērion* in Romans 3:25 has the technical sense "mercy seat" and whether it carries the connotations of propitiation and expiation.

**3.1. Propitiation and Expiation.** Many have repudiated the view that Romans 3:25 pictures Christ's death as propitiatory. O. Hofius (34-39) argues vigorously against that view as contradictory to Paul's understanding of the reconciling event of the cross of Christ. God is only the *subject* in that event (not the object of a propitiating activity). Human beings are only the *objects* (not the subjects of a propitiating activity). He points to various Pauline texts in support of both assertions. "*God* put forth [Christ] as *hilastērion*" (Rom 3:25). "*God* was in Christ reconciling the world to himself" (2 Cor 5:18-21). *God* "did not spare his own Son but gave him up for us all" (Rom 8:32). "*God* demonstrated his love toward us in that while we were yet sinners Christ died for us" (Rom 5:8). In Romans 5:6, 8, 10 human beings are objects of the salvation event of the cross as "sinners," "ungodly" and "enemies* of God" (i.e., those who are at enmity with God, but not, it seems, God with them). Christ's death is not a human being's offering to God which enables God to accept sinners—the cross is not a human achievement; rather it is the act of God in free and gracious love* toward the ungodly. "God . . . reconciled us to himself through Christ" (2 Cor 5:18), and "we were reconciled to God through the death of his Son" (Rom 5:10). *God* is not reconciled to *us*.

Proponents of the view that propitiation is a biblical category do not dispute that the Bible presents God as the subject, namely, of the propitiating action (e.g., Morris, 155, 159-60; Nicole, 150-51), both in the OT (Ps 77[78]:38; and in substance Lev 17:11) and in the NT (Rom 3:25 according to their interpretation of this verse). Thus the caricature of propitiation of God as celestial bribery does not apply. For the biblical scheme does not have the chronological sequence characteristic of the pagan understanding: first the human appeasement of divine wrath, then the divine bestowal of favor on humans. Rather the God of the Bible acts out of love to propitiate God's own wrath; propitiation does not turn divine wrath into love (Nicole, 151). Understood in this way, then, the language of propitiation expresses the Godward aspect of atonement: the cleansing of sin affirms the holiness of God.

Advocates of propitiation claim that Romans 3:25-26, using the term *hilastērion*, expresses this Godward aspect of the atonement in terms of the vindication of

God's righteousness* in God's treatment of the sinner. The purpose of putting Christ forth as *hilastērion* was "for the demonstration of his righteousness, because of the passing over of sins previously committed, through the forbearance of God, so that God might be just and the justifier of the one who has faith in Jesus." Righteousness, *dikaiosynē*, in this reading of the text, is a divine attribute, as in Romans 3:5.

Critics of propitiation as a misleading term, however, read the text differently. They explain the righteousness of God which is demonstrated not as God's judicial righteousness but as the righteousness which is a gift of God to sinners, that is, salvation as in Romans 3:21-22. The meaning of divine righteousness would thus be in line with OT texts like Psalm 97(98):2. According to this view, when Romans 3:26 describes God as the one who is "just and the justifier of the one who has faith in Jesus" it refers to divine righteousness only in this one sense of saving righteousness, not righteousness as an attribute of God. Further, this verse is interpreted to speak not of God's "passing over" *(paresis)* former sins, which would cast doubt on God's judicial "righteousness," but of God's "forgiving" them *(paresis* in the sense of *aphesis,* "forgiveness"), which exhibits God's saving "righteousness." According to this line of thought, Christ's death here has nothing to do with God's judicial righteousness. Christ did not die to satisfy God's wrath as the precondition for reconciliation (see, e.g., Hofius, 34-39). Rather, Christ's atoning death itself *accomplished* reconciliation: "God was in Christ reconciling the world to himself" (2 Cor 5:19; see Hofius 1989, 5, 39; also Hofius 1993).

Proponents of propitiation, however, find it difficult to rid Romans 3:25-26 of the notion of righteousness as a divine attribute. Why does the word *paresis* appear rather than *aphesis,* the ordinary word for "forgiveness" (even if *aphesis* is found in the Pauline corpus only at Eph 1:7; Col 1:14)? Does not the former "forbearance" of God *contrast* with the present demonstration of God's righteousness by dealing with sin? The context seems to move in the direction of the vindication of God's righteousness through Christ's death as a judgment* against sin (Barrett, 79-80). But others understand the righteousness of God which is vindicated not as God's judicial righteousness—as if some abstract ideal of justice is upheld through the satisfaction of divine wrath—but as God's covenant* righteousness in which God fulfills God's covenant obligation by dealing with the covenant people's sin (Dunn, 175). The vindication of God's righteousness would therefore amount to the vindication of God's faithfulness as the God who upholds the covenant with God's people despite their unfaithfulness. This construal of the demonstration of God's righteousness does not imply that Christ's death is propitiatory but expiatory.

Other statements in Paul regarding the death of Christ can be brought to bear on Romans 3:25. God "condemned sin in the flesh*" of Christ on the cross so that sinners might be released from the condemnation of the Law* (Rom 8:3). In his death Christ "became a curse" (Gal 3:13) and suffered the condemnation of God's Law on sinners, for the sinless Christ was "made sin" (2 Cor 5:21) by God, that is, he was caused to stand in the place of sinners. In the view of J. Denney (103), these statements support propitiation because they take Christ's death as divine judgment against sin, judgment which is necessary in order "for God to be at once righteous and a God who accepts as righteous those who believe in Jesus."

Yet Denney wrongly defines divine judgment against sin in terms of propitiation. While it is true that Paul can view Christ's death as the execution of the Law's condemnation which fell on sinners in Christ and as God's own condemnation of sin by delivering the one "made sin" unto death and utter destruction, on the other hand Paul never interprets that divine judgment of sin on the cross as something which appeases an angry, offended God or which inclines God toward sinners. For Paul, God has *always* been inclined toward the ungodly. This is supremely evident in the cross, where "God is in Christ" bearing the transgressions of the world (2 Cor 5:19) and where the love of God is demonstrated "while we were yet sinners" (Rom 5:8). Paul interprets the cross as God's own suffering of the divine judgment against sin, which is the destruction of the sinner's sinful existence that took place in Christ's death.

Now we must consider the more general argument that the wider context of Romans 3:25 suggests that putting Christ forth as a *hilastērion* appeases the wrath of God. Namely, in Romans 1:18 we read: "the wrath of God is revealed from heaven against all ungodliness and unrighteousness." It threatens both Gentile and Jew (Rom 1:18; 2:5). But not only is God's wrath revealed. God's righteousness is also revealed, namely in the gospel (Rom 1:17; 3:21). The way in which Paul parallels wrath and righteousness by using the same verb (*apokalyptetai,* "is revealed") to denote their revelation suggests a relationship between the two: If those who receive the righteousness of God through faith in Christ are saved from the wrath of God, it must be because Christ has appeased that wrath through his death for them (Morris, 167-70).

While the wrath of God is the horrible cloud which hovers over the existence of all sinners and from which they escape only by receiving the gift of God's righteousness in Christ, Paul does not specify here how Christ's death frees them from such a destiny. He does not define the cross in terms of the wrath of God. Paul probably did conceive of Christ's death as the anticipation of the final eschatological judgment and outpouring of divine wrath. And thus he also probably did think that those who are in Christ will be saved from that wrath because Christ suffered it for them on the cross. Romans 5:9 is compatible with this explanation: "Having now been justified by his blood, we will be saved through him from the wrath." But that still does not mean that Christ's death propitiated God. For Paul the wrath of God is God's judgment (see Rom 2:5; 3:5-6) which destroys all unholiness and sin. In the light of the threatening wrath of God, the need of sinners can be said to be not *the transformation of God's attitude toward them* but the transformation of *their sinful existence before God* through its destruction and new creation. This transformation of sinners is precisely the significance Paul sees in the death and resurrection of Christ. And the notion of divine wrath as a judgment consisting in destruction fits well with such a view of the cross. Paul, however, gives us no systematic presentation of the relationship between sin, Christ's death and God's judgment, and the theological questions we might have in that regard can hardly be answered from his letters.

On the other end of the spectrum are those interpreters whose plain distaste for the notion of divine wrath leads them not to hold a propitiatory view of Christ's death. Confronted with the biblical language of divine wrath, they explain it as the ascription to God of what is really impersonal retribution. They point in support to the absolute use of "wrath" (without the qualifying "of God," e.g., Rom 2:5 among many others; see, e.g., Dodd 1932, 20-21). But the NT texts themselves do not support such a separation of wrath from God, which amounts to a kind of fatalism or dualism (Kleinknecht, 423-24) and conflicts with the biblical notion of divine sovereignty (Morris, 133).

In summary, not "propitiatory" but "expiatory" is the more appropriate description of Christ's atoning death as a *hilastērion* since (1) expiation clearly fits the Pauline understanding of that death as God's own gracious initiative in love toward the ungodly (see further below) as well as God's judgment against sin, (2) the idea of the appeasing of a wrathful God is in tension with Paul's understanding of Christ's death, (3) the context of Romans 3:25 does not require propitiation, and (4) the usage of the *hilask-* word group in the LXX suggests a development of meaning toward the connotations of expiation. *Hilastērion* as im-

plying expiation still allows us to understand the death of Christ as a necessary expression of God's holiness in dealing with human sin, yet not to deny that judgment is at once an expression of God's love, because the Son of God is the one who suffered the curse for the sins of all people as God's agent of the reconciliation of sinners to God.

*3.2. Mercy Seat.* Having discussed whether *hilastērion* has the connotations of propitiation or expiation, we now need to ask whether Romans 3:25 alludes to the "mercy seat" (*kappōret*) where the supreme act of atonement took place in the OT sacrificial cult or whether Christ's death is interpreted instead in terms of a noncultic form of atonement. Related questions are: Is Christ's death as *hilastērion* understood as a sacrifice? and What does a cultic understanding of *hilastērion* imply theologically about the death of Christ?

The view that the crucified Christ is identified as the eschatological antitype of the mercy seat of Leviticus 16, where atonement for sin is made once for all and reconciliation with God is accomplished, rendering the Temple cult obsolete, has seemed improbable to some. It is argued that the context in Romans 3:25 lacks any indication that *hilastērion* has the special, technical sense of "mercy seat." *Hilastērion* does not even have a definite article here which would specify it as something familiar to the readers: "*the* mercy seat" (contrast the anarthrous use in the LXX and Heb 9:5). Further, the statement that Jesus was "put forward" as *hilastērion* contrasts with the hiddenness of the OT mercy seat in the holy of holies. And the typological interpretation of "*hilastērion* . . . in his blood" (Rom 3:25) is found to result in a confusing image in which the blood of Jesus is sprinkled on himself as the mercy seat (e.g., Lohse, 151-52).

But some interpreters (notably Manson, accepted and updated by Davies and Reumann, on the basis of the pre-Pauline tradition in Rom 3:24-26; see Martin, 81-89; Stuhlmacher 1986, 96-100) have not found these criticisms fatal. *Hilastērion* can have the technical sense of "mercy seat" even without the usual article since it belongs to arguably traditional material which Paul is quoting in verses 24-26a (some exclude verse 24), material which stems from Jewish Christianity and would have been completely unambiguous in that setting. A grammatical argument for the anarthrous *hilastērion* has also been adduced: according to BDF 252.2 the article can be omitted in formulas and set phrases (noted by Stuhlmacher, but see Friedrich, 62-63). Behind this use of *hilastērion* for the crucified Christ could stand the early Christian critique of the Temple* and the Law,* whose fulfillment and therefore obsolescence was seen in Jesus Christ. Since Christ's death not only corresponds to but supersedes the ritual of atonement in the OT, the public putting forth of Christ as *hilastērion* in contrast to the hiddenness of the mercy seat does not damage the typology but brings out its full force. Finally, the typological language is not problematic because it does not intend to conjure up a picture of Christ's blood literally being sprinkled on Christ's body. The OT ritual was not so concrete as that: the blood of the sacrifice was sprinkled into the smoke rising over the mercy seat in a symbolic gesture of the reconciliation achieved through the atonement (Lev 16:13-15). And after all, the ark of the covenant had disappeared and no longer stood in the holy of holies, and the high priest now performed this ritual over only an imaginary mercy seat. The meaning of this event therefore was not seen in its literal but symbolic value. For this reason also in Hebrews Christ can appear as both offering and high priest, another literally impossible notion.

The competing interpretation of E. Lohse, which defines *hilastērion* in Romans 3:25 in a noncultic sense, appeals to 4 Maccabees 17:21-22. There the martyr death of a few righteous Jews atones for the sins of the whole people. Against Lohse, it is less likely that Jewish Christians would have drawn on this tradition to elucidate the unique and expiatory significance of Christ's death than on the tradition enshrined in the Day of Atonement ritual. The Jewish martyrs' death cannot be set within a firm or long tradition of substitutionary atonement. And this tradition does not easily offer a way to express the singularity of Christ's death (cf. further Stuhlmacher 1986, 101-3).

Given the weakness of the counterarguments and alternatives, the dominance of the meaning "mercy seat" for *hilastērion* in the LXX, and the Jewish-Christian provenance of the pre-Pauline tradition in which this term is embedded in Romans 3:25, it is likely that *hilastērion* here means "mercy seat."

The use of *hilastērion* to describe Christ crucified as a new "mercy seat" thus shows that the traditional material interpreted his death in terms of cultic atonement. Specifically, the Day of Atonement ritual in Leviticus 16 is the theological key to this view of Christ's death, as especially O. Hofius (1989, 39-48) has argued, drawing on H. Gese's and B. Janowski's insights into the OT material. Key elements of Paul's understanding of Christ's death can be linked to this ritual: the atoning death of Christ as an act of God (cf. Lev 17:11), the presence of God in Christ on the cross as reconciler, "inclusive substitution" as the basis of Christ's death for sinners, atonement as a "coming to God through judgment of death," and reconciliation as a new creation.

C. Breytenbach, among others, has recently attacked this interpretation of Christ's death along the line of the Day of Atonement (see esp. Breytenbach 1989, 167-68). While trying to argue that Paul understood reconciliation in noncultic Hellenistic terms, Breytenbach marginalizes the language of atonement in Paul which can easily link the death of Christ with OT cultic atonement. Thus he asserts that it would be unwarranted to take *(ex)hilaskesthai* and its word group as a central category in Paul's thought since Paul does without that terminology until Romans, and in Romans 3:25 Paul is only quoting pre-Pauline tradition; *hilastērion* is not *his* term (Breytenbach 1993, 67). In another step, Breytenbach denies that the pre-Pauline tradition attempts to interpret Christ's death through the Day of Atonement ritual anyway. Such an interpretation is precluded by early Christian rejection of the Temple cult (Breytenbach 1989, 167-68). Stuhlmacher (1991, 349-50) exposes faulty reasoning here, however: while the pre-Pauline tradition does conceive of Christ as the *antitype* of the OT mercy seat—implying its critique of the enduring validity of the Temple cult—nevertheless the tradition's reference to the blood of Christ as the eschatologically effective means of atonement instituted by God alludes to Leviticus 17:11—revealing the positive influence of OT cultic thought categories. Further against Breytenbach, Stuhlmacher (1989, 57) has judged correctly the importance of the traditional material Paul quotes in Romans 3:25-26a: Paul agrees with the tradition describing Christ as *hilastērion* (which he interprets according to his gospel) and incorporates it into the christological *Kernsatz* ("key statement"), which expresses his gospel in Romans 3:25. (For other trenchant criticisms of Breytenbach's view, see Stuhlmacher 1991; Hofius 1990.)

Finally, Romans 3:25 reflects the view of Christ's death as a sacrifice by virtue of its cultic interpretation, though the term *hilastērion* itself of course depicts Christ as the place of God's atoning presence, not the offering.

*See also* DEATH OF CHRIST; FORGIVENESS; PEACE, RECONCILIATION; REDEMPTION; RIGHTEOUSNESS, RIGHTEOUSNESS OF GOD; SACRIFICE, OFFERING; SALVATION; SIN, GUILT; WRATH, DESTRUCTION.

**Bibliography.** C. K. Barrett, *A Commentary on the Epistle to the Romans* (HNTC; New York: Harper & Row, 1957); C. Breytenbach, *Versöhnung. Eine Studie zur paulinischen Soteriologie* (WMANT 60; Neukirchen-Vluyn: Neukirchener Verlag, 1989); idem, "Versöhnung, Stellvertretung und Sühne: Semantische und traditionsgeschichtliche Bemerkungen am Beispiel der paulinischen Briefe," *NTS* 39 (1993) 59-79; W. D. Davies, *Paul and Rabbinic Judaism* (Philadelphia: Fortress, 1955); J. Denney, *The Death of Christ,* ed. R. V. G. Tasker (London: Tyndale, 1956 repr.); C. H. Dodd, "Atonement," in *The Bible and the Greeks* (London: Hodder & Stoughton, 1935) 82-95 (= "*ΙΛΑΣΚΕΣΘΑΙ,* Its Cognates, Derivatives, and Synonyms, in the Septuagint," *JTS* 32 [1931] 352-60); idem, *The Epistle of Paul to the Romans* (New York: Harper & Row, 1932); J. D. G. Dunn, *Romans 1—8* (WBC 38; Dallas: Word, 1988); H.-J. Eckstein, " 'Denn Gottes Zorn wird vom Himmel her offenbar werden.' Exegetische Erwägungen zu Röm 1:18," *ZNW* 78 (1987) 74-89; G. Friedrich, "Römer 3,23-26," in *Die Verküdigung des Todes Jesu im Neuen Testament* (Neukirchen: Neukirchner, 1982) 57-67; N. S. L. Fryer, "The Meaning and Translation of *Hilastērion* in Romans 3:25," *EvQ* 59 (1987) 99-116; H. Gese, "Die Süne," in *Zur biblischen Theologie. Alttestamentliche Vorträge* (München: Chr. Kaiser, 1977) 85-106; J. Herrmann and F. Büchsel, "*ἵλεως κτλ,*" *TDNT* III.300-23; D. Hill, *Greek Words and Hebrew Meanings: Studies in the Semantics of Soteriological Terms* (SNTSMS 5; Cambridge: University Press, 1967) 23-48; O. Hofius, "2 Kor 5,19a und das Imperfekt," in *TLZ* 118 (1993) forthcoming; idem, "Sühne und Versöhnung. Zum paulinischen Verständnis des Kreuzestodes Jesu," in *Paulusstudien* (Tübingen: J. C. B. Mohr, 1989) (= *Versuche, das Leiden und Sterben Jesu zu verstehen,* ed. W. Maas [Munich: Schnell & Steiner, 1983] 25-46); idem, Review of C. Breytenbach, *Versöhnung. Eine Studie zur paulinschen Soteriologie,* in *TLZ* 115 (1990) 741-45; B. Janowski, *Söhne als Heilsgeschehen* (WMANT 55; Neukirchen: Neukirchener, 1982); H. Kleinknecht, et al., "*ὀργή κτλ,*" *TDNT* V.382-447; E. Lohse, *Märtyrer und Gottesknecht* (2d ed.; Göttingen: Vandenhoeck & Ruprecht, 1963); T. W. Manson, "*ΙΛΑΣΤΗΡΙΟΝ,*" *JTS* 46 (1945) 1-10; I. H. Marshall, "The Development of the Concept of Redemption in the New Testament," in *Reconciliation and Hope,* FS L. Morris, ed. R. J. Banks (Grand Rapids: Eerdmans, 1974) 153-69; R. P. Martin, *Reconciliation* (rev. ed.; Grand Rapids: Zondervan, 1990) 81-89; L. Morris, *The Apostolic Preaching of the Cross* (Grand Rapids: Eerdmans, 1974 repr.) 125-85; R. Nicole, "C. H. Dodd and the Doctrine of Propitiation," *WTJ* 17 (1955) 117-57; J. Reumann, "The Gospel of the Righteousness of God: Pauline Reinterpretation in Romans 3:21-31," *Int* 20 (1966) 432-52; P. Stuhlmacher, "Cilliers Breytenbachs Sicht von Söhne und Versöhnung," in *Altes Testament und christlicher Glaube,* ed. B. Janowski et al. (Jahrbuch für biblische Theologie 6; Neukirchen-Vluyn: Neukirchener Verlag, 1991) 339-54; idem, *Der Brief an die Römer* (NTD 6; Göttingen: Vandenhoeck & Ruprecht, 1989); idem, "Recent Exegesis of Romans 3:24-26," in *Reconciliation, Law, and Righteousness* (Philadelphia: Fortress, 1986) 94-109.

J. M. Gundry-Volf

**EXPULSION.** *See* DISCIPLINE.

# F

## FAITH

Paul's emphasis on faith can scarcely be denied. He uses the noun *pistis* 142 times, whereas it occurs but 101 times in all the rest of the NT. He also has the verb *pisteuō* ("to believe") 54 times and the adjective *pistos* ("faithful," "trustworthy") 33 times. Clearly the faith words featured largely in the Pauline vocabulary. O. Michel points out that the demand for faith was something new beginning with the Christians: "neither Qumran, nor John the Baptist, nor yet the ancient zealot movements made any explicit demand of faith"; by contrast, "Christianity is a unique faith-event" (Michel in Becker and Michel, 599, 605). But for Paul trust in God was of central importance. It is significant that he can speak of becoming a Christian as believing (e.g., Rom 1:16; 1 Cor 1:21). He is not referring to a shallow surface experience but to believing in one's heart (Rom 10:9); and its focus is the God* who raised Jesus Christ* from the dead and inaugurated the new age (see Ljungman).

For Paul the great central truth is that God has acted in Christ to bring about the salvation* of sinners (*see* Sin). Salvation cannot be merited or earned; it must be received as a gift of grace.* Sinners cannot merit salvation, they can only trust God or, as Paul puts it, have faith in God (or in Christ). It is a distinctively Christian feature that the verb *pisteuō* ("to believe") is often followed by the preposition *epi* ("on") or *eis* ("into"), and Paul follows this usage. This brings out the truth that Christians rest their faith "on" Jesus or are brought "into" union with him. Bultmann cites Romans 10:9 to show that believing in one's heart and "acknowledgment of Jesus as Lord is intrinsic to Christian faith along with acknowledgment of the miracle of His resurrection" (Bultmann TDNT, VI.209).

Faith has many aspects. "It is response to revelation as contrasted with discovery of new knowledge" (Blackman, 222). It implies our recognition that we are sinners and thus unable of ourselves to forsake evil and to do good. Socrates might hold that knowledge and virtue are much the same, so that to know what is right leads people to do what is right, but Paul would

not have agreed. For him faith implies both that we have come to see ourselves as sinful and also that we have come to recognize that God has provided for our forgiveness* through what Christ's death has done for us. Faith means coupling the recognition of the impossibility of our achieving our salvation with the acceptance of the truth that God has done all that is necessary. The "good news" is "the power of God for salvation to everyone who believes" (Rom 1:16). And faith means commitment. Those who believe have not only come to see their shortcomings, they have committed themselves to be Christ's people.

1. Faith and the Cross
2. Justification
3. Faith and Law
4. Abraham
5. Faithfulness
6. Faith and the Holy Spirit
7. Faith and the Christian Life
8. Faith and Obedience
9. Faith and the Church
10. The Faith

### 1. Faith and the Cross.

God's saving work is done in Christ. Paul constantly emphasizes the centrality of the cross,* sometimes by using just that word, sometimes by using some figure to bring out the truth. Thus he speaks of God as effecting "redemption"* and "propitiation" (*see* Expiation, Propitiation) and immediately adds, "through faith" and "in his blood" (Rom 3:24-25). The latter expression makes it clear that the apostle is referring to the Savior's atoning death,* and the former insists that this does not come to anyone automatically. Faith is the divinely appointed way. Indeed there is "one Lord, one faith" (Eph 4:5); the two go together.

Redemption means the payment of a price to set people free, and we should not miss the importance of freedom* in Paul's understanding of faith. He does not link freedom expressly with the "faith" terminology, but such a passage as Romans 5:16-21 assumes that the believer enters a freedom impossible without faith, which is the gateway to the new age of messianic salvation.

Paul sees what God has done in Christ as central, and he links faith to grace (Rom 4:16). Indeed, he writes to the Ephesians, "by grace you have been saved through faith" (Eph 2:8). Grace is important in understanding faith, for it emphasizes that salvation is a free gift, not a reward for human achievement of any sort, even as a reward for outstanding faith. So, too, it is faith that gives access to the grace in which believers stand and which leads to joy* (Rom 5:2). Paul looks to be of service to the Philippians* for "their progress and joy of faith" (Phil 1:25). And, interestingly, a little later he comments on "the sacrifice and service" of the Philippians' faith (Phil 2:17). Their faith resulted in sacrificial service.* In Christ believers have "boldness and access in confidence through faith in him" (Eph 3:12). Or Paul may stress the divine power*: "that your faith might rest not on human wisdom but on the power of God" (1 Cor 2:5 NRSV; Fee, 96).

## 2. Justification.

Justification* is the process whereby the sinner comes to be accepted by God. Paul sees the Christian understanding of justification as distinctive in that it rests on what God has done, not on any human achievement. It is appropriated by faith, not relying on human merit. The apostle brings out the central message of the Christian way by saying that the gospel* is "God's power for salvation to every one who believes," and he goes on to say that God's righteousness* is revealed "out of [Gk ek] faith into faith"—faith from first to last! He goes on to cite his great text from Habakkuk 2:4, "the one who is righteous by faith will live" (Rom 1:16-17). The "righteousness of God" comes "through faith in Jesus Christ to all the believers" (Rom 3:22).

God is both just and the justifier of anyone who has faith in Jesus (Rom 3:26). People are justified "out of faith," where the preposition ek indicates the origin; it is out of the faith that reposes in God that people are justified. Being justified they experience the peace* of God (Rom 5:1). Or Paul may vary his way of putting it by saying that one is justified "not from works of Law, but through faith in Jesus Christ" (Gal 2:16; see Works of the Law). He puts emphasis on the truth that believers are justified by faith quite apart from "works of Law" (Rom 3:28). Or he can look to the future when he will be found in Christ "not having my own righteousness which is of the Law, but that which is through faith in Christ, the righteousness of God on the basis of faith" (Phil 3:9). Still further in the future, "by faith we eagerly expect the hope of righteousness" (Gal 5:5); this righteousness is the securing of the acquittal on the last great day (see Eschatology) and it is plain that Paul sees faith as important in this connection. This great theme underlines all that Paul wrote. It is basic for him and central to the gospel he spent his life proclaiming. With or without this terminology he constantly puts before his readers the truth it conveys. People can do nothing to merit their salvation, but Paul reiterates the truth that all who come to God in faith receive salvation as a free gift.

## 3. Faith and Law.

To the Jews of the first century it was a matter of great importance that God had given the Law* to their nation of all the nations on the earth. This was a gift to be treasured and made the basis for the whole of life. But Paul points out that God's promise to Abraham and his descendants was "not through Law . . . but through the righteousness of faith" (Rom 4:13). The promise is made sure to all Abraham's descendants, not on the basis of keeping the Law but on that of faith (Rom 4:16). Law may be distinguished from faith, for "the Law is not of faith" (Gal 3:12). As F. F. Bruce puts it, "Law and faith, for Paul, are unrelated: the gospel calls for faith, but law requires works" (Bruce 1982, 162). Paul is very clear on the primacy of faith; thus he says plainly, "We (the pronoun is emphatic: "we Christians" in distinction from non-Christians) have believed in Christ Jesus so that we are justified by faith in Christ and not by works of Law." Then he adds the strong statement, "because from works of Law no flesh will be justified" (Gal 2:16). Paul finds a place for the Law, but only until faith should be "revealed" as the way (Gal 3:23); Paul can say that faith "came" (Gal 3:25); he sees faith as active.

Paul is interested in the salvation of Jews as well as Gentiles.* E. P. Sanders finds it "clear that one of Paul's major concerns is to assert that salvation is for both Jews and Gentiles and that it must be *based on the same ground.* That ground cannot be the law and must therefore be faith" (Sanders, 488). The error of ancient Israel* was that it did not seek to attain righteousness by faith, but rather by the way of Law (Rom 9:31-32). Paul was deeply concerned for Israel (Rom 10:1) and it was devastating for him that the Israelites did not come to God by the way of faith in Christ. Their emphasis on law meant that they stumbled, a lapse for which Paul finds a fulfillment of prophecy (Rom 9:33, citing Is 28:16 and 8:14). He does not mean that no Israelites are saved. After all, he himself was an Israelite and he gloried in the fact; and many of his coworkers were Israelites too. But they are saved in the same way as are Gentiles, by faith (Rom 3:30). Law is not the way to salvation. Law shows that men and women are sinners; it does not bring salvation (2 Cor 3:6-16).

Indeed Paul can speak of "a law of faith," which he specifically opposes to a law "of works" (Rom 3:27). It may be paradoxical to speak of "a law of faith," but the expression brings out something of Paul's strong emphasis on the centrality of faith. If people are going to see a "law" as the way to God, then that law assumes that they come to him by faith and not on account of any merits of their own. If those who come by way of Law inherit the blessing, then the promise made to Abraham* is void and that is unthinkable. It would mean that God's promise meant nothing (Rom 4:14). Scripture, Paul says, "has shut up all things under sin so that the promise by faith in Christ Jesus might be given to those who believe" (Gal 3:22). The very Scriptures that the Jews value so highly emphasize sin in such a way that anyone who reads them rightly must see that people cannot achieve salvation by their own deeds. They must turn to the promise, and the promise implies trust in the God whose faithfulness is demonstrated in his covenant promises made to the patriarch and made good in Christ and the church (cf. 2 Cor 1:17-22; see van Unnik).

### 4. Abraham.

Paul appeals to the example of Abraham,* the progenitor of the people of God (he speaks of him nineteen times). Twice he has a sustained development of the way Abraham was accepted by God, stressing both times that the great patriarch was accepted on no other grounds than faith (Rom 4; Gal 3). For Paul it is significant that Abraham was accepted by God simply because he believed that what God had promised him God would perform. Paul explicitly rules out works as the basis of Abraham's acceptance before God (Rom 4:2). It was Abraham's faith in divine faithfulness that was significant. Genesis 15:6 is a foundation text for Paul and it makes it clear both that Abraham exercised faith and that God accepted him on that basis (Rom 4:3-4; Gal 3:6). If the great patriarch was accepted in this way, then it is obvious to Paul that others who are accepted are accepted in no other way.

The Jews of Paul's day attached enormous importance to circumcision,* a rite which had been introduced for them by Abraham at God's command and as a "sign of the covenant*" (Gen 17:11); indeed, God had said to Abraham, "This is my covenant" (Gen 17:10). But Paul points out that Abraham's acceptance with God took place before he was circumcised, from which sequence he reasons that circumcision does

not have the significance attributed to it by the Jews of his day, that is, as an identity marker and badge of their covenant status (Dunn 1988; see Works of the Law). He can speak of Abraham as "the father of circumcision," but he sees this as a fatherhood not for those who are simply circumcised but for those "who walk in the steps of the faith of our father Abraham which he had in uncircumcision" (Rom 4:12).

Faith was reckoned to Abraham for righteousness (Rom 4:22), a truth that was recorded not simply as a piece of history but "for our sake also who believe on him who raised Jesus our Lord from the dead" (Rom 4:24; see Resurrection). Paul makes this the basis of an argument for the acceptance of Gentiles into the Christian church. It is those who are "of faith [ek pisteōs]" who are "sons of Abraham" (Gal 3:7), those "of faith" who "are blessed with faithful Abraham" (Gal 3:9); this is a truth foreseen in Scripture (Gal 3:8).

Paul regards circumcision as a barrier to salvation when it is claimed as an exclusive privilege (Gal 5:2): it is faith (the faith that works through love) that matters (Gal 5:6). If a person is circumcised out of a zeal for the Law but has no faith, that one is not rightly to be counted among Abraham's children. Not all Abraham's descendants are his true children (Rom 9:7); rather it is those who belong to Christ who are Abraham's offspring and "heirs according to promise" (Gal 3:29). Paul has a noteworthy statement that Christ's redeeming work in becoming "a curse* for us" was "in order that the blessing of Abraham might come to the Gentiles in Christ Jesus" (Gal 3:13-14). Faith is the only way.

### 5. Faithfulness.

"God is faithful" writes Paul, "through whom you were called" (1 Cor 1:9), and this is basic for the whole Christian understanding of God's dealings with his people, in both covenant ages. No human failing can void the faithfulness of God (Rom 3:3). Because God is faithful those whom God calls must reflect the quality they have learned from him, that is, in response to his covenant loyalty. Believers may be referred to as "the faithful in Christ Jesus" (Eph 1:1; cf. Col 1:2). The word pistis is generally translated "faith," but on occasion it can signify "faithfulness" (e.g., Gal 5:22). This is surely the case when Paul asks "shall their unbelief make void the faithfulness [pistin] of God?" (Rom 3:3).

It is more difficult when we come to the expression which could literally be translated as "a righteousness of God through faith of Jesus Christ" (Rom 3:22; cf. Rom 3:26; Gal 2:16, 20; 3:22; Phil 3:9). Most agree that we should understand this as "faith in Jesus Christ," though it is possible to see the meaning as "the faithfulness of Jesus Christ" or as "the faith Jesus Christ exercised," taking the words to point to the perfect humanity of Jesus (*see* Christology). The latter view, which understands the genitive of *pistis Christou* to be a subjective genitive (i.e., "Christ's faithfulness"), has gained some support among scholars, being argued most influentially by R. Hays (1983, 1991; see Howard *ABD*, for history of interpretation). The traditional position has argued that the genitive is objective ("faith *in* Christ"; see, e.g., Dunn 1988, 1991). The issue continues to be debated (for a linguistic and structural perspective on the significance of *ek pisteōs* and *dia pisteōs* and the influence of Hab 2:4, see Campbell), but as Dunn has noted, it is telling that if Paul wished to draw attention to the faithfulness of Christ, he missed some opportunities. In Romans 4, for instance, it is the faith of Abraham that is the model, not Christ's faithfulness (Dunn 1988, 1.166; but cf. Longenecker 1990, 87-88). We should probably understand Paul to be referring to faith in Jesus as object, though the other possibilities remind us both that he was faithful to the Father and that he lived by faith.

Paul includes faith in his list of what he calls "the fruit of the Spirit" (Gal 5:22). This may possibly mean that the Holy Spirit* produces saving faith within the believer, but it is much more likely that in this list the word denotes faithfulness, the quality of complete reliability. This will be the case also when the apostle speaks of a series of gifts made to believers and includes "faith, by the same Spirit" (1 Cor 12:9). As these words are preceded by "to another," the apostle* is not referring to saving faith, for that is the common possession of all Christians and not a gift made by the Spirit to one believer over against another. He may be referring to faithfulness, though, of course, elsewhere he speaks of having "all faith so as to move mountains" (1 Cor 13:2), and it may be that it is some such faith of which he writes here (see O. Wischmeyer's classification of this as *Wunderglaube* over against *Kerygmaglaube*, i.e., faith in God's miraculous power vs. the believer's saving faith in the gospel). W. Schmithals, it is true, holds that this refers to the controversy with the Gnostics who held that only a limited number of Christians are "pneumatics" ("spiritual"), and that Paul is arguing that all Christians have faith and thus are "pneumatics" (Schmithals, 172-73). But apart from objections that may be urged against Schmithals' general position, it seems that he has not paid sufficient attention to the expression "to another." Paul is not describing the position of all true Christians but is speaking of a gift made only to some of them, though it may be that here, as in 1 Corinthians 13:2, we should see the Spirit's endowment or the charism

of healing* power exercised in faith.

### 6. Faith and the Holy Spirit.

Paul sees faith as the necessary prerequisite for the presence of the Holy Spirit* in the believer. He castigates the Galatians for going back on the faith that had marked their earlier experience and had brought them the gift of the Spirit. He says he has only one question: "Did you receive the Spirit from works of Law or from the hearing of faith?" but then he puts it in a slightly different form: "He who provides to you the Spirit . . . (does he do it) from works of Law or from the hearing of faith?" (Gal 3:2, 5). In this passage he takes the Galatians* back to the beginning of their Christian experience and reminds them that at that time they had simply believed and that this had resulted in the gift of the Holy Spirit. Supernatural things had happened then and such displays of miraculous power were the result of the coming of the Spirit in response to faith, not to any keeping of the Law. His use of the present tense implies that these things were continuing. God was still providing them with the Spirit and still doing it by faith rather than Law.

Those who believe are "sealed with the promised Holy Spirit" (Eph 1:13), where the metaphor of sealing marks believers out as God's own. God's mark is on them. The same passage goes on to affirm that the Spirit is "the earnest" or "pledge" (*arrabōn*) of their inheritance. The *arrabōn* was a down payment (*see* First Fruits, Down Payment), a pledge that the rest of what was promised would be paid in due course. Paul uses it to bring out the thought that, while the present gift of the Holy Spirit is evidence of salvation now, there is much more to come in the eschatological future.

Paul further says that Christ "redeemed us from the curse of the Law" and that this was "in order that the blessing of Abraham might come on the Gentiles in Christ Jesus," and he adds a further clause of purpose, "in order that we might receive the promise of the Spirit through faith" (Gal 3:13-14). We should not see faith as a meritorious act which is rewarded by the gift of the Spirit. Rather Paul is saying that there is a divine work in believers and that it is through faith that they receive the gift of the Spirit of God, and so the gift of saving faith (1 Cor 12:3).

He also says that it is "through the Spirit by faith" that believers await "the hope* of righteousness" (Gal 5:5). We should remember also that "faith" is part of the harvest of the Spirit (Gal 5:22) and that God by his Spirit produces the gift of "faith" (1 Cor 12:9). As this gift is made "to another" it is not the saving faith that is the common possession of all Christians that is in mind, but a special gift (*charisma*). But for our present purpose the important thing to observe is that this kind of faith which is exercised in a ministry of miracle-working powers (*see* Signs, Wonders, Miracles) is a gift of the Spirit.

Paul speaks of having "the same spirit of faith according as it is written, 'I believed and therefore I spoke' "; he goes on, "we also believe, therefore also we speak" (2 Cor 4:13). His quotation is from Psalm 116:10 and, as R. P. Martin remarks, "Paul's confidence is traced back to a like assurance he found in the psalmist. . . . He regards his spoken ministry as a testimony to his faith—and the psalmist's—in the triumph of life over death" (Martin, 89). It is not easy to see here a specific reference to the Holy Spirit in the sense normally seen in the NT. But by the same token it is not easy to rule out such a reference, for it is clear that the apostle saw himself as acting and speaking under the inspiration of the Holy Spirit.

### 7. Faith and the Christian Life.

Paul does not see faith as a kind of passport to salvation, as though we must believe if we are to be regarded as among the saved, and that from then on we must live by our own efforts. He speaks of Christ as dwelling in the hearts of believers "through faith" (Eph 3:17), which points to an ongoing activity, not a fleeting visit.

Faith is not static, but must grow. Paul makes it clear that there are different levels of faith. Some believers, for example, have the faith that moves mountains (1 Cor 13:2; the implication is that this is miracle-working faith, not the faith we may expect every Christian to have; see 1 Cor 12:29, where the questions expect the answer no). The apostle speaks of the Corinthians as "abounding" in faith (2 Cor 8:7), and he looks for that faith to increase (2 Cor 10:15). Similarly, he tells the Ephesians that God has made certain gifts to the church for its edification "until we all attain the unity of the faith and of the knowledge of the Son* of God" (Eph 4:13). The faith of the Thessalonians "grows abundantly" (2 Thess 1:3; cf. 2 Cor 10:15). On the other hand he recognizes that some believers are "weak in faith" (Rom 14:1). Worse are those who profess faith but deny that Christ rose from the dead, for if Christ was not raised from the dead, "your faith is empty" (1 Cor 15:14), or "futile"* (1 Cor 15:17). The mention of "sincere faith" (1 Tim 1:5 NRSV) perhaps indicates that a spurious faith was not unknown (see Volf, esp. sec. VII, for this distinction; *see* Apostasy, Falling Away, Perseverance).

Faith is linked with other important Christian qualities, notably with love* (as Philem 5). In a noteworthy trio Paul says, "Now there abides faith, hope,* love, these three" (1 Cor 13:13), where the singular verb links the three very closely indeed (unless it simply agrees with the nearest subject [see BDF 135], or else Paul is grouping the three qualities into a unified subject; see Martin 1984, 54-56). These three qualities are linked elsewhere (e.g., Gal 5:5-6; Eph 1:15-18; Col 1:4-5; 1 Thess 1:3). The linkage of faith with hope and love is apparently a truth to which Paul gave frequent expression. And, of course, he links faith with several important Christian virtues when he lists "the fruit of the Spirit"* (Gal 5:22-23). He prays that Christ may dwell in the hearts of the Ephesian* Christians and goes on to the thought that they are "rooted and grounded in love" (Eph 3:17). He brings the letter to the Ephesians to a close with the prayer* that peace and love and faith "from God the Father and the Lord Jesus Christ" might be with the brothers and sisters (Eph 6:23). Or he may link faith with "the hope of the gospel" (Col 1:23).

We should not think of faith as a virtue Christians produce by their own meritorious act. Believers are sinners and quite unable to produce such a quality as saving faith out of their own resources. God bestows it, gives it as a gift (Rom 12:3; cf. 12:6). This accords with the fact that faith is sometimes seen as the basis of the whole Christian life. "We walk by faith" (2 Cor 5:7): faith pervades the whole of the life of the Christian. And Paul has a notable statement when he says that he has "died to the Law" that he might "live for God" and goes on, "I have been crucified with Christ, and no longer is it I that lives, but Christ lives in me; and what I now live in the flesh I live by faith in the Son of God" (Gal 2:19-20). There are depths in this statement, but for our present purpose the important thing is that Paul can say that his whole life is lived "by faith in the Son of God." Faith is central to all of his life.

Life is not always peaceful and Paul recognizes the inevitability of conflict between good and evil, which involves the people of God. He makes use of the metaphor of armor a number of times and sees "the shield of faith" as important; with it believers can "quench all the flaming arrows of the evil one" (Eph 6:16). From another point of view he uses the thought of conflict when he urges the Philippians to stand firm and strive "for the faith of the gospel" (Phil 1:27; see 10 below).

### 8. Faith and Obedience.

In the opening to Romans Paul speaks of the "obedience of faith" (Rom 1:5; 16:26). This has been understood in a number of ways. It is unlikely that it means "obedience to the faith" (Moffatt; surely the article would be used if this were his meaning). "Obedience which consists in faith" or "obedience which springs from faith" are much more likely. For our present purpose the important point is that faith and obedience are linked; we must not take Paul's emphasis on faith to mean that he is doing away with the importance of obedience. Those who really trust Christ will be obedient to his will. "The word of faith" (Rom 10:8) probably is another demand for obedience, with the meaning "the message that calls for obedience."

Paul does not set forth a series of food* laws, but he lived in an age and a place where food laws were not uncommon among religious people. If a Christian had the faith that enabled one to see that food laws were irrelevant, then that Christian might well eat forbidden foods, but "those who have doubts are condemned if they eat, because they do not eat out of faith" (Rom 14:23; Paul adds, "everything that is not of faith is sin"). Faith (or the lack of faith) determines what we may eat! We are not to think of faith as doing away with ethical conduct (see Ethics). Rather faith leads to ethical responsibility, especially where new Christians are concerned (see Idolatry; Strong and Weak).

### 9. Faith and the Church.

Paul can stress the importance of membership in the heavenly family. "You are all children of God through faith," he writes, and adds, "in Christ Jesus" (Gal 3:26), which is probably to be understood not so much of "faith in Christ" (though that is true) as "children of God" and also people "in Christ Jesus" (so Bruce; see Adoption, Sonship). It is faith and not any human achievement that admits believers to membership of the family of God.

Paul expected his converts to be linked in communities of faith. He speaks of the whole church* as "the household* of faith" (Gal 6:10). What characterizes a group of believers to whom he writes is that they have faith. He rejoices that the faith of the Roman Christians is proclaimed throughout the world (Rom 1:8). He says that he has heard of the Ephesians' faith in the Lord Jesus (Eph 1:15), so their faith was also widely known. And, apostolic leader though he was, he looks to be encouraged by the faith of the Roman Christians (Rom 1:12). He plays down the part played by rival Christian preachers and leaders at Corinth.* He says that he has no authority* over the faith of the Corinthians and says firmly, "for you stand by faith" (2 Cor 1:24). The Corinthian Christians had their direct relationship to God by faith and Paul had no

authority to interpose himself.

The adjective *pistos* signifies "faithful" and is used to make the point that God is faithful (1 Cor 1:9; 10:13). But believers may also be said to be faithful, either believers as a whole (Eph 1:1; 1 Tim 4:12), or individual believers such as Timothy (1 Cor 4:17) or Tychicus (Col 4:7). Indeed, Paul maintains that he himself is faithful (1 Cor 7:25; i.e., trustworthy, cf. 1 Cor 4:2).

### 10. The Faith.

Mostly Paul speaks of faith in terms of trust in Christ or in God. It is the basic attitude that brings people out of their sinfulness into a right relationship with the Deity. So fundamental is faith that the term may be used to categorize the whole Christian way, and the expression "the faith" comes into being, not simply as a way of referring to the trust in Christ that is so basic, but as a means of drawing attention to the whole body of teaching and practice that characterizes the Christian group. It all springs from faith and is an expression of faith, yet it articulates and expresses what Christians believe, their doctrine or "deposit" (a term frequent in the Pastorals*).

Thus Paul can say that he now preaches "the faith" he formerly persecuted (Gal 1:23). He does not mean that he persecuted people for trusting God; he is saying that he persecuted those who accepted the whole Christian system of truth that so strongly emphasized the importance of faith. We should not overlook the fact that faith is so central to Christianity that it can be characterized in terms of that word. But here it is not the simple exercise of trust in Christ that is meant, but the Christian way of belief that results from that trust.

We see this too in such a passage as, "Examine yourselves whether you are in the faith, test yourselves" (2 Cor 13:5). These words seem to mean more than "Test whether you still trust Christ"; they point to an understanding of truth that arises from trust in the Savior. It will be much the same with Paul's exhortation to the Corinthians: "Stand fast in the faith" (1 Cor 16:13), where it is surely the body of Christian teaching that is in mind. The Philippians are urged to contend "for the faith of the gospel" (Phil 1:27), in which we see a very clear use of "the faith" for the doctrinal content of the gospel that was preached (unless we understand the words in the sense "the faith brought about by the gospel"). In the Pastoral letters it is important that people, especially leaders, should be "sound in the faith" (Tit 1:13; 2:2). Paul prophesied that in the last times some "will renounce the faith" (1 Tim 4:1; cf. 4:6). But as his life drew near to its close he could write, "I have kept the faith" (2 Tim 4:7). See also APOSTASY, FALLING AWAY, PERSEVERANCE; CREED; GALATIANS, LETTER TO THE; GOSPEL; JUSTIFICATION; LAW; ROMANS, LETTER TO THE; WORKS OF THE LAW.

BIBLIOGRAPHY. G. Barth, "πίστις κτλ," *EDNT* 3.91-98; F. F. Bruce, *The Epistle to the Galatians* (NIGTC; Grand Rapids: Eerdmans, 1982); O. Becker and O. Michel, "Faith," *NIDNTT* 1.587-606; E. C. Blackman, "Faith, Faithfulness," *IDB* 2.222-34; R. Bultmann, "πείθω κτλ," *TDNT* VI.1-11; idem, "πιστεύω κτλ," *TDNT* VI.174-228; idem, *Theology of the New Testament* (2 vols.; New York: Charles Scribners, 1951, 1955) 1.314-30; D. A. Campbell, "The Meaning of ΠΙΣΤΙΣ and ΝΟΜΟΣ in Paul: A Linguistic and Structural Perspective," *JBL* 111 (1992) 91-103; K. W. Clements, *Faith* (London: SCM, 1981); H. Conzelmann, *An Outline of the Theology of the New Testament* (New York: Harper & Row, 1969) 171-73; J. D. G. Dunn, "Once More, ΠΙΣΤΙΣ ΧΡΙΣΤΟΥ," *SBL Seminar Papers* (Atlanta: Scholars, 1991) 730-44; idem, *Romans* (2 vols.; WBC 38; Dallas: Word, 1988); G. D. Fee, *The First Epistle to the Corinthians* (NICNT; Grand Rapids: Eerdmans, 1988); L. Goppelt, *Theology of the New Testament* (Grand Rapids: Eerdmans, 1982) 2.124-34; D. Guthrie, *New Testament Theology* (Downers Grove, IL: InterVarsity, 1981) 591-94; R. Hays, "ΠΙΣΤΙΣ and Pauline Christology: What Is at Stake?," *SBL Seminar Papers* (Atlanta: Scholars, 1991) 714-29; idem, *The Faith of Jesus Christ: An Investigation of the Narrative Substructure of Galatians 3:1—4:11* (SBLDS 56; Chico, CA: Scholars, 1983); M. D. Hooker, "ΠΙΣΤΙΣ ΧΡΙΣΤΟΥ," *NTS* 35 (1989) 321-42; G. Howard, "Faith of Christ," *ABD* II.758-60; idem, "On the 'Faith of Christ,' " *HTR* 60 (1967) 459-65; A. J. Hultgren, "The *Pistis Christou* Formulation in Paul," *NovT* 22 (1980) 248-63; D. R. Lindsay, "The Roots and Development of the πιστ-Word Group as Faith Terminology," *JSNT* 49 (1993) 103-18; H. Ljungman, *Pistis: A Study of Its Presuppositions and Its Meaning in Pauline Use* (Lund: Gleerup, 1964); R. N. Longenecker, *Galatians* (WBC 41: Dallas: Word, 1990); idem, "The Obedience of Christ in the Early Church," in *Reconciliation and Hope*, ed. R. J. Banks (Grand Rapids: Eerdmans, 1974) 146-47; J. G. Machen, *What Is Faith?* (Grand Rapids: Eerdmans, 1962); R. P. Martin, *2 Corinthians* (WBC 40; Waco: Word, 1986); idem, *The Spirit and the Congregation* (Grand Rapids: Eerdmans, 1984); L. Morris, *New Testament Theology* (Grand Rapids: Zondervan, 1986) 82-84; H. Ridderbos, *Paul: An Outline of His Theology* (Grand Rapids; Eerdmans, 1975) 231-52; E. P. Sanders, *Paul and Palestinian Judaism* (Philadelphia: Fortress, 1977); W. Schmithals, *Gnosticism at Corinth* (Nashville: Abingdon, 1971); W. C. van Unnik, "Reisepläne und Amen-Sagen. Zusammenhang und Gedankenfolge in 2 Korinther 1:15-24," in *Studia Paulina*, ed. J. N. Sevenster and W. C. van Unnik (Haarlem: Bohn, 1953); J. M. Gundry Volf, *Paul and Perseverance* (Louisville: Westminster/John Knox, 1991); O. Wischmeyer, *Der höchste Weg. Das 13. Kapitel des 1. Korintherbriefes* (Gütersloh: Gütersloher Verlag, 1981).

L. Morris

## FAITH OF JESUS CHRIST. See FAITH.

## FAITHFULNESS OF GOD. See FAITH; GOD; RIGHTEOUSNESS, RIGHTEOUSNESS OF GOD.

## FALLING AWAY. See APOSTASY, FALLING AWAY, PERSEVERANCE.

## FALSE APOSTLES. See APOSTLE; JUDAIZERS; OPPONENTS OF PAUL.

## FAMILY. See CHURCH; CHURCH ORDER AND GOVERNMENT; HOUSEHOLDS AND HOUSEHOLD CODES.

## FAMINE RELIEF VISIT. See CHRONOLOGY OF PAUL; ITINERARIES, TRAVEL PLANS, JOURNEYS, APOSTOLIC PAROUSIA; JERUSALEM.

## FATE. See MAGIC; WORSHIP.

## FATHER. See GOD.

## FEAR, REVERENCE

Fear or reverence refers in Paul to the appropriate level of respect and honor to be shown to another, often in light of fulfilling one's service* to God.* It also implies terror at the prospect of failing to fulfill one's obligation. Paul asserts that believers are to show fear or reverence with respect to God and Christ,* the state, and other humans. The relation among these, in Paul's thinking, is that reverence or fear of God constitutes a suitable basis for Christian conduct. Paul's concept of fear or reverence is grounded in the OT idea of fear or reverence not being a completely sinister terror stemming from being subjected to an angry deity. For Paul, fear or reverence reflects an appropriate response in terms of respect, honor and service due to the powerful and holy God who is bound by covenant* to his people. Due reverence demands moral and cultic obedience; disobedience or not showing due respect warrants justifiable terror. Paul uses the words *phobos* and *phobeomai* almost exclusively when referring to this concept. (He never uses *tremō* or *eulabeomai/eulabeia*, found elsewhere in the NT.)

1. Fear and Reverence of God and Christ

### 1. Fear and Reverence of God and Christ.

For Paul fear or reverence of God or Christ is foundational for the Christian's relations to God and humanity. Apart from use of the phrase "fear and trembling" (see 5 below), there are four major contexts that define the Pauline concept of fear or reverence of God and Christ.

In Romans 3:18 Paul establishes the verdict that Jew and Gentile* alike stand condemned under sin*; Paul supports this by quoting from the OT, concluding with Psalm 36:1: "there is no fear of God before their eyes." As Cranfield says, this "is a figurative way of saying" that for an individual condemned under sin "the fear of God has no part in directing his life, that God is left out of his reckoning, that he is a practical, whether or not he is a theoretical, atheist" (Cranfield, 1.195). In Romans 11:20 Paul tells his Gentile Roman readers that they should not be arrogant because God has grafted them into the olive* tree and cut off unbelieving Jews; rather, they should fear. Although the Greek word *phobos* ("fear") is unmodified, in the context "fear of God" is spoken of. The link between fear and reverence as an appropriate response to God and fear or terror for disobedience is well illustrated by these passages.

In 2 Corinthians 5 Paul grounds his confidence regarding the state of believers after death (2 Cor 5:6-10), despite its uncertain nature, in the "fear of the Lord" (2 Cor 5:11). This serves as a transition to his defense of his Corinthian* ministry of reconciliation (2 Cor 5:11-21; see Peace, Reconciliation). Paul concludes with reference to God's promises and the believers' obligation to respond appropriately through cleansing themselves from defilement and perfecting themselves in sanctification, a passage probably influenced by cultic terminology (see Holiness, Sanctification). Sanctification is grounded "in fear of God" (2 Cor 7:1). The word "in" (*en*) refers to the sphere or arena in which sanctification occurs.

In Colossians 3:22 the author commands slaves* to be genuinely obedient, fearing the Lord. The word *lord* (*kyrios*), also used for earthly masters, refers here to Christ, as Colossians 3:24 confirms (O'Brien, 227-28): serving the "Lord" or Christ is the backdrop for all the commands in the Colossian household* code. Similar OT phrasing (e.g., Ex 1:17, 21; Lev 19:14, 32; 25:17; Ps 54:20) is consistent with other features of Yahweh attributed to Christ in Colossians (see Col

1:15-20). Grounding these practical exhortations in the larger sphere of divine service forges links with the OT tradition of service to God. Unlike the chief letters of Paul, and Colossians, Ephesians 5:21 introduces a new "divine" object of fear or reverence by referring directly to being subject to others in the fear of Christ. Even though the believer's fear is directed toward Christ, in distinction from God or the Lord, the sense of "in" (*en*) to describe the sphere or arena in which the action is performed is similar to the use in 2 Corinthians 7:1. Christian submission exists in the realm of fear of Christ.

### 2. Fear and Reverence Directed to the State.

In Romans 13:1-7 Paul commends fear of those who are authorities characterized by justice, "just authorities" (*see* Civil Authority). These authorities are appointed by God to reward good and punish evil behavior. "Just authorities," Paul states, are not an object of terror to the one who does good (Rom 13:3), but are objects of terror to those who do evil (Rom 13:4). In light of these guidelines Paul instructs his readers to give fear or reverence to the one deserving it (Rom 13:7). The relation between fear or reverence as a sign of appropriate behavior, as opposed to fear or terror as a sign of disobedience to God, is well illustrated by the contrasting uses of *phobos* in Romans 13:3, 4 and 7. Scholars do not agree on whether the "fear" in Romans 13:7 is to be given to the authorities or to God. Paul's advocacy of paying taxes, and his general advocacy of standards of Christian behavior in Romans 12—15, argue for fear of the authorities. Paul's preceding statements, which establish the "just authorities" as servants of God, argue for fear of God. The two concepts are not easily separated. When Paul speaks of fear of authorities, he is speaking of authorities who behave justly and are instituted by God. Since they are God's agents of good on earth, defiance of them incurs judgment,* a judgment endorsed by God and worthy of fear or terror.

### 3. Fear and Reverence of Humans.

In 2 Corinthians 7:11 Paul chronicles the results of godly sorrow, listing one of these as fear. Although Paul may be referring here to fear of God, the context of Paul's commendation of the Corinthians' change of heart makes it likely that he is referring to their fear of him as apostle,* whether as God's comforter or punisher (1 Cor 4:21). In Galatians 2:12, in recounting his rebuke of Cephas, Paul attributes Cephas's reaction to fear of the party of the circumcision,* a fear resulting in an inappropriate response.

In Ephesians 5:33 the husband is commanded to

love his wife as himself, but the wife is told to fear her husband, that is, to show an appropriate reverence and respect befitting her service to God. This is the concluding statement of the household code on the reciprocal relations of husbands and wives (Eph 5:21-33). In 1 Timothy 5:20 fear is a means of condemning sin. It is not said what the object of "fear" is. It could be fear of falling into sin, or it could be fear of God.

### 4. Fear as a Personality Trait.

The majority of instances in which Paul speaks of fear or reverence are in contexts of a healthy fear or reverence that motivates appropriate behavior in relation to God or Christ, to the state or to other humans (see 1-3 above). There are several instances, however, where Pauline words often translated "fear" or "timidity" refer to a personality trait. These instances do not permit drawing theological conclusions, such as seeing this trait as having its origin in God's character. In many instances, the trait is simply an unfocused anxiety. In Romans 8:15 Paul contrasts two human spirits, one of servitude and one of sonship (*see* Adoption, Sonship). The former is said to lead "to" (*eis*) fear. In 2 Corinthians 7:5 Paul confesses to afflictions* without and fears within. Whereas scholars are divided over whether Paul's external troubles are human adversaries or adverse circumstances, the consensus regarding his internal fears is that he is anxious over possible failure at Corinth. In 2 Corinthians 11:3 and 12:20 Paul expresses his anxiety regarding the Corinthians' spiritual choices. In Galatians 4:11 Paul expresses anxiety for his readers on the chance that he has vainly labored for them. And in 2 Timothy 1:7, in a discussion of human traits given by God, Paul contrasts those of power,* love* and wisdom* with "timidity" (*deilia*, the only use of this word in the Pauline literature).

### 5. Fear and Trembling.

The phrase "fear and trembling" is unique to the Pauline writings in the NT (1 Cor 2:3; 2 Cor 7:15; Phil 2:12; Eph 6:5).

Many recent commentators, following Michael, have argued for a sociologically based use of "fear and trembling," reflecting an attitude to be displayed toward others. In 1 Corinthians 2:3 and 2 Corinthians 7:15 Paul has "fear and trembling" regarding his own reception by the Corinthians and the Corinthians' rightful performance of their duties toward Titus. This sense is not so evident in the context of Philippians 2:12. After his christological passage of Philippians 2:6-11, regarding Christ's example, Paul tells his audience to be similarly obedient and to work out their salvation with "fear and trembling." Although "salvation"* might mean "spiritual health" (Hawthorne), the normal sense of the Pauline language—supported by the context—is soteriological. Paul is not saying here that, in light of Christ's example of obedience to God, Christians should accomplish their salvation with fear and trembling directed toward other believers; he is endorsing fear and trembling toward God (Silva, 34, "godly fear").

Unlike the above examples, Ephesians 6:5 states that slaves are to show "fear and trembling" toward their earthly masters. The fear is directed toward humans outside the sphere of ecclesial relations, although the addition of the phrase "as to Christ" brings it into harmony with the Colossian household code (see 1 above).

*See also* CIVIL AUTHORITIES; GOD; HOUSEHOLDS, HOUSEHOLD CODES; LORD; SERVANT, SERVICE; SLAVE, SLAVERY.

BIBLIOGRAPHY. C. E. B. Cranfield, *The Epistle to the Romans* (2 vols.; ICC; Edinburgh: T. & T. Clark, 1975, 1979); G. F. Hawthorne, *Philippians* (WBC 43; Waco: Word, 1983); W. Lillie, "The Pauline House-table," *ExpT* 86 (1975) 179-83; A. T. Lincoln, *Ephesians* (WBC 42; Dallas: Word, 1990); R. P. Martin, *2 Corinthians* (WBC 40; Waco: Word, 1986); J. H. Michael, " 'Work out your own Salvation,' " *Expositor* 9th series, 2 (1924) 439-50; P. T. O'Brien, *Colossians, Philemon* (WBC 44; Waco, TX: Word, 1982); S. E. Porter, "Romans 13:1-7 as Pauline Political Rhetoric," *Filología Neotestamentaria* 3.6 (1990) 115-39; M. Silva, *Philippians* (WEC; Chicago: Moody, 1989).

S. E. Porter

## FELLOWSHIP, COMMUNION, SHARING

The relationship of believers to one another in the common experience of salvation* is chiefly presented in Paul by several Greek word groups (including *koinōneō* and its cognates, together with the verbs *metechō* and *merizō*), along with several words having the prefix *syn-* and a number of images (e.g., the body) which express the idea of common participation. The focus of attention in this article will be the *koinōnia* ("fellowship") word group. Much of the key NT teaching on fellowship is found in Paul who uses the verb *koinōneō* five times out of a total eight occurrences, and the noun *koinōnia* thirteen times out of nineteen instances (as well as five examples of *syngkoinōneō* and its cognate noun). *Koinōnia*, which was used so expansively in the Greek world as to lose much of its shape (it covered all types of common enterprise, including a marriage union and bonds of human friendship), had to do with "having *something* in common with *someone*" and was rendered in the NT by "association," "communion," "fellowship," "close relationship," "generosity," "sign of fellowship," "gift," "contribution" and "participation." The NT emphasis is on the participation "in something," particularly objective realities outside and independent of one's existence (Martin), rather than the association "with someone" which is the emphasis on the contemporary notion of "fellowship."

1. Having a Share In
2. Giving a Share In

## 1. Having a Share In.

In several significant Pauline instances of the *koinōnia* word group the dominant idea is of believers sharing together in something, often spiritual realities. So 1 Corinthians 1:9 signifies "the fellowship *with* (literally "of") his Son, Jesus Christ,*" into which the Corinthians have been called by God* (cf. 1 Cor 10:16, where the readers' participation in a common meal is, in some sense, a sharing in the body and blood of Christ). This common sharing of Christ stands over against the party slogans of the Corinthians.* The Philippians,* who share with (*syngkoinōnos*) Paul in the grace* of God (perhaps this is a reference to the grace of his apostleship, Phil 1:7), have experienced "the fellowship of the Spirit" (Phil 2:1; *see* Holy Spirit), an expression which is best understood as a participation in the Holy Spirit (an objective genitive) rather than the fellowship which is created by the Holy Spirit (a subjective genitive). Their common sharing in the Spirit should be a decisive factor in their life together (Phil 2:1-4) as "one body in Christ" (Rom 12:5). Similarly, 2 Corinthians 13:13 is best interpreted as the participation in the Holy Spirit rather than that which is created by the Holy Spirit.

Elsewhere in Paul this language of fellowship is used of those who enjoy certain privileges in common: in Romans 11:17 Gentile believers are sharers along with (*syngkoinōnos*) Jews in the rich inheritance that belongs to Abraham's* children (cf. Rom 15:27), while in 1 Corinthians 9:23 the apostle* speaks of his energetic and single-minded activity "for the sake of the gospel, that I may share (*syngkoinōnos*) in its blessings." Common experiences of a different kind (1 Cor 10:18, 20) can also be described by the adjective *koinōnoi* ("sharers").

In the unique expression, "the fellowship (*koinōnia*) of his sufferings*" (Phil 3:10; cf. 2 Cor 1:7 where *koinōnoi*, "sharers," is used), Paul's own afflictions are an active participation in Christ's "sufferings" (the genitive is objective, denoting that in which one participates). These afflictions do not refer to Christ's redemptive death on the cross but, like the messianic woes of Jewish apocalyptic* thought, designate the trials (*see* Afflictions, Trials) in which all Christians share (cf. Acts 14:22; 1 Thess 3:3, 7). By participating in Christ's afflictions, Paul was entering into a deeper personal relationship with his Lord* and thus becoming more like him every day. This fellowship was evidence that Paul was truly one of the Messiah's people, destined for salvation and future glory* (Phil 1:29; Rom 8:17).

A similar note is struck in Philippians 4:14 where it is asserted that the Philippians had "made common cause with" (*syngkoinōneō*) the apostle in his affliction. By their recent gift (cf. Phil 4:15) they had identified with him in his ministry* and given further evidence of their participation in the apostolic task of proclaiming the gospel* (Phil 1:5).

## 2. Giving a Share In.

Both the noun *koinōnia* and its cognate *koinōneō* are used by Paul in an active sense of "sharing with" another person or group. So the Macedonians assisted the poverty-stricken saints of the Jerusalem* church by their "contribution" (*koinōnia*), that is, "their generosity" (2 Cor 8:4), even when they themselves were in great financial distress (*see* Collection). Paul wants the Corinthians to follow this splendid example (2 Cor 9:13).

Similarly, at Philippians 1:5 the apostle states that he is thankful for the Philippians' "partnership in the gospel" (*euangelion*). This phrase is not to be taken in a passive sense and therefore equivalent to "your faith" (Seesemann), but denotes their active cooperation in the widest sense. *Euangelion* is a noun of agency describing an activity of furthering the gospel mission* to Gentiles.* Several writers take the term *koinōnia* to signify "generosity" here, with the Philippians' financial help being a signal instance of this active cooperation.

In his opening prayer* for Philemon,* Paul prays that his colleague's "generosity or liberality" (*koinōnia*), which arises from his faith, might lead him effectively into a deeper understanding of all the blessings that belong to him and others incorporated into Christ (Philem 6).

Both noun and verb can then designate a concrete form of this generosity and come to signify a "gift," "contribution" (Phil 4:15; cf. Gal 6:6; *see* Financial Support) and even the "collection" for the needy Christians of the Jerusalem church* (Rom 15:26).

*See also* BODY OF CHRIST; CHURCH; COLLECTION FOR THE SAINTS; FINANCIAL SUPPORT; HOLY SPIRIT; IN CHRIST.

BIBLIOGRAPHY. J. Y. Campbell, "κοινωνία and its Cognates in the New Testament," in *Three New Testament Studies* (Leiden: Brill, 1965) 1-28; J. Hainz, *Koinonia. 'Kirche' als Gemeinschaft bei Paulus* (BU 16; Regensburg:

Pustet, 1982); F. Hauck, "κοινός κτλ," *TDNT* III.797-809; J. M. McDermott, "The Biblical Doctrine of *KOINΩNIA*," *BZ* 19 (1975) 64-77, 219-33; R. P. Martin, *The Family and the Fellowship* (Grand Rapids: Eerdmans, 1979); G. Panikulam, *Koinōnia in the New Testament: A Dynamic Expression of Christian Life* (AnBib 85; Rome: Biblical Institute, 1979); H. Seesemann, *Der Begriff KOINΩNIA im Neuen Testament* (BZNW 14; Giessen: 1933); M. J. Suggs, "Koinonia in the New Testament," *Mid-Stream* 23 (1984) 351-62.

P. T. O'Brien

## FINAL JUDGMENT. *See* ESCHATOLOGY; JUDGMENT.

## FINANCIAL SUPPORT

Paul's letters have more to say about the financial support of ministers and fundraising in the church than any other part of the NT. In 1 Corinthians 9 and 2 Corinthians 11—12 Paul explains why he refuses the financial support that is his right as an apostle; and, in his letter to the Philippians, Paul thanks the church for their generous financial support of his ministry. One of the major projects of Paul's ministry was raising money for a collection* that would go to the poor in the Jerusalem* church. He writes extensively about this collection in 2 Corinthians 8—9 and mentions it in Romans 15:25-32, 1 Corinthians 16:1-4 and Galatians 2:9-10. These texts show that for Paul, financial issues always had important theological implications and that requests for money were to be related to the message of the gospel.*

1. Financial Support of Apostles
2. The Collection
3. Money and Mission

### 1. Financial Support of Apostles.

The issue of financial support is raised in Paul's defense of his apostleship in 1 Corinthians 9 and 2 Corinthians 11—12 (*see* Apostle). The most striking aspect of Paul's comments is his refusal to accept support from the Corinthian congregation, a refusal which evidently gave rise to considerable misunderstanding at Corinth. Here the connection between money and authority* is at issue. Paul was accused of not having true apostolic authority because he did not receive the usual apostolic support.

*1.1. Historical Background to the Issue of Support.* The Corinthians probably questioned Paul's authority because they understood Paul's actions in terms of the issue of how teachers and philosophers (*see* Philosophy) ought to be supported. In contemporary Greek society there was much debate about how philos-

ophers and teachers should support themselves. Most philosophers either charged fees or accepted the patronage of a wealthy individual. The major criticism of this method of support was that it placed a philosopher under obligation to a patron and therefore jeopardized the philosopher's freedom to teach the truth. In Hellenistic society the giving and receiving of benefactions was an extremely important component of the social structure. The wealthy expressed their power by becoming patrons, and since benefaction was the basis of friendship, refusing a gift was an act of enmity. Philosophers who wished to avoid this network of obligation could either beg, as the Cynics chose to do, or work. However, since most of Greek society looked down on those who worked at a trade or begged, not many philosophers chose these methods of support. Those who did gained freedom at the expense of social status.

Seen against this background the Corinthians' misunderstanding of Paul's refusal to accept support makes sense. In refusing support from the Corinthians, Paul could be understood as refusing their friendship or refusing to offer them a chance to share in the ministry* of the gospel. Paul could also be seen as demeaning the Corinthians as well as himself by working at a trade rather than accepting their patronage (*see* Tentmaking). It is not just Paul's status as an apostle but the Corinthians' status as a congregation that is at issue here. The Corinthians want their apostle to have honor in society and want to share in that honor by supporting him. So they ask whether or not Paul deserves to be honored as a true apostle if he refuses to accept true apostolic support.

*1.2. Reasons for Financial Support of Apostles.* In 1 Corinthians 9 Paul begins his defense of his apostleship (and his apostolic right to refuse support) by a vigorous defense of an apostle's right to earn a living by the preaching of the gospel.

Paul's authority as an apostle has been challenged, so he starts his defense in 1 Corinthians 9:1-2 by establishing himself as an apostle and reminding the Corinthians that their congregation is the result of his apostolic labors. Paul establishes the fact that he and Barnabas have the same right to material support as the other apostles in 1 Corinthians 9:4-14. Apostles have the right to receive food and drink and to be accompanied by a wife (who would, presumably, also be supported). Like other apostles, Paul has the right not to have to work in order to support himself, but to get his living by the gospel. Paul offers several different arguments to prove his point about an apostle's right to support. He first uses several analogies that show that in everyday life people expect to be supported by their labor. Paul then uses a scriptural example to show that the Law also speaks to this issue and insists that even animals are to be fed from their labors. Even more to the point, he reminds the Corinthians that those who minister in both Jewish and pagan temples get their food from the sacrifices. Supporting those who serve at the altar is part of both Jewish and Hellenistic piety. Christian ministers are no different, which is why the Lord commands that those who preach the gospel are to live by the gospel.

In the argument about apostolic rights to support Paul is defending his apostolic authority. The Greek word *exousia*, translated "right," can also mean "authority."* Understanding that apostolic authority, rather than apostolic rights, is the major focus of Paul's defense helps explain why Paul also argues that he has the authority to give up his apostolic right to material support. In Paul's discussion about apostolic rights, he has not only established his right to be supported but has also affirmed his authority by his refusal of support. This authority is based on the preaching of the gospel, not on taking financial support. Because he preaches the gospel, he has sown spiritual seed among the Corinthians, seed which has clearly resulted in the congregation which now questions his authority. He has the right to their material benefits, but he is not under any obligation to receive their financial support. His primary obligation is to the preaching of the gospel, and it is from the gospel that he receives his apostolic authority.

*1.3. Why Paul Refuses Financial Support.* As an apostle Paul's primary obligation is to the gospel itself. One of the signs of this apostolic authority is that for the sake of the gospel he renounces his right to financial support. Paul gives his reasons for his rejection of financial support in 1 Corinthians 9:12, 15-19, 2 Corinthians 11:7-15 and 2 Corinthians 12:13-18.

The first reason Paul gives for not accepting financial support is that he does not want to put a "stumbling block"* in the way of the gospel. Exactly what this "stumbling block" might be is not made clear in 1 Corinthians 9. In 2 Corinthians 11:9 and 2 Corinthians 12:14-18 Paul says that he does not want to burden the Corinthians or take advantage of them in anyway. As their "parent" in Christ he wants to give to them rather than receive from them. Paul's freedom in preaching the gospel also seems to be an issue in 1 Corinthians 9:15-23. Any appearance of greed or obligation to the Corinthian congregation might hurt the cause of the gospel of Christ.

Paul's second reason for refusing financial support is found in 1 Corinthians 9:15-18. Refusing financial support gives Paul a "ground for boasting*" in the

gospel. Since his primary obligation as an apostle is the preaching of the gospel, he cannot boast about his preaching or the apostolic authority the gospel confers upon him. But he is under no obligation to receive financial support for his preaching. In fact, by refusing financial support he is able to proclaim the gospel even more effectively. This is the reward he seeks. When he preaches the gospel "free of charge" he is a living example of the message he preaches— that God's grace is freely offered to all in Christ. This is why Paul can use his boast of not accepting support to expose the false apostles in 2 Corinthians 11:10-18 (*see* Opponents). These false apostles show that they are not serving the true gospel, and therefore do not have true apostolic status, when they take advantage of the Corinthians financially. When the truth of the gospel is at stake, Paul is able to boast that he serves only the gospel, not his own financial interests. When Paul refuses financial support, he does so because of his own unique apostolic relationship to the gospel he preaches.

The Corinthians think that accepting financial support shows that one has apostolic status. Paul turns this type of thinking around and ties his authority as an apostle to the gospel he preaches. The fact that he offers this gospel free of charge and refuses financial support rather than put a stumbling block in the way of the gospel proves his true apostolic status. Paul's overall concern as an apostle is to avoid misusing his authority and thereby hurting the cause of the gospel. The single passion of Paul's life—all things for the sake of the gospel—is reflected in his renunciation of financial support.

*1.4. Did Paul Always Refuse Support?* Paul's correspondence with the Corinthians makes it clear that he did not accept financial support from the Corinthian church. He also appears to have followed this policy during his time in Thessalonica (1 Thess 2:9). But in 2 Corinthians 11:9 Paul mentions that he received support from Macedonian Christians during the time he spent in Corinth. In Philippians 4:10-20 Paul makes a point of thanking the church for their generous gift to him. Their gift has more than met his need, and Paul assures the Philippians that God will also meet their needs. The Philippian church has been Paul's partner in the gospel from the beginning of his ministry, especially during the time he was at Thessalonica. This financial partnership reflects the close bond between Paul and the Philippian congregation. Philippians 4:15 suggests that the Philippians may have been the only church that supported his ministry, although 2 Corinthians 11:8 implies that other churches may also have supported Paul. Why did Paul

accept financial support from the Philippians and refuse support when he was at Corinth and Thessalonica?

There is no indication that Paul accepted financial
support from the Philippians when he was actually at
Philippi. Their support came after he departed and
went on to establish other churches. In their giving
the Philippians entered into partnership with Paul in
the proclamation of the gospel. It appears that Paul
did not accept support from any church when he was
actively working in that church. But after he had established a church, he expected them to contribute to
the cause of the gospel. This is not inconsistent behavior on Paul's part. It is merely another example of Paul
putting the gospel first and using money in ways that
further the preaching of the gospel rather than hindering it. Even though Paul did not expect financial
support from the Corinthian church for his ministry
at Corinth, he did expect them to support his work
later. This is made especially clear in Paul's pleas that
the Corinthians contribute generously to the collection for the saints at Jerusalem.

## 2. The Collection.

Even though Paul did not ask the churches he worked
in to support him financially, he had no hesitation
about asking them to contribute to one of his ongoing
projects—the collection* for "the poor among the
saints at Jerusalem" (Rom 15:26). The collection is
mentioned in Galatians 2:10 in connection with Paul's
visit to the Jerusalem apostles. As part of the agreement that Paul would go to the Gentiles* and the
other apostles to the Jews (see Israel), Paul agrees to
"remember the poor" (see Rich and Poor). In Romans
15:25-32 Paul tells the church that he is taking a contribution to Jerusalem before he comes to visit them
at Rome. This contribution comes from the saints in
Macedonia and Achaia as a grateful response for the
spiritual blessings they have received and as a tangible
expression of unity between Jew and Gentile in Christ.
In 1 Corinthians 16:1-4 Paul also mentions taking the
collection to Jerusalem and how contributions to the
collection ought to be made. In 2 Corinthians 8 and
9 Paul makes it clear just how important this collection
is to him and why the Corinthians ought to give to it.

Even though this collection was of vital importance
to Paul, it is not mentioned in the rest of the NT. This
is especially surprising in Acts, which does refer to
Paul's meeting with the Jerusalem apostles and his
final journey to Jerusalem. The only time Acts speaks
of Paul bringing money to Jerusalem is in Acts 11:29-
30, where the Gentiles send money to Judea at the
time of the great famine. But this does not seem to be

the collection referred to in Paul's letters, although it
may be the prototype of that collection. The Acts 11
event occurs at the very beginning of the Gentile mission before Paul had even established the churches
he writes to about the collection. The Acts 15 account
of Paul's meeting with the Jerusalem apostles does not
include any reference to money or relief for the poor
at all. The Acts 21 account of Paul's final journey to
Jerusalem sounds very much like the trip Paul mentions in Romans 15:25-32, but again there is no mention of money. Did Paul eventually deliver the collection? Perhaps he did as part of his final journey to
Jerusalem, as he implies in Acts 24:17 in his speech
before Felix. But on the basis of Acts alone it is impossible to be certain. All of our direct information
about the collection comes from Paul's letters.

*2.1. Historical Background to the Collection.* In his
commentary on 2 Corinthians F. W. Danker suggests
that the Hellenistic system of patronage is an important historical background to the collection (see 1.1.
above). A question often asked about the collection is
whether there were any precedents within Judaism for
such an activity. Two antecedents are worth considering: the Temple tax and a votive offering.

K. F. Nickle has explored the parallels between the
Temple tax and the collection. The Temple tax of one
half-shekel was used to support the cult of the Jerusalem Temple. Payment of this tax was obligatory for all
Jewish males over the age of twenty, so that the whole
Jewish people would be represented in the sacrifices
bought with the tax money. In the Diaspora* the tax
was collected in a central location and then sent with
a large retinue to Jerusalem. The parallels between
this tax and Paul's collection are impressive—both
were large sums of money that were delivered to Jerusalem by delegates and both were used to represent
the unity of God's people. But the differences are also
obvious—Paul's collection was for the poor, not the
Temple, and there is no indication that it was repeated or obligatory. H. D. Betz suggests that the collection
also shows many similarities to a votive offering. The
collection can be seen as a thank offering given to
God for blessings received. Gifts of thanks to God
were also bound up with provision for the poor, just
as the collection was.

Neither the Temple tax nor the votive offering
alone provides a convincing precedent for Paul's collection. But taken together, they seem to provide
precedents for most of Paul's concerns for the collection. What is clear is that Paul gets many of his ideas
about money from Judaism and applies those ideas in
the churches he serves.

*2.2. Fundraising for the Collection.* Although Paul

mentions the collection in Romans 15 and Galatians 2, he talks about giving money to the collection only in his correspondence with the Corinthian church. He devotes two entire chapters, 2 Corinthians 8—9, to urging the Corinthians to give generously to the collection. In these two chapters Paul's views of how Christians should use their money to glorify God are clearly set forth.

Paul begins his appeal to the Corinthians in 2 Corinthians 8:1-15 by describing the enthusiastic participation of the Macedonians. The Macedonians' liberality is a sign of the grace of God operating among them despite their affliction and poverty. This gift of money signifies their giving of themselves to God and serves as a model for the Corinthians. Paul challenges the Corinthians to prove that their love is genuine, and that they are generous benefactors like the Macedonians, by completing their contribution to the collection. That the Corinthian church had begun to make contributions is clear not only from this passage, but from 1 Corinthians 16:1-4 where Paul advises them to lay aside money for the collection each week. Paul holds up Christ's love for them as the reason they ought to enrich others as they have been enriched. The other reason they should want to contribute is the matter of equality between Christians—those who have abundance should help those in need. Paul is not asking for their money in order to impoverish them. Giving money is an opportunity to thank God for his abundant gifts, especially the gift of Christ, and a chance to show genuine love* for Christ by helping brothers and sisters in need. Paul understands giving as an act of ministry and as an expression of Christian fellowship.

In 2 Corinthians 8:16—9:5, Paul goes on to explain why Titus is returning to help with the collection. Titus is another generous benefactor who can serve as a model for the Corinthians and he has the best interests of the Corinthians at heart. Paul seems anxious that "no one shall blame us about this liberal gift we are administering." This same concern is reflected in 2 Corinthians 12:14-18. Several scholars have suggested that the Corinthians may have thought Paul was enriching himself at their expense by taking up the collection. They may even have accused him of using the collection to support himself even after he had refused their offer of support. Whatever the case, Paul is exceptionally careful to have others supervise the collection and do what is honorable by human standards. The identity of the "famous" brother and the "earnest" brother are the subjects of much debate; but no firm conclusions about their identities can be stated (see Furnish, 433-38, for a more complete discus-

sion). The purpose of the men's coming is to make sure the Corinthians do earnestly attempt to complete their contributions. Paul reminds the Corinthians that if they fail to give what they have promised they will humiliate not only themselves, but Paul and Christ as well. Generous benefaction increases the prestige of the givers and those with whom they are associated, but parsimonious giving is a source of public shame. The Corinthians' participation in the collection project is a sign of their commitment to Paul, as well as to God. The most theologically interesting part of Paul's fund-raising appeal is found in the extended sowing/reaping metaphor of 2 Corinthians 9:6-15. The recognition of the spiritual and financial dimensions of sowing and reaping was a characteristic emphasis of Hellenistic and Jewish thought. Sowing was seen as a sign of trust in God, who could alone guarantee the harvest. In this context, any gift given to God was understood as a thank offering for blessings received. Since all things come from God, the issue is not whether one should sow, but how much one should sow. A thankful giver gives cheerfully and abundantly, knowing that both seed and harvest come from God. When God gives an abundant harvest, it is not only to bless the one who sows but also to enable further giving. God provides everything, including the means to be generous. In fact, since liberal sowing results in a liberal harvest, one can expect progressively larger harvests as one is provided with more seed to be sown. God will not only provide for the needs of the generous giver, but will multiply the giver's resources for even more generous giving. Generous giving glorifies God by providing for the needs of the saints, showing obedience to the gospel of Christ and results in even more thanks being given to God. It also results in intercessory prayer being offered on behalf of the benefactors because of the grace of God manifested through them. Both Jews and early Christians believed the prayers of the poor were especially powerful, so this would be yet another benefit to the generous giver.

In his use of the sowing/reaping metaphor, Paul sums up all the reasons why the Corinthians should give generously to the collection and does not hesitate to appeal to selfish motives as well as noble ones. Generous giving is an act of worship which gives thanks to God for his gifts. Since material and spiritual wealth are both gifts of divine generosity, one should share with others. Generosity will not leave one impoverished, but will allow God to give even more to the giver. The not-so-subtle threat here is that God will not bless those who refuse to give generously. So giving generously is truly in the Corinthians' best interests. They can glorify God and ensure further blessings for themselves at the same time.

### 2.3. The Theological Significance of the Collection.

As the sowing/reaping metaphor shows, Paul regards giving as a theologically significant activity. What particular theological significance did Paul attach to the collection? Paul's discussion in 2 Corinthians 8—9 uses heavily theological language which points to three possible reasons the collection was so significant for Paul: concern for the poor, concern for the unity of Jew and Gentile in the church and concern for the eschatological significance of the Gentile mission.

Concern for the poor was a dominant element in both Jewish and Christian piety. This kind of concern for the poor characterized the ministry of Christ, who became poor so that those who follow him could become rich. This is why Paul can refer to generous giving as a sign of grace* (*charis*) and as a ministry* (*diakonia*) of the church. Generous giving to the poor is an integral part of a Christian's response to God's gift in Christ and an act of obedience to the gospel of Christ. This is certainly one of the reasons Paul thinks it is important for the Corinthians to give to the collection.

But the collection is not just a collection for the poor, it is a contribution to "the poor among the saints in Jerusalem"—a tangible expression of the unity of Jew and Gentile in Christ. This may be the most important aspect of the collection for Paul and is reflected in his use of the word "fellowship"* (*koinōnia*) to refer to the collection. This relationship between the collection and the unity of the church is clearly seen in Galatians 2:9-10. Here the Jerusalem apostles give Paul the "right hand of fellowship (*koinōnia*)," agreeing that Paul's mission is to the Gentiles and theirs is to the Jews. Paul also agrees to "remember the poor." In the context of the ongoing debate about whether Gentiles should keep the Law, a debate that not only brought Paul to Jerusalem but continued at Antioch* even after his agreement with the Jerusalem apostles, a tangible witness to the grace of God at work in the Gentiles took on tremendous importance. The collection is an expression of the reciprocity that characterizes Jew and Gentile in Christ. The Gentiles have participated in the spiritual blessings of the gospel through the Jews, and they pay off this spiritual debt by being of service to the Jews in material blessings (Rom 15:27). This kind of reciprocity in the gospel reinforced the unity of Jew and Gentile in Christ.

Several scholars, among them J. Munck and K. Nickle, have suggested that the collection also has eschatological* significance as an enactment of Paul's missionary theology (*see* Mission). Paul believed that the whole people of Israel would not embrace the gospel until "the full number of Gentiles* come in" (Rom 11:25). Paul's role as apostle to the Gentiles was to bring the Gentiles into the gospel so that Israel would turn to God. The collection and the Gentile delegates who accompanied it would fulfill the prophecies about Gentiles coming to Zion with gifts in the last days (Is 2:2-3; 60:5-6; Mic 4:1-2). Since the collection was an unmistakable sign of the salvation* of the Gentiles, it could serve both as verification of Paul's Law-free gospel to the Gentiles and as an instrument of the saving grace of God toward Israel. The only problem with this suggestion about the eschatological significance of the collection is that Paul does not ever mention it when he writes about the collection. For him the major significance of the collection lies in its witness to the unity of Jew and Gentile in Christ and in its contribution to the needs of the saints in Jerusalem.

### 3. Money and Mission.

Paul claims the right to ask for and receive money on the basis of his apostolic status. However, if receiving money would interfere with his apostolic task, he also claims the right to refuse it. He apparently did not ask for money from a community in which he was currently working, but he had no hesitation about receiving money for his continuing mission or raising money for others from a community he had already established. Is Paul's teaching about money contradictory and/or inconsistent? Not when one realizes that the controlling force in his requests for and refusal of money was the gospel of Christ. When money is being used to further the preaching of the gospel or to express the unity of all Christians in the gospel, Paul does not hesitate to ask for money. But if the receiving of money meant that the gospel might be abused, Paul is willing to refuse the money and to readjust his life for the sake of the gospel.

In Paul's understanding of money the spiritual and material aspects of giving and receiving are closely related. A minister who sows spiritual seed should receive material support from those who have benefited. Since the Gentiles have received spiritual blessing from the Jews, they should respond by blessing the Jews in material ways. Requests for money are rooted in partnership in the gospel; one gives out of thankfulness for the spiritual benefits received. In Paul's letters it is clear that the way Christians use their money should be an extension of the message of the gospel and the ministry of the church.

*See also* COLLECTION FOR THE SAINTS; FELLOWSHIP, COM-

MUNION, SHARING; JERUSALEM; MISSION; RICHES AND POVERTY; TENTMAKING.

BIBLIOGRAPHY. J. M. Bassler, *God and Mammon: Asking for Money in the New Testament* (Nashville: Abingdon, 1991); H. D. Betz, *2 Corinthians 8 and 9: A Commentary on Two Administrative Letters of the Apostle Paul* (Herm; Philadelphia: Fortress, 1985); N. A. Dahl, "Paul and Possessions," in *Studies in Paul: Theology for the Early Christian Mission* (Minneapolis: Augsburg, 1977); F. W. Danker, *II Corinthians* (ACNT; Minneapolis: Augsburg, 1989); G. D. Fee, *The First Epistle to the Corinthians* (NICNT; Grand Rapids: Eerdmans, 1987); V. P. Furnish, *II Corinthians* (AB; New York: Doubleday, 1984); D. Georgi, *Remembering the Poor: The History of Paul's Collection for Jerusalem* (Nashville: Abingdon, 1992); R. F. Hock, *Tentmaking and Apostleship: The Social Context of Paul's Ministry* (Philadelphia: Fortress, 1980); R. P. Martin, *The Epistle of Paul to the Philippians* (TNTC; Grand Rapids: Eerdmans, 1973); J. Munck, *Paul and the Salvation of Mankind* (Atlanta: John Knox, 1959); K. F. Nickle, *The Collection: A Study in Paul's Strategy* (SBT; Naperville, IL: Alec R. Allenson, 1966).

J. M. Everts

**FIRST ADAM.** *See* ADAM AND CHRIST.

## FIRST FRUITS, DOWN PAYMENT.

Paul found metaphors both in the Temple* and the marketplace to express how God* had pledged himself to believers, not only in giving his Son,* Jesus Christ,* but also the Spirit. Paul describes the Holy Spirit* as a "first fruit" (Rom 8:23) and as a "down payment" (2 Cor 1:22).

1. First Fruits
2. Down Payment

### 1. First Fruits.

The Greek term *aparchē* had a wide currency stretching from the fifth century B.C. through the patristic period. It referred to the first produce or profits that might be given as a gift of thanksgiving. The recipient might be a person or, as in most cases, the Temple. Its use evolved so that any offering—even Temple taxes on the people—could be called *aparchē*.

*1.1. Jewish Temple Sacrifice.* The background for Paul's thought comes from the Temple in Jerusalem. Since the land belonged to God, the Israelites were commanded to offer the "first fruit" (LXX *aparchē*) of flock and field to God for the maintenance of the priesthood and later of the priests and the Temple services (Deut 16:2; 18:4; Num 18:8-12; Neh 10:35-37; 12:44). Once God had received his portion, the people were set free to share in the remainder. The sacrifice

of the part thus effected the blessedness of the whole. The harvest could not be enjoyed until Yahweh's portion had been given. This was worked out in particular during the Feast of Unleavened Bread. The feast began when the sickle cut the first grain (Deut 16:9) and these were given at "the place where the Lord your God shall choose," which later became the Temple in Jerusalem. Leviticus 23:9-14 tells how the priest should wave the first sheaf of the harvest before the Lord.

This concept found ready use in the OT as a metaphor for initial devotion to God. Even male children who opened the womb (thus the firstborn of the family) belonged to the Lord (Ex 13:3; Num 18:15). But this was quickly explained as a symbolic ritual (Num 18:15-16), for such children were not to be sacrificed but redeemed with five shekels of silver. The Levites, in turn, took the place of the firstborn in Israel, performing special service before God (Num 8:18), and in their dedication were presented as a wave offering before the Lord (Num 8:11; cf. Lev 23:9-11). Jeremiah similarly uses first fruits as a symbol of Israel: "Israel was holy to the Lord, the first fruits of his harvest" (Jer 2:3; cf. Jas 1:18).

*1.2. Paul's Use of the Term.* First fruit (*aparchē*) is a Pauline word. Seven of its nine uses in the NT are found in Paul's letters. He draws on this well-known Jewish metaphor in a variety of ways. When he was thinking about evangelism and the first converts of a region he called them "first fruits" (Rom 16:5; 1 Cor 16:15; cf. 1 Cor 1:16). They were the first fruits of the eschatological harvest among the nations, a promise of the complete harvest to come (cf. Israel as first fruits of humanity in Philo *Spec. Leg.* 4.180). When he was thinking of redemption* and resurrection* he naturally referred to Jesus Christ as "the first fruits" of those raised from the dead (1 Cor 15:20, 23; cf. *1 Clem* 24:1; *see* Firstborn).

An important use occurs in Romans 11:16. As the whole of the grain harvest was consecrated by the offering of the first sheaf, and as all of the baked bread of Israel was consecrated when a single cake made from the first-ground flour was offered (Num 15:17-21), and similarly as in Leviticus 19:23-25 fruit trees were called "uncircumcised" until an offering was made for them, so in the same way, Paul argues, Israel—even unbelieving Israel—was consecrated by the first fruits that went before (variously interpreted as the patriarchs, Jewish Christians, all the seed of Abraham or even Jesus Christ).

*1.3. Romans 8:23.* Paul's most interesting theological use of first fruits is found in Romans 8:23 where he refers to the Holy Spirit. *Aparchē* was often considered a foretaste of good things to come (cf. *Barn* 1.7). But here Paul reverses the relationship of giver and recipient. The Spirit serves to reassure and sustain believers as God's partial gift of the whole of salvation* awaiting them. But Paul's emphasis here is *qualitative*: believers can have confidence in the goodness of their salvation because the Spirit represents a portion of what is to come. Indeed, their experience of future adoption* will be just like the Spirit they now possess, but even more so. Paul reserves another term to show the certainty of God's promised gift: *arrabōn*.

## 2. Down Payment.

The Greek term *arrabōn* was a Semitic loanword which stemmed from the commercial vocabulary of Israel (*ʿēraḇôn*). An *arrabōn* was a first installment, a deposit, pledge, or a down payment. It represented a part of the purchase price in advance, "a payment which obligates the contracting party to make further payments" (BAGD, 109).

*2.1. 2 Corinthians 1:22.* Twice in 2 Corinthians Paul strives to build up the confidence of the Corinthians about the certainty of their faith. In 2 Corinthians 1:22 he refers to the Spirit as tangible evidence of God's presence with them and for them. It is a "guarantee" (RSV) that his promises are true. Here, however, he aligns *arrabōn* with "seal" (*sphragis, sphragizomai*), implying that this Spirit is not only a pledge for the future but God's mark of ownership. And in this particular case, it is a seal of apostolic ministry.* Paul is having to defend himself against critics who question the apostolic authority* of his work.

*2.2. 2 Corinthians 5:5.* A second text, 2 Corinthians 5:5, is similar but its theological context is different (contra Martin, 119, who sees eschatological salvation in both 2 Cor 5:5 and 1:22). Paul candidly describes the eschatological tension Christians face as they examine their own mortality ("this earthly tent that will be destroyed") while looking forward to their redemption (the building from God, not made with hands, eternal in the heavens). Here the issue is reassurance in light of death, judgment* and eternal life* (2 Cor 5:1-10). Believers groan and have anxiety as they look forward longingly. But God gives the Spirit as the *arrabōn*, the guarantee of their future destiny, namely, that their mortality will be swallowed up in life (*see* Immortality).

*2.3. Ephesians 1:14.* Paul's most precise description of *arrabōn* and the Spirit appears in Ephesians 1:14. Note again the union of favorite Pauline concepts: hope,* promise, destiny, seal, *arrabōn* and inheritance (Eph 1:11-14). The apostle once again describes the "already/not yet" tension of life and speaks of the Spirit as God's down payment on the believer's future.

The Spirit is a deposit on "our inheritance—until we acquire possession of it." The Spirit for Paul, then, is an interim gift, a prelude and foretaste of the glory that is to come. The Spirit is not simply to comfort and strengthen believers during the trials of the world; the Spirit is also there to remind them of the future, that they possess identity as aliens in this world as they await their complete glorification (*see* Glory) in Christ.

*2.4. Polycarp.* The only occurrence of *arrabōn* among the early patristic fathers is found in Polycarp's *Epistle to the Philippians* 8:1. Here the Bishop of Smyrna in Asia Minor states that Christ becomes the *arrabōn* of believers' righteousness.* Polycarp writes: "Let us therefore hold steadfastly and unceasingly to our hope and the guarantee of our righteousness, who is Christ Jesus, 'who bore our sins in his own body upon the tree.' "

*See also* ADOPTION, SONSHIP; ESCHATOLOGY; FIRSTBORN; HOLY SPIRIT; RESURRECTION.

BIBLIOGRAPHY. B. Ahern, "The Indwelling Spirit, Pledge of our Inheritance," *CBQ* 9 (1947) 179-89; J. Behm, "ἀρραβών," *TDNT* I.475; R. Bultmann, *Theology of the New Testament* (2 vols.; New York: Charles Scribners, 1951, 1955) 2.330-40; F. W. Danker, "Consolation in 2 Corinthians 5:1-10," *CTM* 39 (1968) 552-56; G. Delling, "ἀπαρχή," *TDNT* I.484-86; E. E. Ellis, "2 Corinthians 5:1-10 in Pauline Eschatology," *NTS* 6 (1959-60) 211-24; D. Guthrie, *New Testament Theology* (Downers Grove, IL: InterVarsity, 1981) 549-66; M. J. Harris, "2 Corinthians 5:1-10: A Watershed in Paul's Eschatology?" *TynB* 22 (1971) 32-57; R. P. Martin, "The Spirit in 2 Corinthians in Light of 'The Fellowship of the Holy Spirit,' " in *Eschatology and the New Testament: Essays in Honor of George Raymond Beasley-Murray*, ed. H. Gloer (Peabody, MA: Hendrickson, 1988) 113-28; C. L. Mitton, "Paul's Certainties. The Gift of the Spirit and Life Beyond Death: 2 Cor 5:1-5," *ExpT* 69 (1958) 260-63; H. Ridderbos, *Paul: An Outline of His Theology* (Grand Rapids: Eerdmans, 1975); R. O. Rigsby, "First Fruits," *ABD* II.796-97; A. Sand, "ἀπαρχή," *EDNT* I.116-17; idem, "ἀρραβών," *EDNT* I.157-58; R. de Vaux, *Ancient Israel* (2 vols.; New York: McGraw-Hill, 1961) 2.490-93; N. M. Watson, "2 Corinthians 5:1-10 in Recent Research," *ABR* 23 (1975) 33-36.

G. M. Burge

## FIRSTBORN

The word *firstborn* (*prōtotokos*) appears eight times in the NT; most references are figurative, although a literal sense occurs at Luke 2:7. The term appears in the plural only at Hebrews 11:28 and 12:23 referring to believers; the remaining instances in the singular always refer to Jesus Christ (*see* Christ). In the latter contexts, while priority of time is in view (Rom 8:29; cf. the parallel expressions in 1 Cor 15:20; Acts 26:23; Rev 1:5), the notion of supremacy or priority of rank tends to dominate. "Firstborn" appears on three occasions in Paul's letters in a figurative sense with reference to Jesus Christ: Colossians 1:15, 18; Romans 8:29.

1. Firstborn of All Creation
2. Firstborn from the Dead
3. Firstborn Among Many Brothers

## 1. Firstborn of All Creation.

The expression "firstborn of all creation" (*prōtotokos pasēs ktiseōs*, Col 1:15) occurs in the opening line of the Colossian* "hymn" (*see* Hymns) and speaks of Christ's relationship to the creation.* Stripped from its context and from other Pauline statements about Christ, this phrase might be understood to include him among created things (as simply the "eldest" of the "family": *prōtotokos* in Rom 8:29 has this inclusive sense). The English word *firstborn* is misleading for it normally suggests someone who is born and therefore created. But this cannot be the significance of the term here since the immediately following words (Col 1:16, beginning with *hoti*, "because"), which provide a commentary on the title, emphasize the point that he is the one by whom the whole creation came into being. There are no exceptions, for absolutely everything in creation has been made by him. Further, apart from the incompatibility of this thought with the teaching of Paul in general about the person and work of Christ (*see* Christology), such an understanding is not required by the word *prōtotokos* ("firstborn") itself.

The term *prōtotokos* was frequently used in the LXX (130 times), mostly in genealogies and historical narratives, to indicate temporal priority and sovereignty of rank (e.g., Gen 49:3). Frequently it was employed to denote one who had a special place in the father's love. So Israel* is called "my beloved son" (*huios prōtotokos mou*, literally, "my firstborn son," Ex 4:22), a phrase that expresses the particularly close relation between God and Israel. In Judaism the messianic king, as well as Israel, the patriarchs and the Torah are given this title of distinction (see Str-B and Michaelis).

The title "firstborn," used of Christ in Colossians 1:15, 18, echoes the wording of Psalm 89:27, where God* says of the Davidic king: "I will also make him my firstborn, the highest of the kings of the earth." This title belongs to Jesus Christ not only as the Messiah of David's line, but also as the Wisdom* of God (note the same background to the preceding title "the image* of the invisible God"). While Jewish writers speculated about Wisdom by giving to it a quasi-per-

sonal status (it was present with God from all eternity, Wis 9:9; sharing the divine throne, Wis 9:4; existing before heaven and earth, and according to Philo was the "firstborn son," *prōtogonos huios: Conf. Ling.* 146; *Agric.* 51; *Som.* 1.215; the instrument "through whom the universe came into existence," *Fug* 109), the NT writers knew that they were speaking of a living person, one whom some of them had met personally.

As *prōtotokos* Christ is unique, being distinguished from all creation (cf. Heb 1:6). He is both prior to and supreme over that creation since he is its Lord.*

## 2. Firstborn from the Dead.

"Firstborn" (*prōtotokos*) also occurs in the second section of the "hymn" in the expression "the firstborn from the dead" (*prōtotokos ek tōn nekrōn*, Col 1:18). While formally parallel to the first instance, "firstborn" here stands at the beginning of the soteriological section in apposition to the preceding expression, "He [Christ] is the beginning" (*archē*). *Archē* has to do with primacy, whether in a temporal sense (Mt 19:4, 8; Jn 15:27) or with reference to authority* and sovereignty (Rom 8:38; 1 Cor 15:24; Eph 1:21; 6:12; etc.). In Colossians 1:18 when it is said of Christ that he is "the beginning," it does not mean that he is "the beginning of God's creation" (Rev 3:14) or its first cause, notions that might have applied in the first part of the paragraph (Col 1:15-17), but rather as the one who is "the firstborn from the dead" he is the founder of a new humanity (*see* Adam and Christ). The meaning of *archē* is explained in the words "firstborn from the dead," while *prōtotokos* is here used in an inclusive sense. In Genesis 49:3 the two terms *firstborn* and *beginning* appear together to describe the firstborn as the founder of a people (cf. LXX Deut 21:17 and Rom 8:29). The resurrection* age has burst forth and, as the first who has risen from among those who had fallen asleep in death (*ek tōn nekrōn*), he is the first fruits who guarantees the future resurrection of others (1 Cor 15:20, 23). The hymn had previously asserted Christ's primacy in creation; it now mentions his primacy in resurrection. In both new creation and old the first place belongs to him alone. In accordance with the divine intention he "*has become* preeminent in everything."

## 3. Firstborn Among Many Brothers.

"Firstborn" (*prōtotokos*), which is used inclusively in Romans 8:29, expresses both the unique preeminence of Christ and the fact that he shares his privileges with his brothers and sisters. In a passage which surveys the whole course of God's dealings with his people (Rom 8:28-30), it is affirmed that the new creation, a community of men and women who are being progressively conformed to the image of Christ (who is the image of God, 2 Cor 4:4; Col 1:15), is seen from the beginning to have been the object of God's foreknowledge* and foreordaining mercy.* The Father's purpose ("*in order that* he might be the *firstborn* among many brothers and sisters") was that his only begotten Son (*see* Son of God) might not be alone in enjoying the familial privileges but might be the head of a multitude of brothers and sisters (cf. Ex 4:22 where Israel is God's firstborn son) who have been made God's children through him (*see* Adoption, Sonship). As the resurrected Christ, the first fruits* of those raised from the dead (1 Cor 15:20, 23), he is the pattern of this new humanity of the last age, the firstborn (from the dead) of a new eschatological race of people in whom God's design from the beginning of creation (Gen 1:27; cf. Heb 2:6-7) is at last fulfilled.

*See also* ADOPTION, SONSHIP; CREATION AND NEW CREATION; FIRST FRUITS, DOWN PAYMENT; LORD; PRE-EXISTENCE; SON OF GOD; WISDOM.

BIBLIOGRAPHY. J. D. G. Dunn, *Christology in the Making* (Philadelphia: Westminster, 1980); A. Hockel, *Christus der Erstgeborene: zur Geschichte der Exegese von Kol. 1.15* (Düsseldorf, 1965); E. Lohse, *Colossians and Philemon* (Herm; Philadelphia: Fortress, 1971); W. Michaelis, "πρωτότοκος," *TDNT* VI.871-82; P. T. O'Brien, *Colossians, Philemon* (WBC 44; Waco: Word, 1982); Str-B 3.256-58, 626. P. T. O'Brien

# FLESH

Interpreters have long recognized a complexity in Paul's usage of the Greek word *sarx*, frequently translated "flesh" in English, and modern linguistics has shed more light on the nature of that complexity. Nevertheless, interpreters of Paul are still prone to speak of "Paul's view of the flesh." But to do so is to beg the question of whether by *flesh* we mean: (1) the various notions to which that term refers in English usage; (2) the notions referred to by Paul in his use of the term *sarx*; or (3) one of Paul's more characteristic usages.

Option (1) is of course to be rejected, since it would imply that Paul wrote as a speaker of twentieth-century English. In any event there can be no consistent correlation between the various applications of the English term *flesh* and those of the Greek *sarx* as Paul used it. Option (3) is a better choice since it recognizes that even within a single language a word may have numerous "meanings," some mutually unrelated. To speak of "Paul's view of the flesh" would entail selecting one meaning, or "semantic field," from the array to which *sarx* belongs. This, however, raises the question: Which one? Such a selection would necessitate

a different title for this article (e.g., "humanity" or "human rebellion") and would involve the study of the other terms belonging to the chosen field (e.g., world,* body,* human, sin,* spirit,* promise). Option (2), then, is best here; it provides access to all the fields to which the Pauline term *sarx* belongs. One wonders, however, whether there are other concepts for which Paul might have employed *sarx* in his letters, but for some reason did not.

1. The Represented Semantic Fields
2. Striking Formal Contextual Features
3. Comparison with Other Judeo-Christian Writers
4. Theological Issues

**1. The Represented Semantic Fields.**
Paul uses *sarx* in at least six different applications.

*1.1. Physical Matter.* Paul uses *sarx* to refer to the physical matter that makes up the living bodies of humans and animals. The most obvious instance of this application is 1 Corinthians 15:39, where Paul speaks of the various fleshly materials of animals (always living flesh, as opposed to meat). In this context Paul uses *sōma*, "body," in a manner parallel with *sarx* (1 Cor 15:38-39; cf. Col 1:22). Elsewhere, in Paul's metaphor "thorn in the flesh" (2 Cor 12:7) and in the synecdoche "flesh and blood" (1 Cor 15:50; Gal 1:16; reversed as "blood and flesh" in Eph 6:12; cf. literal use in Wis 12:5), *sarx* itself refers to physical matter. This point is not always noticed, since the entire expression in each case indicates "trouble" or "humanity," respectively. Similarly, in Paul's expression "fleshly hearts" (*kardiais sarkinais*, 2 Cor 3:3) *sarx* is part of an extended metaphor for the lives of the believers. Romans 2:28 (*en sarki peritomē* "circumcision in the flesh"; *see* Circumcision) perhaps also belongs in this category, used here as a euphemism, though it could be included under the next category (see 1.2 below; note the qualifier *en tō phanerō* "externally").

*1.2. Human Body.* By synecdoche *sarx* in 1 Corinthians 6:16 envisions the entire body ("Do you not know that whoever is united to a prostitute becomes one body [*sōma*] with her? For it is said, 'The two shall be one flesh [*sarx*]' " NRSV, quoting Gen 2:24) (cf. Eph 5:29-30; Col 2:1; 1:22?; 2:11?; Sir 25:26; *see* Sexuality). Here *sarx* is placed parallel with *sōma*, and perhaps also with *melos*, "member" (1 Cor 6:15), and is contrasted with *pneuma*, "spirit" (1 Cor 6:17). In this way *sōma* pulls *sarx* into its own realm (contrast 1 Cor 15:38-39 in 1.1 above).

Under this category we should also include 2 Corinthians 7:1, where Paul can contrast flesh and spirit as a person's defilable outer and inner aspects respectively (cf. Col 2:5, and with *dianoiai*, Eph 2:3; *see* Psychology).

*Sarx* as human body is also subject to physiological states (*see* Healing, Illness) and religious rites. Paul first preached in Galatia owing to some bodily ailment (*di' astheneian tēs sarkos*, Gal 4:13-14; *see* Weakness), and his opponents there wish to circumcise the believers so as to boast* in the condition of their bodies (*hina en tē hymetera sarki kauchēsōntai*, Gal 6:13, that condition contrasted with the cross* of Christ in Gal 6:14). Paul's usage in 2 Corinthians 7:5, "our *sarx* had no rest," may be better classed in 1.3 (see the parallel in 2 Cor 2:13-14 where Paul's inner anxieties are the point; cf. Psalm 62:2 LXX [63:1]).

*1.3. Human Person, Human Race.* In imitation of LXX usage, *pasa sarx* ("all flesh") in Galatians 2:16 and 1 Corinthians 1:29 (both of which parallel the expression with a human being), and in Romans 3:20, refers to the whole of humanity, or perhaps to an individual (cf. Mt 24:22). More ambiguous is Romans 8:3b ("God sent his son in the likeness of sinful *sarx*"), which can be read as "in the likeness of sinful humanity." Paul's reference to the entire Jewish nation as "my flesh" (Rom 11:14) arises possibly from certain usages listed under 1.4 (*see* Israel).

*1.4. Morally Neutral Sphere.* Forming a group under this rubric are those passages referring to human relationships based on natural birth processes. All of these passages are concerned in some way with Israel, her traditions and her descendants (1 Cor 10:18; Rom 1:3; 4:1; 9:3, 5, 8). Of these references, the contrast between *sarx* and *pneuma* in Romans 1:3 is between Christ's natural human existence "from the seed of David," on the one hand, and his divine dignity on the other (cf. 1 Tim 3:16; Phil 2:9-11). In this case a negative shadow is not cast on *sarx* as is the case elsewhere (see 1.6 below: rebellious human nature).

The occurrences in Galatians 4:23, 29 are more ambiguous however. Paul contrasts Ishmael, the son of the "slave woman" who was born "according to the flesh" (*kata sarka*), and Isaac, the son of the "free woman" who was born "through the promise." If Paul views Abraham's* first son, Ishmael, as born through his father's rebellious unbelief, *sarx* would carry a sense more in line with the usage described in section 1.6 ("rebellious human nature"). The subsequent contrast in Galatians 4:29 between the one born *kata sarka* and the one born *kata pneuma* (= Holy Spirit*?) tends to confirm this.

To this category also belong references to the natural course and conduct of human affairs: Galatians 2:20, Philippians 1:22, 24, and probably 1 Corinthians 7:28, where a parallel is drawn with *kosmos* ("world"* 1 Cor 7:31). In Philemon 16 Onesimus' relationship to Philemon is said to have a social dimension (*en sarki*, "in the flesh") in contrast to a specifically Christian dimension (*en kyriō*, "in the Lord"). "Our mortal flesh" (*tē thnētē sarki hēmōn*) in which Christ's life is manifested (2 Cor 4:11; cf Col 1:24), may refer to the human body (see 1.2 above; cf. the parallel with *sōma*, 2 Cor 4:10), but more likely it is a reference to Paul's natural earthly life. Paul's usage in Romans 6:19 ("I am speaking in human terms because of the weakness of your flesh," *astheneian tēs sarkos*; contrast Gal 4:13 in 1.2 above) concerns more than bodily weakness (cf. NRSV, "natural limitations"). In 1 Corinthians 9:11 and Romans 15:27 Paul claims that those who impart "spiritual" blessings have a right to fiscal (*sarkikos*) support.

*1.5. Morally Negative Sphere.* Here we refer to Paul's use of *sarx* as applied to the "world," humanity's value systems as they stand in opposition to God's. In Philippians 3:3-4, which prefaces a fine description of a Jewish culture-based value system, and Galatians 6:12 which presupposes it, Paul characterizes the whole as *en sarki* (*see* Jew, Paul the). Another value system, based in Hellenistic culture but perverse like the first, is at issue in 1 Corinthians 1:26. Here Paul can characterize the "wise" (*sophoi*; *see* Wisdom) as *kata sarka*, which he sets in parallel with "world" (*kosmos*) in 1 Corinthians 1:27 (cf. 2 Cor 1:12). Paul is accused of making decisions and living his life by these values (*kata sarka*, 2 Cor 1:17; 10:2). This he denies; one can live in the midst of such a system without patterning one's methods on it (2 Cor 10:3-4). People, even Christ himself, can be evaluated from this false perspective (*kata sarka*, 2 Cor 5:16); and of course, hollow boasting is its natural consequence (2 Cor 11:18).

*1.6. Rebellious Human Nature.* Paul's most characteristic use of *sarx*, and his most frequent, is his application of *sarx* to sinful human nature (*see* Sin). Well over half of these instances occur in Romans,* mostly in Romans 8. All others but one (1 Cor 5:5; cf also 1 Cor 3:3) appear in Galatians.* Correspondingly, in over two-thirds of the many contrasts between *sarx* and *pneuma*, *sarx* refers to fallen human nature. Most of these are found in Galatians 5 and 6 and Romans 8; of the others (Gal 3:3, Rom 7:5, 1 Cor 5:5), Galatians 3:3 is almost programmatic for the whole group (see 4 below).

1 Corinthians 5:5 ("hand this man over to Satan for the destruction of the flesh [*sarx*], so that his spirit [*pneuma*] may be saved on the day of the Lord" NRSV) is distinct in that it employs *pneuma* for the human spirit; nevertheless, *sarx* there does not refer to the body (*see* Discipline). Depending on how one dates Galatians and the Thessalonian letters (*see* Chronology), this application is likely a later development for

Paul. He is not here recommending sickness or death but the destruction of rebelliousness, an effect synonymous with the crucifixion* of the flesh, the Spirit's goal in struggling against it (Gal 5:24, 17).

For Paul the unacceptable alternative for believers is to make opportunity for this rebellion to indulge its desires (Gal 5:13, 16, 19-21; 6:8; Rom 13:14). One lives in the rebellious nature, there is nothing good about it, and through it one serves the law of sin (cf. *sarx* in Rom 7:5, contrasting with Law* and written code; Rom 7:18, in parallel with the ego of Paul himself; Rom 7:25, contrasting with *nous* "mind"). As mentioned earlier (see 1.4 above), in Galatians 4:23, 29 the contrast is between the one born either by his father's rebellious impatience or by the normal process of human reproduction, on the one hand, and the one who was born by the Spirit's intervention in that process, on the other. The contrast in Galatians 4:23 between *sarx* and *epangelia* ("promise") suggests rebelliousness on Abraham's part. Romans 8:1-14 is the classical passage on this subject, where rebellious *sarx* and the life grounded in it are contrasted with life in the Spirit (see 4 below).

Paul's use of *sarkinos* in 1 Corinthians 3:1 reads like an *ad hominem* criticism of gnosticizing believers at Corinth, and probably means "immature" rather than "rebellious."

## 2. Striking Formal Contextual Features.

Several correlations between formal grammatical structure and "semantic field assignment" are notable:

(1) When Paul uses *kata sarka* ("according to the flesh") + VERB (e.g., 2 Cor 1:17; 5:16), the semantic field is that of moral negativity (see 1.5 above). On the other hand, when he uses *kata sarka* + NOUN (e.g., Rom 4:1; 9:3), the semantic field is that of moral neutrality (see 1.4 above). This was noticed by Bultmann (236-37) and is confirmed here (cf. *kata anthrōpon*, "in an ordinary fashion," 1 Cor 3:3).

(2) Every occurrence of *sarx* as morally negative (see 1.5 above) lacks the article. This is probably due to the stereotyped prepositional phrases Paul employs. All formal contexts have either the shape *kata sarka* ("according to the flesh") + VERB (e.g., 2 Cor 10:2, 3) or *en sarki* ("in the flesh") + VERB (e.g., Phil 3:3, 4; Gal 6:12).

(3) All uses of *sarx* in the broad sense of "humanity" (see 1.3 above), except one, are formed on LXX style: *pasa sarx* ("all flesh").

(4) Those uses of *sarx* which refer to human rebelliousness (see 1.6 above) almost invariably appear with the article. To this category also belongs nearly every instance where *sarx* is construed as the subject

or direct object of a verb (the verb usually being in the form of an abstract noun), unless it is qualified by a possessive personal pronoun, in which case it refers to the human body.

## 3. Comparison with Other Judeo-Christian Writers.

In the LXX the term seems never to be used either in a morally negative sense (see 1.5 above) or as a designation for human rebelliousness toward God (see 1.6 above). This contrasts with Paul, for whom these two senses account for half of his usage of *sarx*. The closest parallel to Paul's use of *sarx* in these senses is 4 Maccabees 7:18. But while that document is contemporary with Paul, the usage in that passage is more in line with the Hellenizing ethical dualism of Philo than with Paul's use.

However, "flesh" (Gk *sarx* or Heb *bāśār*) is used in the Qumran scrolls (e.g., 1QS 11:7[?], 9[?], 12; 1QM 4:3) and Jewish apocalyptic (e.g., *T. Judah* 19:4; *T. Zeb.* 9:7) to refer to fallen humanity or a cosmic evil sphere. Oddly, the Apostolic Fathers are nearly in line with the LXX here. Even the rest of the NT does not alter this picture by much: it is used once (?) for moral negativity (Jn 8:15) and five times for rebelliousness (mostly in 2 Pet and Jude; cf. 1 Jn 2:16). The employment of *sarx*, then, to indicate fallen humanity and the evil worldly system of values is a decidedly Pauline phenomenon, with its roots in Jewish apocalyptic.* It is imitated perhaps, but not wholeheartedly adopted by any of the other early Christian writers.

## 4. Theological Issues.

For theological implications of these data, fields 1.1—1.4 and 1.5—1.6 form two distinct groups: the first indicating a natural aspect of creation* and the latter an opposition toward God.*

*4.1. The Flesh as a Natural Aspect of Creation.* The employment of the term *sarx* in 1.1—1.4 (i.e., physical matter, human body, human person/race, morally neutral sphere), especially as the natural sphere in which earthly life is conducted (cf. Rom 1:3), implies that Paul continued to share the Jewish heritage of a high regard for creation. The ontological dualism of Hellenistic thinkers is ruled out in Paul's view, since while the fleshly body, and humanity generally, are weak and open to defilement, they are nonetheless redeemable and subject to resurrection.* On the other hand, Paul's suggestion that *both* the flesh and the (human) spirit can be defiled (2 Cor 7:1) probably means that he entertained no ethical dualism between higher and lower natures coexistent in and natural to a person. The seemingly negative attitude expressed in 2 Corinthians 5:1-10 toward the "body" of earthly existence is not to be taken to imply such a dualistic view.

***4.2. Flesh as Opposition to God.*** R. Jewett has shown how the development of Paul's various conflicts sets the scene for, and explains the inconsistencies in, his use of the term in 1.5 and 1.6 (i.e., morally negative sphere and rebellious human nature).

The following remarks can be made. Galatians 3:2-3 neatly sets forth the dualism which does characterize Paul's peculiar use of *sarx*. It is a dualism between flesh and spirit in the sense of flesh as an independent reliance on one's own accomplishments over against a spirit of dependence on God and submission to his rule (see esp. Rom 8). In the controversy with nomists in Galatians 3:2-3, this translates into a contrast between "works of the Law"* and "hearing with faith.*" Dependence upon human value systems and institutions for securing power and position, as well as libertinistic self-indulgence as a means of attaining "life" (Jewett), are likewise manifestations of a rebellious independence from God's promised provision of life and personal worth through faith in Christ. Ironically, then, by trusting in the "flesh" one attains not life* but death.

This in fact is an apocalyptic dualism which proleptically views the regenerate Christian as already "in the Spirit" and under the rule of God by faith while still living a "fleshly" existence in this present age. The solution to the tension thus created is the continual putting to death of the flesh and its works. But the "death of the flesh" is abhorrent to a person and can only be endured by virtue of God's promise to have already endowed humanity with resurrection life in Christ (cf. Rom 5:12-21). To die this death, and to "put on" Christ, is to place oneself again, as once in Eden, under the protection and provision of God, to become dependent and trusting. It issues furthermore in a love toward other people which arises out of the assurance of one's own security in Christ (cf. Gal 5:22-26).

*See also* Body; Holy Spirit; Psychology; Sin, Guilt; Weakness; World, Cosmology.

Bibliography. F. F. Bruce, *Paul: Apostle of the Heart Set Free* (Grand Rapids: Eerdmans, 1977); R. Bultmann, *Theology of the New Testament* (2 vols.; New York: Scribners, 1951, 1955) 1.232-46; E. R. Goodenough, *By Light, Light: The Mystic Gospel of Hellenistic Judaism* (New Haven: Yale University, 1935); R. H. Gundry, Sōma *in Biblical Theology: With Emphasis on Pauline Anthropology* (Cambridge University Press, 1976); D. Guthrie, *New Testament Theology* (Downers Grove, IL: InterVarsity, 1981); R. Jewett, *Paul's Anthropological Terms: A Study of Their Use in Conflict Settings* (Leiden: E. J. Brill, 1971); K. G. Kuhn, "New Light on Temptation, Sin and Flesh in the New Testament," in *The Scrolls and the New Testament,* ed. K. Stendahl (New York: Harper, 1957) 94-113; G. E. Ladd, *A Theology of the New Testament* (Grand Rapids: Eerdmans, 1974); A. Sand, *Der Begriff "Fleisch" in den paulinischen Hauptbriefen* (Regensburg: Pustet, 1967); E. Schweizer, R. Meyer, F. Baumgärtel, "σάρξ κτλ," *TDNT* VII.98-151; H. Seebass and A. C. Thiselton, "Flesh," *NIDNTT* 1.671-82; W. D. Stacey, *The Pauline View of Man in Relation to Its Judaic and Hellenistic Background* (London: Macmillian, 1956); A. C. Thiselton, "The Meaning of Σάρξ in 1 Corinthians 5:5: A Fresh Approach in the Light of Logical and Semantic Factors," *SJT* 26 (1973) 204-28.

R. J. Erickson

**FOOD LAWS.** *See* Food Offered to Idols and Jewish Food Laws; Purity and Impurity.

# FOOD OFFERED TO IDOLS AND JEWISH FOOD LAWS

With circumcision,* laws and observances regarding food served as important ritual markers of Jewish identity. The literary evidence (both Jewish and non-Jewish) affirms that Jewish identity was in no small measure determined by how food was prepared, what sort of foods were and were not eaten, and with whom one ate or did not eat. Early Christians ate meals together, and with their early identity with and emergence from Judaism came questions about the appropriateness and necessity of these food laws for followers of Christ. A related problem arose over the appropriateness of Christians eating meat which had been sacrificed to pagan gods.

1. The Setting of Early Christian Gatherings
2. Jewish Food Laws
3. The Incident at Antioch and the Jerusalem Council
4. Meat, Idols and the Christian Gathering

### 1. The Setting of Early Christian Gatherings.

The early believers met in houses (cf. 1 Cor 16:19; Rom 16:5; Philem 2; Col 4:15) not strictly by default (i.e., because there was nowhere else to meet) but deliberately, because the house setting provided the facilities which accommodated the practices of the early communities (*see* Church). The one feature of the assembly that necessitated a house setting was the common meal, including the Lord's Supper.* Based on the tradition of the Last Supper (Mk 14:17; cf. 1 Cor 11:17-34), which was held in an "upper room," the early Christian meal was an important aspect of the life of the community. The house, in addition to being at the immediate disposal of the community, furnished the facilities for the preparation of common meals. It is no coincidence that when the meals no longer featured in the gatherings, the house setting was no longer necessary. When food preparation and dining facilities were no longer required, a large hall (and later the basilica) was found to be more appropriate for the growing number of Christians.

The nature of the early Christian gatherings—especially for meals—took on added significance when the Gentile converts were included. For a devout Jew to associate with a Gentile, or "sinner," was perilous, as is readily observed in the Gospels when the Pharisees criticize Jesus for having table fellowship with "sinners." Although Law abiding Jews allowed the possibility of restricted table fellowship between a Jew and a non-Jew (i.e., with proselytes, resident aliens and God-fearers), the rules and regulations were so stringent that they did not promote broad associations (see Dunn, 137-48).

## 2. Jewish Food Laws.

The limits of acceptable table fellowship between a Jew and a Gentile would be determined by two factors: (1) the Deuteronomic laws in Leviticus 11 and Deuteronomy 14:3-21, and (2) the various *halakoth* (*hᵃlākôt*, "ways") of the oral tradition. For the most part these laws and traditions primarily concerned the production and consumption of food and the appropriate environment in which consumption took place. J. Neusner has stressed that during the NT era

> one primary mark of Pharisaic commitment was the observance of the laws of ritual purity outside of the Temple, where everyone kept them. Eating one's secular, that is, unconsecrated food in a state of ritual purity, as if one were a Temple priest in the cult, was one of the two significations of party membership. Moreover, the agricultural laws, just like the purity rules, in the end affected table-fellowship, namely what one may eat. (Neusner 1984, 57)

After a detailed examination of rabbinical traditions concerning the Pharisees, involving 341 case rulings, Neusner concludes that "no fewer than 229 directly or indirectly pertain to table-fellowship, approximately 67% of the whole" (Neusner 1973, 86). In this respect the Pharisees can be called an "Eating Club" (Neusner 1982).

The meals within the context of Christian house gatherings can be seen as an overt manifestation of reconciliation between the Jews and Gentiles in Christ.* W. A. Meeks observes that by abandoning the standard Jewish regulations governing eating, the "Pauline Christians gave up one of the most effective ways by which the Jewish community had maintained its separate identity in the pagan society" (Meeks, 97). The house church was the venue for the cultural disestablishment which was necessary for the founding of the church in a Jewish-Gentile milieu. While the Gentiles were admonished to respect Jewish sensibilities, the meals served in these house churches confirmed the central message of the gospel* in the Christian community, the message of reconciliation (*see* Peace, Reconciliation).

## 3. The Incident at Antioch and the Jerusalem Council.

In Galatians 2:11-14 Paul describes an event in the life of the church at Antioch,* which corresponds to Luke's emphasis on Jewish-Gentile table fellowship in Acts. The events of Galatians 2 should probably be placed chronologically prior to the Jerusalem Council of Acts 15 and subsequent to the mission of Paul and Barnabas described in Acts 13 and 14 (*see* Chronology; Galatians; cf. Jerusalem). On this reading of the evidence, the conference described in Galatians 2:1-10 preceded the one described in Acts 15, and the events of Galatians 2:11-14 necessitated the meeting in Acts 15. The purpose of the apostolic decree (Acts 15) should then be seen as directly related to the social problem which arose during Peter's visit to Antioch. The Christians in Antioch regularly gathered together for meals, including the Lord's Supper. Although the church in Antioch is presented as sympathetic to the Gentile mission (Acts 13:1-3), Jewish Christians also participated in the gatherings and meals. Even Peter regularly met and ate with the Antiochian Christians until the dramatic event described in Galatians 2. Paul testifies that a major breach in the church in Antioch was caused by certain men who came from James,* and by implication, from the Jerusalem church (Gal 2:12).

These men are identified as "of the circumcision" (Gal 2:12). In all likelihood these individuals are to be aligned with those mentioned in Acts 15:1 who came from Judea and were members of the party of the Pharisees (Acts 15:5). However, as in Acts 15, we should be cautious not to associate their position too closely with that of James. After all, James certainly voiced disapproval over their conduct (Acts 15:24). It is probable that they had exceeded the terms of their commission. Paul states that before certain men came from James, Peter was in the habit of regularly eating with Gentile Christians; nevertheless the presence of these Jewish Christians from the circumcision party caused Peter* to begin to withdraw from his regular practice altogether.

Paul portrays the church in Antioch as a unified group until the contingent from Jerusalem arrived. The confrontation exposed the problem: Jewish-Gentile table fellowship. The magnitude of the confrontation is obvious: the other Jewish Christians as well as Peter and Barnabas were affected by the Judaizers. Furthermore, such a retreat was evidently the impetus behind the Galatians' desertion from Paul's gospel (Gal 1:6-7). The pressure upon the Jewish Christians to remain faithful to the Law* and their heritage caused these Jewish Christians to force Gentiles to comply with Jewish laws. R. Jewett suggests that in the late forties and early fifties Jewish Christians in Judea were stimulated by pressure from the Zealots to take up a nomistic campaign among their fellow Christians (*see* Revolutionary Movements). The goal of these Judaizers was to avert the suspicion that they were in communion with lawless Gentiles (Jewett, 205). In Paul's mind they conformed to such pressure in order to "make a good showing in the flesh" and to avoid persecution for the cross* of Christ (Gal 6:12). Regardless of their motives, Paul sees their behavior as blameworthy and intolerable. The truth of the gospel was at stake: in Christ neither circumcision nor uncircumcision is of any avail (Gal 5:6; cf. Gal 6:15), and there can be no distinction based on ethnic heritage, social status or sexual distinction. In Christ all are Abraham's* offspring (Gal 3:26-29).

**3.1. The Cornelius Episode.** In Acts 10:1—11:18 the story of Cornelius's conversion is told twice. This fact and the length of the story indicate its importance to Luke's narrative. Luke presents two events: the outpouring of the Spirit on the Gentiles and the table fellowship in Cornelius's home. The confirmation of the validity of the Spirit's coming is symbolized by Peter's willingness to eat with a Gentile.

It was Peter's willingness to enter Cornelius's home, to eat at his table, and to live with him that alarmed the Jewish Christians in Jerusalem (Acts 11:1-3). After all, the implications drawn from the Cornelius episode—that Gentiles could be admitted into the Christian community *without* undergoing circumcision (Acts 10:45; 11:18) and that table fellowship between Jews and Gentiles was permissible—were avant-garde. In Luke's narrative the obstacle of a Jew associating with the "unclean" was overcome for Peter by the vision he received at Joppa. The Cornelius episode closes with Cornelius, having been baptized with his household, inviting Peter to stay with them for several days (Acts 10:48). Clearly, by portraying Peter's willingness to accept the invitation of hospitality (cf. Acts 16:15), Luke intends to demonstrate to his readers the authenticity of the Gentiles' reception of the Spirit.

Peter's willingness to associate publicly with a Gentile (albeit, a God-fearer) was not welcomed by the Jerusalem church and, in particular, by those of the circumcision. They still held that such behavior was "unlawful" (*athemitos*), just as Peter had so regarded it prior to the vision. Therefore it is important to understand the force of Peter's words in Acts 10:28, which must be interpreted in light of the criticism voiced by the church in Jerusalem and the continued debate in the early church over the issue of table fellowship. Moreover, we must ask on what grounds (if any) Jewish Christians were forbidden to associate with Gentile Christians. What claims did the Law (the breaking of which Peter calls unlawful) have on the lives of Christians (Jewish and Gentile) in light of the gospel message (in this case, revealed in the vision)?

Oepke comments that with *athemitos*, "unlawful," we have a reference to "the Pharisaic standpoint overcome in Christianity" (Oepke, 166). Indeed, this was the case in the Jerusalem church: Jewish-Gentile table fellowship was as forbidden as indulging in non-kosher foods. We must conclude that prior to the vision in Joppa, Peter was convinced that eating with a Gentile (= forbidden foods) was against the tradition and that he had not experienced table fellowship with a Gentile (inasmuch as he had never eaten forbidden meat, Acts 10:14). To associate with or visit a non-Jew was seen as unlawful (Acts 10:28). By *unlawful* Luke was probably referring to the common Jewish antipathy toward associating with Gentiles and not that which is contrary to Torah legislature. Two points lead to this conclusion: (1) Luke is nowhere critical of Jews or Jewish Christians who keep the Law and, although Leviticus 11 makes clear distinctions between clean and unclean foods, the distinction between clean and unclean people is not made (however naturally this might be deduced from passages such as Lev 20:22-26). (2) The commonplace of this association between Gentiles and forbidden foods is seen in our narrative: "Peter's vision, which ostensibly deals with the dissolution of the distinction between clean and unclean foods, . . . is interpreted as signifying the dissolution of the similar, but not identical, distinction between clean and unclean people" (Wilson, 68).

For the Jewish Christians in Jerusalem, however, the issue was not so clear. The implications were obvious to them and potentially damaging to the Jewish traditions. That God had poured out his Spirit on the Gentiles was amazing in its own right. But the legitimacy of Torah was called into question if by this event Jewish believers were to accept (and even have table fellowship with) Gentile Christians—without those Gentiles having undergone circumcision or observed Torah.

This was only the beginning of problems in defining appropriate social relations between Jewish and Gentile Christians. The conflicts reflected in Galatians 2 and Acts 15 were intense and the opinions varied. More often than not, the diverse opinions and tensions resulted in inconsistent behavior even among the leaders. Clearly, a failure to reconcile differences would have nullified the possibility of fellowship, and Christianity would have become as segmented as first-century Judaism.

*3.2. The Jerusalem Council.* In Acts 15 the issue of the Gentile obligation to the Law is once again raised, as though it had never been discussed in Acts 11. Once again it is Peter who defends the inclusion of the Gentiles, citing his summons to preach to the Gentiles as a defense of his position. James recommends that certain levitical obligations (or possibly Noachic ones [Gen 9], in which case the obligations are to be enforced as a pre-Mosaic code binding on all people) be required of the Gentile Christians: that they abstain from certain things which were repulsive to the Jewish-Christians: from eating what is offered in sacrifice to idols, from what is strangled, from blood and from practicing fornication (Acts 15:29). The solution was an accommodation of Jewish sensibilities without jeopardizing the nature of the gospel (cf. 1 Cor 9:19-23; though whether Paul ultimately saw no conflict with his gospel is debated, since he never appeals to the decree in 1 Cor; see Catchpole; cf. Tomson, 269-74).

#### 4. Meat, Idols and the Christian Gathering.

There are indications that the early church leaders uniformly forbade eating meat sacrificed to idols* (Acts 15:20, 29; 21:25; Rev 2:20; *Did.* 6.3). The reason for this was simple: the idol temple seems to have served both as a butcher shop and as a place for sharing a cultic meal. For the most part, meat was either eaten at the temple or sold at the market after a pagan festival, and the association with the pagan gods, which was idolatry to the Christian, was obvious (Theissen, 121-43).

That meat was included in the banqueting in a pagan temple at Corinth is suggested by the dining rooms beneath the Abaton in the Asclepion at Corinth (Murphy-O'Connor, 161-70). Reclining at an idol's temple is envisioned as a problem at Corinth (1 Cor 8:1-10).

Consecrated meat was also included in sumptuous dinners in the homes of the affluent. On occasion this was the case at Corinth (1 Cor 10:27). Plutarch (c. 46-120), who lived near Corinth, records an episode which reflects a private dinner. The venue is the home of Ariston:

Ariston's cook made a hit with the dinner guests not only because of his general skill, but because the cock he set before the diners, though it had just been slaughtered as a sacrifice to Heracles, was as tender as if it had been a day old. (Plutarch *Conv.* 6.10.1)

Recent Gentile converts to Christianity would have found it difficult to consider the issue of meat offered to idols independent of its ritual setting; they would eat with a guilty conscience* (1 Cor 8:7). The invitation to dine in the home of an unbeliever could present a dilemma (1 Cor 10:27-30); while the invitation to dine at a temple would only sharpen the issue (1 Cor 8:10).

Evidently, however, not all the Corinthians shared this frustration. Paul, in writing to the Corinthians, takes note of two Christian responses. First, for some meat that had been sacrificed to idols must be avoided and be viewed as a fundamental contradiction to genuine monotheism. From this vantage, eating consecrated meat was taboo and such flirtatious associations hazardous. Second, other Corinthians claimed a "knowledge"* (*gnōsis*) which denied the existence and/or relevance of idols. The consumption of consecrated meat, from this perspective, did not pose a threat to the monotheism of Christianity (or Judaism) since the existence of other deities was denied: there was only one God.*

In response, Paul affirms monotheism by quoting the Shema (1 Cor 8:4: "There is no God but one" NRSV; *see* Liturgical Elements) and then places Jesus in the middle of this familiar text (1 Cor 8:6: "Yet for us there is one God, the Father, from whom are all things and for whom we exist, and one Lord, Jesus Christ, through whom are all things and through whom we exist" NRSV). In a discussion of meat sacrificed to the idols at Corinth, Paul, it seems, has redefined the Shema christologically, producing what N. T. Wright has called a "christological monotheism" (*see* God; Christology). This reformulation is intended to answer the problem at hand: the theology of the incarnation (through the lens of the Shema) effectively means love* and concern for the members of God's community. This is Wright's proposal: the Corinthians are admonished to put into practice a Christianized view of the Shema: "there is one God, one Lord, and his people are defined as those who love him, and who love their neighbors as themselves. The allowance for the weak is not a mere *ad hoc* concession. It arises from the heart of Christian theology itself" (Wright "One God," 49). And for the Christian, the cross of Christ answers those who insist on their rights: eating the consecrated meat could destroy the believer for whom Christ died (1 Cor 8:11).

Lest his readers miss the point, Paul's self-disclosure is intended to serve as a case in point: while he was at Corinth he had the apostolic right to secure support (1 Cor 9:1-23; *see* Financial Support). Because of the danger of being mistaken for a sophist (*see* Apollos), Paul denied himself the remuneration for the sake of the community of faith.

*See also* CIRCUMCISION; CONSCIENCE; ETHICS; IDOLATRY; JAMES; LAW; PETER; PURITY AND IMPURITY; SOCIAL-SCIENTIFIC APPROACHES TO PAUL; WORKS OF THE LAW.

BIBLIOGRAPHY. D. R. Catchpole, "Paul, James and the Apostolic Decree," NTS 23 (1976-77) 428-44; J. D. G. Dunn, "The Incident at Antioch (Gal 2.11-18)," in *Jesus, Paul and the Law* (Louisville: Westminster/John Knox, 1990) 129-82; P. F. Esler, *Community and Gospel in Luke-Acts: The Social and Political Motivations of Lukan Theology* (SNTSMS 57; Cambridge: University Press, 1987); R. Jewett, "The Agitators and the Galatian Congregation," *NTS* 17 (1970-71) 198-212; W. A. Meeks *The First Urban Christians: The Social World of the Apostle Paul* (New Haven: Yale University, 1983); J. Murphy-O'Connor, *St. Paul's Corinth: Texts and Archaeology* (GNS 6; Wilmington: Michael Glazier, 1983); J. Neusner, *From Politics to Piety: The Emergence of Pharisaic Judaism* (Englewood Cliffs, NJ: Prentice Hall, 1973); idem, "Two Pictures of the Pharisees: Philosophical Circle or Eating Club," *ATR* 64 (1982) 525-57; idem, *Judaism in the Beginning of Christianity* (Philadelphia: Fortress, 1984); O. Oepke, "ἀθέμιτος," *TDNT* I.166; G. Theissen, *The Social Setting of Pauline Christianity: Essays on Corinth* (Philadelphia: Fortress, 1982); P. J. Tomson, *Paul and the Jewish Law: Halakha in the Letters of the Apostle to the Gentiles* (CRINT 3.1; Minneapolis: Fortress, 1990); W. L. Willis, *Idol Meat at Corinth: The Pauline Argument in 1 Corinthians 8 and 10* (SBLDS; Chico: Scholars, 1985); S. G. Wilson, *Luke and the Law* (SNTSMS 50; Cambridge: University Press, 1983); N. T. Wright, "Monotheism, Christology and Ethics: 1 Corinthians 8," in *The Climax of the Covenant* (Minneapolis: Fortress, 1991) 120-36; idem, "One God, One Lord, One People: Incarnational Christology for a Church in a Pagan Environment," *Ex Auditu* 7 (1991) 45-58.

B. B. Blue

**FOOLISHNESS.** *See* CROSS, THEOLOGY OF THE; WISDOM.

## FOREKNOWLEDGE, DIVINE

Paul expresses the concept of divine foreknowledge with the verb *proginōskō*, "to foreknow." He uses the verb twice, both times with reference to God's activity: "Those whom he foreknew, he also predestined to be

conformed to the image of his Son" (Rom 8:29). " 'God has not rejected his people' whom he foreknew, has he?" (Rom 11:2). The prefix *pro-* in *proginōskō* indicates that the action of "knowing" takes place "before," that is, before the world was created (cf. Eph 1:4; 2 Tim 1:9), not just before one's own knowledge of God* (Cranfield, 1.431). This divine foreknowledge has been understood either as God's advance knowledge or as God's choosing. Both interpretations are construed soteriologically, based on the contexts in which the notion of divine foreknowledge appears. It is thus explained either as God's knowing beforehand who would believe, on the basis of which God then elects to salvation,* or as God's recognizing or "knowing" a person before the world began, which is itself an act of electing grace.*

1. Divine Foreknowledge as Foresight of Faith
2. Divine Foreknowledge as Election

### 1. Divine Foreknowledge as Foresight of Faith.

The verb "to foreknow," *proginōskō*, usually means "to know beforehand" (cf. Acts 26:5; 2 Pet 3:17; Philo *Som.* 1.2; see further Bultmann, 715-16). When used of God's action, therefore, it could refer to God's eternal foresight of what will come to pass (cf. Wis 8:8 LXX, where this kind of foreknowledge is ascribed to pre-existent Wisdom*; cf. Anderson, 311-13, on the biblical material on God's knowledge of all things). The two passages where Paul uses the verb also speak about divine predestination or election.* Thus, it is argued, God's prior knowledge of who will have saving faith* is the basis of God's predestination or election (e.g., Godet, 2.107-10). Divine foreknowledge thus explains why God elects some but not others.

Against this view J. Murray (316-17) argues that Paul writes not of God's foreseeing the faith of persons but foreknowing persons: "*whom* he foreknew" (Rom 8:29; 11:2). The idea of the foresight of one's faith is not present in the texts. J. Calvin (180-81) rejects the understanding of divine foreknowledge as prescience, that is, of knowing what humans would do, since God's gracious election is unmerited and springs only from God's good pleasure.

### 2. Divine Foreknowledge as Election.

Rather than referring to speculative or neutral knowledge (i.e., knowledge of who will believe), the Pauline notion of divine foreknowledge is understood by many interpreters as a knowing in the Semitic sense of acknowledging, inclining toward someone, knowledge which expresses a movement of the will reaching out to personal relationship with someone (e.g., Michel, 277). This kind of knowing is illustrated by the meaning of the Hebrew *yāḍa'*, "to know," in texts such as Amos 3:2; Hosea 13:5; and Jeremiah 1:5. The Hebrew verb can come close in meaning to "elect" (see esp. Amos 3:2; also Deut 9:24; Schotroff, 691-94). It is used in the OT for the special relationship of Yahweh to Israel or particular Israelites (see also Ex 33:12, 17; Gen 18:19; Deut 34:10). The Greek verb *ginōskō*, "to know," can also have the sense of acknowledging, recognizing someone (BAGD, 7). It is used this way in Galatians 4:9 and 1 Corinthians 8:3 to refer to God's "knowledge" of human beings which is the basis for their coming to know or love* God: "Now knowing God, or rather being known by God"; "If anyone loves God, that person is known by God." Although *proginōskō* is not used, God's knowing human beings here is clearly prior knowledge (prior to their knowing and loving God).

In Paul's use of *proginōskō* the aspect of pretemporality is added to the Hebrew sense of "know" as "have regard for" or "set favor on." The result is a verb which refers to God's eternal loving election (cf. Bultmann, 715; Sand; the only other NT occurrence of *proginōskō* for God's activity, in 1 Pet 1:20, also has the sense of election or foreordination; there Christ is the object.)

Paul distinguishes between divine foreknowledge and divine predestination in Romans 8:29: "those whom he foreknew, he also predestined." While foreknowledge denotes the exercise of God's will to establish a special relationship with those whom God graciously elects before all time, predestination expresses God's appointing of them to a specific goal before all time (cf. also the related motif of God's eternal purpose, *prothesis*, in Rom 8:28). In Romans 8:29 this goal is conformity with the image of the Son, a reference to the final salvation of the elect (see Gundry-Volf, 9-11). Foreknowledge as divine choice is thus the basis of predestination to glorification with Christ (Michel, 277; *see* Glory, Glorification). Foreknowledge does not have to be understood as foresight of faith in order to be distinguished from predestination.

Again in Romans 11:2 divine foreknowledge has the connotation of God's joining a people to himself in eternity in loving faithfulness. Implicit here is the idea that divine foreknowledge as election implies predestination to salvation. " 'God has not rejected his people' whom he foreknew, has he?" The thought that God might have rejected Israel* is seen to be incompatible with God's foreknowledge of his people. Unbelieving Israel may now be hardened (Rom 11:7), but there is a believing remnant because of God's gracious election (Rom 11:5, 7), and that remnant provides hope that the rest are yet consecrated to God

because of their election (Rom 11:16, 28). The divinely "foreknown" people have a destiny of salvation (see Rom 11:25-26), as unlikely as that may have appeared in Paul's day (contrast Calvin, 239, who takes the foreknown people to be members of Israel subject to God's secret election).

*See also* ELECTION AND PREDESTINATION; GOD.

BIBLIOGRAPHY. B. W. Anderson, "Foreknow, Foreknowledge," *IDB* 2.311-14; R. Bultmann, "γινώσκω κτλ," *TDNT* I.689-719, esp. 715-16; J. Calvin, *The Epistles of Paul the Apostle to the Romans and to the Thessalonians* (Grand Rapids: Eerdmans, 1960); C. E. B. Cranfield, *Romans* (2 vols.; ICC; Edinburgh: T. & T. Clark, 1975, 1979); W. Eichrodt, *Theology of the Old Testament* (Philadelphia: Westminster, 1967) 2.292-93; F. Godet, *Commentary on St. Paul's Epistle to the Romans* (Edinburgh: T. & T. Clark, 1882); J. Gundry-Volf, *Paul and Perseverance: Staying in and Falling Away* (WUNT 2.37; Tübingen: J. C. B. Mohr; Louisville: John Knox/Westminster, 1990); O. Michel, *Der Brief an die Römer* (KEK 4; 5th ed.; Göttingen: Vandenhoeck & Ruprecht, 1955); J. Murray, *The Epistle to the Romans* (NICNT; Grand Rapids: Eerdmans, 1968); A. Sand, "προγινώσκω, πρόγνωσις," *EDNT* 3.153-54; W. Schotroff, "ידע jd' erkennen," *THAT* 1.682-701.

J. M. Gundry-Volf

# FORGIVENESS

Paul makes little use of words for forgiveness compared to his frequent use of other terms that bring out what Christ has done for believers' salvation.* He seems to have preferred positive imagery like justification* or redemption.* Whatever his reason, he does not employ the terminology of forgiveness very much.

1. The Vocabulary of Forgiveness
2. Forgiveness As Grace
3. Forgiveness As Remission

## 1. The Vocabulary of Forgiveness.

Paul uses the verb *aphiēmi*, the normal NT verb for "to forgive," only five times (in the NT it occurs 142 times), and four of those do not refer to forgiveness (they have meanings like "leave"). He uses the corresponding noun *aphesis* twice only out of its seventeen occurrences in the NT. Another verb, *charizomai* (which is connected with *charis*, "grace,"* and which means to "give freely or graciously as a favor" or "remit, forgive, pardon," BAGD) appeals to him more, for he uses it sixteen times, of which ten have the meaning "forgive." We should also notice his use of *paresis* (Rom 3:25), which has the meaning of "passing over" and signifies at least that the sins to which it refers were not punished. We could say the same about *epi-*

*kalyptō,* "to cover," which Paul uses in a quotation from the LXX (Rom 4:7). It cannot be said that Paul overlooks this important aspect of Christianity, but he makes rather less use of it than we might have anticipated.

## 2. Forgiveness As Grace.

Paul uses the verb *charizomai* in the sense of "forgive" mostly to bring out the truth that Christians ought to be forgiving people. Perhaps, as W. Klassen (136-37) suggests, Paul chose *charizomai* because of its resonance with *charis,* "grace," and its personal reference to people rather than to sins.* Thus he writes to the Corinthians about someone they had disciplined and says the man has been punished enough (*see* Discipline). Now, he goes on, "you should rather forgive [*charisasthai*] and comfort him" (2 Cor 2:6-7). As his argument proceeds Paul emphasizes the importance of forgiveness as part of the Christian life. "If you forgive anyone, I do too. For what I also have forgiven, if I have forgiven anything, it is for your sake in the presence of Christ" (2 Cor 2:10). The details of the incident that lies behind these words are not clear. But what is abundantly plain is that Paul sees it as very important that both he and the Corinthians should forgive the offender. It is the way of the world to nurture grudges against those they think have wronged them. It is the way of those forgiven by Christ to forgive freely the wrongs people do to them.

The motivation for this is made clear when Paul writes to the Colossians, "forgiving one another . . . as the Lord forgave you, you do also" (Col 3:13). Christians have been forgiven so much that it ill becomes them to hold grudges against those they fancy have wronged them. Paul has the same thought in Ephesians, "forgiving one another, even as God in Christ forgave you" (Eph 4:32). This time he points out the relevance of the work of Christ to the process of forgiveness. Forgiveness in Christ means forgiveness because of all that Christ is and does. Christ died for the forgiveness of his people; how can they then withhold forgiveness for the petty wrongs done to them?

In the one passage where Paul uses this verb of the divine forgiveness, the apostle* refers to the deadness of sinners on account of their misdeeds and "the uncircumcision of (their) flesh." He goes on, God "has made you alive together with him (i.e., Christ), having forgiven us all our misdeeds" (Col 2:13). This clearly means that it is the work of Christ that brings forgiveness about, though Paul does not here say in what way. But that forgiveness of "all our misdeeds" is important is abundantly clear.

There is one more Pauline use of this verb we

should consider, namely the passage in which he reminds the Corinthians that he had never been a burden to them and adds, "Forgive me this wrong" (2 Cor 12:13). There is heavy irony here, but we should also notice the politeness of the apostle,* and his readiness to seek forgiveness. For him it is very important that believers act in a spirit of forgiveness and he sets the example (*see* Imitation of Paul/of Christ).

## 3. Forgiveness As Remission.

Paul does not make much use of the concept of remission. He sees it as important and speaks of Christ "in whom we have redemption through his blood, the forgiveness (or remission, *aphesin*) of our sins, according to the riches of his grace" (Eph 1:7). The links with redemption and with grace are important, for both are used often to bring out what the death of Christ (*see* Death of Christ) has done for sinners. So here we see that the forgiveness of sins arises from the atoning death of the Savior.* We have a very similar statement in Colossians, though it lacks the reference to grace (Col 1:14). But it does link redemption with "the forgiveness of sins."

In Romans 3:25 Paul, speaking of God's setting forth Jesus as a propitiatory sacrifice (*hilastērion; see* Expiation, Propitiation, Mercy Seat), refers to this act as a demonstration of God's righteousness* in "passing over" or "remitting" (*paresis*) "sins committed in former times." The precise meaning of this verse is debated, with some scholars suggesting that the verse is part of a pre-Pauline formula (Rom 3:24/25-26) originating in Jewish Christianity. The remission of past sins would seem to refer to the sins covered by the sacrificial system of Israel, which God passed over in his forbearance. But now, with the sacrifice of Christ, the final and effective solution has been put forward (see Martin 1990, 84-89; Kümmel).

When he uses the corresponding verb *aphiēmi* Paul mostly has it in the sense of "leave," "forsake." But once he cites Psalm 31:1 for the words, "Blessed are those whose lawlessnesses are forgiven [*aphethēsan*] and whose sins are covered" (Rom 4:7). "Blessed" refers to the highest state of felicity, and Paul sees this as brought about by Christ's dealing with the sins of believers—they are seen no more.

For Paul then forgiveness is important, though he does not often refer to it in set terms. But he sees it as significant that, because of what Christ has done, believers' sins are no longer counted against them. And he sees it as important that they translate this into their manner of life, by forgiving others the wrongs they do to them. Most importantly, forgiveness reveals something about the character of God.* He is a God who pardons, not a grim tyrant who holds sinners everlastingly responsible. He sent his Son to die on a cross to effect forgiveness. This surely means more than the remitting of penalty; it points to the establishment of a warm personal relationship with the forgiving God.

*See also* DEATH OF CHRIST; EXPIATION, PROPITIATION, MERCY SEAT; GRACE; JUSTIFICATION; PEACE, RECONCILIATION; SACRIFICE, OFFERING; SIN, GUILT.

BIBLIOGRAPHY. R. Bultmann, "ἀφίημι κτλ," *TDNT* I.509-12; W. Klassen, *The Forgiving Community* (Philadelphia, 1966); W. G. Kümmel, "Πάρεσις und ἔνδειξις," in *Heilsgeschehen und Geschichte* (Marburg: Elwert, 1965) 260-70 (="*Paresis* and *Endeixis:* A Contribution to the Understanding of the Pauline Doctrine of Justification," *Journal for Theology and the Church* 3 [New York: Harper & Row, 1967] 1-13); H. R. Mackintosh, *The Christian Experience of Forgiveness* (London: Nisbet, 1927); R. P. Martin, "Reconciliation and Forgiveness in Colossians," in *Reconciliation and Hope*, ed. R. Banks (Grand Rapids: Eerdmans, 1974) 104-24; idem, *Reconciliation: A Study of Paul's Theology* (2d ed; Grand Rapids: Zondervan, 1990); A. Richardson, *An Introduction to the Theology of the New Testament* (New York: Macmillan, 1951) 348-50; V. Taylor, *Forgiveness and Reconciliation* (2d ed.; London: Macmillan, 1946); W. Telfer, *The Forgiveness of Sins* (London: SCM, 1959); H. Vorländer, "Forgiveness," *NIDNTT* 1.697-703.

L. Morris

## FORMER LIFE IN JUDAISM. *See* JEW, PAUL THE.

## FREEDOM/LIBERTY

Paul is the "apostle of liberty" (Longenecker). He employs the noun *eleutheria* ("freedom," "liberty"), the adjective *eleutheros* ("free") and the verb *eleutheroō* ("to liberate," "set free"). The use of these terms for proclaiming the gospel* (as distinct from denoting social status, Col 3:11, Eph 6:8) is confined to Galatians, 1-2 Corinthians and Romans; but the concept of liberty permeates all the letters.

1. The Liberating Work of Christ.
2. The Practice of Christian Liberty.

### 1. The Liberating Work of Christ.

The arch-enemy of liberty is Sin* (hereafter capitalized as a personified power), a tyrannical ruler which holds all humanity in bondage (Rom 3:9; Gal 3:22). To maintain its mastery Sin employs several agencies, notably the flesh,* the Law,* the demonic* powers and death (*see* Life and Death). Christ comes to liberate

human beings from slavery* to Sin and all the powers at its command. Those whom he liberates, far from becoming autonomous, are ushered into a new bondage (Rom 6:12-23): they become Christ's willing slaves (*douloi*), he becomes their Lord* (e.g., 1 Cor 7:22; Rom 6; Eph 6:6-7).

*1.1. Christ's Redemptive Death.* "Christ crucified" is "our redemption*" (1 Cor 1:18-31). His death is the ransom price that secures liberation from bondage to Sin (1 Tim 2:6; cf. Tit 2:14). Christians "were bought at a price" (1 Cor 6:20; 7:23)—Christ's sacrificial death (1 Cor 15:3). The final "day of redemption" (Eph 4:30; 1:14; Rom 8:18-25) looks forward to the release accomplished by "his blood" (Eph 1:7; Rom 3:24-25; *see* Death of Christ).

*1.2. Liberation from Bondage to the Law.* To be "under Law" is to be "under Sin" (Gal 3:22-23). To purchase freedom for those "under Law" Christ himself was "born under Law" (Gal 4:4-5) and suffered death, "the curse* of the Law," on their behalf (Gal 3:10-13). Such persons are no longer "under Law" but "under grace*" (Rom 6:14); once enslaved to Law, they are now heirs of God (Gal 3:26—4:7), freed by Christ from a "yoke of bondage" (Gal 5:1). Those once bound to the Law are now married to Christ instead (Rom 7:1-6). The Law itself is not jettisoned but wrested from Sin's grip and placed into the hands of a new master. As a tool of Sin, the Law of God is an instrument of destruction (Rom 7:7-13; 1 Cor 15:56); wielded by Christ the Lord through the empowering Spirit, it becomes a means of grace (Rom 7:7-13; 8:2-8). The Spirit grants liberation, not from the "Law" itself (*nomos*) nor from the "writing" (*graphē*), but from the "letter" (*gramma*) or its "curse" (Gal 3:13)—which is what the Law becomes apart from the Spirit and the Christ in whom the Law reaches its appointed goal (2 Cor 3:4-17; Rom 7:6; 10:4; *see* Law).

*1.3. Liberation from the Powers.* In giving himself "for our sins," Christ rescues us from the powers of "the present evil age" (Gal 1:4). He "disarmed the powers and authorities" by snatching from them the record of lawbreakers' guilt and "nailing it to the cross" (Col 2:13-15; *see* Triumph). Moreover Christ saves persons from the powers' destructive use (through human agencies) of the Law itself, and summons them to purposeful lawkeeping under his headship (Gal 4:3, 8-9; Col 2:16-23). Persons "raised with Christ" are rescued from "the ruler of the kingdom of the air" and the "spiritual forces of evil" at his command (Eph 2:1-10; 6:10-18). The ascended Christ takes the hostile powers captive and liberates their former victims for effective service (Eph 4:7-13; 1:21; *see* Principalities and Powers; Triumph).

**1.4. Liberation from the Flesh.** Paul frequently employs the term *sarx* ("flesh"*) to denote the whole person in rebellion against God and in bondage to Sin. By Christ's incarnation and death, Sin is "condemned . . . in the flesh," and its victims freed from existence "according to the flesh" (Rom 8:3-4). They are no longer "in the flesh" but "in Christ" and "in the Spirit" (Rom 8:1, 9). Persons who belong to Christ "have crucified the flesh with its passions and desires," these being replaced by qualities cultivated by the Spirit (Gal 5:16-26; cf. Rom 8:13). To be freed from the flesh is to be freed from oneself, the fallen self, the self within the old humanity: "Our old self was crucified with [Christ] so that the body under Sin's control might be rendered powerless, that we should no longer be slaves to Sin" (Rom 6:6; *see* Dying and Rising).

**1.5. Liberation from Death.** Sin explains Death's entry into the world (Rom 5:12; *see* Life and Death). As though repaying a debt, Death becomes Sin's vicegerent, exercising dominion over all human beings on Sin's behalf (Rom 5:12-21). The death that results from bondage to Sin is at the same time the effect of God's wrath* (Rom 1:18-32; 2:5-9; Eph 2:1-3). By his sacrificial death Christ rescues his people from "the wrath to come" (Rom 5:9; 1 Thess 1:10; 5:9); by his resurrection from the dead he offers "eternal life" in place of death (Rom 5:21; 6:23). "The last enemy" is not yet destroyed (1 Cor 15:20-26, 42-58); but those united to Christ and indwelt by his Spirit are already granted "newness of life" (Rom 6:4, 13; 8:1-17).

## 2. The Practice of Christian Liberty.

The tension between liberty and Law, or freedom and obligation, which marks the current study of Paul, is evident in the Pauline letters themselves (Barrett, 1-16; *see* Ethics). We shall consider three—Galatians, 1 Corinthians and Romans. Having declared that "Christ has set us free for freedom" (Gal 5:1), Paul enjoins readers not to misuse their freedom (Gal 5:13) but to "fulfill the law of Christ" (Gal 6:2). In 1 Corinthians 8—10 freedom to eat certain meats is qualified by the command to respect the weak. Romans 14—15 addresses a conflict between champions of liberty (the "strong") and defenders of law (the "weak"; *see* Strong and Weak; Rome).

**2.1. Thralldom to Christ.** Slavery to Christ and submission to his Lordship provides the basis for the exercise of liberty.

**2.1.1. Galatians.** "Am I now persuading men, or God? Or am I seeking to please men? If I were still pleasing men, I would not be a slave [*doulos*] of Christ" (Gal 1:10). Christ's slave can logically be slave to no one else. Paul's adherence to this principle and

Peter's violation of it are equally evident during the crisis at Antioch* (Gal 2:11-14). Paul states that Peter withdrew from table fellowship with Gentiles because he feared the members of the circumcision* party (Gal 2:12): their approval, together with that of James's group, was vital (so he thought) for his theological and social security; thus he allowed them to dictate his actions and, in the process, to override his personal convictions. Despite the risks, Paul "opposed [Peter] to his face" (Gal 2:11), because "the truth* of the gospel" demanded it (Gal 2:5, 14-21) and because slavery to Christ left no room for the fear of others (Gal 1:10). By the same token slavery to Christ frees the believers from bondage to self ("the works of the flesh") and binds them instead to "the law of Christ"* and the power of the Spirit (Gal 5:16—6:10; *see* Holy Spirit).

**2.1.2. 1 Corinthians.** As Christ's purchased possession, believers belong neither to themselves (1 Cor 6:20, "you were bought at a price") nor to others (1 Cor 9:19, "free from all people"). Moreover, says Paul, "I myself am not under the Law" (9:20): the *doulos* of Christ cannot be under a second master, even the Law of God. Yet, Paul continues, "I am not free from God's Law but in thrall to Christ's law [*ennomos Christou*]" (9:21). Life "in Christ"* (*en Christō*) provides the essential context for law keeping (*ennomos Christou*). Persons united to Christ are subject to his law.

**2.1.3. Romans.** Christ is Lord* of both weak and strong; the conduct of each is ultimately directed to Christ (Rom 14:3-8). The weak cannot logically be enslaved to both Christ and the Law, nor the strong to both Christ and their liberty. Likewise Christ alone is ultimately responsible for them: "Who are you to judge someone else's servant? To his own master he stands or falls" (Rom 14:4). The weak and the strong are relieved of the arduous and inevitably frustrating task of shaping the other into their own image. Yet each is free to assist the other in becoming conformed to the image* of him who alone is master of both.

**2.2. The Responsible Use of Freedom.** Interlaced with Paul's declarations of liberty are instructions about its proper use.

**2.2.1. Galatians.** Freedom incites "the flesh" to destructive ends (Gal 5:13, 15, 19-21), but under the Spirit's direction freedom is employed to serve and support the needy (Gal 6:1-10).

**2.2.2. 1 Corinthians.** Enlightened as they are by the Spirit (1 Cor 2:6-16), believers recognize that food* and drink are gifts of a benevolent Creator (1 Cor 8:4-8; 10:25-26). "Am I not free?" asks Paul (1 Cor 9:1). He is indeed: he may marry if he so chooses; he has the right to payment for his services; he may enjoy pagan foods without pangs of conscience* (1 Cor 9:3-18; 10:27-30). Yet precisely in face of those gifts Paul sounds a warning: " 'Everything is permissible'—but not everything is beneficial. 'Everything is permissible'—but not everything is constructive" (1 Cor 10:23 NIV; Paul quotes a Corinthian slogan with approval yet qualification). One danger is that believers' freedom will "become a stumbling block to the weak" (1 Cor 8:9), to those who lack the true understanding of God and foods (1 Cor 8:4-8); that they will dare to eat food offered to idols* (1 Cor 8:10); and that they will therefore have acted out of accord with (that is, "violated") their conscience and be "destroyed" as a result (1 Cor 8:7, 11). But there is danger too for Christians whose knowledge gives them liberty to partake of pagan foods. First Corinthians 10:23 applies to these "stronger believers [adelphoi]" as surely as to the "weaker"; indeed, lacking as they do the danger signal of a wounded conscience (1 Cor 8:12), the former may be at greater risk (1 Cor 10:12). While the idols and the sacrifices offered to them amount to nothing, the demons behind them are very real indeed; and they are able to bring people under their dominion and into an intimacy akin to that of the Lord's Supper* (1 Cor 10:19-21). Let both weak and strong learn a lesson from Israel's experience in the wilderness: they all received God's provision and protection; nevertheless the majority fell under judgment on account of their sins (1 Cor 10:1-10). Believers too should be careful how they respond to grace—they who have witnessed its supreme manifestation (1 Cor 10:11). God's grace is at work both in his promise of deliverance (1 Cor 10:13) and in his warning against idolatry (1 Cor 10:14); one cannot rightly claim the word of promise while disobeying the attendant word of command.

*2.2.3. Romans.* The "strong" perceive the ethical implications of the gospel more clearly than do the "weak." The person who "eats everything" and who "considers every day alike" (Rom 14:3, 5) is the more liberated of the two. For this very reason it is to the strong that Paul appeals. "Accept the one whose faith is weak," he counsels them at the outset (Rom 14:1). As in 1 Corinthians it is especially the conscience of the weaker believer that is to be safeguarded (Rom 14:13-23). It is most significant that Paul, himself one of the strong (Rom 15:1), does not employ his apostolic authority* to impose his personal convictions upon the weak. Nor does he counsel the strong to try by whatever means to convert the weak into the strong. Not for a moment does he ask the strong to renounce their liberty (which would be to repudiate their very being as Christians), but he does challenge them to practice it in a certain way. They are free both

to exercise and to restrict their freedom, for they are enslaved to Christ and not to the liberty he has granted them. The strong are free to defend expressions of the very weakness from which they themselves have been liberated. More than that, they are strong enough and free enough actually "to bear the infirmities of the weak" (Rom 15:1 KJV).

*2.3. Bondage to Love.* "A Christian is a perfectly free lord of all, subject to none. A Christian is a perfectly dutiful servant of all, subject to all" (Luther, 344)—"subject to none" with respect to liberty, "subject to all" with respect to love.* Love brings liberty to its fullest expression (Schlier, 500).

*2.3.1. Galatians.* "You, my fellow believers, were called to be free. But do not use your freedom as an opportunity for the flesh; rather, be slaves [douleuete] to one another in love. The entire law is summed up in a single command: 'Love your neighbor as yourself' " (Gal 5:13-14). This is "the law of Christ," now inscribed on the heart by the Spirit (Gal 5:22—6:2; cf. 2 Cor 3:1-3). (On the outworkings of this with respect to the triad of 3:28, see Longenecker 1984, Richardson.)

*2.3.2. 1 Corinthians.* "Knowledge puffs up, but love builds up" (1 Cor 8:1). The gift of the Spirit ("knowledge"*) must not be divorced from the fruit* of the Spirit, especially love (1 Cor 13:1-13). Paul declares: "Though I am free from all, I have made myself a slave [edoulōsa] to all, that I may win the more" (1 Cor 9:19). Normally people are enslaved against their will; here the act of enslavement is voluntary and deliberate, an exercise of Christian liberty: "I have made myself a slave." Now that Paul is "free from all" (for he is Christ's slave), he is free *for* them (he can "become all things to all people," 1 Cor 9:22). Indeed Christ commands that bondage to himself be expressed by bondage to others ("For we do not preach ourselves, but Jesus Christ as Lord, and ourselves as your slaves [douloi] for Jesus' sake," 2 Cor 4:5). Paul is free to eat food offered to idols, but he is also free to abstain. He has freedom not to exercise his freedom: "A truly emancipated spirit such as Paul's is not in bondage to its own emancipation" (Bruce, 432 n.39). In love for the weaker believer, Paul will if necessary become a vegetarian (1 Cor 8:13); he is a slave to Christ, not to food. "Let no one seek his own good, but the good of the other" (1 Cor 10:24). Thus the statements of 1 Corinthians 10:27, 29b-30, are qualified by the parenthesis of 1 Corinthians 10:28-29a. Yet in refraining from food for the sake of the other's conscience, Paul does not violate his own conscience.* He still adheres to the conviction of 1 Corinthians 10:26 (he has not capitulated to the notion that food belongs to idols or to demons), and he still recognizes his right to the food. His right is relinquished, not invalidated. It is precisely as the one who holds these convictions that Paul acts on behalf of the weaker brother. His decision to refrain is not a loss of freedom but an expression of freedom. By the same token Paul is free to relinquish—as he was free to receive—payment for his services (see Financial Support). He has the right to relinquish his right, for the sake of other people (1 Cor 9:7-23).

*2.3.3. Romans.* Christ freely receives the diverse expressions of worship and obedience offered by the Jewish and the Gentile* members of his household* (Rom 14:3-8). Christ's unconditional acceptance of both Jew and Gentile is to be mirrored in the conduct of strong and weak toward each other. "Those who eat must not despise those who abstain, and those who abstain must not pass judgment on those who eat; for God has welcomed them" (Rom 14:3 NRSV). "Welcome one another, then, just as Christ welcomed you" (Rom 15:7). Let the strong stop despising the weak; instead, after Christ's example, let them bear their weaknesses even at risk of insult (Rom 15:1-3). Let the weak stop judging the strong for their perceived lawlessness; instead, let them show them the mercy which the covenant God granted to lawless Gentiles (Rom 15:8-12). Such acceptance entails respect for diverse expressions of liberty. The weak and the strong must accept one another as they are, rather than as potential converts to one's own position. "Disputable matters" (Rom 14:1) are almost certain to remain a matter of controversy. But such diversity in the community provides love (*agapē*, Rom 14:15) its greatest opportunity. Love honors both the liberty which is the concern of the strong (for freedom comes to fullest expression in acts of love), and the law which is the concern of the weak (for "love is the fulfillment of the Law," Rom 13:8-10). The result is the praise of God (Rom 15:5-7).

*See also* AUTHORITY; CIVIL AUTHORITY; CONSCIENCE; ETHICS; FLESH; FOOD OFFERED TO IDOLS AND JEWISH FOOD LAWS; FUTILITY; HOLY SPIRIT; LAW; LAW OF CHRIST; LIFE AND DEATH; LOVE; PRINCIPALITIES AND POWERS; SIN, GUILT; SLAVE, SLAVERY; STRONG AND WEAK; TRIUMPH.

BIBLIOGRAPHY. C. K. Barrett, *Freedom and Obligation: A Study of the Epistle to the Galatians* (Philadelphia: Westminster, 1985); J. Blunck, "Freedom," *NIDNTT* 1.715-21; F. F. Bruce, *The Book of the Acts* (Grand Rapids: Eerdmans, 1956); R. Bultmann, *Theology of the New Testament*, Vol. 1 (New York: Scribner's, 1951); E. J. Epp, "Paul's Diverse Imageries of the Human Situation and His Unifying Theme of Freedom," in *Unity and Diversity in New Testament Theology*, ed. R. A. Guelich (Grand Rapids: Eerdmans, 1978) 100-116; R. N. Longenecker, *New Testament Social Ethics for Today* (Grand Rapids: Eerdmans, 1984); idem, *Paul, Apostle of Liberty* (New York: Harper & Row, 1964); M. Luther, "The Freedom of a Christian [1520]," in *Luther's Works*, Vol. 31, ed. H. J. Grimm (Philadelphia: Muhlenberg, 1957) 327-77; F. Mussner, *Theologie der Freiheit nach Paulus* (Düsseldorf: Aschendorff, 1976); P. Richardson, *Paul's Ethic of Freedom* (Philadelphia: Westminster, 1979); H. Schlier, "ἐλεύθερος κτλ," *TDNT* II.487-502; R. Schnackenburg, "Christian Freedom according to Paul," in *Christian Existence in the New Testament* (South Bend, IN: Notre Dame, 1969) 31-53.

J. K. Chamblin

# FRUIT OF THE SPIRIT

The expression "the fruit of the Spirit" is a metaphor used by Paul to describe virtues* that manifest the realities of life in Christ.* Paul does not speak about the fruit of faith, but he does speak explicitly of the "fruit of the Spirit" (*ho karpos tou pneumatos*). In Galatians 5:22-23 Paul catalogs the components of the "fruit of the Spirit" as "love,* joy,* peace,* patience, kindness, goodness, faithfulness, gentleness and self-control."

1. Similar and Contrasting Metaphors
2. The Context of Galatians
3. Paul's Sources
4. Spiritual Graces
5. Conclusion

## 1. Similar and Contrasting Metaphors.

Galatians 5:22-23 is the only text that refers to the "fruit of the Spirit," but Paul uses a similar metaphor in other places. He views Christian churches and lives as fields and gardens from which the owner who has spent love and time with them may expect positive results, "fruit unto God" (Rom 1:13; 7:4). In Philippians 1:22 Paul indicates that his continued living will result in "fruit" from his labors. He refers to the Philippians' gift to him as a "fruit" of their love.

Closer to the idea of "fruit of the Spirit" is a reference to the "fruit of the light" (*ho karpos tou phōtos*), described as goodness and righteousness* and truth* (Eph 5:9). The gospel produces "fruit," accompanying its intended effect (Col 1:6, 10). The "fruit" of the new life in Christ is righteousness (Phil 1:11) and sanctification (Rom 6:21-22; see Holiness).

In a contrasting metaphor, Paul describes those apart from Christ as "unfruitful" (*akarpos*). Ephesians 5:11 speaks of those who walk in darkness as living unfruitful lives (cf. Rom 6:21). The unregenerate life produces fruit unto death, evidencing negative vices instead of the positive virtues produced by the Spirit (Rom 7:4; Col 3:5-9; Gal 5:19-21).

Paul may well have derived the metaphor of fruitfulness or unfruitfulness from the OT. There Israel is compared to a fruit-bearing tree or vineyard (e.g., Ps 80:8-18; Is 5:1-7; 27:2-6; Jer 2:21; 11:16; 12:10; Hos 14:6; cf. 4 Ezra 9:31-32), and Isaiah can bring indictment against the "vineyard" of the Lord for not bearing its righteous fruit (Is 5:2, 4). When Israel is restored, however, and the Spirit is poured out, the land will be fruitful (Is 32:15-16), and the trees and vine will bear their fruit (Joel 2:18-32).

## 2. The Context of Galatians.

As mentioned earlier, Galatians 5:22-23 is the primary passage outlining the "fruit of the Spirit." Galatians includes Paul's polemical defense of his apostleship* and the tension between the Law* and Spirit.* The Gentile* believers were seemingly engaging themselves with the Law in a way Paul prohibited, for it threatened to jeopardize "the truth of the gospel*" (Gal 2:11-21). Galatians 5:13-26 exhorts the Galatian believers to live/walk by the Spirit and not follow the fleshly* desires characteristic of those outside the believing community. It was necessary for Paul to show that freedom* from the Law does not by any means do away with the obligations of ethical* living. However, the responsibilities of moral conduct must not be shaped by the dictates of Law but by the operation, enablement and sufficiency of the Spirit (on the Galatian context, see Barclay).

### 2.1. Flesh and Spirit.
In Galatians 5:16, 18 a contrast is made to emphasize actions characterized by the Spirit (*pneumati*). The exhortation in Galatians 5:16 is an active construction with the dative (*pneumati peripateite*) translated "walk by the Spirit." The verbal form in Galatians 5:18 is passive, again with the dative, meaning "be led by the Spirit" (*pneumati agesthe*). The two ideas are very similar when one is illumined by the other. "Walking by the Spirit" means not to gratify the desires of the flesh, while "being led by the Spirit" is the opposite of being under the Law.

The exhortation in Galatians 5:16 establishes parameters for life in the Spirit by establishing opposition to fleshly license; Galatians 5:18 excludes legalism as a guide for the believer. The enablement supplied by the Spirit excludes both legalism and license. Legalism and license are further defined by the lists of vices (Gal 5:19-21) and virtues (Gal 5:22-23; *see* Virtues and Vices). Paul uses the terms *desire* (*epithymia*) and *flesh* (*sarx*) to emphasize the contrast in character between the Spirit-controlled life and the life governed by fleshly impulses.

### 2.2. Shape of Life in the Spirit.
The listing of the "fruit of the Spirit" in Galatians 5:22-23 gives positive shape to life in the Spirit, setting it in contrast with the vice list of Galatians 5:19-21. Galatians 5:25, "Since we live by the Spirit, let us walk by the Spirit," provides a summary verse for this section with the repetition of the dative for "Spirit" (*pneumati*). Paul's emphatic summary is best understood as an exhortation to "keep in step [*stoichōmen*] with the Spirit."

The context stresses the Spirit's power for motivation and enablement in Christian living. Paul's view of life in the Spirit takes shape in both positive and negative ways. The virtues (the fruit of the Spirit) are genuine examples of the ethical character produced in those who walk by the Spirit.

## 3. Paul's Sources.

It is highly unlikely that the list of virtues is entirely Paul's creation. One of the strongest influences was the OT. In his letter to the Romans, Paul indicates that love, which is the first virtue in the list of Galatians 5, fulfills the specific commands of the Decalogue (Rom 13:8-10). Paul, however, does not codify in a formal manner the ethical teachings of the OT. Little or no direct influence from the intertestamental period can be firmly established, though it is likely that his overall ethical teaching reflects Paul's rabbinic background (Davies, 177-226). O. Wischmeyer has, however, produced from Hellenistic Judaism an impressive array of parallels to "love."* But as G. D. Fee notes, "the alleged parallels are of dubious value; praise of 'virtue' or 'eros' is not quite the same as an exhortation to ἀγάπη" (Fee, 626).

The list of virtues parallels similar terminology and style in Hellenistic ethics. While the language is similar to Greek thought, Paul does not use the qualities in a Greek way. Some of the concepts and descriptions in the list are more, others less, "specifically Christian." For Paul, however, these virtues are always for the benefit of the community and the upbuilding of the church and not, as in the Greek ethic, merely for character formation. They are always approached from the standpoint of Christian liberty and obedience in Christ.

Although Paul, with the exception of love (*agapē*), adopts conventional terms, they do not represent "virtues" in the traditional sense but manifestations of divine redemption.* They occur in the Christian community as reflections of Christ's presence in the church by means of the Spirit.

## 4. Spiritual Graces.

The graces included in Paul's list of the "fruit of the

Spirit" must be compared with similar lists in Philippians 4:8 and Colossians 3:12-15. These Spirit-prompted graces go beyond the natural bounds of virtue so that believers, for example, demonstrate love by loving their enemies (Rom 12:14; cf. Mt 5:44). The outworking of these virtues demonstrates the work of the Spirit in believers. There may not, however, be a one-to-one correspondence between these lists and progress in the Christian life. V. Furnish suggests they are not designed to portray the Christian ideal toward which all are to strive, but are rather different ways Paul addresses himself to concrete historical situations to explain how the new life in Christ expresses itself (Furnish, 87). Yet these virtues can be seen as evidence of the work of the Spirit in the development of believers in contrast to "works of the flesh" (Gal 5:19-21). To some extent we can say the virtues are definite marks of the Spirit.

Paul lists nine virtues or graces (not to be understood as an exhaustive list), which make up the "fruit of the Spirit"—the lifestyle of those indwelt and energized by the Spirit (Bruce 1982, 251). The "fruit of the Spirit" is obviously intended as a contrast to the "works of the flesh." The phrase "fruit of the Spirit" indicates that the qualities enumerated are not the results of observing a legal code, but are to be attributed to the power* of the Holy Spirit (Fung, 262-63). The ethical characteristics produced by the Spirit are in sharp contrast to the natural activities and attitudes of the self-centered life.

*4.1. Love* (**Agapē**). It is most important that "love"* should stand at the head of the list. This emphasis is present elsewhere in Paul (1 Cor. 13). Love characterizes God,* and when performed by men and women love fulfills the Law (Rom 13:10). It is a self-giving action for the benefit of others, not necessarily an emotion. The best example of such love is, of course, Christ's self-giving on the cross* (Gal 2:20; Eph 5:25).

*4.2. Joy* (**Chara**). Although Paul repeatedly exhorts believers to rejoice "in the Lord" (cf. Phil 3:1; 4:4), the only occurrence of the word joy* in Galatians is here in the listing of the fruit of the Spirit. Even in trials, believers may retain the joy of the Lord, which prevents them from giving way to total despair. While love is clearly attributed to God, joy is not so clearly linked, but its character as a divine gift is obvious in other contexts (e.g., Rom 14:17).

*4.3. Peace* (**Eirēnē**). Genuine Christian existence demonstrates the peace of God because believers have peace* with God (Rom 5:1). Peace, like all graces in the list, is not a precondition of justification; instead, for Paul justification* is the precondition and root from which these qualities grow. Peace is the

tranquillity that is ministered to believers to sustain them in life. H. D. Betz suggests that this initial threefold structure (love, joy, peace) reveals an important element of Paul's ethic: "People cannot be expected simply to act in an ethically responsible way, but they must first be enabled, empowered, and motivated before they can so act" (Betz, 287). Since through the Spirit the love, joy and peace of God are present to believers, they should act appropriately. In Colossians 3:15 Paul's exhortation for peace transcends individual experience. He calls for peace to rule in their corporate experience so that there would be harmony in the congregation (Melick, 301-2).

*4.4. Patience* (**Makrothymia**). Patience is a positive value embracing steadfastness and staying power. Patience, or forbearance, is a quality of God (Ps 103:8), and it is to be reproduced in God's people (1 Cor 13:4; Eph 4:2; Col 1:11; 3:12).

*4.5. Kindness* (**Chrēstotēs**). The Holy Spirit produces in believers the attitude of gentleness, or kindness, putting love in action. Kindness is a quality of God's gracious attitude and actions toward sinners (Rom 2:4; Eph 2:7; Tit 3:4). Christians have no better way to continue in God's kindness than by showing others the kindness of God (Eph 4:32).

*4.6. Goodness* (**Agathōsynē**). Goodness includes the idea of generosity, but focuses on moral excellence. An unusual term, it occurs in the LXX and only four times in the NT. Fung claims that "goodness is an attitude of generous kindness to others, which is happy to do far more than is required by mere justice" (Fung, 268). Such magnanimous generosity is the antithesis to envy (Gal 5:21).

*4.7. Faithfulness* (**Pistis**). *Pistis* may mean either "faith"* or "faithfulness." The context, which lists eight other ethical qualities, indicates that one should expect *pistis* to denote an ethical quality also. Since God is faithful (Rom 3:3), his people also are to be faithful. The word points to the idea of reliability or trustworthiness.

*4.8. Gentleness* (**Praütēs**). This quality combines strength and meekness, denoting strength under control. It lacks any negative sense of an absence of spirit, courage or vigor sometimes associated with the English word *gentleness*. This spiritual grace is best understood as a humble disposition to the divine will (Burton, 317).

*4.9. Self-Control* (**Enkrateia**). This last term is especially important. The idea had been introduced into Greek ethics by Socrates, and by Paul's time the word had become a primary concept in Hellenistic thought. Its place at the end of the list possibly indicates that just as love, the first quality, is the fulfillment of the

Law, Christian self-control fulfills the complete demand of Greek ethics.

### 5. Conclusion.

Whereas the list of vices or "works of the flesh" is unstructured, by contrast the "fruit of the Spirit" are characterized by a structured unity. This unity consists of three sets of three concepts, the most important of which are at the beginning and the end. "Love" at the beginning and "self-control" at the end, represent perfection and completeness. Where the "fruit of the Spirit" are present, it enhances the life of the church and its members. No room remains for the "works of the flesh."

For those at Galatia that fear abandoning Law for Spirit will lead to libertinism, Paul assures that against these things there is no law. Nor are these characteristics to be codified into a new law. These Spirit-given graces do not originate in any form of legalism but are the outgrowth of the Spirit's eschatological activity (Barclay 1991, 119-25).

*See also* ETHICS; FLESH; GIFTS OF THE SPIRIT; HOLINESS, SANCTIFICATION; HOLY SPIRIT; JOY; LOVE; PEACE; SPIRITUALITY; VIRTUES AND VICES.

BIBLIOGRAPHY. J. M. G. Barclay, *Obeying the Truth: Paul's Ethics in Galatians* (Minneapolis: Fortress, 1991); W. Barclay, *Flesh and Spirit: An Examination of Galatians 5:19-23* (Nashville: Abingdon, 1962); H. D. Betz, *Galatians* (Herm; Philadelphia: Fortress, 1979); F. F. Bruce, *Commentary on Galatians* (NIGTC; Grand Rapids: Eerdmans, 1982); idem, *Paul: Apostle of the Heart Set Free* (Grand Rapids: Eerdmans, 1977); E. D. Burton, *The Epistle to the Galatians* (ICC; Edinburgh: T. & T. Clark, 1921); W. D. Davies, *Paul and Rabbinic Judaism* (rev. ed.; Philadelphia: Fortress, 1980); G. D. Fee, *The First Epistle to the Corinthians* (NICNT; Grand Rapids: Eerdmans, 1987); R. Y. K. Fung, *The Epistle to the Galatians* (NICNT; Grand Rapids: Eerdmans, 1988); V. P. Furnish, *Theology and Ethics in Paul* (Nashville: Abingdon, 1968); R. N. Longenecker, *Galatians* (WBC 41; Dallas: Word, 1991); W. Longsworth, "Ethics in Paul: The Shape of Christian Life," in *The Annual of the Society of Christian Ethics* (1981) 29-56; D. J. Lull, *The Spirit in Galatia* (SBLDS 49; Chico, CA: Scholars, 1980); R. R. Melick, Jr., *Philippians, Colossians, Philemon* (NAC; Nashville: Broadman, 1991); E. Schweizer, "Traditional Ethical Patterns in the Pauline and Post-Pauline Letters and Their Development," in *Text and Interpretation*, ed. E. Best and R. McL. Wilson (Cambridge: University Press, 1979) 195-209; O. Wischmeyer, *Der höchste Weg. Das 13. Kapitel des 1 Korintherbriefes* (Gütersloh: Mohn, 1981).

D. S. Dockery

## FULLNESS

Paul uses *fullness* (*plērōma*) with different shades of meaning in both the passive sense "that which is completed or filled" (as object) and the active sense "that which completes or fills up" (as subject).

1. Totality of Space
2. Totality of Quantity
3. Totality of the Law
4. Fulfillment of Time
5. Fullness of Essence

### 1. Totality of Space.

In 1 Corinthians 10:26, 27 Paul quotes Psalm 24:1 LXX to defend his view that "all *contents* of the earth" belong to the Lord,* and thus all kinds of food can be eaten.

### 2. Totality of Quantity.

In Romans 11 Paul refers to "the *full inclusion*" or "*full recovery*" of Israel* (Rom 11:12), which will most probably take place soon after "the *total number* of the Gentiles have come in" (Rom 11:25). In Romans 11:12, although the *plērōma* is morally neutral, the contrasting parallel, *trespass* (Gk *paraptōma*), suggests moral or spiritual consummation. And in Romans 11:25, although it can mean that the Gentiles* have "the *whole time* of the church" all to themselves (cf. Lk 21:24), the parallel phrase "all Israel" (Rom 11:26) points to "until the *great multitude* is completed" (cf. Rev 7:9).

In Romans 15:29 the passive sense is used to refer to Paul's desire that the Roman believers share in "the *full abundance*" of Christ's* blessing" through their financial collection,* not just to bring relief to the famine-stricken in Jerusalem, but also to strengthen the bond between Jews and Gentiles in the church* (Rom 15:24-33).

### 3. Totality of the Law.

Another passive use is Paul's reference to love* as "the *sum* of the Law's demands" (Rom 13:10), which believers fulfill wholly because by God's* provision in Christ through his Spirit (*see* Holy Spirit) sin* has no more power* over them (cf. Rom 8:4, 9-10); the immediate context shows his concern for obedience to the *whole* Torah (Rom 13:8-10). But it is also possible that it has an active meaning: the Torah has been fulfilled and receives its perfection in love. Love for one's neighbor is the *end* or *complete realization* of the Torah (cf. Rom 13:8; Gal 5:14; 6:2; *see* Law).

### 4. Fulfillment of Time.

The active sense of *plērōma* is clearly used with reference to time. In Galatians 4:4 Paul refers to Christ's first advent as "the *completion* of time (*chronos*)." This may be one (or the first) of the times (Gk *kairos*, cf. Lk 21:24; Acts 1:7) or ages (Gk *aiōnes*, cf. Gal 3:20-21; 1 Cor 10:11; Eph 2:7) which will all find their *consummation* in God's ultimate objective of uniting all things in Christ (Eph 1:10). Christ is not only the source and sustainer, but also the goal of the history of the whole cosmos. So here in Galatians 4:4 *plērōma* means the *full realization* of God's predestined plans revealed in the Scripture (Eph 1:10; cf. Mt 5:17; Mk 1:15; *see* Election and Predestination).

### 5. Fullness of Essence.

*5.1.* Significant yet controversial is the usage in Colossians 1:19 and 2:9. Here *plērōma* most likely means "the *whole total* of the Godhead" which was pleased to dwell in the person of Christ (Delling). Some scholars (Lightfoot, Bultmann) think that *plērōma* is used in Colossians 1:19 as a quasi-technical term borrowed from early Gnosticism* to refer to the space in which the *entirety* of intermediary beings exist between the creator and his creation.* This assumes that Paul was using a term taken from the Colossian heretics (*see* Colossians) who, under the influence of gnostic thinking, taught that Christ is only one of the members of the heavenly mediatorial hierarchy. Paul was therefore arguing for the superiority and uniqueness of Christ, that he rules over these beings as the divinity who fills them all.

But apart from the lack of external evidence for early Gnosticism, there is also no internal evidence of a polemic against this alleged false teaching about Christ. So the active sense of *plērōma* seems best for this text: Christ has *all* the divine attributes in himself. This fits the OT and Hebraic usage, where the Hebrew equivalent connotes *completeness* and God who, on the one hand, in his being or glory* fills the whole earth (e.g., Ps 72:19; Jer 23:24; Is 6:3; Ezek 43:5), on the other hand is said to be "pleased to dwell" in a place of his choosing, Zion (Col 1:19, *eudokēsen . . . katoikēsai;* LXX Ps 67:17; cf. LXX Ps 131:13, 14; Is 8:18; 49:20; see O'Brien). Moreover, Jewish wisdom speculation spoke of Wisdom's universal presence and permeation of all things (Wis 7:24). Colossians 1:19 seems to indicate that the fullness the OT attributed to God and Judaism attributed to Wisdom now dwells in the place of God's choosing, Christ. Other aspects of Wisdom christology* may be detected in the statements about the pre-existent Christ and his role in creation in Colossians 1:15-16 (*see* Firstborn; Pre-existence; Wisdom; cf. the appropriation of wisdom concepts in the Johannine logos christology, Jn 1:14, 16).

*5.2.* Another difficult text is Ephesians 1:23 (see Yates, who lists the interpretive options). It seems best to take *plērōma* as a christological title that is used in apposition to "him" in Ephesians 1:22: Christ himself is the one who has the *full measure* of the God who fills everything (cf. 1 Cor 15:28). This harmonizes with the use of the verb *plēroō* in Ephesians 4:10 and the usage in Colossians (Moule).

It seems probable that the passive sense of the church being dwelt in and "*completed* by Christ" may be meant. Though the immediate context can also suggest that "Christ is being *filled* by the church," "the church is being *filled* by Christ" makes better sense since the usage of the imagery of the church as Christ's body (*see* Body of Christ) focuses on the importance of Christ to the church and not vice versa (Eph 4:13). The church is the receptacle being *filled up* with the grace* and gifts* of Christ (cf. Eph 4:7-11).

*5.3.* *Plērōma* is used in the body metaphor of Ephesians 4:13 to denote the *full realization* of the unity of all believers in Christ: it attains "the measure of the stature of the *fullness* of Christ" (RSV) in which Christians are no longer easily swayed by false teachings (Eph 4:14).

*5.4.* The usage in Ephesians 3:19 is possibly similar: the growth in Christian experience is to reach "to the measure of (*eis*) all the *fullness* of God."

*See also* BODY OF CHRIST; ISRAEL; WISDOM.

BIBLIOGRAPHY. P. Benoit, "Body, Head and *Pleroma* in the Epistles of the Captivity," in *Jesus and the Gospel* (London: Darton, Longman and Todd, 1974) 2.51-92; M. Bogdasovich, "The Idea of *Pleroma* in the Epistles to the Colossians and Ephesians," *Downside Review* 83 (1965) 118-30; R. Bultmann, *Theology of the New Testament* (2 vols.; New York: Charles Scribner's, 1951, 1955) 2.149-52; G. Delling, "πλήρης κτλ," *TDNT* VI.283-311; J. Ernst, *Pleroma und Pleroma Christi. Geschichte und Deutung eines Begriffs der paulinischen Antilegomena* (BU 5; Regensburg: Pustet, 1970); A. Feuillet, "L'église plérôme du Christ d'après Éphés., 1, 23," *NRT* 78 (1956) 449-72, 593-610; A. T. Lincoln, *Ephesians* (WBC 42; Dallas: Word, 1990) 72-78; C. F. D. Moule, " 'Fullness' and 'Fill' in the New Testament," *SJT* 4 (1951) 79-86; P. T. O'Brien, *Colossians, Philemon* (WBC 44; Waco: Word, 1982); P. D. Overfield, "*Pleroma:* A Study in Content and Context," *NTS* 25 (1978-79) 384-96; I. de la Potterie, "Le Christ, Plérôme de l'église (Eph 1.22-23)," *Bib* 58 (1977) 500-524; R. Schippers, "πληρόω," *NIDNTT* 1.733-41; R. Yates, "A Reexamination of Eph 1:23," *ExpT* 83 (1971-72) 146-51.                    D. S. Lim

## FUTILITY

In Paul's letters the adjective *kenos*, and the words *mataios* (adjective), *mataiotēs* (noun) and *mataioomai* (verb) are the most prominent terms used to convey the general idea of futility, uselessness, or lack of purpose or result. But other words are also used with various degrees of synonymous meaning: *eikē*, "in vain," "without result"; *dōrean*, "for no reason," "for no purpose"; *akarpos*, "unproductive." *Kenos* and *mataios* are frequently used together in the LXX (e.g., Job 20:18; Is 37:7; Hos 12:1), in classical Greek (e.g., Sophocles *Elec.* 324 and Aristotle *Eth. Nic.* 1.2) and in Hellenistic Greek (e.g., *1 Clement* 6). *Kenos* is used by Paul to signify that which is empty and hollow—hence, pointless and futile. *Mataios* is employed by Paul to signify that which is vain and useless—hence, ineffective and futile.

    1. Futility and the Apostolic Gospel
    2. Futility As Human and Cosmic Plight

**1. Futility and the Apostolic Gospel.**
In Colossians 2:8 Paul uses *kenos* to describe the enticements of those trying to capture believers with a false teaching or "philosophy" (*philosophia*), which is nothing but *kenē apatē*, "empty deceit" or "hollow deception" (cf. Eph 5:6; see 1 Tim 6:20; 2 Tim 2:16 where *kenophonia*, "foolish talk," appears). Paul further characterizes this message as "according to human tradition, according to the elements [or elemental spirits] of the world, and not according to Christ" (Col 2:8).

In contrast, Paul's preaching* was not futile but purposeful and effective because it was about Christ who had died (*see* Death of Christ) and had been raised to life* again (see 1 Cor 15:14). He made the same claim of effectiveness for his labor among believers (1 Thess 2:1). Paul was concerned that neither his labor nor the faith and suffering* of believers be in vain (*kenos,* Gal 2:2; 2 Cor 6:1; *eikē,* Gal 3:4). And he could express confidence that it had not been for nothing, despite threats from within and without (Gal 3:4; Phil 2:16; 1 Thess 3:5; cf. use of *eikē,* "in vain" or "to no result," in Gal 4:11; 1 Cor 15:2). Paul was confident that he had not received God's grace* "to no effect" or "without result" (1 Cor 15:10; Gal 2:2).

Behind this concern that his labor and proclamation not be in vain seems to lie his self-identity as an apostle conceived along the lines of an OT prophet, or more particularly, the Servant of Yahweh (*see* Prophet, Paul As). There is substantial evidence that Paul had reflected deeply on Isaiah 49, where the Servant's call (cf. Is 49:1, 5 and Gal 1:15-16) and dual mission to restore Israel* (Is 49:5-6; *see* Restoration of Israel) and take salvation* to the Gentiles* (cf. Is 49:6 and Gal 2:2) are clearly articulated. There also the Servant expresses doubts about his effectiveness in

the mission: "But I said, 'I have labored in vain [LXX *kenōs ekopiasa*], I have spent my strength for nothing and vanity [LXX *eis mataion*], yet surely my cause is with the Lord, and my reward with my God' " (Is 49:4). The context and use of *kenos* and *eikē* in Galatians suggests that Paul's concern that he not "run" (Gal 2:2) or "labor" (Gal 4:11) in vain echoes the language of the Servant of Yahweh in Isaiah 49:4. The same background may be reflected in Philippians 2:16 (note again the metaphors of labor and running), where the second half of Isaiah 49:4 may stand behind Paul's expression of confidence that his ministry will be vindicated and he will "boast" on the Day of Christ. Thus the purposefulness and effectiveness of Paul's apostolic ministry appear to be directly related to his divine mission to take the good news of God's salvation "to the end of the earth" (Is 49:6) and so serve the eschatological purposes of God. This background may shed further light on Paul's repeated expressions of concern in 1 Corinthians 15 (1 Cor 15:2 [*eikē*], 10, 14 [*kenos* 3 times]) that his apostleship, his message and the Corinthians' response will have been in vain if the message of Christ's resurrection* is misconstrued along the lines the Corinthians* have taken it. For the resurrection of Christ is the first fruit* (1 Cor 15:20) and guarantee of the future resurrection which epitomizes all that is included in the establishment of God's new cosmic order (1 Cor 15:17-28; *see* Eschatology) and the end of all futility.

**2. Futility As Human and Cosmic Plight.**
Paul's use of *mataiotēs* was very likely informed by the LXX, especially Ecclesiastes. Although the adjective *mataios* was regularly employed in Greek literature to describe that which is vain or empty, in extant Greek literature *mataiotēs* is rarely used as compared with the LXX, where it is used frequently with the sense "uselessness," "worthlessness," or "futility" (Bauernfeind, 523). In Ecclesiastes (1:2, 14; 2:1, 11, 15, 17, etc.) the expression appears repeatedly in the negative refrain, *mataiotēs mataiotētōn, ta panta mataiotēs.* This haunting chorus is difficult to render in English translation due to the numerous connotations of *mataiotēs.* The traditional rendering, "vanity of vanities, all is vanity," found in many older translations, is being replaced in newer versions with more creative attempts at capturing the meaning (e.g., "meaninglessness" NIV; "emptiness" NEB; "uselessness" TEV; or "Futility, utter futility, . . . everything is futile," Eccles 1:2 REB). Qoheleth points to the futility of all human endeavors which seek to bring lasting satisfaction in and of themselves. One might as well "try and catch the wind" (Eccles 2:11). A person can find permanent

meaning and lasting contentment only in God, who transcends human existence and with whom there is no *mataiotēs*.

Nowhere in the NT is the kind of futility described in Ecclesiastes so clearly reflected as in Romans 8:20. When Paul speaks of the creation* being subjected to futility, he is focusing on the inability of creation to attain the goal for which it was originally designed (*see* World, Cosmology). When humanity sinned, God subjected creation to the curse of futility and decay (cf. Gen 3:17-19). An alternative view is worth noting, however. C. K. Barrett (166) suggests that *mataiotēs* in Romans 8:20, building on the LXX's use of *mataios* to refer to gods or idols (e.g., LXX Ps 30:6), refers to "inferior spiritual powers," or what Paul otherwise calls the "elements* of the world" (e.g., Gal 4:9), to which the created order has been enslaved.

Creation's "fall" was the result of humanity's disobedience as steward of creation. The subhuman creation thus shares in Adam's fallenness "not of its own will"—but neither is it by chance. God subjected it "in hope," and so the way out from under futility is shown to be the eschatological work of God by which he presently redeems and adopts his children (*see* Adoption), and will ultimately bring them and the created order into the glory* of a new creation, liberated from its slavery to corruption. In the present age, however, all of the creation groans in labor pains as it awaits that redemption.* The children of God groan with the creation (Rom 8:22-23), though by the Spirit they presently experience redemption (Rom 8:15). For the subhuman creation cannot experience its freedom from futility and enter into the newness of the age to come until the "revealing of the children of God" (Rom 8:21) at the end of this age. That coming "glory of the children of God" (Rom 8:21) will be shared by the whole created order; both will be liberated from *mataiotēs*.

In other places Paul used *mataiotēs* to depict the human plight as characterized by a futility that has its source in the thought life of fallen humanity. With the Psalmist Paul can characterize the presumptuous "thoughts of the wise" as being futile, nothingness (1 Cor 3:20, quoting from LXX Ps 93:11). In Romans 1 and Ephesians 4 we find a parallel development of this human plight. In Romans 1:21, using the verb *mataioomai*, Paul argues that the ungodly, having not recognized or honored God, "became futile [*emataiōthēsan*] in their thinking, and their senseless minds were darkened" (NRSV). Likewise, Ephesians 4:17-18 speaks of the nothingness of the purposes of the Gentiles,* who are those living "in the futility of their minds" because "they are darkened in their understanding, alienated from the life of God because of their ignorance and hardness of heart" (Eph 4:17-18, NRSV; cf. Rom 1:21; Wis 13:1). In Romans 1:21-23 Paul's indictment moves from futility to foolishness* to idolatry* ("they changed the glory of the incorruptible God for the likeness of the image of corruptible man, and of birds, . . ." Rom 1:23). Paul's polemic against Gentile idolatry recalls the language of Psalm 106:20, but also that of Isaiah 44:9-20 where the prophet satirizes idols. There, as elsewhere, the LXX associates *mataios* with idols, or the gods of the nations (see above; in Is 44:9 those who fashion idols are *mataioi*; cf., e.g., Jer 10:15; 51:18; Ps 31:6). The thought life of the unregenerate is futile and aimless because it is alienated from the life of God and lacks spiritual insight. Thus it produces a life of purposelessness and ineffectiveness, marked by abandonment to licentiousness, greed, and impurity (Eph 4:19; cf. Rom 1:24-32).

*See also* PROPHET, PAUL AS; WORLD, COSMOLOGY.

BIBLIOGRAPHY. H. Balz, "μάταιος κτλ," *EDNT* 2.396-97; C. K. Barrett, *The Epistle to the Romans* (HNTC; New York: Harper & Row, 1957); O. Bauernfeind, "μάταιος κτλ," *TDNT* IV.519-24; J. D. G. Dunn, *Romans 1-8* (WBC 41; Dallas: Word, 1988); M. Lattke, "κενός," *EDNT* 2.281-82; A. Oepke, "κενός κτλ," *TDNT* III.659-62; E. Tiedtke et al., "Empty, Vain," *NIDNTT* 1.546-53.

P. W. Comfort

# G

**GALATIA.** *See* GALATIANS, LETTER TO THE.

## GALATIANS, LETTER TO THE

Freedom* and unity in Christ are central themes of Paul's letter to the Galatians. His letter addresses Christians, whose preoccupation with keeping the Law* was splitting their churches along racial lines, separating Jews from Gentiles.* Such splits could not be tolerated because "there is neither Jew nor Greek, slave nor free, male nor female; for you are all one in Christ Jesus" (Gal 3:28). This new unity which transcends all racial, social and sexual barriers is based upon the "truth of the gospel*" (Gal 2:5): Christ was crucified to set us free from the curse* of the Law so that we might receive his Spirit (Gal 3:13-14; *see* Holy Spirit). It is the Spirit, not the Law, who gives us our identity as children of God (Gal 4:6; *see* Adoption, Sonship). Believers must protect their freedom from slavery to the Law (Gal 5:1) and yet use their freedom to fulfill the Law by serving one another through love* (Gal 5:13-14). We are no longer under the Law that divides us; we are led by the Spirit who unites us. Paul undergirds these central concepts of freedom through the cross of Christ and unity by his Spirit with other complementary themes: an account of his own call to evangelize the Gentiles (Gal 1:13-16), a record of his loyalty to the gospel for the Gentiles in his relationships with the other apostles (Gal 1:17—2:21), an explanation of justification* by faith, not by works of the Law (Gal 2:16; 3:6-12; *see* Works of the Law), an exposition of OT texts on the Abrahamic* promise and the Mosaic Law in the context of salvation history (Gal 3:6-25; 4:21-31), and a definition of Christian ethics* in terms of the flesh* and the Spirit (Gal 5:13—6:10).

The significance of these central themes in Galatians gives this letter a predominant place in any consideration of Pauline chronology* and theology. The letter has had a profound impact on Christian thought and action throughout the history of the church. Luther called it "my own epistle, to which I have plighted my troth; my Katie von Bora."

1. Galatia

2. Historical Context
3. Literary Forms
4. Contents

### 1. Galatia.

Paul's letter "to the churches in Galatia" (Gal 1:2) rebuked the recipients for being "foolish Galatians" (Gal 3:1). His letter to the Corinthian church instructed that church to do what he had told "the churches of Galatia" to do concerning the collection (1 Cor 16:1). In a letter to Timothy he informed Timothy that "Crescens has gone to Galatia" (2 Tim 4:10). The geographical location of the churches in Galatia and the ethnic origin of the Galatians referred to by Paul is still a topic much debated by NT scholars. Some (notably, J. B. Lightfoot and H. D. Betz), following the majority of patristic, medieval and Reformation commentators, have argued that Galatians was written to Christians of Celtic (Gaulish) descent who were living in or around Ancyra, Pessinus and Tavium, three cities in northern Asia Minor. Others (notably, E. deW. Burton, F. F. Bruce and R. N. Longenecker) argue that the "churches in Galatia" were planted by Paul, as recorded in Acts 13—14, in Pisidian Antioch, Iconium, Lystra and Derbe in southern Asia Minor and consisted of Gentiles from diverse ethnic origins (Phrygians, Pisidians and Lyconians). The references in Acts 16:6 ("the region of Phrygia and Galatia") and Acts 18:23 ("the region of Galatia and Phrygia") have been claimed as support by both sides in this debate. To understand the background for this debate, it is necessary to review three stages in the history of Galatia: the Celtic invasion, Hellenistic Galatia and Roman Galatia.

*1.1. The Celtic Invasion.* When an army of Celts (also called Gauls or Galatians by Greek and Latin authors) invaded and subsequently settled in north-central Asia Minor (modern Turkey), they gave their new homeland their own name, Galatia. Those Celts (or Galatians, as they were usually called in Asia Minor), who were of the same ethnic origin as the Celts of France and Britain, had migrated from central Europe to Greece. According to the Roman historian, Livy (A.D. 23-79), they became "inflamed with desire" to cross into the rich land of Asia. Their opportunity came when they were invited by Nicomedes I, king of Bithynia, who needed mercenaries in his campaign to recapture the greater part of Bithynia. In 278 B.C. some 20,000 Galatians waged war on behalf of Nicomedes until all of Bithynia acknowledged his sovereignty. Livy describes those fierce Galatian warriors, who inspired such terror "that the most distant and nearest alike obeyed their orders: . . . tall bodies, long reddish hair, huge shields, very long swords; in addition, songs as they go into battle and yells and leapings and the dreadful din of arms as they clash shields according to some ancestral customs—all these are deliberately used to terrify their foes" (Livy *Hist.* 38.18.3-9.)

Livy's real purpose in giving this description was to demonstrate the might of Rome in defeating such awesome foes ("how far Roman valor surpasses Gallic madness"). But there must be some truth in his account because other ancient sources describe the way they ravaged western and north-central Asia Minor, and were paid tribute by even the Seleucid kingdom until Attalus I, king of Pergamum, was finally able to defeat them and confine them within fixed boundaries after 232 B.C. Their territory was over 200 miles from southwest to northeast, bounded by Lyconia and Pamphylia to the south, by Bithynia, Paphlagonia and Pontus to the north, by Cappadocia to the east and by Phrygia to the west.

The Galatian people inhabiting this territory consisted of three tribes: the most powerful, the Trocmi, settled in the east around Tavium; to the Tectosages belonged the fortress Ancyra (modern Ankara); the Tolistobogii lived in the area around Pessinus in the western part of the Galatian territory. Each tribe was subdivided into four tetrarchies, each tetrarchy having its own tetrarch, judge, military commander and two subordinate commanders. Representatives from the twelve tetrarchies formed one council which assembled at Drynemetum. The Galatian nobility ruled over the native population. Although the Galatians maintained their own Celtic language, to some extent they adopted the religion of the country. Thus a Celtic invasion from the west was the origin of Galatia in Asia Minor.

*1.2. Hellenistic Galatia.* Writing in the first century A.D. from a Roman perspective, Livy described the Hellenization of the Galatians: "those forefathers of ours had to do with true Gauls, born in their own land; these are now degenerates, of mixed race, and really Gallogrecians, as they are named" (Livy *Hist.* 28.17.9). Although the Galatians became known as the "Gallo-

grecians," Greek-speaking Galatians, they are depicted by the ancient Greek and Latin historians as barbaric warriors, invading and ransacking neighboring countries. They were more influenced by local Phrygian culture and religion than by Hellenization. In Pessinus they participated in the famous ancient temple of the Phrygian goddess, the Mother of gods, called Agdistis. The sanctuary with its porticoes of white marble was an object of great veneration. The priests were called potentates because of the immense power they exercised in their society.

The Galatian form of government became more totalitarian: by 63 B.C. the tribes were no longer ruled by a council and tetrarchs, but by three tribal kings; by 42 B.C. Deiotarus gained control of all Galatia after a civil war. In a series of battles the Galatians fought against the power of Rome. In 190 B.C. they sided with the Seleucid king, Antiochus III, against Rome, but they were defeated at Magnesia in 189 B.C. by Consul Manlius Vulso.

The Galatians began to see the benefits of supporting the Roman cause. So when the Roman general, Pompey, marched against Mithradates V, the Galatians were on Pompey's side. In 64 B.C. Pompey rewarded their support by designating Galatia as a client kingdom and expanding its borders to include regions to the south and east. When in 36 B.C. Galatia was passed to Amyntas, the secretary and general of Deiotarus, the territory included portions of Pisidia and Phrygia. Later Amyntas acquired a large part of Lyconia and was given a section of Cilicia called Cilicia Tracheia and also much of Pisidia and Isauria by Augustus as a reward for his aid in the battle of Actium. As a result the territory of Galatia included a large area in the southern part of Asia Minor that had never been ethnically Galatian. When Amyntas, the last king of Galatia, was killed in battle against the Homanadenses in 25 B.C., Augustus did not entrust the Galatian kingdom to the sons of Amyntas, but instead reorganized it as a Roman province under the authority of a Roman governor. Thus the Galatian kingdom became the Roman province of Galatia.

*1.3. Roman Galatia.* As a Roman province, Galatia included the original territory (the area from Pessinus in the west to Tavium in the east) with major additions from other regions: Phrygia, Isauria and Pisidia. Such cities and villages as Antioch of Pisidia, Iconium, Lystra and Derbe were now within the boundaries of the Galatian province. Portions of Pamphylia formerly belonging to Amyntas were restored by Augustus to Pamphylia and parts of eastern Lyconia and Cilicia Tracheia were transferred to his ally Archelaus, king of Cappadocia. But in 5 B.C. the Galatian province was again enlarged by new annexations: a large section of Paphlagonia to the north was added and about three years later part of Pontus was added and then designated as Pontus Galatica, to distinguish it from the rest of Pontus which did not belong to Galatia.

By analogy with this official Roman designation of Pontus Galatica, it has been inferred that the references in Acts 16:6 and 18:23 should be taken as proper designations for Phrygia Galatica, that part of Phrygia which is included within the province of Galatia, to distinguish it from that part of Phrygia which lay within proconsular Asia (Phrygia Asiana). On this basis, Acts 13:14—14:23 is viewed as an account of the planting of churches in the region of Phrygia Galatica and Acts 16:6 and 18:23 are taken as references to Paul's subsequent visits in the same region. The alternative view that these references in Acts 16:6 and 18:23 describe a visit of Paul in the northern, original territory of Galatia fails to recognize the grammatical construction of these phrases in Acts ("the region of Galatia and Phrygia" indicates one region, not two) and the historical construction of the Roman province of Galatia. It seems that Acts follows the typical Greek practice of describing a Roman province by listing the regions within that province.

Thus in the time of Paul the Roman province of Galatia extended from Pontus on the Black Sea to Pamphylia on the Mediterranean. "The churches of Galatia" addressed by Paul might have been in the northern ethnic territory of the Galatian tribes in the vicinity of the chief cities, Pessinus, Ancyra and Tavium, or they might have been in the southern region of the expanded Roman province of Galatia where, according to the account in Acts 13—14, Paul visited Antioch of Pisidia, Iconium, Lystra and Derbe. Either a North Galatia or a South Galatia address is theoretically possible as a result of the greatly expanded boundaries of the Roman province of Galatia in the first century A.D.

The Greek geographer Strabo describes the population of the province as a mixed one and distinguishes Galatians, Paphlagonians, Phrygians, Pisidians, Lyconians and Isaurians. Most of these ethnic groups maintained their own languages. But whatever their mother tongues or ethnic backgrounds may have been, all inhabitants of the Roman province of Galatia were considered Galatians. Inscriptions bearing the names of slaves refer to them as Galatians even though none of them has a Celtic name. An inscription (1st century A.D.) of Pednelissus, on the southern edge of Pisidia, designates that city as "the city of the Galatians." Another inscription of Apollonia in the Phrygian region of the province called the residents of that city Galatians. In such places as Athens and Rhodes there are numerous inscriptions on tombstones which designate resident aliens as Galatians even though the names are almost uniformly Greek, though some show a Phrygian background.

It seems that the name of Galatians was widely used as a designation for persons of Phrygian as well as Celtic origin. Although this fact is well attested (see esp. Hemer, 299-305), it is disputed by such reputable authorities as W. Bauer's *Greek-English Lexicon* and the *IDB* article on Galatia. The latter insists that "the name of Galatians would hardly be an appropriate designation for all the inhabitants of the Roman province, but rather would evoke special memories of the history of the tribe" (Mellink, 338). But if Galatians were only a designation for pure-blooded Celts, it could only have been applied to a very small number of the Celtic aristocracy. S. Mitchell provides ample evidence to show that

> although the nobility seems to have kept distinct from the subject population, the lower class probably intermarried freely and by the second century B.C. has become at least partly amalgamated with it. It is significant that the peasant population at this date was referred to not as Phrygian but as Galatian, although it is quite clear that most of it was of Anatolian origin. (Mitchell, 1058)

Even where Celtic names are found, they are usually in association with Greek, Roman or Phrygian family name types. So the pure-blooded Celt must have been very rare indeed. The entry in BAGD bases its case on Memmon's frequent use of the name of Galatians for "the people with a well-defined individuality, who came to Asia Minor from Europe." On this basis it is claimed that Memmon "would certainly never address Lycaonians as Galatians" (BAGD, 150). Presumably, we are to infer that Paul would follow the same practice as Memmon (a questionable inference in itself). Memmon, a contemporary of Paul, wrote a lengthy history of his own city, Heraclea Pontica. The purpose of his references to the Galatians was to show how the Celtic invasion in the third century B.C. weakened his city and reduced its territory. So his references do not establish the proper designation for the residents of the Roman province of Galatia in the first century A.D.

The evidence indicates that the name of the Celtic invaders became the name of honor for many diverse peoples of Asia Minor within the expanded borders of the Roman province of Galatia in the first century A.D. So members of churches anywhere in the Roman province of Galatia would have been regarded as Galatians in Paul's time. The question of their location in North or South Galatia cannot be decided one way or the other simply on a geographical basis and must await further treatment in the discussion of Paul's letter to the Galatians.

Near the end of the first century (c. A.D. 74), Vespasian detached most of Pisidia from the Galatian province. In the second century (c. A.D. 137) the Lyconian portion of the province was transferred to Cilicia and Isauria to form an enlarged province of Cilicia. Then near the end of the third century (c. A.D. 297) the remainder of the southern regions of Galatia were transferred to a new province of Pisidia, with Pisidian Antioch as its capital and Iconium as its second city. The province of Galatia was thus reduced to approximately its ancient ethnological dimensions, the original northern territory of the Celtic invaders. It is not surprising, therefore, that patristic commentators, followed by medieval and Reformation commentators, assumed that Paul addressed his letter to churches in North Galatia since that was the only Galatia there was in patristic times.

*1.4. Culture and Religion of Roman Galatia.* Galatia was a rural province. The few major cities, notably Ancyra and Pisidian Antioch, and small villages were separated by vast tracts of countryside. The province was normally able to supply its own needs for food by the production of grain, the basic staple of life. Wool was the product that brought wealth to the province. Much of the central and southern area of the country was a huge sheep farm. Strabo informs us that many people made their fortunes from sheep, especially Amyntas, who had three hundred flocks. Many of the decorated tombstones of Galatia depict the same objects: a yoke of oxen with plow and sickles to portray the planting and harvesting of grain, a distaff and bobbin to indicate the care of sheep and weaving of wool, and a vine or bunch of grapes to show that for many the production of wine was important.

The vast areas of farmland and grazing land were crisscrossed by Roman roads which tied the cities and villages together in a remarkably efficient communications system. The Phrygian cult of the Mother of gods was widespread as were temples to Zeus (see Acts 14:13). When Ancyra became the capital of the Roman province of Galatia, the imperial cult was established there. The remains of the temple of Augustus and Roma can still be seen in Ancyra (now Ankara, the capital of modern Turkey).

## 2. Historical Context.

To understand the central themes of the letter we must consider the historical context: the authorship, addressees and date of the letter.

*2.1. Authorship.* Paul introduces himself in the first line as "Paul an apostle" (Gal 1:1) and underlines the authority of his decision regarding the problem in the Galatian churches with the words, "Behold, I Paul say to you . . ." (Gal 5:2). His authorship is accepted by all except a few radical critics. Almost all scholars view Galatians as the standard example of Paul's style and theology.

*2.2. Addressees.* Paul addresses the recipients as his own children (Gal 4:19). To sharpen our focus on these believers we need to consider their location, Paul's relationship with them and the crisis they faced in their churches.

*2.2.1. Location of the Churches.* Paul addressed his letter to the "churches in Galatia " (Gal 1:2). Scholars are divided regarding the geographical location of these churches (see discussion above). The weight of evidence seems to be in favor of a south Galatian location. In Paul's time Galatia was the name for the entire Roman province, stretching from Pontus in the north to Pamphylia in the south. All the residents of this entire province were properly called Galatians whatever their ethnic origin. Paul normally classified the churches that he founded according to provinces: "churches of Asia" (1 Cor 16:19); "churches of Macedonia" (2 Cor 8:1) or "Achaia" (2 Cor 9:2). So it would be natural for Paul to refer to churches in Antioch of Pisidia, Iconium, Lystra and Derbe (all cities within the Roman province of Galatia) as churches in Galatia and to refer to the members of those churches as Galatians. Indeed, there would be no other single name which would be appropriate for them. Since there is no clear evidence that Paul founded churches in north Galatia, it seems best to take the account of Acts 13—14 as a record of the founding of the churches in Galatia which are addressed in Paul's letter to the Galatians. Acts 16:6 and 18:23 refer to subsequent visits by Paul to strengthen those same churches in Galatia.

*2.2.2. Paul's Relation to the Churches in Galatia.* Paul's description of his first visit to Galatia indicates that he went there because of some repulsive physical illness (*see* Healing, Illness). Nevertheless, when he preached the gospel there his converts received him as if he were an angel of God, as if he were Christ himself. Their response to Paul was extremely generous. Paul says that if it were possible, they would have given him their own eyes (Gal 4:12-15). When Paul portrayed Christ* crucified, they believed and received the Holy Spirit* (Gal 3:1-2).

*2.2.3. The Crisis in the Galatian Churches.* Soon after Paul planted the churches in Galatia, they were infiltrated by "troublemakers" who preached a gospel different from Paul's (Gal 1:6-9). The identity of these troublemakers has been the subject of extensive discussion (*see* Judaizers; Opponents).

It is most likely that they were Jewish Christians who insisted that it was necessary to belong to the Jewish nation in order to receive the blessing of God.* Therefore they required the badges of identity peculiar to the Jewish people: circumcision,* Sabbath observance (*see* Holy Days) and keeping the Mosaic Law. No doubt they appealed to the example of Abraham's* circumcision in their campaign to persuade the Galatian believers that without circumcision it was impossible to participate in the covenantal blessings promised to Abraham. Probably the intruders had preempted Paul's authority by claiming support from the higher authority* of the original apostles in the Jerusalem* church.

The troublemakers were winning the Galatian converts over to their side. Evidently their message met a need in the Galatian churches. They may well have felt a loss of identity since their faith in Christ excluded them from both their pagan temples and from the Jewish synagogues. So they sought identification with the Jewish people to gain a sense of belonging to God's people. It also appears that they wanted to come under the discipline of the Mosaic Law because they believed that the Law would give them clear guidance in their moral struggle. In any case, they were mesmerized by the message of the intruders and had become negative toward Paul.

*2.3. Date.* Paul provides an autobiographical sketch of his life from the time of his conversion to the time of writing this letter. A comparison of this autobiography with his other letters and Acts has led to a number of conflicting hypotheses regarding the place of this letter in the chronology* of Paul's life (*see* Paul in Acts and Letters). These hypotheses can be evaluated on the basis of a consideration of three lines of evidence: (1) the Jerusalem visits; (2) the meaning of "former" in Galatians 4:13; and (3) the location of the churches in North or South Galatia.

*2.3.1. The Jerusalem Visits and the Date.* The basic point of dispute in the discussion of the Jerusalem visits revolves around the matching of Paul's visits to Jerusalem described in this letter and his visits to Jerusalem described in Acts. Only two visits are mentioned in Galatians: (1) Galatians 1:18, first post-conversion visit; and (2) Galatians 2:1-10, conference visit. Five of Paul's visits to Jerusalem are recorded in Acts: (1) Acts 9:26-30, first post-conversion visit; (2) Acts 11:30, famine relief visit; (3) Acts 15:1-30, conference visit; (4) Acts 18:22, quick visit; and (5) Acts 21:15-17, arrest visit. Of the many attempts to relate the visits described in Galatians to those of Acts, two merit special attention: Galatians 2:1-10 = Acts 15:1-30; and Galatians 2:1-10 = Acts 11:30.

*2.3.1.1. Galatians 2:1-10 = Acts 15:1-30.* If we match the Galatians 1:18 (first post-conversion) visit with the Acts 9:26-30 (first post-conversion) visit and the Galatians 2:1-10 conference visit with the Acts 15:1-30 conference visit, then Paul's letter to the Galatians would be placed after the Jerusalem conference described in Acts 15:1-30 (= Gal 2:1-10). Such an equation seems reasonable since both accounts of the conference visit refer to the same issue (the obligation of Gentile converts to keep the Jewish Law), the same participants (Paul and Barnabas* go to Jerusalem to confer with Peter* and James* and others) and the same decision (the requirement of circumcision is not imposed upon Gentile converts).

Two major objections raised against this equation are Paul's omissions under oath in Galatians 1:20 of any reference to the famine relief visit (Acts 11:27-30) or any reference to the "Apostolic Decrees" of the conference (Acts 15:20, 29). Some scholars assert that to hold to the equation of Galatians 2:1-10 and Acts 15:1-20 in the light of these two omissions necessarily involves an attack on the truthfulness of Paul's account or the account in Acts or both. Yet such scholars as J. B. Lightfoot and J. G. Machen, who certainly uphold the reliability of both accounts, argue that these two omissions on Paul's part can be explained on the basis that they are not relevant to his discussion in Galatians and therefore Paul was not obliged to record them. Since the point of Paul's autobiography was to record his relationship with the original apostles in Jerusalem, not simply his visits to Jerusalem, it was not necessary for him to refer to the famine-relief visit (Acts 11:27-30) since he did not meet with the apostles then. At least the account in Acts of that visit makes no mention of such a meeting. And it makes sense that Paul would not refer to the "Apostolic Decrees" since they are not viewed in the Acts account as a negation of the major decision not to require circumcision. Therefore, Paul's claim that "those who seemed to be important . . . added nothing to my message" (Gal 2:6) fits with the record in Acts. Since the Galatian Christians were all too eager to come under whatever decrees came from the Jerusalem church, Paul may have decided that any mention of the "Apostolic Decrees" would have been ill advised, unless absolutely necessary. Since he never appealed to the "Apostolic Decrees" in any of his letters, we may conclude that he did not feel obligated to do so (though some have suggested that he may have been out of sympathy with the Decrees). After all, his authority was not based on decrees from Jerusalem but on "revelation from Jesus Christ" (Gal 1:12).

Another criticism of the Galatians 2:1-10 = Acts 15:1-20 equation is that this equation makes it difficult to explain the withdrawal of Peter and "even Barnabas" from table fellowship with Gentile Christians in Antioch* (Gal 2:11-14) after guidelines for such fellowship were established at the conference according to the Acts account. But even if the conflict in Antioch occurred before the Acts 15 conference, as some scholars suggest, it still is difficult to explain Peter's behavior. We still have to ask why he would withdraw from table fellowship with Gentile Christians in Antioch after the Jerusalem conference described by Paul in Galatians 2:1-10. From Paul's perspective, Peter's conduct is indefensible because it violates the truth* of the gospel which had been defended in the Jerusalem conference.

*2.3.1.2. Galatians 2:1-10 = Acts 11:27-30.* The criticisms of the Galatians 2:1-10 = Acts 15:1-20 equation have led some to suggest another equation: Galatians 2:1-10 = Acts 11:27-30. The benefit of this equation is that it avoids any suspicion that Paul has failed to report all of his visits to Jerusalem after his conversion since in this equation the first two visits in Acts equal the two visits listed in Galatians. And Paul did not refer to the Apostolic Decrees for the simple reason that this letter was written before the Acts 15 conference when those decrees were set forth. This equation also takes at face value the statement in Galatians 1:21, "Later I went to Syria and Cilicia." If Galatians 2:1-20 refers to the Jerusalem conference that came after Paul's mission in Galatia, then Galatia must be read into the statement in Galatians 1:21. But if Galatians 2:1-10 refers to a conference that occurred during the Acts 11:27-30 visit, then the natural reading of the text stands: Paul was only in Syria and Cilicia between the two Jerusalem visits of Galatians 1:18 and 2:1-10.

It is also easy to see similarities between Paul's account of the conflict in Antioch in Galatians 2:11-14 and the conflict in Antioch before the Jerusalem conference described in Acts 15:1-2. Both refer to a conflict over the application of the Jewish Law to Gentile converts and both indicate that the conflict was caused by a delegation from Jerusalem. If these accounts refer to the same event, then it would be reasonable to conclude that Paul wrote Galatians on the eve of the Jerusalem conference of Acts 15:1-20. And if so, then we can identify the conference visit of Galatians 2:1-10 with the famine-relief visit of Acts 11:27-30.

But this identification also faces problems. There is no record of a conference visit in Acts 11:27-30 or even any indication that Paul and Barnabas met with the apostles. Of course, Acts is a selective account, but there is very little evidence in the text for matching the Galatians 2:1-10 visit with the Acts 11:27-30 visit. Even though there are minor differences between Galatians 2:1-10 and Acts 15:1-20, at least both passages seem to describe a conference in Jerusalem. Furthermore, if Galatians 2:1-10 = Acts 11:27-30, then there were two conferences in Jerusalem. Many scholars have thought that it is highly unlikely that there were two conferences where the same people debated the same issue with the same outcome. This duplication of conferences is unnecessary if the Galatians 2:1-10 = Acts 15:1-20 equation stands.

*2.3.2. The "First" Visit and the Date (Gal 4:13).* Paul's reference to the time when he "first preached the gospel" in Galatia (Gal 4:13) has been taken as a clue for the date of the letter. Unfortunately, all sides of the debate claim this clue as support. Even if the term "first" should be taken as a true comparative (the "former" of two), it is by no means clear which visit it designates: it could either refer to the Acts 16:6 visit as the one before the second visit of Acts 18:23, or it could refer to the visit of Acts 13:14—14:23 as the one before the second visit of Acts 16:6, or it could refer to the Acts 13:14—14:21a visit as the one before the return journey of Acts 14:21b-23. So this term does not provide much help in dating the letter to the Galatians.

*2.3.3. The Destination and the Date.* The question of the date of the letter is related to the question of destination. But it must be admitted that a determination of the destination does not necessarily decide the date. If the framework of Acts is accepted, then a destination of north Galatia means that the letter was written after the so-called second missionary journey (after Acts 18:22), sometime between A.D. 53 and 57. If south Galatia was the destination (as seems more likely in light of the discussion above), the letter could have been written immediately after the first missionary journey and before the Jerusalem conference in A.D. 49. But if the equation of Galatians 2:1-10 = Acts 15:1-20 is slightly favored by the evidence as argued above, then the letter was written to south Galatia sometime after the Jerusalem conference, anytime between A.D. 50 and 57.

It has often been noted that a comparison of Galatians with 2 Corinthians and Romans shows a similarity of tone and themes, especially related to the controversy over the role of the Jewish Law in Gentile churches. This similarity may indicate that these three letters were written during the same time, a time when Paul faced a fierce struggle for the freedom of his Gentile churches from pressure to succumb to bondage to the Jewish way of life. But attempts to date the letter on the basis of such theological comparisons with other letters have been used to support early (Longenecker) and late (Lightfoot) dates. The subjective approach of such comparisons and the occasional nature of Paul's letters (each letter responds to a specific occasion) render these attempts at best only secondary lines of support for theories in search of firmer ground.

The dating of Galatians is a notorious and for some a fascinating historical puzzle. But the outcome of the protracted debate about the date has little if any effect on the interpretation of the major themes of the letter.

### 3. Literary Forms.

Considerable attention has been given in recent years to the literary form of Galatians.

**3.1. The Form of the Letter.** A detailed comparison of Galatians to Hellenistic letters (see Letters, Letter Forms) of the same period indicates that Paul used a standard form of letter called the "rebuke-request" form (see Hansen and Longenecker). Unlike his custom in all the rest of his letters, in Galatians Paul does not follow his salutation (Gal 1:1-5) with any form of thanksgiving. Instead, he expresses astonishment and rebuke: "I am astonished that you have so quickly departed from the one who called you by grace" (Gal 1:6).

The expression "I am astonished" was often used in letters of that time as a rebuke for not meeting the expectations of the writer. The expression of rebuke was usually followed by reasons for the rebuke. Paul scolds his readers for their disloyalty to the gospel (Gal 1:6-10) and undergirds that rebuke with an autobiographical account of his loyalty to the truth of the gospel (Gal 1:11—2:21). Then he rebukes them for their foolishness regarding the gospel (Gal 3:1-5) and undergirds that rebuke by explaining the meaning of the gospel in the light of his exposition of the Scriptures (Gal 3:6—4:11). Letters of rebuke contained requests to set things right. Paul begins his request in Galatians 4:12 with the personal appeal to imitate* him in his stand for the freedom of the gospel. This appeal is strengthened by an autobiographical account of his relationship with the Galatian believers (Gal 4:12-20) and an allegorical treatment of the Abraham story (Gal 4:21-31). The request to stand fast for freedom is then spelled out in a series of specific ethical instructions (Gal 5:1—6:10). Paul underlines the main themes of the letter in his own hand-written subscription (Gal 6:11-18).

**3.2. The Structure of the Argument.** Recent rhetorical analyses have attempted to explain the methods and structures of Paul's argumentation in Galatians (see Rhetoric; Rhetorical Criticism). They point to many similarities between the structure of Paul's argument in Galatians and the guidelines for rhetoric in the classical rhetorical handbooks. H. D. Betz classifies Paul's argument as an example of forensic rhetoric since he is viewed as adopting the tactics of persuasion used in the law court to address the judge or jury in order to defend or accuse someone regarding past actions. Paul defends himself against accusations (Gal 1:10); at the same time he accuses his opponents of perverting the gospel (Gal 1:7). Using the categories of classical forensic rhetoric, Betz outlines Galatians as follows:

    I. Epistolary Prescript (Gal 1:1-5)
    II. *Exordium* ("introduction," Gal 1:6-11)
    III. *Narratio* ("narration," Gal 1:12—2:14)
    IV. *Propositio* ("proposition," Gal 2:15-21)
    V. *Probatio* ("confirmation," 3:1—4:31)
    VI. *Exhortatio* ("exhortation," Gal 5:1—6:10)
    VII. Epistolary Postscript-*Peroratio* ("conclusion," Gal 6:11-18)

But Betz has to admit that he is not able to cite parallels to the exhortation section (Gal 5:1—6:10) from the classical rhetorical handbooks. For this reason G. Kennedy argues that Galatians is best viewed as deliberative rhetoric, since it aims to exhort or dissuade the audience regarding future actions by demonstrating that those actions are expedient or harmful. Paul seeks to dissuade the Galatian believers from following the false teachers by pointing to the harmful effects: severance from Christ and grace* (Gal 5:4), exclusion from the kingdom* of God (Gal 5:21) and a reaping of corruption (Gal 6:8). He underscores the expediency of the course of action which he has exhorted them to follow by giving them the promise of the harvest of eternal life (Gal 6:8) and granting them the benediction upon all those who walk according to "this canon" (Gal 6:16).

It seems best to classify Paul's argument in Galatians as a mixture of forensic and deliberative rhetoric. The rebuke section of the letter (Gal 1:6—4:11) has the characteristics of forensic rhetoric, but at Galatians 4:12 a major rhetorical shift to deliberative rhetoric occurs. Paul is no longer so much concerned to accuse or defend as he is to persuade the Galatian believers to adopt a certain course of action. He begins his appeal to this new course of action in Galatians 4:12: "Become as I am." That exhortation is then supported by the command from the Abraham story to "cast out the slave and her son" (Gal 4:30), clarified by authoritative instructions to stand in freedom (Gal 5:1-12) and defined in specific terms in the ethical exhortation to walk in the Spirit (Gal 5:13—6:10). The following pattern thus emerges:

Salutation (Gal 1:1-5)
    Rebuke (Gal 1:6—4:11)
        Autobiography (Gal 1:13—2:21)
        Argument from Scripture (3:6-29)
    Request (Gal 4:12—6:10)
        Autobiography (Gal 4:12-20)
        Allegory from Scripture (Gal 4:21-31)
        Ethical instruction (Gal 5:1—6:10)
Subscription (Gal 6:11-18)

## 4. Contents.

*4.1. Salutation (Gal 1:1-5).* Beyond the standard elements of sender, addressees and greetings, present in all his salutations, this opening paragraph contains two significant theological statements which anticipate central themes of the letter. First, in Galatians 1:1 Paul's designation of himself as an apostle* goes beyond his references to his apostolic position in his other letters. His double denial of any dependence on human agency or authority for the legitimacy of his apostleship and his claim to a divine commission place an emphasis on apostolic authority that will be an important feature in his letter. Second, Paul's declaration that the cross* of Christ is the way to freedom from the present evil age (Gal 1:4) sets the cross in the center of his theology, where it stays through to the very end of the letter (Gal 2:19, 21; 3:1, 13; 4:5; 5:11, 24; 6:12, 14). Paul's central argument is that the cross alone is the way of salvation and therefore all attempts to supplement the work of the cross with works of the Law must be totally rejected.

*4.2. Rebuke (Gal 1:6—4:11).* Immediately after the opening paragraph Paul expresses his rebuke for the Galatians' desertion to a perverted gospel (Gal 1:6) and places anyone who distorts the gospel of Christ under a double curse (Gal 1:7-9). In this way Paul establishes at the outset the ultimate measure of genuine authority: adherence to the one gospel. Paul's recognition that he himself will be judged by the standard of the gospel as a servant of Christ keeps him from seeking human approval (Gal 1:10). The standard of the gospel was not derived from human tradition; it was given by "the revelation of Jesus Christ" (Gal 1:11-12): Jesus Christ is both the source and the subject of the gospel.

*4.2.1. Autobiography (Gal 1:13—2:21).* Paul's autobiography is essentially a portrayal of his faithfulness to the one true gospel: he was called by God to preach the gospel (Gal 1:16); he defended the gospel in the Jerusalem conference (Gal 2:1-10) and in the conflict with Peter (Gal 2:11-14); and he embodied the essence of the gospel (Gal 2:15-21). His record as a loyal representative of the gospel stands as the basis of his authority* as an apostle* and as a sharp rebuke to the Galatian believers' disloyalty to the gospel.

The primary point of Paul's story of his call (Gal 1:13-21; *see* Conversion and Call) is to stress that he was called by God, not by the church, to preach the gospel. Before God's gracious call stopped Paul in his tracks, he was engaged in a campaign to destroy the church of God because of his zealous devotion to the traditions of Judaism (Gal 1:13-14). God's call was not an afterthought; like the prophets of old (see Jer 1:5 and Is 49:1; *see* Prophet, Paul as), Paul had been set aside from his mother's womb (Gal 1:15). Paul heard the call when God revealed his Son to him so that he would preach Christ to the Gentiles (Gal 1:16). When Paul heard the call, he did not confer with "flesh and blood" or go up to Jerusalem to those who were apostles before him; instead he went into Arabia and then returned to Damascus (Gal 1:16-17). It was only three years later that he first had a short visit with Peter in Jerusalem. Except for James, Peter was the only apostle that Paul saw at that time (Gal 1:18-19). And after that visit he was in the regions of Syria and Cilicia, unknown by face to the church in Judea; they only heard that he was now preaching the faith he had previously tried to destroy (Gal 1:21-24). This part of the story defends Paul's independence from the original apostles. God directly commissioned him to be an apostle to the Gentiles.

But Paul did not work independently. As the next episode in his autobiography shows, he had the full support of those considered most important as leaders in Jerusalem (Gal 2:1-10). As a result of the council in Jerusalem, Paul and Barnabas were given the right hand of fellowship by the leaders of the mother church in support of their mission to the Gentiles. The leaders in Jerusalem did not add anything to Paul's message (Gal 2:6-9). But even though Paul worked to establish a consensus with these leaders, he was not willing to allow arch-conservative Jewish "Christians" (counterfeit Christians, in Paul's eyes) to destroy his mission* to the Gentiles. When there was pressure to get his Gentile companion, Titus, circumcised, Paul refused to give in; he stood for "the truth of the gospel." (As he hopes the Galatian believers will also do when they are pressured to be circumcised.)

In the next episode of his autobiography, Paul describes how he confronted Peter in order to defend the truth of the gospel (Gal 2:11-14). When Peter* visited the church in Antioch,* he followed the custom in the integrated congregation of Christian Jews and Gentiles of eating with Gentile Christians. Undoubtedly his presence at table fellowship with Gentiles was taken as an official stamp of approval on the union and equality of Jews and Gentiles in the church. But when some representatives who were sent by James from the church in Jerusalem came to Antioch, they persuaded Peter to stop the practice of Jews eating with Gentiles in the church. According to Paul, Peter gave in to their demand because he feared those who were circumcised, namely, the Jews. This probably means that he became concerned about the detrimental effect that his table fellowship with the Gentiles would have on the mission of the church in Jerusalem to the Jews. If non-Christian Jews in Jerusalem heard that Peter was eating with Gentiles, they might not only turn away from the witness of the church but also become actively hostile to the church for tolerating such a practice (for social background in Palestine *see* Revolutionary Movements).

Peter's withdrawal from table fellowship with the Gentiles split the church into Jewish and Gentile factions and by action if not by word compelled the Gentiles to think that they would have to become Jews if they wanted to enjoy table fellowship with the apostles and the mother church. From Paul's perspective, Peter's action was not a legitimate accommodation for the sake of the gospel; it was a compromise of the essential truth of the gospel. Peter was charged with hypocrisy, not heresy. Peter and Paul did not disagree about the truth of the gospel; but Peter's action was inconsistent with his belief in the gospel. By going along with Jewish adherence to the Law, which required the separation of Jews and Gentiles and implied that incorporation into the Jewish nation was necessary for salvation,* Peter had denied the essence of the gospel, which proclaimed that salvation for both Jews and Gentiles was by way of the cross and incorporation into Christ. The conflict in Antioch was a mirror image of the crisis faced by the Galatian believers, since the issue of compelling Gentiles to live like Jews was precisely the central issue for the churches in Galatia.

Paul wraps up his autobiography with a statement that is both intensely personal and at the same time serves as a paradigm for all Christians (Gal 2:15-21). In his own experience as a Jew by birth (Gal 2:15; *see* Jew, Paul the), he knew that he was justified by faith in Christ, not by works* of the Law (Gal 2:16). By implication it must be clear that those who are Gentile sinners (Gal 2:15) could only be justified by faith* in Christ and not by works of the Law. Paul sought justification* only in Christ, but he was found to be a sinner on the basis of the Law (Gal 2:17) because he was eating with Gentiles. Since his table fellowship with Gentiles was on the basis of common faith in Christ, Christ was blamed for being the agent who caused Paul to break the Law by eating with Gentiles (Gal 2:17). But Paul adamantly rejects any notion that Christ is an agent of sin.* For it is only if the Law which separates Jews and Gentiles were to be rebuilt that then Paul would be proved to be a sinner on the basis of the Law (Gal 2:18). But in fact he has died to the Law, so the Law can no longer be used to condemn table fellowship with Gentiles. His death to Law was accomplished by union with Christ in his death—"I am crucified with Christ" (Gal 2:19).

Death to the Law did not mean moral license but the means for achieving the highest goal—"that I might live to God" (Gal 2:19). This life* to God is empowered by Christ ("Christ lives in me"); it is lived by faith in Christ ("I live by faith in the Son of God"); it is motivated by the sacrificial love of Christ ("who loved me and gave himself for me"). Paul's experience sets forth an either-or choice: either attempt to attain righteousness* "through the Law" and so negate the value of Christ's death (Gal 2:21); or die to the Law by participation in the death of Christ and so live to God by the indwelling life of Christ (Gal 2:19-20; *see* Death of Christ). Paul sets forth his own experience in Galatians 2:15-21 to prove that participation in the events of the gospel, not adherence to the Law, is the source of life and righteousness. In the next chapter he uses the story of Abraham to prove the same thesis.

*4.2.2. Argument from Scripture (Gal 3:6-29).* The Abraham argument is introduced by five barbed questions (Gal 3:1-5) which rebuke the Galatians for their foolishness.* Implied in these questions is the charge that the Galatians have failed to understand the significance of the message of Christ crucified (Gal 3:1) and have not realized the implications of their experience of the Spirit (Gal 3:2-5). Their past (Gal 3:2, 3) and present (Gal 3:5) experience of the Spirit is indisputable evidence that they are already experiencing the full blessing of God. Paul's questions are posed as sharp antitheses so that the Galatians will be compelled by their own experience of the Spirit to choose the right answer: "Not by observing the Law, but by believing what we heard about Christ crucified!"

The Galatians' expected answer is confirmed by the exposition of Scripture (*see* Old Testament in Paul). Paul quotes Genesis 15:6 to redefine the basis of Abrahamic sonship. The sign of the covenant—the true sign of Abrahamic sonship—is faith, not circumcision. His second quote from the Abraham story (Gen 12:3 and 18:18) is interpreted as a prophecy of the present experience of Gentile believers. Because Scripture foresaw that it would be by faith that God would justify the Gentiles, it preached the gospel beforehand to Abraham: Gentiles would be included in the blessing promised to Abraham.

The Galatian believers had been lured into thinking that they could be included in the promised blessing of Abraham by keeping the Law* of Moses. But in fact those who are of faith are already in the circle of blessing (Gal 3:9), while those who rely on the works of the Law are under a curse* (Gal 3:10) because Scripture (Deut 27:26) puts all who do not keep all the things written in the book of the Law under a curse. If the Law keepers themselves are under a curse since even they have not kept all the Law, then the risk of incurring a curse is even greater for Gentile believers who accept only certain items of the Law in order to identify with Israel.* Habakkuk 2:4 proves that righteousness by faith is the way to life (Gal 3:11).

But the Law is not of faith because it demands doing works of the Law as the way to life as the quotation of Leviticus 18:5 proves (Gal 3:13). The Law demands perfect obedience (Gal 3:10) and offers life on the basis of this perfect obedience (Gal 3:12), but the Law is incapable of engendering life or righteousness before God (Gal 3:21). The way to blessing is not though the Law but through the cross of Christ. Christ redeemed us from the curse of the Law by becoming a curse in our place (Gal 3:13-14). The Galatian believers had already received the blessing of Abraham when they received the Spirit by believing in the message of the cross (Gal 3:1-2, 14).

Following this contrast of Law and faith, Paul turns to a contrast of Law and promise by sketching out the flow of salvation history. Since the promise of blessing had been given to Abraham and his seed 430 years before the giving of Law, it could not be modified or annulled by the giving of the Law. This argument from history is designed to destroy the synthesis of the Abrahamic promise and Mosaic law which had led the Galatians to turn to the Law as the way to experience the promised blessing. And Paul's messianic definition of seed (Gal 3:16) removes Jewish national boundaries as the limits of the inheritance of the Abrahamic blessing. The link Paul makes between Abraham and Christ bypasses the Mosaic law and the Jewish nation as channels for the reception of the promises to Abraham, with the result that Christ alone is the channel of the promised blessing.

Two rhetorical questions in Galatians 3:19-21 disclose Paul's own awareness that his argument so far would lead his readers to question whether he has denied any purpose to the law ("Why then the Law? . . . Is the Law therefore opposed to the promises of God?"). Paul's description of the negative purpose,

temporary function and mediated origin of the law leaves the Galatian converts without any sound reason for turning to the Law (Gal 3:19-25). The focus of Galatians 3:26-29 is the union of the Gentile believers with Christ. The equal status of all believers as "children of God," "Abraham's seed" and "heirs" in Christ renders any attempt to gain superior status by circumcision or Law observance of no value whatsoever. At the beginning and end of his argument from the Abraham story, Paul's main point is that the inclusion of Gentile believers in the people of God is based solely upon their identification with Christ. Identification by race, class or sex no longer has any significance because of identification with Christ.

Paul closes the rebuke section of his letter with a dramatic before-and-after picture (Gal 4:1-11) to contrast the slavery* before and the freedom* after Christ was sent by the Father and accepted by the Galatian believers. Now that they have experienced the Spirit who gives them assurance that they are children of God, it is absurd for them to turn back to live as slaves under the Law. Formerly they were slaves to the gods of this world, now they are children of God. Paul's rebuke ends with an expression of fear that his efforts for them may be in vain (Gal 4:11; see Futility).

*4.3. Request section (Gal 4:12—6:10).* Paul turns from rebuke to request. The initial request of Galatians 4:12 ("Become as I am!") really amounts to a call for loyalty to the truth of the gospel and decisive resistance against the troublemakers. Paul developed his autobiography to illustrate how at Jerusalem (Gal 2:3, 5) and at Antioch (Gal 2:11-14) he had remained loyal to the gospel and decisively resisted pressures from Jewish Christians similar to those faced by the Galatian churches. Now he turns to autobiography again to strengthen this initial request by reminding the Galatians of the close relationship which they and Paul enjoyed prior to their departure from the gospel.

*4.3.1. Autobiography (Gal 4:12-20).* Paul's account of the Galatians' previous welcome (as if he were Christ Jesus), even when he was suffering from repulsive illness and their willingness to give him their own eyes, adds great force to his request for renewed identification and imitation. His request that they imitate him is also intensified by contrasting the evil intentions of the intruders with his own concern for his "children" as a mother in labor with unborn children, laboring for them until Christ is completely formed within them (see Pastor).

*4.3.2. Allegory from Scripture (Gal 4:21-31).* Paul's initial request of Galatians 4:12 is now spelled out by quoting an imperative from the Law itself. If the Galatians are so eager to be under the Law, then let them follow the Law. The "punch line" of the allegory is to command the Galatians through the Law to "cast out the bondwoman and her son" (Gal 4:30; Gen 21:10). Paul interprets Genesis 21 within the framework already established in Galatians 3. Within that framework Paul sees a real correspondence between the historical situation of the two sons of Abraham and the two sorts of descendants of Abraham in his own day, those born according to the flesh and those born according to the Spirit.

But Paul moves from typological interpretation built on historical correspondence to allegorical definitions. Here again, however, the key is the theological framework of Galatians 3. For in that argument Gentile converts were identified as true children and heirs of Abraham in the same sense as Isaac on the basis of the promise given to Abraham and their experience of the Spirit. And in that argument there is a contrast between the Abrahamic covenant and the Sinaitic covenant, which leads to slavery. Thus when Paul redefines the terms in his allegorical treatment of Genesis 21, Sarah (and her counterpart, the Jerusalem above, the true mother Zion) is identified as the mother of the Galatian believers in Christ.

Paul's Hagar = Sinai and Sinai = present Jerusalem equations are problematic. The major difficulty with them is their apparent lack of validity in the face of the fundamental Jewish conviction that the Mosaic Law had been given to the descendants of Isaac at Mount Sinai and had nothing to do with Hagar. The most satisfactory explanation of Paul's allegorical equations is simply stated in Galatians 4:25: "for she is in slavery with her children." Slavery is the common feature that links Hagar (the slave woman), the covenant given at Mount Sinai and the present Jerusalem. Paul had already attributed this feature of slavery to the Mosaic Law (Gal 3:22-24; 4:1-10) and to a certain faction at Jerusalem (Gal 2:4). His allegorization must be seen as a counterattack upon that Jewish-Christian faction within the church at Jerusalem which tried to rob Gentile believers of their freedom by requiring them to be circumcised (Gal 2:3-6) and which was now attempting to do the same thing at Galatia (*see* Judaizers). It was this actual experience of "troublemakers" in the church that gave rise to Paul's allegorical treatment of the text and is the key to its interpretation.

While the Hagar-Sarah allegory serves primarily as the basis for Paul's biblical appeal to resist the influence of the intruders, it also sets up a conceptual foundation for the ethical instructions of the rest of the letter. The freedom-slavery and spirit-flesh antitheses presented in the allegory set the stage for the ethical appeal to stand for freedom against slavery under the Law and to walk by the Spirit and so overcome the desires of the flesh.

*4.3.3. Ethical instructions (Gal 5:1—6:10).* The new identity of the Galatian believers leads to a new behavior (see Barclay; *see* Ethics). By grace they are true children of the free woman (Gal 4:31), born by the power of the Spirit (Gal 4:29). Now they must learn to express their new identity in new behavior. Paul gives instructions about their behavior. But he constantly bases his imperatives on the indicatives of grace:

For freedom Christ has set you free (indicative). Stand firm (Gal 5:1)!

You were called to freedom (indicative). Serve one another (Gal 5:13)!

We live by the Spirit (indicative). Keep in step with the Spirit (Gal 5:24)!

After the emphatic declaration in Galatians 5:2-12 that faith and Christ, on the one hand, and circumcision and Law, on the other, are exclusive alternatives, Paul's imperative of Galatians 5:13 echoes the command of Galatians 5:1. In both Galatians 5:1 and Galatians 5:13 there is first an indicative statement regarding freedom in Christ, which is then followed by an imperative and a warning. In Galatians 5:1 Paul commands the Galatians to stand fast; in Galatians 5:13 he exhorts them to serve one another in love. The warning of Galatians 5:1 is against a return to slavery under the Law; in Galatians 5:13 it is against giving opportunity to the flesh.

The fact that in Galatians 5:13 Paul warns that the flesh is the danger to freedom in Christ, instead of slavery to the Law, has led many to suppose that Paul begins to attack libertinism and lawlessness in Galatians 5:13. The description of the warfare between the flesh and the Spirit in the verses which follow is understood to confirm this supposition. But in the allegory which precedes this section, Paul identified slavery with both the Sinaitic covenant and the flesh. Those who are according to the flesh, like Ishmael, are identified with those who are proponents of the Sinaitic covenant. And in the subscription which follows this section those who campaign for circumcision boast in the flesh. So it seems best to interpret Galatians 5:13—6:10 in context. Paul has not changed fronts to fight against libertinism in this section. His attack against the works of the flesh is a continuation of his attack against the works of the Law.

The intruders' campaign for circumcision and the Law evidently led to social disorder and a lack of love in the Galatian community. In Paul's list of the works of the flesh these social sins receive the major emphasis. Paul's description of the opposition of the flesh and the Spirit is developed as a way of explaining the

Christian's relationship to the Law. The Law is still a central factor in Paul's thinking (Gal 5:14, 18, 23, 6:2). His statement that one who is led by the Spirit is not under Law (Gal 5:18) implies that a life under the Law is a life subject to the desires of the flesh. The works of the flesh, then, are to be seen as the result of living under the Law rather than under the guidance of the Spirit. The result of living under the guidance of the Spirit results in the fruit of the Spirit (*see* Fruit of the Spirit), against which there is no Law (Gal 5:23). For love fulfills the Law (Gal 5:14), the "Law of Christ"* (Gal 6:2). It is the Spirit, not the Law, which has the power to liberate one from the desires of the flesh.

*4.4. Subscription (Gal 6:11-18).* In common Hellenistic letters, the author would close the letter by writing a summary of the contents of the letter in his own hand. Paul does that in this letter. The denunciation of the intruders (Gal 6:12-13), the autobiographical statement of personal loyalty to the cross of Christ (Gal 6:14), with the mention of the marks of Christ as evidence of that loyalty (Gal 6:17), and the reminder that circumcision means nothing whereas the new creation means everything (Gal 6:15) all repeat and underscore the main themes of the letter. The first benediction on those who follow his rule, even on the Israel of God (Gal 6:16), his second benediction* (Gal 6:18), the appellation "brothers and sisters" (*adelphoi*) and the final "Amen" all express Paul's confidence that his request to "stand firm" for freedom in Christ by "keeping in step with the Spirit" will be followed by his Christian readers.

*See also* ABRAHAM; ANTIOCH ON THE ORONTES; CHRONOLOGY OF PAUL; CIRCUMCISION; CONVERSION AND CALL OF PAUL; CROSS, THEOLOGY OF THE; CURSE, ACCURSED, ANATHEMA; ETHICS; FAITH; FRUIT OF THE SPIRIT; GENTILES; GOSPEL; HOLY SPIRIT; JERUSALEM; JUDAIZERS; JUSTIFICATION; LAW; LAW OF CHRIST; OLD TESTAMENT IN PAUL; OPPONENTS OF PAUL; PETER; RHETORIC; RHETORICAL CRITICISM; WORKS OF THE LAW.

BIBLIOGRAPHY. **Commentaries:** W. Barclay, *The Letters to the Galatians and Ephesians* (DSB; rev. ed.; Edinburgh: St. Andrews, 1976); H. D. Betz, *Galatians: A Commentary on Paul's Letter to the Churches in Galatia* (Herm; Philadelphia: Fortress, 1979); F. F. Bruce, *The Epistle to the Galatians* (NIGTC; Grand Rapids: Eerdmans, 1982); E. deW. Burton, *A Critical and Exegetical Commentary on the Epistle to the Galatians* (ICC; Edinburgh: T. & T. Clark, 1921); R. A. Cole, *The Epistle of Paul to the Galatians* (TNTC; rev. ed.; Grand Rapids: Eerdmans, 1989); C. B. Cousar, *Galatians* (Int; Atlanta: John Knox, 1982); G. Ebeling, *The Truth of the Gospel: An Exposition of Galatians* (Philadelphia: Fortress,

1985); R. Y. K. Fung, *The Epistle to the Galatians* (NICNT; Grand Rapids: Eerdmans, 1988); D. Guthrie, *Galatians* (NCB; London: Marshall, Morgan & Scott, 1973); G. W. Hansen, *Galatians* (IVPNTC; Downers Grove, IL: InterVarsity, 1994); J. B. Lightfoot, *Saint Paul's Epistle to the Galatians* (1st ed. 1865; repr: Grand Rapids: Zondervan, 1957); R. N. Longenecker, *Galatians* (WBC 41; Dallas: Word, 1990); M. Luther, *A Commentary on St. Paul's Epistle to the Galatians* (repr: Grand Rapids: Baker, 1979); J. G. Machen, *Machen's Notes on Galatians*, ed. J. H. Skilton (Nutley, NJ: Presbyterian & Reformed, 1977); F. Mussner, *Der Galaterbrief* (HTKNT 9; Freiburg, Basel and Vienna: Herder, 1974); W. M. Ramsay, *A Historical Commentary on St. Paul's Epistle to the Galatians* (2d ed.; London: Hodder & Stoughton, 1900); H. N. Ridderbos, *The Epistle of Paul to the Churches of Galatia* (NICNT; Grand Rapids: Eerdmans, 1953); J. R. W. Stott, *The Message of Galatians* (Downers Grove, IL: InterVarsity, 1968). **Studies:** J. M. G. Barclay, *Obeying the Truth: A Study of Paul's Ethics in Galatians* (Edinburgh: T. & T. Clark, 1988); B. H. Brinsmead, *Galatians as Dialogical Response to Opponents* (SBLDS 65; Chico, CA: Scholars, 1982); C. H. Buck, "The Date of Galatians," *JBL* 70 (1951) 113-22; J. W. Drane, *Paul, Libertine or Legalist? A Study in the Theology of the Major Pauline Epistles* (London: SPCK, 1975); J. D. G. Dunn, *Jesus, Paul and the Law: Studies in Mark and Galatians* (Louisville: Westminster/John Knox, 1990); D. French, "The Roman Road System of Asia Minor," *ANRW* II.7.2.698-729; G. W. Hansen, *Abraham in Galatians: Epistolary and Rhetorical Contexts* (JSNTSup 29; Sheffield: Academic, 1989); R. B. Hays, *The Faith of Jesus Christ: An Investigation of the Narrative Substructure of Galatians 3:1-4:11* (SBLDS 56; Chico, CA: Scholars, 1983); C. J. Hemer, *The Book of Acts in the Setting of Hellenistic History*, ed. C. Gempf (Winona Lake, IN: Eisenbrauns, 1990); G. Howard, *Paul: Crisis in Galatia: A Study in Early Christian Theology* (SNTSMS 35; Cambridge: University Press, 1979); D. Lull, *The Spirit in Galatia: Paul's Interpretation of Pneuma as Divine Power* (SBLDS 49; Chico, CA: Scholars, 1980); M. J. Mellink, "Galatia," *IDB* 2.336-38; S. Mitchell, "Population and Land in Roman Galatia," *ANRW* II.7.2.1053-81; W. Ramsay, *The Cities of St. Paul* (London: Hodder & Stoughton, 1907); idem, *St. Paul The Traveller and the Roman Citizen* (London: Hodder & Stoughton, 1896); R. K. Sherk, "Roman Galatia," *ANRW* II.7.2.954-1052; S. Westerholm, *Israel's Law and the Church's Faith: Paul and His Recent Interpreters* (Grand Rapids: Eerdmans, 1988). G. W. Hansen

**GENERAL RESURRECTION.** *See* ESCHATOLOGY; RESURRECTION.

# GENTILES

"Gentiles" is the common English translation of the Greek term *ethnē*, which in Paul and elsewhere in the NT is used to refer to nations other than the nation of Israel.* That God now accepts men and women from all nations into full covenant* relationship without the need for conversion to Judaism is an insight given supremely to Paul, and one which threatened deep splits within the early church.

Paul's attitude to the Gentiles is intimately connected on the one hand with his understanding of the status of Israel, and on the other with his experience of a call to be apostle* to the Gentiles. Controversy sparked off by the influx of Gentiles into the church* forced him to explicate an understanding of the relationship between the two groups in God's purposes.

1. Terminology
2. Relations between Jews and Gentiles
3. The Gentile Mission
4. The Status of Gentile Christians in Paul's Theology

## 1. Terminology.

Neither the Hebrew Bible nor its Greek translation (LXX) developed a specific vocabulary to distinguish the nation of Israel from what we now term the Gentiles. The word *ethnos* (plural *ethnē*), "nation," can be quite general and universal, though already in the pre-Christian period it had developed the significance of "nation other than one's own" (cf. the development of terms such as *ethnarchēs*, "ethnarch," or "ruler of an ethnic minority," and the adjective *ethnikos*, "national," in Polybius and elsewhere). Thus in the LXX it is used to translate *gôy*, "nation," normally used of nations other than Israel; and also the word *'ām*, also "nation," when that word does not refer to the nation of Israel. But the usage is by no means consistent; and that the term has no necessary pejorative connotations may be seen by the dual use in 1 Peter 2:9-12 "you are . . . a holy *ethnos* . . . conducting yourselves well among the *ethnē*."

However, in the Pauline corpus the referent of *ethnos* is always (apart from the quotation of Gen 17:5 in Rom 4:17-18) the non-Jewish nations, sometimes in explicit contrast to Israel (e.g., Rom 3:29; 9:24) and occasionally in contrast to the church (1 Cor 12:2; Eph 2:11).

Other words occur as close synonyms: *laos*, "nation", occurs only in OT citations, generally of the Jewish nation but in the plural in Romans 15:11 in parallelism with *ethnē*. In Romans 9 the referent is transferred from national Israel to the new people of God (see 4 below). *Hellēn*, "Greek," is contrasted with *Ioudaios*, "Jew" (or "Judean"), in Romans 1:16; 2:9; 2:10; 3:9; 10:12; 1 Corinthians 1:22; 12:13; Galatians 3:28; Colossians 3:11. But in Romans 1:14 it is contrasted with *barbaros*, "barbarian," to describe the totality of the Gentile world. The word *akrobystia*, "foreskin," is used by metonymy in Romans 2:26-27; 3:30; 4:9 (?); Galatians 2:7; Ephesians 2:11; Colossians 3:11. In 1 Corinthians 9:21 *anomoi*, "those without [the] Law," are contrasted with *tous hypo nomou*, "those under [the] Law." In 1 Corinthians 6 *adikoi*, "unjust," or perhaps "unjustified," and *apistoi*, "unbelieving," "unfaithful" or "untrustworthy," are used to describe those outside the Christian fold; probably with full awareness of the ambiguities. It is not clear whether this is intended to include or exclude Jews. What is clear is that Paul uses whatever terms lie to hand, with no concern for creating a technical vocabulary. More significant is the conceptual distinction between Paul's own kin, heirs to God's promises, and all others, however described.

## 2. Relations Between Jews and Gentiles.

Although relationships between individuals doubtless covered the full gamut of possibilities, some general perspective is possible.

*2.1. Gentile Attitudes Toward Jews.* Much has been written on the extent of anti-Semitism in the Greco-Roman world (see Kraft and Nickelsburg chapter 4 for a summary and bibliography; and Stern for the texts). Recent European history makes the task of an impartial assessment of the first-century situation difficult in the extreme. An exhaustive investigation would need to distinguish between Jews in Israel viewed as a nation living in their own foreign country; and Jews of the Diaspora* viewed as close and potentially threatening neighbors. It would also distinguish between the various genres of the texts: the sober reportage of a Strabo, the litigious advocacy of a Seneca or the satirical jibes of a professional humorist like Juvenal. And a constant reminder is necessary that only a small fraction of ancient literature has survived, and that the literati may not anyway be representative of commonly held attitudes.

The conventional picture (based on comments by writers such as Juvenal and Seneca) is that Jews were perceived as arrogant and foolish: they refused to work on the Sabbath (which was a sign of laziness); they circumcised their sons (which was revolting); they had strict food laws and they kept themselves to themselves and rejected the gods (which was misanthropy). It is most unlikely that this was either the official view or even a common one (though see Josephus *Ant.* 14.10.1 §§186-88; 16.6.8 §§174-76, which may suggest that attitudes became more negative after the Jewish War of 66-70). Officially Judaism was not only tolerated but awarded specific privileges. Jews could and did attain to high positions in the state. Many earlier references describe Jews as a nation of "philosophers" and witness to widespread interest in the Jewish concept of God. To some Jewish monotheism was tantamount to "atheism," because they refused to worship the gods of the empire, and their own God had no form or image (*see* God). An alternative belief was that they worshipped a man with an ass's head. While there is certainly a great deal in the literature which is deliberately offensive or pokes fun at the Jew, it is also clear that many people were attracted to the lofty ideals which they saw in Judaism.

All apparently anti-Semitic statements in the ancient literature must also be set against a considerable body of comparable statements about other races. While it is possible that (in the main) the Romans did not seem to like the Jews, it is equally true that (in the main) the Romans did not seem to like the Greeks. The diminutive *Graeculus* was contemptuous and derogatory. The problem is not so much a racial one as it is cultural and social. Prejudices are most commonly and most vehemently expressed when the object of that prejudice is perceived as a threat. Many anti-Jewish statements can be located in specific historic contexts which make it unwise to generalize.

*2.2. Jewish Attitudes Toward Gentiles.* Again we must beware of the stereotype picture of Jewish attitudes to "sinners of the Gentiles," and recent studies (for instance, those by Hengel and Novak) provide an important corrective. Because of the nature of the Torah's purity* laws, Jews were almost bound to regard Gentiles as ritually unclean, but such ritual uncleanness was not necessarily a bar to friendship and cooperation. It was, in any event, of major significance only for those who wished to enter the Jerusalem Temple (though it is clear that the purification rituals were also performed away from Jerusalem), and all Pharisees outside Israel had to live somehow with the fact that they were themselves permanently contaminated with corpse-uncleanness. The Rabbinic literature (from a later age, but arguably a time when attitudes had hardened more than in the first century) speaks of Jews and Gentiles trading and eating together as a matter of course (e.g. *b. Ber.* 45a, reinterpreted by the later gemara as referring to uncircumcised proselytes; *m. 'Abod. Zar.* 5:5). Certain groups within Judaism may have maintained a rigid separation, perhaps especially those who regarded Israel itself as corrupt and themselves as the pure remnant. But even these may not have been as rigid as we would like to

think. For all its isolationism, the Qumran* community was clearly in touch with other Jewish groups to whom we may have expected them to be hostile, as some of their correspondence (e.g., 4QMMT) and their center in Jerusalem testify, and it is not inconceivable that contacts with the outside world went wider still. For those living outside the land the probability is proportionately greater.

What non-literary and archaeological evidences we have may be interpreted two ways. Since the epic work of E. R. Goodenough, scholars have been cautiously moving from the earlier perspective (implacable antipathy to all things Hellenistic) toward conceding a far greater tolerance to Greek influence (see Hengel; Goldstein; and, for a spirited defence of the traditional position, Feldman; *see* Hellenism). Paul's positive use of athletic metaphors supports this view, as would his knowledge of pagan authors, if we could be sure that this was more than just quoting what had already become proverbial.

From the Torah onward in Jewish tradition, distinctions were made between various groups of Gentiles, the "resident alien" in particular being awarded special treatment (Lev 17—26). Based on the covenant of Genesis 9 there developed a number of traditions about the divine laws binding on all humankind (*Jub.* 7:20-25; *Gen. Rab.* 34; *b. Sanh.* 56a; *b. 'Abod. Zar.* 8:4; etc.). Despite Novak's claim that "there is no convincing evidence that this doctrine was conceived earlier than the Tannaitic period . . . specifically after the destruction of the Temple and the Christian schism" (29), the range of the traditions suggests that the underlying ideas were much earlier. Varying forms of these "Noachide commandments" included prohibitions such as of idolatry, murder, theft, incest, blasphemy and eating the flesh of living animals, as well as the obligation to institute courts of justice (see the extended discussion in *b. Sanh.* 56a—60a). According to rabbinic traditions (though not for the author of *Jubilees*) Gentiles who adhered to the Noachide commandments might have a place in the age to come. Such "righteous Gentiles" were however in no sense part of the covenant people.

The position of those who sought closer ties with Judaism (so-called godfearers) is more difficult to assess. Kraabel denied the very existence of godfearers as a distinct group in our period, though the Aphrodisias remains appear now to establish their existence beyond question (see Reynolds and Tannenbaum). Such people would in addition to the Noachide commandments be obligated to keep the laws pertinent to the "resident alien," such as abstention from work on the Sabbath (Ex 20:10-11); from blood (Lev 17:10-16);

and from leaven during Passover (Ex 12:18-19). Other food laws, however, and circumcision, are not included in these obligations. Full proselytism was probably more rare and for our purposes is not particularly relevant, since the Gentiles in whom Paul is interested are manifestly not proselytes. It is, however, worth noting that according to the Mishnah (*m. Bik.* 1:4) even the full proselyte was not entitled to call Abraham* "father."

Finally we need to note that Judaism is not one thing, but a multiplicity. The question "who is a Jew?" continues to vex the Israeli authorities, and its answer for the first century is not simple. Samaritans are clearly to be included within the ambit of the heirs of Abraham and Moses, yet Judean-Samaritan relationships may at times have been worse than Jew-Greek (see Kraft and Nickelsburg, chaps. 2 and 3). We simply do not know how the average Pharisee regarded the Essenes, or any of the many other groups which constituted the phenomenon of pre-70 Judaism, but it is not impossible that a devout Gentile might have been more acceptable as, say, a table partner than an irreverent *'am ha-aretz* ("people of the land"), or someone deemed heretical. Nor is it simply a matter of degrees of strictness: where criteria differ, each group will accuse the other of laxity (*see* Holy Days).

### 3. The Gentile Mission.

*3.1. The NT Apart from Paul.* The Gospels record surprisingly few encounters between Jesus and Gentiles. Some sayings appear (humorously?) contemptuous (e.g., Mt 5:47) and there are none even in Luke that are unambiguously positive to Gentiles as a group. It is not unreasonable to suppose that even reports of Jesus' activity in Gentile regions (e.g., Decapolis, Caesarea Philippi) intend the reader to think primarily of activity amongst whatever Jewish groups may have been found there. Peter's response to Cornelius (Acts 10—11) makes clear that whatever Jesus may have taught about the Gentiles, it included none of the Law*-free gospel of Paul. The ending of Matthew's Gospel, however, indicates at the very least a tradition of dominical authority to take the Christian message beyond the bounds of Judaism (cf. also Mk 13:10).

The early chapters of Acts portray no steady move toward acceptance of Gentiles or radical reinterpretation of the Law. Stephen's speech could be regarded as critical of Law observance, but Luke explicitly states that he regards the charge of "changing the customs of Moses" to be false. The acceptance of Cornelius leads to great joy but no clear move toward Gentiles as a group. At the persecution of the Jerusalem church

some took the gospel to Gentiles (*Hellēnas*, Acts 11:20; the alternative reading *Hellēnistas*, "Greek speaking [Jews]," though favored by NA[26], is hard to square with the trend of Luke's narrative). On the first missionary journey Barnabas and Saul go to the synagogues and only turn to the Gentiles when rejected by Jews (Acts 13:46). However, there is no uncertainty about this move, which "the Lord commanded" (Acts 13:47; on Jervell's suggestion that for Luke it was Jewish *acceptance* of the message which stimulated the Gentile mission, see Wilson 222-24).

Luke is aware of opposing views within the church. Although it is difficult to assess how much a Gentile would understand the inter-Jewish debate, or think it important, the picture he presents is both clear and cogent. In Acts 15 the debate is over whether becoming a proselyte is necessary to salvation, and its extent indicates that in Jerusalem* at least, the issue was by no means cut and dried at this stage. The resultant restrictions of the apostolic decree, however, seem closer to some versions of the Noachide commandments than to a summary of the whole Torah. In Acts 21:17-26 the issue is different; James and "all the elders" express concern over rumors that Paul is teaching Diaspora *Jews* to forsake the Torah. The position over Gentiles is reiterated (Acts 21:25), and Paul without demur submits to Jewish *halakah*.

To Luke a Law-free gospel for Gentiles is the mainstream position, unhesitatingly held to by James,* Peter* and all the Jerusalem authorities.

*3.2. Paul and the Gentile Mission.* Paul's own references to his work (Rom 1:5, 13; cf. 15:16-19; 16:26) suggest that he saw himself as having a major role and responsibility in God's plan for the world. To see the crucial status of Gentile Christianity in his thought one need not gloss Romans 11:13 with a claim to be the only apostle to the Gentiles, nor assume that Paul thought that every individual in the areas he mentions had heard the gospel. The autobiographical sections in Galatians, 2 Corinthians and Philippians provide further details about his understanding of the Gentile mission. They indicate that he was certainly not alone in evangelizing Gentile regions, and that at least up to the writing of Galatians (and thus well after the meeting of Gal 2) there was no general agreement as to the content of the Gentile gospel (*see* Mission).

The presence at that meeting of Titus, an uncircumcised Gentile, clearly indicated Paul's belief that circumcision* of Gentiles was no part of the gospel; and, just as clearly, it caused controversy. Whatever the outcome may have been for Titus personally (it is possible that he was indeed circumcised, see the commentaries), the final agreement must have sanctioned

*337*

Paul's continuing to preach his particular message among the Gentiles, even if unauthorized opposition to Paul continued (Phil 3:2; perhaps 2 Cor 11:1-6).

In Romans 9—11 there is a more extended reflection on the significance of the Gentile mission. We should beware of seeing this section as "about" the Gentile mission or "about" the Jews; there are good reasons for supposing that the primary topic of Romans 9—11 is the same as that of the whole letter; namely the righteousness* of God which, at least in part, raises the question whether the influx of Gentiles means that he has abandoned his promises to Israel (Rom 9:6; see Wright, chap. 13; see Restoration of Israel). Paul's response begins with a conventional "remnant" theology; but with a double twist: first, that the failure of Israel is actually part of the purpose (and promise) of God (note almost all of the OT passages cited in Rom 9—11); and second, that this was specifically so that God could demonstrate his mercy* and salvation* for the whole world* (Rom 9:24-26; cf. also the many instances of *pas* ["every," or "all"]). So the ecclesiology of such passages as Ephesians 1:22-23; 2:14-22; 3:9-10, even if they were not written by Paul, only expresses what is already in mind in Romans, and indeed implicit in the "one man" of Galatians 3:28.

The Gentile mission, far from being a contingency plan or reaction to the gospel's failure among the Jews, stands at the heart of the affirmation of the righteousness of the God who "has consigned all of humanity to disobedience, in order that his mercy may extend to all of humanity" (Rom 11:32). Romans 15:7-12 reinforces the point. The Gentile mission is a natural concomitant of the unity of God and of his grace.*

**4. The Status of Gentile Christians in Paul's Theology.** What does not seem to have been clarified at the Jerusalem meeting is the nature of the relationships between Paul's communities and Jewish Christians. The "men from James" clearly felt that accepting hospitality from such Gentiles was impossible for Torah-observant Christians; and if this issue had not been explicitly discussed in Jerusalem, then it is not improbable that they had good arguments to persuade Peter and Barnabas. "Righteous Gentiles" may indeed be acceptable to God through his grace, but they could not be part of Israel, and relationships with them would continue to defile Torah-observant Jewish Christians. With the growing success of the Gentile mission, this problem and the threat it posed to Jewish-Christian self-identity will have grown ever greater.

Paul's own understanding of the grace of God, however, led him to affirm that there could be no distinction before God between the Christian Jew and the righteous Gentile (cf. Rom 3:29-30). Galatians* is a sustained argument that his converts already enjoy all the blessings of the covenant—they are already children of Abraham* (Gal 3:7, 28-29). Hence for Gentiles to accept the yoke of Torah observance is not simply a matter of indifference, but a denial of God's acceptance of them in the gospel, and therefore a denial of Christ (Gal 5:4). In Galatians then—almost certainly one of the earliest extant letters of Paul—we already see not only a fully developed rationale of the Gentile mission but also a deep conviction about the nature of the church* as the true Israel* of God, with Jew and Gentile on equal standing before God and to each other. Within this perspective it is more likely than not that in Romans 11:26 Paul reiterates his *redefinition* of "all Israel" (cf. Rom 9:6) as a new people in Christ, wherein is "neither Jew nor Greek" (Gal 3:28; but *see* Israel).

*4.1. The Origins of Paul's "Gospel of the Uncircumcision."* The incident at Antioch* (Gal 2) indicates that this perspective was something radically new in the church's self-understanding; and the comparatively rapid disappearance of Jewish Christianity as a major force in the church suggests that the careful integration it presupposes was too soon replaced by a mere Gentile takeover. (Rom 11:1 seems to reflect Paul's fear of precisely such an eventuality.) So remarkable was Paul's insight that much effort has been expended to seek its origins. Paul's own answer is clear but unhelpful: "I received it . . . by a revelation of Jesus Christ" (Gal 1:12). Since, according to Luke, a revelation to Peter singularly failed to produce the same effect in his case (Acts 10:1—11:18), it is still worth asking how far we can probe the mechanisms which led to Paul's conclusions (see Conversion and Call). There is no consensus among scholars, and all that can be done here is to suggest some of the factors which may have been influential.

(1) If he did not already inherit it from his Pharisaism, Paul would have derived from his Christian mentors, and his own experience, a realization that descent from Abraham in itself is by no means a sufficient condition for involvement in God's new covenant* (see Jew, Paul the).

(2) Paul's own testimony (Phil 3:5-6; cf. Gal 1:14) indicates that in his eyes there was nothing more that Torah observance could offer for the attainment of true religion. However valid the charge of Pharisaic hypocrisy, it is clear that the Pharisees did represent an acme of Jewish piety. Yet now his Christian expe-

rience introduced him to a community with a far greater knowledge of God than he had had; but one which, albeit Jewish, fell far short of his standards of Torah observance.

(3) Paul does not explain why he persecuted the church, but it is hard to imagine that Deuteronomy 27:26 played no part in his pre-Christian thinking. It was surely appropriate that this blasphemer should have been executed in a way which manifested the curse* of God upon him. If this is so, then a re-assessment of the Torah, and of the status of the Israel which had rejected its Messiah, was essential for the Christian Paul.

Such factors, coupled with the experience of Gentiles already in the church, may perhaps help us to understand how Paul came to realize that the worldwide mission of the church entailed not merely a policy of proselytizing, but an awareness that response to Christ, and only to him, is the basis on which God now calls people of every race to fulfill his purpose for his creation.*

*See also* ABRAHAM; CHURCH; CIRCUMCISION; COVENANT AND NEW COVENANT; CREATION AND NEW CREATION; FOOD OFFERED TO IDOLS AND JEWISH FOOD LAWS; GALATIANS, LETTER TO THE; GOSPEL; ISRAEL; JERUSALEM; JEW, PAUL THE; LAW; MISSION; OLIVE TREE; PEACE, RECONCILIATION; PURITY AND IMPURITY; RESTORATION OF ISRAEL.

BIBLIOGRAPHY. J. G. Gager, *The Origins of Anti-Semitism: Attitudes toward Judaism in Pagan and Christian Antiquity* (Oxford: University Press, 1983); J. A. Goldstein, "Jewish Acceptance and Rejection of Hellenism," in *Jewish and Christian Self-Definition*, volume 2, ed. E. P. Sanders et al. (Philadelphia: Fortress, 1981) 64-87; E. R. Goodenough, *Jewish Symbols in the Greco-Roman Period* (13 vols.; New York: Pantheon, 1953-68); M. Hengel, *Judaism and Hellenism: Studies in Their Encounter in Palestine During the Early Hellenistic Period* (2 vols.; Philadelphia: Fortress, 1974); idem, *Jews, Greeks and Barbarians: Aspects of the Hellenization of Judaism in the pre-Christian Period* (Philadelphia: Fortress, 1980); idem, *The Pre-Christian Paul* (Philadelphia: Trinity Press International, 1991); A. T. Kraabel, "The Disappearance of the 'God-Fearers,'" *Numen* 28 (1981) 113-26; R. A. Kraft and G. E. W. Nickelsburg, ed., *Early Judaism and Its Modern Interpreters* (Atlanta, GA: Scholars, 1986) 57-80; S. McKnight, *A Light Among the Gentiles: Jewish Missionary Activity in the Second Temple Period* (Minneapolis: Fortress, 1991); D. Mendels, *The Rise and Fall of Jewish Nationalism: Jewish and Christian Ethnicity in Ancient Palestine* (New York: Doubleday, 1992); D. Novak, *The Image of the Non-Jew in Judaism: An Historical and Constructive Study of the Noahide Laws* (Toronto: Mellen, 1983); J. Reynolds and R. Tannenbaum, *Jews and Godfearers at Aphrodisias* (Cambridge: Cambridge Philological Society, 1987); M. Stern, *Greek and Latin Authors on Jews and Judaism* (3 vols.; Jerusalem: Israel Academy of Sciences and Humanities, 1974, 1980, 1984); F. B. Watson, *Paul, Judaism and the Gentiles: a Sociological Approach* (SNTSMS 56; Cambridge: University Press, 1986); S. G. Wilson, *The Gentiles and the Gentile Mission in Luke Acts* (SNTSMS 23; Cambridge: University Press, 1973); N. T. Wright, *The Climax of the Covenant* (Minneapolis: Fortress 1991).

D. R. de Lacey

**GIFT OF KNOWLEDGE.** *See* GIFT OF KNOWLEDGE, KNOWLEDGE; GIFTS OF THE SPIRIT.

**GIFT OF PROPHECY.** *See* GIFTS OF THE SPIRIT; PROPHECY, PROPHESYING.

**GIFT OF TONGUES.** *See* GIFTS OF THE SPIRIT; TONGUES.

## GIFTS OF THE SPIRIT

The term "gift(s) of the Spirit" does not occur in the Pauline corpus. Nonetheless, the occasional collocation of "gift" language and Spirit activity (*see* Holy Spirit), especially in Romans 1:11 and 1 Corinthians 12—14, makes the term a legitimate one. The problems are three: (1) to determine what Paul himself might have understood by the words *charismata* and *pneumatika*, since his own usage exhibits a considerable degree of fluidity; (2) to isolate what Spirit activities might legitimately be classified as "gifts of the Spirit," since the texts themselves are neither systematic nor exhaustive; and (3) to identify the nature of the various "gifts" that are mentioned. Part of the problem is to determine whether "gifts of the Spirit" should be limited to the more extraordinary phenomena of 1 Corinthians 12—14 or whether one should also include the "ministries" in Ephesians 4:11, which are called "gifts," but not *charismata*, and are not directly associated with the Spirit.

1. The Linguistic Data
2. The Texts
3. The Charismata

### 1. The Linguistic Data.

In most contemporary interpretation and writing on this subject, especially in popular literature, the term "gift of the Spirit" is associated with Paul's use of the word *charisma;* hence the frequent contemporary use of *charismatic* to describe people or churches who have experienced the phenomena of 1 Corinthians 12—14. This is not altogether wrong, but it can be misleading.

That Paul qualifies *charisma* (gift) with the adjective *pneumatikon* ("spiritual"; i.e., pertaining to the Spirit) in Romans 1:11 is certain evidence that *charisma* does not automatically mean "spiritual gift." Moreover, there is good exegetical reason to believe that the "*charisma* of God," which Timothy is urged to "fan into flame" in 2 Timothy 1:6 is none other than the Spirit himself (see Fee 1993). All of this is further complicated by the several listings of "gifts" in Paul's letters and the variety of language used to designate them.

So, for example, (1) in 1 Corinthians 12:4 Paul speaks of the Spirit's *charismata*, which in 1 Corinthians 12:7 are called "manifestations," while *charismata* appears again in 1 Corinthians 12:9 (and in 1 Cor 12:28, 29) narrowly confined to "healings,"* only to reappear in 1 Corinthians 12:31 to refer to the broader categories; (2) in 1 Corinthians 12:6 the activities of God* are called *energēmata* ("workings") which he *energei* ("works"), yet *energēmata* occurs again in 1 Corinthians 12:10 as one of the Spirit's "manifestations," and in 1 Corinthians 12:11 the Spirit is said to *energein* all these things; (3) in 1 Corinthians 12:5 the activities associated with the Lord are called *diakoniai* ("services"), a word that appears again as a *charisma* in Romans 12:6-7, but in a context where the Spirit is not mentioned; (4) the "workings of miracles" in 1 Corinthians 12:10 is simply "miracles" in 1 Corinthians 12:28-29; (5) one finds the *logos* of "knowledge"* in 1 Corinthians 12:8, "knowing all mysteries* and all knowledge" in 1 Corinthians 13:2, and simply "knowledge" in 1 Corinthians 13:8 and 1 Corinthians 14:6; (6) "prophecy"* is a "manifestation" in 1 Corinthians 12:10; prophets themselves are mentioned in 1 Corinthians 12:28-29 (cf. 1 Cor 14:29, 37); but it is not at all clear that "prophecy" is the private province only of some who are called "prophets" (cf. "teachers" and "teaching"* in 1 Cor 12:28 and 1 Cor 14:6, 26). It is fair to say that in both the scholarly and popular literature far greater confidence is often expressed on some of these matters than the evidence itself warrants. Nonetheless, as a beginning point one must at least look at how Paul uses some key words.

*1.1. Charisma(ta).* The word *charisma* is a distinctively Pauline word (found elsewhere in the NT only in 1 Pet 4:10 and otherwise rarely in Greek literature at all). On its own the word has nothing to do with the Spirit; it picks up Spirit overtones only by context or by clear qualifiers. The noun has been formed from *charis* ("grace"*), referring to *a concrete expression of grace,* which is what it means in its every instance in Paul. Thus in nearly half of its uses *charisma* designates a variety of ways God's grace has been evidenced among his people. It includes such diverse "gifts" as eternal life* (Rom 6:23; cf. Rom 5:15, 16), the special privileges granted to Israel* (Rom 11:29, referring to Rom 9:4-5), celibacy and marriage* (1 Cor 7:7) and deliverance from a deadly peril (2 Cor 1:11).

On the other hand, the word sometimes refers to certain Spirit activities as "gracious gifts," as for example in Romans 1:11 noted above (Fung considers this a "technical" sense, but without warrant). Thus in 1 Corinthians 1:4-7 God's grace (1 Cor 1:4) finds concrete expression in the rich number of *charismata* he has bestowed upon this community (1 Cor 1:5, 7). This same usage is picked up in 1 Corinthians 12 (1 Cor 12:4, 9, 28, 30, 31), with specific reference to the Spirit. But here is where the difficulties also begin. In three of these verses (1 Cor 12:9, 28, 30) Paul uses the phrase "*charismata* ('gifts') of healings," apparently referring to specific instances of physical healing within the community. But in 1 Corinthians 12:4, at the head of this discussion, *charismata* is associated with the Spirit in a way that seems intended to include what in 1 Corinthians 12:7 Paul terms "manifestations of the Spirit." Thus there seems to be little question that the list of "manifestations" in 1 Corinthians 12:8-10 are to be understood as *charismata,* gracious bestowments of the Spirit in the gathered community for the sake of building up the people of God (*see* Church).

More difficult is the recurrence of this word coupled with the imperative at the end of this discussion in 1 Corinthians 12:31, in which Paul urges them "eagerly to desire the greater *charismata.*" For several exegetical reasons (see Fee 1987), this imperative almost certainly does not refer to the preceding potpourri of people, ministries and Spirit manifestations that "God has placed in the church" (1 Cor 12:28). Rather, it is most likely intended to begin the argument on intelligibility and order in 1 Corinthians 14, which is then interrupted so as to place all of these things in the context of love.* When Paul then resumes this imperative in 1 Corinthians 14:1 the word *charismata* is now replaced with *ta pneumatika* ("the things of the Spirit"), which have to do, as in 1 Corinthians 12:4-11, with Spirit manifestations in the community gathered for worship.* It is doubtful, therefore, whether in 1 Corinthians 12—14 Paul intends to refer to such people as apostles* and teachers, or to such ministries as helpful deeds and acts of guidance, as *charismata.* At least in its only specific appearances in this argument the term seems to be limited to Spirit manifestations in the community, and thus probably means something like "concrete expressions of grace manifested through the Spirit's empowering."

The usage in Romans 12:6 is more difficult. Here Paul speaks of "having *charismata* that differ, in keeping with the *charis* given to us," where the clear tie of *charismata* with "grace" is again evident, but the Spirit is not mentioned. Several matters, to be sure, may imply the Spirit's presence: the language about unity and diversity in the body (*see* Body of Christ), which reflects 1 Corinthians 12; prophecy as the first *charisma* mentioned in verse 6, which in Paul is a Spirit gifting par excellence; and the similarities of Romans 12—14 with Galatians 5—6, where the Spirit dominates the discussion.

Nonetheless, despite these associations with the Spirit that come from the larger contexts of Romans,* 1 Corinthians* and Galatians,* it is not at all clear that Paul intended the listing in Romans 12:6-8 to be thought of as "gifts of the Spirit" in the same way as the *charismata* in 1 Corinthians 12—14. This list is so heterogeneous, and covers such a broad range of activities, that the emphasis more likely lies on the "grace of God" here being worked out among the Roman believers in concrete ways (esp. in light of Romans 14—15), rather than on the empowering of the Spirit for such behavior. Thus the list includes two items from 1 Corinthians (prophecy, teaching), plus a further verbal (apparently) *charisma* (exhorting/encouraging), as well as various forms of serving others within the believing community (service, contributing to the needs of others, giving aid and showing mercy). These latter items in particular seem to move away from the idea of "gifts" per se, at least in terms of Spirit manifestations, to Christian behavior (ethics*), in which the fruit of love finds concrete expression in their midst. Therefore, to include these as "gifts of the Spirit" of the same kind and categories as in 1 Corinthians 12—14 seems to be a case of mixing oranges and apples. For Paul they are clearly *charismata;* it is less clear that he thought of them also as Spirit giftings.

Finally, in 1 Timothy 4:14 and 2 Timothy 1:6 the *charisma* (singular) is said to be "in Timothy" and is expressed in contexts referring to Timothy's ministry. In its first instance it probably refers to his "giftedness" for ministry, which came to him through prophetic utterances. In 2 Timothy 1:6, however, the *charisma* seems more likely to refer to the Spirit himself (Fee 1993), although that in turn probably is a metonymy for Timothy's Spirit-given ministry that came to him "through prophetic utterances."

In sum, *charisma* does not necessarily refer to Spirit activity; when it does, it seems to refer to specific visible ways in which the Spirit manifests himself in the believing community, granting them "gracious bestowments" to meet their various needs and thus to build them up as the eschatological people of God.

One should probably, therefore, make a distinction between "Spirit *charismata*" and other expressions of *charismata* that do not necessarily imply visibly evident Spirit activity as such.

*1.2. Pneumatika.* This term (neuter plural of the adjective *pneumatikon;* thus literally, "the things of the Spirit") occurs twice in 1 Corinthians 12—14 (1 Cor 12:1; 14:1). The apparent overlap of *pneumatika* with *charismata* in 1 Corinthians 14:1 (and 1 Cor 12:31) has already been noted. There has been considerable debate about this apparent interchange. Some have suggested that the words are nearly interchangeable, both of them in this context meaning roughly the same thing; others have suggested that one or the other is the more comprehensive term, with the other serving to designate specific Spirit manifestations; and still others have speculated that one of them might be a Corinthian term, related to their apparently unbridled enthusiasm for tongues,* which Paul is here attempting to bring under control partly in a linguistic way (see Fee 1987 for this discussion).

Since there seems to be little question that the two words have a degree of overlap in this particular context, the best solution to this matter probably lies with taking seriously the root meaning of the two words. If the emphasis in the word *charisma* is on God's graciousness toward his people, then the emphasis in *pneumatika* rests with the Spirit nature of the activity to which these various *charismata* bear witness. Paul would thus be referring to the same phenomena. Diverse *charismata* of the one Spirit they are indeed; here is how God is currently at work among his people in a variety of ways for the common good. But in the argument in 1 Corinthians 14 the emphasis now lies on these *charismata* as Spirit manifestations. Here is how the Spirit is at work in them individually (tongues in private for edification; 1 Cor 14:2-3, 14-15) and corporately (prophecy etc.) for their common upbuilding.

This is probably how one is also to understand the ambiguous genitive with which this whole argument begins in 1 Corinthians 12:1 ("now concerning *tōn pneumatikōn*"). There is considerable debate as to whether this means "spiritual gifts" (neuter) or "spiritual people" (masculine). Most likely the term is neuter (as in 1 Cor 14:1), but probably not meaning "spiritual gifts" as such, which is much too narrow an understanding of this word, but "Spirit matters," which includes "gifts" and their abuse by the "pneumatics" in this community.

*1.3. Pneumata.* It is more difficult to determine what Paul meant by three occurrences of the plural *pneumata* (spirits) in 1 Corinthians 12—14: "the discerning of spirits" (1 Cor 12:10), "since you are zealots for spirits" (1 Cor 14:12) and "the spirits of the prophets are subject to the prophets" (1 Cor 14:32). The usage in 1 Corinthians 14:12 is so unusual that most English translations consider it to mean the same as *pneumatika* in 1 Corinthians 14:1 and thus translate it "spiritual gifts" (NIV, NASB, NRSV; cf. GNB, NEB; "manifestations of the Spirit" RSV). That Paul himself believed in a plurality of "good spirits" is emphatically denied by 1 Corinthians 12:4, 8-11: "the same Spirit," "the one Spirit," "the one and the same Spirit." Whether this emphasis also combats a belief in the plurality of spirits on the part of the Corinthians is moot. This curious affirmation in 1 Corinthians 14:12 at least allows as much; but Paul's own use of this language in 1 Corinthians 14:32, where such a meaning does not seem possible, suggests that the meaning lies elsewhere.

The probable solution to these passages is to be found in Paul's apparent conviction that the believer's spirit is the place where, by means of God's own Spirit, the human and the divine interface in the believer's life (*see* Psychology). Thus the key to this usage probably lies with the context of 1 Corinthians 14:32, where "the *pneumata* of the prophets" most likely refers to "the prophetic Spirit" by which each of them speaks through his or her own spirit; thus the prophetic utterance, inspired by the divine Spirit, is subject to the speaker and must be "discerned" by others in the community. Perhaps the inelegant translation "the S/spirits of the prophets" might best capture Paul's own intent. In any case, the term refers to "spiritual gifts" only in the most indirect way.

*1.4. Dorea.* This word, the term for "gift" proper, rarely occurs in Paul, but does appear in Ephesians 4:7. This sentence serves as transition from the Trinitarian basis for unity in Ephesians 4:4-6 (one body, one Spirit, one hope; one Lord, one faith, one baptism; one God) to the several-fold ministries God has given to the church for its own health and service to the world. Since the Spirit is crucial to the church's unity (Ephesians 4:3-4), and since three of the ministries listed in Ephesians 4:11 also appeared in the listing in 1 Corinthians 12:28, it is common to see Ephesians 4:11 as giving us yet one more list of "gifts of the Spirit," this time more specifically narrowed to ministries as such.

While there is every reason to believe that Paul considered all such people and their ministries as Spirit-empowered for the task of building up the community, what remains unclear is whether in considering them as "gifts" to the church, he would also have considered all of these ministries as *charismata* in the sense that word is used in either 1 Corinthians 12 or Romans 12.

## 2. The Texts.

The difficulty with "organizing" Paul in the matter of spiritual gifts lies not only with the linguistic factors noted above, but also (especially) with the purely ad hoc nature of his letters, which reveal considerable ambiguity of both language and listings. For that reason, rather than to superimpose an outside grid on what Paul was about, one should begin with a look at the texts in their contexts.

*2.1. 1 Corinthians 12—14.* The rhetorical (*see* Rhetoric), sometimes polemical, nature of the argument in his passage, especially chapters 13 and 14, suggests that Paul's purpose is primarily corrective, not instructive. Tongues* is clearly the culprit (as 1 Cor 14 makes clear); true spirituality* (in the sense of being a Spirit person) is most likely the issue, and Paul and the Corinthians are at odds on this matter (1 Cor 14:36-37). The latter probably thought of tongues as the language of the angels* (1 Cor 13:1), hence as evidence for the present realization of heavenly existence, with only the sloughing off of the body remaining (hence their denial of the future bodily resurrection,* 1 Cor 15:12). The result was both inordinate zeal for tongues and consequent disorder in their assembly (*see* Worship).

In his effort to curb their misguided zeal Paul first argues for the necessity of diversity—if the community is truly to be "of the Spirit" (1 Cor 12:4-30). He then argues that no gifting counts for anything if love does not motivate (1 Cor 13:1-13), concluding that, in terms of Spirit manifestations, love demands that they seek after intelligible utterances (1 Cor 14:1-25) and order (1 Cor 14:26-40), if the community is to be built up (1 Cor 14:1-19, 26-33) and outsiders are to be converted (1 Cor 14:20-25). In the process Paul has occasion to list various *charismata*, ministries and forms of service at seven different points in his argument (1 Cor 12:8-10, 28, 29-30; 13:1-3, 8; 14:6, 26), no two of which are alike (not even 1 Cor 12:28 and 29-30); not only so, but they appear in ways that make systematizing nearly impossible.

*2.1.1. 1 Corinthians 12:8-10.* The purely ad hoc character of this list is demonstrated both by its order and content. Paul's concern is not with instruction about "spiritual gifts" as such, their number and kinds; rather, he offers a *considerable* and diverse list so that they will stop being singular in their own emphasis. Thus, tailored to speak to their situation, this list is but *representative* of the diversity of the Spirit's manifestations.

Attempts to classify the several items are numerous and varied. It has been suggested that they reflect a descending order of value, while others have rearranged the items conceptually (MacGorman). A popular grouping is (1) gifts of instruction (wisdom* and knowledge*); (2) gifts of supernatural power (faith,* healings,* miracles); and (3) gifts of inspired utterance (prophecy,* discerning spirits, tongues,* interpretation of tongues) (Martin). It will be noted that the seventh item ("discernments of spirits") is the one that tends to give trouble to most of these arrangements. If grouping them is legitimate at all, it is most likely to be found in some clues Paul himself has given, by starting the third and eighth items (faith and tongues) with a different word for "another" and without the connective *de*. If so, then the first two are chosen for very specific ad hoc purposes; "wisdom" and "knowledge" held high court in Corinth. He then adds a random list of five items that have as their common denominator a supernatural endowment of some kind, and concludes with the "problem child" and its companion, tongues and interpretation.

What distinguishes this listing is the concretely visible nature of these items, especially of the last seven. After all, these are not only "gifts," they are *manifestations* of the Spirit's presence in their midst, most likely chosen because they are, like tongues itself, extraordinary phenomena. It would scarcely do for Paul at this point to attempt to broaden their perspective by listing less visible gifts. That will come in time (especially through the analogy of the body and in the lists in 1 Cor 12:28-30); but for now the emphasis is on the supernatural.

On the other hand, it also includes the message [*logos*] of wisdom [*sophia*] and the logos of knowledge [*gnōsis*]. In this case the language seems to be chosen not because Paul has some supernatural endowment in mind, but because these three words (*logos, sophia, gnōsis*) are especially high in the Corinthians' understanding of Spirit activity (see 1 Cor 1—3, 8). But their wisdom and knowledge are described by Paul as worldly and defective. For Paul these words are especially to be understood in terms of the cross (1 Cor 1:18-31; 8:11). Thus Paul uses two of their own terms to begin his list of "manifestations" in the assembly that demonstrate the great diversity inherent in the one Spirit's activities. At the same time he reshapes those terms in light of the work of the Spirit so as to give them a significantly different content from that given by the Corinthians—although it is not at all certain what concrete form these may have taken in Paul's own mind.

The other puzzling item in this list is "discernments of spirit," over which there has been considerable debate, whether it has to do with the ability to discern what is truly of the Spirit of God and what comes from other spirits (e.g., Grudem), or with the phenomenon

noted in 1 Corinthians 14:29, "and let the others discern (judge rightly) what is said," in which the cognate verb of this noun appears (e.g., Dunn, Fee). Most likely, given Paul's own use of language in 1 Corinthians 14, it refers to both, but particularly to the phenomenon of "discerning, differentiating or properly judging" prophecies in 1 Corinthians 14:29. There are two reasons for taking this position: (1) Both 1 Thessalonians 5:20-21 and 1 Corinthians 14:29, the two places where Paul mentions the functioning of prophecy in the church, call for a "testing" or "discerning" of prophetic utterances; it therefore seems likely, given that the noun used in this passage is the cognate of the verb in 1 Corinthians 14:29, that the same is true here, since it immediately follows "prophecy." (2) These two are followed immediately by "tongues" and "interpretation," the same pattern found again in the instructions on order in 1 Corinthians 14:26-29.

*2.1.2. 1 Corinthians 12:27-30.* After twice applying his analogy of the body, with emphasis on the need for diversity (1 Cor 12:15-26), Paul concludes this section of his argument with yet another list of gifts and ministries (*see* Ministry). The emphasis remains the same; the need for diversity. The list itself has several interesting features: (1) He begins with a list of *persons* (apostles, prophets, teachers), whom he ranks in the order of first, second, third. (2) With the fourth and fifth items ("miracles" and "gifts of healings") he reverts to *charismata*, taking two from the list in 1 Corinthians 12:8-10. These are both prefaced with the word "then," as though he intended the ranking scheme to continue. (3) The sixth and seventh items ("helpful deeds" and "acts of guidance"), which are *deeds* of service, are noteworthy in three ways: (a) they are the only two not mentioned again in the rhetoric of 1 Corinthians 12:29-30; (b) nor are they mentioned again in the NT; (c) they do not appear to be of the same kind—that is, supernatural endowments—as those on either side (miracles, healings, tongues).

This list represents a whole range of "ministries" in the church, which were probably chosen for that reason. What one is to make of this mix is not certain. At best one can say that the first three emphasize the persons who have these ministries, while the final five emphasize the ministry itself. That probably suggests that the first three items therefore are not to be thought of as "offices," held by certain "persons" in the local church, but rather refer to "ministries" as they find expression in various persons; likewise the following "gifts" are not expressed in the church apart from persons, but are first of all gracious endowments, given by the Spirit to various persons in the church for its mutual upbuilding.

The question as to whether Paul intended *all* of these to be "ranked" as to their role or significance in the church is moot. Probably not. He certainly intends the first three to be ranked. One might argue also for the rest on the basis of the "then . . . then" that preface the next two. But that seems unlikely, since (1) he drops the enumeration with the sixth item, (2) the fourth and fifth items (1 Cor 12:28-30) are in reverse order from their earlier listing (1 Cor 12:9-10) and (3) there seems to be no special significance as to whether miracles precedes healings, or vice versa, or whether these precede or follow helpful deeds and acts of guidance. The gift of tongues is last, as always, because it is the problem child—included only after the need for diversity is well heard.

Why he ranks the first three is more difficult to answer; probably it is related to his understanding of the role these three ministries play in the church. It is not so much that one is more important than the other, nor that this is necessarily their order of authority,* but that one has precedence over the other in the founding and building up of the local assembly. In light of 1 Corinthians 14:37 and the probability that those who have taken the lead against Paul are considered "prophets," Paul might also be subordinating such people to the apostle, who is giving them "the Lord's command."

It is no surprise that Paul should list "apostles" first. The surprise is that they should be on this list at all, and that he should list them in the plural. Most likely with this word he is reflecting on his own ministry in this church; the plural is in deference to others who have had the same ministry in other churches (cf. 1 Cor 9:5; 15:7-11). In any case, there is no other evidence that Paul thought of a local church as having some among it called "apostles," who were responsible for its affairs. Moreover, there is no place in Paul where there is a direct connection between the Spirit and apostleship. His apostleship is received "from Christ" (Rom 1:5) and "by the will of God" (1 Cor 1:1); he never specifically suggests it to be a "charism" of the Holy Spirit, as though the Spirit gifted him for this "office" (*see* Apostle).

The ranking of "prophets" and "teachers" (which appears here for the first time in his letters) is equally difficult. The question is whether Paul is here thinking of specific groups of people known as "prophets" and "teachers," vis-à-vis "apostles" and other members of the community, or whether these are more functional terms, referring to any and all who would exercise these gifts. The similar language in Ephesians 2:20 (apostles and prophets) and Ephesians 4:11 suggests that the terms here are probably

designations for certain people—although the emphasis would still be on their *function* to build up the community. Thus when these words occur again in 1 Corinthians 14, they do so as "prophecy" and "teaching," apparently as spontaneous utterances (1 Cor 14:6, 26), without concern for the person of the prophet or teacher.

The other two new items on this list, *helpful deeds* and *acts of guidance,* occur only here in the NT. Both appear to refer to what in 1 Corinthians 12:5 Paul called *diakoniai* ("services"); whether they are also *charismata* is moot.

*2.1.3. The Remaining Lists.* For the most part the remaining listings in 1 Corinthians (1 Cor 13:1-3, 8; 14:6, 26) add little that is new, except for two things: (1) One receives added insight into what Paul understands about "knowledge," by his speaking in 1 Corinthians 13:2 of "knowing all mysteries and all knowledge." In 1 Corinthians 14:6 it appears alongside "revelation," which suggests Spirit-inspired understanding of the ways of God. (2) Revelation, which appears first in 1 Corinthians 14:6, also is listed in 1 Corinthians 14:26 as one of the things that happens in the gathering for worship. Its cognate verb appears in 1 Corinthians 14:30, referring to prophecy. Since the prophetic word in 1 Corinthians 14:24-25 also "reveals" the hidden secrets of the heart of the sinner and leads to conversion, it seems likely that this word, in part at least, indicates something of Paul's own understanding of prophecy.

*2.2. Romans 12:6-8.* This passage stands near the beginning of the paraenesis (*see* Teaching, Paraenesis) of this letter. The concern is with a sober estimate of oneself and the need for mutuality and diversity in the community. The three features that make this passage look similar to some things in 1 Corinthians 12—14 are (1) the analogy of the body—as one, with many parts; (2) the fact that the members have *charismata* given to them (for the building up of the body is implied); and (3) the mention of prophecy as the first of the *charismata* and the inclusion of teaching as the third item. But after that, nothing is familiar. In contrast to 1 Corinthians, but in keeping with the issues in the Roman church (*see* Romans), the seven items emphasize not miracles and verbal utterances, but forms of service ("service" itself being one of the items listed). One further item (*paraklēsis,* "exhortation," NRSV, NASB) is probably a verbal gift, but it also might be another form of serving ("encouraging," NIV). Furthermore, each item is qualified as to the manner in which the utterance/service is to be rendered ("according to the rule of faith," "with sincerity, earnestness, cheerfulness," etc.).

The most difficult item on this list is the sixth, *proïstamenos,* which is quite ambiguous in Greek, meaning either "to manage/govern" or "to care for/ give aid to." In 1 Thessalonians 5:12 Paul used the word to describe those in leadership; its appearance here between "giving" and "showing mercy*" suggests that for Paul it usually carries the sense of "caring for" rather than "leading," even when leadership is in view.

All in all, this list obviously expands how one is to view Paul's understanding of the plural *charismata;* but it helps very little in assessing whether Paul would also have thought of all of these as "gifts of the Spirit."

*2.3. Ephesians 4:11.* This list is unique in the Pauline corpus. Three ministries from 1 Corinthians 12:28 are mentioned (apostles, prophets, teachers); these are joined by "evangelists" and "pastors," the latter probably are to be understood in very close relationship with "teacher." Although this list occurs again in a context of Spirit and body (Eph 4:4), these "gifts" are not referred to as *charismata,* nor are they suggested to be "gifts of the Spirit." They are in fact given to the church by Christ; and they are not spoken of as "gifts" per se. Rather, they are people who function in these ways within the church for the singular aim of "equipping the saints," apparently so that the latter can do the "work of the ministry, for the building up of the body."

The burning question in this list is whether these people are to be thought of in terms of their function or as holders of an office (*see* Churches, Pauline). In keeping with the prior lists, when ministries of these kinds are mentioned, the emphasis still seems to be on function. In any case, with this list one moves somewhat beyond Paul's own understanding of *charismata,* either as "Spirit manifestations" or as "forms of service." It is doubtful whether Paul ever considered an "office" in the church as a "spiritual gift," either in terms of a *charisma* or as a special enduement of the Spirit. That seems to be the reading of these texts from a later time.

### 3. The Charismata.

Despite the difficulties involved, the various items from these texts may be conveniently grouped under three major headings: Spirit manifestations within the worshipping community; deeds of service; specific ministries. It should only be noted that, whether or not we understand the term "gifts of the Spirit" in its narrower sense (as applying only to Spirit manifestations), the goal of all *charismata,* in all categories, is the "building up" of the community itself, and individual members within the community. Furthermore, in its first two senses Paul makes a considerable point of the universality of such "gifting" within the Spirit-filled community.

*3.1. Gifts As Spirit Manifestations.* This is the one certain grouping in Paul's letters in which there is a specific connection between the Spirit and *charismata.* These appear chiefly to be supernatural manifestations of the Spirit within the community at worship. They can be further grouped into "miracles" as such, and "verbal utterances."

*3.1.1. Miracles.* Included here are three items from 1 Corinthians 12:9-10, "faith" (= the supernatural gift of faith that can "move mountains"; cf. 1 Cor 13:2), "charismata of healings" (of the physical body; also 1 Cor 12:28, 30) and "workings of miracles" (= all other such phenomena not included in healing). The use of the plurals "gifts" and "workings" for the latter two probably means that these "gifts" are not permanent, but each occurrence is a "gift" in its own right. That such phenomena were a regular part of the apostle's own ministry is evidenced by 2 Corinthians 12:12 and Romans 15:18-19. That they were also the regular expectation of the Pauline churches is evidenced by Galatians 3:5.

*3.1.2. Inspired utterance.* Included here are "the message of wisdom," "the message of knowledge," "prophecy," "the discernments of S/spirits," "tongues" and "the interpretation of tongues" from 1 Corinthians 12:10; "teaching" and "revelation" from 1 Corinthians 14:6; and (perhaps) "exhortation" from Romans 12:8—it might also include "singing" from 1 Corinthians 14:15 and 26 (cf. Eph 5:19; *see* Hymns). Attempts to distinguish some of these items from one another are generally futile, as is any distinction between their "charismatic" or "non-charismatic" expression (e.g., teaching or singing).

The "message of wisdom" and "knowledge," for example, is language created by the situation in Corinth. For Paul the "message of wisdom" is the preaching of the cross* (see 1 Cor 1:18—2:16; the terminology occurs nowhere else). "Knowledge," on the other hand, is closely related to "mysteries"* in 1 Corinthians 13:2 and elsewhere stands close to the concept of "revelation" (1 Cor 13:8-9, 12; 14:6). Similarly, prophecy itself is closely connected to "revelation" in 1 Corinthians 14:6, and especially in 1 Corinthians 14:25, 26, 30. Are these to be understood as distinctively different gifts? Or, as seems more likely, do they suggest different emphases for the expression of the prophetic gift, since that too seems to fluctuate between "revealing mysteries" and more straightforward words of edification, comfort and exhortation (or encouragement)? In any case, the use of uninterpreted tongues in the assembly is what brought forth the whole argument, and Paul uses prophecy as representative of all other intelligible inspired utterances that are to be preferred to tongues in that setting. These two need further comment.

*3.1.2.1. Glossolalia.* Paul's actual term is "different kinds of tongues.*" Enough is said in 1 Corinthians 13—14 to give us a fairly good idea as to how Paul understood it. (1) It is Spirit-inspired utterance; that is made plain by 1 Corinthians 12:7, 11 and 14:2. (2) The regulations for its community use in 1 Corinthians 14:27-28 make it clear that the speaker is not in "ecstasy" or "out of control." Quite the opposite; the speakers must speak in turn, and they must remain silent if there is no one to interpret. (3) It is speech essentially unintelligible both to the speaker (1 Cor 14:14) and to the ungifted hearers (1 Cor 14:16), which is why it must be interpreted in the assembly. (4) It is speech directed basically toward God (1 Cor 14:2, 14-15, 28); one may assume, therefore, that what is interpreted is not speech directed toward others, but the "mysteries" spoken to God. (5) As a gift for private prayer,* Paul held it in the highest regard (1 Cor 14:2, 4, 5, 15, 17-18).

Whether Paul also understood it to be an actual earthly language is moot, but the overall evidence suggests not. He certainly does not envisage the likelihood of someone's being present who might understand without interpretation; and the analogy of earthly language in 1 Corinthians 14:10-12 implies that it is not an earthly language (a thing is not usually identical with that to which it is analogous).

*3.1.2.2. Prophecy.* Of all the Spirit *charismata*, this is the one mentioned most often in the Pauline letters (1 Thess 5:20; 1 Cor 11:4-5; 12—14; Rom 12:6; Eph 2:20; 3:5; 4:11; 1 Tim 1:18; 4:14; and probably "through the Spirit" in 2 Thess 2:2), implying the widest range of occurrence in the Pauline churches (*see* Prophecy). Although it was also a widespread phenomenon in the Greek world (see Aune), Paul's understanding of prophecy was thoroughly conditioned by his own history in Judaism. The prophet was a person who spoke to God's people under the inspiration of the Spirit. In Paul such "speech" consisted either of spontaneous, intelligible messages, orally delivered in the gathered assembly, intended for the edification or encouragement of the people, or of a "revelation" of some kind (Gal 2:2), which at times could expose the hearts of unbelievers and lead them to repentance. Those who prophesied were clearly understood to be "in control" (see 1 Cor 14:29-33).

Although some people are called prophets, the implication of 1 Corinthians 14:24-25, 30-31 is that the gift is available—at least potentially—to all.

But it is also clear that prophecy does not have independent authority. The combined evidence of 1 Thessalonians 5:21-22 and 1 Corinthians 12:10 and 14:29 is that all such prophesying must be "discerned" by the charismatic community. The implication in both texts is that one may believe oneself truly to be "inspired" of the Spirit, but in reality what is said may not come from the Spirit at all. Therefore, the community must test all things, holding fast to the good and dispensing with every evil expression.

*3.1.3. Their Extent in the Pauline Churches.* The very fact that Paul can list all these items in such a matter-of-fact way, especially in 1 Corinthians 12:7-11, indicates that the worship of the early church was far more "charismatic" than has been true for most of the church's subsequent history. Some indeed have tried to make a virtue of this lack, arguing that the more extraordinary phenomena were relatively limited in the early church—they belong to more "immature" believers like the Corinthians—and that they are no longer needed once the NT was canonized. But that quite misses the evidence in Paul, as well as his point in 1 Corinthians 13:8-13 (see Fee 1987). One may as well argue that the other Pauline churches did not celebrate the Lord's Supper,* since it is mentioned only in 1 Corinthians.

In fact the evidence is considerable that a visible, "charismatic" dimension of life in the Spirit was the normal experience of the Pauline churches. That Paul should speak to it in a direct way only twice (1 Thess 5:19-22; 1 Cor 12—14) is the "accident" of history— only here were there problems of abuse. Indeed, the problem in Thessalonica is especially telling, since apparently there was a tendency to play down the prophetic Spirit in their gatherings; but Paul would have none of that.

Even more telling are the offhanded, matter-of-fact ways these phenomena are mentioned elsewhere. For example, in 2 Thessalonians 2:2 Paul knows that someone has falsely informed them under the guise of his authority as to "the day of the Lord" (*see* Eschatology). What he does not know is the source of this false information; one possibility that automatically comes to mind is "through the Spirit" (most likely a "non-discerned" prophetic utterance). Likewise in 1 Corinthians 11:2-16 in the matter of head coverings (*see* Head), Paul refers to worship as "praying and prophesying," the two primary ways of addressing God and people in the assembly. In Galatians 3:4-5 his argument rests on their past ("such remarkable experiences" BAGD) and ongoing experience of the Spirit, including "miracles." And in the case of Timothy's ministry (1 Tim 1:18; 4:14), his own gifting is related to prophetic utterances in the community, prophetic utterances that are so significant for Timothy that he is urged to keep up the fight in light of them (1 Tim 1:18). In none of these instances is Paul arguing for something; rather, the visible, "charismatic" expression of their common life in the Spirit is the presupposition from which he argues for something else.

**3.2. Charismata *As Deeds of Service*.** This category comes from the use of *charismata* in Romans 12:6-8, where he includes "serving," "giving," "caring for" (in the sense of leadership) and "showing mercy." To these one might also add "helpful deeds" and "acts of guidance" from 1 Corinthians 12:28 (the first word implies that some minister to the physical and spiritual needs of others in the community, while the second probably refers to giving wise counsel to the community—as a whole, not simply to other individuals). These are the least visibly "charismatic" of the "gifts," and the least obvious as expressions of corporate worship. In fact they seem to belong rather to Paul's ever-present interest in relationships within the church. Whether Paul himself considered these ministries as gifts of the Spirit is especially moot. In any case, they fit better in discussions of the Pauline understanding of Christian ethics* and community life (*see* Churches, Pauline). As such, they give visible expression to the fruit of the Spirit (*see* Fruit of the Spirit), but Paul himself does not designate them as spiritual gifts (except by our loading the term *charismata* with meaning not inherent to it).

**3.3. *Gifts and Ministry*.** Here is one of the more controverted areas in this discussion. Included here are such items as "apostles," "prophets" and "teachers" from 1 Corinthians 12:28 and Ephesians 4:11, "pastors" and "evangelists" from the latter passage, and Timothy's own charisma of ministry in 1 Timothy 4:14. The difficulties lie in three areas: the ambiguity of language noted above; whether these terms are primarily to be understood in terms of function or office; that Paul himself designates some of these as *charismata*, but not all of them (*see* Ministry).

The clue to this ambiguity is probably to be found in a proper distinction between function and office. For the most part, these terms in Paul's letters seem to be primarily functional, rather than denoting office. That is, Paul is more often concerned with the function of prophecy in the community than he is with a position known as "prophet." In any case, the latter emerges from the former, not the other way about; and this is where the role of the Spirit and

*charismata* terminology fit in. Paul clearly understood his own ministry and that of others to be Spirit-given and Spirit-empowered. When functioning as Spirit ministries, Paul would probably consider such ministries to be *charismata*. Even in what most scholars consider to be the Deutero-Pauline Pastoral Letters (*see* Pastoral Letters), Timothy's charism is clearly not an office. The charisma resides "within him," for the sake of his ministry (so Schatzmann, Fee; contra Dunn et al.).

In sum, the frequent distinction between "charismatic" and "official" is probably a false one (so Käsemann, Fung), partly because all ministry was "charismatic" in the sense of being Christ-given and Spirit-empowered (Käsemann), and partly because the language distinctions come from a later time and have little to do with Paul and his concerns. This does not negate "office"; it merely suggests that such a discussion seems quite foreign to Paul's own use of *charismata* when associated with the Spirit.

*See also* Body of Christ; Fruit of the Spirit; Holy Spirit; Knowledge, Gift of Knowledge; Ministry; Prophecy, Prophesying; Spirituality; Tongues; Worship.

BIBLIOGRAPHY. D. E. Aune, *Prophecy in Early Christianity and the Ancient Mediterranean World* (Grand Rapids: Eerdmans, 1983); A. Bittlinger, *Gifts and Graces* (Grand Rapids: Eerdmans, 1967); D. A. Carson, *Showing the Spirit* (Grand Rapids: Baker, 1987); H. Conzelmann, "χάρισμα," *TDNT* IX.402-406; J. D. G. Dunn, *Jesus and the Spirit* (Philadelphia: Westminster, 1975); G. D. Fee, *The First Epistle to the Corinthians* (NICNT; Grand Rapids: Eerdmans, 1987); idem, *God's Empowering Presence: The Holy Spirit in the Letters of Paul* (Peabody: Hendrickson, 1993); R. Y. K. Fung, "Ministry, Community and Spiritual Gifts," *EvQ* 56 (1984) 3-14; D. Gee, *Concerning Spiritual Gifts* (Springfield: Gospel Publishing, 1947); W. A. Grudem, *The Gift of Prophecy in 1 Corinthians* (Washington: University Press of America, 1982); D. Hill, *New Testament Prophecy* (Atlanta: John Knox, 1979); E. Käsemann, "Ministry and Community in the New Testament," in *Essays on New Testament Themes* (London: SCM, 1964) 63-94; J. Koenig, *Charismata: God's Gifts for God's People* (1978); J. W. MacGorman, *The Gifts of the Spirit* (Nashville: Broadman, 1974); R. P. Martin, *The Spirit and the Congregation* (Grand Rapids; Eerdmans, 1984); S. Schatzmann, *A Pauline Theology of Charismata* (Peabody: Hendrickson, 1986); E. Schweizer, *The Holy Spirit* (Philadelphia: Fortress, 1978).

G. D. Fee

**GLORIFICATION.** *See* Glory, Glorification.

# GLORY, GLORIFICATION

The terminology of glory provides a window on virtually the whole of Paul's theology (the noun *doxa* occurs seventy-six times, the verb *doxazō*, twelve times, predominantly in Romans and the Corinthian letters). Nowhere in the NT are its OT roots more apparent than in Paul's usage.

1. Background
2. God's Eternal Purpose
3. Creation and Fall
4. Christ, the New Creation and the Church

## 1. Background.

In the OT Yahweh's glory (*keḇôḏ yhwh*, "glory of the Lord," is a technical term) is his visible and active presence in the creation (Ps 19:1; Is 6:3) and among the nations (Ps 97:6), especially his covenant people Israel.* Closely related to his grandeur and power as creator and redeemer, glory is often associated with the phenomenon of light or fire, sometimes of such overwhelming brilliance and unendurable intensity that it is shrouded in a cloud (Ex 16:10; 24:17; cf. Ex 33:22-23 and 34:29-35).

God's glory-presence, for salvation or destruction, is prominent in the decisive moments and central institutions of Israel's history: Moses and the Exodus, monarchy and Temple, Exile and return. In the prophets glory takes on an eschatological cast; their hope for the future is summed up in Habakkuk's words, "the earth will be filled with the knowledge of the glory of the Lord, as the waters cover the sea" (Hab 2:14). This final, transforming revelation of the divine glory, through the coming of the Messiah, will bring salvation to all nations (Is 40:5; 58:8; 62:1-2).

The LXX's decision to translate the OT *kāḇôḏ* with *doxa* initiated a process of substantial semantic change in the usage of the latter word in Jewish religious contexts (in secular Greek it meant "opinion," "reputation," "praise"). That change carries through into the NT usage, especially in John and Paul.

## 2. God's Eternal Purpose.

God* is "the Father of glory" (Eph 1:17). Glory begins and ends with him and his plan is to share his glory. "The riches of his glory" (Rom 9:23; Eph 1:18; 3:16; Col 1:27) are displayed in those whom "he prepared beforehand for glory" (Rom 9:23). The mystery*-wisdom*, revealed in Paul's gospel* preaching,* was "predestined before the ages for our glory" (1 Cor 2:7). Election* in Christ* "before the foundation of the world," God's loving predestination, is "to the praise of the glory of his grace" (Eph 1:4-6, 12). The final link in the chain that begins with foreknowl-

edge* and predestination is glorification (Rom 8:29-30).

## 3. Creation and Fall.

"What has been made" is an evident display of "God's invisible qualities—his eternal power and divine nature" (Rom 1:20 NIV); in other words, the entire created order shows "the glory of the immortal God" (Rom 1:23). Uniquely within the creation,* "man . . . is the image and glory of God," and "woman is the glory of man" (1 Cor 11:7; the contrast in Rom 1:23 shows that *doxa* is correlative with *homoiōma* ["likeness"] and *eikōn* ["image"]).

Sin* enters the creation through Adam* (Rom 5:12-19). Consequently, "although they knew God," human beings "neither glorified him as God nor gave thanks" (Rom 1:21); that is, they have withheld worship* and adoration, their due response to the divine glory reflected in the creation around them and in themselves as God's image* bearers. Instead, with futile minds and foolish, darkened hearts (cf. 1 Cor 1:18-25), they have idolatrously exchanged God's glory for creaturely images, human and otherwise (Rom 1:21-23). Having so drastically defaced the divine image, they have, without exception, forfeited the privilege of reflecting his glory (Rom 3:23). This *doxa*-less condition, resulting in unrelieved futility,* corruption and death, permeates the entire created order (Rom 8:20-22).

## 4. Christ, the New Creation and the Church.

The whole of Paul's gospel, centered in Christ's death* and resurrection* (Rom 1:3-4; 1 Cor 15:3-4), may be viewed as a message of restored and consummated glory.

*4.1. Promise and fulfillment.* Sinful human rebellion has not frustrated God's eternal plan. To Israel* belong, as part of the elect nation's privileges, "the adoption and the glory and the covenants* and the giving of the Law* and the promises" (Rom 9:4), and in Christ those covenant promises, "no matter how many," have their fulfillment (their "Yes") "to the glory of God" (2 Cor 1:20).

The highest single concentration of glory vocabulary in Paul's letters (ten occurrences of the noun and verb) is in 2 Corinthians 3:7-11—a contrast between old and new covenants (2 Cor 3:6), with glory as a common denominator. Even the old covenant with its condemning and death-dealing "letter" is invested with divine glory. But the glory of the Law, intervening between the promise and its fulfillment in the interests of that fulfillment (Gal 3:15-18), was transitory (2 Cor 3:11); it is as if the old had none, in comparison with the surpassing, permanent glory of the new covenant (2 Cor 3:10-11).

The new covenant *doxa* in Christ is the climactic revelation of God's glory; it is eschatological* glory. Its full dimensions are especially apparent in 2 Corinthians 4:6 (quoting Gen 1:3): As the God who in the beginning said "Light shall shine out of darkness," so he gives believers "the light of the knowledge of the glory of God in the face of Christ." Christ's glory-light* answers to the light of the original creation; his is the splendor of a new and final creation (cf. 2 Cor 5:17; *see* Creation and New Creation).

*4.2. Righteousness and the Spirit.* 2 Corinthians 3:6-18 expressly associate the glory of the new covenant with its being "the ministry of the Spirit" (2 Cor 3:8) and "the ministry of righteousness" (2 Cor 3:9). Righteousness* and the Spirit,* together with closely related concepts like life* (2 Cor 3:6), freedom* (2 Cor 3:17) and power* (cf. 1 Cor 2:4), form a matrix that constitutes the eschatological glory revealed in Christ.

*4.2.1. Righteousness.* "The gospel of the glory of Christ" (2 Cor 4:4) is the revelation of God's righteousness (Rom 1:17), a righteousness that justifies* (Rom 3:21-26; cf. 2 Cor 5:21). On the cross Christ is "the Lord of glory" (1 Cor 2:8) because his death is a propitiatory sacrifice (Rom 3:25; *see* Expiation, Propitiation), a provision of God's love (Rom 5:8) that removes his just wrath toward sinners (Rom 1:18).

Christ's glory-righteousness, veiled in the cross* of Christ (1 Cor 2:6-8), is openly displayed in his resurrection.* Because he was "obedient unto death," under conditions of humility and abased servitude, uniquely intensified by his being "in the form of God" and "equal with God" (that is, eternally and inherently he is a participant in divine glory), "therefore" (*dio*) God "has highly exalted him" (Phil 2:6-9). Rewarded with life for death, "justified in the Spirit, ... taken up in glory" (1 Tim 3:16), "raised from the dead through the glory of the Father" (Rom 6:4), the humiliated Lord* of glory has become the glorified Lord of glory (*see* Christology).

This movement involved a real, climactic enhancement in glory for Christ personally. In contrast to his preresurrection existence, marked by "perishability," "dishonor" and "weakness," his resurrection body is characterized by "imperishability," "glory" and "power" (1 Cor 15:42-43; Phil 3:20-21; cf. 2 Cor 13:4).

*4.2.2. The Spirit.* Christ's glorification results in a new and unprecedented relationship with the Holy Spirit. "The last Adam became life-giving Spirit" (1 Cor 15:45). In this declaration, central to both Paul's christology* and his pneumatology, (1) the reference is to the Holy Spirit (cf. 1 Cor 2:14-15; Rom 8:11; 2 Cor 3:6), and (2) the word *became* has in view

Christ's resurrection or, more broadly, his exaltation* (as the flow of the argument in chapter 15 shows). Consequently (2 Cor 3:17), "the Lord [= the glorified Christ; cf. v. 18 with 2 Cor 4:4, 6] is the Spirit" (= the Holy Spirit; see 2 Cor 3:6, 8; *see* Holy Spirit). This equation does not miss or deny the personal distinction between Christ and the Spirit; eternal, inner-trinitarian relationships are outside Paul's purview in these statements (*see* God). The identification is functional or eschatological, not ontological; it describes what has happened to Christ, as "the last Adam" (1 Cor 15:45), in history. In being glorified he has been so thoroughly transformed by the Spirit (Rom 1:4; 8:11) and come into such full and permanent possession of the Spirit (Rom 8:9; 2 Cor 3:17) that they are now inseparably one in the activity of giving eschatological life.

*4.3. Present Glory.* Christ's glorification is not only for himself but others, "in order that he might be the firstborn among many brothers" (Rom 8:29). His loving self-sacrifice for the church (Eph 5:25) was in order that, as his bride, it too might be "glorious" (*endoxon*, Eph 5:27). To that end faith is essential; Christ's indwelling presence, through the power of the Spirit, is "through faith," "according to the riches of [God's] glory" (Eph 3:16-17).

The church's glorification takes place specifically as believers are "conformed to the image of his Son" (Rom 8:29); the glory-image, universally defaced and perverted in Adam, is restored and made consummate in Christ and the church.* This conformity is a reality already underway (2 Cor 3:18 in context): As believers, in "the light of the gospel of the glory of Christ, who is the image of God" (2 Cor 4:4), "behold [or 'reflect'] the glory of the Lord"—Christ (who is the Spirit, 2 Cor 3:17), they "are being transformed into the same image from glory to glory." The glorified Christ, as life-giving Spirit, is the source of the ongoing, transforming glorification of the church (*see* Adam and Christ).

This present glory of the church, paradoxically and parallel to the experience of its Lord prior to his resurrection, is veiled by afflictions and adversity. Sharing in "the fellowship of his sufferings" is the way believers experience "the power of his resurrection" (Phil 3:10; cf. 2 Cor 1:5); the condition for those who aspire to be glorified with Christ is that for now "we suffer with him" (Rom 8:17). Paul's prayer* is that believers might be powerfully strengthened "according to the might of [God's] glory" just with a view to the "great endurance and patience" (NIV) they must display (Col 1:11). The present situation, where glory-renewal is being experienced "inwardly" but not "outwardly," involves affliction that is "momentary" and "light" in comparison with the "eternal weight of glory" being produced (2 Cor 4:16-17; cf. Rom 8:18; *see* Afflictions; Suffering).

*4.4. Future Glory.* Christ, indwelling the church, is "the hope of glory" (Col 1:27). The glorification of believers awaits its full realization at his return; "when Christ, our life, is manifested, then you also will be manifested with him in glory" (Col 3:4). Then Christ, "the firstfruits*" of the resurrection-harvest (1 Cor 15:20, 23), will transform the present, humble body of the believer to be "in conformity with the body of his glory" (Phil 3:20); "raised in glory," with a "spiritual body*" like his (1 Cor 15:43-44), believers, outwardly and bodily now, "will bear the image of the heavenly [Christ]" (1 Cor 15:49). This final, open revelation of "the freedom of the glory of the children of God" (Rom 8:21), will be cosmic in scope, including as well the freedom of the entire, non-image-bearing creation, its release from futility and corruption (Rom 8:19-21; *see* Eschatology).

Christ's glorious return will result, for unbelievers, in "eternal destruction," consisting in separation from him and "the glory of his power" (2 Thess 1:9). It will also be the "day" when, definitively, "he comes to be glorified in his saints" (2 Thess 1:10). To that end the apostle's prayer for the church is that even now, until then, "the name of our Lord Jesus Christ may be glorified in you, and you in him." (2 Thess 1:12).

*See also* ADAM AND CHRIST; CHRISTOLOGY; CREATION AND NEW CREATION; ESCHATOLOGY; GOD; IMAGE, IMAGE OF GOD; LIGHT AND DARKNESS.

BIBLIOGRAPHY. H. Hegemann, "δόξα, *EDNT* 1.346-47; G. Kittel, "δόξα, *TDNT* II.233-37, 242-55; C. C. Newman, *Paul's Glory-Christology: Tradition and Rhetoric* (NovTSup 69; Leiden: E. J. Brill, 1992); H. Schlier, "Doxa bei Paulus als heilsgeschichtlicher Begriff," in *Studiorum Paulinorum Congressus Internationalis Catholicus* (2 vols.; AnBib 17-18; Rome: Pontifical Biblical Institute, 1963) 1.45-56; N. Turner, "Glory and Glorification," in *Christian Words* (Edinburgh: T. & T. Clark, 1980) 185-89. R. B. Gaffin, Jr.

**GLORY OF GOD.** *See* GLORY, GLORIFICATION; GOD.

**GLOSSOLALIA.** *See* TONGUES.

# GNOSIS, GNOSTICISM

The Gnostics were followers of a variety of religious movements which stressed salvation* through *gnōsis*, or "knowledge," that is, of one's origins. Cosmological dualism was an essential feature of Gnosticism—an opposition between the spiritual world and the evil, material world. Gnosticism was attacked in the writings of the church fathers, who regarded the various gnostic groups as heretical perversions of Christianity.

Modern scholars believe that Gnosticism was a religious phenomenon which was in some cases independent of Christianity. There is as yet no consensus as to when and how it originated, though many scholars have recently sought to trace the roots of Gnosticism to Jewish fringe elements. One problem that faces this view is the need to explain the anti-Jewish cast given by the Gnostics to the OT, such as the caricature of Jehovah as a foolish demiurge.

1. Sources
2. Gnostic Doctrines
3. Gnosticism and the Pauline Corpus

## 1. Sources.

Texts that are unambiguously gnostic date from after the second century A.D. Those who maintain a pre-Christian Gnosticism assume the early existence of Gnosticism and interpret the NT texts in the light of this assumption.

*1.1. Patristic Sources.* Until recently scholars were entirely dependent upon the descriptions of the Gnostics found in the church fathers. In some cases the patristic sources preserved extracts of the gnostic writings but for the most part they were polemical in nature. Our most important sources include Justin Martyr from Samaria (d. 165), Irenaeus of Lyons (d. *c.* 225), Clement of Alexandria (d. *c.* 215), Origen of Alexandria and Caesarea (d. 254), and Epiphanius of Salamis in Cyprus (d. 403).

Especially valuable is Irenaeus's account, which has been preserved in a Latin translation, *Adversus Haereses*. The *Philosophoumena* of Hippolytus was only discovered in 1842. Clement and Origen were in many ways sympathetic to the gnostic emphases. Though Epiphanius had some firsthand contact with Gnostics in Egypt, his *Panarion*, while comprehensive, is not very reliable. Some of the observations of the fathers, especially of Irenaeus, have been confirmed by the discovery of original gnostic documents at Nag Hammadi, Egypt. On the other hand, we have nothing as yet from the gnostic sources themselves which corresponds to the patristic description of licentious Gnosticism.

The church fathers were unanimous in regarding Simon of Samaria as the arch-Gnostic, though our earliest source, Acts 8, describes him only as a *magos*, "magician." According to the later sources Simon claimed to be divine, and taught that his companion, a former prostitute, was the reincarnated Helen of Troy. Those who accept the patristic view of Simon believe that Acts has not given us an accurate portrayal of Simon. Most scholars, however, believe that the church fathers were mistaken.

According to the church fathers, Simon was followed by a fellow Samaritan, Menander, who taught at Antioch in Syria toward the end of the first century. He claimed that those who believed in him would not die. His claims were nullified when he himself died. Also teaching in Antioch at the beginning of the second century was Saturninus, who held that the "incorporeal" Christ was the redeemer. That is, he held a docetic view of Christ which denied the incarnation (cf. 1 Jn 4:3).

Teaching in Asia Minor in the early second century was Cerinthus, who held that Jesus was but a man upon whom Christ descended as a dove. As Christ could not suffer, he departed from Jesus before the crucifixion. Another early gnostic teacher was Basilides, to whom we have attributed both a dualistic system by Irenaeus and a monistic system by Hippolytus.

An important though atypical Gnostic was Marcion of Pontus (northern Turkey), who taught at Rome from 137 to 144. He contrasted the God of the OT with the God of the NT. Marcion drew up the first canon or closed list of NT books, including a truncated Gospel of Luke. Jesus simply appeared; his body was a "phantom." Marcion's church spread to Egypt, Mesopotamia and Armenia. His docetic teachings were sharply rebuked by Tertullian.

The most famous Gnostic teacher was Valentinus, who came from Alexandria to Rome in 140. He taught that there were a series of divine eons. He divided humankind into three classes: *hylics*, or unbelievers immersed in nature and the flesh; *psychics*, or common Christians who lived by faith; and *pneumatics* or the spiritual Gnostics. The later Valentinians divided into an Italian and an Oriental school over the question of whether Jesus had a psychic or pneumatic body. The many outstanding Valentinian teachers included Ptolemaeus, Heracleon, Theodotus and Marcus. The earliest known commentary on a NT book is Heracleon's on the Gospel of John.

*1.2. Mandaic Sources.* The Mandaean communities in southern Iraq and southwestern Iran are today the sole surviving remnants of Gnosticism. Their texts, though known only through late (seventeenth or eighteenth century) manuscripts, were used by the History-of-Religions scholars and R. Bultmann to reconstruct an alleged pre-Christian Gnosticism. In addition to the manuscripts there are earlier magic bowl texts (A.D. 600) and some magical lead amulets, which may date to as early as the third century A.D. There is no firm evidence to date the origins of Mandaeanism earlier than the second century A.D.

*1.3. Coptic Sources.* In the nineteenth century two Coptic gnostic codices were published: the *Codex Askewianus* containing the Pistis Sophia, and the *Codex Brucianus* containing the Books of Jeu—both relatively late gnostic compositions. (Coptic is a late form of Egyptian written mainly in Greek letters.) A third work, the *Codex Berolinensis*, though acquired in the nineteenth century, was not published until 1955. It contains a *Gospel of Mary* (Magdalene), a *Sophia of Jesus*, *Acts of Peter* and an *Apocryphon of John*—a work mentioned by Irenaeus in A.D. 180.

In 1945 a cache of eleven Coptic codices and fragments of two others were found by peasants near Nag Hammadi in Upper Egypt, 370 miles south of Cairo where the Nile bends from west to east. Unfortunately some of the papyrus leaves and covers were burned in an oven after the lot was brought back to the village of al Qasr. The first translation of a tractate, that of *The Gospel of Truth*, appeared in 1956. After various vicissitudes, an English translation of the fifty-one treatises appeared in 1977, largely through the efforts of J. M. Robinson.

The Nag Hammadi Library, as the collection has been called, contains a variety of texts: non-Gnostic, non-Christian Gnostic, and Christian Gnostic. The most famous example of the latter is *The Gospel of Thomas*, probably composed c. A.D. 140 in Syria. This contains 114 purported sayings of Jesus. In 1897 and in 1904 B. P. Grenfell and A. S. Hunt had discovered at Oxyrhynchus in Egypt non-canonical sayings or the so-called "Logia" of Jesus. We now know that these papyri came from copies of the Greek text of the *Gospel of Thomas*.

Some scholars such as J. M. Robinson and K. Rudolph are convinced that the Nag Hammadi texts have served to confirm R. Bultmann's thesis of a pre-Christian Gnosticism, which is both assumed and attacked by the NT. They have cited especially *The Apocalypse of Adam* and *The Paraphrase of Shem* as non-Christian gnostic works from Nag Hammadi. But the assertion that these are actually non-Christian works has been challenged; they certainly do not appear to be pre-Christian compositions. G. W. MacRae, who believes in a pre-Christian Gnosticism, concedes, "And even if we are on solid ground in some cases in arguing that the original works represented in the [Nag Hammadi] library are much older than the extant copies, we are still unable to postulate plausibly any pre-Christian dates." The weakness of the arguments which have sustained a pre-Christian date for gnosticism have been pointed out by S. Petrement (cf. Yamauchi; *see* Apocryphal Pauline Literature; Paul in Early Church Tradition).

***1.4. Other Sources.*** Other sources such as the *Hermetica* and the Syrian *Odes of Solomon* and the *Hymn of the Pearl* are problematic, both because they are not unambiguously gnostic and because there are question about their dates. Though hermetic texts have been found in the Nag Hammadi Library, the *Hermetica* as a whole are not radically dualistic.

## 2. Gnostic Doctrines.

Because there was no central authority or canon of scriptures, the Gnostics taught a bewildering variety of views. Fundamental to clearly gnostic systems was a dualism, which opposed the transcendent God and an ignorant demiurge (often a caricature of the OT Jehovah). In some systems the creation of the world resulted from the presumption of Sophia (Wisdom). In any event the material creation, including the body, was regarded as inherently evil. Sparks of divinity, however, had been encapsuled in the bodies of certain pneumatic or spiritual individuals, who were ignorant of their celestial origins. The transcendent God sent down a redeemer (Christ), who brought them salvation in the form of a secret *gnōsis* or "knowledge." Most Gnostics were docetics, who held that Christ did not really suffer as he was not truly incarnate. Gnostics hoped to escape from the prison of their bodies at death and to traverse the planetary spheres of hostile demons to be reunited with God. There was for them, of course, no reason to believe in the resurrection of the body.

Since salvation was not dependent upon faith or works but upon the knowledge of one's nature, some Gnostics indulged deliberately in licentious behavior. Carpocrates, for example, urged his followers to participate in all sins; his son Epiphanes taught that promiscuity was God's law.

Most Gnostics, however, took a radically ascetic attitude toward sex and marriage, deeming the creation of woman the source of evil, and the procreation of children but the multiplication of souls in bondage to the powers of darkness. They looked forward to the time when females would be transformed into males.

We know very little about the cult and the community of the Gnostics. Women were very prominent in many of their sects. As a general rule the Gnostics interpreted rites such as baptism and the Eucharist as spiritual symbols of gnosis.

## 3. Gnosticism and the Pauline Corpus.

Despite the lack of gnostic texts prior to Christianity, many scholars (Robinson, Rudolph) have assumed a pre-Christian origin of Gnosticism. They also believe that they can detect references to Gnosticism in the NT, especially in the writings of John and Paul. H. Koester, in his influential introduction to the NT, assumes a gnostic background for Corinthians, Philippians, the Pastorals, but not Colossians. W. Schmithals finds Gnostics almost everywhere in Paul's letters, even in Thessalonians and Galatians (Schmithals 1972).

***3.1. Galatians and Romans.*** R. Bultmann held that a large number of transformed gnostic concepts appeared in Romans,* such as the fall of creation (Rom 8:20-21; Bultmann, 1.174; *see* Futility) and baptism* into the body of Christ (Rom 6:5; Bultmann, 1.141) and reference to the powers of this age (Rom 8:38-39; Bultmann, 1.173). Schmithals has argued that Paul's opponents in Galatia* were Gnostics on the dubious ground that Paul's insistence on his apostolate was based on a concept of the apostle* derived from the Gnostics (Schmithals 1972, 13-64). Most scholars find it quite obvious that Galatians was directed against Judaizers.* Bultmann and Schmithals operate within a hermeneutical circle which assume a pre-Christian Gnosticism, which can only be extrapolated from much later sources.

***3.2. Corinthians.*** Because Paul spoke about *gnōsis* and *sophia* in his letters to Corinth, the possibility of a gnostic background looms the largest here. The thesis that a Jewish Gnosticism characterized Paul's opponents at Corinth has been most fully developed by Schmithals. One of the weightiest evidences cited is Paul's antithesis of *psychikos* ("physical") and *pneumatikos* ("spiritual"; 1 Cor 2:14-15; 15:44-46). But it is quite anachronistic to use Valentinian distinctions to understand Paul's terminology (*see* Corinthians).

Other scholars have concluded that it is not necessary to understand Paul's opponents as Gnostics. R. A. Horsley has attempted to illuminate the "gnosis" of Paul's opponents from Hellenistic Judaism as illustrated by Philo and the Wisdom of Solomon, rather than from Gnosticism. He concludes, "What Paul responds to, therefore, is not a gnostic libertinism, as derived from Reitzenstein, elaborated on by Schmithals and still presupposed by commentators such as Barrett, but Hellenistic Jewish *gnosis* at home precisely in the mission context" (Horsley 48-49). R. McL. Wilson has also come to the same conclusion: "What we have at Corinth, then, is not yet Gnosticism, but a kind of *Gnosis*" (Wilson, 112), that is, a tendency that had not yet become systematized as in the late second century (*see* Corinthians).

***3.3. Philippians.*** Schmithals concludes that the libertines criticized by Paul (Phil 3:19) must be gnostic libertines (Schmithals 1972, 65-122). Others believe that the Christ Hymn of Philippians 2:6-11 may be based on a gnostic prototype (e.g., Bultmann, 1.175-77; Käsemann). On the other hand, Philippians 2:6-11 may be readily explained as an early Christian hymn or an example of exalted Pauline language that is dependent on OT imagery and/or Jewish wisdom* traditions (see Christology). Libertinism may develop from antinomianism rather than Gnosticism. Paul's clear allusion to circumcision (Phil 3:2-3) indicates that his main opponents were Judaizers or Jews (see Philippians).

**3.4. Colossians.** Many scholars, including J. B. Lightfoot in the nineteenth century, have suspected that the Colossian heresy was a form of Gnosticism (e.g., Bornkamm). Some interpreters have expounded the "preeminence of Christ" in Colossians 1:18 against the background of a series of eons, a concept developed in Valentinian Gnosticism (Bultmann, 149-52; Lightfoot, 255-71). But it is quite possible with P. T. O'Brien to interpret Colossians in a way other than postulating a fully developed gnostic system or as combating a non-gnostic heresy. Many scholars have concluded that the Colossian error was neither a gnostic heresy nor a pagan mystery cult, but was related to Jewish mysticism* (e.g., Francis; see Colossians).

**3.5. Ephesians.** Some scholars have interpreted the "dividing wall" of Ephesians 2:14-16 as the opposition of the hostile powers to the ascent of the souls in the divine plērōma (cf. Eph 1:23; see Fullness) of Gnosticism (e.g., Schlier, 18-25). But the simplest explanation would be a reference to the barrier keeping out Gentiles from the inner precincts of the Jerusalem Temple* (Lincoln, 139-43; see Ephesians).

**3.6. Pastoral Letters.** As 1 Timothy 6:20 speaks against a false gnōsis and 2 Timothy 2:18 also speaks against those who have assumed that the resurrection has also occurred, many scholars have concluded that the error combatted in the Pastorals is a form of Gnosticism. The heretics' prohibition against marriage* and the eating of meats (1 Tim 4:3) is also cited as evidence of gnostic asceticism. An incipient or rudimentary form of Gnosticism may well have been combated in the Pastoral letters, but it is anachronistic to read back into the NT period the fully developed Gnosticism of the second century. It is not likely that gnōsis in the Pastorals means a knowledge that will release the soul from enslavement to the material world, that is, "knowledge" in the gnostic sense. There is no evidence of any speculation about eons and archons. The idea that the resurrection had already taken place probably resulted from a faulty understanding of Paul's teaching such as we know it from Romans 6.

See also APOCRYPHAL PAULINE LITERATURE; CHRISTOLOGY; COLOSSIANS, LETTER TO THE; CORINTHIANS, LETTERS TO THE; EPHESIANS, LETTER TO THE; FULLNESS; HELLENISM; JUDAIZERS; KNOWLEDGE, GIFT OF KNOWLEDGE; MYSTERY; OPPONENTS OF PAUL; PASTORAL LETTERS; PAUL AND HIS INTERPRETERS; PAUL IN EARLY CHURCH TRADITION; RELIGIONS, GRECO-ROMAN; WISDOM.

BIBLIOGRAPHY. D. L. Balas, "The Use and Interpretation of Paul in Irenaeus's Five Books *Adversus Haereses*," *Second Century* 9 (1992) 27-40; W. Bauer, *Orthodoxy and Heresy in Earliest Christianity* (Philadelphia: Fortress, 1971); G. Bornkamm, "The Heresy of Colossians," in *Conflict at Colossae*, ed. F. O. Francis and W. A. Meeks (2d ed.; SBLSBS 4; Missoula, MT: Scholars, 1975) 123-45; R. Bultmann, *Theology of the New Testament* (2 vols.; New York: Scribners, 1951, 1955); I. P. Couliano, *The Tree of Gnosis* (San Francisco: Harper & Row, 1992); G. Filoramo, *A History of Gnosticism* (Oxford: Basil Blackwell, 1990); F. O. Francis, "Humility and Angelic Worship in Col 2:18," in *Conflict at Colossae*, ed. F. O. Francis and W. A. Meeks (2d ed.; SBLSBS 4; Missoula, MT: Scholars, 1975) 163-95; J. E. Goehring et al., ed., *Gnosticism and the Early Christian World* (2 vols.; Sonoma, CA: Polebridge, 1990); C. W. Hedrick and R. Hodgson, Jr., ed., *Nag Hammadi, Gnosticism, and Early Christianity* (Peabody, MA: Hendrickson, 1986); R. A. Horsley, "Gnosis in Corinth: 1 Corinthians 8.1-6," *NTS* 27 (1980) 32-51; E. Käsemann, "A Critical Analysis of Philippians 2:5-11," in *God and Christ*, ed. R. W. Funk, *JThC* 5 (New York: Harper & Row, 1968) 45-88; H. Koester, *Introduction to the New Testament II: History and Literature of Early Christianity* (Philadelphia: Fortress, 1982); J. L. Kovacs, "The Archons, the Spirit and the Death of Christ: Do We Need the Hypothesis of Gnostic Opponents to Explain 1 Cor. 2.6-16?," in *Apocalyptic and the New Testament*, ed. J. Marcus and M. L. Soards (Sheffield: JSOT, 1989) 217-36; B. Layton, *The Gnostic Scriptures* (Garden City, NY: Doubleday, 1987); J. B. Lightfoot, *Saint Paul's Epistles to the Colossians and to Philemon* (9th ed.; London: Macmillan, 1890); A. T. Lincoln, *Ephesians* (WBC 42; Dallas: Word, 1990); A. Logan and A. Wedderburn, ed., *The New Testament and Gnosis* (Edinburgh: T. & T. Clark, 1983); G. Lüdemann, "The Acts of the Apostles and the Beginnings of Simonian Gnosis," NTS 33 (1987) 420-26; G. W. MacRae, "Nag Hammadi and the New Testament," in *Gnosis. Festschrift für Hans Jonas*, ed. B. Aland (Göttingen: Vandenhoeck & Ruprecht, 1978) 144-57; G. May, "Marcion in Contemporary Views," *Second Century* 6.3 (1987-88) 129-52; P. T. O'Brien, *Colossians, Philemon* (WBC 44; Waco: Word, 1982); E. Pagels, *The Gnostic Paul* (Philadelphia: Fortress, 1975); B. A. Pearson, "Philo and Gnosticism," *ANRW* II.21.1 (1984) 295-342; S. Petrement, *A Separate God: The Christian Origin of Gnosticism* (San Francisco: Harper & Row, 1984); R. Reitzenstein, *Hellenistic Mystery Religions: Their Basic Ideas and Significance* (Pittsburgh: Pickwick, 1978); J. M. Robinson and R. Smith, ed., *The Nag Hammadi Library in English* (3d rev. ed.; San Francisco: Harper & Row, 1988); J. M. Robinson et al., *The Facsimile Edition of the Nag Hammadi Codices* (12 vols.; Leiden: E. J. Brill, 1972-1984); K. Rudolph, *Gnosis: The Nature and History of Gnosticism* (San Francisco: Harper & Row, 1983); H. Schlier, *Christus und Kirche im Epheserbrief* (Tübingen: J. C. B. Mohr, 1930); W. Schmithals, *Gnosticism in Corinth* (Nashville: Abingdon, 1971); idem, *Paul and the Gnostics* (Nashville: Abingdon, 1972); P. H. Towner, "Gnosis and Realized Eschatology in Ephesus (of the Pastoral Epistles) and the Corinthian Enthusiasm," *JSNT* 31 (1987) 95-124; R. Van Den Broek and M. J. Vermaseren, ed., *Studies in Gnosticism and Hellenistic Religions* (Leiden: E. J. Brill, 1981); D. S. Williams, "Reconsidering Marcion's Gospel," *JBL* 108 (1989) 477-96; R. McL. Wilson, "Gnosis at Corinth," in *Paul and Paulinism: Essays in Honour of C. K. Barrett*, ed. M. D. Hooker and S. G. Wilson (London: SPCK, 1982) 102-14; E. M. Yamauchi, *Gnostic Ethics and Mandaean Origins* (Cambridge, MA: Harvard University, 1970); idem, *Pre-Christian Gnosticism: A Survey of the Proposed Evidences* (rev. ed.; Grand Rapids: Baker, 1983).

E. M. Yamauchi

**GNOSTIC PAUL.** See Apocryphal Pauline Literature; Gnosis, Gnosticism; Opponents of Paul; Paul in Early Church Tradition.

**GNOSTICISM.** See Apocryphal Pauline Literature; Gnosis, Gnosticism; Opponents of Paul; Paul in Early Church Tradition.

# GOD

To try to capture in succinct and synthetic form Paul's understanding of God is an almost impossible task. There are several reasons why this enterprise is risky, even if necessary. For one thing, Paul's thought is never systematic, never speculative. Rather like the composition of his letters his mind moves to express his teaching in response to the needs of his congregations. This makes his "doctrine of God" less part of his reasoned theology and more implicit in his pastoral and pragmatic handling of human situations. Yet he claims at all times to be reflecting "the mind of Christ" (1 Cor 2:16) as he expects the same disposition among his people (Phil 2:5). At the same time God is never far from his mind. He uses the word God so frequently that his use has forty percent of all the NT

references (so Morris, 1986).

Then, Paul's letters have in view the congregations gathered for worship* where they are to be read out (1 Thess 5:27; Col 4:16; and implied in Philem 2). That means the doxological note is sounded throughout his correspondence. Often he will punctuate his writing with outbursts of praise to God and celebration of his grace* and goodness (e.g. Rom 11:33-36; 2 Cor 9:15; Gal 1:5; Phil 4:20; 2 Thess 2:16). Paul's truest teaching on God is mirrored in these liturgical jubilations, notably in his use of creeds,* hymns,* poetic snatches and prayer* speech (*see* Liturgical Elements).

Also, much of what Paul held dearest in his faith* was shared with his ancestral beliefs in Judaism and underlay his whole viewpoint and outlook, rather than coming to written, explicit expression. Hence a brief study of the OT-Jewish background is given in what follows.

1. Some Basic Assumptions
2. God as Creator, Father and King
3. The Attributes of God
4. Summary

## 1. Some Basic Assumptions.

Paul, like the other NT writers, makes no attempt to prove the existence of God. He assumes, based on his Jewish ancestral beliefs and upbringing in a pious home of the Diaspora* (Phil 3:5; 2 Cor 11:22; Gal 1:14; *see* Jew, Paul the), that God exists, that he created humankind and continues to maintain interest in his creation* (1 Cor 11:7-8). Whatever the value of attempting to prove philosophically the existence of God, Paul offers no direct guidance. According to his reported responses and sermons in Acts 14:15-17 and 17:22-31 (*see* Athens), he did argue his case for God's providential care from the evidence in his creation and its preservation. This line of reasoning—that God is known, at least in part, by his created works and his provision for human need—is amplified in Romans 1:19-23. Yet the revelation is only of limited value, since it is met by the human tendency to idolatry and perversion. Natural theology, for Paul, has the effect of increasing and giving focus to human sinfulness (see Hendry).

Paul, like the other writers of the NT, shares the view of God as maker of all, which is seen in the OT. The creation story concentrates on God's creative initiative, and this view of God as originator of the created world is basic to OT thought. Moreover it is assumed that the Creator is also sustainer of his creation. The heavens and earth are the work of his hands and he is seen to possess supreme power within the order of nature. In the intertestamental period the

Jews firmly believed in the same basic creative relationship between God and his world, adding to it the conviction that Torah (Law*) or Wisdom* had served as an intermediary through which God created, a view which came close to personifying the Torah and Wisdom.

In Paul's hands this role of an intermediary is taken over by the pre-existent* Christ,* notably in his redactional use of the christological hymn in Colossians 1:15-20 (see commentaries). Yet it remains the case that Paul's monotheism which retains God's creative act as the sole originator of creation is firm (1 Cor 8:6; 2 Cor 4:4-6), even if it is enlarged to accord a cosmological role to the preincarnate Christ. Such christological monotheism has been regarded as Paul's unique contribution to NT thought about God and the cosmos (Wright *Climax*, 120-36). It probably arose out of Paul's response to incipient gnosticism* at Corinth which placed a vast distance between the high God and the world, and later (at Colossae) the Hellenistic idea of a set of intermediaries separating God and the universe had to be opposed by Paul's insistence that the entire fullness* (*plērōma*) of deity resided in the person of Jesus Christ (Col 2:9), both transcendent and incarnate.

In this way, while Paul starts from the OT view of God as transcendent over his creation, as the holy one, he is able to relate God immanently to the world through the divine presence now located in the figure of the earthly Jesus, supremely in Jesus' death* and resurrection.* This was necessary because of the prevalent transcendental view of God during the intertestamental period. The Most High was removed so far from his own creation that he needed some intermediary to maintain contact with the world (but cf. Abelson, 46-54; Sanders, 44, 212-15; Dunn, 198-99). There is nothing of this remoteness in the NT approach. The NT view of God is linked with the OT revelation, not with current Jewish speculations.

Nevertheless, the transcendence of God finds some support in the majesty and particularly in the holiness of God, which is so characteristic of OT writings, especially of the Prophets. The statement in Isaiah 57:15 illustrates the essential difference between the OT view and much Jewish transcendental theology—"For thus says the high and lofty one who inhabits eternity, whose name is Holy: I dwell in the high and holy place, and also with those who are contrite and humble in spirit" (NRSV). This combination of loftiness and tenderness is an essential feature of the NT, and makes the NT view of God intelligible. This high moral view was in strong contrast to the contemporary multifarious and often immoral deities worshiped by non-Jewish people at the time when the NT came into being. It is impossible to appreciate the NT revelation apart from maintaining its close connection with the OT view of God. Those movements, among which Marcionism was the earliest, which have created a cleavage between OT and NT, begin their approach to NT thought with a serious disadvantage for they have no clue to the understanding of the basic NT view of God. The latter did not arise *ex nihilo*; it was the result of a long period of revelation of which the NT was the consummation.

Paul equally builds on the inherited Jewish conviction of God's covenant love for Israel which is undefeatable and sure (this assurance underlies the tenor of the argument in Rom 9—11; *see* Israel). Once more however, the OT-Judaic confidence that God is one, that he has revealed himself in Torah and has entered into covenant relations with his people Israel received a christological modification by Paul. Yet it is not by denying these fundamental tenets in his ancestral faith that Paul argues for the finality of his new relationship (see Hays). Indeed he maintains his monotheism (Gal 3:20; 1 Cor 8:4, 6; cf. 1 Tim 2:5) and grants to the giving of Torah a glory* that accompanied that event (2 Cor 3:7, 9). Israel is still an elect nation, beloved by God for the Jewish fathers' sake (Rom 11:28). On the other side, God's unity is understood in a way that makes room for the place of Jesus Christ as the "form" (Phil 2:6), or "image"* (2 Cor 4:4-6; Col 1:15) or "Son" (Col 1:13; Rom 8:29, 31) of God. Torah's glory was limited at its inception and is now passing away in the face of the greater glory that came in the new age of Messiah's appearing (2 Cor 3:7-11: see Belleville, Newman). And Israel in rejecting Paul's gospel* stands under divine judgment* at the present and in danger of being rejected as branches broken off (Rom 11:19-20; *see* Olive Tree).

The final word, however, is with God's unchanging love* and purpose (Rom 11:29, 32) in grace,* seen to be displayed and made effectual in Christ the elect one and the embodiment of divine love (Rom 8:29-38). Yahweh's love for Israel, itself uncaused (Deut 7:7-8) and persistent (Hosea) is but a foretaste of God's universal love for the world in its reconciliation (2 Cor 5:18- 21; *see* Peace, Reconciliation) and the church in its destiny (Eph 1:1-10).

## 2. God as Creator, Father and King.
So basic to all parts of the Pauline corpus is the doctrine of God that much of the evidence consists of assumptions rather than specific statements. Nevertheless there are many statements which are highly significant. We shall discuss the following aspects—

God as Creator, the providence of God, God as Father, God as King and Judge, various other titles for God, and then in summary form the attributes of God.

**2.1. God as Creator.** There is no doubt that the Christians assumed without discussion that God is the originator of the universe. They took this over from the OT and also from the teaching of Jesus. In his speech to the Athenians, Paul boldly announced the kind of God whom he worshipped as "the God who made the world and everything in it, being Lord of heaven and earth" (Acts 17:24). His creative power is also seen in the statement that mortals are his offspring (Acts 17:29), reflecting Paul's bid to establish a common ground with his audience, some of whom as Stoics cherished the notion that humans were the family of God (see Cleanthes' Hymn to Zeus, for which *see* Hymns). In his speech at Lystra Paul makes a similar assertion about God's creative power* (Acts 14:15).

In his letters Paul sets a distanc e between Creator and creatures as in Romans 1:25. Moreover, creation is said to reflect the work of the Creator (Rom 1:20). Indeed, it shows something of the character of God (his eternal power and deity). It can do this only because it is the direct work of his hands. There are specific assertions that all things were made by God (Rom 11:36; 1 Cor 8:6; 11:12; cf. Eph 3:9). Those who prohibit what God created for human good (1 Tim 4:3) on the mistaken assumption that God has no direct dealing with matter held to be evil per se—a gnostic trait—are refuted. This is why earlier Paul had appealed to Psalm 24:1 to maintain his teaching that all God's gifts of food and drink are good, provided we receive them with acknowledgement of him as giver (1 Cor 10:26-31; cf. 1 Tim 4:5). Alien teaching that places such activities as eating and drinking, along with marital sexual* relations under a taboo (Col 2:21) is as firmly resisted (Col 2:23). Relations between spouses are honorable and necessary, in normal circumstances (1 Cor 7:1- 7).

Yet Paul reflects the same conviction that the OT shows, that the creation is not coeternal with the Creator nor is creation the product of an inferior deity, as in later gnosticism. God is the author of all that exists, though Paul's interest is chiefly in God's premundane election* of his people. In Ephesians 1:4 the phrase "before the foundation of the world" is used of the choice of God and indicates that the Creator existed apart from the material existence of his creation.

Paul does not discuss the method of creation. He uses a common OT-Jewish imagery (as in Heb 11:3, based on Ps 33:6, 9; cf. Gen 1:3) of a powerful word giving birth to created orders (2 Cor 4:6, based also on

Ps 33). More important than the method is the agent. Whereas in Genesis the agency of the Spirit is mentioned (Gen 1:2), creation is said to have been effected through Christ. This has great significance for christology.* But for our present purpose it serves to put the Pauline view of creation in a somewhat different context from the OT view. The emphasis on the creative activity of Christ in no way lessens the creative activity of God. Indeed, the creative act is seen as a unity. As we have noted, the theme comes in Colossians 1:16—"for in him (i.e., Christ) all things were created, in heaven and on earth . . . all things were created through him and for him." 1 Corinthians 8:5- 6 provides a similar statement, based on a creedal confession, in turn going back to the OT-Jewish *shema* (Deut 6:4; see Wright "One God").

These passages clearly teach not only that God created through (*dia*) Christ but also for (*eis*) Christ, which give some indication of the divine purpose for the created order. The infinite wisdom of the Creator is seen in his making the creation christocentric rather than anthropocentric. The NT does not support the view that the world belongs to humanity, except in the sense fulfilled in Jesus Christ (1 Cor 15:27, based on Ps 8). Paul does hint in one place (1 Cor 3:22) that believers are called to see the world as theirs, even if it is transitory (1 Cor 7:31), and they await the gift of their eternal homeland (Phil 3:20-21) at the parousia. Creation itself is bound up with the human condition, as Paul clearly recognized in speaking of the groaning of creation for deliverance (Rom 8:19-25). Modern concerns over misuse of creation has brought this into focus and has shown the extraordinary relevance of Paul's concept. The whole ecological issue of not wasting nature's resources and avoiding pollution of earth's environment as though it were an end (however laudable and necessary) *in itself* hardly tallies with the view of creation as made "for" Christ.

It is as important to consider Paul's teaching of God's providential dealing with his creation, as to note his basic assumptions about God's creative work. Paul provides an answer to the question of God's continued activity within the created order. No support is given for the view that, having created the world, God left it to its own devices. A very different picture lies behind the apostolic approach. Providence is based on the character of God, who is thought as constantly at work and vitally interested in the well-being of his handiwork. As we noted earlier, Paul's reported speech at Lystra (Acts 14:17) stresses God's control of the seasons and his harvest provision. In Paul's Areopagus address (Acts 17:25) he affirms that God gives to all people and creatures both life and breath (*see* Athens).

God's providence is attested in Paul's life as a missionary in the Acts record, especially in the hazards to which he was exposed and the way God is said to have brought him through (see Acts 27:24-26). The same conviction of a divine superintendence of events, in spite of obvious setbacks and dangers, runs through Paul's recital of a "litany of affliction" (*peristaseis-katalog* is the technical term current in studies on Paul's trials: *see* Afflictions) in 2 Corinthians 4:7-15; 6:4-10; 11:21-29; 1 Corinthians 15:30-32; Philippians 2:17.

Although it is the case that providence embraces all peoples, God's special care is offered to his people in their experience of trial (Rom 5:1-10), and his benign regard for all facets of life is celebrated in Romans 8:28 which is most likely to be rendered with modern translations as "in all things God works for good to those who love God and are chosen," even if they are called on to suffer for his sake. This leads on to the teaching on the fatherhood of God.

*2.2. God as Father.* It is the idea of God as Father which is most characteristic of NT teaching in general and especially of the teaching of Jesus. Whereas the contemporary pagan world held its gods in fear or uncertainty (*see* Worship), the Christian view of God's parenthood brings an unparalleled element of intimacy into human relationship with God. Nevertheless, while there are striking aspects in Jesus' concept of God as Father carried forward into the letters, the idea is not absent from the OT or from Jewish usage. God is conceived of as Father of his people. The Israelite king could be conceived of as an individual son of God (Ps 2; *see* Adoption, Sonship). Israel could be called "my son" (Hosea 11:1). But this tended to be a nationalistic idea rather than an individual relationship, though there is a development in the direction of a personal relationship with God as parent in Sirach 4:10, *Psalms of Solomon* 17:30 and *Jubilees* 1:24-25 (*see* Son of God). At the same time, bearing in mind the Hebrew concept of solidarity, it should be noted that this corporate fatherhood did not exclude the idea of individual relationship. Indeed it prepared the idea for its full development in the NT.

Some of the Psalms, which are expressions of individual piety, come close to the more intimate character of God as seen in the NT, but the father-son relationship is not specifically formulated. The idea of God as shepherd (as in Ps 23; Is 40; Ezek 34), while introducing an amazingly tender view of God, falls short of the full acceptance of God as Father. With the advent of Christ these adumbrations of fatherhood emerge into a view of God which shows that the most intimate form of human relationships (parent-children) is but a reflection of the essential characteristic of God (see comment on Eph 3:14, 15 below).

In the Pauline literature the parenthood of God is seen in three ways. He is Father of Jesus, he is Father of the Christians, and he is Father of all creation. It is important to note that the father-child relationship in reference to God is almost wholly reserved for those who are believers. The relationship is the result of the redemptive activity of God. The creative relationship has already been discussed under the providence of God. Our concern here will be the special relationship with believers.

In the opening salutation in all the letters under Paul's name God is described as Father. It forms a basic assumption behind all that the apostle writes in these letters. Moreover, it is frequently reflected in the course of the discussions, whether doctrinal or practical. Indeed there is no one concept of God which dominates the theology of Paul more than this. Yet the maternal aspects of the divine-human relationship are not overlooked, even if they are only implicit in the way Paul describes his pastoral role (Gal 4:19; 1 Thess 2:7) as reflecting God's care (*see* Pastor, Paul as).

The title "Father" is sometimes qualified to give added richness to the concept. God is many times described as the Father of Jesus Christ, but he is also Father of glory (Eph 1:17), that is, the one whose presence is surrounded by an aura of majesty and might, a numen that both attracts and is mysterious; and "Father of mercies" (2 Cor 1:3), that is, he is known for his compassion, to which Paul appeals, by this use of a phrase drawn from the synagogue liturgy (see Martin 1986, 6-12), to enforce his exhortation to steadfastness under trial (2 Cor 1:4-7). All human fatherhood is said to derive from the fatherhood of God (Eph 3:14-15), which shows that God is not called Father on the basis of a human analogy, as if human fatherhood was the nearest approximation to the relationship between God and humanity. Fatherhood is seen rather to be inherent in the nature of God and in determining all that is highest and holiest in the human relationship of parenthood. Yet this interpretation of Ephesians 3:14-15, while it has support in some ancient authorities like Athanasius and among modern writers such as F. F. Bruce (see the discussion in Lincoln 1990, 201-4), has not gone uncontested; the text may simply mean that God is the Father of all family groupings in heaven and on earth.

But we need to inquire what "fatherhood" means when applied to God. As far as believers are concerned it means that God is the source of their spiritual life and pours his love upon them. God is concerned with their welfare (Rom 8:28) and also with their growth in likeness to his holy, loving character

(Eph 5:1; Col 1:12; 1 Thess 2:12; 4:7, 9). For Paul, then, this characterization of God is the criterion and norm of all that we are to understand by the name God. Supremely God is the Father of Jesus, the Son who is loved (Col 1:13; *see* Son of God). It is the divine purpose to replicate in the lives of Christ's people the image of his Son so that by the Spirit's ministry (2 Cor 3:18) the likeness of his Son is being made increasingly more apparent until at length, at the consummation of their salvation,* they become "conformed to the image" of Christ (Rom 8:29). It may be that in the process they will be called on to experience suffering for Christ (Phil 3:10) in anticipation of the resurrection of the dead (Phil 3:11).

A further observation which is of great importance in any assessment of the Pauline view of God and which distinguishes the NT from any Jewish antecedents is the use of the form *Abba* by Christians in Paul's congregations (Rom 8:15; Gal 4:6), undoubtedly based on Jesus' own use of the term in addressing God (Mk 14:36). This Aramaic form of address (*'abbā'*) to a father was originally a term used by young children as part of nursery speech (though this is debated: see Barr), but it had acquired an extended meaning in familiar usage, roughly equivalent to "my father" or "dear father" (i.e., a caritative form of address). It is a unique form, for it finds no certain parallels either in the OT or in Judaism as an address to God. Its use by Jesus shows how completely his view of God as Father is divorced from any formal approach. The *Abba* form conveys a sense of intimacy and familiarity which introduced an entirely new factor into an approach to God. And the fact that Paul is able to cite it in its Semitic formulation, which is then rendered loosely into Greek, seems to indicate a liturgical origin for the appellation. It is in converse with God in spoken prayer and in a congregational setting that the term is found (note the corresponding verb is *krazein*, to cry, in both texts in Paul), and in the two instances given the work and witness of the Holy Spirit* are invoked. The Spirit is the agency by which believers come to this recognition and acclamation of God as one known and approached intimately. It is the mark of the "spirit of sonship/adoption*" that the Spirit places the seal of his witness on believers as sons/children of God, delivering them from nomistic religion with its uncertainty of God and the pagan fearfulness that is, for Paul, akin to slavery (Rom 8:15-16; Gal 4:5-7). Thus the cry *Abba* becomes for Paul's congregations a point of entry into the experience of a familial relationship to God which is their privilege and inheritance under the new covenant of grace (see Byrne, Scott; *see* Adoption, Sonship).

**2.3. God as King and Judge.** Throughout the NT are traces of the idea of God as king. It comes into focus especially in the phrase kingdom* of God or kingdom of heaven. But clearly the idea of kingdom implies a king who exercises his rule over his subjects. There are many OT passages in which God is seen as king, and this furnishes a solid basis for the NT usage. In the contemporary world of NT times, most kings were tyrants, but this idea is nowhere suggested in the NT as applicable to God. Kingship implies sovereignty, which in its proper function carries with it responsibility. This is not to say that the idea of sovereignty is necessarily the major idea of the kingdom. Indeed the kingdom stands also for the entire blessings of salvation. Yet the two ideas are closely linked, since for believers the sovereignty of God has no meaning apart from the salvation which he has effected. The subjects of the kingdom are those who have committed themselves wholly to carrying out the will of the king.

This idea of kingship springs from the creatorship of God. When the early Christians prayed they acknowledged this fact, addressing God as "Sovereign Lord, who made the heaven and the earth and the sea and everything in them" (Acts 4:24). He who creates has a right to direct. Indeed the creature has no right to question the decisions of the creator. Paul recognized this when he used the potter illustration in Romans 9:19-26 (ideas drawn from Isaiah and Jeremiah as understood in Wisdom of Solomon). Sovereignty is therefore seen to be an inherent part of the creative activity of God.

In harmony with idea of kingship is the use of the title Lord* as applied to God, a lexical feature found often in Paul. This is another title which is prevalent in the OT and assumed in the NT. Lordship and sovereignty demand such rigorous standards of allegiance that the announcement of these themes is sufficiently attested in Paul e.g., Philippians 2:11; Romans 14:11-12. God's sole right to worship and homage is not open to question (announced in Is 45:23 which the two Pauline passages just referred to cite). For humans to act in any other way would result in their falling into temptation and consequently dishonoring God. This is the thrust in Paul's argument in Romans 3:1-6 in answer to those who in a diatribe*-like debate reasoned that God is accountable to human reason (see Moxnes).

In the record of Paul's public preaching in the book of Acts and in the letters the idea of the kingdom is less frequent and consequently the concept of God as king is not as prominent. Yet the attestation is there in Acts 28:31, even if it is true that Paul is said chiefly to have preached Christ (Acts 17:18; cf. 1 Cor 1:23; 15:12; 2 Cor 1:19; Phil 1:15-18: *see* Preaching from Paul). For the early Christians Jesus was seen to be the embodiment of the kingdom. This led to less emphasis on the kingdom itself, but in no sense lessened the conviction that the reign of God had been inaugurated. His kingly function was everywhere assumed rather than expressed.

In his letters there are many indirect indications that the apostle thought of God in terms of sovereignty, that is, under God Christ's kingdom is a present reality (1 Cor 15:25; Col 1:13; Eph 5:5). God is more powerful than the rulers of this age (1 Cor 2:6-8: *see* Principalities). All the powers of evil (the principalities and powers) are incapable of interfering with God's purposes in Christ (Rom 8:37-39). Indeed they have already been conquered (Col 2:15; *see* Triumph). The earlier notice (in Col 1:16) that such cosmic powers were created in and by Christ poses a problem, which is most likely resolved by supposing that in the hands of the Colossian philosophers they were venerated in rivalry to Christ (Col 2:8, 18, 20) and so needed to be overcome and "reconciled." Paul sees the final act of history as God subduing his enemies "under his feet" (Rom 16:20, 1 Cor 15:23-28). In the apostle's thought there is little real distinction between the kingdom of God and the kingdom of Christ, although Christ at the Parousia will deliver his kingdom to God (1 Cor 15:24) thereby transforming the *Regnum Christi* to the *Regnum Dei*. What is central to Paul's thinking in this context is the supreme sovereignty of God over everything (see Martin 1984, 107-25; Kreitzer). The Pastoral Letters contain one statement which clearly brings this aspect to the fore when God is described as "the blessed and only Sovereign, the King of kings and Lord of lords" (1 Tim 6:15).

The concept of king is closely allied to that of judge. For Paul the idea of God as judge was an integral part of his gospel (cf. Rom 2:16). Indeed, there was no doubt in his mind that God would judge the world (Rom 3:6). He speaks positively about "the judgment seat of God" (Rom 14:10; alternately this phrase appears as the judgment seat of Christ in 2 Cor 5:10 with no significant change of meaning; see Roetzel) and uses it as a basis for his verdict on Christians who were judging their fellows. What is not regarded as a legitimate prerogative for human beings—for the reason given in 1 Corinthians 4:3-5—is nevertheless of the essence of the divine nature (see Kuck). It is assumed as right and proper in Paul that the divine king should exercise his prerogative of judgment. There is admittedly a certain element of severity about this aspect of God (Rom 3:5-6, though with the concession made

that Paul is speaking in human terms). Paul, who admits the severe side of God, is nevertheless careful to link it with the kindness of God (Rom 11:22). For that reason it is important to see the judgments of God as refracted through the prism of Paul's christology. God will judge the world in righteousness, as a facet of his righteous character. Yet, according to the speech in Acts 17:31, it is a universal judgment made by the standard set in Christ: "by the man whom he (God) has appointed." The effect of this clause is to recall how Paul's entire theology, his doctrine of God, is shaped by the revelation of God's nature and action that came into focus by the coming of Christ.

### 2.4. Other Titles for God.

*2.4.1. Spirit.* The entire NT presents the nature and character of God in a number of different titles which express various facets, not found in a formal way, but nonetheless significant. As part of the indictment he levels at the propensity to idolatry* once the knowledge of God is perverted by human sinfulness (Rom 1:21-23), Paul takes it for granted that God is not a human creation or invention. His attitude to idols is not easy to systematize. In 1 Corinthians 8:4 he joins with his Corinthian readers to affirm that "there is no God but one"; hence "an idol has no real existence" (RSV: this is placed in quotation marks to signify it is cited from the Corinthians themselves). The idols are then dubbed "so-called" (1 Cor 8:5), since Paul cannot deny that idol worship does exist. Yet in 1 Corinthians 10:14-22 his tone is more serious, since he grants that there is a malign demonic influence that can infect "food offered to idols" and Christians may be exposed to evil forces (otherwise the warnings in 2 Cor 6:4—7:1 would have no meaning). These powers are to be resisted (1 Cor 10:14) since they are rivals to the true God and yet are powerless to thwart his purpose, however much they seek to try by seducing believers (2 Cor 2:11). The "spiritual" essence of Paul's religion is something he assumes without much argumentation (e.g., Phil 3:3 and his teaching on the church as the dwelling place in God in the Spirit in 1 Cor 3:16; cf. Eph 2:18-21).

*2.4.2. Savior.* Although the title "Savior"* is occasionally applied to Jesus Christ in the Pauline tradition, it is also used of God and in this respect tallies with a dominant activity of God the Savior in the OT. The main occurrences of the title are in the Pastorals (1 Tim 2:3; Tit 2:10, 13; 3:4). Although the title is relatively rare in Paul, the activity implicit in the title permeates the whole of Paul's soteriology. Indeed, Christian theology centers in the theme of God saving his people and for Paul the power of God is displayed in the saving work initiated by God and executed in

Christ (e.g., Gal 4:4-5). One notable treatise (by C. A. A. Scott; see too Morris 1986, 172-75) has placed the essential meaning of Pauline Christianity under the rubric of salvation.

*2.4.3. Almighty/Most High.* This is a title of supreme dignity which expresses the superiority of God over all other gods. It is used by the slave girl with a python (oracular) spirit in Acts 16:17. Paul and his party at Philippi see this invocation as idolatrous, however, and the demon in the girl is expelled in the name of Jesus Christ. This vignette is an illustration of the way Paul opposed the deities of contemporary religion and superstition by asserting the lordship of Christ, an office and authority given him by God, the only Lord (see Acts 16:31). "Jesus is Lord" is the Christian confession that is made in the light of the resurrection (Rom 10:9: *see* Creed), which in turn in is, for Paul, the signal proof of the power of God and his approving of his Son's right to rule human lives and cosmic destiny (Phil 2:9-11; Rom 14:9; Eph 1:20-23). The similar title *pantocratōr* in 2 Corinthians 6:18 moves in the same circle of ideas (see commentaries).

*2.4.4. Sovereign.* It is similarly the case with this appellation (found in 1 Tim 6:15), with the addition "the King of (all) kings," that is, world ruler and all powerful emperor. Probably this fulsome description is designed to counter the claims of the emerging emperor cult in the Roman empire, where the emperor* was assuming divine honors and sanctioning the erecting of temples in his name.

### 3. The Attributes of God.

Anyone who seeks an answer to the question "What is the God of Paul's theology like?" will find no formal statements, but a mass of incidental indications, which nevertheless are invaluable in throwing light on many facets of the character of God. There is nothing to suggest that there were differences of opinion in the Pauline circles about the being of God, even when Paul had occasion to defend his gospel (Phil 1:8, 16) and to offer a counterattack on those whom he reproved as teachers who perverted his teaching (Gal 1:6-7; *see* Opponents) and introduced an "alien gospel" (2 Cor 11:13-15; Berger). The closest Paul comes to meet head-on a rival theology is in Colossians, which opposes a bid to reduce his message to a species of Hellenistic philosophy (Col 2:8; see commentaries). Whereas some parts of Paul's theologizing bring certain facets into focus more than other parts, there is no doubt that a unified picture is presented. While it is impossible to arrange the evidence in a systematic form, it will be helpful to group the main ideas under the following considerations—the glory of God, the wisdom of God, the holiness of God, the righteousness of God, the love and grace of God, the goodness of God, the uniqueness of God and the unity of God. Some of the ground has already been covered, but it will be convenient to set the evidence together in this way.

*3.1. The Glory of God.* There is a strong OT background to the frequent references in Paul to the glory* of God. Whereas the Hebrew word for "glory" (*kābôd*) was used of anything which possessed splendor, honor or conspicuousness, it soon came to have a special significance when applied to God. It came in fact to stand for the revelation of God, as when the psalmist maintained that the heavens declare the glory of God (Ps 19:1). OT history is seen as a record of God's revelation of his glory in his activities on behalf of his people. A more developed sense of the same idea is the use of "glory" to denote the presence of God in a theophany, which was later to become known in Jewish theology as the Shekinah (*šᵉkînâ*). But it is the translation of the Hebrew *kābôd* by the Greek *doxa* which provides the key for understanding the Pauline ideas of the glory of God (see Newman). We shall note that in the texts there are two senses in which *doxa* is used, as visible glory (in the sense of seeing the glory of God) and as uttered praise (in the sense of ascribing glory to God).

It is astonishing how frequently the NT writers in general mention the glory and majesty of God. Moreover, men and women are prompted to glorify God. To ascribe glory to God in face of the mysterious working of his power is often spontaneous, yet in Pauline theology the theme is more implicit than fully spelled out. The pattern for measuring human shortcomings is "the glory of God" (Rom 3:23), which implies that sin has made it impossible for humans to be reflectors of God's glory as they should have been, as the way God designed them as part of his image and glory (1 Cor 11:7: see Scroggs). Nevertheless, through the process of justification and renewal Paul sees the possibility of men and women again sharing in God's glory (Rom 5:2; Col 3:10: see commentaries). When describing the glory of Christ, he equates it with the glory shared by Christians (2 Cor 3:18). On one occasion he describes God as the "Father of glory" (Eph 1:17). He includes several doxologies which ascribe glory to God (Rom 16:27; Phil 4 :20; 2 Tim 4:18). All that Christians do must be done to God's glory (cf. Rom 15:7; 2 Cor 4:15; Phil 1:11; 2:11). Moreover, eternal destruction is seen as exclusion from the presence of God and the glory of his might (2 Thess 1:9), which shows that any obscuring of God's glory is the worst possible happening in human experience.

Enough has been said to demonstrate the great importance in Paul's thought of the theme of God's glory as a basic assumption about the nature and character of God. Now we must consider how it bears upon other aspects of God. A vision of his glory cannot fail to promote a reaction of awe. It provides a ready preparation for the view of God's power, which is everywhere assumed in Paul. So glorious a being could never be impotent (cf. Rom 4:21; 11:23; 1 Cor 2:5; 2 Cor 9:8). Indeed the description "the power* of God," when used absolutely, aptly indicates this dynamic aspect of God's character (cf. 2 Cor 6:7; 13:4; 2 Tim 1:8; see Powell).

With so exalted a view of the glory and power of God, it is not surprising that Paul at times alludes to the mysteries* of God (see Caragounis; Harvey). The apostle speaks of "the depths of God" (1 Cor 2:10), which are known only to the Spirit of God. Some have interpreted this reference to the "depths" of God in a gnostic sense (so Wilckens, cited by, but not supported by Conzelmann, 66). Wilckens supposes that "depths" are to be identified with the revealer, but Conzelmann finds this explanation of Paul's words incomprehensible. He contends that Paul is combating this view that humans could plumb the depths of God's being (see also Fee). There is a whole area of knowledge of God which is beyond the finite grasp. God is in a sense incomprehensible, although the Spirit's revelations of him are sufficient for our understanding of his redemptive purposes. There is no question of humans being able to set their own limits on God's nature and attributes. What we know is at most no more than a glimpse of the whole reality. A massive area of mystery must remain (as in the poetic passage, 1 Cor 13:12). Paul can speak of God's servants as "stewards of the mysteries of God" (1 Cor 4:1), which shows that an element of mystery will always attend the proclamation of the gospel. The sense of awe is well brought out by the apostle at the conclusion of Roman 11, where he speaks of the unsearchable character of God's judgments and the inscrutable nature of his ways (verse 33). No one has known the mind of God, as Isaiah 40:13-14, which Paul quotes, so patently implies. The identical thought lies behind the strange report of Paul's own mystical experience in 2 Corinthians 12:1-10, especially in the "journey to heaven" motif (paralleled in rabbinic literature as well as esoteric Judaism) where Paul heard auditions "which cannot be told" (2 Cor 12:3; see commentaries and Lincoln 1979; 1981; see Visions).

*3.2. The Wisdom and Knowledge of God.* The Jewish wisdom writers often speak of wisdom,* but not so much as an attribute of God as an emanation from God (Wis 7:25). She is described as the brightness of his everlasting light (Wis 7:26). She is created, but created before all things (Sir 1:4, 7-9; 24:14) and is in fact the principle of creation (Sir 24:10-34; 42:21; Wis 7:21; 9:2: see Schnabel). This concept is more relevant to the NT understanding of Christ (see Christology); nevertheless, there is the strong implication that this personification of wisdom proceeds from God and therefore witnesses to an essential attribute of God.

The concept of the wisdom of God is especially prominent in Paul. He contrasts the wisdom of God with human wisdom (1 Cor 1:20) and shows its superiority. Human wisdom is in fact turned to foolishness in the light of God's wisdom. This implies that the latter is the standard by which all other wisdom is gauged. In the same letter Paul speaks of the secret and hidden wisdom of God (1 Cor 2:7), which can nevertheless be imparted. It is clear that Paul identifies the wisdom which can be communicated with what the apostles proclaimed. Since in the same passage he identifies Christ as "our wisdom" (1 Cor 1:30), he is evidently thinking of the wise acts of God in the salvation of the church or more specifically of Christ as the embodiment of divine wisdom in human form. This is regarded in NT thought as the supreme manifestation of wisdom. (On the various ways "wisdom," both good and bad, is used in 1 Corinthians see Barrett 1982, 6-14; cf. Ellis 1978.) Indeed, it is through the church that "the manifold wisdom of God" is made known even to spiritual powers (Eph 3:10). What is important for our present purpose is that God's work for his people is seen to spring from his wisdom. It is no wonder that Paul marvels at the depth of the "wisdom and knowledge of God" (Rom 11:33).

Some distinction has to be drawn between wisdom and knowledge in relation to humans, but this distinction is not so appropriate when applied to God. If wisdom is the right use of knowledge, perfect wisdom presupposes perfect knowledge. The NT writers like Paul never doubt the perfect knowledge of God. This unerring knowledge on the part of God is extended in some statements to include foreknowledge.* The extension is a logical development. Paul insists that in the perfect planning of God to provide a people conformed to the image of God, he knew beforehand those who were to share that image (Rom 8:29). Paul's statement has provoked endless debate because it appears to limit man's free will (see Election). But here it may simply be noted that Paul does not discuss systematically the foreknowledge of God; he takes it for granted. He does not doubt that if God knows the present, he must also know the future as he has known the past. This seems to be an essential part of his total picture of God (cf. Eph 1:5), and seems to have its contextual setting, not in speculative theology but in a pastoral concern to answer the needs of people in first-century society who felt threatened by a sense of purposelessness and powerlessness in the face of astrological determination and the role of impersonal fate (Martin 1991, 14-15).

There are certain deductions from this conviction that God is all-wise and all-knowing. Such perfect understanding means that when God wills, his plans and purposes are all-knowing and can never be in error. Indeed, although there are few specific statements in support of this in NT, it does not seem to be questioned. What God says must be true. He never lies (Rom 3:4; Tit 1:2). The absolute truth of God guarantees the consistency of his wisdom and knowledge. There is no suggestion that he ever modifies his plans in the light of his own progressive experience. This aspect of God, which will be expounded more fully in the discussion on the uniqueness of God (see 3.7), is essential if his acts in history are to have continuing validity.

Paul, like the NT writers generally, is conscious of the controlling character and obligatory nature of the will of God. This acceptance of the ruling character of God's will is frequently found in the letters. Paul begins several letters with the declaration of his apostleship "by the will of God" (1 Cor 1:1; 2 Cor 1:1; Eph 1:1; Col 1:1; 2 Tim 1:1). Moreover, his and other people's movements are controlled by God's will (Rom 1:10; 15:32; 1 Cor 16:12, which shows how human decision-making is not ruled out: see Fee, 824). Indeed, even in his approach to those who challenged his change of plans and policies, Paul asserts that God's nature as trustworthy sets the stage for his own dealings with the Corinthians to be treated as reliable (2 Cor 1:15-22, with a word-play on God's fixed nature as the faithful God [with *pistos*, "faithful," reflecting the Heb root *'mn*, as in "Amen," used of God in Deut 7:9 and Is 49:7] and the apostles' declaration of "yes" [Gk *nai* = Heb *'āmēn*] to God's promises validated in Christ whom he proclaimed and certified in the congregational Amen ["it is certain"] at worship; see Martin 1986, 26-27).

He also, at a later point in 2 Corinthians, reverts to this theme and justifies his ministry at Corinth by recalling how he always operated within the limits God imposed on him according to his good will (2 Cor 10:12-18: on this difficult section see Martin 1986, 314-26).

Life for the Christian is life according to God's will even in suffering.* The ever-present problems involved in God's permitting suffering for his people are nowhere discussed. Does this mean that the NT writers like Paul were unaware of the problem? Yet it is hard to think this personal issue ever eluded Paul's notice or that of his congregations (it underlies much of Philippians*). It must be assumed, therefore, that the Christians were convinced about the all-inclusive character of God's wisdom and the perfection of his will. This is bound up with the conviction of God's providential care for his people. If suffering comes, God must have a purpose in it.

Much confusion arises from the fact that it is generally assumed that all suffering should be avoided. The notion that God can use suffering does not come naturally. But the biblical approach to suffering constantly takes it into the sphere of God's purpose. Although it is true that suffering is nowhere explained, there is enough evidence to show what the Christian attitude toward it should be. There is no suggestion that God is less than wise or good because suffering exists. Since the supreme example of suffering lies at the heart of God's redemptive activity in Christ, it cannot be maintained that suffering is alien to the purpose of God. It will always remain a mystery why God chose to redeem humankind the way he did, but this very fact must be taken into account in considering the Pauline view of God.

Arising from the necessity for Christ to suffer comes the problem of suffering for Christians. It is not surprising that in a hostile world Christians will meet with opposition on account of their faith. This is the least problematic aspect of suffering. Paul, in recounting his experiences in 2 Corinthians 4:7—5:10, in no way criticizes God for the hardships he has endured. He sees these hardships as tools in the hand of God. The present momentary affliction is regarded as "slight" (2 Cor 4:17) compared with the weight of glory to follow. Later in the same letter the apostle gives details of his "slight" affliction (cf. 2 Cor 6:4; 11:23—12:10), which consists of a harrowing list of calamities which have been seldom equalled or surpassed and yet he has arrived at a triumphant attitude toward them. There is no hint anywhere in this letter that he resents or questions the wisdom of God in allowing suffering.

Indeed the one place where he does tackle the theodicy question (Why does God allow suffering, when undeserved?) provides Paul the opportunity to bring out the gracious character of God as seen (paradoxically) in the face of human trials. This appears in Philippians 1:19-30. The implicit questions relate to Paul's own imprisonments and prospect of imminent martyrdom and the Philippians share in his trials (Phil 1:7). To those who doubted Paul's authentic apostleship because he was a suffering leader (and in 2 Cor

12:1-10, a failed charismatic who could not heal himself) and to the Philippians who took their suffering as a test of faith Paul responds with a stirring assertion of God's overruling power-in-weakness and uses affliction as a mark of favor (Phil 1:29; see Güttgemanns, Bloomquist). This leads to Romans 5:3, where Paul actually rejoices in suffering because it develops the quality of endurance. In this same context he speaks of God's love being poured out in our hearts. The two things were clearly not incompatible in his mind.

It cannot be said that the writings of Paul answer all the intellectual problems which arise from God's permitting human suffering, but they do enable Christians to face suffering without losing confidence in the perfection of God's wisdom and his loving design to guide and support his people's lives in their times of testing (Rom 8:28-39).

*3.3. The Holiness of God.* One of the most characteristic qualities of God in the OT is his holiness.* Although people and things and places are described as holy, this is in the sense of being set apart for God. Holiness is essentially an attribute of God. It marks him out as being utterly pure in thought and attitude. In the prophecy of Isaiah "the Holy One" is a characteristic name for God (cf. Is 6). It is this quality of holiness which creates at once a barrier in our approach to God, since we become conscious of our lack of holiness in the presence of God. It is because Israel had a holy God that demands were made upon her people to become a holy people, which they certainly failed to fulfill.

Undoubtedly this conviction that God is holy forms an important element in the Pauline account of salvation. It underlies his argument in 1 Thessalonians 4:3-8 that his readers should steer clear of immoral practices and respond to God's call to "live a holy life" (1 Thess 4:7, NIV). Yet this for Paul is only possible and practicable if we have recourse to God's provision in the gift of the Holy Spirit (1 Thess 4:8), who is the sanctifying agent in redemption* (cf. 2 Thess 2:13). Equally, in 1 Corinthians 6:12-20 the insistence of Paul's stringent advice to "flee from sexual immorality" (1 Cor 6:18) is governed and supported by his reminder that the holy Lord will have a holy people whose bodies are the temple of the Holy Spirit.

*3.4. The Righteousness and Justice of God.* So far the only moral characteristic of God which has been mentioned is his absolute truthfulness and his holiness. But more needs to be said about the righteousness* of God, for this is basic to the Pauline plan of salvation. In the OT righteousness in God means more than that God always acts in a morally right way. It

includes also the fact that God acts on behalf of his people when they are unjustly oppressed. In the NT the apostle Paul is the great exponent of this important characteristic of God. He does not question that God is righteous. He begins his exposition in the letter to the Romans* with the assertion that God's righteousness has been revealed (Rom 1:17). This is reiterated in Romans 3:21, 22.

Exegetes debate whether "the righteousness of God" in these contexts concentrates on what can be imparted rather than what is inherent to God. Is the expression intended to refer to a quality in God or not? The genitive may be taken in three ways: (1) as an objective genitive, in which case the righteousness is that which God grants (so Luther); (2) as a subjective genitive, in which case it refers to that which belongs to God; (3) as a genitive of origin, in which case it is God's righteousness, but proceeds from God to humans. There is a notable reluctance among many recent writers to regard righteousness solely as an attribute of God (*see* Righteousness, Righteousness of God). Whatever the conclusion, the association of God and righteousness is clear enough. True righteousness comes from God (cf. Rom 10:3; Phil 3:9). In 2 Corinthians 5:21 Paul even states that Christ was made sin "so that in him we *might become* the righteousness of God"—an unusual expression, which may indicate a taking over by Paul of an earlier statement (see commentaries). Yet we may concede that 2 Corinthians 5:21 makes sense only if God himself is essentially righteous. Indeed Paul describes the Christian's new nature as "created after the likeness of God in true righteousness and holiness" (Eph 4:24), showing righteousness as an essential constituent in God's image, restored to his people in Christ by the Spirit (2 Cor 3:18).

The concept of God's judging in righteousness involves the idea of God's impartiality. It was difficult for Jews to accept this idea, for they were convinced that Israel was a favored nation, which made it superior to the Gentile peoples in the sight of God. It was this strong bias which threatened to cause real problems when Jews and Gentiles had to mix in the early Christian communities.

Paul had already made a *volte-face* when he became a Christian. More than any other he wrestled with the problem of God's special concern for the Jewish people, but as a Christian he never doubted that God was impartial and that both Jew and Gentile* must be included in the plan of salvation on an equal footing. On two occasions he asserted as axiomatic that God shows no partiality (Rom 2:11; Gal 2:6), the second of which deals with the apostolic office. The idea definitely excluded any notion of favoritism with God, which would not be in keeping with absolute justice.

An important side to the righteousness and justice of God is his wrath.* There are sufficient instances of emphasis on God's wrath and judgment in the NT and in Paul in particular to make it important to define its meaning. The precise meaning has been subject to debate (see Morris 1960). Indeed of all the aspects of God in the NT this is perhaps the most questioned. Some reduce wrath (*orgē*) to the effect of human sin, thus getting rid of all notion of anger in God because this is considered to be irrational (Dodd; but see reply in Tasker). But this is an unsatisfactory way of dealing with the NT evidence. In Romans 1:18 the expression "the wrath of God" occurs (cf. Rom 5:9; 12:19; 14:5; cf. also 9:22), and it is impossible in this case to empty the phrase of any relevance to the attributes of God. Paul speaks of a wrath of God which is being revealed (*apokalyptetai*) in precisely the same way as he had just previously stated that God's righteousness is being revealed (Rom 1:17-18). It is inescapable that Paul intended a connection between the two concepts. It seems most reasonable to suppose that "wrath" is the negative aspect of God's righteousness. It does not express anger in the sense in which it is applied to humans, an uncontrolled outburst of passion (which would certainly be an irrational concept), but it must express the revulsion of absolute holiness toward all that is unholy. This is in harmony with the context where "wrath" is explicitly said to be against (*epi*) ungodliness and wickedness. The same may be said of Romans 5:9 where salvation is said to be from "the wrath," which may well denote the wrath of God as an expression of God's rejection of all that is sinful (*see* Enemy).

It is not sufficient to define wrath as the principle of retribution in a moral universe without connecting the principle to its source, the nature of God. Unless we find some place for the moral displeasure of God we shall make light of his judgment, which finds no small place in NT thought. When Paul says in Colossians 3:6 that the wrath of God is coming, he must mean more than that a principle of retribution is approaching. The eschatological aspect is again present in this context and is more explicit than in Romans 1:18 (Martin 1972, 110). Lohse has denied that wrath in Colossians 3:6 indicates an emotion of God, but is God's judgment of wrath (Lohse, 139). Yet God's judgment cannot be wholly detached from his continual reaction against sin. "Wrath" cannot, in short, be received as a term which describes only God's final act of judgment. The expression has more force if the condemnation of the evils mentioned in the previous verse is based on the active opposition of God against them (cf. also Eph 5:6). It should be noted that when the apostle assures the Thessalonians that God has not destined them for wrath (1 Thess 5:9), he is writing to Christians and his words cannot cancel out the statements about God's wrath elsewhere.

*3.5. The Love and Grace of God.* That God is a God of love* is another assumption Paul makes, though he does not make it lightly, writing (Rom 5:8) that God's love is *proved* to believers by the death of his Son. The inference is that what was required is a demonstration of what we would not have imagined possible or conceivable without prior revelation of God, namely that God loves undeserving and guilty sinners. It has a firm basis in the OT and Jewish literature, but takes on a sharper focus and a more dominant role in the NT generally.

Hence, the apostle Paul pursued this line of thought. In the letter which most emphasizes the righteousness of God, he can speak with equal certainty about the love of God. God's love has been poured into believers' hearts through the Spirit (Rom 5:5), a vivid way of speaking of the communicating of God's love to humankind. That love is most seen in God's saving work for sinners (Rom 5:8). The consequence for believers is that they will never be separated from that love (Rom 8:39). Love makes them more than conquerors (Rom 8:37). Indeed the love of God is a familiar part of such benedictions as 2 Corinthians 13:13 (14) (cf. also 2 Cor 13:11) and Ephesians 6:23. It comes in Paul's prayers for the Thessalonians (2 Thess 2:16; 3:5). In the latter prayer the love of God is regarded as the aim to which the Christians' minds should be directed ("may the Lord direct your hearts to the love of God").

There are two other aspects of God which are so closely linked to love that they may properly be considered in conjunction with it. First there is the understanding that God is a God of grace.* The whole concept of grace lies at the heart of Paul's soteriology and in that connection we note that "the grace of God" denotes an essential feature of God's love. When applied to God, the word grace denotes the favor of God toward those who do not deserve his favor, and therefore came to be used particularly of God's saving work in Christ. It has become a basic assumption, so much so that it frequently occurs in the opening salutations and in the concluding benedictions of the Pauline letters. God is seen as one who bestows unmerited favor on the objects of his love. God's grace is more than his gracious acts, although it includes these. It involves his nature. His love is of such a quality that it gives unstintingly. Grace is another name for the outgoing character of his love, especially to sinners and to his elect people. Sometimes God's grace becomes almost objectified in the results that it achieves, as when Paul can say that the Macedonians' response to the challenge to Christian giving is a sign of God's grace in human lives (2 Cor 8:1; cf. 2 Cor 8:7 as a summons to the Corinthians to excel in this "grace" of generosity also).

The apostle Paul was deeply convinced of his personal indebtedness to God's grace. He saw his own calling as an act of grace (Gal 1:15). He had no doubt that Christians are saved by God's grace (Rom 3:24; 5:15; cf. Eph 2:5, 7; Tit 2:11). He sees it as a subject for praise (Eph 1:6). He views it as in some way a communicable gift (e.g., 1 Cor 1:4; 3:10; 15:10; 2 Tim 1:9). Living by grace is diametrically opposed to any religious claim depending on human effort (Gal 2:21; Rom 11:6). "Grace" also provided Paul with the assurance that God would work in his apostolic life (1 Cor 15:10-11); indeed the term becomes almost indistinguishable from "strength" needed to fulfill his missionary task (2 Cor 12:9). In spite of the limitations Paul faced he was able to embrace a way of relying more fully on God's power-in-weakness* (2 Cor 12:10; 13:4).

The second aspect of God closely allied to love is the mercy* of God. The root meaning of "mercy" is compassion, hence its close link with love. It is essentially outgoing love marked by persistence and commitment (as in the Heb *ḥesed*). Mercy is also inseparably linked with grace, but is more specifically connected with righteousness. It is when the righteous judgments of God are considered that his mercy becomes a vivid reality. If he must condemn what is unrighteous because he himself is righteous, he extends mercy to those who would otherwise be condemned because mercy is as much a part of his nature as righteousness. This idea of God's mercy is not unique to the NT. It finds its roots in the OT.

The apostle Paul was deeply aware of the mercy of God (Rom 9:15-16, 18) as part of God's gracious prerogative. He several times speaks, often autobiographically when reflecting on his apostolic calling and mission, of obtaining mercy, which means receiving the results of God's merciful acts (Rom 11:30-32; 1 Cor 7:25; 2 Cor 4:1; 1 Tim 1:16). There is no suggestion that the quality of mercy is alien to God, nor that it conflicts with his essential righteousness. It is part of the apostle's understanding of the total nature of God. Indeed, Paul uses the striking expression "Father of mercies" of God in 2 Corinthians 1:3, which draws attention to his compassionate nature. It echoes Exodus 36:6, Psalm 86:15 and 145:8, which speak of

God as merciful and gracious, and is integral to the synagogue's liturgy in its acclamation of God as kind to Israel, especially in forgiving sins and restoring relations (see Col 2:13-15, which suggestively finds its Jewish background in the New Year prayer of supplication for God's mercy to his people).

Paul sometimes uses another word—kindness (*chrēstotēs*)— when describing the gracious attitude of God. He once links it with the quality of severity (Rom 11:22). It may seem difficult to see how these two facets of God's character can exist in one person, but Paul is not apparently embarrassed by this difficulty. To him both kindness and severity are essential characteristics. He sees God's kindness as intended to lead people to repentance (Rom 2:4), although he recognizes that his Jewish contemporaries have incurred the righteous judgment of God (Rom 2:5). The close connection between God's grace and his kindness is clearly seen in Ephesians 2:7 where God's immeasurable riches of grace are equated with his kindness toward us in Christ. Kindness is therefore practically synonymous with grace. Kindness is further linked with the goodness of God in Titus 3:4, where both are stated to have "appeared" (i.e., in the provisions of salvation by the incarnate presence of Christ).

*3.6. The Goodness and Faithfulness of God.* There are a few significant statements in the Pauline library which focus on the goodness of God and which deserve separate consideration. The concept of goodness is difficult to define but is nevertheless generally recognized to be closely linked with the moral holiness of God. The Gospels' statement "Only one is good, God," makes clear that the character of God is such that it is itself the standard that should determine all human notions of goodness. Whatever goodness anyone else possesses is derived from him. This is supported by such an OT statement as Psalm 53:1, which is cited by Paul in Romans 3:12, and which affirms that no one is good. Paul uses it to demonstrate human need, but he does not bring out so specifically as Jesus had done the unique goodness of God (Mt 19:17; Mk 10:17; cf. Lk 18:18-19).

Although the faithfulness of God is a different kind of attribute from goodness, it may be linked with the sense that were God faithless to his word he could not be good. Paul was deeply impressed with the faithfulness of God. He is faithful in calling people into fellowship with his Son (1 Cor 1:9) and in guarding them against excessive testing of their faith (1 Cor 10:13) or from the attacks of the evil one (2 Thess 3:3). The faithfulness of God is even cited by Paul as a guarantee of the dependability of his own word (2 Cor 1:18). Moreover, God remains faithful even when others are faithless (2 Tim 2:13). There is a rock-like quality to the apostle's conviction of God's reliability.

We may perhaps include in this section a note about the expression "the God of peace" which is particularly familiar through the concluding salutation in Romans 15:33 and in 1 Thessalonians 5:23. The more widely used form of the idea "peace from (*apo*) God" occurs in the opening greetings in all Paul's letters. It appears that the quality which God can impart has become an ascription to him. The form "God of peace" is suggestive because it points to the absence of conflict in God and his solicitude for his people's welfare (*šālôm*). Indeed 1 Corinthians 14:33 brings this out explicitly—"God is not a God of confusion, but of peace." Peace* therefore describes an attitude of God as well as a quality which he imparts. Peace cannot be bestowed "from God" unless it is an integral part of his nature. Humankind in its fallen state is in a perpetual state of enmity and tension until reconciled to God (Rom 5:1-10; cf. Eph 2:1-3, 12). But such a state of tension does not exist in God. There is no suggestion anywhere in NT teaching that God is ever uncertain as to his actions, nor frustrated in his plans. His mind is always in a state of equilibrium. It is no wonder that Paul, in desiring to allay anxiety among Christians, not only exhorts them to commit themselves to God, but also assures them that the peace of God will garrison (*phroureō*, i.e., act as a sentry or patrol, to guard the city gates against invading attack; see Hawthorne, 184) their hearts and minds (Phil 4:7). In the same passage he assures his reader of the continued presence of the God of peace (Phil 4:9).

**3.7. The Uniqueness of God.** Included here will be Paul's hints of teaching concerning the invisibility of God. The mystery conveyed in the expression "no one has ever seen God" is fully in accord with the OT conceptions. This invisibility is one of the ways to find a counterpoint in the revelatory character of the mission of Jesus. Paul makes clear that God the creator has made himself known in his works (Rom 1:19), but in saying this he implies that there are also aspects of God which cannot be known. In 1 Timothy 1:17 is included in the somewhat formalized ascription to God his invisibility, which is specifically mentioned only here in the NT.

Closely linked and occurring in the same statement in 1 Timothy 1:17 is the idea of the immortality of God, which occurs also in Romans 1:23. The concept may be indebted more to Hellenistic than Jewish thought. A God who is changeless must be a God who is immortal. Such a God can rightly be described as "eternal" (Rom 16:26).

**3.8. The Unity of God.** Our purpose here will be to bring together the main NT evidence for the Trinity and then to assess its significance. It must be remembered that although the intertestamental Jews were strongly monotheistic, there are not wanting indications in the OT that God was not regarded as one in the mathematical sense of being unitary (in fact, recent studies have shown how Jewish theology in early Judaism could entertain notions of separate hypostases or personifications within the strict monotheism it cherished and defended; see Segal, Hurtado, Rainbow; more cautiously Dunn, 183-206). Such an expression as "the Lord of hosts" at least implies that God is not alone (cf. 1 Kings 22:19-23; Ps 89:5-8). The armies of heaven or the "sons of God" (as in Job 1:6; 38:7; Ps 29:1; 89:6) show that God has agents. Of greater significance is the frequently mentioned "angel* of Yahweh," who sometimes appears in human form, but is nevertheless recognized as God (cf. Gen 16:7-14; 18:1-22; Ex 3:2- 6). Nevertheless at times the "angel" is distinguished from Yahweh (Ex 33:2, 3). It is certainly significant for the NT teaching about the Trinity, and may have left enigmatic traces in Paul's writing (see Gal 4:14).

An entirely new factor was nevertheless introduced with the emergence of the Christian gospel, which led to a development of the monotheistic approach and ultimately to the doctrine of the Trinity. Of the Trinity there are many adumbrations in the NT, although it cannot be said that the doctrine is explicitly expounded in a formal way. It is significant that none of the NT writers sees the need to speculate about such a doctrine; indeed they seem able to accord divine honors to Jesus without embarrassment (Dunn). They are content to present data which imply the divine nature of both Christ and the Spirit and which naturally give rise to reflections about the unity of God (see Wainwright).

The Pauline evidence may be summarized under three different types of quasi-liturgical passages. First, there are a few passages where trinitarian formulae are used. The passages in view are such as 1 Corinthians 12:3-7; Ephesians 1:3-14; 2:18; 4:4-6; Titus 3:4-6, and are conceivably and suggestively linked with a baptismal and/or initiatory creed.*

Another such passage is 2 Corinthians 13:13 (14), where Paul adds a benediction* involving God, the Lord Jesus Christ and the Holy Spirit. No distinction is made between them and it is a reasonable assumption that Paul regarded them as coequal persons. (On the debate over the genitive, "fellowship of the Holy Spirit" see commentaries.)

These sections are cast in triadic form. In Ephesians 4:4-6, we read of "one Spirit . . . one Lord . . . one God and Father." The threefold form occurs also in 1 Corinthians 12:3-7, where each Person is introduced with the adjective "same" in the sequence Spirit, Lord and God, as in Ephesians 4. Under this category may be included Ephesians 1:3-14, where the flow of the eulogy is marked by a trinitarian format or a salvation-historical sequence of the plan of redemption from its eternal purpose to its execution in human experience (see Lincoln 1990, 8-44; Martin 1991, 13-20).

The second type consists of passages where the three Persons are mentioned together, but without any clear triadic structure. Samples of such passages are Galatians 4:4-6 ("God has sent the Spirit of his Son into our hearts"), Romans 8:1-4; 2 Thessalonians 2:13-14; Titus 3:4-6. The close linking of Father, Son and Spirit in these passages cannot be regarded as accidental.

Third, actions which are normally attributed to God are ascribed to Christ (such as creation: see Col 1:15-20; 1 Cor 8:6) or to the Spirit (e.g., acts of power, e.g., Rom 8:5-11). These add a further dimension to the NT evidence. Although no systematic trinitarian doctrine is stated, Paul furnishes several hints which point in that direction. The problems which confronted later theologians do not seem to have occurred to him, especially as part of his "christological monotheism" or "realigned monotheism" (Dunn, 163) by which he was able to accommodate the risen Lord into his picture of the one God of his Jewish faith, now broadened and deepened to make space for the exalted Lord* who in worship was greeted as on a par with Yahweh and worthy of divine honors and praise (Bauckham). In praise of the living Lord installed as head of the universe and the church Pauline Christians evidently were expected to confess that Jesus could be worshiped alongside (but not in competition with or to the exclusion of) Israel's God. Hence the appellation "God" (theos) for the risen Christ trembles on Paul's lips (Rom 9:5; see Harris).

We have been discussing the adumbrations of the Trinity, but it is under the general heading of the unity of God and some comment must be made concerning this. It must at once be noted that nowhere in the NT is any concern shown over purely speculative ideas about unity. Statements can be found like "the Lord is the Spirit" (2 Cor 3:17) or "our Lord Jesus Christ . . . and God our Father . . . comfort" (sing. verb) in 2 Thessalonians 2:16 or a doxology to Christ as God (Rom 9:5; see commentaries), without any apparent blurring of the distinction between them in the context. Undoubtedly there are deep mysteries in the

NT conception of God, but what must strike the thoughtful reader is the complete absence of any attempt to explain the mysteries. Christian convictions were strong enough to maintain the divine nature of both Jesus Christ and the Spirit without falling into the trap of postulating three gods. The conviction that God was active in Christ and in the Spirit prevented this from happening. It may be said that Paul does not work with a conceptual framework which would lead naturally to speculations about the essence of God. In a study of Paul's theology we cannot go further than the evidence we find. Yet the evidence lays foundations for the later developed doctrine. The problems which that later doctrine grappled with had their roots in the NT itself. Although Paul concentrates more on functions than relationships (as Cullmann's writings show), the latter aspect is certainly not lacking.

### 4. Summary.

Our survey of the Pauline presentation of God has done no more than to erect signposts toward an understanding of what must always retain an air of profound mystery. No outline of names or qualities can present a total picture. But Paul gave abundant indication that what is necessary to know about God can be known. Indeed, this is a basic assumption which colors his entire theological and missionary task (see Gilliland).

Moreover both in the titles and attributes of God found in the NT, there is a remarkable combination of what might at first appear to be opposites. The paradox of the love and wrath of God, his kindness and severity, his mercy and judgment, are examples of apparent antitheses or antinomies which nevertheless are perfectly balanced in the character of God. What in humans would be regarded as real antitheses and unrelieved paradoxes are postulated in God in a way which shows no awareness of any problem.

Another remarkable fact about the evidence is that it includes both transcendent and immanent aspects without any tendency to lay an overemphasis on either. There are no signs, in fact, that the problems which arise from such an overemphasis ever seriously troubled the minds of the early Christians. God is at the same time both majestic and concerned about the human condition. He is never remote, but is at the same time apart from his own creation.

The relevance of a right doctrine of God for an approach to Pauline theology may be illustrated as follows. A God who cares for his creatures is the God who acts to redeem them. A true understanding of the incarnation and therefore of the person of Christ is impossible if a wrong notion of God is maintained (signally at Colossae). Similarly if God were an angry deity who needed to be placated this would naturally color any approach to the doctrine of the mission of Christ. Some indication of the havoc which can be caused within a theology based on wrong assumptions about God can be seen in such issues as the way Paul has been misread as supporting anti-Semitism or (to take a practical yet profound concern) recruited as an ally of the paternalistic-hierarchical structure that demotes and dehumanizes women due to a false deduction regarding male headship.

*See also* CHRIST; CHRISTOLOGY; CREATION AND NEW CREATION; GRACE; HOLINESS, SANCTIFICATION; HOLY SPIRIT; IMAGE, IMAGE OF GOD; JUDGMENT; LORD; LOVE; MERCY; POWER; PRE-EXISTENCE; REDEMPTION; RIGHTEOUSNESS, RIGHTEOUSNESS OF GOD; SON OF GOD; WISDOM; WRATH, DESTRUCTION.

BIBLIOGRAPHY. J. Abelson, *The Immanence of God* (1912); J. Barr, "Abba Isn't Daddy," *JTS* 39 (1988) 28-47; idem, " 'Abba, Father' and the Familarity of Jesus' Speech," *Theology* 91 (1988) 173-79; C. K. Barrett, *Essays on Paul* (Philadelphia: Westminster, 1982); R. Bauckham, "The Worship of Jesus in Apocalyptic Christianity," *NTS* 27 (1981) 323-31; L. L. Belleville, *Reflections of Glory: Paul's Polemical Use of the Moses-Doxa Tradition in 2 Corinthians 3:12-18* (JSNTSup 52; Sheffield: Sheffield Academic, 1991); K. Berger, "Die impliziten Gegner: Zur Methode des Erschliessens von 'Gegner' in NT Texten" in *Kirche*, FS G. Bornkamm, ed. D. Lührmann and G. Strecker (Tübingen: J. C. B. Mohr 1980) 373-400; L. G. Bloomquist, *The Function of Suffering in Philippians* (JSNTSup 78; Sheffield: Academic, 1993); B. Byrne, '*Sons of God'— 'Seed of Abraham': A Study of the Idea of the Sonship of God of all Christians against the Jewish Background* (AnBib 83; Rome: Biblical Institute, 1979); C. C. Caragounis, *The Ephesian Mysterion* (Lund: Gleerup, 1977); H. Conzelmann, *1 Corinthians* (Herm; Philadelphia: Fortress, 1975); O. Cullmann, *The Christology of the New Testament* (Philadelphia: Westminster, 1959); C. H. Dodd, *The Epistle of Paul to the Romans* (New York: Harper & Row, 1932); J. D. G. Dunn, *The Partings of the Ways* (Philadelphia: Trinity Press International, 1991); E. E. Ellis, *Prophecy and Hermeneutic in Early Christianity* (Tübingen/Grand Rapids: Mohr/ Eerdmans, 1978); G. D. Fee, *1 Corinthians* (NICNT; Grand Rapids: Eerdmans, 1987); D. S. Gilliland, *Pauline Theology and Mission Practice* (Grand Rapids: Baker, 1983); L. E. Goodman, *Monotheism* (Allanheld, Osmun, 1981); R. M. Grant, *Gods and the One God* (Philadelphia: Westminster, 1986); E. Güttgemanns, *Der leidende Apostel und sein Herr: Studien zur paulinischen Christologie* (FRLANT 90; Göttingen: Vandenhoeck & Ruprecht, 1966); M. J. Harris, *Jesus as God: The NT Use of Theos in Reference to Jesus* (Grand Rapids: Baker, 1992); A. E. Harvey, "The Use of Mystery Language in the Bible," *JTS* 81 (1980); G. F. Hawthorne, *Philippians* (WBC 43; Waco: Word, 1983); R. B. Hays, *Echoes of Scripture* (New Haven: Yale University, 1989); G. S. Hendry, "Reveal, Revelation" in *A Theological Word Book of the Bible*, ed. A. Richardson (London: SCM, 1950); L. W. Hurtado, *One God, One Lord: Early Christian Devotion and Ancient Jewish Monothesim* (Philadelphia: Fortress, 1988); L. J. Kreitzer, *Jesus and God in Paul's Eschatology* (JSNTS 19; Sheffield: JSOT, 1987); D. W. Kuck, *Judgment and Community Conflict* (NovTSup 66; Leiden: E. J. Brill, 1992); A. T. Lincoln, *Ephesians* (WBC 42: Dallas: Word, 1990); idem, *Paradise Now and Not Yet* (SNTSMS 43; Cambridge: University Press, 1981); idem, "Paul the Visionary: The Setting and Significance of the Rapture to Paradise in 2 Corinthians 12:1-10," *NTS* 25 (1979) 204-20; E. Lohse, *Colossians and Philemon* (Herm; Philadelphia: Fortress, 1971); R. P. Martin, *Colossians: The Church's Lord and the Christian's Liberty* (Exeter: Paternoster, 1972); idem, *2 Corinthians* (WBC 40; Waco: Word, 1986); idem, *Ephesians, Colossians and Philemon* (Int; Louisville: John Knox, 1991); idem, *The Spirit and the Congregation: Studies in 1 Corinthians 12—15* (Grand Rapids: Eerdmans, 1984); L. Morris, "The Apostle and his God," in *God Who Is Rich in Mercy*, ed. P. T. O'Brien and D. G. Peterson (Homebush West, NSW: Anzea, 1986) 165-78; idem, *The Biblical Doctrine of Judgement* (London: Tyndale, 1960); H. Moxnes, *Theology in Conflict: Studies in Paul's Understanding of God in Romans* (NovTSup; Leiden: E. J. Brill, 1980); C. Newman, *Paul's Glory-Christology: Tradition and Rhetoric* (NovTSup 69; Leiden: E. J. Brill, 1992); C. H. Powell, *The Biblical Concept of Power* (London: Epworth 1963); P. Rainbow, "Jewish Monotheism as the Matrix for New Testament Christology," *NovT* 33 (1991) 78- 91; C. J. Roetzel, *Judgement in the Community: A Study of the Relationship between Eschatology and Ecclesiology in Paul* (NovTSup; Leiden: E. J. Brill, 1972); E. P. Sanders, *Paul and Palestinian Judaism* (Philadelphia: Fortress, 1977); E. J. Schnabel, *Law and Wisdom from Ben Sira to Paul* (WUNT 2.16 Tübingen: J. C. B. Mohr, 1985); C. A. A. Scott, *Christianity According to St. Paul* (Cambridge: University Press, 1927); J. M. Scott, *Adoption as Sons of God: An Exegetical Investigation into the Background of ΥΙΟΘΕΣΙΑ in the Corpus Paulinum* (WUNT 2.48; Tübingen: J. C. B. Mohr, 1992); R. Scroggs, *The Last Adam* (Oxford: Blackwell, 1966); A. F. Segal, *Paul the Convert* (New Haven: Yale, 1990); idem, *Two Powers in Heaven* (SJLA 25; Leiden: E. J. Brill, 1978); R. V. G. Tasker, *Biblical Doctrine of the Wrath of God* (London: Tyndale, 1951); A. W. Wainwright, *The Trinity in the*

*New Testament* (London: SPCK, 1962); U. Wilckens, *Weisheit und Torheit* (Tübingen: J. C. B. Mohr, 1956); N. T. Wright, *The Climax of the Covenant* (Minneapolis: Fortress, 1991); idem, "One God, One Lord, One People," *Ex Auditu* 7 (1991) 46-48; idem, *The New Testament and the People of God* (Minneapolis: Fortress, 1992).

D. Guthrie and R. P. Martin

## GOD OF THIS AGE. *See* SATAN, DEVIL.

## GODS. *See* IDOLATRY; RELIGIONS, GRECO-ROMAN.

## GOODNESS OF GOD. *See* GOD.

## GOSPEL

The Greek word *euangelion*, frequently translated "gospel," means "glad tidings," or "good news," and in Pauline usage it refers to the message of God's* saving work in Jesus Christ.* Of the seventy-six instances of "gospel" in the NT, sixty are found in the Pauline corpus (forty-eight in the undisputed letters). There are twenty-one occurrences of the verb *euangelizomai*, "to announce good news" in the Pauline corpus (nineteen in the undisputed letters); two occurrences of the noun *euangelistēs*, "evangelist" (Eph 4:11; 2 Tim 4:5); and a single occurrence of *proeuangelizomai*, "to announce good news ahead of time" (Gal 3:8). *Euangelion* is for Paul the classic expression of the grace* of God, responded to by faith.* Occasionally Paul speaks of "my gospel," but over twenty times he uses gospel without any qualifier. This strongly suggests that his readers were already familiar with the term.

1. The Gospel and Paul
2. The Gospel of God and of Christ
3. The Gospel's Past, Present and Future Tenses
4. The Gospel, Grace and Faith

### 1. The Gospel and Paul.

Since *euangelion* is found in all the traditional Pauline letters except Titus, it should be considered a central feature of the apostle's theological vocabulary. And since the largest portion of occurrences in the NT belong to Paul, some scholars have argued that "it was Paul who established *euangelion* in the vocabulary of the N.T." (Becker, 110). G. Strecker and others have argued that it was Hellenistic usage that influenced Paul, particularly the Hellenistic ruler or Roman emperor* cult, where the noun *euangelion* was used (with the emperor as *sōtēr*, "savior"*) for the announcement of "salvation"* associated with the emperor's rule (Strecker, 71; Friedrich, 725). But this derivation is by no means clear, and arguments have been mounted

to show that Paul may have derived the term from the early church, particularly through the Hellenists, who may have translated the Palestinian church's supposed use of the Hebrew *bᵉśôrâ* ("message of victory/ salvation") into the Greek *euangelion* (see Stuhlmacher).

It appears that Isaiah 40—66, with its theme of the good news of the coming reassertion of God's kingly rule (cf. *euangelizomai* in LXX Is 40:9; 52:7; 60:6; 61:1), had some shaping influence on Paul's use of *euangelion* (though the noun *euangelion* does not appear in Isaiah). Isaiah 52:7 may have been particularly influential (Beker, 116), since Paul quotes from it (perhaps with Nah 2:1) in Romans 10:15, and its theme of peace may be echoed in Ephesians 2:13-18 (Stuhlmacher). Evidence for the significance of Isaiah 52:7 in at least one strand of apocalyptic* Judaism comes from 11QMelch 2:15-16, where the verse is part of a pastiche of proof texts, several of them from Isaiah 40—66. These texts are set forth as testimonies to the year of God's favor and of the eschatological restoration* of Israel (cf. *Pss. Sol.* 11:1; 1QH 18:14). The influence of the Isaianic *euangelion* on Jesus (cf. Lk 4:43; Mt 11:5) and the Gospel tradition is also evident (see Broyles) and may have had a shaping influence on Paul insofar as it was a part of the tradition he inherited (*see* Jesus, Sayings of).

Much discussion has surrounded Paul's infrequent but intriguing references to "my gospel" (Rom 2:16; 16:25; 2 Tim 2:8), including its possible relationship to the origin and nature of the overall NT understanding of *euangelion*. Certainly the phraseology "my gospel" can be construed as speaking of content that has been decisively shaped by Paul. But that is by no means the only possible understanding, especially given the pattern emerging from the rest of the Pauline usage of *euangelion*.

Paul also speaks of "the gospel of God" (e.g., Rom 1:1; 15:16), "the gospel of his Son" (Rom 1:9), "the gospel of Christ" (Rom 15:19; also see below) or simply "the gospel" (without further description). Some of these usages even occur in the general context of the relatively infrequent expression "my gospel" (e.g., Rom 16:25; cf. Rom 15:16, 19 and 2 Tim 2:8; cf. 2 Tim 1:8, 10). Paul can also speak of "our gospel" in 1 Thessalonians 1:5 and 2 Thessalonians 2:14, though we must here consider the fact that Paul shares with Silas and Timothy (cf. 2 Cor 1:19) the prescript of both of these letters (cf. 1 Thess 1:1; 2 Thess 1:1) and that these coworkers* shared with Paul the gospel ministry* that gave birth to the church in Thessalonica* (cf. Acts 17:1-15).

The opposition Paul faced at Galatia* led him to

state that the distinctive nature of his *euangelion* was derived from divine revelation (Gal 1:11-12; cf. 1 Tim 1:11). The integrity of this gospel (Gal 2:5, 14) was to be protected from the subtle and deadly distortion that Paul labeled "a different gospel—which is not really another" (Gal 1:6-7; *see* Opponents). Whatever authority* or credentials a "Judaizer"* might claim, even if it was that of an angel* from heaven (Gal 1:8), that "gospel" was to be rejected if it differed from the gospel Paul had preached to the Galatians. The criterion was not the person nor credentials but the nature of the gospel itself (which Paul can also refer to as "the faith*" in Gal 1:23).

Paul speaks of his divine revelation (*see* Conversion and Call) in terms reminiscent of the calling and commissioning of a prophet of Israel. God had set him apart from his birth (Gal 1:15; cf. Jer 1:5), called him, revealed his Son* to him (Gal 1:16; cf. 1:12) in a heavenly vision* (1 Cor 9:1; 15:8; cf. Acts 9:1-19; 22:3-16; 26:12-18) and sent him on a mission* to proclaim the gospel (*euangelizomai*) to the Gentiles* (Gal 1:16; cf. Is 6:8; Jer 1:7; Ezek 2:3). This self-identity is related to Paul's allusion to himself as a herald of the eschatological "good news" of peace* (Rom 10:13-15; cf. Is 52:7; Nah 1:15; *see* Apostle).

Whatever else might be said about the content or coherent structure (see Becker) of Paul's gospel, it is clear that the eschatological* work of God in Christ* is at its center and that it conveys benefits to Gentiles (*see* Center). Research into Paul has suggested that the logic of his gospel was a natural outworking of his Damascus Road experience (see Kim). In the struggle at Galatia for a Law*-free gospel, in which Gentiles were to be accepted in Christ apart from Jewish rituals and identity markers (*see* Works of the Law), Paul was quick to point out the unusual means by which his gospel had come to him and to accent its distinctive features (see Longenecker, 22-25). But Paul could also speak of having "received" certain traditions* from those who preceded him in the faith (e.g., 1 Cor 11:23-26; 15:3-11), and there is evidence that he adopted and incorporated early Christian confessions into his letters (*see* Creeds). These traditions must have been compatible with the christological and soteriological essence of the gospel that was revealed to him.

Elsewhere Paul felt free to forge a "partnership (*koinōnia*) in the gospel" (Phil 1:5; *see* Fellowship) with the Philippian church (which may have included monetary assistance for Paul's gospel ministry, cf. *koinōnia* in Rom 15:26; 2 Cor 8:4; 9:13; *see* Financial Support). And if he was passionate for the truth* of the gospel at Galatia, it is also noteworthy that the passages in which Paul's usage of *euangelion* is most heavily clustered are among the most passionate and personal in the Pauline corpus (e.g., 1 Cor 9; Phil 1; 1 Thess 2). Indeed, P. T. O'Brien notes Paul's use of *euangelion* in several of his initial prayers* of thanksgiving (Rom 1:9; Phil 1:5; Col 1:6; 1 Thess 1:5-6; *see* Benediction, Blessing, Doxology, Thanksgiving). There Paul observes that the outworking of faith, love* and hope* in believers is evidence that the gospel has carried out its powerful work in the midst of the church at Thessalonica (1 Thess 1:3-5).

## 2. The Gospel of God and of Christ.

The Pauline letters contain seven references to "the gospel of God" and ten to "the gospel of Christ" (or "his Son, the Lord Jesus"). In three contexts mention of "the gospel of God" (Rom 1:1; 15:16; 1 Thess 2:9) is followed closely by "the gospel of Christ" (Rom 1:9; 15:19; 1 Thess 3:2). However, that order is reversed in 2 Corinthians 10:14; 11:7. The Corinthian correspondence contains five instances of "the gospel of Christ" and only one of "the gospel of God" (2 Cor 11:7). On the other hand, 1 Thessalonians includes "the gospel of God" three times and "the gospel of Christ" just once (1 Thess 3:2). There is no clear pattern of Pauline usage of these phrases.

Also at issue is whether the construction "gospel *of God*" or "gospel *of Christ*" should be taken as objective or subjective genitive. If taken as an objective genitive, God and Christ are the content of the gospel message ("the gospel about God/Christ"). If viewed as subjective, the nuance of authorship or source is emphasized (e.g., "the gospel from God/Christ").

For example, the context in which "the gospel of God" appears in Romans 1:1 makes it slightly more likely that the focus is on the gospel's origin (subjective genitive). Perhaps "the gospel of his Son" in Romans 1:9 is best viewed as specifying the content of Paul's preaching (objective genitive). However, as in virtually every occurrence of these phrases in Paul, the genitive makes good sense if it is read either way. Sometimes the context appears to underline the objective aspect, sometimes the subjective, and sometimes either is equally possible. Ultimately, it is true to Pauline theology to say that God in Christ is both the source and the content of the gospel. But a priority seems to be placed on "Christ" (Gal 1:16 [*euangelizomai*]; 2 Cor 1:19; 4:5; Phil 1:15-18), or "Christ crucified" (1 Cor 1:23; cf. Gal 3:1; *see* Cross, Theology of the), as a summary of the content of the gospel Paul preached. Thus "preaching the gospel" and "preaching Christ" seem to be interchangeable (1 Cor 1:17 and 1:23; 1 Cor 15:1, 11 and 15:12; 2 Cor 4:3 and 4:4). In fact, for Paul the "message of the cross" (1 Cor 1:17-

18) or "the message of reconciliation" (2 Cor 5:19) seem also to be interchangeable with "the gospel."

### 3. The Gospel's Past, Present and Future Tenses.

The gospel message is the divinely powerful instrumentality through which God's salvation* and righteousness* are presently revealed (Rom 1:16-17). In this sense it is akin to the biblical notion that God's word is powerful and effective (see Power). This may contribute to explaining why, particularly in Paul's thanksgivings for his churches, euangelion is in some degree synonymous with martyrion ("witness"*), logos ("word") and ho logos tou theou ("the word of God"; see O'Brien). Paul can use euangelion in a manner that suggests its activity, whether in coming (1 Thess 1:5), confirming (1 Cor 1:6) or bearing fruit and increasing (Col 1:6).

But the past and future aspects of the gospel message are also considered by Paul to be critically important. The historical events proclaimed in the gospel necessarily laid its foundation, providing trustworthy roots (1 Cor 15:1-20). But the gospel cannot be severed from the eventualities of the future: Paul speaks of the day when the thoughts of everyone will be judged by the all-knowing God "in accordance with my gospel" (kata to euangelion mou, Rom 2:16). This may mean that Paul's gospel is the basis for his statement regarding the coming judgment* or that his gospel will be the criterion for the judgment. But on a positive note, Paul can speak of the "hope" which is the content of the gospel (Col 1:23), and of the gospel bringing to light the promise of "life* and immortality*" (2 Tim 1:10 NIV). While the benefits of this gospel begin in the here and now of receiving the gospel, they are also the believer's eternal destiny.

The past tense of the gospel also looks back beyond the "good news" of Christ's redemptive death* and resurrection* (1 Cor 15:1-4), even to his "epiphany" as savior* (2 Tim 1:10), perhaps a reference to his incarnation (as in 1 Tim 3:16). Paul can speak of the gospel as having been "promised beforehand (proepēngeilato) through [God's] prophets in the Holy Scriptures" (Rom 1:2 NIV). The apostle specifically asserts that the Scripture (Genesis 12:3) "preached the gospel beforehand" (Gal 3:8 NASB; proeuēngelisato). Thus the blessing God extended to Abraham* (Gen 12:3; Gal 3:14), as well as the promises made through the OT prophets (Rom 1:1-4), are somehow included in the rich substrata of the preaching* of the gospel of Christ, God's Son (Rom 1:9). The most likely explanation of these Pauline references to the "gospel" before Christ is linked to God's plan for the future worldwide spread of the gospel before the end comes (cf. panta ta ethnē in Mt 28:19; also Lk 24:47).

Thus it is quite plausible that Paul's focus on the phrase panta ta ethnē ("all nations") in Galatians 3:8, borrowed from Genesis 12:3, while serving as a corrective to the Judaizers' understanding of how Gentiles were to be included in the blessing of Abraham (the necessity of circumcision), is related to Paul's understanding of the anticipated global impact of the gospel. This theme appears again at the end of Romans in the yoking of "my gospel" and the "preaching of Jesus Christ" (Rom 16:25; kerygma Iēsou Christou) together with "the Scripture of the prophets" and "all the nations" (Rom 16:26 NASB; panta ta ethnē). Whether this concluding doxology of Romans is authentically Paul's or not (Rom 16:25-27; see e.g., Dunn, 912-17), it ably summarizes the central focus of Paul's gospel: the divine plan for the salvation of humankind in Christ.

### 4. The Gospel, Grace and Faith.

The apostle makes it abundantly clear that to alter the gospel message in any way is to desert the God "who called you by the grace of Christ" (Gal 1:6 NIV; cf. 2 Cor 11:4 for the intrusion of a "different gospel"). At least ten other passages in the Pauline literature also find "gospel" and "grace"* employed in the same immediate context, strongly implying that the only salvific channel of divine grace is the pure "truth of the gospel" (Gal 2:5, 14). In fact, the relationship between "gospel" and "grace" is so far-reaching and enduring that Paul tells the church at Corinth that their generosity is related to their "confession of the gospel of Christ" (2 Cor 9:13 NIV) and is an expression of "the surpassing grace (hyperballousan charin) of God" that has been given to them (2 Cor 9:14).

Even as Paul labored unceasingly to safeguard "the truth of the gospel" (Gal 2:5, 14) of "the grace of Christ" (Gal 1:6), he also strove to clarify beyond misunderstanding the appropriate response to the gospel: faith in Jesus Christ, without any diluting mixture of works of the Law (Gal 2:16; see Works of the Law). The "good news" of God's undeserved favor is available, according to Paul, to "everyone who believes" (Rom 1:16), whether Jew or Gentile. God has chosen them for salvation through sanctification (see Holiness, Sanctification) by the Holy Spirit* and "faith in the truth" (pistei alētheias, 2 Thess 2:13), and thus those who are called through the gospel gain the glory* of the Lord Jesus Christ (2 Thess 2:14).

See also AUTHORITY; CENTER OF PAUL'S THEOLOGY; CROSS, THEOLOGY OF THE; GRACE; JESUS AND PAUL; LAW; PREACHING, KERYGMA; TRADITION.

BIBLIOGRAPHY. K. Barth, God, Grace, and Gospel (Edinburgh: Oliver & Boyd, 1959); U. Becker, "Gospel,"

*NIDNTT* 2.110-15; J. C. Beker, *Paul the Apostle: The Triumph of God in Life and Thought* (Philadelphia: Fortress, 1980); C. C. Broyles, "Gospel (Good News)," *DJG* 282-86; C. H. Dodd, *The Apostolic Preaching and Its Developments* (London: Hodder & Stoughton, 1936); idem, *Gospel and Law* (New York: Columbia University Press, 1951); J. D. G. Dunn, *Romans* (2 vols.; WBC 38; Dallas: Word, 1988); J. A. Fitzmyer, "The Gospel in the Theology of Paul," in *To Advance the Gospel* (New York: Crossroad, 1981) 149-61; G. Friedrich, "εὐαγγέλιον κτλ," *TDNT* II.707-37; L. Goppelt, *Theology of the New Testament* (2 vols.; Grand Rapids: Eerdmans, 1982) 2.110-17; S. Kim, *The Origin of Paul's Gospel* (Grand Rapids: Eerdmans, 1981); R. N. Longenecker, *Galatians* (WBC 41; Dallas: Word, 1990); P. T. O'Brien, "The Importance of the Gospel in Philippians," in *God Who Is Rich in Mercy*, ed. P. T. O'Brien and D. G. Peterson (Homebush West, Australia: Lancer, 1986) 213-33; idem, "Thanksgiving and the Gospel in Paul," *NTS* 21 (1974-75) 144-55; E. F. Scott, *The Gospel and Its Tributaries* (Edinburgh, T. & T. Clark, 1928); R. H. Strachan, "The Gospel in the New Testament," *IB* 7.21-28; G. Strecker, "εὐαγγέλιον," *EDNT* 2.70-74; P. Stuhlmacher, *Das paulinischen Evangelium* (FRLANT 95; Göttingen: Vandenhoeck & Ruprecht, 1968); idem, "The Pauline Gospel," in *The Gospel and the Gospels*, ed. P. Stuhlmacher (Grand Rapids: Eerdmans, 1991) 149-72; H. G. Wood, "Didache, Kerygma and Euangelion," in *New Testament Essays: Studies in Memory of T. W. Manson*, ed. A. J. B. Higgins (Manchester: Manchester University, 1959) 306-14.

A. B. Luter, Jr.

**GOVERNMENT.** *See* CHURCH ORDER AND GOVERNMENT; CIVIL AUTHORITY; POLITICAL SYSTEMS.

# GRACE

Nearly two-thirds (100 of 154) of the NT occurrences of *charis*, normally translated "grace," are found in the Pauline letters. The term is found in all thirteen of the traditional Pauline letters, and is heavily clustered in Romans* (twenty-three times) and the Corinthian* letters (eighteen times in 2 Cor; ten times in 1 Cor). In Pauline usage the word *charis* carries the basic sense of "favor" (cf. Heb *ḥēn*, "favor," and *ḥesed*, "loving kindness," in the OT; see Esser, Conzelmann), and when God* or Christ* is its subject, acting in grace toward humankind, it is undeserved favor. This is especially apparent in contexts referring to salvation* or gifts of the Spirit* (where the kindred term *charisma* overlaps with *charis*). Paul employs *charis* as his customary epistolary salutation, but even in that context it appears to carry a theological connotation.

With human subjects *charis* sometimes refers to thanksgiving (to God), to a collection* or offering (recalling divine grace), or to gracious or encouraging speech directed toward others.

1. The Grace of God and Christ
2. The Grace of Salvation
3. Gifts of Grace
4. Greetings of Grace

## 1. The Grace of God and Christ.

The Pauline corpus includes numerous mentions of "the grace of God" (or "his grace") and "the grace of Christ" (or its lengthened version, "the grace of the Lord Jesus Christ"). The last phrase adorns the conclusion of over half of the Pauline letters (e.g., Rom 16:20; 1 Cor 16:23; 2 Cor 13:13[14]), perhaps signaling a climactic summary in linking *charis* to the full divine-messianic title "the Lord Jesus Christ." In 2 Thessalonians 1:12 the expression "the grace of our God and the Lord Jesus Christ" (NIV) indicates the inseparable bond between the *charis* of God and Christ.

F. Fisher goes so far as to assert that Paul understands *charis* as "God acting in accordance with his own character and being" (Fisher, 86), and that "grace" means not merely a divine attribute or attitude but "God himself" (Fisher, 86). Whether or not Paul intended such an identification, a close correlation between God and his grace may be observed in the extended and rhythmic "blessing" (*see* Benediction, Blessing, Doxology, Thanksgiving) of Ephesians 1:3-14. There we read that appreciation of "the riches of his grace" in Christ (Eph 1:7) should result in praise of "the glory of his grace" (Eph 1:6). This "praise" apparently entails a "blessing" (Gk *eulogētos*) of "the God and Father of our Lord Jesus Christ" who has greatly "blessed" (Gk *eulogēsas*) believers in Christ (Eph 1:3). Essentially, to offer praise to his glorious grace is to praise God. A number of passages employ *charis* to express the human response of overwhelming gratefulness translated into thanksgiving to God (e.g., 1 Cor 15:57). Occasionally it is the mention of divine grace in the immediately preceding context that prompts the grateful articulation of human *charis* (thanks) to God (e.g., Rom 6:14, 15, 17; 2 Cor 9: 14, 15). Colossians 3:16 states the ideal, that a song of "gratitude" (NIV; "thankfulness" NASB; Gk *en chariti*) to God should undergird whatever the Colossians* "do in word or deed" (Col 3:17 NASB). The astounding reality of divine *charis* demands an awed response of human *charis* to God.

## 2. The Grace of Salvation.

The Pauline message of grace is neatly summed up in

Ephesians 2:5: "by grace you have been saved." Conzelmann is surely right when he concludes, "In Paul *charis* is a central concept that most clearly expresses his understanding of the salvation event" (Conzelmann, 393). But for Paul, grace is not a previously undisclosed attitude or characteristic of God, as if he had previously been known only as a wrathful deity. Grace speaks of the "wholly generous *act* of God" (Dunn, 202; cf. Bultmann, 288-90), which reflects the wholly generous nature of God.

For Paul the grace of God encompasses a broad arena, reaching back to the grace of God's pretemporal electing purpose (Eph 1:3-6; *see* Election), including his choice of a Jewish remnant (Rom 11:5-6; *see* Israel). It embraces the actual offer of the gospel* message, which Paul can refer to as *charis* in place of (2 Cor 4:15), or interchangeably with (Col 1:5-6), the term *euangelion* ("gospel*"). But fundamentally, grace refers to a pivotal event, God's *eschatological deed* in Jesus Christ (so Bultmann, 289), as it is experienced in the present gift (*dōrea/dōrean*) of eschatological justification,* which comes by divine grace and is appropriated by faith* (Rom 3:24; 4:4-5, 16). Believers continue to experience this grace in the ongoing work of sanctification in their lives (Rom 5:2, 21; 6:1, 14, 15).

Paul himself found a unique personal experience of divine grace in the midst of the weakness* of prolonged suffering* with his "thorn in the flesh" (2 Cor 12:9). Here, as elsewhere in Paul, grace is used synonymously with, or in place of, divine power* (*dynamis*; cf. Rom 5:20-21), and in certain cases seems to be used as a correlative of God's Spirit* (cf. Rom 6:14 and Gal 5:18; see Bultmann, 290-91; Dunn, 203).

A salvation so gracious from beginning to end might be misconstrued as encouraging the continuance of sin in the Christian's life (Rom 6:1), a notion the apostle denounces in the most vigorous terms (Gk *mē genoito*, "By no means!"): those who have died to sin cannot go on living in it (Rom 6:2). Exactly the opposite is true: while works of the Law (Gal 2:16; *see* Works of the Law) have no part in justification, which is solely of grace (Eph 2:8-9), good works are to be the very centerpiece of the life of gratitude, which is to characterize those who have been saved by God's grace (Eph 2:10). The *charis* of God manifested in salvation* (Tit 2:11) has the further effect of training (Gk *paideuō*) believers in a disciplined, godly lifestyle as they await the appearing of their great God and Savior* Jesus Christ (Tit 2:12-13). Their gratefulness for the divine *charis* should motivate a response of zeal* for good works (Tit 2:14).

In writing to the Corinthians, Paul can appeal to the grace of God given to the Macedonian churches which, despite their poverty, had been moved by grace to pour out their offerings to the Jerusalem saints (2 Cor 8:1-4). The Corinthians, who had also received the grace of God in their spiritual gifts (their *charismata* seem to be implied in 2 Cor 8:1) and come to know the supreme model of grace in their Lord Jesus Christ (2 Cor 8:9), are called upon to respond in kind (*en tautē tē chariti*, "in this grace," 2 Cor 8:7). They are to make good on an earlier pledge to come to the aid of the church in Jerusalem in its time of need (1 Cor 16:3; *see* Collection).

### 3. Gifts of Grace.

For the most part, the Pauline literature develops the concept of spiritual gifts around the closely related idea of *charisma*, meaning "a personal endowment with grace," always concrete in its expression (Esser, 121; *see* Gifts of the Spirit). Occasionally, though, *charis* is also used, probably to emphasize the source of divine grace providing and empowering the gifts.

In Romans 12:6 *charis* is found alongside *charisma* to highlight the undeservedness of the diverse spiritual gifts God has provided (Rom 12:6-8). This sense of being "graced" by the various *charismata* (Rom 12:6) was apparently intended to promote the unity of the body of Christ (Rom 12:4-5; see Body of Christ). Following a somewhat different appeal to "the unity of the Spirit" (Eph 4:3) and body (Eph 4:4-6), *charis* and *dōrea*, another word for "gift," introduce (Eph 4:7) the most selective and distinctive of the Pauline passages dealing with spiritual gifts (Eph 4:7-11).

Frequently Paul refers to his own spiritual gift of apostleship (*see* Apostle) and related functions in connection with the "grace" involved in that calling. Against the backdrop of controversy in Galatia, Paul speaks of "the grace" that has been given to him (Gal 2:9). Elsewhere he uses the same language to refer to his grace-given apostolic role as a priest or liturgical officiant serving the gospel in order that the offering of the Gentiles* might be acceptable (Rom 15:15-16). Or he can speak of himself as a master-builder (1 Cor 3:10), as a vehicle of God's revelation (Eph 3:2) and as a servant* and preacher of the gospel to the Gentiles (Eph 3:7-8).

### 4. Greetings of Grace.

Without fail, the Pauline letters all contain *charis* as an initial salutation and part of the normally formal epistolary prologue (*see* Letters). Again, without exception, they all have *charis* as part of their concluding benediction (e.g., Rom 16:20: "The grace of our Lord Jesus be with you"). Such consistent usage has been studied by T. Y. Mullins and others as an element of NT epistolary style. In adopting *charis* as part of his salutation, Paul seems to have been substituting a word rich in theological significance for the customary Hellenistic greeting, *chairein* ("greetings").

The twenty-six instances of this usage are statistically significant enough to be discussed merely as a stylistic feature, but there would appear to be more to it than style. A clue to the significance of this feature may be found in comparing the use of *charis* in the introductions and in the conclusions: While all the letters yoke "grace" and "peace"* (e.g., Rom 1:7; 1 Cor 1:3) in their introductions (although 1 Tim 1:2 and 2 Tim 1:2 insert "mercy" between "grace" and "peace"), only "grace" recurs in the conclusions. This may be simply a feature of Pauline style, but it may also represent a broad *inclusio* structure. The consistent use of the definite article, "*the* grace," in the conclusions (Gk *hē charis*) may also point toward this intention on Paul's part. At the very least, in keeping with a keynote of Pauline theology (see above), the Pauline letters all begin and end by sounding a note of grace. It is not unlikely that the apostle intended all of his writings to be viewed within the all-encompassing framework of divine grace, from beginning to end.

Moreover, within the evangelistic context of Colossians 4:6, Paul cautions that the word of the gospel must always be presented sensitively and graciously (Gk *en chariti*). In Ephesians 4:29 we read that verbal communication between Christians is to focus on edification (Gk *oikodomē*) and needs, especially by purposefully aiming to "give grace" (i.e., spiritual benefit) to those who hear the words. In both cases, such loving concern may be understood as a reflection of divine grace.

*See also* BENEDICTION, BLESSING, DOXOLOGY, THANKSGIVING; COLLECTION FOR THE SAINTS; FINANCIAL SUPPORT; FORGIVENESS; GIFTS OF THE SPIRIT; HOLY SPIRIT; MERCY.

BIBLIOGRAPHY. R. Bultmann, *The Theology of the New Testament* (2 vols.; New York: Scribners, 1951, 1955) 1.288-92; H. Conzelmann, "χάρις κτλ," *TDNT* IX.393-98; J. D. G. Dunn, *Jesus and the Spirit* (Philadelphia: Westminster, 1975) 202-5; H.-H. Esser, "Grace," *NIDNTT* 2.115-24; F. Fisher, *Paul and His Teachings* (Nashville: Broadman, 1974) 85-102; W. Manson, "Grace in the NT," in *The Doctrine of Grace*, ed. W. T. Whitley (London: SCM, 1932); C. L. Mitton, "Grace," *IDB* 2.464-67; J. Moffatt, *Grace in the NT* (New York: Long and Smith, 1932); T. Y. Mullins, "Greeting as a NT Form," *JBL* 87 (1968) 418-26; C. R. Smith, *The Bible Doctrine of Grace* (London: Epworth, 1956); G. P. Wetter, *Charis* (Leipzig: Brandstetter, 1913); R. Winkler, "Die Gnade im Neuen Testament," *ZSTh* 10 (1933) 642-80. A. B. Luter, Jr.

**GRECO-ROMAN RELIGIONS.** *See* RELIGIONS, GRECO-ROMAN.

**GREEK RELIGION.** *See* RELIGIONS, GRECO-ROMAN; HELLENISM.

**GUILT.** *See* SIN, GUILT.

# H

**HALAKAH.** *See* JEW, PAUL THE; OLD TESTAMENT IN PAUL.

**HARDENING.** *See* ELECTION AND PREDESTINATION; ISRAEL; OLD TESTAMENT IN PAUL; RESTORATION OF ISRAEL.

**HARDSHIPS.** *See* AFFLICTIONS, TRIALS, HARDSHIPS; SUFFERING.

**HATRED.** *See* ENEMY, ENMITY, HATRED.

## HEAD

Paul used the term *kephalē* ("head") in ways that demonstrate a variety of meanings, sometimes blending both literal and figurative values in a single passage. In some texts he suggests more than one meaning for the word. "Head" is for him in the first place a literal member of the body (1 Cor 12:21), but the meaning of the term when applied to man in relation to woman, or to Christ,* has been extensively debated (*see* Man and Woman). Paul's use of *kephalē* must be understood against the background of its use in ancient Greek.

    1. Paul's Understanding of *Kephalē*
    2. The Classical View of Head as Source
    3. Headship in the Household
    4. Headship in the Trinity

### 1. Paul's Understanding of *Kephalē*.

Homer and successive generations of writers used the term *head* as a metonymy for the entire person, especially where matters of military census or taxation were concerned. The head was also a synecdoche for the individual upon whom judgment, curses or misfortunes could devolve, a sense we find in Romans 12:20. On occasion, *kephalē* was a synonym for life itself. From Homeric times onward, "head" was employed to refer to a person who had special significance to the speaker, usually one for whom the speaker had deep affection and commitment. Whatever other sense Paul may have attached to the word, this value must always be considered to be present when he refers to Christ

as head (*see* Head, Christ as).

The ancients recognized the head as the most prominent and conspicuous bodily member, by virtue of its uppermost position. This, R. Cervin maintains, is the basic Pauline sense. Paul speaks of the preeminence of Christ as head (Col 1:18) and declares Christ was given to be head over all things to the church,* his body (Eph 1:22; *see* Body of Christ). Philo, the apostle's Jewish contemporary, noted, however, that the head was interdependent with all of the other body parts (Philo *Fug.* 110; 112; *Aet. Mund.* 29; *Spec. Leg.* III.184; *Sacr.* 115), a notion also reflected in 1 Corinthians 12:21.

*Kephalē* became a word used both for an objective or goal to be reached and for its fulfillment, culmination or full fruition. Philo declared, "The head [*kephalē*] of all actions is their goal [*telos*]" (Philo *Sacr.* 115). Paul adopts this sense when he writes of growing up in all things into Christ, who is the head (Eph 4:15), and of believers as being made complete in him who is their head (Col 2:11). *Kephalē* could also indicate the sum total of anything, so that Paul uses the verb *anakephalaiō* to imply the summation of the Law* (Rom 13:9) and of "all things" (Eph 1:10).

### 2. The Classical View of Head as Source.

Plato and Aristotle, among others, maintained that sperm was formed in the brain. The Pythagoreans in particular considered the head to be the source of human generation. They refrained from eating any part of an animal or fish head lest the creature be a reincarnated ancestor and the head the very organ from which they themselves had derived. By the time of Plato, adherents of Orphic religion were using *kephalē* with *archē* ("source" or "beginning"; Kern *Orph. Fr.* 2.nos. 21 a.2., 168; Plato *Leg.* IV.715E and sch; Proclus *In Tim.* II 95.48. (V.322); Pseudo-Aristides *World* 7; Eusebius *Praep. Ev.* 3.9; Deveni Papyrus col. 13, line 12; Stobaeus *Ecl.* 1.23; Plutarch *Def. Orac.* 436D; Achilles Tatius, fr. 81.29), as did the translators of the LXX version of Isaiah 9:14-15.

W. Grudem views *archē* as conveying the sense of

"rule or dominion" when used synonymously with *kephalē*, but this concept did not find wide acceptance among the ancients. Irenaeus equates head with "source" when he writes of the "head and source of his own being" (*kephalēn men kai archēn tēs idias ousias*; PG 7.496. See also Tertullian *Marc.* 5.8). Hippolytus emphasized the productivity of this bodily member when he designated the head as the characteristic substance from which all people were made (PG 16.iii.3138). Philo declared, "As though the head of a living creature, Esau is the progenitor of all these members" (Philo *Congr.* 61). *Kephalē* was considered by Photius to be a synonym for *procreator* or *progenitor* (Photius *Comm. 1 Cor 11:3.* ed. Staab 567.1). The concept of head (*kephalē*) as "source," "beginning" or "point of departure" is readily apparent in the Pauline corpus. *Kephalē* is used in apposition to *archē* in Colossians 1:18. (As an aside, one should recall that the head is the part of the body which is usually born first, a feature that may shed light on Christ as the first-born* of the dead, and the firstborn of all creation* [Col 1:15, 18].)

While there was debate as to whether the head, breast or stomach was the dwelling place of mind and soul, philosophers viewed the head as the organ from which there issued forth that which was important or distinctive of humans—most notably speech. The head resembled a spring, from which power flowed forth to other bodily organs (Philo *Fug.* 182; Aristotle *Prob.* 10 867a). It was placed nearest to the heavens, drawing from thence its power and distributing the life force to every member of the body (Philo *Det. Pot. Ins.* 85; *Praem. Poen.* 125). This concept of the head as source of supply to the whole body is well attested among medical writers and is twice echoed by Paul (Eph 4:15-16; Col 2:19). In Colossians 2:10 Christ is presented as the head ("source") of the originative power and ability needed for the believer's fulfillment as he himself embodies the fullness* of the Godhead (*see* Head, Christ as).

### 3. Headship in the Household.

In 1 Corinthians 11:3 *kephalē* appears to have the sense of "ground of being" or antecedent source. The Son* proceeds forth from the Father and is himself the primal cause of all creation, including every human being. Woman found her origin in man, in an interdependency which now brought forth man from woman. The notion of man as the source of woman is twice repeated in the following verses (1 Cor 11:8, 12). The covered head of the woman not only indicated commitment to her husband but also respected the Jewish obligation for a man to divorce a woman who

appeared in the street with head uncovered (*m. Ketub.* 7:6). Observance of this custom was particularly important in a house church which met next door to the synagogue (Acts 18:7), where "messengers" (*angeloi*) might carry back a report of unsuitable behavior or attire (1 Cor 11:10). In 1 Corinthians 11:16, however, Paul indicates that the church has no such universal custom, and a woman has the right of choice (1 Cor 11:10, *exousia;* cf. 1 Cor 7:37; 8:9; 9:4, 5, 12); but it is mandatory for her to respect the sensibilities of others.

The punishment of the "head" of the household* for the misdemeanors of his family, in the early-Christian *Shepherd of Hermas* (*Similitudes* 7.3) is representative of the prevailing legal structure. According to Roman *patria potestas*, the oldest living male (*paterfamilias*)—whether father, grandfather or great-grandfather—controlled all the other members of the family, regardless of age or political importance. Only the *paterfamilias* was recognized as a full person in the eyes of Roman law and society. As such, he held the power of life and death over other family members and assumed accountability for their behavior. They in turn could not even possess property in their own right, nor were they free to make their own choices in matters of religion. By certain legal procedures it was possible for a younger male to disengage himself from this system, but it was frequently a painful step because of religious and social pressures.

In legal terminology, to have "head" (*caput*) was to be an integral part of one's legitimate family. If a person was adopted into another family, that individual lost "head." In Christ, believers were offered a new head along with their new family, with Christ as head. Paul calls upon his churches to free themselves from familial bondage and to assume moral responsibility for their own behavior, and to establish new households with Christ as head (1 Cor 11:3; Eph 5:31).

Marriages* within the Empire were ordinarily arranged so that the wife remained legally and religiously part of her father's family. Her relatives might with impunity remove her from the marriage and contract another more favorable alliance, even against her will. This system wrought marital instability that Paul countered with a call for men and women to be bound together as one flesh,* head and body, and both as members of Christ's body (Eph 5:30-31; 1 Cor 11:11-12). If a Roman woman was formally attached to her husband's family rather than her own, her legal position became that of a daughter with respect to her own husband. In the transfer to his family, she was said to have forfeited "head" (*capitis deminutio;* Cicero *Topica* III 18. Gaius *Institutes* I.162). In an era when a woman was legally required to have a "head," Paul called upon the woman to join herself in an attitude of both accountability and commitment (*hypotassō*, "to submit to," "identify with" or "assimilate to") to a husband, freed of repressive family hierarchy and responsive to Christ as head.

After stressing the mutuality of submission (Eph 5:21), Paul, in Ephesians 5:23, calls the husband head of the wife "as Christ is head of the church, himself Savior* of the body." The extended passage stresses the concern of Christ, the bridegroom, for the full development of his bride, the church; and husbands are called to a similar concern. As Christ the head brought growth and empowerment to the body of believers (Eph 4:15; Col 2:10), so the husband should be the enabler of the wife for personal growth and empowerment in a society that afforded her few opportunities.

### 4. Headship in the Trinity.
By the Byzantine era *kephalē* had acquired the sense of "chief" or "master." Although the English *head* and Hebrew *rō'š* can have such a meaning, this was rarely true of the Greek *kephalē* in NT times. B. Mickelsen and A. Mickelsen have demonstrated that, with rare exceptions, translators of the Septuagint chose words other than *kephalē* to render the Hebrew *rō'š* when the term implied authority or power. The contemporary desire to find in 1 Corinthians 11:3 a basis for the subordination of the Son to the Father has ancient roots. In response to such subordinationism, church fathers argued vehemently that for Paul *head* had meant "source." Athanasius (*Syn. Armin.* 26.3.35; *Anathema* 26. Migne PG 26, 740B), Cyril of Alexandria (*De Recte Fide ad Pulch.* 2.3, 268; *De Recte Fide ad Arcadiam* 1.1.5.5(2). 63.), Basil (PG 30.80.23.), Theodore of Mopsuestia (*Eccl. Theol.* 1.11.2-3;2.7.1) and even Eusebius (*Eccl. Theol.* 1.11.2-3; 2.7.1.) were quick to recognize the danger of an interpretation of 1 Corinthians 11:3 which could place Christ in a subordinate position relative to the Father. In view of Scripture ascribing coequality of Christ with the Father (Jn 1:1-3; 10:30; 14:9, 11; 16:15; 17:11, 21), John Chrysostom declared that only a heretic would understand Paul's use of "head" to mean "chief" or "authority over." Rather one should understand the term as implying "absolute oneness and cause and primal source" (PG 61.214, 216; *see* Christology).

*See also* CHRISTOLOGY; FIRSTBORN; HEAD, CHRIST AS; MAN AND WOMAN.

BIBLIOGRAPHY. S. Bedale, "The Meaning of *Kephalē* in the Pauline Epistles," *JTS* 5 (1954) 211-15; R. S. Cervin, "Does *Kephalē* Mean 'Source' or 'Authority' in Greek Literature? A Rebuttal," *TJ* 10 NS (1989) 85-112; J. A. Fitzmyer, "Another Look at *ΚΕΦΑΛΗ* in I Corinthians 11.3," *NTS* 35 (1989) 503-11; W. A. Grudem, "Does *Kephalē* Mean 'Source' or 'Authority over' in Greek Literature? A Survey of 2,336 Examples," *TJ* 6 (1985) 38-59; C. C. Kroeger, "The Classical Concept of Head as 'Source' " Appendix 3, in G. G. Hull, *Equal to Serve* (Old Tappan, NJ: Revell, 1987); A. Mickelsen and B. Mickelsen, "The 'Head' of the Epistles," *CT* (February, 20 1981); idem, "What Does *Kephalē* Mean in the New Testament?" in *Women, Authority and the Bible*, ed. A. Mickelsen (Downers Grove, IL: InterVarsity, 1986).                                                                          C. C. Kroeger

## HEAD, CHRIST AS
A particularly significant use of "head" (*kephalē*) in the Pauline letters is in Colossians* and Ephesians* where Christ is designated as "head"* (*kephalē*) in relationship to the church* as "body."*

    1. Head and Body
    2. Head as Christological Metaphor

### 1. Head and Body.
In 1 Corinthians 12:12-31 Paul employs an extensive body metaphor and identifies the Corinthian congregation(s) as the "body of Christ" (1 Cor 12:27). Various anatomical parts, "members," are listed (foot, hand, ear, eye, head, feet), with some of these "mouthing" divisive statements. The head utters one such declaration to the feet: "I do not need you" (1 Cor 12:21). The passage represents Paul's bid to demonstrate the absurdity of attitudes of either inferiority or supremacy on the part of church "members" who have been endowed with a variety of gifts. In the setting of 1 Corinthians 12 the "head" is one body part among others and is not assigned a place of preeminence.

When "head" is taken up again in relationship to the body metaphor in Colossians and Ephesians, it is employed differently. In these two letters Christ is identified as "head" in relationship to the body (Col 1:18; 2:19; Eph 1:22; 4:15; 5:23).

Colossians 1:18 states of Christ, "He himself is the head of the body, the church." This phrase, part of a longer hymn (Col 1:15-20), may represent a revision by Paul of an earlier hymn* which identified Christ as "head" of the cosmic body (see commentaries). Colossians 2:19 once again employs "head" in relation to the body metaphor in describing erring teachers (either actual or rhetorical) as "not holding to the head, from whom [the antecedent of the pronoun is 'Christ'] the whole body, nourished and joined by its ligaments and sinews, grows with a God-given growth."

In Ephesians it is said that God has made Christ

"head over all things for the church, which is his body" (Eph 1:22-23) and that believers are to "grow up in every way into him who is the head, into Christ, from whom the whole body, joined and knit together by every ligament with which it is equipped, as each part is working properly, promotes the body's growth in building itself up in love" (Eph 4:15-16 NRSV). Christ is also identified as "head" in the context of both body and bridal imagery, where the husband as "head" of the wife is compared to Christ as "head" in his relationship to the church, "the body of which he is Savior*" (Eph 5:23).

## 2. Head as Christological Metaphor.

A central question in regard to the use of "head" in Colossians and Ephesians is: Should "head" be understood as a submetaphor of the "body" metaphor? That is, should "head" be viewed anatomically as part of the body or understood as a separated, if related, metaphor?

While it is frequently assumed that "head" in the Colossian and Ephesian letters refers to "head" as an anatomical part, an opposing view has been gaining ground in recent discussion. This view depends on the notation that "head" is used with Christ as referent and not as a part of the body metaphor (Col 2:10 cf. 1 Cor 11:3), and that the phrase "all the body" in Colossians 2:19 and Ephesians 4:16 specifically excludes imagining a headless body. In this view "head" and "body" are two separate metaphors which are related to one another. Such a view may be pressed with regard to other passages in Ephesians. In Ephesians 1:22, 23 it is as "head of all things" rather than as anatomical head of a specific body that Christ is given to the church. And mention of Christ's "feet" (drawn from Ps 110:1) helps to affirm that "head" should not be taken here in the sense of an anatomical part. In Ephesians 5:21-33 both Christ and husbands are called "head." The passage is not suggesting that the ecclesial body, apart from Christ, lacks a head any more than it is stating that wives apart from their husbands are incomplete persons.

How should the designation of Christ as "head" in Colossians and Ephesians be accounted for? Challenges to Christ's uniqueness in the setting of the letter to the Colossians explain the initial designation of Christ as "head." When the theme is picked up in the closely related document, the letter to the Ephesians, it is used in service of that letter's ecclesiology with its understanding of the church not as a local congregation but as the church universal. Coordinated with advanced views of the unity and ministry of this universal body (Eph 4:1-16), the term "head" becomes a

useful way to designate the relationship of Christ to this expansive ecclesial body.

A final comment touches on the nature of metaphor as metaphor. A modern theory of metaphor appreciates metaphor as a useful cognitive vehicle and respects profound or poetic metaphor as incapable of complete paraphrase. When, in the Pauline letters, Christ is designated as "head," it is not as "mere metaphor" but as an important means to communicate the uniqueness and importance of Christ. In other words, the headship metaphor is more christologically* oriented than a part of Paul's ecclesiology.

*See also* BODY OF CHRIST; CHRISTOLOGY; CHURCH; HEAD.

BIBLIOGRAPHY. E. Best, *One Body in Christ* (London: SPCK, 1955); E. Clowney, "Interpreting the Biblical Models of the Church: A Hermeneutical Deepening of Ecclesiology," in *Biblical Interpretation and the Church: Text and Context*, ed. D. A. Carson (Exeter: Paternoster, 1984) 64-109; J. D. G. Dunn, "The Body of Christ in Paul," in *Worship, Theology and Ministry in the Early Church: Essays in Honor of Ralph P. Martin*, ed. M. J. Wilkins and T. Paige (JSNTSup 87; Sheffield: JSOT, 1992) 146-62; G. Howard, "The Head/Body Metaphors of Ephesians," *NTS* 20 (1974) 350-56; A. Perriman, " 'His body, which is the church . . .': Coming to Terms with Metaphor," *EvQ* 62 (1990) 123-42; G. Yorke, *The Church as the Body of Christ in the Pauline Corpus: A Re-Examination* (Lanham, MD: University Press of America, 1991).

J. K. McVay

## HEAD COVERINGS. *See* MAN AND WOMAN.

## HEALING, ILLNESS

The apostle* Paul considers weakness,* sickness and other afflictions as part of the fallen natural order (2 Cor 4:17), as part of his suffering* as a servant* of Christ* (2 Cor 11:23—12:10), as a motivator in preaching the gospel* (Gal 4:13-14) as well as a messenger from Satan* (2 Cor 12:7). Also, sickness is portrayed as God's* judgment* or chastening occasioned by sin* (1 Cor 11:27-32), though Paul never applies this interpretation to his own sickness or suffering. The mention of Luke the beloved physician (Col 4:14) shows Paul's favorable attitude to the medical profession (cf. Sir 38:1-15).

### 1. Illness As Judgment.

In 1 Corinthians 11:30 Paul attributes "weakness" (*astheneia*), "sickness" (*arrōstos*, in the NT, Mt 14:14 par. Mk 6:5, 13; [16:18]; 1 Cor 11:30) and even death (*koimaō*, "falling asleep," cf. 1 Cor 7:39; *see* Life and Death) among the Corinthian* Christians as God's judgment over abuse of the Lord's Supper (*see* Lord's Supper).

Paul does not have in mind any magical effect of the bread and the cup, nor does he indicate that demonic powers (*see* Demons) are involved in the sickness, even though the alternative to drinking the cup of the Lord is to drink the cup of demons (1 Cor 10:21). Rather, in a passage where he plays on the root of the word *judge* (*krin-*), the failure to discern (*diakrinō*) the body and blood of the Lord* brings divine judgment (*krinō*). The divisive and greedy behavior of the Corinthians (1 Cor 11:18-19) amounts to a disregard of the meaning of the crucifixion.* Thus, when the Corinthians meet together they do not eat the Lord's Supper, proclaiming the benefits of his death (1 Cor 11:20, 26). Instead, they proclaim themselves guilty and condemned (cf. Heb 10:29). The purpose of the judgment in sickness is seen to be disciplinary correction so that believers will not end up being condemned (*katakrinō*) along with the world* (cf. Heb 12:9-11).

It cannot be maintained that Paul considers all sickness and death to be related to the abuse of the Lord's Supper. However, Romans 1:18-32 and 1 Corinthians 10:1-14 may indicate that Paul held to a general principle that sickness was sometimes caused by sin.

### 2. Illness As a Messenger from Satan.

In 2 Corinthians 12:7 Paul says that in order to keep him from being too elated by the abundance of revelations (*see* Visions), a thorn in the flesh, a messenger of Satan, was given to him to batter him.

The nature of this thorn (*skolops*) has been much debated. As early as Chrysostom (*On Second Corinthians* 26.2) the view was propounded that the thorn is to be understood as the persecution Paul experienced, including that from his enemies at Corinth. For, the thorn is characterized as an "messenger" or "angel" (*angelos*, 2 Cor 12:7) of Satan, implying a person or group (cf. Satan as "angel of light," 2 Cor 11:14), and "to batter" (*kolaphizō*, 2 Cor 12:7) is a personal activity. Further, the context of the passage is Paul's struggle with his opponents* (2 Cor 10—13) and Numbers 33:55 (LXX) uses the image of a thorn for the enemies of the Israelites. However, on the other hand, the thorn may have been given to Paul near the time of his visions and revelations when he had yet to confront his opponents. Also, the reference to a messenger or angel of Satan does not seem like a reference to a group of opponents, and in 2 Corinthians 11:14-15 his opponents are Satan in disguise as his servants (*diakonoi*) rather than his messengers.

A view from the Middle Ages is that the thorn is

every kind of temptation (cf. Calvin *Commentary*), or sexual temptation in particular. But this does not accord with the list of hardships and weaknesses (*see* Affliction, Trials, Hardships) in 2 Corinthians 11:23-29 and 12:10, and it requires too narrow a view of "flesh."* Also, 1 Corinthians 7:7 implies that Paul did not struggle with sexual temptation (*see* Sexuality).

The majority of interpreters, from Tertullian onward (*Pud.* 13), take the thorn to be some form of physical illness. In favor of this view is the metaphor of a thorn, the connection in ancient times between demonic manifestations and physical illness, and the structure of the 2 Corinthians 12:7-10 passage imitating the narratives of a healing miracle.

Due to the scarcity of data, some scholars do not attempt a diagnosis of the illness. Others have suggested epilepsy (as a result of Paul's conversion experience; *see* Conversion and Call), hysteria, migraine, depression, severe sciatica, rheumatism, poor hearing, leprosy, stammering and solar retinitis (an inflammation of the retina caused by the blinding light at his conversion). Lightfoot used Galatians 4:13, 14 (see 3 below) to interpret the meaning of the thorn as an ophthalmic complaint. Ramsay's view, that Paul contracted recurring malarial fever in Pamphilia, is often accepted since it takes account of the thorn as being a physical disorder, one that is felt continually or often as battering (2 Cor 12:7, *kolaphizē*, present tense), and humiliating while not stopping Paul's rigorous mission work.

In so far as Paul intended the thorn in the flesh to denote a physical ailment (with *sarx*, "flesh," taken to refer to the physical body; *see* Flesh), he expresses a number of his views on illness and healing in this passage. First, the illness humbled Paul, preventing him from becoming conceited. Second, this illness is a messenger from Satan causing pain and humiliation. Yet, third, the use of the passive *edothē* ("was given," 2 Cor 12:7) is a veiled allusion to the illness being given by God. Paul resolves this paradox by saying that the Lord's grace* is shown to be sufficient for him even though his three requests for the thorn to leave him were not answered as he expected. Thus, fourth, Paul does not view illness as something the Lord always heals, though remaining weakness makes the power of Christ more evident in his life to the point of Paul boasting in his weaknesses* (2 Cor 12:9-10).

### 3. Illness As Weakness Yet Opportunity.

In Galatians 4:13 Paul makes a direct reference to a bodily weakness or illness (*astheneian tēs sarkos*) that he suffered. If this passage is taken as closely resembling

2 Corinthians 12:7, it is not unnatural to suppose the allusion is to the same illness (see 2. above). Others, noting that "flesh" (*sarx*) is the only word common to both passages, treat them separately.

Paul's saying that the Galatians* would have plucked out their eyes and given them to him, and the postscript in his own hand being in large letters (Gal 6:11), has led to the suggestion that Paul's eyesight was bad. But, as ancient belief held the eyes to be the most delicate and costly human organ (Deut 32:10; Ps 17:8; *Barn.* 19.9) and that gouging out eyes was an act of self-sacrifice (1 Sam 11:2), notably as a demonstration of friendship (Lucian *On Friendship* 40-41), Paul is probably saying no more than that the Galatians were prepared to give their eyes as we would say we were prepared to give our "right arm" for a friend.

That Paul's condition was a temptation on the part of the Galatians (*humōn*, "your," rather than *mou*, "my," has the greater textual support) to despise or neglect Paul has been thought to mean that for them his illness was likely to be interpreted as demon possession. But, as the context suggests, the Galatians were tempted to reject Paul because his illness was in contrast to the miracles he performed (cf. Gal 3:5). While Paul's illness may not have been severe enough to be listed in the catalog of his trials in 2 Corinthians 11:24-27, it initially caused Paul to preach* to the Galatians, and they received him as Christ (Gal 4:14). Thus, even illness becomes an opportunity to preach the gospel.

## 4. Healing.

Paul does not adopt a triumphalist attitude to illness and healing, though he is convinced that nothing can separate a person from the love* of God (Rom 8:35-39) and that one of the expressions of the presence of the Holy Spirit* is the gift of healing.

*4.1. The Gifts of Healings.* The only place Paul refers directly to the healing of illness is when he mentions gifts, or "charismata of healings" (*charismata iamatōn*), in his lists of gifts of the Spirit (1 Cor 12:9, 28, 30; *see* Gifts of the Spirit).

Having introduced the theme of *charismata* ("gifts," 1 Cor 12:4), and saying that to each one is given an expression of the Spirit's presence, he repeats the word *charismata* (plural) when mentioning healing and says that an individual person (*allos*, singular) receives gifts of healings (plural, cf. 1 Cor 12:28, 30). Paul may be emphasizing that a person does not inherently possess power* to heal but is given charisma for specific and different occasions of healing. As we do not hear of full-time healers from Paul, and the gift of healing is mentioned only in the context of gifts for

the local community of believers, Paul probably does not envisage itinerant healers.

*4.2. Paul As Healer.* Paul gives few direct references to being a healer (cf. Gal 3:5). However, the traditional phrase he uses to describe his work, "signs and wonders" (*sēmeia kai terata*, Rom 15:18-19; 2 Cor 12:12; cf. 2 Thess 2:9), would have been understood to include healings (cf., e.g., Jn 4:48; Acts 2:22; 5:12). In recalling the miracles of the exodus (cf. Ex 7:3; Deut 6:22; 7:19; 26:8) and associating "power" (*dynamis*) with his "signs and wonders" Paul emphasizes that God is the author of his healings. From Paul's perspective these signs and wonders, along with his message, are Christ working through him, and they identify him as an apostle as well as help to win obedience from the Gentiles.*

*4.3. Healing the Demonized.* In the undisputed Pauline letters demons* are only mentioned in 1 Corinthians 10:20-21 (cf. 1 Tim 4:1) as the gods (*see* Religions; Idolatry) pagans worship.* Unlike his contemporary Greeks (*see* Hellenism), Paul did not even attribute the troubles of 2 Corinthians 11:24-27 to demons or evil spirits. Only in 2 Corinthians 12:7 (see 2 above) is it likely that he directly attributed sickness to the demonic. It is in his notion of principalities and powers that much of what Paul thought about evil spiritual beings is contained.

Paul may be expected to include exorcism as one of the *charismata* ("gifts"). The *charisma* of "workings of powers" (*energēmata dynameōn*, 1 Cor 12:10) could mean the acts of power driving out demons. However, these *charismata* are all for the benefit of the body (1 Cor 12:7; *see* Body of Christ). As Paul sees all people in relation to either Satan or Christ (2 Cor 6:14-15; cf. Gal 5:16-26), and the Christian has passed from Satan to Christ (Col 1:13), it would be inconceivable for exorcism to appear in Paul's lists of *charismata*. Nevertheless, Luke's portrait of Paul shows him to be involved in exorcism (see 4.4. below).

*4.4. Acts.* In Acts 14:8-18 a man lame from birth was healed when Paul noticed that as a result of hearing him speak the man had faith or trust to be healed. In Acts 16:16-18 a girl with a spirit of divination (*pneuma pythōna*) is annoying Paul and is said to be healed by him when he orders the spirit to come out of her. According to Acts 19:11-12, God did extraordinary miracles through handkerchiefs or aprons being carried away from Paul's body to the sick, and diseases left them and evil spirits came out. In Acts 20:7-12 Paul raises Eutychus from the dead by bending over him and embracing him. Paul himself is healed from a deadly snakebite, according to Acts 28:1-6. Paul is also reported to have laid hands on, and successfully prayed for, the father of Publius, the chief man of Malta, who lay sick with fever and dysentery so that "the rest of the people on the island who had diseases also came and were cured" (Acts 28:9). Thus, Luke confirms that Paul's activity as a healer is integral to his missionary work.

*See also* AFFLICTIONS, TRIALS, HARDSHIPS; DEMONS AND EXORCISM; GIFTS OF THE SPIRIT; OPPONENTS OF PAUL; SATAN, DEVIL; SIGNS AND WONDERS; SUFFERING; VISIONS, ECSTATIC EXPERIENCE; WEAKNESS.

BIBLIOGRAPHY. W. M. Alexander, "St. Paul's Infirmity," *ExpT* 15 (1904) 469-73; 545-48; H. D. Betz, "Eine Christus-Aretologie bei Paulus (2 Cor 12, 7-10)," *ZTK* 66 (1969) 288-305; V. P. Furnish, *II Corinthians* (AB; Garden City, NY: Doubleday, 1984); J. Jervell, "The Signs of an Apostle," in *The Unknown Paul* (Minneapolis: Augsburg, 1984) chap 5; R. H. Lightfoot, *Saint Paul's Epistle to the Galatians* (London: Macmillan, 1881); T. Y. Mullins, "Paul's Thorn in the Flesh," *JBL* 76(1957) 299-303; R. P. Martin, *2 Corinthians* (WBC; Waco: Word, 1986); S. M. Praeder, "Miracle Worker and Missionary: Paul in the Acts of the Apostles," in *SBL 1983 Seminar Papers,* ed. K. H. Richards (Chico, CA: Scholars Press, 1983) 107-29; W. M. Ramsay, *St. Paul the Traveller and the Roman Citizen* (London: Hodder & Stoughton, 1908) 94-97; G. H. Twelftree, *Christ Triumphant: Exorcism Then and Now* (London: Hodder & Stoughton, 1985).

G. H. Twelftree

## HEART. *See* PSYCHOLOGY.

## HEAVEN, HEAVENLIES, PARADISE

Paul's understanding of heaven and related themes must be placed within the wider context of his total eschatology (see esp. Lincoln 1981). As with other NT writers, Paul reveals a debt to, as well as a development of, both the OT and apocryphal and pseudepigraphical Jewish works, some knowledge of which is essential for an understanding of Paul's thinking.

    1. Background
    2. Heaven
    3. Things Above
    4. Third Heaven, Paradise
    5. Heavenlies

### 1. Background.

Basic to OT understanding is the duality of heaven and earth which together make up the material creation, an idea retained throughout Scripture, culminating in the promise of a new heaven and a new earth (*see* Creation and New Creation). This physical demarcation pointed toward a spiritual distinction: earth as the dwelling place of humankind, the heavens as the place where God* dwells (*see* World, Cosmology). The idea of a third "realm," Sheol, was introduced as the place of the departed, a shadowy realm where knowledge of and fellowship with God was not possible. As the thought of vindication for the righteous beyond the grave arose, culminating in the hope of personal resurrection,* so also Sheol was divided, the righteous waiting for final salvation in a form of paradise.

The word *paradise* (Gk *paradeisos*) was almost certainly a Persian word taken into both Hebrew and Greek, originally referring to a park or garden. It is used only three times in the OT (Song 4:13; Neh 2:8 and Eccles 2:5), but is found forty-seven times in the LXX, notably as a term for the garden of Eden. This paradisal bliss became a model for a hidden paradise, the immediate resting place of the righteous dead (*1 Enoch* 60:8; 61:12), but also of an ultimate resting place (*2 Enoch* 8—9; *2 Bar.* 51:3).

Alongside the present/future dichotomy was an earth/heaven duality in which paradise was sometimes located on earth (*1 Enoch* 32:3-6; 77:3) and sometimes in heaven (*1 Enoch* 60:8; 61:12; 70:3). These ideas are brought together in *2 Enoch* 8. Alongside these developments went another in which the number of "heavens" proliferated; sometimes there were three, or five, or seven or even ten; *2 Enoch* 8:1 and *Apocalypse of Moses* 37:5 locate paradise in the third heaven.

This brief and much simplified account of a complex and often confusing and inconsistent development of ideas puts Paul's thinking into context.

### 2. Heaven.

Paul uses the word *ouranos* twenty-one times, twelve of these in the singular and nine in the plural. It is frequently assumed that the plural uses reflect the Hebrew *šāmayim*, but it is possible that, as in the LXX, where the frequency of the plural increases in the later writings, this is due to the influence of the notion of several heavens (see, e.g., Turner). However, there appears to be no discernible pattern in Paul's usage of singular and plural. He uses the word as:

    (1) Part of a description of the universe as the heavens and the earth (1 Cor 8:5; Eph 1:10; 3:15; Col 1:16)

    (2) The abode of angels* (Gal 1:8)

    (3) The dwelling place of Christ* from which he came down (Eph 4:9; Rom 10:6), to which he returned (Eph 4:10), where he now is (Eph 6:9; Col 4:1; cf. Rom 8:34) and from whence he will return (Phil 3:20; 1 Thess 1:10; 4:16; 2 Thess 1:7)

    (4) The eternal home of the believer (2 Cor 5:1, 2; Phil 3:20; cf. Gal 4:26), where the hoped-for salvation* is being kept (Col 1:5)

### 3. Things Above.

This brief survey demonstrates that heaven was not for Paul a merely future reality; it denotes a spiritual sphere coexisting with the material world of space and time; it is where the exalted Christ now is, seated at God's right hand (*see* Exaltation and Enthronement). Not only that; the believer is united with Christ, is "in Christ,"* and as such belongs already to the company of heaven (Phil 3:20) and can be thought of as being seated with Christ in the heavenly realms (Eph 2:6). Even now the believer's life is "hidden with Christ in God," and "the things above" should be the focus of the believer's attention and should provide the orientation and goal of the Christian's life here and now. Believers live now in this world as citizens* of heaven, seeking increasingly to become what they are in Christ; and as their gaze is fixed on Christ above the life of heaven becomes an increasing reality as they are "being transformed into his likeness with ever-increasing glory*" (2 Cor 3:18). It is similar thinking which lies behind the expression "the Jerusalem* which is above" in Galatians 4:26. Ever since Christ was exalted, he has become the focal point of salvation, in whom is found all the fullness* of salvation once centered upon the earthly Jerusalem. The heavenly realm of Christ's rule is the new city of God of which the believer is a citizen.

It is this fact, of which the Holy Spirit* is the pledge and guarantee (2 Cor 5:5), that enables Paul to face weakness* and suffering* in the present, and even to face the awesome reality of death; for when the present "earthly tent" is taken down, the believer has "a building from God, an eternal house in heaven" (2 Cor 5:1; *see* Body). Here Paul is thinking not so much of corporate citizenship as he is of personal transformation, as in 1 Corinthians 15:35-57 (but see, e.g., Ellis for a corporate interpretation), and also seems to raise the difficult and much discussed question of an intermediate* state. The latter may be a bodiless experience after death, sometimes understood as "sleep" but more likely as real fellowship* with Christ, preceding the reception of the final resurrection* body (cf. Phil 1:23). However, "naked" in 2 Corinthians 5:3 can be understood differently, for example, as referring to appearing before God outside of Christ. Paul's concern might not be with bodiless existence after death, but rather with a desire to be transformed at the Parousia rather than pass through the experience of death, or even with a polemic against a realized eschatology that thought the resurrection state was a present experience and reality (see Martin, ad loc.; *see* Eschatology).

### 4. Third Heaven, Paradise.

Part of the difficulty is precisely that for Paul heaven is not only a future reality; there is a vertical as well as a horizontal dimension to his eschatological understanding. Fellowship with the exalted Christ, citizenship in heaven and eternal life are present realities to such an extent that the border between earthly and heavenly can be crossed even now. In 2 Corinthians 12:1-5, albeit with the greatest reluctance (the third-person narration emphasizes his desire to distance himself from what he describes), Paul recounts an experience in which he was caught up to the third heaven, to paradise. How much of his contemporaries' thinking Paul accepted is not clear, but here his language undoubtedly reflects some of their ideas about the various heavens as outlined above (e.g., *T. Levi* 2—5), and the two modes of heavenly journey in their writings—"in the spirit" or bodily (e.g., *1 Enoch* for the former, *T. Abr.* 8:3B for the latter). Clearly Paul enters the very throne room of God; he goes into the presence of Christ and receives a revelation so sacred or mysterious that it cannot be shared (*see* Visions).

### 5. Heavenlies.

What is significant in 2 Corinthians 12, both for Paul's argument and our understanding of his thinking, is the thorn in the flesh* which was given to him to keep him humble, and his description of it as a "messenger of Satan.*" Several interpreters refer to the experience of four rabbis, reported in the Babylonian Talmud, who were taken up to heaven, of whom only one, Rabbi Akiba, returned unscathed, the others all suffering in some way (*b. Ḥag.* 14b). If, as scholars such as W. Baird have suggested, Paul is speaking of a similar assault upon himself in the heavenly realms, this would suggest that Paul distinguishes between heaven in the ultimate sense of the dwelling place of God, and the heavenly realms which are part of the created order, and which will one day be renewed along with the earth. This would make sense of a unique expression used by Paul five times in Ephesians only—*en tois ouranois*, "in the heavenly realms." The exalted Christ is seated at God's right hand in the heavenly realms (Eph 1:20), and the Christian is seated with him (Eph 2:6) enjoying "every spiritual blessing" (Eph 1:3). But these heavenly realms are also inhabited by "the rulers and authorities" (Eph 3:10) who are further described in Ephesians 6:12 as "the spiritual forces of evil"! The heavenly realms, therefore, refer to the spiritual sphere in which God, Christ, the powers of darkness and the believer exist together, and as well as sharing Christ's reign and receiving the blessings of salvation the believer is involved in spiritual warfare (*see* Principalities and Powers).

There is, therefore, a tension in Christian experience between the earthly and the heavenly, the present and the future; the believer lives in this world while belonging to another, in this age while anticipating the age to come. It is a tension that will be resolved only when Christ "hands over the kingdom to God the Father after he has destroyed all dominion, authority and power . . . so that God may be all in all" (1 Cor 15:24, 28).

*See also* CITIZENSHIP, ROMAN AND HEAVENLY; CREATION AND NEW CREATION; DYING AND RISING WITH CHRIST; EPHESIANS, LETTER TO THE; ESCHATOLOGY; INTERMEDIATE STATE; PRINCIPALITIES AND POWERS; RESURRECTION; VISIONS, ECSTATIC EXPERIENCE; WORLD, COSMOLOGY.

BIBLIOGRAPHY. W. Baird, "Visions, Revelation and Ministry: Reflections on 2 Cor 12:1-5 and Gal 1:11-17," *JBL* 104 (1985) 651-62; C. K. Barrett, *A Commentary on the Second Epistle to the Corinthians* (HNTC; San Francisco: Harper & Row, 1973) 149-61, 305-18; H. Bietenhard and C. Brown, "Paradise," *NIDNTT* 2.760-64; E. E. Ellis, "II Corinthians V.1-10 in Pauline Eschatology," *NTS* 6 (1959-60) 211-24; V. P. Furnish, *2 Corinthians* (ABC; New York: Doubleday, 1984) 253-305, 512-56; M. J. Harris, "2 Cor 5:1-10: A Watershed in Paul's Eschatology?," *TynB* 22 (1971) 32-57; idem, "Paul's View of Death in 2 Corinthians 5:1-10," in *New Directions in New Testament Study*, ed. R. N. Longenecker and M. C. Tenney (Grand Rapids: Eerdmans, 1974) 317-28; J. Jeremias, "παράδεισος," TDNT V.765-73; A. T. Lincoln, *Paradise Now and Not Yet* (SNTSMS 43; Cambridge: University Press, 1981); idem, "A Reexamination of 'the Heavenlies' in Ephesians," *NTS* 19 (1972-73) 468-83; idem, "Paul the Visionary: The Setting and Significance of the Rapture to Paradise in 2 Cor 12:1-10," *NTS* 25 (1978-79) 204-20; R. P. Martin *2 Corinthians* (WBC 40; Waco: Word, 1986) 95-116, 387-424; R. M. Price, "Punished in Paradise: An Exegetical Theory on 2 Corinthians 12:1-10," *JSNT* 7 (1980) 33-40; G. von Rad and H. Traub, "οὐρανός," *TDNT* V.497-543; D. S. Russell, *Divine Disclosure: An Introduction to Jewish Apocalyptic* (London: SCM, 1992); A. F. Segal, *Paul the Convert* (New Haven: Yale University, 1990) 34-71; B. Siede et al., "Heaven, Ascend, Above," *NIDNTT* 2.184-96; N. Turner, *Christian Words* (Edinburgh: T. & T. Clark, 1980) 202-5, 308-12.

J. F. Maile

**HEAVENLY CITIZENSHIP.** *See* CITIZENSHIP, ROMAN AND HEAVENLY.

**HELLENISM**

Hellenism refers to Greek culture, especially that which was spread throughout the Near East after the conquests of Alexander the Great. The word was first popularized by the historian J. G. Droysen in his *Geschichte des Hellenismus* (1836-43). He derived the term from the occurrence of the Hellenists in Acts 6:1.

Alexander's conquests spread the use of the Koine (*Koinē*, "common") dialect, a simplified form of Attic Greek, from Egypt to Afghanistan. Inasmuch as the Torah did not specifically ban such matter as Greek literature, drama, philosophy, art and athletics, most Jews came to varying degrees of accommodation with Greek culture.

1. The Hellenistic Era
2. The Results of Hellenization
3. Scholarship on Hellenism and the NT
4. Hellenization and the NT

**1. The Hellenistic Era.**
The Classical Age of Greek city-states was replaced by the rise of the Macedonians under the leadership of Philip and his son Alexander, who forcibly unified the Greeks and launched a crusade against the Persians.

*1.1. Alexander.* Alexander the Great, who had been privately tutored by Aristotle, became the king of Macedonia in 336 B.C. A brilliant general, he led his army of about 30,000 soldiers into the heart of the Persian Empire. It is ironic that the Macedonians, whom the Athenian orator Demosthenes regarded as "barbarians," were the greatest disseminators of Greek culture. Alexander promoted a fusion of Greek and Persian culture and intermarriage with native women. He established over thirty Greek cities, notably Alexandria in Egypt.

*1.2. The Diadochi.* After Alexander's death in 323, his territories were carved up among his generals, the Diadochi ("the Successors"). After much internecine violence, including murders of all the members of Alexander's family, three major kingdoms were established by 275 B.C.: the Antigonids in Macedonia, the Ptolemies in Egypt, and the Seleucids in Syria.

*1.3. The Ptolemies.* Ptolemy seized Egypt, the wealthiest country in the ancient world. He and his successors inherited a highly centralized administration. Not only in Egypt but also in Palestine, which they controlled until 198 B.C., the Ptolemies exercised rigid controls to exact the maximum amount of taxes from their subjects. Their policies led to inequities in the distribution of properties in favor of the elites who were loyal to them. At first all of the positions of power and prestige were held by the Macedonians/Greeks and their descendants. Native Egyptians were restricted to the lower levels and even had to have special permission to reside in Alexandria.

But gradually with intermarriages on the part of the Greeks and the acquiring of Greek language and culture on the part of the Egyptians, the ethnic distinction became less important than the cultural ones. A turning point came when Ptolemy IV Philopator, in his struggle with the Seleucids, had to recruit 20,000 Egyptians into the army to win the battle of Raphia in 217 B.C.

The Jews constituted an important minority in Ptolemaic Egypt, eventually occupying two of the districts in Alexandria. The evidence from the Jewish papyri indicates that Jews quickly gave up Aramaic in favor of Greek. A most decisive step was taken with the translation of the OT into Greek, the Septuagint, a project beginning under the auspices of Ptolemy II (c. 270 B.C.) and continuing perhaps over a century until it was completed. The *Letter of Aristeas* relates the legend of seventy-two Jewish scholars sent by the Jewish high priest to Egypt to do the translation. Aristeas defended both the Jewish Law and Greek education and culture. The first reference to synagogues are Greek inscriptions which appear in the Ptolemaic era.

Aristobulus, an advisor on Jewish affairs to Ptolemy VI (180-45 B.C.), began the tradition of an allegorical interpretation of passages in the Pentateuch which were deemed offensive to Greek tastes. The climax of this tendency to view the Scriptures through a Hellenistic lens is epitomized in the numerous writings of the Jewish philosopher, Philo of Alexandria (30 B.C.-A.D. 50), who used allegory to reinterpret the Scriptures in terms of Middle Platonism. A Hellenized but still loyal Jew, Philo was chosen to lead a legation to the Emperor Gaius (A.D. 37-42) to protest the ill treatment of the Jews by the governor.

*1.4. The Seleucids.* Seleucus acquired by far the largest territories from Alexander's empire, stretching from the Mediterranean to Persia. Like the Ptolemies, the Seleucids tried to maintain power and privilege in the hands of the Macedonian/Greek elites. A study indicates that even after two generations only 2.5 percent of the positions of authority were held by natives. Seleucus, however, had inherited too much territory with too many diverse populations. By the middle of the third century B.C. Bactria had become an independent kingdom and the Parthians had taken over Persia. The Seleucids failed to recognize their limitations and fought in vain to regain their lost territories. They were finally restricted to the area of Syria.

After a bitter struggle with the Ptolemies, the Seleucids finally gained control over Judea in 198 B.C. Antiochus III (223-187 B.C.) was quite generous to the Jews, asking only that they should pray for his welfare. It was Antiochus IV (176-65 B.C.) who provoked the Maccabean Revolt (165 B.C.) by his policy of a radical replacement of Judaism by Hellenism. The events are recounted in 1—2 Maccabees and Josephus.

The fateful development began in 175 B.C. when Jason, the brother of the incumbent high priest Onias, offered a bribe to Antiochus IV to get himself appointed to that position. Jason then applied for authority to establish a gymnasium and an organization for youth (for *ephēboi*, young men between eighteen and twenty) in Jerusalem (2 Macc 4:7-9). 2 Maccabees 4:10 declares that "When the king assented and Jason came to office, he at once shifted his compatriots over to the Greek way of life" (*pros ton hellēnikon charaktēra*). The gymnasium, which involved male athletes exercising and engaging in wrestling in the nude, was shocking to Jewish sensibilities. Some Jews, who wished to compete, even underwent operations to disguise their circumcision.* The graduates of the gymnasium, the ephebes, wore the broad-brimmed Greek hat.

Antiochus then replaced Jason with Menelaus, who, according to Josephus, was an even more radical Hellenizer. Civil war broke out, with the masses behind Jason, and the Hellenized Tobiads of Transjordan behind Menelaus. At the urging of Menelaus, Antiochus harshly suppressed the uprising. In 167 B.C. his forces occupied Jerusalem and despoiled the Temple, which was then defiled with what Daniel called "The Abomination of Desolation"—the imposition of three meteorite idols on the altar. A garrison called the Akra was placed near the Temple, and plans were underway to establish a Greek polis, Antiochat, in Jerusalem. The Jews were to forsake their laws; they could neither observe the Sabbath nor perform circumcision.

It was not until late 167 or early 166 B.C. that the Jews rebelled against the Syrians under the leadership of Mattathias, a priest from the small town of Modin, and his sons. After defeating the Seleucids under the leadership of Judas Maccabeus, the jubilant Jews celebrated the rededication of the Temple (Hanukkah) in 164. Antiochus V wrote a letter in 163 acknowledging, "We have heard that the Jews do not consent to our father's change to Greek customs but prefer their own way of living." Nonetheless, the Jews declared themselves an independent state in 143 B.C. (*see* Revolutionary Movements).

The Maccabean revolt must not be understood as a rebellion against Hellenism but against paganism. The Hasmoneans, the descendants of Mattathias and his sons, demonstrated their acceptance of many of the non-religious elements of Greek culture. Simon's elaborate mausoleum was built in the Hellenistic style. Many of the Hasmoneans had Greek as well as Hebrew names: Judah Aristobulus, Alexander Jannaeus,

Mattathias Antigonus. Jannaeus inscribed his coins in Greek as well as in Hebrew, and employed Greek mercenaries. Aristobulus called himself a "philhellene," that is, a "lover of Greek culture."

*1.5. The Romans.* The Romans first became acquainted with Greek culture as early as the eighth century B.C. with the establishment of Greek colonies in Italy and Sicily. But it was the later military victories of the Roman legions over the Greek phalanxes in the Macedonian Wars which brought a flood of Greek objects and slaves back to Italy. Perseus, the last king of Macedon, was defeated by the Romans at Pydna in 167 B.C. When the Greek cities of the Achaean League plotted a rebellion, the Romans thoroughly destroyed the city of Corinth in 146 as an example.

Though victorious in war, the Romans were overcome by the superiority of Greek culture in spite of the futile protests of conservatives like Cato against Greek vices such as homosexuality.* There is hardly any aspect of higher culture which was not decisively influenced by the Greeks: art, architecture, literature, drama, medicine, philosophy and religion were all deeply affected by the Greeks. Educated Romans after the second century B.C. were expected to know Greek as well as Latin. It is significant that Philo of Alexandria praised Augustus (Philo *Leg. Gai.* 147) as one "who enlarged Hellas by many a new Hellas and hellenized the outside world in its most important regions."

## 2. The Results of Hellenization.

The results of three centuries of Hellenization can best be demonstrated by the textual evidence provided by papyri, inscriptions, coins and artifacts recovered by archeological excavations of ancient Egypt, Rome and Palestine. From the second century B.C. to the second century A.D., Greek became the most common language of discourse between peoples found in the area east of Italy to the Levant.

*2.1. In Egypt and in Rome.* Jewish texts in Italy and Egypt are overwhelmingly in Greek. With the exception of the Nash Papyrus, all of the papyri from Egypt pertaining to the Jews are in Greek. All but five of the 116 inscriptions from Egypt related to the Jews are also in Greek. In Rome, 405 of 534 Jewish inscriptions are in Greek or seventy-six percent of the total. An analysis of the names of Jewish garrison troops in Egypt indicates that in the third century B.C. seventy-five percent of their names are Greek. In Rome about half the names are Latin and one-third are Greek. Favored names are Dositheos, Theodotus and Theodorus, all referring to God's gift (cf. the Hebrew names Nathaniah, Jonathan).

*2.2. In Palestine.* Hellenization transformed the

areas around Judea such as the Decapolis and urban centers more than it did the Jewish countryside. Gadara, a city in Transjordan, produced Menippus the satirist, Meleager the poet and Philodemus the Epicurean philosopher. Herod the Great (37-4 B.C.) intensified the process of Hellenization in Judea. His secretary was Nicolaus of Damascus, who encouraged Herod to write his autobiography in Greek. According to Josephus (*Ant.* 15.8.1 §§267-70), Herod established quinquennial games in honor of Augustus, built a theater in Jerusalem and an amphitheater in the plain. He built the Temple in Jerusalem in a lavish Greco-Roman style with colonnaded stoas or porticos (cf. Jn 10:23).

It was probably an expression of a rebellion against Greco-Roman paganism that the Jewish rebels in both the First Revolt (A.D. 66-73) and the Second Revolt (A.D. 132-35) used Hebrew inscriptions on their coins. But the letters of Bar Kochba, who led the Second Revolt, indicates his, or his followers, use of Greek as well as Aramaic and Nabataean.

## 3. Scholarship on Hellenism and the NT.

The issue of "Hellenism" has played an important role in the analysis of the development of Christianity and of Pauline theology. Earlier scholars assigned it a decisive factor in the later transformation of Christianity into a kind of Hellenistic mystery religion,* but recent studies have indicated that Hellenistic Judaism was already a factor in the earliest stages of Jesus' ministry and message.

*3.1. The History-of-Religions School.* Scholars of the History-of-Religions School sought to explain Paul's theology on the basis of a contrast between the earliest Palestinian Christians and a later Hellenistic Christianity. W. Heitmüller (1910) proposed that Paul derived his view on the title *kyrios* ("Lord"*), the Eucharist, and Christ mysticism* from Hellenistic Christianity in Antioch. W. Bousset in his celebrated book *Kyrios Christos* (1913, 1921; ET 1970) argued that Jesus was first addressed as *kyrios* not in the primitive community but in Hellenistic Christianity. This view was popularized by R. Bultmann in his influential *Theology of the New Testament* (1951, 1955). F. Hahn in *The Titles of Jesus in Christology* (1963; ET 1969) postulated three stages before Paul: (1) Palestinian Christianity, (2) Hellenistic Jewish Christianity, and (3) Hellenistic Gentile Christianity (*see* Paul and His Interpreters)

*3.2. Martin Hengel.* To protest this artificial dichotomy, M. Hengel produced a notable series of erudite monographs (between 1974 and 1989). After an exhaustive examination of the literary and epigraphic evidences, Hengel concluded that Palestinian Judaism was as much a Hellenistic Judaism as that of the Diaspora.* In his view the alleged distinction between an early Hebraic Christianity and a later Hellenistic Christianity is misguided, a conclusion which had already been reached by I. H. Marshall. Hengel observes: "There is hardly any doctrinal theme in the New Testament which could not also have been thought or taught in Palestine. . . . Even a christology of pre-existence and of the Son of God is intrinsically not 'Hellenistic' nor even 'un-Jewish' nor 'un-Palestinian' " (Hengel 1989, 55).

Though Hengel's erudition is impressive and though his main point may be conceded, he frequently strains his arguments in an effort to maximize the evidence for early Hellenism in Palestine. Even if one should accept as Palestinian such Jewish literature as the elder Philo, the tragedies of Ezekiel, the Tobiad romance, Eupolemus and other fragmentary writings, few would be led to conclude with Hengel that, with the exception of Philo, Jerusalem's literary production was greater than that of the Jews in Alexandria. As evidence of Hellenistic influence he even cites such openly anti-Hellenistic writings as Ben Sirach and the Qumran* Scrolls. But the overwhelming predominance of Hebrew and Aramaic scrolls as opposed to the few Greek fragments at Qumran would indicate that the Qumran community was consciously maintaining a traditional stance against the encroachment of Hellenism.

*3.3. L. H. Feldman.* In L. H. Feldman's view, although the Hellenistic elements were extensive, they were essentially superficial and did not profoundly affect the nature of Judaism. In particular, Feldman is not persuaded that extensive Hellenization had taken place before the Maccabean revolt. The inscriptions cited by Hengel reveal only an elementary acquaintance with Greek. Where Hengel finds Greek influence in Esther, Tobit and Judith, Feldman prefers to see either Egyptian or Persian influence. Where Hengel maximizes the evidence too often, Feldman frequently minimizes the evidence. He points to the fact that Josephus admitted that he needed aid to polish his Greek (Josephus *Ag. Ap.* 1.9 §50). Josephus's mother tongue was Aramaic; his Greek was imperfectly pronounced, but he was certainly able to speak and to write more than adequately in Greek. Feldman points to the fact that inscriptions from Upper Galilee indicate that there was little Hellenization there. But Upper Galilee was a particularly remote area.

## 4. Hellenization and the NT.

The most obvious effect of Hellenization is indicated by the fact that the NT was written in Koine Greek.

Most of the citations of the OT in the NT are from the Septuagint.

*4.1. Acts.* The conflict over the distribution of food between the *hellēnistai* and the *hebraioi* in Acts 6:1-6 was probably a conflict between Greek-speaking Jewish Christians and Aramaic-speaking Jewish Christians. Members of the former would include Jews from the Diaspora areas such as Cyrene, Alexandria, Cilicia and Asia Minor (Acts 6:9). Though both may have been bilingual, each group would use its mother tongue in their own worship. It was the Hellenists, including the deacons Stephen and Philip, who took the lead in spreading the gospel to the Samaritans (Acts 8) and to Gentiles (Acts 11:19-20). Hengel and other scholars have credited the Hellenistic Christians from Jerusalem as those who first made it possible to proclaim the gospel beyond the bounds of Israel.

*4.2. Paul.* Paul was born in Tarsus in Cilicia, a city noted for its Stoic philosophers.* However, as he probably came to Jerusalem at about the age of twelve to study under the famous rabbi Gamaliel, Paul received at most a secondary Hellenistic education. Paul was able to address crowds in the "Hebrew dialect," that is, in Aramaic (Acts 21:40; 22:2; *see* Jew, Paul the). Though Paul eschews the more florid displays of Greek oratory (1 Cor 2:1-4), his letters nonetheless employ such rhetorical devices as: chiasmus (1 Cor 3:17), litotes (Rom 1:28), alliteration (2 Cor 6:3), climax (Rom 8:29-30), oxymoron (2 Cor 6:9) and paronomasia (2 Cor 3:2), and he meets his sophistic opponents (in 2 Cor 10—13) by using their techniques and procedures (e.g., *synkrisis*, "comparison"; *see* Rhetoric).

There are but three certain citations of classical literature in the NT. Paul in his famous Areopagus speech before Stoics and Epicureans at Athens* quoted from Aratus's *Phaenomena* 5 (Acts 17:28), "We are also his offspring." In 1 Corinthians 15:33 Paul cited from Menander's play *Thais*, the line, "Bad company is the ruin of good character." In Titus 1:12 Epimenedes' *De Oraculis* is cited: "The Cretans, always liars, vicious brutes, and lazy gluttons." As these were commonplace sayings, they do not prove that Paul read the literary works or that he attended plays, but they do show that he had enough acquaintance with such works to use them as illustrations in his sermons and in his letters.

*4.2.1. Theaters.* Theaters were invariably built at Hellenistic cities. Herod Agrippa I (A.D. 40-44) generously provided theaters and baths to such cities as Beirut. He was attending the theater at Caesarea (Acts 12:20-23; cf. Josephus *Ant.* 19.8.2 §§343-44) when he was struck with his fatal illness. Philo, as a Hellenized Jew, tells us that he attended the theater in Alexandria

(Philo *Ebr.* 177): "For example, I have often when I chanced to be in the theater noticed the effect produced by some single tune sung by the actors on the stage or played by the musicians." On the other hand, rabbis were opposed to the attendance at the theater inasmuch as Greek tragedy was performed under the auspices of gods such as Dionysus. The magnificent theater at Ephesus was filled with 24,000 Ephesians shouting their praise of their goddess in protest against the missionary efforts of Paul (Acts 19:29).

*4.2.2. Gymnasia.* The Greek ideal of *paideia,* "education," included not only literature and rhetoric, but also music and athletics. The Greek ideal of a person was a sound mind in a beautiful body. Isocrates, an orator, said: "He who shares in our *paideia* is a Greek in a higher sense than he who simply shares our descent."

The gymnasium where male athletes exercised *gymnos,* "nude," was an essential element of a Hellenistic city. Pausanias declared, "No gymnasium, no theater, no public water supply—no city." Gymnasia were established in the far reaches of Alexander's Empire, even in Susa in southwestern Persia and in Afghanistan. It was the attempt to establish a gymnasium in Jerusalem which helped to provoke the Maccabean crisis. Herod the Great established gymnasia in Gentile cities but not in Judea proper.

One of the most prestigious positions in the city was that of the gymnasiarch, or official in charge of the games. The graduates of the gymnasium program, the ephebes, originally served in the army. Later in the Hellenistic Age the ephebes formed a social register which provided the leaders of the city. In the East the gymnasia perpetuated the Greek way of life as a protected island in a sea of barbarians. Ambitious parents enrolled their children on waiting lists to enter the gymnasia. Eventually wealthy, Hellenized nationals were admitted into the charmed circle.

At first Jews had difficulty accepting this alien institution, especially since the games were ordinarily dedicated to a god or to a Greek hero such as Heracles. But eventually the athletic games became such an accepted part of culture that we have inscriptional evidence of Jewish participation in the life of the gymnasia from Hypaepa in Lydia, Iasos in Caria, Coronea in Messenia, Teucheira and Cyrene in Cyrenaica. Claudius (A.D. 41-54) in a famous letter warned the Alexandrian Jews against forcing their way into gymnasiarch games.

Philo of Alexandria saw no problem in attending the games and drawing illustrations from them. It is from the realm of athletics that Paul drew many of his striking illustrations: from the boxing ring (1 Cor 9:26), from the stadium race (Gal 2:2; 1 Cor 9:24; Phil 3:13-14; 1 Tim 6:12), from athletic training (1 Cor 9:25; 1 Tim 4:10) and the athletic crown (1 Cor 9:25; 2 Tim 2:5). Though he recognized the value of physical *gymnasia,* Paul urged Timothy to exercise himself even more spiritually (1 Tim 4:7-8). O. Broneer infers that when Paul was in Corinth he attended the Pan-Hellenic games at nearby Isthmia. Paul's reference to the perishable athletic wreath (1 Cor 9:25) seems to be a specific reference to the withered celery crown of Isthmia.

*4.2.3. Philosophy.* The influence of Greek philosophy* on Jews and on Jewish Christians is much debated. It is most clearly evident in Philo. It has also been claimed that Platonic and Stoic ideas are present in such works as 4 Maccabees and the Wisdom of Solomon. Though some rabbis forbade the teaching of Greek wisdom, Gamaliel II, the grandson of Paul's teacher, had 500 students of Greek wisdom in addition to 500 students of the Torah. The rabbis mentioned only two Greek philosophers by name, Epicurus and Oenomaus of Gadara. Among the 2,000 Greek words in the Talmudic corpus, it is significant that there are no Greek philosophic terms.

H. Koester writes, "but if Paul had any real knowledge of Greek philosophy, it certainly did not influence his theology materially, nor does he ever concern himself critically with any subject matter of the Greek philosophical tradition" (Koester 1965, 187). Koester, following R. Bultmann, believes that Paul's preaching was dependent on the model of the Cynic-Stoic diatribe.* Though there are many parallels, according to E. A. Judge (1972, 32-33) these may be better explained by the common conversational language of the day. Whatever Stoic terms Paul may have used, he gave them a completely un-Stoic denotation (Cornish). When Paul confronted Stoics and Epicureans in Athens (Acts 17:18), he certainly did not modify his message of the bodily resurrection of Jesus— a concept which was completely unacceptable to Greek philosophers.

*See also* APOLLOS; ATHENS, PAUL AT; CHRISTOLOGY; DIASPORA; GENTILES; GNOSIS, GNOSTICISM; JEW, PAUL THE; LORD; PAUL AND HIS INTERPRETERS; PHILOSOPHY; RELIGIONS, GRECO-ROMAN; REVOLUTIONARY MOVEMENTS; RHETORIC; WISDOM.

BIBLIOGRAPHY. E. J. Bickerman, *The Jews in the Greek Age* (Cambridge, MA: Harvard University, 1988); O. Broneer, "The Apostle Paul and the Isthmian Games," *BA* 25 (1962) 2-31; M. L. Cornish, "Pauline Theology and Stoic Philosphy," *JAAR Supplement* 17 (1979) 1-21; W. D. Davies and L. Finkelstein, ed., *The Cambridge History of Judaism* II: *The Hellenistic Age* (Cambridge:

University Press, 1989); L. H. Feldman, "Hengel's *Judaism and Hellenism* in Retrospect," *JBL* 96 (1977) 371-82; idem, "How Much Hellenism in Jewish Palestine?" *HUCA* 57 (1986) 83-111; E. Ferguson, *Backgrounds of Early Christianity* (Grand Rapids: Eerdmans, 1987); J. A. Goldstein, *I Maccabees* (AB; New York: Doubleday, 1976); idem, *II Maccabees* (AB; New York: Doubleday, 1983); idem, "Jewish Acceptance and Rejection of Hellenism," in *Jewish and Christian Self-Definition*, Volume 2, ed. E. P. Sanders et al. (Philadelphia: Fortress, 1981) 64-87; E. R. Goodenough and A. T. Kraabel, "Paul and the Hellenization of Christianity," in *Religions in Antiquity*, ed. J. Neusner (Leiden: E. J. Brill, 1968) 23-68; H. A. Harris, *Greek Athletics and the Jews* (Cardiff: University of Wales, 1976); M. Hengel, *Jews, Greeks and Barbarians* (Philadelphia: Fortress, 1980); idem, *Judaism and Hellenism* (2 vols; Philadelphia: Fortress, 1974); idem, *The "Hellenization" of Judaea in the First Century after Christ* (Philadelphia: Trinity Press International, 1989); E. A. Judge, "St. Paul and Classical Society," *JAC* 15 (1972) 19-36; idem, "Cultural Conformity and Innovation in Paul," *TynB* 35 (1984) 3-24; H. Koester, *Introduction to the New Testament* I: *History, Culture and Religion of the Hellenistic Age* (Philadelphia: Fortress, 1982); idem, "Paul and Hellenism," in *The Bible in Modern Scholarship*, ed. J. P. Hyatt (Nashville: Abingdon, 1965) 187-95; I. H. Marshall, "Palestinian and Hellenistic Christianity," *NTS* 19 (1972-73) 271-87; F. Millar, "Background to the Maccabean Revolution," *IJS* 29 (1978) 1-21; J. N. Sevenster, *Do You Know Greek?* (NovTSup 19; Leiden: E. J. Brill, 1968); V. Tcherikover, *Hellenistic Civilization and the Jews* (Philadelphia: Jewish Publ. Soc. of America, 1961); A. J. Toynbee, *Hellenism* (Cambridge: University Press, 1959 and Westport: Greenwood, 1981); F. W. Walbank et al., ed., *The Cambridge Ancient History* VII, Pt. 1: *The Hellenistic World* (Cambridge: University Press, 1984); H. Windisch, "Ἕλλην κτλ," *TDNT* II.504-16.

E. M. Yamauchi

## HELLENISTIC RELIGION. *See* RELIGIONS, GRECO-ROMAN; HELLENISM.

## HERMENEUTICS/INTERPRETING PAUL

In one sense the development of modern hermeneutics, or principles for interpreting texts, has been strongly influenced by Pauline studies. The basis for the development of grammatical, semantic, background and literary approaches came first from the interpretation of epistolary material and later branched out into narrative, apocalyptic and other genre studies. In this sense the Pauline letters participate in general hermeneutical

issues. Yet there are also problems inherent to their exegesis, such as the occasional nature of his letters, and the letter-form that lies behind them.

1. Recent Hermeneutical Issues
2. Paul's Letters and First-Century Forms
3. Special Issues

### 1. Recent Hermeneutical Issues.

Classical hermeneutics has always identified the goal of interpretation as ascertaining the author's intended meaning. Even in the Middle Ages, with the "four-fold sense" (literal, allegorical, tropological/moral, anagogical), scholars felt they were drawing out the meaning of the text (the "literal sense" on which the other senses were based). Recently, however, this approach has come under increasing attack, as attention has shifted from the author to the text (semiotic theory) and then to the reader (postmodern theories) as the locus of meaning.

*1.1. Foundations: Gadamer and Ricoeur.* The hermeneutical theory of H. G. Gadamer brought about a paradigm shift in the field. Gadamer argued that the act of coming-to-understanding does not unlock the past meaning of a text but establishes a dialectic between reader and text. In what Gadamer called a "fusion of horizons," the reader enters the historical process of tradition and unites with the thought-world of the text. The text, having been detached from the author, is open to new relationships. The reader is not re-creating the author's past situation by reasoning back into the past, but is entering into a relationship with the text in which both text and reader interrogate each other.

P. Ricoeur took Gadamer's theory one step further, arguing that interpretation is symbolic or metaphorical at its core and occurs in front of the text (as the reader is addressed) rather than behind the text (in a reconstruction of the historical meaning). A new world of meaning is created by the text as it engages the reader. For both Gadamer and Ricoeur, the problem of "distanciation" (the distance between the text as originally written and as currently read) demands a "hermeneutic of suspicion," which reckons with the ambiguities of language and the human mind's capabilities for self-deception. With this the hermeneutical emphasis had shifted from an appropriation of the "intended" meaning of the author to a present interaction with the text, now seen as autonomous from the author's intended meaning. For instance, one studies a passage such as Romans 3, dealing with "justification by faith," in terms of its metaphorical or extended meaning rather than its intended Pauline meaning.

*1.2. From Structuralism to Deconstruction.* Following Gadamer several distinct movements have shifted the focus of hermeneutics even more decisively from the author to the text and, finally, to the reader. First, the hermeneutical approach known as *structuralism*, or *semiotics*, has treated the text as an arbitrary system of signs which must be decoded in order to arrive at the meaning. The interpreter works with the "synchronic," or literary, presence of the text itself as autonomous from the author and as controlled by two aspects of the text: the *syntagmatic* (the horizontal framework of the surface text) and the *paradigmatic* (the vertical life-world to which the codes of the text belong). The interpreter charts the *actantial* (basic narrative units) codes behind Romans 3 and determines the structural configuration beneath those surface codes. This is done primarily in terms of identifying binary opposites, that is, a set of oppositions within the surface text. These codes are then recomposed on the basis of transformational rules (primarily derived from N. Chomsky) to derive the "meaning" of Romans 3 for today.

Weaknesses in structuralism (e.g., its lack of a strong philosophical foundation; its overstatement of the place of codes and binary opposites; its overemphasis on the paradigmatic at the expense of the syntagmatic in the production of meaning) has led to a new movement known as *poststructuralism*. Primarily, this represents a shift from the text to the reader as the generating force in interpretation. The text becomes an open system of signs that compels the reader to complete its meaning. As R. Barthes puts it (74-75), the text is art rather than a work. It is dynamic and subversive, cutting across boundaries and open-ended, with an infinite number of possible meanings. The author is no longer present, and the text participates with the reader in determining meaning. Romans 3 no longer contains Pauline themes; rather, it draws the reader into its textual framework, and it is up to the reader to complete its meaning.

Closely connected to this approach are the movements of postmodernism and deconstructionism. *Postmodernism* denies that the text has any objective or referential meaning. Instead the reader discovers meaning by interacting with the text. *Deconstructionism* is the ultimate statement of this perspective. J. Derrida, the father of deconstructionism, building upon Nietzsche and the later phase of Heidegger's philosophy, attacked the very foundations of Western thought by demanding a rhetorical rather than a philosophical approach to communication. There are no fixed norms or dogmas, only metaphorical ones. Metaphor is a "decentering" process involving an infinite

number of sign substitutions. The reader can never reach a "final" interpretation of meaning. This leads to "play" as the readers bring their own interpretive rules to bear on the text. There is no presence of meaning in a text, only "difference" and "absence" as the interpreters are forced to deconstruct the text from all past meaning (not only the author's but also all past understandings) and then reconstruct it by developing their own game on the playground of the text (Derrida, 280-81). Derrida would note the many codes that lie behind the surface of Romans 3 and show how all interpreters have built upon and yet reconstructed the "meanings" of each other regarding the "justification" language of Romans 3. He would then urge the readers to engage in the joyous activity of freeplay in the text.

*1.3. Reader Response.* A similar school, but one built upon slightly different philosophical conceptions, is reader-response criticism. These critics posit the union of text and reader at the moment of response. The "author" of a text is a creation of the reader rather than inherent in the text. In fact, the text itself exists only in the reader's mind, in the sense that the text only takes on life as a formal literary entity when the printed page and the reader converge.

There are two schools of thought within reader-response criticism. The moderate position of W. Iser states that the text plays a mediating role in guiding as well as correcting the interpreter's understanding. Through a series of gaps, the text develops an anticipation which, while still pluri-significant, works with the reading strategy of the interpreter in producing meaning. A more radical type is exemplified in S. Fish, who believes that the reading community dominates the text, which does not truly exist apart from the reader. The text supplies potential meanings, but these are only actualized by the preshaped reading interests brought to bear on the text. For Iser the reader *completes* the text's meaning; for Fish the reader *creates* its meaning. Most biblical reader-response critics (e.g., Culpepper, Fowler, Resseguie) are closer to Iser, attempting to blend reader-response with historical-critical perspectives.

*1.4. Socio-Critical Hermeneutics: Liberation and Feminist.* Socio-critical hermeneutics embraces such diversity as that seen in the writings of J. Habermas, in liberation theology and in feminist hermeneutics. The primary theorists are Habermas and K.-O. Apel. They propose a "critical," or "depth hermeneutics," which posits that interpretation must include a "critique of ideology," that is, the tendency of all communication to manipulate and control others. All texts are the products of a worldview and seek to draw the reader into an acceptance of that social world. Hermeneutics then begins with a critical liberation of understanding from ideology. In other words, one must unmask the worldview behind the text and enter into a critical interaction with that world in coming-to-understanding. Socio-critical theory would seek to uncover the changing social world (i.e., the shift from Judaism to Jesus, then to primitive church and on to Pauline systems) behind the justification teaching of Romans 3, and then critique the social world behind the interpreters who study it.

Liberation and Black theology form another type of socio-critical approach. The basic premise is that Western ideology has used a theology based on heaven and spiritual salvation to oppress the poor by telling them to wait for the next life for their reward. A critical reflection on society, based on praxis, must begin with the plight of the poor. Centering on a view of God as immanent, "in" the world and not just "above" it, justification is redefined as liberation, faith as praxis, and knowledge as the transformation of society (see Gutierrez). In this sense the study of historical meaning in the text takes a back seat to the preeminence of present encounter based on the current social situation. Theory and praxis are fused, and for liberation theologians this demands that one begin with the suffering of the oppressed. Thus the motifs of Exodus and redemption from slavery lying behind the Pauline language of salvation come to the fore. In Romans 3 emphasis is given to the "righteousness* of God" as demanding justice over all oppressive systems.

Finally, feminist hermeneutics utilizes the full spectrum of reader-response and socio-critical theory. The patriarchal nature of all biblical texts and of subsequent theological reflection has oriented Christian theology toward power, domination and exploitation of women. Hermeneutics must be liberated from male-dominated interpretation, and the place of women in church and society must be reinstated before the truth of Scripture and theology can be realized. Thus the femaleness of God and the central role of women in Scripture must be retrieved. The critical norm is seen as women's experience, which R. Radford Ruether sees as "a critical force, exposing classical theology, including its foundational tradition in scripture, as shaped by male experience rather than human experience" (Ruether, 113). The Bible in this sense must be probed from the perspective of the interpreter's social world, not merely of the ancient world. The social framework of biblical thinking, especially in its patriarchal perspective, must be replaced by models that speak to today. For instance, the models of God

as father and king are to be replaced by models of God as mother, lover and friend (see TeSelle McFague). Studies by this school tend to center upon Paul either as a reflection of rabbinic oppression of women (e.g., 1 Cor 11:2-16; 14:34-35; cf. 1 Tim 2:11-15) or as containing the seeds of the emancipation of women (e.g., Rom 16:1-3, 7; Gal 3:28).

*1.5. Intentionality Approaches.* There is a growing number of scholars who stress some type of intentionality approach, that is, a return to author and text as generating meaning. Prominent among these are E. D. Hirsch and his followers (e.g., W. Kaiser, E. Johnson) who see the author's intention as the sole authentic meaning of the text. Hirsch sees two aspects in interpretation—meaning (linked to authorial intent) and significance (as the readers align themselves with the implications of the author's meaning for the present). The former is never changing while the latter changes with the reader's context.

Others build more upon the later phase of L. Wittgenstein's thought and J. Searle's speech-act theory. Searle argues that the heart of interpretation theory is the notion that language is referential more than it is performative. The sentence is an intentional device that brings hearers into the proper arena so that they might apply the correct rules for recognizing the meaning of the utterance. His thesis is: "speaking a language is engaging in a (highly complex) rule-governed form of behaviour" (Searle 1969, 77, 80). K. Vanhoozer (1986, 91-92) notes four factors that guide interpretation: proposition (the data in the text), purpose (the reason communicated), presence (the form or genre of the message) and power (the illocutionary force of the message). He argues that the reader is ethically bound by the text to discover its intended message. Osborne (411-15) calls for a trialogue between author, text and reader. The reader recognizes the guiding presence of preunderstanding and tradition but seeks to place it in front of rather than behind the text, thus allowing the text to correct previous understanding if necessary. This is not done easily but is accomplished by studying past meaning (via historical-grammatical exegesis) and present interpretative possibilities (via the conclusions of competing reading communities). The key is to allow competing possibilities to drive the interpreter back to reexamine the text in a new and open way.

Finally, A. C. Thiselton (597-619) has developed a comprehensive speech-act hermeneutic. Building upon Wittgenstein's theory of language games and J. L. Austin's understanding of performative-language functions, Thiselton argues that texts perform not only locutionary functions (propositional meaning) but also illocutionary acts (calling for commitment and action on the part of the reader). Thus meaning and significance are united in a single act of coming-to-understanding. The text not only communicates its meaning but demands response. While in some ways there is a pluralism of response as the biblical text communicates in many different reading situations, there is not polyvalence (plurality of meanings) in the strictest sense, for the text performs a transforming function, as readers are led to new horizons or life-worlds by the text. For Romans 3 this would involve not only Paul's development of justification by faith, but also the sense in which the readers are called to experience this for themselves.

## 2. Paul's Letters and First-Century Forms.

Genre has been long recognized as an important classification device for determining the rules for interpreting a specific text. To know that Paul's writings fit under the general rubric "Hellenistic letters" helps one to identify certain principles for understanding them. Yet it is also critical to identify more precisely exactly what kind of letters they are. Since Deissmann's epochal essay (224-46), discussion has centered upon whether certain of Paul's letters were personal letters or literary treatises. Yet all agree today that Deissmann's analysis and distinction is too simplistic (see Letters, Letter Forms).

*2.1. Paul and Epistolary Types.* There were many kinds of letters in the ancient world. Stowers (49-173) provides a functional typology based on rhetorical patterns, with six types: letters of friendship (cf. 2 Cor 1:16; 5:3; Phil 1:7-8); family letters; letters of praise and blame (1 Cor 11; Rev 2—3); exhortatory or paraenetic letters (1 Thess; the Pastorals); letters of mediation or recommendation (Phil 2:19-30; Philem); juridical or forensic letters (1 Cor 9:3-12; 2 Cor 1:8-2:13). Aune (162-69) adds three other types: private or documentary letters (letters of request, information, introduction, instruction, family and business); official letters (royal edicts, governmental correspondence); and literary letters (recommendation, letter-essays, philosophical letters, novelistic letters, imaginative letters, letters embedded in biographies).

Some of Paul's letters are personal (e.g., Philemon* as traditionally understood, though not by some modern commentators), some come close to being a treatise (e.g., Romans, Ephesians, in their traditional understandings), and some claim to be public letters (e.g., 1 Thess 5:27, Col 4:16). They speak to specific, occasional situations and yet are meant to be read again and again in the churches. Nearly all go beyond the boundaries of the normal letter (see 2.2 below)

and mix several forms (e.g., 1 Cor: exhortation in chaps 1—3, juridical in 9, apologetic in 15). Paul's letters were more than personal reminiscences; they represented his presence in the community and were meant to be read again and again in the worship service (see Worship). On the basis of Paul's apostolic authority* behind the letters, they possessed almost a creedal authority from the start.

*2.2. Paul and Letter Forms.* While Paul's writings followed the Hellenistic form of letters generally, they went beyond the norm in almost every particular. Introductions follow the pattern of "Paul to _____ , greetings," but often add a lengthy description of his office and purpose in writing. The greetings combine the Greek *charein* and the Hebrew *šālôm* but christianize both, centering upon the divinely bestowed grace* (*charis*) and peace* (*eirēnē*) that God provides. The initial thanksgiving and prayer are even more extensive in Paul. Normally letters in the ancient world began with a brief thanksgiving to the gods and a bestowal of blessing, but for Paul these took on great significance. As O'Brien has noticed (262-63), the introductory prayers* of Paul often embody in embryo the basic themes and atmosphere of the letter. There is a paraenetic, or hortatory, function in these sections (see Benediction, Blessing, Doxology, Thanksgiving).

The body of Paul's letters is often far more extensive than even the more literary ancient letters. Writers like Cicero tended to stay within traditional bounds, but Paul felt less bound to tradition. Thus in the body of his letters he strayed farthest from those conventions, undoubtedly because of the situations he addressed. Certain key phrases are markers for divisions in his letters, like "I want you to know" (Rom 1:13, Gal 1:11), "I do not want you to be ignorant" (2 Cor 1:8), and "I urge/exhort you" (Rom 12:1, 1 Thess 4:1). Prayers (Eph 1:15-19, 3:14-19) and doxologies (Rom 11:36; Eph 3:21) often conclude major sections. Paul's presence via his letters is especially observable in what Funk labels "apostolic parousia" (e.g., Rom 1:8-15; 1 Cor 4:14-21; Gal 4:12-20), centering upon his travel plans (see Itinerary), relationship with the readers, and past and future contacts with them. Paraenesis (see Teaching) or general moral exhortation is at the heart of many of his letters, found at the conclusion of some (1 Thess, Rom, Gal, Eph, Col) and interspersed throughout others (1 and 2 Cor, Phil, the Pastorals). This includes social codes (see Households, Household Codes), and virtue and vice lists (see Virtues and Vices), and often builds upon traditional Jewish and Hellenistic teaching. In addition, there are distinct doctrinal sections (e.g., Rom 9—11, 1 Cor 15, 1 Thess 4:13—5:10) in which Paul counteracts false understandings. These often utilize creeds* or hymns* to present the accepted dogma from which the correction can be made. The latter are also linked with other liturgical elements* like confessions and prayers in worship sections.

The closing section of the letter, like the introduction, more closely follows established patterns of Paul's day. A list of secondary greetings, following the format "*A* greets you, along with *B*" is found in all the letters except Galatians, 2 Thessalonians, Ephesians and 1 Timothy. The normal closing formula (with *errōsō*) is replaced with *charis*, and the traditional "health wish" is replaced by a doxology or benediction. The benediction, with some form of "the grace of our Lord Jesus Christ be with you all," closes all of his letters except Romans and 1 Corinthians.

### 3. Special Issues.

*3.1. Paul and Rhetorical Criticism.* Recently biblical scholars have taken up the study of the modes of communication or persuasion (*see* Rhetorical Criticism). It is impossible to know whether Paul was ever trained in rhetoric,* which was an essential part of Hellenistic education at the secondary level. Whatever his formal training, however, his letters evidence both a knowledge and use of rhetorical techniques. Aristotle (his thought later developed by Quintilian) spoke of three types of rhetoric—judicial (legal), deliberative (political or religious debates) and epideictic (praise or blame). Scholars have debated whether there were four (Mack) or six (Kennedy) elements in proper ancient speech. Here we will utilize six (with the disputed parts in brackets):

(1) The *exordium* (introduction) establishes rapport regarding the subject matter.

(2) The *narratio* (proposition statement) provides a rationale and background to the subject matter.

[(3) The *partitio* (explanation, often seen as part of the *narratio*) enumerates the points to be made.]

(4) The *probatio* (presentation of arguments) cites proof and offers evidence for the argument.

[(5) The *refutatio* (refutation of opponents, often seen as part of the *probatio*) disproves opposing views.]

(6) The *peroratio* (conclusion) summarizes the points and seeks to persuade the reader.

This style, taken primarily from judicial rhetoric, was widely employed in the ancient world and can enhance one's understanding of Pauline argumentation, so long as it is used cautiously and the text is allowed to dictate the final outline. For instance, H. D. Betz's rhetorical analysis of Galatians* identifies it as a judicial or apologetic letter that argues for justification* by faith* rather than by the works* of the Law*;

Kennedy concludes that it is a deliberative work that calls for endurance rather than a return to Judaism; and B. Mack finds Galatians too complex to be relegated to one rhetorical type. The latter is certainly the wiser decision. The task for the rhetorical critic is to study the patterns of persuasion and to elucidate the techniques utilized by Paul. This analysis provides important hermeneutical guidelines as to how Paul marshals his arguments. For instance, Paul employs the diatribe* in Romans, a rhetorical method by which an author presents his argument by first showing the errors of his opponents (often with *mē genoito*, "may it not be so!," as in Rom 3:1-9; 6:1-3, 15-16; 9:14-15), and then demonstrates the true meaning of his own gospel.

In studying the rhetoric of Paul, the interpreter first determines the rhetorical unit (which must have an introduction, a developed argument and a conclusion). It can be a macro-unit (like Galatians or Romans) or a micro-passage (such as those in Rom 9—11 or Rom 9:6-18). Next, one analyzes the rhetorical situation (the purpose or *Sitz im Leben*, "life setting") of the unit. Then one seeks to determine the type of rhetoric employed (judicial, deliberative or apodeictic) and the specific aspects being addressed. This leads to an analysis of the arrangement, technique and style by which the situation is addressed. Finally, the rhetorical effectiveness, that is, the text's movement from the problem to the solution, is evaluated. These steps enable an interpreter more carefully to evaluate and interpret the language and meaning of Paul in specific passages.

*3.2. Creeds, Hymns and Liturgical Material.* Paul's letters are replete with creedal and liturgical material. These contain confessional utterances such as "Abba, Father"; "Maranatha"; "Amen"; doxologies; benedictions*; creeds*; and hymns.* These developed out of two needs: worship* in the house churches and the need for established convictions in the light of increased numbers of false teachers. They were used both to draw the heart to God and to anchor established truth in the mind. The central focus of most creedal material is the person and work of the Christ, primarily his incarnation (Phil 2:6-8), the pattern of humiliation and exaltation* (Phil 2:6-11; Rom 4:24, 8:32), his saving work (1 Cor 15:3-5; Rom 10:8-10) or his exaltation as cosmic Lord* (Col 1:15-20; 1 Tim 3:16). Such material incorporated into Paul's letters may have been quoted from a corpus of creedal and liturgical material, though some of this might certainly have been produced on the spot by Paul himself (*see* Liturgical Elements).

Several formal criteria have been used to detect

creedal and hymnic material. They are often introduced by *hos* ("who") or *hoti* ("that"). Language of "receiving" and "passing on" may be used (e.g., 1 Cor 15:3). There also will often be a series of parallel participial constructions, and the terms utilized might not be common to Paul. There is a certain hymnic or strophic pattern to the style, and the contents usually contain a very high christology. Finally, there may be a discernible sense in which the passage goes beyond the basic needs of the immediate context, such as the incarnation and exaltation theology of Philippians 2:6-11. To be sure, these criteria are not failsafe (see the objections of G. Fee to Phil 2:6-11 as a hymn), but they do represent the consensus of modern scholarship.

It is interesting that Paul's creedal affirmations at times centered on ethical as well as doctrinal issues (e.g., Phil 2:6-11; Rom 10:8-10; see Fowl). One aspect of interpretation centers on the function of the creed or hymn in both its original setting within early Christian worship and its setting within Paul's letter. For instance, Philippians 2:6-8 functions both as a christological hymn of worship and as a paradigm or paraenesis in the context of Philippians 2. This is somewhat unusual, but interpreters must be aware of both possible elements in exegeting a creedal passage.

**3.3. Social Codes and Virtue/Vice Lists.** The *Haustafeln* or "household/social codes" are found in the later (disputed) letters of Paul (Eph 5:21—6:9; Col 3:18—4:1; Tit 2:1-10), as well as in 1 Peter 2:13—3:8 (*see* Households and Household Codes). A precursor is seen in Romans 13:1-7 where Paul takes up the issue of submitting to civil* authorities (a theme found in the house code of 1 Pet 2). These codes are concerned with the reciprocal responsibilities between the members of the household: husband and wife, parents and children, masters and slaves.* Virtue and vice lists, on the other hand, appear in every letter except Philemon and the Thessalonian correspondence. Scholars, noting similarities between Paul's lists and those found in Hellenism and Judaism, have disagreed as to whether these lists stem primarily from Jewish or Hellenistic antecedents. They probably owe something to both cultures.

The household codes reflect one of the primary metaphors for the church, that of the extended family. Since the church itself was a macrocosm of the family (Eph 5:23, 25-27), it followed that its primary unit, the family, should exemplify the ethical unity and equity that was to characterize the church as a whole (see esp. Eph 5:21). Some (e.g., Aune, 196) maintain that the purpose of the codes was entirely apologetic: to show that Christianity was not subversive. However,

the example of 1 Peter 2:12 ("glorify God on the day of visitation") demonstrates a missionary purpose as well. Primarily, however, their purpose was internal: to regulate the social relationships in the church.

The virtue and vice lists (*see* Virtues and Vices) find parallels in the traditional lists known to us from antiquity and have a similar function: to encourage correct conduct along the lines of contemporary mores (but with the deeper expectations associated with the Christian calling, cf. Gal 5:19-23; Eph 4:25-32), to help differentiate between true and false teachers (cf. 1 Tim 6:4-5, 11; 2 Tim 2:22-25), to lay out the conduct expected of church leaders (1 Tim 1:3-11; 6:4-5) and to demonstrate the depravity of the pagan (Rom 1:29-31; 1 Tim 1:9-10). Paul followed Jewish more than Hellenistic parallels in one particular aspect: his lists focused more on corporate (e.g., love,* patience, envy, strife) than on individual virtues and vices (e.g., self-sufficiency).

In the case of both social codes, and virtue and vice lists, the interpreter must bear in mind that the lists are not meant to be exhaustive and rigid. Their purpose is to provide positive moral and ethical guidance. The lists are sometimes tied directly to their contexts (e.g., 1 Cor 5:9-10; 6:9-10) and sometimes draw upon traditional and widely recognized standards of morality (e.g., Rom 1:29-31).

**3.4. The Center of Paul's Theology.** There has been extensive debate recently as to whether a "center"* of Paul's thought can be elucidated. Since the Pauline letters are occasional in nature, and since Paul failed to develop his thought systematically, is it possible to conceive of a Pauline "theology" in the broad sense or of a "center" in the narrow sense? J. C. Beker calls these poles "the dialectic of coherence and contingency" (Beker, 15-19); others prefer to see both unity and diversity in Paul's thought. Most interpreters of Paul seek a balance. One point counts against the search for a center, namely, the tremendous diversity of "centers" that have been found. E. Käsemann finds the center in justification* by faith or, more broadly, lordship (see Way); R. P. Martin in reconciliation (*see* Center of Paul's Theology); J. C. Beker in apocalyptic*; C. J. A. Hickling in the new age and the new life in Christ; and E. P. Sanders in the lordship of Christ and the Gentile mission. It seems as if no one quite agrees on any center. This leads many others to argue that at the core of Paul lies a cluster of themes rather than a single idea or controlling principle (*see* Paul and His Interpreters).

The way out of the maze is to utilize the techniques of biblical theology, especially those of the analytical method. A "bottom-up" approach will follow the themes as they develop from one Pauline letter to another, allowing them to decide their own direction. One begins by tracing and charting these developing themes book by book. From this analysis, archetypal patterns may be discovered that tie together major ideas in each letter and then between letters. As these archetypal patterns coalesce along lines of primary and secondary emphases, the scholar may hope to discover a single idea (or cluster of ideas) from which the others derive. Only then can one demonstrate a "center" for Pauline thought.

*3.5. Development in Paul.* Interpreters of Paul have discussed at some length the extent to which Paul's theology developed from one letter to the next. Some have maintained that Paul's theology was fully formed by the time he began his missionary journeys. Others believe that development can be seen in his letters. Longenecker notes three models for development (24-26): (1) There is a basic unity and identity in development, with later changes being new deductions, applications and explications of foundational ideas (the view of the Alexandrian Fathers). (2) There is organic development with genuine innovation, but always growing out of what is inherent in the original "seed" (the view of the Antiochian Fathers). (3) There are genuine ideological changes, not only innovative but even contradictory, and without any propositional correspondence to earlier ideas (the view of Bultmann and his followers). Most Pauline scholars would hold one of these three views, but the hermeneutical criteria for determining which is correct in a given instance have not been developed.

Pauline eschatology* is the most frequently cited example. On the one hand, it has been hypothesized that 1 Thessalonians 4—5 (resurrection* at the Parousia) derived from Paul's primitive apocalyptic period, 1 Corinthians 15 and 2 Corinthians 5 (resurrection but without strong apocalyptic overtones) from Hellenistic Judaism, and the prison letters (with realized eschatology replacing expectation of the Parousia) from the Hellenistic church. On the other hand, many have also posited a development in which Paul moves from a belief in the resurrection at the Parousia (1 Thess 4, 1 Cor 15) to a belief in the resurrection at death (2 Cor 5). But the larger question is which of the three models of development best explains the data of Paul's eschatological statements, and how does one go about deciding?

The interpreter must consider both semantic and contextual factors. The first hypothesis, in which Paul moves from a primitive apocalyptic to a Hellenistic viewpoint seems to cohere with the third model of development, but it simply does not fit the data. There are apocalyptic aspects in the Corinthian letters (e.g., 1 Cor 15), as well as in the prison letters, which maintain a strong expectation of the Parousia (e.g., Eph 1:14, 5:5; Phil 1:6, 10, 23; 3:21). The second hypothesis, in which Paul's understanding of the timing of the resurrection appears to shift, does seem to suggest development. But which of the three models of development fits this picture? Most would say that Pauline eschatology exemplifies one of the first two models (either a new explication of a basic truth or an organic development of thought), for resurrection at death and at the Parousia are not contradictory if one posits an intermediate state.* In light of an intermediate state, it may be unnecessary to ask whether Paul changed his mind. Paul may have been stressing two different aspects of a larger truth, in each instance addressing a particular contextual situation. In other words, there likely was some development in Paul's thinking and theological understanding, but it is difficult to ascertain it in particular instances due to the paucity of data (Paul's letters taken together would constitute a fairly short treatise by today's standards).

*3.6. Paul and Sociology.* Paul's ministry did not occur in a religious vacuum. Paul's mission was conducted within the socio-economic framework of the Roman empire, and he utilized its institutions and social dynamics in pursuing his mission.* Thus Paul provides an attractive field for sociological analysis. Sociology as a discipline studies the relationships and social settings that shape a society. There are two aspects of its application to the study of Paul: (1) Social description studies cultural factors and customs that lie behind biblical texts in order to understand them better (e.g., the Hellenistic banquet practices behind 1 Corinthians 11:17-34; *see* Social Setting). (2) The application of social-science theory is another matter, applying modern macro-theories to reinterpret the social dynamics behind the development of the early church (e.g., J. G. Gager's use of modern millenarian movements and "cognitive dissonance" theory to explain the movement of the primitive church from apocalyptic to universal mission; *see* Social-Scientific Approaches to Paul).

There are, however, several problems inherent in this approach. Applying a twentieth-century model to a first-century situation can easily lead to a misuse of the data in support of a theory imposed from above rather than one emerging from the data itself. There is a certain revisionist tendency in such approaches. The data is often too scanty to support such theories. Paul was not writing a sociological treatise on Corinth or Thessalonica but producing pastoral letters interacting with local problems. It is often too easy to take a spiritual problem and read it as a social one. For instance, some have seen the problem of meat offered to idols* in 1 Corinthians 8—10 as a social conflict between upper and lower classes rather than as a religious problem between strong and weak. If social conflict is the issue, it will have to be proven from the text itself. The tendency to explain all factors as a result of social forces is reductionistic, based on the untenable assumption that religious phenomena can simply be reduced to human factors. Social theory does have a place in background analysis, but it must be used very carefully, with an eye constantly open to reductionist tendencies. On the whole, social description is more useful than the application of social-science theory, but both can be helpful.

A general consensus has arisen that Paul and his mission were not restricted to the very poor but affected a wide social range, including those in the upper-middle register of the social spectrum. The proconsul of Cyprus was among Paul's first converts (Acts 13:12), and Paul moved freely from rural (typifying a large part of his first journey) to urban (characterizing his second and third journeys) environments. Studies of the more than eighty names found in Paul's letters have shown that a significant number were of the upper class, with homes that hosted house churches and with the mobility that was the backbone of Paul's mission network (see Meeks). R. F. Hock has shown that Paul's mission method was complemented by his leather-making craft (*see* Tentmaking), which provided not only his livelihood but the social setting for much of his missionary contact with individuals, with whom he conversed as he worked. Not only rabbis but also Stoic-Cynic philosophers functioned in this way.

When engaged in sociological research, it is important to observe several hermeneutical cautions. Before beginning the sociological study, exegete the passage thoroughly along grammatical-semantic-syntactical lines. This will provide a control against allowing a revisionist, reconstructed "event" to predominate over the text. Also, one should be comprehensive in compiling the data. It is one thing to suggest a *possible* social background and quite another thing to maintain that this is the *likely* background. The latter cannot be decided until all possible explanations have been explored. It is not enough to show that a Hellenistic, class-oriented meal conflict may lie behind the Lord's Supper* conflict of 1 Corinthians 11; it must be shown to be superior to the traditional understanding. One must study the contexts of the biblical episode and of the possible explanations and see which one coheres best with the NT data. One must not read extrabiblical parallels into the Pauline context any fur-

ther than the data allows. The text itself should determine that theory which best explains it. When these cautions have been observed, sociological research can prove to be an invaluable ally to Pauline studies.

*3.7. Paul and Narrativity.* Many literary critics believe that all genres, including Paul's letters, possess a "narrative world," a fictive aspect that relates a "story" about the life setting behind the work conceived as art. In this sense, it is believed, Paul's writings all possess a plot, a point of view, an ideological framework, a setting, a characterization regarding the implied readers, and a closure. Most scholars distinguish between the historical setting or event behind the text, and the "symbolic universe" portrayed in the text. The former relates to what actually happened, the latter to the fictive re-creation of the event in the text. The latter "story" does not have to conform to the former, for it is a fictional or reconstructed world created by Paul. The reader derives the "story" by reworking the letter to discover the "narrative time" or structural sequence behind the didactic text. Each passage gives a hint regarding "what happened" behind the text, and these are reorganized along story lines to derive the narrative world in the text.

A good example is Petersen's application of narrative and sociological methods to Philemon.* He believes that two "events" dominate the letter, Philemon's obligation to Paul (from which Paul deduces a position of superiority), and Onesimus's debt to Philemon (such that Onesimus plays the role of supplicant). Paul addresses Philemon from the standpoint of Onesimus. He asks not only that Onesimus be forgiven but that he also be freed (with "brother" in Philem 16 having legal as well as social implications). Thus Paul is using his "authority" at once asserted and veiled as well as his closeness to Philemon to demand manumission via Philemon's "obedience" (Philem 21).

Narrative criticism shows promise as a new approach to Paul, but it has to exhibit even greater care in the treatment of letters than it does of the historical books, for it is more a "stranger" to non-narrative texts. Petersen's book represents exciting new possibilities but exemplifies many of the pitfalls of an over-exuberant literary criticism: namely, a facile dichotomy between history and fiction in the text; a failure to develop criteria for distinguishing between the two aspects; an ignoring of the referential in favor of the symbolic dimension; a reductionism that ignores the epistolary genre in favor of narrativity; and reading twentieth-century categories too easily into ancient documents. However, these can be corrected, and there is real potential in this approach to Paul (see Bartchy, 308-9).

### 3.8. Contextualization of Paul.

**3.8. Contextualization of Paul.** Developed by missiologists in the 1970s, contextualization is the process of crosscultural communication, determining the significance of a biblical text for a group distanced from the cultures behind the Bible. The barrier has been called *distanciation*, the historical-cultural gap between the biblical world and our own. The method for overcoming this gap recognizes the form-content dilemma: that the content of Paul's letters provides the core of meaning, but the form by which it is understood (see 1.5 above) changes from culture to culture. This process was true also of the early church. Paul consciously contextualized the Jewish-Christian gospel of the primitive church for his Gentile mission on the basis of his principle of "all things to all people" (1 Cor 9:23). The gospel content was inviolate, but the form that it took in Gentile circles varied. This often caused problems, exemplified in the Jerusalem decree of Acts 15 and the issue of the strong versus the weak in 1 Corinthians 8—10 (*see* Strong and Weak).

Yet the process is the same for us. The move from biblical text to current context is not characterized by a simple one-to-one correspondence but by a dynamic process. Nida and Taber (51-54) developed a translation technique (which applies to contextualization as well as to translation) whereby the translator "back transforms" the surface message of the text to discover the transcultural element behind the passage, the universal truth that applies to every culture. The universal truth is then "forward transformed" to parallel situations today. Some texts cross over intact, like the warnings against pride and dissension of Philippians 2:1-4, 14-18. Other texts demand a deeper transformation at the level of principle, such as Paul's outburst against the Judaizers* in Philippians 3:1-6, 18-19. G. D. Fee and D. Stuart (61-65) note two types of transforming principle: "extended application" (e.g., applying "unequally yoked" [2 Cor 6:14] to marriage with unbelievers) and "particulars that are not comparable" (e.g., meat offered to idols in 1 Corinthians 8—10, which must be applied at the level of principle).

There are six steps in the contextualization process. First, determine the surface message via historical-grammatical exegesis. By combining grammar, semantics and background information, the interpreter seeks to uncover the original meaning of the passage in its ancient context. Second, study the underlying theological or "deep structure" message via biblical theology. This is not structuralism but theological exegesis. As Paul wrote his occasional letters, he consciously chose his surface message from a deeper set of theological truths articulated by Jesus, the early church and himself. The interpreter tries to discover those larger theological categories in order to understand the message of the text in a deeper way. Third, one should study the situation (via background analysis) which caused Paul to emphasize the points in the text. These first three are the historical (or "what it meant") column of the hermeneutical task. The final three constitute the contextual (or "what it means") column. The fourth step is to seek the parallel situation in the modern world, that is, those areas that fit the situation behind the text. One must ask, "If Paul were speaking to my congregation or group on the points of this passage, what issues would he address?" Finally, the interpreter must decide whether to contextualize the passage generally (at the level of principle, step five) or specifically (at the same level as the surface text, step six). This becomes the contextualization of the text.

*See also* CANON; CENTER OF PAUL'S THEOLOGY; LETTERS, LETTER FORMS; LITURGICAL ELEMENTS; PAUL AND HIS INTERPRETERS; PAUL IN EARLY CHURCH TRADITION; PREACHING FROM PAUL; RHETORICAL CRITICISM; SOCIAL-SCIENTIFIC APPROACHES TO PAUL.

BIBLIOGRAPHY. K.-O. Apel, *Hermeneutik und Ideologiekritik* (Frankfurt: Suhrkamp, 1971); D. E. Aune, *The New Testament in Its Literary Environment* (Philadelphia: Westminster, 1987); S. S. Bartchy, "Philemon, Epistle to," *ABD* V.305-10; R. Barthes, "From Work to Text," in *Textual Strategies: Perspectives in Post-Structuralist Criticism*, ed. J. V. Harari (Ithaca: Cornell University, 1979) 73-81; J. C. Beker, *The Triumph of God: The Essence of Paul's Thought* (Minneapolis: Fortress, 1990); R. A. Culpepper, *Anatomy of the Fourth Gospel: A Study in Literary Design* (Philadelphia: Fortress, 1983); A. Deissmann, *Light from the Ancient East* (London: Hodder & Stoughton, 1909); J. Derrida, "Structure, Sign, and Play in the Discourse of the Human Sciences," in *Writing and Difference*, ed. A. Bass (Chicago: University of Chicago, 1978) 79-153; G. D. Fee, "Philippians 2:5-11: Hymn or Exalted Pauline Prose?," *BBR* 2 (1992) 29-46; S. E. Fish, *Is There a Text in This Class? The Authority of Interpretive Communities* (Cambridge, MA: Harvard University, 1980); R. M. Fowler, "Who is 'the Reader' in Reader Response Criticism?" *Semeia* 31 (1985) 5-23; H.-G. Gadamer, *Truth and Method* (2d ed.; New York: Crossroad, 1982); J. G. Gager, *Kingdom and Community: The Social World of Early Christianity* (Englewood Cliffs: Prentice-Hall, 1975); G. Gutierrez, *A Theology of Liberation: History, Politics, and Salvation* (New York: Orbis, 1973); J. Habermas, *Knowledge and Human Interests* (2d ed.; London: Heinemann, 1978); C. J. A. Hickling, "Centre and Periphery in Paul's Thought," in *Studia Biblica III. Papers on Paul and Other NT Authors*, ed. E. A. Livingstone (Sheffield: Academic, 1978) 199-214;

E. D. Hirsch, *Validity in Interpretation* (New Haven: Yale University, 1967); R. F. Hock, *The Social Context of Paul's Ministry: Tentmaking and Apostleship* (Philadelphia: Fortress, 1980); W. Iser, *The Act of Reading: A Theory of Aesthetic Response* (Baltimore: Johns Hopkins University, 1978); E. E. Johnson, *Expository Hermeneutics: An Introduction* (Grand Rapids: Zondervan, 1990); W. C. Kaiser, *Toward an Exegetical Theology: Biblical Principles for Preaching and Teaching* (Grand Rapids: Baker, 1981); E. Käsemann, *New Testament Questions of Today* (Philadelphia: Fortress, 1979); H. C. Kee, *Knowing the Truth: A Sociological Approach to New Testament Interpretation* (Minneapolis: Fortress, 1989); G. A. Kennedy, *New Testament Interpretation through Rhetorical Criticism* (Chapel Hill, NC: University of North Carolina, 1984); R. N. Longenecker, *New Testament Social Ethics for Today* (Grand Rapids: Eerdmans, 1984); B. L. Mack, *Rhetoric and the New Testament* (Minneapolis: Fortress, 1990); R. P. Martin, *Reconciliation: A Study of Paul's Theology* (rev. ed.; Grand Rapids: Zondervan, 1990); W. A. Meeks, *The First Urban Christians: The Social World of the Apostle Paul* (New Haven: Yale University, 1983); E. A. Nida and C. R. Taber, *The Theory and Practice of Translation* (Leiden: E. J. Brill, 1974); P. T. O'Brien, *Introductory Thanksgivings in the Letters of Paul* (Leiden: E. J. Brill, 1977); G. R. Osborne, *The Hermeneutical Spiral: A Comprehensive Introduction to Biblical Interpretation* (Downers Grove, IL: InterVarsity, 1991); N. R. Petersen, *Rediscovering Paul: Philemon and the Sociology of Paul's Narrative World* (Philadelphia: Fortress, 1985); J. Resseguie, "Reader-Response Criticism and the Synoptic Gospels," *JAAR* 52 (1984) 307-24; P. Ricoeur, *The Rule of Metaphor* (Toronto: University of Toronto, 1977); R. R. Ruether, "Feminist Interpretation: A Method of Correlation," in *Feminist Interpretation of the Bible*, ed. L. M. Russell (New York: Blackwell, 1985) 111-24; E. P. Sanders, *Paul and Palestinian Judaism* (Philadelphia: Fortress, 1977); J. R. Searle, *Expression and Meaning: Studies in the Theory of Speech Acts* (Cambridge: University Press, 1979); idem, *Speech Acts: An Essay in the Philosophy of Language* (Cambridge: University Press, 1969); S. K. Stowers, *Letter-Writing in Greco-Roman Antiquity* (Philadelphia: Westminster, 1986); S. TeSelle McFague, *Models Of God: Theology for an Ecological, Nuclear Age* (Philadelphia: Fortress, 1987); A. C. Thiselton, *New Horizons in Hermeneutics* (Grand Rapids: Zondervan, 1992); K. J. Vanhoozer, *Biblical Narrative in the Philosophy of Paul Ricoeur: A Study in Hermeneutics and Theology* (Cambridge: University Press, 1990); idem, "The Semantics of Biblical Literature: Truth and Scripture's Diverse Literary Forms," in *Hermeneutics, Authority, and Canon*, ed. D. A. Carson and J. D. Woodbridge (Grand Rapids: Zon-

dervan, 1986); D. V. Way, *The Lordship of Christ: Ernst Käsemann's Interpretation of Paul's Theology* (Oxford: Clarendon, 1991).

G. R. Osborne

**HISTORICAL JESUS.** *See* CHRISTOLOGY; JESUS, SAYINGS OF; JESUS AND PAUL.

**HISTORY-OF-RELIGIONS SCHOOL.** *See* PAUL AND HIS INTERPRETERS.

## HOLINESS, SANCTIFICATION

On the basis of God's* holy character and behavior, and as a consequence of the salvific work of Christ,* Paul insists that believers also are to be holy or sanctified. For Paul holiness or sanctification includes soteriological status, and—more importantly—ethical* and eschatological perfection.* Not only are the significant passages found in contexts addressed to "believers," the most important sustained Pauline passages occur after Paul has turned from his major soteriological categories to focus on the (ethical) consequences of salvation.* Paul insists upon holy and pure behavior and conduct in the lives of believers in anticipation of the return of Jesus Christ, even though attainment of complete perfection in this life is not envisioned by him.

Although the concept of holiness was important in the OT and early Judaism, its application to the Pauline concept of holiness is limited. First, apart from reference to "the holy" (see 1 below), Paul does not use the language of holiness in predominantly cultic contexts (see 2 Cor 7:1 below as a possible exception). Second, he democratizes the concept by removing it from the domain of the cult and making it the spiritual responsibility of every believer. Third, he delimits the concept, to distinguish it from other concepts that remain more cultic in nature, such as "purity"* (*kathar-*), which is mentioned at 2 Corinthians 7:1, Ephesians 5:26 and Titus 2:14.

1. The "Holy," or "Saints"
2. Sanctification and Justification
3. Sanctification of One's Family
4. The Problem of the Indicative and Imperative
5. Colossians, Ephesians and the Pastorals

### 1. The "Holy," or "Saints."
Members of the Christian community are frequently addressed in the Pauline letters as "the holy" or "saints" (Rom 1:1, 7; 8:27; 15:25, 26, 31; 16:2, 15; 1 Cor 1:2; 6:1, 2; 14:33; 16:1, 15; 2 Cor 1:1; 8:4; 9:1, 12; 13:12; Eph 1:1, 4, 15, 18; 2:19; 3:8, 18; 4:12; 5:3; 6:18; Phil 1:1; 4:21, 22; Col 1:2, 4, 12, 22, 26; 1 Thess 3:13; 2 Thess

1:10; 1 Tim 5:10; Philem 5, 7). That this is more than a formula is seen by occasional linkage of the word "call"* with "saint" (e.g., Rom 1:7; 1 Cor 1:2) and reference to the "people of God" as holy (e.g., 1 Cor 3:17; Eph 2:21). In Paul's eyes holiness is both a condition and a process in which the believer is involved through the work of God, of Christ or of the Holy Spirit* (see Rom 15:16; 1 Cor 1:2; 1 Thess 5:23; Eph 5:26; the verb *hagiazō*, "make holy," "sanctify," always has a member of the Godhead as its primary agent).

Language regarding the holy community of believers and a holy God is reminiscent of the OT. In the LXX the adjective *hagios* ("holy") is used frequently of God (e.g., Lev 19:2) and his people (e.g., Ex 19:5, 6), and verb forms (*hagiazō*, etc.) are used to call the community to right living. Some of Paul's language regarding "the holy," as well as "sanctification," may have cultic overtones derived from his seeing parallels between God's OT people, who were called to conduct lives of purity, and the church (cf. Rom 12:1; 15:16; Col 1:22; 3:12; Eph 1:4; 5:27).

## 2. Sanctification and Justification.

As a result of the Reformation, there is a persistent tendency among Protestants to evaluate Paul's major salvific categories in light of the doctrine of justification.* While it is unwise to impose uncritically on Paul Reformation categories of thought, an evaluation of these passages cannot but reflect these questions. There are two major views of the relationship between sanctification and justification.

*2.1. Sanctification as a Consequence of Justification.* A number of scholars have interpreted Pauline sanctification as a consequence of justification. Hence sanctification is not a synonymous term but a development, actualization or consequence of justification in the believer's life.

*2.1.1. 1 Thessalonians 3, 4.* Assuming that his readers are already believers and giving thanks for this (1 Thess 1:3, 6, 7, 8; 2:4), Paul in 1 Thessalonians 4 turns to ethical instruction regarding living their lives as pleasing to God (4:1—5:22, the paraenesis). He states that "this is the will of God, your sanctification" (1 Thess 4:3), for "God has not called us for the purpose of impurity, but in sanctification" (1 Thess 4:7 NASB). In this context most commentators differentiate between the call of God, and sanctification, or holy and pure behavior. This ethical behavior centers upon sexual* morality (1 Thess 4:3, 4, 5, 6).

As is typical for Pauline paraenesis, his ethical section follows closely upon theological reflection, as seen in 1 Thessalonians 3:13, the concluding verse of the body of the letter. As he ends his discussion of his concern for the Thessalonians (2:17—3:13), Paul adds that he wishes for their love to increase, "so that He [the Lord] may establish your hearts unblamable in holiness before our God and Father at the coming of our Lord Jesus with all his saints" (1 Thess 3:13 NASB). This passage places Paul's subsequent admonitions regarding pure ethical behavior within a context of anticipated eschatological reward. In 1 Thessalonians 3:13 and 4:7 the Greek preposition *en* ("in holiness") indicates that Christians are to live in an atmosphere permeated and surrounded by holiness.

Most recent commentators distinguish between the word used for "holiness" in 1 Thessalonians 3:13 (*hagiōsynē*) as the "state of being holy" and the word for "sanctification" in 1 Thessalonians 4:3, 7 (*hagiasmos*) as "the process of making holy." These are the earliest occurrences of *hagiasmos* ("sanctification") in Christian literature and, according to F. F. Bruce, have a "strong ethical sense" (Bruce, 82). As Marshall states, *hagiasmos* "refers to an active process which leads to the state of holiness which is the goal of Christian living in 3:13" (Marshall, 106). This distinction between *hagiōsynē*, "holiness," and *hagiasmos*, "sanctification," is well in keeping with the uses of these words in their epistolary contexts, with *hagiōsynē* reflecting the doctrinal assumption by Paul of the Thessalonians' status in Christ and *hagiasmos* reflecting his paraenetic exhortation that the Thessalonians conduct lives pleasing to God.

*2.1.2. Evaluation.* V. P. Furnish disputes the above analysis (Furnish, 154-57). First, other passages, he claims, do not reveal the same ordering of ideas (e.g., 1 Corinthians 6:11, "but you were cleansed, but you were sanctified [*hēgiasthēte*], but you were justified in the name of the Lord Jesus Christ"). This argument is not so significant, however, since "cleansed," "sanctified" and "justified" do not seem to be listed sequentially. Second, Furnish contends that justification, more than a forensic act, is a change in one's standing and one's living, and that sanctification is not primarily ethical (as if there were a special "ethical doctrine" at play in Paul's thought) but soteriological. Because there is conceptual overlap between justification and sanctification, however, does not prove that there is no conceptual differentiation of the terms, especially in light of their use in the unfolding argument of Paul's letter. In fact, the context as outlined above appears to demand differentiation between the concepts of holiness and sanctification, depending upon their immediate context.

*2.2. Sanctification as Overlapping with Justification.* Just as justification, reconciliation, etc., are Pauline conceptual labels for the believer's right standing with

God, so too is sanctification, some scholars contend. In other words, the term is primarily soteriological rather than ethical.

*2.2.1. Romans 6:19-23.* Whereas the discussion in 1 Thessalonians 4 reflects Paul's ethical exhortation, in Romans the major passage on sanctification is part of Paul's larger theological or doctrinal argument (Rom 1—8). Paul has already established the sinfulness* of the human condition (Rom 1:18—3:20) and described the solution to this as "justification" and "reconciliation" (Rom 3:21—5:21; *see* Peace, Reconciliation). Within the larger context of discussing "life in the Spirit" (Rom 6:1—8:39), Paul introduces the concept of sanctification in Romans 6:19-23. In Romans 6:19 Paul states that "just as you once yielded your members to impurity and to greater and greater iniquity, so now yield your members to righteousness* for sanctification" (RSV). Furnish, observing that words for "justification" and "sanctification" are used in the passage, claims that this verse might "suggest that sanctification is the 'working out' of justification, the attainment of an even fuller measure of 'righteousness' " (Furnish, 156). This is reflected in some translations (e.g., NASB: "resulting in sanctification") and commentators (e.g., Cranfield, 327). But, Furnish contends, Romans 6:22 makes such a formulation difficult, since " 'sanctification' is used where one might have expected to find 'righteousness' " (Furnish, 156). The RSV renders Romans 6:22: "But now that you have been set free from sin and have become slaves of God, the return you get is sanctification and its end, eternal life."

*2.2.2. Evaluation.* The substitution of "sanctification" for "righteousness" in Romans 6:22 is not as evident as Furnish believes. The train of thought in Romans 6:22 "telescopes," or condenses, Paul's meaning (Cranfield, 328). The Greek distinguishes between "the return you get" (literally "your fruit") and "sanctification." "Sanctification" is preceded by a preposition (*eis*), which indicates direction ("to," "unto"). "What Paul is saying is that they are now obtaining fruit (of their slavery to God) which is a contribution to—indeed, a beginning of—the process of their sanctification" (*hagiasmos*) (Cranfield, 329).

*2.3. Summary.* The Pauline notion of sanctification is complex, complicated by its relation to justification and its use in several different Pauline epistolary contexts. But if one must reduce sanctification to a single notion, it may be summarized in the idea that the believer *both* lives in holiness *and* grows into holiness.

*2.3.1. Semantic Overlap.* Justification and sanctification are used by Paul to describe overlapping (but not contiguous) theological concepts. 1 Corinthians 1:30

joins the two together explicitly: the Corinthians are said to be "in Christ Jesus," who became righteousness and sanctification. On this verse alone one cannot draw a major distinction between the two concepts (Barrett, 60-61). The expressions in 2 Thessalonians 2:13, "sanctification of the Spirit" (possibly human spirit?) and "by belief in the truth," refer to the means by which salvation is procured for the believer. Here sanctification appears to be the initiating event for salvation, which culminates in eschatological salvation (1 Thess 5:9).

*2.3.2. Semantic Distinction.* Despite significant overlap, sanctification is not completely synonymous with any other Pauline term. In Romans 6:19-23, whereas one cannot be the slave* of sin *and* of righteousness, or God (Rom 6:20, 22), once one is freed from sin and presented, or enslaved, to righteousness, or God (Rom 6:19, 22), one is directed toward what ultimately results in sanctification (Rom 6:19, 22). Thus justification emphasizes the initial, or "conversion," experience of the believer, but it is larger than this, including the believer's life "in Christ Jesus our Lord" (Rom 6:23). Sanctification, although it may include initiation (Rom 6:22), is the end (*telos*) toward which the justified strive, eternal life* (Rom 6:22, 23). Sanctification in some sense is "the highest level of justification" (Furnish 157, although he dismisses this). This understanding coincides with traditional analyses of Romans, in which chapters 6—8 speak of the life of the justified believer as sanctification.

If justification in Romans describes for Paul the power of God to make righteous ("rightwising" [Käsemann]), often equated with, though not to be limited to, the believer's initiation into life in Christ, sanctification is used by Paul to describe the ongoing life of the believer dedicated to serve God (Reumann, 83). This has implications for two areas: moral purity* and perfection,* and eschatology.*

*2.3.2.1. Moral Purity and Perfection.* One of the primary Pauline emphases regarding sanctification is moral purity. Impurity when contrasted with righteousness* in Romans 6:19-23 is expressed as lawlessness. In 1 Thessalonians 4:1-18 sanctification is opposed to impurity, exemplified in immoral sexual acts. Likewise in 2 Corinthians 7:1, perhaps the most important passage for seeing cultic overtones of this concept, Paul implores his readers to cleanse (*katharizō*) themselves from defilement and to perfect holiness or sanctification in the fear of God. There is serious debate over whether or not 2 Corinthians 6:14—7:1 is derived from a Judaism such as that represented at Qumran* (see commentaries), which perhaps accounts for its strong disjunctive opposition of believers and unbelievers. Assuming that it has at the least been adapted by Paul for this context, it is a passage that puts sanctification in terms of ritual purity, in which believers are said to be temples* of God and are to be separate from what is unclean (quoting a number of OT passages). Some commentators see the word for "holiness," *hagiōsynē*, in 2 Corinthians 7:1 as merely a static condition, a holiness obtained by observance of cultic practices. But the context is not one of resting content with an unholy life (2 Cor 6:1-2) but one of acting out one's status in Christ (cf. 2 Cor 6:14-18). The present participle *epitelountes*, "perfecting," indicates being involved in a process of perfection.

*2.3.2.2. Eschatology and Expectation.* When Paul speaks of sanctification he expects righteous behavior in light of the return of the Lord Jesus Christ. Paul's address of believers as "the holy," or "saints," indicates his belief in at least positional (if not actual) holiness and sanctification. But the tone in which Paul expresses his desire for sanctification in Romans 6 (e.g., Rom 6:2, 6, 11, 14, 22) and 1 Thessalonians 4 indicates belief that sanctification or perfection of the believer by God (through the Spirit) is an ongoing process. First, Paul couches his words in terms of the continuing struggle of the believer. His address to "the holy" includes churches wrestling with their life in Christ. The contexts in 1 Thessalonians 4 and Romans 6 deal with believers struggling morally or intellectually with proper Christian behavior. Second, whereas Paul indicates that believers are at least positioned to attain perfection and sanctification, he indicates also that the believer has yet fully to attain this (e.g., Rom 6:2, 12). This is particularly clear in autobiographical passages, where Paul admits that he has not attained to sanctification in its fullness (e.g., 2 Cor 9:27; Phil 1:6; 2:12-18; 3:12-15). Complete sanctification, in Paul's eyes, only occurs at the return of Christ (1 Thess 3:13). Furthermore, one of the two sustained discussions of sanctification is in 1 Thessalonians, a letter concerned with eschatology. As Paul says in 1 Thessalonians 5:23, "Now may the God of peace Himself sanctify you entirely; and may your spirit and soul and body be preserved complete, without blame at the coming of our Lord Jesus Christ" (NASB).

Marshall, commenting upon 1 Thessalonians 5:23, aptly states the Pauline perspective: "Just as Paul can refer to believers as saints or holy ones, despite their lack of actual holiness in conduct, so those who have been sanctified or set apart as God's people must increasingly show the appropriate characteristics in goodness and dedication to God's service, and Paul prays that God will work in the lives of his readers to this end" (Marshall, 161).

*2.3.2.3. Reference to the Holy Spirit with Respect to Sanctification.* Scholars disagree over how much to make of Paul's use of the attribution "holy" when referring to the Spirit (*see* Holy Spirit). On the one hand, everything that Paul wants to say regarding the work of the Spirit can be said without making use of the adjective *holy* with *Spirit* (e.g., 1 Cor 12:13; Gal 3:2; Rom 8:9, 14; Rom 8:9; Phil 1:19, etc.), so in Paul's mind in this sense the adjective "holy" adds nothing essential to the quality or character of the Spirit. On the other hand, when Paul does refer to the Spirit in a sustained context that speaks of sanctification, it is with the adjective "holy" (1 Cor 6:19; 1 Thess 4:8). Although nothing is added by the adjective, its use may illustrate Paul's association of a cultic background with the terminology. Just as the Spirit accomplishing God's purpose is holy, or dedicated to God and his service, so the product of his work, sanctification in the believer, is a matter of purity and dedication to him.

### 3. Sanctification of One's Family.

In the context of forbidding mandatory divorce in the case of a mixed marriage* of believer and unbeliever, Paul in 1 Corinthians 7:14 says that the unbelieving husband or wife is sanctified, or made holy, through his or her spouse, and the previously unclean children are now holy. Several solutions have been suggested for understanding this problematic verse. (1) OT views of holiness by association (Ex 29:37) are extended to unbelievers. (2) A corporeal unity between marriage partners results in the unbelieving partner actually being made holy. (3) Marriage to a believing partner removes the marriage from control of the powers of the world. (4) "Sanctification" is used in anticipation of the unbeliever being brought to baptism,* and "holy" refers to infant baptism. (5) Since "sanctification" is a process, "holiness" refers to the behavior of the spouse, reflected also in the children. (6) One of the partners is an unbeliever, so sanctification refers not to sanctification in its full theological sense but to making the marriage relationship pure and thus not warranting dissolution.

The explanation is difficult, so that a few commentators have debated whether the passage is a later interpolation. The most likely view, (6), has the major difficulty that it requires a less theologically rigorous sense for "sanctification," one unparalleled in the rest of the Pauline literature. But in its defense, if Paul were arguing for a salvific transformation of the unbelieving partner, he would surely have made this clearer. The context argues against this, being part of a section detailing the principle of "one husband, one wife" (1 Cor 7:1-16), with no divorce for Christian partners (1 Cor 7:10-11) or for Christians in mixed marriages (1 Cor 7:12-16). As part of Paul's paraenesis to the Corinthians, the ethical side of "sanctification" is probably to the fore, in which Paul is saying that the marital relationship in which these mixed partners are involved, perhaps even by its ongoing maintenance, is made morally pure by the believing partner being in it.

### 4. The Problem of the Indicative and Imperative.
In describing Pauline ethics,* scholars frequently refer to the tension between the indicative and the imperative. This has come to mean two different things. Bultmann proposed that the imperative (ethical command) proceeds out of the indicative (statement of theological truth), with the idea that Christians should "become what they are." E. Käsemann rejects this when he argues that the believer is simultaneously in two realms: obedience is a requirement for maintaining the condition of faith.*

Despite its enshrinement in the secondary literature, indicative/imperative language is potentially misleading, since "indicative" and "imperative" are strictly speaking grammatical labels for two of the Greek verbal mood forms (it was in this sense that they were originally used in discussion of Pauline ethics). Sometimes they are used in parallel constructions, at other times they are not. The indicative-imperative construct is in actual fact a theological paradigm, in which the two grammatical forms play *some* part. In Romans 6:1-23 Paul gives a series of exhortations predicated upon a description of the believer's condition (a passage frequently referred to in illustrating the indicative-imperative terminology). But Romans 6:1-11 contains a variety of verbs used in the description of the Christian, including future forms (which are arguably not "indicatives"), subjunctives (hortatory and other uses), infinitives and participles. And Roman 6:12-23 contains verbs other than imperatives regarding attainment of the believer's anticipated condition. In fact, following the imperatives in Romans 6:12 and 13, there are few other imperatives in the section.

Rather than using potentially misleading indicative-imperative terminology, scholars would be better served by the use of narrative ethics to describe the tension in Pauline ethics between Paul's description of the believer's current condition (as justified) and his ethical appeal (for sanctification). Scholars have been using a form of narrative ethics, despite their terminology, by virtue of the fact that they do not (and cannot) insist upon a strict use of indicative-imperative forms. For Paul, ethical discourse is more than

simply an appeal to grammatical forms to establish moral directives, but a set of directives for behavior which derive from description of the believer's condition in Christ. The force of Paul's directives will be judged on how well he has adequately described (to the satisfaction of his audience) his audience's condition in Christ, or has narrated the story of Christ (*see* Christology).

### 5. Colossians, Ephesians and the Pastorals.
These letters occasionally differ from Paul's chief letters by using a modified vocabulary to describe such notions as holiness or sanctification, and by dealing with these concepts differently.

Colossians 1:28 and Ephesians 4:13 have the same conceptual perspective on sanctification, but use the word *teleios* ("perfect") instead of the more common Pauline words. In the household* code of Ephesians 5:21—6:9 cultic terminology is used at Ephesians 5:26 when it is said that Christ sanctifies (*hagiazō*) the church, purifying (*katharizō*) her by the washing of water by the word.

In the Pastoral* letters holiness and sanctification are always spoken of in terms of defining personal behavior. In 2 Timothy 2:21, *hagiazō*, a frequent Pauline word, modifies the word "vessel," an impersonal use uncharacteristic of Paul's chief letters, even though describing the pure person. In 1 Timothy 2:8 a word translated "holy" (*hosios*) is probably used to describe the hands of men who pray* without anger or dispute. This word, not found in Paul's chief letters, is also used at Titus 1:8 of the overseer. In 1 Timothy 5:22 and Titus 2:5 the moral quality of purity (*hagnos*) is listed as a personal trait. In 1 Timothy 2:15 the author says that women shall be saved through childbirth if *they* remain in faith and love and holiness (*hagiasmos*), with self-control. Faith, love and holiness are distinctively Christian traits, in which case the verse states that salvation for the Ephesian women is conditional upon their remaining believers (*see* Man and Woman; Apostasy, Falling Away, Perseverance).

*See also* DEATH OF CHRIST; ESCHATOLOGY; ETHICS; FLESH; GLORY, GLORIFICATION; HOLY SPIRIT; IMITATION OF PAUL/OF CHRIST; JUSTIFICATION; MARRIAGE AND DIVORCE; NEW NATURE AND OLD NATURE; PURITY AND IMPURITY; RIGHTEOUSNESS, RIGHTEOUSNESS OF GOD; SEXUALITY, SEXUAL ETHICS; SIN, GUILT; SPIRITUALITY; VIRTUES AND VICES.

BIBLIOGRAPHY. C. K. Barrett, *The Second Epistle to the Corinthians* (New York: Harper & Row, 1973); F. F. Bruce, *1 and 2 Thessalonians* (WBC 45; Waco, TX: Word, 1982); R. Bultmann, *Theology of the New Testament* (2 vols.; New York: Scribners, 1951, 1955) 1.332-

33; C. E. B. Cranfield, *The Epistle to the Romans* (Vol. 1; ICC; Edinburgh: T. & T. Clark, 1975); S. E. Fowl, *The Story of Christ in the Ethics of Paul* (Sheffield: JSOT, 1991); V. P. Furnish, *Theology and Ethics in Paul* (Nashville: Abingdon, 1968) 171-76, 224-27; E. Käsemann, " 'The Righteousness of God' in Paul," in *New Testament Questions of Today* (Philadelphia: Fortress, 1969) 168-82; I. H. Marshall, *1 and 2 Thessalonians* (NCB; Grand Rapids: Eerdmans, 1983); R. P. Martin, *2 Corinthians* (WBC 40; Waco, TX: Word, 1986); J. Murphy-O'Connor, "Works without Faith in 1 Cor 7:14," *RB* 84 (1977) 349-61; J. Reumann, *Righteousness in the New Testament* (Philadelphia: Fortress; New York: Paulist, 1982); H. Ridderbos, *Paul: An Outline of His Theology* (Grand Rapids: Eerdmans, 1975) 253-65; R. Tannehill, *Dying and Rising with Christ* (Berlin: Töpelmann, 1967) 7-43; V. Taylor, *Forgiveness and Reconciliation* (2d ed.; London: Macmillan, 1946) 144-88.

S. E. Porter

## HOLINESS OF GOD. *See* GOD; HOLINESS, SANCTIFICATION.

## HOLY DAYS

Judaism was rich in festivals and the observance of other special days. The vagaries of the calendar however led to disputes among Jewish groups; and the rapid self-definition of the church over against its parent increased the problems for the early Christians. It is not certain what special days were observed by Paul and his churches, though it is clear that some observances provided points of friction.

1. Holy Days and Calendar Systems
2. Paul and Holy Days in Acts
3. Holy Days in the Pauline Corpus

### 1. Holy Days and Calendar Systems.

Problems with the calendar stem from the lack of correlation between the day, the lunar month (29½ days) and the year (365¼ days). Several calendars were in use in the ancient world, and people were probably accustomed to using different ones concurrently for different purposes. The stress in the Torah on the importance of keeping religious festivals at the correct time (the three great annual feasts Ex 23:14-17; the new moon Num 10:10; 28:11; etc.; and the observance of a strict rest not merely one day in seven but on the seventh day) adds a theological dimension to the problem of choice. Errors in calculation might be feared to lead to the observance of the wrong day, even to the profanation of the Sabbath. For it is of course the seven-day week rather than the month or year which lies at the heart of Israelite practice. A

proper calendar is consequently of great religious significance.

After the Exile there is likely to have been debate over the nature of the calendar to be used in the restored cultus. The Pharisees and Sadducees, and hence the administration of the Temple, appear to have agreed on a strictly lunar calendar, with an intercalary month ("second Adar") added every third or fourth year (fuller details of this calendar may be found in Schürer 1973, Appendix III). For some, however, such ad hoc adjustment dishonored the divine order of creation (e.g., *1 Enoch* 75:1-2; 82:4-6; *Jub.* 6:36-38). The book of Jubilees (among others) argues for a neat system of a fifty-two-week year (*Jub.* 6:23-38), as used at Qumran, where parts of full calendrical cycles have been found.

That calendrical concerns were not just the preserve of the Essenes is seen from other writings such as *1 Enoch* 72—82, from groups like the Samaritans, and also from a later (and highly implausible) rabbinic tradition that the Pharisees had coerced the Sadducees to observe a Pharisaic calendar for the Temple cultus. In fact rabbinic tradition also witnesses to sharp differences between Pharisees and "Boethusians" on calendrical issues (*m. Menaḥ.* 10:3; expanded in the Talmud and Tosefta). The Book of Revelation appears to use a solar calendar (12 months of 30 days each) in Revelation 11—12, where 3½ years = 42 months = 1260 days. The widely pervasive influence of astrology in the ancient world may well have added a further dimension to Jewish calendrical concerns.

Apart from the annual Day of Atonement, the Torah's calendrical occasions were feasts, not fasts (cf. Hos 2:11). Feast days, the Sabbath and its eve are explicitly excluded from Judith's fast (Judith 8:1-6). Fasting might be called for on specific occasions (e.g., 1 Sam 7:6; Neh 9:1; Joel 2:15; cf. 1 Kings 21:27), and Zechariah (7:3, 5; 8:19) refers to what appear to be four set fasts, one of which is probably the commemoration of the fall of the Temple on 9 Ab. We do not know what the others signified; nor whether by the first century they were still observed. But it is clear both from the gospels (Mt 6:16; 9:14 and par.; Lk 18:12; cf. also Acts 13:2) and from the *Didache* (*Did.* 8) that regular fast days were an integral part of Jewish and Christian piety, and for the *Didache* even a part of Christian self-identity.

### 2. Paul and Holy Days in Acts.

The Book of Acts contains a handful of references to calendrical items, though it is unclear whether they are used to indicate liturgical practice or simply as time markers. Strange though it may seem for a Gentile writer to use the Jewish calendar for the latter purpose, it is difficult to interpret Acts 12:3 in any other way. Similarly in Acts 20:6 we are hardly to understand Paul deciding to stay in Philippi—that least Jewish city of the area—specifically in order to spend the festival there. Acts 20:16 is more problematic. It would certainly make good sense as indicating Paul's desire to make the pilgrimage for the great feast. On the other hand, Pentecost marked the time after which sailing became too hazardous; and Acts 20:16 may indicate simply that Paul had no desire to be trapped in Asia by the weather (cf. Acts 27:9). Since nothing more is said about the festival, it is clear that it is no great concern of Luke (see Itinerary).

The other calendrical references in Acts are all to the Sabbath (Acts 13:14, 27, 42, 44; 15:21; 16:13; 17:2; 18:4; 20:7). M. M. B. Turner argues that Acts is best consonant with a continued Sabbath keeping by the early church, Gentile* as well as Jew; but that at least in the Ephesus area a meeting on Sunday evening was seen as a suitable occasion to celebrate the common meal (see Love Feast).

### 3. Holy Days in the Pauline Corpus.

References to calendrical points are few. Three allusions to "winter" (1 Cor 16:6; 2 Tim 4:21; Tit 3:12) would not of themselves even allow us to determine whether a Babylonian two-season calendar or the more common four-season one is in view. There are no references to fasting, even where we might expect one (e.g., 1 Cor 5). The references to abstention from foods may relate to fasting, but are more likely to relate to concerns not to transgress Jewish food* laws. The only significant passages are the following.

*3.1. 1 Corinthians 5:8; 16:8.* We cannot now tell whether or to what extent the festivals were being observed in Paul's churches, for the redefinition of the leaven in 1 Corinthians 5 clearly indicates that the primary referent here is a metaphorical festival, to be "kept" all year round. Yet this still presupposes some knowledge of the Jewish calendar on the part of the reader (see Lord's Supper).

*3.2. Galatians 4:10.* One major thrust of Paul's polemic in Galatians* is to draw a parallel between Jewish submission to the Law* and Gentile subjection to the "no-gods" which enslaved them. For both, Christ is liberator. Gentiles* were never under the Law, not being involved in the Mosaic covenant*; to seek to submit to it as Christian converts, then, is tantamount to returning to that slavery; to the enfeebled and impotent elements* (*asthenē kai ptōcha stoicheia*, Gal 4:9). This is described as observing "days, months, seasons and years"—surprisingly non-specific terminology (in contrast to Col 2:16), which may be due to Paul's intended parallelism (see Barclay, 61-64). The "observing" might be "studying" such times (as the inclusion of "years" might suggest) rather than "performing" them; and it is clear that astrology was widely pervasive and deeply influential in Greco-Roman (and Jewish) daily life (see Worship). The "elements"* are likely to be either those of earth, air, fire and water (as generally in ancient cosmology) or the heavenly bodies (which controlled fate in ancient astrology). Either way they are closely linked to the sun, moon and seasons. But without some form of "performance" it is hard to see how the matter could have become a specific point of contention; and it may be that, in the context of the other issues in Galatians, such calendrical observation were viewed, at least by Paul's opponents,* as part of the core of the covenant with Israel, or of the self-identity of God's people. In either case Paul views it as a self-submission to the elements which is in direct opposition to the Christian's subjection to Christ.

*3.3. Colossians 2:16.* The overall tone of Colossians* is more eirenic than that of Galatians. Any theological dangers facing the church are potential, not actual. But Christian freedom is reiterated, here freedom from what is obscurely described as a "written document of decrees which was against us" (Col 2:14) and from the "principalities and powers." The switch from "you" to "us" (presumably, "us Jews") suggests that the Law* is again in view. Its calendrical observance is characterized as mere shadow (*skia*) in contrast with the reality (*sōma*), which is Christ, but it is not stated that the two are mutually exclusive. The "judgment" seems to be criticism of the Christians' present practice, apparently of eating and drinking and enjoying Jewish festivals, in contrast to those whose watchword was "do not handle, do not taste, do not even touch" (Col 2:21). It does not however come from an authority figure imposing on them some alternative as a *sine qua non* of Christian life (cf. Rom 14:3). Here then the choice is not set up as one between following Christ and being subject to the world elements (cf. the *hōs* of Col 2:20), and so the issue is treated as one of many *adiaphora* ("matters of indifference").

*3.4. Romans 14:5.* The extent of the oddity of Paul's puzzling introduction of the problem of "days" is rarely noted by commentators. Romans 14:5 breaks the flow of thought despite the fact that it is introduced by a logical connective (*gar*, "for"). Having introduced the issue, Paul fails to tackle it at all, and his general solution ("Let everyone be convinced in his own mind") fails to help a *community* to solve the problem of calendrical observance. The most plausible solution to this problem is to suppose that the calendrical issue was already resolved in Rome (see de Lacey). Paul is referring back to the solution of another bone of contention in order to develop a parallel for the foods problem. If so, then probably all calendrical issues had been tackled, but the parallelism in Romans 14:2, 5 and 6 suggests that it was primarily the "strong"* who observed the days, in which case they would be more likely to be festivals than fasts (though Michel assumes a deliberate chiasmus here to argue the opposite case). It is likely that specifically Jewish festivals would have been more contentious than fasts.

***3.5. 1 Corinthians 16:2.*** Paul's sole reference to the first day of the week occurs in the context of his discussion of the collection.* Scholarly speculation has claimed that this implies regular Christian meetings on Sunday (see Rordorf, 193-95) or on Saturday (Bacchiocchi 90-101), but the context has little to do with church assemblies. What is called for is the private budgeting of an individual. There is no evidence to support Deissmann's suggestion that Sunday was payday; we know only of daily (cf. Mt 20), monthly or annual settlement. It is therefore reasonable to suppose that Paul's advice presupposes some weekly pattern of Christian devotion, but there is no way for us to tell what it was. Bacchiocchi claims that Jews would do no financial transactions on Sabbath; on the assumption that Paul was a strict sabbatarian, Sunday was the first day on which this budgeting could be done. But if Paul sees only the Noachide commandments as relevant (*see* Gentiles) this suggestion becomes less plausible. Little therefore can be deduced from the Pauline corpus about the calendrical observances of his churches.

*See also* LORD'S SUPPER; LOVE FEAST; WORKS OF THE LAW; WORSHIP.

BIBLIOGRAPHY. S. Bacchiocchi, *From Sabbath to Sunday: A Historical Investigation of the Rise of Sunday Observance in Early Christianity* (Rome: Pontifical Gregorian University, 1977); J. M. G. Barclay, *Obeying the Truth: A Study of Paul's Ethics in Galatians* (Minneapolis: Fortress, 1991); D. R. de Lacey, "The Sabbath/Sunday Question and the Law in the Pauline Corpus," in *From Sabbath to Lord's Day*, ed. D. A. Carson (Grand Rapids: Zondervan, 1982) 159-95; J. C. Greenfield and M. Sokoloff, "Astrological and Related Omen Texts in Jewish Palestinian Aramaic," *JNES* 48 (1989) 201-14; O. Michel, *Der Brief an der Römer* (KEK; Göttingen: Vandenhoeck & Ruprecht, 1978); W. Rordorf, *Sunday* (London: SCM, 1968); E. Schürer, *A History of the Jewish People in the Age of Jesus Christ (175 B.C.-A.D. 135)*, rev. and ed. G. Vermes and F. Millar (3 vols.; Edinburgh: T. & T. Clark, 1973-87); E. Schweizer, "Slaves of the Elements and Worshipers of Angels: Gal 4:3, 9 and Col 2:8, 18, 20," *JBL* 107 (1988) 455-68; M. M. B. Turner, "The Sabbath, Sunday, and the Law in Luke-Acts," in *From Sabbath to Lord's Day*, ed. D. A. Carson (Grand Rapids: Zondervan, 1982) 99-157.

D. R. de Lacey

# HOLY SPIRIT

1. The Sources of Paul's Concept of the Spirit
2. The Spirit of God
3. The Spirit and Wisdom
4. The Spirit as Divine Power
5. The Spirit of Christ
6. The Spirit and Mission
7. The Spirit and the Christian's New Life
8. The Spirit and Eschatology
9. The Spirit and Worship

### 1. The Sources of Paul's Concept of the Spirit.

Paul's concept of the Spirit has three main sources: the revelation in the OT canon, intertestamental Judaism and early Christian thought. In addition, Paul's own experience (and that of the Christian communities he founded) no doubt played an important role in his thinking. It must be admitted that only three times in the OT (MT: Is 63:10-11; Ps 51:1) is the Spirit of God called "holy," but this designation became more common in the intertestamental period. The OT roots are evident in the fact that for Paul the Spirit is singular and unique. To speak of the Spirit is to speak of God's presence and power (Is 31:3; 34:16; 40:13). As God is one, so there is only one Spirit of God (1 Cor 12:4-6, 11, 13; Eph 4:4-6). However the term *spirit* (Heb *rûaḥ*, Gk *pneuma*) is increasingly used in later Jewish writing for angels* or demons* (usually in the plural) at Qumran, in rabbinic and apocalyptic* literature (Sekki, chap. 5; Schweizer, *TDNT* VI.375-76). The Spirit is associated from an early time forward with prophecy (Num 11:29; 1 Sam 10:6; 19:20-24; Mic 3:8; Ezek 11:5; Joel 2:28-29; *Sir* 48:12, 24; cf. 1 Thess 5:19-20; 1 Cor 12:7- 11). And, especially in the prophets, the Spirit has a moral character, being associated with justice, judgment and living in covenant (Is 4:4; 28:5-6; 59:21; 63:10; Ezek 36:26-27; 39:27-29; Ps 51:10-11; 143:10). The OT holds out a hope that this Spirit, as the power of prophecy, life and covenant keeping, will be a feature of the future messianic age of blessing (Is 32:15; 44:3; Ezek 36:25-27; 39:28-29; Joel 2:28-29), and this hope persisted into the Second Temple period (*Pss. Sol.* 17:37; 18:7; *T. Levi* 18:7; *T. Judah* 24:2). The Qumran* sectarians apparently believed themselves heirs in some sense of this promise of the

Spirit (Sekki, 79-84). This prophetic promise underlies Paul's view of the Spirit as a normal part of the Christian life.

The association of the Spirit with God's wisdom (cf. 1 Cor 2:10-11) is a thought found a few times in the OT (Ex 31:3; 35:31; Num 11:16-17; Job 32:8; Is 11:2; 42:1-4) and developed further in later Judaism (Wis 7:22-8:1; 1QH 9; 12:11-12, 31-35; in Philo the divine *pneuma* is the source of reason and wisdom in mortals, *Leg. All.* 1.42; *Gig.* 22-24, 27). Two other ideas that Paul inherits from his background, though they are not unique to Hebrew thought, are the association of Spirit with power (2 Kings 2:9-15; Judg 6:34-35; 14:19; 15:14-15) and with life, as the life-giving force that originates with God (Gen 1:2; 6:3; Ps 104:29-30; Job 32:8; Is 42:5; Ezek 37:4-14; on the Spirit in the OT and Judaism see *TDNT* VI.362-63, 365-67, 368-89).

Paul's concept of the Spirit is not, however, simply a continuation of the OT/Jewish viewpoint. For one thing the Spirit has a prominence in Paul's writings which far exceeds its place in the OT. In relative numeric terms, *rûah* refers to the Spirit of God an estimated 90 times in the MT, and *pneuma* does so 100 times in the LXX (Gächter). In contrast *pneuma* refers to God's Spirit 112 to 115 times (depending on the exegesis of some passages) in the much smaller corpus of Pauline letters.

The increased importance of the Spirit in Paul may be explained on the basis of the early Christian communities' experience of the Spirit in their midst (including Paul's own experience), in the perception of God's immanence during worship,* in the working of miracles (*see* Signs) and the inspiration of prophecy,* in the experience of boldness and wisdom to proclaim the gospel even through difficult circumstances, and in the feelings of joy.* These experiences for the early Christians were evidence of the Spirit present and acting. And they understood their experience as the fulfillment of prophetic hopes that in the age of the Messiah, the Spirit would fall on "Israel" (Ezek 36:25-27; Joel 2:28-32; Paul cites from the latter passage in Rom 10:13). Paul shows awareness of this OT eschatological* hope* in referring to the "promise of the Spirit" (Gal 3:14; cf. Eph 1:13). The coming of the Spirit was also a sign for the early Christians that the risen Lord, Jesus, was indeed the Messiah (cf. Acts 2:14-24, 36, 38-39; Jn 16:7-11; see 5 below).

In contrast to much Hellenistic thought, Paul does not see the Spirit as a force or a being at the beck and call of the believer. Unlike "demons" or the magician's helping spirits, the Holy Spirit cannot be controlled by special incantations or actions. He is, however, present to aid the believer in living out God's

will. And while in ancient magic* supernatural aid was only believed to be available to the few with esoteric knowledge (regardless of their motives), the Spirit is given freely to all, on the sole condition of faith in Christ as Lord* (1 Cor 12:3).

### 2. The Spirit of God.

An obvious but important fact is that Paul assumes the Holy Spirit is God's Spirit (*see* God). That is, it is not merely one of a host of intermediaries, but in accord with the OT and intertestamental Jewish literature it is assumed that the Spirit is singular, unique in power and in its relationship to God (e.g., 1 Cor 2:11; Rom 8:9, 11; 2 Cor 3:17; cf. Eph 4:4). Paul always speaks of the Spirit which is given to Christians in the singular: the Holy Spirit or Spirit of God (cf. Rom 8:9; 1 Cor 3:17; 12:4-6; 2 Cor 5:5; Gal 3:5). This singularity of the Spirit can be used as a theological argument for the unity of the church: "we were all baptized* by one Spirit into one body . . . we were all given the one Spirit to drink" (1 Cor 12:13). Paul never speaks of God giving spirits (plural) to believers (1 Cor 14:12 is best taken as Paul's quoting a Corinthian saying, "[we are] zealots for spirits," without endorsing the viewpoint it implies). The Spirit represents God as present among his people—in Paul often in connection with inspired speech (particularly proclaiming the gospel, but also prophecy, encouragement, exhortation, teaching) and with miracles (1 Cor 12:4-11; 1 Thess 1:5; Gal 3:1-5).

Paul never addresses directly the issue of the personality of the Holy Spirit. At times the Spirit and God may overlap, having seemingly identical functions (as in the distribution of spiritual gifts* to different "parts" of the body of Christ, 1 Cor 12:11, 18, 26). At times the Spirit is spoken of as distinct from both God and Christ, as in the triadic formula of 1 Corinthians 12:4-6 or the blessing of 2 Corinthians 13:13 (14), or when God is said to send the Spirit or to seal believers by means of the Spirit (Gal 4:6; 2 Cor 1:21-22; 5:5; Rom 5:5). The Spirit may be described with personal characteristics. He may "lead" believers (Gal 5:18; Rom 8:14; cf. 8:4), "reveal" the mystery* of the gospel* and its implications (1 Cor 2:6-16; Eph 3:5) or help believers in prayer* (Gal 4:6; Rom 8:15, 26-27; cf. 1 Cor 14:14-16). The Spirit has its "desires" (though the "flesh"* does also, without the "flesh" necessarily being a personal force: Gal 5:16-17); and in Ephesians may be "grieved" (4:30). None of these remarks are intended by Paul as comment directly on the personhood of the Spirit, but are incidental to Paul's main point, which is usually more pragmatic than speculative. Some scholars think these remarks no more point to personhood than do remarks which seem to personalize the power of sin or of the flesh. Certainly Paul does not work with definitions of divine "persons" such as arose in later Christian theology. Nevertheless it seems that the seeds of such thought are present here. Whether or not Paul asserts the personhood of the Spirit, he is eager that his churches know what sort of personality the Spirit has: he has the character of God, and more precisely, of Jesus Christ (see 5 below).

### 3. The Spirit and Wisdom.

The Spirit is the only means by which God's wisdom may be communicated to humans, for only the Spirit knows God's mind (1 Cor 2:10-16). Paul denies that any sort of "wisdom"* originating from below, from the side of humanity, may comprehend God and his workings. In 1 Corinthians 1:18—2:16 Paul attacks attempts by Corinthian Christians to "correct" the gospel by revising it in the light of contemporary intellectual currents (whether Jewish or Greco-Roman)—specifically by denigrating the role of Jesus' death* on the cross.* In this passage Paul makes a very important link between the Spirit, the cross and wisdom. The gospel foundations cannot be altered, for not only are human intellectual systems "foolish"* in God's sight (1 Cor 1:18-25); the problem is even more radical. God's working remains mysterious, incomprehensible to the unredeemed, who reject it (1 Cor 2:6-8, 14).

It is precisely the crucified Savior who is the content of God's mysterious wisdom, a wisdom that cannot be grasped apart from the Spirit (1 Cor 1:23-24; 2:2, 6-12). So the Spirit remains as the only possible bridge to knowing God and to accepting the gospel. Those who try to tamper with the role of the cross (or the foundational elements of the gospel) only demonstrate that they are actually people without the Spirit, "carnal" (1 Cor 2:14; 3:1). This last remark is addressed to those at Corinth who regarded themselves as "the spiritual ones," and who were attempting to revise the apostolic message. When seen in its historical and literary context, this passage has continuing relevance for the church, which in every age is faced with demands by the dominant intellectual/religious forces to modify some aspect of the gospel core. 1 Corinthians 2:6-16 is not an announcement of mystical knowledge for a Christian elite; it is a defense of the apostolic gospel as most truly "spiritual," and the Spirit as the one who communicates and expounds it.

### 4. The Spirit as Divine Power.

Paul inherits from the OT and intertestamental Juda-

ism the concept of the Spirit as the power* of God (see 1 above). He attributes his evangelistic success to the Spirit's effective presence, and suggests more than once that miracles attended his own preaching,* though he does not enumerate these (1 Thess 1:4-6; 1 Cor 2:4-5; Rom 15:18-19; Gal 3:2). He expects that at Christian meetings the Spirit will inspire not only the spoken word but "supernatural" skills and events as well (1 Cor 12:7-11; 14; Gal 3:5). Naturally this is only one facet of Paul's understanding of the Spirit and must not be taken in isolation. Never does Paul invoke the Spirit's work merely to impress or entertain. Most of the Pauline passages speaking of the Spirit's power relate it directly to the purpose of evangelism or to living the new life in Christ (on evangelism see 6 below; on the Christian life see 7 below). Other references include the Spirit's power in worship—again, not simply as display but as the power to inform and "build up" Christians (1 Cor 12:7; cf. 14:5, 19, 26), or to discipline* and punish (cf. 1 Cor 5:3-5).

That the reception of the Spirit by believers is sometimes described with terms such as "fill" or "pour out (on)" has led several to claim that the Spirit was conceived by Paul and the earliest Christians as a fluid that physically fills the believer (e.g., Hunter 92), though in the Pauline corpus "fill" is only one image of many, and it occurs just three times (1 Cor 12:13; Eph 5:18; Tit 3:4-5). Such language is evoked in part by purposefully echoing Septuagintal usage, and is best understood as metaphor (cf. Joel 2:28-29, "pour out" the Spirit, echoed at Acts 2:33; and Mic 3:8, "I am filled with power, with the Spirit of the Lord").

In Ephesians the only explicit connection between Spirit and power has been internalized: it is for the "inner self" (see Psychology), and is associated with the indwelling of Christ by faith (Eph 3:16-17). Elsewhere in Ephesians the author speaks of God's power (= the Spirit?) as the instrument of Christ's resurrection* (Eph 1:19-20). Similarly at 2 Timothy 1:7 the Spirit given to Timothy is to be the foundation for a divinely inspired boldness concerning both the gospel and his association with the imprisoned Paul ("therefore do not be ashamed of the testimony about our Lord, nor of me his prisoner," 2 Tim 1:8), as well as the source of divine power to "suffer together (with Paul or with Christ?) for the gospel" (2 Tim 1:8). These functions are reminiscent of the role of the Spirit in the proclamation of the gospel (see 6 below).

### 5. The Spirit of Christ.

The Spirit has the character of Christ. One notable aspect of Paul's teaching on the Spirit which distinguishes it from Israelite and Jewish faith is the intimate association of the Spirit with the risen Lord Jesus, the "Jesus character" of the Spirit (Hermann, 59-66; Dunn 1975, 318-26). Hence it is called the "Spirit of Christ" or the "Spirit of God's Son" (Rom 8:9; Gal 4:6). The Spirit transforms believers from the heart outward to have the character of their Lord Jesus Christ (2 Cor 3:3, 18; Eph 3:16-17). And to be in the fellowship of God's Son, Jesus Christ (1 Cor 1:9), is the same as having fellowship in the Holy Spirit (2 Cor 13:13 [14]; Phil 2:1; see Christology).

**5.1. Spirit of Christ and the Cross.** Because the Spirit is Christ's, he is associated not only with power and blessing, but with the cross of Christ (1 Cor 2:1-16; see 4 above), with lowliness and service to others in line with the character of the master (1 Cor 12—13; see Cross, Theology of the). The Corinthians have to be taught that to be a spiritual person may mean not glory,* but weakness* and suffering* (e.g., 2 Cor 4:7-18 with 3:7-8; 11:16—12:10). Jesus' earthly life is a pattern for the Spirit's working in believers: "For in fact (Christ) was crucified in weakness, but lives by God's power; and indeed we are weak in him, but we will live with him by God's power for your benefit" (2 Cor 13:4). In this verse God's power is tantamount to the Spirit of Christ. This Jesus-character of the Spirit explains why the supreme sign of the Spirit's presence, the principal element of the "fruit of the Spirit" (Gal 5:22), is love. God's greatest act of love was shown to creation in Christ's death for its redemption; and this love is "poured out" into believers' hearts by the presence of the Spirit (Rom 5:5-8).

**5.2. The Spirit of Christ Relating to the Church.** Since his resurrection and ascension Jesus now relates to his church and to the world via the Spirit (see Eschatology). Christ can only be experienced (in this time before his return) through the Spirit. The Spirit marks Christians as members of Christ's body (1 Cor 6:15-20; 12:12-13; see Body of Christ); he signifies that believers do not belong to themselves, but to the Lord who purchased them. Christ, as the church's Lord, leads it by means of the Spirit in prophecy, in the teaching and leadership gifts, or by other means. The Spirit's opposition to the flesh may be seen as one way the Spirit presents Christ's will to the individual. The link between Jesus and the Spirit is so intimate that for Paul it was impossible to have one without the other: "If anyone does not have the Spirit of Christ, that person does not belong to him" (Rom 8:9; cf. 1 Cor 12:12-13). All who have faith* in Christ are on the basis of that faith assured of the eschatological gift of the Spirit (Rom 8:1-2, 9; Gal 3:1-2, 5; cf. Eph 1:13-14; 4:30; and Acts 2:33, 38-39). Hence to be a Christian is to be truly a "spiritual person" (pneumatikos, 1 Cor

2:10-16), indwelt by the Spirit (see Spirituality).

"The first Adam became a living soul; the last Adam became a life-giving Spirit" (1 Cor 15:45) is not meant to be a simple identification of Christ with the Spirit; the point of the saying in the context of the discussion of resurrection is not christological but soteriological (Fee). Adam had life for himself as God's gift; but Christ is able to give life to others (the life of resurrection, of the age to come). And he is able to do this via the Spirit, with whom he is in some sense one (2 Cor 3:17; see Adam and Christ).

In light of the above, it is to be expected that the Spirit is known by the fact that he will promote the confession of Jesus as Lord* (1 Cor 12:3). Anything contrary to that confession cannot be from the Spirit. This is the measure of the authenticity of any manifestation of the Spirit, taking precedence over ecstasy, glossolalia or any other supposed sign (see Visions, Ecstatic Experience).

**5.3. Distinctions between the Spirit and Christ.** At times the Spirit and Christ (as with the Spirit and God) seem to overlap or even become completely interchangeable, as in Romans 8:9-11, where "the Spirit of God," "the Spirit of Christ" and "Christ in you" all refer to the same reality (on 1 Corinthians 15:45 see 5.2 above). Christians may be said to be "in the Spirit" (Rom 8:9; Gal 5:25; cf. Gal 5:16; 1 Cor 12:3) or to have the Spirit in them (Rom 8:11; 1 Cor 3:16; 6:19; Gal 4:6), just as they may be "in Christ"* (2 Cor 5:17) or have Christ in them (Gal 2:20). 2 Corinthians 3:17 should not be taken as evidence for the identity of Jesus and the Spirit ("The Lord is the Spirit; and where the Spirit of the Lord is, there is freedom"). The first occurrence of "Lord" in that passage refers to the wording of Exodus 34:34 LXX (2 Cor 3:16), meaning that when those in this age "turn to the Lord (i.e., God)" as Moses* did at Sinai, a veil of spiritual blindness is lifted from their eyes; only now "Lord" signifies "the Spirit" who is the key to knowledge of God. This is Paul's interpretation of the OT passage's meaning which he applies to his conflict with Jews and Jewish Christians. The next verse must also be understood in this context: it is the work of "the Lord who is the Spirit" to transform believers into the image of Christ, the Last Adam, the pattern of a new humanity (2 Cor 3:18).

In the expression "Spirit of Christ" we cannot take the genitive "of" as simply an equal sign (i.e., an epexegetical genitive phrase, meaning "the Spirit which = Christ"). Paul can clearly distinguish the two: only Jesus is described as the Father's Son* (Rom 1:3; Gal 4:4); only he had a human nature (Rom 1:3; 8:3; Gal 4:4; Phil 2:7); only Jesus Christ died "for our sins"

(1 Cor 15:3; cf. Rom 5:8; 2 Cor 5:15), was raised and is said to be seated at God's right hand (Col 3:3; cf. Phil 2:9). Never are these said of the Spirit. In none of his extant letters does Paul spell out in detail how the Spirit and Christ are related, but a few clues to his thinking may be present:

(1) The Spirit comes only as a result of faith in Christ, and is not otherwise a possession of humanity in general (Gal 3:1-2).

(2) The Spirit is known by the fact that he will promote the confession of Jesus as Lord in the church (1 Cor 12:3), and that he bears witness to the character of and the truth about Jesus (1 Thess 1:6 with 1:8; 4:7-8). The Spirit is recognized because he manifests the character of Christ in himself and in those in whom he dwells.

(3) The Spirit brings to believers in a personal or existential way the reality of their new relation to God as children (*huioi*), a reality which has been accomplished for them by Christ. "God sent his Son . . . to redeem those under Law, so that we might receive adoption as children [*see* Adoption, Sonship]. Because you are children, God sent the Spirit of his Son into our hearts crying 'Abba, Father!' " (Gal 4:4-6; cf. Rom 8:14-16).

(4) The coming of the Spirit for the church is a divine work that is historically subsequent to the work of Christ (Gal 4:4-6) and may be seen as dependent upon what he accomplished.

(5) The Spirit binds all believers to Christ: they are "one Spirit" with him (1 Cor 6:17) and have been baptized* in (or by) the Spirit into the body of Christ, where they serve in the power of the Spirit and at his direction (1 Cor 12:4-13).

(6) On the basis of the 1 Corinthians 12, we see the Spirit as empowering, organizing and directing Christian worship and Christian community; and this direction carries equal authority to that of God (1 Cor 12:11 with 18, 28) or Christ (by implication, since the "body" in which believers serve is Christ's). The functions of the Spirit in relation to Christ may in many ways be said to be analogous to Jesus' relationship to the Father as depicted in the Synoptics. The two may have identical functions, yet are distinct. The Spirit, to use John's phrase, glorifies Christ (Jn 16:12-14; cf. 1 Cor 12:3), just as the earthly Jesus glorified the Father. The Spirit conveys the "mind of Christ" to believers; he communicates the will and direction of their Lord, and an understanding of his gospel. The Spirit's work and the Spirit's coming to believers is dependent on the Son, and ultimately on the Father. Yet the Spirit is not thought of as a lesser emissary, like one of the angels; he is in a real sense the presence of Christ with believers.

The Spirit has a very important place in Paul's theology because it makes possible the uniting of the historical Jesus, who was raised from the dead, with the heavenly Lord, who is at the same time present with his people. The corporeality of a risen Jesus could be potentially troubling in two ways: (1) it might seem to give Jesus a corruptible nature (because he shared in material existence); and just as serious, (2) it might make Jesus a distant figure, exalted* into heaven but separated from the feelings and needs of his people on earth. Paul avoids these pitfalls, preserving Jesus' exalted nature in a new body,* and at the same time his immanent presence with the faithful in the Spirit ("spiritual body," 1 Cor 15:44, does not mean "a body made of spirit" or bodiless existence; rather, it indicates a body fit for the existence of resurrection life—simultaneously corporeal and "spiritual"). To use a modern analogy, the Spirit might be compared to the lines connecting our homes to electricity or to telecommunication networks. These make possible the presence in our homes of power or of communication with other people, without actually having those people or the electricity plant physically present.

Some scholars believe Paul was the first Christian to link Jesus and the Spirit in this way. Although this is especially peculiar to Paul, there is evidence that he developed themes or linkages already present in early Christianity. For instance, in Acts receiving the Spirit is linked with faith in the risen Christ and confession of him as Lord (2:38; 4:29-31; 11:17; cf. Hunter, 95; Goppelt, 1.249), not to mention the gospel traditions about Jesus as the one who would baptize with the Holy Spirit (Mk 1:8 and par.). It is also notable that there is no evidence that any Palestinian or Jewish Christians ever opposed Paul's linking of Spirit and Christ in this fashion, though there was plenty of controversy on other points (one exception may be 2 Cor 11:4, which has the expression "different spirit/Spirit"; see commentaries). This implies that Paul's stance was in harmony with early Palestinian Christianity, even if Paul developed and expanded its less articulated ideas.

### 6. The Spirit and Mission.

As the Spirit of Christ, the Holy Spirit has an intimate connection with the gospel message. The Spirit empowers and impels the Christian mission.* This is vividly portrayed in Acts, where the coming of the Spirit is associated with the beginning of the post-Easter proclamation of the gospel (Acts 2), with its infusion of power (Acts 4:8, 31; 6:10; 8:29; 10:44), and with the directing of Peter, Paul and Barnabas at key points (Acts 10:19-20; 11:12; 13:2-5; 16:6-10). Paul himself writes to the church at Rome that he has been enabled to lead Gentiles* to God "by what I have said and done—by the power of signs and miracles, through the power of the Spirit" (Rom 15:18-19 NIV). He can refer to the apostolic task as a "ministry of the Spirit" (2 Cor 3:8), no small part of which was evangelism. The Spirit accompanied his initial missionary preaching (1) by confirming the truth of the message in his hearers' hearts; (2) by empowering Paul to effect "signs* and wonders" (Rom 15:18-19; cf. 2 Cor 12:12, which may, however, be a Corinthian expression; see commentaries); (3) by filling new believers in such a way that the Spirit's presence was unmistakable. In three of his letters, all to different communities, he reminds the readers of their initial vivid experience of the Spirit in the context of hearing the gospel and conversion (1 Thess 1:4-6; Gal 3:1-3; 1 Cor 2:4-5). Paul assumes such initial encounters with the Spirit serve to confirm the reality of his readers' conversion and the validity of his gospel, as being truly from God. The Spirit gives believers in turn boldness and wisdom to testify about Jesus (cf. 1 Thess 2:2 with 1:5-6).

## 7. The Spirit and the Christian's New Life.

Paul more than any other NT writer links the concept of the Spirit given to indwell believers with living the Christian life. The Spirit is not only the power of God convincing believers of the truth of the gospel, not only promoting its preaching, but the Spirit is the power of new creation to those who have come to faith in Christ (see Creation and New Creation). Christians who were formerly alienated from God have not simply been entered into the heavenly register of the redeemed; the Spirit indwells them and empowers them to live a life pleasing to God (Rom 8:1-4; 12:1; 1 Thess 4:1; to the Lord, 2 Cor 5:9; Eph 5:10). This life is described as being "led by the Spirit" (Rom 8:14) or "walking in the Spirit" (Rom 8:4; Gal 5:16, 25).

*7.1. Flesh and Spirit.* The opposite of walking in the Spirit is to be "in the flesh," and "flesh"* is often contrasted with "Spirit" in Paul. Flesh represents the self in its fallenness; the egotism, self-assertion, willful ignorance of God's will or the outright defying of that will. Such defiance characterizes humanity in Adam, under the old aeon. The Spirit is utterly opposed to the principles of flesh and sin, "for the flesh's way of thinking is death; but the Spirit's way of thinking is life and peace" (Rom 8:6). The Spirit within believers breaks the power of sin so that the Christian may be said to fulfill the Law* (Rom 8:1-4, 12-15).

Just how pervasive the new dominion of the Spirit is in believers, according to Paul, and how far Paul

expected the Spirit-led freedom* from the dominion of sin* and the flesh to be complete, is a matter of scholarly debate. A large part of the debate concerns the meaning of Romans 7 in the context of that letter. Calvin and several modern exegetes (Cranfield, Dunn) understand Romans 7:14-25 as referring to the experience of a believer, and hence modifying the seemingly absolute statements of freedom from the power of the flesh in Romans 8:1-11. The Christian, though redeemed, may still be described as "fleshly," "sold under sin" and helplessly subject to its power until the resurrection. Some would see Romans 7:14-25, along with Romans 7:7-13, as referring to life prior to conversion, with the inevitable victory of sin broken and deliverance shown in Romans 8. Others see Romans 7:14-25 as the experience of a convert who attempts to fight sin by personal willpower, a believer who is spiritually immature and needs to be pointed to the power of the Spirit (Rom 8) that is necessary to triumph over sin (Bruce, 193-98).

Whether Romans 7 is seen as referring to pre- or post-conversion, there is abundant evidence elsewhere in Paul of his awareness that believers can and do sin. This is presupposed by his many warnings against falling into sin and his exhortations to chose the path of life in the Spirit (Rom 8:12-14, a warning and implied imperative; 1 Cor 6:18- 20; Gal 5:16-26; cf. Rom 6:12-16; 1 Cor 5:9-13; 10:11-13, 14, 18-22, 31; and especially 2 Cor 12:21). Though Paul may express surprise and condemnation when members of his churches persist in sinful behavior (1 Cor 5:1-6, 11-12; cf. Rom 6:1-2, 11-12; Gal 6:7-10; Col 2:20-23), he is ready, nevertheless, to admonish those who are "spiritual" (*hoi pneumatikoi*) to deal pastorally and meekly with Christians who do sin (Gal 6:1-2).

Because of humanity's corporate participation in the fallen Adamic nature, the believer's present existence is one of struggle in a life lived in the era between two aeons. The pull of the old nature does not let up, even though the redeemed now belong to the future age, to the new humanity in Christ. "We also, who possess the Spirit as a firstfruits, groan within ourselves as we eagerly expect our adoption, the redemption of our body" (Rom 8:23). Christ's redemption will therefore eventually extend to the complete renewal even of the physical self, when at the parousia Christians are raised from the dead and receive "spiritual bodies" (1 Cor 15:42-54; 2 Cor 5:1-5; *see* Eschatology).

On the other hand, we should take seriously Paul's assumption in Romans 8 that such a choosing of the path of life, to walk in the Spirit and please the Lord, is really possible in the present time. The Spirit provides new possibilities for humanity, and the Spirit's powerful presence characterizes the new existence which is the "indicative" (or statement of a factual condition) upon which the ethical "imperative" is grounded. This is not simply an objective, legal matter to be believed; Paul expected this living in the Spirit to affect their lives in the world in a concrete fashion. "I tell you, live by the Spirit and you will certainly not accomplish the desire of the flesh" (Gal 5:16; cf. 1 Thess 1:4-10; 4:3-8; Rom 8:4, 12-17; see Ethics).

This being-in-the-Spirit expresses itself by the "fruit"* of the Spirit: love, joy, peace, etc. (Gal 5:22-23). The image of fruit accords with the gracious character of the new possibility given by God, like the fruits of the earth which grow by his creative sustaining power. And in Galatians 5:22-23 this fruit is explicitly contrasted with "works of the flesh." If any proof of the Spirit's working and a believer's maturing is to be looked for on the basis of Scripture, surely it is to be found in the fruit of the Spirit, which displays the character of Christ being formed in a person. In 1 Corinthians 13 Paul criticizes the idea that any spiritual manifestation is of value apart from that most important token of the Spirit of Christ, love.*

*7.2. Spirit and Law.* As the Spirit is opposed to the power of flesh, so we find Spirit and Law opposed in several places in Paul (see Law). This is primarily because the Law (i.e., Jewish Torah), though given by God, has become sidetracked by sin and the flesh, so that even Law-keeping can become another sinful enterprise whereby humans idolize their own efforts and keep the living God at bay; or alternatively, attempt to put God under obligation. The Law cannot be kept fully by unregenerate humans, for it is impossible for them to overcome the power of sin. When the Spirit enters in, he begins a transformation into the new humanity which is epitomized by Christ. The Spirit places believers in the position of fulfilling "the righteous requirement of the law" (Rom 8:4) because by his assistance they are able to carry out the original intent of the Law: to love and obey the heavenly Father (cf. Mt 5:48; 22:34-40).

A key function of the Spirit is its power to make the saving events of Jesus' life-death-resurrection present in an effective way for the believer (Wendland, 151, 136-37). The Spirit "presents" the Son to believers: "the one joined to the Lord is one Spirit with him" (1 Cor 6:17). God's sending the Spirit depends on, and makes real to believers, the sending of the Son (Gal 4:4-7). A similar connection may be observed in the prayer in Ephesians: "I pray to the Father . . . that he may cause you to be strengthened with power . . . by his Spirit in the inner person, so that Christ may dwell

in your hearts through faith" (Eph 3:14-17). Related to this function of making Christ and his benefits present to believers, Paul's understanding of the Spirit is continuous with his understanding of justification.* The placement of Romans 8 in the letter's overall structure, as well as the argument of the chapter itself (cf. Rom 5:1-5 with 8:1-4), confirms this. There is no doctrine of Christ without justification or without the Spirit; and no justification without Christ and the Spirit.

Why the ethical quality of Spirit? For Paul this ethical nature of the Spirit, and of his effect on the believer, originates from two main sources. The first is that, like the classical Israelite prophets, Paul sees the Spirit as having the ethical character of God (see 1 above), which he expresses in the appellative "holy."

Paul argues in 1 Thessalonians 4:7-8 that whoever rejects the new lifestyle that is consecrated to God (1 Thess 4:3, 7) is really rejecting "God who also gives his Holy Spirit to you" (1 Thess 4:8). The argument uses the fact that the Spirit is known as the Holy Spirit, supposing that therefore those in whom the Spirit dwells should be characterized by ethical purity.* Similarly in 1 Corinthians 6:19-20, while showing the Corinthians why it is wrong and inconsistent for a Christian to use prostitutes, Paul musters the argument that "your body is a temple* of the Holy Spirit within you, whom you have (received) from God."

A second reason for Paul's emphasis on the ethical nature of the Spirit is the fact that it is the Spirit of Christ. As mediator of the presence of Christ to the Christian, the Spirit promotes desires, attitudes and behavior which are in line with the person and teaching of Christ. He is at work creating the new nature of which Christ is the archetype, and which believers will possess in its perfect form in the age to come (2 Cor 3:17-18).

*7.3. The Spirit and the Church as Body of Christ.* A person does not simply receive the Spirit as an individual. To claim Christ as Lord entails being "baptized by one Spirit into one body" (1 Cor 12:13; see Body of Christ). It means a calling into a corporate existence, becoming part of a new social network directed by the Spirit. Therefore the changes which the Spirit brings about, and the spiritual gifts which he supplies to the individual, are not for self-improvement only; believers are to use these for the benefit of their fellow Christians (1 Cor 12:7; 14:5, 26). The Spirit is the unifying and creative force which brings about Christian community, expressed in the term *koinōnia*, which points both toward a mutual sharing in the Spirit ("participation in" the Spirit) and a fellowship (i.e., community) created by the Spirit (2 Cor 13:13 [14]; see Fellowship). Within this new fellowship the Spirit brings different gifts to different people, who are intended to come together and work with one another, like the diverse parts of a natural body, so forming Christ's body on earth to serve the Lord (1 Cor 12:4-31).

### 8. The Spirit and Eschatology.

Paul regards the Spirit given to believers as an eschatological* sign signifying that God's promised salvation* and restoration* of his people has already begun. Wendland speaks of "the thoroughly eschatological character of the *pneuma*" for Paul (Wendland, 134). This eschatological viewpoint has some precursors in the OT and rabbinic hope for the general giving of the Spirit in the future age, and also in perspectives of the Qumran* literature (Sekki, 82-83). The difference for Paul is that the Spirit represents the inbreaking of the end time in the present.

An eschatological note is sounded in the idea of the Spirit as "first fruits"* and as the "down payment" (*arrabōn*) for believers of what they will receive when the messianic kingdom* has fully arrived, judgment* is past and every enemy* of God is defeated (Rom 8:18-25; 2 Cor 1:22; 5:5; Eph 1:13-14; 4:30; *see* Triumph). Thus in the present the Spirit is simultaneously a portion of the life and power of the future age, and a sign pointing beyond the present, telling believers that the fullness of the messianic age has not yet arrived. "The creation waits in eager expectation for the children of God to be revealed . . . but also we who have the first fruits of the Spirit groan inwardly too, while we eagerly await (our) adoption, the redemption of our bodies" (Rom 8:19, 23). Throughout his letters Paul maintains this tension in his view of the Spirit: it is not itself the fullness of the kingdom of God, yet it is a foretaste of future "glory,"* continually pointing forward to the eschatological redemption of the body (Beker, 281-83). The Spirit is himself an in-breaking of the powers of the age to come and a guarantee of the reality of that age together with the believer's part in it.

This linking of the power and presence of the Spirit with the future age is also manifest in the hope and joy that the Spirit inspires in believers (Gal 5:22; Rom 15:13). This hope is a confidence that believers will not be disappointed, that the down payment of the Spirit will indeed be one day confirmed by participation in God's glory and in the renewal of their entire existence alongside the renewal of all creation (Rom 5:2, 5; 8:23-25). Hence a "hope" that has reference only to this present existence is a cruel joke which ends in meaningless existence (1 Cor 15:19).

The Spirit is also the power of the future age present for believers in their struggle with the forces of this age which are at enmity with God—particularly the flesh and sin. Paul can at the same time say "by the Spirit we eagerly await through faith the hoped-for righteousness*"; yet also enjoin believers to "live by the Spirit, and you will not carry out what the flesh desires" (Gal 5:5, 16). For Christians in the Spirit are set free from the deadly powers of this age (Rom 8:2, 6). Hence we are brought back to ethics and to the Christ-nature of the Spirit, showing how for Paul all these facets are inextricably interwoven.

### 9. The Spirit and Worship.

Paul informs the Corinthian Christians that, both as a whole and individually, they are God's temple*: "Do you not know that you (plural) are God's temple, and God's Spirit lives in you?" (1 Cor 3:16; cf. 6:19). This saying establishes that worship* is not facilitated by a holy site, building or objects, but by the presence of God's Spirit. "For it is we who are the circumcision, we who worship by the Spirit of God, who glory in Christ Jesus" (Phil 3:3). The place of worship is the human heart, cleansed, renewed and accompanied by the Spirit (cf. Jn 4:23-24), or the Christian community as the Spirit's shrine (1 Cor 3:16).

In 1 Corinthians 12 and 14 Paul discusses the significance and purpose of the Spirit's gifts to the body of Christ within the context of worship gatherings. This is the most extensive discussion of early Christian worship we have from the NT period. Paul points to the Spirit as the source of Christians' "gifts,"* whether they appear to be more supernatural or more normal. That the Spirit distributes these gifts means they are benefits given by God's generous grace and may not be used as tokens of one's spiritual status or achievement. They are given out as the Spirit wishes, not as humans wish. We learn from chapter 14 that the purpose of this direction by the Spirit is for Christians to be "edified" (1 Cor 14:1-5, 26)—a term which literally means "built up," as in the construction of a house. "To edify" pictures the Christians as those who learn, mature and are strengthened. Although Paul urges believers to attend to the way in which they use these Spirit-given abilities, ultimately the building up of the body is the work of the Spirit himself.

The most notable class of actions which the Spirit empowers in worship is that of inspired speech of various sorts. Prophecy* is the most obvious (1 Cor 12:10; 14:1-5, 39); it involved instruction, moral exhortation and correction for the congregation (1 Cor 14:3). It is one of the most frequently mentioned of spiritual gifts, closely linked with the Spirit's presence, and Paul encouraged its practice. To denigrate or prohibit it would seem from 1 Thessalonians 5:19-20 to be equivalent to "quenching" the Spirit. Other gifts of inspired speech include a "word of knowledge*" or wisdom (1 Cor 12:8; one or both may be equivalent to teaching, which is not mentioned in this list but is included at 1 Cor 12:28-29); teaching is viewed as inspired by the Spirit as well (1 Cor 12:28-29; 14:19, 26), as is prayer—whether "in the Spirit" or not (1 Cor 14:2, 14-19)—and glossolalia with its accompanying interpretation (1 Cor 14:1-5, 13-19, 39; *see* Tongues). Even the singing of hymns is in the overall context to be understood as something prompted by the Spirit, who leads the church in its worship, inspiring music and praise (1 Cor 14:15, 26). Ephesians 5:18-19 (cf. Col 3:16) also makes a link between being filled with the Spirit, edification and worship (psalms, hymns and songs of the Spirit; *see* Hymns).

These worship settings also demonstrate a concern for the mutual welfare and upbuilding of believers. Other supernatural events during worship are sometimes referred to by Paul in a general way. The reference of Galatians 3:5 to God's supplying the Spirit and working miracles among the Galatians most likely refers to the ongoing worship experience of their churches. And if, on the basis of what is said about the Spirit's work in 1 Corinthians 12:4-11, the gifts are always the Spirit's work, then we may look to the list in Romans 12:6-8 to highlight vividly how for Paul the Spirit inspires even mundane tasks such as administration and charity.

Outside 1 Corinthians there are surprisingly few explicit references to the role of the Spirit in worship. Perhaps this is partly because nowhere else in Paul are problems with the worship assemblies of a church dealt with so extensively. Outside 1 Corinthians the most frequent aspect of worship associated with the Spirit is prayer.* The Spirit who marks Christians as God's children inspires the confident "Abba" prayer of the redeemed (Rom 8:15-16; Gal 4:6). And he aids believers in their prayers, directing them to pray properly (Rom 8:26). At the same time the Spirit himself prays on behalf of those he indwells (Rom 8:27). In Ephesians also "access" to God in prayer is granted by the Spirit (Eph 2:18), and this praying in the Spirit is urged on believers as a constant practice (Eph 6:18). This is the mark of the church* as true Israel,* that the community prays and worships in the Spirit (Phil 3:3). Philippians 1:19 also associates the Spirit's provision with prayer.

Beyond these there are no other explicit connections between the Spirit and worship in Paul. A few other statements may depend upon an oblique reference to believers' experience of the Spirit in worship,

such as the "Abba" prayer already noted. It is possible that references to the peace and joy generated by the Spirit are inspired partly by worship experiences (Rom 15:13), as are those to the love generated by the Spirit (Rom 5:5; Col 1:8), the fellowship created by the Spirit (Phil 2:1; 2 Cor 13:13 [14]) and the Spirit as a "down payment" (2 Cor 1:22; 5:5—as though it were a tangible evidence to believers), though these suggestions are only conjectures. One thing is sure: that the Spirit plays an enormously important role in Christian worship and in every aspect of the believer's experience of God. We must remember the ad hoc nature of Paul's letters, and assume that there is even more to be said about the Spirit's role in worship that he has not thought necessary to mention (hence the need, e.g., to supply the idea of the Spirit's inspiration in Rom 12:6-8 on the basis of what Paul says in 1 Cor 12).

We might summarize by saying that the Spirit empowers various believers with gifts that benefit others and that aid in worship; that he arranges the distribution of gifts according to their need, and inspires believers to use them aright (1 Cor 14:37-40). This does not mean that everything done with the Spirit's aid in worship must necessarily be done spontaneously, for what is done with the mind (1 Cor 14:15), with purposeful and creative forethought, or with faithfulness to apostolic tradition* (as in teaching*), may be just as inspired and spiritual as something done on the spur of the moment (cf. traditional formulas at 1 Cor 15:1-8; 1 Tim 3:16; *see* Creed).

The Spirit encourages believers in prayer to have boldness in speaking to the God with whom they are now reconciled as beloved children. He initiates the impulse from below and brings the Father's loving response from above. Ideally, worship is a Spirit-led symphony of doxology, giving praise to God, proclaiming what he has done and is doing, and what the human response should be.

*See also* ADOPTION, SONSHIP; CHRISTOLOGY; ESCHATOLOGY; ETHICS; FELLOWSHIP, COMMUNION, SHARING; FIRST FRUITS, DOWN PAYMENT; FRUIT OF THE SPIRIT; GIFTS OF THE SPIRIT; GOD; HOLINESS, SANCTIFICATION; IN CHRIST; LITURGICAL ELEMENTS; POWER; PROPHECY, PROPHESYING; SPIRITUALITY; TONGUES; WORSHIP.

BIBLIOGRAPHY. J. C. Beker, *Paul the Apostle: The Triumph of God in Life and Thought* (Philadelphia: Fortress, 1980); F. F. Bruce, *Paul: Apostle of the Heart Set Free* (Grand Rapids: Eerdmans, 1977); R. Bultmann, *Theology of the New Testament* (London: SCM, 1952) §§ 14, 38; C. E. B. Cranfield, *A Critical and Exegetical Commentary on the Epistle to the Romans* (2 vols.; ICC; Edinburgh: T. & T. Clark, 1975, 1979); J. D. G. Dunn, *Jesus and the Spirit* (Philadelphia: Westminster, 1975); idem,

*Romans* (WBC; 2 vols.; Dallas: Word, 1988); E. E. Ellis, *Prophecy and Hermeneutic* (Tübingen: J. C. B. Mohr, 1978); G. D. Fee, *The First Epistle to the Corinthians* (NICNT; Grand Rapids, Eerdmans, 1987); P. Gächter, "Zum Pneumabegriff des hl. Paulus," *ZKT* 53 (1929) 345-408; L. Goppelt, *Theology of the New Testament* (2 vols.; Grand Rapids: Eerdmans, 1981, 1982); I. Hermann, *Kyrios und Pneuma: Studien zur Christologie der paulinischen Hauptbriefe* (Munich: Kösel, 1961); D. Hill, *Greek Words and Hebrew Meanings* (Cambridge University Press, 1967); A. M. Hunter, *Paul and his Predecessors* (rev. ed.; London: SCM, 1961); D. J. Lull, *The Spirit in Galatia: Paul's Interpretation of* Pneuma *as Divine Power* (SBLDS 49; Chico, CA: Scholars, 1980); R. P. Martin, *The Spirit and the Congregation* (Grand Rapids: Eerdmans, 1984); idem, "The Spirit in 2 Corinthians in Light of the 'Fellowship of the Holy Spirit' in 2 Corinthians 13:14," in *Eschatology and the New Testament*, ed. W. H. Gloer (Peabody, MA: Hendrickson, 1988); idem, *Worship in the Early Church* (London: Marshall, Morgan & Scott, 1964); P. Meyer, "The Holy Spirit in the Pauline Letters: A Contextual Exploration," *Int* 33 (1979) 3-18; C. F. D. Moule, *The Holy Spirit* (London: Mowbrays, 1978); A. Schweitzer, *The Mysticism of Paul the Apostle* (2d ed.; London: Black, 1953); E. Schweizer, "πνεῦμα κτλ (New Testament)," *TDNT* VI.396-451; idem, *The Holy Spirit* (London: SCM, 1980); A. E. Sekki, *The Meaning of* Ruah *at Qumran* (SBLDS 110; Atlanta: Scholars, 1989); H.-D. Wendland, "Das Wirken des heiligen Geistes in den Gläubigen nach Paulus," in *Pro Veritate: Ein theologischer Dialog*, ed. E. Schlink and H. Volk (Münster: Aschendorff, 1963) 133-56; W. Wright, Jr., "The Source of Paul's Concept of Pneuma," *CovQ* 41 (1983) 17-26. T. Paige

# HOMOSEXUALITY

Homosexual activity was not uncommon in the Hellenistic world of Paul's day, chiefly in the form of pederastic liaisons between adult males and young teenagers. Some male prostitution was also current. Yet pederasty was no longer as accepted as it had once been in classical Greece, nor did such "Greek love" ever enjoy equal acceptance in Roman life. Female homosexuality is hardly ever mentioned in classical Greek literature, and not often in the Hellenistic era—mostly post-NT.

1. Hellenistic Judaism
2. Romans 1:26-27
3. 1 Corinthians 6:9; 1 Timothy 1:10
4. General Considerations

## 1. Hellenistic Judaism.

Paul and other early Christian writers inherited the strong critique of homosexuality common in Hellenistic Judaism. Israel, it seems, had met the problem only in contacts with the peoples of Canaan. The later encounter with Hellenism led Jewish writers (e.g., Philo and Josephus) to stress the homosexual aspect of the Sodomites' gang rape (Gen 19:5) and, especially under Stoic influence, to condemn same-sex intercourse as contrary to nature.

## 2. Romans 1:26-27.

Most of the references to homosexuality in the NT occur in the Pauline letters. The clearest is Romans 1:26-27. In the context Paul is portraying the moral disorder that accompanies the rejection of the knowledge* of God in the pagan world. Exchanging the creator for the idolatrous worship (*see* Idolatry) of creatures issues in God's abandoning of women and men who then forsake "the natural use" of their bodies for a use "against nature."

The force of this unmistakable presentation of both female and male same-sex intercourse as a mark of godlessness is today often blunted by minimizing arguments. It is claimed, for example, that the condemnation concerns only homosexual depravity inspired by idolatry (e.g., in sacral prostitution) and has no bearing upon same-sex relations in other contexts. But this is to ignore the clear sequence of Paul's text, which cites the unquestionably immoral character of homosexuality, along with "all manner of wickedness," such as envy, murder, slander and disobedience to parents (Rom 1:29-31), as evidence of the consequences of abandoning God.

Even less plausible is the interpretation (of J. Boswell, among others) that limits Paul's reference to those heterosexuals who pursue homosexual unions contrary to their individual heterosexual natures. The passage has no bearing, it is alleged, on people homosexual by nature. This atomistic reading of these verses is artificially strained, for Paul is commenting on human society at large and focuses on behavior itself. A distinction between persons of heterosexual and homosexual orientation was almost certainly unknown to him.

Others again argue that "unnatural" simply means unconventional, contrary to accepted social practice. But the prominence of the theme of divine creation* in the context (especially Rom 1:20, 25) surely requires that defiance of nature be construed of the flouting of sexual distinctions basic to God's creative design. After all, widespread social usage tolerated homosexual intercourse.

Finally, L. W. Countryman thinks that Romans 1:26-27 treats homosexual acts not as sinful but only as

*413*

unclean, "an integral if unpleasantly dirty aspect of Gentile culture" (Countryman, 117). Such a reading, which makes the import of Paul's statements cultural rather than moral, misses the triple parallelism of "God gave them up" in Romans 1:24, 26 and 28, and invests the passage with an implausibly sophistic subtlety.

These varied attempts to rule Romans 1 out of court in modern ethical discussion nearly all miss a feature which attests remarkable insight on Paul's part. These verses contain one of the very earliest combined condemnations of female and male homosexuality alike. Only two earlier texts make the link (Plato *Laws* I.636c; Pseud.-Phoc. *Sentences* 191-92). It is most unlikely that Paul derived it from preformed tradition. The fact that he condemns both female and male malpractice at one and the same time, together with his use of language that does not specifically identify pederasty as the male abuse, gives his statements a generic force. There was no equivalent to pederasty on the female side.

Contrary to frequent assertions, pederasty as such is never mentioned in the NT. Despite the availability of a varied range of words and phrases denoting pederasty in particular, none of the NT references to same-sex disorder specifies pederasty as a form of homosexuality of an exploitive or aggressive or venal character.

### 3. 1 Corinthians 6:9; 1 Timothy 1:10.

These two verses may be discussed together. In whatever sense the Pastorals* may be termed Pauline, the use of *arsenokoitai* in 1 Timothy 1:10 surely betrays a Pauline finger-print, for this Greek noun is not attested before 1 Corinthians 6:9. English translations vary considerably, partly because the obvious derivation of the word from the LXX of Leviticus 18:22; 20:13 for so long went unnoticed (Lev 20:13: *hos an koimēthē meta arsenos koitēn gynaikos*). It denotes (males) "who lie or bed with males" (not, as Boswell argues, "males [prostitutes] who lie with" (males or females), which linguistically is impossible). Whether a Jewish or Christian—even a Pauline—neologism, the term picks up the Levitical ban, which did not have pederasty in view. Even if what Paul has chiefly in mind is pederasty, his choice of this word, at best very rare, depicts it as sinful in the generic context of males having sex with males. (R. Scroggs' attempt to find in the two Pauline uses not merely pederasty alone but quite precise forms of pederasty is rendered highly improbable by his other claim that Paul is merely reproducing preformed tradition.) The Levitical associations of *arsenokoitēs* are borne out by the context of its next oc-

currence, in *Sibylline Oracles* 2:73: "Do not practice homosexuality."

The *malakoi*, literally "soft," who precede *arsenokoitai* in 1 Corinthians 6:9, may well be those who allowed themselves to be misused, rather than took the initiative, in male homosexual acts.

The lists in these two verses are similar in form to the vice-lists found in Hellenistic pagan and Jewish moralists, but the parallel appearance of homosexual abuse in such lists is more often asserted than illustrated. No parallel is cited in H. Conzelmann's commentary on 1 Corinthians (Conzelmann, 106), and this vice is absent from a list of 147 items in Philo's *Sacrifices of Cain and Abel* 32.

### 4. General Considerations.

One net result of the preceding paragraphs is to vindicate greater originality and broader scope for Paul's brief references. Yet Paul does not single out same-sex intercourse as specially perverted or monstrous. He lists it alongside theft, drunkenness and perjury, as well as adultery and murder (*see* Virtues and Vices). The paucity of Paul's references is inconsistent with its being incomparably execrable, but this fact does not imply its relative unimportance. The broader context of his teaching on sexuality supports the view that he saw same-sex activity as so self-evidently contrary to God's creative purpose as to allow of such brief—but eloquent—mention.

Certainly Paul could not have envisaged some facets of contemporary debates, such as "monogamous" same-sex relationships between persons of homosexual preference. It is nevertheless a safe conclusion that, whatever might be said about individual orientations or dispositions, Paul could only have regarded all homosexual erotic and genital behavior as contrary to the creator's plan for human life, to be abandoned on conversion (cf. 1 Cor 6:11; *see* Ethics).

*See also* ETHICS; MAN AND WOMAN; MARRIAGE AND DIVORCE, ADULTERY AND INCEST; SEXUALITY, SEXUAL ETHICS; VIRTUES AND VICES.

BIBLIOGRAPHY. J. Boswell, *Christianity, Social Tolerance and Homosexuality* (Chicago: University of Chicago, 1980); J. J. Collins, *Between Athens and Jerusalem: Jewish Identity in the Hellenistic Diaspora* (New York: Crossroad, 1983) 141-53; H. Conzelmann, *1 Corinthians* (Herm; Philadelphia: Fortress, 1975); L. W. Countryman, *Dirt, Greed and Sex: Sexual Ethics in the New Testament and Their Implications for Today* (Philadelphia: Fortress, 1988); L. M. Epstein, *Sex Laws and Customs in Judaism* (New York: Block, 1948) 134-38; V. P. Furnish, *The Moral Teaching of Paul: Selected Issues* (Nashville: Abingdon, 1979) 52-83; R. H. Hays, "Relations Natural and

Unnatural: A Response to John Boswell's Exegesis of Romans 1," *JRE* 14 (1986) 184-215; R. MacMullen, "Roman Attitudes to Greek Love," *Historia* 27 (1982) 484-502; R. Scroggs, *The New Testament and Homosexuality* (Philadelphia: Fortress, 1983); L. P. Wilkinson, *Classical Attitudes to Modern Issues* (London: Kimber, 1978) 111-42; D. F. Wright, "Homosexuals or Prostitutes? The Meaning of *Arsenokoitai* (1 Cor. 6:9, 1 Tim. 1:10)," *VC* 38 (1984) 125-53; idem, "Homosexuality: The Relevance of the Bible," *EvQ* 61 (1989) 291-300; idem, "Early Christian Attitudes to Homosexuality," *SP* XVIII:2 (1989) 329-34.

D. F. Wright

# HOPE

Hope is an essential characteristic of the Christian life and a central feature of Paul's theology. Every statement Paul makes about Christian hope is also a statement about what God* has given the believer in Christ.* In his letters, especially the letter to the Romans,* Paul explores the ground of Christian hope, what it means to live in hope and the Christian hope for the future.

1. Hope in the OT
2. Hope in the Letters of Paul

## 1. Hope in the OT.

In the OT hope is closely related to the character of God.* Those who hope in God, trust God and his promises. Because God is the hope of the righteous, they can expect good things from God and wait patiently for his help and deliverance. This patient hope is firmly anchored in the history and narrative of Scripture. The God who has fulfilled his promises to Israel in the past will continue to be faithful in the present and future. Hope that does not place its trust in God is false hope which God will eventually overthrow.

Hope in God in the present is also a hope in God's future eschatological* intervention which will put an end to all earthly distress. This eschatological hope expressed itself as a conviction that all of history was in God's hands and that God would fulfill his promise to establish David's throne forever. This aspect of Israel's hope gave rise to the messianic expectation of the OT, apocalyptic* literature and the idea of the resurrection* of the dead. The messianic age was seen as a time when Israel's hope in God's promises would be fulfilled, the kingdom* of God would be given to the saints and the hopes of the ungodly would be destroyed by God's judgment.*

## 2. Hope in the Letters of Paul.

The NT concept of hope is rooted in the OT; Christian hope includes trust in God, patient waiting and confidence in God's future. But the situation of the Christian who hopes is decisively different from that of the OT. Christian hope rests on God's eschatological act of salvation* in Christ. The eschatological dimensions of Christian hope provide the framework for Paul's thinking. Christ's resurrection marks the beginning of the messianic age, the presence of the Spirit is evidence that the end has begun and Christian hope waits for the complete manifestation of the kingdom of God at the Parousia. In Paul's letters the church is addressed as an eschatological community of hope: grounded in God's act of salvation in Christ, living in the power of the Holy Spirit* and moving toward the full realization of the purposes of God.

*2.1. The Ground of Hope.* Paul understands Christian hope as a fulfillment of God's promises to Israel.* This hope is firmly anchored in the history of Israel and in the revealed character of God as one who is faithful to fulfill his promises. Paul delineates this aspect of Christian hope in his discussion of Abraham* in Romans 4.

Abraham is offered as an example of someone who never doubted that God would fulfill his promises. Abraham's hope is grounded in a personal relation with the God whom he trusts. In fact the only ground of Abraham's hope was God's promise. Abraham had no external or historical grounds for his hope; but when that hope was tested by human impossibilities, it grew. This is what is meant by "in hope he believed against hope." Abraham's hope grew because he believed the God of hope, even though all human hope was gone.

Christian hope is directed to the same God who fulfilled his promise to Abraham and who raised Jesus from the dead. What God has done in Christ gives Christians a far greater reason to hope than Abraham had. Christ is the faithful fulfillment of God's promise to Abraham; now even the Gentiles* can be justified* by faith and included in the promise. The resurrection of Christ is the beginning of a new age of hope determined by God's promises in Christ and empowered by God's gift of the Spirit.

*2.2. Living in Hope.* Christians live in the time between the resurrection of Christ and the ultimate realization of the kingdom of God. They are members of an eschatological community determined by the reality of a future that has already begun, but is still awaiting its final consummation. They live in hope because God's promises in Christ so often stand in contradiction to the reality around them. But they have more than God's faithfulness in the past and promises about the future to give them hope. God's gift of the

Holy Spirit provides an experiential basis for hope in the present. In Romans 5:1-5 and Romans 8, Paul writes about what it means for Christians to live in hope.

Like Abraham, Christians must live in hope because the reality of their present circumstances so often stand in direct contradiction to the promises of God and in Christ. In Romans 5:1-5 Paul reminds the Roman church that in Christ they have already been justified by faith, have obtained access to the grace* of God and can rejoice in their hope of sharing the glory of God. Even though it is difficult to embrace hope in the midst of the reality of suffering,* Christians can rejoice even in their suffering since all of Christian experience is illuminated by the reality of the hope of glory.* If Christians hold on to this hope in the midst of suffering, their hope will grow and they will not be put to shame. The reality of Christian hope is based on two things: the reality of God's victory over evil in the death and resurrection of Christ, and the gift of the Holy Spirit. Hope is the source of present strength for believers because it is grounded in what God has done in Christ, is experienced in the power of the Spirit and moves toward the glory that is to be revealed.

The relation between the Spirit and Christian hope is further developed in Romans 8. Here it becomes clear that hope is inseparable from the gift of the Holy Spirit and the new life Christians have as heirs of God. The Holy Spirit assures Christians that they are fellow heirs with Christ because the giving of the Spirit is a sign that Christ has already entered into his inheritance; it is a guarantee that the expectations of those who still wait will be fulfilled.

The suffering that Christians undergo is also part of this guarantee. Those who are joint heirs with Christ must suffer with him before they are glorified with him. But the glory is as sure as the suffering, and the Holy Spirit is a pledge that the suffering is not in vain. The activity of the Spirit is proof that a new age has dawned and that the consummation of the age cannot be long delayed. The suffering which is characteristic of this age is the result of being faithful to Christ in a world that is hostile to him.

The image of groaning and travailing shows that creation's present condition will result in a glorious issue, which includes the redemption* of the cosmos. Christians have a great advantage in this travail because they possess the first fruits of the Spirit and can anticipate their future salvation—their adoption* and the redemption of their bodies. The glory which will be revealed is already present in the gift of the Spirit who intercedes for Christians according to the will of God. The Spirit helps Christians in their weakness by giving them assurance that their hope of glory is not vain. Romans 8:28-30 assures believers that nothing can destroy their ultimate glory; God will triumph.* This is the ground of Christian hope in the face of adverse circumstances.

This close connection between the Spirit and hope is also seen in 1 Corinthians 12 and 13. The pouring out of gifts is part of life in the Spirit. These gifts, when exercised in love,* provide Christians with an overwhelming assurance of their inclusion in a new age that has already dawned. Faith and hope belong with love (1 Cor 13:13; cf. 1 Thess 5:8) in the exercise of spiritual gifts* because these virtues embrace all of Christian existence. Life in the Spirit is a life of trusting God, having confidence about the future and loving one another.

*2.3. Hope for the Future.* Believers in this age live in hope because they know that they will eventually enter into an inheritance of glory (Col 1:5). This future glory exerts influence on the present through the hope it awakens. As Christians hope they anticipate the future and bring it into the present. Hope is not defined by present realities but by God's purposes for the future.

But when Paul writes about this future, it never becomes detached from the present experience of life in Christ (Col 1:27). The future Christians anticipate is a consummation of activity that began in Christ's death* and resurrection and continues in the present experience of the Spirit. The object of Christian hope is the coming manifestation of Christ. What is now the ground of Christian hope will then be fully manifested.

The object of Christian hope is explicitly mentioned in Titus 2:13 as "the appearing of the glory of our great God and Savior* Jesus Christ." Closely connected to the manifestation of glory is eternal life (Tit 1:2; 3:7) and the resurrection of the dead (1 Thess 4:13-18; 1 Cor 15). The most extended discussion of these future realities is found in 1 Corinthians 15. Even though the word *hope* is not mentioned except once (1 Cor 15:19), this chapter is connected to the discussion of hope in Romans 8 by the use of the first-fruits* image. Just as the Spirit's work in the lives of believers is the first fruit of the coming glory, so Christ's resurrection is the first fruit which guarantees the coming resurrection of all who are in Christ. At this time God's final purpose will be fulfilled and the kingdom will come in all its glory. This final resurrection is so certain that to deny the resurrection is to deny the God who has promised this glorious future.

Christian hope only finds meaning as a foretaste of

something greater and more glorious. It sets out from the present reality of God's activity in raising Christ from the dead and giving the Spirit to believers, and proclaims the future of that reality. Hope is an encouragement to believers in the midst of suffering, but it also prevents believers from being content with present circumstances. Hope insists that Christians wait with eager longing for the great day when all of God's promises are fulfilled.

Paul's thinking about hope has had a tremendous impact on modern theologians who have sought to recover the significance of the future for Christian thinking (see Moltmann). The Christian faith lives from the raising of Christ from the dead and strains toward the hope of a future given by God. In the promises of God, the hidden future announces itself and exerts an influence on the present through the hope it awakens. Hope's statements of promise stand in contradiction to present reality; hope leads reality toward the promised transformation. Christians who live in hope are "coworkers" with Christ, loving and striving for the glorious kingdom as well as waiting patiently for it.

*See also* ADOPTION, SONSHIP; CREATION AND NEW CREATION; ESCHATOLOGY; FAITH; FIRST FRUITS, DOWNPAYMENT; GLORY; HOLY SPIRIT; RESURRECTION; SUFFERING.

BIBLIOGRAPHY. C. E. B. Cranfield, *Romans I-VIII* (ICC; Edinburgh: T. & T. Clark, 1975); G. D. Fee, *The First Epistle to the Corinthians* (NICNT; Grand Rapids: Eerdmans, 1987); B. Hebblethwaite, *The Christian Hope* (Grand Rapids: Eerdmans, 1984); P. S. Minear, *Christian Hope and the Second Coming* (Philadelphia: Westminster, 1954); J. Moltmann, *The Future of Hope* (New York: Harper & Row, 1967); C. F. D. Moule, *The Meaning of Hope* (Philadelphia: Fortress, 1963); K. H. Rengstorf and R. Bultmann, "ἐλπίς κτλ," *TDNT* II.517-35; S. Travis, *I Believe in the Second Coming of Jesus* (Grand Rapids: Eerdmans, 1982).

J. M. Everts

# HOUSEHOLDS AND HOUSEHOLD CODES

Among the metaphors Paul drew upon to describe the church,* that of the "household" is certainly one of the most important. Not unrelated is his interest in conduct and relationships proper to that institution and his use of the striking pattern of instruction known as the "household code." Although the emergence of the "house church" may have played a role in determining his literary approach, it was probably the structure of society itself which most inspired Paul.

1. The Household Concept
2. Household Codes in Paul

## 1. The Household Concept.

The basic unit of the Greco-Roman society in which Paul lived and ministered was the household (*oikos, oikia*). Its importance was such that secular ethicists saw the stability of the city-state as dependent upon responsible management of the household. The foundational nature of this institution is further seen in the pattern it provided for the structure and definition of larger political institutions. The emperor* (*see* Caesar's Household) came to be viewed as a father and the state as his household. And many functions or positions in relation to the state were derived from the "household" root: *metoikoi/paroikoi* ("resident aliens"), *oikeios* ("native"), *katoikoi* ("military colonists") *dioiketēs* ("chief financial officer"), *oikonomos* ("administrator").

The household consisted of members of the immediate family and typically extended to include slaves,* freedmen, servants and laborers, and sometimes even business associates and tenants. In principle, the householder ("lord," *kyrios* or *despotēs*) had full authority* over the members of the household. He also had obligations and some legal responsibilities to them. But the cohesiveness of the unit depended more upon the sense of loyalty to the household which stemmed more directly from common economic, social, psychological and religious factors. The household provided members with a sense of security and identity that the larger political and social structures were unable to give (*see* Social Setting).

Given the dominant place of the household concept within the culture of Paul's day, its impact upon his teaching is not surprising. Paul brings to life his descriptions of the church and various relationships within it by drawing on terms and concepts associated with the household.

There are numerous references to the secular household in Paul's letters* (*oikia*: 1 Cor 11:22; 16:15; Phil 4:22; 1 Tim 5:13; 2 Tim 3:6; *oikos*: Rom 16:5; 1 Cor 1:16; 11:34; 14:35; 16:19; Col 4:15; 1 Tim 3:4, 5, 12; 5:4; 2 Tim 1:16; 4:19; Tit 1:11; Philem 2). In some of these the household is identified as the place in which believers met for worship* (Rom 16:5; 1 Cor 16:19; Col 4:15; Philem 2). As distinctions between Judaism and nascent Christianity became pronounced, forcing Christians to separate from the Temple* and synagogues, access to the homes of certain believers led naturally to the development of house churches. And Paul's subsequent references to churches* (*ekklēsia*) are probably to such house churches, whether considered individually or collectively (see 1 Thess 1:1; 2 Thess 1:1).

But it is the use of household terminology to describe the church that sheds most light on Paul's thinking about God's people and their life in relation to God* and one another (*see* Fellowship). 1 Timothy 3:15 describes the church in Ephesus as the "household of God" (*oikos theou*). Rather than referring to a building or meeting place, Paul here draws on the concept of the household as a social unit, made up of various members, each responsible to one another and ultimately to the householder, to emphasize the need for appropriate behavior among the various groups in the church (the church as a whole, 1 Tim 2:1-7; men and women, 1 Tim 2:8-15; overseers, 1 Tim 3:1-7; deacons and deaconesses, 1 Tim 3:8-13). This theme recurs in 2 Timothy 2:20-21, where the church is compared with "a great house" (*megalē oikia*) in which can be found both valuable and common vessels. As the imagery is applied to the church, the master (*despotēs*), for whom the "vessel" should be cleansed in preparation for use, is God.

Although in these two instances Paul applies the household concept to the church to encourage appropriate and responsible behavior as well as respectability and order, the imagery would also call to mind thoughts of another kind. To be a member of a household meant refuge and protection, at least as much as the master was able to provide. It also meant identity and gave the security that comes with a sense of belonging. Paul expressed such ideas in describing particularly Gentile believers as "members of the household of God" (*oikeioi tou theou*, Eph 2:19; or "of faith": *oikeioi tēs pisteōs*, Gal 6:10; cf. 1 Tim 5:8).

The dominance of the household concept in Paul's thought also influenced his perception of the ministry* and the minister. Paul's ministry thus comes under the category of "stewardship" (*oikonomia*, 1 Cor 9:17; Col 1:25), that is, a task entrusted by the master to a member of the household. The one who receives this trust, the minister, is called a "steward" (*oikonomos*, 1 Cor 4:1, 2; Tit 1:7). Such a description emphasizes the need for faithful execution of duties and accountability to the master.

In describing the church (in one way or another), the household metaphor might combine with other metaphors. Ephesians 2:19-22 illustrates this well. Here, along with six terms derived from the *oikos* root (*paroikoi, oikeioi, epoikodomēthentes, oikodomē, synoikodomeisthe, katoikētērion*), Temple* imagery also occurs (*naon hagion*, Eph 2:21). Thus God's household (= God's people) and God's Temple, which signifies above all the place in which God dwells, are brought together. The images are held together by Paul's teaching about the Holy Spirit* (Eph 1:14): the same Spirit which indwelt the Temple now indwells the new community of God. Also present is an emphasis on

the process of "building" (*epoikodomeō*) which leads to the description of the resultant church as a "building" (*oikodomē*). That a meeting place is not in mind is clear from the organic nature of the process ("growing into a holy Temple") and the fact that the description is of a peculiar people. Discussing the growth of the Christian community in 1 Corinthians 3:6-15, Paul combines the image of planting with "building."

The effect of Paul's use of household imagery is to depict the people of God as God's household, a living and growing family whose life together requires mutuality of service and care, recognition of responsibilities, and a sense of identity, belonging and protection. As a household it would be understood that the community of God's people would be comprised of varieties of people, roles and responsibilities, and that to function effectively order would need to be maintained. In this respect Paul's use of the household concept and his choice to use what have been termed "household codes" to encourage appropriate behavior within the church are almost certainly related (*see* Ethics).

**2. Household Codes in Paul.**

Colossians 3:18—4:1 and Ephesians 5:22-33 represent teaching addressed to the various members of the household. What distinguishes these blocks of teaching as a special form is the tendency to address church members according to household role and status (wives/husbands, children/parents, slaves/masters), reciprocity (each member being addressed), the delineation of appropriate behavior with a verb enjoining subordination (*hypotassō*) or obedience (*hypakouō*). These two passages represent the fullest expression of the NT household code. But 1 Timothy 2:1-15; 5:1-2; 6:1-2, 17-19; Titus 2:1—3:8 and 1 Peter 2:13—3:7 also contain teaching very similar in tone and form. And shorter sections of related teaching in 1 Corinthians 14:33-35 (cf. 1 Cor 11:3-16) about men and women (*see* Man and Woman) and in Romans 13:1-7 about the church's posture toward the government appear to come from the same basic source (*see* Civil Authority).

A great deal of effort has gone into attempts to identify the sources of the NT household codes. Secular sources provide numerous examples of teaching in which household members were addressed. Aristotle, the Stoic duty codes, ethical teaching in Hellenistic Judaism (especially Philo) have all been cited at one time or another as sources of the NT convention. Similarly, determinations about function of the form in the earlier extrabiblical settings are brought across to discussions of the NT house codes' intention and meaning. However, no exact formal parallels have been unearthed. And the question about intention is therefore not to be answered on formal grounds.

What can be said about the intention of the NT household code will have to be based on NT usage and some broader conclusions about the culture of that day. For example, it is reasonable to say that the "fixed" pattern of teaching reflects a depth of interest in the household on the part of the early church equivalent to that of the pagan ethical writers. From this it can also be suggested that Paul's use of the Christian household code reflects his (and the church's) sensitivity to wider social expectations. Moreover, the emphasis, especially in the Pastoral Letters, on behavior that is visibly respectable and appropriate would seem to imply that the apostle desired the church to meet those social expectations as far as possible.

If we now ask the question "Why?" we begin to get at the intention of this aspect of Paul's teaching. Did Paul, like the secular ethicists, believe that the household (expanded to include the whole church) formed the fundamental building block of society? Or was this aspect of his teaching a reaction to unsettling emancipation tendencies based upon some enthusiastic but misguided use of Galatians 3:28? We can be certain of neither alternative. The indications allow the conclusion that his aim was to promote a manner of social behavior that was respectable in the eyes of those outside the church (esp. 1 Tim 3:7; 6:1; Tit 2:5, 8, 10; 3:10; cf. 1 Pet 2:12). But Paul's motives in doing so have been open to question. Some have seen in this development (which is attributed not to Paul but to his successors) the beginning of the secularization of the church. Yet it seems characteristic of Paul to endorse the respectable and orderly lifestyle encouraged in the household codes as an aid to the execution of the evangelistic mission* in a potentially hostile world (cf. 1 Thess 4:12).

*See also* BODY OF CHRIST; CAESAR'S HOUSEHOLD, IMPERIAL HOUSEHOLD; CHURCH; ETHICS; MAN AND WOMAN; SLAVE, SLAVERY; SOCIAL SETTING OF MISSION CHURCHES; SOCIAL-SCIENTIFIC APPROACHES TO PAUL.

BIBLIOGRAPHY. D. L. Balch, *Let Wives Be Submissive: The Domestic Code in 1 Peter* (SBLMS 26; Chico, CA: Scholars, 1981); R. Banks, *Paul's Idea of Community: The Early House Churches in Their Historical Setting* (Grand Rapids: Eerdmans, 1980); J. E. Crouch, *The Origin and Intention of the Colossian* Haustafel (FRLANT 109; Göttingen: Vandenhoeck & Ruprecht, 1972); M. Dibelius and H. Greeven, *An die Kolosser, Epheser, an Philemon* (3d ed.; HNT 12; Tübingen: J. C. B. Mohr, 1953); J. H. Elliott, *A Home for the Homeless* (Philadelphia: Fortress, 1981); F. V. Filson, "The Significance of the Early House Churches," *JBL* 58 (1939) 105-12; L. Goppelt, "Prinzipien neutestamentlicher Sozialethik nach dem 1. Petrusbrief," in *Neues Testament und Geschichte*, ed. H. Baltensweiler & B. Reicke (Tübingen: J. C. B. Mohr, 1972) 285-96; L. Hartman, "Some Unorthodox Thoughts on the 'Household-Code Form,' " in *The Social World of Formative Christianity and Judaism*, ed. J. Neusner et al. (Philadelphia: Fortress, 1988) 219-34; E. A. Judge, *The Social Pattern of Christian Groups in the First Century* (London: Tyndale, 1960); A. J. Malherbe, *Social Aspects of Early Christianity* (Baton Rouge: Louisiana State University, 1977); S. Motyer, "The Relationship between Paul's Gospel of 'All One in Christ Jesus' (Gal 3:28) and the 'Household Codes,' " *VoxEv* 19 (1989) 33-48; W. Schrage, "Zur Ethik der NT Haustafeln," *NTS* 21 (1974) 1-22; D. Schroeder, *Die Haustafeln des neuen Testaments (ihre Herkunft und theologischer Sinn)* (Dissertation, Hamburg: Mikrokopie, 1959); G. Theissen, *The Social Setting of Pauline Christianity* (Philadelphia: Fortress, 1982); D. C. Verner, *The Household of God: The Social World of the Pastoral Epistles* (SBLDS 71; Chico, CA: Scholars, 1983); P. Vielhauer, *Oikodome: Aufsatze zum Neuen Testament*, ed. G. Klein (rev. ed.; TB 65; Munich: Kaiser, 1979) 1-168.

P. H. Towner

# HYMNS, HYMN FRAGMENTS, SONGS, SPIRITUAL SONGS

The Pauline churches that meet us in the pages of the NT were worshipping communities of believing men and women. This is clear from the statement of Paul in his letters* (notably 1 Cor 10—14). It is therefore only to be expected that these letters will contain some allusion to a specific part of the Christian cultus, namely, the worship* of God* in religious song since, in both the Jewish background and the religious ethos of the Greco-Roman world (*see* Religions; Worship), hymns to God or gods were well known.

1. Background for This Study
2. Presence of Hymns in the Pauline Corpus
3. Classification and Function of the Hymns

### 1. Background for This Study.

The data for hymns and songs lie mostly beneath the surface of the text and have to be explored by the biblical discipline of form criticism as applied to the NT letters. But there are, in addition to certain explicit references to Christian hymns (in 1 Cor 14:26; Col 3:16; Eph 5:19-20), some encouragements of an inferential character, to which attention should be drawn. We may list these with a brief comment.

First, the origin of the church in the womb of the Jewish faith made it inevitable that the first followers of the risen Lord* Jesus, themselves Jews by birth and tradition, who formed the nucleus of the Jerusalem community, would wish to express their religious devotion in a way to which they were accustomed. This would include the use of religious song. It is this background which leads to the suggestion that the worship of Jewish Christianity cherished and preserved messianic psalms, which are represented in fragmentary form in Romans 11:33-36 as well as creedlike snatches in Romans 1:3-4 (cf. 1 Tim 1:17; 6:15-16).

Then, as the message spread to confront the world of Hellenism,* Gentile* converts entered the church from a religious world which sang hymns to the deities of Greco-Roman religion. There are some superficial correspondences between the literary form and language used in both pagan and Christian hymnody (see the definitive work of Norden), but on the more serious levels of theological content and human aspiration there are fundamental differences. These differences center in the way in which Christian compositions appeal to God whose nature is known in Jesus Christ* as a loving and faithful Father (the nearest we come to this conviction is Cleanthes' *Hymn to Zeus,* but that trails off in a sad identification of the father of the gods and humans with impersonal Fate) and the clear declaration that the God and Father of Jesus Christ is the God who acts in history.

Much of the NT hymnology stands in the OT tradition of confessional statements (e.g., Deut 26:5-8; Ps 105) which celebrate the mighty acts of God in salvation history (see Bradshaw). Pagan prayer* as expressed in personal hymns is largely self-centered and does not break out of the circle of egocentricity (see for a good example the suppliant's appeal to Serapis in Aristides' *Hymn to Serapis,* which does contain some lofty thoughts but without the involvement of personal religion: so Delling, 114; Festugière, 99). NT examples of hymnic prayer are quite different as they focus on objective realities which are at the same time intimately related to the believers' experience in the Christian community—the coming of God's kingdom,* the progress of the gospel* in the world,* and the upbuilding of the church.*

In sum, Christian hymns in the NT church stand in relation to both Jewish antecedents and pagan examples of Greco-Roman religion as the fulfillment stands to the longing which precedes it. That which explains the transition is the gospel of God's grace in Jesus Christ (celebrated in such hymnic pieces as 2 Tim 1:8-10; Tit 3:4-7 as well as the more theologically sophisticated Eph 1:3-14). This good news of human salvation* brought to Christians an awareness of living in days of eschatological* fulfillment; and it was only to

be expected that Christian lips should be opened in praise of the mighty deeds of God in tribute to his goodness. Much closer to the ethos of the apostolic hymns are the confessions of the community at Qumran* (e.g., in 1QS 10:9 and in the Hymn scroll, 1QH 11:3-4). These fine expressions offer examples of personal faith* and a desire to give glory to God for his saving acts. But even these tributes lack the note that is characteristic of the NT hymns. Though parts of the Pauline data are simply creation hymns (Rom 11:33-36), the most distinctive feature is seen in those hymnic confessions of faith which praise the redeeming power* of God in the gospel and share in the element which is taken from the OT and given a richer connotation in the Incarnation and redemption of Israel's Messiah (*see* Christ). As Deichgräber puts it, "The praise of the community is the response to God's saving act" (201), thus making Christian hymns reflexive and expressive of gratitude to God for all that he has done for the world's reconciliation (*see* Peace, Reconciliation). Encouragements like this give added depth to our study, for Christian hymns expose the nerve ends of the Pauline gospel itself, as will be seen.

## 2. Presence of Hymns in the Pauline Corpus.

The detection of hymnic forms in the literature of the NT is a product of comparatively recent scholarly work, and includes the results of an analysis of the literary features which are present in the documents. Direct witness to the presence and use of such liturgical compositions comes in Colossians 3:16 (cf. Eph 5:19-20). There the designations "psalms, hymns and spiritual songs" (i.e., songs inspired by the Spirit) could well refer to different types of composition. "Psalms" would be based on OT precedents; "hymns" might well be a specifically Christian genre devoted to the praise of the risen Lord (a "Christ psalm," in Hengel's description), while "songs of the Spirit" could reflect the spontaneous outburst in rapturous praise or else a song with hortatory appeal; evidence for the last-named comes in Ephesians 5:14 with its address to the newly baptized (see 3.1 below; for a discussion of these passages in Ephesians, see Lincoln). Many interpreters, however, are reluctant to see a rigid demarcation in this way, and, taking the adjective "spiritual" to refer to all three nouns—psalms, hymns, odes—regard the list as not indicating different genres of song but simply employing the most important terms found in the LXX for religious song in general (Hengel).

*2.1. Criteria for Detecting Hymns.* The chief criteria for ascertaining the presence of hymnic forms according to Stauffer are these:

(1) Contextual dislocations, as in Colossians 1:15-20 where the "flow" of epistolary prose is interrupted, thus betraying the insertion of quoted material.

(2) Terminology and style occur that are noticeably different from the prose writing in context and give evidence of an elevated period that is inserted into the context (e.g., 1 Timothy 3:16).

(3) Both introductory phrases, such as "thus it says" (Eph 5:14) and "confessedly" (1 Tim 3:16), and the initial relative pronoun (*hos*, "who," Col 1:15; Phil 2:6) suggest that a preformed composition is being added to illustrate the writer's point.

(4) An antithetic style sets up a contrast, whether on a grand scale (Phil 2:6-11) or within a more restricted soteriological tag (Rom 1:3-4). In the former instance the two stages of Christ's odyssey are delineated presupposing a pretemporal existence in 2:6a (incarnate/cosmological), while in the latter his earthly existence ("according to the flesh") is matched by his subsequent state as "designated Son of God" according to the Spirit (*see* Christology). The couplet formation has been traced throughout Philippians 2:6-11, and is evident more clearly in 1 Timothy 3:16, with anaphora (words linked by similar-sounding openings) and epiphora (similar endings) an obvious literary trait. Rhyme and assonance are thereby produced to indicate how poetic the piece was in its composition. Trochaic rhythms are sometimes seen, for instance, in Ephesians 5:14 with a three-line iambic structure in the original.

(5) As befits the subject matter, the vocabulary is rare, ceremonial, hieratic and full of *hapax legomena*.

*2.2. Discerning Hymns from Other Forms.* The line that divides poetry (e.g., 1 Cor 13; 15:32; Tit 1:12) from hymnody is finely drawn, and indeed the terms overlap. What distinguishes the latter as such is the subject matter that is expressed in poetic form. Invariably the hymn is focused on God or Christ and praises some aspect of the divine nature or activity.

It is just as difficult and delicate a task to separate out a species of Christian hymn from an early confession of faith (*see* Creed), but the chief test (offered by Bultmann, 9) is simply one of length. The creed in early times was short and was used as a baptismal confession of faith (e.g., Rom 10:9). As the creedal statement became lengthened in definition of the person and work of Christ and the character of God—both enlargements even in NT times arose as a result of pressure exerted by false teaching and polemics—so the hymnic forms were drawn into use. Adaptations of Jewish hymns (seen in Lk 1—2 and Rev 15) were insufficient to ward off the strange teachings which threatened the apostolic gospel. The distinctive Chris-

tian hymn was born out of a need to assert: (1) the centrality of Christ in God's saving plan and his unique relationship to God; (2) the true meaning of the Christian life as one of moral excellence and (3) the freedom of believers from all forms of bad religion and superstition which would hold them prey to fears and doubts.

We can sum up the chief enemy as a gnosticizing teaching which quickly challenged the apostolic message and imposed its presence in the churches of the Pauline mission (cf. Martin 1982). The tenets are seen in a denial of the lordship of Christ as the sole intermediary between God and the world (Colossians), the insidious relaxing of the moral fiber which led Christians to be indifferent to bodily lusts and sins (Ephesians), and the uncertainty that underlies the meaning of life since the star-gods still hold sway and need to be placated (*see* Elements/Elemental Spirits). It is not accidental that the main examples of Pauline hymns address the various situations in which the presence of gnostic ideas (*see* Gnosticism) is suspected and form the polemic counterthrust to heretical teaching in the areas of both doctrine and morals (for an elaboration of this thesis, see Sanders).

### 3. Classification and Function of the Hymns.
In light of the above discussions, the following is an attempt to classify the Pauline material which is germane. Apart from some specimens which have been identified as drawn from the synagogues of hellenistic Judaism (e.g., Rom 11:33-36), distinctively Christian compositions may be subdivided as follows:

*3.1. Sacramental.* Here parts of Ephesians (Eph 2:12-19: on this see Martin 1992, 167-76) and the Pastorals (Tit 3:4-7) have been designated as baptismal (*see* Baptism). Ephesians 5:14, the clearest illustration of a NT hymn, also falls in this grouping. It divides naturally into three lines on grounds of style and finds its obvious *Sitz im Leben* in a baptismal setting. The convert is summoned to moral endeavor and promised divine aid to live a life worthy of one's profession. In the context of the letter it challenges the view of an indifferent moral attitude—a wrong-headed notion which was plaguing the Asia minor churches (so Eph 4:17-23; see Martin 1968).

*3.2. Meditative.* Ephesians 1:3-14 is a good example of a Christian rhapsody on the themes of trinitarian faith and redemption.* It is possible that a Jewish pattern drawn from the synagogue in which God is blessed (hence the term *berakah*) lies in the background, but if so it has been dramatically christianized by impressive Christian concepts of election,* salvation and adoption* (Lincoln; Martin 1992, ad loc.).

*3.3. Confessional.* The nature of the Christian life comes to vivid expression when believers are called upon to attest their faith in time of trial. Passages of the Pastorals* (e.g., 2 Tim 2:11-13) read like hymns of the martyrs' confession and illustrate the strenuous quality of Christian living which was expected in the early church in its incipient conflict with the persecuting state.

*3.4. Christological.* Here we touch the heart of the matter, for as we have seen, the NT teaching on the person of Christ is virtually contained in its hymns (*see* Christology). Outstanding specimens in Pauline literature are Philippians 2:6-11, Colossians 1:15-20 and 1 Timothy 3:16. All these texts have been the subject of in-depth studies in recent times and collectively are discussed in detail by Sanders, Deichgräber and Fowl, with individual treatments on Philippians 2:6-11 (Martin, Rissi), Colossians 1:15-20 (Gabathuler) and 1 Timothy 3:16 (Gundry).

Let it suffice to extract a modicum of common teaching. The Christians' Lord* is depicted in a cosmological role in the double sense of that adjective. First, his pre-existence and pretemporal activity in creation are made the frontispiece of the hymns, and from the divine order in which he eternally exists, he "comes down" as the incarnate one in an epiphany. Second, at the conclusion of his earthly life he takes his place in God's presence by receiving the universal homage and acclamation of the cosmic spirit powers (*see* Principalities and Powers), which confess his lordship and so are forced to abandon their title of control over human destiny. His saving work is seen as that of bringing together the two orders of existence (the celestial and terrestrial), and his reconciliation is described in a cosmic setting. The hymns are essentially soteriological in their purpose, and set forth the person of Christ in relation to his world as reconciler and world ruler. But inasmuch, as he accomplished what God alone could do—the pacification (*see* Triumph) of the hostile powers of the universe and the enthronement (*see* Exaltation and Enthronement) of a true lordship, in particular—and has received from the Father's hands the right to rule human life and to be the judge of history, it was but a short step for the early Christians to set him on a level with God in their cultic worship.* Hymnology and Christology thus merge in praise of the one Lord (see Hengel), soon to be hailed after the close of the NT canon* as worthy of hymns "as to God" (Pliny's report of Bithynian Christians' worship, A.D. 112).

*3.5. Ethical/Paraenetic.* Much recent discussion has centered on the role Pauline hymns played in illustrating and enforcing his ethical appeals (*see* Ethics). The chief *crux interpretum* has been Philippians 2:5-11 in which the introductory verse 5 paves the way for a recital of the (preformed and self-contained) hymn in Philippians 2:6-11. Interpretations have to wrestle with some basic issues on the correct or most likely way to translate Paul's elliptical Greek, which lacks a verb in Philippians 2:5b, and thereby to identify the kind of appeal that is made by the subsequent citation of the stately "hymn to Christ." (A brief review of exegetical possibilities for rendering verse 5 is offered in Martin 1976, with some expanded comment in Martin 1983 in response to, e.g., Hurtado: see now Fee.)

The issue turns on whether Paul is moving at verse 5 from a statement of pastoral problems at Philippi in Philippians 2:1-4 to a display of ethical qualities seen in the incarnate and exalted Lord, notably his humility and selflessness (*see* Servant), with a view to providing a pattern for imitation.* Or, as a rival view, Paul is basing his pastoral call to have done with pride and self-centeredness (in Phil 2:1-4) on the Christians' way of life "in Christ" (see NEB at Phil 2:5), that is, as members of his church, and more pointedly on their adherence to his lordship (expressed in Phil 2:9-11). There are refinements offered to both alternatives (Hurtado for the first; in part Fowl for the second, but in danger of losing the basic insight that the "center" of the hymn is in Phil 2:9-11, noted by Käsemann). Above all, recent discussion in the commentaries (Hawthorne, Silva) largely passes over the possibility that the christological emphasis in Philippians 2:6-11 may have had an independent function prior to its being taken over and incorporated into a pastoral letter and that, in taking it over, Paul may well have redacted it (by inserting v. 8c) to bring it into line with his purpose.

If this theory of a two-stage development is so, it may offer a path of agreement which will unite the soteriological and exemplary functions of the present hymn. In its pristine form the hymn will have celebrated the cosmic authority* of the exalted Lord; in adapting it to meet a pastoral situation at Philippi (*see* Philippians) Paul has brought out more clearly the elements of utter humiliation and atonement (since his death was *on a cross*, Phil 2:8c; *see* Death of Christ), and so the language of his lowly condescension in Philippians 2:6-8 matches the need seen in a tension-racked community in Philippians 2:1-4, and provides an additional basis for Paul's ethical/paraenetic appeal. The call is to accept Christ's lordly authority as an antidote to disfigurements in the church with the reminder that Christ came to his throne only along the road of obedience to God (hence Phil 2:12), self-sacrifice and giving of himself in atoning death. Lordship and the "theology of the cross" (*see* Cross, Theology of the) thus merge to form a unified plea for "being conformed" to his way (cf. Phil 3:10).

*See also* CREEDS; LITURGICAL ELEMENTS; WORSHIP.

BIBLIOGRAPHY. J. L. Bailey and L. D. Vander Broek, *Literary Forms in the New Testament* (Louisville: John Knox/Westminster, 1992) 76-82; P. Bradshaw, *The Search for the Origins of Christian Worship* (London: SPCK, 1992) 42-45; R. Bultmann, "Bekenntnis- und Liedfragmente in ersten Petrusbrief," *Coniectanea Neotestamentica* 11 (1947) 1-4; R. Deichgräber, *Gotteshymnus und Christushymnus in der frühen Christenheit* (Göttingen: Vandenhoeck & Ruprecht, 1967); G. Delling, *Worship in the New Testament* (London: Darton, Longman and Todd, 1962); G. D. Fee, "Philippians 2:5-11: Hymn or Exalted Pauline Prose?" *BBR* 2 (1992) 29-46; A. J. Festugière, *Personal Religion Among the Greeks* (Berkeley: University of California, 1954); S. E. Fowl, *The Story of Christ in the Ethics of Paul* (Sheffield: Academic, 1990); H.-J. Gabathuler, *Jesus Christus: Haupt der Kirche—Haupt der Welt* (Zurich: Zwingli, 1965); W. H. Gloer, "Homologies and Hymns in the New Testament: Form, Content and Criteria for Identification," *PRS* 11 (1984) 115-32; R. H. Gundry, "Form, Meaning and Background of the Hymn Quoted in 1 Timothy 3:16," in *Apostolic History and the Gospel*, ed W. W. Gasque and R. P. Martin (Grand Rapids: Eerdmans, 1970) 203-22; G. F. Hawthorne, *Philippians* (WBC 43; Waco, TX: Word, 1983); M. Hengel, "Hymn and Christology," in *Studia Biblica 1978 III: Papers on Paul and Other New Testament Authors*, ed. E. A. Livingstone (JSNTSup 3; Sheffield: Academic, 1980) 173-97 [= idem, *Between Jesus and Paul* (Philadelphia: Fortress, 1983) 78-96]); L. Hurtado, "Jesus as Lordly Example in Phil 2:5-11," in *From Jesus to Paul: Studies in Honour of Francis Wright Beare*, ed. J. C. Hurd and G. P. Richardson (Waterloo, Ont.: Wilfrid Laurier University, 1984) 113-26; E. Käsemann, "A Critical Analysis of Phil 2:5-11," in *God and Christ: Existence and Providence*, ed. R. W. Funk (New York: Harper and Row, 1968) 45-88; A. T. Lincoln, *Ephesians* (WBC 42; Dallas: Word, 1990); R. P. Martin, *Carmen Christi: Phil.2:5-11* (rev. ed.; Grand Rapids: Eerdmans, 1983); idem, *Ephesians, Colossians, Philemon* (Int; Louisville: Westminster, 1992); idem, "An Epistle in Search of a Life Setting," *ExpT* 79 (1968) 296-302; idem, "Hymns in the New Testament: An Evolving Pattern of Worship Responses," *Ex Auditu* 8 (1992) 33-44; idem, *Philippians* (NCB; Grand Rapids: Eerdmans, 1976); idem, *Reconciliation: A Study of Paul's Theology* (rev. ed.; Grand Rapids: Zondervan, 1990); idem, "Some Reflections on New Testament Hymns," in *Christ the Lord*, ed. H. H. Rowdon (Downers Grove, IL: InterVarsity, 1982) 37-49; E. Norden, *Agnostos Theos* (Stuttgart: Teubner, 1956); M. Rissi, "Der Christushymnus in Phil 2, 6-11," *ANRW* II.25.4 (1987) 3314-26; L. Ryken, *The New Testament in Literary Criticism* (New York: Ungar, 1984) 142-46; J. T. Sanders, *The New Testament Christological Hymns* (SNTSMS 15; Cambridge: University Press, 1971); M. Silva, *Philippians* (WEC; Chicago: Moody, 1989); E. Stauffer, *New Testament Theology* (New York: Macmillan, 1956); D. V. Way, *The Lordship of Christ: Ernst Käsemann's Interpretation of Paul's Theology* (Oxford: Clarendon, 1991) esp. 88-100.

R. P. Martin

# I

**IDOL FOOD.** *See* FOOD OFFERED TO IDOLS AND JEWISH FOOD LAWS; IDOLATRY.

## IDOLATRY

Idolatry, the English transliteration of the Greek word *eidōlolatria* (literally, "the worship of *eidōla*, 'idols, images' "), refers to a common pagan religious phenomenon of Paul's day in which images or material symbols of deities or other supernatural powers were the objects of worship.* But the term could also refer to the gods represented by the idol. Paul's critique and guidance regarding questions related to idols and idolatry was rooted in a christological revision of his inherited Jewish monotheism which thoroughly rejected idolatry of any kind.

    1. Idolatry and the OT
    2. Idolatry in the First-Century Mediterranean World
    3. Paul on Idolatry

### 1. Idolatry and the OT.

Idolatry was a problem of special magnitude to the ancient Hebrews because to them had come, "You shall have no other gods besides me," and, "You shall not make for yourself an idol in the form of anything in heaven above, or that is on the earth beneath" (Ex 20:3-4; Deut 5:7-8). Their pagan neighbors, however, had many gods and made material representations of these deities, often distinguished solely by the characteristic emblem of the god or goddess (cf. Gen 31:19, 34; Num 33:52; Deut 29:17). In Egypt, Mesopotamia, and probably in Canaan as well, devotees of the deities considered cultic images to share in the reality of the deity represented, believing that the presence and power and personality of the deity somehow resided in its image so that what happened to the image or idol happened to the deity itself (cf. Is 46:1-2). They built altars to these gods and goddesses, maintained their images, sacrificed to them, partook of feasts of sacrificial food, ate symbolically with the gods, and bowed down in worship before them (cf. Num 25:1-2).

    But such practices were forbidden to Israel. They were to have no other God than the living and true God (cf. Jer 10:10) of Abraham, Isaac, and Jacob, who had revealed himself to Moses by the name Yahweh (Ex 6:2-3) and delivered Israel from slavery to Egypt (and, by implication, from Egypt's gods) at the Exodus. Further, they were to make no material representation—no image or idol—of this one God (Deut 6:4).

    According to the OT Israel did not always obey these commands, and there is some archeological evidence that confirms the use of idols in Israel. The biblical witness is that they forgot the God who gave them birth, abandoned the God who made them, adopted new gods, which in reality were demons,* made idols of these deities, sacrificed to them and worshipped them (cf. Deut 32:15-18; LXX Is 65:11; also Jer 44:15-19; Ezek 8). In response to this apostasy, the prophets declared the impotence of the idols (1 Chron 16:26; Is 40:18-20; Ezek 8:10), called upon the people to return to the Lord (Is 1:16-19), pronounced the impending judgment of God upon them if they failed to do so (Is 10:10-11), and warned them of the catastrophe that would surely come of being expelled from their land and driven among the nations as punishment for their sin of idolatry (Jer 9:15-16; cf. Wis 14:11-21).

### 2. Idolatry in the First-Century Mediterranean World.

By the first century, however, idolatry seems to have been rooted out of Jewish religion (cf. Rom 2:22; Jdt 8:18). The *Shema* of Deuteronomy 6:4 ("Hear, O Israel, the Lord our God, the Lord is One") had become the hallmark confession of Judaism's strict monotheistic faith. For the Jews of the first century, the words of Deuteronomy 6:4 clearly indicated monotheism, not monolatry (the worship of only one of the many gods) or henotheism (belief in one god without denying the existence of others). Thus, there is no mention in the Gospels of Jesus ever speaking out against the sin of idolatry—except in a specialized sense of worshipping Mammon (*mamōnas*, "worldly wealth," Mt 6:24).

    Outside of Judaism, however, idolatry was pervasive.

What had been true of ancient Israel's neighboring nations was equally true of the peoples of the Roman Empire—they had many gods (cf. Acts 17:23): gods to be feared, gods to be appeased, gods to be honored, gods to whom sacrifices were owed, gods whose meal was to be shared by the worshipper (see *OCD*, 787-88). Throughout the entire Greco-Roman world "idols were venerated in temples dedicated to the traditional Gentile gods, in popular magic and superstition, as well as in mystery religions and mystery worship" (Garber, 2, 799; *see* Religions, Greco-Roman). Thus when Paul went out on his missionary journeys into the Gentile world he encountered idols of every sort and people who participated in the worship of these idols. For example, when Paul traveled to Athens, he was "greatly distressed to see that the city was full of idols" (*kateidōlon*, Acts 17:16 NIV). Athens* was typical of other Hellenistic cities that were given over to many forms of idolatry. Ephesus,* for example, was the center for the worship of Artemis (Acts 19:28-36), and Corinth was well known as a religious center, devoted to idolatry and its accompanying evils.

### 3. Paul on Idolatry.

The fullest discussion in the NT on idolatry and idol worship is found in what is now known as Paul's first letter to the Corinthians.* Earlier, in a letter no longer extant, Paul had told the Corinthians not to associate with those who called themselves believers, but who were still practicing idolatry (cf. 1 Cor 5:9-11). In the Corinthians' reply to him about this command they must have put up some resistance to it, or at least asked for clarification about it, for beginning at 1 Corinthians 8:1 and continuing through 11:1 Paul devotes his attention to the topic of idolatry using the vocabulary of the LXX, e.g., *eidōlothyton* ("food sacrificed to idols," 1 Cor 8:1, 4, 7, 10; 10:19; cf. also *hierothytos*, "meat offered in sacrifice," 1 Cor 10:28), *eidōla* ("idols," 1 Cor 12:2) and *eidōleion* ("the temple of an idol," 1 Cor 8:10) and vocabulary not found in the LXX, such as *eidōlolatria* ("idolatry," 1 Cor 10:14) and *eidōlolatrēs* ("idolater," 1 Cor 10:7).

One of the sins that Paul condemned at Corinth and which he was concerned to correct involved those Christians who had turned away from idols (1 Cor 12:2) to serve "the living and true God*" (see 1 Thess 1:9, which may echo early missionary preaching, cf. Acts 14:15). In spite of this conversion, they continued to go back to the idol temples (which, in a city like Corinth, could evidently function as a sort of restaurant) and there eat the food* that had been sacrificed to the idol. Apparently the Corinthian believers were able to do this in good conscience* because they had come to "know" that "no idol in the world really exists" and "there is no God but one" (1 Cor 8:4 NRSV). The suggestion has been made that the Corinthians' "knowledge"* was informed by a Hellenistic-Jewish argument that knowledge of the one true God imbued the knower with a wisdom that allowed them to dismiss pagan idols as religious nonsense (see Horsley, Wright).

On this reading of the text, Paul is agreeing in principle with the Corinthians and anchoring his argument in the *Shema*. But he reinterprets the *Shema* christologically and introduces a duality in the Godhead: "the *Lord* our *God*" of the Jewish confession becomes "one *God* the Father" and "one *Lord*\* Jesus Christ" in contrast with the "many gods and many lords" of the Greco-Roman world. By this God and Lord all things were created and all things exist. There are no other deities, and what appear to be deities are but a part of the created order in rebellion: they are demons (Wright; the view that idols are demons was well known in Judaism, see Str-B 3.48-60; cf. Deut 32:17; Bar 4:7).

What the Corinthians failed to understand was (1) that not all Christians had this knowledge nor the liberty to act toward idols with such freedom* (1 Cor 8:7); (2) that the liberty of those with "knowledge" could become a stumbling block to less knowledgeable Christians, leading these weaker Christians to sin (*see* Strong and Weak) against their conscience by eating food sacrificed to idols (1 Cor 8:9-11); and (3) that the reality behind the idol at whose table these Christians sat and ate was demonic (1 Cor 10:20). Furthermore, as Wright has pointed out, (4) Paul seems to imply that they had overlooked Deuteronomy 6:5, which follows directly on the heels of the *Shema*: "You shall love the Lord your God with all your heart, and with all your soul, and with all your might" (NRSV). In letting knowledge override the interests of the community, they sin against members of their own family and so sin against Christ (1 Cor 8:12). Thus Paul expressly prohibits Christians from eating food offered to idols and eating it *in* the temple of the idol (Fee, 359).

Although the eating of sacrificial food at cultic meals in pagan temples was forbidden by Paul because he believed that those who thus ate became united to demons (1 Cor 10:19-21), Paul had no such word of prohibition for those who purchased the food that had been left over from these events and was later sold in the marketplace. In his judgment, if they ate this food at home, or even in the home of an unbeliever (1 Cor 10:27), they were not participating in the practice of idolatry nor becoming partners with demons (1 Cor 10:20-21). They could eat whatever was sold in the meat market without raising any question of conscience. If, however, in the course of doing so, someone should point out that this was food offered in sacrifice to idols, Paul's word was, "Do not eat it, out of consideration for the one who informed you." To ignore this command of the apostle could result in serious harm being done to the weaker believer (1 Cor 10:28; cf. 8:10-11). Therefore, for the sake of that weaker believer, more liberated Christians, who realized that "the earth and its fullness are the Lord's" (cf. Ps 24:1), were asked to restrain themselves and voluntarily abstain from eating food offered to idols.

In other Pauline letters idolatry is mentioned but not always with the same definition nor with the same extended discussion as that found in 1 Corinthians. Nevertheless, Paul links idolatry in all of its forms, both literal and metaphorical (i.e., the desire for anything more than God; cf. Mt 6:24), with sorcery and other "works of the flesh," against which Christians must constantly be warned and from which they must continually flee (Gal 5:19-21; cf. 1 Cor 10:14).

In Romans 1:18-32, a passage which may reflect Hellenistic-Jewish polemic against idolatry (cf. Wis 11—15), Paul traces sexual immorality (*see* Sexuality, Sexual Ethics) and every other kind of sin, great or small, ultimately back to idolatry. The Gentiles, who should have known that God existed from observing the handiwork of God in creation, nevertheless failed to honor God as God, and instead exchanged the immortal, invisible God for mortal, visible images (idols). Because of this, God gave them up and allowed them to go their own way and do the filthy things their hearts desired (Rom 1:24 TEV). Thus Paul included idolaters among those evil people who will not inherit the kingdom of God (1 Cor 6:9).

From Ephesians 5:5 it is clear that idolaters are not simply those who go to pagan temples and worship idols; idolaters also include those who are greedy or covetous: "No fornicator or impure person or one who is greedy (that is, an idolater), has any inheritance in the kingdom of Christ and of God" (NRSV). The point is that greedy, covetous persons, those who make their desires their object of devotion, are as much idolaters as are any of those who bow before an idol in a pagan temple. Thus *pleonexia* ("covetousness") and *eidōlolatria* ("idolatry") are used synonymously (cf. also Col 3:5).

*See also* ATHENS, PAUL AT; DEMONS AND EXORCISM; FOOD OFFERED TO IDOLS AND JEWISH FOOD LAWS; GOD; RELIGIONS, GRECO-ROMAN; STRONG AND WEAK; WORSHIP.

BIBLIOGRAPHY. E. R. Bevan, *Holy Images: An Inquiry into Idolatry and Image-Worship in Ancient Paganism and Christianity* (New York: AMS, 1979); J. Brunt, "Rejected, Ignored, or Misunderstood? The Fate of Paul's Approach to the Problem of Idol Food in Early Christianity," *NTS* 11 (1964/65) 138-53; F. Büchsel, "εἴδωλον κτλ," *TDNT* II.375-80; A. C. Clarke and B. W. Winter, ed., *One God, One Lord in a World of Religious Pluralism* (Cambridge: Tyndale House, 1991); H. Conzelmann, *1 Corinthians* (Herm; Philadelphia: Fortress, 1975); J. Faur, "The Biblical Idea of Idolatry," *JQR* 69 (1978) 1-15; G. Fee, "*Eidolothyta* Once Again: An Interpretation of 1 Corinthians 8—10," *Bib* 61 (1980) 172-97; idem, *The First Epistle to the Corinthians* (NICNT; Grand Rapids: Eerdmans, 1987); P. L. Garber, "Idolatry," *ISBE* 2.799-800; R. A. Horsley, "*Gnosis* in Corinth: 1 Corinthians 8.1-6," *NTS* 27 (1980) 32-51; H. Hübner, "εἴδωλον κτλ," *EDNT* 1.386-88; R. MacMullen, *Paganism in the Roman Empire* (New Haven: Yale University, 1981); J. E. Stambaugh and D. L. Balch, *The New Testament in Its Social Environment* (Philadelphia: Westminster, 1986); P. J. Tomson, *Paul and the Law: Halakha in the Letters of the Apostle to the Gentiles* (CRINT 3.1; Minneapolis: Fortress, 1990); W. L. Willis, *Idol Meat in Corinth* (SBLDS 68; Chico, CA: Scholars, 1985); B. W. Winter, "Theological and Ethical Responses to Religious Pluralism—1 Corinthians 8—10," *TynB* 41 (1990) 209-26; N. T. Wright, "Monotheism, Christology and Ethics: 1 Corinthians 8," in *The Climax of the Covenant: Christ and the Law in Pauline Theology* (Minneapolis: Fortress, 1992) 120-36.

P. W. Comfort

**ILLNESS.** *See* HEALING, ILLNESS.

## IMAGE OF GOD

The concept of the image of God* appears in the Pauline literature in three distinct contexts: in reference to Christ* (2 Cor 4:4; Phil 2:6; Col 1:15), in reference to males (1 Cor 11:7) and in reference to Christians (Col 3:10). Elsewhere in the NT the term appears only twice, in Hebrews 1:3, where it is used of Christ, and in James 3:9, where it is used in reference to humanity generally (a usage closer to that of the OT than the Pauline senses).

1. In the Pauline Literature
2. In the OT
3. The OT Background and Paul

**1. In the Pauline Literature.**

The terms used are *morphē* (Phil 2:6), usually translated "form," *eikōn* (1 Cor 11:7; 2 Cor 4:4; Col 1:15; 3:10), usually translated "image" (in Heb 1:3 it is *charactēr*, usually translated "stamp, impress," and in Jas 3:9 it is *homoiōsis*, usually translated "likeness"); there is no clear difference among these terms. To these could be added passages where Christians are said to bear the image of Christ (Rom 8:29; 1 Cor 15:49; 2 Cor 3:18, all with *eikōn*).

**1.1. In Reference to Christ.** When Christ is spoken of as the "image" of God, the idea is that he is the visible representation of God. This is particularly explicit in Colossians 1:15, where Christ is "the image of the invisible God," but it is also observable in 2 Corinthians 4:4, where Christ's glory* is seen as an expression of the divine: unbelievers are unable to see "the light of the gospel of the glory of Christ, who is the image of God"—which means to say, as 2 Corinthians 4:6 makes plain, that the "light of the knowledge of the glory of God" is seen "in the face of [Jesus] Christ." (Cf. Heb 1:3 also, where Christ's being "the exact imprint of God's very being" [NRSV] makes him the "radiance" [*apaugasma*] of God's glory.) In Philippians 2:6, on the other hand, there is no explicit use of the terminology of "glory," but the contrast between Christ's existence "in the form of God" and his subsequent adoption of the "form of a servant*" and the "likeness [*homoiōma*] of humans" (Phil 2:7) suggests that the form of God is the very opposite of the humble status of a servant. The "image of God" when used of Christ may therefore refer to his being, but mostly denotes his function as an expression of the divine.

**1.2. In Reference to Males.** In 1 Corinthians 11:7 Paul speaks of males (*anēr*) generally (not Christian men specifically) as "being" (*hyparchōn*) the image and glory of God, and implies that women are not. Because every male "is" God's image and glory (presumably meaning he is created after God's image and expresses God's glory), every female is subordinated to a male and expresses that male's glory.

**1.3. In Reference to Christians.** Colossians 3:10 sees the Christian believer, as the "new human" (*ho neos anthrōpos*), being progressively "renewed" (or, in process of creation) "according to the image of its creator." This image consists of a superior "knowledge" (*epignōsis*) that overlooks or dissolves the boundaries between Jew and Greek, slave* and free, male and female (Col 3:11).

## 2. In the OT.

The background to these varied uses of the concept in the Pauline literature and elsewhere in the NT is the few occurrences of the terms *ṣelem*, "image," and *dᵉmût*, "likeness," in Genesis 1:26, 27; 5:1, 3; 9:6. In Genesis 1:26, 27 humankind, both male and female, is created "in" the image of God and "according to" his likeness. The context allows us to infer no more than that the divine image is the authorization for

human control of the animal world and the physical environment. In Genesis 9:6 murder is prohibited (or rather, capital punishment for murder is prescribed) on the ground that "in his own image God made humankind." This could mean that human life is sacrosanct because it in some way bears the image of God or, preferably, that the taking of human life is sanctioned in certain cases because God has devolved his authority to humans. In Genesis 5:1, 3 the reader is reminded that at the creation God made humankind "in" his likeness, and told that Adam became the father of a son "in" his likeness, "according to" his image (the variation in prepositions from Genesis 1 is probably of no consequence). The meaning apparently is that the image of God is not characteristic only of the first human generation, but of subsequent generations as well. The fact that women are included in the statements of Genesis 1:26, 27 probably does not imply any idea of male and female equality; the text speaks rather of undifferentiated humanity.

The extrabiblical context of the concept of the image of God should also be considered. In the ancient world images were apparently viewed functionally, as a means by which deities became present and visible in the world of humans. A statue or image of a god represented that god on earth, just as the image of a king represented the authority of a king in a land he had conquered. In Genesis, therefore, humanity takes the place of God on earth, a point that becomes clearer if we adopt the suggestion that Genesis 1:26 should not be translated "in our image" but "as our image, to be our image" (understanding the preposition *beth* as the *beth* of essence).

In Egypt the king is several times referred to in literary texts as the image of God, where plainly it is his right to rule that is in view. In Genesis it is not the king but humanity at large that bears that privilege; but here also it is the authority of the creator God that is the principal content of the image. In fact, we should probably translate Genesis 1:26 "Let us make humankind . . . so that they may have dominion."

## 3. The OT Background and Paul.

It is interesting that Paul never uses the concept of "the image of God" in the sense it has in Genesis; only in James is the OT usage continued. For Paul the phrase obviously has important christological overtones, especially within the framework of the New Adam* typology, and it would not have been surprising if he had reserved it for exposition of the role of Christ in creation* and as the expression of the divine. But it is also understandable that in Colossians the term should further be extended to refer to "the new humanity" that is in process of creation. What does not seem to fit so well with Pauline theology is the narrowing of the gender reference of "the image of God" in 1 Corinthians to refer to males exclusively and, furthermore, the absence of any christological connection in its application to males generally.

*See also* ADAM AND CHRIST; CHRISTOLOGY; GLORY, GLORI-FICATION; MAN AND WOMAN.

BIBLIOGRAPHY. J. Barr, "The Image of God in Genesis—Some Linguistic and Historical Considerations," in *Old Testament Papers Read at the Tenth Meeting of Die Outestamentiese Werkgemeenskap in Suidafrika* (Pretoria, 1967) 5-13; idem, "The Image of God in the Book of Genesis—A Study in Terminology," *BJRL* 51 (1968) 11-26; G. C. Berkouwer, *Man: The Image of God* (Grand Rapids: Eerdmans, 1962); P. Bird, " 'Male and Female He Created Them': Gen 1:27b in the Context of the Priestly Account of Creation," *HTR* 74 (1981) 129-59; D. J. A. Clines, "The Image of God in Man," *TynB* 19 (1968) 53-103; idem, "What Does Eve Do to Help? and Other Irredeemably Androcentric Orientations in Genesis 1-3," in *What Does Eve Do to Help? and Other Readerly Questions to the Old Testament* (JSOTSup 94; Sheffield: JSOT, 1990) 25-48; E. M. Curtis, "Image of God (OT)," *ABD* III.389-91; L. Fatum, "Image of God and Glory of Man: Women in the Pauline Congregations," in *Image of God and Gender Models in Judeo-Christian Tradition*, ed. K. Borresen (Oslo: Solum Forlag, 1991); G. D. Fee, *The First Epistle to the Corinthians* (NICNT; Grand Rapids: Eerdmans, 1987); J. Jervell, *Imago Dei. Gen. 1,26f. im Spätjudentum, in der Gnosis und in den paulinischen Briefen* (Göttingen: Vandenhoeck & Ruprecht, 1960); G. A. Jónsson, *The Image of God: Genesis 1:26-28 in a Century of Old Testament Research* (CBOT 26; Lund: Almqvist & Wiksell, 1988); V. Lossky, *In the Image and Likeness of God* (London: A. R. Mowbray, 1975); R. P. Martin, *Carmen Christi: Philippians ii.5-11 in Recent Interpretation and in the Setting of Early Christian Worship* (SNTSMS 4; Cambridge: University Press, 1967) 99-133; T. N. D. Mettinger, "Abbild oder Urbild? 'Imago Dei' in traditionsgeschichtlicher Sicht," *ZAW* 86 (1974) 403-24; M. Miller, "In the 'Image' and 'Likeness' of God," *JBL* 91 (1972) 289-304; L. Scheffczyk, ed., *Der Mensch als Bild Gottes* (Wege der Forschung 124: Darmstadt: Wissenschaftliche Buchgesellschaft, 1969); J. E. Sullivan, *The Image of God: The Doctrine of St Augustine and Its Influence* (Dubuque, IA: The Priory, 1963); H. Wildberger, "Das Abbild Gottes," *TZ* 21 (1965) 245-59, 481-501; R. McL. Wilson, "Genesis 1:26 and the New Testament," *Bijdragen* 20 (1959) 117-25.

D. J. A. Clines

## IMITATION OF PAUL/OF CHRIST

There are relatively few passages in the Pauline corpus where Paul uses the language of imitation (*mimētēs/mimeomai:* 1 Cor 4:16; 1 Cor 11:1; Phil 3:17; 1 Thess 1:6; 2:14; 2 Thess 3:6, 9). The idea of imitation, however, plays a significant (contra Michaelis), though sometimes misunderstood, role in Paul's ethics.

1. 1 Corinthians 4:16
2. 1 Corinthians 11:1
3. Philippians 3:17
4. 1 Thessalonians 1:6; 2:14
5. 2 Thessalonians 3:7-9
6. Misunderstandings of Imitation
7. Imitation and the Cross

### 1. 1 Corinthians 4:16.

There are two specific places in 1 Corinthians* where Paul urges the Corinthians to become imitators (*mimētai*) of him. The first occurs at 1 Corinthians 4:16. This call to become imitators of Paul comes at the end of a list of Paul's tribulations (1 Cor 4:9-13; *see* Afflictions). Paul (and his coworkers) has become a "fool for the sake of Christ*"; he is "held in disrepute"; he is "hungry, thirsty, poorly clothed, beaten and homeless." He closes this list by claiming that he has become like the "garbage of the world."

From the beginning of the letter Paul has been arguing against those in Corinth who believe that the end of the ages in all its fullness, power and freedom has been completed in them (*see* Eschatology). Paul claims that the Corinthians misunderstand the power and freedom of the gospel* because they failed to understand the significance of the cross when they were baptized into Christ and his death (cf. Rom 6:3; *see* Dying and Rising). He reminds them, however, that when he was among them he "knew nothing but Jesus Christ and him crucified" (1 Cor 2:2; see also 1 Cor 1:18, 23). Prior to the consummation of all things, the Christian life, and particularly Christians' conception of true power* and authority,* are characterized by the cross.* Throughout the first four chapters of the letter Paul has sought to reorient the Corinthians' understanding of the power of the gospel by turning their eyes to the cross. In particular he has pointed to his own life as an apostle, as an embodiment of a cruciform existence in the world.*

By reciting his afflictions in 1 Corinthians 4:9-13 Paul hopes to persuade his audience that in his weakness* the true power of the cross is revealed. This is what lies behind Paul's desire that the Corinthians become imitators of him. J. H. Schütz summarizes this point well when he says, "To imitate the weakness and power of Christ is to become the recipient of God's power in one's own weakness" (230). In calling the Corinthians to imitate him, Paul is pointing to his life of weakness as the way to embody the life of the cross. By imitating Paul in this respect the Corinthians will adopt the manner of life needed to live faithfully on this side of Christ's return.

### 2. 1 Corinthians 11:1.

At the beginning of 1 Corinthians 11 Paul again urges the Corinthians to imitate him. This time an additional phrase is added. The Corinthians are to imitate Paul as he imitates Christ. Although this verse begins chapter 11 it really represents the closing of the paragraph that starts at 1 Corinthians 10:23. This call to imitation, therefore, ought to be understood in this light.

There may be some temptation to read Paul's call to imitate him as he imitates Christ in the light of 1 Corinthians 10:31 where he claims that he does not "seek his own advantage, but that of the many so that they might be saved." It is not at all likely, however, that Paul is claiming that he imitates Christ by saving people just as Christ does (see Schütz, 229).

Rather, the guiding theme of this paragraph (and indeed of this whole section on idol worship) is contained in the notion of "building up" the body of Christ (*see* Body of Christ) through seeking the advantage of others rather than one's own advantage (see 1 Cor 10:23-24, 33). The building up of the body is a theme that appears repeatedly throughout the letter (see 1 Cor 8:1; 14:5, 12, 17, 26 and less directly in 1 Cor 11:17-34 and 1 Cor 12:4-27). For the Corinthians to imitate Paul as he imitates Christ, the one who calls the community into being and who sustains it (1 Cor 1:30), they will need to dedicate themselves to the task of building up the body. In terms of concrete action this imitation demands that the Corinthians seek the well-being of others rather than their own.

### 3. Philippians 3:17.

In Philippians 3:17 Paul uses the unusual word *symmimētai* to call the Philippians to become "fellow imitators." Because this is such an unusual word, it is not clear whether Paul wants the Philippians to join with him in being imitators (presumably of Christ) or whether the Philippian congregation is to engage in a collective practice of imitating Paul. The reference at the end of Philippians 3:17 to the "example you have in us" would indicate that it is the latter of these two possibilities.

As a call to imitate Paul, Philippians 3:17 serves as a climax to a discussion about his life which he begins at Philippians 3:4. After reciting all of the reasons he has for boasting,* Paul says that he considers all these things to be rubbish in comparison with knowing Christ (Phil 3:7-8). Indeed, Paul wants to know Christ in a particular way. He wants "to know Christ and the power of his resurrection* and the sharing of his sufferings by becoming like him in his death" (Phil 3:10). Here again Paul sees his life of discipleship as the living of a cruciform life, and it is this which the Philippians are to imitate. Further, as Philippians 3:18 implies, should the Philippians fail to imitate Paul, they run the risk of living as "enemies of the cross of Christ" (*see* Enemy).

In many ways Philippians 3:17 simply reiterates the demands Paul has made of them in Philippians 1:27-30, urging the Philippians to act in ways that conform to Christ's self-emptying, obedient death on a cross (Phil 2:6-8; see also Fowl, Hooker, Stanley). As God vindicated Christ's activity by raising him from the dead and giving him a name above all names, so "[Christ] will transform the body of our humiliation that it may be conformed to the body of his glory" (Phil 3:21; *see* Resurrection).

### 4. 1 Thessalonians 1:6; 2:14.

As part of Paul's greeting to the Thessalonians, he notes that they have become "imitators of us [Paul, Silvanus and Timothy] and of the Lord" (1 Thess 1:6). The basis for such a claim is then spelled out both in terms of the Thessalonians' reception of the gospel amidst tribulation and in regard to their continued faithfulness (1 Thess 1:6-9).

As the letter unfolds, it seems that the Thessalonians are less steadfast than they once were. By accepting Paul's message, they made a radical break with their past. Making such a break would court both social and familial disfavor. The distress and affliction that this disfavor caused new believers seemed relatively common among Pauline churches (see Malherbe, 46-52; DeBoer, 115; *see* Social Setting).

Such a situation in Thessalonica led Paul to encourage and instruct this struggling body. As part of his strategy of encouragement and instruction Paul in 1 Thessalonians 2:13-16 recalls the Thessalonians' initial reception of the gospel. In receiving the gospel as the word of God in the midst of affliction, the Thessalonians became "imitators of the churches of God in Christ Jesus in Judea" (1 Thess 2:14). By noting that the Thessalonians' reception of the word of God in the midst of tribulation imitates the situation of the churches in Judea, Paul hopes to confirm the Thessalonians' faith. "Their persecution has become the index, the credential which authenticates their reception of [the gospel] as the *logos theou*" ("word of God"; Schütz, 226).

In both of these references the imitation that is commended is seen in terms of faithfulness in the midst of suffering and distress (DeBoer, 97-99). This faithfulness is the cruciform life which Paul saw in Christ and took on for himself (see Stanley, 868). In the case of the Thessalonians, unlike the Corinthians, Paul does not have to convince them that this is the only way to live faithfully. Rather, they need to be encouraged and instructed on how to continue in the life of the cross which they took on from the beginning in imitation of the Lord.*

### 5. 2 Thessalonians 3:7-9.

The only other text in the Pauline corpus where Paul explicitly urges imitation of himself occurs in 2 Thessalonians 3:7-9. Here Paul is addressing "disorder" in the Thessalonian church. The source of this disorder is not clear. It may have come from those Christians who believed that the Parousia was so close at hand that they were unwilling to engage in the day-to-day activities needed to keep body and soul together (*see* Discipline). Alternatively, the disorder might have stemmed from some form of proto-gnostic spirituality (DeBoer, 132-35; *see* Gnosis, Gnosticism; Thessalonians). In either case, Paul makes it quite clear that this is not "according to the tradition" which the Thessalonians received from Paul and his coworkers* (2 Thess 3:6). Indeed, rather than characterizing the lives of these Thessalonian Christians in terms of either watchful expectancy or committed spirituality,* Paul calls them "idle." To reinforce his disdain for such lives, Paul points to the example of himself and his coworkers. They not only preached the gospel to the Thessalonians, they also engaged in gainful employment. The Thessalonians themselves ought to imitate this example (*see* Tentmaking).

### 6. Misunderstandings of Imitation.

Having surveyed the relevant texts where Paul explicitly uses the language of imitation in regard to himself, we should note some ways in which this notion can be misunderstood. First, our contemporary notion of imitation (as well as some ancient notions) leads us to think that the imitation should be like the original in as many respects as possible. It should be the mirror image of the original. If we apply this notion of imitation to Paul, not to mention Christ whom Paul imitates, we will miss the point. When Paul calls on Christians to be imitators of himself and of Christ he wants them to incorporate certain specific aspects of his life into their own lives. Without doubt, when Paul calls on the Corinthians, for example, to become imitators of him they did not understand this as a call to become tent-

makers. The contexts in which Paul uses the language of imitation are clear enough that both modern Christians and his original audience can recognize the respects in which Paul is to be imitated. In this sense Paul's language of imitation is not substantially different from other places where Paul calls on believers to do as he does (see 1 Cor 7:7-16; Gal 4:12-20; Phil 4:9).

Secondly, the individualism so characteristic of modernity might well lead us to accuse anyone urging us to imitate them of being extremely arrogant (Best deals with this charge, 69-71). Several considerations should lead us to be cautious in making this judgment in regard to Paul. We must first recognize that the notion of imitating some sort of moral exemplar was quite common in the ancient world. (See, e.g., Isocrates, *Dem.* 4.11; Seneca *Ep. Mor.* 6.5-6; 7.6-9; 11.9; Quintilian *Inst. Orat.* 2.28; Philostratus *Vit. Ap.* 1.19; 4 Macc. 9:23; 2 Macc. 6:27-28. See Best for other examples.)

Further, new converts cannot be expected to have mastered the demands of their new faith and the practices needed to live in accord with these demands in their day-to-day lives. Such converts will need both instruction in their new faith and concrete examples of how to embody their faith in the various contexts in which they find themselves. We can understand this if we think in terms of the ways in which it is essential for an apprentice to imitate a master of a particular craft. For example, in the initial stages of an apprenticeship in silversmithing the apprentice sits directly opposite the master silversmith in order to imitate the master's movements. Years of learning and practice allow the master to work almost instinctively. Apprentices, however, can only hope to develop such instinctual movements through imitating the master. No amount of abstract verbal instruction can bring about mastery of a craft without the concrete example of a master to imitate.

It would have been futile for Paul simply to repeat to the Philippians, for example, the abstract command "Live a cruciform life." Without giving this phrase some concrete content by pointing to his own life and practice, Paul infers that the Philippians* would have been unclear about how to embody such a command. In fact, failure to understand just this aspect of the life of a disciple led some Philippian Christians to succumb to wrong-headed notions, presumably while claiming to live faithfully before Christ. It appears that the Philippians needed to be directed to a concrete example of what a cruciform life might look like in their context if they were to have any expectation of achieving this themselves and if they were to see the ways in which they were not presently achieving this aim.

Hence, rather than reflecting an arrogant desire for

self-aggrandizement, the idea of imitation (in certain respects) was crucial to Paul's moral discourse. For Paul (and for all Christians), the only arrogance surrounding the language of imitation would be the arrogance of those who think that they can walk the path of discipleship without observing, learning from and imitating those who are already further down the path.

### 7. Imitation and the Cross.

Aside from the relatively general reference in 2 Thessalonians 3, the examination of the specific passages in which Paul uses the language of imitation has shown that the language of imitation is closely associated with the cross. For Paul the cross is the sign under which all Christian life this side of the Parousia is judged (*see* Judgment). That the cross should be a sign of such power, that God's power should be demonstrated through a sign of weakness and brokenness, contradicts all of the expectations of both Paul's audience and our own world. The cross is "a stumbling block to the Jews and foolishness to the Greeks" (1 Cor 1:13). It appears that even for those who sought to live faithfully before the God of Jesus Christ, the life of the cross was a source of great puzzlement and dispute. Paul seems to have grasped that it was only through *imitating* one who already had sought to embody—with some degree of success—the cruciform life of a disciple that new disciples could hope to embody the cross in the various contexts in which they found themselves. The strangeness of the cruciform life is what led Paul to urge several of his churches to imitate him as he imitated the life of the cross which he saw in Christ.

*See also* CROSS, THEOLOGY OF THE; DYING AND RISING WITH CHRIST; ETHICS; SERVANT, SERVICE; SUFFERING.

BIBLIOGRAPHY. E. Best, *Paul and His Converts* (Edinburgh: T. & T. Clark, 1988) chap. 3; E. A. Castelli, *Imitating Paul: A Discourse of Power* (Louisville: Westminster, 1991); W. P. DeBoer, *The Imitation of Paul* (Kampen: Kok, 1962); S. E. Fowl, *The Story of Christ in the Ethics of Paul* (JSNTS 36; Sheffield: JSOT, 1990); E. Güttgemanns, *Der leidende Apostel und sein Herr* (FRLANT 90; Göttingen: Vandenhoeck & Ruprecht, 1966); M. Hooker, "Philippians 2:6-11," in *Jesus und Paulus: Festschrift für Werner Georg Kümmel zum 70. Geburtstag*, ed. E. Grässer and E. E. Ellis (Göttingen: Vandenhoeck & Ruprecht, 1975) 151-64; A. J. Malherbe, *Paul and the Thessalonians* (Philadelphia: Fortress, 1987); W. Michaelis, "μιμέομαι κτλ," *TDNT* IV.659-74; J. H. Schütz, *Paul and the Anatomy of Apostolic Authority* (SNTSMS 26; Cambridge: University Press, 1975); D. M. Stanley, "Become Imitators of Me: The Pauline Conception of Apostolic Tradition," *Bib* 40 (1958) 859-77.

S. E. Fowl

# IMMORTALITY

*Athanasia*, a Greek word that literally means, "not subject to death," or "that which will never die," occurs rarely in the NT and is used only by Paul (three times: 1 Cor 15:53, 54; 1 Tim 6:16) to express the idea of immortality. *Aphtharsia* (literally, "not subject to decay"), another uniquely Pauline word, is used much more often by the apostle and conveys a similar if not identical concept (cf. Rom 2:7; 2 Tim 1:10). Frequently, however, *aphtharsia* and its cognate adjective, *aphthartos*, are translated, "imperishable," "the imperishable" or "imperishability" (1 Cor 9:25; 15:42, 50, 52-54; cf. Rom 1:23; 1 Tim 1:17). Immortality in Paul's writings, therefore, must be understood to be an existence that is imperishable, incorruptible, never-dying, never-ending.

1. Immortality in the OT and Judaism
2. Immortality in Paul
3. Conclusion

### 1. Immortality in the OT and Judaism.

The idea of immortality is not one that figures largely in the Hebrew OT canon (cf. Dan 12:2). But certain deductions can be drawn from Genesis 1—3. In Genesis 2:17 death is introduced as the judgment for eating of the tree of the knowledge of good and evil, a judgment enacted in the expulsion from the garden and the consequent denial of access to the tree of life. This tree of life may represent life as an inherently divine quality that was on offer to humankind. In short, Adam may have been "created neither immortal nor mortal but with the potentiality to become either, depending on his obedience or disobedience to God. While he was not created *with* immortality, as far as the divine purpose was concerned he was created *for* immortality" (Harris 1983, 193-94).

The idea of immortality appears frequently in the writings from Qumran and in intertestamental literature, especially in the Wisdom of Solomon. In these writings it is said that human beings are made for eternity, created for immortality and destined for eternal joy in perpetual life (1QH 3:19-36; 1QS 4:7; Wis 2:23; cf. also Wis 3:4; 4:1; 6:19; 8:13, 17; 15:3; see also 4 Macc 9:22; 14:5; 16:13; 17:12). Such texts as these no doubt formed the background for Paul's teaching on the subject, which he modified and clarified and grounded firmly in light of the Christ event.

### 2. Immortality in Paul.

According to Paul, it is God* alone who is immortal

(Rom 1:23; 1 Tim 1:17; cf. Deut 32:40; Sir. 18:1) and to whom immortality truly belongs (1 Tim 6:16). Human beings, on the other hand, do not by nature possess immortality. Instead they are mortal, perishable, made susceptible to corruption because of sin* (Rom 5:12; 1 Cor 15:42, 50; cf. Acts 2:22). And yet, because they have eternity stamped on their souls (cf. 1QH 3:19, 20), they crave immortality and seek to achieve it by good deeds (Rom 2:7) or to attain to it by wisdom (Wis. 8:13, 17). In the final analysis, however, immortality cannot be gained by human endeavor. Rather it is something that is "brought to light through the gospel" (2 Tim 1:10), that is to say, through the appearing of the Savior,* Christ Jesus, who by his life and death and resurrection* abolished death, on the one hand, and provided all who believe with immortality, on the other (2 Tim 1:10).

Immortality, it may be argued, is not intrinsic to humans, affected as they are by the debilitating effects of sin, nor is it attained by human achievement, nor is it a right that inherently belongs to human beings. If such a right ever existed, it was forfeited by rebellion and disobedience to God (cf. Gen 3:1-7, 24; Rom 5:12). Rather, according to Paul, immortality is always for humans a derived state of existence, a gift from God to be received by faith.* Paul would be in harmony with the words of the Wisdom writer, even though he most certainly would wish to modify them christologically: "To know you [O God] is the whole of righteousness, and to acknowledge your power is the root of immortality" (Wis 15:3; cf. 2 Tim 1:10).

Paul may have thought of immortality as something already possessed by believers. This is possible if one assumes that his use of the expression *zōē aiōnios* ("eternal life"; cf. Rom 5:21; 6:23) parallels that of immortality. And it is clear that Paul did not relegate the blessings of the age to come, including the life of the new age (*zōē aiōnios*), exclusively to the future (cf. Rom 5:21; 6:23). Nevertheless, he insisted, contrary to what the Corinthians* themselves may have believed (cf. 1 Cor 4:8, 9; 15:12-19), that the immortality which God has promised to believers (1 Cor 15:53)—immortality in the fullest sense of this term—can only be attained at the resurrection, an event that is still future (1 Cor 15:52-53).

1 Corinthians 15 is the primary source for understanding Paul's meaning of immortality. Here he uses all three words for immortality—*athanasia, aphtharsia* and *aphthartos* (1 Cor 15:42, 50, 52-54). He contrasts immortality with *phthartos* ("that which is bound to disintegrate and die," "perishable," "mortal"). He argues that as there are both earthly bodies and heavenly bodies, and the glory of the one differs from the

other, so in the human realm there is both the earthbound physical body and the resurrection spiritual body, and the difference between these two is striking (*see* Body). The physical human body is marked by weakness, dishonor, perishability, mortality. The resurrection body on the other hand is characterized by glory,* power,* immortality (1 Cor 15:42-44). This contrast spells out a fundamental difference between the first Adam and the second Adam, the man from the earth and the man of heaven (*see* Adam and Christ). Since what is physical, or earthly, cannot inherit the kingdom of God, and the perishable does not inherit the immortal, a radical change is necessary that will result in the perishable putting on the imperishable (1 Cor 15:52)—God's final victory over death. Life, not death, has the last word (1 Cor 15:54-57).

It is also possible that other Pauline texts argue for immortality, at least implicitly. 2 Corinthians 5:1-10 is one of these. Although it is a passage that is difficult to interpret, perhaps because Paul multiplies figures (or metaphors)—house, tent, clothing—in his attempt to explain life after death, yet this much is clear from what he writes: on account of the goodness and action of God (2 Cor 5:1, 5) that which is mortal (*to thnēton*) will eventually be swallowed up by life—mortality will give way to immortality.

Philippians 1:20-21 and 3:20-21 also point in this same direction. In these texts Paul not only hints at the possibility of the believer consciously enjoying the presence of Christ after death, but he states with confidence that the humble, mortal, perishable body of the believer will be radically transformed, and, by implication, made immortal at the Parousia (*see* Eschatology).

### 3. Conclusion.
There are at least three viable schools of thought generated by those who have attempted to interpret Paul's understanding of life after death. These result from differing views of humankind. Traditional Christianity, holding to a dualistic or tripartite view of persons, believes that between death and the resurrection there is some sort of an intermediate state in which the immaterial part of the individual continues in a conscious existence apart from the physical body. Others are persuaded that there can be no separation of soul from body if a person is to continue to be a person. Those who hold to this latter perspective must assume, therefore, that at death God immediately provides the believer with a new spiritual body from heaven. Still others, with this same holistic anthropology, propound a form of re-creationism—a temporary lapse of consciousness at death (soul sleep), which

ends in a new creation at the resurrection of the last day (*see* Intermediate State).

*See also* BODY; ESCHATOLOGY; INTERMEDIATE STATE; LIFE AND DEATH; RESURRECTION.

BIBLIOGRAPHY. F. F. Bruce, "Paul on Immortality," *SJT* 24 (1971) 457-72; R. Bultmann, "ἀθανασία," *TDNT* III.22-25; J. W. Cooper, *Body, Soul, and Life Everlasting* (Grand Rapids: Eerdmans, 1989); O. Cullmann, *Immortality of the Soul or Resurrection of the Dead?* (London: Epworth, 1958); E. E. Ellis, "II Corinthians v.1-10 in Pauline Eschatology," NTS 6 (1959-60) 211-24; idem, *Paul and His Recent Interpreters* (Grand Rapids: Eerdmans, 1961) 35-48; G. D. Fee, *The First Epistle to the Corinthians* (NICNT; Grand Rapids: Eerdmans, 1987) 775-809; G. Harder, "φθείρω κτλ," *TDNT* IX.93-106; M. J. Harris, "2 Cor 5:1-10: A Watershed in Paul's Eschatology?" *TynB* 22 (1971) 32-37; idem, *From Grave to Glory* (Grand Rapids: Zondervan, 1990); idem, *Raised Immortal: Resurrection and Immortality in the New Testament* (Grand Rapids: Eerdmans, 1983); J. Jeremias, "Flesh and Blood Cannot Inherit the Kingdom of God," NTS 2 (1956) 151-59; G. E. Ladd, *A Theology of the New Testament* (Grand Rapids: Eerdmans, 1974) 550-65; A. T. Lincoln, *Paradise Now and Not Yet* (Cambridge: University Press, 1981); D. E. H. Whiteley, *The Theology of St. Paul* (Oxford: Blackwell, 1964) 248-69.

J. J. Scott, Jr.

**IMPERIAL HOUSEHOLD.** *See* CAESAR'S HOUSEHOLD, IMPERIAL HOUSEHOLD; PHILIPPIANS, LETTER TO THE.

**IMPRISONMENT.** *See* PRISON, PRISONER.

**IMPURITY.** *See* PURITY AND IMPURITY.

## IN CHRIST

The phrases "in Christ (Jesus)" and "in the Lord" appear frequently in the Pauline letters. They are nearly absent from the other writings of the NT, except for pronominal references to Christ in the Johannine materials. This concentration of the expression in the Pauline letters has suggested to many interpreters that some or all of its occurrences represent a Pauline formula. It is often thought that such a formula was based on a "local" conception of Christ* as a substance or person. But the variety of ways in which the phrases appear in Paul's letters indicates that they serve as a flexible idiom which may express instrumentality or mode of action as well as locality. While Paul sometimes joins the expression "in Christ" with the image of Christ as an inclusive figure, body* or building, it is not derived from or limited to a "corporate" idea. Paul's language instead partakes of a com-

mon metaphorical use of "space" by which definition or exclusivity is represented. In varying ways, then, the expression "in Christ" conveys Paul's belief that God's saving purposes are decisively effected through Christ.

1. The Usage of the Expression
2. The Origin and Basis of the Expression
3. Theological Aspects of Paul's Usage

### 1. The Usage of the Expression.

A number of variations of the expression are possible for Paul, the most frequent of which are "in Christ," "in Christ Jesus" and "in the Lord." It is probable that the individual forms often represent differing nuances of meaning. The Pauline letters only once use "in Jesus" (Eph 4:21), and never "in Jesus Christ," although otherwise references to "Jesus Christ" regularly appear in the letters. The prominence of "Christ" in the phrase suggests an emphasis on the exalted status and saving role of the Messiah. The frequently attached name "Jesus" may call forth the idea of the earthly figure and his humanity. The alternative form "in the Lord" usually stresses the unique power* and divine authority* of Christ, and hence his right to demand obedience or his ability to deliver from other "powers" (e.g., Phil 1:14, 1 Thess 4:1). These distinctions in meaning may not always be present however (see, e.g., Rom 16:1-16).

Unlike the Johannine literature, which focuses on the mutual inherence of Christ and believers, Paul does not emphasize this reciprocal aspect. The idea that Christ is in or among believers appears in his letters (e.g., Gal 2:19; Rom 8:10; Col 1:27) but is only occasionally brought into association with the thought that believers are in Christ.

The expression is used over a triangular field of meaning rather than in a single, "technical" sense. At one corner of the field one finds the examples of the form "certain ones/churches (are) in Christ," where the phrase takes a local sense. At another corner one finds statements like "God was reconciling the world to himself in Christ" (2 Cor 5:19). Here Christ is viewed as the instrument of God's action (debate on the meaning of this verse notwithstanding). Sometimes "in Christ/the Lord" may stress the manner in which an action occurs ("I speak the truth in Christ," Rom 9:1). Paul's use of the phrases moves between these limits, generally exhibiting a lack of distinction between the three ideas of locality, instrumentality and modality (e.g., "your labor is not in vain in the Lord," 1 Cor 15:58).

As Robertson and others have observed, the instrumental use of the Greek preposition *en* ("in") is a metaphorical extension of the local sense (Robertson,

590). Even when "in Christ"/"in the Lord" is used to describe an instrument or manner of action, "Christ" is understood as a defining "sphere." The "in" phrases bear a more specific sense than the "through" phrases, as Paul's shift from the wording "through a human being" to "in Adam*" and "in Christ" shows (1 Cor 15:21-22). Christ, and no other, is God's instrument for raising humans from the dead, just as death comes through Adam alone. A similar change of meaning emerges in 2 Corinthians 5:18-19 where Paul moves from affirming that he was reconciled to God through Christ, to describing his preaching as asserting that God was reconciling the world to himself in Christ. In the second instance the exclusivity of the proclamation evokes a more definite idea.

Occasionally Paul describes believers or their actions as "in the Spirit" (e.g., Rom 8:9; 9:1; 14:17; *see* Holy Spirit). If we may take Romans 8:1-11 as the determinative context, it is clear that being "in Christ" leads to being "in the Spirit," not the reverse (Rom 8:1, 2). Those who belong to Christ have the indwelling Spirit of Christ, and so are not "in the flesh*" but "in the Spirit" (Rom 8:9).

Twice Paul refers to the Thessalonians as being "in God the Father and the Lord Jesus Christ" (1 Thess 1:1; 2 Thess 1:1). This unusual variation is part of Paul's concentration of references to God* in the Thessalonian correspondence, stemming from his focus on eschatology* and, perhaps, his awareness of their recent conversion from paganism. It may reflect a concern on Paul's part to preserve monotheism while asserting the efficacy of faith* in Christ.

In Colossians* and Ephesians* the frequency of "in Christ/the Lord" increases sharply. Furthermore, a series of new spatial metaphors appears. The fullness* of deity dwells in Christ bodily (Col 2:9). The divine purpose for creation,* redemption and the consummation of all things is comprehended within the "sphere" of Christ (Eph 1:3-10). Believers have been placed in heaven* by being placed in him (Eph 2:6; Col 3:1). They have been made part of a body of which Christ is the head* (Eph 4:15-16). They are being built together as a temple* (Eph 2:21-22). They have put on a new humanity (Eph 4:22-24; Col 3:10). All these images present Christ as the focal expression of deity and the divine purpose, and consequently the basis of the life and unity of the entire church.*

### 2. The Origin and Basis of the Expression.
The local or spatial sense of "in Christ/the Lord" has provided the starting point for most modern scholarly theories of its derivation. Generally these theories depend on a quasi-physical understanding of "Christ" in order to interpret the spatial sense conveyed by the phrases. Some scholars in the earlier part of the twentieth century claimed that Paul, equating Christ with the Spirit, understood him as an all-pervading fluid, like the air which we breathe and in which we live (e.g., Deissmann, Bousset). Others asserted that the background to the local idea lay in the myth of a redeemer figure found in gnostic* writings (e.g., Käsemann). This thesis further provided the means for understanding Paul's statements about participation with Christ in death* and resurrection*: as a member of the redeemer's material body, one shared in his destiny. A. Schweitzer claimed to find the source of Paul's thought in an early Jewish expectation of a real, physical union of the elect with the Messiah.

During the latter decades of the twentieth century, scholars have tended to appeal to the broader notion of a "corporate personality," which is thought to be found in the Hebrew Scriptures and early Jewish literature (e.g., Best, Moule). In this reading Christ is regarded as an all-encompassing "person" with whom the whole community of believers is united in experience and destiny. This frequently used but ill-defined idea has come under justified criticism in recent study (see Wedderburn, Porter).

In some measure the local and quasi-physical understanding of Paul's language has been tempered by several mid twentieth-century studies, especially those of F. Neugebauer and M. Bouttier. Neugebauer denied that "in Christ" or "in the Lord" had any spatial sense, arguing that these expressions convey instead the temporal idea of inclusion in the decisive saving event, Christ's death and resurrection. Bouttier was more impressed by the diversity of Paul's usage, finding instrumental and eschatological ideas as well as the inclusive (local) sense. These studies have brought an increased awareness that in many contexts the primary force of the phrase may be something other than locality.

It remains a question whether Paul's employment of a spatial metaphor demands any of the proposed corporeal images of Christ. Three crucial considerations argue against supposing that the idea of an organic reality lies behind his usage. Paul's references to "in Christ" and "in the Lord" appear to be a special extension of the common and almost unnoticed practice of symbolically representing exclusivity or definition as a locality. Paul, like the psalmist, rejoices and hopes "in the Lord" (e.g., Phil 4:4, cf. Ps 5:11; 9:2; 33:21, 22). He applies similar language to persons who do not fit the model of a universal "corporate personality": the Israelites were baptized "into Moses*" (1 Cor 10:2), God promised to bless the nations "in Abraham*" (Gal 3:8, 9), he raised up Pharaoh to display his power "in him" (Rom 9:15), the Philippians have the struggle they saw and heard "in me" (Phil 1:30), the unbelieving husband is sanctified "in his wife" (1 Cor 7:14). Parallel representations may be found elsewhere in the NT (e.g., Mk 3:22; 14:6), in contemporary Jewish authors ("In him [God], and in no other, was their salvation," Josephus Ant. 3.1.5 §23), in secular papyri (e.g., "There is an additional debt from the price of grain 'in' Ptolemy," cited by Mayser, 2.396), and even in classical Greek sources of the fifth century B.C. (e.g., Sophocles Ajax 518, the captive Tecmessa to Ajax: "In you entirely, I am delivered"). The Greek preposition en, "in," may convey association or instrumentality, but the idea of a defining "sphere" remains in such instances. This wider use of spatial metaphor cautions against requiring a concrete local image behind Paul's language.

Moreover, although the attempt has been made (Schweitzer, Sanders), it is not possible to extend a quasi-physical image of union with Christ into Paul's larger theology. There is a breakdown of the metaphor, which reveals that it is not informed by some more definite corporeal understanding of salvation. Paul derives his ethical demands from what God has accomplished in Christ: "Clean out the old leaven, that you might be a new lump of dough, just as you are unleavened" (1 Cor 5:7); "You were once in darkness, but now you are light in the Lord: walk as children of light" (Eph 5:8). If Paul were operating with an organic concept of salvation, he might speak of degrees of mystical participation (e.g., a process of being filled with "light") but not in the paradoxical formulation he offers here.

Paul's utilization of material symbols is robust yet diverse, suggesting a plurality of metaphors rather than a basic realistic idea. Paul's figure of the "body of Christ" is supplemented by his description of the community of believers as the temple* of God (e.g., 1 Cor 3:16, 17; Eph 2:19-22). He plays upon the image of spirit-body dualism with his description of immersion and infusion with the Spirit uniting believers in one body (1 Cor 12:12, 13). He also occasionally links Christ with the indwelling Spirit (Rom 8:10; 1 Cor 15:45; probably Col 3:11; see Holy Spirit). Yet there is no absolute identification of the two (e.g., Rom 8:11). The statements rather represent metonymy: the Spirit is spoken of as Christ, because the Spirit is the means by which Christ's lordship is effected in believers (e.g., 1 Cor 12:3). It is noteworthy that the expression "in Christ" qualifies the idea of believers as the body of Christ, describing its "sphere" of validity: "We, who are many, are one body in Christ" (Rom 12:5). As Gundry has argued, the body here is a metaphor for the interdependence and unity of believers, not a real entity (Gundry, 223-44).

Although the corporate explanations are not satisfactory, it is clear that for Paul, in some real sense, believers share in Christ's death and resurrection. Life in Christ brings participation with him in his death and resurrection (Rom 6:1-11; 2 Cor 13:4; Gal 3:26-28). Paul's employment of Adam* as an inclusive figure is of fundamental importance in tracing this aspect of his thought. Early Jewish parallels to Paul's references to Adam are especially close, and reveal a conception of destiny based on divine pronouncement which matches Paul's statements. God ordained that the entire human race arise from one human being, to show that one who murders a single human being is guilty of destroying the whole world (m.Sanh. 4:5). With Adam's transgression, condemnation came on the whole of humanity (4 Ezra 3:21; 2 Baruch 23:4; 48:42, 43). The judgment* of God on the deed of the one decides the life or death of the many: as in Adam, so also in Christ, Paul argues (1 Cor 15:22, Rom 5:12-21). Solidarity with Adam stems from the divine will to bless or curse through him, not from physical descent, although in this instance the two converge. Paul's dependence on this larger category is apparent in his interpretation of the divine blessing of the Gentiles "in Abraham," who, of course, were not the physical offspring of the patriarch (Gal 3:8, 9).

Paul's connection of Christ to Adam derives from his understanding of the universal scope of Christ's atoning work on the cross: "One died for all, therefore all died" (2 Cor 5:14, 15). Like Adam, therefore, Christ is the new beginning of humanity (Gal 3:28; Eph 4:22-24; Col 3:9-11). The idea that the destinies of the Messiah and the people of God are linked is not unique (e.g., Dan 7:9-27; 2 Baruch 30), but Paul's explicit messianic universalism is. For him, the figures of Adam and Christ are contrasted in all-embracing judgment and salvation.

The expression "in Christ/the Lord" probably came from earlier Jewish Christianity. The book of Acts provides evidence that, before Paul, the earliest believers in Jerusalem proclaimed Jesus as the decisive "sphere" of God's saving action (Acts 4:2, 12). And as Paul's reliance on a traditional statement in Romans 6:3 shows, prior to him participation in salvation had been expressed in baptism,* through which one was transferred into the "realm of Christ." This language and these ideas came into special prominence and underwent further definition in Paul's letters.

### 3. Theological Aspects of Paul's Usage.

Although there is considerable overlap of the various types, the occurrences of the expression may be divided into five broad thematic categories:

(1) More than one-third of the 151 references affirm something that God has done or does through Christ for salvation (e.g., "the redemption which is in Christ Jesus," Rom 3:24). As we have noted, in Colossians and Ephesians this is expanded to include creation and its consummation.

(2) Approximately another third have to do with exhortation or commendation of behavior or character (e.g., "Rejoice in the Lord always," Phil 4:4; "Prisca and Aquila, my fellow workers in Christ Jesus," Rom 16:3).

(3) About twenty occurrences of the expression describe the present state of believers in view of Christ's saving work (e.g., "we, who are many, are one in Christ," Rom 12:5).

(4) A final dozen or so describe specific persons or particular situations in relation to salvation. Among these are six statements that simply affirm that certain ones are "in Christ" (Rom 16:7, 22, 1 Cor 1:30; Gal 1:22; 1 Thess 3:8; 2 Cor 12:2).

(5) Two references in Colossians have to do strictly with the nature of Christ (Col 1:19; 2:9).

The expansion of the phrases in the vocabulary of Paul's letters and churches is very likely the product of two basic concerns:

(1) In varying ways Paul found it necessary to assert the exclusivity or distinctiveness of God's saving action through Christ. To describe God as having acted "in Christ" or redemption as being "in Christ" succinctly conveyed this thought ("the gift of God is eternal life in Christ Jesus our Lord," Rom 6:23).

(2) It was also important to Paul to define how believers were to live under Christ's saving lordship. In statements which call for, describe or commend obedience, "in Christ/the Lord" communicates simultaneously the gift of salvation and the accompanying divine demand (e.g., "stand firm in the Lord," Phil 4:1). The phrases therefore became a vehicle for Paul to describe the life of faith under Christ's lordship in a world where other powers and temptations were present. To act "in Christ" is to act in faith and obedience in the face of false alternatives: "In Christ Jesus neither circumcision or uncircumcision has any force, but rather faith working through love" (Gal 5:6).

*See also* ADAM AND CHRIST; BODY OF CHRIST; CHRIST; CHRISTOLOGY.

BIBLIOGRAPHY. E. Best, *One Body in Christ: A Study of the Relationship of the Church to Christ in the Epistles of the Apostle Paul* (London: SPCK, 1955); W. Bousset, *Kyrios Christos* (Nashville: Abingdon, 1970); M. Bouttier, *En Christ: Étude d'exégèse et de théologie pauliniennes* (Paris: Universitaires de France, 1962); A. Deissmann, *Paul: A Study in Social and Religious History* (London: Hodder & Stoughton, 1926); R. H. Gundry, Soma *in Biblical Theology* (SNTSMS 29; Cambridge: University Press, 1976); E. Käsemann, "The Theological Problem Presented by the Motif of the Body of Christ," in *Perspectives on Paul* (Philadelphia: Fortress, 1971) 102-21; E. Mayser, *Grammatik der griechischen Papyri aus der Ptolemäerzeit* (Berlin: Walter de Gruyter, 1934); C. F. D. Moule, *The Origin of Christology* (Cambridge: University Press, 1977); F. Neugebauer, "Das Paulinische 'in Christo,'" *NTS* 4 (1957-58) 124-38; A. Oepke, "ἐν," *TDNT* II.537-43; S. E. Porter, "Two Myths: Corporate Personality and Language/Mentality Determinism," *SJT* 43 (1990) 289-307; A. T. Robertson, *A Grammar of the Greek New Testament in the Light of Historical Research* (4th ed.; New York: Hodder & Stoughton, 1923); E. P. Sanders, *Paul and Palestinian Judaism: A Comparison of Patterns of Religion* (Philadelphia: Fortress, 1977); A. Schweitzer, *The Mysticism of Paul the Apostle* (London: Black, 1931); A. J. M. Wedderburn, *Baptism and Resurrection: Studies in Pauline Theology Against Its Graeco-Roman Background* (WUNT 44; Tübingen: J. C. B. Mohr, 1987); idem, "Some Observations on Paul's Use of the Phrases 'in Christ' and 'with Christ,'" *JSNT* 25 (1985) 83-97; N. T. Wright, "Χριστός as 'Messiah' in Paul: Philemon 6," in *The Climax of the Covenant* (Minneapolis: Fortress, 1991) 41-55.

M. A. Seifrid

**INCEST.** See MARRIAGE AND DIVORCE, ADULTERY AND INCEST.

**INSPIRED UTTERANCE.** See GIFTS OF THE SPIRIT; PROPHECY, PROPHESYING; TONGUES.

**INSTITUTIONALIZATION.** See EARLY CATHOLICISM; SOCIAL SETTING OF MISSION CHURCHES.

## INTERCESSION

When Paul and the early Christians reflected on the resurrection* and exaltation* of Christ,* it is not surprising that they thought about Christ's heavenly* role. From its use throughout the NT, Psalm 110 seems to have shaped this picture: "The Lord says to my Lord, 'Sit at my right hand, till I make your enemies your footstool'" (Rom 8:34; 1 Cor 15:25; Eph 1:20; Col 3:1; cf. Mt 26:64; Mk 14:62; Heb 1:3, 13; 8:1; 10:12; 12:2; 1 Pet 3:22). Christ had been enthroned in heaven, and it was clear that as a king his heavenly authority* stood unchallenged as to its ultimate acknowledgement (Phil 2:9-11).

But further inquiry about Christ's salvific work prompted more questions. Did Jesus present the completed work of his sacrifice* to God*? Did he continue to intercede for his people before the Father as their representative? If the Spirit* was indeed Christ's Spirit, did the Spirit have an intercessory role as well? For Paul, the answer to these questions was yes.

1. The Exalted Christ
2. The Holy Spirit

### 1. The Exalted Christ.

Only in two NT texts is the heavenly intercession of Christ explicitly mentioned (Rom 8:34 and Heb 7:25). In each case the term used is *entynchanō* (cf. *hyperentynchanō* and *enteuxis*), the root of which refers to an approach, an entreaty, often a plea on behalf of another. Paul uses this sense in Romans 11:2, describing how Elijah pleaded with God against Israel (cf. Acts 25:24). But generally in the NT the word group refers to prayer (see 1 Tim 2:1; 4:5).

Romans 8:34 appears in Paul's well-known summary of the work of God in Christ on behalf of believers (Rom 8:31-39). In Romans 8:34 he lists the climactic events of Christ's life: "Christ Jesus, who died, yes, who was raised from the dead, who is at the right hand of God, and who intercedes for us." This contributes to Paul's confidence in the unfailing love* which God holds for believers (Rom 8:35). Christ is their advocate who continuously prays on their behalf before God (*see* Prayer).

Considerable debate has always surrounded this issue. (1) Are we to think that Christ's intercession is a continuation of his work of redemption*? Must he eternally plead the efficacy of his cross* before God in order to make salvation a reality for believers? Luther was persuaded that this was the case, and for him, Christ's intercession stood alongside his death* and resurrection as integral works of salvation. (2) On the other hand, some have emphasized the completed work of Christ. Since the mystery* of salvation is concluded at the cross, redemption is accomplished without further mediatorial ministry of the ascended Christ.

This second view has been particularly popular in the Reformed Tradition (see esp. K. Barth and the commentaries by L. Morris and C. E. B. Cranfield). Its premise is that if we posit more requirements for salvation than the death of Jesus, this undercuts the conclusive power of the cross. Most have argued that Christ's presence alone with the Father in heaven achieves this intercession.

This latter view seems true to Paul in terms of the finality of the cross, though some have suggested that it lacks a pastoral quality implicit in Paul's statement. Jesus Christ is ultimately and eternally sympathetic with the condition of believers and forever validates their security in God's plan. Thus Romans 8:35 quickly emphasizes that nothing can separate from the love of God because God's compassion for his own is eternally displayed in heaven in Christ.

### 2. The Holy Spirit.

Intercession, however, is not simply the work of Christ. Paul also believed that the Holy Spirit carried on an intercessory ministry on behalf of believers. Romans 8:26-27 is the only text where Paul makes this clear. As Christ intercedes in heaven, so too the Spirit works on behalf of the saints, interceding for them during the struggles and limits of this earthly life. But it is vital to see how this notion fits into the larger theological argument of Romans 8. After celebrating the glory of life in the Spirit (Rom 8:1-17), Paul lapses into a realistic discussion of the imperfect, limited character of the Christian life. The Spirit of Christ within believers brings transformation, and yet the Spirit cannot bring eschatological perfection* (*see* Holiness, Sanctification). Those who are "in Christ"* continue to live in a world of suffering,* decay, futility* and confusion (Rom 8:18-25). The creation itself longs for its redemption (Rom 8:22). All is still subjected to hope.* And yet within this darkness, even when believers do not know how to speak or pray or worship,* the Spirit facilitates believers to form an appropriate response to God in spite of their fallenness: "The Spirit intercedes for us with sighs too deep for words." God sovereignly draws men and women into his presence, even when they seem too crippled to walk.

Significant debate surrounds whether or not this ministry of the Spirit is actually describing glossolalia (or "speaking in tongues," cf. 1 Cor 12—14; *see* Tongues). "Sighs too deep for words" (Rom 8:26) and "inward groanings" (Rom 8:23) might well be the incomprehensible prayer language that Paul had described as taking place among the Corinthian believers. This is even more likely when we recall the theological function of the Spirit in Romans 8:18-27. The Spirit is a foreign power* that intervenes in our darkness and confusion; a remedy when no cure is at hand. He does not energize human effort in prayer, but, in human weakness* and powerlessness, he fills believers' prayers with completely new content.

K. Stendahl and E. Käsemann are among those who have argued that Romans 8:26 is best viewed "simply as glossolalic utterance" (Käsemann, 131) parallel to that described in 1 Corinthians 12—14. According to them, the phrase *katho dei* ("as we ought") does not modify *ouk oidamen* ("we do not know") as in the RSV. Correct method in prayer is not the issue. Rather, *katho dei* relates to the content of prayer: What, not *how* (*ti*, not *pōs*), we pray is the concern here, since it is only the Spirit that can lead us "according to the will of God." The Spirit supplies sighs which are not "wordless" (*alalētos*), but beyond words, not formulated in human words. For Paul, "prayer is never wordless" (Käsemann, citing Schniewind, 129). Thus, it is a noticeable, audible phenomenon, an utterance likely appearing in assemblies of worship.

The most articulate opponent of Käsemann's view is A. J. M. Wedderburn (see also the remarks of C. E. B. Cranfield, 423-24). For Wedderburn the crux of the issue is the word *alalētos* ("unspeakable"). The term has no metaphorical meaning (there is no precedent for this in Greek), and according to Wedderburn it must mean that these words are literally unuttered. He points to 2 Corinthians 12:4 as support. But this is debatable. 2 Corinthians 12:4 is about heavenly visions* that Paul cannot and must not articulate in human language. On the contrary, Romans 8:26 focuses on the believers' human inability to express what they should pray but cannot because of their finiteness and weakness. Yet had Paul wished to make the allusion to glossolalia unmistakably clear, certain indications, as he provided in 1 Corinthians 12—14, would certainly have been given (see Dunn, 1.479 for discussion). Nevertheless, the thrust of the text is clear. Prayer needs to be formed by the Spirit as well as empowered by the Spirit on this side of the eschaton.

*See also* CHRISTOLOGY; EXALTATION AND ENTHRONEMENT; HOLY SPIRIT; PRAYER; TONGUES.

BIBLIOGRAPHY. O. Bauernfeind, "τυγχάνω κτλ," *TDNT* VIII.242-45; C. Brown, "ἐντυγχάνω," *NIDNTT* 2.882-84; C. E. B. Cranfield, *A Critical and Exegetical Commentary on the Epistle to the Romans* (ICC; 2 vols.; Edinburgh: T. & T. Clark, 1975, 1979) 1.420-44; J. D. G. Dunn, *Christology in the Making* (Philadelphia: Westminster, 1980); idem, *Romans* (WBC 38; 2 vols.; Dallas: Word, 1988); E. Käsemann, "The Cry for Liberty in the Worship of the Church [Rom 8:26]," in *Perspectives on Paul* (Philadelphia: Fortress, 1971) 122-37; G. Ladd, *A Theology of the New Testament* (Grand Rapids: Eerdmans, 1974) 578-84; G. MacRae, "A Note on Romans 8:26-27," *HTR* (1973) 227-30; L. Morris, *The Epistle to the Romans* (Grand Rapids: Eerdmans, 1988) 334-42; K. Niederwimmer, "Das Gebet des Geistes, Röm 8:26," *TZ* 20 (1964) 252-65; K. Stendahl, "Paul at Prayer," in *Meanings: The Bible as Document and as Guide* (Philadelphia: Fortress, 1984) 151-61; A. J. M. Wedderburn,

"Romans 8:26—Toward a Theology of Glossolalia?," *SJT* 28 (1975) 369-77.

G. M. Burge

## INTERMEDIATE STATE

The "intermediate state" is something of a technical term (the German equivalent being *Zwischenzustand*) used to describe the state of the believer between his or her death and the consummation of the created order at the parousia of Christ, at which time a new bodily existence is begun (*see* Eschatology). The phrase is not a NT one and is at best an inference which arises out of key passages dealing with eschatological hope* and resurrection* belief. The problem expressed by the phrase clearly arises out of the eschatological context of Paul's thought, assumes the future bodily resurrection and in one sense might be seen as an attempt to understand, from the strict vantage point of chronological time, the status of the deceased believer in God's eternal presence until the parousia. We could put the essential point which prompts the rise of the idea in the form of a question: What happens to believers at death?

To a great degree the idea of an intermediate state rests on the dualistic assumption that physical death is the separation of soul and body.* This is, of course, an assumption which must be balanced not only by a realization of the somatic nature of the resurrection in Paul's thought, but also by a sensitive handling of temporal considerations in the matter. Only when all three of these facets are held together can a balanced understanding of Paul's contribution to the matter be obtained.

1. Physical Death and Life with Christ
2. Immortality of the Soul or Resurrection of the Dead?
3. Development in Pauline Thought: 1 Corinthians 15 and 2 Corinthians 5
4. The Intermediate State as "Soul Sleep"

### 1. Physical Death and Life with Christ.

Some interpreters note that much of the NT witness on these matters is corporate (and not individualistic) in focus, a fact which may render some of the discussion about the intermediate state of the *individual* believer open to considerable question, or open to the charge of being speculative at best. Nevertheless, at several points within Paul's letters the apostle talks about the physical death of the believer as a means of entry into a fuller participation of life with Christ (*see* Life and Death). Thus in Philippians 1:23 he contrasts continuing life here on earth over against being "with Christ, for that is far better." Similarly in 2 Corinthians

5:6-8 we have a contrast between being "at home in the body" and being "at home with the Lord," with the death of the believer being the transitional event moving him or her from one "home" to the other.

Yet how can this life with Christ be the promised life in its fullest sense, given that according to Paul resurrection life is inherently somatic in nature and the granting of resurrection bodies is closely tied to the future parousia of Christ? The idea of an intermediate state attempts to bridge the chasm created by these two seemingly contradictory theological statements by postulating either an immediate consciousness of "being with Christ" at death or the granting of the resurrection body at death. Thus the intermediate state can be interpreted in terms of either a postmortem embodied existence, or a postmortem disembodied existence; the Pauline materials have been invoked by competent scholars to support both positions.

*1.1. "Sleep."* Two evocative images are used by Paul in seeking to express something of what we have termed the intermediate state. First, Paul uses the verb "to sleep" (*koimaomai*) with reference to the deceased a total of nine times (1 Cor 7:39; 11:30; 15:6, 18, 20, 51; 1 Thess 4:13, 14, 15). This builds upon the established intertestamental idea of Hades as the place of the sleep of the dead (as in *1 Enoch* 91:10; 92:3). Although the verb is clearly used by Paul as a euphemism for dying, it nevertheless carries with it the idea of presence with Christ at death (see below).

*1.2. "Nakedness."* In 2 Corinthians 5:3-4 Paul uses an extended clothing metaphor to describe existence between the time of death and the granting of a resurrection body at the parousia of Christ. Thus "nakedness" is equal to existence without a body (disembodiment) and is something to be abhorred, while "being clothed" is embraced in that it means being granted the heavenly resurrection body (see Sevenster). Some scholars, such as E. E. Ellis, feel that the curious reference to "being away from the body" in 2 Corinthians 5:8 is closely related to this clothing image. The precise meaning of the clothing metaphor is a debated point (as Weigelt observes), although a contrast between earthly life and a postmortem existence is clear. C. F. D. Moule offers an interesting interpretation of the metaphor which, in a way, helps resolve somewhat the tension between 1 Corinthians 15 and 2 Corinthians 5:1-10 concerning the nature of the resurrection body. He argues that in 1 Corinthians 15 the resurrection body is something *superimposed* upon mortal existence, while in 2 Corinthians 5:1-10 the resurrection body is something *exchanged* for it. This subtle distinction, Moule contends, is related to the

clothing metaphor in that there is a correspondingly subtle distinction between the various forms of *endyesthai* and *ependyesthai* used by Paul in 1 Corinthians 15 and 2 Corinthians 5:1-10 respectively (Harris, 220-23, discusses the matter).

Both images (sleep and nakedness) should be recognized as essentially metaphorical in substance, seeking to express the inexpressible, and neither should be made to carry more theological weight than it is able.

### 2. Immortality of the Soul or Resurrection of the Dead?

Some (such as Cullmann) have sought to approach the question of the intermediate state in terms of a straightforward contrast between the Greek view of the postmortem existence and the Judeo-Christian view. According to Cullmann, the former focuses on the immortality of the soul and viewed death as a friend, while the latter focuses on the resurrection of the dead and viewed death as an enemy to be defeated. The resolution such a juxtaposition provides does answer some of the more pressing difficulties raised by the issue of postmortem existence, but it is one which rests on a false dichotomy (as Hanhart notes). It is unlikely that a hard and fast distinction can be made between the Hellenistic and the Judeo-Christian views on the postmortem state, especially given the interpenetration of (so-called) Palestinian and Hellenistic cultures of the NT period (*see* Hellenism). In addition, there are several Christian and Jewish sources (including the Qumran materials) from the time which seem to teach the immortality of the soul (Cavallin provides some discussion of these). The matter cannot be solved by means of such a false contrast as Cullmann's distinction maintains.

While it is true that in Paul's writing immortality is, more properly speaking, a concept applied to the resurrected body (and not to the disembodied soul), this should not be taken as a denial of the truth of immediate presence with Christ at death to which the idea of immortality of the soul points. We must allow that Paul combines his belief in the reality of the intermediate state in heaven together with his expectation of the future resurrection of the dead (as Lincoln argues). At the same time we should recognize that the dichotomy between immortality of the soul and the resurrection of the body implies a distinction between the disembodied and embodied postmortem states respectively. It is highly doubtful that Paul would have conceived of the believer as ultimately disembodied, given his Jewish background which generally viewed the human being as a complete psychosomatic entity.

## 3. Development in Pauline Thought: 1 Corinthians 15 and 2 Corinthians 5.

Some have attempted to expound the significance of the Pauline teaching about the intermediate state in terms of a two-stage development of his eschatological thought. Thus the more traditional teaching on the granting of the resurrection body at the last day (as expressed in 1 Thess 4 and 1 Cor 15) is seen to give way to a greater emphasis on the believer as being immediately in the presence of Christ at the moment of death (as Phil 1:23 and 2 Cor 5:8 suggest). C. H. Dodd, a classic proponent of this approach, takes this shift in Paul's thought to have been occasioned by the apostle's own brush with death, something which took place between the writing of the letters we know as 1 Corinthians and 2 Corinthians; this trauma is perhaps hinted at in 2 Corinthians 1:8 (see R. Yates for a discussion of this crucial verse).

Certainly the fact that the verb "to sleep" (*koimaomai*) is used in 1 Thessalonians and 1 Corinthians but not in 2 Corinthians and Philippians lends some support to the theory of development of thought. Others have contested that such a radical shift in Paul's thought has occurred, or have sought to contain its implications in some way. Moule, for example, explains the difference in emphasis between the two stages as one brought about by the circumstances of the individual letters concerned. Harris explains the difference in the two stages as arising from the fact that the corporate and individualistic facets of Paul's teaching about postmortem existence are being expressed in 1 Corinthians 15 and 2 Corinthians respectively. Certainly too much can be made of the differences between 1 Corinthians 15 and 2 Corinthians 5, and it should be ever kept in mind that Paul's focus of concentration and reason for writing is different in the two letters (as Gillman argues).

In any event, however differently 1 Corinthians and 2 Corinthians might be with respect to the issue of the present postmortem state of the believer, they are united in that they proclaim (or at least imply) a resurrection body for the believer at the parousia of Christ. In that sense both letters assert a transformation of the believer in Christ; but what of the *timing* of that transformation? F. F. Bruce remarks wisely on this matter: "The tension created by the postulated interval between death and resurrection might be relieved today if it were suggested that in the consciousness of the departed believer there is no interval between dissolution and investiture, however long an interval might be measured by the calendar of earthbound human history." (The issue of development in Paul's eschatological thought is usually treated in commentaries on 2 Corinthians, generally within the discussion on 2 Corinthians 5:1-10; see Furnish and Martin.)

## 4. The Intermediate State as "Soul Sleep."

The description of the intermediate state as one of soul sleep is often associated with the thought of the Reformer Martin Luther. Luther described the deceased believer as being unconsciously "asleep" in the arms of Christ until the last day. Effectively Luther's teaching challenged Roman Catholicism with respect to ideas of afterlife (including purgatory) as he shifted the focus of discussion from one of topography to one of christology.* At the same time it should be noted that Luther also recognized that such earthly measurements of time are inadequate to describe fully the status of the deceased believer. As Luther argued, human and divine measurements of time cannot be equated. The sleep image itself has its limitations and should be seen as but one attempt to communicate the believer's assured presence with Christ at death.

The idea of afterlife as soul sleep presents great problems for some modern interpreters of Paul who argue that a proper view of humankind emphasizes the *wholistic nature* of a person (Badham offers some discussion of this).

*See also* BODY; ESCHATOLOGY; LIFE AND DEATH; PSYCHOLOGY; RESURRECTION.

BIBLIOGRAPHY. P. Althaus, *The Theology of Martin Luther* (Philadelphia: Fortress, 1966) 410-17; P. Badham, *Christian Beliefs About Life After Death* (London: Macmillan, 1976); M. C. de Boer, *The Defeat of Death* (JSNTS 22; Sheffield: Academic, 1988); F. F. Bruce, "Paul on Immortality," *SJT* 24 (1971) 457-72; R. Cassidy, "Paul's Attitude to Death in II Corinthians 5:1-10," *EvQ* 43 (1971) 210-17; H. C. C. Cavallin, *Life After Death: Paul's Argument for the Resurrection of the Dead in 1 Cor 15* (ConB 7,1; Lund: Gleerup, 1974); O. Cullmann, *Immortality of the Soul or Resurrection of the Dead?* (London: Epworth, 1958); C. H. Dodd, *New Testament Studies* (Manchester: University Press, 1953) 67-128; E. E. Ellis, "II Corinthians V.1-10 in Pauline Eschatology," *NTS* 6 (1959-60) 211-24; V. P. Furnish, *II Corinthians* (AB 32A; Garden City, NY: Doubleday, 1984); J. Gillman, "A Thematic Comparison: 1 Cor 15:50-57 and 2 Cor 5:1-5," *JBL* 107 (1988) 439-54; K. Hanhart, "Paul's Hope in the Face of Death," *JBL* 88 (1969) 445-57; M. J. Harris, *Raised Immortal: The Relation Between Resurrection and Immortality in New Testament Teaching* (Grand Rapids: Eerdmans, 1983); A. T. Lincoln, *Paradise Now and Not Yet* (SNTSMS 43; Cambridge: University Press, 1981); R. P. Martin, *2 Corinthians* (WBC 40; Waco, TX: Word, 1986); C. F. D. Moule, "The Influence of Circumstances on the Use of Eschatological Terms," *JTS* 15 (1964) 1-15; idem, "St. Paul and Dualism: The Pauline Conception of the Resurrection," *NTS* 13 (1966-67) 106-23; J. N. Sevenster, "Some Remarks on the GYMNOS in II Cor. V.3," in *Studia Paulina in honorem Johannis de Zwaan*, ed. J. N. Sevenster and W. C. van Unnik (Haarlem: Bohn, 1953) 202-14; H. Weigelt, "Clothe, Naked, Dress, Garment, Cloth," *NIDNTT* 1.312-17; R. Yates, "Paul's Affliction in Asia: 2 Cor 1:8," *EvQ* 53 (1981) 241-45.

L. J. Kreitzer

# ISRAEL

Paul confesses openly that he himself is an Israelite, that he loves his kinfolk and desires their salvation.* Despite their present rejection of the gospel,* he refuses to regard them as irretrievably rejected by God.* He sees them as bearers of a spiritual heritage which has now been opened up to Gentiles* also. He never suggests that Gentiles have displaced Israel or that Israel has no role to play in God's future. Rather he sees God's gift to Israel as irrevocable and Israel as occupying an inalienable place in the divine economy of salvation.

1. Introduction
2. Definition and Terminology
3. The Extension of the Covenant with Israel to Gentiles
4. Israel as the Creation of God's Word
5. Israel's Fault
6. Israel's Dual Status: Beloved and at Enmity with the Gospel
7. Paul's Solution: The Restoration of Israel by Means of the Gentile Mission
8. Israel in Contemporary Perspective

## 1. Introduction.

*Israel* was the established name in Scripture for both the covenant* people and the covenanted land. When Paul uses the term he is not using it simply as a general designation of those claiming physical descent from Abraham.* Rather he uses it to designate them as the people of the covenant made with Abraham. Even when Paul refers to the Israel which has rejected his gospel, he can still use the title because he thinks of the people as a whole as a religious entity, the historic people of God. In Romans 2:17, 28-29 and Romans 3:29 Paul speaks of the "Jew," but in Romans 9—11 his clear preference is for "Israel"/"Israelite." One gets the impression that when Paul wants to stress ethnic affiliation, he uses the term Jew, but when he comes to reflect upon their spiritual heritage, Israel/Israelite alone can clearly designate this people as a religious entity.

## 2. Definition and Terminology.

*2.1. Israel of God—New Israel.* The main passages in Paul's letters where Israel is discussed are Galatians 6:16, Romans 9—11 and, to a lesser extent, 2 Corinthians 3:7, 13. In 1 Corinthians 10:18 Paul gives a brief reference to Israel to warn the Christians not to be presumptuous. In 2 Corinthians 3 a contrast is drawn between the old dispensation and the new—a contrast really between degrees of glory,* showing how greatly the new excels the old. Also in 2 Corinthians 11:22 Paul, in face of counterclaims, asserts that he himself is an Israelite. It turns out therefore that Romans 9—11 is the crucial text for our topic and we must devote substantial attention to it. But first we need to consider Galatians 6:16 ("the Israel of God"), which some interpreters have regarded as the first reference to the church as "the new Israel."

At the conclusion of his letter to the Galatians, Paul concludes with a benediction.* In Galatians 6:15 he has asserted that in Christ* "neither circumcision* counts for anything nor uncircumcision, but a new creation." By this he sought to repudiate and to relativize the claims of those who wanted to force his Gentile converts in Galatia* to accept circumcision—the major purpose of his letter. He concludes with a sentence which the RSV translates as "Grace and mercy be upon all who walk by this rule, upon the Israel of God." This translation suggests that the latter phrase, "the Israel of God," is simply in apposition to the former and that Paul's benediction is thereby applied to all those Christians who, like him, regard circumcision as unessential. This would mean that Paul, already at this early stage in the NT era, identifies the Christian church* as "the Israel of God" in opposition to the historical people of God. But this translation is unlikely for several reasons.

The basic problem is that the RSV translation has omitted the *kai* ("and") in the Greek text. The NRSV has corrected this error and now translates Galatians 6:15, "Peace be upon them, and mercy, and upon the Israel of God." The revised NEB unfortunately is similar to the RSV. If Paul had really wished to equate the Gentile believers with "the Israel of God," it seems strange that he first uses the phrase here at the very conclusion of his letter. And even if it be granted that the identification is actually made here between believers and the Israel of God, it is somewhat tenuous to hang so much on one doubtful translation since, apart from this passage, there is no other evidence until about A.D. 160 for the *explicit* identification of the church as "the Israel of God" or "New Israel." This isolated instance would be difficult to explain by itself. Why was it that no one in the next hundred years used this verse to identify the church as "the New Israel?"

It seems better to translate as P. Richardson has suggested: "May God give peace to all who will walk according to this criterion, and mercy also to his faithful people Israel" (Richardson, 84), or as the NIV translates, "Peace and mercy to all who follow this rule, even to the Israel of God."

From this brief survey of the references to Israel in Paul, there is no clear or explicit evidence prior to Romans 9—11 that suggests either an identification of the church with "the New Israel" nor of a theory of displacement of the "old Israel" by the new. Only historical Israel can properly claim the title "Israel of God."

**2.2. An "Israel" within Israel?** The attribution of the title "Israel" and the recognition of her heritage does not imply however that Paul is not fully conscious of the fact that the majority of the people of Israel were currently rejecting his message. The unique aspect of Paul's understanding of Israel is that she is both beloved because of the fathers—the legitimate heir of the promises—and yet at the same time at enmity with the gospel. In order to give a satisfactory explanation of this state of affairs, Paul was forced to take a careful look at the history of Israel in the Scriptures. From this he came to a conclusion that some Jews would have considered radical, even blasphemous—that not all the descendants of Abraham are truly Abraham's children in the sense that they share the same kind of faith as their father Abraham.

Paul's thesis, which has been grossly misrepresented and which has led to unbalanced interpretations of the relation of Jew and Gentile in the gospel is not, on his premises, simply his own novel creation. Within the nation of Israel God has always exercised his prerogative to select people to carry out his purpose. Every Jew admitted this; Ishmael was a child of Abraham but no Jew believed that the Arabs, his descendants, were within the covenant. According to the OT, the children of faith were reckoned through the line of Isaac (Rom 9:8), and this was because the birth of Isaac was not just a matter of ordinary physical generation but the result of the promise of God, accepted in faith by Abraham (Rom 4:18-22). So Paul insists that since in the biblical narrative there were already examples of descendants of Abraham who were not children of promise, then there ought to be no problem in acknowledging in his own day that "not all those descended from Abraham are Israel."

It seems, at least on the surface, that Paul is guilty of redefining "Israel" to suit his own purposes. The issue centers on the definition of "the Israel of God."

In Romans 2:28-29 Paul had already asserted "Not the outward Jew is a real Jew," a parallel to Romans 9:6b—"Not all offspring of Israel are Israel." It seems therefore that some such term as the "real Israel," "true Israel" or "inner Israel" is logically required to express Paul's intent. The true Israel is "of Israel" in terms of physical descent but not coextensive with historical Israel. (We note in passing that having introduced the concept of the "true Israel" we are then forced to introduce a neutral term, i.e., "historical Israel," in order to avoid slipping into the easy equation of Israel with unbelieving or false Israel, i.e., as a symbol of disobedience.)

Paul himself appears to operate with a fluid concept of Israel. This doubtless originates from ancient Semitic concepts of solidarity which modern individualism finds hard to understand because it is so far removed from much contemporary (Western) religious thought.

Paul's thought in Romans needs to be differentiated from his previous discussion in Galatians.* There Paul distinguished two contrasting groups "Israel of the flesh" and "Israel of the Spirit" (Rom 4:29). The closest parallel in Romans* is Romans 4:14-16, where the terms used are *hoi ek nomou* ("those of the Law") and *hoi ek pisteōs* ("those of faith"). But in this chapter the argument runs not on the pattern "either a or b" but "*not only* a *but also* b"—it is inclusive rather than exclusive. Paul insists that since the coming of faith (in Christ), not only those who follow the Law,* the Jews, but also those of faith,* Gentiles, may also be included in the people of God. It could be argued that Paul in Romans 9—11 first frees the concept of Israel from its absolute identification with all of Abraham's descendants and then, having loosed this connection, he proceeds to include Gentiles also within "eschatological Israel."

But we must be careful about what Paul does and does not say. It is true that he argues that not all offspring of Israel are Israel. Then he continues from this to argue from Romans 9:22 and what follows that Gentiles may also be included in the people of God. Yet Paul never suggests a complete displacement of Israel by Gentiles however much he argues for the rights of believers. In the end he maintains that the children of God (*tekna tou theou*) are not merely children of fleshly descent (*tekna tēs sarkos*) but rather children of promise (*tekna tēs epangelias*, Rom 9:8).

Nor does Paul simply equate the Christian community with "spiritual Israel," "Israel *kata pneuma*," and the Jews with "fleshly Israel," "Israel *kata sarka*" (cf. Gal 4:29). His thought is more complex on this issue.

The problem with terms such as *true Israel, spiritual Israel* or even *eschatological Israel* is that all of these may be misused to imply that the church is the only true Israel, and that "historical Israel" is no better than pagan nations, having forfeited her heritage absolutely. It is quite clear that despite Paul's making a radical distinction within Israel and thereby driving a wedge into the historical people of God, he would certainly have insisted that part of historical Israel is also part of eschatological Israel.

### 3. The Extension of the Covenant with Israel to Gentiles.

It is beyond dispute that Paul could not have envisaged an eschatological Israel that contained none of the historical Israel. Paul's thinking is much more concrete and historically oriented than subsequent Gentile-Christian understanding makes it out to be.

Moreover, certain legal and theological factors have to be taken into account. If an inheritance is bequeathed to someone, one cannot legally displace the heir without breaking the terms of the agreement, the covenant. Gentiles have too easily presumed on their access to the heritage of Israel to which they have no inherent right. The theological factor involves our conception of God's faithfulness. If God is a faithful, covenant-keeping God, how then can Israel be fully and finally rejected? If, for whatever reason, Israel's promises are given to others, then Israel has failed and God also has failed in his purpose for Israel (Rom 9:6). Paul is therefore concerned to maintain both that God is free (and hence not determined by Israel), but also that he is committed to Israel in that he will achieve his purposes through this people whether in their cooperation or in their rebellion.

### 4. Israel as the Creation of God's Word.

Both the power and the creative freedom of God are emphasized by Paul in his discussion of Israel in Romans 9—11. By his call God created his people and by his word he accomplishes what he purposes. By this alone is Israel the people of God constituted (and re-constituted). But this does not mean God uses his power in any arbitrary fashion. He does have the power to make children from stones, but in fact what Paul claims in Romans 9:1-22 is that God selects not stones, nor even Gentiles but those from within the people of Israel.

The freedom of the potter is absolute; he can make from the clay whatever vessel he purposes, whether for menial or honorable purposes, and the vessel cannot question the logic of its destiny. Yet we need to remember that God, the divine potter, uses *the Jewish people* as his clay. Granted, the Jew is not *eo ipso* "seed" (*sperma*) or "child of God" (*teknon theou*) but only be-

comes this through the calling (*kalein*) and reckoning (*logizesthai*) of God (Rom 9:7-8). Yet this people, as those historically in covenant with their creator, occupy a unique position. Only since and because of the advent of Christ can Gentiles be included in the people of God through the extension of Israel's covenant; Israel's privilege and priority necessitate that the gospel to the Gentiles can only come by the way of Judaism. Thus Israel occupies an inalienable place in the purposes and plans of God; if Gentiles are to participate in these, they must acknowledge God's prior commitment to Israel and all that this entails (Eph 2:11-22 is an important recognition of this fact).

Until the coming of Christ, God, through his word of promise, creates Israel anew according to his purpose of grace. With the opening up of the promises to Gentiles also the possibility of a "new Israel" or a "renewed Israel" is now a reality. Thus Israel and the church are both the creation of the divine word. From this perspective there is no essential difference between them. However, both historically and theologically, Paul wishes to maintain an awareness of the priority of Israel and warns Gentiles about being too presumptuous lest they forget God's prior engagement with Israel.

### 5. Israel's Fault.

The non-inclusion of part of Israel is attributed by Paul both to God's predestination (*see* Election) and to Israel's failure (Rom 9:6-29). In Paul's thought these elements are neither contradictory nor mutually exclusive. Israel's fault is that most Israelites of Paul's time did not put their faith in Jesus Christ. He had become a stumbling* stone to them (Rom 9:30—10:4). The reason for this failure to accept Christ has traditionally been regarded as "a self-righteous attitude on the part of Jews." "They sought to establish their own righteousness" (Rom 10:3) has been understood to mean that Jews thought that righteousness* could be achieved by *their own* effort, that is, by good works. Hence those who made that effort presumed they had succeeded and became self-righteous as a result. They had a zeal but a mistaken zeal (Rom 10:2).

E. P. Sanders in particular has written much to correct this general view of the fault of Israel. He argues that zeal as such is not wrong. They did not err in *seeking* righteousness but they sought the *wrong kind of righteousness*—righteousness "of their own" in the sense that it was a righteousness peculiar to Jews as a people and the righteousness of a former dispensation prior to the coming of faith (in Jesus Christ). The fault of this righteousness is its exclusivity and the "coming of faith" means that God's salvation is open to everyone who has faith, whether Jew or Gentile; there is no distinction (Rom 10:12). It seems therefore that Paul's gospel was an offense to many Jews who failed to understand and/or acknowledge the new day that had dawned in Jesus Christ. They saw Paul's work and message as an absolute threat to the future and well-being of Israel and they opposed it bitterly as a result. But Paul did not perceive it thus—he sees the coming of Christ as confirmation (Gk *bebaian*, Rom 4:16) of the promises made to Abraham and as an extension of the covenant to include believing Gentiles along with the believing in Israel. He refuses to regard Israel as "rejected" but only as temporarily hardened by God until the full number of the Gentiles comes into the kingdom.*

### 6. Israel's Dual Status: Beloved and at Enmity with the Gospel.

As we have noted already, Paul seems to have had a fluid concept of Israel because he saw the people as one corporate entity irrespective of the merits or failure of particular individuals. His perspective on Israel is both historical and communal (as distinct from some modern views that are theological/symbolic and individualistic). But because his approach is historical and since he discusses the actual, empirical Israel, he has a problem of definition. Israel is opposed to the gospel; particular Jews are enemies of Paul and his message. But the Jews as a whole are the heirs of the promises given to Abraham and confirmed by the coming of Christ.

Paul does not shrink from the full seriousness of this dilemma. Israel's dual status is that she is rejecting the gospel but is still beloved because of the patriarchs.

Various solutions have been offered to this problem. A common one is that God has two different covenants*—a covenant involving Law-keeping for the Jews and a covenant based on faith alone for Gentiles. But Paul's solution differs from this. He neither minimizes the problem by claiming that all Jews will be saved apart from Christ, nor by predicting another covenant to ensure their eventual salvation.

### 7. Paul's Solution: The Restoration of Israel by Means of the Gentile Mission.

The actual situation Paul faced near the end of his ministry was that Gentiles were willing to accept Christ but Jews were not. Some Jews probably still held fast to the traditional view of "Jews first and then the Gentiles," that the gospel could only be allowed to proceed to the Gentiles after Israel had already embraced it. Paul had possibly wrestled with this issue as he first

heard the Hellenists proclaim the Christian message. But when he experienced his Damascus Road vision, he himself had to work out how his own commission related to this perspective (*see* Conversion and Call). Working from the empirical evidence of the reality of the Spirit's work among the Gentiles, Paul came to the conclusion that the order of salvation had been changed. "To the Jew first" now means that while the irrevocable place of Israel is confirmed by the gospel, the order of entry for Jew and Gentile into the new community of faith is in fact reversed.

The new reality is that the Gentiles are preceding the Jews and from this *actual historical sequence* Paul proceeds to argue a theology of the final salvation of Israel succeeding that of Gentiles (Rom 11:12). Just as the rejection of the gospel by Jews had caused it to spread to the Gentiles, so now the reception of the gospel by Gentiles will ensure the turning back of the Jews. Paul came to this conclusion from scriptural, theological and empirical evidence. The empirical evidence of believing Gentiles and unbelieving Jews was plain to see.

The theological evidence Paul developed from his conviction of God's faithfulness. Paul was convinced that Christ's coming demonstrated that God himself is faithful and that he justifies the one who has faith (in Jesus, Rom 3:26). The theology of a "righteous remnant" was frequently used in this discussion. God always retained a faithful remnant to ensure the final success of his purposes. The remnant could be seen as a sign either of judgment* or of mercy,* or even of both. In Romans 9:22-29 and 11:2-6 Paul makes use of this theme. The RSV text of Romans 9:27 (which quotes the prophet Isaiah) reads "Though the number of the sons of Israel be as the sand of the sea, only a remnant will be saved." Although it could be disputed whether the introduction of "only" is justified, we have in the English version an example of the remnant theme reminding us of the divine judgment upon Israel. In Romans 11:2-6 there is no doubt that Paul sees the remnant as a sign of hope*—of *mercy* rather than of *judgment* (although judgment is already presupposed). He again uses a scriptural example: Elijah mistakenly thought he alone was left of God's faithful people, but God reminded him that he had kept for himself seven thousand who had not bowed the knee to Baal. Paul concludes "so too at the present time, there is a remnant, chosen by grace" (Rom 11:5). Paul interprets this present remnant, believing Jews, as first fruits* of the coming harvest—it is a *hopeful* sign. Thus it would be appropriate to translate Romans 11:5 "so too at the present time—there is *already* a remnant." The existence of *some* Jewish believers becomes for Paul a pointer to the salvation of *all* Israel.

How this salvation would take place led Paul to ponder the Scriptures in the light of his own experience. there is a very real possibility that Paul's apostolic commission may actually have included a vision of the restoration* of Israel. The image in Isaiah 49:1 of one set apart from his mother's womb is used by Paul in Galatians 1:15 (cf. Acts 13:47; *see* Prophet, Paul as). The Servant's call in this passage ties together the twin aspects of his universal work—to be an agent of Israel's restoration and a light to the Gentiles. It is therefore inappropriate to view Paul as apostle to the Gentiles with no function in relation to Israel. It is more fitting to see him as the apostle to the Gentiles *for the sake of Israel*, so that there is a necessary connection between Paul's Gentile mission and the restoration of Israel.

It was, however, in Deuteronomy 32 that Paul found Scripture that suggested a way to lead rebellious Israel back to God. When Paul read in Deuteronomy 32:21 "I will make you jealous of those who are not a nation; with a foolish nation I will make you angry," he took this to mean that the Gentiles were "the foolish nation," the "no people"; so he found here a clue which he developed to argue that his Gentile mission would indirectly bring Israel, through jealousy, to acknowledge the truth as he saw it.

R. B. Hays has convincingly demonstrated that in Deuteronomy 32 "Paul finds not only the prophecy of Israel's lack of faith and ultimate restoration but also the prefiguration of God's intention to 'stir them to jealousy' through embracing the Gentiles (Deut 32:43)." Hays goes on to comment, "It is hardly coincidental that Paul quotes both of these verses explicitly (Rom 10:19; 15:10)," and he concludes "Deuteronomy 32 contains Romans 'in nuce' " (Hays, 164). It would appear that Paul, faced with the hardened hearts of the majority of his people, found in Deuteronomy 32 a text which looked inexorably beyond present judgment to future hope. Despite a certain tendency among some scholars to regard Romans 9—11 as stressing *either* judgment or mercy upon Israel, it is plain that in the Deuteronomic tradition it includes both—"Note then the kindness and the severity of God" (Rom 11:22). The severity is for the sake of God's ultimate compassion, and it is perfectly fitting that Romans 11 ends not with the *rejection* but with the *restoration** of "all Israel" (Rom 11:25).

So despite Israel's present obduracy, the ongoing historical process of the Gentile mission will continue until their number is complete—perhaps when the gospel has been "planted" everywhere. The pilgrim-

age of the Gentiles (Is 2:2-5) will not succeed but rather precede the restoration of Israel—the nations do not come because they see Israel's glory,* but Israel comes because she sees the salvation and glory Gentiles have in Christ. Paul was probably the first to propose this sequence but, as Hofius notes, Paul may have found support in certain OT texts which had already suggested it.

A number of items are closely interrelated in Paul's thought: "The Deliverer will come from Zion, he will remove ungodliness from Jacob;" all Israel—in the sense of the totality of the people (not necessarily every single individual)—will be saved, and this will usher in the resurrection* of the dead.

This will be the final deliverance and vindication of Israel expected in Deuteronomy 32:36-43 and, significantly for Paul, when the Gentiles will rejoice with Israel (Deut 32:43). Most important of all, with the restoration of Israel it is not primarily Israel that is vindicated but the faithfulness and honorable name of God.

What emerges from all this is that Paul's mission cannot be viewed in isolation from Israel's restoration. The apostle views his Gentile mission both as a *catalyst* to the *present* salvation of a remnant from within Israel and as an *essential precursor* to the eventual salvation of all Israel; it is only when the "full measure" of the Gentiles comes in that all Israel will be saved (Rom 11:25-26).

Thus in the reverse sequence to earlier traditions, Israel and the Gentiles will both share in God's salvation. Moreover, despite present or future separation between the church and Israel, in the end there can be no absolutely "separate development" because their destinies remain intertwined in the mysterious workings of God's eternal purpose. Thus Israel cannot achieve her restoration until "the fullness of the Gentiles," and the Gentiles cannot participate in the resurrection without the prior restoration of Israel.

## 8. Israel in Contemporary Perspective.

Paul's understanding of Israel is thoroughly eschatological.* Modern Christians frequently do not share his perspective. They want to know precisely where contemporary Jews stand in relation to the kingdom of God—judging more from the perspective of a realized eschatology. Paul was as conscious as anyone of the division between him and his unconverted kinfolk. But he viewed them in the perspective of God's ultimate purpose. From this perspective they are not rejected by God but rather they still remain *potential* members of his eternal kingdom (as all are).

The continuing existence of the Jewish people

should not be viewed simply as a result of their failure to accept the Christian message, that is, as a result of their disobedience. Nor should they be viewed merely as a sort of living object-lesson to Christians of the danger of "blind religiosity" as some extremists might describe them. We dare not insist that everything that happens in this world is directly caused by God, but it would be naive to suggest it is merely an accident of history that the historical people of God, the Jewish race, should continue to exist alongside Christianity.

*See also* ABRAHAM; COVENANT AND NEW COVENANT; ESCHA-TOLOGY; GENTILES; JEW, PAUL THE; OLIVE TREE; RESTORA-TION OF ISRAEL; ROMANS, LETTER TO THE; STUMBLING BLOCK.

BIBLIOGRAPHY. J. C. Beker, "The Faithfulness of God and the Priority of Israel in Paul's Letter to the Romans," in *The Romans Debate*, ed. K. P. Donfried (rev. ed.; Peabody, MA: Hendrickson, 1991); R. Bring, "Paul and the Old Testament: A Study of the Ideas of Election, Faith and Law in Paul with Special Reference to Rom ix:30-x:21," *Studia Theologica* XXV (1971) 21-60; P. M. van Buren, "The Church and Israel: Romans 9-11," *The Princeton Seminary Bulletin*, Supplementary Issue 1, *The Church and Israel: Romans 9-11* (1990) 5-18; W. S. Campbell, *Paul's Gospel in an Intercultural Context* (Frankfurt: Peter Lang, 1992); R. E. Clements, "A Remnant Chosen by Grace, (Rom 11:5)," in *Pauline Studies: Essays Presented to F. F. Bruce*, ed. D. A. Hagner and M. J. Harris, (Grand Rapids: Eerdmans, 1980) 106-21; C. E. B. Cranfield, *Romans* (ICC; Edinburgh: T. & T. Clark, 1979); idem, "The Significance of *dia pantos* in Romans xi:10," Studia Evangelica 2, *Texte und Untersuchungen* 87 (1964) 547-50; N. A. Dahl, "The Future of Israel," in *Studies in Paul: Theology for the Early Christian Mission* (Minneapolis: Augsburg, 1977) 137-58; W. D. Davies, "Paul and the People of Israel" and "Paul and the Gentiles: A Suggestion Concerning Romans 11:13-24," in *Pauline and Jewish Studies* (Philadelphia: Fortress, 1984) 123-63; E. Dinkler, "The Historical and Eschatological Israel in Rom ix-xi: A Contribution to the Problem of Predestination and Individual Responsibility," *JR* (1956) 109-27; K. P. Donfried, ed., *The Romans Debate* (rev. ed.; Peabody, MA: Hendrickson, 1991); J. D. G. Dunn, *Romans* (WBC 38b; Dallas: Word, 1988); L. Gaston, *Paul and the Torah* (Vancouver: University of British Columbia, 1987); M. A. Getty, "Paul on the Covenants and the Future of Israel," *BTB* 17 (1987) 92-99; K. Haacker, "Der Bekenntnis des Paulus zur Hoffnung Israels nach der Apostelgeschichte des Lukas," *NTS* 31 (1985) 437-451; idem, "Der Römerbrief als Friedensmemorandum," *NTS* 36 (1989) 25-41; S. J. Hafemann, "The Salvation of Israel in Romans 11:25-32: A Response to Krister Stendahl," *Ex Auditu* 4 (1989) 38-58; R. B. Hays *Echoes of Scripture in the Letters of Paul* (New Haven: Yale University, 1989); M. Hengel, *The Pre-Christian Paul* (Philadelphia: Trinity Press International, 1991); O. Hofius, "All Israel Will Be Saved: Divine Salvation and Israel's Deliverance in Romans 9-11," *The Princeton Seminary Bulletin*, Supplementary Issue 1 (1990) 19-39; idem, "Das Evangelium und Israel. Erwägungen zu Römer 9-11," *ZThK* 83 (1986) 297-324; D. G. Johnson, "The Structure and Meaning of Romans 11," *CBQ* 46 (1984) 91-103; E. Käsemann, "Paul and Israel," in *New Testament Questions of Today* (Philadelphia: Fortress 1969) 183-87; R. D. Kaylor, *Paul's Covenant Community: Jew and Gentile in Romans* (Atlanta: John Knox, 1988); S. Kim, *The Origin of Paul's Gospel* (2d ed.; WUNT 2.4; Tübingen: J. C. B. Mohr, 1984); R. P. Martin, *Reconciliation: A Study of Paul's Theology* (rev. ed.; Grand Rapids: Zondervan, 1990); W. Meeks, "Judgment and the Brother: Romans 14:1-15:13," in *Tradition and Interpretation: Essays in Honor of E. Earle Ellis*, ed. G. F. Hawthorne with O. Betz (Grand Rapids: Eerdmans, 1987) 290-300; L. Morris, *The Epistle to the Romans* (Grand Rapids: Eerdmans, 1988); J. Munck, *Christ and Israel: An Interpretation of Romans 9—11* (Philadelphia: Fortress, 1967); H. Räisänen, "Paul, God and Israel: Romans 9-11 in Recent Research," in *The Social World of Formative Christianity and Judaism: Essays in Tribute to Howard Clark Kee*, ed. J. Neusner et al. (Philadelphia: Fortress, 1988); P. Richardson, *Israel in the Apostolic Church* (SNTSMS 10; Cambridge: University Press, 1969); E. P. Sanders, *Paul* (Oxford: University Press, 1991); idem, *Paul, the Law and the Jewish People* (Philadelphia: Fortress, 1983); A. F. Segal, *Paul the Convert: The Apostolate and Apostasy of Saul the Pharisee* (New Haven: Yale University, 1990); K. Stendahl, *Paul Among Jews and Gentiles and Other Essays* (Philadelphia: Fortress, 1976); J. Ziesler, *Romans* (TPINTC; Philadelphia: Trinity Press International, 1989).

W. S. Campbell

**ISRAEL OF GOD.** *See* ISRAEL.

## ITINERARIES, TRAVEL PLANS, JOURNEYS, APOSTOLIC PAROUSIA

Paul traveled extensively in the ancient world in fulfillment of his commission from the risen Christ* to be an apostle* to the Gentiles.* Our sources are sufficient for us to outline much of his itinerary and to discuss Paul's motivation for his journeys.

1. Sources
2. The Evidence of Paul's Letters
3. Apostolic Parousia
4. Paul's Motivation for Travel

**1. Sources.**
The primary source for Paul's itinerary must be his letters as these provide firsthand evidence. Since Paul's letters are occasional documents and do not cover all of his career, they do not tell us of all of Paul's travels. On the other hand, Acts, our main secondary source, describes Paul's travels in detail. Methodologically it is important to examine Paul's letters first and ascertain what information they provide. Second, we will outline the evidence of Acts and, finally, we will see to what extent the evidence can be integrated.

**2. The Evidence of Paul's Letters.**
*2.1. The Early Years.* The revelation of Christ to Paul occurred in or near Damascus and from there Paul went into Arabia (Gal 1:16-17). The Nabatean kingdom of Arabia extended east and south of Palestine from the Euphrates to the Red Sea. Paul may have gone to Arabia to begin missionary work, or he may have sought a place of solitude to reflect on his encounter with the risen Christ (*see* Conversion and Call).

Paul then returned to Damascus (Gal 1:17) where he remained until three years after his encounter with Christ (Gal 1:18). At that time he found it necessary to escape from the hands of the provincial governor under King Aretas IV (2 Cor 11:32-33). He then went to Jerusalem* for fifteen days but saw only Cephas (*see* Peter) and James* of the apostles (Gal 1:18-19). Paul then went into the regions of Syria and Cilicia (Gal 1:21). The churches of Judea heard that Paul was preaching the faith he once tried to destroy (Gal 1:23), so we can infer that in Syria and Cilicia he was involved in missionary work.

After fourteen years Paul went up again to Jerusalem with Barnabas* and Titus. The fourteen years could be reckoned either from the time of his encounter with Christ, or from his first visit to Jerusalem. When in Jerusalem he had a private meeting with James, Cephas and John, who gave to Paul and Barnabas the right hand of fellowship and agreed that Paul and Barnabas should go to the Gentiles (Gal 2:1-10). Paul then returned to Antioch* and shortly afterward there occurred the incident in which he accused Cephas and Barnabas of hypocrisy (Gal 2:11-14).

*2.2. Founding the Galatian Churches.* Paul first preached the gospel* to the Galatians because of an illness (Gal 4:13; *see* Healing); he does not relate this founding visit to any other event. That he first visited Galatia before he wrote 1 Corinthians (see 2.4 below) is clear from 1 Corinthians 16:1, but Paul gives us no more information about when this was. It is debated whether Paul visited places like Ancyra and Pessinus (the North Galatian view) or Pisidian Antioch, Iconium, Lystra and Derbe (the South Galatian view). Whether *to proteron* (Gal 4:13, "earlier" or "the first time") indicates that Paul made a second visit before he wrote Galatians is also debated (*see* Galatians).

*2.3. Macedonia and Athens.* In 1 Thessalonians 2:2 Paul tells us that he went to Philippi first and then went on to Thessalonica; Philippians 4:15-16 also implies this order. Paul seems to have spent quite some time in Thessalonica, long enough for him to receive help from the Philippian Christians "more than once" (Phil 4:16; *see* Thessalonians). After leaving Thessalonica Paul went to Athens.* He wanted to return to Thessalonica to visit the church there, but was hindered from doing so by Satan* and thus sent Timothy to strengthen the church. Timothy returned to Paul with a positive report (1 Thess 2:17-18; 3:1-6). As Paul wrote 1 Thessalonians he was praying that he would be able to go to Thessalonica to see the believers there (1 Thess 3:6, 10-11).

*2.4. Ministry in Corinth and Ephesus.* Second Corinthians 1:19 indicates that Paul, Silvanus and Timothy were the first to preach the gospel in Corinth (*see* Corinthians). This probably occurred shortly after the mission in Macedonia and Athens for two reasons. First, when Paul was in Corinth his needs were supplied by believers from Macedonia (2 Cor 11:9). Second, Paul had travelled from Philippi to Athens and then sent Timothy from there to Thessalonica; he met Timothy again at the place where 1 Thessalonians was composed (1 Thess 3:1-2). Silvanus probably accompanied Timothy on the return trip since he joined Paul and Timothy in writing 1 Thessalonians shortly after Timothy returned to Paul (1 Thess 1:1; 3:6; the three share only 1 and 2 Thess). Thus we know that the three people who first preached the gospel in Corinth (2 Cor 1:19) were together just after the mission in Thessalonica when they wrote 1 Thessalonians. This suggests they were in Corinth when they wrote and that we should place Paul's first visit to Corinth shortly after his time in Macedonia. It is clearly a good while after this that Paul wrote 1 Corinthians, since much had happened in the intervening period (Lüdemann, 101-3). This his second letter to Corinth (cf. the "previous letter" mentioned in 1 Cor 5:9 and now lost) was written from Ephesus (1 Cor 16:8, 19), so at some point after his time in Corinth he went on to Ephesus,* where his stay seems to have been a prolonged one.

Paul outlines his future travel plans in 1 Corinthians 16:1-8. He hoped to go to Corinth in connection with the Collection,* and may then accompany those carrying it to Jerusalem (1 Cor 16:3-4; 4:18-19). But first, after Pentecost, he planned to travel from Ephesus to Macedonia and might then spend the winter in Corinth (1 Cor 16:5-6). In the meantime he sent Timothy to Corinth (1 Cor 4:17; 16:10-11). Timothy seems to have returned to Ephesus with the bad news that neither the letter nor Timothy's presence had healed the rift between Paul and the Corinthians. Paul then made a second, "painful" visit to Corinth (2 Cor 2:1-2; 13:2); he was humiliated before the church and returned to Ephesus in great distress (2 Cor 12:21). He then sent Titus to Corinth with his third, "tearful" letter to the Corinthians (2 Cor 2:3-4, 9; 7:8-12; some scholars think that this was 2 Cor 10—13).

Paul then went to Troas where he had planned to meet Titus (2 Cor 2:12-13). When he did not find Titus there, he went on to Macedonia (2 Cor 2:13; 7:5). While there, Titus arrived with encouraging news that the Corinthians mourned their wrongs and longed to see Paul (2 Cor 7:6-7). Titus and two others were then sent on ahead to Corinth with Paul's fourth letter (2 Cor 8:16-24), which was probably 2 Corinthians 1—9, a letter of reconciliation. In the letter Paul also explained his change in travel plans (2 Cor 1:15—2:1; cf. 1 Cor 16:2-4) which had led to the charge that he was vacillating (2 Cor 1:17). Paul himself hoped to follow Titus (2 Cor 9:4-5). He probably then received word that renewed troubles had occurred in Corinth, so he wrote 2 Corinthians 10—13. He was again ready to visit the Corinthians (2 Cor 12:14, 20-21; 13:1-2, 10) for what was his third visit and it seems he did so (and was presumably well received), since he wrote Romans* from Corinth (Rom 16:23; cf. 1 Cor 1:14) and noted in Romans 15:26 that he had already added contributions to the Collection money from churches in Achaia, which would include Corinth.

Before Paul wrote Romans he had preached the gospel in Illyricum (Rom 15:19). We do not know when this was, although it was probably connected with a period in Macedonia.

*2.5. To Jerusalem and Rome.* Paul outlines further travel plans in Romans 15:22-31. Rome* is neither his immediate nor his long-term goal. From Corinth he plans to travel to Jerusalem; this is the third Jerusalem visit he mentions in his letters (see also 1 Cor 16:1-4; 2 Cor 1:16). He will deliver the Collection there (Rom 15:25-27), although he is fearful that he might face trouble from unbelievers in doing so (Rom 15:31; cf. 1 Cor 16:3-4). He will then go to Rome, so that he and the Romans may be mutually encouraged by each oth-

ers' faith (Rom 1:12). But he also notes that since his mission from Jerusalem to Illyricum is complete (Rom 15:19, 23), he plans to go to Spain to begin a new phase of his mission after he has spent some time in Rome. He hopes that the Roman Christians will become partners in his mission to Spain (Rom 15:24, 28).

*2.6. Letters from Prison.* Paul is in prison as he writes Philippians* (1:7, 13) Colossians* (4:3, 10, 18) and Philemon* (1). From Philippians 1:27; 2:24 we know that Paul planned a visit to Philippi if or when he was released from prison. As he wrote Philemon he was looking forward to release from prison and hoped to visit Philemon (Philem 22), who probably lived in the neighborhood of Colossae (Col 4:9). However, the place of Paul's imprisonment is debated for all three letters, with Rome, Ephesus and Caesarea all being possibilities. This lack of consensus makes it difficult to use them as evidence here, and in any case we do not know if Paul was released to travel as he had planned.

*2.7. The Pastoral Letters.* G. D. Fee (3-5), arguing that the Pastorals* are genuinely Pauline and come from a period after Paul's release from prison in Rome (Acts 28), has outlined the most probable order of events portrayed in the Pastoral letters. Paul and Titus evangelized Crete, where Titus remained (Tit 1:5). Paul then traveled with Timothy to Ephesus, where Timothy stayed to combat false teaching (1 Tim 1:3). Meanwhile Paul went on to Macedonia (1 Tim 1:3), where he probably wrote both 1 Timothy and Titus. He planned then to travel to Nicopolis for the winter (Tit 3:12). Paul was probably on his way back to Ephesus (1 Tim 3:14) when he was arrested, perhaps at Troas (2 Tim 4:13-15). At some point he also visited Corinth and Miletus (2 Tim 4:20). When he wrote 2 Timothy he was in Rome, where he expected to die (2 Tim 1:16-17; 2:9; 4:6-8, 16-18).

This outline of events cannot easily be fitted into Paul's ministry as it can be reconstructed from his other letters and Acts, and requires us to assume that Paul undertook further travels after release from Rome, for which we have no other clear evidence. Further, it is noted that if Paul was released from prison in Rome, his plans were to go west, not east, and that Luke would surely have written of such a release. These factors, along with the denial of Pauline authorship of the Pastorals on other grounds, have led to the view that this evidence for Paul's travels should be discounted (*see* Pastoral Letters). However, with Fee one could maintain that Paul could have changed his plans and gone east. If such an argument is accepted, then the travel information given in the Pastoral letters is reliable, but the evidence obviously postdates

Acts and cannot be integrated with Luke's account.

**2.8. Other Travels.** On a number of occasions Paul lists some of the hardships he has endured, and often these refer to his experiences while traveling.* For example, in 2 Corinthians 11:25b-27 he says:

> Three times I was shipwrecked; for a night and a day I was adrift at sea; on frequent journeys, in danger from rivers, danger from bandits, danger from my own people, danger from Gentiles, danger in the city, danger in the wilderness, danger at sea, . . . in toil and hardship, through many a sleepless night, hungry and thirsty, often without food, cold and naked. (NRSV; see also 1 Cor 4:11; 2 Cor 6:4-5)

Since many of these experiences are unknown to us, these passages serve to remind us of how many gaps there are in our knowledge of Paul's life.

**2.9. Summary.** From Paul's occasional letters, which do not cover all of his career, we are able to arrive at the following itinerary (excluding evidence for travel after Paul's Roman imprisonment, since this is debated):

(1) Damascus, Arabia, Damascus, Jerusalem, Syria and Cilicia, Jerusalem, Syrian Antioch

(2) Founding visit to Galatian churches at some point

(3) Philippi, Thessalonica, Athens

(4) Corinth, Ephesus, Corinth, Ephesus, Troas, Macedonia, Corinth, plans to travel to Jerusalem and Rome

## 3. Apostolic Parousia.

**3.1. Definition.** Certain passages in Paul's letters have been identified by Funk on the basis of their form and content as literary units concerned with the theme of the "apostolic parousia," that is, the presence of apostolic authority* and power.* In these passages Paul reminds readers of his apostolic authority by making his presence felt through the letter itself, by reference to the visit of an emissary or to Paul's coming visit. The letter and the envoy are anticipatory substitutes for Paul's own personal presence when he cannot travel, but both function as a means of conveying his apostolic presence.

Thus, these apostolic parousia sections remind the readers of Paul's apostolic authority by making his presence felt in these three related ways. The presence of Paul in person was the primary medium by which he made his apostolic authority effective (1 Cor 4:19; Phil 1:24-25), and he would rather have conveyed his information in person than by letter or via an emissary, but these two substitutes were sometimes necessary. An envoy did not have the same power as Paul himself had, as he implied in 1 Corinthians 4:17-

20: Timothy would remind them, whereas Paul himself would put their power to the test.

**3.2. Form.** Funk identified the following passages as concerned with the apostolic parousia: Romans 1:8-15; 15:14-33; 1 Corinthians 4:14-21; 2 Corinthians 12:14—13:13; Galatians 4:12-20; Philippians 2:19-24; 1 Thessalonians 2:17—3:13; Philemon 21-22. Funk (252-53) suggested that the apostolic parousia had five formal units; however, Jervis (113-14) has since proposed that there are in fact only three functional units of the apostolic parousia. These concern:

(1) Paul's writing of the letter* (including the manner in which he is writing) a reference to Paul's apostolic authority to write, and an appeal to fall into line with his teaching.

(2) Paul's dispatch of an emissary, including the credentials of the emissary and what Paul expects the emissary to do.

(3) Paul's visit and its purpose, along with either (a) the announcement of a visit, including Paul's submission to God's will in this matter, or (b) the desire to visit, including his desire and prayer to see his readers, a recognition that he has been hindered from coming and an expression of love* or concern for the readers.

Each of these units or sub-units need not be present in each passage. In fact the visit unit is the only one that occurs in every letter and only 1 Corinthians 4:14-21 contains all three units.

**3.3. Significance.** Clearly Paul attached great significance to his presence with his congregations and hence to his visits, and this is clear in the content of the apostolic parousia sections and elsewhere. In Galatians 4:20 he writes "How I wish I were present with you now and could exchange my voice [for this letter]." Paul can also speak of his presence in terms of power. In 1 Corinthians 4:19-21 he writes:

> "I will come to you soon, if the Lord wills, and I will find out not the talk of these arrogant people but their power. For the kingdom of God depends not on talk but on power. What would you prefer? Am I to come to you with a stick, or with love in a spirit of gentleness? (NRSV)

In response to the charge that he wrote bold letters but his bodily presence was weak* he replies: "Let such people understand that what we say by letter when absent, we will also do when present" (2 Cor 10:11 NRSV; cf. 2 Cor 13:10). As Funk (265) comments: "Paul's power is bound to the weakness of Christ, it is true, but that power, even in weakness, is capable of making itself felt." Hence he promises to show no leniency when he arrives in Corinth for his third visit (2 Cor 13:1-4).

We see then the significance Paul attached to his actual presence and to the oral word. This is one of the reasons he often prays that he may be able to visit (1 Thess 3:10-11; Rom 1:10; 15:30-32). It is because of his understanding of the significance of his presence that he gathers the items which concern his presence, either in person or via the substitute of a letter or an envoy, into discreet sections in his letters and thus uses the form which has been called the "apostolic parousia."

### 4. Paul's Motivation for Travel.

As apostle to the Gentiles, Paul traveled to proclaim the gospel. As he writes in 1 Corinthians 9:16: "An obligation is laid on me, and woe to me if I do not preach the gospel." This compulsion led Paul to travel across the ancient world to preach the gospel and establish churches (Rom 10:14-15; 2 Cor 2:14, 10:14-16; Col 1:25-29), often while enduring great hardship (2 Cor 11:23-27). In Romans 15:19-20 we see the vision that motivated Paul's travels. He has preached from Jerusalem to Illyricum and has followed his policy of preaching only where Christ was not already known and so not building on another's foundation. As he writes Romans he wants to continue to fulfill this missionary vision by preaching in the West. Yet Paul also had a more detailed strategy of focusing his work in large cities like Ephesus and Corinth. He seems to have used these as large centers for regional outreach through fellow workers (e.g., Col 1:7; 4:12; *see* Coworkers).

Yet Paul traveled not only to preach the gospel and establish churches, but also to nurture and encourage his churches that they might be firmly established. Thus Paul often expressed his longing to see a congregation that he may, for example, supply what was lacking in their faith* (1 Thess 3:10; see also 1 Cor 16:5-7; 2 Cor 13:9-10). This accords well with Acts where Paul regularly revisits congregations to strengthen and encourage them (Acts 14:21-23; 15:36, 41; 16:1-5; 18:23; 20:1-2). Paul also traveled extensively because of the need to attend to difficult situations in his congregations, particularly at Corinth (e.g., the "painful visit," 2 Cor 2:1-2). Further, Paul wanted to travel to Rome, a congregation he had not founded, since as apostle to the Gentiles he had a responsibility to strengthen and enrich Gentile believers (Rom 1:11-12; 15:15-16) and to work for their "obedience of faith" (Rom 1:5; 15:18).

Paul traveled extensively in connection with the Collection* to which he devoted much time and energy (1 Cor 16:1-4; 2 Cor 8—9; Rom 15:25-26). For Paul the Collection symbolized the unity of the churches and the validity of the salvation* of the Gentiles. That Paul was willing to risk his life to deliver the Collection (Rom 15:31) indicates the strength of his motivation in this regard.

There was a good deal of flexibility and change in Paul's travel plans, sometimes because of necessity. He notes his plans were hindered by Satan (1 Thess 2:17-18) and that he was unable to travel to Rome when he wanted to because of his service in the East (Rom 1:13; 15:22). It was because of an illness that he stopped to preach the gospel to the Galatians (Gal 4:13-16). Paul also changed his travel plans to Corinth (1 Cor 16:2-4; 2 Cor 1:15-16, 23; 2:1), and this caused difficulty (2 Cor 1:17).

Paul knew that his travel plans were subject to God's will. To the Corinthians he says: "I will come to you soon, if the Lord wills" (1 Cor 4:19; cf. 16:7; Rom 1:10; 15:32). In Acts the Spirit guides Paul in various ways in his travels, and particularly initiates new phases of mission (Acts 11:27-30; 13:1-3; 16:6-10; 18:9-10).

### 5. Paul's Itinerary in Acts.

#### 5.1. The Sequence of Paul's Travels in Acts.

1. From Jerusalem to Damascus, encounter with the risen Christ, meeting with Ananias, flight from Damascus (Acts 9:1-25)

2. First Jerusalem visit, introduction to the apostles, preaching in Jerusalem (Acts 9:26-29)

3. To Caesarea, Tarsus (Acts 9:30)

4. To Syrian Antioch with Barnabas (Acts 11:25-26)

5. Famine relief visit to Jerusalem, return to Antioch (Acts 11:29-30, 12:25)

6. "First missionary journey": Antioch, Seleucia, Salamis to Paphos on Cyprus, Perga, Pisidian Antioch (actually in Phrygia), Iconium, Lystra, Derbe, Lystra, Iconium, Pisidian Antioch, Perga, Attalia, Antioch in Syria (Acts 13:1—14:28)

7. Third Jerusalem visit for the Council; return to Antioch (Acts 15:1-35)

8. "Second missionary journey": Antioch, Syria, Cilicia, Derbe, Lystra, the Phrygic-Galatic territory, opposite Mysia, Troas, Samothrace, Neapolis, Philippi, Amphipolis, Apollonia, Thessalonica, Berea, Athens, Corinth (for eighteen months), Cenchreae, Ephesus, Caesarea, Jerusalem (a visit to Jerusalem [Paul's fourth] is certainly implied in Acts 18:22), Antioch (Acts 15:36—18:22)

9. "Third missionary journey": Antioch, the Phrygic-Galatic territory, Ephesus (for three years), Macedonia, Greece, Philippi, Troas, Assos, Mitylene, Samos, Miletus, Cos, Rhodes, Patara, Tyre, Ptolemais, Caesarea (Acts 18:23—21:14)

10. Fifth Jerusalem visit (Acts 21:15—23:30)

11. Antipatris, Caesarea, Sidon, Myra, Fair Havens, Crete, Malta, Syracuse, Rhegium, Puteoli, Rome (Acts 23:31—28:31)

*5.2. Issues Arising from the Account in Acts.* Acts is often taken to imply that Paul undertook three "journeys" during which he was continually on the move. However, this is a misleading modern deduction. The account in Acts is too complex to be analyzed simply in terms of three journeys, since Paul actually "settles down" for an extended period in Corinth and Ephesus and in some other places (e.g., Philippi) spends only a short time because of opposition. The Acts picture is better thought of as periods of travel and extended periods in which Paul was resident at one place.

Although we cannot go into the debated question of Luke's sources (particularly in the "we-passages"), it is clear that Luke had more information for some of Paul's travels than for others. In addition, Paul made journeys about which Luke probably knew nothing (2 Cor 11:25-27). Luke also makes no mention of Paul's "painful visit" to Corinth during his Ephesian ministry (2 Cor 2:1; 13:2). Luke's intention was not to provide a continuous "life of Paul" but rather to present selected episodes that furthered the purposes of his narrative.

On some occasions we cannot be certain of Paul's exact route (e.g., Acts 13:14; 15:41—16:1; 17:14-15; 19:1). Acts 16:6-10 creates particular difficulties. Having visited Derbe and Lystra, Paul probably had planned to follow the Via Sebaste westward to Ephesus, but was prevented by the Spirit from entering Asia. As a result they travelled through *tēn Phrygian kai Galatikēn chōran* (Acts 16:6). Taking *Phrygian* as a noun, the phrase would mean that they passed through two regions, Phrygia and then the Galatian country. The latter would refer to the northern part of the province of Galatia and could include Ancyra, Pessinus and Tavium. On the North Galatian view, Paul conducted a mission in these areas at this time. Alternatively, *Phrygian* can be an adjective which, along with *Galatikēn* delimits *chōran*; two adjectives bound by a common article would denote one entity, the *regio Phrygia Galatica*. This would then be the Phrygian territory incorporated in the south of the province of Galatia and would include Pisidian Antioch, Iconium, Lystra and Derbe (*see* Galatians).

Luke tells us that Paul was arrested in Jerusalem and went to Rome for trial. It is debated why Luke ended here; did his source end or did he choose to conclude at this point? To record Paul's vindication and release would have suited Luke's apologetic purpose; that no release is recorded has suggested to

some that Paul was martyred in Rome at the end of this imprisonment (the tradition of the early church is that Paul was eventually martyred in Rome, e.g., *Acts of Paul* 11:1-7; Eusebius *Hist. Eccl.* 2.25.7-8). The prediction of martyrdom in the farewell speech to the Ephesian elders (Acts 20:25, 38) was perhaps intended to indicate what occurred at the end of the two-year period. In *1 Clement* 5:6-7 (c. A.D. 95) it is said that Paul reached "the limits of the west," which could mean Spain, although this may simply be an inference from Romans 15:24.

## 6. Integration of the Letters and Acts.

As T. H. Campbell (80-87) has shown, apart from some omissions (e.g., Acts does not mention Paul's visit to Arabia) there is substantial agreement between Paul's letters and Acts concerning Paul's travels. We turn now to the major issue on which the two sources differ (*see* Chronology).

*6.1. Visits to Jerusalem.* In his letters Paul speaks of only three visits to Jerusalem*:

(1) The acquaintance visit three years after his conversion (Gal 1:18-20)

(2) The Conference visit "after fourteen years" (Gal 2:1-10)

(3) The Collection visit (Rom 15:25-33; 1 Cor 16:1-4; 2 Cor 1:16)

Acts, however, portrays five visits to Jerusalem:

(1) The conversion visit (Acts 9:26-30)

(2) The famine visit (Acts 11:27-30)

(3) The Jerusalem Council (Acts 15:1-30)

(4) The hasty visit (Acts 18:22)

(5) The Collection visit (Acts 21:15-17)

There is general agreement that Galatians 1:18-20 is to be identified with Acts 9:26-30, although there are significant differences between the two accounts. The Collection visit planned by Paul in Romans 15:25-33 and the visit in Acts 21:15-17 are clearly identical, although Luke describes this visit without any mention of the Collection (its purpose is mentioned, but only incidentally, in Acts 24:17).

The main difficulty, however, concerns Galatians 2:1-10. Longenecker (lxxii-lxxxiii) gives the most prominent solutions to this question:

(a) Galatians 2:1-10 is the Jerusalem Council visit of Acts 15:1-30, with the famine visit seen by Paul as unimportant and so not mentioned by him (the traditional view until the early twentieth century).

(b) Galatians 2:1-10 is the famine visit of Acts 11:27-30, with the Jerusalem Council visit occurring after Paul wrote Galatians (Gunther, Bruce, Longenecker).

(c) Galatians 2:1-10 is the Jerusalem Council visit of Acts 15:1-30, which Luke has turned into two visits by misunderstanding the parallel nature of two reports about the Council and so fabricating the visit of Acts 11:27-30 (Lake, Haenchen).

(d) Galatians 2:1-10 is the Jerusalem Council visit of Acts 15:1-30, while Acts 11:27-30 is a misplaced report of the Collection visit which was originally connected with the material of Acts 21:15-17 but which Luke has chosen to place earlier (Beare, Funk).

(e) Galatians 2:1-10 is the Jerusalem Council visit of Acts 15:1-30, but the Council actually took place during the visit of Acts 18:22; Acts 11:27-30 is an invention of Luke's (Knox, Jewett, Lüdemann).

Many scholars point out that for Luke Jerusalem had a key role in the expansion of the church. Hence, Luke had specific theological reasons for presenting Paul as making five trips to Jerusalem (Jewett, 67, 92-93), which for many scholars casts doubt on Luke's historicity at these points. It is argued, therefore, that Paul only made the three visits to Jerusalem mentioned in his letters. However, while Luke's theological and redactional activity has clearly shaped the story he tells, we need to ask if he has altered the story to the extent that is sometimes claimed? Or did Luke's theology arise in part, at least, out of the actual circumstances of Paul's career and other features of the story of the early church? We must turn then to a brief consideration of Luke as a historian.

*6.2. The Historicity of Acts.* Scholars like E. Haenchen and H. Conzelmann have combined interest in Luke as a theologian with rigorous historical skepticism, while in recent years many scholars studying Acts have bracketed off historical questions and focussed solely on literary and theological concerns. However, other scholars have argued that Acts presents a historically reliable picture.

In a study of the earlier parts of Acts, M. Hengel argues that Luke is no less trustworthy than other historians of antiquity. Hengel notes that:

> The radical "redaction-critical" approach so popular today, which sees Luke above all as a freely inventive theologian, mistakes his real purpose, namely that as a Christian "historian" he sets out to report the events of the past that provided the foundation for the faith and its extension. He does not set out primarily to present his own "theology." (Hengel, 67-68)

C. Hemer has shown that many of the background details of Acts receive considerable corroboration from other sources, and he concludes that Luke is much more historically reliable than has often been thought. While accuracy in background details does not necessarily mean that the main plot is accurate, Hemer has shown that where Luke's work can be

checked, it shows a concern for accuracy and care. Marshall notes that Hemer's work leads to a significant conclusion:

> [The] common assumption that theological concern necessarily implies an indifference to history and even a readiness to reconstruct history is extremely dubious; the fact of historical precision in areas that can be tested strongly suggests that there are limits to the way in which theological concern can shape narratives which purport to be historical, and that a concern for history and a concern for theology can be mutually compatible rather than irreconcilable. (Marshall 1992, 90)

G. Lüdemann (1989) has attempted to distinguish between tradition and redaction in Acts and then has sought to analyze the traditional material to determine what may be regarded as historical. In arguing for the necessity of studying the history behind Acts, Lüdemann's work represents a decisive break with the work of Haenchen and Conzelmann. Although questions may be asked about Lüdemann's analysis (see Marshall 1992, 87-88), it is significant that he is far more positive about the historical value of Acts than much of recent scholarship.

Marshall (1990, 44-51; 1992, 91-98) has argued that, while Luke has given a limited picture of Paul and of his theology, and has not slavishly followed Paul to the point of using Paul's own terminology, he has not misrepresented Paul in any serious way.

Thus the case that Acts gives a truer historical picture than many have allowed is a strong one. This does not mean that Luke necessarily always got the story exactly right or that he has not given it his own literary and theological shape. Clearly his perspective and purposes were different from Paul's. Further, as Marshall (1992, 89-90) notes, Luke may have received mistaken or partial information that he could not check, or he may have been affected by conscious or unconscious bias which led him to overlook some things or present others from a tendentious angle. But given the work of Hengel, Hemer and others, we should take the likely historicity of Luke's account of Paul's itinerary seriously.

Thus J. Knox (58) is unjustified when he writes: "I would question anything in Acts involving Paul that is not explicitly or by clear implication indicated also in the letters." While Paul's letters must be the primary source for his itinerary, to dismiss Acts in this way is to be unnecessarily skeptical. In attempting to give an outline of Paul's travels we must begin, as we have done, with the evidence of Paul's letters, but then we can carefully assess the Acts evidence and use it in our reconstruction, provided priority is always given to

Paul's letters. We return then to the relationship between the Jerusalem visit of Galatians 2 and the Acts account of Paul's visits to Jerusalem.

**6.3. Galatians 2:1-10 and the Visits in Acts.** We can note that views (a) and (b) (in 6.1 above) accept the historicity of the Acts framework. With views (c) and (d) Acts has less credibility, and with view (e) Acts is seen as unreliable. Apart from the fact that view (b) takes the likely historicity of Acts seriously, a number of points argue strongly in its favor, as Longenecker (lxxvii-lxxxiii) has recently shown.

**6.3.1. Galatians 2 and Acts 15.** There are strong similarities between these passages. Both concern a meeting at Jerusalem at which the main participants were Paul, Barnabas, Peter and James, and which decided in favor of a Law-free mission to the Gentiles. However, there are some very significant differences. In Galatians 2 Paul is at the center of the meeting; in Acts 15 he is a minor player. In Galatians 2:2 the visit is in response to a revelation; in Acts 15:1-3 it is at the instigation of the church at Antioch. In Galatians 2:2 the meeting is private, small and informal; in Acts 15:6, 12 it is a public Council resulting in an authoritative decision. Are these differences the result of different perspectives and purposes on the part of Luke and Paul, or do the two authors describe different occasions?

We might conclude that the differences are the result of different perspectives if it were not for the fact that there are three factors which question the identification of Galatians 2 and Acts 15. First, if we accept the basic reliability of Acts and identify Galatians 2:1-10 with Acts 15:1-30, we must ask why Paul in Galatians 1—2 has omitted reference to the famine visit of Acts 11:27-30. Given his oath that he is telling the truth (Gal 1:20), such an omission would tend to undermine his argument. To argue that Paul regarded this visit as insignificant and hence not worthy of mention is unconvincing since his opponents would be quick to mention the omission.

Second, again assuming the Acts account is basically reliable, Paul's silence in Galatians about the major decision of the Jerusalem Council argues very strongly against the identification of Galatians 2:1-10 and Acts 15:1-30. Luke (at least) clearly saw the decision as applicable to Gentile believers in general (Acts 16:4; 21:25; cf. Acts 15:23). While Paul may have been reluctant to accept and advocate the four prohibitions (Acts 15:20, 29), it is extremely difficult to see why, if he was writing to Galatia after the Jerusalem Council, he would remain completely silent about the Council's favorable decision which would have clinched his case in the Galatian conflict. This omission strongly suggests that Paul wrote Galatians before the Council of Acts 15 and thus that Galatians 2:1-10 is not Paul's account of that Council. The only other alternative is that Luke's account in Acts 15 of a decision in Paul's favor in which Paul was involved is unhistorical.

A final point concerns Paul's inclusion of the account of his clash with Peter and Barnabas in Galatians 2:11-14. In the incident Peter's and Barnabas's actions favor the position of Paul's judaizing opponents in Galatia. Including an account of the incident in a letter written before the Council is understandable; doing so after the Council, and without reference to it, actually undercuts Paul's whole argument, since the incident shows Paul's recognition of a continuing chasm between himself and the Jerusalem apostles. This suggests Paul wrote Galatians on the eve of the Jerusalem Council, and that the visits described in Galatians 2:1-10 and Acts 15:1-30 are different. Thus there are significant problems with identifying Galatians 2:1-10 with Acts 15:1-30.

**6.3.2. Galatians 2 and Acts 11:27-30.** These factors suggest that Galatians 2:1-10 is to be identified with the famine visit of Acts 11:27-30; the following points argue in this direction.

First, the two accounts are clearly written from different perspectives, but there are significant points of contact. Barnabas had been sent to Antioch* because of the conversion of Gentiles there (Acts 11:19-26), so it would have been natural for him to discuss the Gentile mission with the Jerusalem leaders on his return, even if the trip was primarily concerned with the relief of the famine. This sort of discussion accords well with the clearly private nature of the meeting described in Galatians 2:2. The silence of Acts about this does not exclude the possibility that such discussions occurred. Further, the injunction from the Jerusalem leaders, which can be translated as to "*continue* to remember the poor" (*mnēmoneuōmen*, Gal 2:10), makes good sense in the context of the famine relief visit of Acts 11:27-30.

Second, the most natural reading of Galatians 1:21 is that between his first two Jerusalem visits Paul was *only* in Syria and Cilicia. This is in accordance with the Galatians 2:1-10 visit being the famine visit and not the Jerusalem Council visit (cf. 6.3.3 below).

Third, according to Galatians 2:11-14 Barnabas and Peter gave in to the pressure of Jewish Christians from Jerusalem and separated from the Gentile Christians at Antioch. It is very difficult to believe that Barnabas, a pioneer in the Gentile mission, would have done this after the Jerusalem Council, thus undercutting the Council's decision, in which he played a significant part according to Acts, and his own mission work.

Peter's action is also difficult to explain as having taken place shortly after the Council. The incident at Antioch is much easier to understand as taking place at a time before the Council when there were no agreed-upon guidelines about table fellowship between Jewish and Gentile believers. Again this suggests Galatians 2:1-14 occurred before the Jerusalem Council. This view presupposes that Barnabas and Paul renewed their friendship after the incident of Galatians 2:11-14, so that they went together to Jerusalem for the Council (Acts 15:2).

Identifying Galatians 2:1-10 with the famine visit of Acts 11:27-30 does, however, raise some difficulties. One concerns the time spans of three years and fourteen years of Galatians 1:18 and 2:1, which are difficult to fit into the widely accepted chronological framework established by the crucifixion and Paul's Corinthian ministry, which is dated by Gallio's proconsulship (Acts 18:12). To fit them into this time frame involves assuming that the three years and fourteen years are concurrent and not consecutive (i.e., both are to be counted from Paul's conversion). The other main difficulty is that identifying Galatians 2:1-10 and Acts 11:27-30 compresses the "second missionary journey," since it needs to occur between the Acts 15 Council (probably in 48-49) and the meeting with Gallio in Corinth in 51 after eighteen months there. Again, this is not impossible, particularly on a South Galatian view, but some argue against this identification on the basis of this compression (see Jewett, 89-93). An earlier date for the crucifixion would help (30 rather than 33), but only if we ignore the probable date of 37 for Paul's escape from Aretas (2 Cor 11:32-33), although this is a date on which we should not rely too heavily (Hemer, 264).

Thus the equation of Galatians 2:1-10 and Acts 11:27-30 requires us to make some chronological assumptions, although these are not at all impossible. Given the arguments presented above for identifying Galatians 2:1-10 with Acts 11:27-30, the necessity for making these assumptions does not undermine this view.

*6.3.3. Galatians 2 and Acts 15 and 18:22.* The other main possibility is that Luke did not have sufficient information to enable him to sequence his material clearly. If this was the case, the true setting for the Council of Acts 15 could be the trip to Jerusalem in Acts 18:22, as proponents of view (e) argue, and the visit of Acts 11 would be a tradition that reflected either the Council or Collection visits. This three-visit hypothesis which Jewett (95-104) has worked out in detail, eases the crowding involved in Paul's travels which results from view (b). However, this view has at least three weaknesses:

First, in Paul's letters Barnabas is not connected with Paul's ministry in Macedonia and Achaia (1 Cor 9:6 is no real exception), yet this view requires Paul and Barnabas to be together after this ministry when they travel to the Jerusalem Conference (Gal 2:1). Galatians 2:1-10 certainly suggests Paul and Barnabas were mission partners up until the time of this meeting.

Second, in Galatians 1:21 Paul says he went to Syria and Cilicia between his first two visits to Jerusalem. However, this view requires that he also undertook an extensive mission in Galatia, Macedonia and Achaia during this period. This goes against the natural reading of the verse and seems to discredit Paul's claim to be truthful (Gal 1:20). Further, since Paul is stressing his remoteness from Jerusalem, it seems likely that if he had gone beyond Cilicia he would have said so since it would have further underlined his independence from Jerusalem.

Third, Knox thought the Collection was an obligation laid on Paul at the Jerusalem Conference. Yet if the Jerusalem leaders obliged Paul to undertake the Collection, Paul's fears about its acceptance (Rom 15:25-32) and its likely rejection (judging from Luke's silence) are hard to explain. It is more probable that the impetus for the Collection came from Paul. This would undermine one of Knox's reasons for arguing that the Conference had to be late in Paul's career. Thus, as Longenecker comments:

> It must be concluded that the Knox reconstruction gives a much less satisfactory account of a series of details found in Paul's own letters than does the traditional framework of Acts. . . . It is, therefore, not simple naiveté that causes us to prefer Luke's framework in Acts to Knox's reconstruction. (Longenecker, lxxvii)

*6.3.4. Conclusions.* The most likely view, then, is that Galatians 2:1-10 and Acts 11:27-30 concern the same visit. This results in the following outline of Jerusalem visits:

| | |
|---|---|
| 1. Galatians 1:18-20: | Acts 9:26-30 |
| three years after conversion | (the conversion visit) |
| 2. Galatians 2:1-10: | Acts 11:27-30 |
| "fourteen years later" | (the famine visit) |
| | 3. Acts 15:1-30 |
| | (the Jerusalem Council) |
| | 4. Acts 18:22 |
| | (the hasty visit) |
| 5. Romans 15:25-33; | Acts 21:15-17 |
| 1 Corinthians 16:1-4; | (the Collection visit) |
| 2 Corinthians 1:16 | |

We thus suggest that there were two meetings held to discuss the issue of the place of Gentiles, one which was more informal and private (Gal 2:1-10 and Acts 11:27-30) and the other of a more formal nature, probably called to resolve the problem posed by the Antioch incident (Acts 15:1-30). On this view Paul made five visits to Jerusalem but had no reason to mention visits three and four in his occasional letters. If Galatians was written before Acts 15:1-30, then it was before visits 3 and 4 had occurred. When Paul writes about the Collection visit he does not say it was his third visit, and so it could well have been his fifth; Paul certainly says nothing to indicate that there were no other visits (cf. Knox, 35-40).

***6.4. Summary.*** The accompanying chart summarizes the proposed reconstruction of Paul's itinerary, showing how the information in Paul's letters and Acts may be related (adapted from Campbell, 87):

*See also* CHRONOLOGY OF PAUL; COLLECTION FOR THE SAINTS; CORINTHIANS, LETTERS TO THE; EPHESUS; GALATIANS, LETTER TO THE; JERUSALEM; MISSION; PASTORAL LETTERS; PAUL IN ACTS AND LETTERS; TRAVEL.

BIBLIOGRAPHY. P. Bowers, "Fulfilling the Gospel: The Scope of the Pauline Mission," *JETS* 30 (1987) 185-98; F. F. Bruce, *The Book of the Acts* (rev. ed.; Grand Rapids: Eerdmans, 1988); T. H. Campbell, "Paul's 'Missionary Journeys' as Reflected in His Letters," *JBL* 74 (1955) 80-87; H. Conzelmann, *Acts of the Apostles* (Herm; Philadelphia: Fortress, 1987); B. Corley, ed., *Colloquy on New Testament Studies: A Time for Reappraisal and Fresh Approaches* (Macon, GA: Mercer University, 1983); G. D. Fee, *1 and 2 Timothy, Titus* (NIBC; Peabody, MA: Hendrickson, 1988); J. A. Fitzmyer, *Paul and His Theology: A Brief Sketch* (2d ed.; Englewood Cliffs, NJ: Prentice Hall, 1989); R. W. Funk, "The Apostolic *Parousia*: Form and Significance," in *Christian History and Interpretation: Studies Presented to John Knox*, ed. W. R. Farmer, C. F. D. Moule and R. R. Niebuhr (Cambridge: University Press, 1967) 249-68; J. J. Gunther, *Paul, Messenger and Exile: A Study in the Chronology of His Life and Letters* (Valley Forge: Judson, 1972); E. Haenchen, *The Acts of the Apostles: A Commentary* (Philadelphia: Westminster, 1971); M. Hengel, *Acts and the History of Earliest Christianity* (Philadelphia: Fortress, 1979); C. J. Hemer, *The Book of Acts in the Setting of Hellenistic History*, ed. C. H. Gempf (Winona Lake, IN: Eisenbrauns, 1989); L. A. Jervis, *The Purpose of Romans: A Comparative Letter Structure Investigation* (JSNTSup 55; Sheffield: JSOT, 1991); R. Jewett, *A Chronology of Paul's Life* (Philadelphia: Fortress, 1979); J. Knox, *Chapters in a Life of Paul*, ed. and intro. D. R. A. Hare (Macon, GA: Mercer University, 1987); R. N. Longenecker, *Galatians* (WBC 41; Dallas: Word, 1990); G. Lüdemann, *Paul, Apostle to*

## Paul's Itinerary

| Letters | Acts |
| --- | --- |
| Damascus (Gal 1:17c) | Damascus (Acts 9:1-22) |
| Arabia (Gal 1:17b) | |
| Damascus (Gal 1:17c; 2 Cor 11:32-33) | Damascus (Acts 9:23-5) |
| Jerusalem (VISIT 1; Gal 1:18) | Jerusalem (Acts 9:26-9) |
| Syria and Cilicia (Gal 1:21) | Caesarea, Tarsus (Acts 9:30) |
| | Antioch (Acts 11:26a) |
| Jerusalem (VISIT 2; Gal 2:1-10) | Jerusalem (Acts 11:29-30, 12:25) |
| | Antioch (Acts 13:1-4a) |
| | Cyprus (Acts 13:4b-12) |
| Galatia (Gal 4:13) | South Galatia (Acts 13:13—14:25) |
| Antioch (Gal 2:11-14) | Antioch (Acts 14:26-28) |
| | Jerusalem (VISIT 3; Acts 15:1-29) |
| | Antioch (Acts 15:30-5) |
| | Syria and Cilicia (Acts 15:41) |
| | Derbe, Lystra (Acts 16:1-5) |
| | Phrygic-Galatic region (Acts 16:6) |
| | Mysia, Troas (Acts 16:7-10) |
| Philippi (1 Thess 2:2) | Philippi (Acts 16:11-40) |
| Thessalonica (1 Thess 2:2; Phil 4:15-16) | Thessalonica (Acts 17:1-9) |
| | Berea (Acts 17:10-14) |
| Athens (1 Thess 3:1) | Athens (Acts 17:15-34) |
| Corinth (2 Cor 1:19; 11:7-9) | Corinth (Acts 18:1-18a; for 18 months) |
| | Cenchreae (Acts 18:18b) |
| | Ephesus (Acts 18:19-21) |
| | Caesarea (Acts 18:22a) |
| | Jerusalem (VISIT 4; Acts 18:22b) |
| | Antioch (Acts 18:22c) |
| | Phrygic-Galatic region (Acts 18:23) |
| Ephesus (1 Cor 16:1-8) | Ephesus (Acts 19:1—20:1; for approximately 3 years) |
| Corinth (2 Cor 2:1; 13:2) | |
| Return to Ephesus | |
| Troas (2 Cor 2:12) | |
| Macedonia (2 Cor 2:13; 7:5) | Macedonia (Acts 20:1b) |
| Illyricum (Rom 15:19)? | |
| Corinth (2 Cor 13:1; Rom 15:26) | Greece (Acts 20:2b-3a) |
| | Philippi (Acts 20:3b-6a) |
| | Troas (Acts 20:6b-12) |
| | Miletus (Acts 20:15c-38) |
| | Caesarea (Acts 21:8-14) |
| Plans to visit Jerusalem, Rome, Spain (Rom 15:22-27) | Jerusalem (VISIT 5; Acts 21:15—23:30) |
| | Caesarea (Acts 23:33—26:32) |
| | Rome (Acts 28:14b-31) |

*the Gentiles: Studies in Chronology* (Philadelphia: Fortress, 1984); idem, *Early Christianity According to the Traditions in Acts* (Minneapolis: Fortress, 1989); I. H. Marshall, *The Acts of the Apostles* (NTG; Sheffield: JSOT, 1992); idem, "Luke's View of Paul," *SWJT* 33 (1990) 41-51; G. Ogg, *The Odyssey of Paul* (Old Tappan, NY: Revell, 1968); W. M. Ramsay, *St Paul the Traveller and the Roman Citizen* (8th ed.; London: Hodder & Stoughton, 1905). P. Trebilco

## J

## JAMES AND PAUL

Since the Reformation James and Paul have often been viewed as having contradictory theologies, one focusing on works (*see* Works of the Law) and the other on grace.* An examination of the critical texts shows, however, that in reality the two men used similar terms differently in separate contexts. Modern scholarship generally recognizes this in claiming that James knew only a misunderstood Paulinism.

1. The James-Paul Issue
2. James and Paul on Works
3. James and Paul on Faith
4. James and Paul on Justification
5. Conclusions

### 1. The James-Paul Issue.

Ever since Luther the watchword of Pauline studies has been "justification* by faith alone, not by works." At the same time one can hardly ignore the fact that James 2:24 states, "You see that a person is declared right [or justified] by [their] deeds [works] and not by faith alone." This apparent conflict with Paul's view of justification is further complicated by the fact that both Paul (Rom 4:3, 9, 22; Gal 3:6) and James (Jas 2:23) refer to Abraham* and cite Genesis 15:6 in support of seemingly opposite views. Does this not support the thesis that one writer knew of the other and was deliberately arguing against him?

There are four ways to answer this question. The first is to deny any knowledge of the one man by the other, the likenesses being coincidental. The problem with this position is that Paul (Gal 1:19; 2:9) and Luke (Acts 15; 21:17-26) each mention at least two contacts between the two men in which these issues at the heart of the gospel* must have been discussed. In Paul's version, three years after his conversion he met James briefly (Gal 1:19), but his first substantive discussion with James took place "fourteen years later" (Gal 2:9). At that point James and his colleagues fully endorsed Paul's version of the gospel, while recognizing that Paul and they had differing spheres and styles of ministry. In Galatians 2:12 Paul makes one further

reference to James, but it is unclear from his remarks here whether Peter's actions of withdrawing from table fellowship with Gentiles because of the arrival of "certain people from James" had anything to do with the purpose James himself had in mind in sending them. Hence James's own attitude is not clear. In Luke's version James appears as the leader of the Jerusalem* church and a skilled mediator. In both passages he comes up with a *modus vivendi* by means of which the stricter Jewish-Christians could live in the same church with Gentile* Christians without compromising the beliefs of either group. How the two versions fit together, and their precise chronology, is one of the issues of NT study on which there is no consensus.

The second answer is to argue that Paul is correcting James or a distortion of James' position. This is a possible solution if one can find a Jewish-Christian context for James's writing. While a few scholars have argued for such a background and even fewer (most notably F. Spitta in 1896) for a purely Jewish background, there is no clear evidence that Jews or Jewish-Christians were discussing faith and works using the types of terminology James is using. Furthermore, many scholars cannot see why James would write as he did if Paul had not written first, for while Judaism does not appear to be concerned with James's issues, in particular that of faith and works, Paul does in fact introduce them into theological discussion using terminology which overlaps that of James. Finally, this answer appears to put the letter of James at an impossibly early date, especially if Paul would have had to have read it before writing Galatians. Thus, while this position remains possible, it is unlikely.

The third answer, then, is that James is directly contradicting Paul, perhaps having read Romans.* This, of course, would mean that the letter of James was written after A.D. 56 and probably far later than A.D. 61 (the year of the death of James), to allow sufficient time for the letter to the Romans to make its way to Jerusalem. (Most scholars who give this answer, whether in the modified form of W. Pratscher or in the original form of the older German commentators, see Acts as a deliberate attempt to harmonize the theologies of Paul and James and so they consider the accounts of the relatively harmonious interaction of the two men in Acts 15 and 21 to be unhistorical.)

The fourth answer is to say that James is responding to a misunderstood Pauline teaching. Two time frames make this answer a possibility. The earliest of these is A.D. 40-50, after Paul began preaching to the Gentiles and before the Jerusalem Council occurred (most scholars who take this position consider Acts 15 to be historical). The other time frame is that period after the teachings contained in Romans, and perhaps Galatians*, had circulated widely enough to be distorted (i.e., after A.D. 60) but before the Pauline corpus had reached the author of James (some scholars place this time frame as late as A.D. 96). M. Dibelius, S. S. Laws and M. Hengel all take this latter position.

Of the four answers the first and third are unlikely because, on the one hand, the overlap between James and Paul is too great to make total independence likely. On the other hand, if James had read either Romans or Galatians* he did a colossal job of misunderstanding Paul. Something similar could be said of the second answer; in other words, if Paul had read the written form of James, he misunderstood him. This leaves open the possibility of his having heard an oral distortion of James's teaching. The fourth answer, therefore, appears the most likely.

This conclusion, however, leaves open which version of the fourth answer is the most likely. Either the version that proposes an early date for James or the one that proposes a late date is a possible solution to the relationship between the two leaders. The question about early or late dates must be decided on literary and theological grounds. This conclusion is supported by M. Hengel, who, while certain of the relationship, is vague about what this means for dating the Epistle of James other than that it is "early" (which could mean A.D. 60-66 or A.D. 40-50).

We can clarify our choice of the fourth answer by an examination of how James and Paul use each of the three critical terms of *works, faith* and *justification.*

### 2. James and Paul on Works.

Both James and Paul use the Greek word *erga* ("works" or "deeds"; *see* Works of the Law). In James 2:14-26 the author is clearly arguing for a particular kind of works. The two deeds he cites are (1) Abraham's* offering of Isaac and (2) Rahab's hospitality to the spies. In regard to Abraham's act, in Jewish eyes this offering of Isaac was the culmination of a lifetime of obedience to God and charity toward others (Gen 18; *Jub.* 17:17;

19:8; *T. Abr.* recension A, 1.17; *Tg. Ps.-J.* Gen 21:33; *'Abot R. Nat.* 7 and 32). The fact that Isaac was not offered was seen as a declaration of Abraham's righteousness.* Rahab's deed was also viewed as an act of charity. Furthermore, charity is the issue which begins the argument (Jas 2:14-17). Thus the works James champions are good deeds (charitable acts, generosity, impartiality, control of the tongue, etc.).

It is true that Paul is clearly against "works," but "works" as a means of becoming righteous before God. Such works he calls "the works of the Law." This phrase is also found in the Dead Sea Scrolls, but is never used by James. The phrase "of the Law" (*see* Law) is always present, at least in the near context, when Paul speaks negatively of works. What are these works? The principal one is circumcision,* although he also speaks of the observance of (Jewish) holy days and (Jewish) dietary laws (*see* Food) as concerns of his. In other words, while Paul never mentions generosity and other good deeds in these negative contexts, he is against those cultic acts of the Mosaic Law which set apart a Jew from a Gentile and which could be thought of as necessary acts for one to do to be right with God. This fits the context of the Pauline letters, for the issue he is facing is that some Jewish-Christians are insisting that Gentile believers must become proselytes to Judaism to be saved. Paul denies there is any such need to become Jewish, although there is a need to become godly.

There is, then, no real conflict between James and Paul on the issue of works. Not only does Paul always use a phrase ("works of the Law") James never uses (in fact, it is the lack of reference to the works Paul cites that makes Pratscher and Dibelius reject James as the author of the letter), but in places such as Galatians 5:19-21 Paul can give lists of evil deeds (similar to James' in Jas 3:14-16) and then say "I say to you [now] and I said to you [earlier] that those doing such things will not inherit the kingdom of God." Likewise in places such as Romans 12:9-21 and Galatians 5:22-23; 6:7-10 he affirms good works as James also does. Paul will not separate practical righteousness from eternal salvation.*

### 3. James and Paul on Faith.

When it comes to faith, James gives a clear definition of what he means by "faith alone": "Do you believe that God is one?" (Jas 2:19). This is not only the basic creed of Judaism, but also the creed that Jews believed Abraham discovered. It is an orthodoxy, but in this case an orthodoxy totally separated from obedience to God (Jas 2:18), an orthodoxy which is shared with demons.* Elsewhere in James a different definition of faith appears. The faith referred to in James 1:6 and James 2:1 is that of personal commitment which includes trust and obedience; in contrast, the faith mentioned in James 2:14-26 is the orthodoxy without action which James sees his opponents claiming.

Turning to Paul, one can discern a definition of faith in Romans 10:9-10: a commitment to the living Lord* Jesus and a confession that "Jesus is Lord" (*see* Creeds). This is similar to the relational trust type of faith which James refers to in chapter 1. In Galatians 5:6 Paul goes on to state that in Christ the issue is not one of Jewish ritual deeds (circumcision), but of "faith working through love.*" This faith-love pair is not accidental, for it occurs repeatedly in Paul (e.g., 1 Cor 13:13; 1 Thess 1:3; 3:6). For Paul, then, faith is a commitment to Jesus as Lord which results in a life of love. If the love is lacking (as "the deeds to the flesh*" or "unrighteousness" show), then such a person is no heir of God's kingdom (1 Cor 6:9-10; *see* Kingdom).

Having noted these different emphases, one is not surprised that James and Paul also use the example of Abraham differently. For Paul the critical issue is that Abraham was declared righteous before the rite of circumcision was instituted (Gen 15:6; 17:9-14). Since ritual law is the issue, the fact that Genesis 15 follows after significant acts of obedience by Abraham, such as his leaving home, is not mentioned by Paul, for whom faith is the starting point. For James the critical issue is that the declaration of righteousness in Genesis 22:12 ("now I know that you fear God") shows that the faith referred to in Genesis 15:6 is not mere orthodoxy but a trust leading to actual righteous deeds so that "[his] faith worked together with his deeds and the faith was completed by the deeds" (Jas 2:22). It is important to James that deed precedes God's final declaration; on the other hand, he is not at all concerned about Jewish ritual. In other words, the two men come at the Abraham narrative from different directions, using definitions of faith with different emphases, and as a result argue for complementary rather than contradictory conclusions. Paul stresses that ritual expresses faith, but does not supplement it; yet, as we saw in Galatians 5:19-21, he questions the validity of a "faith" that does not produce good works. James stresses that only a useless type of "faith" does not result in good works; yet, as we noted, he does not comment on the place of Jewish ritual (probably because it was not an issue in his community). Both James and Paul agree on the element of obedience in faith.

Is it possible that James is doing more than this, that he is actually *defending* Paul by correcting a distortion of the Pauline doctrine of grace which rejected the need for works (or what Paul would call the fruit of the Spirit)? That is certainly a possibility, although, as Reumann (157) argues, it is "speculative." What we know for sure is that James is in contact with what sound like Pauline slogans used by a group which rejects the place of works and thus does not have Paul's balance. How conscious James was of the origin of these slogans and thus how consciously he is trying to rehabilitate Paul within his community can only be guessed at.

## 4. James and Paul on Justification.

Perhaps the most misunderstood of the three types of terms used in common by James and Paul is the Greek word group including *dikaiosynē* ("righteousness"), *dikaiōsis* ("justification") and *dikaioō* ("declare righteous" or "justify"). The usual meaning of these words in the LXX is a demonstrated righteousness (i.e., one which a person deserves on the basis of their behavior) or a declaration of such righteousness (e.g., Gen 38:26; Ex 23:7; Deut 25:1), a meaning that Paul also knows (e.g., Rom 2:13). It is these traditional meanings that James invariably uses (he never use *dikaiōsis*, however, which appears in the LXX only in Lev 24:22). Paul, on the other hand, often writes of God's making a sinner righteous (justifying a sinner, Rom 2:24) or of a righteousness obtained by Christ's righteousness being given to the sinner (Rom 5:17) or of the resulting state (justification, Rom 4:25; 5:18; *see* Justification; Righteousness).

Unfortunately, the Pauline meaning (of which James certainly reveals no understanding) has dominated Protestant thinking since the Reformation and has been read by many translations into James (as the KJV, RSV and NIV all do in Jas 2, where, for example, "justified" in Jas 2:24 would be better translated "declared to be just" to avoid overtones of Paul's usage). This results in an artificial conflict between James and Paul. James, on the one hand, is asking how God knew Abraham was righteous when God made the statement "now I know that you fear God" in Genesis 22:12 and therefore how the reader can know that the faith in Genesis 15:6 was a trust in God (or faith) that actually made Abraham righteous. The answer is, one can know this from Abraham's deeds. And without such deeds any claim of righteousness or of faith is empty. Paul, on the other hand, is pointing out that both Jews and Gentiles are equally short of God's standard of righteous judgment and thus the issue is not how a person can demonstrate that their faith is real faith, but how will God make the unrighteous righteous? The answer is, God does so, not through cultic ritual (circumcision, etc.) but through commitment to (or faith in) Jesus Christ. The two authors use their terms in different ways because they address different issues.

Naturally, it is also because of this that "justification" has a different place in their respective theologies. For Paul the concept is central; for James it is simply one of a number of issues and thus not a central focus of his interest.

### 5. Conclusions.

It is clear, then, that James and Paul are moving in two different worlds. In James's world Jewish ritual is not an issue (perhaps because all of those in his church are Jews), but ethics* is. His problems are with those who claim to be right with God on the basis of their orthodoxy (i.e., adherence to the proper creed, including that Jesus is Lord), although they were ignoring issues of obedience, especially charity. Abraham and Rahab, in contrast to the demons, demonstrate that saving faith manifests itself in its deeds. Paul, on the other hand, is concerned in Romans and Galatians with the relationship of Jews and Gentiles in the church; that is, his concern is that a Gentile does not have to become a Jew to enter the kingdom. Commitment to Jesus as Lord (including the obedience which flows from this commitment) is all that is necessary for salvation; those ritual deeds which marked out the Jews as a distinct people are unnecessary for Gentiles (although not prohibited for Jews). In the instances where Paul does address the issue of whether a person can enter the kingdom while living in sin, he emphatically denies that this is possible (1 Cor 6:9; Gal 5:19-21), agreeing with James (Jas 2:14, 17, 26).

Paul himself realized that he was at times misunderstood. Some misinterpreted his denial that legal ritual was needed for salvation. They understood him to say that ethical issues were irrelevant to salvation (Rom 3:8; 6:1; 1 Cor 6:12). Paul strongly repudiated these interpretations of his gospel. While we cannot be certain whether James was contending with an orthodoxy-without-deeds rooted in Judaism (such as rabbis would later attack) or a misunderstood Paulinism (such as Paul himself attacked), both being possible backgrounds, the latter is the more likely. What becomes clear is that James is not attacking any actual belief of Paul's, and that Paul could endorse everything James wrote. Nevertheless, Paul used some terms such as *works* and *justify* differently than James.

If James is dealing with a misunderstood Paulinism, then it is probable that the sermon preserved in James 2:14-26 comes from a period before James met Paul, for it is likely that once they discussed the gospel together James would have cited Paul's own words against anyone who claimed Paul as an authority for such a twisted doctrine as James is countering. This would certainly have been true had James been trying to rehabilitate Paul and even more likely had James been writing after Paul's letters were being circulated.

It is therefore most unlikely that M. Hengel is correct in seeing "anti-Paulinism" behind most sections of the letter, for (1) most of the letter lacks specific Pauline terms and (2) the sections of the letter were originally separate units (sayings or sermons), and it is unlikely that they were all on the same theme. Hengel's theory, which is possible in one context (Jas 2:14-26), is being used to read that passage's concerns into others. This theory is turned on its head by Reumann, of course, who is more likely correct in arguing that far from being anti-Pauline, James is trying to defend Paul.

The James-Paul issue, then, is partially our misunderstanding of Paul (stemming from the fact that Luther was concerned with the earning of salvation through penance and pious deeds rather than with Jewish ritual, thus reading Luther into Paul) and partially a problem of reading Paul into James. In reality, both James and Paul had similar ideas on the role of good works in the Christian life, but since they ministered in different spheres socially and geographically, they addressed different concerns and used their overlapping terminology differently. Even if James is attacking "Paul" (and this is uncertain), it is a misunderstood and distorted Paul that he is targeting; he may well, in fact, be trying to defend the real Paul. Luke does not appear to be incorrect in Acts when he portrays Paul and James as getting along reasonably well (in spite of Acts 21:17-26).

*See also* ABRAHAM; FAITH; JERUSALEM; JUSTIFICATION; WORKS OF THE LAW.

BIBLIOGRAPHY. P. H. Davids, *The Epistle of James* (NIGTC; Grand Rapids: Eerdmans, 1982) 19-21, 120-134; M. Dibelius, *James* (Herm; Philadelphia: Fortress, 1976); J. D. G. Dunn, "The New Perspective on Paul," *BJRL* 65 (1983) 93-122; H. P. Hamann, "Faith and Works: Paul and James," *LTJ* 9 (1975) 33-41; M. Hengel, "Der Jakobusbrief als antipaulinische Polemik," in *Tradition and Interpretation in the New Testament*, ed. G. F. Hawthorne with O. Betz (Grand Rapids: Eerdmans, 1987) 248-78; J. Jeremias, "Paul and James," *ExpT* 66 (1954-1955) 368-71; S. S. Laws, *A Commentary on the Epistle of James* (San Francisco: Harper and Row, 1980); J. G. Lodge, "James and Paul at Cross-Purposes? James 2:22," *Bib* 62 (1981) 195-213; R. P. Martin, *James* (WBC 48; Waco, TX: Word, 1988) 75-101; D. Moo, "Paul and the Law in the Last Ten Years," *SJT* 40 (1987) 287-307; W. Pratscher, *Der Herrenbruder Jakobus und die Jakobus-*

*tradition* (Göttingen: Vandenhoeck & Ruprecht, 1987); J. Reumann, *"Righteousness" in the New Testament* (Philadelphia: Fortress, 1982) 148-58; K. R. Snodgrass, "Justification by Grace to the Doers: An Analysis of the Place of Romans 2 in the Theology of Paul," *NTS* 32 (1986) 72-93; A. E. Travis, "James and Paul: A Comparative Study," *SWJT* 12 (1969) 57-70; R. B. Ward, "James and Paul: A Critical Review," *ResQ* 7 (1963) 159-64.

P. H. Davids

## JEALOUSY, ZEAL

The bulk of the NT usage of the related ideas "jealousy" and "zeal" (associated with *zēlos*, "zeal," and *zēloō*, "strive" or "be jealous") is found in Paul's letters, including several nontechnical instances of "zealot" (*zēlōtēs*). Zeal represents intense effort and emotional energy focused toward a goal, and the zealot is one who single-mindedly pursues the goal, which frequently involves guarding and vindicating the sanctity of that goal. Jealousy is the relational counterpart to zeal, primarily a focusing of emotion toward a person in the desire for a closer or renewed bond, or an envying of another person. Jealousy is often self-centered and destructive, although God is righteously jealous when his right to total allegiance by his people is infringed. Moreover, Paul regards godly jealousy on the human level as quite possible.

1. Paul's Pre-Christian Zeal
2. Paul's Refocused Zeal
3. Destructive Jealousy and Zeal
4. Godly Jealously and Zeal

### 1. Paul's Pre-Christian Zeal.

Perhaps Paul's extensive use of the concepts "zeal" and "jealousy" is due to his background and zealous personality. Acts 22:3 tells of the rigorous training he received in Jerusalem under Gamaliel and his youthful zealotry for the Jewish Law* and for God.* In Galatians 1:14 Paul recalls how he gained advanced standing in Judaism at an early age because of his "extremely zealous" (NIV; Gk *zēlōtēs*) keeping of the traditions of his ancestors (*see* Jew, Paul the). Paul may have considered his zeal as being in the tradition of Mattathias, whose great zeal for the Law and traditions was said to have followed the prototype of Phineas, the grandson of Aaron (1 Macc 2:26, 54; cf. 1QH 14:13-15; Dupont, 184-85). Phineas exhibited zeal for God when he spontaneously slew the Israelite Zimri and the Midianite woman Cozbi, thereby making atonement for the Israelites and averting the plague that had broken out against Israel in its worship of the Baal of Peor (Num 25:1-15).

S. G. F. Brandon's view that there were ties between Jesus or his followers and the Zealot political movement must be rejected as extreme, and the existence of a Zealot sect prior to A.D. 68 is now widely questioned (*see* Revolutionary Movements). But there is a more basic and older sense in which the pre-Christian Paul could be considered a "zealot." As a Pharisee (Phil 3:5), a member of the "strictest sect" of Judaism (Acts 26:5 NIV), he was truly a zealot for the Law of Moses (Phil 3:6), protecting and vindicating its sanctity against all violations (Hengel 1991, 63-68).

While Saul of Tarsus was never involved in seeking the political overturning of Roman rule, as the Zealot movement attempted to do (see Hengel 1989, 83-94), his tireless zeal was just as intensely focused. Following the death of Stephen by stoning (Acts 7:55—8:1), Saul "attempted to destroy" the church* through violent persecution (Gal 1:13). As M. Hengel has argued, this "church" may be a reference to the Jewish Christian "Hellenists" (first in Jerusalem and then in Damascus), who in their criticism of Torah and Temple would have been considered by Saul to be accursed lawbreakers (Hengel 1991, 72-84; Kim, 44-50). Speaking from the perspective of his postconversion experience, Paul considered this fanatical persecution to be the epitome of his pre-Christian zeal (Phil 3:6; Hengel 1991, 71-79). Thus he regarded the zeal for God exhibited by many of his fellow Jews as "not according to knowledge" because they were "ignorant of the righteousness* that comes from God" (Rom 10:2-3; cf. Phil 3:6).

### 2. Paul's Refocused Zeal.

Saul's murderous zeal drove him to pursue Christians as far as Damascus (Acts 9:1-2). But, when he was blinded by a heavenly light on the Damascus Road, there was no escaping the fact that he had been zealously persecuting Jesus,* the Messiah of God, and not just the church (Acts 9:3-5). It took a revelation of God's Son to transform Saul's zeal into that of an equally energetic apostle* of Jesus Christ* (Gal 1:15-17; *see* Conversion and Call).

As a believer in Christ, who was no longer zealously seeking to establish his righteousness through the Law (Phil 3:9), Paul fervently pursued (Gk *diōkō*) the heavenly calling of Christ (Phil 3:12, 14). He did so with a tenacity that was every bit the equal of the "zeal" with which he had previously persecuted (Gk *diōkō*) the church (Phil 3:6; Gal 1:13), only now he lived and worked by the power of Christ's resurrection* (Phil 3:10).

Accordingly, Paul appreciated zealousness for the right purpose (Gal 4:18), and resisted and exposed zeal that was misguided or self-serving (Gal 4:17). Thus Paul urged those who had been redeemed by the grace* of

God to be "zealots" (Gk *zēlotas*) for good works (Tit 2:14).

### 3. Destructive Jealousy and Zeal.

To pursue a life of zeal is to walk a fine line. One may have proper zeal, directed toward an appropriate object or goal (Gal 4:18); but it may just as easily be directed toward "no good" (Gal 4:17; *ou kalōs*), rooted in false teaching or aimed at self-promotion (*see* Judaizers).

Nor does such distorted "zeal" affect only the individual pursuing that course. "Jealousy" is the nuance of *zēlos* in the negative sense that often overflows into relationships with others. Such zeal gone bad is dangerous to the health of a Christian community (Hahn).

The prime NT example of rampant corporate jealousy was the church at Corinth.* Their jealousy spilled over into quarreling (Gk *eris*) so bitter that it equalled that of unbelievers (1 Cor 3:3 *sarkikoi . . . kata anthrōpon*). Paul considered jealousy to be an essential problem behind the factions infecting the Corinthian fellowship (1 Cor 3:4). Even later, after substantial repentance and progress had taken place in Corinth, Paul feared the reemergence of such jealous quarreling with its attendant "outbursts of anger" (2 Cor 12:20) and disputes similar to the party spirit displayed earlier (1 Cor 1:12; 3:4).

This realistic understanding and concern of Paul for the jealous Corinthian congregation should not be mistaken for tolerance or sympathy. The apostle saw such behavior as indicative of prolonged spiritual infancy, of believers acting as if they were still mere unbelieving worldlings (1 Cor 3:1-3). He minces no words in likening the religious factions at Corinth to something non-Christians would do (1 Cor 3:4). Strikingly, in speaking to another aspect of the Corinthians' misguided practice, Paul employs the intensive *parazēloō* ("to provoke to jealousy") in asking the church with language borrowed from the OT: "Are we trying to arouse the Lord's jealousy?" (1 Cor 10:22 NIV). For all their generally commendable zeal for spiritual gifts, they exhibited little interest in edifying the church (1 Cor 14:12).

These symptoms point to the root cause of jealousy in this hurtful sense, namely a lack of love.* Love, as Paul describes it to the Corinthians, is incapable of jealousy (1 Cor 13:4), anger that is related to jealousy, or anything that is "self seeking" (1 Cor 13:5 NIV). Love builds up the community (1 Cor 8:1), while the negative aspects of jealousy never can do so.

Loving behavior is a choice, but it is also the "fruit"* of the Spirit of God who controls the Christian's life (Gal 5:22; *see* Holy Spirit). Jealousy is also a choice,

prominent among the "works of the flesh" (Gal 5:20), that are in continual conflict with the Spirit that indwells the believer.

Paul forcefully warns his readers that fleshly jealousy, and the anger and dissension it so frequently stirs up (Gal 5:20), is unfit for those who will "inherit the kingdom* of God" (Gal 5:21). The alternative lifestyle he points them to is that of living in the power* of the Spirit (Gal 5:16) and of walking by faith (Gal 5:5). As believers "keep in step with the Spirit" (Gal 5:25 NIV), jealousy and other obvious manifestations of the flesh will not occur.

Elsewhere the apostle relates the avoidance of jealousy and other "lusts" of the flesh* (Rom 13:13, 14) to single-mindedly "putting on" the Lord Jesus Christ and the "armor of light" (Rom 13:12, 14). By this Paul seems to be saying that by consistent faith* in Christ, the power of the Holy Spirit brings forth in the believer's life a behavioral pattern dominated by love (Gal 5:5-6), instead of self-indulgent and destructive jealousy (Gal 5:13, 15, 20).

### 4. Godly Jealousy and Zeal.

In the second commandment the Lord God is characterized as "a jealous God" (Ex 20:5; cf. Deut 5:9), demanding a covenant relationship of loving fidelity that excludes idolatry of any sort (Ex 20:4, 6). Accordingly, the Corinthians' unwitting participation in the worship of demons* by eating food* sacrificed to idols* (1 Cor 10:20-21) is understood by Paul as "provoking the Lord to jealousy" (10:22).

This righteous jealousy displayed by God also provokes unbelieving Israel* to jealousy. In the Song of Moses the Lord said that his jealousy had been provoked by Israel's idolatry, and he would in turn make them jealous by reaching out to other peoples (Deut 32:21). Paul cites this passage in Romans 10:19 to demonstrate that it is the righteous jealousy of God which continues to use the conversion of Gentiles* to "provoke [them] to jealousy" (*parazēloō*, Rom 11:11). The apostle's own godly jealousy for Israel is that which makes him earnestly long to provoke his "kinsmen according to the flesh" (Rom 9:3) to accept the same salvation he offered the nations as the apostle to the Gentiles (Rom 11:13, 14).

Paul also spoke tenderly of his "godly jealousy" (2 Cor 11:2 NIV) for the Corinthian church, that their relationship to Christ might be pure. The repentant Corinthians (2 Cor 7:10), out of "godly sorrow" brought forth a zeal (or godly "jealousy"; Gk *zēlos*) for Paul and others (2 Cor 7:7, 11). Though formerly immature, jealous and riddled with strife (1 Cor 3:1-3), that church is commended by the apostle for becoming a model of generous, enthusiastic zeal (2 Cor 9:2). *See also* ISRAEL; JEW, PAUL THE; LOVE.

BIBLIOGRAPHY. S. G. F. Brandon, *Jesus and the Zealots* (Manchester: Manchester University, 1967); T. L. Donaldson, "Zealot and Convert: The Origin of Paul's Christ-Torah Antithesis," *CBQ* 51 (1989) 655-82; J. Dupont, "The Conversion of Paul, and Its Influence on His Understanding of Salvation by Faith," in *Apostolic History and the Gospel*, ed. W. W. Gasque and R. P. Martin (Grand Rapids: Eerdmans, 1970) 176-94; E. M. Good, "Jealousy," *IDB* 2.806-7; H. C. Hahn, "Zeal," *NIDNTT* 3.1166-68; M. Hengel, *The Zealots* (Edinburgh: T. & T. Clark, 1989); idem, *The Pre-Christian Paul* (Philadelphia: Trinity Press International, 1991); S. Kim, *The Origin of Paul's Gospel* (Grand Rapids: Eerdmans, 1982); W. Popkes, "ζῆλος κτλ," *EDNT* 2.100-101; D. Rhoads, "Zealots," *ABD* VI.1044-54; H. N. Snaith, "Jealousy, Zealous," in *A Theological Word Book of the Bible*, ed. A. Richardson (New York: Macmillan, 1950) 115-16; A. Stumpff, "ζηλόω κτλ," *TDNT* II.882-88.

A. B. Luter, Jr.

# JERUSALEM

The relationship of Paul to the Jerusalem church raises a number of difficult questions. One of these involves how we are to relate the accounts found in the Acts of the Apostles with those in the Pauline letters. When apparent contradictions surface, how are they to be handled? How do we balance the various visits of Paul to Jerusalem mentioned in Acts with those mentioned in Galatians*? What is the relationship between the council meeting mentioned in Acts 15 and the meeting mentioned in Galatians 2? What was at stake in the debate? How was it resolved? And what was the perceived role and status of James,* the Lord's brother?

1. The Centrality of Jerusalem
2. Jerusalem and the Early Years of Paul
3. Paul's Visits to Jerusalem
4. The Jerusalem Church Council
5. Subsequent Visits of Paul to Jerusalem
6. The Collection
7. The Demise of the Jerusalem Church

## 1. The Centrality of Jerusalem.

*1.1. In Judaism.* The earliest mention of Jerusalem in the Bible appears to be the reference to "Salem" in Genesis 14:18 (cf. Ps 76:2). Later it is referred to as a Jebusite fortress which was not captured by Joshua (Jos 10:3; 15:63; Judg 1:21). During the reign of David it was captured and made the capital of his kingdom (2 Sam 5:6-10). It also became the religious center of worship by the relocation of the ark of the covenant

in the city (2 Sam 6). With the building of the Solomonic Temple the religious worship of Israel was forever centered in Jerusalem.

The destruction of Jerusalem by Nebuchadnezzar in 587 B.C. had a monumental effect on both the history and religion of the people of Israel (Lam; Ps 137). After the destruction of the Babylonian Empire, the Persian Cyrus permitted the Jewish exiles to return to Jerusalem (Ez 1—3). Led by Sheshbazzar, Zerubbabel and Haggai, the Temple was rebuilt, and as time progressed Jerusalem was rebuilt as well. It was in the reign of Herod the Great (37-4 B.C.), however, that Jerusalem experienced its greatest time of building. Through him the Temple was rebuilt, so that it surpassed in glory even the Solomonic Temple. Jerusalem also experienced beautification. As a result Pliny the Elder could refer to Jerusalem as "by far the most famous city of the East" (*Nat. Hist.* 5.15.70), and Josephus spoke of the Temple as "a structure more noteworthy than any other under the sun" (Josephus *Ant.* 15.11.5 §412).

The place of Jerusalem in the life of Israel can be seen clearly in various Psalms (Ps 24; 46; 48; 76; 84; 87; 99; 118; 122; 125—29; 132—35; 146—47). Despite the loss of political independence after 63 B.C., Jerusalem remained for Jews both in Palestine and in the diaspora the center of worship, "the holy city" (Is 52:1). The ruling body of Israel, the high priest and Sanhedrin, were located there; the leading and most influential sect, the Pharisees, resided there. Above all, however, the Temple was in Jerusalem. Sacrifices, pilgrimages, the yearly Temple tax, all focused attention on Jerusalem. Although more Jews lived in Babylon and Egypt than in Judea, Jerusalem was still the holy city. And for the average Jew her most glorious days lay in the future. In the last days all roads would lead to Zion when the Gentile world would acknowledge Yahweh. This thinking was so pervasive that even the future Christian hope could be framed using the metaphor of the "new Jerusalem" (Rev 12:2-7; Heb 12:22).

*1.2. In Early Christianity.* The centrality of Jerusalem in the life of the early church is apparent from the beginning. It is the place of the resurrection* and the subsequent rise of the disciples' faith* (Mt 28; Mk 16 [but cf. Galilee in Mk 14:28; 16:7]; Lk 24; Jn 20). It is the first home of the apostles and leaders of the church (Acts 15:2; Gal 2:1-2; cf. Rom 15:19, 27), and it is the place from which the new faith would spread (Luke 24:45-53; Acts 1:1-8). Paul reveals a similar understanding in his description of the spread of the gospel through his ministry as being "from Jerusalem to Illyricum" (Rom 15:19). For Paul as well as for Luke

(Lk 24:47), the gospel began in Jerusalem.

Within the mother church of early Christianity the apostles served as leaders and guardians of the Jewish-Christian tradition.* How the apostles passed on that tradition is uncertain. The more radical critical theories allow little or no substantial involvement on the part of the apostles in the passing on of the Jesus tradition. This is in no small part due to the miraculous events embedded in much of the tradition. Eyewitnesses cannot be involved in passing on traditions that are replete with miracles if it is assumed a priori that miracles cannot happen. The "Swedish school" of interpretation (e.g., B. Gerhardsson) has sought to explain the handing down of the Jesus traditions in a manner similar to that found in second- and third-century rabbinic Judaism, where the oral traditions of Judaism were passed on by careful and rote memorization (see Jesus, Sayings of). This explanation is not without its weaknesses, but it at least conceives a central role for the apostles in the process.

According to the Lukan prologue (Lk 1:2), the Jesus traditions were passed on by the ministers and eyewitnesses of the word. Preeminent among these were the apostles.* This process began already in the ministry of Jesus, when they went out to preach the message and do the works of Jesus (Mk 6:30). This teaching continued unabated after the resurrection as the apostles proceeded to witness to what they had seen and heard (Acts 1:8, 22; 2:32; 3:15; 5:32; 10:39-41; 13:31; 1 Jn 1:1-3; 1 Pet 5:1). In this process the base of operations was Jerusalem where the mother church of the new group was located.

In Jerusalem the church consisted of a multi-lingual community (Acts 6:1-6; 2:5-12). It was mandatory that the Jesus traditions be translated into Greek for the Hellenists, or Greek-speaking believers. Whether some of these traditions were already translated into Greek during Jesus' ministry is uncertain, although possible (Mk 7:24-37; Lk 7:1-10), but this took place within weeks, or at most months, of the resurrection. Thus not only the sayings of Jesus but also the pronouncement stories, the miracle stories and the stories about Jesus which the disciples had shared during the ministry of Jesus were translated into Greek. This was done in a bilingual community by the apostles, who were eyewitnesses and had passed on these traditions on numerous occasions during Jesus' ministry. Such a reconstruction of events fits well the words of Luke in Luke 1:1-4.

The reconstruction given above depends heavily on what the Third Evangelist states in Luke-Acts. Luke, of course, had an apologetic purpose in mind in his presentation of this material, for he sought to demonstrate in his twofold work that Jerusalem had a central place in the divine plan. He begins his Gospel in Jerusalem (Lk 1:5-23) and concludes at the same place (Lk 24:33-53). He begins Acts in Jerusalem as well (Acts 1:3-8) and patterns the spread of the gospel along the lines of the paradigm Jerusalem-Judea-Samaria-ends of the earth (Acts 1:8). The centrality of Jerusalem for Luke is also seen in its being the place of the church's origin (Lk 24; Acts 1) and the place where the Spirit came (Acts 2). The church leaders in Jerusalem are portrayed as the founders and supervisors of the church in Samaria (Acts 8:14-25; cf. also its role with regard to the church in Antioch, Acts 11:22). It is the place where key theological issues are discussed (Acts 10—11), where debates are settled (Acts 15) and from where decrees are promulgated (Acts 15:19-35). Yet all this is certainly not a de novo creation on the part of Luke. This Lukan portrayal is not a pure literary fiction but based on reality. From the available evidence, the fact is that Jerusalem was indeed the center and the mother church of the Christian movement. From his prologue (Lk 1:1-4; Acts 1:1-2) the Evangelist clearly expects his readers to interpret Luke-Acts as a serious historical work.

### 2. Jerusalem and the Early Years of Paul.

Although Paul does not refer to his place of birth in any of his letters, there is no reason to doubt the Lukan portrayal of his birthplace as Tarsus of Cilicia (Acts 9:11; 21:39; 22:3). The silence of Paul about Palestine in Philippians 3:5, where he seeks to establish his Jewish pedigree, suggests that he was not born in Judea. If he had been born there, he would almost certainly have mentioned it, for this would have helped establish his being "a Hebrew born of Hebrews" (Phil 3:5; see Jew, Paul the).

When did Paul first come to Jerusalem? The answer depends on how one interprets Acts 22:3. Here Luke quotes Paul addressing the crowd in Jerusalem saying, "I am a Jew, born in Tarsus of Cilicia, but brought up in this city, at the feet of Gamaliel educated according to the strict manner of the law of our fathers." The threefold "born . . . brought up . . . educated" is a well-attested literary unit which provides biographical information of the birth to teenage years of a person's life. The first term refers to one's birth; the second to the earliest years of life; and the third to the education one received as a youth. Luke's understanding of this trilogy is revealed in Stephen's speech of Acts 7:20-22, where after Moses is "born," he is "brought up" as a nursing child (Exod 2:6-9) by Pharaoh's daughter and then is educated in the wisdom of Egypt.

According to Acts 22:3 Paul was born in the city of

Tarsus, but in the earliest months of his life his family moved to Jerusalem ("in this city"; but cf. Hengel, 34, 38-39) where Paul was then brought up. (Note that in Acts 23:16 Paul's sister lived in Jerusalem and that in Acts 26:4 "in my own nation" is better understood as referring to Judea than Tarsus.) Later he was educated under Gamaliel. (The expression "at the feet of Gamaliel" goes best with the verb "educated.") Galatians 1:22, which speaks of Paul not being personally known to the church in Judea, does not refute Luke's biographical description, because it is a general statement and does not mean that Paul's reputation was not known (as Gal 1:23 reveals) or that not a single person within the Judean church knew him. Paul clearly interpreted what he wrote in Galatians 1:22 in light of what he had said in Galatians 1:18, that although he was known to Peter* and James and the others he met during the fifteen days he spent in Jerusalem on his first visit, he was generally unknown. The thrust of Paul's statement in Galatians 1:22 is that Paul had little contact with the Jerusalem church.

During this period of being educated in Jerusalem, Paul studied at the feet of a leading Pharisaic teacher, Gamaliel (Acts 22:3). Although Paul makes no direct reference to this in his letters, this accords well with several of his statements. Certainly, if he studied under Gamaliel he could boast of being "a Hebrew of Hebrews, with respect to the Law a Pharisee . . . and according to the righteousness which comes from the Law blameless" (Phil 3:5-6). Paul's father, who was himself a Pharisee (Acts 23:6), no doubt intended such an education for his son. Such an education placed Paul in a good position later to acquire letters of authority in order to continue his persecution of the church in Damascus (Acts 9:2; 22:5). The main argument against accepting Luke's description of Paul at this point is the argument from Paul's silence on the matter. It is assumed that, if this were true, Paul would have mentioned his having studied under Gamaliel somewhere in his letters. It is precarious, however, to build an argument on silence, and it must be remembered that the Pauline letters are also silent about Paul's place of birth. Yet there are few scholars who doubt that, as Luke says, it was Tarsus.

### 3. Paul's Visits to Jerusalem.

In Galatians 1 and 2 Paul speaks of two visits that he made to Jerusalem after his conversion.* The first took place three years (Gal 1:18) after his conversion (Gal 1:15) and the second fourteen years later (Gal 2:1). (It is unclear whether the fourteen years is measured from his conversion or from his previous visit.) On the first visit Paul was befriended by Barnabas*

(Acts 9:27), who overcame the fear and suspicion others in the Jerusalem church held toward Paul (Acts 9:26). Whether Barnabas was acquainted with Paul previously is uncertain, but from this relationship developed the missionary team (Acts 11:25—15:41; Gal 2:1-10) and a lasting respect of Paul for Barnabas (1 Cor 9:6; Gal 2:13; Col 4:10). This visit involved a short, private meeting "to inquire of" (or "to get acquainted with," *historēsai*, Gal 1:18; for the former rendering see Dunn, 110-13, 126-28) Peter, and on that occasion he saw only Peter* and James,* the Lord's brother. (Luke states that Barnabas brought Paul "to the apostles" [Acts 9:27], but this is probably a general expression for the apostolic leadership. It need not be interpreted as conflicting with Paul's statement that he saw only Peter and James, the Lord's brother. Peter and James were in fact the two leading apostles.) During this visit Paul and Peter surely talked about more than just the weather. The verb *historeō* suggests that Paul went to see Peter in order to gain information. It is quite likely that at this time he received such traditions as he delivered in 1 Corinthians 7:10; 11:23-25; 15:3-7. It may even be that during this visit Paul learned of the resurrection appearances to Peter (1 Cor 15:5) and James (1 Cor 15:7) from these "pillars" (Gal 2:9) themselves. The second visit involved all the apostles and centered on the issues of circumcision* (Gal 2:1-3) and Paul's apostleship (Gal 2:7-10).

Five separate Pauline visits to Jerusalem are recorded in Acts: (1) after his conversion (Acts 9:26-28); (2) a "famine" visit (Acts 11:30; 12:25); (3) a visit involving the issue of circumcision (Acts 15:1, 5) and frequently called the "Jerusalem Council" because it involved the entire church (Acts 15:6, 12, 22); (4) a brief visit after his second missionary journey (Acts 18:22); and his final visit after the third missionary journey, which involved Paul's bringing the collection to the church, his arrest, imprisonment and appeal to Rome (Acts 21:17—25:12).

There are at least eight different ways in which scholars have sought to relate the two sets of accounts:

(1) Galatians 2 = Acts 15

(2) Galatians 2 = Acts 11

(3) Galatians 2 = Acts 11 = Acts 15 (Luke, or his traditions, has misinterpreted what happened in the visit of Galatians 2 and erroneously reported it twice.)

(4) Galatians 2 = Acts 18

(5) Galatians 2 = Acts 15:1-4

(6) Galatians 2 = Acts 11 + Acts 15 (Luke, or his traditions, has misinterpreted what happened in the visit of Galatians 2 and erroneously reported what happened on this occasion as occurring at two separate times.)

(7) Galatians 2 is not reported in Acts

(8) Galatians 2 = Acts 9

Of these views the three that are the most probable are: (1), (2) and (6).

*3.1. Galatians 2 = Acts 11:30; 12:25.* According to this view we have the following pattern: Galatians 1:18 = Acts 9:26-28; Galatians 2:1-10 = Acts 11:30; 12:25; and Acts 15:1-35 is omitted in Galatians, because Paul probably wrote Galatians before this visit took place. According to this view the famine visit of Paul and Barnabas in Acts 11:30; 12:25 is identical with Paul's second visit in Galatians 2. There are several arguments that have been raised in support of this. Most important is the fact that this view does not require Paul's omission in Galatians of a visit to Jerusalem between 1:18 and 2:1-10. Such an omission, which the third view requires (see 3.3 below), would have exposed him to the charge of dishonesty and suppression of facts, and this would have jeopardized his whole argument. This view also avoids the necessity of attributing to Luke an error in his arrangement of the Pauline visits as the next view maintains (see 3.2 below). This view also points out that the apostolic decree of Acts 15:22-29 is not mentioned in Galatians 2:1-10, and this suggests that Luke and Paul are not reporting the same event. In both Acts 11:27-28 and Galatians 2:2 the reason for going to Jerusalem is attributed to a divine revelation. There are furthermore some differences between Acts 15 and Galatians 2, which suggest that these are two different events. According to Galatians 2 Paul and Barnabas met privately with the leaders of the Jerusalem church. Acts 15, however, portrays the meeting as taking place before the whole church. Finally, it is argued that the lapse of Peter reported in Galatians 2:11-14 is far more likely to have occurred prior to the Jerusalem Council of Acts 15 than after it, in other words, Peter's lapse is more easily understood as taking place after the events of Acts 11:30; 12:25 than after Acts 15:1-11.

*3.2. Galatians 2 = Acts 11:30; 12:25 + Acts 15.* The arguments in favor of this view involve the twofold nature of the account in Galatians 2. During the Galatians 2 visit several major issues were decided. One involved the issue of circumcision. Gentiles* did not need to be circumcised in order to become Christians (Gal 2:1-3). This corresponds well with Acts 15:1, 5, 13-21. Also at that visit it was decided that Gentile Christians should be concerned with the needs of the poor in Jerusalem (Gal 2:10). This corresponds with the relief of the poor referred to in Acts 11:30; 12:25. This view also avoids Paul's having omitted a reference to a visit between Galatians 1:18 and 2:1-10 as the next view maintains (see 3.3 below). On the other hand,

this view attributes a serious historical error to Luke.

*3.3. Galatians 2 = Acts 15.* Some of the arguments in favor of this view include the following:

(1) It must be noted that on a simple reading Acts 15 and Galatians 2 look more alike than do Acts 11:30; 12:25 and Galatians 2. Both Acts 15 and Galatians 2 deal with the question of Gentile Christians' responsibility toward the Law and especially with regard to the issue of circumcision. On the other hand, circumcision is not mentioned at all in Acts 11:30; 12:25.

(2) The geographical delineation (cf. Gal 2:7-8 with Acts 15:12, 22-29), the people (Paul, Barnabas, Peter, James), the occasion (Gal 2:4-5; Acts 15:1), the subject matter (circumcision) and, most important, the result (Gentiles not required to be circumcised) are significant points of correspondence between Galatians 2 and Acts 15.

(3) If Galatians was written at approximately the same time as Romans and 1 and 2 Corinthians, it would be strange indeed if, according to the first view (Gal 2 = Acts 11:30; 12:25), Paul would not have mentioned or alluded to the incident of Acts 15. This would have provided considerable support for his argument against his opponents* in Galatians.

(4) In Galatians 4:13 the expression "at first" is best interpreted as referring to two separate visits Paul made to Galatia on two separate journeys. Thus Galatians is better understood as having been written after Acts 15, and, if Galatians 2 = Acts 11:30; 12:25, it is strange that Paul did not mention what happened at the Jerusalem council in his letter.

(5) In Galatians 2:10 when Paul states that he "was eager" to remember the poor, this can only with difficulty be interpreted as referring to something he was already doing, that is, as a pluperfect referring to the "famine" relief visit of Acts 11:30; 12:25. It is most naturally interpreted as referring to something Paul would do in the future, as prospective and not retrospective.

(6) In both accounts Paul and Barnabas give a report of the Gentile mission (Gal 2:7-9; Acts 15:3, 12).

(7) It seems unlikely that on two separate occasions Paul would have met with the Jerusalem church and its leaders to discuss the same issue, whether Gentiles needed to be circumcised, and reach the same conclusion.

Another argument in favor of understanding Galatians 2 as the Pauline version of Acts 15 involves Paul's description of this event. In Paul's description of the incident in Galatians 2, it is clear that he saw himself as the leader. He went up to Jerusalem, and Barnabas went with him (Gal 2:1). Paul (not Barnabas and Paul, and clearly not Barnabas and Saul) also took Titus

(Gal 2:1). Paul then set forth before them the gospel he preached (Gal 2:2). The leaders of the Jerusalem church saw that Paul had been entrusted with the gospel to the Gentiles (Gal 2:7) and that God was at work in Paul's ministry to the Gentiles (Gal 2:8). As a result they gave to Paul and Barnabas the right hand of fellowship* (Gal 2:9). As for concern for the poor, Paul was eager to do this (Gal 2:10). Clearly Paul in Galatians 2 portrays himself as the chief actor and leader. It is true that he is associated with Barnabas, but in Galatians it is not Barnabas and Saul or Barnabas and Paul. It is clearly Paul and Barnabas!

Yet when we read the account in Acts 11:30; 12:25, the situation is reversed. There Barnabas enlists Saul to work with him (Acts 11:25). The church sends Barnabas and Saul to Jerusalem with famine relief (Acts 11:30), and it is Barnabas and Saul who return from Jerusalem (Acts 12:25). The church then sends out Barnabas and Saul (Acts 13:2) on the first missionary journey. The name "Paul" first comes up in Acts 13:9, and only at Acts 13:9 is Paul placed in the forefront of the leadership. The difference in perspective of these two events is major. Luke sees Paul, actually Saul, as the lesser of the team members. Barnabas is the leader. He enlists Saul, not vice versa. In Acts 15, however, Paul is now portrayed by Luke as the leader of the group. It is Paul and Barnabas who debate those advocating circumcision and who are appointed to go to Jerusalem (Acts 15:2), and it is Paul and Barnabas who return to Antioch (Acts 15:22, 35). This portrayal of Pauline leadership fits Galatians 2 better than the portrayal found in Acts 11:30; 12:25.

An additional argument in favor of this view involves Paul's reputation as a missionary. In Acts 11:30; 12:25 his missionary accomplishments still lie in the future. He has yet to go on a missionary journey, and even when he does, the team will be described as "Barnabas and Saul." But in Galatians 2 Paul's fame and success as a missionary is already known and recognized. The Jerusalem pillars acknowledge that what Peter was for the mission to the Jews, Paul was for the mission to the Gentiles (Gal 2:7-8). Yet the Jerusalem pillars could not have recognized this if Galatians 2 = Acts 11:30; 12:25 is correct. There was no basis for recognizing Paul as "the" apostle to the Gentiles. If the church were to recognize anyone in this regard, it would have been Barnabas. The recognition Paul speaks of in Galatians 2:7-9 could not have taken place unless it was being revealed prophetically, but there is no suggestion that this is what took place. On the contrary, the Jerusalem pillars "saw" that God had entrusted this mission to Paul and "recognized" on the basis of what Paul had reported and had already accomplished (Gal 2:2). This could not have occurred during the famine visit of Acts 11:30; 12:25, but it could easily have taken place during the Acts 15 visit after Paul's first missionary journey.

One final argument that can be mentioned involves the chronology* of the early years of Paul. Paul states that three years after his conversion he went for the first time to Jerusalem (Gal 1:18). The next visit took place fourteen years later. Although this could refer to fourteen years after his conversion (or eleven years after the preceding visit), it is more likely that Paul is thinking consecutively: three plus fourteen, or seventeen years after his conversion. The reason for this is that in Galatians 1:18, 21; 2:1 we have a series of three "then(s)" (*epeita*). In all the other instances in which Paul uses this term, except one (1 Cor 15:6, 7, 23, 46; 1 Thess 4:17; the exception is 1 Cor 12:28), he ties what follows to what has immediately preceded. Here it is best to understand him as doing the same. The first "then" (Gal 1:18) must be interpreted as "then three years after Galatians 1:15 (his conversion)" he went to Jerusalem. The second (Gal 1:21) must be interpreted "then after the event of Galatians 1:18 (having gone to Jerusalem)" he went to Syria and Cilicia. The third (Gal 2:1) should therefore also be interpreted similarly, "then fourteen years after the events of Galatians 1:18 and 21 (which took place at the same time)" he went again to Jerusalem. Since it is more likely that the three plus fourteen years add up to seventeen full years than, by figuring the beginning and ending of the two periods being short fractional years, thirteen or fourteen years, to date the event of Galatians 2 at the time of Acts 11:30; 12:25 is less likely than to date it at the time of Acts 15. Chronological considerations make it difficult to date the famine visit seventeen years after Paul's conversion. The Jerusalem Council, however, is much easier to fit within this time frame (*see* Chronology).

In light of the above arguments it seems that unless we reject in some radical fashion the Lukan portrayal of the Pauline visits, it is best to see Galatians 1:18 = Acts 9:26-28; Paul not mentioning the famine visit of Acts 11:30; 12:25; and Galatians 2:1-10 = Acts 15:1-35. According to this view, Paul in telling the Galatians of his visits to Jerusalem had as his purpose the demonstration of his independence as an apostle (*see* Galatians). Thus he told them of his first visit, and that it occurred three years after his conversion. This demonstrated that it was not necessary for him to go to Jerusalem and meet with the apostles. God had ordained him directly to the apostleship of the Gentiles, and as a result he never bothered to go and meet the apostles until three years later. At that time he only met with Peter and James and only for fifteen days. This was certainly not long enough to be trained and commissioned by the Jerusalem apostles, of whom he met only two. The only other visit that had a bearing on his relationship with the Jerusalem apostles took place fourteen years later, when his independent apostleship was acknowledged (Gal 2:6-10) and his view on circumcision was likewise affirmed (Gal 2:1-5; cf. 1 Cor 15:11). Paul has omitted mentioning the famine visit which occurred between these two events, because it was of no consequence to his argument. Only the two visits he records had relevance for demonstrating his apostolic calling.

### 4. The Jerusalem Church Council.

*4.1. The Issues Involved.* In Galatians 2:2 Paul states that when he went up to the Jerusalem Council, he went "according to revelation." Although it is uncertain as to how this revelation came to Paul, why Paul mentions this is clear. (It is most unlikely that this refers to Agabus' prophecy in Acts 11:28, because nothing is mentioned in Gal 2 about a famine.) Paul wants the Galatians to know that he was not summoned or compelled by the Jerusalem church to attend the conference. The driving force which caused him to attend the conference was the leading of the Holy Spirit.* As an independent apostle, Paul was subject to the leading and directing of the Spirit, but he was not subject to the Jerusalem church. From a human perspective the cause of his coming to Jerusalem was the teaching of certain Jewish Christians that apart from circumcision Gentile believers could not be saved (Acts 15:1-2). Yet even here it should be noted that it was the church in Antioch, not Jerusalem, which initiated Paul's going to Jerusalem.

It is clear that Paul had a great concern as to the outcome of the Council. He sensed that his own work and the entire Gentile mission could be "in vain" (Gal 2:2) if the outcome went the wrong way. Exactly what Paul meant by this is unclear. Certainly he did not believe that the truthfulness of his message was at stake or that it could be affected by anything the Council decided, for his gospel was not of human origin nor even from a human source (Gal 1:1, 11) but directly from Christ himself (Gal 1:12). If an angel from heaven could not change that gospel, how much less could the Jerusalem Council. Yet if the Council demanded that circumcision be required of Gentiles, this would have hindered greatly the work of evangelism among the Gentiles. This would be true not only for evangelism by the Jerusalem church but for his own efforts as well. He knew that the demand for circumcision was already causing havoc among his

converts (Acts 15:1-3; cf. Gal 1:7; Phil 3:2). If this demand had the support of the Jerusalem church, the problem would be multiplied many times.

Another possible danger that Paul feared was the splitting of the church. Paul would, of course, continue to preach the gospel (1 Cor 9:16), but the church would be irreconcilably divided. In fact, since out of Jerusalem there would be coming forth a different gospel, which in fact was no gospel at all (Gal 1:6-7), they might not even be able to be considered a true church. The mother church would itself have become apostate! Finally, Paul no doubt feared that the divine purpose of uniting Jew and Greek and the destruction of the dividing wall through the death of Christ might be thwarted by actions of the Council (Eph 2:11-21). Paul's great concern for the collection (see 6 below) reveals his own great desire to further the oneness of Jew and Greek now created in Christ.

For Paul two key issues were at stake. One involved the question of whether Gentile believers had to be circumcised in order to be justified.* Some recent interpreters have sought to interpret this issue in light of the sociological implications involved (see, e.g., Dunn, 215-41, 242-64; *see* Social-Scientific Approaches). Thus they portray the issue as one of acceptance into the Jewish community of believers or of becoming full members in the church. For both Paul and Luke, however, the issue was seen primarily from a theological perspective with soteriological implications. (It may well be that Luther, because of his theological orientation, may have understood Paul better than those who approach the apostle with a more sociological orientation.) The issue for Paul involved how one was justified before God* (Gal 2:16; 3:6; Rom 4:9-12), and, in his understanding of the gospel, for a Gentile believer to become circumcised was to fall from saving grace* (Gal 5:2-4). Luke states even more clearly that the issue involved certain Jewish believers, allegedly representing the Jerusalem church, who claimed that unless the Gentile believers submitted to circumcision, they could not be saved (Acts 15:1). For modern commentators to claim that Luke misunderstood the real issue and that we today can better understand what was at stake is highly questionable.

In Galatians 2:1 Paul states that he brought with him to Jerusalem an uncircumcised believer named Titus. Whether this was simply fortuitous or intentional on Paul's part is uncertain. (Most likely it was intentional, for bringing an uncircumcised Gentile believer to the Jerusalem Council would have been provocative, to say the least.) Regardless, Titus served as a highly visual test case of the issue. "Did Titus have to be circumcised in order to be saved?" Although some did demand his circumcision (this appears to be the meaning of Gal 2:3), Paul states that the decision of the Council was that he did not. The Council agreed with Paul that salvation is through faith alone! (Although the grammar of Gal 2:3 permits the following interpretation: "Titus was not compelled to be circumcised, but he voluntarily submitted himself to this," such an interpretation is ruled out by what Paul says in Gal 5:2-4. Furthermore, Paul's whole argument against his opponents in Galatia would have been undermined if it could have been pointed out that Paul had agreed to circumcise Titus.)

For Paul the other issue which was at stake involved his apostleship (*see* Apostle). Paul certainly did not seek the approval or confirmation of the Jerusalem apostles, for his apostleship had been approved by God (Gal 1:1; Rom 1:5; 1 Cor 9:2). How could they approve his "independence?" Even seeking such approval would defeat his claim to have been called independently as an apostle. What Paul hoped for was that the Jerusalem apostles would recognize that God had indeed called him to be the apostle to the Gentiles.

### 4.2. The Results of the Council.

#### 4.2.1. Salvation apart from Circumcision.
Regardless of how one interprets the Apostolic Decree (see 4.2.3 below), the results of the Jerusalem Council were a clear victory for Paul. The church with one voice recognized that salvation was by grace alone. The Gentiles needed only believe. Those who were troubling them and demanding their circumcision were refuted (Acts 15:14-21; Gal 2:3-5). Yet on what basis was this recognized?

It is difficult for Christians today to appreciate the weight of the argument of those advocating the circumcision of the Gentiles. Two millennia of Christians denying the necessity of this symbol and practice, and the teaching of the NT, which rejects this position, makes the argument of its proponents look very weak. But such was not the case at the time of the Jerusalem Council, for there was no NT canon to which one could refer. The circumcision party probably argued something like this: (1) All of the heroes and leaders of God's people, from the time of Abraham* to the present, had been circumcised. The apostles were all circumcised. Jesus was circumcised! If it was "good enough" for the Son* of God, why should a Gentile complain about following in his steps? (2) Truth is not determined by vote, polls or the desires of Gentiles and their supporters. If this were so, should the church no longer require baptism or repentance if they become unpopular? (3) Jesus never taught that circumcision would no longer be neces-

sary. (4) The covenant which God made with Abraham and by which we are saved (Gal 3:6-9, 29; Rom 4:13-17) has, as an everlasting requirement, circumcision (Gen 17:9-14). According to the Scriptures, the rejection of circumcision cuts one off from this covenant. Thus for Gentiles to enter the saving community they must submit to circumcision.

The weight of the above arguments should not be minimized. Nevertheless the church "recognized" (they did not "decide") that circumcision was no longer required. Luke indicates how this was first recognized in his account of the conversion of Cornelius. In Acts 10:44-48 Peter baptized the uncircumcised Cornelius because Cornelius had received the Spirit (Acts 10:47). Later, when questioned in Jerusalem as to why he shared in table fellowship with this uncircumcised Gentile, Peter explained that the Spirit had come upon Cornelius just as he had come upon them at Pentecost. In light of this fact the church concluded that God was now granting that even Gentiles who repented would receive life (Acts 11:18). At the Jerusalem Council both Peter (Acts 15:7-9) and James (Acts 15:14) recalled this incident, but Luke's readers understood that these brief references involved the entire account of the coming of the Spirit upon Cornelius as recorded in Acts 10—11. Paul also at the Council recalled how God bore witness to the salvation* of the Gentile believers by "signs and wonders" (Acts 15:12). For Luke signs and wonders are understood as a means by which God witnessed to Jesus being the Christ (Acts 2:22), the truthfulness of the gospel (Acts 4:30; 5:12; 14:3) and Stephen being God's spokesperson (Acts 6:8). One of those "signs and wonders" was the coming of the Spirit upon the Gentiles. It should be noted that Paul argues similarly in Galatians 3:2. Since the Galatians received the Spirit by faith while they were uncircumcised, God had accepted them apart from circumcision.

The fact that the Spirit has come upon the believing Gentiles reveals to the church that God has accepted them. Since the Spirit is the seal and first fruits* of divine salvation (2 Cor 1:22; 5:5; Eph 1:13-14; 4:30), the church can only conclude that those who have received the Spirit have been accepted by God into the eschatological community as they are, apart from circumcision. The possession of the Spirit is the infallible witness to salvation (cf. Acts 19:2). Apart from the Spirit one stands outside of Christ (Rom 8:9), but possession of the Spirit indicates that believers have life (Rom 8:10-11) and are children of God (Gal 4:6). Thus the decision of the Jerusalem Council was simple and clear. It was not dependent on pragmatic or missiological considerations but on what God had done (Acts

15:12, 14). God had revealed that he had accepted the Gentiles apart from circumcision on the basis of faith alone. There was thus nothing to vote on or decide. They could only recognize what God had done and was doing. In the new covenant God accepts all who repent and believe in Jesus, whether Jew or Greek (Acts 15:14-21). Thus Paul's message was vindicated, and the circumcision party was refuted. The church had one gospel* (cf. 1 Cor 15:11). Both Jew and Greek are justified by faith alone (Acts 15:11). As to the question of whether Jews needed to be circumcised, such a question was a matter for Jewish Christians and was irrelevant to the pressing issue of the hour.

*4.2.2. Recognition of Paul's Apostleship.* For Paul the Jerusalem Council was also a vindication of his apostolic office. Although Luke does not refer to this in Acts, Paul points out that this took place at a private meeting between him and the leaders of the church (Gal 2:9). This meeting should not be interpreted as contradicting the larger church meeting described in Acts 15:6, 12, 22 but as supplementing it. (What church denominational gathering does not include private meetings involving officials and leaders of the denomination?) At that meeting Paul's message was not only acknowledged (Gal 2:2-6), but his divine calling and apostolic office were likewise recognized. (The giving of the right hand referred to in Gal 2:9 represents the sealing of the contractual agreement described in this and the next verse.)

This recognition went further than simply acknowledging that Paul was a legitimate apostle. That he was qualified to be an apostle was evident. He had seen the risen Lord* (1 Cor 9:1). This was why he included himself in the list of apostolic resurrection appearances in 1 Corinthians 15:5-8. Yet it was a unique kind of apostleship which he had been given. The "grace given to him" (Gal 2:9) involved more than simply apostleship. This expression is also used by Paul in 1 Corinthians 3:10 and Romans 15:15-16 to describe his unique apostleship, and the term "grace"* is used in the same way in Romans 1:5; 12:3; and 1 Corinthians 15:10. At the Council Paul was recognized as "the" apostle to the Gentiles, and his role among the Gentiles was compared and equated to Peter's role among the Jews.

Paul's own understanding of this role can be seen in his letters. He wrote to the church in Rome because the apostleship which he possessed extended to all the Gentiles, and this included the Romans (Rom 1:5-6). Even though he had not founded the church in Rome and even though he did not seek to build upon the foundation of another (Rom 15:20), he had often sought to come to Rome,* because due to his being

"the" apostle to the Gentiles, the Roman church lay within his apostolic jurisdiction (Rom 1:13-15). This responsibility caused him to exhort, admonish and rebuke even the Roman church (Rom 15:15-16). This recognition of Paul's apostleship over the Gentiles by the leaders of the Jerusalem church is best understood as due to their reflection on his mission work recorded in Acts 13:1—14:28 rather than that of Acts 9:20—12:25.

The demarcation of the sphere of Paul's apostleship is described as the "Gentiles" (Gal 2:7-9). It is unclear whether this should be understood geographically (the Gentile world versus Palestine) or ethnically (the Gentiles versus Jews). That Luke understood Paul's call geographically is clear, for Paul's strategy in Acts is to use the synagogues in the cities of the Gentile world as his mission base. It is also apparent that in his churches there were both Gentile (Rom 1:5, 14; 11:13-16, 25-31; Gal 5:2; Eph 2:11-22) and Jewish believers (Rom 2:17—3:20; cf. Rom 16:3 with Acts 18:2). Paul's submission to the discipline of the synagogue (2 Cor 11:24) is inexplicable if his mission avoided contact with Jews, and such passages as 1 Corinthians 9:20 and 1 Thessalonians 2:16 assume Paul's ministry among Jews. It is also unlikely that the Jerusalem church did not minister to Gentiles in Jerusalem and Palestine. Thus, whereas Paul's apostleship should not be interpreted exclusively as geographic or ethnic, the demarcation of missionary spheres both for the Jerusalem church and Paul are probably best understood as being primarily geographic in nature. The purpose of designating these areas was more to focus the various responsibilities of Paul and the Jerusalem church than to impose limitations.

*4.2.3. The Apostolic Decree.* Luke records in his version of the Apostolic Council that a decree was sent out to the Gentile churches which summarized the conclusions of the Council (Acts 15:19-21, 23-29). The decree recognized that circumcision was not required of the Gentiles (Act 15:19, 24-28). On this issue the freedom of the gospel Paul preached to the Gentiles was vindicated (Gal 2:2). Yet there appear to be certain restrictions placed upon the Gentiles by the decree (Acts 15:20, 29; cf. Acts 21:25). The area in which this decree was to be promulgated was Antioch, Syria and Cilicia (Acts 15:23), that is, not so much the "Pauline" churches but the churches in the area in which the circumcision party caused the most trouble (Acts 15:1, 30).

These restrictions are best understood as based on Noachian laws: minimal laws which Jews believed were enjoined by the Scriptures on all people, reaching back to the period prior to Abraham (Gen 9:1-7).

There were seven of them: the prohibition of idolatry,* blasphemy, bloodshed, sexual immorality, theft, eating from a living animal (i.e., eating the blood of an animal) and, on the positive side, the need to establish a legal system of justice. In Acts the non-controversial Noachian laws (blasphemy, murder, robbery, establishment of justice) are omitted. The first three mentioned in Acts refer to food restrictions: things devoted to idols, or food dedicated to idols (cf. Acts 15:20, 29; 21:25 with 1 Cor 8:1-13; 10:14-33), and meat which was non-kosher, that is, meat obtained from animals killed by strangling and from which the blood was not properly drained (Lev 7:26-27; 17:10-14). The fourth requirement was ethical in nature and dealt with sexual immorality. This may refer to either sexual immorality in general or more probably to marriage relationships forbidden in Scripture, for example, marriage between close relatives (Lev 18:6-18). (In Codex Bezae the third requirement, "things strangled," is omitted, and there has been an attempt by the scribe to interpret the regulations as being purely ethical: idolatry-murder-fornication. These restrictions must be understood as ritualistic, however, for if not, then Acts 15:28 would seem to imply that refraining from idolatry, murder and fornication would be the only moral laws that Gentile Christians would have to keep! This variant reading cannot be accepted, for the great weight of textual evidence includes the third requirement.)

Many scholars see these requirements as compromising the Pauline teaching of justification* by faith* alone and have denied that Paul could ever have accepted such a decree. Furthermore it is argued that the requirements of the decree contradict Galatians 2:6, where Paul states that the Jerusalem leaders "added nothing to his message." As a result some scholars deny the historicity of the Jerusalem decree altogether; some argue that the decree took place at a later time (at least after the writing of Galatians); and a great many scholars argue that Paul would never have accepted such a decree for it conflicts with his teachings and practice (1 Cor 8:1-13; 10:25-33). Paul saw all such things as lawful (1 Cor 6:12; 10:23). To have accepted the decree would have compromised his gospel. It would have placed the Gentiles under the Law.*

It must be admitted that if the Jerusalem decree taught that salvation for the Gentiles demanded that they keep certain food restrictions, then Paul in principle lost at the Jerusalem Council. Salvation is either free and through faith alone or it is not free. It cannot be "mostly" free. Yet it is questionable whether the Jerusalem decree should be interpreted in this manner. Luke explains the cause for the establishment of the decree as being due to the fact that "Moses has been preached for generations in every city and has been read each Sabbath in the synagogues" (Acts 15:21). The issue at stake, according to Luke, is not justification but rather social intercourse between Jews and Gentiles. The decree does not add a requirement for Gentiles who are seeking salvation. Rather they are directions given by the Spirit (Acts 15:28) which seek to promote sensitivity on the part of Gentile Christians with respect to issues that were especially offensive to Jews.

If we observe Paul's own practice concerning the scruples of "weaker" brethren, it is quite clear that he always accommodated his personal liberty (see Freedom) and practice in order not to offend the sensitive among his congregations. On several occasions a similar problem arose in his churches. At times it involved eating food* dedicated to idols (1 Cor 8:1-13; 10:23-33); at times it involved those who objected to eating meat (Rom 14:1-15). In such instances, whereas Paul agreed with those advocating freedom, he always surrendered his own freedom in order not to offend the "weak" (see Strong and Weak), and he urged those who had a similar understanding of the freedom of the gospel to do the same. For Paul circumcision was an irrelevant issue in itself, for it only involved the presence or absence of a piece of skin unless one argued that the removal of this piece of skin was a requirement for salvation. Thus when a theological issue was at stake, he refused to have Titus circumcised (Gal 2:1-3); but in the case of Timothy, when it did not involve a theological issue but permitted greater freedom in ministering among the Jews, he was willing to have him circumcised (Acts 16:1-3).

To understand Paul's view of freedom, we must recognize that he was so free that, unless a theological issue was at stake, he could willingly surrender his freedom in order to facilitate the spread of the gospel. This is seen most clearly in 1 Corinthians 9:19-23. Although free, Paul voluntarily became a slave to the weaknesses of others. Among the Jews he lived as under the Law that he might win his fellow Jews (1 Cor 9:20). The Paul of 1 Corinthians 8—10 would have had no problem urging Gentile believers that they should keep the decree when they were in the presence of Jews, for truly free persons are only free when they can surrender their freedom out of love for the weak. For Paul this could even involve taking a Jewish vow, if it helped in his ministry among the Jews (Acts 18:18; 21:26).

**5. Subsequent Visits of Paul to Jerusalem.**
Paul's view of Jerusalem as the mother church of early

Christianity is evidenced by his frequent visits to that city. Three such visits have already been discussed: Galatians 1:18/Acts 9:26-28; Acts 11:30/12:25, which Paul does not mention; and Galatians 2:1-10/Acts 15:1-30. Luke records two subsequent occasions on which Paul again visited Jerusalem.

The first is mentioned only briefly and indirectly. Paul at the end of the second missionary journey left Ephesus and arrived at Caesarea. From there he "went up and greeted the church" (Acts 18:22). There is debate as to which church Paul greeted—the church in Caesarea or Jerusalem. The grammar permits either interpretation. Yet the expression "went up" is frequently used by Luke for going to Jerusalem (Lk 2:4, 42; 18:31; 19:28; Acts 11:2; 15:2; 21:12, 15; 24:11; 15:1, 9), so that for Luke this must refer to Jerusalem. This would also fit well the Lukan portrayal of Paul returning to Jerusalem after each missionary journey. This interpretation receives additional support from an indirect comment found in Acts 18:18. There Luke records that Paul took a vow and cut his hair. If, as seems likely, this was a Nazirite vow (Num 6:1-21; Acts 23:21-26), its fulfillment would have required Paul's offering a sacrifice in the temple in Jerusalem. Other than the implied completion of this vow, Luke gives no additional information as to the nature of this visit.

Paul's final visit to Jerusalem took place after the third missionary journey (Acts 19:21; 20:22; 21:25-26). The expressed purpose of this visit was to bring the collection from the Gentile churches to the church in Jerusalem (see 6 below). Luke alludes indirectly to this in Paul's speech before Felix (Acts 24:17). In the process of fulfilling a vow similar to that of his previous visit (cf. Acts 18:18 and 21:23-26) Paul is involved in a riot, rescued and arrested by the Roman troop which guarded the Temple and was stationed in the Fortress of Antonia (Acts 21:31—22:29). Paul's subsequent defense before the Sanhedrin also results in a riotous division of the Pharisaic and Sadducaic members of that body (Acts 22:30—23:10).

Due to a plot on Paul's life, the tribune sent him to Caesarea under heavy guard. Such concern was afforded him due to his being a Roman citizen* (Acts 22:24-29). For over two years Paul remained under arrest during the governorship of Felix and Festus (Acts 24:27; 24:1—26:32). Finally, having appealed to Caesar, he was sent to Rome to await trial before the emperor* himself (Acts 27:1—28:30; Phil 1:12-14).

## 6. The Collection.

In his three longest letters Paul mentions a collection being made by the Gentile churches for the church in Jerusalem (1 Cor 16:1-4; 2 Cor 8:1—9:15; Rom 15:25-32; see Collection for the Saints). This is probably Paul's response to the request of the Jerusalem church for the Gentiles churches to "remember the poor" (Gal 2:10; see Rich and Poor). (Although it is doubtful that "the poor" was a technical term for the Jerusalem church, it is clear that the collection was to be given to it.) Its importance for Paul is evidenced not only by the amount of space he devotes to this in his letters but also by several other factors. For one, the collection took a great deal of time (at least several years— 2 Cor 9:2) and effort on his part to assemble. During the period of the collection, he had an experience in which he despaired of life itself (2 Cor 1:8), but the collection had to continue. The effort required an offering which was to be collected weekly (1 Cor 16:2), and representatives were to be chosen who would supervise the taking of the collection all the way to Jerusalem (1 Cor 16:3). The offering itself took over a year to complete (2 Cor 8:10) and involved churches in at least three major provinces, Macedonia and Achaia (Rom 15:26; 2 Cor 9:2), and Galatia (1 Cor 16:1; cf. Acts 20:4), and perhaps even Asia (cf. Acts 20:4). Paul furthermore needed to send Titus and another helper to assist in the collection (2 Cor 8:16-24), and it required that Paul postpone his planned mission to Spain (Rom 15:28). Luke mentions seven people who accompanied the offering, and Acts 20:16 suggests that a sufficiently high percentage of the passengers on the ship were accompanying Paul and the collection that the apostle could influence the itinerary. Even plots (Acts 20:3), danger (Acts 20:23) and warnings (Acts 21:4, 10-14) could not dissuade him from carrying out this mission. As for the reception of the collection by the Jerusalem church, this was also a major concern for Paul and weighed heavily on his mind (Rom 15:31).

Paul did not understand the collection as a requirement levied upon the Gentile churches by the Jerusalem Council. Galatians 2:10 was understood as a request rather than a "tax." This is clear from the terminology he uses to describe the collection. It is a "contribution" (1 Cor 16:1); a "generous gift" (2 Cor 9:5); "material blessings" (Rom 15:27); "fruit" (Rom 15:28); "aid" (Rom 15:31; 2 Cor 8:4; 9:1); and a "gracious work" on the part of the Gentile churches (2 Cor 8:6).

The collection served a number of purposes for Paul. It was at the very least an act of love* which met a real need in the Jerusalem church. Whatever the value of the communal sharing of the earliest days (Acts 4:32—5:11), the benefit described in Acts 4:34 was only temporary. The concern of the Hellenists that their widows share in the distribution of goods (Acts 6:1) suggests that only limited resources were available to the church. The famine of Acts 11:28-30 might also have had lasting consequences for the economic health of the church community. The collection was therefore a loving act of kindness in tune with the teachings of Jesus (Mt 5:42; 6:2; 25:31-46; Mk 10:21; Lk 6:34-38; 12:33; etc.) and that of the early church (Rom 12:8, 13; Jas 2:14-17). In this way the collection would also serve as a proof of the Gentiles' faith by demonstrating their love for other Christians (1 Thess 4:9; Rom 12:10; Jn 13:35).

Another reason Paul felt so strongly concerning the collection was that it provided an opportunity to reinforce the bonds of unity between Jews and Gentiles within the church. This was especially important in light of the division caused by his opponents (Gal 2:11-13; 1 Cor 3; Acts 15:1). This unity was, for Paul, not based simply on a voluntary decision or spiritual inclination on the part of Jewish and Gentile Christians. It was based rather on the corporate nature of their being "in Christ."* The collection would help demonstrate that the body of Christ was one. Neither Jew nor Greek could say of the other "I have no need of you" (1 Cor 12:14-26).

If the Gentiles had come to share in the benefits of the gospel (Rom 15:27) and had been ingrafted into the people of God (Rom 11:17-24; Eph 2:11-22), this, Paul argued, was due to Jewish believers (such as Paul, Barnabas and Peter) and the spiritual heritage of the mother church in Jerusalem. What they had "received" (1 Cor 11:23-26; 15:3-8) came from the Lord via the Jerusalem church. Now they could return the favor and minister to the mother church by means of their material blessings through this collection. (Paul may be arguing here similarly to how he argues in 1 Cor 9. Just as a minister has the right to live off the gospel he preaches, so the mother church [personified as a "minister"] has a right on this occasion to share in the material blessings of the Gentile churches to which it has given birth.) This unity would be further strengthened by the fact that the offering would be brought by numerous representatives from the Gentile churches (1 Cor 16:3; Acts 20:4-5) who both safeguarded the collection and would symbolize the oneness of the church when they delivered this offering to the church in Jerusalem.

A third reason why the collection was important for Paul involved the eschatological significance of this event. Paul understood the collection as symbolizing in some way the eschatological ingathering of the Gentiles into the people of God. It is quite unlikely that he thought that the collection would be the means by which the Jews would become jealous and turn in faith to God, that is, he did not think that it would be the event that would bring about the fulfillment of Romans 11:13-27 (see Israel). Yet this collection would symbolize the "first fruits"* of the offering of the Gentiles to God (Rom 15:16). The collection was itself an offering to God (2 Cor 9:12), but in a deeper sense it symbolized that now the Gentile world was coming in faith to God. Salvation had come to the uttermost parts of the earth (Acts 13:47). The collection revealed in an undeniable way that the Gentiles who had not pursued righteousness* had now attained it (Rom 9:30).

### 7. The Demise of the Jerusalem Church.

Although a great deal of information is available concerning the fall of Jerusalem in A.D. 70 and the events leading up to its destruction, not much is known with certainty regarding the Jerusalem church during the decade leading up to this nor in the subsequent decades.

*7.1. The Death of James.* From Acts 12:17; 15:13-21; 21:18; Galatians 2:9 (note the order); and James 1:1, it is apparent that James, the brother of Jesus, was the leader of the Jerusalem church in the decade of the fifties. There is no reason to doubt that he remained its leader until his death in A.D. 62. The two major traditions concerning James' death come from Josephus and Hegesippus. Josephus (*Ant.* 20.9.1 §§199-203) states that after the death of Festus and before the arrival of Albinus, the new procurator, the high priest Ananus convened the Sanhedrin to try "James, the brother of Jesus who was called the Christ." James was condemned and stoned. Ananus was subsequently deposed from the high priesthood for this illegal act (cf. Jn 18:31). There is no major reason for rejecting Josephus's portrayal of this event, for unlike the passage on Jesus in *Antiquities* 18.3.3 §§63-64, this does not appear to be a Christian interpolation. Josephus would also have been in a position to know, in that he was a contemporary of this event.

A somewhat different description of the death of James is given in Eusebius's *Ecclesiastical History* 2.23.3-18 by Hegesippus, a second-century church father. According to Hegesippus, James, called the "Just," was killed by being thrown down from the Temple, stoned and clubbed. No trial before the Sanhedrin is mentioned. In both accounts, however, James is portrayed as being martyred by being stoned in Jerusalem by hostile Jews (see James).

*7.2. The Flight to Pella and the Fall of Jerusalem.* According to the Pella tradition, the Jerusalem church was able to flee the city and escape its terrible fate.

Eusebius (*Hist. Eccl.* 3.5.3-4) states that shortly before the destruction of Jerusalem the church was warned by an oracle to flee to the city of Pella in Perea. It is impossible to prove or disprove this tradition. (Epiphanius refers to this same tradition on three occasions [*Haer.* 29.7,7; 30.2,7; *Weights* 15], but it is quite possible that he is indebted to Eusebius for this information.) The Gospels, however, contain numerous warnings which, if heeded, would have resulted in Christians fleeing Jerusalem before the arrival of Vespasian and the Roman legions (Mk 13:13-23; Lk 21:20-24; Mt 24:15-25).

*7.3. The Loss of Influence of the Jerusalem Church.* The return of Christians to Jerusalem after the destruction of the city in A.D. 70 is witnessed to by ossuaries and tombs, and by Eusebius (*Hist. Eccl.* 4.5), who lists a succession of Jewish bishops from the time of the death of James to the second revolt in A.D. 132-35. Yet the city would never again be the mother church of Christianity. The prohibition of Hadrian barring Jews from living in Jerusalem after the second revolt no doubt hindered Jewish Christians from returning, and the bishops Eusebius (*Hist. Eccl.* 5.12) lists after the second revolt all carry non-Jewish names. The bishopric of Jerusalem remained important, but its power was limited and more nostalgic than real. The center of influence in the church had switched to such major cities as: Caesarea, Ephesus, Antioch, Alexandria, Rome and later Constantinople.

*See also* CHRONOLOGY OF PAUL; CIRCUMCISION; COLLECTION FOR THE SAINTS; GALATIANS, LETTER TO THE; ITINERARIES, TRAVEL PLANS, JOURNEYS, APOSTOLIC PAROUSIA; JAMES AND PAUL; RESTORATION OF ISRAEL; TEMPLE; WORKS OF THE LAW.

BIBLIOGRAPHY. F. F. Bruce, *Paul: Apostle of the Heart Set Free* (Grand Rapids: Eerdmans, 1977); D. R. Catchpole, "Paul, James, and the Apostolic Decree," *NTS* 23 (1977) 428-44; J. D. G. Dunn, *Jesus, Paul and the Law* (Louisville: Westminster, 1990); F. J. Foakes-Jackson and K. Lake, *The Beginnings of Christianity: The Acts of the Apostles* (5 vols.; New York: Macmillan, 1920-33; repr. Grand Rapids: Baker, 1979); G. Fohrer and E. Lohse, "Σιών κτλ," *TDNT* VII.292-338; W. W. Gasque, *A History of the Criticism of the Acts of the Apostles* (Grand Rapids: Eerdmans, 1975); D. Georgi, *Remembering the Poor* (Nashville: Abingdon, 1992); B. Gerhardsson, *Memory and Manuscript: Oral Tradition and Written Transmission in Rabbinic Judaism and Early Christianity* (Uppsala and Lund: Gleerup, 1961); L. Goppelt, *Apostolic and Post-Apostolic Times* (New York: Harper, 1970); M. Hengel, *The Pre-Christian Paul* (Philadelphia: Fortress, 1991); R. Jewett, *A Chronology of Paul's Life* (Philadelpia: Fortress, 1979); W. L. Knox, *St Paul and the Church of Jerusalem* (Cambridge: University Press, 1925); G. Luedemann, *Opposition to Paul in Jewish Christianity* (Minneapolis: Fortress, 1989); J. Munck, *Paul and the Salvation of Mankind* (Richmond: John Knox, 1959); K. F. Nickle, *The Collection* (SBT 48; Naperville: Allenson, 1966); J. D. Purvis, *Jerusalem, The Holy City: A Bibliography* (Metuchen: Scarecrow, 1989 and 1991); W. Schmithals, *Paul and James* (SBT 46; Naperville: Allenson, 1965); J. H. Schütz, *Paul and the Anatomy of Apostolic Authority* (Cambridge: University Press, 1975); M. Simon, "The Apostolic Decree and its Setting in the Ancient Church," *BJRL* 52 (1969) 437-60; R. H. Stein, "The Relationship of Galatians 2:1-10 and Acts 15:1-35: Two Neglected Arguments," *JETS* 17 (1974) 239-42; W. C. van Unnik, *Tarsus or Jerusalem: The City of Paul's Youth* (London: Epworth, 1962); F. Watson, *Paul, Judaism, and the Gentiles* (Cambridge: University Press, 1986); S. G. Wilson, *The Gentiles and the Gentile Mission in Luke-Acts* (Cambridge: University Press, 1973); N. T. Wright, "Jerusalem in the New Testament," in *Jerusalem: Past and Present in the Purposes of God*, ed. P. W. L. Walker (Cambridge: Tyndale House, 1992) 53-77.                              R. H. Stein

**JERUSALEM APOSTLES.** *See* JERUSALEM; JUDAIZERS; OPPONENTS OF PAUL.

**JERUSALEM COUNCIL.** *See* CHRONOLOGY OF PAUL; GALATIANS, LETTER TO THE; ITINERARIES, TRAVEL PLANS, JOURNEYS, APOSTOLIC PAROUSIA; JERUSALEM.

## JESUS, SAYINGS OF

When one moves from the Gospels to the Pauline letters one is immediately struck by the virtual absence of quotations of sayings of Jesus. While Paul makes Jesus Christ* and his work of salvation* the center of his preaching, he hardly ever quotes actual sayings of this Jesus or refers to his deeds, except to his death* and resurrection.* In his paraenesis, or teaching,* he gives instructions similar to those of Jesus, and yet he seldom cites the latter. There may be some allusions to or echoes of Jesus' sayings in the Pauline letters, but they are very allusive, a phenomenon which raises the question of a proper criterion for correctly discerning them. In any case, these allusions and echoes do not seem to be numerous. This state of affairs is puzzling when contrasted with the often observed continuity in theology and attitude between Jesus and Paul. This paucity and allusive character of Paul's references to sayings of Jesus has led some critics to conclude that Paul did not know much of Jesus tradition or that he was not at all interested in the tradition or in the historical Jesus. So our topic constitutes a central element in the "Jesus-Paul debate" (*see* Jesus and Paul)

**1. Certain or Probable References.**

There are six explicit references to "words of the Lord" in Paul's letters: 1 Corinthians 7:10-11; 9:14; 11:23-25; 14:37; 2 Corinthians 12:9; 1 Thessalonians 4:15-17. Among them 2 Corinthians 12:9 obviously refers to the word of the risen Lord, and the "command of the Lord" in 1 Corinthians 14:37 is probably a "prophetic" teaching of Paul who has "the mind of Christ" (1 Cor 2:16). The "minimalists" who allow a minimum number of references, allusions or echoes of the sayings of Jesus in Paul deny a reference to the historical Jesus in 1 Thessalonians 4:15-17, understanding the phrase "in the word of the Lord" exclusively in terms of the OT idiom which the prophets used in order to indicate in whose commission and authority they spoke. They discount also 1 Corinthians 11:23-25, arguing that Paul received and transmitted it as a liturgical tradition. So, for the "minimalists" like F. Neirynck and N. Walter, there are only two explicit references to sayings of Jesus in Paul.

*1.1. 1 Corinthians 7:10-11.* In 1 Corinthians 7:10-11, Paul cites the "command" of the Lord, emphasizing that it is the Lord's and not his own. It is fairly clear that it is a reformulation of Jesus' teaching on divorce preserved in Mark 10:9-12 (par. Mt 19:6, 9); Matthew 5:32 (par. Lk 16:18; *see* Marriage and Divorce). The parenthetical remark in 1 Corinthians 7:11a is often thought to be Paul's "free" modification of Jesus' teaching. But it is more a faithful representation of Jesus' teaching in Mark 10:11 (cf. Mt 19:9) than a "free modification" of it. As D. Wenham has shown, there are two indications that Paul knew Jesus' teaching on divorce in its Synoptic context: (1) In Matthew 19 (par. Mk 10) Jesus bases his teaching on the "one flesh" principle drawn from Genesis 2:24, and precisely this principle is used by Paul in the passage immediately preceding his teaching on marriage and divorce (1 Cor 6:12-20), for his teaching that a Christian, being a member of the body of Christ, cannot join himself to a prostitute; (2) In Matthew 19 Jesus' teaching on divorce is followed by his sayings about those who are eunuchs for the kingdom of God (Mt 19:10-12). These latter sayings are often seen to be echoed in 1 Corinthians 7:7, 32-35 in Paul's teaching on celibacy

as a special gift from God* for more effective service of the Lord. Thus it seems that Paul knew not just an isolated saying of Jesus on divorce but rather his teaching on marriage as a whole, including its "one flesh" principle and its relationship to the service of the kingdom of God.

*1.2. 1 Corinthians 9:14.* In 1 Corinthians 9:14 Paul also cites a "command" of the Lord, in this case "for those who preach the gospel to get their living from the gospel." Again, this is a faithful representation of Jesus' saying in Luke 10:7 (par. Mt 10:10), though not a verbatim quotation of it. D. L. Dungan has shown that just as in 1 Corinthians 7 Paul reflects his knowledge both of Jesus' divorce saying and of its interpretation in the tradition behind the Synoptics, so also in 1 Corinthians 9 he reflects his knowledge both of Jesus' missionary charge itself and its interpretation in the Q tradition. However, Paul's practice of forgoing the apostolic right tends to be viewed by some critics as if it reflected his freedom from Jesus' command or evidencing his disregard for Jesus' sayings in general. But surely Jesus' "command" in this case was intended as a "permission" from the beginning, so that Paul's failure to avail himself of it is hardly a "disobedience" to it (Bruce, 107-8). In fact, Jesus' intention in the "command" was probably so that the apostles might concentrate on preaching the gospel without having to divert themselves to securing their living. In that case Paul's refusal to avail himself of the privilege "in order not to burden" any of his churches, but to preach the gospel more effectively, causing no worldly misunderstanding (1 Thess 2:9-10; 1 Cor 9) is paradoxically a real obedience to his Lord Jesus.

*1.3. 1 Corinthians 11:23-25.* The fact that 1 Corinthians 11:23-25 is a liturgical tradition does not necessarily mean that Paul is unconscious of his transmitting actual sayings of Jesus, or that it is no indication of Paul's interest in the sayings of Jesus. On the contrary, the concrete reference to "the night" and the use of the word *paradidosthai* ("to be delivered up"), which is so characteristic of Jesus' passion announcements (Mk 9:31 par.; Mk 10:33 par.; Mk 14:18 par.; Mt 26:21; Jn 13:21; Mk 14:21 par.) and so prominent in the Synoptic passion narratives, could hardly have failed to make Paul conscious of the historical reality of the event of the Last Supper and of the words spoken by the man who was to be delivered up and crucified. If nothing else, then, at least the word "Do this in remembrance of me" (1 Cor 11:25) must have reminded Paul of the importance of remembering those sayings of Jesus as well as his acts (*see* Lord's Supper).

*1.4. 1 Thessalonians 4:15-17.* Concerning 1 Thessalonians 4:15-17, the OT prophetic idiom of "in the word of the Lord" is now widely recognized. It has been noted that there is a substantial similarity between 1 Thessalonians 4:15-17 and 1 Corinthians 15:51-52, and that in the latter Paul speaks of a "mystery,"* a revelation by the risen Lord. However, there is also a wide recognition of an echo here of Jesus' eschatological saying in Matthew 24:30-31 and parallels. In addition D. Wenham sees here several echoes of the parable of virgins (Mt 25:1-13, e.g.: "with him/the Lord" in 1 Thess 4:14, 17 and the "shout of command"/the "voice of archangel" in 1 Thess 4:16 are matched by "with him" in Mt 25:10 and the "cry" in Mt 25:6 respectively, and the phrase *eis apantēsin*, "to meet," appears both in 1 Thess 4:17 and Mt 25:6). Recently R. H. Gundry has argued that in 1 Thessalonians 4:15-17 Paul is drawing on Jesus' saying (whose original form may have been: "The one who has died will rise, and the one who is alive will never die") embedded in John 11:25-26 and that, prompted by the pre-Johannine tradition of the raising of Lazarus (cf. Jn 12:13-18) and intending to console the grief-stricken Thessalonians more effectively, Paul portrays the future coming of the Lord and the believers' meeting him in terms of the imperial visit (*parousia*) and the citizens' going out to meet the approaching emperor (*apantēsis*) in the Hellenistic world (*see* Eschatology). In view of the undeniable echoes of various sayings of Jesus here, P. Stuhlmacher thinks that Paul is presenting his own prophetic reapplication of Synoptic tradition. However, in arguing that it is uncertain whether Paul is conscious of applying Jesus-tradition, N. Walter suggests that 1 Thessalonians 4:15-17 should be regarded merely as containing Christian insights (Walter, 66). But the several and clear echoes of Jesus' sayings in the passage seem to suggest that Paul must be conscious of the material he is using as Jesus material and therefore that with "the word of the Lord" here Paul is referring to the word(s) of the historical Jesus he is using (cf. Wenham; Gundry; Holtz), rather than a prophetic oracle spoken in the name of the Lord.

*1.5. 1 Thessalonians 5:1-7.* The formulation "You yourselves know accurately" (*autoi . . . akribōs oidate*) in 1 Thessalonians 5:2 may also be an indication that allusions to Jesus' sayings are to be found in 1 Thessalonians 5:1-7. It is widely recognized that verses 2 and 4 echo Jesus' parable of the thief (Mt 24:43 par. Lk 12:39), especially as the metaphor of thief is not applied in an eschatological context in the OT and Jewish literature. Then, as Wenham has shown, there is a close parallelism in vocabulary, structure and meaning between 1 Thessalonians 5:3 and Luke 21:34-35:

| 1 Thessalonians 5:3: | "come upon them suddenly as birth-pangs . . . escape" |
|---|---|
| | (*aiphnidios autois ephistatai . . . hōsper hē ōdin . . . ekphygōsin*) |
| Luke 21:34-36: | "come upon you suddenly as snare . . . escape |
| | (*epistē eph' hymas aiphnidios. . . hōs pagis . . . ekphygein*) |

(*Pagis* ["snare"] and *ōdin* ["birthpangs"] may be translation variants of an original *ḥbl/ḥbl'*, caused by different pointings of the word or, as Wenham argues, the original *pagis* may have been replaced by Paul with *ōdin* under the influence of Is 13:6-7 and Jer 6:14-21.) Paul's exhortation in the 1 Thessalonians passage to be awake and sober, not asleep nor drunk, represents the general tenor of Matthew 24:42-51 (par. Lk 12:41-46) and Luke 21:34-36 (par. Mk 13:33-37).

In view of these clear echoes of Jesus' eschatological sayings, how are we to understand the introductory formula "you yourselves know accurately"? With that unusual introductory formula Paul cannot possibly refer so simply to anything that was taught by anybody other than himself and his coworkers,* even if there had been such a thing within the short interval between his founding the church at Thessalonica and his writing of 1 Thessalonians. Nor can he refer to what was simply his own teaching based on the OT-Jewish tradition. For what the Thessalonians are supposed to "know accurately" in 1 Thessalonians 5:2-10 has already been shown, in part, according to the criteria of dissimilarity and coherence, to contain clear echoes of Jesus' sayings. Nor can he refer to his teaching which was based simply on a common Christian tradition, without any consciousness of the teachings of Jesus himself. Some of the parallels between our passage and the dominical sayings recorded in the Gospels seem too striking for that to be correct. It also is hard to believe that Paul was unaware that the Christian tradition was based on Jesus' own teachings, especially in view of the presence of Silvanus, who surely bore tradition from Jerusalem and was with Paul both at the time of founding the church and of writing 1 Thessalonians.

It may be helpful to compare our passage with 1 Thessalonians 4:2 ("For you know what instructions we gave you through the Lord Jesus"). Here the phrase "through the Lord Jesus" (*dia kyriou Iēsou*) may in itself refer to the origin or inspiration of the instructions. What the Thessalonians are supposed to "know accurately" (1 Thess 5:2) is probably part of the "instructions" Paul gave them *dia kyriou Iēsou*. In giving them that instruction *dia kyriou Iēsou*, was Paul conscious only of being inspired by the Lord Jesus, or was he conscious also of it originating from the actual teaching of the Lord Jesus recorded in the tradition? The clear echoes of Jesus' sayings in 1 Thessalonians 5:2-7 suggest the latter as the more likely case. Paul must have given at least this part of the instruction on the basis of the actual sayings of Jesus, even if he interpreted and adapted them as one standing under the inspiration of the Lord.

The conclusion seems unavoidable: with the introductory formula "you yourselves know accurately." Paul is trying to remind the Thessalonians of the teaching that he delivered to them at the time of founding their church (cf. 2 Thess 2:15; 3:6) on the basis of Jesus' eschatological sayings.

This further strengthens our previous conclusion with regard to the formula "in the word of the Lord" (1 Thess 4:15). For by way of an analogy it points to the following conclusion: just as Paul based the instruction now recalled in 1 Thessalonians 5:2-7 ("through the Lord Jesus") on Jesus' teaching, recognized by its many echoes of that teaching, so also in giving a new instruction in 1 Thessalonians 4:13-18 on the fate of the Christian dead "in the word of the Lord," he bases it on Jesus' teaching so that it too contains many echoes of that teaching.

So the formulas, "in the word of the Lord" and "you yourselves know accurately," which follow each other so closely in the wake of Paul's reminder of his previous instructions "through the Lord Jesus" (1 Thess 4:2), both indicate that in 1 Thessalonians 4:15—5:7 Paul is alluding to the eschatological teachings of Jesus.

*1.6. Romans 14:14.* There is a general consensus that Romans 14:14a ("I know and am convinced by the Lord Jesus that nothing is unclean in itself") is an allusion to a saying of Jesus recorded in Mark 7:15 (par. Mt 15:11) and that Romans 14:20 ("all [foods] are clean") corresponds to the editorial remark of Mark ("he declared all foods clean," Mk 7:19). Between Romans 14:14a and Mk 7:15 there is not only an exact material correspondence, but also a verbal agreement: *ouden koinon/ouden . . . koinōsai.* For this reason some think that with the phrase "by the Lord Jesus" Paul refers to the historical Jesus and seeks to indicate that he is alluding to Jesus' teaching. However, others think that in Romans 14:14a, 20 Paul is giving a general Christian maxim or an insight from his gospel (cf. 1 Cor 6:13; 8:8a), and that the phrase "by the Lord Jesus" is not necessarily a reference to the historical Jesus (cf. Phil 2:19).

This negative judgment is supported by the recent argument of H. Räisänen that Paul's failure to refer to the logion of Mark 7:15 in his controversy with Peter* at Antioch* (Gal 2:11-21) and Luke's failure to refer to it in Acts 10—11; 15:7-9 indicate that Mark 7:15 is inauthentic. But this argument has justly been rejected by H. Merkel and M. Thompson (see below). Furthermore, Thompson appropriately asks how it is possible for Paul simply to declare "Nothing is unclean in itself" and "All [foods] are clean" to an unknown church containing a number of Jewish Christians, to whom he is concerned to show that he is upholding the Law* (Rom 3:13; 7:12) and whose support he is soliciting for his mission to Spain. Unless he knows that a teaching like Mark 7:15 has already been delivered to the church he is treading on dangerous ground. Given the apparent dispute between the "strong"* and the "weak" in the Roman church, it would hardly do for Paul to utter a mere declaration without any accompanying theological justification of what would be taken as simply a corollary of his (disputed) gospel or an opinion ("maxim") of a certain party. So with the phrase "by the Lord Jesus" in Romans 14:14a Paul seems to be alluding to a saying of Jesus (Mk 7:15 par.) in the hope that the Romans would recognize its authority.

*1.7. Romans 12:14-21 and 1 Corinthians 4:11-13.* There is broad agreement that in Romans 12:14-21 and 1 Corinthians 4:11-13 there are a number of clear echoes of the sayings of Jesus. Even N. Walter, a "minimalist," grants this and notes particularly the following sets of correspondences:

| | |
|---|---|
| Romans 12:14 | Luke 6:28a (Mt 5:44b v.l) |
| Romans 12:17a | |
| (1 Thess 5:15a) | Luke 6:29 par. Matthew 5:39b-41 |
| Romans 12:18 | Mark 9:50 par. Matthew 5:9 |
| Romans 12:19-21 | Luke 6:27a + 35 par. Matthew 5:44a |
| 1 Corinthians 4:11a | Luke 6:21a par. Matthew 5:6; 10:9-10; 11:19 |
| 1 Corinthians 4:12b-13 | Luke 6:22-23 par. Matthew 5:11-12; Luke 6:27-28 (Mt 5:44) |

Of course, there are some who doubt one or another of these sets. But there is virtual consensus that Romans 12:14 echoes Matthew 5:44 (par. Lk 6:27-28). J. Piper's conclusion on the basis of the criterion of dissimilarity is entirely convincing: "There need be no doubt that Jesus commanded 'Love your enemies,' . . . we found nothing so explicit and unequivocal in our survey of Jesus' environment; nor is it thinkable that the early church should invent the saying and thus impose upon themselves such a troublesome requirement" (Piper, 56). So Thompson considers Romans 12:14 to be "a virtually certain echo" or "possibly even an allusion" to a teaching of Jesus. Related to this observation is the often observed fact that the series of Paul's exhortations in Romans 12:14-21 is matched by a series of Jesus' sayings that appear in the central section of Luke's Sermon on the Plain (Allison) or Matthew's Sermon on the Mount (Wenham). This provides a strong argument for the view that the Pauline exhortations as a whole are echoes of those sayings of Jesus and therefore that the similar autobiographical remarks in 1 Corinthians 4:11-13 also are echoes of them (Walter; Thompson).

Granting all these points, however, N. Walter thinks that the question might be left open as to "whether Paul, in using these sayings, did so in the consciousness that these were sayings *of Jesus*" (Walter, 56). He maintains there is no indication that Paul considered them as sayings of Jesus but, of course, neither can he give any evidence that Paul did *not* so regard them. Some have seen the imperative *eulogeite* ("bless," Rom 12:14) in a section where Paul otherwise gives his exhortations mostly using participles, infinitives or adjectives in verbless clauses, as evidence of Paul's using Jesus' saying without adapting it to the grammatical style of the context. Having represented a saying of Jesus by "bless (*eulogeite*) those who persecute (you)" (cf. Mt 5:44), Paul may be adding "bless (*eulogeite*) and do not curse (them)," repeating the word *eulogeite* because the use of *eulogeite* in Romans 12:14a "has instantly recalled a more familiar logion" recorded in Luke 6:28. If so, the repetition of *eulogeite* may be an indicator that here Paul deliberately alludes to a saying of Jesus (Thompson). However, whether or not Paul was conscious of the echoes of Jesus' sayings will have to be decided after examining all those passages and considering a number of other factors.

***1.8. Romans 13:8-10 and Galatians 5:14.*** The majority of scholars see also in Romans 13:8-10 and Galatians 5:14 echoes of Jesus' sayings, especially that of Mark 12:28-34 and parallels. Thompson observes them well, and in the following we give a summary of his observations (with our supplement starting with point 5).

(1) Paul's linking of love* and "debt" in Romans 13:8a may reflect Jesus' teaching represented, for example, in his parables of the unforgiving servant (Mt 18:23-35) and of the debtor (Lk 7:36-50) as well as his sayings like Luke 6:36; Matthew 6:12 etc. (cf. Rom 15:1-3; Col 3:13): the recipient of love from God owes a debt of love to others.

(2) The article *to* introducing "love one another" in Romans 13:8a indicates it to be "the well-known command" that the readers are expected to recognize immediately. In view of John 13:34-35; 25:12-13, 17 and 1 John 3:11; 2 John 5; 1 Peter 1:22, it is probable that they are expected to recognize it as a dominical command.

(3) The expression "fulfilling [*plēroō*] the Law" in Romans 13:8b (also Rom 13:10b) and in Galatians 5:14 (especially with its eschatological nuance), while being rare in Jewish literature, is paralleled by Matthew 5:17 (*see* Law).

(4) Paul's exhortation "Bear one another's burdens, and so fulfill the law of Christ" in Galatians 6:2 (cf. also 1 Cor 9:21) should be taken with Galatians 5:14: "For the whole law is fulfilled in one word, 'You shall love your neighbor as yourself' " (Lev 19:18; *see* Law of Christ).

(5) In a very similar formulation to Galatians 5:14, Romans 13:9 also cites Leviticus 19:18 as the epitome of the whole Law. This corresponds to Jesus' answer to the question about the greatest commandment (Mk 12:28-34 par. Mt 22:34-40 and Lk 10:25-28). Scholars have debated the authenticity of the Synoptic logion. Was there a similar practice of summing up the Law in first-century Judaism? If so, the principle of dissimilarity (i.e., that sayings of Jesus that are dissimilar to his environment are more likely to be authentic) would reduce its claim to authenticity. But even if scholars are correct in noting the presence of such summaries of the Law in Judaism, the fundamental difference between the Jewish practice on the one hand and the Pauline and the Synoptic summaries on the other is to be noted. The Jewish practice aims at stating the Law that is logically prior and therefore includes by implication all the rest, in order to facilitate learning and keeping all the stipulations of the law. The Pauline and Synoptic summaries seek to stress "that love is what *really* matters, more so than legal scruples" (Thompson). Further, the combination of Deuteronomy 6:5 and Leviticus 19:18, as in Mark 12:28-34 and parallels, has no analogy in Judaism (Neirynck). So the summary of the Law in terms of love for God (Deut 6:5) and love for the neighbor (Lev 19:18) must be accepted as an authentic teaching of Jesus. If so, in view of the material connection between Galatians 5:14 and 6:2 as observed above (4), the striking formulation "the law of Christ" in Galatians 6:2 should be seen not as merely including a reference to Galatians 5:14, but as concretely designating the summary of the Law in Galatians 5:14 *as the teaching of (Jesus) Christ on the Law* or *as the Law given by (Jesus) Christ*. If this is so, as in Galatians 5:14; 6:2, so also in Romans 13:8-10 Paul is clearly alluding to Jesus' teaching on the Law.

An objection has been raised against this conclusion from the fact that while Jesus summarized the Law in two commandments, Paul does it in only one. Here Thompson answers well: in Romans 13:8-10 (and also Gal 5:14) Paul refers only to the second commandment because in the context(s) he is concerned with giving his readers ethical exhortations for proper behavior toward one another, rather than giving an instruction in Jesus tradition. Romans 12:17 shows how Paul is capable of using only half of a tradition: citing Proverbs 3:4 ("Take care to do what is noble in the sight of the Lord and people"), he leaves out the reference to the Lord because it does not suit his immediate purpose. Furthermore, he has already stated in the opening verses the believers' duty to love God (Rom 12:1-2) as the foundation for the whole paraenetical section of Roman 12—15. In fact it is quite probable that Romans 12:1-2 echoes the first part of Jesus' double summary of the Law.

*1.9. Romans 13:7.* The conclusion that Romans 13:8-10 alludes to Jesus' saying in Mark 12:28-34 (and pars.) strengthens the view that Romans 13:7 echoes the saying of Jesus in Mark 12:17 (and pars.). Those who hold this view derive support not only from the material correspondence between the Pauline injunction and the dominical saying, but also from the fact that the dominical sayings that are echoed in Paul's successive exhortations of Romans 13:7 and 13:8-10 also stand closely connected and in the same order in the conflict stories of Mark 12:13-17, 28-31 and Matthew 22:15-22, 34-40. Those who reject this view, however, point to the uncertainty as to whether the two Synoptic narratives stood together in the pre-Markan collection of conflict stories, and also to the difficulty of the generalizing phrases "Pay (*apodote*) all of them (*pasin*) what you owe. . . . Let not any debt to *anyone* (*mēdeni*) remain unpaid" (Rom 13:7a and 8a). They also point to the absence of anything in Romans 13:7 that corresponds to the second part of Jesus' double saying ("Render unto God the things that are God's"), which is the real point of the whole saying. There is, however, discussion as to whether the phrase in Romans 13:7, "(render) fear to whom fear is due" (*tō ton phobon ton phobon*), refers to that second part of the Jesus logion (Cranfield). It is uncertain. However, Paul's omission of the second part of Jesus' double saying here can be understood exactly the same way as that in Romans 13:8-10: having already stated in the principial declaration of Romans 12:1-2 the duty of rendering unto God what is God's (our whole being), he omits repetition of that in Romans 13, as it does not suit his immediate purpose of instructing his readers about their proper attitude to the civil authorities. (While in Jesus' original saying the second part is stressed, by omitting it in the context of Romans 13 Paul undoubtedly makes the first part prominent. This is probably conditioned by the situation of the Roman Christians or that of the church as a whole at that critical period in its history.) Once this is recognized, the generalizing phrases in Romans 13:7-8 pose no problem. They just indicate that here Paul is applying a generalized form of Jesus' teaching ("Render unto Caesar the things that are Caesar's") to different authorities. Even if Mark 12:13-17 and parallels, and Mark 12:28-34 and its parallels did not stand together in the *pre-*Markan collection of conflict stories, their present connection in Mark and Matthew, corresponding to the connection of Paul's two exhortations in Romans 13:7 and 8-10, is significant. So it is highly likely that Romans 13:7 is an echo of Jesus' saying found in Mark 12:17 and parallels (*see* Civil Authority).

*1.10. Romans 8:15 and Galatians 4:6.* The *abba* address for God* to which Paul refers twice (Rom 8:15; Gal 4:6) is universally recognized as originating in Jesus' teaching. But we should note also the unique formulas: "the Spirit* of his Son*" (Gal 4:6) and "the Spirit of adoption*" (Rom 8:15). Is Paul not referring to the Holy Spirit with these formulas as the Spirit who indwelt Jesus, attesting (making?) him as the Son of God and so enabling him to use this unique form of address for God? If so, when Paul says that this Spirit sent by God into our hearts cries "*Abba* Father!" (Gal 4:6), he may have in mind the fact that Jesus taught his disciples to use that same unique form of address. The Spirit of Jesus the Son of God indwells the hearts of those who by faith* and baptism* unite with the Son of God, Jesus Christ, and who participate in his divine sonship. It is this indwelling Spirit that enables them to use the same form of address for God as Jesus the Son of God used. Thus Romans 8:15 and Galatians 4:6 seem to show Paul's awareness of the full significance of Jesus' *abba* address (*see* Adoption, Sonship).

Further, some commentators wonder whether with "Abba Father!" Paul may not actually be referring to the Lord's Prayer which opens with "*Pater!*" ('*abbā*', Lk 11:2). But the context of Romans 8:12-27 seems to remind us rather of Jesus' prayer at Gethsemane (Mk 14:32-42 pars.; cf. Thompson). Paul introduces the cry "*Abba!*" in the context of describing the reality of Christians' participation in Christ's suffering* in order for them to participate in his glory.* Furthermore, the "groanings" of Christians and the idea of the Spirit's helping them make the right prayer according to God's will are reminiscent respectively of Jesus' anxiety and sorrow, and of his prayer at Gethsemane, "Remove this cup from me; yet not what I will, but what you will."

*1.11. Kingdom of God.* Finally, Paul's references to the "kingdom of God"* (Rom 14:17; 1 Cor 4:20; 6:9-10; 15:50; Gal 5:21; Col 4:10-11; 1 Thess 2:11-12;

2 Thess 1:5; cf. 1 Cor 15:24; Col 1:13; 2 Tim 4:1, 18) must be considered. In view of the fact that in the Synoptics the kingdom of God is the center of Jesus' preaching, while the death (and resurrection) of Jesus Christ is the center of Paul's preaching,* critics tend to emphasize the infrequency with which Paul uses that characteristic expression of Jesus. However, while the thought expressed by the "kingdom of God" was central to contemporary Judaism, the term itself was by no means common in Judaism (let alone to Hellenism*). This observation, considered together with the fact that the total number of occurrences of "the kingdom of God" in the non-Pauline writings of the NT outside the Synoptics is hardly more than those within the Pauline corpus, points out that the eight Pauline references to the kingdom of God are by no means insignificant.

Among the many similarities between Paul's concept of the kingdom of God and that of Jesus (see below), Paul's language of "inheriting the kingdom of God" may be singled out as a sign of his adoption of the characteristic language of Jesus. The phrase "inherit the kingdom of God" is not frequent in the Synoptics (Mt 25:34; cf. Mt 5:5; 19:29), yet it is practically synonymous with the characteristic phrase of Jesus, "enter the kingdom of God" (Mk 10:15 pars.; Mk 10:23-27 pars.; etc.). Both phrases were formed after the OT model of "inheriting" or "entering" the promised land of Canaan (e.g., Deut 4:1; 6:17-18; 16:20; cf. also the phrases reflecting God's "giving" the kingdom [Lk 12:32; cf. Lk 22:29; Mk 4:11 pars.] and the believers' "receiving" it [Mk 10:15 pars.; Lk 18:17]). In the cluster of the synonymous expressions of Jesus (to "enter," "inherit" and "receive" the kingdom of God), Paul seems to have chosen the one of "inheriting the kingdom of God" (1 Cor 6:9; 15:50; Gal 5:21) under the influence of the common Jewish turn of speech, to "inherit" the age to come or eternal life. So it is fairly certain that Paul knew about Jesus' kingdom preaching and that he reflects it in his letters.

### 2. Possible Echoes.
There are also a large number of Pauline texts which may be seen, with a varying degree of probability, as echoing sayings of Jesus. They do not show any direct indication for it, and they are more disputed than those which have hitherto been treated. As space does not allow them to be discussed and evaluated here, they are simply presented in tabular form (see chart). However, some of them will be drawn into discussion in the subsequent sections.

*2.1. 1 Corinthians.* 1 Corinthians is distinguished among Paul's letters by the unique presence of three explicit references to the word/command of the Lord (1 Cor 7:10; 9:14; 11:23-26) and by the relative frequency of echoes of Jesus' sayings. It is also distinguished by Paul's explicit statement that on certain issues he has no *Herrenwort* ("word of the Lord," 1 Cor 7:12, 25, 40) and by the tenfold "Do you not know that? . . ." formula. These characteristics raise several interesting questions concerning Paul's attitude to and transmission of the dominical logia on the one hand, and the Corinthian problems and the nature of 1 Corinthians on the other. (In this article the former question will be taken up at relevant places.)

Paul's use of the "Do you not know that?" formula is quite suggestive and has not received adequate attention in scholarly discussions of Jesus' sayings in Paul. Among its ten occurrences, 1 Corinthians 5:6; 6:2 and 6:3; 6:9 have often been cited as echoes of Jesus' sayings in Mark 8:15-16 and parallels; in Matthew 19:28 (par. Lk 22:29-30); and in Matthew 5:20 respectively. 1 Corinthians 9:13, 24, however, refer to OT practice or common sense. The remaining four cases remain to be explained:

> 1 Corinthians 3:16 ("that you are the temple of God")
> 1 Corinthians 6:15 ("that your members are members of Christ")
> 1 Corinthians 6:16 ("that he who joins himself to a prostitute becomes one body with her")
> 1 Corinthians 6:19 ("that your body is a temple of the Holy Spirit within you")

E. E. Ellis has sought to demonstrate that they refer to Paul's previous teaching to the Corinthians on "body"* and "temple,"* which was based on Jesus' own teaching. To summarize his argument briefly: 1 Corinthians 10:16 and 11:23-24 show that Paul's theology of the body of Christ is partly rooted in the eucharistic sayings of Jesus. 1 Corinthians 6:15 as well as 1 Corinthians 12:12, 27 reflect the same theology of the "body of Christ."* Ephesians 5:30, which also speaks of Christians as "members of Christ's body," grounds the conception in an exposition of Genesis 2:24: "The two shall be one flesh." Precisely this same passage is in Paul's mind in 1 Corinthians 6:15-17. This shows that the Corinthians' knowledge of their being "members of Christ" or of his "body" is based both on the Last Supper teaching of Jesus and on an exposition of Genesis 2:24, which the Corinthians had learned from Paul. It is most interesting then that Genesis 2:24 forms a part of the Synoptic tradition of Jesus' teaching on divorce, to which Paul alludes in 1 Corinthians 7:10-11. This means that Paul's conception of the church as the "body of Christ" is rooted, partly, both in Jesus' Supper teaching and in his mar-

# Possible Echoes of Sayings of Jesus

*Romans*

1. Romans 12:1-2 — Mark 12:17 par.; Mark 12:29-30 par.

2. Romans 12:9-13 — Mark 7:6 par. Matthew 15:7; Mark 12:15 par. Matthew 22:18; Luke 12:56; Matthew 7:5 par. Luke 6:42

3. Romans 13:11-14 — Luke 21:28, 31, 34 (cf. 1 Thess 5; Eph 6)

4. Romans 14:1-13a — Matthew 7:1 par. Luke 6:37 (cf. Rom 2:1-5; 1 Cor 4:3-5)

5. Romans 14:13b — Mark 9:42 par. (cf. 1 Cor 8:13)

6. Romans 15:8-9 — Matthew 15:24; 8:11; Mark 10:45 par. (cf. 1 Cor 9:19; 10:33; 11:1 and Mk 10:44-45 par. Mt 20:27-28)

7. Romans 16:19 — Matthew 10:16

*1 Corinthians*

8. 1 Corinthians 1:18—2:16 — Luke 10:21-24 par. Matthew 11:25, 27; 13:16-17
   1 Corinthians 1:20-25 — Luke 11:29-32 par. Matthew 12:38-42
   1 Corinthians 1:23 — Matthew 11:6 par. Luke 7:23
   1 Corinthians 2:8 — Luke 23:13, 35; 24:20

9. 1 Corinthians 4:1-5 — Luke 12:41-46 par. Matthew 24:45-51; Matthew 25:14-30 par. Luke 19:12-27; Luke 12:37; Matthew 7:1 par. Luke 6.37a

10. 1 Corinthians 7:7 — Matthew 19:12

11. 1 Corinthians 8:13 — Mark 9:42 par.

12. 1 Corinthians 9:19; 10:33; 11:1 — Mark 10:45 par.

13. 1 Corinthians 10:27 — Luke 20:8

14. 1 Corinthians 13:2b — Matthew 17:20; Mark 11:22-23 par. Matthew 21:21

15. 1 Corinthians 3:16; 5:6; 6:2, 3, 9, 15, 16, 19 containing the "Do you not know that?" formula (see below)

*2 Corinthians*

16. 2 Corinthians 4:10 — Mark 9:31 par.; Mark 10:33 par.; Mark 14:21, 41 par.; etc. (cf. Rom 4:25; 8:32; Gal 1:4; 2:20)

17. 2 Corinthians 5:1 — Mark 14:58 par. (see below)

18. 2 Corinthians 6:16 — Mark 15:58 par. (see below)

19. 2 Corinthians 12:12 — Mark 6:7 par. (cf. Mk 16:17-18)

*Galatians*

20. Galatians 1:4; 2:20 — see 16 above

21. Galatians 1:1, 12-16; 2:7-9 — Matthew 16:16-17 (cf. 1 Cor 3:11; Wenham)

*Ephesians*

22. Ephesians 2:19-21 — Mark 14:58 par. (cf. 1 Cor 3:11, 16; 2 Cor 6:16; Gal 2:9; see below)

23. Ephesians 6:10-18 — Luke 21:28, 31, 34-36

*Philippians*

24. Philippians 1:27—2:11 — Mark 10:43-45 par.; Luke 14:11; Matthew 23:12 par. Luke 18:14

*Colossians*

25. Colossians 3:5 — Mark 9:43-48 (cf. Mt 5:29; 18:8-9)

26. Colossians 3:13 — Matthew 6:12 par. Luke 11:4

*1 Thessalonians*

27. 1 Thessalonians 2:2-9 — Matthew 10:10 par. Luke 10:7

28. 1 Thessalonians 4:8 — Luke 10:16 (cf. Mt 10:10; Jn 13:20)

29. 1 Thessalonians 5:15 — Matthew 5:39-40 par. Luke 6:27-29 (cf. Rom 12:17)

30. 1 Thessalonians 2:16 — Matthew 23:32-33

*2 Thessalonians*

31. 2 Thessalonians 2:1-12 — Mark 13 par.

riage/divorce teaching based on Genesis 2:24. The formula "Do you not know that?" in 1 Corinthians 6:15, 16 as well as the references to the Last Supper tradition in 1 Corinthians 11:23-24; 10:16 (perhaps a variant form of the formula "Do you not know that?") then indicate that Paul had previously taught the Corinthians about the church being the "body of Christ" and about divorce on the basis of Jesus' teachings (cf. above).

For an explanation of the origin of the temple typology in 1 Corinthians 3:16 and 6:19 it is helpful to consider 1 Corinthians 3:11 and 2 Corinthians 5:1. The statement "you are the temple of God" (1 Cor 3:16) must somehow be related to the earlier statement that the "foundation" which the apostle Paul has laid is Jesus Christ (1 Cor 3:11). The use of "foundation" (*themelion*) here may reflect the influence of Isaiah 28:16, which is alluded to in Ephesians 2:20-22 and explicitly cited in 1 Peter 2:4-10 in connection with the conception of the church* as the temple of God in both passages. In 1 Peter 2:4-10, Isaiah 28:16 is cited together with Psalm 117(118):22 (the "rejected stone" becoming the "head of the corner"), which Jesus used in his explanation of the meaning of his sign-act at the Temple of Jerusalem (Mk 11:27—12:11 par.; cf. Kim). May it not be that in 1 Corinthians 3:11, 16 Paul reflects Jesus' teaching on the Temple and, in echoing Isaiah 28:16 (cf. Rom 9:33) he has also Psalm 117(118):22 in mind? (Cf. *kephalē gōnias* in Ps 117:22 and *lithos . . . akrogōniaios* in Is 28:16.) The several verbal affinities between 2 Corinthians 5:1 and the Temple saying attributed to Jesus (Mk 14:58 par. Mt 26:61) suggest that 2 Corinthians 5:1 echoes the saying and reflects an interpretation of it which, as in John 2:21-22, identifies Jesus' resurrection body as the new temple. Paul's introductory formula in 2 Corinthians 5:1, "for we know that . . . ," indicates that he had previously taught the Corinthians the temple typology on the basis of Jesus' Temple saying. So they "know" that they are the "temple of God" (1 Cor 3:16) or "that your body is the temple of the Holy Spirit" (1 Cor 6:19).

At this point Ellis's argument needs much supplementing. Elsewhere I have attempted to show that Jesus did predict the destruction of the Jerusalem Temple and promise to build a new temple, and that by the new temple he meant the community of the new people of God he was to create through his vicariously atoning and covenant-establishing death and resurrection. So the new temple was the people of God whom he, as their substitute and representative, embodied, as it were, and it was to come into being with his resurrection. Therefore it was interpreted in terms

of the resurrection "body" of Christ in John 2:21-22, where the body concept is perhaps both individual and collective (in its latter aspect, approaching the Pauline concept of the church as the "body of Christ"). Many Qumran* documents illustrate the Jewish background for Jesus' metaphorical or "spiritual" interpretation of temple, and passages like 1QH 7:4, that use for the community the language of body as well as that of building, illustrate the interpretation of temple as body. Paul seems to reflect both the collective interpretation of the temple (1 Cor 3:16) and its individual interpretation (1 Cor 6:19). The resurrection body which believers are to put on as a "building from God, a house not made with hands, eternal in the heavens" (2 Cor 5:1) is the resurrection body like that of the Last Adam, the "man from heaven" (1 Cor 15:42-49). But this resurrection body has already begun to take on reality in believers, insofar as they have died and risen with Christ through faith-baptism, and as the Holy Spirit* has already taken residence in them and they are being transformed into the glorious image* of the risen Lord (2 Cor 3:18). Hence we find the statement of 1 Corinthians 6:19! Space forbids a substantiation of the thesis in greater detail, but at any rate Paul's temple typology (cf. also 2 Cor 6:16—7:1) is undoubtedly based on Jesus' unique teaching on the Temple which is closely bound up with his kingdom preaching. 1 Corinthians 3:16; 6:19 and 2 Corinthians 5:1 clearly suggest that Paul had previously taught the Corinthians about it.

If this is so, all the cases of the formula "Do you not know that? . . ." in 1 Corinthians (except 1 Cor 9:13, 24) and its variant forms in 1 Corinthians 10:16 and 2 Corinthians 5:1 suggest that Paul transmitted Jesus' teachings to the Corinthian church at the time of his founding the church.

### 3. Continuity/Similarity in Theology and Attitude.
We have seen that in only a few cases does Paul clearly indicate his reference to a saying of Jesus, and even in those cases, as 1 Corinthians 7:10-11 and 9:14 show, he does not quote them verbatim but *re-presents* them in his own language, sometimes using one or two words and/or the form drawn from them. This suggests that verbal parallelism cannot be made the sole criterion for judging whether a Pauline statement reflects a dominical saying or not. The presence of a parallel content or meaning must also be considered. The instances of allusions and echoes listed in sections 1 and 2 above are the result of critical comparisons of the vocabulary, form and/or content of Pauline statements with those of dominical logia preserved in the Synoptics. The critical criteria used are the prin-

ciple of dissimilarity (i.e., a Pauline statement that is similar to a saying of Jesus could have come only from the latter, since the latter is unique, being dissimilar to OT-Judaism and Hellenism) and the principle of coherence (i.e., a Pauline statement should be both similar to and cohere well with a saying of Jesus). (The limited space, however, has prevented the actual display of comparisons for the instances tabulated in section 2.) Undoubtedly this investigation involves a fair degree of subjectivity. Some may wonder whether there may not be more allusions or echoes that have gone undetected, while others may reject many of the above cases. Even where a Pauline statement clearly seems to reflect a saying of Jesus, minimalists will wish to question whether Paul was conscious that it originated with Jesus when he made the statement.

In such a situation can there not be another criterion to provide a more reliable judgment? It is submitted here that the continuity or similarity between Paul and Jesus both in theology and in attitude must be considered as a factor, if not a criterion.

It is widely recognized that there is a real continuity between Jesus' kingdom preaching and Paul's doctrine of justification* (Bultmann; Jüngel). As noted above, the fact that the specific Jesuanic term kingdom of God is used by Paul at all (and over eight times, when elsewhere in the NT outside the Gospels it is rarely used) is significant. Like Jesus, Paul teaches that the kingdom of God is both present (Rom 14:17; 1 Cor 4:20; Col 1:13; 4:11) and future (all other instances). It presents its saving power through the Spirit (1 Cor 4:20 cf. Mt 12:28; Lk 11:20). It will be "inherited" not by natural, sinful people (1 Cor 15:50; Gal 5:21) but only by the righteous or those who are worthy of the kingdom (1 Cor 6:9; 1 Thess 2:12; 2 Thess 1:5; Gal 5:21; cf. Mt 5:20, 10) or by those who have been made God's children and are so privileged to call God *abba* (Rom 8:15-17; Gal 4:6-7; cf. Mk 10:15 par.). Paul's emphasis on divine grace corresponds to Jesus' emphasis on the kingdom's transcendental and grace character exhibited in his language of the kingdom "coming," and on God's "giving" it and people's "receiving" or "inheriting" it. It is also seen in Jesus' parables of the kingdom (Mt 20:1-16; Lk 7:36-50; 15:11-32; 18:9-14; Mk 1:40-45). Jesus' summary of the Law in terms of the double commandments of love for God and for one's neighbor, his critique of the contemporary Jewish understanding of the Law, and his disregard for the laws of the Sabbath, fasting, purity, table-fellowship, etc., find their close correspondence in Paul's teaching on the Law and his criticism of the "works of the Law" as the means of justification. Jesus' blessing the poor and helping the outcasts—the "sinners" accord-

ing to the Law—who respond to his kingdom preaching is not only continuous with Paul's outreach to the Gentiles but also with his doctrine of the "justification of the ungodly" *sola gratia* (Dahl, 115).

It is more true to say that there is a close correspondence between Jesus' teaching centered upon the kingdom of God and Paul's theology as a whole, rather than specifically between the former and Paul's doctrine of justification (*see* Center). For the post-Easter church in general, what Jesus had *promised* through his kingdom preaching, namely to create a people (or children) of God to live in his love and wealth, has been *realized* in his atoning and covenant*-establishing death,* and this has been confirmed by God through his resurrecting Jesus. So the post-Easter church naturally concentrates on preaching the good news of salvation *already wrought* in Christ's death (and resurrection) rather than on simply repeating Jesus' kingdom preaching which had basically the character of a promise and an invitation (see Kim). So also Paul makes Jesus' death on the cross the center of his preaching. He expounds the meaning of salvation wrought in it by various categories or metaphors such as justification, reconciliation (*see* Peace), adoption,* new creation,* life in the Spirit, transformation, etc. He explains its blessings in terms of righteousness,* peace,* joy,* freedom,* hope,* life,* etc. These categories/metaphors and these blessings are those that were explicitly or implicitly promised in Jesus' kingdom preaching. They have now been made available by Jesus' death. Thus *the fact that Jesus' gospel of the kingdom is replaced with Paul's gospel of the death and resurrection of Jesus Christ means no discontinuity between Jesus and Paul.* Rather, the reverse is true: *it had to be so replaced.*

However, in explaining the salvation promised in Jesus' preaching of the kingdom and accomplished by his death and resurrection, could Paul not have continued using the "kingdom" language? If so, why does he do so only on a few occasions? Among the various categories/metaphors which Paul uses in place of kingdom language, justification is the most prominent. At least, those who maintain that the notion of justification is not merely a "subsidiary crater" or something that developed later out of polemical necessity, but rather is the central category of Paul's soteriology, owe an explanation as to why Paul replaced the language of kingdom chiefly with the language of justification. Certainly the reason must be seen against the background of "righteousness" being a central concern of the Jews, whether they were trying to earn salvation or remain in a saving covenant relationship with God by keeping the Law. It may also have something to do with Paul's attempt to avoid a political misunderstanding of his gospel in the Roman world. Further, it is connected also with his own conversion from a zeal for Law-righteousness (see Works of the Law) to receiving God's righteousness in Jesus Christ (Gal 1:13-16; Phil 3:4-11). From that experience, Paul saw clearly God's saving act in Jesus Christ as God's righteousness, and he realized also that righteousness/justification was the best category for bringing out the *grace* character of salvation over against the Jewish conception of Law-righteousness-salvation.

The main reason, however, must lie in his understanding of Jesus' death as the atoning and covenant-establishing sacrifice* that has wrought the salvation promised by Jesus in his kingdom preaching (Rom 3:24-26; 2 Cor 5:21; etc.). Since this *saving event* was the atoning and covenant-establishing *sacrifice* and, furthermore, since Jesus indicated that his death was to bear such meaning and he portrayed it in terms of the *'Ebed Yahweh* ("Servant of the Lord") who was to "pour out his soul to death" as *'ăšām* ("guilt offering"), "making many accounted *righteous*" (Is 53:10-12; Mk 14:17-25 par.), Paul naturally interpreted the salvation wrought through Jesus' death chiefly through the category of righteousness/justification. This category of righteousness/justification, which expresses the concerns of atonement, the forgiveness of sins and the restoration of the proper, or covenantal, relationship to God, had the additional advantage of perfectly bringing out the intention of Jesus' kingdom preaching and his conduct in receiving sinners.

Thus not only the close material connection between Jesus' gospel of the kingdom of God and Paul's gospel of Jesus Christ's death and resurrection, but also Paul's choice of righteousness/justification as the main category of interpretation of salvation in Jesus Christ betrays his intimate knowledge of Jesus' kingdom preaching and Jesus' view of his own death.

We have already noted how Paul echoes Jesus' unique teaching on the temple as well as his unique address for God as *abba*, and his teaching on the adoption of believers into God's family. These teachings of Jesus are in fact closely associated with his kingdom preaching. Jesus' association with sinners, which is seen by many as a basis for Paul's outreach to the Gentiles,* is in fact granted as a foretaste and pledge of salvation, of entrance into the kingdom of God. The close similarity between Paul and Jesus in their eschatological teachings is also often noted (see esp. E. Schweizer on the Pauline kingdom passage of 1 Cor 15:20-28). Jesus' eschatological teaching is given in terms of the kingdom of God. Here the continuity between Jesus' intention of gathering the people of God in solidarity with him in the kingdom and Paul's conception of the church as the people of God and the body of Christ is instructive. These parallels also indicate Paul's intimate knowledge of Jesus' kingdom preaching.

C. Wolff has conveniently surveyed the Jesus and Pauline evidence to compare the conduct of Jesus and Paul under the four headings of deprivation, renunciation of marriage, humble service and suffering persecution. In this area Wolff affirms "some remarkable correspondences" between the two figures, and concludes that Paul as an apostle, a representative of Jesus Christ "displays himself as a true follower" of him. May we not then take this as evidence that Paul knew of Jesus' life and teaching quite well?

Some try to see the similarities between Paul and Jesus in theology and in attitude and conduct as mediated by the *Hellenists* (Wedderburn, 117-43; cf. Hengel; Dunn). Indeed, the Hellenists may have been the first tradents of the dominical tradition. However, it is very unrealistic to suppose that Paul would have been satisfied merely with knowing their teaching and attitude. Since he preached none other than Jesus Christ and God's saving work in him, he would have demanded to know that what the Hellenists claimed to represent about Jesus Christ and his teaching was accurate. For example, if Paul had heard the Hellenists justify their outreach to the Gentiles on the basis of Jesus' attitude to the outcasts, would he not have felt the urge to know how Jesus justified his attitude, especially since it would have been unacceptable to him in his preconversion days? For Paul, Jesus was no legendary ancient hero, but a contemporary of his who had been only recently crucified as a false messiah. Given this fact, it is impossible to think that Paul did not try to learn of Jesus, his life and teaching, more accurately from the primary witnesses like Peter as well as others from Jerusalem such as Barnabas,* Silvanus and John Mark. Nor is it easy to think that the close correspondences between the teaching and conduct of Jesus, and the teaching and conduct of Paul, could have come about if there was anything less than an earnest desire on Paul's part to learn of Jesus.

Therefore, we conclude that the remarkable similarities between Paul and Jesus in theology and attitude may be taken as evidence for Paul's intimate knowledge of Jesus' teaching and attitude. They must be counted then as Paul's reflections of Jesus' sayings, since it is chiefly by means of one's sayings that one's teaching is imparted. If Paul's theology, especially his doctrine of justification, closely represents Jesus' kingdom preaching, we must conclude that he knew it well, and this conclusion implies that he knew well

Jesus' sayings (including the parables) about the kingdom of God.

This consideration of the theological continuity between Jesus and Paul should tip the balance in favor of a positive judgment in the cases (like those considered in 2 above) where there is a dispute about a possible echo of a saying of Jesus in a Pauline statement. A thesis may now be submitted, one analogous to that of J. Jeremias on the question of authenticity of dominical logia in the Synoptics: *When in the Pauline letters an echo of a dominical logion is disputed, the burden of proof lies more heavily on those who would deny it, than on those who would accept it.*

### 4. Theological Loci and Sayings of Jesus.
The sayings of Jesus that we have discerned, whether they be allusions or echoes, are diverse and appear in various contexts of Paul's teaching. The majority of them, however, may be classified as connected with Paul's *ethical** and *eschatological teaching*. It is especially noteworthy that in a number of places Paul echoes the sayings of Jesus which are compiled by Matthew and Luke in the Sermon on the Mount/Plain. D. C. Allison infers from this that Paul knew an early collection of Jesus' logia now preserved in Luke 6:27-38, the central section of the Sermon on the Plain (cf. Mt 5:38-48; 7:12). Ascertaining Paul's "heavy dependence" on the pre-Synoptic eschatological traditions of Jesus, D. Wenham even uses the Pauline echoes as important pieces of evidence in elucidating the history of those Gospel traditions.

One of Paul's explicit references to Jesus' saying is about the apostolic privilege to "get their living by the gospel" (1 Cor 9:14; cf. 1 Thess 2:2-9; *see* Financial Support), and several of Paul's echoes of Jesus' sayings are concerned with *apostleship** and *mission** (Rom 15:8-9; 16:19; 1 Cor 4:1-5; 7:7; 2 Cor 12:12; Gal 1:12-16; 2:7-8; 1 Thess 4:8; etc.). Here one must consider also Paul's close "following" (or imitation*) of Jesus in his apostolic existence of deprivation, unmarried life, humble service and suffering, which, as argued above, implies his knowledge of Jesus' life and of his teaching about such a life. Clearly, as an apostle and missionary, Paul cherished his Lord's teaching on apostleship and mission and his example (cf. 1 Cor 11:1).

Since the words of Jesus at the Last Supper are explicitly referred to by Paul, their influence on Paul's doctrine of the *eucharist* (*see* Lord's Supper) needs no further substantiation. We have also seen some intimations of the influence of Jesus' teachings on the Temple and on marriage/divorce as well as his eucharistic sayings, as they shaped Paul's conception of the *church as the body of Christ.*

Now we turn to the question of whether Paul's christology* and soteriology also echo Jesus' teaching. N. Walter claims that precisely in "expounding the central content of his gospel, in making his important christological or soteriological statements . . . Paul adduces no Jesus-tradition" (Walter, 74). Moreover, he also maintains that "in expounding the gospel of Christ Paul shows no trace of the influence of the theologically central affirmations of Jesus' preaching, in particular of his characteristic 'Jesuanic' interpretation of the kingdom of God" (Walter, 63). Walter concludes that Paul was either not very familiar with Jesus' message or not able "to understand and assimilate these central ingredients of the Jesus-tradition" (Walter, 64).

However, this sort of statement can be made only by the "minimalists" who accept exclusively those few passages in Paul where there is an explicit reference to sayings of Jesus. But as we have seen, there is a strong continuity between Jesus' kingdom preaching and Paul's gospel of God's salvation through the death and resurrection of Jesus Christ and his interpretation of this salvation chiefly through the category of justification. We have tried to show that the replacement of kingdom by justification was not only expedient but also logically required. We have argued that this continuity or unity presupposes Paul's intimate knowledge of Jesus' kingdom preaching and Jesus' view of his own death. Otherwise we cannot explain the theological unity between Paul and Jesus.

In addition to this fundamental consideration, we may, *contra* Walter, point to Paul's references to the kingdom of God, which with similarities to Jesus' kingdom preaching are significant in themselves. We may also point to his citation of the eucharistic words of Jesus, which could hardly have failed to influence his soteriology; to his allusion to Jesus' *abba* address to God, which forms a basis of his Son* christology* and his adoption soteriology as well as his teaching on the testimony of the Spirit in Romans 8; to his use of the language of *paradidomai* ("to be given up," 1 Cor 4:10-11; Rom 4:25; 8:32; Gal 1:4; 2:20), which echoes Jesus' passion announcements; and to his christological and soteriological argument in 1 Corinthians 1:18—2:16, which is full of echoes of Jesus' shout of praise (Lk 10:21-24 par.) and passion. There is no space here to examine whether behind his *kyrios* christology, reconciliation and new creation soteriology, etc., there may not stand some concrete teachings of Jesus. However, enough has been shown to indicate that in his christological and soteriological statements also there are clear echoes of Jesus' teachings.

Certainly it is true that he does not cite any saying

of Jesus as a proof-text for his christological or soteriological statement. But except for 1 Corinthians 7:10-11 and 9:14, he does not use Jesus tradition in that manner for other kinds of theological statements either. In comparison with his ethical and eschatological teachings, Paul shows a greater freedom in interpreting Jesus' teaching as he incorporates it into his christology and soteriology, where he more frequently replaces Jesus' language with his own. This is quite understandable. Our earlier consideration (see 3 above) goes some way toward explaining the reason for this.

So in his christology and soteriology as well as in all the other areas of his theology, Paul echoes Jesus' sayings. That is, *Jesus' teaching provides Paul with a basis for his theology as a whole.*

**5. Narrative Tradition.**
According to N. Walter, there is "no hint that Paul knew of the narrative tradition about Jesus." But again this is a positivistic statement by a minimalist. With M. Hengel, one must realistically consider the *Sitz im Leben* of Paul's missionary preaching: "It was simply impossible in the antiquities to proclaim a man crucified a few years ago, as Kyrios, Son of God and Redeemer, without saying something about who this man was, what he taught and did, and why he died" (Hengel 1971, 34). This consideration should prevent interpreters from dealing cavalierly with various indications in Paul's letters of his knowledge of the narrative tradition about Jesus, simply because they are mere indications and not extended narratives of Jesus' life and deeds such as those found in the Gospels.

In Galatians 3:1 Paul reminds the Galatians of his having "portrayed Jesus Christ as crucified before your eyes" at his first preaching to them. In Galatians 6:17 and 2 Corinthians 4:10 he speaks of his apostolic life in terms of both carrying about the "marks [*stigmata*] of Jesus" in his body and the "putting to death [*nekrōsis*] of Jesus" in his body. Here his use of the name *Jesus* (instead of the more familiar "death of Christ [Jesus]") as well as the terms *stigmata* and *nekrōsis* clearly indicate his consideration of the concrete process of Jesus' crucifixion (Wolff). From this Kleinknecht rightly infers that Paul "must have had a certain visual image" of Jesus' death. We receive the same impressions from Philippians 3:10, where Paul speaks of his resolution to "participate in [Christ's] sufferings, being conformed to his death."

Further, we have already suggested that Paul's use of the *paradidomai* language (2 Cor 4:11; Rom 4:25; 8:32; Gal 2:20; cf. 1 Cor 11:23; Gal 1:4) indicates his knowledge of the passion tradition. 1 Corinthians 2:8

alludes to the Jewish and Roman rulers' crucifying Jesus, and Romans 15:3 probably refers to the "insults" Jesus suffered on the cross (cf. also 2 Cor 13:4). Of course, it would be most arbitrary if the direct and concrete data provided by 1 Corinthians 11:23-25 and 15:3-5 were excluded from consideration of Paul's knowledge of a version of the passion narrative on the ground that they are a liturgical and a kerygmatic formula (*pace* Walter). Walter tries to argue against this overwhelming evidence by granting that Paul "certainly knew something about the event of the passion of Jesus," but at the same time by denying "Paul's knowledge of the passion narrative in the (or a) pre-Synoptic version" (Walter, 63). But this distinction is quite arbitrary. If Paul knew something about the passion of Jesus, then he knew *a* version of the passion narrative. How could it have been otherwise?

Since Paul makes the death and resurrection of Jesus Christ the center of his preaching, it is natural that his allusions to the narrative tradition about Jesus would also be concentrated on the passion narrative. However, indications of his knowledge of other kinds of the narrative tradition are not lacking. Walter asserts again confidently that "Jesus' actions played no role" in Paul's picture of him, "and certainly not his actions as a performer of miracles." However, when Paul speaks of "the signs* of the apostle" in terms of "signs and wonders and mighty works" (2 Cor 12:12; Rom 15:18-19; Gal 3:5; 1 Cor 2:4; 1 Thess 1:5), he seems to reflect Jesus' word of apostolic commission (Mk 6:7-8 par.; cf. Mk 16:17-18). But does not the fact that he regards miracles as a sign of an apostle, as the representative and revealer of Jesus Christ, imply that he knows that Jesus demonstrated the salvation of the kingdom of God through his miracles? Does not precisely this knowledge stand behind Paul's summary description in Romans 15:18-19 of his apostolic ministry: "I will not venture to speak of anything except what *Christ* has wrought *through me* to bring about the obedience of the Gentiles, by word and deed, by the power of signs and wonders, by the power of the Spirit"? (cf. 1 Cor 2:4; 1 Thess 1:5). So Christ *is* a performer of miracles, and the miracles Paul the apostle has performed are in fact the works *of Christ* done *through him.* Unless Paul knew that Jesus was a miracle worker, how could he speak like this? (see below).

In fact, one of Paul's kingdom sayings (1 Cor 4:20) seems to betray his knowledge of Jesus' kingdom preaching as accompanied by miracles (cf. Lk 11:20 par.; G. Haufe). As Jesus actualized through miracles the salvation of the kingdom he preached, so also Paul, his apostle, has actualized through miracles the salvation of the gospel he has preached. But Paul did it in the name of his Lord Jesus Christ, and he was conscious that in this work of his the risen Lord Jesus Christ carried on his work of salvation as during his earthly ministry. Thus Paul reveals, though allusively, his knowledge of a narrative tradition about Jesus as a miracle worker.

Passages such as Romans 15:3, 8-9; 1 Corinthians 10:33—11:1; 2 Corinthians 4:5; 8:9; 10:1; Philippians 2:6-8 clearly reveal Paul's knowledge of Jesus' life as one of poverty and humble service.* The lists of qualities set forth for the Christian life in 1 Corinthians 13:4-7 and Galatians 5:22-23 are "character sketches" of Jesus (Dunn; Wedderburn). Paul exhorts Christians to "put on Christ" (Rom 13:14; Gal 3:27) and speaks of "imitating" him (1 Cor 11:1; 1 Thess 1:6). In these and other instances of his ethical instruction he often thinks of the *example* of Christ, and the exemplary "character of Jesus as Paul understood it is consistent with the character of Jesus as portrayed in the Gospels" (Bruce, 96; cf. also H. Schürmann).

To be sure, when Paul speaks of Christ's example of self-renunciation, service, love, humility, meekness, etc., he has in view not just Jesus' actions during his earthly days but his total existence from his pre-existence through the incarnation and the earthly life to his post-exaltation present status (*see* Christology). But the actions and character of Christ in his supra-historical existence are affirmed in the light of those of the earthly Jesus (or as Wedderburn, 188, puts it, they are "projections backwards and forwards of the patterns of action and the attitudes of the earthly Jesus"). It may be conceivable that without actually knowing anything about the life and character of the historical Jesus, Paul simply attributed those nice qualities to his "Christ." But, as noted above, the "remarkable correspondences" between Jesus and Paul in a life of suffering and humble service suggest that it is more realistic to think that having actually learned of the life and character of the historical Jesus, Paul as his apostle tried to imitate him. This is far more likely than that he gave himself up so totally to deprivation, service and persecution only for a figment of his own imagination (note well the use of the name "Jesus" in 2 Cor 4:5 as well as in 2 Cor 4:10; Gal 6:17). So we must assume on Paul's part an extensive knowledge of a narrative tradition of Jesus' life, ministry and character as standing behind those passages where Paul refers to Christ's example (though the term *example* as an example to be imitated* is debated; see Käsemann, Martin; *see* Hymns).

The continuity between Jesus' welcoming sinners and Paul's mission to the Gentiles also suggests Paul's knowledge of a narrative tradition about the former.

As argued above, this cannot be denied by appealing to a theory of the Hellenists' mediating this aspect of Jesus' ministry as a justification for their outreach to Gentiles. In fact, Romans 12:16b (cf. Rom 15:7) seems to indicate that Paul was conscious of the model character of Jesus' association with the humble (Käsemann 1980, 347; Thompson).

Finally, Romans 1:3-4; 9:5 and Galatians 4:4 (cf. also Gal 1:19: "James the brother of the Lord") hint that Paul would not have been totally ignorant of or uninterested in the family origin of Jesus.

### 6. Paucity and Allusive Character of References.

If our argument so far is sound, in the Pauline corpus there are a considerable number of references to or echoes of the sayings of Jesus and the narrative tradition about him. They are found in all the letters of Paul, and are connected with all the major themes of his theology. However, critics regularly comment that they are "strikingly" few. But the question of whether they are to be evaluated as many or few depends on the terms of comparison. Certainly they are strikingly few and indirect in comparison with Paul's references to the OT or to the habits of the contemporary rabbis and Hellenistic philosophers in their references to the teachings of their masters. However, as is often noted, in comparison to the references to the actions and teachings of Jesus in other NT writings, such as Acts, 1 Peter, the Johannine letters, and James, those in Paul's writings are by no means few.

A. J. M. Wedderburn (117-18) lists some issues in connection with which Paul might be expected to refer to Jesus' teaching but, in fact, he does not: (1) the controversies over observance of certain days (Gal 4:10; Rom 14:5-6); (2) the advice for the "virgins" (1 Cor 7:25-28; cf. Mt 19:10-12?); (3) the attitude toward the authorities (Rom 13:1-7); (4) the question about food* and table fellowship (Rom 14; 1 Cor 8—10; Gal 2:11-14; cf. Mk 7:15, 18-19 par.); and (5) the doctrine of salvation by grace* and not by works (cf., e.g., the parable of the workers in the vineyard, Mt 20:1-16).

However, it has already been argued (1) that in Romans 13:1-7 Paul does echo Jesus' teaching in Mark 12:17 and (2) that in Rom 14:14a, 20 he does allude to Jesus' saying in Mark 7:15, 19. In 1 Corinthians 8—10, he may have avoided referring to Jesus' saying in Mark 7 because the saying was known to the Corinthians and precisely its right interpretation was part of the controversy between the strong and the weak at Corinth. Similarly, in Galatians 2:11-14 Paul may also have been conscious of the different interpretation of the saying by the Jerusalemites as well as of the fact that he could hardly speak as authoritatively on the Jesus tradition as could Peter.

(3) It has been noted that in 1 Corinthians 7:7 Paul probably echoes the saying of Jesus recorded in Matthew 19:12. Then, when he regrets that he has "no command of the Lord concerning the virgins" in 1 Corinthians 7:25, he must have found Jesus' saying in Matthew 19:10-12 irrelevant to the "virgins."

(4) The reason why Paul did not cite the examples of Jesus' working on the Sabbath days in connection with the controversies over observance of certain holy days (*see* Holy Days) may be that he had already taught the Galatians about the real meaning of the Sabbath, citing Jesus' healings on Sabbath days as tokens of his eschatological fulfillment of its true intention (note Paul's reference to his previous "labor" for them in Gal 4:11) or, in the case of Romans 14:5-6, because he regards the Sabbath observance (like dietary observance) as an *adiaphoron* ("a matter of indifference"), so long as it is properly understood as fulfilled in Jesus and not elevated to a meritorious work for salvation.

(5) For us it would have been natural and most effective if he had cited Jesus' parables, such as that of the workers in the vineyard or the prodigal son (Lk 15), in support of his argument for the doctrine of salvation by grace and not by works. The reason he did not do it, however, lies probably in the more thorough interpretation and representation of Jesus' teaching that Paul gave in his own language—a necessity because of the christological and soteriological center of his gospel. Apparently, in his argument for the doctrine of salvation by grace, he judged it to be far more effective to refer to the actual revelation of God's grace in Christ's vicarious death than to refer to his parabolic teaching about it. Taking all of this into consideration it becomes evident that the number of places in which Paul fails to echo a saying of Jesus is, in fact, but few, and the instances are all naturally understandable.

Nevertheless, when one compares Paul's references to the OT Scriptures with the practices of the contemporary rabbis and philosophers as they referred to the words of their teachers, it becomes clear that Paul's references to the sayings of Jesus are incomparably few. Furthermore, while his references to the OT Scriptures are very often explicit and verbatim, although some are allusive, his references to the sayings of Jesus are mostly allusive, often hardly more than an echo and seldom verbatim.

Now the reason(s) for these phenomena must be found. Certainly the great reverence Paul shows for the "command" of the Lord in 1 Corinthians 7:10-11, distinguishing it from his own instruction, and his re-

gret in 1 Corinthians 7:25 not to have a "command" of the Lord for the "virgins" clearly indicate that his lack of interest in or reverence for the sayings of Jesus does not explain the phenomena.

Some try to explain this paucity in terms of a hypothesis in which Paul's opponents* play a significant role. Wedderburn suggests that Paul saw the teaching of Jesus largely held "in enemy hands" and misused in a legalistic way by his Judaizing opponents (Wedderburn, 100). As we have seen, this hypothesis may explain Paul's failure to refer to some sayings of Jesus (cf. Mk 7:15 par.) in a few exceptional cases like Galatians 2:11-14 or 1 Corinthians 8—10. But it is hardly adequate to explain the problem as a whole. H. W. Kuhn speculates that it is a result of Paul's using his theology of the cross to counter the two groups of his opponents at Corinth: one, the Jewish-Christian opponents who concentrated on a Q-type collection of Jesus' sayings, presenting him as a wisdom teacher, and the other, the "enthusiasts" who transmitted the miracle stories of Jesus, presenting him in the style of a Hellenistic "divine man" (*theios anēr*). But Kuhn is then left to explain Paul's reticence about Jesus tradition in his other letters. Why precisely in 1 Corinthians and only there does Paul cite explicitly the sayings of Jesus three times over and refer to the kingdom of God more frequently than in any of the other letters? Ultimately, the "opponents hypotheses" are inadequate for solving our problem.

The only viable solution seems to be one that starts by noticing that Paul's attitude to Jesus tradition is exactly in line with the general phenomenon observable in the NT writings outside the Gospels. Luke in Acts hardly ever refers to the Jesus traditions of his Gospel, and 1 John contains few references to the traditions found in the Gospel of John. In the other non-Pauline letters and Revelation the situation is the same. So the scarcity of Paul's explicit reference to Jesus tradition can hardly mean his lack of knowledge of or interest in it. In this vein B. Gerhardsson has argued that the concrete Jesus tradition was treated as an independent entity and transmitted separately as a unique tradition within the early church (Gerhardsson). This argument is persuasive when one observes the general phenomenon of the letters, Acts and Revelation in contrast with the Gospels. Explicit recountings of Jesus tradition are found only in the Gospels, and the Gospels contain only Jesus tradition. On the other hand James may be taken as an illustration of an early Christian author who works out many of his motifs, phrases and words from the Jesus tradition and yet does not cite sayings of Jesus.

It is also to be observed that like Acts 20:35, the only

case of citation of a saying of Jesus in Acts (an *agraphon*, i.e., not found in the Gospels), so also Paul's citation of Jesus' words in 1 Corinthians 11:23-25 has the character of reminding the Corinthian church of the words that they already know. There, using the Jewish technical terms for the faithful transmission of a tradition, *parelabon* (Heb *qbl*) and *paredōka* (Heb *mśr*), Paul indicates that he had faithfully transmitted the eucharistic tradition to the Corinthians. Similarly, in several other places Paul refers to the "tradition" he transmitted or taught to his churches (1 Cor 11:2; 15:3; Phil 4:9; Col 2:7; 1 Thess 4:1-2; 2 Thess 2:15; 3:6; cf. also Rom 6:17), and to the knowledge they already have about various teachings in the tradition (1 Cor 3:16; 5:6; 6:2, 3, 9, 15, 16, 19; 2 Cor 4:14; 5:1; Gal 2:16; 1 Thess 2:11-12; 3:3-4; 5:2; etc.). We have already seen that several of these passages echo sayings of Jesus.

So it is very probable that his initial preaching at each place included a separate transmission of Jesus tradition (the Antiochian tradition?) as well as the christological and soteriological exposition of the Christ-event and paraenesis based both on the Christ-event and Jesus tradition. Then, in his letters to his converts to whom he had already delivered Jesus tradition, Paul did not have to transmit it again. He needed only to refer to it, if necessary.

Thus the fundamental reason why in Paul's letters, as well as in other NT writings outside the Gospels, the references are fewer in number and more allusive in nature than we might expect may well be that Paul and the other representatives of the early church treated Jesus tradition *separately* as a unique and sacred tradition.

Nevertheless we could imagine that Paul's references to Jesus' teaching would have been more numerous and would have taken the form of an exact citation, had he used it in his argument to *prove* the truth of his gospel or of his paraenesis. But Paul bases his argument for the truth of his gospel on the Christ-event, that is, not on Jesus' teaching but on the *Christ-act*, which is the fulfillment of the promise contained in his teaching (see above). For Paul, Jesus is significant primarily not as a teacher but as the *Christ\** who died and rose again (*see* Resurrection) for the salvation of humankind! Hence the meaning of Jesus as the risen Lord for Paul is essentially and fundamentally different from that of a rabbinic or a philosophic teacher for his pupil. Therefore the manner in which Paul refers to Jesus' teaching in his letters cannot be compared to that of a rabbi's or a philosopher's references to their teacher in the rabbinic or philosophical tractates.

Considering the realistic logic of Hengel's statement cited above, we can well imagine that in his initial preaching at each place, Paul expounded the meaning of the death (and resurrection) of Jesus Christ in relation to Jesus' teaching, which Paul transmitted separately, indicating how the former had fulfilled the promise contained in the latter. In his letters he did not need to repeat this. Since his opponents were not denying the character of Jesus' death as the eschatological atonement or as the accomplishment of salvation promised in Jesus' teaching, Paul was not required to cite elements of Jesus' teaching to prove these points. The "Judaizers" in Antioch, Galatia,\* Philippi\* and elsewhere, took issue with him only because of their insistence that the Gentiles must receive circumcision and take upon themselves the yoke of the Law of the covenant in order to avail themselves of the salvation effected by the death and resurrection of Jesus Christ, the fulfillment of the old covenant. The "enthusiasts" in Corinth irritated Paul with their misunderstanding of the gospel, interpreting it in terms of Hellenistic wisdom and with their over-confident belief that they had already obtained full salvation.

Paul would have found few concrete sayings of Jesus that were directly relevant to his struggle against the "Judaizers" and the "enthusiasts" in his Gentile\* churches. For Jesus it had been largely a case of welcoming Israelite "sinners," not Gentiles, to table fellowship as a token of their entry into the kingdom of God. So instead of *citing* any concrete saying of Jesus, he concentrated on expounding the full significance of Jesus' death for his people (its vicarious character), guided by the general spirit of Jesus' teaching (hence the theological continuity between Jesus and Paul), in order to prove the truth of his gospel of *sola gratia* and *sola fide*, or that of his theology of the cross against a theology of glory (*see* Cross). He backed up his arguments with citations of the Scriptures, which he had come to understand anew in light of the Christ-event.

In paraenesis, unlike in theological argument, one normally does not *prove* the truth of one's teaching, and so is not required to cite its sources. So, as an apostle of Christ who had the mind of Christ (1 Cor 2:16) and spoke under the inspiration of his Spirit (1 Cor 7:40), Paul usually imparted his authoritative apostolic teaching. However, when he was conscious of the opinions or attitudes contrary to his own teachings, he *did* refer or allude to Jesus' teachings in order to support his apostolic teachings with the Lord's authority. Romans 14:14; 1 Corinthians 7:10-11; 9:14; Galatians 5:14 (+ 6:2) and other passages (discussed in 1 above) well illustrate this point. With Paul's eschatological teaching also a similar phenomenon is observable, and 1 Thessalonians 4:15-17; 5:1-7 illustrate this. Thus, Paul *did* use Jesus' sayings in support of his own teaching when he found himself in the situation where he had to *prove* its veracity. In the usual situations, however, he did not need to make any *explicit citation* of the sayings of Jesus. Nevertheless, since as an apostle he had to represent his Lord's teaching, he *re*-presented it in his own language, sometimes alluding to or echoing some of his concrete sayings. This *re*-presentation was necessary in order to make Jesus' teaching more suitable to Paul's changed, post-Easter situation (Goppelt, 42-46), or to his audience in the Hellenistic world. Furthermore, it is to be noted that even in paraenesis he tends to concentrate on the cross and resurrection of Christ as a motivating force rather than on his concrete sayings and deeds. About this, Thompson puts it well: "Why should Paul point to an act [or a command—we may add] of love, humility, or compassion during Jesus' ministry when he could cite his example of total commitment on the cross? Why should he cite a healing act of power, when he could refer to the resurrection? Everything Jesus said and did before his death and vindication paled in significance by comparison to the Christ-Event."

Thus, *the "paucity" and allusive character of Paul's references to Jesus' sayings turn out, partly, to have been necessitated by Paul's living in the post-Easter period, and partly to have been natural. In any case they turn out to be quite understandable. They should no longer be used as evidence for Paul's lack of knowledge of or interest in the Jesus tradition or in the historical Jesus.*

### 7. Summary and Conclusion.

We have ascertained over twenty-five instances where Paul certainly or probably makes reference or allusion to a saying of Jesus. In addition, we have tabulated over forty possible echoes of a saying of Jesus. These are distributed throughout all of the Pauline letters, though 1 Corinthians and Romans contain the most.

There is a real continuity between Jesus' teaching centered around the kingdom of God and Paul's theology as a whole. The replacement of Jesus' gospel of the kingdom with the apostolic gospel of the death and resurrection of Jesus Christ was logically necessitated by the salvation promised in Jesus' kingdom preaching being realized in his death and resurrection. In Paul's central soteriological category of justification, he accurately expressed the intention of Jesus' gospel of the kingdom. The theological continuity between Jesus and Paul is further supported by Paul's concrete echoes of the "kingdom of God" and "*abba*," of his teachings on the Law, the Temple and escha-

tology, of his welcoming sinners, and of other aspects of his attitude and conduct such as renunciation of privilege and humble service.

The close similarities between Jesus and Paul in theology and attitude may be taken as evidence of Paul's intimate knowledge of Jesus' teaching and attitude. This consideration should incline interpreters toward a more positive judgment in those cases where there is a dispute over the presence of an echo of a saying of Jesus, placing the burden of proof more heavily on those who would deny it than on those who would accept it.

Echoes of Jesus' sayings are discernible in all the major themes of Paul's theology. His christology and soteriology are conditioned by Jesus' teaching as much as his other theological *loci*, leading to the conclusion that Jesus' teaching provides Paul with a basis for his theology as a whole.

Paul also provides hints of his knowledge of the narrative tradition of Jesus' passion, his healing ministry, his welcoming sinners, his life of poverty and humble service, his character and other aspects.

The number of contexts in which Paul fails to refer to a saying of Jesus against our expectation is in fact few and explainable. Nevertheless, the fact that Paul's references to Jesus' sayings are not numerous and they are all allusive, a characteristic shared by other NT writings outside the Gospels, requires an explanation. Paul, like the other NT writers, probably treated Jesus tradition as an independent entity and transmitted it separately to his churches at their foundation (cf. Gerhardsson). However, for Paul, as for the post-Easter church as a whole, Jesus was significant primarily not as a teacher but as the Christ who had died and risen. Hence Paul concentrated on the Christ event. He cannot be compared to a rabbi or a Hellenistic philosopher who diligently cites his teacher.

In his letters Paul was called upon not to prove the character of Jesus' death as the fulfillment of Jesus' ministry, but the availability of that salvation to Gentiles apart from works of the Law. So Paul did not need to cite Jesus' kingdom preaching to prove its fulfillment in his death and he would have found few concrete sayings from the Jewish context of Jesus' ministry that were directly relevant to his conflict with Judaizers and enthusiasts in his Gentile churches. Paul, therefore, concentrated on expounding the full significance of Jesus' death, guided by the general spirit of Jesus' teaching, in order to prove the truth of his gospel of the cross, *sola gratia* and *sola fide*.

In paraenesis and eschatology, in order to support his teaching with the Lord's authority in the face of a contrary opinion, Paul occasionally referred explicitly to Jesus' sayings. But usually he did not need to *prove* the truth of his teaching. As an apostle of Christ who had the mind of Christ and spoke under the inspiration of his Spirit, he could simply impart his authoritative apostolic teaching. In this he seldom cited Jesus' sayings explicitly, but *re-presented* them, echoing them in his own language. Although he shows a great reverence for Jesus' sayings and shapes his theology as a whole according to them, he does not use them in a literalistic or legalistic way, but adapts them to the new post-Easter situations and to his Hellenistic audiences, modifying their letter while respecting their spirit.

Against this background the "paucity" and allusive character of Paul's references to Jesus' sayings should no longer be used as evidence for Paul's reputed lack of knowledge of or interest in the Jesus tradition or in the historical Jesus. On the contrary, we are led to search for echoes of Jesus' sayings woven into Paul's statements. Once these echoes as well Paul's allusions to Jesus' sayings are established, we can study in detail the actual method by which Paul used them (cf. Gundry; Ellis) and their relationship to the history of the Synoptic tradition (cf. Dungan; Allison; Kuhn; esp. Wenham).

*See also* CHRISTOLOGY; ESCHATOLOGY; JESUS AND PAUL; JUSTIFICATION; KINGDOM OF GOD/CHRIST; LAW; LORD'S SUPPER; RESTORATION OF ISRAEL; RESURRECTION; RIGHTEOUSNESS/RIGHTEOUSNESS OF GOD.

BIBLIOGRAPHY. D. C. Allison, "The Pauline Epistles and the Synoptic Gospels: the Pattern of the Parallels," *NTS* 28 (1982) 1-32; F. F. Bruce, *Paul: Apostle of the Heart Set Free* (Grand Rapids: Eerdmans, 1977) 95-112; C. E. B. Cranfield, *A Critical and Exegetical Commentary on the Epistle to the Romans*, Vol. 2 (ICC; Edinburgh: T. & T. Clark, 1979); N. Dahl, "The Doctrine of Justification: Its Social Function and Implications," in *Studies in Paul: Theology for the Early Christian Mission* (Minneapolis: Augsburg, 1977) 95-120; D. L. Dungan, *The Sayings of Jesus in the Churches of Paul* (Philadelphia: Fortress, 1971); J. D. G. Dunn, "Mark 2.1—3.6: A Bridge between Jesus and Paul on the Question of the Law," in *Jesus, Paul and the Law* (Louisville: Westminster/John Knox, 1990) 10-31; E. E. Ellis, "Traditions in 1 Corinthians," *NTS* 32 (1982) 481-502; B. Gerhardsson, "The Path of the Gospel Tradition," in *The Gospel and the Gospels*, ed. P. Stuhlmacher (Grand Rapids: Eerdmans, 1991) 75-96; L. Goppelt, *Theology of the New Testament*, Vol 2 (Grand Rapids: Eerdmans, 1982); R. H. Gundry, "The Hellenization of Dominical Tradition and Christianization of Jewish Tradition in the Eschatology of 1-2 Thessalonians," *NTS* 33 (1987) 161-78; G. Haufe, "Reich Gottes bei Paulus und in der Jesustradition," *NTS* 31 (1985) 467-72; M. Hengel, "Between Jesus and Paul: The 'Hellenists', the 'Seven' and Stephen (Acts 6.1-15; 7.54-8.3)," in *Between Jesus and Paul* (Philadelphia: Fortress, 1983) 1-29; idem, "Der Ursprünge der christliche Mission," *NTS* 18 (1971) 15-38 (= "The Origins of the Christian Mission," in *Between Jesus and Paul* [Philadelphia: Fortress, 1983] 48-64); T. Holtz, "Tradition im 1. Thessalonicherbrief," in *Die Mitte des NT*, ed. U. Luz and H. Weder (Göttingen: Vandenhoeck & Ruprecht, 1983); E. Jüngel, *Paulus und Jesus: eine Untersuchung zur Präzisierung der Frage nach dem Ursprung der Christologie* (HUT 2; Tübingen: J. C. B. Mohr, 1962); E. Käsemann, *Commentary on Romans* (Grand Rapids: Eerdmans, 1980); idem, "A Critical Analysis of Philippians 2:5-11," in *God and Christ* (New York: Harper & Row, 1968) 45-88; S. Kim, "Jesus—the Son of God, the Stone, the Son of Man and the Servant: the Role of Zechariah in the Self-Identification of Jesus," in *Tradition and Interpretation*, FS E. E. Ellis, ed. G. F. Hawthorne with O. Betz (Grand Rapids: Eerdmans, 1987) 134-48; idem, "Jesus' Kingdom Preaching and Christian Politics," [in Korean] *Presbyterian Theological Quarterly* 222 (1989) 6-49; K. T. Kleinknecht, *Der leidende Gerechtfertigte: die alttestamentlich-jüdische Tradition vom 'leidenden Gerechten' und ihre Rezeption bei Paulus* (WUNT 2.13; Tübingen: J. C. B. Mohr, 1984); H. W. Kuhn, "Der irdische Jesus bei Paulus als traditionsgeschichtliches und theologisches Problem," *ZTK* 67 (1970) 295-320; R. P. Martin, *Carmen Christi: Philippians ii.5-11 in Recent Interpretation and in the Setting of Early Christian Worship* (SNTSMS 4; Cambridge: University Press, 1967); H. Merkel, "Die Gottesherrschaft in der Verkündigung Jesu," *Königsherrschaft Gottes und himmlischer Kult*, ed. M. Hengel and A. M. Schwemer (Tübingen: J. C. B. Mohr, 1991); F. Neirynck, "Paul and the Sayings of Jesus," in *Apôtre Paul*, ed. A. Vanhoye (Leuven, 1986) 265-321; J. Piper, *'Love Your Enemies': Jesus' Love Command in the Synoptic Gospels and the Early Christian Paraenesis* (SNTSMS 38; Cambridge: University Press, 1979); H. Räisänen, "Zur Herkunft von Markus 7,15," in *The Torah and Christ* (Helsinki: Finnish Exegetical Society, 1986) 209-18; P. Richardson, "The Thunderbolt in Q and the Wise Man in Corinth," in *From Jesus to Paul: Studies in Honour of F. W. Beare* (Waterloo: W. Laurier University, 1984) 91-111; P. Richardson and P. Gooch, "Logia of Jesus in 1 Corinthians," in *Gospels Perspectives 5: The Jesus Tradition Outside the Gospels*, ed. D. Wenham (Sheffield: JSOT, 1985) 39-62; H. Schürmann, " 'Das Gesetz des Christus' (Gal 6,2): Jesu Verhalten und Wort als letztgültige sittliche Norm nach Paulus," in *Neues Testament und Kirche*, ed. J. Gnilka (Freiburg: Herder, 1974) 282-300; P. Stuhlmacher, "Jesustradition im Romerbrief?," *Theologische Beiträge* 14 (1983) 240-50; E. Schweizer, "1.Korinther 15, 20-28 als Zeugnis paulinischer Eschatologie und ihrer Verwandtschaft mit der Verkündigung Jesu," in *Jesus und Paulus,* ed. E. E. Ellis and E. Grässer (Göttingen: Vandenhoeck & Ruprecht, 1975) 301-14; M. Thompson, *Clothed with Christ* (JSNTSS 59; Sheffield: JSOT, 1991); N. Walter, "Paul and the Early Christian Jesus-Tradition," in *Paul and Jesus,* ed. A. J. M. Wedderburn and C. Wolff (JSNTSS 37; Sheffield: JSOT, 1989) 51-80; A. J. M. Wedderburn, "Paul and Jesus: the Problem of Continuity," in *Paul and Jesus,* ed. A. J. M. Wedderburn and C. Wolff (JSNTSS 37; Sheffield: JSOT, 1989) 99-115; idem, "Paul and Jesus: Similarity and Continuity," in *Paul and Jesus,* ed. A. J. M. Wedderburn and C. Wolff (JSNTSS 37; Sheffield: JSOT, 1989) 117-43; D. Wenham, "Paul's Use of the Jesus Tradition: Three Samples," in *Gospel Perspectives 5: The Jesus Tradition Outside the Gospels,* ed. D. Wenham (Sheffield: JSOT, 1985) 7-37; idem, *Gospel Perspectives 4: The Rediscovery of Jesus' Eschatological Discourse* (Sheffield: JSOT, 1984); C. Wolff, "Humility and Self-Denial in Jesus' Life and Message and in the Apostolic Existence of Paul," in *Paul and Jesus,* ed. A. J. M. Wedderburn and C. Wolff (JSNTSS 37; Sheffield: JSOT, 1989) 145-60.

S. Kim

# JESUS AND PAUL

The relationship between Jesus and Paul poses a historical question with huge theological ramifications. Is Paul's theology in harmony and continuity with the teaching and ministry of Jesus, or is there an unbridgeable gulf between them? It is generally held that, if it is to merit the title "Christian," the Christian religion must be recognizably continuous with Jesus' message and the impact of his activity. Yet, both at a popular and at a scholarly level, many would argue that Paul, our earliest Christian witness, departed significantly from the message of Jesus and introduced an alien system of theology. This raises many important historical questions; but, since Paul has been so influential in later Christianity, it also constitutes a major theological challenge.

1. History of the Debate
2. The Teaching of Jesus in Paul
3. The Life of Jesus and His Example
4. Letters and Missionary Preaching
5. Revelation and Tradition
6. The Kingdom of God
7. Israel and the Law
8. Sinners, Outsiders and the Mercy of God
9. Suffering, the Cross and Vindication
10. Continuity and Development

## 1. History of the Debate.

### 1.1. Before 1914.

#### 1.1.1. Ferdinand Christian Baur.
When F. C. Baur opened the modern era of Pauline studies in the nineteenth century, he argued that rigorous historical analysis of the NT indicated that there were significant differences among the various branches of the early Christian church. In particular he emphasized the differences between Paul on the one hand and the Jerusalem* apostles and Palestinian churches on the other. The latter were more influenced by, and more faithful to, the original teaching of Jesus while Paul was consciously independent of such traditions and differed widely from the teaching of Jesus, particularly in his christology* and in relation to the validity of the Law.*

The questions raised by this thesis were discussed in various forms but became the center of an extremely lively debate in the twenty years preceding the First World War. The "Jesus and Paul" question became in these years a focal point of discussion both at an academic and at a popular level, as a number of scholars in Germany and France (H. H. Wendt, M. Goguel, M. Brückner, P. Wernle) suggested that there was a very significant gulf between the teaching of Jesus and the theology of Paul. Some also argued that, for all his organizational and intellectual gifts, Paul should not be allowed to obscure the essential religious truths expressed by Jesus. "Back from Paul to Jesus" became the slogan of such radical critics. Such views were highly alarming both to traditional believers and to liberal Protestant theologians whose theological commitments depended on a synthesis of the teaching of Jesus and Paul.

#### 1.1.2. William Wrede.
This controversy became most sharply focused through the publication in 1904 of W. Wrede's *Paul*, a popular book, brilliantly composed and presenting the radical position with provocative force. Wrede argued that Paul's theology represented a religion of redemption whose centerpiece is the notion of a superhuman being (the Son of God) entering the world in order to break the hold of the powers which keep it in slavery. This theological structure, a system of ideas which he inherited preformed from apocalyptic* Judaism, Paul merged with the story of the death (*see* Crucifixion) and resurrection* of Jesus. What was significant both in Paul's own religious experience and in his system of thought was not the life and teaching of Jesus but only the fact that Jesus was a man, that he died and was raised. Thus, as representative of humanity, Christ* effected an "objective" salvation,* now mediated to those who believe these dogmas and take part in the sacraments.

Wrede insisted that this thought structure was entirely alien to current theological emphases on individual piety and, more particularly, was in a different world altogether from the simple prophetic style of Jesus and the pure moral truths he had so memorably pronounced. Paul's conversion had been through an encounter with the risen Christ, not the earthly Jesus, and indeed, he was only able to describe Christ as a divine figure because he had not known Jesus. For all the points on which Paul and Jesus might agree, and however much Paul may have known about the teaching of Jesus, Paul was not deeply influenced either by the personality of Jesus or by the spirit of his thought. In all important respects, the theological system basic to Paul's thought was worlds apart from Jesus. Thus Wrede reached his oft-quoted conclusion that "Paul is to be regarded as the second founder of Christianity" (Wrede, 179). While Paul rescued the Christian faith from "pining away as a Jewish sect" he did so only by transforming it. One can readily appreciate the theological dynamite packed into this conclusion. The dilemma which it poses for Christian theology is encapsulated in Wrede's observation that "this second founder of Christianity has even, compared with the first, exercised beyond all doubt the stronger—not the better—influence" (Wrede, 180).

*1.1.3. Response to Wrede.* The response to Wrede and to similar radical views was vigorous, both from liberal Protestant theologians in Germany (A. von Harnack, A. Jülicher, A. Resch) and from more conservative voices in the English-speaking world (J. Moffatt, C. A. A. Scott, J. G. Machen). Among the common lines of defense were the following: (1) Paul knew a lot more of the teaching of Jesus than we are inclined to acknowledge and alludes to it often, even if he quotes it rarely. (2) Although Paul rarely refers to the life of Jesus in his letters, the salient facts and even the personality of Jesus must have figured largely in his initial missionary preaching. (3) The supposed gulf between Jesus and Paul in matters of theology has been greatly exaggerated; for instance, Jesus' attitude to the Law was, in his own way, just as critical as Paul's and the implicit christology in his claims is not that far distant from the explicit divine titles and roles accorded him by Paul. (4) In many aspects of their theology Jesus and Paul were entirely at one, for instance, in their doctrine of the fatherly love* of God,* in their perception of eschatology* and in their ethics.* It could be argued that these were the kernel of the Christian religion and that any remaining differences were on merely peripheral matters. (5) It was argued by some that even if Paul's theology was different from that of Jesus, in his religious experience he was

at one with the spirit of Christ and showed clear signs of the influence of the personality of Jesus. (6) Finally, a variety of explanations could be put forward for the difference of atmosphere between the Gospels and the Pauline letters: Paul's rabbinic training (*see* Jew, Paul the), his different personal experience, the needs of the Gentile* mission* and of the battle against Judaizers,* as well as the obvious fact that Paul inevitably views Christ from, as it were, the other side of the cross and resurrection. All these were appealed to as factors of purely external significance, not materially affecting the substance of the inner unity between Paul and Jesus.

By such means there was mounted a strenuous rebuttal of the notion of Paul as "second founder" of Christianity and any implication that he had perverted or substantially altered the gospel announced by Jesus. In the kernel of their thought, Jesus and Paul are in harmony and any development from Jesus to Paul constitutes no more than legitimate interpretation and explication.

*1.1.4. Wilhelm Heitmüller and Albert Schweitzer.* Just before the interruption caused by the First World War, two further contributions heralded important aspects of the debate in its next phases. In 1912 W. Heitmüller probed the question of the Christian sources of influence on Paul's thinking. Whereas previously Paul had been treated largely as an isolated figure, or as drawing what information he had about Jesus from the primitive Palestinian communities, Heitmüller drew attention to the Hellenistic Christian circles in which Paul was nurtured as a Christian, and suggested that his relative neglect of the words and deeds of Jesus was not just an idiosyncrasy but was characteristic of the Hellenized forms of the Christian movement. This not only reinforced those in the history-of-religions school who argued that the really decisive influences on Paul's thought came not from Judaism but from Hellenistic culture. It also pinpointed an important issue in the historical question of continuity between Jesus and Paul: if the Hellenized wing of the early Christian movement already put more emphasis on the risen Lord* than the earthly teacher, the problem cannot simply be framed as "Jesus and Paul" but must incorporate study of this third shadowy entity, "Hellenistic Christianity."

By contrast, in his survey of Pauline scholarship, *Paul and his Interpreters* (1911), A. Schweitzer supported those who discerned the influence of Jewish apocalyptic on Paul. His interpretation of Paul's theology as molded by eschatological "mysticism" was not published until many years later (*The Mysticism of Paul the Apostle,* 1930), but already in his earlier survey it is clear that he considered Paul's thought to be fully explicable from its parallels in Jewish apocalyptic sources. The significance of this is that in his famous *Quest of the Historical Jesus* (1906) Schweitzer had demolished all the liberal attempts to write a biography of Jesus and had presented Jesus not as the spokesperson for liberal piety and morality but as an apocalyptic prophet working within a rigorous apocalyptic timetable. Schweitzer thus suggested a quite different solution to the "Jesus and Paul" question. Instead of the gulf between the liberal Jesus and a Hellenized (or an apocalyptic) Paul, Schweitzer suggested a relatively easy transition from the apocalyptic Jesus to an apocalyptic Paul, separated only by the fact that the eschatological events, to which Jesus had looked forward, Paul now saw as having at least begun in the resurrection of the Messiah.

*1.1.5. Which Jesus and Which Paul?* These contributions at the end of this period of fierce controversy serve to highlight one of its essential underlying problems. In any comparison between Jesus and Paul and any attempt to suggest continuities or correspondences between them, everything will depend on which Jesus is being compared with which Paul. Critical questions about the validity of the gospel material as evidence for the historical Jesus continued to be discussed (the majority discounted John but put confidence in Mark's Gospel); yet most of the participants in the mainstream of this debate took it as axiomatic that the real Jesus was the Jesus of liberal theology, who preached simple but profound moral truths, and highlighted in particular the "fatherhood" of God, the "brotherhood" of all humanity and the infinite value of the human soul. The essence of Christianity (and of religion in general) was contained in Jesus' call for the trusting devotion of the human soul in its God. With this Jesus on one side of the equation, it was simply a matter of arguing whether Paul, in his religion or his theology, had substantially altered or appropriately developed this essential religious vision. When Schweitzer (and J. Weiss) began to shake the foundations of the liberal picture of the historical Jesus, new possibilities for understanding the relationship between Jesus and Paul began to open up.

*1.2. Rudolf Bultmann.* In the next phase of the discussion, from the First World War to the 1950s, R. Bultmann's contributions were of decisive importance. As a major participant in the post-war theological backlash against liberal theology, he moved the debate forward in several significant ways, both in his multifarious individual works on Jesus and Paul and in two seminal essays specifically on the "Jesus and Paul" question.

*1.2.1. Bultmann's Jesus.* Bultmann shared Schweitzer's perception of Jesus as an apocalyptic preacher, who proclaimed the imminent arrival of the kingdom of God. In his form-critical work on the Gospels Bultmann cast doubt on the historicity of much of the material, arguing that the Gospel accounts had been heavily influenced by the faith of the church in the period of oral transmission, as well as by the interests of the individual Gospel writers. This made it impossible, in his view, to reconstruct a convincing portrait of the personality of Jesus or the sequence of events in his life. But (contrary to popular opinion) Bultmann was still confident that he could draw the main contours of the message of Jesus; and that proclamation he saw as decisively molded by an eschatological outlook. The kingdom of God was not a matter of God's rule in the soul (Harnack) but described the moment when God would bring the corrupt world to an end. Jesus thus portrayed God in radical terms as creator and judge and his apocalyptic language could not be dismissed as mere "husk"; thus "whoever finds Paul offensive and uncanny must find Jesus equally so!" (Bultmann 1936, 194).

*1.2.2. Material Congruity with Paul.* In his interpretation of the proclamation of Jesus, Bultmann broke decisively with the liberal emphasis on ethics and on Jesus as a teacher of timeless and universal truths. In probing the meaning of Jesus' eschatological message, and the human situation portrayed in it, Bultmann saw Jesus as issuing a summons, a call to radical obedience. He took Jesus' critique of the Pharisees to represent an attack on any "legalism" which required only partial or external obedience. In his absolute demands Jesus calls for the total dedication of the self to the will of God as the individual surrenders his/her previous self-satisfaction. Moreover, he saw here a real point of correspondence with Paul's theology. At the center of Paul's critique of the Law and in his theology of the cross (*see* Cross, Theology of the), Bultmann saw a penetrating attack on Jewish legalism and on any attempt to secure salvation from purely human resources. "The real sin of man is that he himself takes his will and his life into his own hands, makes himself secure and so has his self-confidence, his 'boast.' " (Bultmann 1929, 228). Thus, with interpretive insights derived from existential philosophy, Bultmann detected a material (*sachliche*) congruity between Jesus and Paul in their understanding of the human condition, even though Paul's theology was more theoretically explicated than that of Jesus. Even in christology Bultmann saw some element of similarity, since Jesus, although he "did not demand faith in his own person, did demand faith in his word. That is, he made his appearance in the consciousness that God had sent him in the last hour of the world" (Bultmann 1936, 195). It was thus inevitable that the proclaimer should become the proclaimed. The only difference (though it is significant) is that what Jesus proclaimed as an imminent act of God, Paul preached as an accomplished work of salvation.

*1.2.3. Historical Continuity?* Bultmann made an extremely important distinction between two aspects of the "Jesus and Paul" debate. It is one question to ask what correspondence there may be between the proclamation of Jesus and the preaching of Paul; it is quite another to inquire if Paul was, either directly or indirectly, influenced by the teaching of Jesus. In regard to this latter question Bultmann saw very little historical connection between Jesus and Paul. He emphasized how little Paul quotes of the words of Jesus and that, even if one allows for all possible allusions, they affect only Paul's ethics*: "it is most obvious that he does not appeal to the words of the Lord in support of his strictly theological, anthropological and soteriological views" in which are contained "the essentially Pauline conceptions" (Bultmann 1929, 223). In such respects Paul is not dependent on Jesus, and "Jesus' teaching is—at least in essentials—irrelevant for Paul." Thus while he saw some important elements of theological congruity between the proclamation of Jesus and the kerygma of Paul, Bultmann found very little by way of historical continuity between them.

*1.2.4. The Historical Jesus and the Kerygma.* Bultmann's treatment of our theme also made one further significant contribution. He took the "Jesus and Paul" question to be representative of a wider theological issue, namely, the relationship between the historical Jesus and the preaching of the church. This issue had been vigorously pressed back in 1892 in M. Kähler's protest against the liberal lives of Jesus—that they attempted to substitute for the Christ of the church's faith a pale, historically uncertain and theologically irrelevant Jesus of history. As a "theologian of the word" Bultmann shared Kähler's conviction that the Reformation principle of "justification by faith" should be applied to theological method: theological truths could never be validated by the limited and insecure results of historical research but were secured by faith alone. Christian theology therefore could never confine itself to, or even take its starting point from, scholars' tentative reconstructions of the historical Jesus. The starting point is always the kerygma—that the crucified Christ was raised from the dead and is to be acknowledged as Lord (*see* Preaching, Kerygma).

Bultmann's interpretation of the NT gave strong support to this theology. In particular he argued that the lack of reference in Paul to the life and teaching of Jesus indicated that the only thing concerning the historical Jesus which was significant for the church's preaching and faith was that Jesus, the crucified one, was a historical fact: everything else that was important about him theologically (e.g., that he died for us, that he was the pre-existent* Son of God [*see* Son of God] and that he is Lord*) was established by the resurrection and by the preaching of the church, not by the facts and events of Jesus' historical life. The significance of the historical Jesus for faith was simply that he lived (*Dass*), not how he lived (*Was*). In Paul's theology "one does not acquire knowledge about the Messiah: one either acknowledges him or repudiates him" (Bultmann 1929, 236). If Jesus is teacher or example, that is only as he is already acknowledged as Lord—"it is not the exemplary character of the historical Jesus that makes him Lord" (Bultmann 1929, 239). Thus Bultmann considered the radical cry—"Back from Paul to Jesus"—theologically dubious. "All that one can do is to go to Jesus through Paul: i.e., one is asked by Paul whether he is willing to understand God's act in Christ as the event that has decided and now decides with respect both to the world and to us" (Bultmann 1936, 201).

*1.2.5. Bultmann's Significance.* In this way Bultmann tackled the question of "Jesus and Paul" not merely at the historical level (how much was Paul actually informed about, or influenced by, or in agreement with Jesus) but also in the context of the larger theological issue of the relationship between the historical Jesus and Christian faith. It is the massive significance of this theological question, and the radical way it was posed and answered by Bultmann, which made his contributions to the debate so important.

It is worth emphasizing also the value of his distinction between historical continuity between Jesus and Paul and theological congruity. Much of the discussion of the "Jesus and Paul" issue before Bultmann had confused these two matters, and some debate since has failed to heed his distinction. It has been easily assumed, for instance, that if agreements in motif or vocabulary between Jesus and Paul can be found which suggest some lines of continuity (e.g., that Paul drew on traditions of the teaching of Jesus in ethics or eschatology), that in itself is proof of close correspondence in their theological perspectives. As NT scholars have learned from many other areas of study, even if parallels are found between two sources, and even if those parallels represent dependence by one upon the other (they sometimes do not), these can be no more than surface phenomena which mask deep differences in the underlying structure of thought. Conversely, as Bultmann himself argued, significant congruity between the thought of Jesus and Paul need not imply continuity in the simple historical sense of traditions about Jesus being passed on to, and received by, Paul. One could still press a historical question as to how such remarkable congruity came about (Bultmann never addresses this), and it would be unwise to separate totally the questions of continuity and congruity. But there is nonetheless considerable value in recognizing the distinction between them.

**1.3. From the 1950s to the Present Day.** Bultmann's dominant position in German NT scholarship had the effect of depressing interest in the historical Jesus. Historically he cast doubt on our ability to recover anything like a rounded picture of the Jesus of history and theologically he considered that, in any case, the results would be largely irrelevant as far as the kerygma was concerned. But when he emphasized these points in a lecture in 1960 he was obliged to defend his position against a contrary trend already gaining ground even among his own pupils. The tide had begun to turn, and it was bound to bring in with it a renewed interest in the old question of Jesus and Paul.

**1.3.1. Joachim Jeremias.** From the 1930s onward, resolutely independent of the Bultmannian school, J. Jeremias had been pursuing fresh and highly successful research on the historical Jesus. He believed that it was possible to recover the central facts about Jesus and even, in some cases, his *ipsissima verba* ("very words"); he also considered that the Jesus thus recovered was, in his consciousness of his status (as seen in the distinctive *Abba*), in his break with the Law and in his redemptive interpretation of his death, entirely at one with later Christian preaching about him. In particular, Jeremias detected a crucial point of similarity between the Jesus who gave a welcome to sinners and outcasts and the Paul who preached the justification* of the ungodly through the grace* of God.

**1.3.2. Werner G. Kümmel.** At the same time W. G. Kümmel kept the "Jesus and Paul" issue alive with important essays on the theme. While considerably influenced by Bultmann's position, and largely agreeing with him on Paul's lack of information about the life and teaching of Jesus, Kümmel analyzed the congruity between Jesus and Paul in terms less dependent on existentialist philosophy. In particular he argued that for Jesus the kingdom was not purely future but was already breaking in during his ministry. Whereas Bultmann (following Schweitzer) had seen an important distinction between Jesus pointing to the imminent future and Paul pointing to the immediate past,

Kümmel saw both Jesus and Paul as conditioned by a very similar tension between the presence of salvation and its future fulfillment (*see* Eschatology). The resurrection and the gift of the Spirit (*see* Holy Spirit) merely widened the effect of the salvation already present in Jesus—and present not just in his word (Bultmann) but in his person. Thus for all the differences in formulation between Jesus' preaching and Paul's, Kümmel insisted that Paul's theology represents no fundamental alteration or falsification of the teaching of Jesus, but only a proper reformulation of its fundamental ideas.

**1.3.3. The New Quest.** However, the "Jesus and Paul" debate could only take on new life with a widespread revival of research on Jesus. The 1950s saw renewed interest in the historical Jesus springing up even among Bultmann's pupils, most notably E. Fuchs, G. Bornkamm and E. Käsemann. While remaining true to the "kerygmatic" principle that the gospel can never be dependent on the uncertain results of historical research, Käsemann made out a powerful exegetical and theological case for what became known as the new quest for the historical Jesus. He warned against the dangers of "docetism" if the Christ preached in the gospel is not firmly linked to the historical Jesus and argued that Bultmann's reduction of this link to the mere historical existence of Jesus was too meager. If Christian scholars did not investigate the character of Jesus' ministry, others certainly would. More importantly, the Synoptic Gospels showed that an important strand of early Christianity did attempt to tie its preaching of the gospel to a life story of Jesus; and even if Paul's kerygma has much less interest in such things, it does focus on the earthly Jesus inasmuch as it emphasizes his crucifixion. Only in this way could Paul combat the Spirit enthusiasm of his converts, for he soon discovered in Corinth that an appeal to the Spirit alone was vulnerable to all sorts of misinterpretations (*see* Corinthians). Thus research into the historical Jesus, while certainly not providing a historical basis for faith, is important as a criterion for distinguishing the true gospel from falsifications of it. In particular, Käsemann's own interpretation of the historical Jesus as one who broke in a decisive way with the Law and removed the distinction between sacred and secular realms gave support for his emphasis on the radical political and social significance of the gospel.

**1.3.4. Eberhard Jüngel.** Although the new quest of the 1950s and 1960s had rather limited results, it did open up again the historical questions about Jesus and thus serve to raise afresh the question of the relationship between Jesus and Paul. The most immediate result was a new presentation of the congruity between Paul and Jesus by E. Jüngel (1962). With a skillful combination of NT exegesis and theological expertise, and drawing effectively on the "new hermeneutic" of his mentor E. Fuchs, Jüngel compared the understanding of the kingdom of God which comes to expression in the parables with Paul's central theological affirmations about the righteousness* of God. For all their differences as forms of speech, Jüngel detected an essential correspondence here: just as in the parables, as "speech-events," God and his kingdom draw near to history and establish a new word over against the old word of the Law, so Paul preaches the arrival of a new era which releases us from the slavery of the Law and from the bondage of the past.

*1.3.5. Omissions and Problems in the Last Thirty Years.* The abstract character of Jüngel's thesis has perhaps made his work more accessible to theologians than to NT specialists. But it is remarkable that there has been virtually no new work on the question of theological congruity between Paul and Jesus in the thirty years since Jüngel's book. The reasons for this neglect are complex but certainly include the following:

(1) In general there has been a parting of the ways between theology and NT study. The theological dimensions of our topic which were so important to Bultmann and his immediate successors have simply eluded or failed to interest most recent NT scholars. At the same time theology has taken much less interest in the NT.

(2) To discuss the congruity between Jesus and Paul requires an analysis of their theologies which can isolate the dominant motifs and discern, within and behind these, the central dimensions of their thought. But in the present climate a large degree of uncertainty prevails concerning such matters regarding both Paul and Jesus.

The Reformation interpretation of Paul, dominant in Germany and also in evangelical theology elsewhere, has long identified justification as the heart of Paul's theology, understanding his critique of the Law as an attack on any attempt of the individual to earn his/her own righteousness. At present, however, under the influence of K. Stendahl and E. P. Sanders, it is now highly debatable whether justification by faith is so easily to be identified as the center of Paul's thought and whether its thrust is to be understood in such individualistic terms (see Justification; Center of Paul's Theology). The last decade in particular has seen a considerable debate on Paul's theology of the Law in which many influential voices present Paul's thought as confused, or wholly confined to issues of practical significance in his Gentile mission. This leaves significantly fewer scholars than in previous generations who are confident about the central dynamic of Paul's theology and thus able to compare this with the central concerns of Jesus.

Meanwhile, although research on the historical Jesus has gained a new lease on life, it has largely cut loose from theological interests—in contrast to the close connections between the "old quest" and liberalism on the one hand and the "new quest" and Protestant existentialism on the other. Thus although there have been substantial advances made in recent years on the historical context of Jesus' ministry and the analogies between his impact on Israel and that of contemporary first-century Palestinian movements (e.g., by J. K. Riches, A. E. Harvey, G. Theissen, M. Hengel, M. J. Borg, E. P. Sanders), these have rarely been accompanied by the sort of theological engagement which seeks to pinpoint the core of Jesus' message and purpose. Although some consensus is emerging on the limits of a plausible picture of Jesus, there is continuing scholarly uncertainty about the authenticity of the sayings material in the Gospels and a large measure of disagreement about the extent to which Jesus challenged central aspects of Judaism. In particular, Sanders has forced a reconsideration of the two points at which Jesus' distinctive message has been most commonly discerned—his critique of the Law and his welcome of sinners. Although many would take issue with Sanders on this, most agree that the decisive questions in relation to the historical Jesus concern his purpose in relation to Israel, and his impact on the religious, cultural and political complex of Palestinian Judaism.

But the more Jesus' life and preaching are placed within his Palestinian context, the harder it appears to find significant points of correspondence with the theology of Paul, which was forged in the light of the cross and resurrection and in the context of the Gentile mission. In fact, the present trend of NT scholarship is largely hostile toward the creation of theological syntheses in general, and any synthesis between Jesus and Paul in particular. It is the diversity, rather than the unity, of the NT which attracts most attention, and there is a general distaste for what are seen as apologetic attempts to paper over the cracks.

The conviction of many Jewish scholars—that Jesus can be accommodated within Judaism, but Paul cannot—was famously propounded in the middle of the century by J. Klausner, and has since been reiterated by G. Vermes and others. Although most Pauline scholars would resist the implication that Paul has been decisively influenced by non-Jewish (mystery-religion [see Religions] or Gnostic [see Gnosis, Gnosticism]) ideas, there is still a general willingness to concede that between the worldview of Jesus and that of Paul there is a considerable gulf. Whereas previous generations were concerned to rebuff Jewish arguments that Christianity was corrupted by Paul, the prevailing atmosphere of pluralism and of sympathetic sensitivity to Jewish perspectives has made Christian scholars altogether less urgent and less polemical in their treatment of this issue.

*1.3.6. Progress in the Last Thirty Years.* If the last three decades have seen little attempt to explore the possible congruity between the messages of Jesus and Paul, there has been considerable attention paid to the question of historical continuity. In the first place, there has been renewed interest in the question of Paul's use of traditions about (and from) the historical Jesus. The conservative British school of thought had been maintained in W. D. Davies' influential *Paul and Rabbinic Judaism* (1948) in which he deduced from the quotations and allusions in Paul's letters that "Paul is steeped in the mind and words of his Lord" (Davies, 140). This was supplemented by the researches of the Scandinavian school (H. Riesenfeld, B. Gerhardsson) which stressed the careful preservation of Jesus material in the first generation. In the case of Paul, much hinges on the detection and evaluation of allusions to the teaching of Jesus. D. L. Dungan's careful analysis of *The Sayings of Jesus in the Churches of Paul* (1971) examined Paul's allusive use of the sayings of Jesus in 1 Corinthians 7:10 and 9:14, and suggested that the Corinthians were already familiar with such material and that there could be many other places where Paul alludes to Jesus' teaching. This has encouraged scholars to pursue further the question of Paul's dependence on eschatological material originating from Jesus and the possibility that Paul knows not just isolated sayings but whole blocks of material (D. Wenham, D. C. Allison, P. Stuhlmacher). New work on the character of echoes and allusions and the proper method for detecting them is being undertaken (M. Thompson), although it must also be acknowledged that a large number of scholars consider this whole enterprise as so fraught with uncertainty as to be of very limited significance.

The second aspect of continuity which presently commands attention is the question of the channel through which Jesus tradition could reach Paul. Most acknowledge that Paul's contact with the immediate disciples of Jesus in the Palestinian churches was not extensive, although argument continues over the proper evaluation of Paul's first meeting with Peter (Gal 1:18). More interest focuses on "the Hellenists," the radical Jewish-Christian group represented by Stephen and Barnabas, who were expelled from Jerusalem, became the target of Paul's persecution and seem to have been the most important influence upon him after his conversion. It is generally accepted that if there is any "bridge" between Jesus and Paul it must lie here. But we are hampered by our lack of direct and reliable evidence about this group. If, in historical terms, the "Jesus and Paul" question cannot be discussed without reference to the "early church" as a third entity, it is frustrating that it is precisely this decisive early period and this crucial "Hellenist" branch of the church which remain so shadowy.

**2. The Teaching of Jesus in Paul.**

As we have seen, there has been considerable debate about the extent and significance of Paul's use of the teaching of Jesus (*see* Jesus, Sayings of). There is no dispute about the occasions on which Paul explicitly quotes the words of Jesus (e.g., 1 Cor 7:10; 9:14; 11:23; 1 Thess 4:15—though the origin of this is uncertain). The argument generally focuses on the question whether in other places, where we can detect parallels with the Gospels, Paul is alluding to or echoing the teaching of Jesus (e.g., the cluster of possible allusions in Rom 12—14). Naturally, those who emphasize the gulf between Jesus and Paul minimize the number of plausible allusions; and those who see a close relation between them tend toward a maximalist reading. Of course, within the wider debate the issue is not just the number of occasions on which Paul quotes or alludes to Jesus' teaching. It also concerns the significance which Paul attaches to the teaching of Jesus. Do the words of Jesus carry a special authority? If he does allude to them, why are they so often mixed in with other material and not specifically identified as the words of Jesus? Further, what significance would Paul's christology give to Jesus as a moral teacher?

**3. The Life of Jesus and His Example.**

The number of facts about Jesus' life which we could glean from Paul's letters is not large: that he was born and lived under the Law (Gal 4:4); that he was of the line of David (Rom 1:3); that he had brothers, one of whom was called James (1 Cor 9:5; Gal 1:19); that he had a meal on the night he was betrayed at which he used certain words (1 Cor 11:23-25). There is no reference to the baptism of Jesus, to his many miracles and parables, to the disputes with Pharisees, the Transfiguration or the Temple incident; there is no indication of the setting of Jesus' ministry, no references to Galilee or Jerusalem. The only facts about Jesus which are constantly referred to are that he was crucified and that he was raised, although even here we must note the absence of detail about time, place and attendant circumstances. The mere fact of Christ crucified seems so to dominate Paul's perspective that everything else recedes into the background.

The cross is also central to Paul's depiction of Jesus' character and his moral example. There are references to the gentleness and meekness of Jesus (2 Cor 10:1) and to his love (Gal 2:20); but these general character traits are illustrated not by any incidents in his life or by his treatment of others but by his self-giving on the cross. When Paul refers to the obedience of Christ (Rom 5:19; Phil 2:5-9) or to his grace in making himself poor (2 Cor 8:9), it appears that he has in mind the whole drama of the Incarnation and the cross (*see* Christology), rather than any specifiable event in his life. And it is probably significant that in referring to the example of Jesus in bearing the burdens of others (Rom 15:3) Paul refers not to any words or deeds of Jesus but to the depiction in the Psalms of the suffering of the righteous.

All this suggests that it would be incorrect to claim that Paul was wholly ignorant of, or uninterested in, the life of the earthly Jesus. But his mind operates in terms of general characteristics rather than specific narratives, and he is concerned to bring out the significance of the story of Jesus as a whole, interpreted in the light of the Scriptures. Alongside the references to his own example, Paul does appeal to the figure of Jesus as an example of obedience, self-giving and love. For instance, despite the objections of some scholars, part of Paul's purpose in citing the hymn in Philippians 2:5-11 does seem to be to provide a moral example (*see* Imitation; Hymns). However, one may observe that such a generalized depiction of virtue is sometimes not as effective in moral exhortation as the dramatic narrative which illustrates the point. Other religious and philosophical groups in the Greco-Roman world cultivated stories of heroes (e.g., Moses, Pythagoras, Diogenes, Socrates) whose lives encapsulated the truths they propounded. One can thus understand the need for, and the popularity of, the detailed Gospel narratives alongside the generalized outlines provided by Paul.

### 4. Letters and Missionary Preaching.

Thus far we have been discussing the evidence of Paul's letters. But it is obvious that these provide only a partial picture of Paul's thought, and it has often been suggested that Paul may (or even "must") have provided a much fuller picture of the life and ministry of Jesus when he carried out his initial evangelism. To draw broad conclusions from the letters alone would thus be misleading. It has been suggested that the

genre of a letter in itself precludes the provision of detailed narratives, and the contrast between the Gospel and the letters of John is sometimes cited as a parallel here. There is also the general consideration that one would expect any preaching of Christ crucified to provoke requests for fuller information both from interested and from hostile audiences.

The problem here is our lack of evidence for the original preaching of Paul. Although Acts gives some of his sermons, scholars continue to debate how much these can be taken as evidence for Paul's preaching and the extent of their recasting by Luke; in any case, even the speech at Pisidian Antioch (Acts 13:16-41) provides very scanty information about the earthly Jesus. In his letters Paul does occasionally refer to the terms of his initial preaching (1 Thess 1:9-10; 1 Cor 2:2), but he does not give any hint of a fuller account of the life of Jesus. Further, in Romans, which Paul writes to a church he did not found and which sets out fully the gospel he preaches, there is none of the expected detail on the life of Jesus. Of course to argue that Paul rarely referred to the life of Jesus because he does not say much about it in his letters is to argue from silence; and arguments from silence are always slightly precarious. Yet to assert that Paul did know much more than he says in his letters, and thus to have to provide one hypothesis or another to explain his silence, is perhaps an even more precarious procedure.

### 5. Revelation and Tradition.

There is an interesting contrast between Galatians 1 and 1 Corinthians 15 in the way Paul describes the origins of his gospel.* In Galatians 1 he insists on his independence from all human authorities and in particular from the apostles in Jerusalem. He suggests that his call and his gospel were received directly through a revelation from Christ (*see* Conversion and Call) and that it was only some three years later that he had occasion to meet Peter.* In 1 Corinthians 15, however, he reminds the Corinthians of the creedal formula he had passed on to them concerning the death and resurrection of Christ, and says that he had himself received this piece of tradition.* In this latter case we see Paul as one who inherits and treasures traditions from those who were Christians before him, including Palestinian eyewitnesses of the resurrection; while in Galatians all the emphasis lies on what he himself has experienced in his call-revelation. The two passages thereby suggest different perceptions of how much Paul would be concerned to find out, and pass on, information about the earthly Jesus.

It would obviously be a mistake to set these two self-portraits in any absolute antithesis. In both passages rhetorical considerations explain a certain onesidedness in Paul's presentation. It would be wrong to conclude from Galatians that Paul was averse to, or embarrassed by, information about the historical Jesus. As C. H. Dodd once quipped, it is hardly likely that at their initial meeting Peter and Paul spent a fortnight talking about the weather (Gal 1:18)! Yet it is also clear that Paul is extremely self-conscious about the manner of his calling. As one who had not seen or followed the earthly Jesus, his authority could only rest on the visionary calling he received on the Damascus Road. There he encountered the risen Christ, whose crucifixion he had previously counted the chief scandal to Jews like himself (see Jew, Paul the). It is understandable, then, that it is these facts about Christ, his crucifixion and resurrection, rather than details of his teaching or ministry,* which impressed themselves most on Paul's mind.

Another verse often referred to in this connection is 2 Corinthians 5:16 where Paul writes: "So from now on we regard no one from a human point of view (kata sarka); even if we once knew Christ from a human perspective (ei kai egnōkamen kata sarka Christon), we know him thus no longer." For a while this verse became a central text in the Jesus-Paul debate, particularly since Bultmann interpreted it to support his view that Paul had little interest in the life of the earthly Jesus. Detailed discussion of whether the phrase kata sarka should go with the noun or the verb tended to obscure the fact that what is said here of Christ is said in the first half of the verse of everyone. One could hardly say that Paul was uninterested in the natural life and circumstances of everyone he encountered! Yet it is also clear in the context (with its talk of dying with Christ [see Dying and Rising] and of the new creation in Christ [see Creation and New Creation]) that Paul's perspective on everyone, including Christ himself, is determined by the world-shattering events of the cross and resurrection. For Paul these were not simply events which concluded Jesus' life; they constituted the death of an old aeon (together with its old ways of perception) and the opening of a new (see Eschatology).

In this sense, any information Paul may have had about the life and ministry of Jesus seems to have been overshadowed by the cross and resurrection. It is sometimes suggested that Paul makes little reference to the life and teaching of Jesus because he felt insecure in citing such facts, which could be used with more confidence by his Palestine-based opponents.* It is also possible that stories of Jesus as a miracle worker were naively invoked by some of his enthusi-astic converts, for instance the Corinthian Christians. But even if either or both of these hypotheses are true, it is more important that the structure of Paul's own theology laid almost exclusive stress on the central facts about Jesus which had caused the dramatic shift in salvation history: that Jesus, the Christ, had been crucified but raised from the dead by God.

### 6. The Kingdom of God.

One theme that provides a particularly clear example of the difference between the theology of Jesus and Paul is the kingdom of God (see Kingdom). On a surface level, in terms of vocabulary usage, it is immediately obvious that this terminology, which is so central to Jesus' message, plays a much-reduced role in Paul. It is still a part of Paul's vocabulary (e.g., Rom 14:17; 1 Thess 2:12; Gal 5:21; 1 Cor 4:20; 6:9) but often in formulae which appear stereotyped and never in the central statements about salvation. It is possible that this reflects a merely superficial change of terminology and that, as Jüngel and more recently Wedderburn have argued, the basic concept is preserved in Paul's talk of the righteousness* of God. However, it is also significant that where Paul uses metaphors of sovereignty, he does so characteristically by reference to the lordship of Christ (see Lord). In this connection 1 Corinthians 15:20-28 is particularly revealing with its reference to Christ's present reign, even though that is only preliminary and ultimately subordinate to the universal rule of God. This passage also makes it clear that Paul understands the lordship of Christ as a consequence of the resurrection.

This would suggest an important dissimilarity between the preaching of Jesus and the theology of Paul. If Jesus spoke of the kingdom of God as breaking in through his ministry, he pointed primarily to the effects of his preaching and healing. From the other side of the cross and resurrection, Paul understood the rule of God as focused in the risen Lord, and thereby highlighted an event and emphasized a christology which are at most implicit in the teaching of Jesus. Given this undeniable difference in perspective caused by the events of the cross and resurrection, we must now consider whether there are still significant points of congruity between the preaching of Jesus and the theology of Paul that would allow us to hold them together as recognizably united in their fundamental concerns.

### 7. Israel and the Law.

Recent research on the historical Jesus has highlighted the question of his purpose and has focused attention on his relationship to the people of Israel.* A consensus has emerged which understands his ministry as devoted to the restoration and reconstitution of Israel: he called twelve disciples, a symbol of the twelve tribes of Israel, in order to gather around himself the renewed core of the people of God. Jesus did not found a church because the church (Israel) was already in existence. But the restoration of Israel (*see* Restoration of Israel) involved a fundamental challenge to its value system. Following on from John the Baptist's call to repentance, Jesus challenged Israel to grasp and to practice the will of God in radical obedience. The object of his attack was not legalism (in the sense of the self-satisfied performance of meritorious works) but the narrowness of vision which confines the perception of the will of God within the boundaries of nation and tradition (*see* Law; Works of the Law). When Jesus spoke of the kingdom of God he consistently broke apart traditional expectations. Although the evidence probably does not allow us to claim that he set himself against the authority of the Torah as a matter of principle, it is sufficiently clear that he challenged the nation to reconsider its priorities and interpreted the Law in such areas as Sabbath, purity and the love command in an open-ended fashion. To insist, for instance, that the Sabbath rest was to be understood as an opportunity for the performance of acts of mercy was to shift the emphasis from the protection of Israel's way of life to her unique calling to demonstrate, even in the tense historical context of Palestine, the unlimited mercy of God.

Paul's theology also has as its focal point the question of God's purposes for Israel. It is now increasingly appreciated that Romans 9—11 is not an appendix but an integral part of the argument of that letter and that Paul's theology of justification has as its immediate horizon not the question of the salvation of the individual but of God's impartiality toward Jews and Gentiles.* Paul then is also concerned with the reconstitution of Israel, the redefinition of the children of Abraham* (*see* Restoration). For Paul, the context in which this is worked out is not the political and religious tensions of Palestine but the social environment of Jews and Gentiles in the cities of the Greco-Roman world (*see* Social Setting). His unique calling to the Gentile mission and its remarkable success necessitated a rethinking of the sufficiency of the Torah as the standard of moral guidance—a much more radical reappraisal than we can detect in the teaching of Jesus. Paul himself looks back to Jesus as one who lived under the Law (Gal 4:4) and his ministry as directed to "the circumcision*" in order to fulfill the promises to the patriarchs (Rom 15:8). But he understands that fulfillment as now entailing a systematic redefinition

of the "Israel of God" (*see* Israel) to include Gentiles who enjoyed freedom from the Law. Paul never invokes the life or teaching of Jesus as a model for his Gentile mission or his selective use of the Law; in this respect it appears that he himself was aware of a significant point of discontinuity between Jesus and himself. But it may still be possible for us to claim that there is a real congruity between the dynamic of Jesus' challenge to Israel and Paul's Law-free mission* to Gentiles; this will require us to investigate more carefully the theological driving force of their respective ministries.

### 8. Sinners, Outsiders and the Mercy of God.

Recent discussion of Jesus and the "sinners" has highlighted the boldness of his association with those who were not just ignorant of the Law but who willfully and repeatedly crossed the boundaries of acceptable Jewish behavior. Prostitutes and tax collectors (renowned for their dishonesty) were apparently among the company whom Jesus welcomed in table fellowship. The rationale for this controversial behavior is made clear in the parables of the lost (Lk 15) and the saying about the doctor (Mk 2:17): Jesus represents his ministry as the decisive opportunity of forgiveness, the moment when the kingdom of God, focused in his activity, is revealed as the unconditional and saving mercy of God. Instead of reinforcing the protective boundaries of the pure and the righteous, Jesus consciously redefined God's love in radically inclusive terms as welcoming the poor, the maimed, the tainted, the "unconvertible" and the enemy. In taking a Samaritan as the model of service to others, in finding the qualities proper to the people of God represented even outside its traditional boundaries (cf. Mt 8:10-12; Mk 7:24-30), Jesus hints that the mercy of God is not necessarily confined to the Jewish race, even if his primary concern is with the revitalization of Israel. In Paul's context "sinners" are not just disobedient Jews but also, and especially, Gentiles. His theology of justification is focused on the question of how even such Gentiles can be included in Abraham's family. The Gentile mission he pursues, together with his own experience of transformation from persecutor of the church to apostle, lie at the root of his characteristic emphasis on the grace of God—a grace extended even to the weak (*see* Weakness), the enemy* and the ungodly (Rom 4:5; 5:6-11; etc.). For all the differences of context and expression, and for all the complexities of the theological argumentation Paul employs, it is here, at the very heart of his theology, where Paul seems to be entirely in tune with the dynamic of the message and ministry of Jesus. For both Jesus and Paul, the core of the good news consists in the radical demolition of restrictive boundaries in the free and gracious activity of a merciful God.

Since Paul never appeals to the example of Jesus in this regard, it is not clear how this remarkable theological congruity can be explained in historical terms. The most likely solution, well argued recently by Wedderburn, is that the Jewish "Hellenist" Christians whom Paul initially persecuted were influenced in their openness to Gentile converts by the memory of Jesus' controversial welcome of sinners and took inspiration from his open-ended emphasis on the merciful forgiveness of God. It was perhaps this atmosphere and these priorities which Paul then absorbed when he joined the Hellenist community which he had formerly tried to destroy.

### 9. Suffering, the Cross and Vindication.

There is good evidence that Jesus consciously adopted a life of poverty and self-denial and understood the measure of greatness to be in service. Because of the suspicion that the Gospel records of Jesus' words have been heavily influenced by subsequent events, many scholars remain agnostic on the question of whether Jesus predicted his own death or what interpretation he may have given to it. However, there is some solid evidence in the well-attested tradition about the Last Supper (*see* Lord's Supper), and in the logion in Mark 10:45, that Jesus knew his life of service would culminate in death and understood that death as being in some sense on behalf of "many." Moreover, given the long tradition of reflection in Jewish theology on the fate of the righteous martyrs and their sure vindication by God, it is entirely plausible to attribute to Jesus some hope that God's purposes would triumph even in and through his impending death.

Looking back from the other side of the cross and resurrection, Paul's perspective is in some respects radically different: in the confidence of Christian experience of the resurrection, he detects the opening of the new era in the resurrection of Christ and his exaltation* to the position of "Lord."* Yet he also sees the life and death of Jesus as characterized preeminently by service and obedience (Phil 2:5-11; Rom 15:3; 2 Cor 8:9). Moreover, like Jesus, he places the pattern of service* and vindication, death and new life, at the very heart of the good news of the gospel. Just as Jesus saw the love of God as expressed in his own self-giving for others and the essence of discipleship in losing one's own life and finding it again (Mk 8:34-37), Paul's theology focuses on the "Son of God who loved me and gave himself for me" (Gal 2:20), and his dominant image of the Christian life is of

"carrying about the dying of Christ in order that the life of Christ might be manifest in our bodies" (2 Cor 4:10; *see* Cross, Theology of the). Like Jesus, although with more explicit focus on the cross, Paul sees this gospel pattern as presenting a radical challenge to the pride, defensiveness and self-sufficiency endemic in human nature (1 Cor 1:18-25; cf. Lk 10:25-37; Mk 10:35-45).

### 10. Continuity and Development.

As our survey of the history of debate has shown, there are important theological presuppositions lying behind many discussions of the "Jesus and Paul" issue. At one extreme lies Bultmann's assertion "that it is the Christ of the kerygma and not the person of the historical Jesus who is the object of faith" (Bultmann 1960, 17). The natural effect of this is to minimize the continuity between the historical Jesus and the theology of Paul and to lay all the emphasis on the Easter faith. At the opposite end of the spectrum is J. W. Fraser's concern that "we cannot rest content with the beliefs of Paul or others; it must be Jesus himself who provided the basis for and the impetus to the whole New Testament understanding of his saving person and work" (Fraser, 29). From this perspective it is important to find as much similarity and continuity between Jesus and Paul as possible.

In fact no one can deny that there are significant changes and developments between the message of Jesus and the theology of Paul. The events of Good Friday and Easter, and the momentum of the Gentile mission, made such developments inevitable and, indeed, necessary. Moreover, quite apart from the different idioms and thought forms used by Jesus and Paul, their very different social and cultural contexts would have made it impossible for Paul simply to repeat the preaching of Jesus. The central question is whether in essence Paul's theology is harmonious with, and a legitimate development of, the message of Jesus. As we have seen, this question cannot be answered simply by discovering or denying the presence of echoes of the words of Jesus in Paul. That issue, which lies on the level of historical continuity between Jesus and Paul, cannot by itself determine whether Paul's theology is congruous with that of Jesus. But there is sufficient evidence to show that, whether consciously or otherwise, Paul did develop the central insights of the teaching of Jesus and the central meaning of his life and death in a way that truly represented their dynamic and their fullest significance.

*See also* CENTER OF PAUL'S THEOLOGY; CHRISTOLOGY; ESCHATOLOGY; ETHICS; IMITATION OF PAUL/OF CHRIST; JESUS, SAYINGS OF; JEW, PAUL THE; KINGDOM OF GOD/

CHRIST; LAW; LORD'S SUPPER; PAUL AND HIS INTERPRETERS; RESTORATION OF ISRAEL; TRADITION.

BIBLIOGRAPHY. M. J. Borg, *Conflict, Holiness and Politics in the Teaching of Jesus* (New York/Toronto: Edwin Mellen, 1984); C. Brown, "Historical Jesus, Quest of," *DJG* 326-41; R. Bultmann, "The Significance of the Historical Jesus for the Theology of Paul," in *Faith and Understanding* I (New York: Harper & Row, 1966 [1929]) 220-46; idem, "Jesus and Paul," in *Existence and Faith* (London: Hodder and Stoughton, 1961 [1936]) 183-201; idem, "The Primitive Christian Kerygma and the Historical Jesus" (1960), in *The Historical Jesus and the Kerygmatic Christ*, ed. C. E. Braaten and R. A. Harrisville (New York/Nashville: Abingdon, 1964) 15-42; W. D. Davies, *Paul and Rabbinic Judaism* (Philadelphia: Fortress, 1948); D. L. Dungan, *The Sayings of Jesus in the Churches of Paul* (Oxford: Blackwell, 1971); J. W. Fraser, *Jesus and Paul* (Appleford, Berkshire: Marcham, 1974); W. Heitmüller, "Zum Problem Paulus und Jesus," *ZNW* 13 (1912) 320-37; J. Jeremias, *The Central Message of the New Testament* (London: SCM, 1965); E. Jüngel, *Paulus und Jesus* (Tübingen: J. C. B. Mohr, 1962); M. Kähler, *The So-Called Historical Jesus and the Historic Biblical Christ* (Philadelphia: Fortress, 1964 [1896]); E. Käsemann, "The Problem of the Historical Jesus," in *Essays on New Testament Themes* (London: SCM, 1964); idem, "Blind Alleys in the 'Jesus of History' Controversy," in *New Testament Questions of Today* (London: SCM, 1969); J. Klausner, *From Jesus to Paul* (London: Allen & Unwin, 1943); W. G. Kümmel, "Jesus und Paulus" (1939) and "Jesus und Paulus" (1963) in *Heilsgeschehen und Geschichte* (Marburg: N. G. Elwert, 1965) 81-106, 439-56; J. K. Riches, *Jesus and the Transformation of Judaism* (New York: Seabury, 1982); E. P. Sanders, *Paul and Palestinian Judaism* (Philadelphia: Fortress, 1977); idem, *Jesus and Judaism* (Philadelphia: Fortress, 1985); A. Schweitzer, *Paul and His Interpreters* (London: A. & C. Black, 1912); M. B. Thompson, *Clothed with Christ: The Example and Teaching of Jesus in Romans 12.1—15.13* (Sheffield: JSOT, 1991); G. Vermes, *Jesus and the World of Judaism* (Philadelphia: Fortress, 1984); A. J. M. Wedderburn, ed., *Paul and Jesus: Collected Essays* (JSNTSup 37; Sheffield: JSOT, 1989); S. G. Wilson, "From Jesus to Paul: The Contours and Consequences of a Debate," in *From Jesus to Paul: Studies in Honour of Francis Wright Beare*, ed. P. Richardson and J. C. Hurd (Waterloo: Wilfrid Laurier University, 1984); B. Witherington, *Jesus, Paul and the End of the World: A Comparative Study in New Testament Eschatology* (Downers Grove: InterVarsity, 1992); W. Wrede, *Paul* (London: Philip Green, 1907).

J. M. G. Barclay

**JESUS TRADITION.** *See* JESUS, SAYINGS OF; JESUS AND PAUL.

## JEW, PAUL THE

In recent years a significant change has taken place in Pauline scholarship. During the first half of the twentieth century the dominant "history of religions" school emphasized a Hellenistic approach to Paul: Paul was understood to be a Hellenized Jew of the Diaspora. For example, R. Bultmann and his followers reasoned the syncretistic Judaism of the Diaspora and the popular philosophy of the time constituted the background of Paul's thought (*see* Paul and His Interpreters). Today, however, NT scholarship finds more and more evidence for the Jewishness of Paul's life and thought. Indeed, this change is part of a general movement in Christian scholarship to rediscover the Jewish roots of Christianity. Concurrently, Jewish scholarship shows a growing interest in reclaiming the Jewishness of Jesus and Paul. Accordingly, the following study emphasizes the Jewish dimension of Paul's life and thought.

Much of the current emphasis on the Jewishness of Paul focuses on his social world. It attempts to go behind his thoughts and words to matters of lifestyle and behavior. For example, Paul shared the apocalyptic hope of primitive Christianity: what did that mean in terms of everyday life, in terms of a group that lived outside the mainstream of life in the Roman Empire? Since the social study of Paul is now a field in itself, it is not possible here to do full justice to this aspect of Pauline scholarship (*see* Social-Scientific Approaches).

A recent study by J. Neyrey, however, demonstrates how cultural anthropology sheds light on the Pauline letters and on Paul the Jew. According to Neyrey, Paul's early upbringing, or socialization, as a strict Pharisaic Jew conditioned his view of the world and reality. Consequently, Paul had a passionate concern for such categories as order, hierarchy and boundaries in matters of purity (*see* Purity and Impurity). Paul's concern for these categories was carried over to his postconversion (*see* Conversion and Call) perspective. Thus Paul was not an entirely new person after his conversion: his Jewish past continued to influence him. This continuity will be further illustrated in the following discussion.

1. Paul's Autobiographical Statements
2. Paul's Formal Education in Judaism
3. Paul's Apocalyptic Worldview
4. Paul's Self-Understanding as a Jew
5. Paul's Mysticism
6. Paul and Torah

## 1. Paul's Autobiographical Statements.

The proper place to begin a study of Paul the Jew is his own autobiographical statements. The most pertinent autobiographical passage is Philippians 3:4-6. This is a polemical passage in which Paul explicitly emphasizes his credentials as a Jew. "If anyone else has reason to be confident in the flesh, I have more: circumcised on the eighth day, of the people of Israel, of the tribe of Benjamin, a Hebrew born of Hebrews; as to the Law a Pharisee, as to zeal a persecutor of the church, as to righteousness under the Law blameless." In this passage Paul makes the point that his Jewish credentials and his zeal for his religion could be matched by few other Jews or Jewish Christians.

Still haunted by a false dichotomy between Palestinian Judaism and that of the Diaspora,* many Pauline scholars refuse to take such autobiographical statements at face value. The scholarship of a previous generation posited a pure, Torah-centered Judaism for Palestine and a syncretistic, Hellenistic Judaism for the Diaspora. And, since Tarsus was located in the Diaspora, Paul was subsumed under the category of syncretistic Hellenistic Jew.

In contrast to the older view, recent archeological and literary finds have demonstrated the rich variety in Palestinian Judaism both in adherence to the Law* and in speaking languages other than Aramaic (see Hellenism). Much the same variety is true of Diaspora Judaism, although Greek was the predominant language spoken. While Greek was the language of Alexandrian and Egyptian Jewry, the language situation in Syria was different; Syria later produced an Aramaic literature. Geographically, Tarsus is quite close to Syria. Also, Jerome reports that Paul's parents came from Gischala in Galilee. If Jerome is correct, Paul could very well have spoken Hebrew or Aramaic in his home.

Philippians 3:4-6, however, reports far more about Paul's Judaism than the fact that he claimed Jewish identity. For example, he claims to be a Benjaminite. Precisely what Paul was declaring by this assertion is not clear. Nevertheless, the following may have been involved in Paul's boast. Jerusalem and the Temple were located within the tribal land of Benjamin. In the separation of the northern kingdom from Judah, Benjamin and Judah remained loyal to the Davidic kings. After the Babylonian exile, Benjamin and Judah were the center of the new community.

Next, Paul claims to be "a Hebrew born of Hebrews." Again, certainty is elusive in defining this phrase (cf. 2 Cor 11:22). He may have meant his blood was pure in that he had no Gentile* ancestry. More probably, he was contrasting himself with Hellenists

or Greek-speaking Jews. Thereby, he was saying that he was taught to speak Hebrew in the home. According to R. N. Longenecker, this interpretation gains in probability if Philippians is read in the light of 2 Corinthians 11:22. There Paul matches his qualifications against those of other Jews or Jewish Christians: "Are they Hebrews? So am I. Are they Israelites? So am I. Are they descendants of Abraham? So am I" (Longenecker, 22).

As a further cause for boasting in Philippians, Paul claims to be a Pharisee. Here the term was defined with precision. The expression "as to the Law a Pharisee" refers to the oral Law. The Sadducees held that only the written Law was binding, while the Pharisees believed God had revealed the oral Law as well as the written Law. In Galatians 1:14 Paul writes that he was "extremely zealous . . . for the traditions of the elders." The Greek for traditions* is a technical expression (*paradosis*) for the oral law. The same Greek word occurs in Mark 7:5 where the Evangelist speaks of the "traditions of the elders." According to E. Rivkin, Paul thereby understood himself as a member of the scholarly class who taught the twofold Law. By saying that the Pharisees sit on Moses' seat (Mt 23:2), Jesus was indicating they were authoritative teachers of the Law. Consequently, the Pharisees claimed to believe that they were the true Israel who knew God's will for the world.

Another basic Pharisaic belief was the resurrection of the dead. If a member of the covenant community (a Jew) or a Gentile convert obeyed the oral and written Law, that person could anticipate being raised to eternal life.

In summary, Paul was saying that he was a Hebrew-speaking interpreter and teacher of the oral and written Law.

A further point should be made in reference to Paul's statement "as to righteousness* under the Law blameless" (Phil 3:6). The uneasy, guilt-ridden conscience of the West, as seen particularly in Martin Luther and his age, should not be read back into Paul's psyche (see Stendahl). The anxieties of one age are not those of another. Paul's biographical statements are best taken at face value—like the Pharisees in the Gospels he understood himself as zealous and righteous (see Jealousy, Zeal).

## 2. Paul's Formal Education in Judaism.

According to Acts 22:3 Paul received formal education in the Judaism of the time "at the feet of Gamaliel." This famous Gamaliel was either the grandson or son of the renowned Hillel who was instrumental in drawing up the exegetical methods (*middôt*) by which Scripture should be studied (cf. *t. Sanh.* 7.11; *'Abot R. Nat.* [A] §37). Recently, some scholars have questioned the claim that Paul was trained under Gamaliel. The dispute cannot be recapitulated here, but a brief consideration of Jewish education in Paul's day illuminates the setting of Paul's early years (see Hengel, 1.78-83).

From the early Hellenistic period we have the renowned Ben Sira's description of his "school" which was designed to teach wisdom to upper-class young men (*Sir* 51:23-28). Sometime later and well into the Hellenistic period there arose a movement to instruct the whole Jewish population in the Law (*b. B.Bat.* 21a). This movement attempted to preserve Judaism from assimilation to Greek learning and language. Even later the attempt to instruct the whole people became a primary goal of Pharisaism. In Paul's generation a network of elementary schools taught the Hebrew Bible, primarily the Pentateuch, to boys who began school at the age of six or seven (*y. Ketub.* 32c, 4). More advanced schools taught young men to interpret the text of the Bible and to explain contradictions and problems found therein. The exegetical methods drawn up by Hillel were applied both to interpreting the text of the Bible as well as to applying Pentateuchal laws to the contemporary needs of Jewish society.

Some insight into Paul's formal education is gained by considering his exegetical skills in a passage such as Romans 9:6-29, where Paul utilizes Hebrew Scripture, midrashic techniques and the exegetical traditions of his day (*see* Old Testament in Paul). In this passage Paul is struggling with a problem faced by early Christians: Why have the majority of Jews rejected their own Christ*? He states the issue in Romans 9:6: "But it is not as though the word of God had failed." He then turns to the Pentateuch for primary passages which address this issue. The initial text to which Paul appeals is Genesis 21:12: "Through Isaac shall your descendants be named" (Rom 9:7). A second supplementary text is cited from Genesis 18:10: "About this time I will return and Sarah shall have a son" (Rom 9:9). In the argument that follows, Paul cites other subordinate texts from the OT. These subordinate quotations are linked to the initial and secondary texts by the use of three catchwords: "descendants" (*sperma;* translated "children" in verse 29), "named" (*kaleō*) and "son" (*huios; see* Adoption, Sonship). E. E. Ellis has outlined the pattern of the use of Scripture in the following manner (Ellis, 155).

| Romans 9:6-7 | Theme and initial text: Genesis 21:12 |
| Romans 9:9 | A second, supplemental text: Genesis 18:10 |

| Romans 9:10-28 | Exposition containing additional citations (Rom 9:13, 15, 17, 25-28) and linked to the initial texts by the catchwords *kaleō* (name) and *huios* (son) (Rom 9:12, 24-26, 27) |
| Romans 9:29 | A final text alluding to the initial text with the catchword *sperma* (descendants and children) |

Paul employed a number of midrashic techniques in composing this unit. The use of a parallel secondary text to supplement and elucidate the primary text is frequently found in later classical midrashim. Also common is the use of a key term in both the initial text and the conclusion of the composition, thereby forming a correspondence of beginning and ending in a discussion (*inclusio*). The use of key words to pull in other passages of Scripture is also well known. In Paul's composition the key word is not always found in the texts that have been quoted. Nevertheless, the key word is always found in the context of the quotation if not in the quotation itself. Similarly, later rabbis did not always quote the key word.

Other elements of midrashic form found here are introductory or citation formulas for Scripture, breaks in thought caused by dealing with an incorrect inference or an imaginary opponent (also found in the diatribe), and the use of words from the initial text in the exposition.

Perhaps the most significant element in this midrash-like unit is Paul's use of contemporaneous exegetical traditions which are preserved for us in later rabbinic works. An example from outside Romans 9:6-29 is found in 1 Corinthians 10:4 where Paul wrote: "For they drank from the supernatural rock which followed them. . . ." The biblical narrative contains no hint that the rock was mobile. How did Paul know this? As Conzelmann states (Conzelmann, 166-67), Paul was making use of a Jewish haggadic tradition that appears in a later work (*t. Sukk.* 3.11; cf. *b. Ta'an.* 9a; *Bib. Ant.* 11.14; Philo *Leg. All.* 2.86).

In Romans 9:6-29 the initial text (Gen 21:12) Paul employs was used in two different ways in later rabbinic works. First, the Babylonian Talmud quotes Genesis 21:12 in several places. The following passage from *Sanhedrin* 59b is typical:

> Circumcision was from the very first commanded to Abraham only. . . . If so, should it not be incumbent upon the children of Ishmael (Abraham's son)? For *in Isaac shall thy seed be called.* Then should not the children of Esau be bound to practice it?—*In Isaac* but not all Isaac. (Soncino edition)

Both Paul and the later Babylonian Talmud use the same text to show who belonged to Israel, and both associated Esau with this text. However, unlike Paul, the Talmud ties "in Isaac" to purely physical descent from Jewish parentage.

But what is even more striking is the way both Paul and the later Genesis *Rabbah* exegete this same text. Here another factor in addition to physical descent is associated with the phrase "in Isaac." (In order to understand the following passage the reader needs to know that in the first century Hebrew letters also had a numerical equivalent: since *bêt* is the second letter of the alphabet, it was also the symbol for the number two.) In *Midrash Rabbah* Genesis 53.12 we read:

> AND GOD SAID UNTO ABRAHAM: LET IT NOT BE GRIEVOUS IN THY SIGHT ... FOR IN ISAAC SHALL SEED BE CALLED TO THEE (XXI, 12): R. Judan b. Shilum said: Not 'Isaac', but IN ISAAC is written here. R. 'Azariah said in the name of Bar Ḥuṭah; the *beth* (IN) denotes two, i.e., [thy seed shall be called] in him who recognizes the existence of two worlds; he shall inherit two worlds [God says]; 'I have given a sign [whereby the true descendants of Abraham can be known] viz. he who expressly recognises [God's judgments]: thus whoever believes in the two worlds shall be called "thy seed", while he who rejects belief in two worlds shall not be called "thy seed." (Soncino edition, 471)

In the above midrash the true descendants of Abraham* believe in two worlds. This is precisely Paul's stance in Romans: physical descent alone is not enough; those who have a certain belief or type of faith* are children of Abraham. In commenting on Romans 9:6-29 Paul writes the following in Romans 9:30-32:

> What shall we say, then? That Gentiles who did not pursue righteousness have attained it, that is, righteousness through faith; but that Israel who pursued the righteousness which is based on Law did not succeed in fulfilling that Law. Why? Because they did not pursue it through faith.

Paul's view of faith is closely related to what we have observed in the *Midrash Rabbah*. As a Pharisee Paul had believed in the two worlds, that is, not only in this present world but also in the resurrection*—the world to come. When Paul met the resurrected Christ on the Damascus Road, he interpreted Christ as the "firstfruits" of the general resurrection to follow. From that point on his belief in a general resurrection became concretized in a specific person through whom he had experienced reconciliation* with God* and all that the term "faith" meant for him.

Before drawing any conclusions, however, another piece must be added to the picture. Genesis *Rabbah* is not the only later rabbinic work in which belief in two worlds is associated with Genesis 21:12. Much the same

interpretation is also found in the Jerusalem Talmud, *Nedarim* 2:10. Here also the *bêt* means "two" and points to a Jew who believes in two worlds.

These two late Palestinian sources raise the possibility of the existence of a Palestinian exegetical tradition which associated the belief in two worlds with Genesis 21:12. As we have seen, the Babylonian Talmud does not know this tradition and construes Genesis 21:12 to mean physical descent alone.

Still, the question remains: How could Paul and this exegetical tradition (if such it was), found in sources "published" hundreds of years after Paul, have interpreted the same verse in such a remarkably similar manner? G. Vermes points us toward a solution (Vermes, chap. 6). He first rejects various possibilities: that the NT depends on the Talmud and Genesis *Rabbah* (they did not exist in NT times); that the later exegetical tradition was learned from Paul; and that the similarities are purely coincidental (there is too much overlap). Rather, he holds open the possibility that the NT and the later rabbinic exegetical tradition both had a common source, namely, traditional Jewish teaching. Exegetical traditions "lived" for hundreds of years. Here Vermes would say that Paul knew the exegetical tradition associated with Genesis 21:12. This tradition "lived" in the schools of Palestine and later resurfaced in the Jerusalem Talmud and in Genesis *Rabbah*. And, of course, this opens the possibility that a Palestinian exegetical tradition was one source of Paul's doctrine of justification* through faith.

In addition, another exegetical tradition was apparently associated with Paul's second text: "About this time I will return and Sarah shall have a son." Genesis 18:10 and the figure of Sarah herself were associated with the theme of the steadfastness of God's work in Genesis *Rabbah* and in other places (see Stegner, 47).

Paul's use of Scripture, of midrashic techniques and of contemporary exegetical traditions in Romans 9:6-29 yielded a highly sophisticated composition. It cannot have been the product of an uneducated mind. If he was not trained by Gamaliel, then he was taught by some other Jewish master. In any case, it seems clear that Paul received a formal education in the Judaism of the time.

### 3. Paul's Apocalyptic Worldview.

Did Paul's apocalyptic (*see* Apocalypticism) worldview constitute a central motif in his thinking and theology? In answering this question scholars sometimes begin by defining the term, then match their definition with passages from Paul and, thereby, conclude that apocalypticism did or did not constitute a central focus in his thinking. However, since definitions vary from one scholar to another, it is better to start with the centrality of Paul's belief in the resurrection of Jesus and work outward from there.

W. Pannenberg is surely correct in pointing out that in first-century Judaism the resurrection could be expressed only in the language of the apocalyptic tradition (Pannenberg, 96). Indeed, the belief in a resurrection was part of the apocalyptic hope and worldview. For example, the disciples already had to have an understanding of resurrection before they could identify Jesus' empty tomb and appearances as constituting a resurrection. The hundreds of ossuaries (receptacles holding bones of the dead) discovered by archeologists in the environs of Jerusalem may be material evidence of this first-century Jewish hope in a future resurrection.

That the resurrection* was a central element in Paul's message is a truism. 1 Corinthians 15 alone illustrates the point, and Paul again and again mentions resurrection: Christ's saving death and resurrection seem to have been the focus of his preaching.*

Moreover, Jesus' resurrection is the first fruits (*see* First Fruits) that foreshadows and authenticates the resurrection of all those who belong to him (1 Cor 15:23). This resurrection will involve a transformation like the transformation that Jesus' body underwent in the tomb. Paul makes this point in Philippians 3:20-21: "We await a Savior, the Lord Jesus Christ, who will change our lowly body to be like his glorious body, by the power which enables him even to subject all things to himself." In apocalyptic fashion Paul is speaking of a "bodily" resurrection and transformation in so far as one can speak of a "spiritual body" as a body* (*see* Immortality).

Further, the resurrection of Jesus as first fruit of the eschaton heightened the expectation for the general resurrection at the end of this age and the accompanying transformation of all creation (*see* Eschatology). Thus Paul believed the end of this age was very near. According to 1 Thessalonians 4:13-18, Paul expected to be alive (1 Thess 4:15) to see Jesus return. Then two related events would occur: first, the "dead in Christ will rise" and, secondly, the living will be transformed (so also 1 Cor 15:51). This raising of the dead and transformation of the living was to be accompanied by the transformation of nature and all creation*: "the creation itself will be set free from its bondage to decay and obtain the glorious liberty of the children of God" (Rom 8:21). This is clearly apocalypticism.

Paul shared the apocalyptic belief in the two ages: this present evil age will be transformed by an act of God into the age to come, or kingdom of God (*see* Kingdom of God). Thus Paul says that "the whole creation has been groaning in travail" (Rom 8:22) and waiting "with eager longing for the revealing of the children of God" (Rom 8:19).

Perhaps the key ingredient in apocalypticism was the category of revelation. Most apocalyptic writings reveal the future. Paul also reveals the future.

In describing God's purpose for the future, Paul, like other apocalypticists, used the word *mystery** (*mystērion*, e.g., Rom 11:25). Paul's use of the term is both Jewish and apocalyptic in background. Generally speaking, the Jewish apocalypses portrayed God's purposes for history as well as the nearness of the end of this age. They used the term *mystery* to designate a purpose or secret of God which could not be known by human reason, but had to be revealed by God.

According to the "mystery" that Paul is revealing, God has formed a new people in Christ and the unbelief of the Jewish people has caused the gospel to be preached to the Gentiles. However, in the end time "all Israel," presumably the Jewish people who do not believe in Christ, will be drawn to faith in him by God.

Many interpreters conclude that Paul was speaking of a secret or revelation that he had received from God. Others are not sure. Regardless of how Paul received the "mystery," this term was the common currency of apocalyptic language.

Nevertheless, in the use of traditional apocalyptic language and imagery there is a difference between Paul and other apocalypticists. In Paul the sharp separation between this age and the age to come is lacking. The resurrection of Jesus, more specifically, his crucifixion* and resurrection, introduced a new factor into the equation. There is an overlap between the two ages: the new age is proleptically present in Christ's work of reconciliation. Indeed, the transformation of believers is secretly taking place within them: "And we all . . . beholding the glory of the Lord, are being changed into his likeness from one degree of glory to another" (2 Cor 3:18).

### 4. Paul's Self-Understanding as a Jew.

The previous discussion of the term *mystery* and its surrounding context in Romans 9—11 introduces another dimension of Paul's Jewishness, namely, his ongoing Jewish self-understanding. Romans 9—11 enables us to enter into Paul's self-understanding as a Jew better than any other Pauline passage.

In introducing his discussion in Romans 9:2-3 he shares his feelings for his "own people," his "kindred according to the flesh." He agonizes over the unbelief of the Jews as only a fellow Jew could (*see* Israel). Troubled by the general Jewish rejection of "the Christ," Paul rejects the possibility that "the word of God has failed" (Rom 9:6). In Romans 11:1 Paul also rejects the proposition that God has "rejected his people." The solution is simple: the unbelief of the Jews has caused the gospel to be preached to the Gentiles, who in turn believed. While Paul was "an apostle* to the Gentiles" (Rom 11:13), he cannot forget his own people. Indeed, the turning of the Gentiles to Christ causes the Jews to become jealous: "Inasmuch then as I am an apostle to the Gentiles, I magnify my ministry in order to make my fellow Jews jealous, and thus save some of them" (Rom 11:13-14). The very vigor with which Paul pursued his Gentile apostolate has suggested to some interpreters that Paul thought he was entering into the very eschatological purpose of God in saving all Israel. Paul not only had "unceasing anguish" for his "kinsmen by race," but he gave himself for their salvation,* a side effect of his Gentile mission being the conversion of Jews.

At this point, recent scholarship has tended to take divergent paths. Some hold that Paul is advocating a two-covenant people of God: the Gentiles approach God through faith, while the Jews approach him through Torah (Gaston, Gager, Stendahl). Surely, the majority of NT scholars are correct in holding that any two-covenant approach founders on the rock of Romans 10 (see Israel, Law).

If the Jews must come to faith in Christ in order to be saved, how will God accomplish this? Paul knows the election of the Jews still holds (Rom 11:28-29), and he knows the secret plan (mystery) of God (note the elements of self-understanding implied here). After "the full number of the Gentiles come in," then "all Israel will be saved" (Rom 11:25-26). Will jealousy over the "full number of the Gentiles" turn the Jews to faith? Will the Second Coming of Jesus occasion such faith? Paul reveals God's overall purpose for Israel, but not the details. Paul continued to understand himself as a (believing-in-Christ) Jew, privy to the plan of God.

Even the notion of the ingathering of the Gentiles at the end of the age was a part of Paul's Jewish heritage. In some apocalyptic scenarios the Gentiles would be converted in the end time and make a pilgrimage to Jerusalem (see Collection). This expectation for the ingathering of the Gentiles seems to lie behind Romans 11:25. However, in the "mystery" that Paul is sharing, God has formed the Jewish Christians and the Gentile converts into a new people of God in Christ. As we have seen, the unbelief of the Jewish people had caused the gospel* to be preached to the Gentiles.

### 5. Paul's Mysticism.

Contemporary scholarship is just beginning to explore Paul's mysticism* (see Visions, Ecstatic Experience). Paul's mysticism is Jewish mysticism and derives from Palestinian Judaism. It must be defined with care.

Paul's mysticism is as well defined by what it is not as by what it is. The attempt of a previous generation to identify Paul with the mystery religions (see Religions) of the Hellenistic world on the basis of his use of the Greek term mystērion was a failure (see Paul and His Interpreters). Further, the older discussion of Paul's "Christ mysticism," related to his repeated use of the phrase "in Christ" (see In Christ; Mysticism), is not the issue contemporary scholars are addressing. Rather, Paul's mysticism is best defined by (1) the experience he describes in 2 Corinthians 12:1-4 and (2) his knowledge* of God's eschatological plan (described above in connection with the term mystery). In 2 Corinthians 12:1 Paul boasts of "visions and revelations of the Lord." He goes on to describe his being "caught up to the third heaven" (2 Cor 12:2) and then "into Paradise" (2 Cor 12:3; see Heaven, Heavenlies, Paradise) where "he heard things that cannot be told, which man may not utter" (2 Cor 12:4).

What is the background for this kind of experience? An emerging scholarly consensus posits Merkabah mysticism (related to Ezekiel's vision of the throne chariot, or merkābâ, of God) as the background for Paul's experience (see, e.g., Bowker, Segal). G. Scholem (EncJud) associates early Merkabah mysticism with certain circles of Pharisees, and particularly with Johanan ben Zakkai, who flourished around A.D. 70, and with the later Akiba.

Today, scholars are dating Merkabah mysticism earlier than Scholem supposed. Among the Dead Sea Scrolls (see Qumran and Paul) fragments of a so-called Angelic Liturgy were found (4Q400-407 = 4QShirShab). These fragments describe the divine throne chariot—a central theme of early Jewish mysticism. This find shows that Paul could have been acquainted with Merkabah mysticism, especially since he was Johanan ben Zakkai's contemporary.

This early Jewish mysticism was centered in Palestine and found expression in apocalyptic literature such as the Enoch tradition (e.g., 1 Enoch 70—71; 2 Enoch 22; 3 Enoch). Certain Pharisaic circles focused on the first chapter of Ezekiel which tells of the throne chariot (the merkābâ) of God. Scholem also reports that the early literature speaks of an "ascent to the Merkabah" (Scholem 1961, 46).

This form of early Jewish mysticism fits together with Paul's autobiographical statements. In Philippians 3:5-6 Paul tells us that he was a zealous Pharisee and blameless "as to righteousness under the Law." In 2 Corinthians 11:22 (a passage immediately preceding his description of his visions), Paul emphasizes his descent from Abraham*: "Are they descendants of

Abraham? So am I." Early Jewish mysticism was practiced in certain Pharisaic circles. Nevertheless, not every Pharisee was permitted to study Ezekiel 1 because of the dangers involved (cf *m. ḥag.* 2:1). If the exegete should see again the vision of the throne chariot and not be in a state of ritual purity, he might die: "You cannot see my face; for man shall not see me and live" (Ex 33:20). Hence Johanan ben Zakkai taught mystical contemplation only to "his most favored pupils." J. W. Bowker has emphasized the importance of the Jewish credentials of the exegete, such as his direct descent from Abraham (Bowker). Paul's credentials well fit these requirements.

However, even more important than Paul's credentials for establishing a connection with Merkabah mysticism are the words he uses in 2 Corinthians 12:1-4. Three expressions stand out: being "caught up" (*harpazō*), "the third heaven" (*tritos ouranos)* and "paradise" (*paradeisos*). J. D. Tabor has shown that these words belonged to the vocabulary of Jewish mysticism and cites the first-century *Life of Adam and Eve* (25:3) as an illustration:

> And I saw a chariot like the wind and its wheels were fiery. I was carried off into the Paradise of righteousness, and I saw the Lord sitting and his appearance was unbearable flaming fire. And many thousands of angels were at the right and at the left of the chariot (*OTP* 2.266-8).

In this excerpt the mystic is not talking about the future, but the dwelling of God in paradise, perhaps in the seventh heaven. Other visions associate paradise with the third heaven.

Finally, the book of Acts records that Paul experienced visions. While all visions are not the same, the overlap in vocabulary plus Paul's credentials indicate that his vision in 2 Corinthians 12:1-4 was the kind associated with Merkabah mysticism. Furthermore, Paul's apocalyptic worldview and his concept of "mystery" (revelation of God's future plan) are additional indications of his orientation to mysticism.

There is a fascinating interplay between the facets of Paul the Jew that we have examined so far. His autobiographical statements disclose his Pharisaism, his zeal and his righteousness under the Law. His writings reveal his exegetical prowess and his appropriation of the exegetical traditions by means of which he interpreted the passages of the Septuagint. All this is evidence of his formal training in the Judaism of his day. Of course, this formal training was a precondition for his instruction in Merkabah mysticism. Moreover, his mysticism and his apocalyptic worldview fit together like hand in glove. Since revelation of God's plan for the future is an essential ingredient in apoc-

alypticism, the one depends on the other.

Two striking observations emerge from the above summary. The first concerns how well Paul fits into the first-century, pre-A.D. 70 (Palestinian) Judaism that we know from other sources. For example, the same combination of zeal for the Law, apocalyptic worldview and mysticism characterized the Qumran sectarians. While not an Essene, Paul stands forth as a devoutly religious Pharisee of the time. The second striking observation concerns how well the pieces all fit together into a harmonious whole. Heretofore Paul has been pictured as a marginal man, living uncomfortably in two worlds—the Hellenistic and the Jewish. Heretofore Paul has been pictured as a man characterized by conflicting goals and serious internal contradictions. This is not the picture that emerges from the above study.

Now we are ready to examine the element that shattered the unity of his preconversion synthesis—his relationship to Torah. Still, nothing more cogently depicts Paul the Jew than his continuing preoccupation with Torah. On the one hand, he cannot reject Torah altogether and, on the other hand, he cannot accept it as he formerly did.

### 6. Paul and Torah.

The literature on the subject of Paul and Torah, or Law, is immense. Our purpose here is not to review this literature (see, e.g., Dunn, Sanders), but to outline the significant issues in the contemporary debate (*see* Law; Works of the Law). Indeed, a new perspective on Paul and the Law is coming into focus out of the contemporary debate.

The dilemma for scholarship is posed by Paul's apparently contradictory statements about the Law. On the one hand, Paul appears to have had a positive view of the Law: "So the Law is holy, and the commandment is holy and just and good" (Rom 7:12). "Do we then overthrow the Law by this faith? By no means! On the contrary we uphold the Law" (Rom 3:31). On the other hand, Paul wrote negatively about the Law and appears to have attacked the Law itself: "By works of the Law shall no one be justified" (Gal 2:16). "For Christ is the end (in the sense of termination) of the Law, that every one who has faith may be justified" (Rom 10:4). Did Paul contradict himself?

According to the traditional view Paul made a radical break with the positive OT view of Law. Paul rejected the Law and saw Christ as the termination or end of the Law. The traditional view is best articulated by R. Bultmann and other German Lutheran exegetes. The Jews obeyed the Law to accumulate merit for themselves and thereby earn salvation. Indeed, the Pharisee was a worse sinner than most because the Pharisee best exemplified the human striving to assert independence from God and to be free of dependence upon God's grace.*

E. P. Sanders has challenged this traditional interpretation of Law in the name of covenantal nomism. After an exhaustive examination of the Jewish literature of the period, Sanders has challenged Bultmann's understanding of first-century Judaism: Bultmann has read Luther's conflict with Catholicism back into the first century. The covenant,* the Law, the special status as elect people of God (hence the term *covenantal nomism*) were all gifts of God's grace to Israel. The Jews did not have to earn what they already had: the Law was simply the means of maintaining their covenantal status.

What then was Paul condemning when he spoke of "works of the Law"? In answering this question, J. D. G. Dunn, who accepts Sanders's understanding of first-century Judaism, carries the argument further than Sanders. Dunn points out that the phrase "works of the Law"* occurs three times in Galatians 2:16. More importantly, the issue is table fellowship between Jewish Christians and Gentile Christians: in this context Paul was opposing Jewish Christians who insist on maintaining the food laws (*see* Food). The heart of the matter for Paul is the inclusion of Gentiles in the messianic community on an equal footing with Jewish Christians. The Jewish Christians, on the other hand, wanted the Gentiles to become Jews before they could share in the table fellowship with observant Jewish Christians. Thus, the issue was not merit-based righteousness so much as racial exclusiveness. According to Dunn, the problem for Paul was those observances of the Law that set Jews apart from Gentiles.

For Dunn the issue Paul addressed was not how one was saved: the issue was sociological. The "works of the Law" were circumcision,* purity and food laws, and Sabbath observance. In the ancient world the pagan writers regarded these very practices as distinctly Jewish. These "works of the law" marked "the boundaries of the covenant people" (Dunn, 193). Paul was saying no to the Law inasmuch as it set boundaries for the covenant people. Thus Paul was saying both no and yes to the Law at the same time. According to Dunn, Paul said no to the Law where it reinforced Jewish nationalism and exclusiveness, but yes to the Law where it expressed the will of God.

How could Paul the Jew do this? How could he say no to some provisions of the Law and yes to other provisions of the same Law? The answer seems to lie in Paul's apocalyptic worldview. A shift had taken place from the old age to the new age in Christ. Law

or Torah was superseded by Christ. Paul's statement in Romans 10:4 is crucial: "For Christ is the end of the Law, that everyone who has faith may be justified." Paul was not speaking of "the end" as termination of the Law, but as the goal or fulfillment of the Law. While the Law still defined God's will, it no longer functioned salvifically. The new age had arrived, and the Law had been superseded by God's new gift: Christ. Thus Paul can write in 1 Corinthians 15:20-22:

> But in fact Christ has been raised from the dead, the first fruits of those who have fallen asleep. For as by a man came death, by a man has come also the resurrection of the dead. For as in Adam all die, so also in Christ shall all be made alive.

The new perspective first advanced by Sanders and then furthered by Dunn does not answer all questions concerning Paul and Torah. But it does answer some. It tends to solve Paul's so-called contradictory attitude toward the Law, as stated above. This new perspective also allows for some continuity between the generally positive attitude toward the Law in the OT and Paul's attitude. Paul opposed the more nationalistic and exclusivistic parts of the Law because God's new act in Christ had extended the covenant to Gentiles: Grace had superseded ritual and race.

Dunn's observation that Paul affirmed the Law where it expressed the will of God is strikingly confirmed by the recent research of P. Tomson. For example, in 1 Corinthians 5:1-5 Paul writes about a man who "is living with his father's wife." The issue is forbidden sexual relationships according to Leviticus 18:1-18 (*see* Sexuality). Paul tells the church to excommunicate the man. Tomson discovers point-by-point agreement between Paul's discussion and later Jewish legal tradition that explicates forbidden sexual relationships. This is only one example of the continuity between Paul's ethical teachings and Jewish legal tradition.

Finally, this new perspective enables us to see Paul more clearly as a first-century Jew. Jewish scholars have long argued that Paul misunderstood Judaism and his view of the Law differed from that of most first-century Jews. Actually, according to Dunn, the German-Lutheran portrayal of Paul has been the problem. Paul was an authentic first-century Jew; there was no serious discontinuity between Paul and his Jewish past. He was a son of Abraham who objected to narrowing the covenant to the Jewish nation: Abraham was to be a blessing to all the families of the earth (*see* Universalism).

Among other questions that still remain is Paul's teaching directed toward Jewish Christianity. Was Paul asking Jewish Christians to abandon the boundary markers of the Law in their own practice? Did he teach that they should cease circumcising their sons and observing the dietary laws in their homes? Or was he speaking about fellowship between Jewish Christians and Gentile Christians in such places as Antioch and other mixed congregations? The question can be asked more pointedly: Did Paul entirely abandon the boundary markers ("works of the Law") for himself? Or did he continue to observe them in so far as they did not interfere with his Gentile apostolate? At this point, there does not seem to be a clear answer to this question.

Only a few Jewish-Christian voices have survived to tell us how Jewish Christianity reacted to Paul's views concerning the Law. Whether those surviving voices are representative of the various groups composing Jewish Christianity, we do not know. However, these few voices, while they stressed the Jewishness of Jesus, regarded Paul as a villain (Flusser, chap. 13). Some Jewish Christians looked upon Peter as their leader and others preferred James,* the leader of the church in Jerusalem.*

Do these few muffled Jewish-Christian voices constitute the last Jewish pronouncements about Paul the Jew? We hope not. With the scholarly rediscovery of the Judaism of Paul's day, perhaps some contemporary Jewish voices with Paul will offer a more positive evaluation of Paul the Jew.

*See also* APOCALYPTICISM; CIRCUMCISION; CONVERSION AND CALL OF PAUL; DIASPORA; HELLENISM; ISRAEL; LAW; MYSTERY; MYSTICISM; OLD TESTAMENT IN PAUL; PAUL IN ACTS AND LETTERS; PURITY AND IMPURITY; QUMRAN AND PAUL; RESTORATION OF ISRAEL; VISIONS, ECSTATIC EXPERIENCE; WORKS OF THE LAW.

BIBLIOGRAPHY. **Texts:** Babylonian Talmud: Sanhedrin (Hebrew-English Edition of the Babylonian Talmud; London: Soncino Press, 1969); Midrash Rabba Genesis (The Midrash Rabba, I Genesis; London: Soncino Press, 1977); *Life of Adam and Eve, OTP* 2.266-68. **Studies:** J. C. Beker, *Paul the Apostle* (Philadelphia: Fortress, 1980); J. W. Bowker, " 'Merkabah' Visions and the Visions of Paul," *JSS* (1971) 157-73; H. Conzelmann, *I Corinthians* (Herm; Philadelphia: Fortress, 1975); J. D. G. Dunn, *Jesus, Paul and the Law* (Louisville: Westminster/John Knox, 1990); E. E. Ellis, *Prophecy and Hermeneutic in Early Christianity* (Tübingen: J. C. B. Mohr, 1978); D. Flusser, *Jewish Sources in Early Christianity* (New York: Adama Books, 1987); J. Gager, *The Origins of Anti-Semitism: Attitudes Towards Judaism in Pagan and Christian Antiquity* (New York: Oxford, 1983); L. Gaston, *Paul and the Torah* (Vancouver: University of British Columbia, 1987); G. F. Hawthorne, *Philippians* (WBC 43; Waco: Word, 1983); M. Hengel, *Judaism and Hellenism* (Philadelphia: Fortress, 1981); R. N. Longenecker, *Paul, Apostle of Liberty* (Grand Rapids: Baker, 1976); J. Neyrey, *Paul, In Other Words: A Cultural Reading of His Letters* (Louisville: Westminster/John Knox, 1990); W. Pannenberg, *Jesus—God and Man* (Philadelphia: Westminster, 1968); E. Rivkin, "Pharisees," *IDBSup* 657-63; E. P. Sanders, *Paul and Palestinian Judaism* (Philadelphia: Fortress, 1977); G. G. Scholem, *Major Trends in Jewish Mysticism* (New York: Schocken Books, 1961); idem, "Merkabah Mysticism," *EncJud* 11. cols. 1386-89; A. F. Segal, *Paul the Convert: The Apostolate and Apostasy of Saul the Pharisee* (New Haven: Yale, 1990); W. R. Stegner, "Romans 9:6-29: A Midrash," *JSNT* 22 (1984) 37-52; K. Stendahl, *Paul Among Jews and Gentiles and Other Essays* (Philadelphia: Fortress, 1976); J. D. Tabor, *Things Unutterable: Paul's Ascent to Paradise in Its Greco-Roman, Judaic, and Early Christian Contexts* (Lanham, MD: University Press of America, 1986); P. Tomson, *Paul and the Jewish Law: Halakha in the Letters of the Apostle to the Gentiles* (Minneapolis: Fortress, 1990); G. Vermes, *Jesus and the World of Judaism* (Philadelphia: Fortress, 1984).

W. R. Stegner

**JEWISH EXEGESIS.** *See* JEW, PAUL THE; OLD TESTAMENT IN PAUL.

**JEWISH GNOSTICISM.** *See* GNOSIS, GNOSTICISM; OPPONENTS OF PAUL.

**JOURNEYS.** *See* ITINERARIES, TRAVEL PLANS, JOURNEYS, APOSTOLIC PAROUSIA.

# JOY

For Paul, Christianity was the religion of joy as much as the religion of grace.* Since all was of grace as far as his justification was concerned, one of the main consequences of his reconciliation with God* was his ability to "rejoice in God through our Lord Jesus Christ" (Rom 5:11), in spite of the afflictions,* hardships and trials that came his way.

    1. The Vocabulary of Joy
    2. Being in Christ
    3. The Fruit of the Spirit
    4. Joy in Suffering
    5. The Eschatology of Joy

### 1. The Vocabulary of Joy.

Of the 326 occurrences of words for joy in the NT, 131 are found in the ten letters that are usually ascribed to Paul, namely forty percent. Even if Ephesians and Colossians are discounted, that would still leave a high percentage of the vocabulary of joy in the NT attributable to Paul. So Paul can well be regarded as the theologian of joy as he undoubtedly was that of grace (88 of the 153 NT occurrences of *charis*, "grace," or fifty-eight percent, are found in Paul). It is significant that the most common cognates for joy (*chara*, "inner joy," and *chairein*, "to rejoice") are derived from the same root *char-* as is the Greek word for "grace," *charis*. There is a very close connection between the two concepts. Those who have come to experience God's grace, as Paul had done, know that, by standing firm in their faith (2 Cor 1:24), they can continue to celebrate the Christian life as a festival of joy (1 Cor 5:8), in perfect freedom from all anxious worries and fears.

**2. Being in Christ.**
As far as Paul was concerned, a Christian is a person who is "in Christ"*; or, as J. Stewart put it, "The heart of Paul's religion is union with Christ" (Stewart, 147). Christianity is a personal relationship with the risen Lord.*

The keynote of the letter to the Philippians is "Rejoice in the Lord" (Phil 3:1; 4:4, 10). What J. Moffatt spoke of as "the history of joy" is described in Philippians 4:4-7, where its implied source is the risen and reigning Lord Jesus Christ. Life's struggle both with external circumstances and with inner anxiety can be endured since "the Lord is at hand". Our safety lies in the fact that we are guarded by God's peace,* which "keeps our hearts and minds in Christ Jesus." The last word, like the first, is a personal relationship, since the history of joy is "simply the history of a man's plain experience with his God in Jesus" (Moffatt).

**3. The Fruit of the Spirit.**
The Christian life is a life of joyful freedom,* since, with the coming of Christ, Law* has been superseded by grace. In contrast to his opponents in Galatia, Paul boldly declared his reliance upon the cross and all it stood for (Gal 6:14). Believers ought to be able to boast* not only in the death* of Christ seen as the outreaching of the love* of God to all human beings, but also in the work accomplished by them in fulfilling the law of Christ (Gal 6:2; *see* Law of Christ) by showing the divine love to others. Of the ninefold fruit of the Spirit in Galatians 5:22-23, joy comes second in the list as one of three virtues of the inner life. It comes as a close second to the greatest of them all, love, and is followed by peace (*see* Fruit of the Spirit).

**4. Joy in Suffering.**
Outward circumstances can be joyfully accepted as factors in the Christian's moral and spiritual progress (Rom 5:3-4). Yet it is in a letter written from prison that

Paul's stress on the duty of celebrating in the midst of suffering* comes to its climax. In spite of all that has happened to him and in spite of his present circumstances, the apostle can still "rejoice in the Lord" and glory in work accomplished for his Lord. As the letter to the Philippians* comes to an end, Paul sums up: "Finally, my brethren, rejoice in the Lord" (Phil 3:1), and then proceeds, after a parenthesis or interpolation, to give the reason for his "joy in the Lord"—"for we are citizens of heaven" (Phil 3:20). The expectation of the coming of the Lord Jesus Christ and of the changing of "our lowly body to be like his glorious body" (Phil 3:21) is enough to keep Christians full of hope* and joy. The message of Philippians was neatly expressed by Bengel: "the sum of the whole letter: I rejoice, rejoice!" (Bengel, 766).

**5. The Eschatology of Joy.**
Over and over again, Paul links joy with the Christian hope. While no human being can boast in the presence of God (1 Cor 1:29), Christians can exult in their hope of sharing the glory* of God in the life to come (Rom 5:2). Such hope can keep a believer joyful (Rom 12:12), for it includes not only the expectation of the coming of the deliverer, the Lord Jesus Christ, to transfigure our physical bodies* (Phil 3:20-21), but also assures us of joy in the world to come. Provided we suffer with Christ here and now, we can expect to participate in his triumph hereafter. Such union with Christ is the heart of Paul's religion.

*See also* FRUIT OF THE SPIRIT; GRACE; HOPE; LOVE; PEACE; PHILIPPIANS, LETTER TO THE; SUFFERING.

BIBLIOGRAPHY. D. J. A. Bengel, *Gnomon Novi Testamenti* (3d ed.; London: Macmillan, 1855); E. Beyreuther and G. Finkenrath, "Joy, Rejoice," *NIDNTT* 2.352-61; H. Conzelmann, "χαίρω κτλ," *TDNT* IX.359-72; J. Moffatt, "The History of Joy," *ExpT* 9 (1897-98) 334-36; W. G. Morrice, *Joy in the New Testament* (Grand Rapids: Eerdmans, 1985); J. S. Stewart, *A Man in Christ* (London: Hodder & Stoughton, 1935).

W. G. Morrice

# JUDAIZERS

There is some evidence in the Pauline letters that certain Jewish Christians had doubts as to whether Gentile* Christians could be regarded as full members of the people of God* if they did not conform to the requirements of Torah (*see* Law). Some may even have attempted to force circumcision* and a Jewish life-style on such converts. There is also evidence in early Christianity that some Gentile Christians were attracted to Judaism. The verb *judaize* and the noun *Judaizer* have been used in relation to both the above groups with a subsequent lack of clarity in meaning.

## 1. Introduction.

At several points in his letters Paul directs his arguments and his anger at opponents* who are misleading or distressing his converts. Such people are probably, in some instances at least, from outside the congregation(s). In Galatians,* 2 Corinthians* and Philippians* we encounter this interaction. One of the questions that has occupied scholars for the last century and a half has been the identity of these opponents. A basic issue has been whether or not to regard such opponents as specific groups peculiar to each local context, or whether to see each instance of opposition as part of a widespread movement. In a famous essay in 1831, F. C. Baur found the identity of Paul's opponents in those who came to Corinth as emissaries of Peter and claiming to be "of Christ." The long-term effect of Baur's contribution was to drive a wedge between Paul and his teaching and that of the primitive church in Jerusalem. A contrast was thus established among interpreters between Gentile and Jewish Christianity, and this contrast has influenced the understanding of Paul's relationship to Jerusalem* even up to the present day (*see* Paul and His Interpreters).

One outcome of this viewpoint is that Paul is seen too much as an isolated apostle who alone truly understands the universalism* and freedom* that Jesus* represented. Apparently in the memory of the other leading apostles this has either been forgotten, misunderstood or compromised. A misleading contrast informed Baur's and many of his followers' theology—they posited an absolute opposition between particularism and universalism; this is typical of a modern cosmopolitan outlook but should not be read back into the NT. However, from this perspective Paul was seen as a lone contender for the universalism of the gospel* in contrast to the primitive church, whose leaders were in varying degrees tribalistic or particularistic in their ongoing commitment to Judaism.

More recent research has uncovered more diversity in NT groups and theologies. The emphasis upon the particularity of each letter, addressed to a specific situation, has, in following the historical interest of Baur, revealed that Paul's enemies are not necessarily all of Jewish background nor should we regard them

as a coherent, organized opposition. Partisanship need not always take the form of an organized party.

## 2. Definition and Terminology.

*2.1. Judaizer.* The term *Judaizer* originates as a transliteration via the Latin of the Greek verb *ioudaïzein* (*ioudaïzō*). The latter is a *hapax legomenon* in the NT (Gal 2:14). The normal meaning of the verb was "to live as a Jew in accordance with Jewish customs." It is found in this sense, for example, in Plutarch (*Cicero* 7.6), Josephus (e.g., J.W. 2.17.10 §454) and Ignatius (*Magn.* 10.3). In Galatians 2:14 it probably means "to become a Jewish convert and to keep the Law" (cf. Gal 5:3). In Galatians 2 we also find a unique NT expression *ioudaïkōs zēn*, "to live as a Jew." Peter's religious status is defined by Paul as being that of a Jew (*Ioudaios hyparchōn*), and yet as one who lives a Gentile life-style (*ethnikōs*, another NT *hapax legomenon*; cf. *ethnikos* in Mt 5:47; 6:7; 18:17; 3 Jn 7).

*Ioudaïsmos* (Judaism) occurs in the NT only at Galatians 1:13-14. The term appears to describe the Jewish way of life as a whole as it is distinct from that of other religions (cf. Ignatius *Phld.* 6.1, where it appears as opposite to Christianity, *christianismos*). One of the difficulties encountered in a discussion of the meaning of Judaizer or judaize is ascertaining where a reference may indicate simply an adherence to the Jewish way of life *without* implying any deliberate intention of forcing it upon Gentiles. Thus Josephus (J.W. 2.18.2 §463) appears to distinguish between the Judaizers (*hoi ioudaïzontes*) and the Jews (*hoi Ioudaioi*). In Christian literature the term *Judaizer* generally characterizes Christians engaged in Jewish practices. For example, Ignatius (*Magn.* 10.3) says "It is absurd to say 'Jesus Christ' and to practice Judaism" (*ioudaïzein*). It is probably correct to maintain that "to judaize" is not quite synonymous with simply living as a Jew (*ioudaïkōs zēn*), but seems rather to describe the somewhat artificial character of new converts (cf. Esth 8:17 [LXX]: "Many of the people had themselves circumcised and practiced Judaism because of their fear of the Jews.")

*2.2. Those of the Circumcision.* According to Galatians 2:12, in the encounter with Peter at Antioch, Paul accused him of being afraid of the Jews, "those of the circumcision" (*tous ek peritomēs; see* Circumcision). Part of the problem is that Paul severely criticized certain believers (Gal 2:14) in addition to Peter.* He also refers to "certain people from James*" (Gal 2:12) whom he did not accuse of hypocrisy. Who are included in these people referred to as "those of the circumcision" (Gal 2:12)? It is possible that the people from James are included, but perhaps Paul also had in mind the Jews in general, including non-Christian

Jews—in fact all those who think according to Jewish patterns.

However, we must be careful to allow for at least some diversity among those who think as Jews. Peter must be included as a Jewish person—so too James and John—but according to Paul, these three pillars did not insist that Gentile Christians should be circumcised. The problem with translating *tous ek peritomēs* as "the circumcision party" is that it does not allow for diversity, but suggests that all who belonged to the "circumcision party" were ideologically committed to promoting circumcision among Gentile Christians and, therefore, inevitably involved in opposition to the Pauline Gentile mission.

In addition to the above group of Jews probably associated with Jerusalem in some sense, we have other references to Judaizers in the Galatian churches. It would be easy simply to identify these with the "circumcision party" as indicated above. However, it is not at all clear that those advocating circumcision for Gentile Christians in Galatia were themselves Jews by birth.

*2.3. Those Who Receive Circumcision.* A key text is Galatians 6:13, where Paul surprisingly claims that "even those who receive circumcision (*hoi peritemnomenoi*) do not themselves keep the Law." On the face of it this looks like a plain case of Gentile Christians who, having recently received circumcision themselves, are now attempting to force it upon other Gentiles. Munck (88) notes how interpreters have tried for a long time to get around this possibility (i.e., that Gentile Christians also agitate for Judaism) by maintaining the traditional view that the agitators in the Galatian churches were Jewish Christians. This is done by making the present participle with the article (*hoi peritemnomenoi*) denote "those belonging to the class of those . . . who are circumcised according to the established custom, 'the class of' Jews who receive circumcision."

Since the present participle of *peritemnō* ("to circumcise") occurs only in two places (Gal 5:3 and 6:13) in the NT and not at all in the LXX or in the Apostolic Fathers, there is little on which to come to a clear understanding of its meaning. However, it is used in Justin's *Dialogue*, 27.5 and 123.1, twice in each place, and in these instances there is no doubt that the meaning is "receive circumcision." Munck argues from this that since the present participle in the middle voice of *peritemnō* never means "those who belong to the circumcision" but everywhere "those who receive circumcision," or "those who get themselves circumcised," then this must be the meaning in Galatians 6:13 as well. Paul's opponents who are agitating for Judaism among the Galatian Gentile Christians

are therefore themselves Gentile Christians. Their circumcision is still in the present, so that all of this judaizing movement is of recent date. (It should be noted, however, that there is strong MS support for the perfect passive participle, *peritetmēmenoi* (*P46* B et al.], "those who have been circumcised," which at least attests to how some early scribes understood the present participle.)

Whether or not we follow Munck entirely in this argument, it is very probable that certain traditional interpretations have little or no weight. It is certainly clear that *tous ek peritomēs* cannot any longer be translated simply as "the circumcision party" (RSV) or even as "the circumcision faction" (NRSV). More precision is needed in the use of terms so that distinctions are drawn between a neutral use of the term circumcision such as Romans 15:8, "Christ became a servant to the circumcised," and other texts in which some degree of commitment to a policy of circumcision for all seems presupposed. We need to distinguish between Jewish Christians who accept Gentiles as *Gentiles* and others who can properly be termed Judaizers in that they insist on circumcision for all. Moreover, Gentile Christianity cannot be viewed as a monochrome entity, and differing attitudes to the Law and the Temple* have to be recognized within it. Before we deal more specifically with the identity of Paul's opponents, we wish to eliminate if possible one traditional source of opposition.

## 3. Paul and Jerusalem: Diversity Within the Early Christian Mission.

F. C. Baur not only regarded all Paul's opponents as part of a single movement, but he also connected them via Galatians 2 and Acts 15 with Jerusalem. However, Paul cannot really be viewed as being in continual opposition to Jerusalem. What he says in conflict with opponents must be distinguished from what he explicitly says of the Jerusalem church.

Paul never connects any of his opponents with Jerusalem. Moreover, he always speaks of the Jerusalem church in positive terms. He calls the Jerusalem Christians "the saints"; he refers to their leaders as "apostles"* and "brothers of the Lord," and to three of them as "pillars" (even if he may do so grudgingly). Paul recognized that Peter's apostolate to the circumcised has been fruitful, just as his own mission to the Gentiles has been. There was certainly a degree of mutual recognition as regards these two spheres of mission.* So although the Jerusalem church differs in its mission from that of Paul, there is agreement in principle that both of their respective missions represent the work of the Spirit. Jerusalem may have regarded itself as restricted in mission to Israel,* but its leaders nevertheless supported Paul's mission to the Gentiles.* What is even more significant is that Paul himself can say "he who worked through Peter for the mission to the circumcised, worked through me also for the Gentiles" (Gal 2:8).

A more balanced view of the Jerusalem church is to see diversity of opinion represented within it just as there was diversity at Antioch and elsewhere. Some people at several points may have been closer to Paul on particular issues than others. But in the end there is solidarity in the gospel of Christ (cf. 1 Cor 15:11), and James eventually shared with Paul in martyrdom for his faith, demonstrating beyond dispute that what he shared with the apostle to the Gentiles was more significant than what joined him to his fellow Jerusalemites.

### 4. Diversity in Opposition: The Variety of Paul's Opponents.

Baur's attempt to portray all Paul's opponents as Judaizers has been gradually modified and to some extent refuted over the years. The oversimplification of dividing early Christianity into two opposing sections and the failure to distinguish between differing emphases within each section was soon found to be lacking in various respects, even in the last century. More recent studies by W. Lütgert, J. Munck and W. Schmithals offer alternative perspectives on the situations Paul addressed. Lütgert drew attention to the existence of spiritual enthusiasts of a gnostic* libertine variety and saw them as Paul's opponents in 1 Corinthians and (in company with Judaizers) also in Galatians.

Munck stressed the particularity of each letter as addressing a specific and therefore probably a different situation. As noted, he saw the Judaizers in Galatians as originating from Gentile converts; nor were there any Judaizers at Corinth or even at Philippi (where at least some of the opposition came from Jews).

In place of what J. D. G. Dunn (1990, 370) calls Baur's "pan-judaizer" hypothesis, W. Schmithals has proposed a "pan-gnostic" hypothesis so that the opponents in Galatians are viewed not as Judaizers but as Jewish-Christian Gnostics, and likewise in Corinthians and Philippians.

As has been shown above, comprehensive hypotheses are not fully adequate to account for the enormous diversity of the first century. Nor is it appropriate to see the heresies that were inflicted upon early Christianity as all emerging from Jewish sources. Current research as exemplified in the studies by D. Georgi, R. P. Martin, J. L. Sumney and C. C. Hill has sought a reappraisal of division within the earliest church. More attention has been devoted to the Hellenists and to their role in opposition to Paul. For example, it may be that Paul faced the same opponents in 1 and 2 Corinthians (though there were developments between the writing of the two letters) and that these opponents were pneumatics. The only real evidence for Judaizers is in Galatians, and, it may be argued that Munck's thesis that they were of Gentile origin is worthy of serious consideration.

*See also* ABRAHAM; CIRCUMCISION; GALATIANS, LETTER TO THE; GENTILES; ISRAEL; JERUSALEM; JEW, PAUL THE; JUSTIFICATION; LAW; OPPONENTS OF PAUL; WORKS OF THE LAW.

BIBLIOGRAPHY. W. Baird, *History of New Testament Research*, Vol. 1, *From Deism to Tübingen* (Minneapolis: Augsburg-Fortress, 1992); idem, "One against the Other: Intra-Church Conflict in 1 Corinthians," in *The Conversation Continues: Studies in Paul and John in Honor of J. Louis Martyn*, ed. R. T. Fortna and B. Gaventa (Nashville: Abingdon, 1990) 116-36; P. W. Barnett, "Opposition in Corinth," *JSNT* 22 (1984) 3-17; C. K. Barrett, "Paul's Opponents in II Corinthians," *NTS* 17 (1970-71) 233-54; F. C. Baur, *Paul the Apostle of Jesus Christ* (London, 1876); H. D. Betz, *Paulus und die socratische Tradition* (BHT 45; Tübingen: J. C. B. Mohr, 1972) 132-37; idem, *Galatians: Commentary on Paul's Letter to the Churches in Galatia* (Herm; Philadelphia: Fortress, 1979); J. D. G. Dunn, *The Partings of the Ways Between Christianity and Judaism and their Significance for the Character of Christianity* (Philadelphia: Trinity Press International, 1991); idem, "Judaizers," in *A Dictionary of Biblical Interpretation*, ed. R. J. Coggins and J. L. Houlden (Philadelphia: Trinity Press International, 1990) 369-71; idem, "The Relationship between Paul and Jerusalem according to Galatians 1 and 2," *NTS* 28 (1982) 461-78; E. E. Ellis, "Paul and his Opponents: Trends in Research," in *Christianity, Judaism and Other Greco-Roman Cults*, Vol. 1, ed. J. Neusner (Leiden: E. J. Brill, 1975) 264-98; G. Friedrich, "Die Gegner des Paulus im II Korintherbrief," in *Abraham unser Vater: Festschrift für Otto Michel*, ed. O Betz et al. (Leiden: E. J. Brill, 1963) 181-215; L. Gaston, "Paul and Jerusalem," in *From Jesus to Paul: Studies in Honour of F. W. Beare*, ed. P. Richardson and J. C. Hurd (Waterloo, ON: Wilfred Laurier University) 61-72; D. Georgi, *The Opponents of Paul in II Corinthians* (Philadelphia: Fortress, 1986); M. Goodman, *The Ruling Class of Judea: The Origins of the Jewish Revolt against Rome, A.D. 66-70* (Cambridge: University Press, 1987); J. J. Gunther, *St. Paul's Opponents and Their Background: A Study of Apocalyptic and Jewish Sectarian Teachings* (NovTSup 35; Leiden: E. J. Brill, 1973); M. Hengel, "Der Jakobsbrief als antipaulinischer Polemik," in *Tradition and Inter-*

*pretation: Essays in Honor of E. Earle Ellis*, ed. G. F. Hawthorne with O. Betz (Grand Rapids: Eerdmans, 1987) 248-78; C. C. Hill, *Hellenists and Hebrews: Reappraising Division within the Earliest Church* (Philadelphia: Fortress, 1992); C. Holladay, *Theios Aner in Hellenistic Judaism: A Critique of the Use of This Category in NT Christology* (SBLDS 40; Missoula: Scholars, 1973); J. Jervell, "Der schwache Charismatiker," in *Rechtfertigung: Festschrift für Ernst Käsemann zum 70 Geburtstag*, ed. J. Friedrich et al. (Tübingen: J. C. B. Mohr, 1976) 185-98; E. Käsemann, "Paul and Israel," in *New Testament Questions of Today* (Philadelphia: Fortress, 1969) 183-87; idem, "Die Legitimität des Apostels: Eine Untersuchung zu II Korinther 10-13," *ZNW* 41 (1942) 33-71; M. Kettunen, *Der Abfassungszweck des Römerbriefes* (Helsinki, 1979); H. Koester, *Introduction to the New Testament*, Vol. 2 (Philadelphia: Fortress, 1982); G. Lüdemann, *Opposition to Paul in Jewish Christianity* (Minneapolis: Fortress, 1989); R. P. Martin, "The Opponents of Paul in II Corinthians: An Old Issue Revisited," in *Tradition and Interpretation in the New Testament: Essays in Honor of E. Earle Ellis*, ed. G. F. Hawthorne with O. Betz (Grand Rapids: Eerdmans, 1987) 279-89; J. L. Martyn, "The Covenants of Hagar and Sarah," in *Faith and History: Essays in Honor of Paul W. Meyer*, ed. J. T. Carroll et al. (Atlanta: Scholars, 1990) 160-92; idem, "A Law-Observant Mission to Gentiles: The Background of Galatians," *SJT* 38 (1985) 307-24; J. Munck, *Paul and the Salvation of Mankind* (Atlanta: John Knox, 1959); W. Schmithals, *Gnosticism in Corinth* (Nashville: Abingdon, 1971); P. Stuhlmacher, *Der Brief an die Römer* (NTD 6; Göttingen: Vandenhoeck & Ruprecht, 1989) 13-14, 49, 222-23; idem, "The Theme of Romans," *ABR* 36 (1988) 31-44; J. L. Sumney, *Identifying Paul's Opponents: The Question of Method in II Corinthians* (JSNTSup 40; Sheffield: JSOT, 1990); M. E. Thrall, "Super-Apostles, Servants of Christ, and Servants of Satan," *JSNT* 6 (1980) 42-57; A. J. M. Wedderburn, *The Reasons for Romans* (Edinburgh: T. & T. Clark, 1989); S. G. Wilson, "Gentile Judaizers," *NTS* 38 (1992) 605-16.

W. S. Campbell

**JUDGE.** *See* GOD; JUDGMENT.

# JUDGMENT

Paul shares with his Jewish antecedents the conviction that God* as Creator has the right to call people to account for their behavior and allot their destinies accordingly.

1. Terminology and Meaning
2. Continuity and Discontinuity with Judaism
3. Judgment and the Gospel of Christ
4. Judgment According to Works
5. Judgment of Christians

## 1. Terminology and Meaning.

Two main word groups occur frequently in Paul's letters. Like the English verb *to judge*, the Greek *krinō* can mean "form an opinion," "decide" (1 Cor 2:2), but commonly refers to the assessment of human beings by others (1 Cor 4:5; 6:1) or by God (Rom 2:16). Related words include *krima* ("judgment," "sentence," Rom 2:2; 13:2); *katakrinō* ("condemn," 1 Cor 11:32); *katakrima* ("condemnation," Rom 5:16). Words derived from *dikē* ("justice," "punishment," 2 Thess 1:9) include *ekdikēsis* ("punishment," 2 Thess 1:8) and *ekdikos* ("punisher," Rom 13:4; 1 Thess 4:6). But Paul expresses his thought also in other images, such as wrath (*orgē*, Rom 1:18), destruction (*phthora*, Gal 6:8; *see* Wrath, Destruction), "paying back" (*antapodidōmi*, 2 Thess 1:6) and reward* (*antapodosis*, Col 3:24).

## 2. Continuity and Discontinuity with Judaism.

In many respects Paul takes over perspectives familiar in Jewish literature. Non-Christian Jews would find nothing strange in Paul's expectation of a final "day" of judgment (Rom 2:16) when all "will appear before God's judgment seat" (Rom 14:10) to be judged "according to their deeds" (Rom 2:6; 1 Thess 4:6; cf. *1 Enoch* 45:3; *4 Ezra* 7:33-44; *see* Eschatology). But they would be shocked by his reversal of common Jewish assumptions about the outcome of judgment. Because God exercises impartiality in judgment (Rom 2:11), Jew and Gentile* alike face both the prospect of judgment and the possibility of salvation* through Christ.*

## 3. Judgment and the Gospel of Christ.

For Paul, the process of judgment is integrally related to his message of salvation through Christ. Although he can speak of God's righteous judgment (Rom 2:5; 2 Thess 1:5), God's wrath (Rom 1:18) and God's judgment seat (Rom 14:10), he regularly associates judgment with Christ. He cites with reference to Christ OT texts which originally referred to judgment by Yahweh (2 Thess 1:9-10; citing Is 2:10, 19, 21). He links judgment with the "day" of Christ's Parousia (2 Thess 1:6-10; 1 Cor 4:3-5), when "we shall all appear before the judgment seat of Christ" (2 Cor 5:10).

The criterion by which people will be judged is their attitude or relationship to Christ: the key question is whether they "believe" (*see* Faith) in him, whether they "know" (*see* Knowledge) God and "obey the gospel* of the Lord Jesus" (2 Thess 1:8, 10).

The outcome of the final judgment also is expressed in terms of relationship to Christ. Unbelievers will suffer "exclusion from the presence of the Lord*" (2 Thess 1:9), while the destiny of believers is to be "at home with the Lord" (2 Cor 5:8; *see* Intermediate State). Paul is quite reticent about going further than this in describing human destiny. He does not use terms such as *Gehenna* (Mk 9:43, 45, 47) or the vivid imagery of some Jewish apocalyptists (*see* Apocalypticism). He prefers more abstract terms such as "life" (*zōē*) and "death" (*thanatos*, Rom 6:23; *see* Life and Death), "destruction" (*olethros*, 1 Thess 5:3; *apōleia*, Phil 3:19; *phthora*, Gal 6:8; *see* Wrath, Destruction). He is more concerned to warn of the danger of missing life in Christ than to explore the precise form which this loss might take.

### 4. Judgment According to Works.

Paul's focus on relationship to Christ is not in conflict with his affirmation of judgment according to works. For he understands people's deeds as evidence of their character, showing whether their relation to God is fundamentally one of faith or unbelief (*see* James and Paul). Judgment according to deeds does not imply degrees of reward or punishment in accordance with the quantity of good or evil works done. In Romans 2:5-11 and elsewhere Paul distinguishes only two groups of people—those who do evil and those who do good—and only two possible destinies (see Snodgrass). When he writes that those whose lives are dominated by sinful acts "will not inherit the kingdom of God" (Gal 5:19-21; cf. 1 Cor 6:9-10; Eph 5:5; *see* Kingdom of God/Christ), he implies that if professing Christians persistently did evil rather than good they would show themselves not to be Christians and to be in danger of condemnation at the final judgment. Christians are not exempt from that judgment precisely because its function is to show, by the evidence of people's deeds, whether they are in relationship to Christ or not (2 Cor 5:10).

### 5. Judgment of Christians.

For Christian believers justification* by grace represents a real, though not irreversible (*see* Apostasy), anticipation of the verdict of the final judgment. Through faith in Christ they have been accepted into relationship with God and are expected to bear the fruit of this relationship in their lives (*see* Fruit of the Spirit). At the final judgment the evidence of their deeds will confirm the reality of this relationship, which will then find its eternal fulfillment in God's presence.

Two passages in 1 Corinthians (1 Cor 5:5; 11:27-34) seem to express the conviction that, when Christians are guilty of serious sin,* God may use illness (*see* Healing, Illness) as a disciplinary judgment (*see* Discipline) to provoke them to repentance. But it would be risky to conclude from this limited evidence either that (in Paul's view) God regularly deals with Christians' disobedience in this way or that Paul normally understands illness as an expression of divine judgment.

Some have argued, on the basis of texts such as 1 Corinthians 3:14-15 and 2 Corinthians 5:10, that Paul believed in a final assessment of Christians leading to degrees of reward in the future life (*see* Rewards). But these tantalizingly unspecific texts are an uncertain basis for such a doctrine. What they do make clear, however, is Paul's willingness to urge human accountability to God as a motive for Christians to take seriously their life and service.

*See also* APOSTASY, FALLING AWAY, PERSEVERANCE; ESCHATOLOGY; JUSTIFICATION; LIFE AND DEATH; REWARDS; RIGHTEOUSNESS, RIGHTEOUSNESS OF GOD; SALVATION; WRATH, DESTRUCTION.

BIBLIOGRAPHY. K. P. Donfried, "Justification and Last Judgment in Paul," *ZNW* 67 (1976) 90-110; F. V. Filson, *St. Paul's Conception of Recompense* (Leipzig: Hinrichs'sche Buchhandlung, 1931); C. J. Roetzel, *Judgment in the Community* (Leiden: E. J. Brill, 1972); K. R. Snodgrass, "Justification by Grace—to the Doers: An Analysis of the Place of Romans 2 in the Theology of Paul," *NTS* 32 (1986) 72-93; S. H. Travis, *Christ and the Judgment of God* (Basingstoke: Marshall Pickering, 1986). S. H. Travis

**JUSTICE.** *See* GOD; JUDGMENT; RIGHTEOUSNESS, RIGHTEOUSNESS OF GOD.

# JUSTIFICATION

Since the time of the Reformation in the sixteenth century, considerable attention has been paid to the theme of justification in Paul. For Martin Luther the doctrine of justification was not merely the center and focus of Paul's thought; it was the "article by which the church stands or falls," the touchstone and heartbeat of all Christian theology and spirituality. That judgment has, however, been subject to intense scrutiny over the last two centuries. Recent discussion of Paul's understanding of justification has tended to focus on a number of major themes, each of which merits careful attention.

1. The Meaning of the Term *Justification*
2. The Relation of Paul's Thought to That of Contemporary Judaism
3. Paul's Understanding of "the Righteousness of God"
4. The Relation Between Faith and Works in Paul's Thought

5. The Importance of Justification to Paul's Thought

The purpose of this article is to explore and explain the present state of scholarly research on these questions. (It will be clear, however, that these issues are not merely of scholarly interest; they are of vital importance to Christian evangelism and spirituality.)

We begin by considering what Paul means by the term *justification* and how this differs from related terms such as *sanctification* (*see* Holiness, Sanctification) and *salvation*.*

### 1. The Meaning of the Term *Justification.*
The Pauline vocabulary relating to justification is grounded in the OT and seems to express the notion of "rightness" or "rectitude" rather than "righteousness."* The OT prefers the verb rather than the noun, presumably thereby indicating that justification results from an action of God* whereby an individual is set in a right relationship with God—that is, vindicated or declared to be in the right. Paul echoes this emphasis, using the verb *dikaioō*, "to justify" relatively often, but generally avoiding using the noun *dikaiōsis* "justification" (Rom 4:25). The verb denotes God's powerful, cosmic and universal action in effecting a change in the situation between sinful humanity and God, by which God is able to acquit and vindicate believers, setting them in a right and faithful relation to himself.

How does justification relate to other Pauline soteriological terms? It is tempting to adopt a simplistic approach to the matter. For example, one could attempt to force justification, sanctification and salvation into a neat past-present-future framework (Donfried), as follows:

Justification: a past event, with present implications (sanctification).

Sanctification: a present event, dependent upon a past event (justification), which has future implications (salvation).

Salvation: a future event, already anticipated and partially experienced in the past event of justification and the present event of sanctification, and dependent upon them.

But this is inadequate. Justification has future, as well as past, reference (Rom 2:13; 8:33; Gal 5:4-5), and appears to relate to both the beginning of the Christian life and its final consummation. Similarly, sanctification can also refer to a past event (1 Cor 6:11) or a future event (1 Thess 5:23). And salvation is an exceptionally complex idea, embracing not simply a future event, but something which has happened in the past (Rom 8:24; 1 Cor 15:2) or which is taking place now (1 Cor 1:18).

It is important to note that not all Paul's statements regarding justification are specifically linked with the theme of faith.* The statements appear to fall into two general categories (Hultgren): (1) those set in strongly theocentric contexts, referring to God's cosmic and universal action in relation to human sin; and (2) those making reference to faith, which is the mark to identify the people of God. This is perhaps best regarded as a difference of emphasis rather than of substance. In its universal sense justification seems to underlie Paul's argument for the universality of the gospel*; there is no distinction between Jews (*see* Israel) and Gentiles.* But in its more restricted sense justification is concerned with the identity of the people of God, and the basis of its membership.

Justification language appears in Paul both with reference to the inauguration of the life of faith and also its final consummation. It is a complex and all-embracing notion, that anticipates the verdict of the final judgment* (Rom 8:30-34) by declaring in advance the verdict of ultimate acquittal. The believer's present justified Christian existence is thus an anticipation and advance participation of deliverance from the wrath* to come, and an assurance in the present of the final eschatological (*see* Eschatology) verdict of acquittal (Rom 5:9-10).

### 2. The Relation of Paul's Thought to That of Contemporary Judaism.
In recent years a considerable debate on the relation of Paul's views on justification to those of first-century Judaism has developed, centering upon the writings of E. P. Sanders. His first major writing to address this theme was *Paul and Palestinian Judaism* (1977), followed several years later by the more important *Paul, the Law and the Jewish People* (1983). Sanders's work represents a demand for a complete reappraisal of our understanding of Paul's relation to Judaism (*see* Jew, Paul the). Sanders noted that Paul has too often been read through Lutheran eyes (a perspective in marked contrast to the Reformed standpoint, associated with Bullinger and Calvin, it stresses the divergence between the Law and the gospel). Luther argued that Paul criticized a totally misguided attempt on the part of Jewish legalists to find favor and acceptance in the sight of God by earning righteousness through performing works of the Law* (*see* Works of the Law). This view, Sanders argued, colored the analysis of such Lutheran writings as Käsemann and Bultmann. These scholars, perhaps unwittingly, read Paul through Lutheran spectacles, and thus failed to realize that Paul had to be read against his proper

historical context in first-century Judaism.

According to Sanders, Palestinian Judaism at the time of Paul could be characterized as a form of "covenantal nomism." The Law is to be regarded as an expression of the covenant* between God and Israel, and is intended to spell out as clearly and precisely as possible what forms of human conduct are appropriate within the context of this covenant. Righteousness is thus defined as behavior or attitudes which are consistent with being the historical covenant people of God. "Works of the Law" are thus not understood (as Luther suggested) as the means by which Jews believed they could gain access to the covenant; for they already stood within it. Rather, these works are an expression of the fact that the Jews already belonged to the covenant people of God and were living out their obligations to that covenant.

Sanders puts it like this. He rejects the opinion that "the righteousness which comes from the law" is "a meritorious achievement which allows one to demand reward* from God and is thus a denial of grace." "Works of the Law" were not understood as the basis of entry to the covenant, but of maintaining that covenant. As Sanders puts it, "works are the condition of remaining 'in,' but they do not earn salvation." If Sanders is right, the basic features of Luther's interpretation of Paul are incorrect, and require radical revision.

So what, then, is Paul's understanding of the difference between Judaism and Christianity according to Sanders? Having argued that Jews never believed in salvation on account of works or unaided human effort, what does Sanders see as providing the distinctive advantage of Christianity over and against Judaism? Having argued that it is not correct to see Judaism as a religion of merit and Christianity as a religion of grace,* Sanders argues as follows. Judaism sees its hope of salvation as resting upon "their status as God's covenant people who possess the law," whereas Christians believe in "a better righteousness based solely upon believing participation in Christ." Paul, like Judaism, was concerned with the issue of entering into and remaining within the covenant. The basic difference is Paul's declaration that the Jews have no national charter of privilege; membership of the covenant is open to all who have faith in Christ and who thus stand in continuity with Abraham* (Rom 4).

Sanders's analysis is important, not least in that it forces us to ask hard questions about Paul's relation to his Jewish background and the relation between the idea of participating in Christ and justification. (Interestingly, both Luther and Calvin made the notion of participating in Christ of central importance to

their doctrines of justification, Calvin to the point of making justification the consequence of such participation). But is Sanders right? The debate over this matter continues and is likely to go on for some time. But the following points seem to be sufficiently well established to note.

First, Sanders is rather vague about why Paul is convinced of the superiority of Christianity over Judaism. Judaism is presented as being wrong, simply because it is not Christianity. They are different dispensations of the same covenant. But Paul seems to regard Christianity as far more than some kind of dispensational shift within Judaism. R. H. Gundry is one of a number of scholars to stress that salvation history does not account for all that Paul says, much less for the passion with which he says it.

Second, Sanders suggests that both Paul and Judaism regard works as the principle of continuing in salvation through the covenant. Yet Paul appears to regard good works as evidential rather than instrumental. In other words, they are a demonstration of the fact that the believers stand within the covenant rather than instrumental in maintaining them within that covenant. One enters within the sphere of the covenant through faith. There is a radical new element here, which does not fit in as easily with existing Jewish ideas as Sanders seems to imply. Sanders may well be right in suggesting that good works are both a *condition for* and a *sign of* remaining within the covenant. Paul, however, sees faith as the necessary and sufficient condition for and sign of being in the covenant, with works (at best) a sign of remaining within its bounds.

Third, Sanders tends to regard Paul's doctrine of justification in a slightly negative light, as posing a challenge to the notion of a national, ethnic election. In other words, Paul's doctrine of justification is a subtle challenge to the notion that Israel* has special religious rights on account of its national identity. N. T. Wright, however, has argued that Paul's doctrine of justification should be viewed positively, as an attempt to redefine who comes within the ambit of the promises made by God to Abraham (Wright 1980 and 1992). Such ideas, which may subsequently be found developed in such essays as J. D. G. Dunn (1983) treat justification as Paul's redefinition of how the inheritance of Abraham genuinely embraces the Gentiles apart from the Law.

### 3. Paul's Understanding of the "Righteousness of God."

There is a close semantic connection between the terms *justification* (*dikaiōsis*) and *righteousness* (*dikaio-*

*synē*) in Paul's thought, making it essential to give at least a brief account of Paul's understanding of righteousness in the present discussion (*see* Righteousness, Righteousness of God). The idea of the revelation of the righteousness of God is obviously of major importance to Paul's conception of the gospel (e.g., Rom 1:16-17). Before exploring this in any detail, a serious difficulty must be noted, arising directly out of the English language. English possesses two words which are regularly used to translate the Greek *dikaiosynē* and the Latin *iustitia*: "justice" and "righteousness." These words have very different associations in English. *Righteousness* tends to mean something like "personal moral uprightness" whereas *justice* tends to bear the meaning of "social and political fairness." The former has individualistic, the latter social and communal, associations. If *dikaiosynē tou theou* is translated as "the righteousness of God," the English translation itself can mislead us regarding Paul's intentions by imposing individualist ideas of righteousness upon God. There is no easy way of avoiding this difficulty other than noting that one could equally well translate the phrase as "the justice of God."

But what does the phrase mean? There is a distinguished history of interpretation of this term, going back to the first centuries of the Christian tradition. Augustine of Hippo argued that "the righteousness of God" did not refer to the personal righteousness of God (in other words, the righteousness by which God is himself righteous), but to the righteousness which he bestows upon sinners, in order to justify them (in other words, the righteousness which comes from God). This interpretation of the phrase seems to have dominated the Western theological tradition until the fourteenth century, when writers such as Gabriel Biel began to reinterpret it in terms of "the righteousness by which God is himself righteous."

The interpretation of the phrase came to be of major importance at the time of the Reformation in the sixteenth century. Luther's theological breakthrough, probably dating from 1515, centers on the question of what it meant to speak of God as righteous. Luther initially believed that it meant that God was himself righteous, and employed that righteousness to reward those who were obedient and punish those who were sinners. As Luther knew himself to be a sinner, he could not see how the revelation of the righteousness of God could conceivably be gospel—good news—for sinners. Gradually, he came to discover that it referred to the righteousness which God imputes to sinners, covering their sins, and enabling them to be counted as righteous in the sight of God (*coram Deo*).

This understanding of the nature of the righteousness of God has continued to find a place in the modern debate, especially on the part of Lutheran interpreters of Paul. Two such interpreters may be considered in detail—R. Bultmann and E. Käsemann.

Bultmann, basing his view especially on Romans 10:3 and Philippians 3:9, argued that the "righteousness of God" was not a moral, but a relational, term. Believers are counted as being righteous by means of their faith. The term "righteousness of God" represents a genitive of authorship. Whereas Judaism regarded the bestowal of this righteousness as part and parcel of the future eschatological hope,* something which would happen at the end of history, Bultmann argued that Paul was declaring that this righteousness is imputed to believers in the present time, through faith.

E. Käsemann subjected Bultmann's interpretation to a penetrating criticism on a number of grounds. First, he argued that Bultmann had fallen into the trap of a radical individualism, based on his anthropocentric approach to theology. Bultmann was mainly concerned with questions of human existence; he ought, according to Käsemann, to have concentrated on the purpose of God. Furthermore, by interpreting "the righteousness of God" as a genitive of authorship, Bultmann had managed to drive a wedge between the God who gives and the gift which is given. Bultmann's approach isolated the gift from the giver, and concentrated on the gift itself rather than on God himself. Käsemann comments thus: "The Gift can never be separated from the Giver; it participates in the power of God, since God steps on to the scene in the gift" (Käsemann 1969, 174).

This lack of balance could be recovered by understanding "righteousness" as referring to God himself, rather than to that which he gives. Käsemann then argues that the "righteousness of God" refers to God in action. It refers to both his power, and to his gift. (Strictly speaking, then, Käsemann is not treating the "righteousness of God" as a statement about God's attributes, but as a reference to God in action.) A cluster of phrases may help convey the sort of things that Käsemann has in mind here: "salvation-creating power"; "a transformation of [our] existence"; "the power-character of the Gift"; "a change of Lordship" (Käsemann 1969, 168-82). The basic theme that recurs throughout Käsemann's discussion is that of God's saving power and action, revealed eschatologically in Jesus Christ. It merges a number of central Pauline themes, including those of victory through Christ, God's faithfulness to his covenant, and his giving of himself in power and action.

Käsemann's approach has been very influential in

recent years, both positively and negatively (see Way). Basing himself on Käsemann, P. Stuhlmacher argues that it is unacceptable to treat the "righteousness of God" as if it were a purely theocentric notion or an exclusively anthropocentric idea. It brings together elements of both, as the embodiment of the saving action of God in Christ, that brings new life for believers in its wake. The righteousness of God is both demonstrated and seen in action in the redemptive event of Christ—both in terms of God's faithfulness to his covenant and in terms of the salvific transformation of the believer.

A much more critical approach is adopted by K. Stendahl, who argued that Käsemann had neglected the importance of salvation history (often referred to in its German form, *Heilsgeschichte*) in his analysis. In fact, Stendahl suggests that Käsemann has virtually lost sight of the fact that Paul locates the event of justification in a specific historical context—namely, the history of God's dealings with his people, Israel. There is every danger that Käsemann's approach could lead to some kind of unhistorical mysticism* by failing to see that Paul discusses justification within the context of "reflection on God's plan for the world." Drawing on a series of passages (most significantly, Rom 9—11), Stendahl argues that Paul seems far more interested in the way in which God enables salvation to come about through history (above all, through the history of Israel) rather than with the abstract idea of justification by faith.

Once more, an important debate is still under way and has yet to be resolved. J. Reumann helpfully suggests that four main lines of interpretation of the "righteousness of God" may be discerned, along with their respective champions, as follows:

1. An objective genitive: "a righteousness which is valid before God" (Luther).

2. A subjective genitive: "righteousness as an attribute or quality of God" (Käsemann).

3. A genitive of authorship: "a righteousness that goes forth from God" (Bultmann).

4. A genitive of origin: "man's righteous status which is the result of God's action of justifying" (Cranfield).

However, there is a general consensus on one point of major importance, which needs to be emphasized. *The "righteousness of God" is not for Paul primarily a moral concept.* Rather, it represents a profound statement about the relevance of God for the human situation. Especially in popular circles, there is often a disturbing tendency to use Pauline texts to construct a picture of God as some kind of moral rigorist and thus impose human conceptions of righteousness

upon God. If Pauline exegesis has achieved anything, it is to remind us of the need to interpret Pauline phrases within their proper context, rather than impose "self-evident" interpretations upon them.

### 4. The Relation Between Faith and Works in Paul's Thought.

It is sometimes remarked that justification by faith implies a devaluing of human works. Or does it? A long and distinguished tradition of interpretation, drawing its inspiration largely from Luther, has seen an absolute contradiction between faith and works. They are held to be mutually exclusive entities designating two radically opposed ways of thinking about and responding to God. The way of works is seen as oriented toward human achievement, centered upon human righteousness and based upon human merit. The way of faith is seen as radically opposite, oriented toward God's achievement in Christ, centered upon the righteousness of God and based upon divine grace.

Yet this is an inadequate understanding of a complex aspect of Paul's understanding of justification. It is unquestionably a simple interpretation of Paul, and possesses all the seductive attractiveness of simplicity. But it is not adequate. It fails to do justice to the nuanced understanding of the relation of faith and works within Paul's thought, most notably expressed in the terse statement that "not the hearers, but the doers of the Law will be justified" (Rom 2:13). Some (e.g., Bultmann) have sought to dismiss this as a vestige of Paul's Jewish phase. But this cannot be maintained in the face of the evidence.

Perhaps the most important issue to emerge from recent Pauline interpretation concerning the relation between faith and works centers on clarifying the relation between Paul's theme of "justification by faith" and "judgment by works" (*see* James and Paul). There seems to be an apparent contradiction here, the resolution of which is made considerably more difficult by the fact that Paul can speak of this future judgment both negatively (as a warning against disobedience) and positively (as an encouragement for obedience). E. P. Sanders argues that Paul reproduces a characteristic first-century Jewish attitude, which could be summarized in the words "God judges according to their deeds those whom he saves by his grace." Justification by faith resonates with the accents of grace—so why are believers going to be judged on the basis of their works (e.g., Rom 2:12; 14:10; 1 Cor 3:15; 2 Cor 5:10), which resonates with the accents of human achievement? But this statement of the problem and its solution fails to deal with the fact that justification is not seen as an event in the past, but as something with future reference (Rom 2:13; 8:33; Gal 5:4-5). It is not simply a case of being justified in the past and judged in the future; there is a "not yet" element to Paul's teaching on justification which Sanders cannot quite explain.

One possible explanation of the way in which justification and future judgment are related involves an enhanced sensitivity toward the different contexts which the Pauline letters presuppose (N. M. Watson). Paul's message of justification is directed toward various audiences with very different backgrounds. The one doctrine finds itself applied practically for very different ends. The Corinthians appeared to be living in a state of bad theology and spiritual arrogance; Paul's objective is to break down their arrogance by warning them of judgment.* Paul does not intend the message of judgment to be his last word, but rather the word they need to hear so long as they remain unaware of the full implications of the gospel. On the other hand, those who exist in a state of spiritual dejection or discouragement need reassurance of the unconditionality of grace. If this understanding of Paul is correct, it implies that the theme of judgment by works is not Paul's final word to his audience; it is his penultimate word, determined by the pastoral situation of his audience, and intended to shake up those who exploit (and thus distort) the gospel proclamation of grace.

This attractive approach to the problem leaves one glad to have been reminded that Paul's letters have indeed been written to different audiences, but profoundly uneasy concerning the idea of a "penultimate word of God." How does one know what is God's final word, and which is merely his penultimate word? The idea of the finality of justification seems to be compromised.

Perhaps the simplest approach to the problem has the most to commend it. In one of his earliest writings, Paul uses the enormously important phrase "work of faith" (1 Thess 1:3). This would most naturally be understood as implying a genitive of origin—that is, "work which comes from faith." Faith is such that it does not merely produce obedience (Rom 1:5 speaks of the "obedience of faith"—that is, assuming a genitive of origin, the obedience which comes from faith) but also activity. Believers are thus justified on the basis of faith, seen not as a human work or merit, but as an expression and result of the grace of God. And believers are judged on the basis of their works, seen as the natural outcome, result and expression of justifying faith. Believers are justified by faith, and judged by its fruit. There is thus a strong connection between the past and future elements of justification—embrac-

ing faith and its outworking. Works are the visible demonstration of a real and justifying faith—not the dead faith of which James complained (Jas 2:14-24). And so these two moments of justification coinhere (*see* James and Paul).

**5. The Importance of Justification to Paul's Thought.**
In conclusion, we may pose the question which continues to remain intensely controversial within Pauline scholarship: how important is justification to Paul's understanding of the gospel? Luther, as is well known, regarded it as central. While some modern writers have endorsed Luther's judgment, others have been more critical. The center of gravity of Paul's thought lies elsewhere, they argue. But where? It is one thing to suggest that justification is *not* the center of Paul's presentation of Christianity (*see* Center). But if it is not, what is? It is actually quite difficult to identify a center to Paul's thought, not least because there is disagreement among scholars as to what the idea of a "center" actually means: a principle of coherence? a summarizing principle? a criterion of authenticity? These difficulties stand in the path of any attempt to reach agreement on the importance of justification to Paul's thought.

Nevertheless, three broad positions may be discerned within recent scholarship on this question.

(1) Justification by faith is of central importance to Paul's conception of Christianity. Among those who adopt this position are G. Bornkamm, H. Conzelmann, E. Käsemann and K. Kertelge. As noted above, this position has strong historical associations with Martin Luther, and it is perhaps not surprising that it is echoed by many modern German Lutheran NT scholars. This school of thought tends to regard justification as the real theological center of gravity within Paul's thought and is critical of any attempt to treat it as being of lesser importance. Justification by faith is not simply concerned with clarifying the Christian gospel in relation to first-century Judaism; it addresses the fundamental question of how sinful human beings can find favor or acceptance in the sight of a righteous God. Within this approach differences can nevertheless be discerned. Bultmann adopts a generally Lutheran position, stressing the positive importance of faith while interpreting Paul's justification language in terms of existentialist categories. C. E. B. Cranfield adopts a more Reformed stance, noting the continuing importance of the Law.

(2) Justification by faith is a "subsidiary crater" (A. Schweitzer) in Paul's overall presentation and understanding of the Christian gospel. The origins of this view may be traced back to the nineteenth cen-

tury, especially to the writings of W. Wrede. Wrede argued that justification by faith was simply a polemical doctrine designed to neutralize the theological threat posed by Judaism. Having neutralized this threat, Paul was then able to develop the positive aspects of his own thought (which, for Wrede, centered on the idea of redemption in Christ). The real emphasis of Paul's thought thus lies elsewhere than justification. Among those who adopt this position, the following may be noted (along with their views on where the center of Paul's thought really lies): A. Schweitzer (the rising and dying of the believer with Christ), R. P. Martin (reconciliation with God) and E. P. Sanders (believing participation in Christ).

(3) A third view may be regarded as a compromise between these two views. Justification by faith is regarded as one of a number of ways of thinking about, or visualizing, what God has achieved for believers in and through Christ. The position adopted by J. Jeremias well illustrates this mediating function. The center of Paul's thought does not lie with justification as such; rather it lies with the grace of God. But justification is one of a number of ways of describing this grace (in juridical terms of unconditional pardon and forgiveness). It is thus central in one sense (in that it is a way of expressing the core of the gospel), and not central in another (in that it is only one way, among others, of expressing this core).

This debate seems set to continue, and it is not clear whether there is any hope of a genuine consensus. It is perhaps worth noting that it is genuinely difficult to classify some approaches to Paul's theology in terms of this neat framework. Nevertheless, both the first and second positions continue to attract supporters.

This, then, represents the state of present scholarship on the main aspects of Paul's theology of justification by faith. It is clear that it is one of the most interesting aspects of Pauline scholarship, attracting writers of considerable skill and commitment. It is likely that the years ahead will witness still further wrestling with this aspect of Pauline thought, to the considerable enhancement both of academy and church; the former, as scholars seek to understand Paul, and the latter, as Christians seek to apply him to the tasks and opportunities of the Christian life.

See also CENTER OF PAUL; LAW; PAUL AND HIS INTERPRETERS; RIGHTEOUSNESS, RIGHTEOUSNESS OF GOD; WORKS OF THE LAW.

BIBLIOGRAPHY. G. Bornkamm, *Paul* (New York: Harper & Row, 1971); C. H. Cosgrove, "Justification in Paul: A Linguistic and Theological Reflection," *JBL* 106 (1987) 653-70; C. E. B. Cranfield, *A Critical and Exegetical Commentary on the Epistle to the Romans* (2 vols; ICC; Edinburgh: T. & T. Clark, 1975, 1979); K. P. Donfried, "Justification and Last Judgement in Paul," *ZNW* 67 (1976) 90-110; J. D. G. Dunn, "The New Perspective on Paul," *BJRL* 65 (1983) 95-122; R. H. Gundry, "Grace, Works and Staying Saved in Paul," *Bib* 60 (1985) 1-38; C. J. A. Hickling, "Centre and Periphery in the Thought of St Paul," in *Studia Biblica III. Papers on Paul and Other NT Authors*, ed. E. A. Livingstone (JSNTSup 3; Sheffield, Academic Press, 1978) 199-214; A. J. Hultgren, *Paul's Gospel and Mission* (Philadelphia: Fortress, 1985); E. Käsemann, *Commentary on Romans* (Grand Rapids: Eerdmans, 1980); idem, " 'The Righteousness of God' in Paul," in *New Testament Questions of Today* (Philadelphia: Fortress, 1969); K. Kertelge, *Rechtfertigung bei Paulus* (Münster: Aschendorff, 1967); A. E. McGrath, *Iustitia Dei: A History of the Christian Doctrine of Justification* (2 vols; Cambridge: University Press, 1986); R. P. Martin, *Reconciliation: A Study of Paul's Theology* (Atlanta: John Knox, 1981); J. Reumann, *Righteousness in the New Testament* (Philadelphia: Fortress, 1982); E. P. Sanders, *Paul and Palestinian Judaism* (Philadelphia: Fortress, 1977); idem, *Paul, the Law, and the Jewish People* (Philadelphia: Fortress, 1983); M. A. Seifrid, *Justification by Faith: The Origin and Development of a Central Pauline Theme* (NovTSup 68; Leiden: E. J. Brill, 1992); K. Stendahl, *Paul Among Jews and Gentiles* (Philadelphia: Fortress, 1976); P. Stuhlmacher, *Gerechtigkeit Gottes bei Paulus* (FRLANT 87; Göttingen: Vandenhoeck & Ruprecht, 1966); idem, "The Apostle Paul's View of Righteousness," in *Reconciliation, Law, and Righteousness: Essays in Biblical Theology* (Philadelphia: Fortress, 1986) 68-93; N. M. Watson, "Justified by faith, judged by works: an antimony?" *NTS* 29 (1983) 209-21; D. V. Way, *The Lordship of Christ: Ernst Käsemann's Interpretation of Paul's Theology* (Oxford: Clarendon, 1991); S. K. Williams, "The 'Righteousness of God' in Romans," *JBL* 99 (1980) 241-90; N. T. Wright, *The Climax of the Covenant: Christ and the Law in Pauline Theology* (Minneapolis: Fortress, 1991); idem, *The Messiah and the People of God* (unpublished D.Phil. thesis, Oxford University, 1980); idem, "The Paul of History and the Apostle of Faith," *TynB* 29 (1978) 61-88; J. A. Ziesler, *The Meaning of Righteousness in Paul* (Cambridge: University Press, 1972).
A. E. McGrath

# K

**KERYGMA.** *See* Center of Paul's Theology; Preaching, Kerygma.

**KING.** *See* God; Kingdom of God/Christ.

## KINGDOM OF GOD/CHRIST

The whole of Paul's theology is conditioned by a perspective which sees the eschatological promises of God as having been inaugurated through the resurrection* of Jesus Christ from the dead. An important feature of this eschatological worldview is the teaching concerning the kingdom of God, which overlaps somewhat with the teaching about the kingdom of Christ in the Pauline materials. This overlap also provides a fertile ground for demonstrating how christology* and eschatology* interlock in Paul's thought.

    1. Statistical Evidence
    2. Is the Kingdom Present or Future?
    3. Is the Kingdom of God the Same As the Kingdom of Christ?
    4. The Deliverance of the Kingdom to God the Father
    5. Transferral into the Kingdom of Christ

### 1. Statistical Evidence.

While the idea of the kingdom of God or kingdom of Christ is certainly foundational to the whole of Paul's thought, it is somewhat surprising to discover the comparative rarity of explicit references to "the kingdom" within the Pauline letters. The term *basileia* ("reign," "kingdom") occurs only fifteen times (Rom 14:17; 1 Cor 4:20; 6:9, 10; 15:24, 50; Gal 5:21; Eph 5:5; Col 1:13; 4:11; 1 Thess 2:12; 2 Thess 1:5; 2 Tim 4:1, 14, 18), while the verb *basileuō* ("to reign") occurs nine times (Rom 5:14, 17 [twice], 21 [twice]; 6:12; 1 Cor 4:8 [twice]; 15:25) and the verb *symbasileuō* ("to reign with") occurs in 1 Timothy 2:12. The phrase "kingdom of God" (or its equivalent) occurs a mere eight times within the Pauline letters (Rom 14:17; 1 Cor 4:20; 6:9; 15:50; Gal 5:21; Col 4:11; 1 Thess 2:12 ["his kingdom"]; 2 Thess 1:5). The reference to "commonwealth in the heavens" (*to politeuma en ouranois*) in

Philippians 3:20 might also legitimately be understood as a parallel expression. Another startling fact is that within the Pauline corpus the kingdom *of Christ** is only explicitly described in Colossians 1:13 and Ephesians 5:5. This is remarkable given Paul's firm commitment to the messiahship of Jesus Christ and the frequent association of the kingdom with God's Messiah in Jewish OT and pseudepigraphal literature (see Kreitzer, 29-91, for details). Several key issues arise as one considers the teaching about the kingdom within the Pauline letters.

### 2. Is the Kingdom Present or Future?

NT scholarship has long discussed the temporal nature of the kingdom of God as it is contained in the sayings of Jesus. A general consensus has been reached, namely that the primary message of Jesus himself was one of an inaugurated kingdom, one which had already begun in his own life and ministry but which was awaiting consummation in the future. Many of the questions about the temporal nature of the kingdom as it is found in the Gospel materials also surface within the Pauline letters, despite the paucity of references to "the kingdom" as such. At times Paul speaks of the kingdom of God as if it were a present reality capable of being experienced by the Christian believers. Notably, two texts are expressive of this, Romans 14:17 and 1 Corinthians 4:20.

At other times Paul speaks of the kingdom of God as if it were a future hope, something which had yet to be awaited by the Christian believers. A good example of this is 1 Thessalonians 2:12: a verse sandwiched between two declarations of the parousia of Christ (1 Thess 1:10 and 2:19). In 2 Thessalonians 1:5 the kingdom of God is described in terms of it being God's future vindication for those who endure suffering* for their faith.*

Again, in keeping with the future dimension of the kingdom of God, Paul often speaks of it as something which will be inherited by the faithful if they demonstrated the necessary character (1 Cor 6:9-10; 15:50; Gal 5:21). The language of future inheritance is also found in Colossians 3:24 (cf. Col 1:12). A similar declaration about inheritance is made in Ephesians 5:5, with the slight alteration that the kingdom is here described as belonging to both God* and Christ.*

In short, the kingdom of God is something which straddles the dimensions of time, being both present and future (as Martin, 109-25, affirms). It is not possible to restrict Paul's teaching about the kingdom of God/Christ to temporal terms. It is true that he tends to speak of the ultimate revelation of the kingdom as a future event, but there is ample evidence to support the contention that the power of this eschatological kingdom is also at work in the life of the Christian community now. Indeed, G. Johnson in his comment on 1 Corinthians 4:20 goes so far as to suggest that "in the last analysis the so-called 'eschatological' dimension of the kingdom has been relegated to a fairly minor place, and its present fact has been translated instead into the great concept of spiritual life" (Johnson, 151). Thus the kingdom of God/Christ might even be described as "life in the Spirit" or "life within the Body of Christ," both much more prominent themes within the Pauline letters.

### 3. Is the Kingdom of God the Same as the Kingdom of Christ?

Some scholars have suggested that Paul maintains a distinction between the kingdom of God and the kingdom of Christ, usually by pointing to 1 Corinthians 15:20-28 as a key text and postulating that the passage hints at a temporary messianic reign on earth which gives way to the kingdom of God in the fullness of time. Such a suggestion parallels a similar distinction between the two kingdoms found in select Jewish and Christian apocalypses of the NT period, namely the *Apocalypse of Weeks* (*1 Enoch* 93:1-10; 91:12-17); 4 Ezra 7:26-30; 12:31-34; *2 Baruch* 29:3—30:1; 40:1-4; and Revelation 20:4-6 (see Kreitzer for a discussion).

A literal interpretation of passages such as these has yielded a "chiliastic" (or "premillennial") strand of eschatology in the history of the Christian church. Some interpreters, such as A. Schweitzer, have appealed to Paul as an advocate of precisely this position, noting that a necessary corollary is a doctrine of two resurrections,* one for the saints who participate in the temporary, messianic, kingdom and the second a general resurrection for judgment before the age to come. Effectively this means that the kingdom of Christ commences with the parousia and concludes with the arrival of the kingdom of God (the age to come) and that the reign of the Messiah is the interval between the two resurrections associated with these two events.

However, it is not at all clear that Paul maintains a rigid distinction between the kingdom of God and the kingdom of Christ throughout his letters; nor that he anywhere teaches a doctrine of two resurrections (although Luke has Paul speak of a resurrection of "the just and the unjust" in Acts 24:15). Consequently most scholars dispute that Paul can be legitimately described as consistently chiliastic in his eschatological viewpoint (if he can be described as chiliastic at all). They point out that more often than not Paul's description of the consummation of God's kingdom is simply associated with the future parousia of Jesus Christ, with no forced dichotomy implied between the two kingdoms. In other words, it is denied that 1 Corinthians 15:20-28 teaches a temporary messianic kingdom, and the passage is effectively harmonized with other passages (such as 1 Cor 15:51-56 and 1 Thess 4:13-18) which describe the parousia of Christ in greater detail (G. Vos is a classic proponent of this approach).

Usually those following this interpretation take Christ's rule over the "kingdom" (which he is said to hand over to the Father in 1 Cor 15:24) to have begun at the cross. This interpretation has the benefit of offering a Paul who is entirely coherent and uniform in his schematization of the future, avoiding presenting Paul as hopelessly confused or inconsistent in his teaching. On the other hand, the passage in 1 Corinthians 15:20-28 is anything but clear in its expression and it is easy to see how a chiliastic interpretation might be derived from it. The question then arises whether we need Paul to be wholly consistent in the way that he describes how the kingdom of God relates to the kingdom of Christ and the parousia. A much more realistic approach is to accept the idea that flexibility of expression is inherent within all eschatological literature, including Paul's letters. Harmonization of eschatological detail, even in the aid of rescuing Paul from (what is perceived to be) a damaging inconsistency, is not the answer. We may be able to iron out all of the eschatological tensions and wrinkles within Pauline theology but in the process distance ourself from Paul himself.

How then, is it that the "kingdom of God" gives way to the "kingdom of Christ" as an expression of eschatological hope? If the basis of Paul's eschatology is the OT proclamation of the kingdom *of God*, how is it that this kingdom becomes explicitly described as the kingdom *of Christ*? Almost certainly this transition takes place as a result of the close association of Jesus of Nazareth and the kingdom of God which he came to proclaim. We see examples of just this sort of christological shift of emphasis in the redaction of the Gospels, and it is likely that the Pauline materials follow suit in this regard. As B. Klappert remarks: "The phrase 'basileia of Christ' and the equation of 'kingdom of God' with Jesus Christ are thus seen to be the result of the change-over from an implicit to an explicit christology" (Klappert, 387).

### 4. The Deliverance of the Kingdom to God the Father.

In 1 Corinthians 15:20-28 we have one of the most difficult passages within the Pauline corpus to interpret, one which is filled with apocalyptic* imagery and language (E. Käsemann's interpretation of Pauline apocalyptic eschatology is heavily dependent upon these verses). Contained within the passage is a curious reference to "the kingdom": "Then comes the end, when he delivers the kingdom to God the Father after destroying every rule and every authority and power" (1 Cor 15:24; see Principalities and Powers). One of the most frustrating features of this highly compressed pericope is the ambiguity of the subject of the verbs. For example, who is the subject of hypetaxen ("he subjected") in 1 Corinthians 15:27? Is it God or Christ? If it is assumed to be God (as in the NRSV) then some difficulties of understanding arise within the rest of the passage. One is never quite sure who is subjecting what to whom. No doubt the referential confusion between God and Christ is partly due to the christologically motivated use of Psalm 110:1 and Psalm 8:7b in verses 25 and 27 respectively (de Boer, 114-20, offers some discussion of this).

A related item of exegetical significance is the connection between "the kingdom" and "the created order" (ta panta) within the passage. M. J. Harris associates the resurrection of the dead and the coming of the kingdom with the re-creation of the created order (see Creation and New Creation); the kingdom, he says "incorporate(s) the rational and the irrational universe" (Harris, 18). Clearly there is an important cosmological dimension to this passage in addition to the more traditional temporal one which has been the focus of scholarly attention in the past.

### 5. Transferral into the Kingdom of Christ.

In Colossians 1:13-14 we have an unusual reference to the kingdom of Christ: "He (God) has delivered us from the dominion of darkness and transferred us to the kingdom of his beloved Son, in whom we have redemption, the forgiveness of sins." The remarkable thing about this passage is that the transferral is described as an act already accomplished, as realized within the life of the believer. This departure from the more characteristic description of the kingdom of God/Christ as a future reality yet to be awaited has led

some interpreters to question Pauline authorship of the letter (see the commentaries by E. Lohse, E. Schweizer and P. T. O'Brien for a discussion of this; see Colossians).

In conclusion, while the explicit expression "kingdom of God/Christ" is not widespread within the Pauline letters, the idea is a fundamental component of Paul's eschatological perspective and underlies the whole of his teaching. The same tension between the present and future dimensions of a kingdom theology found to be present in the teaching of Jesus within the Synoptic Gospels is also contained within the Pauline materials. Perhaps even more significant within the Pauline letters is the fact that the idea of the "kingdom of God" affords an important vehicle for Paul's developing christology wherein the "kingdom of Christ" begins to compete with "kingdom of God" as the focal point of theological concern.

*See also* APOCALYPTICISM; CHRISTOLOGY; CREATION AND NEW CREATION; ESCHATOLOGY; EXALTATION AND ENTHRONEMENT; JESUS AND PAUL; RESURRECTION.

BIBLIOGRAPHY. M. C. de Boer, *The Defeat of Death* (JSNTS 22; Sheffield: Academic, 1988); M. J. Harris, *Raised Immortal: The Relation Between Resurrection and Immortality in New Testament Teaching* (Grand Rapids: Eerdmans, 1983); G. Johnson, " 'Kingdom of God' Sayings in Paul's Epistles," in *From Jesus to Paul: Studies in Honour of Francis Wright Beare*, ed. P. Richardson and J. C. Hurd (Ontario: Wilfred Laurier University, 1984) 143-56; E. Käsemann, "Primitive Christian Apocalyptic," in *New Testament Questions of Today* (Philadelphia: Fortress, 1969) 108-37, esp. 133-37; B. Klappert, "King, Kingdom," *NIDNTT* 2.372-90; L. J. Kreitzer, *Jesus and God in Paul's Eschatology* (JSNTS 19; Sheffield: Academic, 1987) 131-64; R. P. Martin, *The Spirit and the Congregation* (Grand Rapids: Eerdmans, 1984); A. Schweitzer, *The Mysticism of Paul the Apostle* (London: A. & C. Black, 1931); G. Vos, *The Pauline Eschatology* (Princeton: University Press, 1930) 226-60.

L. J. Kreitzer

## KNOWLEDGE, GIFT OF KNOWLEDGE

The term "word of knowledge" (logos gnōseōs) occurs only once in the Pauline corpus, at 1 Corinthians 12:8. There it is listed second in a catalog of nine charisms (charismata, manifestations of divine grace,* or special gifts bestowed by the grace of God*). While no definition is provided for this gift of the Spirit, we are able to reach some understanding of what it was and is by looking at the way Paul addressed himself to the subject of knowledge within the larger corpus of his writings and the Corinthian correspondence in particular (see Gifts of the Spirit).

1. Knowledge
2. Knowledge at Corinth
3. Gift of Knowledge

## 1. Knowledge.

From the Pauline corpus as a whole we understand that Paul frequently referred to knowledge (*gnōsis*) and knowing in the sense of "acquaintance" or "comprehension." One is able to know God* (Rom 1:21; Gal 4:9; Phil 3:10), to know God's will (Rom 2:18), to know the Law* (Rom 7:1) or to know the love* of Christ* (Eph 3:19). *Gnōsis* is also a term Paul used frequently to communicate information he wants his readers to understand (Gal 3:7; Eph 5:5; 6:22; Phil 1:12). But Paul also viewed certain things to be inscrutable or unknowable in themselves, such as the mind of God. He writes that the depths of the riches of God's wisdom* and knowledge are unsearchable (Rom 11:33-34). The human mind unaided is not sufficient to grasp the mind and knowledge of God.*

If God's knowledge is unsearchable in the sense that it transcends the human capacity to comprehend it, it is equally clear, especially from the Corinthian* correspondence, that at times the Holy Spirit* reveals insight into the mind of God. No one comprehends what is God's except the Spirit of God (1 Cor 2:11), and since Christians have received the Holy Spirit, they are now capable of understanding many of the things of God. It is the Holy Spirit's role to make the spiritual things of God comprehensible to the human mind (1 Cor 2:11).

## 2. Knowledge at Corinth.

From the Corinthian correspondence it is clear that knowledge held an important place in the minds of many within that congregation. Paul acknowledged the richness of their endowment with knowledge of all kinds (1 Cor 1:5), and he noted that the Corinthians excelled in knowledge, among other things (2 Cor 8:7), but within the Corinthian context knowledge was being abused. It had come to be identified *ipso facto* as a badge of spirituality,* which only certain Corinthians enjoyed. One can, as does Schmithals, therefore identify a type of proto-gnosticism present at Corinth even in Paul's day (*see* Gnosis, Gnosticism). Paul's discussion of knowledge in 1 Corinthians 8 is telling. Knowledge is much like a double-edged sword. Paul, like the Corinthians, can sing its praises, but he also recognizes that it possesses a dark side. "Knowledge puffs up," he notes, "but love builds up" (1 Cor 8:1 NRSV). It is this selfish use of knowledge that must be avoided. While knowledge can bring freedom* to some because it has succeeded in banishing the fears which result from ignorance, for others the lack of knowledge means that they can easily be offended by those who, apart from wisdom and love, exercise their newly found "knowledge" (1 Cor 8:7-11). Knowledge improperly handled by those who possess it can result in the destruction of those who do not possess it.

Repeatedly Paul's concern at Corinth is that those with knowledge choose not to employ it as somehow symbolic of their own spirituality, but rather employ it for positive, edifying ends. It should serve the congregation and direct its members toward God. Knowledge must be exercised in love.

## 3. Gift of Knowledge.

In spite of this, Paul is clear that there are generally useful words or utterances of knowledge, and that these words may be viewed as charisms, or gifts, freely bestowed by the Holy Spirit in a sovereign manner (1 Cor 12:4, 11). J. D. G. Dunn rightly calls them "rational revelations" (Dunn, 217-19). Their purpose, like the purpose of all such charisms, is to serve the ongoing welfare of the church* (1 Cor 12:7). In 1 Corinthians 8 the knowledge possessed by those Corinthians who were labeled as "strong" appears to have provided them with a "charismatic insight into the real nature of reality" (Dunn, 218). The sovereign action of the Spirit's distribution of these utterances of knowledge, moreover, means that not all Christians have been given this charism (1 Cor 12:11) and, therefore, it is important for those who gain this knowledge from the Spirit to share it with the rest of the body of Christ in such a way as to teach and lead them without injury (*see* Body of Christ). The possession of this knowledge, then, is viewed as having certain limitations.

In 1 Corinthians 13 Paul notes several of the limitations inherent in this knowledge, even if it consists of Spirit-inspired utterances of knowledge. One of these limitations is temporal in nature, for knowledge will ultimately come to an end (1 Cor 13:8). A second, and perhaps more important, limitation is its inability to communicate adequately in words the whole picture. At present our knowledge, even Spirit-inspired knowledge, is only partial or incomplete. It appears merely as a dim reflection in a mirror (1 Cor 13:12), as we ourselves are slowly moving through a process of transformation from one level of glory* to another (2 Cor 3:18) by means of the Holy Spirit. This process of transformation, which also in some way involves a form of divine revelation, will not be complete until the consummation (1 Cor 13:12; 2 Cor 3:18; cf. 1 Jn 3:2). At that time a full knowledge will come, but perhaps more importantly, with it will come the realization that believers have also been the subject of the divine knowledge. They have been fully known by God.

Probably the most important limitation that Paul views as governing knowledge is the limitation placed on it by love. Love edifies (1 Cor 8:1; 13:4-7, 13), and its primary focus seems to be a recognition and an encouragement of others. Any exercise of a manifestation of knowledge apart from love is of no value. It is nothing (1 Cor 13:2). Paul's view of knowledge is expressed in 1 Corinthians 14:6, where knowledge is shown to be parallel with, and to play a role in, teaching.* Teaching, by its very nature, demands an open and trusting relationship characterized by love.

In the contemporary Pentecostal and Charismatic renewal many claims are made regarding the presence and use of the "word of knowledge." Like all charisms, these claims must each be discerned by the community of faith. This charism, like all genuine charisms, is meant to contribute to *the whole community*, bringing its recipients to a new level of maturity by providing insight into the mind of Christ (1 Cor 2:16). Such charisms show their genuine character by the fruit which they bring forth.

*See also* GIFTS OF THE SPIRIT; GNOSIS, GNOSTICISM; PROPHECY, PROPHESYING; TEACHING/PARAENESIS; WISDOM.

BIBLIOGRAPHY. J. D. G. Dunn, *Jesus and the Spirit* (Philadelphia: Westminster, 1975); E. E. Ellis, *Prophecy and Hermeneutic in Early Christianity* (Grand Rapids: Eerdmans, 1978); D. Gee, *Concerning Spiritual Gifts* (rev. ed.; Springfield, MO: Gospel Publishing House, 1972); M. R. Hillmer, "Knowledge: New Age, Gnosticsm and First Corinthians," *McMaster Journal of Theology* 3 (1992) 18-38; W. Schmithals, *Gnosticism in Corinth* (Nashville: Abingdon, 1971); D. Wead, *Hear His Voice* (Carol Stream: Creation House, 1976).

C. M. Robeck, Jr.

**KOINONIA.** *See* FELLOWSHIP, COMMUNION, SHARING; LORD'S SUPPER.

**KYRIOS.** *See* CHRISTOLOGY; LORD.

# L

**LAST ADAM.** *See* ADAM AND CHRIST; CHRISTOLOGY; ESCHATOLOGY.

## LAW

A well-attested feature of Jewish religion in Paul's time was the manner in which the Jewish way of life was being defined in both oral and written form. The foundation of this material was the covenant* which God* communicated to Moses* and made with the people of Israel* at Sinai as it is preserved in the first five books of the Hebrew Bible. Jews of Paul's time, following biblical usage, frequently referred to these foundational writings as the "Law" (Heb *tôrâ*, Gk *nomos*). After Paul's call to preach Christ* to the Gentiles* (Gal 1:15-16; Rom 1:5, 13-14; 15:18; cf. Acts 9:15; 22:21; 26:17) he thought extensively about the relationship between the Jewish Law and faith* in Christ. We find the results of that thinking primarily in the Thessalonian* and Corinthian* correspondence, in Galatians,* Philippians* and Romans,* and to a lesser extent in Colossians,* Ephesians* and the Pastorals.*

No area of Pauline studies has undergone more sweeping revision in the last half century than the apostle's view of the Law. Compelling evidence has required a reassessment of Christian, and especially Protestant, assumptions about the Law in Judaism and therefore about Paul's relationship to this single most important aspect of his ancestral faith. Some understanding of the nature of this revolution in Pauline studies is, therefore, an important prerequisite to a fresh reading of Paul's own comments about the Jewish Law (*see* Paul and His Interpreters).

    1. The Struggle to Understand Paul's View of the Law
    2. The Jewish Law in the Second Temple Period
    3. The Jewish Law in the Context of Paul's Letters
    4. Conclusion

**1. The Struggle to Understand Paul's View of the Law.**
During the period of the Renaissance and Reformation the Roman Catholic Church understood Paul's claim that "by works of the Law no flesh shall be justified" (Gal 2:16) to mean that no one could attain eternal life* without divine help. To the Catholic Church in the several centuries before and after Luther, this dictum did not seem to exclude good deeds from some role in salvation,* and other passages in Paul's letters seemed to indicate that such works were necessary (Gal 5:6; Rom 6:13, 19; cf. Council of Trent, *Decree on Justification*, 6.10-11). Thomas Aquinas, therefore, believed that since human nature in itself required the transforming power of God's grace* in order to inherit eternal life, humanity could not have been saved by its own merits even prior to the Fall. After the Fall God's grace was even more necessary for salvation since humanity was now two removes from God (*Summa Theologica*, I-II.109.2). The OT Law, likewise, operated at a human level and, as good as it might have been, was lacking the requisite grace of God that enabled people to keep its precepts (I-II.98.1-2). The new law of the NT contained this grace, however, and so Christians were able, by means of this grace, to do the works which merited for them eternal life (I-II.108.1; 111.2; 112.1; 114.1-9). Likewise, the Council of Trent claimed that justification was a process of cooperation with divine grace which began with repentance and continued in the form of obedience to the commandments of God and the church (Council of Trent, *Decree on Justification*, 6.10-11).

It was chiefly against this principle of cooperation between grace and works as it was expressed in the doctrine of the merits of the saints, that the Reformers raised the banner of dissent. Prior to his protest against the Roman Catholic Church, Luther feared that neither his own good works, even if done out of love for Christ, nor the merits of his order could save him from God's terrible righteousness. Finally, after reaching a point of near despair, Luther began meditating on such texts as Psalm 31:1-2 and Romans 1:17 and discovered through them that the purpose of God's righteousness* was not to condemn but to save the sinner. Rather than his angry accuser, God, as it turned out, was his rock of refuge and mighty fortress.

This experience informed Luther's reading of

Paul's letters, especially Galatians. There he found ample evidence that no human activity, or "active righteousness," no matter how sincere or vigorous, could save people from God's wrath.* Such salvation could come only through "passive righteousness"—a righteousness provided in its entirety by God himself and appropriated by faith in Jesus Christ. Luther took Paul's use of the word *law* in such passages as Galatians 2:16-21 as a cipher for God's righteous demands and all human attempts to be saved by them. These, he believed, could not save but only condemn and inspire terror: "no matter how wise and righteous men may be according to reason and the divine Law," he says, "yet with all their works, merits, Masses, righteousness, and acts of worship they are not justified" (*LW*, 26:140, commenting on Gal 2:16). The role of the Law is not to justify but to condemn and terrify (*LW*, 26:148-51). Salvation comes by another, entirely separate "law," the Law of grace which gives righteousness to the believer apart from any effort and insulates him or her from the Law's accusations. In the sphere of justification,* therefore, the Law has no place. By putting his or her faith in Christ, the Christian has climbed up into heaven and left the Law far away on the earth below (*LW*, 26:156-57).

It is easy, when reading Luther, to concentrate on the theological argument with the Roman Catholic Church in which he is so energetically engaged and to miss a subtle hermeneutical impropriety in which the great Reformer and theologian has indulged. Especially in his lectures on Galatians, but elsewhere as well, Luther assumes that the Jews, against whose view of the Law Paul was arguing, held the same theology of justification as the medieval Roman Catholic Church. This hermeneutical error would be perpetuated over the next four centuries and eventually serve as the organizing principle for mountains of Protestant scholarship on the OT and ancient Judaism.

It was frequently assumed among OT scholars, for example, that at least from the period of the restoration of the Jews to Israel under Ezra, the history of Judaism was a story of spiralling degeneracy into legalism, hypocrisy and lack of compassion. Similarly, when Protestant scholars discussed rabbinic Judaism they tended to assume that Paul's polemic against Judaism, interpreted through the lens of Luther's reaction against Roman Catholicism, provided a sound basis for systematizing the religion of the Mishnah, Talmud and related Jewish writings of a later era. F. Weber's "popular" description of Talmudic theology (1880) is typical. Keeping the many and peculiar commands of the Law, said Weber, was the means by which the rabbis believed salvation was earned. The

ordinary rabbi, therefore, believed that the goal of rabbinic religion was the search for reward on the basis of merit, that God was a stern judge, and that approaching death brought with it the fear of losing salvation due to a lack of merit.

A large part of this portrait of ancient Judaism found its way into interpretations of the NT generally, and especially into expositions of Paul's writings. Widely used commentaries, such as that of W. Sanday and A. Headlam on Romans (reprinted seventeen times from 1895 to 1952) and influential books about the NT, such as R. Bultmann's popular description of *Primitive Christianity in Its Contemporary Setting* (1949; ET 1956) used this picture of Judaism as the backdrop for their explanations of NT theology. In Sanday and Headlam's commentary, for example, Paul's struggle with the Law in Romans 7:7-25, which they take to be a self-portrait of his preconversion existence, is interpreted as the natural consequence of the "stern" rabbinic view of the Law, which, they claim, "was fatal to peace of mind" (Sanday and Headlam, 189). Similarly, Bultmann, in a section of *Primitive Christianity* titled "Jewish legalism," claimed that the Jewish view of the Law in the first century made "radical obedience" to God impossible because it held that once a certain list of commandments had been kept, one was in the clear and was free to do anything (Bultmann, 69). In addition, said Bultmann, it taught that God would punish sins strictly according to the law of retribution, that salvation was never a certainty, and that even repentance and faith could be transformed into meritorious works (Bultmann, 69-71).

The Lutheran picture of ancient Judaism, now clad in the impressive robes of scholarship, did not go unchallenged among Jewish scholars. As early as 1894 the distinguished Jewish reformer C. G. Montefiore objected forcefully to what he viewed as the tendency of Christian theologians to paint rabbinic Judaism as a dark shadow against which Paul's theology could brightly shine. The rabbinic literature, pleaded Montefiore, reveals a compassionate and forgiving God, ready to lay aside even grievous infractions of the Law at the slightest movement toward repentance by the offending party. It portrays rabbis, moreover, as those who regarded the Law as a gift and delight, who placed a value on faith in God as high as Paul's, and whose daily prayer was "Sovereign of all worlds! not because of our righteous acts do we lay our supplications before thee, but because of thine abundant mercies" (*b. Yoma* 87b). "I wonder," Montefiore asked in an address before England's St. Paul Association in 1900, "if there is the smallest chance that you, unlike the theologians, will believe me when I say that all this business of the severe Judge and the stern Law giver is a figment and a bugbear?"

Montefiore's critique of the Lutheran caricature of Judaism at first fell on deaf ears; but through the work of several influential scholars over the next seventy years, it gradually began to gain the ascendancy not only in Jewish circles but among nearly everyone working in the field. In 1927 G. F. Moore published a two-volume study of rabbinic theology which, in contrast to Weber's work, emphasized the role of grace, forgiveness and repentance in the earliest literature of rabbinic religion. This was followed in 1948 by W. D. Davies's detailed study of *Paul and Rabbinic Judaism* in which Davies argued that Paul's doctrine of justification by faith apart from the Law was only one metaphor among many, probably developed first in the heat of argument (Davies, 221-23), and that the apostle's letters revealed simply a Pharisee for whom the messianic age had dawned (Davies, 71-73; *see* Jew, Paul the).

Without question, however, the pivotal event in bringing Montefiore's complaint from the backwater to main stream was the publication in 1977 of E. P. Sanders's *Paul and Palestinian Judaism*. Sanders's book was so powerful not because its approach was original but because Sanders addressed pointedly and exhaustively the distorted view of Judaism which Lutheran scholarship, and those under its influence, had produced. Sanders made his way step by step through the most influential works of modern NT scholarship in order to show that they disparaged ancient Judaism as a religion in which salvation was accomplished by meritorious achievement. He then embarked on a lengthy journey through not only the rabbinic literature of the first 200 years after Christ but through the Qumran* literature, the apocrypha and the pseudepigrapha as well to determine how those documents answer the question, What must one do to be saved?

His conclusion was that in all of this ancient Jewish literature, with the exception of the atypical document 4 Ezra, salvation came not through achieving a certain number of meritorious works but through belonging to the covenant people of God. The proper response to the covenant was, of course, obedience; but means of atonement were readily available for those who did not obey fully. This "pattern of religion" Sanders called "covenantal nomism" (Sanders 1977, 75; 1992, 262-78), and, he claimed, it bears little resemblance to the descriptions of Jewish "soteriology" in most handbooks of Protestant biblical scholarship.

Largely as a result of this important work, most students of Pauline theology now believe that Montefiore, Sanders and other dissenters from the classic Protestant perspective have proven their case. The problem has now become what to do with Paul, who after all *does* seem to argue loudly against Jews who espouse justification by "works of the Law."* Montefiore's answer to this question in 1894 has become popular among some. He believed that Paul was an aberration whose neglect of the Jewish doctrine of repentance for infractions against the Law was puzzling and whose Judaism, if Judaism at all, must have been heavily influenced by Hellenism. S. Sandmel claims similarly that "Paul's attitude toward the Law is exactly the reverse of the views in all other surviving Jewish writings" (Sandmel 1978, 320) and that the origin of Paul's negative evaluation of the Law lies to a large extent in ideas about the Law which flourished in the fertile soil of Hellenistic Judaism. This brand of Judaism, Sandmel argues, often saw value in the Law only as a guide to other religious ideals and so played down the importance of its literal observance. Paul, therefore, was predisposed to devalue the Law because of his roots in a Judaism heavily influenced by Greek thought (Sandmel 1979, 48-53). This view reaches its extreme in the work of H. Maccoby who, largely on the basis of Galatians 3:19 and 4:9-10, claims that Paul's view of the Law was derived from Gnosticism* (Maccoby, 40-48).

This reading of Paul, as W. D. Davies observed long ago, blunders methodologically and historically by assuming neat divisions between the "orthodox" Judaism of Palestine and a supposedly deviant variety in the Diaspora.* Such neat divisions apparently did not exist. Sanders, then, both in *Paul and Palestinian Judaism* and in two subsequent books on Paul, takes the view articulated by Moore (Moore, II.94) half a century before but not carefully worked out: Paul always began with the premise, which his own experience had made certain to him, that Jesus was the savior* of the world,* and worked backward from this premise to the conclusion that all the world, Jews included, needed to be saved through Jesus. In Sanders's view, therefore, Paul's theology represents a leap out of Jewish covenantal nomism into a different religion.

Sanders contends that Paul had no "theology of the law" but responded in various ways to various circumstances which threatened his mission of announcing to both Jew and Gentile the necessity of participation in Christ for salvation. For practical reasons he considered those parts of the Law which Gentiles viewed as particularly Jewish (circumcision,* Sabbath keeping and dietary observance) to be annulled. They would hinder the Gentile mission and would make it seem to Gentiles that the key to salvation was Judaism when in fact it was participation in Christ. When he felt compelled to give reasons for setting aside the Law, he answered in various ways, some of them incompatible with others. His central explanation, however, seems to be that the Law was given to condemn everyone so that everyone could be saved through Jesus Christ.

Nevertheless, Paul was still enough of a Jew psychologically to be uncomfortable with saying in every situation that the Law was no longer valid. He had firm convictions about right and wrong, propriety and impropriety, derived from his Jewish upbringing. When asked to adjudicate on such matters, as he was for example by the Corinthians, the origin of his answers was often, ironically, the Jewish Law (Sanders 1991, 84-100).

J. D. G. Dunn likewise has accepted the new consensus which Sanders's work represents but criticizes Sanders for not providing a plausible explanation of the fundamental Jewishness of Paul's letters. Sanders, Dunn charges, has so divorced Paul from Judaism that Paul's anguish over his unbelieving Jewish brothers and sisters in Romans 9:1-3 and his concern that Gentile Christians understand their spiritual indebtedness to Israel* in Romans 11:17-24 are enigmas (Dunn, 188; see Romans).

The account of Paul which Dunn proposes as a substitute claims that Paul worked through the details of his view of the Law in the heat of controversy with Jewish Christians who believed that Gentile Christians, in order to maintain a place in the covenant people of God, had to adopt the three "works of the Law"* which served as badges of national Israel: circumcision,* Sabbath keeping (see Holy Days) and dietary observance (see Food). Paul's polemic against "works of the Law," then, is not directed against gaining salvation by doing good works but against believing that salvation was, at least in part, contingent upon belonging to national Israel and observing the Law as a badge of that status (Dunn, 191-96). As a result, Paul's positive statements about the Law are not inconsistent with his more negative statements, for the negative statements are directed against a nationalistic misuse of the Law rather than against the Law itself (Dunn, 200).

This reading of Paul, says Dunn, has numerous advantages. It acknowledges the legitimacy of Sanders's complaint against the Lutheran paradigm for understanding Judaism, but it gives a picture of Paul more plausible than Sanders's own picture. Paul is now firmly rooted within first-century Judaism and his statements about the Law, both positive and negative, are held together by a consistent underlying conviction that the Law, while good, can be misused as an instrument of national pride (Dunn, 200-203).

Another highly influential response to the new consensus comes from the pen of H. Räisänen. Like Dunn, Räisänen accepts Sanders's portrait of ancient Judaism and, like others, attempts to explain Paul's polemic against works of the Law in light of this new perspective. He claims that Paul first developed his postconversion attitudes toward the Law under the influence of the Hellenistic Christian community, a group which played down the necessity of the Law's particularly Jewish aspects in the interest of winning Gentiles to Christianity. Later, in the heat of his own Gentile mission,* and as a matter of convenience, Paul dropped the Law entirely from his evangelistic agenda without clearly thinking through the reasons why (Räisänen 1986, 300-301; cf. 1983, 256-63)

Räisänen suggests that Paul produced his first attempts to explain the relationship between the Law and faith in Christ when the Judaizers* invaded his churches in Galatia. This group was antagonistic to Paul and produced a powerful case, based on straightforward arguments from the Hebrew Scriptures that Gentile Christians should adhere to the Law and so become Jewish. Paul, convinced on the basis of his own experience that such additions to the requirement of faith in Christ were unnecessary hindrances, then began to cast around for arguments to prove his conviction (Räisänen 1983, 256-63). In Räisänen's view he was less than successful. Instead of producing a convincing counterargument, he constructed a series of ad hoc statements, some mutually contradictory and others clear distortions of the Jewish view of the Law.

The Paul of Räisänen's description provides an appropriate summarizing metaphor for the state of current scholarship on Paul's view of the Law. The reexamination of Judaism which began with Montefiore and culminated in Sanders has shifted the ground beneath interpreters' feet so dramatically that no consensus on Paul's theology of the Law has been able to emerge. Is this disarray ultimately the product of the disharmony between Paul's distorted picture of Judaism and Judaism as it really existed? Could it be the result of internal disharmonies within Paul himself, and hence within his letters? An honest answer to these questions will require a fresh reading both of Paul and of the Jewish literature of his era.

## 2. The Jewish Law in the Second Temple Period.
After the Babylonians destroyed Jerusalem, burned the Temple and took many in Israel captive in 586 B.C., most Israelites in exile seem to have adopted the perspective of Jeremiah and Ezekiel and considered the experience as punishment for breaking the covenant

God had made with them at Sinai. To the exiles, the Pentateuch's curses* for disobedience to the covenant must have appeared to be a breathtakingly accurate prediction of the Babylonian invasion and subsequent exile (Lev 26:14-46; Deut 28:43-52, 64-67; 29:22-28; 31:14-29). Thus when the Persians overran the Babylonians and subsequently allowed expatriate Israelites to return to their native land the leaders of the return understandably resolved to adhere strictly to the Law and so to avoid future punishment for disobedience. Their Achilles heel prior to the exile, they believed, was their seduction into idolatry by foreign influences. The road to a restored covenant relationship with God, they reasoned, was a renewed determination to fence themselves off from harmful foreign influences by strictly obeying the Law.

We can see these convictions clearly in Ezra-Nehemiah, where both Ezra and Nehemiah express grave concern over Jewish intermarriage with the Gentile population of Palestine precisely because such actions could lead Israel once again into national apostasy and punishment (Ezra 9:10-15; cf. Neh 10:30). These convictions were still in place two and a half centuries later, as the book of Tobit reveals. There we read of Tobit's awareness that defeat and exile came to Israel as just punishment for breaking the Mosaic covenant (Tob 3:2-6) and of Tobit's determination, while living among Gentiles, to observe the Jewish marriage and dietary customs strictly (Tob 1:9-12; cf. 4:12-13).

The belief that the Law was the distinguishing mark of Israel as God's chosen people intensified in subsequent years as Hellenistic* challenges to Israel's ancestral religion became more frequent and violent, especially under the Seleucid ruler Antiochus IV. The Maccabean books show that Antiochus attempted to force Israel into cultural conformity with the rest of his realm by forbidding the Jews to practice precisely those parts of their Law which distinguished them from other peoples. He outlawed circumcision (1 Macc 1:48), made martyrs of those who refused to eat unclean food (2 Macc 6:18-31) and, most horrific of all, tried to force Jews to worship pagan gods (1 Macc 2:15-28; see Idolatry).

Some Jews folded under such pressure, and a few even welcomed compromise as an opportunity for personal advancement; but many became more resolute than ever in their conviction that they would not again ignore God's Law and consort with Gentile ways. They believed that if Israel were faithful to the Mosaic covenant, God would protect them no matter how overwhelming the foe, but that if, on the other hand, they disobeyed the Law, the Gentiles would defeat them in battle and they would cease to be, in any

meaningful sense, God's covenant people (Jdt 5:17-21; 8:18-23; Pr Azar 6-14). So, like Daniel (Dan 1:1-21; 3:1-30) they determined not to break the Law, especially observance of circumcision (Jub. 15:11-34), dietary restrictions (Jdt 10:5; cf. 12:2) and Sabbath keeping (Jub. 2:17-33), for these aspects of the Law separated them most clearly from the surrounding nations.

The politically minded among these strict adherents to the covenant of Moses turned to open rebellion against a succession of Seleucid rulers and eventually obtained political independence. Others, however, were content to wait upon God to establish the new covenant with his people which Jeremiah (Jer 31:31-34) and Ezekiel (Ezek 36:24—37:28) had predicted, a covenant in which God himself would give them a "new heart" and a "new spirit," removing their "heart of stone" and giving them a "heart of flesh" in its stead (Ezek 36:26). Thus the authors of *Jubilees* and of the Qumran documents frequently echo these passages (*Jub.* 1:22-25; 1QS 4, 5; 1QH 4, 5, 18; 4QShirShabb 2) and witness to a belief that these prophecies were being fulfilled within their communities.

Once the Maccabean family succeeded in throwing off Seleucid rule, observing the Jewish Law was required of all who lived in the land, whether Jewish or not. Under John Hyrcanus I the Idumeans were forced to submit to circumcision and other legal requirements (Josephus *Ant.* 13.9.1 §§257-58), and Hyrcanus' successor, Aristobulus I, forced the Itureans to do the same (Josephus *Ant.* 13.11.3 §318). M. Hengel concludes appropriately that Hyrcanus and Aristobulus took these steps because they regarded all of ancient Israel as God's possession and viewed it as part of their mandate to purge the land of Gentiles, either by forcing them out or by forcing them to become Jews (Hengel, 197). Although written much earlier, Psalm 125:3 must have struck a resonant cord with them: "For the scepter of the wicked shall not stay upon the land apportioned to the righteous so that the righteous might not stretch out their hands to act wickedly." The evil influences of Gentiles in years past had led Israel into exile. That mistake would not be repeated.

By the first century A.D., the last of the Hasmoneans had nevertheless capitulated to Rome, and many Jews were happy within the limits of religious freedom that Rome allowed. Some radical groups arose, however, who claimed to be heirs to the zeal of the Hasmonean family and whose goal was to free Israel from the polluting presence of Gentiles. During the formative years of the early church these groups gained strength until, prompted by the blunders and corruption of a quick succession of Roman procurators, their zeal burst into open rebellion against Rome in A.D. 66 (*see* Revolutionary Movements). Many of those involved in the revolt were concerned, like the Hasmoneans of old, to force conformity to the particularly Jewish aspects of the Law upon everyone who lived on the sacred land of Israel (see, e.g., Josephus *J.W.* 2.17.10 §454; *Life* 12 §§65, 67; 23 §§112-13).

Not all Jews during the five centuries from Ezra to the time of Paul, of course, took an approach this radical, and many sought to achieve some level of compromise with the Gentile world around them. In such writings as the Wisdom of Solomon, Ben Sira and Baruch, for example, the Law was closely identified with "wisdom,"* and was found to encompass the insight which Gentile philosophers and theologians on occasion undeniably possessed. In the Wisdom of Solomon the Jewish Law is said to be given to the world through Israel (Wis 18:4), and in Ben Sira and Baruch true wisdom and understanding are repeatedly coupled with observance of the commandments (Sir 1:26; 6:37; 9:15; 15:1; 16:4; 19:20; 21:11; 23:27—24:1; 24:23-29; 33:2-3; 34:8; 39:1-5; Bar 3:12; 3:36—4:1, 12). Despite these efforts to take Gentile thought seriously, however, there is no doubt that if a choice must be made, the Law, not wisdom, should take priority (cf. Sir 19:20 with 19:24). This literature, moreover, continues to express a profound sense of grief at the plight of oppression into which disobedience to the Law has landed Israel (Sir 49:4-7; Bar 2:27—3:13; 4:12-13).

In other writings of the period the particularly Jewish aspects of the Law were ignored (e.g., *Pseudo-Phocylides*), allegorized (e.g., *Letter of Aristeas* 139-69) or otherwise rationalized (see, e.g., Josephus *Ag. Ap.* 2.173-74, 234; Aristobulus as quoted in Eusebius *Praep. Ev.* 13.12.9-16; 13.13.8) in an effort to emphasize to Gentile readers aspects of Judaism which would be most intelligible and attractive to them. Some Jews even spiritualized the distinctively Jewish aspects of the Law to the extent that they felt literal observance was not necessary. According to Philo (who did not approve of their activity) this group focused its spiritualizing efforts on the laws of Sabbath observance, festival participation and circumcision (Philo *Migr. Abr.* 450).

In sum, from at least the period of the exile in Babylon, most Jews realized that their subjugation to foreign powers was a direct result of their violation of the Law given at Sinai. Many Jews believed, therefore, that the answer to their oppression was renewed commitment to separate themselves from the Gentiles around them by adhering to the Law, especially to those aspects of the Law which marked Israel as a separate people with a distinct way of life. Some within this group sought to cast off Gentile overlords and even to purge Gentiles from the land within the borders of Davidic Israel. Others, believing that God had begun to establish his new covenant within their communities, waited upon God to intervene eschatologically as he had promised in the prophets (*see* Restoration of Israel).

Another group, although probably no less committed to the Law as the distinguishing mark of Israel, believed that contact with Gentile peoples and ideas was not only permitted, but revealed that the best aspects of Gentile life were anticipated in the Mosaic Law. Some Jews were willing to go still further and to become outwardly indistinguishable from monotheistic and morally upright Gentiles by spiritualizing at least the laws governing Sabbath observance, festival keeping and circumcision. The scanty evidence for this last group probably indicates that their numbers were small and their influence insignificant. For most Jews of Paul's era, then, the Law was the distinguishing mark of the Jewish people, to be kept at all costs in order to escape the curse which the Law itself pronounced upon the disobedient, and for some Jews the period in which this happened would mark the fulfillment of the prophetic promise of the new covenant.

### 3. The Jewish Law in the Context of Paul's Letters.

When we turn to Paul's letters we find a large measure of discontinuity, but also a surprising amount of continuity, between Paul and second Temple Judaism on the place of the Law in God's dealings with his people.

*3.1. 1 and 2 Thessalonians.* Paul's Thessalonian* correspondence is widely neglected in the study of the apostle's view of the Law. The word *nomos* ("law") does not, after all, occur in these letters, and they were written before Paul's heated disputes with the Judaizers over the Law had taken place. It has in the past, therefore, seemed safe to move immediately beyond them to the more fertile ground of 2 Corinthians, Galatians, Philippians and Romans. The absence of the word *nomos* from the Thessalonian letters, however, does not mean that we cannot glean some information from them about Paul's view of the Law at this early stage in his letter-writing career. What we can glean turns out to be helpful in understanding Paul's view of the Law in his later, more Law-oriented correspondence.

As T. J. Deidun has pointed out (Deidun, 10-12), Paul's use of the phrase "the church* of the Thessalonians in God the Father and the Lord Jesus Christ" in 1 Thessalonians 1:1 (cf. 2 Thess 1:1), and his description of the Judean Christians as "the churches of

God" in 1 Thessalonians 2:14 come from the OT conception of "the church of God," a status which became Israel's on the day that they assembled to receive the Law from Moses at Sinai (Deut 4:9-14; 9:10; 10:4; 18:16). Israel was to observe this Law, according to Leviticus, both because it gave them a holiness corresponding to the holiness* of God who was present among them and because it distinguished them from the surrounding Gentile nations (Lev 11:45; 18:1-5, 24-30; 19:1; 20:7-8, 23-26). Presumably the new covenant prophesied in Jeremiah 31 and Ezekiel 36—37 would have a similar effect for God's people: it would serve to distinguish his people from the rest of the world.

This is precisely what we find in 1 Thessalonians where the distinguishing mark of the Thessalonians is adherence to the "specific precepts" (*tinas parangelias*, 1 Thess 4:2) which Paul gave to them and which would mark them off from "the Gentiles who do not know God" (1 Thess 4:5; Deidun, 18-28). They are to be "set apart" (*hagiasmos*), for God's Holy Spirit* dwells among them and they are taught by God himself (1 Thess 4:7-9; cf. Jer 31:34). The wicked figure who will arise in the eschaton can, therefore, be described as "the man of lawlessness" (*anomia*, 2 Thess 2:3, 7-8). Paul could hardly be unaware of the echoes which his description of the Thessalonian community contains both of Leviticus and of Jeremiah.

Thus Paul views the Thessalonian congregation as a fulfillment of God's promise to establish a new covenant with his people, one in which the Law would be written on hearts and obeyed. Although the congregation is predominantly Gentile (1 Thess 1:9), Paul regards it as parallel to the Israel of the Mosaic covenant, whose status as "the church of God" originated with the giving of precepts to mark them off as a distinct people. We cannot at this point discern the details of the relationship between the old covenant and the new in Paul's thinking; but that there are parallels between the patterns of the two covenants and that there are differences is clear. Both old covenant and new emphasize sanctity through behavior and for identical reasons; but the new covenant, unlike the old, is not ethnically determined.

**3.2. 1 Corinthians.** Paul's attitude toward the Jewish Law comes into sharper focus when we move to 1 Corinthians.* Although Paul uses the word *nomos* only eight times in this letter (nine if 14:34 is original), like the Thessalonian correspondence, a stance toward the Law is presupposed in much of what Paul says in the letter about sanctity and ethics. Moreover, the few times that Paul explicitly speaks of the Law provide excellent evidence for his attitude toward the Law when the Law itself is not a bone of contention

between himself and his opponents,* as it is in several of his later letters. For these reasons, 1 Corinthians provides a ripe field for gleaning information about Paul's view of the Law.

The first two verses of the letter demonstrate that Paul's emphasis on the continuity between the people of God in the OT and the newly constituted people of God has not weakened since writing to the Thessalonians. Paul addresses the Corinthian believers as "the church of God . . . set apart in Christ Jesus, called to be separate" (1 Cor 1:2), once again echoing the Pentateuch's description of Israel's constitution as the people of God at Sinai. The theme is filled out in 1 Corinthians 3:10-17 where Paul describes the Corinthian church as God's temple,* subject to the most careful maintenance, "for the temple of God, which you (pl.) are, is sacred" (1 Cor 3:17). Because they are God's congregation and God's temple, moreover, the Corinthians should distinguish themselves from "the Gentiles" by abstaining from sexual immorality (1 Cor 5:1; cf. 1 Thess 4:5) and separating themselves from those who claim to be part of God's congregation but refuse to shun immorality (1 Cor 5:10-13). Paul supports his argument for excommunicating those within the church who refuse to separate themselves from Gentile sexual misconduct (*see* Sexuality) by citing a saying which recurs many times in Deuteronomy and makes the same point with respect to Israel: "cast out the evil person from among you" (1 Cor 5:13; cf. Deut 17:7; 19:19; 22:21, 24; 24:7). He is also concerned that they not taint themselves with idolatry* and, as N. T. Wright (120-136) has shown, Paul approaches the subject of eating meat offered to idols from the standpoint of the great Jewish confession, drawn from the Torah, that there is but one God* (1 Cor 8:4; cf. Deut 4:35, 39; 6:4).

Paul also demonstrates in 1 Corinthians that he is aware of the whole story of God's covenant with Israel at Sinai, Israel's failure to keep that covenant, and of the promise of an eschatological covenant (*see* Eschatology). In 1 Corinthians, just as in 1 Thessalonians, he shows that he believes the churches coming into existence through his missionary work and on the basis of faith in Christ are the inheritors of this new covenant. These convictions come most clearly to the surface in 1 Corinthians 10 where, in the course of warning the Corinthian believers against idolatry, Paul reminds them of the story of Israel's failure and its miserable consequences and then makes the telling statement, "But these things happened to them as a pattern and were written in order to admonish us, upon whom the climax of the ages has arrived" (1 Cor 10:11). The Corinthian believers, then, appear in

Paul's thinking to be eschatological Israel, the new "congregation of God" who stand in contrast both to the Gentiles on one side and to "Israel according to the flesh*" on the other (1 Cor 10:18, 32; cf. 12:2).

Most of the points in the letter at which Paul specifically refers to the Law tally well with this picture of believers as the new Israel. In 1 Corinthians 7:19 Paul claims that what really matters in the busy era before Christ's return is not whether one is married or unmarried, slave or free, circumcised or uncircumcised, but whether one "keeps the commands of God," a phrase frequently used in the literature of Paul's era for "observing the Jewish Law" (Ezra 9:4 LXX; Sir 32:23; Mt 19:17-19). In 1 Corinthians 9:8-9 he calls upon "the Mosaic Law" as an authority for his contention that he, like other preachers of the gospel,* has the right to be supported by the community in which he works (see Financial Support). In 1 Corinthians 9:19-23 he claims that he seeks to accommodate everyone, whether Jew or Gentile, whether "under the Law" or not, although he is not himself "outside the Law but within the Law of Christ" (1 Cor 9:21). In 1 Corinthians 14:21 he calls upon "the Law" to prove a point about the role of speaking in tongues in the church's worship* (1 Cor 14:23). Clearly, for Paul, "the Law" was valid in some form for members of the new covenant.

Already in these few references, however, we find clues that Paul's view of the Law is complex. How could Paul claim that what mattered was keeping God's commands but then say that circumcision, one of the Law's most prominent commands, did not matter? What provoked him to say that he could observe or not observe the dietary scruples of "weak" (see Strong and Weak) Jewish Christians because he was not "under Law" but that he was subject to "the Law of Christ"? In what meaningful sense could Paul claim that the Law was authoritative for believers when he ignored these central commands?

1 Corinthians does not provide an explicit answer to this question; but if we add Paul's comments in 1 Corinthians 7:19 to those in 1 Corinthians 9:19-23 we can see a pattern that may help us to understand Paul's thinking about the Law. In 1 Corinthians 7:19 the part of the Law with which Paul is willing to dispense is circumcision; in 1 Corinthians 9:19-23 it is dietary observance (cf. 1 Cor 8:1-13 and 10:1-11:1). Both of these aspects of the Law, as we saw above in our study of the Law in Judaism, were prized by many Jews as particularly Jewish laws, laws which marked the Jews off from the rest of the world as God's special people. It is precisely these highly prized, and ethnically specific, aspects of the Law that Paul considers no longer valid.

If we pause to think about Paul's calling to be the apostle to the Gentiles we can see clearly the reason for his rejection of these laws: they served to limit membership in the people of God to ethnic Jews and those willing to convert to Judaism. As we have seen, Paul affirmed the Law's commitment to separation of the people of God from the rest of the world; but the crucial areas of separation were now no longer the observance of dietary rules and circumcision, but moral behavior motivated by God's sanctifying Spirit.

Paul's view of the Law, however, is more complex still. Another element of its complex structure breaks through the surface in 1 Corinthians 15:56, his final reference to the Law in this letter. Paul has been discussing the necessity of the bodily resurrection* of believers and of Christ from the dead, and has been trying to explain to Greeks unfamiliar with Jewish eschatology the eternal value of the body and what a bodily resurrection will be like. The climax of his argument comes in 1 Corinthians 15:54-55 with a paraphrase of Isaiah 25:8 and a quotation of Hosea 14:4: "Death has been swallowed up in victory. Where, O Death, is your victory? Where, O Death, is your sting?" Paul's next statement comes, like a bolt from the blue, with no warning: "the sting of death is sin, and the power of sin is the Law" (1 Cor 15:56). Sin* has not figured prominently in Paul's argument to this point, and Law not at all. Why does Paul suddenly mention them here?

The surprise which the reader feels at encountering 1 Corinthians 15:56 demonstrates how firmly the Law was connected with sin and death in Paul's mind. Like a runner unable to stop at the finish line, Paul is unable to stop his argument at its most rhetorically effective finish and runs ahead into other subjects which he associates with the Law. This comes as a surprise not only because it raises a new subject within chapter fifteen, but also because what Paul says about the Law in this verse does not immediately appear to be compatible with what he has said about it elsewhere in the letter. Elsewhere it appears as an authority; here it is connected with sin and death (see Life and Death), aspects of the present world which are evil and will pass away. How can Paul hold both positions?

1 Corinthians does not answer this question for us. In Paul's next letter, however, we find some information which helps us to move toward an answer.

*3.3. 2 Corinthians.* By the time Paul wrote 2 Corinthians he had entered a period of stormy relations with the Corinthian believers, apparently aggravated by the arrival in Corinth of a group of Jewish Christians who opposed him. Despite this changed situation, Paul's attitude toward the Jewish Law in 2 Corinthians meshes well with our discoveries in the Thessalonian correspondence and in 1 Corinthians. We still find Paul, for example, appealing to the Law as an authority when discussing how believers should conduct the practical affairs of everyday life (2 Cor 8:15, quoting Ex 16:18; 2 Cor 13:1, quoting Deut 19:15). In 2 Corinthians, as in 1 Corinthians, moreover, one passage does not seem to square with this picture of continuity between the Jewish Law and the new Israel.

The topic under discussion in 2 Corinthians 3:1-18 is the contrast between Paul's style of ministry* and that of his opponents. Specifically, Paul is concerned to refute the notion that letters of recommendation, such as his opponents carry, are necessary credentials for true apostleship (2 Cor 3:1; *see* Apostle). Paul claims to have letters of recommendation, but not ones written with ink or on tablets of stone. His letters were written instead with the Spirit of the living God on the tablets of the human heart (2 Cor 3:2-3). Letters were not, of course, written with ink on stone in Paul's time, but with ink on papyrus. Paul has, however, purposely mixed his metaphors in order to echo the prophetic passages dealing with the new covenant, in which God would replace his people's "heart of stone" with a "heart of flesh," put his Spirit in them (Ezek 36:26-27), and write his Law "on [their] hearts" (Jer 31:33; *see* Prophet, Paul as). Thus, in 2 Corinthians 3:6 Paul claims to be a minister of a new covenant, not like the old, written covenant which "killed" by properly bringing the covenant's curses down upon disobedient Israel, but like the covenant which Jeremiah predicted would at some future time bring forgiveness for sin and a renewed ability to know and to obey God.

Paul's implied conclusion to this argument is that written letters, such as his opponents carry (2 Cor 3:1-2), provide insignificant proof of apostleship when compared to the eschatologically significant "letters" which Paul can bring forward in the form of the Corinthian believers themselves, for the Corinthians joined the eschatological people of God through Paul's ministry and represent the long-awaited fulfillment of the prophetic promise.

In order to drive the point home even more forcefully, Paul, in 2 Corinthians 3:7-11 comments on the superiority of the new covenant, of which he is minister and the Corinthians are proof, to the old. The old covenant, he says, was glorious, so glorious in fact that when Moses* received the covenant stipulations from God, his face was "glorified" to the extent that the Israelites were not able to look at it (2 Cor 3:7; cf. Ex 34:29-30 LXX; *Tg. Onq.* Ex 34:29-30). If such glory*

attaches to "the ministry of death" (2 Cor 3:7) and "condemnation" (2 Cor 3:9), Paul says, how much more glorious must be "the ministry of the Spirit" and "righteousness" (2 Cor 3:8-9). In 2 Corinthians 3:12-18 Paul goes on to describe how Moses veiled his face to prevent the Israelites from seeing that its glory was fading, and comments that the old covenant's obsolescence is still veiled from the unbelieving Jews of Paul's day (2 Cor 3:14).

When we compare 2 Corinthians 3:1-18 with Paul's appeal to the Law as a guide to conduct in 2 Corinthians 8:5 and 13:1 we face the same problem we discovered in 1 Corinthians. Paul at times appears to say that the Law is no longer valid since it is aligned with sin, death and condemnation (1 Cor 15:56; 2 Cor 3:7, 9) and at times seems to regard it, at least in some form, as authoritative. Are these two sides of a complex view of the Law or are they, as Räisänen and others believe, indications that Paul's view of the Law is confused and contradictory?

One hint that these two approaches to the Law form part of a complex but coherent position lies in the consistent presence of the two approaches in different letters. That 1 Corinthians and 2 Corinthians contain both attitudes, although the letters address different situations, shows at least that Paul did not simply make one type of statement when convenient in one situation and another type of statement when convenient in a different situation.

A second indication that Paul's view of the Law is complex and coherent rather than *ad hoc* and contradictory lies in the nature of the negative statements. The most natural background for Paul's statements that the Law is aligned with sin, death and condemnation is the widespread conviction among first-century Jews that the Law had justly condemned Israel to Gentile domination for transgressing its commands. When Paul speaks of the "old covenant" as "made obsolete in Christ" (2 Cor 3:14), he may have in focus not everything the Law contained but the Law's sentence of condemnation upon Israel's transgression of the covenant. This reading gains some support from Paul's description of the Sinaitic covenant as "the ministry of death" (2 Cor 3:7), recalling precisely the penalty for breaking the covenant according to Leviticus 26:25 (LXX) and Deuteronomy 30:15, 19, and his further description, so appropriate in this context, of the Mosaic code as the "ministry of condemnation" (2 Cor 3:9). If this perspective is correct, then Paul does not say in these passages that every aspect of the Mosaic legislation was abolished, but that God himself had abolished the Law's just sentence of condemnation upon his people for their transgressions. As Paul puts it, "God was in Christ reconciling the world to himself by not counting their transgressions against them" (2 Cor 5:19).

In sum, we have discovered so far that Paul clearly believed that the promise of the new covenant had been fulfilled in the coming of Jesus Christ, that the people of God which this new covenant constituted included Gentiles as Gentiles, not Gentiles as converts to Judaism, and that this newly constituted people was, like the old people of God, separated from the world around it by their conduct. We have also found that the specific rules of this separation coincide in many cases with the rules in the Mosaic legislation, and sometimes are quoted from that legislation word for word. Nevertheless, the Mosaic code viewed from the standpoint of its historical role in justly condemning God's people for their sin, Paul says, has been abolished. For Paul, therefore, it is impossible to say that the Mosaic Law, minus a few cultic and ethnic regulations, is still in force. To the contrary, since the Mosaic Law was inextricably bound to a period of time in which the boundaries of God's people were virtually identical with the boundaries of the Jewish people and to a time in which God's people labored under a justly pronounced sentence of condemnation, it has come to its divinely appointed end (see esp. 2 Cor 3:13).

With these discoveries in mind we are now in a better position to understand the statements which Paul makes about the Jewish Law in the letters where the Law is a specific topic of debate. Hopefully our discoveries in the Thessalonian and Corinthian correspondence will help us to understand the more difficult passages in Galatians, Philippians and Romans.

**3.4. Galatians.** Paul's letter to the Galatians* records the apostle's angry response to a group of fledgling churches which had come under the influence of Jewish Christians preaching "another gospel" (Gal 1:8-9). This group, evidently under pressure from zealous and violent Jews in Palestine (Gal 6:12; see Revolutionary Movements), taught that it was necessary to become a full proselyte to Judaism in order to stand justified (see Justification) before God at the final day of reckoning. At issue in particular were the requirements that the Gentile Galatians observe circumcision (Gal 2:3; 5:2-6, 11-12; 6:12-13), Jewish holy days (Gal 4:10) and dietary restrictions (Gal 2:11-14).

The details of Paul's response are compressed and frequently difficult to understand; but it is clear that they flow out of the central convictions that a new era in God's dealings with his creation has dawned and that in this new era God has established a new covenant with a newly constituted people (Gal 1:4; 4:4;

538

4:24, 28; cf. 3:17). Viewed from this perspective, the reintroduction of precisely those barriers which divided Jew from Gentile was nothing short of a defection from the new covenant and a return to the days of the old covenant with its divisions between people (Gal 2:15-21) and its legitimate curse upon Israel's miserable failure to keep the Law (Gal 3:10-14). It was to nullify the effect of Christ's timely coming and death (Gal 4:4; 2:21; 5:4; cf. 3:13-14), to deny the work of the eschatologically supplied Spirit (Gal 3:1-5) and to fall away from the graciously fulfilled promise of God (Gal 5:4). It was, in short, a prodigious error of timekeeping.

From this hermeneutical origin, Paul's discussion of the Law takes two directions. The first, which not surprisingly consumes most of his energy, is that the national markers of circumcision, Sabbath keeping and dietary observances, or "works of the Law"* as Paul calls them (Gal 2:11-16), cannot make one righteous before God. The reason for this is twofold. For one thing, Paul says, no one can keep the whole Law. Paul's opponents themselves demonstrate this by their own inability to do the Law (Gal 6:13); the Galatians will discover it too if they undertake its yoke (Gal 5:3); and the historical experience of Israel with the curse of the Law for disobedience proves it to be true (Gal 3:10-12, cf. Col 2:14). Why is it impossible to keep the Law? Paul hints at what he thinks on this important issue in Galatians 2:16, when he says that "by works of the Law no *flesh* shall be justified." The term *flesh*\* was probably suggested to Paul not only by the physical nature of the circumcisions which his opponents wished to perform on the Galatians but by the use of the word to indicate human weakness in such biblical passages as Genesis 6:3 and 12, Jeremiah 17:5 and Isaiah 40:6. Thus, the term appears to be Paul's shorthand for humanity's vulnerability to sin (Gal 5:19, 24; 6:8). To elevate "works of the Law" to the level of a requirement for living in a harmonious covenant relationship with God, Paul says, is to place such a relationship outside anyone's reach, whether Jew or Gentile, because the human inclination to disobey God prevents "any flesh" from obeying the Law completely (Gal 2:16).

The second reason that "works of the Law" cannot place one within this harmonious covenant relationship with God is that the covenant of which these works are part was temporary. Unlike the promise made to Abraham,* which constituted a permanent covenant fulfilled in Christ (Gal 3:15-18), the Sinaitic covenant was established "on account of transgressions." By this last phrase Paul probably means that God gave the Law at Sinai in order to reveal clearly

Israel's sin, to transform it from something ill defined and inchoate into specific transgressions against God's will. Paul is probably alluding here to a well-known irony: at the very moment God gave the Law to Moses on Sinai, Israel was on the plain below already violating its first stipulation (Ex 32:7-8; cf. *Bib. Ant.* 12.4, c. first century A.D.).

Paul's meaning becomes even clearer when he describes the Sinaitic covenant as a "pedagogue" (*paidagōgos*), the family slave in the Greco-Roman world who served as guardian, disciplinarian and teacher of children until they reached maturity (Gal 3:23-25). Those under the pedagogue's charge sometimes remembered their caretaker fondly; but frequently in satire and in art work he is depicted as a harsh figure, rod in hand, ready to punish any disobedience. As Galatians 3:23 shows, Paul's purpose for comparing the Sinaitic covenant to a pedagogue in this passage is twofold: to emphasize its purpose of identifying and punishing sin and, at the same time, to highlight its temporary nature.

From Galatians 4:1—5:1 Paul uses a series of metaphors to argue that those who want to live under the yoke of the covenant at Sinai are turning the clock back to an era in which both Gentile and Jew were enslaved to sin. The concept which allows these various metaphors to hang together is that of slavery. First Paul compares the Gentile Galatians' former existence under "the elemental things of the world" (*stoicheia tou kosmou*; *see* Elements/Elemental Spirits of the World), a phrase reminiscent of their former idolatrous practices, to the life of the young heir to a wealthy estate who, for the time being, is no different from a slave. For the Galatians to accept the yoke of the Sinai covenant was to return from the era of the eschatological Spirit to that former era in which sin dominated their lives (Gal 4:1-11). Next, Paul compares life under the Sinaitic covenant to Hagar, Abraham's female slave who gave birth to Abraham's first son, Ishmael (Gal 4:21-31). Hagar, he says, stands for the present Jerusalem* (Gal 4:25), and to accept the Sinaitic covenant as binding is to turn away from the eschatological new Jerusalem, with its new covenant of freedom from the Law's curse (Gal 4:24, 26), and to return to the "present" Jerusalem where the curse remains in force (Gal 4:25; cf. 4 Ezra 9:38—10:28; *2 Bar.* 4). It is, therefore, to accept Hagar the slave as one's mother and to live in slavery with her other children (Gal 4:25).

This extensive case against human ability to keep the Mosaic covenant and against that covenant's continuing validity does not, however, exhaust Paul's comments on the Law in Galatians. In a few other passages, Paul's comments take a different direction. In Galatians 5:14 he tells his readers that "the whole Law is fulfilled in one phrase, namely, 'You shall love your neighbor as yourself,' " and in Galatians 6:2 he encourages them to bear each others' burdens "for thereby you will fulfill the law of Christ." These statements seem surprising until we remember (1) that the Corinthian correspondence showed a similar pattern of regarding the Mosaic legislation as obsolete but then referring to the Law in positive ways and (2) that in neither the Corinthian correspondence nor in Galatians does Paul say that each specific command in the Mosaic code is obsolete, but only the code viewed as a whole with its curses for disobedience and its barriers against Gentiles.

Paul's quarrel is with the imposition of old and temporary structures upon the new eschatological age of reconciliation*—structures whose purpose was to condemn sin and to sequester the Jews from the Gentiles (cf. Eph 2:14-18). Some of the content of the Mosaic Law emerges unscathed from Paul's critique, therefore, because it is untainted by the temporal nature of the curses and barriers. These aspects of the Mosaic law, Paul believes, are not only still valid but are fulfilled by believers when they walk in the Spirit (Gal 5:22-23; 6:2; cf. Eph 6:2).

*3.5. Philippians.* Although Philippians,* unlike Galatians, was not written primarily to correct a mistaken notion of the role of the Law in salvation history, the Galatian controversy was nevertheless ringing in Paul's ears as he wrote this letter. In Philippians 3:2-11, therefore, we find a warning against the same Jewish Christians who were trying to turn the clock back to an era in which circumcision, dietary requirements and Sabbath keeping separated Israel from the Gentiles (Phil 3:2-3). Although the group did not yet pose an active threat to the Philippians (Phil 3:2 sounds more like a warning of possible rather than of present danger), Paul had seen enough of the damage they could do to warrant delivering a warning against them to one of his favorite churches (Phil 4:15-16).

Paul's warning, although brief, provides a helpful link between his compressed and forceful statements about the Law in Galatians and his more carefully nuanced comments in Romans. In articulating his case against his opponents, Paul argues, as he had in Galatians, that to demand the fulfillment of these obsolete requirements is to place confidence in "the flesh," humanity's fallen and inadequate ability to do what God requires (Phil 3:3-4; cf. Gal 2:16). In explaining what he means, however, he takes a step beyond Galatians toward his later argument in Romans. To place confidence in one's fleshly circumcision, Jewish lineage and punctilious legal observance, he says, is to rely on one's own inadequate righteousness rather than on the righteousness which comes from God (Phil 3:5-6, 9; cf. Rom 2:1—3:20).

This new twist to his case against the reintroduction of the Sinaitic covenant is grounded in two biblical images. The first is the image of Israel's own inadequate righteousness during the wilderness wanderings, in spite of which God led them into the promised land (Deut 9:1—10:11). As with Israel, Paul's *own* righteousness was based on the broken Sinaitic covenant and therefore was an inadequate means of attaining salvation (literally, "the resurrection from the dead," Phil 3:9; cf. Rom 10:2-3). The second biblical image Paul uses is of God's powerful and effective action to rescue his people from their plight as exiles and to restore them both to their land and to a peaceful relationship with himself. In Isaiah 46:13 and 51:5-8 God refers to this saving activity as "my righteousness." Paul takes up this notion in Philippians 3:9 to say that the biblical expectations of an eschatological display of God's righteousness have been at least partially fulfilled in Jesus Christ, and so to cling to the old, inadequate righteousness based on a broken Sinaitic covenant is to put one's trust in "refuse" (Phil 3:8). This brief comment in Philippians on the relationship between the Law, conceived as the Sinaitic covenant, and "the righteousness from God" will in Romans become a dominant theme.

*3.6. Romans.* Paul's view of the Law in Romans,* like his comments in Galatians, come into sharper focus if we understand something about the situation that provoked the letter. When Paul wrote Romans he was on the verge of delivering his highly prized collection* of relief funds from his predominantly Gentile churches to the Jewish Christians in Jerusalem (Rom 15:25). He was concerned, however, that this offering, purchased at the price of considerable labor, would not be acceptable to the church there, and so he wrote to Rome, in part, to solicit that church's prayer* support for his journey (Rom 15:30-32). Acts shows us that Paul's concern centered upon what some Jewish Christians in Jerusalem had heard about his view of the Law (Acts 21:20-21). Similar rumors had also reached the Roman church, a community which, as A. J. M. Wedderburn (44-65) argues, had close ties to Jerusalem (Rom 3:8; 6:1; 6:15; *see* Rome). Hence Paul's purpose in Romans was probably at least in part to correct misunderstanding about his view of the Law.

As in Galatians, Paul makes both positive and negative statements about the Law. He maintains both that "works of the Law" cannot give righteousness and that the Law, no longer apparently conceived as the Sinaitic covenant, can be fulfilled by Christians. In Romans, however, Paul articulates his critique of the Sinaitic covenant in a slightly different way from what he had in Galatians. In Galatians Paul never mentioned boasting in the Law (although see Gal 6:13-14); but in Romans his argument receives a new twist from the case it makes against "boasting" or "glorying" in the Law as a special possession of the Jewish people (Rom 2:17, 23; 4:2; cf. Phil. 3:3-6).

When Paul begins to describe the gospel which he wants "to preach to you who are in Rome also" (Rom 1:15), among his first points is that mere knowledge* of what God requires does not provide one with a right standing before God. Only obedience to God's requirements, Paul says, can do that. He begins by discussing the Gentile world where many people sin against God (Rom 1:21-31) although they know his awesomeness, power, divinity (Rom 1:20), creative activity (Rom 1:25) and moral standard (Rom 1:32). Nevertheless, their knowledge goes unaccompanied by obedience, and so in spite of their knowledge, God punishes them precisely as their sins deserve (Rom 1:24, 26, 28).

Paul then turns to the Jewish world where God's impartiality (Rom 2:11) requires that the same standard of judgment hold true: "It is not the hearers of the Law who are righteous in God's eyes, but the doers of the Law who will be declared righteous" (Rom 2:13). This standard is so firm, says Paul, that in God's eyes it is appropriate for a Gentile who keeps the Law in spirit but violates its letter by remaining uncircumcised (Rom 2:26, 29) to sit in judgment upon a Jew who boasts (Rom 2:23) in the possession of the Law but does not obey it (Rom 2:14-29). Although this is a complex passage, its fundamental point is clear: it is no use for Jewish Christians to impose a standard upon Gentile Christians which the Jews themselves have historically not been able to keep (cf. Rom 2:24 and Acts 15:10-11). The reason for this is that doing the "just requirements of the Law" (Rom 2:26) and keeping it "inwardly" and "spiritually" (Rom 2:28-29) are what matters before God, not boasting in the possession of the Law (Rom 2:23) and in outward marks like circumcision (Rom 2:25-26).

In Romans 3:9-20 Paul takes the further step of pointing out that no one, whether Jew or Gentile, fully does what the Law requires. Instead, when measured against the standard which the Law demands, all apologetic speeches must cease (Rom 3:19; cf. Job 29:7-10), for everyone stands condemned. All, both Jew and Gentile, are "under sin" (Rom 3:9; cf. 8:7), and boasting in possession of the Law (Rom 3:27) or the careful observance of the Mosaic code's stipulations ("works of Law," Rom 3:28) are of no use. The Mosaic covenant has been broken both nationally and personally by both Jew and Gentile, and only eschatological help from the covenant keeping God ("the righteousness* of God," Rom 3:21) can remedy the situation. This, of course, has happened in Jesus Christ, because of whom all believers, whether Jew or Gentile, stand assured of a favorable verdict at the day of reckoning (Rom 3:21-26).

By this point in the argument Paul has largely made his case. Two important threads, however, remain loose and need attention. First, Paul must address the significant objection that he has nullified the Law, which after all Paul himself believes to be God's Word (Rom 3:31). Paul answers this objection by appealing not to the Sinaitic covenant but to the narrative portion of the Law and specifically to God's covenant with Abraham,* the first "Jew." Paul observes that God reckoned Abraham righteous (Gen 15:6) prior to circumcision (Gen 17:11-14, 23-27), and then claims that circumcision only served as a seal upon a covenant already made on the basis of Abraham's faith.* Hence faith, not "works" prescribed by the Mosaic code, bring righteousness (Rom 4:1, 1-5, 13), and Abraham serves as the prototype not only of the believing (and circumcised) Jew but of the believing (and uncircumcised) Gentile as well (Rom 4:11-12). In this way Paul demonstrates that, far from nullifying the Law, "the righteousness of God" is consistent with the principle of faith found in the Law itself.

A second problem Paul must address is why, if it lends no advantage to the Jew, did God give the Law? Paul points out carefully that nothing he has said should lead to the conclusion that the Law and sin are identical (Rom 7:7). To the contrary, the Law is holy, righteous, good and spiritual (Rom 7:12, 14; cf. 7:22); it is only so closely allied with sin because it shows sin for the evil transgression that it is and condemns the transgressor. It accomplishes this, according to Paul, in three ways. First, it brings knowledge of sin by making God's will explicit so that people can know God's will and understand that they have not done it (Rom 3:20; 4:15; 5:13; 7:7, 21-23). Second, the Law demonstrates how insidious sin is by suggesting to fallen humanity ways in which it can rebel against God (Rom 7:7-12; cf. 5:20). Finally, "the Law brings wrath*" (Rom 4:15; cf. 1:18), for it contains a list of dire consequences which God ordains for those who disobey its commands. Not surprisingly, then, believers are "no longer under," have "died to" and have been "freed from" this "Law of sin and death" (Rom 6:14; 7:4; 7:6; 8:2).

By this point in our study it should come as no surprise that while Paul can unambiguously speak of the abrogation of the Mosaic code, he can at the same time speak of the Law's authority and of its fulfillment among believers. In Romans the tension between these two kinds of statements is at its sharpest, for along with comments about freedom from the Law we read that the Law is God's (Rom 7:22; 8:7), that it is "the law of the spirit of life in Christ Jesus" (Rom 8:2) and that believers fulfill its "just requirement" when they walk in the Spirit (Rom 8:4; cf. 13:8-10), something that unbelievers are not able to do (Rom 8:7).

Evidence from Paul's other letters has so far pointed toward a resolution to this tension in Paul's belief in two covenants, or two laws, one old and the other new. Romans 9:30—10:8 tends to confirm this view. Here Paul explains that most of Israel has failed to believe the gospel because they have pursued the Law "as if it were a matter of works" (Rom 9:32), believing that in spite of God's eschatological provision for rescue from the broken covenant in Jesus Christ ("the righteousness of God," Rom 10:3), they could continue to cling to the Law of Sinai as proof that they were God's people (Rom 10:3; cf. Phil 3:9). To demonstrate that clinging to the Law in this way could not lead to salvation, Paul quotes two passages from "the Law." The first, Leviticus 18:5, reminds the attentive reader that the Mosaic covenant promised life only to those who obeyed it (Rom 10:5), something which anyone who had read Leviticus 26:14-46 knew Israel had not done, and which Paul has just argued energetically that no individual has done either. This Law, Paul says, has reached its climax (telos) in Christ (Rom 10:4; see Wright, 241) and has given way to a new covenant. The second passage features much of the vocabulary of Deuteronomy 9:4 and 30:12, passages which in their original context spoke of obedience to the Mosaic Law. In Paul's hands, however, they have been transposed into a different key and now speak of righteousness by faith in Christ (Rom 10:6-8; Hays, 73-83). The very Law which has come to its climactic end (telos) in Christ can be taken up and remolded to fit the shape of the new covenant.

## 4. Conclusion.

If the portrait of Paul's view of the Law painted here is correct, then at its heart was the conviction that the old covenant made with Israel at Sinai had passed away and the new covenant predicted by Jeremiah and Ezekiel had come. The change of covenants was necessary because no individual could keep the stipulations of the old covenant, a fact which Israel had demonstrated at the national level. The change was also necessary because after the covenant was broken,

Israel used the Law to erect barriers between itself and the Gentile world, barriers which to some became a point of pride and false security. The new covenant maintained the formal structure of the old, including its barrier of separation between those within and those outside. This barrier ceased to be national in character, however, and assumed instead dimensions dictated by the Spirit, dimensions which in their practical outworking coincided in many particulars with the old covenant. This new covenant, moreover, as the prophets had predicted, was written on the heart and could be kept by those who walked in the Spirit.

All of this means, of course, that Paul's view of the Law was to a large measure discontinuous with the view of many Jews during his time. It is hard to imagine that the authors of Tobit and Judith, *Jubilees* and the Qumran Scrolls would have been comfortable in Paul's company. On the other hand, the undeniable element of discontinuity can be overstressed. The conceptual world within which Paul worked would have been familiar to Paul's Jewish contemporaries. They knew that Israel suffered under "the curse of the Law" in the form of Gentile domination because it had broken the covenant, and some of them at least looked for the answer to this plight in the promises of Jeremiah 31 and Ezekiel 36—37. The image of Paul, the aberration, as it appears in the work of Montefiore, Sanders and others is, therefore, hardly fair.

Neither, if our reading is correct, is Räisänen's image of Paul the muddle-head. Paul's conviction that his churches formed the community of the new covenant, with all of the ramifications which that conviction entailed, remains consistent from his earliest correspondence to his latest, from his most placid to his most polemical. Paul did not produce his view of the Law as an expedient in the heat of the moment. Rather it bears the marks of a complex and carefully considered position, worthy of the most painstaking study and of the deepest theological reflection.

*See also* COVENANT AND NEW COVENANT; CURSE, ACCURSED, ANATHEMA; ETHICS; ISRAEL; JUDAIZERS; JUSTIFICATION; LAW OF CHRIST; RESTORATION OF ISRAEL; RIGHTEOUSNESS, RIGHTEOUSNESS OF GOD; WORKS OF THE LAW.

BIBLIOGRAPHY. R. Bultmann, *Primitive Christianity in Its Contemporary Setting* (Philadelphia: Fortress, 1956); W. D. Davies, *Paul and Rabbinic Judaism: Some Rabbinic Elements in Pauline Theology* (4th ed.; Philadelphia: Fortress, 1980); T. J. Deidun, *New Covenant Morality in Paul* (AnBib 89; Rome: Biblical Institute, 1981); J. D. G. Dunn, *Jesus, Paul, and the Law: Studies in Mark and Galatians* (Louisville: Westminster/John Knox, 1990); R. B. Hays, *Echoes of Scripture in the Letters of Paul* (New Haven: Yale University, 1989); M. Hengel, *The Zealots* (Edinburgh: T. & T. Clark, 1989); H. Hübner, *Law in Paul's Thought* (Edinburgh: T. & T. Clark, 1984); H. Maccoby, *Paul and Hellenism* (Philadelphia: Trinity Press International, 1991); C. G. Montefiore, "First Impressions of Paul," *JQR* 6 (1894) 428-75; idem, "Rabbinic Judaism and the Epistles of St. Paul," *JQR* 13 (1900-1901) 161-217; G. F. Moore, *Judaism in the First Centuries of the Christian Era: The Age of the Tannaim* (2 vols.; Cambridge, MA: Harvard University, 1927); H. Räisänen, *Paul and the Law* (WUNT 29; Tübingen: J. C. B. Mohr, 1983); idem, *The Torah and Christ: Essays in German and English on the Problem of the Law in Early Christianity* (SESJ; Helsinki: Finnish Exegetical Society, 1986); W. Sanday and A. C. Headlam, *A Critical and Exegetical Commentary on the Epistle to the Romans* (ICC; 5th ed; Edinburgh: T. & T. Clark, 1902); E. P. Sanders, *Judaism: Practice and Belief 63BCE-66CE* (Philadelphia: Trinity Press International, 1992); idem, *Paul and Palestinian Judaism: A Comparison of Patterns of Religion* (Philadelphia: Fortress, 1977); idem, *Paul, the Law, and the Jewish People* (Philadelphia: Fortress, 1983); idem, *Paul* (New York: Oxford University Press, 1991); S. Sandmel, *The Genius of Paul: A Study in History* (Philadelphia: Fortress, 1979); idem, *Judaism and Christian Beginnings* (New York: Oxford University Press, 1978); F. Thielman, *From Plight to Solution: A Jewish Framework for Understanding Paul's View of the Law in Galatians and Romans* (NovTSup 61; Leiden: E. J. Brill, 1989); P. J. Tomson, *Paul and the Jewish Law: Halakah in the Letters of the Apostle to the Gentiles* (CRINT 3.1; Minneapolis: Fortress, 1990); F. Weber, *Jüdische Theologie auf Grund des Talmud und verwandter Schriften, gemeinfasslich dargestellt* (2d ed.; Leipzig: Dörffling & Franke, 1897; 1st ed., 1880); A. J. M. Wedderburn, *The Reasons for Romans* (Edinburgh: T. & T. Clark, 1988); S. Westerholm, *Israel's Law and the Church's Faith: Paul and His Recent Interpreters* (Grand Rapids: Eerdmans, 1988); N. T. Wright, *The Climax of the Covenant: Christ and the Law in Pauline Theology* (Edinburgh: T. & T. Clark, 1991).

F. Thielman

## LAW OF CHRIST

The meaning of the phrase "law of Christ" (*ho nomos tou Christou*) is notoriously difficult since Paul uses it only once (Gal 6:2) in his letters (although there is the related expression "subject to the law of Christ" [*ennomos Christou*] in 1 Cor 9:21), and since the use of the phrase in Galatians* occurs unexpectedly, without any clear definition. We shall attempt to defend briefly the following definition: The "law of Christ" for Paul includes the moral norms of the OT Law,* focusing particularly on the commandment to love one's neighbor. Paul emphasizes that this Law cannot be fulfilled apart from the powerful working of the Holy Spirit* in the believers' life.

1. Survey of Interpretation
2. The Pauline Texts
3. Conclusion

## 1. Survey of Interpretation.

A survey of the various interpretations will be given here, and though there is some overlap between the various views, we shall attempt to focus on what is distinctive to each.

*1.1. Law of Love.* The most common interpretation, represented in the commentaries on Galatians by F. F. Bruce and R. Y. K. Fung, understands the "law of Christ" as another way of describing the law of love* which is enunciated in Galatians 5:13.

*1.2. Teaching of Jesus.* C. H. Dodd and W. D. Davies claim that the phrase refers to the words of Jesus which function as an authoritative standard for the church.* The instruction given by Jesus becomes the new Torah for the Christian community.

*1.3. Servants like Jesus.* O. Hofius does not understand the "law of Christ" as referring to the teachings of Jesus, nor to the Sinai Torah, nor to the law of love. Rather, he sees it as grounded in the Isaianic Servant Songs in Isaiah 42:1-4 and 52:13—53:12. The Servant as the sin-bearing substitute bears the "burdens," the sins of the sinful. This is parallel to Galatians 6:2 where the one who fulfills the law of Christ "bears the burdens" of others. In light of Galatians 6:1, Hofius thinks the "burdens" are "sins and miseries." Those who have experienced the saving power of God in the gospel* are so gripped by it that they in turn embody the gospel in their relationship with other believers.

*1.4. Pattern of Christ.* Similar to the above view is the one propounded by R. B. Hays and H. Schürmann. What it means to live according to the law of Christ is to live in accordance with the pattern which was exemplified in Christ Jesus, whose self-giving on the cross becomes the paradigm for all people.

*1.5. Borrowed from Opponents.* H. D. Betz contends that Paul uses the phrase "law of Christ" in a polemical fashion in Galatians 6:2. The expression is rare in Paul, and Betz suggests that Paul used the phrase as a counter to the opponents.*

## 2. The Pauline Texts.

*2.1. 1 Corinthians 9:21.* An examination of 1 Corinthians 9:21 reveals that Paul says he is "subject to the law of Christ" to prevent a misunderstanding of his statement that when he is with "those without Law, he is as one without Law." He does not want his readers

to conclude that since he is without Law he is an antinomian. The origin of the expression here is best explained rhetorically. Paul coins it in the course of his discussion to delineate his stance vis-à-vis the Law. Moreover, the context suggests that when Paul says he is "not under the Law" (1 Cor 9:20) and "without Law" (9:21), he is specifically thinking of the Law insofar as it creates a breach between Jews and Gentiles. Thus, specific laws such as circumcision,* food* laws and Sabbath keeping would be particularly in view here. Paul adapts his lifestyle so that he lives as a Jew when with Jews ("under Law") and as a Gentile* when with Gentiles ("without Law") so that he can proclaim the gospel to each. Nevertheless, he wants to stress that he is not "without the Law of God, but is subject to the law of Christ."

This probably means that Paul still abides by the moral norms of the OT Law. He does not consider his freedom* from the Law as a freedom which can violate the moral norms of the Law. The wider context of 1 Corinthians 8—10 supports this observation, for the issue under discussion is food offered to idols (*see* Idolatry). Jews and Jewish Christians would consider such food unclean, while Gentile Christians would tend to view the eating of such foods as a matter of indifference. A confirmation of the interpretation presented here is found in 1 Corinthians 7:19, "Circumcision is nothing and uncircumcision is nothing, but keeping the commandments of God is essential." The ritual law of circumcision Paul can describe as insignificant, but the moral norms and commandments of the Law are still binding.

*2.2. Galatians 6:2.*

*2.2.1. Weaknesses of Other Views.* We have already seen that discussion has been centered on the phrase "law of Christ" in Galatians 6:2. Contrary to Betz, it is hardly clear that the phrase is polemical, especially since Paul uses it in the paraenetic section of the epistle without providing any substantial clue that the phrase should be understood as a response to opponents. It is also unlikely that the words of Jesus constitute a new Torah for Paul. Nowhere in Galatians nor in the near context of 1 Corinthians 9:21 does Paul cite the words of Jesus as a new law for the Christian. And explicit citations of the teaching of Jesus is rare in the Pauline letters (*see* Jesus, Sayings of).

Most would agree that the "law of Christ" involves the "law of love," but the phrase can be interpreted more specifically. Hofius provocatively interprets Galatians 6:2 in the light of the sin-bearing Servant of Yahweh, but such an allusion is not evident in the context of Galatians. And the view of Hays and Schürmann, that the focus is on the paradigmatic self-giving of Christ Jesus, although supported by other passages in the Pauline literature and even in the earlier chapters of Galatians, is too far removed from the immediate context of Galatians 6 to be credible.

*2.2.2. The Law of Christ Defined in Context.* A surprising and little-used phrase, like "law of Christ," is best interpreted in light of its immediate context. In this case the context begins with the paraenesis that extends from Gal 5:13—6:10. Here Paul stresses life in the Spirit. Believers are to "walk in the Spirit" (Gal 5:16), "be led by the Spirit" (Gal 5:18), manifest "the fruit of the Spirit" (Gal 5:22-23), "live by the Spirit" (Gal 5:25), "keep in step with the Spirit" and "sow to the Spirit" (Gal 6:8). Thus, we can conclude that believers can fulfill the law of Christ only by the power of the Spirit. Indeed, this exhortation is addressed (Gal 6:1) to "the spiritual," who live in the strength provided in the Spirit. The emphasis on the Spirit shows that the "law of Christ" cannot be described as legalistic or constraining.

The other link forged in the context is found in the words "law" and "fulfill" (*anaplērōsete*) which recall Galatians 5:14 where "the whole law is fulfilled (*peplērōtai*) in love. It is clear in the latter text that Paul is thinking of the OT Law because he specifically cites Leviticus 19:18. The connection between these two texts suggests the following conclusion. The one who fulfills the law of Christ also fulfills the OT Law, which is summed up in the law of love. From the previous context of Galatians (e.g., Gal 2:11-14; 4:10; 5:2-6) it is evident that food laws, circumcision and the observance of certain days (*see* Holy Days) are no longer binding on believers.

Is the "law of Christ" for believers limited to the law of love? Yes and no. Love is the heartbeat and center of the Pauline ethic. And yet even in Galatians Paul unfolds the true nature of love by delineating what is not loving (Gal 5:15, 19-21, 26) and what is (Gal 5:22-23; 6:1-2, 6-10). A comparison of Galatians 5:14 with Romans 13:8-10 shows that for Paul the moral norms of the OT Law must be included when one is defining love. Otherwise love collapses into sentimentality and vagueness. Nevertheless, the focus must remain on the affections in the heart and the power* of the Spirit so that believers will not be satisfied with outward conformity to a norm.

### 3. Conclusion.
In conclusion, we have found the expression in Galatians confirms and deepens what we discovered in 1 Corinthians. The law of Christ is the law of love, and it includes the moral norms found in the OT Law, although it is not exhausted by those norms. Further-

more, the law of Christ can only be fulfilled by the power of the Holy Spirit.

*See also* ETHICS; LAW; LOVE.

BIBLIOGRAPHY.J. M. G. Barclay, *Obeying the Truth: A Study of Paul's Ethics in Galatians* (Edinburgh: T. & T. Clark, 1988) 126-35; H. D. Betz, *Galatians: A Commentary on Paul's Letter to the Churches in Galatia* (Hermeneia; Philadelphia: Fortress, 1979) 298-301; F. F. Bruce, *The Epistle to the Galatians: A Commentary on the Greek Text* (NIGTC; Grand Rapids: Eerdmans, 1982) 260-61; W. D. Davies, *Paul and Rabbinic Judaism* (4th ed.; Philadelphia: Fortress, 1980) 142-44; C. H. Dodd, "Ἔννομος Χριστοῦ," in *Studia Paulina in Honorem Johannis de Zwaan* (Haarlem: De Erven F. Bohn, 1953) 96-110; R. Y. K. Fung, *The Epistle to the Galatians* (NICNT; Grand Rapids: Eerdmans, 1988) 286-89; R. B. Hays, "Christology and Ethics in Galatians: The Law of Christ," *CBQ* 49 (1987) 268-90; O. Hofius, "Das Gesetz des Mose und das Gesetz Christi," *ZThK* 80 (1983) 262-86; T. R. Schreiner, "The Abolition and Fulfillment of the Law in Paul," *JSNT* 35 (1989) 47-74; H. Schürmann, " 'Das Gesetz des Christus' (Gal 6:2): Jesu Verhalten und Wort als letztgültige sittliche Norm nach Paulus," in *Neues Testament und Kirche* (Festschrift für R. Schnackenburg; Freiburg: Herder, 1974) 282-300; J. G. Strelan, "Burden Bearing and the Law of Christ," *JBL* 94 (1975) 266-76.          T. R. Schreiner

## LAWSUIT
In 1 Corinthians 6 Paul addresses abuses in the Christian community at Corinth. The powerful were using their position and affluence to manipulate cases of civil litigation. Worse, the litigations were contests between believers in front of unbelievers. According to Paul, such behavior and display by certain Corinthians was nothing more than another attempt to magnify their own self-importance.

    1. The Church and the State
    2. Civil Litigation in Roman Corinth

### 1. The Church and the State.
In Romans 13:4 (cf. 1 Pet 2:14), Paul presents the dual function of a ruler: on the one hand, the ruler is seen as God's servant (*diakonos*; cf. *leitourgos*, Rom 13:6) who rewards those who do what is right. Conversely, the ruler, as God's servant,* is the avenger (*ekdikos*) who dispenses punishment on the wrongdoer (*see* Civil Authority).

1 Corinthians 6:1-8 seems to stand in contrast with Romans 13 (and 1 Pet 2; if under Pauline influence which is uncertain); Paul seems to embrace a contrary view of the state in 1 Corinthians 6. The term *servant* is conspicuously absent; rather, we read that author-

ities are "unrighteous" (*adikoi*, 1 Cor 6:1), least esteemed by the church (1 Cor 6:4) and for Christians to appeal to them is categorically wrong (1 Cor 6:6).

The difference of perspective must be explained with reference to the nature of the problems addressed: Romans 13 offers general instruction concerning the role of the ruler, including jurisdiction over criminal cases; 1 Corinthians 6 addresses the nature of civil litigation. Civil suits included claims of legal possession, breach of contract, damage, fraud and injury (Garnsey, Part 3), as contrasted with the more serious criminal offenses (e.g., treason, murder, adultery, etc.). The practice of some at Corinth seems to fall into the category of civil law (v. criminal law): believer summoning believer before a pagan court concerning even a trivial case (*kritērion elachiston*, 1 Cor 6:2; *see* Legal System).

## 2. Civil Litigation in Roman Corinth.

B. Winter has collected the evidence (literary and nonliterary) for the protocols of forensic litigation regarding civil disputes.

(1) At best, civil lawsuits were generally contests between social equals among the powerful and influential of the city. It was not uncommon, however, for the plaintiff to use position and influence against the inferior. "Litigation caused personal enmity and litigation was used to aggravate personal enmity. The proceedings were not conducted dispassionately by the parties but with great acrimony" (Winter, 566). In fact enmity itself was seen as sufficient cause to litigate, and manuals for rhetorical* training elucidated the most effective means of *vituperatio*—how to attack the character of the opponent!

(2) The appointed judge, or magistrate (or in some instances a jury), was chosen from among the leading citizens. An honorary magistrate (*duovir*) would be capable of significant benefaction, and, if assembled, the jury would be comprised of men over the age of twenty-five who were on the census list and held property of more than 7,500 *denarii*.

(3) The appointed judges and juries were notoriously partial. Hence Paul's invective: these judges are unrighteous. Paul is not merely equating them with the unbelievers in 1 Corinthians 6:6 (although they were non-Christians). He seems rather to imply that at this level, the Corinthian courts were corrupt (cf. the supporting documentation in Winter, 562-64).

(4) Judicial bribery was common and jury service was not without reward (cf. Suetonius *Claudius* 15.1; Winter, 564-66). According to Cicero, bribery (*pecunia*) was one of the three forces which frustrated the legal proceedings (Cicero *In Defence of Aulius Caecina* 15.73).

Winter (following Garnsey) concludes: social status and legal privilege were inextricably connected in the Roman Empire: praetors "undoubtedly acted in the interests of the members of higher orders, to which they themselves belonged" (Garnsey, 4). Cicero comments that security and power constitute advantage. "Security is a reasoned and unbroken maintenance of safety. Power [*potentia*] is the possession of resource sufficient for preserving one's self and weakening others" (Cicero *De Inventione* 2.56.169). Moreover, the catalog of virtues which tended to favor the powerful included: public office, money, connections by marriage, high births, friends, country, power and all other things pertaining to this class (Cicero *De Inventione* 2.59.177).

***2.1. Paul's Response to Litigation at Corinth.*** In light of these observations, Paul's stringent response seems intelligible. Enmity was no stranger to Corinth (cf. 1 Cor 1—4). Civil litigation augmented the existing problems, and the corollary—the award of financial damages—was interpreted by Paul as defrauding *brothers and sisters* (1 Cor 6:7-8).

Paul's demand that the wise (*sophos*, 1 Cor 6:5; cf. 1 Cor 1:20, 26; 3:18) present themselves as arbiters is biting criticism at best (Fee, 237). Such lawsuits (*krimata*) are self-defeating, and Paul condemns the Corinthians' behavior. Even if certain Corinthians were capable of plying their skills in civil suits between Christians, Paul does not advocate this practice. Rather, it would be better to suffer, "even to be defrauded" (1 Cor 6:7).

***2.2 1 Corinthians 6: A Contextual Reading.***
Paul denies the Corinthians' insistence on a public exposure of their disputes. This pericope is really an attempt to set this right:

> Paradoxically, on the one hand, the Corinthian church had judged the outsider when they had no right to do so, 5:12, but failed dismally to judge the insider when they should have done so, 5:13. On the other hand, they had allowed the unrighteous outsiders to judge the insiders, 6:1, when they should have resorted to the use of a fellow Christian who, by reason of his legal training, would have had the requisite qualifications to act as a private arbitrator. (Winter, 572)

1 Corinthians 6:1-8 is a scathing criticism of the Corinthians' inability to understand the offense committed. Parading power was a parody of the gospel and must be abjured by Christians.

*See also* CIVIL AUTHORITY; CORINTHIANS, LETTERS TO THE; LEGAL SYSTEM, ROMAN.

BIBLIOGRAPHY. G. D. Fee, *The First Epistle to the Corinthians* (NICNT; Grand Rapids: Eerdmans, 1987); R. H.

Fuller, "First Corinthians 6:1-11—An Exegetical Paper," *Ex Auditu 2* (1986) 96-104; P. Garnsey, *Social Status and Legal Privilege in the Roman Empire* (Oxford: Clarendon, 1970); B. W. Winter, "Civil Litigation in Secular Corinth and the Church: The Forensic Background to 1 Corinthians 6:1-8," *NTS* 37 (1991) 559-72; idem, "The Public Honouring of Christian Benefactors: Romans 13.3-4 and 1 Peter 2.14-15," *JSNT* 34 (1988) 87-103; N. T. Wright, "The New Testament and the 'State,' " *Themelios* 16 (1990) 11-17; W. C. van Unnik, "Lob und Strafe durch die Obrigkeit. Hellenistisches zu Röm. 13.3-4," in *Jesus und Paulus, Festschrift für Werner Georg Kümmel zum 70. Geburtstag,* ed. E. E. Ellis and E. Grasser (Göttingen: Vandenhoeck & Ruprecht, 1975) 334-43.

B. B. Blue

# LEGAL SYSTEM, ROMAN

Roman law in the first century A.D. was surprisingly simple and easy to understand by comparison with our own legal system. Its origins, like many ancient legal systems, was based on specific laws of retaliation for private and public wrongs. These were collected in the Twelve Tables (c. 449 B.C.), known to us only from numerous fragments. As the Roman state expanded and life became more complicated in late Republican times and the early Empire, the laws of the Twelve Tables were expanded by recourse to legislation enacted by the senate (*senatus consulta*), the replies (*rescripta*) of the emperors* to requests for advice, their edicts (*mandata*), and precedents that developed out of the decisions of magistrates at every level. These were codified and circulated as reference works in the first three centuries of the Empire by the famous jurists: Scaevola, Celsus, Gaius, Salvius Julianus, Paulus and Ulpian.

1. The Legal System in Rome
2. The Legal System in the Provinces
3. Paul's Encounters with Roman Law

## 1. The Legal System in Rome.

In order to understand the apostle* Paul's encounters with the law one must gain a clear picture of provincial administration. However, it is not possible to comprehend provincial legal administration without recourse to Roman law in general. Decisions at law were delegated to the office of *praetor* (magistrate) as early as the second century B.C. Most basic to Roman law was the concept that cases would be heard by an individual, usually a praetor, who would render a decision binding on both parties. For lesser offenses the praetor might appoint magistrates of lower rank who would hear cases as an extension of the prerogative of the praetor.

In time there developed the *ordo iudicorum publicorum* ("the body of public legal opinions"). This consisted of laws dealing with major offenses against persons, society and the government. By late Republican times, if the offense was grievous enough in the opinion of the praetor, the case would be assigned to a jury under the jurisdiction of the praetor. These juries became permanent criminal courts, *quaestiones*, that developed out of special inquiries made by the senate and the senior magistrates. By the time of the Augustan principate, however, they had regular jurisdiction over more serious crimes. The jurors, thirty in number, were drawn from senators and knights; but the juries were extensions of the authority of the praetor himself. There was no jury system separate from the authority of the magistrates. In fact, juries were all but eliminated by the first half of the third century A.D. The provincial legal system placed the same priority on the jurisdiction of the individual magistrate as that of the individual magistrates in Rome.

All cases, whether heard by a magistrate or a jury, consisted of three parts. First, there was a free formulation of charges and penalties by the magistrate in the presence of both the plaintiff and defendant. Second, there was a formal accusation before the court. Third, this was followed immediately by a hearing before the magistrate and his assistants. In almost all cases when the decision was rendered, it was final. Only persons of wealth and great influence could appeal the decision of the magistrate to the emperor. The decision by the emperor to hear an appeal was not based so much on the interpretation of the law as it was on the prominence and importance of the individual who had access to the emperor, often through the Senate.

## 2. The Legal System in the Provinces.

In the provinces the senior Roman official, a proconsul in the more settled senatorial provinces, or a procurator in the provinces controlled directly by the emperor, had absolute authority over his realm. In fact *provincia* meant the area ruled by a particular official rather than a defined geographical area. The governor's authority over provincial subjects, his *imperium*, was limited only by laws against extortion and extreme cruelty. He usually followed the precedents of Roman law; at other times, particularly for lesser charges, he allowed local law to be the standard. In capital offenses he had the sole authority for local residents. Roman citizens who resided in a province had right of appeal to the emperor, with or without a trial before the governor, if they had sufficient influence to gain a hearing.

Palestine, which in NT times was part of the province of greater Syria, was a special case. Because of the unruly factions present in Palestine, it was placed under the jurisdiction both of the procurator, a Jewish king and the direct military rule of an imperial legate especially positioned in potentially volatile places like Jerusalem (*see* Political Systems). The legate had *imperium* ("authority") directly from the emperor, but it is unclear in very serious matters whether the legate was required to defer to the procurator or not. When he did defer to the procurator, the evidence is too scanty to say whether he did so for political or legal reasons. In any event, it should be noted that the book of Acts in particular, and the Pauline letters to a lesser degree, are some of the best sources for Roman legal procedure in the time of the early Empire. To be sure, the allusions to the law in the Acts and the letters are limited and the narrative accounts of the trials are greatly condensed, but there is little in them to prompt questions about the historicity of either of these sources. Contemporary Roman legal documents and literature are as full of difficulties for scholars as are the NT sources (see Sherwin-White, 172-93).

In summary, the provincial governor had absolute authority over all the inhabitants of a particular province. He followed precedents of Roman law, especially in that he, the chief magistrate, rather than a jury, adjudicated the law. He could and often did delegate authority to lesser magistrates, and often in lesser matters of law the municipalities were allowed to retain authority over their subjects at the discretion of the governor. The governor's authority was limited only by laws under which he could be charged with extortion or extreme cruelty. He had absolute authority over Roman citizens in the province he governed, except in capital cases. There was, however, precedent but no binding law that a Roman citizen who resided in a province would be returned to the governor of that province for trial rather than be tried by the local governor.

## 3. Paul's Encounters with Roman Law.

*3.1. Ephesus.* Nowhere does the writer of Acts show greater familiarity with Roman provincial administration than he does in regard to the uproar at Ephesus* (19:23—20:1). Paul had connections there with wealthy and powerful friends, the Asiarchs, who were either civil or religious officials of the council of Asia. Their existence in the first century is well documented, although there is some confusion about the precise role they played in government. The authority of the *grammateus* ("the town clerk") over the informal assembly in the temple is appropriate (Acts 19:35), as

is the distinction made in Acts 19:39 between unapproved mob action and an *ennomos ekklēsia* ("a regular assembly"). There is some dispute about the appropriateness of the technical term *tēn Ephesiōn polin neōkoron . . . tēs megalēs Artemidos* ("the city of Ephesus, custodian of the great Artemis," Acts 19:35) for the first century, but the evidence suggests that its historical authenticity is a reasonable probability. Finally, the town clerk reminds the crowd that if they have a legitimate complaint they have the right to bring their complaint to the Roman proconsul in the court. He adds that "anything further," whatever that meant, should be settled in the "regular assembly." The intimation of the latter comment is that matters of local religious dispute should be settled by the council; charges of a more serious nature would be heard by the proconsul. This conforms to Roman procedure in all the provinces. The town clerk suggests further that the ones really in danger of an indictment are the mob and its leaders for fomenting an insurrection.

*3.2. Thessalonica.* At Thessalonica (Acts 17:1-9) the Jews incite a mob against Paul and Silas. Unable to find them, they drag their host, Jason, and other believers of the city before the local authorities. There they accuse them in a vague way of fomenting sedition. "They are all acting contrary to Caesar's decrees, by saying that there is another king, Jesus" (Acts 17:7; *see* Judge 1971; 1972). It would seem that in this incident the civil authorities have jurisdiction only in the city. They receive a bond, presumably cash, from Jason and his followers, then release them. Next, we are told that the believers sent Paul and Silas out of the city by night. The chronology of the arrest of Jason and the other believers is not clear. This much is: the local magistrates have authority over Jason and other residents of the city. They do not have any jurisdiction over Paul and Silas once they leave the city, unless they can bring a charge of sedition before the Roman proconsul. In this instance the local officials apparently consider the charge to be so vague that the Roman provincial administrator would probably refuse to hear it.

*3.3. Berea.* At Berea Paul and Silas are more successful in preaching to the Jews, but troublemakers from Thessalonica follow them there and agitate the crowds. Paul and Silas again leave quickly, presumably to escape the local authorities (Acts 17:10-15).

*3.4. Athens.* At Athens Paul was brought before the local religious authorities at the Areopagus (Acts 17:16-21; *see* Athens). This was not voluntary. The words, *epilabomenoi autou . . . ēgagon* ("they seized him and led him," Acts 17:19) are too strong for a voluntary appearance. The only point to be made out of this incident is that Paul soon leaves the city. As is typical in the semiautonomous cities of the East, once he is outside of Athenian jurisdiction, he is safe.

**3.5. Corinth.** An incident at Corinth (Acts 18:12-17) further defines the matter of jurisdiction. Paul is accused by the Jews before L. Junius Gallio, the proconsul of Achaea, of persuading men to worship God contrary to the law (Acts 18:13). Gallio responded by stating that "if it were a crime or a serious piece of villainy (Can we interpret *adikēma* and *rhadiourgēma* [Acts 18:14] as respectively a crime against the state and a private tort?) he would reasonably listen to that. But since it was an inquiry about words and names and Jewish law, he told them to see to it themselves (Acts 18:15). He did not wish to be a judge of these things. Then he had them driven from the *bēma* (Acts 18:14, 15). Furthermore, Gallio was quite unconcerned when the Jews beat Sosthenes, the ruler of the synagogue* (and possibly a Christian sympathizer, cf. 1 Cor 1:1), in front of him (Acts 18:17). In this incident it is clear that the proconsul was willing to act only in important criminal and civil matters that concerned Rome, and that local authorities were free by his permission to inflict punishment as they saw fit for lesser offenses.

**3.6. Pisidian Antioch, Iconium and Lystra.** Earlier incidents in Asia Minor, recorded in Acts, were probably similar to the ones at Thessalonica, Berea, Athens and Corinth. Paul and Barnabas had great success in their ministry at Pisidian Antioch (Acts 13:14-49) until some Jews incited the religious women and prominent men of the city and instigated persecution against them. Paul and Barnabas simply left the city. No comment is made about any brush with the Roman authorities (Acts 13:50-51).

At Iconium they were more successful in their ministry in the synagogue. However, both Gentiles and "the Jews with their leaders" succeeded in driving them from the city. Then Paul and Barnabas fled to Lystra (Acts 14:6). But Jews from Antioch and Iconium followed them there and convinced the residents of that city to stone Paul and drag him from the city (Acts 14:19). In each instance such confrontation was of no lasting significance from a legal point of view, even though devout women and prominent men of Antioch (Acts 13:50) opposed Paul and Barnabas, and Gentiles cooperated with Jews against them at Iconium (Acts 14:19). We must assume that this was again interpreted by the local magistrates in each city as a conflict between Jews about their own law, because Paul and Barnabas returned immediately afterwards to Lystra and to Iconium, without fear of apprehension by the Roman authorities (Acts 14:21).

**3.7. Philippi.** Luke relates the arrest, beating and imprisonment of Paul and Silas at Philippi in much greater legal detail than in earlier accounts of their conflicts with the authorities (Acts 16:12-40). Is this to serve as a warning for those who would illegally arrest and imprison Christians who were Roman citizens (cf. Acts 22:24-29)? The nuances of this narrative are noteworthy.

Philippi is properly identified as a Roman colony. Its residents were citizens of Rome. Many of them were veterans of Antony's army who had been stripped of their land in Italy by the victorious Augustus Caesar. Typically such a colony consisted of a mixture of veterans of Italian and of provincial origin as well as local Greeks. (A similar population mix was to be found in Corinth, a city that has been carefully studied.)

In the first century A.D. the chief magistrates of such a city were *duoviri legi dicundo* ("two magistrates who administrate the law"), whom Luke calls *stratēgoi* (lit. "generals," here "presidents," Acts 16:20). They had jurisdiction over the lesser crimes of citizens that resulted in fines. Paul and Silas, however, were treated by them not as citizens but as *peregrini* ("foreigners"); being subjected to arrest, beating and imprisonment without a trial.

It should be noted, however, that the charge brought against the apostles was one that could have resulted in the arrest of a provincial in the first century B.C., but not in the first century A.D. By that time Roman authorities had long ceased to attempt to control foreign cults by forbidding the practice of strange and unfamiliar customs or of proselytizing. Only if their adherents were also involved in sedition or violence would the government move against them to arrest them and specifically charge them with violation of the law. This is apparent from the revision of the charges first made against Paul when he was arrested in Jerusalem. Later, when he was transferred from Jerusalem to Caesarea, Tertullus, the lawyer of the Jews, expanded "the charge over questions about the law" (Acts 23:39) to a charge that corresponded closely to the edict of Claudius (c. A.D. 49-50) by which many Jews were driven from Rome for "stirring up insurrections among all the Jews throughout the inhabited world" (Acts 24:5).

The conclusion of Paul's imprisonment at Philippi (Acts 16:19-40) is a textbook example of the benefits of the status of Roman citizens when they were abroad. The *duoviri* ("the magistrates") and their police no doubt assumed that Paul and Silas were Jews involved in a controversy with other Jews about their religion. They did not for a moment entertain the idea that Paul was a Roman citizen (*see* Citizenship), and so they treated him as they would any religious zealot who was causing a civil disturbance. Their concern was the disturbance he had created, not about the existence of the cult or its laws and practices. The *duoviri* joined with the police in seizing Paul and Silas, disrobing and beating them on the spot and throwing them in prison. But after an overnight stay in jail, with the threat of riot past, they ordered them released from prison. Paul did not claim Roman citizenship until the police came to set them free and offer them safe departure from the city in secret. Only then, when Paul complained about the beating he had received despite his Roman citizenship, did the magistrates become greatly distressed. They were all the more eager to escort him from their city without further trouble (Acts 16:39). The text strongly—if not certainly—suggests that the *duoviri* themselves came to beg Paul and Silas to leave. The issue was resolved without recourse to the courts, but Paul's status as a Roman citizen was obviously of great importance and concern to the magistrates, to Luke and to Paul himself.

**3.8. Jerusalem.** The incident at Jerusalem\* (Acts 21:27—26:32), one which ultimately led to Paul's hearings and trials in Jerusalem, in Caesarea and in Rome before Caesar, was related to Paul's earlier ministry in Asia Minor. Jews from that region who had come to Jerusalem stirred up the crowds inside the Temple precinct with an accusation that Paul had desecrated the holy place. They had seen Paul in the city with Trophimus the Ephesian, a Gentile,\* and assumed that he had brought Trophimus into the Temple area. When the crowd, assuming he had violated the Temple, tried to kill Paul, the Roman garrison nearby heard the disturbance, came running, stopped the beating and took Paul into custody. The commander of the troops, a tribune, ordered Paul bound by two chains and brought to the barracks. Before Paul was taken away, he told the tribune that he was a Jew, a citizen of Tarsus. Asking for permission to address the people, he was granted the opportunity. After Paul had spoken at length, the Jews rioted again. The tribune then ordered Paul to be examined by scourging, a standard practice for the examination of slaves and non-Romans of lowly status. Oddly, Paul did not mention that he was a Roman citizen until they began to stretch him out on a rack. It seems to have been a strategy of his that he did not reveal his status as a Roman citizen until he had been unlawfully treated (cf. Acts 16:37). The centurion in charge of the flogging, upon hearing this, consulted with the tribune, who released Paul but ordered a hearing before the

Jews to ascertain the details of their accusations against him. This seems to have been a hearing *extra ordinem* that would have given the military commander considerable freedom to gather evidence before reaching a verdict. The hearing, however, ended abruptly in a heated argument between the Pharisees and Sadducees (Acts 23:9-10). Paul was returned to the barracks. It is clear from all of this that the Jews, even in their formal council meetings, had only as much jurisdiction in determining Paul's fate on a capital charge as the military commander granted to them. On the other hand, the commander, who had much greater jurisdictional latitude, used it more for political advantage than he did for executing Roman law.

Political influence rather than law was even more decisive in the events that followed. Paul learned from his nephew that there was a plot to kill him the next day en route to a hearing before the tribune and the council of the Jews, information that was then delivered to the tribune (Acts 23:16-22). With an extraordinary show of force—200 soldiers, 70 cavalrymen, 200 spearmen—the tribune, Claudius Lysias, sent Paul to the governor Felix at Caesarea (Acts 23:23-24). In a letter to Felix, Lysias made the point that Paul was guilty of nothing that deserved imprisonment or death. He said that he was accused only on questions regarding Jewish law (Acts 23:26-30). Felix held an initial hearing when Paul arrived, but put off a formal hearing until his accusers should come from Jerusalem. In this initial hearing Felix asked the apostle from what province he was. By custom it was typical for a Roman provincial administrator to return a provincial to his own district, in this instance Cilicia, for trial (Acts 23:33-35). We can only speculate that Felix kept Paul at Caesarea because he saw a rare opportunity to satisfy the Jews, to consult with Paul about his faith and to extort money from him.

About five days later, when the Jews arrived from Jerusalem, it became obvious that they had attempted to strengthen their case. In words reminiscent of Claudius' edict that expelled many Jews from Rome, Tertullus, the lawyer for the Jerusalem Jews, argued that Paul was a troublemaker, one who had stirred up insurrections (*staseis*) throughout the inhabited world and a ringleader of the sect of the Nazarenes (Acts 24:1-5). He added the further charge that Paul had attempted to desecrate the Temple (Acts 24:6). But while Paul admitted to being a follower of Christ, he refuted all the other charges. In what follows in Acts it is clear that Felix wanted to satisfy everyone. He put the case off until he could consult with Claudius Lysias, the Roman tribune from Jerusalem (Acts 24:22), and gave Paul considerable freedom while he was under house arrest (Acts 24:23). Both Felix and his wife, Drusilla, a Jewess, heard Paul speak about faith in Christ, but ultimately Felix seemed more interested in improving his own lot. Luke tells us that, as a favor to the Jews, Paul was forced to remain a prisoner for about two years. Moreover, Felix consulted with Paul frequently, hoping that Paul would ultimately give him a bribe (Acts 24:24-27).

In the first century A.D. a provincial administrator's power was limited only by the emperor. Hence he had enormous freedom to dispense justice as arbitrarily as he liked, just so long as he did not fall foul of the emperor. But there was one exception to this "unlimited" freedom—the *leges repetundarum* ("laws against extortion"), the first of which, the *Lex Calpurnia* of 149 B.C., stipulated that a governor could be as harsh and arbitrary as he liked, but he could not extort property or money from provincials. The law, of course, assumed an abuse of power. Felix seems to have contented himself with a delicate political balancing act. On the one hand, he was eager to hear Paul expound Christianity. On the other, he satisfied the Jews by keeping Paul a prisoner while trying to extort money from him without being obvious about it.

When Festus replaced Felix as governor, much the same situation prevailed. He seemed eager to resolve the standoff that had existed for two years until he too held a hearing first in Jerusalem and then in Caesarea (Acts 25:1-8). The Jews in attendance asked that a new trial be held in Jerusalem, all the while planning to kill Paul (Acts 25:2). Luke never tells us if Paul knew of the plot, but when he was confronted with the suggestion that he stand trial in Jerusalem, Paul appealed to Caesar (Acts 25:9-11). In the hearing *extra ordinem* the governor could have freed Paul, since neither he nor King Agrippa at a later hearing could find any crime on which Paul could be convicted (Acts 25:25; 26:31). However, beneath it all is Luke's assertion that Festus, like Felix, was eager to do the Jews a favor (Acts 25:3, 9).

In the end Festus too chose the politically expedient course. He could find no wrong in Paul. In fact, both he and Agrippa, with Agrippa's wife, gave Paul a wide-ranging hearing. Festus satisfied the Jews by sending Paul out of the country to Rome and, by doing so, he protected the apostle from the Jews. Underlying all of Luke's narrative is (1) the Jews' relentless efforts to neutralize the effects of Paul's ministry by putting him to death if necessary; (2) Paul's careful adherence to Roman law; (3) Paul's innocence of charges brought by the Jews; and (4) the moral and legal expediency of the Roman rulers of Judea.

*3.9. Rome.* The book of Acts ends with the notation that Paul was placed under house arrest in Rome while he was awaiting trial. There he lived in rented quarters with a single soldier as his guard (Acts 28:16, 30; Phil 1:13-17). He would have been under the jurisdiction of the praetorian guard while he awaited trial. He could have been heard by the emperor himself or a high official delegated by the emperor to act on his behalf. There is no indication that Paul ever appeared in court at Rome. More than likely he was released, as were many others during the reign of Claudius and the early years of Nero's rule, as a show of clemency at a time when there was a large backlog of appeals to the emperor. It is much less likely that his case was dismissed on the grounds that his accusers did not appear. Roman law was heavily biased in favor of a trial. The weight of the law fell on accusers to appear in court. Cases were not often dismissed because of the absence of one's accusers.

We can only speculate regarding Acts' ending without stating the outcome of Paul's appeal to Caesar. Certainly Luke had made the point that the early Christians scrupulously adhered to Roman law in the face of relentless Jewish legal persecution and Roman political vacillation in the complicated region of Judea.

*See also* ATHENS, PAUL AT; CITIZENSHIP, ROMAN AND HEAVENLY; CIVIL AUTHORITY; EMPERORS, ROMAN; LAWSUIT; POLITICAL SYSTEMS; PRISON, PRISONER.

BIBLIOGRAPHY. F. F. Abbot and A. C. Johnston, *Municipal Administration in the Roman Empire* (Princeton: University Press, 1926); A. Berger, "Law and Procedure, Roman," in *Oxford Classical Dictionary*, ed. M. Cary et al. (Cambridge: University Press, 1949) 484-91; H. Conzelmann, *Acts of the Apostles* (Philadelphia, Fortress, 1987); C. J. Hemer, *The Book of Acts in the Setting of Hellenistic History* (WUNT 49; Tübingen: J. C. B. Mohr, 1989); E. A. Judge, "Decrees of Caesar at Thessalonica: Acts 17:5-7," *RTR* 30 (1971) 1-7; A. N. Sherwin-White, *Roman Society and Roman Law in the New Testament* (Oxford: University Press, 1963).

A. A. Rupprecht

**LEGALISM.** *See* LAW; WORKS OF THE LAW.

## LETTERS, LETTER FORMS

The Greek word *epistolē* ("epistle," "letter") originally referred to an *oral* communication sent by a messenger. The term *letters* was a broad designation for different types of documents in the ancient world, and could include a great variety of commercial, governmental and legal documents, as well as political and military reports, along with other sorts of correspondence, especially of a personal kind. Paul adapted the

Greco-Roman letter models for Christian purposes. His letters, which have fascinated people for generations, were usually constructed along lines similar to that of Hellenistic letters. But the apostle,* who had a sense of freedom in literary matters, was not tied to fixed models, and he often combined non-Jewish Hellenistic customs with Hellenistic Jewish ones.

1. Private Personal Letters?
2. The Form of the Pauline Letters
3. The Use of Other Literary Traditions

### 1. Private Personal Letters?

Since Deissmann's distinction between "letters" (which were understood as natural, daily and situational) and "epistles" (which were understood as mechanical, artistic and literary), there has been considerable scholarly discussion as to whether Paul's letters should be regarded as "private personal letters" or not. They were certainly private as opposed to *literary essays*, which adopted an epistolary form but were written for an unspecified, universal audience, and *official* letters, which were not written in the context of a personal relationship. Galatians,* for example, is a highly personal letter written to a specific group of people in an immediate relationship with Paul. However inclusive is the address, "the churches of Galatia," this letter was sent to a relatively minor group in the Greco-Roman world (Hansen).

But Paul's letters were "more than private." He wrote self-consciously as an apostle, that is, as a representative of the risen Christ* (note the emphasis on apostleship in Gal 1:1, 15, 16; 5:2) in order to instruct, give advice, encourage and reprimand (note 1 Thess 5:27 and 2 Thess 3:14-15 regarding the impact on the church at Thessalonica*). Most of Paul's letters were addressed to communities of Christian believers and were intended for public use within the congregations. They were occasional, contextual writings addressing particular situations (though note Ephesians), and were the substitutes for Paul's personal presence (*see* Itineraries). He was concerned with the life situation of his readers, but never in the impersonal way characteristic of many Hellenistic letters. Paul treated each situation as unique and important. At the same time his letters set forth significant theological teaching and express a Christian understanding of life which reaches beyond the particular historical situation.

### 2. The Form of the Pauline Letters.

Many ancient letters, which were written by professional scribes, were highly stylized with each part basically determined by convention, regardless of the occasion. The general model of the Hellenistic letter included an opening, a body and a closing. The basic Pauline letter form, in which there was a normal progression rather than any stereotyped or mechanical framework, contained the following elements:

*2.1. Opening.* Paul's letters, which follow the usual Hellenistic letter openings of "A to B, greetings," regularly contain expansions of this basic pattern (e.g., Rom 1:1-7; Gal 1:1-5; 1 Thess 1:1; Tit 1:1-4), and these often point to the specific purposes of the letters. The identification of the writer (with coworkers often named) and addressees is followed by expanded descriptions of both in terms of their standing in relation to God in Christ. Paul usually identifies himself with epithets such as "apostle" and "servant,"* while the addressees are called "saints," "beloved" or "the church* of God which is at. . . ." The usual Hellenistic greeting, *chairein* ("greeting"), is replaced by *charis kai eirēnē* ("grace and peace"). This benediction* is both an affirmation regarding the grace* and peace* of God* in which they already participate, and a prayer* that they may appreciate and experience these blessings more fully.

*2.2. Introductory Thanksgiving or Blessing.* On occasion the more intimate letters of the Hellenistic period began with a thanksgiving to the gods for personal benefits received. Paul adopted this Hellenistic epistolary model, frequently using it at the beginning of his letters as he expressed his gratitude to God, the Father of Jesus Christ, for what God had effected in the lives of these predominantly Gentile* readers (e.g., 1 Cor 1:4; Phil 1:3; Col 1:3; 1 Thess 1:2; 2 Thess 1:3; Philem 4). But the apostle was no slavish imitator of this epistolary convention, since his structures were highly developed and sophisticated.

Two basic types of structure occurred in Paul's thanksgiving paragraphs (*see* Benediction, Blessing, Doxology, Thanksgiving). The first, which contained up to seven basic elements, began with the verb of thanksgiving and concluded with a *hina*-clause (or its equivalent) which spelled out the content of the apostle's intercession for the readers (Phil 1:3-11; Col 1:3-14; 1 Thess 1:2—3:13; 2 Thess 1:2-12; 2:13-14; Philem 4-7; cf. Eph 1:15-19). The second was simpler in form. It also commenced with the giving of thanks to God and concluded with a *hoti*-clause which noted the reason for this expression of gratitude (1 Cor 1:4-9; cf. Rom 1:8-10).

While the *structure* of the Pauline thanksgiving periods was Hellenistic, the *contents* (apart from their specifically Christian elements) showed the influence of the OT and Jewish thought. These paragraphs, which open with a statement of thanksgiving to God, have an epistolary function, that is, they introduce and present the main themes of their letters, usually setting the tone and atmosphere. Many have a didactic function so that either by fresh teaching or recall to instruction previously given the apostle sets forth theological matters he considers important (see esp. Col 1:9-14). An exhortatory purpose is also present in several of these passages (e.g., Phil 1:9-11). Further, the thanksgivings and petitions which are included give evidence of the apostle's deep pastoral and apostolic concern for the readers. At the same time Paul reports his *actual* thanksgivings and *actual* petitions for the readers (*see* Prayer).

Using a typically OT and Jewish prayer form denoting praise (cf. the doxological conclusions to the books of the Psalter: Ps 41:13; 72:19-20, etc.), Paul introduces two of his letters (2 Cor 1:3-4; Eph 1:3-14; cf. 1 Pet 1:3-5) with an introductory blessing or eulogy (*eulogētos*, "blessed"). While his introductory *thanksgivings* focus on God's work in the lives of others, his *eulogies* praise God for blessings in which he himself participates. The formula with a Jewish background was apparently more apt when he himself came within the circle of blessing.

*2.3. Body.* The bodies of Paul's letters show considerable variety, for it is here more than anywhere else that they reflect the different epistolary situations. Apparently, the apostle was more inclined to strike out on his own within the bodies of his letters and to be least bound by epistolary structures. There has been some difficulty in determining where the body section begins and ends (for example, in 1 and 2 Thess the body seems to have assimilated entirely to the thanksgiving). However, several possible openings have been identified through the *parakaleō* sentences ("I urge you my brothers," 1 Cor 1:10; 1 Thess 4:1; cf. Rom 12:1; 15:30), the disclosure formula ("I/we want you to know," Rom 1:13; Gal 1:11; Phil 1:12), the joy* expression (Philem 7), the expression of astonishment (Gal 1:6) or statement of compliance (Gal 1:8-9), while the close of the body was occasionally signalled by eschatological* conclusions (Rom 11:25-36; 1 Thess 3:11-13) or the travelog (see 2.4 below; *see* Itineraries).

The clustering of various epistolary formulas at certain strategic points signals significant breaks or turning points in the letter (Mullins). A distinct transition from a more didactic section to a lengthy section of paraenesis is occasionally signalled by a closing doxology and one of the transitional formulas (e.g., Rom 11:36—12:1; Eph 3:21—4:1; 1 Thess 3:11—4:1). Paraenetic or exhortatory materials were by and large traditional materials (they included "household tables": cf. Col 3:18—4:1; Eph 5:22—6:9), deriving from the

OT and Jewish literature as well as from Hellenistic moral traditions (cf. Phil 4:8-9; *see* Households and Household Codes).

Another typical feature of the bodies of Paul's letters is the "apostolic *parousia* (i.e., presence)," in which the apostle speaks of his travel plans, including his intention to be with his readers, and of his past and future contacts with them through his coworkers (1 Cor 4:17-21; 16:5-12; Phil 2:19-30; 1 Thess 2:17—3:11; Philem 22). Because he was unable to be with his readers, Paul's letters were a direct substitute for his personal presence, and were "to be accorded weight equal to [his] physical presence" (Doty).

Epistolary *topoi*, that is, themes and constituent motifs of ancient letters, appear also in Paul's letters. These include the themes of letter writing (Rom 15:14; 1 Cor 4:14), health (2 Cor 1:8-11; Phil 2:25-30), domestic events (1 Cor 5:1—6:11; Phil 4:2-4) and reunion with the addressees (Rom 15:14-33; 1 Thess 2:17—3:13).

*2.4. Closing.* Paul used the typical closing greetings of Hellenistic letters in order to link the congregations with his own traveling ministry (cf. Rom 16:3-16, 21-23; 2 Cor 13:12-13; Col 4:10-17). However, he did not include the customary health wish or Greek word of farewell. Instead, a benediction (1 Cor 16:23; Gal 6:16, 18; Eph 6:23-24; 2 Thess 3:16, 18) or doxology (Rom 16:25-27; Phil 4:20; cf. Heb 13:20-21) served the same function. The final benediction, which brings the letter to a definitive conclusion, often gives expression to Paul's strong desire (e.g., that the grace of the Lord Jesus may be with them, 1 Cor 16:24) and strikes a note of confidence.

Other closing conventions Paul used include references to his writing a phrase or two in his own hand (1 Cor 16:21; Gal 6:11; Col 4:18; 2 Thess 3:17), his use of a secretary (Tertius, Rom 16:22; cf. Richards), and a holy kiss (e.g., Rom 16:16).

### 3. The Use of Other Literary Traditions.

Paul's letters exhibit not only a broad stylistic range; they also employ a variety of other literary traditions, including the contemporary rhetorical* forms and modes of persuasion, chiastic structures, diatribe* style, midrashic exegetical methods where appeal is made to the authority of the OT, as well as early traditional hymnic* material and confessional formulas. Paul appears not to have been bound to any one stylistic convention, whether epistolary, sermonic or oratorical. The letter form which developed in the Pauline letters was richer than either the brief private letters or the more developed letter essays of Hellenism. We note briefly the following:

**3.1. Liturgical Forms.** The apostle's letters were intended to be read aloud to the congregations to whom they were addressed (1 Thess 5:27; Col 4:16). Perhaps this intended setting accounts for the inclusion of liturgical formulas in Christian letters. Recent scholarship suggests that the following belong to this category: (1) "grace"* benedictions, (2) blessings (Rom 1:25; 9:5), (3) doxologies (Rom 11:36; Gal 1:5), (4) hymns* (cf. Col 3:16) and (5) confessions and acclamations (Rom 10:9; 1 Cor 12:3; *see* Liturgical Elements).

**3.2. Greco-Roman Rhetoric.** Paul specifies his primary, apostolic task as the preaching of the gospel (Gal 1:16). When he writes his letters, he does so as a preacher of the gospel. His letters, though real, are nevertheless similar in many ways to oral speech. Accordingly, any epistolary analysis must be supplemented with a rhetorical analysis of his argumentation (*see* Rhetoric; Rhetorical Criticism). The persuasive modes of the classical rhetorical handbooks were well known during Paul's day, and one did not have to be formally trained in rhetoric to use them. Each type of speech could consist of four elements: (1) *exordium* (introduction), (2) *narratio* (statement of facts), (3) *probatio* (argument) and (4) *peroratio* (conclusion). The introduction and conclusion were intended to influence the audience by securing their interest and goodwill, and conclude by recapitulating the arguments and making an appeal. The body of the speech sought to establish the case. Most of the early Christian letters were written with a basically deliberative purpose. Apart from the opening and closing epistolary formulas, Paul's letters consist of three elements: in the first, which is conciliatory, he commends his readers for their past performance. The middle segment consists of advice, while the final section contains paraenesis (Aune).

Longenecker claims that in Galatians (as elsewhere in his letters) "Paul seems to have availed himself almost unconsciously of the rhetorical forms at hand, fitting them into his inherited epistolary structures and filling them out with such Jewish theological motifs and exegetical methods as would be particularly significant in countering what the Judaizers were telling his converts" (Longenecker, cxix).

*See also* BENEDICTION, BLESSING, DOXOLOGY, THANKSGIVING; DIATRIBE; HOUSEHOLDS AND HOUSEHOLD CODES; ITINERARIES, TRAVEL PLANS, JOURNEYS, APOSTOLIC PAROUSIA; HERMENEUTICS/INTERPRETING PAUL; LITURGICAL ELEMENTS; RHETORIC; TEACHING/PARAENESIS.

BIBLIOGRAPHY. D. E. Aune, *The New Testament in Its Literary Environment* (LEC; Philadelphia: Westminster, 1987); G. J. Bahr, "The Subscriptions in the Pauline Letters," *JBL* 87 (1968) 27-41; C. J. Bjerkelund, *Parakalô. Form, Funktion und Sinn der parakalô-Sätze in den paulinischen Briefen* (Oslo: Universitetsforlaget, 1967); A. Deissmann, *Light from the Ancient East* (2d ed.; London: Hodder & Stoughton); W. G. Doty, *Letters in Primitive Christianity* (Philadelphia: Fortress, 1973); R. W. Funk, *Language, Hermeneutic, and Word of God* (New York: Harper and Row, 1966) 250-74; idem, "The Apostolic *Parousia*: Form and Significance," in *Christian History and Interpretation: Studies Presented to John Knox*, ed. W. R. Farmer, C. F. D. Moule and R. R. Niebuhr (Cambridge: University Press, 1967) 249-68; G. W. Hansen, *Abraham in Galatians: Epistolary and Rhetorical Contexts* (JSNT 29; Sheffield: JSOT, 1989); R. N. Longenecker, *Galatians* (WBC 41; Dallas: Word, 1990); T. Y. Mullins, "Formulas in New Testament Epistles," *JBL* 91 (1972) 380-90; idem, "Topos as a New Testament Form," *JBL* 99 (1980) 541-47; P. T. O'Brien, *Introductory Thanksgivings in the Letters of Paul* (NovTSup 49; Leiden: E. J. Brill, 1977); E. R. Richards, *The Secretary in the Letters of Paul* (WUNT 2.42; Tübingen: J. C. B. Mohr, 1991); J. T. Sanders, "The Transition from Opening Epistolary Thanksgiving to Body in the Pauline Corpus," *JBL* 81 (1962) 348-62; S. K. Stowers, *Letter Writing in Greco-Roman Antiquity* (LEC; Philadelphia: Westminster, 1986); J. L. White, "Introductory Formulae in the Body of the Pauline Letter," *JBL* 90 (1971) 91-97; idem, *Light from Ancient Letters* (Philadelphia: Fortress, 1986); idem, *The Form and Function of the Body of the Greek Letter* (SBLDS 2; Missoula, MT: Scholars, 1972).

P. T. O'Brien

**LIBERATION.** *See* FREEDOM/LIBERTY.

**LIBERTY.** *See* FREEDOM/LIBERTY.

## LIFE AND DEATH

Paul uses the terms *life* and *death* in diverse contexts and with more than one referent. But broadly speaking, he sees life and death as opposed to one another, with life the gift from God and death the penalty of sin. Believers pass from the realm of death to life by dying with Christ.

1. Life
2. The Reign of Death
3. Death to Sin
4. Mortality and Corruption
5. Summary

### 1. Life.

Occasionally Paul clearly uses *zōē*, "life," and related forms to refer to present, earthly existence (Rom 5:10; 7:1-2, 9; 8:12-13; 1 Cor 3:22; 7:39; 15:19, 45; Phil 1:20, 22; 1 Thess 4:15, 17; 1 Tim 5:6; 2 Tim 4:1). *Bios*, "daily life," or "material existence," occurs twice, and then only in the Pastorals (1 Tim 2:2; 2 Tim 2:4). More frequently *zōē* is used in Paul to mean something other than mere physical existence; it refers to a unique quality of life which comes through faith* in and union with Christ* (*see* In Christ). Nine times it is combined with *aiōnios* to mean "eternal life," a life qualitatively different from life as it is presently known, a life bestowed by God* as part of the age to come (Rom 2:7; 5:21; 6:22, 23; Gal 6:8; 1 Tim 1:16; 6:12; Tit 1:2; 3:7; *see* Eschatology). "Eternal life" or "life" (2 Tim 1:10) can also be used as a synonym for "immortality" (*aphtharsia*, Rom 2:7; cf. 1 Tim 1:16, 17) or an antonym for "corruption," or "decay" (*pthora*, Gal 6:8).

*Psychē* can be employed in a variety of senses which are often difficult to distinguish from one another (*see* Psychology). Paul uses it in referring to physical existence (e.g., Rom 11:3; 16:4; 1 Cor 15:45; Phil 2:30), although in Philippians 2:30 it may mean more than physical life: Epaphroditus risked his "very being." *Pneuma* can also refer to physical life (as it clearly does in Rev 11:11; 13:15), but Paul does not seem to use it in this way (but cf. *pneuma* and *sarx* in 2 Cor 2:13 and 7:5, where the words seem to refer to inner and outer aspects of the whole person). Nevertheless, the new spiritual life is life by and in the Spirit* of God (Rom 7:6; 8:3-13; 1 Cor 15:45; 2 Cor 3:6; Gal 5:16, 25; 6:8; Phil 1:27).

**2. The Reign of Death.**
"Death," *thanatos* (and its related verbs *apothnēskō*, "die"; *thanatoō*, "kill," "execute"; *apokteinō*, "kill,"; *anaireō*, "kill," "do away with"), may refer to the cessation of earthly, physical, human life (but cf. Eph 2:16). More often it designates the spiritual-physical condition of humanity "in Adam," which came initially through the sin of Adam* (Rom 5:12-21; 1 Cor 15:21-22). "Death," "flesh"* and "sin"* can be used by Paul in close relationship, particularly in Romans 5—7, where they operate in Paul's narrative of life in Adam and life in Christ, as personified powers. Death and sin operate together, with death coming through sin (Rom 5:12) and exercising its universal dominion (Rom 5:12, 17) from Adam to Moses* (Rom 5:14). With the coming of the Law,* sin increased (Rom 5:20), sprang to life (Rom 7:5) and exercised its dominion in death (Rom 5:21). Humanity became enslaved to sin and to death (Rom 6:6, 9, 12, 14, 16, 18, 20), with the two powers operating in alliance (see Beker, 213-34, who interprets them as an alliance of apocalyptic* powers; cf. de Boer). Paul does not speak of eternal separation from God and final punishment as "death" as clearly as does Revelation 21:8 (the "second

death"), but he appears to have this in mind when referring to death as the ultimate wages of sin (Rom 6:23). In Ephesians 2:1, 5 and Colossians 2:13 Paul refers to believers as formerly "dead" in sinful humanity's utter helplessness and need of God's gracious initiative (Eph 2:8) in salvation by which he made them alive with Christ (*syzōopoieō*, Eph 2:5; Col 2:13).

Death is the "last enemy*" (1 Cor 15:26), which at the consummation will be "swallowed up" in Christ's final victory (1 Cor 15:55-57; but cf. 2 Tim 1:10; *see* Triumph). Here again the personification of death is evident, with Paul in 1 Corinthians 15:25-26 listing death as one of the enemies of Psalm 110:1, and in 1 Corinthians 15:54-55 taunting the power of death (cf. Is 25:7; Hos 13:14), which in the OT is sometimes characterized as a cosmic power. The reign of death exceeds humankind and encompasses the cosmos, which longs for its freedom* from bondage to decay (Beker, 221; de Boer).

**3. Death to Sin.**
Paul also uses the concept of death in yet another way. To be freed from domination by the "old nature" and from the dominion of death, one must die to sin (*see* New Nature and Old Nature). This is possible through the death* of Christ, in which believers participate (Rom 6:8-10; *see* Dying and Rising with Christ). At the same time Paul calls for conscious action, to "reckon" or "consider" oneself "dead to sin" and "alive to God" (Rom 6:11), to "yield yourself to God" as those freed from death (Rom 6:13) so that the new life in Christ may have its full effect (Rom 8:1-17).

**4. Mortality and Corruption.**
Natural life, subject to both physical and spiritual death, is "mortal" (*thnētos*). The presence of death also produces a corrupting, rotting effect. The word "corruptible" (*diaphthora*) is associated with Paul's thought only in Acts 13:34-37 (which has been influenced by the LXX of Ps 16:10) to refer either to the decomposition of the physical body in the grave, or possibly to the permanent abandonment of the individual to the realm of the dead (*še'ōl*). Paul employs *phthartos* and *diaphtheirō* in ways that may be translated with such English words as "destroy," "corrupt," "ruin," "deprave," "lead astray" or "waste away." The latter is frequently used to translate *diaphtheirō* in 2 Corinthians 4:16: "even though our outer nature is wasting away" (RSV, NIV, NRSV; cf. "perish" KJV; "decaying" NASB). Here *diaphtheirō* refers to the progressively destructive force at work in our "outer nature," presumably the physical body, although it possibly refers to

the whole sinful nature. The present depraved condition, or the Christian's "former way of life," is corrupt (*phtheirō*, Eph 4:22) and depraved (*diaphtheirō*, 1 Tim 6:5). Even the believer is subject to the corrupting influence of bad company (1 Cor 15:33), unfaithful messengers (2 Cor 7:2) or evil thoughts (2 Cor 11:3).

Paul speaks of life, death, decay and mortality in most of his letters, but four passages are of special importance. Romans 5:12—8:39 focuses on the entrance of sin and death through Adam and the gracious gift of life in a new and superabundant sense coming through Christ by the Spirit. This same theme is sounded in 1 Corinthians 15:12-57 where the defeat of death and the availability of life are linked to the resurrection* of Christ.

2 Corinthians 5:1-10 introduces the comparison of "the present earthly tent" (the physical body), which will be "demolished," or "dismantled," with the "building from God ... eternal in the heavens.*" Here Paul also likens the present state to being "unclothed" and the future with being "clothed." This occurs "in order that the mortal may be swallowed up by life" (2 Cor 5:4). 2 Corinthians 5:6 contains the important statement, "while we are at home in the body,* we are away from the Lord." When read with Paul's personal testimony in Philippians 1:20-24, it appears that Paul is here affirming that at death believers pass immediately into the presence of the Lord. On the other hand, he may only be making a general statement about his postdeath expectation without implying an exact chronological sequence (*see* Immortality; Resurrection).

**5. Summary.**
Paul asserts that humans were created as "living beings" in the fullest sense of the word, but all "died" in the sin of Adam. This "death" is both spiritual and physical, with temporal and nontemporal aspects. Spiritual death began immediately with the entrance of sin into the race and is not bound to time. With it comes separation from God. Death dominates the physical life in the present (Rom 5:14), renders humans helpless (Eph 2:1), and eventuates in the physical and spiritual destruction of the individual.

Spiritual life is available to humans through faith in the saving act of God by the life, death and resurrection of Jesus Christ. It is synonymous with righteousness through Christ (Rom 1:17; 5:17-18; cf. Gal 3:11), who is the source, meaning, reality and goal of spiritual life in both the present and future. Spiritual life is characterized by fellowship and union with God in Christ and is unaffected by physical death. In fact, for the believer physical death makes possible a closer

union with Christ and so a "more real" life. This new life involves "death" to the old nature and a completely new lifestyle springing from the life of the Spirit within. Thus in describing his own understanding of both life and death, Paul says living is, or means, Christ; dying is gain (Phil 1:21).

*See also* ADAM AND CHRIST; BODY; CREATION AND NEW CREATION; DEATH OF CHRIST; DYING AND RISING WITH CHRIST; ENEMY, ENMITY, HATRED; FLESH; IMMORTALITY; INTERMEDIATE STATE; LAW; RESURRECTION; SIN, GUILT; TRIUMPH; WORLD, COSMOLOGY.

BIBLIOGRAPHY. J. C. Beker, *Paul the Apostle: The Triumph of God in Life and Thought* (Philadelphia: Fortress, 1980); W. Bieder, "θάνατος, ἀποθνῄσκω," *EDNT* 2.129-33; M. D. de Boer, *The Defeat of Death* (JSNTSup 22; Sheffield: JSOT, 1988); R. Bultmann and G. Bertram, "ζάω κτλ," *TDNT* II.832-75; R. Bultmann, "θάνατος κτλ," *TDNT* III.7-25; J. A. Burns, "The Mythology of Death in the Old Testament," SJT 26 (1973) 327-40; R. Cassidy, "Paul's Attitude to Death in II Cor 5:1-10," *EvQ* 43 (1971) 210-17; J. W. Cooper, *Body, Soul, and Life Everlasting* (Grand Rapids: Eerdmans, 1989) 147-72; J. D. G. Dunn, *Romans* (2 vols.; WBC 38; Waco: Word, 1988) 242-513; G. D. Fee, *The First Epistle to the Corinthians* (NICNT; Grand Rapids: Eerdmans, 1987) 737-807; A. Feuillet, "La règne de la mort et la règne de la vie (Rom. V,12-21)," *RB* 77 (1970) 481-521; G. Harder, "φθείρω κτλ," *TDNT* IX.93-106; G. F. Hawthorne, *Philippians* (WBC 43; Waco: Word, 1983); R. P. Martin, *2 Corinthians* (WBC 40; Waco: Word, 1986); R. Martin-Achard, *From Death to Life* (London: Oliver & Boyd, 1960); L. Morris, *The Wages of Sin* (London: Tyndale, 1955); L. Schottroff, "ζῶ, ζωή," *EDNT* 2.105-9; D. E. H. Whiteley, *The Theology of St Paul* (Oxford: Blackwell, 1964). J. J. Scott, Jr.

# LIGHT AND DARKNESS

Paul occasionally uses the universal symbols of light and darkness in a manner in keeping with his Jewish heritage. Light originates and is associated with God,* while darkness is associated with the enemy,* Satan.* The world is in darkness until the light of the gospel breaks in and those "in Christ"* are transformed from children of darkness to children of light and live in the "day" rather than the "night."

1. The Symbols of Light and Darkness
2. God's Light and the World's Darkness
3. The Gospel As Light Penetrating Darkness
4. The Children of Light and of Darkness
5. Immortality and Light

**1. The Symbols of Light and Darkness.**
The primary use in Paul of light (*phōs*) and dark(ness)

(*skotia*) is in the figurative sense. The terms are employed as symbols of the opposing principles of good and evil, a pattern of religious usage which goes back to the earliest times. This figurative use undoubtedly developed out of a reflection on the phenomenological differences between day and night and the revealing nature of the day/light compared to the hidden and terror-inducing nature of night/darkness.

The literal use of night and day is present in several places in Paul as a temporal reference (e.g., 1 Thess 2:9; 3:10; 2 Cor 11:25; cf. 1 Tim 5:5; 2 Tim 1:4). The order of night preceding day is typical of the Semitic pattern of reckoning the passing of time. This order, however, is not always maintained in the Bible, as is evident in some of the Psalms (e.g., Ps 32:4; 42:3; 55:10; etc.) and the Prophets (e.g., Is 28:19; 60:11; Jer 9:1; 33:20; etc.).

Night and darkness are regarded by biblical writers, including Paul, as the *context* wherein practices occur which do not represent true godly living. Drunkenness and spiritual sleepiness or insensitivity are associated by Paul with night and darkness (1 Thess 5:7; cf. Eph 5:14 as a baptismal chant to mark the transition to Christ's light; *see* Worship).

### 2. God's Light and the World's Darkness.

The metaphorical use of light and darkness in the Bible, as Paul affirms, has its foundation in the creation* account with God's ordering of light into the realm of darkness and void (2 Cor 4:6; cf. Gen 1:2-5). Together with other biblical writers, as at Qumran,* where the phrase "children of light" served as a self-designation of the sect against their enemies, "sons of darkness" (cf. 1QS 1:9; 2:16; 3:13, 24-25), so Paul's view of the human dilemma in sin* and judgment* is likened to a state of darkness (e.g., Rom 1:21; cf. Ps 107:10-14; Deut 28:29; Mt 22:13; Jn 3:19). Satan, the enemy of God, is portrayed as a pretender to light, but in actuality he is a minister of darkness (2 Cor 11:14). In Colossians and Ephesians evil is pictured in terms of a forceful realm of dark powers (Eph 6:12) from which those in bondage need deliverance (Col 1:13; *see* Principalities and Powers).

### 3. The Gospel As Light Penetrating Darkness.

The creation model of light shining into darkness was adopted by Paul and the early Christians from the OT message of hope* (e.g., Is 9:2; 60:1-3; Ps 18:28; 112:4) and served as a model for the proclamation of the gospel* to a world bound by sin (2 Cor 4:4-6; cf. Mt 4:16; Jn 1:5, 9). Not only is the model of the light penetrating the darkness employed by Paul as a symbol of the power of the gospel in Christ, but it is also used by him as a symbol of hope in the coming of the Lord* and the revealing of the dark and hidden purposes of human hearts (1 Cor 4:5). This use of shining light contrasts greatly with gnostic* ideas (see *Gospel of Truth*) and especially with the later Manichean views, where the shining light of goodness results in the capture of light particles and provides one of the gnostic explanations for the human dilemma (see Jonas, Borchert).

### 4. The Children of Light and of Darkness.

Those who have experienced the inbreaking of the gospel in their lives are called by Paul "children/sons" (*huioi*) of light and day. They are no longer to be categorized in the terms of night and darkness (1 Thess 5:5). Accordingly, they are instructed by Paul to live in anticipation of the end time as the motivation for life; not as those who sleep, as in a moral stupor, but as those who are awake (Rom 13:11; 1 Thess 5:2-6). They are expected to put away the "works" of darkness and take on the protective "armor [*hopla*] of light" (Rom 13:12). This armor in Paul's parallel passage is identified as the breastplate of faith and love and as the helmet linked to the hope of salvation* (1 Thess 5:8; *see* Triumph).

In Ephesians the entire argument concerning the transformed life is expanded as readers are summoned to wake up (Eph 5:14), and to walk as children of light (Eph 5:8), bearing the fruit of light (understood as goodness, righteousness and truth), which is contrasted with the unfruitful works of darkness (Eph 5:7-11) and disobedience (Eph 5:6). These dark works may seem to be hidden now but the light of Christ exposes their dead nature and makes the character of human action visible (Eph 5:12-14). Moreover, after an explication of the reciprocal nature of the Christian household* codes in contrast to the authoritarian codes of the Hellenistic world (Eph 5:21—6:9), the discussion is climaxed with an expanded statement of the armor necessary for the Christian in the war against the dark powers at work in the world (Eph 6:10-17). This section then concludes with a call to be awake and ready for the battle and for the proclamation of the gospel (Eph 6:18-20).

In contrast to the sinful and perverse people of the world, Paul describes Christians as children of God and as "lights [or 'stars,' *phōstēres*] in the world" (Phil 2:15; see commentaries). There is here no attempt to identify believers with being divine or possessing divine seed as in Gnostic thinking, but in this argument Paul calls Christians to responsible living so that his work among them might be fruitful and not result in futility* (Phil 2:12-18). The argument in Colossians concerning "the inheritance of the saints of light" (unless it refers to the angels* in God's presence: see commentaries) must likewise be understood in the context of salvation or deliverance in Jesus and should not be interpreted in terms of later gnostic thinking involving an awakening to one's destiny.

### 5. Immortality and Light.

The references to light in the Pastoral letters provide some interesting ideas. God is described in the creedal formula at 1 Timothy 6:16 as alone "having immortality* [and] dwelling in unapproachable [*aprositon*, used only here in the NT] light." In the creedal formula at 2 Timothy 1:10, Christ Jesus the Savior* is described as having "brought to light [*phōtisantos*, or "made clear") life and immortality through the gospel." Both of these creedal statements are unique in the Pauline corpus and they offer good examples of the early church's wrestling with the meaning of Jesus in a setting of Greco-Roman aspirations for immortality, both in terms of Christ's relationship to God and his work in salvation.

*See also* ESCHATOLOGY; IMMORTALITY; QUMRAN AND PAUL; SATAN, DEVIL.

BIBLIOGRAPHY. S. Aalen, *Die Begriffe "Licht" und "Finsternis" im AT, im Spätjudentum und im Rabbinismus* (Oslo: Det Norske Videnskapsakademi, 1951); E. R. Achtemeier, "Jesus Christ, the Light of the World: The Biblical Understanding of Light and Darkness," *Int* 17 (1963) 439-49; G. L. Borchert, "Insights into the Gnostic Threat," in *New Dimensions in New Testament Study*, ed. R. N. Longnecker and M. C. Tenney (Grand Rapids: Zondervan, 1974) 79-93; H. Conzelmann, "σκότος κτλ," *TDNT* VII.423-45; idem, "φῶς κτλ," *TDNT* IX.310-58; H. Jonas, *The Gnostic Religion* (Boston: Beacon, 1958); E. Lövestam, *Spiritual Wakefulness in the New Testament* (Lund: Gleerup, 1963); L. R. Stachowiak, "Die Antithese Licht-Finsternis. Ein Thema der paulinischen Paränese," *TQ* 143 (1963) 385-421.

G. L. Borchert

## LITURGICAL ELEMENTS

Liturgical elements refers to the corporate expressions of praise to God* or Christ* that were developed into fixed forms through constant and repeated usage in the public worship of the early churches. In the Pauline corpus, the most common liturgical elements mentioned are: creedal* confessions, hymns,* doxologies, benedictions* and prayer* acclamations such as "Amen," "Abba, Father" and "Maranatha."

1. Creedal Confessions
2. Hymns
3. Doxologies
4. Benedictions
5. Prayer Acclamations
6. Conclusion

### 1. Creedal Confessions.

Creeds, in the modern sense, may not have been fully evident in the early church as in later centuries. Fragments of confessional statements (or creedal confessions), however, are present throughout the NT. In the Pauline corpus creedal confessions can be recognized by the presence of an introductory formula such as "so it says" (*dio legei*, Eph 5:14; cf. Eph 4:8) or an expression such as "I receive" (*paralambanō*, 1 Cor 15:3; Col 2:6). The central messages of creedal confessions are usually related to the saving work of Christ (e.g., 1 Cor 15:3-5) and his lordship (e.g., Rom 10:9-10; 1 Cor 12:3). The rise of these confessions is most likely due to evangelistic intention (the proclamation of the gospel*); cultic practice (the expression of corporate praises to the triune God); or apologetic assertion (the defense of the gospel under attack). Creedal confessions were usually uttered at public worship* or a baptismal ceremony (*see* Baptism). As used in Paul, creedal confessions are often found in contexts where he is defending the gospel message or proclaiming the person (*see* Christology) and work of Christ (1 Cor 15:3-5; cf. 1 Tim 3:16) or where he is exhorting believers to practice proper Christian conduct (1 Cor 11:26; 16:22; *see* Creed).

### 2. Hymns.

Singing was a common practice in the corporate worship of the Pauline communities (cf. 1 Cor 14:26; Eph 5:19-20; Col 3:16). While most of the songs were spontaneous expressions of praise to God by different individuals during public worship, some of them were more structured, containing various confessional elements relating Christ's saving work and his lordship, and were recited unitedly. In the Pauline corpus, passages such as Philippians 2:6-11, Colossians 1:15-20, Ephesians 2:14-16, 5:14 and 1 Timothy 3:16 are generally acknowledged as hymnic materials. In origin and usage, hymnic materials and creedal confessions are essentially the same, that is, they were originally devised for evangelistic, cultic, apologetic purposes and carried didactic and hortative functions in their contexts. In style, however, hymnic materials are recognizable by the introductory relative pronoun "who" (*hos*) being followed by a participle prior to the main verb. They are written in poetic or metrical style (*see* Hymns).

### 3. Doxologies.

Doxology is a form of exalted prayer speech directed

to the praise of God. It was an essential element in Jewish worship and was adopted by the early churches in their public worship. In the Pauline letters there are two major types of doxologies. One is expressed by the formula "Blessed (be) God" (Rom 1:25; 9:5; 2 Cor 1:3-11; 11:31; Eph 1:3-14), resembling the form of the *š⁽e⁾môneh ʿeśrēh* (the *Eighteen Benedictions*). The other is expressed by the phrase "to him be glory for ever" (Rom 11:33-36; 16:25-27; Gal 1:5; Phil 4:20; cf. Eph 3:21; 1 Tim 1:17; 6:16; 2 Tim 4:18), which is less formal in structure but more commonly used. There is no particular or fixed location for the insertion of these doxologies except to note that they are not usually tacked-on elements, but are connected with the context, arising out of the preceding words. And their contents, while following a basic formula, are often expressed differently by the addition of new phrases that help to convey didactic messages directly related to the situation of the readers (2 Cor 1:3-11; cf. Eph 1:3-14; Rom 11:33-36; Gal 1:5; *see* Benediction, Blessing, Doxology).

## 4. Benedictions.

Benediction is a form of wish-prayer expressed for the well being of the people for whom the prayer* is offered. In the Pauline corpus each letter is commenced with an introductory benediction, "Grace* to you and peace* from God our Father and Jesus Christ" (see Rom 1:7; 1 Cor 1:3; Gal 1:3; Phil 1:2; Philem 3; Eph 1:2), and concludes with a benediction, "The grace of our Lord Jesus Christ be with you" (see 1 Cor 16:23; Gal 6:18; Phil 4:23; Philem 25; 2 Thess 3:18). The form and location of these benedictions are similar to those used in Jewish worship, but in content Pauline benedictions are distinctly Christian in that additional features such as "grace" and "from our Lord Jesus Christ" are added to the Jewish formula. The content of these benedictions (both the introductory and the concluding) are essentially the same in that they include three basic elements: the wish for blessing, the source of the benefaction and the recipients. But they are not expressed identically in every case. Paul does not simply borrow and insert a stereotyped benediction into each letter; nor does he include benedictions in his letters for the sake of formality. In each letter the introductory or concluding benediction may be written somewhat differently (see 2 Cor 13:13; Gal 6:18; 1 Thess 1:1; Col 1:2).

Besides the introductory and concluding benedictions, Paul at times inserts "wish-prayers" for his readers. These are placed within the content of the letter at places where he wants to express his sincere concern for his readers in relation to problems being

addressed. In such cases the "wish-prayers" are always tailored to address the specific needs of his readers (Rom 15:5, 13, 33; 1 Thess 3:11-13; 2 Thess 1:11-12; 2:16-17; 3:5). Thus Paul's use of liturgical benedictions is not perfunctory (*see* Benediction).

## 5. Prayer Acclamations.

In the Pauline corpus there are three non-Greek liturgical acclamations which are usually connected with prayers that are used by Paul for other purposes. These acclamations are "Amen," "Abba, Father" and "Maranatha."

*5.1. "Amen."* "Amen" (Gk *amēn*) is a transliteration of the Hebrew word *ʾāmēn*, which is derived from the root *ʾmn*, meaning "firmness, certainty." In the OT amen is an expression of affirmation of what has been said, whether in a solemn curse* (Num 5:22; Jer 11:5) or in prayer and praise (1 Chron 16:36; Neh 8:6; Ps 41:13; 106:48). In early Judaism this usage of amen continued (Tob 3:3) and was so firmly established that in time it became a liturgical element in Jewish worship: the congregation responded with an "Amen" at the end of each prayer recited by the leader.

In Paul's letters amen is used in two different ways. The first one is the common usage where it is placed at the end of benedictions (Rom 15:33; 1 Cor 16:24; Gal 6:18; Philem 25), doxologies (Rom 1:25; 9:5; 11:36; 16:27; Gal 1:5; Eph 3:21; Phil 4:20; 1 Tim 1:17; 6:16; 2 Tim 4:18) and prayers of thanksgiving (cf. 1 Cor 14:16) as an affirmation of the prayer or thanksgiving of another person. But Paul does not use amen merely for liturgical purposes. In some instances it is intentionally mentioned to promote the unity of the congregation through their corporate utterance of "Amen" together (cf. Rom 15:33) or to lead the readers into a verbal affirmation of the doctrinal beliefs which they are in danger of abandoning (see Gal 1:3-5). This is indicted by the frequency of references to and the locations of amen in Paul's letters.

The second way of using amen by Paul is found in 2 Corinthians 1:20. In this context (2 Cor 1:15-22) there is no doxology or benediction. Instead, Paul is explaining to the Corinthians his change of traveling plans. In defending his personal integrity in the ministry* of the gospel, Paul refers to God's faithfulness (2 Cor 1:18), which is supported by Christ's faithfulness in fulfilling God's promises (1 Cor 1:19-20). Because Christ is faithful (not "yes" and "no"), God's faithfulness in promising salvation to humanity is fulfilled. The amen in this context is not likely a substitution of "yes" (as Hahn proposes), nor a reference to its semitic meaning "firmness, certainty" (as van Unnik argues). Rather, it is invoked in its liturgical usage (i.e., expressed at the end of prayers) to underscore the faithfulness of Christ in fulfilling God's promise of salvation* which in turn creates the possibility for believers to utter together "Amen" in their corporate worship to the glory* of God. Accordingly, Paul's argument is: He (Paul) is faithful (or trustworthy) just as God is faithful. God is faithful because his son Jesus Christ is faithful in fulfilling his promises. In this light amen is used in 2 Corinthians 1:20 not only directly to affirm Christ's faithfulness, but also indirectly to support Paul's argument for his own trustworthiness. Here we see an example of Paul's creative use of a liturgical acclamation with its familiar meaning for the strengthening of his argument.

*5.2. "Abba, Father."* The original meaning of *Abba* and the original usage of the phrase "Abba, Father" in addressing God have long been discussed among NT scholars. The majority view (following J. Jeremias) considers *Abba* an Aramaic word (*'abbā'*) used by small children in addressing their fathers. It was adopted by Jesus in all his prayers to God and later on introduced by him to his disciples to indicate an intimate relationship between God and the believers. Although this popular view has been challenged by J. Barr, who argues that Abba is actually an adult's word and was used to address God prior to Jesus' use of the term, its unique usage by Jesus to emphasize a relationship of endearment between God and the believers must not be denied (cf. Jn 5:17-18). In Jesus' usage of Abba there is portrayed a direct, individual, filial relationship with God. The double address formula "Abba, Father" appears three times in the NT (Mk 14:36; Rom 8:15; Gal 4:6). This formula most likely originated in the garden of Gethsemane when Jesus, under intense emotional stress, added "Father" to Abba. Evidently, this double address was known among the Palestinian churches and was transmitted to the Gentile churches both in Asia (cf. Gal 4:6) and Italy (cf. Rom 8:15) as a reminiscence of the *ipsissima vox Jesu* (*see* Jesus, Sayings of). It was later used as a liturgical acclamation (perhaps the communal recitation of the Lord's Prayer) during public worship and was also applied by individuals in their private prayers.

In Paul's letters the two occurrences of "Abba, Father" are found in contexts where Paul is presenting theological arguments for Christian conduct (Rom 8:1-17) and the gospel (Gal 3:1—4:31). In Romans 8 "Abba, Father" is mentioned as a proof of the Romans' filial relationship with God (*see* Adoption, Sonship), and on such basis the Romans are obligated to live according to the Spirit (*see* Holy Spirit). In Galatians 4:6 "Abba, Father" is used to reassure the Galatians of their filial relationship with God even without the observance of the Law* (cf. Gal 3:26; 4:5, 7) which the "troublemakers" among them tried to impose. So in both cases this liturgical address, "Abba, Father," with its popular meaning, is used by Paul to convey the theme of his argument.

*5.3. "Maranatha."* One of the unique features in Paul's letters is his inclusion of the Aramaic word *maranatha* at the end of his letter to the Corinthians, immediately before he expresses his customary concluding benediction (1 Cor 16:22). This is the only occurrence of the word in the entire NT, and for this reason there has been much discussion concerning its meaning, origin and function. Linguistically, the Greek *maranatha* can be read as a transliteration of the Aramaic *marana' ta'* (i.e., the first person plural with the pronominal suffix), denoting an imperative cry "Our Lord, come!," or *maran 'eta'* (i.e., the shorter form), denoting an indicative statement "Our Lord has come" or "The Lord will come." Of these three meanings, the first has been understood by most NT interpreters to be the original meaning of the term, based on the fact that two similar prayers for the Lord's future coming are found in Revelation 22:20 (*erchou Kyrie Iēsou*, "Come! Lord Jesus") and in Didache 10:6 (*maran atha*, "Maranatha"). Many interpreters have argued that the *Sitz im Leben* of this invocation was the Eucharist (*see* Lord's Supper), where it served as a prayer for the Lord's immediate presence as well as for his eschatological return (*see* Eschatology). This view draws its support from *Didache* 10:6 where "Maranatha" occurs at the end of the meal in connection with the eucharistic liturgy.

In 1 Corinthians the mention of maranatha in its context is directly related to the particular occasion and purpose of this letter. Being misled by the intruding errorists (*see* Opponents) into believing a realized eschatology, some of the Corinthians thought that they were already in the new age and that there was no need for a future bodily resurrection.* This belief led them to many unacceptable styles of behavior, and Paul is seen making continual emphasis on a futuristic eschatology throughout the letter (e.g., 1 Cor 1:7-8; 3:13; 4:5; 5:5; 6:14; 11:26; 13:12; 15:50-54). Then when he comes to the end of the letter, the pronouncement of a curse, "anathema" (*see* Curse) on those who do not love the Lord (possibly Paul's opponents) and the exclamation "maranatha!" a prayer for Christ's coming, together serve to reinforce the key messages of the letter.

In brief, Paul's use of this liturgical acclamation at the end of his letter accomplishes three possible functions. First, it may express his sincere wish-prayer that the Lord may soon come. After writing a lengthy letter filled with confrontation, correction and instruction, Paul certainly wishes that the Lord will soon come to vindicate what he had said and done as an apostle (cf. 1 Cor 4:3-5). Secondly, it may be used to correct the Corinthians' misconception concerning their status in Christ. The Lord will come again to usher them into the new kingdom with their resurrected or transformed bodies. They are not yet in the new age here and now (1 Cor 15:50-53; 6:14; cf. 4:8). And finally, it may function to exhort them to live worthily before the Lord. Since they will face his judgment* at his coming (1 Cor 3:11-15), a petition for the Lord's coming reminds them to behave constantly in a proper manner, notably in their personal lives but also in their corporate worship. Thus in 1 Corinthians, maranatha is placed in its context for specific purposes and to suit the particular needs of the Corinthian* congregation.

**6. Conclusion.**
The above discussion indicates that Paul's letters are richly endowed with liturgical elements. Since these letters were read in public worship, the frequent inclusion of liturgical elements is to be expected. Yet it is remarkable to find that Paul's use of liturgical elements is never confined to stereotyped usage or content. This is seen in his careful selection of a particular form of liturgical element and his placement of it in a strategic location. In many cases the content of these liturgical elements (e.g., doxologies and benedictions) are tailored to clarify or underline the crucial messages he wants to convey to his readers, either for didactic, hortative or apologetic functions. In similar fashion, the liturgical acclamations "amen," "Abba, Father" and "maranatha," with their popular meanings, are cited in contexts to strengthen his arguments. In sum, liturgical elements are used by Paul in a lively and creative manner. Their presence in public worship becomes meaningful only when they include relevant messages directed to the needs of the worshipers.
*See also* BENEDICTION, BLESSING, DOXOLOGY, THANKSGIVING; CREED; HYMNS, HYMN FRAGMENTS, SONGS, SPIRITUAL SONGS; PRAYER; WORSHIP.
BIBLIOGRAPHY. J. Barr, " 'Abba Isn't 'Daddy,' " *JTS* 39 (1988) 28-47; L. G. Champion, *Benedictions and Doxologies in the Letters of Paul* (Oxford: publ. privately, 1934); W. Dunphy, "Maranatha: Development in Early Christology," *ITQ* 37 (1970) 294-308; J. A. Fitzmyer, "The New Testament *Kyrios* and *Maranatha* and their Aramaic Background," in *To Advance the Gospel* (New York: Crossroad, 1981) 218-35; W. H. Gloer, "Homologies and Hymns in the New Testament: Form, Con-

tent and Criteria for Identification," *PRS* 11 (1984) 115-32; F. Hahn, "Das Ja des Paulus und das Ja Gottes," in *Neues Testament und christliche Existenz: Festschrift für Herbert Braun*, ed. H. D. Betz & L. Schottroff (Tübingen: J. C. B. Mohr, 1973) 229-39; J. Jeremias, *The Prayers of Jesus* (SBT 2/6; London: SCM, 1967) 11-65; idem, *New Testament Theology: The Proclamation of Jesus* (New York: Scribners, 1971) 61-68; H.-W. Kuhn, "ἀββά," *EDNT* 1.1-2; A. MacDonald, *Christian Worship in the Primitive Church* (Edinburgh: T. and T. Clark, 1934); R. P. Martin, "Paul and His Predecessors," in *New Testament Foundations* (2 vols.; Grand Rapids: Eerdmans, 1978) 2.248-75; A. Mawhinney, "God as Father: Two Popular Theories Reconsidered," *JETS* 31 (1988) 181-90; J. T. Sanders, *The New Testament Christological Hymns* (Cambridge: University Press, 1971); W. C. van Unnik, "Reisepläne und Amen-Sagen, Zusammenhang und Gedankenfolge in 2 Korinther 1:15-24," in *Studia Paulina in honorem J. de Zwaan*, ed. J. N. Sevenster und W. C. van Unnik (Haarlem: De erven F. Bohn, 1953) 215-34.

J. L. Wu

# LORD
In Pauline writings as in the rest of the NT, "lord" usually translates the Greek term *kyrios*. The term basically connotes a superiority of the one to whom it is given. When *kyrios* is used vocatively to address a person (*kyrie*), it can be a purely respectful gesture, roughly equivalent to the English polite address "sir" or "mister" (Jesus is frequently addressed as *kyrie* with this sense in the Gospels). The term can also designate a person as "master" of his servants or followers, and was applied to rulers as masters over their subjects. With this connotation of the term, *kyrios* is linguistically paired with *doulos* ("slave," "servant"). Also, *kyrios* was applied to deities, especially among Semitic and other Eastern peoples of the Greco-Roman period (*see* Worship), and came to be applied to Roman emperors* in the late first century and beyond as emperor devotion was more strongly promoted. The Greek *despotēs*, also translated "lord" (or "master"), is found a mere ten times in the NT, and in the Pauline corpus, mainly in household codes,* only in writings whose authorship is disputed, where the term refers to a "master" in a social relationship (1 Tim 6:1, 2; Tit 2:9; 2 Tim 2:21).

*Kyrios* is used by Paul with reference to Christ* most frequently, far less often to designate God,* and in a very few cases to refer to humans in socially dominant roles such as masters of slaves. Along with the more frequently occurring "Christ" and the less frequently occurring "Son of God,"* *kyrios* ("Lord") is one of the major christological titles used by Paul.

Paul's "secular" use of *kyrios* for human masters and his religious use of the term for God reflect the applications of *kyrios* in the Greco-Roman world among both Jews and Gentiles.* It is Paul's use of *kyrios* with reference to Christ that marks Paul as Christian and has drawn the interest of scholars. The central questions have to do with the historical background and influences upon the application of *kyrios* to Christ, the origin of this use of the term in early Christianity, and its use and significance as a christological title in Paul (*see* Christology).

1. Background
2. Origins of Christian Usage
3. Pauline Usage
4. Summary

**1. Background.**

*1.1. General.* As with many other languages, so in ancient Hebrew, Aramaic and Greek the terms for "master" or "lord" were used with reference to humans in socially superior positions, and could also be used as designations for deities (for much more extensive discussion of the linguistic background, see Foerster and Quell). It is this use of *kyrios* as a title for deities that seems most relevant for appreciating Paul's application of the term to Christ. Paul alludes to the pagan use of *kyrios* for divine beings in 1 Corinthians 8:5 with his remark about "many gods [*theoi*] and many lords [*kyrioi*]" in the religious world of his day.

In the wider religious uses in Paul's time, two in particular have sometimes been pointed to as of direct significance for Paul's designation of Christ as *kyrios*: the use of *kyrios* for the deities of various so-called mystery cults, and the application of the term in Roman emperor devotion. Various criticisms have been offered about such suggestions, however, which make it highly improbable that Paul's use of *kyrios* for Christ can be explained as stemming from these circles.

Both the mystery cults and emperor devotion achieved their zenith of popularity in the second century and later, well after the Christian use of *kyrios* for Christ was firmly established. Most importantly, a general and deeply felt antipathy toward, and disdain of, pagan religiousness were characteristic of Jews such as Paul and the others who made up the initial circles of Christian groups (and who continued in leadership positions through the crucial first few decades). This makes it most difficult to understand how pagan religious usage of *kyrios* could have had any direct influence upon early Christian application of the term to Christ.

Consequently, more recent scholarship has tended

to conclude that the pagan use of *kyrios* and similar terms in other languages is probably not the occasion or source that explains the early Christian application of *kyrios* as a title for Christ. Instead, the pagan religious use of the term simply illustrates the wider linguistic context within which the Christian use of *kyrios* is to be seen, showing that the term was widely seen as an appropriate appellation for revered beings, and that pagans would have understood the term as connoting such reverence when Christians used it for Christ. But to understand why Paul and other early Christians acclaimed Christ as *kyrios* and what they meant when they did so, we must turn elsewhere.

*1.2. Jewish.* It is now clear to most scholars that it is the Jewish religious background of early Christianity that provides the most important linguistic sources and precedents for the use of *kyrios* as a christological title (see esp. Fitzmyer). There are two particular features of this Jewish religious background that are directly relevant: (1) the religious use of translation equivalents to *kyrios* in Hebrew and Aramaic, and (2) the use of *kyrios* itself as a religious term by Greek-speaking Jews.

By the time of the origin of Christianity, it appears that religious Jews had already developed a widely observed avoidance of pronouncing the Hebrew name of God, Yahweh, and that various substitutes were used. Indeed, evidence of ancient Jewish texts suggests that substitutes for Yahweh were often used even in written references to God. In Hebrew God was often referred to as "the Lord" using *'ăḏônay*. And in Aramaic, as illustrated in documents from Qumran, the equivalent term, *māryā'* (definite form of *mārēh*), was used similarly. That is, in Jewish circles of the first century, the Semitic equivalents to *kyrios* could be used to designate the God of the Bible, and in the absolute form ("the Lord") could be used as substitutes for the holy name of God (Yahweh).

Among Greek-speaking Jews of the period, there likewise developed the practice of using Greek equivalents of *'ăḏônay* to refer to God in place of using the sacred Hebrew name of God. Josephus, writing toward the end of the first century, seems to have preferred *despotēs* in place of God's name (but he may have wanted to avoid using *kyrios* on account of its having become one of the titles of the Roman emperors under whose sponsorship he worked). Philo (several decades earlier than Josephus) usually employed *kyrios* as the Greek substitute for Yahweh. The NT authors likewise more often than not use *kyrios* in citing OT passages where God's name appears in Hebrew, giving further evidence (1) that Greek substitutes were used for God's name, and (2) that *kyrios* was a popular (preferred?) choice as such a substitute, functioning in Greek the same as Hebrew *'ăḏônay* and Aramaic *māryā'*.

The occurrences of Yahweh in Hebrew characters (*yhwh*) or of the curious combination of Greek characters *pipi* (which seems intended to signal and to resemble the Hebrew characters for Yahweh) in certain early Jewish copies of the Greek OT cannot be used to gainsay these observations. It is almost certain that in the actual reading of these copies of the OT in Greek neither Yahweh nor the *pipi* device was pronounced, and that instead a substitute, very likely *kyrios*, was spoken, the sort of practice demonstrated in the NT and other first-century Greek writings that reflect the Jewish religious background.

To summarize, in addition to the general honorific sense of *kyrios* and the pagan religious application of the term to certain divine figures, there is the specific adoption of *kyrios* into the religious vocabulary of Greek-speaking Jews of the first century as a way of referring reverentially to God, which was paralleled to, and likely facilitated by, the use of *'ăḏônay* and *mārêh* for God among Semitic-speaking Jews. And given the Jewish religious background and theological scruples of Paul and most Christians of the formative decades, the Jewish religious use of *kyrios* and its Semitic equivalents is to be seen as the most directly important linguistic datum in considering the use of *kyrios* in the NT. The Jewish uses of *kyrios* as equivalent to *'ăḏônay* and even as a Greek substitute for Yahweh add significantly to the range of connotative possibilities to be reckoned with, especially when interpreting the application of the term to Christ.

## 2. Origins of Christian Usage.

The earliest Christian writings extant are Paul's letters, and they provide evidence for the origin of a practice of referring to Christ as "Lord" that antedates the apostle (cf. Kramer, whose treatment of this question, however, goes repeatedly against the evidence). From his earliest letters onward, Paul applies *kyrios* to Jesus without explanation or justification, suggesting that his readers already were familiar with the term and its connotation. This is shown also in the "formulaic" or linguistically routinized way that *kyrios* is applied to Christ in phrases such as "the Lord Jesus Christ" (e.g., 1 Thess 1:1), and "our Lord Jesus Christ" (e.g., 1 Thess 1:3), especially common in the letter openings and closings (*see* Letters) which seem to employ greetings and benediction* conventions from the liturgical life of Paul's churches. The frequently occurring reference to Jesus simply as "the Lord" (e.g., 1 Thess 1:6; 4:15) shows how the term had acquired such a famil-

iar usage for Christ that no further identification was necessary. Paul's letters presume a familiarity with the term as a christological title from the earliest stages of his ministry.

And such a usage of the term is a priori unlikely to have been initiated by Paul peculiarly among his own converts. This is confirmed by a number of data. Though Paul insisted on his special calling from God to evangelize the Gentiles and could even refer to "my Gospel" (Rom 2:16), he was also at pains to insist that his proclamation embodied a view of Christ shared by Jewish Christians in Jerusalem* (e.g., Gal 1—2; 1 Cor 15:1-11). His concise summary of faith in Romans 10:9-10, which focuses on Jesus' resurrection and status as *kyrios*, is presented as an uncontested core statement of Christian belief shared by Christians generally. In Paul's references to James* and others as "brother(s) of the Lord" he seems to be using quasi-formal designations of Jesus' relatives that originated in Palestinian Jewish-Christian groups (see, e.g., Gal 1:19; 1 Cor 9:5), in which the risen Jesus was referred to as "the Lord."

But the most direct confirmation of the very early and non-Pauline origin of the reference to Jesus as "Lord" is found in the Greek transliteration of the Aramaic invocation formula, *maranatha*, in 1 Corinthians 16:22 (see Liturgical Elements). Probably to be vocalized *marānā' ṭā*, it means "Our Lord, Come!" This phrase derives from Aramaic-speaking Jewish Christians. It is used here by Paul without explanation or even translation, which suggests that it had been conveyed to the Corinthians earlier by him, likely as a sacred verbal link between Paul's Gentile Christians and their Palestinian predecessors and coreligionists, among whom the risen Jesus was addressed as "our Lord" (*marānā* from *mārêh*). Paul's preservation of the Aramaic form of invocation of God as *abba* ('*abbā'*, Rom 8:15; Gal 4:6) is probably a parallel linguistic and liturgical link with Jewish Christians that Paul gave to his Gentile converts. It is interesting that Paul passed on to his converts the Aramaic liturgical terms used to address both God and Christ, showing the early "binitarian shape" of Christian devotion in both Aramaic-speaking and Greek-speaking churches.

Suggestions by Bousset that *maranatha* was an Aramaic translation of an invocation of Christ that originated among Greek-speaking Christians, or that the "Lord" addressed was not Christ but God, are rightly regarded today as utterly unpersuasive attempts to avoid the obvious historical force of the phrase, which is that the reverential address of Christ as "Lord" can be traced back to the earliest Jewish Christian groups. Furthermore, claims that the use of *mārêh* for Christ among Aramaic-speaking Christians cannot have connoted a reverence of him as divine but only a more general honorific connotation such as "master" are now refuted by Aramaic texts from Qumran in which forms of *mārēh* are used to refer to God. *Mārēh* seems to have been used similarly to the Hebrew *'ădōnay* (and the Greek *kyrios*), including its use as an appellation for God.

When this semantic fact is combined with the observation that the *maranatha* phrase shows Christ addressed as *mārēh* in corporate prayer*/invocation, it is difficult to avoid the conclusion that *mārēh* connotes a reverence of the risen Christ approaching, or on the level with, the reverence shown to God. And this means that Christ first began to be reverenced as "Lord" among the earliest circles of Jewish Christians in terms and actions corresponding to what is slightly later presupposed and everywhere reflected in Paul's letters.

That is, the appellation of Christ as "Lord," connoting a status like God's, seems to have its roots surprisingly early, in fact in the earliest circles of the Christian movement, and is not to be the result of a gradual process of assimilation to pagan models of devotion to various deities. Nor can the attribution of *kyrios* to Christ and the view of him as divine be attributed to the influx of large numbers of Gentiles of pagan background into the Christian movement (contra Casey). Linguistically and historically, the reference to Christ as "Lord" with an exalted connotation seems to have erupted among Jewish Christians of Palestinian provenance. As was also true for Paul, they were somehow able to accommodate such reverence for Christ within their exclusivist monotheism inherited from their Jewish background, producing thereby a distinctive "binitarian" adjustment in this tradition (see Hurtado 1988; *see* God).

### 3. Pauline Usage.

*3.1. OT Citations.* The first observation to make about Paul's use of *kyrios* concerns the figures to whom he applies the term. If (simply to avoid becoming entangled in another issue) we exclude the Pauline writings widely regarded as pseudepigraphical, there are a little more than 200 occurrences of *kyrios* to reckon with (and the following observations would not be altered if the excluded letters were included). In the overwhelming majority of these occurrences (about 180) Paul uses *kyrios* as an appellation for Christ, and it is this use of the term to which we must devote the greater part of the following discussion. But it is worth noting that Paul refers to God as *kyrios* also, though in several passages it is difficult to be sure whether in fact

the reference is to God or Christ.

The certain passages where Paul refers to God as *kyrios* are all in citations of the OT where God is mentioned in the OT text, and *kyrios* is Paul's Greek substitute/translation for the Hebrew Yahweh (the practice customarily followed also in the LXX; *see* Old Testament Citations). We may take God as certainly the referent in the following Pauline passages where *kyrios* translates Yahweh in the Hebrew text of the OT: Romans 4:8 (Ps 32:1-2); 9:28-29 (Is 28:22; 1:9); 10:16 (Is 53:1); 11:34 (Is 40:13); 15:11 (Ps 117:1); 1 Corinthians 3:20 (Ps 94:11); and 2 Corinthians 6:17-18 (Is 52:11; 2 Sam 7:14). In addition, there are several passages where Paul cites the OT and modifies it by supplying an explicit reference to God as *kyrios* that is missing in the Hebrew and LXX: Romans 11:3 (1 Kings 19:10); 12:19 (Deut 32:35); 1 Corinthians 14:21 (Is 28:11). In these latter passages Paul imitates the language of his Greek Bible and shows how familiar he was with *kyrios* as a Greek substitute/translation of Yahweh in referring to the God of the OT among Greek-speaking Jews and Christians. This makes the following passages all the more interesting.

In several places where Paul cites OT references that mention Yahweh, he clearly applies the OT citations to Christ: Romans 10:13 (Joel 2:32); 1 Corinthians 1:31 (Jer 9:23-24); 10:26 (Ps 24:1); 2 Corinthians 10:17 (Jer 9:23-24). There are two passages where the context makes it more difficult to be certain whether it is God or Christ to whom Paul applies the citation (cf. Capes who argues these are references to Christ): Romans 14:11 (Is 45:23); 1 Corinthians 2:16 (Is 40:13). Moreover there are a number of Pauline passages that may well incorporate allusions to OT passages that mention Yahweh where the *kyrios* Paul refers to is clearly Christ (e.g.): 1 Corinthians 10:21 (Mal 1:7, 12); 10:22 (Deut 32:21); 2 Corinthians 3:16 (Ex 34:34); 1 Thessalonians 3:13 (Zech 14:5); 4:6 (Ps 94:2); 2 Thessalonians 1:7-8 (Is 66:15); 1:9 (Is 2:10, 19, 21); 1:12 (Is 66:5). But surely the most striking allusive passage in Paul is Philippians 2:10-11, which is commonly seen as an appropriation of monotheistic language from Isaiah 45:23-25 concerning Yahweh to portray the eschatological acclamation of Christ as *kyrios* "to the glory of God the Father."

If we set aside the ambiguous passages mentioned above, we are still left with a considerable body of evidence that Paul applied to Christ OT language, even passages, that originally quite clearly referred to Yahweh. In these cases at least, it appears that Paul's appellation of Christ as *kyrios* connoted, and was based on the conviction that, Christ was somehow directly and uniquely associated with Yahweh. In Philippians 2:9-11 we read that God has bestowed on Christ "the name above every name" (whether the passage was composed by Paul or appropriated by him, either way he clearly approved of it as a christological statement). This phrase likely reflects the ancient Jewish reverence for God's name (Yahweh), which for ancient Jews represented God's unique status and being. The passage thus refers to a status and endowment given to Christ that can be compared only with God's status and attributes. This seems to be why Isaiah 45:23-25, originally portraying a universal acknowledgment of Yahweh, is drawn upon to predict a universal acknowledgment of Jesus as *kyrios*. *Kyrios* here must be the Greek equivalent of acclaiming Christ as bearing the OT name of God.

Another instance of Paul appropriating an OT passage allusively to make a christological point is in the much studied passage 2 Corinthians 3:15-18. Paul's statement "when one turns to the Lord the veil is lifted" (2 Cor 3:16) adapts phrasing from Exodus 34:34, where the *kyrios* is Yahweh, to refer to Christ. This application of *kyrios* to Christ is not simply wordplay but indicates that Paul sees Christ as the *kyrios* in divine terms. The following verses confirm this, where Christ the *kyrios* is linked with the (divine) Spirit (*see* Holy Spirit) and is referred to as the source of transforming "glory"* (Gk *doxa* = Heb *kābôd*), one of the most important attributes of Yahweh in the OT and here borne by Christ (see also 1 Cor 2:8 which refers to Christ as "the Lord of glory"; and on the christological significance of *doxa*, see Newman).

Other evidence that Paul's reference to Jesus as *kyrios* can connote a direct association of Jesus with Yahweh is found in several passages where Paul uses the OT concept of "the day of the Lord [Yahweh]" to refer to the eschatological victory of Christ (on this see Kreitzer; *see* Eschatology). In 1 Thessalonians 5:2, 2 Thessalonians 2:2 and 1 Corinthians 5:5, Paul simply appropriates the OT phrase, though the context makes it clear that the *kyrios* whose "day" is coming is Christ. In other passages, Paul modifies the phrase to identify Christ explicitly as the *kyrios* (1 Cor 1:8; 2 Cor 1:14; cf. 2 Tim 1:18; 4:8). Capes studied Paul's application of *kyrios* to Christ, emphasizing especially those OT passages applied to Christ where the *kyrios* referred to was originally Yahweh. Unfortunately, his work is flawed at crucial points by his tendency to approach the Pauline texts in terms of the christological controversies of later centuries, occasional distortion of the work of others (esp. 168-74 in his discussion of Hurtado) and dubious claims about pre-Christian Jewish readiness to accept the worship of figures other than God. Though he is not fully consistent, Capes tends to claim that Paul's application of OT Yahweh texts to Jesus means that Paul "considered Jesus to be one with God" (Capes, 165) and that for Paul Jesus was "identified with God" (Capes, 169). These are, however, unfortunate oversimplifications.

Kreitzer focused on the close association between Christ and God in Paul's eschatology and described a "referential shift" of the term *kyrios* in Paul (e.g., Kreitzer, 113), in which Christ is the referent acting in the role of God. Though Kreitzer intended nothing of the sort, his phrase could be misunderstood as implying an emphasis on Christ in Paul at the expense of God, leading to christomonism. Elsewhere (Kreitzer, 116), Kreitzer refers to a "conceptual overlap between God and Christ" in Paul, and this is perhaps a more appropriate way of putting the matter. Linguistically, we might also speak of Christ as enfranchised or incorporated quite prominently and uniquely into Paul's referential field in his use of *kyrios* as a divine title. And, as shown particularly in Paul's application to Christ of OT passages and eschatological actions that originally concerned Yahweh, when Paul refers to Christ as *kyrios* the term can carry a connotation of honor and status deliberately comparable with God's.

*3.2. Creedal Use.* Another particularly important collection of evidence concerning Paul's application of *kyrios* to Christ are the several passages commonly identified by scholars as "creedal," that is, passages probably reflecting early expressions of Christian faith in Christ (*see* Creed). The term *creedal* is perhaps a bit misleading, however, for the phrases in question were neither intended as full confessions of early Christian beliefs nor were they the result of doctrinal deliberations. Instead, these faith expressions likely originated as acclamations in the setting of corporate worship* in Christian circles. The oldest surviving expressions of Christian faith, they all acclaim Christ as *kyrios*.

Perhaps the earliest reference to the acclamation of Christ in the Christian worship setting is 1 Corinthians 12:3. Here, in the midst of a lengthy discussion of proper behavior in Christian worship (1 Cor 11—14), Paul refers to the acclamation *kyrios Iēsous*, and attributes it to the work of the Holy Spirit in Christian believers. We have noted earlier Romans 10:9-10, which is another reference to this early liturgical acclamation of Jesus as *kyrios Iēsous*, probably to be translated as "Jesus is Lord." In Romans 10:9-10 this acclamation is connected to belief in Christ's resurrection,* which was the event that seems to have initiated the conviction that Christ had been given the unique heavenly glory referred to in proclaiming him *kyrios*. This passage shows that Jesus' resurrection continued to be regarded in early Christian groups as the historic basis and demonstration of his exaltation.*

Another passage previously cited, Philippians 2:9-11, likewise must be considered again here. On the basis of the two previous passages just considered, Philippians 2:9-11 also seems to allude to the early Christian acclamation of Jesus as *kyrios*, projecting a future universal participation in this acclamation which now the Christian groups anticipate and prefigure in their worship gatherings.

Two more features of this passage are to be noted. First, the slightly longer formulation *Kyrios Iēsous Christos* (Phil 2:11) is found (with some variation) especially in Paul's letter openings and closings (commonly thought to reflect liturgical formulas used in his churches), such as Philippians 1:2. This fuller formulation shows that there were variations in acclamation wording, this one is likely an attempt at greater sonorousness and christological fullness, and demonstrates at the same time that the core acclamation remained the heralding of Jesus as "Lord." And, as mentioned already, the title here certainly seems to carry the connotation of Jesus having been given the name (thus, status, honor and attributes) of God.

Second, the attempt at fuller christological expression in the acclamation formula is followed in Philippians 2:11 by a phrase conveying more explicit theological precision than the simple acclamation of Jesus as *kyrios*. Specifically, verse 11 makes the acclamation of Jesus as "Lord" (which constitutes acknowledging that Jesus has been given the divine name) redound at the same time "to the glory of God the Father." As Kreitzer observed (Kreitzer, 161), this phrase is evidence that Paul sought to maintain the "integrity" of his monotheistic faith and reconcile it with the breathtaking status of Jesus reflected in the acclamation of him as the *kyrios*. This concern is also reflected elsewhere in Paul in this sort of "clarifying word or phrase" (Kreitzer, 158) added to passages referring to Christ (e.g., 1 Cor 3:23; 11:3; 15:20-28).

In the final "creedal" passage to be considered here, 1 Corinthians 8:5-6, we see another example of how Paul reconciled Christ's exalted status with his inherited monotheism. In contrast to the Greco-Roman polytheistic environment (*see* Religions), Paul affirms a two-part confession of "one God [*heis theos*] the Father," and "one Lord [*heis kyrios*] Jesus Christ" (the latter phrase another example of the longer sonorous reference to Christ noticed above in Phil 2:11). The wording seems to be influenced by Deuteronomy 6:4, "Hear, O Israel: The Lord our God is one Lord" (*kyrios heis estin* [LXX], translating the Hebrew *Yahweh 'eḥāḏ*). That is, Christ is included in a revised procla-

mation of God's uniqueness. By Paul's time Jews were probably using Deuteronomy 6:4 as part of their confession of faith in the uniqueness of their God (the *Shema*). Paul may thus have intended an allusion to this Jewish confessional practice as well, to express the distinctively Christian version of monotheism in which Christ is the "one *Kyrios*," the Greek title by which Yahweh was referred to among Greek-speaking Jews and in the Greek OT. This constitutes an acclamation of Christ in the most exalted degree.

At the same time, we must notice how Paul's two-part ("binitarian") statement of Christian faith in 1 Corinthians 8:6 places the acclamation of the "one Lord Jesus Christ" within and under a continuing commitment to a monotheistic faith. This is the significance involved in the careful use of prepositions in the statement that "all things," including the redemption* of Christians (which is probably what is meant by "we") have come "from" (*ek*) the "one God the Father" and "through" (*dia*) the Lord Jesus Christ.

Nevertheless, although Paul fitted his view of Christ within his monotheistic faith, he clearly felt compelled to regard Christ in an amazingly exalted light, which resulted in a dramatically redrawn monotheism. Indeed, given Paul's fundamentally monotheistic commitment, it is difficult to imagine a more exalted status for Christ without replacing God with Christ, something scarcely imaginable for Paul.

D. R. de Lacey has described 1 Corinthians 8:6 as representing "a significant milestone in the development of New Testament Christology" (de Lacey, 203), and this is surely correct. It is, however, less certain that he is right to make the religious view it expresses Paul's unique christological handiwork, "his own radical re-interpretation of the creed of Israel" through which he "was able to steer the church down the road towards a truly trinitarian faith" (de Lacey, 202).

In Paul's own personal history, to be sure, he experienced a "radical re-interpretation of the creed of Israel" as a result of his christophany experience in which God chose "to reveal his Son" to him (Gal 1:16). And Paul's "revelations" and gifts in thinking through their implications are not to be minimized. The wording of 1 Corinthians 8:6 with its allusions to Deuteronomy 6:4 and to Jewish recitation of the *Shema* may well show Paul's own creativity of expression and rhetorical skill (*see* Rhetoric). But the "significant milestone" de Lacey refers to, the reverence for Jesus as *kyrios*, connoting his divine status but within the limits of the biblical tradition about God's uniqueness and supremacy, seems to have been arrived at by many other Christians in addition to Paul, including Jewish Christians not indebted to him for their faith.*

The evidences of corporate acclamations of Jesus as *kyrios* considered above suggest that Paul's high view of Christ was representative of the Christians with whom he was acquainted and of the churches whose piety he knew. And, as shown earlier, we must include Jewish-Christian groups, both Greek-speaking and Aramaic-speaking ones, as those who confessed and invoked Christ as "Lord" in their gatherings and over their lives.

*3.3. Appellation Formulas.* In addition to the types of usages already mentioned, there are in the seven undisputed letters about another 170 occurrences of *kyrios* (of the approximately 200 total occurrences) which appear in several frequently recurring, somewhat fixed ways of referring to Christ. These may be seen sociolinguistically as "routinizations" in the religious language of Paul and early Christians which show how thoroughly familiar among them was the use of *kyrios* as a christological title.

Of these, in about sixty-five cases (decisions about textual variants in a number of passages will produce slightly differing counts) *kyrios* is used in connection with other christological terms in the following expressions: "Jesus Christ our Lord" (e.g., Rom 1:4; 5:21), "our Lord Jesus Christ" (e.g., Rom 5:1, 11; 16:20; Gal 6:18), "Christ Jesus our Lord" (e.g., Rom 6:23; 1 Cor 15:31), "the Lord Jesus Christ" (e.g., 2 Cor 13:13) and "the Lord Jesus" (e.g., Rom 14:14; 1 Cor 11:23). These constructions are found especially (but by no means exclusively) in the opening and closing sections of Paul's letters, in greetings and farewells, where as already noted Paul is believed to use the greeting and benediction formulas used in early Christian worship assemblies. Here we probably have a glimpse of the deliberately sonorous phrasing of earliest Christian liturgical language.

Syntactically, in these expressions "Jesus," with and without "Christ," identifies the "Lord," and "Lord" defines who Jesus is for Christians and their relationship to him. That is, in these expressions the fundamental force of the term *kyrios* denoting the superior or "master," seems primary. Jesus is the "master" of Christians, to whom in turn they are his followers, his subjects bound to obey him.

In fact the single most frequently found use of *kyrios* in Paul (about 100 times in the letters we are considering here) is as the designation of Jesus without any other title, simply "the Lord" (*ho kyrios*, e.g., Rom 14:6, 8; 16:2, 8, 11, 12, 13; 1 Cor 3:5; 4:4-5). It is as if "the Lord" is a shorthand way of referring to Jesus, and Paul feels he needs no identifying terms to indicate who is designated as "the Lord." As noted earlier, the reference to Jesus simply as "the Lord" seems to have had its equivalent (*māryā'*) in Aramaic-speaking Christian groups, and was likely taken over by Paul from his predecessors in the faith. It is certainly the case that Paul nowhere shows any need to justify or explain such a way of referring to Christ, indirectly suggesting that this is a well-established custom already among Christians of his time.

As with the fuller constructions listed above, so in this absolute form, *ho kyrios*, used of Jesus we are probably to see the primary connotation as "Lord" or "Master." That is, Jesus is the one whom the Christians are to regard as supreme, to whom they are obliged to give obedience, and whom they see as designated by God as the unique agent of redemption and judgment.* Through his death and resurrection Jesus has now been given authority to exercise lordship (Rom 14:9, *kyrieuō*), which Christians recognize freely now in referring to him as "Lord."

Yet it is well to remember that Paul and other Christians applied *kyrios* to Jesus at times with a far more specific connotation that was also more sweeping in import. As noted earlier, in some Pauline passages *kyrios* is applied to Christ with the effect of associating him directly with God, even implying that he shares in the divine name. It may be that this very profound and exalted meaning of *kyrios* was not consciously intended every time Jesus was referred to by Paul in expressions such as "the (our) Lord Jesus Christ" or even "the Lord." But it is reasonable to surmise that an undertone of the more exalted connotation was present even in these formulaic uses. That is, though the emphasis of the term might vary from one occasion to another, it is likely that the various connotations or emphases of *kyrios* mutually colored one another in the living use of the term by Paul and other Christians.

*3.4. Contexts.* In his study of Paul's christological titles, Kramer pointed out that the individual titles each tend to be used in particular kinds of statements and contexts. He noted that Jesus is referred to as *kyrios* especially frequently in hortatory passages in Paul. Kreitzer and Capes have confirmed that references to Jesus as *kyrios* tend to occur in certain kinds of contexts, especially in Paul's hortatory and eschatological passages. In fact, however, we should identify at least three types of statements in which Jesus is referred to as *kyrios*, each of which reflects an important way in which Paul and fellow Christians related themselves to Christ as "Lord." Paul's usage is not rigid, but we can identify a tendency to refer to Jesus as *kyrios* more frequently in these contexts.

*3.4.1. Paraenetic Contexts.* It is certainly the case that Jesus is referred to as *kyrios* in passages where Paul deals with matters of Christian behavior. We may take Romans 14:1-12 as an example, where Paul urges believers who differ over scruples of food and calendar matters not to judge one another harshly. Whether they eat or refrain, whether they regard one day special or all days alike (Rom 14:5-8; *see* Holy Days), Paul encourages them all to believe that their common motivation is that they act "unto the Lord." And he goes on to characterize Christian existence generally as living and dying "to the Lord" to whom they belong (Rom 14:9).

To cite another passage, in 1 Corinthians 6:13—7:40, where Paul deals with a number of questions of sexual relationships (*see* Sexuality), he mainly refers to Jesus as "the Lord." Forbidding the use of prostitutes, Paul proclaims that the Christian's body is "for the Lord" (1 Cor 6:13). It is "the Lord" whose command he either can or cannot cite (1 Cor 7:10-12, 25) in responding to the questions sent to him from Corinth about married and unmarried people (*see* Marriage). (See also 1 Cor 9:14; 14:37 for references to commands of "the Lord.") Indeed, here as in other passages Jesus "the Lord" defines the realm of Christian existence. Christians are called "in the Lord" (1 Cor 7:22); single persons are able with fewer distractions to devote themselves "to the Lord" (1 Cor 7:32-35); and the widow may remarry only "in the Lord" (1 Cor 7:39, i.e., within the Christian fellowship).

In Romans 16:2-20 Paul repeatedly uses the phrase "in the Lord" in referring to people in the context of Christian fellowship* and service* to Christ (Rom 16:2, 8, 11-13). Compare his criticism of certain troublesome people who by contrast "do not serve our Lord Christ" (Rom 16:18). The phrase "the work of the Lord" can serve as Paul's way of referring to Christian involvement in promoting the gospel* (1 Cor 15:58; 16:10). And Paul refers to his personal movements in his ministry as dependent upon the will of "the Lord" (1 Cor 4:19; 16:7).

In 1 Thessalonians 1:6 the Thessalonians are congratulated for having become "imitators of us and of the Lord" in their obedience to the gospel despite affliction. And in 1 Thessalonians 4:1-12, where Paul exhorts the believers to observe ethical instructions previously given, he designates Jesus as "the Lord Jesus" (1 Thess 4:1- 2) or simply "the Lord" (1 Thess 4:6).

We may summarize these examples as showing that Paul tended to refer to Jesus as "Lord" in contexts where Paul instructs his churches in Christian obedience, and, more generally, in referring to Christian life and relationships, and the service involved in spreading the gospel message. As their *kyrios*, Jesus

claimed the obedience of his followers and defined the sphere of their endeavor.

*3.4.2. Eschatological Contexts.* A second type of context and statement in which Paul tends to refer to Jesus as *kyrios* may be identified as eschatological. Consider, for example, the several references to the eschatological return of Jesus in 1 Thessalonians in which the term *kyrios* is used, either alone (four times) or with identifying terms ("the Lord," 1 Thess 4:15-17; "day of the Lord," 1 Thess 5:2; "our Lord Jesus Christ," 1 Thess 5:23; "our Lord Jesus," 1 Thess 2:19; 3:13).

As another example of this usage, in 1 Corinthians 1:7-8 the Corinthians are described as awaiting the eschatological "revelation" and "day" of "our Lord Jesus Christ." And in 1 Corinthians 4:1-5 Paul refers to the eschatological coming of "the Lord" who will render final judgment over Paul and other ministers of the gospel (1 Cor 4:4-5). The little phrase "the Lord is near" in Philippians 4:5 is probably to be taken as a reference to the hope of Christ's imminent return. As 1 Corinthians 15:23 shows, with its reference to the eschatological "coming" of "Christ," there is some variation in the christological terms Paul uses in eschatological references as well as in other kinds of statements. But his general tendency was to use the title "Lord" in passages where Jesus' eschatological manifestation and victory are in view (*see* Eschatology).

To the passages cited here we must add the references listed earlier where Paul appropriates the OT concept/phrase "day of the Lord" to describe Jesus' eschatological appearance, sometimes modifying the OT phrase by the use of formulas such as "Lord Jesus Christ." In fact it is likely that the OT phrase "day of the Lord," and the hope it came to represent in ancient Jewish tradition, influenced Paul's tendency to use "Lord" in references to Jesus' return. And, given Paul's familiarity with the OT, it is also likely that we should see his references to the "day of the Lord (Jesus)" as indications that for Paul Jesus was associated with God and would act in the eschatological role of God.

Thus, to refer to Jesus as *kyrios* in these eschatological statements probably connoted something beyond the basic meaning of "master." In such statements the "Lord" Jesus was clothed with the attributes and functions of Yahweh. His eschatological appearance would involve his judging all things and would bring divine victory over all evil. As Kreitzer has shown, pre-Christian Jewish writings show that there had already developed the notion of a messianic figure acting on God's behalf in eschatological redemption. In this the Pauline references to Jesus carrying out the role that originally was God's has a precedent. It is, however, significant that in Paul (and the NT elsewhere) Jesus not only acts in God's place in the projections of eschatological hope,* but is also frequently referred to as the "Lord" whose "day" of eschatological triumph* is anticipated. This association of Jesus with God, in eschatological action and in title, is not without parallel but seems comparatively more pronounced and consistent in the NT than in the pre-Christian Jewish references to principal agents of God's eschatological victory.

*3.4.3. Liturgical Contexts.* The third type of passage and setting to highlight with regard to Paul's use of the term *kyrios* for Jesus has to do with the worship life of earliest Christian groups. We have already mentioned Pauline passages identified as evidence of early acclamation formulas and practices by which Jesus was confessed liturgically as *kyrios* in Christian worship gatherings (probably collectively). And we have also noted that Paul's letter openings and closings, with their sonorous references to "the (or our) *kyrios* Jesus Christ" (or "Christ Jesus our *kyrios*") in statements of greetings and farewells, are commonly thought to echo the parlance of early Christian worship as well. The point to repeat here is that these uses of *kyrios* all derive from, and give evidence of, the setting of Christian worship gatherings as one of the earliest and most important contexts for, and sources of, the application of *kyrios* to Christ.

In further illustration of this we may consider 1 Corinthians 5:1-5, which concerns the man guilty of *porneia* ("sexual immorality") with "his father's wife." Paul calls for disciplinary action to be taken in the setting of the gathered church (*see* Discipline), and we are particularly concerned to note the way he describes the Christian gathering. We should probably punctuate verses 3-5 with a stop at the end of verse 3, taking "in the name of the Lord Jesus" in verse 4 as referring to the Christian assembly. Thus, 1 Corinthians 5:4-5 are to be read in the following fashion: "When you have assembled in the name of the Lord Jesus, I also present in spirit, with the power of our Lord Jesus you are to hand this man over to Satan for the destruction of his flesh that his spirit may be saved in the day of the Lord."

Though the occasion for this particular assembly may have been unusual, the terms Paul uses to describe the Christian gathering are probably typical, and the point to underscore here is how Jesus is repeatedly referred to as *kyrios*. They gather "in the name of the Lord Jesus," a probable allusion to an invocation and acclamation of Jesus as *kyrios* in the early Christian assembly for which we have already

seen evidence. This phrase and the references to the "power" of the Lord and his eschatological "day" show that *kyrios* is here applied to Jesus with a connotation of transcendent attributes and functions such as are associated with God.

And both the use of *kyrios* to designate Jesus and the transcendent connotation of the title seem typical of the Pauline passages where early Christian worship gatherings are either referred to directly or are indirectly reflected in phraseology taken from this setting. As a final example we may examine 1 Corinthians 11:17-33. The sacred meal of the Christian gathering is "the Lord's supper"* (*kyriakon deipnon*, 1 Cor 11:20; and cf. "table of the Lord" in 1 Cor 10:21). Consistently Jesus is referred to as *kyrios* in the passage (1 Cor 11:23, 26, 27, 32). It is probably both the worship context and the allusion to the eschatological appearance of Christ ("until he comes") that account for the expression "the death of the Lord" in 1 Cor 11:26, a striking contrast to the more typical Pauline tendency to use "Christ"* in references to Jesus' death.

We have, then, three main types of Pauline contexts in which he characteristically uses *kyrios* to designate Jesus, reflecting three early church settings in which particularly Jesus was referred to as *kyrios*. In the Pauline hortatory statements and passages the *kyrios* Jesus is the "master" whose teaching and example are authoritative for Christian conduct. In the references to eschatological expectations, the designation of Jesus as *kyrios* seems to reflect the conviction that Jesus has been designated to act in the eschatological role of God. Finally, in the Pauline references to early Christian worship gatherings and in his liturgically influenced language, *kyrios* designates Jesus as the transcendent, exalted one who has been given the divine "name" and incorporated into the devotional and cultic life of early Christianity.

These three contexts are, of course, not to be separated entirely. We may distinguish varying emphases of the term *kyrios* as applied to Christ in each type of passage, but the connotations were also likely linked in the religious thought of Paul and early Christians generally. In some cases the link is explicit, as in Philippians 2:9-11, where the future universal acclamation, *Kyrios Iēsous Christos*, echoes and is anticipated in the Christian acclamation of Jesus in the worship setting. Or we may again cite 1 Corinthians 11:26, where the present liturgical celebration of the death of the *kyrios* Jesus in the sacred meal is connected with his eschatological appearance. In Paul's references to early Christian worship, Jesus is the *kyrios* whose present authority over the church is both very real and inseparable from his future dominion over all things to be made manifest in the "day of the Lord."

**4. Summary.**
In any attempt to probe Paul's view of Christ, the term *kyrios* must be central. It functions in several ways and is enriched by several connotations in Paul. The term expresses the relationship of Christians to Jesus as subjects and followers to their master, as in the phrase "our Lord Jesus Christ." In Philippians 3:8 Paul speaks of this relationship in very personal terms with the reference to "Christ Jesus my Lord." As *kyrios*, Jesus' example and command are unquestionable authorities for Christian behavior in Paul's letters. Paul reflects the acclamation of Jesus as *kyrios* in the worship setting, which is understood by him as the pattern and anticipation of the universal acknowledgment of Jesus as Lord when he comes in eschatological glory. The divine glory of Jesus the Lord, however, has already been revealed to Paul. As a result, Paul views Jesus in incredibly exalted terms, permitting the application to Jesus of OT passages concerning Yahweh and the portrayal of *kyrios* Jesus as the agent of all creation* and redemption (1 Cor 8:6). In short, in some cases at least, Paul's application of *kyrios* to Jesus connoted the conviction that Jesus had been given to share in the properties and honor of God's "name" (with all that represented in the OT and ancient Jewish tradition) and bore the very glory of God in such fullness and uniqueness that Jesus could be compared and associated only with God "the Father" in the honor and reverence due him.

*See also* CHRIST; CHRISTOLOGY; EMPERORS, ROMAN; EXALTATION AND ENTHRONEMENT; GOD; HOLY SPIRIT; SAVIOR; SON OF GOD.

BIBLIOGRAPHY. W. Bousset, *Kyrios Christos* (Nashville: Abingdon, 1970 [1913]); E. D. Burton, *A Critical and Exegetical Commentary on the Epistle to the Galatians* (ICC; Edinburgh: T. & T. Clark, 1921) 392-417; D. B. Capes, *Old Testament Yahweh Texts in Paul's Christology* (WUNT 2/47; Tübingen: J. C. B. Mohr, 1992); P. M. Casey, *From Jewish Prophet to Gentile God* (Louisville: Westminster/John Knox, 1991); L. Cerfaux, "Kyrios dans les citations pauliniennes de l'Ancien Testament," in *Recueil Lucien Cerfaux: Études d'exégèse et d'histoire religieuse de Monseigneur Cerfaux*, Vol. 1 (Gembloux: Duculot, 1954); O. Cullmann, *The Christology of the New Testament* (Philadelphia: Westminster, 1963 [1957]); N. A. Dahl, "Sources of Christological Language," in *Jesus the Christ*, ed. D. H. Juel (Minneapolis: Fortress, 1991) 113-36; D. R. de Lacey, " 'One Lord' in Pauline Christology," in *Christ the Lord: Studies in Christology Presented to Donald Guthrie*, ed. H. H. Rowdon (Downers Grove, IL: InterVarsity, 1982) 191-203; W. Foerster, G. Quell, "κύριος κτλ," *TDNT* III.1039-98; J. A. Fitzmyer, "The Semitic Background of the New Testament Kyrios-Title," in *A Wandering Aramean: Collected Aramaic Essays* (SBLMS 25; Missoula, MT: Scholars, 1979) 115-42; L. W. Hurtado, "New Testament Christology: A Critique of Bousset's Influence," *TS* 40 (1979) 306-17; idem, *One God, One Lord: Early Christian Devotion and Ancient Jewish Monotheism* (Philadelphia: Fortress, 1988); W. Kramer, *Christ, Lord, Son of God* (SBT 50; London: SCM, 1966 [1963]); L. J. Kreitzer, *Jesus and God in Paul's Eschatology* (JSNTSup 19; Sheffield: JSOT, 1987); C. C. Newman, *Paul's Glory Christology: Tradition and Rhetoric* (NovTSup 69; Leiden: E. J. Brill, 1992).

L. W. Hurtado

# LORD'S SUPPER

Abuses in the holding of the church* meal at Corinth* led Paul to remind the church of its real significance as a memorial of the Lord's* sacrificial death* on the basis of a tradition describing the Last Supper. Recent study has emphasized the importance of social factors in explaining the divisions between rich* and poor in the church. These divisions led to the abuses and the response of Paul which emphasized the meal as a focus of Christian unity and mutual love* which does away with class and other human distinctions. Theories that the Pauline type of meal differed significantly from meals in other areas of the early church are improbable.

1. Introduction
2. Religious Meals in the Ancient World
3. The Church Meal in Corinth
4. Paul's Response to the Situation at Corinth
5. The Pauline Lord's Supper and Practice Elsewhere

**1. Introduction.**
In 1 Corinthians 10:1-3 Paul points out the danger that Christians who think that they stand secure in their faith may fall into severe temptation by participation in idolatry. The people of Israel, who had experienced a remarkable act of divine grace in being liberated from slavery in Egypt, nevertheless fell into idolatry and its accompanying immorality. This was to serve as a warning to the Corinthians. Paul strengthens the parallel he is drawing by tracing an analogy with the way in which the Israelites "were all baptized . . . [and] all ate the same spiritual food and drank the same spiritual drink." Just as their experience with the cloud and the sea is seen in terms of Christian baptism, so too their eating and drinking must be seen as analogous to the Christian meal, which is referred to

later in the same chapter (1 Cor 10:15-17). Here, then, we have the first explicit mention (though some scholars find a possible allusion in 1 Cor 5:6-8) by Paul of the church meal with its spiritual food and drink. (And here, too, we have one of the few places where baptism* and the Lord's Supper are linked together as the two rites practiced in the church. 1 Corinthians 12:13 refers purely to baptism in two parallel expressions and not to baptism with the Spirit [*see* Holy Spirit] and drinking the Spirit at the Lord's Supper, which is a totally unattested idea.)

Later in the same letter Paul refers to a church meal called the Lord's Supper (1 Cor 11:20; cf. "the table of the Lord," 1 Cor 10:20) which was celebrated, manifestly on a frequent basis, in the church at Corinth. References in Acts indicate that an event called "the breaking of bread" was celebrated in the church at Jerusalem, "on the first day of the week" at Troas (Acts 20:7), and by implication in the other churches. Since at Corinth the collection of money for church purposes was also made on the first day of the week (1 Cor 16:2), it is reasonable to suppose that this day had special significance for the church and that a church meeting took place weekly on that day.

Details of what happened at the actual celebration, whether in the Pauline churches or elsewhere, are scanty, and it has often been commented that, if there had not been abuses of the meal in Corinth, we might never have heard about it. However, the fact that the tradition cited by Paul in connection with the occasion contains a command by the Lord to his followers to "do this in memory of him" indicates clearly enough that it was regarded as a duty wherever this tradition was known.

For Paul the origin of the meal lay in the last meal of Jesus with his disciples "on the night when he was betrayed/handed over" to the Jewish authorities, and ultimately by God, and subsequently put to death (1 Cor 11:23). He based his understanding of the meal on this event. However, the nature and theology of the meal in the Pauline churches, and its relationship both to the so-called Last Supper and to Christian meals in general, raise a number of problems.

### 2. Religious Meals in the Ancient World.

Communal meals were important in both Judaism and Hellenistic religions. They served a social purpose in bringing the adherents together, and they functioned religiously in a variety of ways (*see* Food).

For the Jews in general each and every meal was "religious" to the extent that it was accompanied by the giving of thanks to God* for the food. The main evening meal at the beginning of the Sabbath (which commenced at sunset on the previous day) had a special character, and there were special meals associated with Passover and other festivals. Within the religious movement associated with the Pharisees small groups known as *ḥăbûrôṭ* met to celebrate meals as occasions for giving thanks to God and for self-dedication. Jewish daily meals began with a thanksgiving to God associated with the breaking of bread and concluded with a further thanksgiving. Festal meals on special occasions, including Sabbaths, other festivals and guest-meals, included wine (which was not drunk at ordinary daily meals). Thanks were offered for each cup of wine (Klauck 1982, 66-67). At the Passover meal a more elaborate procedure was followed. An important element was an explanation of the symbolism attached to the various parts of the meal (including the lamb, unleavened bread and bitter herbs). This verbal "proclamation" (cf. *katangellō*, 1 Cor 11:26) was intended to make the occasion a remembrance (Ex 12:14; 13:9; cf. *anamnēsis*, 1 Cor 11:24-25) of what God had done for his people.

The situation in the Hellenistic world has been described fairly exhaustively by Klauck (1982), who discusses in turn meals associated with religious offerings and sacrifices, meals held by associations, meals celebrated in the cult of the dead, meals associated with the various mystery religions both in Hellenism* and also in Judaism, and cultic meals in Gnostic* sects. He notes that the communal meals held by associations were particularly important and that they maintained a religious character. Individual Christian converts could well have been familiar with any of these types of meal and also with some of the practices of the different mystery religions (*see* Religions).

There was a complicated mix of religious practices in Corinth. Some members of the church were familiar with meals associated with pagan temples and some of them believed that it was all right to continue to participate in these. It does not, of course, follow that they viewed what happened at these meals and the Lord's Supper in the same way. Further, it is important to note that the very strong explicit criticisms that Paul makes of the Corinthian church meal do not appear to be connected in any way with pagan beliefs or practices that had been carried over into it. It may be that the Corinthian Christians felt that participation in the meal of itself protected them from divine judgment,* but Paul's instruction to them is not about misunderstanding the meal but about refraining from idolatry.* Rather, the abuses at the meal were of a social character and reflected the practices of the secular world in general rather than of pagan religions in particular.

## 3. The Church Meal in Corinth.

Since Paul was the founder of the church, and since he refers to what he had told the church (undoubtedly during the visit to Corinth when the church was established), it follows that the church meal had been introduced by Paul himself but had developed characteristics in his absence from Corinth of which he could not approve. The church was meeting regularly to celebrate the Lord's Supper, but in such a way that Paul denied that the church meal could properly be called the *Lord's* Supper (1 Cor 11:20).

The basic problem appears to have arisen out of tensions in the church between the poor and the rich. Since there were no church buildings, meals were held in the houses of church members. The believers met together in groups of a maximum size dictated by the size of the houses which were at their disposal. It has been convincingly shown that the groups would have met in the homes of the rich (since they alone could accommodate them). These occasions were full meals with plenty of food and drink—at least for some members. The rich brought plentiful food for themselves (including meat), whereas the poorer members had to make do with their own scanty fare (*see* Social Setting; Social-Scientific Approaches).

Closer definition of what went on is disputed. The tradition about the Last Supper suggests that the eating of the bread and the sharing of the cup, which were given special significance by Jesus, were separated from one another by the meal (cf. the words "likewise after supper the cup," Lk 22:20 = 1 Cor 11:25). Nevertheless, the bringing together of the bread and the cup in the tradition and the way in which the words of interpretation were shaped symmetrically indicate that the specific "remembrance of the Lord's death" came to be seen as one action and that it followed the meal proper. However, there is dispute as to whether the juxtaposition had already taken place in Corinth when Paul wrote, and it has been argued that the order bread-meal-cup was followed at Corinth (Theissen; Lampe). Klauck (1982, 295) argues that, since there is no indication that the poorer members of the church were excluded from participation in the bread, the meal must have preceded the use of the bread and cup.

One view of the matter is that the richer members came early and ate and drank copiously before (cf. Gk *prolambanō*) the arrival of the poorer members who would have brought much scantier fare with them (Theissen). It is pointed out that the poorer people would have had to be content with bread and not much besides, whereas the rich would have had meat and a variety of delicacies. Parallels from the Greco-Roman world indicate that there could be at least two levels of eating at one and the same meal, the rich thereby accentuating their difference from their poorer neighbors who also came at their invitation to the church meeting. Thus, although the rich opened their houses to the church, they did so in a way that emphasized social divisions. (It perhaps needs to be mentioned that the fact that the problems at the meal reflected social divisions was recognized long before Theissen [see, e.g., G. G. Findlay, in *EGT* II.879]; what his research has done is to indicate more clearly how the rich carried over the practices of the secular world into the church and sinned against their poorer brothers and sisters.)

Further research has taken up the analogy of Hellenistic meals to which a householder would invite guests; a meal was held in two stages, the main meal being followed by a "dessert" or "symposium" at which there could be further guests who had not been at the earlier stage (Lampe). Lampe argues that the "religious" gathering at Corinth corresponded to the "dessert and drinks" part of the meal, and that it was preceded for the rich by the "main meal" to which each brought their own food (on the analogy of a Greek *eranos*) The poorer members of the church could not come so early (because of their work commitments) nor bring food of the same quality.

An alternative view is that the rich were actually eating their meal in the presence of the poorer members and not sharing out the food with them (Winter; the problem at issue is whether Gk *prolambanō* in 1 Cor 11:21 signifies eating *prior to* other people or, as an intensified form of *lambanō*, "take," means simply "to devour").

Despite uncertainty over the precise circumstances, the main point stands out quite clearly. There was over-indulgence on the part of the rich and feelings of envy on the part of the poor who were made to feel inferior (cf. 1 Cor 12:15). For Paul this was inconsistent with the intended character of the meal. Both hunger and drunkenness were out of place in a church meal. Rowdy festivity and social divisions alike ruined the occasion.

## 4. Paul's Response to the Situation at Corinth.

Paul's teaching in 1 Corinthians 11 was directed against these practices which meant that the meal had lost its character as the *Lord's* meal. As far as practically stopping the abuse was concerned, he commanded that the church members should welcome one another when they came together for their meal. That is to say, the rich should welcome the poor and treat them (as indeed all members of the church should treat one another) courteously and graciously; the occasion was still to be a meal, but the implication may be that there was to be sharing of the food (Winter defends this sense for Gk *ekdechomai* in 1 Cor 11:33) so that nobody felt disadvantaged. Further, Paul laid down that the rich should eat privately in their own houses if they wished to have a larger meal or more expensive fare, and thus avoid importing social divisions into the meeting of the church. Thus Paul was not counseling that the occasion should cease to be a meal and become what it subsequently became in the church generally, namely the token consumption of a morsel of bread and a sip of wine. He had further instructions which he promised to give verbally, but we shall never know what these were.

Paul's main point, which provided the theological undergirding for the practical advice, was made by citing the tradition which he had received concerning the meal and which he had previously passed on to the church by word of mouth. The language used indicates that it was a matter of an accepted, authoritative tradition. Paul says that he received it "from the Lord," which has been understood by some to mean that it came in the form of a private vision or communication directly from the Lord to Paul (Maccoby); it is far more likely to have been a piece of church tradition* which had the authority* of the Lord behind it (cf. the use of words of the Lord, doubtless handed down in church tradition to Paul, in 1 Cor 7:10; 9:14; *see* Jesus, Sayings of).

The tradition described what happened at the Last Supper, when the Lord took bread and the cup and distributed them to his disciples with accompanying sayings that interpreted them as representing his body and the new covenant* in his blood; he gave directions that the disciples were to do "this" (i.e., repeat the practice) in memory of him. The meal was thus intended to be a memorial of his death, through which it would be proclaimed. It followed that conduct which was contrary to the spirit of self-giving seen in the death* of Jesus would negate that proclamation. Hence it was the contempt and lack of love for the poorer members of the church which specifically aroused Paul's anger.

The members of the church should stop before taking part in the meal to be sure that they were not committing this sin* which was a sin against the body and blood of Christ and would bring judgment upon them. Such conduct was "unworthy" and represented a failure to "discern the body" (1 Cor 11:29). The use of "discern" (Gk *diakrinō*) here is difficult, and interpretation depends on whether "body" here stands for "the body [and blood of the crucified Lord]" or for

"the church" (Fee, 562-64). Either Paul is saying that people who eat unworthily are not recognizing that the food symbolizes the body (and blood) of Jesus nor acting as befits the recipients of his salvation; or he is saying that they are failing to recognize that the people gathered together for the meal are present as the body of Christ (made one by sharing in the one loaf, 1 Cor 10:17) and must be treated in Christian love.

In any case, what Paul says here is reinforced by his earlier comment that the "many" who share in the one loaf at the supper are "one body" in virtue of doing so (1 Cor 10:16-17). He sees that those who share in the blood and the body of Jesus are thereby brought into a unity with one another where social distinctions cannot be allowed to exist. Opinions differ as to whether the communion with the body and blood of Christ signifies "a union (sharing) with the risen Christ" (Hauck, 805), or a common sharing between the members that binds them together on the basis of the Lord, his death and his resurrection* (Fee, 564), or a common sharing in the benefits secured for them by the death of Christ (Barrett 1968, 232). However precisely we understand the phrase, Paul emphasizes that sharing in this meal and taking part in idolatrous* meals are incompatible. His stress on the fact that believers are joined together as one by the church meal may suggest that any members who take part in idolatry are contaminating the whole community. But his main thought is probably, as in 1 Corinthians 6, the incompatibility of being joined to Christ and to what is sinful/demonic.*

In 1 Corinthians 11 Paul develops the theological significance of the Supper on the basis of the tradition. He reminds the readers that the body of Christ, represented by the bread, was "for you." This phrase forms part of a series of statements which teach that Christ died for other people (Rom 5:8; 8:32; 1 Cor 15:3; 2 Cor 5:15 [3x]; Gal 2:20; 3:13; Eph 5:2, 25; 1 Tim 2:6; Tit 2:14) and which occur throughout the NT (Mk 10:45 [Gk *anti*]; Jn 10:11, 15; 11:52; Heb 2:9; 9:24; 1 Pet 2:21; 3:18; 1 Jn 3:16). Thus the death of Jesus is seen as his self-giving in death on behalf and for the benefit of other people, so that they might be redeemed from sin and its judgment and be justified. Possibly his self-giving "for you" is intended also to be seen as exemplary (Winter, 79).

The cup is interpreted as signifying the new covenant in the blood of Christ. Against the background of Exodus 24:8 and Jeremiah 31:31-34 this indicates that the death of Jesus is the sacrifice which inaugurates the new covenant between God and his people, thus establishing the new people of God.

There has been much discussion, arising out of contemporary theological differences in the church, as to whether Paul's teaching indicates that the Lord himself is present at the Supper. He appears to regard the food and drink as "spiritual," like the heaven-sent provision for the Israelites in the desert (1 Cor 10:3-4; Wedderburn, 234-39). Roman Catholic interpreters tend to find a presence of the Lord in the bread and the cup on the basis of "This is my body," whereas Protestant interpreters argue that the phrase means rather "This symbolizes my body." The debate turns on 1 Corinthians 10:20-21 where there appears to be an analogy between being partakers with demons through sharing in their cup and table and what happens at the Lord's Supper. However, there is no indication that the two events are precisely parallel, and in any case it is not suggested that the worshippers eat the demons or that the demons are present in the food. Rather, the parallel suggests that, just as those who share in idolatrous feasts are brought into a relationship with demons, so those who share in the Lord's Supper are brought into a relationship with the Lord who is present as host. This language of "host and guests" admittedly goes beyond what Paul explicitly says, but fits in with the background concept of feasts held under the patronage of a god in paganism and feasts celebrated "in the presence of the Lord" in the OT and Judaism (cf. also Rev 3:20). There is no indication that Paul saw the event as sacrificial; it is likened not to the offering of an animal on an altar but to the eating of food at a table, where the partakers receive the symbols that indicate that a sacrificial death has already taken place (at Calvary). It is thus conceived of as a post-sacrificial meal.

There is no explicit reference to the Supper elsewhere in Paul. However, if 1 Corinthians was meant to be read as part of the proceedings at the church meal, the use of the curse* against those who do not love the Lord (1 Cor 16:21) may be seen as reinforcing the sense of community among those who in the meal confessed their love of the Lord and their separation from others, specifically those who proclaimed another gospel* (cf. the similarly placed warning in Rom 16:17-18 and also Gal 1:8-9 for the use of the curse). The kiss of peace, mentioned at the end of several letters, will also have had significance as an expression of unity and love. Finally, the phrase *Maranatha*, which may be understood as a statement or a prayer,* should be taken as an expression of longing for the final coming of Jesus as Lord (rather than as a prayer for his presence in the Lord's Supper; *see* Liturgical Elements).

**5. The Pauline Lord's Supper and Practice Elsewhere.** How is the Pauline material related to other teaching about the Supper in the NT? The Synoptic Gospels uniformly witness to the occasion when Jesus met with his disciples for what is characterized as a Passover meal. He used this occasion to announce to them his imminent decease and to share with them the customary bread of the Passover and one of the cups of wine with accompanying statements that these symbolized his body and his blood. The precise wording of the accounts varies between the Gospels, with Matthew and Mark standing close to one another with essentially the same wording (Mark: "Take, this is my body; this is my blood of the covenant which is poured out for many"), and with Luke offering a form of words close to those preserved by Paul (Luke: "This is my body which is given for you; do this in remembrance of me; this cup is the new covenant in my blood, which is poured out for you"). The somewhat stylized nature of the accounts suggests that the wording had become "fixed" as part of a liturgical statement used in church meetings and was incorporated into the Gospels (*see* Worship).

The variation in wording between Matthew/Mark and Luke/Paul has been variously explained. Perhaps the majority of scholars regard the Markan wording as the older, with the Lukan/Pauline as a development from it, but there is a sizable minority (to which the present writer would join himself) which sees the development moving in the reverse direction. Opinions further differ as to whether this tradition actually goes back to the historical occasion described or has been developed from a simpler form of words which was less pregnant with theological implications. The view that the whole account is a church creation, and that we know nothing historical about a final meal of Jesus with his disciples, need not be taken seriously (see the refutation by Stein).

Communal meals were celebrated widely in the early church and are traced back by Luke to the earliest days of the Jerusalem* church. There is nothing unlikely about this. The first Christians in a Jewish setting appear to have acted in a way analogous to the Pharisees or indeed to any Jewish group which met to eat together. The meal is referred to as "the breaking of bread"—with no mention of drinking wine. Although this phrase refers strictly to the opening act of a meal, the sharing of bread to the accompaniment of prayers of thanksgiving, it is clear that a proper meal is meant. The use of meal imagery in Revelation likewise shows that the religious significance of meals was recognized in its geographical area in Asia.

The question that now arises is whether there was

uniformity of practice throughout the early church. Were there two or more types of meal in the early church, the one a rather more festive type of meal which was known as "the breaking of bread" and which was not a memorial of the Lord's death and not based on the tradition of the Last Supper, while the other was very much tied up with the use of bread and the cup to remember the Lord's death and was the kind of occasion advocated by Paul?

A theory of this kind was developed especially by H. Lietzmann, who argued that the original Jerusalem meal was replaced by the Pauline one. Other scholars have suggested similar theories. (Barrett 1985, 61, 67-68, thinks it possible that it was Paul who made the link between the church's weekly fellowship meal, celebrating the resurrection, and the Last Supper.) However, it has proved impossible to trace the independent existence of the putative Jerusalem meal. The most that can be said is that the phrase "the breaking of bread" in Acts may cover both celebrations of the Lord's Supper and other church meals without wine (which was not normally drunk at ordinary meals). The meal at Corinth included the breaking of bread, and it also included the use of wine. Our sole witness for a Lord's Supper with bread only would be Luke, if that is what he is describing, and the close links of Luke with Pauline Christianity make it very unlikely that he intends to describe anything other than Pauline practice; the case that a post-Pauline writer is describing a "bread-only" meal current in his own time and reading it back into the days of the early church has no basis. Thus we have no historical evidence for the parallel existence of two different kinds of meal.

We therefore have to ask whether there is any evidence which might suggest an evolution in the early church meals from being simply fellowship gatherings to becoming memorials to the death of Jesus with an increasingly elaborate theological significance attached to them and reflected in the varying forms of the so-called "words of institution." The "Last Supper" itself was a reinterpretation of a Passover meal, and this might have suggested an annual celebration of it rather than a weekly one. That some early Christians celebrated an annual "Christian Passover" emerges from 1 Corinthians 5:6-8, but this evidence also shows that Paul had no difficulty in holding together an annual Christian Passover and a weekly Lord's Supper (see Jeremias, 901-4). We are thus thrown back again on the question whether the account of the Last Supper is historically plausible and reliable and whether it influenced the church from its earliest days. So far as Luke is concerned, it is noteworthy that he describes the Emmaus meal with the risen Lord in

a way which suggests that it was a pattern for what was to follow, and he describes it in terms which are reminiscent of the Last Supper. There were evidently no problems in his mind regarding the continuity between them.

The case for development has been defended by Maccoby. He states that at ordinary Jewish meals the opening action was the "breaking of bread" and the sharing of it among the participants with a prayer of thanksgiving in which God was blessed for his provision; however, at ceremonial meals on the Sabbath and at festivals this action was *preceded* by the sharing of wine, with thanks given to God. He then argues that in the Jerusalem church the "breaking of bread" followed the pattern of ordinary Jewish meals. But the last meal of Jesus with his disciples followed the pattern of a festival meal with the order wine-bread, as attested in Luke and *Didache* 9-10. Originally it had a purely "apocalyptic"* theme, as Jesus looked forward to the imminent inauguration of the kingdom* of God. Then Paul had a vision* in which he learned that at the Last Supper Jesus had distributed bread and wine (in that order!) and interpreted them with reference to his death. (This is the tradition received [directly] from the Lord to which reference is made in 1 Cor 11.) Hence arose the text of Luke which shows a secondary combination of the apocalyptic and eucharistic themes, and then the text of Mark which almost entirely suppresses the apocalyptic aspect. Thus the Lord's Supper is a Pauline creation, and is not to be confused with the breaking of bread in Acts.

Maccoby's theory comes to grief on various facts. There is no clear evidence in the NT itself for a church meal with the order wine-bread (1 Cor 10:16-17, to which he rightly does not appeal, has the inverted order to allow Paul to develop the significance of the one loaf), and the *Didache*'s evidence should not be preferred to that of earlier sources. It would be strange if the post-Pauline Acts were to ascribe to Paul a "breaking of bread" (Acts 20) which was different from the Pauline custom known to the author. Paul himself uses the term "breaking of bread" to refer to the Lord's Supper (1 Cor 10:16). And the phrase "the cup of blessing" (i.e., "the cup for which we bless God") used by Paul in 1 Corinthians 10:16 was used for the *third* cup at the Passover meal (Str-B IV.1, 72). The case, in short, is not convincing.

*See also* BAPTISM; BODY OF CHRIST; CORINTHIANS, LETTERS TO THE; FELLOWSHIP, COMMUNION, SHARING; FOOD OFFERED TO IDOLS AND JEWISH FOOD LAWS; LITURGICAL ELEMENTS; LOVE FEAST; SACRIFICE, OFFERING; SOCIAL-SCIENTIFIC APPROACHES TO PAUL; TRADITION; WORSHIP.

BIBLIOGRAPHY. C. K. Barrett, *The First Epistle to the Co-*

*rinthians* (HNTC; New York: Harper & Row, 1968); idem, *Church, Ministry and Sacraments in the New Testament* (Exeter: Paternoster, 1985); G. D. Fee, *The First Epistle to the Corinthians* (NICNT; Grand Rapids: Eerdmans, 1987); F. Hauck, "κοινός κτλ," *TDNT* III.789-809; J. Jeremias, "πάσχα," *TDNT* V.896-904; H. J. Klauck, *Herrenmahl und Hellenistischer Kult: Eine religionsgeschichtliche Untersuchung zum ersten Korintherbrief* (Münster: Aschendorff, 1982); idem, "Lord's Supper," *ABD* IV.362-72; P. Lampe, "Das korinthische Herrenmahl im Schnittpunkt hellenistisch-römischer Mahlpraxis und paulinischer Theologia Crucis (1 Kor 11, 17-34)," *ZNW* 82 (1991) 183-213; H. Lietzmann, *Mass and Lord's Supper* (Leiden: E. J. Brill, 1953-1979); H. Maccoby, "Paul and the Eucharist," *NTS* 37 (1991) 247-67; I. H. Marshall, *Last Supper and Lord's Supper* (Exeter: Paternoster, 1980); P. Neuenzeit, *Das Herrenmahl: Studien zur paulinischen Eucharistiefassung* (München: Kösel, 1960); E. Schweizer, *The Lord's Supper According to the New Testament* (Philadelphia: Fortress, 1967); R. H. Stein, "Last Supper," *DJG* 444-50; G. Theissen, *The Social Setting of Pauline Christianity: Essays on Corinth* (Philadelphia: Fortress, 1982); A. J. M. Wedderburn, *Baptism and Resurrection: Studies in Pauline Theology against Its Graeco-Roman Background* (Tübingen: J. C. B. Mohr, 1987); B. W. Winter, "The Lord's Supper at Corinth: An Alternative Reconstruction," *RTR* 37 (1978) 73-82.

I. H. Marshall

# LOVE

For Paul love is the most important of all the Christian graces and the very heart of Christian ethics.* Motivated by the supreme expression of God's* own love in the sacrificial death* of Christ, it springs from a transformed life filled with God's own Spirit.* The primary focus of love in Paul's writings is its tangible expression within the Christian community.

1. Terminology
2. God's/Christ's Love for Us
3. Our Love for God/Christ
4. Our Love for Others

## 1. Terminology.

There is no Pauline letter in which the term *love* does not figure prominently. Most commonly Paul uses *agapaō* terminology (referring to love based on high regard or appreciation) for both divine and human love: *agapē* ("love," 75 x), *agapaō* ("to show love," 34 x), and *agapētos* ("one who is loved," 27 x). The terms *eleeō* ("to show compassion, mercy," 12 x) and *eleos* ("compassion, mercy," 10 x) apply almost exclusively to God, not humans, in Paul's usage.

A wide variety of *phileō* terminology is employed, though not frequently: *aphilargyros* ("no lover of money," 1 x), *philagathos* ("lover of goodness," 1 x), *philadelphia* ("brotherly, or familial, affection, love," 2 x), *philandros* ("lover of one's husband," 1 x), *philanthrōpia* ("love for people," 1 x), *phileō* ("to love, have affection for," 2 x), *philēma* ("kiss," 4 x), *philotheos* ("lover of God," 1 x), *philoxenia* ("hospitality," 1 x), *philoxenos* ("hospitable person," 2 x), *philostorgos* ("lover of those in close relationship," 1 x) and *philoteknos* ("lover of children," 1 x).

Other words expressing love include *epipotheō* ("to have great affection, yearning," 7 x), *epipothēsis* ("great affection, yearning," 2 x), *epipothētos* ("one who is yearned for," 1 x), *epipothia* ("great affection, yearning," 1 x), *eusplanchnos* ("compassionate person," 1 x), *homeiromai* ("to have great affection, yearning," 1 x) and *splanchna* ("compassion," "affection"; "object of compassion or affection," 8 x). A few words are used negatively, of non-Christian attitudes: *astorgos* ("without love or affection," 2 x), *philargyria* ("love of money," 1 x), *philargyros* ("lover of money," 1 x), *philautos* ("lover of oneself," 1 x) and *philēdonos* ("lover of pleasure," 1 x).

## 2. God's/Christ's Love for Us.

At the heart of Paul's understanding of the gospel* lies the saving love of God (*agapē*) in Christ.* The supreme expression of this undeserved love is Christ's death on the cross as a sacrifice* for sins* (Rom 5:8; Eph 2:4-5; 2 Thess 2:16; cf. Gal 2:20). When Paul speaks of God's (or Christ's) love, it is usually with reference to some aspect of the atonement or Christian salvation.* (Note: the expressions "love of God" and "love of Christ" are notoriously ambiguous. They may refer either to our love for God or Christ [objective genitive], or to God's or Christ's love for us [subjective genitive]. It is only the individual context that determines the meaning, and sometimes it is simply not possible to be sure which Paul intends: e.g., Rom 5:5; 2 Cor 5:14; 2 Thess 3:5.)

God's love is shown both in the cross and in the specific calling and choosing of believers ("In love he predestined us to be his sons through Jesus Christ," Eph 1:4-5; *see* Call, Calling; Election and Predestination). So when Paul speaks of Christians as the "elect" or "chosen," the idea of God's undeserved love is clearly implicit. Indeed, his discussion of predestination in Romans 9 seems to speak of God's love as exclusively for his chosen people (Rom 9:13, 15, 18, 21-24); but he does not press the logic of this point, and writes elsewhere of God's love for all people.

For Paul, having a good grasp of God's saving love

in Christ is crucial. It lies at the heart of all true Christian theology and ethics, and is important for a believer's sense of security. ("Nothing can ever separate us from God's love in Christ Jesus our Lord," Rom 8:31-39). Coming to a full appreciation of this love, then, is one of his strongest desires and prayers* for his young converts (Eph 3:14-21). Indeed, the overpowering sense of Christ's love is one of the chief driving forces in Paul's own life (2 Cor 5:14-15).

### 3. Our Love for God/Christ.

Though implicit throughout, love for God (or Christ) remains strangely unemphasized in Paul's writings. (It is mentioned only in Rom 8:28; 1 Cor 2:9; 8:3; 16:22; Eph 6:24; 2 Tim 3:4; the phrase is ambiguous in Rom 5:5; 2 Cor 5:14; 2 Thess 3:5.) Though the second great commandment is quoted twice, the first great commandment is cited nowhere. The focus is rather on God's (or Christ's) love for us, with the emphasis on grace. The response Paul calls for is not so much one of loving God or Christ, as one of believing in Christ and loving others. The initial response is a receptive one.

This does not mean that the concept of loving God is peripheral in Paul's thinking: it is central to his Jewish heritage and clearly in line with his view of the Christian life as one of utter dedication to God. But why he speaks so little of loving God and builds so little on it remains a mystery.

### 4. Our Love for Others.

For Paul, loving others is the single most important characteristic of the Christian life and the heart of Christian living. Everything one does is to be an expression of love (1 Cor 16:14). More important than the charismatic gifts* that the Corinthians coveted (1 Cor 12:31—13:2), love is listed as first among the "fruit of the Spirit"* (Gal 5:22-23; much of the rest of the list could be taken as a commentary on love) and is the one grace that believers are to seek above all others (Col 3:12, 14). Paul speaks of it as the epitome and essence of the entire OT moral law (Rom 13:8-10; Gal 5:14), the one unending debt that Christians owe others. Indeed, in language most unusual for him, he even speaks of love as the "law of Christ"* (Gal 6:2), in line with Jesus' own emphasis on the law of love. As such, loving others has some bearing on one's welfare on the coming Day of Christ (Phil 1:9-10; 1 Thess 3:12-13; *see* Eschatology). Paul's whole concept of holy living is dominated by love.

*4.1. The Theology of Love.* The terms *faith** and *love* are frequently linked in Paul's writing: together they represent a summary of his greatest theological and ethical concerns. Reference to his readers' faith in Christ and love for one another often occurs in the initial thanksgiving sections of his letters, and it suggests the importance of these two concepts in his thinking (Eph 1:15; Col 1:4; 1 Thess 1:3; 2 Thess 1:3; Philem 4-5; cf. Eph 6:23; 1 Thess 3:6; 5:8; 1 Tim 1:5, 14; 2:15; 6:11; 2 Tim 1:13; 2:22; 3:10; Tit 2:2). Paul reminds the Galatians that what really counts is not the Jewish Law* but "faith working through love" (Gal 5:6)—a phrase that perhaps comes closer than any other to summarizing his view of the Christian life.

Love represents the ethical outworking of the imputed righteousness* bestowed by grace through faith, the outward expression of new life in Christ. There is a necessary correlation, then, between faith in Christ and loving others. And just as faith spells the end of the Jewish Law in a salvific sense (Rom 10:4), so love represents the fulfilling of the Law in an ethical sense (Rom 13:10); in Paul's thinking, together the two essentially replace the focus on Law as the way of righteousness.*

*4.2. The Sources of Love.* Love comes through one's relationship to Jesus Christ (1 Tim 1:14; 2 Tim 1:13), by the gift of the Holy Spirit* (cf. 2 Tim 1:7). Love is possible because faith in Christ brings the believer into a whole new life, dominated no longer by sin and self-desire but by the Spirit of God. As the guarantee of the life to come (2 Cor 5:5; cf. 1:22), the Spirit effects the power of the new age in the believer's life here and now, making a form of eschatological* existence actually possible in the present. Thus, freed from the enslaving powers of sin and the Law, the believer is empowered to produce real "fruit" for God (Rom 7:4), the "fruit of righteousness" (Phil 1:11)—which for Paul is always the "fruit of the Spirit"; and the most important "fruit" is love (Gal 5:22-23; cf. Rom 15:30; Col 1:8; 2 Tim 1:7).

For Paul, then, love is never simply a self-attained virtue; it is the result of a transformed life filled with the Spirit of God, which pours God's own love into the human heart (Rom 5:5; cf. Gal 4:6-7; Phil 1:8). Lack of love therefore calls into question the presence of the Spirit in one's life, and hence one's whole relationship to God (cf. Rom 8:1-14). The fact that Paul's encouragements to love are frequently voiced in the form of a prayer (Phil 1:9; 1 Thess 3:12; cf. 2 Thess 3:5) reflects his conviction that love, like everything good, ultimately derives from God as a gift of grace (2 Cor 8:16; 1 Thess 4:9). The key to loving is being filled with the Spirit of God (Eph 5:18).

*4.3. The Motivation of Love.* Sometimes Paul speaks of love as a simple command to be obeyed—indeed as the most important of all the moral commands

(Rom 13:8-10; Gal 5:14). At other times he encourages love because of the purity demanded on the coming Day of Christ (Phil 1:9-10; 1 Thess 3:12-13; see Eschatology). At still other times he appeals to the story or example of Christ (Rom 15:2-3; 1 Cor 10:31—11:1; 2 Cor 8:8-9; Eph 4:32—5:2; Phil 2:4-8; Col 3:12-14; see Imitation; see Fowl).

But above all, Paul thinks of love as a joyful response to the grace of God in Jesus Christ, motivated by one's personal relationship to the Savior.* It is not so much a matter of submitting to Jesus's teachings, or of imitating his earthly life, as of responding with a grateful heart to the ultimate expression of love in his death on the cross (Rom 12:1-2) and in obedience to him as Lord. Loving others is only the appropriate ethical response to the divine love shown in the gospel. (Even when Paul speaks of imitating Christ, the appeal is not to his earthly life but to some aspect of the sacrificial love shown in his dying.) For Paul, the whole of the Christian life is a joyful response to God's grace in the gospel: it is an expression of gratitude for Christ. Loving others is a way of saying "thank you" for divine love (cf. 2 Cor 8:1-9).

*4.4. The Focus of Love.* Because Paul's major concern is the welfare of the churches, his primary focus is on the expression of love within the Christian community. Though he occasionally speaks of showing kindness to those outside the fellowship (Rom 12:14, 17-21; Gal 6:10; 1 Thess 3:12; 5:15), he is much more concerned with the expression of love among Christians themselves: "Let us do good to all people, but especially to . . . the family of faith" (Gal 6:10).

Because the church* is the body of Christ (see Body of Christ), the fellowship* of God's own people and the temple* of his presence on earth, it is of supreme importance that Christians learn to live together in love. Love is what knits the diverse members of the body together in "perfect harmony" (Col 2:2; 3:14). Without love the body can neither function well nor honor Christ as it ought. The importance of this matter may be seen in Paul's repeated emphasis on love and unity (Rom 12:10, 16, 18; 14:1, 19; 15:5-6; 1 Cor 1:10; 10:16-17; 2 Cor 13:11; Gal 3:27-28; 5:22-23; 6:2; Eph 4:1-6; Phil 1:27; 2:1-4; 4:2; Col 2:2, 19; 3:12-14; 1 Thess 5:13-14) and in his constant caution against anything that would prove disruptive (Rom 12:16; 14:1-23; 16:17; 1 Cor 3:3-4; 4:6; 11:18-22; Gal 5:15, 19-21; Eph 4:25, 31; Phil 2:3-4; Col 3:8-9). As "members one of another," Christians are to care for one another (1 Cor 12:25-26) and to be concerned above all with building one another up (Rom 14:19; 15:2; 1 Cor 8:1; 14:3-5, 12, 17, 26; Eph 4:15-16; 1 Thess 5:11). The placing of Paul's classic discourse on love (1 Cor 13)

in the middle of a discussion on the use of charismatic gifts for the edification of the church shows something of the role of love in his thinking. For Paul the welfare of the community is as important as that of the individual—and that is why love plays such a central role in his writings.

*4.5. The Nature of Love.* The characteristics of love (*agapē*) are spelled out by Paul in 1 Corinthians 13. Love is shown in patience and kindness—not in jealousy, pride, arrogance, rudeness, insistence, irritability, resentment, or a sense of getting even. In other words, real love is not self-centered, but is willing to sacrifice its own desires for the good of others. It is this sense of self-sacrifice for others—modeled by Christ's sacrifice for us—that lies at the heart of Paul's understanding of what real love is (cf. Wischmeyer).

That Christians are not to live for themselves but for others is a theme that runs throughout Paul's writings. Jesus, Timothy and Paul himself all serve as models of this way of life (Rom 9:3; 15:1-3; 1 Cor 9:19-22; 10:33—11:1; 2 Cor 1:6; 4:5; 6:4-6; 8:8-9; 12:15; 13:9; Gal 2:20; Phil 1:20-26; 2:4-8, 17, 19-24; Eph 4:32—5:2; Col 1:24; 1 Thess 2:9; 1 Tim 4:12). This attitude of self-sacrificing care is to be expressed even in the home (Eph 5:25-33; Col 3:19; Tit 2:4). For Paul, then, real love demands self-denial. (In contrast, the "last days" will be marked by the love of self, money and pleasure; 2 Tim 3:2-4.) The refusal to indulge in meat if it would cause others to sin is one of the strongest illustrations of the self-denial demanded by love (Rom 14:15, 20-21; 1 Cor 8:9-13; 10:23-33; see Food Offered to Idols and Jewish Food Laws; Idolatry; Strong and Weak).

One further point: for Paul love is not just a matter of doing, it is also a matter of being (cf. 1 Cor 13:3: "Even though I give away everything I have . . . but don't have love. . . ."). Loving others is not simply a matter of doing good or showing mercy* but is to spring from a sense of genuine care and compassion. It is to be real and heartfelt—merely going through the motions will not suffice. And it must be expressed with a sense of warmth and affection if it is to be truly perceived as love. The importance of this in Paul's thinking may be seen in his urging of his readers to communicate their affection for one another (Rom 12:10; 16:16; 1 Cor 16:20; 2 Cor 2:8; 13:12; 1 Thess 5:26) and in his repeated affirmation of his affection for them (1 Cor 16:24; 2 Cor 2:4; 6:11; 7:3; 11:11; 12:15; Phil 1:7-8; 4:1; 1 Thess 2:8; 3:12; Philem 9). Paul is deeply concerned that the churches know his care and affection for them; and he in turn seems to derive no little comfort from the knowledge of their love for him (2 Cor 7:6-7; 1 Thess 3:6-10). When Paul speaks of love, then, he is thinking not only of practical acts of charity but also of the heartfelt expression of care and affection—both of which are important.

**4.6. The Limits of Love.** Questions are sometimes raised about how consistent Paul is in living out his own ideals, especially in light of the harsh language he uses of those who oppose the gospel (Gal 1:8-9; 5:12; Phil 3:2; cf. his emphasis on gentle responses and gracious words in Rom 12:17-21; Col 4:6!). When the grace of the gospel is jeopardized, theological concerns clearly take precedence in his thinking over considerations of politeness and etiquette. For Paul, the basic tenets of the gospel simply cannot be compromised; and if a church's grasp of those is weakened, tough words and actions may be required for the sake of his readers' salvation. In other words, Paul does not conceive of love as gentleness at any price. Indeed, he insists that it is precisely out of genuine concern for their welfare (i.e., out of love) that such harsh words and confrontive actions arise (1 Cor 4:14; 2 Cor 2:4; 7:8-11; 12:19; 13:2-4, 10; Gal 2:11-14). There are clear theological and moral limits, then, to the validity of some of his statements about the form that love generally takes. When God-given norms are threatened, there are times when love does not endure all things (cf. 1 Cor 13:7), when love does insist on its own way (cf. 1 Cor 13:5), even rather strongly—if that way is identified with God's way (1 Cor 14:37-38; 2 Thess 3:14). And when the doctrine of God's grace is at stake, love does not seem to be of greater importance than faith (cf. 1 Cor 13:13). In Paul's own life, then, the expression of love is clearly conditioned by certain theological and moral considerations of critical importance; and when these are threatened, harsh words may be the truest form of love and not a violation of it (see Opponents).

See also DEATH OF CHRIST; ETHICS; FRUIT OF THE SPIRIT; GOD; MERCY.

BIBLIOGRAPHY. R Bultmann, *Theology of the New Testament* (2 vols.; New York: Scribner's, 1951, 1955); S. E. Fowl, *The Story of Christ in the Ethics of Paul* (JSNTS 36; Sheffield: JSOT, 1990); V. P. Furnish, *The Love Command in the New Testament* (Nashville: Abingdon, 1972); idem, *Theology and Ethics in Paul* (Nashville: Abingdon, 1968); W. Günther et al., "Love," *NIDNTT* 2.542-50; J. P. Louw and E. A. Nida, "Love, Affection, Compassion," in *Greek-English Lexicon of the New Testament: Based on Semantic Domains* (New York: United Bible Societies, 1988) 1.293-96; J. Moffatt, *Love in the New Testament* (London: Hodder & Stoughton, 1929); R. Mohrlang, *Matthew and Paul: A Comparison of Ethical Perspectives* (SNTSMS 48; Cambridge: University Press, 1984); H. Ridderbos, *Paul: An Outline of His Theology* (Grand Rapids: Eerdmans, 1975); G. Schneider, "ἀγάπη κτλ," *EDNT* 1.8-12; C. Spicq, *Agape in the New Testament* (2 vols.; London: Herder, 1963, 1965); G. Stählin, "φιλέω κτλ," *TDNT* IX.114-46; E. Stauffer, "ἀγαπάω κτλ," *TDNT* I.21-55; O. Wischmeyer, *Der höchste Weg. Das 13. Kapitel des 1 Korintherbriefes* (Gütersloh: Mohn, 1981). R. Mohrlang

# LOVE FEAST

The use of the term *agapē* ("love") to refer to a Christian meal is rare, with Jude 12 offering the only explicit reference in the NT. There is no evidence from the NT period to suggest that the love* feast was a separate meal from the Lord's Supper; rather, love feast and Lord's Supper refer to the same event (see Lord's Supper).

1. The New Testament Evidence
2. The Love Feast and the Common Meal
3. The Abuse of the Love Feast

## 1. The New Testament Evidence

In 1 Corinthians 11 Paul is addressing an abuse in the gathering of the local church. It is helpful, therefore, to consider a similar situation indicated in Jude, where the abuse seems to involve certain false teachers who are feasting without fear (Jude 12 NRSV), fattening and indulging themselves. Likewise in 2 Peter 2:13 we find the language of feasting (*syneuōcheomai*, cf. Jude 12) and reference to overt displays of opulence, suggesting riotous misbehavior during the meal. While Jude speaks of deplorable behavior during the love feasts (*agapai*) 2 Peter 2:13 deliberately alters the expression *agapais* to read *apatais* ("dissipation"), thereby presenting a deliberate play on words. (The textual variants at Jude 12 and 2 Pet 2:13 indicate subsequent scribal attempts at harmonization.) According to 2 Peter, this dissipation (a mockery of the love feasts) takes place in the daytime—a further indication of degeneracy (cf *As. Mos.* 7:4, where the godless "feast at any hour of the day").

## 2. The Love Feast and the Common Meal.

Early Christian churches met in houses, which, among other things, offered all that was necessary for the common meal (see Households). Based on the tradition of the Last Supper (Mk 14:17 and par.), the early Christians ate together in their house churches. The meal, or aspects of the meal (including the prayers* of thanksgiving), can be referred to by a variety of terms: "Lord's Supper" (1 Cor 11:20), "breaking of bread" (i.e., the ritual opening of the meal, Acts 2:42, 46; 20:7; cf. Lk 24:35; 1 Cor 10:16), "sharing" (*koinōnia*, 1 Cor 10:16 NRSV; or "participation" RSV, NIV), Eucharist, or "thanksgiving" (1 Cor 11:24, with the verb *eucharisteō*), and "love feast."

The separation of the meal/*agapē* from the Lord's Supper, or Eucharist, was made in the second century. Justin Martyr (c. 150) indicates that by his time the common meal and Eucharist (as sacrament) were separate observances. He speaks of the Eucharist without referring to a meal. Accordingly, a portion of bread accompanied by the water and wine constituted the Eucharist (Justin Martyr *Apol.* 1.65-66).

### 3. The Abuse of the Love Feast (1 Cor 11:17-34).

Food and meals were prominent features in the various associations and religious, or cultic, groups of the Greco-Roman world (Klauck; *see* Food). The early church, unlike many of these associations, was not a homogeneous group; rather, early Christianity displayed a marked internal social and economic stratification (Theissen, 145-74; Judge, 60-62). This stratification offers some clues regarding the nature of the problems that arose in early Christian table fellowship (*see* Social-Scientific Approaches; Social Setting).

All we know from Paul is that the actual celebration of the Lord's Supper was linked with, and perhaps was an extension of, the so-called *agapē*, a common meal, which Christians in a given locality were in the habit of sharing together. Abuses of this practice occurred at Corinth, involving a discrepancy between "haves" and "have nots," which Paul was careful to set right. It cannot be determined beyond all doubt that this common meal was called *hē agapē*, "the love feast." But if it was so called, it was to remind all who partook that lying at the base of their fellowship was *agapē*, "love"—the love of God for them expressed so vividly in the broken bread, and the love of Christian for Christian as seen in their sharing the one loaf.

According to Paul, certain Corinthians "have" while others "lack": one is hungry, another drunk, some have houses, others have nothing. On the one hand there are believers who have plenty of food and drink while others have an insufficient quantity (and quality?) and go hungry. The stark difference between these two groups is dramatized at the table. To further accentuate the difference, the "haves" also have houses where, Paul suggests, they might carry on their selfish behavior if they must. Those who "lack," on the other hand, are without food and, perhaps as day laborers, may be without houses or the security of a larger household, which even slaves* might enjoy during times of austerity.

Paul does not commend the Corinthian gathering for the community meal: "when you come together it is not for the better but for the worse" (1 Cor 11:17). Apparently the abuse was sufficiently abhorrent that the divisions and factions rendered the meal merely one of many and not the Lord's Supper ("it is not really the Lord's Supper," 1 Cor 11:20). Paul's advice was candid: the wealthier Christians who arrive early should not begin eating a private meal which precedes the communal meal, but they should wait and thereby have more to share with those who have nothing. If the wealthy are insistent on gorging themselves they should do so at home (in a private meal) but not at the Lord's Supper, or *agapē*.

During Paul's eighteen months at Corinth (Acts 18:11) he must have established a pattern of practice for the gathering community, particularly for something as important as the Lord's Supper (including the communal meal). Given the social and economic diversity of the church, Paul would surely have addressed the issue of the rich* rubbing elbows with the poor at table. It is highly probable that a severe famine gripped the region in A.D. 51, shortly after Paul's departure. This could have precipitated the problems envisioned in 1 Corinthians 11:17-34, problems which the absent apostle was called upon to address (see Blue; the famine may lie behind the *anangkē*, "crisis," of 1 Cor 7:26; see Winter, 93-94).

Paul's gospel of reconciliation would have brought together people from different religious and socio-economic backgrounds to share the table of the Lord. Regardless of Greco-Roman mores, believers were instructed to share, and not to parade affluence and influence by indulging themselves while others lacked. Blatant disregard for others is not *agapē* but selfishness. The abuses of the meal were a byproduct of a breakdown of *koinōnia*; humiliating to those who had nothing and contemptible to Paul.

*See also* CORINTHIANS, LETTERS TO THE; FOOD OFFERED TO IDOLS AND JEWISH FOOD LAWS; LORD'S SUPPER; RICHES AND POVERTY; SOCIAL-SCIENTIFIC APPROACHES TO PAUL; SOCIAL SETTING OF MISSION CHURCHES.

BIBLIOGRAPHY. R. J. Bauckham, *Jude, 2 Peter* (WBC 50; Waco: Word, 1983); B. B. Blue, "The House Church at Corinth and the Lord's Supper: Famine, Food Supply, and the Present Distress," *CTR* 5 (1991) 221-39; J. Jeremias, *The Eucharistic Words of Jesus* (London: SCM, 1966); E. A. Judge, *The Social Pattern of Christian Groups in the First Century: Some Prolegomena to the Study of the New Testament Ideas of Social Obligation* (London: Tyndale, 1960); H.-J. Klauck, *Herrenmahl und hellenistischer Kult: Eine religionsgeschichtliche Untersuchung zum ersten Korinthbrief* (NTAbh 15; 2d. ed.; Münster: Aschendorff, 1982); I. H. Marshall, *Last Supper and Lord's Supper* (Grand Rapids: Eerdmans, 1980); G. Theissen, *The Social Setting of Pauline Chirstianity: Essays on Corinth* (Philadephia: Fortress, 1982); B. Winter, "Secular and Christian Responses to Corinthian Famines," *TynB* 40 (1989) 86-106.                    B. B. Blue

# M

## MAGIC

Belief in gods, demons,* spirits and various other forms of supernatural powers was a prominent characteristic of the first-century A.D. worldview. Through the widespread practice of magic, one could find protection from this realm and even control it. People who became Christians and joined the early Christian churches would have been tempted to bring their magical beliefs and practices with them, as we see in the Acts account of an incident in Ephesus* (Acts 19:18-19). These people needed perspective on their past and a changed attitude toward it in the light of Paul's interpretation of the gospel.*

    1. Definition of Magic
    2. Sources
    3. Magic and the Spirit World
    4. The Uses for Magic
    5. Jewish Magic
    6. Paul and Magic in Acts
    7. Paul and Magic in the Letters

### 1. Definition of Magic.

In the world of Paul's time, magic was not a form of entertainment consisting of the skilled use of illusory tricks. It was far more serious and corresponds closely with what we might today call sorcery, witchcraft or the occult.

Magic was based on the belief in supernatural powers which could be harnessed and used by appropriating the correct technique. Magic can therefore be defined as a method of manipulating supernatural powers to accomplish certain tasks with guaranteed results. Magicians would not seek the will of the deity in a matter, but would invoke the deity to do precisely as they stated.

There is also a sociological aspect to the definition of magic. Magic was illegal in the Roman Empire and regarded as socially deviant, outside the boundaries of acceptable religious practice. Accusing another person or group of practicing magic was a powerful tool of social dominance in the ancient world. Although the motives of those who accused people of magic and

witchcraft need to be evaluated carefully, the sociological definition of magic by no means exhausts its definition (see Betz 1990, 212-19; pace Segal). Magic was characterized by a set of objective characteristics and its own positive self-definition.

### 2. Sources.

The most important witnesses for our understanding of magical beliefs and practice are a collection of Greek papyri originally discovered in Egypt (abbreviated *PGM*). These have recently been translated into English (see Betz 1986). Most of these papyri date to the third and fourth centuries of our era (although a few date as early as the first century B.C.), but the contents reflect the way magic was practiced during Paul's time and earlier (Luck, 14, 16).

Hundreds of lead curse tablets (*defixiones*) have also been unearthed from throughout the Mediterranean world by archeologists. The tablets using the Greek language date between the fifth century B.C. and the sixth century A.D. and contain formulae similar to the papyri. In addition, numerous magical amulets have been discovered which shed much light on magical practices. Our understanding of magic is also enhanced by the many Greek and Roman authors who describe the practice (see Luck, 3-131).

### 3. Magic and the Spirit World.

The wearing of amulets, recitation of magical formulas and performance of magical rites were carried out in the belief that these words and actions could exert a compelling influence over one or more spirits. Practitioners would try to "conjure" (*orkizō*) well-known deities (e.g., Mithras, Isis, Helios), but more often the "angels"* (*angeloi*) or "assistants" (*paredroi*) of the gods. Note the following magical formula in a recipe that reputedly "accomplishes anything":

> I call upon you, holy, very powerful . . . assistants of the great god, the powerful chief daimons, you who are inhabitants of Chaos, of Erebos, of the abyss . . . dwelling in the recesses of heaven, lurking in the nooks and crannies of houses . . . lead-

ers of those in the underworld, administrators of the infinite, wielding power over earth . . . lords of Fate . . . adverse daimons . . . rulers of daimons . . . do the matter [which I demand]. (*PGM* IV.1345-75)

This formula is to be recited after performing an elaborate rite using, among other things, some fat and hairs from an ass, a female goat and a black bull. The person who performed the rite and uttered the formula would expect the spirits to fulfill the demand if the recipe was followed in precise detail.

Magic also drew on nonpersonal powers and forces for its purposes. It assumed the principle of cosmic sympathy—that the microcosm is bound to the macrocosm in a system of correspondences. What affects one part affects the other in this integrated whole of life forces. The magician would therefore make use of animal viscera, plants, herbs, precious stones and metals, believing that there was a cosmic correspondence. Even the seven vowels in the Greek alphabet had their cosmic counterpart in the seven planetary deities.

### 4. The Uses for Magic.

People who used magic sought self-serving aims. There are no extant examples of people using magic to accomplish the will of a deity. Rather, magic was used precisely to influence the will of a deity or spirit.

*4.1. Protection.* One of the primary uses of magic in everyday life was for protection. In a world thought to be populated by hordes of evil spirits bent on bringing harm in every conceivable way, people sought supernatural protection. This was perhaps the chief use of the magical amulets, which frequently bore the inscription "protect me!" Many recipes for constructing these kinds of amulets appear in the magical papyri as, for example, the following:

The protective charm which you must wear: Onto lime wood write with vermilion this name "[50 Greek letters] Guard me from every daimon of the air on the earth and under the earth, and from every angel and phantom and ghostly visitation and enchantment, me [space for name]." Enclose it in a purple skin, hang it around your neck and wear it. (*PGM* IV.2694-2704)

This text vividly illustrates the fear of evil spirits from which people sought relief.

*4.2. Altering Fate.* In Paul's day many in the Mediterranean world were convinced that the course of their lives was directly affected by the alignment of the stars in the heavens at their time of birth. This reflected the principle of cosmic sympathy and represented the basis for astrology. In the worldview of the masses, however, the stars either embodied or represented

personal powers (*see* Worship). Thus, the names of deities were given to the sun, moon, planets and stars. Magical practitioners believed that a foul fate could be altered by influencing these astral deities through the appropriate magical formula. Also through magical means, a prominent deity could be invoked to thwart the grip of fate. For example, in one text Sarapis is invoked for this purpose:

I call on you, lord, holy, much hymned, greatly honored, ruler of the cosmos (*kosmokratōr*), [Sarapis] consider my birth and turn me not away. . . . Protect me from all my own astrological destiny; destroy my foul fate; apportion good things for me in my horoscope." (*PGM* XIII.618-40)

*4.3. Other Uses.* Magic was also used for less honorable purposes. Spirits could be invoked to compel the physical attraction of another person (aphrodisiacs), to gain favor and influence with people, to heal various kinds of illnesses (*see* Healing, Illness) and to gain an appearance from a deity who could reveal special knowledge. There was also a malevolent kind of magic, represented especially by the curse tablets (*defixiones*). This form of magic sought to inflict pain and harm on opponents and enemies.

### 5. Jewish Magic.

Magic was by no means practiced only by pagans. Jewish magic flourished in antiquity (Alexander, 342). There are many testimonies to Jewish involvement in magical practice in the apocrypha, pseudepigrapha, Qumran, Josephus, the earliest traditions within the Talmud and the midrashim, early Christian writings, pagan authors and even in the NT itself (Acts 19:13-20, "certain itinerant Jewish exorcists"). The Greek magical papyri also contain many magical formulas of probable Jewish origin.

An interesting example of Jewish magic is the *Testament of Solomon* (first to third centuries A.D.). Essentially a manual of magical formulas, the *Testament* ostensibly records how Solomon directed demons to build the Temple at Jerusalem by manipulating them through magical means. Another important early Jewish book of magic, translated into English and published under the title *Sepher ha-Razim* ("Book of Mysteries"), probably comes from the fourth century A.D. However, the book likely contains traditions and reflects the magical practices of certain segments of Judaism dating to the first century A.D. The work describes the seven heavens and gives the names of the angels populating each of the heavens. Within this framework are numerous magical formulas instructing how the angels can be invoked to fulfill the desires of the conjurer. Although the angels appear to take the place of pagan gods (in comparison with pagan magical texts), there are a few examples of invocations directly to the pagan deities (e.g., Helios, Aphrodite, Hermes).

Speaking of the various Jewish magical texts, P. S. Alexander concludes that, "As an indicator of the spiritual atmosphere in which large sections of the populace lived—rich and poor, educated and ignorant—their importance can hardly be overestimated" (Alexander, 342).

### 6. Paul and Magic in Acts.

Luke records one incident in which Paul was confronted with a magician (Acts 13:4-12). This magician was Jewish and yet was attached to the Gentile proconsul of the Island of Cyprus. Paul encountered him on the island at the outset of his first missionary outreach. When the proconsul showed interest in the gospel which Paul preached, Elymas (the magician) strongly opposed Paul. According to Luke, Paul denounced Elymas as a pawn of the devil and the Lord immediately struck the magician with blindness.

Acts recounts another dramatic episode that occurred during Paul's Ephesian ministry (Acts 19:13-20; see Ephesus). Luke narrates a situation involving itinerant Jewish exorcists who invoked the name of Jesus as part of their magical rite for exorcism (see Demons and Exorcism). On one occasion they were tragically unsuccessful as they applied this method to a demonized man. Luke says they were physically assaulted by the man and forced to flee the house naked and bleeding. As word spread among Christians about this incident, those who continued to practice magic came under strong conviction. Gathering all of their expensive books of magical formulas and incantations, they burned them. This account reinforces the reputation of Ephesus as being something of a center for magical practices during the first century. It is also important for understanding the pre-Christian background of many of Paul's converts. Early Christians faced a strong temptation to combine their magical beliefs and practices with their Christianity. It is clear that Luke regards magic as evil and the domain of the devil (see Garrett, 101-9). In this respect, he also accurately reflects the convictions of Paul.

### 7. Paul and Magic in the Letters.

Very little has been written on the theme of magic in relation to Paul's letters. This is probably due to the fact that he explicitly mentions it only once (Gal 5:20) in his undisputed letters. Furthermore, his theology betrays nothing of a magical worldview.

*7.1. "Witchcraft" (Gal 5:20).* If Galatians 5:20 is any indication of Paul's overall attitude toward magic, we can conclude that he believed it to be inconsistent with life in the Spirit. He roundly condemns "magic" (*pharmakeia*) in Galatians 5:20 as on the same level as idolatry; both are acts of the "flesh"* which should have no part in the life of a believer (cf. Rev 21:8 where it is said that those who practice magic will experience the "second death").

*7.2. "Magicians" (2 Tim 3:13).* The text of 2 Timothy 3:13 predicts that "evil men and impostors [*goētes*] will go from bad to worse, deceiving and being deceived" (NIV). The term *goēs* is commonly used in literature as a derogatory reference to a magician—a person who is a charlatan or a swindler. Although it is possible that 2 Timothy 3:13 uses the term in a general sense, it is more likely that a magician is in mind, perhaps of the same sort as Apollonius of Tyana (Philostratus *Vit. Ap.*). This interpretation is rendered more likely because the deceivers are compared in 2 Timothy 3:8 with magicians who opposed Moses (Jannes and Jambres). Here again, the practice of magic is viewed in the worst possible light.

*7.3. Principalities and Powers.* Practitioners of magic were obsessively interested in supernatural powers for utilitarian reasons. Paul's letters, especially Colossians* and Ephesians,* provide his readers with a new outlook on the spirit realm (see Principalities and Powers). Paul never denies the real existence of evil spirits (but cf. 1 Cor 8:4); rather he is careful to describe them as minions under the control of the prince of evil, Satan* (e.g., Eph 2:2). Most importantly, Christ has defeated all these forces by his work on the cross (Col 2:15; see Triumph) and is now exalted far above them to a position of sovereignty (Eph 1:20-22; see Exaltation and Enthronement). Nevertheless, the powers still exert their influence and are hostile to the church. Christ's parousia will bring an end to their tyranny over the world (1 Cor 15:24; Eph 1:10; Col 1:20). Because of their dangerous hostility to the church, these powers are not to be invoked or manipulated by Christians, but rather resisted through the power* of God (Eph 6:10-20).

The terms Paul uses for the powers reflect the wide array of vocabulary shared by people of all religious traditions during the NT era. Some of these terms are used in magical texts (e.g., *dynameis, kosmokratores, thronoi*), although his vocabulary for the powers more closely reflects the angelology and demonology of Second Temple Judaism. Paul draws on this reservoir of terminology with which his readers would be familiar, lumping together all manner of spirits, when he speaks of the supernatural realm of evil (see Principalities and Powers).

**7.4. The "Elemental Spirits."** It is possible that Paul's terminology for "elemental spirits of the world" (*stoicheia tou kosmou*, Gal 4:3, 9; Col 2:8, 20) comes from a background of usage in astrology and magic (of course, it is also possible that the meaning "elementary principles" is more appropriate to these contexts; *see* Elements/Elemental Spirits). The expression appears, for instance, in the astrological section of the *Testament of Solomon* (*T. Sol.* 18:1, 2; cf. also 8:1-4), a portion that probably had an independent existence and use as early as the first century B.C. It is used there to refer to the astral decans, thirty-six spirits controlling every ten degrees of the heavenly sphere. The expression is used similarly in the magical papyri (*PGM* 39.18-21). If Paul was drawing the phrase *stoicheia tou kosmou* from the tradition represented in this literature, he did so strictly because it was part of the wide array of vocabulary shared by Jew and Gentile alike to refer to the spirit world. In this case he may have chosen this particular expression for the powers because it was well known to the readers of Galatians* and Colossians.* Paul does not necessarily give credence to the notion that astral spirits hold the keys of fate; rather, he is more concerned to subsume them under the category of the demonic and assert that by participation in Christ's death, believers have died to their enslaving influence (*see* Dying and Rising).

**7.5. Addressing a Magical Worldview (Ephesians).** Many aspects of the teaching of Ephesians about divine power and supernatural spirits seem particularly appropriate for people who have come to Christ from a background of involvement in magical practices (Arnold 1989, esp. 167-72). That such people were entering the churches is certain because of the widespread use of magic at the time. This is corroborated by Luke's account of the burning of the magical books at Ephesus (Acts 19:18-19), which is especially relevant for understanding the struggles of the Asia Minor churches.

In Ephesians Paul declares the superiority of the power* of God and the supremacy of Christ over all spiritual powers, indeed, over "every name that is named" (Eph 1:19-23; 4:8-10). For those who lived in constant fear of the dreadful workings of evil spirits, this would have provided much comfort. Fate is not in the hands of capricious powers, but rather is determined by the loving Father who "chose us in him before the creation of the world" (Eph 1:3). The will and purpose of this benevolent heavenly Father is being worked out in history (Eph 1:5, 9, 10, 11; 2:10); he is not a deity to be manipulated according to one's carnal whims. One approaches God with humility and thankfulness and prays according to his will (Eph 3:14-19; cf. 1:15-19). In contrast to the self-serving attempts to use divine power in magic, Ephesians stresses the believer's reception of divine power to manifest love* to other people in a selfless manner (Eph 3:16-17; 5:2). The letter also gives a new perspective on the powers by highlighting their collusion with the devil and exposing their objective of attacking the church (Eph 2:2; 4:27; 6:12). Ephesians assures believers of the availability of God's power for resisting these forces. God's power, according to Paul, is not obtained through incantations and formulae, but by virtue of a close union with the resurrected Christ (Eph 2:5-6; 6:10).

*See also* DEMONS AND EXORCISM; ELEMENTS/ELEMENTAL SPIRITS OF THE WORLD; EPHESIANS, LETTER TO THE; PRINCIPALITIES AND POWERS; RELIGIONS, GRECO-ROMAN; SATAN, DEVIL; TRIUMPH; WORLD, COSMOLOGY.

BIBLIOGRAPHY. P. S. Alexander, "Incantations and Books of Magic," in *The History of the Jewish People in the Age of Jesus Christ (175 B.C.-A.D. 135)*, rev. and ed. G. Vermes, F. Millar and M. Goodman (3 vols.; Edinburgh: T. & T. Clark, 1986) 3.1.342-79; C. E. Arnold, *Ephesians: Power and Magic* (SNTSMS 63; Cambridge: University Press, 1989); idem, *Powers of Darkness* (Downers Grove, IL: IVP, 1992); D. Aune, "Magic in Early Christianity," *ANRW* II.23.2 (1980) 1507-57; H. D. Betz, ed., *The Greek Magical Papyri in Translation*, vol. 1: *Text* (Chicago: University of Chicago, 1986); idem, "Magic and Mystery in the Greek Magical Papyri," in *Hellenismus und Urchristentum: Gesammelte Aufsätze* I (Tübingen: J. C. B. Mohr, 1990) 209-29; C. A. Faraone and D. Obbink, eds., *Magika Hiera: Ancient Greek Magic and Religion* (New York: Oxford University Press, 1991); S. R. Garrett, *The Demise of the Devil: Magic and the Demonic in Luke's Writings* (Minneapolis: Fortress, 1989); E. R. Goodenough, *Jewish Symbols in the Greco-Roman Period*, vol. 2 *The Archaeological Evidence from the Diaspora* (BS 37; New York: Bollingen Foundation, 1953); T. Hopfner, *Griechisch-Ägyptischer Offenbarungszauber* (SPP 21; Amsterdam: Adolf M. Hakkert, 1974 [= Leipzig: Haessel, 1921]); G. Luck, *Arcana Mundi* (Baltimore: Johns Hopkins, 1985); A. Segal, "Hellenistic Magic: Some Questions of Definition," in *The Other Judaism of Late Antiquity* (BJS 127; Atlanta: Scholar's, 1987) 79-108; E. M. Yamauchi, "Magic in the Biblical World," *TynB* 34 (1983) 169-200.

C. E. Arnold

# MAN AND WOMAN

No NT writer has been more criticized for his allegedly negative portrayal of women than the apostle Paul. Although Paul's view that "There is neither male nor female in Christ" (Gal 3:28) has been hailed as revolutionary, he has been viewed conversely as merely a child of his culture in other texts in which he appears to subordinate or denigrate women (e.g., 1 Cor 14:34-35). Whether Paul merely reflects his culture's views of women or significantly differs from them (positively or negatively) can only be determined by examining some of the most debated Pauline passages in light of his culture.

    1. Paul and Men's and Women's Roles in General
    2. Paul and Women's Head Coverings
    3. Paul and Wives' Submission
    4. Paul and Women's Ministry

**1. Paul and Men's and Women's Roles in General.**
Paul's letters are occasional letters, that is, they were occasioned by specific circumstances and thus address certain situations as responses to them. Paul's earlier letters (mainly those undisputedly attributed to him) do not deal specifically with women, men or marriage* very frequently, but the topic does come up, especially in 1 Corinthians 7.

In 1 Corinthians 7 Paul addresses Christians who, like a few groups in their culture, have come to value the single lifestyle; their view, however, has created certain complications. One complication is that some of those valuing the single lifestyle are already married, and their pursual of celibacy within marriage provides a danger of sexual temptation to their spouses and possibly themselves as well (1 Cor 7:2, 5; cf. 1 Cor 7:9). Paul may be citing a Corinthian position in 1 Corinthians 7:1, but in 1 Corinthians 7:2-5 Paul's language is quite sensitive to hearers of both genders: he addresses both husbands and wives on equal terms. Jewish marriage contracts stipulated certain duties required of husbands and wives, but Paul focuses on one duty relevant here, intercourse. What is significant is that it is not simply a duty for husbands, as in some Jewish texts; it is a reciprocal duty (1 Cor 7:3-4). Both the Jewish contracts and Paul show special sensitivity for the wife's feelings in this matter, however, quite in contrast with Greek culture's emphasis on male sexual gratification (Keener 1991, 67-82).

Another complication of their lifestyle is that some Christians now wanted to divorce, either due to lack of sexual fulfillment or, more likely, to pursue a celibate lifestyle (or, like Cynic philosophers, a lifestyle free of the encumbrance of marriage, yet not of sexual relations; cf. 1 Cor 6:12-20). In response Paul cites a saying of Jesus: divorce is not permissible (1 Cor 7:10-11; cf. Mk 10:11-12). Having appealed to Jesus' prohibition of divorce, however, Paul goes on to qualify it, without in any sense feeling that he is challenging its authority; it was widely understood that general state-

ments of principle needed to be qualified in certain situations (especially since Jesus' Jewish teaching style often included hyperbole, i.e., rhetorical overstatement; see Keener 1991, 13-28). It is true that the believer is not allowed to initiate the breakup of his or her marriage; if, however, the believer is forced into the situation (Paul's example here covers abandonment and being divorced against one's will; either spouse could unilaterally divorce the other under Roman law), the believer is "not under bondage" (1 Cor 7:15), for there is no guarantee of the unbeliever's conversion (1 Cor 7:16).

Paul's "not under bondage" echoes the exact language of Jewish divorce contracts, meaning that the person's divorce was valid and they were "free" to remarry (see Keener 1991, 50-66). To read "not under bondage" as anything other than freedom to remarry is to ignore how all first-century Jewish readers would have understood it (not to mention ignoring the synonym in 1 Cor 7:27, 39). Throughout this initial discussion on divorce, Paul is careful to maintain his balance of inclusive language, involving husband and wife equally in spiritual responsibility and freedom.*

After exhorting his readers that it is better to remain in their present state (i.e., he prefers remaining single, and more strongly advocates avoiding divorce; cf. 1 Cor 7:17-24), he explains that virgins are probably better off remaining single (1 Cor 7:25-38), although he acknowledges that this is only better for those who are fit for it (1 Cor 7:36; cf. 1 Cor 7:9). In this context he again returns momentarily to the issue of divorce. Digressions were common in antiquity in general and Paul in particular, and the flow of thought in the immediate context leaves no doubt that 1 Corinthians 7:27-28 refers to divorce: "Are you married to a wife? Do not seek a divorce. Are you divorced (the same Greek word as in the preceding line) from a wife? Do not seek to be married again. But if you do remarry, you have not sinned; and the same is true for one who has not been married before." Here Paul's language is temporarily less inclusive, but his point is meant to cover both genders: by 1 Corinthians 7:32-34, he values the spiritual devotion of men and women equally.

1 Corinthians 7:36-38 may be relevant to our discussion if it refers to parentally arranged marriages, as is likely; but scholars are almost evenly divided as to whether a virgin's father or fiancé is addressed here. If the former is in view, Paul simply addresses the father in the cultural situation which then prevailed: parents arranged their children's marriages, usually with input from the children. If the latter is in view, we have no earlier cultural parallels to the situation

addressed here. On either reading, however, Paul apparently suggests sensitivity to the girl's wishes (1 Cor 7:36).

We must now turn to the more specific questions of head coverings, and authority relationships in marriage and in the church, the most frequent issues of debate concerning women's roles in Paul.

## 2. Paul and Women's Head Coverings.

Some commentators have managed to deny Pauline authorship to nearly all the controversial passages in Paul concerning women, but the textual evidence for this attempt in 1 Corinthians 11:2-16 is so weak that few scholars support it; most writers have concerned themselves instead with the more rigorous task of understanding the text. The text clearly refers to a custom of women covering their heads, at least in worship*; often a shawl (covering only the hair) was employed for this, but in some places face-veils were also used. There are so many contexts in which head coverings were used, however, that one must question which context Paul addresses. For instance, people covered their heads due to mourning or shame; but since this practice was used for both men and women, it is unlikely that Paul has this practice directly in view.

Although Greek women had traditionally been secluded in the home to a great extent, there is not much evidence for frequent head coverings among them in this period, certainly not among the well-to-do. East of Greece, however, the custom was prevalent, including in Palestine and southern Roman Asia (e.g., Tarsus; see MacMullen); further, Roman women (like Roman men) covered their heads in worship, in contrast to Greek women and men. The Corinthian church, located near a major port and born in a synagogue (Acts 18:4, 7-8), probably included a number of Eastern immigrants for whom the covering was an important practice. Evidence from Egypt indicates that many Jewish women covered their heads outside Palestine, even if they were Hellenized in many other respects (Philo; Joseph and Asenath). But more is probably involved than merely a clash of cultural icons; the head covering was a cultural issue, but it symbolized certain values that went deeper than the symbol itself.

Women's hair was a prime object of male lust in the ancient Mediterranean world (Apuleius *Met.* 2.8-9; *Sifre* Num. 11.2.3); societies which employed head coverings thus viewed uncovered married women as unfaithful to their husbands, that is, seeking another man (cf. *m. Ket.* 7:6; virgins and prostitutes, conversely, were expected not to cover their heads, since they were looking for men). Women who covered their heads could thus view uncovered women as a threat; uncovered women, however, undoubtedly viewed the covering custom as restrictive and saw the way they dressed their hair as their own business. Significantly, the uncovered women probably include the cultured women of higher status, whose family homes hosted most of the house churches. Statues show that well-to-do women pursued fashionable hairstyles and uncovered heads, styles that poorer women probably considered seductive. Given the class conflict in the Corinthian church evident from other passages in 1 Corinthians (e.g., 1 Cor 11:21-22; see Theissen), this would easily have flared into a major issue of controversy (see Keener 1992, 22-31; cf. Thompson)

Both the Book of Acts and Paul's own letters present him as a skilled debater, conversant in the logic and rhetoric* of his culture. In ancient rhetoric, one's arguments for a position need not be the same as the reasons for which one actually held the position. Paul's purpose in advising head coverings may have been the unity of the church, but his arguments are those which would work best to persuade his readers. He proposes four main arguments for his position: family values, the creation order, the example of nature and of propriety as dictated by custom.

First, Paul argues from family values and a pun (plays on words were common in ancient argumentation, both Jewish and Greek): the husband is the wife's head, so if she dishonors her head by uncovering it in a culture where that is dishonorable, she dishonors her husband (1 Cor 11:2-6). By drawing an analogy between uncovered and shaven heads (this is the rhetorical technique *reductio ad absurdum*: Paul says, "If you want to be uncovered, why don't you go all the way with it?"), Paul reinforces this sense of shame; when a woman's hair was cut short or shaved, it was a great dishonor and symbolized the loss of her femininity.

Although Paul is arguing from a play on words, modern interpreters have often fastened on the single word *head* (Gk *kephalē*) and debated what Paul meant when he called the husband the wife's "head." Some scholars have argued that the term means "authority" or "boss"; the Hebrew for "head" (*rō'š*) could mean this, and occasionally *kephalē* means this in the Septuagint (Grudem; Fitzmyer). Other scholars have disputed this meaning, noting that the translators usually bent over backward to avoid translating the Hebrew *rō'š* with the Greek term *kephalē*; *kephalē* does not normally mean "authority" or "boss" in Greek. These latter scholars often argue for the meaning "source," which it does mean in some texts (Mickelsen in Mickelsen, 97-117; Scroggs, 284). Scholars favoring the "authority" meaning, however, respond that "source" is an even rarer meaning of *kephalē* in the Septuagint than "authority." Both groups of scholars are undoubtedly right in what they affirm but may fall short in what they deny; the term sometimes means "source" and sometimes means "authority," at least in "Jewish Greek" influenced by the rhythms of the Septuagint.

The question is, what sense should be attributed to the term in 1 Corinthians 11:3? Given the allusion to Adam as Eve's source in 1 Corinthians 11:8, it is very likely that Paul speaks of the man (Adam) as his wife's "source," just as Christ had created Adam and later proceeded from the Father in his incarnation (in which case 1 Cor 11:3 is in chronological sequence; see Bilezikian, 138). (In Eph 5:23, by contrast, the wife is to submit to her husband as her "head," i.e., one in authority* over her [although the husband is simultaneously expected to define headship in terms of his sacrificial service for his wife]. Even Ephesians 5, however, does not give us a transcultural view of the husband's authority; the husband's authority in this passage reflects the status of women in a society where they were already subordinate to their husbands, and modifies it in a more progressive direction. See our discussion of this passage below.)

Secondly, Paul argues from the creation order (1 Cor 11:7-12); essentially Paul says, "Adam was created before Eve, therefore women should wear head coverings." This argument does not work well on modern logic, but undoubtedly made the point admirably to the Corinthians. Although Paul knew from Genesis 1:26-27 that man and woman together represented God's image* (cf. Rom 8:29; 2 Cor 3:18), he points out that woman, taken from man, also reflects man's glory (1 Cor 11:7) and therefore can distract men from worship; this may relate to the danger of typical male lust in that culture. But once Paul has made his argument from the creation order, he takes it back: it is true that woman comes from man, but it is also true that men come from women; both are really dependent on one another in the Lord* (1 Cor 11:11-12). Although Paul only needs woman's derivation from man to support his point, he qualifies his argument so that no one will press more meaning into it than he himself intends: he uses this only as an ad hoc argument for head coverings, not for everything one might extrapolate from it.

Paul concludes argument two with an allusion so brief that it has generated a considerable variety of interpretations: "Therefore it is proper for a woman to exercise authority over her head [not, to have authority 'on' her head, as in many translations; see

Hooker], because of the angels" (1 Cor 11:10). The angels* may be (1) lusting angels, as in the most common Jewish interpretation of Genesis 6:2 (cf. also 2 Pet 2:4; Jude 6; probably 1 Pet 3:19-22), although Paul presumably would have made more of these angels here and elsewhere in his writings had he believed them a current threat; (2) angels who were present for worship, as witnessed in texts from Qumran,* who might be offended by a breach of propriety that culturally signified disregard for one's family's honor; or (3) angels who ruled the nations, but which Christians would someday judge; in this case, Paul is exhorting the women to recognize their authority over their heads but to use it responsibly (cf. 1 Cor 6:3). In any case, the Greek construction indicates that Paul recognizes the woman's authority over her head; he reasons with her to cover it for the sake of propriety, but his argument is no more forceful than this.

Third, Paul argues from nature, that is, from the natural order of things (1 Cor 11:13-15). Stoics normally argued from nature, and other writers often joined them. Paul may here be arguing from current Greek and Roman custom (other peoples in Paul's day and Greeks in an earlier period wore their hair long), although "nature" usually means something stronger than this; or he may be arguing that women's hair naturally grows longer than men's.

Finally, Paul employs a classic argument of both early Jewish and other Greco-Roman rhetoric: "That's just the way things are done" (1 Cor 11:16). One group of philosophers,* called the Skeptics, only accepted arguments from custom; most other thinkers accepted this as a supporting argument. With arguments that related to all his readers (those influenced by Jewish, Stoic and perhaps some Skeptic thought), Paul concludes with an argument related to his real purpose for writing the arguments: to avoid contention (cf. Keener 1992, 31-47, for further documentation for this section).

A few points are clear here. One is that Paul engages the issues with which his congregation is struggling, including gender issues from the culture. He also upholds the importance of the Christian family and church unity; further, while providing arguments for propriety of dress to keep the church unified, he seeks to persuade the woman who hears his letter read in the church to keep these arguments in mind without questioning her right to dress as she will (1 Cor 11:10), a far cry from stronger arguments elsewhere in the letter (1 Cor 4:18—5:5; 11:29-34). Perhaps most significant for our discussion, however, is what he omits: Paul nowhere in this text subordinates the woman, failing even to touch on that issue.

**3. Paul and Wives' Submission.**

Although several Pauline passages address the subordination of women in the home (Eph 5:22-33; Col 3:18; 1 Tim 5:14; Tit 2:4-5), we will examine in detail only the longest of these passages, since all four share the same cultural milieu, and the two references in the Pastorals may reflect the social situation depicted in our treatment of 1 Timothy 2:9-15, below. (That the social situation influences the directives is clear from a sample comparison of, say, 1 Tim 5:14 and Prov 31:10-31.)

*3.1. The Social Situation.* Before examining Paul's meaning in Ephesians 5:22-33, we should note that even the most restrictive interpretation of this passage would portray Paul as no more conservative than his culture in general. Although women were experiencing some upward mobility in this period (anything would have been an improvement over classical Athens!), and women in some areas (e.g., urban Roman Asia and Macedonia) experienced more freedom than in other areas, women nowhere enjoyed the social freedom recognized as their right today.

Influential ancient male attitudes toward women often sound harsh to modern ears; to some early Jewish teachers, women were inherently evil (cf. Sir 42:12-14; *m. 'Abot* 2:7); Josephus claimed that the Law prescribed their subordination for their own good (Josephus *Ag. Ap.* 2.24 §§200-201). Philo complains that women have little sense (Philo *Omn. Prob. Lib.* 117), and praises one exception, the Empress Livia, for becoming "intellectually male"! Likewise, Plutarch, one of the more progressive writers on the subject, positively suggests that women can learn philosophy from their husbands—but negatively bases this on the datum that they will pursue folly if left to their own devices (Plutarch *Bride and Groom* 48; *Mor.* 145DE). Such attitudes naturally affected their treatment in ancient households, where men always held the power. Roman law vested complete authority over wife, children and slaves* to the male head of the household, known as the *paterfamilias*. The wife's quiet submission was viewed as one of her greatest virtues throughout Greco-Roman antiquity (e.g., Sir 26:14-16, 30:19; Greek marriage contracts).

Perhaps due to the proliferation of female infanticide (this detail is debated), there seems to have been a shortage of women in Greek society, and the marriage of men in their thirties to girls in their early and mid teens was thus a standard practice. Until their thirties men normally had intercourse with slaves, prostitutes or one another (*see* Homosexuality); when men in classical Athens married, many of them found their wives (just entering puberty) less intellectually challenging than prostitutes. While the situation was not this dismal throughout the Empire of Paul's day, and tomb inscriptions testify to an abundance of genuine love between husbands and wives, the very structures of ancient society militated against husbands perceiving their wives as potential equals.

From the time of Aristotle, in fact, it had been customary for moral philosophers to advise their male readers how to govern wives and other members of the household* properly; these instructions have come to be known as "household codes" (or in their German title common in scholarly literature, the *Haustafeln*). Aristotle and many subsequent moralists classified the three main categories subordinate to the male householder as (1) wives, (2) children and (3) slaves (Aristotle *Pol.* 1.2.1, 1253b); although he allowed that the character of their subordination differed (male children, for instance, required less subordination as they grew older; cf. Aristotle *Pol.* 1.5.12, 1260b), he argued that their subordination was a matter of their nature, not merely of culture (on women, Aristotle *Pol.* 1.2.12, 1254b). Such moral themes appealed to the Romans, whose culture emphasized duty and order, and who were suspicious of any potential threats to their social order (e.g., the socially disruptive cult of Dionysus in the second century B.C.).

In the first and early second century, many aristocratic Romans (e.g., Petronius, Juvenal) found reason to disparage religious groups from the East, especially when these groups converted Roman women and subverted traditional Roman values. In the first century major scandals concerning women misled by Jews and followers of Isis in Rome led to severe reprisals from the government (Tacitus *Ann.* 2.85; Josephus *Ant.* 18.3.4 §§64-80). To prove that they were not subversive to traditional Roman family values after all, suspected groups often produced their own sets of "household codes" modeled after those of the moral philosophers: instructions as to how each householder should govern his wife, children and slaves (Josephus *Ag. Ap.* 2.25-31 §§201-17; see Balch for a thorough treatment of household codes from Aristotle through Josephus).

*3.2. Ephesians 5:22-33.* Some scholars have argued that the original Paul (as reflected in Rom 16:3-15; Phil 4:2-3) preserved Jesus' spirit of egalitarianism, but the second and third generations of his disciples (reflected in Colossians* and Ephesians,* and the Pastorals,* respectively) increasingly subordinated women's roles to fit the standards of their culture. While such a view has some evidence to support it, it rests on two hypotheses requiring proof: first, that the later canonical Pauline writings are not genuine; and second, a particular reading of these later letters. The question of these letters' authenticity is examined elsewhere in this volume (*see* Canon); the question of their meaning, however, is examined here. The text of Ephesians itself actually does not support the contention that its writer has become more chauvinistic than the Paul of the earlier letters.

Assuming that Ephesians is written by Paul, it is written by a prisoner in Rome well aware of Roman attitudes toward "Eastern cults" like worshipers of Isis and Dionysus, plus Judaism in both its Christian and non-Christian forms (what we today call Christianity and Judaism, respectively). Paul is also well aware that the social ostracism Jews and Christians often faced could become much worse if the outcome of his own trial set a negative precedent for Christians elsewhere (cf. Phil 1:7, addressed to a congregation that includes some Roman citizens like himself). Like representatives of other mistrusted religious groups in the Roman Empire, Paul had good strategic reason to uphold traditional Roman family values.

At first sight, it may appear that Paul has done just that. Given the social situation, it is hardly surprising that Paul presents household codes in their familiar three basic categories: relations between wives and husbands, children and fathers, and slaves and masters. But contrary to our expectations, Paul significantly adapts the list. Yes, wives, children and slaves are to submit, and thus to silence cultural objections to the gospel (submission here is "for the Lord's sake," Eph 5:21; 6:5-8). But for Paul a truly Christian ethic compatible with Jesus' teaching and example of servanthood goes beyond this: the male householder is also to submit. That Paul requires this of the *paterfamilias* is implied in a number of ways, and the distinction between his view and the more usual ancient injunction that the householder govern should have been clear to ancient readers.

First, Paul begins this three-part structure in a very unusual way. As the climax of his exhortations describing a Spirit*-filled life (Eph 5:18-21), Paul calls on all believers to submit to one another (Eph 5:21). It is true that the following context delineates different ways to submit according to differing societal roles; but the very idea of "mutual submission" strained the common sense of the term "submission": householders were sometimes called to be sensitive to their wives, children and slaves, but they were never told to submit to them. That Paul envisions the same sort of mutual submission to cover the slave and master relationship is clear from his exhortation in Ephesians 6:9: after explaining how and why slaves should submit (Eph 6:5-8), he calls on masters to "do the same

things to them," an idea which, if pressed literally, goes beyond virtually all other extant writers from antiquity.

Second, the duties are listed as reciprocal duties. Whereas most household codes simply addressed the head of the household, instructing him how to govern other members of his household, Paul first addresses wives, children and slaves. Far from instructing the *paterfamilias* how to govern his wife, children and slaves, he omits any injunction to govern and merely calls on him to love his wife (undoubtedly a common practice, but rarely prescribed), be restrained in disciplining his children and to regard slaves as equals before God.* This is hardly the language of the common household code, although some ancient philosophers also exhorted moderation and fair treatment of subordinates. The wife, children and slaves are to regulate their *own* submission voluntarily.

Third, Paul does not describe the duties that are attached to submission. An ancient reader could therefore have been tempted to read a wife's submission as meaning all that it could mean in that culture—which, as we have noted above, involves considerably more subordination than any modern Christian interpreters would apply to women today. (Applying the text in this way would return women to rarely being able to attend college, to disallowing them voting privileges, etc.) However, Paul does define the content of the wife's submission once, in quite a strategic place: at the concluding summary of his advice to married couples. The wife is to "respect" (*phobeomai*, Eph 5:33) her husband. Although the term usually translated "submission" (*hypotassō*) could be used in the weaker sense of "respect," household codes demanded far more of wives than mere respect; Paul's view of women's subordination even in this social situation could not be much weaker than it is.

Finally, the wife's subordination to her husband is directly parallel to the slave's subordination to his or her master. In both cases one submits as "to Christ"— who is compared with a slave's master no less than with a wife's husband. Most interpreters recognize today that Ephesians 6:5-9 does not address the institution of slavery; it simply gives advice to slaves in their situation. Like some Stoic philosophers, Paul could recommend securing one's freedom where that was possible (1 Cor 7:21-22); like the rare philosophers whom Aristotle chastised for suggesting that slavery was against nature and therefore wrong, Paul clearly regarded the subordination of humans as unnatural (Eph 6:9). Whereas the OT enjoined children's obedience to morally sound parental instruction (Deut 21:18-21), the OT nowhere explicitly enjoins the submission of wives and slaves (although they regularly appear in subordinate cultural roles, which God sometimes contravened). Paul does call on wives and slaves in his culture to submit in some sense; but he does not thereby approve of the institutions of patriarchal marriage or slavery, both of which are part of the authority of the *paterfamilias* and the household codes he here addresses.

That Paul's instructions to wives and slaves are limited to wives and slaves culturally subordinated to the male householder has often been noted (e.g., Martin, 206-31; Giles, 43). The objection that Paul could have rejected the institution of slavery but clearly would support the institution of marriage (Knight, 21-25) simply begs the real question. It is not the institution of marriage per se, but the institution of *patriarchal* marriage, that Paul addresses here; that was what appeared in the household codes. Paul elsewhere calls on believers in normal circumstances to submit to all who are in authority (Rom 13:1-7; *see* Civil Authorities), as Peter does (1 Pet 2:13-17); but this does not mean that he regards the particular authority structures (e.g., kingship) as necessary for all cultures. Because Paul's instructions specifically address institutions as they existed in Paul's day, interpreters of Paul who do not insist on reinstituting slavery or the monarchy should not insist on patriarchal marriages which subordinate wives, either. Indeed, given Paul's weak definition of the wife's submission as "respect" (Eph 5:33; see above), it appears that Paul advocated her submission in only a limited manner even for his own social situation.

### 4. Paul and Women's Ministry.

*4.1. Passages in Which Paul Approves Women's Ministry.* Although some Greek and Roman women became philosophers, higher education in rhetoric and philosophy was usually reserved for men. In a society where most people were functionally illiterate (especially much of the rural peasantry, estimated at perhaps 90 percent of the Empire's population), teaching roles naturally would fall on those who could read and speak well. Nearly all of our Jewish sources suggest that these roles were, with rare exceptions, limited to men.

Although inscriptions from ancient synagogues indicate that women filled a prominent role in some synagogues (see Brooten), the same inscriptions indicate that this was the exception rather than the norm. Our sources indicate that most Jewish men, like Philo, Josephus and many later rabbis, reflected the prejudice of much of the broader Greco-Roman culture. Josephus (*Ant.* 4.8.15 §219) and the rabbis in most cases dismissed the trustworthiness of women's witness, and, with the possible exceptions of Beruriah, wife of R. Meir, and the women followers of Jesus (Mk 15:40-41; Lk 8:1-3; 10:38-42), women seem never to have been accorded the role or status of teachers or their disciples (see Swidler). While the roles of women varied from region to region, certain Pauline passages make it clear that he was among the more progressive, not the more chauvinistic, writers of his day.

In a brief letter of recommendation at the conclusion of Romans, Paul commends the bearer of his letter whom the Romans may trust to explain it to them (Rom 16:1-2). Phoebe is "servant" of the church at Cenchreae, the port city of Corinth; the term may refer to a "deacon" (*diakonos*), apparently a person with administrative responsibility in the early church, but which in Paul's letters usually refers to a minister of God's word, such as himself. He also calls her a "helper" (*prostatis*) of many, a term which normally referred in antiquity to patrons, some of whom were women. As a patron, she would own the home in which the church met and hold a position of honor (see further Keener 1992, 237-40).

In Paul's following greetings (Rom 16:3-16), he lists about twice as many men as women, but commends more than twice as many women as men (*see* Coworkers, Paul and His). This may indicate his sensitivity to the opposition women undoubtedly faced for their ministry in some quarters. Among the most significant ministers he lists is Prisca (a diminutive form of Priscilla), possibly mentioned before her husband Aquila because of her higher social status (Rom 16:3-4). Luke also portrays her as a fellow-minister with her husband, joining him in instructing another minister, Apollos (Acts 18:26).

Paul also lists two fellow-apostles (this is the most natural way to construe "notable among the apostles," since Paul nowhere else appeals to commendations from "the apostles"), Andronicus and Junia. "Junia" itself is clearly a feminine name, but writers inclined to doubt that Paul could have referred to a female apostle have proposed that this is a contraction for the masculine "Junianus." But this contraction does not occur in our inscriptions from Rome and is by any count quite rare compared to the common feminine name; the proposal rests on the assumption that a woman could not be an apostle, rather than on any evidence inherent in the text itself.

In another letter Paul refers to the ministry of two women in Philippi, who, like his many male fellow-ministers, shared in his work for the gospel* there (Phil 4:2-3). Macedonia was one of the regions where women were accorded more prominent religious roles

(Abrahamson), and this may have made it easier for Paul's women colleagues to assume a position of prominence (cf. also Acts 16:14-15).

Paul, who ranks prophets* second only to apostles* (1 Cor 12:28), assumes the existence of prophetesses and demands only that they, like other women in the congregation, cover their heads (1 Cor 11:5). In this he follows the tradition of the OT (where women filled the prophetic office far less than men, but nonetheless could assume positions of prominence and authority, e.g., Ex 15:20; Judg 4:4; 2 Kings 22:13-14) and other elements of early Christianity (Acts 2:17-18, 21:9).

These passages alone establish Paul among the more progressive writers of his culture, but other passages must be examined before one can determine *how* progressive he was. It is these passages, therefore, which have stirred the greatest controversy.

### 4.2. Passages in Which Paul Seems to Restrict Women's Ministry.

Although both the following passages have been subjected to a bewildering array of interpretations, neither of them is universally held to be Pauline. Not only the authorship of 1 Timothy, but also that of 1 Corinthians 14:34-35, has been called into question. On the basis of some (admittedly slender) textual evidence, some prominent text critics have denied that the latter passage is actually Pauline, thinking that it was inserted instead by a later hand (Fee, 699-705). While this position is possible, the passage can be explained as a Pauline digression on a specific aspect of church order relevant to the Corinthian church (*see* Church Order and Government).

Some have argued instead that Paul here quotes a Corinthian position (1 Cor 14:34-35), which he then refutes (1 Cor 14:36); but 1 Corinthians 14:36 does not read naturally as a refutation of 1 Corinthians 14:34-35. Others have suggested that the church services were segregated by gender like the synagogues, thus rendering any communication between the sexes disruptive; but this view is refuted both by the architecture of synagogues in this period (Brooten) and that of homes like that in which the Corinthian church met. Still other scholars, examining the context, have suggested that Paul addresses Corinthian women abusing the gifts of the Spirit, or a problem with judging prophecies. While both of these views can be argued from the context, both ancient writers in general and Paul in particular were fond of digressions, and 1 Corinthians 14:34-35 may simply represent a digression concerning a specific issue of church order, distinct from other matters of church order in the context.

More likely is the view that Paul is restricting the only kind of speech directly addressed in these verses: asking questions (Giles, 56). It was common in the ancient world for hearers to interrupt teachers with questions, but it was considered rude if the questions reflected ignorance of the topic (see Plutarch *On Lectures*). Since women were normally considerably less educated than men, Paul proposes a short-range solution and a long-range solution to the problem. His short-range solution is that the women should stop asking the disruptive questions; the long-range solution is that they *should* be educated, receiving private tutoring from their husbands. Most husbands of the period doubted their wives' intellectual potential, but Paul was among the most progressive of ancient writers on the subject. Paul's long-range solution affirms women's ability to learn and places them on equal footing with men (see more fully Keener 1992, 80-85).

Whatever reconstruction one accepts, however, two points are clear. First, Paul plainly does not enjoin total silence on women, since earlier in the same letter he expects them to pray* and prophesy publicly along with the men (1 Cor 11:4-5); he thus must enjoin only the silencing of a particular form of speaking. Second, there is nothing in the context to support the view that Paul refers here to women teaching the Bible. The only passage in the entire Bible that could be directly adduced in favor of that position is 1 Timothy 2:11-14.

In 1 Timothy 2:8-15 Paul (on authorship, *see* Pastoral Letters) apparently addresses the proper decorum of men and women in prayer. Paul first addresses the men in the Ephesian churches, who are apparently involved in conflict inappropriate for worshipers of God (1 Tim 2:8). Then, in a more lengthy passage, he turns to problems with the women in these congregations. As noted above, women of the lower economic ranks in the East frequently covered their heads; but the urban congregations of Ephesus would have included women of higher social status, who would flaunt their status by the ornate ways they decorated their hair. To poorer women in the congregation, the wealthier women's wardrobe represented both ostentation and potential seduction, so Paul rules against it, borrowing language common among moralists of his day (1 Tim 2:9-10; Scholer, 3-6; Keener 1992, 103-7).

After calling on the women in the congregation to adorn themselves properly, he forbids them to "teach in such a way as to take authority" (reading "teach," *didaskō*, and "take authority," *authenteō*, together as many scholars do, although they could also be read as separate prohibitions). The precise meaning of the rare Greek term here used for "take authority" has been questioned. Some scholars suggest that it normally means simply "have authority" and that the passage thus excludes women from exercising any authority in the church at all. Other scholars have shown that it is often used more strongly than that in this period, and may mean, "seize authority"; on this reading, Paul merely forbids women to grasp for authority overbearingly, in the same way he would have forbidden it to men. Still other scholars have appealed to other examples within the semantic range of the term to argue for meanings like "domineer in a murderous way" or "proclaim oneself originator." Since some second-century Gnostics saw Eve as the originator of Man, 1 Timothy could be refuting a gnostic myth (Kroeger argues this case with impressive erudition, and even suggests that part of this passage quotes a gnostic* source in order to refute it). This case works well if 1 Timothy is written by another writer in Paul's name in the second century (which many scholars believe, although Kroeger does not); if it was written by Paul or his amanuensis, however, the term probably means to "have authority" or (more likely) "seize authority."

The social situation of the letter may represent a more fruitful basis for resolving the meaning of the text than the broad lexical possibilities, however; both Paul and his readers assumed this situation when reading the text, and the situation which elicited Paul's response is thus part of his intended meaning. Clues in the text indicate the following situation: male false teachers (1 Tim 1:20; 2 Tim 2:17) have been introducing dangerous heresy into the Ephesian church (1 Tim 1:4-7; 6:3-5), often beginning by gaining access to its women, who would normally have been difficult to reach because of their greater restriction to the domestic sphere (2 Tim 3:6-7). Because the women were still not well trained in the Scriptures (see above), they were most susceptible to the false teachers and could provide a network through which the false teachers could disrupt other homes (1 Tim 5:13; cf. 1 Tim 3:11). Given Roman society's perception of Christians as a subversive cult, false teaching that undermined Paul's strategies for the church's public witness (see above on Eph 5—6) could not be permitted (cf. 1 Tim 3:2, 7, 10; 5:7, 10, 14; 6:1; Tit 1:6; 2:1-5, 8, 10; cf. Padgett, 52; Keener 1991, 85-87; Verner).

Whether because the women were uneducated and thus particularly susceptible to error, or because their seizing authority would have injured the church's witness in a tense social situation, or (most likely) both, the specific situation Paul addresses invites his specific response. Paul again provides a short-range solution and a long-range solution. The short-range solution is: They should not take ruling positions as teachers in the church. The long-range solution is: Let them learn. Again, Paul affirms their ability to learn, and he proposes educating them as a long-range solution to the current problem. That they are to learn "quietly and submissively" may again reflect their witness within society (these were characteristics normally expected of women), but it should be pointed out that this was the way all novices were supposed to learn, and also characterizes the desired behavior of the whole church (1 Tim 2:2). That Paul addresses these admonitions to the women rather than to the men is as determined by the social situation as his admonition to the men to stop disputing (1 Tim 2:8); he hardly wanted the women to dispute, but addressed only those involved in the problem.

This solution might be so obvious as to render debate superfluous, except for Paul's following argument, in which he appears to predicate his admonitions to women on the roles of Adam and Eve (1 Tim 2:13-14). What one must ask is whether Paul adduces these examples as the basis for his point, or merely as an ad hoc argument to support it. His argument from the creation order is no more straightforward here (1 Tim 2:13) than it was when in 1 Corinthians 11:7-9 he used it to contend that women should wear head coverings. His argument from Eve's deception is even more likely to be ad hoc. If he argues that Eve's deception prohibits all women from teaching, he is arguing that all women, like Eve, are more easily deceived than all men; if the deception does not apply to all women, neither could his prohibition of their teaching. It is far more likely that Paul instead uses Eve to illustrate the plight of the particular women he addresses in Ephesus, who are easily deceived because they are untrained. Paul elsewhere uses Eve for *anyone* who is deceived, not just women (2 Cor 11:3). Finally, it is possible that 1 Timothy 2:15 is meant to qualify the preceding verses, though there is considerable debate on its meaning (salvation coming through Mary's childbirth, perhaps as the new Eve; through women submitting to traditional roles like childbearing; or simply a woman being brought through childbirth safely, challenging the curse in Eden).

Other passages in Paul which clearly demonstrate his approval of women's ministry of God's word (above) indicate that 1 Timothy 2:9-15 (if, as we assume here, it is genuinely Pauline) cannot prohibit women's ministry in all situations, but is limited to the situation in Ephesus and perhaps some other congregations facing similar crises in this period of the church's history. Pauline texts addressing the roles of women in both church and home suggest that Paul be ranked among the most progressive of ancient writers. *See also* AUTHORITY; COWORKERS, PAUL AND HIS; HEAD; HOUSEHOLDS AND HOUSEHOLD CODES; MARRIAGE, DIVORCE, ADULTERY, INCEST; SEXUALITY, SEXUAL ETHICS.

BIBLIOGRAPHY. V. A. Abrahamsen, "The Rock Reliefs and the Cult of Diana at Philippi" (Th.D. dissertation, Harvard Divinity School, 1986); D. L. Balch, *Let Wives Be Submissive: The Domestic Code in 1 Peter* (SBLMS 26; Chico, CA: Scholars, 1981); G. Bilezikian, *Beyond Sex Roles: What the Bible Says About a Woman's Place in Church and Family* (Grand Rapids: Baker, 1986); B. J. Brooten, *Women Leaders in the Ancient Synagogue: Inscriptional Evidence and Background Issues* (Chico, CA: Scholars, 1982); G. D. Fee, *The First Epistle to the Corinthians* (NICNT; Grand Rapids: Eerdmans, 1987); J. A. Fitzmyer, "Another Look at KEPHALE in 1 Corinthians 11.3," *NTS* 35 (1989) 503-11; J. Gardner, *Women in Roman Law and Society* (Bloomington: Indiana University, 1986); K. Giles, *Created Woman: A Fresh Study of the Biblical Teaching* (Canberra: Acorn, 1985); W. A. Grudem, "Does *kephale* Mean 'Source' or 'Authority Over' in Greek Literature? A Survey of 2,336 Examples," *TJ* n.s. 6 (1985) 38-59; N. A. Hardesty, *Women Called to Witness: Evangelical Feminism in the 19th Century* (Nashville: Abingdon, 1984); M. D. Hooker, "Authority on Her Head: An Examination of I Cor. XI.10," *NTS* 10 (1964) 410-16; P. K. Jewett, *Man as Male and Female: A Study in Sexual Relationships from a Theological Point of View* (Grand Rapids: Eerdmans, 1975); C. S. Keener, *And Marries Another: Divorce and Remarriage in the Teaching of the NT* (Peabody, MA: Hendrickson, 1991); idem, *Paul, Women and Wives: Marriage and Women's Ministry in the Letters of Paul* (Peabody, MA: Hendrickson, 1992); G. W. Knight, III, *The NT Teaching on the Role Relationship of Men and Women* (Grand Rapids: Baker, 1977); R. S. Kraemer, *Maenads, Martyrs, Matrons, Monastics: A Sorcebook on Women's Religions in the Greco-Roman World* (Philadelphia: Fortress, 1988); R. C. Kroeger and C. C. Kroeger, *I Suffer Not a Woman: Rethinking 1 Timothy 2:11-15 in Light of Ancient Evidence* (Grand Rapids: Baker, 1992); M. R. Lefkowitz and M. B. Fant, *Women's Life in Greece and Rome* (Baltimore, MD: Johns Hopkins, 1982); R. MacMullen, "Women in Public in the Roman Empire," *Historia* 29 (1980) 209-18; C. J. Martin, "The Haustafeln (Household Codes) in African American Biblical Interpretation: 'Free Slaves' and 'Subordinate Women,' " in *Stony the Road We Trod: African American Biblical Interpretation*, ed. C. H. Felder (Minneapolis: Fortress, 1990) 206-31; W. A. Meeks, "The Image of the Androgyne: Some Uses of a Symbol in Earliest Christianity," *History of Religions* 13 (1974) 165-208; A. Mickelsen, ed., *Women, Authority and the Bible* (Downers Grove, IL: InterVarsity, 1986); A. Padgett, "The Pauline Rationale for Submission: Biblical Feminism and the *Hina* Clauses of Titus 2:1-10," *EvQ* 59 (1987) 39-52; J. Peradotto and J. P. Sullivan, ed., *Women in the Ancient World: The Arethusa Papers* (SUNY Series in Classical Studies; Albany, NY: State University of New York, 1984); S. B. Pomeroy, *Goddesses, Whores, Wives, and Slaves: Women in Classical Antiquity* (New York: Schocken, 1975); B. Rawson, "The Roman Family," in *The Family in Ancient Rome: New Perspectives*, ed. B. Rawson (Ithaca, NY: Cornell, 1986) 1-57; S. Safrai, "Home and Family," in *The Jewish People in the First Century*, ed. S. Safrai et al. (CRINT 1.2; Philadelphia: Fortress, 1976) 728-92; D. M. Scholer, "Women's Adornment: Some Historical and Hermeneutical Observations on the New Testament Passages," *Daughters of Sarah* 6 (1980) 3-6; R. Scroggs, "Paul and the Eschatological Woman," *JAAR* 40 (1972) 283-303; A. B. Spencer, *Beyond the Curse: Women Called to Ministry* (Peabody, MA: Hendrickson, 1989); L. Swidler, *Women in Judaism: The Status of Women in Formative Judaism* (Metuchen, NJ: Scarecrow, 1976); G. Theissen, *The Social Setting of Pauline Christianity* (Philadelphia: Fortress, 1982); C. L. Thompson, "Hairstyles, Head-Coverings and St. Paul: Portraits from Roman Corinth," *BA* 51 (1988) 101-15; D. C. Verner, *The Household of God: The Social World of the Pastoral Epistles* (SBLDS 71; Chico, CA: Scholars, 1983).

C. S. Keener

# MAN OF LAWLESSNESS AND RESTRAINING POWER

The man of lawlessness is mentioned in just one passage in the whole of Scripture, namely the place where Paul writes to the Thessalonians to correct the view that "the day of the Lord" has already arrived (2 Thess 2:2). Paul assures his readers that before the Lord's* return "the man of lawlessness" (2 Thess 2:3, 8; KJV "the man of sin") must appear. He says further that this lawless one is "the son of perdition," that he is strongly opposed to God,* that he even sits in the Temple* claiming to be God, that there is a power restraining him and that when that power is removed the Lord Jesus will destroy him (2 Thess 2:3-8). This man has not appeared, Paul argues, and therefore "the day of the Lord" could not have come.

1. The Man of Lawlessness
2. The Restraining Power

### 1. The Man of Lawlessness.

At the Reformation some held that the man of lawlessness was the papacy (see the Preface to KJV), but this polemical view is not now held. Some have thought that Paul meant the Roman emperor* (Caligula? Nero?) or perhaps the whole line of emperors. The emperors were certainly opposed to the church and they even claimed divinity. Caligula wanted to have an image of himself set up in the Temple at Jerusalem, but he died before this could be done (A.D. 41; cf. Mt 24:15; Dan 9:27; 11:31; 12:11). But in any case, setting up an image is not the same as sitting there himself. Moreover Paul was clearly referring to an eschatological figure, one who will appear at the end of the age, not to a contemporary. Other suggestions are that he would be an incarnation of Satan* or someone falsely claiming to be the Messiah. But none of these suggestions carries conviction. We do not know enough to say more than that Paul was referring to the supreme embodiment of evil and that it will take place at the end of this age when there will be a great apostasy* from the church and when evil will be strong (*see* Apocalypticism; Eschatology).

## 2. The Restraining Power.

Paul says that his readers know "what restrains, so that he may be revealed in his own time" (2 Thess 2:6). "What restrains" is neuter (*to katechon*) in verse 6, but "he who restrains" in verse 7 is masculine (*ho katechōn*). This seems to many to point to the Roman Empire, which might be spoken of in itself (neuter) or in the person of its emperor (masculine). One of the emperors, usually Nero, is sometimes seen as the man of lawlessness. The emperor in question could not make his appearance on the world stage until his predecessor was removed from the scene. But is this Paul's meaning? Nothing the apostle says really indicates contemporary Rome, and in fact not only Nero but the whole Roman empire has now passed away and the end of this age has not come.

Another view is that Paul was referring to some contemporary view about the end time. Various myths are cited to show that many people expected great conflicts at the end of time, and Paul is held to refer to one such speculation. In the nature of the case this cannot be decisively refuted. But we know of nothing in ancient literature that fits what Paul is saying and to speculate that something of what has perished would give the necessary identification is hazardous. As far as our knowledge goes, there was nothing in contemporary speculation that would fit Paul's words.

O. Cullmann (supported, for example, by A. L. Moore and J. Munck) suggests that the church's missionary preaching is in mind; Paul's mission* to the Gentiles* must be completed before the end comes. Perhaps. But who is "*he* who restrains?" Cullmann suggests the apostle himself, but this is unconvincing. We have no reason for thinking that Paul held that he

himself was holding back the man of lawlessness. And the preaching of the gospel* scarcely presupposes a great falling away. I. H. Marshall has introduced a variation of this view in suggesting that the "present opportunity for preaching and hearing the gospel" is that which restrains, and "he who restrains" is "the angelic* figure who is now in charge." When this figure withdraws, "the power of evil . . . will be openly manifested so as to produce the final showdown" (Marshall, 199-200). But Paul is otherwise silent about such an angelic figure.

C. H. Giblin has argued that what is meant is a force of evil, "a present and persistent threat to faith" (Giblin, 230). But it is not easy to see the restraining power as a force for evil. One would have thought that a force for evil would be something that prepares the way for Satan rather than something that must be removed before the evil one's henchman makes his appearance.

B. B. Warfield, identifying the man of lawlessness sitting in the temple of God with Jesus' reference to the "abomination of desolation" (Mt 24:15) and the fall of Jerusalem* (cf. the divine wrath* to befall the "Jews" in 1 Thess 2:16), thought of the Jewish state as the restraining power with perhaps James* of Jerusalem as the masculine restrainer (Warfield, 471-74). But it is not easy to see how either could hold back the coming of the man of lawlessness. Warfield saw the line of Roman emperors as the persecuting power let loose by the destruction of the Jewish state. But despite the learning with which this case is argued, it seems impossible to accept it.

It has sometimes been held that what is meant is the presence of the church* and of the Holy Spirit* in the church. But it is not easy to see either the church or the Spirit in Paul's words and it is more than a little difficult to see how or why the Holy Spirit should be taken away.

Probably our best understanding is that the restrainer of evil is the principle of order. The neuter would refer to the general principle and the masculine to its personification. In Paul's day the principle was seen in the Roman system of law and its personification in the emperor (*see* Legal System, Roman). Similar applications are evident in other systems of law. The rule of "the man of lawlessness" will take place when the rule of law ceases to operate. "The civil power is set up as a bulwark against the powers of chaos, but it can only keep these powers in check, never really subdue them. The fight against them will never come to an end, and in the end it must succumb to their final onslaught" (Stauffer, 85).

Paul sees the climax of Satan's opposition to the

things of God as coming at the end of time. And he is confident that God will then defeat all the forces of evil.

*See also* APOCALYPTICISM; ESCHATOLOGY; THESSALONIANS, LETTERS TO THE; TRIUMPH.

BIBLIOGRAPHY. R. D. Aus, "God's Plan and God's Power: Isaiah 66 and the Restraining Factors of 2 Thess 2:6-7," *JBL* 96 (1977) 537-53; O. Betz, "Der *Katechon*," *NTS* 9 (1962-63) 279-91; W. Bousset, *The Antichrist Legend* (London: Hutchinson, 1896); F. F. Bruce: *1 & 2 Thessalonians* (WBC 45; Waco: Word, 1982); O. Cullmann, "Le caractère eschatologique du devoir missionnaire et de la conscience apostolique de saint Paul. Étude sur le κατέχον (-ων) de 2 Thess. 2:6-7," *RHPR* 16 (1936) 210-45; D. Ford, *The Abomination of Desolation in Biblical Eschatology* (Washington, DC: University Press of America, 1979); C. H. Giblin, *The Threat to Faith* (AnBib 31; Rome: Pontifical Biblical Institute, 1967); I. H. Marshall, *1 and 2 Thessalonians* (NCB; Grand Rapids: Eerdmans, 1983); A. L. Moore, *The Parousia in the New Testament* (NovTSup 13; Leiden: E. J. Brill, 1966); L. Morris, *The First and Second Epistles to the Thessalonians* (NICNT; 2d ed.; Grand Rapids: Eerdmans, 1991); J. Munck, *Paul and The Salvation of Mankind* (Atlanta: John Knox, 1959) 36-42; E. Stauffer, *New Testament Theology* (London: SCM, 1955); W. Trilling, *Der Zweite Brief an die Thessalonicher* (EKKNT; Neukirchen-Vluyn: Neukirchener, 1980) 81-105; G. Vos, *The Pauline Eschatology* (Grand Rapids: Eerdmans, 1953); C. A. Wanamaker, *1 & 2 Thessalonians* (NIGTC; Grand Rapids: Eerdmans, 1990) 249-57; B. B. Warfield, "The Prophecies of St. Paul" [1886] in *Biblical and Theological Studies*, ed. S. G. Craig (Philadelphia: Presbyterian & Reformed, 1952) 463-502.

L. Morris

**MANUSCRIPTS.** *See* TEXTUAL CRITICISM.

**MARANATHA.** *See* LITURGICAL ELEMENTS.

**MARCION.** *See* CANON; PAUL IN EARLY CHURCH TRADITION.

## MARRIAGE AND DIVORCE, ADULTERY AND INCEST

Paul did not write treatises on the subjects of marriage, divorce, adultery or incest, and, were it not for problems in some of the churches he had founded that specifically concerned these matters, he might have made no reference to any of them at all. But there were problems and there were questions, and as a result Paul, as an apostle* of Jesus Christ, addressed these problems and questions and gave his answers to them.

1. Background
2. Marriage
3. Divorce
4. Adultery
5. Incest

### 1. Background.

Paul was born, lived, worked and traveled in the Greco-Roman world. Although it is a matter of debate as to how much of Paul's thinking was shaped by this world, one should at least take passing note of its views about marriage, divorce, adultery and incest.

*1.1. Greco-Roman World.* Marriage in Roman times was held to be monogamous and for life, "a life-long partnership, and a sharing of civil and religious rights" (Modestinus *Digesta* 23.2.1). And yet marriage, while it was usually terminated by death, could also be brought to an end by the will of one or both of the parties involved if marital affection (*affectio maritalis*) ceased to exist between them. Legal divorce proceedings were not required—a simple oral or written notification was sufficient, and under the Empire divorce was as readily available to the wife as to the husband. Adultery, usually rather narrowly defined as sexual intercourse of a married woman with a man other than her husband, was viewed as a serious crime, perhaps because it was thought to be a gross invasion of a husband's property rights, and was punished with severe penalties—at times with death to the wife and her partner or more often with the banishment of both from home and community (cf. *Lex Iulia de adulteriis coercendis*, c. 18 B.C.). Laws were enacted that forbade the marriage of one class of people to another. Of special interest here are those laws or sanctions that prohibited persons from marrying other persons of near relationship, whether natural or adoptive—this kind of *conubium* was not acceptable in a well-ordered society (see *OCD*, 8, 539-540; *RE* 14.2259-86).

*1.2. Judaism.* Although Paul was born into the Roman world, he was also born into a Jewish home that rigidly adhered to Jewish beliefs and customs (Phil 3:5-6), and for whom the Torah was the prime source of instruction. He attended the school of Hillel, studied under Rabbi Gamaliel (Acts 22:3) and joined the order of strict observance of the Law,* the Pharisaic order (cf. Phil 3:5-6). So although Paul may indeed have been acquainted with what was taught and practiced in the Greco-Roman world of which he was a part, yet it is likely that both his thinking and his way of life were shaped more by a Judaism informed principally by the OT than they were shaped by Greco-Roman ideas (*see* Jew, Paul the).

*1.2.1. Marriage.* For the discussion here it is important to note that the OT writers held to a high view of marriage. No doubt this was true because they understood marriage to be the perpetuation of that fundamental social unit which God was said to have created when he formed one man from the dust of the ground and fashioned one woman from him and brought her to him to be his sole partner, thus becoming "one flesh" with him (Gen 2:21-24; cf. 1:27-28). It is true that customs and practices are recorded in the OT that fall far short of this ideal, such as polygamy, concubinage, the wife considered to be the property of her husband, the husband seen as the master of his wife. Nevertheless the accounts of monogamous marriages of significant persons such as Noah, Isaac and Joseph, the numerous narratives of husbands treating their wives with love, respect, equality and faithfulness, and the many statements indicating that domestic happiness and prosperity are tied directly to monogamy, fidelity and respect show that the ideal was never lost and that many of God's people strove to make this ideal a reality in practice (cf. 2 Kings 4:8-25; Ps 128; Prov 31; Eccles 9:9; Mal 2:14; cf. also Sir 25:1, 8; 26:1-4, 13-18).

*1.2.2. Divorce and Remarriage.* Hence, divorce was perceived as something contrary to God's original intent for the welfare of the covenant community and as an action hated by God (Mal 2:16 NIV). Nevertheless, the OT did make allowances for the willful stubbornness of human beings (cf. Mk 10:5), and thus both divorce and the remarriage of divorced persons were permitted (Deut 24:1-4). It seems that in the history of ancient Israel divorce proceedings could only be initiated by the husband (but cf. Ex 21:11), for rather unspecified reasons and with relative ease. Note the following: If the husband were to find "some indecent thing" (Heb *'erwaṭ dābār*, LXX *aschēmon pragma*) in his wife, he was simply required to write her a certificate of divorce and send her from his house (Deut 24:1-4; cf. Is 50:1; Jer 3:8; see Hos 2:2 for a simple form of such a certificate).

*1.2.3. Adultery.* Quite contrary to modern ideas and practice, adultery in the OT was not considered to be grounds for divorce. Rather, death—usually by stoning, but also by burning (Lev 20:10; Gen 38:24)—was the consequence for such infidelity both for the adulterous wife and her paramour (Deut 22:22-24). The severity of this punishment was because adultery struck against "the foundations and personal rights of marriage and family" and "against the law of God (Ex 20:14) and so threatened the basis of the people's existence" (Reisser, 582-83) as the covenant people of God (see Deut 22:22).

*1.2.4. Forbidden Marriages.* OT Law forbade marriage to and the having of sexual intercourse with any close relation (cf. Lev 18:6-18). After the return from the Exile the leaders of Israel ruled against marriage to "outsiders" and took a vow on behalf of the citizens of the nation of Israel that they would not permit their daughters to be given in marriage to the sons of the people of the nations around them, nor would they permit the taking of the daughters of these foreigners for their sons (Neh 10:30). Such marriages, it was believed, posed a deadly threat to Israel's faith in the one true God (cf. Ex 34:16; Ezra 10:5; Neh 13:23-27; Mal 2:11).

*1.3. Jesus.* Paul was also familiar with the tradition about Jesus. Hence, what Jesus said about marriage and divorce and adultery must also have provided background for the answers he gave to his churches (*see* Jesus, Sayings of).

*1.3.1. Marriage.* Jesus reaffirmed the ideal for marriage laid down in the beginning. He passed over all intervening history and what may have happened or had been sanctioned in this interim and took his questioners and listeners back to creation. Jesus said to them, "In the beginning he [God] made them male and female. For this reason a man will leave his father and mother and will be joined to his wife, and the two will be one flesh, so that they are no longer two but one flesh" (Mk 10:6-7; cf. Gen 1:27; 2:24). And then he added his own new word of command based on what was implied but not made explicit in the ancient biblical texts, "No one ever is to break apart that which God has linked together" (Mk 10:9). Jesus thus taught that marriage was a divine institution, owning the blessing of God. It was to be monogamous, lifelong and an unparalleled spiritual oneness of two people— a man and a woman—so united by God that they are no longer two but one.

*1.3.2. Celibacy.* Singleness, or celibacy, was also an option for Jesus. According to the gospel records he chose that way of life for himself. He never married. And he taught that others, too, had the ability to accept celibacy for the sake of the kingdom of God. From all existing data Jesus did not advocate this as the preferred way of life. Rather he viewed celibacy as a *charism*, as a gift bestowed (*dedotai*) on certain people by God (see Mt 19:10-12).

*1.3.3. Adultery.* Jesus stood with the Law against adultery, fully supporting the ancient command, "Thou shalt not commit adultery!" But he went beyond it in two significant ways: (1) Jesus said that the man who looks at a woman for the express purpose of lusting for her (*pros to epithymēsai autēn*) has already committed adultery with her (Mt 5:27-28). Thus for him such a culpable act as adultery can be committed in the mind as well as in the bed. And (2) Jesus also said that any man who divorces his wife and marries another woman commits adultery, or any woman who divorces her husband and marries another man commits adultery (cf. Mk 10:11).

In sum, Jesus saw the ideal for marriage as two people, a man and a woman, being yoked together in a union so permanent and inviolable that only God has the right to dissolve it. Hence he deplored divorce and forbade remarriage. And yet one should be careful not to treat these words of Jesus as unyielding, iron-clad, legal prescriptions that permit no exceptions ever. For already within the Gospel record this high standard was modified when the ideal was applied to real-life situations where all the characteristic human frailties, even of Christians, came to light (Mt 19:9; cf. Mt 5:32).

As a person acquainted with the Roman world of which he was a citizen, as a person who was a Jew by birth and training, and as a devoted follower and apostle of Jesus Christ,* Paul was heir to all these traditions. From them he forged his ideas about marriage, divorce, adultery and incest.

## 2. Marriage.
Paul's view of marriage is multifaceted and somewhat complex. His remarks need careful examination.

*2.1. Marriage as Inviolable and Permanent.* In simplest terms Paul considered that marriage was for life and that this union was to be maintained as inviolable. This idea of marriage was so much a part of Paul that almost without thinking he could use it as an illustration while discussing another subject altogether. He wrote: "Are you unaware, my brothers and sisters, that the law lords it over a person as long as that person is alive. For example, the Law binds a woman to her husband as long as her husband is living, . . . but if her husband dies she is free from that law" (Rom 7:1-3).

Paul reiterates this same understanding of the life-long permanence of the marriage union, repeating and affirming the law of Christ (for that seems to be *the* law he had in mind in Rom 7:1-2; see Law of Christ) concerning such a union, when he addresses problems in the Corinthian church: "I issue this command to those [Christians] who are married—no, not I, but the Lord—a wife is not to separate herself from [divorce?] her husband; but if she does separate herself from him, she must remain unmarried or be reconciled to her husband, and the husband must not divorce his wife" (1 Cor 7:10-11; cf. Mk 10:11; but see Murphy-O'Connor, 601-2).

*2.2. Headship and Mutuality in Marriage.* For the purposes of establishing order within any Christian societal group, small or large, Paul was prepared to say that within the marriage relationship the husband is the head* of his wife (1 Cor 11:3; see Man and Woman). Here he reflected the cultural customs of his times and his own understanding of the divine order. He nevertheless rejected any notion that the husband thus was lord over or master of his wife with the right to do to her or with her as he wished. On the contrary, he cut across many of the cultural norms of his day and stressed the equality that exists between husband and wife and the mutual responsibility that each has to the other. He wrote "The husband must give his wife what is due to her, and the wife equally must give the husband his due. The wife cannot claim her body as her own; it is her husband's. Equally, the husband cannot claim his body as his own; it is his wife's" (1 Cor 7:3-4 NEB). "For Paul the marriage bed is both unitive (cf. 6:16) and an illustration that the two belong to one another in total mutuality" (Fee, 280).

This idea of mutuality within the marriage bond is once again articulated in Ephesians where both Christian husbands and Christian wives are urged to subject themselves to one another out of reverence for and obligation to Christ (Eph 5:21)—wives to husbands (Eph 5:22) and, by implication, husbands to wives in love (Eph 5:25). But it seems clear from the whole of this passage that once again

> mutual submission coexists with a hierarchy of roles within the [Christian] household. Believers should not insist on getting their own way, so there is a general sense in which husbands are to have a submissive attitude to wives, putting their wives' interests before their own. But this does not eliminate the more specific [role] in which wives are to submit to husbands. (Lincoln, 366; but see Kroeger, 267-83)

On the other hand, a Christian husband, described here as "head of his wife," to whom his wife is to submit (see also Col 3:18; Tit 2:5; cf. 1 Pet 3:1), is not given license to rule his wife, but he is ordered to love* his wife with self-sacrificing love—the same kind of love that Christ had for the church.* In this sense, then, the husband in actuality also submits himself to his wife as she to him, for he puts himself at her service.* According to Paul, then, any exercise of headship on the part of the husband in relation to his wife is to be actualized not through self-assertion but through self-sacrifice.

*2.3. Marriage, Christ and His Church.* Further, it is also clear from Ephesians 5:22-33 that Paul's view of the marriage relationship is extremely high. The OT prophets had magnificently and boldly described the covenantal union between God and Israel in terms of marriage (cf. Ezek 16:8), thus heralding the sacredness and honorableness of marriage. In this same tradition Paul proclaims the sacredness and honorableness of marriage by boldly using the marriage bond between husband and wife as an analogy of the bond that has been forged between Christ and the believing community. "This is a profound mystery," he writes about marriage, "but I am talking about Christ and the church" (Eph 5:32). Why, of all human institutions that existed at that time, did he select the institution of marriage to illustrate the relationship between the believing community and its Lord? The answer would seem to be that Paul held marriage in high esteem as the perfect example of *henōsis*, a "oneness" forged between two by the unifying power of love.

*2.4. Marriage or Asceticism?* Because Paul held marriage in high regard and was true to his own Jewish heritage ("It is not good for a man to be alone," Gen 2:18), he considered the married state to be the normal and expected state for people within the Christian church (cf. Eph 5:22-33; Col 3:18-19; 1 Tim 3:2). For this reason he struck out against those who forbade people to marry (1 Tim 4:3). Hence, the abruptly introduced words in 1 Corinthians 7:1, literally: "It is good for a man not to touch a woman" (meaning, "It is good for a man not to have sexual intercourse with a woman," cf. Gen 20:6 [LXX]; Ruth 2:9 [LXX]; Prov 6:29 [LXX]) must *not* be understood as reflecting Paul's own position on marriage. Rather, it is a slogan expressing the view of some within the church at Corinth who were advocating strict asceticism, even to the point of sexual abstinence within the marriage relationship (see Scroggs, 293-303). Paul strongly rejected this notion and forbade its implementation because of the counter-Christian and destructive practices (*porneias*, 1 Cor 7:2) he knew could result if it were adopted as the norm (cf. 1 Cor 6:13-16). Thus he struck a blow against such unnatural abstinence within the marriage bond by saying, "Let each husband be having [a euphemism for 'sexual intercourse with'; cf. Ex 2:1 LXX; Is 13:16 LXX] his own wife, and each wife be having her own husband" (1 Cor 7:2). "Thus he means, 'Let each man who is already married continue in relations with his own wife, and each wife likewise.' And that means a *full* conjugal life," which is precisely what he argues for in detail in the verses that follow (Fee, 279).

*2.5. Marriage and Church Leaders.* Paul's high evaluation of marriage is also seen in the guidelines he lays down for the one who is to fill the office of bishop. A bishop, he wrote, "must be *mias gynaikos andra*"

(1 Tim 3:2; Tit 1:6; cf. 1 Tim 5:9)—an expression that is literally translated, "husband of one wife." But this is a notoriously difficult expression, and as a consequence has led to various translations and interpretations. These are: (1) "the husband of one wife" (KJV, NASB), a translation that has been understood to mean that the bishop *must* be a married person; (2) "married to one wife only" (cf. NIV, Phillips), a translation that has been understood to mean that a polygamist could not be a bishop; (3) "married only once" (cf. NRSV, Goodspeed, Moffatt), a translation that has been understood to mean that no bishop was permitted to marry a second time, if his first wife should die; (4) "faithful to his one wife" (cf. NEB), a translation that has been understood to mean that of all people the bishop must lead an exemplary life as a married person.

Of these possible translations and interpretations the last seems best. It allows room for a bishop to be a person like Paul himself—unmarried (1 Cor 7:7; cf. 7:25-38), but at the same time, in light of Paul's high estimation of marriage, and in contradiction to the position of his opponents (1 Tim 4:3), it commends marriage to the bishop. It not only stresses the importance of marriage but at the same time strikes out against polygamy, at least implicitly, as well as divorce and remarriage. Further, it best fits the context in which it appears (1 Tim 3:2; Tit 1:6), for the emphasis here is not so much on the status of the bishop as upon the character of the bishop (see Houlden, 78; Scott, 31; *see* Church Order and Government; Ministry).

*2.6. Marriage and Times of Crisis.* While Paul championed the normalcy of marriage, even counseling younger widows to re-marry (cf. 1 Tim 5:14), he nevertheless envisioned times of crisis or distress when marriage might not be the best course of action for people to take (1 Cor 7:26). What kinds of crises Paul had in mind when he gave such advice may have been clear to the Corinthian* church, but it is no longer clear to any who might read this same letter today. Hence, it is presumptuous to state what these particularly stressful situations might have been for the purpose of providing some sort of rule book for contemporary action. The most one can do is to point out that Paul, without surrendering his high view of marriage, did on occasion advise against it, when certain grave circumstances warranted that kind of restraint, and to use such advice simply as a guiding principle for life in the church, not as a binding rule for any segment of its people.

*2.7. The Option of Celibacy.* Like Jesus, Paul also believed and taught that celibacy instead of marriage was a legitimate option for Christians. He taught that celibacy provided advantages to the one who would choose such a way of life for the sake of the kingdom of God, advantages not always available to the one who is married (1 Cor 7:32-35; cf. Mt 19:10-12). Paul himself was celibate and free from those legitimate and requisite responsibilities of caring for a wife that of necessity would have restricted his activity as an apostle. But he, no doubt familiar with the words of Jesus, also recognized that celibacy was a *charism*, a gift* from God (1 Cor 7:7), and that it was not for everyone, even though he might wish it were for everyone in light of his understanding of the vastness of the mission* and the shortness of the time available (1 Cor 7:26-35, esp. 7:26 and 29; cf. Mt 19:11).

*2.8. Marriage with an Unbeliever.* In the tradition of some of the writers of the OT, Paul stood firmly opposed to mixed marriages—marriages between believers and unbelievers—and no doubt for precisely the same reason that burdened his OT predecessors. Like those ancient writers, perhaps, he too foresaw far greater potential for the believing spouse being turned away from following after God by the one who had no faith than for the believing partner converting the unbelieving partner (cf. Deut 7:3-4; Ezra 9:12; Neh 10:30; 13:25). This was a tragedy he wished Christians to avoid at all costs. Hence his words opposing such a union come in the form of a harsh negative command and a rhetorical question: "Do not be yoked together (*mē ginesthe heterozygountes*) with unbelievers. For what do righteousness and wickedness have in common? Or what fellowship can light have with darkness?" (2 Cor 6:14 NIV). Such an interpretation of this Corinthian text may be putting too fine a point on it, narrowing it too severely (as Martin, 197, cautions). Nevertheless, it is interesting to note that the word translated here, "yoked together" (better, "mis-yoked," *hetero-zygeō*), has essentially the same root as the word Jesus used when, in speaking of marriage, he said "That which God yoked together [*sy-zeugnymi*] no person must break apart" (Mk 10:9). So it is correct to see marriage as at least one kind, if not the only kind, of mismating that Paul had in mind.

## 3. Divorce.

Paul had little to say about divorce, simply because for him marriage was a lifelong covenant relationship between husband and wife that found its basis in the Genesis account of the creation of man and woman (Gen 2:24; cf. Rom 7:2-3).

*3.1. Marriage: Ideals and Concessions.* Like Jesus before him, however, Paul realized that life brings people situations in which the ideal is not always attain-

able, even by the redeemed. Hence, when he addresses a particular impending crisis (*ean chōristhē* [1 Cor 7:11; cf. BDF 373]) where one of the women in the Corinthian church seems to have been about to "separate herself/divorce herself" (*chōristhēnai*) from her husband (1 Cor 7:10), he counters this threat with a word of Jesus and an implication drawn from it: "she is not to divorce herself from her husband (cf. Mk 10:12); but if she does she must remain unmarried" (1 Cor 7:10-11).

From this statement of Paul it may be inferred that when the church moved out into the Greco-Roman world, Christian women, like their pagan counterparts, found themselves culturally free to divorce their husbands. This freedom had not been a part of the Jewish milieu from which Christianity sprang, where the privilege of divorce belonged only to the husband (cf. *m. Yebam.* 14:1). This same statement also makes it clear that, although women in general were culturally free to divorce their husbands, women as Christians were not free to do so. The word of Jesus, their Lord, that forbade divorce stood as a command (*parangellō*) against their exercise of such freedom— a command that applied equally to Christian husbands as to wives (1 Cor 7:11).

Paul, while holding to the ideal situation—"no divorce"—nevertheless concedes (as did Jesus) that it is possible that a divorce will take place in spite of any command against it. What then? Once more Paul advocates the same standard that was set forth by Jesus under similar circumstances: if divorce does take place (is permitted) then there is to be no re-marriage (so as to avoid committing adultery, cf. Mk 10:11-12; Mt 5:31; 19:9; Lk 16:18). The divorced person must remain unmarried. And if this state of affairs cannot be endured, then the apostolic authoritative command is for the parties to be reconciled, she to her husband and he to his wife (1 Cor 7:11). This then is the goal for marriage set out by Jesus (preserved for us in Mark's Gospel) and toward which Paul emphatically encouraged all Christians to strive: No divorce; but if divorce occurs, then no remarriage to a different partner.

*3.2. The Exceptions.* But just as the ideal for marriage that Jesus set forth (cf. Mk 10:8-12) was early modified by an exception (cf. Mt 5:31; 19:9), thus freeing the "innocent" partner from the marriage bond and providing legitimate grounds for remarriage, so Paul establishes still another exception for similarly troubled Corinthian Christians. What happens if a husband who comes to faith in Christ now finds himself married to a wife who does not share that same faith? Or what if a believing wife now finds herself married to an unbelieving husband? Paul's answer to this question is consistent with what he said earlier: believers must initiate *no* change in their marital status—not even in situations like this that might cause them to think (incorrectly) that they have grounds for divorce (cf. 2 Cor 6:14; cf. 1 Cor 6:15-16). The believer is still bound to his or her spouse until that bond is dissolved by death as long as the unbelieving partner agrees to live together as husband or wife with the Christian partner. But it is at this point that Paul, by inspiration, allows still one more exception to the marriage ideal. He writes, "If an unbelieving husband (or wife) initiates a divorce, breaks (*chōrizetai*) the marriage union [this must be at least part of Paul's meaning here in light of Jesus' word about marriage in Mark 10:9—"Let no person break it apart" (*mē chōrizetō*)], and abandons his or her marriage partner, the Christian is to let the break take place and let that partner go. In situations such as this the Christian husband or wife is *not bound* [*ou dedoulōtai*]" (1 Cor 7:15).

These two words of Paul, "not bound," the new exception now added to the rule "No divorce! But if divorce does occur, no remarriage," have generated considerable debate (see bibliography). There is no consensus about precisely what Paul meant. Nevertheless, they are taken here to mean that Paul was saying to the Christian husband or wife, "If you find yourself in circumstances like this—abandoned by your non-Christian spouse—you are no longer bound by the constraints of the divinely given laws that govern marriage. You are free to marry again" (but see Fee, 303, who argues rather extensively against such an interpretation only to conclude his remarks by writing, "All of this is not to say that Paul *disallows* remarriage in such cases; he simply does not speak to it at all").

The exception to the marriage ideal that Paul offers here was the apostle's solution to a particular real-life situation that had arisen in a particular church in a particular place at a particular time. Therefore, one cannot help but ask whether it is possible that Paul may have authorized still other exceptions to the marriage ideal when very different, but equally serious ruptures of the union between husband and wife, were brought to him for an authoritative answer? Is it possible to infer from the fact that two exceptions to the marriage ideal are already found within the boundaries of the sacred canon—one in Matthew's Gospel (Mt 5:32; 19:9) and one here in Paul's letter to the Corinthians, both of which reinforced the sanctity of marriage by dissolving travesties against it—that other exceptions might also fall in line with these? Marital unfaithfulness (*porneia*, Mt 19:9, a word with a wide range of meaning; see Blomberg, 195-96) and

the abandonment of the believing partner by the unbeliever were seen as destroying and dissolving the marriage union and freeing the wronged or abandoned partner to remarry without committing adultery. Is it possible to extrapolate from this that other such marital travesties, although not identical to these (e.g., cruelty, desertion, physical abuse, the systematic psychological destruction of one's marriage partner, and the like), might also have been included as exceptions to the ideal had only authoritative responses to such abuses been written down and preserved by the church?

There is no agreed-upon answer to these questions. It is sufficient to say that, although the exception which Paul added to the one in the Jesus tradition may seem to point in the direction of the possibility of other exceptions being envisioned, there is no evidence within the Pauline corpus of the slightest encouragement for Christians to act unilaterally in such matters and to decide to divorce on their own initiative. Therefore, from this it may be inferred that any plan to divorce must not be made independently of the community of faith or apart from the advice and support of the authorized leaders of the church (*see* Church Order).

## 4. Adultery.

Paul says very little about the subject of adultery, perhaps because he knows that as heirs to the OT people of God Christians for the most part are already quite convinced that adultery is out of bounds for them. But what Paul does say makes it clear that he considers adultery to be a destructive perversion of the divine ideal and stands under God's curse.*

Paul never defines adultery. But if he had, he most certainly would have expanded its definition beyond that of sexual intercourse between a married woman with a man other than her husband. He would also have defined adultery as sexual intercourse between a married man with a woman other than his wife—quite contrary to the norms of sexual morality in the Roman world (see 1.1 above). Paul never tolerated a double standard—one for the husband, another for the wife—when it came to matters of conjugal rights and responsibilities that each shared with the other (1 Cor 7:3-4). From this it may correctly be inferred that "the apostolic message from the very outset made it clear to the churches that the full marital fidelity of both spouses is an unconditional divine command" (Hauck, 734; cf. 1 Cor 6:9; *see* Sexuality).

Because Paul held to the same high ideal of marriage to which Jesus held, he likewise, with one exception (see above), considered that the remarriage of a divorced man or the remarriage of a divorced woman was the equivalent to committing adultery (cf. Rom 7:3 with Mk 10:11-12). Thus he added his apostolic authority* to that of Jesus, whose critique of adultery reached a level never before articulated.

The tragic seriousness of adultery, in that it is a violation of the will of God, can be seen from Paul's severe pronouncement that those who commit adultery will not inherit the kingdom* of God (1 Cor 6:9). The severity of his judgment is because adultery destroys the very fabric of the marriage union, tears asunder the *henōsis*, the oneness, that God had planned for marriage, and is one thing that has the potential of fracturing what Jesus said no one ever should break apart. It must be noted, however (not to alter in the least Paul's view of the heinousness of adultery, or to weaken the harshness of his judgment against it) that always his severity was tempered by the tender heart of a pastor who wished for and strove to bring about the repentance of the sinner and the sinner's full restoration to the believing community (*see* Discipline). This was the case even for the sinner whose sin may have been that of sexual perversity (cf. 1 Cor 5:1-5 with 2 Cor 2:5-9; see Martin, 33-38; Lampe, 353-54; cf. also 2 Cor 12:21).

## 5. Incest.

There is only one instance recorded in Paul's letters where incest is addressed: "a man has his father's wife" (1 Cor 5:1), meaning, no doubt, that after the death of his father, a Christian man had married his father's widow, his stepmother (the expression *'išaṭ 'ab* [Gk *gynē patros* ], "father's wife," is an OT and rabbinic designation for a stepmother; cf. Lev 18:8, Str-B 3.343, noted by Conzelmann, 96). Paul's reaction to this sexual relation is one of dismay, anger and judgment.* (1) He terms this union *porneia*—not itself the word for incest, but a word, while wide-ranging in its meaning, nevertheless primarily describes grievous, perverse, unlawful sexual acts, that would include incestuous acts. Christians must flee from *porneia*, for it is counter to the holy Law of God and comes under his judgment (cf. 1 Cor 6:13, 18; 2 Cor 12:21; Gal 5:19-21; Eph 5:3; Col 3:5; 1 Thess 4:3). (2) He speaks of the sin* of this man as being so perverse that it does not even occur among pagans. Even the Romans had laws which forbade such action (see 1.1 above). (3) And finally, because of the seriousness of this sin, he instructs the church corporate to put this person out of the fellowship, into the realm of wrath, and into the hands of Satan.* He is to be given over to death (cf. 1 Cor 11:30; see Käsemann). Once again, it is important to note that such severity always has a redemptive

purpose in mind—so that the church may be maintained pure and so that the sinner may be saved (1 Cor 5:5, 7).

*See also* ETHICS; HEAD, HEADSHIP; HOMOSEXUALITY; HOUSEHOLDS, HOUSEHOLD CODES; MAN AND WOMAN; SEXUALITY, SEXUAL ETHICS.

BIBLIOGRAPHY. C. J. Barber, "Marriage, Divorce or Remarriage: A Review of the Relevant Religious Literature," *Journal of Psychology and Theology* 12 (1984) 170-77; C. L. Blomberg, "Marriage, Divorce, Remarriage, and Celibacy," *TJ* 11 (1990) 161-96; V. P. Boyer, *Divorce and Remarriage* (Stow, OH: Cre-Com, 1976); H. Conzelmann, *I Corinthians* (Philadelphia: Fortress, 1975); J. D. M. Derrett, *Law in the New Testament* (London: Darton, Longman and Todd, 1978); G. Duty, *Divorce and Remarriage* (Minneapolis: Bethany Fellowship, 1967); J. K. Elliott, "Paul's Teaching on Marriage in 1 Corinthians: Some Problems Considered," *NTS* 19 (1972-1973) 219-25; S. A. Ellisen, *Divorce and Remarriage in the Church* (Grand Rapids: Zondervan, 1977); G. D. Fee, *The First Epistle to the Corinthians* (NICNT; Grand Rapids: Eerdmans, 1987); D. E. Garland, "The Christian's Posture Toward Marriage and Celibacy: 1 Corinthians 7," *RevExp* 80 (1983) 351-62; F. Hauck, "μοιχεύω κτλ," *TDNT* IV.729-35; W. A. Heth, "The Meaning of Divorce in Matthew 19:3-9," *Churchman* 98 (1984) 136-52; idem, "The Changing Basis for Permitting Remarriage after Divorce for Adultery: The Influence of R. H. Charles," *TJ* 11 (1990) 143-59; J. L. Houlden, *The Pastoral Epistles* (New York: Penguin, 1976); E. Käsemann, "Sentences of Holy Law in the New Testament," in *New Testament Questions of Today* ( Philadelphia: Fortress, 1969) 66-81; C. S. Keener, *And Marries Another: Divorce and Remarriage in the Teaching of the New Testament* (Peabody, MA: Hendrickson, 1991); C. C. Kroeger, "The Classical Concept of *Head* as 'Source,' " in *Equal to Serve*, ed. G. G. Hull (Old Tappan, NJ: Revell, 1987) 267-83; G. W. H. Lampe, "Church Discipline and the Interpretation of the Epistles to the Corinthians," in *Christian History and Interpretation*, ed. W. R. Farmer (Cambridge: University Press, 1967) 353-54; A. T. Lincoln, *Ephesians* (WBC 42; Dallas: Word, 1990); R. P. Martin, *2 Corinthians* (WBC 40; Waco: Word, 1986); J. Murphy-O'Connor, "The Divorced Woman in 1 Corinthians 7:10-11," *JBL* 100 (1981) 601-6; H. Reisser, "μοιχεύω," *NIDNTT* 2.582-83; E. F. Scott, *The Pastoral Epistles* (New York: Harper, n.d.); R. Scroggs, "Paul and the Eschatological Women," *JAAR* 40 (1972) 283-303; D. L. Smith, "Divorce and Remarriage: From the Early Church to John Wesley," *TJ* 11 (1990) 131-42; G. J. Wenham, "Gospel Definitions of Adultery and Women's Rights," *ExpT* 95 (1984) 330-32; B. Witherington, "Matthew 5:32 and

19:9—Exception or Exceptional Situation?," *NTS* 31 (1985) 571-76. G. F. Hawthorne

**MARS HILL.** *See* ATHENS, PAUL AT.

**MATURE.** *See* PERFECT, MATURE.

**MEALS, RELIGIOUS.** *See* FOOD OFFERED TO IDOLS AND JEWISH FOOD LAWS; LORD'S SUPPER; SOCIAL-SCIENTIFIC APPROACHES TO PAUL.

## MERCY

The God* Paul worshiped* and about whom he preached* is a God who is "rich in mercy" (Eph 2:4). It is fundamental to the apostle's thinking that all are sinners* (Rom 6:23) and therefore deserving of judgment,* totally unable to achieve salvation* by their own merits. When anyone is saved it is only because God is merciful. The mercy of God underlies Paul's whole message.

But God is not just merciful: he is "rich in mercy." He is "the Father of mercies and the God of all consolation" (2 Cor 1:3). We are not to think of him as one who occasionally has merciful impulses: for Paul God is essentially and wholeheartedly merciful.

1. OT Background
2. Mercy on Israel
3. Mercy as Incentive to Service

### 1. OT Background.

In the LXX the noun *eleos* is normally used for the Hebrew *ḥesed*, which has to do with the attitude of a human or of God arising out of a mutual relationship (see Andersen). *Ḥesed* is chiefly used of God's relationship with his people in which the notion of grace rather than obligation is prominent. God's *ḥesed* issues in his covenant with Israel,* and by it he refuses to abandon Israel when the nation is faithless.

God's mercy consistently manifests itself in his saving acts which consist of his forgiveness* of individuals and the nation (e.g., Deut 13:17; Ps 25:6; Hos 1:6-7), his deliverance of Israel* from enemies (e.g., Ps 69:16-18; Is 30:18) and his restoration* of the exiles (e.g., Deut 30:3; Is 49:10, 13; Jer 12:15; Ezek 39:25). God's mercy also has an eschatological dimension, for from God's *ḥesed* will flow the final forgiveness and redemption of his people (e.g., Is 54:8; 55:3; Jer 33:26).

Less frequently (six times), *eleos* is used in the LXX for the Hebrew *raḥᵃmîm* (as is *oiktirmoi*, etc.), a term which seems to denote the feeling of kinship between those born from the same womb or the maternal feeling of a mother who has given birth (*reḥem*, "womb").

### 2. Mercy on Israel.

God's dealings with Israel form for Paul the supreme example of mercy. When he is discussing the position of Israel* (Rom 9—11) he uses the verb *eleeō*, "to have mercy," eight times and the noun *eleos*, "mercy," three times. He finds God's treatment of the nation a superb illustration of his sovereign exercise of mercy.

Paul sees the divine mercy as extending to all peoples, not only to Israel. He emphasizes God's freedom to act as he wills. In making the point that salvation is God's free gift and that we sinners can do nothing to merit it, Paul quotes words of God: "I will have mercy on whom I have mercy and I will have compassion on whom I have compassion" (Rom 9:15; citing Ex 33:19). It is the mercy of God that matters, not any human will or endeavor. Indeed Paul says explicitly, "So then it is not of him who wills nor of him who runs but of God who shows mercy" (Rom 9:16). And a little later he comes back to the theme with "he has mercy on whom he wills" (Rom 9:18). No human merit avails before God. Our salvation is due to the wonder of the divine mercy.

Paul wrestles with the problem of the divine choice of some while others are subjected to "the wrath* of God" (*see* Election). He does not produce theoretical reasons why some are saved and others are lost, but he insists that there are "vessels of wrath" which, he says, are "fitted for destruction." Over against them are "vessels of mercy which God has prepared beforehand for glory" (Rom 9:23). Paul leaves no doubt about the importance of mercy for the people who are saved. They are saved not on account of merit, but because God is merciful.

It is clear from Romans 9-11 that Paul suffered agonies over the failure of his own nation to embrace the gospel* (but cf. 1 Thess 2:16). The Jews were the people of God and it was inconceivable to him that they should fail at the last. There was no doubt about their rejection of the gospel in Paul's own day, but he sees this as part of the plan of God. The Gentiles were formerly disobedient to God but have "now obtained mercy because of the disobedience" of the Jews (Rom 11:30). The Jews were "enemies"* for the sake of the Gentiles* (Rom 11:28), which appears to mean that their rejection of the gospel was the means of its being preached to the Gentile nations and of the Gentiles obtaining mercy (Rom 11:31). The Gentiles should be duly appreciative of their high privilege, and Paul looks to them to "glorify God for his mercy" (Rom 15:9). Mercy is the keynote of the whole passage.

But the Jews are also "according to election beloved on account of the fathers" (Rom 11:28). This does not mean that every individual Israelite will be saved (any more than the preaching to the Gentiles means that all Gentiles will be saved). But it does mean that in the providence of God salvation will in due course reach the Jews and they too will know the divine mercy: "God has shut all up to disobedience that he may have mercy on all" (Rom 11:32).

### 3. Mercy as Incentive to Service.

Paul speaks of himself and his coworkers* as those who had their ministry* as people who had "obtained mercy" (2 Cor 4:1), and thus that they are not to lose heart. The mercy of God has been shown to them; therefore they should engage in the service* of God. In a very different context Paul gives an opinion on "virgins" in a matter where he has no divine command to which to appeal. He gives his advice "as one who has obtained mercy from the Lord to be faithful" (1 Cor 7:25). Those who have received mercy can speak because of that mercy, and the reception of mercy leads to faithfulness. It is on the grounds of "the mercies of God" that Paul makes his appeal to the Romans (Rom 12:1).

Paul recognizes that he had not been an ideal person prior to becoming a Christian and says that he had obtained mercy "so that in me as the foremost sinner Christ might demonstrate his longsuffering" (1 Tim 1:12-16). If God could show mercy to such a one as Saul the persecutor, he can show it to anyone! At the same time Paul recognizes that his ignorance was a mitigating factor (1 Tim 1:13).

Paul finds mercy in the ordinary affairs of life. He prays for mercy (Gal 6:16), especially in his greetings (1 Tim 1:2; 2 Tim 1:2; Tit 1:4). He prays for Onesiphorus's household to find mercy (2 Tim 1:16, 18). And he sees evidence of God's mercy in the recovery of Epaphroditus from a serious illness (Phil 2:27; *see* Healing). Mercy is a quality believers should show as well as receive (Col 3:12). And Paul is anxious that they should show mercy cheerfully and not as a grim duty (Rom 12:8).

In addition to the words we naturally understand as mercy, Paul makes use of the word for "entrails" (*splanchna*), which was used for the deepest feelings and often denoted mercy. Paul mostly uses it for love and similar terms. He uses it almost in the sense of mercy when he speaks of longing for the Philippians with "the compassion of Jesus Christ" (Phil 1:8; cf. 2:1).

*See also* FORGIVENESS; GRACE; LOVE.

BIBLIOGRAPHY. F. I. Andersen, "Yahweh, the Kind and Sensitive God," in *God Who Is Rich in Mercy*, ed. P. T. O'Brien and D. G. Peterson (Sydney: Lancer, 1986) 41-48; R. Bultmann, "ἔλεος κτλ" *TDNT* II.477-87; C. H.

Dodd, *The Bible and the Greeks* (London: Hodder & Stoughton, 1935) 55-69; H.-H. Esser, "Mercy, Compassion," *NIDNTT* 2.593-601; N. Glueck, *Das Wort ḥesed im alttestamentlichen Sprachgebrauche als menschliche und göttliche gemeinschaftgemasse Verhaltungsweise* (Geissen: Alfred Töpelmann, 1927); H. Köster, "σπλάγχνον κτλ," *TDNT* VII.548-59; N. H. Snaith, *The Distinctive Ideas of the Old Testament* (London: Epworth, 1944) 94-130; H. J. Stoebe, "Die Bedeutung des Wortes Häsäd im Alten Testament," *VT* 2 (1952) 244-54.

L. Morris

**MERCY SEAT.** *See* EXPIATION, PROPITIATION, MERCY SEAT.

**MERIT.** *See* JUSTIFICATION; LAW; WORKS OF THE LAW.

**MERKABAH MYSTICISM.** *See* JEW, PAUL THE; MYSTICISM; VISIONS, ECSTATIC EXPERIENCE.

**MIDRASH.** *See* JEW, PAUL THE; OLD TESTAMENT IN PAUL.

**MIND.** *See* PSYCHOLOGY.

## MINISTRY

For the apostle* Paul, ministry included all that the exalted Christ* did and is doing through his people for the building of his church.* This involved the proper exercise of gifts* for ministry which Christ bestowed upon all his people, as well as the ministry of those who, like Paul, had been divinely appointed to establish and nurture churches. It also included those appointed by human agency to exercise leadership roles in the churches.

1. Ministry in the Pauline Churches
2. Paul as Minister
3. Eschatological Evaluation of Ministry

### 1. Ministry in the Pauline Churches.

The churches founded by Paul were "charismatic" communities, made up of individuals each of whom had received gifts of ministry to be exercised for the common good (1 Cor 12:7, 11). Some persons were appointed directly by God* to have a leadership role in the church, and their function was to equip the other members to exercise their own ministries. There is also evidence of more "official" ministries; those of bishops (overseers), elders and deacons, and of apostolic delegates as well, whose appointment was by human agency (*see* Apostle; Church Order and Government).

*1.1. Pauline Churches as "Charismatic" Communities.*

That Paul's churches were "charismatic" communities is implied in a number of places in his letters. In Galatians 3:5 the apostle asked his converts, "Does he who supplies the Spirit to you and work miracles among you [do so] by the works of the Law, or by [the] hearing of faith?" Paul's question would have had no point unless the presupposition underlying it were true, that is, that God was supplying them with the Spirit and working miracles* among them (see Holy Spirit). In 1 Thessalonians 5:19-21 Paul exhorted his readers: "Do not quench the Spirit; do not despise prophecies; but test everything." Such an exhortation presupposes a prophetic ministry inspired by the Spirit in the church at Thessalonica.* Paul's extended treatment of the *charismata* in 1 Corinthians 12—14 was in response to problems that had arisen in respect of "charismatic" ministry exercised in the church at Corinth* (see Worship).

*1.2. All Believers as "Charismatic" Ministers.* When dealing with the problems related to "charismatic" ministry in 1 Corinthians, Paul pointed out that all believers had been given one of a variety of manifestations of the Spirit to be used for the common good (1 Cor 12:4-11). These manifestations of the Spirit included the utterance of wisdom,* the utterance of knowledge,* faith,* gifts of healing,* working of miracles, prophecy,* discerning of spirits, various kinds of tongues* and the interpretation of tongues (1 Cor 12:7-10). In Romans 12:4-8 Paul stressed that believers had different gifts according to the grace* given to them. Those he listed include gifts of prophecy, service,* teaching,* exhortation, giving, leading and showing compassion. These lists were probably not meant to be exhaustive but illustrative of the manifold gifts of God to his people to facilitate the building up of his church. And this occurred when each part was working properly (Eph 4:16 NRSV), when each member of the church is using his/her gift for the common good (see Body of Christ).

*1.3. Women in Ministry.* There are many indications in the Pauline corpus that women labored alongside men in the cause of the gospel. First, there is the outstanding example of Priscilla. She and her husband, Aquila, were coworkers with Paul, and they risked their necks for his life. It was in their house that the church met, and for them all the churches of the Gentiles gave thanks (Rom 16:3-4; cf. 1 Cor 16:19; 2 Tim 4:19). Then there were Euodia and Syntyche, Paul's fellow-workers in the gospel who labored in the congregation at Philippi (Phil 4:2-3), the deacon Phoebe who served the church in Cenchreae (Rom 16:1-2), and Tryphaena and Tryphosa, workers in the Lord to whom Paul sent greetings (Rom 16:12). In addition, there was possibly a person named Junia, who, with her partner Andronicus, was "outstanding among the apostles" (Rom 16:7, although this text could be read: "They are people well known to the apostles"). Further, there is the assumption in 1 Corinthians 11:4-5 that women prophesied and prayed in the congregation.

While Paul affirmed women's ministries, texts such as 1 Corinthians 11:2-16; 14:33b-35 and 1 Timothy 2:11-15 suggest that he expected them to exercise their ministries in ways that did not undermine the headship* of their husbands at least, if not male headship in general (see Man and Woman).

*1.4. Divinely Appointed Ministers.* While Paul spoke of all believers having gifts of ministry, he also believed that certain ones had been divinely appointed to have a leadership role in the church. Thus in 1 Corinthians 12:28, for example, he says that God appointed in the church first apostles, second prophets, third teachers (and then deeds of power, gifts of healing etc.). Such a view is also reflected in Ephesians 4:11-13, where it is said that the gifts of Christ are that some would be apostles, some prophets, some evangelists, some pastors and teachers, whose task was to equip the saints for the work of ministry, for building up the body of Christ. The ministers mentioned here have a role vis-à-vis the rest of the members of the church, and function to equip them for their ministries (see Lincoln ad loc.).

*1.5. Ministers Appointed by Human Agency.* In the Pastoral* letters instructions were given to Timothy and Titus concerning the qualifications of those to be appointed as bishops, deacons and elders (1 Tim 3:1-7, 8-13; Tit 1:5-9). Such ministers were appointed by Paul and his delegates (Tit 1:5; cf. Acts 14:23). The task of the bishop involved teaching and managing the household* of God (1 Tim 3:2, 5). It would appear that the task of elders was to rule the church (1 Tim 5:17a) and that some of them also labored in preaching, teaching and refuting error (1 Tim 5:17b; Tit 1:9). No information is given concerning the actual task of deacons.

Because of the closeness of the descriptions of the tasks of bishops and elders, and because the words *elders* (*presbyteroi*) and *bishops* (*episkopoi*) appear to be used as synonyms in Titus 1:5, 7, it has generally been thought that in NT times these words were different terms for the same office. In recent times this identification has been called into question. Attention has been drawn to the fact that the early churches were house churches. Therefore, it has been suggested, the heads of households came to have supervisory responsibilities for the churches which met in their houses, and that these were the bishops of the early church (so, e.g., Theissen, Holmberg, Giles). Further, it has been suggested that as elders in the Jewish community were not synagogue officials but community leaders, so too early Christian elders were community leaders not church officials. Thus elders are to be distinguished from bishops in the NT. Bishops were the hosts of the house churches and they exercised a supervisory role over the church meeting in their houses. Elders were leaders in the Christian community, but were not necessarily hosts of house churches as well. There is the possibility that one person was both an elder (community leader) and a bishop (host of a house church) which accounts for the overlapping of the descriptions of the tasks of elders and bishops in the Pastoral Letters (Giles). If this suggestion could be shown to be correct, it would throw light upon the references to elders who rule only (community leaders only), and elders who also labor in teaching (hosts of house churches as well as community leaders).

*1.6. The Ministry of Apostolic Delegates.* Timothy and Titus appear to have functioned as delegates of the apostle Paul (1 Tim 1:3; Tit 1:5; *see* Coworkers). Timothy was instructed to counteract erroneous teaching (1 Tim 1:3-11), to order public worship* (1 Tim 2:1-15), to appoint bishops and deacons (1 Tim 3:1-13), to regulate the enrollment of widows on the list for financial* support (1 Tim 5:9-16), to ordain elders, but not hastily, (1 Tim 5:22), ensuring that they were properly remunerated and that no flippant charges were brought against them (1 Tim 5:17-21). Timothy's overall responsibilities are summed up in the instruction: "What you have heard from me through many witnesses, these things entrust to faithful people who will be able to teach others as well" (2 Tim 2:2). In other words, he was responsible to ensure the faithful handing-on of apostolic tradition to the next generation. Titus was instructed to appoint elders who were able to preach sound doctrine and refute those who contradicted it (Tit 1:5-9) and to do the same himself (Tit 1:10—2:2). He was to exhort the members of the Christian community to behave in ways that adorned the doctrine of God our Savior,* to be devoted to good works and avoid dissensions (Tit 2:3—3:11). Titus himself was to model what he taught (Tit 2:7-8).

*1.7. Charisma and Office.* Two interrelated questions are involved here. First, were the earliest Pauline churches dependent for their ministry upon "charismatic" individuals alone, there being no "official" ministers (i.e., those appointed by human agency) as well? The evidence of 1 Corinthians 12—14 seems, on first reading, to reflect a congregation that was min-

istered to only by those who were spontaneously endowed with various *charismata*. Further, Romans and 2 Corinthians give no indication that there were "official" ministers in the churches to which these letters were addressed. One might then be tempted to conclude that "official" leadership roles appeared only in a later, even post-Pauline, period when the ministry had developed away from the charismatic and spontaneous form it had earlier on (so, e.g., von Campenhausen).

However, there are difficulties with this view. For example, Paul's letter to the Philippians was addressed to the bishops and deacons (Phil 1:1), and in 1 Thessalonians 5:12 the apostle appeals to his readers to respect those who labored among them and who had charge of them. They were to esteem them highly because of their work. In 1 Corinthians 16:15-16 reference is made to the devoted service of Stephanus and others, to whom the Corinthians were urged to subject themselves. All this suggests that there were "official" ministries existing alongside the charismatic ministries in the Pauline churches from the earliest period.

This leads to a second question. If there were both charismatic and official ministries in the Pauline churches, were they antithetical to one another, as has sometimes been suggested? It is not easy to answer this question because of the scarcity of evidence. However, there are a few hints to be found, and these suggest that no such antipathy existed. For example, in the concluding chapter of his letter to the "charismatic" churches of Galatia, Paul says: "Let him who is taught the word share in all good things with the one who teaches" (Gal 6:6). This exhortation to supply the needs of the teacher is unlikely to be a request for assistance for Paul himself; such a request would be out of keeping with his overall stance as far as personal financial support is concerned. It is more likely to be an exhortation that one who was recognized as a teacher of the Galatian churches be supported by those who were taught by him. This suggests that the teacher was someone who had been set apart for this task; someone who exercised a kind of official ministry among the charismatic Galatian churches.

Another hint is found in 1 Thessalonians 5:12-13 where Paul says: "Recognize those who labor among you, and have charge of you in the Lord and admonish you; esteem them very highly in love because of their work." In this same letter, just a few verses later, Paul urges his readers not to quench the Spirit or despise the words of the prophets, but to test everything (1 Thess 5:19-21). So here, found side by side, we have references to those who "have charge of you" and to the ministry of Spirit-inspired prophets, without any hint of antipathy between them.

Finally, it is significant that there is included in the lists of gifts in both Romans and 1 Corinthians a reference to the ministry of leadership (Rom 12:8; 1 Cor 12:28). That this gift is listed among others of a more charismatic nature suggests that Paul saw no antipathy between what we might call charismatic and official ministries (so, e.g., Holmberg, Martin 1979).

*1.8. The Church and the Ministry.* One of the issues that has been much debated is the relationship of the ministry to the church. All agree that ultimately it must be Christ himself who commissions people for ministry in his church. The disagreement comes in respect of the means by which this commissioning is done. Is it (1) directly by God's call; or (2) by human agency, in any way the church chooses; or (3) by those who have themselves been commissioned by duly authorized persons? As far as the Pauline corpus is concerned, there appears to be no evidence that could be adduced in support of the second approach, but there is some evidence for the first and third approaches.

In support of the first, it may be noted that Paul himself claims to have been commissioned as an apostle by direct call of God and the revelation of Jesus Christ, without any involvement by those who were apostles before him (Gal 1:1, 15-16). In 1 Corinthians 12:28 he speaks of the appointment by God of apostles, prophets, teachers and other gifted individuals to minister to the church (cf. Eph 4:11-12). In all this there is no hint of any human commissioning. In these texts it appears that the bestowal of ministerial gifts by God constitutes the commission to use them, and the church's role is to recognize the gifts God has bestowed and to allow for their use (cf. 1 Thess 5:19-21).

In support of the third position, it may be noted that the Pastoral letters reveal that Paul himself appointed Timothy and Titus to act as his delegates in Ephesus and Crete respectively, and that they in turn were to appoint bishops, elders and deacons. Within the Pauline corpus, it is only in the Pastoral letters that any reference is made to the qualifications (aside from the brief designation of "those approved"—if not used ironically—in 1 Cor 11:19) and appointment of these ministers; however, the existence of such ministries is reflected in Philippians 1:1 and 1 Thessalonians 5:12 as well. The Pauline corpus leaves us completely in the dark as far as the involvement of the churches themselves in the process of the appointment of their bishops, elders and deacons, apart from the lists of desirable and necessary credentials and characteristics in 1 Timothy 3 and Titus 2.

## 2. Paul as Minister.

Paul saw his ministry primarily as an apostle of Christ, charged with the responsibility of bringing about the obedience of faith among the Gentiles. It was a ministry in which the exalted Christ himself was actively involved; a ministry carried out by word and deed and in the power of the Holy Spirit. His ministry was motivated primarily by a realization of the love* of Christ for all (2 Cor 5:14) and an awareness of the obligation he was under to fulfill the commission that had been given to him (1 Cor 9:16-17).

*2.1. An Apostle of Jesus Christ.* While Paul referred to himself variously as a minister of Christ (Rom 15:16; 2 Cor 11:23), a minister of the gospel (Eph 3:7; Col 1:23) and a minister of the church (Col 1:24-25), he saw himself primarily as an apostle* of Jesus Christ, one called and commissioned by the risen Lord to bring about the obedience of faith among the Gentiles* (Rom 1:5; Gal 1:15-16).

As an apostle, Paul acted as an ambassador for Christ, one through whom God made his appeal to people to be reconciled to him (2 Cor 5:20). Paul also spoke of this ministry in priestly terms. He was "a minister of Christ Jesus to the Gentiles, serving the gospel of Christ as a priest, so that the offering [consisting] of the Gentiles may be acceptable, sanctified by the Holy Spirit" (Rom 15:16). It was possibly in response to Jewish suspicions about the "cleanness" of his Gentile converts that Paul was prompted to speak of his ministry in this way. He saw himself as a priest responsible for the offering of the Gentiles, and particularly for the purity of that offering. He presided over the offering of the Gentiles, and by his preaching and teaching ministry endeavored to ensure that they were an offering acceptable and well pleasing to God.

*2.2. The Essential Elements of Paul's Ministry.* The fundamental element of Paul's ministry was the preaching* of the gospel* (1 Cor 1:17). This, he recognized, was the means by which God had chosen to make himself known to people (1 Cor 1:21); this was the power of God for salvation* (Rom 1:16; 1 Cor 1:18). He was under obligation to preach this gospel, and faced dire consequences if he did not (1 Cor 9:16-17). The only option he had was whether or not to preach it free of charge, and he consistently chose to do it free of charge (1 Cor 9:18; 2 Thess 3:8).

Paul's gospel preaching was accompanied by the performance of the signs of an apostle: "signs and wonders and mighty works"* (2 Cor 12:12: evidently a Corinthian slogan taken over by Paul, see commentaries). In Romans 15:18-19 the apostle gave a summary description of his evangelistic ministry: "For I will not dare to speak of anything except what Christ has accomplished through me to [bring about] the obedience of the Gentiles, by word and deed, by the power of signs and wonders, by the power of the Spirit [of God]." From this statement, reminiscent of the Synoptic descriptions of the public ministry of the historical Jesus, we can infer that the exalted Christ continued to accomplish through Paul's ministry what he had begun to do as the historical Jesus (*see* Jesus and Paul).

Paul's ministry to people did not cease once he had brought them to initial obedience of faith. He felt under obligation to teach, encourage and warn, so that his converts might reach maturity in Christ (Col 1:28). This involved him in continual anxiety over the churches, especially when he saw their members faltering in their Christian walk (2 Cor 11:28-29; Gal 4:19). In a striking metaphor Paul describes himself as one who betroths people to Christ: "I feel a divine concern for you, for I betrothed you to one husband, to present you as a chaste virgin to Christ" (2 Cor 11:2). Through his apostolic preaching of the gospel he betrothed people to Christ. Then he was responsible to do all in his power* to ensure the continuance of their devotion to Christ until the day of Christ's coming. Such devotion was under threat when their thoughts were led astray by false teaching, and so the apostle sought by all means to make plain to them the truth of the gospel.

Prayer,* too, was an essential element of Paul's ministry. His letters abound with references to his prayers for his converts and others for whom he was responsible as apostle to the Gentiles (Rom 1:8-10; Eph 1:15-19; 3:14-19; Phil 1:3-5, 9-11; Col 1:9-12; 2 Tim 1:3; Philem 4-6). The burden of these prayers was that believers might know the hope to which they were called and the greatness of God's power at work in them (Eph 1:17-19); that they might be strengthened by the Spirit and comprehend the surpassing love of Christ (Eph 3:16-19); that their love might overflow in greater insight to know what is best, and so be blameless on the day of Christ (Phil 1:9-11), and that they might know God's will and so lead lives worthy of their Lord (Col 1:9-10).

A further aspect of Paul's ministry was conscious modeling of the sort of life believers should live. When the Corinthians had become puffed up with their own importance through what appears to have been overrealized eschatological notions, Paul urged them rather to be imitators of him, and to facilitate this he sent Timothy to remind them of his ways in Christ (1 Cor 4:16-17). Concluding his response to the Corinthian problem of eating meat offered to idols,

Paul urged his readers to "give no offence to Jews or Greeks or the church of God." Rather they should be imitators of Paul, trying to please everyone in everything so that some might be saved (1 Cor 10:32—11:1; cf. 9:22). When warning the Philippians against those who lived as enemies* of the cross* of Christ, Paul urged them to "join in following my example, and observe those who live according to the example you have in us" (Phil 3:17). The Thessalonian believers were told to keep away from those who were living in idleness, and reminded of how Paul had worked day and night rather than be a burden to anyone, "in order to make ourselves an example for you, that you might imitate us" (2 Thess 3:7-9). It is not surprising, then, that we find in the Pastoral letters exhortations that Timothy and Titus should also set an example for the believers to follow (1 Tim 4:12; Tit 2:7; *see* Imitation).

*2.3. The Involvement of the Exalted Christ.* One of the striking things to emerge from a study of Paul's letters is his strong conviction that the exalted Christ was actively involved in his ministry. Paul ascribed the successes of his mission* to "what Christ has accomplished through me to [bring about] the obedience of the Gentiles" (Rom 15:18). It was the voice of Christ himself that was heard through the proclamation of the apostle and his colleagues (2 Cor 5:20; cf. Eph 2:17). Christ was the author of the "living letters" written in the hearts of men and women, but this he achieved through the "scribal" ministry of Paul and his colleagues, to whom was entrusted the precious "ink" of the Spirit (2 Cor 3:1-3). It was none other than Christ himself, Paul believed, who inspired him with the energy needed for the preaching and teaching ministry by which he sought to present men and women mature in Christ (Col 1:28-29).

*2.4. Paul's Defense of his Ministry.* Paul's apostolic ministry was called into question in both Galatia and Corinth (and maybe Philippi; see commentaries). In Galatia,* it would appear, Paul's opponents, the Judaizers,* had suggested that he had not been faithful to the commission they believed he had received from the Jerusalem* apostles, because he failed to include in his preaching the demand for circumcision.* In defense of his apostolic integrity and the truth of the gospel which he preached, Paul insisted that both his commission as an apostle and his understanding of the gospel for the Gentiles had been received neither from men nor through a man (Gal 1:1, 11). It had been given to him directly by a revelation from God (Gal 1:12, 15-17), and therefore, it is implied, there was no basis to any charge that he had been unfaithful to a commission received from the Jerusalem apostles.

In fact it was not until three years after his conversion-commissioning experience that he had his first contact with Peter* (Gal 1:18-21). And it was only after fourteen years that he laid the gospel he had been preaching before the Jerusalem apostles, and at that time they had added nothing to it (Gal 2:1-10). For this reason also, it is implied, he could not rightfully be accused of unfaithfulness to any commission received from Jerusalem.

In Corinth Paul experienced a strong attack upon his apostolate. This was made by those to whom he referred as "false apostles" (see Opponents). They accused him of being "bold" while absent and at a safe distance, but of being "timid" when present (2 Cor 10:1). He lived by worldly standards (2 Cor 10:2). He used to frighten people with stern letters from afar, but in person he was unimpressive and his speaking amounted to nothing (2 Cor 10:9-10). They criticized Paul's apostolate, saying it was inferior to their own, because he was not a trained speaker (2 Cor 11:5-6), he lacked proper Jewish ancestry (2 Cor 11:22), his apostolate was not based on visions and revelations (2 Cor 12:1) and "the signs of an apostle" were not performed by him (2 Cor 12:11-12). They also attacked Paul's personal integrity in financial matters, insinuating that his refusal to accept financial support from the Corinthians (as they themselves obviously did) was both evidence that Paul did not really love his converts (2 Cor 11:7-11), and a smokescreen behind which he intended to extract an even greater amount for himself through the ploy of the Collection* (2 Cor 12:14-18).

For the sake of the Corinthian church Paul felt obliged to point out that, although he might not be skilled in speaking, he did not lack knowledge* (2 Cor 11:6) or authority* (2 Cor 13:2-3, 10). He pointed out also that he had experienced visions* and revelations of God (2 Cor 12:1-5), that he did perform signs and wonders (2 Cor 12:11-13), and that he could show evidence that Christ spoke through him (2 Cor 13:2-3). However it is patently clear that Paul rejected this whole approach to evaluating claims to apostleship, and the triumphalist criteria involved. For Paul the marks of true apostolic ministry were its fruit (i.e., churches planted, 2 Cor 3:2-3), the character in which it is carried out (i.e., in accordance with the meekness and gentleness of Christ, 2 Cor 10:1) and the sharing of Christ's sufferings* (2 Cor 4:8-12; 11:23-33). Far from regarding his sufferings as something which disqualified his claim to apostleship, he actually appealed to them as legitimatizing evidence (cf. Gal 6:17).

**2.5. The Simultaneity of Weakness and Power.** Paul claimed to be the agent through whom God worked. His opponents in Corinth asserted that his lack of a commanding presence and his unimpressive speech (2 Cor 10:10) were inconsistent with this claim (see Rhetoric). Since the Corinthians had listened to his opponents in this matter, Paul wrote: "I said before . . . that if I come again I will not spare, since you desire proof that Christ is speaking in me," and he added, "he is not weak toward you, but is powerful among you. For he was crucified in weakness, but lives by the power of God" (2 Cor 13:2-4a). And then, to defend the "weakness"* of his own presence and ministry, while at the same time asserting that divine power was manifested through it, he wrote: "For we are weak in him, but in dealing with you we shall live with him by the power of God" (2 Cor 13:4b). Clearly we are here confronted with a paradox. The apostle implies that he is simultaneously identified with the Jesus who was crucified in weakness and with the Christ who now lives by the power of God.

The *locus classicus* for this teaching of power-in-weakness is 2 Corinthians 12:9-10: "He [the Lord] said to me, 'My grace is sufficient for you, for [my] power is made perfect in weakness.' I will all the more gladly boast of my weaknesses, that the power of Christ may rest upon me . . . for when I am weak, then I am strong." Paul's words here indicate the simultaneity of weakness and power; it is in the very weakness of the apostle that the "epiphany" of God's power takes place. Thus, against his opponents in Corinth, Paul argued that while true apostolic ministry does involve the manifestation of the power of Christ, that power is manifested through the weakness of the apostle.

**2.6. Motivation for Ministry.** Paul's motivation was multifaceted. He was essentially driven by a realization of the love of Christ for himself personally and for all humanity (2 Cor 5:14-15; Gal 2:20). Alongside this was his sense of obligation to carry out the apostolic commission which had been given to him (Rom 1:14-15; 1 Cor 9:16-17), and a realization that he must give an account of his life and work to God (1 Cor 4:1-5; 2 Cor 5:9-10). The apostle was motivated by a strong desire to see fellow Jews brought to a saving knowledge of Christ (Rom 9:1-3; 10:1), and he hoped that his ministry among the Gentiles would make them jealous and so save some of them (Rom 11:13-14). Paul developed a strong affection for his converts, and this made him want to share with them, not only the gospel but his own self also (1 Thess 2:8). This affection made him want to visit them and pray for them (1 Thess 2:17-20; 3:9-10), and to spend both his resources and himself for them (2 Cor 12:15).

### 3. Eschatological Evaluation of Ministry.

Paul's ministry came under much criticism. The genuineness of his apostleship was called into question in Galatia, Corinth and Philippi. While he defended his apostolate against his critics for the sake of the truth of the gospel, ultimately he seems to have laid little store by the evaluations made of his ministry by his converts or anyone else (1 Cor 4:3), even the Jerusalem apostles (Gal 2:6). For Paul what counted was the evaluation to be made of his ministry when the Lord comes (*see* Eschatology).

The first hint of Paul's conviction about eschatological evaluation of ministry is found in 1 Thessalonians 2:19-20. Here the apostle expresses the hope that his converts will be his joy and crown of boasting* on the day of the Lord. A similar hint is found in Philippians 2:14-16, where Paul urges his readers to live blameless lives so that in the day of Christ he may be proud that he had not run in vain nor labored in vain (*see* Futility).

The most developed form of this teaching is found in 1 Corinthians. In this letter Paul declares that he is not accountable to the Corinthians, asserting that for him it was a very small thing that he be judged by them or any human court (1 Cor 4:3). No judgment should be pronounced "before the Lord comes." When he comes all things will be brought to light and people will receive their commendation from God (1 Cor 4:5). Even clearer teaching is found in 1 Corinthians 3:10-15, where, using a building metaphor (with its fabulous as well as mundane building materials), Paul asserts that everyone's ministry will be tested by fire on the last day (1 Cor 3:13). It is possible that some Christians' ministries will not survive the testing, but even so they themselves will be saved (1 Cor 3:15). However, those whose ministries do survive the testing will receive rewards (1 Cor 3:14). Here we see the principle of eschatological validation, which Paul previously applied to his own ministry, extended to apply to the ministries of all those who take it upon themselves to build up the church.

*See also* APOSTLE; CHURCH; CHURCH ORDER AND GOVERNMENT; COWORKERS, PAUL AND HIS; GIFTS OF THE SPIRIT; PASTOR, PAUL AS; SERVANT, SERVICE; WEAKNESS.

BIBLIOGRAPHY. *Baptism, Eucharist and Ministry* (Faith and Order Paper No. 111; Geneva: World Council of Churches, 1982); N. Baumert, "Charisma und Amt bei Paulus," in *L'Apôtre Paul: Personnalité, Style et Conception du Ministère*, ed. A. Vanhoye (Leuven: Leuven University, 1986) 203-28; H. von Campenhausen, *Ecclesiastical Authority and Spiritual Power in the Church of the First Three Centuries* (London: Adam & Charles Black, 1969); E. E. Ellis, *Pauline Theology: Ministry and Society* (Grand Rapids: Eerdmans, 1988; Exeter: Paternoster, 1988); K. Giles, *Patterns of Ministry among the First Christians* (Melbourne: Collins Dove, 1989); A. T. Hanson, *The Pioneer Ministry* (London: SPCK, 1975); B. Holmberg, *Paul and Power: The Structure of Authority in the Primitive Church as Reflected in the Pauline Epistles* (Philadelphia: Fortress, 1980); C. G. Kruse, *New Testament Models for Ministry: Jesus and Paul* (Nashville: Thomas Nelson, 1985); A. T. Lincoln, *Ephesians* (WBC 42; Dallas: Word, 1990); R. P. Martin, *The Family and the Fellowship: New Testament Images of the Church* (Grand Rapids: Eerdmans, 1979); idem, *The Spirit and the Congregation: Studies in 1 Corinthians 12—15* (Grand Rapids: Eerdmans, 1984); L. Morris, *Ministers of God* (London: Inter-Varsity, 1964); P. Perkins, *Ministering in the Pauline Churches* (New York: Paulist, 1982); E. Schillebeeckx, *Ministry: A Case for Change* (London: SCM, 1981); G. Theissen, *The Social Setting of Pauline Christianity* (Edinburgh: T. & T. Clark, 1982); B. Witherington, *Women in the Earliest Churches* (SNTSMS 59; Cambridge: University Press, 1988).

C. G. Kruse

**MIRACLES.** *See* CORINTHIANS, LETTERS TO THE; SIGNS, WONDERS, MIRACLES.

## MISSION

Since the time of F. C. Baur the modern debate on Paul has repeatedly used the remarkable missionary expansion of first-century Christianity as an essential backdrop for understanding the conflicting forces out of which early Christianity took shape (*see* Paul and His Interpreters). And since the earliest Christian literature assigns to Paul a significant role in that expansion, the Pauline mission has also featured prominently in modern attempts to arrive at a comprehensive picture of early Christian development.

Even more so has Paul's mission proven foundational for understanding the apostle* himself. The outlines of his career, the contents of his letters and the structures of his thinking are all substantially determined by implications of his missionary vocation.

The modern study of Paul has focused on his mission principally in terms of his life and work, while consideration of that mission as an integral element of his *thinking* remains underdeveloped. An adequate assessment of Paul and his mission requires attention to both dimensions.

1. Paul's Missionary Activity
2. Paul's Missionary Thought

### 1. Paul's Missionary Activity.

Paul's permanent historical significance is commonly

taken to be that he was the first to give theological articulation to the early Christian proclamation and to work out reflectively the issues which it raised. But the historical significance of Paul's missionary labors must not be underestimated. At all points the apostle's theological articulations were called forth from within the context of his Gentile* mission. By means of that mission Paul also contributed to the remarkably early transposition of the new faith from the limited sphere of Judaism into the broader frame of the Gentile world, thereby making it possible for Christianity to survive and flourish as a distinct movement after A.D. 70. And in the process Paul's mission became for all religious history a preeminent model of organized missionary outreach.

Nevertheless, in his missionary labors Paul himself achieved the planting of the gospel only in certain principal cities along the northeastern arc of his Mediterranean world. He neither inaugurated the opening of the faith to Gentiles, nor did he originate the active proclamation to Gentiles, nor did he initiate their inclusion in the Christian communities. Nor can Paul even be credited with accomplishing the principal portion of the missionary expansion during the first generation. What then did Paul do in his missionary career?

*1.1. Historical Career.* Paul's missionary effort has become a dominant model in the history of Christian expansion not least because the author of Luke-Acts chose to highlight the Pauline mission, and did so with often vivid and lively narrative. The question of what indeed happened in the Pauline mission has therefore become bound up with questions about appropriate sources for the study of Paul, and especially with contentions about the historical reliability of Acts.

Yet one should note that, with respect to the general outline of Paul's missionary career, it is the traditional *chronology* which the recent debate has called most prominently into question, not the geographical locations which Paul visited during his career nor the larger sequences of his movements through those areas—except for questions about the "first tour" in southern Asia Minor (Acts 13—14) and the well-known uncertainties regarding Galatia (*see* Chronology; Itineraries). The consequence, significantly, is that the still-disputed modern reconstructions of Paul's missionary career tend to reschedule that career rather than reroute it.

This is so not least because both in the general scheme of Paul's missionary movements, as well as in their details, at those points where Paul's letters can serve as a check, the record available in Acts is found

to be in fairly close and sometimes quite precise accord with the letters. This fact has suggested to many (including Cadbury, Dibelius, Haenchen) that, at least with respect to the itinerary of the Pauline mission, the writer of Acts often had access to dependable information.

Thus with reference to the general scheme of Paul's mission, both the letters and Acts place Paul in the same area of the Mediterranean world and in the same provinces, and take him through these provinces in the same general sequence. That is to say, Paul's area of mission in all the sources is the northeastern Mediterranean world, ranging between Judea and the Adriatic. And he moves through this area roughly from east to west, touching Syria and Cilicia, Macedonia, Achaia and Asia—and touching them in that order (as well as Galatia at some point along the way).

That Paul was conscious of this geographical pattern in his missionary career is made explicit in his summation at the end of his Aegean period: "From Jerusalem and as far round as Illyricum I have fully preached the gospel of Christ" (Rom 15:19). At this point both the Roman letter and the narrative of Acts (Acts 19:21) indicate that Paul intended to travel to Jerusalem* and then to Rome. Only Acts reports subsequent visits to Jerusalem and Rome,* whereas only in Romans* do we encounter Paul's plans for going on further west beyond Rome to Spain—because, as he states, he no longer had "any room for work in these regions" (Rom 15:22; cf. 2 Cor 10:12-16). Thus Paul both proceeded in his missionary activities and surveyed them in a manner confirming the presence of a geographical factor in his conception of what he was about. Mission was for Paul in part a geographically definable accomplishment.

The sources also bear witness to a second defining dimension of the Pauline mission, namely Paul's commitment to founding and nurturing Christian communities as the central goal of his missionary endeavors in any particular region. Paul did indeed engage in missionary preaching stage by stage in his journeys. And he actively sought individual conversions as part of his calling. But these evangelistic functions were pursued as necessary preliminary steps in a larger missionary objective to form communities of believers region by region throughout his part of the world. It is hardly accidental that Paul did not picture himself as a maker of bricks but as a builder of buildings (cf. 1 Cor 3:10). His mission was focused on corporate achievement.

Yet even the emergence of such communities proves an insufficient measure of Paul's missionary intentions. Paul repeatedly displays a sense of obligation not only to founding but also to nurturing such communities, not only to begetting but also to rearing, not only to planting but also to cultivating. For this reason he regularly revisits churches he has previously founded, and shows an inclination to pursue a residential ministry* of edification wherever possible. As Paul explains about his activities cut short at Thessalonica: "You know how, like a father with his children, one by one we exhorted you and encouraged you and charged you to walk worthy of God" (1 Thess 2:10-12). Paul's missionary commitment to nurturing his newly founded churches is most directly demonstrated by the existence of the very letters themselves. These letters are not evangelistic pieces: the Paul who is available to us at first hand is available almost exclusively in the community-nurturing dimension of his missionary role.

These indications accord with Paul's representation to the Colossians of his missionary assignment: "We proclaim [Christ], warning everyone and teaching everyone in all wisdom, so that we may present everyone mature in Christ" (Col 1:28). Likewise, Paul characterizes his letter and his proposed visit to the Roman community as edificatory in intent, and then expressly justifies this intention by referring to the nature of his missionary vocation (Romans 1:5-15; 15:14-21). A distinguishing dimension of the Pauline mission is that it found its fullest sense of completion neither in an evangelistic preaching tour nor in individual conversions but only in the presence of firmly established churches (Bowers 1987).

Both from these broader characteristics, and from details recoverable from the sources, one can propose certain predominant patterns in Paul's missionary career. (1) Paul is committed to introducing the gospel* where it has not yet been heard, to a pioneering function at the frontiers of the Christian expansion. (2) He understands this commitment to imply geographical movement in the proclamation of the gospel. (3) He conceptualizes such movement in terms of specific geographical areas. (4) Paul attempts to canvass these areas in a roughly contiguous sequence, from east to west. (5) Within that compass Paul seeks to establish Christian communities in the main population centers of each region. (6) Paul's missionary commitment includes nurturing such communities toward mature stability. (7) Once he takes this to be accomplished, Paul feels that he has "no more room" for his particular missionary calling in these areas, and is prepared to move on.

*1.2. Methods and Strategy.* In attempting to discern the contours of Paul's missionary approach, we must recognize at once that Paul was by no means the only figure engaged in religious propaganda in his day. If Paul traveled about among urban centers, preaching publicly and soliciting converts in synagogue and marketplace and private dwelling, such methods of religious attraction turn out on fuller inquiry to have been a widespread feature of the Greco-Roman world. The itinerant preachers of Hellenism,* the devotees of the mysteries and the faithful of the Jewish synagogue were all engaged in religious propaganda of one form or another, as of course were many early Christians besides Paul. One contribution of the *religionsgeschichtliche* ("history-of-religions") emphasis earlier in this century was to throw fresh light on the Pauline mission by exploring those methods which Paul apparently utilized in common with the numerous other examples of religious outreach in his day (Cumont, Nock 1933).

But it has not yet been sufficiently recognized that the Pauline model also diverges from each of these other examples of first-century religious propaganda in important aspects, and that these differences help to define more effectively the nature of the Pauline mission (Bowers 1980). Such divergence is apparent not least with regard to the geographical dimension of Paul's missionary conception and the ecclesial focus of his endeavors. Thus the deliberateness with which Paul pursued a geographically definable expansion of the faith unexpectedly proves on closer review to be an approach to religious outreach apparently lacking effective parallel in his day. And the focus of Paul's missionary efforts on founding and nurturing believing communities also appears to lack exact equivalent among other examples of religious propaganda of his world.

Recent studies have tended to confirm these distinctions in several important respects. For example, the latest reassessments of the Jewish proselyte movement raise serious doubts whether one should speak of Jewish "missionaries" during the Second Temple period, or even of a Jewish "mission" at that time (McKnight, Goodman). Even if the case may prove to be somewhat more nuanced, the cautionary implications for comparisons with the Pauline mission are salutary.

Likewise the conventional depiction of the "missionary expansion" of the mystery religions throughout the Roman world has now been subjected to authoritative challenge (MacMullen 1981, 98-99, 111-12; cf. Nilsson, 670, 699-700; Nock 1972, 81). On closer inquiry this expansion proves not to have been so diffuse, and to have occurred principally by the relocation of existing converts rather than by any deliberate outreach (*see* Religions, Greco-Roman).

Indeed, the degree to which the early Christian mission itself may have proceeded by patterns familiar from the Pauline model, both in the first and in succeeding centuries, has also been questioned (MacMullen 1984, 34, 136 n.29; cf. Beskow, Congar). The public evangelist seeking to plant churches territory by territory is hardly discernible in early Christian history after Paul. In short, recent reassessment is supporting the suggestion that the first-century world was not widely populated by "missionaries" of the Pauline type.

Scholarship in general has yet to reckon with the degree to which these clarifications seriously undermine the accepted depictions of religious propaganda in the time of the Early Empire. This would apply not least to the extensive and still influential description worked out by D. Georgi. Georgi argues that Paul found himself competing with a whole class of early Christian "missionaries" modeled on types familiar from Hellenistic Judaism and pagan Hellenism. But on closer scrutiny the evidence offered for discerning such deliberately "missionary" types substantially vanishes, making a reexamination of the entire question desirable. At the very least one must now expect a much more cautious precision than exhibited by Georgi and others in sorting out the variant models of religious propaganda in Paul's time.

While the inquiries of comparative-religion scholarship earlier in this century were useful in drawing attention to these movements and to their similarities with the early Christian mission, no systematic and comprehensive study is yet available which treats with sufficient sensitivity and precision the rich variety of approaches to religious expansion in the first-century world. Such investigations would help considerably to sharpen and refine the scholarly characterizations of Paul's own missionary activity and its particular place in early Christian development.

The emerging sociological approach in NT studies has fruitfully taken up certain lines of this inquiry. For example, G. Theissen (1982) has sketched out a suggestive distinction between the "itinerant charismatic" preachers of early Palestinian Christianity and what is taken to be the more orderly and sophisticated mission of Paul as a "goal-oriented community organizer." According to Theissen, the former were devoted to proclamation but not to community formation. And while they traveled constantly, their itinerancy was not organized in a manner that could sustain proclamation to distant lands.

Theissen has also helpfully illumined economic dimensions of the early Christian mission, while R. F. Hock has contributed to a better understanding of the social context of Paul's tentmaking* vocation in relation to his missionary role. Most of the principal sociological inquiries in Pauline studies have, however, tended more to illuminate the results of the Pauline mission, including the social status of the members of his communities, the structures of those communities and Paul's troubled relationships with them, rather than the dynamics of the mission itself (Meeks et al.; *see* Social Setting of Mission Churches; Social-Scientific Approaches to Paul).

Those sociological analyses which have ventured into interpreting the Pauline mission itself have not been entirely successful. Writers have variously interpreted the early Christian mission in terms of a "millenarian movement" or a "conversionist sect," based on models drawn from the sociology of religion. Relying on some of these materials, F. Watson has vigorously promoted a not altogether novel paradigm for the origins of Paul's mission and theology. According to Watson, Paul turned to the Gentiles only after he had failed as a Christian missionary to his fellow Jews (Gal 5:11). To ensure that the second venture would not also fail, Paul found it expedient to discard the normal legal requirements for Gentile inclusion, which led in turn to separation from the Jewish community. Thus whereas Christianity had hitherto functioned as a reformist movement within Judaism, in Paul's mission it became transformed into a dissident sect outside of Judaism, and one therefore requiring its own legitimating rationalizations. Paul's theological perspectives on Judaism and the Law derive from these sociological necessities.

Watson can only achieve this reconstruction by overlooking fundamental inconveniences to his theory. Thus he fails to clarify why, if Paul was so capable of missionary expediency, he did not first engineer a radical accommodation of his message for his hesitant Jewish hearers, sufficient to avert the failure of that earlier mission. Nor can Watson offer supporting examples where a Jewish preacher, rejected by his own people, promptly compensated by turning to the Gentiles. The link with social theory claimed for the inquiry is also only minimally in evidence. Watson has raised useful questions about the origins of the Pauline mission and about its resulting implications for Pauline theology, but the answers he proposes fall short of persuasiveness.

The methodology of much recent sociological analysis of the NT has now been subjected to a careful assessment by Holmberg, who severely criticizes the tendency often found in such studies to handle sociological models as factually determinative rather than as interpretively suggestive. Holmberg particularly discredits the adequacy of millennial, conversionist and sectarian models as currently deployed. Sociological interpretations of the missionary phenomena in the first century, including the Pauline mission, will likely have much to offer, but have yet to be worked out with sufficiently credible methodological discipline.

W. D. Davies, discussing territoriality in early Christianity, criticizes the persisting notion that the Pauline mission must have functioned on the basis of a larger strategy (Davies 1974, 180-82), a perception first given prominence in the writings of W. M. Ramsay nearly a century ago. In Ramsay's view, the missionary efforts of Paul the Roman citizen disclose the operations of a conscious "imperial" strategy to render the Christian faith coextensive with the Empire. Ramsay points especially to Paul's evident predilection for the strategic cities and roads of the Roman world. But most material and ideological commerce would have flowed inevitably along these very lines, not owing to any conscious strategy but by the necessity of the available routes and the locations of major populations (*see* Itineraries, Travel Plans, Journeys, Apostolic Parousia; Travel in the Roman World).

In an often cited article, J. Knox (1964) has suggested that underlying Paul's choice of words in surveying his mission in Romans 15:19 is the hint of a larger missionary plan to proceed in circuit right around the Mediterranean world. In terms of this more comprehensive plan Paul is claiming so far to have completed the first leg up to Illyricum, and is projecting a second leg to Spain. The lexical hint that forms the basis of Knox's proposal is very slender at best, and no supporting indications exist that Paul ever entertained missionary intentions toward Egypt or other parts of the southern Mediterranean coast.

If a comprehensive strategy or plan is not demonstrable for Paul's mission, he did certainly perceive the scope of his assignment in broad terms. Thus the spreading gospel is "bearing fruit and growing in the whole world" (Col 1:6), and his own apostleship is "for obedience of faith among all the nations" (Rom 1:5). And the presence of Spain in Paul's missionary plans probably also indicates, at least in part, a desire to attain to "the ends of the earth" of OT eschatology. In antiquity Spain was conceived to lie at the western edge of the inhabited earth, and of the four extremities of popular conception it was the only one within the Empire and hence relatively accessible. Given the already generally westward orientation of his missionary movement, Paul may have come to look on Spain as an eschatologically meaningful objective for his mission, so that by preaching in Spain he would have traversed his world with the gospel, from its place of origin at the eastern edge of the empire right across to earth's western boundary.

Nevertheless, the inherited outlook of Paul's Roman citizenship may have acted as a limitation upon his practical geographical interests. The known world of Paul's day was considerably larger than the Roman Empire, and not least in Jewish consciousness since a significant portion of the Diaspora* was resident in the East. Luke's inhabited world apparently stretched at least from Ecbatana to Rome (Acts 2:9-11), and contemporary references to India and the Ganges were not uncommon. Yet the boundaries of Paul's active missionary interest appear rather to have been essentially from Jerusalem to Gades, entirely within the confines of the Empire. The reference to Arabia in Galatians 1:17, if relevant, is not an exception, since Arabia fell within the sphere of Roman suzerainty. Paul may speak of barbarians and Scythians, but there is neither word nor movement that even hints at projected travel outside the jurisdictions of the Empire. In that sense Paul was not a "foreign" missionary, and the operational world of his missionary vision as available to us was apparently something less than the known world of his day.

*1.3. Conversion and Call.* The complex of issues relating to Paul's Damascus experience admit of at least one fixed point, namely that Paul believed that Jesus had appeared to him alive (1 Cor 15:8; *see* Conversion and Call). Pauline scholarship has long busied itself with the various theological consequences that might flow from such an experience, especially in light of what may have been Paul's pre-Christian dispositions and activities. But the pivotal significance of the Damascus experience for Paul is not exhausted by reference to the encounter alone. The relevant data indicate a close correlation in the apostle's thinking between his sense of encounter and his sense of personal calling. God revealed his Son in him, Paul declares, "in order that I might preach him among the Gentiles" (Gal 1:15-16).

The modern study of Paul has often attempted to explain Paul's sense of missionary calling as an inevitable theological derivative of his vision. The Damascus event precipitated a sequence of soteriological insights resulting in the acknowledgement that a Lawfree gospel must by its nature be universal in applicability. This universalistic perception led in turn to a conviction of the legitimacy and even the necessity of a Gentile mission. One must, however, discount this conventional explanation of Paul's sense of missionary calling for at least two reasons.

In the first place, Paul understands his call to Gentile mission as a specific individual assignment, which he grounds not in a common experience in Christ but in a unique personal experience which set him apart. Had he arrived at his sense of vocation based on his soteriology, he would have understood that vocation to be applicable to all believers in general. The evident particularity of his sense of vocation renders inadequate any attempt to explain his call simply as a necessary theological consequence of his conversion.

In the second place, the theological connections which are supposed to have led inevitably from encounter to call cannot be sustained. A resurrection* appearance would certainly require the sort of christological* reorientation evident in Paul, and this should imply a new valuation of the cross* and the Law,* and hence a new soteriology. But if the new soteriology would permit a universalizing ingredient, does it require it? It is arguable that soteriological universalism* is not inevitably implied in a Law-free gospel. But even more to the point, mission is not an inevitable derivative of soteriological universalism. A belief in universal *access* does not inexorably lead to a sense of universal *mission*. A conviction that a message is applicable to everyone, and a conviction that one is obliged to make that message known to everyone are two different beliefs—without necessary correlation, as the subsequent history of Christianity itself has repeatedly demonstrated.

Given the available evidence, it would seem better to understand Paul's Damascus experience as both encounter and call, as an encounter with the risen Christ which Paul understood to include a special commission to Gentile mission. Once this duality of Paul's initial experience is acknowledged, the contours both of his missionary career and of his theological development can be appropriately clarified. The resurrection appearance called forth certain theological adjustments, adjustments which were then worked out within the specific framework of a Gentile mission vocation, and which moved toward solutions to questions arising from within that historical context.

It is useful to note that, while an encounter with Jesus in resurrected glory could not help but bear revolutionary theological implications for Paul as an unconverted Pharisee, a divine summons to Gentile outreach by itself would not have required a similar radical reorientation for such a person (*see* Jew, Paul the). Since the Jewish community of Paul's day generally maintained an openness toward Gentile accessions, a simple assignment to Gentile outreach of itself should not have proved especially incompatible with Paul's pre-conversion disposition. It was the christological encounter that provided the creative force in Paul's theological renovation, and the commission that determined its direction of development. Either without the other cannot adequately account for all the historical and theological data involved.

That is not, of course, to conclude that everything happened at once for Paul: encounter, call, a specific focus on Gentiles, the energetic Pauline mission, and a developed Pauline mission theology. The sources suggest otherwise. Subsequent decisive experiences at Jerusalem* and Antioch,* and indeed in his missionary travels, certainly also fundamentally shaped Paul's later sense of his missionary vocation. (For the place of Paul's outreach within the development of the early Christian mission, see now especially Hengel 1983.)

Although S. Kim's extensive analysis of Paul's Damascus experience and its theological consequences provides useful access to the issues and literature in the modern debate, the incompleteness of the inquiry bears notice. While Kim argues for the duality of the initial event, he fails to provide any detailed consideration of Paul's apostolic self-understanding and universal mission, acknowledging in the conclusion that this aspect must yet await his attention. The limitation for the entire enterprise implied by this omission should not be overlooked.

## 2. Paul's Missionary Thought.

Whatever the impact of Paul's missionary career on the subsequent history and literature of Christianity, his *thinking* about mission (as distinguished from his *activity* in mission) has received relatively meager elaboration in modern scholarly study. From F. C. Baur to A. Schweitzer to R. Bultmann and E. P. Sanders, the mission of Paul as a historical reality is used to provide essential backdrop for assessing the structure and content of Pauline theology. But, with notable exceptions, the apprehension of Paul's mission within his theological reflection, as one of its integral and even generative features, can only be found at the margins of the scholarly discussions or in some underlying assumptions. This deficiency is yet to be addressed adequately even within contemporary Pauline research.

Yet given Paul's evident preoccupation with his vocational mission, we may rightly suppose that no adequate understanding of Pauline theology will be achieved until his perspective on mission has been integrated into the larger interpretation of his theology, showing the place and relationships of the Gentile mission within his theological reflection. Without such an achievement, we will not have an adequate understanding either of Paul's mission or of his theology.

**2.1. The New Perspective on Paul.** In his path-breaking inquiry *Paul and Palestinian Judaism* (1977), E. P. Sanders offered a two-part answer to the question of a proper starting point for understanding Paul's thinking, the central locus (*see* Center) from which all the rest may be explained: "There appear to me to be two readily identifiable and primary convictions which governed Paul's Christian life: (1) that Jesus Christ is Lord, that in him God has provided for the salvation of all who believe, . . . and that he will soon return to bring all things to an end; (2) that he, Paul, was called to be the apostle to the Gentiles" (Sanders 1977, 441-42). From these two generative foci Sanders believes he can explain the entire complex of Pauline reflection. Thus in one of the most influential contemporary studies on Paul, the issue of the Gentile mission in Paul's theology has been fundamentally reasserted.

Sanders did not go on in this study to elaborate the role of the Pauline mission in Paul's theology, since his particular concern was Paul's attitude towards Judaism and the Law. But Sanders does suggest that Paul's call to Gentile mission played a pivotal role in that question. It was Paul's sense of calling that required him to understand that the salvation* available in Christ was for all, both Jew and Gentile (Sanders 1977, 442-43). His resulting attitude toward Judaism and its Law thus arose from his prior conviction of the *universal* nature of the salvation offered in Christ. "It is the Gentile question and the exclusivism of Paul's soteriology which dethrone the law" (Sanders 1977, 497). Sanders's follow-up study, *Paul, the Law, and the Jewish People* (1983), in further considering Paul's attitude toward Judaism, asks how Paul understood himself and his work, and addresses in some detail the question whether Paul's mission included an outreach to Jews, which Sanders denies (see the balanced assessment of this in Hultgren, 137-43).

In the lively debate which has followed Sanders's new perspective, although the proposal regarding the formative place of the Gentile mission in Paul's theology has largely remained a suggestive pointer for future discussion, some have seen in this particular theme a helpful basis for addressing the larger questions of current Pauline research. This approach appeared first in a remarkably suggestive contribution by N. T. Wright (1978), and has since been elaborated in some detail by J. D. G. Dunn in a series of publications beginning with "The New Perspective on Paul" in 1983. Dunn proposes that early Christians were faced with the question of how, with the coming of Jesus the Messiah, they should relate to their covenantal* obligations under Judaism. Should the people of God still be defined, and should the Gentiles be incorporated, on terms of distinctively Jewish national identity? According to Dunn, it is on just this point that Paul's answer develops, namely that the advent of Christ has introduced the time of the covenant's fulfillment, the realization of God's eschatological purpose as proclaimed to Abraham*: "In you shall all the nations be blessed." The fulfillment of the covenant therefore requires that covenantal participation no longer be established by legalistic badges of national identity (*see* Works of the Law).

Sanders and those engaged in the debate precipitated by his proposals have by no means been the first to affirm the significance of Gentile mission in Paul's theology. At least four strands of the scholarly discussion have previously attended to the question in one form or another.

**2.2. Mission in Biblical Perspective.** The modern western missionary movement, in its search for a credible biblical undergirding, has from time to time called forth certain contributions of merit from the scholarly community, which have in turn secured a place within the general debate on Paul and his theology. Among the more notable examples have been the classic treatment by F. Hahn, *Mission in the New Testament* (1963), and the broader inquiry by D. Senior and C. Stuhlmueller, *The Biblical Foundations for Mission* (1983) (also, e.g., Allen, Kuhn, Blauw, Green, Haas, Hinson, Gilliland, Bosch). While these studies have usually been elicited by interests external to modern Pauline research, and have tended more to offer summary and synthesis of scholarly findings than to break new ground, they have nevertheless played a fruitful role in keeping alive relevant questions about the early Christian mission.

**2.3. Paul's Universalism.** From Baur onward the recurrent pattern in Pauline scholarship has been to assume that the place of mission in Paul's theology is adequately addressed by attending to the issues relating to Paul's "universalism."* Thus Baur identified the heart of Paul's controversy with Jerusalem in terms of a struggle between a Jewish-Christian particularism and a Pauline universalism. Paul's apostolic mission was but the outward expression of his conviction that in the new faith the exclusiveness of Judaism must be abandoned, the nationalistic distinction between Jew and Gentile must be systematically rejected, and the principle must be established that salvation is for all people. It is in order to establish this fundamental universalism that he denies the validity of salvation by works of the Law. Such an approach assumes rather than demonstrates that Paul's mission is theologically explicated by reference to his universalism.

But can one find in Paul's universalistic soteriology

the generative theological explanations for his mission? The assumed linkage of concepts suffers in the first place from a persisting looseness in defining "universalism." The various notions evident from religious history which scholars so easily combine under the rubric of universalism in fact represent a considerable diversity of perspectives. Thus what appears on first glance in Paul to represent a dramatic removal of distinctions, a sweeping universalizing of religion, proves on closer inspection to be no more than a redefined particularism. What we actually find in Paul could be termed a universal access to a particularistic community. Everyone may enter, but those who do so have entered into a distinct group which is not universal, but only representatively universal. If "universalism" means universal access to a particularistic community, then one must note that the term could as well be applied to the Judaism of Paul's day. Where Paul differed from contemporary Judaism was not in offering access without ethnic distinctions, but in offering a means of access and a resulting community that were not linked to ethnic exclusiveness.

But the more substantial deficiency in the analysis of Pauline universalism and mission which Baur inaugurated lies in the fact that "universalism" does not explain mission. In the actual history of religions, universalism can exist without mission, and mission can exist without universalism. There is no necessary correlation. The conviction that anyone may be admitted is not at all the same as the conviction that everyone must be actively invited. Therefore, the presence in some form of a universalistic religious conviction in Paul may be congenial to his mission, but it neither requires that mission, nor does it explain its emergence. And once the inquiry has gone further to distinguish the nature of the Pauline mission as a deliberate aggressive outreach, then the inadequate explanatory power of Pauline universalism becomes readily apparent. While there may be many instances in religious history where a universalistic conviction has generated a missionary impulse, there are undoubtedly as many or more instances where it has not, where the attitudes of acceptance ("if anyone knocks, we will open") and of availability ("if anyone asks, we will answer") have not inevitably been followed by, or given rise to, a sense of compulsion to move out persuading and inducing others to knock and to ask. And hence when all discussion of Pauline universalism is concluded, the question of the place of Paul's mission in his theology remains unresolved.

In the *religionsgeschichtliche* phase of Pauline studies, these issues of particularism and universalism became submerged. With the presumption that the Hellenistic world and its religious energies furnished the essential setting for interpreting Paul, the particularistic preoccupations of the world of Judaism dropped easily from view. Baur's supposed struggle between the Jerusalem church's exclusivism and Paul's inclusivism no longer offered the consequential key for interpreting early Christian development. Within the new interpretive framework any missionary effort *per se* appears as an interesting but inconsequential historical accessory to the central theological questions, and the more so on the supposition that comparable missionary undertakings were a pervasive feature of the Hellenistic religious world. On such terms Paul's mission, far from requiring theological explanation, seemed sufficiently comprehensible simply as another reflection of Paul's Hellenistic milieu.

In his *Paul and Rabbinic Judaism* in 1948, W. D. Davies carefully reasserted the significance of Paul's Jewish religious background for any adequate interpretation of Paul, including any assessment of Paul's Gentile-mission thinking. According to Davies, postexilic Judaism gradually gave up the OT prophetic expectation that the Gentiles would be included in the blessings of the messianic kingdom, while increasingly accommodating an exclusivist nationalism. The result was an uneasy conscience respecting the Gentiles, evident not least in the rise of the proselyte movement as an alternative solution to their fate. Yet Judaism remained ambivalent toward the results of that approach. Although the Rabbis maintained an open door to accessions from among the Gentiles, a persisting lack of enthusiasm toward the process is also evident.

For Davies this tension at the heart of late Judaism, the struggle between a narrow nationalism and a concern for the fate of the Gentiles, is directly reflected in Paul's own attitudes. Universalism, Davies states, was implicit in Paul's conversion experience; in Christ he found his nationalism necessarily transcended. "To be converted had meant for Paul to be a missionary to the Gentiles" (Davies, 58). Yet Paul the apostle to the Gentiles could never entirely shake off the ethnic particularism of his heritage, even as he courageously worked his way toward a true universalism. Whatever else one may make of the inner contradictions of his arguments in Romans 9—11 respecting Jews and Gentiles in the divine economy, they are but one more confirmation of the significance of his Jewish background for understanding the man and his theology.

In Bultmann the issues of Jewish particularism and Pauline universalism were transposed from a question of ethnic identity into a question of existential individualism. Under the requirements of Bultmann's hermeneutical enterprise, legalistic Jewish exclusivism comes to represent for Paul not a corporate particularism but a universal individualism, the assertive self seeking to achieve its own salvation. Once Judaism is taken as the symbol of a universal religious stance, issues of ethnic exclusivism and inclusivism as perceived by Paul and the Judaism of his day can no longer be relevant categories of analysis. And under such interpretive impulses it is not surprising that, whereas in his treatment of the development of early Christian theology Bultmann everywhere presupposes the historical process of the early Christian mission, any need for explaining Paul's singular missionary preoccupation within an exposition of his theology goes unattended.

*2.4. The Käsemann/Stendahl Debate.* E. Käsemann was the first to break with the mold of Bultmann's interpretive enterprise, arguing against an exclusively individualistic focus, and asserting the cosmic and apocalyptic* dimensions of Paul's soteriological theology. In doing so Käsemann reopened the possibility of addressing the place of mission in Paul's theology, within a context of fresh and fruitful insights. But Käsemann could not break entirely from Bultmann's conception that Paul was opposing Jewish legalism, nor from an individualistic conception of salvation by faith.* And he therefore initiated a celebrated debate with K. Stendahl, directed against Stendahl's influential 1963 investigation, "The Apostle Paul and the Introspective Conscience of the West" (see Stendahl 1976).

Stendahl had argued that Paul's theology took its central orientation not from the question of Law and gospel but from the question of the place of the Gentiles in God's plan. Paul's problem is not the anguished guilty conscience seeking divine grace; that is the problem of an Augustine or a Luther. For Paul the vital concern was how his call to Gentile outreach could be interpreted within God's age-old salvific operation.

Käsemann took stern exception to this approach (see Käsemann 1971), in part because he thought its *heilsgeschichtliche* flavor to be dangerous for modern Christianity, and in part in order to defend the traditional Reformation perception that justification* by faith functions at the center of Paul's theology. The contention was sharp and not always clarifying, not least because both men sometimes allowed their variant twentieth-century agendas to intrude inordinately upon their historical judgments.

Nevertheless, by breaking the grip of Bultmann's powerful exposition, Käsemann allowed the study of

Paul to resonate once again with elements in the apostle's thinking otherwise elusive to existentialist interpretation. And Stendahl, by breaking with the "Lutheran" exposition of Paul, and pointing toward the formative issue of Gentile inclusion in Paul's thought, allowed Pauline research to assess with much greater flexibility the inner structure of Paul's theology. Equally important, the Käsemann/Stendahl debate served to bring the then-dominant existential approach to Paul into a necessary and creative interaction with an alternative eschatological interpretation of Paul, and it did so specifically with respect to questions of the Gentile mission. The full implications of this development, reinforced almost immediately by Sanders's decisive intervention in the interpretation of Paul, are still being worked out in current Pauline studies.

*2.5. Paul's Eschatological Self-Understanding.* While A. Schweitzer's influential 1911 critique of previous Pauline research urged an interpretation of Paul worked out consistently from within the framework of Jewish eschatology, the issue of Paul's mission featured in the presentation only marginally. But when Schweitzer's own constructive exposition of Paul's theology, *The Mysticism of Paul the Apostle*, finally appeared after long delay in 1930, it included a pioneering attempt to take Paul's mission into account within a systematic exposition of his theology (Schweitzer, 177-87).

According to Schweitzer, Paul's commitment to Gentile mission arose from his particular theological conviction that the coming of the End awaited the ingathering of the "full number" of the elect from among the Gentiles. To achieve this Paul felt himself compelled to carry the knowledge of Christ to Gentile lands. And since he was alone in perceiving this specific need, he came to recognize himself as "the God-appointed apostle to the Gentiles." Paul also insisted upon the Law-free gospel for his converts because only as their Gentile status was maintained could they still be counted within the required eschatological quota for elect Gentiles.

The delay in publication of Schweitzer's study meant that, when it finally did appear, readers did not always find it "in step" with the contemporary state of discussion. Perhaps this is why Schweitzer's creative attempt to explain Paul's mission within the context of his eschatology was never widely noticed in the subsequent literature.

In modern Pauline studies the most sustained and influential discussion of the place of Paul's mission in his theology took its rise from an article by O. Cullmann in 1936. Like Schweitzer, Cullmann directed attention to Paul's eschatology. His theme was the eschatological character of Paul's missionary self-consciousness, and he based his presentation on a controversial suggestion that the mysterious "restrainer" in 2 Thessalonians 2:6-7 was the apostle himself in his mission (*see* Man of Lawlessness and Restraining Power), a suggestion which probably helped obscure the seminal contribution of the article as a whole.

Nevertheless, Cullmann's more fundamental insights were taken up in other studies, and in particular by J. Munck in 1954 in his *Paul and the Salvation of Mankind*. Munck began with a systematic critique of what he took to be the continuing influence of the Tübingen interpretation of Paul and of early Christian history. He then sought to replace this with a consistent interpretation of Paul centered on his eschatological self-consciousness as the apostle to the Gentiles. "Paul's apostolic consciousness in its eschatological form stands in the center of his personality and theology" (Munck, 42). The scholarly response to Munck's study on Paul was extensive, and focused principally on his negative critique of Tübingen influence, which it found inadequate. Most scholarship also found unpersuasive Munck's positive attempt to place Paul's eschatological self-consciousness at the center of his theology.

But Munck's exposition of Paul's eschatological understanding of his missionary vocation has proved of more enduring influence. Once one makes allowance for the sometimes eccentric exegesis, and for the tendency to overstate a case, the central elements of Munck's assessment of Paul's vocational self-consciousness remain defensible and illuminating. And indeed when Sanders refers to Paul's sense of missionary vocation as one of the two generative convictions for his theology, it is Munck whom he singles out in particular for positive reference (Sanders 1977, 442). Munck investigates a series of Pauline texts in order to demonstrate that Paul took his Gentile mission vocation to be decisively connected with the events of the consummation. His call was to fulfill the OT eschatological expectation of the ingathering of the nations, and to this end he undertook to proclaim the good news to the ends of the earth before the final day. Munck proposed that it is within this framework of eschatological beliefs that Paul's sense of mission is to be sorted out and clarified (*see* Eschatology).

But Munck's full formulation incorporated significant excesses requiring correction, a process which in fact can serve the more exact delineation of Paul's eschatological self-understanding. According to Munck, Paul saw himself not only as a key participant but in fact as the pivotal figure in the eschatological drama: "Paul regards himself as the one on whom the arrival

of the Messianic age depends" (Munck, 41). The completion of his own Gentile mission assignment would thus precipitate the final events leading to the Parousia. This in turn explains the intensity of Paul's vocational self-consciousness and of his missionary endeavor. Such a formulation is defective in at least two consequential respects.

First, the evidence is plentiful enough that Paul entertained a heightened sense of his vocational significance. Thus having referred to the other apostles, he can say: "His grace toward me was not in vain; on the contrary, I worked harder than any of them" (1 Cor 15:10). He takes his assignment to be on a par with that of Peter (Gal 2) and does not hesitate to place it on superior footing to that of Moses (2 Cor 3). Yet the two passages on which Munck must principally depend in order to establish a uniquely decisive eschatological role for Paul fail in the purpose, either because the text is incapable of any assured interpretation and very likely not this one (2 Thess 2), or because the crucial element of unique decisiveness must be read *into* the text (Rom 11). Munck also ignores the numerous signals that Paul clearly recognized the limitation and interdependency of his vocation. Thus his own mission characteristically functioned as a collaborative rather than an individual effort (Ollrog; *see* Coworkers). And when Apollos,* not apparently at that time part of the Pauline team, carried forward the work that Paul had begun at Corinth, Paul readily described their ministries as complementary under God (1 Cor 3:4-9). Indeed Paul's sensitivity to spheres of labor, and his annoyance at violation of such spheres, is itself an acknowledgement of the limits of his own contribution in the spread of the gospel (2 Cor 10:12-16; Rom 15:18-21). And even when he is imprisoned, he can accept with equanimity the provocative endeavors of his opponents, so long as the proclamation continues (Phil 1:15-18). Paul understood his part in the eschatological mission to be consequential, but not uniquely decisive.

Second, and even more important, Munck assumes a uniformly future orientation for the eschatological dimension of Paul's missionary understanding. Yet clearly for Paul the most decisive event of the End had already taken place in Jesus Christ, and the determinative experience for his own life and mission had been when this recognition had been forced upon him by a personal messianic encounter and commission. Throughout his letters the references and allusions to his sense of mission habitually take orientation from this consciousness. For him the End had already arrived, eschatological expectation had given way to eschatological experience, and the long-expected ingathering of the nations was now being fulfilled. He conceived of his Gentile mission as eschatological in nature principally not by virtue of some connection with a yet future event but by virtue of its evident connections with a past one.

For this reason Paul can boldly describe his assignment as a direct extension of the messianic mission which God* has already initiated: "God was in Christ reconciling the world to himself, and has committed to us the message of reconciliation. So we are Christ's ambassadors, God making his appeal through us" (2 Cor 5:19-20; *see* Peace, Reconciliation; Center). That Paul did see a link between the Gentile mission and the Parousia is evident from Romans 11, but the exact nature of the relationship is left unemphasized and obscure in Paul's treatment, and no other Pauline texts clearly take up this particular theme. That is to say, contrary to Munck, Paul in his mission is much more demonstrably working *from* an eschatological event than *toward* one.

**2.6. Conclusion.** Whether or not we touch the generative springs of Paul's theology as a whole by focusing upon his eschatological self-understanding, it would appear that in that eschatological self-understanding we are nevertheless provided central explanatory sources for Paul's thinking on mission. Paul's theology of mission is a theology of his own mission, and he understood that mission as an eschatological event. To discern Paul's thinking on mission we must explore his vocational self-understanding, and to do that we must address his eschatology. It is here that we are likely to find the most appropriate matrix within which to understand the place of mission in Paul's theology. Within such a framework particularism is understood by Paul to be giving way to universalism, not by way of struggle and contradiction but as an intended expansion and fulfillment. "You were grafted in," Paul tells his Gentile readers, "to share the rich root of the olive tree" (Rom 11:17; *see* Olive Tree). And it is here as well that the contours of Paul's soteriological universalism find their most effective interpretive setting, no longer as the source of Paul's missionary commitment but as one of its theological consequences.

And to the extent that Paul's larger theological frame is structured as well by underlying assumptions concerning the outworking of the redemptive drama, he and his assigned mission fit within that larger frame as a feature of those eschatological events which are understood to proceed from the first advent and prepare for the second. What has now already been made available at the end of time in the Messiah is to be made available by Paul himself in a geogra-

phically defined outreach to the nations, in fulfillment of the OT eschatological promises, and it is to be realized in representative communities which demonstrate the life of the new age. By thus fulfilling the eschatological promise of blessing to the nations, Paul in his mission helps to complete that task which in the divine economy is to precede the final denouement.

So far as the modern task of apprehending the place of Paul's mission within his theology is concerned, the flood of fresh studies provoked by Sanders has led the modern discussion of Pauline theology in promising directions that have yet to be fully exploited. While Sanders did identify Paul's sense of call to Gentile mission as one of the two basic convictions underlying Paul's theological reflection, and directed particular attention to Munck for a suggestive assessment of this dimension of Pauline thought, the interest of the subsequent discussion has generally concentrated on Sanders's original theme, namely the question of the Law in Paul and in Judaism. Nevertheless, by supporting a renewed awareness of issues about Gentile inclusion, the modern discussion is offering a more congenial climate in which to address the related (but not identical) questions surrounding the place of Paul's mission in his theological reflection.

Whether these latter questions will be effectively addressed within that larger discussion remains yet to be seen. But one must suspect that the way forward in the study of Paul and his mission lies not least in achieving a greater precision both in discerning what exactly Paul was doing in his eschatological mission, and in understanding how that eschatological mission functioned within his larger theological reflection.

*See also* ANTIOCH; APOSTLE; CENTER OF PAUL'S THEOLOGY; CHRONOLOGY OF PAUL; CONVERSION AND CALL OF PAUL; COWORKERS, PAUL AND HIS; DIASPORA; EPHESUS, PAUL AT; ESCHATOLOGY; FINANCIAL SUPPORT; GENTILES; GOSPEL; ITINERARIES, TRAVEL PLANS, JOURNEYS, APOSTOLIC PAROUSIA; JERUSALEM; JUDAIZERS; MINISTRY; OPPONENTS OF PAUL; PAUL AND HIS INTERPRETERS; PAUL IN ACTS AND LETTERS; RELIGIONS, GRECO-ROMAN; SOCIAL-SCIENTIFIC APPROACHES TO PAUL; SOCIAL SETTING OF MISSION CHURCHES; TENTMAKING; TRAVEL IN THE ROMAN WORLD; UNIVERSALISM.

BIBLIOGRAPHY. R. Allen, *Missionary Methods: St Paul's or Ours? A Study of the Church in the Four Provinces* (London: World Dominion, 1912); P. Beskow, "Mission, Trade and Emigration in the Second Century," *SEÅ* 35 (1970) 104-14; J. Blauw, *The Missionary Nature of the Church: A Survey of the Biblical Theology of Mission* (London: Lutterworth, 1962); D. Bosch, "Mission in Paul: Invitation to Join the Eschatological Community," in

*Transforming Mission: Paradigm Shifts in Theology of Mission* (Maryknoll: Orbis, 1991); P. Bowers, "Paul and Religious Propaganda in the First Century" *NovT* 22 (1980) 316-23; idem, "Fulfilling the Gospel: The Scope of the Pauline Mission" *JETS* 30 (1987) 185-98; idem, "Church and Mission in Paul" *JSNT* 44 (1991) 89-111; Y. Congar, "Souci du salut des païens et conscience missionnaire dans le christianisme postapostolique et préconstantinien," in *KYRIAKON. Festschrift Johannes Quasten*, ed. P. Granfield and J. A. Jungmann (Münster: Aschendorff, 1970) 1.3-11; O. Cullmann, "Le caractère eschatologique du devoir missionnaire et de la conscience apostolique de S. Paul" *RHPhR* 16 (1936) 210-45; idem, "Eschatology and Missions in the New Testament," in *The Background of the New Testament and Its Eschatology*, ed. W. D. Davies and D. Daube (Cambridge: University Press, 1954) 409-21; F. Cumont, "Why the Oriental Religions Spread," in *Oriental Religions in Roman Paganism* (New York: Dover, 1956) 20-45; N. A. Dahl, *Studies in Paul: Theology for the Early Christian Mission* (Minneapolis: Augsburg, 1977); W. D. Davies, *Paul and Rabbinic Judaism: Some Rabbinic Elements in Pauline Theology* (4th ed.; Philadelphia: Fortress, 1980); idem, *The Gospel and the Land* (Berkeley: University of California, 1974); J. D. G. Dunn, "The New Perspective on Paul" *BJRL* 65 (1983) 93-122; D. Georgi, *The Opponents of Paul in Second Corinthians* (Philadelphia: Fortress, 1986); D. Gilliland, *Pauline Theology and Mission Practice* (Grand Rapids: Baker, 1983); M. Goodman, "Proselytising in Rabbinic Judaism," *JJS* 40 (1989) 175-85; M. Green, *Evangelism in the Early Church* (Grand Rapids: Eerdmans, 1970); O. Haas, *Paulus der Missionar. Ziel, Grundsätze und Methoden der Missionstätigkeit des Apostels Paulus nach seinen eigenen Aussagen* (Münsterschwarzach: Vier-Türme, 1971); F. Hahn, *Mission in the New Testament* (London: SCM, 1965); M. Hengel, "The Origins of the Christian Mission" in *Between Jesus and Paul: Studies in the Earliest History of Christianity* (Philadelphia: Fortress, 1983) 48-64; E. G. Hinson, *The Evangelization of the Roman Empire: Identity and Adaptability* (Macon, GA: Mercer University, 1981); R. F. Hock, *The Social Context of Paul's Mission* (Philadelphia: Fortress, 1980); B. Holmberg, *Sociology and the New Testament: An Appraisal* (Minneapolis: Fortress, 1990); A. J. Hultgren, *Paul's Gospel and Mission: The Outlook from His Letter to the Romans* (Philadelphia: Fortress, 1985); E. Käsemann, "Justification and Salvation History in the Epistle to the Romans," in *Perspectives on Paul* (Philadelphia: Fortress, 1971) 60-78; H. Kasting, *Die Anfänge der urchristlichen Mission* (Munich: Chr. Kaiser, 1969); S. Kim, *The Origin of Paul's Gospel* (2d ed.; Tübingen: J. C. B. Mohr, 1984); J. Knox, "Romans 15:14-33 and Paul's Conception of His Apostolic Mission," *JBL* 83 (1964) 1-11; K. G. Kuhn, "Das Problem der Mission in der Urchristenheit," *Evangelische Missionszeitschrift* (Stuttgart) 11 (1954) 161-68; S. McKnight, *A Light Among the Gentiles: Jewish Missionary Activity in the Second Temple Period* (Minneapolis: Fortress, 1991); R. MacMullen, *Christianizing the Roman Empire (A.D. 100-400)* (New Haven: Yale University, 1984); idem, *Paganism in the Roman Empire* (New Haven: Yale University, 1981); W. A. Meeks, *The First Urban Christians: The Social World of the Apostle Paul* (New Haven: Yale University, 1983); J. Munck, *Christ and Israel: An Interpretation of Romans 9—11* (Philadelphia: Fortress, 1967); idem, *Paul and the Salvation of Mankind* (Atlanta: John Knox, 1977); M. P. Nilsson, *Geschichte der griechischen Religion* (München: Beck, 1941-50); A. D. Nock, *Conversion: The Old and the New in Religion from Alexander the Great to Augustine of Hippo* (New York: Oxford University Press, 1933); idem, *Essays on Religion and the Ancient World* (2 vols.; Cambridge: Harvard, 1972); W.-H. Ollrog, *Paulus und seine Mitarbeiter* (Neukirchen-Vluyn: Neukirchener, 1979); W. M. Ramsay, *St. Paul the Traveller and Roman Citizen* (11th ed.; London: Hodder & Stoughton, 1895); E. P. Sanders, *Paul and Palestinian Judaism* (Philadelphia: Fortress, 1977); idem, *Paul, the Law and the Jewish People* (Philadelphia: Fortress, 1983); A. Schweitzer, *The Mysticism of Paul the Apostle* (London: Black, 1931); D. Senior and C. Stuhlmueller, *The Biblical Foundations for Mission* (Maryknoll: Orbis, 1983); K. Stendahl, *Paul Among Jews and Gentiles* (Philadelphia: Fortress, 1976); G. Theissen, *The Social Setting of Pauline Christianity: Essays on Corinth* (Philadelphia: Fortress, 1982); F. Watson, *Paul, Judaism and the Gentiles: A Sociological Approach* (Cambridge: University Press, 1986); N. T. Wright, "The Paul of History and the Apostle of Faith" *TynB* 19 (1978) 61-88.

W. P. Bowers

**MISSIONARY JOURNEYS.** *See* CHRONOLOGY OF PAUL; ITINERARIES, TRAVEL PLANS, JOURNEYS, APOSTOLIC PAROUSIA; MISSION; PAUL IN ACTS AND LETTERS.

**MITHRAISM.** *See* RELIGIONS, GRECO-ROMAN.

**MONEY.** *See* COLLECTION FOR THE SAINTS; FINANCIAL SUPPORT; RICHES AND POVERTY; TENTMAKING.

**MONOTHEISM.** *See* CHRISTOLOGY; GOD.

**MONTHS.** *See* HOLY DAYS.

**MORTALITY.** *See* IMMORTALITY; LIFE AND DEATH; RESURRECTION.

# MOSES

References to Moses in the Pauline Corpus are few in number. Yet it is through these few references that one catches an important glimpse of Paul's hermeneutical method and gains a crucial understanding of the relationship between the old and new covenants.*

1. As a Historical Figure
2. Identified by His Work As Lawgiver
3. Illustrative Use of Moses
4. Typological Use of Moses
5. Reflective Use of Moses
6. Use of Mosaic Haggadah and Lore
7. Theologically Significant Uses

## 1. As a Historical Figure.

Paul clearly sees Moses as a historical figure and recounts several significant events in Moses' life. Mention is made of the duplication of Moses' miracles by Pharaoh's court magicians (2 Tim 3:8), of the revelation of God's* sovereign character to Moses while in the cleft of the rock (Rom 9:15) and of the descent of Moses from Mt. Sinai with the Law* (2 Cor 3:7-11). Moses is also used to mark a historical period of time. In Romans 5:14 Paul makes the claim that "death reigned from Adam until Moses."

## 2. Identified by His Work As Lawgiver.

Moses is primarily identified in Paul by his work as lawgiver. The Law was "put into effect through angels by the hand of a mediator"—who by implication was Moses (Gal 3:19). The splendor of the Law was transferred to Moses' face as he descended from Mt. Sinai (2 Cor 3:7). Paul can therefore refer to the Law as "the Law of Moses" (1 Cor 9:9). So closely, in fact, are Moses and the Law linked that they become virtually interchangeable. Citations from the Law are prefaced by "Moses writes" (Rom 10:5; cf. Rom 10:19; see Old Testament in Paul). "The reading of the old covenant" (2 Cor 3:14) becomes "when Moses is read" (2 Cor 3:15). And the period when the Law was given is called the "time of Moses" (Rom 5:14).

## 3. Illustrative Use of Moses.

The most frequent contexts in which "Moses" appears are illustrative ones. Timothy is warned that in the last days there will be those who oppose the truth "just as Jannes and Jambres opposed Moses" (2 Tim 3:1-9). The church at Corinth is cautioned against following the idolatrous (see Idolatry) example of the wilderness generation, which had been "baptized into Moses" (1 Cor 10:1-22).

Moses himself is used as an example at several points. The custom of Moses' removing the veil from his face on entering the tabernacle to speak with the Lord* (Ex 34:34) becomes an example for Paul of the action that the Jews in his own day needed to take (2 Cor 3:15-17). For only if "someone turns to the Lord" as Moses did, will "the veil be removed" as Moses' veil was (2 Cor 3:16). Moses' request to be blotted out of Yahweh's book for the sake of Israel* (Ex 32:30-35) is probably behind Paul's willingness to be cut off from Christ* for the sake of his Jewish kinspeople (Rom 9:3).

A number of Paul's illustrative uses are contrastive ones. Yet these references are not to Moses per se but to his "old covenant" ministry or to his office as lawgiver, over against which the apostolic ministry* and the new covenant are set. The gospel* minister, Paul claims, is very open and forthright in manner, "and not as Moses who placed a veil over his face, so that the sons of Israel could not stare intently down to the last glimmer of that which was fading" (2 Cor 3:12-13). This, Paul states, is because of the character of the ministry that each represents ("because we have such a hope," 2 Cor 3:12). For the ministry of Moses, though it came with overwhelming glory* (2 Cor 3:7), was nonetheless a ministry of "death" (2 Cor 3:7; see Life and Death), "condemnation" (2 Cor 3:9) and "fading glory" (2 Cor 3:11), while the apostolic ministry is of "the Spirit" (2 Cor 3:8; see Holy Spirit), "righteousness"* (2 Cor 3:9) and "permanence" (2 Cor 3:11). As was fitting for such a ministry, Moses customarily covered his face (Ex 34:35), whereas the face of the gospel minister is "unveiled," thereby reflecting a glory that, far from fading, is constantly increasing (2 Cor 3:18).

## 4. Typological Use of Moses.

Paul nowhere employs Moses as a type of Christ. This is probably because of the parochial nature of the Mosaic ministry as contrasted with the universal character of the gospel. Yet, like other NT writers, Paul finds in Moses and the wilderness generation a pattern or "type" for his own day (see Old Testament in Paul). To the church at Corinth Paul writes that what happened to the wilderness generation took place as "types" (typoi; 1 Cor 10:6). The suggestion is that the many visible blessings that God bestowed on Israel (e.g., the crossing of the Red Sea, the miraculous provision of food and water) occurred as prefigurements of the far greater blessings that the church experiences through Christ (e.g., salvation,* the Lord's Supper,* baptism*). Among these blessings Paul includes Israel's being "baptized into Moses."

## 5. Reflective Use of Moses.

More often Paul found that current events shed light

on events of the past. This is especially true for Moses and the wilderness generation. Seen through the perspective of salvation in Christ, Paul could claim that the rock that followed Israel through the wilderness "*was* Christ" (*ēn ho Christos*, 1 Cor 10:4). And he could assert that what was thought to have been written by Moses out of concern for the ox who labors in the field, could now be understood as God's concern for the gospel minister who labors on Christ's behalf (1 Cor 9:9-12). It is salvation *en Christō* ("in Christ") that leads Paul to the recognition that the Mosaic covenant has become "old" (2 Cor 3:14) and that Israel pursued the Law-righteousness about which "Moses wrote," but never attained (Rom 10:1-5; *see* Law). And it is the overwhelming response of the Gentiles* to the gospel that allows him to identify what Moses obscurely referred to as "those who are not a nation" (Rom 10:19). It is also the corresponding Jewish lack of response to the gospel that leads Paul to speak of divine election* by grace* (Rom 9:15) and prompts him to seek an explanation for this response in Moses' veiled face and the resultant dulling of Israel to the transient character of the Law "until this very day" (2 Cor 3:13-15).

### 6. Use of Mosaic Haggadah and Lore.

Scholarship is coming more and more to the realization that Paul was dependent on the vast body of extrabiblical Jewish lore that developed around the major OT figures. This dependence is brought home clearly when one investigates Paul's Mosaic references. Paul incorporates such Mosaic lore as the opposition of Jannes and Jambres to Moses (2 Tim 3:8; cf. CD 5:17-19), angels* giving the Law to Moses (Gal 3:19; cf. *Jub.* 1:27-29), Israel's inability to look at the glory of the face of Moses when he descended Mt. Sinai (2 Cor 3:7; cf. Philo *Vit. Mos.* 2.70), the fading character of Moses' facial splendor (2 Cor 3:7; cf. *Zohar* 3.58a), the reason Moses veiled his face (2 Cor 3:13; cf. *Bib. Ant.* 12.1-3) and the rock that followed Israel through forty years of wilderness wandering (1 Cor 10:4; cf. *Bib. Ant.* 11.15).

### 7. Theologically Significant Uses.

A number of the Pauline Mosaic references function in theologically significant ways. One of the blessings that Paul recalls from Israel's history is that "all were baptized into Moses" (*pantes eis ton Mōusēn ebaptisthēsan*, 1 Cor 10:2). "Baptism *into*" elsewhere in Paul is used of the believer's incorporation into and union with Christ (e.g., Rom 6:3; Gal 3:27; *see* In Christ). Paul finds a parallel to the Christian experience of baptism in Israel's crossing the Red Sea, which becomes her "baptism" or means of corporate identification with Moses ("into Moses") as leader of Israel.

A notoriously difficult problem is determining the basis for Paul's verdict in Romans 5:14 that death "reigned from Adam until Moses," as this sentence of death was prior to the Mosaic standard for judging sin* (Rom 5:13; *see* Adam and Christ). This has become a critical text for subsequent theological doctrines such as the imputation of guilt to all of Adam's descendants by virtue of their corporate solidarity with Adam, as well as for the argument regarding the pre-Mosaic existence of the Law, a conclusion bearing significant implications for the role of Law in salvation history.

Paul's references to Moses in 2 Corinthians 3:6-18 are of critical importance. For it is here that one finds some of his strongest statements regarding the fundamental discontinuity between Christianity and Judaism. The Jews are blind to the fact that their covenant has become "old," is temporary in function and, as an external code, kills and condemns. By contrast the Christian covenant is "new," permanent and, through the internal working of the Spirit, brings life* and righteousness. It is just such an understanding that eventually led to the separation of the church from the synagogue.

*See also* ABRAHAM; ADAM AND CHRIST; COVENANT AND NEW COVENANT; LAW; OLD TESTAMENT IN PAUL.

BIBLIOGRAPHY. L. Belleville, *Reflections of Glory. Paul's Polemical Use of the Moses-Doxa Tradition in 2 Corinthians 3:12-18* (Sheffield: Academic, 1991); P. Démann. "Moïse et la loi dans la pensée de saint Paul," in *Moïse, l'homme de l'Alliance*, ed. H. Cazelles (Paris: Desclée, 1955) 189-242; R. P. C. Hanson, "Moses in the Typology of St. Paul," *Theology* 48 (1945) 174-77; R. E. Nixon, *The Exodus in the NT* (London: Tyndale, 1963); T. Saito, *Die Mosevorstellungen im Neuen Testament* (Bern: Peter Lang, 1977).

L. L. Belleville

## MYSTERY

The word *mystery* in modern speech means a sublime or unclear truth that is marvelled at but only partly understood. The Greek *mystērion*, however, describes any divine or heavenly* reality which is regarded as hidden or secret and can be known only when revealed by the gods.

    1. Background
    2. Mystery in Paul

### 1. Background.

In Paul's world *mystērion* ("mystery") was employed in the ancient pagan cults, philosophy,* secular usage and Gnosticism. Recent biblical scholarship has focused attention on the OT and Judaism, particularly the wisdom* literature, apocalyptic* literature (e.g., *2 Apoc. Bar.* 81:4; 4 Ezra 14:5; *1 Enoch* 51:3; 103:2; 104:10) and Qumran (e.g., 1QpHab 7:4, 8, 13; 1QM 3:8; 16:9; 1QS 3:21-23; 4:18; 11:34; 1QH 7:27; 10:4; 11:9, 16), as the proper background for understanding the NT writers' use of the "mystery" language.

*Mystērion* corresponds to the Aramaic *rāz* ("secret"), frequently found in the book of Daniel (Dan 2:18, 19, 27-30, 47), which denotes "an eschatological mystery, a concealed intimation of divinely ordained future events whose disclosure and interpretation is reserved for God alone" (Bornkamm, 814-15).

## 2. Mystery in Paul.

*Mystērion* appears twenty-one times in Paul's letters out of a total of twenty-seven NT occurrences. Usually it points not to some future event hidden in God's plan, but to his decisive action in Christ here and now. Paul normally employs the term with reference to its disclosure or its being revealed (Rom 16:25-26; 1 Cor 2:10; Col 1:26-27; Eph 1:9; 3:3, 5).

### 2.1. Earlier References.

*2.1.1. 1 Corinthians 2:1, 7.* Apart from the earliest reference to *mystērion* in 2 Thessalonians 2:7 in a negative sense ("the mystery of lawlessness which is at work"; *see* Man of Lawlessness), the apostle* offers some important insights into his view of revelation in his early use of this word in 1 Corinthians 2. After indicating that the only knowledge* he proclaimed as he set forth "the mystery of God" (1 Cor 2:1 *v.l.*) at Corinth was Jesus as the crucified Messiah (*see* Christ), Paul states: "we speak God's wisdom* in a mystery." The gift of wisdom is for the *teleioi*, "the mature," not the initiates of the Hellenistic mystery religions. Rather it is for those who by their attitude and behavior show they are spiritual rather than carnal and thus are ready for "solid food" (1 Cor 3:1-4). The mystery which focuses on salvation* through the cross of Jesus Christ is not new, for God* had decreed it "before the ages" (1 Cor 2:7; *see* Election and Predestination). It has been kept hidden from "the rulers of this world" (1 Cor 2:8; *see* Principalities and Powers): only ignorance of the mystery can explain their crucifixion* of "the Lord of glory." But now the mystery of God's salvific plan, which includes the divine inheritance, is being revealed through his Spirit (1 Cor 2:10; *see* Holy Spirit); it completely escapes human perception, but God has prepared it for all who love* him (cf. Rom 8:28-30).

*2.1.2. 1 Corinthians 4:1; 13:2; 14:2.* The plural *mysteries* appears here, perhaps for polemical reasons or

because it draws attention to the essential elements of the one mystery. As an apostle Paul is a steward of "the mysteries of God" (1 Cor 4:1). In 1 Corinthians 13:2, where "all mysteries" include everything that transcends human power of conceiving, he may be rebuking those who thought they had a superior understanding of Christian teaching—after all, only God understands "*all* mysteries." "Mysteries" (perhaps hidden truths of God, 1 Cor 14:2), spoken in a tongue, are unintelligible and of little value unless interpreted (*see* Tongues).

*2.1.3. Romans 16:25; 11:25.* In the concluding doxology of Romans (Rom 16:25) there is a correlation between the disclosure of the mystery and Paul's preaching* of Jesus Christ. The connection between the mystery and the salvation of the *Gentiles** is a feature that is developed in Ephesians* and Colossians.* An element of new teaching may be in view in Romans 11:25 where the "mystery" points to the salvation of the *Jews* (cf. 1 Cor 15:51; *see* Israel).

### 2.2. Colossians and Ephesians.
Some of the most significant Pauline references to *mystērion* occur in Colossians and Ephesians.

*2.2.1. Colossians 1:26-27; 2:2; 4:3.* The "mystery" has to do with God's decisive action in Christ in the here and now (Col 1:26-27). It is characterized by "riches," for in it the wealth of God was lavished in a wonderful way, and "glory"* which suggests that it shared in the character of God himself. Its content was "Christ in you [Colossians], the hope of glory": he now indwelt these Gentiles who had believed its proclamation. They are to come to a deeper understanding of Christ, God's mystery, for in him all the treasures of wisdom were available (Col 2:2). Finally, the Colossians are to pray for Paul so that he might proclaim this divine mystery in a clear manner (Col 4:3; cf. Eph 6:19).

*2.2.2. Ephesians 1:9; 3:3, 4, 9; 5:32; 6:19.* Ephesians has been called the "epistle of the mystery." Paul uses the term six times in the letter and in Ephesians 3:2-11, in the context of his stewardship, he presents the fullest NT expression of this concept. Many key theological terms in Ephesians are associated with "the mystery." In Ephesians 1:9 *mystērion* refers to God's plan to unite in Christ all things in heaven* and earth (Eph 1:22-23; *see* Peace, Reconciliation), and this refers to subduing everything, especially hostile "powers," under his lordship. "Christ is the one who will consummate all things by providing ultimate redemption for believers and pacifying the opposing forces" (Arnold). The focus of the mystery which was made known to Paul on the Damascus road is Christ (Eph 3:4; *see* Conversion and Call), for in him the unseen God is fully revealed. As a steward of the mystery Paul knows that the Gentiles were destined to be fellow heirs, members of the same body and partakers of the same promises as Israel (Eph 3:6). In the reconciliation (*see* Peace, Reconciliation) of Jews and Gentiles in one body the manifold wisdom of God is unfolded (Eph 3:10; *see* Body of Christ). The very existence of the church bears witness to the "administration of the mystery," which further implies the defeat and ultimate overthrow of the powers. In Ephesians 5:32 the "mystery" points to the union of Christ and the church, the meaning of which (perhaps like Gen 2:24) is hidden.

The situation of "perceived demonic hostility in western Asia Minor may have provided a partial motivation" for Paul's emphasis on the cosmic aspect of the mystery in Ephesians (Arnold). It could have stood in deliberate contrast to the Lydian-Phrygian "mysteries," which were so popular, so as to be a polemic against the possible influence of these mysteries in the churches. According to PGM I.128-32 a pagan mystery initiation involved receiving "the lord of the air" (cf. Eph 2:2) as the indwelling deity!

The mystery revealed in Ephesians, however, was the opposite of the pagan mysteries. Christ bringing "all things" under his head implied the impending doom of the so-called deities invoked in magic and the mystery religions. It is inadequate to claim that the content of the mystery in Ephesians is defined solely in terms of God's acceptance of the Gentiles and their union with Jews on an equal footing in Christ (Eph 3:3-4). Christ is the starting point for a true understanding of the notion of "mystery" in this letter, as elsewhere in Paul. There are not a number of "mysteries" with limited applications, but one supreme "mystery" with a number of applications (Caragounis).

*2.3. 1 Timothy 3:9, 16.* Mystērion appears twice in the Pastorals, that is, in 1 Timothy 3:9, 16. Many claim that in its first occurrence, the "mystery of faith" (1 Tim 3:9), *mystērion* here has lost its characteristically Pauline sense and describes what transcends ordinary comprehension. However, it is best to understand the phrase as referring to the corpus of Christian teaching. This is a logical inference from the earlier usage of speaking about the saving plan of God. Essentially the expression is akin to the truth of the gospel, particularly the saving character of Christ's death, which was previously hidden but not revealed by the Spirit (1 Cor 2:6-16). "Faith" is here used in an objective sense so that "the mystery of faith is what is believed, as the mystery of the gospel is what is preached" (Brown).

In 1 Timothy 3:16 the unusual expression "the mystery (*mystērion*) of godliness" ("our religion," NRSV)

appears. "Godliness," a favorite term in 1 Timothy, which usually refers to "the duty which people owe to God," is here understood in an objective way to refer to the content or basis of Christianity. What follows in the hymn expresses something of the content of the "revealed truth" of this godliness which has been committed to God's people (Fee). The hymn's focus is upon Christ's humiliation and exaltation, and Christians' ongoing praise of him as the exalted and glorified One. This double emphasis may stand in contrast to the Christology of the false teachers in Ephesus, with the hymn preparing the way for Paul's censure that follows. At the same time the apostle exhorts his colleague Timothy to stand firm and in sharp contrast to the false teachers (1 Tim 4:6-16).

*See also* Cross, Theology of the; Gentiles; Gnosis, Gnosticism; Religions, Greco-Roman; Wisdom.

BIBLIOGRAPHY. C. E. Arnold, *Ephesians: Power and Magic* (SNTSMS 63: Cambridge: University Press, 1989); M. N. A. Bockmuehl, *Revelation and Mystery* (WUNT 2/2; Tübingen: J. C. B. Mohr, 1990); G. Bornkamm, "μυστήριον, μυέω," *TDNT* IV.802-28; R. E. Brown, *The Semitic Background of the Term "Mystery" in the New Testament* (FBBS 21; Philadelphia: Fortress, 1968); C. C. Caragounis, *The Ephesian Mysterion: Meaning and Content* (ConNT 8; Lund: Gleerup, 1977); J. Coppens, " 'Mystery' in the Theology of St. Paul and Its Parallels at Qumran," in *Paul and Qumran,* ed. J. Murphy-O'Connor (London: Chapman, 1968) 132-58; G. Fee, *1 and 2 Timothy, Titus* (NIBC; Peabody, MA: Hendrickson, 1984); A. E. Harvey, "The Use of Mystery Language in the Bible," *JTS* 81 (1980) 320-36.

P. T. O'Brien

**MYSTERY RELIGIONS.** *See* Religions, Greco-Roman.

## MYSTICISM

The attempt to understand Paul in terms of "mysticism" has been very popular in the past, but has inevitably run into difficulties of definition. "Mysticism" can be understood broadly as "a generic term covering an enormous range and variety of experience. . . . All the great figures in the history of religion were, basically, mystics" (S. G. F. Brandon, 462-63). On this description, Paul was undoubtedly a mystic. However, this criterion tends to obscure rather than illuminate. Accordingly, we prefer R. C. Tannehill's clearer and more specific definition of "mysticism" as "the doctrine that the individual can come into immediate contact with God through subjective experiences which differ essentially from the experiences of ordinary life" (Tannehill, 4). Two questions, therefore, arise: Was Paul a "mystic?" Does he have a mystical theology?

1. Earlier Views
2. Paul's Conversion
3. Dying and Rising with Christ
4. Being "in Christ"
5. Sharing Christ's Sufferings
6. Paul's Contentment
7. Glossolalia
8. Conclusions

### 1. Earlier Views.

Significant earlier studies understood Paul's interpretation of Christian existence in terms of "mysticism." A. Schweitzer claimed Paul's mysticism was unique since it took the form of union with Christ ("Christ-mysticism") rather than direct union with God. The apostle's teaching on "being-in-Christ" (see "In Christ") which provided the clue to his entire thought, was founded on theology, and was essentially eschatological.* A. Deissmann and J. Schneider spoke of Paul's "passion mysticism" as they focussed attention on his experiences of suffering within the context of the dying* and rising with Christ theme. "Ontological mysticism" has been used of A. Wikenhauser's presentation and refers not to an experience but to an objective state of all Christians; it is for Wikenhauser, "the mysterious union between Paul—and indeed all Christians—and the person of Christ Triumphant" (Wikenhauser, 19).

Each of these earlier interpreters was attempting to come to grips with several important motifs in Paul, including his teaching about dying* and rising with Christ and being "in Christ." The following issues are relevant to our inquiry:

### 2. Paul's Conversion.

Paul uses the language of revelation (Gal 1:12, 16) and mystery* (Eph 3:3, 4, 9) to describe his conversion-commissioning on the Damascus road (see Conversion and Call). The gospel* came to him through a revelation of Jesus Christ* (Gal 1:11-12). God was pleased to reveal his Son* in him in order that he might preach him among the Gentiles* (Gal 1:15-16). Paul stresses the inward and personal character of God's revelation: it was *"in me."* Yet for him inward illumination and outward vision* coincided. Stressing the objectivity of the latter he states that Christ appeared to him (*ōphthē* is the language of christophany, 1 Cor 15:8), and so he *saw* Christ (1 Cor 9:1). A. F. Segal has attempted to understand Paul as an ecstatic visionary who underwent a mystical conversion akin to the experiences found in the Jewish mystical tradition exem-

plified in the Qumran* Angelic Liturgy, 1 Enoch and later medieval Merkabah mysticism. While valuable insights may be gained from viewing Paul's visionary experience against this more clearly defined environment of Jewish mysticism, with its theme of the ascent to heaven, Segal's rereading of Paul's language of justification and spiritual transformation (e.g., "His faith in Christ, based on his conversion experience, made him feel righteous and justified him"; Segal, 130) does violence to Paul's emphasis on the objectivity of Christ and his salvific work. Even if Paul is thought of as a mystic on Tannehill's definition, the Damascus christophany does not support the notion of a mystical theology.

### 3. Dying and Rising with Christ.

The apostle's dying and rising with Christ was a personal, life-changing experience (Gal 2:20; cf. Rom 6:3-6; Col 2:11-12, 20; 3:1-4; see Dying and Rising). He, like other believers, was personally united with his Lord in the salvation-historical acts of the cross* and resurrection.* But this important event is misunderstood when dissolved into a subjective, mystical experience. The apostle does not isolate the individual and focus on the inner experience as mysticism does. Consequently, any attempt to understand this dying and rising motif in terms of mysticism fails to come to grips with its corporate nature or Paul's eschatological teaching about the two ages, while mysticism obscures the connection of this motif with other basic themes of his thought.

### 4. Being "in Christ."

Phrases such as "in Christ"* (cf. Phil 1:13; 2:1, etc.) or "in the Lord" (cf. Phil 1:14; 2:24, etc.) are characteristic of Paul, and it is the notion which they express that is often in view when people speak of "Pauline mysticism" (cf. Schweitzer). These phrases, which focus on the fact that Christians are fellow members of the body of Christ, have nothing to do with individual mysticism (it is even doubtful whether the expression "the mystical body of Christ" is appropriate). The corporate significance of being in Christ is regularly stressed by Paul, both in relation to what God has done on behalf of his people and the responsibilities believers have to Christ and to one another. All believers are incorporated into the body* of Christ by the Holy Spirit* (1 Cor 12:13), and his presence, by which they are empowered for new life, is in fulfillment of the OT promises about the outpouring of the Lord's Spirit on his people in an unprecedented way (cf. Ezek 36:24-27; Joel 2:28-29).

### 5. Sharing Christ's Sufferings.

The notion of "sharing in Christ's sufferings*" is part

of Paul's wider teaching on dying and rising with Christ and is not to be interpreted along mystical lines. The background to this teaching is the messianic woes of OT and Jewish apocalyptic* thought which would usher in the end time. With the death and resurrection of the Lord Jesus the coming age has already been inaugurated, even though the present age still continues. Christians living between the first and second comings of Christ already experience these afflictions and sufferings, for it is through them that they enter the kingdom* of God (Acts 14:22; 1 Thess 3:3, 7). The exalted Christ in heaven continues to suffer in his members, not least in Paul himself. The sufferings which he experienced in his apostolic* ministry* were "Christ's afflictions" (Phil 3:10; Col 1:24) and were endured on behalf of other Christians like the Colossians.* The more Paul bore in his own person the more his fellow-believers would be spared (cf. 2 Cor 4:12).

### 6. Paul's Contentment.
The mystic tends to be self-sufficient (*autarkēs*) in his religious life, or he can become so when the circumstances require it. Paul, who insists on the common life in the body of Christ where members are interrelated and interdependent with each contributing to the welfare of others and to the whole, speaks of sufficiency: "I have learned to be *content* in whatever circumstances I find myself" (Phil 4:11). But his *autarkeia* was not Stoic self-sufficiency, the cultivated attitude of the wise person who could face life and death with equanimity because of his own inner resources; rather, Paul's independence of external circumstances was only because he was totally dependent upon God. He is able to be content in all things because of his relationship with Christ who gives him strength (Phil 4:12-13). The apostle's contentment is different from the *sufficiency* (*autarkeia*) of the mystic.

### 7. Glossolalia.
Paul makes special reference to glossolalia (*see* Tongues), but it was not necessarily bound up with mysticism, for the one could exist without the other. The person speaking with tongues "utters mysteries in the spirit"; but he is not communicating anything "for no one understands him" (1 Cor 14:2). It is the source and content of the utterance which is important rather than the simple fact of its being inspired. Paul himself practiced glossolalia (1 Cor 14:18; 2 Cor 5:13, possibly), but he downplays this gift in favor of prophecy* which edifies the congregation.

### 8. Conclusions.
In light of the above-mentioned definition Paul may be spoken of as a "mystic" (cf. his visions 2 Cor 12:1-4), but he does not have a mystical theology. His theology was not based on experiences which might be called mystical, but "on Jesus, the fulfiller of God's promise and purpose of salvation; Jesus, the crucified and exalted Lord; Jesus, the divine wisdom, in whom God creates, maintains and brings to consummation everything that exists; Jesus, who here and now lives within his people by his Spirit" (Bruce, 75). So, Paul's all-consuming passion was "the incomparable value of knowing Christ Jesus my Lord" (Phil 3:8).

*See also* CONVERSION AND CALL OF PAUL; DYING AND RISING WITH CHRIST; IN CHRIST; SUFFERING; TONGUES; VISIONS, ECSTATIC EXPERIENCE.

BIBLIOGRAPHY. S. G. F. Brandon, ed., *A Dictionary of Comparative Religion* (New York: Scribner's, 1970); F. F. Bruce, "Was Paul a Mystic?" *RTR* 34 (1975) 66-75; L. Cerfaux, *The Christian in the Theology of St. Paul* (London: Chapman, 1967); A. Deissmann, *Paul: A Study in Social and Religious History* (London: Hodder & Stoughton, 1926); J. D. G. Dunn, *Jesus and the Spirit* (Philadelphia: Westminster, 1975); A. T. Lincoln, "Paul the Visionary: the Setting and Significance of the Rapture to Paradise in 2 Corinthians 12:1-10," *NTS* 25 (1979) 204-20; J. Schneider, *Die Passionsmystik des Paulus* (Leipzig: Hinrichs, 1929); A. Schweitzer, *The Mysticism of St. Paul* (London: A. & C. Black, 1931); A. F. Segal, *Paul the Convert: The Apostolate and Apostasy of Saul the Pharisee* (New Haven: Yale, 1990); J. D. Tabor, *Things Unutterable: Paul's Ascent to Paradise in Its Greco-Roman, Judaic, and Early Christian Contexts* (Lanham, MD: University Press of America, 1986); R. C. Tannehill, *Dying and Rising with Christ: A Study in Pauline Theology* (BZNW 32; Berlin: Töpelmann, 1967); A. Wikenhauser, *Pauline Mysticism: Christ in the Mystical Teaching of St. Paul* (Edinburgh: Nelson, 1960).

P. T. O'Brien

# N

**NAG HAMMADI.** *See* APOCRYPHAL PAULINE LITER-
ATURE; GNOSIS, GNOSTICISM.

## NAME

Of some 225 NT uses of the noun "name" (*onoma*),
only twenty-one are found in Paul's letters. However,
the verb "to name" (*onomazō*), which is found nine
times in the NT, appears six times in the Pauline letters. Paul's usage of "name" always speaks of more
than a topical identification. It is a description of the
one to whom reference is made. In many cases
"name" is virtually equivalent to a person or being. In
that regard, "the name above all names" (Phil 2:9)
means the person higher than any rival beings: the
Lord* Jesus Christ.* The verbal examples range from
a description that presumes the reality of the character implied in a name to a personal identification with,
or trust in, the person being "named."

1. Human Names.
2. God's Name.
3. Christ's Name.
4. The Name Above All Names

### 1. Human Names.

In dealing with the factions in the church* at Corinth* that were short-sightedly following leading per-
sonalities, Paul asks pointedly: "Were you baptized
into the name of Paul?" (1 Cor 1:13 NIV). The similarity of expression between this passage (see also 1 Cor
1:15) and the trinitarian formula for baptism* in Matthew 28:19, and particularly the compressed statement
in Acts 2:38, strongly suggests that Paul is concerned
about improper identification with, or adherence to,
his person. Paul's "name" thus stands for his person,
which could never take the place of the person of
Christ (1 Cor 1:13). Similarly, Paul's later mention of
his coworkers* "whose names are in the book of life"
(Phil 4:3) has the same force. It is clearly the eternal
destiny of people like Euodia, Syntyche, and Clement
(4:2-3) that is meant here.

Three examples of the verb "to name" are of significance at this point. The Greek phrase *adelphos onoma-*
*zomenos* in 1 Corinthians 5:11 may speak of a "so-called
brother" (NASB)—one outwardly "named" a Christian,
but lacking inward reality—or, more naturally in the
context, one whose behavior belies his "name" as a
believer. Ephesians 5:3 urges that immoral or impure
actions not even be "named" among Christians, apparently meaning that there be no "hint" (NIV) that such
behavior is actually taking place. We find an analogy
elsewhere in the NT where the name *Christianos*,
"Christian," was apparently a name given by outsiders
to identify believers as "followers of Christ" (Acts 11:26;
26:28). While this name may first have been used in
ridicule of believers by those outside the Christian
community, for Christians it came to imply the honor
of bearing Christ's name (1 Pet 4:16) in a life consistent
with Christ. In a broader sense, Ephesians 3:15 speaks
of every *patria*, every "nation," "family" or "clan" "in
heaven and on earth" as being "named" only by God,*
the "Father" (*patēr*, Eph 3:14). Here Paul seems to be
speaking of every grouping of spiritual ("heaven") and
human ("earth") beings. Their assignment of a
"name" is solely a divine prerogative and an expression of God's sovereignty over every power in the cosmos (see Arnold, 58-59; Lincoln, 201-4).

### 2. God's Name.

In Romans the common OT usage of "name" in connection with God is drawn upon most clearly among
Paul's writings. OT citations in Romans 2:24, 9:17 and
15:9 all support the equivalence between the name of
God and his person. Romans 10:13, quoting Joel 2:32,
extends the same parallel to "the name of the Lord,"
which in Joel refers to God, while in Romans it speaks
specifically of Christ (Rom 10:10).

The two other instances in the Pauline corpus
where name refers to God are in the Pastorals. 1 Timothy 6:1 provides an example of the name of God as
a way of speaking of the divine person. In 2 Timothy
2:19 the verb and noun forms are combined in the
phrase "naming the name of the Lord" (*onomazōn to*
*onoma kyriou*; cf. Is 26:13), which in its context means
identifying fully with God and his sovereignty and

turning "away from wickedness."

### 3. Christ's Name.

Eleven of the twenty-one uses of the noun *name* refer to Jesus Christ (with an additional instance of *ōnomasthē*, "named," in Romans 15:20). The apostle's earliest uses of the term *name* are in the Thessalonian letters. His prayer* that "the name of our Lord Jesus be glorified in you" (2 Thess 1:12 NIV) is to express the desire that Jesus Christ, as a person, may receive the glory* he deserves. In 2 Thessalonians 3:6 the command given "in the name of the Lord Jesus Christ" draws upon the sovereign authority of his person, not some magical quality Paul attributes to Christ's name.

Interestingly, the two examples of the name of Jesus Christ in Romans are found in the introduction (Rom 1:5) and biographical epilogue (Rom 15:20). Romans 1:4-5 states that it is in the resurrection* power* of "Jesus Christ our Lord" that Paul extended his apostleship* to "all the nations for his name's sake" (*hyper tou onomatos autou*). This means, in essence, that Paul carried out his apostolic ministry* to glorify the person of Jesus Christ. In Romans 15:20 Paul speaks of "proclaiming the gospel not where Christ has already been named [*ōnomasthē*]." The verb *named* could initially be taken as a superficial hearing of the gospel,* but the context seems to demand a deeper knowledge of, response to and possibly worship* of the person of Christ (Rom 15:19-20).

1 Corinthians employs the term *name* four times in connection with Jesus Christ (1 Cor 1:2, 10; 5:4; 6:11). As with most of Paul's other references to the name of Christ, "Lord"* (*kyrios*) occurs as a title of highest authority,* further emphasizing the worship and obedience due his person. Paul appeals to the Corinthians as those "who call on the name of the Lord Jesus Christ" (1 Cor 1:2). Thus agreement and unity between them is possible in Christ's "name" (1 Cor 1:10). Their justification* and sanctification* came about "in the name of the Lord Jesus Christ" (1 Cor 6:11), and their church* "assembled in the name of our Lord Jesus" (1 Cor 5:4). In each case it is Christ's person or authority, or both, that is in focus with the use of "name."

The remaining three references to Christ's name are found in the prison letters. In contexts that contain a striking number of parallel terms, Colossians 3:17 and Ephesians 5:20 both include "the name" of the Lord Jesus Christ in the midst of admonitions for God-empowered relationships with other Christians and for constant thanksgiving before God. Everything that is said or done is to be carried out "in the name

of the Lord Jesus" (Col 3:17). Thus all of life is to be lived under the conscious authority of Christ and in active, thankful allegiance to his magnificent person (Col 3:17; Eph 5:20). Such a perspective takes on cosmic and eternal dimensions in Philippians 2:10-11. Despite the ongoing debate over the structure and significance of the Christ hymn in Philippians 2:6-11 (see Martin 1983), it is clear that "the name of Jesus" deserves and demands universal worship: "in heaven and on earth and under the earth" (Phil 2:10).

### 4. The Name Above All Names.

In Ephesians 1:20 Paul strongly asserts that Christ, in his glorious post-resurrection status (Eph 1:20), is far above "every name named" (*pantos onomatos onomazomenou*, Eph 1:21). A number of significant studies have posited that the "powers" (Eph 1:20) over which the Lord Jesus is exalted (Eph 1:21) are societal or political structures. But it is much more likely that the letter is addressing a cultural milieu in which supernatural demonic* beings are regarded with fear (so Arnold; *see* Principalities and Powers). The phrase "every name named" would thus include every possible power that might be named by those who call upon deities or spirits whether for the practice of magic* or in worship (in either case, the "name" of the spiritual power plays an important role).

The usage of the verbal form (*onomazein*) and the noun form (*onoma*) in Acts 19:13, in the context of an attempted exorcism at Ephesus, is generally parallel to Ephesians 1:20-21 and lends some credibility to the view that Ephesians is addressing a similar situation in Asia Minor in which the relationship between Christ and the demonic powers is a concern (*see* Ephesus). Also, like Philippians 2:10-11, Christ's unrivaled supremacy over any and every being that could be mentioned exists "not only in the present age but also in the age to come" (Eph 1:21). Though it is not yet seen clearly in earthly terms, the surpassing greatness of Christ's name means "all things" have been placed under his feet (Eph 1:22), in fulfillment of such messianic texts as Psalm 110:1 and 8:5-7 (*see* Exaltation, Enthronement; Triumph).

The most significant christological use of "name" in Paul occurs in Philippians 2:9 where "the name above every name" is given to Christ. The exaltation of Christ Jesus (Phil 2:9-11) follows his ignominious humiliation on the cross* (Phil 2:5-8). His subsequent elevation by God "to the highest place," or "office" (Phil 2:9), is matched by his receiving the highest "name" (or title) in all creation (Phil 2:10). What is this name? From the context two possibilities are frequently suggested: "Jesus" (Phil 2:10) or "Lord" (*kyrios*, Phil

2:11). Here the OT background of the exalted name of Yahweh (LXX *kyrios*) must be kept in mind, and the influence of Isaiah 45:23 ("to me [Yahweh] every knee shall bow, every tongue shall swear") is observed in the immediately following verse (Phil 2:10). The exalted Christ shares the universal lordship known of Yahweh, and is thus given the title "Lord." But his humiliation to the extent of death on the cross has given new meaning to lordship: the true character of the one who bears the "name" has been indelibly shaped by servanthood in the historical person of Jesus.

*See also* BAPTISM; CHRISTOLOGY; LORD; MAGIC; PRINCIPALITIES AND POWERS.

BIBLIOGRAPHY. R. Abba, "Name," *IDB* 3.506-8; C. E. Arnold, *Ephesians, Power and Magic* (SNTSMS 63; Cambridge: University Press, 1989); H. Bietenhard, "ὄνομα κτλ," *TDNT* V.270-83; H. Bietenhard and F. F. Bruce, "Name," *NIDNTT* 2.648-56; L. Hartman, "ὄνομα," *EDNT* 2.519-22; G. F. Hawthorne, *Philippians* (WBC 43; Waco: Word, 1983); A. T. Lincoln, *Ephesians* (WBC 42; Dallas: Word, 1990); R. P. Martin, *Philippians* (NCB; rev. ed.; Grand Rapids: Eerdmans, 1980); idem, *Carmen Christi: Philippians 11:5-11 in Recent Interpretation and the Setting of Early Christian Worship* (rev. ed.; Grand Rapids: Eerdmans, 1983).

A. B. Luter, Jr.

## NARRATIVE CRITICISM. *See* HERMENEUTICS/INTERPRETING PAUL.

## NARRATIVE TRADITION. *See* JESUS, SAYINGS OF.

## NEW COVENANT. *See* COVENANT AND NEW COVENANT.

## NEW CREATION. *See* CREATION AND NEW CREATION.

## NEW ISRAEL. *See* ISRAEL; RESTORATION OF ISRAEL.

## NEW NATURE AND OLD NATURE

Paul can contrast what believers were "in Adam" and what believers are after receiving the gift of salvation in Christ in terms of their "old" and "new nature" (*see* Adam and Christ).

1. Terminology
2. Romans
3. Ephesians and Colossians
4. Theological Significance

### 1. Terminology.
Few words are more dangerously ambiguous than

"nature." Because of this there has been considerable misunderstanding of the phrases "old nature" and "new nature" (see Rom 6:6; Eph 4:22; Col 3:9). Numerous popular explanations of Paul's doctrine of the Christian life argue, or assume, that the apostle distinguishes with these phrases between two parts or natures of a person. Following this misguided thinking is the debate as to whether the "old nature" is replaced by the "new nature" at conversion, or whether the "new nature" is added to the old (*see* Psychology).

The interpretation that *ho palaios anthrōpos* and *ho kainos anthrōpos* refer to parts, or natures, of a person is wrong and misleading. These terms rather designate the complete person viewed in relation to the corporate whole to which he or she belongs. Thus these terms are better translated as "old person" and "new person." The translation "old self" and "new self" (NIV, NRSV) is too individualistic, since the idea certainly means the individual Christian (Rom 6:6), but is much more than merely individual. "Old person" and "new person" are not, then, ontological but relational in orientation. They speak not of a change in nature, but of a change in relationship.

The "old person" is not the sin* nature which is judged at the cross* and to which is added a "new person." The "old person" is what believers were "in Adam" (in the old era). The "old" points to everything connected with the fall of humanity and with the subjection to the distress and death of a transitory life, separated from God (*see* Life and Death). Within the context of Paul's theology, this concept carries with it deep undertones of God's wrath* and the wages of sin. The "new person" is what believers are "in Christ" (in the new era). Paul directs us to the completely new, to the salvation* and healing that believers receive when they are crucified* with Christ and raised with him (cf. Rom 6:3-6; *see* Dying and Rising with Christ).

### 2. Romans.
In Romans 6:6 Paul argues that the old person (the individual believer) was crucified with Christ.* The reference to the crucifixion is a startling message indicating the vast distance separating Paul's theology of dying and being raised with Christ from the mysticism* of the mystery religions* of his day (see Cranfield, 1.309). The "old person" was crucified with Christ in baptism.* For in baptism believers received the divinely appointed sign and seal of the fact that by God's* gracious decision the old person was, in God's sight, crucified with Christ on Golgotha. Paul's language denotes the unity between baptized believers and the person of Christ himself in his redemptive

action (see Beasley-Murray, 134). Yet believers, by putting off the old person, still have to fulfill on the moral level the death that in God's gracious act and in the symbol of baptism they have already experienced. This is Paul's emphasis in Ephesians and Colossians.

### 3. Ephesians and Colossians.

Behind the contrast between the "old person" and the "new" is the contrast between Adam and Christ (1 Cor 15:45; see Ridderbos, 223-31). These phrases indicate the solidarity of people with the heads of the two contrasting eras of salvation history. Paul employs the term with a corporate meaning in Ephesians 2:15 and Colossians 3:10-11, showing that Jews and Greeks, the circumcised* and the uncircumcised, are united into one new humanity.

In Colossians 3:9-11 Paul explains that believers have taken off the "old person" with its practices and have put on the "new." This does not merely mean that Christ demands a new standard of life from his redeemed people. It means that everything associated with distorted humanity is to be put to death (Col 3:5-8) because it has been transformed according to the perfect model, Christ himself (Col 1:15-20; 2:6), and therefore there is no excuse for such distorted behavior (Wright, 137-38; Melick, 286-99).

The metaphor of "putting off" and "putting on" clothes (Col 3:8-10; Eph 4:22-24) does not simply mean promising to behave differently. Rather it is the gracious action of God's Spirit* moving believers into a different sphere where the new rule of life obtains. Paul may be alluding to the familiar picture of the candidate for baptism, who by exchanging old clothes for new symbolizes the transfer of solidarities.

These two pictures of what believers *are* and what they *should become* are not in conflict. Christians have been transferred from the old era of sin and death to the new era of righteousness and life. The powers of the old age must continually be resisted (thus the imperative infinitives *apothesthai* and *endysasthai* in Eph 4:22-24). At the center of the contrast between the old and the new is the eschatological tension between the inauguration of the new age in the life of believers (cf. 2 Cor 5:17) and the consummation of the new age in glory (cf. Rom 8:17, 19-23; Beker, 288-89; Moo, 392). What believers were in Adam remains no more, but the struggle of life between the inauguration and consummation of the new age continues (see Eschatology).

### 4. Theological Significance.

Life in the new age for the "new person" is to be lived out between the polarities of what has been redemptively accomplished by the historical achievement of the death of Christ and what is yet to be fully realized in the consummation of God's redemptive program. Believers live in this temporal tension between the "already" and the "not yet," and between the indicative (what they *are*) and the imperative (what they *should become*). Believers live in this "not yet" age, but their life pattern and standard of conduct are not to be those of this age, which are essentially human-centered and prideful, but of the age to come. Yet the struggle continues. While living as a "new person" in the new age, the basis for new life should be remembered. It is through the death and resurrection of Jesus Christ that the Spirit applies the benefits of the "new" life to the lives of believers. Life for the "new humanity" is living out, by the Spirit's empowerment, what believers are because of Christ.

*See also* ADAM AND CHRIST; BAPTISM; CREATION AND NEW CREATION; DYING AND RISING WITH CHRIST; ESCHATOLOGY; ETHICS; RESURRECTION; SPIRITUALITY.

BIBLIOGRAPHY. M. Barth, *Ephesians* (AB; Garden City: Doubleday, 1974); J. Baumgarten, "καινός κτλ," *EDNT* 2.229-32; G. R. Beasley-Murray, *Baptism in the New Testament* (Grand Rapids: Eerdmans, 1962); J. Behm, "καινός κτλ," *TDNT* III.447-54; J. C. Beker, *Paul the Apostle: The Triumph of God in Life and Thought* (Philadelphia: Fortress, 1980); C. E. B. Cranfield, *A Critical and Exegetical Commentary on the Epistle to the Romans* (ICC; 2 vols.; Edinburgh: T. & T. Clark, 1975); D. S. Dockery, "An Outline of Paul's View of the Spiritual Life," *CTR* 3 (1989) 327-40; D. Guthrie, *New Testament Theology* (Downers Grove, IL: InterVarsity, 1981); H. Haarbeck, "Old," *NIDNTT* 2.713-16; M. J. Harris, *Colossians and Philemon* (Grand Rapids: Eerdmans, 1991); R. Melick, *Philippians, Colossians, Philemon* (NAC; Nashville: Broadman, 1991); D. J. Moo, *Romans 1-8* (WEC; Chicago: Moody, 1991); H. Ridderbos, *Paul: An Outline of His Theology* (Grand Rapids: Eerdmans, 1975); P. Tachau, *'Einst' und 'Jetzt' im Neuen Testament* (Göttingen: Vandenhoeck & Ruprecht, 1972); R. C. Tannehill, *Dying and Rising with Christ* (Berlin: Töpelmann, 1967); N. T. Wright, *Colossians and Philemon* (TNTC; Grand Rapids: Eerdmans, 1986).

D. S. Dockery

# NEW PERSPECTIVE ON PAUL. See LAW;
PAUL AND HIS INTERPRETERS; ROMANS, LETTER TO THE.

# O

**OBEDIENCE.** *See* Abraham; Adam and Christ; Ethics; Faith; James and Paul; Justification; Law; Works of the Law.

**OFFERING.** *See* Death of Christ; Sacrifice, Offering.

**OLD NATURE.** *See* New Nature and Old Nature.

## OLD TESTAMENT IN PAUL

Although many Jews in the first century saw the Christian gospel* as antithetical to their faith, Paul regarded his message as the fulfillment of God's promises to Israel.* His letters are therefore filled with OT references used to clarify and defend the gospel. This feature, unquestionably, is of central importance to understanding Paul's teaching, but it also raises many questions. Sometimes we come across *textual* problems, caused in part by the fact that Paul, who was writing in Greek, naturally made use of the Septuagint (LXX), and this translation does not always correspond precisely with the Hebrew text. In addition his exegesis of some OT passages is puzzling to the modern reader: can we follow that pattern in our interpretation of the Bible? Moreover Paul's use of Scripture has profound theological implications, and these have caused heated debate throughout the history of Christianity, such as the church's conflicts with Marcion in the second century, the sixteenth-century debates among Protestants regarding the continuing validity of the OT Law,* the more recent disagreements between covenant theologians and dispensationalism, and so on. This article seeks to provide a survey of the textual data and to shed light on Paul's principles of biblical interpretation.

1. Explicit Citations
2. Allusions
3. Paul and Jewish Exegesis
4. Biblical Interpretation in Paul's Writings

### 1. Explicit Citations.

Discussions about Paul's use of the OT have focused primarily—in certain cases exclusively—on the apostle's explicit citations. This approach, though understandable, can prove misleading. As will be pointed out below, it is possible that a particular quotation, though explicit and verbatim, may play only an illustrative role and thus will not tell us very much about Paul's fundamental conceptions. Conversely, some of the apostle's arguments that do not contain any apparent citations reflect a very deep insight into, and dependence upon, OT themes. In spite of these caveats, however, there is a certain usefulness and convenience in using explicit citations as a starting point for further study.

*1.1. The Data.* We should begin by listing those passages that are generally recognized as quotations from the OT. Unfortunately, there is no unanimity among researchers, particularly as they seek to distinguish between quotations and allusions. The accompanying chart of OT citations in Paul, based primarily on the work of Michel, Ellis and Koch, are meant to be as inclusive as possible: if two of these scholars agree on a reference, that reference is included. In addition, the half-dozen citations found in Ephesians and the Pastorals, though excluded by Michel and Koch (the latter also excludes the ones in 2 Cor 6:16-18), are included here; scholars who do not recognize these letters as authentically Pauline can eliminate them easily enough.

Rather than present the data in raw form, an attempt has been made to group the quotations into useful categories. The first group consists of passages that are free of significant textual difficulties. In these cases the LXX renders the Hebrew text in a generally reliable and fairly "literal" way, while Paul's citation in turn conforms with the LXX rendering in all matters of substance.

In many passages, however, the MT and the LXX give different readings. (At least three factors, individually or in combination, can account for the differences: free translation, mistranslation and the translators' use of Hebrew MSS that differed at points from what would later become the MT.) These passages can

# Old Testament Citations in Paul

Note: All OT references are keyed to the chapter/verse numbers of the English Bible. In the Psalms, the Hebrew and the English are frequently off by one or two verses; beginning with Psalm 10, the Hebrew and the LXX are off by one chapter, so that, for example, Psalm 24 in the Hebrew and English is Psalm 23 in the LXX. Discrepancies of this sort outside the Psalms are noted in parentheses.

## 1. Paul = LXX = MT.

| | |
|---|---|
| (1) Rom 2:6 | Ps 62:12 |
| (2) Rom 3:4 | Ps 51:4 |
| (3) Rom 3:13a | Ps 5:9 |
| (4) Rom 3:13b | Ps 140:3 |
| (5) Rom 3:18 | Ps 36:1 |
| (6) Rom 4:17 | Gen 17:5 |
| (7) Rom 4:18 | Gen 15:5 |
| (8) Rom 7:7 | Ex 20:17 (= Deut 5:21) |
| (9) Rom 8:36 | Ps 44:22 |
| (10) Rom 9:7 | Gen 21:12 |
| (11) Rom 9:12 | Gen 25:23 |
| (12) Rom 9:13 | Mal 1:2-3 |
| (13) Rom 9:15 | Ex 33:19 |
| (14) Rom 9:26 | Hos 1:10 (2:1) |
| (15) Rom 10:5 | Lev 18:5 |
| (16) Rom 10:13 | Joel 2:32 (3:5) |
| (17) Rom 10:19 | Deut 32:21 |
| (18) Rom 13:9a | Deut 5:17-21 (cf. Ex 20:13-17) |
| (19) Rom 13:9b | Lev 19:18 |
| (20) Rom 15:3 | Ps 69:9 |
| (21) Rom 15:9 | Ps 18:49 (cf. 2 Sam 22:50) |
| (22) Rom 15:11 | Ps 117:1 |
| (23) Rom 15:21 | Is 52:15 |
| (24) 1 Cor 3:20 | Ps 94:11 |
| (25) 1 Cor 5:13 | Deut 17:7 et al. |
| (26) 1 Cor 10:7 | Ex 32:6 |
| (27) 1 Cor 10:26 | Ps 24:1 |
| (28) 1 Cor 15:27 | Ps 8:6 |
| (29) 1 Cor 15:32 | Is 22:13 |
| (30) 1 Cor 15:45 | Gen 2:7 |
| (31) 2 Cor 4:13 | Ps 116:10 (LXX 115:1) |
| (32) 2 Cor 6:2 | Is 49:8 |
| (33) 2 Cor 6:16 | Lev 26:12 (cf. Ezek 27:37) |
| (34) 2 Cor 6:17 | Is 52:11 + Ezek 20:34 |
| (35) 2 Cor 8:15 | Ex 16:18 |
| (36) 2 Cor 9:9 | Ps 112:9 |
| (37) Gal 3:8 | Gen 12:3 + 18:18 |
| (38) Gal 3:12 | Lev 18:5 |
| (39) Gal 3:16 | Gen 13:15 (cf. Gen 12:7; 17:7; 22:18) |
| (40) Gal 4:30 | Gen 21:10 |
| (41) Gal 5:14 | Lev 19:18 |
| (42) 1 Tim 5:18a | Deut 25:4 |

## 2. Paul = MT ≠ LXX.

| | |
|---|---|
| (43) Rom 1:17 | Hab 2:4 |
| (44) Rom 11:4 | 1 Kings 19:18 |
| (45) Rom 11:35 | Job 41:11 (3) |
| (46) Rom 12:19 | Deut 32:35 |
| (47) 1 Cor 3:19 | Job 5:13 |
| (48) Gal 3:11 | Hab 2:4 |
| (49) 2 Tim 2:19a | Num 16:5 |

## 3. Paul = LXX ≠ MT.

| | |
|---|---|
| (50) Rom 2:24 | Is 52:5 |
| (51) Rom 3:14 | Ps 10:7 (LXX 9:28) |
| (52) Rom 4:3 (9, 22) | Gen 15:6 |
| (53) Rom 4:7-8 | Ps 32:1-2 |
| (54) Rom 9:29 | Is 1:9 |
| (55) Rom 10:16 | Is 53:1 |
| (56) Rom 10:18 | Ps 19:4 |
| (57) Rom 10:20-21 | Is 65:1-2 |
| (58) Rom 11:34 | Is 40:13 |
| (59) Rom 12:20 | Prov 25:21-22 |
| (60) Rom 14:11 | Is 45:23 (+ 49:18?) |
| (61) Rom 15:10 | Deut 32:43 |
| (62) Rom 15:12 | Is 11:10 |
| (63) 1 Cor 6:16 | Gen 2:24 |
| (64) 2 Cor 13:1 | Deut 19:15 |
| (65) Gal 3:6 | Gen 15:6 |
| (66) Gal 4:27 | Is 54:1 |

## 4. Paul ≠ LXX ≠ MT.

| | |
|---|---|
| (67) Rom 3:10-12 | Ps 14:1-3 (cf. Ps 53:1-3) |
| (68) Rom 3:15-17 | Is 59:7-8 |
| (69) Rom 9:9 | Gen 18:10, 14 |
| (70) Rom 9:17 | Ex 9:16 |
| (71) Rom 9:25 | Hos 2:23 (25) |
| (72) Rom 9:27-28 | Is 10:22-23 (+ Hos 1:10?) |
| (73) Rom 9:33 | Is 8:14 + 28:16 |
| (74) Rom 10:6-8 | Deut 9:4 + 30:12-14 (cf. Ps 107:26) |
| (75) Rom 10:11 | Is 28:16 |
| (76) Rom 10:15 | Is 52:7 |
| (77) Rom 11:3 | 1 Kings 19:10 (cf. v. 14) |
| (78) Rom 11:8 | Deut 29:4 (+ Is 29:10) |
| (79) Rom 11:9-10 | Ps 69:22-23 |
| (80) Rom 11:26-27a | Is 59:20-21 |
| (81) Rom 11:27b | Is 27:9 |
| (82) 1 Cor 1:19 | Is 29:14 |
| (83) 1 Cor 1:31 | Jer 9:24 (23) |
| (84) 1 Cor 2:16 | Is 40:13 |
| (85) 1 Cor 9:9 | Deut 25:4 |
| (86) 1 Cor 14:21 | Is 28:11-12 |
| (87) 1 Cor 15:54 | Is 25:8 |
| (88) 1 Cor 15:55 | Hos 13:14 |
| (89) 2 Cor 3:16 | Ex 34:34 |
| (90) 2 Cor 6:18 | 2 Sam 7:14 (+ v. 8; cf. 1 Chron 17:13) |
| (91) 2 Cor 9:7 | Prov 22:8 (LXX only) |
| (92) 2 Cor 10:17 | Jer 9:24 |
| (93) Gal 3:10 | Deut 27:26 |
| (94) Gal 3:13 | Deut 21:23 |
| (95) Eph 4:8 | Ps 68:18 |
| (96) Eph 5:31 | Gen 2:24 |
| (97) Eph 6:2-3 | Ex 20:12 (cf. Deut 5:16) |

## 5. Debated.

| | |
|---|---|
| (98) Rom 3:20 | Ps 143:2 |
| (99) Rom 9:20 | Is 29:16 (45:9) |
| (100) Rom 11:1-2 | Ps 94:14 |
| (101) Rom 12:16-17 | Prov 3:7 |
| (102) 1 Cor 2:9 | (Is 64:4 + 65:16?) |
| (103) 1 Cor 15:25 | Ps 110:1 |
| (104) 2 Cor 8:21 | Prov 3:4 |
| (105) 2 Cor 9:10 | Is 55:10 + Hos 10:12 |
| (106) Gal 2:16 | Ps 143:2 |
| (107) 2 Tim 2:19b | Is 26:13? (+ Sir 35:3?) |

[Ellis also notes 1 Tim 5:18b (= Mt 10:10?) because of the introductory formula at the beginning of the verse.]

be further subdivided on the basis of Paul's agreement with one or the other. Accordingly, the second group below consists of a handful of instances in which Paul agrees with the Hebrew (i.e., the MT) over against the LXX. More frequently, Paul follows the LXX over against the Hebrew, as shown by the passages listed under the third category.

Two additional categories round out the lists. The fourth group consists of passages where Paul's citation differs from both the Hebrew and the LXX, whether or not these two agree. The fifth and last category brings together a series of citations that are problematic, either because the source of the citation is debated and/or because only one of the three scholars mentioned above regards it as a citation rather than an allusion.

It needs to be stressed that a strong subjective element affects some of the decisions reflected in the lists, particularly when one must determine whether a variation is significant enough to be noted as such. Differences between Paul and LXX are here regarded as significant primarily if they appear to reflect a different Greek version of the OT or a different understanding of the Hebrew. Similarly, variations between LXX and MT are noted if the Greek rendering suggests a misunderstanding of the Hebrew text or presupposes a Hebrew text different from the MT. Not everyone, however, will apply these criteria in the same way. For example, 2 Corinthians 13:1, quoting Deuteronomy 19:5, is included in the third group below because Paul follows the LXX (against MT) in adding the word "every" (*pan*), but someone could argue that such an addition is almost required for Greek stylistic reasons. Similarly, not everyone will agree that Paul's citation of Habakkuk 2:4 in Romans 1:17 and Galatians 3:11 should be placed in the second category (contrast Smith, 272).

Complicating the discussion is the fact that sometimes a particular quotation could be listed under two different headings. As mentioned above, 2 Corinthians 13:1 is normally regarded as closer to the LXX than to the MT because of the addition of the Greek word *pan*; however, in the same quotation Paul—against both MT and LXX—fails to repeat the phrase "by the mouth." Note also Romans 9:17, where Paul's choice of a verb departs from the LXX in a way that approximates the Hebrew of Exodus 9:16; at the same time, Paul accepts the phrase *en soi*, "through you," added by the LXX. Understandably, this passage has been included under the fourth category, yet it may be misleading to suggest that Paul's citation agrees with neither the MT nor the LXX.

In spite of these problems, however, the rough cate-

gorizations of the accompanying chart should prove sufficiently reliable to form a broad picture of the relevant data.

*1.2. Textual Problems.* What emerges from the material, more than anything else, is the fact that Paul's quotations of the OT do not follow a simple pattern. Certainly the apostle feels no compulsion in every instance to reproduce texts exactly. On the other hand, it would be a mistake to infer that he attached no significance to the details: when appropriate or necessary, he could focus on the actual wording in support of his teaching (the best known example is his emphasis on the singular of the word "seed" in Gal 3:16).

We also find a lack of uniformity with regard to Paul's textual source. His dependence on the current Greek translation of his day is clearly established, but there is good reason to think that he was familiar with the original Hebrew and that the latter, in at least some cases, determined how he used the OT. This general question, unfortunately, becomes tangled in the technical problems of textual transmission. The LXX translators would of course have used Hebrew MSS produced at about their time (two or three centuries before Christ), when the textual situation was somewhat unstable; by A.D. 100, however, the Hebrew text had become more standardized, and it was not until some centuries later that the particular form available to us (the MT) took definitive shape.

Could some of the differences in the lists above be accounted for by such changes in the Hebrew textual tradition? Someone might argue, for example, that the addition of the words *pas anthrōpos* ("every person") in Deuteronomy 27:26 LXX = Galatians 3:10 reflects a Hebrew text that contained the corresponding phrase and that such a text was used by the LXX translators as their *Vorlage* (master-copy). Indeed, the Hebrew biblical MSS found in Qumran and other areas of the Judean desert confirm that peculiar LXX renderings occasionally reflect a Hebrew *Vorlage* different from the MT. Most discrepancies between the MT and the LXX, however, arise from other factors (such as the translators' method of work, their exegesis, their style, etc.). In any case, there is no hard evidence that differences in the passages cited by Paul resulted from the lack of uniformity among Hebrew MSS.

To complicate matters further, the OT Greek text itself was not uniform. What we (naively) call the Septuagint, or LXX, is really a collection of various translations done at different times by different people who had differing skills and different approaches. Moreover, major revisions and even competing new Greek translations affected the subsequent transmission of the text. As a result, determining what may have been the actual form of the so-called "Old Greek," and thus whether that was the form used by Paul, can be a challenge. For example, at the end of Romans 9:33 Paul quotes the LXX of Isaiah 28:16, "he who believes in him will not be ashamed." The words "in him" do not appear in the MT; however, they are also missing from an important Greek MS, Codex Vaticanus (B). In this case, and usually when there is evidence of competing traditions, Paul's wording conforms to the "standard" and probably original Greek text, which in the book of Isaiah is best represented by Codex Alexandrinus (A).

Occasionally, however, Paul's quotations seem to reflect a mixed text. Romans 9:27-28 cites Isaiah 10:22-23 in a form that is very close to Codex A, but instead of *theos* ("God") Paul has *kyrios* ("Lord"), which is the reading of Codex B (however, since the divine names are so easily interchanged, it seems wise not to put too much weight on this variation). Outside Isaiah the textual alignments are somewhat different, but we can find other cases where Paul's wording may reflect, not his own changes, but a variant reading. The original Greek translation of Deuteronomy 27:26 probably contained the relative pronoun *hostis* (cf. J. W. Wevers' edition of Deuteronomy in the Göttingen *Septuaginta*), but when Paul quotes this passage in Galatians 3:10 he uses the pronoun *hos*, which is also attested in various LXX MSS.

These technical details are of importance for the following reason. If Paul quotes an OT passage in a form that differs from the "standard" Greek text but that is attested in isolated LXX MSS or in a later translation, most scholars would explain the divergence as having originated not with Paul but with a competing textual tradition (the most common example is 1 Cor 15:54, where Paul's citation of Is 25:8 departs from the LXX and agrees with a later version attributed to Theodotion). However, if Paul's text form is not attested in a LXX MS or in another Greek version, should we assume that Paul himself is responsible for the change? In 1 Corinthians 3:19, where Paul quotes Job 5:13, he departs from the LXX in several ways that bring the text a little closer to the MT. Since no LXX MSS preserve the rendering used by Paul, it is often assumed that Paul himself is responsible for it. Possibly so. Interestingly, however, one of the features of that rendering (the use of *panourgia*, "craftiness," for Heb *'ormāh*) has led several scholars to argue that a competing version was available to Paul and used by him (the translation attributed to Symmachus, which may reflect an earlier tradition, used the same rendering at Prov 8:12). This option cannot be ruled out.

One final complicating issue is textual variation in the Pauline letters themselves (*see* Textual Criticism). For example, in 1 Corinthians 9:9 Paul quotes Deuteronomy 25:4, but the verb he uses for "muzzle" is *kēmoō*, whereas the LXX uses *phimoō*. It turns out that the vast majority of NT MSS, including P⁴⁶ ℵ A, also have *phimoō*. Because scribes would naturally have adjusted the quotation in the NT to the Greek OT text with which they were familiar, modern textual critics rightly judge *kēmoō* to be the original reading in 1 Corinthians 9:9, even though it is found only in a handful of MSS (including Codex B; incidentally, note that the same OT verse is quoted in 1 Tim 5:18, but there the original reading is almost certainly *phimoō*).

*1.3. Exegetical Significance.* When Paul's citation varies from either the LXX or the MT (or both), the reason need not be significant. Just as we may sometimes refer to a passage without quoting it exactly, so might Paul. For example: "Jesus said that we cannot do anything without him" is a reliable reference to John 15:5, even though the exact quotation (from NIV) would be: "apart from me you can do nothing." The difference in the personal pronouns ("me" becomes "him"; "you" becomes "we") is due to the very character of an indirect quotation, while the other changes (the word order; the difference between "nothing" and "not anything") are not intended to communicate something special—nor do they imply that the speaker considers the actual words to be unimportant. Similarly, many of Paul's citations belong in this category (cf. Rom 3:15-17 = Is 59:7-8). In short, the mere fact that they contain verbal differences is not a clue to Paul's hermeneutics.

But there are also many other quotations where verbal differences do have exegetical significance. A very interesting example is 1 Corinthians 2:16, where Paul quotes the LXX of Isaiah 40:13a, "Who has known the mind [*nous*] of the Lord?" even though the Hebrew text has the word "spirit" (Heb *rûaḥ*) rather than "mind." The rendering of the LXX translator can perhaps be defended as an attempt to clarify the meaning of the original. But whatever we may think of the translator's technique, Paul could surely have changed the Greek *nous*, "mind," to *pneuma*, "spirit," if he had wanted. His choice was probably intentional, and it gives us an important insight into his use of Scripture, namely, the role played by the LXX in Paul's theological reflection.

As it turns out, 1 Corinthians 2 focuses on the Spirit (*see* Holy Spirit) as the one who makes it possible for us to know God* (see especially 1 Cor 2:11). As Paul draws that discussion to a close, he appeals to Isaiah 40:13 and concludes with the statement "But we have the mind of Christ." The use of the word "mind" here links this last comment with the LXX quotation, but the Hebrew original, as well as the context of Paul's discussion more generally, makes clear that what the apostle means is "We have the Spirit of Christ and therefore we really know Christ." Could it be then that the LXX's interpretive rendering itself became a source for the development of Paul's teaching?

Clues for understanding Paul's use of Scripture, however, go far beyond mere verbal changes. Many passages that contain verbatim citations can reflect important interpretive principles. Conversely, passages that do not even contain an explicit citation at all may be especially revealing of Paul's exegesis. Before discussing the broader hermeneutical questions, therefore, we need to survey Paul's allusions to the OT.

### 2. Allusions.
As already suggested, the distinction between citation and allusion is not hard-and-fast, and the NT writers (who did not have quotations marks available to them!) appear to have been quite unconcerned about the issue; certainly, there is little to be gained by attempting to formulate a definitive criterion to decide this question. Moreover, the category of "allusion" itself can cover a rather broad range of scriptural uses: loose quotations, references to events, intentional appeals to specific passages, verbal similarities used (perhaps unconsciously) to express a different idea, broad undercurrents of themes, even totally unintentional correspondences. Since hardly a paragraph in the Pauline corpus fails to reflect the influence of the OT on the apostle's language and thought, a complete list of these allusions would be very long indeed; in Romans 9—11 alone, for example, more than one hundred quotations and allusions have been identified (so Hübner, 149-60). The most useful way to survey the material, therefore, is not to produce such a list, but rather to discuss briefly a select and representative number of items.

Philippians,* for example, is conspicuously absent from the list of explicit citations, but it would be a grave mistake to infer that this letter shows no OT influence. A fairly obvious dependence on the OT may be seen in the way Paul describes the monetary gifts he received from the Philippian church: "They are a fragrant offering, an acceptable sacrifice, pleasing to God" (Phil 4:18). This language, of course, comes from various ceremonial passages, such as Exodus 29:18; moreover, a figurative shift is already present in Ezekiel 20:41, "I will accept you as fragrant incense when I bring you out from the nations." This

detail must be understood against a larger theological framework, for Paul elsewhere uses priestly language to describe Christian service (cf. *leitourgia*, "service," and related words in Phil 2:17, 25, 30). In effect, the ceremonial system of Israel is viewed as having been transformed and transferred to the Christian church, which properly fulfills the significance of that system. A few scholars have even suggested that Paul sees himself as the priest who, serving in the church as the true temple* of God, receives the Christians' offerings (*see* Financial Support).

Another well-known allusion is in Philippians 2:9-11, where Paul states that the purpose of Christ's exaltation* is that "every knee should bow . . . and every tongue confess that Jesus Christ is Lord." In Isaiah 45:23, after God has repeatedly affirmed his oneness and uniqueness, he adds: "By myself I have sworn, . . . Before me every knee will bow; by me every tongue will swear" (the last verb is translated by the LXX with the same verb used by Paul, *exomologēsetai*, "will confess"). Although not an explicit or precise quotation, this use of Isaiah is especially significant because of its profound implications for Paul's conception of Christ* (this would be true whether or not the so-called Christ hymn* was originally composed by Paul).

Close attention to the LXX reveals other interesting allusions to the OT in Philippians. A few verses later, Paul addresses the problem of grumbling and complaining (Phil 2:14), a theme reminiscent of the experience of the Israelites in the wilderness. That comment leads him to speak of the Philippians as "children of God without fault in a crooked and depraved generation" (Phil 2:15), a phrase that reproduces half a dozen words from Deuteronomy 32:5 LXX. Since the OT passage (which is exegetically difficult) speaks of the Israelites themselves as a crooked people and thus not God's children, Paul here gives a provocative, possibly ironic, twist to the phrase in Deuteronomy: it is the Gentile* Christians of Philippi, not the unbelieving Jews, who may be regarded as God's children, and therefore the Philippians need not be intimidated by the Jewish-based opposition they are experiencing (cf. Phil 3:1-3; *see* Opponents).

Another allusion which is easy to miss unless one refers specifically to the LXX text is at Philippians 1:19, "what has happened to me will turn out for my deliverance." The Greek here is *touto moi apobēsetai eis sōtērian* (lit., "this will lead to salvation for me"), a verbatim quotation from Job 13:16 LXX. Most commentators, even if they notice the striking verbal correspondence, appear to see little significance in it. And, to be sure, it is possible that Paul has simply—and perhaps even unconsciously—borrowed the language of Job to express quite a different idea, his hoped-for deliverance from prison (the connection would have been aided by the parallel between Job's accusers and the individuals Paul mentions in Phil 2:17; cf. Hays, 21-23). There is much to be said, however, for the view that what Paul has in mind is the more profound issue of his relationship with God and thus his spiritual destiny. Since the context of Job 13:13-18 deals precisely with matters of eternal import, Paul's use of that passage may be more than a casual allusion.

In other instances conceptual rather than strict verbal correspondences suggest that Paul has an OT passage or theme in mind. For example, some scholars have argued that the clause "made himself nothing" (*heauton ekenōsen*, lit., "emptied himself") in Philippians 2:7a alludes to Isaiah 53:12, which says that the Servant* of the Lord "poured out his life unto death." Since, as we have seen, Paul definitely uses Isaiah later in the passage (Phil 2:10-11), and since he refers to Jesus as *doulos* ("servant," Phil 2:7b), it may well be that the Suffering Servant motif has played a role in the formulation of the Christ hymn. If so, however, the allusion is rather subtle, and therefore one would want to be cautious about reading too much into the meaning of the phrase.

Even more subtle is the suggestion that Philippians 2:12, where Paul encourages his readers to continue their obedience whether or not he is present with them, is an allusion to Moses'* words in Deuteronomy 31:27, "If you have been rebellious against the Lord while I am still alive and with you, how much more will you rebel after I die!" Three verses later, as already noted, Paul certainly alludes to a statement in the close context of Moses' exclamation (Deut 32:5); moreover, Paul seems to have his own death in mind at Philippians 2:17. The possibility that Deuteronomy 31:27 may have affected the apostle's writing can hardly be excluded, but it is difficult to determine whether the allusion was a conscious one and, if so, how much significance should be attached to it.

One reason for focusing on Philippians (and there are perhaps another half dozen allusions not mentioned above) is to show that even a letter that has no citations in the usual sense may reflect Paul's great dependence on the OT. In the case of letters that do include citations, readers usually concentrate on those citations to the exclusion of the less obvious ways in which Paul uses Scripture. A good case in point is 2 Corinthians. Paul quotes Psalm 116:10 (LXX 115:1) in 2 Corinthians 4:13, "I believe; therefore I have spoken," in support of his own attitude to his apostolic ministry. What commentators usually fail to note, how-

ever, is that in that Psalm there are several references to humiliation and death, recurring themes in 2 Corinthians; that Psalm 118, which also has references to death, speaks of affliction* (Ps 118:5), God's power* (Ps 118:15-16, LXX *dynamis*; cf. 2 Cor 6:7) and discipline (Ps 118:18, LXX *epaideusan*; cf. 2 Cor 6:9); and that there are some other light parallels in nearby Psalms. Several important allusions to other parts of Scripture are also present in 2 Corinthians. As Paul relates his ministry to the problems in Corinth, he shows "that he has 'lived in the Bible' to the point where the Bible has formed his whole outlook on how the world is and what his place in it might be. Those who idly suppose that Scripture is important only when Paul uses it in argument in Galatians and Romans have a superficial view of the situation" (Young and Ford, 63, though not all of the parallels mentioned on 64-68 are convincing).

### 3. Paul and Jewish Exegesis.

As an educated and religious first-century Jew, Paul would of course have been familiar with the range of principles and techniques employed by his contemporaries (*see* Jew, Paul the). We have already seen his indebtedness to the interpretive tradition preserved in the LXX. It is also reasonable to think that Paul would have learned from the targumic tradition, that is, the Aramaic interpretive renderings of the Hebrew Bible that were part of the synagogue liturgy (whether written targumim were available to him is debated). The most convincing example of targumic influence is found in one of the disputed letters, Ephesians 4:8 (= Ps 68:18), which uses the verb "gave" as in the targum, whereas both MT and LXX have "took" (see commentaries). Some scholars have also tried to explain Paul's use of Deuteronomy 30:12-14 in Romans 10:6-8 by appealing to a targumic tradition, but even this instance is debatable. At any rate, the ancient versions do not contain explicit exegetical reflection (except perhaps for some of the expansive glosses of the Palestinian targumim), and so we turn to other sources.

*3.1. Alexandrian Exegesis.* Jews living in the Diaspora were constantly faced by the twin tasks of confronting pagan culture and accommodating to it; survival required learning how neither to compromise their own faith nor to reject Greek thought altogether. This challenge would of course affect their use of Scripture. The very existence of the LXX (a Greek document) is evidence of that fact. Philosophical currents would moreover exert their influence in the self-understanding of Hellenistic Judaism. One important element in Greek philosophy, as it turns out, was the need to reinterpret the old Homeric stories (the *Iliad* is sometimes referred to as the Bible of the Greeks) in the light of cultural changes. The Stoics in particular, offended by some elements in those stories, resorted to allegorization: Homer was salvaged by nonliteral interpretation.

The allegorical approach was borrowed by Hellenistic Jewish thinkers, especially in Alexandria. Best known among them was Philo (c. 13 B.C.-A.D. 45), who used this method as a means of synthesizing Hebrew and Greek thought. Whether Paul was familiar with Philo's work is impossible to prove or disprove, but attempts have been made to demonstrate a connection between them. Passages in Paul that some have considered allegorical include 1 Corinthians 9:9 (where he applies to Christian workers the principle of not muzzling the ox), 1 Corinthians 10:3 (which identifies the wilderness rock with Christ), 2 Corinthians 3:12-16 (where the veil over Moses' face is applied to Jewish unbelief) and especially the Sarah-Hagar analogy in Galatians 4:21-31.

This last passage actually contains the Greek verb *allēgoreō* (Gal 4:24), a feature that some consider conclusive, but that word could be used quite broadly and one can hardly assume that Paul intended it in the rather technical sense in which the English word *allegorize* is often used today. The apostle neither dehistoricizes the Genesis narrative—on the contrary, he clearly assumes its historical character—nor does he seek to integrate the narrative into a philosophical scheme, the two features that most clearly distinguish Philonic interpretation. In fact, even a superficial acquaintance with Philo's usual exegetical mode highlights its differences from, rather than similarities to, Pauline hermeneutics. Attempts to find an organic connection between Paul's use of Scripture and Alexandrian exegesis have not been persuasive.

*3.2. Qumran Exegesis.* The discovery of the Dead Sea Scrolls in the late 1940s, and subsequent findings elsewhere in the Judean desert, have greatly affected our understanding of Jewish life and thought in the first century (*see* Qumran and Paul). Although the NT makes no direct reference to the religious groups that produced this literature, we may reasonably assume that the early Christians would have had some knowledge of the ideas held by those sects. Some scholars have even argued, though not successfully, for a relatively close connection between Christianity and Qumran. (According to one theory, the "Damascus" where Paul went upon his conversion was none other than Qumran!)

This question is particularly relevant to the present article because biblical interpretation is very common

in the Dead Sea Scrolls and is in fact one of the most interesting and distinctive features in Qumranic thought. The most obvious feature common to both Qumran and Paul is the use of certain expressions to introduce explicit citations from the OT, in particular the formula "as it is written" (in various constructions). At a more substantive level, Fitzmyer has pointed out that both Qumran and the NT, over against Alexandrian exegesis, use the OT in a generally—but not strictly—literal way; that both often "modernize" the OT text by applying its general sense to a contemporary situation (sometimes going so far as to "accommodate" the text by, in Fitzmyer's judgment, wresting it out of its original context); and that both make use of "eschatological" exegesis by identifying the "last days" of certain OT passages with the expectations of the respective communities. Fitzmyer concludes, however, that such similarities "do not affect anything more than the periphery of their theologies. Both depend on the Old Testament, but both have certain presuppositions in the light of which they read the Old Testament. It is these presuppositions which distinguish the two groups despite the similarities in their exegetical procedures" (Fitzmyer, 332).

The eschatological* exegesis in Qumran is especially evident in the *pesharim*, which comment on the biblical text more or less "verse-by-verse." After citing a portion of text, the comments are introduced with the formula "its interpretation is" (*pišrô*, or a comparable expression). The word for "interpretation" is in fact *pesher* (*pēšer*), and the commentary normally consists in identifying the words of the OT prophets with a contemporary event.

Undoubtedly there is a rough parallel between this approach and the conviction of the NT writers, including Paul, that the coming of Jesus Christ was to be understood as the fulfillment of the OT prophecies. Both communities had a heightened sense of expectation based on God's promises to Israel,* and this common frame of mind sheds light on their use of Scripture. But the contrasts are fundamental. Apart from the obvious, yet crucial, fact that the events they identified as the fulfillment of the prophecies were completely different, other factors figure prominently. The letters of Paul, for example, do not include sustained, verse-by-verse interpretations of the OT, a Qumranic approach that led to highly arbitrary applications. More significantly, the apostle shared with the other NT writers the belief that Jesus' death* and resurrection* constituted the manifestation of God's kingdom,* whereas the community in Qumran was much more preoccupied with the yet-to-come deliverance. Although Paul's thought certainly includes a strong sense of expectation (cf. Rom 8:18-25), his dominant perspective is the conviction that the age to come is already here (cf. 1 Cor 10:11).

*3.3. Rabbinic Exegesis.* If Philo's work was geographically and conceptually distant from Palestinian Judaism, and if the teachings of Qumran (and other sectarian groups) were somewhat removed from "mainstream" Jewish thought, can we find a more fruitful area of study in the rabbinic materials? On the assumption that such documents as the Talmud (the basic storehouse of Jewish folklore and law, which includes the Mishnah) and the midrashim (rabbinic expositions of Scripture) give an accurate picture of first-century Pharisaism, many scholars have in fact drawn striking parallels between Pauline and rabbinic exegesis and even argued that the apostle was in some important respects indebted to the latter.

Formally, rabbinic citations of OT texts are introduced, as in Qumran and Paul, with an authoritative formula, though the precise expressions are often somewhat different (e.g., the rabbis prefer forms of the verb "say" rather than "write"). Again, scholars have detected a similarity between Paul's occasional stringing of quotations (e.g., Rom 9:25-29, citing successively Hos 2:23; 1:10; Is 10:22-23; 1:9), which may be related to one another by the use of significant words, and a rabbinic method known as *ḥāraz* ("to string," figuratively "to draw parallels between passages"). Another possible feature is Paul's structuring of texts-plus-exposition in a way reminiscent of some (later) rabbinic commentaries that fall into a category known as *Yelammedenu rabbenu*, "May our master teach us." Ellis (in Mulder, 708) gives the possible example of Galatians 4:21-31, which begins with a general reference to a basic text (Gen 16 and 21); the exposition includes a secondary reference (Is 54:1); and the application quotes another passage (Gen 21:10) that relates to the other texts both verbally and conceptually. A few other literary techniques have been suggested.

In addition to noticing formal characteristics, scholars have paid much attention to exegetical principles and methods found in the rabbinic literature. An explicit set of rules attributed to Hillel, a very influential teacher who lived just prior to the ministry of Jesus, may have been known to Paul. The very first rule, known as *qal wāḥômer* ("light and heavy"), establishes a relationship between two ideas, one of which is more significant than the other. Such an approach may be reflected in 2 Corinthians 3:7-11, where Paul draws a contrast between the Mosaic Law* and the gospel by arguing that if the former, which was a ministry* of death, was glorious, then we should expect the ministry of the Spirit to be all the more glorious.

Other principles of exegesis, attributed to later rabbis, have also been suggested as parallels to Pauline interpretation. For example, a rule clearly formulated by R. Ishmael in the second century states that when two texts appear to be contradictory, one may appeal to a third to resolve the tension. Now in Galatians 3:11-12 Paul sets Habakkuk 2:4 in contrast to Leviticus 18:5 (does one live by faith or by doing what the Law says?), and H. J. Schoeps argued that Genesis 15:6, cited by Paul earlier in the context, provides the solution (Schoeps, 178-79; differently, Bonsirven, 316-17 with 201). Many additional examples could be adduced.

In spite of the massive efforts expended in this field of study, the results are ambiguous. One basic obstacle is chronological: the rabbinic literature available to us dates back only as far as the beginnings of the third century, and even the older oral tradition to which that literature refers developed mostly after the destruction of Jerusalem in A.D. 70. According to some scholars, there is little (if any) significant connection between the Pharisees of Jesus' day and the later rabbinic school that flourished in the second century and thereafter became "mainstream" Judaism. This position surely goes too far; there is no need for an extreme skepticism regarding the historical value of rabbinic literature. Nevertheless, great caution and tentativeness is required when attempting to draw parallels. Because the antiquity of specific rabbinic statements can no longer be assumed, concrete reasons need to be offered in support of using those statements as evidence of first-century thought and practice.

Another serious obstacle is the relative vagueness of some of the adduced parallels. It is immediately apparent, for example, that the *qal wāḥômer* argument simply reflects the general logical principle of arguing *a fortiori*, a technique present in a wide variety of cultures at both popular and sophisticated levels. Indeed, one would be hard-pressed to find an exegetical example in Paul's writings that is distinctively rabbinic; that is, some technique that could not be paralleled elsewhere.

One particularly ambiguous term is the adjective *midrashic*, which is frequently applied to various portions of the NT, such as 1 Corinthians 10:1-5 and 2 Corinthians 3:6-16. The Hebrew noun *midrash* (*midrāš*) can have a very general meaning, suggesting nothing more than our own term *interpretation*; when capitalized, the Hebrew term has a very specific meaning, namely, a particular type of rabbinic literature consisting of collections of biblical expositions (it is generally agreed that no NT book can be described as a midrash in this sense).

Between these two meanings, *midrash* is commonly used as shorthand for "distinctive Jewish interpretation," but just what is distinctive about it? In the view of some scholars, it is the tendency to embellish narratives; for others, it is the presence of exegetical moves that do not conform to the grammatico-historical method. A less prejudicial definition that has become widely accepted focuses on the way that Jewish interpretation actualizes the text—for the rabbis the Bible was a living text, and its interpretation could not be divorced from application. True enough, but has not such a focus also characterized the reading of Scripture in most Christian communities? Although a few modern writers are careful to define midrash more concretely and precisely, the term continues to be used by others in a way that is either pejorative or sloppy, and it seldom serves to clarify Pauline exegesis.

To be sure the numerous similarities between Paul and the later rabbis, when taken cumulatively, create the strong presumption that the apostle does reflect the Jewish culture of which he is a part (and which developed into what we call Rabbinic Judaism). The importance of that insight must not be underestimated. Increased familiarity with first-century Jewish interpretation is of inestimable help, at least in a general way, as we seek to appreciate Paul's use of Scripture. Nevertheless, the appeal to later rabbinic literature remains problematic; its evidential value is only indirect, and thus its function is largely limited to illustrative, not probative, uses.

*3.4. Other Sources.* In addition to the bodies of literature already considered, there are many other documents produced during or before the NT period that shed light on the Jewish use of Scripture. The so-called apocryphal and pseudepigraphic books (some of which, incidentally, are represented among the Qumran findings) are full of allusions to the OT. Some of these works consist of "retellings" of biblical narratives, often with considerable expansion and embellishment; at least implicitly, they reveal certain hermeneutical commitments. The same is true even of writings that are more self-consciously historical, such as Josephus' *Antiquities.* (For a discussion of biblical interpretation in such documents, see the relevant chapters in Mulder.) While these works have been exploited for their relevance to Pauline studies with regard to theology, less has been done with regard to exegetical practice—surprisingly so, in view of their close chronological proximity to the NT writings.

Finally, it should be pointed out that Paul, though first and foremost a Jew, had direct and sustained contact with Greco-Roman culture. Apart from the debated question whether his childhood was spent in Tarsus or in Jerusalem, he certainly ministered for at least a decade in Syria and Cilicia (Gal 1:18—2:1); his use of the Greek language and his obvious familiarity with current Greek thought are further evidence of the extent to which he was influenced by Hellenism.* Considerable attention has been paid to parallels between Paul's style of argumentation and the rhetorical* techniques of the day, but an issue that needs addressing is the possible influence of Greco-Roman literary interpretation on his handling of Scripture (at the formal level, cf. Stanley).

### 4. Biblical Interpretation in Paul's Writings.

The present article is concerned with Paul's principles and methods of interpretation rather than with the actual content of that interpretation. Of course, exegesis and theology are intimately related and so the lines tend to blur (*see* Hermeneutics/Interpreting Paul). Nevertheless, no attempt will be made here to summarize Paul's teaching, as that teaching arises from his use of the OT, on the various relevant topics (for which the reader should consult the appropriate articles; *see,* e.g., Abraham, Adam, Covenant, Creation, Eschatology, Law, Wisdom).

*4.1. Foundational Concepts.* Although, as we have noted, many of the OT citations are not verbally exact, it is apparent to virtually all students of Paul that he regarded the Scripture (*hē graphē*) as proceeding from God himself and therefore as enjoying ultimate authority. In polemical contexts he explicitly invokes the OT as the final court of appeal; such is in fact the point of the introductory formulas—to say "as it is written" in effect settles the argument. Not surprisingly, then, the explicit quotations appear almost exclusively in the *Hauptbriefe* (chief letters): Romans,* 1-2 Corinthians* and Galatians.* The significance of this distribution is not, as A. von Harnack once argued, that the appeal to Scripture was forced upon Paul by the Judaizers'* arguments and that he really had no desire to bind the Gentile churches to a book. As we have seen, Paul's dependence on the OT is just as clear in those passages where he makes no direct appeal to it. Moreover, Harnack's theory does not really do justice to the fact that the greatest concentration of quotations is found in Romans. Whatever polemical element we may rightfully see in this letter, its great significance lies in the fact that here Paul gives a sustained exposition of his gospel (Rom 2:16), and for that purpose nothing is more important than to show the consistency of his message with that of Scripture (Rom 1:2; 3:31; 9:6; etc.).

Of special interest is the way in which Paul depends

on the OT even (especially?) when he appears to view it negatively. Galatians 3, for example, is a sustained rejection of the view that the Law* can give life,* yet he directly appeals to the Law itself in support of his position. Paul can even combine those two perspectives within one statement: the Law is a primary witness to the fact that righteousness* comes apart from the Law (Rom 3:21); indeed, the Law itself led him to die to the Law (Gal 2:19).

A related issue is Paul's use of Scripture to deal with the serious problem of why the Jewish nation as a whole had failed to receive the gospel (*see* Israel). The early Christians faced no greater challenge to the validity of their message than the negative Jewish response. If the gospel is indeed God's fulfillment of his promises, is it conceivable that God's own people would not see it? Would not that imply that God's purposes have been thwarted—that his word has failed (Rom 9:6)? Both the problem and the solution to it can already be seen in the ministry of Jesus. In explanation of his use of parables, for example, the Synoptic Gospels record Jesus' appeal to Isaiah 6, which stresses the hardening of Israel within the context of God's providence (Mk 4:12 and par.). The Gospel of John, which focuses sharply on the fact that "his own did not receive him" (Jn 1:13), also depends on Isaiah 6, in combination with Isaiah 53, to account for that unbelief (Jn 12:37-41).

Very probably this background is part of the reason why the book of Isaiah, as the lists of citations indicate, figures most prominently in Paul's quotations. It also helps us to understand why Romans 9—11, far from being a "parenthesis" in the argument of the letter, constitute its very heart—indeed, the climax to which the earlier chapters were building (cf. esp. Rom 2:28-29 and 4:11, anticipating Rom 9:6-8). Having already quoted or alluded to Isaiah in Romans 9:20, he does it again in Romans 9:27-28, which is followed by another Isaiah quotation in Romans 9:29 and still another one in Romans 9:33 (this last one combining two different passages from Isaiah). But that is not all: Romans 10 includes four more quotations from the same book, and Romans 11 another four! Undoubtedly, the prophecies of Isaiah provided Paul with the ammunition he needed to fight one of his fiercest battles.

There is a positive side, however, to the sobering truth of Israel's hardening, namely, the glorious reception of the Gentiles* into God's fold. This is the "mystery"* that had been hidden throughout the ages but is brought to light with the coming of Christ (Rom 16:25-26; 1 Cor 2:7; Eph 3:2-11; Col 1:25-27). The church* as the eschatological community that Christ has established through his Spirit becomes therefore a focal point for Paul's hermeneutics (for the view that Paul's use of Scripture is primarily "ecclesiocentric," see Hays, chap. 3). But this concept reflects a view of redemptive history that also functions as an interpretive principle, as the next section will make clear.

*4.2. Guiding Principles.* It should be evident from what has already been said that Paul's use of the OT was not motivated by antiquarian interests. The Scriptures were intensely practical for him. However, the moment we use an earlier writing to meet a current need, we of course transfer that writing to a new historical context and thus unavoidably involve ourselves in shifting its meaning (cf. Rom 15:21, where Paul applies the messianic words of Is 52:15 to his own ministry). Just how much shifting goes on and, more important, in what way that shifting takes place, is perhaps the fundamental problem in the field of hermeneutics.

It is precisely because Paul is never content with merely restating the original, historical meaning of an OT text, but rather applies it to his present situation, that the perennial and troublesome question arises, "Can we use Paul's exegesis today?" The very formulation of the problem can be misleading. Usually what is in view is whether Paul's methods of interpretation are compatible with "scientific," grammatico-historical exegesis. But this concern often ignores some fundamental obstacles. In the first place, Paul never gives us an exegetical discussion in the usual sense. We find no sustained Pauline exposition of any one OT passage. He never explicitly raises the question, What does such or such a passage mean? Even in sections where he appears to be arguing exegetically (e.g., Gal 3:10-14), he never stops to consider alternate interpretations of the texts. When we further consider the possibility that at least some of Paul's references to Scripture are not intended as doctrinal proofs but serve primarily to heighten the emotive thrust of his words (e.g., 2 Cor 13:1), the difficulties in answering our question become clearer.

To put it differently: there is no evidence that Paul or his contemporaries ever sat down to "exegete" OT texts in a way comparable to what today's seminary students are expected to do—that is, to produce an exposition that focuses on the historical meaning. Nevertheless, many of Paul's actual uses of Scripture are acknowledged by all concerned to be consistent with such a historical meaning. In other words, there is plenty of evidence that the apostle reflected carefully and thoughtfully on OT texts in their contexts. Even in the case of quotations that appear somewhat arbitrary, patient consideration of the broad context can be enlightening.

For example, in the middle of the Sarah-Hagar analogy Paul quotes Isaiah 54:1, which at first blush may look like a violent use of the text. Isaiah's words, however, are strongly reminiscent of the description of Sarah's barrenness in Genesis 11:30 LXX. Moreover, Isaiah had earlier referred to the (true) children of Sarah as the inhabitants of Zion who "pursue righteousness and who seek the Lord" (Is 52:1-3). In between these two chapters, of course, is the Suffering Servant passage, which Paul seems to allude to in Galatians 3:1 (cf. Gal 3:2 with Is 53:1 LXX; see Jobes). These and other features suggest that Paul is in fact exploiting important associations present in the OT itself. Yet one does not usually hear complaints that the OT prophets are guilty of using allegorical exegesis; nor is it common to argue that, in their view, Scripture contained a *sensus plenior* ("fuller meaning"). We simply recognize that they knew how to exploit their literary tradition.

The emotive power of literary associations can be great, and so a good writer or speaker will use them as a method of persuasion. Such a "technique" implies neither disrespect for the OT as a source of doctrine (quite the opposite) nor lack of concern for its historical meaning, though admittedly that original sense may sometimes recede into the background in the interests of contemporary needs. In addition, we as modern readers are not always privy to ancient interpretive traditions that perhaps fill the logical gaps that we are so quick to detect. Of course, this principle applies also to rabbinic interpretations. All too often Christian interpreters have tried to salvage Paul by emphasizing the "fantastic" interpretations of the rabbis. The latter, however, were quite capable of careful, literal exegesis; at other times, they could be simply playful. More important, however, their writings are greatly compressed: two or three words might call to mind a whole passage of Scripture, plus other parallel passages, plus a body of tradition that linked those passages with the point being made. Similarly, our inability to identify all the logical steps that might have led Paul to use an OT text for a particular purpose may reflect nothing more than our ignorance (cf. Silva, 159-61).

Finally, Paul's use of Scripture was guided by the conviction that God was the Lord of history. Scholars use different adjectives to describe and nuance this approach: typological (because it may focus on correspondences between OT and NT events or individuals), eschatological (because it emphasizes the coming of Christ as bringing in the end times), canonical (because it considers that the full meaning of a text depends on the teaching of Scripture as a whole) and so on. As already mentioned, the point is simply—but profoundly—that redemptive history came to a climax with the people of the new covenant,* for whom the OT events were recorded as "examples" (1 Cor 10:11). That last word translates the Greek *typos*, and, though it is doubtful that it reflects the heavy theologizing associated with the modern use of the English word *typology*, we may be sure that the apostle saw a fundamental and organic connection between OT history and the eschatological realities of Christ's coming. And because the same God who ruled over that history inspired the biblical writers, it is inevitable that the text of Scripture would include a certain undercurrent—a "deeper meaning"?—that could only become clear after the fulfillment of the promises.

Such a view of redemptive history, of course, implies that the whole OT was a witness to Christ, and for that reason Paul's use of the Bible was most distinctively guided by his christological* orientation. Whatever else may be said about the subject, the hermeneutics of the apostle to the Gentiles was ultimately rooted in Christ "in whom are hidden all the treasures of wisdom* and knowledge*" (Col 2:3).

*4.3. Habakkuk 2:4 as a Test Case.* Some of Paul's quotations raise difficult exegetical problems that cannot be treated adequately in a reference work such as this one. The present article, instead, has sought to provide general guidelines that may help the reader work through those problems in a satisfactory way. Nevertheless, it will be useful to pull together at least a few of the threads by covering one sample passage in greater detail.

In Galatians 3 the apostle is seeking to demonstrate that the true children of Abraham* are those who believe as Abraham believed (Gal 3:6-7; cf. the concluding words in Gal 3:29); these believers are sharply contrasted with those who are "of the works of the Law" (Gal 3:10). In Galatians 3:11 Paul states the crucial thesis that "through the Law no one is justified,*" and as proof for that thesis he quotes Habakkuk 2:4, "the righteous one will live through faith*" (*ho dikaios ek pisteōs zēsetai*). So fundamental is this statement that it becomes the programmatic verse in Romans (Rom 1:17), a book that can be viewed as a systematic expansion of the message of Galatians.*

This citation provokes some interesting questions. For example, it would be possible to construe the prepositional phrase (*ek pisteōs*) with the subject rather than with the verb, which yields the translation "he who through faith is righteous will live," but this problem does not directly affect our main concerns. Another issue of secondary importance has to do with textual variation, since the Hebrew includes a pronoun, "his faith," which the LXX mistranslated with the first-person pronoun, "my faith"; Paul's omission of the pronoun has the effect of bringing the quotation closer to the Hebrew (though some argue that it deliberately renders the reference ambiguous).

The main problem with this citation, however, is the fact that the word for "faith" (*pistis*) translates the Hebrew *'emûnâh*, which normally means "steadiness, faithfulness" (thus implying obedience to the Law), yet Paul uses this text precisely to attack the notion of justification by the works* of the law. It seems bad enough that Paul should use this verse in a way not originally intended—namely, to propound a distinctively "Pauline" doctrine—but even worse that his meaning appears to be exactly the opposite of the original. And if Paul was being careless or dishonest, how could the Christian church use this text as a basic argument for the biblical doctrine of salvation*? In short, we are faced with a major exegetical and theological problem.

The Hebrew text of Habakkuk, in spite of some textual and interpretive problems, is quite clear. The prophet had uttered a complaint to God regarding wickedness in Judah (Hab 1:4, "the wicked hem in the righteous"). The divine response was that the Babylonians would destroy Judah, but that response raised an even more serious problem regarding God's justice and thus we have a second complaint: how can God, who cannot look upon evil, be silent while the wicked swallow up those more righteous than they (Hab 1:13)? The answer is delayed by a verse that creates considerable suspense (Hab 2:1). The setting is then further dramatized by the instruction to write down the message and by an emphatic word that, in spite of apparent delay, the prophecy will come to pass, and so the prophet must wait for it (Hab 2:3). Finally, Habakkuk 2:4 discloses the awaited revelation, which we may paraphrase: "Behold, the unrighteous Babylonians are wicked and proud, but the righteous one will live by his faithfulness." The clause in question, which may be parenthetical (cf. NIV), is followed by a detailed prophecy of the destruction of the wicked.

How did the earliest readers understand this verse? The LXX translator faltered at various points, obscured the syntax and ended up with the view that God's faithfulness is the basis of salvation (a popular Jewish belief still common today). The Jewish community at Qumran interpreted the herald ("reader") of Habakkuk 2:2 as the Teacher of Righteousness and applied Habakkuk 2:3b and 4b to the doers of the Law in Judah, whom God will deliver from condemnation because of their suffering and their faithfulness or

loyalty to the Teacher of Righteousness (1QpHab 6:12—8:3). The writer of the Epistle to the Hebrews, for his part, followed the LXX, but with some important changes that emphasize the concept of *pistis* as faithful perseverance (Heb 10:36, a theme developed in Heb 11).

In view of all this evidence, Paul appears to be the "odd one out." In fact, he seems to use Habakkuk to support a notion of faith that he gets from elsewhere, namely Genesis 15:6, "He [Abraham] believed God and it was credited to him as righteousness." But is it true that the Genesis passage addresses a different issue? A quick look at the Hebrew text suggests that Genesis and Habakkuk may in fact be dealing with the same thought, since the lexical parallels can hardly be a coincidence (the roots *'mn* and *ṣdq* appear in both passages). The point to appreciate is that Habakkuk himself was involved in biblical interpretation. Though his method may appear subtle to the English reader, the prophet surely was exhorting the people of Judah to follow the footsteps of Abraham, whose faith was not a momentary experience, but a whole life of persevering in obedience (cf. esp. Gen 22, which is the basis for Jas 2:21-24). Faith involves waiting for fulfillment and thus is always in danger of being shaken; therefore, steadiness and constancy are of its essence.

In other words, for Habakkuk there was no such dichotomy between faith and faithfulness as we often assume (similarly, Hebrews emphasizes their connection; cf. Heb 3—4). That the apostle Paul did not view justifying faith as excluding obedience to God's commandments is suggested in Galatians itself (see esp. Gal 5:13-26), but the organic link between these two concepts is extensively developed in Romans. Indeed, in his letter to Rome, after describing his gospel as the fulfillment of the OT promises (Rom 1:2) and appealing to Habakkuk 2:4 as a key to understanding that gospel (Rom 1:16-17), Paul spends considerable time elaborating on the significance of Abraham's faith (Rom 4; note especially the emphasis on his perseverance, Rom 4:18-21), and then devotes a major section to the doctrine of the believer's sanctification (Rom 6—8; *see* Holiness, Sanctification). Far from manipulating the Habakkuk citation as a convenient proof text for a view that contradicted that of the prophet, Paul was genuinely indebted to that text as a source for his teaching; moreover, his own theological formulations strengthened and advanced the prophetic message (*see* Prophet, Paul as).

*4.4. Conclusion.* It is plain, then, that Paul was not careless when he quoted the Scriptures. True, the apostle's use of his Bible did not in every respect conform to methods that modern exegesis considers appropriate, but only a superficial reading of his letters could lead one to regard that use as invalid or irresponsible. Quite the contrary, the very categories with which he presented his understanding of Christ's work clearly arose from a serious study of the OT that was both meticulous and comprehensive. Guided not only by the text's historical meaning, but also by its divine authority, by the need to actualize the biblical message, by the power of literary associations and by a christological view of redemptive history, Paul succeeded both in setting forth the truth of the gospel and in teaching God's people how Scripture should be read.

*See also* HERMENEUTICS/INTERPRETING PAUL; JEW, PAUL THE; LAW; PREACHING FROM PAUL TODAY; QUMRAN AND PAUL.

BIBLIOGRAPHY. J. W. Aageson, "Paul's Use of Scripture: A Comparative Study of Biblical Interpretation in Early Palestinian Judaism and the New Testament: With Special Reference to Romans 9—11" (D.Phil. diss., Oxford University, 1983); idem, *Written Also for Our Sake: Paul and the Art of Biblical Interpretation* (Louisville: Westminster/John Knox, 1993); J. Barr, *Old and New in Interpretation: A Study of the Two Testaments* (London: SCM, 1966); J. Bonsirven, *Exégèse rabbinique et exégèse paulinienne* (Paris: Beauchesne, 1938); W. D. Davies, *Paul and Rabbinic Judaism: Some Rabbinic Elements in Pauline Theology* (4th ed.; Philadelphia: Fortress, 1980); D. R. Denny, "The Significance of Isaiah in the Writings of Paul" (Ph.D. diss., New Orleans Theological Seminary, 1985); C. H. Dodd, *According to the Scriptures: The Sub-structure of New Testament Theology* (London: Fontana, 1952); E. E. Ellis, *Paul's Use of the Old Testament* (Edinburgh: Oliver & Boyd, 1957; repr. Grand Rapids: Baker, 1981); J. A. Fitzmyer, "The Use of Explicit Old Testament Quotations in Qumran Literature and in the New Testament," *NTS* 7 (1960-61) 297-333; L. Goppelt, *Typos: The Typological Interpretation of the Old Testament in the New* (Grand Rapids: Eerdmans, 1982); A. T. Hanson, *Studies in Paul's Technique and Theology* (Grand Rapids: Eerdmans, 1974); A. Harman, "Paul's Use of the Psalms" (Th.D. diss., Westminster Theological Seminary, 1968); R. B. Hays, *Echoes of Scripture in the Letters of Paul* (New Haven; Yale University, 1989); H. Hübner, *Gottes Ich und Israel. Zum Schriftgebrauch des Paulus in Römer 9—11* (FRLANT 136; Göttingen: Vandenhoeck & Ruprecht, 1984); K. H. Jobes, "Jerusalem, Our Mother," *WTJ* 55 (1993) 299-320; W. C. Kaiser, Jr., *The Uses of the Old Testament in the New* (Chicago: Moody, 1985); D.-A. Koch, *Die Schrift als Zeuge des Evangeliums. Untersuchungen zur Verwendung und zum Verständnis der Schrift bei Paulus* (BHT 69; Tübingen: J. C. B. Mohr, 1986); B. Lindars, *New Testament Apologetic: The Doctrinal Significance of the Old Testament Quotations* (Philadelphia: Westminster, 1961); R. N. Longenecker, *Biblical Exegesis in the Apostolic Period* (Grand Rapids: Eerdmans, 1975); O. Michel, *Paulus und seine Bibel* (1929; repr. Darmstadt: Wissenschaftliche Buchgesellschaft, 1972); M. J. Mulder, ed., *Mikra: Text, Translation, Reading and Interpretation of the Hebrew Bible in Ancient Judaism and Early Christianity* (CRINT 2.1; Philadelphia: Fortress, 1988); D. A. Oss, "Paul's Use of Isaiah and Its Place in His Theology: With Special Reference to Romans 9-11" (Ph.D. diss., Westminster Theological Seminary, 1992); H. J. Schoeps, *Paul: The Theology of the Apostle in the Light of Jewish Religious History* (Philadelphia: Westminster, 1961); M. Silva, "The New Testament Use of the Old Testament: Text Form and Authority," in *Scripture and Truth*, ed. D. A. Carson and J. W. Woodbridge (Grand Rapids: Zondervan, 1983) 147-65; D. Moody Smith, "The Pauline Literature," in *It Is Written: Scripture Citing Scripture. Essays in Honour of Barnabas Lindars, SSF*, ed. D. A. Carson and H. G. M. Williamson (Cambridge: University Press, 1988) 265-91; C. D. Stanley, *Paul and the Language of Scripture: Citation Technique in the Pauline Epistles and Contemporary Literature* (SNTSMS 69; Cambridge: University Press, 1992); P. J. Tomson, *Paul and the Jewish Law: Halakha in the Letters of the Apostle to the Gentiles* (CRINT 3.1; Minneapolis: Fortress, 1990); S. Westerholm, *Israel's Law and the Church's Faith: Paul and His Recent Interpreters* (Grand Rapids: Eerdmans, 1988); F. Young and D. F. Ford, *Meaning and Truth in 2 Corinthians* (Grand Rapids: Eerdmans, 1988).

M. Silva

## OLIVE TREE

1. Setting
2. Pauline Usage
3. Theology of the Olive Tree Analogy
4. Summary

### 1. Setting.

In order to develop his argument concerning the proper relationship of Gentile* Christians to Jewish Christians and of both of these to Judaism, Paul introduces in Romans 11:16b-24 an analogy from oleiculture. The olive tree played an important role in the culture of people in the Mediterranean region and also enjoyed wide symbolic usage, for example, signifying fruitfulness or athletic success. In the long-established imagery of Israel* as God's* planting, the people had occasionally been likened to an olive tree as in Jeremiah 11:16 or Hosea 14:6, though other plant images were more frequent. The reason why Paul chose the olive tree rather than any other figure is most likely that he wanted to make use of the process of engrafting. The essence of the grafting process is the implanting into an established root or trunk of a new scion. In modern times we are more familiar with the implanting of a cultivated scion into a wild root or stem to provide a tree capable of producing good quality fruit. But another process has also been practiced in which a new scion is grafted into an aged trunk or root to rejuvenate the tree. In both cases the desired result is the same, that the tree produces a good harvest of useful fruit.

## 2. Pauline Usage.

In Paul's use of the olive tree what is basic is the image of an ancient trunk from which some (*tines*) branches *have been broken off*. (The passive verb *exeklasthēsan* in Rom 11:17, 19 is a circumlocution for divine action.) Among (*en autois* and not as in NRSV, "in their place") the remaining branches of this cultivated olive tree, wild olive shoots (lit. "wildlings" Rom 11:17, 24) are grafted. Since the wild olive (*oleaster* in Latin, *kotinos* in classical Greek) is almost certainly not a different species from the cultivated (on this see Baxter and Ziesler), there is no natural obstacle to the process Paul describes. The rejuvenation of aged stock by engrafting was known and practiced in the ancient world.

The basic grafting process itself is unnatural (cf. the contrast *kata/para physin*, Rom 11:24) only in the sense that it is an interference with the natural order, but when Paul goes on to speak of the grafting in again of branches that had been deliberately cut off, he is referring to something which has no parallel in normal oleiculture.

The context in Romans 11 into which the olive tree analogy is introduced is one in which Gentile Christians are directly addressed (Rom 11:13-25). Hence the application of the analogy must have its primary reference to them. The resumption of the diatribe* style, with its repeated second-person address, is directed against the presumptuous boasting* of Gentile Christians: the echo of earlier rebukes of Jewish presumption is deliberate. Apparently the Roman* Gentile Christians have misunderstood God's dealings with Israel and also their own place in the divine plan. From the fact that the majority of Jews have failed to accept Paul's gospel,* the Gentile Christians have come to the erroneous conclusion that God has rejected the Jews irretrievably. Moreover they saw themselves as displacing the broken-off branches and boasted in their new-found status. Some may even have believed that God had deliberately cast off the Jewish branches to make way for Gentile believers as if the divine choice were determined on purely ethnic grounds.

Paul uses the olive tree analogy to make several important points.

(1) The branches remain in, or are incorporated into, the tree only by faith (not because of ethnic or any other qualities).

(2) The branches, even those grafted in, do not support the root but are entirely dependent on it; the life is in the root, branches of themselves can never constitute a tree.

(3) The branches grafted in are brought in to *share* (Rom 11:17) the richness of the root—not to monopolize it or to displace all the other branches.

(4) The in-grafted branches are not different in kind from the other branches because if they do not live in humble dependent faith they too will be broken off.

(5) Even the broken-off branches (normally destined to wither or even to be burned), if they do not continue to disobey will be grafted in again—a truly unnatural, even miraculous activity.

The function served by the analogy here is primarily that of deflating the pompous self-image of the Gentile Christians, to insist that arrogance stands in contradiction to faith, to reaffirm the divine election of Israel and to maintain the unity of all God's people whether Jew or Gentile.

## 3. Theology of the Olive Tree Analogy.

This passage, its immediate context in Romans 11, and indeed Romans 9—11 as a whole, are not negative with respect to Israel; nor are they a finely balanced mixture of judgment* and mercy* (cf. the goodness and severity of God, Rom 11:22); rather the overall emphasis is upon divine mercy and the dominant note is one of hope*—God has the power to graft in again even the branches broken off (Rom 11:23). In Romans 11:25-36 we find Paul's final blow against Gentile-Christian conceit when he goes on to reveal that Israel's hardening is temporary, preliminary to the salvation of "all Israel," "the full number" of Israel (*see* Fullness).

The imagery of God as an olive cultivator implies a concern to keep the tree alive, to make it bear fruit and to use whatever means necessary to reinvigorate it. Gentiles are only allowed access to the people of God by the extension of God's covenant* with Israel. It is not the grafted branches in and of themselves that invigorates but their ingrafting that rejuvenates the tree. In the image of the olive tree the continuity (and to a lesser extent the discontinuity) of the people of God is underlined. There is no total destruction of the old tree, nor is the planting of an entirely new tree envisaged. The implication is that the root is still healthy and certainly not incapable of bearing further fruit. Although human response and responsibility are stressed here, there is an underlying emphasis upon divine freedom. God takes human behavior into account but he is not determined by it. He is free to graft in Gentile branches, free to break off Jewish branches, and he maintains the prerogative to make his gifts and call* irrevocable (Rom 11:29).

From this analogy, we can conclude that Paul rejected the notion of the church* having displaced Israel and likewise the concept of an exclusively Gentile Christianity not cognizant of its dependence upon the Jewish root. For Paul this means that the church cannot be in relationship with the God of Israel without at the same time seeing herself as somehow also related to the historical Israel of God.

There may also be implicit in Paul's use of the olive tree analogy, as W. D. Davies has noted, a criticism of Gentile culture and a positive appreciation of God's historic revelation to Israel. Contrary to normal Hellenistic expectation, in Paul's analogy it is the (believing) Jews who are represented in the cultivated olive and the Gentiles who are equated with the wild olive (*agrielaios*), a notoriously unproductive and profitless shrub. Perhaps Paul was turning the tables on proud Gentile Christians who were tending to make culture rather than the gospel the dominant factor in social relations. Paul displays a positive regard for the heritage of Israel even though in his day the majority rejected his message ("If the root [probably Abraham*] is holy, so are the branches," Rom 11:16).

### 4. Summary.

Paul's concern in his use of the olive tree is to stress the continuity in God's community of salvation.* God's historic relation to Israel cannot be ignored by the church: The church has to be kept in genuine continuity with its own origins. Only thus can it arrive at true self-understanding and only thus can the church be prevented from deteriorating into some ancient or modern form of gnosticism* or other such ideology. Only as the church sees itself in continuity with Israel and learns from God's interaction with Israel as recorded in the Scripture can the church truly designate itself the "people of God."

*See also* GENTILES; ISRAEL; RESTORATION OF ISRAEL.

BIBLIOGRAPHY. A. G. Baxter and J. A. Ziesler, "Paul and Arboriculture: Romans 11:17-24," *JSNT* 24 (1985) 25-32; P. M. van Buren, "The Church and Israel: Romans 9-11," *The Princeton Seminary Bulletin*, Supplementary Issue 1 (1990) 5-18; W. S. Campbell, *Paul's Gospel in an Intercultural Context* (Frankfurt: Peter Lang, 1992); C. E. B. Cranfield, *Romans (ICC;* Edinburgh: T. & T. Clark, 1975, 1979); W. D. Davies, "Paul and the People of Israel" and "Paul and the Gentiles: A Suggestion Concerning Romans 11:13-24," in *Pauline and Jewish Studies* (Philadelphia: Fortress, 1984) 123-63; J. D. G. Dunn, *Romans* (WBC 38; Dallas: Word, 1988); O. Hofius, "All Israel will be Saved: Divine Salvation and Israel's Deliverance in Romans 9-11," *The Princeton Seminary Bulletin*, Supplementary Issue 1 (1990) 19-39; J. Munck, *Christ and Israel: An Interpretation of Romans 9—11* (Philadelphia: Fortress, 1967); W. M. Ramsay, "The Olive Tree and the Wild Olive," *Expositor*, 6th Series, 11 (1905) 16-34, 152-60.

W. S. Campbell

**ONESIMUS.** *See* PHILEMON, LETTER TO.

## OPPONENTS OF PAUL

Opposition is often presupposed in Paul's letters, which are not theoretical treatises but reasoned replies to living situations in the churches. Paul's epistolary responses are often in rebuttal of opposition, whether to his person or to his teachings. Sometimes these are general and merely imply the existence of local resistance to Paul's doctrines, in which case they are deemed to lie outside the scope of this article. At other times, however, Paul refers to opponents from outside who have infiltrated the churches established by him with a view to overturning his doctrines and influence. In what follows we will limit our discussion to outsiders who have penetrated the Pauline assemblies.

Scholars have devoted considerable effort in identifying such opponents. So important is the question of the identity of the opponents in 2 Corinthians that C. K. Barrett declared it to be "one of the crucial questions for the understanding of the New Testament and the origins of Christianity," a view with which we concur.

2 Corinthians, where opposition to Paul comes into clearest focus, has been submitted to intense investigation and has proved to be the most appropriate point at which to begin.

1. Survey of Opinion
2. Paul's Opponents at Corinth: "Servants of Righteousness"
3. Paul and the Jerusalem Apostles
4. Opponents in the Galatian Churches
5. Paul's Opponents: A Profile
6. The Judaizers, James and Paul

7. Opposition at Colossae: Jewish Gnosticism
8. Opposition at Philippi: Judaizers
9. Opposition in the Pastoral Letters.

### 1. Survey of Opinion.

The range of opinion on the identity of Paul's opponents is usefully summarized by E. E. Ellis and J. J. Gunther. Broadly speaking, the identity of the opponents in 2 Corinthians has been classified in three ways.

*1.1. Judaizers.* This view has been classically expressed by F. C. Baur and repeated with refinements by C. K. Barrett, M. E. Thrall and R. P. Martin. It argues that the newcomers to Corinth were Palestinian Jews bent on bringing the Gentile* Corinthians within the framework of Judaism. There is much to be said for this hypothesis.

However, based on 1 Corinthians 1:12, Baur also argued that the opponents were emissaries of Peter who came to Corinth claiming to be "of Christ*" (2 Cor 10:7). Moreover, Baur drew a distinction between the false apostles (*pseudapostoloi,* 2 Cor 11:13-15) and the exalted apostles (*hyperlian apostoloi,* 2 Cor 11:5; 12:11) from whom the false apostles came, namely the Jerusalem* apostles (*see* Apostle).

Against this it should be noted, first, that neither Peter* nor James* is mentioned within 2 Corinthians, although Paul does not hesitate to refer to them by name—and sometimes in negative terms—on other occasions (Gal 1:18-19; 2:9, 11-14; 1 Cor 1:12; 9:5).

Moreover, the differentiation of *hyperlian apostoloi* from *pseudapostoloi* appears to be arbitrary. Bultmann argued that the transition from *pseudapostoloi* (2 Cor 11:1-4) to the *hyperlian apostoloi* (2 Cor 11:5) is far too abrupt to make sense. The distinction is perhaps necessitated by Baur's own thesis. Baur would not go so far as to suggest that Paul would call Peter and James "false apostles . . . disguising themselves as apostles of Christ . . . servants [of Satan]" (2 Cor 11:13, 15 RSV). The less sinister sounding *hyperlian apostoloi* is more of a tribute paid to the Jerusalem leaders.

Furthermore, the one explicit reference to *pseudapostoloi* is sandwiched between the two references to *hyperlian apostoloi* in a part of the letter (2 Cor 10—12) where Paul utilizes the idea of *hyper* ("better") ironically. Paul uses words prefixed with *hyper* to attack the *pseudapostoloi* for their missionary imperialism (*over*-extending themselves, *hyperektenein,* 2 Cor 10:14) into lands *beyond* (*ta hyperekeina,* 2 Cor 10:16), for their boast of *abundance* of revelations, (*tē hyperbolē tōn apokalypseōn,* 2 Cor 12:7) and the resulting *super*-elation (*hyperairesthai,* 2 Cor 12:7). To expose their boastfulness Paul himself boasts ironically of being a "better"

(*hyper*) servant of Christ in terms of the sufferings* which he catalogues (2 Cor 11:23-33; *see* Afflictions). The close association of *hyper* words with *pseudapostoloi* makes it likely that the *hyperlian apostoloi* and the *pseudapostoloi* are the same people.

*1.2. Gnostics.* Diametrically opposed to the Baur thesis is the opinion that the opponents were "gnostic pneumatics" who minimized the earthly Jesus in favor of a heavenly Lord and who pushed Paul's doctrines of grace to antinomian extremes. This theory holds that since the opponents preached "another spirit" (2 Cor 11:4) they must have been antinomian, since Law* and Spirit (*see* Holy Spirit) are mutually exclusive. 2 Corinthians 6:14—7:1 is held to be Paul's reaction against their antinomianism. They despise Paul's inferior *gnōsis* (2 Cor 11:6) and self-confessed weakness (2 Cor 10:10) and present themselves as offering a higher *gnōsis* supported by miraculous and visionary "signs" (*see* Visions). This hypothesis regards the opposition to Paul in 2 Corinthians as an extension of the gnosticizing tendencies evident in 1 Corinthians.

An early advocate of this theory was W. Lütgert (see Gunther) who saw the opponents' background in liberal diaspora Judaism. Lütgert in turn influenced the more recent expositions of R. Bultmann and W. Schmithals.

This view is undermined by the strongly Hebraic/Israelite character of those who oppose Paul (2 Cor 11:22) and by their message which appears to have focused on Moses* and therefore the Law (2 Cor 3:4-16). Furthermore, it is far from certain that Gnosticism (*see* Gnosis, Gnosticism) was as clearly defined during Paul's time as this hypothesis would require.

*1.3. Divine Men* (**Theioi Andres**). More recently D. Georgi has developed the hypothesis that Paul's opponents claimed—on the basis of their gifts and signs—to be "divine men" in succession to Jesus and Moses, who both were charismatic, wonder-working figures. These were itinerant Hellenistic Jewish missionaries whose methods and beliefs arose from a Hellenistic milieu. Their confident claims and strong demands made on the Corinthians were part of their legitimacy as *theioi andres* which they insisted upon over against the manifest weaknesses* of Paul.

A variation of this theory may be found in that of G. Friedrich who holds that the models to which the newcomers pointed were not drawn from the Hellenistic world but from early Christianity. According to Friedrich, Stephen and Philip, the miracle-working Hellenist leaders of Acts 6, gathered supporters who have now come with similar powers to Corinth to present Jesus as a triumphant second Moses, as opposed to the suffering figure preached by Paul.

Georgi's theory suffers from the problem that the *theioi andres* are not the clearly defined type he presupposes, and reference to them generally comes from texts later than the NT (see Blackburn). His argument for their claim to "being sufficient," "sufficiency" (*hikanos, hikanotēs*, 2 Cor 2:16; cf. 2 Cor 3:5) does not necessitate self-presentation as "divine men"; mere superiority over Paul would suffice.

Friedrich's hypothesis, while helpfully suggestive, does not reckon on the many points at which Stephen's theology may have anticipated and indeed been the source of Paul's doctrines rather than being antipathetic to them.

While the growing knowledge of the world of the NT will doubtless stimulate further theories of their identity and intentions, given that we only meet Paul's opponents in his own passing rebuttal of them, it is unlikely that a scholarly consensus will be reached. The evidence from Paul's letters is too unsystematic and indeed polemical to permit ultimately secure historical decisions.

### 2. Paul's Opponents at Corinth: "Servants of Righteousness."

*2.1. Evidence from 2 Corinthians.* The key to the identity of Paul's opponents in Corinth is to be found in his statement:

> For such men are false apostles,
>> deceitful workmen,
>>> disguising themselves as apostles of Christ . . .
>>>> [Satan's] servants
> also disguise themselves as *servants of righteousness*
> (2 Cor 11:13-15).

In terms of their self-presentation the opponents came as "apostles of Christ," "workmen" and "servants," that is, on the same terms as Paul (2 Cor 11:12), having a vocabulary of ministry* identical with Paul's. Their "deceit," their "disguise" was that they purported to be "servants of righteousness*" (*diakonoi dikaiosynēs*).

Earlier Paul had contrasted two ministries (*diakoniai*)—of Moses and of Christ (2 Cor 3:4-18). The former, a "written code" which "kills," the latter—"a new covenant"—"[written] in the Spirit," "gives life*" (2 Cor 3:6). The former is a "ministry (*diakonia*) of condemnation," the latter "a ministry (*diakonia*) of righteousness" (*dikaiosynēs*, 2 Cor 3:9).

How does "this ministry," which Paul says he "has" (2 Cor 4:1), mediate "life" and "righteousness"? It is by Christ's death, Paul declares, that "God made him to be sin . . . that in him we might become the *righteousness* (*dikaiosynē*) of God" (2 Cor 5:21). This is "the

ministry (*diakonia*) of reconciliation . . . the message of reconciliation" (*see* Peace, Reconciliation) which God has entrusted to Paul (2 Cor 5:18-19; cf. 2 Cor 6:3).

Paul, therefore, is a *diakonos* in the *"diakonia* of righteousness" through the cross of Christ (*see* Cross, Theology of the) while the opponents are *diakonoi* of Moses' *diakonia* of righteousness through "the written code" which, however, brings not "righteousness" but "condemnation" (2 Cor 3:7). The opponents' "deceit" lies in their "message" to the Corinthians that God imputes righteousness by the "written code" rather than through the cross. In proposing to the Corinthians an alternative to the death of Christ as the means of "the righteousness of God" (*see* Righteousness of God) Paul declares these men to be "servants of Satan*" (2 Cor 11:15).

The phrase "servants of righteousness," therefore, is critical in the identification of Paul's opponents in Corinth. Since theirs was "the ministry . . . of the written code," that is, of "Moses" (2 Cor 3:6-7), we take it that these men were indeed Judaizers* and that their version of the "righteousness of God" by means of the "written code" lay at the heart of their message and was their chief point of difference from the apostle to the Gentiles.

Unfortunately, we may only speculate about their precise message. Once more, however, the word *righteousness* may come to our assistance. *Righteousness* occurs not at all in the Thessalonian letters and only once in 1 Corinthians. The single appearance of *righteousness* to this point, in a letter written to a Greek church, suggests that the issues associated with righteousness had not been raised in Macedonia or Achaia until the writing of 2 Corinthians in about A.D. 56.

*2.2. Evidence from Romans.* By general agreement Romans* was written in Corinth around A.D. 56 or 57, not long after the writing of 2 Corinthians from Macedonia. There we find *righteousness* occurring forty-nine times with numerous occurrences of the closely related words *justify* (*dikaioō*) and *righteous* (*dikaios; see* Justification). Since the *righteousness* family of words lies at the heart of the argument of Romans (see the key text Rom 1:17), it is likely that Paul is there addressing the same issues and the same (kind of) opponents as in 2 Corinthians. Although Paul makes no mention of circumcision* in 2 Corinthians, it is quite possible that circumcision was part of the dispute at Corinth. It was certainly prominent in both Romans and Galatians.*

The Romans letter may well be Paul's more measured response to the issue of righteousness so painfully raised in Corinth and passionately but unevenly addressed in 2 Corinthians. Certainly polemical echoes may still be heard in Romans which may relate to the same opponents as in 2 Corinthians. There are those who "slanderously charge" Paul with saying "why not do evil that good may come?" (Rom 3:8; cf. Rom 6:1; Gal 2:17). His defensive comments about the Jews (Rom 3:1, 9; 4:1; 9:3-5; 11:1) are consistent with accusations that might arise from a Judaizing apostolate whose message focused on righteousness through the keeping of the works of the Law (cf. Rom 3:21—4:3, 16; 10:3-4). Possibly "those who create dissensions and difficulties in opposition to the doctrines you have been taught" (Rom 16:17) represents Paul's general warning to Roman Christians about the Judaizing message arising out of problems recently encountered in Corinth.

*2.3. Newcomers at Corinth.* It is evident from 2 Corinthians that Paul's opponents in Corinth were a group ("many," 2 Cor 2:17) of persons (*hoi kapēleuontes,* "hucksters" or "peddlers," 2 Cor 2:17) who had "come" to Corinth (2 Cor 11:4-5) from outside (their "letters of commendation," 2 Cor 3:1) where they and their message had been "received" (2 Cor 11:4, 20).

It emerges from 2 Corinthians that these newcomers legitimated their *diakonia* in Corinth by "boasting" (*kauchasthai,* 2 Cor 10—12 passim) of their achievements, "contrasting" (*synkrinein,* 2 Cor 10:12) their strengths with Paul's weaknesses. In their missionary journey to Corinth they have come a greater, Paul a lesser, distance (2 Cor 10:13-14). They have "letters of commendation" (from Jerusalem?); Paul has none (2 Cor 3:1-3). They are "sufficient," triumphant figures (*see* Triumph); Paul is inadequate, a sorry figure as he limps from place to place in defeat (2 Cor 2:14—3:5; 4:1, 16). Extrapolating from remarks Paul makes about himself, some scholars affirm that these experiences were being claimed by his opponents. They are men of divine power* ("beside" themselves, 2 Cor 5:13), "caught up . . . out of the body . . . into paradise" (*see* Heaven) where they see "visions" and hear "revelations" of what "cannot be told" (2 Cor 12:1-5; *see* Visions), whereas Paul is mundane, a minister without power, worldly and weak (2 Cor 10:3-6; 12:1-10; cf. 2 Cor 5:12-13). Possibly they performed "the signs of an apostle" (2 Cor 12:12) whereas, they allege, Paul did not. They are powerful in speech (2 Cor 11:5-6) and in wisdom* whereas he is in speech "unskilled" and in general "a fool" (2 Cor 11:1—12:13). In all things he is "inferior" (cf. 2 Cor 11:5), whereas they are superior, "better" (*hyper,* 2 Cor 11:23).

Herein lies the difficulty of identifying these opponents as Judaizing "Hebrews" bent on imposing "Moses" (the Law) on the Corinthians (2 Cor 11:22; 3:4-16). Corinth was a Greco-Roman metropolis. How can we account for "Hebrews" having sufficient style to find acceptance with such an audience and, moreover, displaying proficiency in the rhetorical arts (*see* Rhetoric; Rhetorical Criticism) of "boasting" and "comparison"? These "Hebrews" would appear to be behaving like Greeks.

The two main theories about the opponents—that they must have been Judaizers *or* Gnostics—are perfectly understandable given the apparent contradiction implicit in the evidence about them in 2 Corinthians.

New information is available, however, which changes our whole idea of life in first-century Judea. On the basis of funerary inscriptions M. Hengel has argued that there may have been as many as 16,000 Greek-speaking Jews in Jerusalem out of an estimated population of 100,000 (Hengel, 10; *see* Hellenism). He reasons that many of these must have enjoyed a high level of classical education. It is quite conceivable, therefore, that the "Hebrews" who came to Corinth spoke polished Greek and possessed skills in rhetoric. Saul/Paul himself was not altogether without abilities in these areas, to say nothing of his coworker Silas/Silvanus (*see* Coworkers), the Jewish-Christian prophet of Jerusalem to whom is attributed the stylishly written 1 Peter (Acts 15:32; 2 Cor 1:19; 1 Pet 5:12).

What then of the paranormal ecstasy, visions, revelations and miracles on which Paul's opponents depended, in part at least, for their acceptance in Corinth? Study of the history of Judea in the period A.D. 44-66 reveals a milieu of political disintegration, revolutionary activism and apocalyptic fervor which was expressed in prophetic inspiration and miraculous signs (see, e.g., Josephus *J.W.* 2.13.4 §§258-59). It is quite possible that Judea at the time represented the kind of religious milieu from which the *pseudapostoloi* could have come. It is unnecessary, therefore, to require a gnostic provenance for these newcomers.

**3. Paul and the Jerusalem Apostles.**

If the newcomers in Corinth, as reflected in 2 Corinthians, were Judaizers, were they emissaries of the Jerusalem apostles, as F. C. Baur suggested? Paul's relationship with the Jerusalem church and its apostles is set out most clearly in Galatians, particularly in chapters 1—2. Contrary to Baur's thesis, it emerges from these chapters that while tension existed between Paul and the Jerusalem apostles, they are distinct from his opponents, both in Jerusalem and Antioch.*

Paul outlines his relationship with the Jerusalem apostles by referring to four critical occasions in his own ministry. He writes autobiographically but so as to establish with the Galatians the delicate nature of relationship with "those who were apostles before" him in Jerusalem (Gal 1:17).

First he refers to his "call" on the way to Damascus (Gal 1:15-17; *see* Conversion and Call of Paul). It was God,* not the Jerusalem apostles, who "called" Paul and "revealed his Son" to him that he "might preach him among the Gentiles" (Gal 1:16). Not even after his call did Paul "confer with (literally, "seek corroboration from") flesh* and blood," that is, the apostles in Jerusalem. He went away to Arabia and then to Damascus. Paul's knowledge of the risen Christ has been mediated directly to Paul by God.

The second occasion was in Jerusalem (Gal 1:18-21). Only "after three years" from his "call" did Paul go up to Jerusalem "to visit Cephas" with whom he remained fifteen days (Gal 1:18). Paul's word *visit* (Gk *historēsai*), whose meaning is much debated, could be interpreted "meet" or perhaps "inquire of," suggesting some indebtedness to Cephas for information about the historical (*see* Jesus and Paul), as opposed to the heavenly, Christ. Paul underlines his apostolic autonomy by commenting in passing, "I saw none of the other apostles except James the Lord's brother," suggesting no more than a courtesy call. His carefully chosen words are highlighted by his solemn assurance, "In what I am writing to you, before God, I do not lie" (Gal 1:20; but cf. Acts 9:26-30). "Still not known by sight to the churches of Judea" (i.e., in and around Jerusalem) he went to Syria and Cilicia (Gal 1:21-22; cf. Acts 9:30).

The third occasion, also in Jerusalem, occurred "after fourteen years" (Gal 2:1-10), that is fourteen years from his great watershed "call" en route to Damascus. Concerned to know of the acceptability to James, Cephas and John "of the gospel which [he] preach[es] among the Gentiles," a gospel which did not require circumcision of Gentiles, Paul brought with him as a test case the uncircumcised Titus. While Paul's apostolic authority* was independent of Jerusalem, it was important that his circumcision-free Gentile converts were accepted, along with believing Jews, as spiritual heirs of Abraham.*

Despite the attempts of "false brethren" (Gk *pseudadelphoi*, Gal 2:4) to have Titus circumcised, the "pillar apostles"—James,* Cephas and John—made no such demands on Paul's Gentile companion (Gal 2:6). Rather, the three Jerusalem apostles formally *recognized* that Paul had been "entrusted [i.e., by God] with the gospel* to the uncircumcised" whereupon they *joined hands* with Paul and Barnabas* in a gospel "fellowship" whereby Paul and Barnabas should "go to the Gentiles" and the Jerusalem triumvirate should "[go] to the circumcised" (Gal 2:7-9).

In other words, the Jerusalem apostles recognized two apostolates, one to Jews led by Peter, the other to Gentiles led by the Antioch delegates Paul and Barnabas. Despite the decision to approve two racially distinct apostolates, there was overarching agreement in the fundamentals of the gospel based on the death and resurrection* of Christ (see 1 Cor 15:3-5, 11).

The fourth occasion was at Antioch in Syria, a church of mixed Jew-Gentile membership (Gal 2:11-14; *see* Social Setting). Cephas had come (from Jerusalem) to Antioch where he had shared table fellowship with Gentile members (including the Lord's Supper?; *see* Lord's Supper), something he had presumably been prepared to do following the conversion of Cornelius (Gal 2:14; cf. Acts 10:28). Though a Jew, Peter now "lived like a Gentile" (Gal 2:14), that is, he had eaten with Gentiles which meant eating what they ate (*see* Food).

But a serious division along racial-religious lines developed within the church in Antioch with the dramatic arrival of "certain men . . . from James" (in Jerusalem, Acts 15:23-24; cf. Acts 15:1), whom Paul calls "the circumcision party." Cephas "drew back and separated himself" [from eating with the Gentile members of the church]. The rest of the Jewish members, including even Barnabas, acted "insincerely" (literally "hypocritically"). Paul "opposed [Cephas] to the face because he stood condemned" for withdrawing into an exclusively Jewish table fellowship. It was hypocritical for Peter to "live like a Gentile" but now by this action "compel the Gentiles to live like Jews" (Gal 2:14).

At stake at Antioch was "the truth of the gospel" (Gal 2:14), which was raised by the demand that the Jewish Christians *must* eat separately from Gentile believers, which had the effect of demanding that Gentiles adopt Jewish eating practices. Paul used the telling phrase "the truth of the gospel" in the previous incident in Jerusalem when he opposed the *necessity* of the circumcision of the Gentile Titus (Gal 2:5). In other words "the truth of the gospel" is preserved when circumcision and Jewish food laws are regarded as extraneous to the gospel and nonmandatory for Gentiles.

This long autobiographical passage (Gal 1:15—2:14), covering a decade and a half of Paul's life, is invaluable for identifying the degrees of difference between Paul and various persons within the Jerusalem church. We are able to distinguish between "those who were apostles before him" in Jerusalem—with whom certain tensions may be recognized—and others with whom there is outright opposition. Thus Paul insists that his "call" to be an apostle to the Gentiles was mediated directly by God and after some years formally recognized by the "pillar" apostles of Jerusalem. He expresses deference to Cephas in one situation but fierce opposition in another. In regard to James there is a certain ambivalence. At his first visit to Jerusalem he merely "saw" James. He acknowledges by his order of names the primacy of James at the second meeting in Jerusalem, while implying criticism of James because the trouble in Antioch was caused by "men who came from James."

Nonetheless, Cephas and James are not "opponents." No qualifying remarks are used in regard to the "false brethren secretly brought in who slipped in to spy out our freedom . . . that they might bring us under bondage" (Gal 2:4). They may be associated with or more probably identified with the "men who came from James" to Antioch and who had such a dramatic effect on the eating practices of Cephas, Barnabas and the Jewish believers (Gal 2:12-13).

The same distinction is to be found in the Acts of the Apostles. On one hand there are the "apostles and elders" of the Jerusalem church (Acts 15:2, 6, 22, 23), among whom are named Peter (Acts 15:7) and James (Acts 15:13), while on the other are "believers who belonged to the party of the Pharisees" who said, "It is necessary to circumcise [Gentiles] and to charge them to keep the Law of Moses" (Acts 15:5; cf. Acts 15:1). Whether or not we identify the meeting of the Antioch delegates and the "pillar" apostles (Gal 2) with the so-called Jerusalem Council (Acts 15), it is probable that the "false brethren" of Galatians 2:4 are to be equated with the "believers of the party of the Pharisees" of Acts 15:5.

Acts 15:5, therefore, supplies the precious clue, which is found nowhere else, and which goes a long way toward solving the mystery of the identity of Paul's opponents in Jerusalem. These "false brethren" of Jerusalem, these "men who came from James [from Jerusalem to Antioch] . . . the circumcision party" (Gal 2:4, 12) were "*believers who belonged to the party of the Pharisees.*"

What, then, was the relationship between the "pillar" apostles of the Jerusalem Church—James, Cephas and John—and these men?

### 4. Opponents in the Galatian Churches.

Scholars are divided over the dating of the Letter to the Galatians.* Some place it in the late forties, following hard on the dispute in Antioch (Gal 2:11-14) on the eve of the Jerusalem Council. Others date the letter at about the same time as 2 Corinthians and Romans, that is, around the mid-fifties. Certainly the "righteousness" vocabulary is very prominent in the letter, suggesting that the same issues were at stake as in 2 Corinthians and Romans. But this does not necessarily demand that Galatians was written in the mid-fifties. Paul may have used the "righteousness" vocabulary whenever the Judaizing question was raised.

Unlike Antioch and Corinth there is no mention of anyone from outside coming to the Galatian churches (2 Cor 11:4; Gal 2:12). The churches were being troubled by a group of Jews led by an unidentified individual (Gal 5:10, 12; 3:1; 1:7, 9) who said that circumcision was a prerequisite for membership in the Israel* of God (Gal 3:6-14; 6:16). These "agitators" and their leader were putting pressure on other Jewish believers to compel the Gentile members to be circumcised (Gal 6:12). They claimed that Paul really owed his authority to the Jerusalem apostles (Gal 1:15—2:9) and that Paul himself "preached circumcision" (Gal 5:11).

Were these agitators and their leader indigenous to the Galatian region or had they in fact come there from somewhere else? The letter of the Jerusalem Council to the "brethren in Antioch, Syria and Cilicia" acknowledges that "some persons from us have troubled you" (Acts 15:23). If such agitators had come from Jerusalem to Cilicia, it would have been no great surprise had they travelled on to southern Galatia. Since the focus of Galatians is on circumcision related to Christian freedom (see, e.g., Gal 5:1-2), a theme which is also prominent in the autobiographical section where "false brethren" in Jerusalem "spy out our freedom . . . that they might bring us into bondage" by having Titus circumcised (Gal 2:3-5), it is reasonable to argue that those who came to the Galatian churches were in fact the "false brethren" of Jerusalem, the "believers who belonged to the party of the Pharisees" (Acts 15:5).

### 5. Paul's Opponents: A Profile.

A pattern emerges from the study of 2 Corinthians, Romans and Galatians which enables us to define more closely Paul's opponents in Corinth as reflected in 2 Corinthians. The supersession of the "written code" associated with Moses by means of "a new covenant" (*see* Covenant and New Covenant), "a *diakonia* of righteousness," along with Paul's rejection of the opponents in Corinth as "servants of righteousness," suggests that the newcomers had come on a Judaizing mission to bring the Gentile Corinthians under obligation to the written Mosaic code. The proliferation of *righteousness* and related words in Romans and Galatians, concerned as they are to rebut righteousness arising from the works of the Jewish Law, add confirmation to the profile of the opponents in Corinth as Judaizers.

Galatians assists us to see that while significant tensions existed between himself and the Jerusalem apostles, it is important to differentiate these from persons Paul calls "false brethren . . . the circumcision party" whom we have been able to more closely identify as "believers from the party of the Pharisees."

The "false brethren" who are also "false apostles" are one and the same group as the "superlative apostles" (*hyperlian apostoloi*, 2 Cor 11:5; 12:11). It emerges from 2 Corinthians that their claim to superiority is based, in part, on their boast that they have traveled as far as they have, possibly that they have traveled further than Paul (2 Cor 10:13-18). Paul rejects this claim in the terms of the missionary agreement made in Jerusalem in the late forties by the "pillar" apostles with Paul and Barnabas (Gal 2:7-9). In their coming to Corinth the "superlative apostles" have crossed the line of demarcation and entered Paul's sphere of agreed missionary labor (*see* Mission): ministry to the Gentiles. They have "overextend[ed] themselves . . . [not kept] to the limits God has apportioned . . . boasted of work already done in another's field."

From 2 Corinthians there emerges a fascinating profile of these men, their mission and their means of legitimating their mission. Driven in all probability by a heightened religious zeal arising from the rapid deterioration of Roman-Jew relationships in Judea under Felix's notorious regime, these "superlative apostles" have apparently armed themselves with an array of paranormal abilities calculated to impress the Gentiles in Corinth so as to supplant Paul as their apostle. Their determination to overturn Paul is perhaps also indicative of their awareness of his success in establishing messianic assemblies among the Greeks. But, so far as they were concerned, such assemblies, though connected to the Messiah Jesus, were schisms from Israel, because they gave no real place for Moses and the Law (Acts 15:1, 5).

In their counter-mission Paul's opponents have, by any measure, shown zeal comparable with his own. They have opposed him in Jerusalem and traveled from there to churches in Antioch, Syria-Cilicia, Galatia and now they have come all the way to the city of Corinth in Achaia. This is a remarkable historical phenomenon. They claimed, he says, to be "servants of Christ" (2 Cor 11:23) yet, from his viewpoint, so misguided as to the ministry of "righteousness" that he calls them "[Satan's] servants" (2 Cor 11:14). Their mission and activities have constituted a major threat to the survival of Paul's churches and have provoked him to write letters which are among his most powerful. It is fair to say that lack of appreciation of their identity and zealous program by modern readers significantly hinders our grasp of Paul's argument in those letters where he is responding to their doctrines.

### 6. The Judaizers, James and Paul.

It is clear from the above argument that we may not too closely associate the name of Peter with Paul's opponents. The incident at Antioch (Gal 2:11-14) shows that Peter was susceptible to their influence, but not the source of it. But what of James, the brother of the Lord, an "apostle before" Paul, who by the late forties had emerged as the preeminent "pillar" apostle of the Jerusalem church? Was James the source of the opposition which flowed from Jerusalem to the churches of the Gentiles?

James had been a member of the Jerusalem church from its beginning until his death in A.D. 62, a period of about thirty years. At first the leader was Peter, supported by John Zebedee. By the late forties, however, James, not Peter, was the leader (Gal 2:9; Acts 15:13-22). At that time there were both apostles and elders at Jerusalem (Acts 15:2, 4, 6, 22, 23). However, when Paul came for the last time to Jerusalem in about A.D. 57, there was no reference to "apostles"; only the Jerusalem elders remained, with James the clear leader.

Over this thirty-year period the Jerusalem church became more conservatively Jewish, doubtless reflecting the rise of Jewish religious nationalism in the face of worsening Roman-Jew relationships in Judea (Josephus *J.W.* 2.12.1—13.7 §§223-271 passim). First, the Hellenists emigrated in the thirties, and by the late forties they were followed by Peter (and John?) and possibly the other apostles. The final glimpse of the Jerusalem church given by Acts at the time of Paul's final visit is of a thoroughly Jewish enclave.

Despite the good face Acts gives to the meeting, it is clear enough that the Jerusalem elders expressed profound unhappiness with Paul. No speech of gratitude for the collection* from the Gentile churches is mentioned, though Luke knew of the collection's existence (Acts 24:17). Rather, the elders pointedly remark on the size and thorough Jewishness of the believing community in Jerusalem, whose widely held conviction it is that Paul has betrayed the cause of Judaism in the Diaspora. It is their understanding that Paul has taught Jews to abandon Moses and not to circumcise their children (Acts 21:21), and he has not required Gentiles to uphold the decisions of the Jerusalem Council over ritual and moral matters (Acts 21:25).

These accusations are instructive since they clearly reflect the views of the Jerusalem elders. Yet these opinions are continuous with and closely resemble the commitment to Moses of the men from Judea who a decade and a half earlier went from Jerusalem to the Gentiles in Antioch insisting on circumcision as a prerequisite to salvation and who, we have argued, were "believers who . . . belonged to the party of the Pharisees" (Acts 15:1, 5).

It is not suggested they were necessarily the same men. Rather, that there was from at least the forties a strongly held theological viewpoint within the messianic community in Jerusalem, which, influenced by Pharisaism, promoted a nationalistic and therefore a Mosaic version of the faith and which therefore regarded Paul's mission to the Gentiles with profound unease. The rising tide of religious nationalism during the crises in Judea of the forties and fifties, together with the decreased influence of more liberal leaders like Stephen, Philip, John and Peter and the emergence of James as the undisputed leader—the brother of the Lord no less—created an environment in which there arose a mission to counter Paul's influence in the Diaspora. But these persons are never named, either by Paul or in Acts. They remain "certain men" (*tines*, Acts 15:1, 5; Gal 2:12) who on account of their assault on the doctrines of Christ, Paul will portray as "false brothers," "false apostles" and even "[Satan's] servants."

James must have been a significant figure in Jerusalem by the late fifties since he presided over such a large religious community (Acts 21:18-20). In his account of James's death in A.D. 62, Josephus corroborates this impression. The high priest Ananus II seized the opportunity presented by the unexpected death of the procurator Festus to have James stoned. Clearly James must have been important to pose a threat to the high priest. But his death provoked a protest by those Jerusalemites who were "considered the most fair-minded and who were strict in their observance of the Law" (Josephus *Ant.* 20.9.1 §201), which can only mean citizens of Pharisaic sympathy.

Thus James appears to have enjoyed significant respect within the wider community of Jerusalem. From his viewpoint, as a leader of a messianic community in Jerusalem, Paul's mission to Gentiles in the Diaspora must have raised acute difficulties for relationships between the messianic Jewish community and the wider Jewish community at a time of rapidly increasing religious nationalism.

From Paul's perspective there may have been a degree of nervousness about the Lord's brother since his opponents appear to have come from James's community. It is true that Paul refuses to allow that his apostleship is derived from James (Gal 1:19; cf. Gal 1:17) and to a degree he deprecates the authority of the Jerusalem apostles (Gal 2:6-9), and indeed he voices an angry complaint about "the men who came from James" creating division in Antioch (Gal 2:12). Nonetheless,

Paul acknowledges James's apostleship and indeed his primacy as a Jerusalem apostle (Gal 1:19; 2:9). There is no good reason to believe that the "letters of recommendation" brought by the newcomers to Corinth (2 Cor 2:17—3:1) bore the name of James. Paul is hardly likely to have persevered with the collection for the Jerusalem church if James was the well-spring for the opposition which flowed out from Jerusalem to the Pauline churches. Indeed, one of Paul's motives for the collection* may have been to maintain a gospel fellowship* between his apostolate to the Gentiles and that other apostolate, which was directed to Jews and which was based at Jerusalem where James was the undisputed leader.

A comparable impression of James may be discerned in Luke's account of the council in Jerusalem. James does not demand circumcision of the Gentiles, and he denies that those who have gone from Jerusalem "unsettling" the Gentiles in Antioch, Syria and Cilicia did so on his authority (Acts 15:19, 23-24). At Paul's final and tense visit to Jerusalem, the complaints about the apostle to the Gentiles come from the mouths of the elders, not from James (Acts 21:18-25).

### 7. Opposition at Colossae: Jewish Gnosticism.

Mindful of the major theories that Paul's opponents were either Judaizers or gnostics, a neat solution would be to identify Paul's opponents, particularly those in Corinth, where so much is said about them, as Jewish gnostics. The existence of such people is made probable by Paul's rebuttal of what is generally regarded as some species of Jewish gnosticism within the Colossian church (*see* Colossians). Unquestionably, there was a version of Christianity at Colossae which was characterized by circumcision, asceticism, Jewish calendrical observance, mysticism and worship of angels (Col 2:8-23).

These elements are largely missing from Paul's rejection of the teaching of his opponents in Corinth. Paul's presentation of Christ's person and work (*see* Christology) to the Corinthians—in terms of his fulfillment of the promise and righteousness of the Law (2 Cor 1:19-20; 3:4-9; 5:18-21)—has a very different emphasis from the cosmic Christ of the Colossians letter (Col 1:15-20; 2:9-10, 19; 3:1-3).

There is no hint in Colossians about the origin of this Jewish gnosticism, whether it was indigenous or imported. It is, however, well known that Judaism flourished even in remote regions of Anatolia such as the Lycus Valley. The most probable explanation is that a local version of Jewish gnosticism had found its way into the life of the Christian church at Colossae. In any case Paul had not visited this region. The more typical Judaizers seem to have been attracted to churches directly established by the apostle.

### 8. Opposition at Philippi: Judaizers.

According to many scholars Paul wrote his letter to the Philippians from Rome in the early sixties. Once again opposition to Paul from Jewish believers is evident. But the nature of the opposition to Paul at Philippi is debated (see Philippians). Paul's imprisonment has encouraged the "brethren" in Rome to "speak the word of God" (Phil 1:14). Some of these, however, do so "from envy and rivalry . . . out of partisanship, not sincerely, but thinking to afflict me in my imprisonment" (Phil 1:15, 17). In all probability these are "those who mutilate the flesh" (Phil 3:2), the circumcisers of Gentile believers, "whose god is the belly" (Phil 3:19), that is they observe Jewish food regulations.

As with other letters—Galatians and Romans— where the imposition of circumcision on Gentiles is being promoted, we notice the apostle's use of "righteousness . . . the righteousness of God which is through faith in Christ" (see Phil 3:6, 9 bis).

From the time of the arrival of believers in the world capital there had been problems within the large Jewish community (see Rome and Roman Christianity). It was forced to withdraw from Rome in A.D. 49 "on account of Chrestus" (Suetonius Claudius 25.4; cf. Acts 18:1), a probable misspelling of Christus. It is likely that the conversion of Jews to Jesus the Christ had created such turmoil within the Jewish community that Claudius expelled all the Jews. The accession of Nero in A.D. 54 meant that Jews could return to the city, doubtless fearful that further disturbances might mean more reprisals from the authorities. Known to be a storm center wherever he went, it is possible that Paul's Jewish-Christian opponents in Rome even resorted to preaching Christ—their version, of course—to precipitate unrest within the Jewish community and so prejudice the impending hearing of Paul's case.

There is no hint that these persons had come from Jerusalem to Rome to harass Paul. Possibly the Judaizing movement, like Paul's own mission, had by then developed its own momentum so that it had no direct connection with the mother city, Jerusalem. This may support the argument that the Judaizing program is not directly associated with James, who would have been dead by the time Paul wrote to the Philippians.

### 9. Opposition in the Pastoral Letters.

We have limited our discussion to opponents from outside who penetrated the churches established by Paul. In our opinion the false teachers and other opponents referred to in the Pastoral Letters (see Pastoral Letters) were indigenous to the churches. In this we follow E. E.

Ellis: "Unlike the earlier letters, the opponents appear to include a considerable number of former co-workers whose apostasy creates an especially bitter situation" (Ellis, 214).

See also APOSTLE; CIRCUMCISION; GNOSIS, GNOSTICISM; JERUSALEM; JUDAIZERS; LAW.

BIBLIOGRAPHY. F. A. Agnew, "Paul's Theological Adversary in the Doctrine of Justification by Faith: A Contribution to Jewish Christian Dialogue," JES 25 (1988) 538-54; P. Barnett, "Opposition in Corinth," JSNT 22 (1984) 3-17; C. K. Barrett, "Paul's Opponents in II Corinthians," NTS 17 (1971) 233-54; B. Blackburn, "Miracle Working THEIOI ANDRES in Hellenism (and Hellenistic Judaism)," in Gospel Perspectives 6: The Miracles of Jesus, ed. D. Wenham and C. Blomberg (Sheffield: JSOT, 1986) 185-218; J. D. G. Dunn, "The Relationship between Paul and Jerusalem according to Galatians 1 and 2," NTS 28 (1982) 461-78 [= Jesus, Paul and the Law: Studies in Mark and Galatians (Louisville: Westminster/John Knox, 1990) 108-26]; E. E. Ellis, "Paul and his Opponents," in Christianity, Judaism and Other Greco-Roman Cults, ed. J. Neusner (Leiden: E. J. Brill, 1975) 264-98; C. Forbes, "Paul's Opponents in Corinth," Buried History 19 (1983) 19-23; D. Georgi, The Opponents of Paul in Second Corinthians (Philadelphia: Fortress, 1986); J. J. Gunther, St. Paul's Opponents and Their Background (NovTSup 35; Leiden: E. J. Brill, 1973); M. Hengel, The "Hellenization" of Judaea in the First Century after Christ (Philadelphia: Trinity, 1989); D. Kee, "Who were the 'Super-Apostles' of 2 Corinthians 10-13?" RQ 23 (1980) 65-76; C. G. Kruse, "The Offender and the Offence in 2 Corinthians 2:5 and 7:12," EvQ 60 (1988) 129-139; idem, "The Relationship between the Opposition to Paul Reflected in 2 Corinthians 1-7 and 10-13," EvQ 61 (1989) 195-202; S. E. McClelland, " 'Super-Apostles, Servants of Christ, Servants of Satan': a Response," JSNT 14 (1982) 82-87; R. P. Martin, "The Opponents of Paul in 2 Corinthians: An Old Issue Revisited," in Tradition and Interpretation in the New Testament, ed. G. F. Hawthorne with O. Betz, (Grand Rapids: Eerdmans, 1987) 279-89; J. Murphy-O'Connor, "Pneumatikoi and Judaizers in 2 Cor 2:14-4:6," ABR 34 (1986) 42-58; D. W. Oostendorp, Another Jesus: A Gospel of Jewish Christian Superiority in II Corinthians (Kampen: Kok, 1967); E. P. Sanders, "Paul on the Law, His Opponents, and the Jewish People in Philippians 3 and 2 Corinthians 11," in Anti-Judaism in Early Christianity 1, ed. P. Richardson and D. Granskou (Waterloo: Wilfred Laurier University, 1986) 75-90; J. Sumney, Identifying Paul's Opponents (JSNTSup 40; Sheffield: JSOT, 1990); idem, "The Role of Historical Reconstructions of Early Christianity in Identifying Paul's Opponents," PRS 16 (1989) 45-53;

M. E. Thrall, "Super-Apostles, Servants of Christ, and Servants of Satan," *JSNT* 6 (1980) 42-57.

P. W. Barnett

**ORDER.** *See* CHURCH ORDER AND GOVERNMENT; PASTORAL LETTERS.

**ORDINATION.** *See* CHURCH ORDER AND GOVERNMENT; MINISTRY; PASTORAL LETTERS.

# P

**PAGANISM.** *See* IDOLATRY; RELIGIONS, GRECO-ROMAN.

**PARADISE.** *See* HEAVEN, HEAVENLIES, PARADISE.

**PARAENESIS.** *See* TEACHING/PARAENESIS.

**PAROUSIA.** *See* ESCHATOLOGY.

**PARTICULARISM.** *See* ELECTION AND PREDESTINATION; UNIVERSALISM.

**PASSOVER.** *See* LORD'S SUPPER; SACRIFICE, OFFERING.

## PASTOR, PAUL AS

1. Pastor Paul
2. Paul as Parent
3. Paul's Pastoral Care
4. Pastoral Authority
5. Shared Pastoral Responsibilities

### 1. Pastor Paul.

*1.1. Paul as Pastor.* Paul's letters are a clear testimony to his pastoral heart. Indeed his letters* are a product of his pastoral care, for through them Paul exercised a pastoral role in regard to the churches which he or his converts had founded. Paul was no academic theologian, far removed from the realities of church life; rather it was his concern for the churches which proved to be the springboard for his theology. Nor was Paul a single-focus evangelist, intent only on winning people for Jesus Christ; rather it was his concern to remain in relationship with the churches he planted. V. P. Furnish helpfully pointed out that Paul's pastoral ministry* was in fact rooted in the character and meaning of his gospel.* For the obedience to Christ he sought to win from Gentiles* (Rom 15:18) involved their becoming one in Christ* (Gal 3:26-28), members of Christ's body* (Rom 12:4, 5; 1 Cor 12:12-27), bound to one another as members of God's family (cf. Gal 6:10).

*1.2. Paul as Teacher.* In view of his pastoral heart, it is perhaps somewhat surprising to discover that Paul nowhere uses the term "pastor" of himself. Indeed, in the *Corpus Paulinum* the term "pastor" occurs only once in Ephesians 4:11, where the office of pastor is described as one of the gifts* of the risen Christ to his church. The fact that one definitive article is used for both "pastor" and "teacher" indicates that the pastoral office is here closely linked with teaching or "feeding" the flock. In Luke's record of Paul's speech at Miletus, the Ephesian elders are charged to "watch over the flock, of which the Holy Spirit has made you overseers, to shepherd the church of God" (Acts 20:28). If the context is a guide, then preaching* and teaching* would appear to be a major element in such pastoral care. Although Paul does not actually use the pastoral imagery of himself, the context suggests that he too had been engaged in the pastoral task.

*1.3. Paul as Church Planter.* On the other hand, Paul was more than simply a pastor. Paul was a pioneer, with his eye always on fresh fields to conquer: for instance, he hoped that his projected visit to Rome* would be a staging post for a mission* to Spain, providing him as well with an opportunity for securing the support of the Christians at Rome for this mission (Rom 15:28). Primarily a church planter, Paul was content to leave the task of watering to others (1 Cor 3:6); he was far more concerned to break new territory (Rom 15:20). It was perhaps for this reason that at Corinth he left the task of baptizing (for the most part) to others: it was not that he considered baptism* unimportant (see Rom 6:3, 4), but rather because Christ had called him to "proclaim the gospel" (1 Cor 1:17); moreover, the inevitable link between baptizer and the baptized would have made pastoral care by the local church leaders easier in the future.

### 2. Paul as Parent.

*2.1. The Parent-Child Relationship.* Paul's preferred imagery for the pastoral task is found in the parent-child relationship. To the Corinthians Paul declared: "For though you might have ten thousand guardians in Christ, you do not have many fathers. Indeed, in Christ Jesus I became your father through the gospel"

(1 Cor 4:15). Paul regarded himself as the founding father of not only the church in Corinth (1 Cor 4:15; 2 Cor 6:13; 12:14), but also of the churches in Philippi (Phil 2:22) and Thessalonica (1 Thess 2:11). Paul could also be a spiritual father to individuals, as well as to churches: during Paul's imprisonment he had become "father" to Onesimus (Philem 10); Timothy is "my beloved son and faithful child in the Lord" (1 Cor 4:17: similarly Phil 2:22; 1 Tim 1:2, 18: 2 Tim 1:2; 2:1); Titus, too, is his "loyal child" (Tit 1:4). Indeed, Paul could even apply the metaphor of a mother to describe his relationship with his churches (1 Cor 3:1-3; Gal 4:19; 1 Thess 2:7). When writing to Rome and to Colossae, however, churches he had not founded, he carefully avoided the parental—and thus the pastoral—tone.

*2.2. Parental Love.* It is this parental imagery that underlies his expressions of love* and concern for the churches which are in his care. Thus in 2 Corinthians 11:28, 29 it is almost certainly in his role as a "founding father" that Paul experiences the daily pressure of "anxiety for all the churches"; hence he "burned" with indignation born of love as he saw his spiritual children made to stumble. Indeed the logic of 2 Corinthians 11 suggests that for Paul it was pastoral care of this kind—and not the performance of wonders—which was the truest sign of being an apostle (cf. 2 Cor 12:12). Second Corinthians 6:11-13 (cf. 2 Cor 7:13) provides another telling insight into Paul's pastoral heart: there he tells his children in the faith (2 Cor 6:13) that his heart is "wide open" to them and that there is no restriction to his affection for them (2 Cor 6:12). Paul cared deeply for his converts. His letters are full of expressions of love for their recipients: for example, he has "abundant love" for the Corinthians (2 Cor 2:4); the Philippians, who are his "crown and joy,*" he regards with "love" and "longing" (Phil 4:1, see also Phil 1:7); because of his "deep care" for the Thessalonians (1 Thess 2:8), he longs "with great eagerness" to see them face to face (1 Thess 2:17). Paul frequently calls his converts his "beloved" (1 Cor 4:14; 15:58; Phil 2:12; Philem 16; 2 Tim 1:2). Undoubtedly it was precisely because of his love for his churches that he was so indignant when he felt they were threatened (see Gal 1:6-9; 4:16-20; 2 Cor 11:13-14). Similarly, it was his love for his churches which accounted for the intensity of his prayers for them: so he "constantly prays with joy" for all the members of the church at Philippi (Phil 1:4); similarly he prays "night and day . . . most earnestly" for the church in Thessalonica (1 Thess 3:10). Love—as of a parent for a child—was the bedrock of Paul's pastoral care.

*2.3. The Parental Metaphor in Jewish and Greek Thought.* This metaphor of parenthood was well known both to Jews and Greeks alike. The terms *father* and *son* with reference to a master and his disciple appear as early as 2 Kings 2:12 (of Elijah and Elisha respectively). In the Wisdom literature the term "my son" is used for the one who is instructed in the way of wisdom (see e.g., Prov 1:8, 10; 2:1; 3:1; 4:1 etc.; Eccles 12:12; Sir 2:1; 3:1 etc.). The rabbis likewise used the metaphor: it was, for instance, customary for a rabbi to call his pupil "my son" (cf. Mt 23:9-10). Although in this usage there was no thought of begetting, the notion is present in the statement of the Babylonian Talmud: "he who teaches the son of his neighbor the Torah, Scripture ascribes it to him as if he had begotten him" (*b. Sanh.* 19b). It was said that the Jew who wins another to his faith satisfies in an ideal manner the injunction to be fruitful and multiply, which according to the rabbis was laid on all male Jews as a supreme command.

A. J. Malherbe has drawn attention to a number of similarities between Paul and the hellenistic philosophers of his day (*see* Philosophy). Paul's description of his pastoral care in 1 Thessalonians 2:1-12, where he speaks of himself as a father and as a mother to his charges, is reminiscent of the ideal philosopher in Dio Chrysostom's *Discourses* 32.11-12. Similarly Paul's literary style in 1 Thessalonians is typical of the paraenetic devises employed by hellenistic philosophers, who sought to confirm their audiences in what they already knew (cf. 1 Thess 1:5; 2:1, 2, 5, 11; 3:3, 4; 4:2; 5:2) by reminding them of it (1 Thess 2:9; 3:6), complimenting them on what they had already accomplished and encouraging them to continue in their practice (1 Thess 4:1, 10; 5:11). On the other hand, Malherbe recognizes that there are significant differences: whereas these philosophers drew attention only to their words and deeds, Paul draws attention to the gospel, whose divine power is exhibited in his ministry (1 Thess 1:5, 6). Furthermore, Paul differs from these philosophers, in so far as his goal is to form communities of believers rather than only to bring about change in individuals (1 Thess 3:12; 4:9).

*2.4. Paul as Mother.* The maternal metaphor is rich in imagery. In 1 Thessalonians 2:7, 8 Paul likens his pastoral care for the Thessalonians to that of a nursing mother "tenderly caring for her own children." Unlike certain itinerant Cynic philosophers, gentleness was the hallmark of his ministry. Indeed, so great was his affection for them that he was determined to share his very life with them (cf. 2 Cor 12:15).

In Galatians 4:19, 20 Paul expresses his concern for his children in the faith in terms of childbirth: once already he, like a mother, had suffered at their birth, and now he found himself in labor again. Anguish and tenderness are bound together. The imagery, however, is somewhat confusing: for whereas initially Paul envisages the Galatians as embryos still in the mother's womb and yet to be delivered, Paul then moves on to represent the Galatians as the pregnant mother, with Christ as the developing embryo.

The maternal image is also to be found in 1 Corinthians 3:1-3, where Paul speaks of having to feed his converts with milk and not with "solid food." E. Best reminds us that while fathers today may bottle-feed their babies, in the ancient world babies were breast-fed. However, the emphasis in this passage is less on Paul's maternal care as on the Corinthians' failure to develop and grow in the faith. Interestingly, whereas elsewhere Paul uses the word *teknon* ("child") in a positive sense to describe his relationship with his converts (1 Cor 4:14-16; 2 Cor 6:13; Gal 4:19; Phil 2:22; 1 Thess 2:7, 11; Philem 10), here Paul uses *nēpios*—"mere infant"—in a pejorative sense to bring out the Corinthians' failure to develop in the faith.

*2.5. Paul as Father.* There are a number of aspects to Paul's pastoral role which emerge from his use of this parental imagery. For Paul's role as a "father" is not limited to bringing individuals to faith: rather, as a result of his evangelistic activity, Paul enters into a relationship which involves ongoing pastoral responsibilities. Thus it is precisely because he is their "father-in-God" that Paul can exhort the Corinthians to "be imitators of me" (1 Cor 4:14-16). It is significant that while he can issue an exhortation to churches in general to follow Christ (e.g., Rom 15:1-7; Col 3:13), it is only those churches that he had founded that he can exhort to follow him (1 Cor 4:16; 11:1; Gal 4:12; Phil 3:17; 1 Thess 1:6; 2 Thess 3:7, 9) as he follows Christ (1 Cor 11:1).

In the secular world of Paul's day sons were expected to imitate their fathers: for instance, Demonicus is exhorted to follow the example of his father Hipponicus: "I have produced a sample of the nature of Hipponicus, after whom you should pattern your life as after an example, regarding his conduct as your law, and striving to imitate and emulate your father's virtue" (Isocrates, *Dem.* 4.11). Similarly Plato regarded education as the visible practice of example (Plato *Leg. All.* 5.729b,c) and said that sons must be able to see the walk of their fathers as in a mirror (Plutarch *Lib. Educ.* 20). Not surprisingly in the church it was to be "like father, like son." The call to imitation was not a mark of spiritual arrogance on the part of Paul, but rather an indication of a close pastoral relationship (*see* Imitation).

Similarly it was in his role as "father" that Paul

sought to promote spiritual growth in the churches. Just as a father in the world of his day was responsible for the education of his children, so too Paul saw himself as responsible for the education of his children in Christ. Although, with the exception of the Pastorals (see 1 Tim 2:7; 2 Tim 1:11), Paul never specifically referred to himself as a "teacher," he did see himself as having a teaching role, a role which was contained within the father imagery (see 1 Cor 4:17: also Eph 4:21; Col 1:28; 2:7; 2 Thess 2:15). Thus as he expected fathers to bring up their children "in the discipline and instruction of the Lord" (Eph 6:2), so in similar fashion he sought to bring up his spiritual children. Paul clearly believed that both encouragement (1 Thess 2:11, 12) and correction (1 Cor 4:14-21) were necessary for healthy development within the Christian family.

On the one hand, there were occasions when encouragement was called for: thus Paul "like a father with his children" urged and encouraged and pleaded with the Thessalonians to lead a life worthy of God (1 Thess 2:11, 12). This approach to pastoral care is reflected in 1 Thessalonians in particular (see 1 Thess 4:12; also 5:12, 14), as also in his letters in general.

On the other hand, there were occasions when correction was called for: to the Corinthians Paul wrote, "I am writing this to admonish you as my beloved children" (1 Cor 4:14). Whereas the primary effect of "teaching" is directed to the intellect, "admonishing" (*noutheteō*) describes an effect on the will and disposition and involves correction. Indeed in 1 Corinthians 4:12 Paul refers to the possibility of his wielding "the rod of correction" (see Ex 21:20; 2 Sam 7:14; Prov 10:13; 22:15; Is 10:24; Lam 3:1). For Paul discipline* was not reserved as a final resort for gross moral error, but rather was perceived to be an essential part of Christian nurture by which individuals and churches were built up in the faith (see Col 1:28). Discipline was a form of pastoral care. Needless to say, such discipline, however, was always born of love (2 Cor 2:24), love which could be likened to that of a father for his child (1 Cor 4:14-21).

A further expression of "fatherly" care is to be found in Paul's refusal to accept financial help from his churches (*see* Financial Support). Although entitled to an apostolic right (1 Cor 9:1-14), Paul refuses financial support from the Corinthians on the basis that it was not the duty of children to lay up money for their parents, but rather parents for their children (2 Cor 12:14). It is of interest to see how Paul's parental role here takes precedence over his apostolic role. Furthermore Paul, in his parental role, was also concerned to give to his converts an example of honest toil (see

1 Thess 4:11; 2 Thess 3:6-12). Unlike the Cynics who were renowned for greedily making money out of their philosophizing, Paul was at pains to ensure he put no "obstacle in the way of the gospel of Christ" (1 Cor 9:12).

### 3. Paul's Pastoral Care.

*3.1. Paul's Care for Individuals.* Paul was concerned not just for the corporate health of the churches in his care, but also for the well-being of individuals. People mattered to Paul: hence in Romans 16 Paul takes the trouble of greeting over twenty-seven people by name. In 1 Thessalonians 2:11 Paul declared: "We dealt with *each one of you* like a father with his children," implying that he had concerned himself with his converts on an individual basis. Similarly Paul emphasized the personal character of his work in Colossians 1:28: he sought to promote individual maturity by "warning and teaching *everyone* in all wisdom." All this is in line with Luke's account of Paul's speech to the Ephesian elders, which suggests that his normal practice was to combine preaching to the church at large together with the visiting of individual church members (Acts 20:20). Significantly, Paul commended this kind of pastoral care to the Thessalonians: their mutual care for one another was to take place on an individual basis (1 Thess 5:11).

*3.2. Paul's Care for Churches Other Than His Own.* So far we have been noting Paul's concern for those churches which stood in a special relationship to him. However, Paul's "eagerness" to remember the poor in Jerusalem (Gal 2:10) throws an interesting light on his concern for the needs of those who were not in one of his churches. Although this "collection for the saints"* is often interpreted as evidence of Paul's concern for the unity of the church (see Gal 2:6-10), Paul himself never explicitly mentions this as a factor when encouraging his Gentile churches to give generously to the Jerusalem church (see, e.g., 2 Cor 8 and 9, though some find it implied in 2 Cor 8:24 and Rom 15:27). Paul is rather concerned because of the poverty of his brothers and sisters in the Jerusalem church, and therefore as a matter of equality urges the Corinthians to give (2 Cor 8:14; *see* Rich and Poor).

### 4. Pastoral Authority.
Paul was a forceful person who expected obedience from the churches in his care (e.g., 2 Cor 10:6; Phil 2:12; Philem 2). His letters are full of instructions on how his readers are to live their lives together. Thus he writes to the Corinthians, "Now in the following instructions I do not commend you. . . . About the other things I will give instructions when I come"

(1 Cor 11:17, 34: see also 1 Thess 4:2; 2 Thess 3:6-15). He tells the Corinthians that the "authority" which the Lord has given him is for "building up" the church and not for "tearing down" (2 Cor 10:8; 13:10: cf. 12:19)—for it is only arguments (2 Cor 10:3-5), and not people, which he seeks to destroy.

It has often been assumed that Paul based his authority on his calling to be an apostle* (*see* Conversion and Call). However, at no point do we find Paul issuing instruction on the basis of his apostleship. It is much more likely that his sense of authority* was derived from his position as founding father of his churches. In this respect it should be borne in mind that for Jews and Greeks alike the father relationship was perceived as one of authority. For a Jew to honor one's father (Ex 20:12; Deut 5:16) inevitably involved obedience (see 2 Kings 16:7: "your servant and your son"). Epictetus declared: "To be a son is to regard all one's possessions as the property of the father in all things, never to blame him before anyone, to support him with all one's power" (Epictetus *Diss.* II.107). In Roman society a father retained control over his children even after they were grown and married.

However, Paul puts limits upon his own authority. He much preferred to "appeal" (e.g., Rom 12:1; 15:30; 16:7; 1 Cor 1:10; 4:16; 16:16; 2 Cor 5:20; 6:1; 10:1; 13:11; Eph 4:1; Phil 4:2; 1 Thess 2:11; 4:1, 10; 5:14; 2 Thess 3:12; Philem 8-9) rather than to "command," which in turn implies that he preferred not to impose his own will upon the churches, but rather to encourage them to make their own decisions. Hence he writes to the Corinthians that he does not seek to "lord it over your faith" (2 Cor 1:24), and reminds the Galatians, "You were called to freedom, brothers and sisters" (Gal 5:13). The churches he founded may have been his spiritual children, but they were to be no longer babes in Christ. In this respect Paul's model is the parent-adult child, and not the parent-infant child. Thus although he is clear about the form of discipline which should be exercised at Corinth toward the man committing incest, he prefers that it is the church itself which exercises that discipline* (1 Cor 5). Paul does not want his children to be overly dependent upon him.

### 5. Shared Pastoral Responsibilities.
Although Paul regarded himself as having a special pastoral relationship with his churches, this did not cause him to operate as a solo pastor. Rather Paul constantly surrounded himself with colleagues who could share in the pastoral task (*see* Coworkers). It is reckoned that, if one adds all the names found in Acts and in the *Corpus Paulinum*, then at various times

some one hundred people were associated with the apostle. Unlike the itinerant philosophers, Paul was always accompanied by others (e.g., Barnabas,* Luke, Silas and Timothy) on his missionary journeys. His letters were sent out not only in his name, but in the name of others too (see, e.g., 1 Cor 1:1; 2 Cor 1:1; Phil 1:1; Col 1:1; 1 Thess 1:1; 2 Thess 1:1). Some of his associates were sent out on difficult pastoral missions: Timothy was sent to Corinth to remind the church of Paul's "ways in Christ Jesus" (1 Cor 4:17); Titus was likewise sent to Corinth, ostensibly with a view to organizing the collection for the Jerusalem poor (2 Cor 8:6), but no doubt also to report back to Paul on the church's overall progress (2 Cor 7:6, 7).

If Acts 14:23 is any guide, then it would appear that Paul appointed leaders to be responsible for the on-going life of the church after Paul had left (see Church Order and Government). Certainly Paul recognized and encouraged local leadership: for example, he urges the church at Corinth to submit themselves to Stephanas and others who had devoted themselves to the "service of the saints" (1 Cor 16:16); similarly he appeals to the Thessalonians to respect those who "have charge of you in the Lord" (1 Thess 5:12). At Corinth he by and large left the task of baptizing to others (1 Cor 1:14-17). In this respect Best is not fair in suggesting that, though Paul desired his converts to behave in orderly fashion (1 Cor 4:33, 40), he did singularly little to organize them. This is all the more true, if we accept the evidence of the Pastoral Letters.*

Paul also encouraged his converts in general to be involved in pastoral care. Likening the church to a body,* he spoke of the members having "the same care for one another" (1 Cor 12:25), so that "if one member suffers, all suffer together with it; if one member is honored, all rejoice together with it" (1 Cor 12:26; cf. Rom 12:15). Paul urged the Galatians to "bear one another's burdens," which in turn involved caring for those straying from the faith, restoring the backsliders (Gal 6:1, 2). The Thessalonians were to "encourage one another and build up each other" (1 Thess 5:11). Indeed Paul expected the Thessalonians to share in every aspect of pastoral care: "admonish the idlers, encourage the faint-hearted, help the weak" (1 Thess 5:14). Similarly the Colossians were "to teach and admonish one another in all wisdom" (Col 3:16). Pastoral care was not exclusively conferred to a particular cadre in the church: all were involved in "the work of ministry" (see Eph 4:12, 15, 16).

See also APOSTASY, FALLING AWAY, PERSEVERANCE; APOSTLE; AUTHORITY; BODY OF CHRIST; CHURCH; CHURCH ORDER AND GOVERNMENT; COWORKERS, PAUL AND HIS; DISCIPLINE; FINANCIAL SUPPORT; IMITATION OF PAUL/OF CHRIST; MINISTRY; MISSION; PASTORAL LETTERS; SOCIAL SETTING OF MISSION CHURCHES.

BIBLIOGRAPHY. R. Banks, Paul's Idea of Community (Exeter: Paternoster, 1980); E. Best, "Paul's apostolic authority—?," JSNT 27 (1986) 3-25; idem, Paul and His Converts (Edinburgh: T. & T. Clark, 1988); W. E. Chadwick, The Pastoral Teaching of St. Paul (Edinburgh: T. & T. Clark, 1907); D. Coggan, Paul: Portrait of a Revolutionary (London: Hodder & Stoughton, 1984); H. Doohan, Leadership in Paul (Wilmington, DL: Michael Glazier, 1984); E. E. Ellis, "Paul and His Co-workers," NTS 17 (1970-1971) 437-52; idem, Pauline Theology: Ministry and Society (Grand Rapids: Eerdmans, 1989); V. P. Furnish, "Theology and Ministry in the Pauline Letters" in A Biblical Basis for Ministry, ed. E. E. Shelp and R. Sunderland (Philadelphia: Westminster, 1981) 101-44; S. M. Gilmour, "Pastoral Care in the New Testament Church," NTS 10 (1964) 393-98; T. R. Glover, Paul of Tarsus (London: SCM, 1926); P. Gutierrez, La Paternité Spirituelle selon Saint Paul (Paris: Gabalda, 1968); D. R. Hall, "Pauline Church Discipline," TynB 20 (1969) 3-26; B. Holmberg, Paul and Power: The Structure of Authority in the Primitive Church as Reflected in the Pauline Epistles (Philadelphia: Fortress, 1978); J. Knox, "The Ministry in the Primitive Church," in The Ministry in Historical Perspective, ed. H. R. Niebuhr and D. D. Williams (New York: Harper & Row, 1956) 1-25; J. T. McNeill, A History of the Cure of Souls (New York: Harper & Row, 1951); A. J. Malherbe, "Gentle as a Nurse: The Gnostic Background to 1 Thess 2," NovT 12 (1970) 203-17; idem, Paul and the Thessalonians: The Philosophic Tradition of Pastoral Care (Philadelphia: Fortress, 1987); idem, " 'Pastoral Care' in the Thessalonian Church," NTS 36 (1990) 375-91; E. M. Martinson, "Paul as Pastor," BR 9 (1924) 350-70; J. R. W. Stott, The Preacher's Portrait: Some New Testament Word Studies (Grand Rapids: Eerdmans, 1961); D. J. Tidball, Skilful Shepherds: An Introduction to Pastoral Theology (Leicester: Inter-Varsity, 1986); W. Wuellner, "Paul as Pastor: The Function of Rhetorical Questions in First Corinthians," in L'Apôtre Paul: Personnalité, Style et Conception du Ministère, ed. A. Vanhoye (Leuven: Leuven University, 1986) 49-77.

P. Beasley-Murray

## PASTORAL LETTERS

First Timothy, Second Timothy and Titus, termed the Pastoral Epistles since the eighteenth century, are, with Philemon,* letters of the Pauline corpus addressed to individuals. Like other NT literature written under Paul's name, they employ the letter form to convey not just personal communications but primarily teachings and exhortations, some of them preformed traditions already in use in Pauline congregations (Ellis, *Making*). In the face of defections and of the depredations of false teachers they emphasize instructions on ministry,* church order* and related themes in order to protect the apostle's congregations in Asia Minor and Greece during the final years of his life.

1. Canonicity and Authorship
2. Occasion and Date
3. Historical Setting
4. Composition: Literary Criticism
5. Outline
6. Themes

### 1. Canonicity and Authorship.

In the patristic church the reception of the letters into the NT canon was tied to their Pauline authorship for, as Serapion (died c. A.D. 211) bishop of Antioch put it, "we receive both Peter and the other apostles as Christ, but pseudepigrapha in their name we reject" (Eusebius *Hist. Eccl.* 6.12.3). This judgment was virtually unanimous, explicitly witnessed by the Muratorian Canon and Irenaeus (c. A.D. 180; *Haer.* 1.16.3; 2.14.7; 3.14.1), and probably to be inferred from earlier quotations (cf. Theophilus *Autol.* 3.14; Polycarp *Phil.* 4.1) and allusions (cf. Ignatius *Eph.* 14:1). The Pastorals (along with 2 Thess and Philem) are lacking only in one incomplete manuscript of Paul's letters ($P^{46}$; c. A.D. 200), and were rejected only by certain heretical teachers: 1—2 Timothy by Tatian and Basilides (cf. Clement *Strom.* 2.11, end; Jerome *Commentary on Titus, Preface*) and all three by Marcion (cf. Tertullian *Marc.* 5.21). However, they encountered serious objections in the literary criticism of the nineteenth century.

*1.1. The Baur School.* In 1835 F. C. Baur, drawing upon earlier literary questions about the Pastorals, concluded that they reflected a post-Pauline context and identified them, in his Hegelian reconstruction of early Christian history, as second-century forgeries (cf. Ellis, "F. C. Baur and his School," in *Making*). His views were elaborated by H. J. Holtzmann, who summed up the objections to Pauline authorship: (1) the historical situation, (2) the gnosticizing false teachers condemned, (3) the stage of church organization, (4) the vocabulary and style, and (5) the theological views and themes. Baur was ambivalent about the effect of his criticism on the canonicity of the Pastorals, but most of his followers thought that it should have no effect, asserting against the evidence that in antiquity pseudonymity was an innocent device (see Ellis, "Pseudonymity," in *Theology and Criticism*). They often attributed the Pastorals to "disciples" of

Paul and cited as precedents the schools of Pythagoras and Plato, who wrote letters in the names of those philosophers. However, there is no evidence that a "school" of Paul existed after the apostle's death: The earliest postapostolic writers, such as Clement of Rome, Papias, Ignatius and Polycarp, cite or appeal to various apostles and display no knowledge of any "school" tendency to transmit only teachings of a particular apostle (*see* Paul and His Interpreters).

*1.2. The Nineteenth-Century Debate.* J. B. Lightfoot and T. Zahn countered the Baur school with the observations that (1) the changed historical circumstances and (2) the more advanced church organization were well accounted for if some years separated Paul's earlier letters from his writing of the Pastorals, that is, after his release from his first Roman imprisonment, a release well attested in *1 Clement* 5 (c. A.D. 95, Lightfoot) and in second century literature (Muratorian canon; *Acts of Peter* [*Vercelli*]). Anticipating twentieth-century criticism, Lightfoot argued that (3) gnosticizing false teachers were already present during the ministry of Paul (cf. Ellis 1993, 89-95), and he also attributed (4) changes in vocabulary, style and (5) in theological emphasis to the origin of the Pastorals in the last years of the apostle's ministry.

In the nineteenth century both traditional and speculative scholars assumed that Paul himself penned his letters* or dictated them verbatim. They consequently supposed that if the major letters were taken as a touchstone, the genuineness of the others could be determined by internal criteria of vocabulary, style and theological motifs. They differed only as to whether variations in such matters were sufficient to exclude Pauline authorship (the Baur/Holtzmann tradition) or lay within the literary range of a versatile writer like the apostle (the Lightfoot/Zahn tradition). The debate, which has continued and developed through the present century, was something of a standoff (Prior; Ellis 1979). However, the pseudepigraphal viewpoint was undermined by three new insights of twentieth-century criticism: the role of the secretary; the function of cosenders; and the presence of a considerable number of preformed, non-Pauline pieces in almost all of Paul's letters (see Creeds; Hymns; Liturgical Elements).

*1.3. Developments in the Twentieth Century.* The problem of the Pastorals continued in the minds of many to lie in their vocabulary and style, in their more developed church order and in the difficulty of "placing" them within the Pauline missions in Acts.

*1.3.1. Vocabulary.* With respect to *vocabulary* it was not just the divergence from the terminology of the recognized Pauline literature but also the absence of many word groups common to Paul (e.g., *apokalyptō, energeō, kauchaomai, perisseuō, hypakouō, phroneō*) and the use of different terminology for the same concepts in eschatology* (*epiphaneia* vis-à-vis *parousia*), church organization (*presbyteroi* vis-à-vis *prohistamenoi* and *poimenes*) and soteriology (cf. Dibelius). At the same time many Pauline expressions in these letters were evident to all.

Three attempts were made to resolve this problem. Writers in the Baur/Holtzmann tradition ascribed the Pauline traits to a conscious attempt by the forger to imitate Paul, either to gain apostolic authority for his deception (Donelson) or, reworking certain Pauline traditions, to offer under the apostle's name what he thought Paul might have taught had he been there (Wolter). Some in the Lightfoot/Zahn tradition contended that the role of the secretary and Paul's use of traditions composed by others accounted for the differences in the Pastorals' style, vocabulary and theological idiom (see 4 below). A few scholars early in the twentieth century argued that the Pastorals were genuine Pauline letters supplemented by second-century interpolations, mainly on church order (Harnack), or that they were early second-century products incorporating some genuine Pauline fragments (Harrison). The fragment hypothesis failed to convince very many because it could not explain why and how a forger would have used the fragments in such a strange way (Guthrie; Dibelius). The interpolation hypothesis was a possibility in its day. But with the advances in textual criticism and in the understanding of writing practices of the Greco-Roman world, it lost credibility.

As was the custom in antiquity (cf. Cicero *To Friends* 7.25.1; Richards, 6-7.), Paul retained a copy of his letters both for subsequent reference (cf. 1 Cor 5:9-10; 2 Cor 7:8; 2 Thess 2:15) and because of the danger of loss or damage in transit (cf. Cicero *Friends* 16.18. end). It is also likely that he allowed the church where he was writing to make a copy of the letter for its own use and that he permitted or instructed the recipients to make copies for themselves or for neighboring congregations (cf. 2 Cor 1:1, Achaia; Gal 1:2; Col 4:16). In this way the apostle himself initiated, virtually at the outset, different textual traditions with inevitable variations in the wording of his correspondence. Therefore,

> it appears to be quite impossible that an interpolator, who anywhere in the stream of tradition arbitrarily inserted three verses, could force under his spell the total textual tradition (which we today have before our eyes in a way quite different from any generation before us) . . . so that not even one contrary witness remained. (Aland, 141)

What is said here of Romans applies also to the Pastorals. Any theory that certain verses were later additions must produce some manuscript that omits the verses, or it will lack all historical probability. The sections that Harnack thought were later interpolations are not absent from any manuscript and were, therefore, in all likelihood a part of the Pastorals from the beginning.

*1.3.2. Church Organization.* The Baur tradition (and also Harnack) supposed that the qualifications demanded for the ministry of "bishop" or "overseer" = ? "elder" (1 Tim 3; 5; Tit 1) reflected a "developed" church order that was post-Pauline. It rested its case on the twin assumptions that the earliest congregations had no structured ministries and that early Christian (theology and) praxis moved forward gradually and stage-by-stage as a block. These assumptions were deeply embedded in nineteenth-century consciousness from theories of egalitarianism, of historical and social progress and of biological evolution. But they do not accord either with the variegated church order of the apostolic congregations nor with the present-day recognition that "development" may be either gradual or extremely rapid (*see* Ministry; Church Order and Government).

From the beginning the congregations of all the apostolic missions had some measure of church order. The church at Jerusalem with its leadership of resident apostles, especially Peter* (c. A.D. 33-42; Gal 1:18; Acts 2:14; 3:12; 5:3; 8:14; 9:32; 12:17) and James* (c. A.D. 42-62; Gal 2:9; Acts 12:17; 15:13; 21:18) and elders (Acts 11:30; 15:2; 21:18; cf. Jas 5:14) had a more structured organization, probably similar to that of the synagogues and of the Qumran* community (e.g., Lk 7:3; CD 13:9-10; 1QS 6:14-15, 19-20: $m^c \underbar{b}aqq\bar{e}r, p\bar{a}q\hat{\imath}d$; cf. Schürer II.427-39; Thiering; Weinfeld). According to 1 Peter (1 Pet 5:1-3; cf. 1:1; c. A.D. 64) and Acts (Acts 14:23; 20:17, cf. 20:28; c. A.D. 65), certain churches in Asia Minor and Greece founded by the Petrine and Pauline missions also had a recognized church order, even if the term *elders* (*presbyteroi*) in Acts is a Lukan idiom for ministries given different designations in Paul's earlier letters. These letters disclose established ministries of administrative and teaching leadership, although they identify them more often as activities (Rom 12:8; 1 Cor 12:28; Gal 6:6; 1 Thess 5:12-13) than as appointed offices (cf. Phil 1:1). The Pastorals give more prominence to appointed ministries and to the qualifications for them because, among other things, of the increasing threat to Paul's churches by false teachers (Ellis, *Ministry*, 92-107; idem, *Prophecy*, 113-15). They represent an understandable development of his earlier usage.

**1.4. Conclusion.** The role of the secretary (Richards, Roller) and the use of preformed traditions (see 4.3 below) in the composition of the Pastorals cut the ground from under the pseudepigraphal hypothesis with its mistaken nineteenth-century assumptions about the nature of authorship. They require the critical student to give primary weight to the opening ascriptions in the letters and to the external historical evidence, both of which solidly support Pauline authorship.

## 2. Occasion and Date.

Proponents of Paul's authorship of the Pastorals usually, though not always (Reicke, Robinson), presuppose the tradition that Paul was released from his first Roman imprisonment (Acts 28), rightly regarded by Harnack (I.240n) as "a certain fact of history," and afterwards had a second Aegean ministry in which 1 Timothy and Titus could be placed. The tradition is supported by two considerations: (1) second-century accounts underlying the *Acts of Paul* (9-11; c. A.D. 170-190) of the apostle's final trip to Rome and martyrdom under Nero on a route different from that in Acts 27—28 (Rordorf; Zahn, II.84) and (2) very early evidence for a post-Acts 28 Pauline mission to Spain.

**2.1. Paul's Mission to Spain.** The probability of a missionary journey to Spain arises largely (1) from the anticipation of such a task in Romans 15:24, Acts 1:8 and Acts 13:47, and (2) from the evidence for it in *1 Clement* 5.7 (c. A.D. 70, cf. Robinson), the *Acts of Peter* (*Vercelli*) 1-3, 40 (probably Asia Minor, c. A.D. 160-180) and the Muratorian Canon (Rome, c. A.D. 170-190). The last two are independent witnesses to a widespread second-century tradition that Paul journeyed from Rome to Spain and, in the *Acts of Peter*, that he returned to Rome for martyrdom.

Clement of Rome knows of seven imprisonments of Paul, calls Paul and Peter "our good apostles," and, according to Irenaeus (*Haer.* 3.3.3; c. A.D. 180), Clement sat under their teaching. He speaks of Paul's preaching in the West, which for a writer in Rome would mean Spain or Gaul (cf. 2 Tim 4:10), and of his reaching "the extreme limits of the West" (*to terma tēs dyseōs*). The latter phrase, like "to the end of the earth" (*heōs eschatou tēs gēs*, Acts 1:8), referred in the usage of the time to the region of Spain around Gades (= Cadiz), where the apostle probably traveled after he was set free from his first Roman imprisonment (cf. Ellis 1991 "End of the Earth"). These sources are supported by later traditions of Paul's release and of his post-Acts 28 ministry (Eusebius *Hist. Eccl.* 2.22.1-8: *logos echei*, 2). Since Paul's Spanish sojourn was apparently unknown to Origen (cf. Eusebius *Hist. Eccl.* 3.1.3) and

produced no churches in Spain that claimed Pauline origins, it may have been a brief mission (c. A.D. 63-64), undertaken soon after his release (cf. Zahn, II.64-66), from which he returned to his churches in the Aegean area.

**2.2. The Situation of 1 Timothy and Titus.** The situation of 1 Timothy and Titus differs from that of Paul's earlier Aegean ministry (c. A.D. 53-58; cf. Kelly, 6-10). His mission had now extended to Gaul (2 Tim 4:10; Zahn, II.25-26), and his congregations around the Aegean had multiplied and now encompassed Crete, Miletus and Nicopolis (Tit 1:5; 3:12; 2 Tim 4:20). They were increasingly endangered by a judaizing-gnostic countermission (1 Tim 1:3-7, 19-20; 4:1-2; 6:20; 2 Tim 4:3-4; Tit 1:10-16; cf. Ellis, *Prophecy*, 92-93; 113-15) that included church leaders and probably former coworkers* (2 Tim 1:15-18; 2:16-17; 3:6-9; 4:10; Tit 3:9-14). Some house churches were ravaged and near collapse, as Paul's instructions to Titus indicate: "Restore the things that remain, and appoint elders in each city. . . . For many deceivers . . . especially the circumcision party . . . are overthrowing whole houses" (Tit 1:5, 10-11). This threat may have occasioned Paul's return from Spain.

To meet the problem, Paul adopted a new strategy for his writing. He continued as before to work from a hub-city, perhaps Corinth (2 Tim 4:20), with several visits to a number of churches, for example, in Macedonia (1 Tim 1:3), Crete (Tit 1:5), Nicopolis (Tit 3:12), Miletus (2 Tim 4:20) and Ephesus (1 Tim 1:3; 3:14; 4:13; 2 Tim 1:15-18; 4:19; but see Zahn, II.17-19). But he could not, as he did earlier (1 Cor 4:17; 2 Cor 7:6, 12-13; Eph 6:21-22; Col 4:7-8; cf. Phil 2:25), send a letter to each of the many congregations, along with a colleague to explain and apply it. Instead, he sent letters to trusted coworkers, Titus in Crete and Timothy in Ephesus, which served both as instruments of personal communication and encouragement and also as vade mecums to give apostolic authorization for their teaching.

For the itinerary* of his second Aegean ministry one is left largely to conjecture, for Paul's letters and other sources offer little help. The apostle probably returned there from Spain only in late A.D. 64 and labored in Crete (Tit 1:5) and Macedonia (1 Tim 1:3) as well as in Achaia for a year or so, spending the winter of 65-66 (or 66-67) at Nicopolis in Epirus (Tit 3:12; Zahn, II.27-35, 66). He composed 1 Timothy and Titus fairly early in this period, probably in 65. In the late spring of 66 or 67 he visited Miletus, where he left Trophimus (2 Tim 4:20), and Troas, where he left his winter coat and a number of books and notebooks (*membrana*), which probably included copies of his previous letters and traditional materials useful in his teaching and in composing new letters (2 Tim 4:13, 20; cf. Richards, 158-60). From Troas, apparently, he departed for Rome with the intention of returning before winter.

*2.3. The Situation and Date of 2 Timothy.* Paul took his last missionary journey from the Aegean to Rome, where he was again imprisoned, wrote 2 Timothy and soon thereafter was beheaded on the Ostian Way (2 Tim 4:6-7; *Acts of Paul* 11; Eusebius *Hist. Eccl.* 2.25.5-8). He may possibly have been arrested in Ephesus (Spicq, I.141) or Troas (Fee, 244-45) and taken to Rome a prisoner. More likely, in accordance with second-century traditions used in the *Acts of Paul* (9-10), he returned to Rome a free man (Rordorf, 323; cf. Zahn, II.67) to minister to a church that was suffering "repeated calamities and reverses" (*1 Clement* 1:1) due to the continuing persecution of Nero. He may have traveled by the Egnatian and Appian Ways (Troas—Philippi—Apollonia—Brundisium—Rome), about a three week journey, or again following second-century traditions, by a route from Troas via Philippi to Corinth and from there to Italy and Rome (cf. 2 Tim 4:20; Rordorf).

According to Eusebius's *Chronicle* (c. A.D. 303; cf. Jerome, *Vir.* 1; 5; 12), Paul was martyred together with Peter in the fourteenth year of Nero, 67-68. However, neither *1 Clement* 5 nor the *Ascension of Isaiah* (4:2-5; c. A.D. 90) suggests that both apostles died together, and Dionysius, bishop of Corinth (c. A.D. 170; cf. Eusebius *Hist. Eccl.* 2.25.8), says only that they were executed at about the same time. Probably Peter suffered death near the beginning of the Neronian pogrom in the winter or spring of 65 and Paul in late 67, or at any rate before the suicide of Nero on June 9, 68 (cf. Zahn, II.61-67; Edmundson, 147-52; otherwise: Harnack, I.240-43). If so, he would have composed 2 Timothy in the late summer or fall of A.D. 67.

## 3. Historical Setting.

*3.1. Congregations.* The churches had no special buildings in Paul's day, and they usually met in the homes of affluent members (*see* Social Setting). Some of these homes could accommodate a (standing) congregation of between 100 and 200 people in the main room (*atrium*) or in a colonnaded garden (*peristylium*) further back in the house (cf. Ellis 1989, 139-45, 144). Paul's Aegean congregations had affluent members, as is evident also in the Pastorals from his comments on slaves* and masters, and on proper attitudes for wealthy Christians (1 Tim 6:1-7, 17-19; cf. Rom 16:23; Eph 6:5-9). Such house churches are probably in view in the references to "households"* (1 Tim 3:15; 2 Tim

1:16; 4:19; Tit 1:11; ? 1 Tim 5:13).

Pliny (*Ep.* 10.96.9-10; c. A.D. 110), governor of Bithynia-Pontus, reported that extensive conversions to Christianity had virtually emptied pagan temples of the province "for a long time" (? c. A.D. 100). In the mid-sixties the Pastorals suggest that conversions around the Aegean had already been extensive. Paul's earlier letters disclose that even in the fifties there were at least two house churches in Colossae (Philem 2; Col 4:15) and two in Ephesus (1 Cor 16:19; cf. 2 Tim 1:16; 4:19), and probably four at Corinth (Rom 16:23; 1 Cor 1:11; 16:15-16; Acts 18:7-8). There were four or five at Rome (Rom 16:5, 10-11, 14-15; cf. Phil 4:22). When one house church is specified, at least one other is implied. While many numbered their members in the dozens, some probably had congregations of 100 to 150, including the household servants. The size and impact of the church at Ephesus is reflected by the uproar of the silversmiths (Acts 19:23-40), who would hardly have reacted so strongly to a minor threat to their sales.

In the mid-sixties the church at Rome suffered the martyrdom of "a great multitude" (*1 Clement* 6.1; cf. Tacitus *Ann.* 15.44) and Paul's Aegean churches had suffered defections, as the Pastorals attest. However, in the decade of 57-67 the Pauline congregations of Greece and Asia had greatly increased both in numbers and in area, and their total membership is probably to be counted in the thousands.

*3.2. Coworkers.* The coworkers* of Paul include a number who are mentioned in Acts (Trophimus) and in his earlier letters: Apollos, Demas, Erastus, Luke, Mark, Priscilla and Aquila, Timothy, Titus, Tychicus. Others appear only in Titus (Artemas, Zenas) or in 2 Timothy (Claudia, Crescens, Eubulus, Linus, Onesiphorus, Pudens, ? Carpus), where they are workers in the church at Rome or participants in Paul's continuing mission outreach.

*3.3. Opponents.* The opponents* represent the same type of opposition throughout the Pastorals (Kelly, 10-11; Dibelius, 65-67), that is, indeed, only a more developed form of the false teaching that plagued Paul's and other apostolic missions virtually from the beginning. They originated as a "judaizing" segment of the ritually strict *Hebraioi*, that is, "the circumcision* party" of the Jerusalem church (cf. Acts 11:2 with Tit 1:10; *see* Judaizers), which combined a demand for Gentile adherence to the Mosaic regulations and an ascetic ritualism with a zeal for visions of angels* and, at least in the Diaspora,* with gnosticizing tendencies to promote an experience of (a distorted) divine wisdom* and knowledge,* and to depreciate matter and physical resurrection* and redemption* (cf. 1 Cor 15:12

with 2 Tim 2:18; *see* Gnosis, Gnosticism). At times their vaunted asceticism produced an arrogance primed for a subtle sexual licentiousness (cf. Gal 4:9; 5:13-21; Col 2:18, 23 with 1 Tim 4:3; 2 Tim 3:6-7; Tit 1:10, 15). While Paul argued that in the messianic age the OT ethical laws remained valid but its ritual laws were passé (Col. 2:17; cf. Gal 4:9-10) and were no longer binding (Rom 10:4; 13:8-10; Gal 3:24-25), his opponents argued that the ritual laws remained binding and yet they vitiated the ethical commands by their conduct (cf. Ellis 1993, 36-38, 51-52, 61, 80-115, 116-28, 230-36; *see* Law).

In the Pastorals the gnosticizing judaizers were known as "the circumcision party" (Tit 1:10) and continued their claim to be "teachers of the Law" (1 Tim 1:7), although they apparently no longer stressed, as in Galatians, the duty of circumcision. They forbade marriage, promoted food laws and claimed to impart a spiritual "knowledge" (*gnōsis*) whose source was, in the words of an oracle applied to them, demonic* spirits (1 Tim 4:1-3; 6:20). They represented one stage of a continuing counter-mission, which appears in Ignatius (*Magn.* 8-11; *Trall.* 9; c. A.D. 110) as a kind of "Judaism crossed with Gnosticism" (Lightfoot) that denied not only Christ's resurrection but also his physical incarnation and death, and which later in the second century developed or merged into the full-blown Gnostic heresies. While some of the opponents originated in the mission of "the circumcision party," others were teachers in Pauline congregations and defectors from a Pauline theology, including former associates or coworkers (1 Tim 1:3-5; 2 Tim 1:15-16; Tit 1:10-11).

### 4. Composition: Literary Criticism.

Literary questions about the Pastorals have addressed their letter form, the role of the secretary and, perhaps most significant, their use of preformed traditions (cf. Ellis, *Making*; Ellis 1989, 104-7).

*4.1. Letter Form.* Early in this century Paul's "letters," understood as non-literary products intended solely for the addressees, were distinguished from more formal literary "epistles" intended for a larger circle (G. A. Deissmann). More recently they have been the subject of attempts to identify the "letter" as a literary genre (*see* Letters). Deissmann's distinctions were at best oversimplified and probably mistaken, and the later attempts at classification were misleading (cf. Ellis, *Making*; but see Malherbe, *ANRW* II.26.1, 192-93, 325-26). In fact, in antiquity letters could take virtually any form, as P. L. Schmidt pointed out (*KP*, II.325), and according to Cicero (*Friends* 2.4) they were simply "of many kinds," although he classified his own as

newsletters and as the "familiar and sportive, and the grave and serious."

The apostle's letters were intended to be used by more people than the immediate addressees (see 1.3.1 above) and were specifically to be "read in church" (Col 4:16; 1 Thess 5:27; cf. 1 Cor 7:1, 25; 8:1; 12:1; 16:1, 12). In the light of his Jewish background in which not even Targums but only canonical Scripture could be read "in church" (*b. Meg.* 32a; cf. Alexander, CRINT 2.1. 238-39), they were written and received as "the Word of God," that is, as inspired and normative authority for the churches (cf. 1 Thess 2:13 with 2 Thess 2:15). They were teachings of an apostolic prophet that, unlike other prophetic teaching and writing in the congregations, were not subject to "testing" or vetting by other prophets (1 Cor 9:3, *anakrinō*; 1 Cor 14:29, *diakrinō*, with 1 Cor 14:37-38). That is, they were teaching pieces clothed in the form of letters: Philemon addresses a specific personal question; others, like 1 Corinthians, give attention to immediate congregational problems or, like Romans and Ephesians, to more general theological motifs; 1 Timothy and Titus (and to some extent 2 Tim) are virtual manuals of tradition that have genre affinities with Qumran's *Manual of Discipline*. The apostle utilizes the letter form for a number of reasons, not least that by it he can combine personal communication and relationships with his primary purpose of teaching and upbuilding believers in the truth of the gospel of Christ.

*4.2. Secretary.* A secretary was a practical necessity in antiquity for all but the briefest letters, since the poor quality of pen, ink and paper made writing slow and laborious (cf. Quintilian *Inst. Orat.* 10.3.31; 10.3.19-22) and could require more than an hour to write a small page (Roller, 13-14, 6-9). The secretary ordinarily would record first on a wax or wood tablet in shorthand, which was used in first-century Greek and Latin writing (Richards, 24-43), and then would transcribe in longhand onto papyrus. Such a helper is explicitly mentioned in Romans 16:22 and is implied where Paul, in accordance with the custom, adds a marginal note (e.g., Philem 19a; 1 Cor 14:34-35; Ellis 1989, 67-68) or an ending (e.g., 1 Cor 16:21-24; Gal 6:11-18; Col 4:18; 2 Thess 3:17; cf. 1 Tim 6:20-21; 2 Tim 4:19-22; Tit 3:15) to a completed secretarial composition. For the Pastorals a secretary may be inferred from numerous verbal and stylistic peculiarities, and he has been plausibly suggested to be Luke (2 Tim 4:11; cf. Strobel, 210; Moule, 434; C. Spicq, I.199; Knight, 51: perhaps; but see Metzger, 10-16). The secretary's work could range from taking dictation to being a coauthor, and in the Pastorals he appears to have had a greater input than in certain other

Pauline letters (cf. Richards, 23-24, 193-94). However, more significant for the literary form of the Pastorals are the numerous preformed traditions, largely non-Pauline, that are employed in them.

**4.3. Traditions.** Traditions* in the Pastorals have long been recognized in a few passages, such as the confession at 1 Timothy 3:16 and the five "faithful word" (*pistos ho logos*) sayings (see 4.4.1 below). In other passages they can also be identified by the use of acceptable criteria. Some preformed pericopes were composed by Paul and some by others whom he recognized to be prophetically gifted to mediate divine revelation.

Criteria to identify a cited or traditioned piece (*see* Creed; Liturgical Elements) include: (1) a formula that elsewhere introduces or concludes quoted material (e.g., 1 Tim 4:1; cf. Acts 20:23; 28:25; Heb 3:7); (2) the self-contained character of the passage; (3) a relatively large number of *hapax legomena* and an idiom and style that differ from the rest of the letter and from other writings by the same author; and (4) a strikingly similar passage in another writing where no literary dependence is probable. One criterion alone may not be significant since a different vocabulary or idiom may point only to a change of subject matter, to a different secretary or to a different time of writing. Also, a quotation might not be transmitted tradition (e.g., Tit 1:12), and transmitted traditions might be paraphrased and incorporated without a formula of quotation. Nevertheless, several criteria in a given passage provide guidelines for measuring probabilities.

**4.4. The Classification of Traditions.** Preformed pieces embrace a variety of topics and literary forms (cf. Ellis, *Making*). Among them are doxologies (1 Tim 1:17; 6:15-16; *see* Benediction), a vice list (1 Tim 1:9-10; *see* Virtues and Vices), congregational regulations for the conduct of wives (1 Tim 2:9—3:1a) and qualifications for ministries (1 Tim 3:1b-13), predictive prophecies (1 Tim 4:1-5; 2 Tim 3:1-5), confessions that are sometimes hymnic (1 Tim 2:5-6; 3:16; 2 Tim 1:9-10; Tit 3:3-7; cf. 1 Tim 1:15) and other hymns* (1 Tim 6:11-12, 15-16; 2 Tim 2:11-13; Tit 2:11-14). Some of these are in the form of implicit and explicit midrash, that is, commentary on OT texts (1 Tim 1:9-10; 2:9—3:1a; 5:17-18; 2 Tim 2:19-21; cf. Ellis 1993, 188-97, 147-237: "prophecy as exegesis"). One passage combines midrash and a hymnic form (Tit 3:3-7), both of which are characteristic of early Christian prophecy* (cf. Aune, 453-55; "the prophetic hymn").

Some traditions may also be identified and classified in terms of three formulas that introduce or conclude them: "faithful is the word" (*pistos ho logos*), "knowing this that" (*touto ginōskein/idein hoti*) and

"these things" (*tauta*). Such passages are relatively independent of their contexts and are distinguished by other criteria listed above.

*4.4.1. "Faithful is the Word."* This formula introduces (1 Tim 1:15; 4:9-10; 2 Tim 2:11-13) or concludes (1 Tim 2:9—3:1a; Tit 3:3-8a) five passages which, with the exception of 1 Timothy 2:9—3:1a, are confessional statements of Pauline soteriological themes, whose vocabulary is generally Pauline. The formula is absent from Paul's earlier letters (but see 1 Cor 10:13) and apparently had its origin among Jewish apocalyptic prophets or at Qumran (cf. 1Q27 1:8). However, it was employed in the Johannine mission (Rev 22:6) and came to be used by Paul and his coworkers during his Caesarean or first Roman imprisonment. On the analogy of Ben Sira's use of "faithful" (Sir 46:15; 48:22) to designate the prophecies of Samuel and Isaiah, the formula governs a word that is no mere saying but that is a prophetic word of God to the hearers. Therefore, the teaching elder (= bishop) is required to "hold to the faithful word" (Tit 1:9), and Timothy in his ministry is said to be nourished on such "faithful words" and is urged to mediate them to his congregations (2 Tim 2:11-13, 14). Given their Pauline themes and vocabulary, most "faithful Word" sayings were probably Paul's compositions, but 1 Timothy 2:9—3:1a (and perhaps Tit 3:3-8), composed by others, is a variant of a tradition used in common with the Petrine mission (cf. 1 Pet 3:1- 5, 18-22; 1 Cor 14:34-35).

*4.4.2. "Knowing this that."* This and similar phrases do not always have a formulaic significance (e.g., 1 Thess 1:4-5), but they are sometimes used elsewhere as formulas to introduce a paraphrastic biblical quotation (Acts 2:3, cf. Ps 132:11; cf. Polycarp *Phil* 4:1) and other cited traditions (Rom 6:6; Eph 5:5; cf. 1 Cor 6:9-10). In the Pastorals they are used as formulas to introduce a vice list paraphrasing the Fifth to the Ninth Commandments (1 Tim 1:9-10) and a transmitted prophecy (2 Tim 3:1-5).

*4.4.3. "These things."* This formula is found at the conclusion of cited material and introduces its application to the current situation. It appears at the end of pericopes identified above as traditioned pieces (1 Tim 4:6, 11; 2 Tim 2:14; cf. Tit 1:15-16; 2:1). It also occurs at the end of a regulation on ministry* (1 Tim 3:1b-13, 14; cf. Tit 1:7-9) that is distinct from its context (Harnack, I.482-83; Kelly, 231) and of congregational and household* rules (1 Tim 5:5-6, 9-10, 17-20; 6:1, 2; Tit 2:2-14, 15), which are probably also preformed traditions incorporated into the letters.

*4.4.4. Conclusion.* A number of other passages are probably reworked traditional material: hymnic confessions (1 Tim 2:5-6; 2 Tim 1:9-10), a doxology (1 Tim

1:17), a commission + doxology (1 Tim 6:11-16) and other sayings (1 Tim 6:7-8, 10a; 2 Tim 1:7). Together such preformed materials make up about forty-three percent of 1 Timothy, sixteen percent of 2 Timothy and forty-six percent of Titus (Ellis, *Making*).

## 5. Outline.
### 5.1. 1 Timothy.
I. 1:1-20 Introduction
  1:1-2 Greeting
  1:3-20 A Charge to Oppose the Gnosticizing
    Judaizers
      1:3-7 Their Errors
      1:8-11 The Right Use of the Law
      1:12-17 Paul's Example
      1:18-20 Timothy Contrasted with the False
      Teachers
II. 2:1—4:10 Congregational Regulations
  2:1-8 Prayers and Their Purpose
  2:9—3:1a "A Faithful Word" for Husbands and
    Wives
  3:1b-13 Qualifications for Overseers and
    Ministers
  3:14-16 Their Purpose and Christological Basis
  4:1-10 A Prophetic Warning and Its Application
III. 4:11—6:2 Instructions for Timothy
  4:11—5:2 His Example to Others
  5:3—6:2 His Congregational Supervision:
    Widows, Elders, Slaves and Others
      5:23 A Personal Aside: Purity Does Not
      Require Asceticism
IV. 6:3-19 Final Admonitions
  6:3-10 Concerning False Teachers and Their
    Money Motives
  6:11-16 Concerning the Motives and Conduct
    of "The Man of God"
  6:17-19 Concerning Affluent Believers
V. 6:20-21 Admonition and Benediction in Paul's
  Hand

### 5.2. Titus.
I. 1:1-4 Greeting
II. 1:5-16 Instructions for Titus
  1:5-9 Qualifications for Overseers
  1:10—2:1 Concerning False Teachers
III. 2:2-15 Congregational Supervision and Its Basis
IV. 3:1-11 Responsibilities of Believers
  3:1-2 Concerning Civic Life
  3:3-8 Its Basis in a Faithful Word
  3:9-11 Concerning the False Teachers
V. 3:12-15 A Concluding Word
  3:12-13 Concerning the Coworkers
  3:14 A Repeated Admonition

3:15 Greetings and Benediction in Paul's Hand

### 5.3. 2 Timothy.
I. 1:1-5 Greeting and Thanksgiving
II. 1:6—2:13 Appeal to Timothy
  1:6—2:7 For Faithful Witness in the Face
    of Opposition
  2:8-13 In the Light of Paul's Example
III. 2:14—4:5 Warnings Against False Teachers
  2:14-26 Avoid Their Vain Ways
  3:1-9 A Prophecy Concerning False Teachers
    and Its Application
  3:10-17 The Reason and Way to Counter False
    Teachers
  4:1-5 An Exhortation to Faithful Ministry
IV. 4:6-21 Paul's Situation and Prospects
  4:6-8 His Approaching Death
  4:9-16 His Need For Timothy to Come
  4:17-18 His Confidence in God's Presence and
    Final Redemption
V. 4:19-22 Greetings and Benediction in
  Paul's Hand

## 6. Themes.
The teachings of the letters are largely contained in the (reworked and) transmitted traditions and their application. They concern (1) the errors of the false teachers and the proper response to them (1 Tim 1:3-20; 4:1-10; 6:3-10; Tit 1:10—2:1; 3:9-11; 2 Tim 2:14—4:5) and (2) the strict qualifications for ministries in the light of the opponents' activities (1 Tim 3:1b-13; Tit 1:5-9). Not unrelated to this situation are (3) other regulations on church order (1 Tim 2:1—3:1a; 5:3-25; Tit 2:1-14) and on the conduct of believers (1 Tim 6:1-2; Tit 3:1-8). As is the case in the other Pauline letters, all the teachings are given (4) a christological* basis in salvation history (1 Tim 3:16; Tit 2:11-14), including Christ's identity with God* (Tit 2:13), pre-existence* (1 Tim 1:15, *erchomai*), human Davidic descent (2 Tim 2:8), faithful ministry (1 Tim 6:13), saving work (1 Tim 2:5-6a; 2 Tim 1:9-10), resurrection (2 Tim 2:8) and future coming and reign (1 Tim 6:14; 2 Tim 2:11-12; 4:8, 18).

*See also* CANON; CHRONOLOGY OF PAUL; CHURCH ORDER AND GOVERNMENT; EARLY CATHOLICISM; PAUL IN ACTS AND LETTERS; PAUL IN EARLY CHURCH TRADITION.

BIBLIOGRAPHY. **Commentaries:** M. Dibelius and H. Conzelmann, *The Pastoral Epistles* (Herm; Philadelphia: Fortress, 1972); G. D. Fee, *The Pastoral Epistles* (Peabody, MA: Hendrickson, 1988); D. Guthrie, *The Pastoral Epistles* (TNTC; 2d ed.; Grand Rapids: Eerdmans, 1990); H. J. Holtzmann, *Die Pastoralbriefe* (Leipzig: Engelmann, 1880); J. N. D. Kelly, *The Pastoral Epis-*

*tles* (London: Black, 1963); G. W. Knight III, *The Pastoral Epistles* (NIGTC; Grand Rapids: Eerdmans, 1992); T. D. Lea and H. P. Griffen, Jr., *1, 2 Timothy, Titus* (NAC; Nashville: Broadman, 1992); W. Lock *The Pastoral Epistles* (ICC; Edinburgh: T. & T. Clark, 1958 [1924]); A. Schlatter, *Die Kirche der Griechen im Urteil des Paulus* (Stuttgart: Calwer, 1958 [1936]); C. Spicq, *Les Épîtres Pastorales* (2 vols.; Paris: Gabalda, 1969). **Studies:** K. Aland, "Neutestamentliche Textkritik und Exegese," *Wissenschaft und Kirche. FS E. Lohse*, ed. K. Aland (Bielefeld: Luther, 1989) 132-48; D. E. Aune, "The Odes of Solomon and Early Christian Prophecy," *NTS* 28 (1982) 435-60; F. C. Baur, *Die sogenannten Pastoralbriefe* (Tübingen: Gotta, 1835); L. R. Donelson, *Pseudepigraphy and Ethical Argument in the Pastoral Epistles* (Tübingen: J. C. B. Mohr, 1986); G. Edmundson, *The Church in Rome in the First Century* (London: Longmans, 1913); E. E. Ellis, " 'The End of the Earth' (Acts 1:8)," *BBR* 1 (1991) 123-32; idem, *The Making of the New Testament Documents* (forthcoming); idem, *Theology and Criticism* (Edinburgh: T. & T. Clark, 1994); idem, "The Pastorals and Paul," *ExpT* 104 (1992-93) 45-47; idem, *The Old Testament in Early Christianity* (Tübingen: J. C. B. Mohr, 1991); idem, *Pauline Theology: Ministry and Society* (Grand Rapids: Eerdmans, 1989); idem, *Prophecy and Hermeneutic in Early Christianity* (4th ed.; Grand Rapids: Baker, 1993); idem, *Paul and His Recent Interpreters* (5th ed.; Grand Rapids: Eerdmans, 1979) 49-57; D. Guthrie, *Introduction to the New Testament* (rev. ed.; Downers Grove, IL: InterVarsity, 1990) 636-46; A. Harnack, *Geschichte der altchristlichen Literatur*, Teil II: *Chronologie* (2 vols.; Leipzig: Hinrichs, 1958 [1904]) 1.480-85; P. N. Harrison, *The Problem of the Pastoral Epistles* (London: Oxford University Press, 1921); J. B. Lightfoot, "The Date of the Pastoral Epistles" and "The Close of the Acts," in *Biblical Essays* (London: Macmillan, 1893) 399-437; W. Metzger, *Die letzte Reise des Apostels Paulus* (Stuttgart: Calver, 1976); C. F. D. Moule, "The Problem of the Pastorals: A Reappraisal," *BJRL* 47 (1964-65) 430-52; M. Prior, *Paul the Letter-Writer* (JSNTSup 23; Sheffield: JSOT, 1989); B. Reicke, "Chronologie der Pastoralbriefe," *TLZ* 101 (1976) 82-94; E. R. Richards, *The Secretary in the Letters of Paul* (Tübingen: J. C. B. Mohr, 1991); J. A. T. Robinson, *Redating the New Testament* (London: SCM, 1976); O. Roller, *Das Formular der paulinischen Briefe* (Stuttgart: Kohlhammer, 1933); W. Rordorf, "Nochmals: Paulusakten und Pastoralbriefe," in *Tradition and Interpretation in the New Testament. FS E. E. Ellis*, ed. G. F. Hawthorne with O. Betz (Grand Rapids: Eerdmans; Tübingen: J. C. B. Mohr, 1987) 319-27; A. Strobel, "Schreiben des Lukas? Zum sprachlichen Problem der Pastoralbriefe," *NTS* 15 (1968-69) 191-210; B. E.

Thiering, "*Mebaqqer* and *Episkopos* in the Light of the Temple Scroll," *JBL* 100 (1981) 59-74; M. Weinfeld, *The Organizational Pattern and the Penal Code of the Qumran Sect* (Göttingen: Vandenhoeck & Ruprecht, 1986); M. Wolter, *Die Pastoralbriefe als Paulustradition* (Göttingen: Vandenhoeck & Ruprecht, 1988); T. Zahn, *Introduction to the New Testament* (3 vols.; Minneapolis: Klock, 1977 [3d ed. 1909, 1st ed. 1899]) II.1-133.

E. E. Ellis

**PAUL AND HIS COWORKERS.** *See* COWORKERS, PAUL AND HIS.

## PAUL AND HIS INTERPRETERS

The story of Paul's interpretation stretches from his contemporaries to the present and includes such notable figures as Augustine, Luther, Calvin and Wesley. This article focuses on modern research on the life and letters of Paul, which has burgeoned exponentially since the days of F. C. Baur and the "Tübingen School" that grew up around him. Nevertheless, despite the increased volume of studies, the basic perspectives of the Tübingen School provided both the framework and presuppositions for the modern study of Paul's writings until the mid-1970s. Hence, as a result of the agenda set by Baur's work, Pauline research in the twentieth century has predominantly focused on the interrelated questions of the center* of Paul's thinking, Paul's view of the Law* and the nature of Paul's opponents.* Moreover, the central questions raised by Baur concerning Paul's theology and his place in the history of the early church still remain to be resolved.

1. F. C. Baur and the Tübingen School
2. The Identity and Theology of Paul's Opponents
3. Paul's View of the Law
4. The Center of Paul's Theology
5. Prospects for the Future

### 1. F. C. Baur and the Tübingen School.
F. C. Baur was professor of NT at the University of Tübingen from 1826 until his death in 1860. At the heart of Baur's work was his conviction that the traditional Christian view of a transcendent, personal God could no longer be accepted. The concept of revelation as the disclosure of God's will, and miracles as the act of a personal God in history, must therefore also be rejected. In mid-career Baur became convinced that this traditional Christian view must be replaced by the new speculative philosophy of Hegel, which to Baur's mind offered the most coherent and comprehensive explanation of history and the nature of reality. But in the final fifteen years of his life Baur

came to reject Hegel's abstract view of God as an infinite Spirit or eternal Idea, which in the evolving process of history was emerging from its own previous finite manifestation. Baur then returned to a simpler rationalism that emphasized universal ethical principles as the meaning of life and the value of Christianity. Nevertheless, it was the Hegelian orientation of Baur's earlier and formative understanding of Paul and early Christianity that became determinative for subsequent scholarship.

*1.1. Baur's Paradigm.* In 1831 Baur published his seminal essay, "Die Christuspartei in der korinthischen Gemeinde, der Gegensatz des petrinischen und paulinischen Christenthums in der ältesten Kirche, der Apostel Petrus in Rom" ("The Christ-party in the Corinthian Church, the Conflict Between Petrine and Pauline Christianity in the Early Church, the Apostle Peter in Rome"; *TZT* 4 [1831] 61-206). In it he laid out the foundation for his understanding of Paul and the history of the early church by applying the dialectical, evolutionary approach of Hegel's philosophy to 1 Corinthians 1:11-12. Based on this text Baur posited a *fundamental opposition* between Gentile Christianity, represented by Paul and the party of Apollos,* with its universal, Law-free, Hellenistically determined gospel, and Jewish Christianity, represented by Cephas and the "Christ-party," with its particular, Law-orientated, Jewish-bound interpretation of the significance of Jesus. According to Baur the "Christ-Party" was a Jewish-Christian faction which followed Peter and emphasized its own direct relationship to the historical Jesus through the original apostles whom Christ had appointed.

First Corinthians 1:11-12 thus provided a basic framework for understanding the conflict within early Christianity and the inner dynamic of Paul's writings. Paul's Law/gospel contrast was seen to reflect the opposition within early Christianity between Paul and Gentile Christianity on the one side, and the Jewish Christianity supported by Peter, James and the rest of the Jerusalem* apostles on the other. It was against the continual attacks of his Jewish-Christian opponents, therefore, that Paul developed his doctrine of justification by faith as the center of his theology. Moreover, according to Baur this original and bitter conflict between Peter and Paul not only dominated the rest of the writings of the NT, it also drove the historical development of the early Church until the end of the second century, when it was eventually resolved by the emerging unity of the hierarchial catholic church.

The height of the Tübingen school was reached in 1845 with the publication of Baur's *Paulus, der Apostel*

*Jesu Christi. Sein Leben und Wirken, seine Briefe und seine Lehre* (published in English in 1875 in two volumes as *Paul, the Apostle of Jesus Christ, His Life and Work, His Epistles and His Doctrine*). As the capstone of his work on Paul, Baur now argued that the authentic Paul could only be found where the conflict between Jewish (Petrine) and Gentile (Pauline) Christianity was evident, *and* where Paul's doctrine of a law-free justification by faith was explicitly presented in response. Those writings attributed to Paul that evidence an attempt to mediate this conflict by finding a middle ground were regarded as a second stage in the development of the early church. Furthermore, any documents which reflected an authoritarian and ecclesiological attempt to resolve this conflict were considered part of the eventual catholic resolution of the Jewish-Gentile Christian conflict around A.D. 200, which came about only in response to the common threat of Gnosticism.*

Armed with this paradigm, Baur concluded that only Romans,* Galatians* and the Corinthian* letters could be considered authentic. On the other extreme, the Pastorals* were clearly inauthentic, late-second-century documents written against Gnostics and Marcionites. The Prison letters and Philemon,* although sometimes disputed in terms of authorship and theology, were also in reality aimed at Gnostic opponents and written between A.D. 120 and 140 as late examples of the Pauline school. 1 and 2 Thessalonians were written in the generation after Paul (A.D. 70-75), but were of no particular significance, since they were of inferior quality theologically. They had no trace of the Pauline doctrine of justification by faith, nor of the conflict between Peter and Paul, while their eschatology conflicted with 1 Corinthians 15. Following his lead, Baur's students and followers then applied this basic scheme to the rest of the NT writings by interpreting and categorizing them according to their theological "tendency" (*Tendenz*) as either Pauline (e.g., Hebrews, 1 Peter), Petrine-Judaizing (e.g., James, Matthew, Revelation), mediating and conciliatory (e.g., Luke-Acts; Mark) or catholicizing (2 Peter, Jude, John; *see* Early Catholicism).

*1.2. Baur's Impact.* As time went on scholars completely rejected the Tübingen School's evaluation of the late date and character of the majority of the Pauline letters. Its analysis of the rest of the NT and the second century as a continuation of the conflict between a Pauline and Jewish Christianity has also proved unconvincing, since it was based on the groundless identification of Simon the Magician in the Pseudo-Clementine *Homilies* with Paul(!). Most NT scholars have also rejected Baur's historical skepticism and philosophical rationalism, which as a matter of principle excluded the supernatural from history. Nor has the Tübingen School's complete skepticism concerning the historical Jesus gained wide acceptance, beginning as it did with D. F. Strauss's *Life of Jesus* in 1835 and the decisive break it posited between the life and teachings of Jesus and the Jerusalem apostles on the one hand, and Paul on the other.

But in spite of the weakness of his historical and theological judgments, Baur's consistent attempt to provide a comprehensive and coherent understanding of the history of the early church on the basis of historical reasoning alone, without recourse to supernatural interventions or to explanations based on the miraculous, did propel biblical scholarship into the modern world. Moreover, Baur's work also set the stage for the debate in the twentieth century over the relationship between the life and teaching of the historical Jesus and the theology of Paul (*see* Jesus and Paul). Most importantly, however, Baur's treatment of Paul raised the three interrelated interpretive questions with which all subsequent students of Paul have had to wrestle in attempting to work out a comprehensive picture of Paul's life and theology: (1) the identity and perspective of Paul's opposition as a key to his own life and thought; (2) Paul's view of the Law and its relationship to his own understanding of the Gospel; and (3) the search for the generating center of Paul's theology (if indeed it is possible to talk about one such generative principle within Paul's varied writings).

It is these three questions, above all, which have determined the interpretation of Paul and his place within the history of the early church for the last 150 years. How one answers any one of them will greatly influence, and be greatly influenced by, one's understanding of the others. But for the sake of clarity, the three issues will be treated separately, since the interpreters of Paul since Baur have usually entered the debate by one of these three avenues.

## 2. The Identity and Theology of Paul's Opponents.

No aspect of Pauline studies has received more attention in the twentieth century than the question concerning the identity and arguments of Paul's opponents (*see* Opponents of Paul). And nowhere has the disagreement been more far reaching. Since the work of Baur there have been at least eight major theories proposed for Galatians, and in the more difficult cases such as 2 Corinthians and Philippians, no less than thirteen and eighteen different proposals have been made respectively (see Gunther, 1-5). Despite the multitude of proposals, however, the current debate con-

cerning the identity of Paul's opponents in his various letters still centers on the validity of Baur's understanding of the conflict between Jewish and Gentile Christianity during Paul's day and on its *extent* within the Pauline corpus, since Baur was the first modern scholar to make Paul's opponents the key to interpreting the whole of Paul's writings.

*2.1. The Polarization of Views in the Nineteenth Century.* Of course, Baur's view was not new, nor was it uncontested. Ever since the Reformation most Protestant exegetes have held that Paul's opponents were "Judaizers"* who advocated the necessity of keeping the Mosaic Law and of circumcision* for Christians. But already in the seventeenth century some scholars argued that Paul's opponents were gnostics, while others maintained that Paul's opponents were not simply comprised of Judaizers or gnostics, but included those who mixed legalistic and gnostic and/or enthusiastic elements. And just prior to Baur's work, Edward Burton offered in 1829 the most thoroughgoing presentation to date of the thesis that Paul's opponents were gnostics. Hence, the debate in the first half of the twentieth century had its immediate roots in the polarization that took place during the previous century between those who presented Paul's opponents as gnostics and those who, following Baur, saw them as Judaizers. Moreover, the debate centered primarily on the identity of Paul's opponents in Corinth because of its pivotal role in Paul's ministry and the difference in subject matter between 1 and 2 Corinthians and the other Pauline letters. If Baur's thesis was to stand, it must be able to account for Paul's theology and opposition in 1 and 2 Corinthians, where the issue of the Law does not appear to be central but where, especially in 2 Corinthians, the focus of Paul's apologetic is still on his own legitimacy as an apostle.

*2.2. Lightfoot, Lütgert and the History of Religions School.* In nineteenth-century Germany the overwhelming majority of scholars thought that Baur was right, even in regard to the issues at stake in the Corinthian correspondence. But outside of Germany the reaction to Baur was significantly different. This was especially true in England, where J. B. Lightfoot led the way with his critique of Baur entitled "St Paul and the Three" (in his *St. Paul's Epistle to the Galatians*, 5th ed., 1884, 292-374), in which he maintained that Paul did not stand in opposition to the chief "apostles of the circumcision," James,* Peter* and John. Moreover, Lightfoot argued that the opponents of Paul were not rival Christians associated with the "Pillar" apostles (Gal 2:9). Rather, the opponents behind Colossians, Romans, 1 Corinthians and the Pastorals were part of a "Christian Essene" movement which was more gnostic in orientation than the traditional Pharisaic Judaizers whom Paul opposed in Galatians, 2 Corinthians and Philippians. In contrast to the situation in Germany, Lightfoot's influence in the English-speaking world thus mitigated Baur's impact, since it kept scholars from interpreting Paul's letters as reflecting only one type of Judaizing heresy.

Within Germany the first significant break with Baur did not come until the beginning of the twentieth century, with the publication in 1908 of W. Lütgert's *Freiheitspredigt und Schwärmgeister in Korinth*. In Lütgert's view Paul's opponents in his various writings could all be subsumed under the overarching rubric of "gnostics," or "pneumatics," whose background was a liberal, Alexandrian Judaism that taught a gnosis in the form of a haggadic exposition and expansion of Scripture. Only in Galatians could Paul's opponents clearly be identified as Christian, Pharisaic Judaizers. But even in Galatia there was still a pneumatic opposition present, so that in his letter to the Galatians Paul was fighting against two fronts at once.

But it was the rise of the *Religionsgeschichtliche* ("history of religions") School, with its emphasis on a gnostic, mystery-religion backdrop to early Christianity, which appeared to deal the death-blow to the reign of Baur's position. The History of Religions School crystallized around the works of W. Bousset, especially his 1913 work, *Kyrios Christos, Geschichte des Christusglaubens von den Anfängen des Christentums bis Irenaeus* (ET *Kyrios Christos: A History of the Belief in Christ from the Beginnings of Christianity to Irenaeus*, 1970) and R. Reitzenstein's study of the ancient mystery religions, *Die hellenistischen Mysterienreligionen* (1927³, ET *Hellenistic Mystery-Religions: Their Basic Ideas and Significance*, 1977). As a result of these works and others from this perspective, the attention of NT scholars was now forcefully directed to the conceptual world of Hellenism.* In addition, the History of Religions School offered for the first time a reconstruction of the development of early Christianity that was just as comprehensive and extensive as that of Baur. Prior to this time the concept of gnosticism had been used merely as a general description for certain theological tendencies. With the rise of the history-of-religions approach, this formerly vague term was now given the concrete and well-defined content needed to compete with the Tübingen School's ability to define the precise nature of Jewish-Christian legalism.

It was precisely the well-defined nature of gnosticism offered by the History of Religions School, however, that also brought about its own demise. In fact, the last serious attempt to argue that Paul's opponents in 2 Corinthians were gnostics was R. Bultmann's 1947 essay *Exegetische Probleme des Zweiten Korintherbriefes zu 2 Kor 5:1-5; 5:11-6:10; 10-13; 12:21*, written in response to E. Käsemann's influential article, "Die Legitimität des Apostels, Eine Untersuchung zu II Korinther 10-13" (*ZNW* 41 [1942] 33-71). Käsemann had concluded that Paul's opponents in Corinth were simply pneumatics who belonged to an association of Palestinians in the Diaspora who in their preaching emphasized their own spiritual exploits and accomplishments. In Käsemann's view, to say more than this, especially to attempt to understand them as gnostics, was to go beyond the evidence of the text. In response, Bultmann argued that Paul's opponents in 2 Corinthians were in fact the same Christian gnostics whom Paul had opposed in 1 Corinthians 15. But what is most evident in Bultmann's response is his determination to maintain at all costs the theory of the existence of a pre-Christian gnosticism. Bultmann's desperate attempt eventually failed, along with the entire History of Religions School's program of interpreting early Christianity against the backdrop of the gnostic mystery religions. There was simply no evidence to justify their extension of the incipient gnostic tendencies apparent in some parts of the NT into a reconstruction of a full-blown pre-Christian gnosticism like that first attested only in the second and third centuries.

*2.3. The Bornkamm-Georgi Hypothesis.* The collapse of the Bousset-Reitzenstein-Bultmann hypothesis thus freed scholarship from the burden of its past bias toward gnosticism as the key to Paul's thought, while at the same time allowing it to retain the History of Religions School's sound insight that early Christianity must be interpreted in the light of its surrounding religious context. Ultimately this continuing interest in Paul's religious environment and his opponents in Corinth culminated in the massive work of Dieter Georgi, *Die Gegner des Paulus im 2. Korintherbrief* (1964; ET *The Opponents of Paul in Second Corinthians*, 1986). Georgi's work was an extension and substantiation of the position of his mentor, Günther Bornkamm, whose overall understanding of Paul's life and thought was summarized in his now classic study, *Paul* (original German ed., 1969; ET 1971).

Georgi concluded that Baur's earlier adversaries had not been able to offer an adequate alternative because they had not taken seriously enough the Jewish origins and aspects of Paul's opposition. Georgi's own study of the terminology in 2 Corinthians 10—13 led him to the conclusion that Paul's opponents were Jewish-Christian missionaries and apostles of Palestinian origin who utilized the propaganda methods of the Hellenistic Jewish apologists. Georgi's extensive study of the missionary activities of Hellenistic Jews thus sought to provide the history-of-religions foundation Lütgert and Bultmann had failed to produce in order to combat Baur's extensive depiction of Palestinian Judaism and Judaizers. The result of Georgi's surveys of the Hellenistic-Jewish sources is a picture of Paul's opponents as Hellenistic-Jewish pneumatic missionaries whose self-understanding was based on the "divine man" (*theios anēr*) tradition within Hellenistic Judaism.

The publication of Georgi's work finally confronted Baur's thesis concerning Paul's opponents with an equally systematic and comprehensive antithesis. Thus, if Lütgert had ended the *dominance* of Baur's position, Georgi appeared to have called into question its very *legitimacy*! Baur's traditional picture now seemed to be a thing of the past. The only remaining task, apparently, was to refine Georgi's position, which many scholars since then have attempted to do.

*2.4. Oostendorp, Barrett and the Revival of F. C. Baur.* This new surge of optimism was premature. Not only was Georgi's work severely criticized for his methodology and use of sources, but the position of Baur itself still remained very much alive, despite the rise of the History of Religions school. In an ironic reversal of roles, however, it was now two scholars from outside Germany, D. W. Oostendorp and C. K. Barrett, who rose up to defend Baur's classic thesis, albeit with certain significant modifications.

Oostendorp modified Baur's Judaistic hypothesis sufficiently to incorporate the central significance of the Spirit (*see* Holy Spirit), which Baur had excluded and which had repeatedly become the basis upon which he was attacked. According to Oostendorp (*Another Jesus: A Gospel of Jewish Christian Superiority in II Corinthians*, 1967), the Judaizers in Corinth, as in Galatia, had connected the work of the Spirit with the observance of the Law (cf. Gal 5:13-26), so that Paul's purpose was to contrast the Law and the Spirit (cf. Gal 3:1-5; 2 Cor 3:6) in such a way as to contradict their teaching. Though largely overlooked, Oostendorp's work was thus able to integrate the question of the reception and role of the Spirit with the issue of obedience to the Law both in the theology of Paul's opponents and in Paul's own understanding. Oostendorp brought together what, in the more traditional approach to Paul's opponents, had always been kept apart: the Spirit and the Law.

But of even greater significance for the history of the debate is the fact that Baur's position has also been strongly represented by one of the most influential of the recent interpreters of Paul in the English-speaking world, C. K. Barrett. In 1953 Barrett laid the foundation for his future work in his article "Paul and the 'Pillar' Apostles" (in *Studia Paulina, FS Johannis de Zwaan*, ed. J. N. Sevenster and W. C. Van Unnik, 1953, 1-19). Ten years later Barrett built upon this foundational study with a corresponding reexamination of the references and possible allusions to Peter in 1 and 2 Corinthians entitled "Cephas and Corinth," (in *Abraham unser Vater, Juden und Christen im Gespräch über die Bibel, FS Otto Michel*, ed. Otto Betz, et. al., 1963, 1-12). In this study Barrett concluded not only that it was probable that Cephas had visited Corinth, but that therefore the "man" who was building on Paul's foundation in 1 Corinthians 3:10-17 was either Peter himself or someone acting in his name. Like Baur before him, Barrett thus posited the existence in Corinth of a Jewish-Christian "Cephas-Party" in opposition to Paul.

But why then was Peter not mentioned in 2 Corinthians? Because, according to Barrett, and contrary to Baur's view, Paul still retained some respect for the original Jerusalem apostles. For this reason Paul released all of his "vigorous antipathy" on the "other agents" at work in Corinth under the guise of the authority* of Peter, that is, the "false apostles" of 2 Corinthians 11:13-15. Thus for Barrett, as for Käsemann before him, a distinction must be made between the "false apostles" and the eminent Jerusalem apostles of 2 Corinthians 11:5 and Galatians 2:9. Furthermore, the key to the situation in 2 Corinthians is the same as that in Galatians 2:12: Peter's heart was in the right place, but he was easily frightened and used by others! At Corinth Peter had once again become an easily manipulated figurehead whose name and authority were being used by impostors. As in Galatians 2, Paul was therefore once again in the uncomfortable position of not being able to repudiate Peter, while at the same time having to deal with those who wanted to destroy his work in Peter's name. From this point on Barrett's subsequent work was aimed at strengthening this basic position.

*2.5. The Deadlock in Recent Scholarship.* After more than 150 years of scholarship the result of Barrett's extensive work was to destroy any notion that a general consensus had been reached concerning the identity and theology of Paul's opponents. By the mid-1970s the camps were equally divided. The very fact that Barrett could argue for Baur's position so persuasively in the face of its most serious challenge made it clear that scholarship was at a stalemate. The two basic positions were now both firmly entrenched and seemed to be well fortified with a strong supply of documented arguments and counter-arguments.

But equally devastating to the modern debate has

been the serious doubt raised concerning the historical reality which is said to undergird both of these positions. Georgi's evidence for the very existence of a "divine man" in Judaism, as the key to the opponents' self-understanding, has been seriously called into question. Others have criticized Georgi's attempt to interpret "servants of Christ" in 2 Corinthians 11:23 in the sense of "envoys," while still others have rejected Georgi's entire enterprise by maintaining that Jewish parallels to the missionary motives and methods of Paul do not exist. On the other hand, those who want to maintain that Paul's opponents were in some sense "Judaizers" must now contend with the challenges of E. P. Sanders and the "new perspective on Paul" which it has produced (see 3.2 below). Indeed, many from this perspective doubt if Paul's polemics have anything to do with the real position of his opponents at all! Hence, like the gnostic hypothesis of a previous generation, both of these remaining and basic hypotheses now stand under the shadow of serious questions concerning their historical reliability.

Finally, the current stalemate is a direct and natural result of the methodology employed in attempting to determine the nature of Paul's opposition. The inconclusive and internally contradictory history of Pauline studies since Baur has demonstrated that the temptation to reconstruct some grand hypothesis based on isolated fragments and "catch words" from Paul's letters, which are then filled out by recourse to distant parallels, must be resisted. For the simple fact is that there is no direct evidence from any of Paul's opponents themselves, unless James is read as an anti-Pauline polemic, which is certainly questionable.

Sumney's recent proposal of a "minimalist approach" to identifying Paul's opponents is therefore to be welcomed for its emphasis on the priority of exegesis in a "text-focused method," for its insistence upon a sound evaluation and use of proper sources, together with a "stringently" limited application of the "mirror technique" (i.e., reading the position of Paul's opponents directly out of Paul's own assertions as their opposite), and for its rejection of the attempt to approach the text with a previously determined, externally based, reconstruction. But it is significant in view of the history of research that when Sumney himself applies his method to 2 Corinthians, he offers no new insights into the identity of Paul's opponents. If progress is to be made in breaking the current deadlock it will thus come about only when such a text-oriented approach to the problem is combined with a renewed analysis of Paul's view of the Law and the center of his thinking as they impinge upon and are determined by the opposition which he faced not only in

Corinth, but in Galatia, Antioch* and Jerusalem as well. Essential to such a renewed study is the recognition that in countering his opponents Paul drove a wedge between the "Pillar Apostles" and those who worked in their name by underscoring his essential unity with the Jerusalem apostles (cf. Gal 2:1-10; 1 Cor 15:1-11; 2 Cor 11:5-6), while at the same time opposing those who claimed to represent them.

### 3. Paul's View of the Law.

Baur's understanding of the conflict in the early church between a Law-free, Pauline, Gentile Christianity and its Judaizing, Petrine, Jewish Christian counterpart was wedded to and supported by his acceptance of the Reformation understanding of Paul's Law/gospel contrast (*see* Law). But as Douglas Moo observed in 1987, following the insight of Robert Jewett, "scholarship on Paul and the Law in the last ten years has witnessed a 'paradigm shift' " (Moo, 287). All of the traditional "assured results" concerning Paul's Law/gospel contrast are now being so seriously called into question that, after a long period of dormancy characterized only by minor refinements of the reigning paradigm, Paul's understanding of the Law is currently the most debated topic among Pauline scholars.

*3.1. Antecedents to the Paradigm Shift in Recent Scholarship.* This recent destruction of the modern consensus concerning Paul's Law/gospel contrast corresponds to the earlier but largely unheeded dissatisfaction in our century with the traditional Reformation understanding of the centrality of justification by faith in Paul's theology (see 4 below). Nor could Johannes Munck turn the tide with his explicit and sustained critique (in his *Paul and the Salvation of Mankind*, 1959 [German, 1954]) of the continuing influence of Baur on modern scholarship. To argue as Munck did that the only substantive difference between Paul and the Jerusalem apostles was over mission strategy, based on Paul's conviction that the Gentiles must be won to Christ *first* as a prelude to the salvation of Israel,* did not seem to account for Paul's critique of the Law itself (*see* Mission). Moreover, Munck's contention that Paul was convinced that the arrival of the messianic age depended upon his own ministry,* so that Paul himself becomes the central figure in salvation history, was viewed not only as an overstatement of the case, but as an untenable denial of the centrality of Christ in Paul's eschatology.* Munck's supporting thesis that Paul's opponents were *Gentile* Judaizers has also garnered little support. Nevertheless, Munck's interpretation of Paul is insightful at many points, and his strong rejection of Baur's conflict theory concerning the relationship between Paul and the rest of the primitive church, based upon a supposed difference in their fundamental perspectives concerning Jesus and the Law, is a lasting contribution of his work. For Munck there was no essential theological conflict between Paul and Jewish Christianity.

On the other hand, H. J. Schoeps's *Paul: The Theology of the Apostle in the Light of Jewish Religious History* (1961; German, 1959) and W. D. Davies, *Paul and Rabbinic Judaism* (1948; see now the revised 4th ed., 1980), sought in different ways to challenge the traditionally negative view of Judaism and the supposed antagonism between Paul and the Jewish-Christian apostles against which Paul had been interpreted since Baur. But Schoeps did not deny the basic Reformation understanding of the Law in Paul. He merely sought to show its irrelevance to the "mainstream" Judaism of Paul's day, since in Schoeps's view Paul was in essence attacking only a distortion of Judaism represented by the Hellenistic Jews of the Diaspora. Conversely, Davies discounted Paul's critique of the Law too readily as mere polemic, and therefore as not essential to Paul's otherwise normal "rabbinic" views. In other words, Schoeps's Paul was not Jewish enough to win the day, and Davies's Paul was too Jewish to be accepted.

However, the modern consensus was significantly attacked again in 1964 in C. E. B. Cranfield's now programmatic article, "St. Paul and the Law" (*SJT* 17 [1964] 43-68). Cranfield did not deny the centrality of justification by faith for Paul's theology or the Reformation understanding of Paul's opponents. Rather, his burden was to redefine the focus of Paul's criticism of the Law in terms of a criticism of its *perversion* into legalism, this perversion being represented by the unique Pauline phrase "works of the law"* (cf. Rom 3:20, 28; Gal 3:2,10 etc.). According to Cranfield, Paul coined this new terminology because no designation was available in Greek to represent "legalism." Hence, when Paul speaks negatively of the "works of the Law," or simply the "Law," he is not opposing the Law itself but its perversion into works-righteousness. Conversely, Paul's positive statements concerning the Law refer to the Law freed from this legalistic misuse. In arguing this, Cranfield's overall intention was to counter the axiom of the modern consensus that, for Paul, Christ had abolished the Law. For although Christ had abolished legalism, he was, for Paul, the "goal" (*telos*) of the Law itself (Rom 10:4). In 2 Corinthians 3:6 it is thus the "legalistic misunderstanding and perversion of the law," not the Law itself, which kills.

Cranfield's view has won many followers and has been refined in many directions (see now his two-volume commentary on Romans, and the studies of C. F. D. Moule, Ragnar Bring and, most importantly, D. P. Fuller). But this position has also been severely criticized for its reliance on what appears to many to be a self-confirming hypothesis in which Paul's negative statements concerning the Law are simply taken really to be about legalism, even when the full phrase "works of the Law" is not used (cf., e.g., Gal 3:10-12, 17-19). Others have pointed to its apparent failure to incorporate adequately some of Paul's statements concerning the abolition of the Law itself (e.g., Gal 3:12, 15-20; Rom 6:14; 7:4). And now, with the advent of E. P. Sanders's work, NT scholars increasingly regard the historical basis for Cranfield's view to be a phantom (but see his self-defense, Cranfield 1991).

Finally, although from a very different perspective on Paul's theology as a whole, a revitalized interest in biblical theology has led Hartmut Gese and Peter Stuhlmacher to reject the traditional Reformation understanding of the Law/gospel contrast as a theological distinction between two competing ways of salvation (see P. Stuhlmacher, "Paul's View of the Law in the Letter to the Romans," *SEÅ* 50 [1985] 87-104; his *Reconciliation, Law, and Righteousness*, 1986; and his recent commentary on Romans, 1989). Instead, the Law and the gospel are seen to represent an eschatological contrast between two periods in God's salvation history. Though still retaining the Reformation understanding of the centrality of justification by faith in Paul and his corresponding critique of the Law apart from faith, this approach views the Law itself as also in need of "redemption" from its role within the old covenant as the "Sinai Torah." Through the atonement of Christ and by the power of the Spirit, God has therefore redeemed not only humanity, but the Law as well from the power of sin. As the freed, eschatological "Zion Torah," God gives back to the Law its original function of giving life which it had in paradise. But to date, this approach has not been fully developed. In addition, the refinement it offers either goes too far for the traditional view, or not far enough for those seeking to replace the old consensus with a new one, since its criticism of the more traditional view does not strike at its essence.

*3.2. The "New Perspective" on Paul.* Hence, though substantial critiques of the reigning paradigm could certainly be found prior to 1977, these attacks on the prevailing consensus were primarily attacks on the Reformation understanding of Paul rather than an assault on its perception of Paul's Judaizing opponents. But as long as the traditional view of Paul's opponents remained substantially in place, the attempt to rethink Paul's own view could be dismissed not only as theologically or exegetically unsound, but also as historically misguided. Moo is therefore right in dating the destruction of the modern consensus to the advent of Sanders's contribution to the debate, beginning with his *Paul and Palestinian Judaism* in 1977. Sanders's view of Paul is, of course, in and of itself worthy of note and demands a response. But this is not what turned the tide in Pauline studies.

Sanders changed the course of scholarship on Paul because he succeeded in forcing scholars to rethink *fundamentally* the nature of the opposition Paul faced in his churches, and consequently the character and content of the criticism he raised against it. He accomplished this feat by presenting his own portrayal of Paul against the backdrop of a comprehensive and polemically forceful understanding of Palestinian Judaism as a religion of non-legalistic "covenantal nomism." According to Sanders, rather than demanding a perfect "works-righteousness" as the basis of one's salvation and as the prerequisite for entering into the covenant, the "covenantal nomism" pervasively found throughout Palestinian Judaism "is the view that one's place in God's plan is established on the basis of the covenant* and that the covenant requires as the proper response of man his obedience to its commandments, while providing means of atonement for transgression" (Sanders, 75). Thus, for Palestinian Judaism at the time of Paul, "the intention and effort to be obedient constitute the *condition for remaining in the covenant*, but they do not *earn* it" (Sanders, 180, emphasis his). Sanders's conclusions concerning Palestinian Judaism, though certainly not new (cf., e.g., the work of G. F. Moore before him) and not without their critics, could not be ignored, combined as they were with a corresponding reinterpretation of Paul's polemic against the Law.

For the vast majority of scholars, Paul's world had suddenly changed, and with this change came the need to rethink Paul's view of the "problem" of Law itself in view of the "solution" now offered in Christ. For if Sanders and his followers are right about the nature of Palestinian Judaism in Paul's day, then the traditional Reformation view of "Paul's polemic is left hanging in mid-air, and it is necessary either to accuse Paul of misunderstanding (or misrepresenting) his opponents, or to find new opponents for him to be criticizing" (Moo, 293). Once accepted, the effects of the paradigm shift regarding Judaism precipitated by Sanders are thus both far-reaching and decisive for the way in which Paul will be read in the decades ahead.

As is always the case, however, it is easier to tear down than to build up. Since the early 1980s the study of Paul's view of the Law has been marked by a flurry of studies seeking to work out the implications of Sanders's work for "the new perspective on Paul," to quote the title of the 1983 article written by J. D. G. Dunn, who has become one of the leading voices of this radical reorientation. In addition to Dunn's many studies (e.g., his collection of essays, *Jesus, Paul, and the Law: Studies in Mark and Galatians*, 1990, and his two-volume commentary, *Romans*, 1988; *see* Romans), most important among these new voices have been the works of Heikki Räisänen, especially his *Paul and the Law* (1983), Sanders's own subsequent works on Paul and Judaism (see especially his *Paul, the Law, and the Jewish People*, 1983; *Judaism: Practice and Belief, 63BCE-66CE*, 1992; and *Paul*, 1991; as well as Reinhold Liebers, *Das Gesetz als Evangelium, Untersuchungen zur Gesetzeskritik des Paulus*, 1989). Often at odds with one another on individual points of exegesis, these studies are unified only by their common conviction concerning the non-legalistic nature of first-century Judaism and their corresponding rejection of the traditional Reformation understanding of the Law/gospel antithesis as the key to Paul's view of the Law and the theology of his opponents, especially in view of the fact that 2 Corinthians apparently lacks this debate over the Law entirely.

**3.3. The Current Diversity of Proposals.** Dating from Sanders's initial work in 1977 a forceful and, in part, successful attack on the traditional understanding of Paul's view of the Law, stemming from Baur, has thus been mounted. But the plethora of new proposals spawned by this paradigm shift suffers as much from internal dissent as from external critique, since no consensus has yet emerged concerning the reason(s) why Paul actually rejected Judaism and the "works of the Law," nor concerning the actual meaning of "works of the Law" in Paul's writings. Morevoer, the earlier positions represented by Cranfield and Stuhlmacher continue to win adherents, while the recent studies of Charles H. Cosgrove, *The Cross and the Spirit: A Study in the Argument and Theology of Galatians* (1988); Roman Heiligenthal, *Werke als Zeichen, Untersuchungen zur Bedeutung der menschlichen Taten im Frühjudentum, Neuen Testament und Frühchristentum* (1983); Frank Thielman, *From Plight to Solution: A Jewish Framework for Understanding Paul's View of the Law in Galatians and Romans* (1989); and Peter J. Tomson, *Paul and the Jewish Law: Halakha in the Letters of the Apostle to the Gentiles* (1990), offer great promise due to their recognition of the positive role that obedience to the Law plays in the soteriological structures of both Judaism and Paul. Moreover, although the pendulum of opinion is now swinging toward the new perspective, recent proponents of the more traditional view, such as F. F. Bruce, Seyoon Kim, G. Lüdemann (who has once again picked up and argued extensively and explicitly for the validity of the Tübingen School's perspective), Otfried Hofius, Martin Hengel, Robert H. Gundry, Thomas R. Schreiner, Brice L. Martin and in part S. Westerholm, continue to argue strongly that the "paradigm shift" in Pauline studies has been misguided and that "there is more of Paul in Luther than many twentieth-century scholars are inclined to allow" (Westerholm, 173).

As with the question of the identity and nature of Paul's opponents, the positive result of this great diversity among scholars today is that it drives interpreters back to the text itself. Students of Paul are now approaching his writings with eyes wide open and a healthy skepticism concerning *all* paradigms as they search for fresh insight into passages which suddenly look new again. And here too, Paul's emphasis on his essential unity with the Jerusalem apostles as the conduits of the teaching of Jesus and the positive role which the Law played "in Christ"* and under the power of the Spirit must play a decisive part in the forging of a new consensus (cf. Gal 5:1—6:16; Rom 8:1-8; and the use of the Law in Pauline ethics). Furthermore, the centrality of Paul's eschatological conviction that Christ has initiated the beginning of the new creation* with the establishment of the new covenant, in fulfillment of Jeremiah 31:31-34 and Ezekiel 36:26-27, needs to be taken seriously as a key to Paul's understanding of the Law. For it is against this backdrop that the question of the exact locus of the "problem" with the Law as it functioned under the old covenant, as well as its role in the new, must be raised. But to raise the question of the impact of Paul's eschatology* on his view of the Law is to call attention to the larger question of the center of Paul's theology as such, which is the last and most important question raised by Baur's work.

## 4. The Center of Paul's Theology.

Until the mid-1970s most German scholarship maintained an inextricable link between its traditional Reformation understanding of Paul's Law/gospel contrast and the overriding conviction that the center of Paul's thinking was the concept of the righteousness* of God* as encountered in the doctrine of justification.* This view was then bolstered by the corresponding understanding of Paul's opponents as predominantly Judaistic legalists who insisted that, in addition to faith in Christ, adherence to the Law was necessary for gaining and/or maintaining a righteous standing

before God.

But as with the other pillars of Baur's perspective, this too was not without its challengers within Germany, while Anglo-Saxon scholarship was never dominated by this position or controlled in the same way by this question. Instead, outside of Germany some of the leading scholars sought to understand Paul's doctrine of justification as merely one aspect of a larger panorama of theological themes. The various aspects of Paul's theology were not organized, therefore, as derivatives of this one generating center of Paul's thought. Rather, Paul's thought was analyzed either according to the traditional structure of systematic theology (e.g., creation, anthropology, sin, redemption, christology, eschatology etc; for a prime example of this approach, see the works of D. E. H. Whiteley, *The Theology of St. Paul*, 1964, and Herman Ridderbos, *Paul, An Outline of His Theology*, 1975 [original Dutch ed., 1966]), or within the structure of some other organizational principle (cf., e.g., Richard N. Longenecker, *Paul, Apostle of Liberty*, 1964, who took the broader issue of "legality-liberty" as the organizational framework for displaying Paul's thought; and F. F. Bruce's, *Paul: Apostle of the Heart Set Free*, 1977, who presented Paul's theology within the historical outline of Paul's missionary travels). And yet, due to the influence of the Reformation and its questions on the study of Paul and the leading role that German scholarship played for the first seventy years of the twentieth century, the dominant question within Pauline studies has remained, Is justification by faith the conceptual center of Paul's thought (*see* Center)?

*4.1. Challenges to the Traditional View.* Already in 1904 W. Wrede had argued in his book, *Paulus*, that the doctrine of justification was not the generating principle of Paul's thinking but merely a polemical doctrine (*Kampfeslehre*) aimed at the Judaism of his day. The generating principle of Paul's theology, Wrede maintained, was his eschatological conviction that Christ had ushered in the proleptic beginning of the kingdom* of God. But it was left to Albert Schweitzer to take Wrede's emphasis on eschatology and understand it as the *framework* of Paul's thought. This was Schweitzer's argument in his influential book, *Die Mystik des Apostels Paulus* (1930; ET *The Mysticism of the Apostle Paul*, 1931), which was to that date the most convincing and thoroughgoing alternative to the traditional view. Schweitzer combined Wrede's emphasis on eschatology with Adolf Deissmann's earlier development of Paul's "Christ-mysticism" (*see* Mysticism), which Deissmann had argued was "the characteristic expression of his Christianity," as evidenced in the 164 times that the formula "in Christ" appears in Paul's writings (see his *Paulus*, 1911 and 1926; ET *Paul: A Study in Social and Religious History*, 1912, 1927, 140 for quote and evidence). Hence for Schweitzer, being "in Christ" was not merely a cultic reality as Deissmann had emphasized, but an eschatological reality which was experienced physically and sacramentally and brought about by the inaugurated eschatological kingdom of God now present with the turn of the ages. Viewed in this way, Paul's "mysticism" was the key to his thinking. The title of Schweitzer's book is thus misleading, since for Schweitzer this mysticism was not the result of some immediate and timeless "oneness" with Christ. Nevertheless, Schweitzer relegated the doctrine of justification by faith to a mere "subsidiary crater" (*Nebenkrater*) of Paul's thought, since it was found only in certain letters (predominantly in Galatians and Romans) and then only in reference to the specific problem of the Law as raised by Paul's controversy with the Judaizers.

But the work of Wrede, Deissmann and Schweitzer did not win the day in the German speaking world. Nor did W. D. Davies's rejection of the centrality of the Law/gospel contrast and the doctrine of justification, argued in his *Paul and Rabbinic Judaism*, gain a hearing outside of England and America. It was not until the seminal writings of Krister Stendahl and E. P. Sanders that these earlier protests found a foothold in scholarship. Ever since the work of Stendahl and Sanders, however, the traditional understanding of the center of Paul's thought has been increasingly called into question.

Stendahl's programmatic essays, "The Apostle Paul and the Introspective Conscience of the West" (1960) and "Paul Among Jews and Gentiles" (1963), were originally written in Swedish and were published in English in his *Paul Among Jews and Gentiles and other Essays* (1976). Stendahl's reinterpretation of Paul's theology grew out of his conviction that, due to Reformation theology and the grid of Luther's own conversion experience, Paul's teaching concerning justification by faith had been removed from its original setting and transposed into the very center of his teaching about salvation.* Rather than addressing the status of Gentiles* within God's plan for the world, as it does in Paul's writings, the doctrine of justification by faith was now seen to be the abstract doctrinal response to the despair and failure of humanity brought about by the attempt to live up to the moral demands of the Law or by the pride caused by humanity's attempt to justify itself by the Law. The ultimate result of this loss of the original focus of justification is that the Pauline problem of the relationship between Jews and Gentiles becomes captive to the Western problem of the introspective conscience.

As a corollary to this misunderstanding of the role of justification in Paul's thought, Paul's Damascus Road experience has thus been wrongly universalized as an experience of conversion, rather than rightly understood as Paul's specific call to be the apostle to the Gentiles (*see* Conversion and Call). Hence, for Stendahl, "Paul's argument about justification by faith neither grows out of his 'dissatisfaction' with Judaism, nor is intended as a frontal attack on 'legalism,' " but instead was "hammered out by Paul for the very specific and limited purpose of defending the rights of Gentile converts to be full and genuine heirs to the promises of God to Israel. Their rights were based solely on faith in Jesus Christ" (Stendahl, 130, 2). For Stendahl, therefore, Paul's view of justification by faith served merely as an apologetic doctrine which " 'justified' the status of Gentile Christians as honorary Jews" (5, cf. 130). As such, the doctrine of justification by faith can lay no claim to being the pervasive or organizing principle of Paul's thought.

In much the same way, E. P. Sanders's reexamination of the pattern of Judaism and the central issue of the relationship between Jews and Gentiles in Paul's thinking has also led him to reevaluate the driving force of Paul's theology. Just as Paul's opponents can no longer be understood as legalistic Jews who held to a form of works-righteousness, so too must justification by faith be given up as the clue to Paul's thought (*Paul and Palestinian Judaism*, 438). Instead, following Schweitzer, the dominant conception of salvation in Paul's letters is the transfer from one sphere of lordship (sin, death, the Law) to another (righteousness, life, the gospel), so that being saved both entails, and is brought about by, becoming one with Christ. If the pattern of Judaism in Paul's day can be called "covenantal nomism," the pattern of Paul's religion can thus be described as "participationist eschatology" (*Paul and Palestinian Judaism*, 552).

There have also been those who, like H. Räisänen, have stressed that due to the occasional nature of Paul's theology it is asking too much to seek *the* center to Paul's thinking to begin with. Indeed, the fact that Paul was not a systematic theologian in his approach to doctrine, or in his mode of presentation, is widely acknowledged today. But for Räisänen, not only is Paul not systematic in his framework, his thinking itself is characterized by internal contradictions concerning the relationship between the Law and his gospel, from that of hostility and mutual exclusion in Galatians, to that of compatibility and inclusion in Romans. Räisänen's understanding of Paul as fundamentally inconsistent in his thought has not carried the day, nor should it. It is one thing to recognize the occasional nature of Paul's letters, but it is quite another to conclude that Paul's thinking lacks an internal coherence or conceptual focus.

*4.2. The Debate Within and Against the Traditional View.* The traditional interpretation of justification by faith as the center of Paul's thinking has also undergone a significant development of its own in the last fifty years. The internal debate has focused on the meaning of the corresponding concept of the "righteousness of God" in Paul's thought (cf. Rom 1:17; 3:21-22, 26; 10:3; 2 Cor 5:21; Phil 3:9) and on the relationship of Paul's doctrine of justification to his other central affirmations. Above all, scholars have sought to understand more precisely the interplay between justification by faith and the new creation, the role of the Spirit, the expectation of moral transformation in Christ, the coming judgment by works, and Paul's hope for the future consummation and vindication at Christ's return.

The starting point for the modern debate is the work of Rudolf Bultmann, no doubt the most influential NT scholar of the twentieth century. As an extension of Luther's basic position, Bultmann argued in his *Theology of the New Testament* (2 vols.; 1948, 1953; ET 1951, 1955, §§28-30) that for Paul the righteousness of God, granted to the *individual* upon his or her justification by *faith*, was a forensic concept. As such, it is not an ethical change brought about in a person, but an eschatological reality which, although originally related to the end times, is now, for Paul, already experienced by the believer as a pure gift of God's grace,* rather than as a result of one's obedience to the Law.

Bultmann's view was based on his reinterpretation of Paul's theological categories into existential terms in which God was viewed not as an external subject, but only from the perspective of his relationship to humanity, while humanity was equally viewed only in relationship to God. For Bultmann, therefore, history is the arena in which God encounters us directly and individually in order to call for a decision in response to the preaching of the gospel, rather than being the working out of God's redemptive plan on the way toward an ultimate consummation at the return of Christ.

The legitimacy for this reinterpretation of Paul's view of history and eschatology was found in Paul himself, whom Bultmann saw continuing to demythologize the Jewish apocalyptic* gospel of Jesus as the Messianic Son of Man as originally preached by the early church, into a kerygma concerning Jesus as the divine Son of God (*see* Son of God), which could then be preached and understood in a Hellenistic context. For Bultmann, Paul's letters consequently show hardly a trace of the historical Jesus or of the Jewish and Palestinian tradition of the early Christians, since Paul received the Christian tradition as it had already been altered through the filter of the Hellenistic Church (*see* Jesus, Sayings of). In line with this reconstruction, Bultmann saw Paul's opposition to be a Judaistic legalism based on the Law itself, which for Bultmann not only could not be kept perfectly, but which *itself* brought about sinful boasting by its very demand for obedience. Paul thus opposed the Law and those Jewish Christians who held to it for both quantitative reasons (no one can keep the Law perfectly) *and* qualitative reasons (the very attempt *itself* to keep the Law is already sin). Luther's Law/gospel contrast therefore reaches its apex in Bultmann's reading of Paul.

In stark contrast, Ernst Käsemann argued in his paradigmatic 1961 article, "Gottesgerechtigkeit bei Paulus" (*ZThK* 58 [1961] 367-78; ET "The Righteousness of God in Paul," in *New Testament Questions of Today*, 1969, 168-82), that for Paul the righteousness of God was not primarily a gift, but a cosmic and creative *power,** under which one is brought to live as part of the *corporate* people of God as a result of having been freed in baptism from the power of sin* and death (*see* Life and Death). For Käsemann, Paul's thought must not be conceived of primarily in existential terms, but in apocalyptic categories in which the content of the righteousness of God is the rule of Christ over the world and his people in anticipation of God's final cosmic triumph.* Salvation is not therefore fundamentally the experience of receiving God's righteousness, but of being brought back into obedience to the righteousness of God in Christ. Rather than referring to a righteousness which *comes* from God as a gift, as Bultmann argued, for Käsemann the righteousness of God is God's *own* righteous behavior, expressed in his saving activity as an outworking of his covenantal faithfulness to his creation and to his people (*see* Way).

The most important contribution to this ongoing debate has been the further development of Käsemann's basic perspective in the work of Peter Stuhlmacher, beginning with the 1966 revised form of his dissertation, *Gerechtigkeit Gottes bei Paulus* (*The Righteousness of God in Paul*). Against the backdrop of the OT and Jewish apocalyptic understanding of the righteousness of God, Stuhlmacher has argued that the righteousness of God in Paul's thought must be understood in view of the fact that for Paul the new age of the righteousness of God has already broken in with Christ, so that God's people are now living in the overlapping of the ages. The present experience of the righteousness of God does not refer, therefore, primarily to some forensic transaction in heaven which transcends time. Rather, Paul could speak of the present reality of the righteousness of God in the lives of his people precisely because God's power to save and to vindicate, in accordance with his faithfulness to his covenant, was already being poured out in the world through Christ. The righteousness of God is thus first and foremost the power of God which brings one into the new world of the kingdom of God. In turn, the believer's experience of God's righteousness is made possible by the "forensic situation" brought about by the cross of Christ and realized in the world through participation in the body of Christ.

Stuhlmacher consequently solves the tension between the theological categories of imputed and effective, or real, righteousness by emphasizing that the ontological bridge which makes possible the Pauline assertions concerning one's real participation in the righteousness of God is the concept of the Spirit. Hence, in contrast to the view of Schweitzer and those who follow him, mystic union with Christ and justification are bound together into one reality for Paul, rather than being in conflict or distinct from one another. For according to Stuhlmacher, being justified includes, for Paul, being put into the realm of and experiencing the reality of the Spirit as a proleptic realization of the future new creation (cf. Rom 8:2-17; 1 Cor 12:13; Rom 8:10-11).

Käsemann's fundamental paradigm, based on the conviction that apocalyptic thinking is the "mother" of all Christian theology, has now been further developed and applied consistently to all of Paul's thought in J. Christiaan Beker's, *Paul the Apostle: The Triumph of God in Life and Thought* (1980). Beker too recognizes with the majority of modern scholars that Paul's thought is not systematically developed or presented. Beker's distinct contribution is to argue, however, that for Paul the apocalyptic triumph of God which has now been brought about proleptically in the Christ-event, but which will reach its final victory in the imminent future triumph of God, is nevertheless the coherent and *symbolic* (not doctrinal!) center of Paul's gospel. For Beker the center of Paul's thought is thus neither an abstract doctrine on the one hand, nor a life changing experience on the other. According to Beker, it is "a mistake to define Paul's coherent center *either* in terms of a too-narrow conceptual definition, that is, in a petrified conceptuality ('justification by faith,' 'sacramental participation,' etc.), *or* in terms of a too-general characterization ('being in Christ,' 'the Lordship of Christ')" (Preface to the 1984 ed., xvii; see too the review of Beker's work by R. P. Martin, *JBL* 101 [1982] 463-66). Instead, "Paul's coherent center must be viewed as a symbolic structure in which a primordial experience (Paul's call) is brought into language in a particular way. . . . That language is, for Paul, the apocalyptic language of Judaism, in which he lived and thought" (Beker, 15-16).

In Beker's view, the genius of Paul is his corresponding ability to correlate and apply this overarching and consistent apocalyptic theme to various and distinct situations, without dissolving the coherence of the gospel. Beker thus argues that for Paul "in nearly all cases the contingent interpretation of the gospel points—whether implicitly or explicitly—to the imminent cosmic triumph of God" (Beker, 19). Hence, Beker rejects Bultmann's attempt to remove the apocalyptic elements from Paul's gospel (i.e., to demythologize them into an existential self-understanding) as an attempt to remove the very content of the gospel itself. But unlike Käsemann and Stuhlmacher, Beker also rejects the conclusion that the theme of the righteousness of God is the central theme of Paul's writings. For Beker, it too is merely one of the many expressions of the underlying symbolic theme of the coming triumph of God. "Thus, righteousness must be viewed as *one* symbol *among* others and not as *the* center of Paul's thought" (Beker, 17).

As scholarly investigation and proposals from Wrede to Beker demonstrate, the challenge now is to rethink Paul's theology in such a way that the centrality of eschatology in Paul's thought is brought together with Paul's actual assertions on a doctrinal and personal level concerning what *God in Christ* has accomplished in history and for the believer. But at the same time, to pursue the question of the center of Paul's theology is also to ask what it means for the *believer* to be living in the kingdom of God which, although *already* inaugurated, has *not yet* been established in all its fullness. Within this context, and in anticipation of the coming triumph and judgment* of God, the need to delineate both the meaning of the righteousness of God and the means of the justification of God's people, now and in the future, still remains the crux for interpreting Paul's letters.

### 5. Prospects for the Future.

The history of Pauline research since Baur has highlighted the crucial importance of determining the historical context within which Paul's thought was developed and expressed. As a consequence, recent studies of Paul have increasingly focused on the study and classification of Paul's rhetoric* (apart from H. D. Betz's *Galatians*, 1979, and his earlier work, *Der Apostel*

*Paulus und die sokratische Tradition, Eine exegetische Untersuchung zu einer 'Apologie' 2 Korinther 10—13,* 1972, these contributions are found mostly in journal articles dedicated to specific passages) and on the sociology* of Paul's communities (see Wayne A. Meeks, *The First Urban Christians: The Social World of the Apostle Paul,* 1983, and the many works of Gerd Theissen, especially *The Social Setting of Pauline Christianity,* 1982; *see* Social-Scientific Approaches). Nevertheless, such studies remain merely helpful subsidiaries in service of the main task of interpreting the *content* of Paul's own thought as it was expressed in response to the needs of his communities and the opposition that he faced. The history of Pauline research since Baur has also made it clear that one's view of Paul will be determined, above all, by whether one interprets his letters predominantly against the Greco-Roman philosophical and religious world of Paul's day, as Bultmann argued over fifty years ago, or in light of the Hellenistic-Jewish world of the first century and its Scriptures, as Adolf Schlatter proposed in the early decades of this century. This is true despite the fact that modern scholarship has shown the great degree to which the Judaism of Paul's day had already been influenced by Hellenism,* so that it is a historical mistake to view Paul as *either* Jewish *or* Hellenistic in his thought. Paul was clearly a Hellenistic Jew (*see* Jew, Paul the). Nevertheless, the fundamental issue still to be resolved in Pauline studies is the determination of the *primary* religious and theological context within which Paul's thought is to be understood. This is the great watershed among students of Paul.

How one decides this issue will determine how one reads Paul. And how one reads Paul will determine how one evaluates the relationship between Jesus and Paul on the one hand (*see* Jesus and Paul), and the place of Paul in the development of the early church on the other. Baur saw Paul as the great "Hellenizer of Christianity," so that Paul's opponents became the other apostles themselves. Those who likewise look first to the religions* and philosophies* of the Greco-Roman world to explain Paul's thought must also posit a gap, if not hostility, between Paul and the early church in Jerusalem.

Against the backdrop of this decision, it is worth remembering the words of Ritschl. Already in 1856 he recognized that the enduring value of Baur and the Tübingen School would be in the counter-reactions which it would evoke: " 'The Tübingen School has fallen to pieces and its initiative will only deserve recognition in the measure that it leads to opposition against the system of early Church history as presented by Baur and Schwegler, and as it furthers the cultivation of Biblical Theology more than has been the case up to now' " (quoted by Harris, 108-9).

After 150 years of Pauline studies there still remains a need for a comprehensive developmental, rather than conflict, model of Paul's life and thought, and for the corresponding cultivation of a biblical theology which incorporates Paul's apostolic role and theology within the history of the early church. This need has been underscored by the study of Paul from an explicitly Jewish perspective (in addition to the work by Schoeps, see Samuel Sandmel, *The Genius of Paul: A Study in History,* 1958; Schalom Ben-Chorin, *Paulus, Der Völkerapostel in jüdicher Sicht,* 1970; and now Alan F. Segal, *Paul the Convert: The Apostolate and Apostasy of Saul the Pharisee,* 1990). But even adherents to the "New Perspective" on Paul, who have worked hard to renew our understanding of Paul within the Judaism of his day, have often not taken the Jewish matrix of Paul's own thinking seriously enough as the decisive conceptual source for Paul's thinking. Moreover, at the heart of the debate concerning the Law and the role of justification in Paul's thought is the question of Paul's understanding of redemptive history (cf. Gal 3—4; 2 Cor 3:7-18; Rom 3:21-16; 9—11), which itself can only be solved by a renewed study of Paul's use and understanding of the OT within the larger question of the relationship of Paul and his gospel to Israel* as the old covenant people of God (*see* Restoration of Israel). Such a study is only now beginning to be undertaken (see, e.g., the recent works of Dietrich-Alex Koch, *Die Schrift als Zeuge des Evangeliums, Untersuchungen zur Verwendung und zum Verständnis der Schrift bei Paulus,* 1986; Richard B. Hays, *Echoes of Scripture in the Letters of Paul,* 1989; N. T. Wright, *The Climax of the Covenant: Christ and the Law in Pauline Theology,* 1991; and the various recent motif studies and treatments of particular key passages in which Paul quotes, alludes to, or relies upon the OT explicitly for his self-understanding and theology, such as Seyoon Kim, *The Origin of Paul's Gospel,* 1981, James M. Scott, *Adoption as Sons of God,* 1992, and Karl Olav Sandnes, *Paul—One of the Prophets,* 1991; *see* Old Testament in Paul; Prophet, Paul As). The future of Pauline studies at this juncture in its history is dependent upon just these kinds of studies if we are to move forward in our understanding of Paul as he understood himself: the Jewish apostle to the Gentiles, whose message came from the history of his people, their Scriptures, and the history of Israel's Messiah.

*See also* CENTER OF PAUL'S THEOLOGY; HERMENEUTICS/ INTERPRETING PAUL; JESUS AND PAUL; JUSTIFICATION; LAW; OPPONENTS OF PAUL; RIGHTEOUSNESS, RIGHTEOUSNESS OF GOD; WORKS OF THE LAW.

BIBLIOGRAPHY. J. Becker, *Paulus. Der Apostel der Völker* (Tübingen: J. C. B. Mohr, 1989); R. Bring, "Paul and the Old Testament: A Study of the Ideas of Election, Faith and Law in Paul, with Special Reference to Romans 9:30-10:30," *ST* 25 (1971) 21-60; C. Colpe, *Die religionsgeschichtliche Schule. Darstellung und Kritik ihres Bildes vom gnostischen Erlösermythus* (Göttingen: Vandenhoeck & Ruprecht, 1961); C. E. B. Cranfield, *The Epistle to the Romans* (2 vols.; ICC; Edinburgh: T & T Clark, 1975, 1979); idem, " 'The Works of the Law' in the Epistle to the Romans," *JSNT* 43 (1991) 89-101; N. A. Dahl, *Studies in Paul* (Minneapolis: Augsburg, 1977); W. D. Davies, *Paul and Rabbinic Judaism: Some Rabbinic Elements in Pauline Theology* (4th ed.; Philadelphia: Fortress, 1980); J. D. G. Dunn, "The New Perspective on Paul," *BJRL* 65 (1983) 95-122; E. E. Ellis, *Paul and His Recent Interpreters* (Grand Rapids: Eerdmans, 1961); idem, "Paul and His Opponents: Trends in Research," in *Prophecy and Hermeneutic in Early Christianity: New Testament Essays* (WUNT 18; Tübingen: J. C. B. Mohr, 1978) 80-115; E. J. Epp and G. W. MacRae, eds., *The New Testament and Its Modern Interpreters* (Philadelphia: Fortress, 1989); D. P. Fuller, *Gospel and Law: Contrast or Continuum? The Hermeneutics of Dispensationalism and Covenant Theology* (Grand Rapids: Eerdmans, 1980); idem, *The Unity of the Bible: Unfolding God's Plan for Humanity* (Grand Rapids: Zondervan, 1992); J. J. Gunther, *St. Paul's Opponents and Their Background: A Study of Apocalyptic and Jewish Sectarian Teachings* (NovTSup 30; Leiden: E. J. Brill, 1973); H. Harris, *The Tübingen School: A Historical and Theological Investigation of the School of F. C. Baur* (Grand Rapids: Baker, 1990); H. Hübner, "Paulusforschung seit 1945. Ein kritischer Literaturbericht," in *ANRW* II.25.4.2649-2840; W. G. Kümmel, *The New Testament: The History of the Investigation of Its Problems* (Nashville: Abingdon, 1972); D. Moo, "Paul and the Law in the Last Ten Years," *SJT* 40 (1987) 287-307; C. F. D. Moule, "Obligation in the Ethic of Paul," in *Christian History and Interpretation: Studies Presented to John Knox*, ed. W. F. Farmer et al. (Cambridge: University Press, 1976) 313-35; S. Neill and T. Wright, *The Interpretation of the New Testament 1861-1986* (2d ed.; New York: Oxford, 1988); E. P. Sanders, *Paul and Palestinian Judaism, A Comparison of Patterns of Religion* (Philadelphia: Fortress, 1977); A. Schweitzer, *Paul and His Interpreters: A Critical History* (London: Adam & Charles Black, repr. 1948, 1912); idem, *The Mysticism of Paul the Apostle* (New York: H. Holt, 1931); K. Stendahl, *Paul Among Jews and Gentiles and Other Essays* (Philadelphia: Fortress, 1976); J. L. Sumney, *Identifying Paul's Opponents: The Question of Method in 2 Corinthians* (JSNTSup 40; Sheffield: Sheffield Academic, 1990); J. M. Gundry Volf, *Paul and Perseverance* (WUNT 2/37; Tübingen: J. C. B. Mohr, 1990); D. V. Way, *The Lordship of Christ: Ernst Käsemann's Interpretation of Paul's Theology* (Oxford: Clarendon, 1991); S. Westerholm, *Israel's Law and the Church's Faith: Paul and His Recent Interpreters* (Grand Rapids: Eerdmans, 1988).

S. J. Hafemann

# PAUL IN ACTS AND LETTERS

1. Sources
2. Paul's Career
3. Paul's Missionary Policy and Message
4. Paul's Abiding Influence

### 1. Sources.

There are two main sources for our knowledge of Paul—his own writings and the Acts of the Apostles. These two sources are apparently wholly independent. Paul's writings display him as a letter writer—he is in fact one of the great letter writers of world literature—whereas Acts says nothing of him in this regard. The majority opinion is that Acts makes no use of his letters, although his authentic letters were all in existence (though not yet collected) when Acts was written.

A subsidiary body of source material includes the contemporary evidence bearing on social, political and religious life in those parts of the Mediterranean world where Paul moved and worked, from Judea to Rome.

*1.1. Paul's Letters.* Paul's letters provide primary evidence for our knowledge of the man himself. Most of them were written to churches* he had planted, dealing with issues that had arisen in them during his absence. They are usually second-best substitutes for his presence and spoken word (*see* Authority). In Galatians 4:20, for example, he expresses the wish that he could be with his readers so that they could gather the intensity of his emotions from the tone of his voice as they could not from his writing. On one occasion, however, he deliberately did not visit the church of Corinth when he could have done so because he could express himself more severely in writing than he could have done in speech: he evidently found it difficult to be severe in the presence of his friends and converts and wanted to spare both them and himself the embarrassment of a face-to-face confrontation (2 Cor 1:23—2:4).

The outstanding exception to the rule that Paul's letters were sent to his own churches is the letter to the Romans (*see* Romans). (The letter to the Colossians is not really an exception: it was sent to a church in Paul's mission field, one founded by his lieutenant

Epaphras.) The letter to the Romans was sent to the Christian community in Rome, when Paul was about to pay his first visit to their city. He wished not only to prepare the Roman Christians for his visit but also to enlist their sympathetic involvement in his further apostolic enterprise, both in his projected evangelization of Spain and in the discharge and continuation of his commission to the Gentile* world at large. The main letters of his apostolic prime—those to the Galatians, Corinthians and Romans, are sometimes called his four "capital" letters; they provide our chief source of information for the content and purpose of his message. The "captivity," or "prison," letters (Philippians, Ephesians, Colossians, Philemon) are so called because he appears to have been undergoing some kind of imprisonment when they were written (*see* Prison, Prisoner). Traditionally, they have been dated during his two years of house arrest in Rome; this is most frequently held to be the case with Philippians, but arguments have been presented for dating Philippians and the other captivity letters during his period of custody in Caesarea (Acts 24:27; *see* Philippians) or during the earlier, not explicitly recorded, imprisonment in Ephesus (*see* Ephesus).

One of the captivity letters, the personal note to Paul's friend Philemon of Colossae (*see* Philemon), interceding for Onesimus, Philemon's slave and now Paul's convert, shares the same life setting as Colossians (see Col 4:9 with the references to Archippus in Philem 2 and Col 4:17). Another, the letter to the Ephesians, is not associated with one particular church: the phrase "in Ephesus" (Eph 1:1), from which the traditional title is derived, is probably not part of the original text (*see* Ephesians). This letter has the character of a testament to Paul's mission field, especially in proconsular Asia, viewing his ministry to the Gentiles as a means to the fulfillment of God's eternal purpose, to unite the universe in Christ (*see* Peace).

The Pastoral Letters (1 and 2 Tim and Tit; *see* Pastoral Letters), of uncertain date, include a number of personal notes (especially 2 Tim), but 1 Timothy and Titus largely resemble early manuals of church order, while 2 Timothy has the nature of a personal testament.

Paul's letters were regularly dictated to amanuenses (the name of one of these, Tertius, has been preserved in Rom 16:22). Paul was accustomed to authenticate them by adding the last sentence or two in his own hand (cf. Gal 6:11). Occasionally, but not usually, this autographic addition included his name (cf. 1 Cor 16:21; Col 4:18; 2 Thess 3:17; also Philem 19).

In the opening salutation Paul frequently associates with himself one or more friends who might be with him at the time of writing; only occasionally, however, does internal evidence suggest that one of these was a responsible joint author, like Silvanus in 1 and 2 Thessalonians or Timothy in Colossians. In 1 and 2 Thessalonians those passages are evidently Paul's where we find the singular pronoun "I" (e.g., "I Paul" in 1 Thess 2:18).

Most of Paul's letters are "occasional documents" in the sense that they were called for by some local need where Paul was not present to deal with the situation firsthand. Only once, to our knowledge, did he deal with a critical situation by letter in preference to on-the-spot action (2 Cor 1:23—2:4). Even Romans is an occasional letter because it was sent in view of Paul's plan to visit Rome as soon as he had completed the delivery of relief money to Jerusalem (Rom 15:23-32; *see* Collection for the Saints), although he took the opportunity to present the Roman Christians with an orderly statement of the gospel* as he understood and preached it (*see* Preaching, Kerygma).

*1.2. Acts of the Apostles.* In the Acts of the Apostles, the second part of Luke's history of Christian origins (the sequel to the Third Gospel), Paul is introduced at an early stage. His call to be Christ's worldwide witness is first related in Acts 9:1-20, and from Acts 15:40 to the end of the book he dominates the narrative, until he arrives in Rome and spends two years there in custody. After the record of Acts ends we have only scanty and uncertain hints about the remainder of his life. If the author of Acts was, as seems most probable, an acquaintance and occasional companion of Paul, then Acts has claims to be recognized as a primary source of information about Paul.

Indeed, a collection of occasional letters written by some figure of history at crucial epochs in his career, will have a value and directness of their own, by giving his personal perspective on persons and events and (in a man who wore his heart on his sleeve, as Paul did) by providing insight into his mind and motives. Such a collection, however, cannot take the place of an orderly account of events in which he played a major part, written from the more objective point of view of a writer who had access to the material from reliable informants and from personal involvement, and set in the context of contemporary history.

*1.3. Comparison of the Letters and Acts.* Although these two main sources for our knowledge are apparently independent of each other, there are impressive parallels between their respective portrayals of Paul.

In both sources Paul supports himself by his own labors so as not to be financially burdensome to his friends and converts (*see* Financial Support). His policy recorded in Acts of visiting the local synagogue first, in place after place to which he comes, is in line with his insistence in Romans 1:16 that the gospel is directed "to the Jew first." Besides, apostle* to the Gentiles as he knew himself to be, he found that the Gentile sympathizers who attended the synagogue services presented the most promising nucleus for a Christian community. Plainly, he did not regard visiting the synagogue to make contact with them a breach of his agreement with the Jerusalem church leaders, by which they were to concentrate on evangelizing Jews and he and Barnabas on the Gentile mission (Gal 2:7-9). In any case, he was not the man to keep silent about Jesus while in Jewish company; he was under a debt to his kinsfolk by race as well as to all others (*see* Israel).

In Acts, Paul is the most adaptable of people. He is equally at home with Gentiles and religiously observant Jews. This is the Paul who in 1 Corinthians 9:19-23 claims to live like a Jew among the Jews, in order to win Jews, and like a Gentile among Gentiles, in order to win Gentiles.

From the point where he assumes a major role in the narrative of Acts, Paul is Luke's hero. He is indeed a man "of like nature" with other human beings (Acts 14:15), but in Luke's portrayal he dominates the situation. He is always sure of himself; he always triumphs. The Paul of the letters includes himself among his fellow Christians when he describes them as "more than conquerors" through Christ (Rom 8:27); but there is little triumphalism in his own account of his apostolic activity (*see* Triumph). He is "led in triumph" in Christ (2 Cor 2:14)—led in Christ's triumphal procession—and he can thank God that by his grace* he has worked harder than any of the others called to the same evangelistic task (1 Cor 15:10), but even when he contemplates with satisfaction his preaching the gospel "from Jerusalem and as far round as Illyricum" (Rom 15:19), he claims no credit for himself but for Christ working through him. In himself he is a cheap, expendable earthenware vessel, but to that vessel the surpassing treasure of the gospel has been entrusted "to show that the transcendent power belongs to God" and not to Paul or any of his fellow preachers (2 Cor 4:7; *see* Power).

If he was a hero to Luke, Paul was no hero in his own eyes. In his letters he is too often the prey of conflicting emotions, "fightings without and fears within" (2 Cor 7:5). He confesses that he has neither the self-assurance nor the self-assertiveness of some of his rivals—of those intruders, for example, who tried to supplant his authority in the church of Corinth. Those intruders may exploit his converts, while

he himself hesitates to claim his rights among them as their spiritual father, and some of them despise him for his "weakness"* (2 Cor 10:1—12:13). At times indeed he did assert his authority, although the reader of his letters may suspect (as some of his converts realized) that he found it easier to do this by letter from a distance than in words spoken face to face. The side of Paul shown in Acts is the side that can readily assert authority, the charismatic person of power. But Paul was a many-sided personality, and his letters expose many other sides than that shown in Acts. The most revealing side disclosed in the letters is probably that which says, "I will all the more gladly boast of my weaknesses, that the power of Christ may rest upon me. For the sake of Christ, then, I am content with weaknesses, insult, hardships, persecutions and calamities; for when I am weak, then I am strong" (2 Cor 12:9-10).

## 2. Paul's Career.

*2.1. Family and Citizenship.* Paul was born into a religiously observant Jewish family of Tarsus in Cilicia, apparently in the first decade of the first century A.D. According to Jerome (*Vir.* 5), his family came from Gischala in Galilee (*see* Jew, Paul the). It traced its descent from the tribe of Benjamin, and Paul was given the name Saul, borne by the most illustrious member of that tribe in history—Saul, the first king of Israel. The name Paul, by which he is commonly called, was part of his triple name as a Roman citizen (*see* Citizenship): it is the Roman cognomen Paullus.

It is not known for how many generations the family had lived in Tarsus, but the family business of tentmaking* (or perhaps, more generally, leatherworking) evidently prospered. Paul was born a citizen of Tarsus—"a citizen of no mean city," in his own words (Acts 21:39)—and this implied a certain level of wealth. The property qualification for Tarsian citizenship was 500 drachmae (Dio Chrysostom *Or.* 34.23). In addition to the wealth requirement, the practice of Judaism must have been a further obstacle in the successful quest for citizenship. If the citizens of Tarsus were organized into tribes, like the citizens of many Hellenistic cities, membership of such a tribe involved practices which Jews would have found offensive; possibly the Jewish citizens of Tarsus were enrolled in a tribe of their own, though there is no positive evidence for this.

But much more important than the family's possession of Tarsian citizenship was its acquisition of Roman citizenship—an honor rarely granted to provincials. Paul inherited Roman citizenship at birth: his father or grandfather may have been so honored for conspicuous services rendered to a military proconsul such as Pompey or Antony. Paul would have been registered as a Roman citizen by his father at the public record office in Tarsus. Roman citizenship carried with it several privileges of which Paul was able to avail himself during his career—the right to a fair trial, for example, exemption from degrading penalties like scourging, and most notably the right to appeal from the jurisdiction of a lower court to that of the emperor of Rome* ( Acts 16:37; 22:25; 25:11).

*2.2. Education at Jerusalem.* Although he was born in a Greek center of culture, it was not in any of the schools of Tarsus that Paul was educated. It was probably at a later stage that he acquired the measure of literary knowledge and Stoic thought (*see* Philosophy) that is attested in his writings and speeches. By his own account he was educated according to his ancestral traditions, surpassing many of his contemporaries in the study and practice of Judaism (Gal 1:14). In his Jerusalem speech of Acts 22:3 he says more precisely that, while born in Tarsus, he was brought up in Jerusalem* and "trained in the school of Gamaliel according to the strict interpretation of our ancestral law."

Gamaliel, a leading Jewish teacher of his day, is said by later tradition to have been head of the rabbinical school founded by Hillel, c. 10 B.C., if not indeed a member of Hillel's family. But the earliest traditions which reflect some direct memory of Gamaliel and his teaching do not associate him with the school of Hillel; they speak rather of others as belonging to the school of Gamaliel, as though he founded a school of his own. Even if Gamaliel was a follower of Hillel, however, it would not follow that Paul was a Hillelite. Paul's writings do not yield sufficient evidence to show certainty whether, before he became a Christian, he was a Hillelite or an adherent of the rival school of Shammai. His statement that anyone who submits to circumcision* "is bound to keep the whole Law*" (Gal 5:3) might be thought to reflect the stricter Shammaite doctrine, but such a conclusion cannot safely be drawn from a statement made in a polemical context. His zeal as a persecutor of the church presents a sharp contrast to the temporizing policy advocated by Gamaliel in Acts 5:34-39, but the explanation may simply be that Paul saw more clearly than Gamaliel the serious implications of the Christian movement for the life and health of Judaism.

*2.3. Persecutor of the Church.* According to his letters and to Acts, Paul was an active persecutor of the church before he became a Christian. He assaulted the infant church with the utmost violence in his attempt to destroy it (Gal 1:13). This was the negative aspect of his zeal for the Law and traditions of Israel,

which perhaps found a positive outlet in the proselytization of Gentiles. His words, "If I . . . still preach circumcision, why am I still persecuted?" (Gal 5:11), have been thought to point in that direction.

When he says that he "persecuted the church of God" (1 Cor 15:9), it is natural to think primarily of the Jerusalem* church. The "church of God" would hardly have been found as a recognizable body anywhere else than in Jerusalem in the first two or three years after the resurrection of Christ. This is plainly attested by the record of Acts, which describes him as "entering into houses, dragging out men and women and committing them to prison" (Acts 8:3), and, when the persecution led to dispersal, harrying the refugees even beyond the frontiers of the province of Judea. Reading between the lines, one can infer that "Hellenists" (*see* Hellenism) rather than "Hebrews" (cf. Acts 6:1) were the principal targets for this attack. The apostles remained unscathed in Jerusalem (Acts 8:2).

*2.4. Call to Apostleship.* It was while Paul was on his way to Damascus, armed with the high priest's commission, to round up some who had sought refuge from the persecution there, that he was confronted by the risen and exalted Christ,* turned right around in his tracks and called to be Christ's ambassador to the Gentile world (*see* Conversion and Call of Paul). This personal encounter with Christ determined the whole course of Paul's subsequent thought and action.

Until that moment Paul had taken it as axiomatic that one who had died the death (*see* Crucifixion) on which the divine curse* was pronounced by the Law (Deut 21:23) could not be the Messiah, the elect one of God,* as his followers claimed. Their claim was blasphemous. But now their claim was manifestly true. He had seen and heard Jesus, the crucified one, alive and glorified (*see* Glory, Glorification). But it was his devotion to the Law that had made him such a zealous persecutor—that is, as he now realized, his devotion to the Law had led him into the most sinful course of all: he had been fighting against God, his Son (*see* Son of God) and his people. The Law had done nothing to show him the sinfulness of his course. The Law had proved itself bankrupt. But Christ, whose grace wiped out his guilt and empowered him to be his special envoy, displaced the Law's former centrality in Paul's life. For him, henceforth, "to live was Christ" (Phil 1:21). It was then that Paul first knew himself to be set right with God through the redemptive act of Christ and not through his own works of righteousness (*see* Works of the Law). The very death which incurred the curse of God turned out to be the deliverance of the people of Christ from the curse of a broken Law (Gal 3:10-14).

*2.5. Apostle to the Gentiles.* Paul quickly responded to his call to evangelize the Gentiles by traveling to the nearby territory of the Nabatean Arabs, where his activity seems to have aroused the hostility of the authorities (Gal 1:17; 2 Cor 11:32-33). From there he returned to Damascus and then went up to Jerusalem to visit Peter.* He also met James,* the Lord's brother, all the other apostles being evidently absent from Jerusalem. It was doubtless during this visit that Paul learned how Jesus had appeared in resurrection* to Peter and James, as he records in 1 Corinthians 15:5, 7. They in turn would hear how he himself had met the risen one.

After two weeks he returned to his native Tarsus and spent several years in the united province of Syria and Cilicia, actively propagating the faith he had once endeavored to root out (Gal 1:21-24). While he was thus engaged, he was invited by Barnabas* to join him in directing the new forward movement which had recently been launched in Antioch* on the Orontes, where Gentiles in large numbers were making a positive response to the gospel (Acts 11:19-26).

Paul claimed to be an "apostle* of Jesus Christ"; where necessary, he insisted on this designation. But in what sense was he an apostle? The term is used in a variety of ways in the New Testament: Luke, for his part, generally confines it to the Twelve (with Matthias replacing Judas Iscariot). If a qualification for apostleship was to have remained in Jesus' company throughout his public ministry (Acts 1:21-22), then Paul did not satisfy that qualification. In one section of his narrative (Acts 14:4, 14) Luke uses the plural "apostles" of Barnabas and Paul together; this usage may have been taken over from his source at this point. Otherwise, he does not call Paul an apostle. Paul may very well have recognized Barnabas as an apostle. By "those who were apostles before me" (Gal 1:17) he probably means the Twelve; but he almost certainly looks on James, the Lord's brother, as an apostle (Gal 1:19), together with "all the apostles" who saw the risen Lord in sequence from James (1 Cor 15:7) and who seem to be distinct from the Twelve, mentioned along with Peter in 1 Corinthians 15:5. When he speaks of Andronicus and Junia, whose faith in Christ antedated his own, as "of note among the apostles" (Rom 16:7), he probably means that they were apostles themselves. (The "apostles," or envoys of the churches, mentioned in 2 Cor 8:23, are in quite another category.)

If to be an apostle is to have seen the risen Lord and to have been called and commissioned by him to be his witness and messenger, then Paul was preeminently an apostle of Jesus Christ, accredited as such by the apostolic "signs" which attended his ministry (1 Cor 9:1-2; 2 Cor 12:12). Paul was called and commissioned to be an apostle to the Gentiles (Rom 11:13; Gal 1:16), and his Gentile apostolate appears to have been acknowledged by the leader of the Jerusalem church (Gal 2:7-8). But there was no other witness at hand when the Lord commissioned him. Anyone who refused to recognize this apostleship could appeal to the absence of independent testimony.

Paul could produce nothing like the credentials of the Twelve. His credentials were the converts he had won and the churches he had planted—more than adequate credentials, in all conscience. He had worked harder and preached more extensively than any of those who had seen the risen Christ before he did; he had planted churches more widely and observed the harvest of the Spirit growing in the lives of those who had turned to Christ through his ministry. It is almost incredible that intruders should invade his own mission field and try to persuade his converts that his apostolic standing was questionable, and that they should even find some to lend them an ear. In such situations Paul's argument was practical: his converts were the last people who could question his apostleship, for they owed their new existence in Christ to his apostolic ministry—they were its seal and guarantee (1 Cor 9:2). But what is important is not the title he held but the work he did. In the light of his achievement Paul can safely rest his case before the bar of history—not to speak of a more august bar which he kept constantly in view, as he set himself to discharge his commission in such a way that the day of Christ would reveal that he had "neither run in vain nor labored in vain" (Phil 2:16).

*2.6. Conference at Jerusalem.* The church of Antioch, a mainly Gentile church, was not long in being established. Its members showed their quality by sending a sum of money to the mother church in Jerusalem to help it at a time of food scarcity in Judea, appointing Barnabas and Paul to convey the gift (Acts 11:27-30). This may have provided an occasion for the conference described by Paul in Galatians 2:1-10 (*see* Jerusalem). Barnabas and Paul were received by the leaders of the Jerusalem church, James (the Lord's brother), Peter and John, the three so-called pillars. It was agreed that Barnabas and Paul should continue to concentrate on the Gentile mission, while the Jerusalem leaders would devote themselves to gospel witness among Jews. It is not implied that two different versions of the gospel were involved: Paul laid his Law-free gospel before the Jerusalem leaders, and they evidently found it acceptable. The difference lay rather in the two mission fields and in the presentation of the message. The agreement concealed several ambiguities, and these might lead to tension if full confidence were not maintained between the two sides. At the request of the Jerusalem leaders, Barnabas and Paul undertook to remember the poor (*see* Riches and Poverty) in the mother church—an undertaking which Paul took very seriously.

*2.7. With Barnabas in Cyprus and Anatolia.* On returning to Antioch, Barnabas and Paul were released by the church there to embark on a missionary campaign which took them to Cyprus and then to central Anatolia—to the Pisidian, Phrygian and Lycaonian regions of the Roman province of Galatia. The churches planted in the course of this mission in the cities of Pisidian Antioch, Iconium, Lystra and Derbe are probably among the "churches of Galatia" addressed in Paul's letter to the Galatians.

The historicity of this campaign has been questioned: it has been interpreted as a "model journey," setting forth the way in which Luke conceived that a missionary campaign should be conducted, including the way in which the gospel should be presented both to a synagogue congregation, as in Paul's address at Pisidian Antioch (Acts 13:16-41), and to a pagan audience, as in Barnabas and Paul's confronting the idolatrous Lystrans with the revelation of the true God in his works of creation and providence (Acts 14:15-17). But the details of the journey, when examined in the light of historical geography, make a strong impression of factual truth. There is, moreover, a marked similarity between the missionaries' remonstrance against idolatry at Lystra and Paul's reminder to the Thessalonian Christians of how they had "turned to God from idols to serve a living and true God" (1 Thess 1:9; *see* Idolatry).

*2.8. Terms of Gentile Admission to the Church.* When Barnabas and Paul returned to Antioch on the Orontes, they found themselves before long involved in controversy. The agreement recently concluded at Jerusalem was perhaps understood differently by the two parties. Paul apparently soon began to feel that its spirit was not being observed by the Jerusalem leaders. There was a clash between him and Peter at Antioch, when Peter was spending some time with the church there. To begin with, Peter ate quite freely with the Gentile Christians, but some messengers from James in Jerusalem persuaded him to change his ways and withdraw from table fellowship with Gentiles. In Paul's eyes the implications of Peter's conduct threatened the foundations of the gospel of grace. But other Jewish Christians in Antioch, including even Barnabas, sided with Peter, and Antioch could no longer provide Paul with a base for his missionary activity.

A disagreement on this scale, affecting the unity of the church and indeed the very nature of the gospel, could not be left unresolved: Peter himself, we may be sure, was not happy with the embarrassing situation in which he was placed. A meeting of the Jerusalem apostles and elders, commonly called the Council of Jerusalem, was convened to consider the issue, and observers from the church of Antioch were invited to attend. Those members of the Jerusalem church who maintained that Gentile converts should be circumcised and submit to Mosaic Law were given an opportunity to express their views, but the apostles and elders resolved that no such conditions should be imposed—that Gentile Christians should simply be required to abstain from eating blood or the flesh of animals sacrificed to pagan divinities (*see* Food), and from fornication, including perhaps marital unions within bounds forbidden by Jewish rules (Acts 15:23-29). If Gentile Christians agreed to those terms, the barrier to table fellowship would be removed; and most of them agreed very readily.

Peter must certainly have welcomed this resolution of the dilemma. When Paul, however, was later consulted by his converts at Corinth about the eating of meat sacrificed to idols, he replied that eating such meat was harmless unless it violated one's own conscience* or scandalized a fellow Christian. As for the ban on fornication, Paul agreed that fornication (*see* Sexuality) contravened the order of creation and frustrated the purpose of God in creating the human race male and female (*see* Man and Woman).

*2.9. In Macedonia and Achaia.* One of the messengers chosen by the Jerusalem church to convey the findings of the Council to the Gentile churches of Syria and Cilicia was Silas or Silvanus, in whom Paul found a congenial companion. He invited him to join him in a missionary expedition to the west. Traveling by land through Asia Minor, they first visited the churches which Paul and Barnabas had planted a few years earlier. At Lystra Paul found Timothy, a young convert of his, whom he invited to accompany him; Timothy became his devoted and lifelong lieutenant (*see* Coworkers). Their westward journey would have taken them to Ephesus, which may have been Paul's goal, but they were diverted from this course in circumstances which they recognized to be tokens of the Holy Spirit's (*see* Holy Spirit) guidance, and proceeded in a northwest direction until they reached the Aegean Sea at Alexandria Troas. There they took ship for Neapolis in Macedonia.

In Macedonia they preached the gospel and planted churches in three cities, Philippi, Thessalonica and Berea; but after a short stay in each they were forced to leave when riotous demonstrations had been stirred up against them—in Philippi because of their alleged interference with citizens' property rights and in the other cities through the activity of opponents within the Jewish community.

Philippi (*see* Philippians) and Thessalonica (*see* Thessalonians) stood on the great Egnatian Way, linking the Aegean with the Adriatic; and Paul may have thought of going on to its western terminus and crossing over to Italy. This would have been one of the many occasions when he planned to visit Rome (as he tells the Roman Christians in Rom 1:13). If so, his inability to continue farther west was providentially ordered, for had he gone on he would have met Jews (including Jewish Christians) traveling east because of Claudius's expulsion edict of A.D. 49 (see Acts 18:2). As it was, Paul had to turn off the Egnatian Way, and soon found himself compelled to leave Macedonia altogether. He was taken away from Berea for his own safety by his friends in that city and, after a short stay in Athens, proceeded to Corinth.

Paul's brief mission in Macedonia proved in fact to have been amazingly successful; the churches of Macedonia gave him much cause for encouragement and thanksgiving. But at the time the Macedonian venture must have seemed a failure, in spite of the clear signs of divine guidance which led him and his colleagues to undertake it. He left Macedonia in deep depression and arrived in Corinth, as he confessed, "in weakness and fear and much trembling" (1 Cor 2:3). If Macedonia had shown itself so unwelcoming, Corinth would surely be more so: its public reputation promised no receptive soil for the gospel seed. But nevertheless Paul was able to spend eighteen months in Corinth, preaching the gospel and building up the church, with no serious molestation (*see* Corinthians).

Here Paul met Priscilla and Aquila, a married couple who had left Rome when Claudius expelled the Jews of the city. In them he found helpful and devoted friends for life (cf. Rom 16:3-5).

One serious attempt was made to put an end to Paul's activity during his Corinthian ministry. Some Jewish leader in the city charged him before Gallio, lately arrived as proconsul of the province of Achaia, of propagating a form of religion not authorized by Roman law. A decision by so authoritative an imperial officer would have much greater weight than a ruling by a city magistrate. Had Gallio sustained the charge, the progress of the gospel would have been impeded not only in Achaia but elsewhere throughout the empire. Having heard the charge, however, he concluded that it involved a dispute about interpretations of the Jewish Law and refused to take it up. Negative

as Gallio's action was, it worked to Paul's advantage: he continued his work unhindered.

The mention of Gallio in Acts 18:12 provides a fixed point for the chronology of Paul's career. An inscription at Delphi, recording a directive issued by Claudius within the first seven months of A.D. 52, refers to Gallio as recently proconsul of Achaia. The implication is that he became proconsul in the early summer of 51. We know from other sources that because of poor health he did not remain in the office long. Paul's eighteen-month stay in Corinth may safely be dated between the fall of 50 and the spring of 52.

By the time the work in Corinth was finished, Paul had left behind a large and gifted Christian community, although there were times in the following years when he had to regret its deficiency in moral ballast.

*2.10. In Ephesus and Proconsular Asia.* Paul's next base of operations was the city of Ephesus, in the province of Asia, where he settled for the greater part of three years (*see* Ephesus). Those years mark one of the most fruitful phases of his whole apostolic ministry. The evangelization of the province was accomplished through the activity of Paul and several of his colleagues. One of these, Epaphras, served as the evangelist of the Lycus valley, where his labors resulted in the founding of churches in Hierapolis, Laodicea and Colossae (Col 1:7-8; 4:12-13).

The work was not accomplished without hazards; some of these are recorded by Luke, and others are alluded to by Paul himself. They may have included one or two of the frequent imprisonments which he mentions in 2 Corinthians 11:23. It is doubtful, however, if any of his prison letters is to be dated during an Ephesian imprisonment. Luke describes in graphic detail the riotous demonstration against Paul and his preaching in the great theater of Ephesus (Acts 19:19-41). Paul's activity was perceived as an economic threat to those tradesmen who depended for their livelihood on the cult of Artemis, the great goddess of the city whose temple was one of the seven wonders of the ancient world. But the greatest personal danger which he encountered in those years, toward the end of his Ephesian ministry, is referred to by Paul himself in 2 Corinthians 1:8-10. He speaks of a situation so threatening that death seemed inevitable, and when, against all odds, deliverance finally came, he greeted it as a token of God's power to raise the dead. It has been argued that this perilous occasion was connected with the crisis resulting from the assassination of M. Junius Silanus, in the latter part of A.D. 54. The situation was probably so unfavorable for Paul that an appeal to Caesar, the course which normally lay open to a Roman citizen, would have been counterproductive.

It was almost certainly this experience that brought home to him the likelihood that he would not survive to witness the Lord's Parousia (*see* Eschatology). In earlier references to the Parousia and the attendant resurrection* he tends to include himself among those who would still be alive then; from now on he tends to include himself rather among those who will be raised from the dead. For the first time, so far as the evidence goes, he considers seriously what his condition will be immediately after death (*see* Intermediate State): his conclusion, as set out in 2 Corinthians 5:1-10, is that he will not remain in a state of "nakedness" for one moment; he will be "clothed upon" forthwith with the housing even now reserved for him in heaven. By "nakedness" he means the lack of all means of communication with the environment, and for Paul the believer's environment immediately after death is summed up in the words "at home with the Lord" (2 Cor 5:8).

Some Pauline students, notably C. H. Dodd, have envisaged what they describe as Paul's "second conversion" around this time. This is not simply a matter of the shift in eschatological perspective just mentioned: Dodd draws attention to a change of temper in the later letters. Paul is less sharp in his polemic, less insistent on his status, more relaxed in his attitude toward those fellow Christians who tried to make his apostolic task more difficult than it need be. The contrast has often been pointed out between Paul's unrestrained denunciation of the intruders in the churches of Galatia (Gal 1:6-9; 5:10, 12) and his charitable reference to those Christian opponents (in Rome, possibly) who thought they could rub salt into his wounds by taking advantage of his imprisonment to preach the gospel the more energetically (Phil 1:15-18). True, the difference in the two situations must not be overlooked, but the change of temper is unmistakable. Whether the change was gradual, or precipitated by some crisis like that described in 2 Corinthians 1:8, cannot be said with confidence. But a passage like Philippians 3:7-16 helps us to "see most clearly what experience had made of this naturally proud, self-assertive, and impatient man" (Dodd, 81).

Another experience which profoundly influenced Paul's attitude to life was one which he dates several years before this, although it is only now—at the end of his Ephesian ministry—that he records it (2 Cor 12:2-10). A mystical experience left him with a physical disability, which he calls a "thorn in the flesh" (*see* Visions, Ecstatic Experience). Whatever its precise nature was, it evidently threatened to incapacitate him from continuing his apostolic activity, and he prayed three times that it might be taken away. Instead of

having his prayer answered, he received the assurance that the grace of Christ would enable him to live with it; in fact, he learned to rejoice in it because it helped him to be more completely reliant on the power* of Christ at work in his weakness.*

*2.11. The Collection for Jerusalem.* Toward the end of his Ephesian ministry Paul was busily engaged in organizing in the churches he had planted east and west of the Aegean a collection for the relief of the chronic poverty of the Jerusalem church (*see* Collection for the Saints). On the occasion when he and Barnabas met James, Peter and John in Jerusalem, those three "pillars" urged on them that they should "remember the poor" in the mother church (Gal 2:10). Paul treated this as a solemn obligation both then and subsequently throughout his ministry. As for this special collection, one impelling force behind it was his strong desire to bind the Gentile churches and the Jerusalem church more closely together. The Gentile churches probably imagined that they could get along quite well without Jerusalem, and many members of the Jerusalem church looked with serious misgivings on Paul's preaching of a Law-free gospel and on the Gentile churches founded on the basis of that preaching. If a bond of gratitude, confidence and love* could be forged between Jerusalem and the churches of his own mission field, Paul would feel that his ministry had been truly worthwhile. A generous gift would persuade the mother church that the Gentile's commitment to the gospel was genuine and practical. So he urged his converts by letter and, where practicable, by personal visits to give as generously as possible to this good cause. He also encouraged a spirit of competition when, for example, he depicted the Macedonian churches' sacrificial generosity in glowing terms to the Corinthians, and praised the Corinthians' prompt response to the Macedonians.

In Paul's eyes, moreover, the delivery of the collection in Jerusalem would be the climax of his apostolic service thus far, the visible sign of that "offering of the Gentiles" which he planned to present to God in Jerusalem as the crown of his "priestly service" (Rom 15:16). He hoped to consummate his thanksgiving for the past and his dedication for the future by an act of worship* in the Temple, where the Lord had appeared to him many years before and sent him "far away to the Gentiles" (Acts 22:21).

*2.12. Arrest in Jerusalem; Trial in Caesarea; Journey to Rome.* After his long and fruitful ministry in the province of Asia Paul revisited the churches of Macedonia and Achaia. He and some of his colleagues, especially Titus, helped them to complete their contributions to the collection. It was probably at this time, too, that he traveled west along the Egnatian Way and turned north in the direction of Illyricum (Rom 15:19).

After spending the winter of 56-57 in Corinth he set sail for Judea in company with representatives of the Gentile churches appointed to carry their churches' contributions to Jerusalem. The presence of these men, Paul hoped, would be a further witness to the Jerusalem church of the divine blessing on his Gentile mission. But Paul's final visit to Jerusalem turned out disastrously. In the Temple precincts he was set upon by some of his old enemies from proconsular Asia who accused him of sacrilege (polluting the sacred area by bringing Gentiles into it). He was taken into custody by the commander of the Roman garrison in the Antonia fortress and sent to Caesarea to stand trial before the procurator Felix. After two years' procrastination on the part of his detainers, he exercised the privilege of a Roman citizen and appealed to have his case transferred to the hearing of the emperor in Rome (see Emperors), and was sent there to have his appeal dealt with. After two years under house arrest in Rome, he was summoned to appear before the supreme court when at last his case came up for hearing. What the outcome was cannot be determined with certainty. The record of Acts comes to an end just before the hearing. Paul's letter to the Philippians, written apparently when court proceedings were imminent, shows that he was equally prepared for a favorable or unfavorable outcome—acquittal (followed by liberty for further ministry) or conviction (followed by execution)—although he thought it more probable that he would be acquitted.

That he was in fact acquitted and eventually realized his hope of preaching the gospel in Spain is assumed or implied by several writers from Clement of Rome onward (Clement does not actually mention Spain, but it is difficult to see what else he could have meant by "the limit of the west" which, in *1 Clement* 5.7, he says that Paul reached before he was "taken up into the holy place"). But it is not clear that any of these had firm evidence for this belief, other than an inference from Romans 15:23-29, where Paul speaks of his plan, after the delivery of the Jerusalem relief fund, to begin the evangelization of Spain and to visit Rome on the way.

There is a tradition (accepted by Eusebius and Jerome) that after being acquitted when his appeal was heard, Paul was arrested again and subjected to the more rigorous imprisonment and trial in Rome to which reference is made in 2 Timothy 1:16-18; 4:16-18. There was no acquittal this time; he was convicted and beheaded with the sword at the third milestone on the Ostian Way, at a place called Aquae Salviae,

and buried on the site covered by the basilica of St. Paul Outside the Walls—a probably authentic location. These last proceedings against him may well have been an incident in Nero's proceedings against Christians about A.D. 65.

**Chronological Table.**

| | |
|---|---|
| c. 33 | Call to apostleship; mission in Arabia (Gal 1:15-17) |
| 35 | Short visit to Jerusalem (Gal 1:18-20) |
| 35-45 | In Cilicia, Syria, Antioch |
| 46 | Conference with "pillars" in Jerusalem (Gal 2:1-10); famine relief delivered from Antioch (Acts 11:27-30) |
| 47-48 | Paul and Barnabas in Cyprus and Anatolia (Acts 13:4—14:28) |
| 48/49 | Council of Jerusalem; apostolic decree (Acts 15:6-29) |
| 49-51/52 | Paul and Silas/Silvanus in Macedonia and Achaia; churches of Philippi, Thessalonica, Berea and Corinth planted (Acts 16:9—18:18) |
| 51/52 | Paul's hasty visit to Jerusalem, Antioch and Anatolia |
| 52-55 | Paul in Ephesus (Acts 19:1—20:1) |
| 55-57 | Paul in Macedonia, Illyricum and Corinth (Rom 15:19; 16:23) |
| 57 | Last visit to Jerusalem; arrest and loss of liberty (Acts 21:17—23:35) |
| 57-59 | Imprisonment in Caesarea (Acts 23:35—26:32) |
| 59-60 | Journey to Italy (Acts 27:1—28:15) |
| 60-62 | House arrest in Rome (Acts 28:16-31) |
| ? 62 | Paul's hearing before Caesar |
| 64 | Great fire of Rome |
| ? 65 | Death of Paul |

### 3. Paul's Missionary Policy and Message.

Paul's missionary policy (see Mission) was to win as much of the Gentile world for Christ as was possible within his lifetime, and when it began to be evident that the task would not be completed within his lifetime he tried—not without success, it appears—to bring the Christian community of Rome to share his vision (see Romans).

*3.1. The Mission of the Apostle.* The carrying out of this policy did not require the presentation of the gospel to every individual in the areas which he evangelized; it did require the planting of local churches to serve as self-propagating cells in those areas (see Church). His plan involved pioneer evangelism, preaching the gospel, as he said, "not where Christ has already been named" (Rom 15:20-21), but laying the foundation himself.

A combination of strategic planning and responsiveness to divine guidance was called for. The whole enterprise was undertaken "by the power of the Holy Spirit" (Rom 15:19), and the Spirit's guidance was experienced at special junctures, as when his steps were diverted from the westward road to Ephesus and directed toward Troas and so to Macedonia (Acts 16:6-10). Paul may have discerned the Spirit's overruling, too, in the repeated obstacles placed in the way of his plan to visit Rome up to the time of his writing to the church of that city (Rom 1:13; 15:22). On the other hand, he discerned supernatural interference from a different source at times: "Satan* hindered us" is his explanation of the factors which prevented him from returning to Thessalonica after his forced and hasty departure from it (1 Thess 2:18).

When he wrote to the Roman Christians, he regarded his work east and west of the Aegean as completed: "I no longer have any room for work in these regions" (Rom 15:23).

His achievement during those years, as "from Jerusalem and as far round as Illyricum" he "fully preached the gospel of Christ" (Rom 15:19), is impressive on any showing. As R. Allen has put it, in A.D. 47 there were no churches in the provinces of Galatia, Asia, Macedonia and Achaia. Now, ten years later, these four provinces had been evangelized so thoroughly that Paul could speak of his work in that part of the world as done, and he was planning to repeat a similar program in the Western Mediterranean.

Paul's evangelistic work was thus extensive rather than intensive. He concentrated on the principal cities situated along the main roads, assisted at times by colleagues working either in those cities or in neighboring ones. During his Ephesian ministry, for example, his colleagues worked in outlying parts of the province of Asia (like Epaphras in the Lycus valley), while he himself was active in Ephesus, so that "all the residents of (proconsular) Asia heard the word of the Lord, both Jews and Greeks" (Acts 19:10).

*3.2. The Mission of the Churches.* The local churches planted by Paul throughout these provinces may have preserved some family likeness to the synagogue although, being based on a Law-free gospel, they were separate from the synagogue. In some measure they resembled other private associations for religious or charitable purposes, attested in various parts of the Hellenistic world (*see* Social Setting). But Paul maintained a continuing pastoral care for them, for his aim was that each church should be an extension of his apostolic ministry. Once he had established a church and given it basic teaching, his hope was that he could pass on to another place in the confidence that it would take up his gospel witness and spread the message. Thus, only a few weeks after he left Thessalonica, he could praise the young church he had left behind there because, as he said, "not only has the

word of the Lord* sounded forth from you in Macedonia and Achaia, but your faith in God has gone forth everywhere" (1 Thess 1:8).

Such a church was not encouraged to think of itself as "a garden walled around," mainly concerned to prevent any encroachment by the surrounding wilderness; rather, it was its business to take over more and more of the surrounding wilderness.

The Roman world had to be evangelized as soon as possible. The time was limited. Paul knew himself to be the Lord's special agent in the enterprise. His was not the only mission to the Gentiles, but he "worked harder than any of them" (1 Cor 15:10). He might not live to finish the task, but he would do as much as he could while he could, planting one "colony of heaven" (Phil 3:20) after another, so that in every area within the apostolic sphere allotted to him Christ might be represented, proclaimed and glorified. The churches were to "shine as lights in the world" (Phil 2:15); thus an ever-increasing number of people would come to see "the light of the gospel of the glory of Christ" (2 Cor 4:4).

*3.3. Apostolic Authority and the Churches.* The Pauline churches do not appear to have been linked together in any formal or visible organization (*see* Church Order). Paul was their founding apostle, and it was through his apostolic authority that the authority of Christ, the Lord of all the churches, was conveyed to them and accepted by them. But the one example of anything that could be called organization among Paul's churches is his organizing of the relief fund for the poor of the Jerusalem church (1 Cor 16:1-4, etc.). The care and practical wisdom which are so manifest in the organization of the relief might have been exercised in organizing the life and administration of individual churches, or of groups of churches. But Paul evidently was little concerned about this kind of organization. He was concerned, indeed, that in each of his churches there should be some members who were qualified to provide spiritual guidance for the others. He preferred to let such an aptitude develop and become apparent in the course of time (weeks or months rather than years). And if he thought that a church was slow in recognizing the qualities of leadership in this person or that, he would draw attention to them. The church of Corinth is urged, for example, to take note of the household of Stephanus, who "have devoted themselves to the service of the saints," and to "be subject to such people and to every fellow worker and laborer" (1 Cor 16:15-16).

The Corinthian Christians were perhaps impatient of anything in the nature of authority.* In the church of Philippi, on the other hand, an orderly administration of "overseers (bishops) and deacons" was established within ten or twelve years from its foundation (Phil 1:1). But even in writing to the Philippian church Paul can recommend a man like Epaphroditus as specially worthy of honor because of his self-sacrificing devotion to the work of Christ (Phil 2:29-30).

The Pauline churches tended naturally to have features in common, but no attempt was made to impose conformity by regulation. Paul deprecated one of his churches for stepping completely out of line with the others; but if it insisted on doing so, all he could say was, "If any one is disposed to be contentious, we recognize no other practice, nor do the churches of God" (1 Cor 11:16)—in other words, if there are those who are determined to be out of step, let them recognize that that is what they are.

Individual members might in an extreme case be excommunicated from the local fellowship (*see* Discipline), like the incestuous man at Corinth whose public life subverted the ethics of the gospel and brought the Christian name into disrepute in a permissive pagan city—though even so this drastic measure was designed for his ultimate salvation (1 Cor 5:5). But there was no means of unchurching a church—not that Paul would have contemplated such a self-defeating thing as the disowning of a group of his own spiritual children, the "seal" of his "apostleship in the Lord" (1 Cor 4:14-16; 9:2).

In all these things, discipline, administration and others, the presence and directive power of the Holy Spirit* were so real to Paul that he implies them even where he does not explicitly mention them. If he did not trust his converts, corporately or individually, to advance along the lines he laid down for them, his "ways in Christ" (1 Cor 4:17), he trusted the Holy Spirit to work in his converts.

The Pauline communities were thus equipped to carry on his ministry in the world. They were not debarred by food restrictions or the observance of sacred days from sharing meals or other forms of social fellowship with their pagan neighbors (1 Cor 10:27-30; *see* Food). Only unambiguous idolatry or sexual immorality were barred. Not by segregation but by participation could they most effectively shine among their neighbors "as lights in the world, holding forth the word of life" (Phil 2:15-16).

*3.4. Baptism and the Lord's Supper.* Baptism* and the Lord's Supper (*see* Lord's Supper) were two primitive institutions in the church which Paul "received" from those who were in Christ before him and which he perpetuated in the churches of his own founding.

Baptism was initiatory. It might have been inferred from Jesus' words to the apostles, "John baptized with

water, but . . . you shall be baptized with the Holy Spirit" (Acts 1:5; 11:16), that baptism in water would be superseded by baptism in the Spirit; but in fact it turned out otherwise. Baptism in water acquired a new significance from its association with the gift of the Spirit. "In one Spirit," Paul reminds his Corinthian converts, "we were all baptized into one body, . . . and we were all watered (*epotisthēmen*) with one Spirit" (1 Cor 12:13). Baptism is no individual experience: "All of us who have been baptized into Christ Jesus were baptized into his death, . . . so that . . . we too might walk in newness of life" (Rom 6:3-4); "as many of you as were baptized into Christ have put on Christ; . . . for you are all one in Christ Jesus" (Gal 3:27-28). To be baptized in the Christian sense involves becoming a member of Christ corporate—through the Spirit sharing the life of the exalted Christ together with all others who are united with him by faith.*

Paul might not have left us his understanding of the Lord's Supper if his converts, more particularly in Corinth, had not conducted themselves at times in such a way as to give the lie to its significance. It was a meal in which they celebrated from time to time their fellowship with Christ and with one another. But those members of the church who ostensibly participated in Christ at "the table of the Lord" and also felt free to share a meal in a pagan temple, under the patronage of the divinity worshipped there, effectively denied their Christian profession (1 Cor 10:14-22). So too, those who ostensibly celebrated their fellowship with their brothers and sisters in Christ at the common memorial meal but acted uncharitably or inconsiderately toward some of them, especially the poorer or underprivileged, were "guilty of profaning the body and blood of the Lord" and brought judgment, not blessing, on themselves by their eating and drinking (1 Cor 11:17-32).

Neither baptism nor the Lord's Supper serves as a supernatural prophylactic against divine judgment,* somehow counteracting the law of sowing and reaping. They signify and seal God's pardoning grace, with its ethical implications in believers' lives; those who think that they stand firm must therefore take heed lest they fall (1 Cor 10:11).

**4. Paul's Abiding Influence.**

*4.1. In the Early Centuries.* Paul was venerated as a saint, apostle and martyr throughout most of the church after his death. There were indeed some judaizing traditions which execrated his memory—those, for example, whose influence can be traced in the pseudo-Clementine literature of the third and fourth centuries—but they did not affect the main stream of

Christian thought (*see* Paul in Early Church Tradition).

The Roman church laid a special claim to him because it was in Rome that he spent his closing days and consummated his apostolic career in martyrdom. His funerary monument on the Ostian Way was pointed out with some pride by Roman Christians toward the end of the second century as though it enhanced the apostolic authority of their church. Indeed, Paul was accorded the honor of being joint-founder, along with Peter, of the Roman church—an honor which Paul himself would have deprecated. And nearly all the churches with which he is associated in the NT record made the most of that association (only in Ephesus did his name tend to be overshadowed by that of "John, the disciple of the Lord").

But while Paul's memory was revered, his message was to a large degree simply not comprehended. To know oneself to be freely justified by the grace of God and to rejoice in the liberty of the Spirit were experiences enjoyed by all too few Christians in the post-Pauline generations. Ignatius of Antioch did not enjoy them, as he hoped that his final acceptance with God would be secure when his bones were crunched by the teeth of the wild beasts. On his more pedestrian level Hermas did not enjoy them, as he anxiously feared that by some misdemeanor or other he might have irretrievably forfeited the divine forgiveness.

Paul's Law-free gospel does not readily commend itself to many religious people who prefer to direct their lives, and the lives of others, by rules and regulations. So he was domesticated: the apostle who spoke so "dangerously" (as some thought) of freedom from the Law was transformed into a moralist, not to say a legalist. Until the end of the second century the one man known to us who understood what Paul meant by freedom from the Law was Marcion—and, in Harnack's words, "even in his understanding he misunderstood him" (*History of Dogma* I [London, 1894], 89). Marcion's heresy consisted largely in his pressing Paul's antithesis between grace and Law to what he judged to be its logical conclusion, to the point where the OT, together with the God revealed in the OT, was dismissed as irrelevant to the gospel of Christ, the revealer of the hitherto unknown Father. Because of his heresy, Marcion was unable to transmit his insight into Paul's message to the Christian world: Marcion's teaching was repudiated *in toto*.

Marcion refused to undergird the ethics of the gospel with legal sanctions. When Christian moralists like Tertullian, writing a couple of generations after Marcion's death, asked rhetorically why Christians might not, in the absence of such sanctions, abandon themselves to an extravaganza of sin, Marcion's only answer was "God forbid!" (*absit*)—an answer on which Tertullian poured scorn (*Marc.* 1.27). It is plain that here Marcion was echoing Paul's indignant question, "Are we to sin because we are not under Law but under grace?" and reacting with the Pauline answer "God forbid!" (Rom 6:15). Perhaps Tertullian knew this quite well but could not resist the temptation to score a debating point. Even so, his argument invited the retort: "And is *your* only reason for abstaining from sin your fear of wrath to come?"

It was through the experience and thought of Augustine that an appreciation of Paul's gospel of grace revived in the church. When Augustine, in his friend's garden at Milan, heard a child singing "*Tolle, lege!*" ("Take up and read!"), it is no accident that it was words of Paul (Rom 13:13-14) that his eyes lighted on, flooding his soul with clear light and dispelling the darkness of doubt (A.D. 386). Others had written about the grace of God before Augustine, but none so fully and systematically and none in such depth. Augustine knew himself, as Paul did, to be the undeserving recipient of divine grace. This appears supremely in his *Confessions* (397-401) rather than in his more formal treatises on grace, in which at times the logic of his arguments and the demands of systematization threaten to impose limits on the inherently limitless freedom and sovereignty of the grace of God.

Even in the *Confessions*, however, a non-Pauline note is struck. In the *Confessions* Augustine has given us perhaps the first great essay in world literature on spiritual introspection. Augustine certainly found Paul speaking eloquently to his own condition, but for this reason there has been an unwarranted tendency to suppose that Paul in his pre-conversion days was prey to the same kind of divided conscience as Augustine. Paul, in fact, gives no hint that he suffered from such an inward conflict. Even while he was actively persecuting the church he maintained a good conscience because he was convinced he was serving God. After his conversion, indeed, when he realized the sinfulness of the course he had been pursuing, he magnified the grace of God which had pardoned him and called him to be an apostle (see Stendahl, 78-96). So Augustine's transmission of the doctrine of grace to the Middle Ages was Pauline in part but not in purity.

*4.2. In the Later Centuries.* On the theological side, the sixteenth-century Reformation in Europe marked an unprecedented revival of the Pauline message, or at least of one important aspect of it. Martin Luther tells how he was frustrated in his attempt to grasp the argument of Romans by the expression "the righteousness of God" (Rom 1:17). This he took to mean "the righteousness whereby God is righteous and acts righteously in punishing the unrighteous." But when, with further study of Scripture, he "grasped the truth that the righteousness of God is that righteousness whereby, through grace and sheer mercy, he justifies us by faith," then, he says, "I felt myself to be reborn and to have gone through open doors into paradise" (*Luther's Works*, American edition 34 [Philadelphia, 1960], 336-37). As K. Stendahl points out, Luther, like Augustine, found relief from an inner conflict in Paul's message. Luther's conflict was spiritual whereas Augustine's was moral, and in neither respect did they reproduce an experience of Paul's, but God's justifying grace speaks to the widest variety of human conditions.

It may be that Luther's understanding of justification by faith took insufficient account of other aspects of the believer's participation in Christ, including the ethical aspects.

Luther's discovery played a full part in the Evangelical Revival of the eighteenth century, although other influences were also at work, so that it proclaimed a more comprehensive version of the gospel of Paul, in which there is an insistence on "scriptural holiness" alongside the acceptance of justification by faith.

The most important of these other influences was a booklet published in Scotland in 1677, *The Life of God in the Soul of Man*, by Henry Scougal, a discovery and exposition of Paul's understanding of the Christian life as "a union of the soul with God, a real participation of the divine nature, the very image of God drawn upon the soul, or, in the apostle's phrase, it is 'Christ formed within us' (cf. Gal 4:19)."

It was the reading of *The Life of God in the Soul of Man* that led to George Whitefield's conversion in 1733, and it was another expositor of Paul who precipitated similar experiences in Charles and John Wesley in 1738. Charles was gripped by his first reading of Luther's commentary on Galatians; the words of Galatians 2:20 came home to him with power: "who loved *me* and gave himself for *me*." A few days later took place John Wesley's Aldersgate Street experience, when he felt his heart "strangely warmed" as he listened to a reading from Luther's preface to Romans. In his own words, "I felt I did trust in Christ, Christ alone, for salvation; and an assurance was given me that he had taken away *my* sins, even *mine*, and saved *me from the law of sin and death*" (*Journal*, I, 103). This was Paul's gospel manifesting its abiding vital power in personal life, with profound consequences for social life. It was perhaps the combination of two essential elements in Paulinism—the initial appropriation of God's justifying grace and the progressive work of the Spirit, reproducing the Christlikeness in the be-

liever's life—that gave the evangelical revival such a well-balanced quality: concentration on the one without the other produces a lopsided religion.

One might go on into the twentieth century and recall how Karl Barth, starting to read and expound Romans, felt like a man who, clutching in the dark at a rope for support, finds that he has pulled on a bell-rope and made a noise fit to wake the dead. When the first edition of his *Römerbrief* appeared in 1918, it fell, said a Catholic theologian, "like a bomb on the theologians' playground" (K. Adam; *see* Paul and His Interpreters).

The explosive force of this "bomb" was the voice of Paul himself; and in all the forward movements of the Spirit which we have surveyed, and in others too, it has been the voice of the authentic Paul, the Paul of the capital letters, that has sounded out, making effective his perennial message of liberation. Being dead, Paul continues to speak.

*See also* CHRONOLOGY OF PAUL; JEW, PAUL THE; MISSION; OPPONENTS OF PAUL; PASTOR, PAUL AS; PAUL AND HIS INTERPRETERS; PAUL IN EARLY CHURCH TRADITION; SOCIAL SETTING OF MISSION CHURCHES.

BIBLIOGRAPHY. R. Allen, *Missionary Methods: St. Paul's or Ours?* (2d ed.; London: Word Dominion Press, 1930); C. K. Barrett, *Essays on Paul* (London: SPCK, 1982); J. C. Becker, *Paul the Apostle* (Philadelphia: Fortress, 1980); G. Bornkamm, *Paul* (New York: Harper & Row, 1971); F. F. Bruce, *Paul: Apostle of the Heart Set Free* (Grand Rapids: Eerdmans, 1977); W. D. Davies, *Paul and Rabbinic Judaism* (3d ed.; Philadelphia: Fortress, 1980); C. H. Dodd, "The Mind of Paul," in *New Testament Studies* (Manchester: Manchester University, 1953) 67-128; V. P. Furnish, *Theology and Ethics in Paul* (Nashville: Abingdon, 1968); J. J. Gunther, *Paul: Messenger and Exile: A Study in the Chronology of His Life and Letters* (Valley Forge: Judson, 1972); R. Jewett, *A Chronology of Paul's Life* (Philadelphia: Fortress, 1979); S. Kim, *The Origin of Paul's Gospel* (2d ed.; Grand Rapids: Eerdmans, 1984); J. Knox, *Chapters in a Life of Paul* (New York: Abingdon-Cokesbury, 1950); L. de Lorenzi, ed., *Paul de Tarse: Apôtre du [sic] Notre Temps* (Rome: Abbaye de S. Paul h.l.m., 1979); G. Luedemann, *Paul, Apostle to the Gentiles: Studies in Chronology* (Philadelphia: Fortress, 1984); J. Munck, *Paul and the Salvation of Mankind* (London: SCM, 1959); E. P. Sanders, *Paul, the Law, and the Jewish People* (Philadelphia: Fortress, 1983); idem, *Paul* (Oxford: University Press, 1991); H. J. Schoeps, *Paul* (Philadelphia: Westminster, 1961); K. Stendahl, *Paul among Jews and Gentiles* (Philadelphia: Fortress, 1976); A. Suhl, *Paulus und seine Briefe* (Gütersloh: Mohn, 1975); F. B. Watson, *Paul, Judaism and the Gentiles* (SNTSMS 56; Cambridge: University

Press, 1986); A. J. M. Wedderburn, ed., *Paul and Jesus: Collected Essays* (JSNTS 37; Sheffield: JSOT, 1989); D. E. H. Whiteley, *The Theology of St. Paul* (Oxford: Basil Blackwell, 1964).          F. F. Bruce

## PAUL IN EARLY CHURCH TRADITION

The question of Paul's place in the traditions of the early church is closely tied to the question of the authorship of the disputed Pauline letters. If Paul is not the author of 2 Thessalonians, or Colossians, or Ephesians, or 1—2 Timothy and Titus, then the study of "Paul in Early Church Tradition" should begin with the apostle Paul as presented in those letters. If he is the author, however, or even if the question of authorship is left open, so that "Paul" is consciously defined as the Paul of the canonical NT, then the study of Paul in early church tradition begins where the canon* ends.

The latter course is the one adopted here. This means that the traditions we are examining are based on a very complex figure. The data include the Paul who speaks in the unquestionably genuine letters, the Paul of the disputed letters and the Paul of the book of Acts (*see* Paul in Acts and Letters). These diverse images of Paul have shaped the even more diverse images to be found in the ancient church. Even in the NT itself there is evidence that Paul's views were subject to conflicting interpretations, and that a correct understanding of Paul's teaching was already being seen by some writers as a matter of life and death (cf. 2 Pet 3:15-16, where those who distort Paul's writings are said to do so "to their own destruction").

1. The Apostolic Fathers
2. The Marcionite and Ebionite Paul
3. The Ascetic and Gnostic Paul
4. The Orthodox Paul

### 1. The Apostolic Fathers.

Thus the story of Paul in early church tradition begins with the so-called Apostolic Fathers. Here it is evident that Paul's life and personality made a stronger impact on the next few generations than did his ideas.

*1.1. Clement of Rome.* Clement of Rome mentions Paul, with Peter,* as a hero who had to contend all his life with "jealousy,"* "envy" and "strife" (*1 Clem.* 5.2, 5). "Seven times he was in bonds," Clement writes, "he was exiled, he was stoned, he was a herald both in the East and in the West, he gained the noble fame of his faith, he taught justice to the whole world, and when he had reached the limits of the West he gave his testimony before the rulers, and thus passed from the world and was taken up into the Holy Place—the greatest example of endurance" (*1 Clem.* 5.6-7). Clement

later cites Paul as one who wrote "with true inspiration" when he warned against factionalism in his letter to the same Corinthian church to which Clement was now writing (*1 Clem.* 47.1-5; cf. 1 Cor 1:10-12). Clement's point is that "even then you had made yourselves partisans" (*1 Clem.* 47.3), but that it was worse now because the Corinthians had become partisans not of apostles or of those of noble reputation (like Paul, Cephas or Apollos,* as in 1 Cor 1:12), but of far lesser figures (*1 Clem.* 47.4).

*1.2. Ignatius.* Ignatius, too, saw Paul as a hero. Writing to the Ephesians in imitation of Paul's style, he said, "I am condemned, you have obtained mercy; I am in danger, you are established in safety [cf. 1 Cor 4:10]; you are . . . fellow initiates with Paul, who was sanctified, approved, who gained a good report, who was right blessed, in whose footsteps may I be found when I shall attain to God" (Ignatius *Eph.* 12.1-2). His admiration of Paul's life was greater than his knowledge of Paul's letters, for he continued that "in every Epistle [Paul] makes mention of you in Christ Jesus" (Ignatius *Eph.* 12.2). In his letter to the Romans, Ignatius wrote: "I do not order you as did Peter and Paul; they were Apostles, I am a convict; they were free, I am even until now a slave" (Ignatius *Rom.* 4.3).

*1.3. Polycarp.* In the same generation as Clement and Ignatius, Polycarp viewed Paul, like the other apostles, as a model of endurance (Polycarp *Phil.* 9.1) and admitted that "neither am I, nor is any other like me, able to follow the wisdom of the blessed and glorious Paul, who when he was among you in the presence of the men of that time taught accurately and steadfastly the word of truth, and also when he was absent wrote letters [sic] to you, from the study of which you will be able to build yourselves up into the faith given you" (Polycarp *Phil.* 3.2). Like Ignatius, Polycarp was eloquent about Paul the man but somewhat vague about the content of his letters (cf. Polycarp *Phil.* 11.3).

### 2. The Marcionite and Ebionite Paul.

Ironically, the aspects of Paul's thought which have made the greatest impact in the West since the Reformation—his teachings about the Law* and faith,* and about the salvation* of Jew (*see* Israel) and Gentile*— were first noted and accented by segments of the church later regarded as heretical. The prime example among those sympathetic with Paul is Marcion, and among those hostile to him the Jewish-Christian Ebionites.

*2.1. Marcion.* To Marcion, Paul was more than an apostle*; he was the *only* apostle. Marcion's canon consisted of a collection of Paul's letters plus an expurgated edition of Luke's Gospel. Marcion extended Paul's radical distinction between law and grace (e.g., in Galatians) into a radical gulf between the God* of the Hebrew Bible and the God of Marcion's Christian Bible. Irenaeus charged that for the sake of this distinction Marcion "dismembered the Epistles of Paul, removing all that is said by the apostle respecting that God who made the world, to the effect that He is the Father of our Lord* Jesus Christ,* and also those passages from the prophetical writings which the apostle quotes, in order to teach us that they announced beforehand the coming of the Lord" (Irenaeus *Haer.* 1.27.2, in *ANF* 1.352). Thus Marcion appropriated what many later theologians have judged to be the core of Paul's theology (*see* Center), yet in the process eliminated the nuances and qualifications that have made Paul's thought so complex and challenging to later readers. The judgment of F. Overbeck and A. von Harnack (itself an oversimplification) was that "Marcion was the only one in the second century who understood Paul . . . and he misunderstood him."

*2.2. Ebionites.* Marcion is not the only one, however, to whom Harnack's judgment applies. To a considerable extent, the Paul of Marcion is also the Paul of the Ebionites, perhaps the second-century descendants of Paul's opponents* in Galatians.* The difference is that Marcion saw Paul in this way and liked what he saw, while the Ebionites emphatically did not. If Paul was to Marcion the supreme true apostle, he was to the Ebionites the supreme false apostle, a messenger of Satan.* They saw him as the enemy of Peter (cf. Gal 2:11-14) and destroyer of the Law of Moses.* In the so-called *Kerygmata Petrou* (Hennecke-Schneemelcher-Wilson, 2.102-27), Paul was viewed as the one "who first went to the Gentiles," while Peter was "the one who came after him, appearing as light after darkness, as knowledge after ignorance, as healing after sickness. Thus, as the True Prophet told us, first a false gospel must come through a certain deceiver, and then, after the destruction of the holy place, a true gospel must be propagated secretly in order to rectify the existing heresies" (Pseudo-Clementine *Homilies* 2.17, trans. by Meeks, 180). In the present form of the text Peter's opponent is "Simon" (i.e., Simon Magus), but what is predicated of him makes it clear that this "deceiver" was originally understood to be Paul.

### 3. The Ascetic and Gnostic Paul.
Paul's statements about the body and the present and future aspects of the resurrection* were embedded in an eschatological framework (*see* Eschatology) and were written in the concrete situations of his own struggle to articulate the truth of the gospel* in the face of misunderstanding and opposition. Viewed through

new paradigms of thought and struggle, the subtleties of the canonical Paul were skewed to support two opposing perspectives.

*3.1. The Ascetic Paul.* It was the image of Paul in the canonical Acts of the Apostles that provided a foothold for a view of Paul in apocryphal traditions as a traveling preacher and miracle worker (*see* Apocryphal Pauline Literature). This heroic picture of Paul is similar to that of Clement, Ignatius and Polycarp, except that the apocryphal Paul is seen as a messenger not only of Christ but of the ascetic way of life. This Paul is described in the *Acts of Paul and Thecla* as "a man small of stature, with a bald head and crooked legs, in a good state of body, with eyebrows meeting and nose somewhat hooked, full of friendliness; for now he appeared like a man, and now he had the face of an angel" (*Paul and Thecla* 3). He gives to the "house of Onesiphorus" (cf. 2 Tim 1:16; 4:19) his own version of the Beatitudes: "Blessed are the pure in heart, for they shall see God. Blessed are they who have kept the flesh pure, for they shall become a temple of God. Blessed are the continent, for to them God will speak. Blessed are they who have renounced this world, for they shall be pleasing to God. Blessed are those who have wives as if they had not [cf. 1 Cor 7:29], for they shall inherit God," and so on (*Paul and Thecla* 4-5).

In the story of Thecla, conversion to Paul's gospel means that a woman renounces sexual intercourse (*see* Sexuality, Sexual Ethics) with her husband and is then protected from the anger of her family and miraculously delivered from death by wild beasts. These Acts represent a radicalization of the Paul of 1 Corinthians 7, and on several points stand opposed to the Paul of the Pastoral Letters (e.g., 1 Tim 2:11-15; 4:3; 5:14-15). Yet they agree with the Pastorals in endorsing a future resurrection against those who say that the resurrection "has already taken place in the children whom we have" or "in that we have come to know the true God" (*Paul and Thecla* 14, Hennecke-Schneemelcher-Wilson, 2.357; cf. 2 Tim 2:18). Far from being excluded, the future resurrection is held out as the reward of the celibate life. Paul's opponents in these stories denounce him as one who "deprives young men of wives and maidens of husbands, saying: 'Otherwise there is no resurrection for you, except ye remain chaste and do not defile the flesh, but keep it pure'" (*Paul and Thecla* 12; Hennecke-Schneemelcher-Wilson, 2.256).

The ascetic view of Paul was later denounced by church fathers in the East and the West (e.g., Irenaeus, Clement, Hippolytus, Jerome) as the "Encratite" heresy (from the Greek word *encrateia*, "continence" or "self-control"). Such Pauline passages as Colossians 2:16-23 and 1 Timothy 4:1-5 afforded them a canonical basis for this judgment. The fathers traced the Encratite perspective to Tatian in the mid-second century, whose harmony, or *Diatessaron,* of the four Gospels became the one Gospel in the canon of Syrian Christianity until the fifth century. Whatever its origin, an ascetic form of Christianity, and therefore an ascetic view of Paul, seems to have characterized the Syriac-speaking churches almost from the beginning.

**3.2. The Gnostic Paul.** If the Encratites and their opponents alike maintained Paul's expectation of a future resurrection (as expressed, e.g., in 1 Thess 4:13-17 and 1 Cor 15:12-58), there were others in the second century who attributed to Paul the contrary notion that the resurrection had already taken place (the view of his opponents according to 2 Tim 2:18; *see* Gnosis, Gnosticism). The Valentinian *Epistle to Rheginos,* building on the Pauline idea that "the Savior swallowed death" (*Rheginos* 45.15; cf. 1 Cor 15:53-55), cites "the Apostle" (clearly Paul) as having said, "We suffered with him, and we arose with him, and we went to heaven with him" (*Rheginos* 45.25-28; contrast the future formulations in Rom 6:8; 8:17 and 2 Tim 2:11). Without referring to the actual texts, this tradition extended and expanded on Paul's analogy between Christian baptism* and the death and resurrection of Christ (*see* Dying and Rising) as developed in Colossians 2:12-13 (cf. Col 3:1) and in Ephesians 2:5-6.

**4. The Orthodox Paul.**

Whatever the issue at stake, it was the ambiguities and tensions in the teaching of the canonical Paul that gave rise to conflicting interpretations of him in later centuries. The second century was a time in which the church's desire to claim the Jewish Scriptures for its own won out over Marcion's appeal to cut all its ties with the past. Because Paul was an authentic martyr and hero of the faith, and could not be transformed (as the Ebionites had done) into a false apostle, it became necessary to emphasize the positive side of his attitude toward the law of Moses—for example, as a schoolmaster or tutor preparing humanity for the coming of the Christ (Gal 3:23-24, especially in Clement of Alexandria).

**4.1. The Law and the Unity of Scripture.** Paul's stark contrast between the Law and faith was no longer useful once the mainstream of the church became overwhelmingly Gentile, with nothing more to fear from the requirement of circumcision or detailed legal observance. Instead, distinctions foreign to Paul began to be introduced within the law itself—for example, between the law in its literal and its spiritual sense (Origen), or between the ceremonial law, which the coming of Jesus abolished, and the moral law, which the

coming of Jesus confirmed (Tertullian and others). Such distinctions gave a more positive role to the law in the Christian life, and consequently a greater measure of unity between OT and NT in a Gentile church increasingly in need of a canon.

**4.2. The Resurrection of the Flesh.** On the issue of when the resurrection of believers took place, Paul's dominant emphasis on its futurity (e.g., 1 Thess 4; 1 Cor 15; Rom 8) won out over those texts (e.g., in Rom 6, but above all in Ephesians and Colossians) which applied the language of resurrection to baptism or to present Christian experience in the Spirit (*see* Eschatology).

As to the nature of that resurrection,* many of the church fathers sought to qualify Paul's accent on discontinuity between the present physical body* and the body that will be raised (cf. 1 Cor 15:35-53). "Flesh* and blood," he had said, "cannot inherit the kingdom of God; neither does corruption put on incorruption" (1 Cor 15:50). The Gnostics highlighted this discontinuity in order to emphasize the evil of physical existence in contrast to the spirituality of the resurrection. Origen too accented the discontinuity, but most others, like Irenaeus and Tertullian, were concerned to show that Paul's pronouncement did not exclude an actual physical resurrection. All Paul was saying was that human nature by itself, apart from the work of the Spirit of God (*see* Holy Spirit), could not enter heaven.* Moreover, the expression "flesh and blood" was given a moral rather than a physical meaning. Irenaeus took it to imply the sinful "works of the flesh" mentioned in Galatians 5:19-21.

Such interpretive strategies, in the face of the threat of Gnosticism and Hellenistic dualism, allowed the church to emphasize continuity rather than discontinuity between present and future existence, and so to speak of the "resurrection of the flesh" (a term Paul had never used). Paul, for his part, had emphasized discontinuity and transcendence in the face of very different kinds of threats, possibly from charismatic perfectionists in Corinth (*see* Corinthians) who believed they were already in the age to come. For Paul the questions about the time and the nature of the resurrection of believers had been intertwined. Once they became separated, it was inevitable that many of Paul's interpreters would come to a different set of answers.

On some issues, the interpretation of Paul among the church fathers followed no single or simple pattern. For instance, on the alternatives of marriage and celibacy, Clement of Alexandria (*Strom.* 3) maintained the tension so evident in 1 Corinthians 7 by recognizing that Paul had affirmed the legitimacy of both. But as in the case of the law and the resurrection, others came down on one side or another of the tension. New issues that Paul had not faced created new ambiguities and barriers to understanding the Paul of history and of the NT. Such barriers were by no means a problem only for the ancient church and church fathers. They still exist, and still make the study of the apostle Paul a formidable, fascinating challenge (*see* Hermeneutics/Interpreting Paul).

*See also* APOCRYPHAL PAULINE LITERATURE; GNOSIS, GNOSTICISM; PAUL AND HIS INTERPRETERS; PAUL IN ACTS AND LETTERS.

BIBLIOGRAPHY. W. Bauer, *Orthodoxy and Heresy in Earliest Christianity* (Philadelphia: Fortress, 1971); E. C. Blackman, *Marcion and His Influence* (London: SPCK, 1948); E. Hennecke, W. Schneemelcher, and R. McL. Wilson, *New Testament Apocrypha II* (Philadelphia: Westminster, 1965); D. R. MacDonald, *The Legend and the Apostle: The Battle for Paul in Story and Canon* (Philadelphia: Westminster, 1983); W. Meeks, ed., *The Writings of St. Paul* (New York: Norton, 1972) 151-213; E. Pagels, *The Gnostic Paul: Gnostic Exegesis of the Pauline Letters* (Philadelphia: Fortress, 1975); A. Souter, *The Earliest Latin Commentaries on the Epistles of St. Paul* (Oxford: Clarendon, 1927); T. F. Torrance, *The Doctrine of Grace in the Apostolic Fathers* (Grand Rapids: Eerdmans, 1960); C. H. Turner, "Greek Patristic Commentaries on the Pauline Epistles," *HDB* 5.484-531; H. E. W. Turner, *The Pattern of Christian Truth: A Study in the Relations between Orthodoxy and Heresy in the Early Church* (London: A. R. Mowbray, 1954); M. F. Wiles, *The Divine Apostle: The Interpretation of St. Paul's Epistles in the Early Church* (Cambridge: University Press, 1967).

J. R. Michaels

# PEACE, RECONCILIATION

Reconciliation is the Pauline concept in which enmity between God* and humanity, or between human groups, is overcome and peaceful relations restored on the basis of the work of Christ* (*see* Death of Christ). This concept refers to an objective state of peace, not simply a feeling of peacefulness. Although the strictly secular usage is found in 1 Corinthians 7:11, 15, where Paul speaks of peace being restored to a married couple in the case where one is a believer and the other is not, most of his usage of these terms is distinctively theological. Paul depends upon two word groups, often used together; the more important one includes *katallagē* or *katallassō* ("reconciliation"), and the other *eirēnē* and its cognates ("peace"). The fact that the almost exclusive provenance of *katallagē* and *katallassō* is Greek secular literature, or literature heavily influenced by the Hellenistic world, makes the

Greek milieu foundational to understanding the concept of reconciliation. The Greek terms for reconciliation derive from words for exchange, in which by extension enmity is exchanged for peaceful relations. In confirmation of its Greek background, the words are found only once in the OT outside of the apocrypha (LXX Jer 31:39 [MT 48:39]), and four times in 2 Maccabees (2 Macc 1:5; 5:20; 7:33; 8:29), texts which have no Hebrew antecedent. The relation between Greek *eirēnē* ("peace") and Hebrew *šālôm* ("peace") is discussed in more detail in section 3 below.

1. Chief letters
2. Colossians and Ephesians
3. Superscriptions

## 1. Chief Letters.

Two major passages delimit Paul's thought regarding reconciliation or the establishment of peace between God and humanity.

*1.1. 2 Corinthians 5:18-21.* In support of his belief that the work of Christ means the coming of a new age (2 Cor 5:16-17), Paul proclaims what God has done through Christ (2 Cor 5:18-21). Some scholars claim that Paul has here supplemented traditional material (i.e., a soteriological credo supplemented by adding "not reckoning against them their trespasses" and "we beg you on Christ's behalf, be reconciled to God"), since this theological section, with its kerygmatic idioms suited to preaching* the gospel,* comes while addressing pastoral problems (Martin, 1981, 93-97; Käsemann 1971). But two objections may be raised. First, this analysis of the letter does not fully appreciate that its body (2 Cor 1:8—9:15) is mainly given over to Paul's discussion of his apostolic ministry (2 Cor 1:12—2:13; 2:14—7:16). Second, this analysis does not affect our understanding of the concept of reconciliation, since the traditional material (especially 2 Cor 5:21) is placed within the larger context of distinctly Pauline language: God's reconciling work is accomplished by or through Christ (2 Cor 5:18-19), and the ministry of reconciliation consists of the proclamation of this work of Christ (2 Cor 5:20-21).

In 2 Corinthians 5:18-19 God is the agent and instigator of reconciliation "through Christ." Although the main clause of verse 19 is grammatically problematic, the best rendering is that "God was reconciling the world to himself through Christ." Paul is the first attested Greek author to speak of the offended party (God) initiating reconciliation, using the active voice form of the verb.

The object of reconciliation is "us" (2 Cor 5:18) or "the world" (2 Cor 5:19), probably referring to those of the fallen world* who are reconciled (cf. 2 Cor

5:20). The question of when this reconciliation occurred is established by the phrases "through [*dia*] Christ" and "by [*en*] Christ." "Through Christ," as Bultmann suggests, is equivalent to "through the death of his [God's] Son," a phrase used explicitly in Romans 5:10 and described in more detail in 2 Corinthians 5:14-15 and indicating Christ's sacrificial* death.

Most commentators understand 2 Corinthians 5:20-21 as Paul's appeal to the Corinthian church to be reconciled to God, taking Paul's use of first person plural ("we," "us") as an "epistolary plural," that is, the singular "I" is meant even though the plural form is used. But in light of the context, in which Paul sees himself as allied with his audience of believers, the passage is better understood as a concerted appeal to the unreconciled: "We therefore are ambassadors for Christ, as God makes his appeal through us: 'We beg you on Christ's behalf, be reconciled to God.' " Paul includes himself with other Christians ("we") as ambassadors on behalf of Christ. The message of 2 Corinthians 5:20b is addressed to those to whom the Corinthian believers are ambassadors, to those being called to reconciliation.

The command of 2 Corinthians 5:20, "be reconciled," agrees with the Pauline pattern found in 2 Corinthians 5:18-19 (cf. Rom 5:10, as well as other Greek usage of this verb), in which God is not only the agent or instigator of reconciliation, but is the goal toward whom reconciliation is directed. In all uses of the verb of reconciliation in 2 Corinthians 5 (verses 18, 19 and 20) the object or goal of the action is God. As Furnish states, "reconciliation is not ["only"?] of God but from and to God" (Furnish, 335).

Several commentators have noted that the passage makes no explicit reference to the enmity of God or of humanity. While this passage does not explicitly refer to human antagonism except by alluding to "transgressions" (2 Cor 5:19), it may be inferred that God's righteousness* provides the basis for reconciliation. There is reference in 2 Corinthians 5:14, 15 to humans living for themselves and requiring Christ's death, as well as the defining phrase in verse 19 regarding the nonimputation of sin* and the reference in verse 21 to Christ becoming sin. These point toward a God who condemns sinful rebellion and yet makes provision for it in effecting reconciliation.

*1.2. Romans 5:8-11.* The place of Romans 5 within the argument of Romans* is notoriously difficult to determine. Whether one associates Romans 5 with Romans 1—4 or with Romans 6—8, or detects a division between Roman 5:11 and 12, many recent commentators recognize Romans 5 as a convergence

point of important material (Kaye). There are several noteworthy verbal parallels, or overlaps in meaning, between peace, reconciliation and justification.* In some instances justification (Rom 5:1, 9) is parallel with reconciliation (Rom 5:10b); in others having peace and being reconciled are parallel (Rom 5:1 and 10a). In Romans 5:8-9 Paul says that Christ died for us, and now that we are justified we shall be saved; in Romans 5:10 Paul says that we were reconciled to God, and now that we are reconciled we shall be saved (*see* Salvation). (See similarly Rom 14:17, where Paul describes the kingdom* of God as "righteousness and peace and joy in the Holy Spirit.")

In Romans 5:1-11 having peace with God (Rom 5:1) and being reconciled to God (Rom 5:10) are equated. Although many scholars believe that the sense of "peace" (*eirēnē*) depends upon the OT sense of external or material well-being, the Greek sense denoting a time or state without hostility or war fits the context better. In Greek thought "peace" is a relational word which speaks of a state of objective well-being, leading to harmonious relations between people or nations. The creation of peace (Rom 5:1, 10a) is directed toward God, with whom humans are at odds. R. P. Martin looks to the love of God mentioned in Romans 5:5 and 8 as the basis of reconciliation. Although the love* of God is in harmony with the relational language, and certainly forms part of the divine character that prompts reconciliation, especially in terms of the death of Christ, God's character itself—of which love is a part—is the fundamental basis of the reconciling process (*see* God).

The means for these actions are stated explicitly. In Romans 5:1 and 11 it is said that we have peace or reconciliation "through our Lord Jesus Christ," in Romans 5:8 that "Christ died for us," and in Romans 5:10 that reconciliation is "through the death of his Son." Almost half of the verses of Romans 5:1-11 (Rom 5:1, 8, 9, 10 and 11) mention the work of Christ explicitly: God acts to bring about reconciliation through or by means of the work of Jesus Christ.

In the parallel phrasing of Romans 5:8 and 10 Paul equates being a sinner with being an enemy* of God. The scholarly controversy surrounding C. H. Dodd's understanding of Paul's view of divine wrath* in Romans is well known. Dodd argued that, for Paul, God's wrath is an "objective principle and process in the moral order" (Dodd, 77). On the contrary, however, Paul understands wrath as God's personal repulsion at evil, whether displayed in the present age or revealed at the final judgment. This is the logic of Romans 5:8-11, where the wrath from which one is saved is related to being a sinner and an enemy of God. Romans

1:18—3:20 prepares readers for the reference to humans as sinners. Humans constitute themselves as God's enemies not only by their sin but also by their disdain (the active sense of "enmity") for godly things. Human sin, therefore, precipitates God's wrath, thereby severing his relationship (the passive sense of "wrath") with humanity. As I. H. Marshall states, God does put "away the wrath which he has toward men and women on account of their sins so that there is no longer any barrier on his side to fellowship with them" (Marshall, 128).

Paul closes this section with an appropriate sense of exultation (Rom 5:11; cf. 5:2, 3). Believers jubilantly exult through their Lord Jesus Christ, their mediator, in what God has done: reconciliation (Rom 5:11b). As Cranfield says, "It is through Christ . . . through whom we have already received the gift of reconciliation with God, that we exult; for this gift which we have received through him is ground enough for ceaseless exultation" (Cranfield, 1.268-69). These ideas are caught up "under the catchword of the reconciliation that exists in the eschatological present" (Käsemann, 1980, 139) as a culmination of the past work of God and a hope for future salvation. The life set on the Spirit* is life and peace (Rom 8:6).

## 2. Colossians and Ephesians.

The language of reconciliation in Colossians 1:20-22 and Ephesians 2:16 is slightly different from that in Paul's chief letters. The verb translated "make peace" (*eirēnopoieō*) is used in its only instance in the Pauline letters. The verb for reconciliation, *apokatallassō*, here in its earliest attested usage in Greek literature, is an emphatically prefixed form of the verb (*katallassō*) used in 2 Corinthians 5:18-21 and Romans 5:8-11.

*2.1. Colossians 1:20-22.* Discussion of this passage is often linked to analysis of the reputed "hymn"* of Colossians 1:15-20. Despite arguments on all sides, it cannot be conclusively determined how or whether the "hymn" pre-existed (*see* Colossians). Thus G. B. Caird rightly states that its pre-Colossian function is "totally irrelevant" (Caird, 175) for interpreting its function here, including its contribution to understanding reconciliation. Reconciliation is mentioned in the second half of the "hymn" (Col 1:18b-20) and then restated in the following section (Col 1:21-23; there are textual variants regarding the verb *apoka-tēllaxen*, "be reconciled," in Col 1:22).

Both God and Christ are said to be the primary agents or initiators of reconciliation and peace. In Colossians 1:20 God is the unstated subject of the verb "reconcile," and thus the understood agent ultimately responsible for making peace. Whereas God may also

be the subject of the verb in Colossians 1:22 (in conformity with Romans and 2 Corinthians), the context perhaps more clearly indicates that Christ (or the Son) is the understood subject of the verb and thus also a primary agent of reconciliation (on Ephesians, see 2.2 below).

The relation between these two emphases is best understood through the bipartite argument of Colossians 1:18b-22. The first section, Colossians 1:18b-20, recounts the means and scope of reconciliation. The fullness of divinity (a circumlocution for God; *see* Fullness) was pleased to dwell in Christ and through Christ to reconcile all things to Christ, making peace through the blood of his cross.* It seems best to take all of the pronouns in Colossians 1:19-20 as referring to Christ. The first (*en autō*) provides a place for the fullness of divinity to dwell ("in Christ"), the second (*di' autou*) the means by which reconciliation is enacted (parallel to the instrumental phrase with the same preposition, *dia* ["through"], referring to "the blood of his cross"), and the third (*eis auton*) its goal ("to Christ"). The third pronoun, in the phrase "to him," might be construed as "himself" with reference to God, but this pronoun has no direct grammatical antecedent ("all the fullness of divinity" is a circumlocution for God), and creates an unnecessary break in the parallelism with reference to Christ. Consequently its reference to God is not accepted by most commentators.

We conclude, then, that whereas the goal of reconciliation in the other Pauline literature is God, in Colossians 1:20 it is Christ. This is in keeping with the general tenor of this section of Colossians, in which actions are predicated of Christ that are usually predicated of God, including his creating the cosmos (Col 1:16; *see* World, Cosmology), his sustaining the created order (Col 1:17), and quite possibly his pre-existence* (Col 1:15, 17). In the second portion, Colossians 1:21-23, Christ then assumes the function of reconciler in presenting the personal objects of reconciliation, those who were formerly strangers and enemies, to God. As Martin states, "The link between 1:15-20 and 1:21-23 is close-knit, with the personal pronoun at verse 21, 'And you' and the verb at verse 22, 'he has now reconciled by his death' standing in an unusual and emphatic position" (Martin 1981, 115).

Most commentators understand God as the subject of reconciliation in Colossians 1:22, in which case God is said to reconcile and present strangers and enemies to himself. Although a case can be made for this understanding, its attractiveness to interpreters is probably due more to its conformity with Paul's chief letters than to an analysis of the text itself. Our analysis of the text has shown (1) that Christ is the subject of the main clauses of Colossians 1:15, 17, 18; (2) that he plays the key role in reconciliation in Colossians 1:19-20; (3) that divine functions are applied to Christ in Colossians 1:15-20; and (4) that the structure of Colossians 1:21-22 is closely tied to the preceding verses. We conclude, then, that Christ is better interpreted as the subject of the verb of reconciliation in Colossians 1:22, with the goal now seen as presenting the former enemies before God, the latter being a theme in conformity with Pauline usage in his chief letters. (The textual variant with the verb for reconciliation in Col 1:22 indicates that others have struggled with how to understand it in this context.) The emphasis upon the direct role of Christ is continued in Colossians 3:15 with reference to the "peace of Christ."

The work of Christ as a sacrifice upon the cross is the means or instrument by which reconciliation is brought about (Col 1:20a, 20b, 22). The reference to blood in Colossians 1:20 is unique to Colossians but not unique to reconciliation passages (cf. Rom 5:9). Reference to "the body of his flesh" in Colossians 1:22 calls attention to the fact that it was a physical body* that was involved, and a specific one ("his"). The following instrumental phrase is used to state what happened to this body of flesh* (i.e., physical body): it died.

In speaking of the resolution of enmity between parties, Paul uses the word *eirēnopoieō*, "make peace," a word implying a well-known Greek concept of hostility that requires pacification (*see* Triumph). Furthermore, enmity is implied by reference to the blood of his cross (Col 1:20b), and this alienation is applied to "us," the personal recipients of reconciliation. E. Schweizer states the essential minimum when he says, "in the whole of the NT it is always the individual person, not God, who needs to be reconciled" (Schweizer, 92). It is humans who are characterized as "strangers and enemies in understanding in their evil works." The modifying phrase "in understanding" brings the active sense of enmity to the fore, since "understanding" specifically locates animosity in the human mental activity.

Many commentators understand the language of reconciliation in Colossians as addressed only to Gentiles, since the condition of being strangers "can be said only of former Gentiles and not of Jews" (Lohse, 62). But this is too restrictive. The argument encompasses the time from before creation* to the present (Col 1:16-18), including the time of the church* (Col 1:18), with reference to God's reconciling work affecting "all" (cf. Col 1:20). The word "all" in Colossians 1:20 is explicated as "either things upon the earth or

things in heaven." Interpreters have defined these words in various ways: to include the world of humans (upon the earth) and angels* (in the heavens); the breach between humans and God brought about by sin; subjection of the cosmic powers, which by nature are evil; the rupture between heaven and earth; and the world of humankind. On the basis of the grammar, the contrasting structure and the context of the work of Christ extending from before creation to reconciliation on the cross, the antithetical elements apparently form a comprehensive or inclusive statement, that is, embracing all the things in heaven, upon the earth, seen and unseen, thrones, principalities,* rulers and powers (Col 1:16). Although this passage may imply universal* salvation, in which things are reconciled against their will, that interpretation overlooks the larger argument. Colossians 1:18-20 establishes the general principle of God's cosmic reconciling activity. Its specific application to humanity ("strangers and enemies") does not occur until Colossians 1:21-23.

*2.2. Ephesians 2:14-17.* The phrase "for he is our peace" (Eph 2:14), equating Christ with peace, forms a title for the entire passage. The purpose of Christ being "our peace" is to create one new person by reconciling both Jews and Gentiles* in one body to God through the cross, and so effecting peace by killing the hostility in humankind.

Whereas Colossians 1:20-22 presents the work of Christ in its cosmic implications, here the emphasis is on breaking down a wall which separated Jews and Gentiles (Eph 2:11-13). Paul employs a metaphor probably drawn from the wall in the Jerusalem Temple,* or the Temple itself, which prevented Gentiles from proceeding into the inner courts. This was reinforced by the "Law* of commandments, condemning in its requirements [*en dogmasin*]" (Eph 2:15). Through reconciliation Jews and Gentiles are said to become "one new person" and "one body" (Eph 2:15, 16), being created into a third entity, a body without ethnic boundaries. As M. Barth points out, "The pacification carried out by Jesus Christ is an act of creation" (Barth, 1.308) whereby the two are made into something entirely new (*see* Creation and New Creation). This act of reconciliation is defined in both positive and negative terms. Reconciliation consists of making peace, and of killing animosity. The first phrase explains the title of this section: Jesus Christ can be called "our peace," since he is a peacemaker. This positive message forms the basis of the proclamation of peace to all, those both far and near (Eph 2:17; cf. 6:15; see also Col 1:18-22). The enmity which calls for reconciliation is defined in terms of two human groups, Jews and Gentiles. In that the Law excluded Gentiles, it was the source of their enmity. The animosity is said to be "killed" by Christ's work on the cross, and to constitute the new condition of Christian existence (cf. Eph 4:3; Rom 11:15; *see* Triumph).

In overcoming this separation, Christ is the agent of reconciliation and God is its goal (see 2.1 above). As Barth says, in Ephesians 2:16 "the Messiah rather than God is denoted as the one who reconciles" (Barth, 1.266). Although Christ is the one who effects reconciliation (as the primary agent), his work on the cross is still seen as the means or instrument used to produce reconciliation (Col 1:13, 15, 16, 18).

### 3. Superscriptions.

Paul often uses a form of the word "peace" (*eirēnē*) in the superscriptions of his letters. It virtually always appears with "grace" in the Pauline letters (Rom 1:7; 1 Cor 1:3; 2 Cor 1:2; Gal 1:3; Eph 1:2; Phil 1:2; Col 1:2; 1 Thess 1:1; 2 Thess 1:2; Philem 3; Tit 1:4), and with the word "mercy"* in 1 Timothy 1:2 and 2 Timothy 1:2. In using "grace"* (*charis*) Paul has adapted a cognate word (*chairein*, "greeting") used in the usual superscription of Hellenistic letters. There has been widespread speculation, however, regarding his use of the word "peace." Most scholars take it as a Semitism, translating the Hebrew word for "peace" (*šālôm*). This is not a certainty, although it is a possibility. There is little substantive evidence from Greek Jewish letters of the time that superscriptions with "peace" were used as a convention that Paul might have borrowed (but cf. LXX Dan 4:1; *2 Apoc. Bar.* 78:2; *b. Sanh.* 11b). If Paul was using a Semitic superscription, he risked misunderstanding by his predominantly Gentile, Greek-speaking churches.

A more plausible explanation is that Paul has consciously created his own superscription to emphasize the comprehensive work of God: it is one of gracious giving and forgiveness for previous hostility. This is fully in keeping with Paul's use of "peace" language in his major reconciliation passages and reflects a Greek background which in this case speaks of an objective state of peace with God. Too much theological emphasis, however, should probably not be placed upon a highly formulaic feature of Paul's adaptation of the Hellenistic letter.

Paul often uses similar language in the close of his letters (Rom 15:33; 16:20; 2 Cor 13:11; Phil 4:9, cf. 4:7; 1 Thess 5:23; 2 Thess 3:16), where he speaks in terms of the God (or Lord) of peace (and love) being with his readers. This may be related to Paul's listing of peace in Galatians 5:22 as a fruit* of the Spirit, since he also includes love,* joy and faithfulness, language reminiscent of his extended discussion of peace elsewhere. Too much weight, however, should not be put upon what for Paul is probably a formulaic epistolary closing (*see* Letters).

*See also* CENTER OF PAUL'S THEOLOGY; DEATH OF CHRIST; ENEMY, ENMITY, HATRED; GENTILES; JUSTIFICATION; PRINCIPALITIES AND POWERS; TRIUMPH; UNIVERSALISM; WORLD, COSMOLOGY.

BIBLIOGRAPHY. M. Barth, *Ephesians* (2 vols.; Garden City, NY: Doubleday, 1974); R. Bultmann, *The Second Letter to the Corinthians* (Minneapolis: Augsburg, 1985); G. B. Caird, *Paul's Letters from Prison* (Oxford: University Press, 1976); C. E. B. Cranfield, *The Epistle to the Romans* (Vol. 1; Edinburgh: T. & T. Clark, 1975); C. H. Dodd, *The Epistle of Paul to the Romans* (MNTC; New York: Harper & Row, 1932); V. P. Furnish, *II Corinthians* (Garden City, NY: Doubleday, 1984); E. Käsemann, *A Commentary on Romans* (Grand Rapids: Eerdmans, 1980); idem, "Some Thoughts on the Theme 'The Doctrine of Reconciliation in the New Testament,' " in *The Future of Our Religious Past*, ed. J. M. Robinson (New York: Harper & Row, 1971) 49-64; B. N. Kaye, *The Thought Structure of Romans with Special Reference to Chapter 6* (Austin: Schola, 1979); E. Lohse, *Colossians and Philemon* (Philadelphia: Fortress, 1971); I. H. Marshall, "The Meaning of 'Reconciliation,' " in *Unity and Diversity in NT Theology*, ed. R. A. Guelich (Grand Rapids: Eerdmans, 1978) 117-32 (= *Jesus the Saviour: Studies in New Testament Theology* [Downers Grove, Il: InterVarsity, 1990] 258-74); R. P. Martin, *Reconciliation: A Study of Paul's Theology* (Atlanta: John Knox, 1981); idem, "Reconciliation and Forgiveness in Colossians," in *Reconciliation and Hope*, ed. R. Banks (Grand Rapids: Eerdmans, 1974) 109-16; P. T. O'Brien, *Colossians, Philemon* (WBC 44; Waco: Word, 1982); S. E. Porter, *Καταλλάσσω in Ancient Greek Literature, with Reference to the Pauline Writings* (Cordoba: Ediciones El Almendro, forthcoming); E. Schweizer, *The Letter to the Colossians* (Minneapolis: Augsburg, 1982).

S. E. Porter

## PEDAGOGUE. *See* ABRAHAM; LAW.

## PERFECT, MATURE

In Paul's writings perfection or maturity entails several ideas related to the concept of fulfillment, reaching a goal or attaining completion. The English word *actualized* captures an important nuance in Paul's thinking on this subject: that which is perfect or mature has fulfilled its intended goal. Paul generally uses the Greek adjective *teleios* ("perfect," "complete," "mature") to convey the concept, though several cognate words also contribute to make the complete picture: *teleioō* ("make perfect, complete or mature"), *teleō* ("to complete," "to end"), *telos* ("end," "result," "purpose," "completely") and *teleiotēs* ("maturity," "perfection"). Paul's concept includes four distinct aspects: (1) simple maturity or the attainment of a goal; (2) spiritual perfection as the status of all Christians "in Christ"; (3) a position of relative perfection attainable by Christians in this life; and (4) the state of ultimate perfection that Christians hope to experience in the age to come.

1. Maturity, Having Attained the Goal
2. Spiritual Perfection as Existence "in Christ"
3. Relative Perfection in this Life
4. Ultimate Perfection in the Age to Come

**1. Maturity, Having Attained the Goal.**
In several places Paul speaks of maturity in a non-theological sense. He encourages the Corinthians to think as do adults—mature people—not as do children (1 Cor 14:20). He insists, possibly in irony, that mature Christians exercise a kind of sober judgment (Phil 3:15). Christ's power,* he argues, fulfilled its intended goal or was truly operative when Paul was at his weakest (2 Cor 12:9; *see* Weakness). At the point of death Paul could affirm that he had successfully completed (or actualized) his assignment as a Christian apostle* (2 Tim 4:7).

**2. Spiritual Perfection as Existence "in Christ."**
Parallel to the sense of reaching the goal, becoming a Christian leads to becoming perfect, or complete. So Paul alludes to the Corinthians as "perfect," or "mature" (1 Cor 2:6) because to them God's Spirit revealed his wisdom* that is "not of this age" (1 Cor 2:6, 10). The Corinthians stand in contrast to those without the Spirit (1 Cor 2:12, 14), who possess no spiritual discernment. God's goal for his people is that they should be perfect, and achieving this goal energizes Paul's apostolic ministry.* Convinced that God wants all to be saved, Paul desires nothing less than to present "every person" mature in Christ (Col 1:28). His ministry, whether it be exhorting, teaching or some other means, serves that one intended aim (see Du Plessis, 198-99).

Though salvation itself brings a status of perfection, the new life in Christ needs to be actualized. What is its intended goal? For Paul the goal is perfection, on both an individual and a corporate level. And perfection has two stages: a relative kind of perfection that Christians work to attain in this life, and a final state of absolute sinless perfection realized only in the life to come.

**3. Relative Perfection in This Life.**
First, Paul holds out the prospect of perfection for individual believers. Paul urges Christians who have been so greatly graced by God's salvation* to seek what is perfect (Rom 12:2). God's will is "perfect," and believers, by the renewing transformation of their minds accomplished by God's Spirit,* can know God's will. God purposes nothing short of the goal that his people should perfectly accomplish his will. Along the same lines Paul insists that perfection, or maturity, derives only from living according to God's will (Col 4:12). These are present goals for Christians to seek.

Second, on the corporate side Paul urges the church* to maturity—to become fully grown adults in all their ways. In Ephesians 4:13 Paul calls not individuals but the entire church to God's goal for its existence: the fullness* of Christ (cf. Eph 3:19 for fullness of God).

Maturity also entails the church's corporate expression of unity characterized by faith* and love.* Though "in Christ" the church already exists as God's new, mature person (Eph 2:15), yet it must pursue these virtues with the aid of the ministers Christ has given it (Eph 4:16). This fits Paul's stress on love in Colossians 3:14, where love binds and unites the gifts* and efforts of church members. Pursuing love, Paul says, produces perfection. The church thus becomes what God determined it to be. Here Lietzmann's dictum proves helpful in explaining Paul: "become what you are." "Work out ethically all that is involved in being in Christ" (Flew, 59).

**4. Ultimate Perfection in the Age to Come.**
Though perfection remains the goal for Christians in this life, and a relative perfection might be achieved, Paul envisioned an eventual state of entire perfection for those who are in Christ. This constitutes in a paramount sense "the end" or "the complete state." In this age, as holy or loving as any individual or church may become, absolute perfection remains elusive because it belongs to the age to come. Everything is "in part" until the perfect comes (1 Cor 13:10). Even the best qualities or actions believers can presently exhibit—including the exercise of the most impressive spiritual gifts—fall short of God's final intention for his people. But at the end, when Christ returns and the church secures its final destiny, perfection or completeness reigns (*see* Eschatology). Paul sees that destiny as a prize at the finish line, and he works earnestly to attain that perfection (Phil 3:12-14). He recognizes that he is not yet perfect, yet that consummate state serves to inspire his present life. When the resurrection comes, he will attain the prize. Then

Christians will truly be all God designed them to be—perfect.

Did Paul believe that believers could ever approximate in this life the final perfection of sinlessness? Though it is not extensive, the evidence does suggest that Paul never envisions that Christians could achieve a state of sinlessness in this life. He never claims as much for himself, nor does he ever hold up any other Christians as models of sinlessness. At the same time, Paul clearly sees sin* as a defeated foe. Though Christians may never become completely sinless in this life, God intends that they should and must avoid sinning. And Paul teaches that it is possible for Christians *not to sin*. In Galatians 5:16-26 he champions the power of the Spirit over the sinful nature, and in Romans 6:2, 6, 11-14, 18, 22 he clearly insists that resisting sin is not only possible, it is the required response of those whom God justified. The point is not that Christians reach a state in which they cannot sin, but that God has empowered them so that they need not sin.

*See also* APOSTASY, FALLING AWAY, PERSEVERANCE; ESCHATOLOGY; FULLNESS; GLORY, GLORIFICATION; HOLINESS, SANCTIFICATION; SIN, GUILT; SPIRITUALITY.

BIBLIOGRAPHY. A. Deissler and F. Mussner, "Perfection," *EBT* 2.658-67; G. Delling, "τέλος κτλ" *TDNT* VII.49-87; R. N. Flew, *The Idea of Perfection in Christian Theology* (London: Oxford University Press, 1934); P. J. Du Plessis, Teleios: *The Idea of Perfection in the New Testament* (Kampen: Uitgave, 1959); H. K. La Rondelle, *Perfection and Perfectionism* (Berrien Springs, MI: Andrews University, 1971); R. Schippers, "τέλος," *NIDNTT* 2.59-66; R. Schnackenburg, "Christian Adulthood according to the Apostle Paul," *CBQ* 25 (1963) 254-370; B. B. Warfield, *Perfectionism*, Vol. 1 (New York: Oxford University Press, 1931); J. A. Ziesler, "Anthropology of Hope," *ExpT* 90 (1979) 104-9.

W. W. Klein

**PERSECUTION.** *See* AFFLICTIONS, TRIALS, HARDSHIPS.

**PERSECUTOR, PAUL AS.** *See* JEALOUSY, ZEAL; JEW, PAUL THE; PAUL IN ACTS AND LETTERS.

**PERSEVERANCE.** *See* APOSTASY, FALLING AWAY, PERSEVERANCE; FAITH.

**PERSON, THE.** *See* PSYCHOLOGY.

**PESHER INTERPRETATION.** *See* JEW, PAUL THE; OLD TESTAMENT IN PAUL.

## PETER

Paul never refers to the apostle* Peter by his original name of *Simon* (*Simōn*, as frequently in the Gospels) or *Simeon* (*Symeōn*, as in Acts 15:14 and the preferred text of 2 Pet 1:1). Only twice (Gal 2:7, 8) does he use the name *Peter* (*Petros*, or "Rock") given to Simon by Jesus (Mt 16:17-18; Mk 3:16 par. Lk 6:14; Jn 1:42). In the eight other instances in which Paul refers to Peter (1 Cor 1:12; 3:22; 9:5; 15:5; Gal 1:18; 2:9, 11, 14), he does so with the Aramaic equivalent, Cephas (i.e., *kēpha*, or "rock," identified as *Petros*, "Peter" in Jn 1:42). A possible explanation for this is that Paul regarded *Cephas* as a real name, not a nickname, and consequently not to be translated. The exceptional use of *Peter* in Galatians 2:7, 8 could then be viewed as Paul's accommodation to the wording of an actual agreement drawn up at Jerusalem* regarding the mission* to Jews (*see* Israel) and Gentiles.*

It has been seriously argued (e.g., Lake, Ehrman) that Simon Peter and Cephas were not the same person. Yet even apart from the explicit identification in John 1:42, it is difficult to imagine two different figures in the ancient church, each with a name meaning "rock," each mentioned first among those who saw the risen Christ (in 1 Cor 15:5, within a confessional statement antedating Paul, and in Lk 24:34) and each identified as one sent "to the circumcision" (Gal 2:7-8, with v. 9).

1. Peter in Galatians
2. Peter in 1 Corinthians

### 1. Peter in Galatians.

Paul speaks of "Cephas" only in Galatians and 1 Corinthians. Each time "Cephas" is mentioned in Galatians (i.e., Gal 1:18; 2:9, 11), "Peter" occurs as a variant reading in some manuscripts (e.g., in Codex D [Claromontanus], the Old Latin versions and the majority of later Greek manuscripts; *see* Textual Criticism). A likely reason for this is the unquestioned occurrence of "Peter" in Galatians 2:7, 8. The tendency of later scribes would have been to achieve consistency by conforming the less familiar to the more familiar name.

The purpose of Paul's personal history in Galatians 1:13—2:10 is to minimize his contacts with Peter, not to emphasize them. But Paul admits that three years after receiving a revelation (*see* Conversion and Call) from God* he went to Jerusalem to get acquainted with Cephas and spent fifteen days with him there (Gal 1:18). Fourteen years later he returned with Barnabas* and Titus (*see* Coworkers), not on his own initiative but in obedience to another divine revelation (Gal 2:1-2). Paul insists that the leaders of the Jerusalem church "added nothing" to the gospel* he was already proclaiming (Gal 2:6), but that "James,* Cephas and John" endorsed his ministry by giving him and Barnabas "the right hand of fellowship" (Gal 2:9). It was agreed that Paul and Barnabas would go to the Gentiles, while Cephas and his two associates in Jerusalem would continue their mission to the Jewish people (lit., "the circumcision,*" Gal 2:9; cf. the reference to "Peter" in Gal 2:7, 8). The only stipulation was that Paul and Barnabas "should continue to remember the poor [especially among Jewish Christians, cf. Rom 15:26], the very thing I was eager to do" (Gal 2:10).

Paul encountered Cephas again at Antioch* (Gal 2:11-14) and "opposed him to his face, because he was clearly in the wrong" (Gal 2:11 NIV). Cephas had been eating freely with Gentile Christians until some messengers came from James. At this time, Paul claims, Cephas "drew back and separated himself because he feared those who belonged to the circumcision group" (Gal 2:12). This hypocrisy, as Paul calls it, influenced other Jewish Christians, including Barnabas, to break off table fellowship (see Food) with the Gentile believers in Antioch. Paul's consequent rebuke to Cephas serves as an introduction to his main argument in Galatians (Gal 2:14-21). "If you, being a Jew," Paul begins, "live like a Gentile and not like a Jew, how can you compel the Gentiles to live like Jews?" (Gal 2:14). It is not clear at what point Paul's words to Cephas end and his written words to the Galatians begin, but it is likely that at least Galatians 2:15-17 is intended to fit the context of the confrontation just described. Paul rebuked Cephas precisely because he was convinced that they both agreed in principle. Both had in common the fact that they were "Jews by birth and not Gentile sinners" (Gal 2:15), and both shared in the knowledge that "one is not justified by the works of the Law but by faith in Jesus Christ" (Gal 2:16). Paul's charge was that Cephas had failed to live up to his own convictions.

Quite possibly it was the record of this disagreement that made some later writers (e.g., *Epistle of the Apostles* 2; Clement of Alexandria, in Eusebius *Hist. Eccl.* 1.12.2) reluctant to conclude that Cephas and the apostle Peter were the same person. This evidence is another reason why modern scholars who have attempted to draw a distinction between the two are on shaky ground.

### 2. Peter in 1 Corinthians.
"Cephas" is mentioned four times in 1 Corinthians (1 Cor 1:12; 3:22; 9:5; 15:5), and in none of these instances is "Peter" introduced into the manuscript tradition. Paul states that some in Corinth were saying "I belong to Cephas" (1 Cor 1:12), just as others were saying "I belong to Paul," "I belong to Apollos*" or "I belong to Christ" (see Corinthians). This verse (1 Cor 1:12) carries no necessary implication that Peter's adherents took a particular theological stance over against that of Paul. Their allegiance could have been simply a personal attitude on the part of some who admired Peter, or Peter could have represented in Corinth the authority of the Twelve or of the Jerusalem church. It is difficult to say. The same is true in 1 Corinthians 3:22, where Cephas is mentioned again, along with Paul and Apollos, as someone of importance to the Corinthian community and probably not just to his own faction.

Paul introduces Cephas as an example for yet a third time (1 Cor 9:5) in a list of those who had a right to support from the churches so that they would not have to worry about earning a living or being separated from their wives: "Don't we have the right to food and drink?" Paul asks. "Don't we have the right to take a believing wife along with us, like the rest of the apostles, and the Lord's brothers, and Cephas? Or is it only I and Barnabas who have to work for a living?" (1 Cor 9:4-6). Again Peter is singled out, either because of his following in Corinth or because he represented the Twelve. The phrase "the rest of the apostles" probably includes all Christian missionaries known to Paul (except Barnabas), and within this group Paul wants to call attention particularly to "the Lord's brothers" and (possibly) the Twelve originally chosen by Jesus. By singling out Peter, Paul could be implying that Peter was married, but he does not say so explicitly. Clearly, he is not pronouncing on the marital status of all "the Lord's brothers" and "the rest of the apostles." What Paul is saying is that Peter and the others had the right to marry (see Marriage) and enjoy the support (see Financial Support) of the churches for themselves and their wives, and Paul wants to claim that same right for himself—even if he made no use of it.

Paul's last reference to Cephas in 1 Corinthians comes in his list of witnesses to the resurrection* (1 Cor 15:5). Christ* "appeared to Cephas, then to the Twelve, then he appeared to five hundred at once, . . . then he appeared to James, then to all the apostles" (1 Cor 15:5-7). The recurrent "then" (*epeita*) suggests that Paul was interested in the order of the appearances, yet he did not characterize the appearance to Cephas as "first" (in contrast to an appearance "last of all . . . to me" in 1 Cor 15:8). Paul was evidently following a tradition similar to that of Mark (Mk 16:7) or Luke (Lk 24:34) or John (Jn 21:15-17), in which an appearance to Peter is distinguished from an appearance to the Twelve as a group. Possibly there is a tacit acknowledgment in the tradition Paul was following that the "first" appearance of the risen Christ was to women at the tomb (as in Mt 28:9-10 and Jn 20:14-17). At any rate, Paul assigns no preeminence to Cephas for having been the first to see the risen Lord.*

Paul's references to Cephas in Galatians and 1 Corinthians are all distant and somewhat guarded. Aside from the confrontation described in Galatians 2:11-14, there was no hostility between the two apostles, but Paul was always careful to maintain the principle that Peter "added nothing" (Gal 2:6) to the revelation that Paul himself had received. As for Peter, in the canonical letters attributed to him, Paul is mentioned only once (2 Pet 3:15-16), and with similar reserve. The author of 2 Peter believed that "our beloved brother Paul," when rightly interpreted, was in agreement with Peter, but this author did not have the same confidence in Paul's followers. Paul's letters were "hard to understand" and therefore easily distorted by the "ignorant and unstable." Even though they were classed among "the Scriptures" (2 Pet 3:16), they needed the clarification that the voice of the apostle Peter was able to supply.

*See also* ANTIOCH ON THE ORONTES; GALATIANS, LETTER TO THE; JERUSALEM.

BIBLIOGRAPHY. R. E. Brown and J. P. Maier, *Antioch and Rome* (New York: Paulist, 1983); R. E. Brown, K. P. Donfried, J. Reumann, *Peter in the New Testament* (Minneapolis: Augsburg; New York: Paulist, 1973); O. Cullmann, *Peter: Disciple, Apostle, Martyr* (2d ed.; Philadelphia: Westminster, 1962); B. D. Ehrman, "Cephas and Peter," *JBL* 109 (1990) 463-74; W. R. Farmer and R. Kereszty, *Peter and Paul in the Church of Rome* (New York: Paulist, 1990); K. Lake, "Simon, Cephas, Peter," *HTR* 14 (1921) 95-97.

J. R. Michaels

**PHARISEES.** *See* DISCIPLINE; JEW, PAUL THE; RESTORATION OF ISRAEL; REVOLUTIONARY MOVEMENTS.

## PHILEMON, LETTER TO

Philemon is the shortest (335 words in Greek) and most personal of the letters belonging to the Pauline corpus. Despite the literary, historical and interpretive problems the letter raises for modern scholarship, it offers a fascinating window not only on a corner of the social world of the first century, but on Christian principles at work in a particular setting within the early church.

1. History of Interpretation
2. Continuing Questions of Interpretation
3. Theological Significance

### 1. History of Interpretation.

*1.1. Historical-Critical Method.* Although there are some older critical theories which tended to question the letter's authenticity and purpose (F. C. Baur, for example, regarded it as a second-century "fictional romance" seeking to address the issue of slavery in the early church), the interpretation given by most commentators who follow the historical-critical method and the "natural" meaning of the text, is that this letter was written somewhere between A.D. 58 and 60 while Paul was in a Roman prison. It appears that the letter is addressed to Philemon (Philem 1), who was a wealthy Gentile Christian in Colossae who became a believer under Paul's ministry* (Philem 19). Its divisions include Paul's greetings (Philem 1-3); thanksgiving and prayer* (Philem 4-7); intercession for Onesimus (Philem 18-22); final greetings and benediction* (Philem 23-25).

The heart of the letter centers upon Onesimus, Philemon's slave* who had somehow wronged his master (Philem 18), made his way to Paul in prison (Philem 9), was converted (Philem 10) and became a useful partner (*see* Coworkers) with Paul in the gospel* (Philem 11, 13). But under the existing laws governing slavery, Paul knows that Onesimus must be returned to his rightful owner. In the letter, Paul implores Philemon not only to receive (Philem 17), forgive (Philem 18; *see* Forgiveness) and acknowledge Onesimus' new status as a fellow believer (Philem 16), but to relinquish all claims upon Onesimus so that he can continue serving with Paul (Philem 13, 21).

In the opening greetings (Philem 1-3) Paul identifies Philemon as a "dear friend and fellow worker" (NIV). We have no way of knowing how the two became acquainted and whether Philemon 19 should be taken to imply that Philemon was converted by Paul. If so, it probably was during Paul's stay in Ephesus* and in similar circumstances when Epaphras, another resident of Colossae, came under Paul's ministry (Col 1:7; 4:12). Nor is there any way of knowing whether Apphia was Philemon's wife and Archippus his son.

The thanksgiving and prayer (Philem 4-7) focus on Philemon, who is commended for his faith* in Christ* and his love* for the saints. Both of these virtues have "refreshed" (*anapauō*) the saints and given joy and encouragement to the apostle.* The accent is on Philemon's spirit of love and not on any specific actions. It is the same word (*splangkna*) that Paul uses in verse 20 where he anticipates the effect of Philemon's response.

Paul's request—or intercession—on behalf of Onesimus (Philem 8-22) takes the reader through a series of agonizing delays because Paul just does not seem to get to the point (the opening, "I appeal to you for my son Onesimus" in verse 10, is not completed until verse 17). But Paul is careful to use diplomacy and tact in handling this rather delicate matter. He needs to state the request strongly but yet have the decision be voluntary. He wants Philemon to act out of conviction, not out of compulsion (Philem 14). Thus Paul approaches Philemon as a friend and coworker and not with apostolic authority.*

Although the circumstances surrounding Onesimus' arrival at the place of Paul's imprisonment and his conversion to the Christian faith are uncertain, this section clarifies the strong attachment that Paul has developed for his spiritual "son" (Philem 10) and "brother" (Philem 16) and the appreciation for Onesimus' ministry to him while under house arrest.

All this puts Paul on the horns of a dilemma: Onesimus, whose name means "useful," can only be of value to his master if he returns, and to Paul if he stays. In spite of Paul's tact in approaching Philemon, it is obvious that he wants Philemon to release Onesimus so that he can retain him for his own service. This appears to overshadow the other concern Paul had that Philemon forgive Onesimus and receive him as a Christian brother (Philem 16). Paul's confidence of his release and plan to visit Philemon (Philem 22) may be related to both of these requests. Could it be that Onesimus returned to Colossae before Paul, that he was forgiven by Philemon, and then released to Paul when the apostle visited Colossae?

The final greetings (Philem 23-25) are almost identical to the closing section of Colossians (Col 4:12-18). The plural form of you (hymōn) in the benediction ("The grace of our Lord Jesus Christ be with your spirit") carries a singular meaning and does not necessarily confirm the public nature of the letter.

The letter to Philemon and the letter to the Colossians* are closely related. Both are written from the same place, addressed to the same church, were carried to Colossae by Tychicus (Col 4:8-9), both mention similar circumstances about Paul's imprisonment (Col 4:3; Philem 1, 13) and have an almost identical list of personal greetings. It is most likely that the two letters were kept together as Paul's correspondence to Colossae. Unfortunately, the relationship of these two letters was lost when the compilers of the NT separated them in the canon.*

*1.2. Knox's Reconstruction.* J. Knox's provocative study of Philemon broke with the traditional interpretation at a number of points. First, he identifies Archippus as the recipient of the letter and thus Onesimus' master. The "work" (NIV) or "ministry" (RSV) which Paul admonishes Archippus to complete (Col

4:17) refers to the way he was to receive and handle Onesimus. Philemon is an "overseer" of the churches in the Lycus Valley with a probable residence in Laodicea. Second, he equates "the letter from Laodicea" which Paul wants read in Colossae (Col 4:16) as "the epistle to Philemon." Third, Knox believes that the restored slave Onesimus is the same person who became bishop of Ephesus and may have been responsible for collecting Paul's letters in the second century (Ignatius *Eph.* 1.3). This, claims Knox, could account for the preservation and inclusion of this brief and personal letter in the canon.

Reaction to Knox's reconstruction varies among scholars. While most regard it as novel, interesting and/or ingenious, much of his reconstruction is generally dismissed as lacking sufficient evidence to be taken seriously. It seems more natural to conclude that Philemon, the first person addressed in the letter, is the recipient and the one to whom Paul is interceding on behalf of Onesimus. Neither can the letter referred to in Colossians 4:16 be identified with certainty as our letter to Philemon. On the other hand, Knox's proposal regarding the preservation and function of this letter remains intriguing.

*1.3. Rhetorical Criticism.* This approach analyzes the letter of Philemon through the categories of ancient rhetoric.* F. Forrester Church, for example, believes that Paul is employing such classical rhetorical devices as "pathos," "ethos" and "forensic rhetoric" in order to persuade Philemon to accept his request. "The key" to deliberative rhetoric, writes Church, "is to demonstrate love or friendship and to induce sympathy or goodwill, in order to dispose the hearer favorably to the merits of one's case" (Church, 19-20). In rhetorical categories, Philemon would be divided into the exordium (Philem 4-7), proof (Philem 8-16) and peroration (Philem 17-22; *see* Rhetorical Criticism).

This method does not necessarily challenge the interpretation of Philemon given above. Its proponents believe that it provides further insights into the shape and design of Paul's letters (see White; *see* Letters, Letter Forms). The fact that a common rhetorical device was used to "conceal the ultimate objective" so that the hearers or readers may find it for themselves may account for the ambiguous and puzzling way Paul actually makes his request to Philemon (Derrett).

*1.4. Legal Analogies.* S. Winter has examined Philemon for parallels to legal forms and language used in Paul's day and believes that there are significant analogies which help to explain certain phrases in the letter. Paul's appeal in Philemon 10 (*parakalō . . . peri*), for example, is like a formula used in legal petitions; *anapempō* in Philem 12 ("I am sending him . . . back to you . . .") is a legal term better understood as referring Onesimus' case "to the proper higher authority"; and the idea of the partnership (*koinōnia*) between Paul and Philemon, notes Winter, has more of the elements of a "consensual association," a *societas* in which partnership was legally binding. Paul's plea to Philemon is that Onesimus be received into this *societas* as an equal partner (Winter 1987, 7).

*1.5. Literary Criticism and the Social Sciences.* The most extensive and significant work on the letter to Philemon from this perspective belongs to N. Petersen who draws upon sociological and anthropological models (those of, e.g., Levi-Strauss, Evans-Pritchard, Berger, Eco) and insights on the sociology of the NT (the writings of J. Elliott, B. Malina, W. Meeks and G. Theissen; *see* Social-Scientific Approaches).

Basically, Petersen transfers the letter into a story in order to create a "narrative world" in which Paul is the narrator and Philemon the actor. This narrative is played out in the midst of two social realities—the church* and the world.* The heart of the letter, according to Petersen, centers upon the sociological categories of "kinship" and the tension Philemon faces when confronted with values of kinship in the world and in the church. Paul is forcing Philemon to decide between the two.

The historical and literary approaches outlined above are not mutually exclusive. Rather, they are positive attempts by several disciplines to discover the nature and purpose of this letter. And, even though the letter to Philemon may not necessarily be written as a legal or rhetorical document, there are insights, when combined with the historical-critical method, that are helpful.

## 2. Continuing Questions of Interpretation.

Scholarly debate continues around issues where the text is ambiguous or for which there is no conclusive proof. These include the recipient of the letter (Philemon or Archippus), the address of the recipient (Colossae or Laodicea) and the place of Paul's imprisonment (Rome, Ephesus or Caesarea). Speculation also abounds on how and where Onesimus was converted, if he actually was returned to Philemon, if Paul was able to retain him as a coworker and whether or not he became the bishop of Ephesus. Two major concerns, however, merit special mention.

*2.1. Onesimus: "Runaway Slave" or "Sent Messenger"?* The traditional interpretation among commentators is based on the inference that Onesimus was a runaway slave who probably stole something from his master (Philem 11, 18). This view was doubted by Knox, whose doubts are amplified by Winter who proposes

that Onesimus was "sent" to Paul by the Colossian congregation in order to meet some of Paul's physical needs while Paul was under house arrest. Onesimus' departure and consequent separation (Philem 15) from Philemon need not imply that he ran away. The situation could be similar to the one that brought Epaphroditus from Philippi to Paul while Paul was in prison (cf. Phil 2:22-30).

Winter's conclusions are based on several observations: first, she believes that Paul's commendations of Philemon in the thanksgiving section (Philem 4-7) express the apostle's gratitude for sending Onesimus to him; second, she interprets certain phrases to mean that Paul's "hearing" of Philemon's faith (Philem 5) came from Onesimus, that the "good thing" (*pantos agathou*, Philem 6; *see* Wright) and the "sharing of your faith" (*koinōnia*, 6) is Paul's response to having Onesimus sent by Philemon (Winter, 3-4). Some of this exegesis is questionable and lacks support from the main body of the letter.

All this, however, does not necessarily mean that Onesimus was a runaway slave in the traditional sense of being a fugitive or deserter (cf. Bruce, 197). P. Lampe argues that the situation of Onesimus does not fit the legal category of a "fugitive" (*fugitivus*). Under certain conditions of Roman law governing slavery, it was possible for a slave to seek out an advocate or intercessor to mediate a grievance with the master. In this case Onesimus legally makes his way to the place of Paul's imprisonment to seek help (Lampe; Bruce, 197; Bartchy; *see* Slave, Slavery).

Is it reasonable to suggest the following scenario? Onesimus would have known Paul from the contacts that Philemon had with the apostle (in visits to Ephesus?) and may even have become Paul's friend. Some serious domestic grievance destroyed the relationship between slave and master and Onesimus, who knew his civil rights, believed that Paul could intercede for him. While visiting with Paul and attending to his needs while he was under house arrest (Philem 11, 13), Onesimus became a believer (Philem 10). Paul, then, wrote this "letter of intercession" trusting that Philemon would forgive the "wrong" (*adikeō*), cancel any debt ("owes you anything," Philem 18, 19), accept Onesimus as a "brother in the Lord" (Philem 16) and release Onesimus into Paul's service (Philem 21). We need not infer from Philemon 18 and 19 that Onesimus had stolen money from Philemon other than, perhaps, enough to finance his journey to Paul (cf. O'Brien, 299-300). It could also be that Philemon loaned Onesimus to Paul (a modification of the "sent" theory) so that the "debt" refers to time and not monetary compensation (Patzia, 114).

**2.2. The Letter: Private or Public?** Some scholars conclude that the brevity, personal appeal to one person and the delicate way Paul handles his request, confirm that this is a private letter. However, several factors favor its public nature: (1) the length exceeds that of most private letters; (2) the greetings are extended to more than one person and, in fact, include a house church; (3) it was customary to read Paul's letters to the entire church in worship*; (4) the legal and technical language are more characteristic of a public document than a private letter; (5) it has all the characteristics of Paul's longer letters addressed to churches, such as the inclusion of Timothy as a cosender, salutation, thanksgiving, body and greetings; (6) the designations "fellow worker" (*synergos*), "sister" (*adelphē*) and "fellow soldier" (*systratiōtes*) in Philemon 1-2 suggest church titles.

Finally, one cannot help but feel that Paul's request and the issue of social relationships involves the entire Christian community and not just one person. Lohse, quoting Wickert, notes that "in the Body of Christ personal affairs are no longer private" (Lohse 187 n. 9). "In short," concludes Martin, "this brief epistle is to be seen not so much as a private letter of Paul as an individual . . . but as an apostolic letter about a personal matter" (Martin, 144). In other words, Paul is referring his case to the entire church. This public nature may also account for its value in the collection and canon of Paul's letters (*see* Canon).

### 3. Theological Significance.
The literary, historical and interpretative problems which remain should not detract from the beauty and meaning of this letter. Basically, it contains no explicit theological or ethical doctrines; it attacks no heresies in the church. Nevertheless, it presents a number of important truths that should not go unnoticed.

First, it opens a window on the nature of Paul's imprisonment and the personal relationship that he enjoyed with his friends and coworkers* (Philem 23, 24; Col 4:12-14). It ends by showing the optimism that Paul had for his release and desire to visit his beloved friend Philemon.

Second, it provides a small commentary on slavery in the ancient world. When read together with Colossians 3:22—4:1, we begin to appreciate how conversion to the Christian faith broke down all social, racial and economic barriers (Patzia, 91-93). Although Paul does not speak directly for the abolition of slavery, this letter exemplifies, as much as any other writing of his, the truth of Galatians 3:28: "There is neither Jew nor Greek, slave nor free, male nor female, for you are all one in Christ Jesus" (NIV). A new relationship and partnership has been formed in this situation where master, slave and apostle are all part of one family in Christ (Philem 16). The church as a whole should be characterized by such virtues as love, forgiveness, equality and fellowship.*

Third, it is a masterpiece of pastoral diplomacy (*see* Pastoral). Paul's request is not reinforced by expressions of compulsion, constraint or coercion. The reconciliation* between Philemon and Onesimus is based on the principles of Christian love and forgiveness and not Roman law or apostolic authority. The release of Onesimus for Paul's ministry must be a voluntary action leading to the highest good for all parties concerned. Paul is confident that he will succeed in motivating Philemon "to do even more" than he has requested (Philem 21).

Finally, as W. Barclay so aptly wrote, "here is one of the great romances of grace in the early Church" (Barclay, 316). Although we do not know how the story ended, there is enough reason to suspect that Paul's confidence (Philem 21) in Philemon was honored and that the former slave Onesimus, now a brother in Christ, continued to serve Paul.

*See also* COLOSSIANS, LETTER TO THE; SLAVE, SLAVERY.

BIBLIOGRAPHY. **Commentaries:** W. Barclay, *The Letters of Timothy, Titus and Philemon* (Philadelphia: Westminster, 1960); F. F. Bruce, *The Epistle to the Colossians, to Philemon, and to the Ephesians* (NICNT; Grand Rapids: Eerdmans, 1984); J. Gnilka, *Der Philemonbrief* (HTKNT 10.4; Freiburg, Basel, Vienna: Herder, 1982); E. Lohse, *Colossians and Philemon* (Herm; Philadelphia: Fortress, 1971); R. P. Martin, *Colossians and Philemon* (rev. ed.; NCB; Grand Rapids: Eerdmans, 1981); P. T. O'Brien, *Colossians, Philemon* (WBC 44; Waco: Word, 1982); A. Patzia, *Ephesians, Colossians, Philemon* (NIBC; Peabody, MA.; Hendrickson, 1991); P. Stuhlmacher, *Der Brief an Philemon* (2d ed.; EKKNT 18; Zürich: Neukirchener, 1981); A. Suhl, *Der Brief an Philemon* (ZBNT 13; Zürich: Theologischer Verlag, 1981). **Studies:** S. S. Bartchy, "Philemon, Epistle to," *ABD* V. 305-10; F. F. Church, "Rhetorical Structure and Design in Paul's Letter to Philemon," *HTR* 71 (1978) 17-33; J. D. M. Derrett, "The Function of the Epistle to Philemon," *ZNW* 19 (1988) 85; J. Knox, *Philemon Among the Letters of Paul* (New York: Abingdon, 1959); P. Lampe, "Keine Sklavenflucht des Onesimus," *ZNW* 76 (1985) 135-37; N. R. Petersen, *Rediscovering Paul: Philemon and the Sociology of Paul's Narrative World* (Philadelphia: Fortress, 1985); J. White, *The Structural Analysis of Philemon: A Point of Departure in the Formal Analysis of the Pauline Letter* (SBLASP; Missoula: Scholars, 1971); S. Winter, "Methodological Observations on a New Interpretation of Paul's Letter to Philemon," *USQR* 35

(1984) 203-12; idem, "Paul's Letter to Philemon," *NTS* 33 (1987) 1-15; N. T. Wright, "*ΧΡΙΣΤΟΣ* as 'Messiah' in Paul: Philemon 6," in *The Climax of the Covenant* (Minneapolis: Fortress, 1991) 41-55.

A. Patzia

**PHILIPPI.** *See* PHILIPPIANS, LETTER TO THE.

## PHILIPPIANS, LETTER TO THE

Philippians is a letter the apostle Paul wrote to the church in the city of Philippi in Macedonia, the first church* he founded in Europe. It is the most personal of all of his letters. Although not a theological treatise, Philippians does have a great deal to say about God* and his ways with people, about Christ* Jesus and about Christians and how they should live in this world. The terms "overseers" and "deacons" (1:1) occur here for the one and only time in Paul's letters, but without any elaboration on what these people did or about what kind of authority* they exercised within the church.

1. Contents
2. The City and Its Citizens
3. The Church and Its Apostle
4. Some Critical Questions
5. Theological Themes

### 1. Contents.

*1.1.* The letter begins with a salutation that is both like (e.g., "A to B, greetings!") and unlike (e.g., "from God our Father and the Lord Jesus Christ") letters that were typical of first-century letter forms (1:1-2) (*see* Epistle, Epistolary Forms).

*1.2.* Paul then thanks God for the Philippians, reminds them of his constant prayer* and affection for them, of his confidence in God concerning them, gives a brief account of his imprisonment and the unexpected positive effects it has had and informs them of the likelihood that he will be released from prison* and reunited with them (1:3-26).

*1.3.* Paul turns from thanks to plead with the Philippians to live in a manner worthy of the gospel* of Christ: harmoniously with one another, striving for the faith of the gospel, unafraid of opponents of the gospel, willing to suffer for the gospel, eager to imitate Christ Jesus in seeking the welfare of others with humility, carrying out responsibilities without murmuring or grumbling and keeping themselves pure and holy, blameless children of God (1:27—2:18).

*1.4.* Paul tells them of his desire to send Timothy to them, but until he is able to do so, of his intention instead to send back to them Epaphroditus, one of their own people, their messenger to him—a man who had risked his life in order to bring their gifts to him (2:19—3:1).

*1.5.* The letter changes tone at this point. Paul now begins a bitter attack on those who would subvert the Philippians—upon people who are "enemies of the cross* of Christ." He counters whatever influence they may have had with an assertion of his own authority based not on status but sacrifice, taking the Christ of the Christ hymn* as his model (cf. 3:4-11 with 2:6-11), not on his own self-worth but the exceeding worth of Christ Jesus (3:2-21).

*1.6.* In conclusion, Paul pleads for unity in the church, especially among its leaders, gives his advice about how Christians are to feel and think and act, relieves the Philippians of any sense of guilt they may have had for those times when they were not able to send him aid, gives them thanks for their renewed generosity and brings the letter to a close with a doxology* to God, greetings to all and a benediction* (4:1-23).

### 2. The City and Its Citizens.

Philippi was already a very old and historic city when Paul arrived and later wrote his letter to the Christians there. Philip of Macedon had built it in 358-57 B.C. on the site of an ancient Thracian city located eight miles from the sea in a spring-filled, fertile region. He fortified it and named it after himself. Later Philippi became part of the Roman Empire and was made one of the stations along the main overland route connecting Rome with the East. Destroyed by wars, it was rebuilt by the Emperor* Octavian, who established it as a military outpost, populated it with veterans of his wars, made it a Roman colony and gave it the *ius italicum*—the highest privilege obtainable by a provincial municipality (*see* Legal System, Roman). Consequently, as the citizens of Rome, so the citizens of Philippi could buy and sell property, were exempt from land tax and the poll tax and were entitled to protection by Roman law. Thus it was that when Paul made his first journey to Europe, he purposely neglected the port city of Neapolis to begin preaching the gospel in the small but more important city of Philippi of the first district of Macedonia (Acts 16:12).

Philippi was inhabited predominantly by Romans, but many Macedonian Greeks and some Jews lived there as well. Its people were proud of their city, proud of their ties with Rome, proud to observe Roman customs and obey Roman laws, proud to be Roman citizens* (cf. Acts 16:21). Twice in this brief letter Paul makes statements that capitalize on this fact: "Only conduct yourselves in a manner worthy of the gospel of Christ" (1:27), where the verb he uses for "conduct yourselves," *politeuesthe*, literally means "to live as a citizen, to live as freepersons," even "to take part in government." By choosing this word Paul seems to be appealing to their pride as Roman citizens, and to be extending this idea now to the church, the new community to which they belong, and of which they must be responsible citizens, abiding by its law of love. Paul's other statement is in 3:20: "For our citizenship [*politeuma*] is in heaven. . ." Here again his choice of the word *politeuma* recalls what he said in 1:27 and suggests that once more he is reflecting on the civic status of Philippi as a Roman colony, and reminding the Philippians that they now belong to a higher, more important, more enduring commonwealth. Choosing Philippi, thus, as the place to launch the gospel on European soil fitted in with Paul's mission strategy of selecting important cities of repute and strategic location as ideal centers from which the good news of the gospel might radiate out.

### 3. The Church and Its Apostle.

Paul came to Philippi as the result of a vision he had while he was in Troas. He saw a "man of Macedonia" and heard him say "Come over . . . and help us." Immediately after the vision Paul and his party left off their attempts to go into Bithynia and decided instead to go into Macedonia, concluding that God had called them to preach the gospel there (Acts 16:9-10). According to the Acts account the first convert to Christianity in Philippi was a woman, Lydia. Although Lydia was a pagan, she nevertheless was a God-fearing person who had been attracted to the lofty ideals of the Jewish religion (Acts 16:14). But when she heard Paul preach the gospel and, as Luke said, God opened her heart, she put her faith in Jesus Christ and along with her household was baptized (16:14-15). These people became the nucleus of the church at Philippi, and while meeting in the home of Lydia they showed great kindness in their generous hospitality to Paul and his companions, prevailing upon them to come and join this household and stay with them (Acts 16:15).

The only other Philippian converts mentioned in Acts were the Roman soldier, who guarded the jail where Paul had been put in prison, and his household (Acts 16:30-33). But the extraordinary circumstances in which the jailer became a Christian generated within him such affection for Paul and Silas that he washed their wounds, brought them into his house and spread his table with food for them to eat.

The reactions of these two people, one a distinguished and wealthy woman and one a Roman soldier, and of those around them toward the apostle set the tone for the relationship that was to endure between the church at Philippi and Paul. It is obvious from this brief letter, no doubt one of several he wrote to the Philippians (see Polycarp's *Letter to the Philippians* 3.2), that not only did he have a deep affection for the Philippians, but they as well for him (cf. 1:7; 4:16). When he addresses them he does not do so as "Paul the apostle" but only as a servant of Christ Jesus—he had no need to convince them of his authority. This is not to say, however, that there were not things happening in this church that grieved Paul and against which he raised his voice. Apparently there were divisions between groups of people there (1:27; 2:2), with people who were selfish, conceited and looking out only for their own interests (2:3-4). There were people who were murmuring and grumbling (2:14) and people who simply could not get along with others (4:2)—and all within the church. In a gentle fashion, holding up before them the way of the Christ, he graciously calls them back to harmony and mutual concern one for another.

Little else is known about the composition of the church in Philippi, but names such as Epaphroditus, Euodia, Syntyche and Clement—all mentioned by Paul as members of this church (Phil 2:25; 4:2-3)—indicate that this first Christian church on European soil was made up largely of Greeks. Furthermore, it is safe to infer that from its inception women played an important role in this church, even in its leadership. Not only was its first convert a woman, a woman of wealth and influence (Acts 16:14), but it is possible that all the other women who had met with Lydia for prayer by the riverside even before Paul came to Philippi (Acts 16:13) also were led to faith in Jesus Christ by her example and testimony. It is a fact worthy of note that of the four Philippians mentioned by name in this letter, two of them are women and are designated by Paul as women who worked hard alongside him in the proclamation of the gospel (Phil 4:3) (*see* Man and Woman).

### 4. Some Critical Questions.

*4.1. Authorship.* Although the letter to the Philippians opens with the words "[From] Paul and Timothy" (1:1), it is clear that whatever may have been the reason for Timothy's name being linked together with that of the apostle, it was Paul alone who was responsible for this letter and its contents. The tone of the letter is far too personal to be otherwise. For example, Paul's use of the singular personal pronouns "I," "me," "my"—occurring fifty-one times in such a short letter—alone argues for this. But, in addition, Timothy's name reappears again only in 2:19 and not at all, as might be expected, in the final salutation. In effect, therefore, it is Paul alone who lays claim to being the author of Philippians.

Historically the church has accepted this claim without question—Polycarp of Smyrna, Irenaeus, Clement of Alexandria, Tertullian and others not only quoted from Philippians but assigned it solely to Paul (*see* Paul in Early Church Tradition). In the nineteenth century, however, some thinkers began to doubt that Paul had written Philippians. The most articulate of these thinkers was F. C. Baur (*Paul, the Apostle of Jesus Christ*). Baur's historical studies led him to the conclusion that Paul wrote none of the letters that bear his name, including Philippians, except Romans, 1 and 2 Corinthians and Galatians. In spite of the great power and erudition with which Baur argued, his arguments were not convincing nor widely adopted. Eventually they fell into disuse and essentially disappeared. From time to time, however, other scholars have attempted to revive his thesis, but with little or no success. It is thus safe to say that the vast majority of those who study the NT today are certain that Paul was responsible for Philippians and that the question of the genuineness of this letter has only historical significance.

*4.2. Unity.* Is Philippians a single letter, or is it in reality a composite of several letters written by Paul? In the second century A.D. Polycarp, bishop of Smyrna, wrote to the church at Philippi mentioning that Paul had sent them "letters" (3.2). This remark of Polycarp's, combined with the following features within Philippians itself, are sufficient reasons for many to regard this single letter in reality to be two or more letters fused together into one: 1) the quiet, orderly preparation for the conclusion of the letter at 3:1; (2) the radical change of tone from the rest of the letter beginning at 3:2 and continuing through 4:3; (3) the observation that 3:1 fits together so exactly with 4:4; and (4) the fact that Paul waits to the end of the letter to thank the Philippians for their generosity to him.

The reasons for considering Philippians a composite letter are weighty—as are those against such a consideration: (1) The fact that there is a disjointedness about Philippians and that Paul does interrupt himself at 3:2 should not be surprising in a personal, conversational letter, perhaps not all written or dictated at one time, by a person accustomed to abrupt shifts of style without notice (cf. Rom 16:16-19; 1 Thess 2:13-16). (2) There are no Greek manuscripts, no matter how far back one goes, nor is there any early Church Father offering the slightest indication that Philippians ever appeared in a form different from that which now exists. (3) It is difficult to isolate one part of the letter from another because the same terms, word-roots and motifs pervade all of its so-called parts. Fur-

thermore, the development of Paul's argument in one part of the letter often depends on what he has said in another part (cf. especially 2:6-11 with 3:7-11; and 2:6-11 with 3:20-21; see Hooker, 331-333). (4) If 3:1 and 4:4 fit together so perfectly that chapter 3 must be considered a separate letter, it is difficult to explain why any thinking scribe intent on unifying the various letters would have placed it here where it seemingly fractures the unity of the whole. The same goes for the so-called letter of thanks (4:10-20). Why would an intelligent scribe, desiring to weave the Philippian letters together into a single letter, place this particular "letter" at the end and not at the beginning?

There is thus no compelling reason to doubt that Philippians came fresh from Paul as a single letter and not as several letters later made into one by some anonymous redactor. Hence, Philippians should be treated by interpreters as a unified whole.

*4.3. Place and Date.* The place and time of Paul's writing the letter to the Philippians are important questions with a bearing on the interpretation of the text, particularly the issues of the identity of Paul's opponents and the nature of their opposition.

*4.3.1. Place.* Before it is possible to determine the provenance of Philippians, several factors must first be kept in mind: (1) that Paul was in prison when he wrote (Phil 1:7, 13, 17); (2) that he faced a trial that could end in his death (1:19-20; 2:17) or acquittal (1:25; 2:24); (3) that there was a praetorium where he was held (1:13), as well as people who belonged to Caesar's household* (4:22); (4) that Timothy was with Paul (1:1; 2:19-23); (5) that extensive, effective evangelistic efforts were going on around him (1:14-17); (6) that Paul planned to visit Philippi when he was acquitted (2:24) and (7) that apparently several trips—possibly as many as four—back and forth between Philippi and the place from which Paul wrote Philippians were made by different people within the time span of his imprisonment.

*4.3.1.1. Rome.* As the hypothetical place from which Paul wrote Philippians, Rome not only meets most of these criteria, but is the oldest and longest-held view, dating from as far back as the second century A.D. and the Marcionite prologues. Paul was a prisoner in Rome under house arrest for at least two years (Acts 28:30). Here he had soldiers guarding him (28:16), yet he was given a certain degree of freedom to receive guests and gifts and to write and send off letters (28:17, 30). Here he was free to preach the gospel (28:31). Here he would stand before Caesar and here his fate would ultimately be decided. Here were the praetorium (Phil 1:13) and "the people of Caesar's household" (4:22), which included the imperial guard and the slaves and free persons in the employ of the emperor. Here also was a church sufficiently large and not all that loyal to Paul, not having been founded by him, which might have divided into the factions Paul refers to in his letter (cf. Phil 1:14-17).

And yet to identify Rome as the place from which Paul wrote Philippians is not without its problems: (1) the distance between Rome and Philippi makes it difficult, some would argue, to fit the number of trips between these two cities into the time frame of Paul's prison term. (2) There is no indication in the Acts account that Timothy was with Paul in Rome, whereas Philippians 1:1 makes it clear that Timothy was with him wherever it was he wrote this letter. (3) Paul's intent was to visit Philippi upon his release from prison (2:24), and yet his earlier-stated plan was to quit the East and focus on mission fields in the West, especially Spain (Rom 15:24-28). (4) It has been inferred from 1:30 and 4:15-16 (cf. also 2:12, 22) that Paul is stating here that he had not returned to Philippi since he and Timothy had founded the church there—a statement he could not have made were he writing from Rome, since he had been to Philippi twice between the establishment of the Philippian church (Acts 16) and his journey to Rome (Acts 20:1-6).

*4.3.1.2. Ephesus.* Modern scholarship has suggested that Ephesus* was the place from which Paul wrote Philippians. The following reasons are given in support of this hypothesis: (1) Reference to the praetorium can point to the residence of any provincial governor in Ephesus or elsewhere (cf. Mt 27:27; Jn 18:28, 33). (2) Timothy was with Paul in Ephesus (Acts 19:22; Phil 1:1). (3) The distance between Ephesus and Philippi is minimal in comparison with that between Rome and Philippi and eliminates the time problem that requires several journeys back and forth between Philippi and the place of Paul's imprisonment. (4) Extensive evangelistic activity went on in and around Ephesus while Paul was there (Acts 19:10, 25-26; cf. Phil 1:12-14) as well as contention over Paul and his teaching (Acts 19:2-9; cf. Phil 1:15). (5) Paul refers to his being imprisoned on several occasions (2 Cor 11:23). Consequently, the fact that Acts makes no mention of his being put in prison in Ephesus is not necessarily an argument against the possibility that he was indeed imprisoned there (cf. 1 Cor 15:32; 2 Cor 1:8).

The Ephesian hypothesis, although it enjoys increasing popularity, is not without serious objections: (1) It rests mainly on inference from those texts just cited. (2) Nothing is said in Philippians about the "collection"* for the poor in Jerusalem*—certainly a matter of immense importance to Paul during his Ephe-

sian stay—and for Paul to accept gifts for himself from the church at Philippi during this period of fund raising for the Jerusalem church is inconceivable (Phil 2:25; 4:10-20). (3) The church in the city from which Paul wrote was a divided church—divided over him (Phil 1:15-17)—a fact that does not at all fit the picture of the church in Ephesus (Acts 19; 20:17-31). (4) Paul speaks rather harshly about all the Christians around him except for Timothy (Phil 2:19-21), a strange feature when his best friends, Priscilla and Aquila, were in Ephesus when he was (Acts 18:2, 18, 24-26; 1 Cor 16:19).

*4.3.1.3. Corinth.* Several factors suggest the possibility of Corinth as the place from which Philippians was written: (1) Corinth was in close geographical proximity to Philippi, closer even than Ephesus. (2) A proconsul was in Corinth (Acts 18:12), and consequently a praetorium and a "household of Caesar" was there. (3) Apparently Paul wrote Philippians before his polemic with Jewish Christians who came from James in Jerusalem (cf. Gal 2:12), for there is no mention of his apostleship in this letter; thus it was probably written before 1 Corinthians* (a letter Paul wrote from Ephesus) while he was still in Corinth. (4) The severe opposition Paul faced in Corinth, even mortal danger, and the night vision of encouragement that came to him because of it (Acts 18:10), paralleling that which came to him while in prison in Jerusalem (Acts 23:11), allows one to infer that Paul's enemies had had him arrested, put in prison and threatened with death. But comforted by this nocturnal call to courage he could be confident of release and could assure the Philippians of this fact (Phil 1:25; 2:24).

The objections to this hypothesis are similar to those raised against the Ephesian hypothesis: (1) The hypothesis is totally based on conjecture, and (2) Paul's harsh remarks about those around him (2:19-20) make no sense when one realizes that Priscilla and Aquila were also with Paul when he was in Corinth (Acts 18:1-2, 18).

*4.3.1.4. Caesarea.* Another suggested provenance for Philippians—that of Caesarea—though late in its formulation, makes a great deal of sense and harmonizes with most of the essential facts: (1) Luke specifically says that Paul was imprisoned in Caesarea in the praetorium of Herod (Acts 23:35)—the residence of the Roman procurator (*see* Political Systems) and headquarters for the Roman garrison in Palestine. (2) Paul's imprisonment in Caesarea was a long one (Acts 24:27) allowing time for several communications to travel* back and forth from Caesarea to Philippi. (3) Although Paul was kept in custody, he was nevertheless given considerable liberty with opportunity to be aided by his friends (Acts 24:23; cf. Phil 2:25-30; 4:10-20). (4) Philippians 1:7 implies that Paul had already been given a hearing and had made a defense for himself and his gospel, while 1:16 indicates that Paul still lay in prison in spite of his defense. This harmonizes with the events that took place in Caesarea (Acts 24:1-27), whereas the story of Paul in Rome concludes by describing him as a prisoner, leaving no hint that he had made any defense of any kind (Acts 28:16-31). (5) When Paul wrote to the Philippians he was confident he would be released from prison (1:24-26) and would visit them on his journey west (2:24; cf. Rom 1:13-15; 15:23-29). Here again is a close correlation between the statements in Philippians and those in Acts (19:21; 23:11). Paul's plans to move west were large in his thinking because he believed his work in the east was done (Rom 15:20, 23-24). To assume then that he later changed his mind and made plans to return east from Rome would be a perplexing assumption and one without foundation in fact. It is not unreasonable, however, to assume that Paul would want to return to Philippi on his way from Caesarea westward, in order to see his loyal and generous friends.

The objections to Caesarea are not sufficient to eliminate the assumption that this was the place from which Paul wrote to the Philippians: (1) The objection that the distance from Caesarea to Philippi is too great for the number of communications back and forth is overruled in part by the length of Paul's stay in the Caesarean prison. Too much, thus, may have been made of this matter of distance when considering either Rome or Caesarea. (2) The objection that wherever Paul was when he wrote Philippians he was facing the very real possibility of death is also not a valid objection to Caesarea (cf. Acts 21:31, 36; 22:22; 23:30). It is true that as a Roman citizen Paul had the right of appeal to Caesar, but if the Jews could have proved that he had violated their Temple* by bringing a Gentile into that part of the Temple forbidden to Gentiles, thus desecrating their holy place, then even as a Roman citizen he would, under Jewish Law, have been liable to death at the hands of the Jews (cf. Acts 25:11, and see Josephus, *J.W.* 5.193-94; *Ant.* 15.417).

Not all questions can be answered in this matter, and in reality there is no possibility of knowing with absolute certainty where it was that Paul wrote Philippians. Yet for the sake of trying to understand this letter, and especially in the interest of trying to identify the opponents mentioned in it, it may be argued that Caesarea fits the evidence as well as, or perhaps better than, any other theory of the letter's provenance.

*4.3.2. Date.* If Paul wrote the letter to the Philippians

from Rome, then he wrote it sometime in the early 60s, between A.D. 60 and 63; if from Ephesus, between A.D. 54 and 57; if from Corinth, about A.D. 50. But if he wrote this letter from Caesarea, then he wrote it sometime in the period A.D. 58-60.

*4.4. Opponents.* The opponents* mentioned in Philippians cannot be understood as a single group of people, but as several. One group opposed Paul himself, and though they preached Christ, they did so for the purpose of adding to Paul's sufferings while he was in prison. These were fellow Christians, irrespective of such a hostile attitude on their part, for Paul calls them "brothers" (1:14-15). These Christians may have had a divine-man theology that made them view such matters as humility, meekness, imprisonment and suffering—things that Paul advocated or was experiencing—as proof that he knew nothing of the triumphant power of Christ and hence was an unworthy candidate for a Christian leader who might be emulated. Or they may have been Judaizers,* who taught not only the need for faith in Christ but the necessity also of keeping the Jewish Law,* including circumcision* and regulations about food* and drink, and who thus were at odds with Paul since he held tenaciously to the necessity of faith in Christ but rejected the necessity of keeping the Law.

But there was also a second group of opponents—people very different from those in the group mentioned above. These had threatened the Philippians, had made them afraid because of their threats and had tried to undermine the firmness of the Philippians' faith in the gospel (1:27-29). Very likely this group was the same as those Paul would call "dogs," "evil workers," "mutilators" (3:2), "enemies of the cross of Christ" (3:18), people "whose end is destruction" (3:18). They can hardly be identified as Judaizers—that is, Jewish *Christians*—but rather as Jews, Jewish missionaries in particular, who aggressively pushed for converts at Philippi, even with force. They proclaimed a message that righteousness* and perfection were attainable "now" (cf. Phil 3:12-15) by submitting to circumcision and complying with certain ritual laws (3:19)—a message that offered visible and tangible tokens of God's favor in the present, not in the future and invisible world. Paul's exceedingly harsh words in 3:2 probably reflect his own frustration over the fanatical and unrelenting opposition he was encountering from the Jews both in Jerusalem and Caesarea (Acts 21:37—26:32; cf. 28:19).

*4.5. The Christ-Hymn.* Philippians 2:6-11 is the prime example of an early Christian hymn. But who wrote it and what was the source of the ideas expressed here? Many scholars consider that Paul was its author (cf. Martin 1960) and this has been the traditional view. The way in which this section dovetails so perfectly into Paul's argument in chapter 2 and into the whole tenor of the letter does not immediately lead one to look for another writer. Some scholars, however, have seen features of style, vocabulary and doctrine in the hymn that suggest a composer other than Paul. But whether it was the work of Paul or some other Christian hymn writer makes little difference, since it fits Paul's purpose at this point, harmonizes with his own thinking as he writes to the Philippians and is incorporated into his letter without reservation.

Scholars have looked in many different directions for the source of the ideas in this hymn. Some have suggested the background of the Gnostic* "Redeemed-Redeemer" myth that describes the descent into this world of a "light-person," who comes to bring knowledge to the sons of light, appears in human form and endures misery, pain and suffering like other humans until he leaves this world and returns to the world of light (Bultmann, 1.167).

Others have looked to the Adam theme from the Old Testament (see Adam). Both Adam and Christ were human beings made in the image of God (Gen 1:26; Phil 2:6, "image" and "form" being treated as synonymous), but whereas Adam disobeyed and grasped after being like God, Christ obeyed God and instead of grasping for equality with God chose the way of servanthood and mortality. As a consequence the first Adam was cast out of paradise because of his self-seeking, but the last Adam, Christ, was exalted by God and given the highest place because of his self-giving (Dunn, 114-21; but contrast Wright).

Perhaps one does not need to look so far afield as these scholars have suggested. There is recorded in the gospel tradition (Jn 13:3-17) an incident from the life of Christ that provides an almost perfect model for the movement of the Christ hymn of Philippians 2. Both the Fourth Evangelist and Paul begin what they have to say in a similar fashion. John starts his narrative by saying that Jesus washed his disciples' feet (the work of a slave/servant) because he knew that the Father had given everything into his hands and that he himself had come out from God and was going back to God (John 13:3; cf. Hawthorne 1983, 78-79). The Philippian hymn begins by stating "that Jesus, being in the form of God and yet not taking advantage of his being equal with God, took the form of a slave, and did the work of a servant (Phil 2:6-8). The entire hymn preserves the descent-ascent motif that is prominent in the Gospel story (13:3-17)" (Hawthorne 1987, 65).

## 5. Theological Themes.

Because of its theological themes, the influence of the letter to the Philippians on the church seems to be out of all proportion to its size. Perhaps this in large part is due to the exquisite Christ hymn (2:6-11), a hymn that elegantly sums up Paul's teaching about the person of Jesus Christ *and of the nature of God* (see Christology).

While providing a magnificent description of Jesus Christ—pre-existent,* equal with God, becoming incarnate, a human being, a servant, totally obedient to God, in turn exalted by God to the highest place in heaven or on earth, the object of worship* for all created beings to the glory of God the Father—this hymn also articulately describes who God really is. For Jesus Christ, who shared the very nature of God and acted out of that nature, showed by what he chose to do and by what he in fact did that God's true nature is not characterized by seizing, grasping or attaining, but rather by sharing, by open-handed giving and by pouring oneself out for others in order to enrich them.

Whether or not Paul composed this hymn, it undoubtedly was an integral part of the letter and not a later interpolation because by it Paul provides the Philippians with the basis of his ethical* appeal. He begs them to live humbly, generously, unself-consciously, while being thoughtfully concerned for the welfare of those around them (2:1-5), for this was the attitude that Christ Jesus possessed and that governed all of his conduct—an attitude to be emulated by all who call themselves by his name.

The Christ hymn is not the only factor contributing to the influence of Philippians. Here in this letter one also finds Paul's motto for life, which in turn has become the life motto for many Christians ever since: "For me to live is Christ; to die is gain" (1:21). These two statements, coupled with the one that follows, namely that "to depart and to be with Christ is a very much better thing [than living]," have had great theological significance. They suggest that the condition of Christians who die in the Lord is one of conscious happiness beyond anything experienced on earth. If indeed they do make such a suggestion, they then raise the question of the need for the resurrection* of the body* or for a new body from heaven* (see Cullmann; but see also Phil 3:20-21) (see Immortality; Intermediate State).

Furthermore, there is in Philippians the often-quoted remark of Paul, "work out your own salvation* . . . for it is God who is at work in you" (2:12-13). This remark, rarely put in its context so as to be properly understood, has influenced the thinking both of those who argue for the sovereignty of God, and of those who champion the free will of human beings. In the context of Philippians 2, Paul is not using the word *salvation* to refer to eschatological salvation, the salvation of one's eternal soul, but rather to the *health* of the Christian community in Philippi. Torn apart by conceit, pride and selfishness (2:3-4) the Philippians hear in these words the urging of the apostle to follow the example of Christ (2:5-11), to humble themselves and to take the role of the servant, to work obediently at bringing healing (i.e., "salvation") to their church and to work at this task until it is accomplished. If they do this, they will discover that they have only been cooperating with God, who is already at work among them giving them these desires for wholeness and the energy to fulfil their desires.

In all of Paul's letters, perhaps the most important single statement having to do with the doctrine of sanctification* is found in Philippians 3:8-16. Holiness* described here is an ever-increasing apprehension of the surpassing worth of Jesus Christ by the Christian, with nothing whatsoever allowed to destroy or diminish this apprehension. In turn it is also an apprehension of the Christian by Jesus Christ. Both elements are present—the work of God or Christ, and the work of the Christian. Sanctification for Paul, therefore, allows room for growth, increase, advancement and progress on the part of the Christian (1:9, 25). As the many imperatives present throughout this letter indicate, sanctification in fact demands progress (e.g., 4:8-9; see Beker, 218-19).

Finally, the theme of joy* that runs throughout Philippians has had a profound influence on Christians through the centuries, drawing them back to this letter again and again. Here one learns that joy is not so much a feeling as it is a settled state of mind characterized by peace, an attitude that views life—including all of its ups and downs—with equanimity. It is a confident way of looking at life that is rooted in faith in the living Lord of the church (1:25; 3:1; 4:4, 10). For Paul joy is an understanding of existence that makes it possible for one to accept both elation and depression, to accept with creative submission events that bring either delight or dismay, because joy allows one to see beyond any particular event to the sovereign Lord who stands above all events.

*See also* CAESAR'S HOUSEHOLD, IMPERIAL HOUSEHOLD; CHRISTOLOGY; IMITATION OF PAUL/OF CHRIST; JOY.

BIBLIOGRAPHY. **Commentaries:** K. Barth, *The Epistle to the Philippians* (Richmond: John Knox, 1962); F. W. Beare, *A Commentary on the Epistle to the Philippians* (HNTC; New York: Harper, 1959); J.-F. Collange, *The Epistle of Saint Paul to the Philippians* (London: Epworth, 1979); J. Gnilka, *Der Philipperbrief* (HTKNT 10/3; Freiburg: Herder, 1976); G. F. Hawthorne, *Philippians* (WBC 43; Waco: Word, 1983); J. B. Lightfoot, *St. Paul's Epistle to the Philippians* (London: Macmillan, 1894); R. P. Martin, *The Epistle of Paul to the Philippians* (TNTC; Grand Rapids: Eerdmans, 1959); idem, *Philippians* (NCB; Grand Rapids: Eerdmans, 1976); J. H. Michael, *The Epistle to the Philippians* (MNTC; London: Hodder and Stoughton, 1928); P. T. O'Brien, *The Epistle to the Philippians* (NIGTC; Grand Rapids: Eerdmans, 1991); M. Silva, *Philippians* (WEC; Chicago: Moody Press, 1988). **Studies:** J. M. Bassler, ed., *Pauline Theology* vol I: *Thessalonians, Philippians, Galatians, Philemon* (Minneapolis: Fortress, 1991); F. C. Baur, *Paul, the Apostle of Jesus Christ*, 2 vols. (London: Williams and Norgate, 1875); J. C. Beker, *Paul the Apostle* (Philadelphia: Fortress, 1980); R. Bultmann, *Theology of the New Testament*, 2 vols. (New York: Scribners, 1951); O. Cullmann, *Immortality of the Soul or the Resurrection of the Dead* (London: Epworth, 1958); J. D. G. Dunn, *Christology in the Making* (Philadelphia: Westminster, 1980); D. E. Garland, "The Composition and Literary Unity of Philippians: Some Neglected Factors," *NovT* 27 (1985) 141-73; G. F. Hawthorne, *Word Biblical Themes: Philippians* (Waco: Word, 1987); M. D. Hooker, "ΠΙΣΤΙΣ ΧΡΙΣΤΟΥ," *NTS* 35 (1989) 331-33; L. Hurtado, "Jesus as Lordly Example in Phil. 2:5-11," in *From Jesus to Paul: Studies in Honour of Francis Wright Beare*, ed. J. C. Hurd and G. P. Richardson (Waterloo: Laurier University Press, 1984); R. P. Martin, *An Early Christian Confession: Philippians ii. 5-11 in Recent Interpretation* (London: Tyndale Press, 1960); idem, *Carmen Christi: Philippians ii. 5-11 in Recent Interpretation and in the Setting of Early Christian Worship*, rev. ed. (Grand Rapids: Eerdmans, 1983); D. F. Watson, "A Rhetorical Analysis of Philippians, and Its Implications for the Unity Question," *NovT* 30 (1988) 57-88. N. T. Wright, "Harpagmos and the Meaning of Philippians ii.5-11," *JTS* 37 (Oct 1986) 321-52.

G. F. Hawthorne

## PHILO. *See* PHILOSOPHY.

## PHILOSOPHY

There were four main philosophies that held the intellectual field in the first century A.D.: the Middle Platonists, the (Later) Stoa, the Peripatetics and the Epicureans. In addition there were Cynics who begged for a living and mixed with the people, offering moral advice on a popular level. In the ancient world philosophy was considered a normal part of the education that would prepare a youth for a public career or even military leadership. Hence philosophy's influence was widespread among the upper classes and people of wealth who could afford an education. Few studied to be professional philosophers or read more than a tiny selection of primary texts, but digests of a school's dogma such as we find in Diogenes Laertius were a common source of knowledge. Paul's hometown of Tarsus boasted a flourishing school of philosophy. Though it is unlikely that he attended, it is reasonable to suppose that Paul met with some philosophy in his youth, even if his training may have been in Jerusalem.* Jewish literature of the Hellenistic era shows the influence of Greek philosophy (*see* Hellenism).

1. Schools of Philosophy
2. Paul and Hellenistic Philosophy

## 1. Schools of Philosophy.

*1.1. Common Elements.* Platonism, Aristotelianism and Stoicism shared some common characteristics with one another and with Hellenistic thought generally. All maintained that there was a supreme deity above and behind every other supernatural force, yet the reality of the traditional pantheon of gods was seldom challenged. These were regarded as the children or servants of the highest deity, and were sometimes called *daimones* (*see* Demons). Philosophy in the late Hellenistic and Imperial eras was rarely atheistic; the ancient philosopher studied what we would call "theology" together with physics, logic and other subjects. Cicero even complained that the Stoics were "pitiably and distressingly superstitious" (*De Div.* 2.86). Most philosophers of these three schools from the first century B.C. onward supported a rationalized version of traditional belief in the gods (*see* Religions). Still, Hellenistic philosophy remained aloof from popular piety and was critical of the myths of the gods, particularly their anthropomorphism and portrayal of the gods in trivial quarrels, human passions and immoral activities.

The Middle Platonists and Peripatetics held that God was utterly transcendent, an immaterial divine force, pure mind or rationality. God's will was performed by lesser gods in order to avoid contact with matter. His dwelling place was beyond the moon, in the sphere of serene order where the stars moved. The Stoics, however, were immanentists in their view of God. All three schools held the highest and most divine attribute of God to be mind (*nous*) or reason (*logos*). Hence the reasoning portion of the human soul was also regarded as divine, a portion or "seed" of God.

*1.2. Epicureans.* The Epicureans, though believing in the gods as "blessed and immortal beings," tended to live as though religion were irrelevant. They explained everything in terms of natural forces, and believed everything to be composed of "atoms" (Diogenes Laertius *Vit.* 10.38-44). The random collision of atoms was the cause of every natural event, and chance predominated. They also upheld the validity of free will in opposition to fatalism. The goal of philosophy was to free people from all fears or trouble, enabling tranquility of mind to flourish (*ataraxia*; Diogenes Laertius *Vit.* 10.82, 117, 120, 131-35).

Epicureans became infamous for defining pleasure as the primary good that was to be pursued in life (Diogenes Laertius *Vit.* 10:128-29). Though Epicurus qualified this by noting that excess (whether in eating or in immorality) was incompatible with true pleasure and *ataraxia*, his followers were frequently lambasted by other philosophers as effeminate or profligate.

*1.3. Middle Platonists.* Plato had held that the rational element of the human soul was immortal. While this reason was bestowed by the God who formed the universe (the Demiurge), the formation of the rest of the human person was entrusted to lesser gods who were themselves creations of the Demiurge (Plato *Tim.* 40a, 41a-43a). These lesser gods also contributed the mortal parts of the soul—the "irrational passions" and appetites. By the first century A.D. even the Demiurge was thought to be a lesser god, making the supreme deity vastly remote from the material world. This tended to lead to a denigration of material things as inferior substances, and the body especially as a hindrance to progress toward God. The body, however, was rarely held to be evil in nature (*see* Body).

The universe of Middle Platonism was peopled with a host of intermediary beings who acted as servants of the supreme God, who were also involved in oracles and who attended sacrifices and mystery celebrations (Plutarch *Def. Orac.* 416d-417b; *Fac. Lun.* 944c-d). A person's ascent toward deity, intended to free the soul from its cycle of reincarnation and attachment to a body, was made via the pursuit of philosophy (Plato *Tim.* 90b-c; cf. Plutarch *Fac. Lun.* 943d; *Gen. Socr.* 593d-594a). Divine reason, such as was implanted in humans, had also been put into different sorts of "bodies" which became stars or demigods. Thus in the Platonic tradition we have already a basis for developments in later astral religion and Gnosticism (*see* Gnosis, Gnosticism).

*1.4. Peripatetics.* The Peripatetics followed Aristotle (384-322 B.C.), the disciple of Plato. Aristotle was much more empirical and inductive in his method than Plato. He rejected Plato's immaterial soul, believing soul to be inseparable from the body except for the power of thought. Though Aristotle's works began enjoying a revival among philosophers in the late first century B.C., the Peripatetic school had assimilated a great deal of Platonism and for our purpose is of little importance.

**1.5. Stoics.** Stoicism could be characterized as a religious materialism which was pantheistic. The Stoa rejected "immaterial substance"; for them all that was real was material—including God. God was variously described as "fire," "reason" (*logos*) or "spirit" (*pneuma*). "Spirit" for the Stoic, though, was a material substance, very unlike the Jewish-Christian Holy Spirit (*see* Holy Spirit). God was said to exist in everything throughout the universe, sometimes as "spirit." He shapes Fate and all reality according to divine reason. Despite its materialism Stoicism was not atheism, and it could express profound reverence for God and his wisdom in shaping nature. It is from a Stoic poet who was also a fellow Cilician, Aratus, that Paul is said to quote in his Areopagus speech: "We are his offspring" (Acts 17:28; *see* Athens). Several other Stoic teachers came from Paul's hometown of Tarsus, including Athenodorus who was close to the emperor Augustus, and who in his later years returned to Tarsus to become its leading citizen.

Stoicism became for a short time the leading philosophy of the early empire, a favorite with the Romans. Though the early Stoa had a wide range of interests, by the first century A.D. ethics seems to have almost completely dominated the school's interest. The overarching question became, "How can the wise man live in accordance with nature?" The life according to nature included the thought of a life lived rationally, in concord with the rational-divine part of human nature and in acceptance of one's fate from God (which was inevitable anyway). This was believed to lead to a virtuous life, and virtue was the only absolute "good" which the Stoa recognized. All else, including health, wealth, strength, beauty, even life or death (*see* Life and Death), was termed "indifferent" (*adiaphora*) because, it was said, such things made no difference to the wise person's virtue or happiness. The ideal Stoic life was a highly individualistic, self-centered pursuit of "virtue" in complete independence from any external supports. The Stoa developed the ethical diatribe (*see* Rhetoric), which was adopted by many who did not consider themselves Stoics—including Plutarch and Paul.

**1.6. Cynics.** Cynicism was a predecessor of Stoicism; it is often thought to have been more a way of life than a philosophy (Diogenes Laertius *Vit.* 6.103), and Malherbe notes the Cynic lifestyle was combined with philosophies quite disparate in essence. The key to Cynic thought is a consistent life lived "according to nature." This is interpreted to mean an independence from all external props, living only with the barest essentials. The famous Diogenes of Sinope (founder of Cynicism) lived in a barrel with only a cloak and a cup to his name, eventually giving up the cup as well. The Cynic was known by his ragged cloak and his begging (though some were said to work). Typically they rejected social norms and were proud of their "shamelessness," though they saw themselves as moral reformers. The Cynic ideal of "boldness" (*parrēsia*) in speech was displayed by public preaching which was often caustic, abusive and arrogant in exposing the "sins" of the audience. They compared their manner to surgery on a patient with gangrene. They seem never to have been interested in speculative thought, limiting their attention in general to ethics. Of all the schools the Cynics were the ones most willing to work with common people.

**1.7. Philo of Alexandria.** Philo (c.30 B.C.-C.A.D. 45) was a Jewish scholar who wrote extensively on the Pentateuch, using the allegorical method to make the texts present lessons in philosophy and ethics. His works show a thorough acquaintance with classical literature, philosophy and rhetoric. In his philosophical outlook he was primarily a Middle Platonist (cf. Philo *Op. Mund.*; *Migr. Abr.* 2.9; 11.62), though heavily influenced by Stoicism in his ethics (cf. Philo *Omn. Prob. Lib.*; *Migr. Abr.* 22.127-28; 36.197; *Abr.* 1.5-6), and in his appropriation of the Stoic concepts of the logos of God and the world-"spirit" (*pneuma*). The latter two concepts were reshaped in Philo under the influence of his Judaism, so as to become much more personal than they were in Stoicism.

Though Philo's philosophy was very Greek, he remained loyal to Judaism, upholding monotheism and the divine inspiration of the Jewish Law.* He still regarded the literal meaning of the Law as a necessary companion to its allegorical meaning, and obedience to the Law as necessary to following the path of spiritual perfection (*Migr. Abr.* 16.93; 25.457—26.458). Like Paul, Philo saw Abraham* (along with Isaac and Jacob) as an important model for the virtuous person, as somehow superior to the Law. Abraham is said to have achieved a perfect life "according to nature"; the patriarchs were "living laws," while the Mosaic code is merely a record of their lifestyle (*Abr.* 1.5-6; 11.52; 46.276; *Migr. Abr.* 22.127—23.131). And Abraham represents not simply a historical person but the journey of every soul which seeks God (*Abr.* 14.66; 15.68; *Migr. Abr.* 1.2). For Philo the virtuous life was a journey of the soul which ends in a closer communion with the divine "powers" which are God's intermediaries in the world; some might say Philo believed in a mystical union with God (*see* Mysticism). He certainly believed in prophecy* and in ecstatic divine possession (*see* Visions, Ecstatic Experience; *Migr. Abr.* 7.34-35).

## 2. Paul and Hellenistic Philosophy.

### 2.1. General Observations.

It can be seen from this survey that there were many items Paul held in common with the philosophers as well as many differences. Nearly all who thought deeply about the subject held God to be a moral being whose actions are justifiable even if we cannot always explain them. Paul had in common with Platonists the conception of God as an immaterial being, but he did not see God as remote from the material world. Paul conceived of God as involved in his creation* where he reveals himself, calls* people to repentance and faith* in his Son Jesus Christ* and saves. The foundation for all this was laid in the life and death of Christ,* and upon this are based God's continuing dealings with humankind via preaching* and the Holy Spirit* (e.g., 1 Thess 1:4-6, 9-10; Gal 1:3-4; 1 Cor 1:18-25, 30; 2 Cor 5:17-21; Eph 1:3-14). In this respect Paul bears outward similarity with the Stoic view of God as immanent, though Paul never identified God with nature or the universe as the Stoa did. Thus Paul can say "all things are from him and through him and for him"—a very Stoic-sounding phrase (Rom 11:36; cf. Col 1:16). Yet God remains transcendent over the world he has created (1 Cor 8:6; Col 1:15-19; Eph 4:6). To Hellenistic philosophers the supreme deity could be said to be a craftsman or shaper of the universe, but he does not create from nothing (*see* World, Cosmology); matter is coeternal with him (or in the case of Stoicism, nature is coextensive with him). In light of this view of matter it is interesting that Paul regards Jesus not only as God's instrument in creation, but as having preceded the physical universe: "he is before all things" (Col 1:17).

A major difference between Paul and contemporary philosophers was their approach to the knowledge* of God. Whereas philosophy asserted that reasoning from certain first principles was the proper manner to attain knowledge of God and the world, for Paul this knowledge could only be received as revelation from God, mediated through the Spirit and proclaimed in preaching (1 Cor 1:17-18; 2:6-16). "Wisdom"* cannot be obtained from below. This may be in part because all such reason is tainted with sin, but the explanation Paul gives is that in this way all humanity is placed in need of God's grace,* utterly bereft of any means of self-exaltation (1 Cor 1:19-25).

The only place in Paul (or the NT) where the term *philosophy* occurs is at Colossians 2:8, "Watch out that

no one take you captive through the philosophy and empty deception that is in line with human traditions, with the elements of the world, and is not in line with Christ." What Paul had in view here is not the "standard" philosophies but the speculative mixture of ideas from Judaism, Hellenistic religion and philosophy that were apparently current at Colossae (*see* Colossians). Paul answers it with an assertion of the tradition "in line with Christ" (*kata Christon*)—that is, it is a tradition both about Christ and one which befits his person.

Paul's best-known encounter with philosophy is recorded in Acts 17:16-34. There Luke portrays Paul in the Athenian agora, where he draws the attention of some Epicureans and Stoics. Luke's account echoes the Athenians' rejection of Socrates: like Socrates, Paul speaks with anyone in the agora; is accused of introducing "new gods" (*kaina daimonia*; cf. Plato *Apol.* 24b-c) and is rejected by many (*see* Athens). Paul built the first part of his message around the existence of one God who created the world, who cannot be properly said to live in temples* or idols (Acts 17:24-27, 29; *see* Idolatry). This God is the source of human life, making all people of one family (Acts 17:26, 28-29). Similar sentiments are known to have existed in Greek philosophy, so that there is nothing exclusively Christian about the first half. Yet neither is it unchristian; it establishes a point of contact between the philosophers and Paul, who even quotes two lines of Greek poetry in his support (Acts 17:28): "for in him we live and move and exist" (Epimenides), and "for we are also (members) of his family" (from the Stoic Aratus *Phaen.* 5).

Toward the end of the speech, the themes of forgiveness* and repentance are introduced (Acts 17:30), which entail a day of judgment* over which Jesus will preside (Acts 17:31), who is not named here but is referred to as "a man whom [God] has appointed," the proof of which is his resurrection* from the dead (Acts 17:31). If considered apart from its literary function in Acts, the speech is a good example of early Christian preaching adapted to a Hellenistic Gentile audience.

Many scholars maintain that Acts 17 is incompatible with the Paul who wrote Romans 1—3, excluding natural theology. But there is nothing in Acts 17 which assumes a saving knowledge of God; and in any case the two audiences (Roman Christians and Athenian pagans) demand a somewhat different address. We must assume that in speaking to Gentiles* Paul would have taken a different point of departure than the OT, and the speech of Acts 17 can be seen to incorporate several common Pauline themes, including the typical apocalyptic elements of resurrection and coming judgment associated with Jesus (cf. 1 Thess 1:9-10; see Stonehouse).

### 2.2. Paul and Platonism.

The idea that things which can be grasped only by the intelligence are more divine than those which are open to sensory examination was a Platonic notion which became an altruism in the Hellenistic era. Thus Paul states "we set our gaze not on what is seen but what is not seen" (2 Cor 4:18, also 2 Cor 5:7; Col 1:5); the idea of invisibility at 1 Timothy 1:17; 6:16, though similar, arises from OT traditions (e.g., Ex 20:4; 33:20). Likewise, the concept of a heavenly archetype, or "idea," on which earthly particulars are modeled comes from the Platonic universe. It is used by Philo (e.g., *Leg. All.* 1.31) and influences the "allegory" of Galatians 4:24-26, though any Platonic influence on Paul there has doubtless been mediated through Judaism (cf. 1 Cor 15:48-49; Phil 3:21). The "inner man" (*see* Psychology) of 2 Corinthians 4:16 has a formal parallel in Plato's *Republic* (IX 589A), but for Plato it is a rational power of will, while Paul's concept is broader than mere rationality and includes an eschatological hope of resurrection existence in wholeness (*see* Eschatology).

### 2.3. Stoic Influence in the Letters.

The numerous similarities between Paul's language and Stoic language and thought, especially that of Seneca, has long been noted (e.g., Rom 1:19-20, 26; 11:36; 12:1; 1 Cor 3:21-23; 6:12; 7:31; 9:1, 19; 12:12-27; Col 1:16; Eph 4:6; 5:22-6:9). Sevenster and others have demonstrated that in the latter case most similarities are only formal, and that beneath the language lie very different concepts of God, humanity and the relationship between the two. Some view the similarities as a coincidence from the use of a common language, but it is quite possible that Paul was consciously reworking popular Stoic concepts in light of Christian theology. So *autarkeia*, "self-sufficiency" (2 Cor 9:8), and *autarkēs*, "self-sufficient" (Phil 4:11), are used as technical terms in Cynic and Stoic dogma to express the contentment of the wise person with a "life in accord with nature" which is achieved by long training and severing any dependence on human society or material goods. In this fashion the wise Stoic becomes a heroic figure who rises even above the gods in achieving independence. But Paul posited for the Christian an *autarkeia* which is paradoxically a dependent existence flowing from the grace of God. It resembles Cynic or Stoic independence in its renunciation of the need for material wealth, but internally it is very different: it takes its strength not from resolution of will but from the assurance of the favor and presence of God. And it is not self-centered, but is a "contentment" that enables one to be of service to others.

1 Timothy 6:6-8, 12 sounds more Stoic in its concentration on renunciation and the theme of "struggle," though even these are Christianized by being linked with piety (1 Tim 6:6, 11) and faith (1 Tim 6:11, 12)—an ugly word for a philosopher. Another instance is the "natural theology" of Romans 1:19-20. The Stoa greatly developed the theme of the knowledge of God's existence through observation of a rational and purposive order in the universe. However, the Stoic influence here is probably mediated through a Jewish wisdom source, as can be seen from Paul's use of "wrath" (Rom 1:18; *see* Wrath, Destruction), "what can be known of God" (Rom 1:19, implying also an unknowable essence) and "from the creation of the world" (Rom 1:20). Paul's practice of deliberately using Stoic themes in redefined ways is an early Christian attempt at crosscultural communication, even more significant if Stoicism or a Stoicizing influence were at work in the Gentile churches.

### 2.4. Paul and Cynic Moral Exhortation.

A. Malherbe has demonstrated several thematic and verbal parallels between parts of Paul's letters and the ideal of the "mild" Cynic philosopher as idealized especially by Dio Chrysostom. Most notable is his description of his ministry* in 1 Thessalonians 2. The philosopher who is abused by the crowd, yet speaks "boldly," "without guile," with "purity of mind" (cf. 1 Thess 2:2-3) and attacks the charlatans who deceive their hearers from impure motives (cf. 1 Thess 2:3, 5) was idealized by Dio and others. Even the theme of gentleness in correction was known to some of the milder Cynics (cf. 1 Thess 2:6-8). Again, as with Stoic parallels Paul used available material but in a reoriented framework. His boldness was not due to self-confidence and independence, but to his sense of God's calling—a dependence that might well have repelled a Cynic. The content of his preaching was the gospel, not natural law or asceticism for its own sake.

### 2.5. Paul and Philo.

Most scholars believe Paul was not directly influenced by Philo, though there are some similarities which can be explained by reference to a common Jewish Wisdom* tradition older than either of them. This would explain such things as circumcision* having a symbolic meaning (Philo *Migr. Abr.* 16.92); or that humanity and the world are "foolish" in comparison to God's understanding and purpose (*Migr. Abr.* 24.134-38; cf. 1 Cor 1:18-29). Recently some have proposed that the Corinthians had drawn on Philo or a Philonic-type conception of spiritual perfection through a philosophic use of the Law (1 Corinthians; e.g., R. Horsley, J. Davis); or for an understanding of Moses as a glorious, charismatic,

717

Spirit-filled man (2 Corinthians; cf. Philo *Vit. Mos.* 2.69-70; Martin, 63-64). This is highly unlikely for the situation in 1 Corinthians, where the problems of the mostly Gentile converts have no demonstrably Jewish basis. There may have been, however, some Philonic-type concepts brought into the church by the Jewish-Christian intruders by the time 2 Corinthians was written.

*2.6. Summary.* While Paul may have used philosophical vocabulary for his apologetic or didactic purposes, he was not constrained by the content or method of the philosophies in vogue. As a man of his era, he was aware of intellectual currents, but he was not concerned as Philo was to reconcile his message with philosophy. Paul holds the gospel to be the only means to divine wisdom (1 Cor 1:21; 2:6-16; cf. Eph 1:15-18).

*See also* HELLENISM; MYSTERY; RELIGIONS, GRECO-ROMAN; WISDOM.

BIBLIOGRAPHY. R. Bultmann, *Theology of the New Testament* (2 vols.; New York: Charles Scribner's Sons, 1951, 1955); H. Conzelmann, *1 Corinthians* (Herm; Philadelphia: Fortress, 1975); J. Davis, *Wisdom and Spirit* (New York: University Press of America, 1984); J. Dillon, *The Middle Platonists* (London: Gerald Duckworth, 1977); J. D. G. Dunn, *Romans* (WBC 38a-b; Dallas: Word, 1988); R. A. Horsley, "Pneumatikos vs. Psychikos: Distinctions of Spiritual Status among the Corinthians," *HTR* 69 (1976) 269-88; T. Irwin, *A History of Western Philosophy*, vol. 1: *Classical Thought* (Oxford: University Press, 1989); A. A. Long and D. N. Sedley, *The Hellenistic Philosophers* (2 vols.; Cambridge: University Press, 1987); A. J. Malherbe, *Paul and the Popular Philosophers* (Minneapolis: Fortress, 1989); R. P. Martin, *2 Corinthians* (WBC 40; Waco: Word, 1986); T. Paige, "Stoicism, ἐλευθερία and Community at Corinth," in *Worship, Theology and Ministry in the Early Church*, ed. M. J. Wilkins & T. Paige (JSNTSup 87; Sheffield: JSOT, 1992) 180-93; F. H. Sandbach, *The Stoics* (London: Chatto and Windus, 1975); J. N. Sevenster, *Paul and Seneca* (SNT 4; Leiden: Brill, 1961); N. B. Stonehouse, *Paul Before the Areopagus and Other NT Studies* (London: Tyndale, 1957).

T. Paige

**PLATONISTS.** *See* PHILOSOPHY.

# POLITICAL SYSTEMS

Paul the Hebrew of Hebrews (Phil 3:5) and the Roman citizen* (Acts 16:37-38; 22:25-29; 25:7-12) lived within both the Jewish and Roman political systems. Paul's doctrine that one should be obedient to earthly authorities as to God (Rom 13:1-7) indicates that he held himself accountable to both Jewish and Roman political systems (*see* Civil Authority).

1. Jewish Political System
2. Roman Political System

**1. Jewish Political System.**
While the Mediterranean world was under Roman rule and Paul called himself a missionary to the Gentiles,* Paul himself was a member of the Jewish Diaspora* and worked in dialogue with the Jewish population. While under Roman rule, Diaspora Jews were accountable to local synagogue rulers, who served as local agents of the Jewish political system. Above them were the Sanhedrin and the high priest. This political system worked to maintain Jewish distinctives within Palestine and the Diaspora and it also taxed Mediterranean Jewry for the Jerusalem Temple. The first function is illustrated by the warnings Paul received that the Jews in Jerusalem would hold him accountable for his mission* work in the Diaspora (Acts 21:4, 10-11). Also, Paul's letter to the Romans* is written with concerns of Jewish authorities in mind (Rom 2:17—3:8, 31; 6:1; 9:1-9; 11:25-36). The second function of the Jewish political system was guaranteed by Augustus's edict in 12 B.C. that the Jews could send money to Jerusalem. This support for the Jerusalem Temple provides the ideological background for Paul's own collection* for the Jewish Christians in Jerusalem* (2 Cor 8—9; Rom 15:25- 31).

*1.1. Synagogues and Synagogue Rulers.* As communities with official recognition by the municipal and provincial authorities, Jewish citizens were fully under the secular political system. We have the record of the Jewish communities in Alexandria and Sardis being called *politeuma* in the first century B.C., the term for an organized body of citizens within a Hellenistic city. In Alexandria this *politeuma* was governed by a council called the *gerousia*. For the most part, however, the political matters unique to Diaspora Jews were conducted through the local synagogue. During Paul's ministry synagogues retained the status of *aedes sacrae* (sacred buildings) in Roman law. Synagogues without a permanent fixture for the Torah ark could function as meeting houses of the Jewish community for nonreligious matters. Here thefts would be reported, slaves* would be released, the poor would be fed and decisions about community life would be made. Many synagogues also functioned as schools for the religious education of the Jewish youth. The synagogue ruler (*archisynagōgos* in the NT) functioned as a local political ruler with regard to Jewish affairs. There were a number of synagogue rulers for each synagogue (ten according to an inscription dating from

A.D. 56 in Cyrene, SEG 17.823). According to Acts, Paul habitually began his mission outreach in any Hellenistic city by preaching in the synagogue (Acts 9:20-22; 13:5,14; 14:1; 17:1-3). In Acts 13:15 we see the synagogue rulers asking Paul and Barnabas if they would like to speak. Acts 18:8,17 seems to indicate that two synagogue rulers in Corinth (Crispus and Sosthenes) believed in Christ (cf. 1 Cor 1:1).

*1.2. Sanhedrin.* The Sanhedrin (*synedrion* in the NT) in Paul's day was composed of seventy-one men who were both the religious and political rulers of Jerusalem. The council included the high priest (Acts 23:1-5; Josephus *Ant.* 4.8.14 §218). In light of the link made by Tannaitic rabbis between the Sanhedrin and the seventy elders who worshipped God at Sinai with Moses (Ex 24:1, 9-11; *t. Sanh.* 1.6), to stand before the Sanhedrin was not a small matter (cf. Mt 5:22). While the Talmud allowed for Jewish councils in cities outside of Jerusalem (*t. Sanh.* 1.6; e.g., Josephus, *J.W.* 2.20.5 §§570-571), in the biblical record Paul does not stand trial before any except the Jerusalem Sanhedrin. This Sanhedrin included both a priestly component and a component of scribes, or teachers of Torah. The former were Sadducean in orientation and the latter were primarily Pharisees. This accounts for Paul's ploy of splitting the council on the issue of the resurrection, a point of disagreement between the two groups (Acts 23:6-9). A third component within the Sanhedrin were the "elders," prominent men who were respected as leaders, though they were not of religious vocation (Mk 15:1; Acts 4:5, 8, 27-28; 23:14; 24:1; 25:15). Acts first presents Paul as a passive but approving accomplice of the Sanhedrin-led stoning of Stephen (Acts 6:12; 7:58; 8:1). It is after years of ministry that he is then a defendant before the Sanhedrin (Acts 22:30-23:9), and later seeks to avoid a death plot in which the Sanhedrin was implicated (Acts 23:12-22).

*1.3. High Priest.* The high priesthood secured for itself a political function during the Maccabean period. From this time and throughout the ministry of Paul, the high priests were Sadducees. The influence that a high priest (*archiereus* in the NT) held in Diaspora communities can be seen by Josephus's account (*Ant.* 14.10.20 §§241-242), in which it is evident that the high priest in Jerusalem sent documents on behalf of Jews in Laodicea, so that they would be able to live with fully Jewish distinctives. Acts confirms such influence of the high priest outside of Palestine, for Acts 9:1-2 describes how Paul had received arrest warrants for Jewish Christians in Damascus from the high priest. Acts 23:1-5; 25:2 show an older Paul, after years of Christian ministry, on the other side of the high priest's favor.

## 2. Roman Political System.

Officially still a republic, the Roman empire was in Paul's day an imperial system. Referred to as the early Empire, or the Principate, Rome ruled its provinces with a strong hand. Though tradition informs us that Paul was executed by the Romans, there is no reason to doubt Acts' presentation of the Roman political system as generally a positive force in Paul's missionary efforts. Acts typically describes the Romans rescuing Paul from Jewish hands, thus allowing him to continue his witness (Acts 18:12-17; 21:27-40; 23:12-24). Also, it is at Roman expense that Paul traveled to Rome, a trip he had long anticipated (Rom 1:11-13; Acts 27:1—28:16). In the provinces the Romans allowed native rulers to exercise authority so as to maintain order.

*2.1. Native Rulers.* Rome's efficiency during Paul's lifetime meant that it did not maintain a standardized bureaucracy with each province. Instead it managed the native rulers of various cities and provinces. Because of this one sees a variety of offices that correspond with the NT record of Paul's ministry.

*2.1.1. City Magistrates.* Unnamed city officials (*archontes*) appear in the Acts record of Paul's ministry. The rulers of Philippi handed Paul and Silas over for imprisonment (*see* Prison) after the latter pair had deprived some citizens of their demonically based means of livelihood (Acts 16:16-24). City rulers (*politarchēs*) who were troubled by the disturbance raised in opposition to Paul's ministry are also mentioned in the account of Paul's visit to Thessalonica (Acts 17:8-9). "Some of the Asiarchs" are mentioned in Acts 19:31, counseling Paul not to appear before the violent Ephesian mob. These Asiarchs were probably native rulers of that area of Asia Minor who were entrusted by the Romans to rule it. The clerk (*grammateus*) of the Ephesian assembly is described in Acts 19:35-40 as talking his fellow citizens out of mob violence against Paul. (See the commentaries for local background to these titles, accurately reproduced in Acts.)

*2.1.2. Ethnarch of Aretas.* The Nabataean ruler Aretas IV was ruling Damascus around the time of Paul's conversion. Herod Antipas married Aretas's daughter, but later divorced her. The latter action led to Aretas's impulsive attack on Peraea and defeat of Antipas. A Roman force under L. Vitellius was preparing to counterattack Aretas for this strike, but it withdrew at the news of Tiberius's death in March of A.D. 37. It was Gaius Caligula, the next emperor, who gave Aretas jurisdiction over Damascus. Paul's description in 2 Corinthians 11:32 indicates that Aretas's deputy in charge (*ethnarchēs*) of the Jewish community there was poised to arrest Paul. This attempt to arrest him led to

*719*

Paul's escape over the wall of Damascus (Acts 9:23-25).

*2.1.3. Agrippa II.* Marcus Julius Agrippa II lived in the court of the Emperor Claudius until around A.D. 49. At this time he was made the king of Chalcis (*Ituraea*). Then in A.D. 53 Agrippa's rule was moved to the territory formerly ruled by Herod Philip: Auranitis, Trachonitis, Batanaea, Gaulanitis and Paneas. Abilene and Arcene were added at that time, and later Nero added parts of Galilee and Peraea to his rule. Agrippa's capital was Caesarea Philippi, though he called it Neronias in honor of the emperor. Agrippa maintained a close working relationship with the Jewish leaders, since it was his responsibility to appoint the high priest and oversee the Jerusalem Temple's finances. His position as native ruler in that region explains how he came to visit the Roman procurator Festus (Acts 25:13). Agrippa may have helped Festus draft the legal brief that was sent with Paul to Rome. His familiarity with Judaism accounts for Paul's appeal to Agrippa's belief in the OT prophets and Agrippa's sympathetic response to Paul (Acts 26:27-32).

*2.2. Centurion.* This military officer (*hekatontarchēs* in the NT) served to enforce Rome's political rule in the provinces. There were five or six centurions per cohort. (Each cohort contained from 500 to 1000 men; there were ten cohorts per legion.) During the early Principate most centurions were legionaries who were elevated to the post of centurion. Some, however, were those of the equestrian order, who were attracted to the post because of the high salary and retirement benefits. In the NT record of Paul's travels, centurions appear as favorable officers who rescue Paul from the mob (Acts 21:32), help him escape beating (Acts 22:25-26), guard him (Acts 24:23) and take him to Rome (Acts 27:1). The only centurion named is Julius of the Sebastian cohort (Acts 27:1), which probably indicates that he was from an auxiliary cohort with the honorific title *Augusta*. Paul must have come into frequent contact with centurions during his imprisonments (Phil 1:13-14).

*2.3. Military Tribune.* The *tribunus militum* (*chiliarchos* in the NT) served as leader of a Roman legion. There were usually six tribunes per legion. During Paul's time these officers were taken from either senatorial or equestrian orders. Acts shows a tribune rescuing Paul from a mob (Acts 21:31-33; 24:7), respecting Paul's citizenship (Acts 22:29), listening readily to the report of a plot against Paul (Acts 23:18-22) and attending Paul's speech before Festus and Agrippa (Acts 25:23). The only tribune named in the NT record about Paul is Claudius Lysias (Acts 23:26; 24:7, 22). The exchange he has with Paul about citizenship (Acts 22:26-28) indicates that he was a freedman of the emperor Claudius who had been granted equestrian status. The "large amount of money" (Acts 22:28) does not refer to a price he paid for his freedom but rather a bribe to officials in Caesar's bureaucracy or the provincial government, who put his name on the list of people to be granted citizenship. The demand for Roman citizenship and its privileges led to a lucrative business for some imperial officials (Tacitus *Ann.* 14.50.1). The importance of the tribune's office is seen by Felix's comment that he will wait until Lysias the tribune arrives to pass judgment on Paul's case (Acts 24:22).

*2.4. Proconsul.* Both the titles of proconsul (*anthypatos* in the NT) and procurator (see 2.5 below) designate officials who functioned as governors of Roman provinces. The proconsuls functioned as independent administrators of Roman provinces under the Senate's rule in one-year terms of office. Selected by lot, proconsuls in the Republic and Principate were typically ex-consuls or ex-praetors, therefore of senatorial order. As representative of the consuls, this post was officially under authority of the Roman senate rather than the emperor, at least through Paul's lifetime. But this in no way means that the proconsuls functioned as deputies of the senate. Their appointment as proconsuls gave them *imperium*, or ultimate administrative power, including the power to inflict capital punishment. Invested with *imperium*, the proconsul had no obligation to consult with the Roman senate for his decisions. Practically, as long as he did not offend the wealthy citizens in his province, he had no worries about censure from Rome. Indeed the common provincial had little recourse in the face of a proconsular decision. The only legal constraints on a proconsul's decisions in the first century were laws against extortion and treason and part of the *lex Iulia* that protected citizens from undeserved execution. The proconsul's influence over the provincials was also limited by the manner in which his year-long administration of a province was conducted. Proconsuls typically moved on a circuit of the major cities in their provinces to hear litigants. This meant that there was no center for efficient administration of the whole province. Paul's appearance before Gallio, proconsul of Achaia (Acts 18:12), shows that the plaintiffs were sufficient in number or persistence to get a hearing. This is noted because there was no guarantee that litigants' cases would be heard, given the proconsul's itinerant court that could move on to the next judicial center before all of one city's cases were heard. Besides his judicial function, proconsuls also inspected public buildings for needed repairs, maintained the water supply for the province through aqueducts or other means, and participated in municipal governance when they wanted. Both proconsuls mentioned in Acts are portrayed in a manner consistent with the book's agenda of showing the helpfulness of Roman authorities in the spread of the gospel.

*2.4.1. Sergius Paulus.* Sergius Paulus was the proconsul of Cyprus described in the record of Paul's first missionary journey (Acts 13:6-7). This proconsul is not attested in pagan literature, but we do find his name on ancient coins of Cyprus (*Cat. Greek Coins*, "Cyprus," 119-21). The Sergii Pauli were a senatorial family of the first century; the name therefore fits one of consular status. The account in Acts tells us that this proconsul believed the message of Paul and Barnabas after seeing the divine judgment Paul brought against Elymas the magician (Acts 13:8-12).

*2.4.2. Gallio.* Lucius Annaeus Novatus Gallio was a proconsul of Achaea, the province that included Corinth. The brother of Seneca the philosopher, Gallio had been adopted by the senator Lucius Junius Gallio, and therefore took his patron's name. After Seneca's political ruin, Gallio of necessity committed suicide. Paul's appearance before Gallio (Acts 18:12-17) is a crucial starting point for constructing a chronology* of his ministry, since we know from an inscription (*SIG* 2.801) that Gallio was proconsul in A.D. 52. Gallio is amply attested in pagan literature (Dio 61.35.2-4; 62.20.1; Seneca *Ep.* 104.1; Tacitus *Ann.* 15.73.4).

*2.5. Procurator.* This title (*hēgemōn* in the NT) designates a post in the lesser Roman provinces equivalent to that of governor. The title had been used earlier of financial administrators in provinces under senatorial rule, but its use as the title for governor is the only way it is used in the NT. The procurator was normally of the equestrian order and directly appointed by the emperor to rule as his agent in the province for as long as the emperor wished.

*2.5.1. Felix.* Marcus Antonius Felix was procurator of Judea when Paul stood trial before him (Acts 24:1-21). Felix agreed to try Paul even though Paul was not from the geographical area under Felix's responsibility (Acts 23:34-35) because it was probably under the imperial legate of Syria, who did not need to be bothered by an individual's case. Also, Paul's home city of Tarsus was considered a free city, which meant that its citizens were not required to stand trial in their own provincial courts. A freedman of Emperor Claudius's mother Antonia, Felix may have come to Samaria in A.D. 52 as procurator. Felix's brother Pallas was in charge of the emperor's financial accounts and managed to obtain equestrian ranking for his brother and positions normally held by this order, such as procurator. This promotion of a freedman to the equestrian

order and appointment to posts in the normal equestrian career were scandalous in the highly stratified Roman society (Suetonius *Claudius* 25.1.28) and illustrates how easily Claudius was influenced by those in the imperial household. Like Paul, Felix was also accused by the Jews of wrongdoing. He was appointed procurator for Judea, but social upheaval increased during his tenure, and he was replaced by Festus in A.D. 59.

*2.5.2. Festus.* Porcius Festus took over from Felix the responsibility for Paul's trial (Acts 25:1-8) when he relieved the latter of his post as procurator of Judea. His plan to try Paul in Jerusalem formed the pretext for Paul's appeal for trial before Caesar (Acts 25:9-12; *see* Citizenship). Festus led battles against militant Jewish opposition and took part in a dispute between King Agrippa II and Jewish leaders. He died in A.D. 62; his position as procurator of Judea was then filled by Albinus.

*2.6. Praetorians.* From the time of Sejanus's gathering of the praetorian guard in one area in A.D. 23, the praetorians became a political force in Roman life. In A.D. 41, after the murder of Gaius, it was the praetorians who saluted Claudius as emperor while the Senate was considering reinstatement of the republic. By this action they ensured that the Principate would continue and that Claudius would be the next emperor. Elite soldiers who were paid very well, the praetorians served for terms of sixteen years. The praetorians guarded the Emperor and his family members in Rome and abroad. Paul's statement that the cause of his imprisonment was well known throughout the whole praetorian guard (Phil 1:13) is strong but not by itself sufficient evidence for the Roman provenance of Philippians.* The leader of the praetorian guard, the praetorian prefect, had a great deal of political power. Since Nero had announced at the beginning of his reign that he would not judge cases personally (Tacitus *Ann.* 13.4.2), it is thought that the praetorian prefect took this responsibility. If Paul appeared in Caesar's court for trial soon after the time period covered in Acts, it is very likely that the praetorian prefect was his actual judge.

*2.7. Caesar's Household.* This term designates the slaves and freedmen who served in both personal and political capacities for the imperial family (*see* Caesar's Household). There was a significant distinction in status within this household; slaves or freed persons entrusted with financial matters held highest status and were most upwardly mobile. From the reign of Augustus these slaves and freed persons were entrusted with power previously reserved for men of equestrian or senatorial orders. The resulting status dissonance disturbed Roman nobility and began undermining the highly structured Roman social order. Caesar's household thus constituted the elite civil service, as is shown by the phenomenon that freeborn women would marry men of servile classes in this household.

Paul's mention of Caesar's household in Philippians 4:22 is another piece of evidence for the Roman provenance of the letter, though members of the imperial household did serve in other cities of the empire. It also shows that the Christian message had made significant inroads into the imperial court. At least two groups mentioned in Romans 16 may designate members of the imperial household. "Those of Aristobulus" (Rom 16:10) might refer to the former slaves of Aristobulus, the younger brother of Agrippa I. Since he was a member of the Herodian family and the immediately preceding name is Herodion, this identification is quite likely. Aristobulus lived in Rome and was a friend of Claudius (Josephus *Ant.* 18.5.4 §§133,135). If he passed on his property to the emperor, his slaves would have been members of Caesar's household when Paul wrote Romans. "Those of Narcissus who are in the Lord" (Rom 16:11) may signify the family of Tiberius Claudius Narcissus, a rich freedman who wielded much influence in Claudius's imperial household. Nero executed Narcissus shortly after he came to power (Tacitus, *Ann.* 13.1.4; Dio, 60.34), but his slaves would still have remained in Caesar's household.

*2.8. Caesars.* Four emperors* reigned during Paul's lifetime. He was born during the reign of Tiberius (A.D. 14-37), converted to Christianity during the reign of Gaius Caligula (37-41), and ministered mostly during the reigns of Claudius (41-54) and Nero (54-68). By the time of Paul the office of emperor (*kaisar* in the NT) was not simply "first among equals," but dictator. Claudius and Nero are the emperors most significant in the consideration of Paul's ministry and letters.

*2.8.1. Claudius.* Tiberius Claudius Nero Germanicus (10 B.C.—A.D. 54) received little notice in the reigns of Augustus or Tiberius. While alternate consul with his nephew, Gaius Caligula, the latter did not mark him as successor. His accession in A.D. 41 was therefore a surprise, brought on by the political muscle of the praetorians (see 2.6 above). Claudius's daughter Octavia was Nero's first wife. Claudius was known for being easily swayed by his wives and those closest to him in the imperial household. Paul met Priscilla and Aquila as a result of Claudius's edict that expelled Jews from Rome (A.D. 49; Acts 18:1-2). While this edict might be partially due to Claudius's love of Roman distinctives and religion, one must note that Claudius exerted sig-

nificant effort to end the social upheavals in Alexandria and Judea resulting from Gaius's anti-Semitism. Paul's missionary effort (Rom 15:17-24) may have been influenced by Claudius's expansionistic drive that resulted in adding provinces and extending citizenship. In any event, Paul at least uses language of Roman military policy when he describes his apostolic commission in Romans 1:5.

*2.8.2. Nero.* Nero Claudius Caesar (A.D. 37-68) was the emperor first known to have persecuted Christians (Tacitus, *Ann* 15) and was reigning at the time of Paul's execution. When Nero acceded to the throne in A.D. 54, he was under the influence of his powerful mother, Agrippina. Seneca and the praetorian prefect Burrus did much to lead the empire during the first five years of his reign. Helpful legislation was enacted (Tacitus *Ann.* 13.51) and competent governors were appointed. It must be noted that Paul wrote Romans 13:4 in the context of his directives on civil obedience during this period of Nero's reign. But in A.D. 59, after his matricide of Agrippina, the death of Burrus and Seneca's retirement, Nero began to lead as he wished, establishing games, founding a *gymnasium* and singing in public. Those closest to him were of low birth or freedmen of Greek or Asian descent. They were known for their arrogance. Nero's lavish spending on himself and the cost of wars in Armenia and Britain induced him to take money from the rich. By A.D. 62 people at a variety of levels in Roman society hated him. In 64 Nero was suspected of starting the great fire in Rome in order to build a bigger palace. He blamed the fire on Christians and began executing them (Tacitus *Ann.* 15.44). It is probable that Paul was executed c. A.D. 64-65 after trial in Nero's court. Then a conspiracy to assassinate Nero and install Calpurnius Piso as emperor was discovered in A.D. 65 and Nero executed all who were implicated. Paranoid of rebellion from this time on, he killed anyone whom he suspected. In A.D. 67 he toured Greece, granting it freedom. He was summoned back to Rome after the city had experienced famine and there was increasing dissatisfaction with his reign. Arriving in Rome in January of 68, he was unable to reverse the political tide. Beginning in March, three officials in various parts of the empire revolted. When the praetorians removed their support from Nero, he left Rome on June 9, A.D. 68, and committed suicide. Paul's martyrdom in Nero's court was certainly tragic in its time, though Glover's comment that the day would come when men would name their sons Paul and their dogs Nero shows the justice that the passage of time brings.

*See also* CAESAR'S HOUSEHOLD, IMPERIAL HOUSEHOLD; CITIZENSHIP, ROMAN AND HEAVENLY; CIVIL AUTHORITY; DIAS-

PORA; EMPERORS, ROMAN; LEGAL SYSTEM, ROMAN.

BIBLIOGRAPHY. F. F. Bruce, *Paul: Apostle of the Heart Set Free* (Grand Rapids: Eerdmans, 1977); P. A. Brunt, "Procuratorial Jurisdiction," *Latomus* 25 (1966) 461-89; G. P. Burton, "Proconsuls, Assizes and the Administration of Justice under the Empire," *JRS* 65 (1975) 92-106; P. Garnsey and R. Saller, *The Roman Empire: Economy, Society and Culture* (Berkeley: University of California, 1987); N. G. Hammond and H. H. Scullard, ed., *Oxford Classical Dictionary* (2d ed.; Oxford: University Press, 1970) passim; E. Lohse, "συνέδριον," *TDNT* VII.860-71; F. Millar, "The Emperor, the Senate and the Provinces," *JRS* 56 (1966) 156-66; A. Momigliano, *Claudius: The Emperor and His Achievement* (Oxford: Clarendon, 1934); A. M. Rabello, "The Legal Condition of the Jews in the Roman Empire," *ANRW* 2.13 (1980) 662-762; S. Safrai and M. Stern, ed., *The Jewish People in the First Century*, Vol. 1 (CRINT; Philadelphia: Fortress, 1974); A. N. Sherwin-White, *Roman Society and Roman Law in the New Testament: The Sarum Lectures 1960-1961*, (Oxford: University Press, 1963; repr. Grand Rapids: Baker, 1978); P. R. C. Weaver, *Familia Caesaris: A Social Study of the Emperor's Freedmen and Slaves* (Cambridge: University Press, 1972).
M. Reasoner

**POOR.** *See* COLLECTION FOR THE SAINTS; RICHES AND POVERTY.

**POSTAL SERVICE.** *See* TRAVEL IN THE ROMAN WORLD.

**POVERTY.** *See* RICHES AND POVERTY.

# POWER

In Pauline theology the cross represents the ultimate manifestation of the power of God.* In the death,* resurrection* and exaltation* of Jesus, God manifested his superior power against evil, especially as represented by sin,* death (*see* Life and Death) and the realm of Satan.*

Paul's favorite term for power is *dynamis* (and its cognates) which occur throughout his writings. On occasion he also uses the words *kratos* and *ischys* to speak of inherent or derived capability. Paul uses *exousia* usually in the sense of the right or authority* to exercise power and *energeia/energeō* to refer to the actualization of power in concrete circumstances. Paul's concept of power is certainly not restricted to a set of power-denoting terms. When Paul speaks of the Spirit (*see* Holy Spirit), he often has in mind the supernatural power of the Spirit. Similarly, his use of the expressions "grace,"* "glory,"* "fullness"* and even "in

Christ"* often convey the notion of divine power as part of their contextual meanings.

1. Power to Save
2. Power Against "the Powers"
3. Power to Serve
4. Power in Weakness
5. The Role of Faith and Prayer
6. God's Powerful Triumph over Evil

## 1. Power to Save.

The God of creation* who rescued his people from their slavery in Egypt has once again exercised his power for the salvation* of humanity from its bondage to sin and the cosmic powers (*see* Principalities and Powers). The essence of Paul's gospel consists of this message of salvation. The gospel* is thus "the power (*dynamis*) of God for the salvation of everyone who believes" (Rom 1:16; cf. also 1 Cor 1:18). God acted through Christ* to release people from the bondage of death, sin, flesh* and the Law* (Rom 5:12—8:39) and to blunt the influence of the realm of Satan against the church* (Col 2:15). Because of the life-transforming capability of the gospel resulting in the reconciliation* of people to God, the apostle* devoted his life to the propagation of this powerful message.

Paul speaks of the Holy Spirit as the dynamic presence of God dwelling within believers. The Spirit works to transform people into conformity to God's standards of holiness.* The Spirit thus enables believers to rid themselves of evil thoughts and deeds (Rom 8:13). Believers need divine strength to resist the supernaturally powerful influence of the principle of sin (1 Cor 15:56) and the ongoing enticement of the inner evil impulse, which Paul calls the "flesh" (Rom 8:13).

## 2. Power Against "the Powers."

Believers also face personal supernatural opponents who tend to exploit the "flesh" and the world structures (Eph 2:1-3) leading people into rebellion against God's purposes. Although believers have been rescued from the all-encompassing tyranny of Satan's kingdom, his evil forces are still actively hostile to the redeemed people of God. This demonic hierarchy of "principalities and powers"* seeks to cause the demise of the church by promoting impurity, dissension and deviant teaching (Eph 6:10-18; 4:27). God promises to impart his power to believers so they can resist these influences and thus "stand" pure and blameless before him.

## 3. Power to Serve.

Paul zealously devoted himself to the proclamation of

the gospel of the Lord* Jesus Christ. He affirms that he carried out his ministry* "through the power of the Spirit" (Rom 15:19; cf. also 1 Tim 1:12). He tells the Colossians* that he labored to bring all of his converts to maturity in Christ, "toiling strenuously with all the energy and power of Christ at work in me" (Col 1:28-29 NEB; Eph 3:7). This power enabled Paul to continue proclaiming the gospel and building the church even in the most hostile of circumstances (2 Tim 4:17).

In his teaching Paul endeavored to root the faith of his converts in God and his power. The Corinthians,* however, were tempted to be more impressed with the form and style of delivery (perhaps such as they saw in the Sophists; see Rhetoric) rather than the content of the message. Paul thus calls them to focus on the content of the preaching—Jesus Christ and him crucified—and the demonstration of the Spirit's power in his preaching, evident in the transformed lives of the converts (1 Cor 2:1-5; see Cross, Theology of the).

The same divine power that strengthened Paul also empowers other believers in their service to the church. Paul admonished Timothy not to be timid, but to draw on the power which God provides, viz. "the grace that is in Christ Jesus" (2 Tim 1:7; 2:1). The "grace" of God is imparted to believers primarily in the context of the ministry of the various members of the body of Christ to one another. The Holy Spirit works through the individual parts of the body for the building up of the whole (1 Cor 12; see Body of Christ). There is a strong emphasis in Paul's thought on divine empowerment taking place chiefly in the context of Christian community.

God's power will enable believers to manifest love to one another and also to those outside the Christian community (1 Cor 13; Eph 5:1-2). This is possible because God has enabled believers to know and experience the unsurpassed love* of Christ (Eph 3:16-19).

### 4. Power in Weakness.

"When I am weak, then I am strong!" was a guiding principle in Paul's ministry (2 Cor 12:10). Although he regarded his human body as possessing a measure of ability, he was painfully aware of its frailty and inherent limitations (2 Cor 1:8). He even compared his body to a clay pot in its fragility (2 Cor 4:7). Yet, in spite of these constraints, he was able to serve the church in ways that surpassed his innate weakness.* He attributes his ability to the "grace" of God (1 Cor 12:9; Eph 3:7), that is, the power of God working in him and through him. Specifically, it is Christ himself who indwells Paul and enables him to carry out a life of service (2 Cor 12:10; Eph 3:16-17; see Servant, Service).

Paul needed God's empowering to endure suffering.* He saw suffering as integral to knowing Christ—he who suffered to death for his people (2 Cor 4:10; 13:3-4; Phil 3:10). Because Paul experienced God's inner strength, he was able to endure a level of suffering that went far beyond mere human ability to endure (2 Cor 4:7-12; cf. also Col 1:11; 2 Tim 1:8). Because he trusted in a God who could accomplish anything he purposed through his frail human servants (Eph 3:20-21), Paul could tell the Philippians* that he could endure any set of circumstances because of the empowering divine presence (Phil 4:13).

Paul also experienced God's power to help him continue his service in spite of the debilitating effects of what he called his "thorn in the flesh" (2 Cor 12:7-10). Most likely manifested as some physical disability, Paul regarded the thorn as the work of an angelic ambassador of Satan. Although the thorn was inherently evil, it served a good purpose by ensuring Paul's humility. Most importantly, it was an opportunity for God to display his mighty power through the weakness of the apostle (see Black).

### 5. The Role of Faith and Prayer.

Paul speaks of faith* as the essential prerequisite and means for acquiring divine strength (Eph 3:16-17). He regards prayer* as a concrete manifestation of faith in God. Thus, in his famous passage on "spiritual warfare," Paul depicts faith as the shield by which all the attacks of the devil can be thwarted (Eph 6:15). Furthermore, he highlights prayer as the most prominent of the weapons and presents it as foundational to the deployment of each of the other weapons (Eph 6:18-20). Paul has already modeled this to his readers by praying for their heightened comprehension of the vastness of the divine power available to them (Eph 1:15-23) and also by directly praying for God to strengthen them in their innermost beings (Eph 3:14-21).

### 6. God's Powerful Triumph over Evil.

There was no thoroughgoing dualism in Paul's theology. He was convinced that God would triumph* over the cosmic powers in the end. Paul speaks of a definite end to this evil age in which Christ destroys the hostile principalities and powers and, ultimately, death itself (1 Cor 15:24-26). Believers can thus be assured of God's victory over evil and of their own life after death. This is certain because God has already demonstrated his power by raising Jesus from the dead (Rom 8:11; 1 Cor 6:14; 15:43; Eph 1:20-23).

See also AUTHORITY; CROSS, THEOLOGY OF THE; HOLY SPIRIT; MAGIC; PRINCIPALITIES AND POWERS; SALVATION;

TRIUMPH; WEAKNESS.

BIBLIOGRAPHY. C. E. Arnold, *Ephesians: Power and Magic* (SNTSMS 63; Cambridge: University Press, 1989); D. A. Black, *Paul, the Apostle of Weakness: Astheneia and Its Cognates in the Pauline Literature* (New York: Lang, 1984); W. Grundmann, "δύναμαι κτλ," *TDNT* II.284-317; idem, *Der Begriff der Kraft in der Neutestamentlichen Gedankenwelt* (Stuttgart: Kohlhammer, 1932); R. P. Martin, *2 Corinthians* (WBC 40; Dallas: Word, 1986); H. Nielsen, "Paulus' Verwendung des Begriffes *Dunamis*," in *Die Paulinische Literatur und Theologie*, ed. S. Pederson (Århus: Aros, 1980) 137-58; C. H. Powell, *The Biblical Concept of Power* (London: Epworth, 1963). C. E. Arnold

**POWERS.** See COLOSSIANS, LETTER TO THE; ELEMENTS/ELEMENTAL SPIRITS OF THE WORLD; PRINCIPALITIES AND POWERS; TRIUMPH.

**PRAISE.** See HYMNS, HYMN FRAGMENTS, SONGS, SPIRITUAL SONGS; PRAYER; WORSHIP.

# PRAYER

Paul's apostolate began in prayer and, according to tradition, ended in prayer as he was martyred. His whole ministry* was grounded in, and developed from, prayer. For Paul, the Christian experience was essentially (and unceasingly) an act of prayer. Those redeemed and hence overwhelmed by the sovereign grace of the "God and Father of our Lord Jesus Christ," intentionally and purposefully pour out their lives as a perpetual act of thanksgiving, ever conscious of dependence on an omnipresent and omnipotent God,* as they are motivated and empowered by the Holy Spirit.* Apart from prayer, life as a redeemed bondservant* of Christ* was both inconceivable and impossible.

1. Prayer in Paul's Life: Acts and Letters
2. Analysis of Pauline Prayer Material
3. Pauline Prayer Vocabulary
4. Pauline Prayer Theology

## 1. Prayer in Paul's Life: Acts and Letters.

*1.1. Spiritual Roots in Judaism.* Before his conversion* Saul of Tarsus belonged to "the strictest sect" of first-century rabbinic Judaism (Acts 26:5). The young Pharisee was "extremely zealous for the traditions" of his Jewish ancestors (Gal 1:14), and viewed himself as "faultless" regarding legalistic righteousness* (Phil 3:6; see Jew, Paul the). Because of these assertions, we may assume this earnest rabbi participated fully in the prayers prescribed by Pharisaic Judaism. Prayers of praise, blessing, thanksgiving, confession, petition

and intercession* were all part of Saul's daily routine (see Benediction, Blessing, Doxology, Thanksgiving). Among pious rabbis, formal set public prayers were associated with meals, life transitions such as birth, marriage and death, the reading and study of the Law,* local synagogue worship,* national religious festivals and Jerusalem temple rituals. The OT evidences considerable spontaneity and intimacy in private prayer (see the psalms of David, for example), but Pharisaism conformed much personal prayer to fixed forms such as the Shema (š°ma', Deut 6:4-9; 11:13-21 and Num 15:37-41), repeated morning and evening at the third and ninth hour (cf. Ezra 9:5; Dan 9:21) along with several prescribed introductory and concluding benedictions, and the Tephillah (t°pillāh), or Eighteen Benedictions (š°mōneh 'eśrēh), apparently repeated three times each day (see Ps 55:17 and Dan 6:10; cf. Acts 10:9). It has been argued that the spirituality of first-century Judaism may have been far more varied than commonly supposed, inasmuch as the Qumran* scrolls and extant synagogue liturgies evidence considerable variation in Jewish prayer forms. We may be certain, however, that prayer was extremely important to Pharisees like Saul: according to Rabbinic tradition, without a systematic, disciplined and structured prayer life one could not achieve personal righteousness. It is evident at many points, however, that Paul's dynamic prayer experience owes more to the ethos and examples of the OT Psalter and the passion of Israel's prophets than to rabbinic ritualism.

*1.2. Insights from the Book of Acts.* Luke's narrative in Acts stresses the central role prayer played in Paul's life. The apostle's initial conversion,* commission, baptism* and missionary* work were linked to prayer. Saul heard the dying Stephen's prayers to the "Lord Jesus" (Acts 7:59-60; 22:20). Shortly thereafter, on the Damascus road, he spoke directly to the risen Christ, calling him "Lord"* (Acts 9:5). During the three-day period of prayer and fasting which followed (Acts 9:11), Saul first came to understand that "Jesus is the Son of God" (Acts 9:20). Following Ananias's communication of his apostolic commission, Saul was immediately baptized while "calling upon his [Jesus'] name" in prayer (Acts 22:16; cf. 9:19; Rom 10:9-10, 14). The apostle later received personal guidance from Christ while "praying" in the Jerusalem Temple (Acts 22:17; cf. 9:26-30; 16:9-10). It was during a period of "prayer and fasting" that the Holy Spirit instructed the church at Syrian Antioch to set apart Barnabas* and Saul for evangelistic work (Acts 13:2-3). The two missionaries similarly confirmed elders in the fledgling churches at Lystra, Iconium and Pisidian Antioch through "prayer and fasting" (Acts 14:23). Near Philippi, at a Jewish "place of prayer," Paul met Lydia, his first convert in Macedonia (Acts 16:13, 16). The Philippian jailer was converted following an earthquake, apparently a miraculous response to the midnight "praying and singing hymns to God" by the imprisoned Paul and Silas (Acts 16:25). The final trip to Jerusalem* occasioned a sorrowful time of prayer and weeping with the Ephesian elders (Acts 20:36-37), and later a poignant scene of prayer with "all the disciples, their wives and children" kneeling on the beach at Tyre (Acts 21:5). It is likely that encouraging visitations by Christ (Acts 23:11) and an angel* (Acts 27:23) were also associated with prayer. Acts draws to a close with Paul interceding for others: Luke says, "after prayer" the apostle placed his hands on and healed the ailing father of Publius, the chief official of Malta. This scene was surely repeated, because "the rest of the sick on the island came and were [also] cured" (Acts 28:8-9).

*1.3. Reflections of Paul at Prayer in the Letters.* Strictly speaking, the Pauline letters contain almost nothing that can be described as personal or public prayer. The NT letters represent a literary genre quite different from the narratives of the Gospels and Acts or John's visions in Revelation. Directly addressing God while writing to others was ruled out by the conventions of ancient letter* writing. What we find in Paul's letters are references, allusions and reports about his prayers.

*1.4. Requests for Prayer.* G. P. Wiles rightly says Paul's "dynamic ministry involved a triangular relationship between God (known in Christ and through the Holy Spirit), himself as commissioned apostle,* and the churches for which he was responsible" (Wiles, 2). As a result, several times the apostle urges his readers to "join me in my struggle by praying to God for me" (Rom 15:30; cf. 1 Thess 5:25). His prayer requests are both direct and indirect, and often quite specific. 2 Thessalonians 3:1-2 summarizes the concerns most commonly mentioned: "Brothers, pray for us that the message of the Lord may spread rapidly and be honored, just as it is with you. And pray that we may be delivered from wicked and evil men, for not everyone has faith." The focus in Romans 15:30-32 is twofold: (1) that the apostle would be delivered from unbelieving Jews in Judea who wished harm both to him and to the Gentile mission; and (2) that the collection gathered from the predominantly Gentile* churches of Asia, Macedonia and Achaia would be received positively by the impoverished but more conservative Jewish Christians in Jerusalem.

Elsewhere Paul expresses confidence that he will be delivered from "deadly peril" as the believers in Corinth help him by their prayers (2 Cor 1:8-11). Ephe-

sians 6:19 sounds a more urgent note, the apostle asking for intercession that "whenever I open my mouth, words may be given me so that I will fearlessly make known the mystery* of the gospel." The request for courage is repeated in Ephesians 6:20: "Pray that I may declare it fearlessly, as I should." The pattern is repeated in the apostle's final exhortations to the Colossians*: "Pray for us too, that God may open a door for our message. . . . Pray that I may proclaim it clearly, as I should" (Eph 4:3-4). With those he knows better, Paul seems more confident: telling the Philippians* he expects to be delivered from Roman imprisonment "through your prayers" (Phil 1:19) and assuring Philemon, "Prepare a guest room for me, because I hope to be restored to you in answer to your prayers" (Philem 22). The instruction in 1 Timothy 2:1-8 urging intercession for "everyone" should be viewed as an implicit request for personal prayer support, inasmuch as verse 7 stresses Paul's divine appointment as "herald, apostle and teacher" in connection with the Gentile mission.

## 2. Analysis of Pauline Prayer Material.

*2.1. Trends in Research.* Research on Pauline prayer material has been surveyed by R. Gebauer. Helpful digests have also been provided by P. T. O'Brien and G. P. Wiles. However, as compared with concerns such as christology* or soteriology, scholarly interest in NT prayer material has been relatively slight. There are several probable reasons for this. Spirituality* was a concern to several early church fathers, but in the postapostolic period, prayer was not a major issue for church councils, and it was virtually ignored by those who framed the creeds. In the modern period formal study of prayer in Scripture has been discouraged by three discernible trends in Christendom.

(1) From approximately 1900 onward researchers were increasingly uncomfortable with the assumptions of ancient authors concerning the existence of the supernatural. To pray and write as Paul did assumes a so-called pre-scientific worldview in which is assumed the existence of an omnipotent, yet personal living God, who is actively involved in the outworking of his will on earth, and who responds to prayer. Modern historical-critical biblical scholarship has tended to erode the theological underpinnings of petitionary prayer along with the church's certainty about biblical miracles, predictive prophecy and the divinity of Christ.

(2) Following World War I philosophical existentialism exerted a powerful influence on NT scholarship. R. Bultmann said, "How a man prayed concerns no other man, not even the historian. And whoever al-

lows himself to judge how fervently or deeply Jesus prayed, proves only that he neither understands nor respects Jesus' conception of prayer. For whoever so judges either sees prayer merely as a psychological phenomenon which can become the object of interesting analysis [Bultmann's reaction to F. Heiler's work], or he arrogates himself to God's own right. For according to Jesus, prayer is talking with God; whoever assumes he can evaluate any prayer presumes to stand in the place of God." Such views, expressed so forcefully by scholars of significant influence, made the study of NT prayer seem illegitimate. It is notable that the groundbreaking studies of Pauline prayer by H. Greeven, G. Harder and P. Schubert were undertaken in the face of such discouragements.

(3) During an age when social, political and economic issues have dominated large parts of the church there was a tendency to regard biblical spirituality as "other worldly" and irrelevant. The fact that the revolutionary apostolic activist whose ministry "turned the world upside down" (Acts 17:6 RV) drew great power from prayer has been largely overlooked. Despite the fact that recent decades have seen several excellent contributions (see esp. the work of R. Gebauer, P. T. O'Brien and G. P. Wiles), academic study of Pauline prayer material continues to be truncated due to on-going scholarly misgivings about the apostolic authorship of 2 Thessalonians, the Prison letters and the Pastorals.* When prayer does become the focus of serious research, it is often held at arm's length: atomized, analyzed and categorized in ways which rarely seem to reflect the power and passion of apostolic spirituality.

*2.2. General Classification: Prophetic Prayer.* F. Heiler's *Das Gebet*, a study of the history, phenomenology and psychology of the human prayer experience, assigns prayer to six fundamental classes: primitive, ritual, Greek, cultural, philosophical, mystical and prophetic. Despite those who regard Paul as a mystic (often largely on the basis of his descriptions of believers as being "in" or "into" Christ; *see* In Christ), it is evident the apostle prayed in continuity with the "prophetic," or biblical, rather than the "mystical" prayer traditions. Paul's spirituality never seeks to "merge" with divinity; and his letters contain no instruction which can be rightly understood as providing a mystical prayer ladder to (a nonpersonal) God—either through visions in association with asceticism or on the basis of illumination gained through the impartation of (secret) esoteric knowledge. Mysticism* generally asserts that as spirituality matures petition and supplication will be replaced by so-called higher forms of prayer, such as meditation and contempla-

tion. By contrast, the Pauline prison letters evidence ongoing, vigorous supplication and intercession in the apostle's own prayer life, and exhortations that his readers "in everything, by prayer and petition with thanksgiving, present your requests to God" (Phil 4:6). The Pastorals continue these themes: "I urge . . . that requests, prayers, intercession and thanksgiving be made for everyone . . ." (1 Tim 2:1).

*2.3. Classification by Content.* True prayer is a fluid (some would say *spontaneous*) expression of the human spirit which does not readily lend itself to precise analysis or assignment to rigid categories. Nevertheless, both Scripture, worship* and culture have each contributed to the ways Christians pray. As a result, patterns and characteristics are discernible, and attempts at classification are useful aids to study and spiritual formation. Biblical prayer material may be categorized by content as: (1) praise, thanksgiving, worship, adoration; (2) contemplation, meditation; (3) confession, lamentation, penitential prayer; (4) entreaty, petition, supplication, intercession; (5) declaration, affirmation vow, oath; (6) invocation, doxology, benediction; (7) complaint, imprecation (prayer asking for vengeance, curse). There are no undisputed examples of Pauline prayer material in categories (2) and (3). Categories (1) and (4) are most frequent: thanksgiving and intercession predominate. Similar emphases are seen in the Gospel accounts of the prayers of Jesus.

*2.4. Classification by Form.* Since the time of G. Harder and P. Schubert, scholars have generally categorized the bulk of Pauline prayer material as either (1) wish prayers or (2) prayer reports.

*2.4.1. The Wish Prayers.* Wish prayers refer to God obliquely, using the third person, and the optative of the Greek verb: "May our God and Father himself and our Lord Jesus clear the way for us to come to you. May the Lord make your love increase. . . . May he strengthen your hearts . . ." (1 Thess 3:11-13). Similar forms are found in Romans 15:5-6, 13; 1 Thessalonians 5:23-24; 2 Thessalonians 2:16-17; 3:5, 16; 2 Timothy 1:16, 18; 2:25; 4:16b (cf. Heb 13:20-21). An optative is implied in Romans 15:33, and other wish prayers using the future indicative may be observed in Romans 16:20; 1 Corinthians 1:8-9 and Philippians 4:19.

G. P. Wiles includes in this category the epistolary greetings, or "benedictions," which open and close the Pauline letters. With minor modification all contain an initial wish prayer similar to that of Romans 1:7: "[May there be] grace and peace to you from God our Father and from the Lord Jesus Christ." (It is not uncommon for scholars to label texts like Eph 1:3-4, which begin with "praise be" or "blessed be" [*eulogein*] with the Hebrew term *berakoth* [*beʿrāḵôṯ*], a classification used for extended blessings in the OT and other Jewish texts. In the case of thanksgivings, another Hebrew term, *hodayoth* [*hôḏāyôṯ*], is sometimes used to refer to those beginning with "thanks be" [*eucharistein*]. See Bradshaw.)

Though wording varies considerably, all of the Pauline letters close with wish-prayer benedictions. 2 Corinthians 13:14 is a classic example, "May the grace of the Lord Jesus Christ, and the love of God, and the fellowship of the Holy Spirit be with you all." Scholars also include in the wish-prayer category the so-called curse* in 1 Corinthians 16:22, "If anyone does not love the Lord, [may] a curse be on him" (cf. 1 Cor 5:3-5 and Gal 1:8-9). (The AV and NKJV render 2 Tim 4:14b as a prayer for divine retribution, "May the Lord repay him according to his [evil] works." But the best Greek texts have the verb in the future active indicative, indicating the apostle's confidence in God's justice, "the Lord will requite him for his deeds," rather than a prayer-wish for revenge.) Also included is the pronouncement blessing of Galatians 6:16, "Peace* and mercy* to all who follow this rule, even to the Israel* of God."

*2.4.2. Prayer Reports.* Although a few prayer reports mention Paul's prayers for others (Rom 10:1) or the prayer of others for his readers (2 Cor 9:14), most material usually classified under this heading consists of references to the apostle's thanksgiving and/or intercession for his readers. Prayer reports are prominent features of the introductory portions of most Pauline letters. 2 Corinthians begins with the famous doxological exclamation, "Praise be to the God and Father of our Lord Jesus Christ, the Father of compassion and God of all comfort" (2 Cor 1:3), whereas Galatians, 1 Timothy and Titus, documents apparently written under urgent circumstances, have no equivalent.

References to thanksgiving and intercession are often mixed, as in Romans 1:8-10, "First, I thank my God through Jesus Christ for all of you, because your faith is being reported all over the world. God, whom I serve with my whole heart in preaching the gospel of his Son, is my witness how constantly I remember you in my prayers at all times; and I pray that now at last by God's will the way may be opened for me to come to you." Some introductory prayer reports (see, e.g., Col 1:3-14) tend to merge with content of the letter proper. Specific criteria for discerning transitions have been proposed by P. Schubert and J. T. Sanders, but this is a difficult matter. Analysis of the prayer reports is also complicated by the apostle's

preference for lengthy syntax: Ephesians 1:16-23, for example, is one continuous Greek sentence.

In several of Paul's prayer reports, one form of prayer begins before a preceding type concludes. Texts such as 2 Corinthians 9:11-13 evidence the overlap of doxology and thanksgiving; and 1 Corinthians 14:16 shows a merging of blessing and thanksgiving. In some reports (see Col 1:3-14 and 2 Thess 1:3-12) the apostle mentions prayer but seems to move into straightforward teaching, returning to prayer again at the close. Scholars have adopted the expression *period* to designate a portion of a letter generally recognized as an extended prayer report (thus in scholarly literature one will come across references to, e.g., "Pauline thanksgiving periods").

*2.4.3. Introductory Thanksgiving Periods.* The introductory thanksgiving periods have occasioned the most scholarly discussion. P. Schubert's generally accepted syntactical analysis discerned two basic forms:

(1) The most frequent begins with the expression "I thank God" (usually, *eucharistō tō theō*) as the main clause, with the main verb modified by one, two or three participles which follow. The participles are always nominative masculine, making it clear that the apostle himself has offered the prayer. The period concludes with a final subordinate purpose or result clause (introduced with *hina*, *hyper* or *eis to* followed by an infinitive).

(2) Schubert's second type is simpler, but also less personal: It too begins with a main clause of "I thank God," but is followed by a subordinate causal-*hoti* clause, and concludes with a subordinate result clause. In at least three cases (Rom 1:8-15; 1 Thess 1:2-10 and 2 Thess 1:3-12) the two form categories are intermixed.

*2.4.4. Form and Function.* Schubert's analysis led him to conclude that the essential function of the Pauline thanksgivings was simply "to indicate the occasion for and the contents of the letters which they introduce" (Schubert, 27). He reached this deduction by detailed form analysis of all known uses of the verb *eucharistein* ("to give thanks") in non-Pauline NT material, the LXX, Philo, and Greek epistolary papyri and inscriptions. Since many nonbiblical Hellenistic parallels are evident, Schubert confidently concluded, "beyond a shadow of a doubt," that the apostle was not so much a Jew of the Diaspora who was "exposed" to the culture and language of Greece, but a thoroughgoing "Hellenist of Hellenists," who employed the epistolary thanksgiving form "strictly" (and merely) as a convenient literary device to indicate why he was writing a particular letter and to introduce themes he would develop later in the body of the letter (Schubert,

183-84). Schubert admitted that Paul did not slavishly imitate Hellenistic literary forms (some aspects of the Pauline thanksgivings are much more developed structurally than many examples in extant Greek letters). But on this view one is left, as P. T. O'Brien says, to "wonder whether Paul actually gave thanks (or offered petition) for the churches concerned at all" (O'Brien, 13).

Schubert's *Form and Function* was published in 1939, prior to the Qumran discoveries and their enrichment of biblical and historical studies. Following the publication of the Qumran* Scrolls, both J.-P. Audet and J. M. Robinson demonstrated that the prayer and liturgical influences of the Greek and Jewish cultures of the NT period were not as isolated as Schubert believed. J. A. Fitzmyer (223-25) and G. Delling (51-54) have suggested, contra Schubert, that although the structure of Paul's introductory thanksgivings is manifestly Hellenistic in form, their content (although obviously Christian) is clearly influenced by, and indebted to, Judaism. The apostle's own claim to be a "Hebrew of Hebrews" (Phil 3:5) from the Hellenistic city of Tarsus squares well with this conclusion.

Many NT scholars now believe Paul's use of convenient and culturally appropriate Hellenistic epistolary prayer forms has neither dominated nor determined the content of the thanksgiving-intercessory periods. In recent decades researchers have taken the study of Pauline thanksgiving and intercessory material beyond the analysis of form, structure and function to consider seriously their purpose as prayers and their role in the apostle's ministry. An extensive critique of Schubert's work and exegetical analysis has been done by P. T. O'Brien. His *Introductory Thanksgivings in the Letters of Paul* (1977) and subsequent articles clearly establish a number of conclusions:

(1) Paul's "thanksgiving and petitionary prayer reports are evidence of the Apostle's deep pastoral and apostolic concern for the addressees" (O'Brien, 262).

(2) The Pauline thanksgiving periods and intercessory prayer reports also have a didactic function. When the letters were read in a congregation, they would remind the worshippers of the apostle's preaching in their city. The prayers emphasize the faithfulness of God and stress vital elements in Paul's teaching on the believers' life in Christ. As such, they would also serve as a "model for their own giving of thanks when remembering fellow-believers before God" (O'Brien, 1977, 14; cf. 262-63).

(3) The introductory prayer material also often seems to "prefigure" the paraenetic (exhortation, admonition or advice) material which becomes an important emphasis later in the letter. This feature is especially prominent in the intercessory prayer reports. (Analysis of this aspect was a major emphasis in the groundbreaking work of G. P. Wiles, *Paul's Intercessory Prayers* [1974].)

(4) O'Brien draws an important distinction between the paraenetic function of the prayer reports and their more obvious epistolary function "to introduce and indicate the main theme(s) of the letters." He concludes that Paul's "prayer reports" are just that: they are not just an interesting and appropriate literary device, but rather are accounts (or perhaps summaries) of actual thanksgivings and petitions offered by the apostle for his churches. O'Brien stressed the prayer reports' immediate relevance to genuine historical contexts and emphasized their accurate reflection of Paul's theological convictions and personal pastoral compassion for his converts. In this O'Brien echoes Wiles, who concluded:

"In Paul's hands, the conventional usages of ancient letter style turned out to be weighted with new meaning and the prayers were found to give concentrated living expression to his deeply responsible love, his vital anxieties and burning hopes. Each of the prayers was evoked by and adapted to a particular context; the lines of concern flowed together through each threatening occasion, through the letter composed for that situation, and through the prayer passages that reflected it." (Wiles, 293)

"Prayer buttressed all his mission work—in advance of visits, during them and after he had departed. All his plans were conceived under the constant sense of the guidance and will of God. None of his bold advances would have seemed worthwhile to him apart from continual undergirding by the prayers of the apostle and his associates. Taken together, then, the intercessory prayer passages offer impressive documentation of Paul's unfailing reliance upon the ministry of supplication, his own and that of fellow believers." (Wiles, 296)

### 3. Pauline Prayer Vocabulary.

*3.1. Terminology.* The Pauline prayer vocabulary is the richest in the NT, and the apostle uses prayer terms more frequently than any other writer. R. Morganthaler's NT word statistics indicate that 16 different words for prayer appear 105 times in the 13 canonical Pauline letters. (In comparison: Mt has 8 words used 30 times; Mk only 5 used 18 times; Lk has 10 terms used 46 times; Jn only 3 words used 18 times; Acts has 6 words used 36 times; Heb has 3 words, each used once. In the remainder of the NT 11 prayer terms are used 36 times.) The apostle's penchant for thanksgiving is striking: *eucharisteō* ("to give thanks") appears 23 times; and *eucharistia* ("thanksgiving") 12 times. O'Brien has shown that "Paul mentioned the subject of thanksgiving more often per page than any other Hellenistic author, pagan or Christian" (O'Brien 1980, 61). The apostle's preferred words for petition are: *proseuchomai* ("to pray"), 19 times; *proseuchē* ("prayer"), 14 times; *deēsis* ("request, entreaty"), 12 times; and *epikaleō* ("to call upon"), 6 times. G. P. Wiles discerned no unique terms for intercession: "Instead Paul uses general words for prayer in such a way as to imply that the prayer is on behalf of others" (Wiles, 18). In several places nonprayer terminology is used to refer to prayer (see, e.g., Rom 15:30, *synagōnizomai* ("assist"); 2 Cor 1:11, *synypourgeō* ("help"); 1 Thess 1:2, *mneia* ("mention"); 1 Thess 1:3, *mnēmoneuō* ("remember").

*3.2. Sources and Roots.* Paul's prayer language contains terms that would have been familiar to virtually all first-century Greek-speaking readers—even those recently converted from paganism. Yet he uses these words in expressions which indicate his spiritual life had deep roots in OT Scripture, particularly the Psalms. Similarities with Qumran texts have been suggested, and parallels with the LXX, used among Hellenistic Jews, have been noted. A growing number of scholars discern links between Paul's prayer language and the liturgical formulations of early Christian worship. There is a discernible tendency for commentators to regard full-orbed christological expressions in the prayers, for example: "God, the Father of our Lord Jesus Christ" (Col 1:3; cf. Eph 1:2), as evidence of post-apostolic authorship. Yet very similar language may be found in prayer contexts in the chief letters (*Hauptbriefe*) of Paul: "as you wait for the revealing of our Lord Jesus Christ; who will sustain you to the end, guiltless in the day of our Lord Jesus Christ. God is faithful, by whom you were called into the fellowship of his Son, Jesus Christ our Lord" (1 Cor 1:7-9 RSV; cf. 2 Cor 1:3). O'Brien concludes that "phrases from the wish-prayer of 1 Thess 3:11-13 were probably used in pre-Pauline Christian worship" (O'Brien 1977, 264). Those familiar with research on the themes and expressions of the primitive kerygma are immediately struck with the repetition of many characteristic motifs in Paul's prayers. Terms such as *proclaim, gospel,\* receive* (a tradition\*), *witness,\* the word of God, grace,\* faith,\* hope\** and *love\** are common in early Christian preaching. In the "fruit-bearing" language of Colossians 1:10, O'Brien discerns echoes of Mark 4:19, 13-20. There are parallels with "fruitfullness" concepts in the OT (cf. Is 5:1-4 and Ps 80:14-15), and those who posit an original *Sitz im Leben* for Mark's parable in the

earthly ministry of Jesus, find here evidence for a link between Paul's prayer language and the teaching of Jesus.

## 4. Pauline Prayer Theology.

*4.1. Prayer Results from a Theocentric Worldview.* Paul's life was lived in moment-by-moment consciousness of the eternal existence of a holy, sovereign God, "the blessed and only ruler, the King of kings, Lord of lords, who alone is immortal and who lives in unapproachable light, whom no one has seen or can see" (1 Tim 6:15-16 NIV; cf. 1 Tim 1:17). Since "from him and through him and to him are all things" (Rom 11:36), it was impossible for the apostle to conceive of any human activity apart from God: "For in him we live and move and have our being" (Acts 17:28). This totally theocentric worldview fundamentally shaped Paul's spiritual life and prayer.

*4.2. Prayer As a Creaturely Obligation.* Prayer, especially thanksgiving, is a logical, natural and necessary consequence of the apostle's understanding of reality. About those who do not acknowledge God's existence nor their accountability to a holy creator, he says "they neither glorified him as God nor gave thanks to him, but their thinking became futile and their foolish hearts were darkened. Although they claimed to be wise, they became fools" (Rom 1:21-22 NIV; cf. 2 Tim 3:2). Paul's basic theology of prayer was thus constructed on the rational certainty that God exists and personally and providentially sustains the creation (cf. Col 1:16-17). Yet his motivation to pray stems from considerably more than creaturely obligation to glorify the creator.

*4.3. Thanksgiving Motivated by Salvation.* Saul the Pharisee was certainly conscious of human moral accountability to God. But after his conversion Paul asserted that "there is no one righteous" (Rom 3:10) and, what is more, no human effort or legal system could enable one to measure up to "the glory\* of God" (Rom 3:20; 5:12; 8:3). Paul's personal opposition to Christ and persecution of the primitive church are the basis for the claim that he was "once a blasphemer and a violent man," "the worst of sinners" (1 Tim 1:13, 15-16, cf. Acts 9:4-5). One might speculate that the root of the apostle's passion to pray came directly from his awareness that although he was "wretched," "helpless" and "condemned" before God because of the guilt of his sin,\* he "was shown mercy because," as he confesses, "I had acted in ignorance and unbelief. The grace of our Lord was poured out on me abundantly along with the faith and love that are in Christ Jesus" (1 Tim 1:13-14 NIV). It is this which produces the exclamation: "Thanks be to God—through Jesus

Christ our Lord!" (Romans 7:25). Forgiveness of sins, redemption* and justification* by God's grace through faith left no room for human "boasting." But in Paul's mind, being turned from darkness to light,* from the power of Satan* to God—receiving full rights as God's child—was so astounding that it virtually compelled ceaseless thanksgiving: "Be joyful always, pray continually; give thanks in all circumstances, for this is God's will for you in Christ Jesus" (1 Thess 5:16-18 NIV). Hence, Christians are characterized as "always giving thanks to God the Father for everything in the name of our Lord Jesus Christ" (Eph 5:20).

It has been suggested that those who pray "in the name of Jesus" will eventually pray *to* Jesus. Since Paul repeatedly affirms the divinity of Christ, and had observed prayer offered to Jesus (Acts 7: 59), it is notable that his wish prayers, prayer reports, doxologies and benedictions do not evidence prayer to Christ, either as petition or intercession (nor is there a hint of prayer offered to the Holy Spirit). It seems that Paul would affirm as normative the often stated maxim: "Prayer is a co-operation between God and the believer in that it is presented to the Father, in the name of the Son, through the inspiration of the indwelling Holy Spirit" (Thompson, 960; cf. Clowney, 133-73). Yet it is clear that Paul did not adhere to this schema rigidly. 1 Corinthians 16:22 contains his famous use of the Aramaic exclamation *Maranatha* ("Our Lord, come!"; cf. Rev 22:20; *see* Hymns).

*4.4. Prayer Essential to Service.* Paul's personal experience of the "surpassing greatness of knowing Christ Jesus my Lord" (Phil 3:8) reinforced his apostolic commission and commitment to the proclamation of the gospel. Naturally, his "heart's desire and prayer to God for the Israelites is that they may be saved" (Rom 10:1). And it seems reasonable to assume that he prayed similarly for the Gentiles. He requested prayer (Eph 6:19-20; Col 4:3-4) that God would: (1) open a door for the word of the gospel; (2) give him uninhibited boldness or confidence in preaching; and (3) give him facility of speech in his proclamation. Prayer to God was essential in the apostle's understanding of evangelistic work. On a purely human level, even the most eloquent gospel message was "veiled to those who are perishing. The god of this age has blinded the minds of unbelievers so that they cannot see the light of the gospel of the glory of Christ, who is the image of God" (2 Cor 4:3-4 NIV; cf. 1 Cor 2:14). It was neither the preacher nor the convert, but God who supernaturally intervened through the Spirit's call and justified those who believed. Prayer was also expected on the convert's part.

*4.5. The Role of the Mind in Prayer.* Romans 10:9-14 connects salvation* with faith, confession and prayer. The reference to prayer (using the Semitic idiom "to call upon the name of the Lord," cf. Gen 12:8; Ps 99:6) is extremely important. It emphasizes the individual's responsibility to respond to the gospel, it reveals Paul's understanding of faith, and it clarifies the role he assigned to the mind in prayer. In Romans 10:14 the apostle unmistakably links (1) knowledge* of God, (2) faith based on that knowledge and (3) prayer which proceeds from such faith. It is evident that Paul did not regard the faith from which authentic prayer issues as a kind of blind leap in the dark. For him, prayer comes from an intelligent or rationally informed faith and is grounded in the certainty that God is not "unknown" (cf. Acts 17:22-28) but rather, has revealed himself in creation, history, Christ, Scripture and the gospel. Modern tendencies to divorce faith from reason find no support here.

A similar emphasis on the use of the intellect when praying occurs in 1 Corinthians 14:14-17: "For if I pray in a tongue, my spirit prays, but my mind is unfruitful. So what shall I do? I will pray with my spirit, but I will also pray with my mind; . . . . If you are praising God with your spirit, how can anyone in the position of an outsider who does not understand [tongues] say 'Amen' to your thanksgiving, since the outsider does not know what you are saying. You may be giving thanks well enough, but the other person is not edified." The apostle thanked God that he spoke in tongues "more than all of you" (1 Cor 14:18), and in 2 Corinthians 12:1 he claims "visions and revelations" (perhaps associated with prayer) during which he heard "inexpressible things." But he seems to have regarded a rational mental state as less open to abuse or misunderstanding when praying, especially in public meetings (cf. 1 Cor 14:32-33).

*4.6. Prayer Essential to Perseverance.* Paul saw the Christian life in this world as an unending struggle against "rulers, against the authorities, against the powers of this dark world and against the spiritual forces of evil in the heavenly realms" (Eph 6:12; cf. 2 Cor 2:11; *see* Principalities and Powers). He saw persecution and life-threatening opposition to his ministry (*see* Opponents) as manifestations of this hostility and asked for prayer for deliverance (Rom 15:30; 2 Cor 1:8-11). He was convinced that believers needed the supernatural armor of God to resist temptation and "stand against the devil's schemes." He thus exhorts: "Pray in the Spirit on all occasions with all kinds of prayers and requests. With this in mind, be alert and always keep on praying for all the saints" (Eph 6:18). Paul does not, however, believe that perseverance (*see* Apostasy, Falling Away, Perseverance) is ultimately dependent on human ability: His prayers express certainty that God "will keep you strong to the end, so that you will be blameless on the day of our Lord Jesus Christ" (1 Cor 1:8). He prays for the Philippians, being "confident" that God "who began a good work in you will carry it on to completion until the day of Christ Jesus" (Phil 1:6; cf. 1:9). But knowing the human inclination toward "quarreling, jealousy, outbursts of anger, factions, slander, gossip, arrogance and disorder," he tells the Corinthians, "I am afraid when I come again my God will humble me before you, and I will be grieved over many who have sinned earlier and have not repented of the impurity, sexual sin and debauchery in which they have indulged" (2 Cor 12:20-21). He exhorts them to "test" themselves, and says, "we pray to God that you will not do anything wrong" (2 Cor 13:5, 7).

*4.7. Offering Converts to the Returning Christ.* The apostle regarded the whole Gentile mission* as an act of worship and expected to present his converts as an "offering acceptable to God, sanctified by the Holy Spirit" (Romans 15:16). "What," he asks the Thessalonians, "is our hope, or joy, or the crown in which we will glory in the presence of our Lord Jesus when he comes? Is it not you? Indeed, you are our glory and joy*" (1 Thess 2:19-20). In his letters Paul connects this theme with prayer in three ways:

(1) The steadfast faithfulness of his converts results in praise to God: "How can we thank God enough for you in return for all the joy we have in the presence of God because of you?" (1 Thess 3:9).

(2) Their need for spiritual growth motivates the petition that he might visit them as he prays earnestly "night and day . . . that we may see you again and supply what is lacking in your faith. Now may our God and Father himself and the Lord Jesus clear the way for us to come to you" (1 Thess 3:10).

(3) His long-term concern about their state at the parousia (*see* Eschatology) motivates many of his intercessory and wish-prayers: "May the Lord make your love increase and overflow for each other and for everyone else, just as ours does for you. May he strengthen your hearts so that you will be blameless and holy in the presence of our God and Father when our Lord Jesus comes with all his holy ones" (1 Thess 3:12-13).

Paul wanted his converts to "eagerly wait for the Lord Jesus Christ to be revealed" (1 Cor 1:7), and his concern for their holiness, given the immediacy of Christ's return, is a prominent feature of many of the intercessory prayer reports.

*4.8. The Spirit of Adoption.* The Pauline understanding of Christian prayer places major emphasis on the believer's relationship with, and personal access to, God as Father. This privilege is an aspect of the Christian's "adoption" as God's child (*see* Adoption and Sonship), and is grounded solely in the finished work of Christ: "in him and through faith in him we may approach God with freedom and confidence" (Eph 3:12). This opportunity transcends race and culture. Through Christ, Jew and Gentile "both have access to the Father by one Spirit" (Eph 2:18). The apostle says, "God sent the Spirit of his Son into our hearts, the Spirit who calls out *Abba*, Father" (Gal 4:6; cf. Rom 8:15), and he relates the "Spirit of adoption" with the believer's ability to pray as Jesus did (cf. Mk 14:36), with childlike personal intimacy (see Bruce, 199-201). For Paul prayer originates in the indwelling Holy Spirit who gives the believer assurance of adoption. Those who take prayer seriously will pursue holiness and strive to avoid sin which "quenches" or "grieves" the Spirit (1 Thess 5:19; Eph 4:30). In Romans 12:1-2 he connects (1) holiness, (2) service to God and (3) nonconformity to the [sinful] pattern of the world, with the renewing of the mind—clearly implying that Christian obedience facilitates discernment ("testing and approval") of God's will (cf. Jn 14:21).

*4.9. Prayer and the Will of God.* For Paul the "struggle" of prayer was not an attempt to wrestle God into changing his will. Praying according to God's will was critical to Paul because he understood all activity in the world in terms of good and evil. Through prayer, one declares that God and his world are in constant conflict. Prayer is "in essence rebellion—rebellion against the world and its fallenness, the absolute and undying refusal to accept as normal what is pervasively abnormal. [Prayer is] . . . the refusal of every agenda, every scheme, every interpretation that is at odds with the norm as originally established by God" (Wells, 124). Thus prayer truly is a struggle.

But Paul does not envision a striving with God to bend his will to personal desires or to the needs of others. Rather prayer is part of the believer's struggle to discern, affirm and participate in doing God's will against the pervasive influence of the power of evil (see Arnold 1989 and 1992, 148-59). Commitment to living as well as to praying according to God's will constitutes the essence of what Paul means when he calls his readers to pray "in the name of Jesus" (Eph 5:20). Believers are admonished not just to pray, but to lift up hands which are "holy" (1 Tim 2:8). Because of the apostle's high view of God's sovereignty, he did not envision that answers to human prayer could ever be contrary to God's will. He told the Romans, "I pray that now at last by God's will the way may be opened for me to come to you" (Rom 1:10); and later he urged them to pray "that by God's will I may come to you with joy and together with you be refreshed" (Rom 15:32).

The priority of God's will was underscored for the apostle by the reality of importunate, persistent, yet unanswered prayer in his own life. "Three times I pleaded with the Lord," he says in 2 Corinthians 12:7-10, that a "stake in my flesh, a messenger of Satan, to torment me" might be taken away. Through this type of experience he came to understand that (1) adversity, suffering, insults and persecution were opportunities for God's power to be made "perfect," or completely manifest, through human weakness. Furthermore, (2) suffering in the will of God produces perseverance, character and hope which does not disappoint (Rom 5:3-5). And, finally, (3) suffering and "our light and momentary troubles are achieving for us an eternal glory that far outweighs them all" (2 Cor 4:17; cf. Rom 8:18). He thus urges "patience" as Christians wait and pray for the final realization of "our adoption as children (*huiothesia*), the redemption of our bodies" (Rom 8:23).

The apostle recognizes the seriousness of suffering in a fallen world and acknowledges in Romans 8:23 that believers "groan inwardly" because of it. He exhorts the church to "carry one another's burdens" (Gal 6:2), an expression often popularly explained, with appeal to Psalm 55:22, as an exhortation to intercession. But we should probably give more emphasis to the aspect of mutual concern in Christ, expressed in shouldering burdens such as the temptations of others (cf. Gal 6:1). Paul's famous blessing in 2 Corinthians 1:3-4, which describes God as "the Father of compassion and the God of all comfort, who comforts us in all of our troubles, so that we can comfort those in any trouble," seems to support this. Yet intercession is important in the apostle's discussion of suffering.*

*4.10. The Intercession of the Spirit.* Paul reveals in Romans 8:26-27 that "the Spirit helps us in our weakness.* We do not know *what we ought to pray*, but the Spirit himself intercedes (*see* Intercession) for us with groans that words cannot express. And he who searches our hearts knows the mind of the Spirit, because the Spirit intercedes for the saints in accordance with God's will" (NIV, emphasis added). The central point here, namely the assurance that prayer offered by the Spirit is according to God's will, is rightly emphasized by the NIV quoted above. By rendering *to gar ti proseuchōmetha* "how to pray," the RV, RSV, NASB and NEB wrongly focus on prayer technique, methods or procedures. For Paul, asking in accordance with God's will (cf. 1 Jn 5:14-15) is the primary issue (for a survey of the exegetical issues see Cranfield, 1.421-23).

The Spirit's intercession from within believers on earth is paralleled by ongoing intercession for believers by Christ himself in heaven* (Rom 8:34). The expression "unspoken groanings" (RSV) in Romans 8:26 is often taken as an allusion to tongues*-speaking by believers during prayer in difficult circumstances. But it seems best to regard *stenagmois* ("with sighs, groans") as a prayer activity of the Spirit, who discerns the believer's deepest needs and communicates them in a unique way directly to God (see Cranfield, 1.423-25; cf. Käsemann 239-41).

If this is correct, then Paul's reference elsewhere to praying "in the Spirit" (Eph 6:18) should probably also not be interpreted as a reference to tongues: a Spirit-inspired "prayer language" (so Peterson, 98; cf. Barrett, 319-20). To pray "in the Spirit" means "to pray in that awareness of God which the Spirit brings, to be able to approach him in simple trusting confidence as a child to his father" (Mitton, 228). As A. T. Lincoln puts it, in Ephesians 6:18 "the writer is calling for prayer inspired, guided and made effective through the Spirit" (Lincoln, 452).

*4.11. The Pauline Prayer Focus: Eternal Rather Than Temporal.* 1 Timothy 2:2 urges prayer for political stability "that we may live peaceful and quiet lives" in an environment which fosters the progress of the gospel. And the apostle gives instruction concerning prayer which touches on practical issues such as worship (1 Cor 11:5; 14:13-17) and table grace (Rom 14:6; 1 Cor 10:30; 11:24; 1 Tim 3:3-5). But it is striking that in the reports which constitute our major window into Paul's patterns of prayer, we see virtually no petition for many practical things such as daily bread, health or healing, improved economic conditions, etc. This is especially obvious in the two lengthy intercessory prayer periods of Ephesians 1:15-23 and 3:14-21.

The apostle's priorities come to the fore when he encourages the Corinthians to "fix our eyes not on what is seen, but on what is unseen. For what is seen is temporary, but what is unseen is eternal" (2 Cor 4:18). This is paramount when he prays. Hence his initial intercession asks for greater knowledge of God, spiritual enlightenment, better understanding of what it means to be "in Christ" and certainty of God's "incomparably great power." The latter theme is reemphasized in Ephesians 3 where God's power is first linked with the strengthening of believers, "so that Christ may dwell in your hearts through faith" (Eph 3:17) and, secondly, to total comprehension of Christ's love which surpasses knowledge. His ultimate goal is that his converts may mirror Christ, being "filled to the measure of all the fullness of God" (cf. Eph 3:19 with Col 1:19). This emphasis on spiritual well-being is seen throughout the Pauline letters. The missionary-pastor is neither ascetic nor unmindful of the importance of the practical affairs of daily living. But in terms which recall the words of Jesus, he urges believers to live (and pray) in ways which give first priority to the values of the present and coming kingdom: "Physical training is of some value, but godliness has value for all things, holding promise for both the present life, and the life to come" (1 Tim 4:8; see Carson 1992; for exegetical issues see Lincoln 1990, 196-221).

The apostle's intercession in Ephesians concludes with a doxology (Eph 3:20-21) well summarizing Paul's certainty about the efficacy of all prayer offered in the Spirit according to God's will: "Now unto him who is able to do immeasurably more than all we ask or imagine, according to his power that is at work within us, to him be glory in the church and in Christ Jesus throughout all generations, for ever and ever! Amen."

*See also* BENEDICTION, BLESSING, DOXOLOGY, THANKS-GIVING; HOLY SPIRIT; INTERCESSION; LITURGICAL ELEMENTS; MYSTICISM; SPIRITUALITY; TONGUES; VISIONS, ECSTATIC EXPERIENCE; WORSHIP.

BIBLIOGRAPHY. C. E. Arnold, *Ephesians: Power and Magic* (SNTSMS 63; Cambridge: University Press, 1989); idem, *Powers of Darkness* (Downers Grove, IL: InterVarsity, 1992); J.-P. Audet, "Literary Forms and Contents of a Normal *Eucharistia* in the First Century," *Studia Evangelica*, vol. 1, ed. F. L. Cross (Berlin: Akademie, 1959) 643-62; C. K. Barrett, *The First Epistle to the Corinthians* (New York: Harper & Row, 1968); P. F. Bradshaw, *Daily Prayer in the Early Church* (London: SPCK, 1981); F. F. Bruce, *Epistle to the Galatians* (NIGTC; Grand Rapids: Eerdmans, 1982); R. Bultmann, *Jesus and the Word* (New York: Scribners, 1934); D. A. Carson, *A Call to Spiritual Reformation: Priorities from Paul and His Prayers* (Grand Rapids: Baker, 1992); idem, ed., *Teach Us to Pray: Prayer in the Bible and the World* (Grand Rapids: Baker, 1990); E. P. Clowney, "A Biblical Theology of Prayer," in *Teach Us To Pray: Prayer in the Bible and the World*, ed. D. A. Carson (Grand Rapids: Baker, 1990) 133-73; D. Coggan, *The Prayers of the New Testament* (London: Hodder & Stoughton, 1967); C. E. B. Cranfield, *Romans* (2 vols.; ICC; Edinburgh: T. & T. Clark, 1975, 1979); O. Cullmann, "La prière selon les Epîtres pauliniennes," *TZ* 35 (1979) 90-101; G. Delling, *Worship in the New Testament* (Philadelphia: Westminster, 1962); A. Dietzel, "Beten im Geist: Eine religionsgeschichtliche Parallele aus den Hodayoth zum paulinischen Gebet im Geist," *TZ* 13 (1957) 12-32; F. Fisher, *Prayer in the New Testament* (Philadelphia: Westminster, 1964); J. A. Fitzmyer, "New Testament Epistles," in *Jerome Biblical Commentary*, ed. R. E. Brown et al. (Englewood Cliffs, NJ: Prentice-Hall, 1968); R. Gebauer, *Das Gebet bei Paulus* (Basel: Brunnen, 1989); E. F. von der Goltz, "Das Beten des Apostels Paulus," in *Das Gebet in der Ältesten Christenheit* (Leipzig: J. C. Hinrichs, 1901) 81-122; H. Greeven, "δέομαι κτλ," *TDNT* II.40-42; idem, "ἐρωτάω κτλ," *TDNT* II.685-89; idem, "προσκυνέω," *TDNT* VI.758-66; idem, "Paulus," in *Gebet und Eschatologie im Neuen Testament* (Gütersloh: Bertelsmann, 1931) 133-85; A. Hamman, "La Prière chez Saint Paul," in *La Prière. I. Le Nouveau Testament* (Tournai: Desclée, 1959) 245-333; G. Harder, *Paulus und das Gebet* (NTF 1.10; Gütersloh: Bertelsmann, 1936); F. Heiler, *Das Gebet* (5th ed.; München: E. Reinhardt, 1969); idem, *Prayer* (London and New York: Oxford University Press, 1958); E. Käsemann, *Commentary on Romans* (Grand Rapids: Eerdmans, 1980); A. T. Lincoln, *Ephesians* (WBC 42; Dallas: Word, 1990); C. L. Mitton, *Ephesians* (NCB; Grand Rapids: Eerdmans, 1981); E. A. Obeng, "The Origins of the Spirit Intercession Motif in Romans 8:26," *NTS* 32 (1986) 621-32; P. T. O'Brien, "Ephesians 1: An Unusual Introduction to a New Testament Letter," *NTS* 25 (1979) 504-16; idem, *Introductory Thanksgivings in the Letters of Paul* (NovTSup 49; Leiden: E. J. Brill, 1977); idem, "Romans 8:26, 27: A Revolutionary Approach to Prayer?" *RTR* 46 (1987) 65-73; idem, "Thanksgiving and the Gospel in Paul," *NTS* 21 (1974-75) 144-55; idem, "Thanksgiving within the Structure of Pauline Theology," in *Pauline Studies*, ed. D. A. Hagner and M. J. Harris (Grand Rapids: Eerdmans, 1980) 50-66; D. G. Peterson, "Prayer in Paul's Writings," in *Teach Us To Pray: Prayer in the Bible and the Modern World*, ed. D. A. Carson (Grand Rapids: Baker, 1990) 85-101, 325-28; J. M. Robinson, "Die Hodajot-Formel in Gebet und Hymnus des Frühchristentums," in *Apophoreta: Festschrift für Ernst Haenchen*, ed. W. Eltester and F. H. Kettler (BZNW 30; Leiden: E. J. Brill, 1964); J. T. Sanders, "The Transition from Opening Epistolary Thanksgiving to Body in the Letters of the Pauline Corpus," *JBL* 81 (1962) 348-62; H. Schönweiss et al., "Prayer," *NIDNTT* 2.855-86; P. Schubert, *Form and Function of the Pauline Thanksgivings* (BZNW 20; Berlin: Töpelmann, 1939); K. Stendahl, "Paul at Prayer," *Int* 34 (1980) 240-49; J. R. W. Stott, "Paul Prays for the Church," *Themelios* 2 (1976) 2-4; J. G. S. S. Thompson, "Prayer," *New Bible Dictionary*, ed. J. D. Douglas (2d ed.; Wheaton, IL: Tyndale, 1982) 958-61; D. F. Wells, "Prayer: Rebelling Against the Status Quo," in *Perspectives on the World Christian Movement* (Pasadena: William Carey Library, 1981) 123-26; G. P. Wiles, *Paul's Intercessory Prayers: The Significance of the Intercessory Prayer Passages in the Letters of St. Paul* (SNTSMS 24; Cambridge: Cambridge University, 1978).          W. B. Hunter

## PREACHING, KERYGMA

In his letter to the Corinthians Paul declared the priority of preaching in his ministry*—"For Christ did not send me to baptize, but to preach the gospel" (1 Cor 1:17). This gospel* was the "power* of God" leading to the salvation* of all who believed (Rom 1:16). Preaching was not a role Paul had chosen for himself. He spoke of being "compelled to preach" and confessed, "Woe to me if I do not preach the gospel" (1 Cor 9:16; cf. Acts 20:24; Jer 20:9). To the Romans he wrote of his "priestly duty of proclaiming the gospel of God" (Rom 15:16).

1. Terminology
2. The Message Paul Preached
3. Paul the Preacher
4. Twentieth-Century Scholarship

### 1. Terminology.

The two major verbs in Paul's letters for preaching are *kēryssō* and *euangelizomai* (each over twenty times). It is generally true to say that *kēryssō* tends to emphasize the activity of preaching and *euangelizomai* the quality of the message. However, the word groups overlap in such passages as Romans 16:25 ("Now to him who is able to establish you by my gospel [*euangelion*] and the proclamation [*kērygma*] of Jesus Christ." For other combinations see Gal 2:2; Col 1:23; 1 Thess 2:9). But Paul also uses other words in contexts where they are in some degree synonymous with *kēryssō* and *kērygma*. These include the verbs "to make known" (*gnōrizō*, Eph 6:19); "to portray" (*prographō*, Gal 3:1); "to proclaim" (*diangellō*, Rom 9:17); "to proclaim throughout" (*katangellō*, Rom 1:8); "to bear witness*/testify" (*martyreō*, 1 Cor 15:15); "to teach" (*didaskō*, Rom 2:21) and the nouns "news," or "report" (*akoē*, Rom 10:16-17); "testimony" (*martys*, 1 Cor 1:6); "word" (*logos*, Col 3:16). In addition to the passages using *euangel-* and *kēry-* words, and their various synonyms, Paul's sermon at Pisidian Antioch (Acts 13:16-43) and his presentation before the Areopagus (Acts 17:22-31; *see* Athens) provide an important secondary witness to Paul's preaching.

### 2. The Message Paul Preached.

Paul's message centered on the person of Christ* (Gal 1:16), specifically, "Christ crucified" (1 Cor 1:23) and risen from the dead (1 Cor 15:12; cf. Acts 13:30-37; 17:31; *see* Resurrection). The content of his message is described by a variety of terms such as "the word of faith*" (Rom 10:8), "Jesus Christ as Lord*" (2 Cor 4:5), "the gospel*" (Gal 2:2; Col 1:23) or "the gospel of God*" (1 Thess 2:9; 2 Cor 11:7; 1 Thess 2:8), "the faith" (Gal 1:23), or "the unsearchable riches of

Christ" (Eph 3:8). In Acts Paul is said to have preached "the kingdom*" (Acts 20:25), or "the kingdom of God" (Acts 28:31). This gospel is the only real gospel; anyone preaching "another gospel" is accursed (Gal 1:6-8; 2 Cor 11:4, 13-15).

Paul understood that the gospel had been entrusted to him by God (Tit 1:3). Therefore he avoided all flattery and deceit and spoke openly as a man "approved by God to be entrusted with the gospel" (1 Thess 2:4-5). It is instructive that the ancient Greek *kēryx*, or herald, was to be a person of integrity who would proclaim to the people exactly what the king wanted to make known. To add to or subtract from that message was considered treason. Paul served as an "ambassador" for Christ through whom God has made known the message of reconciliation (2 Cor 5:20; *see* Peace, Reconciliation; Apostle).

### 3. Paul the Preacher.

Paul considered himself to be a servant* of the gospel (Col 1:23). This entailed hard work (1 Cor 15:10; 2 Cor 11:24-28), facing strong opposition (1 Thess 2:2), suffering* (2 Tim 1:8) and even imprisonment (Phil 1:16; Eph 6:19-20; Philem 13; *see* Prison). Yet he was eager to preach the gospel especially in places where it had not been heard (Rom 1:5; 15:20; 2 Cor 10:16).

From birth Paul had been set aside for the purpose of preaching the gospel (Gal 1:15-16; cf. Rom 1:1). At the proper time God by his grace* called Paul and revealed to him his Son,* Christ Jesus (Gal 1:15-16). It was Paul's specific task to preach the gospel to the Gentiles* (Gal 2:7).

Paul's preaching did not rely upon "eloquence or superior wisdom*" (1 Cor 2:1). He did not preach the gospel with "words of human wisdom, lest the cross of Christ be emptied of its power" (1 Cor 1:17). It was crucial that faith rest on the power of God rather than on human wisdom or rhetorical proofs (*apodeixis*, 1 Cor 2:4-5; cf. 1 Thess 1:5; *see* Rhetoric). Thus Paul could speak of "miracles, signs* and wonders" attending his proclamation of the gospel (Rom 15:18-19; cf. 2 Cor 12:12). It was by the open declaration of God's redemptive act in Christ that listeners were brought to faith. The divine origin of the gospel (Gal 1:11-12) mandated a supernatural means of communication. Paul served only as the human instrument in that process. Apart from God's active involvement in preaching, the message would come as a stumbling block* to the Jews (who demanded miraculous signs) and foolishness* to the Gentiles (who looked for wisdom). At this point the content and activity of preaching correspond, for both are marked by "foolishness" (1 Cor 1:21-25). Only to those who believe does it bring salvation (1 Cor 1:21-23). The minds of unbelievers have been blinded so that they are unable to see the light of the gospel of the glory* of Christ (2 Cor 4:4).

### 4. Twentieth-Century Scholarship.

In 1936 C. H. Dodd's seminal study on the preaching of the apostles was published. There he defined preaching as "the public proclamation of Christianity to the non-Christian world" (Dodd, 7). He arrived at an outline of the primitive *kērygma* by comparing the early sermons in Acts with the pre-Pauline creedal fragments in Paul's letters. A later study of the *kērygma* described the apostolic preaching as "a proclamation of his death, resurrection and exaltation of Jesus that led to an evaluation of His person as both Lord and Christ, confronted man with the necessity of repentance, and promised the forgiveness of sins" (Mounce, 84). All of these aspects of preaching are clearly seen in the preaching of Paul in Acts. For example, the importance of the resurrection is pivotal in both of Paul's sermons recorded in Acts (13:27-31; 17:31). A similar message is suggested by 1 Thessalonians 1:9-10, which may sum up Paul's gospel as it was first preached to the Thessalonians: turn from idols* to serve the living and true God *; it is his Son who died and whom God raised from the dead [and exalted* to heaven*], this Jesus will come from heaven to rescue his people from the coming wrath.*

Dodd's emphasis on the content of the kerygma was in response to R. Bultmann's understanding of the kerygma as the active and effective Word, rather than content, that addresses men and women in their existential situation and elicits a response of faith. According to Bultmann, Paul's knowledge and interest in the historical Jesus were minimal and did not constitute the kerygma. Thus the existential and the salvation-historical perspectives on kerygma were squared off against one another, and the term *kērygma* and question of its precise character took on far greater weight than it is given in the NT itself.

In recent decades various aspects of the issue have been pursued. Some scholars have revisited the question of Paul's familiarity and interest in the historical Jesus and his use of Jesus tradition in his preaching. Bultmann's claim, based on his tendentious interpretation of 2 Corinthians 5:16, has been discredited in the view of many scholars. Hence, G. N. Stanton's study of the place of Jesus of Nazareth in early Christian preaching concludes that "the possibility must be allowed that Paul laid greater emphasis on the pre-crucifixion events and the character of Jesus in his preaching than he does in his epistles" (Stanton, 113;

see too Lemcio). While Paul's explicit references to sayings of Jesus are relatively few, the possible allusions are, by some accounts, numerous (*see* Jesus, Sayings of). This phenomenon might be due to the Jesus tradition having been transmitted in the setting of Paul's initial missionary preaching and teaching.

Consideration of the varied settings and activities of communication within the early Christian communities questioned whether preaching can be sharply distinguished from other forms of communication. What sort of distinction should be drawn between mission* and community *kērygma*? More importantly, has too rigid a distinction been drawn between *kērygma* and *didachē* ("teaching")? Paul seems to indicate a relationship between the two in Romans 2:21, where the content of *kērygma* seems to be defined as *didachē*. J. I. H. McDonald has suggested that the distinction between *kērygma* and *didachē* lies in the "situation" and "posture" of the communicator "rather than the substance of the message, . . . preaching and teaching are properly regarded as being broadly complementary and as denoting the whole process of communicating the appropriate message" (McDonald, 5). McDonald has examined *kērygma* within the context of the *koinōnia* of the community, where *didachē* ("teaching"), *prophēteia* ("prophecy," "inspired utterance"), *paraenesis* ("moral exhortation"), *paraklēsis* ("exhortatory preaching" to the community) and *paradosis* ("tradition*") all play a role and have varying degrees of overlap and interrelationship (*see* Teaching/Paraenesis).

The content of the Pauline kerygma, or gospel, inasmuch as it shares the same concerns as the larger question of the coherence of Paul's theology (*see* Center), has led some scholars to question whether it ever achieved a final and static form. Did it not develop over time? Is it perhaps better understood as being fluid, having a coherent substratum that was capable of varied contingent expressions according to circumstances (Beker)? Should the structure of Paul's kerygma be summed up as an integrated set of propositions, or should it be construed as a narrative of Jesus Messiah? Was Paul's kerygma (however it might be defined) one of a number of diverse *kērygmata* of the early church, some of which Paul would have found compatible with his own kerygma and others which he would have disavowed as "another gospel" (Dunn)? And to what extent was the kerygma of Paul continuous with or dissimilar from the kerygma of Jesus (*see* Jesus and Paul)? These questions continue to prod research into Paul and the early church and reveal a lack of consensus regarding the coherence, or center, of Paul's gospel, much less of a kerygma of the early church.

Finally, the relationship between Paul's kerygma and his self-understanding as an apostle* as well as the social reality of his mission and ministry is being actively explored (*see* Social-Scientific Approaches to Paul). Clearly, Paul's theology of the cross shaped his apostolic lifestyle, the way in which he envisioned his mission and the definition of his gospel over against that of some of his opponents.*

*See also* APOSTLE; ATHENS, PAUL AT; CENTER OF PAUL'S THEOLOGY; CHRISTOLOGY; CREEDS; CROSS, THEOLOGY OF THE; DEATH OF CHRIST; GOSPEL; JESUS, SAYINGS OF; JESUS AND PAUL; MINISTRY; MISSION; PREACHING FROM PAUL TODAY; RHETORIC; SOCIAL-SCIENTIFIC APPROACHES; TEACHING/PARAENESIS; TRADITION; WITNESS.

BIBLIOGRAPHY. W. Baird, "What is the Kerygma? A Study of 1 Cor 15:3-8 and Gal 1:11-17," *JBL* 76 (1957) 181-91; C. K. Barrett, *Biblical Problems and Biblical Preaching* (Philadelphia: Fortress Press, 1964); J. C. Beker, *Paul the Apostle: The Triumph of God in Life and Thought* (Philadelphia: Fortress, 1980); C. H. Dodd, *The Apostolic Preaching and Its Developments* (London: Hodder & Stoughton, 1936); J. D. G. Dunn, *Unity and Diversity in the New Testament* (2d ed.; Philadelphia: Trinity Press International, 1990); C. F. Evans, "The Kerygma," *JTS* 7 (1956) 25-41; H. H. Farmer, *The Servant of the Word* (London: Nesbet, 1942); G. Friedrich, "κῆρυξ κτλ," *TDNT* III.683-718; L. Goppelt, *Theology of the New Testament* (2 vols.; Grand Rapids: Eerdmans, 1982) 2.107-18; F. W. Grosheide, "The Pauline Epistles as Kerygma," in *Studia Paulina*, ed. J. N. Sevenster and W. C. van Unnik (Haarlem: De Ervem F. Bohn, 1953) 139-45; J. Knox, *The Integrity of Preaching* (New York: Abingdon, 1957); E. E. Lemcio, *The Past of Jesus in the Gospels* (SNTSMS 68; Cambridge: University Press, 1991); J. I. H. McDonald, *Kerygma and Didache: The Articulation and Structure of the Earliest Christian Message* (SNTSMS 37; Cambridge: University Press, 1980); O. Merk, "κηρύσσω κτλ," *EDNT* 2.288-92; R. H. Mounce, *The Essential Nature of New Testament Preaching* (Grand Rapids: Eerdmans, 1960); B. Reicke, "A Synopsis of Early Christian Preaching," in *The Root of the Vine*, ed. A. Friedrichsen et al. (New York: Philosophical Library, 1953) 138-41; J. Reumann, *Variety and Unity in New Testament Thought* (New York: Oxford University Press, 1991); G. N. Stanton, *Jesus of Nazareth in New Testament Preaching* (SNTSMS 27; Cambridge: University Press, 1974); J. S. Stewart, *Heralds of God* (London: Hodder & Stoughton, 1946); J. R. W. Stott, *The Preacher's Portrait* (Grand Rapids: Eerdmans, 1961); P. Stuhlmacher, "The Pauline Gospel," in *The Gospel and the Gospels*, ed. P. Stuhlmacher (Grand Rapids: Eerdmans, 1991) 149-72; H. G. Wood, "*Didache, Kerygma* and *Euangelion*," in *New Testament Essays: Studies in Memory of T. W. Manson*, ed. A. J. B. Higgins (Manchester: Manchester University, 1959) 306-14.

R. H. Mounce

# PREACHING FROM PAUL TODAY

Contemporary preaching from Paul's letters is a natural extension of their original use in first-century churches. For Paul not only addressed these letters to specific churches, he also requested that they be read in the church addressed (1 Thess 5:27; cf. 2 Thess 3:14) and be shared with other churches (Col 4:16). The link to contemporary preaching comes into view when one considers that these letters were not only to be read in the churches but also explained by the letter carriers (Doty, 30, 37). Preachers must be acquainted with several issues in order to do justice to Paul's letters in contemporary preaching.

1. The Nature of Paul's Letters
2. The Form of Paul's Letters
3. Rhetorical Structures
4. Selecting a Suitable Preaching Text
5. Analyzing the Preaching Text
6. Crossing the Historical-Cultural Gap
7. Designing the Sermon
8. Preaching Christ

### 1. The Nature of Paul's Letters.

Paul's letters are ideal sources for contemporary preaching because of their kerygmatic nature. For not only are these letters relevant communications, some also contain the actual preaching* of the apostle Paul, and all may be characterized as a special form of preaching and as the Word of God.*

*1.1. Relevant Communications.* It is clear from Paul's letters that for the most part they were written originally for specific occasions. For example, the letter to the Galatians* was written because Paul had heard that church members were "turning to a different gospel,*" that of the Judaizers* (Gal 1:6 RSV throughout); 1 Thessalonians* was occasioned by Timothy's return from Thessalonica and his report to Paul (1 Thess 3:6); 2 Thessalonians was written to counter a pseudo-Pauline letter circulating in Thessalonica claiming "that the day of the Lord has come" (2 Thess 2:2); and Colossians* was written to head off the threat of a deceitful philosophy* (Col 2:8). Because Paul's letters were written for specific occasions, they have been called "occasional documents." This designation is homiletically significant because it reminds preachers that these letters were inherently relevant in the first century and that this relevance can be uncovered today only by way of historical investigation and interpretation.

**1.2. Summarized Sermons.** In addressing the immediate concerns that occasioned his letters, Paul also recorded here and there summaries of his typical sermons. R. Longenecker writes:

> Probably . . . we should view the body of Romans (1:18-15:13) as something of a précis of Paul's preaching in Jewish synagogues of the Diaspora and at Jewish-Gentile gatherings, with that précis during the course of his missionary activities having become more and more polished in literary form. . . . The so-called Letter to the Ephesians . . . likely . . . was originally meant to be a précis of Paul's teaching on redemption in Christ and the nature of the church, and was sent out as something of a circular tractate letter to churches in the Roman province of Asia, of which Ephesus was the capital. (Longenecker, 104-5)

In the dictation of other letters, too, Paul would quite naturally have included previous sermonic material.

**1.3. Long-Distance Preaching.** Paul's letters may also be characterized as long-distance preaching. They were like preaching not only because they addressed specific needs in early churches but also because they were primarily oral communications. Except for brief conclusions (2 Thess 3:17; Gal 6:11; 1 Cor 16:21; Col 4:18), Paul did not write these letters but dictated them to secretaries (amanuenses; cf. Rom 16:22) for the purpose of public reading in the churches. Like preaching, therefore, these letters were a form of oral communication. Moreover, in the Greek letter-writing tradition, a letter was a stand-in for the presence (parousia) of its author (*see* Itineraries). Since Paul was "unable to be present in person, his letters were a direct substitute, and were to be accorded weight equal to Paul's physical presence" (Doty, 36; cf. 1 Cor 5:3-4; 2 Cor 10:11). Listening to Paul's letter being read, therefore, was the same as hearing Paul himself speak—except that this speaking was long-distance and was committed to writing.

**1.4. The Word of God.** Paul wrote to the Thessalonians, "We also thank God constantly for this, that when you received the word of God which you heard from us, you accepted it not as the word of men but as what it really is, the word of God, which is at work in you believers" (1 Thess 2:13). If the hearers heard Paul speak not only in his preaching but also in his letters, one may assume that they would also have accepted Paul's letters as "the word of God." This assumption was confirmed subsequently when the church acknowledged these letters to be canonical. As the Word of God, Paul's letters are the authoritative kerygma, eminently suitable as the normative source for preaching today. As the letter carriers originally received "authority to convey the letters, to expand upon them, and to continue Paul's work" (Doty, 37), so contemporary preachers may continue Paul's work by expounding his letters. But to do so with authority,* they will have to do justice to the inspired words of Paul (see Greidanus, 1-16).

**2. The Form of Paul's Letters.**
In order to do justice to Paul's words, preachers will have to take into account, among other things, the location of Paul's words: whether they function in the opening section, the body of the letter, or in some other section. For just as letters today have a standard form (Heading, Greeting [Dear Sir], Body, Complimentary Close [Sincerely yours], Signature), so Paul's letters reveal a standard form (*see* Letters, Letter Forms). The homiletical significance of Paul's letter form becomes apparent when one compares Paul's form with that of contemporary Greek letters.

**2.1. The Standard Form of Greek Letters.** The ancient Greeks had developed a standard letter form which consisted of three main parts:

1. An introduction, prescript, or salutation, which included the name of the sender, the name of the addressee, greetings and often a wish for good health.

2. The body or text of the letter, introduced by characteristic formulae.

3. A conclusion, which included greetings to persons other than the addressee, a final greeting or prayer sentence, and sometimes a date (Longenecker, 103).

**2.2. Paul's Changes in the Standard Form.** In writing his letters to various churches, Paul modified the standard Greek form in various subtle ways but particularly by developing two major sections: a section of thanksgiving (*see* Benediction; see O'Brien; Aune, 177, 186) and a section of exhortations. Thus Paul's letters usually follow a five-part form:

1. Opening: Sender, Addressee, Greeting
2. Thanksgiving to God for the Addressee's Faithfulness (missing in Galatians)
3. Body
4. Exhortations ("paraenesis")
5. Closing: Peace Wish, Greetings, Warnings, Benediction

**2.3. The Homiletical Significance.** The changes Paul introduced in the standard Greek letter form provide several hints for preachers on how these letters demand to be preached.

**2.3.1. Major Changes.** Paul changed the opening greeting of his letters from the standard Greek *chairein* (greeting) to *charis* (grace) and, probably in imitation of the *shalom* of Jewish letters, added the word "peace" (Doty, 22, 29). The neutral Greek "Greeting" thus becomes the profound Christian greeting, "Grace to you and peace from God our Father and the Lord Jesus Christ." Paul also changed the conclusion to a peace wish and variations of "The grace* of the Lord* Jesus Christ* and the love* of God and the fellowship* of the Holy Spirit* be with you all." The whole letter is thus enveloped in the *inclusio* of God's grace and peace*: "(opening) grace and peace, (closing) peace and grace" (Roetzel, 37). (Echoes of the opening and closing of Christian worship* services are probably not accidental; *see* Liturgical Elements.)

Further, the new section of thanksgiving to God immediately focuses the listeners' attention on God's grace as it comes to expression in the church.* Moreover, the new section of exhortations *follows* the thanksgiving and the body of the letter; that is, in all of Paul's letters, God's indicative precedes the imperative (*see* Ethics). In short, Paul's major changes have made his letters God-centered. The homiletical implication is clear: to be true to Paul's letters, one will have to preach God-centered, relevant sermons. The reverse also holds true: anthropocentric and legalistic or moralistic sermons do not do justice to Paul and are possible only by isolating the preaching text from its context in Paul's letter.

*2.3.2. Subtle Changes.* Paul's more subtle changes provide clues for understanding the concrete issues he was addressing. His variations in the formal opening frequently provide initial hints of the issues addressed. For example, in his letter to Philemon,* which seeks unheard-of forgiveness* and acceptance for the runaway slave* Onesimus, Paul describes himself humbly as "Paul, a prisoner* for Christ Jesus." By contrast, in his letter to the Galatians* who questioned his apostleship* and rejected his gospel of grace, Paul opens with, "Paul an apostle—sent neither by human commission nor from human authorities, but through Jesus Christ and God the Father" (Gal 1:1 NRSV). Similar clues to the letter's concern may be found in the description of the addressees.

The thanksgiving section provides even clearer clues to the reason(s) for writing and the major concerns of the letter. For example, the thanksgiving section to Philemon concentrates on Paul's love for the saints (Philem 5, 7). Not surprisingly, in the body of the letter Paul appeals for acceptance of Onesimus "for love's sake" (Philem 9). Paul's letter to the Galatians, by contrast, omits the thanksgiving section—an omission which speaks loudly of Paul's deep disappointment at their desertion of the gospel of grace. Paul jumps in immediately, "I am astonished . . ." (Gal

1:6). Since Paul tends to repeat his major concerns in various parts of his letter, he provides a string of clues to the main issues addressed and thus forces contemporary preachers to understand each issue in the context of the whole letter.

### 3. Rhetorical Structures.

Paul's letters reveal intricate rhetorical structures (*see* Rhetoric, Rhetorical Criticism). The existence of these structures in dictated letters can be accounted for by two facts: First, Paul made use of structured traditional materials such as hymns,* creeds,* ethical lists and doxologies (*see* Benediction), as well as his own standardized sermons. Second, Paul dictated these letters with a view to their being heard. For contemporary preaching, one needs to pay attention to these rhetorical structures.

> Good preaching not only presents the text but attends to how the text itself preaches. The Scriptures are not a shapeless mass, a lump of dough, to be divided and shaped into sermons and lessons. The texts already have shapes and contours, reflecting the writer's concern for the arts of persuasion, for the listeners' need to remember what is read to them, and for ways of communicating which are congenial to the nature of the message; in other words, for communication that respects and cares for the listeners as thinking, feeling, deciding, believing human beings. (Craddock, 166-67)

*3.1. Repetition.* Repetition is still used today by teachers and preachers who are sensitive to the demands of oral/aural communication. Paul uses repetition at different levels. He frequently repeats major issues (e.g., Christian freedom in Gal 5:1 and 13). At other times he simply repeats a single word (e.g., the sevenfold repetition of one in Eph 4:4-6, "There is *one* body and *one* Spirit . . ."). Then again he strings together a series of questions (e.g., Rom 6—7). Repetition may serve simply to recall and/or elaborate a point, or to emphasize a point, or to provide continuity for the hearers. Since repetition still serves the same functions in oral communication, preachers should not only pay attention to Paul's repetitions but follow suit in their own preaching.

*3.2. Parallelism and Chiasm.* Parallelism (e.g., A B Á B′) and chiasm (e.g., A B C B′ Á)˜ are both forms of repetition and both are found in Paul's letters. For example, in 1 Corinthians 15:55 Paul quotes the synonymous parallelism of Hosea,

O death, where is thy victory?

O death, where is thy sting?

In 1 Corinthians 12—14 Paul uses a simple A B Á chiasm:

A. Spiritual gifts (1 Cor 12:1-31a)
   B. Love, the greatest gift (1 Cor 12:31b—13:13)
A'. Spiritual gifts: prophecy and tongues (1 Cor 14:1-40)

Parallelism served not only as an aid to memory but also to emphasize and present the point from different angles. True chiasm, in addition, served to focus literally on the central issue, the turning point. Preachers today can use these ancient rhetorical structures, which are detected especially in the Greek NT, to gain a clearer understanding of a passage by comparing the parallel lines, to discern the focal point in the heart of a chiasm and to discover the limits of a section that makes for an ideal preaching text (*see* Greidanus, 58-67, 319-22).

*3.3. Diatribe.* As was customary in his time, Paul used "the device of *diatribe* by which a speaker or writer enters into imaginary debate with an interlocutor, raising points which he would make and objections he would voice, which are then answered and refuted" (Martin, 247). *Diatribe* gave the hearers a voice in the debate and thus sought to persuade. For example, Paul used the following *diatribe* in Romans 3:27-31: "Then what becomes of our boasting? It is excluded. On what principle? On the principle of works? No, but on the principle of faith. . . . Do we then overthrow the law by this faith? By no means! On the contrary, we uphold the law" (for more examples, see Malherbe, 129-34). Awareness of this ancient rhetorical device will help preachers not only in tracing the course of Paul's argument but also in retracing in their own sermons the rhetorical trail laid down by Paul.

**4. Selecting a Suitable Preaching Text.**
One cannot cut up Paul's letters into random snippets and still have confidence of doing justice to Paul. In selecting a preaching text, preachers interested in proclaiming the thoughts of Paul will wish to show respect for the shape as well as the content of Paul's letters. This respect calls for the selection of preaching texts that are appropriate passages, literary units, and that include, if feasible, the original issue, Paul's answer and defense, and his goal.

*4.1. An Appropriate Passage.* Before settling on a preaching text, preachers ought to raise the question of what goal, what objective they are seeking to accomplish with the sermon. If they desire to move their congregation to repentance, they will require a passage where Paul aims at that goal; if they wish to comfort, they will require a passage where Paul aims to comfort; if they wish to stir people to greater love, they will require a passage where Paul aims at that very goal. Coordinating one's goal with that of the apostle Paul will prevent the dissonance that results when a passage of Paul is used for a different objective from what he had in mind.

*4.2. A Literary Unit.* To do justice to the shape and content of Paul's letters, one should select as preaching text at least a literary unit rather than an isolated verse or phrase. Paul's rhetorical devices frequently identify such units, for chiasm and inclusio encompass rhetorical units, and diatribe and repetition, such as the key word technique, continue as long as one is in the same unit of thought. The content, of course, provides the most obvious clue: a change of content means a different unit of thought. Selecting anything shorter than a literary unit is to chop up Paul's original units of thought. For example, to select Ephesians 1:4a, "even as he chose us in him before the foundation of the world," to preach a sermon on predestination (*see* Election and Predestination) distorts Paul's construction and thought. For Paul continues in Ephesians 1:4b, "that we should be holy and blameless before him." And this verse, in turn, is but part of a single Greek sentence that runs from Ephesians 1:3 to 1:14. Since the units and sections in each letter are closely interrelated, the most appropriate treatment of Paul's letters would be a brief series of sermons on a specific letter.

*4.3. The Issue, Response and Substantiations.* Whenever feasible, a reference to the historical issue that gave rise to the text should be included in the preaching text. When the text is a response to a specific issue, combining in one text the original question and its answer can only benefit genuine hearing. Moreover, Paul's substantiations for a claim or demand should be included in the preaching text, for they are part of the thought unit. For example, instead of selecting as text only Romans 8:28, "We know that in everything God works for good with those who love him, who are called according to his purpose," one ought to include the substantiations of this claim that follow in Romans 8:29-30 (Liefeld, 70-71). The inclusion of the issue and substantiations would generally argue against selecting a preaching text from the opening of Paul's letters. Although the sender and greeting sections sometimes anticipate the burden of the letter, since the issue and Paul's answer and substantiations are stated much more elaborately in the thanksgiving and especially in the body of the letter, the latter deserve priority in selection for preaching texts.

*4.4. Paul's Goal.* Whenever possible, Paul's aim should be included as part of the text, for this goal expressed the relevance of this passage in the past—a relevance that can function as a bridge to contemporary relevance. For example, in preaching on Philippians 2, preachers have selected as their text the Christ hymn and preached on Christ's states of humiliation and exaltation.* But what is the aim of such sermons? Paul clearly states his goal in Philippians 2:5 when he introduces the hymn with the words, "Let the same mind be in you that was in Christ Jesus"(NRSV). Paul's aim, as the preceding verses also show, is to stir the Philippians up to love and selfless service (Fowl; see Servant, Service). And that goal is still worth pursuing by preachers today.

**5. Analyzing the Preaching Text.**
After selecting the text to be used in preaching, one ought to study it in its literary and historical contexts.

*5.1. The Literary Context.* The common advice to read through the whole letter in one sitting is good counsel, for that is the way letters are usually read. As one reads through the letter, perhaps several times and aloud in different translations, one should gain a sense of the whole document, its recipients, its occasion, its parts and its overall theme and goal.

*5.2. The Historical Context.* Since Paul's letters are occasional documents, written to respond to specific historical needs in the early church, it stands to reason that one cannot fully understand his letters without understanding the underlying historical background. Therefore, preachers need to determine the occasion that gave rise to the letter. The question is, What is the historical question to which this particular text is the answer?

Sometimes Paul himself identifies the question explicitly. For example, in 1 Thessalonians 4:13 he says that he will deal with the question "concerning those who are asleep." In 1 Corinthians* he lists a whole series of questions starting with 1 Corinthians 7:1, "Now concerning the matters about which you wrote," and answers each in turn (see 1 Cor 7:25; 8:1; 12:1; 16:1). However, Paul responds not only to their written questions but also to other issues: for example, 1 Corinthians 5:1, "It is actually reported that there is immorality among you"; and 1 Corinthians 11:18, "I hear that there are divisions among you." Where such explicit identification of the historical question is lacking, it must be painstakingly gleaned from the letter itself and other sources.

*5.3. The Text Itself.* Reading the whole letter in its historical context has set the stage for analyzing the specific message of the preaching text. This is the time for careful grammatical-historical exegesis of the Greek text. It is also the time for comparing the message of the text with similar messages elsewhere in this letter, as well as in other letters and other books

of Scripture (*analogia Scripturae,* "analogy of Scripture").

Reading the text in its literary contexts will keep one from preaching, say, exhortations in isolation, for the imperative cannot be proclaimed without the divine indicative stated or assumed earlier in the letter (see Greidanus, 325-27). Reading the text in its historical context will make one aware of the intense relevance of Paul's letters for the churches addressed. However, this very relevance brings one face to face with the historical-cultural gap, for questions of circumcision,* eating food offered to idols (see Food) and master-slave relations (see Slave, Slavery) are hardly burning issues in the West today.

**6. Crossing the Historical-Cultural Gap.**
How can one preach relevantly to a twentieth-century Western church a message intended originally for the first-century church of Corinth?

*6.1. Overarching Continuity.* Without denying the reality of the historical-cultural gap, one ought first to appreciate the continuity between past and present—a continuity rooted in the faithful covenant God. God's plan for redeeming his fallen creation (Gen 3:15; Rom 8:19-23) results in the history of the coming kingdom of God (1 Cor 15:22-24; see Kingdom). In this history God calls into being one covenant people, the church (Gal 3:8, 29).

Since the churches Paul addressed and churches today are essentially one church under God, living in the same NT epoch of kingdom history, God's message addressed to first-century churches is relevant for churches today (Greidanus 169-73, 330-31). This continuity accounts for the fact that so much in Paul's letters is directly applicable to the church today. Then as well as now, God's people were and are called to faith,* hope* and love.* Nevertheless, preachers will frequently find themselves obstructed by the historical-cultural gap, for Paul spoke relevantly to churches that lived in a different culture and at an earlier stage of the NT epoch.

*6.2. Analogies.* A major bridge across the historical-cultural gap is provided by analogies between the church Paul addressed and the church today. These analogies are not figments of our imagination, for they exist by virtue of the fact that there is basically but one church and but one Word of God. Preachers, therefore, need not construct analogies but uncover existing ones. This search requires a thorough understanding of both the church addressed by Paul and the church today. It requires cognizance of the question behind the text—the question to which Paul responded.

Why was the church then in need of correction, comfort or encouragement? And is there a genuine analogy between that situation and the situation in the church today so that Paul's answer is an authentic response to the present need for correction, comfort and encouragement? One must be careful to search out real analogies. It will not do simply to draw an analogy between Judaizers in Galatia and conservatives or ritualists in the church today and redirect Paul's words for Judaizers at contemporary conservatives. Before drawing such an analogy to people today, one should at least take into account that Judaizers denied the gospel of grace by insisting on works (*see* Works of the Law) for inclusion among God's people.

*6.3. Principle and Practice.* If the issue is so culturally specific that no direct analogy can be found in the present church, it may be helpful to view the message as a particular cultural application of a biblical principle and seek to discover precisely what this underlying principle is. Once discovered, the question is how to apply this biblical principle today in an analogous way to its biblical application (Fee and Stuart, 62-70). For example, when Paul demands in 1 Corinthians 11:2-16 that women must be veiled when they pray or prophesy, his command is clearly culturally conditioned. Preachers today would miss the point if they insisted in our culture that women be veiled. But the biblical principle behind this application, the principle of appropriate dress for women and men in the worship service (1 Cor 14:40), may open the way for contemporary application.

> The search for the points of analogy is a risky task. This is so since there can be no total identity. History never repeats itself completely. . . . Thus preaching is a creative art. It is not a cool application but a creative vision for analogies. Risky it is, and that is why the preacher must seek the guidance of the Spirit as the sermon grows out of study and meditation. (Stendahl, 307)

## 7. Designing the Sermon.

After considering these issues, one is ready to begin designing the sermon.

*7.1. Paul's Goal.* One of the first questions that needs to be raised concerns Paul's goal or aim. Why is Paul writing this passage to this particular church? Is he aiming to teach, or reprove, or correct, or train in righteousness* (2 Tim 3:16), or comfort or encourage? The question behind the text together with the text will help answer the *why* question.

*7.2. The Sermon's Goal.* The sermon's goal cannot always be identical with Paul's goal but should at least be in harmony with it. Preachers should ask them-

selves, Why am I preaching this sermon? This question will reveal one's goal. The sermon's goal will guide the preacher in designing the sermon, perhaps in selecting a fitting introduction and certainly in formulating a pertinent conclusion.

*7.3. Paul's Theme.* Along with the *why* question about Paul's aim, one needs to ask the *what* question about Paul's message. What is Paul's theme in this text? What is the main idea that encompasses all subsidiary ideas? This theme should be formulated in a brief sentence: subject and predicate.

*7.4. The Sermon's Theme.* Next, Paul's message needs to be compared with other Scripture passages to see if it can be preached as it is or needs some adjustments or qualifications. Usually Paul's message can be preached as is, but sometimes his message is one-sided and needs to be balanced by other passages before it can be preached as God's word for his people today. For example, Paul's message in Romans 13:1-7, "Be subject to the government because it is God's servant," needs to be balanced by Acts 5:29 and Revelation 13:1-10 before it can be preached today. Thus the sermon theme may need to be changed to something like, "Be subject to the government when it is God's servant."

Other passages are so culturally specific that their themes need to be recast to communicate to the church's present situation. For example, Paul's message in 1 Corinthians 8, "Christians may eat food offered to idols unless it causes a brother to fall" will need to be recast into a contemporary issue or the more general sermon theme, "Christian freedom is limited by the well-being of fellow Christians." The functions of the sermon theme are to keep the sermon on the right track and to ensure its unity as well as movement (Greidanus 139-40).

*7.5. The Form of the Sermon.* The form of a sermon on Paul's letters can vary from deductive to inductive development to a combination of both, and from a didactic form to a narrative form. Most appropriate is a form which closely conforms to the text itself by following its flow: for example, its development of ideas, its line of argumentation, or its repetition of words, phrases or questions.

*7.6. The Relevance of the Sermon.* As Paul's letters were intensely relevant for the early church, so sermons on his letters can be intensely relevant for the church today. This relevance can be achieved by taking clear aim as Paul did. Moreover, preachers can follow Paul in addressing the whole person—intellect, will and emotions—and in showing the relevance of their message for the whole of life—physical as well as spiritual and public as well as personal. Further help for relevant preaching is provided by Paul's metaphors which range from putting on "the whole armor of God" with all of its parts (Eph 6:11-17) to running the race to obtain the prize (1 Cor 9:24), and from "justification"* to "redemption" (*see* Redemption), and "adoption"* to "liberty" (*see* Freedom). Preachers can use these metaphors to make abstract truths concrete and living for their hearers.

**8. Preaching Christ.**

Finally and most importantly, preachers are to preach Christ crucified and risen as Paul did (*see* Christology). Paul told the Corinthians, "I decided to know nothing among you except Jesus Christ and him crucified" (1 Cor 2:2; *see* Cross, Theology of the). Contemporary recommendations to use Paul's letters to preach biographical sermons on Paul are obviously contrary to his intentions. Yet, as his letters show, Paul's preaching of Christ is not simply a constant retelling of Jesus' life, death and resurrection (Rom 10:9). Rather, Paul takes his *starting point* in Jesus Christ and preaches Christ as his person and work illumine all other vital issues and questions. "Jesus Christ and him crucified" is the heart of God's plan of redemption; from this heart, renewing power pulses into every area of life.

In the light of Colossians 1:15-20, preaching Christ means to preach the God through whom and for whom "all things" were created and through whom "all things" are being reconciled. Ultimately, preaching Christ has to do with "all things." Therefore, contemporary preaching from Paul's letters may rightly address any area of life and any vital issue, but all issues must be viewed and preached in the light of Christ and his redemptive work. This transforms one's preaching into the good news of which Paul said, "I am eager to preach the gospel. . . . For . . . it is the power of God for salvation to everyone who has faith" (Rom 1:15-16).

*See also* CENTER OF PAUL'S THEOLOGY; GOSPEL; HERMENEUTICS/INTERPRETING PAUL; PREACHING, KERYGMA.

BIBLIOGRAPHY. D. E. Aune, *The New Testament in Its Literary Environment* (Philadelphia: Westminster, 1987); F. B. Craddock, "Preaching to Corinthians," *Int* 44 (1990) 158-68; W. G. Doty, *Letters in Primitive Christianity* (Philadelphia: Fortress, 1973); G. D. Fee and D. Stuart, *How to Read the Bible for All Its Worth: A Guide to Understanding the Bible* (Grand Rapids: Zondervan, 1982); S. F. Fowl, *The Story of Christ in the Ethics of Paul* (JSNTSup 36; Sheffield: Academic Press, 1990); S. Greidanus, *The Modern Preacher and the Ancient Text: Interpreting and Preaching Biblical Literature* (Grand Rapids: Eerdmans, 1988); L. E. Keck, *Paul and His Letters* (Philadelphia: Fortress, 1979); W. L. Liefeld,

*New Testament Exposition: From Text to Sermon* (Grand Rapids: Zondervan, 1984); R. N. Longenecker, "On the Form, Function, and Authority of New Testament Letters," in *Scripture and Truth*, ed. D. A. Carson and J. D. Woodbridge (Grand Rapids: Zondervan, 1983) 101-14; A. J. Malherbe, *Moral Exhortation, A Greco-Roman Sourcebook* (Philadelphia: Westminster, 1986); R. P. Martin, "Approaches to New Testament Exegesis," in *New Testament Interpretation: Essays on Principles and Methods*, ed. I. H. Marshall (Grand Rapids: Eerdmans, 1977) 220-51; F. J. Matera, "Preaching Paul," *Chicago Studies* 24 (1985) 323-38; J. Murphy-O'Connor, *Paul on Preaching* (New York: Sheed & Ward, 1964); P. T. O'Brien, *Introductory Thanksgivings in the Letters of Paul* (NovTSup 49; Leiden: E. J. Brill, 1977); H. Ridderbos, *Paul: An Outline of His Theology* (Grand Rapids: Eerdmans, 1975); C. J. Roetzel, *The Letters of Paul: Conversations in Context* (Atlanta: John Knox, 1975); K. Stendahl, "Preaching from the Pauline Epistles," in *Biblical Preaching: An Expository Treasury*, ed. J. W. Cox (Philadelphia: Westminster, 1983) 306-26.

S. Greidanus

**PREDESTINATION.** *See* ELECTION AND PREDESTINATION.

**PRE-EXISTENCE**

The term *pre-existence* refers to the idea of an entity having a heavenly existence before its earthly, historical or eschatological* manifestation, sometimes even before the creation* of the world. Pre-existence is attributed to Christ* in a number of NT passages (e.g., Jn 1:1-18; Heb 1:1-3), including several Pauline passages, according to most scholars. But there is disagreement about which, if any, Pauline passages express the doctrine of the pre-existence of Christ, about the conceptual sources of this doctrine, and about what the expressions of Christ's pre-existence meant. As well, Paul's letters suggest what may be an allied concept of the precosmic divine predestination of believers (*see* Election and Predestination).

1. Ancient Jewish Tradition
2. Christ's Pre-existence
3. Conclusions

**1. Ancient Jewish Tradition.**

*1.1. Background.* There is today a virtual consensus among scholars that the pre-Christian Jewish tradition provides the most important background for the idea of pre-existence in the NT. (For a fuller discussion, see Hamerton-Kelly 1966.) In addition to specific examples of pre-existence, two general concepts are to be noted: (1) that certain historical phenomena are earthly manifestations of heavenly realities, which gives to the historical phenomena a transcendent validity and significance, and (2) that God* foresees and has even ordained history and/or a plan of salvation from the beginning (see Foreknowledge, Divine).

Both in the OT and in the wider ancient Near Eastern cultures, we encounter ideas that there is a heavenly, transcendent realm in which matters of earthly importance have ideal and prior reality; for example, the wilderness tabernacle is designed according to the heavenly pattern shown to Moses in Exodus 25:9, 40; 26:30; 27:8; Numbers 8:4, showing that it is no mere human contrivance but a model of a heavenly reality. Such an outlook is especially clear in OT material designated as priestly tradition, in Ezekiel (e.g., Ezek 43:10-12), in extracanonical literature (e.g., the Angelic Liturgy from Qumran [4Q400-407; 11Q5-6]; T. Levi 3:4-8), and in the NT (e.g., Rev 4—5). Jubilees likewise claims that Sabbath (Jub. 2:30) and the Feast of Weeks (Jub. 6:17-18) were observed in heaven from the creation.

In apocalyptic* thought God's eschatological blessings are often described as waiting in heaven, as in 2 Apocalypse of Baruch 4:2-7, which states that the heavenly Jerusalem* and Temple* were created with the world but taken to heaven after Adam's sin, to be held there until the eschaton. Paul's reference to "the Jerusalem above" (Gal 4:26) suggests a similar notion (and see Rev 21:9-14).

The conviction that God foreknows all things and (in some passages) has foreordained things before their earthly, historical appearance is frequent in OT prophetic books (e.g., Is 42:9; 46:8-11; Jer 1:4), and is fundamental in apocalyptic thought (e.g., 1QS 3:15-16; "all that is and shall be" answers to God's preordained design). Paul says that God "foreknew" and "predestined" believers "to be conformed to the image of his Son" (Rom 8:29-30), which suggests that the divine salvific purpose, the identity of believers and "the Son" (Christ) had some sort of (precosmic) heavenly reality (in the mind of God?). And Ephesians* (Pauline authorship widely doubted) states that God chose believers "in Christ before the foundation of the world" (Eph 1:3-6).

*1.2. Pre-existent Personages.* The *Testament of Moses* claims that God "created the world on behalf of his people" (*T. Mos.* 1:12-13), and that Moses was "prepared from the beginning of the world, to be the mediator of [God's] covenant" (*T. Mos.* 1:14). In 4 Ezra the Messiah "who will arise from the offspring of David" is kept by God "until the end of days" (4 Ezra 12:32); and 4 Ezra 13:25-26 states that the messianic man from the sea of 4 Ezra 13:3 is "he whom the Most

High has been keeping for many ages." Similarly, *1 Enoch* 48:1-7 describes a messianic figure whose "name was named" and who was "chosen and hidden . . . before the world was created." In *The Prayer of Joseph*, Jacob appears to be described as the historical manifestation of a pre-existent angelic being.

It is sometimes difficult to determine whether in a given text the figure has an independent, heavenly existence or some other kind of prior reality in the mind or plan of God, so to speak. Nevertheless, the evidence shows that in ancient Jewish tradition there was a freedom, a tendency perhaps, to link particular characters of exceptional importance to the heavenly and pretemporal state.

*1.3. Wisdom.* It is a scholarly commonplace that ancient Jewish tradition about personified divine wisdom* may have been a conceptual source the early Christians drew upon in attributing pre-existence to Christ in the NT, especially where Christ is associated with creation of the world (e.g., Col 1:15-16; Heb 1:2; Jn 1:3, 10). In Proverbs 8:22-31 wisdom is pictured as created before all else and as God's companion in the creation of the world and humankind. The same idea is reflected also in Sirach 24:9, and in Wisdom of Solomon we are told that wisdom is "the fashioner of all things" (Wis 7:22) and "an associate in all his [God's] works" (Wis 8:4) who was present in the creation of the world (Wis 9:9). The identification of divine wisdom and the Torah (Law*) reflected in Sirach 24:23 permitted rabbis later to emphasize Torah as pre-existent and the plan/agency of creation.

## 2. Christ's Pre-existence.

In recent scholarly study there has been spirited debate over which (if any) Pauline passages attribute pre-existence to Christ and precisely what was intended in those passages where one sees the doctrine. It is undisputed that the doctrine developed in the first century and is found in the NT. The debate about the Pauline evidence (the earliest extant Christian writings) concerns how early the doctrine emerged. To cite the extreme positions: on the one hand, J. D. G. Dunn has argued that no real doctrine of Christ's personal pre-existence and Incarnation is found in the Pauline writings but only in late first-century NT writings (Heb 1:1-4; Jn 1:1-18); on the other hand, S. Kim has credited Paul with being the specific initiator of this doctrine.

*2.1. Philippians 2:6-11.* The most intense locus of the debate has been Philippians 2:6-11, especially verses 6-7. With a few others, Dunn (114-21) has insisted that these verses allusively contrast Christ with Adam (see Adam and Christ), and that no heavenly pre-existence of Christ is spoken of in the passage. In this view, the "form of God" is synonymous with Adam as being in God's "image" (Gen 1:26-27). Christ's choice not to grasp "equality with God" but to "empty" himself and take the path of slavery (*see* Servant) and obedience is seen as contrasting with the temptation of Adam to be "like God" (Gen 3:5). And Dunn argues that for the analogy with Adam to work, the text must describe the decision of the earthly Jesus to serve God faithfully.

Once it has been pointed out, the contrast between Christ and Adam that can be inferred here is evocative. But, as L. D. Hurst has observed, even granting an intended comparison/contrast of Christ with Adam, it may be a logical fallacy to assume that this requires that Christ's actions be set, like Adam's, entirely within earthly existence. Indeed, a heavenly figure who forgoes grasping at equality with God and voluntarily descends to a human life of servitude and obedience might have been seen as quite a telling contrast with the human Adam understood as having vainly sought to rise above his status as creature.

But it may be unwise to allow an alleged intentional contrast of Christ and Adam to control overmuch the exegesis of the passage. It must be noted that the Adamic allusions are none too explicit. There is no direct use of phrasing from known Greek OT translations of relevant passages in Genesis. It is perhaps too easily claimed by some that the *morphē theou* ("the form of God," Phil 2:6) is to be taken as alluding to the "image of God" of Genesis 1:27. The term *eikōn* is consistently preferred over *morphē* in the Greek OT in passages where Adam is described as made in God's "image."

Most scholars see Philippians 2:6-7 as reflecting a belief in a heavenly pre-existence of Christ. Given this view, two important further observations present themselves. First, if Philippians 2:6-11 is Paul's adaptation of an early Christian hymn* (as is commonly, though not unanimously, thought), it is valuable evidence that the pre-existence of Christ was celebrated liturgically in his churches and affirmed also by Paul (*see* Worship). Second, whether Philippians 2:6-11 is original with Paul or an adaptation of a hymn, to take verses 6-7 as a condensed expression of Christ's pre-existence means that by the time of the composition of this letter (c. 55-65) the idea was already sufficiently familiar among Paul's churches as to require no explanation (*see* Christology).

*2.2. Shorter Texts.* In one or more shorter Pauline passages, most scholars find additional evidence that Christ's pre-existence and Incarnation was a familiar idea among Paul's churches, and supporting evidence

for seeing pre-existence in Philippians 2:6-11. Of these passages 1 Corinthians 8:6 is perhaps the most confidently offered text, where Christ, "through whom are all things and through whom we exist," is taken as the agent of creation, similar to personified wisdom in Jewish sapiential literature. The Greek prepositional phrases used here ("from whom," "through whom") seem to echo cosmological language that originated in pagan circles but had probably become more common linguistic property by Paul's day. A more allusive mention of Christ's pre-existence is often found in 2 Corinthians 8:9, Christ as "rich" and "poor" taken respectively as references to his heavenly and earthly existence. As with Philippians 2:5-11, this passage portrays Christ's self-abasement as a moral basis/example for Christian behavior (*see* Imitation).

But some texts are not as plausible or as widely supported as references to Christ's pre-existence, such as 1 Corinthians 10:4, more likely a christological interpretation of Israel's "rock" in Deuteronomy 32:4, 15, 18, 30-31, used here to "Christianize" the wilderness events for ethical exhortation (cf. Heb 11:26). And Romans 15:3, 8 may simply allude to the tradition of Christ's earthly ministry as a servant (*see* Old Testament in Paul).

*2.3. Colossians 1:15-20.* Of the key christological passages in the Pauline corpus, Colossians 1:15-20 is among the most honorific, and is easily the most explicit and emphatic in linking Christ with the creation of all things. And, like Philippians 2:6-11, this passage is taken by most as an adaptation of an early Christian hymn. Some, such as J. Habermann, who view Colossians as written in Paul's name by someone after Paul's death, take Colossians 1:15-20 as an adaptation of a Christian hymn circulating in the 60s or later. But if Colossians is a genuine letter of Paul (as many scholars hold; *see* Colossians), the passage reflects an even earlier stage of christological belief and devotion in Pauline Christianity.

Christ is here described as the "image [*eikōn*] of the invisible God," and "first born* [*prōtotokos*] of all creation" (Col 1:15). The term *eikōn* reminds one of the status of Adam in Genesis 1, but it is also applied to personified wisdom in Wisdom of Solomon 7:26, and wisdom tradition may be more relevant here. "First born of all creation" resembles the pre-Christian Jewish references to personified wisdom* as the beginning point of creation* (e.g., Prov 8:22-25; Sir 24:9). And in Colossians 1:16 the claim that everything (pointedly specified by types of creatures) was created "in [or by] him [Christ]" (*en autō*) and "through him" (*di' autou*) seems most readily to be taken as expressing the idea that Christ was somehow the agent of creation, similar to some descriptions of personified Wisdom (e.g., Wis 7:22; 8:4; cf. Ps 104:24). The final claim of Colossians 1:16, however, that all things were created "for him" (*eis auton*) goes beyond wisdom tradition and resembles what is said of God in 1 Corinthians 8:6. This phrase may also echo elements of Jewish tradition where Israel or the elect are referred to as the ones for whom God created the world (e.g., 4 Ezra 6:55; T. Moses 1:12-13).

Dunn (187-96), who takes Colossians as from Paul, has suggested that Colossians 1:15-20 was not intended to attribute to Christ real pre-existence and an active role in creation. Instead, he reads the passage as indicating "the continuity between God's creative power and Christ" who is portrayed here as "the one predetermined by God to be the fullest expression of his wise ordering of the world" (Dunn, 190). Doubtless, Dunn has identified some implications of Colossians 1:15-20, but it is less certain that his suggestions adequately convey the full force of the passage. The emphatic language seems more naturally to reflect convictions about Christ's priority in time as well as in significance. Indeed, the ancient Jewish tradition seems to give ample evidence that the two forms of priority were quite often linked. Granting that Paul and other Christians of the earliest decades were heavily influenced by such tradition, it seems quite likely that, in principle, they would have found pre-existence to be a proper attribute of a figure they regarded as the uniquely appointed agent of God's eschatological triumph.* What is remarkable is that early Christians attributed such a significance to a man who was not a great figure of the past but a near contemporary and one who had suffered a shameful death (*see* Cross, Theology of the) and been rejected by the religious leadership of his people.

**3. Conclusions.**
Pre-existence appears in Paul's letters as an attribute of Christ. As his undisputed letters are dated c. A.D. 50-60, the view that Christ is the historical manifestation of a pre-existent (indeed, precosmic) divine reality must, therefore, have begun remarkably early. Moreover, the casual way in which the topic is mentioned suggests that this was an uncontested and familiar view of Christ in Paul's churches. The ancient Jewish tradition provided the basic language and concepts that entities of ultimate and/or eschatological significance could have pre-existence in the divine realm, and that the divine purpose or intention for creation could be personified and understood as having preceded, and participated in, the creation of the world.

But pre-existence was not attributed to Christ simply through a process of intellectual adaptation or speculative thought. Fundamental was the conviction, born of Jesus' career and the subsequent powerful religious life of the earliest Christian groups, that Christ personally and uniquely embodied the divine salvific purpose and bore surpassing significance. And the Pauline writings show that the pre-existence of Christ was meaningful in the practical purposes of ethical exhortation (e.g., Phil 2:5-11; 2 Cor 8:9; *see* Ethics) and religious identity-formation (Col 1:15-20).

*See also* ADAM AND CHRIST; CHRISTOLOGY; FIRSTBORN; IMAGE, IMAGE OF GOD; WISDOM.

BIBLIOGRAPHY. E. Andrews, *The Meaning of Christ for Paul* (New York/Nashville: Abingdon, 1949); F. B. Craddock, *The Pre-existence of Christ in the New Testament* (Nashville: Abingdon, 1968); O. Cullmann, *The Christology of the New Testament* (Philadelphia: Westminster, 1963); N. A. Dahl, "Christ, Creation and the Church," in *The Background of the New Testament and Its Eschatology*, eds. W. D. Davies and D. Daube (Cambridge: University Press, 1964) 422-43; J. D. G. Dunn, *Christology in the Making: A New Testament Inquiry into the Origins of the Doctrine of the Incarnation* (Philadelphia: Westminster, 1980); J. Habermann, *Präexistenzaussagen im Neuen Testament* (Europäische Hochschulschriften, Series XXIII, Vol. 362; Frankfurt am Main: Peter Lang, 1990); R. G. Hamerton-Kelly, "The Idea of Pre-Existence in Early Judaism: A Study in the Background of New Testament Theology," (Th.D. diss.; Union Theological Seminary, New York, 1966); idem, *Pre-Existence, Wisdom, and the Son of Man: A Study of the Idea of Pre-Existence in the New Testament* (SNTSMS 21; Cambridge: University Press, 1973); L. D. Hurst, "Re-enter the Pre-existent Christ in Philippians 2:5-11?" *NTS* 32 (1986) 449-57; S. Kim, *The Origin of Paul's Gospel* (WUNT 2/4; 2d ed.; Tübingen: J. C. B. Mohr, 1984 [1981]); R. P. Martin, *Carmen Christi: Philippians 2:5-11 in Recent Interpretation and in the Setting of Early Christian Worship* (rev. ed.; Grand Rapids: Eerdmans, 1983 [1967]); C. F. D. Moule, *The Origin of Christology* (Cambridge: University Press, 1977); J. T. Sanders, *The New Testament Christological Hymns* (SNTSMS 15; Cambridge: University Press, 1971).

L. W. Hurtado

# PRINCIPALITIES AND POWERS

The two terms, *principalities* and *powers*, are shorthand for a variety of terms Paul employed to refer to powers that were created by God* but in some way are hostile to Christ* and his church.* The precise meaning of these terms in their various contexts has been a matter of twentieth-century scholarly debate. Most would agree, however, that Paul was speaking of a spiritual dimension of the created order (objective and personal powers, some would add) who, being inimical to Christ and his church, were in some way opposed and either neutralized or conquered by Christ. A promising approach is to view them from the perspective of the OT tradition of holy warfare.

1. Interpretation of the Powers
2. Terminology, Context and Background
3. The Nature of the Powers
4. Christ and the Powers

## 1. Interpretation of the Powers.

The interpretation of the powers has been discussed within a hermeneutical horizon shaped by political and social concerns. Whereas Bultmann's existential approach viewed the powers as mythic projections of human dis-ease within the cosmos, O. Cullmann, speaking from the context of Europe shortly after World War II, represented an interpretation of Romans 13 and 1 Corinthians 2:6-8 which saw the powers as both spiritual and civil authorities and thus gave a theological accounting for the potential good and evil of the state (see also Morrison). But a particularly influential line of interpretation has been that Paul demythologized the powers and employed the language to refer to the structures of earthly existence such as tradition, morality, justice and order (Berkhof). This approach has been adapted by others who have argued that Paul was referring to both the sociopolitical structures of society and spiritual forces behind and within those structures (Yoder, Mouw).

The most comprehensive study of the subject has been undertaken by W. Wink, who surveys the whole range of Paul's usage of the language of power (not just where it ostensibly refers to nonhuman entities or dimensions of reality). He concludes that Paul employed the imprecise and interchangeable language of power to refer simultaneously to the "inner and outer aspects of any given manifestation of power" (Wink, 5). While Paul himself believed in the ontological reality of an invisible spirit world, Wink finds Paul's perspective far more subtle than has previously been appreciated. Paul had already taken steps toward the demythologization of that worldview by expanding the list of enemies of Christ and his people to include Law, sin, flesh and death. The "powers are both heavenly and earthly, divine and human, spiritual and political, invisible and structural" (Wink, 100). As such they are capable of being "depotentiated" and "neutralized"—even redeemed—in God's plan for cosmic restitution (Wink, 50-53; see critique in Arnold 1989, 48-51, 129-34; 1992, 198-201).

The notion that Paul's usage of the language of principalities and powers was always in reference to good angels* in the service of God, not hostile powers, has been argued at some length by W. Carr. But his interpretation of texts such as Colossians 2:14-15 and the exegetical expedient of concluding that Ephesians 6:12 was not part of the original text, have led most interpreters to dismiss his proposal (see Wink, O'Brien, 125-28). Attention has also been devoted to the relationship between Paul's reference to the powers and the demonology implicit in the magical texts of the period (see Arnold).

## 2. Terminology, Context and Background.

The range of terminology Paul employed in speaking of powers was varied and in some cases is ambiguous to modern interpreters.

*2.1. Designations of Power and Authority.* A large portion of the terms Paul employs hold certain features in common: (1) They are not proper names (e.g., Belial, Beelzebul), nor do they reflect particular abilities (e.g., Deception, Strife, Error in *T. Sol.* 8:3), but appear to be titles or nominal classifications, the most prominent of which are based on abstract qualities of power and authority. (2) The terms employed are potentially ambiguous to modern interpreters because for the most part they depend upon their contexts to define whether they refer to human or non-human leaders and potentates—or, less plausibly, both. (3) They most frequently occur in the plural or their plurality is implied (e.g., *pasan archēn*, 1 Cor 15:24; Eph 1:21; Col 2:10), and thus they seem to refer to classes of beings. (4) In most cases they appear in a series of like names. (5) The names themselves suggest some possibility that they refer to echelons of power within the spiritual world, but if that is the case, the evidence is insufficient to determine their ranking. (6) These powers, unlike those called "demons,"* are not said to inhabit humans or idols,* nor reside "under the earth"; when their domain is indicated or implied, it is "heaven and earth," "this age" and in the "heavenlies." This implies that their power is cosmic in extent.

*2.2. Contexts.* Within the Pauline corpus only four letters use these terms in contexts implying that they are nonhuman powers (excluding for the moment the more problematic *stoicheia tou kosmou*, "elements of the world,"* which appear twice in both Galatians and Colossians): Romans, 1 Corinthians, Colossians and Ephesians. Of these, only Romans and 1 Corinthians are of undisputed Pauline authorship, and by far the greatest concentration is found in Colossians (eight instances) and Ephesians (eleven instances). It is argued that the expanded emphasis on the "powers" in these letters may reflect specific cultural and religious situations being addressed, either in Paul's day (e.g., magic* at Ephesus; see Arnold 1989) or the post-Pauline era.

**2.3. Specific Terms.** The meaning of these terms relies primarily on Paul's own usage. But the broader context of their usage in other extant literature—particularly Jewish literature—predating or roughly contemporary with Paul, offers light on the meanings Paul may have employed in his own usage. But the evidence must be considered with care. Claims for these terms referring to cosmic powers have frequently been based on evidence that postdates Paul by a century or more.

*2.3.1. Archai* ("principalities" or "rulers": Rom 8:38; 1 Cor 15:24; Eph 1:21; 3:10; 6:12; Col 1:16; 2:10, 15). *Arch-* was the most frequently used prefix for Greek words denoting positions of human power (Wink, 13). In Daniel 7:27, where the rulers of earthly kingdoms serve the Most High, Theodotion's Greek text speaks of them as *archai* (LXX *exousiai*). The possibility that the Ethiopic equivalent of *archai* is found in 1 Enoch 61:10, where it refers to spiritual powers in the service of God, is more problematic, but likely (see Wink, 153 n. 2).

*2.3.2. Archontes* ("rulers," 1 Cor 2:6, 8). This term commonly referred to human rulers, a sense Paul himself used when he spoke of rulers as civil authorities (*archontes*) in Romans 13:3 (where they bear the sword and collect taxes). Interpreters are divided over whether 1 Corinthians 2:6, 8 refers to human or to spiritual powers, with some suggesting a dual reference. In light of this, the argument for a reference to cosmic powers calls for support.

The possibility of *archontes* referring to spiritual powers is illustrated by the Greek texts of Daniel. Where the Masoretic text uses the Hebrew *śar*, both the LXX and Theodotion (late second century but probably relying on a much earlier Greek text) speak of Michael, the archangel of Israel, as *heis tōn archontōn tōn prōtōn* ("one of the prominent rulers") in Daniel 10:13. Theodotion also uses *archōn* (singular) of Michael in Daniel 10:21 and 12:1, where the LXX has *angelos*. Moreover, in Daniel 10:20-21, where the LXX speaks of the spiritual ruler (*śar*) of Persia and of Greece as *stratēgos*, Theodotion consistently uses *archōn*. The Hebrew term *śarîm*, meaning "chiefs," "princes," "captains" or "rulers," as malevolent spiritual powers of this age, may very well stand behind Paul's usage of *archontes* in 1 Corinthians 2:6, 8 (cf. *śar* in the positive sense as angelic "Ruler/Prince of Light" who has been appointed for Israel's defence against the Satan* or the Angel of Darkness in 1QM

13:10; 1QS 3:20). In 1 Corinthians 2, where Paul speaks of the *archontes tou aiōnos toutou* ("rulers of this age"; cf. 1 Cor 4:4) who are coming to naught (*tōn katargoumenōn*, 1 Cor 2:6), and who did not comprehend God's secret wisdom* and so crucified* the Lord* of glory (1 Cor 2:7-8), there is a compelling context for understanding *archontes* to refer to spiritual powers (but see Fee, 103-5). One need not appeal to a gnostic* or protognostic cosmology to account for this usage. If Paul bore in mind the Danielic cosmology of spiritual powers lying behind the nations, he would quite easily have used *archontes* as a general term for the hostile spiritual powers who, as the chief tradents of the wisdom of this age, were oblivious to the wisdom of God's plan for the ages (cf. Eph 3:10) and so crucified the Lord of glory. The presence of the motif of Satanic opposition to Jesus as it is recorded in the Gospel tradition—an opposition culminating in their leading Jesus to the cross (e.g., Lk 22:3, 53)—probably represents a widespread early Christian understanding of the spiritual conflict that stood behind the human opposition that led Jesus to the cross (cf. the use of *archōn* in reference to Beelzebul in Mk 3:22 par.).

*2.3.3. Exousiai* ("powers" or "authorities": 1 Cor 15:24; Eph 1:21; 2:2; 3:10; 6:12; Col 1:16; 2:10, 15). This term is most frequently used in the NT for the right or authorization to use power bestowed by an office, as is clearly illustrated in Paul's usage of the word in Romans 13:1-3 (Wink, 15, 45-47; cf. Morrison). In LXX Daniel 7:27 the earthly rulers who are subject to and obey the most high are called *exousiai* (contrast Theodotion's *archai* in 2.3.1. above). An example of usage of the word roughly contemporary with the NT, and with a reference to spiritual beings, is found in *Testament of Levi* 3:8. Here the *exousiai* occupy the highest heaven and are privileged, along with the *thronoi* ("thrones"), to be in the very presence of God (cf. also *1 Enoch* 61:10; *2 Enoch* 20:1). In this case, of course, they are servants of God and not of evil.

*2.3.4. Dynameis* ("powers": Rom 8:38; Eph 1:21). In LXX Daniel 8:10 the "powers of heaven" (*dynameis tou ouranou*) and "the stars" are cast down to the earth and trampled by the "little horn" (cf. Is 34:4; Mk 13:25). Philo frequently used *dynameis* to refer to angelic powers (e.g., Philo *Migr. Abr.* 181), and in *Jubilees* 1:29 it is used of "powers of the heaven" (cf. "of the heavens" in *1 Enoch* 61:10 and as part of the heavenly army of the seventh heaven in *2 Enoch* 20:1). In the LXX *kyrios tōn dynameōn* ("Lord of powers"), rather than *kyrios tōn stratiōn* ("Lord of armies"), is used to translate Yahweh Sabaoth, "Lord of Hosts" (where "hosts" refers to Yahweh's heavenly army). This may reflect the frequent use of *dynameis* in Jewish texts to refer to military forces (cf., e.g., Ps 102:21; see Wink, 159-61). This militaristic association suggests that the same connotation might be present in the use of *dynameis* in Romans 8:38 and Ephesians 1:21, where the powers are opposed to God.

*2.3.5. Kyriotētes* ("dominions," "lordships": Col 1:16; Eph 1:21 [singular *kyriotēs*]). It is not clear whether *kyriotētes* lies behind the Slavonic term for the "dominions" that are part of the heavenly army of the seventh heaven in *2 Enoch* 20:1 (cf. *1 Enoch* 61:10; Wink, 20). It may be plausibly argued that the Hebrew term *memšelet*, used of the dominion of Belial in 1QS 1:18; 2:19; 1QM 14:9; 18:1; 4Q 286-87, is the equivalent of *kyriotēs* (Wink, 20; though note the possible parallel to Qumran usage in *tēs exousias tou skotous* of Col 1:13). In speaking of idolatry, Paul can refer to "many gods and many lords [*kyrioi*]" (1 Cor 8:5), which, by implication, he associates with "demons" (1 Cor 10:20). One possible connotation is that the *kyriotētes* represent spheres of spiritual influence formerly understood to be ruled by the gods of the nations.

*2.3.6. Thronoi* ("thrones": Col 1:16). This term appears to be a metonymy for the spiritual power that occupies the throne (cf. *Asc. Isa.* 7-8). In LXX Daniel 7:9 *thronoi* refers to the thrones set in place in the heavenly tribunal of the Ancient of Days, clearly indicating positions of transcendent authority. And in *2 Enoch* 20:1 they are called the "many-eyed thrones" who with the cherubim, seraphim and heavenly forces occupy the seventh heaven. In *Testament of Levi* 3:8 they occupy the highest heaven and are privileged with the *exousiai* to be in the very presence of God. The use of the term in Colossians* may be attributed to the particular set of beliefs Paul challenged at Colossae, perhaps associated with the "worship of angels" (Col 2:18).

*2.3.7. Kosmokratores tou skotous toutou* ("cosmic rulers of this darkness": Eph 6:12). *Kosmokratōr* is used of the god Sarapis in the magical texts (*PGM* XIII.618-40). In Ephesians the evil nature of these powers is emphasized by the phrase *ta pneumatika tēs ponērias en tois epouraniois* ("spiritual forces of evil in the heavenlies": Eph 6:12).

*2.3.8. Angeloi.* In at least one case Paul speaks of *angeloi* ("angels" or "messengers") in a context suggesting they are evil powers who might attempt to thwart the purposes of God (Rom 8:38), and in other instances they appear to be in some sense culpable and to be judged by believers (1 Cor 6:3). More problematic is the usage in Colossians 2:18, where the angels are either the objects of misplaced devotion or their worship* of God is an object of human religious

aspiration (note the ambiguity of the genitive in the phrase *thrēskeia tōn angelōn*, "worship *of* angels": if an objective genitive it means worship directed toward angels; if a subjective genitive it refers to angelic worship of God, or worship led by angels).

*2.3.9. Inclusive Phrases.* Paul also employs four phrases which are broadly inclusive of every imaginable power. In Romans 8:39, in a series of contrasting pairs, he uses a spatial image, "neither height nor depth (*oute hypsōma oute bathos*), which may refer to the zenith and nadir of the heavenly bodies and thus encompass the full sweep of celestial powers (cf. *1 Enoch* 18:3, 11). Or it may simply refer to any powers that might occupy the height of heaven or the underparts of the earth—or any space between.

In Colossians 1:16 "all things in heaven and on the earth, things seen and unseen" (*ta horata kai ta aorata*) are said to be created by Christ. These are then enumerated as "thrones, dominions, principalities and powers."

In Philippians 2:10, in speaking of the exalted Christ (*see* Exaltation), Paul depicts the universal submission to the sovereign Lord by using a spatial image of a three-tiered universe: "every knee . . . in heaven and on earth and under the earth [*epouraniōn kai epigeiōn kai katachthoniōn*] should bow." Here Paul (or the hymn writer) seems to include every rational being—human and spiritual, good and evil—as ultimately (or presently) submissive to the rule of Christ (for reference to demons "of the air, on the earth and under the earth" see *PGM* IV.2694-2704). The echo of Isaiah 45:23 recalls the OT context of the enforced submission of earthly powers (cf. Is 45:24 and 24:21) as apocalyptic symbols.

Finally, in Ephesians 1:21, as the conclusion to a list of four names of evil powers, we find a global reference to "every name named, not only in this age but in the age to come" (*pantos onomatos onomazomenou ou monon en tō aiōni toutō alla kai en tō mellonti*). If this is taken as authentically Pauline, it is further evidence that Paul never intended to exhaust the possibilities of names. Against a cultural background in which the successful magical manipulation of evil powers was commonly believed to be predicated on the knowledge of the power's name, Ephesians emphasizes the triumph* and sovereignty of Christ over every power—known or unknown, real or imagined, present or future.

### 3. The Nature of the Powers.

Within the Pauline corpus the powers are mentioned in a variety of specific contexts, most notably those corresponding to decisive episodes in the story of

Christ: they were brought into existence by the pre-existent* Christ in his creative role (Col 1:16); led in triumphal procession as defeated enemies at the cross (Col 2:15 and possibly 1 Cor 2:6, 8); subjected to the triumphant, exalted and reigning Christ (Eph 1:21; cf. Col 2:10; Phil 2:10); and will be destroyed at his eschatological consummation of God's plan (1 Cor 15:24).

*3.1. The Powers as Created Through Christ.* Colossians 1:15-16 asserts that Christ was instrumental in the creation* of "thrones," "dominions," "principalities" and "powers"; along with "all things in heaven and earth, visible and invisible," they were created "in" (*en autō*), "through" (*di' autou*) and "for" (*eis auton*) him. The powers were originally a divine creation and were to find their goal in Christ. Yet the same christological* hymn* of which this statement is a part asserts that Christ reconciled all things to himself in the cross (Col 1:20). We may legitimately assume that Paul and the author of the hymn (if it is non-Pauline in origin) shared the basic biblical premise that the original creation was good and in harmony with God's purposes. The necessity for peace to be made, along with the later assertion of Christ's victory over the powers at the cross (Col 2:15), implies that something had gone wrong and the powers had turned hostile to God and his purposes. As to the circumstances of this transformation we are left to guess. Some interpreters have maintained that from Paul's perspective the problem with the powers is that they had been wrongly regarded by the Colossians as rivals to Christ (Col 2:8, 20). They are a specter of a superstitious religious imagination from which believers in Christ have been set free. But as we have already observed, the understanding of powers existing as angelic servants of God is well represented in texts reflecting the Judaism of Paul's day, and the notion that some of these are "fallen," hostile spiritual beings is also found. It seems likely that Paul understood the powers to belong to the latter category, and that he did attribute to them a spiritual, ontological existence, if not perhaps in exactly the same sense as did the Colossians.

*3.2. The Powers as Enemies of God, Christ and His People.* Palestinian Judaism of Paul's day was faced with a longstanding but monumental problem: the occupying power of the Romans who challenged the sanctity of her Temple, Torah and sacred territory. More than a social and political problem, this was a theological problem demanding a theodicy. From the apocalyptic* perspective of a sectarian Judaism (from the latter decades of the first century B.C.) comes an answer that sheds light on Paul's language of the powers: the War Scroll of Qumran (11QM, 4QM491-496).

Expanding on the account of eschatological battle found in Daniel 11:40—12:3, the scroll depicts a war in which the righteous of Israel, called the "Sons of Light," are assisted by Michael and the angelic forces in overthrowing the "Sons of Darkness," the latter being assisted by Belial and his powers of darkness. In this battle various traditional opponents of Israel (Edom, Moab, Ammon, Philistia, 1QM 1:1-2) would first be defeated, with the final battle pitched against the "Kittim of Asshur" (1QM 1:1-14; 11:11; cf. Num 24:24), probably a reference to the Romans and their encroachment on Palestine during the second half of the first century B.C. The War Scroll's appropriation of the language and imagery of divine warfare and of the traditional names of Israel's enemies, now fortified by demonic powers, suggests an avenue for understanding Paul's depiction of the powers.

As a former Pharisaic Jew (*see* Jew, Paul the), Paul professed to have been zealous for the cause of Israel* (Gal 1:13-14; Phil 3:5-6), a passion transformed by his encounter with the risen Lord (e.g., Rom 9:1-5). With Paul's conversion* came a radical reassessment of the place in God's redemptive plan of Torah, Temple and territory of promised inheritance. Moreover, the Gentiles,* being formerly reckoned as enemies* of God's purpose in history, were now the very people to whom he was called to proclaim the good news (*see* Gospel) of eschatological peace* initiated by Messiah Jesus. No longer were the Gentiles enemies of God (Rom 5:10; 8:7; 11:28; Col 1:21).

In Paul's theology we find evidence of a hermeneutical shift by which the traditional symbols of Israel were reinterpreted, including Torah, Temple, sacrifice, purity, the people of God and even the inheritance of land (Col 1:12-14). Likewise, it appears that the themes of Yahweh the divine warrior and the traditional enemies of Israel were transformed. The Gentiles, who had once been "far off," aliens and enemies (Eph 2:17; cf. Col 1:21), had now become the focus of God's saving grace.* They could no longer be regarded as flesh and blood enemies, the objects of the Old Covenant "ban" (*ḥērem*) of divine warfare. That penalty, paradoxically, had been visited upon the Messiah himself as he hung on the cross (Gal 3:10-14) and opened up the way for Jews and Gentiles to become one new eschatological person in Christ (cf. Eph 2:14-18). The true enemies were no longer the Romans, but the spiritual powers that lurked behind the human faces of the authorities and empires of this world.

Here Paul could find precedent in the OT: "When the Most High apportioned the nations, when he divided humankind, he fixed the boundaries of the peoples according to the number of the sons of God; the Lord's own portion was his people, Jacob his allotted share" (Deut 32:8-9 NRSV; cf. Sir 17:17; *Jub* 15:31-32). The gods and idols* of the nations were in reality demons* (Deut 32:17; cf. 1 Cor 10:20) who were to be judged by the Judge of all the earth (Ps 82; Is 24:21). This understanding of the spiritual powers behind the nations had been further developed in the vision of the monstrous beasts representing empires in Daniel 7:2-8 and the "Prince" of Persia and Greece fought by "the one like a man" and Michael, the Prince of Israel, in Daniel 10:13, 20-21. And there is evidence that Paul was joined by other Jews in this world view (cf. *Jub.* 15:30-32; *1 Enoch* 89:59-61; 90:20-25 where the seventy shepherds seem to represent the angels of the nations; cf. Is 24:21).

The immediate context of 1 Corinthians 15:24 leaves no doubt about whether Paul ever spoke of the powers as being evil, for there they are listed among the eschatological "enemies" (*echthroi*, 1 Cor 15:25-26; cf. Eph 6:12), including death (*see* Life and Death). The powers also populate the backdrop of this drama of redemption:* appearing among the potential barriers to the love of Christ, they are, nonetheless, ultimately powerless to thwart the final triumph of Christ (Rom 8:38). In Ephesians they are even more boldly presented as the enemies of Christ who oppose the church in the present age (Eph 6:12). From their vantage point "in the heavenlies" (*see* Heaven), they also observe God's wisdom unfolding in his plan for the ages (Eph 3:10).

### 4. Christ and the Powers.

Paul utilized the story of Israel to tell the story of Christ. The progressive pattern of warfare, victory, kingship, temple building and celebration, evident in the OT (and ancient Near Eastern mythic patterns) was transposed by Paul. Messiah Jesus, who had engaged the enemy and was victorious (Col 2:15; cf. Col 1:12-14), was now exalted and reigning as heavenly king (1 Cor 15:24-26; Phil 2:9; Col 3:1; Eph 1:20-22; 1 Tim 3:16), building his new temple* (1 Cor 3:16-17; 2 Cor 6:16; Eph 2:19-22) and receiving praise and obeisance (Phil 2:10-11). The enemy for Paul consisted not of Romans or Greeks, but of "principalities and powers" (as well as sin,* flesh,* death and even the Law*), so named perhaps to accent the authority and dominion they exercised in this age. Like the kings of the Gentile nations who would become the footstool for the Davidic king (Ps 110), the principalities and powers were already and would finally be placed under Christ's feet (1 Cor 15:24-28). Whether Paul spoke of these powers as being stripped of power and

brought into the service of Christ or as utterly defeated and ultimately to be annihilated, is a question that has been debated. However, the language Paul employs in 1 Corinthians 15:24 to speak of their end (*katargeō*, used also of defeat of death in 1 Cor 15:26) strongly suggests their utter defeat or annihilation with no possibility of redemption. Here again the language reflects the "ban" (*ḥērem*) of Yahweh's warfare.

If the powers played such a role in Paul's narrative of Christ, they were also recognized as the hostile cosmic powers of the universe that gripped with fear the hearts of many in the Roman world of Paul's day. Whether through association with magic,* the mysteries or astrology, popular religion of the first-century Mediterranean world conceived of a cosmos haunted by spirits in the heavens, on the earth and beneath the earth. Paul addressed this situation by announcing that the powers of darkness had been defeated by Christ on the cross. Though their power was still real and potent, they were not to be feared by those "in Christ" (Rom 8:37-39). Thus when Paul spoke of the hostility of the powers in this age and their defeat by Christ, he spoke a language that was not only fundamentally Jewish in its echo of OT archetypes and the pattern of redemption, but one that resonated in the hearts of his Gentile audience.

Ephesians develops the theme of the hostility of the powers to the church. In Ephesians 6:12-17 the earthly struggle of the church is portrayed in imagery reminiscent of the holy warfare of Israel. But here the enemy is not "flesh and blood" but spiritual; the warfare is waged "against the principalities, against the powers, against the spiritual forces of evil in the heavenly realms" (Eph 6:12). These powers are under the direction of their leader "the devil," whose schemes (*methodeiai*) they carry out against the church. The weapons of the church are both the defensive armor and shield (Eph 6:13-17), and the offensive "sword of the Spirit" (Eph 6:17). The power* of the church militant is found "in the Lord and in his mighty strength," and represents the benefits of Christ's work. The church thus resists the enemy and advances from a position of power founded on the "already" of the defeat of the devil and his forces. While the terminology of military paraphernalia is taken from the Roman world, the archetype of warfare is clearly Israelite.

The full picture of conflict and victory in Paul's theology must also take into account his statements about the "elements" or "elemental spirits of this world," Satan, demons and his describing sin, flesh, death and the Law as enemies of Christ. But the essential features of his perspective are clear in his statements about the principalities and powers.

*See also* ANGELS, ARCHANGELS; DEMONS AND EXORCISM; ENEMY, ENMITY, HATRED; ELEMENTS/ELEMENTAL SPIRITS OF THE WORLD; FLESH; LIFE AND DEATH; LAW; SATAN, DEVIL; SIN; TRIUMPH.

BIBLIOGRAPHY. C. E. Arnold, *Ephesians: Power and Magic: The Concept of Power in Ephesians* (SNTSMS 63; Cambridge: University Press, 1989); idem, *Powers of Darkness: Principalities and Powers in Paul's Letters* (Downers Grove, IL: InterVarsity, 1992); H. Berkhof, *Christ and the Powers* (Scottdale: Herald, 1977); M. Black, "πᾶσαι ἐξουσίαι αὐτῷ ὑποταγήσονται," in *Paul and Paulinism*, ed. M. D. Hooker and S. G. Wilson (London: S.P.C.K., 1982) 74-82; G. B. Caird, *Principalities and Powers* (Oxford: Clarendon, 1956); W. Carr, *Angels and Principalities: The Background, Meaning and Development of the Pauline Phrase HAI ARCHAI KAI HAI EXOUSIAI* (SNTSMS 42; Cambridge: University Press, 1981); O. Cullmann, *The State in the New Testament* (London, 1957); M. Dibelius, *Die Geisterwelt im Glauben des Paulus* (Göttingen: Vandenhoeck & Ruprecht, 1909); J. Y. Lee, "Interpreting the Powers in Pauline Thought," *NovT* 12 (1970) 54-69; G. H. C. Macgregor, "Principalities and Powers: The Cosmic Background of Paul's Thought," *NTS* 1 (1954-55) 17-28; O. Merk, "ἄρχων," *EDNT* 1.167-68; C. D. Morrison, *The Powers That Be* (SBT 29; Naperville, IL: Allenson, 1960); R. J. Mouw, *Politics and the Biblical Drama* (Grand Rapids: Eerdmans, 1976); P. T. O'Brien, "Principalities and Powers: Opponents of the Church," in *Biblical Interpretation and the Church*, ed. D. A. Carson (Nashville: Thomas Nelson, 1984) 110-50; H. Schlier, *Principalities and Powers in the New Testament* (Freiburg: Herder, 1961); J. S. Stewart, "On a Neglected Emphasis in New Testament Theology," *SJT* 4 (1951) 292-301; K. Weiss, "ἀρχή," *EDNT* 1.161-63; W. Wink, *Naming the Powers* (Philadelphia: Fortress, 1984); J. H. Yoder, *The Politics of Jesus* (Grand Rapids: Eerdmans, 1972).

D. G. Reid

# PRISON, PRISONER

The fact that Paul was imprisoned on more than one occasion is well attested. For the reasons, circumstances and results of those imprisonments we are dependent on the evidence from Acts and chiefly Paul's letters, with an occasional allusion in the early Church Fathers (e.g., *1 Clem.* 5.6: Paul was "seven times in chains"). Of particular significance is Paul's apostolic perspective on imprisonment, whether it be his own or that of his coworkers. The question of the possible locations from which Paul wrote his prison letters is discussed in the articles on Philippians, Colossians, Philemon and Ephesians.

1. Prison
2. Paul the Prisoner
3. Prisoners of War

### 1. Prison.

In Acts we read of Saul of Tarsus imprisoning men and women when he was persecuting the church (Acts 8:3; 22:4, 19; 26:10; cf. Acts 9:4-5). But as an apostle of Jesus Christ, he suffered imprisonment for the sake of Jesus Christ. Ironically, on the occasion of his final visit to Jerusalem it was a Roman prison that protected him from the hands of his Jewish persecutors (Acts 21:33-34). When Paul cataloged his afflictions* in 2 Corinthians 6:4-5 and 11:23-29 he alluded to his "imprisonments" (2 Cor 6:5), which numbered "far more" (2 Cor 11:23) than those of the "false apostles" who opposed him (*see* Opponents of Paul). This statement implies that by the time of his writing 2 Corinthians (A.D. 55-56), just prior to his arrest (A.D. 57) and successive imprisonments in Jerusalem,* Caesarea and Rome,* Paul had been put in prison on more occasions than the one imprisonment related in Acts, that at Philippi (Acts 16:23-40).

The description of Paul and Silas's imprisonment at Philippi provides a valuable glimpse into a prison in a Roman colony. After Paul and Silas had suffered a severe beating with rods, the jailor was ordered by the magistrates to "keep them securely." The jailor (*desmophylax*) complied by placing Paul and Silas in the "innermost cell," chained, with their feet fastened in stocks, which served as an instrument of torture since the legs were painfully stretched. This cell is described as being in a building at least partially designated as a prison (alternately called *phylakē*, Acts 16:23, 24, 27, 37, 40, and *desmōtērion*, Acts 16:26), occupied by a number of prisoners, and under the direction of a jailor whose residence appears to have adjoined the prison, possibly upstairs from the prison (Acts 16:34).

But an official prison was not necessarily the norm; parts of buildings largely devoted to other uses could serve as prisons. At Jerusalem Paul was bound in two chains and held in the "barracks" (*parembolē*, Acts 21:37; 23:16) adjoining the Temple area, presumably in the fortress of Antonia. Later, at Caesarea, Paul was held under guard in Herod's palace (*praitōrion*, Acts 23:35). The narrative of Acts suggests a more relaxed detainment at Caesarea than at Jerusalem. After being transferred as a prisoner to Rome, Paul was kept for two years under house arrest (*custodia libera*) at his own expense (Acts 28:30), guarded by a Roman soldier (Acts 28:16) and restrained by a light chain (*alysis*, Acts 28:20). There he was granted the freedom to entertain numerous guests (Acts 28:17, 23, 30) and carry on his preaching and teaching (Acts 28:17-31). Both at Caesarea and at Rome, Paul's imprisonment paradoxically gave him access to audiences he would not otherwise have reached, especially if Philippians 1:13-14 and 4:22 relate to either of these captivities.

In the Roman world imprisonment was legally not a penalty for a crime. Prisons were sort of "holding tanks" used to detain those awaiting trial (*custodia reorum*) or execution (see Ramsay, 273-74). And, as Paul's recorded imprisonments indicate, the circumstances could vary: on the one hand, he was brutally scourged and then locked in stocks in the darkness of an innermost cell; on the other hand, he could experience the relatively humane detention of guarded house arrest.

### 2. Paul the Prisoner.

Paul employs several words to speak of prison and being a prisoner. He can speak of "chains" (*desmoi*, always plural in Paul), by which he means "imprisonment." He frequently refers to them as "my chains" (Phil 1:7, 13, 14, 17; Col 4:18) and sometimes uses them to speak of his situation "in prison" (Philem 10, 13; 2 Tim 2:9). In 2 Corinthians, when speaking of his afflictions as an apostle,* he refers to being *en phylakais*, "in prison" (2 Cor 6:5; 11:23). In Ephesians 6:20 and 2 Timothy 1:16 the apostle's imprisonment is indicated by the word *halysis*, "chain," and in Colossians 4:3 Paul speaks of being "bound" (*dedemai*).

Paul's repeated references in Philippians 1 to "my chains" offer insight into his experience and how he reconciled it with his calling as apostle, presumably questioned at Philippi by those who supposed that a suffering* apostle was a contradiction (see Bloomquist). Paul speaks from his imprisonment with a note of joy,* untarnished by self-pity, and confident that though he is confined to prison, the word of God is not confined. Hence the frequent mention of "my imprisonment" functions rhetorically as apologetic. Through his imprisonment it has "come to light" (*phanerous ginomai*) in all the praetorium and among those outside the praetorium that his imprisonment is *en Christō*, "for Christ" (Phil 1:13; *see* Caesar's Household). This effect, Paul implies, is due to divine providence, to which he appeals as a theodicy. Some of his fellow believers have found in Paul's imprisonment more confidence and motivation to preach the gospel* (Phil 1:14), knowing that Paul is held in prison so that he might give his defense of the gospel (Phil 1:16). Sadly for their sake, but happily for the gospel, others have been motivated out of selfish ambition to preach the gospel with the hope of increasing Paul's suffering in prison (Phil 1:17), perhaps by insinuating

that he was not a true apostle since he was in jail and under sentence (Phil 1:22-23). But the Philippians, even at a distance, partake of Paul's ministry* by their prayers* and gifts, and so they too partake of the divine grace* of Paul's apostolic commission in its Christ-like afflictions (Phil 3:10) and defense of the gospel (see Hawthorne, 23; O'Brien, 70).

When Paul speaks of himself as "prisoner" (*desmios*), it is always as "prisoner of Christ* Jesus" (Philem 1, 9; Eph 3:1), "prisoner in the Lord*" (Eph 4:1) or "prisoner of him [our Lord]" (2 Tim 1:8). Though the phrase "prisoner of Christ Jesus" and its equivalents appears three out of five times in the contested Pauline letters, its presence in Philemon calls for it to be reckoned as an authentic piece of Pauline vocabulary and self-understanding. Does the genitive in the expression *desmios Christou Iēsou* ("prisoner *of* Christ Jesus") indicate that Paul sees himself as one taken prisoner by Christ or as one who suffers imprisonment for the sake of Christ? Most commentators have understood it in the latter sense, appealing to Philippians 1:29-30. This seems to be the most likely meaning, with the implied nuance that it is Christ who is truly sovereign over Paul's circumstances. In Philemon 13 Paul refers to his *desmoi tou euangeliou*, which can scarcely be rendered "imprisonment of the gospel" and must be read "imprisonment *for* the gospel," an emphasis similar to that of Colossians 4:3, where Paul writes that he is in prison (*dedemai*, lit. "bound") for declaring the "mystery* of Christ." In opening the letter to Philemon with the words "Paul a prisoner of Christ Jesus," Paul is substituting this identification for his more usual "called to be an apostle," "an apostle* of Christ Jesus" and "a slave* of Christ Jesus." Whereas Paul elsewhere can pair "apostle" and "slave," in Philemon 9 he speaks of himself as "ambassador" (*presbytēs* should probably be so translated rather than "old man," see commentaries) and "prisoner" (cf. Eph 6:20, *presbeuō en halysei*, "I serve as ambassador in chains"). The situation from which Paul writes to Philemon is by all indications an actual imprisonment, so while "prisoner" does take on metaphorical overtones, it is rooted in Paul's simultaneous situation as a literal prisoner.

Paul's self-identification as a "prisoner of Christ Jesus" plays a rhetorical* function in Paul's appeal to Philemon* (as it does in Philippians for a different reason; see above). The humility Paul enacts in his submission and obedience to Christ—to the point of imprisonment—is the very humility Paul expects of Philemon as he responds to Onesimus "in the Lord" (see Petersen, 124-28). Clearly, Paul views his imprisonment as part of his apostolic activity. Inasmuch as his imprisonments are among his trials and afflictions as an apostle, he lives out his commitment to the "word of the cross*" as a prisoner of Jesus Christ, who took upon himself the end-time messianic woes. In his cruciform "weakness"* he finds and displays the power* of God (cf. 2 Cor 13:1-4). Thus Paul's identity as a prisoner serves both as an emblem of Christ's humiliation upon the apostle's life and as a symbol of Paul's apostolic authority.* Thus when he asks the Colossians to "remember my bonds" (Col 4:18), it is "not chiefly a matter of pathos but of authority" (Moule, 139). The rhetorical function of the prisoner theme is also evident in Ephesians 4:1: "I, therefore, the prisoner in the Lord, beg you to lead a life worthy of the calling to which you have been called." Here the pastoral* appeal of the letter is underscored by the costly commitment of the apostle, who was imprisoned for the sake of the Gentiles* now addressed (Eph 3:1; see Lincoln 234, cf. 171-72).

The interpretation of R. Reitzenstein bears mention here. Reitzenstein explained Paul's status as a "prisoner of Christ Jesus" not as literal imprisonment but as a metaphor shaped by the mystery religions in which the devotee was purportedly detained (*katochē*), or "imprisoned," prior to initiation. Paul, it was reasoned, regarded his imprisonment as preparation for entrance into the final mystery of Christ (Phil 1:23). Apart from the unproven influence of the mystery religions on Paul (*see* Religions), such an interpretation comes to grief on Paul's view of his imprisonment in Philippians, where he clearly wrestles with the possible outcomes of his imprisonment as either life or death (Phil 1:19-24), the desirable outcome being life and the opportunity to visit the Philippians again (Phil 1:25-26; 2:24; cf. Philem 22; see Kittel 43).

### 3. Prisoners of War.

Paul can use *synaichmalōtos* ("fellow prisoner [of war]") of certain coworkers* (Rom 16:7, Andronicus and Junia; Col 4:10, Aristarchus; Philem 23, Epaphras). Though he never uses *aichmalōtos* of himself (the closest allusion, if not the actual term is 2 Cor 2:14; see Hafemann, 18-39), he implies that he considers himself a prisoner of war by consistently speaking of *synaichmalōtos mou*, "*my* fellow prisoner"—these individuals are fellow prisoners of war with Paul. This military metaphor seems to fit well with Paul's occasional invoking of the warfare metaphor to speak of the work of Christ, the struggle of the church and the ministry of an apostle of Jesus Christ (*see* Triumph). It could be that *synaichmalōtos* was a rank of honor that Paul reserved for those who had borne with him the particular affliction of imprisonment for gospel min-

istry. But if so, it is notable that whereas in Philemon 23-24 Epaphras is called *synaichmalōtos* and Aristarchus is counted among Paul's "fellow workers" (*synergoi*), in Colossians it is Aristarchus who is called *synaichmalōtos* (Col 4:10) and Epaphras, who initially brought the gospel to Colossae (Col 1:7, note "Epaphras our beloved fellow servant," *Epaphra tou agapētou syndoulos hēmōn*), is called a "servant of Christ [Jesus]" (*doulos Christou [Iēsou]*, Col 4:12; *see* Coworkers).

In Ephesians 4:8 the related verb *aichmalōteuō* ("take into captivity") and noun *aichmalōsia* ("captivity," "prisoners of war") are found in an adaptation of Psalm 68:18 (LXX 67:19), which many interpreters have understood as a reference to Christ's having taken spiritual powers captive and led them into captivity. In Romans 7 the verb *aichmalōtizō* ("take captive in war") is used to speak of the "law of sin*" taking "me" captive (Rom 7:23), and in Galatians 3:23 Paul speaks of the Law holding prisoners (*ephrouroumetha synkleiomenoi*) before faith* was "revealed." In 2 Corinthians Paul writes that he takes every thought captive for Christ (2 Cor 10:5). Finally, in 2 Timothy reference is made to those who enter households and take "silly women" captive, or ensnare them (2 Tim 3:6).

*See also* COLOSSIANS, LETTER TO THE; EPHESIANS, LETTER TO THE; LEGAL SYSTEM, ROMAN; PHILEMON, LETTER TO; PHILIPPIANS, LETTER TO THE; SUFFERING; TRIUMPH.

BIBLIOGRAPHY. M. Barth, *Ephesians* (AB; Garden City, NY: Doubleday, 1974); L. G. Bloomquist, *The Function of Suffering in Philippians* (JSNT 78; Sheffield: Academic, 1993); S. J. Hafemann, *Suffering and the Spirit* (WUNT 2.19; Tübingen: J. C. B. Mohr, 1986); G. F. Hawthorne, *Philippians* (WBC 43; Waco, TX: Word, 1983); G. Kittel, "αἰχμάλωτος κτλ," *TDNT* I.195-97; idem, "δεσμός, δέσμιος," *TDNT* II.43; A. T. Lincoln, *Ephesians* (WBC 42; Dallas: Word, 1990); E. Lohse, *Colossians and Philemon* (Herm; Philadelphia: Fortress, 1971); C. F. D. Moule, *The Epistles to the Colossians and to Philemon* (CGTC; Cambridge: University Press, 1957); P. T. O'Brien, *Colossians, Philemon* (WBC 44; Waco, TX: Word, 1982); idem, *Philippians* (NIGTC; Grand Rapids: Eerdmans, 1991); N. R. Petersen, *Rediscovering Paul: Philemon and the Sociology of Paul's Narrative World* (Philadelphia: Fortress, 1985); W. M. Ramsay, *The Letters to the Seven Churches of Asia* (London: Hodder & Stoughton, 1904); R. Reitzenstein, *Hellenistic Mystery Religions* (Pittsburgh: Pickwick, 1978); F. Staudinger, "δεσμός," *EDNT* 1.288-90.

D. G. Reid

**PROMISE AND FULFILLMENT.** *See* ABRAHAM; LAW; OLD TESTAMENT IN PAUL.

# PROPHECY, PROPHESYING

Prophecy is one of the "gifts" *(charismata)* of the Holy Spirit* described within the Pauline corpus, especially in 1 Corinthians 12—14. Its action or use is prophesying (*see* Gifts of the Spirit). It consists of a word or oracle given or revealed by God* through the initiative and inspiration of the Holy Spirit and conveyed by a willing medium or participant sometimes designated as a "prophet" or as "one who prophesies." A prophecy is given in order to meet one or more needs within the Christian community for guidance and direction, edification, encouragement, consolation or witness, and it ultimately points back to the One who gives this gift.

1. Paul and OT Prophecy
2. Paul's Personal Experience with Prophecy
3. Paul's Reflections on Prophecy
4. The Limits of Prophecy
5. Appeals to Paul in Contemporary Claims to Prophecy

## 1. Paul and OT Prophecy.

The nature of prophecy for Paul is clearly informed by the nature of prophecy as it is expressed by the literary prophets of Israel. As one who had read, indeed, studied the prophetic writings of Israel's prophets, Paul attempted repeatedly to show that the Christian gospel stands in continuity with their message (*see* Prophet, Paul as). Critical to his argument are three factors.

(1) God has spoken through the prophets of Israel (Rom 1:1-2; 11:3; 16:26). Basic to the Hebrew term *nābî'* in the OT, which is typically translated as "prophet," is the idea that the *nābî'* is a person who speaks on behalf of another. The prophet of Yahweh served as a mouthpiece for God by proclaiming God's message to those who were to receive it. Paul affirmed repeatedly the idea that God had spoken through the OT prophets.

(2) The word or message of the literary prophets was considered to be authoritative. It was a word or message which originated with Yahweh and ultimately came to occupy an important position in Israel's own self-understanding of the relationship between Israel and Yahweh. It is true, as Paul observed, that Israel did not initially embrace the prophets or their messages. Indeed, Israel had killed prophets with unwelcome messages (Rom 11:3; 1 Thess 2:15). Ultimately, however, Israel came to recognize the genuine authoritative character of the prophetic words, even though the people did not always perceive their full meaning at the time in which they were given. The prophets were thus granted a special position along-

side the Torah. The Law* and the Prophets were viewed as working in tandem with one another (Rom 3:21-22), and the prophets found their place among the holy writings (*en graphais hagiais,* Rom 1:2) of Scripture.

(3) The oracles which are found embedded within OT literature were originally directed toward a large community, a small group or an individual. Sometimes the message is predictive of a future event, while on other occasions it serves as an exhortation. On the whole, though, Paul regards the OT prophetic literature as having achieved at least two things: (1) the prophets have borne witness to the righteousness* of God (Rom 3:21) and (2) they have predicted, or promised beforehand, the good news (*to euangelion; see* Gospel) of God in Jesus Christ* (Rom 1:1-6).

The method by which the OT prophets received their message is described only indirectly by Paul. In Romans 16:25-26 he notes that it is a message which came by means of revelation *(apokalypsis),* but that its meaning had been mysterious* and kept secret until Paul's own day. Only recently had God made known the real meaning of the prophetic writings. In short, it is to divine revelation that Paul attributed genuine prophetic activity in the OT (*see* Old Testament in Paul).

## 2. Paul's Personal Experience with Prophecy.

*2.1. Luke-Acts.* According to Acts, Paul's first encounter with Christian prophetic activity occurred immediately after his encounter with the risen Lord on the road to Damascus (*see* Conversion and Call). Ananias, described by the writer of Luke-Acts simply as a "disciple" who lived in Damascus, is seldom, if ever, acknowledged as a prophetic figure. Two things suggest, however, that the role Ananias played with respect to Saul was, indeed, a prophetic one. First, it is said that the Lord spoke to him in a vision *(en horamati),* providing specific instructions for him to go to Saul (Acts 9:10-16). Second, Ananias went to Saul and gave him this message: "The Lord Jesus, who appeared to you on your way here, has sent me so that you may regain your sight and be filled with the Holy Spirit" (Acts 9:17). In short, the reception of a divine word of instruction by means of a vision and the conveyance of this message to Paul are clearly indicative of prophetic activity consistent with OT precedent. The OT prophet *(nābî)* had originally been called a seer *(rō'eh)* precisely because of the significant role visions and dreams often played in prophetic activity (1 Sam 9:9).

Shortly after Saul's conversion, Barnabas went to Tarsus to meet Saul and to take him to Antioch in

Syria (Acts 11:22-26). Upon their arrival in Antioch, Barnabas and Saul began a ministry which lasted over a year. It was during this period that a group, or guild, of prophets, including one named Agabus, first came upon the scene. They had traveled from Jerusalem* to Antioch,* where Agabus "foretold [esēmanen] by the Spirit" that a great famine would soon engulf the world (Acts 11:27-28). The response of this congregation to Agabus's revelation was quick and tangible. They took an offering designated for the relief of Christians living in Judea, and they empowered Barnabas and Saul to convey the offering to the elders of Judea (Acts 11:29-30).

The Agabus story marks the first explicit occasion in which Saul came into personal contact with a Christian prophet. The prophetic act was predictive in its content, and the writer of Luke-Acts indicates that this prediction was fulfilled while Claudius was emperor (Acts 11:28; see Chronology). The themes of prophecy and fulfillment were deeply rooted in the religious life of Israel,* and the expectation that prophetic oracles, including predictive prophecies, should be tested was an injunction affirmed by the Mosaic Law (Deut 18:21-22). The action of this congregation at Antioch is unexplainable apart from certain testing which must have gone on once the prediction was made. The text is silent on who tested, interpreted or applied the oracle, or what tests were imposed to determine the genuine character of the oracle, but Paul's role in conveying the offering to Judea is sufficient evidence of his acceptance of Agabus's prediction as a genuine prophetic word. Barnabas* and Saul, having traveled to Jerusalem and delivered the offering, returned to Antioch and resumed their role in a Christian community in which both prophets and teachers were present (Acts 13:1). The writer of Acts notes that it was in the context of worship that the Holy Spirit indicated that Barnabas and Saul should be singled out for a specific ministry to which they had been called (Acts 13:2-3).

It is very likely that the Holy Spirit spoke through one of the prophets who was present at the time. While the text does not indicate clearly that this is what happened or that testing was undertaken, the presence of these prophets and the time of prayer and fasting suggests that this was a period in which the validity of this call could be and was tested. Once again, the fact that Barnabas and Saul acceded to the request, and that others laid hands upon them and sent them out, suggests that Saul understood this word of personal guidance to be a genuine oracle of the Holy Spirit.

A third incident in Luke-Acts is recorded in Acts 21:8-14. This incident takes place about a decade later than that mentioned in Acts 11. Once again Agabus appears upon the scene. Paul was on an extended journey to Jerusalem which eventually took him through Caesarea, where he found lodging with Philip the evangelist (Acts 21:8). Philip's four unmarried daughters were all known to prophesy (Acts 21:9). While Paul was visiting with these believers in Caesarea, Agabus came with a message for Paul regarding his intention to travel to Jerusalem. Agabus predicted that the Jews in Jerusalem would bind Paul and hand him over to the Gentiles* (Acts 21:11).

In this incident, the prophetic word was interpreted differently by Paul than it was by those who were accompanying him. Those who were with Paul understood this prediction to be a warning intended to serve a prescriptive purpose: "Do not go." As a result, they begged Paul to terminate his trip. Paul, on the other hand, viewed this oracle as informative or *predictive*, not as *prescriptive*: "Go, but know that you will not return." Ultimately, Paul's resolve to continue his journey to Jerusalem was acknowledged, and the believers prayed that the Lord's will would be done (Acts 21:14).

Some have argued from this passage that Paul resisted God's prescriptive warning and as a result paid the ultimate consequence in his capture and death. In support of this position they cite Acts 21:4, which states that at Tyre, certain Christians had told Paul explicitly, "through the Spirit," not to go to Jerusalem. Others, however, argue that Paul was not disobedient because he had been "bound in the Spirit" (Acts 20:22) to go to Jerusalem. Furthermore, in Acts 20:23 Paul acknowledged that as he advanced on his itinerary* to Jerusalem, the Holy Spirit in every city he visited had testified that he would undergo imprisonment and afflictions upon his arrival in Jerusalem. They argue that the apparent prohibition in Acts 21:4 should be understood as a mixture of genuine prophetic prediction and of mistaken interpretation, but that the mistake lies not with Paul, but with Paul's friends. In either case, it is clear from the Acts account that Paul had firsthand contact with Christian prophets over an extended period of time and that he took their ministries seriously.

*2.2. Prophecy in the Pauline Corpus.* Paul wrote of his own encounter with prophets, and for the purposes of this and subsequent discussions, Ephesians* and the Pastorals* are included under this heading. While incidents behind the letters are less graphic than are those found in Acts, they are no less informative. Paul, after all, had been in the company of prophets in Antioch, in Caesarea and presumably elsewhere. Paul understood prophets to be gifts which God had placed (*etheto*, 1 Cor 12:28) in or bestowed (*edōken*, Eph 4:11) upon the church, and that they had an ongoing ministry* to perform.

The language Paul adopts when he refers to prophets and prophesying is occasionally ambiguous. As a consequence, some scholars have concluded that while Paul maintained in theory that all Christians had the potential to prophesy, a goal toward which Paul seemingly exhorted all the Corinthians to move, in reality only a limited number of individuals ever did so, and these few occupied the *office* of prophet. Paul himself *never* uses the term *office* to describe the position of the prophet, but seems rather easily to alternate between using the noun for "prophet" (*ho prophētēs*) and a substantive participle, "the one who prophesies" (*ho prophēteuōn*). This suggests a fluidity during this period in which a variety of individuals, including both women (1 Cor 11:5) and men (1 Cor 11:4; *see* Man and Woman), or even groups such as elders (1 Tim 4:4), were prepared to speak on behalf of God under the inspiration of the Holy Spirit. While within particular congregational settings some may have prophesied more frequently than others, Paul was aware of a wide range of such persons. Clearly, some seem to have been identified with their local congregations (1 Cor 14:29) while others appear to have engaged in a more itinerant form of ministry (e.g., Agabus).

One particular incident involving prophetic activity is described repeatedly in 1 and 2 Timothy. According to Acts 16:1-3, while staying in the city of Lystra, Paul met Timothy and asked this young believer to accompany him as he ministered throughout Asia Minor. Acts notes that the believers in Lystra and the neighboring town of Iconium "spoke well" of Timothy. It is likely that the description of Timothy's commission to the ministry is to be understood precisely in this context.

In 1 Timothy 1:18 a series of instructions are given to Timothy in keeping with the prophecies (*prophēteiai*) which had previously been made regarding him. The occasion during which these prophecies had been made appears to have been a meeting or council of elders or presbyters (*see* Church Order and Government). On this occasion one or more of them had laid hands upon Timothy (1 Tim 4:14). The result of this laying on of hands and the utterance of a prophetic oracle apparently can be linked to a divine call and the bestowal upon Timothy of a gift (*charisma*) of ministry. If this incident occurred in Lystra, as is likely, then Paul was present at the time. The statement in Acts 16:2 that the believers spoke well of Timothy may be Luke's way of describing the call and

gifting of Timothy. Paul's presence at that event would also lend authority to Paul's repeated appeal for Timothy to remember this prophetic event (1 Tim 1:18; 4:14; 2 Tim 1:6-7).

Paul himself was no stranger to the phenomena frequently linked to prophetic activity. Acts tells us that he was the recipient of visions* (Acts 9:12; 16:9; 18:9) and trances (Acts 22:17) and that he was privy to angelic* appearances (Acts 27:23-25). In his letters he claims to have received revelations (2 Cor 12:1, 7; Gal 1:12) through the Spirit (1 Cor 2:10). Occasionally he speaks of a "command" (*entolē*) of the Lord (1 Cor 14:37) or a "word" (*logos*) of the Lord (1 Thess 4:15), and he views himself as one who had been called to pass on the meaning of what had previously been "hidden" or "mysterious" but which was now to be revealed and declared (1 Cor 4:1; 15:15; Eph 3:3-4; 5:32; 6:19; Col 4:3). Furthermore, Paul claimed to know of a man, in all likelihood himself, who was "caught up into Paradise" (2 Cor 12:4; *see* Heaven, Heavenlies, Paradise), where he heard unspeakable things. Acts portrays Paul as one "full of the Holy Spirit" (Acts 13:9) and as "bound in the Spirit" (Acts 20:22), and in 1 Corinthians Paul claims to "have the Spirit of God" (1 Cor 7:40) in the sense that he believed his reflections to be totally in line with those of God. In short, the evidence from Acts and the letters is that Paul was clearly at home with a range of prophetic phenomena, and as such his teaching on the subject reflects his own experience.

### 3. Paul's Reflections on Prophecy.

*3.1. Prophecy as Charism.* In two Pauline passages, 1 Corinthians 12—14 and Romans 12, the subjects of prophets and prophesying occur in conjunction with a uniquely Pauline term, *charisma* and its plural *charismata*. Outside the Pauline corpus this term occurs only in 1 Peter 4:10, and then with a distinctively Pauline flavor given to it. Rooted in the Greek term for "grace"* (*charis*), *charisma* suggests the "result or manifestation of divine grace" or "a special gift bestowed by the grace of God." A second concept which is shared by these two passages in which the gift of prophecy is mentioned is the metaphor frequently chosen by Paul to describe the nature of the church*: the body of Christ (*see* Body of Christ).

While the term *charisma* is absent from Ephesians 4, it also refers to prophets (Eph 4:11) and embraces the metaphor of the church as the body of Christ (Eph 4:12-16). Furthermore, Ephesians 4:11 notes that Christ "gave" (*edōken*) this "gift" (*dōrea*, Eph 4:7) as one of several to the church. It is likely, then, that in Ephesians 4 the terms *dōrea* and *doma* ("gift" Eph 4:8; cf.

LXX Ps 67[68]:19) serve as synonyms for *charismata*. In any event, the Pauline corpus is consistent in its attribution of the gift of prophecy to the grace of God. The consistent metaphorical portrayal of the church as the body of Christ in conjunction with the gift of prophecy suggests that the interrelationship between the various parts of the body working together in their unity and diversity is the locus in which this grace is most richly manifested.

It is clear from Paul's Corinthian* correspondence that the emphasis of many of the Corinthians was upon diversity at the expense of unity. Their emphasis was upon the ability to speak in tongues regardless of how this activity affected the rest of the community. Their undue emphasis upon speaking in tongues* as the manifestation of the so-called *pneumatika* ("spiritual gifts," 1 Cor 12:1) was misguided. The Corinthians mistakenly understood this to be a sign of Spirit possession and, by extension, of their own spirituality.* Their insistence that such activity need have no communal value for the church was also misinformed. By changing the focus of the discussion from *pneumatika* to *charismata* (cf. 1 Cor 12:1, 4), Paul underscored the fact that the various manifestations of the Spirit were gracious gifts of God and was thus able to recommend some concrete guidelines for their use within the Christian community. In short, he removed these manifestations of the Spirit, including prophecy, from a context of selfish and prideful individualism and set them in a context of community, accountability, mutual development, good order, intelligible worship* and ministry on behalf of others.

The charism of prophecy, then, becomes much more beneficial as a manifestation of the Holy Spirit within the community than does the ability to speak in tongues, except when the tongue is interpreted (1 Cor 14:5), precisely because it builds up the body. It is a gift that is bestowed "for the common good" (1 Cor 12:7 RSV). As a manifestation of God's grace, the ability to prophesy may be used for the "upbuilding and encouragement and consolation" (1 Cor 14:3 NRSV) of others.

For Paul the church is preeminently a charismatic community (Dunn). Prophecy as a manifestation of God's abiding, sustaining and operative grace must, therefore, be viewed as having corporate or community dimensions. Prophecies are intended to be shared with the community. Failure to do so is tantamount to quenching the Spirit (1 Thess 5:19), to manipulating individuals or, for that matter, the entire congregation (1 Cor 14:36-38; cf. *Shepherd of Hermas* Mandate 11). It is the sharing of the Holy Spirit by each member of the Christian community that creates the *koinōnia*, "fellowship," or participation in the lives of one another. This participation defines the charismatic community over against the world. The community, then, becomes the primary place where the Spirit-inspired speech of prophecy is intended to be given, for the good of the community (1 Cor 12:7; 14:4-5).

*3.2. Prophecy as a Community Phenomenon.* The prophet appears to have stood second only to the apostle if the Pauline order is to be taken seriously (1 Cor 12:28; Eph 4:11; 2:20). Paul's instructions to the Corinthians clearly demonstrate that he viewed prophecy as providing a major corrective to an otherwise dysfunctional appeal to tongues (1 Cor 14:5). Prophecy was a gift whose pursuit Paul encouraged and whose exercise was intended to be governed by the principle of love* (1 Cor 14:1). In spite of its significance, Paul was equally clear that it had its limitations. It was at best both partial and temporary (1 Cor 13:8-9), but nonetheless Paul extolled its value. It could edify, encourage and console (1 Cor 14:3); it could communicate a message directly understandable by all (1 Cor. 14:5), including a message of reproof or accountability (1 Cor 14:24). Its very exercise might be all that was sufficient for an outsider to recognize the presence of God in the midst of the Christian community (1 Cor 14:25). It acted as a sign of God's presence and of eschatological reality that the new age was inaugurated.

In order for such a gift to function properly, then, Paul established certain guidelines for its usage within the Christian community. Edification must play a central role (1 Cor 14:26). On occasion several persons might have a prophetic word to deliver at a single gathering, but order must reign (1 Cor 14:32-33). This order, consistent with the nature of the giver of the gift, might be maintained by limiting the number of individuals who would be allowed to prophesy (1 Cor 14:29). Or those intending to speak might exercise self-control (1 Cor 14:32), even to the point of deferring to another individual who, while sitting in their presence, receives what appears to be a spontaneous revelation (1 Cor 14:30). Like all other charisms, the presence of the prophetic gift is neither to be despised, thereby quenching the Spirit (1 Thess 5:19-20), nor accepted without question (1 Cor 14:29; 1 Thess 5:20-22), nor allowed to dominate the body of Christ at the expense of other charismatic manifestations (1 Cor 14:25-31) and in violation of the Lord's* command (1 Cor 14:37-38). Within the body of Christ prophecy might play an important role, but God had given other gifts as well and these deserved adequate time for expression.

*3.3. Prophecy, Revelation and Mystery.* A significant

amount of discussion in recent years concerns the relationship between prophecy and apocalyptic. Attention has been focused primarily on the role which apocalyptic played as a successor to prophetic activity, particularly during the intertestamental period. In the NT attention has regularly been directed to John's Revelation which claims both to be "the revelation [apokalypsis] of Jesus Christ" (Rev 1:1) and "the words of the prophecy [tous logous tēs prophēteias]" (Rev 1:3). That a NT writer saw a relationship between revelation and prophecy, then, is fairly clear. The nature of apocalyptic* as a genre and the nature of both mystery and revelation as part of that larger genre, as well as the relationship between the apocalyptic and prophetic genres, have been the primary focus of the discussion.

In the Pauline corpus the verb apokalyptō, "to reveal," appears thirteen times and the noun apokalypsis, "revelation," occurs ten times. In several instances it is used to speak of the divine eschatological disclosure of the presently operative righteousness (Rom 1:17) or wrath* (Rom 1:18) of God, or the future glory* (Rom 8:18). In other words, the term suggests something eschatological* in nature that is being or will be made known. Within the context of prophetic discussion, however, these terms appear to have a more specific nuance, one which may form the basis of the content to be revealed.

In Paul's most explicit treatment of prophecy, he employs this group of words, "prophecy/revelation," three times. In 1 Corinthians 14:6 he asks, "How will I benefit you unless I speak to you in some revelation or knowledge or prophecy or teaching?" (NRSV) This statement appears to form a chiasmus, which, if it does, connects revelation with prophecy and knowledge* with teaching. In 1 Corinthians 14:26 the word apokalypsis occurs, and prophesying is left unmentioned. Still, within the immediate context other forms of inspired speech, such as a "tongue" or "interpretation," are mentioned, as is the designation "teaching."* Again, in 1 Corinthians 14:30-31 Paul clearly links together prophecy and revelation by mentioning revelation in the midst of his very specific discussion of prophecy. Prophecy, it appears, comes by way of revelation. The revelation when spoken forms the basis of the prophecy. And both revelation (1 Cor 2:10) and prophecy (1 Cor 12:8) come by means of the Holy Spirit (dia tou pneumatos).

Of equal importance is Paul's linkage of these terms to the idea of "mystery."* Paul understood himself to be a steward of God's mysteries (1 Cor 4:1), but he was not alone. He suggests that those who possess prophetic abilities and who understand all mysteries and knowledge (as though they might be the same person) but do not possess love are of no account (1 Cor 13:2). The concept of mystery for Paul is not something that remains hidden or secret, but something that is made known or revealed (Eph 1:9; 3:3). In Romans 16:25-26, then, he notes that the very gospel of Jesus Christ which he preaches was formerly a "mystery," but it is now "disclosed," or "revealed," through the "prophetic writings."

### 4. The Limits of Prophecy.

*4.1. The Sovereignty of the Spirit's Distribution.* In a sense, Paul viewed the prophetic gift as unlimited. If the Holy Spirit who distributed such gifts were present in all who believe (Rom 8:9), then theoretically all who believe should have the potential to prophesy. The Pauline wish that the Corinthians might earnestly desire the ability to prophesy (1 Cor 14:1) is by no means, then, a vapid rhetorical wish. It was a genuine possibility which stood in continuity with Moses' prayer that all of God's people might be prophets (Num 11:29), with Joel's prediction that the Lord's Spirit would be poured out on all persons, thereby enabling the sons and daughters of Israel to prophesy (Joel 2:28 [= MT 3:1]), and with Peter's identification of the Pentecost event (Acts 2:14-18) as the fulfillment of that for which Moses had longed and which Joel had predicted.

The limits of prophecy, however, were fixed not so much by possibility as by reality. In one sense the appearance of the prophetic gift, like all other gifts, was dependent upon the sovereign distribution of the gift by the Spirit of God (1 Cor 12:11). It was, after all, only one manifestation within the body of Christ. But it may also have been limited by the faith to receive and to act upon the inspiration which the Holy Spirit manifested (Rom 12:6). Paul is clear that there is no limitation of this gift on the basis of gender. Both men and women might prophesy (1 Cor 11:4-5), but they needed to be people whom the Spirit inspired to speak and people who chose to obey the Spirit's promptings.

To be sure, Paul viewed prophecy as providing a valuable corrective to the abuses of the Corinthian congregation. Its primary value was not so much individual as communal. It was intended to build up the community (1 Cor 14:3-5). Still, this gift was not the only gift granted to the church. Indeed, like all other gifts it was an imperfect one (1 Cor 13:9) with temporal limitations. And it needed to be exercised with restraint. Diversity within the one body of Christ anticipated that. The Holy Spirit distributed not only the prophetic gift but others as well. Paul recommended, therefore, that when the community gathered, only two or three prophetic utterances be given. Such a limitation would allow other individuals with other gifts adequate space to minister to the body (1 Cor 14:26). It would also make possible sufficient time for the various prophetic words to be given and to undergo the scrutiny of others (1 Cor 14:29).

But who are the "others" to whom Paul made reference here? Many have suggested that Paul envisioned a group of "prophets" who might weigh or test the oracle, but it is more likely that Paul saw a role for the entire congregation in this regard. Paul's injunction in 1 Thessalonians 5:20-21 that prophecy should not be despised but tested is not limited to a group of testing "prophets." It appears to be a congregational mandate. Regardless of who engaged in the discernment process, the important issue seems to have been that all claims to prophetic inspiration be limited to those who have been appropriately reviewed and accepted by the larger body.

*4.2. Prophecy and the Need for Discernment.* In every age there have been those who claim to have prophetic inspiration. Some claims may be true, while others are not. In Paul's day there were those who were designated as false prophets, such as Bar Jesus or Elymas (Acts 13:6, 8). There were also those such as the young slave girl at Philippi who had a spirit of divination and was engaged in soothsaying (Acts 16:16), an activity which had been condemned in the strongest of terms in the OT (Deut 18:10-12). Jesus had warned even his disciples that there would eventually arise false prophets who were actually wolves in sheep's clothing (Mt 7:15-20). It should come as no surprise, then, that Paul, who wrote about the gift of prophesying, should also address himself to the subject of verification. Prophetic claims, after all, are easily made. Besides, genuine prophetic activity demands a response. It is important, therefore, to see that those who anticipate genuine prophetic activity in their midst are granted the necessary tools to distinguish between genuine and illegitimate prophetic claims.

Paul's approach to this was twofold. On the one hand he spoke of another gift, the discerning of spirits (*diakriseis pneumatōn*, 1 Cor 12:10), which had been given to the body of Christ. In a sense, this gift should be viewed as a partner gift to the gift of prophecy. It too is a gift which is sovereignly bestowed upon certain individuals according to the will of the Spirit. It appears to be an ability to identify the source of the prophetic utterance, but that ability may also include the weighing of prophetic content. Paul himself may have exercised this gift when, "filled with the Holy Spirit," he identified the true character of Elymas the sorcerer (Acts 13:6-11). Similarly, he may have em-

ployed this gift at Philippi when he addressed the young woman with the spirit of divination (Acts 16:16-18). On the other hand, Paul provided some practical advice which could enable the body of Christ to distinguish true from false prophecy. Since the gift of prophecy was a charism bestowed upon the church, it is natural to begin the discernment by knowing who it is that makes prophetic claims. Genuine prophecy is more likely to be given by members of the body of Christ, that is, by members of the Christian community rather than by those outside. As members of the community, those who prophesy will also exhibit certain characteristics, or fruit of the Spirit (Gal 5:22-23), a test also found in *Didache* 11—13.

Paul was concerned to stop certain behavior at Corinth, including unquestioned prophetic claims which could lead to an abuse of power. The gifts of God must reflect the nature and character of God, bringing peace* rather than confusion (1 Cor 14:33) in a manner which is decent and orderly (1 Cor 14:40). In the case of the gift of prophecy, order includes the willingness of the person who prophesies to allow his or her utterance to undergo the scrutiny of others (1 Cor 14:29). Paul referred to this as a "command" of the Lord (1 Cor 14:37).

Associated with the requirement of order is Paul's clear understanding that a genuine prophet had a distinct prophetic consciousness. Unlike some who might claim the loss of their identity swallowed up in ecstasy, Paul viewed the genuine, gifted Christian prophet as one in full control of himself or herself. "The spirits of prophets are subject to prophets," Paul maintained (1 Cor 14:38). There was no excuse for unrestrained behavior or uncontrolled speech. There was no reason to accept the argument that the Spirit who had inspired the prophet had simply overwhelmed the prophet, robbing him or her of self-control or of his or her identity. Prophetic activity which reflected the character of God would be decent and orderly, and it would attract the notice of the unbeliever, drawing their attention not to the prophetic individual, but to the God who granted the gift (1 Cor 14:24-25).

The realization that prophetic activity was ultimately under the control of those who prophesied meant that this particular work of the Holy Spirit could also be quenched. Paul's instruction to the church at Thessalonica that they not quench the Spirit nor despise prophesying suggests that some Christians would rather deny a place to continuing or spontaneous prophecy than deal with the problems it might potentially raise (1 Thess 5:19-22). Paul's advice was to hear it out, then make a decision or test it *(dokimazete)*, accepting what was valuable while discarding the rest. The assessment of prophetic content was also an important aspect of weighing the prophecy. Paul is clear that a primary purpose for prophecy is to edify or build up the body of Christ. But it is also for the encouragement and consolation of the body (1 Cor 14:3-5). Elsewhere in Scripture prophecy might even be understood as a means of calling others to account (cf. 2 Sam 12:1-15) or of disclosing the secrets of an individual heart (cf. Jn 3:16-19).

The Thessalonian congregation may have been troubled by prophetic claims which robbed them of hope or otherwise confused them. Paul wrote to them that they were not to let certain individuals, whether by Spirit *(dia pneumatos)* or by word *(dia logou),* trouble them with the claim that the Day of the Lord had already come (2 Thess 2:2; *see* Eschatology). These phrases suggest some prophetic activity or claim to prophetic inspiration in which a message had already been given within the Thessalonian context. The fact is that when he was with them Paul had already spoken to the Thessalonian Christians regarding the coming of the Lord (2 Thess 2:5). And in 1 Thessalonians 4:15 he refers to a "word of the Lord" *(logos kyriou)* that when the Lord returned those who had died in Christ would be raised first, then those who were yet alive would be caught up in the clouds together with those who had died in Christ, in order to be with the Lord forever (1 Thess 4:15-17). Paul's use of the designation "word of the Lord," a phrase used repeatedly in the OT to describe prophetic activity (e.g., Jer 1:2; Ezek 1:3; Hos 1:1; 4:1; Joel 1:1, etc.), and his exhortation to the Thessalonians to encourage, or comfort *(parakaleō),* one another with these words, an explicit function of prophecy articulated in 1 Corinthians 14:3, suggest that this passage possesses a prophetic character (Dunn). To say all of this, however, is merely to build a case by which 1 Thessalonians 4:15-17 may be understood as an actual prophetic oracle cited by Paul within his larger argument which seeks to allay the fears of the Thessalonian Christians.

Other interpretations of this passage are possible however. D. Hill, for example, has pointed out that the phrase "word of the Lord" need not be understood as a reference either to a revelatory word made known by the Spirit or a logion of the risen Lord. It may be a simple reference to an otherwise unknown saying of Jesus, or even a generic reference to the apocalyptic teaching of Jesus (cf. Wenham; *see* Jesus, Sayings of).

Regardless of the interpretation one adopts for 1 Thessalonians 4:15-17, Paul's concern is clear. There are limits to the genuine expression of prophetic activity, and these limits can and must be discerned by the community of the faithful who are both gifted and capable of doing their part. For the community to fail to discern the voice of the Lord, or for the so-called prophet to refuse the community its role in the discerning process is for the gift and its purpose to be thwarted.

## 5. Appeals to Paul in Contemporary Claims to Prophecy.

During the twentieth century the rise of Pentecostalism and the charismatic renewal movement has raised new questions regarding the gift of prophecy. The Reformers, Luther and Calvin, limited the spontaneous character of prophecy by defining this gift as the proper exposition of the Scriptures, hence, they popularized the idea of prophecy as preaching. During this century Benjamin B. Warfield's well-known "cessation theory" and Dispensationalist arguments, based upon a reading of 1 Corinthians 13:8-10 which suggests that the "perfect" has come in the form of Scripture, thereby ending the need for any continuing form of revelation, has led many to argue that if genuine prophecy exists at all today, it can only be understood as the exposition of a previously existing authoritative text, namely, Scripture.

If prophecy is viewed as revelatory in nature, or as in any way providing for new revelation, regardless of content, it is said to conflict with the role of Scripture as the canon by which all Christian life and thought is to be judged. Any hint of the possibility of new revelation is thought to make Scripture less authoritative than Protestants claimed in the Reformation cry of *sola Scriptura,* and makes possible the arguments or claims for subsequent "scriptures" such as the *Book of Mormon* (so Chantry).

Pentecostals and those Christians who align themselves with the charismatic movement tend to share some of these same ideas and concerns but differ on some of them as well. The exposition of Scripture in teaching and preaching, when undertaken with the Holy Spirit as one's guide, seems to parallel Paul's understanding of prophecy as the revelation of the mystery of God now made known (Eph 1:9; 3:3; Rom 16:25-26), although Dunn is probably correct in identifying this as inspired proclamation, a charismatic form of preaching, but not as prophecy per se. While some prefer to view the Spirit's role in prophetic preaching as limited to sermon preparation, others view it as something done with spontaneity, including a sudden illumination or application of the text made clear by the Holy Spirit during the act of preaching or teaching. Pentecostals and members of the charismatic renewal, however, are less concerned by the possibility that the value of Scripture in some way will be subverted by spontaneous oracles. On the whole they value the place of the spontaneous oracle alongside preaching as a genuine manifestation of prophecy which continues to appear within the contemporary church (cf. Yocum, Grudem, Cullmann). Such utterances are believed to play a role that may be both revelatory and authoritative, but these believers take their cue from Paul by emphasizing the need for discernment by the community of faith (1 Cor 14:29-33; 1 Thess 5:19-22).

At least three concerns continue to exist. First, such oracles appear to have limited value for specific people at a specific time and in a specific place. These utterances are not understood to possess the same universal authority of Scripture. They are a form of inspired speech which "ceases when the words cease" (Dunn). Second, these oracles are assessed according to the Pauline guidelines found in 1 Corinthians 12—14, Ephesians 4, Romans 12 and 1 Thessalonians 5. Because these oracles are scrutinized in the light of Scripture as it is understood by the believing community, the oracles are understood to be subservient to Scripture, which provides the norm by which all prophetic activity is to be assessed. Third, the purpose or purposes of such spontaneous oracles must be consistent with the God who reveals them; that is, they must be given in a decent, orderly and edifying manner. Prophetic claims that do not meet these criteria are disregarded. In the end, then, prophetic activity within the modern Pentecostal and charismatic movements functions at its best when it is submitted to the guidance of Scripture and follows the limitations and guidelines expressed by Paul.

*See also* APOCALYPTICISM; BODY OF CHRIST; GIFTS OF THE SPIRIT; HOLY SPIRIT; KNOWLEDGE, GIFT OF KNOWLEDGE; MYSTERY; MYSTICISM; PROPHET, PAUL AS; TONGUES; VISIONS, ECSTATIC EXPERIENCE.

BIBLIOGRAPHY. D. E. Aune, *Prophecy in Early Christianity and the Ancient Mediterranean World* (Grand Rapids: Eerdmans, 1983); E. M. Boring, *Sayings of the Risen Christ: Christian Prophecy in the Synoptic Tradition* (SNTSMS 46; Cambridge: University Press, 1982); idem, *The Continuing Voice of Jesus: Christian Prophecy and the Gospel Tradition* (Louisville: John Knox, 1991); W. Chantry, *Signs of the Apostles* (2d ed; Edinburgh: The Banner of Truth Trust, 1976); T. M. Crone, *Early Christian Prophecy: A Study of Its Origin and Function* (Baltimore: St. Mary's University, 1973); O. Cullmann, *Early Christian Worship* (London: SCM, 1953); G. Dautzenberg, *Urchristliche Prophetie* (Stuttgart: W. Kohlhammer, 1975); J. D. G. Dunn, *Jesus and the Spirit* (Philadelphia: Westminster, 1975); E. E. Ellis, *Prophecy and Hermeneutic in Early Christianity* (Grand Rapids: Eerdmans, 1978); D. Gee, *Concerning Spiritual Gifts* (rev. ed.; Springfield, MO: Gospel Publishing House, 1980); W. A. Grudem, *The Gift of Prophecy in 1 Corinthians* (Washington, D.C.: University Press of America, 1982); idem, *The Gift of Prophecy in the New Testament and Today* (Westchester, IL: Crossway Books, 1988); H. A. Guy, *New Testament Prophecy: Its Origin and Significance* (London: Epworth, 1947); A. J. Heschel, *The Prophets* (2 vols.; New York: Harper & Row, 1962); C. Hill, *Prophecy Past and Present: An Exploration of the Prophetic Ministry in the Bible and the Church Today* (Ann Arbor: Servant, 1989); D. Hill, *New Testament Prophecy* (Atlanta: John Knox, 1979); G. Houston, *Prophecy: A Gift for Today?* (Downers Grove, IL: InterVarsity, 1989); E. C. Huber, *Women and the Authority of Inspiration* (Lanham, MD: University Press of America, 1985); J. Lindblom, *Prophecy in Ancient Israel* (Philadelphia: Muhlenberg, 1973); U. B. Müller, *Prophetie und Predigt im Neuen Testament* (SNT 10; Gütersloh: Gerd Mohn, 1975); J. Panagopoulos, Ἡ Ἐκκλησία τῶν προφητῶν: Τὸ προφητικόν χάρισμα ἐν τῇ ἐκκλησίᾳ τῶν δύο πρώτων αἰώνων (Athens: Historical Publications, 1979); idem, *Prophetic Vocation in the New Testament Today* (NovTSup 45; Leiden: E. J. Brill, 1977); J. R. Pridie, *The Spiritual Gifts* (1921); C. M. Robeck, Jr., "Canon, *Regulae Fidei*, and Continuing Revelation in the Early Church," in *Church, Word and Spirit*, ed. J. E. Bradley and R. A. Muller (Grand Rapids: Eerdmans, 1987) 65-91; idem, "The Gift of Prophecy in Acts and Paul, Parts I & II," in *StBT* 5 (1975) [5.1] 15-38; [5.2] 37-54; F. Rousseau, *L' Apocalypse et le Milieu Prophétique du Nouveau Testament* (Tournai: Desclée & Cie, 1971); C. Rowland, *The Open Heaven: A Study of Apocalyptic in Judaism and Early Christianity* (New York: Crossroad, 1982); D. Wenham, "Paul and the Synoptic Apocalypse," in *Gospel Perspectives 2: Studies of History and Tradition in the Four Gospels* (Sheffield: JSOT, 1981) 345-75; A. C. Wire, *The Corinthian Women Prophets: A Reconstruction Through Paul's Rhetoric* (Minneapolis: Fortress, 1990); B. Yocum, *Prophecy: Exercising the Prophetic Gifts of the Spirit in the Church Today* (Ann Arbor: Word of Life, 1976).

C. M. Robeck, Jr.

## PROPHET, PAUL AS

Although nowhere in the NT is Paul ever explicitly called a prophet, scholars have nevertheless compared the apostle to the OT prophets. It has been observed that not only has Paul adopted some of the vocabulary of the prophetic call and ministry,* he has also adopted the hermeneutical principles employed by the prophets of the OT. It is likely, then, that in some sense Paul understood his apostleship in terms of the OT prophetic tradition.

1. Relationship between Apostle and Prophet
2. Prophetic Call
3. Prophetic Gospel
4. Prophetic Comparison
5. Prophetic Criticism

### 1. Relationship Between Apostle and Prophet.

Recent research has rightly recognized the close relationship between apostle* and prophet (Agnew, 90-96; Sandnes, 17-20). By definition, prophets are those who have been "sent" (Heb *šālaḥ*; Gk *apostellō*) by Yahweh. Isaiah, Jeremiah and Ezekiel are "sent" by God to the people of Israel (Is 6:8; Jer 1:7; Ezek 2:3). Throughout Israel's history God has sent his "servants the prophets to them" (Jer 7:25). Malachi prophesies that God will "send [his] messenger" (Mal 3:1) and "will send Elijah the prophet" (Mal 4:5). Similar language is employed in the NT, in reference both to OT prophets and to Jesus' disciples/apostles (Mt 23:37; Mk 1:2; Lk 9:2; 10:3; 13:34; 22:35; Jn 1:6; 3:28; Rom 10:15). In later traditions, the prophets are called "apostles" (cf. *Mek.* on Exod 12:1 [*Pisha* §1], where God says to Jonah: "I have other apostles [*šᵉlûḥîm*] like you"). The great lawgiver and prophet Moses is "sent" (Ex 3:10, 12, 13, 14, 15; 4:28; 7:16; Deut 34:11). In later Jewish and Samaritan traditions Moses is also called a *šāliaḥ* (*Mek. R. Sim. Yoh.* on Ex 3:10-11; *'Abot R. Nat.* A §1; *Exod. Rab.* 3.4 [on 3:12]; 3.14 [on 4:10]; *Memar Marqa* 5:3; 6:3).

### 2. Prophetic Call.

In Galatians Paul adopts prophetic language in describing his apostolic calling. His reference to God "who set me apart from my mother's womb and called me through his grace . . . that I might preach him among the Gentiles" (Gal 1:15-16) is clearly reminiscent of the call of Jeremiah (1:5: "Before I formed you in the womb I knew you . . . I appointed you a prophet to the Gentiles") and of the language found in Isaiah (49:1, 5: "He called my name from my mother's womb . . . to gather Jacob and Israel to him"). Even Paul's criticism of his Galatian opponents* (Gal 1:6-9: "there are some who trouble you and wish to distort the gospel of Christ . . . But even if we, or an angel from heaven, should preach to you a gospel contrary to that which we preached to you, let him be accursed") likely echoes biblical language employed against false prophets and others who would encourage God's people to worship false gods (LXX Deut 13:12-18: "And if . . . evil men in one of your cities . . . say, 'Let us go and worship others gods, . . .' you will curse it"; cf. Deut 13:1-5, 6-11; 20:17-18). Prophetic language is also

found in Paul's description before Herod Agrippa II of his Damascus Road experience (compare Acts 26:16-17 with LXX Jer 1:7-8; Ezek 2:1-3). Although the speech is a Lukan composition, the language may accurately reflect Paul's sense of a prophetic call (*see* Conversion and Call).

There is evidence, moreover, that prior to the Galatian crisis Paul understood himself as a prophet and that he did not adopt this vocabulary *ad hoc* to deal with the problem he faced in the churches of Galatia. His language in 1 Thessalonians, which is probably his earliest extant letter, suggests that Paul's prophetic self-understanding originated with his apostolic calling. His expression of sincerity (1 Thess 2:4: "even as we have been tested by God . . . to please God who tests our hearts") echoes the words of Jeremiah (LXX Jer 11:20: "Lord, who judges justly, testing the reins and the hearts . . ."). Both Paul and Jeremiah uttered these words in the face of opposition (cf. 1 Thess 2:2 with Jer 11:19). Later Paul again takes up the theme of persecution (1 Thess 3:4: "For when we were with you, we told you beforehand that we were to suffer affliction, just as it has come to pass"; cf. 2 Cor 11:23-27), which recalls the tradition of the suffering and persecuted prophet (cf. Lk 13:33-34; *Pesiq. R.* 26.2: "Jeremiah said, 'Master of the universe, I cannot prophesy to them. What prophet ever came forth to them whom they did not wish to slay?' "). Paul's eschatological warning (1 Thess 5:3: "When people say, 'There is peace and safety,' then sudden destruction will come upon them as travail comes upon a woman with child") echoes similar solemn warnings found in the OT prophets (cf. Jer 6:14, 24; 8:11, 21; 14:13-14; Ezek 13:10, 16; Hos 14:1; *see* Afflictions, Trials, Hardships).

Finally, it is important to observe that the very nature of Paul's conversion invites comparison with the prophets. Just as the prophets received revelations and visions of God and/or heaven, particularly in connection with their call to prophetic office (Is 1:1; 6:1-13; Ezek 1:1; 8:4; Obad 1; Nah 1:1; Hab 2:2), so also Paul received revelations and visions* (1 Cor 15:8; 2 Cor 12:1-4; Gal 1:12, 16; 2:2; cf. Acts 9:3-9; 22:6-11; 26:13-20).

### 3. Prophetic Gospel.

Paul's understanding of the apostolic obligation to proclaim the gospel is informed by the words of Isaiah 52:7: "And how can they preach unless they are sent? As it is written, 'How beautiful are the feet of those who preach good news' " (Rom 10:14-17; cf. Is 53:1; Dinter, 48). Moreover, when Paul says "Woe to me, if I should not preach the gospel" (1 Cor 9:16), he echoes the exclamations of the OT prophets (Is 24:16; Jer 13:27; Hos 9:12). Paul's anguish (Rom 9:2: "I have great sorrow and unceasing anguish in my heart"; Rom 11:1: "Has God rejected his people?") also is reminiscent of prophetic anguish: "Hast thou utterly rejected Judah?" (Jer 14:19; *see* Gospel).

Paul's allusion to and application of Isaiah 64:3 in 1 Corinthians 2:9 ("what eye has not seen") coheres with rabbinic discussion of the divine source of the prophetic message: "No eye has seen what God . . . will work for him who waits for him" (*b. 'Abod. Zar.* 65a). "All the prophets prophesied only for the messianic age, but in the world to come the eye has not seen, O Lord, beside you [what he has prepared for him who waits on him]" (*b. Šabb.* 63a).

### 4. Prophetic Comparison.

Despite the fact that relatively few Israelites had responded in faith to the gospel message, Paul was convinced that God* had not rejected Israel* (Rom 11:1-2). He grounds this conviction on the example of Elijah (Rom 11:3-4; cf. 1 Kings 19:10, 18) and on Isaiah's remnant theology (Rom 9:27-29; 11:5; cf. Is 1:9; 10:22). What is interesting here is Paul's comparison with Elijah. Evidently the apostle saw himself very much like Elijah of old, who felt alone and threatened. Just as God had preserved a remnant of the faithful in Elijah's time, so now in the eschatological period God once again has preserved a faithful remnant (*see* Restoration of Israel).

It is important to note too that Paul did not regard himself as an apostate from Judaism (Rom 11:1: "I myself am an Israelite, a descendant of Abraham, a member of the tribe of Benjamin"), but rather as an apostle (and prophet) to an apostate Israel, even as Elijah the prophet had been sent to an apostate Israel (*see* Jew, Paul the).

### 5. Prophetic Criticism.

Paul's application of Scripture to his own generation is similar to the hermeneutics of prophetic criticism employed by the "true" prophets of the OT (Evans 1984, 560-70). "True prophecy," as J. A. Sanders has explained (87-105), is theocentric, not ethnocentric. Unlike most of the "false prophets," who prophesied peace and safety, the true prophet understood sacred tradition and history from the divine point of view. Nowhere can this be seen more clearly than in the prophets' respective interpretations of Israel's sacred tradition. Ezekiel warns his contemporaries not to assume, as false prophets would have them believe, that since "Abraham was only one man, yet he got possession of the land, [then] we [who] are many" will surely

be able to possess the land (Ezek 33:24). Jeremiah tells his contemporaries not to listen to the false prophets who assure the inhabitants of Jerusalem that there is nothing to fear because of the presence of the Temple: "Do not trust in these deceptive words: 'This is the Temple of the Lord' " (Jer 7:4); "No evil shall come upon you" (Jer 23:17). One of the most startling examples comes from Isaiah, who alludes to two of David's great victories over the Philistines: "The Lord will rise up as on Mount Perazim [cf. 2 Sam 5:17-21], he will rage as in the valley of Gibeon [cf. 2 Sam 5:22-25]; to do his deed—strange is his deed! and to do his work—alien is his work!" (Is 28:21; Evans, 1986, 96-97). But unlike the false prophets, Isaiah does not find in these victories assurance that Israel will once again be victorious against her enemies. On the contrary, Isaiah has "heard a decree of destruction from the Lord God of hosts" (Is 28:22). God is angry and ready to defeat sinners on the field of battle; only this time the sinners are the Israelites, not their enemies (*see* Triumph).

"Paul's understanding of God's continuing activity was prophetic and dynamic. God could, as in the days of Isaiah, do a 'new thing' " (Is 43:19; Dinter, 52). The new thing that God was doing in Paul's time was to take a noncovenant people and make a people of God out of them (Rom 9:25-26; cf. Hos 1:10; 2:23; *see* Covenant). Imprecations originally uttered against Israel's enemies are applied against Israel itself: "Let their table become a snare and a trap, a pitfall and a retribution for them" (Rom 11:9-10; cf. Ps 69:22-23; Evans 1984, 567-68). This remarkable application of the sacred tradition is not anti-Jewish—for Paul is a loyal Jew (cf. Rom 9:1-5; 11:1-2)—but rather prophetic in the same sense as that which we have seen in prophets like Isaiah, Jeremiah and Ezekiel. Paul is no more anti-Jewish than were these great prophets of old. If Paul's interpretation and application of the Scripture of Israel are to be properly understood, it will be necessary to take into account the apostle's prophetic self-understanding.

*See also* APOSTLE; CONVERSION AND CALL OF PAUL; FUTILITY; GOSPEL; ISRAEL; PROPHECY, PROPHESYING; OLD TESTAMENT IN PAUL; RESTORATION OF ISRAEL; VISIONS, ECSTATIC EXPERIENCE.

BIBLIOGRAPHY. F. H. Agnew, "The Origin of the NT Apostle-Concept: A Review of Research," *JBL* 105 (1986) 75-96; P. Dinter, "Paul and the Prophet Isaiah," *BTB* 13 (1983) 48-52; C. A. Evans, "Isaiah's Use of Israel's Sacred Tradition," *BZ* 30 (1986) 92-99; idem, "Paul and the Hermeneutics of 'True Prophecy': A Study of Romans 9—11," *Bib* 65 (1984) 560-70; T. W. Gillespie, "A Pattern of Prophetic Speech in First Corinthians," *JBL* 97 (1978) 74-95; T. Holtz, "Zum Selbst-verständnis des Apostels Paulus," *TLZ* 91 (1966) cols. 321-30; J. M. Myers and E. D. Freed, "Is Paul also Among the Prophets?" *Int* 20 (1966) 40-53; J. A. Sanders, "Hermeneutics in True and False Prophecy," in *From Sacred Story to Sacred Text* (Philadelphia: Fortress, 1987) 87-105; K. O. Sandnes, *Paul—One of the Prophets? A Contribution to the Apostle's Self-Understanding* (WUNT 2.43; Tübingen: J. C. B. Mohr, 1991); J. M. Scott, "Coherence and Contingency: The Function of Scripture in 2 Corinthians 6.14—7.1," in C. A. Evans and J. A. Sanders eds., *Paul and the Scriptures of Israel* (JSNTSup 83; SSEJC 1; Sheffield: JSOT, 1993) 187-220; P. Stuhl-macher, "The Pauline Gospel," in *The Gospel and the Gospels*, ed. P. Stuhlmacher (Grand Rapids: Eerdmans, 1991) 149-72.                    C. A. Evans

## PROPHETIC PRAYER. See PRAYER.

## PROPITIATION. See DEATH OF CHRIST; EXPIATION, PROPITIATION, MERCY SEAT.

## PSEUDEPIGRAPHY. See CANON; EARLY CATHOLICISM; EPHESIANS, LETTER TO THE; PASTORAL LETTERS.

# PSYCHOLOGY

The term *psychology* is based on Greek (*psychē* ["soul"] + *logos* ["word"]) but is not Pauline. It is useful for denoting aspects of Paul's anthropology, so long as we recognize that Paul views the human being as a psychosomatic unity in whom rational, emotional and physical functions are fully integrated. We shall give our attention chiefly to Paul's use of *kardia* ("heart"), *nous* ("mind"), *pneuma* ("spirit"), *psychē* ("soul," "life"), *sarx* ("flesh") and *esō anthrōpos* ("inner person").

1. Pauline Psychology in Modern Study
2. The Person as God's Creation
3. The Person in Bondage to Sin
4. The Person Made Whole

### 1. Pauline Psychology in Modern Study.

The history of research into each of Paul's anthropological terms has been chronicled (to about 1970) by R. Jewett. The following points survey the principal issues that have occupied researchers in this field.

*1.1. Dichotomy or Trichotomy?* From the days of the Church Fathers until about 1850 this question was the main focus in discussions of Paul's anthropology: Does the person consist of two parts (body and soul) or of three (body, soul and spirit)? The Greek fathers favored the latter option, the Latin fathers the former. Through the influence of Augustine and the Protestant reformers, dichotomy became the established

view in Western theology; but the debate has continued (Berkouwer, 194-233; Hoekema, 204-10). In one version of trichotomy God inhabits the spirit ("the inner person"), releasing it from bondage to the soul ("the outer person") and the body ("the outermost person") and making them subservient to the spirit instead. Dichotomy, however, remains the dominant view. J. G. Machen, for example, affirmed that the Bible "unquestionably . . . recognizes the presence of two distinct principles or substances in man—his body and his soul" (Machen, 143); *soul* and *spirit* denote the same reality (Machen, 159-73). More recently Hoekema, however, has rejected the word *dichotomy* ("to cut in two"), arguing that "the Bible describes the human person as a totality, a whole, a unitary being" who "in this present life cannot be so cut" (Hoekema, 210).

*1.2. The Ancient Setting.* Modern scholarship has rightly insisted that Paul's anthropology be interpreted in the light of his own historical and cultural milieu.

*1.2.1. The Hellenistic Setting.* Early in this century some scholars contended that Paul was strongly influenced by non-Jewish philosophy and popular religion, ideas perhaps mediated to him through Hellenistic Judaism or the Hellenistic church (*see* Hellenism). Among the suggestions in favor of this dependence, or at least influence, are: (1) Paul's use of *sarkikos* (and *sarkinos*, "fleshly"*), *psychikos* ("physical," "natural") and *pneumatikos* ("spiritual"), and his message about the renewal of the *nous* and the saving of the *pneuma* through *gnōsis* ("knowledge"*) and *sophia* ("wisdom"*) in 1 Corinthians 2:6-16; 3:1-4; 5:5, show his alleged indebtedness to gnosticism.* (2) The Pauline theme of warfare between the *sarx* and the *pneuma* (Gal 5:16-26; Rom 8:1-17) recalls the metaphysical dualism of Plato (spirit is good, matter is evil) and has antecedents in gnosticism and the mystery religions. (3) The distinction between the "outer self" and the "inner self" (e.g., 2 Cor 4:16) may be traced to a Hellenistic anthropological dualism. Yet all these positions have been challenged.

*1.2.2. The Hebraic Setting.* The latter half of the twentieth century has seen a growing scholarly consensus: (1) that Paul antedated or opposed much of the non-Jewish teaching on which he had allegedly depended, and (2) that the decisive influences upon him (apart from Jesus and early Christianity) were the OT and Palestinian Judaism (*see* Jew, Paul the). Some of the emphases are as follows: (1) As in the OT, Paul's concern is not human nature but its relationship to God* (Jacob in Dihle et al., 630-31; Stacey, 3). (2) *Sarx* in Paul does not denote the "earthly part" of the person over against the "divine part." Instead, like

765

its OT counterpart *bāśār, sarx* signals the radical difference between God and humans, and the relationship between them: "flesh" depicts the whole person as a weak, vulnerable creature utterly dependent on God (Schweizer and Baumgärtel, 123). (3) In the vast majority of instances in Paul, *pneuma* designates not the human spirit but the Holy Spirit*—the essential source of life and power, like the OT's *rûaḥ Yahweh*. *Pneumatikos* (e.g., 1 Cor 2:15) identifies a person "who knows God's saving work by virtue of the Spirit of God" (Schweizer in Kleinknecht et al., 436). "Spiritual body" (*sōma pneumatikon*) "is to be understood, not as one which consists of *pneuma*, but as one which is controlled by the *pneuma*" (Schweizer in Kleinknecht et al., 421; cf. 1 Cor 15:44-45). (4) In Paul, as in the OT, *kardia* denotes the center of the person as a rational, emotional and volitional being (Baumgärtel and Behm 606-7; Jacob in Dihle et al., 626-28). (5) In Paul *psychē* is not the "soul," but the life or being of the whole person—as in Genesis 2:7, "man became a living being [Heb *nepeš*, LXX *psychē*]" (NKJV, as against KJV's "living soul"). *Psychikos* (1 Cor 2:14) denotes the "natural person" bereft of God's Spirit. Correspondingly, all who are in Adam* and who experience the life and mortality of present existence possess a "natural body" (*sōma psychikon*; 1 Cor 15:42-46). (6) Firmly rooted in the OT is Paul's usage of anthropological terms, starting with *anthrōpos* ("human") itself, to designate corporate solidarities (e.g., *sōma* in 1 Cor 12:12-13 and often [cf. Robinson, 49-83]; *pneuma* and *psychē* in Phil 1:27; and "old and new self" in Col 3:9-10 and Eph 4:22-24 [together with the references to Adam and Christ in Rom 5:12-21 and 1 Cor 15:21-22, 45-47]).

*1.2.3. A Twofold Indebtedness.* Recognizing the interlacing of Greek and Hebrew thought in Paul's day, and Paul's awareness of both strands, many scholars think his anthropology owes something to both.

(1) Some detect a shift within Paul's writings from a Judaic outlook to a Hellenistic perspective. In a work on Paul's anthropology published in 1872, H. Lüdemann argued that redemption in Galatians (expressive of Paul's earlier, Jewish outlook) rests upon God's juridical verdict of acquittal, whereas in Romans 5—8 (Paul's mature, Hellenistic view) redemption "was an ethical-physical transformation from 'flesh' to 'spirit' through communion with the Holy Spirit" (Ellis, 24). In an article published in 1934, C. H. Dodd argued that Paul's eschatology became less Jewish and more Hellenistic between the writing of 1 Corinthians 15 (the resurrection of a "spiritual body" at Christ's return) and 2 Corinthians 5 (the reception of "an eternal house in heaven" at death; cf. Ellis, 32).

(2) Some perceive in the letters an ongoing tension between Hebraic and Hellenistic elements. According to Bultmann, Paul opposes some of the gnostics' cherished notions (such as their depreciation of the body) but sees "so deep a cleft within man, so great a tension between self and self . . . that he comes close to Gnostic dualism" (Bultmann, 1.199). Similarly, says Bultmann, while Paul primarily uses *psychē* in the OT sense of "life" or "person," his use of the term "in a depreciatory sense" in contrast with *pneuma* betrays gnostic influence (Bultmann, 1.204).

(3) W. D. Stacey's more general thesis (Stacey, 39) is that Paul's anthropology was fundamentally Christian; that he normally used Jewish language (such as *kardia* and *sarx*) "because his Gospel sprang out of the Old Covenant"; that Hellenism sometimes offered a more adequate term (such as *nous*, "mind," or *syneidēsis*, "conscience"*); and that he was not consciously joining two cultures (Judaism and Hellenism) but seeking to express his Christian view of humanity in the best language available.

(4) R. Jewett argues that a principal reason for the presence of Hellenistic elements in the letters alongside those elements inherited from the OT and Judaism, is that Paul, for polemical purposes, frequently "borrowed anthropological terms from his conversation partners, redefining them to suit the needs of his argument" (Jewett, 447).

*1.2.4. Monism or Dualism?* Related to the preceding issue is the question whether Paul's anthropology is monistic or dualistic: do persons consist of one substance or two (see Machen under 1.1 above), or, as some prefer to put the question, are soul and body indivisible (though conceptually distinguishable) or divisible (though ideally inseparable)? Many, probably most, contemporary scholars choose the first option, some form of monism. A cosmic or eschatological or moral dualism is seen in Paul (*see* Cosmology; Eschatology), but his anthropology is said to be monistic, or basically so (any evidence of dualism is minimal and extraneous, a vestige of Greek influence; cf. the discussions in Whiteley, 32-34; Jewett, 82-95; Ridderbos, 29-32). This is the view, for instance, of Bultmann ("Man does not consist of two parts [*sōma* and *psychē*], much less of three [*sōma, psychē* and *pneuma*], 1.209) and of Stacey ("The separation of *psychē* from *sarx* means . . . extinction for Paul," Stacey, 126).

Two arguments are commonly enlisted in support of this view: (1) While some expressions of Judaism in Paul's day were dualistic owing to Greek influence (Sjöberg in Kleinknecht et al., 377; Lohse in Dihle et al., 635-37), OT anthropology, the principal source of Paul's thinking on the subject, is monistic. Jacob maintains that "older distinctions between dichotomy and trichotomy must be abandoned so far as OT anthropology is concerned. Israelite anthropology is monistic. . . . The unity of human nature is not expressed by the antithetical concepts of body and soul but by the complementary and inseparable concepts of body and life" (Jacob in Dihle et al., 631). (2) In accord with the OT's *nepeš* (see 1.2.2 above), *psychē* in Paul never denotes the higher part of the person (Paul never joins *sōma* and *psychē* together as the two parts of the whole) or a disembodied, immortal "soul" (Jewett, 334-46; Schweizer in Dihle et al., 650, 655-56; Guthrie, 165). Paul "cannot conceive even of a future human existence after death . . . as an existence without *sōma*," and "does not know the Greek-Hellenistic conception of the immortality of the soul (released from the body)" (Bultmann, 1.192, 203; cf. Ellis, 24).

That reading of Paul has been challenged by Gundry and Cooper. According to Gundry "anthropological duality," not "monadic unity," best describes Paul's view (Gundry, 79, 83): the whole person ("human," *anthrōpos*) consists of a corporeal side (for which Paul's favorite term is *sōma*, "body") and an incorporeal (whose various functions are described by *pneuma, psychē, kardia, nous, esō anthrōpos,* etc.); "there is an ontological duality, a functional pluralism, and an overarching unity" (Gundry, 84; cf. 156). Cooper's terms for Pauline and the biblical anthropology generally (Cooper, 50, 179) are "functional holism" (as opposed to "ontological holism") and "holistic dualism" (as opposed to "holistic monism").

Some of the arguments in support of this conclusion are:

(1) Like the OT, Paul represents the human being as a fully integrated whole, in which psychological and physical functions are joined inextricably together but remain ontologically distinct. Terms for a corporeal or incorporeal function (such as *sōma* or *pneuma*) may be applied by synecdoche to the whole person; but what represents the whole is not equated with the whole.

(2) In the OT and in Paul (also in most intertestamental Judaism) "persons are not merely distinguishable from their earthly bodies, they are separable from them and can continue to exist without them" (Cooper, 77); so Paul teaches in 2 Corinthians 5:1-10; Philippians 1:21-24. (For these two arguments, see Gundry, 117-56; Cooper, 36-103, 147-72.)

(3) Paul's "holistic dualism" is utterly opposed to other kinds of dualism in the ancient world (so that Gundry prefers "duality"), in which *sarx* or *sōma* is inherently evil, the human *psychē* or *pneuma* is inherently good, and salvation consists in the release of the soul from the body. Paul dreads entry into a bodiless state at death (2 Cor 5:1-5) because it is unnatural and abnormal, entailing a "cutting in two" (a "dichotomy") of what God created as a unified whole (which may explain why Paul never applies *psychē* to such an existence). That period is indeed an "intermediate state"*; ultimate salvation* awaits the reintegration of the person at the resurrection* of the body (1 Cor 15:42-58; Phil 3:20-21; see Gundry, 149-54, 159-83; Cooper, 89-103, 152-63, 173-95).

*1.3. Contemporary Thought.* These efforts to interpret Paul in the light of his own day also witness to the impact of modern currents of thought. A number of intellectual movements have shaped perceptions of Pauline psychology.

*1.3.1. Idealism.* The nineteenth-century theologian F. C. Baur, influenced by the idealism of G. W. F. Hegel, taught that the war between *sarx* and *pneuma* represented the conflict between the "finite and relative" and the "infinite and absolute" (Ridderbos, 16). Some advocates of "panpsychism" (a variety of idealistic monism according to which persons consist of just one metaphysical element—soul, mind or spirit) believe in the body's extinction but the soul's immortality (Cooper, 21 n.36; 51 n.26; 236-37).

*1.3.2. Liberalism.* H. Lüdemann and H. J. Holtzmann typify classical liberalism by explaining the conflict between flesh and spirit in terms of ethical dualism: for them *sarx* is "the outer man struggling against the inner, spiritual man" (Jewett, 52-55). "Thus 'spirit' is no longer taken . . . as the antithesis of the finite and the human (as with Baur), but as the antipode of the sensual. . . . The spirit [= *nous*] as the leading rational principle in man must gain victory over the lower sensual nature (*sarx*) and hold it in subjection" (Ridderbos, 18).

*1.3.3. Existentialism.* Bultmann argued that the Pauline conception of conflict between *sarx* and *pneuma* is far deeper than liberalism realized. In Galatians 5 and Romans 8 *pneuma* refers to God's Spirit, not human spirit (where Paul speaks of the latter, it is "not some higher principle within him or some special intellectual or spiritual faculty of his, but simply his self," 1.206); and *sarx* is not the lower, sensual part of the self but the whole self oriented toward itself and independent of God—a self-centeredness which expresses itself both in rebellion against God and in zeal for religion (Bultmann, 1.232-46; cf. Phil 3:3-6; Schweizer and Baumgärtel, 131-34). Every person must decide whether to live "according to the flesh" (a self-reliant, self-confident, worldly pursuit of one's own ends for one's own glory) or "according to the Spirit" (in which God is the center of attention and acknowledged to be the source of life and power, and Christ instead of self becomes the object of faith* and boasting*).

*1.3.4. Materialism.* In this form of monism (opposite to that of idealism, see 1.3.1 above) human beings are thought to consist solely of matter and its functions. In behaviorism and epiphenomenalism, for example, "the mind and soul are no more than the combination of . . . brain-caused states" (Cooper, 18-19).

*1.3.5. Psychology.* By "psychological exegesis" G. Theissen seeks to discover Paul's relevance to current discussions in the field of psychology. For example, as religion entails confrontation with the unconscious, it is fruitful to explore such subjects as the disclosures of the heart at the last judgment* (1 Cor 4:1-5; Rom 2:16); the elucidation of the language of the unconscious (tongues*) through interpretation and prophecy* (1 Cor 14); and Christian enlightenment (by the gospel* and the Spirit) as the means whereby matters submerged in the unconscious (Phil 3:4-6) are brought to consciousness (Rom 7:7-23; 1 Cor 2:6-16), their threats removed and their beneficent aspects enrolled in the service of Christ.

*1.3.6. Monism versus Dualism.* Neither the monism of idealism that reduces the person to soul nor the monism of materialism that reduces the person to body is compatible with Paul. Nor are those contemporary forms of dualism which encourage (1) the saving of the soul and the depreciation of the body, (2) inattentiveness to the psychosomatic unity of the person and (3) a dichotomy between grace and nature (cf. Hoekema, 222-26). At the same time "the diagnosis fusing illicit dualisms with the body-soul distinction is mistaken" (Cooper, 209, cf. 198-209).

*1.4. The Present Stance.* This section may be concluded by indicating the standpoint from which this article is written.

(1) Scholars have long debated the extent to which the letters ascribed to Paul may be used as sources of Paul's own thought. Jewett, for example, excludes Colossians,* Ephesians* and the Pastorals* from his analysis; Bultmann excludes these five and 2 Thessalonians.* The following discussion takes account of all thirteen letters. A fuller study would need to consider how the distribution and the usage of the terms relate to the question of authorship.

(2) Paul uses the anthropological terms in the awareness of both Hellenistic and Hebraic settings (his indebtedness to the latter being by far the greater), for the singular purpose of propagating the Christian gospel* and explaining salvation* in Christ (thus too Stacey, 235-41; cf. 1.2.3 above). To reflect this perspective the terms will be joined together in a topical approach. A more detailed treatment would need to ask

(i) what the distribution of terms reveals about Paul's theological and pastoral concerns, and (conversely) what light these concerns shed on the meaning of the terms (cf. Jewett); and (ii) what the chronological order of the letters discloses about developments in Paul's anthropology.

(3) Pauline psychology, like that of the Bible generally, is "practical rather than scientific" (Wright in Brown et al., 567); these letters do not teach "a theoretical anthropology or psychology" and may be called "pre-philosophical" (Cooper, 112, 180). Yet "although Scripture does not teach philosophy, it provides a normative framework for a Christian anthropology" (Cooper, 197). The view with which Pauline psychology is most compatible is "anthropological duality" or "functional holism" and "holistic dualism" (see 1.2.4 and 1.3.6 above). It will thus be necessary to give some attention to anthropological terms (notably *sōma*) treated elsewhere in this volume.

## 2. The Person as God's Creation.

A consideration of the self before the Fall will help us better to understand what Paul says about the impact of sin* and of Christ* respectively.

*2.1. The Person's Diversity in Unity.* In accord with both Hebrew and Greek antecedents, Paul views the person as both corporeal and incorporeal. His favorite word for the former is "body"* (*sōma*). He also uses "flesh"* (*sarx*) in this same sense: "always carrying around in our body [*sōma*] the death of Jesus . . . that the life of Jesus may be manifested in our mortal flesh [*sarx*]" (2 Cor 4:10-11). Being "absent in body" (1 Cor 5:3) is the same as being "absent in flesh" (Col 2:5; cf. Col 1:22, "the body of his flesh"). The "weakness of the flesh" (Gal 4:13-15) and the "thorn in the flesh" (2 Cor 12:7) describe the same (?) physical infirmities (*see* Healing, Illness).

Paul describes incorporeal activity by various terms whose meanings overlap considerably (Gundry, 156; Kümmel, 43). There is no significant difference between the apostle's presence "in spirit [*pneuma*]" (1 Cor 5:3) and his presence "in heart [*kardia*]" (1 Thess 2:17). One reasons and understands with "the mind [*nous*]" (1 Cor 14:14-16), but the heart (*kardia*) may likewise be "enlightened" (2 Cor 4:6; Eph 1:18), and "the spirit [*pneuma*] of the person" understands "the things of the person" (1 Cor 2:11; cf. Eph 4:23, "the spirit [*pneuma*] of the mind [*nous*]"). In 2 Corinthians 6:11-12 *splanchna* (NIV "affection") and *kardia* are synonymous expressions of love.* Obeying "from the heart [*kardia*]" (Rom 6:17; 1 Tim 1:5) is the same as obeying "from the soul [*psychē*]" (Eph 6:6, Col 3:23; NIV "heart") and serving "with my spirit *[pneuma]*" (Rom 1:9; NIV "whole heart"). To stand "in one spirit *[pneuma]*" is to struggle "with one soul *[psychē]*" (Phil 1:27), though Paul's concern here is not personal psychology but believers' harmony of purpose.

Paul distinguishes the incorporeal from the corporeal in several ways. He speaks of being devoted to the Lord "in body *[sōma]* and spirit *[pneuma]*" (1 Cor 7:34); of "being absent in body but present in spirit" (1 Cor 5:3), and of being separated "in person, not in heart *[kardia]*" (1 Thess 2:17 NRSV). He exhorts readers to purify themselves "from every defilement of flesh *[sarx]* and spirit *[pneuma]*" (2 Cor 7:1).

To the above we join Paul's distinction between the internal and the external. True circumcision* is not "outward" but "inward," not "in the flesh" but "of the heart" (Rom 2:28-29). Man's spirit is "in him" (1 Cor 2:11). Certain persons "boast in outward appearance and not in the heart" (2 Cor 5:12 NRSV). The corporeal dimension obviously embraces the internal as well as the external, the hidden organs as well as the visible ones. Moreover Paul describes certain incorporeal functions with terms which could also denote bodily organs—for example, the literal *kardia* (heart) or *splanchna* (variously the intestines, the liver, the kidneys, the lungs or the heart; cf. Baumgärtel and Behm, 606-11; Köster, 548-53).

In this light two points call for equal emphasis. (1) Paul never confines an incorporeal function to a particular bodily organ. In the verses cited above, *kardia* stands not for the literal heart but for "the whole of the inner being of man in contrast to his external side" (Baumgärtel and Behm, 612). In 2 Corinthians 3:3 "fleshly hearts" is no more literal than the handwriting of the Spirit. Paul's interest in *splanchna* is not physiological. This is "the most expressive term available to indicate the source of human emotion" (Silva, 55); by metonymy, Paul focuses on the emotion itself (the *splanchna* of Philem 12 may be translated "heart" or "love," BAGD). (2) Paul never dissociates the internal-incorporeal from the internal-corporeal. "An essential part of the original [i.e., literal] meaning has been retained to the degree that *splanchna* concerns and expresses the total personality at the deepest level" (Köster, 555). *Kardia* likewise stands for "the whole of the inner being" in both its corporeal and incorporeal dimensions. Thus fear, or anger or excitement causes the heart to beat rapidly.

**2.2. The Person's Unity in Diversity.** The self's diversity in unity must be kept in view as we proceed. But there is far greater emphasis in Paul's letters upon the self as an integrated whole.

In Paul the *kardia* is "the integrating center of man

as a rational, emotional, volitional being" (Dunn 1988, 100; cf. 2.1 above; Baumgartel and Behm, 612; Ladd, 475). Thus the heart may be enlightened (Eph 1:18); it may experience anguish (2 Cor 2:4); and it is from the heart that one obeys (Rom 6:17).

Paul frequently denotes the whole self by means of terms which in other contexts designate an aspect or dimension of the self. In doing so he is not contradicting the other usage, or confusing the part with the whole. Rather, by synecdoche he is viewing the whole person from a particular standpoint, or stressing the contribution of a particular aspect to the functioning of the whole.

To present "your bodies *[sōmata]* as living sacrifices" (Rom 12:1) or to offer "your members" (Rom 6:13, 19; NIV "the parts of your body") is to offer "yourselves" (Rom 6:13, 16). In Romans 12:1 *sōma* denotes "the person in his corporeality, in his concrete relationships within this world; it is because he is body that man can experience the world and relate to others" (Dunn 1988, 709; cf. Gundry, 50). Yet *sōma* is not equated with the whole person; mind and will are active in the offering of the body (Rom 12:1-2).

Similarly *sarx* may denote the whole human being or all of humanity (*see* Flesh), in certain respects—as beings who (1) are by nature creaturely, limited and weak (Rom 6:19; "flesh and blood," Gal 1:16; 1 Cor 15:50; Eph 6:12); (2) devise and adhere to certain standards ("not many wise according to the flesh," 1 Cor 1:26); (3) belong to a physical lineage (e.g., Rom 1:3; 4:1; 9:3); and (4) stand in relationship both to other human beings and to God (Philem 16, "both in the flesh and in the Lord"; Rom 3:20). In none of these passages is the *sarx* depicted as inherently sinful (but see 3 below; cf. 1.2.2 above; Thiselton, 674-75).

*Psychē* ("soul" in earlier examples) may likewise denote one's whole life or, by metonymy, the whole person. "We loved you so much that we were delighted to impart to you not only the gospel of God but our own lives *[psychai]* as well" (1 Thess 2:8). Epaphroditus "almost died for the work of Christ, risking his life *[psychē]*" (Phil 2:30): his whole earthly or natural life was in danger, not just his "soul" (see also Rom 2:9; 11:3; 13:1; 16:4; 2 Cor 1:23). Such usage is thoroughly Hebraic (Jacob in Dihle et al., 620). Like *sōma*, *psychē* designates the person from a particular point of view: "man as a thinking, working, and feeling person" (Ladd, 460); "the ego, person, or personality . . . the whole man, with all that he believes, hopes and strives for" (Harder, 683). Similarly *nous* can mean "the whole thinking man, man as a creature capable of understanding" (Guthrie, 169).

While the corporeal and the incorporeal are distinguished, the dynamic activity between them witnesses to the unity of the person. The distinction between *sōma* and *psychē* is strictly anthropological, not ethical: the body is not intrinsically evil (it is integral to God's good creation*); and the soul is not a "higher self" which is by nature protected from temptation and sin. Moreover within creation the soul, far from being destined to overrule or escape the body, fulfills its purpose precisely in relation to the body. The "life" denoted by *psychē* is a bodily existence—which helps to explain why *psychē* can be employed by synecdoche for the whole person. *Psychē* is the person's vitality "from the point of view of his body and flesh" (Ladd, 460), as with *nepeš* in the OT (see Jacob in Dihle et al., 620). "Because of their interpenetration the soul *is* the animation of the body and the body *is* the incarnation of the soul. The soul *has* a body and the body *has* a soul and man as a whole *is* both, a psycho-physical unity." (Gundry, 121).

Much the same can be said of body and spirit. Paul does not view the *pneuma* "as a divine spark (the real 'I') incarcerated in the physical, 'the ghost in the machine' " (Dunn in Kamlah et al., 694). The self which, as spirit, experiences communion with God, is a bodily being. At the very moment Paul distinguishes the *sōma* from the *pneuma*, he unites them in devotion to Christ (1 Cor 7:34). Salvation* embraces both body (1 Cor 6:12-20; 15) and spirit (1 Cor 5:5). Similarly the offering of the *sōma* entails the renewal of the *nous* (Rom 12:1-2).

Paul likewise unites the flesh (*sarx* as a synonym of *sōma*) to the spirit. Both must be purified if the person is to become holy (2 Cor 7:1). It is instructive to juxtapose two texts: "I had no rest [*anesin*] in my spirit [*pneuma*], because I did not find my brother Titus there" (2 Cor 2:13); "For when we came into Macedonia, our flesh [*sarx*] had no rest [*anesin*], but we were distressed in every way—conflicts without, fears within" (2 Cor 7:5). "Spirit" and "flesh" are not interchangeable: the turbulence "within" (*pneuma*) affects the "outside" (*sarx*); "Paul carefully chooses his terms after the pattern of an anthropological duality" (Gundry, 144). Yet he describes one experience; his anxiety over Titus and the Corinthians affects his whole being.

1 Thessalonians 5:23, with its triad "spirit [*pneuma*], soul [*psychē*] and body [*sōma*]," appears to divide the person into three parts. But Paul's intention is just the opposite: "May God . . . sanctify you through and through [*holoteleis*]. May your whole [*holoklēron*] spirit, soul and body be kept blameless" at Christ's return. Far from dissecting the person, Paul expresses the hope that believers may, by God's sanctifying work, be saved from disintegration and preserved as whole (*holos*) beings. He joins the three terms together (here only in his letters) "for emphasis rather than for definition" (Guthrie, 165; cf. Deut 6:5; Mt 22:37).

**2.3. The Person's Experience of Knowledge.** As creatures made in the divine image, human beings have a unique capacity for knowing God. Knowledge entails the exercise of the *nous*. "My mind" knows that the Law* is good and wants to obey it (Rom 7:14-23). Decisions about special days call for rational deliberations: "Let all be fully convinced in their own minds" (Rom 14:5 NRSV). The heart (*kardia*) too has intellectual capacities. The Israelites' "minds [*noēmata*] are made dull," because "a veil covers their hearts [*kardia*]" (2 Cor 3:14-15)—where Paul describes not the effect of one organ on another, but the blunting of the heart's own cognitive powers (*kardiai* and *noēmata* are again closely parallel in Phil 4:7). If truth* about God is to be grasped, the *kardia* must be enlightened (2 Cor 4:1-6; Eph 1:17-19). Moreover the conscience* (*syneidēsis*) makes rational judgments when appraising one's actions (Rom 2:15).

Yet knowing is not purely cognitive. In Paul the *nous* is a place of moral judgments whose deliberations always affect the will (Behm, in Behm and Würthwein, 958-59; Ladd, 476; Bultmann, 1.211). The renewal of the *nous* is requisite for knowing and doing God's will (Rom 12:1-2). Being "convinced in one's own mind," affects behavior (Rom 14:1-8) and issues in a life of holiness* (Eph 4:20-32). Similarly the verb *phroneō* denotes an attitude of mind which finds expression in the will (Bultmann, 1.214). Once the believers' "attitude" is like Christ's (Phil 2:2, 5, where *phroneō* occurs three times), they will become obedient like him (Phil 2:6-11). When Christians "set their minds" on things above (Col 3:2, *phroneō*), their conduct will become holy (Col 3:5-17). The "mindset" (*phronēma*) of the flesh or the Spirit (Rom 8:6-7) determines a whole way of life (Rom 8:1-17). Insights of the *kardia* are likewise wed to conduct. Gentiles demonstrate "the work of the Law in their hearts" by doing what the Law requires (Rom 2:14-15). "Each of you should give as you have decided in your heart to give" (2 Cor 9:7). Obedience to apostolic teaching arises "from the heart" (Rom 6:17).

*Pneuma* designates the self's capacity for three kinds of knowledge:

(1) Knowledge of self. "For what human being knows what is truly human except the human spirit [*pneuma*] that is within?" (1 Cor 2:11 NRSV). Within the one question, *pneuma* represents both the whole self (what the human spirit knows, the human knows) and the internal or incorporeal dimension of the self

("the human spirit that is within").

(2) Knowledge of others. "For though absent in body [sōma] I am present in spirit [pneuma]; . . . When you are assembled, and my spirit [pneuma] is present" (1 Cor 5:3-4 NRSV). While distinguishing the corporeal from the incorporeal, Paul says that he himself will actually participate in the church's life; his pneuma is present and active by the agency of the divine pneuma, who works through the letter Paul is writing.

(3) Knowledge* of God. Galatians 6:18, "The grace of our Lord Jesus Christ be with your spirit, brothers and sisters," is just as comprehensive as 1 Thessalonians 5:28, "The grace of our Lord Jesus Christ be with you." Or, as we may also put it, the pneuma is that dimension of the self through which the whole person engages in communion with God: "The Spirit [pneuma] testifies with our spirit [pneuma] that we are God's children"; through the Spirit's agency "we cry, 'Abba, Father' " (Rom 8:16, 15). Similarly 1 Corinthians 5:5 ("that the spirit [pneuma] may be saved") speaks not of the incorporeal to the exclusion of the corporeal (cf. 1 Cor 15) but of "the whole person as oriented towards God" (Fee, 212). (On the oscillation in Paul's use of pneuma between "person" and an "aspect" or a "dimension" of the person in communion with God, see Dunn in Kamlah et al., 693-94.)

There is a kind of knowledge that is distinct from the cognitive. "If I pray in a tongue, my spirit [pneuma] prays but my mind [nous] is unfruitful" (1 Cor 14:14). Such a prayer is unintelligible to the reason (whose activity is temporarily suspended), but the person is in genuine communion with God ("If you are praising God with your spirit," 1 Cor 14:16 NIV) and is thus edified (1 Cor 14:2, 4). Again speaking of prayer,* Paul affirms that "the peace of God, which surpasses all understanding [nous], will protect your hearts [kardiai] and your minds [noēmata] in Christ Jesus" (Phil 4:7). This is not descriptive knowledge about "the peace of God" (the faculties of the nous are superseded), but intimate knowledge of that reality (the peace of God is experienced in the heart). Paul prays that Christians "may know [ginōskō] the love of Christ, which surpasses knowledge [gnōsis]" (Eph 3:19).

### 3. The Person in Bondage to Sin.

Paul speaks of sin* (hamartia) much more often as a power than as an action. Sin is a ruthless tyrant which entered the world and established its rule through the transgression of Adam (Rom 5:12-21) and has henceforth held the whole of humanity in terrible bondage (Rom 3:9; 6:20; Gal 3:22). (When hamartia is depicted by Paul as a power, the capitalized "Sin" will be used in the following.)

In Paul, as with the equivalent term and usage in the OT, sarx signals creaturely impotence (see 2.2 above). But Paul also employs sarx to denote "man's being and attitude as opposed to and in contradiction to God and God's Spirit" (Bornkamm, 133; cf. Schweizer and Baumgärtel, 132; Thiselton, 675-76). The sarx has sworn allegiance to another power: "By means of the flesh I am enslaved to the law of Sin" (Rom 7:25). The sarx of every person from Adam onward, Jesus alone excepted (Rom 8:3), has been Sin's habitation and slave.

By means of the flesh, Sin subjugates the whole person. In the garden of Eden Sin's main appeal, through the serpent, is not to physical desire but to human reason and pride (Gen 3:1-6); Eve is deceived by the serpent's cunning (2 Cor 11:3; 1 Tim 2:14). So too, while "the works of the flesh [sarx]" (Gal 5:19-21) include what we would call fleshly sins such as sexual immorality and drunkenness, the catalog is dominated by sins of the mind and spirit: "hatred, discord, jealousy, anger, quarrels, dissensions, factions and envy" (see Virtues and Vices). Again by synecdoche Paul uses a term for a part of the self (sarx) to designate the whole person viewed in a certain way, namely in rebellion against God and in bondage to the powers of "the present evil age" (Gal 1:4), the chief of which is Sin.

Accordingly, neither the pneuma nor the nous nor the kardia escapes Sin's clutches. Believers must purify themselves "from every defilement of flesh [sarx] and spirit [pneuma]" (2 Cor 7:1)—that is, both corporeally and incorporeally. Where sarx wars against pneuma, it is invariably the human sarx, including its spiritual dimension, versus the divine pneuma: "those who sow to their own flesh [sarx] will from the flesh reap corruption; but those who sow to the Spirit [pneuma] will from the Spirit reap eternal life" (Gal 6:8; cf. 5:16- 26). The human pneuma, far from offering salvation, itself needs to be saved (1 Cor 5:5; cf. Kümmel, 44). (In Rom 8:10 pneuma denotes the Holy Spirit; with NRSV, against NIV.)

Paul speaks of "the mind [nous] of the flesh [sarx]" (Col 2:18), that is, the mind possessed by the flesh as the tool of Sin. The moral standing of the nous "is determined by what is dominating it, either the Spirit of God or the flesh" (Guthrie, 169). When ruled by the devil (see Satan, Devil), "we lived in the passions of our flesh [sarx], fulfilling the desires of the flesh [sarx] and of the thoughts [dianoiai]" (Eph 2:2-3). In this text it seems likely that the first sarx is broader than the second, and that the second sarx and dianoiai represent two ways "the passions of the flesh" find expression—sensually and intellectually (cf. Eph 5:3-5, akin to Gal

5:22-23; Behm in Behm and Würthwein, 966-67).

God judged those who "suppress the truth" by accelerating their descent into error: "they became futile in their thinking and their foolish hearts [*kardia*] were darkened"; "since they did not see fit to acknowledge God, he gave them over to a depraved mind [*nous*]" (Rom 1:18-21, 28). By the darkening of "their foolish [*asynetos*] heart" (1:21), Paul means "not merely a chance lack of knowledge . . . [but] a sign that a man in his deepest being rejects God. . . . [The] lack of insight must be regarded as culpable behaviour" (Goetzmann in Harder and Goetzmann, 132). The effect of the hardening of the heart is culpable "ignorance" (*agnoia*), a "darkened understanding [*dianoia*]" and "futility of mind [*nous*]" (Eph 4:17-18). While in Romans 1:14 the *anoētoi* ("foolish") are "the simple and uneducated whose power of thought is undeveloped," elsewhere in Paul (Gal 3:1, 3; Tit 2:3; 1 Tim 6:9) the term denotes "adverse religious and moral judgment" (Behm in Behm and Würthwein, 962). The sense of right and wrong is therefore blunted: "Both their [non-believers'] minds [*nous*] and consciences [*syneidēsis*] are defiled" (Tit 1:15; cf. 1 Tim 4:2).

In keeping with the unity of mind and will noted earlier (see 2.3 above), a depraved *nous* (and a foolish *kardia* produce "every kind of wickedness" (Rom 1:18-32). "Hostility of mind" toward God is joined to "evil works" (Col 1:21); those whose hearts are hardened and whose understanding is darkened predictably "indulge in every kind of impurity" (Eph 4:18-19). Talk among persons "of corrupt mind [*nous*], who have been robbed of the truth," inevitably leads to envy, avarice and the like (1 Tim 6:3-5; cf. 2 Tim 3:8).

In Paul's usage the *sōma* ("body") never belongs to itself but always to a master (Bornkamm, 131). By virtue of creation, the body belongs to God; but in consequence of the Fall it becomes the subject of Sin. The body is not inherently sinful; "the body of sin" is the body possessed by Sin (Rom 6:6; 5:12). Such a person habitually offers "the parts of [his/her] body to Sin, as instruments of wickedness" (Rom 6:13). "The deeds of the body [*sōma*]" which need to be destroyed are committed by persons who live "according to the flesh [*sarx*]" (Rom 8:13). "The body is not meant for sexual immorality" (*see* Sexuality), but this is exactly how it behaves as Sin's slave (1 Cor 6:12-20).

*Psychē* still means "natural life" but such life in its fallen state. The "natural person" (*psychikos anthrōpos*) is unable to understand spiritual realities (1 Cor 2:6-16); the "natural body" (*sōma psychikon*) is destined to perish (1 Cor 15:42-55).

Slavery to Sin offers no escape from personal responsibility. The self does not resist but readily submits to Sin's assaults. It is by the mind's own suppression of truth and the heart's willful disobedience that Sin establishes and maintains its mastery. The body readily gives itself—"yields its members"—to Sin's servitude (Rom 6:13; 7:23). Persons enslaved to Sin are nonetheless "held accountable to God" for their decisions and are "deserving of death" for their actions (Rom 1:32; 3:9, 19). As the ally of Sin (Rom 5:12-21), Death (*see* Life and Death) causes the disintegration of the self in flagrant violation of the magnificent unity in diversity which God created. Despite his assurance that "to be away from the body [is to be] at home with the Lord," Paul dreads bodiless existence (2 Cor 5:1-10; see 1.2.4 above). A. T. Lincoln observes that "what is to be seen here . . . is not an ultimate anthropological dualism but rather a temporary duality brought about by sin and death, which until the consummation of salvation continue to mar the wholeness of human existence" (Lincoln, 70).

### 4. The Person Made Whole.

Christ and the Spirit act to undo and to reverse the ruin and destruction which Sin and Death visited upon their victims.

*4.1. New Creation.* "The first man Adam became a living being [*psychēn zōsan*]; the last Adam, a lifegiving spirit [*pneuma zōopoioun*]" (1 Cor 15:45)—not *pneuma zōn*, "living spirit" (*see* Adam and Christ). Dunn comments, "The contrast is between man the recipient of the breath of life which constitutes him a living being, and Christ the giver of the life of the age to come, the life of the Spirit" (Dunn 1980, 108). Moreover, like the first Adam the last Adam is an inclusive being, the very place of new life (1 Cor 15:21-22, 48-49). The "old self" (*palaios anthrōpos*) (Rom 6:6)—humankind in Adam (Rom 5:12-21)—is crucified, so that persons may be joined to the risen Christ (Rom 6:4-11). To "put on" the new humanity is to embrace Christ himself (Rom 13:14; Gal 3:27). The "one new humanity [*kainon anthrōpon*]" of Ephesians 2:15 is the corporate Christ—Christ himself together with all those united to him in his death and resurrection.* On this reality is founded the ethical imperative: "put away . . . your old self [*palaion anthrōpon*], corrupt and deluded by its lusts, . . . clothe yourselves with the new self [*kainon anthrōpon*], created according to the likeness of God in true righteousness and holiness" (Eph 4:22-24 NRSV; cf. Col 3:9-10).

To be understood in the same way, in my judgment, is "the inner being" (*ho esō anthrōpos*) (Eph 3:16 NRSV): this phrase identifies the person in Christ, in contrast to "the outer nature," the person in Adam and destined to perish. "Though our outer nature [*exō* *anthrōpos*] is wasting away, our inner [*esō*] nature is being renewed day by day" (2 Cor 4:16 NRSV), anticipating the full realization of the new humanity in the heavenly glory* (2 Cor 4:17-18; *see* Creation and New Creation). By the same token "the inmost self" of Romans 7:22 is equivalent to the "new self" implied in Romans 6:6 (for this understanding of "the inner self," see Barrett, 145-47; Dunn 1988, 394; Kim, 321-26). Others (e.g., Gundry, 135-40) take "inner and outer self" (as distinct from "old and new self") to denote the incorporeal and the corporeal aspects respectively.

**4.2. The Renewal of the Person.** The person united to Christ is transformed as a total being.

Death to Sin (Rom 6:1-14) entails death to the flesh (Rom 8:1-17; *see* Dying and Rising). Paul never speaks of the resurrection of the *sarx*, only of its destruction. 1 Corinthians 5:5 speaks not (or not necessarily) of the physical death of the incestuous man but of the end of his rebellion against God—as when in Galatians 5:24 Paul calls for the "crucifixion of the flesh with its passions and desires" (cf. Fee, 212; *see* Discipline). "Human commands and teachings" do not restrain but only encourage the *sarx* (Col 2:23). The power* of the Holy Spirit* is essential for conquering the flesh (Gal 5:22-26; Rom 8:1-17). Paul longs for "fleshly" (*sarkinoi, sarkikoi*) persons, still vulnerable to the *sarx* as the agent of Sin, to become "spiritual" (*pneumatikoi*) persons dominated by the Spirit, the agent of Christ (1 Cor 2:14—3:3). "Where the NT differs from behaviourist psychology is over the actual reality of the work of the Spirit" (Wright in Brown et al., 568).

Because the *kardia* is the integrating center of the person, renewal occurs from the heart outward. God causes the light* of the gospel* of the glory of Christ to "shine in our hearts" (2 Cor 4:4-6). It is here that Christ dwells (Eph 3:17), here that his peace* reigns (Col 3:15) and here that Christians are enlightened about God's saving purpose (Eph 1:18). It is the heart that receives the Holy Spirit (2 Cor 1:22), into the heart that God pours his love* by the Spirit (Rom 5:5) and "from a pure heart" that acts of love arise (1 Tim 1:5). Similarly it is Christ who explains Paul's "affection" (*splanchna*) for his people (Phil 1:8; Köster, 556). Corresponding to the depth of their former commitment to Sin, Christians believe the gospel "in the heart" (Rom 10:9-10) and obey apostolic teaching "from the heart" (Rom 6:17).

As part of the same process believers are "transformed by the renewing of [their] mind [*nous*]" for discovering God's "good, pleasing and perfect will," and for employing his gifts* in the church (Rom 12:2-

8; cf. Col 1:9-10). Persons once duped by "the wisdom* of this age" are given "the wisdom of God" for understanding (if only in part) the person and work of Christ, and God's saving purpose for both humanity and creation (1 Cor 1:18—2:16; Col 1:15—2:5; Eph 1:8-19). In place of the futile mentality and darkened understanding which marked existence in Adam, persons incorporated into Christ are "renewed in the spirit of [their] minds" for growth "in true righteousness and holiness" (Eph 4:17-24). "The law of my mind" (Rom 7:23) is God's law,* to which the mind, now liberated, gives its hearty approval (see 4.3 below); the attitude of mind imparted by the Spirit is able and willing to obey God's law, and to resist the assaults of the flesh (Rom 8:1-17).

The believer's present *sōma* ("body") is mortal. "God will destroy" the food that the stomach receives, and the stomach itself (1 Cor 6:13), for this body belongs to a perishable order (1 Cor 7:29-31; 15:42-44). Yet the *sōma* itself is destined for resurrection (1 Cor 6:13-14; 15:20-23). At the end the perishable will be clothed with the imperishable, and the believer's lowly body transformed into a glorious body like that of Jesus himself (1 Cor 15:42-57; Phil 3:20-21). Yet it is this perishable body which Jesus has purchased and now calls into his service (1 Cor 6:12-20; Rom 6:11-23; 12:1). The body's mortality offers not the slightest excuse for indulging its cravings or yielding it to Sin's directives.

Given the self's unity in diversity, the experiences of the *psychē* and the *pneuma* are bound up with those of the *sōma*. *Psychē* still denotes "natural life" within the present order of existence. The believer is no longer a "natural person" (*psychikos anthrōpos*) but "spiritual" (*pneumatikos*) (1 Cor 2:14-15); yet the believer retains a "natural body" (*sōma psychikon*), another name for the "mortal, corruptible body" (1 Cor 15:42-44). The *psychē* will share in the transformation at the End (1 Thess 5:23). Till then the *psychē* is no less vulnerable than the *sōma* to the hazards of a deteriorating order and the lures of "the present evil age." Yet as with the body, it is this very "life" that Christ calls into his service: "Whatever your task, put yourselves [*psychē*] into it, as done for the Lord and not for your masters" (Col 3:23 NRSV); "as slaves of Christ, doing the will of God from your heart [*psychē*]" (Eph 6:6 NRSV); "we were delighted to impart to you . . . our lives [*psychai*] . . . because you had become so dear to us" (1 Thess 2:8). By the same token the human spirit (*pneuma*) is destined for final salvation (1 Cor 5:5; 1 Thess 5:23); can still experience the defilements of sin (2 Cor 7:1); can already experience deep communion with God through the Spirit (Rom 8:16; 1 Cor 14:2,

14-15); and is, together with the body, to be devoted to the Lord's service (1 Cor 7:34).

We have already observed that slavery to Sin, far from affording escape from personal responsibility, comes about through the self's willful surrender to Sin's demands. The same holds true (*mutatis mutandis*) for the slaves of Christ. Ethical* decisions matter; believers shall be answerable for them on the day of judgment* (1 Cor 3:12-15; 2 Cor 5:10). Moreover just as Sin exploited the self's unity in diversity, so Christ calls for the dedication of the whole person to the life of obedience. The proof of "knowledge and depth of insight" is righteous* conduct (Phil 1:9-11; cf. Col 1:9-11).

*4.3. The Divided Self.* We turn finally to Romans 7:14-25, a crucial passage for Pauline psychology, indeed for Paul's theology as a whole. We would argue that these verses describe a Christian's struggle, one that is exclusively Christian, and one in which Paul represents Christians generally. (For a recent defense of this view see Dunn 1988, 387-99, 403-12; for another view, see Moo, 448-98.)

*4.3.1. Two Views of the Self.* From one standpoint the self is a fleshly being. The words "that is, in my flesh" (Rom 7:18) serve to define rather than limit the "I" as here conceived. So should we also understand Romans 7:14. From the standpoint of one's participation in Adam (Rom 5:12-21), and one's continued vulnerability to Sin's agents, the "I" as a Christian is still "fleshly" (*sarkinos*), still subject to Sin's power (cf. 1 Cor 3:1). Behind the words "sold as a slave to sin" (Rom 7:14) lies the perfect participle *pepramenos* ("sold"), denoting a condition that began before conversion and carries over into Christian experience. From another viewpoint the self is renewed. In setting "the law of my mind [*nous*]" over against "the law of sin which is in my members" (Rom 7:23), Paul is not describing warfare between two segments of the self. Rather "my mind" designates the whole person as renewed by Christ and the Spirit, and "my members" the whole person as threatened by slavery to Sin (Rom 7:25). "The inner self" (Rom 7:22) is the self in Christ, what Paul elsewhere calls "the new self" (see 4.1 above); "the law of my mind" (Rom 7:23) is God's law, to which the person, now renewed by Christ, gives its allegiance (Rom 8:1-8). The non-believer's doing so was adversely affected by Sin's use of the law, or by one's own perverse motives (Rom 10:3). But whereas the *nous* used to capitulate to Sin's seductive uses of the law (Rom 7:7-11; Gal 3:22-23), it now resists (Rom 7:23). Paul the Christian knows what he does, and he understands what he does (Rom 7:15) and why (Rom 7:17-18). But he does not acknowledge the legitimacy

of what he does. Even when succumbing to the dictates of Sin, he repudiates and loathes what he does; he recognizes that Sin's claims are illegitimate (Rom 6).

*4.3.2. Two Kinds of Slavery.* A servant* (*diakonos*) can serve more than one master, but a slave* (*doulos*) cannot (Mt 6:24). Yet consider Romans 7:25: "So then, I myself [*autos egō*] am enslaved [*douleuō*] to the law of God with the mind, but to the law of Sin with the flesh." "I myself" do both; *douleuō* governs both parts of the sentence. The explanation is that "I myself" participate in two humanities (represented by Adam and Christ respectively) and in two realities (the present evil age and the age to come). I am capable of giving myself totally to each, not alternately but simultaneously. This interpretation is supported by the order of clauses in Romans 7:24-25. First comes the cry "What a wretched man I am!" (Rom 7:24a), and finally the recognition of a deeply divided self (Rom 7:25b). In between stands the question "Who will rescue me from this body of death?" (Rom 7:24b) and the exclamation "Thanks be to God—through Jesus Christ our Lord!" (Rom 7:25a). Significantly this unmistakable reference to Christian experience is integral to the present discussion, not appended to it. The cry of Romans 7:24a is echoed in the more sober statement of Romans 7:25b. The verb of Romans 7:24b (*rhysetai*) is a true future: Jesus Christ "will rescue me from this body of death" at the resurrection (Rom 6:5, 8; 8:10-11). It is not merely the struggle against Sin (Rom 7:25b) which accounts for the anguish (Rom 7:24a). To have tasted the "already" of salvation creates a longing that is not fully satisfied until the "not yet" becomes a reality (Rom 8:18-25; 13:11-14). Assurance of eventual rescue prevents anguish from degenerating into despair; and the very division within the self shows that Sin is being effectively resisted in anticipation of final victory (*see* Eschatology).

*See also* ADAM AND CHRIST; BODY; CONSCIENCE; ESCHATOLOGY; ETHICS; FLESH; HOLY SPIRIT; IMMORTALITY; INTERMEDIATE STATE; LAW; LIFE AND DEATH; NEW NATURE AND OLD NATURE; SIN; SPIRITUALITY; WEAKNESS.

BIBLIOGRAPHY. C. K. Barrett, *The Second Epistle to the Corinthians* (New York: Harper & Row, 1973); F. Baumgärtel and J. Behm, "καρδία κτλ," *TDNT* III.605-14; J. Behm and E. Würthwein, "νοέω κτλ," *TDNT* IV.948-1022; G. C. Berkouwer, *Man: The Image of God* (Grand Rapids: Eerdmans, 1962); G. Bornkamm, *Paul* (New York: Harper & Row, 1971); C. Brown, H. Vörlander and J. S. Wright, "Man," *NIDNTT* 2.567; R. Bultmann, *Theology of the New Testament*, Vol. 1 (New York: Scribner's, 1951); J. K. Chamblin, *Paul and the Self:*

*Apostolic Teaching for Personal Wholeness* (Grand Rapids: Baker, 1993); J. W. Cooper, *Body, Soul, and Life Everlasting* (Grand Rapids: Eerdmans, 1989); A. Dihle et al., "ψυχή κτλ," *TDNT* IX.608-66; C. H. Dodd, "The Mind of Paul: Change and Development," in *New Testament Studies* (Manchester: University Press, 1953 [1934]) 67-128; J. D. G. Dunn, *Christology in the Making* (Philadelphia: Westminster, 1980); idem, *Romans 1-8* (WBC; Dallas: Word, 1988); E. E. Ellis, *Paul and His Recent Interpreters* (Grand Rapids: Eerdmans, 1961); G. D. Fee, *The First Epistle to the Corinthians* (Grand Rapids: Eerdmans, 1987); R. H. Gundry, Sōma *in Biblical Theology, with Emphasis on Pauline Anthropology* (SNTSMS 29; Cambridge: University Press, 1976); D. Guthrie, *New Testament Theology* (Downers Grove: InterVarsity, 1981); G. Harder and C. Brown, "Soul," *NIDNTT* 3.676-89; G. Harder and J. Goetzmann, "Reason, Mind, Understanding," *NIDNTT* 3.122-34; A. A. Hoekema, *Created in God's Image* (Grand Rapids: Eerdmans, 1986); H. J. Holtzmann, *Lehrbuch der Neutestamentlichen Theologie*, Vol. 2 (2d ed.; Tübingen: J. C. B. Mohr, 1911); R. Jewett, *Paul's Anthropological Terms* (Leiden: E. J. Brill, 1971); E. Kamlah et al., "Spirit, Holy Spirit," *NIDNTT* 3.689-709; S. Kim, *The Origin of Paul's Gospel* (Grand Rapids: Eerdmans, 1982); H. Kleinknecht et al., "πνεῦμα κτλ" *TDNT* VI.332-455; H. Köster, "σπλάγχνον κτλ," *TDNT* VII.548-59; W. G. Kümmel, *Man in the New Testament* (Philadelphia: Westminster, 1963); G. E. Ladd, *A Theology of the New Testament* (Grand Rapids: Eerdmans, 1974); A. T. Lincoln, *Paradise Now and Not Yet* (SNTSMS 43; Cambridge: University Press, 1981); H. Lüdemann, *Die Anthropologie des Apostels Paulus und ihre Stellung innerhalb seiner Heilslehre* (Kiel: University, 1872); J. G. Machen, *The Christian View of Man* (Grand Rapids: Eerdmans, 1937); D. Moo, *Romans 1-8* (WEC; Chicago: Moody, 1991); H. Ridderbos, *Paul: An Outline of His Theology* (Grand Rapids: Eerdmans, 1975); J. A. T. Robinson, *The Body: A Study in Pauline Theology* (SBT 5; London: SCM, 1952); E. Schweizer and F. Baumgärtel, "σάρξ κτλ," *TDNT* VII.98-151; M. Silva, *Philippians* (WEC; Chicago: Moody, 1988); W. D. Stacey, *The Pauline View of Man* (London: Macmillan, 1956); G. Theissen, *Psychological Aspects of Pauline Theology* (Philadelphia: Fortress, 1987); A. C. Thiselton, "Flesh," *NIDNTT* 1.671-82; D. E. H. Whiteley, *The Theology of St. Paul* (Oxford: Blackwell, 1964).

J. K. Chamblin

# PURITY AND IMPURITY

The Pauline texts that relate to purity are found in those sections concerning controversies over food* (Gal 2:11-19; 1 Cor 8; 10:14—11:1; Rom 14:1—15:13);

sections concerning sexual sin within the churches (1 Cor 5); and isolated texts in the Pastoral Letters that speak of the pure heart and the pure conscience.* Paul looks at purity and impurity from two viewpoints, that of the ceremonial purity of Mosaic Law* and moral purity.

1. Ceremonial Purity and Impurity
2. Moral Purity and Impurity
3. Background

## 1. Ceremonial Purity and Impurity.

Paul's stance on questions of ceremonial purity represents an enlightened viewpoint. He is careful to distinguish between his own view of the purity of food and others' scruples that are still based on Jewish food laws.

*1.1. Paul's Own Stance on Issues of Ceremonial Purity and Impurity.* As one who has died to the Mosaic Law (Gal 2:19), Paul no longer sees the Jewish food laws as binding on the Christian. Thus he accepts the teaching of Jesus that no food can be called unclean. The term *koinon*, meaning "common," or "unclean," which he uses in Romans 14:14, clearly refers to an unclean status in view of Jewish laws of ceremonial purity (cf. 1 Macc 1:47, 62). Because Paul is convinced that no food is unclean, he takes a liberal view on meat offered to idols* (1 Cor 10:25-26). The Christian Paul does engage in purification rites related to special vows, but this is done to placate those who saw him as completely antinomian (Acts 21:21-26).

*1.2. Paul's Stance Toward Those Who Followed Ceremonial Purity Laws.* Despite his enlightened view toward food, Paul is careful to respect the consciences of those who clearly feel defiled by ceremonially unclean food. While Paul thinks that no food is actually ceremonially unclean (Rom 14:14, 20; 1 Cor 8:4, 8; 10:25-26), he does recognize that if someone feels ceremonially defiled by a given food, for that person the food is to be considered unclean (Rom 14:14). This respect for another's conscience on questions of ceremonial purity leads Paul to place great responsibility on the strong in conscience to avoid offending the weak (*see* Strong and Weak). Thus he tells the Corinthians to abstain from food when they know a table partner will be troubled by seeing them eat it (1 Cor 10:28). Similarly, Paul tells the Romans to avoid consuming any food that will offend another Christian (Rom 14:21; *see* Rome).

## 2. Moral Purity and Impurity.

Paul's writings on moral purity deal with the subject both in an individual sense and in a corporate sense.

*2.1. Paul's Stance on Moral Purity for Individuals.*

Paul's teaching on individual purity includes both physical and spiritual levels (2 Cor 7:1). Thus we see strong words on the necessity of remaining pure in physical behavior (Rom 13:13-14; 1 Tim 5:22; Tit 2:5). The ground of Paul's appeals for physical purity is his understanding of the individual's body as "for the Lord" and as a temple* of the Holy Spirit* (1 Cor 6:13, 18-19).

More common in Pauline literature are encouragements for inner purity. Thus in the Pastorals we have references to purity of conscience (1 Tim 3:9; 2 Tim 1:3) and in Philippians and the Pastorals references to purity of heart or mind (Phil 4:8; 1 Tim 1:5; 2 Tim 2:22). Paul's major contribution to the idea of moral purity comes with his teaching that ceremonial impurity does not affect moral purity (1 Cor 8:4; Rom 14:14). This represents a major step beyond the decision of the Jerusalem* council (Acts 15:20). Paul's doctrine of individual moral purity must also be understood in light of his own sense of moral responsibility to carry the message of the risen Christ to others. Thus we read his attestations of innocence, or being undefiled by others' blood (Acts 18:6; 20:26). Paul is concerned with the question whether he is contaminated by the unbelief of others, but considers himself pure, or guiltless, in that he has delivered the message with which he was commissioned. Such attestations come from Paul's understanding of his call (*see* Conversion and Call) in light of the prophetic responsibility to deliver God's message completely (Jer 1:5,17; Ezek 3:16-21; Acts 9:15; 22:21; 26:16-20; 1 Cor 9:16; *see* Prophet, Paul As).

*2.2. Paul's Stance on Moral Purity for the Church.* Because of his view of the church* as the body of Christ (*see* Body of Christ), Paul taught that impurity in one member can contaminate a given body of believers (1 Cor 5:6-7, 13). It is because of this that members must be watchful to preserve the corporate purity, something for which Paul later commends the Corinthians* (2 Cor 7:11). The goal of this emphasis on purity is Paul's presentation of a pure church to Christ (2 Cor 11:2). Here we see a motivation for purity that arises out of eschatological* hope.* This is seen more clearly in 1 John 3:1-3 and is evident also in the Dead Sea Scrolls (1QS 5:13-20; 8:4-10; 9:3-6; *see*

Qumran). Paul's emphasis on purity is not primarily motivated by this eschatological hope, however (except perhaps at Rom 13:11-14). It is rather based on his sense of God's election* of Christians to be like Christ (Rom 8:29-30). To follow Christ involves putting off moral uncleanness in order to be purified by the atoning work of Christ (Rom 3:21-26; 6:19) and the power of the Holy Spirit (1 Thess 4:7-8; cf. 2 Thess 2:13). Paul understands baptism* to be the symbol of this purification process (Rom 6:3-4; Eph 5:26).

**3. Background.**

The background of Paul's teachings on purity is his knowledge of the historical Jesus, and not Greek views of purity (*see* Jesus and Paul; Jesus, Sayings of). Paul's statement in Romans 14:14 that he knows "in the Lord Jesus that nothing is unclean in itself" may be directly related to traditions now preserved in Mark 7:15-19. This view that impurity did not reside in a given object is also reflected in one strand of early Judaism (*Tanḥuma Ḥuqat* 26: *Pesiqta de Rab Kahana*), so one cannot say that this teaching was viewed as unique in first-century Palestine. The perception of things as pure to the pure in Titus 1:15 seems related to Jesus' logion now preserved in Matthew 6:22-23.

*See also* BAPTISM; CONSCIENCE; ETHICS; FOOD OFFERED TO IDOLS AND JEWISH FOOD LAWS; HOLINESS, SANCTIFICATION; HOLY SPIRIT; JERUSALEM; IDOLATRY; LAW; SEXUALITY, SEXUAL ETHICS; SIN, GUILT; TEMPLE.

BIBLIOGRAPHY. B. Janowski and H. Lichtenberger, "Enderwartung und Reinheitsidee: Zur eschatologischen Deutung von Reinheit und Sühne in der Qumrangemeinde," *JJS* 34 (1983) 31-59; J. Neusner, *The Idea of Purity in Ancient Judaism* (SJLA 1; Leiden: E. J. Brill, 1973); M. Newton, *The Concept of Purity at Qumran and in the Letters of Paul* (SNTSMS 53; Cambridge: University Press, 1985); J. Neyrey, *Paul, In Other Words: A Cultural Reading of His Letters* (Louisville: Westminster/John Knox, 1990); W. Paschen, *Rein und Unrein: Untersuchung zur biblischen Wortgeschichte* (SANT 24; Munich: Kösel, 1970); J. P. Sampley, 'And the Two Shall Become One Flesh': A Study of Traditions in Ephesians 5:21-33 (SNTSMS 16; Cambridge: University Press, 1971). M. Reasoner

# Q

## QUMRAN AND PAUL

In 1947 a Bedouin boy, looking for lost goats in the caves overlooking the Dead Sea near the arid ruin of Khirbet Qumran, came upon a cache of scrolls which W. F. Albright soon pronounced to be "the greatest manuscript find of modern times." The first discovery led to a "scroll rush" of Bedouin and archeologists who found eleven caves with scrolls at Qumran and other caves throughout the Judean desert and at the mountain fortress of Masada. While the term *Dead Sea Scrolls* can refer broadly to all the finds, it is popularly used for those belonging to the distinctive community at Qumran. The Dead Sea Scrolls afford us the surest contemporary evidence of the Judaism from which first-century Christianity emerged. Knowledge of these scrolls is crucial to any careful study of the apostle Paul and his times.

1. Understanding the Qumran Community and Scrolls
2. Revelation
3. Interpretation of Scripture
4. God's Reign
5. The New Covenant
6. The Messianic Age

### 1. Understanding the Qumran Community and Scrolls.

Since their discovery the Qumran Scrolls have evoked varied and sometimes bizarre theories as to the origin of the community that penned them and its relationship to individuals and groups known from the NT.

*1.1. Identity of the Sect.* By the late 1950s a consensus among scholars identified the Qumran sect with the Essenes mentioned by Josephus, Pliny and Philo of Alexandria. Further, it was claimed that the Essenes took rise from the Hasidean reaction to Hellenization* of Judaism under the Seleucid kings such as Antiochus IV and the Jewish Hasmonean priest-kings who replaced them. The "Wicked Priest" who persecuted the sect's founder, the Teacher of Righteousness, was identified as the Maccabean priest-king Jonathan (152-142 B.C.) or Simon (142-134 B.C.). The

"seekers after smooth things" (CD 1:18) were identified with the Pharisees, who split from the Essenes and subsequently allied themselves with the Hasmonean and Herodian regimes.

Since 1970 several well argued reconstructions, not to mention several speculative proposals, have complicated this scholarly consensus. Archeological data do provide a *terminus a quo* of the mid-second century B.C. and a *terminus ad quem* of the Jewish Revolt in A.D. 66-73 (*see* Revolutionary Movements). However, analysis of Qumran texts like the *Damascus Covenant* and the *Temple Scroll* suggest a longer prehistory to the movement than that focused on the Maccabean era. The collection at Qumran of nonsectarian apocalypses like *1 Enoch*, the Aramaic *Testament of Levi* and *Jubilees* suggests that the Essene movement predates and subsumes the group at Qumran, as Josephus claimed. A newly published "halakic letter" (4QMMT) strengthens the view that the primary cause of the withdrawal to Qumran was a dispute over legal and calendrical rulings. The new text has also led one leading scholar (L. H. Schiffman) to conclude that the sect was not Essene in origin but Sadducean.

Despite the complexity of Qumran origins, the large overlap between Josephus's description and the Qumran texts themselves still favors the Essene hypothesis, but publication of new texts may force a change in the scholarly consensus.

*1.2. Contents of the Library.* The 800-plus scrolls from the Dead Sea caves comprise OT texts (including Tobit, Sirach and Baruch from the Apocrypha), pseudepigraphal works and sectarian compositions. All the books of the OT canon are represented except Esther, reflecting an intermediate stage of canon formation. It is unclear, however, what status the Essenes granted to patriarchal revelations such as *1 Enoch* or "deuteronomic" restatements of the Law like the *Temple Scroll*.

The earliest scrolls published from cave 1 were, on the whole, the most complete because they were preserved in jars. They represent different genres: (1) sectarian rules, such as the *Manual of Discipline* (1QS); (2) exegesis, such as the *pesher* commentaries on the Prophets; (3) prayers and liturgies, such as the *Hymns* (1QH); and (4) messianic visions and plans, such as the *War of the Sons of Light and the Sons of Darkness* (1QM), the *Messianic Rule* (1QSa) and the *New Jerusalem* texts (e.g., 1Q32, 2Q24, 5Q15).

Much of the community library was deposited in the more vulnerable cave 4; the massive collection of fragments from this cave has been published over the past twenty-five years. Numerous manuscripts of *The Book of Enoch* written in Aramaic were published in 1976. The most startling discovery from the Aramaic versions of *1 Enoch* is that an original "Book of Giants," detailing the escapades of the bastard sons of the "Watchers" (Gen 6:1-4), was replaced by the "Similitudes of Enoch" (*1 Enoch* 37—71) in the first century A.D. Since the latter book makes the most overt connection between a heavenly "son of man" and messiah, its relevance for NT Christology* is a matter of renewed debate. Several large scrolls have been published since the late 1970s. The *Temple Scroll*, confiscated by the Israelis in 1967 and published in 1978, appears to be an "inspired" revision of biblical Law, adapting earlier Essene legal rulings to the expected messianic age. In 1985 the full collection of the angelic liturgy texts, entitled *Songs of the Sabbath Sacrifice*, saw the light of publication. The scholarly logjam to publishing the remaining Qumran scrolls seems to have broken up, and we should expect to have the entire Qumran corpus available by the end of the century. These new texts will sharpen our knowledge of the sect and Second Temple Judaism and thus further supplement our knowledge of NT background.

*1.3. Qumran and Paul: Method of Study.* Studies of Paul and Qumran have taken two directions. Earlier studies emphasized specific parallels between particular words and ideas in the two bodies of writings. For instance, strong similarities can be found in 2 Corinthians 6:14—7:1 to the Qumran exclusivist dualism of light* and darkness, God* and Belial. Pauline phrases like "righteousness of God"* (Rom 1:17/1QS 11:12), "works of the Law"* (Gal 2:16/4QFlor [4Q174] 1-2), "church* of God" (1 Thess 2:14/1QM 4:10), and "sons of light" (1 Thess 5:5/1QS 1:9 et al.) and "son of God"* (Rom 1:4/4QpsDan).

Parallels are particularly strong in the case of Ephesians* and Colossians* with their Semitic phraseology such as "a share in the lot of the saints in light" (Col 1:12/1QS 11:7-8). The elaborate introduction in Ephesians 1 reflects the style of *Manual of Discipline* as well as its idea that God's predestined yet mysterious plan has been fulfilled in the community.

On the strength of these parallels, some scholars would claim that Paul and his associates were influenced by the Essenes. Others would argue that we do not have sufficient comparative data to determine to what extent Paul and the Qumran texts were drawing from a common pool of contemporary Jewish usage (*see* Jew, Paul the).

A second, more recent approach has been to compare the "patterns of religion" between Paul's gospel* and the Essene covenant. E. P. Sanders emphasizes the overarching "covenantal nomism" which the Qumran sect shares with all other forms of Judaism in contrast with Paul's experience of salvation. A. F. Segal, developing Käsemann's claim that "apocalyptic is the mother of all Christian theology," points out the similar social psychology of messianic conversion in Paul and the Essenes. In another direction, J. Neusner rejects the idea of one normative pattern and emphasizes the distinctiveness of "Judaisms" in the period just before and after the destruction of the Second Temple.

The approach taken here is, without accepting fully any of these theories, to identify several major themes which appear in the theology of Paul and the Dead Sea Scrolls and to compare how they work within the worldview of their particular community.

## 2. Revelation.

A striking common note of the apocalyptic* writings of Qumran and Paul's letters is their claim to be a response to divine revelation.

*2.1. Mysteries at Qumran.* The Essenes were noted for the gift of prophecy (Josephus *J.W.* 1.3.5 §§78-80; 2.7.3 §§111-13; *Ant.* 15.10.4-5 §§371-79). While Josephus's examples of Essene prophecy are addresses to political leaders, he also mentions that they "kept the names of the angels" (Josephus *J.W.* 2.8.7 §142). This description corresponds to the practice of the Qumran community: revelations were to be kept secret from outsiders (1QS 10:24-25).

While the sect clearly shared in the apocalyptic tradition of Daniel and the pseudepigrapha, they attributed a fundamental role to the insight of the Teacher of Righteousness (CD 1:11; 1QpHab 7:4). In the *Hymns* the Teacher confesses: "Thou hast unstopped my ears to marvelous mysteries" (1QH 1:21). These mysteries include matters of creation, including all-important matters of astronomy and calendar, of the spirits of good and evil and their predestinated end, of the true interpretation of Torah and Prophets, and of the coming end of the evil age and restoration* of Israel.

The publication of the *Songs of the Sabbath Sacrifice* has placed the community within a larger framework of Jewish mysticism. The 13 Sabbath Songs describe in hypnotic detail the worship of the angels in the heavenly temple and the movement of the divine throne-chariot (*merkabah*), and they seem to provide a communal context in which visions or auditions might be received.

*2.2. Paul's Vision of Christ.* Paul claims that his own ministry* was founded on a revelation, when God "was pleased to reveal his Son in me" (Gal 1:15-16; Acts 9 par.). From this conversion experience Paul derives the essential elements of his Gospel (*see* Conversion and Call). He also describes a subsequent experience when as "a person in Christ" he was caught up to paradise in the third heaven and heard inexpressible things (2 Cor 12:2-4; *see* Visions). Were these two revelations equivalent?

The discovery of a vital apocalyptic mysticism at Qumran has reinforced the view of Albert Schweitzer that the essence of Paul's Gospel was the experience of "being in Christ," though not as Schweitzer thought of it (*see* In Christ; Mysticism). However, it should be noted that Paul's reticence about his rapture to heaven* is in strong contrast with his insistence that he always preached the gospel publicly and freely (Gal 3:1). In this respect his Damascus Road conversion is more like a prophetic call in which the vision is prolegomenon to the message (1 Cor 9:1, 16; *see* Prophet, Paul As). In the doxological summary of the gospel in Romans 16:25-27, the "revelation of the mystery*" seems clearly linked to the public proclamation of salvation* by faith* to all nations (cf. Eph 6:19).

### 3. Interpretation of Scripture.

While claiming decisive new insight into God's truth, the Qumran community and Paul were both deeply biblical in their conviction that the Scriptures were the oracles of God addressed to the end of the ages.

*3.1. Text and Canon.* The Qumran library has enriched immeasurably our knowledge of the biblical text and the textual traditions of the time of Jesus and Paul. The Qumran manuscripts include various text types, predominantly of the Masoretic type which underlies our Hebrew text but with representation of Septuagint and Samaritan types. By contrast, late first-century manuscripts from other Dead Sea caves and Masada are almost exclusively of the Masoretic type.

The community practice of copying and storing biblical texts is a mark of its reverence for Scripture as an inspired word. The supplement to the Psalms Scroll (11QPsaᵃ), known as the "words of David," explains that David wrote 4,050 compositions and that "all these he uttered through prophecy which was given him from before the Most High." This text also suggests the existence of writings not in our present canon, and the Psalms scroll in fact include eight such psalms. While the covenanters revered works now called apocrypha and pseudepigrapha, they did not make commentaries on them, which may suggest that the distinction between canon and other inspired writings was already in existence.

While revering the letter of Scripture, the Qumran exegetes exercised considerable liberty in introducing variant readings for purposes of clarification of the text. In the Habakkuk commentary on Habakkuk 1:5, it seems virtually certain that where the MT reads "look *among the nations* (*baggôyim*)," the commentator introduced the variant "look at the traitors" (*bōgᵉḏîm*), with the sense that God is condemning the community's enemies.

There are thus general similarities in matters of canon and text between Qumran and Paul. Both look primarily to the canon of Law, Prophets and Psalms. Paul's citations are exclusively from the canonical OT, although he is willing to paraphrase and makes allusion to apocryphal texts and legends. In terms of text, Paul does not quote from one text type but shows awareness of LXX and MT texts as well as eclectic readings.

*3.2. Methods of Interpretation.* The Scrolls exhibit the most contemporary examples of Jewish exegetical method to the time of Paul (*see* Old Testament in Paul). Qumran exegesis is strongly literal, that is, it cites and interprets the actual words of Scripture. The earliest known targum (or Aramaic paraphrase), on the book of Job, is clearly not just a translation device but a form of meditation on the text. Legal application (*halakah*), seen preeminently in the *Temple Scroll*, works from specific Pentateuchal texts. The *Genesis Apocryphon* (1QapGen) is distinctive in its interspersing of haggadic legend with literal citation from Genesis.

The most distinctive Qumran method is that of *pesher*, which begins with the letter and discovers in it an eschatological meaning. More than a dozen continuous *pesharim* were found in portions of the prophetic books (and Ps 37). Thematic collections of *testimonia* were also found, which draw together proof-texts from various OT books. Finally, isolated *pesher* texts appear throughout the rules, suggesting a larger body of authoritative exegesis known to the community. Finally, in the Qumran hymns and wisdom writings, one finds unselfconscious reproduction of biblical style and thought.

A significant issue raised for Pauline studies is whether Paul employed specific exegetical techniques or to what extent both Paul and the Qumran exegetes exhibit an "intertextual" consciousness that allows them to make citations and allusions without recourse to a particular method of exegesis. In this respect the use of Scripture in the Qumran rules may present the closest parallels to Paul's letters. The rules demonstrate an eclectic use of Scripture, including quotation, allusion and paraphrase in the context of pastoral exhortation.

*3.3. Eschatological Hermeneutic.* The Qumran exegetes were convinced that the "hidden things," especially the cryptic words of the Prophets, had been revealed to their founder, the Teacher of Righteousness, and to his priestly descendants (CD 3:13-19; 1QpHab 7:1-17). In all the sectarian texts there is a consistent appropriation of Scripture, not as past history but as present fulfillment. Of particular interest is their deuteronomic typology. They see themselves as the remnant, the "penitents of the desert" who are waiting expectantly for redemption. Yet in a sense it is not a new dispensation but a recovery of the truth and perfection of the original Law of Moses (1QS 1:1-10).

Paul likewise sees the gospel as the eschatological fulfillment of Scripture (1 Cor 15:3) and the church as fulfilling the role of Israel* at the turn of the ages. But the gospel is not just a new insight but a new act of God* in Christ's death* and resurrection.* This new act, "what eye hath not seen nor ear heard," causes Paul to reorder the priorities of the old covenant,* most strikingly the role of Law observance, and it gives him a kind of exegetical virtuosity which differs from the studied insights of the priestly expositors at Qumran. Secondly, while for both the Essenes and Paul Scripture forms the way of life of a covenant community, the Pauline community operates on a new constitution, that of inclusion of the Gentiles* in the new Adam.* Qumran interpretation, despite its condemnation of those outside, is more in line with the exegesis of other Jewish groups as represented by Philo and the rabbinic writings.

## 4. God's Reign.
Paul shared with the writers of the Scrolls the monotheistic faith of Israel (*see* God). At the same time, comparison of Paul's theology and that of Qumran discloses a considerable flexibility in depicting the uniqueness of the one God and his governance of the world.

*4.1. God and the Archangels.* The "two spirits treatise" (1QS 3:13—4:26), which encapsulates the peculiar teaching of the Qumran sect, begins with a strong assertion of God's omnipotence and omniscience: "From the God of knowledge comes all that is and shall be. Before ever they existed he established their whole design . . . and they accomplish their task without change." As is suggested in many apocalyptic works, God's laws of creation and covenant overlap perfectly, and thus the courses of the sun and stars accord exactly with the community's 364-day festival calendar. Similarly, God's perfection of way extends to his predestination of history, mysterious though this may be (see 4Q180).

The two spirits treatise juxtaposes this strong monarchianism with a modified dualism which many scholars believe to have filtered down from Iranian sources: "He has created humankind to govern the world, and has appointed for them two spirits" (1QS 3:18-19). While these spirits have their psychological influence, they are primordially angels: the Prince of Light and the Angel of Darkness (1QS 3:20-21).

In other texts the public and esoteric names of these two angels* appear: Michael, the archangel of Israel, who is also called Melchizedek (*Melkîṣedeq,* "king of righteousness," 11QMelch), and his counterpart Belial, whose secret name is Melchiresha (*Melkîrešaʿ,* "king of wickedness," 4Q280-82). What is unusual in Qumran angelology is the supremacy granted to these opposite "princes" in the world. The Melchizedek scroll identifies the good archangel as Elohim, the agent of eschatological judgment* (11QMelch 24-25). This overlap of language for God and his angel is reminiscent of the "angel of the Lord" texts of the OT (e.g., Judg 6:11-24) and may anticipate later rabbinic discussions of "two powers in heaven" (see Segal, 40-52).

*4.2. God and Christ.* Paul's evangelical version of monotheism is captured in his reformulation of the OT Shema: "for us there is but one God, the Father . . . and one Lord, Jesus Christ" (1 Cor 8:6). The Damascus Road encounter with the Lord* of glory* provided a primary occasion for the development of Paul's christology.* This initial revelation has much in common with Jewish throne, or merkabah, visions* (e.g., *3 Enoch*), like the one that Paul alludes to in 2 Corinthians 12:2-4. According to L. W. Hurtado, apostolic christology may represent a "mutation" in Jewish monotheism, which was assisted by the "divine agency tradition" which included the role of principal angels like Michael (Hurtado, 71-92).

Paul accuses his Colossian* opponents of "worship of angels" (Col 2:18). While it is unlikely that the Colossian heretics were Essene or that they literally advocated worshiping angels, they manifest a confusion between the "many lords" of the cosmic realm and the one Lord who is a legitimate object of worship,* at whose name "every knee should bow" (Phil 2:10). In their very pretension to God's authority, the powers are a "dominion of darkness" (Col 1:13; 2 Cor 4:4) whom Christ triumphed* over by his cross (Col 2:15).

*4.3. God's Spirit and the Human Spirit.* In its remarkable fusion of determinism and dualism, the two spirits treatise goes on to identify two predestined communities or "lots" (*gôrāl*), the sons of light and sons of darkness, who walk according to the two angelic spirits and reap the appropriate eternal reward (*see* Light and Darkness). However, the cosmic battle is also waged within the individual soul according to each person's spiritual portion. In a fragmentary physiognomic text (4QCryptic), each individual's character is judged by the balance of nine parts between the "House of Light" and the "House of Darkness." In this way no doubt, they could explain the fundamental separation of the elect as well as the differentiated ranks within the sect.

Even the most pious Essene was aware of the moral chasm between flesh and spirit: the sectarian *Hymns* contain moving confessions of sin and pollution (e.g., 1QH 1:21-23). The Holy Spirit is closely identified with God's attribute of mercy* but also with God's truth, the gift of insight into the Law (1QH 12:11-23). The sect looks forward to the day of visitation when God by his Spirit will "refine for himself the human frame" by imparting to the elect the angelic wisdom of Eden (1QS 4:20-26). In the meantime the community members are confident that they can "establish the spirit of holiness according to all truth" for Israel (1QS 9:3).

Paul's doctrine of humanity and the Spirit is intimately connected with his new perspective on Christ (2 Cor 5:16). If Paul's argument in Romans 1:16—3:20 reflects his pre-Christian viewpoint, then we can see a pattern similar to Qumran doctrine: the human race is fallen into sin* and idolatry,* and God will punish sin with disease and death (Rom 2:9; *see* Life and Death). The delusion of the Law-observant Jew, even as Paul describes his former life (Phil 3:6), is in confusing the insight that the Law is spiritual with the "boast"* that the flesh* can obey it (Rom 3:17-20; 7:14).

Paul's doctrine of the Spirit (*see* Holy Spirit) is based on the incarnation of Christ as "the last Adam,* a life-giving Spirit" (1 Cor 15:45; Rom 1:4). The Holy Spirit cannot now be separated from the unity of God in Christ (Eph 4:3-6). The "flesh," epitomized by circumcision,* now becomes the marker of life under the old dispensation, to which the believer must die (Col 2:11-12; Gal 5:24). This death to all the elements* of this age, including the Law, frees the believer to walk by the Spirit (Rom 8:1-2).

Paul uses the form of exhortation from the "two ways" tradition of Judaism, though now reinterpreted in terms of one's status in Christ. He can speak of two "minds" (Rom 8:5), or of the fruit* of the Spirit and the works of the flesh (Gal 5:19, 22). He also expresses the awareness that Christian moral choice involves wrestling with unseen principalities* and powers (Eph 6:12) and the temptation to revert to the former life of the flesh (Gal 3:3).

## 5. The New Covenant.

One of the striking parallels between the NT and the Dead Sea Scrolls is the Essene claim to be the community of the new covenant (CD 6:19; 19:33; 20:12). It is important to determine in what way the religion of Qumran is new and how this new pattern compares with Paul's Gospel.

*5.1. Law Keeping at Qumran.* The sectarians of Qumran frequently referred to themselves as "covenant-keepers" (1QS 5:2) because they, like Abraham, kept the commandments of God (CD 3:2). While the halakah at Qumran are more directly biblical than Pharisaic/rabbinic rulings, it does seem that the sect distinguished between biblical laws, certain hidden laws revealed for the present evil age, and ideal laws to be instituted in the messianic age. M. O. Wise has proposed that the *Temple Scroll* is the messianic Law mediated by the Teacher as the eschatological prophet. If true, this thesis shows that the new covenant was a version of covenantal nomism even stricter than that of the OT, with wider application of purity rules and absolute exclusion of foreigners from Israel. Nevertheless the covenant was understood to be essentially continuous from creation to the end time.

E. P. Sanders and others have rightly insisted that Jewish Law* keeping is not to be caricatured as "legalism." The sect referred to the "covenant of grace" (1QS 1:8), and the *Hymns* make clear that "righteousness is not of humankind . . . except by the spirit which God created for them to make perfect a way for the children of humankind." (1QH 4:30-31). At the same time "keeping the covenant" involves exact performance of legal precepts as interpreted by the priests. Thus the pesher on Habakkuk 2:4 interprets "faith" as faith in the Teacher of Righteousness (i.e., in his exegetical insights and legal rulings).

The Essenes were renowned for their attention to ritual purity, and this feature of their life has been confirmed by archeologists' discovery of a massive water system at Qumran. Forgiveness of sins follows from entry into the community, acceptance of its secret knowledge and perfect obedience to its rules (1QS 1:6-11). By its corporate obedience, the community hoped to "atone for the land" and hasten the messianic age (CD 4:6-12).

*5.2. Paul and the Law.* Whereas the new covenant at Qumran is seen as a fuller unveiling of the Mosaic Law, Paul can speak of the discontinuity between the covenants of promise to Abraham* and of Law given to Moses* (Gal 3:17-18; 4:24-31). Paul recognized by revelation that zeal for God's Law had led not to righteousness* but to a legal curse* borne by Christ on the cross* (Gal 3:13). Thus Paul evaluates the Law differently as a Christian from what he did as a Pharisee: the Law brings knowledge of sin to both Jew and Greek that all may receive mercy through faith in Christ (Rom 3:20-31). Interpreters differ sharply as to what ongoing and positive role for the Law Paul may have seen for Jewish and Gentile Christians (*see* Law).

While Paul would agree fully with the Qumran Teacher that righteousness belongs to God alone, he would differ radically on the means by which the elect appropriate that righteousness. For Paul the role of faith* is part of the new revelation of the gospel, even though some like Abraham and Habakkuk had received it by anticipation (Rom 1:16; 4:18). Hence his use of Habakkuk 2:4-5 is fundamentally different from the Qumran *pesher*. Paul interprets the prophet as not calling for renewed faithfulness to covenant Law but for faith in God's new cosmic act of redemption,* which will initiate a new relationship with God in the Holy Spirit (Rom 5:1-11). While the church has a ministry of reconciliation (*see* Peace, Reconciliation), it is not a matter of "perfection of way" but of persuading others to believe that Christ died for all (2 Cor 5:11-15).

## 6. The Messianic Age.

The dawn of the messianic age in Qumran thought is, above all, the act of God in the unfathomable mystery* of his will. The term *messianic* can be used in the narrow sense of the expected Davidic savior of Israel or in the broad sense of an eschatological age of God's intervention in creation and history. While not all Jews maintained equal hope for both a messiah and a new age, the Qumran community did, though the picture is not simple, given the long history of the sect and the subsequent redactions of its documents.

*6.1. The Messiah.* Some texts which may predate Qumran suggest the coming of a single Davidic messiah (1QDibHam; 4QPBless). The community rules seem to foresee the messianic age ushered in by a prophet (the Teacher of Righteousness) and the "messiahs of Aaron and Israel" (e.g., 1QS 9:10-11; 1QSa). This dual anointing is in continuity with postexilic prophecy and the theocratic vision of the Chronicler (Zech 4:14; 6:12-13; Neh 8:8-9). While most

scholars have seen the reference to a messiah of Aaron as special sectarian pleading, the emphasis in the use of "anointed" may be more a matter of perspective than polemics. The priestly author of the *Temple Scroll*, for instance, specifies the duties of the ideal king in the perfected theocracy without mention of the messiah of Aaron.

The idea of messiah as God's son does not go beyond the biblical sources (4QFlor). Neither is there any certain indication of a supernatural birth or vicarious death of the messiah (despite an ongoing debate over two obscure readings in 1QSa and 4Q285). The role of the Davidic figure in the final battle is unclear in the War Scroll; it is the archangel Michael whom God sends to deliver Israel, and his victory will have cosmic reverberations: "[God] will raise up the kingdom of Michael among the gods [i.e., angels] and the realm of Israel in the midst of all flesh" (1QM 17:7-8).

While Paul is aware of the political dimension of messiah as son of David, it is Jesus' resurrection which dominates his view of Christ* (Rom 1:3-4; 2 Cor 5:16; *see* Son of God). All his references to Davidic anointing have become metaphorical (Rom 1:5). Interestingly, Paul can portray Christ as an eschatological warrior in a supra-mundane battle (1 Thess 4:16; *see* Triumph).

*6.2. Eschatology.* The Qumran writers, like many other apocalypticists, were interpreters of the times and especially the end of the age. The *Damascus Rule* (CD 1) gives an authoritative history of the community which sees it as the remnant foreseen by the prophets during the 390-year exile (c. 200 BC). The penitential movement struggled for twenty years until God sent the Teacher of Righteousness. While the Teacher laid the foundations of the community, the sect continued to be tested by enemies down to the present.

The community saw itself living between the time of revelation and fulfillment. Several scholars have seen in Qumran eschatology a spiritualizing of sacral imagery, especially that of the Temple (1QH 6:12-20; 1QS 11:8-9; cf. 1 Cor 3:9). In their observance of the Law they sought to abide by Temple purity rules extended to messianic dimensions. The messianic age, as imagined in the *Temple Scroll* and *Messianic Rule*, would involve restoration of the Law as interpreted at Qumran and a new Temple built along Ezekielian lines. Their vivid sense of standing in rank with the angels (1QH 3:22) may explain Josephus's comment that the Essenes believed in immortality of the soul (Josephus *J.W.* 2.8, 11 §§154-58). Hippolytus reports that the Essenes believed in resurrection, and by the "glory of Adam" they may envision a millennial life span (1QS 4:23; CD 7:6).

Paul's summary of salvation history is less speculative and yet depicts a more dramatic crisis of the ages: "When the time had fully come, God sent forth his Son" (Gal 4:4-5). The end time has already come (2 Cor 5:17); the church* as Christ's body* has taken over the Temple and festival imagery of Israel (1 Cor 3:9-15; 5:7-8; see Sacrifice), even though Paul sees a continuing identity for Israel* and its heritage (Rom 9:4-5).

Their sense of new access to God through Christ led some early Christians to "realize" the heavenly* realm by means of angelic glossolalia (1 Cor 13:1; Col 3:16; see Tongues) and liken their love feasts* to heavenly manna (1 Cor 10:2). Sexual* abstinence was now considered a spiritual gift* (1 Cor 7:7) and perhaps led to the thought that the old age had completely passed away, replaced by the resurrection* life. In Paul's tortuous argument exhorting women to wear an "authority"* in worship "because of the angels" (1 Cor 11:10), he may be reminding them that the angelic "rulers of this age" are still responsible for decent and orderly conduct between the sexes.

Finally, Paul reaffirms the resurrection of Jesus as the decisive event of history but adds that there is more history to come under his reign until he subjects himself to the Father and God is all in all (1 Cor 15:28; see Eschatology; Kingdom).

See also APOCALYPTICISM; ESCHATOLOGY; JEW, PAUL THE; LAW; OLD TESTAMENT IN PAUL; RESTORATION OF ISRAEL.

BIBLIOGRAPHY. D. Dimant, "Qumran Sectarian Literature," in *Jewish Writings of the Second Temple Period: Apocrypha, Pseuedepigrapha, Qumran Sectarian Writings, Philo, Josephus*, ed. M. E. Stone (CRINT 2.2; Assen: Van Gorcum) 483-550; J. A. Fitzmyer, *The Dead Sea Scrolls: Major Publications and Tools for Study* (rev. ed.; Atlanta: Scholars Press, 1990); L. W. Hurtado, *One God, One Lord* (Philadelphia: Fortress, 1988); J. M. Murphy-O'Connor and J. H. Charlesworth, *Paul and the Dead Sea Scrolls* (New York: Crossroad, 1990 [1968]); C. A. Newsom, *Songs of the Sabbath Sacrifice: A Critical Edition* (HSS 27; Atlanta: Scholars, 1985); H. Ringgren, *The Faith of Qumran: Theology of the Dead Sea Scrolls* (Philadelphia: Fortress, 1963); E. P. Sanders, *Paul and Palestinian Judaism: A Comparison of Patterns of Religion* (Philadelphia: Fortress, 1977); L. H. Schiffman, "The Significance of the Scrolls," *BibRev* (Oct. 1990) 19-27; A. F. Segal, *Paul the Convert: The Apostolate and Apostasy of Saul the Pharisee* (New Haven: Yale University, 1990); G. Vermes, *The Dead Sea Scrolls in English* (3d ed.; Sheffield: JSOT, 1987); M. O. Wise, *A Critical Study of the Temple Scroll from Qumran Cave 11* (SAOC 49; Chicago: University of Chicago, 1990); idem, "Dead Sea Scrolls," *DJG* 137-46.

S. F. Noll

# R

**RABBINIC BACKGROUND.** *See* Jew, Paul the.

**READER-RESPONSE CRITICISM.** *See* Hermeneutics/Interpreting Paul.

**RECONCILIATION.** *See* Center of Paul's Theology; Peace, Reconciliation.

## REDEMPTION

Paul uses the concept of redemption primarily to speak of the saving significance of the death* of Christ.* It is one of several Pauline metaphors for the work of Christ and is firmly rooted in the story of God's covenant relationship with Israel.*

    1. Background
    2. Redemption and the Cross
    3. The Life of the Redeemed
    4. Redemption and the Future

### 1. Background.

The fundamental idea of redemption in antiquity took its origin in such practices as when in warfare the victor in a battle would take prisoners and let it be known that he was ready to release them on payment of a price. The process was called redemption and the price paid was the ransom.

The Greco-Roman background for redemption was argued by A. Deissmann, who pointed out that slaves could be liberated by a procedure that entailed the fictitious transaction of paying or depositing money in the sanctuary of a god, notably at Apollos' shrine at Delphi. By this transaction, Deissmann argued, they became "slaves of Apollo" (see Deissmann, 319-30). But Deissmann's interpretation of the contracts of manumission inscribed on the wall at Delphi has been rejected by recent scholarship, which argues that the priests (and thereby the god Apollo) functioned as no more than intermediaries and public guarantors of the contracts of manumission (see Bartchy, 121-25).

The OT provides three special areas of interest, all relevant to Paul's thinking regarding redemption.

First, the most important background is seen in the OT imagery of the Exodus, God's redemption of the people Israel from Egyptian servitude to become the community of God's covenant. One text (Ex 8:23 NRSV marg.) neatly sums up the basic Hebrew thought of this episode. Yahweh says "I will set redemption" between Israel and the Egyptians, thus claiming Israel as God's own possession as they are set free from tyranny and oppression, and are bound to God's covenant obligation and treaty (Ex 12—24). In the Exodus story God's strength and delivering activity in history are brought to the fore as the means of redemption (cf. Deut 7:8; 9:26; Ps 74:2; 77:15).

Second, because Israel was God's firstborn* (Ex 4:22) whom he had redeemed from helpless bondage, Israel in its life before God was also to redeem people and property from various situations from which they could not otherwise break free (*see* Adoption, Sonship). On occasion it could take the form of Israelites redeeming impoverished kinfolk who had sold themselves into slavery (Lev 25:47-49) or of redeeming a family's inheritance of land that had been sold (Lev 25:25-26). On the other hand, if a man owned an ox known to be dangerous and he let it escape and it killed someone, the ox and its owner must be put to death. But this was not willful murder, and provision was made for redemption: the man could pay a ransom and go free (Ex 21:29-30).

But as a regular practice, the firstborn redemptive status of Israel before Yahweh was to be reflected in Israel's "redeeming" and consecrating the firstborn males "of every womb," whether livestock or human, for Yahweh (Ex 13:12-16). Further, the Levites served as consecrated and "redeemed" representatives for the firstborn nation as they stood in for Israel's firstborn males (with the number of firstborn Israelites that exceeded the number of Levites being "redeemed" at the price of five shekels per person, Num 3:11-51).

Third, the ancient practice of prisoners in captivity being set free by payment of a ransom or an act of clemency on the part of the ruling authority is notably seen in the exiles being restored by Cyrus' decree (Ezra 1). Isaiah 45:1-25 speaks of a return celebration in which Cyrus is the agent who releases the Babylonian exiles, but the redeemer is God (Is 52:3). This release from Exile is spoken of as a new Exodus, an event likened to God's redemption of his people through the first Exodus from Egypt (e.g., Is 43:1-4, 14).

## 2. Redemption and the Cross.

Paul assumes the creation story which sees people as originally in right relationship to God.* But the coming of sin made them slaves to sin* (Rom 6:6) and liable to the sentence of death (Rom 6:23). One way of viewing what was done at the cross of Christ was to see it as the paying of a price (1 Cor 6:20; 7:23), specifically a ransom (1 Tim 2:6) that frees people from slavery* or the death sentence (*see* Life and Death). Releasing people from bondage with the payment of a price is just the sort of thing that the ancient world saw as redemption. Paul sees salvation* as a process of redemption.

Paul does not use the customary word for ransom (*lytron*), but he does employ a stronger term to denote the price (*antilytron*, 1 Tim 2:6). There is perhaps no great difference in meaning, but the compound strengthens the idea of substitution. Christ took the place of humans, undergoing death to set them free. We should perhaps notice that neither here nor anywhere else in the NT is there mention made of any recipient of the ransom price. To try and identify the one to whom the ransom was paid is to press the words beyond what they are meant to convey. The term indicates that redemption was costly, not that there was someone such as Satan* or demons* demanding that a price be paid.

The apostle makes a good deal of use of the unusual word *apolytrōsis*. This word is used ten times in the NT (seven times in Paul) and it is cited about the same number of times in all the rest of Greek literature. It may be that by the choice of this unusual word the Christian writers were hinting that the redemption of which they wrote was not the ordinary redemption with which everyone was familiar, but a very special redemption. Paul indicates something of this when he speaks of Christ "in whom we have redemption through his blood" (Eph 1:7, where he has "the forgiveness* of trespasses" in apposition; the identical expression is found in Col 1:14, except that most MSS omit "through his blood"). "His blood" means the death of Jesus, and again we have the thought that a high price was paid to set believers free from the consequences of their sins.

Paul links redemption with justification* when he speaks of "being justified freely by his grace through the redemption that is in Christ Jesus" (Rom 3:24). The expressions are not to be identified; they are two ways of looking at the salvation Christ effected. Christ brought about acquittal (justification); he also set believers free (redemption).

In writing to the Galatians Paul twice links redemption with freedom from the Law.* In a striking statement he says that Christ "redeemed us from the curse of the Law, having become a curse for us," and he goes on to quote Deuteronomy 21:23, "cursed is everyone who hangs on a tree" (Gal 3:13). Paul has already said that everyone who does not continue in all that is written in the Law is accursed (Gal 3:10; so Deut 27:26; cf. 28:58). He is now saying that sinners stand under a curse* because they have broken the Law of God, but that Christ redeemed them, paid the price for setting them free (but *see* Law; Restoration of Israel).

The other passage is that in which Paul says that God sent his Son to be "born under Law in order that he might redeem them that are under Law" (Gal 4:4-5). We should notice that God initiated the process, and that the purpose of Jesus' coming was the redemption of those "under Law." In this place the reference will not be to Jews only, but to all those who have failed to keep God's Law and who thus are under a curse. Redemption means paying the price to release sinners. This truth is also behind the words to Titus, that Jesus "gave himself for us in order that he might redeem us from every iniquity" (Tit 2:14).

## 3. The Life of the Redeemed.

Paul reminds the Corinthians that they had been "bought with a price"; therefore, he says: "glorify God in your body" (1 Cor 6:20). We are not to think of redemption as some remote, ethereal process. Redemption has effects in everyday experience and living. This comes out again with another reference to being bought at a price, followed this time with "Do not be slaves of human masters" (1 Cor 7:23). The redeemed belong to God; they should not seek to have themselves enslaved to human opinions.

Twice Paul speaks of "redeeming the time" (Eph 5:16; Col 4:5). While in these cases the "redemption" is different from that wrought by Christ, it points to the conduct Paul sees as appropriate in the redeemed. They are to make the most of the time given them, the opportunities of service they encounter day by day. So also redemption is to result in "the praise of his glory*" (Eph 1:14).

## 4. Redemption and the Future.

In this life believers do not experience the fullness of

redemption. Paul speaks of those who have received the Spirit as awaiting "sonship, the redemption of our body" (Rom 8:23; *see* Adoption, Sonship). Life's choices here and now will not be overlooked in the resurrection at the end of the age. Redemption extends to that era. This will be in mind also in Paul's reference to being "sealed [by the Holy Spirit*] unto the day of redemption" (Eph 4:30).

*See also* CROSS, THEOLOGY OF THE; DEATH OF CHRIST; EXPIATION, PROPITIATION, MERCY SEAT; FORGIVENESS; JUSTIFICATION; PEACE, RECONCILIATION; SACRIFICE, OFFERING; SALVATION.

BIBLIOGRAPHY. G. Aulén, *Christus Victor* (London: SPCK, 1931); S. S. Bartchy, *MALLON CHRESAI* (SBLDS 11; Missoula, MT: Scholars, 1973); C. Brown et al., "Redemption," *NIDNTT* 3.189-223; F. Büchsel, "ἀντίλυτρον κτλ," *TDNT* IV.351-56; A. Deissmann, *Light from the Ancient East* (New York: Harper, 1927) 319-30; J. G. Gibbs, *Creation and Redemption: A Study in Pauline Theology* (Leiden: E. J. Brill, 1971); K. Grayston, *Dying, We Live: A New Enquiry into the Death of Christ in the New Testament* (New York: Oxford University Press, 1990); D. Hill, *Greek Words and Hebrew Meanings: Studies in the Semantics of Soteriological Terms* (SNTSMS 5; Cambridge: University Press, 1967); K. Kertelge, "ἀπολύτρωσις," *EDNT* 1.138-40; idem, "λύτρον," *EDNT* 2.364-66; S. Lyonnet and L. Sabourin, ed., *Sin, Redemption and Sacrifice* (AnBib 48; Rome: Pontifical Biblical Institute, 1970); I. H. Marshall "The Development of the Concept of Redemption in the New Testament," in *Reconcilation and Hope*, ed. R. J. Banks (Exeter: Paternoster, 1974) 153-69 (= *Jesus the Savior: Studies in New Testament Theology* [Downers Grove, IL: InterVarsity, 1990] 239-57); L. Morris, *The Apostolic Preaching of the Cross* (3d ed.; Grand Rapids: Eerdmans, 1965) 11-64; idem, *The Atonement* (Downers Grove, IL: InterVarsity, 1983) 106-31; H. W. Robinson, *Redemption and Revelation* (London: Nisbet, 1942).

L. Morris

# RELIGIONS, GRECO-ROMAN

The adjective *Greco-Roman* indicates that the cults discussed in this article are those which were practiced in the ancient Mediterranean world during the Hellenistic* and Roman periods (i.e., from the late fourth century B.C. through the fifth century A.D.). These were periods of complex political and cultural change and syncretism in which first the Greeks and then the Romans provided the dominant political and cultural frameworks for life in the ancient Mediterranean world. Thus Greco-Roman religions include not only those public and private cults which had developed out of archaic and classical Greek and Roman religious practices, but also the many native cults and mystery religions which had arisen on ancient Near Eastern soil and which had subsequently spread to the major urban areas of the Mediterranean world, including early Judaism and early Christianity.

1. Political and Cultural Setting
2. Greek Religion
3. Roman Religion
4. Hellenistic Religions
5. Paul and Greco-Roman Religion

**1. Political and Cultural Setting.**
The political and cultural situation of the Mediterranean world changed radically following the victorious campaign which Alexander the Great, king of Macedonia, waged against the massive Persian empire beginning in 334 B.C. when Alexander invaded Anatolia with a force of 37,000. His father, Philip II, had earlier defeated the Greeks at the battle of Chaeronea in 338 B.C., and upon his death in 336 he was succeeded by his son Alexander III. Alexander was successful at the battle of Granicus in Anatolia in 334 B.C., where he first clashed with the Persian army under Darius and won decisively; the final blow was delivered at the battle of Gaugamela near the Ganges river in 331 B.C. Following the premature death of Alexander in 323 B.C., his empire crumbled.

The *diadochoi*, or Greek "successors," of Alexander fought among themselves in the attempt to gain control of ever larger parts of the vast region which Alexander had conquered. The more important among these successors were able to found dynastic kingdoms in which a Greco-Macedonian elite ruled over extensive native populations until the Roman conquest of the eastern Mediterranean. Ptolemy founded the Ptolemaic dynasty, which ruled Egypt (and Palestine until 201 B.C.); Seleucus founded the Seleucid dynasty, which ruled the territories from Syria to India; Antigonus founded the Antigonid dynasty, which ruled Macedonia, shorn of its empire; and Lysimachus and his successors ruled Armenia and Thrace.

After Rome had taken control of most of Italy shortly after the beginning of the third century B.C., she embarked on a series of wars with Punic Carthage in North Africa for control of the western Mediterranean. Following Roman victories in the First Punic War (264-241 B.C.) and the Second Punic War (220-201 B.C.), Rome turned to the eastern Mediterranean, initially to punish Philip of Macedonia for the military assistance he had provided to Hannibal, the Carthaginian general. Rome fought a series of three Macedonian wars (214-205, 200-196 and 148-146 B.C.). After the conclusion of the Third Macedonian War in 146 B.C.

(which included the complete destruction of Hellenistic Corinth in 146 B.C.), Rome turned Macedonia and Greece into Roman provinces. At the same time Rome permanently eliminated the economic competition afforded her by Carthage by completely destroying this Punic North African city in 146 B.C.

After the decisive Roman victories over Macedonia, Greece and Carthage in 146 B.C., Rome slowly began annexing the Hellenistic kingdoms which had achieved independence following the crumbling of Alexander's Greco-Macedonian empire. The last Hellenistic kingdom to be defeated was Ptolemaic Egypt; Octavian, the Roman general who was later to become the first Roman emperor and assume the titular name Augustus (meaning "venerable"), defeated Mark Antony and Cleopatra VII (the last Ptolemaic dynast) at the Battle of Actium in 31 B.C. At this point the Romans began to refer to the Mediterranean as *mare nostrum* ("our sea").

Rome had undergone profound changes since the city was founded c. 753 B.C. (the date preferred by the Roman antiquarian Varro, 116-27 B.C.). The period of the monarchy lasted from 753 to 509 B.C., when Tarquinius Superbus, the last of seven kings, was overthrown. The monarchy was succeeded by the Republic which lasted from 509 until it collapsed during the political and military chaos of 133-31 B.C. Following the Battle of Actium in 31 B.C., Octavian took firm control of political and military affairs in Rome. In 27 B.C. he became the first of a series of Roman emperors to rule until the collapse of the western empire in A.D. 476, when the last Roman emperor Romulus Augustulus was deposed.

## 2. Greek Religion.

The Greek world consisted of hundreds of *poleis*, or "city-states," on the Greek peninsula and islands, on the west coast of Asia Minor, Sicily and in Magna Graecia in Italy. Each *polis* was fiercely independent. Each had its own distinctive internal political and religious structure. Originating c. 750 B.C., perhaps linked to the transition from monarchy to aristocracy throughout much of the Greek world, the *polis* reached a fully developed form by the late sixth century, and typically included such features as an acropolis, walls, a market, temples, a theater and a gymnasium (Pausanias 10.4.1). There were, in addition, a number of interstate religious institutions and sanctuaries which did not function primarily for the benefit of a particular *polis*. These institutions provided the hundreds of Greek communities, separated both by distance and topography, with a variety of cult centers which, along with the use of a common language (in

many dialects), contributed to the development of Hellenic national consciousness (Herodotus 8.144). The religious and cultural institutions accessible to all Greeks included the panhellenic games held at intervals of from two to four years (the Olympian games, the most famous, were held every four years beginning in 776 B.C.), the oracle of Apollo at Delphi, the healing cult of Asclepius at Epidauros and the Eleusinian mysteries at Eleusis in Attica. Another panhellenic religious development was the institution of the civic cult of the Twelve Gods instituted in a number of Greek cities beginning in the late sixth century B.C. In general, Greek religion was not organized around a set of coherent doctrines, but rather centered in the observance of traditional rituals such as processions, prayers, libations, sacrifice and feasting (*see* Worship).

*2.1. The Gods.* The Greek notion of deity contrasts sharply with traditional Jewish and Christian conceptions. For the Greeks the gods were not transcendent and passive, but rather immanent and active. They did not create the cosmos (which was thought to be eternal), but came into being after the cosmos. Consequently gods such as the sun, moon and stars were considered "eternals," while gods such as Zeus, Hera and Poseidon were considered "immortals." Though the Greek gods were thought to be more powerful than humans, both were subject to *moira* ("fate"). Further, gods were sustained by ambrosia and nectar, usually inaccessible to mortals, and "ichor" rather than blood flowed in their veins. Though considered very powerful and very wise, they were neither omnipotent nor omniscient. Human beings were considered mortal, while the Greek gods were considered immortal; in archaic and classical Greek religion, immortality was not a possibility for mortals. The scores of deities worshiped by various Greek cities were placed into a comprehensive genealogical relationship by Hesiod in his *Theogony*. In the *Iliad* and *Odyssey*, epic poems probably created by a series of bards collectively designated "Homer," a synthetic presentation of the many originally local divinities was depicted as a pantheon of Olympian gods (though chthonic deities such as Demeter and Dionysus are not mentioned). The cult of Twelve Gods, however, first appears in the late sixth century; literary and archeological evidence indicates that an Altar to the Twelve Gods was dedicated c. 520 B.C. (Herodotus 6.108; Thucydides 6.54.6; Plutarch *Niceas* 13.2). However, this group of Twelve, while they were probably major Attic deities, was not identical with the later pantheon of twelve Olympians (which typically included Zeus, Hera, Poseidon, Hades, Apollo, Artemis, Hephaestus, Athena, Ares, Aphrodite, Hermes, Hestia). The earth deities Demeter and Dionysus (absent from Homer) are sometimes substituted for Hades and Hestia. The earliest complete list of the Twelve Olympians comes from 217 B.C. in connection with the list of gods honored at the *lectisternium* (a sacred banquet where the gods were made guests at a meal; Livy 22.10.9-10; Quintus Ennius *Annales* 7.240-41).

The Greeks recognized three kinds of deities: Olympian gods, chthonic ("earth") gods and heroes. Some of the Olympian gods were of Indo-European origin and were brought with the Greeks when they migrated into the Greek peninsula c. 2000 B.C. The most important Greek deity, for example, was Zeus (the genitive form is Dios, a cognate of the old Sanskrit term *dyaus*, "bright sky"), who corresponds to the central Roman god Jupiter (derived from *Dius + pater*, i.e., "Zeus father"). Other Olympians, such as Athena, Apollo, Artemis and Poseidon, were indigenous to the Greek peninsula or western Anatolia. Most of the chthonic gods, including Demeter and Dionysus, appear to have been deities indigenous to the Greek world and associated with the earth, crops and the underworld. The heroes were thought originally to have been mortals (usually with one divine parent) who were deified upon death and received cultic honors at the supposed site of their tomb. The major exception to this generalization is Heracles, a mythological figure who was worshiped as a god in some places, but as a hero in others, even though he had no known tomb (Herodotus 2.43-45; Apollodorus 2.7.7). Some heroes appear to have originally been considered gods who subsequently "faded" to heroic status (e.g., Asclepios, Helen), some are mythical (e.g., Perseus, Achilles, Orestes, Oedipus, Theseus; on the last two see Sophocles *Oedipus at Colonus* 1590-1666; Plutarch *Theseus* 35-36), while yet others are historical (the Spartan heroes Brasidas and Lysander).

In general the Greeks were extremely open to new deities and cults, and often identified their own deities with some of the major foreign deities which they encountered. During the long contact that the Greeks had with Egypt, they developed an *interpretatio Graeca*, "Greek interpretation," of Egyptian religion in which they regarded various native Egyptian deities as identical with traditional Greek deities. For example, Demeter was thought to be the Greek equivalent of Isis, Athena of Thoeris, Zeus of Ammon and Hermes of Thoth. The pantheon of Olympian gods was the creation of the Homeric poet(s), who produced a synthetic assembly of divinities unknown before the seventh century B.C.

**2.2. Prayer.** From Homer on, Greek prayer involved formulas that were intended to ensure that the god addressed would not be offended by an incorrect invocation. The hymn of Zeus in the *Agamemnon* of Aeschylus is introduced in this manner: "Zeus, whoever he is, if this name pleases him in invocation." Here the liturgical formula *hostis pot' estin*, "whoever he is" occurs (lines 160-61). An earlier example of this formula occurs in *Odyssey* 5.445: "Hear, Lord, whoever you are." In Plato *Cratylus* 400d-e, a distinction is made between the names which the gods use of themselves, which are unknown to humans, and the customary names which humans use in prayers since the true names of the gods are unknown. Prayers were uttered aloud in connection with great public sacrifices, at the beginning of public assemblies (Aristophanes *Thes.* 295-305) and before battle (Aeschylus *Sept. c. Theb.* 252-60; Thucydides *Hist.* 6.32).

**2.3. Sacrifice.** The primary type of sacrifice practiced in Greek religious rituals was the slaughter of approved types of domestic animals, part of which was burned on an altar and part of which was consumed by those who offered the sacrifice. Such sacrifices could be part of domestic or public religious ritual. Certain animals were thought to be required of particular divinities. Cows were sacrificed to Athena, while pigs were sacrificed to Demeter. In the Greek protocol of sacrifice a distinction was made between sacrifices made to Olympian and to chthonic (earth) deities. Sacrifices to Olympians were made on a raised altar (*bomos*) during the day; the sacrificial animals were light colored; their throats were slit upward so that the blood would spurt toward the sky before running down on the altar. Sacrifices to chthonic deities, on the other hand, were made on a low altar (*eschara*) during the evening; the sacrificial animals were dark colored; their throats were slit downward so that the blood would spurt down upon the low altar or pit. The central event of many of the great civic religious festivals, such as the Hyacinthia at Sparta or the Panathenaia at Athens, was a great procession in which the priests and civic officials led the sacrificial victims to the altar, followed by the citizens. After the ritual slaughter, parts of the victims were burned on the altar, while the edible portions were divided up equally among the populace. These portions of meat were sometimes cooked and eaten on the spot or were taken to private homes for cooking and eating.

**2.4. Festivals.** In the *polis* of Athens, about which most is known, approximately 120 days of the calendar were devoted to religious festivals, and the number may have been even greater. Most of these festivals originated as rural, agricultural celebrations. The single festival found more frequently than any other throughout the Greek world was the Thesmophoria, celebrated in honor of Demeter, an indigenous Aegean earth goddess.

*2.5. Temples.* The Greek temple, a free-standing architectural form, originated in the early eighth century B.C., perhaps in conjunction with the rise of the *polis*. Most temples were rectangular (the Telesterion of Demeter at Eleusis was square), and in a central room, called the *cella*, was located a cult-statue of the divinity to whom the temple was dedicated, usually larger than life-size. The temple functioned primarily as a house for the god. Inside the temple various types of offerings and dedications to the deity were stored, and incense was burned in honor of the god. Altars where animals were sacrificed were always located in the open air, usually in front of the temple. Worshipers gathered outside the temple for festivals and sacrifices, never inside.

*2.6. Divination.* Oracles and divination played an important role in the lives of the Greeks from the archaic period until the triumph of Christianity in the fourth century A.D. Divination is the art or science of interpreting symbolic messages from the gods; often these messages are of an unpredictable or even trivial nature. Some of the more typical forms of divination included cleromancy (casting lots), ornithomancy (observing the flight of birds), hieromancy (observing the behavior of sacrificial animals and the condition of their internal organs before and after sacrifice), cledonomancy (interpreting random omens or sounds) and oneiromancy (dream interpretation). The general Greek term for the diviner was *mantis*, a word which is translated "diviner," soothsayer," "seer" and "prophet." Greeks and Romans often distinguished between "technical divination" (the interpretation of signs, sacrifices, dreams, omens and prodigies) and "natural divination" (the direct inspiration of the *mantis* through trance, ecstasy or vision), though in practice there was no rigid distinction between these two types of divine revelation.

The term "oracle" could refer both to the verbal response of a god to a query as well as to the sacred place where the god was consulted. Local oracles were of several types: lot oracles, incubation oracles and inspired oracles. One of the most famous incubation oracles of antiquity was the sanctuary of Asclepius at Epidauros. There healing was believed to be accomplished through the nocturnal appearance of the god to the patient, who was often given instructions about what he or she must do to be cured. The most famous inspired oracle of ancient Greece, which was combined with a lot oracle, was the panhellenic oracle of Apollo at Delphi. There on the seventh day of each month, inquirers could pose questions to the Pythia,

a priestess believed to be the spokesperson for Apollo when seated on Apollo's throne-tripod. The male priests who assisted the Pythia would convey her responses, often in verse, in oral or written form to the inquirer. Apollo gave advice on such matters of state concern as the founding of colonies, the waging of war and issues of sacrificial ritual and protocol, and on such private matters as business trips, occupations, marriages and the whereabouts of stolen property. Thousands of such oracles have survived, most of them in literary sources, though most of them are not authentic. Since oracles were often phrased enigmatically, oracle interpreters (*chresmologoi*) would explain their meaning for a fee.

*2.7. Domestic Cults.* The ancient Greek extended family (the *oikos*, or household) was the context for a form of cult which focused on the hearth and the tomb. The hearth was the place where meals were cooked over a fire that was kept burning for an entire year. It was ritually extinguished each year only to be rekindled again the same day for the next year. Prayers were said before the hearth at the beginning and end of each day, and libations (drink offerings usually consisting of a mixture of wine and water) were poured out on the ground or on the hearth, which functioned as a domestic altar (Hesiod *Op.* 722-24). The male head of the household functioned as a priest, and such offerings were often made to deceased ancestors, who had been made divine upon death. Offerings to these ancestors were also made at the site of their tombs, located on land owned by the family.

**3. Roman Religion.**

Though Rome was a single city-state which became the political seat and administrative center of an enormous empire which surrounded the Mediterranean Sea and extended north and northeast into Europe, native Roman religious cults and cultic practices were never adopted in any significant way by those who were not Roman citizens. Even when citizenship was extended to all adult male inhabitants of the Roman empire by the emperor Caracalla in A.D. 212, the practice of the traditional Roman forms of public worship (religious rituals performed on behalf of the state by members of the college of priests and the magistrates, and rituals celebrated by all citizens) and private worship (the *sacra domestica*, "domestic worship," practiced by families and clans) remained almost exclusively the concern of those who were ethnically Roman. The following description of the public and private aspects of Roman religion focuses on the stage of development which had been reached by the reign of Augustus (27 B.C.-A.D. 14).

**3.1. Central Features.** One of the central features of Roman religion throughout its long history was an emphasis on the *pax deorum* ("peace with the gods"), that is, the conviction that the maintenance of a harmonious relationship with the gods was the basis for temporal prosperity and success. All public disasters were assumed to have been caused by a breach in the relationship between the Roman people and the gods and the reasons for these breaches must be diagnosed through divination and rectified by specific cultic measures. The *pax deorum* was maintained by following a number of measures: (1) deities must be placated by sacrifice and prayer, (2) all vows and oaths must be fulfilled exactly, (3) the city must be preserved from hostile influences by the ritual of *lustratio* and (4) strict attention must be paid to all outward signs of the will of the gods. By the imperial period, the most important aspect of the *pax deorum* was the support and protection of the emperor by the gods.

**3.2. Roman Deities.** The ancient Romans recognized three categories of divine beings. The first type was composed of the autonomous divinities, often arranged in triads (following the Etruscan model), such as Jupiter, Mars and Quirinus, or Jupiter, Juno and Minerva. These deities had a relatively fixed character and were individually honored but (unlike Greek divinities), though they could be called "Father" and "Mother," they did not have marital relationships or offspring. Consequently, the Romans had no native mythology recounting the adventures of the gods (Dionysius of Halicarnassus *Ant. Rom.* 2.19-20), though they later absorbed Greek myths about the gods, and their deities could never be arranged genealogically. Roman mythology took the form of historical accounts with a pervasive legendary component (e.g., Virgil's account of the origins of Rome in the *Aeneid*). The most important Roman god, Jupiter Optimus Maximus ("Jupiter Best and Greatest") had two partners (not wives), Juno and Minerva. Archaic Roman religion grouped Jupiter with Mars and Quirinus. There is evidence attributed to Quintus Ennius (early second century B.C.) for the introduction of the Greek grouping of Twelve Gods in Rome, called *di consentes* ("united gods"), under the names Juno (= Hera), Vesta (= Hestia), Minerva (= Athena), Ceres (= Demeter), Diana (= Artemis), Venus (= Aphrodite), Mars (= Ares), Mercury (= Hermes), Jupiter (= Zeus), Neptune (= Poseidon), Vulcan (= Hephaestus) and Apollo (Ennius *Annales* 7.240-41). During the terrifying days of Hannibal's invasion of Italy in 217 B.C. during the Second Punic War, the Greek municipal cult of the Twelve Gods was incorporated into the *lectisternium* of the Twelve Gods in Rome (previous *lectisternia* honored

only six gods). A *lectisternium* was a "sacred banquet," held only at times of political or social crisis, at which the images of the Twelve Gods were placed in pairs on each of six couches (Livy 22.10.9-10); *lectisternia* were celebrated until at least A.D. 166 (see *Scriptores Historiae Augustae, Marcus Antoninus*, 13.1-2).

The second type of Roman divinity was the countless numbers of secret beings which were jealous of their anonymity and which were constantly helping or hindering the Roman people in their various undertakings, though the Romans were at a disadvantage because they were unable to name them and so control them through the appropriate ritual.

The third category of divinities were the so-called *indigitimenta*, teams of minor deities (existing in extensive lists) each with a minor function in assisting or hindering in each activity or fraction of various human activities, particularly those characteristic of rural areas and those involving private life (Tertullian *Nat.* 11; *De An.* 37-39; Augustine *Civ. D.* 4.11).

**3.3. Priests.** There were two different terms for "priest" in Roman religion, *pontifex* (a member of a college of priests holding supreme authority in public religious matters in Rome, and later a term for an inferior grade of priest) and *flamen* (a priest charged with carrying out the sacrificial ritual of a particular deity, and in the imperial period a priest of a deceased or living Roman emperor). The offices of priest and magistrate were not mutually exclusive, so that all priesthoods, with two exceptions (the *rex sacrorum*, "king of sacrifices," and the *flamen Dialis*, "priest of Jupiter"), were part-time positions which could be held for life (with the exception of the six Vestal virgins, who held office for thirty years). These customs ensured that no priestly class ever developed in Rome, just as none had developed in Greece.

During the late period of the Republic and the Empire there were four main colleges of priests that developed: (1) the *collegium pontificum*, or "college of priests," consisted eventually of sixteen *flamines*, including three *flamines maiores*, "major priests," the *flamen Dialis*, "priest of Jupiter" (Aulus Gellius *Noc. Att.* 10.15), the *flamen Martialis*, "priest of Mars," and the *flamen Quirinalis*, "priest of Quirinus" (reflecting the archaic triad of Jupiter, Mars and Quirinus), together with twelve *flamines minores*, minor priests. Other members of this college included the *rex sacrorum*, "king of sacrifices" (a survival of one function of the Roman kings) and six *virgines vestales*. This college was under the jurisdiction of the *pontifex maximus*, "high priest" (Cicero *Phil.* 11.18), an office regularly held by the emperor during the imperial period. (2) the college of sixteen *augures*, (3) *quindecemviri sacris faciendis*, a college of fifteen men "for conducting sacrifices," and (4) the *septemviri epulones*, a college of seven, and later ten "supervisors of public feasts"). Only the emperor could belong to all of the priestly colleges simultaneously (Augustus *Res Gestae* 7.3).

Public divination, the *ius divinum*, was an important part of Roman civic religion, for divination was the primary means for diagnosing the causes which were thought to have interrupted "peace with the gods" and for interpreting prodigies, signs sent by the gods. There were three types of public diviners whose chief task was to proclaim divine approval or displeasure by interpreting various types of symbolic messages sent by the gods: the *augures*, who interpreted the flight of birds and the meaning of thunder and lightning (Cicero *De Leg.* 2.30), *haruspices*, who interpreted the entrails of sacrificial animals, and the *quindecimviri*, who kept and interpreted the Sibylline books.

*3.4. Prayer.* The invocation of a god or gods by name is a universal feature of prayer. When Romans prayed or sacrificed, they always did so with their heads covered. In the polytheistic system of Roman religion, it was necessary to discover which deity one wanted to influence through invoking his or her name (Varro in Augustine *City of God* 4.22; Horace *Odes* 1.2.25-26). The Romans used a kind of "to whom it may concern" prayer formula so that their prayers would be properly addressed. This formula is usually phrased *sive deus sive dea*, or *si deus si dea*, "whether a god or goddess" (Livy 7.26.4; Cicero *Rab. Perd.* 5; Aulus Gellius *Noc. Att.* 2.28.3) or *sive quo alio nomine te appellari volueris*, "or whatever name you want to be called" (Virgil *Aeneid* 2.351; 4.576; Catullus 34.21-22). A regular part of the structure of ancient prayer was the reasons given why a deity should respond favorably to the request. Two common reasons were: (1) because the god had done so in the past, and (2) because it was within his competence to do so now. In Roman religious ritual, Janus was the first deity invoked in prayers and invocations (followed by Jupiter, Mars and Quirinus), while Vesta was the last.

*3.5. Sacrifice and Temples.* Sacrifice was one of the most important aspects of Roman religion, both public and private. One invariable rule was that male animals were offered to male deities and female animals to female deities. It was considered a good sign if animals went willingly to their slaughter. According to the Roman antiquarian Varro, the early Romans worshipped the gods without statues or temples for 170 years (Augustine *Civ. D.* 4.31), when the Etruscan king Tarquinius Priscus vowed to erect a temple to Jupiter on the capitol (Livy 1.38.7). Roman temples were usually rectangular buildings constructed on a raised plat-

form and had four main features: (1) the inner room, or *cella*, contained the statue of the god to whom the temple was dedicated, together with an altar for the burning of incense; (2) a room or rooms behind the *cella* for the preservation of treasures; (3) an anteroom located in front of the *cella*, surrounded by (4) a roofed colonnade, oblong in Italian temples, but square in Romano-Celtic temples. A stone altar was usually located in front of the temple, where animal sacrifices were made. With the sacrifice of smaller animals, such as goats or lambs, the priest and the sacrificers could eat the edible portions of the sacrifice. The sacrifice of larger animals, such as oxen, provided a feast for a larger number of people, and often the excess meat was sold to the public in the market.

*3.6. The Imperial Cult.* The antecedents of the Roman imperial cult are to be found in the civic cults of the Hellenistic kings (see 4.2 below). The Hellenistic period is characterized in part by a tendency to blur the traditional Greek distinction between mortal and immortal. From the end of the third century B.C. on, there were many cults of Roman magistrates instituted by the Greek cities they controlled. The deified Julius Caesar and the deified Augustus, who were consecrated by official acts of the Roman senate, became part of the official pantheon of the Roman people. The imperial cult was of far greater importance in the provinces than in Rome itself. In Roman Asia in particular, the imperial cult provided a presence for an absent emperor. In the traditional form of the imperial cult, the emperor was worshiped as a god only after his death and apotheosis. In the imperial cults in Anatolia, the divinized emperor was usually associated with other, more traditional, gods such as Dea Roma or various groups of Olympian deities (*see* Emperors).

## 4. Hellenistic Religions.

*4.1. Introduction.* The Hellenistic period began with the conquests of Alexander the Great during the late fourth century B.C. Technically it concluded with the Roman conquest of the last independent Hellenistic kingdom, Ptolemaic Egypt, at the Battle of Actium in 31 B.C. Nevertheless, it actually continued on into the Roman period because of the enormous cultural influence which the Greeks had on their Roman conquerors. The immense political, social and cultural changes accompanying the conquests of Alexander meant that the tension between continuity and change was one of the central features of the Hellenistic age.

*4.2. Hellenistic Ruler Cults.* The development of the ruler cult of Alexander the Great, followed by the cults of subsequent Hellenistic kings, was in many respects an adjustment to the political reality that the cities were no longer independent. As such they required a type of cult appropriate to their subordinate status. One of the major forms of this adjustment is reflected in the development of the ruler cult. Such cults (with priests, processions, sacrifices and often games) were founded in honor of various Greek rulers such as Lysander of Sparta and Dion of Syracuse. Alexander the Great both requested and was granted a cult with divine honors. Greek cities often benefited from various privileges and benefactions from those Hellenistic rulers in whose honor they established cults. Cities normally took the initiative in founding ruler cults and these cults were integral to the affairs of each city-state. After the death of Ptolemy I (c. 280 B.C.), his son and successor Ptolemy II Philadelphos arranged for the formal deification of his father Ptolemy I and his mother Berenike, as *theoi sōtēres*, "savior* gods." In the 270s, Ptolemy II and his wife Arsinoe II were officially deified while yet living as *theoi adelphoi*, "sibling gods," and were offered divine worship in the shrine of Alexander the Great. After Ptolemy II, each successive Ptolemaic king and queen was deified upon accession and worshiped as part of the royal household.

***4.3. Private Associations.*** During the Hellenistic and Roman period there were three types of voluntary associations (*collegia*), each of which had a religious character: (1) professional corporation or guilds (fishermen, fruit growers, ship owners, etc.), (2) funerary societies (*collegia tenuiorum*), and (3) religious or cult societies (*collegia sodalicia*), which centered in the worship of a deity.

***4.4. Mystery Religions.*** *Mystery religion* is a general term for a variety of ancient public and private cults which shared a number of common features. The term *mystery* is based on the Greek term *mystēs*, meaning "initiant," from which is derived the term *mystērion*, meaning "ritual of initiation," that is, the secret rites which formed the center of such cults. In contrast to the public character of most traditional cults of the Greek city-states, the mystery religions were private associations into which interested individuals could be initiated by undergoing a secret ritual. The mystery religions did not appear suddenly in the Mediterranean world during the Hellenistic period, though the period of their greatest popularity appears to have been the first through the third centuries A.D. Many of the mystery cults in the Greek world were profoundly influenced by the oldest of all mystery cults (referred to as "*the* mysteries"), the Eleusinian mysteries with their cult center in Eleusis in Attica. While very little is known about these rituals of initiation (called *teletē*), they appear to have consisted of

three interrelated features of a mystery cult initiation ritual: (1) *dromena*, "things acted out," or the enactment of the myth on which the cult was based; (2) *legomena*, "things spoken," or the oral presentation of the myth on which the cult was based; and (3) *deiknymena*, "things shown," or the ritual presentation of symbolic objects to the initiant. Initiants who experienced the central mystery ritual became convinced that they would enjoy *sōtēria*, "salvation," both in the sense of health and prosperity in this life as well as a blissful afterlife (Firmicus Maternus *De Errore Prof. Rel.* 22.1). Mystery religions were once thought to share a common focus in a divinity who represented the annual decay and renewal of vegetation through his or her death and restoration to life. In recent years the great diversity among those cults formerly lumped together as "mystery cults" has become increasingly apparent. Though there were many mystery cults in antiquity, only the Eleusinian Mysteries and the Mysteries of Mithra will be summarized.

***4.4.1. The Eleusinian Mysteries.*** This cult was native to Attica until it was taken over by Athenians upon the unification of Attica under Athens. Originating as early as the fifteenth century B.C., the cult continued to flourish until the Telesterion, the rectangular temple in Eleusis which served as the center for the cult, was destroyed by the Goths in A.D. 395. The earliest literary evidence for this cult is found in the Homeric *Hymn to Demeter*, which originated c. 550 B.C. A story about the goddess Demeter and her daughter Persephone served as the central myth of the cult. Hades, the god of the underworld, seized Persephone and took her down into the underworld as his wife. Grieving for her daughter, Demeter sought her whereabouts for nine days, when Helios (the sun god) revealed to Demeter what had happened to her daughter. In anger Demeter left Olympus and caused a drought which deprived humans of food and gods of sacrifices. Zeus therefore sent Hermes to strike a compromise with Hades. Persephone was returned to her mother on the condition that she spend one-third of every year in the underworld with Hades. In this myth Demeter is literally the "earth mother," while Persephone represents grain. Persephone's presence with her mother for two-thirds of the year represents the rainy season (primarily during the winter) when crops flourish, while her descent to Hades each year represents the dry, dormant season of the year (Hesiod *Op.* 582-88).

These vegetation deities were understood as metaphors for life and death, and those initiants who voluntarily participated in this cult believed that their ritual identification with Persephone would guarantee them a blissful afterlife (Isocrates *Paneg.* 28-29). One fragment of Sophocles (found in Plutarch *How to Study Poetry* 22F) emphasizes the salvific benefits of initiation: "Thrice blest are those who go to Hades after beholding these rites. For them alone is there life there; for all others there is only evil" (see also Pindar in Clement of Alexandria *Strom.* 3.3.17).

Initiation into the Eleusinian mysteries was a voluntary, two-staged process. The first stage involved initiation into the Lesser Mysteries celebrated annually during the month Anthesterion. After the interval of at least one year, a candidate could be initiated into the Greater Mysteries, which took place during the month Boedromion (September/October). The ritual began in Athens with a gathering of the initiants and the offering of a sacrificial pig in honor of Demeter. Thereafter there was a torchlight parade to Eleusis culminating at the Telesterion, or "hall of initiation." The initiation concluded when the initiants were led into the Telesterion, and to the innermost room of that temple called the Anaktoron. There the initiation was completed. Though ancient sources divulge very little information about the specific character of the initiation ritual, the *dromena* ("things enacted") probably consisted of a nocturnal drama depicting Demeter's sufferings, the *legomena* ("things spoken") possibly consisted of a recitation of a myth similar to that preserved in the Homeric *Hymn to Demeter*, and the *deiknymena* ("things shown") may have consisted of the display of symbolic ritual objects such as an ear of grain.

*4.4.2. The Mysteries of Mithra.* Mithras was worshiped as the sun god, and the name is of Iranian origin. The actual Iranian connections of this cult are dubious, however. Though the earliest datable evidence for the existence of the Mithraic mysteries is the first century A.D., it is likely that this cult originated in the first century B.C. This mystery cult flourished in the second through the fourth centuries A.D., after which the triumph of Christianity resulted in its ultimate disappearance. Information about this cult is primarily available through archeological evidence, which suggests that it was particularly popular in Italy and in the region of the Danube. Epigraphical evidence indicates that members of the cult included soldiers, bureaucrats, merchants and slaves (women were excluded). The central focus of the cult was the preparation for astral salvation, which would be realized upon death when the soul would ascend through the seven planetary spheres to the place of its origin. Members of the cult were initiated into seven ascending levels or grades of initiation, each of which had the protection of a planetary god: (1) *corax*, "raven" (Mercury); (2) *nymphus*, "bride" (Venus); (3) *miles*,

"soldier" (Mars); (4) *leo*, "lion" (Jupiter); (5) *Perses*, "Persian" (Moon); (6) *heliodromus*, "courier of the sun" (Sun); and (7) *pater*, "father" (Saturn). This cult worshiped in artificial caverns, structures called mithraea (fifty-eight of which have been identified by archeologists), located below grade. Every Mithraeum had an artistic representation of the *tauroctony*, or "bull-slaying" scene, in which Mithras is portrayed as slaying a bull, and it was probably the experience of this event, presented through the medium of a ritual, that constituted the central salvific events for adherents to the cult.

## 5. Paul and Greco-Roman Religion.

*5.1. Introduction.* Though there is little doubt that Paul must be understood primarily in terms of Judaism (he claims to have been an observant Jew and a Pharisee in Phil 3:5-6), it must also be recognized that he was a Hellenistic Jew from Tarsus who spoke and wrote fluent Greek and who lived in a context in which Judaism had undergone the process of Hellenization to various extents (*see* Jew, Paul the). Paul was fully aware that his pagan contemporaries recognized many gods and many lords (1 Cor 8:5). Both the Pauline letters and the Acts of the Apostles, the two primary sources for our knowledge of Paul, reflect the ways in which aspects of Hellenistic and Roman religious beliefs and practices had an effect on Paul and his missionary* activity.

*5.2. Paul and the Mystery Religions.* During the late nineteenth and early twentieth centuries, representatives of the German "history-of-religions school" maintained that early Christian sacramentalism (particularly the baptismal* experience of sharing the death* and resurrection* of Christ* reflected in Rom 6) was derived from the dying-and-rising god figure who was supposedly a central feature of Hellenistic mystery cults. Following R. Bultmann, several scholars have argued that Paul formulated part of his argument in Romans 6 and 1 Corinthians 15 in opposition to a Hellenistic sacramental theology which had been adopted by some segments of early Christianity (*see* Paul and His Interpreters). This theology consisted of a form of realized eschatology* understood in terms of the present realization of a resurrection mode of existence.

A. J. M. Wedderburn has provided a series of convincing arguments concerning the mystery cults and Paul's relationship to them: (1) The mystery cults were widespread in the first century A.D., and not primarily in the second century and later as some scholars have argued. (2) The mystery cults had no standard theology centering on the promise of immortality through the ritual experience of sharing the death-and-resurrection experience of the cult deity. (3) The view that the mysteries offered immortality through the ritual identification of the initiate with a dying-and-rising deity is not verified by the surviving evidence about the significance of such mystery initiations. (4) The close connection between baptism* and the Spirit* of God has no analogy in the mysteries.

Some scholars (H.-J. Schoeps; L. Goppelt; H. Böhlig) have proposed that Paul was, at least indirectly, influenced by the particular form of mystery cult found at Tarsus, the annual public festival in honor of the vegetation god Sandon-Heracles. During this festival an image of the god was burned on a funeral pyre. This cult reportedly centered on the dying of nature caused by the intense heat of the summer sun and its resurrection to new life when the rainy season began. In this cult Sandon-Heracles was celebrated as "savior," and the title "Lord" was also applied to him, supposedly in a way similar to Paul's use of the designation "Lord"* for Christ. More recent evidence suggests, however, that the cult of Sandon-Heracles cannot be considered a mystery cult, and it seems likely that the Pauline use of the titles "savior"* and "Lord" were derived from Jewish religious language rather than from the admittedly analogous use of religious language in the Greco-Roman world. However, there are what appear to be a number of words and phrases in Pauline vocabulary which seem to have been derived ultimately from the language used to describe aspects of the mystery cults. These terms, which include "wisdom"* (1 Cor 1:17-31), "knowledge"* (1 Cor 8:1; 13:8), "spiritual person" contrasted with "psychic person," (1 Cor 2:14-16), "to be initiated" (Phil 4:12), "mystery"* and "perfect"* or "mature" (1 Cor 2:5-6), "unutterable" (2 Cor 12:4), do not appear to be drawn *directly* from the mystery cults but had much earlier passed into the common fund of figurative religious language. In particular instances it appears that Paul actually adopted the language of his opponents in his attempt to refute them (e.g., 1 Cor 2:6-13).

*5.3. Paul and the Imperial Cult.* The imperial cult was particularly influential throughout Asia Minor, including the eastern region where Tarsus was located. Beginning with the divine Augustus, Roman emperors* were frequently lauded with such titles as *kyrios* ("Lord"*) and *sōtēr* ("savior"*), and these titles were also used of Jesus by Paul and other early Christians (Rom 1:4; 4:24; 16:2; Phil 2:11; 3:20). While these titles are used of God frequently in the Greek OT, they would have had clear associations with the imperial cult to many ancient Mediterraneans. While the title

"Son of God"* was certainly derived from the OT (2 Sam 7:14; Ps 2:7), the phrase *divi filius* ("son of god") was used of Augustus (referring to his adopted father Julius Caesar) and was a title taken over by other Roman emperors to underline their filial relationship to their divinized predecessors, so that this designation would also have had associations with the imperial cult for many ancients.

*5.4. Paul and Pagan Sacrifices (1 Cor 8:1-13; 10:14-33).* Since observant Jews had scruples against idolatrous* practices and followed dietary laws based on the Torah, which prohibited the consumption of meat from unclean animals or even clean animals not killed in a ritually appropriate manner, Jews and Jewish Christians were naturally reluctant to eat the meat of animals sacrificed to pagan deities (2 Macc 6:7, 12; 7:42; 4 Macc 5:2; *m. 'Abod. Zar.* 2.3; Acts 15:20, 29; 21:25; Rev 2:14, 20; *Did.* 6:3; Aristides *Apol.* 15:5; Justin *Dial. Tryph.* 35; *see* Food). While part of the victims sacrificed in Greek temples was consumed on the premises by priests and worshipers, the rest was sold to the public in the market place. The practice of eating "meat sacrificed to idols*" (*eidōlothyton* in 1 Cor 8:1, 4, 7, 10; 10:19; or *hierothyton* in 1 Cor 10:28), could refer to participation in a sacral meal in a temple or during the distribution of sacrificial meat in the course of a public religious festival, or to the practice of eating meat purchased at the marketplace but which had originally been part of a pagan sacrifice. Paul thought that when people sacrificed to idols they were really sacrificing to demons (1 Cor 10:20), a view common in Judaism (Deut 32:17; Ps 19:5; *Jub.* 1:11; 11:4-6; *1 Enoch* 19:1), and even found among some pagans such as the philosopher Celsus, though for him *daimones* were petty deities (Origen *Contra Celsum* 8.24).

*5.5. Paul in Acts.* In the narrative world of Acts the ubiquitous presence of a variety of Greco-Roman religious traditions and cults become the backdrop for Paul's missionary activity in Anatolia and Europe. In Philippi Paul exorcised a *pneuma Pythōna*, or "spirit of divination," from a young female slave used as a fortune teller by her owners (Acts 16:16-18; *see* Demons, Exorcism). While in Ephesus* (a famous ancient center for the practice of magic*), those who responded to the gospel reportedly rejected sorcery and burned their magical books (Acts 19:18-19). These clashes with paganism are either used by Paul as opportunities for proclaiming the existence and claims of the one true God, or reflect pagan hostility in response to Paul's successful proclamation of the gospel.*

*5.5.1. Deities in Disguise (Acts 14:11-13).* Following the narrative of the healing of a cripple at Lystra by

Barnabas* and Paul, the onlookers make the acclamation "The gods have come down to us in human form," and they called Barnabas Zeus and Paul Hermes (cf. Acts 28:6). The priest of the local temple of Zeus then brought oxen and garlands with the intention of sacrificing to Barnabas-Zeus and Paul-Hermes. From Homer on, Greek tradition entertained the possibility that gods could disguise themselves as human beings (*Iliad* 24.345-47; *Odyssey* 1.105; 2.268; 17.485-87; Homeric *Hymn to Demeter* 94-97, 275-81; Plato *Soph.* 216b; *Rep.* 2.20 [381b-382c]; Silius Italicus 7.176; Ovid *Metam.* 8.626), though such disguises were not usually maintained very long and were generally followed by a recognition scene. Zeus and Hermes were occasionally paired since Zeus had chosen Hermes as his herald and spokesperson (Diodorus Siculus 5.75.2; Apollodorus 3.10.2; Iamblichus *De Myst.* 1.1). Paul was identified by the onlookers with Hermes precisely because he was the chief speaker (Acts 14:12). The closest mythological parallel recounts how Zeus and Hermes, disguised as mortals, were barred from a thousand homes until welcomed by the aged farm couple Baucis and Philemon (Ovid *Metam.* 8.611-724). In Greek tradition the appearance of a deity is traditionally the occasion when divine honors are instituted, a fact which accounts for the behavior of the priest of the temple of Zeus in Acts 14:13.

*5.5.2. The "Unknown God" (Acts 17:23).* In the context of a visit to Athens* narrated in Acts 17:16-34 (a section in which the author of Luke-Acts reveals a familiarity with philosophical traditions and language), Paul visits the Areopagus and, in the manner of an ancient philosopher, directs an apologetic speech to the Epicurean and Stoic philosophers present. In the introduction to this speech (the *captatio benevolentiae*), he congratulates the Athenians for their piety and then refers to an altar in the vicinity with an inscription "to an unknown god," claiming that it is this God whom he is now proclaiming to them. The German classical scholar E. Norden discussed this passage in detail on the basis of the evidence of the unknown gods of antiquity and claimed that the conception of an unknown god is oriental rather than Greek; this view has been refuted by P. W. van der Horst. Jerome thought that Paul had rephrased the inscription (Jerome *Comm. in Tit.* 1.12; *Ep.* 70), a view held by many modern scholars. Pausanias reports the existence of altars to "unknown gods" (in the plural) in Athens and Olympia (Pausanias 1.1.4; 5.14.8). Important cult centers such as Athens, Olympia and Pergamon had dozens of altars to traditional Greek gods (Zeus, Athena, Hermes, etc.), to less traditional deities (e.g., Helios, "sun," and Selene, "moon"), to abstrac-

tions (e.g., Pistis, "fidelity," and Arete, "virtue") and (in an attempt to be complete, i.e., to have a *pantheos peribōmismos*, a "precinct for altars of all gods without exception") to "unknown gods" and (safer still) to "all the gods." Though no inscription has been found which exactly reproduces the phraseology of Acts 17:23, it is quite possible that such inscriptions actually existed.

*5.5.3. Artemis of the Ephesians (Acts 19:23-41).* In this episode (perhaps alluded to in 1 Cor 15:32 and 2 Cor 1:8-11), Paul's success in proclaiming the gospel in the Roman Province of Asia is perceived as threatening the livelihood of the silver-workers guild, which made miniature silver replicas of the temple of Artemis to be sold as souvenirs or amulets (Acts 19:24). The temple of Artemis in Ephesus* was one of the seven wonders of the world (Strabo 14.1.20-23; Pausanias 2.2.5; 4.31; Achilles Tatius 7-8; Xenophon Eph. *Ephesian Tale* 1.1-3), and the city was given the title *neōkoros*, "temple-keeper" (Acts 19:35), as a major center of the imperial cult. The acclamation "Great is Artemis of the Ephesians" (Acts 19:28) reflects a popular title of the goddess (Xenophon Eph. *Ephesian Tale* 1.11).

*See also* ATHENS, PAUL AT; DEMONS AND EXORCISM; ELEMENTS/ELEMENTAL SPIRITS OF THE WORLD; EMPERORS, ROMAN; EPHESUS, PAUL AT; FOOD OFFERED TO IDOLS AND JEWISH FOOD LAWS; GNOSIS, GNOSTICISM; HELLENISM; IDOLATRY; MAGIC; PHILOSOPHY; WORSHIP.

BIBLIOGRAPHY. H. Böhlig, *Die Geisteskultur von Tarsos im augusteischen Zeitalter mit Berücksichtigung der paulinischen Schriften* (FRLANT 19; Göttingen: Vandenhoeck & Ruprecht, 1913); W. Burkert, *Ancient Mystery Cults* (Cambridge: Harvard University, 1987); idem, *Greek Religion* (Cambridge: Harvard University, 1985); F. Cumont, *The Mysteries of Mithra* (New York: Dover, 1956); idem, *Oriental Religions in Roman Paganism* (New York: Dover, 1956); E. J. Edelstein and L. Edelstein, *Asclepius: A Collection and Interpretation of the Testimonies* (Salem: Ayer Company, 1988); J. Ferguson, *The Religions of the Roman Empire* (Ithaca: Cornell University, 1970); J. Finegan, *Myth & Mystery: An Introduction to the Pagan Religions of the Biblical World* (Grand Rapids: Baker, 1989); J. Fontenrose, *The Delphic Oracle: Its Responses and Operations* (Berkeley: University of California, 1978); P. W. van der Horst, "The Altar of the 'Unknown God' in Athens (Acts 17:23) and the Cult of 'Unknown Gods' in the Hellenistic and Roman Periods," *ANRW* II.18.2 (1989) 1426-56; J. H. W. G. Liebeschuetz, *Continuity and Change in Roman Religion* (Oxford: Clarendon, 1979); G. Luck, *Arcana Mundi: Magic and the Occult in the Greek and Roman World* (Baltimore: Johns Hopkins, 1985); J. G. Machen, *The Origin of Paul's Religion* (New York: Macmillan, 1921); R. Mac-

Mullen, *Paganism in the Roman Empire* (New Haven: Yale University, 1981); A. D. Nock, *Conversion: The Old and the New in Religion from Alexander the Great to Augustine of Hippo* (London: Oxford University, 1933); D. Ulansey, *The Origins of the Mithraic Mysteries: Cosmology and Salvation in the Ancient World* (New York: Oxford University Press, 1989); A. Wardman, *Religion and Statecraft among the Romans* (Baltimore: Johns Hopkins, 1982); A. J. M. Wedderburn, *Baptism and Resurrection: Studies in Pauline Theology Against Its Graeco-Roman Background* (WUNT I.44; Tübingen: J. C. B. Mohr, 1987); L. B. Zaidman and P. S. Pantel, *Religion in the Ancient Greek City* (Cambridge: University Press, 1992).                                        D. E. Aune

**REMARRIAGE.** *See* MARRIAGE AND DIVORCE, ADULTERY AND INCEST.

**REMNANT THEOLOGY.** *See* ISRAEL; RESTORATION OF ISRAEL.

## RESTORATION OF ISRAEL

Paul's attitude toward his people Israel* often seems quite contradictory. In one of his earliest letters, Paul comes down hard on "the Jews," affirming that "the wrath* of God has come upon them *eis telos*" (in one translation, "finally"; 1 Thess 2:14-16). In one of his latest letters, however, he expects that "all Israel will be saved" (Rom 11:26). Did Paul's view of Israel's future develop over the course of time or perhaps change periodically according to the missionary* situation with which he was confronted? In order to understand Paul's perspective on the future of Israel it is essential to appreciate the OT and Jewish background, for Paul's appropriation of the OT and his understanding of it provide the framework of his theology. Paul's Jewishness and immersion in biblical thought would have rendered him incapable of developing his theology apart from his traditional and biblical heritage. Against this background, furthermore, the apparent contradictions in Paul's perspective on Israel and her future tend to dissipate.

1. The Restoration of Israel in OT and Jewish Tradition
2. The Restoration of Israel in Paul

### 1. The Restoration of Israel in OT and Jewish Tradition.

For the purposes of this survey, the background of Paul's thinking can be traced to the two main streams of tradition which flowed out of the exilic and post-exilic situations.

*1.1. The Exilic and Post-exilic Situations.*

*1.1.1. The Exile.* The exile which came upon the northern kingdom in 722 B.C. and upon the southern kingdom in 587 B.C. represents a tragic phase in Israel's history and religious self-concept. A fundamental tenet of the ancient Israelite faith was that Yahweh had promised Israel land and statehood as signs of his special covenant relationship with her. These institutions included a capital city and a formal sanctuary where sacrificial worship was carried out. All these had been attained during the reigns of David and Solomon. Consequently the annexation of Israel to the Assyrian empire and of Judah to the Babylonian empire came as a direct challenge to the professed heritage of ancient Israel.

The prophets' response to this situation both before and after Israel's exile was basically to call their audience back to allegiance to Yahweh. The people were challenged to fulfill their responsibilities as his covenant people. From the prophetic perspective the exile was an act of God that was both punitive and redemptive. For, on the one hand, the prophets preached that the Exile was a judgment of God for Israel's failure to live up to her obligations as Yahweh's chosen people. The deportations of both Israel and Judah were understood to be Yahweh's way of dealing with the sins of his people. On the other hand, however, the prophets preached that if the people repented, there was hope of restoration for Israel in the future.

*1.1.2. The Post-exilic Situation.* When the Persians gained control of the Babylonian empire, they attempted to secure peace among a large and diverse mix of nationalities and cultures. This was done by allowing deported peoples to return to their homelands and to set up theocracies (i.e., political institutions that had priestly leadership). The edict of Cyrus allowed for the return of deported Jews to the homeland, as well as for the rebuilding of the city of Jerusalem and the Temple. Many Jews, however, who had been exiled to Babylonia did not take the opportunity to return to Palestine, for life there had become quite comfortable. And none of the ten tribes of the northern kingdom ever returned. A Davidic prince, Sheshbazzar, led the first group of those who returned, but he was not successful in reestablishing a new Jewish community in the homeland. An ambitious nephew, Zerubbabel, followed and sought to reopen the temple at Jerusalem to be a national and religious focal point. He was eventually removed by the Persian governor, who took measures to discourage further displays of royal ambitions. It was at this stage that the high priest of Jerusalem (Joshua ben Jehozadak) was vested with whatever leadership powers were deemed appropriate by the Persian governor. In 515 B.C. a modest temple was completed, which did not compare with the splendor of the former Solomonic Temple.

*1.2. Streams of Tradition: The "Already" and the "Not Yet."* From this point in Israel's history, two major streams of tradition developed which differed radically in their interpretation of the postexilic situation (see Steck 1968; Hengel 1973, 321-22). According to one pervasive Jewish interpretation, the promised restoration had *already* occurred, as evidenced by such events as the return from Exile and the rebuilding of Jerusalem and the Temple. This perspective was based on the theocracy, centered on the Temple and the priesthood, and stressed the putative continuity with the preexilic cult. According to another influential interpretation, however, the restoration had *not yet* occurred and could still be expected in the eschatological future. For although the Israelites could return from exile, a restoration of all twelve tribes did not occur; although the Israelites could again live in the promised land, they did so under foreign rulers; and although the Temple was rebuilt, it was not the center of a unified people in its own land. Hence the theological ambiguity of the events at the turn of the postexilic period allowed for both of these mainstream traditions to flourish, which they did throughout the Second Temple period and beyond.

*1.2.1. The Theocratic Stream.* The stream of tradition associated with Temple circles had as its theological agenda the establishment of the postexilic cult. According to Ezra 1:1, the seventy years of exile with which 2 Chronicles ends (36:16-21) are now over, and Yahweh has raised up Cyrus. Thus Israel is separated from the dark period of Exile, in which Yahweh requited the guilt of the last preexilic generation; the land has in between received the Sabbath years which were denied it; Israel stands again in continuity with the salvific dealings of God before the Exile. If Israel falls into sin, the cult can provide forgiveness and atonement. It does not matter that the northern tribes never returned from exile, nor even that most Judeans remained in the Diaspora, nor that all Israel (even those in Judah and Jerusalem) remain under foreign rule. The restoration has already been realized. For according to this perspective, there is only one theologically relevant factor: whether they adhere to the Jerusalem cult.

The theocratic tradition displays the "pattern of religion" which E. P. Sanders has called "covenantal nomism," identifying it as the common denominator of the various expressions of Palestinian Judaism from 200 B.C. to A.D. 200. "Briefly put," writes Sanders, "covenantal nomism is the view that one's place in God's

plan is established on the basis of the covenant and that the covenant requires as the proper response of man his obedience to its commandments, while providing means of atonement for transgression" (Sanders 1977, 75). "All those who are maintained in the covenant by obedience, atonement and God's mercy belong to the group which will be saved" (Sanders 1977, 422). Unfortunately, however, Sanders has so stressed continuity in the covenantal relationship between God and his people, and readily available atonement for sin by means of repentance, that another major stream of tradition in Palestinian Judaism, which emphasizes prolonged *discontinuity* in the relationship as punishment for sin, has gone practically unnoticed. In no way can it be said that the "business-as-usual" approach of the theocratic stream prevailed in every quarter.

*1.2.2. The Eschatological Stream.* This stream of Jewish tradition takes the position that Israel has not yet been restored, but rather remains, until the eschatological restoration, under the wrath of God which came upon the people in 722 and 587 B.C. for their disobedience. From this perspective the Second Temple and its cult has no efficacy for atonement. In fact the Second Temple is often either considered polluted or deficient (cf. Dan 3:38 LXX; Sir 36:14; *1 Enoch* 89:73; 90:28-33; Tob 14:5; *T. Levi* 16:1-5; 17:10-11; *2 Apoc. Bar.* 68:5-7; *T. Moses* 4:8) or passed over altogether (cf. Yadin, 1:182-87). Many penitential prayers of the Second Temple period lament the present plight of Israel as a nation (e.g., Dan 9:4-19; Ezra 9:6-15; Neh 9:5-37; Bar 1:15—3:8; Pr Azar; Sir 36:1-17; see further Scott "Gal 3:10"). The people are seen as continuing under the judgment and curse of God. Theologically speaking, "all Israel is still in Exile just as before, whether she now finds herself in the Land, which others rule, or in the Diaspora" (Steck 1968, 454). Furthermore, this condition of Exile would last until God intervenes in the eschatological future, which is now recognized as a time well beyond the seventy years which Jeremiah had envisioned (cf. Dan 9:24: 70 x 7 years). Because God's judgment and curse on Israel persists, the whole sinful history from the Exodus on, which led to this judgment, also continues on the people. Therefore, the penitential prayers repeatedly acknowledge Israel's national guilt in order to declare the justice of God for the ongoing judgment (cf. von Rad). The earlier salvific deeds of God can now be only a pledge for the urgent plea that the expected restoration might come in order to bring an end to the present curse and remove the guilt of the people.

The eschatological stream is in no way limited to a

few penitential prayers; it pervades Second Temple literature. Especially from the Seleucid period onward, this stream of tradition occupied an important place in postexilic theological history. It had become apparent from both the apostasy within Israel and the persecution of Antiochus from without that the idea of a realized restoration did not correspond to reality (cf. Neusner). As Nickelsburg comments:

> The destruction of Jerusalem and the Exile meant the disruption of life and the breaking up of institutions whose original form was never fully restored. Much of post-biblical Jewish theology and literature was influenced and sometimes governed by a hope for such a restoration: a return of the dispersed; the appearance of a Davidic heir to throw off the shackles of foreign domination and restore Israel's sovereignty; the gathering of one people around a new and glorified Temple. (Nickelsburg, 18)

Of particular importance to the eschatological stream is the Deuteronomic view of Israel's history, a pervasive OT/Jewish tradition which covered the whole history of Israel from its initial election to its ultimate salvation (cf. Steck 1967). By the final stage of its development (in the period from Antiochus IV to *2 Baruch*), the Deuteronomic view of Israel's history was still a living tradition capable of a certain fluidity of expression, but it had also become a relatively fixed conceptual framework containing the following six elements:

(1) The Deuteronomic view of Israel's history begins with the affirmation that Israel has been persistently "stiff-necked," rebellious and disobedient during its whole long history. For example, the second-century B.C. national confession of sin in Baruch 1:15—3:8, which contains the Deuteronomic tradition, commences with the words: "*We* have disobeyed him [the Lord], and have not heeded the voice of the Lord our God, to walk in the statutes of the Lord that he set before us. From the time when the Lord brought our ancestors out of the land of Egypt *to this day* (cf. Deut 9:7; 29:3, 27; 2 Kings 17:23; 1 Esdr 8:73-74; 2 Esdr 9:7; Neh 9:32; Bar 1:13, 19; 2:6; Ezek 2:3; 20:31), *we* have been disobedient to the Lord our God, and *we* have been negligent, in not heeding his voice" (Bar 1:18-19). As is characteristic of other national confessions of sin in this period which reflect the Deuteronomic perspective, the contemporary generation of Israelites identifies with the sins of the fathers by means of the first person plural (cf. Scharbert; Steck 1967, 114, 119, 120-21, 124-27), just as Moses includes the Israelite community before the conquest with the exile and restoration of future generations by means of the sec-

ond person plural (cf. Deut 4:25-31). This is because Deuteronomy and the Deuteronomic tradition view Israel as a unity in a historical continuum.

(2) After establishing the persistence of Israel's sin right up to the present, the Deuteronomic view of Israel's history goes on to affirm that God constantly sent his messengers, the prophets, to call his people to repentance and obedience.

(3) Nevertheless, Israel continued in its obduracy and rejected the message of the prophets. Again, the words of the national confession of sin in Baruch 1:15—3:8: "*We* did not listen to the voice of the Lord our God in all the words of the prophets whom he sent to us, but all of us followed the intent of our own wicked hearts by serving other gods and doing what is evil in the sight of the Lord" (Bar 1:21-22). Some texts which are framed by the Deuteronomic tradition stress that Israel not only rejected the message of the prophets but actually persecuted and killed them (e.g., Neh 9:26; *Jub.* 1:12; *1 Enoch* 89:51).

(4) Therefore, in view of Israel's intransigence, the wrath of God burned against Israel; judgment came upon them starting in (722 or) 587 B.C.; and the people were sent into Exile. According to the Deuteronomic view of Israel's history, the condition of Exile lasted all through the Second Temple period and even beyond, because the sin of the people and therefore their guilt did not abate (cf. Steck 1967, 122; idem 1968, 453-54). Thus, as the narrative introduction to Baruch shows (1:1-14), the prayer in Baruch 1:15—3:8 was to be prayed on behalf of Jerusalem, because "*to this day* the anger of the Lord and his wrath have not turned away from us" (Bar 1:13). The confession itself goes on to state, in obvious allusion to Deuteronomy 27—32: "So *to this day* there have clung to us the calamities and the curse which the Lord declared through his servant Moses . . ." (Bar 1:20). And similarly, somewhat later in the same confession: "See, *we* are today in our exile where you have scattered us, to be reproached and cursed and punished for all the iniquities of our ancestors, who forsook the Lord our God" (Bar 3:8).

(5) The Deuteronomic view of Israel's history holds that during the protracted exile Israel still has the chance of repenting of sin. Thus the national confession of sin in Baruch 1:15—3:8 affirms, again referring to the latter section of Deuteronomy,

> Yet you have dealt with us, O Lord our God, in all your kindness and in all your great compassion, as you spoke by your servant Moses on the day when you commanded him to write your Law in the presence of the people of Israel, saying, "If you will not obey my voice, this very great multitude will surely turn into a small number among the nations

where I will scatter them. For I know they are a stiff-necked people. But in the land of their exile they will come to themselves and know that I am the Lord their God. I will give them a heart that obeys and ears that hear; they will . . . turn from their stubbornness and their wicked deeds." (Bar 2:27-33)

The confession goes on to implore the mercy of God, for although the petitioners are repentant, they are still in Exile (Bar 3:1-8). The point of much Second Temple literature is, however, that the obduracy of Israel persisted all during the protracted Exile (cf. Steck 1967, 187).

(6) If the people repent, then, according to the Deuteronomic view of Israel's history, God will restore them to the land and to a covenantal relationship with himself. Thus the national confession of sin in Baruch continues with the divine promise:

I will bring them again into the land that I swore to their ancestors, to Abraham, Isaac and Jacob. . . . I will make an everlasting covenant with them to be their God and they shall be my people; and I will never again remove my people from the land that I have given them. (Bar 2:34-35)

The "everlasting covenant" and the covenant formula allude here to Jeremiah 32:38, 40, which in turn recalls the "new covenant" and the covenant formula of Jeremiah 31:31-34. In other texts with the Deuteronomic perspective, the sixth element includes the expectation of an eschatological pilgrimage of the Gentiles to Zion to share in the restoration of Israel (cf. *Pss. Sol.* 17:30-35; *2 Apoc. Bar.* 68:5; Tob 13:11; 14:6-7; *1 Enoch* 90:30-36). Other texts emphasize that, along with the enemies of Israel, unrepentant Israel will fall under the final judgment of God.

## 2. The Restoration of Israel in Paul.

Does Paul's concept of the restoration of Israel agree with either one of these two divergent mainstreams of Jewish tradition? To answer this question it will be necessary to consider Paul's Pharisaic background, his apostolic self-concept and his use of Scripture.

*2.1. Paul's Pharisaic Background.* When Paul the apostle sought to list the reasons he might have for putting confidence in the flesh, he mentioned his Pharisaic background (Phil 3:5; cf. Acts 22:3; 23:6; 26:5; *see* Jew, Paul the). Although it is extremely difficult to ascertain the content of Pharisaic teaching before A.D. 70, and Pharisaism developed over time, splintering into factions (cf. Hengel 1973), nevertheless Steck (1967, 210-11) suggests that the Pharisees were probably bearers of the Deuteronomic tradition. This would correlate in general with Acts 23:6-10 (cf.

Acts 24:15-16; 26:6-7; 28:20), where Paul is able to rally Pharisaic support for his cause in the Sanhedrin when he identifies himself as a Pharisee who is on trial for "the hope*" of Israel* and "the resurrection* of the dead" (Acts 23:6), two closely related themes in OT/ Jewish tradition on the restoration of Israel (cf. Haacker).

*2.2. The Apostle to the Gentiles for the Sake of Israel.* Even after he became a believer and was spurned by his compatriots, Paul affirmed his Jewish ancestry and heritage (Phil 3:5; 2 Cor 11:22; Rom 11:1), and he called the Israelites his own people and kindred (Rom 9:3). Paul's starting point is that the Messiah of Israel (Rom 9:5) came to be the hope* of both Jews and Gentiles* alike (Rom 15:8-13). In true solidarity with his people, therefore, Paul mourned Jewish unbelief and hardening and wished that he himself could be cut off from Christ* and accursed on their behalf (Rom 9:2-3). Paul's heart's desire and prayer* to God* for Israel was that they may be saved (Rom 10:1).

Paul's concern for the salvation* of his people stems not merely from patriotism, but more particularly from the call of God upon his life. Most scholars assume (cf. Sandnes, 61-65) that Paul's description of his apostolic call (*see* Conversion and Call) in Galatians 1:15 ("But when he who has set me apart from my mother's womb and called me by his grace . . .") alludes to the calling of the Servant* in Isaiah 49:1 ("From my mother's womb he has called my name") and 49:5 ("the Lord, who formed me from the womb to be his own servant, to gather Jacob and Israel to him"; *see* Prophet, Paul as). If this is so, then Paul's apostolic commission must have included from the start a vision for the restoration of Israel (cf. Kim, 97), even though the universalistic purpose of his call is stressed in Galatians 1:16 (cf. Is 49:6, which ties together both aspects of the Servant's call—as an agent of Israel's restoration and as a light to the nations; *see* Universalism).

Paul might have been primarily the apostle* to the Gentiles (Rom 1:5; 11:13; cf. Gal 1:15-17; 2:7-8), but he was the apostle to the Gentiles for the sake of Israel. Even the gospel—the good news of Israel's restoration (cf. Is 52:7, cited in Rom 10:15)—which Paul was commissioned to preach was to the Jew first and also to the Greek (Rom 1:16). As a result, Paul would sometimes try to win Jews directly (1 Cor 9:20). More often, however, he would try to win them indirectly through his Gentile mission: "Inasmuch then as I am an apostle to the Gentiles, I magnify my ministry, in order to make my fellow Jews jealous, and thus save some of them" (Rom 11:13-14; cf. 10:19 [citing Deut 32:21]; 11:11). Not only does Paul view his Gentile mission as a catalyst to the present salvation of a remnant from Israel, he also views it as an essential precursor to the eventual salvation of all Israel; for it is not until the full number of the Gentiles comes in that all Israel will be saved (Rom 11:25-26). Hence Paul's driving passion is to bring the gospel to the Gentiles as quickly as possible, even as far as Spain (Rom 15:18-29), and to raise the collection for the saints (*see* Collection).

If Paul casts his Gentile mission as an effort to provoke Israel to jealousy,* it is not just a desperate attempt to demonstrate to Jewish Christians in Rome that he really is concerned for Israel after all (contra Räisänen, 187-88). For Paul bases this understanding of the role of Gentiles in the restoration of Israel on the eschatological* hope of Deuteronomy 32:21. In other words, Paul conceives his ministry as fitting within the framework of the aforementioned eschatological stream of Jewish tradition, particularly the Deuteronomic view of Israel's history.

### 2.3. The Deuteronomic Framework of Paul's Restoration Theology.

*2.3.1. Deuteronomy and Paul's Use of Scripture.* It has often been observed that Paul confines his citations of the OT to certain letters, and that he tends to gravitate toward certain OT books more than others (*see* Old Testament in Paul). Of the approximately one hundred explicit citations of the OT in the Pauline corpus, almost all appear in the *Hauptbriefe* ("chief letters," cf. D. M. Smith). In fact, among the uncontested letters of Paul, not only are the explicit citations confined to the *Hauptbriefe*, but fully half are found in Romans* alone. And fully half of the OT quotations in Romans are found in chapters 9—11. To match this uneven distribution of OT citations in Paul is an uneven selection of OT books cited. Paul obviously has a preference for citations of Isaiah, Psalms, Genesis and Deuteronomy. According to Dietrich-Alex Koch (33), Paul cites Isaiah twenty-eight times, Psalms twenty times and Genesis and Deuteronomy fifteen times each. No other book is quoted more than five times.

What attracts Paul to these specific OT books? On the one hand, the reason behind Paul's attraction to Isaiah is relatively clear. In the words of R. Hays,

> Isaiah offers the clearest expression in the Old Testament of a universalistic, eschatological vision in which the restoration of Israel in Zion is accompanied by an ingathering of Gentiles to worship* the Lord; that is why the book is both statistically and substantively the most important scriptural source for Paul. (Hays, 162)

This is true, according to Hays (46), even when Paul cites Isaiah 52:5 in Romans 2:24 ("For, as it is written, 'The name of God is blasphemed among the Gentiles

because of you' ") and imaginatively assumes thereby that the present-day Israel that he is castigating is in exile, for the quotation of Isaiah 59:20 and 27:9 in Romans 11:26-27 shows that the apostle sees beyond the exile to Isaiah's words of hope and restoration.

On the other hand, what attracts Paul to Deuteronomy is perhaps less clear. Hays calls Deuteronomy "the most surprising member of Paul's functional canon within the canon" (Hays, 163). For, as he goes on to argue,

> One might expect this book of conditional blessings and curses to bear witness—as it apparently does in Gal 3:10, 13—to precisely the sort of performance-based religion that Paul wants to reject. In fact, however, none of Paul's other references to the book is pejorative in character; nowhere else is Deuteronomy disparaged as a retrograde voice of legalism. Instead, . . . the words of Deuteronomy become [in Romans] the voice of the righteousness from faith . . . [and] a prefiguration of Paul's gospel. (Hays, 163)

Hays never resolves the tension between Paul's uses of Deuteronomy in Galatians and Romans. He does, however, emphasize the key importance of the Song of Moses in Deuteronomy 32. In fact, Hays goes so far as to say that "Deuteronomy 32 contains Romans *in nuce*" (Hays, 164), a statement which he substantiates by two considerations:

(1) Deuteronomy 32 contains the salvation-historical scheme appropriated in Romans: God's election* and care for Israel (Deut 32:6-14), Israel's rebellion (Deut 32:15-18; cf. 32:5), God's judgment upon them (Deut 32:19-35) and ultimately God's final deliverance and vindication of his own people (Deut 32:36-43).

(2) Deuteronomy 32 contains both the prophecy that God would stir Israel to jealousy through the Gentiles, cited in Romans 10:19 (cf. Deut 32:21), and the invitation to the Gentiles to join with God's people in praise, cited in Romans 15:10 (cf. Deut 32:43).

For Hays, therefore, Deuteronomy is used by Paul in much the same way as Isaiah, that is, as a part of "his typological reading strategy" to find a scriptural basis for a universalistic, eschatological vision in which the restoration of Israel is accompanied by the inclusion of Gentiles to worship the Lord.*

There can be no question that Hays is fundamentally correct: Deuteronomy is crucial to Paul's thinking. As was discussed above, however, much of Second Temple literature is heavily influenced by Deuteronomic tradition. How does Paul square with this tradition? Although Hays recognizes that Paul's "typological reading strategy extends a typological trajectory begun already in the texts themselves" (Hays, 164), he does not follow through with this idea by showing how Paul's use of Deuteronomy is mediated by OT/ Jewish tradition. In the following, it will be shown how Deuteronomic tradition is taken up by Paul in letters as early as 1 Thessalonians* and as late as Romans.

*2.3.2. Paul's Use of Deuteronomic Tradition in 1 Thessalonians 2:15-16.* In the polemic against the Jews in 1 Thessalonians 2:15-16 (which many have dismissed as a later, post-Pauline addition despite the fact that Rom 9:22 repeats the same idea), Paul appropriates a Hellenistic Jewish-Christian tradition which adapts the Deuteronomic view of Israel's history to include the death of Jesus (*see* Death of Christ) as the culmination of Israel's rejection of the prophets (cf. Steck 1967, 274-78). Beginning in 1 Thessalonians 2:14, Paul compares the persecution which the Thessalonians experienced from their fellow citizens to that which the churches in Judea suffered* at the hands of "the Jews." Then in 1 Thessalonians 2:15-16 he goes on to describe the Jews in more general terms as those

> who killed both the Lord Jesus and the prophets, and drove us out; they displease God and oppose all people, by hindering us from speaking to the Gentiles so that they might be saved. Thus they have constantly been filling up the measure of their sins; but God's wrath has come upon them *eis telos* (lit. "finally" or "completely").

Here, as in the first element of the Deuteronomic perspective (see 1.2.2 above), the historic sin of the people is seen as ongoing even to the present. In fact the sin is steadily filling up to its full measure (cf. Mt 23:32). Here, as in the third element of the Deuteronomic perspective, the violent rejection of the prophets is seen as symptomatic of the continuing guilt and obduracy of the Jews. For Paul the Jewish people have been as unrepentant and recalcitrant in the face of his message (cf. 2 Cor 11:24-25) as they have always been toward the prophets during the long history of Israel. Hence, as in the fourth element of the Deuteronomic perspective, the wrath* of God came upon the people at a historical point in the past, most likely at the destruction of Jerusalem in 587 B.C. and the Babylonian Exile, and they still displease God. The ongoing "wrath" of God on Israel in Exile is a constant theme of the Deuteronomic perspective in OT/Jewish tradition (cf. Steck 1967, 364; McCarthy 1974).

If 1 Thessalonians 2:16 stresses the wrath of God which has come on Israel, that does not necessarily mean that the apostle views his people as doomed forever. While this may depend to a certain degree on whether *eis telos* (1 Thess 2:16) is translated "at last," "forever," "completely" or "to the end," Paul could have a positive outlook on Israel's future even if the phrase should be translated "forever." For even in the ultimately positive perspective in Romans 9—11, Paul cites Psalms 68:24 in Romans 11:10, which apparently pronounces eternal judgment* on the Jews (*dia pantos*). Furthermore, if Paul sees himself in 1 Thessalonians 2:15 (as elsewhere, cf. Sandnes) in the line of the OT prophets, and that particularly within the Deuteronomic tradition of the violent rejection of the prophets, then Luke's portrayal of Paul as a Deuteronomic-style preacher of repentance to Israel (cf. Moessner) gains credibility. Although Paul's verdict on the Jews in 1 Thessalonians 2:16 fails to express elements 5 and 6 of the Deuteronomic view of Israel's history (the traditional hope of repentance and restoration for Israel), this could reflect the apostle's contingent situation (cf. Acts 17:1-15; 2 Cor 11:24-25; Gal 5:11) rather than the coherence of his theological beliefs. The very fact that Paul appropriates the Deuteronomic tradition, which looks inexorably beyond present judgment to future hope, may indicate his basically positive conviction about Israel's future. In that case, there would be no fundamental contradiction or development between this passage and Romans 11:25-32, especially in light of the fact, as will be shown below, that Romans 9—11 is also framed by the same Deuteronomic tradition. Moreover, it is possible that Paul realized already in 1 Thessalonians 2:16— and not first in Romans 11:25-26—that Israel's complete and final salvation depends on the prior inclusion of the full number of the Gentiles, for his negative remarks about Israel's present standing with God follow directly upon his statement that the Jews are hindering him from preaching to the Gentiles that they might be saved.

*2.3.3. Paul's Use of Deuteronomic Tradition in Galatians 3:10.* Scholars have long been baffled about what kind of assumption lies behind Paul's citation of Deuteronomy 27:26 (+ 29:19) in Galatians 3:10: "For as many as are of works of the Law are under a curse*; for it is written, 'Cursed is every one who does not abide by all things written in the book of the law, to do them.'" How can Paul cite Deuteronomy in support of his point? Was Deuteronomy 27:26 not merely a warning of what would happen if Israel violated the covenant stipulations? How could Paul assume that the curse of Deuteronomy had indeed come upon Israel?

The Deuteronomic view of Israel's history provides the most plausible solution to this question (see Scott "Gal 3:10"). Paul's use of Deuteronomy in Galatians 3:10 assumes the same perspective that lies behind 1 Thessalonians 2:15-16, and behind the national confession of sin in Baruch 1:15—3:8, and especially behind the closely related prayer of Daniel 9:1-18. Just as Daniel 9:11 acknowledges that "the curse (*katara*) has come upon us, and the oath that is written in the law of Moses the servant of God, because we have sinned," so also Paul assumes in Galatians 3:10 that the "curse" (*katara*) "written" in Deuteronomy has come upon Israel because of the nation's sin. In fact the likeliest explanation as to why Paul considers Israel to be "under" a curse is that the Deuteronomic "curse" to which Daniel 9:11 refers came "upon" the people. For Paul Deuteronomy 27:26 is not a "retrograde voice of legalism." Paul evidently assumes the Deuteronomic perspective which was prevalent in Second Temple literature and reflected in Daniel 9, that the divine judgment begun in 587 B.C. continues on Israel, that the Jewish people remain in exile until the time of the restoration (cf. also N. T. Wright 1992, 140-41, 146). In other words, the use of Deuteronomy 27:26 (29:19) in Galatians 3:10 is another example of the *exilic* perspective which Hays has already noticed in the citation of Isaiah 52:5 in Romans 2:24.

As in Paul's citation of Isaiah 52:5 in Romans 2:24, however, his quotation of Deuteronomy 27:26 (29:19) in Galatians 3:10 sees beyond Israel's exilic situation. For the subsequent context of Galatians 3—4 goes on to make clear that Christ reverses the effects of the curses of Deuteronomy (cf. Dan 9:24-27) and thereby brings the redemption and restoration expected in Isaiah. According to Galatians 3:13, "Christ redeemed us from the curse of the Law, having become a curse for us; for it is written: 'Cursed is every one who hangs on a tree.' " Here Paul cites Deuteronomy 21:23 in combination with Deuteronomy 27:26, in order to adapt it to the previous citation of Deuteronomy 27:26 both lexically and materially. Paul's use of Deuteronomy in Galatians* is totally subordinated to the Deuteronomic tradition which reflects the situation of Israel since 587 B.C. From Paul's point of view, however, "the fullness of time has come" and the messianic Son of God has redeemed those who were under the curse of the Law (Gal 4:4-5). The fact that Galatians 3—4 moves from "curse" to "redemption" from the curse through Christ, and from there to the integrally related reception of the "Spirit"* and divine adoptive sonship (*see* Adoption and Sonship), shows unequivocally that Paul partakes here of restoration tradition. Thus Galatians 3:10 should be seen together with Galatians 3:13-14 as the negative side of the traditional hope—already articulated in Deuteronomy 27—32—which looks forward to the inclusion of the Gentiles in the restoration of Israel (cf. Deut 32:43, cited in Rom 15:10). Seen in this light, Paul's exilic understanding of the Deuteronomic curse in Galatians 3:10 parallels

that found in Jewish inscriptions of Asia Minor (cf. Trebilco, 60-69), which may help to explain why the Galatian addressees could be expected to follow the rather enthymatic argument here.

*2.3.4. Paul's Use of Deuteronomic Tradition in Romans 9—11.* Here, again, the Deuteronomic view of Israel's history provides the framework for Paul's thinking. In Romans 9—11 Paul presents a sustained theological argument to solve the problem of Israel which was raised in the first eight chapters of the letter. That problem is as follows: although the gospel* is to the Jew first (Rom 1:16), most of Israel is closed to the gospel (Rom 10:16) and therefore has not received salvation (cf. Hofius, 175-78). Has God's promise to Abraham* and his seed been annulled (Rom 9:6)? Has God rejected his people (Rom 11:1-2)? These are the questions which, as an Israelite motivated by supreme love for his people (cf. Rom 9:2-3), Paul seeks to answer in this section, showing that "the gifts and calling of God are irrevocable" (Rom 11:29). Paul's salvation-historical argument in Romans 9—11 is framed by the six traditional elements of the Deuteronomic perspective (see 1.2.2 above).

(1) As in the first element of the Deuteronomic view of Israel's history, Paul affirms in Romans the recalcitrance and guilt of the Jewish people. He makes this point already in Romans 2:1-29, often alluding to Deuteronomy, and carries this thought forward in Romans 9—11. In Romans 9:31, for example, Paul states: "Israel who was pursuing the law of righteousness has not attained to that Law." In Romans 10:21, furthermore, Paul brings out the historical dimension of Israel's guilt by the citation of Isaiah 65:2: "But of Israel he [Isaiah] says, '*All day long* I [God] have held out my hands to a disobedient and contrary people.' " In this citation, Paul thrusts forward the phrase "all day long" in order to stress the constancy with which God has graciously appealed to his people, most recently in announcing to them the gospel message. As Bultmann correctly observes,

> When Paul characterizes Israel according to Isaiah 65:2 as "a disobedient and contrary people" (Rom 10:21), he understands the history of Israel as a whole, that is, as a unified history of sin. And this sin is, so to speak, concentrated—and thereby in its essence manifested—in the Jews' lack of faith in Christ and the Christian message. All the accusations of the Jews and threats of the prophets are applied to the present time (Rom 9:25—11:10). (Bultmann, 100)

Thus Bultmann, who immediately before this comment denies that a Deuteronomic view of Israel's history is found in Paul, unwittingly makes a strong argument for its existence in Romans 9—11! For, as Steck (1967, 193) has shown, the Deuteronomic view brings the whole sinful history of Israel to bear on the present. As in 1 Thessalonians 2:15-16, Paul is saying here that Israel has been continually disobedient and obstinate.

(2-3) As in the second and third elements of the Deuteronomic view of Israel's history, Romans 9—11 features Israel's violent rejection of the prophets, at least tangentially. For in showing that God has not rejected his people totally and finally (cf. Rom 11:1-2a), Romans 11:2b-5 adduces 1 Kings 19:10, 14:

> Do you not know what the scripture says of Elijah, how he pleads with God against Israel? "Lord, they have killed your prophets, they have demolished your altars, and I alone am left, and they seek my life." But what is God's reply to him? "I have kept for myself seven thousand who have not bowed the knee to Baal." So too at the present time, there is a remnant, chosen by grace.

Although Paul's main point in citing this text is that now as always God has preserved a remnant in Israel (cf. Rom 9:27-29), the fact that the apostle thrusts forward the statement about the killing of the prophets suggests that he also wants to stress, as in 1 Thessalonians 2:15, the continual obduracy of Israel to the prophetic message, including his own gospel message (cf. Rom 10:16; 15:31). The Deuteronomic view of Israel's history traditionally uses Israel's violent rejection of the prophets as an indication of Israel's continual obduracy. In fact, *1 Enoch* 89:51 alludes to 1 Kings 19:10, 14 in the context of the Deuteronomic framework (cf. Steck 1967, 155 n. 5). Therefore, the reference to Israel's killing of the prophets in Romans 11:3 should be seen, along with that in 1 Thessalonians 2:15, as an element of the Deuteronomic perspective (pace Steck 1967, 278 n. 2).

(4) As in the fourth element of the Deuteronomic view of Israel's history and 1 Thessalonians 2:16 which appropriates this perspective, Romans affirms the wrath of God on the Jewish people (Rom 2:6-8; 3:5, "on us"). Furthermore, as Hays has observed, the quotation of Isaiah 52:5 in Romans 2:24—"The name of God is blasphemed among the Gentiles because of you"—works in Paul's argument only if the Jewish readers castigated by the text take on the role of Israel in Exile. This does not require Jewish readers to strain their own imaginations, for the Deuteronomic tradition which Paul appropriates assumes that the Jewish people remain under judgment in Exile long after the sixth century B.C. and indeed until the time of the restoration.

The concept of the judgment on Israel is developed in more detail in Romans 9—11. Already in Romans 9:1-3 Paul implies that divine judgment rests on Israel, for, with great sorrow and anguish for his people, the apostle expresses the wish that he were "accursed and cut off from Christ for the sake of my own people, my kindred by race." Paul's anguish for his people stems from the realization, which he articulates in the subsequent context, that the majority of Israel remains under the condemnation of God, at least for the time being. The presence of a "remnant" may show that God has not abandoned his people (Rom 11:1-6), but the fact remains that the "rest" of Israel who are not included in the remnant stand under condemnation. For according to Romans 11:10, David's curse applies to "Israel" which "failed to obtain what it sought" (Rom 11:7; cf. 10:3): "let their eyes be darkened so that they cannot see, and keep their back forever bent" in servitude. Moreover, Romans 11:15 presupposes that God has rejected the majority of Israel. Romans 11:17-24 pictures Israel as an olive tree (*see* Olive Tree) whose branches are cut off because of their "unfaithfulness" (Rom 11:17, 19-22; cf. 3:3). The image stems from Jeremiah 11:16-17 (cf. Hos 14:6), which prophesies that as an olive tree Israel's branches would be broken for violating the covenant—a possible reference to the judgment in 587 B.C.

In view of this evidence, there is much to commend Wright's observation (1980, 218) that in Romans 9—11 Paul is "working out the exile-theology of Moses' closing speech in Deuteronomy, applying it to his new situation as others had applied it to the exile itself (Jeremiah) or the Maccabean crisis (Qumran, the apocalyptists), and would apply it to the events of A.D. 70 (4 Ezra, the Rabbis)."

(5) As in the fifth element of the Deuteronomic view of Israel's history, Romans 2:4-5 makes it clear that God wants to lead Israel to repentance before the final judgment, but that Israel has had a hard and impenitent heart (cf. Deut 31:27). Romans 9—11 elaborates on this point by arguing that Israel's present rejection of the gospel reflects their continual obduracy to the message of the prophets. During the period that God has been showing his wrath, he "has endured with much patience the vessels of wrath made for destruction . . ." (Rom 9:22; cf. 1 Thess 2:16). Paul writes in Romans 10:16, citing Isaiah 53:1: "But they have not all obeyed the gospel; for Isaiah says, 'Lord, who has believed what he has heard from us?' " In other words, what Isaiah could say in his day applies equally in Paul's day because of the continual obduracy of the people. Likewise in Romans 11:7b-8 Paul states, citing Deuteronomy 29:3 (+ Is 29:10): "The elect obtained it, but the rest were hardened, as it is written,

'God gave them a spirit of stupor, eyes that should not see and ears that should not hear, down to this very day.' " Thus Paul affirms, in accordance with the Deuteronomic perspective, that Israel has always been recalcitrant and continues to be so. Moreover, as Paul goes on to say in Romans 11:25: "a hardening has come upon part of Israel, until the full number of the Gentiles has come in." Yet Paul also argues on the basis of Deuteronomy 32:21, a text about Israel's experience in exile, that God seeks to make Israel jealous by means of the Gentiles in order to provoke Israel to repentance and emulation (cf. Rom 10:19; 11:11, 14).

Hence the apostle to the Gentiles has a twofold purpose in evangelizing the Gentiles as quickly as possible: First, he hopes thereby to provoke his fellow Jews to jealousy and thus bring some of them to salvation (Rom 11:13-14). If they do not persist in unbelief, the Jews will be grafted in, for God has the power to graft them in again (Rom 11:23). But, second, he also hopes to bring in the full number of the Gentiles and so bring about the parousia, when all Israel will be saved (Rom 11:25-26).

(6) As in the sixth element of the Deuteronomic view of Israel's history, Romans 9—11 expects the national restoration of Israel in conjunction with the eschatological pilgrimage of the Gentiles. In Romans 11:25-32 Paul reiterates that the salvation of Israel follows the salvation of the Gentiles (cf. Rom 11:11-15), and that the Gentile Christians are not to be conceited (cf. Rom 11:17-24). Paul is confident that the natural branches will be grafted back into their own olive tree (Rom 11:24). He then takes this a step further by describing how Israel will eventually be saved.

First, the hardening of Israel will continue "until the fullness* of the Gentiles comes in" (Rom 11:25), which implies an ongoing historical process which will be completed in the future. In accordance with the OT/Jewish concept of the "eschatological measure," the fullness of the Gentiles (cf. Rom 11:12) refers to a particular number of Gentiles who are predestined to be saved. In other words, as long as Israel remains hardened and thus fills up the measure of their sin* (cf. 1 Thess 2:16), the Gentiles would fill up another measure, according to the sovereign plan of God. Paul probably thought that once the Spanish mission was completed the full number of the Gentiles would be reached (cf. Riesner).

The idea of the Gentiles' "coming in" implies the OT/Jewish expectation of the pilgrimage of the Gentiles to Zion in the messianic time. If the image of the pilgrimage of the Gentiles in Isaiah 2:2-5 has been used here, the order has been reversed: The nations do not come to Israel because they see Israel's glory; rather, Israel comes to the nations because she sees the salvation and glory which they have in Christ. As Hofius (324) suggests, however, Paul may have in mind certain OT texts which put the eschatological pilgrimage of the Gentiles before the restoration of Israel. When the full number of the Gentiles comes in, then, second, all Israel, including the previously impenitent and hardened majority, will be saved at the parousia (cf. Hofius, 319-20). Thus Romans 11:26-27 states, citing Isaiah 59:20 and 27:9: "And so all Israel will be saved, just as it is written: The Deliverer will come from Zion, he will remove ungodliness from Jacob"; "and this will be my covenant with them when I take away their sins."

Interpreters often wonder whether "all Israel will be saved" means every single Israelite or only a full and proper representation of Israel. The answer may be neither, for according to the Deuteronomic tradition which frames Romans 9—11, Israel is a unity in a historical continuum (cf. 1.2.2. above). Therefore, Romans 11:26 probably has in view the people of Israel taken as a whole from their initial election to their ultimate salvation. This will be the time of the resurrection of the dead (cf. Rom 11:15), which is closely associated with the restoration of Israel (cf. Haacker). This will also be the time of the new covenant,* when God will restore the covenantal relationship with his people and forgive Israel's sins (Jer 31:31-34; cf. 1 Cor 11:25-26; 2 Cor 3:1-18; 6:14—7:1). Finally, this will be the time of the deliverance and vindication of Israel expected in Deuteronomy 32:36-43, when the Gentiles will rejoice with Israel (Deut 32:43). Interestingly enough, Paul cites Deuteronomy 32:43 LXX in Romans 15:10 for the benefit of Gentile believers. The fact that the Gentiles participate in the restoration of Israel was signaled already by the quotations of Hosea 2:25; 2:1 (LXX) in Romans 9:25-26.

E. P. Sanders (1985, 91-119) finds in Romans 9—11 such compelling evidence of traditional restoration eschatology that he suggests Paul can be adduced, together with John the Baptist, to show that the expectation of the restoration stands at the conclusion as well as at the beginning of Jesus' ministry. For Sanders, however, Paul's concept of restoration is a somewhat desperate expedient to solve what he calls Paul's "fundamental theological problem," that is, how to hold together and/or reconcile the two dispensations of election/Law and faith, and thus to save God's reputation from the charge of arbitrariness (Sanders 1991, 117-28; cf. also Räisänen, 196). Sanders thinks that Paul is caught in a dilemma—how to reconcile God's promises to Israel with the promise of salvation to those who have faith* in Christ—which cannot be solved as long as the apostle is considering the present age. Hence Paul changes categories by "lateral thinking," relegating the solution to the future, when God will save everyone and everything.

The problem with assuming such a dilemma, however, is that it ignores the fundamental question: Why did Israel need a restoration in the first place? Sanders fails to see that, according to the Deuteronomic view of Israel's history which Paul appropriates in Romans 9—11, there was a plight: Israel had apostatized from the covenant and this led to their judgment in exile; covenantal nomism had ceased to be a viable option after 587 B.C.

*See also* APOCALYPTICISM; COVENANT AND NEW COVENANT; CURSE, ACCURSED, ANATHEMA; ESCHATOLOGY; ISRAEL; JUDGMENT; LAW; WRATH, DESTRUCTION.

BIBLIOGRAPHY. R. H. Bell, "The Origin and Purpose of the Jealousy Motif in Romans 9-11: A Case Study in the Theology and Technique of Paul" (Dr. theol. dissertation, Eberhard-Karls-Universität, Tübingen, 1990); O. Betz, "Die heilsgeschichtliche Rolle Israels bei Paulus," *Theologische Beiträge* 9 (1978) 1-21; R. Bultmann, "Geschichte und Eschatologie im Neuen Testament," in *Glauben und Verstehen. Gesammelte Aufsätze* (2d ed.; Tübingen: J. C. B. Mohr, 1962) 3.91-106; N. A. Dahl, "The Future of Israel," in *Studies in Paul: Theology for the Early Christian Mission* (Minneapolis: Augsburg, 1977) 137-58; K. Haacker, "Das Bekenntnis des Paulus zur Hoffnung Israels nach der Apostelgeschichte des Lukas," *NTS* 31 (1985) 437-51; S. Hafemann, "The Salvation of Israel in Romans 11:25-32: A Response to Krister Stendahl," *Ex Auditu* 4 (1989) 38-58; M. Hengel, *Judaism and Hellenism* (2 vols.; Philadelphia: Fortress, 1974); idem, *The Pre-Christian Paul* (Philadelphia: Trinity Press International, 1991); O. Hofius, "Das Evangelium und Israel. Erwägungen zu Römer 9-11," *ZThK* 83 (1986) 297-324; S. Kim, *The Origin of Paul's Gospel* (2d ed.; Grand Rapids: Eerdmans, 1984); B. W. Longenecker, "Different Answers to Different Issues: Israel, the Gentiles and Salvation History in Romans 9-11," *JSNT* 36 (1989) 95-123; D. J. McCarthy, "The Wrath of Yahweh and the Structural Unity of the Deuteronomistic History," in *Essays in Old Testament Ethics (J. Philip Hyatt, In Memoriam)*, ed. J. L. Crenshaw and J. T. Willis (New York: Ktav, 1974) 99-107; D. P. Moessner, "Paul in Acts: Preacher of Eschatological Repentance to Israel," *NTS* 34 (1988) 96-104; J. Munck, *Paul and the Salvation of Mankind* (Atlanta: John Knox, 1959); J. Neusner, *Self-Fulfilling Prophecy: Exile and Return in the History of Judaism* (Boston: Beacon, 1987); G. W. E. Nickelsburg, *Jewish Literature Between the Bible and the Mishnah: A Historical and Literary Introduction* (Philadelphia: Fortress, 1981); G. von Rad, "Gerichtsdoxologie," in *Gesammelte Studien zum Alten Testament*, ed. R. Smend (Munich: Chr. Kaiser Verlag, 1973) 2.245-54; H. Räisänen, "Paul, God and Israel: Romans 9-11 in Recent Research," in *The Social World of Formative Christianity and Judaism: Essays in Tribute to Howard Clark Kee*, ed. J. Neusner et al. (Philadelphia: Fortress, 1988); R. Riesner, *Die Frühzeit des Paulus. Studien zur Chronologie, Missionsstrategie und Theologie des Apostels bis zum ersten Thessalonicher-Brief* (WUNT; Tübingen: J. C. B. Mohr, forthcoming); E. P. Sanders, *Jesus and Judaism* (Philadelphia: Fortress, 1985); idem, *Paul* (Oxford: University Press, 1991); idem, *Paul and Palestinian Judaism: A Comparison of Patterns of Religion* (Philadelphia: Fortress, 1977); K. O. Sandnes, *Paul—One of the Prophets? A Contribution to the Apostle's Self-Understanding* (WUNT 2.43; Tübingen: J. C. B. Mohr, 1991); J. Scharbert, "Unsere Sünden und die Sünden unserer Väter," *BZ* 2 (1958) 14-26; J. M. Scott, *Adoption as Sons of God: An Exegetical Investigation into the Background of* ΥΙΟΘΕΣΙΑ *in the Pauline Corpus* (WUNT 2.48; Tübingen: J. C. B. Mohr, 1992); idem, " 'For as many as are of works of the law are under a curse' (Gal 3:10)," in *Paul and the Scriptures of Israel*, ed. C. A. Evans and J. A. Sanders (Sheffield: JSNT, forthcoming); D. M. Smith, "The Pauline Literature," in *It Is Written: Scripture Citing Scripture. Essays in Honour of Barnabas Lindars*, ed. D. A. Carson and H. G. M. Williamson (Cambridge: University Press, 1988); O. H. Steck, *Israel und das gewaltsame Geschick der Propheten. Untersuchungen zur Überlieferung des deuteronomistischen Geschichtsbildes im Alten Testament, Spätjudentum und Urchristentum* (WMANT 23; Neukirchen-Vluyn: Neukirchener, 1967); idem, "Das Problem theologischer Strömungen in nachexilischer Zeit," *EvT* 28 (1968) 445-58; P. R. Trebilco, *Jewish Communities in Asia Minor* (SNTSMS 69; Cambridge: University Press, 1991); N. Walter, "Zur Interpretation von Römer 9-11," *ZThK* 81 (1984) 172-95; N. T. Wright, "The Messiah and the People of God: A Study in Pauline Theology with Particular Reference to the Argument of the Epistle to the Romans" (D. Phil. thesis, University of Oxford, 1980); idem, *The Climax of the Covenant: Christ and the Law in Pauline Theology* (Minneapolis: Fortress, 1992); Y. Yadin, *The Temple Scroll* (Jerusalem: The Israel Exploration Society/The Institute of Archaeology of the Hebrew University of Jerusalem/The Shrine of the Book, 1983). J. M. Scott

**RESTRAINING POWER.** *See* MAN OF LAWLESSNESS AND RESTRAINING POWER.

# RESURRECTION

The resurrection of Jesus Christ from the dead is foundational to the Christian faith. It is referred to explicitly in seventeen books of the NT and is implicit in most of the remaining ten. Nearly all of the letters within the Pauline corpus refer to it (the exceptions are 2 Thess, Tit, Philem). Indeed, Romans 10:9 makes confession of the resurrection the equivalent of acceptance of the lordship of Jesus Christ and a necessary condition of salvation,* and 1 Corinthians 15:14 demonstrates how closely connected it is in Paul's mind to his own kerygmatic ministry.* In Romans 4:25 Paul decisively grounds the doctrine of justification* upon Christ's resurrection when he says that Jesus was "raised for our justification" (*dia tēn dikaiōsin hēmōn*); while in Philippians 3:11 he equates "knowing Christ" with knowing "the power of the resurrection." It is no surprise that the longest single chapter in the Pauline letters (1 Cor 15) is given over completely to a discussion of the resurrection.

The resurrection of Jesus Christ stands as the central motif in Paul's eschatology* insofar as it inaugurates the age to come and provides the basis for future hope. The Christ event is, in the evocative words of McDonald: "the Archimedean point that has levered the world of Jewish religion into a new order" (McDonald, 28). The resurrection of Christ and the resurrection of the faithful on the last day are related, the hope of the latter being based upon the certainty of the former.

Two remarks about the resurrection of Jesus Christ as it is portrayed in the Pauline letters need to be made at the outset. First, it is important to note that Paul never attempts to prove the historicity of the resurrection to any of the congregations to which he addresses his letters (contra Bultmann's views on 1 Cor 15:3-8). He simply asserts the resurrection as a fact (presumably believed by them) and seeks to draw out its implications for their life and faith. Paul is not concerned with philosophical questions of how subjective faith and objective history interrelate; this is predominantly a post-Enlightenment issue which is driven by positivistic concerns not a part of Paul's outlook. Modern attempts to argue for the historical verification of the resurrection of Jesus Christ based upon the Pauline materials are therefore misdirected, even though they are generally motivated by the best apologetic concerns (Ladd offers a readable discussion of this issue).

Second, Paul nowhere describes the actual resurrection of Jesus Christ itself, nor does he seek to provide an account of it simply as a historical event to be put alongside other events of history. The resurrection is historical, yes, but it is also more than historical (or to use McDonald's term, "meta-historical"; McDonald, 138). What descriptions Paul does offer about the risen Christ are postresurrectional appearances of the Lord

which are taken to be illustrative of the event and serve as circumstantial guarantees of its historicity. Thus he begins his longest discussion of the resurrection theme by citing a traditional formula which summarizes the kerygma (1 Cor 15:3-4) and then proceeds to list the witnesses to these postresurrectional appearances of the Lord Jesus (1 Cor 15:6-8). The appeal to pre-Pauline tradition highlights the centrality of the resurrection proclamation from the earliest period of the Christian movement (see Kloppenborg and Murphy-O'Connor for a discussion of this passage).

Both of these considerations should be kept in mind in all apologetical concerns focusing on the resurrection as the basis of Christian faith.

1. The Origins of a Doctrine of Resurrection
2. Paul and Pharisaic Belief in the Resurrection
3. Terminology of the Resurrection
4. Images of the Resurrection
5. Co-Crucifixion and Co-Resurrection in Christ
6. The Resurrection: Some Issues of Interpretation

### 1. The Origins of a Doctrine of Resurrection.

Most scholars agree that the doctrine of bodily resurrection is a fairly late development within the writings of Judaism. The first unambiguous declarations in the OT of resurrection from the dead occur in Daniel 12:2 and (possibly) Isaiah 26:19, although there are antecedents of it in the miracles of resuscitation performed through Elijah and Elisha (1 and 2 Kings), and in images of a national revival within OT prophetic literature (notably Hos 6:1-2 and the vision of the valley of dry bones contained in Ezek 37:1-14). A bodily resurrection from the dead is also proclaimed in a number of Jewish apocryphal and pseudepigraphal texts, including 2 Maccabees, 4 Ezra, *1 Enoch* and *2 Baruch*. There are also important background materials, at least to do with postmortem life, within the classical tradition of Platonism, usually as an image of the spiritual awakening or the transmigration of the soul (see Perkins, 37-69). The matter has been well researched by scholarship and need not be rehearsed here (see Nickelsburg and Greenspoon for detailed studies of Jewish background texts).

While Paul's letters are the earliest Christian writings to mention the resurrection of Christ, there is every indication that the idea was part of Jesus' own belief and expectation. All four Gospels record reference to it in virtually all strata (some may deny it is expressed in 'Q'). Paul may have taken over the centrality of the resurrection as a theological idea from Jesus himself (see Witherington), although it certainly was present within the Pharisaic party of Judaism of which he was a member.

## 2. Paul and Pharisaic Belief in the Resurrection.

Paul's membership within the Pharisaic party of Judaism is asserted in both his letters (Phil 3:5) and by Luke (Acts 23:6; 26:5). In Acts the disagreement between the Sadducees and the Pharisees over the doctrine of a bodily resurrection is a prominent theme (Acts 4:2; 23:6-8; 24:21; cf. Acts 26:6; 28:20). It is reasonable to assume that Paul accepted the traditional Pharisaic view of the resurrection of the body and understood his encounter of the risen Lord Jesus Christ in light of it. As Sider states, "as a good first-century Pharisee, Paul could not conceive of the resurrection of the dead in purely immaterial terms" (Sider, 438; for further discussion see Davies, 285-320).

## 3. Terminology of the Resurrection.

There are several different words and phrases which are used to describe the idea of resurrection or associated concepts within the Pauline letters. The verb *anistēmi* ("raise up") is used a total of five times with reference to the resurrection, both of Christ (1 Thess 4:14; cf. Rom 15:12) and of the believer (1 Thess 4:16; Eph 5:14). The verb *egeirō* ("raise," "cause to rise") appears a total of thirty-eight times with reference to the resurrection (Rom 4:24, 25; 6:4, 9; 7:4; 8:11 (twice), 34; 10:9; 13:11; 1 Cor 6:14; 15:4, 12, 13, 14, 15 (twice), 16 (twice), 17, 20, 29, 32, 35, 42, 43 (twice), 52; 2 Cor 1:9; 4:14 (twice); 5:15; Gal 1:1; Eph 1:20; 5:14; Col 2:12; 1 Thess 1:10; 2 Tim 2:8); and the compound verb *exegeirō* ("raise up") once in reference to the resurrection of believers (1 Cor 6:14). In addition the noun *anastasis* ("resurrection") is used eight times (Rom 1:4; 6:5; 1 Cor 15:12, 13, 21, 42; Phil 3:10; 2 Tim 2:18) and the noun *exanastasis* ("resurrection") occurs once (Phil 3:11). These terms are used of both the resurrection of Jesus Christ himself and the raising of the believers which the Lord's resurrection guarantees (Dahl provides a chart detailing the use of the terms in the NT).

Some have argued that there is a difference in meaning between these two word groups (*egeirō* and *anistēmi*) and on that basis have attempted to trace a development in the use of the terms within the Pauline materials. Coenen, for example, suggests that a close examination "shows that *egeirō*, especially in the pass., is used predominantly for what happened at Easter, i.e. the wakening of the Crucified to life, while *anistēmi* and *anastasis* refer more specifically to the recall to life of people during the earthly ministry of Jesus and to the eschatological and universal resurrection" (Coenen, 276). However, an absolute distinction seems rather arbitrary and difficult to sustain (both 1 Cor 15:12-13 and 15:42 appear to use the two verbs interchangeably and Eph 5:14 includes both verbs within its citation of Is

60:1). It seems that Paul does not intend that any substantial difference be maintained between the two, although the use of *egeirō* may be more traditional and related to an underlying Palestinian source (it does appear frequently within passages often taken to contain creedal declarations such as 1 Cor 15:4; *see* Creed).

In Romans 6:10 and 14:9 the verb *zaō* ("to live") is used with reference to Jesus' resurrection. It is similarly used in 2 Corinthians 13:4 and is explicitly contrasted with the verb *stauroō* ("crucify"); the verse also applies the verb *zaō* to the Christians who will share in Christ's resurrection. The compound verb form *syzēsomen* ("we will live with [him]") in Romans 6:8 and 2 Timothy 2:11, as well as *syndoxasthōmen* ("we may be glorified with [him]") in Romans 8:17 are used to the same end. The use of the verb *zōopoieō* ("to give life to") also builds on a resurrection idea and occurs six times (Rom 4:17; 8:11; 1 Cor 15:22, 36, 45; 2 Cor 3:6), usually within the context of the ultimate resurrection of the saints and the manifestation of the glory* of God. Similarly the verb *synegeirō* ("to rise up together") in Colossians 2:12; 3:1 and Ephesians 2:6, as well as *synezōopoiēsen* ("he made alive together with [him]") in Colossians 2:13 and Ephesians 2:5 continue this theme, expressing the union of the church in Christ's death. The verb *anagō* ("to bring up") occurs once in Romans 10:7 with reference to the resurrection of Jesus Christ from the dead (*Christon ek nekrōn anagagein*, "to bring Christ up from the dead").

The use of *anabainō* ("to go up, ascend") in Ephesians 4:8, 10 and *anelēmphthē* ("he was taken up") in 1 Timothy 3:16 may also reflect an underlying resurrection theme, demonstrating how closely connected is the language of ascension and resurrection. This is particularly evident in pre-Pauline materials, such as those contained in Romans 1:4; 8:34; Philippians 2:9 and 1 Thessalonians 1:10 (Baird discusses this at some length).

## 4. Images of the Resurrection.

It is important to note that the English phrase "resurrection from the dead" evokes a rather different mental picture than does its Greek equivalent *anastaseōs nekrōn* (Rom 1:4; cf. Phil 3:11 which has *ek nekrōn*, lit. "out from the dead ones"). In English something of the dynamism of the phrase is lost due to the fact that we take "dead" to be a state of being or the place of habitation of those who are departed, almost as if it were a singular, abstract noun. In Greek, however, the noun behind *nekrōn* is a plural one, which means the phrase *anastasis nekrōn* may be translated literally as "resurrection from out of dead ones" (cf. Phil 3:11). The Greek expression contains a much more dynamic image, conjuring up a

*807*

picture of "the standing up from the midst of corpses," and lending weight to the somatic nature of the resurrection body. But it is essential to observe that Paul does not proclaim a "resurrection of the flesh," as subsequent Christian writers were to do (including the author of *2 Clement* and Justin Martyr). Paul maintains a distinction between *sarx* ("flesh") and *sōma* ("body") when it comes to his teaching about the resurrection.

It is important to show that Paul draws upon several different ideas in an effort to communicate the meaning of this resurrection, which he describes as "a mystery"* (*mystērion*) in 1 Corinthians 15:51. The wide variety of images employed is revealing in its own right; demonstrating the limitations of language when it is put into the service of attempting to describe the indescribable. There is an open-endedness, a flexibility of expression, within Paul's description of the resurrection which is both exhilarating and frustrating to interpreters. The images may be discussed under eight headings.

*4.1. Resurrection as Transformation.* At several points Paul uses the language of transformation in his description of the future resurrection awaited by the Christian. In Philippians 3:10 a participial form of the verb *symmorphizō* ("to take on the same form") occurs in precisely this context: "that I may know him and the power of his resurrection, and may share his sufferings, becoming like him (*symmorphizomenos*) in his death." At the conclusion of the same chapter the image is expanded and linked directly with the revelation of the Lord Jesus Christ as savior* from heaven (Phil 3:20). In Philippians 3:21 the language of transformation appears twice: "(Jesus Christ) will change (*metaschēmatisei*) our lowly body to be like (*symmorphon*) his glorious body." One of the clearest expressions of resurrection as transformation occurs in 1 Corinthians 15:51-52, where the apostle twice uses the verb *allagēsometha* ("we shall be changed") to describe what awaits the believing community at the parousia of Christ. This future transformation is described in verse 52 as instantaneous (*en atomō, en rhipē ophthalmou*, "in a moment, in the twinkling of an eye"). Such transformation language is different in emphasis from that contained in passages from earlier letters, such as 1 Thessalonians 4:13-18 where a spatial metaphor ("caught up together") dominates the action associated with the parousia. Gillman describes the shift such a difference represents as a move from the implicit to the explicit and suggests the "rapture" imagery of 1 Thessalonians 4 is fully compatible with the transformation motif in 1 Corinthians 15.

It is important to note that in 1 Corinthians 15:51-54a Paul is dealing with the matter of the transformation of those who happen to be alive at the parousia of Christ.

Here the apostle teaches a universal transformation of all who are in Christ, both living and dead, but maintains that this does not mean that all will be resurrected. Only those who have died are in need of resurrection; for those who are alive at the parousia the transformation is sufficient to grant immortality in the age to come. Some NT commentators, notably J. Jeremias (following the lead of A. Schlatter), have taken the contrasting phrases in 1 Corinthians 15:50b-c to imply a similar distinction between those believers alive at the parousia and those who have already died (see 4.3 below for additional details). In any event the future transformation is clearly in view in 1 Corinthians 15.

By contrast we find eschatological transformation being described as *presently* taking place in 2 Corinthians 3:18. Here the present passive verb *metamorphoumetha* ("we are being transformed") is used in the midst of an extended passage in which Paul contrasts the glory of Moses with the glory of Christ (2 Cor 3:12—4:6). A similar use of the verb occurs in Romans 12:2, again emphasizing the present process of transformation.

The suggestion that transformation can be dualistically conceived (both present and future) demonstrates the tension inherent within Pauline eschatology as a whole. Despite this E. E. Ellis insists that Paul does not really present us with a true dualism since *moral* transformation is a present process, while *mortal* transformation awaits the granting of the resurrection body at the parousia of Christ; what unites the two aspects of transformation is a corporate existence, the fact that the believer is "in Christ." The idea of resurrection as expressing the present spiritual transformation of the believer in Christ can also be found in Romans 6:1-11; 2 Corinthians 4:10-12; 5:15; 13:4; Galatians 5:24-25; 6:14-45; Colossians 2:12 and Ephesians 2:5-6 (as Harris, 101-5, argues). Once again the close connection between the believers' unity with Christ in his resurrection and their ethical conduct is asserted.

*4.2. Resurrection as Incorruption.* In the midst of his extended treatise on the subject in 1 Corinthians 15 Paul uses a number of contrasting terms and images to describe how resurrection life differs from the present order of existence. Included are the contrasting pairs, perishable/imperishable (1 Cor 15:42); dishonor/glory (1 Cor 15:43); weakness*/power* (1 Cor 15:43); physical body/spiritual body (1 Cor 15:44; *see* Body); man of dust/man of heaven (1 Cor 15:47-49). In 1 Corinthians 15:50 Paul again asserts the first of these contrasting pairs, perishable/imperishable, when he says: "flesh and blood does not inherit the kingdom of God, nor does the perishable inherit the imperishable." The relevant Greek terms (*phthora* and *aphtharsia*) provide quite a powerful image and are better translated as "corruptibility" and "incorruptibility" respectively. The term *aphtharsia* occurs seven times in the NT, all within the Pauline corpus (Rom 2:7; 1 Cor 15:42, 50, 53, 54; Eph 6:24; 2 Tim 1:10), while four of the seven instances of the cognate term *aphthartos* ("imperishable") in the NT are also found in Paul's letters (Rom 1:23; 1 Cor 9:25; 15:52; 1 Tim 1:17). There is a close connection between *aphtharsia/aphthartos* and the resurrection of Jesus Christ throughout, a vivid demonstration of the eschatological significance of the term.

In addition to the instances occurring within the extended discussion on the resurrection in 1 Corinthians 15, the revelation of *aphtharsia* through the destruction of death by means of Christ's resurrection is the focus of the assertion in 2 Timothy 1:10; *aphtharsia* is associated with eternal life in Romans 2:7; and *aphthartos* is used figuratively of the resurrection body within the confines of an athletic image in 1 Corinthians 9:25. Exceptions include Ephesians 6:24, where the term *aphtharsia* is used to describe Christian love of the Lord ("*undying* love"), and Romans 1:23 and 1 Timothy 1:17 where *aphthartos* is used as an attribute of God.*

Jeremias offers an interesting, if disputed, interpretation of 1 Corinthians 15:50, suggesting that a distinction be made between the metamorphosis of the living believer (1 Cor 15:50b) and the deceased one (1 Cor 15:50c), and that a contrast be drawn between Paul's language of corruption/incorruption and mortality/immortality.* In effect Jeremias says that the phrase "flesh and blood cannot inherit the kingdom of God" refers to those who are alive at the parousia, and argues that "nor does the perishable inherit the imperishable" refers to those who have died before the parousia and are presently corpses in decomposition. He goes on to suggest that a similar distinction between the living and the dead is found in 1 Corinthians 15:50-53. However, the proposed distinction is almost certainly a forced one (or at least a limited one), and most scholars have not followed Jeremias in rigidly maintaining it (H. Conzelmann is a good representative of those who disagree with Jeremias).

An essential part of Jeremias's argument is the use of another term in 1 Corinthians 15:53-54, immortality (*athanasia*), a term usually used to describe, as in 1 Timothy 6:16, an attribute of God himself (Harris, 273-75, provides a full terminological discussion of *aphtharsia* and *athanasia*, both of which he renders as "immortality"*). Some have taken the language of investiture in 2 Corinthians 5:2-4 also to imply this distinction between the deceased believer and the believer who is alive at the parousia of Christ.

*4.3. Resurrection as Immortality.* Paul uses another interesting term to describe the resurrection in 1 Corin-

thians 15:53b-54. Here he describes it as the mortal nature (*to thnēton*) taking on immortality (*athanasia*). The resurrection is the means whereby Christians gain immortality, and death is, in the poetic image drawn from Isaiah 25:8, "swallowed up in victory." The distinction between *athanasia* and *aphtharsia* is not always easy to define, but the association of both with the resurrection of the body is sure. Harris argues persuasively that while immortality (either *athanasia* or *aphtharsia*) and resurrection are intimately linked, the former is consistently presented as a *future* possession granted at the parousia of Christ to those who belong to him. In any event, immortality and resurrection both belong in Paul's thinking and are seen as related but distinct ideas (as Harris notes). Both are grounded in Paul's belief that the eschatological hope of the believer is somatic in nature and future in temporality.

*4.4. Resurrection and Exaltation.* In several places in Paul's letters there is a close connection drawn between Jesus' resurrection from the dead and his exaltation* to the right hand of God. Several of the passages which juxtapose these two images are considered by many to reflect pre-Pauline traditions, namely Romans 1:3-4 and Philippians 2:9-11. In the case of the Philippian hymn the fact that there is movement from the death of Christ (Phil 2:8) to his exaltation (Phil 2:9-11) is somewhat unusual. This has caused many to consider that the original Christian proclamation about the resurrection was in fact a theological message of his vindication before God and not a historical message about his bodily resurrection from the dead. However, such a distinction is falsely conceived (as Harris points out). Exaltation is clearly set forth as following the resurrection at several other places within the Pauline letters (Rom 8:34; Eph 1:20; 2:6; Col 3:1). While it is true that resurrection and exaltation should not be viewed as synonymous, there is an essential theological linkage between them. The exaltation is not so much a theological interpretation of the resurrection as the inevitable consequence of it, the logical result to which it is leading. As Harris states, "(Jesus') resurrection was the prerequisite and means of his exaltation and the exaltation was the outcome of his resurrection" (Harris, 85-86).

Strictly speaking, Paul does not relate detailed descriptions of Christ's physical ascension as such; in the NT this is found only in Luke/Acts and in veiled terms using traditional material (such as 1 Tim 3:16). Rather, Paul's letters tend to express the postresurrectional state of Jesus Christ in terms of both the Lord's exaltation and his glorification. Paul does, however, imply that the believers will experience a physical ascension to heaven at the parousia (1 Thess 4:16-17).

*4.5. Resurrection and Glorification.* The ultimate revelation of the glory of God is a well-established feature of Jewish eschatology. Paul also uses the language of glorification at several points to describe the implications of the resurrection for the Christian believer (see Glory, Glorification). 1 Thessalonians 2:12 associates the kingdom of God and glory, while 2 Thessalonians 2:14 unites the Christian calling and the future attainment of the glory of Jesus Christ. In Romans 5:2 the hope of sharing in the future glory of God is a matter of rejoicing for Paul, and in 2 Corinthians 4:17 he uses the poetic phrase "the eternal weight of glory" (aiōnion baros doxēs) to describe what lies in store for the faithful believer. In Romans 8:11-17 and 2 Corinthians 4:10-18 both "mortal bodies" (ta thnēta ta sōmata) and "mortal flesh" (thnētē sarx) are spoken of being eventually glorified as a result of the union between Christ and his church. In Romans 8:30 Paul even uses a series of aorist verbs, including edoxasen ("he glorified"), to proclaim the certainty of salvation based upon the union between Christ and believers. This description of the glorification associated with the resurrection as something in the past anticipates the language of the later letters (Col 1:27; 3:1, 4).

*4.6. Resurrection and Eternal Life.* In Galatians 6:8 we have an illustration of sowing/reaping used by Paul in which the Spirit is said to impart eternal life to the believer. This image is certainly eschatological in meaning and is probably best taken to be synonymous with future resurrection life. The phrase "eternal life" (zōē aiōnios) also occurs in passages concerned with the results of belief in Jesus Christ (Rom 5:21; 6:22-23; 1 Tim 1:16; 6:12; Tit 1:2; 3:7) and with the righteous final judgment* (Rom 2:7). Whereas some images of resurrection in Paul clearly allow the focus to be on the present dimension of life in Christ, the granting of eternal life in all its fullness is (like immortality) something which lies in the future.

*4.7. Resurrection and Conformity to the Image of Christ.* The "image* of Christ" is a key means of expressing christological truth in Paul, particularly within the bounds of the Adam/Christ analogy (see Adam and Christ). The assertion that the believer is also in the process of being conformed to the image of God (in Christ) is mentioned at several points (Rom 8:29; 2 Cor 3:18; Col 3:10). In each instance there is an overlap of imagery involved; "conformity to the image of Christ" is the Christian's eschatological goal and as such might be taken to be an overlap with resurrection. This is further evidenced by the fact that in 1 Corinthians 15:49 the Christian's resurrection hope is described as "bearing the image of the man from heaven." The heavenly dimension of Paul's eschatological thought is an important ingredient within his understanding of cosmic redemption* (as Lincoln argues).

*4.8. Resurrection and Redemption of the Body.* Paul's teaching about the bodily resurrection arises out of a Jewish anthropology in which the "soul" (Heb nepeš; Gk psychē) is the animating principle of human life (see Psychology). In mainstream Jewish thought human beings do not *have* souls, they *are* souls. This anthropological underpinning has tremendous implications for a doctrine of the resurrection in that it refuses to surrender the somatic component of a human being. Resurrection involves the redemption of the physical body, although (as we noted above) the somatic nature of that resurrection existence gives scope for some of Paul's most creative thinking in 1 Corinthians 15:35-49. Given this background it is perfectly understandable how in Romans 8:23 Paul describes the effects of the resurrection in terms of the ultimate "redemption of our bodies" (tēn apolytrōsin tou sōmatos hēmōn). A similar idea is expressed in Philippians 3:20-21, this time where the resurrection body of the believing community is closely tied to that of the risen Lord Christ. Other instances of the idea of redemption (apolytrōsis) within the Pauline corpus (Rom 3:24; 1 Cor 1:30; Eph 1:7, 14; 4:30; Col 1:14) should be seen within the context of the resurrection of Jesus Christ and its implications for both humankind and the cosmos (see World, Cosmology).

## 5. Co-Crucifixion and Co-Resurrection in Christ.

So certain is Paul of the unity which exists between Christ and his church that the believers can be described (within the confines of the image of baptism) as participating in Christ's death and resurrection (Rom 6:3-4, 8; Gal 3:27; Col 2:12; see Dying and Rising with Christ). A similar declaration is contained in Colossians 3:1 where the verb synegeirō ("to raise up with") is used in a first-class conditional clause (assuming the truth of the statement). This union with Christ in his death and resurrection also means that Christian existence (the resurrection life) can be described as "walking in newness of life" (Rom 6:4; cf. Rom 8:13; 2 Cor 5:15; Gal 5:24). Similarly in Philippians 3:10 Paul associates "knowledge of Christ and the power of his resurrection" with participation in his sufferings, pointing to the importance of Christ's resurrection for an ethical lifestyle which endures trial. The aim of such conduct, Paul continues, is the attainment of the resurrection (Phil 3:11). In 2 Corinthians 4:10 another provocative image is used when Paul describes the believer as carrying the death of Jesus around bodily so as to manifest the resurrection.

## 6. The Resurrection: Some Issues of Interpretation.

Historically speaking, several important theological

questions have been raised concerning resurrection. These issues particularly involve the exegesis of key Pauline passages or the interpretation of particular themes. Early evidence of the importance of Paul in these interpretative matters can be seen in the fact that Gnostic* writings very often based their teaching on materials contained in his letters. It would be true to say that the complicated Pauline teaching about the resurrection body became one of the mainstays for the beliefs of Gnostic Christians in the second and third centuries. A classic Gnostic text which wrestles with these issues in typically Pauline language is the *Epistle to Rheginos*, an anonymous work otherwise known as *The Treatise on the Resurrection* (see Pagels).

Three issues call for reflection:

**6.1. The Resurrection and the Messiahship of Jesus.** Several important passages within the Pauline corpus associate the messiahship of Jesus with his resurrection from the dead (Rom 1:3-4; 1 Cor 15:4; 2 Tim 2:8; *see* Christ). Although it would be going too far to suggest that for Paul the resurrection is the act that inaugurates Jesus' messiahship, it certainly would be true to say that his messiahship is vindicated and proclaimed by means of it. Indeed, it is possible to see the resurrection of Jesus as demonstrating not only his messiahship but his cosmic lordship (as Beasley-Murray argues; *see* Lord).

Nonetheless, it is possible to believe in the resurrection of Jesus from the dead without necessarily affirming that this divine act confirmed his messiahship. This may come as a surprise to many Christians since the two are sometimes taken to be equivalent. A good example of this viewpoint is the Jewish scholar P. Lapide, who accepts the historicity of Jesus' bodily resurrection, but does not therefore describe himself as a Christian (by definition, one who affirms Jesus as Messiah). For Lapide the resurrection of Jesus is part of God's preparatory work, making the world ready for the future revelation of the Messiah. The example of Lapide is a case in point for the too-casual assumption that the resurrection of Jesus is at the same time the self-evident proclamation of him as Messiah. At the same time, Lapide's argument offers an interesting insight into one of the peculiarities of modern NT interpretation. In an age when many competent Christian scholars find reason to deny the historicity of the bodily resurrection of Jesus and yet retain their Christian faith, here we have a Jewish scholar who strongly affirms the bodily resurrection and yet seeks to claim no faith on the basis of it. It is a salient lesson about the messianic content of the resurrection faith as Paul proclaims it.

**6.2. The Resurrection and the Empty Tomb Motif.** All four Gospels mention the empty tomb within their resurrection narratives (Mt 28:6; Mk 16:6; Lk 24:2; Jn 20:4-

7). On the other hand, while Paul does explicitly mention the burial of Jesus (1 Cor 15:4; cf. Rom 6:4), he nowhere mentions the empty tomb in connection with the resurrection. Cranfield, however, feels it is "almost certainly implied" (Cranfield, 168) by the mention of Christ's burial between "died" and "he was raised" in 1 Corinthians 15:4. It could simply be an accident of circumstance that Paul never mentions the empty tomb, although R. H. Stein has put forward the suggestion that the omission is due to apologetic concerns on the part of Paul: "When it came to the resurrection appearances, the apostle could argue on equal terms with the other disciples. He, too, had seen the Lord! He could not, however, say the same about the empty tomb" (Stein, 12).

In any event, within the NT the empty tomb is never adduced as proof of the resurrection of Jesus from the dead. This has led some to drive a wedge between the resurrection of Jesus and the evidence of the empty tomb, with a view to denying the historicity of the resurrection itself. The resurrection is capable of thereby being "spiritualized," and its basis in history is seriously undermined if not jettisoned altogether. In recent years in Britain this line of argumentation has been popularly associated with the Bishop of Durham, David Jenkins (see Harris [1985] for details). The guarantee of the resurrection (so the argument goes) is not the empty tomb but the presence of the risen Lord in the lives of the believing community (see Harris, 37-44, and Walker). The Pauline materials, particularly 1 Corinthians 15, are at the heart of much of this modern discussion. It is unlikely that Paul would have accepted the truth of the resurrection of Jesus from the dead without also accepting that a corollary of this is an empty tomb. Barrett's comment succinctly makes the point about how faith in the historicity of the empty tomb must be delicately poised: "Faith . . . would be destroyed by the discovery of the dead body of Jesus, but it cannot be created simply by the discovery of an empty tomb" (Barrett 1968, 349).

A growing number of scholars affirm the historicity of the empty tomb and Paul's knowledge of it (see, e.g., Craig, 1985). The reason that the empty tomb is not explicitly discussed in Paul should not be taken as evidence of its historical unreliability, but of its unimportance as a matter of Christian proclamation.

**6.3. The General Resurrection.** Paul nowhere explicitly discusses a general resurrection for *all* people, although there are indications scattered throughout the letters that all (both believers and nonbelievers, the living and the dead) will face judgment* (Rom 2:6-11; 2 Cor 4:5; 5:10; 2 Thess 1:6-10; 2 Tim 4:1). The nearest place that Paul comes to suggesting a general (or universal) resurrection is in 1 Corinthians 15:22b: "in Christ shall all be made alive" (*en tō christō pantes zōopoiēthēsontai*). However, this declaration comes in the midst of Paul's Adam/Christ analogy and must be so interpreted (it is "all *in Christ*" who will be resurrected). Some have based a Pauline belief in general resurrection upon the words attributed to the apostle in Acts 24:15, but this is viewed as methodologically suspect by many. The idea of a universal resurrection cannot be dismissed out of hand, however. Allison argues that the whole of early Christianity, including Paul, associated Christ's rising from the dead with a general resurrection and understood the Lord's resurrection to have inaugurated the onset of it (Allison is attempting to counter interpretations which overemphasize the importance of a realized eschatological viewpoint in early Christian belief).

*See also* BODY; CHRISTOLOGY; DYING AND RISING WITH CHRIST; ESCHATOLOGY; EXALTATION AND ENTHRONEMENT; IMMORTALITY; INTERMEDIATE STATE; JUDGMENT; LIFE AND DEATH; POWER.

BIBLIOGRAPHY. D. C. Allison, *The End of the Ages Has Come* (Philadelphia: Fortress, 1985); W. Baird, "Ascension and Resurrection: An Intersection of Luke and Paul," in *Texts and Textuality: Critical Essays on the Bible and the Early Church Fathers*, ed. W. E. March (San Antonio: Trinity University, 1980) 3-18; C. K. Barrett, *The First Epistle to the Corinthians* (New York: Harper & Row, 1968); idem, "Immortality and Resurrection," in *Resurrection and Immortality: Aspects of twentieth-century Christian belief*, ed. C. S. Duthie (London: Samuel Bagster, 1979) 68-88; idem, *Essays on Paul* (London: SPCK, 1982); P. Beasley-Murray, "Romans 1:3f: An Early Confession of Faith in the Lordship of Jesus," *TynB* 31 (1980) 147-54; R. Bultmann, "The New Testament and Mythology," in *Kerygma and Myth I & II*, ed. H. W. Bartsch (London: SPCK, 1972) 1-44; H. C. C. Cavallin, *Life After Death: Paul's Argument for the Resurrection of the Dead in 1 Cor 15* (ConB 7.1; Lund: Gleerup, 1974); L. Coenen, "Resurrection," *NIDNTT* 3.259-309; W. L. Craig, "The Bodily Resurrection of Jesus," in *Gospel Perspectives 1: Studies of History and Tradition in the Four Gospels*, ed. R. T. France and D. Wenham (Sheffield: JSOT, 1980) 47-74; idem, "The Historicity of the Empty Tomb of Jesus," *NTS* 31 (1985) 39-67; C. E. B. Cranfield, "The Resurrection of Jesus Christ," *ExpT* 101 (1990) 167-72; O. Cullmann, *Immortality of the Soul or Resurrection of the Dead?* (London: Epworth, 1958); M. E. Dahl, *The Resurrection of the Body* (London: SCM, 1962); W. D. Davies, *Paul and Rabbinic Judaism* (4th ed.; Philadelphia: Fortress, 1980); J. D. G. Dunn, "I Corinthians 15:45—last Adam, life-giving spirit," in *Christ and Spirit in the New Testament: Studies in Honour of C. F. D. Moule*, ed. B. Lindars and S. Smalley (Cambridge: University Press, 1973) 127-41; idem, *The Evidence for Jesus* (Philadelphia: Westminster, 1985); E. E. Ellis, "II Corinthians V.1-10 in Pauline Eschatology," *NTS* 6 (1959-60) 211-24; J. Gillman, "Signals of Transformation in 1 Thessalonians 4:13-18," *CBQ* 47 (1985) 263-81; L. J. Greenspoon, "The Origin of the Idea of Resurrection," in *Traditions in Transformation: Turning Points in Biblical Faith*, ed. B. Halpern and J. D. Levenson (Winona Lake, IN: Eisenbrauns, 1981) 247-317; M. J. Harris, *Raised Immortal: The Relation Between Resurrection and Immortality in New Testament Teaching* (Grand Rapids: Eerdmans, 1983); idem, *Easter in Durham: Bishop Jenkins and the Resurrection of Jesus* (Exeter: Paternoster, 1985); J. Jeremias, "Flesh and Blood Cannot Inherit the Kingdom of God," *NTS* 2 (1955-56) 151-59; J. Kloppenborg, "An Analysis of the Pre-Pauline Formula I Cor 15.3b-5 in the Light of Some Recent Literature," *CBQ* 40 (1978) 351-67; G. E. Ladd, *I Believe in the Resurrection of Jesus* (Grand Rapids: Eerdmans, 1975); P. Lapide, *The Resurrection of Jesus: A Jewish Perspective* (London: SPCK, 1984); A. T. Lincoln, *Paradise Now and Not Yet* (SNTSMS 43; Cambridge: University Press, 1981); J. I. H. McDonald, *The Resurrection: Narrative and Belief* (London: SPCK, 1989) 25-51; C. F. D. Moule, "St Paul and Dualism: The Pauline Conception of the Resurrection," *NTS* 13 (1966-67) 106-23; J. Murphy-O'Connor, "Tradition and Redaction in 1 Cor 15.3-7," *CBQ* 43 (1981) 582-89; G. W. E. Nickelsburg, *Resurrection, Immortality and Eternal Life in Intertestamental Judaism* (HTS 26; Cambridge, MA: Harvard University, 1972); E. Pagels, *The Gnostic Gospels* (New York: Random House, 1982) 35-54; B. A. Pearson, *The 'Pneumatikos-Psychikos' Terminology in 1 Corinthians* (Missoula, MT: Scholars, 1973); P. Perkins, *Resurrection* (London: Chapman, 1984); R. J. Sider, "The Pauline Conception of the Resurrection Body in I Corinthians XV.35-54," *NTS* 21 (1974-75) 428-39; R. H. Stein, "Was the tomb really empty?" *Themelios* 5 (1979) 8-12; D. A. Walker, "Resurrection, Empty Tomb and Easter Faith," *ExpT* 101 (1990) 172-75; B. Witherington, *Jesus, Paul and the End of the World* (Downers Grove, IL: InterVarsity, 1992).              L. J. Kreitzer

**REVELATION.** *See* CONVERSION AND CALL OF PAUL; JESUS, SAYINGS OF; JESUS AND PAUL; MYSTERY; PROPHECY, PROPHESYING; VISIONS, ECSTATIC EXPERIENCE.

**REVERENCE.** *See* FEAR, REVERENCE.

# REVOLUTIONARY MOVEMENTS

Paul's missionary work among the Gentiles* occurred at a critical epoch in the history of Judea, the symbolic center of Judaism. His Gentile mission* must be seen against the background of the volatile political situation of Judea and the various revolutionary movements which were present at that time.

1. Paul's Critical Ministry Period
2. General Background to Revolutionary Movements
3. Immediate Background to Revolutionary Movements: Principes, Procurators and High Priests
4. Revolutionary Movements and Their Causes (A.D. 44-60)

## 1. Paul's Critical Ministry Period.

Our most complete information about Paul relates to the fifteen-year period (approximately) from the time of his ministry in Antioch in the mid-forties (Gal 1:21; Acts 9:30; 11:25-26) until his domicile in Rome in the early sixties (Acts 28:30). Only fragmentary data exist for the earlier period between his commission/conversion c. A.D. 34 and his arrival in Antioch c. 46 and the later period after his imprisonment in Rome prior to his death c. 60-65 (*see* Chronology).

Paul's own letters are the primary source for this well-illuminated period, supplemented by the Acts of the Apostles, whose chief character is Paul (cf. Acts 8:1; 9:1-31; 11:19-30; 12:25—28:31)—as the one *sent* to the Gentiles (Acts 9:15; 22:21; 26:17; *see* Apostle).

Within that decade and a half Paul ministered with Barnabas* in the church in Syrian Antioch and, in partnership with Barnabas and other colleagues, established and maintained links with churches in Galatia, Macedonia, Achaia and Asia. It is clear from (some of) his letters, however—as well as from Acts— that a Jewish mission or (missions) arose, in all probability from Judea (cf. Gal 2:2), whose delegates visited a number of Paul's churches to correct or even overturn his doctrines, replacing them with their own (*see* Opponents).

Since this countermission appears to have arisen in Judea, it is of interest to know as much as possible about the general history and currents of thought in Judea when Paul was active in Gentile regions. Specially significant are the revolutionary movements of that era since they may have influenced the countermission(s) against Paul in the churches of the Gentiles.

## 2. General Background to Revolutionary Movements.

It seems probable that the events and circumstances of the eastern Mediterranean in the previous centuries and decades significantly shaped the life and attitudes of the people of Palestine.

*2.1. The Hellenistic Era.* From the time of the Macedonian conquests of the East in the late fourth century B.C., led by Alexander, the Jews of Palestine found themselves an island in a Hellenistic sea. Specifically, they were subject for two and a half centuries to the hegemony of the Hellenistic kingdoms, first of Ptolemaic Egypt and then of Seleucid Syria. The pressures of Hellenism* on Jewish religious and national culture were generally all-pervasive and subtle but occasionally violent and confrontative. In reaction to this intrusive pagan influence, there arose the pietistic culture of groups like the Pharisees and the Essenes, but also expressions of zealous violence, as at the time of the Maccabean revolt (167 B.C.), when the Seleucids had attempted to compromise and therefore destroy Judaism.

*2.2. The Roman Era: Herodian Rule.* From the second century B.C., however, the eastern Mediterranean region—which had been subject to the Hellenistic kings—progressively succumbed to the eastward expansion of the Romans. By the end of the second century B.C. the Romans had secured and provincialized the Greek archipelago and western Anatolia. By the sixties (B.C.) the Roman legions had asserted their authority in Syria and Judea, and by the thirties (B.C.) Egypt had come within the sphere of Roman power.

In the case of Jewish Palestine the Romans were content at first to rule the Jews of Palestine at arm's length through local Jews whose loyalty they had secured and whom they appointed "client" rulers over an indigenous people with a complex religious culture. Specifically they worked through the Idumean Antipater in the first instance, but then as greater opportunity arose, through his son Herod, whom they appointed "king of the Jews" in Rome in 40 B.C. Herod first pacified the country which was ravaged by war, whereupon he took up unchallenged rule over the Jews of Palestine in 37-4 B.C. Throughout his long and repressive rule Herod effectively kept in check the pious groups such as the Pharisees and the Essenes. One exception was the refusal of six thousand Pharisees to give an oath of loyalty to Herod and Augustus in 7 B.C. (Josephus *Ant.* 17.2.4 §42; cf. 15.10.4 §369). Manifestations of zealous violence, however, do not appear to have arisen until the last year of Herod's rule when forty disciples of the rabbis Judas and Simon, heedless of the dire consequences, tore down from the gate of the Temple a giant effigy of an eagle which the king had erected. They suffered martyrdom for this act (Josephus *J.W.* 1.33.1-4 §§648-655).

Immediately after the death of Herod, the heir-designate Archelaus lost control of Jerusalem during the Passover, only restoring order by a brutal pogrom. When Archelaus and his brother Antipas traveled to

Rome for Augustus to settle the disputed will of the late king, civil wars erupted in the three major regions of Herod's realm. Three charismatic pretenders opportunistically seized power—Judas in Galilee, Simon in Perea and Athronges in Judea—each claiming to be a "king." The legions of Varus, legate of Syria, were forced to march from Antioch to put down these uprisings and enable the three Herodian princes—Archelaus, Antipas and Philip—to assume power in their regions as designated by Augustus.

**2.3. The Roman Era: Judea a Province (A.D. 6-41).** After nine years Archelaus was dismissed as ethnarch of Judea-Samaria. Augustus took a momentous—but logical and ultimately inevitable—step. He annexed Judea as a Roman province subject to a military prefect. Galilee-Perea and Gaulanitis, however, were permitted to remain under the rule of the princes Antipas and Philip. These were allocated a set revenue from taxes,* some of which, presumably, was remitted to Rome. Judea, however, was subjected to a census and property assessment preparatory to the imposition of a head tax, payable directly to Rome. A zealous, violent movement arose, led by Judas the Galilean (Acts 5:37) and Saddok, a Pharisee (Josephus *J.W.* 2.8.1 §118; *Ant.* 18.1.1 §§3, 9-10). These leaders deemed the Roman action deeply offensive to their religious scruples, teaching that Roman domination was tantamount to handing over the kingship of Yahweh to the Gentile. Their zealous watch-cry was "No master except God." As in 4 B.C. Roman forces were again needed to put down what was, in effect, a rebellion against Roman rule. Judas was killed; nothing more is known of Saddok.

Convincing evidence is lacking to support theories (such as advocated by Brandon and Hengel) that a structured revolutionary organization existed throughout the Roman era A.D. 6-66. Rather, there seems to have been an *attitude* of religious zeal which would respond violently at the cost of one's own life, if that was necessary, when provoked by blasphemous acts by Gentiles. This mindset is referred to by Josephus as a "fourth philosophy," which he (incorrectly) says originated with the insurrection of Judas and Saddok over the imposition of a Roman head tax in A.D. 6-7 (Josephus *Ant.* 18.1 §§1-10; 18.6 §§23-25). The reaction of *zeal* for Yahweh can be seen earlier in the Maccabean revolt at Modein in 167 B.C., and the martyrdom of the rabbis and their disciples under Herod in 4 B.C.

Josephus may be correct, however, in suggesting that the more typical Jewish (Pharisaic) attitude was piously and passively to accept the awful circumstances of the moment as the deserved punishment of God, which of itself would—without violent action—

bring the kingdom of God to them (*As. Mos.* 6; 9:7—10:3).

There is little information about life in Roman Judea under the Prefects Coponius (A.D. 6-9), Ambivius (A.D. 9-11), Rufus (A.D. 11-14) or Gratus (A.D. 15-26).

In the case of Pontius Pilate (A.D. 26-36?), however, much more is known both about him as *praefectus* and also about the circumstances in Judea during his tenure. Although appointed during the principate of Tiberius (A.D. 14-37), the first five years of Pilate's prefecture coincided with the notorious praetorian prefect L. Aelius Sejanus who de facto ruled Rome and the provinces (A.D. 26-31). Sejanus was reputed to be anti-Semitic (Philo *Leg. Gai.*, 159-61), perhaps creating—directly or indirectly—an environment in which the newly arrived prefect of Judea would also act against the indigenous provincials. Occasional data support that general hypothesis, whether in the case of the unprecedented attempt to introduce into Jerusalem the military standards with their idolatrous insignia, or the seizure of money from the sacred treasury of the Temple for aqueduct construction (Josephus *Ant.* 18.3.1-2 §§55-62), or the minting of coins with pagan imagery or the slaughter of Galileans in the act of sacrificing the Passover lambs (Lk 13:1-2). The execution of Jesus of Nazareth occurred soon (?) after an "uprising" (Gk *anastasis*, Mk 15:7) in which Barabbas played a critical role. Possibly the "thieves" (Gk *lēstai*) crucified with Jesus were part of that uprising. It is likely that, as at other times of threat to their religious culture, this insurrection was motivated by zeal for Yahweh in response to the provocative actions of Pilate, the Gentile governor. For his part Pilate probably viewed Jesus as a revolutionary "king" like Judas the Galilean a quarter of a century earlier and fit for nothing but crucifixion* (Lk 23:1-3).

At the death of Tiberius in A.D. 37, Gaius (nicknamed Caligula) became emperor. Caligula lacked the sympathy for the Jews shown by his imperial predecessors, whether his great-grandfather Augustus or his granduncle Tiberius. Under Flaccus, prefect in Egypt, the large Jewish population of Alexandria began to suffer progressively in the face of local hostility so that serious riots broke out in the city in A.D. 38. Shortly afterwards an altar erected in Jamnia in Judea, celebrating Caligula's military victories in Germany, was demolished by the Jews. Incensed by this event, Caligula, who had become convinced of his own divinity (*see* Emperors), ordered that a gigantic statue of himself be erected within the Temple of God in Jerusalem. Suddenly Jews and Romans were at the brink of war. Nothing so potentially serious had happened since Antiochus Epiphanes had erected an altar to the

Olympian Zeus in the Temple in 167 B.C. An uprising of monumental proportions was only averted in the short term by the intercession of Agrippa and finally by the assassination of Caligula in January, A.D. 41. Once again we observe that an assault upon deeply held Jewish religious tradition precipitated a reaction of zealous violence.

*2.4. The Roman Era: Agrippa King of Judea (A.D. 41-44).* Herod Agrippa I, grandson of Herod the Great, was brought up in Rome, in all probability as a pagan. Through the direct intervention of his childhood friend Caligula, he was appointed "king" first in A.D. 37 over Philip's tetrarchy and subsequently in A.D. 39 over Antipas' tetrarchy. The new princeps, Claudius— also a boyhood friend—secured Agrippa's royal appointment in A.D. 41, now to Judea in place of the prefects. Although apparently a Gentile at heart, Agrippa convinced the Jews that he was a devoutly observant Jew, committed to their national and religious cause. Part of this program, apparently, was to assault those Jews who had recently offered salvation* in the name of the false messiah, Jesus, to Samaritans and Gentiles, as Peter and John Zebedee had recently done (Acts 8:14-25; 10:24-48). Hence Agrippa had James Zebedee killed (in the absence of his brother, John?) and Peter arrested with a view to execution, because "he saw that it pleased the Jews" (Acts 12:1-5).

Not for many years had circumstances seemed so propitious to the Jews. The Roman prefect had decamped from Caesarea, and with him went the legionaries, the offensive Roman coinage and the payment of direct head tax to the Roman princeps. Instead, a Jewish king—apparently pious as well as zealous—sat on the throne. True, he was grandson of the hated Herod. But he was also descended from the heroic defenders of the faith, the Maccabees, through his grandmother Mariamne. His sudden and untimely death at Caesarea Maritima in A.D. 44 at the age of fifty-four must have been a severe blow to Jewish hopes. Not least, his special relationship with the principes Caligula and Claudius was seriously missed. His intercessions with Caligula A.D. 40 effectively delayed the planned desecration of the Temple. Had Agrippa survived, who knows what problems might have been averted between Claudius and the Jews during Claudius' principate (A.D. 41-54)?

**3. Immediate Background to Revolutionary Movements: Principes, Procurators and High Priests.**
The revolutionary movements in Judea which occurred during the height of Paul's missionary career (c. A.D. 46-60) must be viewed against the background of the two emperors Claudius (A.D. 41-54) and Nero

(A.D. 54-68), and their policies as they affected that Roman province.

*3.1. Claudius (A.D. 41-54).* Although a friend of Agrippa, Claudius did not prove to be specially sympathetic to the Jews at large. In his famous letter to the Alexandrians, written in A.D. 41, in the aftermath of the racial riots, the emperor granted no favors to the Jews beyond those they had enjoyed as a tolerated secondary community within Alexandria. Instead he insisted that they should not agitate for access to individual privileges reserved for the citizens of Alexandria. In the same year he forbade the now multitudinous Jews in Rome from meeting regularly (Dio Cassius *Roman History* 60.6). A few years later, in A.D. 49, when disturbances arose within the Jewish community in Rome over "Chrestus"—a reference to Christ,* either Jesus Christ or another messianic figure (?)—Claudius took the drastic, if not unprecedented, step of expelling the entire Jewish population from Italy (Suetonius *Claudius* 25.4)! Jews everywhere, including within Judea, would have felt that the measure of protection enjoyed under Augustus and Tiberius had been somewhat diminished under Claudius.

In matters of provincial administration Claudius made changes which effectively altered the relationships of the Jews with Rome. When Judea was first annexed as a province to Rome the governors were titled prefects, signifying a predominantly military role. Under Claudius, however, they were called procurators, indicating a shift to a more fiscal role. Roman governors were, as a class, notoriously corrupt in their dealings with the provincials. In a cynical fable Tiberius argued against the rapid turnover of prefects, likening them to voracious flies sucking the blood from a dying man. Under Claudius's procurators it is likely that there were even greater opportunities for venality.

Another significant change made by Claudius related to the manner of appointing the high priest, upon whose style of religio-political leadership the stability of Judea so much depended. In the earlier period of annexation (A.D. 6-41), the prefect appointed the high priest, providing a direct chain of command from princeps to prefect to high priest. Moreover, for the greater part of that period the pontificate was held by one dynasty, that of Annas. Through all but two or three of those years the position of high priest was held either by Annas, his son-in-law Caiaphas, or his sons Jonathan and Theophilus. The pragmatism of that dynasty probably contributed to the relative stability of the earlier period.

Claudius, however, placed the appointment of the high priest in the hands of minor Herodians, first

Herod of Chalcis (A.D. 44-48) and thereafter Herod Agrippa II, who became king of (part of) Galilee in A.D. 54. This method not only deprived the emperor of direct influence through his governor, it is equally probable that the appointment opened up a greater measure of bribery by those dynasties competing for the lucrative position.

The era on which we are concentrating (c. A.D. 45-60) was dominated by one incumbent high priest, the corrupt Ananias (A.D. 48-59). Ananias's name survives in the Talmud as one who seized sacrifices from the Temple for his own use (b. Pesaḥ. 57a), a practice which would be extended by his successor, Ishmael ben Phabi (Josephus Ant. 20.8.8 §§180-81). As an ex-high priest, Ananias was notorious for his bribery of Roman officials and the incumbent high priest as well as for his abuse of the poorer priests (Josephus Ant. 20.9.2 §§205-6). One of his last acts as high priest was his attempt to secure the conviction of Paul (Acts 23:1-5; 24:1-2). The long tenure of this venal person as the high priest of the Temple cannot but have contributed to the expressions of zealous violence during this period.

*3.2. Nero (A.D. 54-68).* Little is known of Nero's policies toward Judea during the first part of his principate. While his neglect of the provinces in the sixties is well known (cf. Josephus J.W. 2.13.1 §§250-51), such evidence as there is points to reasonably responsible attitudes during the fifties. In any case, the procurator Felix had been appointed by Claudius, a position he held until the end of the decade. Apart from adding Galilean territories to Agrippa II on his accession in A.D. 54, there is little evidence of Nero's attitudes to or involvement with the Jews of Judea during the fifties. That, however, would dramatically change in the sixties as crisis was added to crisis, igniting the flames of war between Jews and Romans in A.D. 66.

**4. Revolutionary Movements and Their Causes.**
Revolutionary movements among the Jews in this period did not arise in a historical vacuum. Rather, a potential for such movements was created three and a half centuries earlier by the Hellenizing of that part of the world to which Judea belonged, but also, more immediately, by its annexation as a Roman province in A.D. 6. The Hellenization and the overlapping Romanization of Judea generally heightened the religious nationalism of the Jews. Specific events like the emergence of a military or prophetic leader with his following tended to occur by way of reaction to specific events which were seen as an assault on Israel's religious tradition, in particular assaults on the Torah or the Temple. This, rather than a theory of a standing revolutionary faction ready to spring into action, is a more likely interpretation of the historical situation.

*4.1. Theudas the Prophet.* The reannexation of Judea, a bitter blow after the years of Agrippa's rule, occurred in A.D. 44 and with it the annexation of Galilee for the first time, at least until Agrippa II was appointed king in A.D. 54. The first procurator under reannexation was Cuspius Fadus (A.D. 44-46). Fadus faced the immediate difficulty of adjudicating in a frontier dispute between the Jewish village of Zia in Perea and the Gentile settlement of Philadelphia, in which he favored the Gentiles. Again, he was forced to hunt down and execute the "bandit-chief" Ptolemy, who had been attacking Idumeans and Arabs but not Jews. Moreover, he attempted unwisely, and as it happened, unsuccessfully, to regain custody of the high priest's vestments as a means of controlling the Jews.

In these troubled times a self-declared prophet named Theudas arose (in Jerusalem?) and persuaded a great crowd to follow him—with their possessions—to the Jordan where, at his word of command, the waters would part, giving them a dry passage to the wilderness (Josephus Ant. 20.5.1 §§97-98). Fadus, however, heard of this proposal and had many of Theudas's followers killed. Theudas was captured and executed. Theudas, whom we take to be a different person from that mentioned in Acts 5:36, seems to have regarded himself as a latter-day Moses or Joshua. His action appears to have attempted to activate the hand of God to rerun the conquest of the land at a time of occupation.

*4.2. Jacob and Simon, Sons of Judas the Revolutionary.* The next procurator was Tiberius Alexander (A.D. 46-48) who, though a member of a noted Jewish family from Alexandria, was an apostate. To any problems which might have arisen from this insensitive appointment was added the far-reaching social consequences of the severe famine which began during his procuratorship. Evidence from the period shows a sharp increase in grain prices throughout the eastern Mediterranean. Relief is known to have been sent to Judea from the royal family of Adiabene in Mesopotamia, who were proselytes to Judaism, and from the nascent Christian church in Antioch (Acts 11:27-30).

Jacob and Simon, sons of Judas the Galilean who led the insurrection over the imposition of Roman taxation in A.D. 6-7, were crucified—presumably for leading an insurrection (Josephus Ant. 20.5.2 §102). Famine created desperate people who would resort to violence. However, their father Judas is referred to as a "rabbi," suggesting that he was a pious, not merely opportunistic, leader (Josephus J.W. 2.8.1 §§117-18).

His sons may have been similarly devout, not merely brigands. Theirs may have been a banditry inspired by "zeal."

The private meeting in Jerusalem between Barnabas and Saul, delegates from the church in Antioch,* and James, Cephas and John, the "pillars" of the Jerusalem* church, probably occurred during the procuratorship of Tiberius Alexander. Shortly after their return to Antioch, Barnabas and Saul set out on a mission to Cyprus and from there into central Anatolia. When they returned to Antioch a serious dispute between Paul and Cephas occurred, precipitated—apparently—by the arrival of "certain men from James" from Jerusalem (Gal 2:11-14; Acts 15:1-2). It may have been about that time when Paul heard that troubles over judaizing* had arisen in the newly established Galatian* churches, quite possibly also from emissaries from Jerusalem (cf. Acts 15:23-24). The Galatian churches were "troubled" by a man who led a group of Jews (Gal 5:10, 12; 3:1; 1:7, 9) who urged that circumcision* was a prerequisite for membership in the Israel* of God (Gal 3:6-14; 6:16). These "agitators" and their leader were putting pressure on other Jewish believers to force Gentile members to be circumcised (Gal 6:12).

The Jerusalem Council met soon afterwards to resolve the question of Gentile observation of Jewish practices. The believers from among the Pharisees advocated the circumcision and the full observance of the Law* of Moses (Acts 15:5). Significantly, the Pharisees were involved—whether actively or passively—in the struggles and crises of the times between Jews and Romans. The religious nationalism of the Pharisees cannot but have flowed over into questions raised by Paul's mission to the Gentiles. The times in which mission work among Gentiles began in earnest, therefore, coincided with difficult times in Judea, which appear to have flowed back into the Gentile churches, especially through believers from the Pharisaic brotherhoods (*see* Opponents).

*4.3. Near Rebellion Under Cumanus.* Under the next procurator, Cumanus (A.D. 49-52), the Jews' religious scruples were again scandalized. In one incident during the Passover when Roman troops were having difficulties controlling the crowd in the precincts of the Temple, a soldier blasphemously exposed his genitals. In the ensuing uprising thousands of Jews were killed (Josephus *Ant.* 20.5.3 §112). In another incident near Beth Horon, during a military reprisal expedition on villages suspected of robbery, a soldier blasphemously tore up a copy of the Torah. Fearing further uprisings Cumanus executed the offending soldier. A third incident involved a skirmish between

some Galilean Jews passing by a Samaritan village en route to a festival in Jerusalem. Bribed by the Samaritans—traditional religious enemies of the Jews—Cumanus failed to avenge the Jews who had perished in the fracas. Jewish raiding parties against the Samaritan villages ensued, which were joined by the notorious and long-term arch-brigand Eleazar ben Deinaeus.

Ultimately, Quadratus, legate of Syria, was drawn into an out-of-control situation. In his judgment the Samaritans were the guilty party. Cumanus and Ananias the high priest, with others, were dispatched to Rome for Claudius to decide the matter, while Quadratus visited Jerusalem to calm the populace. In Rome Cumanus was exiled and his military tribune, Celer, executed.

For the greater part of Cumanus's era the apostle Paul was traveling through Anatolia to Troas, then across to Macedonia, establishing churches in Philippi,* Thessalonica* and Berea. Thereafter he sailed to Achaia. He stopped briefly in Athens, and for a year and a half he worked at establishing a church in Corinth.* After a rapid round-trip, making only brief visits to Caesarea, Jerusalem and Antioch, Paul traveled overland through central Anatolia to Ephesus for a period of extended ministry. His arrival in Ephesus (c. A.D. 52) coincided with the beginning of Felix's turbulent era as procurator of Judea.

*4.4. The Rise of Sicarii and Sign Prophets During the Time of Felix.* Under Antonius Felix affairs in Judea were to deteriorate to a degree unprecedented in its years as a Roman province. No governor to this point—with the possible exception of Pilate—had provoked such a level of disturbance.

Felix's shortcomings are noted by Tacitus. Even allowing for his bias against the Julio-Claudians and the appointment of freedmen as officials, Tacitus' comments are quite damaging:

> Claudius . . . took advantage of the death or declining fortunes of the Jewish kings to commit the government of the provinces to Roman knights or freedmen. One of these, Antonius Felix, played the tyrant with the spirit of a slave, plunging into all manner of cruelty and lust. (Tacitus *Hist.* 5.9; cf. *Ann.* 7.54)

Felix, a mere freedman (a former slave), owed his appointment to his brother Pallas, Claudius' financial secretary. Something of Felix's aspirations may be observed from his successive marriages into royal families, of which the third was the Herodian. Felix married the teenaged Drusilla, sister of Agrippa II, who divorced her first husband for that purpose, something the Jews would have found offensive.

*817*

Like Fadus, Felix set about ridding the province of robber bands, in particular Eleazar ben Deinaeus, whom he apprehended and sent to Rome for trial. A notorious arch-bandit, Eleazar had in recent times become involved in the Jewish counterassault against the Samaritans but had "ravaged the land" for twenty years, that is, back to the time of Jesus. While Josephus presents Eleazar as nothing more than a fierce brigand, later writings point to him as dominant in his generation, as one who "sought to hasten the end" (*Midr.* Song 2.7); that is, by his violent actions he sought to force the hand of God to bring in his kingdom (cf. Mt 11:12). Contrary to Josephus' careful misrepresentations, Eleazar may well have been a popular and devout figure of the times. Josephus adds: "Of the brigands whom [Felix] crucified, and of the common people who were convicted of complicity with them and punished by him, the number was incalculable" (Josephus *J.W.* 2.13.2 §253).

Josephus mentions three "movements" which arose in Felix's time and which he appears to connect with the governor's extreme policies.

First, he describes the rise of the *sicarii*, so named after the Latin curved dagger (Josephus *J.W.* 2.13.3 §254). Although no leader or organization for the *sicarii* is known, their *modus operandi* was to murder individuals with the concealed *sica*, usually operating in broad daylight at times of the great feasts. Their targets were noted Jews, known to be sympathetic to Roman interests. Their most famous victims were the ex-high priests Jonathan and Ananias. Thus the *sicarii* appear to have been politically motivated, murdering those known to have been pro-Roman in order to intimidate others from such loyalty.

The term *sicarii* appears to have developed a more generalized use subsequently, being used by Luke of the supporters of the Egyptian prophet (Acts 21:38) and by Josephus of the supporters of Menahem and Eleazar ben Jair in the capture and defense of Masada (Josephus *J.W.* 2.17.6 §426; 7.8.2 §275). Nonetheless, the *sicarii* are not mentioned as participating in the war in Jerusalem in A.D. 66-70. The *sicarii* are to be distinguished from the "Zealot" faction which arose only after the war began and whose known activities were confined to Jerusalem, in particular the Temple precincts. (There were individual "zealots" in earlier times, including one among the followers of Jesus [Lk 6:15]. The pre-Christian Paul may have been such a "zealot" [Gal 1:14; Acts 22:3; cf. Phil 3:6]). As the war approached and then erupted there was a proliferation of military factions, some of whose leaders—such as John of Gischala, Eleazar ben Simon, Simon bar Giora—are known; others are not known. These factions dissipated their energies, warring with one another rather than against the common enemy, Rome.

Second, Josephus writes of "sign prophets" at that time who, "under the pretence of divine inspiration fostering revolutionary changes, they persuaded the multitude to act like madmen, and led them out into the desert under the belief that there God would give them signs of liberation" (Josephus *J.W.* 2.13.4 §259). Josephus does not say what those promised "signs" were. Given that the locale was the "desert"—so evocative in the salvation history of Israel—it is likely that the "signs" would include those performed by Moses and Joshua at the time of the exodus-conquest. The "liberation" would have been a reenacted defeat—Joshua-like—of the enemies of the moment, the Roman occupying force.

Another "sign prophet" to arise under Felix was the Egyptian prophet, who, collecting a large following, went to the Mount of Olives, promising that at his command—again, Joshua-like—the walls of Jerusalem would collapse, after which he would become "the ruler of the people" (Josephus *J.W.* 2.13.5 §§261-62).

These prophetic figures, who arose in reaction to Felix's excesses, appear to have been inspired by the examples of Moses and Joshua, and by their promised "signs" to have attempted to move the hand of God for the deliverance of his people. For their part, the Romans took these prophets seriously, dispatching troops and killing large numbers of their supporters, who appear to have been unarmed. (Other "sign prophets" arose in the sixties—both before and during the war, as well as afterwards [Josephus *Ant.* 20.8.10 §188; *J.W.* 6.5.2 §§284-86; 7.11.1 §438]).

Third, Josephus refers to some kind of an alliance between the prophetic figures and various brigands (*lēstrikoi*) in actions of a political—but religiously inspired—nature (Josephus *J.W.* 2.13.6 §§264-65). In a frenzied manner these organized themselves in companies, threatening to kill any who submitted to Roman rule. They moved through the countryside, murdering those who supported Rome, putting fire to many houses.

Such was the milieu of Judea in about A.D. 52-60, during the first five years of which the apostle Paul was engaged in ministry in the Aegean provinces. It was from this troubled environment, apparently, that Paul's opponents bound for Corinth set out in the mid-fifties. Judea under Felix was subject to political disintegration, revolutionary activism and apocalyptic fervor. These things most probably influenced and, to a degree inspired, Paul's opponents in their countermission against him in Corinth. Nationalistic Jews, including Christian Jews, must have been subject to great cultural and religious pressure at that time, which in turn they exerted on the messianic assemblies established by Paul among the Gentiles. To them Paul's mission to the Gentiles would easily have appeared to betray the cause of Israel (Acts 21:20-21). For his part, Paul devoted extensive parts of his second canonical letter in responding to their claims against him (2 Cor 2:17—4:6; 10:12—12:12).

But this was also the hostile world to which the apostle Paul returned in the late fifties, bringing the collection* for the Jerusalem church, while Felix was still the procurator of Judea. Paul was mistaken for the Egyptian prophet (Acts 21:38), which is ironic, granted that such prophets probably contributed indirectly to the problems Paul faced at the hands of the counter-missionaries who came from Judea to capture his churches.

*See also* APOCALYPTICISM; CHRONOLOGY OF PAUL; CIRCUMCISION; EMPERORS, ROMAN; HELLENISM; JEW, PAUL THE; JUDAIZERS; OPPONENTS OF PAUL; POLITICAL SYSTEMS; RESTORATION OF ISRAEL.

BIBLIOGRAPHY. E. Bammel and C. F. D., Moule, ed., *Jesus and the Politics of His Day* (Cambridge: University Press, 1984); P. Barnett, "The Jewish Sign Prophets," *NTS* 27 (1981) 679-97; idem, "Opposition in Corinth," *JSNT* 22 (1984) 3-17; idem, *Behind the Scenes of the New Testament* (Downers Grove, IL: InterVarsity, 1991); S. G. F. Brandon, *Jesus and the Zealots* (Manchester: University Press, 1967); F. F. Bruce, *New Testament History* (Garden City, NY: Doubleday, 1969); W. J. Heard, "Revolutionary Movements," *DJG* 688-98; M. Hengel, *The Charismatic Leader and His Followers* (New York: Crossroads, 1981); idem, *The Zealots* (Minneapolis: Fortress, 1989); R. A. Horsley and J. S. Hanson, *Bandits, Prophets and Messiahs* (New York: Winston, 1985); D. M. Rhoads, *Israel in Revolution 6-74 C.E.* (Philadelphia: Fortress, 1976); S. Safrai and M. Stern, *The Jewish People in the First Century* (CRINT 1.1; Philadelphia: Fortress, 1976); E. Schürer, *The History of the Jewish People in the Age of Jesus Christ (175 B.C.—A.D. 135)*, rev. and ed. G. Vermes and F. Millar (3 vols.; Edinburgh: T & T Clark, 1973-79); M. Smith, "Zealots and Sicarii: Their Origins and Relations," *HTR* 64 (1971) 1-19.

P. W. Barnett

# REWARDS

For Paul rewards comprise both the enjoyment of all the blessings that are in Christ* and a future tangible recognition of service* in the furtherance of the gospel.* To continue to experience the former, diligence in running the race is essential; to receive the latter, one's works must survive the fiery testing at the final judgment.* Such teachings, however, have at times posed problems for the church.

1. Rewards as Christ's Blessings
2. Rewards as Recognition of One's Works
3. Conclusion

## 1. Rewards as Christ's Blessings.

This ongoing benefit finds its focus in an intimate fellowship* with Christ,* a gain of such surpassing worth that by comparison even the finest human accolades are a loss, no better than rubbish (Phil 3:8-11). Paul describes this fellowship also as the prize awarded to those who successfully finish the Christian race (1 Cor 9:24-27). While these blessings are enjoyed in part now, their full experience awaits the life to come (Phil 1:21, 23; 3:14).

*1.1. The Problem of Works.* Paul's insistence that failure to run the race single-mindedly threatens one with disqualification (1 Cor 9:27; cf. 2 Cor 13:5), the loss of salvation* itself, seems to encourage a works-righteousness, the amassing of deeds that God will find sufficiently meritorious to deserve his blessings. But Paul also firmly denies such a possibility: salvation is by faith* alone, apart from works* in which people can boast (Rom 3:27-28).

*1.2. The Solution.* Understanding the motivation of the runners resolves the difficulty. Were Paul to see their striving for the prize as calculated to earn God's favor through self-effort, a problem would exist. But this is not the case; the race is to be run in dependence upon Christ who enables the Christian to be victorious (2 Cor 12:9-10; Gal 2:20; Phil 2:12-13). And the works that are done en route, far from being meritorious, are works of faith (1 Thess 1:3; 2 Thess 1:11 RSV), done because the runner is convinced that to trust and obey is the essential condition for the enjoyment of fellowship with God (Phil 2:12). What motivates these works therefore is simply the desire to continue to enjoy the blessings God has promised. It is self-interest—and things done for one's own benefit can lay no claim to consideration as meritorious.

*1.3. The Problem of Self-Interest.* But does not this appeal to self-interest counter Paul's own exhortation not to seek one's own good but that of others (1 Cor 10:24; Phil 2:4)? Unquestionably his setting forth both positive and negative motivation—the continuing enjoyment of the blessings of the gospel versus their loss and thus the loss of salvation itself—does have one's own welfare in view.

*1.4. The Solution.* It is important, however, to differentiate between self-interest and selfishness. The latter is clearly objectionable because it promotes one's own welfare at the expense of others. But self-interest centered in the desire for fellowship with Christ can scarcely be faulted. Moreover this fellowship fills Paul with such joy* that he is impelled to bring as many others as possible to share in it (1 Cor 9:19-23). Thus far from being undesirable, to use the reward of Christ's blessing as an appeal to self-interest results in the greatest possible good—winning many more to him.

### 2. Rewards as Recognition of One's Works.

This second aspect of rewards is reserved for the life to come and will recognize the extent of one's accomplishments in the furtherance of the gospel (1 Cor 3:8, 10-14). Of necessity then rewards will be tangible so that the gradations may be visible to all. Here Paul defines them only as "praise from God" (1 Cor 4:5), but elsewhere he speaks of "crowns" that he equates with those he has won for Christ (Phil 4:1; 1 Thess 2:19). An attractive possibility therefore is that the tangible rewards will be literal crowns, representing in some manner his converts. And that Paul does consider his converts a part of his reward is evident from his summation of his life work as the gaining (*kerdainō* "to procure advantage or profit") of as many as possible for Christ (1 Cor 9:19-22 RSV; see Daube).

Not all, however, will receive these crowns, and here again Paul makes use of a negative appeal to self-interest. Those whose works do not endure the testing at the judgment will suffer loss (1 Cor 3:15). Though not the loss of salvation itself, this will clearly be a diminution of one's eternal happiness. Thus here too Paul's appeal to self-interest functions as an incentive to win men and women for Christ.

*2.1. The Problem of Pride.* But if degrees of accomplishment are displayed for all to see, this would seem inevitably to lead to pride and boasting on the part of those with more impressive crowns. How can this be harmonized with Paul's insistence that boasting is excluded, and God alone to be praised (Rom 3:27; 1 Cor 1:31)?

*2.2. The Solution.* The reason Paul sees pride in one's accomplishments as impossible is that the rewards do not reflect the glory* of those to whom they are given but the glory of the giver. For it is the joy of fellowship with him, and confidence in his integrity in keeping his promises, that provides the motivation. Furthermore, Paul's rule of life is that every thought, word and deed is to enhance the glory of God (1 Cor 10:31), to demonstrate that he is truly the *summum bonum* of life and thus worthy of worship.* Differing degrees of rewards then reflect not the relative worth of the individual per se but the extent to which each one has found delight in fellowship with God, and has

thus been dedicated to the doing of his will.

### 3. Conclusion.

Rewards as Paul views them therefore play a most important role in encouraging Christ's followers to be faithful and diligent in the ministries to which each is called. Far from being questionable in any way, they are a most gracious provision by God to motivate his children to run the race successfully, and so to enjoy both in this life and in that to come the blessings of salvation.

*See also* APOSTASY, FALLING AWAY, PERSEVERANCE; ESCHATOLOGY; JUDGMENT; JUSTIFICATION; WORKS OF THE LAW.

BIBLIOGRAPHY. P. C. Boettger and B. Siede, "Recompense," *NIDNTT* 3.134-44; D. Daube, "Κερδαίνω as a Missionary Term," *HTR* 40 (1947) 109-20; F. V. Filson, *St. Paul's Conception of Recompense* (Leipzig: Hinrichs'sche Buchhandlung, 1931); R. M. Fuller, "A Pauline Understanding of Rewards" (unpublished Ph.D. dissertation, Fuller Theological Seminary, 1990); J. M. Gundry Volf, *Paul and Perseverance: Staying in and Falling Away* (Louisville: John Knox/Westminster, 1991); W. Pesch, "μισθός," *EDNT* 2.432-33; J. Piper, *Desiring God* (Portland: Multnomah, 1986); H. Preisker, "μισθός κτλ," *TDNT* IV.695-728; J. E. Rosscup, "Paul's Teaching of the Christian's Future Reward" (unpublished Ph.D. dissertation, University of Aberdeen, 1976). R. M. Fuller

## RHETORIC

The world of Paul's day was deeply enamored with public oratory by virtuoso rhetors known as sophists. Because Christianity placed such an emphasis on public preaching, its speakers would inevitably be judged by sophisticated audiences according to the canons of rhetoric. Therefore, as a missionary, Paul needed to determine whether classical rhetoric was essential for Christian proclamation.

1. Paul's Training in Rhetoric
2. Paul's Use of Judicial Rhetoric
3. Paul's Renunciation of Rhetoric for Preaching
4. A Corinthian Critique of Paul's Rhetorical Presentation

### 1. Paul's Training in Rhetoric.

No direct information is provided on Paul's training in rhetoric. Although born in a noted center for rhetoric, Tarsus, he was educated in Jerusalem in the Jewish tradition at the feet of Gamaliel (Acts 22:3). This statement does not preclude his training in rhetoric, including the tertiary level, at one of the Greek schools which operated in Jerusalem from the third century B.C. It is more likely that he received such training in his early years rather than after his conversion (*see* Paul).

## 2. Paul's Use of Judicial Rhetoric.

According to Acts 24:1-21 Paul defended himself in a Roman court before Felix, the governor, against Jewish opponents represented by a professionally trained forensic rhetor, Tertullus (Acts 24:1). The latter mounted a seemingly formidable case of political agitation and insurrection in worldwide Jewry against Paul, a Roman citizen (*see* Citizenship). Paul reduced the serious criminal charge to a theological issue, the resurrection, which was the only comment he made before the Sanhedrin (Acts 23:6). He prescribed the limits of evidence to events in Jerusalem,* proscribed the charges of absent Asian Jewish accusers, used the forensic structure with an *exordium* (introduction), *narratio* (statement of facts), *confirmatio* (establishment of facts), *refutatio* (refutation) and *peroratio* (conclusion), and displayed his knowledge of the little-known right of appeal to Caesar (Acts 25:11). Legal training by means of forensic rhetoric was an essential part of Greek education, and this summary of Paul's defense reflects his professional forensic skills.

## 3. Paul's Renunciation of Rhetoric for Preaching.

The Corinthians loved public orations (Dio Chrysostom *Or.* 37.33). Paul saw the use of "the wisdom of rhetoric" (1 Cor 1:17) as the means of "emptying" the preaching of the cross,* for it was more interested in the skillful structuring and delivery of a speech than in its content (Epictetus *Diss.* 3.23.23-25). By citing the OT in 1 Corinthians 1:19 (citing Is 29:4; Ps 33:10) and 1 Corinthians 1:31 (citing Jer 9:22-23), he argued that God determined that "the debater of this age," that is, the virtuoso rhetor, or sophist (Philo *Det. Pot. Ins.* 1-5), as well as the Greek philosophers (*see* Philosophy) and Jewish teachers (1 Cor 1:20) did not bring people to the knowledge of God.*

Paul explained why he had renounced in his modus operandi all formal conventions whereby a foreign rhetor established his credentials when he first came to a city (1 Cor 2:1-5). He tells why he would not proclaim the gospel* using the superior presentation of rhetoric or wisdom* (1 Cor 2:1). While rhetors sought topics from their audience on which to declaim in order to demonstrate their prowess in oratory, Paul was concerned only to proclaim Jesus, the crucified Messiah (1 Cor 2:2; *see* Christ; Death of Christ).

Orators used three accepted proofs to persuade their audience: *ethos*, acting out a character; *pathos*, manipulating his audience's feeling; and *demonstra-tion*, arguments. Paul uses none of these. He came "in weakness,* and in fear and in much trembling" (1 Cor 2:3)—the absolute antithesis to the powerful and commanding presence of the virtuoso rhetor (Philodemus *On Rhetoric* 1.194-200). His speech and his preaching did not make use of "persuasive rhetoric." It was a demonstration, not of rhetorical proofs, but of the Spirit (*see* Holy Spirit) and power* (1 Cor 2:4). It was a radical and costly step on the part of Paul to refuse to use the much admired rhetoric of his day in preaching.* His renunciation was motivated by the desire that his converts' faith* must not rest on human wisdom but on the power of God (1 Cor 2:5).

## 4. A Corinthian Critique of Paul's Rhetorical Presentation.

Following Paul's denunciation of contemporary rhetoric in preaching for theological reasons (1 Cor 1:17—2:5), his rhetorically minded opponents made a stinging critique of his oratorical abilities or lack of them (2 Cor 10:10). While conceding his letters were "weighty and strong" in rhetorical presentation, they said he failed as a public orator because he lacked "presence" (*hypokrisis*), that is, a beautiful body and a pleasant-sounding voice with appropriate gestures to match. His physical appearance was weak (tradition says he had crooked legs, a long nose and eyebrows which met, *Acts of Paul and Thekla*) and his voice lacked timbre (2 Cor 10:10; 11:6). Not preaching like a public orator, he called himself a "layperson" (i.e., a person trained in oratory but not making use of it—such is one meaning of *idiōtes*, see Isocrates *Antidosis* 204). However, as the Corinthians* well knew from his letters, he could use rhetoric with devastating effect (e.g., his skillful use of the device of the covert allusion in 1 Cor 4:6-13; *see* Rhetorical Criticism).

*See also* CROSS, THEOLOGY OF THE; DIATRIBE; RHETORICAL CRITICISM; WEAKNESS; WISDOM.

BIBLIOGRAPHY. H. D. Betz, "Rhetoric and Theology," in *L'Apôtre Paul; Personnalité, Style et Conception du Ministère*, ed. A. Vanhoye (BETL 73; Louvain: Louvain University/Peeters, 1986) 16-48; G. W. Bowersock, *Greek Sophists in the Roman Empire* (Oxford: University Press, 1969); C. Forbes, "Comparison, Self-praise and Irony: Paul's Boasting and Conventions of Hellenistic Rhetoric," *NTS* 32 (1986) 1-30; M. Hengel, *The Pre-Christian Paul* (Philadelphia: Trinity Press International, 1991); E. A. Judge, "Cultural Conformity and Innovation in Paul: Some Clues from Contemporary Documents," *TynB* 35 (1984) 3-24; idem, "Paul's Boasting in Relation to Contemporary Professional Practice," *AusBR* 16 (1968) 37-50; G. A. Kennedy, *The Art of Rhetoric in the Roman World* (Princeton: University Press,

1972); D. A. Russell, *Greek Declamations* (Cambridge: University Press, 1983); J. Weiss, "Beiträge zur paulinischen Rhetorik," *Theologischen Studien B. Weiss* (Göttingen, 1897) 165-247; B. W. Winter, "The Importance of the *Captatio Benevolentiae* in the Speeches of Tertullus and Paul in Acts 24:1-21," *JTS* 42 (1991) 505-31; idem, "Philo and Paul among the Sophists: A Hellenistic Jewish and a Christian Response" (unpublished Ph.D. dissertation, Macquarie University, 1988).

B. W. Winter

## RHETORICAL CRITICISM

Though Paul said that his preaching was not marked by the use of persuasive rhetoric (1 Cor 1:17—2:5), and his critics agreed (*see* Rhetoric), his letters were considered "weighty and forceful" even by those critics (2 Cor 10:10). Since Paul wrote his letters to be read aloud to the churches, there is a close connection between the forms of his letters and features of oration. In terms of an Aristotelian definition of rhetoric, Paul's letters are examples of the "faculty of discovering the possible means of persuasion." For this reason rhetorical criticism has often been used to clarify the rhetorical objectives, structures, style and techniques of his persuasive letters.*

1. Hellenistic Rhetoric
2. New Rhetoric
3. Conclusion

### 1. Hellenistic Rhetoric.

*1.1. Rhetorical Handbooks.* In *The Art of Rhetoric* (mid-4th century B.C.), Aristotle summarized and expanded discussions of rhetoric by such notable predecessors as Gorgias, Protagoras and Plato. Aristotle's work was the fountainhead for a stream of Greek and Latin handbooks on rhetoric down through the first century A.D. The most useful ones to survive are the *Rhetoric to Herennius* in Latin (c. 84 B.C.), Cicero's work *On Invention* and his *Partitions of Oratory* (c. 87 B.C.), and the major work of Quintilian, *On the Education of the Orator* (A.D. 92). Since these handbooks provide encyclopedic surveys of the theory and practice of rhetoric in Paul's time, they are frequently used by modern interpreters in the analysis of Paul's letters. Recent expositions of these handbooks on classical rhetoric are found in works by G. Kennedy and E. Corbett, and are summarized by L. G. Bloomquist.

Numerous comparisons of Paul's letters and the rhetorical handbooks of his day demonstrate that Paul employed the art of Hellenistic rhetoric to present his arguments. The extent of correspondence is too great to think otherwise. Yet, the point of using the classical handbooks in an analysis of Paul's letters is not to prove his dependence upon them but to be guided by them in a description of Paul's arguments. Classical rhetoric was based upon an inductive description of the elements of persuasive speech. Quintilian affirms that "it was then nature that created speech, and observation that originated the art of speaking. Just as men discovered the art of medicine by observing that some things were healthy and some the reverse, so they observed that some things were useful and some useless in speaking, and noted them for imitation or avoidance" (Quintilian 3.2.3). Since the classical rhetoricians were thorough in their observation and organization of almost every feature of argumentation, it should not be surprising that many of the features of Pauline argumentation are described in their handbooks. Rhetorical criticism of Paul's letters uses the parallels which are applicable from the rhetorical handbooks as descriptive tools.

*1.2. Theoretical Concepts.* According to Aristotle (*Rhetoric* 1.2.3), persuasion depends upon three factors: the moral character of the speaker (*ethos*), the emotions aroused in the hearers by the speech (*pathos*) and the logical arguments in the speech (*logos*).

Logical arguments are either inductive, by means of examples (*paradeigmata*), or deductive, by means of an enthymeme. What is known in logic as a syllogism includes a full statement of a major premise, a minor premise and a conclusion. But speakers and writers usually assume either the major premise or the minor premise. A deductive argument that omits either the major or minor premise is called an enthymeme. When an enthymeme runs from premise to conclusion it is often introduced by such signals as "therefore," "hence" or "thus" (Gk *gar, ara, oun*); when an enthymeme moves from conclusion to premise it may be introduced by "since," "for" or "because" (Gk *hoti*). Galatians 3:6-7 is an enthymeme: Paul assumes the major premise that God* will deal with all people as he dealt with Abraham*; his explicit minor premise states that "Abraham believed God, and it was reckoned to him for righteousness*" (Gal 3:6); the logical conclusion (signaled by *ara*) states that "those who are of faith are the children of Abraham" (see Hansen 1989, 112).

Three species of rhetoric are described in the classical tradition: *forensic, deliberative* and *epideictic*. Forensic speech defends or accuses someone regarding past actions; deliberative speech exhorts or dissuades the audience regarding future actions; epideictic discourse affirms communal values by praise or blame in order to affect a present evaluation. These three rhetorical genres seek different kinds of response from the audience. Forensic: Is it just? Deliberative: Is it expedient? Epideictic: Is it praiseworthy?

In Betz's opinion, Paul's letter to the Galatians* should be classified as an example of forensic rhetoric: Paul's objective is a defense of himself (a self-apology) and his gospel* against the attack of the intruders. Others have argued that Galatians is comparable to deliberative speech since Paul's primary aim is to exhort his readers to be true to the gospel and to dissuade them from accepting the false gospel of the Judaizers* (see Kennedy, Hall, Smit, Lyons). It is probably best to see Galatians as a mixture of the forensic and deliberative kinds of rhetoric (see Hansen, Longenecker). In the first half of the letter (Gal 1:6—4:11), Paul defends himself against accusations and accuses his opponents* of perverting the gospel. But in the second half of the letter (Gal 4:12—6:18), he seeks to persuade the Galatian believers to adopt a new course of action.

Similar attempts have been made to determine the rhetorical genre of Paul's other letters. G. A. Kennedy classifies 1 Thessalonians* as deliberative rhetoric (Kennedy 1984, 142); R. Jewett identifies it as epideictic (Jewett, 71-78). F. F. Church's study of Philemon* demonstrates Paul's use of deliberative rhetoric. M. M. Mitchell argues that the unity of 1 Corinthians* can be demonstrated when it is seen as deliberative rhetoric convincing the Corinthians to be reconciled to God and to Paul, and D. F. Watson argues similarly for the unity of Philippians (Watson 1988). G. A. Kennedy labels 2 Corinthians as forensic rhetoric, except for chapters 8 and 9 which are deliberative (Kennedy 1984, 87). W. Wuellner shows how discussion of the Law in Romans* can be clarified by observing the epideictic aim (not forensic, as in Galatians) of the letter. Rhetorical criticism of Philippians* suggests that it is either deliberative (Watson 1988, 59; Bloomquist, 120, but with more than one *genus*) or epideictic (Kennedy 1984, 77). It is probably composed of mixed rhetorical *genera* or types (so Black).

The structure of a speech, as described in the classical rhetorical handbooks, consists of six parts: (1) the *introduction*, which defines the character of the speaker and the central issue addressed; (2) the *narration*, which narrates the events related to the central issue; (3) the *proposition*, which summarizes the central theses to be proved; (4) the *confirmation*, which sets forth the logical arguments; (5) the *refutation*, which refutes the opponents' arguments; and (6) the *conclusion*, which recapitulates the basic points and evokes a sympathetic response. The structure of deliberative rhetoric and epideictic rhetoric is usually a simplified version of these six parts. Often in the practice of the

rhetorical criticism of Paul's letters, the Latin terms of classical rhetoric are used to designate these six parts: *exordium, narratio, propositio, probatio, refutatio, peroratio*. Betz uses these terms for his outline of Galatians:

I. Epistolary Prescript (Gal 1:1-5)

II. *Exordium* (Gal 1:6-11)

III. *Narratio* (Gal 1:12—2:14)

IV. *Propositio* (Gal 2:15-21)

V. *Probatio* (Gal 3:1—4:31)

VI. *Exhortatio* (Gal 5:1—6:10)

VII. Epistolary Postscript (*Peroratio*, Gal 6:11-18).

Style received a major share of attention from the classical rhetoricians. The theory of style was based on an analysis of diction, the choice of words, and composition, the arrangement of words. Paul often chose a *metaphor* to express his thought. For example, the Law* is a jailkeeper with the power* to lock up and hold prisoners (Gal 3:23), and the Law is a tutor (*paidagōgos*) with the power of supervision (Gal 3:24-25). Sometimes Paul seems to use hyperbole to emphasize his point. According to J. D. G. Dunn, Paul's use of the words of Psalm 19:4 to assert that the gospel has gone "into all the earth" and "to the ends of the world" (Rom 10:18) provided "a hyperbolic vision of the full eschatological sweep of the gentile mission" (Dunn, 624). When Paul exhorts his readers to "present your bodies as a living sacrifice" (Rom 12:1), his choice of the word "body"* to represent the whole person is an example of *synecdoche*, a part for the whole. The NIV translation of "your bodies" as "yourselves" accurately interprets this synecdoche.

In his composition Paul often arranges words in the form of *antitheses*. "Hate what is evil; cling to what is good" (Rom 12:9). "We know that a person is not justified by observing the Law, but by faith in Jesus Christ" (Gal 2:16). Paul also works out his thoughts in a chiastic pattern. A *chiasm* is a crisscross pattern of words resembling the Greek letter X (*Chi*), and hence its name. For example, "the *first* shall be *last* and the *last first*." Words or concepts are stated in the order A B C and then repeated with important expansions in the reverse order C B A. Lightfoot observed the form of a chiasm in Galatians 4:4-5.

A   The Son of God was born a man.

   B   He was born under the Law,

   B   to redeem those under the Law,

A   that all men might become sons of God.

J. Bligh used this central chiasm as the starting point for outlining the chiastic nature of the entire letter of Galatians. However, the frequency of Bligh's changes in the text has made it appear that the chiastic patterns which he "finds" are actually imposed upon the text.

Another common element in Paul's style is his use of *rhetorical questions*: "Do we then nullify the Law by this faith?" "What, then, was the purpose of the Law?" "Is the Law, therefore, opposed to the promises of God?" These rhetorical questions (Rom 3:31; Gal 3:19, 21) prepare the way for Paul to make some of his most significant statements about the Law.

*1.3. Methodology.* Kennedy provides a helpful guide to the practice of rhetorical criticism (Kennedy 1984, 33-38). He outlines five stages of analysis.

First, determine the rhetorical unit to be studied. Usually, an entire letter of Paul is the rhetorical unit under observation. In some cases a clearly delineated passage within a letter (such as 2 Cor 10—13) may be the rhetorical unit chosen for examination.

Second, define the rhetorical situation. In the description of the persons, events and relations of the rhetorical situation, special attention must be given to the rhetorical problem faced by Paul in his relation to his audience. It is helpful at this stage to define the *stasis*, or basic issue, of the case. Was the basic issue about a question of fact, of definition, of quality or of jurisdiction? The species of rhetoric (forensic, deliberative or epideictic) used by Paul will also be defined at this stage.

Third, consider the arrangement of material in the text. What are the major subdivisions? What is the flow of the argument?

Fourth, list the devices of style and define their function in context.

Fifth, evaluate the impact of the entire rhetorical unit on the rhetorical situation.

## 2. New Rhetoric.

A recent approach in the application of rhetorical criticism to Paul's letters is the description of rhetorical techniques employed by Paul in his argumentation. A wide variety of rhetorical techniques is described by C. Perelman and L. Olbrecht-Tyteca in what Kennedy calls "the most influential modern treatise on rhetoric," *The New Rhetoric: A Treatise on Argumentation* (1969). The application of the categories of new rhetoric to Paul's letters is not anachronistic since the categories of the new rhetoric are derived from a thorough analysis of both ancient and modern examples of argumentation.

The five rhetorical techniques described here are illustrated by an application to Paul's letter to the Galatians (see Hansen, 79-93).

*2.1. Argument by Authority.* An argument that depends upon the prestige, reputation or moral charac-

ter of the orator is an argument from authority.* Paul's double denial of any dependence on human agency or authority for the legitimacy of his apostleship and his claim to a divine commission (Gal 1:1) signal that his entire argument will be structured by this emphasis on authority. Yet Galatians 1:6-9 is not, as might have been expected, a direct development of Paul's claim to apostolic* authority. Instead Paul moves to a definition of the gospel which excludes any possible alternative versions. He then subordinates both himself and any angel* from heaven* to the one true gospel (Gal 1:8-9). Thus Paul responds to a challenge to his authority by establishing one ultimate measure of genuine authority: adherence to the gospel which he preached. In his autobiography (Gal 1:11—2:21) and in his interpretation of the Abrahamic promise (Gal 3:1—4:11) he demonstrates his faithfulness to this standard, in contrast to those who deviated from it. His adherence to the "truth of the gospel" in his life as well as his preaching (Gal 2:19-20; 6:14-15) makes his authority invulnerable. So he has the authority to appeal for his converts' allegiance, issue his apostolic decree (Gal 5:2) and establish the canon for the Israel* of God (Gal 6:15-16).

*2.2. Argument by Definition.* Paul's argument in Galatians is structured by the way he develops his definition of the gospel. When the gospel is first introduced as the focus of the problem in the Galatian churches, the quality of uniqueness is attributed to it. In all the successive stages of the argument the definition of the gospel is elaborated with the use of other key terms such as promise, faith, Law and works* of the Law.

*2.3. Argument by Dissociation of Ideas.* That Paul's argument in Galatians is structured by the dissociation of ideas is evident from his explication of antithetical pairs: curse/blessing, works/faith, flesh/spirit, Law/Christ, Law/Spirit, slavery/freedom.

*2.4. Argument by the Severance of the Group and Its Members.* Paul's dissociation of ideas in his argumentation also involves the dissociation of the group and its members by the use of the rhetorical technique of severance. Paul's argument is designed to drive a wedge between the Galatian believers and the false teachers so as to split them apart. The false teachers are perverters of the gospel (Gal 1:7); therefore, they are under a curse* (Gal 1:8-9); they are guilty of witchcraft (Gal 3:1); they do not seek the Galatian believers for good (Gal 4:17); they are children of Hagar, the bondwoman (Gal 4:29); they have obstructed the Galatians in the race (Gal 5:7); they are leaven in the lump (Gal 5:9); they seek to avoid persecution for the cross* of Christ (Gal 6:12); they do not keep the Law themselves (Gal 6:13). Paul's autobiographical remarks (Gal 1:11—2:21; 4:12-20) and his extended scriptural exposition are designed to validate the expulsion of the false teachers from the Galatian churches.

*2.5. Argument by Sacrifice.* In argumentation by sacrifice, sacrifice is presented as evidence of the value of the thing for which the sacrifice is made. Paul frequently points to the sacrifice* of the cross as the basis for the value of the freedom* in Christ which the false teachers were attempting to destroy (Gal 1:4; 2:4; 2:20, 21; 3:1, 13-14; 4:4; 5:1).

## 3. Conclusion.

Rhetorical criticism of Paul's letters enables the readers to engage in a detailed analysis of the structures and techniques of argumentation employed by Paul. If such analysis leads to a preoccupation with form over substance, then rhetorical criticism may be an obstacle to understanding the meaning of Paul's letters. But if the goal is clear exposition of *what* Paul meant by his arguments, then this methodology may be helpful by clarifying *how* Paul developed his arguments, just as historical criticism may be helpful by throwing light on *why* Paul wrote his letters.

*See also* DIATRIBE; GALATIANS, LETTER TO THE; HERMENEUTICS/INTERPRETING PAUL; LETTERS AND LETTER FORMS; RHETORIC.

BIBLIOGRAPHY. H. D. Betz, *Galatians* (Herm; Philadelphia: Fortress, 1979); idem, "The Literary Composition and Function of Paul's Letter to the Galatians," *NTS* (1975) 353-80; C. C. Black, "Keeping Up with Recent Studies: 16. Rhetorical Criticism and Biblical Interpretation," *ExpT* 100 (1989) 252-58; J. Bligh, *Galatians in Greek: A Structural Analysis of St. Paul's Epistle to the Galatians with Notes in Greek* (Detroit: University of Detroit, 1966); L. G. Bloomquist, *The Function of Suffering in Philippians* (JSNTSup 78; Sheffield: Academic, 1993); H. W. Boers, "The Form-Critical Study of Paul's Letter: 1 Thessalonians as a Case Study," *NTS* 22 (1976) 140-58; B. H. Brinsmead, *Galatians—Dialogical Response to Opponents* (SBLDS 65; Chico, CA: Scholars, 1982); F. F. Church, "Rhetorical Structure and Design in Paul's Letter to Philemon," *HTR* 71 (1978) 17-33; E. Corbett, *Classical Rhetoric for the Modern Student* (New York: Oxford University, 1971); idem, ed., *Rhetorical Analyses of Literary Works* (New York: Oxford University, 1969); P. B. Duff, "Metaphor, Motif, and Meaning: The Rhetorical Strategy behind the Image 'Led in Triumph' in 2 Corinthians 2:14," *CBQ* 53 (1991) 79-92; J. D. G. Dunn, *Romans* (WBC 38; Dallas: Word, 1988); B. Fiore, " 'Covert Allusion' in 1 Corinthians 1—4," *CBQ* 47 (1985) 85-104; B. R. Gaventa, "Galatians 1 and 2: Autobiography as Paradigm," *NovT* 28 (1986) 309-26; R. G. Hall, "The Rhetorical Outline for Galatians: A Reconsideration," *JBL* 106 (1987) 277-87; G. W. Hansen, *Abraham in Galatians—Epistolary and Rhetorical Contexts* (JSNTSup 29; Sheffield: Sheffield Academic, 1989); J. D. Hester, "The Rhetorical Structure of Galatians 1:11—2:14," *JBL* 103 (1984) 223-33; R. Jewett, *The Thessalonian Correspondence* (Philadelphia: Fortress, 1986); G. A. Kennedy, *New Testament Interpretation Through Rhetorical Criticism* (Chapel Hill, NC: University of North Carolina, 1984); P. E. Koptak, "Rhetorical Identification in Paul's Autobiographical Narrative: Galatians 1:13—2:14," *JSNT* 40 (1990) 97-115; B. C. Letegan, "Is Paul Defending His Apostleship in Galatians?," *NTS* 34 (1988) 411-30; R. N. Longenecker, *Galatians* (WBC 41; Dallas: Word, 1990); G. Lyons, *Pauline Autobiography: Toward a New Understanding* (SBLDS 73; Atlanta: Scholars, 1985); A. Malherbe, "Exhortation in First Thessalonians," *NovT* 25 (1983) 238-56; M. M. Mitchell, *Paul and the Rhetoric of Reconciliation* (HUT 27; Tübingen: J. C. B. Mohr, 1991); C. Perelmann and L. Olbrechts-Tyteca, *The New Rhetoric: A Treatise on Argumentation* (Notre Dame: University of Notre Dame, 1969); J. P. Sampley, "Paul and his Opponents in 2 Corinthians 10—13 and the Rhetorical Handbooks," in *The Social World of Formative Christianity and Judaism: Essays in Tribute to Howard Clark Kee*, ed. J. Neusner et al. (Philadelphia: Fortress, 1988) 162-77; E. Schüssler Fiorenza, "Rhetorical Situation and Historical Reconstruction in 1 Corinthians," *NTS* 33 (1987) 386-403; R. Scroggs, "Paul as Rhetorician: Two Homilies in Romans 1—11," in *Jews, Greeks and Christians: Essays in Honor of W. D. Davies*, ed. R. Hamerton-Kelly and R. Scroggs (Leiden: E. J. Brill, 1976) 271-98; J. Smit, "The Genre of 1 Corinthians 13 in the Light of Classical Rhetoric," *NovT* 33 (1991) 193-216; idem, "The Letter of Paul to the Galatians: A Deliberative Speech," *NTS* 35 (1989) 1-26; F. Vouga, "Zur rhetorischen Gattung des Galaterbriefes," *ZNW* 79 (1988) 291-92; D. F. Watson, "1 Corinthians 10:23—11:1 in the Light of Greco-Roman Rhetoric: The Role of Rhetorical Questions," *JBL* 108 (1989) 301-18; idem, "The New Testament and Greco-Roman Rhetoric: A Bibliography," *JETS* 31 (1988) 465-72; idem, ed., *Persuasive Artistry: Studies in New Testament Rhetoric in Honor of George A. Kennedy* (JSNTSup 50; Sheffield: Sheffield Academic, 1991); idem, "A Rhetorical Analysis of Philippians and Its Implications for the Unity Question," *NovT* 39 (1988) 57-88; A. C. Wire, *The Corinthian Women Prophets: A Reconstruction Through Paul's Rhetoric* (Minneapolis: Fortress, 1990); W. Wuellner, "Paul as Pastor: The Function of Rhetorical Questions in First Corinthians," in *L'Apôtre Paul: personnal-*

*ité, style et conception du ministère*, ed. A. Vanhoye (BETL 73; Leuven: Leuven University, 1986); idem, "Paul's Rhetoric of Argumentation in Romans," *CBQ* 38 (1976) 330-51; idem, "Where Is Rhetorical Criticism Taking Us?" *CBQ* 49 (1987) 448-63.

G. W. Hansen

# RICHES AND POVERTY

Neither the appropriate use of riches nor the plight of the economically deprived are dominant concerns for Paul, who usually spiritualizes the vocabulary of riches. Where Paul does display concern about economic issues, his teaching for the most part reflects standard Jewish piety.

1. Riches
2. Poverty

## 1. Riches.

The lack of attention in the Pauline letters to the rich and to the appropriate use of riches is remarkable. The subject is common in intertestamental Jewish wisdom literature and among contemporary Greco-Roman moralists, and of course the Synoptic Gospels and James evince considerable concern about the dangers of wealth. The evidence of Acts (e.g., Acts 16:14; 17:12; 18:7-8) and analysis of names mentioned in Paul's correspondence (e.g., Rom 16:1-23) suggest that there were many early converts who were well-to-do. Yet Paul scarcely touches on the subject of riches, and the only extended treatment is 1 Timothy 6:6-10, 17-19.

Admittedly, the use of wealth falls somewhat outside the scope of the interpersonal and intercommunity issues most characteristic of Pauline ethics.* It is possible that Paul's own "freedom from worldly concerns" (1 Cor 7:28-35; 8:1-27), his "contentment in any state" (Phil 4:10-13), rendered him less aware of the issue for others. Conversely, he may have been so sensitive to the issue that he gave instructions only verbally to individuals. Still, the fact that Paul was an itinerant who presumably lived with minimal possessions and yet required nothing like this for others, suggests that his expectations for rank-and-file believers were modest by comparison.

*1.1. The Spiritualization of Riches.* Among writers roughly contemporary with Paul, only Philo of Alexandria approaches Paul's spiritualization of the vocabulary of wealth. The character of God* in his bestowal of salvation* is described in terms of his "riches," especially in Romans* (Rom 2:4; 9:23; 10:12; 11:33) and Ephesians* (Eph 1:7, 18; 2:4, 7; 3:8, 16; cf. Phil 4:19; Col 1:27). Accordingly, God "enriches" the saints (Rom 11:12; 1 Cor 1:5; 2 Cor 6:10; 9:11; Col 2:2; 3:16; Tit 3:6).

In 2 Corinthians 8:9 Christ is said to have moved from wealth to poverty in order to make others "rich" spiritually. Christ's "impoverishment" here is usually understood as a reference to his exchange of a heavenly state for an earthly state at the Incarnation, but it is possible that it reveals a literal renunciation of wealth on the part of Jesus—or at least highlights the low economic level endured in his earthly ministry. Paul uses a similar line of argument in 2 Corinthians 6:10, contending that his own (economic) poverty leads to the (spiritual) wealth of the Corinthians.*

The inconsistency between Paul's titular status as a Roman citizen (probably indicative of a prosperous family; *see* Citizenship) and his life as an itinerant evangelist may provide a clue to his other-worldly view of riches: in Christ (*see* In Christ), as worldly measures of value are transformed, so worldly terminology must be redefined. 1 Timothy 6:17-19, with its wordplay on "rich," may represent the fullest development of Paul's thought in this regard.

*1.2. Economic Level of Paul's Constituency.* 1 Corinthians 1:26 indicates that "not many" Corinthians were in positions of power or nobility, but recent studies have shown that it is a mistake to take this as an indicator of a low economic level in the Pauline churches. "Not many" allows for significant exceptions (cf. Acts 18:7-8; Rom 16:23), and people could possess riches without prestige or rank. Indeed, Paul criticizes members of the church for social pretensions (1 Cor 11:19) and social prejudice (1 Cor 11:17-22), and his extended appeal for financial aid (*see* Financial Support) assumes their ability to support the cause of helping the Jerusalem poor (2 Cor 8—9; esp. 2 Cor 8:13-15). The emerging consensus is that Pauline churches represented a fair cross-section of urban society: few extremes on either end of the socioeconomic scale, and a preponderance of artisans and traders at various levels of income. Those with money but without other means of status may have been attracted to Christianity in part as a status-enhancing mechanism within the local community (*see* Social Setting).

*1.3. Responsible Use of Riches.* The personal economic ethic of the Pauline corpus reflects standard Jewish piety of the period. This includes warnings against greed (1 Cor 5:11; 1 Tim 3:8; Tit 1:7), avoidance of poverty by industry (Rom 13:8; 1 Thess 4:11-12; cf. 2 Thess 3:6-12), priority in giving to one's own household (Gal 6:10; 1 Tim 5:8; cf. Acts 11:27-30) and liberality toward others (Rom 12:8, 13; 1 Cor 16:2; 2 Cor 8:2; Eph 4:28). The focus of liberality for Paul is the collection for the saints (*see* Collection for the Saints), which appears to have taken the place of the Jewish Temple tax as a Pauline expression of solidarity with the Jerusalem* church (Rom 15:25-29; 1 Cor 16:1-4; 2 Cor 8—

9; perhaps Gal 2:10). More specifically, the rich themselves are enjoined to generosity, which will result in spiritual blessings in this life (2 Cor 9:10-15; Phil 4:14-20) and the next (1 Tim 6:19).

Along with these Jewish features, there are also some Greek elements in Paul's teaching (especially in 2 Cor 8—9). The warning against "love of money" (1 Tim 3:3; 6:6-10; 2 Tim 3:2) is common in contemporary Greek literature. In Philippians 4:11-13 Paul argues for "self-sufficiency" in all circumstances (autarkēs, Phil 4:11; cf. 1 Tim 6:7-8), a term common among Stoics and Cynics (see Philosophy). In Cynic practice and in later Christian monasticism, autarkeia implied not only spiritual freedom or detachment but also voluntary reduction to a minimal economic level. Paul's teaching—and certainly his example—allow for such a radical degree of liberality on the part of the rich. Indeed, 1 Corinthians 13:3 alludes to those who "give away all" (provided they have love). But the fact that Paul does not make explicit such a demand suggests that his expectations for liberality are limited to such expressions of solidarity as the collection and provision for the subsistence of needy believers (Eph 4:28).

## 2. Poverty.
Paul has even less to say about the poor than he does about the rich. This may be due to Paul's own detachment, as suggested above. It may also be due in part to the lack of direct relevance of poverty to the Pauline churches. Among the urban artisans, traders and even slaves who comprised the early communities, there may have been very few who were poor by first-century standards; that is, without any means of livelihood apart from charity.

*2.1. Responsibility to the Poor.* To the extent that poor people can be found, they are the appropriate recipients of Christian liberality (Eph 4:28; cf. Acts 11:27-30), and Paul himself affirms that it is part of his commission to "remember" the poor (Gal 2:10; cf. instructions about widows in 1 Tim 5:3-16). The instructions regarding work in 1 Thessalonians 4:11-12 and 2 Thessalonians 3:6-12 imply a negative view of poverty that results from laziness. Elsewhere, we might infer a measure of sympathy for the plight of the needy from Paul's injunctions to kindness and love* for fellow believers, but poverty per se is not a concern. Paul draws attention to his own poverty not to call for financial assistance, which he forgoes (1 Cor 9:15; 2 Cor 11:10), but to highlight the spiritual riches his ministry bestows (2 Cor 6:10; cf. 1 Cor 4:9-13). He draws attention to the poverty of the Macedonians only as a rhetorical device to highlight their exemplary generosity (2 Cor 8:2).

*2.2. "The Poor Among the Saints in Jerusalem."* Romans 15:26 affirms the gifts of Macedonia and Achaia to "the poor among the saints at Jerusalem" (RSV). Since this is clearly a reference to the Pauline collection, which is not described elsewhere as social relief, it may be best to take the expression here as explicative: "the poor *who are* the saints in Jerusalem." This is consistent with the use of the title *poor* as a self-designation of the Jews, especially the Qumran sectaries (see 1QpHab 12:3, 6, 10; 1QM 11:9, 13; 4Q171 37:2-10; cf. Ps 69:32; 72:4), in contemporary literature. In this sense it is not *primarily* an economic designation but a signifier of the longing for the *spiritual* riches of salvation. This is in line with Paul's spiritualization of the terminology of riches, and it may indicate a noneconomic connotation in the reference to Paul's remembering the poor in Galatians 2:10. On the other hand, if believers in Jerusalem, or a subgroup of them, had suffered economically, the title may indicate economic deprivation. Some may have suffered from despoliation at the hands of antagonistic Jews (Heb 10:32-34), from famine (Acts 11:27-30) or from voluntary depletion of capital (Acts 4:32-37).

*See also* COLLECTION FOR THE SAINTS; SOCIAL SETTING OF MISSION CHURCHES; SUFFERING.

BIBLIOGRAPHY. E. Bammel, "πτωχός κτλ," *TDNT* VI.885-916; D. Georgi, *Remembering the Poor* (Nashville: Abingdon, 1992); F. Hauck and W. Kasch, "πλοῦτος κτλ," *TDNT* VI.318-32; M. Hengel, *Property and Riches in the Early Church* (Philadelphia: Fortress, 1974); B. Holmberg, *Paul and Power* (Lund: CWK Gleerup, 1978); L. E. Keck, "The Poor Among the Saints in the New Testament," *ZNW* 56 (1965) 100-129; R. M. Kidd, *Wealth and Beneficence in the Pastoral Epistles* (SBLDsss 122, Missoula: Scholar's, 1990); W. Meeks, *The First Urban Christians* (New Haven: Yale University, 1983); K. F. Nickle, *The Collection: A Study of Paul's Strategy* (London: SCM, 1966); G. Theissen, *The Social Setting of Pauline Christianity: Essays on Corinth* (Philadelphia: Fortress, 1982). T. E. Schmidt

# RIGHTEOUSNESS, RIGHTEOUSNESS OF GOD
In the Pauline corpus the teaching about the righteousness of God* and the related doctrine of the justification* of the sinner* hold an important place. Though the centrality of these concepts in Pauline thought has in recent times been questioned (Schweitzer, Fitzmyer, Sanders; *see* Center; Justification; Paul and His Interpreters), they have in the past been the object of vigorous discussion, especially since these terms have been widely affirmed as a key

to Paul's understanding of salvation.* But while there has been broad scholarly consensus about the significance of these terms in Paul's thought, there has not been agreement as to the precise meaning these terms have in Paul's usage.

1. Terminology, Background and Issues
2. Righteousness in Paul
3. History of Interpretation
4. God's Righteousness as Relation-Restoring Love

## 1. Terminology, Background and Issues.

The voluminous discussion has been focused largely on two questions: (1) how is the genitive construction *dikaiosynē theou* ("righteousness of God") to be interpreted, and (2) what does it mean in the overall context of Paul's thought? Is it to be understood in the so-called objective sense (somewhat straining the grammatical definition of objective genitive but frequently used by commentators to label this sense), that is, the righteousness which is valid before God? Or is it to be interpreted as a subjective genitive, referring either to God's own righteousness, describing his being (he is righteous) or God's action (God acts justly)? Further, is righteousness, or God's righteousness through Christ, received by impartation or imputation? Does this righteousness give juridical standing, a new status, or a new nature? And from the human side, is the righteousness of God experienced as ethical power, a new relationship with God, or a change of lordship? Is Paul using these terms within the context of Greco-Roman jurisprudence, where righteousness means "justice" or "righteous judgment" (in a legal sense), or is he using them in light of OT meanings?

*1.1. Philological Concerns.* In the interpretation of the theme righteousness of God, the problem begins when one considers the meaning of words. Words neither exist by themselves without a context, nor are texts written as free-floating packages of meaning without a historical basis or a place in their cultural milieu. The language Paul used was Greek, but as a Jew he participated in a culture that was Hebrew as well as Greco-Roman. Since Paul quotes passages of the OT throughout his letters, one must understand Paul as writing within the tradition of the Hebrew Bible. By reason of Paul's frequent use of the Septuagint version of the Hebrew Bible, the same concepts in the LXX should be given due consideration. In English translation the words *righteousness* or *justification* are used to translate the Greek *dikaiosynē*. These words may or may not connote the same meaning as the Greek term. These are just some of the linguistic issues that lie at the foundation of interpretation. If one couples the linguistic possibilities with various theological presuppositions, the interpretive options increase (*see* Hermeneutics, Interpreting Paul).

*1.1.1. Etymology.*

*1.1.1.1. Hebrew.* G. Quell provides an excellent introduction to the issues that are at the basis of the Hebrew understanding of righteousness. The concept of righteousness in the Hebrew Bible emphasizes the relational aspect of God and humanity in the context of a covenant. Among the various Hebrew word groups associated with righteousness, *ṣedeq* ("straightness," "justness," "rightness") and *ṣᵉdāqâ* ("justice," "straightness," "honesty") suggest a norm. In the LXX *dikaiosynē* ("righteousness") is used 81 times for *ṣedeq*, 134 times for *ṣᵉdāqâ*, and six times it renders freely the adjective *ṣaddîq* ("just," "righteous," "honest"). There are eight instances in which *dikaiosynē* ("righteousness") renders *ḥeseḏ* ("loving-kindness," "mercy," "piety," "goodwill"; e.g., Gen 19:19). Other Hebrew words meaning "genuine," "good," "evenness," "purity" and "simplicity" are occasionally translated by *dikaiosynē*. *Dikaios* ("observant of right," "righteous," "fair") renders the Hebrew *ṣaddîq* 189 times. In sum, of the predominant Hebrew terms the root *ṣdq* is the only one to be rendered mainly by *dikē* ("right," "law") and its derivatives, especially *dikaiosynē*, while other synonymous Hebrew terms such as *ḥeseḏ* are not given their due when the LXX translates them by *eleos* ("pity," "mercy"), which introduces an emotional element not present in the Hebrew. *Dikaiosynē* would have been a more accurate rendering of these words as well.

The common Hebrew word for righteousness is *ṣedeq*, or its feminine form *ṣᵉdāqâ*, which occurs in the OT 117 and 115 times respectively. The Hebrew meaning of justice means more than the classical Greek idea of giving to every one their due. Usually the word suggests Yahweh's saving acts as evidence of God's faithfulness to the covenant. For this meaning of righteousness of God, *dikaiosynē* is not as flexible as the Hebrew word.

In the Tannaitic literature of rabbinic Judaism there was a theological and semantic shift restricting *ṣedeq* and *ṣᵉdāqâ* to proper behavior, with *ṣᵉdāqâ* being used primarily for almsgiving (Przybylski, 75). God's righteousness was increasingly understood as God's willingness to protect and provide for the poor. This association was already present within the Hebrew Bible; for example: "They have distributed freely, they have given to the poor; their righteousness endures forever" (Ps 112:9).

*1.1.1.2. Greek.* The richness of the Hebrew usage is generally well reproduced in the LXX (Quell). Of the relatively few instances in which *ṣedeq*, *ṣᵉdāqâ* and *ṣaddîq* are not translated by *dikai-* words, *eleēmosynē* and *eleos* ("alms," "mercy") are employed for *ṣᵉdāqâ* (cf. LXX Is 1:27; Ziesler, 59-60). Similar evidence of this is found in the NT at Matthew 6:1, where the variant readings of later MSS read *eleēmosynēn* for *dikaiosynēn* (see Przybylski, 78).

*1.1.1.3. Latin.* In the Western Roman Empire, the Old Latin versions of the NT displaced the Greek NT, and Paul was consequently understood via the Latin translation. The Old Latin and later Latin Vulgate rendered *dikaiosynē* by *iustitia* ("justice"). The legal connotation of this term in Roman Law was superimposed upon the word *dikaiosynē*, which Paul had employed. The Roman legal understanding of justice was in a distributive sense: to give to each their due, the bestowal of rewards and punishments according to merit. The OT sense of righteousness as grounded in covenantal relationship was weakened, and its place was taken by the courtroom image of the sinner before God's tribunal. Although righteousness in the OT had a legal aspect, it was that of a litigant being adjudged righteous by God before their enemies. The biblical image of the covenant between God and humanity faded into the background, while the Latin context called to mind stark legal realities of the court. The shift in language from Hebrew to Greek to Latin resulted in an alteration in theological content as the words that were employed either overlaid the earlier meaning or signified something new in the receptor language.

*1.1.1.4. English.* Modern English partakes of a double portion of Indo-European languages: a Germanic base from Anglo-Saxon as well as Latinate words from the Norman Conquest. Because of this characteristic of English, one can say either "to be righteous" (from the Anglo-Saxon verb *rightwisen* meaning "to make right, to rightwise"), or "to be justified" (a verbal form derived from *ius, iuris* and *iustitia,* meaning "to be declared just"). The semantic ranges of the two are not identical.

*1.1.2. Worldviews.*

*1.1.2.1. Hebrew.* An essential component of Israel's religious experience was that Yahweh was not only Lord of Law but also the one who was faithful to it. God was faithful to the covenant.\* God's righteousness was shown by saving actions in accordance with this covenant relationship. A person was righteous by acting properly in regard to the covenant relationship with Yahweh. One's relationship with others reflected the relational aspect of the covenant with Yahweh. Righteousness was understood in terms of being in proper relation to the covenant rather than in terms of "right" or ethical conduct as determined by some abstract standard. When Jacob says of Tamar, "She is more righteous than I," he is referring to her being righteous in her pursuit of covenantal, familial responsibility (Gen 38:26).

*1.1.2.2. Greco-Roman.* The gods of the Greco-Roman pantheon were thought to be subject to forces beyond their control (*see* Religions). This understanding later degenerated into a sort of inexorable fate to which even the gods were subject (*see* Worship). The Hellenistic theory of universal law meant that both the gods and humanity had to comply with these overarching norms in order to be righteous. Giving others their due was the basis of righteousness; one acted in accordance with a norm (Plato). In Greek thought, righteousness was a virtue. According to Aristotle, righteousness was the correct functioning of all the virtues. In Roman Civil Law, justice (*iustitia*) was done when one acted toward another in accordance with one's respective status established by tradition and the Roman legal corpus.

*1.2. OT Background.* While the OT uses righteousness terminology in numerous contexts involving all areas of life, the touchstone of righteousness is Israel's covenantal relationship with Yahweh. It is based on the standard of God's covenant faithfulness. Righteousness is not primarily an ethical quality; rather it characterizes the character or action of God who deals rightly within a covenant relationship and who established how others are to act within that relationship. "Shall not the judge of all the earth do what is right?" (Gen 18:25). The covenant faithfulness of God, the righteousness of God, is shown by Yahweh's saving acts. This salvation is variously experienced as Israel's victory over enemies, or personal vindication of one's innocence before God in the presence of one's enemies, and it involves both soteriological and forensic elements (*see* Triumph).

In the classical prophets of the eighth century, there is a greater emphasis on the juridical and ethical views of *ṣedeq*. Amos, on behalf of the poor, associates righteousness with doing justice (*mišpāṭ,* Amos 5:7, 24; 6:12). Corrupt judges who do not judge rightly do not reflect the righteousness of the covenant relationship. Their oppression of the poor is the antithesis of righteousness. Hosea, emphasizing divine love, links righteousness with loving-kindness and mercy as well as justice (Hos 2:19; 10:12). Micah refers only to God's righteousness as being his faithfulness to act within the covenant to save Israel from her enemies and to vindicate the penitent (Mic 6:5; 7:9). Isaiah associates the righteousness of the people and God's righteousness with just decisions (Is 1:26; 16:5; 26:9). God's faithfulness to deliver Israel is seen in the Servant of the Lord and Cyrus as God's chosen leaders/deliverers (Is 42:6; 45:8, 13, 19). Covenant relationship is the basis of righteousness (Is 51:1). God promises to bring righteousness, which is often understood as deliverance or vindication (Is 51:5, 8; 62:1, 2). In sum, the covenant understanding of righteousness in the classical prophets relates persons to the living God and his covenantal purposes in restoring order to his creation, not to an abstract norm of conduct (see Scullion).

### 1.3. Intertestamental Literature.

*1.3.1. LXX.* The Hellenistic idea of righteousness as a virtue, a meeting of the norm, was replaced with the idea of meeting God's claim in this covenant relationship (Schrenk). Thus the semantic range for *dikaios* in LXX Greek was enlarged due to the influence of the Hebrew background. In fourteen instances the Hebrew word *ṣᵉdāqâ*, which could have been translated by *dikaiosynē*, was rendered by *eleēmosynē* (meaning "pity," "mercy"; e.g., Is 1:27; 59:16; Ps 34[35]:24). This added emotional element also limited the semantic value of *dikaiosynē* in later Judaism to almsgiving.

*1.3.2. Apocrypha.* In addition to the understanding of righteousness in the Hellenistic manner as personal virtue, there are Stoic virtues "associated" with righteousness: integrity, courage, constancy, even in the midst of personal woe, and self-control. In the apocryphal works there is an increasing interest in good works and the merits of the righteous. Tobit's farewell advice to his son Tobias portrays charity (*eleēmosynē*) as bringing safety rather than fulfilling the prayers of the poor: "For charity delivers from death and keeps you from entering the darkness" (Tob 4:10). In Tobit the focus is on the individual rather than on the community. We further find an emphasis on the relation between suffering and righteousness (Wis 3:1-5). The belief that the merits of some will assist others to gain righteousness appears in the Maccabean literature (2 Macc 12:38-46).

*1.3.3. Pseudepigrapha.* In the apocalyptic literature such as the *Testaments of the Twelve Patriarchs*, the *Book of Enoch* and *Jubilees*, the idea is prominent that the righteousness of God will characterize the end time (e.g., *T. Dan* 5:7-13). In this literature God not only is faithful to the covenant, but beyond the present difficulty God will vindicate the covenant people in the eschatological future.

Characteristic of apocalyptic* is an added sense of the distinction between the righteous and the unrighteous. And righteousness is seen as an eschatological reality in that Yahweh will vindicate the righteous (*1 Enoch* 95:7). The righteousness of God will be shown in the vindication of the persecuted righteous. Thus there is a coupling of the motif of the suffering

righteous with the traditional Hebrew understanding of God as the one who vindicates (Ps 26; 31:14-18).

*1.3.4. Qumran.* In the documents from Qumran* we find references to God's righteousness providing salvation and forgiveness. "And when I stumble, the mercies of God are always my salvation. When I stagger because of the evil of my flesh, my justification is in the righteousness of God which exists forever" (1QS 11:12). In the *Thanksgiving Psalm*, the righteousness of God shows God's faithfulness to the community: "You forgive the unjust and purify people from guilt by your righteousness" (*ṣᵉdāqâ*, 1QH 4:37). In *The War of the Children of Light*, Yahweh is able to bring them to the joys of future vindication through the righteousness of God (1QM 18:8). "Essentially it means the covenantal faithfulness of God which is being revealed especially in the eschatological warfare for the rule of God's justice" (Kuyper).

## 2. Righteousness in Paul.

The noun "righteousness" (*dikaiosynē*), its related adjective "righteous" (*dikaios*), and the verb "to justify," "to pronounce/treat as righteous" or "put right" (*dikaioō*) are found in the Pauline writings over 100 times. The sheer volume of occurrences in their various usages and meanings indicates the central place they had in the theology of the apostle.

We will present the meaning of Paul's language of righteousness/justification in its various contexts, bearing in mind that not every instance of "the righteousness of God" carries the same meaning. We will then proceed to explain these terms within the history of interpretation, the currents of contemporary scholarship, and summarize our own conclusions regarding this central Pauline affirmation.

### 2.1. Dikaiosynē.
Paul uses this word both in relationship to God and to human beings. In the latter case its ultimate origin is without exception the character and/or action of God. The term is used in various contexts or associations.

*2.1.1. Righteousness Declared.* A distinctive usage is found where Paul states that righteousness in believers is the result of a word, or declaration, of God. In Romans 4, where Paul interprets Abraham's* relationship with God as a scriptural foundation for his understanding of believers' "justification by faith" (explained in Rom 1—3), righteousness is said to be "reckoned to" (RSV) or "credited to" (NIV) Abraham by God on the basis of Abraham's believing/trusting in God (Rom 4:3, 5, 6, 9, 11, 22), rather than on the basis of his works. In Galatians 3:6 Abraham's faith in God is "reckoned to him as righteousness." Here, Abraham's trusting submission to God is evaluated as "righteousness."

*2.1.2. Righteousness as Gift.* Closely related are those usages where righteousness is stated to be a gift of God reigning in the believer (Rom 5:17, 21). Here it is seen as a new reality which dominates or directs the life in Christ (cf. Rom 8:10). According to Galatians 2:21, this righteousness results from God's grace, for if it were possible to achieve it via obedience to the Law, Christ's death would have been in vain. In Galatians 3:21 righteousness (in us, or as our new situation "in Christ") is equated with life, which the Law* is powerless to produce.

*2.1.3. Righteousness of Faith.* Righteousness, based on God's word and work in Christ, a gift of God's grace,* comes to believers in the context and through the instrumentality of faith.* Where righteousness and faith are related by Paul, it is almost always contrasted with a legalistic, or Law-oriented, righteousness. Thus in Romans 4:11, 13-14 the "righteousness of faith" is said to be based neither on circumcision* nor on the deeds of the Law. In Romans 9:30-32; 10:4-6, 10 the righteousness that comes by faith is contrasted with that which is based on the Law and the doing of the works of the Law. Only the former leads to life, to salvation. Philippians 3:9 speaks of the righteousness that results from faith in Jesus, rather than "my own righteousness" based on Law. This righteousness by faith is of course the righteousness from God, "which depends on faith." This conviction is affirmed by Paul in contrast to his own former experience where, on the basis of Law-based righteousness, he judged himself as "blameless" (Phil 3:6). Such moral perfectionism* as that which Paul had by pedigree and personal endeavor does not, however, bring one into right relationship with God. According to Titus 3:5 believers are saved, not because of deeds done in righteousness (here righteousness means "legal obedience"), but by God's merciful,* atoning work in Christ.

*2.1.4. Righteousness of Obedience.* A final context is the use of righteousness in an ethical sense, characterizing the life of obedience of those who have been justified. Romans 6:13, 18, 19, 20 contrast lives/bodies as instruments or slaves of wickedness with lives yielded to God as instruments of righteousness. What is clearly in view here is the expected result of life lived in relationship with Christ, right living that is in keeping with God's purposes. Righteousness (together with peace* and joy*) is that which marks the believer's relationship with others (rather than judging or offending others) and is the result of God's reign.

This view of righteousness is expanded in a number of Pauline passages. In 2 Corinthians 6:7, 14 it is given as a mark of the Christian life (acting rightly, justly,

morally), in contrast with evil, falsehood, inequality (*see* Ethics). Righteousness is that quality of life which bears fruit in generous giving (2 Cor 9:10) or in purity* and blamelessness (Phil 1:11). In Ephesians 4:24 righteousness is paired with holiness* as resembling God, in contrast to corrupt, deceitful living. It is one of the marks of those who are "children of light*" in distinction from those who perform "unfruitful works of darkness" (Eph 5:9). In the Pastorals there are the exhortations to "aim at righteousness" (1 Tim 6:11; 2 Tim 2:22) and to receive "training in righteousness" (2 Tim 3:16); the context is clearly that of moral, ethical living. Finally, on the basis of faithful service, "the crown of righteousness" is granted at the eschatological* judgment* by God, "the righteous judge" (2 Tim 4:8).

*2.2. Dikaios.* The adjective *dikaios* ("upright," "just," "righteous") is ascribed to both human beings and to God. When applied to persons, it defines them as those whose lives are in keeping with God's purposes (Eph 6:1); who live before him in faithfulness (Rom 1:17; Gal 3:11); who are obedient to God's commands (Rom 2:13; 3:10; 1 Tim 1:9); live good, upright, virtuous lives (Rom 5:7; Phil 4:8; Tit 1:8); and exercise fairness and justice (Col 4:1).

Several times God is defined as "righteous" in his nature and action as the just one, the one who can be counted on to mete out justice and do what is right (Rom 3:26; 2 Thess 1:5-6; 2 Tim 4:8). Related to this is the conviction that God's Law is "holy, righteous and good" (Rom 7:12).

Paul's conviction (Rom 5:19) that Christ's obedience to God (in contrast to Adam's disobedience) will result in "many being made righteous" must be understood within the context of God's Law, which reveals the righteous purposes of God. In terms of God's will for humanity, the goal of God's work in Christ is to transform humans into those who are righteous, whose lives are aligned with God's purposes, and who, therefore, are in conformity with the image* of Christ (2 Cor 3:18).

*2.3. Dikaioō.* The verbal form of the noun *righteousness*, (*dikaioō,* "to justify" RSV, NIV, NEB; "to put right" TEV) is used almost always to describe that divine action which affects the sinner in such a way that the relation with God is altered or transformed (either ontologically, as a change in nature; or positionally, resulting from a judicial act; or relationally, as one who was alienated and is now reconciled [see 3 below]). Everywhere this action of God, emerging from his nature as the righteous one, is seen as an act of grace and takes place in the context of the exercise of faith, or trust or believing in Jesus.

Romans 3:21-31 is the most thorough statement of this distinctive Pauline theme. Its validity is grounded by Paul in the story of Abraham (Rom 4). Further reflection is given to it in such central theological texts as Romans 5:1, 9 and Galatians 2:17; 3:8, 24. The negative formulation of this truth is in the contrasting affirmation that no one is justified "by the Law." In Romans 3:20; 4:2 and Galatians 2:16; 3:11 Paul states categorically the impossibility of receiving this justifying action of God by means of successfully keeping the requirements of the Law.

There are several texts where this action of God is addressed not to the sinner but to those who are already "justified." The setting for this action is always eschatological judgment (Rom 2:13; 8:33; Gal 5:4-5). The issue in these instances is not salvation (either by works or by faith). Rather, those who have been justified (by grace through faith) appear before "the judgment seat of Christ" (2 Cor 5:10) where "the empirical reality of one's life before God as 'works' will be revealed and evaluated" (Cosgrove, 660; *see* Judgment; Rewards).

*2.4. Dikaiosynē Theou.* The concept of God's righteousness, its nature, function and result, is central to Paul's teaching on the justification of the sinner. The genitive construction *dikaiosynē theou*, "righteousness of God" (Rom 1:17; 3:5, 21, 22; 10:3; 2 Cor 5:21), or *dikaiosynē autou*, "his righteousness" (Rom 3:25, 26), or *hē ek theou dikaiosynē*, "righteousness from God" (Phil 3:9) are found ten times. Most of these are located in Romans,* Paul's fullest discourse on God's redemptive work in Christ.

Romans 1:16-17 is foundational for understanding the meaning of this concept. For Paul the gospel—the event of the life, death and resurrection of Christ—is the historical manifestation of divine redemptive power. In that gospel "God's righteousness is revealed." Here God's righteousness and the gospel (God's saving work in Christ) are virtually synonymous (with the revelation of the saving righteousness of God being contrasted with the revelation of the wrath of God in Rom 1:18). Faith responds to God's act of righteousness and life results.

In contrast to human faithlessness and wickedness (Rom 3:3-5), God remains faithful, and in that faithfulness his righteousness is manifested. This faithfulness (or righteousness) is given its historical particularity (according to Paul's sustained presentation in Rom 3:21-31) in the sacrificial atonement of Christ's death (Rom 3:24-25). It is explicitly stated that in this redemptive act God's righteousness has been manifested (Rom 3:21, 25, 26; *see* Death of Christ).

In all three passages in Romans (Rom 1; 3; 10), as well as in Philippians 3:9, the apprehension of God's righteousness and of its coming into the sphere of human experience is related to faith in Jesus and understood as a gift of God's grace. In addition, all the texts explicitly include a rejection of "works of the Law"* as a valid instrument for attaining or receiving this righteousness of, or from, God.

The use of "righteousness of God" in 2 Corinthians 5:21 is in a context which does not share all the elements of those in Romans and Philippians. References to the instrumentality of faith or works are absent here. The context is the new creation brought into being through God's work in Christ (2 Cor 5:17). This new creation consists of those who have been reconciled to God (2 Cor 5:18-19) and who at the same time become instruments of that reconciling work within the yet-existing old creation* (2 Cor 5:19-20; *see* Center; Peace, Reconciliation). Paul climaxes this passage with the affirmation that the purpose of Christ's identification with us in our sin-bound existence (2 Cor 5:21a) is so that we, in relationship with Christ, "might become God's righteousness" (2 Cor 5:21b). It is highly significant for the overall understanding of this term that Paul does not say that we in Christ "might become righteous" or "might receive God's righteousness," but rather "that we might become God's righteousness" (see 4 below).

### 3. History of Interpretation.
A. E. McGrath's study of the history of the doctrine of justification is instructive for discerning some of the reasons why the West has understood Paul's theology of God's saving action in Christ largely in terms of justification rather than relying on the varied richness of the biblical understanding of salvation in Christ. Several complex reasons for this include the interest in Paul evidenced by the rise in Pauline scholarship during the theological renaissance of the twelfth century, especially the use of Pauline commentaries as vehicles of theological speculation. Coupled with this, the Western church had a high regard for classical jurisprudence, which made possible the semantic relationship between *iustitia* (justice) and *iustificatio* (justification), and allowed theologians of High Scholasticism to find in the cognate concept of justification a means of rationalizing the divine dispensation toward humankind in terms of justice. Luther interpreted the scholastics as understanding the righteousness of God as that by which God punishes sinners (WA 54.185.18-20). Therefore, Luther could not see how the gospel revealing the righteousness of God could be "good news." Luther's "discovery" of the free imparting of the righteousness of God to believers is instructive in

explaining why the Reformation came to be perceived as inextricably linked with the doctrine of justification. The Roman Catholic desire to establish a Catholic consensus on this issue resulted in the discussion at the Council of Trent of the reconciliation of humanity to God under the aegis of the doctrine of justification.

**3.1. Patristic-Medieval: East.** In the East Paul's concept of the righteousness of God and the justification of the sinner was not a prominent means for understanding God's saving acts in Jesus Christ. J. Reumann notes that the apostolic fathers maintain the biblical view of righteousness as what God does, but they show a greater interest in the human response. Rather than giving importance to the righteousness of God and justification, Eastern Christianity emphasized the divine economy and the condescension of the Son, which led to human participation in the divine nature understood as deification (rather than justification). McGrath sees the theological differences between East and West as due to their different understandings of the work of the Holy Spirit: the West tended to subordinate the work of the Holy Spirit to the concept of grace interposed between God and humanity; the Eastern church holds to the immediacy of the divine and one's direct encounter with the Holy Spirit expressed as deification. With this emphasis it is natural that the Eastern Church did not evidence the Western commitment to justification as the fundamental soteriological metaphor.

**3.2. Patristic-Medieval: West.** In the Latin fathers and Origen, the righteousness of God is understood as distributive justice: God gives to all their due, rewarding the good and punishing the wicked. The Reformers turned to Augustine for his views on the righteousness of God.

**3.2.1. Augustine.** Augustine thought the righteousness of God was not the righteousness characterizing God's nature, but rather that by which God justifies sinners. His idea of faith involved an intellectual aspect: to believe is to affirm in thought. Augustine coupled faith with love (Augustine *Serm.* 90.6; 93.5; *Ep.* 183.1.3). The love of God is the theme dominating his view of justification, whereas the Reformers would coin the slogan *sola fide* ("by faith alone") to characterize justification and their understanding of the righteousness of God. In his work *On the Trinity*, Augustine makes the statement that true justifying faith is accompanied by love (*De Trin.* 15.18.32). In his comments on 1 Corinthians 13:2 he remarks that genuine faith always works through love (recalling Gal 5:6: see Crabtree). Augustine, along with some Greek fathers, underscored the gift aspect of justification. He believed that one's nature was changed through this gift.

**3.2.2. Roman Catholicism.** In the Roman tradition the righteousness of God was understood more as that which was demanded by God. The medieval understanding of the nature of justification referred not merely to the beginning of the Christian life, but to its continuation and ultimate perfection, in which the Christian is made righteous in the sight of God and the sight of others through a fundamental change in nature (McGrath). The prevailing pre-Reformation view in the West of the righteousness of God was that of a distributive justice whereby God judges justly according to God's holiness. A common theological position was that righteousness of God was a subjective genitive, God's holiness being the norm by which all would be judged. Luther's personal struggle with the inexorable righteousness of God resulted in an understanding of the righteousness of God that was deeper than his tradition had grasped. In Catholic thought, justification was not considered something in the present as much as a process leading to the ultimate future judgment.

**3.3. The Reformation.** Generally the Reformers and their theological heirs have interpreted the righteousness of God as a so-called objective genitive (see 1 above) in all instances in Paul's writings, with the possible exceptions of Romans 3:5, 25, 26. The righteousness of God was understood from the viewpoint of the individual, as that righteousness which God gives to people, and on the basis of which the sinner is approved by God. The theocentric OT meaning of the righteousness of God in the sphere of covenant relationship was displaced by an anthropocentric focus. The reformers and their successors often interpreted the righteousness of God from the human aspect because they had replaced the biblical basis of covenant relationship with the Hellenistic theory of universal law which both God and humanity had to fulfill in order to be regarded as righteous. The emphasis on the individual under universal law rather than in covenant relationship contributed to the later "legal fiction" theory whereby those who believe in Jesus are justified, deemed righteous, even though they are not actually righteous. In this view faith in Jesus takes the place of actual righteousness.

**3.3.1. Luther.** Luther's concern was personal and pastoral. The fine theological distinction maintained by the Roman Catholic magisterium did not "trickle down" to villages parishes. Luther interpreted the righteousness of God distinctively as a so-called objective genitive, rendering the Greek term *dikaiosynē tou theou* in Romans 1:17 as righteousness "which counts before God." Luther states the righteousness of God is the cause of salvation, and thus it is not the righteousness by which God is righteous in himself but the righteousness by which we are made righteous by God. This happens through faith in the gospel. Luther points to Augustine for the sense that the righteousness of God is that by which God imparts and makes people righteous. Luther emphasized the immediacy of justification. A person is at once just and unjust: this suggests a composite view of Luther's new understanding of the righteousness of God, in addition to the traditional understanding of the distributive justice of God.

For Luther works are the result of the righteousness given by God. Sanctification is a process that will not be consummated in this life. Luther clearly separated justification from regeneration and sanctification. This perspective gave rise to the understanding of justification as a new status before God: "Thus in ourselves we are sinners, and yet through faith we are righteous by God's imputation. For we believe Him who promises to free us, and in the meantime we strive that sin may not rule over us but that we may withstand it until He takes it from us" (WA 56.271). In Catholic thought, God responds to those who do what they can by giving them enabling grace which then leads to saving grace. Luther broke with this tradition in that he found that God provided the preconditions for justification (see Watson).

*3.3.2. Calvin.* Calvin in his *Commentary on Romans* presents his understanding of the righteousness of God in Romans 1:17 as that which is approved before God's tribunal. Calvin associated sanctification with justification and described sanctification in terms of being in Christ. According to Calvin, God communicates his righteousness to us. In a nearly mystical sense, through faith Jesus communicates himself to those who believe. Works have no place in the justification of sinners. Calvin refutes the notion of a fiction involved in the justification of sinners. God provides all that is necessary. He cautions not to understand righteousness as a quality; we are righteous only in so far as Christ reconciles the Father to us. Calvin, more so than Luther, emphasizes the relational aspect of the righteousness of God. Luther's view of the righteousness of God seems to contain the aspect of acquittal. Calvin emphasizes the marvelous nature of the communication, or imparting, of God's righteousness to us.

*3.4. Post-Reformation.* Just as the Western Church experienced the scholasticism of the twelfth century, Protestant Orthodoxy shifted from Calvin's christological emphasis to other matters, such as predestination, federal theology and the perseverance of the saints. Lutheranism shifted its emphasis from justification of sinners and the righteousness of God to deal with these developments within the Reformed camp. The Pietist movement within Lutheranism was a reaction against a strictly forensic understanding of righteousness. The pastoral aspects of Pietism later influenced Lutheranism to emphasize practical aspects of righteousness, reflecting an interest in promoting personal piety.

John Wesley argued for the Pietist position in his emphasis on personal righteousness subsequent to justification. In his sermon on "The Lord Our Righteousness" he adheres to imputation but understands the Holy Spirit to have a sanctifying aspect upon the believer. The believer's basis of justification is the righteousness of Christ "implanted in everyone in whom God has imputed it." He maintains there is no true faith—justifying faith—which does not have the righteousness of Christ for its object. Wesley sees faith in Jesus' death, and hence the imputation of his righteousness, as the cause, end and middle term of salvation.

*3.5. Currents of Recent Discussion.* The variations within the history of interpretation reflect two basic views: (1) that God's righteousness is a quality of God (or Christ) imparted, making the sinner righteous; (2) that God, the righteous one, declares the sinner to be righteous in a legal transaction (imputed). These dominant views have increasingly been challenged (*see* Paul and His Interpreters). J. Reumann contends that there is a stronger basis in Christian hymnody for these views than in the NT. For Paul does not speak of Christ's merits or God's righteous essence being so imputed to us. G. E. Ladd contends that forensic (declared) righteousness is real righteousness because our relationship with God is just as real as one's subjective ethical condition. One is in fact "righteous" (defined as right relationship with God) based upon what has been done for us objectively in Christ. The ethical content follows on its heels. Ladd maintains that righteousness as acquittal and right conduct belong together.

H. Cremer (1900) launched scholarship in a new direction by pointing to the OT understanding of ṣᵉḏāqâ ("righteousness") as covenant faithfulness, and seeing this meaning as the subjective genitive, not in the ontological sense, but as referring to God's saving activity as Redeemer.*

Some scholars, such as R. Bultmann, attempted to combine both the objective and subjective aspects of the righteousness of God, suggesting a "genitive of the author" to describe God's righteousness which is given to believers as the basis of one's relationship with God. The righteousness of God is the gift which makes possible this new existence for the individual. His existential interpretation involves the kerygmatic reality of the individual: one continues to appropriate God's "rightwising" verdict in obedient existential decision and becomes what one is declared to be. Bultmann's inattention to OT background and to Paul's apocalyptic understanding of history resulted in an anthropocentric and individualistic orientation of the righteousness of God.

There have been various attempts to reevaluate the meaning of the righteousness of God in Paul's writings (see bibliographical details in Brauch). In 1954 J. Bollier, a critic of the legal fiction theory of justification, suggested that God requires a person to be righteous, to recognize God's sovereignty and to submit to God's Lordship. Under the old covenant as well as the new, God has graciously offered faith as the way a person may recognize God as one's Lord and so gain God's approval. Faith is the appropriate human response to the self-revelation of God. Faith actually is righteousness, for it is the way in which one may fulfill this obligation toward God within the covenant relationship. Thus Paul speaks of the "righteousness of faith" in Romans 4:11, 13. Bollier opted for a subjective genitive, maintaining that the righteousness of God is God's own inherent righteousness rather than the righteousness of which God is the author and which he approves. Anticipating E. Käsemann, Bollier further posited that this righteousness of God has a transcendent as well as an immanent aspect, for one is directly affected by the manifestation of this righteousness.

E. Käsemann has had a great impact on the discussion. Although he sees the righteousness of God in Romans 3:5, 25-26 as referring to God's character, he emphasizes that Paul's view of the righteousness of God accents its gift-character against the backdrop of Jewish apocalypticism. "The gift itself has the character of power, salvation-creating power" (Käsemann). The gift is never a personal possession separated from the giver. In this way Käsemann captures the eschatological nature of the relationship of God with creation in a forward orientation toward the consummation of God's saving acts in Jesus Christ. God's faithfulness is faithfulness to the creation, not simply to the individual (cf. Bultmann). God's sovereignty over the universe is established eschatologically in Jesus. A person within that framework experiences a change in lordship. Johannine and Pauline language now go hand in hand, since by "abiding" in Jesus, believers become what they are. The righteousness of God is God's power in Christ reaching out to the world. Salvation is experienced in the sphere of Christ's lordship, which is entered in response to God's righteousness (Käsemann; on this see Way, 177-236).

The subjective genitive is also maintained by two of Käsemann's students, C. Müller and P. Stuhlmacher. Müller (1965) agrees with Käsemann, but places his emphasis on the eschatological victory of God, the final cosmic trial at which creation submits to God (see Eschatology). God's ultimate victory reveals his righteousness and is acknowledged by humanity. That final victory is anticipated in the present, where God's lordship is a reality in everyday life. P. Stuhlmacher stresses the saving aspect of the righteousness of God in that the creator makes right the world on account of his creation-faithfulness, even by raising the dead. The righteousness of God is God's creating power fostering faith and recreating the world. Stuhlmacher sees the righteousness of God as the center* of Pauline theology whereby Paul shows a complete correlation between judicial and ontological ideas of righteousness. Thus justification refers to a divine creative activity, the actualization of the righteousness of God as a "Word event" which creates a new being at baptism.* Stuhlmacher understands justification for Paul to mean the obligating, renewing call of the individual, by the power of God, into the realm of encounter with God which has been opened by Christ. The renewed calling culminates in service.

The Roman Catholic scholar K. Kertelge follows a similar line of thought to Stuhlmacher. The righteousness of God denotes God's redemptive activity and not God's gift of righteousness to us which leads to salvation. This reality consists of nothing except the new relationship between God and humanity created by God, which from the divine side is lordship and from the human side is obedience. For Paul the present and the future character of God's eschatological redemption are essentially identical, because both have their basis in the Christ event. Righteousness is by faith, not as a possession, but as a relationship in which one acknowledges God's claim upon one's life.

H. Brunner understands the OT material regarding righteousness to refer to a comprehensive order corresponding to God's will, which encompasses both nature and humanity. In Paul the theme is the change from alienation to reconciliation (2 Cor 5:17-21), from the old world to the new, from the old creation to the new. Humans are re-created by Christ: his death means his subjection to sin, namely the power of alienation from God; but it also means believers' becoming "God's righteousness." They become transformed by God's power into the people of the reestablished created order, the reconciled new world of God's people of the new covenant. In Romans 1 Paul speaks of the will of the creator being obscured by human rejection, but the gospel has revealed God's power for redemption. The righteousness of God is God's redemptive saving act. God's saving action has always been at work, as evidenced in the OT, but has now been clearly revealed in the Christ event. For those who believe in Christ, the reality and power of sin have been put aside. God's new created order, which is the removal of the alienation of sin, has been brought into being. To be righteous or declared righteous is neither a juridical act nor an ontological transformation, but a state of being restored to right relationship with God because the alienating reality of sin has been set aside.

**4. God's Righteousness as Relation-Restoring Love.** The history of interpretation, including the recent perspectives sketched above, reveals two facets; (1) that the understanding of the righteousness of God has been largely dominated by Greek and Latin categories, where righteousness as a quality of God's character is either given to us and makes us righteous, or is the basis for God's judical pronouncement, declaring us righteous; (2) that the more recent discussion, in seeking to take more seriously Paul's grounding in the OT, has found the earlier understanding to be an inadequate explication of Paul's meaning. Particularly important has been the insistence on the OT covenantal context of the righteousness of God as an interpretive background for the Pauline formulations.

Within that OT context, and beside other meanings and nuances (Brunner), the idea of God's righteousness appears prominently in salvation texts, where God's redemptive action toward his covenant people is defined by this term. It is God's righteousness which saves from enemies, from threatening situations, from the state of alienation from God. In such settings God's righteousness is frequently defined by the terms "steadfast love" and "faithfulness" (e.g., Is 11:5; 16:5; Ps 5:7-8; 89:13-14; 98:2-3). These relational attributes are in some contexts virtually synonymous with "righteousness" and "salvation" (e.g., Ps 85:7-13). Thus, God's righteousness may be rendered as "saving deed" or "relation-restoring love.*"

Paul's use of righteousness of God may best be understood against the background of this particular OT concept. For Paul "unrighteousness" results from disobedience, whether of persons generally, who refuse to acknowledge God (Rom 1:28), and obey unrighteousness and disobey truth* (Rom 2:8), or of God's people who refuse to acknowledge God, and are disobedient within the covenant relationship (Rom 3:3-5; 10:21).

It is the reality of alienation, defined synonymously as "faithlessness" (Rom 3:3) and "unrighteousness" (Rom 3:5), which Paul knows to have been addressed by the revelation (Rom 1:16-17) or manifestation (Rom 3:21-26) of God's righteousness. In both texts the concrete historical expression of "God's righteousness" is the event of Christ: defined in Romans 1:16 as "the gospel" and "the power* of God for salvation"; and in Romans 3:24 as "the redemption which is in Christ Jesus."

Paul contends that God is faithful to his creation/ covenant relationship (Rom 3:3-4), his action is righteous (Rom 3:26), and it is this action in response to his rebellious creation which Paul therefore calls the righteousness of God. The term designates that act of God which restores the broken relationship. "Righteousness" in this context is not an attribute of God, but designates God's forgiving love and redemptive intervention in the world through Christ.

The righteousness of God understood as God's relation-restoring love is central to Paul's argument in Romans 3:21-26. The incarnation of the righteousness of God in the redemptive work of the cross leads to forgiveness*; and forgiveness restores broken relationships. Because this is purely the act of God, Paul calls it a gift. Since a gift is ineffective unless appropriated, it must be "received by faith." The result of this gracious act of God is the justification ("setting right") of the sinner. The passage says nothing about an essential or judical transaction; rather, it declares the restoration of the divine-human relationship through what Christ did by his death (see Expiation, Propitiation, Mercy Seat).

The language of "submitting to the righteousness of God" in Romans 10:3 confirms Paul's understanding of it as God's relation-restoring intervention. The attempt to establish one's own righteousness—one's own position before God—is a rejection of the coming of God's righteousness in Christ, God's way of saving the world. For to submit means to acknowledge one's severed relation with God and to confess the lordship of Christ (Rom 10:7; see Lord).

The difficult expression of 2 Corinthians 5:21, that in (relationship with) Christ "we might become the righteousness of God" further underlines a relational rather than a judicial or ontological meaning. The text is concerned with reconciliation to God in and through Christ (see Center; Peace, Reconciliation) and calls those who are reconciled to become instruments of that reconciling work (2 Cor 5:18-19). In that context, the phrase "to become God's righteousness" means that believers become participants in God's reconciling action, extensions of his restoring love.

For Paul, then, God's righteousness is God's saving deed. In continuity with OT expressions of God's righteousness as God's faithfulness and steadfast love toward Israel, Paul sees this divine action finally expressed in the life, death and resurrection of Jesus. The acceptance of that divine condescension through the act of faith justifies us (makes us right) with God. Righteousness is present in this restored relationship when life is lived in conformity with God's purposes.

*See also* CENTER OF PAUL'S THEOLOGY; CREATION AND NEW CREATION; CROSS, THEOLOGY OF THE; ESCHATOLOGY; EXPIATION, PROPITIATION, MERCY SEAT; FAITH; GOD; JUDGMENT; JUSTIFICATION; LAW; LOVE; MERCY; PAUL AND HIS INTERPRETERS; PEACE, RECONCILIATION; RESTORATION OF ISRAEL; ROMANS, LETTER TO THE; SALVATION; TRIUMPH; WRATH, DESTRUCTION.

BIBLIOGRAPHY. O. Betz, "Der gekreuzigte Christus: unsere Weisheit und Gerechtigkeit (der alttestamentliche Hintergrund von 1 Kor 1—2," in *Tradition and Interpretation in the New Testament*, ed. G. F. Hawthorne with O. Betz (Grand Rapids: Eerdmans, 1987) 195-215; P. Blaser, "Paulus und Luther über Gottes Gerechtigkeit," *Catholica* 36 (1982) 269-79; J. A. Bollier, "The Righteousness of God," *Int* 8 (1954) 404-13; M. T. Brauch, "Perspectives on 'God's Righteousness' in Recent German Discussion," in E. P. Sanders, *Paul and Palestinian Judaism* (Philadelphia: Fortress, 1977) 523-42; H. Brunner, "Die Gerechtigkeit Gottes" *ZRG* 39 (1987) 210-25; R. Bultmann, "ἔλεος κτλ," *TDNT* II.477-87; C. H. Cosgrove, "Justification in Paul: A Linguistic and Theological Reflection," *JBL* 106 (1987) 653-70; A. B. Crabtree, *The Restored Relationship* (London: Carey Kingsgate, 1963); H. Cremer, *Die Paulinische Rechtfertigungslehre im Zussammenhang ihrer geschichtlichen Voraussetzungen* (1900); J. A. Fitzmyer, *Pauline Theology* (Engelwood Cliffs, NJ: Prentice-Hall, 1967); E. Käsemann, " 'The Righteousness of God' in Paul," in *New Testament Questions of Today* (Philadelphia: Fortress, 1969) 168-82; K. Kertelge, *"Rechtfertigung" bei Paulus* (NTAbh n.s. 3; 2d ed.; Münster: Aschendorf, 1971); idem, "δικαιοσύνη," "δικαιόω," *EDNT* 1.325-34; L. J. Kuyper, "Righteousness and Salvation," *SJT* 30 (1977) 233-52; G. E. Ladd, "Righteousness in Romans," *SWJT* 19 (1976) 6-17; E. Lohse "Die Gerechtigkeit Gottes in der Paulinischen Theologie," in *Die Einheit des Neuen Testaments* (Göttingen: Vandenhoeck & Ruprecht, 1973) 209-27; A. E. McGrath, Iustitia Dei: *A History of the Christian Doctrine of Justification* (2 vols. Cambridge: University Press, 1986); R. K. Moore, "Issues Involved in the Interpretation of *Dikaiosyne Theou* in the Pauline Corpus," *Colloquium: The Australian and New Zealand Theological Society* 23 (1991) 59-70; C. Müller, *Gottesgerechtigkeit und Gottesvolk* (FRLANT 86; Göttingen: Vandenhoeck & Ruprecht, 1964); J. Piper, "The Demonstration of the Righteousness of God in Romans 3:25, 26," *JSNT* 7 (1980) 2-32; B. Przybylski, *Righteousness in Matthew and His World of Thought* (SNTSMS 41; Cambridge: University Press, 1980); G. Quell and G. Schrenk, "δίκη κτλ," *TDNT* II.174-225; J. Reumann, "Justification of God: Righteousness and the Cross," *Moravian Theological Seminary: Bulletin* (1964) 16-31; idem, "Righteousness (Early Judaism-New Testament)," *ABD* V.736-73; idem, *Righteousness in the New Testament: Justification in the United States, Lutheran-Roman Catholic Dialogue* (Philadelphia: Fortress, 1983); idem, "The 'Righteousness of God' and the 'Economy of God': Two Great Doctrinal Themes Historically Compared," in *Askum-Thyateira*, ed. G. Dragas (London: Thyateira House, 1985) 615-37; L. Sabourin, "Formulations of Christian Beliefs in Recent Exposition on Paul's Epistles to the Romans and Galatians," *RSB* 1 (1981) 120-36; A. Schweitzer, *The Mysticism of the Apostle Paul* (London: A & C Black, 1931); J. J. Scullion, "Righteousness (OT)," *ABD* V.724-36; M. L. Soards, "The Righteousness of God in the Writings of the Apostle Paul," *BTB* 15 (1985) 104-9; P. Stuhlmacher, *Gerechtigkeit Gottes bei Paulus* (FRLANT 82; Göttingen: Vandenhoeck & Ruprecht, 1965); idem, *Reconciliation, Law, and Righteousness* (Philadelphia: Fortress, 1986); P. Watson, *Let God Be God* (London: Epworth, 1953); D. V. Way, *The Lordship of Christ: Ernst Käsemann's Interpretation of Paul's Theology* (Oxford: Clarendon, 1991); S. K. Williams, "The 'Righteousness of God' in Romans," *JBL* 99 (1980) 241-90; J. A. Ziesler, *The Meaning of Righteousness in Paul: A Linguistic and Theological Inquiry* (SNTSMS 20; Cambridge: University Press, 1972).

K. L. Onesti and M. T. Brauch

**RISING WITH CHRIST.** *See* BAPTISM; DYING AND RISING WITH CHRIST; RESURRECTION.

**ROADS AND HIGHWAYS.** *See* TRAVEL IN THE ROMAN WORLD.

**ROMAN CHRISTIANITY.** *See* ROME AND ROMAN CHRISTIANITY.

**ROMAN CITIZENSHIP.** *See* CITIZENSHIP.

**ROMAN LEGAL SYSTEM.** *See* LEGAL SYSTEM, ROMAN.

**ROMAN POLITICAL SYSTEM.** *See* POLITICAL SYSTEMS.

**ROMAN RELIGION.** *See* RELIGIONS, GRECO-ROMAN.

## ROMANS, LETTER TO THE

Romans is both the least controversial of the major NT letters and the most important. Least controversial, at any rate, in the "who wrote what when to whom" questions which make it so difficult to gain a firm handle on most of the other NT writings. It is most important as being the first well-developed theological statement by a Christian theologian which has come down to us, and one which has had incalculable influence on the framing of Christian theology ever since—arguably the single most important work of Christian theology ever written. This double feature of Romans is important since it means that discussion of the letter can quickly leave behind such preliminary questions and can focus on its substantive theological content without too much distraction from nagging introductory unknowns.

1. Author, Date and Place of Origin
2. Recipients
3. Purposes
4. Literary Form and Coherence
5. The Issues at Stake
6. The Argument of the Letter

### 1. Author, Date and Place of Origin.

*1.1. Author.* There has never been any dispute of real significance over the authorship of Romans. It was written by Paul (Rom 1:1). More to the point is what the letter tells us about this Paul—particularly his sense of commissioning (*see* Conversion and Call) as an apostle* and consequent commitment to preaching the gospel* (Rom 1:1, 5, 12-17; 15:15-24). It is the fact that Paul the Jew,* or preferably, Paul the *Israelite* (Rom 11:1), believed himself thus commissioned as apostle to the *Gentiles** (Rom 11:13), which gives the letter its distinctive character and cutting edge.

*1.2. Date.* As to date, the most significant fact is that Paul wrote his letter at a time when he thought he had completed a major phase of his work—his evangelization of the northeastern quadrant of the Mediterranean (Rom 15:19, 23; *see* Mission). The information that he was about to embark on a visit to Jerusalem* (Rom 15:25) ties in with the larger picture in Acts* of a final visit to Jerusalem at (what proved to be) the close of his work in Asia Minor and Greece (Acts 20). This certainly points to a date in the mid-50s (55-57), though a minority of scholars have argued implausibly for a date as early as 51/52 (*see* Chronology). The fact that in Romans 13:6-7 Paul felt it necessary to provide a theological rationale for paying taxes (*see*

Civil Authority) may also reflect some unrest in Rome* on questions of taxation early in Nero's reign, that is, about the same period (56-58; Tacitus *Ann.* 13). The issue of precise date, however, is of minor significance beside the clear implication that the letter marks a climax in Paul's missionary work.

*1.3. Place of origin.* The correlation of Romans 15:25 with Acts 20 also suggests the place of origin, since Acts 20:3 speaks of three months spent in Greece at the beginning of the final journey to Jerusalem. That suggests Corinth, Paul's main headquarters in Greece, and fits with the information provided by chapter 16: Phoebe came from Cenchreae, one of Corinth's ports (Rom 16:1-2); and Gaius and Erastus (Rom 16:23) probably lived in Corinth (1 Cor 1:14; *NewDocs* 4.160-61). More to the point, a period of three months centered in a single location would give Paul the time to reflect, compose and dictate what is certainly the most carefully thought through and constructed of his letters.

### 2. Recipients.

There is as little dispute over the "to whom" question. The reference to "Rome" in Romans 1:7 is omitted by some manuscripts, but such omission is best explained by subsequent generalizing usage of a letter intended originally for a more specific audience. The more important issue is who the Christians in Rome were, and why Paul, who had never visited Rome, should think it necessary to write to them.

*2.1. "Jews First . . ."* The fact is that we simply do not know how Christianity began in Rome* and who, strictly speaking, its founding apostles were. We do know, however, that there was a large Jewish community in Rome in the first century (estimated at between 40,000 and 50,000). We also know that there was an active Christian mission among "the circumcised" (Gal 2:9), and that even the Gentile mission must have found its most fruitful ground among the Gentile proselytes and God-fearers who attached themselves to many Diaspora* synagogues* (as indicated also by Acts, and Paul's continuing identification with the synagogue implied by 2 Cor 11:24). Furthermore, we have the interesting information that many Jews were expelled from Rome in (probably) 49 because of disturbances "instigated by Chrestus" (Suetonius *Claudius* 25.4), where "Chrestus" is almost universally taken as a reference to Christ. And the number of slave names among those greeted in chapter 16 (at least fourteen out of twenty-four) suggests that not a few of those descended from the Jewish captives brought to Rome, particularly following Pompey's subjugation of Palestine in 62 B.C., came to believe in Jesus as Messiah (*see* Christ).

The obvious implication, then, is that Christianity first took root in Rome within and among the many Jewish synagogues of Rome. This would explain both how Peter could plausibly be regarded as the founder of the church in Rome, and, more to the point, why Paul's letter is so dominated by the motif "to Jew, but also to Gentile" (Rom 1:16; 2:9-10; 3:9, 29; 9:24; 10:12).

*2.2. ". . . Also Gentiles."* That Gentiles were drawn in to the church at Rome sooner or later in the earliest years is clearly implied in the letter itself, particularly Romans 11:13-32 and 15:7-12 (see also Rom 1:6, 13; 15:15-16). That means being drawn in to share in an essentially Jewish patrimony, inevitably raising questions as to Jewish and Christian identity. This alone is sufficient to explain some of the characteristic elements and themes in the letter: for example, "who/what is a Jew?" (Rom 2:25-29); who are "the elect of God"? (Rom 1:7; 8:33; 9:6-13; 11:5-7, 28-32); and the climactic position of Romans 9—11 and Romans 15:8-12. Whether the disturbances within the Jewish community of 49 were simply between Jews who believed Jesus to be Messiah ("Chrestus") and those who denied it, or between Jews who welcomed Gentiles and those (including Christian Jews) who did not, we cannot tell.

Moreover, if indeed many Christian Jews were among those expelled in 49 (cf. Acts 18:2), we may draw the further inference that the Roman churches were at that time shorn of much of their Jewish leadership and membership. Gentile leadership would have become more the norm. And when Christian Jews began to return to Rome as Claudius's rescript began to lapse, some tensions between old and new may well have arisen. This is just the circumstance which seems to be reflected in the exhortations in Romans 14:1 and 15:1, 7.

*2.3. The Social Context.* Two other factors are important in filling in the background behind the letter, so far as that is possible. One is that the Jewish community was both influential in Rome and deeply despised, not to say hated, by the most influential voices of the Roman intelligentsia. This was partly because of its sheer size, partly because of the preferential treatment they had received from Julius Caesar and Augustus, and, probably more important, because of the numbers of Gentiles who were attracted to Judaism. These will also no doubt have been factors in the tensions between Jew and Gentile evident in the letter, and will help explain such emphases as Romans 1:16 and 12:14—13:7.

We also know that the Jewish community had no central authority in Rome (as was the case in Alexandria; *see* Diaspora). This indicates a more fragmented organization and, probably, a fair diversity among the different synagogues. Corresponding to this is the implication that the Christian community was equally lacking in organizational homogeneity (implied by the unusual fact that Paul does not speak of the "church,"* singular, in Rome). As we know the names of ten or so synagogues, so we know of several house churches (five may be implied in Rom 16:5, 10-11, 14-15).

All this suggests that the Christian groups formed something of a spectrum (some more Jewish in composition, some more Gentile, most mixed), which overlapped substantially with the spectrum of synagogues (*see* Social Setting). Paul knew enough of the people and the circumstances (Rom 14:1—15:7; 16:3-15) to frame his teaching and paraenesis accordingly. Among other things he would be aware that his letter would be read not to one single huge gathering of Christians (apart from anything else, such a gathering would be too dangerous in an imperial capital nervous of unlicensed gatherings), but repeatedly to the various house churches, where different facets of his exposition would resonate with different force among the different congregations. This would help explain the combination of general teaching and specific exhortation which is a feature of the letter.

### 3. Purposes.

Among introductory questions related to Romans the most lively discussion in recent years has centered on Paul's purpose(s) in writing it. Three in particular have been strongly canvassed.

*3.1. A Missionary Purpose.* This emerges especially from Romans 15:18-24, 28: Paul as "apostle to the Gentiles," eager to bring in "the full number of Gentiles" (Rom 11:13-15, 25-26), writes to the capital of the Gentile empire (*see* Mission).

Some draw the inference that Paul was seeking to evangelize Rome itself (Rom 1:13-15). This cannot mean that he did not recognize a Christian presence already in Rome (contrast Rom 1:8; 15:14). It has been argued on the basis of Romans 15:20, however, that he saw the Roman churches as lacking an apostolic foundation and sought to fill the gap. But this is equally unlikely, since Paul regarded church founding as an apostolic work (1 Cor 9:1-2), and the slight embarrassment evident in Romans 1:11-12 is just what we would expect from Paul writing to churches in whose founding he himself had played no part.

More plausible is the thesis that Paul wrote to Rome with a view to the churches there providing a support base for his projected mission to Spain. This indeed is what Paul says explicitly (Rom 15:24, 28), and there is no cause to doubt it; the church in Philippi in particular had already served in such a role. In that case the letter would be Paul's attempt to set out the gospel which he had preached so successfully so far and which he intended to preach in Spain (Rom 1:16-17). At the end of the first (or preceding) phase of his great missionary strategy (Rom 15:19, 23) he uses the opportunity to set out in complete terms the theology of the gospel on the basis of which he would be asking the Roman Christians for support.

*3.2. An Apologetic Purpose.* The implication of such passages as Romans 1:16; 3:8 and 9:1-2, not to mention the repeated recourse to diatribe style, is that Paul felt himself and his understanding of the gospel under attack and needing to be justified. Hence the obvious conclusion has been drawn that the letter functions as Paul's apology for his gospel, and therefore also as a self-apologia, since his whole life's-work was bound up with the gospel he preached (*see* Center).

The apology is directed to Rome; by means of the unusually expanded introduction of Romans 1:2-6, including what seems to be a common creedal formula in Romans 1:3-4 (*see* Creeds), Paul presents his "calling card" and his *bona fides*. Was this simply because he looked to the Roman Christians for support in the next phase of his mission (to Spain)? Or did he already have an inkling that the Christian groups in Rome, itself the imperial capital, were bound in due course to become increasingly influential in relation to Christian work elsewhere in the empire? Also plausible is the suggestion that Paul set out a full statement of his gospel as a dress rehearsal for his self-defense in Jerusalem, and thus hoped to recruit the Roman congregations to his support in any confrontation in Jerusalem. The likelihood of such a confrontation, and not simply with his "unbelieving" fellow Jews, was very much in his mind, as is clearly indicated in Romans 15:31. Whether he thought the Roman congregations could actually send support, or was simply asking for their prayers (a real support in Paul's eyes) is left unclear by Romans 15:30.

*3.3. A Pastoral Purpose.* In recent years the section Romans 14:1—15:6 has assumed a central significance in attempts to clarify Romans' purpose: that Paul was writing to heal potential or real divisions among the churches in Rome (*see* Pastor). This makes good sense of the exhortations of Romans 14:1 and 15:7, especially when set against the background sketched above (particularly 2.2 above). Such attempts have been weakened by too casual identifications of "the weak" and "the strong" (as simply Jews and simply Gentiles; *see* Strong and Weak) and by hypothesizing too clearly distinct groups and too sharp differen-

tiations between Jews and Christians. The probability is rather, as indicated above (see 2.3), that there were Jewish synagogues attended by both God-fearing Gentiles and Christian Jews and Gentiles, and that there was a diverse spectrum of Christian groupings, some with more Gentiles (Gentiles more dominant, though not necessarily less attracted to the synagogue), and others with more Jews (Jews more dominant, though not necessarily more conservative toward Jewish traditions and customs).

This would certainly help explain the character of the letter as a whole, and of Romans 14:1—15:6 in relation to the rest, namely: that Paul set out to explain the "both Jew and Gentile" character of the gospel and of the promises to Israel,* not exclusively, but also not least, to encourage his Roman auditors to work out in the experience of everyday what the gospel and these promises must mean in practice. Above all it would give proper significance to what is obviously a climactic expression and rounding-off conclusion of the letter's main theme in Romans 15:7-13. In contrast, attempts to read Romans 12:1—15:13 simply as generalized, all-purpose paraenesis, lifted in part from Paul's experiences with the Corinthian church, hardly explains the distinctiveness of Romans' paraenesis (*see* Teaching/Paraenesis), or the passion with which Paul writes, or, indeed, once again, the climax of Romans 15:7-13.

In addition, assuming that Romans 16 is part of the original letter, it is evident that Paul had some close contacts with various members of the Roman churches and would therefore have a fair knowledge of the character of the Roman churches and of their circumstances. From chapter 16 we can also see that Paul was writing to introduce and commend Phoebe (Rom 16:1-2); but that would be a subsidiary purpose and of itself could hardly explain the whole letter.

*3.4. The Purposes of Romans.* The fact that each of the above reasons for Romans can find such clear support from within the letter itself points to the obvious conclusion: that Paul had not simply one but several purposes in view when he wrote. Indeed, such a conclusion is more or less required by the character of the letter itself; no single suggested reason on its own can explain the full sweep of the document. On the contrary, it was presumably because Paul had several purposes in view that he found it desirable to set out his understanding of the good news of Christ so fully, including its practical implications. As he stood at one of the most important transition points in his whole ministry he saw both the need and the desirability of such a fully worked-out statement—to indicate to others clearly *what* was the gospel he preached, *why* as a Jew he preached it, and *how* it should come to expression in daily life and community. It is the completeness of the statement, as required by the multiplicity of purposes served, which lifts the letter above the immediacy of the circumstances in which and for which it was written and gives it, if not a timeless quality, at least its timeless significance.

### 4. Literary Form and Coherence.

*4.1. The Literary Form.* A second area of debate in recent years has been over the literary character of the letter (*see* Letters, Letter Forms). Much of it has been inconclusive and a somewhat pointless dispute about suitability of categories drawn from other literary and rhetorical forms—"epideictic" (demonstrative), "deliberative" (persuasive), "ambassadorial," to name but three (*see* Rhetoric; Rhetorical Criticism). But since these are hardly "pure types" themselves, and since different categories can be (and have been) applied to Romans, the point of the exercise becomes unclear. The fact is that whatever conventions Paul knew or used, the form he constructed is distinctive and unique in character and content. That being said, the inquiry into literary form and rhetorical parallels has contributed several points of significance to current understanding of Romans.

*4.1.1. Introduction and Conclusion.* One is greater clarification of the letter character of the document indicated by its beginning and end. The literary parallels show that Paul was quite aware of current conventions and that he was concerned to use a medium which would, at least initially, be familiar to his audience, however much he adapted it to his own ends. He writes, therefore, as the wise teacher, leading his audience through familiar forms to the real point of the letter. Equally important for the modern commentator, the literary parallels to the writing's introduction and conclusion show not only how Paul conformed to convention but also where and how he departed from it. The more standard were these conventions, the more distinctive his additions and modifications would be seen to be by his auditors. In particular, the considerable elaboration (Rom 1:2-6) of the normal greeting (Rom 1:1, 7) would indicate clearly enough to a literate audience what the thrust of the letter was to be.

*4.1.2. Epistolary Framework and Body.* Another point to emerge from the study of literary form is the importance of the relation between the epistolary framework and the body of the letter. It is not simply a matter of recognizing that the framework is important for interpreting the whole (Romans is not merely a dogmatic treatise, beginning at Rom 1:17). As we have already noted, the insertion of Romans 1:2-6 into the normal greetings structure gives these verses the force of a prologue to the whole letter. So too the fact that Romans 1:16-17 serves both as the climax to the introduction and the thematic statement for what follows indicates a concern on Paul's part to integrate the framework into the body of the letter. The same conclusion follows from Paul's repetition of his travel plans (Rom 1:8-15; 15:14-33; *see* Itineraries), as indeed of his self-claims to the grace* of God* in Romans 1:2-6 and 15:14-15, that is, after as well as before the body of the letter. Thus he indicates that the intervening exposition is both an expression of that grace (cf. Rom 1:12) and the theological basis of the specific request for support with which he concludes the restatement of his travel plans (Rom 15:30-33).

*4.1.3. Diatribe.* The third point of significance to emerge from studying Romans as a rhetorical form is the renewed appreciation of the diatribe* style used by Paul (dialogue with an imaginary interlocutor)—a feature at key phases in his argument (Rom 2:1-5, 17-29; 3:27—4:2; 9:19-21; 11:17-24). Characteristic of the diatribe is the attempt to criticize arrogance and correct pretension. Stowers in particular has pointed out that the typical function of the diatribe was not as polemic against an opponent but, in a philosophical school context, as a critical questioning of a fellow student intended to lead him to the truth. Thus awareness of contemporary rhetorical convention alerts the modern reader to the danger of reading passages like Romans 2 as the expression of out-and-out polemic against an "opponent"* or as indicating a complete break between two monolithic entities ("Judaism" and "Christianity"). What the diatribe passages indicate, rather, is Paul engaged in a critical dialogue with his fellow Jews and fellow Christian Jews about the significance of the new "philosophical sect" within Judaism (Christianity) as to its relation with its parent Judaism and with the other Judaisms of the time.

*4.2. Literary Coherence.* The a priori likelihood that Paul used or adapted material or themes which he had used in earlier teaching (cf., e.g., Acts 19:8-10) has resulted in various suggestions that some of this previous material can be distinguished as coherent blocks: for example, chapters 5—8 as a distinct homily, or chapters 9—11 as preformed material incorporated here somewhat awkwardly. Such hypotheses can never be proved or disproved since there is no clear line of distinction between re-use of oral patterns never before written down and re-use of written material. All we need say is that the various sections of the argument of Romans cohere with sufficient closeness and, indeed, with such a high degree of integration, that such hypotheses add nothing to our understanding of the letter. The same degree of coherence and integration, however, tells decisively against more complex dissections of the text or elaborate theories of substantial redaction, which unfailingly create more problems than they solve or leave us with a simplistic and monochrome Paul.

The one major issue raised by textual criticism (*see* Textual Criticism) is whether Romans 16 belonged to the original text dictated by Paul. A strong minority opinion continues to hold that chapter 16 was a separate letter written to Ephesus. This is unlikely. In particular, a letter ending with Romans 15:33 and without a "grace" benediction* (Rom 16:20) would be quite unlike Paul; Romans 16:1-23 has all the marks of an epistolary conclusion; and it is hardly implausible that Paul should know so many in Rome as the greetings indicate (the Jewish community was substantial, and the movements of Prisca and Aquila indicate that there was a fair amount of travel* to and from Rome, as might be expected in relation to the imperial capital).

The presence of Romans 16:25-27 at different places in the manuscript tradition (also after Rom 14:23 and after Rom 15:33), however, suggests that shorter forms of the letter were circulated. The consensus is that under Marcionite influence (*see* Canon) the letter was abbreviated (to Rom 1:1—14:23), to which Romans 16:25-27 was then added to provide a fitting conclusion. Early copyists would also see less point in transcribing all the names of chapter 16 and probably circulated a more general version ending at Romans 15:33, to which Romans 16:25-27 was also added. It is equally understandable that the very fitting conclusion, Romans 16:25-27, should likewise become attached to the full version in successive copyings. At all events, there is a strong consensus that Romans 16:25-27 is a later addition to the letter.

## 5. The Issues at Stake.

### 5.1. The New Perspective on Paul.
Traditionally Romans has been treated as a work of systematic theology, "a compendium of Christian doctrine" in Melanchthon's words, a more or less timeless statement of what the gospel means (*see* Paul and His Interpreters). But the recent recognition that the letter is related to the particular emphases and circumstances of Paul's mission (see 3 above) carries with it the corollary that the issues addressed in the letter must also have been conditioned in greater or less measure by the same emphases and circumstances. What is at stake in Romans is not the gospel in general or in the abstract, but the gospel in particular as embodied by

Paul's own life and work—a Jewish gospel for Gentiles, and the strains and tensions which stemmed from that basic conviction.

This perspective on the letter has been reinforced by the new perspective on Paul and on the Jewish context from which he emerged. Traditionally in Protestant exegesis Judaism has been seen as the foil to Christianity, as that which Christianity brought to an end or showed to be bankrupt, as that from which Paul was converted when he became a Christian. Read in that light the antitheses in Romans, particularly between sin* and grace,* death and life (*see* Life and Death), law* and faith,* though surprisingly less so between flesh* and Spirit (*see* Holy Spirit), appeared as antitheses between Judaism and Christianity. "The Jew" became the classic type of religion gone wrong, of religion understood in terms of human achievement, rather than as the expression of gratitude for, and response to, the initiative of divine grace.

Now, however, more scattered protest against such stereotyping of "the Jew" and Judaism has reached a climax, particularly in English-speaking scholarship from the Christian side, in the work of E. P. Sanders. It is he who more effectively than anyone else in the English-speaking world has succeeded in getting across the message that early Judaism at its heart was a religion of grace: its starting point, God's free choice of Israel and rescue from slavery; its system one which focused on repentance, atonement and forgiveness*; its emphasis on Law keeping, the appropriate response of gratitude and faithfulness on the part of the elect people. From this new perspective the theological issues at stake in Romans take on a different hue. In that sense Sanders marks a new epoch in the study of Paul, and commentaries on Romans can be categorized as pre- and post-Sanders—at least to the extent that one can assess work on the theology of Romans by whether it takes serious account of the new perspective (even if to disagree with it).

### 5.2. The New Perspective on Romans.
In light of the new perspective on Paul the issues at stake in Romans receive a fresh clarity. The various themes are already sounded in the substantial elaboration of the more common introduction (Rom 1:2-7): (1) the gospel of God; (2) continuous with the prophecies of the Holy Scriptures; (3) focusing on Jesus, both Son of David and Son of God (*see* Son of God); (4) with his resurrection* marking out a new eschatological epoch (*see* Eschatology); (5) and his lordship (*see* Lord) validating its outreach, not least by Paul himself, to all the Gentiles; (6) among whom the Roman believers in particular are to be counted as numbered among the elect and beloved people of God. Hence the overarching

emphasis on the gospel for Jew *and* Gentile already noted (see 2.1-2 above), is sounded both in the initial thematic statement (Rom 1:16) and in the climax of Romans 15:7-12. Hence also the repeated emphasis is on the gospel for *all*—"all who believe" (Rom 1:16; 3:22; 4:11; 10:4, 11-13), "all injustice" (Rom 1:18, 29), all under sin (Rom 3:9, 12, 19-20, 23; 5:12), "all the seed" (Rom 4:11, 16), "all Israel" (Rom 11:26). The issue is not so much the universality of human need and of the gospel's sufficiency as whether and how the gospel, Jewish in origin and in character, reaches beyond the Jewish nation to include the nations beyond ("all" = Gentile as well as Jew, Rom 1:18—5:21). And conversely, the issue is whether the gospel now drawing in Gentiles in such numbers remains a Jewish gospel and is still the gospel for the Jews ("all" = Jew as well as Gentile, Rom 9—11).

Of course this is a particular expression of the larger theological claim about the universality of human sin and of the gospel's provision, and it is wholly legitimate to validate such a larger theological claim from Romans. But it is important to recognize that the larger claim is derived from this particular expression, that is, both to recognize its historical specificity (including the continuing Jewish character of the Christian gospel), and to be alert to the possibility that individual elements in this particular expression are determined primarily by that context and thus are less amenable to generalization.

*5.3. The Faithfulness of God.* Within this overarching emphasis (Jew and Gentile) several other key themes in the letter fall into place. One is the issue of theodicy ("the gospel *of God*"). This is indicated at once in the centrality of "the righteousness of God" (particularly Rom 1:17; 3:5, 21-26; 4:1-25; 9:30—10:13; *see* Righteousness). The theme is through-and-through Jewish, its Pauline usage in direct continuity with the usage of the Psalms and Isaiah 40—66. The issue is twofold. (1) How the saving action to which God committed himself on behalf of Israel includes those outside Israel. The answer is given partly in terms of the correlated thematic word "faith": that this always was the human medium through which God exercised his saving righteousness (so again particularly Rom 4:1-25 and 9:30—10:17, also 14:22-23). And partly in terms of the new, climactic phase in God's purpose (the same purpose) marked by Christ's ministry (particularly Rom 3:22-26 and again Rom 9:30—10:13).

(2) What the Jewish gospel for Gentiles says about the faithfulness of God to his original promises to Israel. This theme is obscured somewhat by the fact that the Jewish motif of divine faithfulness is translated into Greek in two different ways: God's faithfulness

(Rom 3:3; but perhaps also Rom 1:17 and 3:25) and God's truth (particularly Rom 1:25; 3:7; 15:8). The issue is clearly articulated in Romans 3:1-8, but Paul is able to address it in detail only in Romans 9—11, where it is posed in the key question of whether the word of God has failed (Rom 9:6). The importance of Romans 15:7-13 (here Rom 15:8) as summing up Paul's concerns and thus indicating what these concerns were in the letter is again underlined.

Somewhat surprisingly, christology* does not seem to be part of the issue. It is fundamental to the gospel, of course (Rom 1:3-4), but the fulcrum expression of it in Romans 3:21-26 is brief, probably makes use of pre-formed material, and seems to be noncontroversial (hence the brevity). The christology as such seems to be common ground. The universal significance of Christ is the presupposition of Romans 5—8 rather than the theme. And though Christ is presented as the stumbling-stone in Romans 9:32-33, it is striking that in the final resolution to the problem of Israel's unbelief a distinctively Christian (as distinct from Jewish) messianism is lacking (Rom 11:26; *see* Christ). Characteristic of the letter at this point is, once again, the climax of Romans 15:8: "Christ has become the servant of the circumcised for the sake of God's truth (faithfulness)."

*5.4. The Subtheme of the Law.* The other theme which falls into place in the light of the new perspective is the role of the Law* in Romans. The traditional view tended to see the Law as belonging wholly on the negative side of the antitheses posed by Paul—a hostile power, like sin and death (understandably in view of Rom 5:20 and 7:5), characterizing Judaism as legalistic, a religion of achievement, giving ground for human pride (cf. Rom 3:27-28; 9:11, 32; 11:6). The fact that Paul seems equally concerned to mount an apologetic in relation to the Law (Rom 3:31; 7:7-25; 8:3-4; 13:8-10) fitted ill with this understanding, but on the traditional view it was not easy to see any solution. The new perspective has shaken up the negative side of the equation, but for some (Sanders, Räisänen) the result has been only to increase the incoherence of Paul's overall position.

However, within the new perspective both on Paul and on Romans (see 5.1-2 above), a more coherent solution is possible. For where the primary issue is the tensions caused by a Jewish gospel being offered to Gentiles, the problem of the Law is likely to relate to that issue. The Law is then most naturally seen as a principal hindrance which prevents Gentiles from accepting the gospel. And so we find in Romans. It is the Jewish claim to have the Law and thus to have a privileged position before God (Rom 2:12-29) which focuses the problem of Israel's election* (Rom 3:1). It is the Jewish boast in this privileged status as marked out by their obedience to the Law which Paul seeks to counter by his focus on faith (Rom 3:27-31; 4:1-25). It is the Law, not as evil, but as weak and used as a cat's-paw by sin, which he attempts to defend (Rom 7:7-8:4). It is the Law typified by Jewish works and a focus of Jewish zeal (*see* Jealousy, Zeal) which Paul sees to have been ended by Christ, not "the Law of righteousness" (9:30—10:4); "the Law of sin and death," not "the Law of the Spirit of life" (Rom 8:2-4). Properly understood in the new light of Christ, therefore, what the Law calls for is not the "works" (*see* Works of the Law) which mark off Jew from Gentile (particularly, though by no means exclusively, circumcision* and food laws, Rom 2:25-29; 4:9-12; 9:10-13; 14:1-12), but love* of neighbor (Rom 13:8-10; 14:13—15:6).

In a word, then, it is not the Law as expression of human *achievement* which Paul questions, but the Law as expression of Jewish *privilege*. The solution to "the problem of the Law" in Romans lies not in a "demonizing" of the Law; nor in throwing up one's hands at Paul's "contradictions"; nor in distinguishing ceremonial law from moral law, though Paul's teaching can be worked out in these terms. Paul's concern was more with a nationalizing of the Law than with its ritualizing. It was because the Law could be so identified with Israel, and that identification focused so much in distinctive Jewish rites (particularly circumcision and food laws), that Paul found it necessary to distinguish fulfillment of the Law's requirements from doing such "works." Evidently, in the tensions caused by his proclamation of a Jewish gospel to Gentiles, it was only by so arguing that he could defend both features of the gospel—both its Jewish character and its openness to all nations (*see* Universalism).

### 6. The Argument of the Letter.
We are now in a position to appreciate the thrust and movement of Paul's thought in Romans. Since the main body of the letter is set out so systematically, a brief survey of it provides an invaluable synopsis of Paul's theology as he stood at this climax to his missionary career.

*6.1. Introduction (Rom 1:1-17).* We have already noted how the expanded greetings (Rom 1:1-7) allow Paul to introduce his theme while still at the stage of friendly introductions (see 5.2 above). We also noted that the personal explanations which follow, with their typical features of thanksgiving and prayer* (Rom 1:8-15; *see* Benediction, Blessing, Doxology, Thanksgiving), both root the letter as a whole firmly into the particular historical setting of its composition, and lead into the

key thematic statement for what follows (Rom 1:16-17). Here the principal terms of the letter are clearly enunciated—the gospel as God's power* for salvation,* all who believe, Jew first and Greek, the righteousness* of God being revealed from faith* to faith—together with the supporting OT text (Hab 2:4).

*6.2. The Human Condition—Gentile and Jew (Rom 1:18—3:20).* In a manner followed in subsequent centuries by countless restatements of the Christian gospel or monographs on theology, Paul finds it necessary to define the human condition to which the gospel provides an answer.

*6.2.1. Human Beastliness (Rom 1:18-32).* He begins by characterizing what classically has been described as human depravity (*see* Sin). That is now too heavy or distancing a formulation, particularly when we appreciate that he rounds off his indictment with a description which includes the everyday nastiness and petty selfishnesses of human pride and ruptured relationships (Rom 1:29-31). Such negative features mark the breakdown of human society, features which all people of goodwill would deplore ("what is not fitting," Rom 1:28). The gospel starts by taking such things seriously (Rom 1:32).

Two other elements help explain the build-up to that climax. One is the strong echo of the Adam stories in Genesis 2—3 (Rom 1:19-23). The basic flaw in the make-up of human society is that the human creature has failed to live in accord with its creatureliness, has failed to acknowledge its dependence on God,* has sought to usurp the role of the creator. The consequence has been the opposite—not a rise above human creatureliness, but a fall below humanity to a level of beastliness, marked by idolatry, unnatural sexual practices (*see* Homosexuality; Sexuality) and the nastiness already mentioned. The other is the strong echo of characteristically Jewish polemic against Gentiles and particularly Gentile religion (Rom 1:24-27)—precisely as characterized by idolatry* and debased sexuality (cf. Wis 11—15). Thus at once Paul highlights the tension between Jew and Gentile as central to his concerns.

*6.2.2. Jews Too (Rom 2:1-29).* Romans 2 has caused more difficulties than any other chapter for commentators, particularly because it seems to envisage final justification as depending on human deeds rather than on faith, and because its argument seems to depend on a far too sweeping indictment of Jews at large. The key is to note that the chapter is framed, on the one side, by a typically Jewish attack on Gentile lifestyle (Rom 1:18-32) and, on the other, by a protest that Jewish privilege has been undermined (Rom 3:1). What is in view in Romans 2, therefore, is almost certainly the very sense of Jewish privilege and distinctiveness which was so clearly echoed in Romans 1.

This is confirmed by the first appearance of the characteristic diatribe form in Romans 2:1-5. Paul thus engages not with any imaginary onlooker but precisely with the typical Jew who would commend the typically Jewish indictment of Romans 1. The echoes of such Jewish reasoning as we find in *Psalms of Solomon* 15:8 and Wisdom 15:1-6 (Rom 2:3-4), as well as the explicit quotation of the Jewish theologoumenon in Romans 2:6, confirm that Paul has in view a Jewish rationalization which could justify or excuse in itself what it condemned in others (Rom 2:1-11).

The picture becomes clearer in Romans 2:12-16 as Paul attempts to undermine the confidence of those who think that because they have the Law they are advantaged in the judgment over those without the Law. On the contrary, Jewish teaching is precisely that doing the Law is more important than merely hearing it; the argument is *ad hominem*. The pride and presumption of "the Jew," by virtue of possessing the Law, becomes explicit in Romans 2:17-24. The intention of the forthright indictment of the typical Jewish interlocutor is not to condemn all Jews out of hand, but rather to argue that when the typical Jew breaks the Law in his presumption he undermines the whole basis of his privileged position. The point is brought to sharpest focus in circumcision,* that which is so much the mark of "the Jew" that Jews as a whole can be called simply "the circumcision." The failure to distinguish an outward, ethnic identity marker from the hidden work of the Spirit in the heart, and to play down the importance of the former in favor of the latter means that the typical Jew is in no better (indeed, maybe worse) standing before God than the Gentile (Rom 2:25-29).

*6.2.3. Awkward Corollaries (Rom 3:1-8).* Such an uninhibited attack on Jewish self-confidence in Israel's privileged status before God raises problems which Paul cannot ignore—particularly in relation to Israel's* election,* and thus also to God's faithfulness to the people he chose. It is to be noted that Paul does not wish to query the fact of that election, but also that his one-sentence defense of God's faithfulness looks beyond God's role as Israel's covenant* partner to his role as creator and judge. Thus he hints that the resolution to the tensions of "Jew and Gentile" will be to set Israel's covenant status before its God within the larger picture of the world's status before its creator. But such lines of thought can only be hinted at here.

*6.2.4. Conclusion: All Under Sin (Rom 3:9-20).* The summary gathers all humanity under the same indictment. But the target is still primarily Jewish presump-

tion that "the Jew" is exempt. Thus the catena of OT texts which follows (Rom 3:10-18; *see* Old Testament in Paul) consists mainly of passages which assume that those condemned are "them" and not "us." Paul's point is that such an assumption is itself an expression of the power of the sin it condemned. The trust in privileged position, the boast in the Law (circumcision especially) as marking out Jew from Gentile, is itself an expression of the fleshliness (in this case, ethnic identity) which distances humankind from God (Rom 3:19-20).

*6.3. The Gospel Answer (Rom 3:21—5:21).* Again, providing a pattern for countless sermons and monographs, Paul, having indicted humanity as a whole, turns to the answer given by the gospel.

*6.3.1. Through Faith in Christ (Rom 3:21-26).* In a remarkably brief section (compared with the length of the indictment) Paul points to the death of Christ as the answer. The logic is not spelled out in any detail (why faith in Christ should provide the answer) and seems to draw on an accepted Christian formulation. So the answer must have been an already established Christian conviction which Paul did not need to elaborate.

Significant, however, is the emphasis again on complete continuity with what had gone before (Rom 3:21; Christ's death as a sacrifice, Rom 3:25). Presupposed therefore is the Jewish theology of sacrifice and of the need for an unblemished animal to act as a sin offering, with the probable implication that the animal's death served to put away or cover the sin, or indeed to kill off (in a representative way) the sin-affected offerer (*see* Expiation/Propitiation/Mercy Seat). For a reason not given in the text, Christ's death could be seen not just as such a sacrifice, but as a climactic sacrifice which was effective for all humankind past and present, Gentile as well as Jew, and thus by implication as a sacrifice which ended all further need for sacrifice and as such became the means by which all human relationship with God could be restored (*see* Justification).

*6.3.2. To Jew and Gentile (Rom 3:27-31).* Indicative of Paul's concern is the way he immediately (Rom 3:27) picks up the theme of "the Jew's" boasting* indicted in Rom 2:17, 23. As already clearly implied, it is a boasting in Jewish privilege and prerogative which Paul condemns, a boasting which in effect regards God as "the God of Jews only" (Rom 3:29). The twin recognition that God is one (the Jewish credo), and that God accepts human beings on the basis of faith, shatters any such presumption. This universalism* (Gentile as well as Jew) is what is now effective through the death of Jesus Christ (Rom 3:21-26). But since it is also (properly speaking) a Jewish universalism, it does not contradict the terms of the initial offer of that grace to Israel; that is, the gospel of Jesus Christ stands opposed to the Law characterized by the works of Jewish prerogative, but confirms the Law as calling for the obedience of faith (Rom 3:31).

*6.3.3. Abraham as a Test Case (Rom 4:1-25).* To sustain this central claim Paul takes up the challenge of the precedent provided by "father Abraham."* The test case was crucial, since Abraham was widely regarded within Judaism as the model of piety. Already it was being said that he had observed the Law in its as-yet-unwritten state (e.g., Gen 26:5; CD 3:2). In particular, he was regarded as a paradigm of *faithfulness* to the covenant, because he came through so strongly when he was tested in the matter of the offering of Isaac (e.g., Jdt 8:26; Sir 44:19-21). It was in the light of this faithfulness that Genesis 15:6 was understood: Abraham was counted righteous on the basis of this faithfulness (1 Macc 2:52; so Jas 2:22-23).

Paul's response is to expound Genesis 15:6 afresh: "Abraham believed God, and it was reckoned to him for righteousness." This is one of very few extended expositions of a text from a first-century Jew (Philo excepted) and can thus be counted as a classic example of early Jewish midrash (*see* Old Testament in Paul). It proceeds simply by first announcing the text (Rom 4:3), then analyzing each of the key words in turn—"reckoned" (Rom 4:4-8) and "believed" (Rom 4:9-21)—and finally restating the text thus expounded (Rom 4:22) with its corollary (Rom 4:23-25).

"Reckoned," Paul notes, must have a different meaning in describing a divine-human relationship from its use in a human contract—a claim somewhat fortuitously but appropriately confirmed by the verb's appearance in Psalm 32:1-2. The exposition of "believed" is more tortuous, but builds on three points: the fact that Abraham's believing was prior to and fully effective before he was circumcised (or subsequently "tested") (Rom 4:9-12); the fact that it was faith in promise (Rom 4:13-17); and the fact that the promise was so impossible of fulfillment by any degree of Abraham's contriving (or faithfulness; Rom 4:17-21). This believing could be only trust in God, confidence in God's power alone, that and nothing more—*faith*, not faithfulness. The faith called for in the gospel is precisely the same faith in the life-giving power of God (Rom 4:23-25).

*6.3.4. Conclusion: What This Means for Individual Believers (Rom 5:1-11) and for Humankind (Rom 5:12-21).* Having made his case that the gospel of God's acceptance is for all through faith, Paul rounds off this central section of his argument by spelling out the consequences. For individual believers it means peace with God (*see* Peace, Reconciliation), an experience of grace which will shape the character through suffering,* and a secure basis of hope* for the future (Rom 5:1-11). The initiative of God, its overwhelmingly gracious character, and the experience of that love already manifested in Christ's death and in the gift of the Spirit (*see* Holy Spirit), is the firm rock on which the believer can face both present and future in complete confidence (the same confidence that Abraham had displayed in his paradigmatic believing).

Christ's death thus marks a whole new beginning, not just for individuals, but for all humankind (Rom 5:12-21). The tragedy which began to unfold with Adam, as implied in Romans 1:19-23 (see 6.2.1 above) and Romans 3:23, has been answered by another story (*see* Adam and Christ). The disobedience of Adam was the ancient way of explaining how the harsh reality of sin and death entered the world* and gained such domination over it. But now the obedience of Christ has opened the way and provided another model for human existence. Sin and death need not have the last word in human affairs.

These two men—Adam and Christ—sum up in themselves the two chief possibilities for humanity. That is also to say that they sum up the argument from Romans 1:18 onwards—from the condemnation of life "in Adam" and under the domination of sin and death, to the offer of life "in Christ" under the reign of grace. The whole opening section of the body of the letter (Rom 1:18—5:21) thus has an impressively rounded and global quality—from Adam to Christ as a comprehensive summary of human history. But the passage also brings to the fore the negative factors brought into play by Adam, sin and death, with the role of the Law as a further complicating factor (Rom 5:20-21), and what effect the gospel has on them requires further clarification.

*6.4. The Problem of Sin, Death and the Law (Rom 6:1—8:39).* Paul has essentially set out two principal alternatives for human existence and indicated that the individual believer can in effect transfer from one to the other in terms of basic motivation and character formation. The question at once arises, whether the transfer can be total. Paul's answer is summed up in terms of an already/not-yet formula (*see* Eschatology). Something decisive has *already* happened (Rom 5:1-11), but so long as life lasts within the transitoriness and weakness* of this bodily existence the outworking of that decisive act of God is *not yet* complete. That is to say, sin and death continue to exert an influence which believers cannot escape and to which they are in some measure (the measure of his human Adam-ness) still subject, but which they must continue to resist in the strength of the Spirit.

This is the basic line which Paul elaborates in the next three chapters—in relation first to sin, then to the Law, and finally to flesh and death. In each case he begins by stating clearly the new reality already made effective by God's action in Christ, before going on to indicate how the new reality must be lived out in the "not-yet" conditions of the still sinful flesh—the indicative of God's grace as the inspiration and enabling of human commitment and obedience.

*6.4.1. The Problem of Sin (Rom 6:1-23).* The claim that grace had more than accounted for sin gives rise to the ribald response: if sin results in grace, then the more sin the better. Paul's answer is to point to the decisive cut-off point for sin and death in the death of Jesus. Sin and death could reach as far, but no farther: "the death he died, he died to sin once and for all" (Rom 6:10). For those who have identified themselves with Christ in his death (through baptism*; *see* Dying and Rising), therefore, there can be no question of tolerating or cooperating with sin. The motivating center of their living is now directed toward and determined by the Christ on whom sin has no hold whatsoever.

Sin remains a reality, however, for believers have not yet shared fully in Christ's resurrection; they still must experience the outworking of fleshly corruption and death. Sin thus still has a foothold in them, and its wiles and enticements must be resisted until that end. But in the temptation of the not yet, the already of Christ's victory (*see* Triumph) is the basis and source of strength to resist and overcome, to live out their initial commitment in the renewed commitment of every day.

*6.4.2. The Problem of the Law (Rom 7:1-25).* Underlying the first critique of Paul's gospel outlined in Romans 6:1 was a Jewish suspicion that Paul's gospel meant abandoning the Law.* It was precisely the Law which served as a bulwark against the power of sin, did it not? But Paul's attack on Jewish presumption as focused in works of the Law could easily be heard by his fellow Jews (and modern commentators!) as an attack on the Law itself. It is this problem that Paul now addresses.

He begins, once again, by stating his position in bald terms. The (Jewish) Law is so much identified with the period before Christ that the new possibility of existence brought about by Christ is like a being freed from the Law. In terms of the earlier indictment (Rom 2—3), the Law has become the occasion for Jewish presumption, and thus the instrument of the very sin which it was intended to thwart. Thus the transfer from old to new, from Adam to Christ, from sin and death to grace, has become also a transfer from the legal code which defines Israel to the new life of the Spirit.

But surely such a treatment of the Law is tantamount to identifying the Law with sin. Paul's answer is that the Law is not to blame. It—and the "flesh"* (*sarx*, i.e., human frailty and finitude)—have been manipulated by sin. The reality of the already/not-yet tension between what has begun with and in Christ and the salvation yet to be completed is reflected in a double split—both in the individual who yearns to do the will of God but yet remains in "the flesh," and in the Law which expresses the will of God but is still the tool of sin and death.

*6.4.3. The Problem of the Flesh and Death (Rom 8:1-39).* The third restatement of the outworking of the gospel for the individual once again begins with strong emphasis on the divine indicative. What was impossible for the Law in the face of the power of sin and death and the weakness of human flesh, God has accomplished in Christ. Those who have received the Spirit of Christ thus have a completely other "base of operations" than simply the flesh. It is from this base that they must live and act. They must live out the reality of the sonship which they already experience through the Spirit and share with God's Son (Rom 8:1-17).

This does not mean that the flesh has been left behind or that death has been avoided. On the contrary, the reality of the human condition means continuing weakness and, not least, suffering, a condition which will continue until the completion of the redemption process in the resurrection of the body. The present tension is uncomfortable, but it is one shared with the whole of creation, likewise caught in the overlap of the ages between what has been and what will be, between Adam and Christ. And it is made bearable by the fact of the Spirit already present, already active in and through that weakness, the ground of a sure hope (Rom 8:18-30).

The section is rounded off with a shout of glowing assurance, all equivocation and qualification put aside. Whatever the continuing power of sin and death, the continuing weakness of the flesh, and the continuing hostility of this age, God's triumph is sure. God's purpose in Christ has already secured the victory. Neither death itself nor any other power can separate believers from the love of God in Christ (Rom 8:31-39).

*6.5. What of Israel? (Rom 9:1—11:36).* The issue of Jew and Gentile which dominated the first two main sections of the letter (Rom 1:18—5:21) had been largely lost to sight in the last section (chap. 7 apart) as Paul focused on the outworkings of the gospel in both global (Adam/Christ) and personal terms. But the language used had again and again been drawn from that of Israel's covenant promises. And the final assurance of God's faithfulness to his "elect" begged the whole question of God's faithfulness to his earlier covenant partner, Israel.* As the problem of the Law indicated, a division of history into before and after Christ ran the danger of dumping Israel as a whole into the Adam phase. What then of God's promises to Israel? How could the faithfulness of God to believers be asserted while his faithfulness to Israel was being thus discounted? This is the issue which Paul now addresses in one of the most tensely argued passages in all his writing.

*6.5.1. Introduction (Rom 9:1-5).* Paul begins by reasserting his personal concern for his own people and reminding his readers of Israel's covenant privileges in which they were now participants—that is, in *Israel's* covenant privileges.

*6.5.2. The Call of God (Rom 9:6-29).* He then proceeds to state his primary thesis: God's word (to Israel) has not failed. The failure has been (by implication on Israel's part) to recognize the character of Israel's election and calling—that is, what constituted Israel as Israel. That election was a wholly gracious act of God without respect for physical descent or for the works which had come to be seen as marking out covenant identity.

The negative side of this view of election is that there is a "non-Israel"—those whose function is to highlight the gracious character of Israel's election. This harsh, almost predestinarian view of history, is Paul's attempt to explain what he sees to be the simple fact of a chosen people within a hostile world, that the overall picture has many darker hues. The main point of the discussion, as becomes steadily more apparent, however, is not to dictate a doctrine of predestination (*see* Election and Predestination) but to undermine Israel's own doctrine of predestination. It is Jewish confidence that Gentiles are by definition "non-Israel" which he seeks to challenge. By citing Israel's own Scriptures, as now also being fulfilled through his own mission, Paul is able to argue that whoever non-Israel might be, the chosen people include both Jews and Gentiles.

*6.5.3. Israel's Failure (Rom 9:30—10:21).* Israel's failure, then, has been to understand its calling and privileges in a too narrow and restrictive way—a law understood in terms of works rather than faith, a righteousness understood as exclusively theirs from which Gentiles were excluded. The coming of Christ has put an end to such misunderstanding. He is the prophesied "stone of stumbling" (*see* Stumbling Block) in whom all may believe. The faith which is the only possible response to the completely gracious character of God's calling cannot be restricted within the confines of an exclusively Jewish Law. It now finds expression more fully in the word of preaching which is truly universal in scope, the call for faith in Jesus as Lord.* This is the word which is now being preached, not least by Paul himself, and which is being accepted by Gentiles. Israel, failing to recognize that this universal outreach expresses the same gracious character of its own calling, is refusing to receive this gospel, and thus is fulfilling its own Scriptures.

*6.5.4. The Mystery of God's Faithfulness (Rom 11:1-32).* The fact is that in the already/not-yet overlap period, Israel itself is as much split as the believer or the Law (Rom 7:7-25). There are some within Israel who have recognized the gracious character of Israel's election and responded in terms of that grace, like the Gentile believers. But the bulk have failed to recognize that standing with God is a matter of grace from start to finish. Ironically, unbelieving Israel thus finds itself in the role of non-Israel, the negative role filled by Esau and Pharaoh in Romans 9:13 and 17.

And thus begins to become clear the mystery of the divine purpose of mercy* and judgment.* As it was necessary for Pharaoh to play his negative role in order for the graciousness of God's redemption of Israel to be made clear, so it has been necessary for the bulk of Israel to refuse the gospel in order that the gracious character of the gospel for Gentiles as well as Jews might be made plain. Paul's hope is that the sight of so many Gentiles entering into Israel's covenant blessings will spur Israel to jealousy*; that is why he pursues his own mission to the Gentiles with such dedication. If Israel's failure has brought such blessing to Gentiles, what will be the blessing for the whole world when Israel as a whole accepts its own heritage in Christ (Rom 11:11-16)!

This in turn indicates that an equivalent warning to the Gentile believers is called for. The degree to which the blessings of Israel have passed to Gentiles gives no more cause for pride and presumption to the latter than Israel's original election did to Jews. God has not discarded Israel and started afresh. Gentiles are incorporated into Israel and remain part of Israel only so long as they maintain the fundamental grace-faith character of the relationship (Rom 11:17-24; *see* Olive Tree).

The fact of the divine faithfulness is that God's original calling of Israel remains constant, and constant in terms of grace and faith. The mystery* of the divine faithfulness is that the pre-Christian Jew-and-not-Gentile expression of election and the current Gentile-and-not-Jew response to the gospel are both phases in the larger divine purpose. God's purpose is that all Israel be saved. The perplexing disobedience shown in this phase of God's purpose is but the preliminary, and in some sense the means to realizing the ultimate purpose of showing mercy to all.

*6.5.5. A Concluding Hymn of Adoration (Rom 11:33-36).* Fittingly, Paul rounds off this exposition of high theological ideal and hope with a hymn* of praise to the one creator God, that is, of both Jew and Gentile.

*6.6. The Practical Outworking of the Gospel (Rom 12:1—15:13).* Having thus redefined the Israel of God it becomes necessary to spell out how this Israel should live. Israel defined simply in terms of the Jewish people knew at once the answer: the Law provided the guidelines for life lived within the covenant. But Paul's earlier critique and redefinition of the role of the Law (Rom 2:1—3:31; 7:1-25) must have left his auditors wondering where to find the guidelines for Christian living.

*6.6.1. The Basis for Responsible Living (Rom 12:1-2).* Paul therefore begins by calling for a commitment in daily living which is the Christian's equivalent to the discipline and order previously provided by the Jerusalem cult. Such committed openness to the Spirit of God allows the possibility of immediacy of knowledge of the divine will which the Scriptures themselves had always held out as the ideal.

*6.6.2. The Community of Faith (Rom 12:3-8).* In the new order the social equivalent of corporate Israel (Judaism) is the body of Christ (*see* Body of Christ). Life within ethnic Israel had involved the usual representative roles and functions of any national body. The body of Christ has its equivalent roles and functions, as determined and enabled by the Spirit. No member should think that he or she lacks a role or that there are only a few set roles to which all must aspire.

*6.6.3. Love As the Norm for Social Relationships (Rom 12:9-21).* As for the Christians' mutual relationships and relationships with the wider world, the norm is given by love. Paul illustrates what this will mean in practice. Then, turning to the wider relationships with outsiders, he draws on the accumulated wisdom of Diaspora Judaism on how to live within strange and hostile societies. Here peaceable good-neighborliness must be the rule.

*6.6.4. Live As Good Citizens (Rom 13:1-7).* In particular, and particularly living as they do within the imperial capital, the Roman Christians should endeavor to be as fully law-abiding as possible—including the payment of taxes levied on them (*see* Civil Authority).

*6.6.5. Love Your Neighbor (Rom 13:8-10).* The whole exhortation is summed up in the love command. It will be no accident either that this was also recognized within the rest of Judaism as a summary of the Law, or that the Gospels recall Jesus as giving it similar prominence (Mk 12:31 etc). Here, in other words, Paul indicates his desire to show that the Law still provides guidelines for living and how it does so—that is, by hearing it in the light of Christ's own teaching and ministry.

*6.6.6. The Imminence of the End as Spur (Rom 13:11-14).* Ever in the background of Paul's thought was the confidence that the already/not-yet overlap period would not be long drawn out, in terms either of personal salvation (Rom 7:24; 8:23) or of Israel's salvation (Rom 11:13-15). The same perspective should help provide a spur to live out of the new reality and motivation of being "in Christ" and not in terms of the self-indulgent, decaying flesh.

*6.6.7. The Problem of Food Laws and Holy Days (Rom 14:1—15:6).* The whole issue expounded in principle and practice in the preceding chapters comes to particular focus in an issue which was bound to create tensions in any mixed community of Jews and Gentiles. Wherever there were Jews who continued to identify themselves with the heritage of the Maccabees and the Judaism of the succeeding decades, observance of the food* laws was bound to be a matter of personal and national integrity (cf., e.g., 1 Macc 2:62-63). The same would apply to Gentile proselytes or God-fearers who had found themselves religiously by identifying with the Judaism of the synagogue. Such Christians would find it hard to dispense with the Jewish food laws. Other Jews, like Paul, would have come to regard such works of the Law as too restrictive of the grace of God and would have abandoned them in greater or lesser degree. Many Gentiles converted under such preaching would see no reason to subscribe to these laws. In mixed communities, where table fellowship was a fundamental expression of community, the tensions set up by these differences would be considerable. Presumably Paul knew of such tensions from his personal contacts in Rome, particularly within churches in Rome now mainly Gentile in character to which Christian Jews were returning after the period of expulsion under Claudius. The issue, it should be noted, was a serious one, since bound up with it was the whole question of the identity of the new movement—as a sect within Judaism, or what? Hence the prominence given to it by Paul.

Paul in effect addresses the two main groupings in

turn. To the "weak," that is the more scrupulous, Law-abiding (mainly) Christian Jews who were defined as "weak" by the others who saw strength in their liberty from such scruples, Paul gives a simple warning: Do not make your own conscience the measure for others; recognize that God may be heard speaking differently to different people on such matters; you cannot condemn those whom Christ accepts (Rom 14:3-12; *see* Strong and Weak).

To the self-styled "strong," whose views Paul shares, Paul's advice is that they should hold strongly to conclusions reached in faith, but that they should be willing to limit their liberty (*see* Freedom) of practice if there was a real danger that their freer practice would cause genuine distress and harm to the faith of other members (Rom 14:13-23). The model for such behavior is Christ himself (Rom 15:1-6)—a confirmation that the teaching and example of Jesus provided the basic hermeneutic for this earliest Christian reinterpretation of the Law.

*6.6.8. Concluding Summary (Rom 15:7-13).* Paul neatly integrates this plea to mutual acceptance and tolerance into the overarching theme of the whole letter. Christ was a Jew, both to confirm God's faithfulness to the Jews, and to open the door of grace and faith to the Gentiles, in fulfillment of God's overall purpose as indicated in Scripture.

*6.7. Conclusion (Rom 15:14—16:27).* Paul rounds off his letter by reverting to the themes of the introduction. He describes in more detail his mission, indicating its continuity with the cultic ministry of the Jerusalem Temple and the successful conclusion of its eastern phase. Then he turns again to his plans for the future, indicating more clearly his reasons for wanting to visit his readers in Rome and the reasons for his delay. He ends by indicating his alarm at the possible outcome of his visit to deliver the collection in Jerusalem and asking for their prayers* (Rom 15:14-33; *see* Collection for the Saints).

The final section is a note of commendation for Phoebe, deacon and patron of the church in Cenchreae, and a lengthy list of greetings to those he knows personally or by name in the Roman churches, among whom several women leaders are prominent. A final stereotyped warning about dangers of dissension and a few greetings from others brings this most important of Paul's letters to a close (Rom 16:1-23).

*See also* CENTER OF PAUL'S THEOLOGY; ISRAEL; JUSTIFICATION; LAW; OLIVE TREE; PAUL AND HIS INTERPRETERS; PAUL IN ACTS AND LETTERS; RESTORATION OF ISRAEL; RIGHTEOUSNESS, RIGHTEOUSNESS OF GOD; ROME AND ROMAN CHRISTIANITY; WORKS OF THE LAW.

BIBLIOGRAPHY. **Commentaries:** C. K. Barrett, *Romans* (BNTC; 2d ed.; London: Black, 1991); C. E. B. Cranfield, *Romans* (2 vols.; ICC; Edinburgh: T. & T. Clark, 1975, 1979); J. D. G. Dunn, *Romans* (2 vols.; WBC 38; Dallas: Word, 1988); E. Käsemann, *Romans* (Grand Rapids: Eerdmans, 1980); O. Kuss, *Römerbrief* (3 vols.; Regensburg: Pustet, 1957, 1959, 1978); O. Michel, *An die Römer* (KEK; 14th ed.; Göttingen: Vandenhoeck & Ruprecht, 1978); D. Moo, *Romans 1-8* (WEC; Chicago: Moody, 1991); H. Schlier, *Römerbrief* (HTKNT; Freiburg: Herder, 1977); U. Wilckens, *An die Römer* (3 vols.; EKK; Zürich: Benziger/Neukirchen: Neukirchener, 1978, 1980, 1982); D. Zeller, *An die Römer* (RNT; Regensburg: Pustet, 1985); J. Ziesler, *Romans* (TPINTC; Philadelphia: Trinity, 1989). **Studies:** W. S. Campbell, *Paul's Gospel in an Intercultural Context: Jew and Gentile in the Letter to the Romans* (Frankfurt: Peter Lang, 1991); K. P. Donfried, ed., *The Romans Debate. Revised and Expanded Edition* (Peabody, MA: Hendrickson, 1991); J. D. G. Dunn, *The Partings of the Ways: Between Christianity and Judaism and Their Significance for the Character of Christianity* (Philadelphia: Trinity, 1991); N. Elliott, *The Rhetoric of Romans. Argumentative Constraint and Strategy and Paul's Dialogue with Judaism* (JSNTSupp 45; Sheffield: JSOT, 1990); R. D. Kaylor, *Paul's Covenant Community: Jew and Gentile in Romans* (Atlanta: John Knox, 1988); P. Lampe, *Die stadtrömischen Christen in den ersten beiden Jahrhunderten* (WUNT 2.18; 2d ed.; Tübingen: J. C. B. Mohr, 1989); B. W. Longenecker, *Eschatology and the Covenant. A Comparison of 4 Ezra and Romans 1-11* (JSNTSupp 57; Sheffield: JSOT, 1991); H. Räisänen, "Paul, God and Israel: Romans 9-11 in Recent Research," in *The Social World of Formative Christianity and Judaism*, ed. J. Neusner et al. (Philadelphia: Fortress, 1988) 178-206; E. P. Sanders, *Paul and Palestinian Judaism* (Philadelphia: Fortress, 1977); idem, *Paul, the Law, and the Jewish People* (Philadelphia: Fortress, 1983); S. K. Stowers, *The Diatribe and Paul's Letter to the Romans* (SBLDS 57; Chico: Scholars, 1981); F. B. Watson, *Paul, Judaism and the Gentiles: A Sociological Approach* (SNTSMS 56; Cambridge: University Press, 1986); A. J. M. Wedderburn, *The Reasons for Romans* (Edinburgh: T. & T. Clark, 1988); N. T. Wright, *The Climax of the Covenant: Christ and the Law in Pauline Theology* (Edinburgh: T. & T. Clark, 1991).

J. D. G. Dunn

## ROME AND ROMAN CHRISTIANITY

As the center of the Mediterranean world, Rome was a pivotal city in Paul's mind. Already during the lifetime of Paul the Roman church, composed largely of Gentiles,* was gaining prominence in the Christian world. This motivated Paul to write to it and visit it, so that it would be considered among his spheres of service and aid him in his projected mission to Spain.

1. Rome in the First Century A.D.
2. Roman Christianity

## 1. Rome in the First Century A.D.

With a population of about one million people, the city of Rome in the first century A.D. drew people from every corner of the Empire and beyond. During Augustus's reign (27 B.C.-A.D. 14) an urban police force (*cohortes urbanae*) and fire prevention units (*vigiles*) were added to keep order in the growing city. Like the great cities of today, Rome was the place to visit in the imperial period. Paul's declaration that he had purposed many times to visit the Roman Christians before writing his letter to them (Rom 1:13) was therefore very similar to what any provincial would say before making final arrangements for a trip to Rome.

*1.1. Ethnic Diversity in Rome.* From at least the third century B.C. Rome had been a drawing point for people of a variety of ethnic backgrounds. The immigration of provincial Italians and Greeks that was occurring under the Republic was eclipsed in the early Principate by immigration from Syria, Asia Minor (modern Turkey), Egypt, Africa, Spain, and later Gaul and Germany. Juvenal's statement that "Long ago the Orontes has overflowed into the Tiber" (Juvenal *Sat.* 3.62) shows his perception of the high number of Semitic people living in first-century Rome. Most significant for a study of Roman Christianity are the Jewish immigrants. Record of a Jewish presence in Rome dates from 139 B.C., and it is known that the number of Jewish residents in Rome increased when in 62 B.C. Pompey brought back a large number of Jewish captives for use as slaves. By the time Cicero defended Flaccus in 59 B.C., it appears that the Jews were a significant political interest group in Rome (Cicero *Pro Flacco* 66). In the civil war that began in 49 B.C., the Jews in Rome and throughout the Mediterranean world supported Julius Caesar against Pompey. This explains why we read of Jews mourning the death of Caesar in 44 B.C. (Suetonius *Julius* 84.5). It is estimated that there were at least 40,000 Jews in Rome during the first century A.D. (*see* Diaspora). Literary sources from the late Republic and early Empire show that these foreign residents in Rome (*peregrini*) were not fully accepted and experienced racial discrimination. Greeks received slurs (Cicero *Ep.* 16.4.2; *Tusc.* 2.65; *De Orat.* 1.105; 2.13). Africans were also despised (Livy 30.12.18; Sallust *Iug.* 91.7). The Jews certainly were not exempt from such discrimination (Cicero *Pro Flacco* 66-69; Horace *Sat.* 1.9.71-72). The ethnic diversity in Rome gives rise to Paul's scope in his letter to the Romans,* where he is concerned about God's dealings with all of humanity, both Jew and Gentile (Rom 1:16; 1:18—2:29), both civilized and uncivilized (Rom 1:14). The diversity also makes it clear why the apostle* to the Gentiles would want to minister in Rome.

*1.2. Roman Religion.* Roman religion and the state's policies toward religion* affected the reception that the Roman people gave to foreign religions, including Christianity. Roman religion also affected the way Paul framed his gospel* when writing Romans (*see* Religions, Greco-Roman; Worship).

*1.2.1. Features.* It is important to know that Roman religion was closely bound up with the government of Rome. The priests of this state religion served as advisors to the senate. They were consulted for discerning the divine will through signs and for purifying significant areas (*augures*), setting the calendar and establishing religious law (*pontifices*), making war in religiously correct ways (*fetiales*), and keeping and interpreting the *Sibylline Books* (*duoviri* [later *decemviri*] *sacris faciundis*). Priests, by their function of interpreting foreign books (especially in the third century B.C.), served to call for the acceptance of certain foreign religions into Rome. At the end of the Republican age the *haruspices* (lit. "soothsayers") were organized as a priestly college. Its members were trained to discern the divine will from the entrails of sacrificial animals. Everywhere in first-century Rome there were reminders of the gods. On the hill known as Capitolium a large temple was dedicated to Jupiter, Juno and Minerva in the first year of the Republic. Though it burned in 83 B.C., a new temple was built in 69 B.C. This was repaired and embellished by Augustus in both 26 and 9 B.C. The temple therefore dominated the city when Christianity first made inroads there. On the southern border of the political center, the Forum, were temples of Saturn, the Castores, Vesta and the office spaces of the *pontifices* and another member of their priestly college, the *rex sacrorum* ("king of sacred things," a religious post representing the ancient kings of Rome). Privately, the *lares* (shrines for dead family members) and *di penates* (gods of the family cupboard) were constant reminders in the home of the connection in the Roman religious mind between this world and the other (*see* Worship).

Participation in religious ritual was a way of life for Romans. The possibility of choosing a religion and joining a group defined only for its religious identity was unknown. Groups that were organized solely for religious purposes, with the exception of vocational priesthoods in the state religion, synagogues and later the churches, were unknown. Though there were *collegia* named after certain deities, the members of such associations were joined by a common occupation or ethnic background. The churches in Rome arguably showed their faith as the organizing principle more than synagogues, since the churches likely consisted of a greater variety in ethnic and class backgrounds.

*1.2.2. Legal Orientation.* In public and in private, Roman religion was in essence the performance of ritual. Hence the great emphasis on the proper observance of ritual (Pliny *Nat. Hist.* 13.10). The organization of the priesthoods so closely with the legislative government and the elaborate rules within Roman religion point to the essential legal character of religion. Indeed, far from espousing a personal relationship with the gods, Roman religion taught that if one followed the rituals correctly, a contract would be made that obtained the "peace of the gods" (*pax deorum*). Paul's statement that believers have "peace* with God" on the basis of faith (Rom 5:1-2) thus gains significance when we know the impersonal and contractual connotation of such an idea in the background of his audience. Since the Romans considered religion as in essence a legal matter, it is possible that Paul had to present his gospel* to the Romans in legal terms, covering God's general moral law (Rom 2:14-16), Torah (Rom 3:21; 10:4) and political law (Rom 13:1-7). So his focus in the letter to the Romans on questions of law (Rom 2:12-27; 4:13-16; 7 passim) and his acknowledgement that his readers "know law" (Rom 7:1) are not simply reflections of the Jewish preoccupation with Torah nor the high percentage of secular lawyers in Roman society, but show Paul's recognition that Romans viewed religion as a matter of law.

*1.2.3. Emphasis on Rationality.* The Roman emphasis on "legal etiquette" in religion presupposed that the gods were rational, a point not shared with most foreign cults introduced to Rome. The religious vow of 217 B.C. (Livy 22.10) illustrates how a Roman priest could treat the gods as rational bargaining partners, much as one person would reason with another. Paul must have known of this rational emphasis, for it is his letter to the Romans that most emphasizes being rational in religion. The rational God hands over those who ignore him "to an unfit mind" (Rom 1:28); acting against one's mind is perceived as acting against God (Rom 7:20-24) and presenting one's body to God is reasonable religion, accompanied by a renewed mind (Rom 12:1-2).

*1.2.4. Roman Policies and Attitudes to Foreign Religions.* As one of the later foreign religions to seek entrance into Rome, Christianity inherited stereotypes and government policies developed from past encounters between the Roman government and foreign religions. Any study of church-state relations must not only begin with the state religion of Rome, but must also include the reception Rome gave to the foreign religions that antedated Christianity. It is first of all necessary to make clear that foreign religions could not be introduced in Rome without official approval from the senate. As seen above with Roman state religion, the Romans viewed religion as a concern of the state. Since the late Republic, Rome looked at all foreign religions with much suspicion. At the same time it was ready to attempt the introduction of a foreign religion when it perceived that cults offered a solution to an unmet need in Rome. For example the Asclepius cult (known in Rome as *Aesculapius*) was brought from Epidaurus to Rome when in 293 B.C. the Roman priests who kept the *Sibylline Books* called for its importation to quell a plague. Its temple on the island of Tiber was dedicated on January 1, 291 B.C. The minor deity Hygieia was also worshiped there, to whom the Romans later attached the name of their Italian goddess, Salus.

The official importation of a new cult did not mean that the state religion was somehow abandoned. There was actually no mechanism in Roman religion for abolishing any traditional practice. Rather, new cults were brought to Rome and new interpretations of state religion were made as history progressed. Religious exclusivism, such as was found in Judaism and Christianity, was therefore unheard of to the Roman religious mind. While Rome could bring in new religions for its people, it did not do this regularly after an event in 186 B.C. that raised the government's suspicions about foreign religions. In this year the Roman Senate acted to forbid the practice of the Dionysian *orgia*, or *bacchanalia*, as they are called in Latin. This cult had entered Rome from Campanian Italy. In response to the Senate's measures (*CIL* 1.196; *ILS* 18), the people of Rome reacted violently and an outbreak of crime spread through the city (Livy, 39.8-18). This incident, known now as the Bacchanalia, helped shape the Roman stereotype that foreign religions inevitably brought disorder. It stands to reason, then, that when Christianity entered Rome it was viewed with suspicion.

*1.2.5. Judaism in Rome.* Judaism had been accorded the status of a legal religion (*religio licita*) by Julius Caesar and then Augustus. This meant that the Jewish people were given permission to meet for religious purposes in their synagogues, and the Jews' observance of the Sabbath could not be used to their disadvantage. It is true that Jews were expelled from Rome in 139 B.C. (Valerius Maximus *Fact. ac dict.* 1.3.2), in A.D. 19 (Josephus *Ant.* 18.3.5 §§81-84; Tacitus *Ann.*

2.85.5; Suetonius *Tiberius* 36; Dio Cassius *Hist.* 57.18.5) and in A.D. 49 (Suetonius *Claudius* 25.4; Acts 18:1-2). The first two cases were probably a Roman response to active proselytizing by the Jews; the third was probably due to unrest within the Jewish community about Christianity (on the basis of Suetonius's "at the instigation of Chrestus" [*impulsore Chresto*]). But these expulsions were not permanent measures and at least in the latter two cases probably did not apply to Jews who were Roman citizens.

It is also necessary to realize that Judaism in Rome was closely tied to Judaism in Jerusalem.* Around 140 B.C. the high priests in Jerusalem had sent emissaries to Rome in order to offset the power of the Seleucid Empire. Later, ruling priests in the first century B.C. politically endorsed Julius Caesar (and not Pompey, who had entered the Temple in 63 B.C.) and Herod the Great was in political alliance with Augustus. In the first century A.D. princes in the family of Herod such as Agrippa II (who would later hold the rights of appointing high priests in Jerusalem) were raised in Rome under imperial patronage. Far from being an unruly cousin of Judaism in Jerusalem, then, Judaism in Rome was rather its devoted child. It was within the synagogues of Rome that Christianity first gained its inroads there.

## 2. Roman Christianity.

Although Christianity first appeared as a sect of Judaism, the Roman church by the time of Paul's initial visit (A.D. 60) was beginning to make the break with Judaism, a break that must have been complete by A.D. 64 when Nero focused persecution on Christians. The churches in Rome represented a body of Christianity that Paul could not ignore. Their strategic potential came from their close connection with Jerusalem, their location in the world capital, and their connections with the rest of the empire through people groups represented in Rome's congregations.

*2.1. Origins.* The connection between the Jews in Rome and Jerusalem and the Jewish element within early Roman Christianity lead to the probable conclusion that Christianity was brought to Rome by Jewish Christians from Palestine. This is confirmed by the note that Jews from Rome were in Peter's audience in Jerusalem at Pentecost (Acts 2:10). Jewish Christians most probably entered into dialogue with fellow Jews, and this resulted in tumultuous encounters and some conversions. One such encounter occurred in A.D. 49, when Claudius expelled the Jews from Rome. Suetonius's brief description of this event (see 1.2.5. above) is generally taken to mean that the Jews were arguing among themselves about Christ. The identification of

Priscilla and Aquila as Jewish Christians who left Italy when Claudius expelled the Jews from Rome confirms this reconstruction (Acts 18:2).

It is generally accepted that Christianity in Rome arose not in a single church but in a plurality of house churches. The Jewish component in early Roman Christianity suggests that these house churches may have developed in association with various synagogues. Evidence for this plurality of churches comes from Paul's greeting given not to a church (cf. 1 Cor 1:2; 2 Cor 1:1) but to "all those who are in Rome, beloved of God, chosen saints" (Rom 1:7).

*2.2 Characteristics.* The Jewish presence in the Roman church and its ascetic element (see 2.2.3 below) presented both challenges and opportunities for Paul. The slaves who made up part of this church did not deter him from scaling theological heights in the presentation of his gospel, since Paul held that in Christ there is no slave or free (Gal 3:28) and considered himself bound to communicate his gospel to all (Rom 1:14-15).

*2.2.1. Jewish Presence.* Because of its likely origin in the synagogues of Rome, Jewish Christianity retained a close connection with its Jewish roots in Jerusalem. Paul's letter to the church is evidence for this (Rom 1:16; 3:1-30; 9-11). Half a century later, when Tacitus describes Christianity, he links it to Judea (Tacitus *Ann.* 15.44.2). Roman Christianity must have included a distinctly Jewish element. Theologically such a presence within the church most representative of the world's peoples forced Paul to outline his gospel in a manner that accounted for God's dealings with all people (Rom 2:1-16; 15:7- 13). Apologetically a letter and visit to this church provided opportunities for Paul to defend himself to people with close ties to the groups that most criticized and resisted Paul's ministry, the Judaism and Christianity of Jerusalem. Thus we see Paul working to defend before the Romans his theology (Rom 6:1-2) and mission* strategy (Rom 15:14-24). His upcoming visit to Jerusalem is explained and addressed to them as a worthwhile and spiritual endeavor (Rom 15:25-32). While Roman Christianity was primarily composed of Gentiles, as Paul's letter shows, it is probable that there was an ethnically Jewish presence in the Roman churches.

*2.2.2. Servile Presence.* Since many Jews first came to Rome as slaves, it is likely that some of the Jews within the Roman churches were of the servile classes (either slaves or freedmen and freedwomen; *see* Slavery). The slaves in Rome were primarily of foreign origin in the first century of the Principate. While there were certainly some freeborn foreigners in Rome, the possibility that many were servile foreigners fits with Suetonius's conviction that Nero administered Roman law properly when crucifying Christians (Suetonius *Nero* 16.2; 19.3), since Roman law prohibited crucifixion* of its citizens. Further evidence for the servile nature of the Roman church are the references to those of certain "households"* (Rom 16:10-11), a standard euphemism for the servile classes.

*2.2.3. Asceticism.* La Piana has suggested an ascetic element within the first-century Roman church. This seems fully in accord with extra-biblical evidence and indications in Paul's letter to the Romans. Vegetarianism was taught in the school of Quintus Sextius in the early first century. The philosopher Sotion led Seneca to practice vegetarianism for a time (Seneca *Ep.* 108.22). Another philosopher who was very influential during the reign of Nero, Musonius Rufus, also taught vegetarianism (*Peri Trophes* ed. Hense, 95). Vegetarianism is reflected in *1 Clement* 20.4, while asceticism in dress is mentioned in 17.1 of the same letter. Biblical evidence for asceticism in Roman Christianity comes from Hebrews 13:9 and Romans 14:1-3, 21. In the latter reference the "strong"* and "weak" are differentiated within the Roman church by different postures toward ascetic practice. The mind/body dualism common to ascetics is found in Romans 1:24; 6:19; 7:23-24; 12:1-2. Later we see the ascetic tendencies of Roman Christianity worked out in one of its leaders, Tatian (fl. in Rome A.D. 160-172). The ascetic movement within the Roman church at the time Paul wrote his letter prompted him to delineate an ethic of responsibility in which the "strong" in conscience was to respect the "weak," more ascetic, Christian (Rom 14:14-17; 15:1-3).

*2.3. Influence.* By the time Paul wrote Romans, it is clear that the Roman church was ascendant in influence among churches of the Mediterranean world. Paul's uncharacteristic desire to visit the church in Rome that he had not founded is evidence of this (Rom 1:9-13; cf. 15:20). His need for the Roman church's endorsement and support (Rom 15:22-24) also shows the influence that this church carried in the Mediterranean world. Extra-biblical evidence for the influence of Rome comes as early as A.D. 96, when a letter from the church at Rome to the church at Corinth, *1 Clement*, was written. In this letter we see the Roman church expecting its directives to its sister church in Corinth to be followed (*1 Clement* 7.1-3; 62.1-3; 65.1, cf. Ignatius *Rom.* Introduction).

*2.4. Paul's Relationship with Roman Christianity.* Though the church in Rome was not founded by an apostle, Paul is associated with its early history. As apostle to the Gentiles, he considered this within his sphere of ministry (Rom 1:11-15). His relationship

with Roman Christianity certainly bore fruit from his presence there and continues to do so through his letter to the Romans.

*2.4.1. Before A.D. 60.* One's understanding of the relationship that Paul had with Roman Christianity before his visit in A.D. 60 affects not only one's conception of early church history, but also one's interpretation of the letter to the Romans.* For if Paul knew some of the Roman Christians and the circumstances of the churches there, his letter must be read not simply as a general theological treatise, but as an occasional letter to a particular body of believers. While it is true that Romans is the most systematic of Paul's letters, its occasional nature cannot be denied. The influence that Roman Christianity enjoyed likely meant that Christians throughout the Empire knew something about the Roman church. Paul's statement "Your faith is announced throughout the whole world" (Rom 1:8) is certainly more than epistolary flattery. Paul met Christians from Rome at least by A.D. 50, after Aquila and Priscilla had come to Corinth from Rome (Acts 18:1-2; cf. Rom 16:3-5). Christians in Pauline circles no doubt had associations with other Christians in Rome. The best evidence for this is Romans 16. While this chapter has been assigned an Ephesian destination by T. W. Manson, later works by Gamble, Lampe and Ollrog have conclusively demonstrated the integrity of this chapter as a part of the original letter. On the basis of Romans 16, then, it is most probable that Paul knew a number of people in Rome. The letter is written in order to strengthen an already existing relationship.

*2.4.2. After A.D. 60.* Paul arrived in Rome c. A.D. 60 (Acts 28:14-16) in order to stand trial before Nero's representative, the Praetorian prefect (*see* Political Systems). By the time Paul arrived in Rome, Nero had murdered his mother, his advisor Burrus had died and Seneca had retired. Rumors were probably spreading that the imperial government did not seem as stable as in the earlier part of Nero's reign. According to tradition Paul was freed after his first trial. From *1 Clement*'s testimony that Paul "reached the limits of the West" (*1 Clement* 5:7), it is possible that Paul then reached Spain as intended (Rom 15:24). It is then most likely that Paul was arrested and imprisoned again at Rome, where he was executed sometime between A.D. 64-67. *First Clement* 5:2-5, in citing "pillars of the church," mentions Peter first and then Paul as examples of endurance under suffering. Today one can see a carving of both apostles baptizing their jailers in the Mamertine Prison (Rome's state prison), another testimony to the tradition that both men suffered for their faith in Rome. The details of Paul's second trial (if he had one) and martyrdom are unknown. Tradition tells us that he was beheaded on the Ostian Way at about the same time and place as Peter (Eusebius *Hist. Eccl.* 2.25.7-8). While the account of milk spurting out of his beheaded body is obviously legendary (*Acts of Paul* 11.5), Paul's association with Roman Christianity continues to provide both milk and solid food (1 Cor 3:2) for Christians throughout the world.

*See also* CAESAR'S HOUSEHOLD, IMPERIAL HOUSEHOLD; CITIZENSHIP, ROMAN AND HEAVENLY; EMPERORS, ROMAN; LEGAL SYSTEM, ROMAN; PASTORAL LETTERS; POLITICAL SYSTEMS; RELIGIONS, GRECO-ROMAN; ROMANS, LETTER TO THE; STRONG AND WEAK.

BIBLIOGRAPHY. M. Beard and M. Crawford, *Rome in the Late Republic* (London: Duckworth, 1985) 25-39; R. E. Brown and J. P. Meier, *Antioch and Rome: New Testament Cradles of Catholic Christianity* (New York: Paulist, 1983); H. Gamble, Jr., *The Textual History of the Letter to the Romans* (Grand Rapids: Eerdmans, 1977); P. Garnsey and R. Saller, *The Roman Empire: Economy, Society and Culture* (Berkeley: University of California, 1987); P. Lampe, *Die stadtrömischen Christen in den ersten beiden Jahrhunderten: Untersuchungen zur Sozialgeschichte* (WUNT 2.18; 2d ed.; Tübingen: J. C. B. Mohr, 1989); G. La Piana, "La primitiva communità cristiana di Roma e l'epistola ai Romani," *Ricerche Religiose* 1 (1925) 209-26; 305-26; idem, "Foreign Groups in Rome during the First Centuries of the Empire," *HTR* 20 (1927) 183-403; H. J. Leon, *The Jews of Ancient Rome* (Philadelphia: Jewish Publication Society of America, 1960); T. W. Manson, "St. Paul's Letter to the Romans—and Others," in *The Romans Debate*, ed. K. P. Donfried (Minneapolis: Augsburg, 1978) 1-16; J. A. North, "Conservatism and Change in Roman Religion," *PBSR* 44 (1976) 1-12; idem, "Religion in Republican Rome," in *CAH* 7.2.573-624; W.-H. Ollrog, "Die Abfassungsverhältnisse von Röm 16," in *Kirche*, FS Günther Bornkamm, ed. D. Lührmann and G. Strecker (Tübingen: J. C. B. Mohr, 1980) 221-44.

M. Reasoner

**RULER CULTS.** *See* EMPERORS; RELIGIONS, GRECO-ROMAN.

**RULERS.** *See* CIVIL AUTHORITY; EMPERORS, ROMAN; POLITICAL SYSTEMS; PRINCIPALITIES AND POWERS.

# S

**SABBATH.** *See* HOLY DAYS.

## SACRIFICE, OFFERING

In the world into which Christianity was born animal sacrifice was almost universally the central feature of worship.* The religions* of antiquity had marked differences from one another, but the offering of sacrifice to the deity, or gods/goddesses, featured in every cultus. The Christians formed a solitary group with their total rejection of the offering of animals.

    1. The Sacrifice of Christ
    2. Rejection of Customary Sacrifices
    3. Christian Sacrifice

### 1. The Sacrifice of Christ.

Paul emphasizes that Christ has made the perfect sacrifice that puts away the sins* of humankind. He sometimes speaks of that sacrifice in general terms, as when he says that Christ loved us and "gave himself for us, an offering and a sacrifice to God" (Eph 5:2). Or he may select one specific sacrifice—for example, Christ as the "first fruits"* (1 Cor 15:20, 23), an expression that refers to the first sheaf of the harvest which was brought to the Temple* and offered in sacrifice to God (Lev 23; Deut 16). It is clear that, for Paul, Christ had offered the perfect sacrifice that put away sins once and for all, and because of this there was no longer a place for any of the customary offerings. This makes the sacrifice of Christ of critical importance. It is that sacrifice on which the forgiveness* of all the sins of all the believers depended.

In 1 Corinthians 5:7 Paul, rebuking the Corinthians for their failure to discipline erring members, likens the immorality in their midst to the little yeast that leavens a "whole batch of dough." Prior to the Jewish celebration of Passover, all leaven was to be removed from the house. The church now was to "clean out the old yeast," which served in this case as an image for evil (cf. Gal 5:9; Mt 13:33; Lk 13:20-21), and be the "new batch" which they have already become (1 Cor 5:7). This has taken place by divine initiative, symbolized by Christ, "our Passover" (*to pascha hēmōn*) who

has already been sacrificed. The original Passover delivered Israel from death to life, in which the ways of Egypt had no place. Paul uses the image of Passover only glancingly, but it echoes the early-Christian tradition that Jesus chose to die at Passover and ate his Last Supper with the disciples as a Passover meal. Now Paul can enjoin his fellow-believers to "keep the feast . . . with the unleavened bread of sincerity and truth" (1 Cor 5:8). In all likelihood Paul is using "the feast" as a metaphor for holy living based on the reality of Christ's saving death. But some interpreters have caught an allusion to the Lord's Supper,* or primitive Christian liturgy of Passover, which Paul is enjoining the Corinthians to keep without "the yeast of malice and evil" (see Jeremias, 901).

Sacrifice is in mind when Paul says that God set forth Christ as "a propitiation, through faith, in his blood" (Rom 3:25; *see* Expiation, Propitiation, Mercy Seat). The passage refers to the divine wrath* against sin, a wrath which is dealt with by Christ's offering of himself. "Blood" here will have sacrificial connotations as well as its customary meaning of the infliction of death. It is possible also to see a reference to the sin offering in Paul's statement in Romans 8:3 that God sent his Son* "in the likeness of sinful flesh and *for sin*" (*peri hamartias*; NIV translates "to be a sin offering"; cf. 2 Cor 5:21, where "made him to be sin" also suggests a sin offering). The expression "for sin" is the usual rendering of "sin offering" in LXX. It is far from certain that this is the meaning in Romans 8:3, but it is a possibility, and it certainly is the case that Christ's death accomplished all that to which the "sin offering" pointed. Some interpreters have called attention to the sacrifice, or "binding" (*'Aqedah*) of Isaac (Gen 22), which in early Judaism (particularly in the Palestinian Targums) was understood to have an atoning sense (see Daly, though the currency of this idea in pre-A.D. 70 Judaism has been questioned; see Davies and Chilton, Alexander). This background might stand behind Paul's reference to God, "who did not withhold his own Son, but gave him up for all of us" (Rom 8:32 NRSV; cf. Gen 22:16 LXX).

## 2. Rejection of Customary Sacrifices.

Paul is clear that the sacrifices customary in the religions of his day were of no avail to meet human need. Worshipers in the Roman world held that they were offering their sacrifices to a variety of deities (see Yerkes), but for Paul it was clear that those deities were not real (so 1 Cor 8:4-6, in spite of Paul's *ad hominem* argument in 1 Cor 10:20-22). There is only one God* and the one sacrifice he recognizes is the sacrifice of Christ. But Paul says more than that the sacrifices in the religions were simply useless. They were worse than that, for the demons* were the recipients of these sacrifices; in effect the sacrifices were offered to the demons (1 Cor 10:20; *see* Idolatry; Religions).

We see this in Paul's rejection of the use of food* that had been offered to an idol. The practice in most animal sacrifices in antiquity was that part of the animal was burnt on the altar, part was eaten by the worshipers at a solemn meal in the temple, and part was given to the priests for their own use or to be sold in the market. Some Christians evidently held that since an idol is nothing it did not matter that meat had been offered to it. Paul agrees that an idol is nothing (1 Cor 8:4), but that does not mean that Christian converts might continue to eat meat offered in idol sacrifices. Christians invited to dinner by an idol worshiper might well find meat set before them that had been offered to an idol before being sold on the market. Paul agrees that an idol is nothing and that there can be no contamination in such meat. So believers might well eat it without question. But if someone with a weak conscience* were to point out to them that the meat had been part of a sacrifice, then they should not eat it. It is no longer good food that has come to them by unknown paths, but the end result of idol worship, i.e. worship that is offered to demons. Christians should therefore have no part in eating such meat (1 Cor 8:4-13; 10:19-22, 25-30).

## 3. Christian Sacrifice.

Paul uses the terminology of sacrifice to teach important truths about Christian service. Thus he exhorts the Romans to present their bodies "a living sacrifice" (Rom 12:1), a vivid and forceful way of indicating the need for the complete offering of the worshiper to God. Christians are to be totally committed to God. Similarly Paul speaks of "the offering [*prosphora*] of the Gentiles*" as "acceptable, sanctified in the Holy Spirit*" (Rom 15:16; on whether by "offering *of* the Gentiles" we should understand the Gentiles to be the offering [cf. Is 66:20] or the offering made by the Gentiles [i.e., their priestly ministry] see commentaries).

The apostle applies the terminology of offering and sacrifice to himself, saying to the Philippians that he is "offered [the verb *spendomai* means 'poured out as a drink offering,' cf., e.g., Lev 23:37] on the sacrifice [*thysia*] and service of your faith" (Phil 2:17). He combines the thought of his own giving of himself in sacrificial service (or in his death) with that of Philippians' service. He returns to sacrificial imagery when he speaks of the gifts the Philippians had made to him as "a sacrifice" (Phil 4:18). As could other sectors of Second Temple Judaism (e.g., 1QS 9:3-5; 4QFlor 1:6-7), Paul spiritualizes the sacrificial idioms of the OT cultus.

Paul also uses the imagery of first fruits.* He brings out the thought that ultimately all Israel will be saved by reminding the Romans that "if the part of the dough offered as first fruits is holy, then the whole batch is holy" (Rom 11:16 NRSV). The Jewish patriarchs are seen as the first fruits, and Paul sees this as having its consequences. The first part of the dough offered in sacrifice makes the whole from which it is taken holy.* The Jewish patriarchs likewise have sanctified the whole nation. When he speaks of individual Christians as first fruits (Rom 16:5; 1 Cor 16:15) Paul is saying that their coming to believe carried with it the thought that there would be other believers; they in some sense sanctified the local church.* There is a not dissimilar thought when, in discussing the resurrection,* Paul speaks of Christ as "the first fruits" (1 Cor 15:20, 23). His resurrection carries with it the implication that there would be others resurrected in the end time purpose of God.

*See also* CROSS, THEOLOGY OF THE; DEATH OF CHRIST; EXPIATION, PROPITIATION, MERCY SEAT; FIRST FRUITS, DOWNPAYMENT; LORD'S SUPPER; REDEMPTION; WORSHIP.

BIBLIOGRAPHY. P. S. Alexander, "Aqedah," in *Dictionary of Biblical Interpretation*, ed. R. J. Coggins and J. L. Houlden (Philadelphia: Trinity Press International, 1990) 44-47; J. Behm, "θύω κτλ," *TDNT* III.180-90; R. J. Daly, *The Origins of the Christian Doctrine of Sacrifice* (Philadelphia: Fortress, 1978) 59-65; idem, "The Soteriological Significance of the Sacrifice of Isaac," *CBQ* 39 (1977) 45-75; P. R. Davies and B. D. Chilton, "The Aqedah: A Revised Tradition History," *CBQ* 40 (1978) 514-46; G. D. Fee, "II Corinthians vi.14—vii.i," *NTS* 23 (1976-77) 140-61; E. Ferguson, "Spiritual Sacrifice in Early Christianity and Its Environment," *ANRW* 2.23.2.1151-89; M. Hengel, *The Atonement: The Origins of the Doctrine in the New Testament* (Philadelphia: Fortress, 1981); J. Jeremias, "πάσχα" *TDNT* V.896-904; E. L. Kendall, *A Living Sacrifice* (London: SCM, 1960); H.-J. Klauck, "Kultische Symbolsprache bei Paulus," in *Gemeinde—Amt—Sacrament: Neutestamentliche Perspek-*

*tiven*, ed. H. J. Klauck (Würzburg: Echter, 1989) 348-58; J. Lambrecht, " 'Reconcile Yourselves' . . . A Reading of 2 Cor 5:11-21," in *The Diakonia of the Spirit (2 Cor 4:7—7:4)* (Rome: Benedictina, 1989); S. Lyonnet and L. Sabourin, *Sin, Redemption and Sacrifice* (AnBib 48; Rome: Pontifical Biblical Institute, 1970); L. Morris, *The Atonement* (Downers Grove, IL: InterVarsity, 1983) 43-67; F. Thiele and C. Brown, "Sacrifice etc.," *NIDNTT* 3.415-38; H. Thyen, "θυσία, θύω," *EDNT* 2.161- 63; R. K. Yerkes, *Sacrifice in Greek and Roman Religions and Early Judaism* (New York: Scribners, 1952); F. M. Young, *Sacrifice and the Death of Christ* (London: SCM, 1975).

L. Morris

# SALVATION

*Salvation* is a general term, denoting deliverance of varying kinds. It may be used of the healing of disease, of safety in travel and of preservation in times of peril. It may apply to people or to things. In the OT, when Israel was threatened by hostile nations, the term is used of God's protection. In the Gospels it is often used of Jesus' healings ("Your faith has saved [i.e., healed] you"). But the term is also used for deliverance from sin and for the ultimate deliverance when the saved enter bliss with Christ at the end of the age.

In the Pauline writings the important thing is deliverance from sin and from the consequences of sin,* though it is much more common for Paul to speak simply of salvation than to say what people are saved from. He uses the verb *sōzō* ("to save") twenty-nine times (which is more than anyone else in the NT), the noun *sōtēr* ("savior") twelve times (exactly half its NT occurrences), *sōtēria* ("salvation") eighteen times, *sōtērion* ("salvation") and *sōtērios* ("bringing salvation") once each. He uses *rhuomai* ("to rescue") eleven times. Such statistics show that Paul is interested in the concept of salvation, more so, indeed, than any other NT writer.

Salvation has a wide range of meaning and there are different emphases in different parts of the NT. In the Gospels, for example, we often have stories of Jesus doing miracles accompanied by such words as "your faith has saved you." In such contexts salvation has a strong physical component (though we would be wise not to exclude a spiritual component even in such passages). But this is not a Pauline usage (except in a few possible places, e.g., 1 Tim 2:15: see 3 below). For Paul "salvation" refers to what Christ has done in his great saving act for sinners; all the Pauline passages bear on this act in some way. It is central to the Pauline understanding of Christianity, for salvation is the very purpose of the incarnation of the Son of God:

"Christ Jesus came into the world to save sinners" (1 Tim 1:15). Salvation is a comprehensive word bringing out the truth that God in Christ has rescued people from the desperate state that their sins had brought about.

1. "God Our Savior"
2. Human Agents in Salvation
3. Who Will be Saved?
4. Salvation in the Past
5. Salvation Now
6. A Future Salvation

## 1. "God Our Savior."

In the Pastoral* Letters there are several references to "God* our Savior*" (1 Tim 1:1; 2:3; Tit 1:3; 2:10; 3:4), or to "Christ* our Savior" (2 Tim 1:10; Tit 1:4; 2:13; 3:6). No great deal of difference should be made between these two groups of passages, for the accepted NT teaching that God acted in Christ is summed up in Paul's own words: "God was in Christ reconciling the world to himself" (2 Cor 5:19). From one point of view it is clear enough that salvation originated with the Father, and from another it was the Son* who did what was necessary to bring about salvation.

Paul writes that God did not destine the Thessalonians for wrath* but for salvation "through our Lord Jesus Christ" (1 Thess 5:9). It is Jesus who "delivers us from the wrath to come" (1 Thess 1:10), or to put it slightly differently, it is "through" Christ that believers shall be saved from the wrath (Rom 5:9). Paul develops this thought by saying that sinners were God's enemies* but that they have now been reconciled through the death of the Son and, having been reconciled, "we will be saved in his life" (Rom 5:10; *see* Peace, Reconciliation). It is unlikely that we should understand the apostle to mean that the death* of Jesus effects one form of salvation and his resurrected life another. He is referring to one great act of salvation involving the death and the resurrection* of Jesus, a salvation that delivers the saved from wrath and gives them continuing life. If the preposition "in" is significant, Paul is saying that our full salvation means being saved "in" the life of Christ. As he often speaks of being "in" Christ, this may well be the meaning here. It is explicit when he writes of people obtaining salvation "in Christ Jesus" (2 Tim 2:10). He can also refer to the importance of the Scriptures which can make us "wise unto salvation through faith in Christ Jesus" (2 Tim 3:15).

That salvation has its origin in God is brought out by speaking of God's "call"*: God "saved us and called us with a holy calling" (2 Tim 1:9). The idea of call is an important one for Paul, and here it brings out the truth that salvation comes as a result of a prior divine initiative. Or it may be linked with grace to bring out the fact that salvation is for all (Tit 2:11). This means that salvation is available to all, not that every individual is saved (*see* Universalism).

Paul uses a number of expressions that bring out the thought that salvation comes "through" the Christian message. Thus God was pleased to save believers "through the foolishness of what was preached" (1 Cor 1:21). Later in the same letter Paul makes known "the gospel . . . through which you were saved" (1 Cor 15:1-2). In both cases the preaching clearly means the preaching of what Christ has accomplished in dying for sinners. They are saved by what he has done. Paul can equate "the word of truth" with "the gospel of your salvation" (Eph 1:13), which underlies the reliability of the gospel* proclamation. The gospel tells of divine truth.* And it tells of divine action. The reference to the person who "will be saved, but so as through fire" (1 Cor 3:15) envisages a believer who has achieved so little in the Christian life that on the day of judgment* his or her work will be "burned up." But, being on the foundation Christ laid, that person will be saved. It is Christ who brings salvation, not human effort. It is the sure foundation, not the uncertain work, that is ultimately important.

Nowhere does Paul speak of a salvation brought about by human effort. He does indeed speak of himself and his coworkers* as being "afflicted"* for the salvation of the Corinthians (2 Cor 1:6; cf. Col 1:24), but this means no more than that the evangelists had to undergo troubles to bring the message of salvation to people; it certainly does not mean that their troubles merited the salvation of their hearers. This passage also speaks of the apostle as being encouraged, but it was not the encouragement Paul received that brought salvation. Salvation always comes from God. Another passage indicates that the troubles of the early believers were a token of their salvation (Phil 1:28).

Paul uses the language of salvation to bring out aspects of the great truth that when sinners could do nothing to escape the results of their evil deeds, God took action to deliver them. "By grace you have been saved," he writes to the Ephesians (Eph 2:8), an expression that follows "and he has made us alive in Christ when we were dead in our transgressions" (Eph 2:5). The implication is that sins bring death, but that Christ brings life to people who are dead in sin. So we find that it is "not of works of righteousness that we have done, but according to his mercy he saved us" (Tit 3:5).

The initiative in salvation is with God: "God chose us . . . for salvation" (2 Thess 2:13). Indeed almost every passage dealing with salvation could be cited, for characteristically Paul (like the other NT writers) puts before his readers information about a salvation in one sense already brought about by Christ and in another sense to be consummated in the age to come. In neither is there the slightest suggestion that human effort avails. It is relevant that Paul prays for the salvation of Israel* (Rom 10:1), for if their salvation is a matter for prayer,* then clearly it is to be a gift of God. Salvation is brought about by God in Christ. Christians are "the saved" (1 Cor 1:18; 2 Cor 2:15), not "saving ones" or people saved by their own efforts. This is so also when faith is linked with salvation (Rom 10:9; 1 Cor 1:21; Eph 2:8), for faith means trusting in Christ or in God, not relying on one's own efforts.

## 2. Human Agents in Salvation.

There are some passages where human agency is named in the bringing about of salvation, though this, of course, does not mean that people can save one another. When Paul, for example, speaks of himself saving some of the Israelites (Rom 11:14) he does not mean that his efforts will effect salvation, but only that he brings a message which he hopes will cause some of his own nation to turn to God and thus enter the salvation God alone can give. A similar comment should be made about a woman saving her husband and a man saving his wife (1 Cor 7:16). Paul is not claiming that people can effect the salvation of family members, but rather that a Christian wife or husband can so live as to cause the partner to turn to God and receive salvation from him. Paul sees the principle as of universal application among Christians. He concludes a passage on eating food* offered to idols* by telling his correspondents that whatever they eat or drink, indeed whatever they do, they should do all things for God's glory. He claims that he himself pleases everyone in all he does; he does not look for personal profit, but for that of the many "in order that they may be saved" (1 Cor 10:31-33).

Timothy is urged to remain in "the teaching." By doing this he will save himself "and those who hear you" (1 Tim 4:16). The reference to "the teaching" shows that the writer is not referring to some meritorious activity, but to the teaching that Christ is Savior. And those who hear this will be with Timothy in salvation. Again there is the thought of human effort leading to the salvation of other people. But it is God in Christ who saves.

## 3. Who Will Be Saved?

The fact that salvation is a divine deliverance does not mean that everybody will be saved. Paul quotes from

Isaiah the words, "If the number of the children of Israel be as the sand of the sea, it is the remnant that will be saved" (Rom 9:27). The article is important; Paul does not say "a" remnant but "the" remnant. He is referring to the biblical remnant, the remnant that God has spoken of through his prophets. This remnant is the real people of God, and salvation comes to them, not to the multitudes of the nation, careless as these multitudes are about the things of God.

We should notice that while Paul looks to God to bring salvation to Israel, this does not mean that he sees himself as excused from doing anything to help his nation. Indeed, he regards his ministry* to the Gentiles* at any rate, as in one respect a means of commending the gospel to the Jews. He refers to his position as "the apostle* of the Gentiles" and trusts that his labors in that capacity "will provoke my own flesh and I will save some of them" (Rom 11:13-14). "My own flesh*" is unusual in the sense of "member of the same nation," but it emphasizes Paul's sense of kinship with the nation Israel. And he is expressing the hope that the success of his labors among the Gentiles will have its effect on the Jews so that "some of them," too, will be saved.

He regards it as a principal count against the Jews that they forbade the Christian preachers "to speak to the Gentiles so that they might be saved" (1 Thess 2:16). In another context he speaks of becoming "all things to all people so that by all means I may save some" (1 Cor 9:22). It is clear that for the apostle the bringing of salvation to people everywhere was of the first importance and that, though his own ministry was largely to the Gentiles, this did not mean that he had ceased to care about Israel. His agonizing over his nation in Romans 9—11 should never be forgotten.

We should probably understand the statement that God wills "all people to be saved" (1 Tim 2:4) in this connection. It is the negation of all exclusivism, be it that of the Jews or of the later Gnostics* (who confined salvation to those who had special enlightenment). "All" is to be understood in the same way as it is in the following sentence, which speaks of Christ as giving himself "as a ransom for all" (1 Tim 2:6). We should certainly not take it in the sense that God sets his will on the salvation of the whole human race and is disappointed. Another passage of the same sort is that in which God is referred to as "the Savior of all people, especially believers" (1 Tim 4:10). We should perhaps understand "Savior" here as "Preserver" (for God does "save" us all in some sense), but the emphasis on believers shows that the salvation that matters comes only to people of faith. We should remember that the Philippians were exhorted, "With fear* and trembling work out your salvation" (Phil 2:12). The plural may mean that the whole church is being exhorted to work hard at its spiritual wellbeing. If it is applied to the individual the meaning must be much the same. Paul never sees salvation as the result of the individual's own efforts, and it would be perverse to find such a meaning here (see Hawthorne, 98-100).

In a very difficult passage we are told that "the woman was deceived" (a reference to Eve), but that "she will be saved through the childbearing . . . if they abide in faith" (1 Tim 2:14-15). The plural shows that Paul is speaking of Christian women generally, not confining his remarks to Eve, but it is not easy to see how childbearing brings salvation ("this would be a very odd form of salvation by works," Ward, 53). Some interpreters have held that we should emphasize "the" childbearing (i.e., the bearing of *the* child) and see a reference to Christ, others that Christian women are assured of safe delivery. Paul later speaks of people who forbade marriage* (1 Tim 4:3), and it may well be that he is opposing false teaching and saying that women will be saved (provided, of course, that they "abide in faith and love and sanctification," 1 Tim 2:15) in the normal course of life, giving birth to children in marriage.

### 4. Salvation in the Past.
There is a sense in which salvation has already taken place. Paul can say, "in hope we were saved" (Rom 8:24), where the past tense looks back to the beginning of the Christian life.

"By grace you have been saved through faith and this not of yourselves; it is the gift of God, not of works lest anyone should boast. For we are his workmanship, created in Christ Jesus" (Eph 2:8-10). This is the typical position in Paul's writings. Salvation is something brought about by God (or Christ) and there is nothing human endeavor can do to produce this result. Paul piles expression on expression to emphasize the truth that salvation has been achieved by God only; it is never the result of human initiative or human achievement. We see this also in the reference to Christ as "the head* of the church" and as "the Savior of the body" (Eph 5:23).

There is both a backward and a forward look when Paul writes "For we were saved in hope,* but hope seen is not hope" (Rom 8:24). This intriguing passage recognizes that there is a sense in which salvation is in the past: "we were saved." Paul looks back to the death of Christ for sinners and to the faith repentant sinners exercised when they came to Christ. But he also speaks of hope, and that points to the future when believers will experience to the full all that salvation means.

Salvation is past when the apostle says that God, "when we were dead in trespasses, gave us life in Christ—by grace you have been saved" (Eph 2:5). A little later he repeats the essential thought, "By grace you have been saved through faith" (Eph 2:8), where again the perfect tense points to a salvation already accomplished. The aorist of an event in the past is found when we read, "Not from works of righteousness that we have done, but according to his mercy he saved us" (Tit 3:5). Again, Christ "delivered us from the power of darkness" (Col 1:13). Paul leaves his readers in no doubt as to the reality of salvation as an accomplished fact. It happened in the past.

### 5. Salvation Now.

But in another sense Paul emphasizes that salvation is here and now. The gospel is "the power* of God for salvation" and God's righteousness* is being revealed in it (Rom 1:16-17). The tenor of the apostle's writings and the manner of his living show that this is a reference to a present happening. Again, he quotes Isaiah 49:8, referring to God's help in a day of salvation, and proceeds, "Look, now is the acceptable time; look, now is the day of salvation" (2 Cor 6:2). The doubled "now" conveys a sense of urgency; salvation is not to be deferred to some convenient time in the future. Salvation is now. The gospel must be accepted now.

A present salvation is meant when Paul speaks of the gospel as "the power of God to us who are being saved" (1 Cor 1:18), and when he refers to "those being saved" (2 Cor 2:15). "With the mouth one confesses for salvation" (Rom 10:10) is another indication of a present salvation, not only one that is looked for in the future. This is probably the case also with the "godly grief" that "works repentance" leading to salvation (2 Cor 7:10). Salvation is in the present when Paul asks rhetorically, "Who will deliver me from this body of death?" and answers, "Thanks be to God through Jesus Christ our Lord" (Rom 7:24-25). Paul is referring to this mortal body* and to the constant temptations to sin that such a body provides. And he exults in the deliverance Christ brings. In the battle of life, salvation may be said to be the "helmet" (Eph 6:17), or the helmet may be "the hope of salvation" (1 Thess 5:8). Either way, salvation is now a critical part of the Christian's armor.

The apostle's attitude to the salvation of Israel also reveals a longing for something to happen now. He speaks of his affectionate goodwill toward his nation and adds that his prayer is for their salvation (Rom 10:1). While, of course, there is an eschatological dimension to the salvation for which he prays, the emphasis in this passage is present: he wants Israel to be saved now! That salvation is present is seen in another reference to Israel, namely that it is due to Israel's transgression that salvation has come to the Gentiles (Rom 11:11).

### 6. A Future Salvation.

Paul is certain that salvation is a present reality and that it is a life-changing experience. But he is equally certain that the best we know of it now does not exhaust the subject. He looks for a future salvation when "all Israel will be saved" (Rom 11:26), or again when he urges, somewhat mysteriously, that a certain sinner be "delivered to Satan for the destruction of the flesh so that the spirit may be saved in the day of the Lord" (1 Cor 5:5; see Eschatology). There is much that is obscure to us in this passage, but salvation "in the day of the Lord" certainly looks for the ultimate salvation. This is very clear also in the apostle's reference to our citizenship* as being in heaven, "from where we await a Savior, the Lord Jesus Christ" (Phil 3:20). The idea that salvation is nearer than when we first believed (Rom 13:11) also points to a future happening. The statements that "all Israel will be saved" and that "the Deliverer will come out of Zion" (Rom 11:26) may be understood of the present or of the future. Whichever way we take them, there can be no doubt that Christ is the deliverer and that he is seen as having full heavenly authority.

Paul does not see this future salvation as coming to all, and we must remember that there are passages in which, for example, he sets those who are saved over against "those who are perishing" (1 Cor 1:18; 2 Cor 2:15; 2 Thess 2:10). "The wrath*" (Rom 5:9) from which Paul is saved points forward to the ultimate disaster. Judgment day will test realities. The work of some will survive the fire, whereas that of others will be burned up; of such a one Paul says, "That person will be saved, but so as through fire" (1 Cor 3:15). Paul is here referring to believers and pointing to the difference between those who have built well and those who have built badly. But anyone who has built on the foundation Christ laid will be saved. Clearly this is the future salvation.

In his treatment of "the man of lawlessness"* at the end of the age, Paul says that the Lord Jesus will destroy that wicked one. He also says that this evil being will operate "with every deceit of unrighteousness in them that are perishing, because they did not receive the love of the truth so that they might be saved" (2 Thess 2:10). This is an unusual way of putting it but is a reminder that "the love of the truth" is important. Right up to the last days people will perish because they did not love the truth.

Paul looks forward to the day when the Lord "will save me into his heavenly kingdom*" (2 Tim 4:18). That also is the implication of the remark that the justified* "will be saved through him from the wrath" (Rom 5:9). There is a future dimension in salvation, which is important, for Paul is clear that ultimately sinners will face the wrath of God. But there is ultimate deliverance for those who have put their trust in God. Paul quotes the prophet Joel for the assurance that "Everyone who calls on the name of the Lord will be saved" (Rom 10:13). "Calls"* does not mean calls in a superficial manner, as of one who simply wishes to avoid the personal consequences of sin. "Calls" here means a genuine calling on the Lord which proceeds from the conviction that God can and will save and that the caller is in desperate need.

From all this we see that salvation is the comprehensive term that includes a multiplicity of aspects. Sometimes more than one of these aspects occur together, as when the apostle says that Christ *has delivered* us "from so great a death" and who *will deliver*, and adds that this is the one "on whom we have set our hope that he *will still deliver*" (2 Cor 1:10). For Paul it was important that sinners be delivered from the condemnation their sin deserved, and he gives a good deal of attention to justification, the process of acquittal when believers stand at the bar of God's justice. But he also thinks of the present power of the Holy Spirit* in the lives of believers; salvation includes an ongoing triumph* over the forces of evil. And Paul looks forward to the end of this age and sees salvation as having its effect throughout eternity. We should not think of salvation as simply negative, as "deliverance from . . ." It is that, but it is more. It involves wholeness, wellness, health, goodness. Thus Paul says that Christ "delivered us from the power of darkness," but immediately adds, "and transferred us into the kingdom of his beloved Son" (Col 1:13).

*See also* CREATION AND NEW CREATION; DEATH OF CHRIST; ESCHATOLOGY; GENTILES; GRACE; HOPE; ISRAEL; JUSTIFICATION; PEACE, RECONCILIATION; RESTORATION OF ISRAEL; SAVIOR; TRIUMPH; UNIVERSALISM; WRATH, DESTRUCTION.

BIBLIOGRAPHY. W. Foerster and G. Fohrer, "σώζω κτλ," *TDNT* VII.965-1024; E. M. B. Green, *The Meaning of Salvation* (London: Hodder, 1965); R. Haughton, *The Drama of Salvation* (London: SPCK, 1976); G. F. Hawthorne, *Philippians* (WBC 43; Waco: Word, 1983); D. Hill, *Greek Words and Hebrew Meanings: Studies in the Semantics of Soteriological Terms* (SNTSMS 5; Cambridge: University Press, 1967); W. L. Liefeld, "Salvation," *ISBE* 4.287-95; H. R. Mackintosh, *The Christian Experience of Forgiveness* (London: Nisbet, 1927); L. Newbigin, *Sin and Salvation* (London: SCM, 1956); C. A. A. Scott, *Christianity According to St. Paul* (Cambridge: University Press, 1927); R. A. Ward, *Commentary on 1 & 2 Timothy & Titus* (Waco: Word, 1973).

L. Morris

## SANCTIFICATION. *See* HOLINESS, SANCTIFICATION.

## SANHEDRIN. *See* POLITICAL SYSTEMS.

## SATAN, DEVIL

Paul refers to a personal, evil, spiritual being whose purposes are opposed to God, his people and his cosmos. "Satan" (or "Devil" occurring only in Ephesians and the Pastorals) are the most familiar terms Paul uses, but there are others. The OT and, more particularly, the varied Judaism of Paul's day help shed light on the terminology and understanding of Satan common to Paul and many of his contemporaries.

    1. Background
    2. Pauline Terminology
    3. Satan As Hostile Enemy
    4. Satan As Conquered Enemy

### 1. Background.

In the OT the Hebrew noun *śāṭān*, meaning "accuser" (with the nuance of "adversary" or "slanderer" in certain contexts; see Hamilton, 985-86), is used of both human (cf. 1 Sam 29:4; 1 Kings 11:14, 23, 25) and transcendent beings. The latter reference is found in three notable instances. In Job "the satan" appears before God acting as a sort of public prosecutor, possibly a member of the divine council, who brings accusation against Job. He is given only limited power to afflict Job and his family (Job 1—2). In 1 Chronicles 21:1 a "satan" incites David to take a census of the people, though in the parallel story of 2 Samuel 24:1 the same event is attributed to the influence of Yahweh. In Zechariah 3:1-2 "the satan" brings accusation against the high priest Joshua, as the latter stands before the angel of Yahweh. Yahweh "rebukes" (*gā'ar*) the satan, a powerful word of command with which Yahweh is known to overcome his enemies (e.g., Ps 18:15; LXX 17:16; cf. 1QapGen 20:28-29; 1QM 14:9-10). In none of these cases do we find a being clearly defined as a cosmic adversary who defies divine sovereignty and authority. But these three canonical contexts seem to have laid the foundation for a later development in Jewish thought in which an evil, transcendent spiritual being, known by various names, maintains a spiritual kingdom that is opposed, but ultimately subject, to God. Many scholars believe this development was due to the influence of Iranian thought in the intervening centuries, but this influence is difficult to prove. Whatever its origin, by the first century a dualistic cosmology seems to have been widely accepted.

Within this worldview intelligent beings, whether physical or spiritual, were ultimately aligned with either God or Satan, light or darkness (see Light and Darkness), good or evil (1QS 4:15-16). Whereas in the OT ancient Israel had been faced off against the nations, a deeper dimension was now added in literature outside the OT, though no doubt indebted to Daniel's visions (cf., e.g., Dan 10:1—11:1). Behind the story of Israel and the nations was a transcendent drama in which God* and angels* were set over against Satan and his minions. Moreover, just as the OT depicted rebellion and apostasy taking place within Israel itself, some now saw the spiritual battle lines dividing Israel and extending into a battleground of the individual heart, ultimately distinguishing the true children of light from the children of darkness (1QS 4:22-24; though *Jub.* 16:25-34 puts confidence in circumcision* as the sign of those who belong to God rather than Beliar/Mastema; cf. *Jub.* 48:2-4). This new perspective was accompanied by a mythology which traced the course of conflict, accounted for the origin of demons* (the spirits of the offspring of angels and human wives, *Jub.* 5:1-11; 10:1-14; *1 Enoch* 15:8-9; cf. Gen 6:1-5) and retold Israel's history, now set off in relief by a host of spiritual forces. On this accounting, for instance, it was Satan, known as Mastema, who aided the magicians of Egypt and incited the Egyptians to pursue the Israelites (*Jub.* 48:9-12; *see* Magic).

In broad strokes, Satan was understood to be a personal spiritual being of the highest order (*Life of Adam and Eve* 12:1), originally created by God for good purposes (but cf. 1QM 13:11, "you created Belial for the pit") but now engaged as the leader of a cosmic rebellion (*Life of Adam and Eve* 12—16). While he exercises his power on earth (*Life of Adam and Eve* 16:1), he does not seem to have been barred from appearing in the courts of heaven, and either he or his delegates appear in heaven to bring accusation against God's people (*1 Enoch* 40:7; cf. *T. Job* 8:1-3; *3 Enoch* 30:1-2). He rules over a destructive force of fallen angels or spirits (1QM 13:12; *T. Jud.* 25:3; *T. Zeb.* 9:8), leads the Gentile nations astray (1QM 1:1-2; *1 Enoch* 69:28; *T. Job* 2:1—3:7), and actively and strategically works evil against God's people, whether as individuals, leaders (*Mart. Is.* 1:8-9), sect or nation (*Jub.* 1:19-21). Israel, or at least the righteous remnant within Israel, is protected by God or his archangelic agent, typically Michael, the Prince of Israel (1QM 13:9-11; 1QS 3:18—4:1; cf. 11QMelch). And both individuals and corporate Is-

rael are enjoined to resist Satan's falsehoods, his malevolent schemes and his dangerous assaults (*T. Reub.* 4:11; 1QS 4:15-18). In due course Satan will be defeated and subdued by God (1QM 18:1-2; *T. Levi* 18:12; *T. Jud.* 25:3; *T. Mos.* 10:1), either single-handedly by the divine warrior or by means of an angelic prince (1QM 13:10-11; *1 Enoch* 54:6). In either case, according to some apocalyptic scenarios the angelic warriors and the "children of light" might be pressed into service (11QM).

In Jewish literature of the Second Temple era a number of titles were given to this spiritual archopponent of God and his people: Satan (*T. Job* 3:6; 6:1—8:3; 1QH 4:6; 45:3; 1QSb 1:8), or Satanael/Samael (e.g., in Slavonic/Greek versions of *3 Baruch* 4:8; cf. *2 Enoch* 18:3[J]); the Devil (*T. Job* 3:3; LXX Job 1:6-8, 12; 2:1-7; Zech 3:1, 2); "the enemy" (*T. Job* 47:10); Belial (1QM 13:11; 14:9; 1QS 1:18, 24; 2:5, 19) or Beliar (*T. Levi* 3:3; 18:12; 19:1), from the Hebrew *b°liyā'al* ("ruin," "destruction," "wickedness," cf. Nah 1:11); Azazel (*1 Enoch* 8:1; 10:4; *Apoc. Abr.* 13:6-14; cf. Lev 16:8); Mastema ("hatred," "enmity," from the verb root *śṭm*, "hate"; Jub. 10:8; 11:5; 17:16; 19:28; cf. 1QM 13:4); "the spirit" or "angel of darkness" (1QS 3:20-24); and perhaps *Melkîrešaʿ* ("king of wickedness," 4Q280-82, in contrast with *Melkîṣedeq*, "king of righteousness"; 11QMelch). In addition, the Gospels provide evidence for the name "Beelzebul," known as "the ruler of the demons" (Mt 12:24; Mk 3:22; Lk 11:15).

## 2. Pauline Terminology.

Within the Pauline corpus we also find an array of names or descriptive titles or phrases referring to this archenemy.

### 2.1. Satan.
"Satan" (*ho satanas* Rom 16:20; 1 Cor 5:5; 7:5; 2 Cor 2:11; 11:14; 12:7; 1 Thess 2:18; 2 Thess 2:9; cf. 1 Tim 1:20; 5:15), a transliteration of the Hebrew *śāṭān* (e.g., Job 1:6-8, 12; 2:1-7; Zech 3:1, 2) is the term most commonly used to refer to the supernatural adversary of God and his purposes. In addition, various other terms are used.

### 2.2. Devil.
The term, "devil" (*diabolos*), is found in Ephesians 4:27 and 6:11, and is used with some frequency in the Pastorals (1 Tim 3:6, 7; 2 Tim 2:26; 3:3; Tit 2:3). A Greek term, meaning "slanderer" or "adversary," *diabolos* is used in the LXX to translate the Hebrew *śāṭān*. But the term "devil" can be used in more than one sense. In 1 Timothy 3, while the devil is presented as one who condemns and ensnares church leaders (1 Tim 3:6, 7), the instruction is given that women deacons "must be serious, not slanderers [*diabolous*], but temperate, faithful in all things" (1 Tim

3:11 NRSV). On the other hand, in the Pastorals we also find reference to "Satan" (1 Tim 1:20; 5:15) and once to "the enemy" (*antikeimenos*, 1 Tim 5:14). This provides evidence of the interchangeability of the names Satan and Devil among early Christians, a phenomenon attested elsewhere in the NT in the Gospels (cf. Mt 4:1, 5, 8, 11 and 4:10; Mk 4:15 and Lk 8:12) and Revelation (where *satanas* appears eight times and *diabolos* five times).

**2.3. Other Terms.** Outside of Ephesians and the Pastorals Satan is alluded to as "Beliar" (2 Cor 6:15) or the "god of this age" (*ho theos tou aiōnou toutou*, 2 Cor 4:4; cf. Acts 26:18) who blinds unbelievers, keeping them from seeing the "light of the glory* of the gospel* of Christ." He is also called the "serpent" (*ophis*, 2 Cor 11:3; cf. *1 Enoch* 69:6; *2 Enoch* 31:6; *Apoc. Abr.* 23; *Life of Adam and Eve* 9; *Apoc. Mos.* 17), "the tempter" (*ho peirazōn*, 1 Thess 3:5; cf. Mt 4:3) and the "evil one" (*ho ponēros*, 2 Thess 3:3; cf. Eph 6:16 and Mt 5:37; 13:19, 38; Jn 17:15; 1 John 2:13-14; 3:12; 5:18-19). And in keeping with these sinister titles, in Colossians he is implied as controlling the "power of darkness" (Col 1:13) who stands in contrast with the "the holy ones in the light" (Col 1:12), perhaps a reference to the angels. Elsewhere when Paul refers to "darkness" in contrast with "light" (cf., e.g., Rom 13:12; 1 Thess 5:4, 5), we may infer that he (in a manner reminiscent of the conflict between light and darkness described in the Qumran* scrolls) has in mind the realm and influence of Satan. For Paul, however, Satan is not always so easily identified, for he may cross over into the camp of God's people disguised as an "angel (*angelos*) of light" (2 Cor 11:14; cf. Apoc. Mos. 17:1; Life of Adam and Eve 9:1).

Ephesians offers a particularly rich selection of descriptive titles. He is called the "prince (or "ruler," *archōn*) of the power of the air" (Eph 2:2; cf., e.g., Jn 16:11), the "spirit [*pneuma*] now at work among those who are disobedient" (Eph 2:2), the "evil one" (Eph 6:16; cf. 2 Thess 3:3) and "the devil" (Eph 4:27; 6:11).

## 3. Satan As Hostile Enemy.

Paul's references to Satan always occur in the course of meeting the demands of his apostolic ministry*; nowhere in the Pauline corpus is there any apparent attempt to set forth a systematic "satanology." But the picture which emerges from the fragments of evidence preserved in the Pauline letters seems in most respects compatible with that which we find in the common "satanology" of Judaism—though in Paul these themes are transposed into a Christian framework. Some have even suggested that the descent and ascent of Christ in the hymn of Philippians 2:6-11 is

a mirrored counterimage of the story of Satan's attempt to grasp equality and glory with God, and his subsequent punishment, based on Isaiah 14.

**3.1. The God of This Age.** Paul clearly distinguishes between two kingdoms in the present age: the kingdom* of Christ and the kingdom of Satan. In 2 Corinthians 4:4 Paul maintains that the "god of this age (*aiōn*)" keeps his human subjects (*hoi apistoi*) from the gospel by blinding their minds from seeing "the revealed splendor of the gospel of the glory of Christ who is the image of God." That "good news" of a triumphant and exalted Christ, the glorious second Adam* in the image* of God, heralds the dawn of a new age and the passing of the old along with its dark lord. There may be a twist of irony in this allusion to the work of Satan, for the first-century A.D. *Life of Adam and Eve* (12—16) recounts that Satan fell when he refused to worship the image of God in the newly created Adam. In his rebellion he assailed Eve and so brought about Adam and Eve's expulsion from paradise and his own loss of glory. Satan, transformed as a bright angel (cf. 2 Cor 11:14), returned to her and led her astray with a false assurance of divine forgiveness. When Paul refers to "unbelievers" (2 Cor 4:4) he may have in mind false teachers who carry out Satan's work (cf. 2 Cor 11:13-15). The underlying point is that Satan is vested with a sovereignty, however limited it might ultimately be, that is powerful, compelling and clearly opposed to the work of God in Christ.

Such an understanding also surfaces in 2 Corinthians 6:15 where Paul warns the Corinthians not to be yoked with unbelievers, for "what agreement does Christ have with Beliar?" This passage (2 Cor 6:14—7:1), with its contrasts between Christ and Beliar, righteousness and lawlessness, light and darkness, believer and unbeliever, temple* of God and idols,* clean and unclean, resonates with language similar to that found in the Qumran scrolls. This has led some interpreters to suggest that Paul has here appropriated and reworked a passage of Essene origin (see Martin, 1986, 190-95, 199-201), thus explaining why this is the only occurrence of *Beliar* in Paul and the NT. Whether Paul appropriated it or not, Paul affirms the distinction between the two realms headed by Christ and Belial.

The same perspective is found in the contested Pauline letters of Colossians and Ephesians. In Colossians 1:13 the dominion (*exousia*) of darkness (implied to be Satan's) is contrasted with the kingdom of Christ. In language reminiscent of the exodus tradition, we read that believers have been rescued from the authority of darkness and delivered into the kingdom of God's Son.* In Ephesians 2:2 the archruler of this age is called "the ruler of the power [or realm, *tēs exousias*] of the air, the spirit that is now at work among those who are disobedient." The believers who are addressed were once slaves to the world order of this age, "dead" in their trespasses and sins (note the dual themes of liberation and forgiveness* in Col 1:13-14). But there is a new element in Ephesians, with the Devil (the term used in Eph 4:27; 6:11) being associated with the "air" and being called a "prince" or "ruler" (*archōn*). The "air" may refer to the lower reaches of the heavens,* believed by some in Paul's day to be just above the earth (cf. 2 Enoch 29:4-5). This lower atmosphere seems to be related to the "heavenly realms" which, according to Ephesians 3:10 and 6:12, are inhabited by the principalities and powers (*see* Principalities and Powers), who are in a power alliance with the Devil (Eph 6:11-12; see Lincoln, Arnold).

Finally, in Romans 8:19-23 Paul speaks of the subjection of the created order to "futility"* (or "vanity," *mataiotēs*, Rom 8:20) and the "bondage of decay" (Rom 8:21) in which it "groans in labor pains" (Rom 8:22) as it awaits its liberation. The suggestion has been made that Paul is here alluding to the created order's subjection to the power of Satan as the "god of this age," or to his agents. There is surely something to be said for this, for Paul ends his train of thought with a confident statement that no power of the cosmos can keep believers from the love of God in Christ (Rom 8:37-39; see Martin 1981, 53-54), and in Romans 16:20 he looks forward to the defeat of Satan in terms clearly echoing Genesis 3:15 (see 4 below).

*3.2. Satan the Aggressor.* There is active engagement between the kingdom of Christ and the kingdom of Satan. If Satan strives to maintain humans in his thrall, he also attempts to regain those who have been lost to Christ and he resists Paul, a leading opponent in the battle for human lives.

Among believers (both as individuals and in Christian community), we find that Satan brings sexual temptation to those who lack self-control (1 Cor 7:5) and he can outwit believers and leaders by taking advantage of unforgiving attitudes and discord in the community (2 Cor 2:11). Just as the serpent deceived Eve, Satan cunningly leads believers astray from a pure devotion to Christ by introducing "another gospel" (2 Cor 11:3) and even disguising himself as an angel of light (cf. Gal 1:8; *Life of Adam and Eve* 9:1; on Satan taking a guise, see *T. Job* 6:4). Here Paul is contemplating the fact that his opponents* at Corinth disguised themselves as ministers of righteousness when they were in fact false apostles* and ministers

of Satan (2 Cor 11:15). It is interesting, however, that Paul never speaks of Satan "entering" someone (cf. Lk 22:3; Jn 13:27). On the other hand, trouble may also come in the form of persecution inflicted from outside the community, and the fear of an apostle is that in his absence new believers will be shaken by such events (1 Thess 3:1-4). This too Paul can attribute to the work of Satan, as the tempter (*peirazōn*), and consequently the work of a minister of the gospel might be in vain (1 Thess 3:5). From Paul's perspective, it was Satan who repeatedly thwarted his apostolic plans to return to Thessalonica (1 Thess 2:18).

In Ephesians and the Pastorals many of the same concerns come to the fore. The Devil is wily, and his stratagems must be resisted by divine armor (Eph 6:11). Anger and an unrepentant or unforgiving spirit is a foothold for the Devil (Eph 4:27). Believers, and particularly church leaders, must be on the lookout for the "snare (*pagis*) of the devil" (1 Tim 3:7; 2 Tim 2:26). For an *episkopos* who is a recent convert, conceit can lead to condemnation by the devil (1 Tim 3:6). Some, perhaps Hymenaeus and Philetus who have "swerved from the truth" (2 Tim 2:18 NRSV), have already fallen into that snare and have been held captive (2 Tim 2:26). They may still, by the ministry of Timothy, be granted repentance and knowledge of the truth. Young widows, (presumably because of sexual unfulfillment, idleness or for lack of a living,) should marry so as to close a door of opportunity for the adversary (*antikeimenos*) to do his work (1 Tim 5:14). Indeed, "some have already turned away to follow Satan" (1 Tim 5:15).

Finally, Paul tells the Thessalonians that prior to the parousia of the Lord an eschatological rebellion, led by the "man of lawlessness,"* will occur in accord with the working of Satan (*kat' energeian tou satana*, 2 Thess 2:9). The "mystery of lawlessness" is already at work in Paul's day (2 Thess 2:7), but in its final crystallization of evil it will be accompanied by "power, signs, lying wonders, and every kind of wicked deception" (2 Thess 2:9-10).

*3.3. Satan As an Instrument of Divine Will.* Satan's opposition is carried out under the sovereignty of God. The theological perspective that evil can be used for divine purposes, even as a means of executing divine wrath* and discipline, is a theme familiar from the OT. On the one hand, Assyria and Babylon execute the divine judgment against Israel and Judah; on the other, Satan may be given permission to afflict an individual such as Job for a divine purpose.

Paul speaks of a "thorn in the flesh," a messenger (*angelos*) of Satan, which was permitted by God to afflict him (2 Cor 12:7). While this affliction (most likely a physical disability, see Martin, 1986, 410-17) was evil in itself, and "battered" Paul, it was allowed (*edothē*, "given") within God's providence and was not taken away despite Paul's fervent prayers. It was, in fact, instrumental in bringing home a message at the heart of Paul's theology of the cross*: "God's power is made perfect in weakness."

On another level Satan plays a role in community discipline.* Paul instructs the Corinthians that a certain man, guilty of incest, should be delivered over "to Satan for the destruction of his flesh, that his spirit may be saved in the day of the Lord" (1 Cor 5:5). This passage has puzzled interpreters, for it is not clear whether this is a remedial measure (with the expectation that the man will repent) or whether it was intended that his death would be his salvation (see Roetzel). One thing seems clear: that the individual, in being excommunicated from the blessings of community "in Christ"* (note that the community is to be gathered "in the name of the Lord," 1 Cor 5:4) by the "power of the Lord Jesus" would be placed outside, into the domain of Satan. In this case Satan perhaps is understood to operate like the forces who executed Yahweh's covenant curses* and wrath upon unfaithful Israel in exile. Like Israel, who was cut off from the blessings of the land of promise, this individual's flesh* (e.g., his propensity for sin) through suffering would be destroyed and thus he would be saved on the Day of the Lord (when the Lord would return to execute his final triumph over the enemy). In 1 Timothy 1:20 we find that Hymenaeus and Alexander have been turned over to Satan so that they may learn not to blaspheme.

### 4. Satan As Conquered Enemy.

In Romans 16:20 Paul expresses his victorious confidence that "the God of peace will soon crush Satan under your feet." The influence of Genesis 3:15 is clearly to be seen here. But whereas Genesis 3:15 speaks of the seed of the woman striking the head of the seed of the serpent, Paul speaks of "the God of peace," not Christ, who will defeat the enemy. In speaking of God as the subject and Satan "under your feet," Paul seems to be blending Genesis 3:15 with Psalm 110:1 and/or Psalm 8:6. The latter is the more likely text being echoed here, since it speaks of God placing the created order under the superintendence of humankind. On this reading Paul would be saying that in defeating Satan, who leads and epitomizes creation in rebellion, God will be restoring to the children of the Last Adam (the "seed of the woman") their role of dominion and eschatological shalom. That this will happen "soon" (*en tachei*) may be an

indication of Paul's confidence in the coming triumph* of God. But it may also arise from his confidence that believers in Rome will soon experience divine victory over the present threat of "those who cause dissensions and offenses" and "deceive the hearts of the simple-minded" (Rom 16:17-19).

While the Gospels point to the defeat of Satan in the cross and resurrection* (cf., e.g., Lk 22:1-6, 53; Jn 12:31; 14:30; 16:11), Paul looks back to Christ's triumph at the cross over the "principalities and powers"* (Col 2:15; cf. 1 Cor 2:6-8). It is difficult to imagine that Paul would not have affirmed a proleptic triumph over Satan at the cross, for he speaks confidently of the defeat at the cross of the personified powers of sin,* death,* flesh* and even the Law* (*see* Triumph). Moreover, texts such as Galatians 1:4 ("he delivered us from the present evil age") and Colossians 1:12 ("he has rescued us from the power of darkness") imply a defeat of Satanic power reminiscent of God's victory in the Exodus.

But this defeat, though real, is only provisional. Satan is still a potent and aggressive force of evil seeking to thwart and upset the work of God in Christ. In the present Paul encourages his churches to look forward to the final crushing of Satan (Rom 16:20) and to rely on divine faithfulness and power, for "he will strengthen you and guard you from the evil one" (2 Thess 3:3). In Ephesians 6 the theme of divine weaponry, an image also employed in 1 Thessalonians 5:8 and Romans 13:12, is developed in memorable fashion (see Arnold). Paul points out that the enemy of the church does not consist of "flesh and blood" enemies (like those of the old Israel). God's people are now engaged with enemies in the form of principalities, powers and "the spiritual forces of evil in the heavenly realms" (Eph 6:12). These powers are under the direction of their leader "the devil," whose schemes (*methodeiai*) they carry out against the church. While Israel was organized and regulated as the army of God in the wilderness, dependent on the victorious power of Yahweh, the church is outfitted in spiritual weaponry and finds her strength in the Lord and in the power of his might (Eph 6:10). With the "shield of faith" believers can "quench all the flaming arrows of the evil one" (Eph 6:16).

*See also* ANGELS, ARCHANGELS; DEMONS AND EXORCISM; ELEMENTS/ELEMENTAL SPIRITS OF THE WORLD; PRINCIPALITIES AND POWERS; TRIUMPH.

BIBLIOGRAPHY. C. E. Arnold, *Ephesians: Power and Magic* (SNTSMS 63; Cambridge: University Press, 1989); H. Bietenhard et al., "Satan, Beelzebul, Devil, Exorcism," *NIDNTT* 3.468-77; O. Böcher, "βελιάρ," *EDNT* 1.212; idem, "διάβολος," *EDNT* 1.297-98; P. L. Day, *An*

*Adversary in Heaven: Satan in the Hebrew Bible* (HSM 43; Atlanta: Scholars, 1987); M. Dibelius, *Die Geisterwelt im Glauben des Paulus* (Göttingen: Vandenhoeck & Ruprecht, 1909); W. Foerster, "βελιάρ," *TDNT* I.607; idem, "διαβάλλω, διάβολος," *TDNT* II.71-81; idem, "σατανάς," *TDNT* VII.151-63; N. Forsyth, *The Old Enemy: Satan and the Combat Myth* (Princeton: University Press, 1987); V. P. Hamilton, "Satan," *ABD* V.985-89; R. Leivestad, *Christ the Conqueror: Ideas of Conflict and Victory in the New Testament* (London: SPCK, 1954); A. T. Lincoln, *Ephesians* (WBC 42; Dallas: Word, 1990); idem, *Paradise Now and Not Yet* (SNTSMS 43; Cambridge: University Press, 1981); R. P. Martin, *2 Corinthians* (WBC 40; Waco: Word, 1986); idem, *Reconciliation: A Study of Paul's Theology* (Atlanta: John Knox, 1981); C. J. Roetzel, *Judgement in the Community: A Study of the Relationship between Eschatology and Ecclesiology in Paul* (NovTSup; Leiden: E. J. Brill, 1972); J. B. Russell, *The Devil: Perceptions of Evil from Antiquity to Primitive Christianity* (Ithaca, NY: Cornell University, 1977); idem, *Satan: The Early Christian Tradition* (Ithaca, NY: Cornell University, 1981); G. H. Twelftree, *Christ Triumphant: Exorcism Then and Now* (London: Hodder & Stoughton, 1985); idem, "Demon, Devil, Satan," *DJG* 163-72; R. Yates, "The Powers of Evil in the NT," *EvQ* 52 (1980) 97-111.

D. G. Reid

## SAVIOR

The letters of Paul contain twelve of the twenty-four NT uses of the word *sōtēr* ("savior"). Ten of the twelve instances are in the Pastorals,* of which six are in Titus. In the Pauline literature, as in the overall NT usage, savior (*sōtēr*) means "one providing salvation," and often includes the related meanings of "deliverer" or "protector." The salvation that the savior brings is principally spiritual and usually eternal in scope, but it is also linked to the physical dimension. In the Pauline corpus the term *savior* is always applied either to Jesus Christ (six times) or to God (six times). Thus the question arises as to how both God* and Christ* can function as savior.

1. Savior in Hellenism and Judaism
2. Savior in Ephesians and Philippians
3. Savior in the Pastorals

### 1. Savior in Hellenism and Judaism.

Paul lived and ministered in a cultural environment where the term *savior* could be ascribed to gods, heroes and humans. Gods such as Zeus, Asclepius, Serapis, Isis and Sandon-Heracles (of Paul's native Tarsus) could be called "savior" for their reputed ability to deliver from the seasonal "death" of nature or from

disease, mortality and other afflictions of life (*see* Religions). In the Hellenistic ruler cults that followed after Alexander the Great divine honors were attributed to rulers in life and in death. Thus after the death of Ptolemy I (c. 280 B.C.), he and his wife Berenike were honored as *theoi sōtēres*, "savior gods." And Ptolemy II and his wife Arsinoe II were deified while yet living. Likewise, beginning with Augustus, the Roman emperors* were given the titles "lord"* and "savior" in the emperor cult, which particularly prevailed in the cities of Asia Minor. In the case of rulers, their power as savior was evident in ending war and serving as the great benefactor (*euergetēs*) in bringing peace and prosperity (the news of this peace was frequently called *euangelion*, "good news"). Thus a wide range of deific associations attended the word *sōtēr* (see Bousset, Foerster and Fohrer, Nock, Wendland). But while the history of religions school attributed early Christianity's use of *savior* (and *lord*) to Hellenistic mystery religions (e.g., Serapis and Isis; see Bousset), such a genetic relationship has since been discredited (see Lord; Paul and His Interpreters; Religions). To whatever extent *sōtēr* was used of gods, heroes and humans in the first century, it should be seen as evidence of how the term could be used of a revered or transcendent figure, as a salutary reminder of how the term *sōtēr* might be misunderstood when attributed to Jesus, and as a contrast with the claims early Christians made of Christ.

The more likely background for savior in the Pauline corpus is the use of the term in the OT. There it is primarily God who is called "Savior" or identified as the one who brings salvation* (e.g., Deut 32:15; Mic 7:7; Hab 3:18), particularly in the Psalms (e.g., Ps 24:5; 27:1; 62:2) and in Isaiah (e.g., Is 12:2; 45:15, 21; 60:16; 63:8). Though humans may be called saviors, they serve only as agents of God's salvation (e.g., Judg 2:16; 3:9, 15; 2 Kings 13:5; Neh 9:27). The coming Davidic king was never identified as "savior," though Zechariah could speak of him as "having salvation" (Zech 9:9; cf. Servant, Is 49:6). The LXX regularly uses *sōtēr* to translate the Hebrew *yᵉšû'â* ("salvation"), *yēša'* ("deliverance," "rescue," "salvation") and the participle *môšîa'* ("savior"). The Greek texts of early Judaism do not use *sōtēr* of a messianic figure but limit it to God (Wis 16:17; Sir 51:1; Bar 4:22; 1 Macc 4:30; 3 Macc 6:29, 32; 7:16; *Pss. Sol.* 8:33).

### 2. Savior in Ephesians and Philippians.

Outside the Pastorals the term savior appears only in Ephesians 5:23 and Philippians 3:20. In considering these passages it is instructive to compare the usage in Acts 13:23, where Luke records Paul's early preaching.*

*867*

In Acts 13:16-41 Paul addresses Jews and Gentile God-fearers in the synagogue at Pisidian Antioch (Acts 13:14) on his first missionary journey. He proclaims Jesus as the "Savior" whom "God has brought to Israel" (Acts 13:23 NIV) from David's line (Acts 13:22-23). Paul's "message of salvation" (*ho logos tēs sōtērias*, Acts 13:26), that is, of Jesus as Savior, focuses on the death* and resurrection* of Jesus, the Son of God,* the Messiah, in fulfillment of the prophetic Scriptures. Although there is no evidence that savior was a messianic title in the NT period (Foerster, 1014), nevertheless Jesus is set forth as the Savior (Acts 13:23) who provides forgiveness* of sins* and justification,* which are to be received through faith in him and his victorious redemptive work (Acts 13:38-39). This is consistent with Peter's preaching in Acts 5:31 (cf. 2 Pet 1:1, 11; 2:20; 3:2, 18), as well as with the angel's proclamation in Luke 2:11 (cf. Lk 1:47) and the significance attached to Jesus' name in Matthew 1:21 ("he will *save* his people from their sins").

In Philippians 3:20 savior is used in an eschatological* context. Paul reminds the Philippian believers that their primary citizenship* is in heaven,* from which they "await a Savior, the Lord Jesus Christ" (cf. 1 Thess 1:10). His coming will be accompanied by the glorious transformation of the believers' "body* of humiliation" to be conformed to the "body of his glory,*" a working of the same power* by which he subjects all things to himself (Phil 3:21; cf. Phil 2:9-11). The eschatological context of the title squares with Paul's use of the term *salvation*\* to refer to the completion of God's saving work in the end. From a critical perspective, this is the only use of savior in the generally acknowledged Pauline letters. And some have argued that the use of savior in Philippians 3:20 is due to Paul's use of pre-Pauline tradition at this point (see commentaries) or that Paul, having developed the metaphor of earthly and heavenly citizenship, or commonwealth (*politeuma*), wishes to contrast Christ the coming heavenly Savior with the earthly emperor as "savior."

Ephesians 5:23-32 develops the relationship of Christ to the church as the body of Christ (*see* Body of Christ). Paul discusses the way husbands should love and cherish their wives (Eph 5:25-32) by analogy with Christ, who is head* of the church* and—he adds—"is himself the Savior of the body" (Eph 5:23).

The significance of Christ as "Savior of the body" seems clear enough: it is summed up in his loving death for the church, his cleansing it from sin (Eph 5:26), his presenting it spotless to God (Eph 5:27) and his providing for its welfare (Eph 5:29). Here the Savior's work is seen as realized eschatology.* Ephesians 5:23-32 paints a picture of Christ as Savior that includes both the ideas of salvation from destruction, sin and death, and of protection and provision. But a point of comparison may be drawn between Ephesians 5:23 and Philippians 3:20: in both contexts the theme of subjection appears with the title Savior, as does the title "Lord" (cf. Phil 3:20; Eph 5:22) In Philippians 3:21 his future action on behalf of believers will be by the same power* with which he subjected "all things"; in Ephesians 5:24 the church is subjected to Christ, a theme reminiscent of Ephesians 1:22-23, where the church is the manifestation of the future subjection of all things to Christ.

The future benefits of the Lord Jesus as Savior described in Philippians 3:20 are given a predominantly present-tense focus in Ephesians 5:23, where the emphasis lies on Christ the Savior's provision and protection.

### 3. Savior in the Pastorals.

There is a notable shift from the rare appearance of *sōtēr* outside the Pastorals* to ten occurrences within the Pastorals. Six of these instances refer to God as Savior—three in 1 Timothy (1 Tim 1:1; 2:3; 4:10) and three in Titus (Tit 1:3; 2:10; 3:4). Jesus Christ also is called "Savior" (2 Tim 1:10), and sometimes both God and Christ are referred to as Savior in close proximity to each other (i.e., the frequent use of God as "Savior," especially as "Savior of all people," in the Pastorals: 2 Tim 1:3, 4; 2:10, 13; 3:4, 6). Foerster is representative of those who understand this emphasis on the "Savior of all people" against the backdrop of an emerging Gnosticism* that claimed that salvation was only for the few (Foerster, 1017). However, the presence of full-blown Gnosticism during the NT period has been widely questioned.

A more plausible alternative is to understand the designation of God as Savior as derived from the OT (see 1 above; see Fee). The expression, "God our Savior," occurs five times in the Pastorals (1 Tim 1:1; 2:3; Tit 1:3; 2:10; 3:4). The repeated use of "our" seems to indicate an appropriation of OT language to speak of God's spiritual deliverance of and provision for Christians. But the formulation may intentionally provide a counterpoint to the growing influence of the emperor cult.

God is also called "the Savior of all people" (*sōtēr pantōn anthrōpōn*) in 1 Timothy 4:10 (cf. Tit 2:10-11). Such a designation, however, is not intended to communicate a universalism* in which all people will ultimately be saved. Rather, this expression is tempered by the statement that God as *sōtēr* "desires (*thelei*) all people to be saved" through Jesus Christ (1 Tim 2:3-

4). Such salvation is freely offered to all through the channel of preaching (Tit 1:3), but it is only actualized fully in the lives of those who believe (1 Tim 4:10). God's grace as Savior has been displayed to all people (Tit 2:10-11), and spiritual renewal and justification come only through "Jesus Christ as Savior" (Tit 3:6).

Jesus Christ is also called "our Savior" in Titus 1:4, 3:6; 2 Timothy 1:10, and probably in Titus 2:13 (cf. Schneider and Brown, 220). Because of the appearance (*epiphaneia*) of Christ as Savior in history (2 Tim 1:10), God's grace is made available through the apostolic gospel* (2 Tim 1:9-11). Christ as Savior is likewise involved in the application of divine saving grace* in the believer's rebirth and justification (Tit 3:4-7). The future appearing (*epiphaneia*) of Jesus as Savior is the Christian's "blessed hope*" and generates a lifestyle of godly gratitude (2 Tim 2:11-14). Thus the references to Christ as Savior in the Pastorals can speak of the past, present and future of God's salvation in Christ (cf. Eph 5:23; Phil 3:20; cf. Acts 13:23).

That God and Christ are both seen as *sōtēr* and closely interrelated has significance for the developing theological perspective in the Pauline literature and the entire NT. In Titus 1:3-4 "God our Savior" (Tit 1:3) is closely followed by a reference to "God the Father and Christ Jesus our Savior" (Tit 1:4 NIV). In Titus 3:4-6 "the love of God our Savior" (Tit 3:4) becomes a concrete reality in the Christian's life (Tit 3:5) "through Jesus Christ our Savior" (Tit 3:6). Titus 2:13 even appears to equate God and Savior with Jesus Christ (see Harris; Schneider and Brown, 220; *see* God). Certainly there is no developed doctrine here, but the delicate balance of the distinction between persons (Tit 1:4) and roles (Tit 3:4-6), and the apparent equality of God and Christ as Savior (Tit 1:3-4; 3:4, 6) and Deity (Tit 2:13) may be seen as a further development of the Pauline ascription of the attributes of God to Christ (*see* Christology; God).

*See also* CHRISTOLOGY; EMPERORS, ROMAN; GOD; LORD; RELIGIONS, GRECO-ROMAN; SALVATION.

BIBLIOGRAPHY. W. Bousset, *Kyrios Christos* (Nashville: Abingdon, 1970) 310-17; R. Bultmann, *Theology of the New Testament* (2 vols.; New York: Scribners, 1951, 1955) 2.292-306; J.-F. Collange, *The Epistle of St. Paul to the Philippians* (London: Epworth, 1979); O. Cullmann, *The Christology of the New Testament* (rev. ed.; Philadelphia: Westminster, 1963) 238-45; M. Dibelius and H. Conzelmann, *The Pastoral Epistles* (Herm; Philadelphia: Fortress, 1977) 100-103; G. D. Fee, *1, 2 Timothy, Titus* (GNC; San Francisco: Harper & Row, 1984); W. Foerster and G. Fohrer, "σώζω κτλ," *TDNT* VII.965-1024; R. H. Fuller, *The Titles of Jesus in Early Christology* (London: Lutterworth, 1969); M. J. Harris,

*Jesus as God: The NT Use of* Theos *in Reference to Jesus* (Grand Rapids: Baker, 1992); G. F. Hawthorne, *Philippians* (WBC 43; Waco: Word, 1983); A. D. Nock, *Early Gentile Christianity and Its Hellenistic Background* (New York: Harper & Row, 1964 [1928]) 35-44; J. Schneider and C. Brown, "Savior," *NIDNTT* 3.219-23; V. Taylor, *The Names of Jesus* (London: Macmillan, 1953); P. Wendland, "Σωτήρ," *ZNW* 5 (1904) 335-53.

A. B. Luter, Jr.

**SCHOOL OF TYRANNUS.** *See* EPHESUS.

**SEA TRAVEL.** *See* TRAVEL IN THE ROMAN WORLD.

**SEED.** *See* ABRAHAM.

**SELF.** *See* PSYCHOLOGY.

**SENDING.** *See* CHRISTOLOGY; SON OF GOD; WISDOM.

## SERVANT, SERVICE

Various types of service are mentioned in Paul's letters: the service rendered by slaves; the service of Paul, his colleagues and believers generally, and also of those appointed to fulfill special functions within the Christian communities; the service rendered by governing authorities.

1. Serving as a Slave
2. Servants of God

**1. Serving as a Slave.**

In the Pauline letters slavery* terminology (*doulos, douleuō*) is used only of those who are slaves of human masters and in reference to Paul's own service as an apostle.* (There is only one exception to this rule: 2 Tim 2:24, which says the Lord's slave must not be quarrelsome, but kindly to all and an apt teacher.)

*1.1. Slaves of Human Masters.* Paul offers no theological justification for slavery in principle; on the contrary, he instructs believers not to become slaves by selling themselves into slavery (1 Cor 7:23), and (on one reading of 1 Cor 7:21; the majority understand the incomplete Pauline sentence, "But if you are able even to become free make the most of _____ ," to be supplied with a word like "your freedom"; see Bartchy, Trummer) encourages those who are slaves to obtain their freedom if they can. However, he recognizes that some of those to whom he writes must serve as slaves, and to these he offers encouragement and gives exhortation.

Paul encourages believing slaves to think of themselves as the Lord's freed persons, just as those who were free when they became believers are now

Christ's slaves (1 Cor 7:22). He reminds Philemon* that his runaway slave, Onesimus, having become a believer, is no longer just a slave but also a brother in Christ (Philem 16). He assures slaves that by serving their human masters they serve Christ* and that they will receive their reward* (Eph 6:8; Col 3:24). In serving their human masters well they do the will of God (Eph 6:5-8) and adorn the gospel* (Tit 2:9-10).

*1.2. Paul as a Slave.* Paul frequently refers to himself as a slave (*doulos*) of Christ (Rom 1:1; Gal 1:10; Phil 1:1; cf. Tit 1:1). In the LXX *doulos* is used not only to denote slaves of human masters, but also to describe kings and prophets as servants of the Lord. Therefore, Paul's description of himself as a slave of Christ probably has a double meaning: it reflects not only his understanding of the serving nature of his apostolate, but also his privileged status as an apostle* (see Sass). Paul speaks of himself as the slave of his converts (2 Cor 4:5) and of those to whom he preached the gospel (1 Cor 9:19), but they were not his masters. He acknowledged only one master, Christ, and he served others for his sake (2 Cor 4:5).

## 2. Servants of God.

In his letters Paul refers to various forms of service to God rendered by different people. In describing these forms of service he does not use the *doulos* word group. For the most part he uses two other word groups (*diakonos, diakoneō, diakonia* and *leitourgos, leitourgeō, leitourgia*).

*2.1. Paul and His Colleagues as Servants.* People such as Apollos, Archippus, Epaphras, Phoebe, Stephanus, Timothy and Tychicus are mentioned as those who, like Paul, labor in the service of God (*see* Coworkers). In some cases the nature of their service is unspecified (Eph 6:21; Col 1:7; 4:17), while in others it is clear what is involved, activities such as gospel ministry* (Phil 2:22; Col 4:10-11) and meeting the needs of Paul himself (Phil 2:25, 30, used of Epaphroditus of Philippi).

Paul speaks of himself as a servant (*diakonos*) of Christ (1 Cor 3:5; 2 Cor 11:23). His service consisted primarily of the ministry of the gospel to the Gentiles* (Rom 1:5; 11:13; 15:16). It was a ministry of the new covenant,* of the Spirit and justification* (2 Cor 3:7-9), through which people were brought to faith* in Christ (1 Cor 3:5). Alongside this gospel service Paul involved himself deeply in the ministry of relieving the needs of the poor believers in Jerusalem (see 2.4 below).

Paul never, in his own writings, identifies himself explicitly with the Isaianic Servant of the Lord (only in Acts 13:47); like others in the primitive church Paul seems to have identified the Isaianic Servant christologically* (Rom 4:25/Is 53:4-5; Rom 5:19/Is 53:11). However, there are hints in his writings (Rom 15:21/Is 52:15; Gal 1:15/Is 49:1; Phil 2:16/Is 49:4) that he understood the Isaianic Servant's sufferings to have prefigured his own sufferings as well as Christ's.

*2.2. Believers as Servants.* The apostle speaks of believers generally as servants of God. They perform various functions in accordance with the gifts each one has received from God (Rom 12:4-8; 1 Cor 12:4-6), and it is through their service that the church is enabled to grow in maturity (Eph 4:7-16; Col 2:18-19). Seeing that all believers (Jews as well as Gentiles) are servants of God, no one is to pass judgment upon another, remembering that it is before their own Lord that each servant (*oiketēs*) stands or falls (Rom 14:4).

*2.3. Deacons.* In several places in the Pauline letters the word *diakonos* is used of individuals who exercise a special function within the church. Phoebe is described as a deacon (servant) of the church in Cenchreae in Romans 16:1. Deacons (servants) are included among the addressees of the letter to the Philippians (1:1), and 1 Timothy 3:8-13 includes detailed prerequisites for those who might be appointed as deacons (servants), stating that those who serve well in this capacity gain a good standing for themselves and great boldness in the Lord. However, the Pauline letters give no indication concerning the exact nature of the service to be rendered by these appointees (*see* Church Order).

*2.4. The Collection as Service.* Paul devoted a large portion of his time and energy, and much space in his letters, to one particular piece of service: arranging the collection of contributions from his Gentile churches to relieve the need of poor Jewish believers in Jerusalem (Rom 15:25-32; 1 Cor 16:1-4; 2 Cor 8—9; Gal 2:10). This service was intended not only for the relief of need, but also as a recognition of the Gentile believers' indebtedness to Jewish believers (Rom 15:27). The contributions were also to be proof of the genuineness of the faith of the Gentiles, which would result in much thanksgiving to God (2 Cor 9:13-14). The acceptance of the collection by the Jewish believers in Jerusalem would also constitute a recognition on their part of the validity of Paul's mission* (cf. Rom 15:30-31; *see* Collection for the Saints).

*2.5. The State as Servant.* In Romans 13 Paul describes governing authorities as God's servants for good. They have been instituted by him (Rom 13:1). They approve those who do good and execute God's wrath* upon those who do evil (Rom 13:3-4). Because they are God's servants, Paul says, believers should pay them the taxes that are due (Rom 13:6-7; *see* Civil Authority).

See also APOSTLE; LORD; MINISTRY; SLAVE, SLAVERY; SUFFERING.

BIBLIOGRAPHY. S. S. Bartchy, MALLON CHRESAI: First-Century Slavery and the Interpretation of 1 Corinthians 7:21 (SBLDS 11; Missoula: Scholars, 1973); W. Beyer, "διακονέω κτλ," TDNT II. 81-93; D. Georgi, The Opponents of Paul in Second Corinthians (Philadelphia: Fortress, 1986); E. Kamlah, "Wie Beurteilt Paulus sein Leiden?" ZNW 54 (1963) 217-32; C. G. Kruse, New Testament Models for Ministry: Jesus and Paul (Nashville: Thomas Nelson, 1985); D. B. Martin, Slavery as Salvation: The Metaphor of Slavery in Pauline Christianity (New Haven: Yale University, 1990); R. Meyer and H. Strathmann, "λειτουργέω κτλ," TDNT IV.215-31; G. Sass, "Zur Bedeutung von δοῦλος bei Paulus," ZNW 40 (1941) 24-32; J. E. Stambaugh, "Social Relations in the City of the Early Principate: State of Research," (SBLSP 19; Chico, CA: Scholars, 1980) 75-99; D. M. Stanley, "The Theme of the Servant of Yahweh in Primitive Christian Soteriology, and Its Transposition by St Paul," CBQ 16 (1954) 385-425; P. Trummer, "Die Chance der Freiheit: Zur Interpretation des mallon chresai," Bib 56 (1975) 344-68.

C. G. Kruse

## SERVICE. See SERVANT, SERVICE.

## SEXUAL ETHICS. See SEXUALITY, SEXUAL ETHICS.

## SEXUALITY, SEXUAL ETHICS

1. Paul's Experience
2. Basic Instruction
3. Responding to Problems
4. Conclusions

### 1. Paul's Experience.

Of Paul's own sexual experience little is known. It has been argued (e.g., by R. H. Gundry), on the assumption that Romans 7:7-25 is to be read autobiographically, that in Romans 7:7-8 Paul recalls the awakening of his sexual desire at the onset of puberty. When, as a young teenager, Paul assumed personal responsibility to keep God's Law* (with or without the formality of the later ceremony of bar-mitzvah), it was the tenth commandment that sin seized to stir up sexual lust. But both a general and a particular uncertainty attend this interpretation: in general, an uncertainty whether Romans 7:7-25 should be viewed as Paul's own story, and in particular, an uncertainty whether the "coveting" (NIV) of verses 7-8 has a sexual force.

Subsequently all we know is that Paul was single (1 Cor 7:7-8), but whether as a widower (cf. 1 Cor 9:5) or as one who never married or even as one whose wife left him on his conversion cannot be ascertained. He recognized God's gift (charisma) in enabling him to remain single, without suffering from inordinate sexual desire (1 Cor 7:9).

### 2. Basic Instruction.

Paul never addressed the subject of human sexuality in a systematic manner, but said much about it in response to particular questions. Nevertheless, 1 Thessalonians 4:1-8 suggests that his basic teaching to a community of new converts covered sexual behavior. This was only to be expected in the Greco-Roman world where various forms of sexual license were common. Paul now reminds the Christians at Thessalonica that God's will for their sanctification required abstinence from porneia (1 Thess 4:3, "sexual immorality" NIV). This Greek word and its cognates as used by Paul denote any kind of illegitimate—extramarital and unnatural—sexual intercourse or relationship. The Thessalonians must not yield to their sexual passions like Gentiles* ignorant of God* (1 Thess 4:4-5), but control their bodies (or possibly, sexual organs) but keep to or acquire their own wives, as 1 Thessalonians 4:4 may be variously interpreted. 1 Thessalonians 4:6 ("in this matter no one should wrong his brother") may suggest that adultery was particularly in view.

### 3. Responding to Problems.

*3.1. Avoiding* Porneia. The greater frequency of references to sexual issues in Paul than in the Gospels reflects the laxer sexual mores of Hellenistic society. Paul stresses the incompatibility between a life of sexual license and the kingdom* of God: "no pornos ('immoral') or impure person . . . has any inheritance in the kingdom of Christ and of God" (Eph 5:5). Some of the Christians at Corinth, before being "washed, sanctified and justified in the name of the Lord Jesus Christ and by the Spirit of our God," had been pornoi (prostitutes?), adulterers and homosexually active (1 Cor 6:9-11; see Homosexuality). The inclusion of idolaters among these different sexual offenders (1 Cor 6:9) indicates the gravity of their sinfulness (see Sin). Foremost among "the acts of the sinful nature" (see Flesh) are "porneia ('sexual immorality'), impurity and debauchery" (Gal 5:19; cf. 1 Cor 10:8). It was chiefly in the disordered sexual vices of the Gentile world that Paul discerned God's judgment* on the godless (Rom 1:18-27; see Wrath).

Paul is consequently keenly concerned that the Christian congregations be kept free of such corruptions: "among you there must not be even a hint of sexual immorality (porneia), or of any kind of impurity, or of greed, because these are improper for God's holy people" (Eph 5:3). Paul is outraged that the Corinthian church is tolerating, rather than disciplining, a member indulging in incest with his father's wife (probably not the man's own mother, but his stepmother or his father's divorced or widowed wife. But the brevity of the reference counts against Countryman's view that Paul's interest lay chiefly in the breaching of family hierarchy.) Such *porneia* was not even countenanced among Gentiles (1 Cor 5:1-2). The offender must be expelled (1 Cor 5:11-13), which meant being handed over to Satan* for the purging of his "sinful nature" (NIV; *sarx*, 1 Cor 5:5; *see* Discipline). Paul's language betokens the gravity of such lawless sexuality—and of the Corinthians' vaunted Christian freedom.* Both were inconsistent with their new creation* in Christ* (1 Cor 5:6-8). 2 Corinthians 12:21 reveals Paul's persisting fear that on returning to Corinth he will find the sexually licentious still impenitent.

Less flagrant sexual problems at Corinth than incest evoked Paul's most extended discussions of sexuality. It appears that the Corinthians' distorted eschatology*—which had them exulting prematurely in the final completeness of salvation* here and now (cf. 1 Cor 4:8)—led some to be libertine, wielding the slogan "everything is permissible for me" (1 Cor 6:12), and others to be ascetic, under the banner "it is good for a man not to have sexual relations with a woman" (1 Cor 7:1 NIV margin). In meeting these challenges, of which the ascetic party seems to have been by far the stronger, Paul lays the groundwork for a suggestive and flexible Christian sexuality.

**3.2. Sex, Self and Christ.** For Paul sexual intercourse is not on a par with the satisfying of other natural appetites like eating. To that extent his approach is as inimical to the post-Christian West's obsession with unbridled sexual gratification as it was to Corinthian licentiousness. Sexual intercourse is uniquely expressive of our whole being. "All other sins a person commits are outside his body, but he who sins sexually sins against his own body" (1 Cor 6:18). To deal with a blatantly intolerable perversion of Christian freedom (unlike the subtler ascetic alternative), Paul applies his richly articulated concept of "body"* (*sōma*), which may mean—almost at one and the same time—a person's physical nature ("the body is not meant for sexual license," 1 Cor 6:13), the whole human self ("your bodies are members of Christ himself," 1 Cor 6:15; "your body is a temple* of the Holy Spirit," 1 Cor 6:19) and the church as Christ's body. According to Paul, "there is clearly something wrong in having *both* an intimate relationship with Christ as a member of his body and also a relationship which is intimate in an-

other sense with a prostitute, especially if she is a temple prostitute" (Whiteley, 215). Abusing the body in this way conflicts also with its destiny to be raised from the dead (1 Cor 6:13-15; *see* Resurrection).

Undergirding such teaching lies Paul's distinctive anthropology, in which the flesh,* or body, is no mere external expression or instrument of the true person that resides in some inner essence (*see* Psychology). For Paul it is truer to say that a human being *is* a body rather than *has* a body. In the Corinthian context this is a way of speaking about a Christian both as a sexual being and as a being "in Christ,"* a member of his church-body. Hence, when Paul declares *porneia* to be uniquely a sin against our own body (1 Cor 6:18), he is not referring merely to the misuse of our sexual organs. Nor is he distinguishing sexual sins on the grounds that drunkenness or gluttony, for example, involve things outside the body—drink and food in this case. He may be picking up a notion advanced by some libertine Corinthians, that nothing one does sexually or physically can touch the inner citadel of the soul. (Such sentiments are found among later Christian gnostics.*) For Paul nothing could be further from the truth. Because sexual activity embodies the whole person, sinful union with a prostitute—or adultery or other extramarital intercourse—desecrates a Christian's bodily union with Christ. "The association between Christ and the believer is regarded as just as close and physical as that between the two partners in the sex act" (Schweizer, 1065).

**3.3. Sex in Relationship.** Paul cites Genesis 2:24 ("the two will become one flesh") to demonstrate what is involved in the seemingly casual one-night stand with another woman; you become one body with her (1 Cor 6:16; note that Paul substitutes his own favorite *sōma* for the Septuagint's *sarx*). It is the peculiar dignity of the one-flesh union of heterosexual marriage,* on the other hand, that not only is it quite compatible with spiritual union with the Lord (1 Cor 6:17), but also it expresses the *mystērion* ("mystery"*) of the union between Christ and his church (Eph 5:31-32; 2 Cor 11:2). The analogy covers not merely reciprocal mutual love, respect and care but the union itself. A couple's becoming "one flesh," which entails sexual congress whatever else it may entail, is comparable to the bonding between Christ and believers. They become members, limbs, of his body, just as a husband loving his wife loves his own body, his own self (Eph 5:28-30). There is a close affinity between the teaching of 1 Corinthians 6—7 and Ephesians 5.

**3.4. The Goodness of Sex-in-Marriage.** But if 1 Corinthians 6 responds to an antinomian "permissiveness" current in Corinthian Christianity, 1 Corinthians 7 deals with issues reflecting a more ascetic streak. At the outset Paul cites a statement from the Corinthians' letter (so most commentators agree), "It is good for a man not to touch a woman" (1 Cor 7:1; NIV margin, "not to have sexual relations with." See Col 2:21-23 for a possible parallel.)

The teaching this evokes from Paul is concerned solely with marriage and sexual relations within marriage. The assertion Paul quotes almost certainly expresses the conviction of some Corinthian Christians that sexual activity between male and female, even if married (hence NIV's rendering "good . . . not to marry," 1 Cor 7:1, is misleading), had no place in the Christian's life. (Perhaps teaching such as 1 Cor 6:15-16 had been misunderstood as warranting this conclusion. See also 1 Tim 4:1-5 for a reaffirmation of God's good creation of marriage.) The fact that Paul proceeds to speak only about marriage is highly significant: for him there is no acceptable context for sex except within marriage. Yet the issue is not marriage as such but sexual intercourse—or perhaps better still, marriage as inseparably entailing sexual relations.

Paul neither wholly rejects nor wholly endorses the Corinthians' sentiment (as with "everything is permissible for me" at 1 Cor 6:12 ; cf. 10:23). Yet his response is more "no, although" than "yes, but." It presents an elucidation of marital sexuality that is principled, yet nuanced and realistic.

Marriage (i.e., monogamy) is needed and right because *porneia* as an outlet for sexuality is intolerable (1 Cor 7:2). The implication is clear: the satisfying of sexual desires is not wrong, and marriage is its appointed setting. (The parallels with 1 Thess 4:3-5 exclude the reduction of marriage to merely a cover for uncontrolled sexual gratification.) Moreover, sex is not a dispensable dimension of marriage; like responsible love* and respect (cf. above on Eph 5), it is one of the mutual obligations of husband to wife and wife to husband (1 Cor 7:3). For within marriage neither partner retains sole ownership of his or her own body (1 Cor 7:4). Sex within marriage must exemplify what Paul teaches later in 1 Corinthians: "In the Lord, however, woman is not independent of man, nor is man independent of woman" (1 Cor 11:11; *see* Man and Woman).

The parity of authority and duty in conjugal sexual relations that Paul here ascribes to husband and wife alike is one fulfillment of Galatians 3:26-28: "You are all children of God, . . . for all of you who were baptized into Christ have clothed yourself with Christ. There is neither . . . male nor female, for you are all one in Christ Jesus." With the implications of this new parity between men and women in Christ for spheres

such as church ministry or public service we are not here concerned. If Paul displays its outworking in Christian marriage in 1 Corinthians 7:2-5, 32-34, it is also possible that a radical exaggeration of it in asexual terms may be partly responsible for the ascetic refusal of sexuality that Paul counters in this chapter. We will return to this possibility.

**3.5. A Place for Abstinence.** From the perspective established by Paul in 1 Corinthians 7:2-4, the issue is no longer "is sex (within marriage) ever good?" but "when, if ever, is abstinence from sex within marriage right?" Paul sets out three criteria: (1) mutual consent, (2) for a limited time only, and (3) for religious purposes (1 Cor 7:5). And even this provision for abstinence is a concession—for verse 7 (Paul's recognition that singleness—involving abstinence—is possible by divine gift alone) suggests that the "concession" of verse 6 refers to verse 5, and not to verse 2-4. The underlying assumption is that by divine appointment marriage and sexual relations go together, as do singleness and abstinence from sex; what God has joined together, humans should not separate. Hence the concessionary character of verse 5, perhaps with the Corinthian ascetics particularly in mind.

The teaching of this chapter so far obviously disallows an understanding of sexual intercourse as intended solely for procreation. Even if artificial means of contraception are not in view, the accent falls unambiguously on sexual relations as expressive of selfless mutuality between married partners, of their belonging in the Lord to each other, not to him- or herself.

1 Corinthians 7:8-9 adds little to the picture painted so far. For reasons that Paul will spell out later, at 1 Corinthians 7:29-35, his preference is for the unmarried and widowed to remain so, like himself. But for those who lack the *charisma* of sex-free singleness, it is much better to marry than be consumed with inward desire—even, it seems, if that desire is controlled and not given vent in *porneia*. It is important to record that Paul is not ranking celibacy/virginity above marriage on some absolute scale. He is asserting that the sexless life is "good" only for those endowed with God's *charisma*, in the face of clamor at Corinth to make it a universal rule, with Paul's own example perhaps cited in its favor. It seems to be assumed that marriage-and-sex is "good" for all others—who apparently need no *charisma*.

**3.6. Eschatological Perspectives.** The "virgins" of 1 Corinthians 7:25 appear to be single women, and perhaps men also, who have had no sexual experience. The advice Paul gives them is consistent with what he has already taught in the letter. Because of the critical situation (the phrase in 1 Cor 7:26 seems to be clarified by verse 29a), the advantages of remaining single are obvious. Paul cites the matter-of-fact realities of married life, again, as in 1 Corinthians 7:3-4, maintaining scrupulously the parity of male and female in marriage (1 Cor 7:32-34).

The counsel of 1 Corinthians 7:29, "From now on those who have wives should live as if they have none," cannot override 1 Corinthians 7:2-5. 1 Corinthians 7:31 ("this world in its present form is passing away") combined with verse 29a ("the time is short") may suggest a reminder that marriage belongs to this order alone (cf. Mk 12:25). In the light of this eschatological perspective, spouses are called, not to sexual abstinence, but to "live in a right way in undivided devotion to the Lord" (1 Cor 7:35), to "use the things of the world [including marriage], as if not engrossed in them" (1 Cor 7:31).

The possibility was raised above that an extreme ascetic (encratite, perhaps) interpretation of "neither male nor female in Christ Jesus" (cf. Gal 3:28) may have been influential at Corinth. If, as commentators seem generally agreed, a major root of the Corinthian Christians' troubles lay in their believing that the age to come had already been consummated, and in their behaving accordingly, they—or at least the more ascetic among them—may have anticipated the fulfillment of Mark 12:25 (par. Lk 20:34-36: no marital relations in heaven; we may leave aside the question of the precise import of Jesus' words) and misrepresented Paul's teaching (cf. Gal 3:28) in support. The life of the world to come, according to such a standpoint, would be not only marriageless but even free of gender, and hence sexual, distinctions. But there is no basis in Paul or elsewhere in the NT for linking the expectation of Mark 12:25 with Galatians 3:28, which denotes parity of acceptance and status before God. It carries no ontological force and does not erode the distinctive gender-based sexual natures of male and female. (These sexual natures, to be sure, must in turn be distinguished from cultural developments or expressions of their differentiation. Does the omission of "neither male nor female" in the parallels to Galatians 3:28 at 1 Corinthians 12:13 and Colossians 3:11 suggest that it had been peculiarly prone to misunderstanding? Since 1 Corinthians 7:17-24 also deals with the other two pairs of Galatians 3:28—Jew and Greek, slave and free—the chapter may be viewed as clarifying, and correcting misreadings of, what it affirms.) There are no Pauline or NT grounds for holding that the destiny of redeemed humanity is to be androgynous, unisex, sexually undifferentiated. Paul goes no further than 1 Corinthians 7:29, which as we have

seen is not concerned with abstinence from sex in marriage.

1 Corinthians 7:36-38 still finds commentators divided. The NIV rendering cuts various exegetical knots by opting for what seems, all things considered, the most plausible interpretation. (As far as this article is concerned, the issues are little different if the man is not a fiancé but a father. 1 Corinthians 7:2-5 rules out the interpretation that identifies the present relationship between the two as a "spiritual [i.e., sexless] marriage.") Among the questions the Corinthian letter had posed about "virgins" was the wisdom of engaged couples proceeding to get married. We note the implication of the description of the fiancée as "his virgin"; it is assumed (and no doubt the ascetics' interest hinges on this) that an engaged woman is a virgin until married. Again Paul has to emphasize that those who marry commit no sin (1 Cor 7:36; cf. 1 Cor 7:28), but in present circumstances there is advantage in not going through with the marriage (1 Cor 7:38-39; 7:8, 26, 28-35)—if, that is, they have the *charisma* to refrain.

### 4. Conclusions.

The prevalent sexual license of Western society makes Paul's teaching both peculiarly relevant—for it was addressed to Christians in a world in this respect not too dissimilar to ours—and painfully sharp. He allows no compromise of the restriction of sexual activity to (heterosexual) monogamous marriage. Such an ethic must seem almost utopian to our sex-besotted age, in which it appears at times that one's identity is made to reside in one's sexual organs and their untrammeled exercise. Paul espouses an altogether higher view of sex that could never allow it to be casual or promiscuous, simply because it is an act uniquely expressive of one's whole being. From a Pauline perspective a cavalier freedom in sexual behavior can be bought only at the cost of trivializing the human person. His emphasis on mutuality, including sexual mutuality, within marriage—so marked an advance on the practice and precept of contemporary Hellenism* and Judaism—is attractive in a day of increasing sexual violence and exaggerated insistence on individual sexual rights.

And if for Paul the eschatological urgency accentuated the advantages in remaining unmarried—but only with God's enabling *charisma*—he provides an example of a teacher on sexuality sensitive to differences of circumstances and persons. If his situation heightened the note of sexual discipline, it is arguable that it was in every way healthier—spiritually, psychologically, physically—than alternatives offered and promoted today.

*See also* BODY; ETHICS; FLESH; HOMOSEXUALITY; MAN AND WOMAN; MARRIAGE AND DIVORCE, ADULTERY AND INCEST.
BIBLIOGRAPHY. H. Baltensweiler, "ἐνκράτεια," *NIDNTT* 1.494-97; C. K. Barrett, *The First Epistle to the Corinthians* (HNTC; New York: Harper & Row, 1968); J. Calvin, *The First Epistle of Paul to the Corinthians* (Grand Rapids: Eerdmans, 1960); D. R. Cartlidge, "1 Corinthians 7 as a Foundation for a Christian Sex Ethic," *JR* 55 (1975) 220-34; L. W. Countryman, *Dirt, Greed and Sex: Sexual Ethics in the New Testament and Their Implications for Today* (Philadelphia: Fortress, 1988); G. D. Fee, *The First Epistle to the Corinthians* (NICNT; Grand Rapids: Eerdmans, 1987); V. P. Furnish, *The Moral Teaching of Paul* (Nashville: Abingdon, 1979) 30-51; R. H. Gundry, "The Moral Frustration of Paul Before His Conversion: Sexual Lust in Romans 7:7-25," in *Pauline Studies: Essays Presented to Professor F. F. Bruce on His 70th Birthday*, ed. D. A. Hagner and M. J. Harris (Grand Rapids: Eerdmans, 1980) 228-45; W. Günther et al., "Marriage, etc.," *NIDNTT* 2.575-90; F. Hauck and S. Schulz, "πόρνη κτλ," *TDNT* VI.579-95; B. Malina, "Does Πορνεία mean Fornication?," *NovT* 14 (1972) 10-17; W. E. Phipps, "Is Paul's Attitude Toward Sexual Relations Contained in 1 Cor. 7.1?" *NTS* 28 (1982) 125-31; H. Reisser, "πορνεύω," *NIDNTT* 1.497-501; E. Schweizer and F. Baumgärtel, "σῶμα κτλ," *TDNT* VII.1024-94; D. E. H. Whiteley, *The Theology of St. Paul* (2d ed.; Oxford: Basil Blackwell, 1974).

D. F. Wright

## SHARING. *See* FELLOWSHIP, COMMUNION, SHARING; LORD'S SUPPER.

## SIGNS, WONDERS, MIRACLES

In the early church Paul had a reputation as an exorcist and healer, as well as being involved in miracles. Paul's testimony is that miracles occurred wherever he proclaimed the good news and that they remained essential to the life of the church.

1. Signs and Wonders
2. Miracles in Paul's Mission
3. Signs of an Apostle
4. The Gift of Miracles
5. Miracles of Paul in Acts

### 1. Signs and Wonders.

For Greek writers a "sign" (*sēmeion*) could be, among other things, a ship's ensign (Euripides *Iphigeneia at Aulis* 253), a symptom of sickness (Philo *Det. Pot. Ins.* 43) or something in which a god was understood to communicate to a person (Plutarch *Alex.* 25.1). In the LXX *sēmeion* is almost always used of God showing himself to be the Almighty and Israel to be his chosen

people through the events associated with Moses leading the Israelites out of Egypt (e.g., Deut 26:8; Jer 32:20-21; cf. Philo *Vit. Mos.* 1.210; Josephus *Ant.* 2.12.3—2.13.1 §§274-80).

A "wonder" (*teras*) was that which caused fear and trembling in people and indicated the proximity of and human dependence on the divine (Homer *Iliad* 4.408; Josephus *J.W.* 4.5.5 §287). For Philo and Josephus wonders, especially those performed by Moses, assisted those who witnessed them in knowing God's sovereignty (e.g., Philo *Vit. Mos.* 1.90, 95; Josephus *Ant.* 2.13.3 §§286-87). An explanation of a wonder was required to provide correct insight (Philo *Agric.* 96; Josephus *J.W.* 6.5.3-4 §§288-310), for charlatans could also perform wonders and mislead people (Josephus *Ant.* 20.8.6 168). In the LXX *teras* almost always translates *môpēṭ* which meant something extraordinary from God which demanded attention (e.g., Ex 7:9; 1 Kings 13:1-5; Ezek 12:1-16) and sometimes revealed God's will (e.g., Ex 7:4). *Teras* became rare in Greek and Jewish literature in the NT period and the word does not occur in the NT without *sēmeion*. In the NT *dynamis* ("power") seems to replace *teras*, perhaps in order not to compromise the important element of autonomy in the miraculous activity of Jesus and the early Christians (cf. e.g., Lk 24:19; see 4 below).

The phrase "signs and wonders" (*sēmeia kai terata*) is first known in Polybius (*Hist.* 3.112.18) and refers to the superstitious rites of the Romans (cf. Plutarch *Alex.* 75:1). Plutarch uses the words synonymously (Plutarch *Mor.* 2.149C; cf. Josephus *Ant.* 10.2.1 §28). In the LXX the phrase is generally confined to the wonders associated with Moses' leading God's people to freedom, and Philo only takes up the phrase as a traditional description of miracles in Egypt (e.g., *Spec. Leg.* 2.218). Josephus uses the phrase once of God warning and directing his people and once of imposters deceiving people ("wonders and signs," *Ant.* 20.8.6 §168). He more often used "signs" for these latter events (e.g., *Ant.* 2.12.3 §274), probably to dissociate the work of Moses from the suspicion of magic (cf. *Ant.* 2.13.3 §284).

### 2. Miracles in Paul's Mission.

In light of the strong association between "signs and wonders" and the miracle stories of the Exodus tradition, the "signs and wonders" performed by Paul to win the Gentiles* (Rom 15:19) cannot refer only to Paul's sufferings,* nor can they be of merely secondary importance to him (as Käsemann maintains). Rather, as reluctant as Paul was to draw attention to his miracles in the way his opponents* did (1 Cor 1:22; 2 Cor 12:12), "signs and wonders" were the miracles he performed empowered by the Spirit* and integrally associated with his preaching to form part of the new Exodus to the freedom possible in the age of Christ. Thus the gospel* is, in part, the miracles that were performed (cf. Rom 15:18-19; 1 Thess 1:5).

The function of miracles in Paul's mission can be seen in, for instance, 1 Corinthians 2:1-5 where Paul explains that while he came to the Corinthians in weakness,* fear* and trembling, without lofty words or wisdom* to proclaim only Jesus Christ and him crucified,* his message came in the "demonstration" (apodeixis, only here in the NT) of Spirit and power, in order that their faith* would rest not in human wisdom but in the power* of God.* In Greek rhetoric an apodeixis was a technical word for a compelling conclusion to be drawn from a reasoned argument (e.g., Plato Tim. 40E; 4 Macc 3:19). However, the compelling proof of Paul's message was not in his rhetoric* but in the demonstrations "of Spirit and of power" (1 Cor 2:4). As "Spirit" and "power" can be interchangeable in Paul's writing (cf. Rom 15:13, 19; 1 Thess 1:5), both words here are likely to signify the same reality. In contrasting his weakness, fear and spoken word with the demonstration of the gospel, Paul is probably referring not only to the Corinthians' encounter with God's power to transform their lives in conversion, including the reception of the Spirit accompanied by spiritual gifts, but also to the miracles involved in his mission as the demonstration or proof of his gospel (cf. 2 Cor 12:9-10; 1 Thess 1:9). For in Romans 15:19 the power of the Holy Spirit is paralleled with the power of signs and wonders, and when the Galatians received Paul's message they experienced the gift* of the Spirit and miracles (dynameis, Gal 3:5; see 4 below). Also, in 1 Thessalonians 1:5, perhaps defending himself against a charge of bringing a message without demonstrating its efficacy, Paul says that his gospel came to them not only in word but also in power and in the Holy Spirit and in full conviction or assurance (en plērophoria pollē; cf. Rom 4:21; 1 Clem. 42.3) showing he considered his mission to involve not only proclamation, but also miracles and the inward conviction produced by the Holy Spirit.

### 3. Signs of an Apostle.

Paul's opponents may have denied he was able to perform miracles (cf. 2 Cor 10:1, 10; 11:5) and accused him of being ill (2 Cor 12:7-10). Defending his apostleship* before the Corinthians Paul says "the signs [sēmeia] of an apostle [tou apostolou] were performed among you in all patience, with signs and wonders and mighty works [sēmeiois te kai terasin kai dynamesin]"

(2 Cor 12:12; cf. 13:3; 1 Cor 1:22). The first occurrence of sēmeia here probably means "indication" or "confirmation" and encompasses the second use which is one of three words (all in the dative) referring to miracles. The phrase "signs of an apostle" may have come from the Corinthians or perhaps from his opponents. As Paul's opponents seem to have performed miracles, Paul does not rely entirely on them as evidence of his apostleship and the truth of his message (cf. Rom 15:19; 1 Cor 2:4; 1 Thess 5:9; see 2 above). In 2 Corinthians Paul has already based the authenticity of his apostleship on his holy life of dependence on God (2 Cor 5:18-21; cf. 3:1-3), as well as on his own spiritual experience (2 Cor 1:12; 2:17; 4:2; 7:2), his suffering and weakness through which the power of God is seen (2 Cor 4:7-15; 6:4-10; 11:21-33), and the reconciliation that has taken place between the Corinthians and God (2 Cor 12:1-6). In any case, Paul is unlikely to rest his case entirely on the miraculous, for in 2 Thessalonians 2:9 he says the lawless one's attempt to deceive those who are to perish will be through "signs and wonders" empowered by Satan (cf. Josephus Ant. 20.8.6 §168; see Man of Lawlessness). Thus, the miracles along with his life of patient suffering in proclaiming the gospel and the experience of the Corinthians are the proof of his apostleship and the truth of his message, for in all of these the power of God can be seen (2 Cor 12:9).

### 4. The Gift of Miracles.

Paul describes one of the manifestations of the presence of the Spirit in a believer (1 Cor 12:7) as "workings of powers" (energēmata dynameōn, 1 Cor 12:10) or simply "powers" (dynameis, 1 Cor 12:28, 29). The word dynameis was commonly used for miracles (e.g., 1 Sam 14:48; Mt 7:22; Acts 2:22; 8:13), and Paul was no exception (cf. 2 Cor 12:12; Gal 3:5 and Acts 19:11), for miracles were understood as demonstrations of divine power (cf. P.Oxy 1381.21-26). The gift of miracles is distinguished from healing* (1 Cor 12:9), though it could refer to exorcisms (Dunn; see Demons, Exorcism). More likely the dynameis are miracles of nature, for, in relation to God, energeia ("working," or "power") was generally used of God's direct intervention in events through miracles (e.g., 2 Macc 3:29; 3 Macc 4:21; 5:28). Paul did not think that every one would be given the ability to perform miracles (1 Cor 12:19). The change in the way the gifts are listed in 1 Corinthians 12:28 (cf. 1 Cor 12:8-10) could mean that the gift of miracles is less closely associated with particular believers than God's appointment of apostles, prophets and teachers. But, miracles are sufficiently important to be listed immediately after these primary ministries (*see* Gifts of the Spirit).

### 5. Miracles of Paul in Acts.

A prominent feature of the portrayal of Paul in Acts is the miracle stories associated with him. In Acts 13:4-12 the proconsul believed when he saw Elymas the magician temporarily blinded by Paul for opposing him. In Acts 14:8-18, as a result of healing a cripple, Paul and Barnabas are hailed as gods having come down in human form, and they then take the opportunity to speak about the good news. In Acts 16:16-18 the exorcism of a spirit of divination from a slave girl brought the eventual conversion of the prison warden and his family. Acts 19:11-12, a summary of Paul's ministry, mentions his handkerchiefs being taken to the sick so that they were healed or freed from evil spirits. This contributes to the word of the Lord growing and prevailing mightily (Acts 19:20). In the raising of Eutychus from the dead in Acts 20:7-12, Paul is portrayed as a man of God like Elijah (1 Kings 17:17-24) and Elisha (2 Kings 4:32-37). As a result of Paul healing the father of Publius of fever and dysentery in Acts 28:7-10, the rest of the people on Malta are reported as bringing their diseased for curing. Paul is also portrayed as the object of miracles: he is healed from blindness (Acts 9:8, 18; 22:11-13), released from prison (Acts 16:25-34) and unharmed by a deadly snake (Acts 28:3-6). These stories, which embody theological themes in Acts, do not depict Paul as a miracle worker alone nor for its own sake but, as in the letters of Paul, show him to be proclaiming a gospel that involves both the miraculous and a message about the power of God.

*See also* AFFLICTIONS, TRIALS, HARDSHIPS; APOSTLE; DEMONS, EXORCISM; GIFTS OF THE SPIRIT; HEALING, ILLNESS; HOLY SPIRIT; MAGIC; POWER; VISIONS, ECSTATIC EXPERIENCE; WEAKNESS.

BIBLIOGRAPHY. J. D. G. Dunn, *Jesus and the Spirit* (Philadelphia: Westminster, 1975); G. D. Fee, *1 Corinthians* (NICNT; Grand Rapids: Eerdmans, 1987); J. Jervell, "The Signs of an Apostle: Paul's Miracles," in *The Unknown Paul* (Augsburg: Minneapolis, 1984) 77-95; E. Käsemann, "Die Legitimität des Apostels. Eine Untersuchung zu II Korinther 10—13," *ZNW* 41 (1942) 33-71; R. P. Martin, *2 Corinthians* (WBC; Waco: Word, 1986); C. F. D. Moule, ed., *Miracles: Cambridge Studies in their Philosophy and History* (London: Mowbry, 1965); F. Neirynck, "The Miracle Stories in the Acts of the Apostles: An Introduction," in *Les Actes des Apôtres: Traditions, Rédaction, Théologie*, ed. J. Kremer (Gembloux: Duculot, 1979) 169-213; S. M. Praeder, "Miracle Worker and Missionary: Paul in the Acts of the Apostles," *SBLSP* (1983) 107-29; K. H. Rengstorf, "σημεῖον

κτλ," *TDNT* VII.200-61; idem, "τέρας," *TDNT* VIII.113-26; M. Whitaker, " 'Signs and Wonders': The Pagan Background," *SE* 5 (1968) 155-58.

G. H. Twelftree

## SILENCE OF WOMEN. *See* MAN AND WOMAN.

## SIN, GUILT

There are more than thirty words in the NT that convey some notion of sin, and Paul employs at least twenty-four of them. He makes very little use of the "guilt" terminology in the psychological sense, but it may fairly be said that many of the things he says about sin include the thought that sinners are guilty people. After all, to commit a sin is to be guilty of that sin. While it cannot be said that Paul has a morbid preoccupation with sin, it can be pointed out that he recognizes that the evil that people do is a barrier to fellowship with God* and that unless some way is found of dealing with the problem of sin, all people as sinners face a time of moral accountability (Rom 2:16; 1 Cor 4:5; 2 Cor 5:10). But with this we must also say that Paul's prevailing attitude is not one of unrelieved gloom and pessimism. Rather, he continually rejoices that in Christ sin has been defeated so that the believer has nothing to fear in this world or the next. (For the argument that Paul's thought moves "backward," from the solution of salvation in Christ to human human plight, see Sanders 1977, 442-47; 474-511; cf. Wright, 258-62.)

Paul presents a massive treatment of the problem of sin in his letter to the Romans,* where he uses the noun for "sin" (*hamartia*) forty-eight times, the noun "trespass" (*paraptōma*) nine times, the verb "to sin" (*hamartanō*) seven times, "sinner" (*hamartōlos*) four times, "bad" (*kakos*) fifteen times, and "unrighteousness" (*adikia*) seven times. In addition Paul uses a number of other words with similar meanings which individually do not occur frequently, but which when taken together add up to a significant part of Romans. This concentration of words about evil cannot be paralleled elsewhere in the NT. In this very weighty letter the problem of sin is examined very closely and some important statements are made in the light of his programmatic announcement of the good news of God in Romans 1:16-17.

Paul does not define sin, but clearly he does not see it as primarily an offense against other people; for him sin is primarily an offense against God (cf. Rom 8:7; 1 Cor 8:12). The disruption of a right relationship with God has its results in hindering right relationships with people, but it is the offense against God that is primary.

### 1. The Fall.

Paul does not give much attention to the origin of evil; he does not, for example, speak in set terms of the fall as though he could *explain* the origin of evil. The one place where he describes the stage setting of humankind's fall is 2 Corinthians 11:3 (cf. 1 Tim 2:13-15), which in common with Jewish thinking traces Adam's* fall to Eve's influence (cf. Sir 25:24; *Life of Adam and Eve* 3). But he has an important treatment of Adam (Rom 5) in which he makes it clear that he accepts the truth that sin was no part of the original creation.* Romans 8:19-23 may suggest that the cosmos is affected by man's, or even Satan's,* downfall (*see* Futility). He sees sin as having been brought into the world by Adam and as having been practiced by the whole human race ever since, for "all have sinned" (Rom 3:23). All commit their own sins, to be sure, but in some way all are also caught up in the sin of Adam, for "by the one man's trespass the many died" (Rom 5:15). Paul does not see sin as part of human nature as God created it. God is not responsible for a flawed creation. It is this that made Adam's sin so serious. It meant the bringing of sin into a creation that originally was unflawed. Paul could have expressed himself in the words of 4 Ezra 7:118: "O Adam, what have you done? For though it was you who sinned, the fall was not yours alone, but ours also who are your descendants" (NRSV). Yet Paul never apostrophizes in this way.

### 2. The Universality of Sin.

As he begins Romans the apostle has a strong argument in which he shows that Jews and Gentiles* alike are all "under sin"; he quotes Scripture, "there is none righteous, not even one" (Rom 3:10). The whole human race is involved in sin. Paul does recognize that people on occasion act kindly and do good (Rom 2:7-10, 14). But that is not a problem. Sin is. And it is no minor problem, for it covers the whole human race and has calamitous consequences for every sinner (see Hooker).

### 3. Sin and the Law.

As a faithful Jew* Paul had accepted the Law* as a gift

from God, a mark of divine favor. But as a Christian he came to recognize that the Law taught some uncomfortable things about sin. The Law makes all the world guilty before God: "As many as are of works* of Law (i.e., depend on the Law) are under a curse" (Gal 3:10). Through the Law comes the recognition of sin (Rom 3:19-20); indeed Paul would not have known what sin is apart from the Law (Rom 7:7). He does not see the function of the Law as the prevention of sin, and he can even say that it multiplied sin (Rom 5:20). Its function was to make clear what sin is; its sharp definition of right and wrong made it plain that many things were sinful which people in every age have been quite prepared to overlook. The Law could not bring them salvation,* but it could bring them to Christ so that they could be justified* by faith* (Gal 3:24; cf. Wright, 193-216, who understands the role of the Law as concentrating sin on Israel so that it might be dealt with in the Messiah, Israel's representative, once and for all).

### 4. The Effects of Sin.

Paul sees a link between sin and death; indeed he says that "death came through sin," and further that, since all have sinned, death comes to all (Rom 5:12; *see* Universalism; Life and Death). He recognizes that, although some people's sins are not like Adam's transgression, nevertheless death reigned over all the race (Rom 5:14; cf. 5:21) because all humankind seems to be represented in Adam (Rom 5:12; on this verse see commentaries and Williams). Elsewhere he says simply, "the wages of sin is death" (Rom 6:23). He was once alive apart from the Law, but "when the commandment came, Law sprang into life and I died" (Rom 7:9-10; cf. Gen 4:7). In Romans 7:11, 13 Paul repeats the thought that sin, conceptualized as a power (perhaps with the intimation that sin is like a demon, or monster) killed him. Indeed, the theme of sin as an alien, potent and active power recurs in Roman 5—7 (cf. Rom 5:12, 21; 6:6, 11, 12, 14, 16-18, 20; see Sanders *ABD*; Beker, 213-34; Röhser). In Ephesians Paul reminds his readers that they had been dead in their "trespasses and sins" (Eph 2:1). The apostle leaves no doubt that sin is death-dealing, cutting people off from that life that is life indeed (Eph 4:18).

Paul brings out the seriousness of sin in another way by insisting that sinners are slaves to sin (see Martin). They may fancy that when they commit an evil act, they are free and are doing what they choose to do, but Paul would not agree. He reminds the Romans that in their pre-Christian state they were "sin's slaves" (Rom 6:17, 20). He says that he himself is "fleshly, sold under sin" (Rom 7:14) and "captive to the law of sin" (Rom 7:23). Echoing Ovid, he remarks that he wants to do good, but he still does evil (Rom 7:19). With the mind he may serve the Law of God, but with the flesh* he is "a slave to the law of sin" (Rom 7:25). Even when he wants to do good, evil is with him, indeed sin "dwells" in him (Rom 7:20-21).

Sin creates a gulf between sinners and God, as Paul makes clear in Romans 1:21-25. He specifically speaks of being "alienated from the life of God" (Eph 4:18), and says that the Colossians had been "alienated and enemies* in their minds and engaged in evil works" (Col 1:21). In any case it is obvious enough that when created beings sin against their creator, they erect a barrier between God and themselves.

They also disrupt relationships with one another as, for example, the list of sins in Romans 1 makes clear: covetousness, envy, murder, strife, deceit, insolence, covenant breaking and the rest. Humans may be united in sin, but that does not make them united to one another.

Paul offers a unique insight in pointing to an alienation from creation that sin brings and on which he dwells in Romans 8:19-23. Informed by this teaching Christians do well to care for their environment, not only because of the urgings of modern secular environmentalists, but because this is God's world and Christians look forward to the time when the whole creation "will be freed from the bondage of corruption" (Rom 8:21).

Throughout his writings it is clear that Paul sees sin, however it may be described, as a serious matter and as something that is to be found throughout the whole human race. He sees this as persisting to the end, for when he is dealing with the end time he speaks of the coming of an evil being he calls "the man of lawlessness"* (2 Thess 2:3; traditionally he is called "the man of sin"). Clearsightedly, Paul sees sin as operative throughout the human race and as something that will last through the whole of the race's history.

If he sees sin as universal through the whole human race, he also sees it as pervasive through the whole human person. People have sometimes regarded sin as to be found in the bodily functions only, the "heart" or "mind" or "spirit" being unsullied. But there is no way this can be derived from the apostle (see Psychology). It is true that he says that the sexual* sinner "sins against his own body" (1 Cor 6:18). He also speaks of the flesh as opposed to the Spirit* and goes on to give a dreadful list of "the works of the flesh" (Gal 5:17-21; see Virtues and Vices). But his list includes such things as enmity and envy, which make it clear that he is speaking of sins of the human spirit as well as of those of the human flesh. Paul's writings

as a whole demonstrate that he saw sin as involving the whole person, not one part only. To take an example at random, "the love of money" is not a fleshly activity, but it involves "all kinds of evil" (1 Tim 6:10).

### 5. The Death of Jesus.

Paul has a great deal to say about the death* of Jesus, far more in fact than any other NT writer. And he frequently says that the Savior's* death was due in some way to sin. Thus he says that Christ "died for our sins" (1 Cor 15:3; this creedal* statement, he says, "is of first importance"), and that he "gave himself for our sins" (Gal 1:4). He tells the Romans that Jesus "was delivered up for our offenses" (Rom 4:25), and again that "the death he died, he died to sin once for all" (Rom 6:10). There is not the slightest doubt that for Paul the death of Jesus was connected with humanity's sins, both in that human sins put Christ to death and that his death was designed to deal with sins.

He further says that Jesus' death was for sinners: Christ* "died for ungodly people" (Rom 5:6). In a noteworthy passage Paul tells us that "God shows his own love for us in that while we were still sinners Christ died for us" (Rom 5:8). "His own love" is important; it would be easy to say that the cross* demonstrates the love* of Christ, but Paul is making the point that, while that is true, it is also true that the love of the Father is demonstrated in the death of the Son.* And this death took place "while we were still sinners." It is not that we were somehow cleansed from sin and then the divine love was manifested. That divine love worked sacrificially to deal with the problem of human sin. In two further noteworthy statements Paul says, "one died for all" (2 Cor 5:14) and Christ "died for us" (1 Thess 5:10). The former statement brings out the truth that the death of Jesus is of universal application, the second that it is efficacious for believers. Paul can carry this latter thought a little further with his moving reference to "the Son of God who loved me and gave himself up for me" (Gal 2:20). The influence of Isaiah 53 as well as early creedal formulations is evident in these Passion texts (see Creed; see Popkes).

In an important passage Paul says, "Him who knew no sin he [i.e., the Father] made sin for us so that we might become the righteousness* of God in him" (2 Cor 5:21). This is often misquoted as a passive, "was made sin," which leaves the impression of an impersonal process. But Paul is referring to what the Father did as well as to the Son's saving action. The Father is involved in the solution to the problem of sin as well as the Son. It is important to be clear on this. Paul does not regard the Father as an indifferent spectator in the process of dealing with sin. He was there and the saving act was in accordance with his will. "Made sin" is not an easy expression but it surely indicates an identification with sin and sinners. Christ's death (like the offering of Is 53:6) was the sacrifice* that takes away sin.

Paul writes to the Colossians that in Christ we have "the forgiveness* of sins" (Col 1:14). The expression is in apposition with "the redemption*" and clearly points us to the cross again. It means much to the apostle that Christ has dealt with all the evil human beings have done and has brought forgiveness of sins to believers.

### 6. Christian Opposition to Evil.

Paul recognizes the pervasiveness of sin, yet he does not acquiesce in its inevitability. Constantly he urges believers not to give way to evil, but rather to do what is good. He prays that the Corinthians may do no wrong (2 Cor 13:7), and he urges the Colossians to put to death the evil that is within them (Col 3:5). He urges the Romans not to retaliate when evil is done to them but rather to overcome evil with good (Rom 12:17, 21), and he has a very similar exhortation for the Thessalonians (1 Thess 5:15). It is important to bear in mind that love, which of course should characterize all Christians, does not keep accounts of wrongdoing (1 Cor 13:5).

Paul does not confine himself to denouncing evils in the strictly religious area. He informs Timothy that "the love of money is a root of all kinds of evil" (1 Tim 6:10). He urges the Romans to do what is good and so to merit the approval of rulers (Rom 13:3) and reminds them that love works no evil to a neighbor (Rom 13:10).

### 7. Overcoming Sin.

That sin is all-pervasive and that Christ has died to deal with its effects are two points that Paul makes with some emphasis. He also has a number of statements that make it clear that he does not envisage Christians as people who continue to sin (Rom 6:1, 15; Gal 5:13), though with the added knowledge that their sin is forgiven. He is well aware that sin is so firmly rooted in human nature that in this life it is presumptuous to claim to be free of every sin. But he is also clear that "sin will not lord it over you" (Rom 6:14), adding, "for you are not under Law but under grace.*" It is not the submission to some set of rules (like the Jews with their claim to have kept the Law as an identity marker or badge of election) that marks the Christian, but the presence of the grace of God. It is by

grace that the believer is saved, and it is by grace that the whole Christian life is lived. Indeed Paul can go as far as to say that Christians, now freed from sin's domination, have "become slaves of righteousness" (Rom 6:18).

### 8. The Judgment of Sin.

Sin inevitably leads to final judgment.* Some anticipation of the future is a present judgment, for to commit sin means to make oneself a sinner. The dreadful consequence of being a sinner is brought out in the threefold "God gave them up " in Romans 1:24, 26, 28, with its horrifying lists of the consequences of sin here and now (*see* Wrath). Paul further makes it clear that "the wages of sin is death" (Rom 6:23). He also points out that we reap what we sow and that to sow to the flesh means to reap corruption (Gal 6:7-8). This means that sin brings judgment here and now.

But Paul also insists that sin will be finally dealt with at the judgment at the tribunal of Christ, a truth he brings out forcefully in, say, Romans 2:1-12, 16. This judgment is part of Christian truth and points to the final dealing with evil (1 Cor 4:4-6).

*See also* ADAM AND CHRIST; CONSCIENCE; CURSE, ACCURSED, ANATHEMA; DEATH OF CHRIST; FLESH; FORGIVENESS; HOLINESS, SANCTIFICATION; IDOLATRY; JUDGMENT; JUSTIFICATION; LAW; LIFE AND DEATH; MAN OF LAWLESSNESS AND RESTRAINING POWER; NEW NATURE AND OLD NATURE; PURITY AND IMPURITY; RIGHTEOUSNESS, RIGHTEOUSNESS OF GOD; SATAN, DEVIL; VIRTUES AND VICES; WRATH, DESTRUCTION.

BIBLIOGRAPHY. J. C. Beker, *Paul the Apostle* (Philadelphia: Fortress, 1980); R. Bultmann, *Theology of the New Testament* (2 vols.; New York: Scribners, 1951, 1957); C. E. B. Cranfield, "On Some Problems in the Interpretation of Rom 5:12," *SJT* 22 (1969) 324-41; W. Günther and W. Bauder, "Sin," *NIDNTT* 3.573-87; M. D. Hooker, "Adam in Romans 1," in *From Adam to Christ: Essays on Paul* (Cambridge: University Press, 1990); S. Lyonnet and L. Sabourin, ed., *Sin, Redemption and Sacrifice* (AnBib 48; Rome: Pontifical Biblical Institute, 1970); B. F. Malina, "Some Observations on the Origin of Sin in Judaism and St. Paul," *CBQ* 31 (1969) 18-34; D. Martin, *Slavery as Salvation* (New Haven: Yale University, 1990); L. Morris, *The Epistle to the Romans* (Grand Rapids: Eerdmans, 1988); W. Popkes, *Christus Traditus: Eine Untersuchung zum Begriff der Dahingabe* (ATANT 49; Zurich: Zwingli Verlag, 1967); G. Quell et al., "ἁμαρτάνω κτλ," *TDNT* I.267-335; G. Röhser, *Metaphorik und personification der Sünde* (WUNT 2.25; Tübingen: J. C. B. Mohr, 1987); E. P. Sanders, *Paul and Palestinian Judaism* (Philadelphia: Fortress, 1977); idem, "Sin, Sinners (NT)," *ABD* VI.40-47; J. Schneider, "παραβαίνω κτλ," *TDNT* V.736-44; C. Ryder Smith, *The Bible Doctrine of Sin* (London: Epworth, 1953); F. R. Tennant, *The Origin and Propagation of Sin* (Cambridge: University Press, 1902); idem, *The Concept of Sin* (Cambridge: University Press, 1912); A. J. M. Wedderburn, "The Theological Structure of Romans 5:12," *NTS* 19 (1972-73) 339-54; N. P. Williams, *The Ideas of the Fall and of Original Sin, Bampton Lectures, 1927* (London: Longmans, 1927); N. T. Wright, *The Climax of the Covenant: Christ and the Law in Pauline Theology* (Minneapolis: Fortress, 1991).

L. Morris

**SINNERS.** *See* FORGIVENESS; JESUS AND PAUL; JUSTIFICATION; SIN, GUILT.

## SLAVE, SLAVERY

1. Slaves and Slavery in the Greco-Roman World
2. Slaves and Slavery in Paul

### 1. Slaves and Slavery in the Greco-Roman World.

The Greco-Roman slave system was an integral part of every aspect of life in Paul's time. Estimates are that 85-90 percent of the inhabitants of Rome and peninsula Italy were slaves or of slave origin in the first and second centuries A.D. Facts and figures about slavery in the provinces are sketchy by comparison with those in Italy, but the existing evidence suggests a comparable percentage (see Patterson, 105-31).

By law slaves were what Aristotle called "human tools." Nevertheless, in the first century they were granted many rights. They could worship as members of the extended family of their owner. They could marry. Such marriages, however, were called *contubernium* rather than *matrimonium*. This meant that the offspring of slaves became the property of the owner. Therefore, this may have been the largest source of slaves in the time of the early Empire. During the late Republic slaves were usually prisoners of war. Only very early in Roman history was slavery the result of debt. Slaves also were allowed to accumulate money of their own, the *peculium*, that often could be used by them to purchase their freedom or to start a business when once they were manumitted, that is, set free by their owners.

In addition to being farm workers or semiskilled laborers, slaves were also artisans, workers in crafts, architects, physicians, administrators, philosophers, grammarians, writers and teachers (*see* Tentmaking). Frequently they worked for industrial or building corporations for daily wages that were then paid in part (about two-thirds) to their owners. Sometimes slaves worked alongside freed persons, and freeborn workers. Such competition depressed wages and eliminated inflation from the fourth century B.C. to the end of the first century A.D.

Freed persons, that is slaves who had been manumitted, played an important role in society, if for no other reason than that by the beginning of the first century their numbers had increased dramatically. As a consequence Caesar Augustus saw to it that laws were passed governing the number and the ages of slaves who could legitimately be set free (Bartchy *ISBE* 4.545; ABD). Often these freed persons entered into business partnerships with their former owners. Usually such partnerships were informally negotiated between the two parties involved at the time of the slave's manumission. Cicero says that a slave could expect freedom in seven years, but in any case, under Roman law, persons in slavery could expect to be set free at least by the time they reached age thirty.

Because of the revolt of the Germanic slaves led by Spartacus in 73 B.C., the Romans showed a decided preference for slaves of eastern origin. Slaves from the north and west were given the most difficult tasks. They were the farm laborers who worked in chain gangs by day and were housed in *ergastula* ("workhouses") at night. The use of the *ergastulum* was a particularly hideous aspect of Roman life. It was a flat, solid structure, built low enough to the ground so that the slaves could not stand up in it. Slaves of eastern origin, on the other hand, enjoyed great popularity at Rome. They were the trusted household servants, teachers, librarians, accountants and estate managers. They were manumitted by the thousands in the late Republic and early Empire. One of the reasons for this was a sharp decline in the freeborn population during these periods. No doubt there were both slaves and masters in many of Paul's churches (cf. Philem; 1 Cor 7:21; Eph 6:5-9; Col 3:22—4:1; 1 Tim 6:1-2; also 1 Pet 2:18-21; *see* Households; Social Setting). "Often overlooked are the slaves included in the phrases, 'those of the household of. . .' (Rom 16:10-11), 'Chloe's people' (1 Cor 1:11) and 'the household of Stephanas' (1 Cor 1:16; see Acts 11:14). These phrases cover the same kind of extended households designated by the Latin term *familia*" (Bartchy *ISBE* 4.544-45). Jewish slaves had been brought to Rome by the tens of thousands from the time of Pompey's conquest until the destruction of Jerusalem in A.D. 70.

### 2. Slaves and Slavery in Paul.

Paul refers by name to slaves or former slaves who were believers. He tangentially discusses the status of slaves in 1 Corinthians and Philemon. He also describes salvation by grace through the imagery of slavery.

**2.1. A Theological Metaphor.** Three key words—redemption,* justification* and reconciliation*—reveal the powerful role that the metaphor of slavery played for Paul in giving expression to his theology: redemption, literally the setting free of a slave, is used by him to say that Christ has liberated believers from their sin; justification, the act of being judged and found not guilty, is used to describe the Christians' freedom as the complete freedom a slave received upon manumission; and reconciliation, the bringing together of those who had been separated from each other, is used to convey the idea that as the slave, excluded from the rights and privileges of a free society, became a member of that society upon his manumission, so the one who comes to Christ becomes now a member of God's family. Redeemed, justified, reconciled—the believing person thus is lifted from the lowest level of a slave to that of a child and heir of the promised salvation by the grace of God (*see* Adoption, Sonship).

**2.2. Slaves in Paul's Letters.** The names of those mentioned in Romans 16 suggest that many had been slaves. Andronicus and Urbanus were exclusively slave names in the literature and inscriptions of Paul's day. Moreover, the references to the households of Aristobolus and Narcissus would almost certainly include slaves, probably in large numbers. They were both very wealthy men with powerful political connections.

Inscriptions from the two Jewish catacombs at Rome exhibit the phenomenon of Jewish slaves at Rome who raised their social status by changing their names. Most of the burials can only be determined to be Jewish by the presence of a star of David or a menorah above them. The deceased usually have lofty Roman names that give no hint of their Jewishness. Junius (Junias or Junia), identified as a compatriot of Paul in Romans 16:7 is no doubt a Christian Jew with an aristocratic Roman name. Rufus (Rom 16:13) could also be another of these, particularly if he is the Rufus of Mark 15:21.

In two significant passages Paul makes pronouncements on the status of slaves rather than slavery in the abstract. However, both instances are too enigmatic to be the basis for a definitive statement of Paul's views on this subject.

In 1 Corinthians 7:20-22 Paul writes: "Each one should remain in the situation which he was in when God called him. Were you a slave when you were called? Don't let it trouble you—although if you can gain your freedom, do so" (NIV). The expression "do so" is a translation of the Greek words *mallon chrēsai*, which could better be rendered, "make the most of,

take advantage of." Commentators both ancient and modern have divided almost evenly between understanding these words to mean, "make the most of your slavery," or "make the most of your freedom" (cf. Bartchy: "Were you a slave when you were called? Don't worry about it. But if, indeed, you become manumitted, by all means [as a freed person] live according to [God's calling]"; Bartchy 1973).

A definitive answer to the question of which of these two interpretations is the better lies beyond the scope of this article. But the principle for interpreting 1 Corinthians is perhaps to be found in Paul's other remarks concerning a slave's personal circumstances—the letter to Philemon.* There Paul, an old man, begs for Onesimus' freedom because he was useful to him in his ministry (Philem 8-16). In making his request Paul couches it in a pun, for the word "useful" (*euchrēstos*) and "useless" (*achrēstos*) sound similar to the name of Christ (*christos*). However, in both of these passages (1 Cor 7:20-22 and Philem 8-16) the emphasis is on usefulness in ministry.* Thus the test for freedom for slaves was not an abstract moral imperative calling for the abolition of slavery, but an answer to the question "Given the fact of slavery, what are its advantages for the proclamation of the gospel?" (but see also Bartchy, Finley, Martin). Otherwise, Paul seems to be saying in 1 Corinthians that social, economic and religious standing are of no significance in the church. Believers should live without anxiety in their present circumstances whether married to a believer or an unbeliever; whether they had come to Christ as Jews or Gentiles; whether they were slaves or free; whether men or women.

Paul uses the imagery of slavery with some frequency in his letters. He identifies himself as a slave of Christ in the salutations of Romans and Philippians. He amplifies this idea in Romans 6:15-23. In answer to the question "Shall we sin because we are not under Law but under grace?" (Rom 6:15; cf. Rom 6:1), he answers, "You are slaves to the one whom you obey—whether you are slaves to sin, which leads to death, or to obedience, which leads to righteousness" (Rom 6:16). For Paul the one who is truly free is the person who is a slave of Christ (*see* Servant). That person is as free as mortal and dependent human beings can become, for not only does this new slave-master relationship result in freedom from sin, that destructive tyrant that leads its captives to destruction, but it also results in obedience to Christ, who leads his "slaves" into holiness, goodness and eternal life. The paradox is very strong. The one who is enslaved to Christ is ultimately free; free from sin and death and free to do the will of God and live.

*See also* HOUSEHOLDS AND HOUSEHOLD CODES; PHILEMON, LETTER TO; REDEMPTION; SERVANT, SERVICE; SOCIAL SETTING OF MISSION CHURCHES.

BIBLIOGRAPHY. J. M. G. Barclay, "Paul, Philemon, and the Dilemma of Christian Slave Ownership," *NTS* 37 (1991) 161-86; S. S. Bartchy, *Mallon Chresai: First Century Slavery and the Interpretation of 1 Corinthians 7:21* (SBLDS; Missoula, MT: Scholars, 1973, repr. 1985); idem, "Slavery: In the New Testament," *ISBE* 4.543-46; idem, "Slavery (New Testament)," *ABD* VI.65-73; W. W. Buckland, *The Roman Law of Slavery* (Cambridge: University Press, 1908); M. I. Finley, *Ancient Slavery and Modern Ideology* (New York: Viking, 1980); D. Martin, *Slavery as Salvation* (New Haven: Yale University, 1990); O. Patterson, *Slavery and Social Death: A Comparative Study* (Cambridge: Harvard University, 1982); W. L. Westermann, *The Slave Systems of the Greek and Roman Antiquity* (Philadelphia: American Philosophical Society, 1955). A. A. Rupprecht

**SOCIAL INSTITUTIONS.** *See* SOCIAL SETTING OF MISSION CHURCHES; SOCIAL-SCIENTIFIC APPROACHES TO PAUL.

## SOCIAL SETTING OF MISSION CHURCHES

The churches founded by Paul were not abstract theological entities formed in a social vacuum but real life communities of men and women who inhabited particular social settings. The term *social setting* is a general one which includes matters of the social context of the churches; the social class of converts; the dynamics involved in the formation and development of the Christian communities; social aspects of Paul's own ministry; and social factors in the formation of early Christian doctrine, usually known as the sociology of knowledge. The contemporary discipline of sociology is useful in raising questions and pinpointing issues as well as providing models for analysis and explanation. But sociology needs to be used with caution since the material in question comes from the first century A.D. and is not necessarily open to present-day research.

NT scholarship is showing increasing awareness of the questions of the social setting of the Pauline churches. The approach is already bearing fruit not only in shedding light generally but in illuminating some specific matters of exegesis.

1. The Urban Environment
2. The Social Context of Paul's Mission
3. The Formation and Development of the Communities
4. Social Institutions
5. Social Composition

6. Social Factors in the Formation of Belief

### 1. The Urban Environment.

The mission* undertaken by Paul led to a remarkable social shift in the early Christian church. It moved away from being a predominantly Palestinian and rural movement to being a Gentile and urban movement. Paul's horizons were dominated by the ethos of the city not the countryside.

R. F. Hock (27) has calculated that Paul traveled nearly 10,000 miles on his missionary journeys; traveling having been made easier and safer by the *Pax Romana* (*see* Travel). The cities he visited lay on the East-West trade routes. Antioch* in Syria was the early base for his operations (Acts 13:1-3; 14:26-27; Gal 2:11). A city of a quarter of a million population, it was a city of some prosperity. It had been granted freedom by Pompey, a status later confirmed by Caesar, and so had become a thriving commercial center. Commercial activity was enhanced by its location on the main thoroughfare from Rome* to the Persian border and beyond to the East. Antioch served as the capital of the imperial province and was, in addition, an intellectual focal point. It had a large and long-standing Jewish population. It was a place where Eastern and Western cultures met, and its environment had a significant impact on the development of Paul's mission.

The other cities visited by Paul were nearly all centers of trade, and relatively prosperous. Laodicea, together with Hierapolis and Colossae, was the center of the wool trade (*see* Colossians). Philippi differed from the other cities of Paul in maintaining more of a Latin character and being primarily a center of agriculture rather than commerce (*see* Philippians). Ephesus* was a government center and was well known for its harbor, as well as being famous for its temple of Artemis. Like Ephesus, Corinth (*see* Corinthians) and Thessalonica (*see* Thessalonians) were important trading cities. The identification of "Galatia" is uncertain (*see* Galatians), but if by it Paul means Antioch in Pisidia, Iconium and Lystra, these too, like Philippi and Corinth, were Roman colonies.

The cities shared a common language in Greek and a common orientation toward Rome. They were all conveniently located for travel by land or sea. Their size would have varied, with Antioch being among the largest and Philippi among the smallest. With much space given over to public facilities, their residential areas were tightly packed. Privacy was rare. They contained a number of readily identified ethnic quarters, the most significant of which for the Pauline mission were the Jewish quarters. Five to six million Jews lived in the Diaspora.* They guarded their religious rights jealously but were otherwise politically quiescent. They could be found in most occupations and distributed widely through the status system.

The religious stage was already well populated when Christianity entered the ancient world (*see* Religions). Numerous cults were devoted to the worship of Olympian gods, the reigning emperor,* mystery religions or oriental deities. The cults were important for the economies of the cities, and their temples were prominent buildings within them. Their festivals provided them with public holidays and shaped the annual calendar. The imperial cult was a vehicle for reinforcing political allegiance and cohesion. But it was the more popular devotions which functioned to provide the masses with emotional satisfaction. Syncretism was common.

Cities had much greater potential for the Pauline mission than villages. This is not only because of their obvious value in terms of communication, as a result of their common language and favorable location on the trade routes for spreading the good news, but for deeper reasons to do with their character. Villages were conservative in character and evinced little openness. They were subsistence economies with no opportunities for upward social mobility. Cities were much more open. They possessed both power and potential for change. They would have within them more independently minded people who were open to the new message of the gospel* of Jesus Christ.

## 2. The Social Context of Paul's Mission.

Various estimates are given concerning Paul's own social status. A. Deissmann's early view stressed Paul's occupation and so placed Paul, not without difficulty, at the lower end of the social scale. But more recent estimates have been more generous (*see* Paul in Acts and Letters). Paul was a product of Tarsus and had apparently received a good education there. He had easy access to high authorities in Jerusalem, and although his writing was not of the highest classical quality, neither was it coarse or vulgar, as might be expected from one of low class origin. Whatever his class, largely an economic issue, his status is clear. As a Roman citizen (*see* Citizenship) he enjoyed many privileges and made use of them when the occasion demanded (Acts 16:37; 22:22-29). The reason for his citizenship is a matter of speculation, but it has been suggested that it may have been granted to his father (see Acts 22:28) for services rendered to the Roman army.

On entering a city Paul's mission* strategy was to make contact with people by using the existing social networks to which he related. So, originally, he made

his way to the synagogue (Acts 13:5, 14; 14:1; 17:2; 18:4; 19:8) or, in its absence, the place of prayer* (Acts 16:13) to meet other Jews. Similar links with other expatriates and people who worked at the same trade (including Priscilla and Aquila) were also exploited, especially when the synagogues turned against his message. In each location Paul sought to establish a household as the base of his missionary endeavors and as an ongoing means of support for himself and his newly formed Christian community (Acts 16:15; 17:7; 18:1-3, 7-8; 1 Cor 16:15).

Attention has recently been focused on the significance of the household and the workshop for Paul's missionary activities. Households* were not the private residences of today but were most likely to be large houses which provided shops at the front and living accommodations at the rear. There would also have been room for workshops and living quarters for dependents and visitors. Such an arrangement would have ideally suited Paul's purposes by both enabling him to finance his mission through his work as a tentmaker (Acts 18:3; 20:34, 35; 1 Thess 2:9; *see* Tentmaking) and by providing him with a ready-made platform from which preaching and teaching could be conducted daily among the many who would have been around the workshop. The significance of the workshop has been brought into focus by research into the methods of other itinerant philosophers like the Cynics of Paul's day. Rather than viewing manual labor as demeaning, the Cynics adopted it as an ideal way of life and as the means by which a teacher could model his philosophy to his disciples.

R. F. Hock, A. J. Malherbe and W. A. Meeks have set the apostle Paul in the wider context of other itinerant philosophers. Their work serves two purposes. On the one hand it provides the key that unlocks a number of exegetical problems. It illuminates, for example, Paul's attitude to receiving money from the Corinthians (1 Cor 8—9; 2 Cor 11:7-11; *see* Financial Support); his use of boasting* and folly (*see* Foolishness) in 2 Corinthians 11:16—12:11; his use of a phrase like "gentle . . . like a nurse" (RSV) in 1 Thessalonians 2:7 and his approach to ethics.* On the other hand it highlights the distinctiveness of Paul, especially in the message he preached. So, although superficially, the ethical codes he pronounces (Gal 5:19-23; Eph 5:21—6:9; Col 3:5-14, 18—4:4; 1 Thess 4:1-12) seem to be similar to other contemporary codes, with nothing remarkable about the qualities demanded, they are distinguished by the motivations Paul sets out for this behavior, for example, "to please God" and "in the Lord Jesus" (1 Thess 4:1), and by the power* offered through which a believer in Jesus Christ could meet the requirements. These things set Christians apart from those outside the church.*

### 3. The Formation and Development of the Communities.

Paul's primary interest was not in the conversion of individuals but in the formation of Christian communities. In a large city, such as Rome or Corinth, several communities may well have been brought into existence, each based on a different household. The language of Romans 16:10, 11, 14, 15, 23; 1 Corinthians 14:23 and 16:15 suggests a distinction between individual groups which met in particular households and "the whole church" which was composed of a number of such household groups meeting together occasionally. Furthermore, archeological evidence, as reported by J. Murphy-O'Connor (156), confirms that the average household could have only accommodated fifty (a realistic starting figure for the Christians we can actually identify with the church in Corinth) with difficulty. It is more probable then that they would have more regularly met as subgroups in smaller numbers. But the question here is how were such groups formed and their identity maintained?

*3.1. Language.* The language we speak plays an important role in interpreting and shaping the world in which we live. It is never neutral and always filters reality for us so that we always see reality through its eyes. Language plays a particularly important role in giving groups an awareness of their own identity, in maintaining cohesion and marking out boundaries. So Paul's letters are full of the language of kinship.

Christians are "children of God" and "brothers" and "sisters" to each other. The Christian family replaces the natural family. Body language (1 Cor 12:12-27) and other imagery makes for solidarity. There is also evidence of in-group language, such as *Abba* or *maranatha.* Other language sharply differentiates Christians from the wider society. Thus, just to take the example of 1 Thessalonians 1:9-10, Paul speaks of them having undergone a radical conversion which separated them from their fellow citizens. The use of the language of outsidership (1 Cor 5:12, 13; Col 4:5; 1 Thess 4:12) sharply separates Christians from others. As does also Paul's frequent references to unbelievers as members of "the world,*" "dead in sin,*" "a crooked and depraved generation" or other such terminology. The positive description of Christians as "saints," "beloved" or "coworkers with God" further reinforces their internal cohesion and external separation.

*3.2. Rituals.* Actions also contribute toward the formation and maintenance of distinct communities.

Both baptism* and the Lord's Supper* are rituals associated with the death, burial and resurrection* of Christ, events which mark clear boundaries in the life of Christ and, consequently, in the life of those who are in union with him by faith.

Baptism is a ritual which symbolizes and effects a dramatic break with the candidates' former way of life and their incorporation into the church (Rom 6:1-4; 1 Cor 12:13; Gal 3:26-28). The use made of clothing imagery (cf. Eph 4:22-24; Col 3:9, 10), which probably had its origins in the baptismal rite, also served to reinforce the believers' new identity in Christ.

The Lord's Supper has been termed by Wayne Meeks as a "ritual of solidarity." It separates genuine believers from unbelievers and stresses the exclusivity of serving Christ (1 Cor 10:21). It reenacts the Last Supper Jesus had with his disciples (1 Cor 11:23) and emphasizes the believers' participation not only in Christ (1 Cor 10:16; 11:24-26) but with one another. That is why Paul denounces the Corinthians for turning what was meant to be a ritual reenactment of their unity into an instrument of social division (1 Cor 11:17-22). G. Theissen (121-140) helpfully suggests that social factors may have caused this division, with the strong being higher in the social scale than the weak. Other rituals, such as the weekly offering (1 Cor 16:2), not only strengthened their belonging to one another in the local community but gave the early Christians a vision of belonging to a worldwide community of faith (2 Cor 8—9). Ritual, as the symbolic reenactment of what the community believed about itself, played a significant role in both forming and maintaining community identity.

*3.3. Communitas.* The Pauline communities were not rigidly structured hierarchical organizations but were characterized by *communitas. Communitas* refers to patterns of relationship which are marked by a high degree of participation on the part of its members and a strong sense of belonging (see Sampley). They are antihierarchical brotherhoods which value spontaneity and are loose on structures. The pattern of worship* (1 Cor 14:26-33; Col 3:15-16); the emphasis on every believer receiving gifts* of the Spirit (Rom 12:3-8; 1 Cor 12:1-30; Eph 4:7-13); and the command to accept one another and practice hospitality (Rom 12:13; 15:17; cf. 1 Tim 3:2; 5:10; Tit 1:8) combine with the radical teaching that faith in Christ completely undermines social distinctions (1 Cor 7:21-22; Gal 3:28; Eph 6:5-9) to paint a portrait of Paul's churches as having the typical traits of *communitas.*

No group can exist for long on a level of pure *communitas* and some structural elements are evident in the Pauline community from the beginning (*see*

Church Order). Elders and deacons were appointed. Worship was to be conducted "in a fitting and orderly way" (1 Cor 14:40). E. Käsemann has pointed out how the gifts of the Spirit contain an implicit ordering according to the use made of them by the body. It is likely that the wealthier householders who hosted the church would have played some inevitable leadership role. Nonetheless, in spite of any qualifications, Paul's communities were predominantly characterized by *communitas,* especially when compared with the more structured worship of the Jewish synagogues.

*3.4. External Conflict.* Conflict may have an adverse effect on the survival and development of groups but, providing the members of the group are given satisfactory explanations that legitimate their position, it may be highly constructive for the group's life. So it was for the Pauline churches. Opposition (*see* Opponents) was their recurring experience and consequently Paul frequently taught or wrote to explain why it should have been so (Acts 14:22; Phil 1:12-14, 29-30; 1 Thess 2:14-20; 3:4; 2 Thess 1:4-10; 2 Tim 3:10-14). The existence of conflict can strengthen a group by defining its boundaries, disciplining its members, bonding them together in more intense relationships against a common enemy,* demanding total adherence and heightening the sense members have of belonging. As well as energizing a group, it calls forth creative leadership and even makes a group attractive to nonmembers. All this is evident in the churches of Paul.

*3.5. Institutionalization.* Over time, and given the habitual nature of its activities, a group becomes institutionalized. That is, it loses its original purity and creativity and becomes more mixed in its purposes and motives and less flexible in its relationships and actions. The second generation of members are never as clear-sighted or totally committed as the original founders of a movement. Vested interests enter. Charismatic openness is channeled in certain expected and routinized ways. Worship adopts more predictable patterns. Ethical positions become less demanding and boundaries with the world are blurred. Paradoxically, ethical freedom* in the Spirit (*see* Holy Spirit) is gradually supplanted by the letter of the law. Leadership becomes more concerned with positions, hierarchy and offices. The organization develops and becomes more structured, less responsive to new needs and new times and less versatile (*see* Early Catholicism).

Many have detected the evidence of institutionalization in the NT, especially the Pastoral letters. M. MacDonald has traced its development in detail from the original Pauline communities of Galatia, Phi-lippi, Thessalonica and Corinth, through the pastorally led communities represented by Ephesians and Colossians, to the Pastoral letters. She traces the development of institutionalization in terms of attitude to the world/ethics, ministry, ritual and belief.

To some extent the process was inevitable. Paul himself, the charismatic leader, was ultimately removed from the scene. His churches were conversionist sects, that is, voluntary religious groups which saw themselves as uniquely offering the way of salvation,* demanding great commitment from their members and seeing themselves in opposition to the world but intent on converting it. The desire to convert people from the world builds in an inescapable tension as it brings the Christians into contact with others, so giving opportunity to a host of temptations; it softens the boundaries between the sect and the world and leads toward compromise. The tension is evident in, for example, 1 Corinthians 5:9-10; 8:1-13; 14:23 and 1 Thessalonians 4:11-12. Even so, it is possible to overestimate the process of institutionalization and to let the theory outrun the evidence. The theory is highly dependent on particular views concerning the dating of the letters and if not careful, the argument becomes circular: here is evidence of institutionalization, so the letter must be of a late date; this letter is dated late, and so we must interpret it in terms of institutionalization.

*3.6. Authority and Governance.* No group can exist for any length of time without some form of authority structure. Much of what we learn about the exercise of authority* in the Pauline churches we learn by inference because of the tensions and disputes between Paul and competing authorities. Acts records the tensions which arose between the Pauline mission and the church at Jerusalem* that resulted in the eventual recognition of both as independent and yet in a mutual and continuing relationship with one another (Acts 15:1-35). Other insights arise from Paul's handling of itinerant apostles* who were claiming the allegiance of the church at Corinth (2 Cor 10—13). Further insights come from observing the handling of internal disputes, handling deviance within the community or tensions between settled community organizers and charismatic itinerants (*see* Opponents).

What was the basis for Paul's authority and apostleship? M. Weber classically defined three means by which authority is legitimated: those of legality or rationality, tradition and charisma. Most analyses of Paul's authority have taken place within that framework, although Theissen (51-54) has added the further concept of functional authority. These types of authority never exist in pure terms. Paul shows some concern to claim a traditional basis for his authority (1 Cor 11:23; 15:3) but not to justify his role by reference to the traditional center of Jerusalem (Gal 1:11—2:10). It is most appropriate to see Paul's authority as an institutionalized and rationalized form of charisma (Holmberg).

Paul's is not a pure type of charismatic authority since in the innovative work of the charismatic the pure charismatic points to himself as the one to follow while Paul stresses that his authority is derived from Jesus Christ and is not his own (2 Cor 10:3; 1 Thess 4:2). He limits his authority. He acts as father to the churches rather than as prophet, the archetype of charismatic authority. He refuses to accept financial support (1 Cor 9:1-18; 2 Cor 11:7-9; *see* Financial Support). He gives reasons for the instructions he gives and supports other churches not of his group, like Jerusalem, through the collection.* And he has a place for tradition. And yet, in his radicalism and innovativeness, in his putting himself forward as a model to be imitated, in his formation of communities, in his presentation of himself and his claims, he demonstrates some of the typical traits of the charismatic.

Unfortunately none of this has led to any agreement as to how authoritarian Paul was in practice and evaluations differ widely. Some stress his emphasis on liberty (1 Cor 10:23; Gal 5:1), his restricted use of authority (1 Cor 7:25; 2 Cor 10:8) and his desire to encourage the local church to assume responsibility for its own actions (1 Cor 5:1-5). Others highlight his directiveness and even accuse him of using manipulative techniques (1 Cor 7:17; 14:37-38; Phil 3:15).

Paul exercised his authority in a number of ways: through return visits, letters, locally appointed leaders and through sending his representatives, who carried his delegated authority, on visits (Eph 6:21; 1 Thess 3:2; Tit 1:5). While no clear pattern of local church leadership emerges, it seems that Paul appointed elders on his own authority (Acts 14:23) and that churches recognized elders and deacons (Phil 1:1). The word elder (*presbyteros*) seems synonymous with bishop (*episcopos*); the difference between them perhaps reflecting a more predominantly Jewish (for *presbyteros*) or Gentile (for *episcopos*) social context (*see* Church Order and Government).

It is often suggested that the early churches experienced tension between appointed leaders in structured positions and those itinerating or exercising the charismatic gifts of tongues* and prophecy, with each vying for authority. But it is easy to overdraw the contrast here and to present too simplistic a picture. Meeks (120-21) has drawn attention to some of the complexities: tongue speaking is learned behavior;

Paul accepts the value of tongues (1 Cor 14:18), even if he wishes to discipline their use, and we dare not assume that the ones who spoke in tongues were too distinct from the leaders. Throughout the period of the Pauline mission there is a concern for both structural authority (see, for example, the early reference to elders in Acts 14:23) and for spiritual gifts (note, for example, the late references in 1 Tim 4:14 and 2 Tim 1:6-7).

Whatever questions remain unresolved about authority and leadership in the Pauline communities, and they are many, it is clear that the real authority was Jesus Christ (2 Cor 4:5; Eph 4:15) and human authorities played only a limited role. 2 Corinthians 1:24 captures the spirit of Pauline leadership, which inevitably leads the churches to being more egalitarian in form than most groups in the ancient world: "Not that we lord it over your faith, but we work with you for your joy. . ." (*see* Pastor).

**4. Social Institutions.**
It was not possible for new religions to set up novel institutions in the Roman Empire. They required a license. The emergence of the Christian church was made possible and its growth and continuance were made secure by the way in which it used existing social institutions and adapted them to its own ends. Three institutions are particularly relevant.

*4.1. The Synagogue.* Christianity entered the ancient world as a sect within Judaism which thereby afforded it legal protection in its formative years. The synagogue provided Paul with an immediate platform for his message and served in many ways, but not all, as a model for the emerging churches. The early churches imitated the synagogue in their Scripture reading and exposition, prayers and common meals and in the absence of sacrifices which were common among pagan cults. Other parallels can be seen in handling their own internal disputes, money raising, care for their members and their vision of belonging to a worldwide people of God. Perhaps also some organizational features were borrowed from the synagogue, such as the role of elders and patrons. But there were also many differences. Christians practiced baptism and not circumcision.* Their worship included prophecy* and tongue* speaking. Women had a much greater role. And churches were not formed on the basis of race.

*4.2. The Household.* Early households* were large, inclusive communities consisting not only of a principal family but of slaves and friends, tenants, partners or clients who would have been involved in a common commercial or agricultural enterprise. In the absence of buildings they provided ideal meeting places for the early Christians. The household was a hierarchical body under the authority of the father. Such people appear to have become patrons of the early Christian communities (Rom 16:4, 5, 14, 15, 23; 1 Cor 1:11; 16:19; Col 4:15, Philem 2). The fact that Christian groups were often located in households affected the way in which churches developed.

For this reason Theissen (107) has termed the Pauline communities "love-patriarchies." By doing so he has drawn attention to the role of the household patron in the early church and the shape it gave to social relations. Although, he argues, the gospel ameliorated social differences, the social differences were taken for granted, and respect and subordination were enjoined on those in the lower orders in the church toward their superiors. Evidence of this is found in the codes of household ethics (Col 3:18—4:1; Eph 5:22—6:9; 1 Tim 2:9-10; *see* Households and Household Codes). But love-patriarchalism would be in tension with the more radical and egalitarian claims of the gospel (Gal 3:28), and not all would think there is sufficient evidence to substantiate Theissen's view.

Other implications of the Pauline communities being located within households include questions of conversion, division and growth. The individualism of contemporary Western society would have been quite foreign to the way of thinking in Paul's day. Decisions would have been taken corporately, or more probably, by the leading member of the household on behalf of others. Hence we read of household conversions and baptisms (Acts 16:15, 31-34; 18:8; 1 Cor 1:16). When such a joint decision was taken it would not necessarily call forth equal acceptance, commitment or understanding by all who were involved. Negatively, the existence of various house churches in any one town would lead to a tendency to division; with one house fellowship* owing allegiance to one teacher and others to different teachers. It may be that this is the situation underlying Paul's words in 1 Corinthians 1:10-17. Positively, the household was ready-made to serve as the "basic cell" of the church and the primary unit for mission as it used its existing network of relationships outside its own membership to spread the gospel.

*4.3. Voluntary Associations.* The Roman Empire witnessed the growth of many and varied voluntary associations. These were private clubs to which admittance was gained by an initiation ceremony and were often based around a particular trade or objective. They existed to provide people with opportunities for festivity and frequently centered around meals. The associations provided people with the religious and emotional satisfaction which was lacking in the more public or official cults. Some existed as burial societies. For the most part they were tolerated by Rome but, in view of the secrecy of their activity, they had the potential to be politically subversive and so on occasions they were under scrutiny or restriction by the authorities.

Rome seems to have viewed Judaism, for legal purposes, as a voluntary association, albeit as an association with a difference in view of its international size. It is not surprising therefore that the early Christian communities should have been viewed also as a voluntary association. There are similarities in that they had private meetings, a voluntary membership, practiced initiation rituals, frequently met for meals, or the meal of the Lord's Supper, and had a degree of exclusivity about them. But there were also some marks which distinguish the early Christian communities from other voluntary associations. Paul's churches were much more socially inclusive and enjoyed equality of status within them, between males and females (*see* Man and Woman), slaves and free (*see* Slavery). With Judaism, the church shared an international membership. The commitment expected from members was also more demanding than that of most voluntary societies. There is no evidence of early Christian burial practices (except in the catacombs, of an uncertain date) and the terminology of the associations is absent from Paul's writings. Furthermore, voluntary associations did not usually concern themselves with ethical teaching. But the fact that Paul's churches could be seen to be nothing unusual enabled them to be accommodated by the Roman world.

**5. Social Composition.**

*5.1. Social Stratification.* The terminology of social class needs to be read back into the NT with extreme caution. Contemporary analysis of class is essentially a post-industrial analysis of people's economic position. In the world of Paul, birth and legal status were more significant. A number of ranks were clearly defined, namely, the senatorial aristocracy, the equestrian orders, various degrees within the municipal bureaucracies, plebs, freedmen and slaves. Status, therefore, seems to be a more useful analytic tool and realistically enables measurement of people's social position to take place on a number of dimensions, including those of power, wealth, education, occupation, family connections and so on.

Taking their cue from Paul's comments in 1 Corinthians 1:26 scholars used to argue that the early Christian churches were composed mainly of slaves and inconsequential people from the lower classes. A. Deissmann's work seemed to lend support to this view. His investigations into the language and literature of the NT led him to assert that the early church was nonliterary in nature, "a movement among the weary and heavy-laden, men without power and position . . . the poor, the base, the foolish, as St Paul with a prophet's sympathy describes them." Other contemporary comments by critics of Christianity seem to reinforce that view.

However, in recent days a new consensus has emerged from a fresh examination of the evidence which advances the view that early Christian communities were socially mixed communities with perhaps only the uppermost and lowest ranges of the social stratification system missing (*see* Rich and Poor). The consensus is the result of investigations into the names mentioned in the Acts and Pauline epistles, excluding the Pastorals, which amount to nearly eighty in all. Of these we may tentatively say something about the social status of thirty of them. Among those are clearly persons of some means. Some have an ability to travel which would have required finance. Some, like Lydia (Acts 16:14), we know to have been in the merchant classes. Others had houses sufficiently large to accommodate Christian meetings, such as Priscilla and Aquila (Rom 16:4-5), Gaius (Rom 16:23; 1 Cor 1:14), Nympha (Col 4:15) and Philemon (Philem 2). Some we can identify by the office they held like Crispus, the ruler of the synagogue (Acts 18:8; 1 Cor 1:14). Synagogue rulers were normally men of some substance. Erastus was the *oikonomos tēs poleōs* (Rom 16:23) at Corinth, a term which probably means either the city treasurer or director of public works. It would have been a position of consequence, if not wealth. While Stephanus (1 Cor 16:15) was by inference wealthy enough to act as a patron to the Pauline mission. The families of Aristobulus and Narcissus (Rom 16:10-11) both had good imperial connections.

The Pauline churches were not uniformly composed of such people. Among the names listed were many that were common slave names. The ethical sections concerning masters and slaves would have been superfluous unless slaves had joined the church as well as masters. Other passages about the life of the early church, such as those about giving (2 Cor 8 and 9), only make sense if social diversity is assumed. This is particularly true, as Theissen has shown, of 1 Corinthians. His analysis along lines of social stratification of the weak and the strong (1 Cor 8:1-13; *see* Strong and Weak) and the divisions at the Lord's Table, which he sets in the context of similar meals known to have taken place in voluntary associations,

is especially illuminating.

Attempts to ally the use of the more expressive gifts exercised in Corinth with the poorer and less articulate members of the church are frequent but less successful. At least from the standpoint of contemporary Pentecostal and charismatic movements it is not possible to tie the exercise of charismatic gifts of tongues, healings and prophecy too tightly to social or economic deprivation.

Evidence then, of a direct and inferential nature, suggests that the early church was a socially diverse body.

*5.2. Status Inconsistency.* A particular theory about the social status of the Pauline converts, that of status inconsistency, has been put forward by W. A. Meeks (22-23, 174, 191). Status inconsistency occurs when the various dimensions by which status is measured are not in agreement with one another and a "criss-crossing of categories" takes place. So, a person may be wealthy but of low rank, educated but a slave, in a powerful position but a woman. The major source of tension occurs when a person's "achieved status," through wealth, occupation or education, is in conflict with one's "accredited status" due to one's race, sex or birth. A number of Paul's converts might be said to be suffering from status inconsistency. Among them were independent women of some wealth, rich Jews in a pagan society, skilled or wealthy freed people who were stigmatized by their former slavery and Gentile* God-fearers who had attached themselves to the synagogue.

The theory is used to explain why some people appeared to be more open to conversion than others and why there were particular attractions in apocalyptic* or millenarian preaching. Those whose status was consistent were more likely to be well integrated into their own appropriate social networks. But those whose status was inconsistent, like people who were socially mobile, were likely to be much less integrated into particular social circles. Consequently, they were more likely to be open to receive new teaching. Moreover, the dissonance such a person experienced might find expression and resolution in religious activities or beliefs. Meeks points out that millenarian teaching, with its symbolism of a world out of joint and its promise of radical transformation, might be particularly attractive to those whose own experience of life was ambiguous.

Meeks (68-70) further uses the theory to criticize Theissen's view of the weak and the strong in 1 Corinthians 8 as too simplistic and to suggest that those who showed signs of status inconsistency might have been those most partial to speaking in tongues.

The theory has its critics because of its imprecision and the slender basis of the evidence which supports it. Most evidence is drawn from 1 Corinthians. C. A. Wanamaker, in a recent commentary on 1 and 2 Thessalonians, has pointed out that although it should be ideal for explaining the situation at Thessalonica, we have no information about individuals there to determine if the theory is relevant or not. He further points out that other explanations for the acceptance of Paul's millenarian teaching at Thessalonica, such as its similarity to the Cabirus cult which had been robbed of its popularity by its incorporation into the civic cult, are more plausible (*see* Thessalonians). The theory, however, is not likely to be so easily disposed of and, given that many of the converts of Paul whom we can name seem to be converted from the ranks of the Jews or God-fearers rather than directly from paganism, it seems to hold some water.

### 6. Social Factors in the Formation of Belief.

A social science perspective on the NT is likely to reject what it sees as the fallacy of idealism, that is, that the determining role in historical development is played by ideas, in favor of a view that ideas are constructed on the basis of the social realities that underlie them. The social reality, in the case of Paul, is the situation of his mission churches, and attention is paid to ways in which that has shaped his theology. Many, who would give weight to this general approach, would wish to express it more cautiously than Holmberg (1980) who, in Watson's words (184), argues that, "Paul's theology is in fact 'a secondary reaction' to 'primary, concrete phenomenon in the social world.' "

This approach owes much to the writings of P. Berger and T. Luckmann who argue that, in spite of appearances, our interpretation of reality is not fixed but that all of us are engaged in the enterprise of constructing a universe of meaning. In their view, all that we encounter as reality is in fact socially constructed. Once it is admitted that all reality is constructed in this way it is not possible to dismiss particular constructions as "merely" socially constructed. The validity of all social constructions has to be judged on other grounds. It does not therefore, properly understood, lead to reductionism nor to a relativization of Paul's theology. Three issues illustrate the approach with reference to Paul.

*6.1. Sectarian Legitimation.* Both Esler, primarily in relation to Luke-Acts, and Watson, primarily in relation to Galatians and Romans, have developed the perspective of the sociology of knowledge to expound Paul's ministry in terms of the legitimation of a sectar-

ian movement. Christianity began, they argue, as a reform movement within Judaism before becoming a distinct sect (see 3.5) sharply distinguished from Judaism. Judaism then became a hostile opponent of Paul's mission churches, to say nothing of the more generally unpropitious environment in which they found themselves. But it is characteristic of sects to find themselves encountering hostility, and consequently to have to shore up the wavering commitment of their members. To do this sects engage in a process of legitimations, that is, explanations and justifications which legitimate their beliefs. These legitimations take a number of recognizable forms, including locating the sect meaningfully within the unfolding of history; looking backward and looking forward and reinterpreting past understandings, so that its beliefs are not seen to be radical, creations out of nothing, but traditional, what was meant or to be expected all along.

The central issue for Paul is the inclusion and place of Gentile* Christians within the church and the relationship of Christianity to Judaism with the problems it raised about covenant,* circumcision,* Law,* works (*see* Works of the Law), food* and table-fellowship. Paul seeks to show that the covenant of grace* is not in conflict with older covenants which appeared to major on the role of obedience to the Law but that the central feature of all covenants was that they depended upon faith* in God's promise (Rom 4:1-25; Gal 3:6-25). Thus, his gospel was not a radical departure from the old but a consistent development of the old. The more general question about persecution and the continuing success of evil and evildoers is also very evident, giving rise to his eschatological* and apocalyptic teaching.

When placed in the context of these social realities, the traditional Lutheran interpretation of Paul's views on justification* by faith is called into question, and further support is given to the recent interpretation of E. P. Sanders and others on the role of the Law* within the covenant.

*6.2. Apocalypticism.* Recent studies have highlighted the apocalyptic* strain to be found in Paul's teaching. For Paul the age in which he lived was the last age and one which would be brought to a sudden conclusion by the imminent return of the Lord Jesus Christ who would bring an end to its rebellion against God, render judgment* on the wicked, vindicate the elect (*see* Election) and bring their salvation* to its consummation. Investigation into the social setting of Paul's teaching draws attention to the social realities that lay beneath it and also sets it in the wider framework of millenarian movements.

Millenarian movements, as summarized by J. Gager, have five basic traits: the promise of heaven on earth; the overthrow or reversal of the present social order; a terrific release of emotional energy; a brief life span and the central role of a messianic, prophetic or charismatic leader. With only a little modification these can be found as basic tenets of faith in Paul's churches. The new millennium will dawn at the return of Jesus Christ and the present social order will be transformed (Rom 8:18-23; 1 Cor 7:29-31; Gal 6:14; Eph 1:10; 1 Thess 1:10; 4:16; 2 Thess 1:6-10; Tit 2:12-14). The emotional energy generated can be seen in the movement's zeal for evangelism, the intense relationship between Paul and his converts (2 Cor 7:2; Phil 4:1; 1 Thess 2:17) and in the place given to the exercise of charismatic gifts (1 Cor 12:1-9; 14:1-40). In Paul's case the movement did not have a brief life span, but its continuity depended on it undergoing organizational change (see 3.5). The central messianic figure throughout was Jesus Christ, but Paul himself played a crucial role as a charismatic leader with authority derived from Jesus Christ.

People are open to become members of millenarian movements when there is a deeply felt dissatisfaction with the current situation and where there is a discrepancy between people's legitimate expectations and their current experience in society. Meeks has traced this to the status inconsistency suffered by members of Paul's churches (see 5.2). But wider factors of perceived deprivation, such as economic hardship, lack of political freedom or power, the failure by existing religious rituals to satisfy or low social status are also evident among Paul's converts.

*6.3. Cognitive Dissonance.* The theory of cognitive dissonance hypothesizes that when a specific belief held by a group is subjected to specific disconfirmation, the members of the group may not ease their mental discomfort (or dissonance) by giving up the belief but rather by holding it more firmly and vigorously propagating it in the hope that others will come to share it too. Their activism and success in gaining converts lessens the discomfort felt. As originally propounded by L. Festinger and others to contemporary movements, and applied by Gager to the early church in Jerusalem, whose expectation of the imminent arrival of the kingdom* (Acts 1:6) was, he says, disappointed, it was a theory with precise criteria. There had to be (1) a commitment to a belief, (2) which was held to be important and (3) subject to disconfirmation; (4) the disconfirmation must occur and be seen to occur and (5) the belief must be held by a group and shared by others. It is, however, now in common use as an explanation of the behavior of the early Christians and

has consequently lost its precision and in turn some of its value. The generalized nature of its use makes it difficult to confirm or falsify. Meeks, for example, speaks of apocalyptic movements providing relief from cognitive dissonance and as having implications for the status inconsistency of some members and the socially mixed nature of the church but without spelling out the connections between them at all.

*See also* SOCIAL-SCIENTIFIC APPROACHES TO PAUL.

BIBLIOGRAPHY. R. Banks, *Paul's Idea of Community* (Grand Rapids: Eerdmans, 1980); P. Berger and T. Luckmann, *The Social Construction of Reality: A Treatise on the Sociology of Knowledge* (Garden City, NY: Doubleday, 1966); C. S. Dudley and E. Hilgert, *New Testament Tensions and the Contemporary Church* (Philadelphia: Fortress, 1987); P. Esler, *Community and Gospel in Luke-Acts* (SNTSMS 57; Cambridge: University Press, 1987); L. Festinger, H. Riecken and S. Schachter, *When Prophecy Fails* (New York: Harper & Row, 1956); J. Gager, *Kingdom and Community: The Social World of Early Christianity* (Englewood Cliffs, NJ: Prentice Hall, 1975); R. F. Hock, *The Social Context of Paul's Ministry: Tentmaking and Apostleship* (Philadelphia: Fortress, 1980); B. Holmberg, *Paul and Power: The Structure of Authority in the Primitive Church as Reflected in the Pauline Epistles* (Philadelphia: Fortress, 1980); idem, *Sociology and the New Testament: An Appraisal* (Minneapolis: Fortress, 1990); E. A. Judge, *The Social Pattern of Christian Groups in the First Century* (London: Tyndale, 1960); H. C. Kee, *Christian Origins in Sociological Perspective* (Philadelphia: Westminster, 1980); M. Y. MacDonald, *The Pauline Churches: A Socio-Historical Study of Institutionalization in the Pauline and Deutero-Pauline Writings* (SNTSMS 60; Cambridge: University Press, 1988); A. J. Malherbe, *Paul and the Thessalonians* (Philadelphia: Fortress, 1987); idem, *Social Aspects of Early Christianity* (Baton Rouge: Louisiana State University, 1977); B. Malina, *The New Testament World: Insights from Cultural Anthropology* (Atlanta: John Knox, 1981); W. A. Meeks, *The First Urban Christians: The Social World of the Apostle Paul* (New Haven: Yale University, 1983); idem, *The Moral World of the First Christians* (Philadelphia: Fortress, 1986); J. Murphy-O'Connor, *St. Paul's Corinth: Texts and Archaeology* (GNS 6; Wilmington, DE: Michael Glazier, 1983); J. P. Sampley, *Pauline Partnership in Christ: Christian Community and Commitment in Light of Roman Law* (Philadelphia: Fortress, 1980); J. H. Schütz, *Paul and the Anatomy of Apostolic Authority* (SNTSMS 26; Cambridge: University Press, 1975); J. Stambaugh and D. Balch, *The Social World of the First Christians* (Philadelphia: Fortress, 1986); G. Theissen, *The Social Setting of Pauline Christianity: Essays on Corinth* (Philadelphia: Fortress, 1982); D. Tidball, *The So-*

*cial Context of the New Testament: A Sociological Analysis* (Grand Rapids: Zondervan, 1984); C. A. Wanamaker, *Commentary on 1 and 2 Thessalonians* (NIGTC; Grand Rapids: Eerdmans, 1990); F. Watson, *Paul, Judaism and the Gentiles: A Sociological Approach* (SNTSMS 56; Cambridge: University Press, 1986).

D. J. Tidball

**SOCIAL STRATIFICATION.** *See* Social Setting of Mission Churches.

## SOCIAL-SCIENTIFIC APPROACHES TO PAUL

1. The Legitimacy of a Social-Scientific Approach
2. The Advantages of Social-Scientific Interpretation
3. Problems in Social-Scientific Interpretation
4. Case Studies in Social-Scientific Interpretation
5. Conclusion

**1. The Legitimacy of a Social-Scientific Approach.**
The interpretation of Paul and his letters is a necessarily (though by no means exclusively) historical task. The apostle Paul was a historical figure. The letters,* as ancient Greek texts of a recognizable epistolary form, are human artifacts from a particular time and place in antiquity. Furthermore, the content of the letters (including the ideas, events, problems and persons to which they make reference), their highly occasional character, and the readers to whom they were directed all invite and justify historical and literary-historical analysis. This is not to say that the truth to which Paul and his letters bear witness is confined to what can be determined by historical method. This would restrict unjustifiably the authority* of Paul's apostleship and the truth* of his gospel* to what is ascertainable according to the canons of contemporary, secular historiography—as if, for example, the truth of Paul's message about a "new creation*" through the crucified and risen Christ* were a matter only of the historical evidence for the crucifixion* and the empty tomb. Nevertheless, there can be no doubt for modern readers of Paul that an adequate interpretation of his letters and of the theology they express requires the historical perspective that the historical method aims to give.

But if history is important (something which is recognized widely already), so are the human sciences in general (something which is not yet recognized so widely). There are several reasons for this. First, more than any other texts of the NT, Paul's letters give us unique access to the apostle as an individual and complex personality. In a way that the gospels do not do

for Jesus, the letters give us Paul at first hand. It is natural and legitimate, therefore, to see whether or not approaches from psychology and psychoanalysis may not deepen our understanding of the type of person Paul was, the nature of his experience of call (or "conversion"*), the way he behaved as a leader, the kinds of instruction he gave and the manner in which he gave it, and so on. If, as many agree, it is difficult to put Paul in his place, it may be that conscious or unconscious factors in Paul's make-up had a part to play. It may be the case also that psychological factors help to explain the complexities of the interaction between Paul, his followers and his opponents.

Second, there can be no doubt that Paul was involved deeply with the society of his day and that his letters are directed explicitly to groups of believers to whom he felt bound by strong ties of spiritual kinship. Paul, in other words, cannot be understood adequately in purely individual terms. His identity and self-understanding were bound up with those to whom he himself felt bound—to Christ as "Lord,"* to the people of Israel,* his "kinfolk by race" (Rom 9:3), to the groups of believers whom he had fathered in the faith, to his fellow workers in the apostolic ministry, to authority figures in Jerusalem* and to authority figures in Rome.* So in addition to a psychological dimension to the interpretation of Paul and his letters, there is an important sociological dimension also. This calls for the use of the kind of models which make sociological analysis possible. Such models are likely to be as relevant to the understanding of the situation of Paul's addressees as to the understanding of Paul's own situation.

Third, Paul's engagement with the society of his day often took the form of a provocative reinterpretation of his society's dominant cultural symbols. One only has to bring to mind the sharp controversy Paul generated in one context or another over matters such as Torah observance, circumcision,* table fellowship, the place of women (*see* Man and Woman) in the Christian assembly and the legitimacy or otherwise of eating meat offered to idols,* to see how subversive Paul appeared to supporters of the cultural *status quo.* But attempts to gauge the meaning and significance of these cultural symbols, both for Paul and for his opponents, are likely to lack precision if they fail to make use of critical tools for the analysis of culture. Such tools are those which have been developed and practiced in the discipline of social (or cultural) anthropology. Thus, as well as psychological and sociological dimensions to the interpretation of Paul, there are important anthropological dimensions also.

**2. The Advantages of Social-Scientific Interpretation.** Before proceeding to specific case studies of the application of the social sciences to the interpretation of Paul, it may be worth summarizing at a general level the advantages and disadvantages of the method. I begin with the advantages.

*2.1. Synchronic Relations.* As implied already, social-scientific interpretation is a natural development of the historical interpretation of Paul. If historical and literary-historical method helps us to decipher not only the meaning of Paul's letters but also the world of people and events to which the letters refer, then these other human sciences help us to take that process further. They make possible what anthropologist C. Geertz calls "thick description" in the interpretation of the world behind the text. Thus, where historical analysis focuses on *diachronic* relations, on relations of cause-and-effect over time, social-science analysis draws particular attention to *synchronic* relations, to the way meaning springs from interpreting the relation of one social actor to another within the complex web of culturally-determined social systems and patterns of communication.

For example, where historical criticism of Paul's letters seeks to answer questions of authorship, chronology,* sequence, place of writing, identity of addressees and the like, social-science criticism seeks to determine why Paul writes letters at all, what function letters play in relation to Paul's identity and authority as an apostle,* who needed letters of recommendation and for what purpose (cf. Rom 16:1-2), what factors influenced Paul's decision to write rather than visit in person (cf. 2 Cor 10:1-12) and what factors influenced how Paul's letters were received (see further, Petersen 1985).

*2.2. A Corrective to "Theological Docetism."* Social-science criticism offers a corrective to interpretations of Paul which suffer from what has been called "theological docetism": the assumption that what are important about Paul and his letters are the theological ideas irrespective of their being embedded in the lives of people and communities—ideas like justification* by faith,* or reconciliation (*see* Peace, Reconciliation), or new creation* in Christ, or the gifts* of the Spirit,* or the church* as the body of Christ.* The tendency to abstract these doctrines from their concrete historical, social and cultural setting in the lives of Paul and his fellow believers is countered in a very positive and illuminating way by the determination of a social-scientific analysis to find the bodies in the body of Christ, to see how slave-master relations are affected by reconciliation, to see how justification affects who eats with whom and who sleeps with whom, and to observe whether women understand and practice the new creation in Christ differently from men and if so, why. In other words, Pauline Christianity comes to be seen no longer as a kind of first-century theological seminary, but much more as an identity and commitment which groups of people are developing in the context of a common life, where the things that are important are, not just beliefs absorbed somehow on their own, but beliefs which shape (and in turn are shaped by) the concerns, experiences, politics and obligations of everyday life (see further, Elliott 1981, 1-20).

*2.3. Models for Filling the Gaps.* The social sciences are important also in helping to fill the gaps in our understanding of Paul and his letters. Precisely because our knowledge is based on fragmentary texts—some of Paul's letters plus the second-hand evidence of the Acts of the Apostles and subsequent letters from members of the Pauline school—it is useful to have models of interpretation which allow the fragments to be pieced together into a larger explanatory whole in a way which, though hypothetical, is nevertheless subject to the controls of the interpretative models themselves and the analogies used. For example, the sociology of the sect has been deployed to help answer such questions as, What was it like to become a Christian in the first century? Why are the language and thought forms of apocalyptic* so prevalent in Paul's letters? How did conversion affect household* relations? Why is there such a tension in Paul's teaching between freedom and conformity? Why is eating meat offered to idols so controversial, and why does Paul take an accommodating line (cf. 1 Cor 8) whereas the writer of the Apocalypse is so adamant in his opposition (cf. Rev 2:14, 20)? By drawing attention to the importance of boundary definition and boundary maintenance for the survival of small religious groups, the social sciences make possible a more holistic interpretation of Pauline Christianity as well as opening up fresh insights on old and often unresolved problems.

*2.4. Understanding Ourselves as Readers.* Another gain from the social sciences is the contribution they make to our self-understanding as *the readers* of Paul's letters. The temptation for any reader of Scripture is to find there a reflection of their own image. The Lutheran is likely to find the apostle of justification by faith; the charismatic will find the Paul who teaches about "spiritual gifts"; the Protestant will find Paul the preacher and teacher of the crucified Christ; the Roman Catholic will find Paul the apostle who, along with Peter and the other apostles, establishes the Church and teaches the sacraments; the feminist is likely to find Paul the liberationist or Paul the misogynist; and so on. Because the social sciences draw systematic attention to the sociological dimensions of the world behind the text, they raise simultaneously the question, What are the sociological dimensions of the world *in front of* the text, the world of the reader? To what extent are the ways we read and interpret Paul affected by the social determinants of our own identity, such as gender, class, race and religion? An awareness of this kind helps the reader avoid unconscious ethnocentric or "tribal" interpretations of Paul, while at the same time opening up the possibility of appropriating Paul more responsibly.

*2.5. Gains for Theology and Ethics.* A final advantage worth mentioning is the gain for theology and ethics.* Given the pivotal place of Paul in the formation of the beliefs, practices and self-understanding of followers of Christ, both in the first century and subsequently, it is essential for the integrity of Christian faith and discipleship that the truth of Paul's testimony to Christ, in all its dimensions, be subject to the scrutiny of all the disciplines of critical inquiry, including the social sciences. Faith seeking understanding (to use Saint Anselm's definition of theology) must include faith seeking social-scientific understanding. At some points this may help interpreters to see that the truth of Paul's testimony stands up to scrutiny well—as, for example, the primacy he gives to love (*agapē*) as *the* defining characteristic of Christian community (cf. 1 Cor 13). At other points it may lead interpreters to question the truth of Paul's testimony—as, for example, the teaching he gives on male "headship"* and symbols of gender differentiation, in 1 Corinthians 11:2-16 and 14:33-36.

### 3. Problems in Social-Scientific Interpretation.

If there are clear gains in using social-science models as heuristic devices in Pauline interpretation, there are difficulties and dangers as well—though these are not necessarily unique to social-scientific interpretation.

*3.1. Anachronism.* One problem is that of anachronism, of using sociological models and methods which have taken shape in the analysis of modern organizations, groups or societies and using them as tools of analysis for the interpretation of groups and societies in Mediterranean antiquity. This criticism has been made, for example, of attempts such as that of J. G. Gager to describe earliest Christianity as a millenarian movement on the analogy of nineteenth- and twentieth-century cargo cults studied by anthropologists like K. Burridge and P. Worsley. It has been made also of the application of E. Troeltsch's sect-

church typology (taken further by H. R. Niebuhr and B. Wilson, among others) to developments in social patterns in the early church.

*3.2. Circular Reasoning.* A second problem is methodological also: that of circularity, of beginning with a social-scientific model and finding that the model is strangely self-authenticating, especially when the evidence is fragmentary. E. Gellner has argued persuasively that psychological and psychoanalytic theories are prone to this danger, not least because evidence which might appear counter-factual can be explained away within the terms of the theory itself, as "resistance" or "transference" or "regression" or, more generally, a manifestation of "the unconscious." The issue here, of course, is that the theory is not open to falsification. By being able to explain so much, it is in danger of not explaining anything at all. As another example of circularity, attempts to interpret Paul in terms of M. Weber's sociology of charismatic authority suffer from the problem that Weber's typology is itself rooted in his own study of primitive Christianity.

*3.3. Claiming Too Much.* Another problem for social-scientific exegesis is its proneness to claim too much, the result of which is to *reduce* a particular historical-religious phenomenon to its purported sociological determinants. Functionalist sociology is especially open to this problem, as can be seen in W. Meeks' innovative attempt to explain conversion to Paul's churches as a function of members' experiences of "status inconsistency" in the wider world (Meeks 1983). On this view, the outsiders who were attracted to Paul's gospel joined the Christian gatherings because they found there an ethos and identity which resolved the tensions of status and identity they experienced outside the gatherings. Such an hypothesis is valuable in so far as it draws attention to the possible—even likely—influence of hidden psycho-social and socio-economic forces on converts to Christianity. It is problematic, however, to the extent that it draws attention away from the participants' own ways of seeing things and plays down the intellectual, spiritual/ mystical and emotional dimensions of the transformation which conversion doubtless involved (cf. 1 Thess 1:9-10; Gal 1:6-17; Phil 3:2-11).

*3.4. The Limitations of Statistics.* A related problem is that social science theories tend to operate on the basis of statistically assessed judgments about what is normal in a group or society—hence the importance of the questionnaire in social-science data gathering. Not only is it obvious that such procedures are difficult to apply in the study of antiquity: it is also the case that such procedures have an in-built bias against the unique, the particular and the creative role of the individual. Thus, for example, while Marxist social theory may be illuminating in setting the rise and development of Christianity within the macro-social context of a purported class struggle in the ancient world, it is likely to do less than justice to the interpretation of the gospel and mission of that most idiosyncratic figure, Paul.

*3.5. Post-Enlightenment Presuppositions.* Finally, it is important to be aware of the fact that, like all theories of interpretation, the social sciences have a history. Their roots lie in post-Enlightenment atheism and the hermeneutics of suspicion, according to which theology and religion have an epiphenomenal status only as the products of other forces and interests, whether the human unconscious (Freud), class conflict (Marx), the maintenance of society (Durkheim), the legitimation of patriarchal domination (feminism) or whatever. Interpreters of Paul who stand within a Christian faith tradition need to be aware of this history. Such an awareness might have at least two effects. On the one hand, it will act as a safeguard against allowing the agenda in Pauline interpretation to shift unwittingly in a secularizing direction, away from the evangelical imperatives of every community of faith for which the letters of Paul are part of the canon of Scripture and a constant source of inspiration. On the other hand, in so far as atheism and the hermeneutics of suspicion have developed often as a reaction against what J. Bowker calls religion's "licensed insanities," then it may be that the interpreter of Paul will welcome hermeneutical insights from the social sciences which make possible a more clear-sighted engagement with the truth of Paul's testimony and with perversions of it.

### 4. Case Studies in Social-Scientific Interpretation.

Perhaps the best way to see what is involved in this kind of approach to Paul is to take specific examples as case studies. Other surveys of this kind tend to proceed by looking at the work of leading scholars in the field of social-scientific exegesis (e.g., Garrett). The present account will consider instead a series of topics or themes in Paul's letters.

*4.1. Paul's Theology of the Cross.* The message of the cross and Christ crucified is central to Paul's understanding of the gospel (cf. 1 Cor 1:17—2:5; Rom 8:31-34; *see* Cross, Theology of the). For the contemporary theologian this is a foundational doctrine of the Pauline corpus, and rightly so. From the perspective of the social sciences, however, the doctrine of the cross is also and at the same time a *social construct*, part of a web of meanings embodied in social patterns and social relations. The power* of the message of the cross

to "save" (1 Cor 1:18) is not only a spiritual/mystical power: it is cultural and social as well. Its structure, novelty and rhetorical* force as the negation, reversal or transformation of the dominant cultural values of Paul's world (cf. 1 Cor 1:22-25) provided the basis for developing an alternative symbolic world and an alternative society (the *ekklēsia*) with its own group boundaries, social patterns, leadership structure, ethos, moral order, vocabulary, worship and behavioral norms.

Furthermore, if we ask why it is so central to the preaching and self-understanding of *Paul*, and why he defends his gospel so vigorously on this score, the answer may be seen to be a matter, not only of what Paul regarded as the truth about God and Christ, but also a matter of Paul's social relations with the various Christian communities in which he claimed authority* as an apostle. Paul's gospel and Paul's authority are entwined inextricably (cf. Gal 1:6-17). His doctrine of the cross and his role and status in the Christian societies as an *apostolos* are two sides of the same coin; and Paul's authority depended upon his ability to mediate effectively the message of the cross along with its cultural and socio-economic corollaries. This he attempted to do by preaching it (with whatever lack of rhetorical finesse, cf. 1 Cor 2:3-4), teaching and writing letters about it, and by embodying it in his own apostolic lifestyle and person. It is no coincidence, therefore, that Paul "boasts" of his experiences of suffering* and humiliation (cf. 1 Cor 4:9-13; 2 Cor 4:7-12; 6:3-10; 11:21b-33), for it is these experiences which allow him to align himself most closely with the crucified Christ and to claim the authority to mediate Christ most effectively to his fellow-believers. This he does through the *imitatio Pauli*—"Be imitators of me, as I am of Christ" (1 Cor 11:1; cf. Phil 3:17; 4:9; *see* Imitation).

The limits of this kind of approach become apparent if it is claimed that Paul's preaching of the cross is a matter *only* of his personal authority as an apostle, and that the truth of the message is a matter *only* of its effectiveness in making possible social innovation. But this kind of reduction along functionalist lines is not integral to the approach per se. On the other hand, the potential benefit of a social-science reading is that the interpreter is provided with a method which opens up the cultural and social corollaries and connections of Paul's gospel. From being an important but rather disembodied doctrine, the cross comes to be seen also as a social reality embodied (both metaphorically and literally) in the self-understanding and social patterns of the first Christians and one of their leading apostles (see further, Barton 1982; Meeks 1982).

*4.2. The Resurrection of Christ.* Paul's doctrine of the resurrection* of Christ may be interpreted also in social-scientific terms. Traditionally this doctrine has been approached in terms of questions of historicity (the "what actually happened?" type of question) or of systematic theology (the "what does this tell us about God/Christ/eschatology/etc.?" type of question). These are central and entirely legitimate concerns to do, at least in part, with the truth claims of Christian faith for which the witness of Paul is crucial. But it is legitimate also to ask whether the meaning and significance of Christ's resurrection is *exhausted* by these traditional approaches. Is not Paul's belief in the resurrection of Christ as much a part of the *social reality* of Paul and his churches as the doctrine of the cross and, if so, in what sense? These are social-science questions, and a number of answers are possible (cf. Meeks 1982; Barton 1984).

First, the resurrection of Christ by God provides the *raison d'être* of the fundamental innovation in social patterns represented by the Christian community. In Romans 4:16-25 Paul argues that, just as the "resurrection" of the "dead" (i.e., impotent) bodies of Abraham* and Sarah made possible the creation of an elect people, so the resurrection of the dead Jesus makes possible the fulfillment of the promise to Abraham in the creation of the community of faith consisting now of Gentiles as well as Jews. The God "who gives life to the dead and calls into existence the things that do not exist" (Rom 4:17) is the God who has called into existence this new, universalist community of the justified, believed hitherto to be an ideal attainable only in the eschatological future. In terms of the sociology of knowledge, therefore, the resurrection constitutes the "sacred canopy" (so P. Berger) of the Christian conventicles. It legitimates their existence by reference to an act of God, and provides the foundation for their charismatic and novel form of society.

Second, the particularity of Paul's resurrection belief—that God had raised none other than *Jesus*—gives a particularity to the community. The elaboration of the meaning of the resurrection for Jesus is, at the same time, an elaboration of its meaning for the community of believers in Jesus. To put it another way, the community's self-understanding is mirrored in and enlarged by its representations of the crucified and risen Christ. Thus, according to Romans 1:4, Jesus was "designated Son of God" by his resurrection from the dead. It is noteworthy that the name given to believers corresponds directly. They are "sons of God," "children of God" and "fellow heirs with Christ" (Rom 8:14-17; *see* Adoption, Sonship). The identity of the risen one is determinative of the identity of the communities of believers in him. Furthermore, authority in the community is of a particular kind also. It lies in the hands of those who can claim to have been witnesses of the resurrection (cf. 1 Cor 9:1; 15:8-9).

Third, the resurrection, as a resurrection of one who had been crucified shamefully, serves as a powerful theodicy. The anomic threats to community life posed by the death of Jesus and by the suffering and death of other community members are overcome. The crucified leader is *reincorporated* into the community as its risen and heavenly Lord; and his triumph over death, repeatedly affirmed in creed,* hymn* and (baptismal) ritual, becomes a powerful symbol, both of the truth of the gospel and of the continuity and integrity of the community.

Finally, belief in the resurrection functions as a stimulus to social and cultural change in Pauline Christianity. The binary pattern, death-resurrection, is conducive to this, for it provides a structure of thought particularly amenable to the depiction of alternatives, progressions and transformations, all of which help to mark out the boundaries and contours of the new community. This transformation has a somatic aspect (cf. Rom 6:12-14). Necessarily, therefore, it also has a social aspect (cf. 1 Cor 6:12-20). But too much change or change of the wrong kind can be harmful: so it is noteworthy where Paul *refrains* from appealing to resurrection faith. A case in point may be Romans 13:1-7, where a pragmatic and conservative doctrine of political obedience is based on appeals to the sovereignty of God and the voice of conscience,* rather than to the perhaps more subversive doctrine of the resurrection (*see* Civil Authority).

More work needs to be done in this area, but once again it can be seen that the possibilities raised by questions from the social sciences are unhelpful only if they fundamentally skew the sense of Paul's letters or distract from their real meaning. The suggestions made here in relation to the resurrection, however, show to the contrary that the social sciences make an important contribution to what Meeks has termed the "hermeneutics of social embodiment" (Meeks 1986).

*4.3. Financial and Material Support.* To turn from the cross and resurrection to Paul's means of financial and material support may appear as a move from the sublime to the banal. But appearances may be deceptive; and it is precisely the social sciences which help the interpreter of Paul to see, not only *that* this is an important issue, but also *why* it is so (*see* Financial Support).

The careful reader of Paul's letters will be surprised, perhaps, by the extent of references to money matters and related issues such as patterns of subsistence. The great theologian of grace* and reconciliation seems unduly concerned with mundane matters of financial policy and employment (cf. 1 Thess 2:1-12; 1 Cor 4:8-13; 9:1-18; 2 Cor 8-9; 11:7-11). Why is this so? Why do money and work matter to Paul? Is it a clue to an important aspect of Paul's self-understanding as an apostle of Christ which we have overlooked in our one-eyed focus on Paul the theologian?

The subject surfaces very early in Paul's surviving correspondence. In 1 Thessalonians 2:3-12 Paul defends the authenticity of his gospel by claiming that he does not preach for pecuniary gain. His words are not a "cloak for greed"; and he does not use his apostolic authority to make financial and material demands upon his audience. So there is a clear link in Paul's apostolic self-understanding between the legitimacy of his message and the pattern of his material subsistence. Paul knows that *money speaks*. Above all, by maintaining his financial independence, Paul is able to protect and assert the independence and integrity of his gospel. It is "the gospel *of God*" (1 Thess 2:2) and is neither subject to nor influenced by financial transactions: so it is not vulnerable to the charge of being shaped and fashioned in order "to please people" (1 Thess 2:4). Further, Paul himself is an "apostle *of Christ*" (1 Thess 2:6). He does not belong to a human benefactor, but to a heavenly benefactor; and his financial independence helps to express and guarantee that. Paul knows very well that money is a source of power and influence, that accepting and giving money creates obligations between people and binds them together in relations of subordination and domination. So he works for himself: "we worked night and day, that we might not burden any of you, while we preached to you the gospel of God" (1 Thess 2:9).

More analysis of a social-scientific kind needs to be done in what we can see now to be a highly illuminating aspect of Paul's missionary* practice. The most important contributions so far have been made by B. Holmberg (1978), R. Hock (1980) and G. Theissen (1982). They show that Paul's means of support are related intimately to the integrity of his gospel and the legitimacy of his apostleship, and that, by working sacrificially to support himself, Paul established a consistency between his own practice and the gospel he preached (cf. 1 Thess 2:8). Gospel and apostle are one: and Paul's refusal to conform to cultural norms which disparaged manual labor as demeaning, both expressed and embodied the culture-transforming insights of the gospel he preached. Furthermore, by offering the gospel "free of charge" (1 Cor 9:18) on the basis of his own labors in the workshop as a tentmaker* or leatherworker, Paul was able to reach those at the bottom of the social scale. For here was a gospel which did not entail entry into a burdensome financial tie, and it was offered by one who was himself a manual worker. Is it surprising, therefore, that the apostle who is able to step down in the world in order to gain the majority of people (i.e., the poor), is the one who also undertakes another financial obligation—the collection—for the impoverished believers in the Jerusalem church (cf. 2 Cor 9)? Perhaps it is worth observing that at this point in the interpretation of Paul, a significant convergence of interest between the social sciences and the theology of liberation becomes possible in a way which might not otherwise have been the case.

*4.4. Food and Table Fellowship.* Another mundane matter which appears to demand a considerable amount of Paul's attention has to do with food,* eating and meals. Such matters seem almost to dominate Paul's dealings with the Christians at Corinth (cf. 1 Cor 8:1-13; 9:4, 7, 8-12, 13-14, 22; 10:1-31; 11:17-34); but are not confined there, as Romans 14 shows. Traditionally, and quite properly, interpretation of these texts has focused on a range of important issues. First, there are historical-exegetical issues, such as, Who are the "weak" and the "strong"?* or, What is the nature of the purported gnostic heresy which Paul is attempting to combat? and so on. Second are theological issues, such as Paul's understanding of the Lord's Supper* in 1 Corinthians 10 and 11, or Paul's idea of the role of conscience* in the life of Christian discernment, or Paul's doctrine of the church.* Third, there are moral and pastoral issues to do with the problem of "the weaker brother" and the limits of Christian freedom, or the question of the limits of the believer's accommodation with "the world." Such concerns are entirely valid. From a social-science perspective, however, an important dimension is missing, a dimension which may throw new light on *why* questions relating to food and meals are given the prominence they are in Paul's letters, why such issues generate the *anxiety* that they do, and why Paul responds in the ways he does.

From a social-scientific point of view, food and meals are a fundamental symbolic means by which a group or society expresses its values and identity. What is *natural* (food and the bodily ingestion of food) is transformed into something *cultural* by being made to carry and express social meanings. As social anthropologists like C. Lévi-Strauss, M. Douglas and E. Leach have shown, food constitutes a system of communication, and cooking and eating constitute a kind of language through which a group defines itself. There is a symbolic relationship between the food ingested into the physical body and the identity and self-understanding of the social body. To put it another way, food dealings are a barometer of social relations and a mechanism for creating or destroying sociability. How food communicates—the *semiotics* of food—is enormously various. But, in general, it has to do with: (1) the type of food and drink consumed or abstained from—"clean" or "unclean," meat or vegetable, cooked or raw, alcoholic or non-alcoholic, etc.; (2) the time and frequency of eating (or fasting); (3) the time of and time taken for meal preparation; (4) the quantity of food consumed; (5) with whom meals are shared and who is excluded from the meal; (6) the symbolic geography of the meal—who sits where and why, where women sit in relation to men, whether the meal is taken in private or in public, etc.; (7) the clothes worn by participants; (8) appropriate sounds or silences at the meal; and so on (see further, Barton 1986).

When seen in this light, the degree of attention Paul gives to instructing his groups in the right ordering of their table fellowship becomes much more intelligible. We see, for example, that where eating meat consecrated to idols* is in danger of conveying the message that the all-important boundary between allegiance to idols and allegiance to the lordship of Christ has been compromised, Paul calls for extreme vigilance and, where necessary, separation. Where the believers' meals express only faction and division, Paul calls for a table fellowship which fosters and expresses solidarity. Where the meals become an opportunity for conspicuous consumption in a way which separates the rich members from the poor, Paul calls for self-control and other-regarding hospitality. Above all, Paul institutes a different kind of meal: the "Lord's meal" (*kyriakon deipnon*). This meal functions, anthropologically speaking, as a ritual of incorporation. The eating together, the recitation of the Last Supper tradition, the sharing of "the bread" and "the cup," the remembering and proclaiming, and the acts of moral and social self-examination enable people from separate (and potentially competing) household groups to renegotiate their patterns of allegiance without the threat of humiliation and to reconstitute themselves as members of a new society which they could represent as a single, transformed household of faith based upon love.*

A social-science reading of Paul in this way is likely to be unhelpful only if it distracts from the profound theological, ecclesiological and ethical questions which are raised in a letter like 1 Corinthians. It can

be argued to the contrary, however, that far from being a distraction, such a reading makes possible a greater depth in interpreting and appropriating Paul because the bones of Pauline doctrine are given flesh and blood and come to life in their social and cultural milieu. To shift the metaphor slightly, the body of Paul's thought is able to be related to Paul and his fellow believers as individual bodies and to Paul and his fellow believers as "the body of Christ"* within the larger body of the cities and societies in which they lived. An important lead in this direction in the interpretation of Paul has been provided in the last decade or so by B. L. Malina (1981), G. Theissen (1982), W. A. Meeks (1983), L. W. Countryman (1988) and J. H. Neyrey (1990).

*4.5. Apostolic Authority and Church Order.* As a final case study, the theme of Paul's apostolic authority and the question of order in Paul's churches is worth attention. This is an important theme theologically and ecclesiologically. Theologically, it bears on the authenticity of Paul's gospel and his witness to Christ and the weight to be accorded his letters and those letters attributed to him in the canon.* Ecclesiologically, it bears on the legitimacy of the whole Reformation tradition and the associated and subsequent attempts to define church order in terms of charisma rather than office, spirit rather than law.

What is striking if a social-scientific approach is taken, however, is how strongly the traditional scholarly debate has focused on Paul's *ideas*, and how little attention has been given to *social phenomena*—as if to imply that Paul's ideas somehow emerged unconnected and floating free from his social and historical context. The kinds of phenomena to which the social scientist draws attention are: (1) the distribution of power in and between Paul's groups, including the effects of the all-pervasive system of patron-client and benefactor relations in Roman antiquity; (2) relations between Paul's groups and the Jerusalem* church, including the significance of Paul's collection* for Jerusalem; (3) the effects of differences of wealth, rank, status, gender and ethnicity on roles and functions in the churches; (4) the influence on the churches of patterns of social relationship and communal order practiced in the society at large—whether those of the city (*polis*) or the voluntary association (*collegium, synagōgē*, etc.) or the household* (*oikos*); (5) the role of Paul's coworkers,* emissaries and local representatives; (6) the means of communication and their relative efficacy, including Paul's own letters and his visits in person; (7) the evident willingness of Paul to adopt a conspicuously liminal lifestyle—culturally anomalous, socio-politically provocative, financially independent, transient, physically dangerous and so on.

Important contributions of both a social-history kind (e.g., Martin 1990) and a social-scientific kind (e.g., Holmberg 1978; Petersen 1985; Watson 1986; MacDonald 1988) have been made in this area in the last two decades especially. The benefits are evident. First, such approaches reveal the complexity of Paul's apostolic authority and of church order in Paul's groups (*see* Church Order). They show that attention to what Paul *teaches* is not a sufficient basis for an adequate interpretation of Pauline ecclesiology. Indeed, from a social-science perspective, to use a category like "ecclesiology" is to risk at the outset reducing a very complex and multifaceted social reality to a one-dimensional, doctrinal frame of reference.

Second, such approaches help counter an often apologetic and polemical *idealizing* of Paul's apostolic authority and of the life of Paul's groups. This is a very strong tendency among those for whom Paul as "apostle of liberty" or "apostle of the free Spirit" can be appealed to as a basis for justifying—rightly or wrongly—informal, small-group religion over against hierarchical, institutionalized religion (*see* Early Catholicism). It is a strong tendency also among those who want to denigrate one kind of church as "legalistic" or "tradition-bound" (after the pattern imagined to be that of the Jerusalem church) in favor of another kind of church which is "Spirit-led" and "participatory" (after the pattern imagined to be that of Paul and his groups).

Third, social-science approaches allow us to see that the process of institutionalization or (to use M. Weber's term) routinization which is evident in the Pauline and post-Pauline period is not necessarily a retrograde development, a fall from a charismatic golden age. On the contrary, the charismatic authority of Paul was related intimately to traditional and institutional kinds of authority (in Antioch and Jerusalem) from the very beginning; and it can be argued that routinization may have been essential if the originating impulse and impetus of the gospel was to be preserved and passed on.

**5. Conclusion.**
Approaches to NT interpretation from a social-science perspective are burgeoning and have begun to make a significant impact on our understanding of Paul and his letters (see further, Barton 1992). It remains here to venture a suggestion for continuing debate and possible ways forward. The proposal is that more attention needs to be given to *the history and practice of Pauline interpretation* from a specifically social-scien-

tific point of view. In other words, sociological interpretation of Paul needs to be accompanied by sociological interpretation of Paul's readers and interpreters.

Such a process may make us more aware of how, in times past and present, the apostle Paul and the churches of Paul have been made captive—wittingly and unwittingly, for good and ill—to the ideological interests of his interpreters. K. Stendahl made an important beginning in this regard in his essay, "Paul and the Introspective Conscience of the West" (1963, in Stendahl 1977), where he argues that Paul's doctrine of justification* has been misrepresented by being made captive to an Augustinian and subsequently Lutheran and (later still) Freudian anthropology focused on the introspective conscience of the individual. More recently, feminist and liberation interpreters have used insights drawn from sociology of knowledge to question the adequacy of (respectively) androcentric and First-World interpretations of Paul and to make possible a process of "conscientization" in ways that have potentially radical implications (cf. Fiorenza 1983).

In a quite new way, then, the social sciences and the related hermeneutics of suspicion confront the interpreter of Paul with the problem of *the theology and ethics of interpretation*. This calls in turn for a degree of hermeneutical self-awareness on the part of interpreters which is both demanding and invigorating (cf. Thiselton 1992). The struggle to define the "center"* of Paul's theology and self-understanding as an apostle in *his* social and political context comes to be seen now as part of the struggle of the interpreter and the various communities of interpretation to define the center of *their* theology and self-understanding in *their* social and political contexts. What constitutes validity in this interpretative process has to do partly with the validity of the methods of interpretation used—and here models from the social sciences have their part to play alongside other methods of a historical and literary-exegetical kind. But it has to do also with (to use D. Kelsey's term) certain "policy decisions" on the part of the interpreter and the community to which he or she belongs. That is where the theology and ethics of interpretation are involved and where, again, the social sciences have a significant role to play.

*See also* APOSTLE; AUTHORITY; BODY OF CHRIST; CHURCH ORDER AND GOVERNMENT; CROSS, THEOLOGY OF THE; ESCHATOLOGY; FINANCIAL SUPPORT; FOOD OFFERED TO IDOLS AND JEWISH FOOD LAWS; HERMENEUTICS/INTERPRETING PAUL; SOCIAL SETTING OF MISSION CHURCHES.

BIBLIOGRAPHY. S. C. Barton, "Paul and the Cross: A Sociological Approach," *Theology* 85 (1982) 13-19; idem, "Paul and the Resurrection: A Sociological Approach," *Religion* 14 (1984) 67-75; idem, "Paul's Sense of Place: An Anthropological Approach to Community Formation in Corinth," *NTS* 32 (1986) 225-46; idem, "The Communal Dimension of Earliest Christianity: A Critical Survey of the Field," *JTS* 43 (1992) 399-427; L. W. Countryman, *Dirt, Greed and Sex* (Philadelphia: Fortress, 1988); J. H. Elliott, *A Home for the Homeless* (Philadelphia: Fortress, 1981); E. S. Fiorenza, *In Memory of Her* (New York: Crossroad, 1983); J. G. Gager, *Kingdom and Community: The Social World of Early Christianity* (Englewood Cliffs, NJ: Prentice-Hall, 1975); S. R. Garrett, "Sociology of Early Christianity," *ABD* VI.89-99; R. F. Hock, *The Social Context of Paul's Ministry* (Philadelphia: Fortress, 1980); B. Holmberg, *Paul and Power* (Lund: Gleerup, 1978); M. Y. MacDonald, *The Pauline Churches* (Cambridge: University Press, 1988); B. L. Malina, *The New Testament World* (Atlanta: John Knox, 1981); D. B. Martin, *Slavery as Salvation* (New Haven: Yale University, 1990); W. A. Meeks, "The Social Context of Pauline Theology," *Int* 37 (1982) 266-277; idem, *The First Urban Christians* (New Haven: Yale University, 1983); idem, "A Hermeneutics of Social Embodiment," *HTR* 79 (1986) 176-86; J. H. Neyrey, *Paul, in Other Words* (Louisville: Westminster/John Knox, 1990); N. R. Petersen, *Rediscovering Paul: Philemon and the Sociology of Paul's Narrative World* (Philadelphia: Fortress, 1985); K. Stendahl, *Paul Among Jews and Gentiles* (Philadelphia: Fortress, 1976); G. Theissen, *The Social Setting of Pauline Christianity* (Philadelphia: Fortress, 1982); A. C. Thiselton, *New Horizons in Hermeneutics* (Grand Rapids: Zondervan, 1992); F. Watson, *Paul, Judaism and the Gentiles* (Cambridge: University Press, 1986).

S. C. Barton

# SON OF GOD

The divine sonship of Jesus is a major component of Paul's christology,* though in Paul's letters the references to Jesus as God's "Son" (seventeen times in the entire traditional Pauline corpus and only four instances of the full title "Son of God") are considerably fewer than Paul's many designations of Jesus as "Lord"* and "Christ."* Some have alleged that the idea of Jesus' divine sonship was an appropriation of pagan religious traditions, and that Paul thereby presented Jesus after the fashion of Greco-Roman cult deities (*see* Religions, Greco-Roman), but the evidence concerning the pagan religious background and Paul's use of the divine "Son" language goes against this.

Paul did not employ the language of divine sonship primarily to claim that Jesus was divine. Essentially Paul's references to Jesus as God's "Son" communicate Jesus' unique status and intimate relationship with God.* But the contexts of these references supply several additional and more particular nuances to the term. In some passages Jesus is presented as God's regally enthroned Son, drawing upon OT traditions of the Davidic king as "Son" of God (e.g., Ps 2:6-7; *see* Exaltation and Enthronement). In others Paul seems to allude to the offering of Isaac (Gen 22) to represent Jesus' death as the supreme act of redemptive love (e.g., Rom 8:32). Also Paul presents God's Son as the one sent forth to provide the standing with God for which the Torah was incapable. And Paul also portrays Jesus' divine sonship as the pattern for, and basis of, the enfranchisement of Christians as "sons of God."

    1. Background
    2. Jesus
    3. Jesus' Divine Sonship Outside Paul
    4. Paul's Usage

## 1. Background.

*1.1. Pagan.* In older history-of-religions scholarship, as represented by Bousset, Paul's references to "the Son of God" were taken as intended to denote Jesus as a divine being after the fashion of allegedly prominent pagan traditions about sons of gods with which Paul's Gentile converts would have been familiar (Bousset, 206-10). Though others (e.g., Schoeps) have repeated this viewpoint, it is not persuasive in the light of the main body of scholarly analysis which has on the whole confirmed Paul's fundamental conceptual indebtedness to his Jewish tradition and his disdain for pagan religion (e.g., Blank, Hengel, Kim).

Moreover, Bousset's idea that to communicate his message among his pagan converts Paul misguidedly appropriated pagan traditions that produced a fundamentally new christology is not borne out by a careful reading of what Paul says about Jesus or by the relevant evidence from Greco-Roman pagan religion. As Nock (1972) and Hengel (21-41) have shown, it is difficult to find true Greco-Roman parallels that would account for Paul's view of Jesus as God's "Son" or render it more intelligible to Paul's Gentile converts. The human race could be referred to as offspring of Zeus or other gods, but this generality seems irrelevant to the particular significance Paul attached to Jesus as God's unique Son. A great man (e.g., Alexander the Great) might be styled as a son of a god, but this appears to have been essentially an honorific gesture in recognition of some quality in the man such as wisdom or military prowess, and it is not clear that the man so designated was really thought of as anything other than an exceptionally impressive human being.

In fact the designation "son of god" was not common in Greco-Roman paganism and seems to have been used as a title only by Roman emperors (Latin *divi filius* rendered in Greek as *theou huios*). The deities of the so-called "mystery cults," for example, to which the early history-of-religions school attached such importance, were not referred to as "son of god." Any influence of Roman emperor devotion upon early christology was probably much later than Paul and likely involved Christian recoil from what was regarded as blasphemous rather than as something to be appropriated (e.g., Cuss). Nock's judgment concerning the Pauline use of "Son of God" still holds, ". . . the attempts which have been made to explain it from the larger Hellenistic world fail" (Nock 1964, 45).

*1.2. Jewish.* Consequently, most scholars have turned to the Jewish sources as more directly relevant background for Paul's references to Jesus' divine sonship. In Paul's Bible, the OT, the language of divine sonship is used with three types of referents. In passages that likely reflect an older usage, angels are referred to as "sons of God" (e.g., Gen 6:2-4; Deut 32:8; Ps 29:1; 89:6). Although in a number of cases in the LXX the Hebrew or Aramaic phrase "son(s) of God" is rendered in Greek as "angel(s) of God" (e.g., Deut 32:8; Job 1:6; 2:1; Dan 3:25), this is not consistently done (cf. Deut 32:43 LXX), showing that heavenly beings could still be referred to as "sons of God" among Greek-speaking Jews of the Greco-Roman period.

In some OT passages the Davidic king is referred to as God's "son" (2 Sam 7:14; Ps 2:7; 89:26-27). Psalm 2:7 refers to God having "begotten" the king, but it appears that this poetic language was a way of asserting his divine legitimation, with his enthronement being taken as a kind of divine adoption.

Royal Davidic traditions issued into Jewish messianic hopes of Paul's time. There is, however, no unambiguous evidence that the expression "son of God" was a messianic title, and it is difficult to say how widely the concept of divine sonship was a part of messianic expectation. The document known as 2 Esdras or 4 Ezra has several references to a messianic "son" of God in the surviving versions of this writing (e.g., Latin *filius* in 7:28; 13:32, 37, 52; 14:9), but it is now commonly accepted that these all are Christian translations of the Greek term *pais* ("servant"), which in turn may have rendered the equivalent Hebrew term *'ebed.* Similarly 2 Baruch 70:9 refers to "my Servant, the Anointed One."

The Qumran* text 4Q174 (4QFlorilegium) contains a commentary on 2 Samuel 7:11-14, where God promises to make David's descendant God's "son," and the commentary applies the passage to the royal messiah.

Since first notices of its existence in 1972, the Qumran document 4Q246 has received a great deal of attention because it refers to a ruler who will be acclaimed with the titles "son of God" and "son of the Most High," the same titles given to Jesus in Luke 1:32-35 (see, e.g., Fitzmyer, 90-94). Owing to the fragmentary nature of the document, it is difficult to be certain, but the eschatological flavor makes it quite possible that this document furnishes further evidence that the attribution of divine sonship, including the use of the title "son of God," was part of the messianism of at least some Jews.

One of the ways Philo refers to the Logos is as God's "firstborn son" (e.g., Philo *Som.* 1.215; *Conf. Ling.* 146), but there seems to be no direct connection between this and Paul's use of the term for Jesus. Instead, Philo exhibits an independent appropriation of an OT designation of the king (Ps 89:27) and of Israel (Ex 4:22), which, however, may illustrate how biblical imagery and concepts could be adapted to later religious belief, as seems to be the case also in the NT.

In fact the most common applications of the concept of divine sonship in ancient Jewish texts are with reference to the righteous individual, righteous Jews collectively and Israel as God's chosen people. In a number of OT passages Israelites are called God's "sons" (Deut 14:1; Is 1:2; Jer 3:22; Hos 1:10) and collectively God's "firstborn" (Ex 4:22) and "son" (Hos 11:1). And in extra-canonical Jewish texts these applications are frequent: Wisdom 2:18; 5:5; Sirach 4:10; Psalms of Solomon 13:9; 18:4 (righteous individuals); Wisdom 12:21; 16:10, 26; 18:4, 13 (Israel). In *Joseph and Asenath*, likewise, the righteous Israelites are called "sons" of "the living God" or "the Most High" (*Jos. and As.* 16:14; 19:8), and Joseph (who seems to be an idealized representation of the righteous Jew or of Israel) is acclaimed several times as "son" and "firstborn son" of God (*Jos. and As.* 6:3-5; 13:13; 18:11; 21:4; 23:10).

Vermes (206-11) has cited rabbinic texts in which ancient Jewish holy men are referred to as a "son" of God in the sense of being especially favored by God. With due caution about using such late texts to illustrate first-century Jewish religion, we may take the rabbinic figures Vermes cites as examples of the application to particular righteous individuals of the category of divine sonship as affirmed in Wisdom of Solomon and Sirach mentioned earlier.

## 2. Jesus.

It is widely accepted among scholars that Jesus spoke of God as "Father" (Aramaic *'abbā'*) in ways that expressed unusual familiarity and intimacy, and that he conducted himself in ways that reflect a profound sense of a special status and responsibility toward God. It is reasonable, therefore, to consider whether these features of Jesus' ministry might have influenced the view of Jesus as God's Son in Paul and early Christianity. For the present purpose we can make only a few relevant observations.

First, it seems likely that Jesus' own religious parlance and practice would have been of intense interest and relevance for his followers, both during Jesus' ministry and, especially in light of the conviction that he had been resurrected,* in the early years afterward. Second, Paul's preservation of the Aramaic term *abba* in his Greek-speaking churches and his use of it in contexts mentioning Jesus' divine sonship (Rom 8:15; Gal 4:6, the earliest Christian references to the term) are probably best accounted for as indications that traditions about Jesus' relationship with God were known and were in fact influential in shaping the early Christian view of him as God's Son.

Early christology of course was mainly driven by the conviction that the crucified Jesus had been resurrected and exalted to heavenly glory. But it is likely also that the traditions stemming from Jesus' ministry encouraged especially the identification of him as God's "Son," though the meaning attached to that identification seems to have grown far more exalted in the light of his resurrection and heavenly glorification than was ever explicit or even possible in Jesus' own ministry.

### 3. Jesus' Divine Sonship Outside Paul.

*3.1. Pre-Pauline Tradition.* A number of scholars have argued that Paul's references to Jesus' divine sonship show earmarks of "pre-Pauline" belief in Jesus as God's "Son," especially Romans 1:1-4; 1 Thessalonians 1:10; Galatians 4:4-6; and Romans 8:3. It is, however, misleading to speak of a christological "formula" of the divinely-sent-forth Son in Paul, which some have alleged in Romans 8:3 and Galatians 4:4. These two Pauline references use different Greek verbs, and have in common only the concept of the Son being divinely sent from God, an obvious enough way of referring to a figure seen as operating on a divine mandate.

As for Romans 1:3-4, Hengel (59) and Scott (236) have noted that attempts to reconstruct the actual wording of a pre-Pauline creedal statement (*see* Creeds) from Romans 1:3-4 have amounted to unverifiable (and divergent) hypotheses. Nevertheless, the passage may well preserve basic pre-Pauline convictions about Jesus as Davidic heir by physical descent (*kata sarka*) now "appointed [*horisthentos*] the Son of God in/with power [*en dynamei*]" by virtue of his resurrection [*ex anastaseōs*]. Likewise, 1 Thessalonians 1:9-10, which refers to Jesus as God's Son who has been resurrected to heavenly status and will come as deliverer from eschatological wrath,* is widely regarded as evidence of "pre-Pauline" divine Son christology. But if these passages do preserve "pre-Pauline" tradition, Paul's appropriation of the traditions shows that he saw no essential discontinuity between his view of Jesus and that of his predecessors and of the Jewish-Christian churches such as the one in Jerusalem.

*3.2. After Paul.* Jesus' divine sonship is of considerable importance in the Synoptic Gospels, which were written after Paul's letters, and carries varying connotations in each of the Evangelists. In Matthew Jesus' divine sonship, though infrequently mentioned, has a very strong messianic connotation and connection (e.g., Mt 16:16), and the disciples acclaim him as God's Son (e.g., Mt 14:33). A similar messianic connotation to divine sonship appears in Luke (e.g., Lk 1:32-35). In Mark, however, the claim is closely connected with the secrecy of Jesus' true (transcendent) identity and (with the ironic exception in Mk 15:39) only God (Mk 1:11; 9:7) and demons (e.g., Mk 3:11; 5:7) recognize Jesus' divine sonship.

Jesus' divine sonship is important also in Hebrews, where his status as Son distinguishes him above prophets (Heb 1:1-2) and also angels (Heb 1:3-14; 2:5). Indeed, in Hebrews 1:2 the Son is "heir of all things," giving his sonship a cosmic-scale significance.

It is, however, in John that Jesus' divine sonship has a transcendent connotation expressed with an explicitness and emphasis unmatched in any other NT writing. From the Baptist's confession (Jn 1:34) to the climactic purpose statement in John 20:31, the Fourth Evangelist emphasizes that Jesus is to be recognized as God's Son. And he makes it explicit that the Son is of heavenly origin (e.g., Jn 1:14; 17:1-5). In John, Jesus' claim to be God's Son amounts to a claim to divinity, as illustrated by the charges of blasphemy from Jewish characters in the story (Jn 5:18; 10:36; 19:7).

This Johannine emphasis flowered in the faith of Christianity subsequently, for "Son of God" became the most favored way of referring to Jesus as divine and was used to distinguish Jesus' divinity from his human nature, as seen already in Ignatius (*Eph.* 20:2). As Dunn has noted, no other christological expression "has had both the historical depth and lasting power of 'Son of God'" (Dunn, 12). But we must be careful to determine Paul's connotations in referring to Jesus as God's Son without reading into it the way the term was used by later Christians.

## 4. Paul's Usage.

In the thirteen writings attributed to Paul in the NT, the title "the Son of God" is neither fixed nor frequently used, appearing only four times and in varying Greek word order (Rom 1:4; 2 Cor 1:19; Gal 2:20; Eph 4:13). In the remaining thirteen references to Jesus' divine sonship, we find "his Son" (Rom 1:3, 9; 5:10; 8:29, 32; 1 Cor 1:9; Gal 1:16; 4:4, 6; 1 Thess 1:10), "his own Son" (Rom 8:3), "the Son" (1 Cor 15:28) and "the Son of his love" (Col 1:13). The conviction that Jesus is God's Son was apparently what mattered to Paul, not so much the christological title or fixed verbal formulas to express that conviction.

In all of his references to Jesus as God's Son Paul uses the Greek definite article, not always easily represented in translations. The connotation of the definite article is that Paul views Jesus' divine sonship as unique, and does not accord Jesus membership in a class of other figures who may be regarded as sons of God such as we encounter in the Jewish or pagan sources (e.g., angels,* the righteous, great men, wonder workers; but see 4.5 below).

It is also important, as Hengel has pointed out, that Paul refers to Jesus as God's Son mainly (eleven times) in Romans and Galatians (Hengel, 7). Both the comparative infrequency and the distribution of Paul's references to Jesus as God's Son suggest that for Paul Jesus' divine sonship did not constitute an appropriation of a pagan mythological concept as the crucial means of justifying the worship* of the man Jesus among Gentile converts (contra Bousset, 208-9). Instead, Paul refers to God's Son in terms adapted from the Jewish background to make boldly exclusivist christological assertions in ways and contexts that interact directly with traditional Jewish concerns. These included the Torah (see Law), the unique significance of Israel,* messianic hopes and the fundamentally monotheistic outlook which Paul continued to share and promote in his churches (see God).

From the entire fabric of Paul's christology, it is apparent that Paul saw Jesus as participating in God's attributes and roles, as sharing in the divine glory* and, most importantly, as worthy to receive formal veneration with God in Christian assemblies (see Worship). So we may say that the one Paul called "the Son of God" was regarded by him as divine in some unique way. But neither in the Jewish background of Paul nor in his own usage (unlike John's) did the language of divine sonship in itself attribute divinity. In Paul's Jewish tradition to call a human figure God's "Son" meant primarily to attribute to him a special standing, status and favor with God. Paul's references to Jesus as the "Son" of God meant that Jesus possessed a unique standing, status and favor with God.

In order to determine specifically what Jesus' sonship connoted for Paul, we must look more closely at the references in question. We shall concentrate on references in the letters whose Pauline authorship is almost universally accepted (though Col 1:13 and Eph 4:13 in fact fit the categories established in the undisputed letters). We shall try to establish Paul's meaning by paying attention to the contexts.

*4.1. The Gospel and the Son.* In Romans 1:9 Paul refers to "the gospel* of his [God's] Son," an unusual phrase in Paul (in addition to the numerous references to "the gospel," cf. "the gospel of God," Rom 1:1; 15:16; 2 Cor 11:7; 1 Thess 2:2, 8, 9; and "the gospel of Christ," Rom 15:19; 1 Cor 9:12; 2 Cor 2:12; 10:14; Gal 1:7; Phil 1:27; 1 Thess 3:2). It appears that the phrase is connected with the nearby references to Jesus as God's Son (Rom 1:2-4), and with the larger discussion in Romans in which Jesus' divine sonship is mentioned a number of times (seven of the seventeen instances in the traditional Pauline corpus; cf. 2 Cor 4:4, where the unique phrase "the gospel of the glory of Christ" appears to be linked similarly with the contextual discussion of Christ's divine glory in 2 Cor 3:12—4:6). But, though unique here in Paul, "the gospel of his Son" shows that Paul could refer to his message and ministry* as concerned with Jesus' divine sonship. And the prominence given to Jesus' sonship in Romans and Galatians further suggests that the identification of Jesus as God's Son was more important to Paul than might at first be assumed, especially in portraying Jesus' redemptive significance in theocentric contexts and vis-à-vis Jewish religious themes.

This suggestion is underscored by Paul's description in Galatians 1:15-16 of the experience that turned him from opponent to apostle* of Jesus: God "was pleased to reveal his Son to me [en emoi]" (Gal 1:16). To be sure, Paul elsewhere refers to having seen "Jesus the Lord" (1 Cor 9:1) and includes himself in a list of those to whom "Christ" appeared (1 Cor 15:1-8). But Galatians 1:15-16 indicates that the experience in question included the realization that Jesus is God's unique Son (ton huion autou) and that his calling was to proclaim God's Son (Gal 1:16) specifically among the Gentiles.* Paul had certainly already heard Jewish-Christian claims about Jesus, which he probably regarded as repugnant glorification of a false prophet, and which likely formed part of his reason for zealously opposing Jewish Christians in the name of Jewish tradition (Gal 1:13-14). In ancient Jewish tradition to hail a despised figure as a son of God was to accede to the figure's divine legitimation and righteousness (e.g., Wis 2:12-20; 5:1-8). Paul's reference to the revelation that Jesus is the Son of God (*ton huion autou*), therefore, can be taken as connoting that the experience involved for Paul a direct reversal of his view of Jesus, from false prophet to God's unique representative.

*4.2. The Royal Son.* In several passages Paul portrays Jesus in a royal status and role, drawing upon OT Davidic traditions and applying them to Jesus as royal-messianic "Son" of God. We have already noted two of these passages as possible evidence of "pre-Pauline" christology. In Romans 1:3-4 there are echoes of 2 Samuel 7:12-14. As "seed [*sperma*] of David," Jesus was "raised up [*anastasis*] from the dead" by God (cf. the LXX of 2 Samuel 7:12: "I will raise up [*anastēsō*] your seed [*to sperma sou*]"). And Jesus' appointment in power as divine Son in Romans 1:4 may echo God's promise in 2 Samuel 7:14, "I will be father to him and he will be to me a son." As well, we may have here an allusion to Psalm 2:7, where God announces that he has "begotten" the king as his Son (a symbolic description of the king's enthronement). And Paul's reference to his mission* to secure "obedience of faith among all the nations/Gentiles [*ethnesin*]" (Rom 1:5) may allude to God's promise to the royal "Son" in Psalm 2:8 to give "the nations [*ethnē*] as your inheritance."

In 1 Thessalonians 1:9-10, as in Romans 1:4, Jesus' sonship is mentioned in connection with God having resurrected [*ēgeire*] him from death. Although we do not have allusions to OT Davidic passages here, nevertheless as the divine Son who delivers from (divine) eschatological wrath (1 Thess 1:10), Jesus is given a messianic role that can be compared with messianic expectations at Qumran and in such documents as *Psalms of Solomon* 17—18. This eschatological flavor, plus the contrast between pagan "idols"* and "the living and true God" (1 Thess 1:9) all reflect strongly the Jewish religious background, providing further indication that the divine "Son" here who acts on God's behalf is, as in Romans 1:3-4, God's messianic representative.

Another reference to God's Son with a royal-messianic flavor is found in 1 Corinthians 15:24-28. Royal imagery abounds, with mention of a "kingdom"* (1 Cor 15:24), Christ reigning (1 Cor 15:25) and the putting of all "enemies under his feet" (1 Cor 15:25, an allusion to Ps 110:1, a Davidic royal psalm frequently cited and alluded to in the NT). After "all things" (including death, 1 Cor 15:26) have been subjected to this royal Son, he will then "be subjected" to God (1 Cor 15:28), a thought which further shows that the Son here is not a new and rival deity after the fashion of pagan mythology but functions (as the OT

king and the messiah figures) on God's behalf. And, if Colossians be accepted as from Paul, the reference in Colossians 1:13 to "the kingdom of the Son of his [God's] love" likewise alludes to Jesus in royal-messianic dress.

Certainly the scope and basis of Jesus' sonship in Paul's references are far beyond that of the OT Davidic kings. In Jewish messianic expectations it is perhaps only in the "Elect One" of 1 Enoch (37—71) who sits on God's throne and seems to be clothed with transcendent attributes that we find anything approaching Paul's references to Jesus, the glorious and heavenly Son. And there is absolutely no parallel for the idea that the messianic figure was to be resurrected and thereby constituted God's Son who exercises divine power* and authority.* But in the passages considered Paul uses motifs, language and imagery from the Jewish royal-messianic tradition in expressing these bold beliefs about Jesus' exalted place in God's plan.

*4.3. The Sacrificed Son.* In at least three other passages Paul refers to Jesus as God's Son explicitly as given over, or having given himself, to redemptive death.* A striking example is Romans 8:32, where Paul says that God "did not withhold his own Son but gave him up for us all." The statement is made even more stunning theologically if one notices that "gave up" (*paradidōmi*) is the same verb Paul uses sonorously three times in Romans 1:24-28 to refer to God giving up sinful humanity to judgment,* making Jesus' death just as much a deliberate and solemn act of God as the divine wrath against human sin referred to in Romans 1. In Romans 8:32, however, the Son is given up for the sake of sinful humans, and provides assurance that they will not be condemned and separated from God.

But what is the significance of designating as God's "Son" the one given over in Romans 8:32? In Romans 4:25 Paul uses the verb *paradidōmi* to refer to "Jesus our Lord" being given up to death "for our transgression," and in Romans 8:34, shortly after the statement we are examining, Paul mentions "Christ Jesus who died," illustrating Paul's flexibility in language and christological titles referring to Jesus' death. The reason for the choice of "Son" in Romans 8:32 seems to be that Paul here wishes to emphasize God's personal investment, so to speak, in Jesus' sacrificial death: It is the death of God's Son (see Schweizer, 384).

Paul appears to have used a bold scriptural allusion to underscore this point. The phrase "did not withhold [*ouk epheisato*] his own Son" in Romans 8:32 seems intended to recall the words of the angel to Abraham,* "you have not withheld [*ouk epheisō*] your son, your only son" (Gen 22:12, 16), likening thereby God's offering up of Jesus to Abraham's offering of Isaac.

It is this emphasis on what Jesus' death represented for God that also likely accounts for Paul's reference to "the death of his [God's] Son" in Romans 5:10. The context illustrates Paul's general tendency to use the title "Christ" in references to Jesus' death (Rom 5:6, 8; and cf. the fuller "our Lord Jesus Christ" in Rom 5:11), especially in christocentric statements that portray the death as an act of Jesus. But Romans 5:10-11 has a theocentric focus on reconciliation* of God's "enemies"* to God, and on God-directed rejoicing (Rom 5:11) in consequence of this reconciliation. That this has taken place through the death of God's Son emphasizes how much God has been directly involved in accomplishing this reconciliation.

In Galatians 2:20 Paul refers to "the Son of God who loved me and gave himself up [*paradidōmi*] for me," a statement emphasizing Jesus' active role in a larger christocentric context (Gal 1:15-21). The textual variant, "God and Christ" in place of "Son of God," though supported by several important Greek manuscripts, is probably a corruption of the original text. And so we are left to try to determine the significance of mentioning "the Son of God" here when seven other times immediately preceding and following Galatians 2:20 Paul calls him "Jesus Christ" (Gal 2:16), "Christ Jesus" (Gal 2:16) and "Christ" (Gal 2:16-19, 21).

The expression "the Son of God" emphasizes the very high divine favor and honor of the one whose love and self-giving is stated. And this description of Jesus also implicitly makes God a party to Jesus' redemptive actions, as is confirmed in the following statement (Gal 2:21) where Paul refers to "the grace of God" in connection with Jesus' death.

Given that Romans 8:32 shows that Paul could liken the death of God's Son to the offering of Isaac, it is also possible that Paul's reference in Galatians 2:20 to the self-giving of the Son of God shows an acquaintance with Jewish tradition about the story. Though the Genesis account is silent about Isaac's attitude, ancient Jewish tradition attributes to him an eager willingness to offer himself in obedience to God (e.g., Pseudo-Philo *Bib. Ant.* 18:5; 32:2-4; 40:2; Josephus *Ant.* 1.13.2-4 §§225-36).

*4.4. The Son and the Torah.* Scholars frequently point to Romans 8:3 and Galatians 4:4 as examples of a christological "formula" in which the Son is referred to as "sent" by God. But, as has already been indicated, the identification of a verbal "formula" in these passages is dubious. It is far more relevant that both of these references to the Son being sent are in con-

texts dealing with the Torah, the Jewish Law.* The sending of the Son in Romans 8:3-4 is precisely to overcome the inability of the Torah to save as described in Romans 7, and to make possible the fulfillment the Torah's "just requirement" in the freedom* of the Spirit* given through the Son. And Galatians 4:4 mentions the Son being sent forth "to redeem those who were under the law" (the limitations of which are emphasized in Galatians 3:1—4:1) and to make possible their "adoption* as sons."

As well, in Romans 8:3 and Galatians 4:4 Paul emphasizes that the divine Son appeared in human form, which may allude to the idea of Jesus being an "incarnation" of the "pre-existent"* Son. But the humanity of the Son also means that the divinely initiated deliverance from the Torah's condemnation was effected by the Son within the sphere of human existence, specifically through his death.

*4.5. The Son and God's Sons.* Though he consistently designates Jesus as the divine Son with an exclusivity connoted, in several passages Paul implicitly or explicitly refers to the enfranchisement of the redeemed into fellowship* with Jesus and into a filial relationship with God patterned after Jesus' sonship (on this see esp. Byrne). Galatians 4:5 gives as the purpose of the sending of the Son "that we might receive sonship [*huiothesia*]" (*see* Adoption, Sonship), and the following verses refer to Christians as God's "sons" (*huioi*) who have received "the Spirit of his Son," who join the Son in calling upon God as "Abba, Father," and are now God's heirs. (And, as Gal 3:27-28 makes clear, the "sons" of God include both female and male on equal terms [hence one can, with the NRSV, translate *huioi* as "children"].)

In Romans 8 as well, Paul explicitly connects Jesus the Son with the sonship of Christians. After referring to the sending of the Son in Romans 8:3, Paul mentions the bestowal of the Spirit (Rom 8:5-13, explicitly linked with Jesus, "the Spirit of Christ," Rom 8:9), and refers to Christians as "sons of God" (Rom 8:14) who call to God as "Abba, Father" (Rom 8:15) and are "fellow heirs with Christ." And in Romans 8:18-27 Paul elaborates both present and future consequences of divine adoption. Then comes Romans 8:28-30, a very theocentric passage emphasizing God's redemptive initiative, in which the redeemed are said to have been "predestined to be conformed to the image of his Son, in order that he might be the firstborn within a large family" (Rom 8:29 NRSV). That is, the one divine Son here is the prototype as well as the agent through whom others are enfranchised as sons of God. The uniqueness of Jesus the Son is not restrictive but redemptive. The term *firstborn** may allude to Exodus 4:22, applying to Jesus a title of Israel and connoting that he has become the basis of God's reconstituted people that includes both Jew and Gentile.

The remaining Pauline references to the Son reflect this idea of God enfranchising others through the unique Son into a standing likened to his. 1 Corinthians 1:9 describes Christians as called by God into the "fellowship/participation [koinōnia] of his Son," which suggests that their status is both dependent upon the Son and also a partaking in his filial status. And 2 Corinthians 1:19-20 probably is to be seen as alluding to something similar. The divine "yes" is in Jesus, the Son of God (2 Cor 1:19), because "all the promises of God find their Yes in him" (2 Cor 1:20). And this means that Christians are enfranchised as God's own through the Son (2 Cor 1:20b) and given the Spirit as guarantee of full eschatological salvation* (2 Cor 1:22). (The "knowledge of the Son of God" in Eph 4:13 is probably also an allusion to the idea of the redemption of the elect being patterned after Jesus' divine sonship.)

This idea of other sons or children of God is interesting in light of the strong connotation of the uniqueness of Jesus' divine sonship we have noted earlier. The resolution to the apparent tension seems to be that Paul consistently refers to the sonship of Christians as derived sonship, given through and after the pattern of Jesus, whereas Jesus is the original prototype, whose sonship is not derived from another.

See also ADOPTION, SONSHIP; CHRIST; CHRISTOLOGY; DEATH OF CHRIST; EXALTATION AND ENTHRONEMENT; FIRSTBORN; GOD; HOLY SPIRIT; IMAGE, IMAGE OF GOD; LORD; PRE-EXISTENCE.

BIBLIOGRAPHY. J. Blank, Paulus und Jesus (SANT 16; Munich: Kösel, 1968); W. Bousset, Kyrios Christos (Nashville: Abingdon, 1970 [1921]); B. Byrne, "Sons of God"—"Seed of Abraham" (AnBib 83; Rome: Pontifical Institute, 1979); O. Cullmann, The Christology of the New Testament (London: SCM, 1963); D. Cuss, Imperial Cult and Honorary Terms in the New Testament (Paradosis 23; Fribourg: University of Fribourg, 1974); J. D. G. Dunn, Christology in the Making (2d ed.; London: SCM, 1989); J. A. Fitzmyer, A Wandering Aramean: Collected Aramaic Essays (SBLMS 25; Missoula, MT: Scholars, 1979); M. Hengel, The Son of God (Philadelphia: Fortress, 1976); S. Kim, The Origin of Paul's Gospel (2d ed; WUNT 2/4; Tübingen: J. C. B. Mohr, 1984); W. Kramer, Christ, Lord, Son of God (SBT 50; London: SCM, 1966); O. Michel, "Son," NIDNTT 3.607-68; A. D. Nock, " 'Son of God' in Pauline and Hellenistic Thought," in Essays on Religion and the Ancient World, ed. Z. Stewart (Oxford: Clarendon, 1972) 2.928-39; idem, Early Gentile Christianity and its Hellenistic Background (New York: Harper & Row, 1964); H. J. Schoeps, Paul (Philadelphia: Westminster, 1961); E. Schweizer et al., "υἱός, υἱοθεσία," TDNT VIII.334-99; J. M. Scott, Adoption as Sons of God (WUNT 2/48; Tübingen: J. C. B. Mohr, 1992); G. Vermes, Jesus the Jew (New York: Harper & Row, 1973).

L. W. Hurtado

**SONGS.** See HYMNS, HYMN FRAGMENTS, SONGS, SPIRITUAL SONGS.

**SONS OF ABRAHAM.** See ABRAHAM.

**SONSHIP.** See ADOPTION, SONSHIP; SON OF GOD.

**SOUL.** See PSYCHOLOGY.

**SPIRIT (HUMAN).** See PSYCHOLOGY.

**SPIRIT OF CHRIST.** See HOLY SPIRIT.

**SPIRIT OF GOD.** See HOLY SPIRIT.

**SPIRIT WORLD.** See ANGELS, ARCHANGELS; DEMONS, EXORCISM; HOLY SPIRIT; MAGIC; PRINCIPALITIES AND POWERS; SATAN, DEVIL.

**SPIRITUAL GIFTS.** See CORINTHIANS, LETTERS TO THE; GIFTS OF THE SPIRIT.

**SPIRITUAL SONGS.** See HYMNS, HYMN FRAGMENTS, SONGS, SPIRITUAL SONGS.

## SPIRITUALITY

Spirituality in Paul can best be summarized as an expression of affirmation to God,* a grateful "Yes" from the heart of a believer which, in the power of the Spirit, is manifested in act and attitude. The glory and the possibility of this "Yes" are grounded in God's "Yes" to the believer in Jesus Christ,* a "Yes" experienced and expressed by Paul (2 Cor 1:17-20) and set out in Romans 8 as the thrust of his life and teaching.

The affirmations of Pauline spirituality may be pictured as an ellipse representing the believer's life. The Holy Spirit* as the effective power at work in the believer elicits the believer's "Yes" to God, a "Yes" that is expressed in the interactive poles of the ellipse—(1) the privileged responsibilities of the child of God (especially the triad of prayer,* word and community, culminating in worship*), and (2) the comprehensive obedience represented by the fruit* of the Spirit.

1. Background
2. The Spirit of God and Spirituality

## 1. Background.

However one understands and defines the spirituality of Paul, there is general agreement that it was both noteworthy in itself and critical in shaping the spirituality of the Christian church. Paul called Christian believers to imitate* his apostolic life and service* to Christ—which he experienced in the power* of the Spirit—even as he was an imitator of Christ (e.g., 1 Cor 11:1; cf. 1 Thess 1:6). Other than Jesus Christ, worshiped and served as Lord over all, no other person has had a greater impact upon *Christian* spirituality than Paul.

The importance of Paul notwithstanding, the modern quest to understand Pauline spirituality takes place in a paradoxical setting. On the one hand, the word *spirituality*, though widely used today, finds no consensus regarding its general definition, let alone Pauline spirituality. (Indeed, *spirituality* often seems to be subject to mutually exclusive definitions.) Just as Christianity historically has been marked by considerable confessional and other differences, so there have been divergent understandings of Pauline spirituality. In fact, the variety of Christian denominations can plausibly be attributed to divergent interpretations of Pauline spirituality. Although some NT scholars locate the differences within Paul himself, the spirituality of Paul, like his theological perspective, has a coherence that is frequently overlooked.

The history of Pauline interpretation has unveiled the depth and breadth and complexity of Pauline thought—whether observed as theology or ethics* or spirituality. No one of these three perspectives on Paul stands in isolation from the others. The complexity of Paul is exemplified in the failure of Pauline scholars even to approach a consensus regarding the "center"* of Pauline thought. Since there is widespread agreement that "spirituality" has to do with the central and most urgent aspects of (Christian) existence, uncertainty regarding the so-called *centrum Paulinum* suggests the likelihood that interpreters will diverge in their understanding of Pauline spirituality. However, the problem runs deeper than this. Interpreters have not been unified in the way they approach the immediate reference point of *spirit-* in the term *spirituality*. Should those who wish to comprehend Pauline spirituality understand *spirit-* to refer to the *human* spirit or to the *Holy* Spirit? Surely the Pauline answer is the Holy Spirit.

Although the entire Pauline corpus must naturally provide the grist for understanding Pauline spirituality, Paul's letter to the Roman church, as the mature summary of his theology, ethics and spirituality, is the touchstone for interpreting Pauline spirituality.

## 2. The Spirit of God and Spirituality.

If Paul himself is allowed to determine the meaning of the word *spirituality* in Christian usage, then one cannot speak of "the spirituality" of Paul apart from recognizing that Pauline spirituality (both words are to be emphasized here) is grounded in and determined by the divine, trinitarian community—God the Father, Jesus Christ the Son* and the Holy Spirit (*see* God). For Paul the glory and the basis of the *human* spirit is established and directed by the *Holy* Spirit (Rom 8:1-17; 1 Cor 2:12-16; 12:1-11; 2 Cor 1:21-22; 5:5; Gal 3:1-6; 4:1-7).

Paul's proclamation of salvation* and his instruction regarding the mission of God in the world* is predicated on the understanding that the Holy Spirit, promised in the OT as a decisive aspect of the eschatological time of salvation, is powerfully at work in the world (*see* Eschatology). This is most decisively evident in the Spirit's raising Jesus, God's Messiah, from death* to life and now mediating the presence of the risen, exalted* Christ to the believing community (Gal 4:1-6; Eph 1:13). The apostle also associates the Holy Spirit with the believer's initial act of faith* (Gal 3:1-6; 4:1-7; 1 Cor 12:3; Rom 8:12-17), as well as the continuing confirmation and establishment of believers as sons and daughters of God in a community of the Spirit (2 Cor 13:13; cf. 1 Cor 12; 14) from whose hearts and lips arise the prayer, "Abba, Father" (Rom 8:15; Gal 4:6; *see* Adoption, Sonship; Liturgical Elements).

## 3. Pauline Spirituality: "Yes to God."

The spirituality of Paul may be defined as the grateful and heartfelt "Yes to God," the response of the child of God to the call of God in the Spirit. Expressed both in act and attitude, the believer lives in obedience to and imitation of Jesus Christ, the true Son of God, and walks in the disciplined and maturing pattern of love's obedience to God.

This human response is called forth by and founded on God's own overwhelming "Yes" to the believer—a "Yes" that is supremely manifested in and through God's Son (2 Cor 1:18-22). This "obedience of faith" (Rom 1:5; 16:26) working through love* (Gal 5:6) is enabled by the Spirit of God (Rom 8:1-17), who both makes Christ present to the believer and makes the divine will effective and fruitful in the lived-out faith of the believer (Gal 5:22-23).

Enabled by the indwelling Spirit of God to live in union with Christ, the child of God is ever being transformed into the image* of Christ (Rom 8:29; 1 Cor 15:49; 2 Cor 3:18), the true Son of God. Although in Pauline spirituality the pattern of life called forth by the sovereign, creator God effectively touches the whole of human existence, the Spirit of God has entrusted the believer with special means of grace which nurture a "disciplined" (see 10-11 below) relationship to the trinitarian community—the Father, the Son and the Holy Spirit. Through the use of these gracious means, the believer is enabled to live out the whole of life in the world in faithfulness to God. Thus the spirituality of the believer may be pictured as an ellipse with the two interactive poles representing (1) the exercise of the privileged responsibilities of the child of God and (2) a comprehensive pattern of obedience leading to a growing harvest of the fruit of the Spirit.

**4. The Experiential Foundation of Pauline Spirituality.** Two experiences were especially critical in shaping the spirituality of Paul: (1) his initial Israelite religious heritage and practice rooted in the OT and shaped by his Pharisaic commitment, (see Jew, Paul the) and (2) his encounter with the living Christ on the road to Damascus (see Conversion and Call).

*4.1. Paul's Israelite Heritage.* Paul's obedience to the ways of God set forth in the OT Scriptures established in him a pattern of prayer, direction by the Word of God in Scripture, and life lived in the context of a covenant community characterized especially by its devotion to God expressed in prayer and attentive listening to Scripture (e.g., Ps 1). This triad of prayer, Word of God and community of faith was conjoined in the central activity of the worship of God. Paul was, in his own understanding, an obedient child of God in the way of Israelite faith. For Paul as a pious Israelite the Scriptures everywhere made clear the total claim of God upon the faithful; they were called to walk in righteousness* as the people of a holy God.

*4.2. Paul's Damascus Road Experience.* As important

as Paul's earlier religious experience is for understanding his postconversion pattern of spirituality, his earlier practice was deepened and utterly transformed by his initial encounter with the risen Christ (1 Cor 15:8-11; Gal 1:11-17). Prominent aspects of this new pattern of spirituality included: (1) An awareness of the presence in and among his people of the risen Jesus, now reigning as Lord (Rom 4:24-25; 5:21; 6:23; 8:31-39). (2) The experience of the grace of God—by one who was weak and sinful and an enemy* of God (see Rom 5:6-10; 1 Cor 15:10). (3) The "call" of God to faith in and through the risen Jesus (1 Cor 15:12-19; Rom 10:6-17). (4) The life, suffering,* death, resurrection* and glorification* of Jesus validated by God as the way of righteousness—with all that this means for believing existence (Gal 6:17; 2 Cor 4:5-12; 6:4-10; 12:23-31). (5) A new experience of the presence of God through the empowering action of the Holy Spirit, who brings the believer into union with Christ as an heir of salvation, and places in the believer's heart and mouth the prayer, "Abba, Father" (Rom 8:15; Gal 4:6).

Following Paul's encounter with Christ, his prayer took place within a new, essentially trinitarian framework. Prayer* was now offered to God in the name of the Son of God and mediated by the Spirit of God within the community of the Spirit (see Liturgical Elements), wherein believers constantly uphold one another in fervent prayer (Rom 15:30-33; 2 Cor 13:13; Eph 3:14-21; Col 1:3-10; 1 Thess 1:2-8). Again, just as Paul experienced through faith in Jesus Christ the coming of the Spirit promised in the OT, he also found that the Spirit newly illumined the OT in the context of the new creation in the Spirit, and raised up within the community of the Spirit gifted interpreters of that Word (2 Cor 3:1-18; 4:1-6; see Old Testament). The new community of the Spirit experienced the power of the Spirit in its midst, decisively characterized by faith working through love, expressed in forgiveness,* humility and mutual burden bearing, all functioning to sustain and build up the one body of Christ as the *koinōnia* of the Spirit (see Body of Christ).

**5. Union with Christ.**
The believer's transcendent experience of Christ in the present time has been characterized as "union with Christ"—a term which has often shaped discussions of the spirituality of Paul (see Dying and Rising). The term "union with Christ" reflects the extensive Pauline teaching regarding Christ dwelling in and with the believer, and the believer being in and with Christ (see In Christ). But this must be understood from the dual vantage points of the incarnate and

risen presence of God in Christ (cf. 2 Cor 5:16), and in the believing community. For Paul, life in the Spirit is directed both from *within* and from *without* history. The Spirit of Jesus draws one into conformity to the pattern and model of the incarnate Lord* (2 Cor 3:18), whose obedience to God was lived out within the setting of first-century Palestine. Arguments that Paul was not interested in the incarnate ministry of Jesus collapse in the face of Paul's admission that he had persecuted the early followers of Jesus and his subsequent proclamation of the same Jesus as risen (Gal 1:13, 23); there was, for Paul, no separation between the incarnate and risen Lord (*see* Jesus, Sayings of; Jesus and Paul). Paul teaches that the believer is united in the present with the same Jesus who, in the power of the Spirit, became one with humankind, lived in obedience, and suffered and died on a cruel cross outside Jerusalem. But this union with the risen Christ also has a future dimension of glorification with Christ (Rom 8:17-25; 1 Cor 15:35-41; 2 Cor 4:16-17; Phil 3:17-21).

Paul knew himself to be mysteriously united with Jesus in his suffering and death and risen life—but also joined to all those who, by faith in Jesus, were by the Spirit adopted into the family of God as co-heirs with Jesus Christ. Paul was at once dependent upon the disciples of Jesus and upon the Jerusalem* church for their witness to Jesus' life and teaching. But he was also an "independent" apostle,* who knew himself to be called of God and entrusted with the gospel of Christ to the Gentiles,* along with the fuller explication of the meaning of that gospel. Pauline spirituality is simultaneously determined by his experience of Christ within the community of faith and in his more immediate, revelational experience of the risen Lord.

### 6. The Practice of the Spirit.

The spirituality of Paul, whether in life or teaching, rests on the foundation of God's gracious work through the divine Son, a grace* mediated to believers by and in the power of the Spirit of God. Paul understands that the Spirit is "poured out" (Rom 5:5) in the life of the believer in and through the response of faith (Gal 3:1-6; 4:1-7). From the moment of faith, Christ is present in the believer through the agency of the Spirit who is the Spirit of Jesus (2 Cor 3:17). But the coming of the Spirit is not simply a personal and individual event, or even a larger, "ecclesial" event within the boundaries of the people of God. Rather, the believer is brought into the new creation in Christ, in which all things are made new (2 Cor 3:6; 5:17-19; Gal 6:15; Eph 2:15; *see* Creation and New Creation). But this newness is realized only as the believer continues to walk in the Spirit, whose sanctifying work transforms the believer into the image of the Son.

"Walking in the Spirit" (Rom 8:4; Gal 5:16) is a vivid image of Pauline spirituality, one rooted in OT Scripture (e.g., Deut 10:12; 13:5; 26:17; 28:9) and in Jesus' "way" of discipleship (cf., e.g., Mk 1:17; 2:14; 8:34; 10:21). But the decisive role of the Spirit in directing Christian existence makes it useful to characterize the spirituality of Paul as *the practice of the Spirit* (as in Gal 5:25 NIV). *Practice of the Spirit* makes more explicit the *intentionality* and *discipline* anticipated by Paul's language of "walking." *Practice* here is understood as a comprehensive pattern of action governed by one's basic perspective. For Paul this perspective is theological and spiritual. It should be noted that although Paul can use the Greek equivalent (*prassō/praxis*) of our word *practice* (verb and noun) in a positive way (e.g., 1 Cor 7:9; 9:17; Eph 6:21; Phil 4:9; 1 Thess 4:11), he often uses the same term with strong negative connotations (e.g., Rom 1:32; 2 Cor 4:2; Eph 4:19; Col 3:9).

The preposition "of" in "the practice of the Spirit," lends a pragmatic (but valid) ambiguity to the expression. "Of the Spirit" may be understood simultaneously as a subjective and as an objective genitive. As a subjective genitive the practice is a pattern of action understood from the standpoint of its origins in the Spirit (a practice that comes from the Spirit); it is a practice determined by the Spirit as the divine agent seeking and establishing a community of saints who will walk in the ways of holiness* and righteousness.* As an objective genitive it characterizes the obedience of faith which opens itself to the impulses of the Spirit, an obedience which diligently seeks to use the means instituted by the Spirit in order to "walk in the Spirit."

Although the spirituality defined as the practice of the Spirit is decisively "from above," it is also a spirituality "from below." The Spirit acts "from above," originating, determining and enabling the believer's walk in the Spirit. The believer acts "from below," walking obediently, but freely, from the heart. The believer walks not in the flesh,* as a self-determined being, but in the Spirit, as a being willing and seeking to be determined by the Spirit of God, who is creator and sovereign over all. Within this framework, in the obedience of faith, the believer is illumined and empowered to walk truly in the Spirit, and to be transformed into the image of Jesus Christ, the prototype of life in God. Spirituality is the lived experience of the believer. But its life-giving center and righteous form is experienced as a gift from God through the Spirit of Jesus. This experience and truth shapes all other aspects of the believer's life (see 14 below).

## 7. Spirituality and Sanctification.

As the person and work of the Spirit stands at the beginning and center of Pauline spirituality, so the reality of sanctification as a continuing work of the Spirit is critical to Pauline spirituality (*see* Holiness, Sanctification).

In the divine work of sanctification the Spirit works to effect a two-fold human response. On the one hand, the Spirit calls believers to present or give themselves to God (see Rom 12:1; 6:15-22; 1 Thess 4:1-8). This involves a hearty obedience to the will of God (Rom 6:17) and, above all, a focus on Jesus Christ the Son of God, into whose image the believer is being transformed by the Spirit. On the other hand, there is a negative side to sanctification involving death to sin* (Rom 6:12-23), renunciation of the way of "the flesh*" (Gal 5:16-24; Rom 8:2-14) and full surrender of selfish autonomy to the holy will of God as it is brought to light through the agency of the Spirit.

How are spirituality and sanctification interrelated? Sanctification precedes, begets and undergirds spirituality, even as the new life of the believer comes from the Spirit of God who also sustains that life. Here two Pauline perspectives on the work of the Holy Spirit are important. On the one hand, the Pauline doctrine of sanctification stands as a "declaration" of the believer's location "in Christ"* and "in the Spirit," as an adopted* son or daughter of God. The believer is "called out" of, separated from, the world, and adopted into the holy family of God. At the same time, the Pauline understanding of sanctification anticipates a process of growth and maturation in and through the Spirit (1 Cor 3:6-7; 2 Cor 10:15; Eph 2:21; 4:13-16; Col 2:19), of being made perfect by the indwelling Spirit of Christ (Rom 12:2; 2 Cor 7:1; 13:9; 1 Thess 3:13).

Pauline spirituality is determined by one's status as a believer subject to the sanctifying work of the Spirit, whereby one is transformed into the image of Christ. As set apart (sanctified) to God, as a child of God, the believer is privileged to address God in the communion and conversation of prayer. The believer is also privileged to be addressed by the Word and promise of God; the one who first loves addresses his beloved children. And as a member of the family of God, the believer is blessed not only to know God as Father, but to live in a mutually supportive community of brothers and sisters in Christ.

But the believer's privileged status as a child of God brings responsibility. The gift (*Gabe*) and the believing response (*Aufgabe*) are always interrelated. Although God is a sovereign who claims the total obedience of the entire creation, Pauline spirituality may be understood as the "privileged responsibility" of the adopted children of God. They are called to the obedience of faith enacted through calling upon God in prayer, listening attentively to the divine Word, and living as responsible members of the household* of God. This triadic responsibility is expressed in the community's central act of worship and focused in the Lord's Supper* fellowship meal (1 Cor 10:16-22). Each aspect has many configurations; together they constitute the dynamic center of growth and perfection in grace.

The relationship of spirituality and sanctification may be pictured as a spiral. On the one hand, it is only as one is a child of God, sanctified in the Spirit of Christ, that the privileges embodied in the spiritual exercises are available. At the same time, believers realize the full meaning of that privilege only as they pray to God without ceasing, are open and obedient to the word of God, and live in love as members of the household of faith. Sanctification embodies a call to spirituality; spirituality realizes the promise of sanctification.

## 8. Sin and Sanctification.

For Paul, Jesus Christ is the mediator of the divine response to sin, the locus of the justification* of the sinner. God in Christ brings people into the new world of the Spirit. But, until the consummation of all things, the new life goes on in the midst of an old, dying world wherein weakness* and corruption, sin* and death (*see* Life), still assault the believer (Rom 7). Paul's constant and urgent call to sanctification is a divine antidote for the continuing hostility and power of sin.

Believers, indwelt by the Spirit, are called to a life of response to the Spirit, a new life in the Spirit that ever transcends the old life of the flesh. In this life, with God's own Spirit working in the weakness of the church, believers are called both to put to death the works of the flesh, and to dedicate themselves to God and live unto righteousness. This pattern of dying and rising with Christ is at the center of Paul's understanding of sanctification (as in Rom 6), and of his instruction to believers (above all, see Rom 6—8).

The continuing reality of sin and the call to sanctification means that both the individual believer and the believing community must employ all the means of grace established by the Spirit so as to walk in the Spirit and not quench the Spirit (1 Thess 5:19; cf. Rom 12:11). Thus, discernment (1 Cor 2:14), exhortation (Rom 12:1; 1 Thess 2:11; 4:1; 2 Tim 4:2), and repentant, prayerful turning to God (Rom 2:4; 2 Cor 7:9-10) are essential to the process of sanctification in the community of the Spirit.

## 9. Imitation and Discipleship.

The normative form of the practice of the Spirit is seen preeminently in Jesus Christ, the Lord of the church. Thus Paul exhorts believers to "the imitation of Christ," pointing to himself as an imitator of Christ and calling believers to follow him as he follows Christ (1 Cor 4:15-16; 11:1; Phil 3:12-17; 1 Thess 1:6; 2 Thess 3:9-12). In turn, believers themselves provide an example which others may imitate (1 Thess 1:6-7; 2:14). In spite of the distortions that the NT pattern of imitating Christ has suffered, the antidote is not to abandon the call to imitation, but rather to heed Paul's call to imitate Christ. To be sure, this is not a call to "mere imitation." It is a call to the *obedience of faith*, subjecting oneself to the pattern of Jesus' incarnate and continuing existence, so that the illumining and empowering work of the Spirit can effectively imprint the life of Jesus in the life of a believer (*see* Imitation).

For Paul the meaning of the incarnation is not limited to the suffering and death of Jesus, and neither is his understanding of imitation. Although Paul's references to the sayings and life of Jesus are primarily allusive, it is clear that Paul could not—and did not—separate the "historical" Jesus from the risen Christ. The power of the Spirit that transformed the life of the crucified into a glorious exalted existence is the same Spirit that works in the believer (Rom 1:3-4; 8:11; cf. 1 Cor 15:42-50). The risen Lord Jesus, in his exalted existence, is united to the children of God in their daily existence, an existence which he himself shared in his humiliation. The imprint of Jesus on the life of the apostle is a recurring theme in Paul. The fruit* of the Spirit in the believer is the imprint of that same life which was manifest in the incarnate Lord (2 Cor 4:7-12). This life placed before the churches in the fullness of the church's preaching* (*kerygma*), teaching* (*didachē*) and tradition* (*paradosis*). And Paul replicates the pattern of his Lord in his own prayerful existence, in his utter dependence upon the word of God in Scripture, and in his obedient life and suffering and dying for the sake of the people of God.

The imitation of Christ is the post-Easter continuation of discipleship to Jesus. Even though Paul does not use the specific language of "discipleship," his experience of the risen Christ on the way to Damascus transformed him into a *disciple* of the one whose disciples he had persecuted, and whose incarnate life and ministry became a central aspect of Pauline christology* (see Phil 2:1-11; Rom 5:6-21, esp. Rom 5:6-10). In spite of continuing scholarly reservations regarding any equation of "following" Jesus in the Gospels

and imitating Jesus in Paul, it is apparent that the apostle uses the language of imitation to convey the essential meanings found in the way of discipleship to Jesus in the Gospels. Just as obedience to the historical Jesus was a primary mark of discipleship, so the Pauline theme of imitating Christ entails a central act of obedience to the call of God in Jesus Christ. This obedience brings believers into the presence of Christ and constant communion with him, making them subject to his person, way, and teaching, and uniting them with the Lord who walks in the way of suffering and death. To imitate Christ after Easter is to walk in the way of discipleship to the risen Lord. Thus, Pauline spirituality is joined with the way of discipleship to Jesus; and discipleship to Jesus finds its extension and fulfillment in the pattern of imitating Christ which Paul himself models.

## 10. The Triad of Prayer, Word and Community.

Paul's experience of the risen Christ in the power of the Spirit transformed and empowered the triad of prayer, Word of God and covenant people of God which he inherited from Judaism. Where Paul does not mention this interrelated triad, it can nonetheless be assumed as an abiding premise of Pauline spirituality. Each element of this triple practice is essential to both the solitary life of the individual believer and the corporate life of the body of Christ. The elements of this triad are embraced in the worshiping life of the community, and in this triadic practice the community expresses itself in the worship of Jesus Christ as Lord, the Son of God. Service and witness are also a reflex of this triad, with both emerging from the community at worship.

For Paul, life in prayer, life in the Word of God and life in community of the Spirit, are each and together a creation of the Spirit of God. The Spirit brings the deep prayer, "Abba, Father," to the heart and mouth of the believer (Rom 8:15; Gal 4:6) and sustains the believer, afflicted by a besetting weakness in prayer (Rom 8:26; see 11 below). The Spirit inspires (2 Tim 3:16) and illumines the Word of God (2 Cor 3:1-18). And the Spirit creates and builds up into Christ the community of faith (1 Cor 12; 14; esp. 1 Cor 12:3-13; 14:1-5). Through these means the Spirit continually nurtures an authentic "Yes" to God in the hearts of believers. In the divinely wrought symbiosis of prayer, Word and community, the believer, walking in the Spirit, grows in faith and is strengthened in faith (Phil 1:25; Col 2:7; 1 Thess 3:1-10; Rom 1:11; 16:25; 1 Thess 3:2), is perfected in holiness (2 Cor 7:1; Phil 1:6) and is transformed into the image of the Son (Rom 8:29; Col 3:10).

*911*

**11. Prayer as a Primary Paradigm of Spirituality.**
Through the centuries virtually all Christians have understood prayer to lie at the heart of their spirituality. This finds firm rooting in the practice and writings of Paul. The apostle's letters typically begin and conclude with notes and reports on prayer, and the contents of his letters underscore the great importance of prayer. We can note here only a representative sample of the Pauline data. The apostle shows that true prayer is from the heart (Rom 8:27; Phil 1:7); at the same time, he links effective prayer to the mind and to the spirit (1 Cor 14:14-15). A variety of expressions is used to describe the manner and significance of praying, such as persevering, wrestling, thankfulness and joyfulness. Paul regularly reports at the beginning of his letters his own prayer for the faithful (e.g., Rom 1:8-10; 1 Cor 1:4; Phil 1:3-12; 1 Thess 1:2-3; 3:9-10), and he likewise entreats their prayer for himself and for other believers near and far (Rom 15:30; Col 4:2-4; 1 Thess 2:5; 2 Thess 3:1). Paul reports that he prays "day and night" (1 Thess 3:10; note that Paul also works for Christ day and night, 1 Thess 2:9; 2 Thess 3:8), and he encourages all believers to pray without ceasing (1 Thess 5:17; Eph 6:18) and in every place (1 Tim 2:8).

Paul understands Christian existence as a new way of being in God, through Christ in the power of the Spirit, and so he specifically and sharply differentiates Christian existence from the religious experience of the surrounding Greco-Roman world. The apostle, along with the earliest Church, was encouraged and emboldened by the eschatological presence of the Spirit of Jesus to address God in the intimate pattern of Jesus—"Abba, Father" (Rom 8:15; Gal 4:6).

In Romans 8:26-27 Paul opens a window into his own understanding of the mystery of the Spirit's active presence in the believer's life in prayer. The following aspects of this passage merit mention with respect to Paul's experience, practice and teaching about prayer. (1) It is highly significant that Paul appeals to prayer in the heart of a critical discussion of the Christian experience of the Spirit. (2) As important as prayer is for Paul, he confesses human weakness and inability in praying—even as the entire creation in general (Rom 8:19-22), and the children of God in particular (Rom 8:23), live in a sinful, dying world, awaiting the promised redemption. (3) But Paul knows, as part of the experience of faith, that God's own Spirit assists the believer in prayer—even as God is for the believer in all things (Rom 8:31-39)—and that the Spirit, knowing the heart of the believer, intercedes on behalf of the believer. It is the Spirit, then, who enables "the practice of the Spirit." These three things—the prayer-

ful practice of the Spirit, the human experience of spiritual weakness and transcendent enablement—characterize Pauline spirituality generally.

**12. The Locus of Spirituality.**
In light of peculiar ideas regarding the terms *Spirit*, *spiritual* and *spirituality* which have bedeviled the life of the church through the centuries, it is important to clarify Paul's own understanding of the *locus* of the Spirit in the individual and corporate life of faith.

Although the Pauline letters provide abundant resources for determining the locus of spirituality, Romans 12:1—13:7 notably and usefully summarizes the scope of Paul's instruction of the young churches. In Romans 8 Paul shows that the breadth and depth of the Christian life is generated by and subject to the trinitarian community. Romans 9 offers further commentary on the grace of God and the imperative of obedience to God. Then, beginning with Romans 12, Paul exhorts the Roman Christians by the mercy* and grace* of God to accept a pattern of life appropriate to those who are united to Christ and dwell in him by the power of the Spirit. Although interpreters have often discussed Romans 12:1—13:7 under the rubric of "Christian life" or "ethical imperative," the context and content also place this passage within the scope of spirituality, including the practice of the Spirit (see Rom 12:11). Clearly Paul is giving important instruction regarding the righteousness of the "sanctified" person who belongs to God and exercises the privileges and responsibilities of a child of God. Paul points to a transformed life in which the godless existence of the ungrateful person described in Romans 1:18-32 is transformed into the life of the believer dedicated to God. The very language of Romans 12:1-2 mirrors the thrust of Romans 6, a pivotal text in Paul's instruction regarding the sanctified life.

In successive textual units of Romans 12:1—13:7, Paul points to the following as loci of the Spirit's working in those who are in Christ. (1) Their *bodies** (Rom 12:1) are to be presented to God as a living sacrifice. (2) Their *minds* (Rom 12:2) are to be submitted to God who—in the Spirit of Jesus—transforms them, establishing them in the pattern of Jesus' own life of obedience (note Rom 5:19 and Rom 15:3-4; *see* Psychology). (3) Believers as *selves* (Rom 12:3) before God and other members of the body of Christ, are to regard their selves as under divine Lordship, humanly frail and dependent upon God. (4) Believers are to take an active role within *the corporate body of Christ* (Rom 12:4-8) and according to the particular gifts given to them. (5) In the pattern of Jesus, and according to the reconciling action of God, believers are exhorted to produce the fruit of the Spirit, peace,* while living in *a hostile world* (Rom 12:14-21). (6) Finally, living within a world of political structures and powers (Rom 13:1-7), believers are ultimately subject to the lordship of God, who is sovereign over all (*see* Civil Authority).

A survey of the Pauline corpus quickly reveals the comprehensive perspective as well as the depth-dimensions of Pauline spirituality. There is no place where believers are outside the reign of the Lord who is the Spirit (2 Cor 3:17-18); walking in the Spirit of Jesus means that the whole person in its whole context is subject to the Spirit of God.

### 13. The Fruit and Gifts of the Spirit.

The fruit* of Spirit and the gifts* of the Spirit are two significant aspects of Paul's description of the practice of the Spirit. Since both aspects are the work of the one Spirit of God, it is imperative that we understand them in relation to one another. The fruit of the Spirit is to be evident in the common life of the believer (see 14 below) and in the exercise of the "privileged responsibilities" of prayer, listening to the Word and participating in the life of the body (see 10 and 11 above). The exercise of the gifts of the Spirit is subject to the control of the righteous fruit of the Spirit. And the fruit of the Spirit is caused to flourish and grow within the community wherein the gifts of the sanctifying Spirit are exercised. This symbiotic relationship between fruit and gift fosters the fulfillment of the divine intention that the gifts of the Spirit should sanctify and upbuild the church. Pauline spirituality, the practice of the Spirit, is the believer's "Yes to God," whose righteous fruit and gifts are to be sought, embraced and lived out in the community of the Spirit and in the world.

*13.1. The Fruit of the Spirit.* Galatians 5:22-23 is the *locus classicus* for Paul's teaching concerning the fruit of the Spirit. Although the catalog of the fruit of the Spirit does not appear to be "systematically" developed, that is, it represents but a part of the righteous fruit of the Spirit in human life as Paul understands it, the first three fruits—love,* joy,* peace*—play a major role in Pauline teaching. Statistically and generally this triad of righteous fruit far outweighs other fruits noted by the apostle. Within Romans, for instance, several passages (Rom 5:1-5; 12:9-21; 14:1—15:13, 30-31) directly or implicitly highlight this triad in a way that reflects its primary position in the formal listing of Galatians 5:22-23. Paul's exhortations and prayers generally focus on the necessity of this fruit in the lives of believers. It has often been suggested that love, joy and peace may be viewed as embodying all the other fruit. Paul's declaration in 1 Corinthians 13

that love is the greatest gift is everywhere reflected in the Pauline teaching—above all in Romans 5:5-10 and Romans 8:15-16, 8:26-27 and 8:28-39.

*13.2. The Gifts of the Spirit.* Paul's teaching regarding the gifts of the Spirit has been intensely studied in modern times, above all with an interest in the way in which the church is made fruitful in its mission through the gifts of the Spirit. Four points are of special importance with respect to spirituality as the practice of the Spirit. (1) The gifts of the Spirit are richly varied and are lavished on the community, which is being built up in the world. In Romans 12:4-8 Paul makes clear the varied nature of the gifts; in particular, gifts kindred to functions in common life—service and generosity and mercy—appear alongside gifts more kindred to the privileged responsibilities of prayer, Word and community, viz. prophecy,* teaching, exhortation and leadership. The former seem to be a concrete expression of the fruit of the Spirit. Only as the church recognizes the surpassing value of each gift, and of all the gifts of the Spirit working together, is the body of Christ built up. (2) The gifts are given to be exercised as a privileged responsibility (see esp. Rom 12:4-8). This accords with the structure of the Christian life as the obedience of faith and is congruent with spirituality as the believer's "Yes to God." (3) The exercise of the gifts is the fertile ground upon which the fruit of the Spirit flourishes. Proclamation, faithful teaching, exhortation, leadership—all exercises of the gifts of the Spirit—lead to a rich bounty of spiritual fruit in the community of the Spirit. (4) Believers are enabled to gauge the authenticity of their practice of the Spirit by the measure in which the fruits of the Spirit are evident in their lives. Exhortation in the power of the Spirit provides the believing community the wisdom* by which to judge the efficacy of its own practice of the Spirit.

### 14. The Spirit and the Common Life.

Paul understands the Christian way as "life in the Spirit" or "walking in the Spirit." The totality of Christian existence is subject to the Spirit of God, who is Creator and Lord of all life. Thus in his apostolic exhortation Paul repeatedly emphasizes the concrete shape of life in the Spirit. Rather than pass in review the full catalog of Pauline concerns, five critical intersections of the Spirit and common life may be noted: (1) daily human relationships; (2) everyday conversation; (3) eating and drinking; (4) money and goods; (5) sexual attitudes and relationships.

*14.1. Daily Human Relationships.* Just as Paul can proclaim that the love of God is poured out in believers' lives through the Spirit (Rom 5:5), so love, the most prominent fruit of the Spirit (1 Cor 13), sets the tone for the practice of the Spirit. In 1 Corinthians 13 Paul, in a hymnic style that resonates with his appeals for believers to pattern their lives after Jesus, outlines the contours of the Christian walk in the Spirit as a walk in love. In two major Pauline textual units, Romans 14:1—15:13 and Philippians 2:1-11 (see Thompson), Paul shows how the Christian's Lord models the pattern of love, providing the template (Rom 15:5) for their own life in the Spirit. Jesus, who is the incarnate mediator of divine love (see Rom 5:6-10), did not please himself (Rom 15:3) but opened his heart to the world (Rom 15:7) in redemptive service on behalf of weak, sinful, even hostile, humanity (Rom 5:8, 10). In Philippians Paul appeals to the exhortation in Jesus (Phil 2:1) and the *koinōnia* ("fellowship"*) in the Spirit, encouraging believers to share a common mind and love in the pattern of Jesus Christ, the mediator of their salvation, who took the form of a servant. Paul's abiding description of the spiritual life is that of humble and self-emptying service to one's neighbor. This accords with the Pauline understanding that the Spirit who indwells believers is the Spirit of Jesus.

*14.2. Everyday Conversation.* One of the most overlooked emphases in the Pauline letters is his exhortation concerning the spirituality of ordinary human speech. In Ephesians 4:25—5:20 and a parallel passage in Colossians (Col 3:5-17), we find the strongest possible language—both negative and positive—exhorting believers to give heed to their speech. The Ephesians passage is longer and more detailed: those who have "put on the new nature" (Eph 4:24; *see* New Nature) are not to lie, but to speak the truth (Eph 4:25); not to employ evil talk, but to use fitting, edifying speech which imparts grace to those who hear (Eph 4:29); not to be bitter or to slander, but to be tenderhearted, without malice, and forgiving (Eph 4:31-32); not to employ filthy or silly talk, but to give thanks (Eph 5:4). In keeping with the Pauline emphasis upon the urgency of thanksgiving (see 15 below), Paul concludes his commentary on Christian speech with an appeal to thanksgiving—"always and for everything, giving thanks in the name of our Lord Jesus Christ to God and the Father." This is the way of "true righteousness and holiness" (Eph 4:24); it is the fruit of having been taught in the way of Jesus, the Christ (Eph 4:20-21); it is life lived in imitation of God (Eph 5:1) and in the pattern of Christ (Eph 5:2). It is the fruit of the life which has been "sealed with the promised Holy Spirit" (Eph 1:13), so that the believer is "a dwelling place of God in the Spirit" (Eph 2:22).

*14.3. Eating and Drinking.* In Pauline perspective the simple act of eating and drinking is laden with spiritual import, for all of life is illumined and empowered by the Spirit of Jesus. Thus in Romans 14:1—15:13 Paul reveals a number of perspectives on eating and drinking. To be sure, Paul clearly declares that the kingdom of God has to do, not with "food and drink but righteousness and peace and joy in the Holy Spirit" (Rom 14:17). Nonetheless, he surrounds that declaration with a formidable array of specific comments regarding the meaning of eating and drinking. In eating and drinking, one may honor or dishonor the Lord (Rom 14:6). Eating and drinking are an occasion for the attitude and expression of gratitude to God (14:6). In eating and drinking one lives unto the Lord and dies unto the Lord (Rom 14:7-9). Eating and drinking can be an instance of walking in love, or not walking in love (Rom 14:15-16)—as well as of living or not living in peace with others (Rom 14:19), or of edifying or not edifying the other (Rom 14:19). Of special interest is the section's concluding appeal to Jesus (Rom 15:7): "Welcome one another, therefore, just as Christ has welcomed you." It is impossible to suppose that Paul, who called believers to follow him in imitating Christ, did not have in mind the common meals in which Jesus participated—often with the rejected ones of contemporary society (*see* Food; Love Feast).

It is significant that all these "meanings" of Christian eating and drinking are otherwise closely associated with the Spirit in Paul (love, peace, edification, gratitude and honoring the Lord). Other Pauline passages, most notably significant elements of 1 Corinthians 9—11 where the Lord's Supper* and common meals are conjoined, offer parallel instruction. In *all* eating and drinking, the Christian believer is called to be "spiritual," not "unspiritual" (1 Cor 2:14-16), instructed in the mind of Christ (1 Cor 2:16).

*14.4. The Handling of Money and Goods.* One of the significant aspects of the ministry of Paul was the collection* for the saints which he solicited from Greek Christians in order to bring aid to poor Christians in Jerusalem.* In this collection the apostle, who otherwise was wholly devoted to the proclamation of the gospel and sought nothing for himself (1 Cor 9:3-15; 2 Cor 11:7-9; 1 Thess 2:9), nonetheless understood the ministry of proclamation and the ministry of collection as joined in service to Christ in the power of the Spirit. Thus in Romans 15:26 he speaks of the collection as a *koinōnia* in which the spiritual legacy of Israel* and the material assistance of the Gentiles are a unity. In 2 Corinthians 8—9 Paul speaks of the spiritual significance of the money which the Greeks are giving. It demonstrates genuine love (2 Cor 8:8), follows in the pattern of the self-giving Lord Jesus Christ

(2 Cor 8:9) and honors the Lord (2 Cor 8:21, 23; 9:13). The love of God rests upon the cheerful giver (2 Cor 9:7) whose giving is a "good work" (2 Cor 9:8) which issues in thanksgiving (2 Cor 8:16; 9:11-12, 15) and manifests grace (2 Cor 8:1, 6, 19-20; 9:14-15; *see* Financial Support).

*14.5. Sexual Attitudes and Actions.* The apostle Paul emphasized sexual attitudes and actions as strongly as any contemporary writer—but in his own way (*see* Sexuality; Homosexuality). For the apostle, the body—formed by God in a great creative act—was of great importance. This is especially clear in his arresting note in Romans 8:23, that the great adoption awaited by the children of God "who have the first fruits of the Spirit" is "the redemption of our bodies." In line with this understanding Paul declares that the body is "a temple* of the Holy Spirit" and that anyone who is united with the Lord will not violate the Lord's temple with illegitimate sexual attitudes and relationships.

Paul understands the power of sexuality—and enjoins the believers to allow that power its proper place in the proper marital relationship (1 Cor 7:1-7; *see* Marriage and Divorce). On the other hand, because of the power of sin (Rom 7:8-13), by which the righteous intentions of God the creator are sinfully subverted, Paul places the great stress on the sanctification of the body (Rom 12:1; 1 Cor 6:18-20; 7:34; 2 Cor 7:1; 1 Thess 4:4). It is a profound misunderstanding of the apostle to interpret Paul's warnings about sexual sin and his exhortations to sanctification of the body in respect to sexual attitudes and conduct as a derogation of human sexuality. On the contrary, it is in the practice of the Spirit, who as the Spirit of life sanctifies the human body as a temple of the Spirit, that the believer recognizes and honors the divine intentions in respect to human sexuality. For Paul, there is an intimate interrelationship between sexuality and spirituality; the right understanding and exercise of this relationship is a profoundly important aspect of love's obedience.

### 15. Gratitude: The Heartbeat of Pauline Spirituality.

Gratitude permeates Paul's life and holds a prominent place in his letters to the young churches (*see* Blessing). Gratitude is not only the apostle's response to his overwhelming experience of the grace of God; it is also the prospective attitude that he carries—and exhorts believers to carry—into their daily life in the world. For Paul, thanksgiving marks the dividing line between belief and unbelief, between the obedient and the disobedient heart. It is in the expression of gratitude that one truly honors God as the creator and Lord of the world (Rom 14:6). On the other hand, a lack of gratitude is a primary sin against God (Rom 1:21).

Thanksgiving—gratitude experienced and expressed—is "the heartbeat" of Pauline spirituality. In the Pauline experience and understanding, thanksgiving is the deepest expression of recognition for the direct experience of God's grace (1 Cor 1:4; 15:57; 2 Cor 2:14; 9:15; Phil 1:3)—as well as of grace experienced through others (see esp. Phil 1:5-26; 4:14-20). But the righteous person also gives thanks for the simple blessing of daily sustenance (Rom 14:6; 1 Cor 10:30).

Prayer, faith at work in the front line of Pauline spirituality, is shaped by gratitude in tone and content (Rom 1:8; 14:6; 1 Cor 1:4). Thanksgiving stands at the opposite end of the spectrum from anxiety, which expresses a lack of faith in God (Phil 4:6). Where the peace of Christ rules, there is thanksgiving (Col 3:15). Those established in the faith abound in thanksgiving (Col 2:7). Paul's prayer of thanksgiving is ever and always rising to God (1 Cor 1:4; Col 4:2; 1 Thess 1:2; 2:13; Col 1:3; Philem 4); and the apostle likewise exhorts the Christian community to give thanks to God in all things (1 Thess 5:18; Eph 5:20; Col 3:17). As grace is multiplied, thanksgiving is increased (2 Cor 4:15; 9:11). Thanksgiving is a "peak moment" in Christian experience and appropriately comes to expression in hymns* and songs, in which the whole person expresses deep gratitude to God for great grace (see Eph 5:18-20; Col 2:14-17).

If Pauline spirituality can be summarized in the words "Yes to God," then thanksgiving to God, especially expressed in and through prayer, but in all activity devoted to God, is the believer's most fundamental acknowledgement of the experience of grace—grace experienced in one's self, and grace recognized in its abundant manifestation outside one's own life. At the forefront of the practice of the Spirit is the practice of thanksgiving for all that God is doing.

### 16. Summary.

The deep and abiding mystery of the gracious presence of God in the indwelling Spirit, and the comprehensive reach of that grace, pervade Pauline spirituality as the practice of the Spirit. However, several particular facets can be isolated as summarizing and characterizing Pauline spirituality.

(1) Pauline spirituality is the spirituality of faith. Paul's letters are addressed to *believers*, and in his address he ever and again makes clear the imperative of the obedience of faith. Pauline spirituality is not an "extra" to be sought beyond simple faith but the pattern in which faith is received, nurtured and ex-

pressed in social relationships.

(2) Pauline spirituality takes shape in the believer's grateful "Yes to God" expressed in loving obedience to God in the whole of life and in the privileged responsibilities of the child of God.

(3) Paul ever sets before himself and believers the incarnate and exalted Lord Jesus whom the apostle imitates and exhorts believers to imitate—and to exemplify to others.

(4) Spirituality is the practice of giving one's self wholly to the sanctifying work of the Spirit, so that there is a constant dying to sin and living unto righteousness, as manifest supremely in Jesus Christ, into whose image the believer is being transformed.

(5) Spirituality ever embraces faithfulness in the Spirit-given and interrelated triad of praying to God, receiving the Word of God, and living together as the people of God, so that the life of the individual and the community of faith is constantly being built up in the faith and turned toward the worship of God.

(6) Spirituality comes to expression in an ever growing manifestation of the good fruit of the Spirit, the evidence of which is a critical means of testing and discerning the authenticity of the practice of the Spirit.

(7) Within the context of a growing awareness of the great goodness and grace of God, Pauline spirituality is characterized by a rising hymn of thanksgiving to the gracious God; this alone is the gateway of Christian entry into fruitful engagement with a world which has not yet experienced the reason for that gratitude which rises from a life in which, in the power of the Spirit, faith is working through love.

In the final analysis, the Christian life in Paul is a life in which the believer is ever subject to the practice of the Spirit. From this standpoint, it would seem that "Christian spirituality" and "Christian life"—neither expression actually appearing in Paul—are one and the same thing. This is surely true when the Christian life is perfected in the practice of the Spirit. Short of that perfection, "spirituality" as "the practice of the Spirit" serves as a useful expression for describing the conscious and intentional obedience to God of the heart seeking after a more perfect love for God.

*See also* ADOPTION, SONSHIP; BODY OF CHRIST; CHRISTOLOGY; CHURCH; CREATION AND NEW CREATION; CROSS, THEOLOGY OF THE; DYING AND RISING WITH CHRIST; FEAR, REVERENCE; FELLOWSHIP, COMMUNION, SHARING; FLESH; FRUIT OF THE SPIRIT; GIFTS OF THE SPIRIT; GOD; HOLINESS, SANCTIFICATION; HOLY SPIRIT; IMITATION OF PAUL/OF CHRIST; IN CHRIST; JOY; LORD'S SUPPER; LOVE; MYSTICISM; NEW NATURE AND OLD NATURE; PEACE, RECONCILIATION; PERFECT, MATURE; PRAYER; PSYCHOLOGY; SERVANT, SERV-

ICE; SUFFERING; TONGUES; VISIONS, ECSTATIC EXPERIENCE; WEAKNESS; WORSHIP.

BIBLIOGRAPHY. K. Barth, *The Christian Life* (Grand Rapids: Eerdmans, 1981); G. Bornkamm, *Paul* (New York: Harper & Row, 1971); idem, *Early Christian Experience* (New York: Harper & Row, 1969); L. Bouyer, *The Spirituality of the New Testament and the Fathers* (New York: Seabury, 1982); R. Bultmann, *Theology of the New Testament* (2 vols.; New York: Scribners, 1951, 1955); J. D. G. Dunn, *Romans* (WBC 38; Waco, TX: Word, 1988); G. D. Fee, "Some Reflections on Pauline Spirituality," in *Alive to God: Studies in Spirituality Presented to James Houston,* ed. J. I. Packer and L. Wilkinson (Downers Grove, IL: InterVarsity, 1992) 96-107; idem, *The First Epistle to the Corinthians* (NICNT; Grand Rapids: Eerdmans, 1987); M. Griffiths, *The Example of Jesus* (Downers Grove: InterVarsity, 1985); C. Jones et al., ed., *The Study of Spirituality* (London: Oxford University, 1986); R. P. Martin, *The Spirit and the Congregation* (Grand Rapids: Eerdmans, 1984); J. K. S. Reid, *Our Life in Christ* (Philadelphia: Westminister, 1963); H. Ridderbos, *Paul: An Outline of His Theology* (Grand Rapids: Eerdmans, 1975); W. Schrage, *The Ethics of the New Testament* (Philadelphia: Fortress, 1988); L. Smedes, *Union with Christ* (Grand Rapids: Eerdmans, 1983); J. Sudbrack, "Spirituality," in *Encyclopedia of Theology* 1623-29; M. B. Thompson, *Clothed with Christ: The Example and Teaching of Jesus in Romans 12:1—15:13* (JSNTSup 59; Sheffield: Academic, 1991); E. J. Tinsley, *The Imitation of God in Christ* (London: SCM, 1960).

R. P. Meye

**STOICS.** *See* PHILOSOPHY.

**STRENGTH.** *See* POWER; TRIUMPH; WEAKNESS.

# STRONG AND WEAK

In 1 Corinthians 8—10 and in Romans 14—15 Paul addressed problems between "strong" and "weak" Christians. The strong were exercising their rights and freedom* to the detriment of more scrupulous believers whom they considered had a weak conscience* (1 Cor) or weak faith* (Rom). Although a common issue in both cases was the appropriateness of eating certain foods,* and Paul adopted a similar strategy in responding, the two letters reflect different situations.

1. Corinth
2. Rome
3. Paul's Responses

## 1. Corinth

At Corinth Christians were divided over the question

of whether and where one could eat food* offered to idols* (*eidōlothuta* 1 Cor 8:1, 4, 7, 10; 10:19). The "strong" (a term not used in 1 Cor 8—10, but synonymous with "those who think they stand," 1 Cor 10:12) ate confidently in the knowledge that monotheism meant that idols have no real existence (1 Cor 8:1-6; *see* God). The weak had no such assurance, their conscience* (*syneidēsis*) preventing them from eating despite social (Willis), economic (Theissen) and religious pressure to do so. *Eidōlothuta* may refer specifically to food eaten in a pagan temple (Fee) or more generally to sacrificial food which could be eaten in a variety of places. In any case, the strong affirmed their right (1 Cor 8:9) to partake, even though this led the weak into the temptation of joining in what they believed to be an idolatrous act (1 Cor 8:10-13).

## 2. Rome

Many see Romans 14—15 as simply general paraenesis developed from Paul's earlier correspondence with the Corinthians (e.g., R. J. Karris in Donfried). A growing number of scholars, however, think Paul was speaking to specific circumstances in Rome (Donfried, Tomson, Wedderburn). The references to vegetarianism (Rom 14:2; because of the difficulty of getting certifiably kosher meat? cf. Josephus *Life* 3 §§13-14; *see* Rome), the observance of holy days* (Rom 14:5-6) and abstinence from wine (Rom 14:21; possibly hypothetical) are unparalleled in 1 Corinthians. The distinctive nuance of *koinos* ("unclean") in Romans 14:14 and *katharos* ("clean") in Romans 14:20 reflects disputes over Jewish scruples (cf. Rom 14:1; *see* Purity); neither word appears in 1 Corinthians, while the *eidōl-* and *syneidēsis* language frequent in 1 Corinthians 8—10 is absent in Romans. Furthermore, the close connection of Romans 15:7-13 to Romans 14:1—15:6 (cf. *proslambanesthe*, "welcome," in Rom 14:1 and 15:7), coupled with the overall argument of the letter, points toward disunity primarily between Jewish and Gentile* Christians.

Thus, against a background of anti-Semitism common in first century Rome, apparently some Gentile believers ridiculed more conservative Jewish Christians, whom they perceived as weak in faith (Rom 14:1) for their dietary and calendrical scruples (*see* Holy Days); the weak responded by passing judgment* on the strong (Rom 14:3-4, 10; cf. 2:1-11?). They felt no compulsion to abandon their Jewish heritage, and their differences made communal meals and worship* occasions of conflict (Rom 14:1). Paul did not doubt their motivation (Rom 14:6). Had the weak insisted that all Christians keep the Law, we would expect a response similar to that found in Galatians.*

## 3. Paul's Responses.

In both cases Paul clearly agreed with the strong that food in itself is religiously indifferent (1 Cor 8:8; Rom 14:14; 15:1). But Paul did not try to persuade the weak (apart from warning the Romans against judging the strong); his aim was mutual respect and acceptance of one another. Paul was not making the strong captive to the foibles of the weak. The strong were to refrain from eating meat not because others objected or were offended, but because the weak were in danger of compromising their integrity by succumbing to the temptation to adopt practices they fundamentally believed to be wrong (1 Cor 8:10; Rom 14:14-15). Paul prohibited the eating of idol food within pagan temples (1 Cor 10:14-22).

To act in a way that lays a stumbling block* (1 Cor 8:9, 13; 10:32; Rom 14:13, 20-21) before another for whom Christ died (1 Cor 8:11; Rom 14:15) is not to walk according to the way of love* which builds up both the individual and the community (1 Cor 8:1; 10:23; Rom 14:15, 19; 15:2). Behind the call to set the neighbor's interests above one's own lies the example and teaching of Jesus* (Thompson). Paul's refusal of his right as an apostle to material support (1 Cor 9; *see* Financial Support) illustrates the character of self-sacrificial love involved in becoming a servant* to all for their salvation* (1 Cor 9:19; cf. Mk 10:44). This ultimately is to serve Christ (1 Cor 8:12 negatively; Rom 14:6-8, 18), to imitate* him (1 Cor 10:33—11:1; Rom 15:3-6) and to glorify God (1 Cor 10:31; Rom 15:6-7, 9).

*See also* CONSCIENCE; DEMONS AND EXORCISM; FOOD OFFERED TO IDOLS AND JEWISH FOOD LAWS; IDOLATRY; LOVE; PURITY AND IMPURITY; ROME AND ROMAN CHRISTIANITY; SOCIAL-SCIENTIFIC APPROACHES TO PAUL; STUMBLING BLOCK.

BIBLIOGRAPHY. D. A. Black, *Paul, Apostle of Weakness: Astheneia and Its Cognates in the Pauline Literature* (AUS 7/3; New York: Peter Lang, 1984); K. P. Donfried, ed., *The Romans Debate* (rev. ed.; Peabody, MA: Hendrickson, 1991); G. D. Fee, "*Eidōlothuta* Once Again: An Interpretation of 1 Corinthians 8—10," *Bib* 61 (1980) 172-97; L. De Lorenzi, ed., *Freedom and Love: The Guide for Christian Life (1 Co 8-10; Rm 14-15)* (MSB; Rome: St. Paul's Abbey, 1981); W. Meeks, "Judgment and the Brother: Romans 14:1—15:13," in *Tradition and Interpretation in the New Testament*, ed. G. F. Hawthorne with O. Betz (Tübingen: J. C. B. Mohr, 1988; Grand Rapids: Eerdmans, 1987) 290-300; G. Theissen, "The Strong and the Weak in Corinth: A Sociological Analysis of a Theological Quarrel," in *The Social Setting of Pauline Christianity: Essays on Corinth*, ed. J. H. Schütz (Philadelphia: Fortress, 1982) 121-43; M. B. Thompson,

*Clothed with Christ: The Example and Teaching of Jesus in Romans 12.1—15.13* (JSNTSS 59; Sheffield: JSOT, 1991) 161-236; P. J. Tomson, *Paul and the Jewish Law: Halakha in the Letters of the Apostle to the Gentiles* (CRINT 3.1; Minneapolis: Fortress, 1990); A. J. M. Wedderburn, *The Reasons for Romans* (Edinburgh: T. & T. Clark, 1988); W. Willis, *Idol Meat in Corinth: The Pauline Argument in 1 Corinthians 8 and 10* (SBLDS 68; Chico CA: Scholars, 1985).

M. B. Thompson

**STRUCTURALISM.** *See* HERMENEUTICS/INTERPRETING PAUL.

## STUMBLING BLOCK

Two Greek roots in Paul's letters are sometimes translated "stumbling block" or "to cause to stumble." Both roots are more serious than their translations may suggest, connoting occasions that can lead to spiritual ruin. Paul uses the terms in two basic contexts: with reference to Christ and the cross as an occasion for stumbling, and with reference to Christians who stumble, particularly with regard to the eating of food.*

    1. Background
    2. *Proskomma/Proskoptō*
    3. *Skandalon/Skandalizō*

### 1. Background.
The image of stumbling or causing someone to fall is part of the common Jewish metaphor describing life as a walk or a path to follow. In the OT, language of stumbling describes either the action of stumbling or the cause of a fall. Insofar as an object which causes stumbling can be said to be in one's way, a "stumbling block" could be understood as a "hindrance" or "obstacle," but it is difficult to find examples where only these meanings are intended; an element of danger is always present. Stumbling often refers to idolatry* in its various forms and the enticement to ruin which it offered (e.g., Ex 23:33; 34:12). The metaphor was common in other Jewish writings (e.g., 1QS 2:12, 17; 11:12; 1QH 17:23; *b. Sanh.* 55a, *m. B. Meṣ.* 5:11; *b. Pesaḥ.* 22b), a number of which echo Leviticus 19:14.

### 2. *Proskomma/Proskoptō*.
The noun most commonly rendered "stumbling block" is *proskomma*, a term Paul used five times, four of which are in Romans. In their pursuit of righteousness* based on the Law* instead of faith* in Christ,* Paul says Israel* had stumbled (*proskoptō*) over the stumbling stone (*proskomma*) which is Christ (Rom 9:32). The quotation that follows in Romans 9:33 is a conflation of Isaiah 28:16 and Isaiah 8:14, and its un-

usual form is paralleled in 1 Peter 2:8, suggesting that Paul was citing a shared piece of early Christian tradition.

Elsewhere Paul used *proskomma* and *proskoptō* in admonitions to "strong"* Christians not to cause "weaker" Christians to stumble, particularly with reference to food (Rom 14:13, 20-21; 1 Cor 8:9). The weak were being tempted to compromise their integrity and participate in what they considered to be idolatry (1 Cor 8:7, 10) or impurity (Rom 14:14). Paul's strong language in 1 Corinthians 8:11 and Romans 14:15, 20, 22-23 reflects the gravity of the danger the strong were setting before the weak.

### 3. *Skandalon/Skandalizō*.
Coming over into English as "scandal," this root *skandal-* is more difficult to translate. Sometimes rendered "stumbling block" or "offense," the very rare term *skandalon*, like *proskomma*, signifies something which leads to disastrous temptation or spiritual ruin. In the LXX it most often renders the Hebrew for "trap" or "snare," and connotes a cause for falling, at times with the nuance of enticement to sin.

The word *skandalon* appears with *proskomma* in Romans 14:13, where translations such as "hindrance" (RSV/NRSV) and "obstacle" (NIV) reflect confusion about its meaning and have misled some interpreters. By *skandalon* Paul was not referring to attempts by the weak to foist their dietary restrictions on the strong; instead he was emphasizing the spiritual trap created when confident behavior by the strong (in effect) enticed weaker Christians to sin by acting contrary to their conscience,* as the parallel in 1 Corinthians 8:7 reveals (cf. Rom 14:15). In such cases Paul counseled the strong to govern the exercise of their freedoms by love for the weak. Paul was ready to forgo his rights rather than to risk destroying others by tempting them to do what they believed was wrong (Rom 14:21; 1 Cor 8:13). In his concern for the weak, Paul could not help but be deeply agitated when they were "scandalized" (2 Cor 11:29).

In Romans 16:17 Paul warns his readers to take note of those who create dissensions and *skandala* in opposition to the teaching they had learned. The translations "offenses" (NRSV), "difficulties" (RSV) and "obstacles" (NIV) are all too tame here, given the word's significance. Paul's strong language is strikingly similar to Jesus' stern warning against "scandalizing" one of the little ones (Mt 18:6 par. Mk 9:42 and Lk 17:2), and to other dominical sayings about *skandala* (Mt 18:7 par. Lk 17:1; Mt 13:41-42; 16:23).

Although Christ himself is never called a *skandalon* in the Synoptics, the use of *skandalizō* in the Gospels with reference to him consistently depicts Jesus as the occasion for danger, either through one's rejection of him or by persecution for his sake. It is not a long step from Jesus' declaration "Blessed is the one who is not 'scandalized' by me" (Mt 11:6 par. Lk 7:23; cf. Jn 6:61-64) to Paul who speaks of the *skandalon* of Christ crucified (1 Cor 1:23). For the Jews the cross was a stumbling block or snare (Gal 5:11) because they saw one hanged on a tree as under a curse rather than as a bringer of life (Deut 21:23; Gal 3:13). To those who, like the Pharisees, sought signs, Christ himself could become an occasion of spiritual ruin when encountered without faith (1 Cor 1:22; cf. Mk 8:11-12). So, in the quotation from Isaiah 8:14 in Romans 9:33, Christ is the *petran skandalou*, the "rock that will make them fall" (RSV/NRSV; "makes them fall" NIV).

*See also* CONSCIENCE; CROSS, THEOLOGY OF THE; ISRAEL; STRONG AND WEAK.

BIBLIOGRAPHY. H. Giesen, "σκανδαλίζω," "σκάνδαλον," *EDNT* 3.248, 249-50; J. Guhrt, "Offence, Scandal, Stumbling," *NIDNTT* 2.705-10; H.-S. Lie, *Der Begriff Skandalon im Neuen Testament und der Wiederkehrgedanke bei Laotse* (Europäische Hochschulscrhriften XXIII/24; Bern: Herbert Lang; Frankfurt: Peter Lang, 1973); J. Mateos, "Analisis semantico de los lexemas skandalizo y skandalon," *FN* 2/1 (1989) 57-92; J. Moffatt, "Jesus upon 'Stumbling-Blocks,' " *ExpT* 26 (1914-15) 407-9; J. H. Moulton, "Σκάνδαλον," *ExpT* 26 (1914-15) 331-32; K. Müller, *Anstoss und Gericht: Eine Studie zum jüdischen Hintergrund des paulinischen Skandalon-Begriffs* (SANT 19; München: Kösel, 1969); G. Stählin, "σκάνδαλον, σκανδαλίζω" *TDNT* VII.339-58; M. B. Thompson, *Clothed with Christ: The Example and Teaching of Jesus in Romans 12.1—15.13* (JSNTSup 59; Sheffield: JSOT, 1991) 174-84.

M. B. Thompson

# SUFFERING

The questions of the inevitability and purpose of suffering in the life of Christians in general, and in the life of Paul as an apostle* in particular, are recurring themes of great significance throughout Paul's letters. In addition to the issues of death, his own imprisonment, and other specific instances of hardship and persecution, Paul speaks of affliction* and suffering *per se* over sixty times. In doing so, Paul employs the word groups for "suffering" (*pathēma, paschō*, etc.) and "affliction" (*thlipsis, thlibō*) interchangeably (cf., e.g., the alternation in 2 Cor 1:4-8 and Col 1:24), together with the general category of "weakness"* (*astheneia*), all three of which Paul can also use to describe the suffering and death* of Christ (cf. Phil 3:10; Col 1:24; 2 Cor 13:4). Paul's most sustained treatment of the subject occurs in 2 Corinthians, where he defends his apostleship against those who maintained that his suffering called into question the legitimacy of his own apostleship (cf. esp. 2 Cor 1:3-11; 2:14-17; 4:7-12; 6:3-10; 10-13).

1. Paul's Suffering as an Apostle
2. The Suffering of Believers
3. The Question of the Correct Interpretive Framework

## 1. Paul's Suffering as an Apostle.

According to Acts 9:15-16, Paul's call was inextricably linked to the fact that he would suffer greatly "for the sake of (the Lord's) name." The reality of this is attested throughout the book of Acts and reflected in every one of Paul's letters. Indeed, following the common Jewish notion that all suffering was part of death, Paul could look at his life and exclaim, "I die every day!" (1 Cor 15:31). Moreover, of all Paul's afflictions, he counted the pressure of his daily anxiety on behalf of his churches to be the climax of what he had to endure as a result of his calling (2 Cor 11:28; cf. 2 Cor 2:4, 13). Hence, rather than questioning the legitimacy of his apostleship because of his suffering, Paul considered suffering to be a characteristic mark of his apostolic ministry* (Gal 6:17; 1 Cor 2:1-5; 2 Cor 11:23-29; Phil 1:30; 2 Tim 1:11-12; 2:9; etc.), and an aspect of his own mortal life concerning which he was content, in which he rejoiced and about which he could appropriately "boast" (2 Cor 11:30; 12:10; Phil 1:19-26). Indeed, Paul willingly entered into suffering as a result of his decision to support himself financially when necessary (cf. 1 Cor 4:8-13, which Hock has shown reflects the descriptions of suffering typical of artisans such as Paul in the ancient world; 9:8-18; 2 Cor 2:17; 11:7-11; 12:14-16; *see* Tentmaking).

Paul's reason for this evaluation of suffering, however, was not experiential but theological. Paul understood that as an essential part of his calling to be an apostle, God* himself was continually leading him into situations of suffering, like one sentenced to death in the Roman arena or led to death in the Roman triumphal procession (cf. 1 Cor 4:9; 2 Cor 1:9; 2:14; 4:11; 2 Tim 1:11-12). God's purpose in doing so was to reveal his divine power* and to demonstrate the reality of the cross* and resurrection* of Christ in and through Paul's life (1 Cor 2:1-5; 2 Cor 2:14; 4:11), while at the same time making it clear that the age to come had not yet arrived in all its fullness (1 Cor 4:8-13; *see* Eschatology). Paul could thus interpret his suffering in terms of the cross of Christ, while his ability to endure it or God's action of deliverance from it, were an expression of the same divine power revealed in Christ's resurrection (cf. 1 Cor 4:8-13; 2 Cor 1:3-10; 4:7-12; 6:4-10; Phil 3:10-11; 2 Tim 3:10-11). The wisdom* and power of God first made known through the cross and resurrection of Christ were therefore now being further manifest and revealed publicly through Paul's own suffering as an apostle. In Galatians 3:1 Paul is thus referring to his own suffering as an embodiment of the gospel* and as the vehicle for displaying the truth of the cross when he reminds the Galatians that Jesus Christ was publicly portrayed as crucified before their very eyes.

Viewed from this same perspective, Paul's statement in Colossians 1:24 that his suffering "completes what is lacking in Christ's afflictions" does not refer to the concept of a certain amount of "messianic suffering" or "woes of the messiah" that must be fulfilled before the age can be consummated, as commonly interpreted (cf. Dan 12:1; *1 Enoch* 47:1-4; *2 Baruch* 30:2; Mt 24:8; Mk 13:8; see, e.g., O'Brien). Nor does Paul view his suffering as having an atoning significance in 2 Corinthians 4:7-12 (contra Güttgemanns). For Paul, Christ's suffering stands alone as unique and sufficient (cf. Col 2:13-14; Gal 1:4; 1 Cor 1:18-31; 2 Cor 5:16-21; Rom 3:21-26; etc.). Rather, Paul completes what is "lacking" in Christ's afflictions on behalf of the church in the sense that his ministry *extends* the knowledge and reality of the cross of Christ and the power of the Spirit (*see* Holy Spirit) to the Gentile* world (Col 1:23; cf. Eph 3:13). Paul's suffering also functioned to make it clear, therefore, that the power and knowledge of the gospel was God's and not his own, so that those who encountered Paul would place their faith* in the power of God and not in the person of the apostle (1 Cor 2:1-5; 2 Cor 4:7; 12:9-10). Whatever Paul's much debated (and still unclear) "thorn in the flesh" actually was, it too functioned in this way by keeping him from boasting in the abundance of the revelations that he had received (2 Cor. 12:7).

## 2. The Suffering of Believers.

The fact that others not only accepted Paul as a genuine apostle in spite of his suffering, but were also willing to imitate* him by joyfully continuing in faith,* hope* and love* in the midst of their own afflictions, became a sign for Paul of the legitimacy of their standing in Christ, even as it was a sign of his own legitimacy as an apostle (Gal 4:12-15; Phil 1:3-7; 4:14-15; 1 Thess 1:6; 3:1-5; 2 Tim 1:8). In addition, Paul's willingness to suffer on behalf of his churches also provided a model of Christian love, so that Paul could call his churches to follow his example of giving up their rights for others, even when this meant undue suffering and hardship (1 Cor 4:8-13; 6:7; 9:1-27; 12—14).

Yet unlike the martyrdom theology of the later centuries, Paul stops short of teaching that all believers are *called* to suffer in the same way that he was as an apostle. Rather, Paul recognizes that all Christians simply *will suffer* as a result of identifying themselves with Christ (Rom 8:17; Phil 1:29-30; 2 Tim 3:12) and, to varying degrees, as a result of their distinct circumstances, since such suffering is inevitable in this evil age (cf. 1 Cor 7:28; 12:26; 1 Tim 5:23).

Nevertheless, for Paul, whenever Christians *do* suffer, they too must meet their suffering with joy,* knowing that their affliction is not senseless, but becomes the divinely orchestrated means by which God strengthens their faithful endurance and hope by pouring out his own love and Spirit to sustain or deliver them in their distress (Rom 5:3-5; 8:12-39; 2 Cor 1:6). As a result, they too come to embody the cross and resurrection in their lives as a witness to others of the truth of Christ, especially as this is seen in their ability to love others even when they are experiencing affliction (2 Cor 8:1-2; 1 Thess 1:2-7; 2 Thess 1:3-5). Paul can therefore encourage his readers to be patient and to endure in the midst of adversity, which is the outworking of their faith (Rom 12:12; 2 Tim 4:5), since he knows that only those who suffer with Christ in the endurance of faith will also be glorified with Christ (Rom 8:17; *see* Glory, Glorification). Finally, then, because of the faith and love made real in their lives through suffering, all believers will join Paul in experiencing not only the power of God made known in the cross of Christ as God sustains them in the midst of their adversities, but also the resurrection power of God as he uses their suffering as the pathway to sharing in Christ's glory (Rom 8:35; 2 Cor 4:14; 2 Thess 1:7). It is this hope which keeps one persevering in faith (Rom 4:18-25; 8:18-25; 1 Cor 15:20-34, 58; 2 Cor 4:16-18). As for those who do not share Christ's suffering by identifying with him, but who persecute those who do, they will experience suffering on the day of judgment* (2 Thess 1:6-10; Rom 2:9).

## 3. The Question of the Correct Interpretive Framework.

Apart from the interpretation of these crucial passages themselves, the scholarly debate in recent decades has focused on ascertaining the correct conceptual framework for understanding Paul's statements concerning the role of suffering in the believer's life, especially his own suffering as an apostle (*see* Bloomquist). This debate has been sparked primarily by the fact that, as Bultmann made clear, Paul presents his suffering in 1 Corinthians 4:8-13 and 2 Corinthians 4:7-12; 6:3-10; 11:23-29 in four "catalogues of suffering" (*peristasis* catalogues; *see* Afflictions) which seemingly parallel the kinds of lists found in popular Greco-Roman moral and philosophical portraits of the sufferings of sages and Stoics, as well as those in other walks of life (cf., e.g., Plutarch *Mor.* 326D-333C; 361E-362A; 1057D-E; Epictetus *Diss.* 2.19.12-32; 4.7.13-15; Seneca *Ep. Mor.* 85.26-27). This has led those such as J. T. Fitzgerald to argue that Paul's primary frame of reference is to this standard philosophical and rhetorical* form of testifying to one's legitimacy. Against this backdrop Paul's goal is to picture himself as the ideal sage and philosopher, whose virtue has been revealed by his perseverance of character in the midst of suffering. On the other hand, others such as Kleinknecht have argued that, although Paul may use the general form and some of the common vocabulary for afflictions as found in the *peristasis* catalogues, the backdrop for his thinking is that of the tradition of the suffering of the righteous in the OT and Judaism, as that was embodied in the suffering of the righteous one, Christ.* In making this case they point to the many OT allusions throughout the context of these sections and the direct quotes of Psalm 115:1 LXX in 2 Corinthians 4:13 and Isaiah 49:8 in 2 Corinthians 6:2. Paul's goal is thus to picture himself as suffering in the train of the OT righteous and, finally, of Christ himself as one of those who demonstrated their faith by their endurance in the midst of adversity.

Recently Garrett has questioned the either/or dichotomy in this debate and has attempted to show Paul's reliance both on Stoic philosophy* and on Jewish apocalyptic* thought, such as that found in the *Testament of Job*, in which Satan* and his allies are seen as the ultimate cause of Paul's troubles, with Paul's endurance being the sign that he is confident in God's ultimate victory. Though Garrett is certainly correct to emphasize the overlap between Hellenism* and Judaism in Paul's day, the attempt to derive Paul's thought in these contexts in any significant measure from the philosophical traditions of his day still remains unconvincing in view of Paul's explicit reliance on the Old Testament* and his christology.* Moreover, the wide gulf between Paul's understanding of God and his relationship to humanity and that of the Stoics adds to the difficulty of this attempt. It is still questionable whether there is, in fact, a significant conceptual parallel between Paul's endurance in the midst of adversity, as an expression of his dependence upon God's sovereign leading and working in his life, and the Stoic virtue of enduring hardship for the sake of a greater cause as an expression of one's character and self-mastery.

*See also* AFFLICTIONS, TRIALS, HARDSHIPS; APOSTLE; CROSS, THEOLOGY OF THE; CRUCIFIXION; IMITATION OF PAUL/OF CHRIST; TENTMAKING.

BIBLIOGRAPHY. H. D. Betz, *Der Apostel Paulus und die sokratische Tradition* (BHT 45; Tübingen: J. C. B. Mohr, 1972); D. A. Black, *Paul, Apostle of Weakness: Astheneia and Its Cognates in the Pauline Literature* (New York: Lang, 1984); L. G. Bloomquist, *The Function of Suffering in Philippians* (JSNTSup 78; Sheffield: Academic, 1993); J. T. Fitzgerald, *Cracks in an Earthen Vessel: An Examination of the Catalogues of Hardships in the Corinthian Correspondence* (SBLDS 99; Atlanta: Scholars, 1988); S. R. Garrett, "The God of this World and the Affliction of Paul, 2 Cor. 4:1-12," in *Greeks, Romans, and Christians, FS for A. Malherbe*, ed. D. L. Balch et al. (Philadelphia: Fortress, 1990) 99-117; E. Güttgemanns, *Der leidende Apostel und sein Herr. Studien zur paulinischen Christologie* (FRLANT 90; Göttingen: Vandenhoeck & Ruprecht, 1966); R. F. Hock, *The Social Context of Paul's Ministry: Tentmaking and Apostleship* (Philadelphia: Fortress, 1980); S. J. Hafemann, *Suffering and Ministry in the Spirit: Paul's Defense of His Ministry in II Corinthians 2:14-3:3* (Grand Rapids: Eerdmans, 1990); K. T. Kleinknecht, *Der leidende Gerechtfertigte. Die alttestamentlich-jüdische Tradition vom 'leidenden Gerechten' und ihre Rezeption bei Paulus* (WUNT 2.13; Tübingen: J. C. B. Mohr, 1984); P. T. O'Brien, *Colossians, Philemon* (WBC 44; Waco: Word, 1982).

S. J. Hafemann

**SUFFERING SERVANT.** *See* CHRISTOLOGY; DEATH OF CHRIST; FUTILITY; OLD TESTAMENT IN PAUL; SERVANT, SERVICE.

**SUFFICIENCY.** *See* CORINTHIANS, LETTERS TO THE; MYSTICISM; PHILOSOPHY; RICHES AND POVERTY.

**SUPER-APOSTLES.** *See* APOSTLE; CORINTHIANS, LETTERS TO THE; OPPONENTS OF PAUL.

**SYNAGOGUE.** *See* DIASPORA; POLITICAL SYSTEMS; SOCIAL SETTING OF MISSION CHURCHES.

# T

**TABLE FELLOWSHIP.** *See* FOOD OFFERED TO IDOLS AND JEWISH FOOD LAWS; JESUS AND PAUL; LORD'S SUPPER; LOVE FEAST; SOCIAL-SCIENTIFIC APPROACHES TO PAUL.

**TARSUS.** *See* JEW, PAUL THE; PAUL IN ACTS AND LETTERS.

**TEACHING OF JESUS.** *See* JESUS, SAYINGS OF; JESUS AND PAUL.

## TEACHING/PARAENESIS

Paraenesis is the technical term (the Greek word for "advice," sometimes spelled parenesis) for traditional moral exhortation concerned with practical issues of living. In some Pauline letters paraenesis is concentrated in a concluding section (Rom 12:1—15:13; Gal 5:1—6:10; 1 Thess 4:1—5:22; Col 3:1—4:6; Eph 4:1—6:20); in others it appears throughout the letter (1—2 Cor; Phil; the Pastorals). Paul's paraenetic teaching reflects the influence of Jewish, Hellenistic and Christian tradition(s).*

1. Characteristics
2. Forms
3. Determining Influences

### 1. Characteristics.

Paraenesis addressed themes or topics (*topoi*) of moral concern, such as friends, sex, money, parents, food, etc., offering clear, down to earth counsel. J. I. H. McDonald and D. E. Aune characterize paraenesis as (1) consisting of traditional ethical material, expressing conventional wisdom* approved by society; (2) general in nature, applicable to many situations; (3) so familiar it is often presented as a "reminder"; (4) illustrated by the use of individuals as examples or models of virtue; and (5) given by persons who claim to be more experienced than their audience.

### 2. Forms.

A *topos* could be treated with a simple imperative ("Be at peace among yourselves," 1 Thess 5:13), or it might be lengthened by adding contrasts, illustrations, similes, proverbs or quotations. Jewish paraenesis often included the distinctive "two ways" motif (Prov 4:18-19; Ps 1:6; *T. Asher* 1:3-5; 1QS 3:13—4:26). This ethical dualism is reflected in Paul's language of walking in the Spirit* (vs. the flesh*), or in the light* (vs. darkness), and in the call to put off and put on certain characteristics (Col 3:8-17; Eph 4:22-24), which Paul summarizes as putting on Christ (Rom 13:14).

Catalogs of virtues* and vices were a common device in the ancient world to delineate community values. Aune notes that, in contrast to the individualistic emphasis of typical Hellenistic exhortation, Paul's lists tend to focus on social virtues and vices, such as envy, strife or malice (Gal 5:19-23; Rom 1:29-31; 13:13; 1 Cor 5:9-13; 6:9-10; 2 Cor 6:6-7; 12:20; Col 3:5-17; Eph 4:2-3, 31-32; 5:3-5; 1 Tim 6:4-5; Tit 1:7-10).

Household* codes (often referred to by the German *Haustafeln*, "house-tables") specified reciprocal duties between husbands and wives, parents and children, and masters and slaves* (Col 3:18—4:1; Eph 5:21—6:9; Titus 2:1-10; 1 Tim 2:1-15; 5:1-8; 6:1-2; cf. 1 Pet 2:11—3:7). The Jewish roots of the *Haustafeln* appear in the fourth commandment and in the wisdom literature. J. E. Crouch argues that the household codes reflect concern in the later church to maintain stability and order in the face of enthusiastic tendencies and heresy. P. H. Towner has shown that the aim of the theology and paraenesis of the Pastoral* letters was not to preserve a bourgeois status quo, but to promote mission; it was thus consistent with a goal of paraenesis in earlier Pauline letters.

### 3. Determining Influences.

In the past, Pauline paraenesis attracted little attention from scholars, but the situation is changing. E. G. Selwyn's case for a primitive catechism or holiness code underlying early Christian paraenesis has never been conclusively proved or refuted. More recently, A. J. Malherbe has emphasized parallels with Cynic and Stoic thought, which Paul would have met in the Hellenistic culture of his birthplace, Tarsus (Acts 22:3;

*see* Jew, Paul the; Philosophy). Although comparisons with Greco-Roman rhetorical techniques appear fruitful in the analysis of Paul's method, the content of his paraenesis reflects his Jewish background (cf. especially Rom 13:8-10). P. J. Tomson's study draws out the links between the apostle's exhortations and the *halakah* Paul inherited as a Pharisee. M. B. Thompson argues that the example and teachings of Jesus* provided the orientation for Paul's paraenesis.

The traditional nature of paraenesis was sometimes cited to show that Paul simply tacked it onto his letters without any tangible connection between his theology and ethics.* D. G. Bradley suggested that Paul drew his *topoi* from a "bag of answers" without the intention of thereby addressing specific needs in the community. V. P. Furnish, A. J. Malherbe and others have corrected this view, observing that Paul shaped most of his material for its recipients. Lists of vices addressed the problems of particular Pauline churches (1 Cor 5:9-10; 6:9-10; 2 Cor 12:20-21; *see* Virtues and Vices). Some recent studies of Romans* have argued that even in Paul's most general letter (to a congregation he had never visited), his paraenesis was conditioned by the circumstances of his readers.

Although he used traditional forms and content, the imperatives of Paul's moral teaching are rooted in the indicatives of what God has done in Christ, as seen in Christian baptism* (Rom 6:1-10, 11-23). They were shaped by Paul's awareness of Christian freedom* in the Spirit, by the mandate of Christian witness* to the world, and especially by the character of Christ, seen most clearly in the cross.*

*See also* ETHICS; HOLY SPIRIT; HOUSEHOLDS AND HOUSEHOLD CODES; JESUS, SAYINGS OF; NEW NATURE AND OLD NATURE; PHILOSOPHY; TRADITION; VIRTUES AND VICES; WISDOM.

BIBLIOGRAPHY. D. E. Aune, *The New Testament in Its Literary Environment* (Philadelphia: Westminster, 1987); D. G. Bradley, "The Topos as a Form in the Pauline Paraenesis," *JBL* 72 (1953) 238-46; J. E. Crouch, *The Origin and Intention of the Colossian Haustafel* (FRLANT 109; Göttingen: Vandenhoeck & Ruprecht, 1972); V. P. Furnish, *Theology and Ethics in Paul* (Nashville: Abingdon, 1968); J. I. H. McDonald, *Kerygma and Didache: The Articulation and Structure of the Earliest Christian Message* (SNTSMS 37; Cambridge: University Press, 1980); A. J. Malherbe, *Moral Exhortation: A Greco-Roman Sourcebook* (Philadelphia: Westminster, 1986); W. A. Meeks, *The Moral World of the First Christians* (Philadelphia: Westminster, 1986); E. G. Selwyn, "On the Inter-Relation of I Peter and Other N.T. Epistles," in *The First Epistle of St Peter* (London: Macmillan, 1946) 365-466; M. B. Thompson, *Clothed with Christ: The Example and Teaching of Jesus in Romans 12.1—15.13* (JSNTSup 59; Sheffield: JSOT, 1991); P. J. Tomson, *Paul and the Jewish Law: Halaka in the Letters of the Apostle to the Gentiles* (CRINT III.1; Minneapolis: Fortress, 1990); P. H. Towner, *The Goal of Our Instruction: The Structure of Theology and Ethics in the Pastoral Epistles* (JSNTSup 34; Sheffield: JSOT Press, 1989).

M. B. Thompson

# TEMPLE

Paul very clearly uses temple language at several points in his letters, and interpreters have drawn attention to other possible temple allusions. Paul primarily applied the imagery to the people of God,* both individually and corporately, and seems to have used its associated imagery to speak of Christ.*

1. Background
2. Terminology
3. Temple and People of God
4. Temple and Christology

## 1. Background.

The Temple of Jerusalem* was one of the principal symbols of the Jewish faith and worldview (along with the symbols of Torah, land and ethnic identity; see Wright, 224-32; Dunn, 18-36). In pre-A.D. 70 Judaism the Temple represented the one place God had chosen to be uniquely present among his elect people; and it was the place where Israel's cultic worship* was focused, so much so that the prayers of the Synagogue were timed to the Temple hours of morning and evening sacrifice. The Temple was not only a place and symbol of immense religious importance, it was also a political and economic center, the control of which had deep implications for parties and sects within Judaism (see Dunn, 31-36). When Jews thought of their past, present or future, the Temple occupied a central place in their minds (cf. Ezek 40—48; *1 Enoch* 90:28-29; 5Q15; 11QTemple), and Jesus' own attitude toward the Temple was a matter of interest and controversy in his day (e.g., Mk 11:15-17; Mk 14:49, 58; Mt 17:24-27; 23:37-39 par. Lk 13:34-35; see Wise). Acts shows Paul the apostle acknowledging an ongoing significance for the Jerusalem Temple (Acts 21:26-30; 22:17; 24:18; 25:8; 26:21). It was perhaps inevitable that when Paul spoke of God's new work in Christ,* he would appropriate temple imagery in some way. This was not only because of his Jewish heritage, but also because Paul carried out his mission* in a Greco-Roman world in which temples and sanctuaries of deities were well represented, with notable examples in Corinth* and Ephesus* (*see* Religions, Greco-Roman).

## 2. Terminology.

Paul used two different Greek words to speak of temple: *naos* and *hieron*. In terms of the Jerusalem Temple, *naos* refers to the building, the place of God's dwelling, and *hieron* refers to the entire area, or precincts, including the sanctuary (Michel, 880-90). Generally speaking, *naos* was used to designate the inner section of the Temple known as the holy place and the holy of holies, whereas *hieron* designated the outer court and the Temple proper. Fee summarizes, "The distinctions between the two words do not necessarily hold in all the Greek of the NT period, but the usage in the LXX, where the distinction is common, seems to have influenced Paul" (Fee, 146 n.6).

In Paul's letters the word *naos* appears six times (1 Cor 3:16-17; 6:19; 2 Cor 6:16; Eph 2:21; 2 Thess 2:4) and *hieron* once (1 Cor 9:13). In these verses Paul maintains the distinction of definition noted above. In 1 Corinthians 9:13 Paul, addressing the issue of whether "those who proclaim the gospel should get their living by the gospel," uses the analogy of the actual physical temple. He uses the word *hieron* to indicate the place where the priests offered up animal sacrifices* on the altar (1 Cor 9:13), which was situated in the outer court (see Ex 27—29, 40). And when Paul referred to the abominable act of the "man of lawlessness"* who usurps God's place in the temple, he used the word *naos*—the word that designates the place of the deity's presence (1 Thess 2:4).

In all the other Pauline passages, *naos* is used metaphorically—to depict a human habitation for the divine Spirit. In one instance the sanctuary image is used to describe the individual believer's body (1 Cor 6:19); in every other instance the sanctuary depicts Christ's body, the church (1 Cor 3:16-17; 2 Cor 6:16; Eph 2:21).

## 3. Temple and People of God.

*3.1. 1 and 2 Corinthians.* In arguing for sexual* purity Paul asked the Corinthians, "Do you not know that your body is a temple [sanctuary] of the Holy Spirit* within you, which you have from God, and that you are not your own?" (1 Cor 6:19 NRSV). It is possible that some of the Corinthian believers still frequented the pagan temples and had intercourse with the temple prostitutes; in so doing, Paul argued, they became one body with a prostitute (1 Cor 6:16). But Christ had redeemed them so that they might become united to him, for "anyone united to the Lord becomes one spirit [with him]" (1 Cor 6:17). Each person who has been spiritually united to the Lord is his holy dwelling place; his or her body belongs to the Lord* and must not be given to or joined with a prostitute. Those sanctified by the Lord are now his holy temple (as contrasted with a pagan temple), where he dwells by means of the Holy Spirit.

1 Corinthians 6:19 is the only Pauline passage that describes the individual believer as God's temple. Mistakenly, it is sometimes thought that 1 Corinthians 3:16-17 also speaks of the individual. According to the Greek text, it is unquestionably clear that Paul in 1 Corinthians 3:16-17 was not speaking about the individual but the local church in Corinth when he said, *ouk oidate hoti naos theou este kai to pneuma tou theou oikei en hymin* ("do you [plural] not know that you [plural] are God's temple and that the Spirit of God dwells in you [plural]?"). 1 Corinthians 6:19 should not be read back into 1 Corinthians 3:16 "as if it were a word of warning to individual Christians as to how they treat their bodies or live out their individual Christian lives. Both the context and the grammar disallow such interpretations" (Fee, 149). In the same vein, Paul in 2 Corinthian 6:16—7:1 speaks of believers corporately as "the temple of the living God" and applies to them Ezekiel's rendition of the old covenant's promise of the divine presence in Israel's midst (Ezek 37:27). Because they are inhabited by the holy God, they must live in holiness.*

When the Corinthians heard Paul's analogy in 1 Corinthians of the church as God's sanctuary, they would have understood the image from their knowledge of pagan temples. But Paul probably had in mind the one temple in Jerusalem. The Gentiles* had many gods with many temples in many cities; the Jews had one God with one temple in one place that he had chosen (cf. Deut 12). In the history of Israel this had helped to preserve the unity and identity of the people of God. The Corinthians needed spiritual unity; they were fragmented due to their individual preferences (see 1 Cor 1:10-13). In the context of the letter Paul emphasizes the need for the Corinthians to see that God was producing one spiritual habitation in Corinth. God had given them many workers (such as Paul and Apollos*) to lay the foundation (*themelios*; cf. Ps 118:22; Is 28:16; Eph 2:20-22) for this sanctuary (1 Cor 3:9-15); it was their responsibility to build (*oikodomeō*) with the right materials and not destroy the building by being divisive.

Finally, E. E. Ellis has suggested that when Paul writes in 2 Corinthians 5 of the destruction of the earthly "tent" (*skēnē*) and its replacement by a "building [*oikodomē*] from God . . . a house [*oikos*] not made with hands, eternal in heaven," he is speaking not of individual bodies but of the corporate "body" of Christ conceived as a new temple (*see* Body). In so doing Paul reflects the tradition of Jesus that he would destroy "this temple" and build one "not made by hands" (Mk 14:58; cf. Jn 2:19) and the early Christian tradition that God does not live in houses built by hands (Acts 7:48-49) and was now rebuilding David's "fallen tent" (Acts 15:16-18; cf. Amos 9:11-12; see Ellis).

*3.2. Ephesians.* In Ephesians 2:14-15 Christ is said to have destroyed the "dividing wall of hostility," referring to his abolishing the enmity between Jews and Gentiles and making them into one "new humanity." Commentators frequently identify the "wall" with the barrier in the Temple dividing the Court of the Gentiles from the Court of Women. This barrier, beyond which no Gentile was to venture on pain of death, has been figuratively torn down in Christ.

The Ephesian passage goes on to speak of the local churches as living, organic entities which are all (corporately speaking) growing "into a holy sanctuary [*naon hagion*] in the Lord" (Eph 2:21). This interpretation depends on the textual variant *pasa oikodomē* (supported by א * B D 33 1739* and the text printed in NA²⁶), which could be rendered as "every building" (i.e., every local church). The other reading, *pasa hē oikodomē* (found in א¹ A C P 1739ᶜ), translated as "all the building" (referring to the universal church), is a scribal correction. Paul pictured each local church as providing God with a spiritual habitation in that locality (Eph 2:22) and as growing together with all the other churches into one holy, universal sanctuary for the Lord's indwelling. (Note, however, that A. T. Lincoln accepts the reading *pasa oikodomē*, but translates it "all the building" or "the whole building," arguing that it represents "a Hebraism which has affected Koine usage" [Lincoln, 124, 156]). The several words derived from *oikos* ("house") in Ephesians 2:19-22 (*paroikoi, oikeioi, epoikodomēthentes, oikodomē, synoikodomeisthē, katoiketērion*) suggest that the "building" metaphor was closely associated with that of "temple" (cf. 1 Tim 3:15; note 2 Sam 7 where "house" is used alternately of David's home and dynasty, and the house David proposes to build for Yahweh; cf. Is 66:1; Jer 12:7; Hos 9:8, 15; Zech 9:8; 1QS 5:6; 8:5, 9; CD 3:19; *see* Household).

#### 4. Temple and Christology.

Finally, Paul seems to apply one aspect of temple imagery to Christ. In Colossians 1:19 Paul speaks of Christ as the one "in whom all the fullness* was pleased to dwell," and in Colossians 2:9 he writes "in him all the fullness of deity dwells bodily." The language of God being "pleased to dwell" is used in Psalm 68:16 (LXX 67:16; cf. Deut 12:5) of Zion, the mountain where God would reside forever, and it is later appropriated to speak of divine Wisdom* taking up residence in Zion (Sir. 24:3-12). In the OT the glory* of God which is said to "fill" the whole earth (Ps 72:19; Jer 23:24; Is 6:3) comes to "fill" his Temple (Ezek 43:5). So the "fullness" of God being "pleased to dwell" in Christ suggests an application of the temple metaphor to the incarnation.

*See also* CHRISTOLOGY; CHURCH; FULLNESS; HOUSEHOLDS AND HOUSEHOLD CODES; JERUSALEM; JESUS, SAYINGS OF; TRIUMPH.

BIBLIOGRAPHY. J. Coppins, "The Spiritual Temple in the Pauline Letters and Its Background," *SE* 6 (1973) 53-66; J. D. G. Dunn, *The Partings of the Ways: Between Christianity and Judaism and Their Significance for the Character of Christianity* (Philadelphia: Trinity Press International, 1991); E. E. Ellis, "II Corinthians V.1-10 in Pauline Eschatology," *NTS* 6 (1959-60) 211-24; G. Fee, *The First Epistle to the Corinthians* (NICNT; Grand Rapids: Eerdmans, 1987); B. Gärtner, *The Temple and the Community in Qumran and the New Testament* (SNTSMS 1; Cambridge: University Press, 1965); A. T. Lincoln, *Ephesians* (WBC 42; Dallas: Word, 1990); R. J. McKelvey, *The New Temple: The Church in the New Testament* (Oxford: University Press, 1969); I. H. Marshall, "Church and Temple in the New Testament," *TynB* 40 (1989) 203-22; O. Michel, "ναός," *TDNT* IV.880-90; E. P. Sanders, *Judaism: Practice and Belief 63 BCE-66CE* (Philadelphia: Trinity Press International, 1992); G. Schrenk, "ἱερός," *TDNT* III.221-47; M. O. Wise, "Temple," *DJG* 811-17; N. T. Wright, *The New Testament and the People of God* (Minneapolis: Fortress, 1992).

P. W. Comfort

## TENTMAKING

There are a number of references to Paul working to support himself, both from his own letters (1 Cor 4:12; 9:1-18; 2 Cor 6:5; 11:23, 27; 1 Thess 2:9; 2 Thess 3:8) and from the Acts (18:3; 20:34-35). By so working Paul supported himself (*see* Financial Support) and "those who were with [him]" (Acts 20:35).

Only one of these references, however, identifies the nature of Paul's work—tentmaking (Gk *ēsan . . . skēnopoioi tē technē*, Acts 18:3). The Greek *skēnopoios* literally means "tentmaker" or "leatherworker."

1. The Nature of Tentmaking
2. Paul: Tentmaker and Apostle
3. Paul's Reasons for Working
4. Problems Caused by Paul's Work
5. The Rabbis and Work

#### 1. The Nature of Tentmaking.

Scholars are divided over the kind of material on which Paul worked. Many scholars from earlier generations suggested it was the rough cloth made of goats' hair, known as *cilicium*, which took its name from Paul's native province, Cilicia. Understandably, they have readily connected this local cloth with the Cilician Paul's "tentmaking," suggesting he may have learned this trade as a youth in Tarsus.

A majority today, however, noting that *cilicium* was used widely for purposes other than tentmaking, and that the patristic interpretations of *skēnopoios* point in the direction of leather goods, believe that tents were generally made of leather (Hock 1980, 20-21). It is now held that the material with which Paul worked was leather. "Tentmaking" may have taken its name from its primary task but have included manufacture and repair of a range of leather and woven goods. A problem with this view, however, is that if the tanning of leather was a despised trade among the Jews (Jeremias, 303-12), would not any kind of leatherworking have shared the same reputation? Moreover, the staining of hands through this work may have rendered Paul unacceptable in the upper-class circles in which he sometimes moved (e.g., Acts 17:12, 19; 19:31; Rom 16:23; but cf. "these hands" of Acts 20:34).

Aquila and Priscilla, tentmakers recently arrived in Corinth after Claudius' expulsion of the Jews from Rome,* appear to have been entrepreneurial manufacturers and traders in tents and related goods, who moved from city to city. At least, so far as the meager evidence about them goes, we see them first in Rome, next in Corinth (*see* Corinthians), then in Ephesus* and finally again in Rome (Acts 18:1-3, 26; Rom 16:3-4). Each of the places Paul is known to have "worked"—Thessalonica, Corinth or Ephesus—was a great urban center. Why would tents be needed in these well-developed cities? The many travelers to these great cities may have purchased, as well as sought the repair of, tents and similar items as they passed through. Sailors in these port cities would also have lived in tents while on shore. It is possible that "tentmakers" may have manufactured and repaired various kinds of booths, canopies and awnings for city use.

## 2. Paul: Tentmaker and Apostle.
It is clear that Paul's work was physical and arduous. Paul writes of "labor and toil . . . we worked night and day" (1 Thess 2:9; cf. 2 Thess 3:8; Acts 20:35) and of "working with our own hands" (1 Cor 4:12; cf. Acts 20:34). We gain an impression of one whose daily life was characterized by hard physical labor, which began before sunrise.

Hock has shown that, far from being peripheral to Paul's life, tentmaking was central to it. "More than

any of us has supposed, Paul was *Paul the Tentmaker*. His trade occupied much of his time. . . . His life was very much that of the workshop . . . of being bent over a workbench like a slave and of working side by side with slaves" (Hock 1980, 67; *see* Slave, Slavery).

Fundamental to those passages where Paul catalogs his apostolic sufferings (*see* Afflictions, Trials, Hardships) we find references to Paul's "labor." Comparing himself with the Corinthians, he writes, "We are weak, but you are strong. You are held in honor, but we in disrepute. To this present hour we hunger and thirst, we are ill clad and buffeted and homeless, and *we labor working with our own hands*" (1 Cor 4:10-12; cf. 2 Cor 11:27).

Significantly, Paul connects his work with his ministry.* He reminds the Thessalonians, "Night and day *working* . . . we proclaimed . . . to you the gospel of God" (1 Thess 2:9). This probably means that Paul talked to people while he worked and also, almost certainly, that on some days, or during part of the day, he laid aside his apron and tools and taught the gospel* (Acts 19:9-11). His lifestyle was characterized by both work *and* preaching.*

## 3. Paul's Reasons for Working.
Greco-Roman culture was accustomed to traveling philosophers (*see* Philosophy) and teachers who would be paid a fee for their efforts or, alternatively, given hospitality and other benefits by wealthy patrons, sometimes under circumstances that generated scandal (*see* Stumbling Block). It was not uncommon for itinerant lecturers to enjoy an evil reputation (Philostratus *Vit. Ap.* 1.13; Lucian *Herm.* 59; Dio Chrysostom *Disc.* 8.9). Paul certainly enjoyed the patronage of the wealthy and could easily have sought and received payment (e.g., Acts 17:4, 12; Rom 16:23; 1 Cor 1:14; Acts 19:31).

There are three reasons in particular why Paul worked to support himself.

First, conscious that he may have been perceived as just one of many itinerant lecturers, some of whom were none too scrupulous, Paul may have worked to support himself out of concern lest his ministry and the message of the gospel be associated with other traveling philosophers (cf. 1 Thess 1:5; 2:3-6; 1 Cor 9:12; Acts 20:33-35). Paul contrasts with himself the newly arrived opponents in Corinth as "those who peddle (*kapēleuontes*) the word of God" (2 Cor 2:17), "[who] tamper (*dolountes*) with God's word" (2 Cor 4:2) and who "prey upon" (*katesthiei*, literally "devour") the Corinthians (2 Cor 11:20). This vocabulary implies the receipt of improper payment, the watering down of the message and the exploitation of the hearers. For his part Paul was true to the message, working rather than accept payment for his ministry, and caring for his congregations (cf. 1 Thess 2:5-10; *see* Pastor).

Second, Paul regarded idleness, which was endemic in Greco-Roman society, as inappropriate for the Christian believer. So he deliberately set the example of hard work to support himself and called upon his converts to imitate him (1 Thess 5:14; 2 Thess 3:6-13; *see* Imitation). The practical values of life in Christ were concretely exemplified in his own consciously executed lifestyle in which he supported himself by work (Eph 4:28; cf. Acts 20:35).

Third, as one called to be the apostle to the Gentiles,* Paul had no option but to obey God's call to preach the gospel. *God* called him, and so Paul made "the gospel free of charge" to the people to whom he came (1 Cor 9:16-18). His obedience to God would have been diminished by receiving payment from others. His pay was to receive no pay. His work was between him and God; he would not be paid for it.

**4. Problems Caused by Paul's Work.**
Paul's contemporaries generally regarded work as appropriate for slaves, but not for free citizens. Artisans and manual workers were looked down upon. Cicero commented that a workshop was no place for a free man (*De Offic.* 1.150). Members of churches established by Paul would probably have regarded his manual labor as remarkable and quite possibly offensive. There are hints from Paul himself that his work required a degree of condescension and "abasement" (2 Cor 11:7). That he was born as a Roman citizen (*see* Citizenship) is usually taken to imply an affluent background in provincial Cilicia (Acts 22:28).

It is evident from 2 Corinthians 11:7-10; 12:14-18 that Paul's defense for working to support himself in 1 Corinthians 9:15-18 had proved unconvincing to the Corinthians. It is probable that by working to support himself Paul had broken the conventions of patronage whereby the wealthy would provide for the visiting lecturer. Paul appears to have been guilty of a serious slight on the Corinthians, for which throughout the seven years of their active association, they never forgave him. His "sin" was compounded because he was prepared to receive assistance from the Macedonians (2 Cor 11:9).

**5. The Rabbis and Work.**
From late Jewish sources we learn that rabbis were expected to support themselves by some form of labor. Rabbi Zadok said, "Make not of the Torah . . . a spade wherewith to dig . . . whosoever derives a profit for himself from the words of the Torah is helping his

own destruction" (*Pirqe 'Abot* 4.7). Rabbi Gamaliel III declared, "An excellent thing is the study of the Torah combined with some secular occupation, for the labor by them both puts sin out of one's mind. All study of the Torah which is not combined with work will ultimately be futile and lead to sin" (*Pirqe 'Abot* 2.12).

Based on these texts it is commonly assumed that Paul learned his tentmaking as a pupil rabbi (*see* Jew, Paul the). Although Hock has questioned this assumption, there is good reason to accept it. Otherwise, how can we explain a member of the provincial elite having such a menial trade?

*See also* APOSTLE; FINANCIAL SUPPORT; WEAKNESS.
BIBLIOGRAPHY. F. Hauck, "κόπος, κοπιάω," *TDNT* III.827-30; R. F. Hock, "Paul's Tentmaking and the Problem of His Social Class," *JBL* 97 (1978) 555-64; idem, *The Social Context of Paul's Mission* (Philadelphia: Fortress, 1980); G. H. R. Horsley, *New Documents Illustrating Early Christianity* (North Ryde, NSW: Macquarie University, 1982) 2.17; J. Jeremias, *Jerusalem in the Time of Jesus* (Philadelphia: Fortress, 1969); P. Marshall, *Enmity in Corinth: Social Conventions in Paul's Relations with the Corinthians* (Tübingen: J. C. B. Mohr, 1987); W. Michaelis, "σκηνοποιός," *TDNT* VII.393-94.
P. W. Barnett

# TEXTUAL CRITICISM

Textual criticism, the art and science that seeks to reconstruct the original text of a document, is necessary in the Pauline letters because the autographs have perished and the extant copies differ from each other. It involves three major tasks: (1) gathering and organizing the evidence; (2) developing a methodology by which to evaluate and assess the significance and implications of the evidence in order to determine which of the variant readings most likely represents the original text; and (3) reconstructing the history of the transmission of the text, to the extent allowed by the surviving evidence. In addition, it makes a contribution to the questions of the formation of the Pauline corpus (*see* Canon) and of the integrity of the letters.

1. The Evidence
2. Textual Traditions
3. Methodology
4. The Textual History of the Pauline Corpus
5. Later Redaction or Interpolations?
6. Examples

**1. The Evidence.**
The textual evidence for the Pauline letters is extremely good. The traditional (if somewhat arbitrary) classification provides a convenient means to survey

the more important witnesses. (For a listing by textual tradition see 2.1-4 below.)

**1.1. Papyri.** The earliest copy of the Pauline corpus, $P^{46}$, is also one of the most important. Dating from c. 200, and somewhat carelessly written by a professional scribe, it preserves a very old form of a very good textual tradition. The not-insignificant value of the other twenty-five Pauline papyri, which include portions of all but two (1 and 2 Timothy) of the traditional fourteen letters, is diminished by their fragmentary state of preservation.

**1.2. Uncials.** In the Paulines, the leading uncial witnesses include ℵ A B and C. On the other hand, D/06 F/010 and G/012 form a trio of important Greek/Latin diglot witnesses that often preserve very early readings. Other noteworthy non-Byzantine MSS include P/025 Ψ 075 and 0150.

**1.3. Minuscules.** While the mass of minuscules are Byzantine in character, a number preserve, despite their relatively late dates, valuable testimony. Chief among them is 1739, a tenth-century copy of a fourth-century copy of an old MS very closely related to $P^{46}$ In addition to the well-known 33, other important (and often undervalued) minuscule witnesses include 81 365 1175 1241 1506 1881 and 2464.

**1.4. Lectionaries.** Relatively little is known about the lectionary text(s) of the Pauline letters, which in any case are more important for the later history of the text than for recovering the original.

**1.5. Versions.** Because the roots of the early versions antedate the great uncials, they comprise potentially significant witnesses to the text. But the contributions of the versions to Pauline textual criticism remain largely to be made, for the following reasons: the *Itala* (or Old Latin) is one of the most important of the early versions, yet a critical edition is available only for Ephesians through Hebrews. Of the Syriac translations, the Old Syriac and the Philoxenian versions of the Pauline letters have not survived, and the Peshitta and Harclean revisions are largely Byzantine in character. The many Coptic versions, by virtue of their close association with the history of Christianity in Egypt, are very important witnesses to the Greek textual tradition but remain largely unexplored. Later versions are less significant, as they almost always are based on another version rather than a Greek text, and thus are only indirect witnesses.

**1.6. Patristic Citations.** Citations by Marcion, Irenaeus, Tertullian and Clement of Alexandria, though not numerous, are very helpful in illuminating both the original wording and history of the text of the letters, as are those of Origen and Cyprian. But much work in this area remains to be done before the full value of the patristic evidence can be realized.

## 2. Textual Traditions.

The development of clearly differentiated text types did not occur until the third or early fourth centuries, and the MSS of the earlier period are distinguished from one another as much or more by the care (or lack thereof) with which they were copied and revised as by any distinctive textual characteristics. Yet it is possible in many instances to trace connections between earlier MSS and leading representative MSS of the later text types, which suggests that these MSS belong to a common textual trajectory or tradition. Three of these textual traditions have been identified to date in the Pauline letters: an Alexandrian, a Western and a Byzantine.

**2.1. Alexandrian Witnesses.** Primary Alexandrian witnesses include $P^{46}$ ℵB 1739 Clement of Alexandria and Origen. Secondary witnesses include $P^{11}$ $P^{13}$ $P^{16}$ $P^{27}$ $P^{32}$ $P^{40}$ $P^{49}$ $P^{61}$ $P^{65}$ (?) A C H/015 I 048 0243 33 81 104 1175 1506 1881 the Coptic versions, and later Alexandrian fathers.

**2.2. Western Witnesses.** Witnesses which are Western in the strict sense of the term—that is, those which are from the western part of the Roman Empire—include the Greek-Latin bilinguals D/06 F/010 G/012 Tertullian, the Old Latin and non-Vulgate quotations in Latin fathers.

**2.3. Byzantine Witnesses.** These encompass most of the later uncials, over eighty percent of the minuscules and most of the Greek fathers. Representative earlier witnesses include K/018 L/020 049 056 0151 424 945 and, among the versions, the Peshitta and Harclean Syriac.

**2.4. Other Important Witnesses.** Not all MSS fit into the three traditions identified thus far. These other important witnesses include $P^{30}$ P/025 Ψ 075 0150 6 323 365 614 629 630 1241 2464 2495.

**2.5. Relative Value of the Traditions.** It has been observed that certain combinations of witnesses and/or textual traditions preserve original readings more often than others. Variants supported by both the Alexandrian and Western textual traditions generally will prove to be superior to other readings; an Alexandrian-Byzantine combination is almost as good. Variants with Western and Byzantine support are very ancient, but often not original. Readings found only in the Alexandrian tradition stand a good chance of being original; indeed, it is not unusual for a small group of primary Alexandrian witnesses to be original over against all other witnesses. Either the Western or Byzantine tradition alone can preserve an original reading, but this happens only rarely.

**3. Methodology.**

*3.1. General Considerations.* The classical method of textual criticism relied heavily upon a stemmatic or genealogical approach that sought to reconstruct a stemma or family tree of surviving MSS and thereby to determine the "best manuscript" upon which to base an edition. But in the case of the NT this classical approach has proven to be unworkable due to (1) the large number of MSS involved and (2) the ubiquitous presence of mixture (or "cross-pollination") within the textual tradition. This means that even the most reliable MSS are sometimes wrong, and conversely even a MS of very poor quality may occasionally preserve a true reading. Consequently, there has emerged an approach that is best described as a *reasoned eclecticism.*

This approach applies, on a passage by passage basis, all the tools and criteria developed by the classical method. No one rule or principle can be applied nor any one MS or group followed in a mechanical or across-the-board fashion; each variation unit must be approached on its own merits.

*3.1.1. External and Internal Evidence.* Differences in method today are largely a matter of differing judgments as to the relative weight to be given to external evidence (i.e., that provided by the MSS and other witnesses) over against internal evidence (i.e., considerations having to do with scribes or authors; cf. 3.2.1 below), although there are a few notable exceptions. One is the so-called *rigorous eclecticism* which relies almost exclusively on internal considerations and places little if any weight on external evidence, treating the MSS basically as a storehouse of readings to be evaluated on other grounds. On the other extreme is the *majority text method* which seeks to eliminate entirely any appeal to internal evidence, arguing that a variant which is supported by a majority of the MSS ought to be accepted as original. This amounts to a substitution of counting witnesses for reasoned criticism, and fails to realize that a thousand copies of a mistake do not make it any less a mistake.

*3.1.2. History of the Textual Tradition.* What the "Majority text" and the "rigorous eclectic" approaches have in common is a disregard for the history of the textual tradition. But when the history of the text is taken seriously, it becomes impossible to rely entirely on either external or internal criteria alone. Instead, depending upon the facts in a given instance, a reasoned eclecticism applies a combination of internal and external considerations, evaluating the character of the variants in light of the MSS evidence and vice versa in order to obtain a balanced view of the matter.

*3.2. The Fundamental Guideline.* One overarching guideline governs all other considerations: *the variant most likely to be original is the one which best accounts for the existence of the others.* That is, when confronted with a set of variant readings, one should ask: "Which one best explains, in terms of both external and internal evidence, the origin of the others?" (For examples see 6.1-2 below.) It is important to note that "best accounts for" is here defined in terms of both external and internal considerations, because prerequisite to reaching a judgment about a variant is the reconstruction of its history. This is where both the "majority text" and "rigorous eclectic" approaches fall short, in that they repeatedly contend for the originality of readings which cannot account for the historical (i.e., manuscript) evidence. Only the variant that can best account for all the evidence can seriously be considered as original.

*3.2.1. Additional Factors.* Within the framework established by the fundamental guideline, several factors must be taken into consideration. Exactly which ones ought to be considered and how much weight is to be given to each depends upon the facts and circumstances in a given case. The relevant evidence falls into two broad types. External evidence takes into account (1) the relative date of the witnesses, (2) their geographical distribution, (3) genealogical relationships between the MSS and (4) the relative quality of the witnesses. Internal evidence is of two kinds: transcriptional (dealing with the habits and practices of scribes and editors) and intrinsic (dealing with the author's style, vocabulary, argument, etc.). Intrinsic factors are often the most subjective kind of evidence the textual critic must take into account. In the case of the Pauline letters, however, more often than elsewhere, such exegetical considerations frequently are decisive in judging between variants.

*3.2.2. A Final Consideration.* The importance of exegesis for Pauline textual criticism is a reminder that it, like other historical disciplines, is not a branch of mathematics or an area in which the evidence may be processed in a mechanical fashion according to rigid rules. Each variant presents a potentially unique set of circumstances and must be approached on that basis.

**4. The Textual History of the Pauline Corpus.**

*4.1.* Due to the fragmentary and incomplete state of the evidence, any reconstruction of the transmission history of the Pauline letters involves a high degree of conjecture and hypothesis. It is also closely associated with the formation of the Pauline corpus. For clarity it will be helpful to distinguish three broad stages in the transmission process.

*4.2. The Pre-Corpus Stage.* Initially, some letters appear to have circulated independently, while others circulated from the first only as part of a collection. Small collections in individual churches grew through the exchange of copies until by mid-second century (c. A.D. 180 at the latest) the full fourteen-letter corpus was in existence, though not yet with any standardized order of the letters (*see* Canon).

Two seemingly contradictory observations call for explanation during this stage. First, the presence of shared errors in nearly all surviving copies suggests the existence of a common archetype of the corpus, which must have been created at a very early stage in the transmission process in order to have infected virtually the entire surviving tradition. But second, the survival of genuine readings in a few isolated MSS or one small part of the tradition suggests the possibility of access to independent copies uninfected by the errors of the archetype of the corpus—a circumstance which would, however, refute the very concept of an archetypal corpus. Zuntz suggests, therefore, that there must have existed an archetype equipped with variant readings drawn from MSS available to the editor who compiled the archetype, probably in Alexandria, possibly as soon as the very early second century. This would account for the presence of shared distinctive readings in otherwise widely separated branches of the textual tradition. Alternatively, the initial formation of smaller collections out of which a relatively fixed corpus eventually emerged is a very likely hypothesis.

*4.3. From the Corpus to Text-Types.* From the mid-second to mid-fourth century, the letters were widely copied in a largely uncontrolled manner in a sometimes hostile environment. Most MSS were copied in a relatively normal fashion, subject only to the usual slips, errors and vicissitudes of the copying process. Some, however, were copied—one might even say edited or revised—in a fairly free manner, while a much smaller number appear to be the work of trained and supervised scribes, possibly in a scriptorium. The result was a variety of MSS of widely varying quality and characteristics.

*4.4. The Rise of Text-Types.* Following the Diocletianic persecutions (303-311, during which many MSS perished) and the toleration of Christianity under Constantine (313), the church experienced much growth in numbers and ecclesiastical control. In this environment MSS supplied by influential bishops in Antioch and Alexandria, which naturally reflected the distinctive character of the MSS created or preserved by the exegetical schools in these cities, came to dominate the East and Alexandria, respectively. Here are to be found the origins of the Byzantine and Alexan-

drian text-types. The Byzantine tradition reflects the stylistically polished text attributed to Lucian, while in Alexandria a MS or MSS closely related to B became, due to Athanasius' influence, the model for Egypt.

*4.5. Later Developments.* Though both these traditions continued to develop, their essential characteristics had by now been established. The most significant later development was the eventual dominance of the Byzantine text-type (due largely to the reduction, following the Arab conquests, of Greek-speaking areas to the region dominated by Byzantium) and the steady infringement of Byzantine readings into other branches of the tradition.

## 5. Later Redaction or Interpolations?

Suggestions that one or more of the present letters are a composite of two or more originally separate letters, and/or that the letters were edited (sometimes extensively) or interpolated in the late first or early second century have long been a part of the textual and literary criticism of the letters. Recently it has been argued that the presence of interpolations should be assumed as a working principle, and that the burden of proof lies with those who would disagree.

The textual history of the letters, however, suggests a different perspective. In view of the circumstance that Romans certainly and other letters probably circulated independently prior to the formation of the corpus, the essential uniformity of the existing tradition is remarkable. This means that since the manuscript tradition began, the letters always have had the same form they now exhibit. (The one letter which does exist in multiple forms, Romans,* is the exception which proves the rule, since clear traces of later editorial activity are visible in the tradition.) Therefore any editorial activity, such as that proposed by partition or interpolation hypotheses, must have occurred prior to a letter's entrance into the textual tradition. The burden of proof lies on those who suggest otherwise, and any proposal regarding post-publication textual alterations which is unsupported by evidence of disruption of the textual tradition is inherently implausible.

## 6. Examples.

The following examples illustrate some of the points discussed above (cf. especially 3.2, 3.2.1 and 3.2.2). Details about signs and abbreviations used may be found in the introduction to the United Bible Societies' *Greek New Testament* (3rd ed. [corrected], 1983).

*6.1. 1 Timothy 3:16.* What is the initial word of the hymnic fragment in this verse? The MSS present three variants: (1) OC (*hos*, "who," referring to Jesus), read by ℵ A C F G 33 and 365 among others, two forms of the Syriac, and several church fathers, including Origen, Jerome and Epiphanius; (2) O (*ho*, "which," referring to "mystery"), read by D 061, the Old Latin and Vulgate, and several Latin fathers, including Pelagius and Augustine; and (3) ΘC (the abbreviation for *theos*, "God"), read by K L P Ψ 81 1739 and many others, including the Byzantine tradition, later correctors of ℵ A C D, Gregory of Nyssa, Didymus, Chrysostom and Theodoret. (The Harclean and Peshitta Syriac, and Sahidic and Bohairic Coptic versions read either "who" or "which.")

With regard to external evidence, one may say that (1) has excellent early support from at least two regions (Egypt and Syria); (2) finds its support almost entirely in the West, among Latin MSS and fathers; (3) receives widespread but relatively late support from a large number of Byzantine and other MSS, and from several fathers, the earliest of whom dates from the last third of the fourth century.

Looking at internal evidence, we may say that it appears that reading (2), "which" (neuter pronoun), arose as a scribal "correction" of (1), "who" (masculine pronoun), to bring it into agreement with the immediately preceding word in Greek, *mystērion* ("mystery," a neuter noun). Thus all witnesses reading "which" indirectly support "who" as the earlier reading. In evaluating (1) (OC, "who") and (3) (ΘC, "God"), one may note that scribes very frequently strengthened christological statements, but seldom weakened them; thus a change (due to either accidental misreading or deliberate alteration) from OC to ΘC is much more probable than the reverse.

Summarizing, variant (1) has the support of early MSS and all ancient versions, while there is no trace of (3) prior to the latter part of the fourth century, and (1) was more likely to have been changed to (3) than vice versa. In view of the fundamental guideline given above (3.2), OC must be accepted as the original reading because it best accounts for, in terms of both external evidence and transcriptional probability, the existence of the other two variants.

*6.2. 1 Corinthians 2:1.* Did Paul write about the "testimony" (μαρτύριον, *martyrion; see* Witness) or the "mystery"* (μυστήριον, *mystērion*) of God? The latter reading is found in *P*[46] ℵ* A C 88 436 two Latin MSS, Peshitta, Bohairic and two fathers, while virtually all other evidence (including ℵ² B D G 33 1739 Origen) supports the former.

The external evidence is indecisive. While "testimony" has broad and strong support, the more limited evidence favoring "mystery" is perhaps even earlier and is geographically widespread.

In turning to internal evidence, we may adduce two points in favor of "mystery": first, its presence here prepares the way for its use in 1 Corinthians 2:7 and, second, the presence of "testimony" in 1 Corinthians 1:6 has led scribes to substitute that term here. On the other hand, 1 Corinthians 1:6 is rather distant to have had such influence, and the usage there ("testimony of Christ") is different. Further, to use "mystery" here does not so much anticipate 1 Corinthians 2:7 as rob the use of the word in that place of much of its impact. Finally, "testimony" is a less common and less colorful term than "mystery," and therefore more likely to be replaced by, than to replace, the latter.

In short, although it is possible to explain how the variant "testimony" might have arisen if "mystery" were original, the reverse seems much more probable. Thus "testimony" is, in view of the basic guideline, most likely the original reading.

*6.3. Ephesians 1:1.* This variant affects the interpretation of not only the destination and nature of Ephesians,* but also its place and role in the formation of the Pauline corpus.

While most MSS read "to the saints who are in Ephesus and faithful in Christ," some very significant (and the very earliest) witnesses (including *P*[46] ℵ B 6 1739 Origen) omit "in Ephesus," and Marcion apparently knew the letter under the heading "to the Laodiceans."

If the reading "in Ephesus" is original, it is not easy to explain the rise of the variant. The phrase without the place name is difficult (if not impossible) to translate; if "in Ephesus" was deliberately omitted, it is odd that a few additional words were not also omitted, so as to produce a readable text (cf. Col 1:2). But because the grammar seems to demand a place name, and similar Pauline greetings (cf. Phil 1:1) typically have a place name at this point, it is easy to see how a scribe, once the superscription "to Ephesus" was attached to the letter, might insert "in Ephesus" into the text.

It appears, therefore, that the reading without "in Ephesus" is the earliest surviving form of the text. But in view of its severe grammatical and logical difficulties (a saint is by definition faithful; to speak of "saints who are *also* faithful" is nonsensical), it is unlikely that it is the original reading.

The most widely accepted explanation of these circumstances is that Ephesians is a circular letter, intended for several churches (this would account for the observation that whereas Paul ministered extensively at Ephesus, this letter contains no personal greetings and the author does not know the addressees personally; cf. Eph 1:15; 3:2; 4:21). On this view a gap was intentionally left in the original, to be filled in with the appropriate location in the copies produced for distribution. Ephesus, as the best known of the churches that received a copy, eventually excluded the names of the other recipients, while a copy sent to Laodicea (cf. Col 4:16) would account for Marcion knowing it as "to the Laodiceans."

But while there are ancient examples of duplicate copies being sent to multiple locations, there are no known instances of a letter with a gap in lieu of the place name. Moreover, there are additional grammatical irregularities to be accounted for, including the problematic *kai* ("and" or "also") before "faithful." Of the various attempts to explain these points, the least unlikely suggests that the letter was originally sent to two cities, Laodicea and Hierapolis. On this view the text without any place name is the result of efforts to create a more universal form of the letter (analogous to the 14- and 15-chapter forms of Romans) for liturgical or other use; it may even have been part of a "catholic" or "departicularized" collection composed of Romans, Hebrews, 1 Corinthians (cf. the variant at 1:2b) and Ephesians. The insertion of "in Ephesus" would represent a later development (but why Ephesus, since on this view Ephesus did not, in contrast to the "circular letter" view, receive a copy?).

To summarize, while the earliest surviving text is the one lacking "in Ephesus," it is a matter of continuing debate whether that is the original text. Clearly the last word about Ephesians 1:1 has not yet been spoken. Nevertheless, the preceding discussion of it and the other two variants serves to exemplify the practice and significance of textual criticism in the Pauline letters.

*See also* CANON.

BIBLIOGRAPHY. K. Aland, "Die Entstehung des Corpus Paulinum," in *Neutestamentliche Entwürfe* (Munich: Kaiser, 1979); K. Aland and B. Aland, *The Text of the New Testament: An Introduction to the Critical Editions and to the Theory and Practice of Modern Textual Criticism* (2d ed., rev. and enlarged; Leiden: E. J. Brill/Grand Rapids: Eerdmans, 1989); H. Gamble Jr., *The New Testament Canon* (Philadelphia: Fortress, 1985) 36-46; idem, *The Textual History of the Letter to the Romans* (Studies and Documents 42; Grand Rapids: Eerdmans, 1977); B. M. Metzger, *The Text of the New Testament. Its Transmission, Corruption, and Restoration* (3d, enlarged ed.; New York and Oxford: Oxford University Press, 1992); D. Trobisch, *Die Entstehung der Paulusbriefsammlung: Studien zu den Anfangen christlicher Publizistik* (Fribourg: Editions universitaires/Göttingen: Vandenhoeck & Ruprecht, 1989); W. O. Walker Jr., "The Burden of Proof in Identifying Interpolations in the Pauline Letters," *NTS* 33 (1987) 610-18; G. Zuntz, *The Text of the*

*Epistles: A Disquisition Upon the* Corpus Paulinum (The Schweich Lectures, 1946; London: The British Academy, 1953).

M. W. Holmes

**TEXTUAL HISTORY.** *See* TEXTUAL CRITICISM.

**TEXTUAL TRADITIONS.** *See* TEXTUAL CRITICISM.

**THANKSGIVING.** *See* BENEDICTION, BLESSING, DOXOLOGY, THANKSGIVING; LITURGICAL ELEMENTS.

# THESSALONIANS, LETTERS TO THE

Paul and Silas, accompanied by their assistant, Timothy (*see* Coworkers, Paul and His), took the first steps toward the establishment of a Christian community in Thessalonica as part of the first Christian mission to the province of Macedonia. Thessalonica was one of the major cities of the Roman Empire. The missionaries' subsequent contact with the Thessalonian church included two letters (*see* Letters, Letter Forms), which are probably the oldest Christian documents that we possess. Despite their brevity and their relative lack of significantly developed theological themes compared to the other letters in the Pauline corpus, the two letters to the Thessalonian Christians have become the object of much recent scholarly examination, particularly in the areas of rhetorical criticism (*see* Rhetoric, Rhetorical Criticism), sociological analysis (*see* Social Setting) and the early development of Pauline theology.

1. Contents of the Letters
2. The City of Thessalonica
3. The Pauline Mission
4. The Writing of the Letters
5. Literary and Historical Questions
6. Early Pauline Theology

**1. Contents of the Letters.**

Both 1 and 2 Thessalonians identify themselves in their prescripts (1 Thess 1:1; 2 Thess 1:1-2) as co-authored by Paul, Silas (called Silvanus in the letters) and Timothy. But we can probably assume on the basis of Paul's later letters (and see 1 Thess 3:6) that Paul at least played the leading role in their composition.

*1.1. 1 Thessalonians.* In 1 Thessalonians Paul thanks God* for the Thessalonian Christians, remembering in particular how they "received the word" preached by Paul and his coworkers "in the midst of much suffering*" (1 Thess 1:6) and thus became an example for others who would hear the gospel* (1 Thess 1:7-

10). He goes on to recall for them the difficult circumstances and the earnest sincerity that characterized the initial apostolic mission (*see* Apostle) to Thessalonica (1 Thess 2:1-12). He does so apparently to set forth himself and his coworkers as examples of blamelessness for his readers. Paul then returns to thanksgiving (*see* Benediction, Blessing, Doxology, Thanksgiving) for the Thessalonians' reception of the gospel. He sets them on one side of a divide between God's suffering* people and the persecuting rejectors of God's Word, the latter exemplified by the "the Jews" (1 Thess 2:13-16). He then tells of how his love for them and concern for their steadfastness has led him and his coworkers to seek renewed contact with the Thessalonians. Now, with Timothy successfully returned from Thessalonica, news of their steadfastness has arrived and has brought rejoicing (1 Thess 2:17—3:10; *see* Joy).

A prayer for continued contact, love* and blamelessness (1 Thess 3:11-13) closes out the first major section of the letter (1 Thess 1—3). In this section Paul has drawn strong continuities between the Gentile* Christians of Thessalonica (see 1 Thess 1:9) and others among the people of God, including the OT prophets (1 Thess 2:15) and especially the missionaries who brought the gospel to Thessalonica. By this emphasis on their place in the people of God and their links with the apostolic mission, Paul gives the Thessalonian Christians a way of thinking about themselves that will enable them to stand with certainty in the adversity that they are experiencing. This in turn lays the foundation for the second major section of the letter, in which Paul will repeatedly refer to traditions and instructions that the Thessalonians have received from the missionaries (1 Thess 4:1, 2, 9, 11; *see* Teaching/ Paraenesis).

The second section (1 Thess 4—5) begins with an exhortation to holy living (1 Thess 4:1-12), the main focus of which is sexual morality (*see* Sexuality). Paul then deals with Christ's return (1 Thess 4:13—5:11; *see* Eschatology), which provides the basis for an exhortation to alert and sober living, to faith,* love* and hope,* and to mutual encouragement (1 Thess 5:4-8, 11). His main motivation in penning this eschatological section appears, however, to have been concern on the part of some Thessalonian Christians about the fate of those of their number who had died before Christ's return (1 Thess 4:13-18; *see* Immortality; Resurrection). The letter closes with general admonitions and benedictions (1 Thess 5:12-28).

*1.2. 2 Thessalonians.* Paul's thanksgiving in 2 Thessalonians (2 Thess 1:3-12), like that in 1 Thessalonians, mentions the Thessalonian Christians' characteristic steadfastness in suffering and their example to others. Once again eschatology is the framework in which Paul views both their suffering and their accomplishments.

2 Thessalonians also reveals that central to Paul's concerns for the Thessalonian Christian community were questions regarding eschatology (2 Thess 2:1-12). Here the problem seems to be that some believed that "the day of the Lord" had already occurred (2 Thess 2:2). Paul answers this belief by speaking of events that must take place before "that day" (2 Thess 2:3-12). As in 1 Thessalonians, having answered these initial concerns Paul returns to thanksgiving for the Thessalonians (2 Thess 2:13-17). A particular problem addressed in the general admonitions in 2 Thessalonians (2 Thess 3:1-15) is the refusal of some in the church to work (2 Thess 3:10-12); here the practice of the apostolic missionaries is offered as an example of labor and economic self-sufficiency (2 Thess 3:7-9; *see* Tentmaking). The letter closes with benedictions and Paul's personal greeting (2 Thess 3:16-18).

**2. The City of Thessalonica.**
Thessalonica was a populous city enjoying good fortune throughout most of the Hellenistic and Roman period. It was founded (at or near the site of Therma) at the head of the Thermaic Gulf (now called the Gulf of Salonika) about 315 B.C. by Cassander, formerly a general of Alexander the Great and, when the city was founded, king of Macedonia. As an important military and commercial port, it became the principal city of Macedonia. It was designated the capital of one of the four administrative districts into which Rome divided Macedonia in 168 B.C. In 146 B.C. it became the capital of the now-unified province of Macedonia. In the same year the Egnatian Way, connecting Asia Minor with the Adriatic Sea (and Rome beyond the Adriatic), was put through. It was on this road that Paul and his coworkers traveled from Philippi to Thessalonica (Acts 17:1; *see* Travel). In return for its support of Antony and Octavian, Thessalonica became a free city in 42 B.C. It remained the most important and populous city of Macedonia into the third or fourth century A.D. As Salonika it is the second largest city of modern Greece and still an important seaport.

Archeological sites in the city include parts of the Roman city wall, a first-century Roman forum and an older Hellenistic agora, a hippodrome, three spans of the triumphal arch of Galerius and a number of Byzantine churches. The Vardar Gate, which spanned the Egnatian Way at the west side of the city as the arch of Galerius spanned it at the east end of the city, was dismantled in the nineteenth century. An inscription from the gate, dating from the late first century B.C. to the early second century A.D., uses the Greek word *politarchēs* ("civic official"), otherwise found only in the Acts account of the Pauline mission to the city (Acts 17:6). Inscriptional evidence of Jewish settlement in the city dates from the late Roman period; a Samaritan synagogue inscription dates from an earlier period, perhaps the third century B.C.

## 3. The Pauline Mission.

*3.1. The Account in Acts.* The Jewish setting of the initial Christian mission to Thessalonica is prominent in the Acts account (Acts 17:1-10). The mission of Paul and Silas, which took place mostly or entirely in a Jewish synagogue, was focused on proving to Jews from their Scriptures that Jesus was the Messiah (*see* Christ). The first converts included some Jews, a large portion of the local Gentile worshippers of the God of Israel* and a number of prominent women (who were probably also among the Gentile worshippers of Israel's God). Opposition to the mission began at the initiative of Jews (cf. Acts 17:13), though it quickly spread to Gentiles, first to an unruly mob, and then to the city officials. Apart from the difficulty it brought on the new Christian community, this opposition made it prudent for Paul and Silas (and Timothy, though he is not mentioned in Acts) to move on. Thus Jews who opposed the Pauline mission were successful before the officials in blaming their intended victims, the Christians, for a disturbance that the Jews themselves had actually created.

But Paul's letters to the Thessalonian Christians do not seem, at first examination, to support the Acts account of the beginnings of their church.* Despite Paul's argument in person from the Scriptures (so Acts 17:2-3), neither letter quotes the OT; there are only occasional vague echoes, the most significant being of Daniel 11:36 in 2 Thessalonians 2:4. This is not what we would expect from a writer steeped in the Scriptures, the writer of Galatians* and Romans,* least of all when that person was writing to people who had only recently been all habitués of a synagogue. Furthermore, the readers are reminded how they turned "from idols" (*see* Idolatry) to await God's Son (*see* Son of God) from heaven* (1 Thess 1:9-10). Nowhere in the letters is it even hinted that any of the readers had any positive and meaningful contact with Judaism before they met Paul and Silas, much less that any of them were Jews. (The contrast is at least less certain with regard to their opponents: In Acts the opposition is ultimately both Jewish and Gentile; in 1 Thessalonians the opponents are the Christians' "own countrymen" [1 Thess 2:14], and this designation might

well include some Jews.) For these reasons it has been thought by many that the Acts account of the mission in Thessalonica is inaccurate or at least that it is part of its author's broader portrayal of Paul's mission strategy (*see* Mission) and of Jewish-Christian relations (cf. Acts 13:44-50; 14:19; 18:12-17; etc.).

*3.2. The Picture Suggested by the Letters.* The Acts account might, indeed, describe only one side of a mission that also (and even more significantly) touched Gentiles who had not been influenced by Judaism. By referring to his own physical labor in both letters (1 Thess 2:9; 2 Thess 3:7-9), Paul gives us a clue concerning this other side of the mission: His workplace may have been where many non-judaized Gentiles in the city heard the gospel (*see* Tentmaking). This would be in accord with the methods used by other preachers and popular philosophers (*see* Philosophy) of the day (Hock, 38-41; Malherbe 1987, 17-20). That Paul did enter into some sort of craft-business arrangement in Thessalonica (as in Corinth, Acts 18:2-3) suggests a longer stay in the city than the three weeks or a little more that might be inferred from the Acts account (Acts 17:2). It was more than once that the Philippian Christians sent Paul material assistance while he was in Thessalonica (Phil 4:15-16; *see* Financial Support); this points to the same conclusion.

But it may be that the situation was more complex not only than Acts suggests but also than what we might infer from the letters by themselves. Perhaps Paul sought to downplay what Jewish influence there was on some of the Thessalonian Christians. As it is, the belief structure reflected in the letters is a messianic-apocalyptic form of Judaism (*see* Apocalypticism; Eschatology), even though the letters never refer to the Jewish Scriptures (*see* Old Testament in Paul). They also include a strongly worded anti-Jewish polemic (1 Thess 2:14-16) and emphasize (perhaps even exaggerate) the pagan origin of the addressees (1 Thess 1:9)—possibly because of the circumstances under which the Thessalonian church began or because of Paul's reaction against Judaism coming out of his own call to Christian faith and apostleship (on the latter cf. Gager, though he does not extend his argument back to 1 Thessalonians).

Any attempt to say more about the Thessalonian Christians on the basis of the letters must reckon with the observation that Paul apparently preached a message with a strong eschatological orientation and that this orientation was apparently taken to an extreme by some members of the community (1 Thess 4:13—5:11; 2 Thess 2:1-12). Perhaps this eschatological excitement was great enough to prompt charges of political subversion (Acts 17:6-7). Sociological study of eschatologically focused, or millenarian, groups has emphasized that a new experience of relative deprivation arising from changes within society's structures and patterns of relationships generally lies behind this kind of eschatological interest. Paul's preaching of the gospel offered just such an eschatological faith. Was there a social situation at Thessalonica that would have made Paul's gospel attractive?

Even if the Thessalonian Christians were not at ease with the status quo, we would be mistaken to suppose that all of them were at the bottom of society. Indeed, W. Meeks suggests (173-74) that some of Paul's converts would have been people of some wealth experiencing "status inconsistency" or "status dissonance" because their social standing did not match their wealth. This inconsistency lay behind their attraction to the eschatological faith preached by Paul. A community consisting of both poor and rich persons is suggested by two lines of evidence: the decision of some to quit working (2 Thess 3:11) and Acts' references to "leading women" and to the householder Jason (Acts 17:4-5; *see* Social Setting).

R. Jewett (113-32) has suggested specific social factors at Thessalonica that may have played a role in certain Thessalonians responding to Paul's message. Jewett speaks of the absorption of the Cabirus cult into the city cult of Thessalonica during the first century A.D. (*see* Donfried). The Cabirus cult was a local eschatological redeemer cult once popular among the lower classes and with some superficial structural similarities to the Christian gospel. Some of the Cabirus cult's original adherents, having lost what their recently co-opted faith had provided for them, may have found a suitable substitute in the gospel. Jewett also points to changes in Thessalonian society that had occurred with the shift to Roman power and the coming of new people who bore governmental and commercial power. This shift in power would have contributed to a social situation in which Paul's eschatological gospel would been viewed with favor.

However we picture its origin, the Thessalonian church apparently remained stable and on friendly terms with Paul and his coworkers: Acts 20:4 mentions two men of Thessalonica among the representatives of the Gentile churches accompanying Paul on his last journey to Jerusalem. 2 Timothy 4:10 mentions a "Demas" who deserted Paul and went to Thessalonica; this brief note is not enough to imply that the church there had become disaffected from the apostle.

### 4. The Writing of the Letters.
The letters to the Thessalonian Christians were apparently written not long after the departure of Paul,

Silas and Timothy from Thessalonica and their arrival in Athens (1 Thess 2:17; 3:1; Acts 17:10-15). Paul's attempts to return to Thessalonica were hindered (1 Thess 2:18), perhaps by the guarantee that he would not come back, a guarantee forced out of the Thessalonian Christians by the city officials (Acts 17:9). But he did manage to send Timothy back (1 Thess 3:2).

A written message no doubt accompanied Timothy, but we do not have it, unless it is what we call 2 Thessalonians (which would then be the earlier of the two letters; so Wanamaker, 37-45; see below on the order of the letters). At any rate, 1 and perhaps 2 Thessalonians were written after Timothy's return from Thessalonica with good news concerning the stability of the Christian community there (1 Thess 3:6). Paul still hoped to return to Thessalonica (1 Thess 3:10-11). In the meantime he and his associates sent these two letters to encourage and exhort the fledgling church to attempt to clear up some confusion concerning the eschatological expectation that they had proclaimed and to address a problem of vagrancy on the part of some members.

The Thessalonian letters have often been viewed as arising out of a situation of particular ideological conflict. This situation has usually been defined under the influence of the interpretation of other, more clearly polemical letters of Paul (in different ways by, e.g., Schmithals, 123-218, and Jewett, 149-57). But such an approach is often part of an incorrectly monolithic picture of Paul's opponents* or of ancient religious currents (*see* Gnosticism; Judaizers). Furthermore, it is usually dependent on tenuous connections drawn between Pauline exhortations and other statements and phenomena in the ancient world or between the different letters of Paul (e.g., 1 Thessalonians and 2 Corinthians) and on a questionable identification of some parts of the Thessalonian letters as polemical (see 5.1 below). We are on the most secure ground if, generally speaking, we think of the problems in the Thessalonian church as arising from the possibilities within Pauline Christianity itself, not from any ideological corruption emanating from outside the community.

Within that framework, it does appear that an over-realized eschatology* was advocated by at least some in the Thessalonian church. The eschatological confusion Paul addresses was apparently centered upon questions concerning the time remaining before the expected return of Jesus. Some members of the community had already died, and those remaining were unsure how the dead could benefit from Christ's return (1 Thess 4:13-18). In this situation some of the community had perhaps found solace in believing that the expected eschatological return had, in some sense or another, already occurred (2 Thess 2:1-3; *see* Resurrection).

Paul does not indicate the reasoning that lay behind the refusal of some to work (1 Thess 4:10-12; 5:14; 2 Thess 3:6-12) or even that there was reasoning behind it. He does not even say or clearly imply that this pattern of behavior arose subsequent to their conversion to Christianity. So the common suggestion that this vagrancy was motivated by their new eschatological beliefs and that it was thus another manifestation of the eschatological confusion addressed in the letters (e.g., Marshall, 117, 218) is little more than a guess.

It has also been suggested that the problem of Christian preachers claiming support from their audiences was showing its face in this refusal to work (Trilling 1972, 96-98). But this problem, in which Paul wished to avoid any suggestion of involvement, whether in Corinth or in Thessalonica (1 Thess 2:9; 2 Thess 3:7-9; 1 Cor 9), and which the *Didache* (*Did.* 12) addresses, was associated with *itinerant* preachers. 1 and 2 Thessalonians, however, address a problem of vagrancy among the resident members of the community.

It has commonly been thought that 1 Thessalonians 2:1-12 answers charges that Paul and his associates were hypocritical, motivated not by loyalty to God and love for the Thessalonians but by love for money (e.g., Bruce, 27-28), or that it responds to charges that Paul neglected charismatic gifts (cf. 1 Thess 1:5; 2 Cor 10:10; 11:6; Schmithals, 139-40, followed by Jewett, 102-3; *see* Gifts of the Spirit). But it has been shown that this passage is merely an example of a common ancient rhetorical pattern in which the speaker or writer provides an example to be emulated by describing his own behavior in antithetical terms ("not that, but this") (Lyons, 184; Malherbe 1970, 1983).

It has also been claimed that some aspects of the hortatory material in 1 Thessalonians addressed specific problems in the Thessalonian Christian community (e.g., Jewett, 100-102 on 1 Thess 5:19-22, 103-4 on 5:12-13; Bruce, 87 on 1 Thess 4:3-8). It is clear that this is the case for the problem of vagrancy in 2 Thessalonians and, by extension, in 1 Thessalonians. But in the other exhortations, those concerning adultery and other forms of sexual immorality (1 Thess 4:3-8), and respect for church leaders (1 Thess 5:12-13, perhaps with 2 Thess 3:14-15), Paul is using standardized exhortations expressed in rhetorically normal patterns with no suggestion that particular problems are addressed.

## 5. Literary and Historical Questions.

### 5.1. Form Criticism and Rhetorical Criticism.
Most of Paul's letters contain an "epistolary thanksgiving" after the salutation (e.g., Rom 1:8-15; 1 Cor 1:4-9; Phil 1:3-11), and in this they resemble other Hellenistic letters (*see* Letters, Letter Forms). Both 1 and 2 Thessalonians are anomalous in that they have what can be described as two thanksgiving sections each (1 Thess 1:2-10; 2:13-16; 2 Thess 1:3-4; 2:13-14), and later in 1 Thessalonians we encounter another renewal of thanksgiving (1 Thess 3:9-10). The presence of two thanksgivings in 2 Thessalonians is taken as evidence that it is a non-Pauline imitation of 1 Thessalonians (see below on the question of its authorship).

In 1 Thessalonians, however, this anomaly has been dealt with by adjustments of the normal form-critical categories (e.g., by speaking of the interpenetration of letter body and thanksgiving), by identifying 1 Thessalonians as the result of conflation of two letters (Schmithals) or by identifying 1 Thessalonians 2:13-16 as a post-Pauline interpolation into Paul's letter (e.g., Pearson, Schmidt). The interpolation view has also focused on the contrast between what Paul says in 1 Thessalonians 2:14-16 about "the Jews" (*see* Israel) and the high regard he shows for non-Christian Jews in Romans 9—11, including his statement regarding their future salvation* (Rom 11:26). The interpolation view has also focused on other arguments based on the content and structure of the "second thanksgiving."

It is usually taken for granted that the strongly worded polemics we see in 1 Thessalonians 2:13-16 arose out of a highly combative situation, but this assumption is undermined by the evidence for the general use of strongly worded polemics in the ancient world, both within Judaism and the church (see Johnson). Furthermore, Romans 9—11 itself seems to build on a negative assessment of the present situation of non-Christian Jews (particularly Rom 11:7-10). And if form criticism takes its place as a descriptive, rather than defining, tool, then it becomes difficult to build on it any argument for interpolation (or for regarding 1 Thess as a product of conflation). The same can be said regarding arguments that other passages in the Thessalonian letters were interpolated (e.g., 1 Thess 5:1-11).

Form criticism allows us to isolate the uniqueness, and therefore the special concerns, of the first three chapters of 1 Thessalonians, which are, in the most general terms, Paul's desire to return to thanksgiving as he thinks about his initial work among the Thessalonians (see Simpson). The renewal of thanksgiving in 2 Thessalonians 2:13, however it may be described in form-critical terms, allows the writer to contrast "those affecting you" (2 Thess 1:6) and "those perishing" (2 Thess 2:10) with the addressees and to bracket words about the former with thanksgiving for the latter.

Generally, rhetorical criticism of the letters has consisted of identifying the ancient rhetorical components (e.g., *exordium, partitio, narratio,* etc.; *see* Rhetoric, Rhetorical Criticism) of the letters and viewing the purposes of the sections and of the letters as wholes as the generalized functions associated with the rhetorical terms. In this way the letters are thought of as oratory set within epistolary frameworks. The increasing attention to the rhetorical structure of the letters has not led to complete agreement (see Jewett, 63-87, 221, 225; Wanamaker, 48-52). But it has allowed for more flexible approaches and new ways of understanding the functions of and relationships among the different parts of the letters, including 1 Thessalonians 2:13-16, particularly in comparison with thematic and form-critical analyses. Rhetorical analysis has also raised anew the question of the genre and focus of each of Paul's letters. The disagreements described above with regard to the purpose of 1 Thessalonians 2:1-12, for instance, have come increasingly to be described in rhetorical terms.

*5.2. The Authorship of 2 Thessalonians.* Many scholars working with the Thessalonian letters have concluded that though Paul and his coworkers wrote 1 Thessalonians to the Thessalonian Christians, a post-Pauline Paulinist wrote 2 Thessalonians, using the genuine letter as a model. The arguments for this view have usually been centered around an understanding of 2 Thessalonians as a conscious correction of an overheated apocalypticism partly inspired by the genuine letter. 2 Thessalonians 2:2 and 3:17 are regarded as attempts to cover the tracks of the forgery and to denounce 1 Thessalonians, and the direct appeal to apostolic authority in 2 Thessalonians 2:15 is seen as a mark of a post-Pauline setting.

But the difference in eschatology between the two letters has been exaggerated. That the parousia would be unexpected (1 Thess 5) and that signs would precede it (2 Thess 2) were, in fact, beliefs held together in the earliest church (e.g., Mk 13). 2 Thessalonians 3:17 would be, as a false claim to authenticity, far from convincing, since no other Pauline letter has anything like it. The appeal to apostolic authority in 2 Thessalonians 2:15 is not stronger, just more explicit, than what we find in 1 Thessalonians.

Trilling's influential arguments against Pauline authorship of 2 Thessalonians (see Trilling 1972) have shifted attention away from eschatology and the references to a previous letter and focused on other issues: (1) a number of stylistic and theological differences between 2 Thessalonians and 1 Thessalonians together with the other unchallenged Pauline letters, (2) the difference in tone between the two letters and (3) the lack of personal references in 2 Thessalonians.

The claim of 2 Thessalonians to be written by Paul and his coworkers still does not face any argument that, taken by itself, comes close to making post-Pauline authorship a compelling conclusion. Trilling's separate arguments, particularly that from stylistic differences, have carried little weight with some scholars who have examined them in detail. The different tone of the letters, which must be related to the lack of personal references in 2 Thessalonians, might point, not to different addressees, but to differing amounts of information about the same situation—which, under the assumption that both are Pauline, brings up the question of their chronological order.

*5.3. The Order of the Letters.* The canonical order (*see* Canon) of 1 and 2 Thessalonians matches the most-favored view of their chronological order, but is itself of no importance as an argument for it, being based simply on the length of the letters. What does matter is, first, the differences in how the same concerns are addressed in the two letters and, second, whatever clues about movements of people and letters can be found in the two letters. Is it more likely that the manner in which the concerns with eschatology and vagrancy are addressed developed from 1 to 2 Thessalonians, or the reverse? What shall we make of the references to persecution as, it seems, an experience of the past in 1 Thessalonians (1 Thess 1:6; 2:14; 3:3) but presently occurring in 2 Thessalonians (2 Thess 1:4-7)? Timothy no doubt carried some written communication with him on the journey described in 1 Thessalonians 3:2-8; was it what we call 2 Thessalonians? Or is 1 Thessalonians the letter mentioned in 2 Thessalonians 2:2? Has a deteriorating situation led from the friendly and grateful-to-God tone of 1 Thessalonians to the more "official" tone of 2 Thessalonians, or did a better understanding of the situation (through Timothy's report; cf. 1 Thess 3:6) lead to that more thankful tone?

Strong arguments can be built for the priority of both 1 Thessalonians (Jewett, 24-30) and 2 Thessalonians (Wanamaker, 37-45). Which came first is a question for which we do not have a clear answer. Therefore, we have no sure basis on which to build a theory of the setting of the letters. As is so often the case, what is available to us is the content of the letters and not knowledge of their origin in the amount that we might desire.

## 6. Early Pauline Theology.

Much of the value of 1 and 2 Thessalonians as documents of Pauline theology is based on their apparent closeness to Pauline mission preaching. The two letters are addressed to a church that has been in existence just a short time. Much of both letters speaks of the work of proclamation to which the church owes its beginnings, and little of their content is prompted by special situational concerns, at least in comparison with other letters of Paul. To a large extent they seek merely to encourage the members of the new Christian community in their new standing. Even where they do respond directly to special situational concerns—in the eschatological sections and in the words about the obligation to work—they do so in language that was probably used in the primary gospel proclamation and which is certainly no more than an expansion of themes in that proclamation.

1 Thessalonians 1:9-10 in particular allows us to see something of the general pattern of Paul's early preaching to Gentile audiences. The focus of this preaching was on the one God* and Jesus, the coming one, the mediator to humankind of divine redemption (cf. Acts 17:23-31; 1 Cor 8:6). The one God was essential to any Judaism, and the message of the apocalyptic end of the age was at home in much of Judaism, though, of course, the place of Jesus (see Jesus and Paul) in Paul's preaching went beyond most Judaism.

1 Thessalonians 1:9 also shows that Paul's preaching of Jewish monotheism (see God) included the standard Jewish polemics against pagan idolatry* (cf., e.g., Jer 10:1-10; Wis 13—15). This one God Paul identified as the "father" of Jesus and of Christians (e.g., 1 Thess 1:2-3, 9-10). Paul the preacher also spoke of Jesus' death (1 Thess 1:6; 2:15; 5:10; see Cross, Theology of the), resurrection* (1 Thess 1:10; 4:14) and expected eschatological return (1 Thess 1:10; 2:19; 3:13; 5:23—these references apart from the specific eschatological sections of both letters; see Eschatology). The main motivation given for accepting Paul's message (for "receiving the word of God," 1 Thess 2:13) was that faith in Jesus, "our Deliverer from the wrath* to come," is the way of escape from coming divine judgment* (1 Thess 1:10; 5:9; 2 Thess 2:13).

Though the letters do not make explicit any developed christology,* Jesus, "the Lord," is placed alongside God the Father as the source of the Thessalonian church's existence (1 Thess 1:1; 2 Thess 1:1), as the guide of the apostolic mission (1 Thess 3:11) and as the giver of Christian comfort and hope* (2 Thess 2:16). He is also seen as a model member of the suffering people of God (see Imitation), along with the prophets, the apostles and the Thessalonian Chris-

tians (1 Thess 1:6; 2:15). But his suffering and death have a greater significance: it is that which brings about believers' eternal life* "together with him" (1 Thess 5:10, 17).

This prospect of life with Christ (2 Thess 2:1-2) sets apart Christians as people who have hope (1 Thess 4:13, 18). This life will begin with the divine initiative in Jesus' descent from heaven* and the archangel's call (1 Thess 4:16; cf. 1 Cor 15:52); believers who have died will be resurrected and those living will be lifted up into the clouds so that both may share life with him (1 Thess 4:14-17; 5:10). This, the coming of Jesus and "our assembling together with him" (2 Thess 2:1), will be preceded by a manifestation of evil so great that it will attempt to take the place of God himself as the one who is worshipped, backing its claims with miracles and so convincing nonbelievers (2 Thess 2:3, 9-10; see Man of Lawlessness and Restraining Power). Such evil is already at work, though its effectiveness is now limited (2 Thess 2:6-7). When it does come to its full manifestation, it will do so only as part of God's plan for judgment (2 Thess 2:11-12) and only to be destroyed by Christ in his coming for believers (2 Thess 2:8).

Christ's coming will be unexpected by unbelievers, and no timetable can be set for it (1 Thess 5:1-3). For believers it is not only the focus of hope but also the fundamental motivation for right living and the building up of the community (1 Thess 5:4-11). Nothing in the details of Paul's moral exhortations to the Thessalonians is distinctively Jewish or Christian; all of it could be found among Gentile preachers and moral philosophers of the time (see Malherbe 1987; see Ethics; Virtues and Vices). But for Paul the basis of ethical exhortation is different: It is God's call "into his own kingdom and glory*" (1 Thess 2:12; cf. 2 Thess 1:11), God's will (1 Thess 4:3), knowledge* of God through the Christian proclamation (1 Thess 4:5) and expectation of God's ("the Lord's": perhaps Jesus') judgment (1 Thess 4:6). The call was to holiness* (1 Thess 4:3-4, 7; cf. 5:23) and to a relationship with God enjoyed by those who partake of his Spirit* (1 Thess 4:8; 5:19; 2 Thess 2:13).

Faith in the gospel had brought about a community that was to be focused on mutual love (1 Thess 3:12; 4:9; 2 Thess 1:3) and admonition (1 Thess 5:11; 2 Thess 3:15). The spread of the gospel to new areas was a major concern of the church and, even more, of its missionaries (1 Thess 1:8-9; 2 Thess 3:1). The letters grant little insight into the church structures that had emerged by this early stage, but Paul makes clear that both the missionaries and the local leaders were regarded as having authority* in the lives of believers. A significant function of both local and apostolic leaders was providing ethical example and exhortation (1 Thess 2:11-12; 5:12-13; 2 Thess 3:4, 14-15), but this responsibility was borne also by the rank and file of church members (1 Thess 5:11).

The centrality in Paul's theology of the suffering* of the proclaimers of the gospel, particularly of Paul himself, apparently received much of its formation in connection with the church of Thessalonica (see especially 1 Thess 2 and cf. in particular 2 Cor 10—13; Phil 3; Gal 4:12-19; 5:11). Imitation is the link between those coming to faith and their suffering leaders and predecessors in the faith (1 Thess 1:7; 2:14; cf. 2 Thess 1:4), and suffering is the inevitable experience of both the preachers and the Christian community (1 Thess 3:3-4).

*See also* ESCHATOLOGY; MAN OF LAWLESSNESS AND RESTRAINING POWER.

BIBLIOGRAPHY. **Commentaries:** F. F. Bruce, *1 and 2 Thessalonians* (WBC; Waco, TX: Word, 1982); I. H. Marshall, *1 and 2 Thessalonians* (NCBC; Grand Rapids: Eerdmans, 1983); L. Morris, *The First and Second Epistles to the Thessalonians* (NICNT; Grand Rapids: Eerdmans, 1959); B. Rigaux, *Saint Paul: Les Epîtres aux Thessaloniciens* (EB; Paris: Gabalda, 1956); W. Trilling, *Der zweite Briefe an die Thessalonicher* (EKK; Neukirchener-Vluyn: Neukirchener, 1980); C. A. Wanamaker, *1 and 2 Thessalonians* (NIGTC; Grand Rapids: Eerdmans, 1990). **Studies:** J. M. Bassler, ed., *Pauline Theology* Vol. 1: *Thessalonians, Philippians, Galatians, Philemon* (Minneapolis: Fortress, 1991); R. F. Collins, *Studies on the First Letter to the Thessalonians* (BETL 66; Louvain: Peeters/Louvain University); K. P. Donfried, "The Cults of Thessalonica and the Thessalonian Correspondence," *NTS* 31 (1985) 336-56; J. G. Gager, "Some Notes on Paul's Conversion," *NTS* (1981) 697-704; R. F. Hock, *The Social Context of Paul's Ministry: Tentmaking and Apostleship* (Philadelphia: Fortress, 1980); F. W. Hughes, *Early Christian Rhetoric and 2 Thessalonians* (JSNTSS 30; Sheffield: JSOT, 1989); R. Jewett, *The Thessalonian Correspondence: Pauline Rhetoric and Millenarian Piety* (FF; Philadelphia: Fortress, 1986); L. T. Johnson, "The New Testament's Anti-Jewish Slander and the Conventions of Ancient Polemic," *JBL* 108 (1989) 419-41; G. Lyons, *Pauline Autobiography: Toward a New Understanding* (SBLDS 73; Atlanta: Scholars) 177-221; A. J. Malherbe, "Exhortation in First Thessalonians," *NovT* 25 (1983) 238-56; idem, " 'Gentle as a Nurse': The Stoic Background to 1 Thess. II," *NovT* 12 (1970) 203-17; idem, *Paul and the Thessalonians: The Philosophical Tradition of Pastoral Care* (Philadelphia: Fortress, 1987); W. Meeks, *The First Urban Christians: The Social World of the Apostle Paul*

(New Haven: Yale University, 1983; B. A. Pearson, "1 Thessalonians 2:13-16: A Deutero-Pauline Interpolation," *HTR* 64 (1971) 79-94; D. Schmidt, "1 Thess 2:13-16: Linguistic Evidence for an Interpolation," *JBL* 102 (1983) 269-79; W. Schmithals, *Paul and the Gnostics* (Nashville: Abingdon, 1972) 123-218; J. W. Simpson, "Problems Posed by 1 Thessalonians 2:15-16 and a Solution," *HBT* 12 (1990) 42-72; W. Trilling, *Untersuchungen zum zweiten Thessalonicherbrief* (Leipzig: St. Benno, 1972). J. W. Simpson Jr.

**THESSALONICA** *See* THESSALONIANS, LETTERS TO THE.

**THIS AGE.** *See* ESCHATOLOGY; WORLD, COSMOLOGY.

**THORN IN THE FLESH.** *See* HEALING, ILLNESS; SUFFERING; VISIONS, ECSTATIC EXPERIENCE.

**TIMOTHY, 1 AND 2.** *See* PASTORAL LETTERS.

**TITUS.** *See* PASTORAL LETTERS.

# TONGUES

The phenomenon called "tongues" is mentioned by Paul only in the catalog of charisms (*charismata*, "gifts") found in 1 Corinthians 12:8-10 and in the ensuing discussion regarding its proper use in 1 Corinthians 12—14 (*see* Gifts of the Spirit).

1. Terminology
2. The Prevalence of Tongues in the Early Church
3. Tongues at Corinth

**1. Terminology.**
Generally, this "gift of the Holy Spirit*" is represented in the NT by the combination of the verb *laleō*, meaning "to speak," and the noun *glōssa*, especially in its instrumental case, meaning "in," or "with," "tongues" (cf. 1 Cor 12:30; 13:1; 14:5, 18, 23, etc.). Occasionally Paul also employs the participial forms *ho lalōn glōssē* or *ho lalōn glōssais* when referring to the person or "the one who speaks in a tongue or tongues" (cf. 1 Cor 14:2, 4, 5, 6, 13, etc.). The modern anglicized version of these terms has yielded the term *glossolalia*.

In 1 Corinthians 12:10 the phrase *heterō genē glōssōn* has been translated as "various kinds of tongues" (so the RSV and NRSV), "different kinds of tongues" (so the NIV, which also always supplies the alternate reading of "languages" for "tongues"), "divers kinds of tongues" (AV/KJV and ASV), and even "ecstatic utterance of different kinds" (NEB). The diversity in translations of the noun *glōssa*, from the generic "tongue" to the alternate reading "language," or the interpretation "ecstatic utterance," represents the diversity of presuppositions embraced by various translation committees. The reading "languages" suggests that the Pentecost event described in Acts 2:5-11, in which the crowd heard the 120 speaking in various human languages (*xenolalia*) other than their own, provides the background for this reading. On the other hand, the translation "ecstatic utterances" reflects the conclusions of modern social-scientific studies (e.g., Samarin, Kildahl; cf. Gundry).

Those within the classical Pentecostal movement, as well as the charismatic renewal, speak in tongues, but only very rarely has there been sufficient documentary evidence to substantiate xenolalic claims. Social-scientific study, while not necessarily denying the legitimacy or benefit of certain modern glossolalic claims, tends to view them in terms of psychological and/or sociological influences (e.g., Malony/Lovekin). Paul's mention of the "tongues of mortals and of angels*" in 1 Corinthians 13:1 (NRSV) makes possible this wide variety of interpretations for *glōssais lalein*. Cultural, historical and theological biases against present-day claims for xenolalia undoubtedly influence such diverse translations as well.

## 2. The Prevalence of Tongues in the Early Church.

That Paul does not mention speaking in tongues in any letter other than 1 Corinthians has given rise to two possible yet conflicting explanations. Either (1) this phenomenon was so widespread among NT churches that Paul saw no need to mention it except where it was being abused (at Corinth), or (2) Paul chose not to mention this "problematic" charism to the Romans (Rom 12:6-8) or the Ephesians (Eph 4:11) when he addressed other charismatic phenomena, because he did not want to encourage the use or spread of this gift. Those who argue for the widespread presence of this charism appeal not only to the presence of tongues in Corinth, but to such passages as Acts 2:1-4 (Jerusalem), Acts 10:44-48 (Caesarea) and Acts 19:1-6 (Ephesus). Paul's expression of thankfulness for his own experience of speaking in tongues (1 Cor 14:18; though some commentators see this as irony), as well as his desire that all would speak in tongues (1 Cor 14:5), are also used to develop this case.

Those who argue that Paul did not care to see this charism spread to other congregations cite Paul's preference for intelligible prophetic phenomena (1 Cor 14:1-5, 18-19) alongside his silence on the subject where it might otherwise have seemed to be appropriate (e.g., Rom 12; Eph 4). Evidence from the patristic period suggests that while speaking in tongues did occur in many places, the church, in keeping with Paul's greater concern for the edification of the Christian community, generally encouraged prophetic activity over speaking in tongues.

## 3. Tongues at Corinth.

*3.1. The Corinthian Situation.* The Corinthian context provides a unique opportunity for a case study of speaking in tongues in the early church. Several facts are clear from Paul's discussion of this charism. First, it is apparent that the Corinthians placed a high value on speaking in tongues. Paul's repeated attempts to provide a meaningful context for the appropriate manifestation of this gift point clearly in this direction. Beginning in 1 Corinthians 12:1 he appears to borrow the vocabulary of the Corinthians by turning their attention to matters concerning *ta pneumatika*, literally to "the spirituals" (i.e., "spiritual persons") or "spiritual things." But Paul quickly redirects the focus away from *pneumatika* toward the *charismata*. This shift takes the emphasis off the one who manifests such "spiritual things" (*pneumatika*), with its implication that the individual is "spiritual" simply because he or she manifested these phenomena. Instead, it sets the emphasis on the giver of these *pneumatika* since they are in fact *charismata*, "manifestations of grace*" (1 Cor 12:4).

Second, Paul repeatedly demands that any manifestation of speaking in tongues within the congregation must also receive an interpretation. He does this by mentioning "speaking in tongues" in tandem with its complementary gift *hermēneia glōssōn*, the "interpretation of tongues" (1 Cor 12:10), and by making explicit the importance of using both charisms together (1 Cor 14:5, 13, 27). Furthermore, the fact that he illustrates repeatedly the fruitless nature of an uninterpreted outburst of tongues in a public setting (1 Cor 14:2-4; 6-12; 13-19; 23-25) suggests that the presence of uninterpreted tongues in the Corinthian community was indeed the central concern of his address. A simple retreat into a glossolalic utterance was no clear demonstration of one's spirituality. On the contrary, within the community context it was a selfish act which denied others the ability to enter fully into that experience which, if interpreted, was intended to build up the entire community of believers.

Genuine spirituality* would be demonstrated in more subtle ways. Speaking in tongues, as Paul describes it, is a genuine manifestation of God's grace, which is sovereignly bestowed by the Holy Spirit (1 Cor 12:8-11). But speaking in tongues is only one among a number of such manifestations. For someone to insist upon the gift of tongues as if it were the only legitimate charism of the Spirit is for that person to deny the legitimacy of other Christians who manifest other equally legitimate charisms but do not speak in tongues. Paul's question "Do all speak in tongues?" (1 Cor 12:30) is more than simply rhetoric. It anticipates a decidedly negative response. Speaking in tongues is, indeed, a legitimate manifestation of the Spirit who gives it to various members of the body of Christ. Paul's use of this metaphor, the body of Christ (*see* Body of Christ), for the community of faith in 1 Corinthians 12:12-27, is significant because it suggests that any legitimate expression of the charism within that body should (1) point toward the giver rather than toward its recipient, since it is a manifestation of divine grace; (2) be exercised according to the law of love* (1 Cor 13:1—14:1); and (3) seek the greatest good by contributing to the edification of those in whose presence it is manifest (1 Cor 14:2-5; 12-19). Apart from love, the ability to speak in tongues is a decidedly unspiritual act (1 Cor 13:1).

*3.2. Paul's Instruction.* In order to redirect the thinking of his Corinthian audience, which was clearly given over to divisive behavior of several types, Paul encouraged them to live up to their calling as saints (1 Cor 1:2) by uniting together with a singleness of mind and purpose (1 Cor 1:10). He reflected on the theological character of speaking in tongues, and he set forth some general guidelines for its most fruitful use, describing its use in the context of his important metaphor of the body of Christ.

*3.2.1. The Value and Limitation of Tongues.* Paul recognized from first-hand experience that the ability to speak in tongues was a good thing. He claimed to speak in tongues himself (1 Cor 14:18), and he coveted such an experience for all those to whom he addressed this letter (1 Cor 14:5). He understood that the very act of speaking in tongues edified the one who engaged in it (1 Cor 14:4). After all, they were addressing God (1 Cor 14:2) even though it be in mysteries.* This gift was a type of prayer,* prayed in a preconceptual or transrational mode (1 Cor 14:14; cf. Montague), which when properly interpreted could enable the community of faith to bless, thank or praise God in a truly Spirit-inspired way (1 Cor 14:15-17). The parallels between this passage and Romans 8:26-27 have led many to suggest that some speaking in tongues may also be intercessory in nature and that Paul had speaking in tongues in mind when he penned Romans 8:26-27 (cf. Käsemann).

In spite of its value, the gift of tongues had distinct limitations as well. In an ultimate sense, it had only a temporary value. Unlike love, the ability to speak in tongues will ultimately come to an end (1 Cor 13:8).

Exercised apart from love it could become nerve shattering (as a gong or cymbal, 1 Cor 13:1), a boastful, arrogant, rude, selfish and irritating expression of insensitivity to the community (1 Cor 13:4-7). Exercised in community but without an appropriate interpretation, any manifestation of speaking in tongues, whether by an individual or in concert by the entire Christian community, would lead to confusion (1 Cor 14:17, 23). And God* is not a God of confusion but a God of peace* (1 Cor 14:22).

*3.2.2. Guidelines for Exercising the Gift.* For the gift of tongues to be exercised to its fullest intended potential, Paul maintains that certain basic guidelines should be considered. The manifestation of grace bestowed by the Holy Spirit should reflect the character of the giver. If God is a God of peace, then the use of this gift should reflect that quality. It should not contribute to division or confusion, or to insensitivity to the needs of others. Indeed, the exact opposite should be true. It should contribute to unity and understanding, and it should be exercised in ways that are sensitive to the needs of others. Exactly how did Paul envision this?

The fact that Paul chose the metaphor of the body of Christ to describe the Christian community worked in his favor. This metaphor was consistent with his recognition that believers are called to *koinōnia*, often translated as "participation in" or "in fellowship with," a concept central to what it means to live as disciples of Jesus Christ* (1 Cor 1:9). It was an idea to which Paul had appealed repeatedly in 1 Corinthians 10:14-22, and in light of which he had observed that while everything was lawful, it was not necessarily beneficial or edifying, and that those who were called into *koinōnia* should seek the advantage of "the other" (1 Cor 10:23-24). There should not be dissension within the body (1 Cor 12:25a), but rather edification (1 Cor 14:12), peace (1 Cor 14:33), decency and order (1 Cor 14:40). Paul did not favor abandoning the gift of speaking in tongues on any grounds (1 Cor 14:39). To do so would surely make him guilty of something he did not condone, namely, quenching the Spirit (1 Thess 5:19), who sovereignly chose to bestow this charism upon certain individuals within the body of Christ (1 Cor 12:11). But he did believe that there was a need to recognize that any manifestation of a charism in or through an individual involved a cooperative effort between the Holy Spirit and the recipient of the charism (*see* Worship). Pauline theology makes it clear that while the ability of an individual to speak in tongues may bring personal edification (1 Cor 14:4), that individual should participate with the Spirit for the greater good of the congregation by choosing to limit his or her own action in certain ways.

No legitimate claim could be made that the Holy Spirit had simply overpowered the one who spoke in tongues. This is clearly evident in several ways. There appears to be something akin to a "prophetic consciousness" in those who speak in tongues, a consciousness which permits them to start and stop at will. Paul's observation that the spirits of the prophets* are subject to the prophets (1 Cor 14:32) appears to apply equally well to those who speak in tongues. The fact that (1) limitations can be placed upon the number of people who should speak in tongues during any particular meeting of the Christian community (generally no more than two or three), that (2) they can each take their turn in an orderly fashion, and that (3) they can choose to be silent, speaking quietly to God (1 Cor 14:27-28), all seem to indicate that those who speak in tongues are in complete control of their faculties. They can make conscious decisions regarding their behavior, and they can act in ways that ultimately contribute to the overall good of the community.

Paul's guidelines, which he claims are nothing less than a "command of the Lord" (1 Cor 14:37), place primary responsibility for "speaking in tongues" squarely on the shoulders of the speaker. The person who has the ability to speak in tongues also possesses the power to bring about confusion or to build up anyone who is present when he or she exercises that charism. Paul's repeated exhortation to do that which builds up and to be ruled by love may be the key to the whole of 1 Corinthians (cf. 1 Cor 8:1). Just as the church is not to forbid speaking in tongues (1 Cor 14:40), so too the person who manifests this gift is to act only in a manner which benefits the whole church as well as the outsider who may be present (1 Cor 14:1, 5, 12, 26, 40).

If an interpreter is not present, but a person believes that he or she has been inspired to speak in a tongue, that individual has two legitimate alternatives which will benefit the church:

(1) The person can take responsibility to ask God for the ability to interpret (1 Cor 14:13). Requesting the charism which would render the utterance in tongues intelligible to the community does not necessarily mean that the gift will be given. The Spirit who distributes such charisms is, after all, sovereign over their bestowal (1 Cor 12:11). But if the need is genuine and the Spirit chooses to intervene, there is clearly no harm in asking. For one to do so is not to be guilty of presumption. The congregation might ultimately be edified (1 Cor 14:5).

(2) The speaker can silently pray to God (1 Cor 14:28) a prayer which brings edification to the speaker and addresses God, but does not contribute to disorder and confusion in the congregation. The fact that Paul mentions such an option has led some to regard speaking in tongues as having a legitimate role as a private "prayer language" (e.g., Hayford).

The latter use of this gift, expressed without the need for interpretation because it does not intrude into the life of the community in the same way as would a loud vocal expression, may well be Paul's intent. Paul's own speaking in tongues may in fact have been expressed most frequently in precisely this silent manner. He celebrated the fact that he spoke frequently in a tongue (1 Cor 14:18), but his personal preference was not to do so within the context of a community meeting (1 Cor 14:19). This clearly suggests that when Paul spoke in tongues it was in a nondisruptive manner when he was in a community setting or in private as part of his personal devotional life.

The one exercise of tongues that Paul clearly condems as illegitimate is the very thing the Corinthian Christians seem to have embraced—speaking in tongues for the sake of speaking in tongues, without interpretation and without regard for the life and participation of the community.

According to Paul, speaking in tongues also has value as a "sign." The Corinthians thought tongues played a positive role as a sign of spirituality. Paul, on the other hand, was much more concerned about the potentially negative role the otherwise good gift could play apart from its appropriate context and practice. In Israel's past "strange tongues" had served as a sign of God's judgment. Paul's citation of Isaiah 28:11-12 in 1 Corinthians 14:21 was intended to provide a specific example of this. When the Assyrians overwhelmed Judah, their foreign tongue in the presence of Judah could be viewed as nothing less than God's judgment on Judah's unfaithfulness. So too, for a stranger to enter a meeting in which the babbling of strange tongues was being manifest apart from any interpretation, the very act of speaking in tongues held the potential of confirming that unbeliever in a failure to discern any presence of God (1 Cor 14:23). The judgment by the stranger or outsider that these people were mad rather than that God was present could prevent the stranger from further contact with these people, and ultimately serve as a negative sign of judgment upon the stranger.

It is important to note that nowhere does Paul argue that speaking in tongues is anything other than a *charism*, a gift of the Holy Spirit; Paul does not talk, as do many modern-day Pentecostals, of speaking in tongues as a sign or evidence of baptism in the Spirit. Within the context of 1 Corinthians 12—14 Paul does note that "in one Spirit we were all baptized into one body . . . and we were made to drink of one Spirit" (1 Cor 12:13), a clear indication that he has in mind the concept of conversion-initiation (so Dunn). On the whole, Pentecostals typically interpret this as a reference to the Spirit's role of placing believers into the body of Christ rather than as an outpouring of the Spirit by Christ (Brumback). As a result, they too insist that when Paul asks the question "Do all speak in tongues?" (1 Cor 12:30), he legitimately anticipates a negative response. All parts of the body of Christ are not to be understood as manifesting the same *charism* (1 Cor 12:14-27).

The insistence by many Pentecostals that the ability to speak in a tongue acts as a sign or the evidence of baptism in the Spirit that is available to all Christians (so Brumback) is not based upon Paul; rather, it relies heavily upon the writings of Luke, most notably upon Acts 2:1-39 (cf. also Acts 10:44-48; 19:1-6; and possibly Acts 8:9-19). This distinction does not differentiate between two *phenomenologies*; rather, it appeals to a single phenomenology with multiple purposes. Peter is understood to view speaking in tongues as a sign or evidence of the immanence of God's Spirit which has just been poured out, as the answer to Joel's prophecy (Acts 2:16-21 = Joel 2:28-32). Paul understood the gift of tongues also to point to the presence of God in grace, enabling the speaker to pray in a Spirit-inspired manner. When it was misused in public, however, it could act in a way which was contrary to its divine intent. It could become a sign of judgment against the unbeliever who interpreted it solely as a manifestation of madness (1 Cor 14:23). Paul's concern was that this charism be used in a positive, edifying manner, and not as a negative sign. As a result, when considering the proper conduct of Christians gathered for public worship Paul commended intelligible speech which involved the mind (1 Cor 14:19), and especially the gift of prophecy (1 Cor 14:1, 3-5).

In the end, Paul's discussion of speaking in tongues is clarified when we understand his concern that whenever any charism is manifest within the Christian community it is intended to build up that community. Any undue emphasis upon individual experience, flights of ecstasy or manifestations which are unintelligible to the whole community are to be avoided as misappropriations of God's grace in the life of the Christian community and as inconsistent with the very character of God who sovereignly bestows them upon various members of the church.

*See also* GIFTS OF THE SPIRIT; HOLY SPIRIT; PROPHECY, PROPHESYING.

BIBLIOGRAPHY. C. Brumback, *What Meaneth This?* (Springfield, MO: Gospel Publishing House, 1947); D. A. Carson, *Showing the Spirit* (Grand Rapids: Baker, 1987); D. Christie-Murray, *Voices from the Gods: Speaking with Tongues* (New York: Routledge & Kegan Paul, 1978); G. B. Cutten, *Speaking with Tongues* (New Haven: Yale University, 1927); J. D. G. Dunn, *Jesus and the Spirit* (Philadelphia: Westminster, 1975); G. D. Fee, *The First Epistle to the Corinthians* (NICNT, Grand Rapids: Eerdmans, 1987); R. G. Gromacki, *The Modern Tongues Movement* (Philadelphia: Presbyterian & Reformed, 1967); R. H. Gundry, "Ecstatic Utterance, NEB," *JTS* n.s. 17 (1966) 299-307; J. Hayford, *The Beauty of Spiritual Language* (Dallas: Word, 1992); E. Käsemann, *Perspectives on Paul* (Philadelphia: Fortress, 1971); M. T. Kelsey, *Tongue Speaking* (Garden City, NY: Doubleday, 1964); J. P. Kildahl, *The Psychology of Speaking in Tongues* (New York: Harper & Row, 1972); K. McDonnell and G. T. Montague, *Christian Initiation and Baptism in the Holy Spirit* (Collegeville, MN: Liturgical Press, 1991); H. N. Maloney and A. A. Lovekin, *Glossolalia: Behavioral Science Perspectives on Speaking in Tongues* (Oxford: Oxford University, 1985); R. P. Martin, *The Spirit and the Congregation* (Grand Rapids: Eerdmans, 1984); W. E. Mills, ed., *Speaking in Tongues* (Grand Rapids: Eerdmans, 1980); idem, *A Theological/ Exegetical Approach to Glossolalia* (Lanham, VA: University Press of America, 1986); G. T. Montague, *The Holy Spirit: Growth of a Tradition* (New York: Paulist, 1976); C. M. Robeck, Jr., "Tongues, Gift of," *ISBE* 4.871-74; W. J. Samarin, *Tongues of Men and Angels* (New York: Macmillan, 1972); R. P. Spittler, "Glossolalia," in *Dictionary of Pentecostal and Charismatic Movements*, ed. S. M. Burgess and G. B. McGee (Grand Rapids: Zondervan, 1988) 335-41; C. G. Williams, *Tongues of the Spirit* (Cardiff: University of Wales, 1981).

C. M. Robeck Jr.

**TORAH.** *See* JEW, PAUL THE; LAW; WORKS OF THE LAW.

# TRADITION

Like Jesus, Paul contrasted human tradition (*paradosis*) with revelation from God* (Col 2:8; Gal 1:14; cf. Mk 7:8-9, 13). Still, Paul's letters show us that the apostle* valued and used traditions, including those he inherited from the OT,* from the sayings of Jesus,* and from the creeds,* hymns* and catechisms of early Christian communities. For Paul, the Spirit* did not supplant traditions, but supplemented their application, guided their production, and spoke through their use.

1. Tradition and Revelation
2. Use of Tradition

## 1. Tradition and Revelation.

Paul insisted that he received his gospel* and other revelations from God (Gal 1:11-12, 15-17; 2:2; 2 Cor 12:1-7), but the content of his faith did not differ essentially from the faith of those who were Christians before him. After his conversion* he preached the faith he once sought to destroy (Gal 1:23; cf. Gal 2:6-9; 1 Cor 15:11). His emphasis on divine revelation in Galatians* came in response to those who insisted on requiring Gentile* Christian converts to keep Jewish traditions (circumcision,* food* laws, etc.). Writing to those who esteemed revelations, Paul reminded the Corinthians* of the traditions he had passed on to them (1 Cor 11:23; 15:3-11). He believed that the Spirit of the risen Lord* spoke through Christian traditions, including his own teachings (Cullmann). Paul admonished his readers to hold fast the traditions they had received from him (2 Thess 2:15; 3:6) and he commended his readers for doing so (1 Cor 11:2; cf. 1 Thess 4:1; Col 2:6-7). Many scholars (e.g., Wegenast) conclude that the emphasis in the Pastoral* letters on teaching (*didaskalia*) and keeping/guarding traditions reflects a post-Pauline situation, although more recent research has increasingly shown the profound influence and importance of tradition for Paul (Ellis; *see* Pastoral Letters).

## 2. Use of Tradition.

Although Paul used semi-technical Jewish terminology for receiving (*paralambanō* = *qbl*) and delivering (*paradidōmi* = *msr*) traditional material, he did not simply transfer his former rabbinic approach to the Christian message. Convinced of the Spirit's guidance, Paul rarely felt the need to quote his predecessors. Confidence and freedom in the Spirit (e.g., 2 Cor 3:17) led him to adapt earlier traditions in order to speak more directly to his congregations. This makes it difficult for us to identify precisely where he used traditions (apart from recognizable quotations), but subtle clues such as unusual vocabulary and theological emphases, changes in style, introductory formulae such as "Do you not know?" and tradition words such as "confess" or "testimony" can help us to isolate probable instances.

*2.1. OT Traditions.* Paul's letters indicate that he tended to cite the OT more frequently when writing to Jewish Christian congregations. He quoted it when establishing his gospel of grace* (over against others' insistence on the keeping of Jewish particulars) and when providing examples or summaries of moral teachings (Gal 5:14; Rom 13:9; 15:4; 1 Cor 10:11). For Paul, the OT was not so much the interpreter of Christ, but rather Christ became the hermeneutical key for his use of the OT (e.g., Gen 15:6 in Gal 3 and Rom 4; cf. 2 Cor 3:14-17). Paul fully accepted the authority of the OT; where he appears critical of the Law,* like Jesus he is responding to others' misuse of it. Whether he had a "testimony book" of messianic proof texts or simply shared in early Christian oral traditions of OT interpretation remains an open question (*see* Old Testament in Paul).

*2.2. Jesus Traditions.* Although like all other early Christian writers (apart from the Evangelists) Paul rarely alludes to Jesus' teachings (1 Cor 7:10; 9:14; 11:23-24; 1 Thess 4:15-17) and example (Rom 15:3; Phil 2:5-8), his letters echo a number of dominical sayings (e.g., 1 Thess 5:2-3; 1 Cor 13:2; Rom 12:14; 13:8-10; 14:14). The silence is not due to ignorance or a lack of interest (Thompson). Paul knew Jesus' teachings as such and distinguished between them and the inner promptings of the Spirit (1 Cor 7:12, 25), but he did not use the traditions as a new law (*see* Jesus, Sayings of).

*2.3. Christian Traditions.* Paul inherited a number of specifically Christian traditions, such as liturgical* (?) acclamations and confessions (1 Cor 12:3; Phil 2:11; Rom 10:8-9), creedal* formulations (1 Cor 15:3-5; Rom 1:3-4; 3:24-26; 4:24-25?; 1 Thess 1:9-10?; 2 Tim 2:8; cf. Rom 6:17) and hymns* (Phil 2:6-11; Eph 5:14; Col 1:15-20?). Paul's moral teaching or paraenesis (as found in, e.g., Rom 12:1—15:13; Gal 5:1—6:10; 1 Thess 4:1—5:22; Col 3:1—4:6) contains traditions from several sources, including Cynic and Stoic moralists, Jewish *halakah*, and dominical teachings, but most likely also reflects early Christian catechetical material (Selwyn). The authority of the Spirit within himself and other Christians (1 Cor 2:12-13; 14:31, 37) offered yet another source of traditions. Prophecies were tested, apparently by their coherence with fundamental traditions received from Jesus, the OT and the prior witness of the Spirit in the Christian community (1 Thess 5:20-21; 1 Cor 14:29).

*See also* CREEDS; HYMNS, HYMN FRAGMENTS, SONGS, SPIRITUAL SONGS; HOUSEHOLDS AND HOUSEHOLD CODES; JESUS, SAYINGS OF; LITURGICAL ELEMENTS; LORD'S SUPPER; OLD TESTAMENT IN PAUL; TEACHING/PARAENESIS.

BIBLIOGRAPHY. F. F. Bruce, *Tradition: Old and New* (Exeter: Paternoster, 1970); K. Chamblin, "Revelation and Tradition in the Pauline *Euangelion*," *WTJ* 48 (1986) 1-16; O. Cullmann, "The Tradition," in *The Early Church*, ed. A. J. B. Higgins (London: SCM, 1956) 59-99; E. E. Ellis, "Traditions in I Corinthians," *NTS* 32 (1986) 481-502; R. P. C. Hanson, *Tradition in the Early*

*Church* (London: SCM, 1960); A. M. Hunter, *Paul and His Predecessors* (rev. ed.; London: SCM, 1961); G. E. Ladd, "Revelation and Tradition in Paul," in *Apostolic History and the Gospel*, ed. W. W. Gasque and R. P. Martin (Grand Rapids: Eerdmans, 1970) chap 14; J. I. H. McDonald, *Kerygma and Didache: The Articulation and Structure of the Earliest Christian Message* (SNTSMS 37; Cambridge: University Press, 1980) 101-25; E. G. Selwyn, "On the Inter-Relation of I Peter and Other N.T. Epistles," in *The First Epistle of St Peter* (London: Macmillan, 1946) 365-466; M. B. Thompson, *Clothed with Christ: The Example and Teaching of Jesus in Romans 12.1—15.13* (JSNTSS 59; Sheffield: JSOT, 1991); K. Wegenast, *Das Verständnis der Tradition bei Paulus und in den Deuteropaulinen* (WMANT 8; Neukirchen, 1962); idem, "Teach," *NIDNTT* 3.759-75.

M. B. Thompson

**TRANSFORMATION.** *See* CREATION AND NEW CREATION; PSYCHOLOGY.

## TRAVEL IN THE ROMAN WORLD

One of the most important contributions to civilization made by the Roman Empire was the establishment of an elaborate and comprehensive network of travel and communications. Recent developments in archeological techniques have meant that our knowledge of the construction of roads and ports in the Roman world is greatly enhanced. The construction of roads connecting the far reaches of the Empire and the regularization of sea lanes undoubtedly helped facilitate the spread of the gospel by the followers of Jesus Christ. In a very real sense the *Pax Romana* could be seen as a divine preparation for the evangelistic activity of the church (*see* Mission).

Paul, as the "apostle to the Gentiles," was perhaps the most traveled person within the NT world and benefitted enormously by the ease of travel in the Roman Empire (*see* Paul in Acts and Letters). Assuming for the moment that he made the three missionary journeys from Antioch (Acts 13:1—21:17), the trip to Rome (Acts 27:1—28:16) and several other minor excursions, we arrive at a total distance covered of approximately 6,200 miles. The apostolic ministry of Paul was aided by the travel and communication links in the Roman world on three distinct fronts.

1. Overland Roads and Highways
2. Sea Routes
3. Postal Services

### 1. Overland Roads and Highways.

There is certainly a truth in the words of the adage "All roads lead to Rome." To highlight this point, it is worth noting that Dio Cassius (*Hist.* 54.8.4) tells us that in 20 B.C. the emperor Augustus constructed a "Golden Milestone" (*miliarium aureum*) in the Forum in Rome and that official distances were calculated from it. The Roman world was crisscrossed by a network of some 50,000 miles of main military highways and approximately 200,000 miles of secondary roads (over 4,000 milestones along the principal roads of the Empire have been recorded). Many of the most famous of these roads have their origins in public building projects and bear the name of their benefactor. One of the first was the Via Appia running south from Rome to Capua, begun by Appius Claudius in 312 B.C. These roads became the main thoroughfares for movements of Roman legionaries and later served as important trade routes for goods throughout the Empire. Their construction was of such high standards that many of them still survive today and form the basis of many modern transport systems.

The most common means of travel on the network of overland roads would have been by foot, making a good day's journey about twenty miles. Travel by animals, either by riding them or in a drawn carriage, would have yielded a rate of about five to six miles per hour.

Many of the main trade highways were used by Paul in his travels, such as the Egnatian Way which connected the Adriatic Sea with the East. Paul followed a portion of this highway in his second and third missionary journeys as he traveled from Neapolis to Philippi* and Thessalonica.* In Acts 28:14-16 we are told that Paul followed the Via Appia into Rome following his landing at Puteoli.

Paul occasionally uses travel imagery in describing the Christian journey of faith* (as in 1 Cor 12:31 and 1 Thess 3:11). In 2 Corinthians 8:19 he applies the designation "traveling companion" (*synekdēmos*) to an unnamed colleague (the same term is used in Acts 19:29 of Gaius and Aristarchus, the Macedonian companions of Paul).

### 2. Sea Routes.

The emperor Augustus (27 B.C.-A.D. 14 ) declares in *Res Gestae* 25, "I made the sea peaceful and freed it of pirates." The problem of piracy in the Mediterranean was a long-standing one which perplexed both imperial interests and those of local areas alike. Nevertheless, by the NT period, with the establishment of permanent Roman fleets at Misenum, Ravenna and elsewhere, a sense of stability in the matter had been won, and the sea lanes were open for both travel and commercial traffic (Starr gives details of this). The use of sea routes was especially important for the transport of food, such as corn from Egypt, to the major centers of population like Rome* and Antioch. The sea lanes were the commercial arteries of the Roman Empire and many coastal cities, like Tyre, Caesarea and Ostia (serving the city of Rome), were dependent upon the sea traffic.

Several kinds of ships were used for travel in the NT period. Warships, including biremes and triremes, were fitted with banks of oars and manned by rowers as an important means of locomotion. Most commercial ships were sailing vessels and were dependent on the winds and weather in their journeys, with winter travel being particularly hazardous. For reason of safety most sea voyages were undertaken during the day, with regular stops at night; this meant that established sea routes tended to follow coastlines. The main trans-Mediterranean route was the grain run from Rome to Alexandria, a journey of about 1,000 nautical miles which could be negotiated in approximately ten or twelve days. The return route for these ships, because of the prevailing winds of the Mediterranean, tended to follow the coast of Phoenicia, Asia Minor and Greece and could take up to two or three months (Casson 1971, provides table charts of distance, times and speeds based on Pliny's *Nat. Hist.* 19.3-4).

Paul made use of travel by sea in all four of his major journeys. His longest journey by sea was that from Caesarea to Rome. According to Acts 27:1—28:16 Paul traveled on a series of merchant sailing ships in this journey, which took him around Cyprus, Rhodes, Crete, Malta (where he was shipwrecked) and Sicily before landing in Italy. We gain some index to the hazards presented by sea travel from hints contained in 2 Corinthians 11:23-27. Coins of the ancient world remain one of the most interesting primary sources of information about the ships and harbors of the time, including places with which Paul almost certainly would have been familiar (Kreitzer).

Philo's *Embassy to Gaius* offers an interesting parallel to Paul's journey to Rome. It gives details of a journey made by a Jewish leader so as to appear before Caligula in A.D. 39 and present the case of the persecuted Jewish population in Alexandria to the emperor.*

### 3. Postal Services.
The organization of regular and reliable routes of travel also aided the establishment of a regular postal system in the Roman world (Casson 1974, discusses this at some length). The apostle Paul, along with others, was able to use this to great effect in maintaining contact with his friends and delivery of his letters to the recipient churches (*see* Letters). Timothy, Tychichus and Epaphroditus are all described as couriers of Paul in this regard (1 Thess 3:2; Col 4:7; Phil 2:25).

*See also* ITINERARIES, JOURNEYS, APOSTOLIC PAROUSIA.

BIBLIOGRAPHY. L. Casson, *Ships and Seamanship in the Ancient World* (Princeton: University Press, 1971); idem, *Travel in the Ancient World* (London: George Allen & Unwin, 1974); T. Cornell and J. Matthews, *Atlas of the Roman World* (Oxford: Phaidon, 1982); D. French, "The Roman Road System of Asia Minor," *ANRW* II.7.2.698-729; L. J. Kreitzer, "Nero's Rome: Images of the City on Imperial Coinage," *EvQ* 61 (1989) 301-10; S. V. McCasland, "Travel and Communication in the NT," *IDB* 4.690-93; A. McWhirr, "Transport by Land and Water," in *The Roman World*, ed. J. Wacher (2 vols.; London: Routledge & Kegan Paul, 1987) 2.658-70; W. M. Ramsey, *St. Paul the Traveller and the Roman City* (14th ed.; London: Hodder & Stoughton, 1920); G. Rickman, *The Corn Supply of Ancient Rome* (Oxford: Clarendon, 1980); C. G. Starr, *The Roman Imperial Navy (31 B.C.-A.D. 324)* (Cambridge: W. Heffer, 1960).                                          L. J. Kreitzer

**TRAVEL PLANS.** *See* ITINERARIES, TRAVEL PLANS, JOURNEYS, APOSTOLIC PAROUSIA.

**TRIALS.** *See* AFFLICTIONS, TRIALS, HARDSHIPS.

## TRIUMPH
The theme of triumph in Paul may well be rooted in the OT theme of God as a divine warrior. In the OT this theme encompasses the broader aspect of cosmic conflict, but more frequently it occurs in the context of God's covenant* relationship with Israel* and so-called holy warfare. It is a theme that demanded resolution in Paul's understanding of the climax of God's dealings with Israel, the nations and the cosmos. It is part of the subtext, or implied story, that lies beneath the situational discourses of Paul's letters and occasionally it appears in a variety of contexts and metaphorical extensions.

1. The Triumph of the Divine Warrior in the OT
2. The Triumph of the Divine Warrior in Judaism and in Paul
3. Triumph over Principalities and Powers
4. Triumph over Sin, Flesh, Law and Death
5. Triumph at the End of the Age
6. Prisoners and Soldiers of Christ

### 1. The Triumph of the Divine Warrior in the OT.
The main features of the theme of Yahweh as a divine warrior may be summarized under three headings.

*1.1. The Divine Warrior's Triumphs on Behalf of Faith-*

*ful Israel.* The archetype of Yahweh's warfare against Israel's enemies was the deliverance of Israel from bondage in Egypt, in which Yahweh overcame the imperial forces of Egypt and, by implication, Egypt's gods. The Exodus was celebrated in the "Song of Moses," where the hymnic celebration of Yahweh's victory over Pharaoh's army includes the acclamation "Yahweh is a warrior!" (Ex 15:3). Yahweh's covenant with Israel at Sinai was the covenant of a heavenly suzerain with his people, sealed by the promise of blessing and victory for Israel's faithfulness, and of curse and defeat for Israel's unfaithfulness. Within Israel's traditions a vocabulary of imagery and symbolism was employed to speak of the divine warrior and his work. For example, Yahweh is depicted as riding his cloud chariot (e.g., Ps 68:4; 104:3-4; Is 19:1; cf. Dan 7:13), a feature found also in the Canaanite Baal texts (cf. *ANET*, 134). In the Book of Numbers a prevailing image of the people of God is Israel as the army of God on the march to take the land of promise. The ark of the covenant, possibly representing Yahweh's footstool or portable throne, symbolized the presence of Israel's heavenly warrior-king as he encamped in Israel's midst and led the people through conquest to the land of their inheritance and his sacred mountain sanctuary, Zion (cf., e.g., Ex 15:17; Num 10:35-36). The wars of faithful Israel were occasions in which Israel (e.g., Deut 20), the heavenly army (e.g., 2 Kings 6:17) and creation (e.g., Josh 10:1-15; Judg 5:19-21) took part, but such warfare was clearly the divine prerogative, and it was Yahweh who led Israel into battle and brought the victory (e.g., Gen 14:19-20; 15:1; Josh 10:40; Judg 5:4-5; cf. 1QM 11:4-5).

*1.2. Yahweh Fights Against Unfaithful Israel.* The divine warrior's judgment against unfaithful Israel (Lam 2:5; Amos 2:6-16) was the reflex of the covenant blessing of victory in the shape of a covenant curse in which Yahweh deployed Israel's enemies to defeat his people (cf. Deut. 28:15 and 28:7; Is 10:5-19). In the wars of conquest it was illustrated by Israel's defeat by Ai (Josh 7). But its most poignant expression was the reversal of the Exodus, Judah's defeat and exile at the hands of the Babylonians. This was Yahweh's "strange deed" (Is 28:21), when the Lord rose up and turned his warrior's strength against his own people, who had continued in their unfaithfulness.

*1.3. The Coming Day of Triumph.* A final stage of the divine warrior's activity is the Day of the Lord. This is the sovereign warrior's day of conquest, in which Yahweh will defeat Israel's enemies, even those who formerly acted as the rod of his wrath (e.g., Assyria, Is 10:5-19). On this day he will restore Israel and inaugurate new dimensions of the covenantal blessings

of land, community and divine presence. It is a conflict and triumph that will transcend the limits of Yahweh's former battles. The outcome, memorably portrayed later by Isaiah as a new Exodus (e.g., Is 40:1-5), would encompass the future of the nations and the emergence of a new creation. Israel, a disciplined and restored new Adam, will enter a blissful life of shalom in a new paradise, with the nations subdued (Is 60—66). Yahweh's universal and glorious sovereignty will be manifested visibly (Is 60:1-3; 62:1-2), and all evil will be subjected to the *ḥērem*, or "ban," of Yahweh's war (Is 63:1-6; 66:15-16, 24).

### 2. The Triumph of the Divine Warrior in Judaism and in Paul.

The Judaism in which Paul was raised knew this story well and, at least by some contemporary accounts, there were those who placed Israel in the paradoxical situation of being resident in the land of promise and yet still in exile, under Gentile dominion (*see* Restoration of Israel). For Jews who held this perspective the restoration of Israel had not yet occurred, the curse had not yet been exhausted, and Israel awaited the definitive triumph of God in which he would defeat the nation's enemies, resurrect his "dead" nation and usher in the age to come. The several Judaisms of Paul's day were not of one mind regarding how the Day of the Lord might be enacted, whether as the exclusive act of the divine warrior or by the agency of his Messiah, or a principal angel such as Michael or Melchizedek (11QMelch), or by some combination thereof (e.g., the Qumran *War Scroll*). But the hope of a future day of divine conquest and vindication of Israel was widely and popularly held.

Paul's understanding of Messiah Jesus was that God* in Christ* was reconciling (*see* Peace, Reconciliation) the world to himself and effecting a new creation* (2 Cor 5:17-19). The gospel was the revelation of the eschatological righteousness* of God, God's covenant faithfulness, by which he was powerfully setting the world right (Rom 1:17) and revealing his wrath* (Rom 1:18). Both aspects of God's work were presently operative and revealed to the eyes of faith; both aspects would be manifested clearly at the end of the age.

Paul's story of the triumph of God in Christ is portrayed in two episodes: the past event of his death/resurrection and the future hope of the Day of the Lord (*see* Eschatology). Christ in his death and resurrection engaged the enemy,* was victorious in an epochal battle (Col 2:15; cf. Col 1:12-14), and was exalted to God's right hand, where he reigns as cosmic Lord* (1 Cor 15:24-26; Phil 2:9-11; Col 3:1; Eph 1:20-22;

1 Tim 3:16). Like the divine warrior in the OT (and the pattern of divine conflict and triumph in ancient Near Eastern mythology), Christ's conquest is followed by building his new temple* (1 Cor 3:16-17; 2 Cor 6:16; Eph 2:19-22) and receiving universal praise and obeisance (Phil 2:10-11; *see* Worship). He will come again at the end of the age and seal his triumph over his enemies, who will have waged a final revolt (2 Thess 2:8). In the end death, the final enemy, will be defeated along with every other hostile power, and Christ will hand over his kingdom* to God (1 Cor 15:24-28). But in the meantime the people of the Messiah live between these two episodes and are engaged in eschatological warfare, enjoying the benefits and advantage of Christ's defeat of the enemy at the cross (Rom 8:37) and yet beset by a hostile foe (Eph 6:10-17) as they await their Lord to descend from heaven* on the final day (1 Thess 4:16-17).

This story of conflict and triumph presumes the existence and power of enemies, and Paul selected and fashioned a rich vocabulary to describe them in their various aspects. These enemies consisted not of Romans or Greeks, but of sin,* flesh,* death (*see* Life and Death), Law,* principalities* and powers, and a Satanically inspired enemy called the "man of lawlessness."*

### 3. Triumph over Principalities and Powers.

In Paul's story of salvation* the principalities and powers are equivalent to the enemy "nations" of Israel's story, seen from the perspective of cosmic warfare (*see* Principalities and Powers). The spiritual powers, or "demons,"* that Israel had understood as standing behind the nations and their gods (Deut 32:8-9, 17; Dan 7; cf. *Sir.* 17:17; *Jub.* 15:31-32) were now conceived as the opponents of Christ and his people.

*3.1. Enemies Under His Feet.* In speaking of Christ's triumph over the powers Paul adopts the image of the triumphant Davidic king seated at the Lord's right hand with Israel's flesh-and-blood enemies depicted as a footstool for his feet (Ps 110:1). Moreover, Paul builds on a Jewish self-understanding of Israel as God's new Adam* (e.g., 1QS 4:23; CD 3:20; 1QH 17:15; see Wright, 23-25) in the divine plan to redeem the cosmos, and he understands Christ as representing this new Adam/Israel.* Because the Davidic king represents Israel, when Paul speaks of the exalted Christ he freely combines the imagery of the triumphant Davidic Messiah (Ps 110:1) with that of the reigning "Adam" under whose feet God has placed "all things" (Ps 8:6). In Jewish apocalyptic interpretation of history the nations, as the enemies of God and Israel, could be depicted as "beasts," eventually to be brought into subjection to Israel's vice-regency over God's new creation (cf. Dan 7, where monstrous beasts represent Gentile empires and the Adamic "son of man" represents Israel). Thus in 1 Corinthians 15:22-28 Paul can compare Christ with Adam and then speak of Christ's triumph over the powers, in one breath alluding to the subjection of the "enemies" of Psalm 110:1 and "everything under his feet" from Psalm 8:6 (cf. Eph 1:19-22 and Col 3:1-11; in the latter an allusion to Ps 110:1 leads into the theme of the new humanity/Adam in Christ; cf. Heb 1:3, 13; 2:8; 1 Pet 3:22). All of this is set within the context of the eschatological work of God in which the effects of Adam's "death" are reversed by "resurrection,"* and a new cosmic order emerges. The divine purpose of creation is vindicated in the eschatological triumph. Thus the Pauline theme of the exaltation* and enthronement of Christ symbolizes the triumph of God in Christ.

*3.2. Triumph at the Cross.* Colossians 2:15 is the text where Paul most clearly alludes to the event of Christ's triumph over the powers. Here we find one of the two occasions (cf. 2 Cor 2:14) in which Paul uses the verb *thriambeuō.* This verb is correctly translated "lead in triumphal procession," for it is the Greek term for leading a Roman triumphal march (Latin *triumpho*) in which a victorious general or ruler in ceremonial dress would drive his captives—usually those who formerly had authority and power—and the spoils of war before him into Rome (see Hafemann, Versnel, Williamson; cf. Egan). Having arrived at the god's temple, the prisoners, or representatives of their number, would be executed. In this processional the glory and power of the Roman *imperium* was celebrated, with the triumphant general made up as Jupiter, the god who had blessed the warrior with victory in battle (cf. Josephus *J.W.* 7.5.6 153-55). But although the foreground imagery of Colossians 2:15 is Greco-Roman, its substructure seems to be the Jewish archetype of the divine warrior vanquishing his foes.

In 1 Corinthians 2:6-8 Paul alludes to the story behind the scene of the victory at the cross: the "rulers of this age" did not comprehend the mystery of the divine wisdom of the cross, "for if they had, they would not have crucified the Lord of glory." *Archontes,* "rulers," a term commonly used of human rulers (so Rom 13:3), here refers to spiritual, cosmic powers (cf. LXX Dan 10; *see* Principalities and Powers). These hostile spiritual powers were oblivious to the wisdom of God's plan for the ages (cf. Eph 3:10) and so they crucified the Lord of glory. This was their monumental folly, and Colossians 2:15 alludes to the circumstances of their defeat.

Colossians 2:14-15 speaks of what happened at the

cross. The subject of these two verses, we would argue, is Christ (see Yates). A crucial issue in understanding Colossians 2:15 is the meaning of the verb *apekdysamenos* (the aorist participle of *apekdyomai*, "to strip"). This verb should be understood as a true middle in voice (intransitive, with the subject acting upon itself), meaning Christ stripped himself of something (not an active, transitive verb, as some commentators maintain). The verb occurs twice in Colossians, here in Colossians 2:15 and in 3:9, and its related noun, *apekdysis*, occurs once (Col 2:11); these words occur nowhere else in the NT. In Colossians 2:11 the noun *apekdysis* speaks of the believer's circumcision* in the "stripping off [*apekdysis*] of the body of flesh," a metaphorical removal of flesh in some manner, called the "circumcision of Christ." This circumcision (with *Christou* as an objective genitive) most likely refers to Christ's death* on the cross, in which believers participate by baptism (Col 2:12). In Colossians 3:9 Paul uses *apekdysamenoi*, indisputably as a true middle participle, to refer to something that takes place in the experience of believers: those who are in Christ are to undergo an ethical renewal (Col 3:8), logically implied in their having "taken off" their old humanity (*ton palaion anthrōpon*, Col 3:9) and having "put on" (*endysamenoi*) their new humanity in Christ (Col 3:10; cf. *ekdyō* in 2 Cor 5:4 [5:3 in some MSS] used of taking off "this tent" [= body] at death). It seems unlikely that Paul would use *apekdysamenos* in Colossians 2:15 in the active sense (Christ stripping the powers of weaponry, power etc.), for Christ's action on the cross would seem to form the basis for Paul's appeal in Colossians 3:8-9. In their participation with Christ believers too have "stripped off" their old humanity. But many commentators do not understand Colossians 2:15 in this way and read *apekdysamenos* in the active, transitive, sense, suggesting that Christ divested the powers of their authority or weapons.

How could Christ have stripped himself of the powers—as if they were a garment? An unstated premise seems to stand behind this text. It was Christ's body* that was nailed (*proseloō*, Col 2:14) to the cross (metaphorically portrayed as a "hand written document" *cheirographon*), and his body was the very point at which his divine nature met in solidarity with Adam (see Lightfoot, 190; Robinson, 34-48). Indeed, twice previously in Colossians Paul has spoken of Christ as the one in whom "all the fullness [of God] was pleased to dwell" (Col 1:19; 2:9, with minor variations). This is a christological application of language alluding to Yahweh's taking up residence in Israel, on Mount Zion (cf. Deut 12:5; LXX Ps 67[68]:16, where it is the divine warrior who chooses for his residence

Mount Zion]; Sir 24:3-12; *see* Fullness).

In terms of the story of Israel, recapitulated and brought to a climax in Christ, we may conceive Paul's thinking as follows: The powers unleashed their assault on Christ's body, in a climactic expression of the nations attacking Zion, and on the cross they destroyed his "body of flesh" (Col 2:11; cf. Scott, 34-35). But this was a pyrrhic victory. Christ absorbed and exhausted their fury in his death (with his vindication in the resurrection implied) and so he triumphed over the powers (Col 2:15). In his death as obedient second Adam, Christ represented Israel under the curse, and thereby he stood in for humankind. The powers unwittingly played their part in executing the divine plan; their attack on the faithful and guiltless representative of Israel was their defeat, and Christ marched them in his own triumphal procession on the cross, publicly displaying (*edeigmatisen en parrēsia*, Col 2:15) their defeat and exposing them to shame. All of this may suggest Paul's familiarity with the early Christian tradition that Jesus spoke of the destruction of "this temple," "his body" (Jn 2:18-22), a saying perhaps garbled in the charge brought against Jesus at his trial and in the mocking at the cross (cf. Mk 14:57-58; 15:29-30; Mt 26:61; 27:40). In shifting from the imagery of Christ as "temple" to that of "body," Paul exchanged the metaphor of destruction for that of circumcision—a cutting off of flesh (cf. "not made by hands," *acheiropoiētos*, Mk 14:58; Col 2:11; 2 Cor 5:1, speaking of the heavenly "house" ["temple"?]). The imagery, on this reading, is not gnostic* (though it was later adopted by gnostic interpreters, see *Gospel of Truth* 20.20-30), but a thematic transposition of Jesus' reference to himself as temple and his death as its destruction.

The metaphor of victory is, at its heart, not simply the victory of a superior power, but the triumph of holy, righteous and creative love* over the destructive forces of evil and the reclaiming of a creation gone astray. It is an eschatological victory to be sure, in which is demonstrated the apocalyptic* judgment of the cross on all human sinfulness and the pretense of spiritual powers, and in it redemptive history is brought to a climax. But Paul elsewhere makes plain that the cross was not the last chapter in the warfare against the powers of this age. The enemy is still hostile and active, posing a threat to the church (Eph 6:10-18). On the final day this battle will reach its resolution when "every dominion, and every authority and power will be destroyed," along with the final enemy, death (1 Cor 15:24, 26; cf. 2 Tim 1:10). Such is the story of triumph as Paul saw it spelled out in Christ's salvific act. But in Paul's Hellenistic mission he was able to apply it to situations where the practice of magic, or the worship of angels,* or the grip of local or astral deities held people in fear and bondage (e.g., Eph, Col; see Arnold 1989). It is notable that many of the passages in Paul that speak of Christ's conquest or triumphant enthronement have been identified (with varying degrees of plausibility) as pre-formed hymnic* praises of Christ (Eph 1:20-22; 2:14-16; Phil 2:6-11; Col 2:14-15; 1 Tim 3:16). This suggests that, like Israel, early Christians associated with the Pauline mission celebrated the triumph of Christ in their worship,* and hailed a (future) eschatological event as present reality.

### 4. Triumph over Sin, Flesh, Law and Death.

Four powers—sin, flesh, Law and death—constitute the Pauline perspective on the human plight viewed from within the history of Israel as the story of the world. Sin entered the world through the first Adam, and death through sin. Israel, the new Adam, had been given the Law at Sinai. But no sooner had the Law been given, than sin was operative in Israel, and death struck down thousands in the wilderness. In the end sin, working through the Torah, brought death to Israel. In the course of Israel's history this death was spelled out, as with Adam and Eve, in forced exile from the divine presence and the Edenic land. The paradox of Israel's existence is this: though Israel was to be the agent of salvation for the world, it too became trammeled in sin and death by the very gift of divine Law (Wright, 193-216). This story lies behind Paul's narrative of sin, flesh, death and Law in Romans 5—7, in which they seem to function as person-ified forces opposed to divine redemption. The reign of sin and of death are intertwined, with sin reigning in death (Rom 5:21) and sin the "master" over human-kind, the "slave" (Rom 5:6, 14). Moreover, sin finds its foothold in the flesh (Rom 6:12; cf. 8:7), and its sol-diers wield "weapons" (*hopla*) of wickedness rather than weapons of righteousness (Rom 6:13; 2 Cor 6:7). Sin preys on people, awaiting the opportunity to make the Law a "bridgehead" (*aphormē* in Rom 7:8 can carry this military sense) into humans and so "wages war" (*antistrateuomai*, Rom 7:23) and "takes prisoners" (*aichmalōtizō*, Rom 7:23). Those caught in the bondage of these powers cry out, like Israel in lament, for a deliverer; thankfully, deliverance comes through "Je-sus Christ our Lord" (Rom 7:24-25; cf. 1 Cor 15:57). In Christ believers "are more than conquerors through him [Christ] who loved us," a love that no earthly or cosmic power can sever (Rom 8:37-38).

God initiated the deliverance by sending his own Son in the likeness of sinful flesh (*sarx*, Rom 8:3; cf.

Col 2:11), and in so doing the Son entered sin's sphere of dominion. But when sin pressed its claim upon Christ, he, being guiltless, condemned sin in the flesh. So Christ, coming as the Last Adam, conquered sin on its own ground and reversed the condemnation sin had brought upon Adam (Rom 5:18). The "con-demning" of sin may refer to the execution of judg-ment in the decisive defeat of the power of sin in the death of Christ. This drama of deliverance is similar to the new Exodus motif found in Galatians 1:4 (". . . who gave himself for our sins to rescue us from the present evil age") and Colossians 1:13-14 (". . . who rescued us from the dominion of darkness and trans-ferred us into the kingdom of his beloved Son, in whom we have redemption, the forgiveness of sins").

*4.1. Death.* The theme of death (*see* Life and Death) as a personified enemy is found in ancient Near East-ern mythology, where death could be viewed as a hos-tile cosmic power in the drama of divine conflict. Paul draws on an OT expression of this mythic theme when in 1 Corinthians 15:54-55 he taunts death by adapting lines from Hosea 13:14. But Paul introduces Hosea with a line from Isaiah 25:8, "Death is swal-lowed up in victory" (see commentaries for Paul's ad-aptation of Isaiah). These words are drawn from a hymn of thanksgiving that follows Isaiah's vivid pic-ture of the divine warrior's epiphany on the Day of the Lord (Is 24). In Isaiah these words follow shortly after a description of Yahweh's defeat and punishment of "the powers in the heavens above and the kings on the earth below" (Is 24:21). Paul's use of Isaiah 25:8 at this point supports his own ordering of eschatolog-ical events—the powers will be defeated first (1 Cor 15:24-25), and then death (1 Cor 15:26)—and further confirms that he is reinterpreting divine warrior tra-dition and identifying the principalities and powers with the nations and their gods. The divine conquest of death recalls the OT hymnic theme of the rejoicing and renewal of creation at the triumph of the divine warrior (e.g., Ps 98:4-9).

*4.2. Law.* The notion of the Law* being an "enemy" to be overcome is a paradox. Though Paul views the Law in and of itself as holy and good (Rom 7:12), when seen from the perspective of the human plight the Law serves and empowers sin (Rom 7:8, 11; 1 Cor 15:56). The Law increases the consciousness of sin (Rom 3:20), brings wrath (Rom 4:15), makes sin ev-ident (Rom 5:13) and abundant (Rom 5:20), and pro-vokes further sin (Rom 7:7-25). Within the experience of Israel it served to "heap up" and consolidate sin in one place, where it could be dealt with (Wright, 151-53, 196, 209). Sin perverted the Law, and what the Law was powerless to do, overcome the flesh, God did in sending his Son* (Rom 8:3). The Law was a circumstantial accomplice in a cosmic revolt. And within the polemical context of Galatians, the Law is seen to be "added because of transgressions" (Gal 3:19). It acts as a jailor (Gal 3:22-23) and works its curse* upon Israel (Gal 3:10). Such was Israel's history under the Law, a history which led to the covenant curse of exile under which the nation still languished when God sent his Son.

In Galatians 4:1-7 Paul employs a new Exodus typology. In the eschatological fullness of time God again delivered his people, this time not from bondage to Egypt but from enslavement to the Law and the elemental spirits (Gal 4:3-5). The thought is parallel with Galatians 1:4—"to rescue us from the present evil age." But just as significant is Paul's unique expression in Galatians 3:13 of Christ's death bearing the curse of this Law. The means of redemption is Christ's taking on himself the curse of the covenant (Gal 3:13). "Hanging on a tree" (Gal 3:13) though directly quoted from Deuteronomy 21:23 (in the context of capital punishment), is a practice also evident in Israel's conquest and dispatch of the kings of Canaan. In a reversal of that imagery, Paul speaks of Christ absorbing the curse, or *ḥērem*, of the divine warrior against Israel, and so bringing redemption for his people and in turn for the world. Christ (like a warrior king) died hanging on a tree in his own land, a death and exposure reminiscent of that of the king of Ai (Josh 8:29) and the five kings of the Amorites (Josh 10:26). Seen from the perspective of divine warfare, the picture is a strange reversal of the expected norm. The divine warrior's covenant curse fell upon this representative of Israel, God's Son, upon whom the sins of the nation had been accumulated—and for Paul this is to say that God in Christ absorbed the *ḥērem*, or covenant curse. Here is the eschatological climax of a theme deeply imbedded in covenant Law and the Prophets: the divine warrior against Israel (*see* Prophet, Paul as). From this act emerges a new creation (Gal 6:15) for the Israel of God (Gal 6:16). The exile and restoration of Israel were transmogrified into the death and resurrection of Christ (Wright, 145-48).

Ephesians 2:14-15 is the one other place in the Pauline corpus where the Law is cast as an enemy, and it is the only place where Christ is said to have "destroyed" (*katargeō*) the Law or "rendered it powerless" (cf. Rom 3:31). The Law is here likened to a "barrier," or "dividing wall of hostility," a reference to the role of the Law in forming a barrier of racial and ethnic hostility (Eph 2:14, 16) between Jews and Gentiles* (cf. *Letter of Aristeas* 139). Commentators frequently find an allusion here to the balustrade in the Jerusalem Temple, a wall that separated the court of the Gentiles from the inner courts of Israel. But this Temple wall, part of a microcosmic representation of Israel's view of the world (cf. *m. Kel.* 1:6-9; Dunn, 31-41), was a Torah-inspired spatial representation of the distinction between Israel and the nations. Yahweh dwelt on Zion, with Israel encircling his dwelling and protected by walls from the nations. This dividing wall, the "law of commandments and regulations," Christ "destroyed" (Eph 2:15), "killing" (*apokteinō*, Eph 2:16) the enmity "in his body" (Eph 2:16).

Jesus' death as temple destruction may once again form the background, but it is worth noting that the most frequent reference to walls in the OT is to military fortifications surrounding cities, walls that are either defended or assaulted and torn down during warfare (e.g., Jericho). Further, Paul has already referred to the Gentiles as those once "separated" from Israel and "aliens" to the covenants (Eph 2:12). By the old covenantal standards they were "uncircumcised," "strangers to the covenant of promise," "in the world" and outside the "commonwealth of Israel," the land of promise. As Gentiles "far off," they had been potential enemies of Israel, subject to the assault of Israel and her divine warrior should they reject an offer of peace (see Deut 20:10-15 and instructions for warfare with nations outside the land; cf. mission of the seventy, Lk 10:1-20). But now they had been brought "near" by the blood of Christ (Eph 2:13) who is "our peace" (Eph 2:14). The Law, which had separated foreigners from the promise of Israel and made distant Gentiles the object of covenant curse and warfare, had been assaulted and destroyed by God's Messiah. And this Messiah had come and proclaimed peace to those "far" (Gentiles, cf. Deut 20:10-15) and to those "near" (Israel, cf. Is 57:19; Eph 2:17). The result is a new creation seen now in "one new humanity" (*kainos anthrōpos*, Eph 2:15) and the building of God's new temple (Eph 2:19-22).

The ancient pattern of conflict, triumph and temple building is recapitulated, and Ephesians 4:8-9 seems to extend this story by telling how Christ has outfitted his temple-body for ministry (Eph 4:11-16). Reciting the words of Psalm 68:18 (a psalm replete with the themes of divine warfare), Paul applies the imagery of the victorious divine warrior's ascent to his mountain sanctuary, with captives in his victorious train, to Christ's victorious ascension to his heavenly home, with captives in his triumphal procession. But whereas the divine warrior of the psalm *receives* gifts, Christ *gives* gifts. This reinterpretation of the psalm may have been suggested by Jewish interpretation (cf. *Midr. Tᵉhillim* on Ps 68:11 and *'Abot R. Nat.* 2.2a, where

Moses ascends and *gives* the Law; see commentaries) and the use of Psalm 68 as part of the synagogal readings for Pentecost. But its use in Ephesians (and early Christian tradition? cf. Acts 2:32-36, where Ps 110:1 appears) fits nicely the larger Pauline plot of Christ's triumph.

### 5. Triumph at the End of the Age.

When Paul spoke of the Day of the Lord (e.g., 1 Cor 5:5; 1 Thess 5:2, 4; 2 Thess 1:10; 2:2) he quite naturally used the imagery of the divine warrior's day of triumph (*see* Eschatology). The *parousia*, or "arrival," of Christ was a christological interpretation of the coming of the divine warrior. The overall impression is of the Lord Jesus acting as the eschatological agent of God the Father (cf. 1 Cor 15:23-28; 1 Thess 1:10; 4:14, 16; 5:9; but cf. Tit 2:13; Kreitzer, 112-28). God acts in Christ, and so Paul can readily ascribe the imagery of the divine warrior to the coming of Christ. The visual imagery includes fire (2 Thess 1:7; cf. Ps 104:4; Is 29:6; 30:30; 66:15-16; Dan 7:9); angels, or "holy ones" (1 Thess 3:13; 2 Thess 1:7; cf. Deut 33:2; Zech 14:5; *1 Enoch* 1:9; Jude 14); and clouds, most likely an oblique reference to the cloud chariot of the divine warrior (Ps 68:4; Dan 7:13; Mk 13:26; cf. 2 Kings 2:11-12; see 1.1 above). The event of "meeting" (*apantēsis*) the Lord in the air (1 Thess 4:16-17) appears to be the greeting of Christ the arriving warrior to welcome and escort him in his triumphal approach (cf. Ps 68:24-35; Mt 25:6), as in the triumphal entry of Jesus into Jerusalem. The "loud command," the "call" of the archangel (1 Thess 4:16; cf. Josh 6:5; Judg 7:20; Zeph 1:16; 1 Macc 3:54) and the "trumpet call of God" (1 Cor 15:52; 1 Thess 4:16; cf. Num 10:9; Josh 6:5; Zeph 1:16; 1 Macc 3:54) all reflect a summons to battle. The cumulative picture recalls the processional of the divine warrior to his holy mountain and Temple to reclaim his territory. If 2 Thessalonians 2:3-12 should be understood as a continuation of this story, Christ finds on his arrival a usurping power seated in the "Temple of God" (2 Thess 2:3-4). This "man of lawlessness,"* who has led many astray by his counterfeit Parousia and is inspired by Satan* (2 Thess 2:9-10), is overthrown at the Parousia of Christ the divine warrior (2 Thess 2:8; cf. Is 66:6). This compressed episode in which the enemy is "destroyed" (*anaireō*) by "breath"/ "spirit" (*tō pneumati*; cf. 4 Ezra 13:10) and "annihilated" (*katargeō*) by "splendor" (*tē epiphaneia*) recalls the victory of the messianic conqueror of Isaiah 11:4 (cf. 1QSb 5:24) and is replete with images of divine warfare.

Paul is clear in speaking of humanity's enmity, or hostility, toward God (Rom 5:10; Col 1:21), a condition that makes them objects of divine wrath* (Eph 2:3; Col 3:6). It is from this condition that believers have been rescued by divine initiative (Rom 5:10; Col 1:21-22). But as God's people they now face opposition from his enemies (1 Thess 2:2, 14-15; cf. Rom 11:28). Presently the powerful, salvific righteousness of God is at work in the gospel (Rom 1:16-17), but so also is the wrath of God (Rom 1:18). In the end God's wrath will overtake with eternal destruction those who persist in their enmity, who "do not know God" and "do not obey the gospel* of our Lord Jesus" (2 Thess 1:8). This includes Jews who have actively resisted the advance of the gospel of Christ (2 Thess 2:16, in a dramatic reversal of the fate of the Amorites in Gen 15:16). But faithful believers "are not destined for wrath but for obtaining salvation" by virtue of Christ's work (1 Thess 5:9-10). They await the coming of the Son from heaven, who rescues them from the coming wrath (1 Thess 1:10; cf. 11QMelch 8-9, 13). At this point the imagery of divine triumph and sacrifice meet: the drawing down of the covenant curse, or warrior's wrath of God, on the representative of God's people, who takes upon himself their sin, will save his people from the coming wrath that will reach all who do not stand under the shield of divine grace.*

Ultimately, it is Satan who stands behind this human opposition, whether it be the ongoing opposition to the gospel (1 Thess 3:5) or the final revolt (2 Thess 2:9). Paul tells the Romans that God will "soon crush Satan under your feet" (Rom 16:20), an allusion to divine triumph in which he incorporates Adamic imagery (cf. Gen 3:16; Ps 8:6) and the hope of a new creation.

### 6. Prisoners and Soldiers of Christ.

The Roman triumph was an image that Paul not only applied to Christ's work on the cross, but also to his apostolic ministry. In 2 Corinthians 2:14 Paul speaks of himself as being led in the triumphal procession of Christ. Here Paul is not one of the high ranking officers in Christ's army, but is himself being led in triumph (*thriambeuonti hēmas*) as a former enemy and persecutor of Christ, who has been conquered and is now marched as a captive, being constantly led to his death (cf. 2 Cor 4:10; Hafemann, 16-34; Duff).

By this metaphor he sets forth the paradox of his apostolic ministry: in his weakness and cruciform suffering the power of the triumphant Christ is made manifest (2 Cor 12:10). The triumph of God in Christ is not the triumph of brute force, as if to assert a cosmic principle of "might is right." It is a triumph of grace in which divine love goes forth in sacrifice (see Moule). God in Christ has absorbed the divine judgment due Israel and the world, and the peace of a new creation is offered to Israel and the world in the word of the cross and the ministry* of the apostle* (*see* Cross, Theology of the).

Yet Paul can speak of himself as engaged in a battle. He fights "in truthful speech and in the power* of God [*en dynamei theou*]; with weapons [*hoplōn*] of righteousness in the right hand and in the left" (2 Cor 6:7). Or again, he wages war (*strateuometha*), but not as the flesh* does. The weapons (*hopla*) of his warfare (*tēs strateias*) have divine power (*dynata tō theō*) to demolish strongholds (*ochyrōmatōn*; cf. Prov 21:22 LXX), arguments and pretension, and he takes captive (*aichmalōtizontes*) every thought to make it obedient to Christ" (2 Cor 10:3-5). At Ephesus Paul "fought wild beasts" (*ethēriomachēsa*, 1 Cor 15:32), perhaps an allusion to battle with human opponents of the gospel, behind whom Paul perceives demonic "beasts" (Dan 7; *T. Naph.* 8:4, 6; *T. Jos.* 5:2; cf. Ex 23:29; Hanson, 120). This perception of gospel ministry as warfare is reflected in the title of Epaphroditus and Archippus as "fellow soldiers" (*systratiōtēs*, Phil 2:25; Philem 2), and in Paul's comparison of his "working for a living" to someone in military service (*strateuetai*) paying their own expenses (1 Cor 9:7). In the Pastorals* Timothy is encouraged to "endure hardship with us like a good soldier of Christ Jesus" (2 Tim 2:3-4). In three instances Paul uses the term *synaichmalōtos*, "fellow prisoner of war": in Romans 16:7 of Andronicus and Junia, in Colossians 4:10 of Aristarchus and in Philemon 23 of Epaphras. Whether this allusion refers to those who, like Paul, have been taken captive by Christ or have been taken captive (imprisoned) in the course of gospel warfare is uncertain, but the metaphor of warfare is clearly present (*see* Prison, Prisoner).

The imagery of warfare is of course applied to all believers, who in the period between the cross and Parousia face spiritual opponents. They are to be armed for warfare (1 Thess 5:8), offer their "members" as weapons of righteousness (Rom 6:13, 23) and put on the armor of light (Rom 13:12). Most memorably, in Ephesians 6:10-17 believers are to take on defensive spiritual armor and shield (cf. Gen 15:1, 6), and the offensive weapon of the "sword of the Spirit," in their conflict with the devil, principalities, powers and spiritual forces of evil. Although the terminology is borrowed from the Roman world, it is in essence the armor of Yahweh the divine warrior (Eph 6:13; cf. Is 58:16-18; Wis 5:17-20), and the battle is engaged in "his mighty strength" (Eph 6:10).

*See also* DEATH OF CHRIST; DEMONS AND EXORCISM; ENEMY, ENMITY, HATRED; ESCHATOLOGY; EXALTATION AND ENTHRONEMENT; LAW; MAGIC; POWER; PRINCIPALITIES AND POWERS; PROPHET, PAUL AS; RESTORATION OF ISRAEL; SATAN, DEVIL; WRATH, DESTRUCTION.

BIBLIOGRAPHY. C. E. Arnold, *Ephesians: Power and Magic: The Concept of Power in Ephesians* (SNTSMS 63; Cambridge: University Press, 1989); idem, *Powers of Darkness: Principalities and Powers in Paul's Letters* (Downers Grove, IL: InterVarsity, 1992); G. Aulén *Christus Victor* (New York: Macmillan, 1969); J. C. Beker, *Paul the Apostle: The Triumph of God in Life and Thought* (Philadelphia: Fortress, 1980); M. Black, "πᾶσαι ἐξουσίαι αὐτῷ ὑποταγήσονται," in *Paul and Paulinism*, ed. M. D. Hooker and S. G. Wilson (London: S.P.C.K., 1982) 74-82; M. C. de Boer, *The Defeat of Death* (JSNTSup 22; Sheffield: JSOT, 1988); G. B. Caird, *Principalities and Powers: A Study in Pauline Theology* (Oxford: Clarendon, 1956); P. B. Duff, "Metaphor, Motif and Meaning: The Rhetorical Strategy behind the Image 'Led in Triumph' in 2 Corinthians 2:14," *CBQ* 53 (1991) 79-92; J. D. G. Dunn, *The Partings of the Ways* (Philadelphia: Trinity Press International, 1991); R. B. Egan, "Lexical Evidence on Two Pauline Passages," *NovT* 19 (1977) 34-62; S. J. Hafemann, *Suffering and Ministry in the Spirit: Paul's Defense of His Ministry in II Corinthians 2:14—3:3* (Grand Rapids: Eerdmans, 1990); A. T. Hanson, "Militia Christi," in *The Paradox of the Cross in the Thought of St. Paul* (JSNTSup 17; Sheffield: JSOT, 1987); L. J. Kreitzer, *Jesus and God in Paul's Eschatology* (JSNTS 19; Sheffield: JSOT, 1987); R. Leivestad, *Christ the Conqueror* (London: SPCK, 1954); J. B. Lightfoot, *St. Paul's Epistles to the Colossians and Philemon* (London, 1879); M. C. Lind, *Yahweh is a Warrior* (Scottdale, PA: Herald, 1980); T. Longman III, "The Divine Warrior: The New Testament Use of an Old Testament Motif," *WTJ* 44 (1982) 290-307; G. H. C. Macgregor, "Principalities and Powers: The Cosmic Background of Paul's Thought," *NTS* 1 (1954-55) 17-28; P. D. Miller, *The Divine Warrior in Early Israel* (HSM 5; Cambridge: Harvard University, 1973); C. F. D. Moule, "Reflections on So-called 'Triumphalism,' " in *The Glory of Christ in the New Testament: Studies in Christology in Memory of George Bradford Caird*, ed. L. D. Hurst and N. T. Wright (Oxford: Clarendon, 1987) 219-27; P. T. O'Brien, "Principalities and Powers: Opponents of the Church," in *Biblical Interpretation and the Church*, ed. D. A. Carson (Exeter: Paternoster, 1984); J. A. T. Robinson, *The Body: A Study in Pauline Theology* (SBT 5; London: SCM, 1952); H. Schlier, *Principalities and Powers in the New Testament* (New York: Herder & Herder, 1961); C. A. A. Scott, *Christianity According to St. Paul* (Cambridge: University Press, 1961); S. Versnel, *Triumphus* (Leiden: E. J. Brill, 1970); L. Williamson, "Led in Triumph: Paul's Use of *Thriambeuo*," *Int* 22 (1968) 317-32; W. Wink, *Unmasking the Powers: The Invisible Forces that*

*Determine Human Existence* (Philadelphia: Fortress, 1986); N. T. Wright, *The Climax of the Covenant* (Minneapolis: Fortress, 1992); R. Yates, "Colossians 2.15: Christ Triumphant," *NTS* 37 (1991) 573-91.

D. G. Reid

# TRUTH

A good deal of the discussion of truth centers on whether the NT writers followed the Hebrew idea, which stressed reliability, firmness and the like, or the Greek concept, in which the thought was that of reality as against appearance. For NT writers the antithesis is probably too sharply drawn, for they were heirs of both worlds. The only safe procedure is to study what they have said in their writings themselves and not to read them through Semitic or Hellenistic spectacles (see Thiselton).

Paul puts a good deal of emphasis on truth. He uses the noun *alētheia* forty-seven times, and eight times he uses the related words: the adjectives *alēthēs* ("true," "honest," "genuine" four times) and *alēthinos* ("true," "honest," "dependable"), the verb *alētheuō* ("tell the truth," "be truthful," twice) and the adverb *alēthōs* ("truly," "actually"). The noun *alētheia* occurs in every one of his letters except 1 Thessalonians and Philemon. He knows, of course, that truth is accuracy over against falsehood, and he can refer to speaking the truth just as we commonly do (Eph 4:25; 1 Tim 2:7; etc.). But more often he uses the word with a richer and fuller meaning.

1. The Truth of God
2. The Truth and the Gospel
3. Truth in Christian Living

## 1. The Truth of God.

On a number of occasions he refers to "the truth of God*" (i.e., God in his self-revelation, Rom 1:25; 3:7; 15:8) or "the truth of Christ*" (2 Cor 11:10); once he refers to speaking the truth in Christ (Rom 9:1). The judgment* of God is "according to truth" (Rom 2:2); human judgments might be biased according to class or creed, but with God truth is the only consideration. Paul speaks of the preachers as commending themselves "in the word of truth" which he immediately follows with "in the power* of God" (2 Cor 6:7). We should also consider here the apostle's recognition of "the form of the knowledge of the truth in the Law" (Rom 2:20). He denounced those who proclaimed salvation* by way of the Law,* but that did not prevent him from acknowledging the divine truth enshrined in the Law. Paul finds divine truth (which people reject) in creation as well as in Law (Rom 1:18-20).

Paul has an unusual expression when he says "as truth is in Jesus" (Eph 2:21). This is often rendered "the truth as it is in Jesus" (e.g., REB), but this is surely a misunderstanding. Paul is not saying that truth is many-sided and that he is concerned with that aspect of truth that we see in Jesus. Rather he is saying that real truth, ultimate truth, is to be found in Jesus and that we find it nowhere else. It is a claim that the revelation of truth in Jesus is utterly reliable. Often Paul has the thought that people have not received the truth. They suppress it in unrighteousness (Rom 1:18), exchange it for "the lie" (Rom 1:25). They refuse to obey it (Rom 2:8; Gal 5:7; 2 Thess 2:12). They did not receive a love for it and so lost salvation (2 Thess 2:10). Sinners turn away from truth (2 Tim 4:4; Tit 1:14). They are bereft of the truth (1 Tim 6:5). God has revealed the truth, indeed has sent his Son to live it and to proclaim it, but sinful people have refused to listen (*see* Sin, Guilt).

## 2. The Truth and the Gospel.

Paul can speak of "the word of the truth of the gospel*" (Col 1:5) and again of "the truth of the gospel" (Gal 2:5). He refers to "the word of truth, the gospel of our salvation" (Eph 1:13). The truth that is so closely bound up with God finds its expression here on earth in the gospel, which sets out the ultimate truths of the love* of God especially as shown in the cross,* the sinfulness of the human race, and the provision God has made for salvation. The gospel and truth are closely connected. This is so also in the passage in which Paul speaks of God's will for people "to be saved and come to the knowledge of truth" (1 Tim 2:4).

But while there is this clear revelation of the truth and this provision for sinners to be saved through the truth of the gospel, Paul regretfully sets forth the truth that sinners often refuse to receive the truth. They have missed it or turned from it (2 Tim 2:18). They resist it like Jannes and Jambres of old (2 Tim 3:8). Paul himself was "for the truth" and declared that he could not do anything against it (2 Cor 13:8), but he had to recognize that the sinners to whom he preached did not always emulate him. The truth of the gospel is real, but in the conditions of this world it is always possible for people to decline to receive it.

## 3. Truth in Christian Living.

English does not have a verb "to truth," but Paul uses such a verb, *alētheuō*, when he urges the Ephesians that " 'truthing' in love" they should grow in Christ in all things (Eph 4:15). We might understand this as "speaking the truth in love," but more probably we should see truth as a quality of action as well as of speech. Paul wants his converts to live the truth as well as to speak it.

Paul says that he himself speaks truth (2 Cor 7:14; 12:6), and of course he looks for a similar practice in his converts. He calls on the Corinthians to keep the feast (*pascha*, "Passover") "with the unleavened bread of sincerity and truth," which he contrasts with "malice and evil" (1 Cor 5:8). Just as the Jews cleared out all leaven before their Passover, so believers must be rid of malice and wickedness since Christ, their Passover, has already been sacrificed (*see* Sacrifice). He points out that love "rejoices with the truth" (1 Cor 13:6); real love can take no pleasure in falsehood and unrighteousness, but truth and love go together. "The new self" he says, "is created in righteousness and holiness of truth" (some MSS, "and truth," Eph 4:24; cf. "sons of truth" in Dead Sea Scrolls, e.g., 1QS 4:2; see Murphy- O'Connor, 208-10). The "belt of truth" is part of the Christian's armor (Eph 6:14; cf. Is 11:5); it protects against the attacks of evil (cf. 2 Cor 4:2). When Paul asks the Galatians who has prevented them from "obeying the truth" (Gal 5:7), he is referring to the "truth of the gospel" (cf. Gal 2:5, 14) for which he has just argued (Gal 2—4). The truth of the gospel does not merely call for intellectual agreement. It is to be obeyed and to characterize the new life in Christ (see Barclay, 94).

*See also* GOSPEL; KNOWLEDGE, GIFT OF KNOWLEDGE; WISDOM.

BIBLIOGRAPHY. J. M. G. Barclay, *Obeying the Truth* (Minneapolis: Fortress, 1991); R. Bultmann et al., "ἀλήθεια κτλ," *TDNT* I.232-51; H. Hübner, "ἀλήθεια κτλ," *EDNT* 1.57-60; J. Murphy-O'Connor, "Truth: Paul and Qumran," in *Paul and Qumran*, ed. J. Murphy-O'Connor (London: Geoffrey Chapman, 1968) 179-230; D. J. Theron, "*Alētheia* in the Pauline Corpus," *EvQ* 26 (1954) 3-18; A. C. Thiselton, "Truth," *NIDNTT* 3.874-902.

L. Morris

**TÜBINGEN SCHOOL.** *See* PAUL AND HIS INTERPRETERS.

**TYPOLOGY.** *See* ADAM AND CHRIST; MOSES; OLD TESTAMENT IN PAUL.

# U

**UNCIRCUMCISION.** *See* CIRCUMCISION; GENTILES; ISRAEL.

**UNCLEAN.** *See* PURITY AND IMPURITY.

## UNIVERSALISM

The notion that all intelligent, moral creatures (angels, humans, devils) will be saved in the end is called *universalism*. But commonly universalism refers specifically to the salvation* of all human beings. A number of Pauline texts have been thought to point toward universalism. Other Pauline texts speak of some perishing and have a particularistic understanding of salvation (restricted to the elect and/or believers). Some interpreters deal with this tension by trying to show how the universalistic sounding texts are compatible with the particularistic texts, or vice versa. Still others see inconsistency in Paul's statements, which they usually try to resolve in one of several ways. Any solution to the problem must first grapple with the exegetical issues involved in the key Pauline texts.

1. The Separation of the Saved and the Lost
2. The Universal Scope of Christ's Saving Work
3. Evaluating the Evidence

### 1. The Separation of the Saved and the Lost.
On the one hand, Paul thinks in terms of two possible ultimate destinies: to receive eternal life* and be with the Lord* forever, or to incur wrath, affliction and "eternal destruction," and to perish, be away from the Lord, and excluded from the kingdom (see, e.g., Rom 2:5-10; 5:9; Phil 1:28; 3:19; 1 Thess 1:10; 2 Thess 1:6-10; Gal 5:21). People will go to their respective destinies when Christ* returns in judgment.* Paul assumes that some *will*, not just *could*, perish. This thought is terrible for many modern readers to countenance, especially when conceived in terms of the eternal punishment of the lost. The phrase "eternal destruction" (*olethros aiōnios* ) at 2 Thessalonians 1:9, however, may not refer to eternal suffering but "destruction that lasts forever," or annihilation (Marshall 1983, 178-79).

Already the separation is taking place: some are being saved and others are perishing (1 Cor 1:18; 2 Cor 2:15; 4:3). The response to or rejection of the gospel* is the criterion for this separation. Those who believe in the gospel are saved; those who stumble over it in opposition and unbelief, whose minds are blinded by the god of this age (2 Cor 4:4; *see* Satan), perish. Without standing firm in the gospel one can have no assurance of salvation (Gal 5:2; cf. Rom 10:1-4; see Gundry Volf, 159-229; see E. Boring, 271-72, however, for a discussion of attempts to interpret such texts in a way compatible with universalism). The double outcome of judgment which we find in Paul as well as in the rest of the NT—the division of humanity into two groups consisting of the saved and the lost—corresponds to the OT-Jewish worldview: there are two ways, one leads to life, the other to death (e.g., Deut 30:15-20; Jer 21:8). Universalism is foreign to this thought world (Oepke, 392).

### 2. The Universal Scope of Christ's Saving Work.
Nevertheless, Paul's understanding of the comprehensiveness of the saving work of Christ leads him to make statements that appear to speak of a final restoration of all. (Contrary to the view initiated by Origen, the phrase *apokatastasis pantōn* in Acts 3:21 does not denote the conversion of all persons but the "restoration of all *things*" [for the sense of *pantōn* as neuter, see Oepke, 391], or the universal renewal of the earth, a hope of the OT prophets to be fulfilled through Jesus Christ at his Parousia, according to Peter's sermon.) Did Paul leave behind his inherited particularism and move toward universalism at a later stage? Does he really express the view that all will be saved? Did he hold more than one view at the same time?

*2.1. Romans 5:12-21.* Romans 5:12-21 probably offers the greatest potential support for universalism of any text in the undisputed Pauline letters. Referring to Christ's death,* Paul makes the following statements: "through the righteous act of one, unto [*eis*, i.e., results in] justification of life for [*eis*] all people" (Rom 5:18); "through the obedience of the one, the many will be made righteous" (Rom 5:19); "the grace* of God and the gift in grace, which is of the one man Jesus Christ, abounded to many" (Rom 5:15). The thrust of the passage is that the deed of one person fundamentally determined the nature of human existence. Adam's sin* resulted in the reign of sin and death for all. Christ's obedience to the point of death, on the other hand, resulted in the reign of grace and life for all. Both deeds have a universal effect, but Christ's is greater. Who are the "all" and "many" whom Christ's deed affects? How does it affect them? And how is Christ's deed greater than Adam's deed?

The universalist position takes "all" (*pantes*) literally and, seeing the parallelism between "all" and "many" in the text (see Rom 5:12, 15, 16, 18, 19), argues that "many" (*polloi*) is a Semitism with an inclusive, not exclusive, sense referring to all who are not a few in number (i.e., the many who cannot be counted, Jeremias, 536-45). By contrast, E. P. Sanders (473) takes "many" in Romans 5:19 to be a restrictive modification of "all" in Romans 5:18. The Adam/Christ analogy has pushed Paul to a stronger conclusion than he can maintain, for, while Adam's deed resulted in the sin and death of all, Christ's deed results in the salvation of *some*, as other texts in Paul indicate (*see* Adam and Christ).

Others explain Paul's universalistic language here in terms of the wider context of his argument: Christ is the universal Savior* of all, whether Jews or Gentiles. *All* refers not to individuals but to groups. And even if it is true that *all* individuals sin and die as a result of Adam's transgression, *not all* individuals are saved as a result of Christ's death—there is thus an asymmetry in Paul's argument. Since faith is necessary for salvation according to Paul (as Romans 4 has just made plain), the *all* affected by Christ's death here are presumed to be believers: "all in Christ," who have been "transferred" to the sphere of Christ by faith.* Paul may be thinking of all who belong to Christ who will be raised to eternal life at the end (cf. 1 Cor 15:22), but not of unbelievers raised in a general resurrection.*

In support of the view that Paul has *all believers* in mind, some point to Romans 5:17, where he describes those affected by Christ's death as "those who receive the abundance of grace and of the gift of righteousness." The participle *hoi lambanontes*, "those who receive," implies the decision of faith (Bultmann, 1. 302-3). Christ's death takes saving effect only in individuals who have faith in him. E. Boring (286-87), however, argues that the verb has a passive sense ("receive"), not an active one ("take"), and does not imply belief in the gospel. But I. H. Marshall (1990, 316-17)

refutes Boring, citing references in which *lambanō* is used in clear conjunction with faith (Gal 3:2, 14) and where *lambanō* implies the decision of the recipient (e.g., Christ's taking the form of a servant, Phil 2:7).

Rather than understanding the "all" who are saved by Christ's death to be all who are actually in Christ by faith, C. K. Barrett argues that for Paul there are two ways of looking at humanity: as "in Adam" and thus under condemnation, and as "in Christ" and thus justified. Both are "universal possibilities, and even universal actualities, in the sense that they point to a dialectical truth which is valid for mankind as a whole, and for each individual man" (Barrett 1958, 116-17; cf. Barth, 181-82). Since this explanation still does not tell us whether Paul thought all would be saved at the last day, Barrett adds that the resolution of the dialectical duality lies with the merciful God. Barrett thus implies universalism.

E. Käsemann incorporates both universalistic and particularistic aspects of Romans 5:12-21 into his interpretation. The era of Christ and the reign of life and grace has replaced the era of Adam, dominated by sin and death. Nevertheless, grace must be seized unceasingly in renunciation of the old aeon (Käsemann, 156-57). While the point of the text is justification for believers, the motif of all-powerful grace suggests that unbelievers will not remain outside the scope of salvation, as Käsemann sees other texts to imply (these will be discussed below). Eschatological universalism is implicit in Käsemann's remarks, for "cosmology overshadows anthropology" (similarly, Beker, 193).

It is debatable, however, whether Paul saw the greatness of God's grace to imply universalism. Romans 11:32 does state God's intention "to have mercy on all," but the context clearly indicates that Paul is thinking of people groups: both Jews and Gentiles. No people is beyond the scope of God's grace, though all are shut up to disobedience. And Romans 5:15 says that grace abounded to all, but Paul seems to mean by this that grace was more than enough to deal with all of human sin and put a stop to the universal power of death, and that all can avail themselves of this abundant grace (Rom 5:17). The superiority of Christ's deed in comparison with Adam's (*pollō mallon*, "much more," Rom 5:15) consists in its replacing death with life. Of course Paul also makes the point that Christ's death affected all, just as Adam's sin affected all—but this is equivalence, not superiority, so it cannot explain the "much more" of Christ's work.

How then can Christ's death have affected all if it did not result in universal salvation? On the one hand Paul seems to be saying more than that the cross is sufficient for the salvation of all. It was an act of salvation: its result was "justification of life" (Rom 5:16, 18) and by it many will be constituted righteous (Rom 5:19). Sinners were reconciled to God through the death of his Son (Rom 5:10). God reconciled the world to himself in Christ (2 Cor 5:19). This interpretation of Christ's death highlights the graciousness of salvation. Paul's theology of the cross* comes to expression best in affirmations of "universal salvation" through Christ's death, which lacks nothing in its power and grace. Yet when Paul thinks concretely of the salvation of individuals, he recognizes the need for humans to appropriate by faith the benefits of Christ's death. It is doubtful that we should divorce Paul's theme of reconciliation (see Peace, Reconciliation) through the cross from that of justification* by faith. (Some universalists would argue that all will indeed eventually turn to God in faith, see Bauckham, 51-54.) The completeness of Christ's saving work dominates Romans 5:12-21, however, because Paul is at pains to show that God has provided a comprehensive solution to the problem of universal sin and death elucidated in Romans 1:18-32.

E. Boring (283-84) thinks Paul's universalism in this text (Rom 5:12-21) is the logical inference of the dominant image used to describe salvation here, namely, the image of the conquering king: sin and death are conquered, God alone is Lord, and nothing remains outside of his lordship. Yet when Boring says "all welcome the conqueror as the liberator from an alien tyrant," he is developing the image in a way Paul does not. By contrast, J. C. Beker speaks of the "destruction, judgment or torment of nonbelievers" as the necessary hermeneutical "consequence of the theme of the *triumph* of God" (194, emphasis added; see Triumph). Paul customarily distinguishes between those who believe in this Lord and those who do not. But according to Boring (287-92), Paul's characteristic insistence on faith belongs to a different image for salvation, which pictures God as a judge who separates people into saved and lost. He explains that the juridical image is logically incompatible with the image of royal conquest, but both express important truths. Neither of these images amounts to Paul's "real view." In the end, however, Boring wants to understand the destruction awaiting those outside of Christ as merely the "soft implication" of the juridical image of the salvation of believers through Christ (i.e., one can speak of salvation only if one also speaks of its opposite). Boring thus finds an implicit universalism in Paul (implicit in the image of God the king), and relegates Paul's explicit particularism to its being a necessary extrapolation of the image of God as judge. The tension is thus resolved in favor of universalism.

Instead of regarding the images Paul uses for salvation as logically incompatible, however, we might consider that Paul meant them to be interpreted in the light of each other and of the whole context of his teaching on salvation, including the need for the response of faith. This does not mean, however, that Paul's statements should be forced into a systematic-dogmatic construal (cf. Beker, 193).

**2.2. 1 Corinthians 15:22.** Here Paul uses the same Adam/Christ analogy, which leads him to an assertion similar to that of Romans 5:12-21: "as in Adam all die, so also in Christ shall all be made alive." But the parallelism is plainly asymmetrical, for the context shows that Paul is contemplating the resurrection of "those who belong to Christ" (*hoi tou Christou*, 1 Cor 15:23), a designation for believers (cf. 1 Cor 3:23). While Paul thinks of all humanity as being in Adam and thus subject to death, he apparently does not think of all humanity as being in Christ and thus destined to share his resurrection life. The destiny of those apart from Christ does not enter the picture here ("then the end," 1 Cor 15:24, probably does not mean "then the rest" [will be raised]). Rather Paul is concerned to assert that Christians still await resurrection, for Christ is the "first fruits* of those who sleep" (1 Cor 15:20). Boring, nevertheless, argues that universal salvation is supported by verse 28: "that God might be all in all." This monistic picture of the eschatological state, in which all is united under God's reign, does not allow for hell or annihilation (Boring, 280-81). The operative image of God the king here accounts for this one-group thinking. But, against Boring, Paul speaks in terms of all things being "subjected" to Christ and to God, which does not necessarily entail salvation (cf. Marshall 1990, 316), although it may (subjection is linked with transformation in Phil 3:21). Paul mentions the subjection and even destruction of antagonistic powers (1 Cor 15:24, 26-28), but they neither exclude the similar subjection of unbelievers, nor imply their salvation (see Principalities).

**2.3. Philippians 2:10-11.** Philippians 2:10-11 also uses the motif of the universal lordship of Christ. God exalted Christ "that at the name of Jesus every knee might bow, whether in heaven or on earth or under the earth, and every tongue might confess that Jesus Christ is Lord" (see Exaltation and Enthronement). The hymn* from which this quotation comes intends to affirm something about Christ in order to encourage the church: despite appearances, Christ is Lord of all by virtue of God's exaltation of him to the position of cosmic Lord. The universal acknowledgment of his lordship could coincide with his enthronement, as a present but not-yet-manifested reality, or it could refer to a still future event which will take place at the Parousia. The acknowledgement of Jesus Christ as Lord probably comes from the spiritual powers representing rival lordships, not human beings. The powers are subject to Christ; he is Lord of lords. Thus the hymn does not intend to indicate the extent of salvation, whether universal or particular (Marshall 1990, 318).

Boring, nevertheless, argues that the image of universal lordship in Philippians 2 points beyond the intention of the text itself to universal salvation. Otherwise, he reasons, one has the difficulty of positing that those who acknowledge Christ grudgingly will still be cast into the abyss, or that the spirit-powers are forced to acclaim Christ, but human beings are free to accept or reject him (Boring, 282-83). Neither of these implications may have concerned Paul, however, and we cannot determine his view by engaging in this kind of speculation. Furthermore, Boring's comments show that the image of God the king does not necessarily lead to a one-group eschatology *in which all are saved*, for the one group may consist of those who acknowledge Christ grudgingly as well as those who do so in genuine faith.

We now turn to three Pauline texts that describe Christ's reconciling work as having cosmic scope.

*2.4. 2 Corinthians 5:19.* Here Paul says that "God was reconciling the world to himself in Christ." The *kosmos*, "world,"* must be the human world, since Paul goes on to speak of God's "not counting their trespasses against them" (probably explicative of "reconciling"). But the reconciliation which was accomplished on the cross must now be preached and received: "We beseech you, . . . be reconciled to God!" (2 Cor 5:20). For some interpreters this constitutes evidence that the "reconciliation of the world" does not amount to universal salvation, rather that reconciliation is effective for a person only if it is received in faith (Murray, 23). The "reconciliation of the world" by Christ means that Christ is the only reconciler, not that all are effectively reconciled (Marshall 1990, 320). Others, however, argue that because reconciliation is effective for all, it should be preached and believed.

*2.5. Colossians 1:20; Ephesians 1:10.* The other two texts which speak of all-inclusive reconciliation through Christ are Colossians 1:20 and Ephesians 1:10, but many do not consider these letters authentically Pauline. According to Colossians 1:20 God purposed "through him [Christ] to reconcile (*apokatallaxai*) all things to himself." The reference is to Christ's death ("having made peace through the blood of his cross"). Marshall (1990, 321) thinks that "all things" refers primarily to the human world (cf. Col 1:22),

though he does not rule out a reference to the powers defeated by Christ on the cross. In support of the latter referent, in Colossians 1:16 "all things" refers to all "created" things, "whether in heaven or on earth," and includes the "principalities and powers." These are named in Colossians 2:15 as those whom Christ "led in triumph," enemies defeated in his death (*see* Triumph).

What then is the nature of the reconciliation which Christ's death accomplished? Healing of the breach between human beings and God? Subjection or pacification of cosmic powers? Or, more generally, the establishing of cosmic peace* and order over the universe under Christ's headship*? P. T. O'Brien favors the third explanation (O'Brien, 55-56). Reconciliation would thus be a broad term embracing both the aspects of salvation and subjugation (Murray, 7). The significance of cosmic reconciliation for the readers is that they belong to the supreme Lord, and all other powers in the universe are under his lordship, though their resistance still makes itself known (cf. Marshall 1990, 319). But universal salvation does not appear to be the clear implication of this text. Paul is writing here of the salvation of the readers only (Col 1:21-22) and exhorts them toward steadfastness (Col 1:23; Murray, 18). Thus Marshall (1990, 321) and O'Brien (56-57) conclude that acceptance of reconciliation in repentance and faith is a necessary human response in order to be saved from judgment and assured of eternal salvation.

Ephesians 1:10 speaks of God's purpose "to sum up, bring together (*anakephalaiōsasthai*) all things in Christ, things in the heavens and things on earth." The verb used here is an alternative to "reconcile" (Bruce, 261). In Christ the diverse elements of the cosmos are integrated and harmony is restored. This summing up may be a past event, referring to the exaltation of Christ to the position of cosmic Lord (Lincoln, 34-35). Or it may refer to the future Parousia. The uniting of all things in Christ removes the grounds for fear of hostile cosmic powers: "no aspect of this universe . . . is outside the scope of God's redemptive purpose" (Lincoln, 35). Marshall (1990, 322), however, comments that there is no basis for saying that those hostile toward God will be reconciled. Rather the point of the text is that God's will for the whole universe is realized in Christ.

*2.6. Pastorals.* Finally, the Pastoral Letters contain a few references to the salvation of all. God "wills all people to be saved" (1 Tim 2:4). God "is the Savior of all people, especially of believers" (1 Tim 4:10). "The grace of God has been manifested for the salvation of all people" (Tit 2:11). Some interpreters see here the

Pauline thought that the gospel has a universal scope over against the heretical restriction of salvation to an elite, or the mistaken assumption that some are outside the pale of God's redemptive purposes. Salvation is effective, however, only for believers (e.g. Fee, 64, 106). This interpretation complements the assumption in the Pastorals that some will not be saved. The verses quoted can thus be taken to express God's antecedent or absolute will for the salvation of all, which differs from God's consequent or conditioned will according to which only those who believe are saved. Following Barth, Barrett (1963, 51), on the other hand, sees universal salvation through election* to be possible here.

### 3. Evaluating the Evidence

There is no detectable chronological development in Paul away from particularism toward universalism (as argued by Dodd, 118-26; so Boring, 271; see Marshall's [1990, 325] critique of Stauffer's attempt to find such a development). The evidence that Paul did sometimes express the view that all will be saved is slight, if it exists at all. Some describe it simply as a "final hope" or "final tendency of the divine work of salvation" (Oepke, 392).

Those who see some ground for universalism in Paul have wrestled with the problem of Paul's consistency. What is to be made of the particularistic texts—short of merely discounting them as wrong? J. C. Beker (194) attributes the tension between universal and particular salvation in Paul to contextual differences: "the universalistic thrust of Paul's thought cannot be logically pressed, because the context decides at every turn Paul's argumentative stance." In D. Patte's structuralist approach (Patte, 193, 254-55), Paul's affirmations of particularistic salvation belong to his convictional logic (what Paul "really" thinks, the deep structure of his thought), and statements about universal salvation belong to his argumentative logic (the surface structure of his thought). The contradiction is only formal. E. Brunner (180-84) resolves the issue by redefining the function of Paul's statements about final condemnation and universal salvation. As predictions or pieces of information they are contradictory. But we ought to take them instead as threats or invitations intended to provoke belief and acceptance of God's will to save. Both final condemnation and universal salvation are "true" in the context of existential encounter.

Universalism may perhaps be best defended as an *implication* of some statements in Paul, or a "fuller insight" rooted in but going beyond Scripture (e.g., the notion that the love of God as portrayed in Scripture

must logically entail the salvation of all, cf. Robinson). Marshall (1990, 325-26), however, warns against a methodology which seeks to ground universalism in something beyond the revelation of God already made known in the crucified Christ and accessible in Scripture. Even then, universalism would have to be understood as deliverance from a really possible judgment* so as not to brush aside the texts that speak of a future judgment or dispose of the scriptural teaching of God's justice.

See also ADAM AND CHRIST; APOSTASY, FALLING AWAY, PERSEVERANCE; DEATH OF CHRIST; ELECTION AND PREDESTINATION; ESCHATOLOGY; HEAVEN, HEAVENLIES, PARADISE; IMMORTALITY; JUDGMENT; PEACE, RECONCILIATION; RESURRECTION; SALVATION; TRIUMPH; WRATH, DESTRUCTION.

BIBLIOGRAPHY. C. K. Barrett, *A Commentary on the Epistle to the Romans* (HNTC; New York: Harper & Row, 1958); idem, *The Pastoral Epistles* (Oxford: Clarendon, 1963); K. Barth, *The Epistle to the Romans* (6th ed.; London: Oxford University, 1933); R. J. Bauckham, "Universalism: A Historical Survey," *Themelios* 4 (1979) 48-54; J. C. Beker, *Paul the Apostle: The Triumph of God in Life and Thought* (2d ed.; Philadelphia: Fortress, 1984) 193-94; M. E. Boring, "The Language of Universal Salvation in Paul," *JBL* 105 (1986) 269-92; F. F. Bruce, *The Epistles to the Colossians, to Philemon, and to the Ephesians* (NICNT; Grand Rapids: Eerdmans, 1984); E. Brunner, *Eternal Hope* (London: Lutterworth, 1954) 170-84; R. Bultmann, *Theology of the New Testament* (2 vols.; New York: Scribner's, 1955); W. V. Crockett, "The Ultimate Restoration of All Mankind: 1 Corinthians 15:22," in *Studia Biblica 1978: III. Papers on Paul and Other New Testament Authors,* ed. E. A. Livingstone (Sheffield: JSNT, 1980) 83-87; C. H. Dodd, "The Mind of Paul: II," in *New Testament Studies* (Manchester: University Press, 1953) 83-128; C. S. Duthie, "Ultimate Triumph," *SJT* 14 (1961) 156-71; G. D. Fee, *The Pastoral Epistles* (Peabody, MA: Hendrickson, 1988); J. Gundry Volf, *Paul and Perseverance: Staying In and Falling Away* (WUNT 2.37; Tübingen: J. C. B. Mohr; Louisville: John Knox/Westminster, 1990); J. Jeremias, "πολλοί," *TDNT* VI.536-45; E. Käsemann, *Commentary on Romans* (Grand Rapids: Eerdmans, 1980); A. T. Lincoln, *Ephesians* (WBC 42; Dallas: Word, 1990); I. H. Marshall, *1 and 2 Thessalonians* (NCB; Grand Rapids: Eerdmans, 1983); idem, "Does the New Testament Teach Universal Salvation?" in *Christ in Our Place: The Humanity of God in Christ for the Reconciliation of the World: Essays Presented to Professor James Torrance,* ed. T. A. Hart and D. P. Thimell (Allison Park, PA: Pickwick, 1989) 313-28; W. Michaelis, *Versöhnung des Alls* (Gümlingen [Bern]: Siloah, 1950); J. Murray, "The Reconciliation," *WTJ* 29 (1966) 1-23;

P. T. O'Brien *Colossians* (WBC 44; Waco: Word, 1982); A. Oepke, "ἀποκαθίστημι, ἀποκατάστασις," *TDNT* I.387-93; D. Patte, *Paul's Faith and the Power of the Gospel* (Philadelphia: Fortress, 1983); J. A. T. Robinson, "Universalism—Is it Heretical?," *SJT* 2 (1949) 139-55; E. P. Sanders, *Paul and Palestinian Judaism: A Comparison of Patterns of Religion* (Philadelphia: Fortress, 1977) 472-74; R. J. H. Shutt, "The New Testament Doctrine of the Hereafter: Universalism or Conditional Immortality," *ExpT* 67 (1955-56) 131-35; J. Stott and D. L. Edwards, *Evangelical Essentials: A Liberal-Evangelical Dialogue* (Downers Grove, IL: InterVarsity, 1988) 306-31; N. T. Wright, "Towards a Biblical View of Universalism," *Themelios* 4 (1979) 54-58.

J. M. Gundry-Volf

**UNKNOWN GOD.** *See* ATHENS, PAUL AT; RELIGIONS, GRECO-ROMAN.

**URBAN ENVIRONMENT OF PAUL'S MISSION.** *See* SOCIAL SETTING OF MISSION CHURCHES.

# V

**VANITY.** *See* FUTILITY.

**VICES.** *See* VIRTUES AND VICES.

## VIRTUES AND VICES

Lists of virtues and vices appear in all the Pauline letters except 1 Thessalonians, 2 Thessalonians and Philemon. They are by no means unique to the Pauline corpus since similar lists are found in other writings, and in some cases those in the Pauline letters appear to be adaptations to a greater or lesser extent of these.

1. The Function of Paul's Ethical Lists
2. The Background of Paul's Ethical Lists

### 1. The Function of Paul's Ethical Lists.

The ways the lists are used in the Pauline letters fall into essentially five categories: to depict the depravity of unbelievers, to encourage believers to avoid vices and practice virtues, to expose or denounce the failures of false teachers, to describe what is required of church leaders and to advise a young pastor.

*1.1. To Depict the Depravity of Unbelievers.* The list of vices in Romans 1:29-31 is used to depict the depravity of those (Gentiles) who suppress God's truth. In 1 Corinthians 5:9-11 Paul, when seeking to correct a misunderstanding arising from his "previous letter," lists various types of immoral people. He had not meant that his readers should dissociate themselves from all such immoral persons, but only from Christians who lived immorally.

*1.2. To Encourage Believers to Avoid the Vices and Practice the Virtues.* This is the predominant use made of the lists in the Pauline letters. In Romans 13:13 Paul lists those things which believers must lay aside as they seek to live honorably as people of the new day. Various types of wrongdoers are listed in 1 Corinthians 6:9-10 to warn the Corinthians (some of whom were defrauding one another and taking one another to court; *see* Law Suit) that wrongdoers will not inherit the kingdom* of God. In 2 Corinthians 12:20 Paul lists a variety of moral failures he feared he might still find among the Corinthians when he paid his third visit.

In Galatians 5:19-23 Paul reminds his readers that freedom* from the Law* was no excuse to gratify the desires of the flesh* (listed in Gal 5:19-21); it should lead rather to the manifestation of the fruit* of the Spirit (listed in Gal 5:22-23). The lists of virtues and vices found in the Prison letters (Eph 4:25-32; 5:3-5; Phil 4:8-9; Col 3:5, 8, 12) all function as incentives to urge the readers to have done with the vices listed, and to practice the virtues. Several lists are included in Titus as part of the behavioral instructions to be passed on to various groups within the Christian community on Crete: the older women (Tit 2:3-5); the younger men, for whom Titus is to be a model (Tit 2:6-8); and slaves (Tit 2:9-10). Titus 3:1-3 includes virtues to be pursued by all believers, as well as vices to be shunned which were a part of their behavior before they were saved (*see* Pastoral Letters).

*1.3. To Expose/Denounce the Failure of the False Teachers.* Twice in 1 Timothy lists are included in advice about dealing with false teachers: In 1 Timothy 1:3-11, Timothy is told to curb the activities of certain false teachers who were ignorant of the fact that the Law is not intended for the innocent but the lawless, an illustrative list of whose characteristics is then given (1 Tim 1:9-10); and in 1 Timothy 6:4-5 a list of the vices of the false teachers themselves is provided.

*1.4. To Describe What Is Required of Church Leaders.* In 1 Timothy 6:11 there is a list of the virtues which Timothy, as a servant* of God, should pursue, and 2 Timothy 2:22-25 lists the vices which he is to avoid and other virtues which he is to pursue. The virtues required of, and the vices to be avoided by, those appointed as bishops, deacons, elders are set out in 1 Timothy 3:2-7, 8-13; and Titus 1:6-8 respectively.

*1.5. To Advise a Young Pastor.* A list of vices is used to warn Timothy of the behavior he will encounter in the last times (2 Tim 3:2-5), and a list of virtues is included to remind him of the way in which his mentor, Paul, conducted his life (2 Tim 3:10).

### 2. The Background of Paul's Ethical Lists.

Writing in 1932 B. S. Easton said: "It is now generally

recognized that the catalogs of virtues and vices in the New Testament are derived ultimately from the ethical teaching of the Stoa." He also noted that such lists were fairly abundant in Hellenistic Jewish literature (esp. Philo). If this was the case, then the Pauline lists could be influenced by Stoicism directly or through Hellenistic Judaism.

In more recent times other suggestions have been put forward. Wibbing notes similarities between the NT lists and those found in the Qumran* literature (esp. 1QS), though he admits that there are features of the Pauline lists which distinguish them from the Jewish lists, including those of Qumran.

Kamlah divides Paul's virtue and vice lists into two categories, the paraenetic catalogs (e.g., Col 2:20—3:17) having a background in the Hellenistic syncretism of the mystery religions, and the descriptive catalogs (e.g., Gal 5:19-23) having, he claims, a background in ancient Iranian religion. However, the dualistic cosmology of ancient Iranian religion has no place in the Pauline understanding of virtues and vices (nor in ethical teaching of other Christian or Jewish writings).

Martin, following Schroeder, argues for a return to the OT-Jewish tradition as the preferred background for Paul's lists of vices and virtues.

*2.1. Paul's Lists of Vices.* Paul's lists resemble, in some cases, those developed in Hellenistic Judaism to depict the depravity of the Gentile world (cf., e.g., Rom 1:29-31; Wis 14:25-26). These lists had a regular form in which idolatry* is seen as the root cause of many other vices. Paul appears sometimes to include such lists without much adaptation to the context (e.g., 1 Cor 6:9-10). On other occasions his lists are adapted (to a lesser or greater extent) to the context (Gal 5:19-21; Eph 4:25-32; 5:3-5; Col 3:5, 8).

*2.2. Paul's Lists of Virtues.* Unlike his vice lists, Paul's lists of virtues have very few parallels in Hellenistic Judaism, but have significant parallels in Greek literature. Dibelius notes that the virtues required of a bishop in 1 Timothy 3:2-7 closely parallel those the tactician Onosander set down for a general. Other lists in the Pauline letters reveal greater selection and adaptation. In 1 Timothy 6:11 the Christian virtues of faith* and love* are introduced, and in 2 Corinthians 6:8 there is clear adaptation to describe the nature of Paul's ministry.* The lists in Galatians 5:22-23 and Colossians 3:12-14 are heavily influenced by typically Christian virtues.

*2.3. Significance of the Parallels for Exegesis.* If it is true that the lists of virtues and vices in the Pauline corpus are influenced to greater or lesser extent by similar lists in other literature, and if such lists have sometimes been incorporated with little adaptation to their context within his letters, then care will need to be taken not to overinterpret such lists, especially some of the vice lists, as if they were intended to be accurate descriptions of the conduct of those to whom they refer.

*See also* ETHICS; FRUIT OF THE SPIRIT; HOUSEHOLDS AND HOUSEHOLD CODES; NEW NATURE AND OLD NATURE.

BIBLIOGRAPHY. J. E. Crouch, *The Origin and Intention of the Colossian Haustafel* (FRLANT 109; Göttingen: Vandenhoeck & Ruprecht, 1972); M. Dibelius and H. Conzelmann, *The Pastoral Epistles* (Herm; Philadelphia: Fortress, 1972); B. S. Easton, "New Testament Ethical Lists," *JBL* 51 (1932) 1-12; E. Kamlah, *Die Form der katalogischen Paränese im Neuen Testament* (Tübingen: J. C. B. Mohr, 1964); R. P. Martin, "Virtue," *NIDNTT* 3.928-32; D. Schroeder, "Lists, Ethical," *IDB* Supplementary Volume (1976) 546-47; E. Schweizer, "Traditional Ethical Patterns in the Pauline and Post-Pauline Letters and Their Development," in *Text and Interpretation*, ed. E. Best and R. McL. Wilson (Cambridge: University Press, 1979) 195-209; S. Wibbing, *Die Tugend—und Lasterkataloge in Neuen Testament und ihre Traditionsgeschichte unter besonderer Berücksichtigung der Qumran-Texte* (BZNW 25; Berlin: Töpelmann, 1959).
C. G. Kruse

# VISIONS, ECSTATIC EXPERIENCE

While Paul undoubtedly had visionary experiences, he rarely mentioned them. Greek has two terms for "vision," *optasia* and *horama*. *Optasia* is found only once in Paul's letters (2 Cor 12:1) and *horama* is not found at all. *Apokalypsis*, "revelation," and *apokalyptō*, "to reveal," are more frequent, but only occasionally do they contain a visionary component. Consequently it is difficult to describe the content of Paul's visions or to fix the role they played in his personal piety. While his own call to ministry* came in visionary form (Gal 1:11-12, 16), he plainly rejected visions as a criterion of apostolic authority* (2 Cor 12:12; *see* Apostle).

1. Pauline Visions in Acts
2. Paul's Own View
3. The Journey to Heaven in 2 Corinthians 12:1-4

## 1. Pauline Visions in Acts.

In the narrative of Acts Paul's Damascus Road experience is described three times (Acts 9:1-9; 22:6-11; 26:13-19); in two of these instances Paul himself describes the event, and elsewhere in Acts Paul is described as a man encouraged, driven and guided by ecstatic or vision-like experiences (Acts 9:12; 16:9-10; 18:9-11; 22:17-21; 23:11; 27:23-24). It is important to understand these reports in their connection with Luke's theological agenda, which was different from Paul's.

## 2. Paul's Own View.

Paul's own attitude toward visions can be contrasted with that of Luke. Luke emphasized the visions as part of his apologetic for the Gentile* mission*: this can only be the work of God and so visions corroborate the Pauline ministry in its call and fulfillment. Paul defends the Gentile mission and his role within it on the grounds that the Word has been proclaimed and the church established (2 Cor 3:2-3; 12:12; Rom 15:18-20). Ecstatic experiences are of value only to the extent that they carry forward that work (1 Cor 14:26, 30-33). For this reason they assume a secondary role in Paul's understanding of ministry.

Paul is willing to mention visions when he comes under attack, though always with reticence. In Galatians 1:12, 16; 2:2 he mentions revelations in response to the accusation that he lacked proper credentials from Jerusalem* (saying, in effect, "my commission came from the Lord"). In 2 Corinthians 12:1-4, he shifted the emphasis by creating an ironic parody of the claims being made by the "superlative apostles" whose representatives opposed his work; Paul is respectful to the leaders, if condemnatory of those who claimed to be their representatives (2 Cor 11:5, 13-15; 12:11; see Opponents). In that context, Paul claims an "abundance of revelations" (2 Cor 12:7). Chief among these is the journey to heaven* (*harpagenta . . . heōs tritou ouranou*) in 2 Corinthians 12:1-4.

## 3. The Journey to Heaven in 2 Corinthians 12:1-4.

It is generally agreed that the experience described in 2 Corinthians 12 is not the same as the Damascus Road experience of Acts; the dates do not match, and the Acts account was a commission to preach (Acts 26:16), whereas the 2 Corinthians 12 account contained a prohibition against speaking (2 Cor 12:4). A number of questions remain, including the relationship of the passage to its context, the nature of the attack brought against Paul, possible parallels in rabbinic Judaism of rabbis caught up to paradise (see Heaven, Heavenlies, Paradise), the cosmology of the heavens, the nature of the "thorn in the flesh" with which the vision is associated and the significance of vision as accreditation for ministry.

*3.1. Context.* This pericope falls in the middle of Paul's "fool's speech," 2 Corinthians 10—13, in which he answers specific challenges brought by opponents in Corinth. When we find him boasting of the revelations in 2 Corinthians 12:1-10, then, it must be in response to charges of inadequate spirituality* on his part. This charge would have made sense to the Corinthians, whose tastes ran toward the charismatic and who had seen little evidence of this in Paul's ministry. Whatever the date of 2 Corinthians 10—13, the vision Paul describes as having taken place fourteen years earlier (2 Cor 12:2) must have occurred prior to his founding the Corinthian church, yet Paul had never mentioned it to them despite their hunger for the visionary.

*3.2. Literary Antecedents and Cosmology.* Paul does not feed the Corinthians' appetites. His clear reticence about disclosing the details of his vision (2 Cor 12:2-4) leaves enormous room for speculation, of which the apocryphal* *Apocalypse of Paul* is a prime example. The idea of a heavenly ascent is widely found in ancient literature, both Jewish and Greek. The cosmology here is Jewish (see World, Cosmology). Mention of a "third heaven" (2 Cor 12:2) parallels *2 Enoch* 8:1-8 and the *Apocalypse of Moses* 40:2. Many interpreters and commentators adduce parallels in Jewish Merkabah mysticism* (e.g., Bowker, Young, Segal).

*3.3. The Thorn in the Flesh.* The nature of Paul's thorn in the flesh remains unclear (see Healing, Illness). R. Price argues that in the Merkabah traditions, unworthy visitors to the throne of God* are buffeted by angels,* and that this is the reason for the language in 2 Corinthians 12:7 of a "messenger of Satan, sent to harass" Paul. Whatever its nature, Paul uses the thorn to repel any hint of self-aggrandizement. This is consistent with his ironic "refusal" to boast in his visions and his insistence that visions do not constitute a legitimate criterion for apostolic authority (see Healing).

*3.4. The Rhetorical Structure.* The tone of the entire fool's speech is clearly ironic (see Spencer), and some interpreters go so far as to say that it is derisive. Paul claims he will not boast, then does exactly that. He criticizes his opponents for measuring themselves against one another (2 Cor 12:12), then measures them against himself. The effect would be a kind of inverted understatement, were it not for Paul's obvious indignation (cf. 2 Cor 10:1 with 10:10). C. Forbes relates this to Hellenistic rhetorical* practice: one may use irony to attack an opponent, but not in self-defense. Here Paul is on the attack; he does not intend merely to defend his own authority, but to challenge theirs. The ironic tenor of the entire fool's speech parodies the claims the "superlative apostles" or their representatives are making on their behalf.

*3.5. Visions and the Qualifications for Ministry.* By repelling any self-aggrandizement, Paul calls attention to the error into which his opponents have fallen: he can match them point for point, but these are the wrong points. To secure that position, he offers his "defense" with great reluctance (we may note here the third person singular [2 Cor 12:2-5a]; the repeated recourse to apologies in 2 Cor 11:30-33; 12:1, 5 and 6; and the counterbalancing emphasis on humiliation, suffering and weakness* [2 Cor 11:32-33; 12:7-9, 10] typified in the crucified [2 Cor 13:1-4]). In the end, it is these limitations, and not visions, which represent the proper credentials for ministry.

*See also* APOSTLE; CROSS, THEOLOGY OF THE; HEAVEN, HEAVENLIES, PARADISE; JEW, PAUL THE; MYSTICISM; WEAKNESS; WORLD, COSMOLOGY.

BIBLIOGRAPHY. W. Baird, "Visions, Revelation, and Ministry: Reflections on 2 Corinthians 12:1-5 and Galatians 1:11-17," *JBL* 104 (1985) 651-62; E. Benz, *Paulus als Visionäer* (Wiesbaden: Steiner, 1952); H. D. Betz, *Paul's Apology: II Corinthians 10—13 and the Socratic Tradition* (Berkeley: Center for Hermeneutical Studies in Hellenistic and Modern Culture, 1975); J. Bowker, " 'Merkabah' Visions and the Visions of Paul," *JSS* 16 (1971) 157-73; C. Forbes, "Comparison, Self-Praise and Irony: Paul's Boasting and the Conventions of Hellenistic Rhetoric," *NTS* 32 (1986) 1-30; A. T. Lincoln, " 'Paul the Visionary': The Setting and Significance of the Rapture to Paradise in II Corinthians xii.1-10," *NTS* 25 (1979) 206-20; S. E. McClelland, " 'Super-Apostles, Servants of Christ, Servants of Satan': A Response [to M. E. Thrall]," *JSNT* 14 (1982) 82-87; R. Price, "Punished in Paradise (An Exegetical Theory on 2 Corinthians 12:1-10)," *JSNT* 7 (1980) 33-40; H. Saake, "Paulus als Ekstatiker: Pneumatologische Beobachtung zu 2 Kor. 12, 1-10," *NovT* 15 (1973) 152-60; P. Schaefer, "New Testament and Hekhalot Literature: The Journey into Heaven in Paul and in Merkevah Mysticism," *JJS* 35 (1984) 19-35; A. F. Segal, *Paul the Convert: The Apostolate and Apostasy of Saul the Pharisee* (New Haven: Yale University, 1990); A. B. Spencer, "The Wise Fool and the Foolish Wise: A Study of Irony in Paul," *NovT* 23 (1981) 349-60; R. P. Spittler, "The Limits of Ecstacy: An Exegesis of 2 Corinthians 12:1-10," in *Current Issues in Biblical and Patristic Interpretations*, ed. G. F. Hawthorne (Grand Rapids: Eerdmans, 1975) 259-66; B. Young, "The Ascension Motif of 2 Corinthians 12 in Jewish, Christian and Gnostic Texts," *GTJ* 9 (1988) 73-103.

J. Camery-Hoggatt

**VISITS TO JERUSALEM.** *See* CHRONOLOGY OF PAUL; ITINERARIES, TRAVEL PLANS, JOURNEYS, APOSTOLIC PAROUSIA; JERUSALEM.

**VOLUNTARY ASSOCIATIONS.** *See* SOCIAL SETTING OF MISSION CHURCHES.

# W-Z

**WEAK.** *See* ROMANS, LETTER TO THE; STRONG AND WEAK; WEAKNESS.

## WEAKNESS

In Pauline literature, the term *astheneia* ("weakness") plays a distinctive role. In classical Greek usage, in the LXX and in other NT writers, the term almost always has the meaning "illness" or "powerlessness." In Paul, however, the word is developed into a significant theological concept, especially in his major writings: 1 and 2 Corinthians, and Romans. The term *astheneia* and its cognates (*astheneō, asthenēma, asthenēs*) occur fifteen times in 1 Corinthians, fourteen times in 2 Corinthians, eight times in Romans, but only seven times in all of Paul's other letters. Weakness as a significant theological motif is developed most fully in the Corinthian correspondence, where Paul argues against certain Jewish-Christian opponents* who boasted of their knowledge and sufficiency compared with Paul's apparent inadequacies. In the face of this opposition, Paul takes up their charges about his "weakness" and turns it to his own purpose of defending his gospel* and ministry.*

1. The Pauline Weakness Motif
2. Weakness, Apostleship and Christian Spirituality

### 1. The Pauline Weakness Motif.

Paul develops his concept in three basic ways: anthropologically, christologically and ethically.

Anthropologically, weakness presupposes that a person's whole being is dependent upon God* and is subject to the limitations of all creation (1 Cor 2:3). Weakness also involves the inability of human beings to attain God's favor by themselves (1 Cor 9:22).

Christologically,* weakness becomes a badge of honor for the believer "in Christ"* and the platform from which the power* of God is exhibited in the world.* For Paul, human weakness provides the best channel for divine power. The greatest revelation of this occurred in the person and work of Jesus Christ in the midst of his earthly and human existence (1 Cor 1:25—2:6). Paul has become like Christ in that the power of Christ has been revealed in Paul's own weakness (2 Cor 10—13).

Finally, at the ethical level Paul emphasized against his opponents that, due to the priority of love* over knowledge* and gift,* believers must hold their Christian freedom* in check in deference to the sensibilities of weak Christians (1 Cor 8—10). In the service* of Christ there is no place for selfish individualism, no matter how great or impressive one's abilities may be. The weaker members of the church actually are indispensable for the proper functioning of the body, just as the human body is dependent upon its weaker internal organs (heart, lungs), whose only protection is that which the stronger members afford. Hence a failure to help the weak (1 Thess 5:14) is a failure to recognize the mutual dependence of every member of the unity that characterized Christ's body (1 Cor 12:12-13; *see* Body of Christ).

Paul's concept of weakness is, in sum, markedly theocentric. God depends neither on human strength nor on human achievements, not even in the church. Instead, he seeks out the weak, the ungodly and the hostile to redeem them and to fit them as vessels of his own strength. Weakness is—as the Lord himself had expressed it to Paul—the place where *God's* power is perfected (2 Cor 12:9). Thus between Christ and the believer there is such an intimate identification in weakness that both can be said to live "by the power of God" (2 Cor 13:4).

### 2. Weakness, Apostleship and Christian Spirituality.

Paul's view of weakness is not to be understood only as an abstract doctrine, for it was developed in view of actual conditions. In the first place, weakness speaks of the reality of human finiteness and dependence upon God. It is just this that Paul declares when he says he is weak. He can claim no credit for any of his successes, for he knows that he has been sustained by God. If he has achieved anything, it is only because of God's power working through a weak but consecrated vessel (cf. 2 Tim 2:20-21).

Likewise, Paul teaches that God's way of exhibiting

power is altogether different from human ways. Men and women try to overcome their weaknesses; God is satisfied to use weakness for his own special purposes. God's means of working, rightly understood, is not by making people stronger, but weaker and weaker, until the divine power alone is seen in them.

Finally, for Paul weakness is the greatest sign of apostleship because it identifies him with his crucified Lord.* By his death* Christ proved that God's weakness was stronger than human strength. This same Christ is now the example Christians are to follow (*see* Imitation). By living under the cross* of Christ and dying* daily with him, they participate in the weakness of Christ. This identification with their crucified Lord enables them not merely to endure their weaknesses but to glory* in them.

*See also* AFFLICTIONS, TRIALS, HARDSHIPS; CROSS, THEOLOGY OF THE; POWER.

BIBLIOGRAPHY. D. A. Black, *Paul, Apostle of Weakness: Astheneia and its Cognates in the Pauline Literature* (New York: Lang, 1984); idem, "Paulus Infirmus: the Pauline Concept of Weakness," *GTJ* 5 (1984) 77-93; E. Fuchs, "La Faiblesse, Gloire de l'Apostolat Selon Paul (Etude sur 2 Co 10-13)," *ETR* 2 (1980) 231-53; E. Güttgemanns, *Der leidende Apostel und sein Herr* (FRLANT 90; Göttingen: Vandenhoeck & Ruprecht, 1966); M. Rauer, *Die "Schwachen" in Korinth und Rom* (Freiburg: Herder, 1923).

D. A. Black

# WISDOM

Paul acknowledged that his preaching* was "not in plausible words of wisdom," yet he called his proclamation of the gospel* "wisdom of God" as Christ* himself is "the wisdom of God" (1 Cor 2:1-5, 7; 2 Cor 1:24, 30). Research on wisdom in Paul began with E. Grafe (1892) and since the 1960s (since A. Feuillet) has assumed considerable proportions as a result of increased interest in the wisdom tradition of the OT and early Judaism.

1. Criteria for Determining "Wisdom"
2. Wisdom Material in Paul's Traditions
3. Christology
4. The Gospel
5. Ethics
6. Eschatology

## 1. Criteria for Determining "Wisdom."

Paul referred to *wisdom* (*sophia*) more than any other writer in the NT (forty-four of the seventy-one occurrences). The notion of wisdom is not restricted to the occurrence of the term *wisdom*, however.

Equivalents which constitute the semantic field "wisdom" (Heb *ḥokmâ, ḥākām;* Gk *sophia, sophos*) include *synesis* ("what is understood," "understanding," "insight," "intelligence"); *phronēsis* ("thoughtful planning," "way of thinking," "outlook," "capacity to understand," "wisdom"), *epistēmē* ("ability to understand and evaluate," "intelligence," "understanding"), *gnōsis* ("information," "acquaintance," "the content of what is known," "knowledge," "perception," "understanding"; *see* Gnosis), *aisthēsis* ("capacity to perceive clearly and hence to understand"), *boulē* ("plan," "intention," "purpose"), *paideia* ("instruction with the intent of forming proper habits of behavior," "training in accordance with proper rules of conduct and behavior," "discipline"), with additional words appearing in close syntactical relationship with "wisdom," such as "teaching"* (*didaskō/didachē/didaskalia, katēcheō, noutheteō, paradidōmi, paralambanō, paradosis*), "prudence" (*sōphrosynē, sophos*), "plan" (*thelō/thelēma, protithemai/prothesis, gnomē*), "advice" (*symbouleuō, paraineō, symbibazō*), "perception" (figurative *horaō/ophthalmos; noeō, syniēmi/synesis*) and "success" (*euodoomai, teleō/teleioō, plēroō, plērophoreō, ōpheleō*).

The actual meaning of *wisdom* in the context of the OT and early Judaism can be divided into the three aspects of thought, discourse and action (von Lips):

(1) *Thought.* There is the act of perceiving wisdom with the focus on the acquisition of knowledge* and on the comprehension of life and reality. This includes psychological observations as well as observations on attitudes and frame of mind; human relations including charity, peaceableness, retaliation and slander; social affairs such as kingship, family and clan, legal and economic matters including wealth and poverty; observations on the conditionality of man and woman as God's creation as evident, for instance, in their mortality; the position of other nations; animate and inanimate nature, and orders of creation.

(2) *Discourse.* Wisdom is communicated with the focus on teaching, exhortation and evaluation of conduct. Besides experience and God's revelation which convey wisdom, teaching and education are the other major means for acquiring wisdom (Prov 13:20; 19:20; 23:19; Job 33:33; Wis 6:10; Sir 6:18; 39:1).

(3) *Action.* Wisdom can be viewed as action-related with the focus on conduct as a consequence of right perception, proper behavior in everyday life and capable workmanship. The sages often emphasize the mastering of the tongue, the ability to remain silent at the proper time, self-control in everyday life (restraint versus anger, humility versus pride, moderation in drinking, sexual ethics), prudence in everyday behavior (industry versus laziness, avoidance of evil) and familial solidarity. Thus wisdom has been defined as

"the reasoned search for specific ways to assure well-being and the implementation of those discoveries in daily existence" (Crenshaw).

A remarkable element of the sapiential tradition is the personification of wisdom (Prov 8; Job 28; Sir 24; Wis 8—9), particularly its function as mediator of creation. Wisdom is the first creation or firstborn (Prov 8:22-31); wisdom was created "from eternity, in the beginning" (Sir 24:9); wisdom was present when God made the world (Prov 8:27-30; Wis 9:9); God founded the earth by wisdom (Prov 3:19; 8:30); wisdom is an "initiate in the knowledge of God and an associate in his works" (Wis 8:4). Scholars used to regard this wisdom figure as an instance of a hypostasis, the ascription of material or spiritual existence to a concept. More recently it has been argued that this divine wisdom, sometimes called Dame Wisdom, must not be understood as an intermediary being between God and creation, since wisdom is not given the status of an independent entity. The wisdom "from above" is rather a vivid poetic personification expressing God's nearness, God's acts and God's personal call.

In considering the question of wisdom influence in Paul, there are four lines of investigation: (1) the direct quotations from OT and early Jewish wisdom literature, recognizing that allusions to traditional wisdom texts do not automatically constitute sapiential influence and that connections with wisdom thinking need to be determined on the basis of the relevant contexts; (2) the use of genres which derive from the sapiential tradition, bearing in mind that detection of "sapiential style" is problematic on account of imprecise definitions; (3) the religion-historical analysis of sapiential terminology, themes, motifs and concepts; and (4) the tradition-historical analysis of the origins and communication of sapiential tradition.

## 2. Wisdom Material in Paul's Traditions.

*2.1. OT Wisdom.* Canonical wisdom texts include Proverbs, Job, Qohelet, certain Psalms (e.g., Ps 37; 39; 49; 73) and the wisdom influence which has been detected in Isaiah (cf. Is 9:6; 11:2, 9; 28:23-29; 31:2), Amos, Micah, 2 Samuel and 1 Kings (the succession narrative), Genesis (the Joseph narrative) and in other books. Wisdom genres or forms include hymns, dialogues, proverbs, riddles, admonitions, allegories, noun lists, didactic narratives and autobiographical narratives.

Paul quotes from Job (Rom 11:35; 1 Cor 3:19), wisdom psalms (2 Cor 9:9), Proverbs (Rom 2:6; 12:20; 2 Cor 9:7) and Qohelet (Rom 3:10; *see* Old Testament in Paul). As to wisdom genres, Paul employs proverbs and aphorisms (e.g., Gal 4:16, 18; 5:9; 6:7) as well as

admonitions (e.g., Rom 12—13), then also allegory/parable (Rom 5:12-21; Gal 4:22-31), instructional discourse (e.g., Rom 7:7-25; 13:1-7; 1 Cor 10:1-13), instructional hymns* (the Christ hymns of Phil 2:6-11 and Col 1:15-18), dialogue (Rom), lists (vices, virtues,* household* codes, gifts* of the Spirit, fruit* of the Spirit and beatitudes (Rom 4:6-8; 14:22; 1 Cor 7:40).

The semantic field of "wisdom" can be observed in diverse contexts in most of Paul's letters: in sapiential perception (Rom 1:14; 11:33; 1 Cor 1:19, 21; 2:6, 8; 2 Cor 11—12; Col 1:9; 2:3), in communicative wisdom (1 Cor 1:17; 2:1, 4, 6, 13; 6:5; 12:8; Col 1:28; 3:16; 4:5-6; 2 Tim 3:15) and in action-related wisdom (Rom 16:19; 1 Cor 1:30; 3:10; Eph 5:15-20; Col 1:9-11; 3:16; 4:5).

*2.2. Early Jewish Wisdom.* Early Jewish wisdom texts include Baruch (3:9—4:4), Sirach and the Wisdom of Solomon, and numerous passages in the apocalyptic and Qumran literature as well as in Philo.

As to quotations from wisdom in Paul's letters, 2 Timothy 2:19 has been considered (Sir 17:26). Allusions are more numerous: Nestle-Aland (NA[26], 769-74) detects twenty-six allusions to Sirach, three to Baruch, thirteen to the *Testaments of the Twelve Patriarchs,* forty to Wisdom of Solomon (besides seven in the Areopagus speech of Acts 17:22-31; *see* Athens) and allusions to other Jewish writings which show sapiential influence.

*2.3. Sapiential Motifs.* Wisdom themes are numerous in the Pauline letters, encompassing various areas of life and cosmos, from phenomena of creation to human individuals in their personal behavior and their interpersonal and social relationships.

Examples from Romans are: Romans 1:19-21 (self-revelation of creation); Romans 1:21-25 (misguided perception of God from creation, with idolatry and immorality as consequence); Romans 2:6 (retribution after deed): Romans 2:14-15 (perception of God's will with the conscience*); Romans 5:3-5 (chain reasoning); Romans 10:6-7 (word/wisdom is near); Romans 11:33-36 (praise of God's wisdom); Romans 12:3, 16 (sober judgment versus conceit); Romans 12:8 (charity); Romans 12:10 (admonition to show honor); Romans 12:11 (warning against indolence); Romans 12:12 (virtue of perseverance); Romans 12:13 (hospitality); Romans 12:15 (sharing joy* and sorrow with others); Romans 12:17-20 and 14:19 (endeavor to live peaceably); Romans 13:1-7 (respect for political power, social structures; *see* Civil Authority).

*2.4. Dualistic Wisdom?* The contrast of flesh* and Spirit (*see* Holy Spirit) which determines the existence of humanity before God (Rom 7:7-25; 1 Cor 15:35-58; Gal 5:16-26) has been explained on the background of Jewish-Hellenistic "dualistic" wisdom, as represented by Philo (Brandenburger). The fundamental conception of Philo, the dualism of God* and the world,* is seen to be the basis of his anthropology and ethics: the human spirit is a divine effluence, as God has breathed his spirit into humankind (Philo *Det. Pot. Ins.* 22); the human body is the prison in which the divine spirit is confined, it is the source of all evil (Philo *Leg. All.* 3.14); sin is innate in humankind as all sensuality is evil (Philo *Vit. Mos.* 2.29). The highest ethical principle is the radical renunciation of sensuality, the determined eradication of desire and passion. These bear obvious affinities to Stoic ethics.

It is being questioned, however, whether it is helpful to explain basic elements of Paul's anthropology on the background of the Jewish-Hellenistic "dualistic" wisdom of Philo (von Lips): (1) the Jewish sapiential tradition includes dualistic elements of an entirely different character as well (cf. the teaching about the two spirits in the *T. 12 Patr.*); (2) the contrast of flesh and Spirit implies conceptions of diverse provenance, including, for example, an interpretation of Genesis 1—2; (3) the assumed reconstruction of the origins of the dualism in Jewish wisdom is problematic; (4) Paul can encompass a variety of sapiential elements (cf. 1 Cor 1—2) which cannot be subsumed under the label "dualistic wisdom." Thus Paul's anthropology should not be analyzed in terms of dualistic wisdom.

*2.5. The Jesus Tradition.* The link between the wisdom tradition and Paul is not only a direct one; it was mediated through the sayings of Jesus as well (*see* Jesus, Sayings of; Jesus and Paul). This is apparent in the quotation of the dominical saying of Acts 20:35 (cf. Lk 6:30), which adapts a Greek proverb (Thucydides 2.97.4; Plutarchus 2.173d). Some Pauline admonitions which are also known in the sapiential tradition (*T. Jos.* 18:2; *T. Benj.* 3:6; Prov 3:4; *T. Benj.* 5:1) can be seen, likewise, as influenced by sayings of Jesus: the admonition to bless rather than to curse one's enemies (Rom 12:14; cf. Lk 6:28), the admonition to repay evil with good (Rom 12:17-21; cf. Mt 5:38-42) and the admonition to live in peace* with all if possible (Rom 12:18; cf. Mt 5:9; Mk 9:50).

# 3. Christology.

Jesus himself described his mission, if not his person, in terms of traditional divine wisdom: entrusted with the secrets of God, revealing them to humanity and being rejected by many but accepted by the poor and the unlearned (Mt 11:19 par.; 11:25-30 par.). Thus it is not surprising (Hengel, Gese) to see Paul articulating the significance of the person and the mission of Jesus Christ in terms of wisdom (acknowledged since

the work of Windisch).

It is not impossible to surmise that Paul arrived at this identification of divine wisdom and Jesus Christ as a result of the Damascus revelation at his conversion (*see* Conversion and Call): as he saw Jesus as the Lord* exalted by God and sitting at the right hand (*see* Exaltation), he came to realize that Jesus was the Son of God (*see* Son of God) not only in the messianic sense but in the sense of standing in an intimate relationship with God from the beginning, being the image of God and his agent in creation* and now in salvation* (Kim).

*3.1. Christ and Wisdom in 1 Corinthians 1—4.* These chapters have the highest concentration of the word group *sophia/sophos* in the Pauline corpus (twenty-six occurrences). It is only here that Christ is explicitly called *sophia* (1 Cor 1:24, 30). Paul's formulation is not a polemical reaction against a gnostic *sophia* christology (Wilckens; *see* Gnosis, Gnosticism) nor a reaction against a Torah-centristic wisdom teaching in Corinth (Davis; *see* Corinthians), but should probably be understood in the context of his discussion with supporters of Jewish-Hellenistic wisdom speculation (Wilckens 1980). Whether Paul's wisdom language reflects the vocabulary and conceptuality of his opponents* or whether it is independently chosen is unclear.

In order to preserve the threatened unity of the church* (1 Cor 1:10-13), Paul established that the formation of inner-church groupings had no basis in his ministry as founder of the church nor in the gospel as such. He had baptized only a few of the Corinthians (1 Cor 1:14-17; *see* Baptism), and his teaching was not worldly wisdom teaching where one teacher may be superior to the other. On the contrary, he had promulgated the gospel (1 Cor 1:18—2:16)—proclaimed by himself and his fellow apostles* who were nothing but servants* of Christ responsible to God (1 Cor 3—4). Paul emphasized the dissimilarity between the word of the cross and "wisdom of speech" (1 Cor 1:17; *see* Cross, Theology of the) which is the "wisdom of the world" (1 Cor 1:20), "human wisdom" (1 Cor 2:5), the "wisdom of this age," which is the wisdom of the earthly "rulers of this age" (1 Cor 2:6)— mere "human wisdom" (1 Cor 2:13).

If the gospel is combined with such wisdom, it is emptied of its power* (1 Cor 1:17). Human wisdom, whether it be rhetorical skill (*see* Rhetoric) or human understanding as speculative grasp of reality, invalidates the cross of Christ since it understands Christ's death merely as a symbol of a universal truth or a transition stage in the drama of salvation. Thus Christ's death is stripped of its uniqueness and therefore of its effectiveness (Weder). A christology in which the cross, on account of a sapiential matrix, is not central lacks the fundamental reference to history. It loses the climax of salvation history, the revelation of the mystery* of God (1 Cor 2:1, 7-10). In the logic of human wisdom the cross of Christ is foolishness (1 Cor 1:18), but in reality the apparent weakness* of God is a demonstration of his power (1 Cor 1:24-25).

On a positive note Paul used the formulation "wisdom of God" to describe Christ and God's plan of salvation in Christ. God in his wisdom so arranged things that he cannot be grasped through human wisdom (1 Cor 1:21). A God derived by human wisdom is a source of pride and becomes God only for the elite and the deserving (Fee). The wisdom of God has become personified in Christ who is, for humanity, "the wisdom of God" (1 Cor 1:24) and "the wisdom from God" (1 Cor 1:30). The crucified Christ is the embodiment of God's plan of salvation, the true measure and the climactic expression of God's wisdom and power (Dunn). Therefore, the message of the gospel is "God's wisdom" (1 Cor 2:7), divine wisdom derived from the Creator whose previously hidden plan of salvation has become reality through the crucifixion* (1 Cor 2:8). Thus the proclamation of the gospel of Christ who is God's wisdom has the power to lead to faith* and the bestowal of the gift of the Spirit (1 Cor 2:4-5; see Holy Spirit).

*3.2. Christ and Attributes of Wisdom.* Paul transfers to Christ attributes of Wisdom which speak of her being and nature. We notice this transfer in the Christ hymns in Philippians 2:6-11 and Colossians 1:15-20 where Jewish wisdom theology has been recognized as part of the hermeneutical context (cf. Prov 8:22-25; Sir 1:4; 24:9; Wis 7:26; 9:4, 9-10).

The designation of Christ as being "in the form of God" and "being equal to God" (Phil 2:6) draws upon the thought of Wisdom being near to God, sharing in God's nature and existing before creation. The pattern of humiliation-exaltation and the concept of pre-existence* is reminiscent of the Wisdom of Solomon (cf. Wis 2:12-20; 5:1-6; 6:18-19; 9:4-10).

The description of Christ as "the image* of the invisible God," "the first born* of all creation," "the beginning" and dwelling place of "all the fullness*" (Col 1:15, 18, 19) also takes up attributes of personified Wisdom: the Son is the manifestation of God in creation, he enjoys precedence in both rank and existence over creation, he is the effective presence of the divine power of creation, and he is the perfect manifestation of the attributes and activities of God.

*3.3. Christ and the Functions of Wisdom.* Along with the attributes of wisdom Paul also transferred functions of wisdom to Christ when he describes his work.

With the confession that Jesus Christ is Lord "through whom are all things and through whom we exist" (1 Cor 8:6), Paul stressed his conviction that Christ is the mediator of both creation and salvation (as the new creation). In Jewish wisdom theology divine wisdom was described as mediating creation (Prov 8:27, 30; Wis 7:12, 22; 9:9; 14:2) and as having a soteriological role (cf. Sir 24:8-12; Wis 10:15-21).

Paul's midrash on the exodus tradition in 1 Corinthians 10:1-4 draws decisively on the wisdom literature and Philo (see Old Testament in Paul). In Wisdom 10:17-18; 11:4 the cloud which guided the Israelites in the wilderness was identified with *sophia*. Philo equated the rock from which they drank with *sophia* (and the *Logos;* Philo *Det. Pot Ins.* 115-118), and the spiritual interpretation of bread and water as gifts of wisdom is also sapiential (Prov 9:1-6; Sir 15:3). Thus the statement "they drank from the supernatural rock which followed them, and the rock was Christ" (1 Cor 10:4) implies that Christ is pre-existent and that Christ is understood in terms of divine wisdom both as mediator of God's life-giving salvation and revelation in the history of Israel.

The function of wisdom as mediator of creation and God's "master workman" (Prov 8:27-30; Sir 1:4; 24:9; 43:26; Philo *Rer. Div. Her.* 189, 199; *Fug.* 112; *Quaest. in Gen.* 2.118) was transferred to Christ in Colossians 1:16: "In him all things were created," that is, Christ is the sphere within which the work of creation takes place; "all things were created through him," that is, Christ is the instrument of creation; "all things were created for him," that is, Christ is the goal of creation and therefore of history (cf. Eph 1:10; see Creation and New Creation).

*3.4. Pre-existence and Wisdom.* Paul speaks of Jesus Christ as pre-existent (see Pre-existence) and as savior.* The link between pre-existence (Habermann) and the work of salvation becomes understandable on the background of the wisdom tradition.

*3.4.1. Mediator of Creation and Salvation.* The preexistent Christ is the mediator of creation and the incarnated Christ is the mediator of salvation (1 Cor 8:6; Col 1:15-20). This correlation of creation and salvation resumes the cosmological foundation of salvation in part of the wisdom tradition. The Christ hymn in Colossians 1 is particularly relevant: just as wisdom had been described as "image of God" (Wis 7:26; Philo *Leg. All.* 1.43), Paul calls Christ "the image of the invisible God" (Col 1:15; see Image); as wisdom was first creation, or "firstborn"* (Prov 8:22-29; Sir 1:4; 24:9; Wis 9:9; Philo *Quaest. in Gen.* 4.97; *Virt.* 62), Paul calls Christ "the firstborn of all creation" (Col 1:15); as wisdom was God's creative power in the creation of the world (Prov 8:27-30; Sir 1:4; 24:9; 43:26; Philo *Rer. Div. Her.* 189, 199; *Fug.* 112), Paul emphasizes that "in him all things were created" (Col 1:16) and "in him all things hold together" (Col 1:17). And Christ is the *plerōma*, the cosmic presence of God (Col 1:19; cf. Prov 8:12-14; Bar 3:38; Sir 24:4-11; *see* Fullness).

The objections of J. D. G. Dunn to the view that Paul's christological assertions in Colossians 1 presuppose pre-existence run contrary to the evidence. Whether we take the prepositional phrase "in him" (*en autō*) in an instrumental sense (cf. the similar constructions with *dia* in Col 1:16, and compare 1 Cor 8:6 and Jn 1:3; see Lohse) or in a broader sense as indicating the "sphere" within which the work of creation took place (Bruce), Paul asserts in Colossians 1:16a that the act of creation (aorist *ektisthē*) depended causally on Christ—an assertion which does not make sense if Christ was not present at creation.

*3.4.2. Incarnation.* The pre-existent Christ humbled himself by becoming human (Phil 2:6-11). The notion of incarnation may find a point of contact with the wisdom tradition in the Similitudes of Enoch (*1 Enoch* 48:1-7) where the messianic Son of Man, who is given traits of the pre-existent Wisdom, is said to establish God's kingly rule on earth (Schimanowski).

*3.4.3. Sending.* The notion of the sending of the Son into the world (Gal 4:4-5; Rom 8:3-4) is compared to the wisdom motif of God sending pre-existent Wisdom from the throne of his glory* (Schweizer). In Wisdom 9:10 the writer calls for wisdom to be sent forth (*exaposteilon*) "from the holy heavens" and correlates the giving of wisdom with the sending of the Holy Spirit "from on high" (Wis 9:17). Paul uses *exapostellō* only in Galatians 4:4, 6 where we also find the sending of the Son linked with the sending of the Spirit. As Wisdom 9:10 describes Wisdom dwelling with God before creation, so Paul obviously presupposes the existence of the Son in God's presence before his coming into the world.

*3.5. Christ, Wisdom and the Law.* It has been suggested that the identification of Jesus with pre-existent Wisdom as mediator of salvation replaced the traditional identification of Law* and wisdom (Merklein).

On the basis of the theology of Deuteronomy (cf. Deut 4:6-8; 30:11-14; 33:14) and certain wisdom psalms (Ps 1; 19; 119) the early Jewish wisdom tradition identified Law (Torah) and wisdom. Ben Sira, Torah scholar and wisdom teacher, formulated and implied this correlation repeatedly (e.g., Sir 15:1; 17:11; 19:20; 21:11; 24:23). Law and Wisdom are one in that they are both God's gift to Israel. The objective of both Law and wisdom is submission to God's will, both summarized in the concept of the "fear* of the Lord." Those who keep the commandments practice wisdom, and the sages obey the Law. Both Law and wisdom focus on leading the individual and the nation to a pious and successful life in the presence of God in the context of the world created by him. Both Law and wisdom reveal the will of God for humanity, and both are compared with light which gives orientation (Sir 24:32; 45:17). The scribe as *sōpēr* ("scholar") and *ḥākām* ("wise man") studies and teaches both the Law and the wisdom traditions (Sir 38:34—39:3).

It seems unlikely, however, that Paul's identification of Jesus Christ with Wisdom, thus establishing Christ's pre-existence, was derived from the traditional Jewish correlation of Law and wisdom. Paul never describes Christ in terms of Law (notice how he eliminates all references to the Torah when he uses Deuteronomy 30:12-14 to describe the presence of Christ in Romans 10:6-8). Rather, Paul describes and defines the Law in terms of Christ: the Law comes under the rule of Christ (Gal 6:2; 1 Cor 9:21; cf. Rom 3:27; 8:2). Paul apparently sought to avoid the misunderstanding that Christ, as the embodiment of God's will, brought a new Torah which humans must fulfill, replacing the old Torah. As Christ has fulfilled the Torah in his death and resurrection* "for us," the soteriological function of Torah (cf. the sacrifices) as a way to righteousness* has come to an end. Since Paul asserted that the Torah has lost all salvific significance with the death and the resurrection of Christ, it is doubtful that he would have transferred soteriological functions of Torah to Christ and thus have correlated Christ and the Law (Schnabel). It was possible for Paul to transfer functions of divine wisdom to Christ without having to introduce wisdom's correlation with Torah.

**4. The Gospel.**

*4.1. Gospel and Wisdom in Romans 10:6-8.* Quoting part of Deuteronomy 30:12-14, where Israel has been told that she does not have to climb up to heaven to discover God's will nor does she need to go beyond the sea or descend into the abyss as God has stooped down to reveal his will in the Law, Paul interpreted the passage by means of the pesher method. Where the quotation speaks about the Law, Paul speaks about Christ. Scholars have observed links between Paul's exegesis and the sapiential motif of the hiddenness of wisdom and of the impossibility of ascending to heaven and coming down (Job 28; Prov 30:4; Bar 3:29-30; Sir 1:3, 6; 24:3-7; 51:19). What Moses* had said of the divine Law and what the Jewish tradition had interpreted in terms of Wisdom, Paul says of Christ. God's Wisdom is no longer exclusively accessible in the Torah since the gospel, the goal of the Torah, is now universally available by faith in Christ. Although Christ is not present on earth, he is far from hidden or unattainable; he is present in the proclamation of the gospel of righteousness by faith.

*4.2. The Revelation Scheme.* Paul's theme of the mystery* of God which was formerly hidden but has now been revealed in the gospel of Jesus Christ (1 Cor 2:6-14; Eph 3:4-11; Col 1:26-27; Rom 16:25-26; 2 Tim 1:9-11; Tit 1:2-3) has affinities with the sapiential conception of the hiddenness of wisdom which is revealed in the Law (Wolter).

### 5. Ethics.
Because wisdom deals with the comprehension of life and reality, with exhortation and with proper behavior in everyday life, it is not surprising to observe the presence of the sapiential tradition in the ethics* of Paul.

*5.1. Lists and House-Tables.* Both the lists, or "catalogs," of vices and virtues (Rom 1:29-32; 1 Cor 5:9-11; 6:9-10; 2 Cor 12:20; Gal 5:19-21, 22-23; Eph 5:5; Phil 4:8; Col 3:5, 8, 12; 1 Tim 3:1-13; Tit 1:5-9; *see* Virtues and Vices) and the household codes, or *Haustafeln* (Eph 5:21—6:9; Col 3:18—4:1; 1 Tim 2:8-15; 6:1-2; Tit 2:1-10; *see* Households and Household Codes), have been compared with similar forms and concepts in the OT and early Jewish (Hellenistic) wisdom tradition (cf. Prov 6:17-18; Wis 14:23-26; Sir 7:18-28). The links with wisdom are evident in those areas where Paul characterizes specific behavior which is not covered by the commandments of the Decalog.

The lists of hardships, or *peristaseis* catalogs (1 Cor 4:9-13; 2 Cor 4:8-9; 6:4-10; 11:23-28; 12:10; cf. Rom 8:35-39; Phil 4:11-12; 2 Tim 3:11; *see* Afflictions, Trials, Hardships), share features found in similar lists of vicissitudes in the Greek tradition, particularly in Stoicism, where the true sage is the suffering sage, established as such by his endurance. These lists aim at magnifying the sage's endurance (*askēsis*) and serenity (*ataraxia*), proving that he is a *sophos* who cannot be prevented from acting virtuously by even the most dire calamities. Paul's *peristaseis* catalogues, at least in 2 Corinthians, appear to have a similar revelatory function: the hardships, which are attributed to God, show that he is a true apostle* and a person of proven integrity (2 Cor 6:4). However, his self-commendation by means of listing his hardships is far removed from egocentric boasting which sees endurance as a demonstration of one's own strength. When Paul boasts of his hardships he "boasts in the Lord" (1 Cor 1:31; *see* Boasting), as they provide the occasion for demonstrating the power of God (Fitzgerald).

*5.2. Individual Exhortations.* Paul's ethical exhortation shares numerous elements with the wisdom tradition, both in form (substantiated admonitions, e.g., 1 Thess 4:11-12; 2 Cor 13:11; Col 4:3-4; Phil 4:5; series of short, unsubstantiated admonitions: Rom 12:9-21; Gal 5:25—6:10; Phil 4:4-9; 1 Thess 4:1-12; Col 4:2-6; Eph 5:15-20) and in content.

*5.3. Orientation for Living.* Paul's ethics can be described in terms of the horizon of the traditional early Jewish correlation of Law and wisdom being fused with the horizon of God's salvific action in and through Jesus Christ. The Christian is called and enabled to submit to God's will as revealed in the Law, in the words of Jesus Christ and in the pronouncements of the apostles. At the same time he has the responsibility to realize God's will in the diverse situations of everyday life (Schnabel). This responsibility, as it is observed in Paul's letters, shares many links with wisdom theology (cf. Rom 16:19; Phil 1:9-10) as well as with Stoicism.

The affinities with Stoic ethics (e.g., the appeal to reason in Rom 12:2; 14:5; *autarkeia/autarkēs* in 1 Tim 6:6; Phil 4:11) are due both to Paul's cognizance of contemporary Hellenistic ethics as well as to the Hellenistic influences in contemporary Judaism (cf. Wisdom of Solomon, Aristobulos, 4 Maccabees, Philo). Such parallels must not obscure the fact that the basic structures of Stoic ethics (*see* Philosophy) are utterly distinct from Paul's ethics: Stoic ethics was fundamentally rationalistic, viewing humankind as the ultimate measure of morality, and pursuing the ideal of the autonomous and autocratic personality which could arrive at moral perfection in its own strength and on the basis of innate standards.

The following sapiential elements may be examined:

(1) Reference to social conventions, to what is generally accepted, necessary and befitting (Rom 12:2, 9; 13:3; 14:16; 15:2; 1 Cor 11:13; Eph 6:1; Phil 1:10; 4:8; Col 3:18, 20; 1 Thess 5:15; 1 Tim 2:10; Tit 3:8, 14), including consideration for the reaction of outsiders (Rom 14:18; 1 Cor 10:32; 1 Thess 4:12).

(2) The Spirit as guide for right decisions in discerning what is wise behavior in specific circumstances (Col 1:9-10).

(3) Christian love as leading to knowledge and insight in settling questions regarding behavior (1 Cor 3:18; Phil 1:9-10).

(4) Appeal to the cognitive faculties of the believer: reason which perceives what is good and right in specific situations (Rom 12:2; 14:5; 2 Cor 10:5; cf. the verb *noutheteō* "to put in the right mind, encourage" in Rom 15:14; 1 Cor 4:14; 1 Thess 5:12, 14; etc); discernment as critical choice and a practical testing for what is

satisfactory (1 Thess 5:21; Rom 12:2; 14:22-23; Gal 6:2-5; Phil 1:9-11); and reflection on what is the appropriate attitude and action (Phil 4:8).

(5) Appeal to the conscience which is (partially) based in God's universally revealed Law/wisdom (Rom 2:15), which is, among other factors, motivated by God's orders of creation (Rom 13:5) and which functions, apart from being the tribunal which reminds of God's judgment,* as critical self-evaluation and self-judgment as to one's moral conduct (cf. 1 Cor 4:4; 2 Cor 1:12; Rom 13:5).

(6) Admonition with motivation, as Paul does not look for blind obedience but aims at understanding. This links Paul's ethics as apostolic teaching with practical admonition and wisdom (cf. Col 1:28; 3:16).

### 6. Eschatology.

When Paul discusses Israel's role in God's plan of salvation (Rom 9—11), arguing that when "the full number of the Gentiles" has come in "all Israel will be saved" (Rom 11:25-26; *see* Israel), his argument shows affinity with both apocalyptic* and sapiential thought. This confluence of apocalyptic and wisdom has been analyzed as enabling Paul to maintain a balanced tension between God's impartial treatment of all and God's faithfulness to Israel (Johnson). The wisdom theme of a potter and two types of vessels shows how God elects with purpose to demonstrate his wrath,* power* and glory* (Rom 9). The sapiential correlation of divine wisdom and Torah helps to show that the gospel as the new locus of God's will is universally available (Rom 10; cf. Rom 3:2). The mystery of Israel's salvation, which is a mystery of God's wisdom (Rom 11:25), leads Paul to a hymn in praise of God's wisdom and glory (Rom 11:33-36).

*See also* CHRISTOLOGY; ETHICS; FIRSTBORN; GOSPEL; HOUSEHOLDS AND HOUSEHOLD CODES; LAW; PHILOSOPHY; PRE-EXISTENCE; VIRTUES AND VICES.

BIBLIOGRAPHY. E. Brandenburger, *Fleisch und Geist* (WMANT 29; Neukirchen: Neukirchener, 1968); J. L. Crenshaw, *Old Testament Wisdom* (Atlanta: John Knox, 1981); J. A. Davis, *Wisdom and Spirit* (Lanham: University Press of America, 1984); J. D. G. Dunn, *Christology in the Making* (Philadelphia: Westminster, 1980); G. D. Fee, *The First Epistle to the Corinthians* (NICNT; Grand Rapids: Eerdmans, 1987); A. Feuillet, *Le Christ Sagesse de Dieu d'après les Épîtres Pauliniennes* (Paris: Gabalda, 1966); J. T. Fitzgerald, *Cracks in an Earthen Vessel* (SBLDS 99; Atlanta: Scholars, 1988 [1984]); H. Gese, "Die Weisheit, der Menschensohn und die Ursprünge der Christologie als konsequente Entfaltung der biblischen Theologie," *SEA* 39 (1979) 77-114; J. Habermann, *Präexistenzaussagen im Neuen Testament* (EHS 23/362; Bern/Frankfurt: Lang, 1990); R. G. Hamerton-Kelly, *Pre-existence, Wisdom, and the Son of Man* (SNTSMS 21; Cambridge: University Press, 1973); M. Hengel, "Jesus als messianischer Lehrer der Weisheit und die Anfänge der Christologie," in *Sagesse et Religion* (Paris, 1979) 148-88; E. E. Johnson, *The Function of Apocalyptic and Wisdom Traditions in Romans 9-11* (SBLDS 109; Atlanta: Scholars, 1989); S. Kim, *The Origin of Paul's Gospel* (WUNT 2/4; 2d ed; Tübingen: J. C. B. Mohr, 1984 [1981]); H. von Lips, *Weisheitliche Traditionen im Neuen Testament* (WMANT 64; Neukirchen-Vluyn: Neukirchener, 1990); J. P. Louw and E. A. Nida, *Greek-English Lexicon of the New Testament Based on Semantic Domains* (2d ed.; New York: United Bible Societies, 1989 [1988]); H. Merklein, "Zur Entstehung der urchristlichen Aussage vom präexistenten Sohn Gottes," in *Zur Geschichte des Urchristentums*, ed. G. Dautzenberg (Freiburg: Herder, 1979) 33-62; G. von Rad, *Wisdom in Israel* (Nashville: Abingdon, 1972); G. Schimanowski, *Weisheit und Messias* (WUNT 2/17; Tübingen: J. C. B. Mohr, 1985); E. J. Schnabel, *Law and Wisdom from Ben Sira to Paul* (WUNT 2/16; Tübingen: J. C. B. Mohr, 1985); E. Schweizer, "Zum religionsgeschichtlichen Hintergrund der 'Sendungsformel' Gal 4.4f., Röm 8.3f., Joh 3.16f., 1Joh 4.9," in *Beiträge zur Theologie des Neuen Testaments* (Zürich: Zwingli, 1970) 83-89; H. Weder, *Das Kreuz Jesu bei Paulus* (FRLANT 125; Göttingen: Vandenhoeck & Ruprecht, 1981); U. Wilckens, *Weisheit und Torheit* (BHT 26; Tübingen: J. C. B. Mohr, 1959); idem, "σοφία κτλ," *TDNT* VII:496-526; idem, "Das Kreuz Christi als die Tiefe der Weisheit Gottes: Zu 1.Kor 2.1-16," in *Paolo a una chiesa divisa (1 Cor 1-4)* (Rome: St. Paul's Abbey, 1980) 43-81; H. Windisch, "Die göttliche Weisheit der Juden und die paulinische Christologie," in *Neutestamentliche Studien, Festschrift G. Heinrici*, ed. A. Deissmann and H. Windisch (Leipzig: Hinrichs, 1914) 220-34; M. Wolter, "Verborgene Weisheit und Heil für die Heiden," *ZTK* 84 (1987) 297-319.                    E. J. Schnabel

**WISDOM CHRISTOLOGY.** *See* CHRISTOLOGY; LORD; PRE-EXISTENCE; WISDOM.

**WISH PRAYERS.** *See* PRAYER.

**WITCHCRAFT.** *See* EPHESIANS, LETTER TO THE; MAGIC.

## WITNESS

In Greek the noun *martys* can refer to a witness who can certify facts, especially in a court of law. *Martyreō* can refer to the act of bearing witness; *martyria*, to the witness itself; and *martyrion* to the objective evidence or testimony provided. In the Pauline letters *witness* terms are used in a variety of ways.

1. Gospel and Witness
2. Apostleship and Witness
3. Inner Witness and Public Witness

### 1. Gospel and Witness.

It is instructive to begin by noting that the noun for "testimony" (*martyrion*) appears in Paul's letters as a synonym for the gospel.* Paul speaks of "the testimony about God" (1 Cor 2:1 NIV, if this is the correct textual reading), "our testimony about Christ" (1 Cor 1:6 NIV) or simply "our testimony" (2 Thess 1:10). The Pastorals* urge Timothy not to "be ashamed of your testimony to our Lord" (2 Tim 1:8 REB; cf. Rom 1:16) and observe that Christ's "testimony" was "borne at the proper time" (1 Tim 2:6 NASB).

Paul also mentions the testimony furnished by the Scriptures (cf. Jn 5:39; Acts 10:43; *see* Old Testament in Paul). Thus the righteousness* of God, which is revealed in the gospel, is "attested" by the Law* and the Prophets (*martyroumenē*, Rom 3:21). On the other hand, in the Pastorals the gospel is said to be "attested" by a good reputation (1 Tim 3:7) and by good deeds (1 Tim 5:10).

### 2. Apostleship and Witness.

The integrity of Paul's apostleship* and the truth* of the gospel were closely identified. Witness terminology thus plays an important role when Paul speaks of his apostleship.

*2.1. Bearing Witness.* Paul highlights the fact that he and the other apostles "testified" that God* raised Christ* from the dead (1 Cor 15:15). He uses *martyreō* repeatedly to insist on the truth of his assertions (e.g., Rom 10:2; 2 Cor 8:3; Gal 4:15). Here Paul attests respectively to the "zeal" for God" which the Jews display, the generosity of the Macedonian churches and the former helpfulness of the Galatians. More generally, Paul "testifies," or declares, a spiritual principle to the Galatians (Gal 5:3) and "solemnly warns" his hearers when this is necessary (*diamartyromai*, 1 Thess 4:6).

*2.2. Credible Witness.* Paul recognized that Christian witness required integrity. He appealed to the Thessalonians, reminding them: "You are witnesses, and so is God, of how holy, righteous and blameless we were among you who believed" (1 Thess 2:10 NIV). This is one of many places where he stresses his sincerity (Rom 9:1; 2 Cor 2:17; 11:10, 31; 12:19). Paul's life backed up the teaching of his lips. Both offered credible testimony to the gospel (1 Thess 1:5).

*2.3. False Witness.* Paul abhorred false witness, as he

shows in drawing out the terrible consequences which follow if there is no resurrection* of Christ (1 Cor 15:12-19). The reference in 1 Corinthians 15:15 to the possibility of Paul as an apostle being found to be one of the "false witnesses" is striking (*pseudomartyres*, cf. Mt 26:60), for it recalls the strong OT prohibitions against false witness (Ex 20:16; Deut 5:20; Prov 21:28). It emphasizes the tremendous importance Paul placed on the resurrection of Jesus as the indispensable foundation for the Christian faith.

*2.4. Pastoral Witness.* Initial witness was not enough, for new Christians required discipling and encouragement (hence Paul's letters; *see* Pastor). For example, Paul instructed the Thessalonians about a Christian lifestyle (1 Thess 4:1-12). Because his converts misunderstood his witness, he had to write a second letter to warn them against idleness and irresponsible conduct. Nevertheless, he is able to rejoice "because you believed our testimony to you" (2 Thess 1:10 NIV). Paul's witness to them, and to the other communities where he worked, was no "flash in the pan." He cared deeply for the spiritual welfare of those he led to Christ, and he sought to instruct and nurture them in the things of God.

*2.5. Multiple Witness.* Paul applies the Jewish law of multiple witness, "that at the mouth of two or three witnesses every matter may be established" (2 Cor 13:1; cf. 1 Tim 5:19), to his warnings to the Corinthian church (perhaps associating the two or three witnesses with his second and promised third visit to Corinth; but see commentaries). This is clearly an important principle in both the OT and NT and is also evident in the Dead Sea Scrolls and the Talmud (Num 35:30; Deut 17:6; 19:15; 1 Kings 21:13; Mt 18:16; Jn 5:31-32; 8:13; Heb 10:28; cf. 1QS 9:16—10:3; *b. Sanh.* 9b).

*2.6. Divine Witness.* Repeatedly Paul calls on God as a "witness" (*martys*) to apostolic truthfulness and integrity (Rom 1:9; 2 Cor 1:23; Phil 1:8; 1 Thess 2:5, 10). The cognate verb *martyromai* is used to mean "solemnly charge" or "testify" (1 Thess 2:12; Eph 4:17), and the compound verb *diamartyromai* is employed (1 Thess 4:6); in the Pastorals this verb appears in impressive religious contexts: "I *solemnly charge* you in the presence of God and of Jesus Christ" (1 Tim 5:21 NASB; 2 Tim 2:14; 4:1).

### 3. Inner Witness and Public Witness.

*3.1. Conscience as a Witness.* In several passages Paul refers to the conscience* as a witness (Rom 2:14-15; 9:1; 2 Cor 1:12). In 2 Corinthians 1:12 Paul defends his trustworthiness in the face of slanderous opposition to his apostleship. He appeals to the witness (*martyrion*) of his conscience, that he has "behaved in the world with frankness and godly sincerity, not by earthly wisdom* but by the grace of God"—and "all the more" toward the Corinthians.

Similarly Paul mentions the conscience in Romans 2:14-15 and in Romans 9:1, where the conscience "bears witness with" something else (perhaps the divine law) in accusing or vindicating a person's integrity (*symmartyreō* is used). Here the conscience "joins in giving evidence" which will secure the acquittal or the vindication of the person concerned. The conscience of the Christian can function as a reliable witness, for it is capable of being illumined by the Holy Spirit* (Rom 9:1). Here again Paul insists on his veracity and truthfulness: "I speak the truth in Christ—I am not lying."

In Romans 8:16 the Holy Spirit "bears witness with" the Christian's own spirit that he or she is a child of God (*see* Adoption). This consentient divine witness undergirds the Christian's own testimony and is clearly a use of the formal principle of multiple witness which is employed by Paul elsewhere (2 Cor 13:1; cf. 1 Tim 5:19). Here the Spirit functions as an advocate in the inner court of the believer, testifying to his or her adoption into the divine family.

*3.2. Public Witness.* The witness theme is present in Romans 10: 9-10, where public "confession" of Christ is involved. This testimony is in keeping with the demand for open acknowledgement of commitment that is found in the teaching of Jesus (Mt 10:32; Lk 12:8; cf. Rev 3:5). Similar public testimony to Christ appears in the Pastorals, where Paul has spoken "before many witnesses" (2 Tim 2:2 RSV) and Timothy has made "the good confession in the presence of many witnesses" (1 Tim 6:12 RSV). Timothy's model is Christ himself, who made "the good confession," giving his witness in solemn court "before Pontius Pilate" (1 Tim 6:13).

*See also* APOSTLE; CONSCIENCE; GOSPEL; HOLY SPIRIT; TRUTH.

BIBLIOGRAPHY. J. Beutler, "μαρτυρέω κτλ," *EDNT* 2.389-91; idem, "μαρτυρία," *EDNT* 2.391-93; idem, "μάρτυς," *EDNT* 2.393-95; H. von Campenhausen, "Das Bekenntnis im Urchristentum," *ZNW* 63 (1972) 210-53; O. Michel, "ὁμολογέω κτλ," *TDNT* V.199-220; T. Preiss, "The Inner Witness of the Holy Spirit," *Int* 7 (1953) 259-80; H. Strathmann, "μάρτυς κτλ," *TDNT* IV.474-514; A. A. Trites, *The New Testament Concept of Witness* (SNTSMS 31; Cambridge: University Press, 1977); idem, *New Testament Witness in Today's World* (Valley Forge, PA: Judson, 1983); A. A. Trites and L. Coenen, "Witness," *NIDNTT* 3.1036-51; H. van Vliet, *No Single Testimony: A Study in the Adoption of the Law of Deut 19:15 par. into the New Testament* (STRT 4; Utrecht: Kemink & Zoon, 1958).

A. A. Trites

**WOMAN.** *See* HEAD; MAN AND WOMAN.

**WOMEN IN MINISTRY.** *See* MAN AND WOMAN.

**WONDERS.** *See* SIGNS, WONDERS, MIRACLES.

**WORKS.** *See* JAMES AND PAUL; JUDGMENT; LAW; WORKS OF THE LAW.

## WORKS OF THE LAW

The phrase "works of Law" (*erga nomou*) is used eight times in Paul. He affirms that no one can be justified by "works of Law" (Gal 2:16; Rom 3:20, 28), that the Spirit (*see* Holy Spirit) was not received by "works of Law" but by responding to the gospel* in faith* (Gal 3:2, 5) and that those who are characterized by "works of Law" are cursed (Gal 3:10; *see* Curse). The meaning of the phrase is widely debated in contemporary Pauline scholarship. This article will argue that when Paul used the phrase "works of Law" he referred to *doing what the Law* commanded. Paul maintained that no one can be justified (*see* Justification) before God* *by doing what the Law commands,* for no one can do everything which the Law demands and, should they experience some measure of success, they would sin* in their pride of achievement. Moreover, forgiveness is now only obtained through the death of Christ (*see* Death of Christ) on the cross, not through the OT cultus. Thus, those who seek to be justified by doing the "works of Law" end up cursed; the only way to receive the Spirit is not by obeying the Law (for no one can obey it fully) but by faith in Jesus. This definition and perspective on Paul is far from a consensus in NT scholarship. At least five other views must first be considered.

1. Nomistic Service
2. Jewish Nationalism
3. Legalism
4. Subjective Genitive
5. Human Inability
6. Human Inability, Legalism and Salvation History

**1. Nomistic Service.**

E. Lohmeyer claimed that "works of Law" does not refer primarily to the performance of the specific deeds commanded by the Law. Instead, the focus is on the religious context of existence in which the Law is kept. J. B. Tyson, drawing on the work of Lohmeyer, has argued for a similar view. The focus is not on "Law" as the demand of God which must be fulfilled; instead, the emphasis is on the condition of life under Torah, particularly the demand to observe food* laws and to be circumcised (*see* Circumcision).

Tyson describes such a way of life as "nomistic service," as "Jewish existence." Paul rejects "works of Law" for salvation-historical reasons. "Works of Law" are not excluded because they cannot be fulfilled nor because they lead to meritorious works-righteousness. The coming of Jesus marks the turn of an era; the era of separation between Jews and Gentiles* has ended.

## 2. Jewish Nationalism.

J. D. G. Dunn advocates a position similar to Lohmeyer's in many respects, but he sharpens it further. "Works of Law" does not focus on the Law in general but on "identity markers"—particularly circumcision, food laws and Sabbath keeping (*see* Holy Days)—which functioned to separate Jews from Gentiles. Contrary to Reformation exegesis, Paul was not criticizing self-achievement, legalism or the doing of the Law. What Paul had in mind when he wrote of "works of Law" was the social function of the Law insofar as it divided Jews and Gentiles. The problem was with Jewish *nationalism* and *particularism*, not with *legalism* or *activism*. Those who insisted on Gentiles observing the "works of Law" were requiring that Gentiles become Jews in order to enter the people of God (*see* Church), thereby limiting the people of God on racial and ethnic grounds.

The conclusions of E. P. Sanders and F. Watson are similar to Dunn's in some respects. Sanders stresses that Paul argued from *solution to plight*. In other words, Paul was convinced that "works of Law" do not save because, as a Christian, he believed that salvation* comes only through Jesus Christ. If salvation comes solely through Christ,* then it follows that obedience to Law is not crucial for salvation. Paul's real problem with Judaism, according to Sanders, was that it was not Christianity. To put it another way: Sanders rejects the idea that Paul excluded salvation by "works of Law" because the Law could not be obeyed or because such obedience was legalistic. Instead, the reason Paul ruled out salvation by "works of Law" was because he was persuaded that salvation is available only through Christ.

F. Watson, in contrast with Sanders, emphasizes the social setting of Paul's ministry. Paul's view of the Law, according to Watson, has for too long been understood through the lens of Reformation exegesis. Paul's exclusion of salvation by "works of Law" is best understood sociologically. Paul insisted that salvation does not come via the Law because he wanted his congregations to separate from the Jewish community (*see* Social Setting). Thus Paul's negative statements about the Law served an ideology that supported the separation of

Pauline congregations from the Jewish community.

## 3. Legalism.

D. P. Fuller argues that "works of Law" focuses primarily on laws such as circumcision and food laws, but he sees the underlying problem as *legalism*. In Galatians 3:10 Paul is not saying that *no one can* obey the Law perfectly, and that this imperfect obedience explains the reason for the curse. Such traditional exegesis reads an unwarranted proposition into the text. Rather, the verse claims that "those who are of the works of the Law are cursed" because those who are characterized by "works of Law" are guilty of the sin of bribing God. They think they can pile up merit before God and thereby escape the curse. Such exegesis is confirmed, says Fuller, by *2 Baruch* 48:38; 57:2; Romans 10:3 and Philippians 3:9, where the fundamental sin consists in establishing one's own righteousness.* Moreover, Galatians 2:15-21 confirms such an interpretation, according to Fuller, for there the focus on the ritual Law shows that the problem is with Jewish pride and notions of superiority. Fuller emphasizes that Paul's polemic against "works of Law" was not a polemic against the OT Law per se, but was directed against the Judaizers'* legalistic distortion of what the OT Law teaches.

H. Hübner's understanding (representative of the Bultmann school) of "works of Law" is quite similar to Fuller's. He also sees legalism as the central problem Paul was resisting, the attempt to earn favor in God's sight by performing the Law. The distinctive feature in Hübner's (and the general Bultmannian) position is the contention that even if people could obey the Law perfectly, they would still be cursed. Such perfect obedience would still be sinful because it would be motivated by legalism, the attempt to merit favor with God by good works.

## 4. Subjective Genitive.

L. Gaston has concluded that *nomou* in the phrase *erga nomou* should be taken as a subjective genitive and translated "works which the Law does." A number of texts are marshalled in support of this interpretation: the Law produces wrath* (Rom 4:15), knowledge* of sin comes from the Law (Rom 3:20), the Law produces death (Rom 7:10; *see* Life and Death) and the Law deceives (Rom 7:11). Thus, when Paul says that no one can be justified by "the works of the Law," the point is that the Law produces sin and unrighteousness, and therefore it cannot make a person righteous.

## 5. Human Inability.

S. Westerholm maintains that when Paul uses the

word *works* (*erga*) in the phrase "works of the Law," he does so in a general sense. Paul is arguing that no one can be right before God or receive the Spirit by doing what the Law commands, for no one obeys the Law perfectly. Paul excludes "works of Law" as a way of salvation *not* because they are a legalistic attempt to amass merit before God. It is not legalism which Paul opposes but human imperfection: the inability of people to do everything the Law demands.

### 6. Human Inability, Legalism and Salvation History.
The view favored in this article is that Paul denied the possibility of righteousness by "works of Law" for three reasons: (1) no one can obey the Law perfectly; (2) any attempt to obey the Law to gain righteousness is legalistic and contrary to the principle of faith; and (3) the salvation-historical shift which took effect with the death and resurrection of Jesus Christ.

*6.1. The Problem of Reductionism.* Watson is probably right in detecting some sociological factors which contributed to Paul's understanding of "works of Law." But he unfortunately uses sociology in a reductionistic way and for all practical purposes eliminates the theological dimensions of Paul's thinking. Paul's own explanation for excluding "works of Law" as a way to righteousness is rooted in his theology (see 6.2-3 below). Watson attempts to circumvent Pauline theology by explaining Paul's view solely from a sociological perspective. A better approach would take more seriously the theological foundation of Paul's thinking.

Sanders' position is reductionistic in another way. He sees Paul as arguing from an a priori theological premise that salvation cannot come by "works of Law." He rightly argues that Paul rejected the Law as a way of salvation because of the change in dispensations. Paul no longer believed OT sacrifices atoned for sin. Salvation was available only through the death of Christ (Gal 2:21). Only he could remove the curse which remained on those who did not observe the Law (Gal 3:13). Nonetheless, Sanders' solution is not comprehensive enough, for Paul thought "works of Law" did not save because a shift had taken place in salvation history and because human beings could not keep the Law. R. H. Gundry has demonstrated that both of these convictions—the change in dispensations and human experience—were factors in Paul's dismissal of the Law as a way of salvation.

*6.2. The Argument for Human Inability.* The fundamental flaw of some of the positions described above (esp. Dunn's) is the limited focus assigned to the word *erga* in the phrase "works of Law." For example, to say that the focus in "works of Law" is on certain ritual laws (i.e., circumcision, food laws and Sabbath) col-

lapses upon further reading of Galatians. Paul does not exclude righteousness based only on "works of Law," he also excludes righteousness by Law in a general sense (Gal 2:21; 3:11-12; 5:4). And since much of Galatians* centers on the temporally limited nature of the Mosaic covenant (Gal 3:15—4:7; *see* Covenant), it is strained to argue that only part of the Law is in focus when Paul speaks of "works of Law." Moreover, to say that Paul's emphasis when he refers to "works of Law" is on the ceremonial law is even harder to sustain in Romans, for the failure to be justified by "works of Law" in Romans 3:20 is due to the Jewish failure to obey the *moral claims of the Law,* not adherence to the ritual Law for nationalistic reasons. This last point is clearly supported by Romans 2:17-29 where the Jews are rebuked for failure to obey the Law, *even though* they are circumcised.

Moreover, both D. J. Moo and Westerholm have persuasively argued that the expression "works" (*erga*) in Paul refers to "deeds that are performed," and thus "works of Law" signifies the "deeds" or "actions" demanded by the Mosaic Law. The key to their argument is that in Romans 3—4 "works of Law" and "works" cannot be distinguished. Thus, in Romans 4:1-5 Paul says that Abraham* was not justified by his "works" (Rom 4:2) nor by "working" (Rom 4:4-5), and these cannot be limited to "identity markers" since Abraham lived before the arrival of the Mosaic Law. The example of Abraham is brought in to confirm what Paul has said earlier about justification by faith, and thus there is direct connection between the phrase "works of Law" in Romans 3:20, 28 and the concept of "works" developed in Romans 4:1-8. That Paul ruled out works generally as a way of obtaining salvation is also clear in Romans 9:11-12 where "works" are defined as "doing anything good or evil" (cf. Rom 11:6).

The connection between Paul's use of "works of Law" and "works" also undercuts Gaston's view that "works of Law" is a subjective genitive, for it is clear that "works" in Romans 4:1-5 refers to the good deeds done by Abraham. Moreover, the views of Lohmeyer and Tyson are also seriously called into question since the word *works* refers to concrete and specific actions which are performed; not just to a context of existence (cf. in Jewish literature *2 Bar* 4:9; 57:2; 4QFlor 1:7; 1QS 5:21; 6:18; 1QH 1:26; 4:31).

Thus we agree with Fuller in affirming that Paul counters legalism, but disagree with his claim that Paul does not say that no one can obey the Law perfectly. The point of Romans 1:18—3:20 seems to be that no one can be justified because no one obeys the demands of the Law. The problem identified is not merely a wrong attitude toward the Law but a failure to obey it. The same conclusion is most naturally derived from Galatians 3:10. The reason "those who are of the works of the Law are under a curse" is that no one can obey the Law perfectly, for Deuteronomy 27:26 pronounces a curse on those who do not "abide by *all things* written in the book of the Law." So again, the problem cannot be limited to a wrong attitude, whether legalism (Fuller) or nationalism (Dunn). The fundamental error of those who seek to be righteous before God by "the works of the Law" is that they do not and cannot do everything which the Law demands.

Hübner's understanding that people will be cursed *even if* they obey the entire Law, because such obedience would be legalistic, is contradicted by Paul. The apostle clearly states that *if* one could obey the whole Law, then that person would live (Gal 3:12, 21; Rom 10:5; cf. Lev 18:5). Of course, Paul believes such perfect obedience is a practical impossibility, and thus no one can be justified by doing the "works of Law."

*6.3. The Argument for Legalism.* Thus far we have defended the notion that Paul says no one can be righteous by Law because no one can obey everything the Law commands and because Christ initiated a shift in salvation history. But Paul's polemic against "works of Law" also seems to be a polemic against legalism. Legalism, as defined here, has two characteristics: (1) The attempt to earn righteousness by Law-obedience and (2) human pride in the obedience accomplished. The first characteristic of legalism is logically required by Paul's polemic against "works of Law" as we have defined it above. If "works of Law" describes deeds that are done in accordance with the Mosaic Law, and if Paul says that no one can be righteous or receive the Spirit by "works of Law," then it logically follows that Paul is saying that no one can earn or merit right standing with God by obeying the Law. Today many scholars argue that no Jew or Jewish Christian would have held that righteousness could be attained by doing the Law. They would have maintained that God's grace is prior to any adherence to the Law. But it is improbable that Paul was arguing against an opponent who did not exist. In that case, one of the main points of his argument would have related to no one.

Furthermore, the probability that Paul was arguing against legalism is strengthened by considering Paul's words about boasting.* Boasting is excluded, writes Paul, because righteousness does not stem from "works of Law" (Rom 3:27-28) or "works" (Rom 4:1-5). But surely if one did keep the Law, then one would be tempted to boast and take pride in one's perform-

ance. Again, it seems likely that Paul is addressing a real human problem (cf. Phil 3:4-11) and not simply making a theoretical statement. Otherwise, if no one struggled with this problem, it would seem pointless to exclude boasting. Knowledge of human nature also confirms that boasting in performance is natural to human beings. Of course, such boasting would be legitimate if people could actually do what the Law says. We have already seen, however, that Paul's foundational argument is that no one can obey the Law perfectly, and thus righteousness can never be attained by "works of Law." Thus, any boasting in human works is a perverse delusion since good works are lacking in any case, but those who are trying to impress God with their good works do not come to grips with their failures, thinking they have done enough good to merit favor from God. Such boasting lies at the root of human sin, the desire to heap glory and praise upon oneself instead of giving glory,* thanks and praise to the one and only God (Rom 1:21-23).

*See also* ABRAHAM; BOASTING; GALATIANS, LETTER TO THE; JAMES AND PAUL; JUDAIZERS; JUSTIFICATION; LAW; LAW OF CHRIST; RIGHTEOUSNESS, RIGHTEOUSNESS OF GOD; ROMANS, LETTER TO THE.

BIBLIOGRAPHY. J. D. G. Dunn, "The New Perspective on Paul," *BJRL* 65 (1983) 95-122; idem, "Works of the Law and the Curse of the Law (Galatians 3.10-14)," *NTS* 31 (1985) 523-42 [= *Jesus, Paul and the Law* (Louisville: Westminster/John Knox, 1990) 183-206; 215-36]; D. P. Fuller, "Paul and 'the Works of the Law,' " *WTJ* 38 (1975) 28-42; L. Gaston, "Works of Law as a Subjective Genitive," *SR* 13 (1984) 39-46 [= *Paul and the Torah* (Vancouver: University of British Columbia, 1987) 100-106]; R. H. Gundry, "Grace, Works and Staying Saved in Paul," *Bib* 66 (1985) 1-38; H. Hübner, "Was heisst bei Paulus 'Werke des Gesetzes'?," in *Glaube und Eschatologie: Festschrift für Werner Georg Kümmel zum 80. Geburtstag*, ed. E. Grässer and O. Merk (Tübingen: J. C. B. Mohr, 1985) 123-33; E. Lohmeyer, "Gesetzeswerke," *ZNW* 28 (1929) 177-207; D. J. Moo, " 'Law,' 'Works of the Law,' and Legalism in Paul," *WTJ* 45 (1983) 73-100; E. P. Sanders, *Paul, the Law, and the Jewish People* (Philadelphia: Fortress, 1983) 17-64; T. R. Schreiner, "Paul and Perfect Obedience to the Law: An Evaluation of the View of E. P. Sanders," *WTJ* 47 (1985) 245-78; idem, " 'Works of Law' in Paul," *NovT* 33 (1991) 217-44; F. Thielman, *From Plight to Solution: A Jewish Framework for Understanding Paul's View of the Law in Galatians and Romans* (Leiden: E. J. Brill, 1989); J. B. Tyson, " 'Works of Law' in Galatians," *JBL* 92 (1973) 423-31; F. Watson, *Paul, Judaism and the Gentiles: A Sociological Approach* (SNTSMS 56; Cambridge: University Press, 1986); S. Westerholm, *Israel's Law and the Church's Faith* (Grand Rapids: Eerdmans, 1988).

T. R. Schreiner

## WORLD, COSMOLOGY

In the Pauline corpus seven words are included in this semantic area, *kosmos* ("world," forty-seven times), *aiōn* ("age," thirty-one times), *gē* ("earth," "land," fourteen times), *oikoumenē* ("inhabited world," once), *kairos* ("time," thirty-one times which sometimes overlaps the temporal aspects of *aiōn*) and "creation"* (*ktisis*, cf. the verb *ktizō*) which is also called *ta panta*, "the all". This rich fund of language is derived from both the Jewish and Greek traditions.

Paul's understanding of the origin and structure of the world (cosmology) was dependent on the biblical teaching of creation and could have made use of a variety of mythical traditions concerning the origin and nature of the world. It is frequently suggested that the NT writers thought of the earth as a disc upon which the heavens rest like a dome and under which the waters of the deep formed the sea. But it could be a mistake to interpret such imagery as scientific description rather than as poetic portrayal. From the time of Aristotle the Greeks understood the world to be a sphere (Aristotle *Cael* II.2 p. 285a, 32) and perceptive attempts were made to calculate the circumference of the earth, though the debate persisted concerning whether the earth or the sun circled the other. Because the "world" is not treated systematically in the Pauline corpus, gaps must be filled in from what we suppose was commonly known. The task of dealing systematically with Pauline thought is made difficult by uncertainty about the authenticity of a number of letters and the recognition that all of the letters are occasional writings, not the expression of a unified systematic theology.

1. Terminology
2. The World of Space
3. The Temporal World
4. Perspectives in the Pauline Letters

### 1. Terminology.

*Kosmos* is sometimes understood as planet earth, at times with a special focus on its human inhabitants, but also in a wider sense as the universe. In this latter sense it has the same meaning as the OT "heaven and earth" (Heb *haššāmayim wᵉhā'āreṣ*), meaning the creation. Writers dependent on the OT used this language instinctively even though *kosmos* had become part of the vocabulary of Greek speaking Jews. The OT has no word comparable to *kosmos* and the translators of the LXX naturally translated the Hebrew "heaven and

earth" as *ouranos kai gē*. Only in the later books composed in Greek, such as Wisdom of Solomon, 2 Maccabees and 4 Maccabees, was *kosmos* used (nineteen times, five times and four times respectively). Paul, after John, is the most prolific user of *kosmos* in the NT. He, like John, shows a preference for *kosmos* over *gē*, although *gē* is predominant in the NT. When *gē* occurs in the Pauline corpus it is often in an OT quotation. In Paul the creation of the heavens and the earth (Gen 1:1) finds expression in terms of the creation of the *kosmos* (Rom 1:20) or the creation of all things (*ta panta*, Eph 3:9; Col 1:15-17; cf. Eph 1:10). This idiom (*ta panta*) is characteristic of Stoicism (*see* Philosophy), the *Corpus Hermeticum* and Gnosticism.* In Colossians 1:16, 20 the reference is to "all things in heaven and earth," combining Greek and Jewish idioms. The notion of creation (*ktisis, ktizō, ktisma*, "creation") has its roots in Judaism. The language of Romans 11:36 and 1 Corinthians 8:6 is more ambiguous, raising the question of influences on the development of this language.

Four other expressions overlap the use of *kosmos*. *Oikoumenē*, which is short for *oikoumenē gē* ("inhabited earth"), was used in the LXX to translate the Hebrew *tēbēl*. In poetic works *tēbēl* is frequently used in parallel with *'ereṣ* ("earth"). *Oikoumenē* is used in this way (in parallel with *gē*) in Romans 10:18 (Paul's only use) where it is a quotation from Psalm 19:4. By Paul's time *oikoumenē* had come to mean "the inhabited world," which was sometimes considered to be coterminous with the Roman empire. *Kosmos* is used in this sense in Romans 1:8 and Colossians 1:6. *Aiōn* was used to translate the Hebrew *'ôlām*. Both words have a reference to time, and the expression "this age" has substantially the same meaning as "this world." Some of Paul's uses of *kairos* have much the same meaning. The notion of creation is important in the Pauline corpus where the verb *ktizō*, ("create") is used ten times (fifteen times in NT), the nouns *ktisis* ("creation") eleven times (nineteen in NT) and *ktisma* ("creature") once (four in NT). Paul's focus on creation reflects aspects of Hellenistic Judaism.

### 2. The World of Space.

The extensive nature of the world is expressed in Romans 10:18 (Ps 19:4) where "to the ends of the world (*oikoumenēs*)" parallels "to every land (*gēn*)." In Romans 9:17 (Ex 9:16) *gē* is used ethnically, not of planet earth as it is in the phrase "heaven and earth" (1 Cor 8:5; Eph 1:10; 3:15; Phil 2:10; Col 1:16, 20; and implied in Col 3:2, 5), the Jewish idiom for the whole creation. Heaven represents the realm of God and earth the sphere of human activity. Reference to the Lord performing his word on earth, a quotation of Isaiah 1:9 in Romans 9:28, is also a reference to planet earth. There is an instance where *kosmos* is apparently used of the promised land (Rom 4:13; cf. Gen 17:4-8; 12:3; 18:18; 22:17-18), while elsewhere it is used of the Gentiles* (Rom 11:12, 15).

### 3. The Temporal World.

*3.1. Creation.* The temporal nature of the world, with a definite beginning, is asserted in the teaching about creation (Rom 1:20, 25; 8:19-22, 39; 1 Cor 11:9; 2 Cor 5:17; Gal 6:15; Eph 2:10, 15; 3:9; 4:24; Col 1:15, 16, 23; 3:10; 1 Tim 4:4), which is expressly creation *ex nihilo* (Rom 4:17; 1 Cor 1:28). Ephesians 1:4 envisages the plan and action of God* before the foundation of the world (*pro kataboles kosmou*). This Jewish expression is found four times in the Gospels (Mt 13:35 = Ps 78:2; Mt 24:21; Mk 10:6; 13:9) and with "before the ages" (*pro tōn aiōnōn*, 1 Cor 2:7) means "before the creation."

*3.2. This Age* (Gk *aiōn*; Heb *'ōlām*). The notion of the two ages, this age and the age to come, has its roots in apocalyptic* Judaism (4 Ezra). "This age" is conceived as evil and Paul exhorts, "Do not be conformed to this age" (Rom 12:2; cf. 1 Cor 1:20; 2:6, 8; 3:18; 2 Cor 4:4; Eph 1:21). "This age" is comparable to "this world" (1 Cor 3:19; 5:10); and "the age of this world" (Eph 2:2) is contrasted with the coming of age (Eph 1:21; 2:7). The present age is evil (Gal 1:4), being ruled by the "elemental spirits of the world"* (*ta stoicheia tou kosmou*, Gal 4:3, 9; Col 2:8, 20), "the rulers of this age" (*tōn archontōn tou aiōnos toutou*, 1 Cor 2:6; cf. Jn 12:31), "the god of this age" (*ho theos tou aiōnos toutou*, 2 Cor 4:4), "the prince of the power of the air, of the spirit now working in the sons of disobedience" (Eph 2:2; *see* Satan, Devil), the "devil," "rulers," "powers," the "world rulers (*kosmokratores*) of this darkness," the evil spiritual powers in heavenly places (Eph 6:11-12; *see* Principalities and Powers). "This age" may also have the sense of "the present time"(*ho nun kairos*, Rom 3:26; 8:18; 11:5; 2 Cor 6:2; 8:13) and "the present age" (*ho nun aiōn*, 1 Tim 6:17; 2 Tim 4:10; Tit 2:12). This age/world is evil and opposed to God. It is ruled by spiritual powers and to it fallen, unredeemed humanity belongs (1 Cor 1:20, 21, 27, 28; 2:12; 3:19; 5:10; 6:2; 11:32; 2 Cor 7:10; Gal 4:3; 6:14; Eph 2:2; Col 2:8, 20) and is in need of redemption* (Rom 3:6, 19; 2 Cor 5:19). Here Paul gives expression to an apocalyptic worldview in which no explanation is given for the "fallen" world, unlike certain forms of Gnosticism where the coming into being of this world is itself understood as a fall which can only be reversed by a return to the original heavenly state.

*3.3. The Coming Age.* The notion of the coming age, explicit in Ephesians 1:21; 2:7 and implicit in Romans 8:18-25 and 1 Corinthians 15:20-28, implies the fulfillment of God's purpose in creation when evil and corruption will be overcome. For Paul creation is an eschatological* doctrine. That Christ is the meaning of creation is the point of the parallel statements about the creation and reconciliation (see Peace, Reconciliation) of *ta panta* ("all things") in Colossians 1:16, 20. The explicit essential connection between creation and redemption seems to have been a distinctive early Christian insight.

### 4. Perspectives in the Pauline Letters.

The major aspects of the theme of the world are found in the first four undisputed letters. Ephesians and Colossians add a christological and cosmic focus. 1 and 2 Thessalonians have an eschatological orientation similar to 1 Corinthians 15, though with more attention to the events leading up to the end time. The Pastorals* are also concerned with the degeneration preceding the end.

*4.1. Romans.* The understanding of God in creation (Rom 1:20, 25; 8:19-22, 39) as the basis of revelation has its roots in the Wisdom* tradition. Those who do not worship* God are without excuse (Rom 1:20). But in spite of the revelation, sin* entered the world, and as a consequence death (Rom 5:12; *see* Life and Death). Though sin was already in the world (Rom 5:13), the Law* was introduced to silence all appeals so that the whole world (*pas ho kosmos* is here a reference to humanity, fallen and guilty before God) would be accountable to God (Rom 3:19). Human sin also had consequences for the natural world because the judgment of God in response to human sin (Rom 1:18-31) subjected the world to futility* (*mataiotēs*). This judgment* has as its goal the redemption of the world, a theme given extensive treatment in Romans 8:18-25. The present age, subject to futility, corruption and suffering,* will be released in the coming age. God's purpose is redemption, in which the whole creation will participate through the revelation of the children of God (see Adoption) and the liberation (*see* Freedom) of the creation from the bondage of corruption. Similarly, God's judgment in casting away Israel* leads to the reconciliation of the Gentiles* (*kosmos*, Rom 11:12, 15; *see* Romans). Like corruption and suffering, this casting away is part of the paradoxical purpose of God for the redemption of all. The state of the world is a consequence of human sin and the consequent judgment of God. There is no reference to the powers of evil as in other letters. The theocentricity of Romans finds expression in the doxology of Romans

11:36. Here Paul affirms God to be the source (*ex autou*), the means or mediator (*di' autou*) and goal (*eis auton*) of all things (*ta panta*). (Contrast the subordinate christological focus in 1 Cor 8:6; 15:28; Eph 1:10, 22; Col 1:16, 20.)

*4.2. 1 Corinthians.* Here the world (this world/age) takes on an alien and hostile character (*see* Enemy, Enmity, Hostility). It is opposed to God just as the wisdom of the world is opposed to the wisdom of God. God chose the foolish,* the weak* and the despised, and even those considered nonentities according to this world, which turn out to be the wisdom and power* of God in the fulfillment of his purpose (1 Cor 1:18-28; 2:6-13; 3:18-19; 4:9, 13). The rulers of this age (*hoi archontes tou aiōnos toutou*) lead the forces opposed to God (1 Cor 2:6, 8), and the spirit of the world is opposed to the Spirit* of God (1 Cor 2:12). The redemption of the world, treated in Romans 8:18-25, is picked up in 1 Corinthians 15:20-28, but from a new perspective. The resurrection of Christ is here portrayed as the first fruit* of the new creation. The reign of the risen Christ continues until all enemies (death is the last of these) have been subjected at the "coming" of Christ (*see* Triumph). For Paul the time for this event was growing near (1 Cor 7:29; 10:11) and this is the basis for his distinctive brand of asceticism (1 Cor 7:29-31). The urgency of the moment calls for denial, not because the physical world is evil in itself (1 Cor 10:26) but because the form of this world is passing away (1 Cor 2:6; 7:31) and the new age is dawning. Attachment to things of this world is not appropriate.

With the completion of the Son's saving purposes, the Son himself becomes subject to the one who subordinated all things to him, that God may be everything to every one (1 Cor 15:28; *see* Kingdom of God/Christ). Although the end is God, there is an important subordinate christological* focus. Christ is the means by which God achieves his sovereign purpose. This is reflected in the doxology of 1 Corinthians 8:6: "But for us there is one God the Father from whom are all things [*ex hou ta panta*], and we are for him [*eis auton*], and one Lord* Jesus Christ through whom are all things [*di' hou ta panta*] and we are through him." Though God is here the source of creation, Christ is the means or mediator of God's creative work. That mediation is affirmed twice, concerning all things and in the affirmation, "we are through him." The affirmation concerning God is not "we are from him" but "for him" (*eis auton*). This is generally translated "we live/exist for him." But as the first preposition *ex* relates to source/origin it is likely that the *eis* refers to the goal. We come from God and we go to God. Ultimately God will be "all in all." Then the saints will

judge the *kosmos* (heaven and earth), including angels* (1 Cor 6:2-3).

*4.3. 2 Corinthians.* With the phrase "the god of this age/world" (2 Cor 4:4) the theme of the alien world is announced. This age has values opposed to God (2 Cor 7:10). A step beyond the mediatorial role of Christ in 1 Corinthians is taken by asserting, "God was in Christ reconciling the *kosmos* to himself" (2 Cor 5:19). Here it is uncertain whether *kosmos* means only sinful humanity or involves the whole creation, a theme taken up in Ephesians and Colossians. More likely it is the former.

*4.4. Galatians.* By giving himself for us, Christ has redeemed us from the present evil age according to the will of God our Father (Gal 1:4). Those belonging to this age are in bondage to the "elemental spirits of the world"* (*ta stoicheia tou kosmou*, Gal 4:3, 9 and cf. Col 2:8, 20). Redemption from this age and the spirits that control it involves death (crucifixion) to the world (Gal 6:14). The Jewish Law* seems to be part of the system of the world and thus has no place in the life of the believer who lives in the power of the Spirit of God and by faith.*

*4.5. Ephesians.* Like Romans, Ephesians* lays strong stress on creation, God as creator (Eph 2:10, 15; 3:9; 4:24), and the purpose of God originating before the foundation of the world (Eph 1:4). That purpose has a christological focus coming to fulfillment in the recapitulation (*anakephalaiōsasthai*) of all things (*ta panta*) in Christ (Eph 1:10). "All things" specifically includes what is in heaven* and what is on earth. This recapitulation is the reassertion of God's purpose for creation. It involves the overcoming of the evil powers in control of this present age (Eph 2:2; 6:11-12) and of the enmity manifest in human life (Eph 2:14-22). Consequently Ephesians sets the work of Christ in the context of God's eternal purpose and expounds its cosmic consequences into which humanity is caught up. Christ is the meaning and goal of creation. For a variety of reason many scholars deny the authenticity of Ephesians. Whether or not by Paul, Ephesians has a Pauline understanding of the world and its purpose, though this is set in a wider perspective than in the uncontested letters.

*4.6. Colossians.* Colossians* also has a strong emphasis on creation and the most detailed cosmology (Col 1:15-20) in the Pauline corpus. This cosmology can be illuminated by appeal to Jewish wisdom* tradition, some form of Gnosticism* or a combination of the two. It can also be attributed to false teachings at Colossae upon which Paul has drawn in framing his response (*see* Colossians). The present age is ruled by the power/authority of darkness (Col 1:13; *see* Light and Darkness), by the elemental spirits of the world (*ta stoicheia tou kosmou*, Col 2:8, 20). Creation and redemption (*apolytrōsis*), the forgiveness* of sins, have been wrought by Christ (Col 1:14) who is called God's beloved Son* (Col 1:13) and designated the image of the invisible God (*eikōn tou theou tou aoratou*, Col 1:15; cf. 2 Cor 4:4; Wis 7:26; Philo *Vit. Mos.* 2.65; *Leg. All.* 1.43; *Conf. Ling.* 97, 147). Although recapitulation language is not used, the theme is implied. "All things" (*ta panta*) were created in/by (*en*) him and reconciled through (*dia*) him (Col 1:16, 20; *see* Peace, Reconciliation). Though *en* (Col 1:16) might have had a local sense in the false teaching (according to Philo *Op. Mund.* 17, 20, the Logos was the place [*topos*] of the eternal ideas [the *kosmos noētos*]), Paul is talking about the creation of the material world and *en* thus has an instrumental sense ("by"). This is confirmed by the reiteration in Colossians 1:16 which uses *dia* ("through"). All things were created not only *through* him but also *for* him (*eis auton*). This might seem to be contrary to Romans 11:36, but the mediatorial role of the Son here runs parallel to the role of God in Romans. The passage is framed by the parallelism of the two assertions (Col 1:16, 20) concerning the creation and reconciliation of "all things," which include the things in heaven and on earth. The Son is called the "firstborn* (*prōtotokos*) of creation" (Col 1:15) and the "firstborn of the dead" (Col 1:18). But between creation and reconciliation the world is depicted as alienated from and at enmity with God, dominated by the power of evil. The point of the parallelism is that reconciliation restores the purpose of creation. The Creator and reconciler is the Son. The cosmology is concerned with the relation of the Son to the Father. So that no separation from the Father can be envisaged, the Son is described as the image (*eikōn*) of the invisible God, emphasizing his mediatorial role. It is from this point of view that the goal of the preeminence of the Son is to be understood (Col 1:18).

*See also* CHRISTOLOGY; CREATION AND NEW CREATION; DEMONS AND EXORCISM; ELEMENTS/ELEMENTAL SPIRITS OF THE WORLD; ESCHATOLOGY; FIRSTBORN; FULLNESS; HEAVEN, HEAVENLIES, PARADISE; PEACE, RECONCILIATION; PRINCIPALITIES AND POWERS; SATAN, DEVIL.

BIBLIOGRAPHY. J. C. Beker, *Paul the Apostle: The Triumph of God in Life and Thought*, (Philadelphia: Fortress, 1980) 135-81; R. Bultmann, *Theology of the New Testament* (2 vols.; New York: Scribners, 1951, 1955); idem, "The Understanding of Man and the World in the New Testament and in the Greek World," in *Essays Philosophical and Theological* (London: SCM, 1955) 67-89; G. B. Caird, *Principalities and Powers* (Oxford: Clarendon, 1956); W. Carr, *Angels and Principalities: The Background, Meaning and Development of the Pauline Phrase* HAI ARCHAI KAI HAI EXOUSIAI (SNTSMS 42; Cambridge: University Press, 1981); J. G. Gibbs, *Creation and Redemption* (Leiden: E. J. Brill, 1971); G. Gloege, "Welt," *RGG* VI. 1595-1603; G. Johnston, "*Oikoumene* and *kosmos* in the New Testament," *NTS* 10 (1963-64) 352-60; J. T. Sanders, *The New Testament Christological Hymns: Their Historical Religious Background*, (SNTSMS 15; Cambridge: University Press, 1971); R. Schnackenburg, *Christliche Existenz nach dem Neuen Testament* I (1967) 157-85 and II (1968) 149-85; H. Sasse, "αἰών, αἰώνιος," *TDNT* I.197-209; idem, "γῆ, ἐπίγειος," *TDNT* I.677-81; idem, "κοσμέω, κόσμος κτλ," *TDNT* III.868-95.　　　　J. Painter

## WORSHIP

1. Background
2. Contemporary Setting
3. Pauline Teaching

### 1. Background.

While there is no formal definition of what the worship of God means or entails in biblical literature, it can safely be said that in both testament ages worship originates in the understanding of God as creator and redeemer. (The scriptural references that follow are drawn mainly from the Pauline corpus.) God* is hailed as the sovereign Lord* who brought the world* into existence (Rom 4:17) and is the author of all that is (Rom 11:36; 1 Cor 8:6). He acted through the agency of his Son (Col 1:15-20; *see* Son of God) both to create and to rescue, taking action in salvation* to restore the universe once it had fallen from its original state and to save humankind implicated in sin* (Rom 5:1-21; 8:18-23). Notes of praise are sounded to herald the dawn of a new age of God's reconciling and renewing activity (2 Cor 5:17-21; *see* Peace, Reconciliation), and the church* of Jesus Christ is viewed both as the object of redemption (Eph 1:1-14) and the locus where God's saving activity is rehearsed and displayed (Eph 3:9-10). The scene is both terrestrial and set in the heavenly realms (*see* Heaven), brought together by the work of the regnant Christ* who is at once the unifier of heaven and earth and the means by which earth's praises connect with the heavenly, angelic worship.

The key, then, to worship in the Pauline churches is found in Paul's central affirmations concerning the primacy of divine grace* to meet the human and cosmic need and the pivotal role assigned to Jesus Christ, the once-crucified (*see* Crucifixion) and now risen (*see* Resurrection), ascended and glorified Lord* as head of the church and ruler of all creation (Phil 2:6-11; cf.

1 Tim 3:16). These twin assertions lie at the heart of Paul's practice of worship, seen in his praises, prayers* and confessions of faith* and addressed in the kind of celebratory activity in which he expected his congregations to engage.

## 2. Contemporary Setting.

*2.1. Greco-Roman Religion and Cult.* The ministry of Paul was set in a culture and civilization that had long since acknowledged the place of the gods and goddesses and responded to the elemental awareness of the divine (in the sense of *numen,* divine influence or eerie sensation felt by worshipers). In the ancient Greek world the deities of Homer and Hesiod were accepted as superior beings, linked with virtues and requiring obedience. They formed a society located on Mount Olympus and were presided over by Zeus, the father and king of the gods. Paul's tribute in 1 Corinthians 8:5 refers to deities "in heaven," presumably of the Homeric pantheon, and "on earth," relating to manifestations of the divine in fertility spirits or possibly deified kings and rulers.

At the center of traditional Greek religion was the idea that the gods were guardians of the moral order and were to be reverenced by offerings in a cultus as well as by prayer to secure a favorable "lot" in this world and in the underworld of Hades. The largely unpredictable "fate" awaiting the departed contributed to an uncertainty and fear which made worship at the shrines and temples a fitful experience. The linkage of the cultus with the cycle of nature and the desire for good harvests made religious practice an important feature of everyday life. But it added only to the uncertainty of life should the harvests fail and the herds be stricken with disease. A lot of traditional religion had a prophylactic element, that is, to ensure prosperity by warding off disease and danger.

The advent of Rome* as a military and world-embracing power gave opportunity for the Homeric deities to be associated with the national aspirations and (later) the ruling emperors. The Roman genius for government and political action promoted a sense of duty to the state and obligation on the part of the citizens. Hence "religion" took on its function according to its true etymology, that is, *religare* in Latin, meaning "to bind," namely, humanity to the gods. Religious observances, both domestic and on state occasions, served this wider interest. There was both a corporate and a contractual obligation, and traditional and customary ways of life were related to the various gods and their consorts in a non-exclusive, syncretistic way. Notions of uncertainty were reinforced by the admission that *tychē* ("luck," "chance") was at

the heart of things, and the gods were often treated in a superstitious manner as averters of one's fortune. Household gods (the *lares* and *penates*) were regarded as guardians of hearth and home against evil influences or capricious "fate." A wonderfully revealing picture of the Superstitious Man is drawn by Theophrastus in his *Characters* (the text is given and commented on in Martin 1978, 2.36-38).

Hymns, prayers, votive offerings and sacrifices, at festival time and in conjunction with the shrines, are attested, with various deities being appealed to as a source of life and welfare and a giver of healing (notably of the cult of Asclepius) and prosperity. Divine guidance was sought at centers such as Delphi where the oracle in the hands of the priestesses of Apollo yielded direction to the inquirer. Tributes of praise called aretalogies are on record, addressed to the deities such as Apollo and Zeus (the notable Cleanthes' *Hymn* is a fine example; cited in Martin 1978, 2.42).

With the world-shaking conquests of Alexander in the fourth century B.C. the ancient world was to know changes of an irreversible character. Life was never to be the same, and notably in the matter of religious influence and worship. Two factors came into play. (1) There were political confusions that followed in the wake of Alexander's global influence and its sudden decline. The wars and the disturbances of the balance of power brought an unsettlement to the lives of ordinary people across the Mediterranean world and the Syrian Levant. This contributed to the sense of futility that fell across the spirit of Hellenistic society (*see* Hellenism) in the decades prior to Paul's mission (*see* Mission). (2) But there was a more serious dimension to the human condition in Paul's world that directly influenced the sense of worship.

A new view on the cosmos (*see* World, Cosmology) had been introduced by Greek scientists, with direct repercussions on the traditional theology of Homer that located the deities on Mount Olympus. At a single stroke they were rendered otiose as far as endeavoring to locate them in a mundane sphere; they were banished to the outer regions of starry space. With the fateful exploiting of these astrological and theological novelties by the astrologers and occult-practitioners from the oriental world, religion entered a new phase, one largely of pessimism and despair. Once the existence of personal gods and goddesses was either denied (but with little evidence of atheism in the modern philosophic sense) or "demythologized" (by reducing and explaining away their personal identity, as in Plato), no alternative seemed left but the sad conclusion that all things happen by chance. The next move was that the goddess Tychē (luck) was placed on the throne vacated by Zeus (Pliny *Nat. Hist.* 2.5.22: "We are so much at the mercy of chance that Chance is our god"). So it came about that everything in the cosmos—earthly, subterrestrial and in the heavenly sphere—was placed under the control of the star gods that controlled and determined the lot of humankind. Men and women were made to feel impotent and helpless, and religion was marked by a "failure of nerve" (to use G. Murray's phrase).

But escape was promised and sought along certain paths, all with their distinctive ethos and practice of worship. First, fellowship with a mighty god who was stronger than "necessity" was offered in the mystery religions that practiced an elaborate initiatory rite, as part of a baptismal and meal-event cultus. Second, the worship of Serapis, Isis and the healer Asclepius included the promise that worshipers could gain victory over their fate and be given hope. Third, by a life of renunciation and asceticism as well as the practice of magic, a yearning for salvation and harmony with the eternal world was expressed and celebrated in praise, ritual, sacrament and experience—with special emphasis on a knowledge of secret lore that would offer a passport to a union with the divine and a bridging of the gap that separated the worlds above and below. What Paul in Acts 17:22 said of the Athenian philosophers would be true of a wider constituency representing men and women throughout the Greco-Roman world: "I see that in every way you are very religious."

### 2.2. Jewish Practices.

*2.2.1. Temple and Home.* During the period when Palestine came under the influence of Alexander, the most notable change to Jewish worship was registered by the increasing Hellenization of Jewish ancestral culture. Greek influence, especially in education and thought forms, can be seen in the life of the synagogues. Although there were many challenges to Israel's theocracy, especially emerging from the Maccabean struggle of the mid-second century B.C., once the political threat was withdrawn, the cultural changes to Jewish life served only to enhance belief in one God and the sanctity of his house, the Temple at Jerusalem. Henceforth the creed* of "one God, one land" would be embedded in all kinds of liturgical praise.

The Jerusalem shrine remained the focal point of national worship, since (it was said) the world rests on the threefold foundation of Torah, Temple service and the practice of almsgiving (*m. 'Abot* 1:2). The Law* was the basis of postexilic Judaism, and its central place in the liturgy was unchallenged. It provided a divine revelation of all needed truth and its study and obedience was the gateway to salvation and holy living. The Temple was the focal point for corporate worship and offered the physical meeting point at which the celebration of the annual festivals and feasts could take place. The latter were prescribed in the Law and were obligatory to all Jews living in Israel and the Dispersion. Three great pilgrim feasts (Passover, Pentecost, and Booths or Tabernacles) could only be observed in the holy land. The result was that loyal Jews came to Jerusalem* to share in these occasions (see Acts 2:5-11; and for Paul himself, Acts 20:16).

Part of the Jewish way of life was Sabbath observance. The seventh day of creation was regarded with special esteem as God's gracious gift to his people and a time of gladness. It was often thought of as a picture of the age to come, as well as imposing an identity marker on Jews as a separate people in society. Domestic worship made much of preparation for Sabbath, a duty that fell to the Jewish mother and housewife, notably in lighting the Sabbath lamp as a symbol of her role in providing a model of godly living.

At Passover this motif was particularly prominent in a solemn searching out of leaven as a prelude to Paschal observance that allowed only unleavened bread to be in the home and kitchen (see Paul's application in 1 Cor 5:1-13). Passover commemorated the deliverance of Israel from Egypt, with a personal rehearsal and dramatization of the redemption in every age, and a pointing ahead to Israel's hope of Messiah's coming to set them free (*m. Pesaḥ.* 10). These two ideas of commemoration and anticipation were to be taken over in the Pauline account of the Lord's Supper (*see* Lord's Supper), set in a Passover framework (1 Cor 11:17-34).

The annual Day of Atonement was, in reality, a fast whose details are elaborated in the Mishnaic tractate *Yoma* based on Leviticus 16. Paul makes little use of this language, except at Romans 3:24-26, which may be an edited form of a Jewish-Christian credo (*see* Creeds; for details, see Martin 1989, 81-89).

In Colossians 2:16, 23 Paul knows the ways in which cultic practices, part Jewish, part pagan, can distort what are for him the essentials of faith. His employment of Temple cultus ideas and idioms is invariably spiritualized with some important results: The Temple* becomes the new Temple of God's habitation in the church (Eph 2:21) as the body of Christ (1 Cor 3:16-17; 6:19-20; *see* Body of Christ) and the shrine of the Spirit (*see* Holy Spirit). And the sacrificial idioms are now linked to the worship of the spirit (Rom 12:1-2) and the tangible expressions of giving to the apostolic mission (Phil 4:18-20) and to the collection for the Jerusalem poor (2 Cor 8—9; *see* Collection; on the profusion of cultic terms now lifted into a new setting see the commentaries).

*2.2.2. Synagogue.* The two loci of Jewish worship so far considered are the Temple and the home. In the latter category we must remember that Christian church buildings did not appear until the fourth century. Up to that point Christian believers met for worship in their houses, a practice that goes back to the scenes in Acts 2:42, 46-47; 16:15, 34, 40; 20:7-12 as well as an attested feature of Pauline house churches (see Col 4:15-16; Philem 2; cf. Rom 16:5; *see* Church).

The third setting for Jewish worship was the synagogue. Itself the venue for much that characterized Jewish community life and affairs in the first century A.D.—as a school, a law court and a town forum—the synagogue originated (it is assumed) in the historical development of Judaism as a meeting place for worship on the Sabbath and other set days in the week, usually market days. The format of worship is largely known from later sources, once Jewish sages had codified and elaborated the distinctive role of the synagogue in maintaining the national way of life. But, even if precise details are not given in any contemporary document, some valuable sources of information are provided in Luke 4:15-21 and Acts 13:13-43. Three main elements formed the genius of synagogue worship: praise, prayer and instruction. As Paul's understanding of Christian worship, notably at Corinth (1 Cor 12—14), is often thought to incorporate those features, it is worth turning to observe the chief emphases.

*Praise.* Corporate praise is the note that opens the service. The later Talmudic principle is thus enunciated: We "should always first utter praises, and then pray." It is illustrated in the synagogue liturgy for morning prayer called *'Alenu:* "It is our duty to praise the Lord of all things." Worship is thereby directed to the covenant God of Israel as maker of all things and one worthy to receive the homage of his people.

*Prayers.* These prayers fall into two parts. The first group comprise two special concerns. The *Yôsēr* (meaning "He who forms") takes up the theme of God as creator, while the *'Ahᵃbâ* (a term for love) is related to the fact of God's love for Israel and requires their answering pledge of love to him. In prayers like these, God is "blessed," that is, his name is honored and extolled with some following description of his attributes and character. Hence, "Blessed are you, O Lord, who chose Israel your people in love." In Paul's letters the exordium, or opening, will often announce God's activity as an incentive to praise and supply reasons for the invocation of blessing (2 Cor 1:3-7; Eph 1:3-10) as well as communicate the epistolary theme to be developed in the body of the letter (*see* Benediction, Blessing). Part of the reasons for this rhetorical feature is to secure a good relationship with his readers by inviting them to join in a rehearsal of praise; part also is in the reminder that Paul's letters were meant to be read out in public assembly as the congregations gathered in homes for a liturgical service and assembly (see 1 Cor 5:3-5; Col 4:16; 1 Thess 5:27; Philem 2).

In synagogue worship, immediately following these prayers comes the Jewish creed, the Shema, which is both a confession of faith and a glad benediction. The title for the Shema derives from the opening word in Deuteronomy 6:4: "*Hear (šᵉma'),* O Israel, the Lord our God is one Lord." The term *one* emphasizes the unity and sole reality of God that has always been a central Jewish affirmation. It receives, then, a special prominence in the liturgy—as, indeed, it is picked up and carried forward into Pauline theology (Rom 3:30; 1 Cor 8:6; 12:5; Gal 3:20; cf. 1 Tim 2:5) and doxology (Rom 11:36; Phil 2:9-11). (On Paul's wrestling with Jewish monotheism as a frame for his christology, see Hurtado; *see* God.)

The second division of synagogue prayers begins with a reminder that God's promises are sure and dependable; such reminder is expressed in the prayer titled "True and firm" (cf. 2 Cor 1:18-22 for Paul's exploiting of this conviction as an apologetic ploy; and in Rom 3:4; 2 Cor 11:31; Gal 1:20 he can call on the same attribute of God, in doxological form). At this juncture the synagogue leader summons a member of the assembly to lead in the "Prayer proper," that is, the Eighteen Benedictions (*šᵉmōneh 'eśrēh*), which laud the character of God in blessing as his benefits and mercies to Israel are recalled. The Eighteen Benedictions cover a wide range of themes. They are partly an expression of praise, partly supplication for those in need (exiles, judges, counselors and the chosen people). In the Pauline corpus a parallel may be seen in 1 Timothy 2:1-4, as well as in Paul's concern for good government and a stable social order (Rom 13:1-7; Col 3:18-4:6; cf. 2 Thess 3:6-13; *see* Civil Authority).

*Instruction.* Once the prayers are said, the service assumes a form and shape that has given the synagogue its distinctive ethos. Indeed, the Jews themselves call the synagogue a "house of instruction" (*bēt hamidrāš*), for nothing is more in keeping with Jewish worship than the emphasis that is placed on Scripture reading and exposition. Instruction is given by two means. First, the Law and the Prophets are read by members of the congregation who come up to the rostrum to share the task. Historically, as the ancient language of Hebrew was not understood by all the people present, a translator would turn the Scripture lessons into the vernacular, usually Aramaic. Second, a homily followed that was based on the passages read (e.g., Lk 4:20-21; Acts 13:15-16; 1 Tim 4:13, 16 for duties devolving upon the Pauline pastor). Any person in the assembly who was considered suitable was invited to deliver this sermon, as in the instances at Nazareth and Pisidian Antioch. The service concluded with a benediction and congregational "Amen" (attested to in 1 Cor 14:16; 2 Cor 1:20) to confirm the truthfulness of all that the service has conveyed to the faithful who utter a word of agreement and application in line with the OT precedent (e.g., Neh 5:13).

The issue of whether psalm singing was a feature in Palestinian synagogues is still unresolved (Bradshaw, 22-24). There is no clear attestation. It has been proposed (Hengel, 78-79) that in contrast to Hellenistic synagogues in the world of the Diaspora, where singing is reported and confirmed by Philo of the sect of the Therapeutae (*Vit. Cont.* 80) and at Qumran (1QS 10:9; 1QH 11:3-4), singing was not allowed by the Pharisees. They would have regarded the practice as heretical, since it was practiced by groups they judged to be deviant. By contrast again, Paul's one description of a rudimentary worship service (at Corinth) includes the use of religious song as a "hymn" (*psalmos*) brought to the assembly (1 Cor 14:26; cf. Eph 5:19-20; Col 3:16-17; *see* Hymns). If strict etymology is the determining factor, *psalmos* would suggest compositions akin to the Hebrew Psalter, the headings for which in the LXX read *psalmoi* (cf. Lk 24:44). But in a Hellenistic environment such as Corinth there is no certainty that *psalmos* would be interpreted according to its LXX background, and in any case the "hymn" of 1 Corinthians 14:26 seems clearly to be a newly produced composition made available by a gifted member of the church. Such tributes were evidently meant to be sung (as in 1 Cor 14:15), though the rubrics of Colossians 3:16 and Ephesians 5:19 emphasize that the melody is to find an echo "in the heart" and be a true expression of inner devotion, not just an unthinking act of praise. The musical terms in 1 Corinthians 13 do not appear as germane to our knowledge of early Christian praise (see Smith).

A final word may be added on the question of Jewish holy days. Obviously the Sabbath took pride of place, observed on a weekly cycle as a token of God's creatorial work and as a factor in redemptive history (Deut 5:12-15). The displacement of the Jewish seventh day by the Christian "first day" of the week is a thorny matter, since it seems that the transition was made only slowly. There can, however, be little doubt that the locus shifted from a memorial motif (Ex 20:8) to a day of celebration as a direct consequence of an

appreciation of what Jesus did "on the first day." He was raised to new life and shared a meal with his followers as the living Lord (cf. the Gospel accounts of post-resurrection appearances, and the *Gospel of the Hebrews* with its record of a dominical word to James, "My brother, eat your bread, for the Son of Man is risen from among those who sleep"). As far as the Pauline records go, there is an awareness that "the first day of the week" is the time for the Corinthian gathering (1 Cor 16:1-2) which will involve the bringing of money to the assembly. J. Héring's proposal that the first weekday was a pay day at Corinth is not likely to command assent (Héring, 183). Paul, more likely, is investing a secular day with theological overtones as a tribute to the day as "the Lord's," just as he can commandeer the place of the agape-Lord's Supper as "the Lord's table" (1 Cor 10:21; see Rordorf, 274-75).

According to Acts 20:7-12, the believers at Troas gathered "on the first day of the week" in order to share a meal and to hear Paul speak. Evidently this was an evening-time occasion since (1) the hapless Eutychus was overcome by sleep as he sat at the window, and (2) Paul's resumed speech took him and his audience until daybreak before they dispersed. Later developments in the post-Pauline church gave a more reasoned conviction to the holy day as the start of a new age (*Barn.* 15:9; *Did.* 14:1; Rev 1:10) and placed the setting of the worship at dawn (Trajan-Pliny correspondence [*Ep.* 10.96] dates the *synaxis* "before daylight"), probably to herald the sunrise in christological terms (cf. the early Christian hymn, "Hail, gladdening light").

Yet the cameo of Acts 20:7-12 did play a more determinative role in the evolution of Christian worship, namely it set a pattern of the twofold shape of the liturgy—the preaching and the breaking of bread, the *missa catechumenorum*, open to all, followed by the *missa fidelium*, restricted to the believers—that by the mid-second century (Justin *Apol. I* 66) became standard procedure. The dual pattern of a liturgy of the Word and a liturgy of the upper room, as it is sometimes called, goes back to its genetic origin in Acts 20 and Paul in 1 Corinthians 11—14, with one member also directly traceable to the synagogue and the other taking its rise from the eucharistic tradition (1 Cor 11:23-26) Paul inherited and passed on to the Corinthians.

### 3. Pauline Teaching.

There is no systematized statement of what Paul understood to be a fitting worship practice, nor is there anything resembling a set of rubrics in later service books. Paul's teaching is scattered throughout his correspondence, and while there are some suggestions that he incorporated parts of a set pattern of worship (see the bold attempt of Cuming to construct a NT order of service) there is nothing definite. The one possible indication is seen in 1 Thessalonians 5:16-24, which is capable of being arranged in lines, each line purporting to be a service heading. (The arrangement, first proposed by J. M. Robinson, is set down by R. P. Martin 1975, 135-38, and since approved in part by D. Hill, 119-20. But see now the cautions voiced in Bradshaw, 30-55.)

In 1 Thessalonians 5:16-22 short sentences are carefully constructed. The verb stands last, and there is a predominance of words beginning with the Greek letter p, thus producing a rhythm. The sequence is noteworthy. First the note of glad adoration is sounded ("Rejoice always"). Prayer and thanksgiving are coupled—a linkage that derives from the synagogue. Christians are counseled to give the Spirit full rein, especially in allowing prophetic utterances to be heard (cf. *Did.* 10:7), but cautioned that they must test the spirits. Above all, nothing unseemly must enter the assembly, suggesting a control on unbridled worship practices. The closing part of this putative "church order" has a comprehensive prayer for the entire group (1 Thess 5:23) and an expression of confidence in God (1 Thess 5:24).

Parallels with 1 Corinthians 14 are suggested, with praise and "hymning" linked, and prayer and thanksgiving joined (1 Cor 14:13-18). There is the need to control prophecy and Spirit-inspired speech, especially by women prophets (1 Cor 14:34-36; *see* Prophecy, Prophesying). And in both accounts the need for good order prevails (1 Cor 14:40).

Procedurally it is easier to set down Paul's teaching under simpler headings, namely (1) evidence for the use of liturgical components in his churches; (2) corrective measures Paul took to deal with what he regarded as abuses and distortions; and (3) extrapolation of his theology of worship from the data thus displayed. These are not separate issues, and will be treated in passing as well as in sections.

*3.1. Evidence of Worship Forms and Speech.* At a later stage we shall need to clarify the ways Paul took over preformed liturgical pieces and allusions to incorporate them into the epistolary flow of his writing (see 3.1.1. and 3.1.2. below). It will become clear, we hope, that he did this to establish a rapport with his readers who were not always well disposed to him, his apostleship and his theology. If he can demonstrate acquaintance with a shared creed or well-accepted hymn, he has immediately put himself on common ground, even if he found it needful to redact the tra-

dition to underscore a point or bring it into line with his own position. Yet another possible reason for his citing of liturgical specimens is seen in the use he intended for his letters. They were his *alter ego*, making up for his enforced absence yet conveying the immediacy of his person to those whom distance or circumstance kept apart (see 1 Cor 5:1-12; Col 2:5). To draw on a common fund of hymn, prayer, baptismal reminder or catechesis would again make his presence vividly known to his readers who often (apparently) concluded he had forgotten (2 Cor; Phil) or deserted them (1 Thess).

*3.1.1. Traditional Forms.* One of the most obvious indices of Paul's borrowing from the liturgical treasury comes at 1 Corinthians 16:22. The strange-sounding *maranatha* would be equally as puzzling to the Corinthian Greek speaker as to the modern reader. The expression lies in the text without comment, translation or application. Its very meaning is a source of debate, either "the Lord is coming" or "our Lord, come!" are possible, with recent linguistic discussion (see Fitzmyer) tipping the scale in favor of the second rendering (as in Rev 22:20). The use of an Aramaic prayer call can only be satisfactorily explained on the assumption that it belonged to the liturgical vocabulary of an early Palestinian or bilingual setting. It became embedded in the liturgy of the *Didache* (10:6) as part of a service preparatory to the Lord's table (as it may function in the letter ending of 1 Cor 16:22-24: see Bornkamm and J. A. T. Robinson). It must surely reflect current usage at Corinth; else why would Paul deliberately confuse his readers with an unexplained term? The significance, however, is what counts. The evidence of this ancient watchword throws a flood of light on the way Jewish Christians worshiped their Lord. Here is the earliest recorded Christian prayer, ascribing to the church's Lord highest honors and giving indication of a cult centered on him. It also indicates that those who had previously invoked the name of their covenant God in the synagogue liturgy now came to apply the same divine title to Jesus the Messiah.

"Calling on the name of the Lord" was also an appellation used to describe both the initiation of believers (Rom 10:12-17) and a self-designation of the church (1 Cor 1:2) as a group of men and women who prayed to the Lord (Jesus; cf. 2 Cor 12:1-10; Acts 7:55-60; 9:14; 22:16). Prayers to Jesus and in the name of Jesus were easily associated in a way we may find paradoxical, but the tension was evidently allowed to remain in Pauline circles, while strict monotheism and a worship directed to the risen Lord stood together with little attempt to correlate them (cf. Phil 2:9-11).

Triadic forms of prayer-praise-confession were also permitted to appear side by side (e.g., 2 Cor 1:20-21; 1 Cor 12:4-11; Eph 4:4-6), as the persons of the godhead (as they later were formulated) were associated with various ministries and offices. In Ephesians 1:3-14 there is (on one reading of the text) a trinitarian format as the Father is said to choose believers, the Son of his love to redeem, and the Spirit to authenticate salvation in human experience by applying the experiential seal (Eph 4:30; cf. 2 Cor 1:20-22; 5:5 in baptism?; *see* God).

Specific forms of prayer and praise occur mainly in the opening sections of Paul's epistles, and have been intensively studied (see Schubert; O'Brien; *see* Prayer). The consensus is that Paul used this device to state the epistolary context of what was to follow, and to encourage mutual goodwill by establishing friendly relation with his readers (Gk. *philophronēsis*). Linguistic evidence in constructions like the stringing together of participles, the use of relative pronouns and the fulsome expressions (e.g., Eph 1:6, "to the praise of his glory") all seem to indicate Paul's indebtedness to a liturgical vocabulary (e.g., 2 Cor 1:3; Col 1:9-14; Eph 1:3-14; 1:15-23; on the Greek forms of blessing God, see Bradshaw, 44-45).

*3.1.2. Hymns and Creeds.* The habit Paul has of inserting hymnic and/or creedal pieces into the epistolary sequence of his writing is well known, and there are certain criteria that betray the presence of quoted material (*see* Hymns). Though there has recently been some resistance to this idea of Paul's taking over preformed hymnic, poetic or confessional matter (see Lash), the main conclusions already established by E. Stauffer (338-39) and O. Cullmann in their seminal discussions (and now supplemented by monographs such as Deichgräber) do not seem to be shaken. The combined data of unusual and dignified vocabulary, use of rhetorical features such as participles, relative pronouns and figures of speech, and the way in which the hypothetically inserted material can be detached from the context—all these signs point to Paul's drawing on traditional forms in order to buttress his hortatory appeal (e.g., Phil 2:6-11 in the setting of Phil 2:1-4, 12-13) and to use "the story of Christ" to serve as a paradigm for ethical action (2 Cor 8:9, again in context of generous giving and service).

The main examples are Philippians 2:6-11; Colossians 1:15-20; 1 Timothy 3:16 (most recently grouped together and studied by S. E. Fowl). Aside from the paraenetic function served by those citations, attention is focused on the insight these hymnic compositions give into a Christian cultus in the Pauline churches.

The ruling motif may be said to be the cosmological-redemptive work of Christ, the church's Lord who came from God and as God. He achieved a cosmic reconciliation by his death and exaltation (*see* Exaltation and Enthronement), thereby uniting the disparate realms of heaven and earth (and so meeting the need evident in Greco-Roman religion, as noted earlier) and causing his triumph to be acknowledged in the underworld of demons and cosmic powers (thereby bringing all parts of the universe under his sway; *see* Principalities and Powers). The twin emphases of his pre-existence with God and his role in creation, on the one side, and his eschatological subjugation of all alien powers, especially the "elemental spirits" (*stoicheia tou kosmou*, Col 2:8, 20), served to assure the church that no hostile power can come between God and the world (Rom 8:38-39). The problem addressed in these hymnic/confessional tributes to the lordship of Christ (Rom 10:9-10; Phil 2:11) is that posed by gnostic dualism which made parts of the universe alien and hostile (*see* Gnosis, Gnosticism). God's rule in Christ, now established, and celebrated in song and creed, was the Christian response. Paul's unique contribution was (1) to anchor redemption and reconciliation in the deed of love* at the cross, not in a cosmic fiat (Phil 2:8; Col 1:20; cf. Col 2:15), and (2) to steer the church that sang these hymns and uttered these confessions away from a false triumphalism (*see* Triumph) that denied the continuing reality of evil as it telescoped the future into the present (*see* Eschatology). In its place Paul inserts the eschatological proviso of a "not-yet" factor (1 Cor 15:20-28) and maintains that hymns of triumph offered in worship must be tempered by a realistic assessment of ongoing struggle in anticipation of a future reign, now begun but not yet fully and finally achieved. The element of tension remains in Paul's soteriology, and some of the warning signs in his handling of worship problems are directed to this false emphasis, only too apparent when worship is unrestrained and too exuberant, as at Corinth (1 Cor 4:8; 12—14).

One specimen of Pauline hymnody (in Eph 5:14) is a reminder that not all worship forms were strictly theocentric and directed to the praise of God. Here the introductory words, "Therefore it is said," read as though they were added expressly to prepare for a citation of a familiar passage (otherwise unknown; not in the OT). Style, with a swinging trochaic rhythm and a rhetorical device whereby the ends of the first two lines match by assonance, prove this to be a carefully composed hymn. But it is addressed to believers, presumably newly converted and probably recently baptized, to call them to action and to promise them

Christ's illumination. The idioms of awake/sleep and resurrection/death, along with light/dark (*see* Light and Darkness) indicate the setting in an initiatory rite to which these lines are the accompanying chant. They are words that would indelibly fix the meaning of baptism on the minds of the new believers.

*3.1.3. Baptism.* The appreciation of baptism* was evidently an important feature in the catechetical instruction offered to recent converts and adherents in the churches on a Pauline foundation. Sometimes (at Corinth) there was need to disabuse the people of wrongheaded notions regarding the practice of baptism (1 Cor 1:13-17; 10:1-17; 15:29). More prominently, Paul takes for granted the reality of what baptism entailed, and builds on it (Rom 6:1-14; Col 2:12). For Paul, baptism which is the believing, obedient individual's response to the word of the gospel* (Rom 1:16; 10:9-10) was regarded as the means of entry into the community of the new Israel, akin to the role played by circumcision* in a faith context (Rom 2:27-29; 1 Cor 7:19; Col 2:11-12). So 1 Corinthians 12:13 and Galatians 3:27 are most naturally to be understood. Membership of the elect community was signified by the rite of passage involving the use of water as lustration and initiation. Paul can therefore base an ethical appeal on the reality of his readers' having been baptized (Rom 6:15; 13:14; Col 3:10; cf. Eph 4:24). Their being identified with Christ in his death and new life is reenacted in baptism (*see* Dying and Rising), and is to be played out in the call to "die daily" (2 Cor 4:11-12). At baptism there is for Paul a genuine sacramental action in which God is at work (Col 2:12). God applies to believers the saving efficacy of Christ's death and resurrection in which they died and were raised, and puts them in a sphere of divine life (Gal 2:19-21) in which sin is conquered (Rom 6:7, 9-11). Henceforth, the Christian is bidden to work out the implications of what baptism means (Rom 6:12-14), just as the circumcised Israelite needed to make good his circumcision by a life of obedience within the covenant. The importance of confession at baptism (Rom 10:9-10; Eph 5:25-27) is thus given prominence. But sacramental action can be misrepresented when it is confounded with a gnosticized fiat without moral considerations. Hence the warnings Paul gives in 1 Corinthians 10.

*3.1.4. Lord's Supper.* Paul took over and enriched several traditions to do with a supper meal (*see* Lord's Supper), held in obedience to the Lord's intention "in the night he was handed over" to death (1 Cor 11:23). At an earlier (i.e., pre-Pauline) stage of development it looked as though the framework of the supper consisted of the following elements: a common meal based on Jewish table-fellowship custom and incorporating, we presume, the Jewish prayers for food and drink (with a Christian flavor seen in *Did.* 9—10); as bread and cup were taken, following the pattern of the upper room model, the Lord's presence was recalled "in remembrance of me"; and the simple rite pointed beyond itself to a future hope in the coming kingdom of God (*see* Kingdom). What Paul did in direct response evidently to social problems at Corinth was to enrich and apply these basic ideas with one practical consequence, namely the separation of the love feast (of a shared meal) from a more solemn eucharistic service. The reason for this disjunction lay in the abuses prevalent at Corinth, where too much food and drink led to indulgence and the late arrival of the poor believers meant that they would not share in the social meal (1 Cor 11:17-22). Divisions within the community had led to a breakdown in *koinōnia* (*see* Fellowship) and a refusal to accept one another in a Christian way (1 Cor 11:18-19, cf. 1 Cor 1:10-11; 3:3-4, 21). Paul finds the answer to this malady in a reemphasis on the "one bread" which betokens "one body" (1 Cor 10:16-17), and shows the way whereby the horizontal dimension of "fellowship in the body and blood" of the Lord sounds the death-knell to the party spirit and selfish concern for one's own interests.

The motif of "remembrance" is present in the Pauline account (1 Cor 11:24-25). He goes on to interpret this in the words "you proclaim the Lord's death." Equally, the future hope is stressed and held out in the reference "until he comes" (1 Cor 11:26). Both Pauline additions are to be understood against a Passover background (cf. 1 Cor 5:1-8) and enhance for Paul both the soteriological emphasis of Christ's dying for sins (1 Cor 15:3-5; Rom 5:1-10; 2 Cor 5:18-21; Gal 3:13) to procure a redemption greater than the Exodus deliverance and the eschatological reminder that the end is not yet (1 Cor 15:20-28) but will come at the Lord's parousia (1 Cor 16:22; *see* Eschatology). The latter will be both a final coming and an anticipation of the ultimate reality as he visits his people at the table.

*3.2. Paul's Corrective Measures.* The Pauline teaching on worship includes the unusual feature that certain beliefs and practices in his churches caused him to enter a set of protests with a view to reformation and correction. His countermeasures fall into two categories.

First, certain creedal and hymnic texts were taken over and edited in the process by Paul before he saw fit to include them in his epistolary instruction. Additions such as those in Philippians 2:8, "even the death of the cross," and Colossians 1:18, "the church" to explicate the sense of "he is the head of the body," show the thrust of these revisions, namely to enforce the centrality of the cross and to counteract any gnosticizing emphasis. In the creedal Romans 3:24-26 he evidently redacted a Jewish-Christian atonement formula (*see* Expiation/Propitiation/Mercy Seat) to highlight the universality of faith.

Then, at Corinth Paul confronted a volatile situation in which worship had become completely disorganized and marred by features he reprobated. His concern was to (1) check undue exuberance caused by a false concept of "spirit" (1 Cor 12:1-3; *see* Holy Spirit) and a realized eschatology that denied a future eschaton on the mistaken assumption that the kingdom was here in its fullness (1 Cor 4:8; 15:20-28); and (2) to insert controls to maintain good order, to curb unrestricted glossolalia without interpretation (*see* Tongues), to elevate prophecy to a high office, and to silence the unguarded and alien utterances of women (prophets) in the assembly (for details see the commentaries and Martin 1984, chaps. 5-7).

*3.3. Paul's Distinctives.* The way Paul tackled the problems at Corinth was primarily to accentuate the positive elements in Christian worship. In the main he did this by introducing the threefold criteria to test all spiritual gifts (*charismata*) that were exercised in the worshiping assembly (cf. Dunn, 293-97; Martin 1982, 194-200). They were:

(1) The firm nexus between the Jesus tradition and the Christ of experience (1 Cor 12:1-3), a connection which placed the cross at the center (1 Cor 5:6-7; 11:26; *see* Cross, Theology of the) and indicated that the church lives always between the times of the two advents and in a state of unfulfilled expectation that only the parousia and final kingdom will bring to fruition. In the interim believers have the Holy Spirit to indwell and inspire them in worship (1 Cor 3:16-17; 6:19; 12:3), and he is the first fruits (*see* First Fruits/ Down Payment) of the coming redemption which is promised, but not yet actualized. No view of baptism that promotes the notion of an already attained resurrection* can be right for Paul since it denies the futurity of resurrection hope (Phil 3:10-15).

(2) The primacy of love (Gk. *agapē*, found in Paul 75 times out of 116 NT occurrences) means that all spiritual exercises stand under the power of an energy that is God's gift in Christ (Rom 5:1-10; 2 Cor 5:14) and is to regulate and direct all the motions and demonstrations of worship into channels that are consonant with the divine character and design for his people's lives (Eph 5:1-2).

(3) The goal of worship on the horizontal plane is edification (Gk. *oikodomē*) which, for Paul, is more

than a feeling of well being or an ecstatic experience. Rather, *oikodomē* (in 1 Cor 14:3, 12, 17, 26; cf. 1 Cor 12:7) is a determined effort to promote God's will in human lives, our neighbor's no less than our own (1 Cor 8:9; 10:33; Rom 15:2 in the liturgical context of 15:5-6; Phil 2:3-4 in the context set by the hymn of Phil 2:6-11). At worship believers are actively to seek the good of the entire church, and thereby to glorify God (1 Cor 10:31) and enjoy his presence, while at the same time recalling that God is really among them in holy judgment* and renewing grace* (1 Cor 14:25; cf. 1 Cor 5:3-5; 11:29-32; 16:22).

*See also* BAPTISM; BENEDICTION, BLESSING, DOXOLOGY, THANKSGIVING; HYMNS, HYMN FRAGMENTS, SONGS, SPIRITUAL SONGS; LITURGICAL ELEMENTS; LORD'S SUPPER; PRAYER.

BIBLIOGRAPHY. G. Bornkamm, *Early Christian Experience* (London: SCM, 1969); P. F. Bradshaw, *The Search for the Origins of Christian Worship* (London: SPCK, 1992); A. Cabaniss, *Pattern in Early Christian Worship* (Macon: Mercer University, 1989); G. J. Cuming, "The New Testament Foundation for Common Prayer," *StudLit* 10 (1974) 88-105; R. Deichgräber, *Gotteshymnus und Christushymnus in der frühen Christentum* (Göttingen: Vandenhoeck & Ruprecht, 1984); G. Delling, *Worship in the New Testament* (London: Darton, Longman & Todd, 1962); C. W. Dugmore, *The Influence of the Synagogue on the Divine Office* (London: Oxford, 1944); J. D. G. Dunn, *Jesus and the Spirit* (Philadelphia: Westminster, 1975); J. A. Fitzmyer, "Kyrios and Maranatha and their Aramaic Background," in *To Advance the Gospel* (New York: Crossroad, 1981) 218-35; S. E. Fowl, *The Story of Christ* (Sheffield: Academic, 1990); F. Hahn, *The Worship of the Early Church* (Philadelphia: Fortress, 1975); M. Hengel, "Hymns and Christology," in *Between Jesus and Paul* (Philadelphia: Fortress, 1983) 78-96; J. Héring, *Commentary on First Corinthians* (London: Epworth, 1962); D. Hill, *New Testament Prophecy* (Atlanta: John Knox, 1979); L. W. Hurtado, *One God, One Lord* (Philadelphia: Fortress, 1988); C. J. A. Lash, "Fashionable Sport: Hymn-Hunting in 1 Peter," *SE* 7 [TU 126] (1982) 293-97; R. P. Martin, *Carmen Christi: Philippians 2:5-11* (Grand Rapids: Eerdmans, rev. ed. 1983); idem, *New Testament Foundations*, vol. 2 (Grand Rapids: Eerdmans, 1978); idem, "Patterns of Worship in New Testament Churches," *JSNT* 37 (1989) 59-85; idem, *Reconciliation: A Study of Paul's Theology* (Grand Rapids: Zondervan, 1989); idem, *The Spirit and the Congregation: Studies in 1 Corinthians 12-15* (Grand Rapids: Eerdmans, 1984); idem, *Worship in the Early Church* (Grand Rapids: Eerdmans, 1975); idem, *The Worship of God* (Grand Rapids: Eerdmans, 1982); C. F. D. Moule, *Worship in the New Testament* (London: Lutterworth,

1961); G. Murray, *Five Stages of Greek Religion* (Oxford: University Press, 1925); P. T. O'Brien, *Introductory Thanksgivings in the Letters of Paul* (Leiden: Brill, 1977); J. A. T. Robinson, "The Earliest Christian Liturgical Sequence," in *Twelve New Testament Studies* (London: SCM, 1962) 154-57; J. M. Robinson, "Die Hodajot-Formel in Gebet und Hymnus des Frühchristentums," in *Apophoreta*, ed. W. Eltester (Berlin: Töpelmann, 1964) 194-235; W. Rordorf, *Sunday. The History of the Day of Rest and Worship in the Earliest Centuries of the Christian Church* (London: SCM, 1968); P. Schubert, *Form and Function of the Pauline Thanksgivings* (Berlin: Töpelmann, 1939); W. S. Smith, *Musical Aspects of the New Testament* (Amsterdam: Kok, 1962); E. Stauffer, *New Testament Theology* (New York: Macmillan, 1956).

R. P. Martin

# WRATH, DESTRUCTION

In the NT the Greek words for wrath, *orgē* and *thymos*, are basically interchangeable. In the Pauline corpus, however, *thymos* is primarily related to human anger and is used in lists of negative human actions (2 Cor 12:20; Gal 5:20; Eph 4:31 and Col 3:8), with the exception of Romans 2:8, where it refers to divine anger and judgment. In the case of *orgē* most of the uses can be read as the "wrath of God," even if the designation "of God*" is not present. When we turn to the idea of destruction, it quickly becomes evident that there is a rich variety of Greek words in Paul which carry the meaning of destroying, such as *apollymi* and *apōleia* (basically implying "hopelessness" and "ultimate loss"), *olethros* ("corruption," "ruin," and "death"; cf. *olothreutēs*, "destroyer, 1 Cor 10:10), *katalyō* and *kathairesis* ("tear down" or "take apart"), *katargeō* ("put an end to," "invalidate"), *phtheirō* ("ruin," "destroy") and *portheō* ("lay waste"). In the use of these words only the context will determine whether the destroying is speaking of human activity, Satanic* work, or the judgment* of God.

1. God's Wrath
2. Human Wrath
3. Destruction

## 1. God's Wrath.

In Paul the treatment of the wrath of God is most fully explicated in Romans* where God's wrath is said to be directed against human wickedness (Rom 1:18; 2:5-8). The prevailing thought is that the wrath of God which will be fully and finally revealed on the eschatological "day of wrath" (Rom 2:5; cf. 1 Thess 1:10; 5:9) is, like the saving righteousness* of God in the gospel,* already being revealed from heaven (Rom 1:18). In interpreting Paul, the eschatological nature of the wrath

of God, with its roots in the OT and Judaism, must be recognized.

In the OT the wrath of God is not viewed as an essential attribute of God, but as an expression of his will as he deals with sinful and rebellious humankind in the context of history. Yahweh's wrath, as an expression of his holiness, his omnipotence and his sovereign, kingly rule, is executed against the nations who have rebelled against his sovereignty (e.g., Ex 15:7; Ps 2:1-6; Amos 1:2—2:5; see Herion). Yahweh's wrath is also aimed at Israel for failing to live by the covenant which Yahweh established with the chosen nation (e.g., Ex 32:10; Num 11:1, 33; Amos 2:6), a work that Isaiah calls Yahweh's "strange deed" (Is 28:21). A day will come when Yahweh will finally establish his sovereignty in history and defeat his enemies. That will be a "day of wrath" (e.g., Zeph 1:15, 18; 2:2-3). The question of how Israel will finally be delivered from the wrath of God was a lingering question in Paul's day. Some Jews apparently maintained that Israel still remained under the curse of exile and thus was not yet delivered from the wrath of God (*see* Restoration of Israel).

This background should inform the debate of whether Paul understands the wrath of God as emotional in nature (affective), or the necessary consequence of a holy God encountering sin* (effective). Any solution to the problem must account for both the judgment and the love* of God in his dealings with Israel and humankind in general, and must exclude any notion of malicious or capricious anger on the part of God. C. H. Dodd, noting that "Paul never uses the verb, 'to be angry,' with God as subject" and that *wrath* when used of God is "curiously impersonal," propounded the influential view that wrath is "not a certain feeling or attitude of God toward us, but some process or effect in the objective realm of facts" (Dodd, 21-22). In other words, wrath is the inevitable result, or consequence, of human sin in a moral universe—a calculable effect of certain behaviors or attitudes—and not the activity of God against sinners (Dodd, 23-24; cf. Hanson). But Paul seems to maintain that wrath is not simply something that can be attributed to the way the world is, but that it originates in God and is an activity of God (Dunn, 55). Already the wrath of God is being revealed "from heaven" in the wayward degeneration of humankind, whether Gentile or Jew (Rom 1:18—3:20).

Paul's argument is that no one remains untouched by sin (Rom 3:23) and therefore whether it is a matter of Jew or Greek, none is righteous (3:9-10) and thus all are liable to the wrath of God. Indeed, in Ephesians the readers in their pre-Christian state were "disobedient" and "by nature children of wrath," a Hebraic way of indicating a class of people doomed to suffer God's wrath because of their sinful disobedience (Eph 2:3; 5:6). According to Paul, all people are justified* by the sacrifice of Jesus Christ and will be saved from God's wrath (Rom 5:8-9). Neither Law* nor circumcision* serves as a refuge from wrath because law codes and physical signs such as circumcision are not the means of acceptance by God (Rom 2:25-28). Abraham's* life witnessed for Paul that acceptance preceded both circumcision and Mosaic Law. Indeed, without faith* the Law produces, or brings God's wrath into effect (*katergazetai*, Rom 4:15), in that it heaps up transgressions (Rom 5:20).

Paul views wrath as both a present reality and a future expectation. It is at this point that judgment and destruction intersect with wrath (cf. *orgē* and *dikaiokrisia*, "righteous judgment," in Rom 2:5). The present wrath is indicated by its present revelation from heaven (Rom 1:18) and in the threefold "handing over" (*paradidōmi*) by God of Gentiles to their abysmal lifestyles in which heart, passions and mind are all given over to wickedness (Rom 1:24, 26, 28) and an absence of covenantal relationship with God. Likewise, although the Jews have the commands of God (Rom 3:2), they are judged no better in actuality because of their disobedience (Rom 3:20). Thus, all—Jew and Gentile—stand under judgment. But the wrath of God at this point in the process is not final (Rom 5:9 and 1 Thess 1:10; cf. Col 3:6) but awaits a future manifestation, just as salvation is not yet complete, and will not be fully experienced (Rom 5:21; 6:22) until the last day.

The means by which believers escape the eschatological wrath is through God's action in Christ Jesus (Rom 5:8-9; cf. 1 Thess 1:10). Specifically, this involves the death* of Christ, a subject Paul has already developed with reference to the *hilastērion* of Romans 3:25. The question has been widely debated whether Paul uses the term *hilastērion* to refer to an expiatory sacrifice,* which focuses on the obliteration of sin, or a propitiatory offering, which in some way satisfies the divine wrath directed against sin. Some interpreters suggest that the term refers to Christ as the mercy seat where the blood of atonement was applied in the OT cultus. If propitiation is in mind, the idea is that Christ, having taken sin upon himself, substitutes or stands in for Israel and humanity in general, thus satisfying the holy wrath of God against sin. God in Christ bears, in love and mercy, the judgment of divine wrath upon himself (*see* Expiation, Propitiation, Mercy Seat).

### 2. Human Wrath.
Paul's concern is that Christians evidence a lifestyle of love (Rom 12:9) in response to Christ and leave vengeance to God (Rom 12:19). Salvation and wrath are for Paul polar opposites; Christians are not destined for wrath but for salvation (1 Thess 5:9). Accordingly, they are to avoid all semblance of evil, including all destructive types of human anger and wrath (*thymos*, 2 Cor 12:20; etc.). Some types of anger (*parorgizō*) may seem to have positive results (Rom 10:19), and in Ephesians it is suggested that one might indeed become angry (*orgizomai*), but it must not be indulged and permitted to develop into sin (Eph 4:26; see Lincoln, 301-2). Otherwise human anger and wrath are condemned by Paul.

Christians are likewise to be faithful citizens and therefore should not need to fear either the wrath of God or that of political authorities who rule with justice (Rom 13:4-5; cf. 1 Pet 2:13-17; *see* Civil Authorities). Even when the state is unjust, the assumption is that suffering Christians will still remain steadfast in their faith (cf. Rev 13:7-10), awaiting God's vindication of his people. Paul's conviction is that living authentically Christian lives and witnessing for Jesus is the role of the believer, which may indeed result in persecution. But he is convinced that the enemies of the gospel will at length (*eis telos*) experience the wrath of God (1 Thess 2:16).

### 3. Destruction.
Those who choose to live their lives in their own way quite apart from God's will are designated by Paul as "vessels fit for destruction" (Rom 9:22). Destruction in Paul has several meanings, and some words, like *olethros*, can mean simply "pain" or even "death," as in the "destruction of the flesh" (1 Cor 5:5; *see* Discipline). On the other hand, *olethros aiōnios* in 2 Thessalonians 1:9 seems to mean "eternal destruction" or the opposite of eternal life. In 1 Thessalonians 5:3 *ephistatai olethros*, "sudden destruction," evidently implies some irretrievable loss or catastrophic event in history. In 1 Timothy 6:9 the rich are said to fall into a pattern of life that leads to "ruin and destruction" (*olethron kai apōleian*), seemingly indicating the temporal consequences of a wayward life. As in determining the meaning of any word, so with *destruction* the interpreter must rely on context.

In the case of words like *apollymi*, the usual meaning in Paul is "final and hopeless judgment." For Paul, believing in the resurrected Christ Jesus is the foundation of the faith (1 Cor 15:14). Even though such believers should die, they have the hope of salvation and need not fear an ultimate destruction (1 Cor 15:17-18). But when Paul speaks of those who offend the sensibilities of weaker brothers and sisters by eating meat (offered to idols* in 1 Cor 8), he warns the "strong"* and those of robust conscience* that by their eating in such a manner they are contributing to the destruction (*apollymi*, perhaps in the sense of eschatological ruin) of the weak for whom Christ died (Rom 14:15; 1 Cor 8:11; see Dunn, 38b, 821). In another context Paul speaks of the dual effect of believers' lives. They are the "aroma" of Christ both to those who are being saved and to those who are being destroyed; "to the one a fragrance from death to death, to the other a fragrance from life to life" (2 Cor 2:15-16).

For Paul the threat of destruction, the figure of Satan* or the Son of Destruction, and the hostile principalities* and powers are realities, even as evil in the world and the human rejection of God's love are realities (2 Cor 4:3-4; 2 Thess 2:3-10; cf. Phil 3:19). The task of the Christian is to confront in Christ and through the power* of God all evil and its destructive results (Rom 6:6; 1 Cor 6:13-15; 2 Cor 10:8; Phil 1:27-28). Like Paul, Christians must not lapse from their commitment or take up their old way of life (Gal 1:23), because they are no longer blinded by the god of this world whose activities lead to destruction (2 Cor 4:3-4; 11:14-15).

*See also* CURSE, ACCURSED, ANATHEMA; ENEMY, ENMITY; ESCHATOLOGY; EXPIATION, PROPITIATION, MERCY SEAT; FORGIVENESS; GOD; JUDGMENT; LOVE; MERCY; RIGHTEOUSNESS, RIGHTEOUSNESS OF GOD; SIN, GUILT; TRIUMPH.

BIBLIOGRAPHY. G. L. Borchert "Romans, Epistle to," in *Mercer Dictionary to the Bible* (Macon, GA: Mercer, 1990) 772-74; G. Bornkamm, "The Revelation of God's Wrath," in *Early Christian Experience* (London: SCM, 1969) 47-70; F. Büchsel, "θυμός κτλ," *TDNT* III.167-172; C. E. B. Cranfield, *The Epistle to the Romans* (2 vols.; ICC; Edinburgh: T. & T. Clark: 1975, 1979); C. H. Dodd, *The Epistle of Paul to the Romans* (MNTC; New York: Harper & Row, 1932); J. D. G. Dunn, *Romans* (WBC 38; Dallas: Word, 1988); A. T. Hanson, *The Wrath of the Lamb* (London: SPCK, 1957); G. A. Herion and S. H. Travis, "Wrath of God," *ABD* VI.989-98; H. Kleinknecht et al., "ὀργή κτλ," *TDNT* V.382-447; A. T. Lincoln, *Ephesians* (WBC 42; Dallas: Word, 1990); G. H. C. MacGregor, "The Concept of the Wrath of God in the NT," *NTS* 7 (1960-61) 101-9; L. Morris, *The Biblical Doctrine of Judgment* (Grand Rapids: Eerdmans, 1960); A. Oepke, "ἀπόλλυμι," *TDNT* I.394-97; H. Ridderbos, *Paul: An Outline of his Theology* (Grand Rapids: Eerdmans, 1975) 91-149; J. Schneider, "ὀλεθρεύω κτλ," *TDNT* V.167-71; R. V. G. Tasker, *The Biblical Doctrine of the Wrath of God* (London: Tyndale, 1951); S. H. Travis, *Christ and the Judgement of God* (Basingstoke: Marshall Pickering, 1986); D. E. H. Whiteley, *Theology of St. Paul* (Philadelphia: Fortress, 1964) 61-72.

G. L. Borchert

**YEARS.** *See* HOLY DAYS.

**ZEAL.** *See* JEALOUSY, ZEAL.

**ZEALOTS.** *See* JEALOUSY, ZEAL; REVOLUTIONARY MOVEMENTS.

**ZION.** *See* JERUSALEM.

# Pauline Letters Index

# Subject Index

783, 785, 786, 792, 793,
796, 798-802, 804-806, 810,
815, 818-820, 826-837, 844,
847, 849, 858-862, 866-869,
871, 872, 877, 878, 880-
883, 886, 890, 900, 906-
908, 914, 917, 936, 948,
950, 952, 954, 956-960,
969-971, 973, 975-978, 982,
984, 988, 992
Salvation History 14, 17, 31,
138, 145, 182, 195, 224,
232, 237, 323, 332, 367,
420, 500, 519, 521, 539,
619, 621, 624, 629, 665,
671, 672, 736, 783, 800,
802, 805, 818, 970, 975-978
Sanctification 40, 41, 43, 45,
108, 194, 227, 241, 292,
316, 319, 368, 371, 373,
397-401, 412, 437, 518,
627, 641, 701, 713, 770,
776, 834, 860, 871, 880,
907, 910, 913, 915, 916
Sanctuary 324, 784, 789, 796,
924, 925, 947, 951
Sanders, E. P. 6, 7, 9, 18, 41-
43, 45, 92, 93, 95, 144, 147,
153, 183, 197, 213, 286,
291, 339, 355, 368, 388,
393, 397, 421-423, 435,
436, 443, 446, 497, 503,
509-511, 518, 519, 521-523,
531, 532, 542, 553, 560,
613, 614, 616-619, 652,
671-673, 675, 679, 691,
728, 734, 746, 764, 765,
778, 781, 783, 797, 804,
805, 827, 837, 842, 843,
850, 877, 878, 880, 881,
890, 925, 957, 961, 976-
978, 982
Sanhedrin 119, 141, 142,
215, 463, 472, 473, 505,
511, 718, 719, 799, 821
Sarah 1, 5, 8, 180, 182, 183,
333, 505, 506, 516, 592,
636, 640, 896
Satan 21-23, 28-30, 32-34, 42,
44, 50, 57, 58, 105, 131,
155, 168, 170, 186, 210,
211, 216, 217, 236-238,
247, 261, 262, 265, 274,
304, 378-382, 447, 450,
516, 555-557, 568, 582,
583, 593, 600, 646, 652,
653, 688, 693, 723, 724,
731, 733, 748, 751, 752,
771, 785, 861-867, 872,
876, 878, 880, 921, 952,
953, 956, 964, 965, 980,
982, 991, 993
Savior 32, 80, 97-100, 102,
115, 191, 231, 285, 290,
312, 359, 369, 371, 373,
377, 378, 406, 416, 432,
507, 531, 557, 569, 577,
604, 694, 782, 786, 792,
794, 808, 858-862, 867-869,
879, 957, 959, 970
Saying of Jesus 102, 265,
351, 464, 474-480, 482,

483, 485-491, 498, 503,
524, 584, 736, 761, 776,
909, 918, 943, 944, 969
Scandal 113, 193, 201, 500,
918, 919, 926
School of Tyrannus 251
Schoolmaster, Pedagogue
232, 539, 694
Schweitzer, A. 27, 34, 35, 78,
82, 93, 99, 253, 254, 269,
413, 434-436, 493, 494,
496, 503, 522, 523, 525,
526, 613, 616, 619, 624,
625, 674, 675, 677, 679,
779, 827, 837
Scourging 140, 215, 549, 682,
753
Scribe 21, 27, 215, 244, 471,
514, 551, 578, 606, 633,
701, 709, 719, 925, 928-
931, 971
Scripture 2, 9, 15, 18, 65, 89-
91, 109, 115, 129, 134, 136,
138, 178, 182, 187, 191,
204, 208, 209, 224, 272,
287, 320, 329-332, 352,
353, 368, 371, 377, 381,
384, 390, 397, 410, 415,
434, 441, 442, 445, 446,
469, 470, 471, 488, 489,
499, 504-506, 532, 542,
591, 592, 630, 633-642,
644, 655, 663, 669, 678,
691, 694, 703, 726, 727,
730, 731, 739, 741-743,
755, 761, 762, 764, 765,
768, 777, 779, 780, 799,
800, 803, 805, 842, 848-
850, 858, 868, 878, 887,
893, 895, 908, 909, 911,
934, 960, 974, 985
Scythian 64
Sea travel 945, 946
Seed 2-4, 7-9, 17, 18, 49, 75,
109, 180-182, 215, 232,
270, 296, 298-300, 304,
332, 368, 394, 443, 505,
506, 556, 632, 685, 714,
802, 843, 866, 904, 906
Seed of Abraham 8, 17, 18,
49, 232, 300, 368, 906
Seleucia 36, 450
Self-control, discipline 32,
72, 166, 213, 273, 316, 318,
319, 401, 693, 758, 760,
830, 865, 898, 967
Seneca 19, 35, 77, 78, 335,
430, 717, 718, 721, 722,
854, 921
Septuagint, LXX 3, 4, 5, 6,
12, 16, 20, 22, 42, 45, 46,
68, 69, 73, 76, 98, 106, 109,
124, 138, 169, 170, 181,
187, 199, 209, 212, 226,
227, 239, 271, 277-280,
282-284, 300, 302, 304,
305, 310, 312, 318-322,
335, 348, 369, 375, 377,
379, 381, 384, 386, 398,
405-407, 414, 420, 424,
425, 459, 509, 513, 514,
536, 537, 554, 563, 585,

586, 595, 597, 601, 628,
630, 632-635, 640, 641,
699, 728, 730, 748, 749,
754, 758, 763, 766, 779,
797, 804, 828-830, 856,
862, 863, 867, 870, 872,
875, 901, 904, 918, 921,
924, 925, 948, 949, 953,
966, 979, 986
Sergius Paulus 120, 721
Servant 20, 64, 98, 104, 106,
107, 109, 113, 134, 137,
170, 172, 191, 208, 242,
247, 293, 314, 315, 321,
330, 373, 378, 422, 427,
431, 445, 478, 484, 491,
514, 543, 544, 551, 560,
589, 608, 635, 640, 645,
657, 708, 712, 713, 724,
725, 735, 737, 741, 742,
745, 754, 762, 774, 798,
799, 802, 829, 843, 867,
869-871, 882, 883, 901,
914, 916, 917, 957, 962
Servant of the Lord/Yahweh
64, 113, 208, 321, 484, 543,
829, 870, 871
Servants 23, 25, 58, 83, 134,
135, 155, 171, 173, 183,
210, 236, 237, 265, 277,
292, 361, 379, 417, 516,
543, 560, 644-646, 649-653,
662, 671, 714, 724, 748,
750, 763, 869, 870, 881,
965, 969
Service 10, 42, 64, 81, 83, 98,
118, 129-135, 137, 140,
142, 143, 151, 186-188,
192, 202, 205, 219, 221,
234, 247, 251, 267, 271,
274, 286, 291-293, 299,
300, 313, 341-345, 347,
378, 391, 400, 407, 418,
431, 450, 475, 484, 485,
487, 490, 501, 502, 517,
545, 567, 586, 596, 601-
604, 608, 634, 658, 678,
686, 688, 704, 705, 717,
722, 724, 731, 732, 741,
742, 747, 748, 751, 768,
773, 774, 785, 808, 819,
831, 835, 851, 857, 863,
869, 870, 873, 907, 911,
913, 914, 916, 953, 966,
975, 976, 984-989
Sexual ethics 217, 275, 379,
401, 414, 592, 600, 693,
776, 871, 875, 933, 967
Sexual immorality 57, 173,
217, 246, 247, 363, 426,
471, 535, 568, 689, 771,
772, 871, 936
Sexuality 10, 57, 75, 217,
256, 267, 275, 303, 379,
401, 414, 426, 510, 535,
567, 592, 599, 600, 684,
693, 772, 776, 844, 871-
874, 915, 933
Shalom 98, 391, 739, 866,
947
Shame 77, 155, 216, 298,
406, 416, 585, 633, 746,

949, 974
Shema 309, 356, 424, 425,
565, 725, 780, 985
Sheol 32, 381
Ships 472, 684, 792, 875, 946
Sicarii 817-819
Sidon 451
Sign prophets 817-819
Signs 30, 34, 49, 51, 55, 58,
87, 169, 175, 211, 215, 231,
236, 289, 296, 367, 380,
381, 389, 405, 409, 469,
486, 493, 605-607, 645,
647, 683, 685, 735, 789-
791, 796, 818, 851, 865,
875-877, 889, 919, 930,
937, 988, 992
Silas 124, 140, 183, 185-188,
369, 547-549, 647, 658,
684, 687, 719, 726, 752,
932, 934, 935
Silvanus 49, 183, 186, 188,
429, 447, 476, 484, 647,
680, 684, 687, 932
Sin 9, 10, 12, 13, 15, 17, 18,
37, 41, 45, 50, 59, 60-64,
71-73, 99, 110-112, 148,
155, 160, 166, 178, 189,
190, 193, 196, 205-208,
210, 211, 219-221, 228,
230, 236, 237, 246, 259,
262, 265, 271, 273, 279-
283, 285, 287, 290, 292,
293, 303-306, 313, 314,
316, 319, 331, 348, 360,
363, 364, 373, 378, 379,
399, 401, 406, 409-411,
424-426, 432, 460, 476,
494, 517, 518, 536-541,
543, 553-556, 572, 576,
577, 592, 600, 621, 628,
629, 646, 672, 674-676,
690, 691, 696-698, 701,
716, 723, 730, 732, 744,
747, 751, 752, 754, 765,
768, 770-776, 781, 782,
785, 786, 797-799, 801,
802, 804, 806, 810, 832,
834-836, 842-847, 856, 858,
859, 861, 862, 866, 868,
871, 872, 874, 877, 878,
879-882, 885, 904, 907,
910, 915, 916, 918, 927,
946, 948, 950, 952, 954,
957, 958, 969, 975-978,
980, 982, 989, 991-993
Sinai 22, 124, 129, 169, 178,
180, 181, 232, 333, 407,
529, 533-535, 538, 539,
541, 543, 620, 621, 672,
719, 947, 950
Sinews 377
Sinners 13, 28, 37, 41, 62,
76, 93, 99, 111, 158, 206,
207, 215, 224, 228, 229,
280-283, 285-287, 289, 307,
312, 313, 318, 331, 336,
344, 349, 364, 365, 459,
483, 484, 487, 489, 490,
492, 496, 497, 501, 502,
510, 520, 529, 600-602,
696, 697, 702, 730, 764,

# Articles Index